P9-BIL-047

3 1427 00048 6363

CHILTON'S
IMPORT CAR REPAIR MANUAL 1983

Import Cars from 1976 through 1983

Editorial Director	Alan F. Turner
Managing Editor	Kerry A. Freeman, S.A.E.
Senior Editor	Richard J. Rivele, S.A.E.
Project Coordinator	Dean F. Morgantini, S.A.E.
Editorial Staff	A. Lindsay Brooke
	Mark F. Devlin, S.A.E., N.I.A.S.E.
	David F. Gordon, N.I.A.S.E.
	Martin Gunther
	David H. Lee, S.A.E., N.I.A.S.E.
	Tony Molla
	Larry Stovey, N.I.A.S.E.
	Ron Webb
Production Manager	Warren Owens
Assistant Production Manager	Nancy A. Thomas
Mechanical Pasteup	Dru Brown
	Geraldine M. Basso
	Donna P. Fisher
	Robin S. Miller
	Margaret A. Stoner

OFFICERS

President	William A. Barbour
Executive Vice President	James A. Miades
Vice President & General Manager	John P. Kushnerick

 CHILTON BOOK COMPANY
Chilton Way, Radnor, PA 19089

Manufactured in USA
© 1982 by Chilton Book Company
ISBN 0-8019-7240-X
Library of Congress Card No. 76-648878

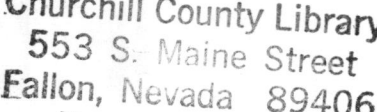

HOW TO USE THIS MANUAL

This manual is arranged in two sections:

Car Section

Car sections are grouped by manufacturer (Audi, BMW, etc.) and arranged in alphabetical order. The text and illustrations that comprise the service procedures in each Car Section are arranged in the following order of systems and components: Tune-Up, Engine Electrical, Engine Mechanical, Engine Lubrication, Engine Cooling, Emission Controls, Fuel System, Manual Transmission, Clutch, Automatic Transmission, Transaxle, Drive Axle, Rear Suspension, Front Suspension, Steering, Brakes, Heater, Radio, Windshield Wiper, Instrument Panel and Fuse Box.

Specification charts are always located at the front of each section. All illustrations are located as close as possible to the pertinent text. Procedures are for all models in the particular section unless specifically noted otherwise.

Unit Repair Section

The Unit Repair Section contains troubleshooting and overhaul procedures for the major components and systems of your car. This portion of the book is intended to be used in conjunction with the Car Sections.

For example: If your car's engine is misfiring and you do not know the cause, use the "Troubleshooting" portion of the Unit Repair Section to find the cause and its remedy. If the cause should prove to be defective piston rings which are allowing oil to foul the spark plugs, the remedy is to overhaul the engine. Then turn to the proper Car Section to find the procedure for removing the engine from the car. After you have removed the engine, turn to the "Engine Rebuilding" chapter in the Unit Repair Section and follow the steps listed there to overhaul the engine.

Every major Unit Repair Section contains an Identification or Application chart to correlate the information contained in that section. The sections are usually arranged by brands, manufacturers or types of components rather than models of cars.

All overhaul procedures in the Unit Repair Section begin with the component removed from the car. The reason for this division of material is an economic one. The steps involved in overhauling an engine are virtually the same for all engines. However, the operation of removing the engine from the car varies greatly from model to model. By combining where possible, and separating where necessary, we are able to publish the maximum amount of information.

Locating Information

The Table of Contents, at the front of the book, lists the beginning of each Car and Unit Repair Section in the manual.

The Index, also at the front of the book, is a comprehensive listing of all major mechanical sections and systems for every section in the book. The Index contains listings for Car Sections as well as for corresponding Unit Repair Sections. Car Section pages are prefixed with the letter "C." Unit Repair Sections are prefixed with the letter "U."

To find where a particular Car Section is located in the book, you need only look in the Table of Contents. Once you have found the proper section, you may wish to find where specific procedures are located in that section. Turn to the Index and read across the top of the page until you reach the appropriate Car Section. When the proper manufacturer's column has been found, read down the side column to the procedure or system for which you are looking. The intersection of the two columns will provide the page number(s) where the procedure is located.

Safety Notice

Proper service and repair procedures are vital to the safe, reliable operation of all motor vehicles, as well as the personal safety of those performing repairs. This manual outlines procedures for servicing and repairing vehicles using safe effective methods. The procedures contain many NOTES, CAUTIONS and WARNINGS which should be followed along with standard safety procedures to eliminate the possibility of personal injury or improper service which could damage the vehicle or compromise its safety.

It is important to note that repair procedures and techniques, tools and parts for servicing motor vehicles, as well as the skill and experience of the individual performing the work vary widely. It is not possible to anticipate all of the conceivable ways or conditions under which vehicles may be serviced, or to provide cautions as to all of the possible hazards that may result. Standard and accepted safety precautions and equipment should be used when handling toxic or flammable fluids, and safety goggles or other protection should be used during cutting, grinding, chiseling, prying, or any other process that can cause material removal or projectiles.

Some procedures require the use of tools specially designed for a specific purpose. Before substituting another tool or procedure, you must be completely satisfied that neither your personal safety, nor the performance of the vehicle will be endangered.

Part Numbers

Part numbers listed in this book are not recommendations by Chilton for any product by brand name. They are references that can be used with interchange manuals and aftermarket supplier catalogs to locate each brand supplier's discrete part number.

CONTENTS

Car Section

Unit Repair Section

INDEX

	Audi	BMW	Capri	Chrysler/Mitsubishi	Datsun/Nissan	Fiat	Fiesta	Honda	Isuzu	Mazda	Mercedes-Benz	MG
Alternator	C13	C64	C118	C166	C222	C288	C344	C386	C429	C479	C549	C615
Automatic Transmission	C36	C87	C137	C186	C252	C315	—	C410	C451	C508	C590	—
Axle Shaft	C41	C90	C140	C191	C257	C320	C360	C408	C453	C511	C594	C634
Ball Joints	C44	C99	—	C194	C261	C326	C366	C413	C457	C516	C597	—
Belt Tension	C30	—	C118	C167	C223	—	—	C386	—	—	—	—
Brake Adjustment	C47	—	C148	C198	C264	C331	—	C416	—	C519	C602	C640
Brakes	C47	C103	C148	C198	C264	C331	C369	C416	C460	C519	C601	C640
Breaker Points and Condenser	C8	C60	—	C162	C215	C282	—	C381	—	C474	C541	—
Camshaft	C25	C74	C124	C172	C234	C297	C349	C394	C437	C495	C560	C620
Carburetor	—	C84	C132	C182	C246	C308	C355	C404	C446	C504	C583	C629
R & I and Adjustment	—	C84	C132	C182	C246	C308	C355	C404	C446	C504	C583	C629
Overhaul	—	U23	U23	U23	U23	U23	U23	U23	U23	U23	U23	U23
Chassis Electrical	C49	C108	C150	C199	C266	C334	C370	C418	C462	C521	C604	C641
Clutch	C34	C87	C136	C184	C251	C313	C359	C409	C450	C507	C589	C630
Combination Switch	C46	C99	—	C197	C264	C329	C368	C415	C459	C517	—	—
Cooling System	C28	C77	C128	C178	C237	C300	C351	C399	C440	C491	C569	C623
Cylinder Head	C18	C66	C121	C170	C226	C292	C347	C391	C433	C492	C552	C617
Diesel Injection	C32	—	—	—	C248	—	—	—	C427	—	—	—
Diesel Service	U15	—	—	—	U15	—	—	—	U15	—	U15	—
Differential	—	C90	C141	C191	C256	C322	—	—	C454	C511	C595	C634
Distributor	C12	C62	C117	C165	C220	C287	C344	C385	C428	C478	C549	C614
Drive Axles	C38	C90	C140	C189	C255	C319	C360	—	C452	C478	C593	C632
Driveshaft	C38	C91	C140	C190	C255	C319	C362	C408	C452	C511	C593	C632
Dwell Angle	C9	—	—	C162	C216	C283	—	—	—	C477	C541	—
Electronic Ignition	C9	C60	C116	C162	C216	C281	—	—	C425	C474	—	C612
Emission Controls	C30	C78	C128	C179	C237	C302	C351	C399	C441	C496	C569	C623
Engine Cooling	C28	C77	C128	C178	C237	C300	C351	C399	C440	C491	C569	C623
Engine Lubrication	C27	C76	C126	C176	C235	C298	C351	C398	C438	C490	—	C622
Engine Mechanical	C15	C65	C119	C169	C225	C290	C346	C388	C431	C481	C550	C616
Engine Rebuilding	U255	U255	U255	U255	U255	U255	U255	U255	U255	U255	U255	U255
Exhaust Manifold	C21	C71	C122	C170	C230	C294	C348	C395	C435	C489	C558	C618
Firing Order	C3	C55	C112	C156	C207	C277	C340	C375	C422	C467	C531	C609
Front Cover	C22	C73	C123	C172	C230	C295	C348	C396	—	C493	—	C618
Front End Alignment	C45	C99	C144	C195	C263	C327	C365	C414	C459	C516	C599	—
Front Suspension	C42	C94	C143	C193	C261	C325	C365	C412	C455	C514	C596	C636
Fuel Filter	—	C83	C131	C182	—	C307	—	C402	C446	C504	C582	C629
Fuel Injection	C31	C85	—	—	C248	C310	—	—	—	—	C586	—
Fuel Injectors	C31	C86	—	—	—	C311	—	—	—	—	—	—
Fuel Pump	C31	C82	C131	C182	C244	C307	C354	C403	C446	C504	C583	C626
Fuel System	C31	C82	C131	C182	C244	C307	C354	C402	C446	C504	C582	C626
Fuse Box	C52	C110	C152	C202	C272	C338	C372	C420	C464	C523	C606	C642
Heater	C49	C108	C150	C199	C266	C334	C370	C418	C462	C523	C604	C641
Idle Speed and Mixture	C11	C61	C117	C164	C219	C286	C344	C385	C426	C478	C544	C613
Ignition Lock and Switch	C46	C100	C145	C198	C264	—	C368	C415	—	C517	C605	C640
Ignition Timing	C9	C61	C115	C163	C217	C283	C343	C383	C425	C475	C542	C612
Instrument Cluster	C51	C110	C152	C201	C270	C337	C372	C419	C463	C522	C604	C642
Intake Manifold	C20	C70	C122	C170	C229	C294	C348	C395	C434	C489	C558	C618
Lower Control Arm	C44	C97	C144	C194	C263	—	C366	C414	C459	C514	C598	C636
MacPherson Strut R & I	C42	C94	C143	C194	C261	C325	C365	C413	—	C514	—	—
MacPherson Strut Overhaul	U201	U201	U201	U201	U201	U201	U201	U201	—	U201	—	—

Removal and Installation

Peugeot	Porsche 911, 912, 914, 930	Porsche 924, 928, 944	Renault	SAAB	Subaru	Toyota	Triumph	Volkswagen Rear Wheel Drive	Volkswagen Front Wheel Drive	Volvo	
C656	C692	C723	C760	C795	C833	C883	C950	C994	C1052	C1101	Alternator
C674	—	C742	C773	C813	C850	C917	C971	C1023	C1073	C1134	Automatic Transmission
C676	C703	C742	—	—	C853	C921	C972	—	C1076	C1139	Axle Shaft
C678	C708	C746	—	C816	C858	C928	C978	C1031	C1080	C1142	Ball Joints
C667	C692	—	—	C795	C834	C883	C951	C995	C1053	C1101	Belt Tension
C680	—	C748	C780	—	C860	C934	C980	C1034	C1085	C1146	Brake Adjustment
C679	C710	C748	C780	C819	C860	C934	C980	C1034	C1085	C1146	Brakes
C649	C688	—	C756	—	C830	C877	C946	C989	C1046	C1096	Breaker Points and Condenser
C663	—	C732	C767	C802	C840	C900	C958	C1003	C1060	C1116	Camshaft
C670	—	—	—	—	C848	C911	C967	—	C1067	—	Carburetor
C670	—	—	—	—	C848	C911	C967	—	C1067	—	R & I and Adjustment
U23	—	—	—	—	U23	U23	U23	—	U23	—	Overhaul
C680	C712	C749	C780	C819	C862	C936	C981	C1036	C1086	C1148	Chassis Electrical
C673	C703	C738	C773	C812	C851	C916	C969	C1019	C1072	C1133	Clutch
C679	C709	—	C779	C818	C859	C931	C979	C1032	C1083	C1143	Combination Switch
C667	—	C734	C768	C803	C843	C903	C961	C1011	C1062	C1119	Cooling System
C658	C694	C726	C762	C798	C839	C888	C954	C998	C1057	C1106	Cylinder Head
C672	—	—	—	—	—	—	—	C1019	C1070	C1131	Diesel Injection
U15	—	—	—	—	—	—	—	U15	U15	U15	Diesel Service
—	—	—	C775	—	—	C923	C972	—	—	C1139	Differential
C655	C691	C722	C759	C790	C832	C882	C949	C992	C1051	C1100	Distributor
C676	C703	—	—	C814	C853	C920	C972	—	C1076	C1138	Drive Axles
C676	C703	—	—	C814	C855	C920	C972	C1024	—	C1138	Driveshaft
C650	C688	—	C756	—	C831	C877	C947	C989	C1046	C1096	Dwell Angle
C650	C688	C720	C756	C792	C831	C877	C947	C989	C1046	C1097	Electronic Ignition
C668	C701	C735	C768	C805	C844	C904	C961	C1014	C1063	C1121	Emission Controls
C667	—	C734	C768	C803	C843	C903	C961	C1011	C1062	C1119	Engine Cooling
C666	—	C733	C767	C803	C842	C902	C959	C1008	C1061	C1117	Engine Lubrication
C657	C693	C725	C761	C797	C837	C885	C953	C997	C1054	C1104	Engine Mechanical
U255	U255	U255	U255	U255	U255	U255	U255	U255	U255	U255	Engine Rebuilding
C660	C695	C728	C764	C800	C839	C895	C956	C999	C1058	C1110	Exhaust Manifold
C645	C683	C716	C753	C786	C826	C869	C943	C985	C1042	C1092	Firing Order
C660	—	C729	C765	—	C840	C896	C956	C1007	C1058	C1112	Front Cover
C679	C708	C747	C779	C817	C859	C930	C979	C1032	C1081	C1143	Front End Alignment
C677	C706	C745	C777	C816	C858	C926	C977	C1028	C1080	C1141	Front Suspension
C669	—	C737	—	C810	C848	C909	—	—	—	C1126	Fuel Filter
C671	C702	C738	C770	C808	—	C914	C967	C1016	C1069	C1127	Fuel Injection
C671	—	—	C771	C809	—	C914	—	C1018	C1069	C1128	Fuel Injectors
C669	C702	C737	—	C807	C848	C910	C966	C1016	C1066	C1126	Fuel Pump
C669	C702	C737	—	C807	C848	C909	C966	C1016	C1066	C1126	Fuel System
C680	C714	C750	C782	C820	—	C940	C982	C1038	C1088	C1150	Fuse Box
C680	C712	C749	C780	C819	C862	C936	C981	C1036	C1086	C1148	Heater
C653	C691	C721	C758	C789	C832	C880	C948	C991	C1049	C1099	Idle Speed and Mixture
C679	C709	C748	C779	C820	C860	C931	C979	C1032	C1083	C1143	Ignition Lock and Switch
C652	C688	C720	C757	C788	C831	C878	C947	C990	C1048	C1097	Ignition Timing
C680	C714	C750	C781	C820	C864	C939	C982	C1037	C1088	C1150	Instrument Cluster
C660	—	C728	C764	C800	C839	C893	C956	C999	C1058	C1110	Intake Manifold
—	C708	C746	C777	C816	C859	C929	C978	C1030	C1080	C1141	Lower Control Arm
C677	C705	C745	C778	—	C858	C926	C977	C1028	C1080	C1141	MacPherson Strut R & I
U201	U201	U201	U201	—	U201	U201	U201	U201	U201	U201	MacPherson Strut Overhaul

(Continued on next page)

INDEX

R & I: Removal and Installation

Peugeot	Porsche 911, 912, 914, 930	Porsche 924, 928, 944	Renault	SAAB	Subaru	Toyota	Triumph	Volkswagen Rear Wheel Drive	Volkswagen Front Wheel Drive	Volvo	
U5	U5	U5	U5	U5	U5	U5	U5	U5	U5	U5	Maintenance
C679	C709	C748	C779	C818	C860	C932	C979	C1033	C1083	C1143	Manual Steering Gear
—	C702	C741	C772	C812	C850	C914	—	C1023	C1070	—	Manual Transaxle R & I
—	U141	U141	U141	U141	U141	U141	—	U141	U141	—	Manual Transaxle Overhaul
C672	—	—	—	—	—	C914	C969	—	—	C1133	Manual Transmission R & I
U49	—	—	—	—	—	U49	U49	—	—	U49	Manual Transmission Overhaul
C680	C710	C749	C780	C819	C861	C934	C980	C1034	C1085	C1146	Master Cylinder R & I
U215	U215	U215	U215	U215	U215	U215	U215	U215	U215	U215	Master Cylinder Overhaul
C675	—	C742	C774	C814	C852	C918	C972	—	C1075	C1137	Neutral Safety Switch
C666	—	C733	C767	—	C842	C902	C959	C1010	C1061	C1117	Oil Pan
C666	—	C734	C767	C803	C842	C903	C960	C1009	C1062	C1119	Oil Pump
C666	—	C733	C767	C803	C842	C902	C960	C1010	C1062	C1118	Oil Seal
C680	C711	C749	C780	C819	C861	C935	C980	C1036	C1086	C1147	Parking Brake
C664	—	C732	C766	C802	C841	—	C959	C1001	C1060	C1117	Piston and Connecting Rod
C679	—	—	—	C818	C860	—	—	—	—	C1144	Power Steering Gear
C679	—	—	—	C818	C860	C932	—	—	—	C1144	Power Steering Pump
C680	—	C749	C781	C820	C863	C937	C982	—	—	C1149	Radio
—	—	—	C775	C815	C854	C922	—	—	—	C1139	Rear Axle
C666	—	C733	C767	C803	C842	C902	C960	C1010	C1062	C1118	Rear Main Oil Seal
C677	C704	C743	C775	C815	C856	C924	C975	C1025	C1078	C1140	Rear Suspension
C657	C693	—	C761	C796	C834	C883	C951	C995	—	C1102	Regulator
C659	C694	—	C764	—	C839	C893	C955	C999	—	C1110	Rocker Shafts
C643	C681	C715	C751	C783	C821	C865	C941	C983	C1039	C1089	Serial Numbers
C677	C705	C744	C777	C815	C857	C925	C976	C1027	C1079	C1140	Shock Absorber
C649	C687	C720	C756	C788	C830	C877	C946	C988	C1045	C1096	Spark Plugs
C643	C682	C715	C752	C785	C825	C866	C942	C984	C1040	C1090	Specifications
C677	C704	—	C777	C816	—	C924	C975	C1027	C1078	C1140	Springs
C657	C692	C724	C761	C796	C835	C884	C951	C996	C1053	C1103	Starter
C679	C708	C747	C779	C818	C859	C931	C979	C1032	C1082	C1143	Steering
—	—	C735	C768	—	C843	C904	C961	C1013	C1062	C1121	Thermostat
—	—	C729	—	—	—	C897	—	C1007	C1058	C1112	Timing Belt
C660	—	C729	C765	—	C840	C896	C956	C1007	C1058	C1112	Timing Belt/Chain Cover
C661	—	—	C765	C800	—	C897	C957	—	—	C1114	Timing Chain/Tensioner
—	C702	C741	C772	C812	C850	C914	—	C1023	C1070	—	Transaxle
U275	U275	U275	U275	U275	U275	U275	U275	U275	U275	U275	Troubleshooting
C649	C687	C720	C756	C788	C830	C877	C946	C988	C1045	C1096	Tune-Up
C660	—	C728	—	C811	—	—	—	—	—	C1111	Turbocharger R & I
U45	U45	U45	U45	U45	—	—	—	—	—	U45	Turbocharger Service
C679	C709	C748	C779	C818	C859	C931	C979	C1032	C1083	C1143	Turn Signal Switch
—	—	—	—	—	—	C920	C972	C1024	—	C1138	U-Joints
—	—	—	C777	C816	—	C930	C978	C1030	—	—	Upper Control Arm
C652	C690	C721	C758	C788	C831	C879	C947	C990	C1049	C1097	Valve Adjustment
C643	C681	C715	C751	C783	C821	C865	C941	C983	C1039	C1089	Vehicle Identification
C657	C693	—	C761	C796	C834	C883	C951	C995	—	C1102	Voltage Regulator
C667	—	C734	C768	C804	C843	C903	C961	C1013	C1062	C1119	Water Pump
C679	C708	C747	C779	C817	C859	C930	C979	C1032	C1081	C1143	Wheel Alignment
C679	C711	C747	—	C817	—	C934	C980	C1034	C1081	C1147	Wheel Bearings (Front)
C676	C711	—	—	C815	C855	—	C980	—	—	C1139	Wheel Bearings (Rear)
C680	—	—	—	—	—	C935	C980	C1035	C1086	—	Wheel Cylinders
C680	C713	C750	C781	C820	C864	C938	C981	C1037	C1087	C1149	Windshield Wipers

ACKNOWLEDGMENTS

AB Volvo, Göteborg, Sweden

American Honda Motor Company, Moorestown, New Jersey

American Isuzu Motors, Inc., Whittier, California

A Pierburg Auto- & Luftfahrt/Geratebau KG (Zenith Carburetors), Neuss-Rhein, Germany

Arnolt Corporation (Solex Carburetors), Warsaw, Indiana

BMW of North America, Inc., Montvale, New Jersey

Champion Spark Plug Company, Toledo, Ohio

Chicago Rawhide Mfg. Company (Fuel/Water Separators), Elgin, Illinois

Chrysler Motors Corporation, Detroit, Michigan

Fiat Motors of North America, Inc., Montvale, New Jersey

Ford Motor Company, Dearborn, Michigan

Gabriel Division, Maremont Corporation, Carol Stream, Illinois

Jaguar, Rover, Triumph, Ltd., Leonia, New Jersey

Lincoln-Mercury Division, Ford Motor Company (Capri), Dearborn, Michigan

Mazda Motors of America, Inc., Compton, California

Mercedes-Benz of North America, Inc., Montvale, New Jersey

Mitsubishi Motor Sales, Inc., Fountain Valley, California

Nissan Motor Corporation of USA, Carson, California

Peugeot, Inc., Clifton, New Jersey

Porsche-Audi, Division of Volkswagen of America, Inc., Englewood Cliffs, New Jersey

Racor Industries (Fuel/Water Separators), Modesto, California

Renault, Inc., Detroit, Michigan

Robert Bosch Corporation, Long Island City, New York

SAAB-Scania, New Haven, Connecticut

Shockley Motors Volkswagen, Devon, Pennsylvania

Subaru of America, Inc., Pennsauken, New Jersey

Toyo Kogyo, Ltd., Hiroshima, Japan

Toyota Motor Sales, USA, Inc., Torrance, California

Volkswagen of America, Inc., Englewood Cliffs, New Jersey

Volvo Inc., Rockleigh, New Jersey

Audi

SERIAL NUMBER IDENTIFICATION

Vehicle

100 and 5000

The chassis number is on the plate on top of the instrument panel, clearly visible through the driver's side of the windshield. It is also stamped into the upper right corner of the firewall. The vehicle identification plate is mounted on the right wheel housing. The chassis number follows the words "Fahrgest.-Nr." on this plate.

4000

The vehicle identification number (VIN) is located on the left (driver's side) windshield pillar and in the engine compartment on the ledge.

Fox

The chassis number is on a plate on the left windshield pillar, clearly visible through the driver's side of the windshield. It is also stamped into the top center of the firewall. The vehicle identification plate is on the right wheel housing. The chassis number follows the words "Fahrgest.-Nr." on this plate.

Engine

100 and 5000

The engine number is stamped on the left side of the engine block (clutch housing).

In addition to the engine number, an engine code number is also stamped on the starter end of the cylinder block, just below

the cylinder head. This number indicates the exact cylinder bore of the particular engine.

4000

The engine number is located on the left side of the cylinder block, below the cylinder head and next to the distributor.

Fox

The engine number is stamped on the left side of the engine block, just above the fuel pump.

In addition to the engine number, an engine code number is also stamped into the left front side of the cylinder block, just above the water pump. This number indicates the exact cylinder bore of the particular engine.

GENERAL ENGINE SPECIFICATIONS

Year and Model	Engine Displacement Cu. In. (cc)	Fuel Delivery	Horsepower @ rpm	Torque @ rpm (ft. lbs.)	Bore × Stroke (in.)	Compression Ratio	Normal Oil Pressure (psi)①
'76–'77 100	114.2 (1871)	F.I.	92 @ 5500	106 @ 3300	3.31 × 3.32	8.0:1	14–85
'76–'79 Fox	97 (1588)	F.I.	79 @ 5500	89 @ 3300	3.13 × 3.15	8.0:1	64–74
'80 4000	97 (1588)	F.I.	78 @ 5500 (76 Calif.)	84 @ 3200 (83 Calif.)	3.13 × 3.15	8.0:1	28②
'81–'83 4000	105 (1715)	F.I.	74 @ 5000	89.6 @ 3000	3.13 × 3.40	8.0:1③	28②
'82–'83 4000 Diesel	97 (1588)	F.I.	52 @ 4800	71.5 @ 2000	3.01 × 3.40	23.0:1	28②

C1

GENERAL ENGINE SPECIFICATIONS

Year and Model	Engine Displacement Cu. In. (cc)	Fuel Delivery	Horsepower @ rpm	Torque @ rpm (ft. lbs.)	Bore × Stroke (in.)	Compression Ratio	Normal Oil Pressure (psi)①
'82–'83 4000 Turbo-Diesel	97 (1588)	F.I.	68 @ 4500	98 @ 2800	3.01 × 3.40	23.0:1	N.A.
'80–'83 Coupe (4000 5 cyl.)	130.8 (2144)	F.I.	100 @ 5100	112.3 @ 3000	3.12 × 3.40	8.0:1③	14–75
'78–'83 5000	130.8 (2144)	F.I.	103 @ 5500④ (100 Calif.)	110 @ 4000⑤	3.13 × 3.40	8.0:1③	14–75⑥
'79–'81 5000 Diesel	121 (1986)	F.I.	67 @ 4800	86.4 @ 3000	3.09 × 3.40	23.0:1	28②
'82–'83 5000 Turbo–Diesel	121 (1986)	F.I.	84 @ 4500	127 @ 2800	3.01 × 3.40	23.0:1	N.A.
'80–'83 Turbo	130.8 (2144)	F.I.	130 @ 5400	142 @ 3000	3.12 × 3.40	7.0:1	N.A.
'82–'83 Quattro	130.8 (2144)	F.I.	156 @ 5500	181 @ 3000	3.12 × 3.40	7.0:1	N.A.

N.A.—Not available at time of publication
① Idle—5,500 rpm
② Min @ 2,000 rpm
③ 1982–83: 8.2:1
④ 1980–83: 100 @ 5,100
⑤ 1980–81: 122.3 @ 4,000
   1982–83: 112.3 @ 3,000
⑥ 1978: 14–85

DIESEL ENGINE TUNE-UP SPECIFICATIONS

Model/ Year	Engine Displacement Cu. In. (cc)	Warm Valve Clear (in) In	Warm Valve Clear (in) Ex	Intake Valve Opens (deg)	Injection Pump Setting (deg)	Injection Nozzle Pressure (psi) New	Injection Nozzle Pressure (psi) Used	Idle Speed (rpm)	Compression Pressure (psi)
'79–'81 5000 Diesel	121 (1,986)	.008–.012	.016–.020	N.A.	Align Marks	1849	1706	700–800	398–483
'82–'83 5000 Turbo-Diesel	121 (1,986)	.008–.012	.016–.020	N.A.	Align Marks	2248	2098	700–800	398–483
'82–'83 4000 Diesel	97 (1,588)	.008–.012	.016–.020	N.A.	Align Marks	1885	1740	770-870	398–483
'82–'83 4000 Turbo-Diesel	97 (1,588)	.008–.012	.016–.020	N.A.	Align Marks	2248	2098	900–1000	398–483

GASOLINE ENGINE TUNE-UP SPECIFICATIONS

Year and Model	Engine Displacement Cu. In. (cc)	Spark Plugs Type	Spark Plugs Gap (in.)	Distributor Point Dwell (deg)	Distributor Point Gap (in)	Ignition Timing (deg)	Intake Valve Opens (deg)	Pressure Fuel Pump (psi)	Idle Speed (rpm)	Valve Clear (in.) In	Valve Clear (in.) Ex
'76–'77 100	114.2 (1,871)	N7Y	.027–.035	44–50	.016	6A @ Idle	5B	4.8–5.4	850–1000	.008–.010	.016–.018
'76–'79 Fox	97 (1,588)	N8Y	.028	44–50	.016	3A @ Idle	4B	4.8–5.4	850–1000	.008–.012	.016–.020

GASOLINE ENGINE TUNE-UP SPECIFICATIONS

Year and Model	Engine Displacement Cu. In. (cc)	Spark Plugs Type	Spark Plugs Gap (in.)	Distributor Point Dwell (deg)	Distributor Point Gap (in)	Ignition Timing (deg)	Intake Valve Opens (deg)	Pressure Fuel Pump (psi)	Idle Speed (rpm)	Valve Clear (in.) In	Valve Clear (in.) Ex
'80 4000	97 (1,588)	N8Y ①	.028	44–50②	.016②	3A @ Idle	4B	64–74	850–1000 ③	.008–.012	.016–.020
'81–'83 4000	105 (1,715)	N8Y ①	.028	ELECTRONIC		3A @ Idle	6B	64–74	850–1000 ③	.008–.012	.016–.020
'80–'83 Coupe (4000 5 cyl)	130.8 (2,144)	N8Y ①	.028 ⑤	ELECTRONIC		3A @ Idle⑦	6B	64–74	850–1000 ④	.008–.012	.016–.020
'78–'83 5000	130.8 (2,144)	N8Y	.035 ⑥	ELECTRONIC⑧		3A @ Idle⑦	6B	64–74	850–1000 ④	.008–.012	.016–.020
'80–'83 Turbo	130.8 (2,144)	N8Y	.028	ELECTRONIC		21B @ 3,000	N.A.	72–82	880–1000	.008–.012	.016–.020
'82–'83 Quattro	130.8 (2,144)	SEE UNDERHOOD SPECIFICATIONS STICKER									

NOTE: The underhood specifications sticker often reflects tune-up specification changes made in production. Sticker figures must be used if they disagree with those in this chart.
N.A. Not available at time of publication
IN Intake
EX Exhaust
A After top dead center
B Before top dead center
① Calif: N8GY
② Calif: Electronic ignition system; not adjustable

③ Calif: 920–960
④ 1980–81 Calif: 880–1000
   1982–83 All: 775–925
⑤ 1980: .035
⑥ 1981–83: .028
⑦ 1982–83: 6B @ idle
⑧ 1978–80 models have adjustable air gap; set to .01 in.

FIRING ORDERS

FIRING ORDER 1-3-4-2

100

FIRING ORDER 1-3-4-2

Fox and 4000 (4 cyl)

FIRING ORDER 1-2-4-5-3

Coupe (4000 5 cyl), 5000 and Quattro

CAPACITIES

Year/ Model	Engine Displacement cu.in.(cc)	Crankcase (qts) With Filter	Crankcase (qts) Without Filter	Transmission (pts) Manual 4-spd	Transmission (pts) Manual 5-spd	Transmission (pts) Automatic	Gasoline Tank (gals)	Cooling System (qts)
'76–'77 100	114.2 (1,871)	4.3	—	4.2	—	6.0	15.3	8

CAPACITIES

| Year/Model | Engine Displacement cu.in.(cc) | Crankcase (qts) | | Transmission (pts) | | | Gasoline Tank (gals) | Cooling System (qts) |
| | | With Filter | Without Filter | Manual | | Automatic | | |
				4-spd	5-spd			
'76–'79 Fox	97 (1,588)	3.7	3.2	3.4	—	6.4	12.0	6.3
'80–'83 4000	105 (1,715)	3.7	3.2	3.4	3.4	6.4	15.9	7.4
'80–'83 Coupe (4000 5cyl)	130.8 (2,144)	4.8	4.3	—	5.5	6.4	15.9	8.6
'82–'83 4000 Diesel/Turbo-Diesel	97 (1,588)	3.7	3.2	—	3.4	6.4	15.9	6.6
'78–'83 5000	130.8 (2,144)	4.8	4.3	3.4	5.2①	6.4	19.8②	8.6
'79–'83 5000 Diesel/Turbo-Diesel	121 (1,986)	4.8	4.3	—	5.2①	6.4	19.8	9.9
'80–'83 Turbo	130.8 (2,144)	4.8	4.3	—	—	6.4	19.8	9.9
'82–'83 Quattro	130.8 (2,144)	4.8	4.3	—	5.5	—	23.8	9.8

① 1980–83: 5.5
② 1978: 15.9

CRANKSHAFT AND CONNECTING ROD SPECIFICATIONS

(All measurements are given in inches)

| Year/Model | Crankshaft | | | | Connecting Rod | | |
	Main Brg. Journal Dia.①	Main Brg. Oil Clearance	Shaft End-Play	Thrust on No.	Journal Diameter①	Oil Clearance	Side Clearance
'76–'77 100	2.3622	.0020–.0040	.003–.007	3	1.8898	.001–.003	.004–.009
'76–'79 Fox	2.1260	.0010–.0030	.003–.007	3	1.8110	.0011–.0034	.010
'80 4000	2.1587	.0010–.0030	.003–.007	3	1.8387	.0011–.0034	.015
'81–'83 4000	2.1247	.001–.003	.003–.007	3	1.8098	.0011–.0034	.015
'82–'83 4000 Diesels	2.1248	.001–.003	.003–.007	3	1.8807	.0011–.0034	.014
'78–'83 5000, Coupe (4000 5 cyl), Turbo, Quattro	2.2834	.0006–.0030	.003–.007	4	1.8110	.0006–.0020	.016
'79–'83 5000 Diesels	2.3187	.0006–.0030	.003–.007	4	1.9107	.005–.0024	.015

① Standard size

VALVE SPECIFICATIONS

Model	Seat Angle (deg)	Face Angle (deg)	Stem to Guide Clearance (in.) Intake	Exhaust	Stem Diameter (in.) Intake	Exhaust
100	45	45°15′	0.001	0.002	0.3507	0.3499
Fox, 4000 & 5000 (All)	45	45	0.039① MAX.	0.051 MAX.	0.3140	0.3130

NOTE: Valve guides are removable.
① 5000 Diesel: 0.051

TORQUE SPECIFICATIONS
(All readings in ft. lbs.)

Year/ Model	Cylinder Head Bolts*	Rod Bearing Bolts①	Main Bearing Bolts	Crankshaft Pulley Bolt	Flywheel-To- Crankshaft Bolts	Manifold Intake	Exhaust
'76–'77 100	65	25–31	58②	130–180	65	18	18
'76–'83 Fox, 4000	54③	25④	47	58	36⑤	18	18
'82–'83 4000 Diesels	54③	33	47	58⑧	54	18	18
'78–'83 5000, Coupe (4000 5 cyl), Turbo, Quattro	54③	36⑥	47	250	54	18	18
'79–'81 5000 Diesel	65⑦	33	47	253	54	18	18

* Cold
① Use new bolts
② 24 ft. lbs. on No. 5
③ In sequence: 1) 29 ft. lbs.; 2) 43 ft. lbs.; 3) 54 ft. lbs. and $\frac{1}{4}$ turn (90°) more
④ 1981 and later: 33 ft. lbs.
⑤ 1981 and later: 54 ft. lbs.
⑥ Turbo and Quattro: 47 ft. lbs.
⑦ 1979–80: In sequence: 1) 35 ft. lbs.; 2) 50 ft. lbs.; 3) 65 ft. lbs. and $\frac{1}{4}$ turn (90°) more
1981–83: same as ③
⑧ Replacement bolt and washer: 108 ft. lbs.

PISTON AND RING SPECIFICATIONS
(All measurements in inches)

Year/ Model	Piston Clearance	Ring Gap Top Compression	Bottom Compression	Oil Control	Ring Side Clearance Top Compression	Bottom Compression	Oil Control
'76–'77 100	.0010	.039	.039	.039	.0060	.0060	.0060
'76–'83 Fox, 4000	.0011	.012–.018	.012–.018	.012–.018①	.0008–.002	.0008–.002	.0008–.002
'82–'83 4000 Diesels	.0011	.012–.020	.012–.020	.010–.016	.002–.004	.002–.003	.001–.002
'78–'83 5000, 4000 (5 cyl), Turbo, Quattro	.0011	.010–.020	.010–.020	.010–.020	.0008–.003	.0008–.003	.0008–.003

PISTON AND RING SPECIFICATIONS

(All measurements in inches)

Year/ Model	Piston Clearance	Ring Gap			Ring Side Clearance		
		Top Compression	Bottom Compression	Oil Control	Top Compression	Bottom Compression	Oil Control
'79–'83 5000 Diesels	.0011	.012–.020	.012–.020	.010–.016 ①	.002–.0035	.002–.003	.001–.002

NOTE: Three oversizes of pistons are available to accommodate overbores of up to .040 in.
① Fox: .010–.016

TORQUE SEQUENCES

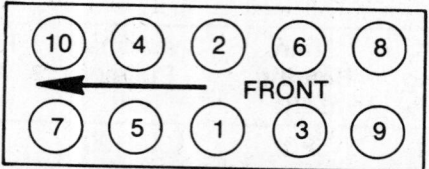

4000 cylinder head tightening sequence

100 cylinder head tightening sequence

Fox cylinder head tightening sequence

Coupe (4000 5 cyl), 5000 and Quattro cylinder head tightening sequence

BRAKE SPECIFICATIONS

(All measurements given are in. unless noted)

Model	Lug Nut Torque (ft. lbs.)	Master Cylinder Bore	Brake Disc ③		Brake Drum			Minimum Lining Thickness	
			Minimum Thickness	Maximum Run-Out	Diameter	Max. Machine O/S	Max. Wear Limit	Front	Rear
'76–'77 100	85	0.813①	0.36 ②	0.002	7.870	7.890	7.910	0.078	0.098
'76–'83 Fox, 4000	65	0.825	0.413②	0.002	7.870	7.890	7.910	0.078	0.098

BRAKE SPECIFICATIONS

(All measurements given are in. unless noted)

Model	Lug Nut Torque (ft. lbs.)	Master Cylinder Bore	Brake Disc③		Brake Drum			Minimum Lining Thickness	
			Minimum Thickness	Maximum Run-Out	Diameter	Max. Machine O/S	Max. Wear Limit	Front	Rear
'78–'83 5000 (all but Turbo and Quattro)	80	0.875	0.807	0.004	10.157	9.005	9.094	0.078	0.098
'80–'83 Turbo and Quattro	80	0.875	0.807	0.002	9.645④	0.335⑤	0.002⑥	0.551	0.472

NOTE: Minimum lining thickness is as recommended by the manufacturer. Due to variations in state inspection regulations, the minimum allowable thickness may be different than recommended by the manufacturer.

①0.874 — 1976–77
②With ventilated discs — 0.768 after refinishing 0.728 in. —discard thickness
③Federal law requires that the minimum rotor thickness be stamped in the disc
④Rear disc diameter
⑤Rear disc min. thickness
⑥Rear disc max. runout

WHEEL ALIGNMENT

Model	Caster		Camber		Toe-in (in.)	Wheel Pivot Ratio	
	Range (deg)	Pref Setting (deg)	Range (deg)	Pref Setting (deg)		Inner Wheel	Outer Wheel
'76–'77 100 LS	0°11'N to 0°29'P	0°0'	0°20'N to 0°20'P	0°	0.00	20	19°40' to 20°20'
'76–'77 100 LS, Power Steering	0°19'P to 0°59'P	0°39'	0°20'N to 0°20'P	0°	0.00	20	19°40' to 20°20'
'76–'77 Fox	0 to 1P	0°30'P	0°5'P to 0°55'P③	0°30'P②	0.00–0.08	20	18°36' to 19°36'
'78–'79 Fox	0 to 1P	½P	0 to 1P	½P	1/16 to 1/8①	20	18°36' to 19°36'
'80–'83 4000 (all)	0–1'P	30'P	1°10'N to 10'N	40'N	0–20'P	—	—
'78–'83 5000 (all)	5/6N to ½P	1/6N	1N to 0	½N	1/8 out to 1/16 in	—	—
'80–'83 Turbo④	30'P to 1°50'P	1°10'P	1°N to 0	30'N	5'P to 10'N	—	—

N Negative
P Positive
— Not Available
①Toe-out

②0°30'N (Rear wheel) not adjustable
③In-0° (Rear wheel) not adjustable
④Quattro specifications not available at time of publication

TUNE-UP PROCEDURES

All the tune-up steps should be followed, as each adjustment complements the effects of the other adjustments. If the tune-up specifications sticker in the engine compartment disagrees with the "Tune-up Specifications" chart, the sticker figures must be followed.

Spark Plugs

1. Disconnect each saprk plug wire by pulling on the rubber cap, not on the wire.
2. Wipe the wires clean with a cloth dampened in kerosene and wipe them dry. If the wires appear to be cracked, they should be replaced.
3. Blow or brush the dirt away from each of the spark plugs.
4. Remove each spark plug with a spark plug socket. Be careful that the socket is all the way down on the plug to prevent it from slipping and cracking the porcelain insulator.
5. Evaluate the condition of the plugs. In general, a tan or medium gray color on the business end of the plug indicates normal combustion conditions. Refer to the "Tune-Up Specifications" chart for the proper spark plug type.
6. If the plugs are to be reused, file the center and side electrodes with a small, fine file. It is often suggested that plugs be tested and cleaned on a service station sandblast-

Check the spark plugs with a wire feeler gauge

ing machine; however, this piece of equipment is becoming rare. Check the gap between the two electrodes with a spark plug gap gauge. The round wire type is the most accurate. If the gap is not as specified, use the adjusting device on the gap gauge to bend the outside electrode to correct. Be careful not to bend the electrode too far, because excessive bending may cause it to weaken and possibly fall off into the engine. This would require cylinder head removal to reach the broken piece, and could result in cylinder wall and ring damage.

7. Clean the plug threads with a wire brush. Crank the engine with the starter to blow out any dirt particles from the cylinder head threads.

8. Put a drop of oil on the threads and screw the plugs in finger tight. Tighten them with the plug socket. If a torque wrench is available, tighten them to 22 ft. lbs.

9. Reinstall the wires. If there is any doubt as to their proper locations, refer to "Firing Order."

Breaker Points and Condenser

FOX, 100 AND 1980 4000 (49 STATES ONLY)

The condenser should be replaced each time the points are replaced. After every breaker point adjustment or replacement, the ignition timing must be checked and, if necessary, adjusted. No special equipment other than a feeler gauge is required for point replacement or adjustment, although a dwell meter should be used to ensure the accuracy of the adjustment.

1. Detach the two spring clips securing the distributor cap. Remove the cap.

2. Clean the cap inside and out. Check for cracks and carbon paths. A carbon path shows up as a dark line, usually from one of the cap sockets or inside terminals to a ground. Check the condition of the button inside the center of the cap and the four inside terminals. Replace the cap if necessary.

3. Pull the rotor up and off the shaft. Clean off the metal end if it is burned or corroded. Replace the rotor if necessary. Remove the dust cap, if there is one.

4. The manufacturer states that the points must be replaced, not reconditioned. Experience also shows that it is more economical and reliable in the long run to replace the point set while the distributor is open, than to have to do this at a later (and possibly more inconvenient) time.

5. Pull the flat plug terminal on the wire from the point set. Remove the point set hold-down screw, being very careful not to drop it into the inside of the distributor. If this happens, the distributor will probably have to be removed to get at the screw. If the screw is lost elsewhere, it must be replaced with one that is no longer than the original to avoid interference with distributor workings. Remove the point set.

Lubricate at (1) with a drop of oil and at (2) with a high melting point grease

6. Remove the condenser by removing the screw and pulling the assembly out. Detach the lead from the coil. The condenser, wire, flat plug connection, and plastic sealing boot are a single assembly.

7. Install the new condenser, attaching the lead to the coil.

8. Apply a small amount of high melting point grease to the pivot side of the point set rubbing block.

9. Replace the point set and tighten the screw tightly. Replace the flat plug terminals.

10. Check that the contacts meet squarely. If they do not, bend the tab supporting the fixed contact.

11. Turn the engine until a high point on the cam that opens the points contacts the rubbing block on the point arm. This is easier if the spark plugs have been removed.

12. There is a screwdriver slot and two raised lugs near the contacts. Insert a screwdriver and lever the points open or closed until they appear to be open about the correct gap.

13. Insert the correct size feeler gauge and adjust the gap with the screwdriver until you can push the gauge in and out between the contacts with a slight drag but without moving the point arm. Another check is to try the gauges 0.001–0.002 in. larger and smaller than the setting size. The larger one should disturb the point arm, whereas

Adjust the point gap with a screwdriver

the smaller one should not drag at all. Tighten the point set hold-down screw snugly. Recheck the gap, because it often changes when the screw is tightened.

14. After all the point adjustments are complete, pull a white business card through (between) the contacts to remove any traces of oil. Oil will cause rapid point burning.

15. Replace the dust cap.

16. Push the rotor firmly down into place. It will go on only one way. If it is not installed properly, it will probably break when the starter is operated.

17. Replace the distributor cap and install the spring clip.

18. Check the dwell with a meter. Dwell can be checked with the engine running or cranking. Decrease dwell by increasing the point gap; increase by decreasing the gap. Dwell angle is simply the number of degrees of distributor shaft rotation during which the points stay closed. Theoretically, if the point gap is correct, the dwell should also be correct or nearly so. However, dwell is a more accurate setting. If dwell varies more than 3 degrees from idle speed to 2500 engine rpm, the distributor is worn.

NOTE: Some tachometers, dwell meters, and oscilloscopes will not work with the capacitive discharge ignition system. Some may be damaged. Check with the manufacturer of your test equipment if there is any doubt.

19. Start the engine. If it won't start, check:

   a. That all the spark plug wires are in place.

   b. That the rotor has been installed.

   c. That the wire inside the distributor is connected.

   d. That the points open and close when the engine turns.

   e. That the gap is correct and the hold-down screw is tight.

   f. That the condenser lead to the coil is attached.

20. After the first 200 miles on a new set of points, the point gap often closes up due to initial rubbing block wear. For best performance, recheck the gap or dwell at this time.

21. Since changing the point gap affects the ignition timing setting, the timing should

be checked and adjusted if necessary after each point replacement or adjustment.

Electronic Ignition

With the exception of the Fox and the 1980 4000 (49 state), all gasoline engined Audis from 1978 are equipped with electronic ignition. Audi has used two different types of electronic ignition systems from 1978–80. The 5000 has used an electronic ignition system that consisted of a distributor with an impulse generator, an ignition coil and an electronic control unit. As of 1981, all Audis use an electronic ignition system with a Hall generator instead of an impulse generator. The Hall generator was also used on the 4000 (Calif.), the 5000 Turbo and the 4000 (5 cyl.) in 1980.

Because no points or condenser are used and the dwell is determined by the control unit, no adjustments are necessary. Ignition timing is checked in the usual way, but unless the distributor has been disturbed it is unlikely to change.

Service consists of an inspection of the distributor cap, rotor and ignition wires. In addition, the air gap between the impulse rotor and the permanent magnet should be checked periodically. The air gap on the models equipped with a Hall generator is not adjustable.

AIR GAP ADJUSTMENT

1978–80 5000

1. Release the two clips with a screwdriver and remove the distributor cap.
2. Remove the ignition rotor (not the impulse rotor) by pulling straight up.
3. Rotate the engine by the starter or by turning a wrench on the crankshaft pulley bolt and align the impulse rotor tooth with the tooth on the permanent magnet.
4. Using a non-metallic gauge, the gap should measure 0.010 in. (.25 mm). If adjustment is necessary, carefully bend the tooth on the impulse rotor until the proper gap is achieved.

Checking the air gap on the impulse generator; the arrow indicates the feeler gauge

Ignition Timing

STATIC

A basic timing adjustment can be made in the following manner. Turn the engine until the basic ignition timing mark is aligned with the ignition timing pointer and the distributor rotor points towards the No. 1 cylinder mark on the rim of the distributor body. Timing marks are on the flywheel on the 4000, 5000 and Fox, and the crankshaft pulley on the other models. This will put No. 1 cylinder at TDC (0°T). Connect a 12 volt test lamp between the ignition coil terminal, No. 1 connected to the distributor clockwise until the lamp goes out. Turn the distributor counterclockwise until the lamp just lights, and tighten the clamp on the distributor at that point. The ignition timing is now approximately set. As soon as possible, check the adjustment with a timing light.

The distributor rotor (L) aligned with the No. 1 cylinder mark (M) on the rim of the distributor body. The dust cap is removed

DYNAMIC

To check with a timing light, connect a timing light to No. 1 cylinder and connect a tachometer.

NOTE: Some tachometers, dwellmeters, and oscilloscopes will not work with the capacitive discharge ignition system. Some may be damaged. Check with the manufacturer of your test equipment if there is any doubt.

Loosen the distributor clamp screw until it is just possible to turn the distributor by hand. Run the engine at idle speed and point the timing light at the pulley (flywheel on the 4000, 5000 Quattro and Fox). Turn the distributor until the specified notch (on the flywheel or pulley) aligns with the pointer. Disconnect the vacuum hoses and on most 1981 and later models the idle stabilizer must be bypassed. To bypass the idle stabilizer, disconnect its two electrical leads

100 series timing marks

Fox timing marks—5000 series similar

Bypass the idle stabilizer unit by connecting the two plugs together (arrow)

and plug them together. This must be done with the ignition turned off or it could ruin the entire system. Check the timing at 2500, 2750 or 3000 rpm if specified. Adjust as necessary.

NOTE: Certain late models have an impedance transformer installed on top of the ignition control unit in place of an idle stabilizer. DO NOT disconnect plugs of the transformer when setting timing.

NOTE: Timing should always be checked both at idle and at 2500, 2750 or 3000 rpm if specified.

Valve Lash

ADJUSTMENT

100

The valve clearance should be adjusted in firing order, with the engine at normal operating temperature. See the specifications for the proper clearances. Remove the air filter and rocker cover. Set the engine at TDC on No. 1 cylinder by aligning the 0°T mark on the crankshaft pulley with the timing cover pointer and aligning the distributor rotor with the No. 1 cylinder mark on the rim of the distributor body. Turn the engine in the normal direction of rotation. The valve clearance of cylinder No. 1 should be adjusted when the valves of No. 4 cylinder overlap, i.e. when both arms move in opposite directions simultaneously. When

100 Series valve location: "A" equals intake; "E" equals exhaust. The arrow points forward.

Tach. Conv. Chart.

Use this chart to convert the 4-cylinder tachometer reading to the true idle speed on 5-cylinder 5000 models

this occurs, the exhaust valve is closing and the intake opening.

Adjust as follows:

1. Valve clearance of cylinder No. 3 at overlap of cylinder No. 2
2. Valve clearance of cylinder No. 4 at overlap of cylinder No. 1
3. Valve clearance of cylinder No. 2 at overlap of cylinder No. 3

When making adjustments, tighten the self-locking adjustment nut until it is just possible to remove the feeler gauge.

4000, 5000, Coupe and Quattro

Audi recommends checking the valve clearance at 1000 miles and then every 15,000 miles thereafter. The overhead cam acts directly on the valves through cam followers which fit over the springs and valves. Adjustment is made with an adjusting disc which fits into the cam follower. Different thickness discs result in changes in valve clearance.

NOTE: Audi recommends that two special tools be used to remove and install the adjustment discs. One is a pry bar (VW 546) to compress the valve springs and the other a pair of special pliers (US 10-208) to remove the disc. If the purchase of these tools is not possible, a flat metal plate can be used to compress the valve springs if you are careful not to gouge the camshaft lobes. The cam follower has two slots which permit the disc to be lifted out. Again, you can improvise with a thin bladed screwdriver. An assistant to pry the spring down while you remove the disc would be the ideal way to perform the operation if you must improvise your own tools.

Checking valve clearance with a feeler gauge—4000, 5000 and Coupe

Valve clearance is checked with the engine moderately warm (coolant temperature should be about 95°F (35°C).

1. Remove the accelerator linkage, the upper drive belt cover and any hoses or lines which may be in the way.

2. Remove the cylinder head cover. Valve clearance is checked in the firing order (1-3-4-2 for the four cylinder and 1-2-4-5-3 for the five cylinder engines) with the piston of the cylinder being checked at TDC of the compression stroke. Both valves will be closed at this position and the cam lobes will be pointing straight up.

NOTE: When adjusting the clearances on the diesel engine, the pistons must not be at TDC. Turn the crankshaft ¼ turn past TDC so that the valves do not contact the pistons when the tappets are depressed.

Remove the adjusting discs with a special pry bar and pliers—don't press on the disc itself, but on the lip of the disc holder. Note the position of the camshaft lobes on no. 1 cylinder. This is the correct position for measuring valve clearance

3. Turn the crankshaft pulley bolt with a socket wrench to position the camshaft for checking.

— CAUTION —

Do not turn the camshaft by the camshaft mounting bolt, this will stretch the drive belt. When turning the crankshaft pulley bolt, turn it clockwise only.

4. With the No. 1 piston at TDC (¼ turn past for the diesel) of the compression stroke, determine the clearance with a feeler gauge. Intake clearance should be 0.008–0.012 in., exhaust clearance should be 0.016–0.020 in.

5. Continue on to check the other cylinders in the firing order, turning the crankshaft to bring each particular piston to the top of the compression stroke (¼ turn for the diesel). Record the individual clearances as you go along.

6. If measured clearance is within tolerance levels (0.002 in.), it is not necessary to replace the adjusting discs.

7. If adjustment is necessary, the discs will have to be removed and replaced with thicker or thinner ones which will yield the

Quattro, Coupe and 5000 valve location

Fox and 4000 valve location

correct clearance. Discs are available in 0.002 in. increments from 0.12 in. to 0.17 in.

NOTE: The thickness of the adjusting discs are etched on one side. When installing, the marks must face the cam followers. Discs can be reused if they are not worn or damaged.

8. To remove the discs, turn the cam followers so that the grooves are accessible when the pry bar is depressed.

9. Press the cam follower down with the pry bar and remove the adjusting discs with the special pliers or the screwdriver.

10. Replace the adjustment discs as necessary to bring the clearance within the 0.002 in. tolerance level. If the measured clearance is larger than the given tolerance, remove the existing disc and insert a thicker one to bring the clearance up to specification. If it is smaller, insert a thinner one.

11. Recheck all valve clearances after adjustment.

12. Install the cylinder head cover with a new gasket.

13. Install the accelerator linkage, the upper drive belt cover and any wires or lines which were removed.

Fox

The valve clearances should be checked in firing order, with the engine at normal operating temperature.

1. Remove the camshaft cover and the distributor cap.

2. Set the engine at TDC on No. 1 cylinder by aligning the 0°T mark on the flywheel with the pointer and aligning the distributor rotor with the No. 1 cylinder mark on the rim of the distributor body.

NOTE: Always turn the crankshaft in the normal direction of rotation. There is a hole in the body behind the front license plate through which a wrench can be used on the crankshaft.

3. The valve clearances of cylinder No. 1 should be checked when the valves of No. 4 cylinder overlap, i.e. when both No. 4 cylinder valves move in opposite directions simultaneously. You may have to move the crankshaft slightly to find this position. When this happens, the exhaust valve is closing and the intake opening. Check and note the clearance of both the intake and exhaust valves for No. 1 cylinder. Use a feeler gauge between each valve tappet and camshaft lobe.

4. Turn the crankshaft 180° (90° at the distributor rotor) in the normal direction of rotation. Check and note the valve clearances of cylinder No. 3 at the overlap position of cylinder No. 2.

5. Turn the crankshaft 180°. Check and note the valve clearances of cylinder No. 4 at the overlap position of cylinder No. 1.

6. Turn the crankshaft 180°. Check and note the valve clearances of cylinder No. 2 at the overlap position of cylinder No. 3.

7. Now the crankshaft has been turned two complete revolutions (one for the distributor rotor) and all the valve tappet-to-camshaft lobe clearances have been noted. Compare the noted clearances with those listed in the "Tune-Up Specifications" chart. Normal wear usually results in the clearances becoming too small. Adjustment is made by replacing the tappet clearance disc in the top of each tappet. These are available in 26 sizes ranging from 3.0 mm (0.119 in.) to 4.25 mm (0.166 in.) in increments of 0.05 mm (0.002 in.). The thickness of each disc is marked on the bottom.

NOTE: If a valve clearance deviates 0.–002 in. or less from the specified clearance, it need not be adjusted.

8. To remove a tappet clearance disc, turn the cylinder to TDC and press down the tappet so that the disc can be lifted out. Audi dealers have special tools that make this operation much easier. Once the disc is removed, check its size and determine what size will be needed to produce the required adjustment.

NOTE: Before depressing the tappets, turn them so their openings are at right angles to the camshaft.

9. Install the required disc and turn the tappet back to its normal direction. When all the clearances have been corrected, check them again to catch any possible error caused by worn discs.

Carburetor

IDLE SPEED ADJUSTMENT

NOTE: On later models, the idle speed should be adjusted in conjunction with the % CO. In these cases, it is suggested that the work be performed by a qualified service technician with the proper equipment.

100 and Fox

1. Operate engine at normal operating temperature.

2. With high beams on and A/C on, ignition timing set to 3A with vacuum hose connected, adjust to 850–1000 rpm.

Idle speed adjustment screw—4000 and Fox

4000 and 5000 Except Turbo and Calif. Models

NOTE: The timing must be set to specifications before adjusting the idle speed.

1. Connect a dwell/tachometer according to the manufacturer's instructions.

2. Run the engine until the oil temper-

Idle speed adjustment screw—5000

ature is above 140°F (60°C). The radiator fan must come on at least once.

3. Turn the headlights on the high beam.

4. Disconnect the PCV valve.

5. Locate the idle adjusting screw in the throttle valve housing on the back of the intake manifold and adjust the idle to specifications.

NOTE: The radiator fan must not run while adjusting the idle.

6. Adjust the % CO.

4000 and 5000 Calif. Models and Turbo

NOTE: The timing must be set to specifications before adjusting the idle speed.

1. Connect a dwell/tachometer according to the manufacturer's instructions.

2. Turn off all electrical accessories.

3. Run the engine until the oil temperature is above 175°F (80°C). The radiator fan must come on at least once.

4. Turn the ignition off.

5. Disconnect the PCV valve.

6. Disconnect the plug for the oxygen sensor wire by the manifold.

7. Unplug both wire leads at the idle stabilizer and connect them together.

8. Start the engine.

9. Locate the idle adjusting screw in the throttle valve housing on the back of the intake manifold and adjust the idle to specifications.

NOTE: The radiator fan must not run while adjusting the idle.

10. Turn off the engine and reconnect the PCV valve, the oxygen sensor wire and the idle stabilizer.

11. Recheck the idle speed. If it has changed, the idle stabilizer will probably require replacement.

12. Adjust the % CO.

Diesel

1. Place an engine RPM sensor (US 1324 or 3606) on cylinder head cover and attach to battery.

2. Connect a dwell/tachometer according to the manufacturer's instructions.

3. Run the engine until the oil temperature reaches 122–158°F (50–70°C).

4. Turn the idle speed control knob on the instrument panel counterclockwise until it stops (5000 only).

Idle speed adjustment screw—diesel

5. Locate the idle speed adjusting screw on the injection pump and adjust the idle to specifications.

6. Lock the screw and seal it with paint.

CO ADJUSTMENT

4000 and 5000

NOTE: An exhaust gas analyzer or a CO meter will be required for this procedure. These are not common, everyday tools; adjustment of the CO is impossible without one of them. If you do not have access to these tools you will have to have the adjustment made by your dealer or a service station. If you do have one of them, please read on.

1. The ignition timing and the idle speed must be properly adjusted before proceeding.

2. Disconnect the PCV valve.

3. Turn the headlights on high beam (all but Turbo and Calif. cars).

4. Turn off the ignition and disconnect the oxygen sensor wire and bypass the idle stabilizer as detailed in the "Idle Speed Adjustment" section (Turbo and Calif. cars only).

CO adjusting tool and locations—Fox and 4000

5. Hook the exhaust gas analyser to the tailpipe on all 5000 models or the CO meter to the probe receptacle on all 4000 models. The probe receptacle is located on the front of the exhaust manifold.

NOTE: The hoses must fit snugly so that there is no exhaust leakge or you will get an improper reading.

6. Remove the plug from the fuel distributor and insert the Special Tool P377.

NOTE: While adjusting the CO, the radiator fan must not come on.

7. Adjust % CO to the proper level by turning the Special Tool clockwise to raise % CO or counterclockwise to lower % CO.

---— CAUTION ———

When adjusting CO, do not push the adjusting tool down. Do not accelerate the engine with the tools in place. Remove the tool after each adjustment and accelerate the engine briefly before reading the % CO. Always adjust CO from lean to rich.

CO adjusting point—5000

8. Reconnect the PCV valve (all but Turbo and Calif. cars).

9. Readjust the idle speed if necessary (all but Turbo and Calif. cars).

The remainder of this procedure deals only with the Turbo and any Calif. cars.

10. Readjust the idle speed if necessary.

11. Reconnect the oxygen sensor wire and check that the % CO is still at the proper level.

12. Remove the exhaust gas analyzer or the CO meter, reconnect the PCV valve and adjust the idle speed if necessary.

13. Turn the ignition off and reconnect the idle stabilizer.

14. Start the engine and check the ignition timing.

15. Load the engine by switching on all electrical accessories and check that ignition timing advances. If not, the idle stabilizer will probably require replacement.

ENGINE ELECTRICAL

Distributor

REMOVAL AND INSTALLATION

100 and Fox

Remove the air cleaner. Pry back the retaining clips and remove the distributor cap. Mark the relationship between the distributor body and the engine block. Make a mark on the distributor body to denote the position of the rotor tip. Disconnect the wiring at the ignition coil. Detach the vacuum line, being careful not to damge the plastic tube. Remove the bolt at the retaining clamp and pull the distributor from the housing. If the distributor is difficult to remove, the rubber seal is probably sticking. Carefully pry the distributor loose with a screwdriver.

Distributor installation is the reverse of

removal. When installing the 100 series distributor, the projections on the shaft, at the bottom of the distributor, must engage the slots in the oil pump driveshaft. Turn the rotor slightly until the two engage. The projections and grooves have been milled off center, making it impossible to install the distributor incorrectly.

The gear-driven Fox distributor has a slot at the bottom which mates with a dog on top of the oil pump driveshaft. Lubricate the seal with a small amount of oil before installation. Align the marks made on removal, then tighten the clamp bolt.

NOTE: If the engine has been turned while the distributor was out, or if a new distributor is being installed, refer to the "Static Ignition Timing" procedure.

4000, 5000, Coupe and Quattro

1. Disconnect the wiring harness connector and any other connectors from the distributor cap.
2. Remove the static shield (if so equipped).
3. Disconnect and note the position of the vacuum lines.

Rotor/distributor alignment for the no. 1 cylinder

4. Undo the two retaining spring clips and remove the distributor cap.
5. Note the position of the rotor in relation to the base. Scribe a mark on the base of the distributor and on the engine block to facilitate reinstallation. Align the marks with the direction the metal tip of the rotor is pointing. Note the approximate position of the vacuum advance unit in relation to the engine.
6. Remove the distributor hold-down bolt and clamp.
7. Lift the distributor assembly from the engine.

To install:

1. Insert the distributor shaft and assembly into the engine.
2. Line up the marks on the distributor and on the engine with the metal tip of the rotor.
3. Make sure the vacuum advance unit is pointed in the same direction as it was pointed originally. If the marks on the distributor and the engine are lined up properly, this will be done automatically.
4. Install the distributor hold-down clamp and bolt.
5. Install and secure the distributor cap.

6. Install the vacuum lines in their original places.
7. Install the static shield.
8. Install the wiring harness connector and any other connectors previously removed.
9. Start the engine. Adjust the dwell angle (breaker point ignitions) and set the ignition timing.

NOTE: If the crankshaft has been turned or the engine has been disturbed in any manner (i.e., disassembled and rebuilt) while the distributor was removed, or if the marks were not drawn, it will be necessary to initially time the engine. Follow the procedure given below.

The oil pump driveshaft must be parallel to the crankshaft on the 4000

1. It is necessary to place the No. 1 cylinder in the firing position to correctly install the distributor. To locate this position, the ignition timing marks on the flywheel and the clutch housing are used.
2. Remove the spark plug from the No. 1 cylinder. Turn the crankshaft until the piston in the No. 1 cylinder is moving up on the compression stroke. This can be determined by placing your thumb over the spark plug hole and feeling the air being forced out of the cylinder. Stop turning the engine when the timing mark on the flywheel is aligned with the lug on the flywheel housing.
3. Remove the upper drive belt cover.
4. Align the mark on the camshaft sprocket with the upper edge of the drive belt cover or with the upper edge of the cylinder head cover gasket.
5. Align the oil pump drive pinion lug so that it is parallel to the crankshaft (4000 only).
6. Oil the distributor housing lightly where it bears on the cylinder block.
7. Install the distributor so that the rotor, which is mounted on the shaft, points to the mark on the distributor housing for the No. 1 cylinder.
8. When the distributor shaft has reached the bottom of the hole, move the rotor back and forth slightly until the drive lug on the oil pump shaft enters the slots cut into the end of the distributor shaft, and the distributor assembly slides down into place

(4000 only).
9. Clean the distributor cap and check for signs of cracking or carbon tracks. Replace the cap and continue from Step 6 of the installation procedure, engine undisturbed.

Alternator

ALTERNATOR PRECAUTIONS

All Audi models are equipped with alternators. When performing any service to the alternator or alternator system the following precautions should be observed.

A. Leads or cables to any part of the charging circuit should be disconnected only after the engine has been switched off and has stopped running.

B. When working on the electrical system, always disconnect the lead from the negative battery terminal.

C. When performing tests with the engine running, the battery must always be connected.

D. Temporary connections should never be made to the alternator. Always make firm connections.

The alternator warning light on the instrument panel should go out when the engine reaches idle speed, or shortly after.

REMOVAL AND INSTALLATION

1. Disconnect the battery ground strap.
2. Disconnect all the leads to the alternator, tagging them first. Various arrangements of plug-in or bolt-on connections have been used. On some models the wiring may be unplugged from the back of the alternator; on others, it must be unplugged at the voltage regulator on the right front wheel-housing.

NOTE: Current models have a voltage regulator built into the alternator.

3. Remove the belt tensioning bolt from the slotted adjusting bracket.
4. Remove the drive belt.
5. Unbolt and remove the alternator.

To install the unit:

6. Install the hinge bolts. On 100 models, made sure that the head of the rear bolt is to the rear of the car.
7. Install the drive belt and the belt tensioning bolt.
8. Adjust the belt tension.
9. Replace all the electrical connections, making sure that they are installed in their original locations.
10. Connect the battery ground strap.

BELT TENSION ADJUSTMENT

The alternator drive belt is correctly ten-

Exploded view of a typical alternator (w/integral regulator)

sioned when the longest span of belt between pulleys can be depressed about ½ in., by moderate thumb pressure. To adjust, loosen the slotted adjusting bracket bolt on the alternator. If the alternator hinge bolts are very tight, it may be necessary to loosen them slightly to move the alternator. Move the alternator in or out by hand to get the correct tension, then tighten the adjusting bolt.

NOTE: Be careful not to overtighten the belt, as this may damage the alternator bearings.

Regulator

The earlier models have a voltage regulator on the right front wheelhousing in the engine compartment. If there is none there, as on current models, it is built into the alternator.

REMOVAL AND INSTALLATION

To remove the regulator, disconnect the battery ground cable, disconnect the three-pronged plug, and unscrew the unit from the wheelhousing. Be careful to make a good ground connection on reinstallation. The manufacturer does not recommend any adjustments to the regulator.

Starter

REMOVAL AND INSTALLATION

100

Disconnect the battery ground lead. Remove the oil filter.

NOTE: When the oil filter is removed, a certain amount of oil will escape.

Disconnect both leads from the upper terminal of the solenoid. Remove the open cable shoe lead from the lower solenoid terminal. The screw need only be slightly opened to permit removal. Unbolt the starter from the mounting flanges and remove it forward.

Installation is the reverse of removal. Be sure that all leads are positioned correctly and are not pinched. If necessary, replace the lower mounting bolt with the head to the front of the car. Thoroughly clean the seal and oil filter sealing surface. Lightly lubricate both surfaces and tighten the oil

filter to approximately 14–18 ft. lbs. or about one turn by hand. Replace the oil that escaped and run the engine, checking the filter for leaks.

CAUTION

Some starters are equipped with an additional terminal (16) which is under full battery voltage, with a direct connection to the ignition coil. This connection bridges the ignition coil series resistor to create higher ignition voltage.

Fox, 4000 and 5000 (All)

1. Disconnect the negative battery cable.
2. Jack up the right front of the car and support it with jack stands.
3. Mark with tape and then disconnect the two small wires from the starter solenoid. One wire connects to the ignition coil and the other to the ignition switch.
4. Disconnect the large cable which comes from the battery and position it out of the way.
5. Remove the starter support bracket bolts (4000 only). Remove the starter mounting bolts from the back of the starter (all models).
6. Remove the starter.
7. Installation is in the reverse.

STARTER DRIVE REPLACEMENT

NOTE: In order to complete this procedure you will need a pair of circlip pliers and Special Tool US 1078; a gear puller.

1. Remove the starter.
2. Remove the solenoid.
3. Remove the two long housing screws and remove the end plate.
4. Lift the brushes to free them from the commutator and remove the brush holder.
5. Tap the field coil housing lightly with a wooden mallet and remove it from the starter drive housing.
6. Remove the nut and bolt that serves as a pin for the shift lever. Be careful to retain all the associated washers.
7. Remove the shift lever.
8. Slide the armature/starter drive assembly out of the starter drive housing.
9. Press the stop ring down and remove the circlip from the end of the armature shaft.
10. Remove the stop ring using the Special Tool US 1078.
11. Slide the starter drive off of the armature shaft.

To install the drive:
1. Lubricate the drive pinion lightly with multi-purpose grease and slide the starter drive onto the armature shaft.
2. Install the stop ring and press it over the circlip groove.

NOTE: When installing the stop ring, the groove must always be on the side

closest to the front of the starter (the side nearest to the starter drive).

3. Install the circlip and using the Special Tool US 1078, pull the stop ring up into place against the circlip.

4. Lightly grease the shaft.

5. Install the armature/starter drive assembly into the starter drive housing.

6. Install the shift lever.

7. Ease the field coil housing over the armature assembly and fit it into the starter drive housing.

8. Install the brush holder and the end plate.

9. Install the solenoid.

ENGINE MECHANICAL

Engine

Removal and Installation

100

The transmission and engine must be lowered from the car as a unit. The following procedure is for manual transmission cars; see "Automatic Transmission Removal and Installation" for details on items that must be disconnected on the automatic transmission.

1. Remove the hood (only if using a hoist to remove the engine).

2. Unbolt and remove the apron just below the front bumper.

3. Remove the negative connection from the battery. Remove the air cleaner and carburetor breather hose at the air filter. Drain the coolant. Disconnect all hoses between the radiator and engine and the heater and engine. Disconnect the fuel hose at the fuel pump and plug the end of the line. Remove the power brake unit vacuum hose at the intake manifold.

4. Disconnect the speedometer cable at the transmission, the clutch cable at the mount and the gearshift linkage at the transmission.

5. Disconnect the accelerator linkage at the carburetor mounting point and connecting rod, and remove the throttle shaft.

6. Separate the brake line at the body mount and plug the line to prevent loss of fluid.

7. Remove the guard plate from the right engine mount.

8. Disconnect the following electrical wiring from the engine and transmission: ignition leads, idle cut-off valve (if installed), temperature switch, four pole plug of regulator, oil pressure switch, starter connections, backup light switch and ground leads.

9. Remove the radiator and the fan support together with the fan and stop pad.

1. Mounting bracket	9. Solenoid
2. End cap screws	10. Disc
3. Housing screws	11. Mounting housing
4. Cupped washer	12. Drive pinion
5. End plate bushing	13. Stop ring
6. Brushes	14. Solenoid bolt
7. Field coil housing	15. Starter bolt and nut
8. Armature	16. Circlip

Exploded view of typical starter

When installing the 100 series engine, the distance (y) between the pulley and the front of the side member must be the same on both sides. Maximum deviation is .08 inch

When installing the 100 series engine, the distance (x) between the brake discs and the control arms must be the same on both sides. Maximum deviation is .08 inch

NOTE: This operation is only necessary if working with a frame contact hoist or in a pit where the opening in the pit is not large enough to permit lowering the engine with the fan attached. If the opening is large enough, unscrew the stop only.

10. Remove the front exhaust pipe at the exhaust manifold and at the primary muffler.

11. Unbolt the driveshaft flange at the brake disc. Do not lose the thin insulator from between the brake disc and the flange. Turn the driveshaft flange slightly in the direction of the wheel and wire it to the upper wishbone.

12. Detach the stabilizer from the lower wishbone, left and right.

13. Position the jack or lifting apparatus and lift the weight from the engine mounts. Remove the bolts retaining the rear crossmember to the body. Remove the retaining nut at the right engine/transmission mount. Note the position of the washers and sleeve on the right engine/transmission mount.

14. Remove the retaining nut from the left engine/transmission mount, but do not move the locknut. Lower the engine/transmission unit from the car.

15. Installation procedures are the reverse of removal. The engine and transmission unit must be aligned in such a way that the same distance between brake disc and wishbone exists on each side. The distance between the pulley and front end of the side-member must also be the same on each side. After installation, bleed the brakes.

Fox

This procedure explains how to lift the engine out of the chassis. If the car has air-conditioning, it will be necessary to lower the engine, transmission, and front suspension from the car as a unit.

1. Remove the hood and disconnect the battery ground cable. Detach the starter wires.

2. Remove the air cleaner.

3. Disconnect the accelerator linkage and the fuel cutoff solenoid wire.

4. Disconnect the ignition coil primary and secondary wires, the oil pressure sending unit, and the coolant temperature sending unit.

5. Loosen the clutch cable adjusting nuts and disconnect the cable. Disconnect the fuel line at the pump. Unplug the alternator.

6. Remove the grille.

7. Remove the bolts holding the panel.

On air-conditioned models, it is necessary to lower the engine, transmission, and front suspension from the car as a unit.

1. Raise the car, allowing the front wheels to hang down. Disconnect the battery ground cable.

2. Drain the coolant.

3. Disconnect all connections between engine, transmission, and body as explained for models without A/C.

4. Remove the radiator.

5. Disconnect the gearshift rod coupling at the transmission.

6. Detach the front engine mount at the engine block.

7. Use a removal tool to separate the tie rod ends from the steering levers.

8. Push the brake pedal down about 1½ in. and fasten it in place to keep the system from draining. Disconnect and plug the brake lines at the brackets on the wheel housing.

9. Attach a framework to keep the assembly steady to a sturdy floor jack and clamp it to the crossmember. Lift slightly and disconnect both coil spring units from the wheel housings. Unbolt the crossmember.

10. Disconnect the backup light switch wire and lower the engine, transmission, and front suspension assembly.

11. On installation, tighten the coil spring units to the body to 16 ft. lbs. and the crossmember to the body to 33 ft. lbs.

4000 Except Coupe and Diesel

NOTE: Though not necessary, removal of the hood will make engine removal easier. Be sure to mark the location of each hood hinge to facilitate reinstallation.

1. Disconnect the negative battery cable. Steps 2–13 refer to cars equipped with air conditioning.

2. Remove the two clips on the top of the grille. Remove the screw on the bottom and remove the grille.

3. Loosen the right and left sides of the condenser and tilt it away from the radiator.

4. Remove the air duct from the throttle valve housing.

5. Remove the hose from the air duct to the auxiliary air regulator.

6. Remove the fuel distributor, the air flow sensor, the fuel injectors and the air cleaner as one unit.

NOTE: Leave all fuel lines connected; protect injectors and cold start valve with caps.

7. Remove the front engine mount bolts and remove the mount.

8. Loosen the nuts on the outer half of the crankshaft pulley and remove the V-belt.

9. Discharge the refrigerant.

10. Remove all lines from the compressor and plug all open connections.

11. Remove the crankcase ventilation hose from the valve cover.

12. Move the air conditioning hoses away from the engine.

13. Remove the mounting bolts (2 upper and 3 lower) and remove the compressor.

14. Open the heater control valve all the way (cold position).

15. Remove the cap on the expansion tank and drain the coolant.

16. Remove the upper and lower radiator hoses from the radiator.

17. Disconnect the plug from the radiator fan.

18. Disconnect the plug from the radiator thermoswitch.

19. Remove the radiator rubber mounts and remove the radiator complete with the fan and the fan shroud.

20. Disconnect the clutch cable.

21. Tag and disconnect all wiring from the engine.

22. Remove the control pressure regulator (above the oil filter) leaving all the fuel lines connected.

23. Remove the air hose from the back of the alternator if so equipped.

24. Unplug the blue wire from the alternator at the plug located between the battery and the rear of the engine.

25. Remove the charcoal filter hose at the intake air duct.

26. Remove the heater hoses.

27. Remove the throttle cable.

28. Tag and remove all vacuum hoses.

29. Pull out the fuel injectors and remove the cold start valve from the top of the intake manifold.

NOTE: Leave all fuel lines connected; protect the injectors and the cold start valve with caps.

30. Remove the hose running from the auxiliary regulator to the air duct.

31. Remove the three upper engine/transmission bolts.

32. Remove the right and left engine mount nuts.

33. Remove the exhaust pipe attaching bolts from the manifold and remove the exhaust pipe.

34. Remove the cover plate bolts and remove the cover plate.

35. Remove the front engine mount bolts and remove the mount.

36. Tag and disconnect the starter cables and remove the starter.

37. Remove the two lower engine/transmission bolts.

38. Loosen the right and left engine mount nuts on the sub-frame.

39. Remove the bolt from the front exhaust pipe support.

40. Support the transmission.

41. Lift the engine until the weight is taken off of the engine mounts and carefully pry the engine and transmission apart.

42. Remove the engine.

Proceed in the reverse order for installation and note the following:

1. Tighten the engine/transmission bolts to 40 ft. lbs.

2. Tighten the bolt for the front exhaust pipe support to 18 ft. lbs.

3. Tighten the starter bolts to 14 ft. lbs.

4. Hand-tighten the front engine mount bolts.

5. Tighten the front cover plate bolts to 7 ft. lbs.

6. Hand-tighten the right and left engine mount nuts.

7. Tighten the cold start valve bolts, the control pressure regulator bolts and the radiator mounting bolts to 7 ft. lbs.

NOTE: Tighten the engine and subframe mounting bolts while the engine is running at idle. Tighten the front engine mount bolts to 18 ft. lbs. and the right and left engine mount bolts to 25 ft. lbs.

4000 Diesel and Turbo-Diesel

1. Disconnect the negative battery cable.

2. Remove the engine and transmission cover plates.

3. Open the heater control valve fully and then open the cap on the expansion tank.

4. Drain the coolant.

5. Detach the radiator cowl from the radiator and remove complete with both fans (A/C models only).

6. Remove the grille and then detach the condenser from the radiator (A/C models only).

7. Disconnect the plugs from the fan and the thermoswitch. Remove the radiator with the fan.

8. Disconnect and remove:
   a. fuel supply and return lines from the injection pump
   b. accelerator cable from pump lever and bracket from pump body
   c. cold start cable at pin
   d. wire from fuel shut-off solenoid
   e. gear shift light switch complete with all wiring from the bracket.

9. Tag and disconnect the wiring from the:
   a. oil pressure switch
   b. coolant temperature sensors
   c. glowplugs
   d. thermoswitch.

10. Disconnect the coolant hose.

11. Loosen the clutch cable and unhook it from the clutch lever.

12. Loosen the right and left engine mounts at top.

13. Disconnect the vacuum hose from the vacuum reservoir.

14. Disconnect and remove the alternator.

15. Remove the front engine stop bolts.

16. On models with A/C, remove the front engine stop bolts. Detach the compressor belt after removing the pulley nuts. Remove the top and bottom compressor brackets. Remove the compressor and position it out of the way.

17. Remove the exhaust pipe from the manifold.

18. Disconnect the starter cable and detach it from the intermediate plate.

19. Remove the exhaust pipe from the front transmission support.

20. Remove the starter.

21. Remove the bottom two transmission-to-engine bolts. Remove the flywheel cover plate.

22. Support the transmission with a jack or install transmission support bar VW 785/1B.

23. Attach a lifting apparatus to the engine and raise the engine/transmission until the transmission housing touches the steering rack.

24. Raise the transmission jack or adjust the support bar and then remove the upper three transmission-to-engine bolts.

25. Pry the engine/transmission apart and lift the engine out of the engine compartment.

26. Installation is in the reverse order of removal. Please note the following:
   a. place the intermediate plate on dowel sleeves and stick to engine block with grease
   b. place the starter on the engine carrier before installing engine

─────── **CAUTION** ───────

Do not interchange fuel supply and return pipe union screws. For identification, the fuel return pipe union screw is marked OUT on the screw head.

──────────────────────

   c. connect the starter cable so it cannot touch the engine
   d. install the engine mounts free of tension (align by shaking engine).

27. Tightening torques for installation are as follows:
   a. cover plate-to-transmission/engine—7 ft. lbs.
   b. exhaust pipe-to-transmission—18 ft. lbs.
   c. front engine stop-to-engine block—18 ft. lbs.
   d. stop housing-to-front cross member—18 ft. lbs.
   e. engine mounts—25 ft. lbs.
   f. engine-to-transmission (12 M)—40 ft. lbs.
   g. starter bolts—14 ft. lbs.

5000, Coupe, Turbo and Quattro

1. Disconnect the negative battery cable.

2. Open the heater control valve all the way (cold position).

3. Remove the cap on the expansion tank and drain the coolant.

4. Remove all radiator and heater hoses. Disconnect the intercooler from the turbo charger on the Quattro.

5. Remove the control pressure regulator.

─────── **CAUTION** ───────

Do not disconnect any fuel lines.

──────────────────────

6. Remove the cold start valve.

7. Pull out the fuel injectors and lay them aside.

NOTE: Protect the fuel injectors and the cold start valve with caps.

8. Loosen the air duct and vacuum hoses from the throttle valve assembly.

9. Remove the air cleaner cover with the filter.

10. Pull the hood latch cable guide off of its bracket.

11. On cars equipped with air conditioning, remove the two clips on the top of the grille and the screw on the bottom and remove the grille, then loosen the condenser mounting bolts and tilt it away from the radiator.

12. Remove the power steering pump leaving the hose connected.

13. Remove the vacuum amplifier.

14. Remove the ignition coil.

15. Remove the EGR control valve.

16. Remove the windshield washer reservoir from its holder.

17. Remove the power steering reservoir from its holder.

18. Remove the distributor cap, the rotor and the ignition wires.

NOTE: Tape the distributor dust cap on to prevent it from falling off.

19. On cars equipped with a manual transmission, take off the circlip and remove the throttle cable.

20. On cars equipped with an automatic transmission, remove the throttle pushrod.

21. Disconnect the oil pressure and the water temperature senders.

22. On air-conditioned cars, remove the compressor mounting bolts. Leaving the hoses connected, tie back the compressor with wire.

23. Remove the exhaust pipe-to-manifold bolts. On turbocharged models, remove the exhaust pipe-to-wastegate connector.

24. Remove the exhaust pipe support bracket from the transmission.

25. Remove the front engine mount bolts and remove the mount.

26. Tag and disconnect all wires from the starter and remove the starter.

27. Tag and disconnect all wires leading from the alternator and remove the alternator.

28. On cars equipped with an automatic transmission, remove the torque converter mounting bolts from the drive plate. This can be done through the starter hole.

29. Remove the lower engine/transmission bolts.

30. Support the transmission.

31. Remove the upper engine/transmission bolts.

32. Remove the left engine support bracket.

33. Loosen the right engine bracket from the right engine mount.

34. Lift the engine until the V-belt pulley is behind the grille opening.

35. Carefully detach the engine from the transmission.

36. Remove the engine completely, turning it to the right as you lift it out.

Proceed in the reverse order for installation and note the following:

1. Tighten the engine/transmission bolts to 43 ft. lbs.

2. Tighten the bolt for the exhaust pipe support bracket to 22 ft. lbs.

3. Tighten the torque converter-to-drive plate bolts to 4 ft. lbs.

4. Tighten the starter bolts to 14 ft. lbs.

5. Hand tighten all engine mount bolts.

6. Tighten the air conditioner mounting bolt to 29 ft. lbs.

7. Tighten the power steering pump bolts and the control pressure regulator bolts to 14 ft. lbs.

NOTE: Tighten the engine and subframe mounting bolts while the engine is running at idle. Tighten all bolts to 32 ft. lbs.

5000 Diesel and Turbo-Diesel

1. Disconnect the negative battery cable.

2. Remove the air cleaner.

3. Remove the cover plates underneath the engine and the transmission.

4. Remove the front grille.

5. Remove the windshield washer reservoir from its holder.

6. Remove the hydraulic fluid reservoir from its holder.

7. Pull the hood latch cable guide out of its bracket.

8. Remove the cap on the expansion tank and drain the radiator.

9. Remove all radiator and heater hoses.

10. Remove the V-belt for the power steering pump and remove the power steering pump with the hoses connected.

11. On cars equipped with air conditioning, loosen the condenser mounting bolts and tilt it away from the radiator.

12. Remove the auxiliary radiator.

13. Remove the fuel filter and plug the fuel lines.

14. Detach the accelerator cable.

15. Tag and disconnect all electrical wiring coming from the cylinder head.

16. Loosen the fuel return pipe on the injection pump.

17. Disconnect the idle speed control cable from the injection pump lever.

18. Remove the cover plate for the right engine mount.

19. Remove the front engine mount bolts and remove the mount from the crossmember.

20. Tag and disconnect all wiring from the alternator and then remove the alternator and its bracket.

21 Remove the exhaust pipes from the manifold.

22. Remove the exhaust pipe support bracket from the transmission.

23. Tag and disconnect all wiring from the starter and remove the starter.

24. On cars equipped with air conditioning, remove the compressor mounting bolts along with the mount. Leave the hoses connected and tie the compressor out of the way with wire.

25. Remove the lower engine/transmission bolts.

26. Remove the flywheel cover plate from the transmission.

27. Support the transmission.

28. Remove the left engine bracket.

29. Lift the engine/transmission up until the transmission housing touches the steering housing.

30. Remove the upper engine/transmission bolts.

31. Carefully pry the engine/transmission apart.

32. Turn the engine to the right and lift up at the same time.

33. Turn the engine 90 degrees and lift it completely out.

Proceed in the reverse order for installation and note the following:

1. Tighten the engine/transmission bolts to 43 ft. lbs.

2. Tighten all engine mount bolts to 33 ft. lbs.

3. Tighten the exhaust pipe-to-manifold bolts to 22 ft. lbs.

Cylinder Head

REMOVAL AND INSTALLATION

100

1. Drain the coolant from the radiator. Disconnect the spark plug wires.

2. Remove the sheet metal cover from the exhaust manifolds. Remove the intake and exhaust manifolds.

3. Disconnect the hose from the thermostat housing.

4. Remove the valve cover. Loosen the valve rocker arm adjusting nuts and remove the pushrods. Note their original locations; they must all go back in the same place.

5. Loosen the cylinder head bolts in the same order as shown for tightening. Remove the bolts. A metric Allen wrench is required for the head bolts.

NOTE: Do not loosen the head bolts until the engine has thoroughly cooled.

6. Remove the head. It if sticks, operate the starter to loosen it by compression or rap it upward with a soft hammer. Do not force anything between the head and block. Check the head for warpage.

7. Reinstallation of the head is made easier by the use of guide studs installed in opposite corners of the block. These can be made by cutting the heads off two bolts of the same size as the head bolts.

8. Put the gasket in place on the block.

9. Guide the cylinder head into place.

10. Coat the head bolt threads with a graphite lubricant. Install them finger tight.

11. Tighten the bolts in the sequence shown in four stages until the proper torque is reached. The bolts should be torqued again after the first 500–1000 miles.

12. Install the pushrods in their original locations. Make a preliminary valve lash adjustment.

13. Replace the valve cover, using a new gasket. Replace the manifolds. Connect the coolant hoses and the spark plugs wires.

14. Refill the cooling system.

15. Run the engine until it reaches normal operating temperature, watching for leaks. Make a final valve adjustment with the engine warm.

16. On overhaul, if the rocker studs and pushrod guide plates have been removed, the guides must be aligned so that the pushrods will not contact them. The cylinder head must be heated to 248°F in an oven in order to install or remove the valve guides.

Fox

1. Disconnect the battery ground cable.

2. Drain the coolant. Disconnect the hoses.

3. Unbolt the exhaust pipe from the manifold.

4. Disconnect the electrical wires. Detach the accelerator linkage.

5. Remove the alternator belt and the timing belt.

6. Loosen the cylinder head bolts in the reverse of the order shown for tightening. Remove the bolts. A metric Allen wrench is required for the head bolts.

―――――――― CAUTION ――――――――
Don't loosen the head bolts until the engine is thoroughly cool. Don't loosen the camshaft bearing cap nuts.
―――――――――――――――――――――――

7. Remove the head. If it sticks, loosen it by compression or rap it upward with a soft hammer. Do not force anything between the head and block. Check the head for warpage.

―――――――― CAUTION ――――――――
Do not attempt to remove the camshaft from the head without checking the "Camshaft Removal and Installation" procedure. Special tools are required.
―――――――――――――――――――――――

8. On installation, make sure that the head gasket is installed with the word OBEN up and to the left side of the engine. Put the head in place and install the right front and left rear head bolts first.

9. Tighten the bolts in the sequence shown in four stages until the proper torque is reached. The bolts should be torqued again after the first 300 miles.

10. On overhaul, valve guides must be pressed out or in from above. The cylinder head must be heated to 176–212°F in an oil bath or an oven to install new valve guides.

NOTE: New cylinder head bolts and a new, soft head gasket are available to correct coolant leakage problems. The new bolts are marked 12.9 and should be torqued to normal specifications. Anytime there is a leakge problem, both the head and block should be checked for warpage.

NOTE: Later model Fox cars come equipped with a new type head bolt. These bolts have a 12 point recessed "polygon" head. The manufacturer states that these bolts require no retorquing during their

service life. These bolts may be used as replacements on older engines, but only in complete sets.

11. Make sure to align the timing belt and sprockets as explained under "Timing Belt Removal and Installation."

─── **CAUTION** ───

Do not attempt to start the engine until you are sure of this alignment.

For cylinder head overhaul, see "Engine Rebuilding" in the Unit Repair section.

Left, new style, right old style Fox head bolts

4000, 5000, Coupe, Turbo and Quattro

NOTE: Cylinder head removal should not be attempted unless the engine is cold.

1. Disconnect the negative battery cable.
2. Drain the cooling system.
3. Disconnect the air duct from the throttle valve assembly on all models except the Turbo and Quattro. On the Turbo and Quattro, remove the hose which runs between the air duct and the turbocharger.
4. Disconnect the throttle cable from the throttle valve assembly.
5. Remove the air duct for the injector cooling fan on the Turbo and Quattro.
6. Clean and remove the fuel injectors and all other fuel lines.

NOTE: Protect the fuel injectors and the cold start valve with caps.

7. Tag and disconnect all vacuum and PCV lines.
8. Remove the hose which runs from the intake manifold to the turbocharger on the Turbo and Quattro.
9. Tag and disconnect all electrical lines leading to the cylinder head.
10. Unbolt and remove the intake manifold.
11. Disconnect all radiator and heater hoses where they are attached to the cylinder head. Position them out of the way.
12. Tag and remove all spark plug wires and then remove the spark plugs.
13. For all models but the 4000, remove the distributor. To aid in reinstallation, scribe

1. Camshaft bearing caps	3. Gasket	5. Oil seal	7. End plug
2. Camshaft cover	4. Valve adjusting disc	6. Cam follower	8. Camshaft

Exploded view of the Fox cylinder head—4000 similar

a mark on the body of the distributor and the cylinder head.

14. Unbolt and separate the exhaust manifold from the exhaust pipe.

NOTE: Exhaust pipe detachment differs slightly on the Turbo and Quattro. First the exhaust pipe must be unbolted from the turbocharger and then it must be unbolted from the wastegate, towards the rear of the engine.

15. Disconnect the EGR valve and the oxygen sensor (if so equipped) from the exhaust manifold.
16. Remove the heat deflector shield on the 4000 models.
17. Unbolt and remove the oil lines (2) from the turbocharger.
18. Unbolt and remove the exhaust manifold.

NOTE: When removing the exhaust manifold on the Turbo and Quattro, the manifold, turbocharger and wastegate should all be removed as one unit.

19. Remove the air hose cover from the back of the alternator (if so equipped) on the 4000.
20. Tag and disconnect all wires coming from the back of the alternator and then remove the alternator and the V-belt.
21. Disconnect and plug the hoses com-

ing from the power steering pump (if so equipped).

22. Remove the power steering pump and the V-belt (if so equipped).
23. Remove the drive belt cover and the drive belt.
24. Remove the cylinder head cover.
25. Loosen the cylinder head bolts in the reverse order of the tightening sequence.
26. Remove the bolts and lift the cylinder head straight off.

─── **CAUTION** ───

If the head sticks, loosen it by compression or rap it upward with a soft rubber mallet. Do not force anything between the head and the engine block to pry it upward; this may result in serious damage.

27. Clean the cylinder head and engine block mating surfaces thoroughly and then install the new gasket without any sealing compound. Make sure the words TOP or OBEN are facing up when the gasket is installed.
28. Place the cylinder head on the engine block and install bolts No. 8 and 10 first. These holes are smaller and will properly locate the gasket and the head on the engine block.
29. Install the remaining bolts. Tighten them in three stages.

CAMSHAFT BEARING CAPS

2 MKG (14 FT LB)

WOODRUFF KEY

CAMSHAFT

OIL SEAL

VALVE ADJUSTING DISC

CAM FOLLOWER

8 MKG (58 FT LB)

VALVE SPRINGS
REPLACE ONLY IN PAIRS

VALVE STEM SEAL

VALVE SPRING SEAT

VALVE GUIDE

CYLINDER HEAD

VALVES

5000 cylinder head assembly

30. Installation of all other components is in the reverse order of removal.

4000 and 5000 Diesels

NOTE: Cylinder head removal should not be attempted unless the engine is cold.

1. Disconnect the negative battery cable.
2. Drain the cooling system.
3. Remove the air cleaner.
4. Clean and disconnect the fuel (injector) lines.
5. Tag and disconnect all electrical wires and leads.
6. Disconnect and plug all lines coming from the brake booster vacuum pump and remove the pump.

7. Unbolt and remove the intake manifold.
8. Disconnect and plug all lines coming from the power steering pump and remove the pump and V-belt (if so equipped).
9. Separate the exhaust pipe from the exhaust manifold and then remove the manifold.
10. Disconnect all radiator and heater hoses where they are attached to the cylinder head and position them out of the way.
11. Remove the drive belt cover and the drive belt.
12. Remove the injection pump belt cover and remove the belt.
13. Remove the PCV hose.
14. Remove the cylinder head cover.
15. Loosen the cylinder head bolts in the reverse order of the tightening sequence shown in the illustration.
16. Remove the bolts and lift the cylinder head straight off.

17. Clean the cylinder head and engine block mating surfaces thoroughly and then install the new gasket without any sealing compound. Make sure the words TOP or OBEN are facing up when the gasket is installed.

NOTE: Depending upon piston height above the top surface of the engine block, there are three gaskets of different thicknesses which can be used. Be sure that the new gasket has the same number of notches and the same identifying number as the one being replaced.

18. Place the cylinder head on the engine block and install bolts No. 8 and 10 first. These holes are smaller and will properly locate the gasket and the head on the engine block.
19. Install the remaining bolts. Tighten them in three stages (see "Torque Specifications") using the sequence shown in the illustration.
20. Installation of all other components is in the reverse order of removal.
21. After reassembly, start the engine and let it run until it reaches normal operating temperature (when the radiator fan switches on). Stop the engine, remove the cylinder head cover and check to see that all bolts are still at the proper tightness.
22. After 1000 miles, remove the cylinder head cover and loosen the cylinder head bolts 30 degrees (⅓ of a turn). Then retorque them to the proper specifications. This is done one bolt at a time, in the proper sequence (5000 only).
23. After about 1000 miles, remove the cylinder head cover and retighten the cylinder head bolts, turning the bolts in sequence ¼ turn (90°) WITHOUT loosening them first. This is done one bolt at a time, in the proper sequence, without interruption.

Intake Manifold

REMOVAL AND INSTALLATION

100 and Fox

1. Drain the coolant.
2. Remove the air cleaner.
3. Disconnect the coolant hoses from the manifold and the automatic choke. Remove the wire from the electric choke.
4. Disconnect the vacuum hose and the lead to the idle cutoff valve. Detach the fuel line and the accelerator linkage.
5. Remove the manifold nuts and the manifold support.
6. Pull the manifold off the studs. If it

sticks, rap it with a soft hammer. Do not force anything between the manifold and the cylinder head. Discard the gaskets.

7. Installation is the reverse of the removal procedure. New gaskets must be used. Tighten the nuts to 18 ft. lbs. After refilling the cooling system, start the engine and check for leaks.

4000, 5000, Coupe, Turbo and Quattro

1. Disconnect the negative battery cable.
2. Drain the cooling system.
3. Disconnect the air duct from the throttle valve assembly on all models but the Turbo. On the Turbo, remove the hose which runs between the air duct and the turbocharger.
4. Disconnect the throttle cable from the throttle valve assembly.
5. Remove the air duct for the injector cooling fan on the Turbo.
6. Clean and remove the fuel injectors.
7. Disconnect the cold start valve.

NOTE: Protect the fuel injectors and the cold start valve with caps.

8. Tag and disconnect all vacuum and PCV lines.
9. Tag and disconnect all electrical lines leading to the cylinder head.
10. Remove the hose which runs from the intake manifold to the turbocharger (intercooler on the Quattro) on the Turbo.
11. Remove the auxiliary air regulator.
12. Remove the manifold.
13. Installation is in the reverse order of removal.

4000 and 5000 Diesels

1. Disconnect the negative battery cable.
2. Drain the cooling system.
3. Disconnect the hose that runs between the air duct and the turbocharger (turbo-diesel only).
4. Remove the air cleaner.
5. Disconnect and plug all lines coming from the brake booster vacuum pump and remove the pump.
6. Disconnect the PCV line.
7. Disconnect and remove the blow-off valve and then disconnect the hose which runs from the intake manifold to the turbocharger (turbo-diesel only).
8. Remove the manifold.
9. Installation is in the reverse order of removal.

Exhaust Manifold

REMOVAL AND INSTALLATION

100 and Fox

1. Disconnect the heated air intake hose from the manifold.

100 series exhaust manifold gaskets. (d) is the type with the oval opening which must be installed with the notched side down. (e) has a round opening. Both types must have the beaded edge around the opening facing outward.

2. Unbolt the exhaust pipe from the manifold.
3. Remove the sheet metal cover.
4. Remove the manifold nuts. Pull the manifold on the studs. If it sticks, rap it with a soft hammer. Do not force anything between the manifold and the cylinder head. Discard the gaskets.
5. Installation is the reverse of the removal procedure. New gaskets must be used. If the gaskets are the type with round openings, they must be installed with the beaded side outward from the head and the notched edge down. Gaskets with oval openings must be installed with the beaded edge outward from the head. Tighten the manifold nuts to the specified torque. Torque the front exhaust pipe flange nuts to 18–22 ft. lbs. in steps. A new gasket should also be used between the exhaust pipe and the manifold.

4000, 5000 (Inc. Diesel) and Coupe

Although it is not imperative to remove the intake manifold in order to remove the exhaust manifold, you may find that it makes everything more accessible.

1. Unbolt and separate the exhaust pipe from the exhaust manifold.
2. Disconnect the EGR valve and the oxygen sensor (if so equipped) from the manifold.
3. Remove the heat deflector shield on the 4000.
4. Disconnect the CO probe receptacle tube (if so equipped).
5. Remove the manifold.
6. Installation is in the reverse order of removal.

NOTE: Always replace old gaskets.

Turbo, Quattro and Turbo-Diesels

1. Remove the hose which runs between the air duct and the turbocharger.
2. If the intake manifold has not been removed, disconnect the hose which runs from the intake manifold to the turbocharger or intercooler.
3. Unbolt the exhaust pipe from the

turbocharger.
4. Unbolt the exhaust pipe from the wastegate on the rear of the manifold (gasoline engines only).
5. Disconnect the EGR valve and the oxygen sensor from the manifold on gasoline engined models.
6. Remove the oil lines (2) from the turbocharger.
7. Remove the line from the bottom of the turbocharger to the intercooler (Quattro only).
8. Remove the manifold.

NOTE: The manifold, the turbocharger and the wastegate can all be removed as one unit.

9. Installation is in the reverse order of removal.

Turbocharger

REMOVAL AND INSTALLATION

1. Removal of the intake manifold (as detailed earlier) is not absolutely necessary but will greatly aid in the accessiblity of all related nuts and bolts.
2. Loosen the hose clamps and remove the hose which leads to the intake manifold (intercooler on Quattro).
3. Loosen the hose clamps and remove the hose which leads to the air cleaner.
4. Unbolt the oil supply (upper) and return (lower) lines and position them out of the way.
5. Remove the four exhaust pipe mounting nuts and pull the exhaust pipe away from the turbocharger.
6. Remove the four turbocharger mounting nuts and pull the turbocharger off of the exhaust manifold.
7. Installation is in the reverse order of removal. Note the following:
   a. Use new gaskets.
   b. Tighten turbocharger-to-exhaust manifold bolts to 43 ft. lbs.
   c. Tighten turbocharger-to-exhaust pipe bolts to 22 ft. lbs.

Turbocharger Wastegate

REMOVAL AND INSTALLATION

Turbo and Quattro

1. As suggested in the turbocharger removal procedure, intake manifold removal is a prudent idea for wastegate accessibility.
2. Remove the wastegate-to-exhaust pipe connecting tube (three bolts top and three bolts bottom).
3. Remove the mounting bolt for the tube leading from the wastegate to the exhaust manifold.
4. Remove the vacuum line from the

end of the wastegate.

5. Remove the four mounting bolts and remove the wastegate from the exhaust manifold.

6. Installation is in the reverse order of removal.

Turbo-Diesels

The wastegate on the 4 cylinder engine is a press—fit cannot be removed. The wastegate on the 5 cylinder engine is removed by disconnecting the air hose and then unbolting it from the turbocharger itself.

Timing Chain Cover

REMOVAL AND INSTALLATION

100

1. Place the car on a lift or pit.
2. Remove the apron under the front bumper.
3. Have an assistant place the car in first gear and hold the brake on. Remove the crankshaft pulley nut. On cars with automatic transmissions, the nut can be removed by affixing a heavy wrench and rapping the wrench with a hammer. The nut must be unscrewed in the opposite direction of normal engine rotation.
4. Loosen the fan and alternator adjustments and remove the belts.
5. Remove the pulley, rapping it with a soft hammer if necessary. Be careful not to lose the shaft key.
6. Drain the oil.
7. Remove first the oil pan, then the timing chain cover.
8. Reverse the procedure to install, using new gaskets. Timing chain cover bolt torque is 7 ft. lbs.

TIMING CHAIN COVER OIL SEAL REPLACEMENT

100

Current models have the lip retaining the oil seal in the cover to the inside. Thus the oil seal is pressed in from the front of the cover. Older models have the retaining lip toward the outside of the cover; the seal is pressed in from the inside of the cover. The result of this is that the oil seal may be replaced with the cover in place on the current models, while on older models the cover must be removed to replace the seal. The only way to determine which cover is installed is by inspection, after removing the crankshaft pulley. Virtually all US models use the current type. The seal can be replaced without removing the engine.

To replace either type:

1. Remove the timing chain cover on older models. Follow Steps 1–6 of the "Timing Chain Cover Removal and Installation" procedure for current models.

2. Carefully pry out the old seal with a screwdriver, being careful not to damage the housing.

3. Apply grease between the lips of the seal and apply a little oil to the outside edge.

4. On older models press in the seal from the inside of the cover. Press or drive it in with a seal installer or a suitable improvised tool, until it bottoms on the retaining lip. If there is no retaining lip, press the seal in until it is flush with the inside of the cover.

5. On current models, press or drive the seal in with the metal side out until it bottoms on the retaining lip. A good way to do this is to tighten a flat plate against the seal with a pulley retaining nut.

6. Reverse the procedure followed in Step 1 to reassemble the engine.

Timing Chain and Tensioner

REMOVAL AND INSTALLATION

100

1. Remove the timing chain cover.
2. All engines have a hydraulic chain tensioner. Bend open the lock plate, unscrew the chain tensioner plug, insert a Phillips screwdriver and turn counterclockwise. If this is not done, the chain tensioner will fly apart as it is removed. On some models, the tensioner must be held together while it is removed. Unbolt and remove the tensioner.
3. Remove the camshaft sprocket retaining bolt. Some way to keep the sprocket from turning will have to be devised.
4. Remove the camshaft sprocket, chain, and crankshaft sprocket together, using a puller on the crankshaft sprocket. Be careful not to lose the key for the crankshaft sprocket.

Use a Phillips screwdriver, as shown, to prevent the 100 series chain from coming apart when it is removed

5. On reinstallation, heat the crankshaft sprocket to 140° F in an oven. Do not heat it with a flame, as it will be warped. Install the shaft key and slide the sprocket into place until it rests against the stop.

6. Align the No. 1 cylinder mark on the distributor body rim with the rotor. Set No. 1 cylinder precisely at top dead center. Place the camshaft sprocket on the camshaft and align the sprocket punch mark with the notch in the chain guide rail.

7. Remove the camshaft sprocket, being careful not to turn the camshaft.

8. Place the timing chain over the crankshaft sprocket and place the camshaft sprocket in the chain, so that the camshaft sprocket can be installed without moving either the camshaft or the crankshaft.

100 series timing chain alignment. The arrows show the camshaft sprocket punch mark, the notch in the chain guide rail, and the dowel which aligns the camshaft sprocket and camshaft.

NOTE: The factory specifies that timing chains with indented links should not be reused. They must be replaced with a straight-link chain.

9. Torque the camshaft sprocket to bolt to 58 ft. lbs.

10. Assemble and install the chain tensioner, torquing the bolts to 9 ft. lbs. Turn the chain plunger clockwise to release it. Current production models have a self-releasing chain tensioner. Make absolutely sure that the hydraulic chain tensioner is free to move. Install the tensioner plunger and lock plate.

11. Replace the timing cover.

Timing Belt Cover

REMOVAL AND INSTALLATION

Fox and 4000 (4 Cylinder)

1. Loosen the alternator adjusting bolts. Pivot the alternator over and slip the V-belt off.

2. If equipped with air conditioning, loosen the compressor mounting bolts and slip off the V-belt.

3. Unscrew the retaining nuts and remove the upper timing belt cover. Take care not to lose any of the washers or spacers.

4. Using the large bolt on the crankshaft sprocket, turn the engine until the No. 1 cylinder is at TDC of the compression stroke. At this point, both of the valves will be closed and the 0 mark on the flywheel will be aligned with the pointer on the clutch housing.

5. Unscrew the crankshaft pulley retaining bolts (4) and then loosen the crankshaft sprocket bolt.

NOTE: To remove the crankshaft sprocket bolt you will need a friend. Put the car in 4th gear and apply the brake, this will enable you to loosen the bolt.

6. Remove the crankshaft pulley.

7. Unscrew the water pump pulley retaining bolts (3) and remove the pulley.

8. Unscrew the retaining nuts and remove the lower timing belt cover. Take care not to lose any of the washers or spacers.

9. Installation is in the reverse order of removal.

4000 (5 Cylinder), 5000, Turbo and Quattro

1. Loosen the alternator adjusting bolts and remove the V-belt.

2. Loosen the power steering pump adjusting bolts and remove the V-belt (if so equipped).

3. If equipped with air conditioning, loosen the compressor adjusting bolts and remove the V-belt.

4. Unscrew the retaining nuts and remove the timing belt cover. Take care not to lose any of the washers or spacers.

5. Installation is in the reverse order of removal

4000 and 5000 Diesels

There are two drive belts on the 5000 Diesels; one at the front of the engine and one at the rear, therefore there are two covers to remove. The front cover on all models is removed in the same manner as the gasoline engined 5000's with two exceptions, the cover has an upper and a lower half. To remove the upper half, follow the procedure for the 5000 above. To remove the lower half, use the following procedure.

1. Remove the upper cover.

2. Unscrew the crankshaft pulley retaining bolts and remove the pulley.

3. Unscrew the retaining nuts and remove the lower cover.

4. Installation is in the reverse order of removal.

To remove the rear timing belt cover on 5000 Diesels, use the following procedure.

1. Remove the outside half of the vacuum pump pulley and remove the V-belt.

2. Unscrew the retaining bolts and remove the rear timing belt cover. Take care not to lose any of the washers or spacers.

3. Installation is in the reverse order of removal.

1. Alternator belt 3. Timing gear cover 5. Intermediate sprocket 7. Tensioner
2. Belt pulleys 4. Crankshaft sprocket 6. Drive belt 8. Camshaft sprocket

Fox timing belt

Timing Belt

REMOVAL AND INSTALLATION

Fox

1. Remove the grille.

2. Remove the alternator belt and the timing belt cover.

3. Loosen the belt tensioner locknut and turn the tensioner counterclockwise (facing it) to release the belt tension.

4. Slide the belt off the camshaft sprocket.

5. Belt installation is easier if the water pump pulley is removed.

6. Set the flywheel timing mark at TDC (0°T).

7. Make sure that the camshaft is positioned so that the No. 4 cylinder valves are overlapping; i.e. the exhaust valve is opening and the intake closing. If there is a punch mark on the back of the camshaft sprocket, align it with the camshaft cover gasket (left side).

8. Turn the intermediate shaft so that the distributor rotor points to the No. 1 cylinder mark on the rim of the distributor body. If there is a notch on the crankshaft

Crankshaft pulley and intermediate shaft sprocket alignment on the Fox and 4000

pulley, it should now align with the punch mark on the front of the intermediate shaft sprocket.

9. Taking care not to disturb any of the three sprockets, install the timing belt.

NOTE: Special tools are available, which can be used to hold the sprockets in alignment. It can also be used to check alignment on early engines which do not have the punch mark on the back of the camshaft sprocket and the notch on the crankshaft sprocket.

Camshaft sprocket alignment on the Fox and 4000

10. Recheck that the No. 1 (and 4) cylinder is at TDC, that the camshaft is in the No. 4 cylinder overlap position, and that the distributor rotor is in the No. 1 cylinder firing position.

11. Turn the belt tensioner clockwise (facing it) until it is just possible to turn the longest span of belt about 90° with your thumb and forefinger. Lock the tensioner in place.

NOTE: It is not necessary to recheck the belt tension during the normal life span of the belt (about 60,000 miles).

12. Again recheck the alignment as in Step 10 and replace the belt cover, water pump pulley, alternator belt, and grille. Check the ignition timing when the job is complete.

4000 (4 Cylinder)

1. Remove the upper and lower timing belt covers.

2. While holding the large hex nut on the tensioner pulley, loosen the smaller pulley lock nut.

3. Turn the tensioner counterclockwise to relieve the tension on the timing belt.

4. Carefully slide the timing belt off of the three sprockets and remove the belt.

5. Using the large bolt on the crankshaft sprocket, turn the engine until the No. 1 cylinder is at TDC of the compression stroke. At this point, both valves will be closed and the 0 mark on the flywheel will be aligned with the pointer on the clutch housing.

V-belt pulley alignment on the 5000

6. Check that the timing mark on the rear face of the camshaft sprocket is aligned with the upper edge of the rear timing belt cover. If it's not, turn the sprocket until they align.

7. Replace the crankshaft pulley and check that the notch on the pulley is aligned with the mark on the intermediate shaft sprocket. If not, turn them until they align.

CAUTION

If the timing marks are not correctly aligned with the No. 1 piston at TDC of the compression stroke and the belt is installed, valve timing will be incorrect. Poor performance and possible engine damage can result from the improper valve timing.

8. Remove the crankshaft pulley. Observe its location on the crankshaft sprocket so that it can be replaced in the same position.

9. Slide the timing belt back onto the sprockets and check for the proper tension (see ''Tension Adjustment'').

10. Installation is in the reverse order of removal.

4000 (5 Cylinder), 5000, Turbo and Quattro

1. Remove the alternator and air conditioning compressor from their mounting brackets and position them out of the way.

2. Remove the front cover bolts and lift off the cover.

3. Loosen the water pump bolts and turn the pump clockwise.

4. Slide the drive belt off the sprockets.

5. Turn the camshaft until the notch on the back of the sprocket is in line with the left side edge of the camshaft housing flange.

6. Align the TDC ''0'' mark on the flywheel with the lug cast on the clutch housing.

7. Install the drive belt and turn the water pump counterclockwise to tighten the belt. Tighten the water pump bolts to 14 ft. lbs.

NOTE: The belt is correctly tensioned when it can be twisted 90° with the thumb and index finger along the straight run between the camshaft sprocket and the water pump.

8. Install the front cover and tighten the bolts to 7 ft. lbs.

9. Install the alternator and compressor and tighten the belts. These belts are correctly tensioned when they can be depressed ⅜″ along their longest straight run.

4000 Diesels

NOTE: This procedure will require a number of special tools and a certain expertise with diesel engines. You may wish to have the work performed by an authorized Audi service technician.

1. Remove the timing belt cover. Remove the cylinder head cover.

2. Turn the engine so that No. 1 cyl-

inder is at TDC and fix the camshaft in position with tool 2065A. Align the tool as follows:

—turn the camshaft until one end of the tool touches the cylinder head

—measure the gap at the other end of the tool with a feeler gauge

—take half of the measurement and insert a feeler gauge of this thickness between the tool and the cylinder head; turn the camshaft so that the tool rests on the feeler gauge

—insert a second feeler gauge of the same thickness between the other end of the tool and the cylinder head.

3. Lock the injection pump sprocket in position with pin 2064.

4. Check that the marks on the sprocket, bracket and pump body are in alignment (engine at TDC).

5. Loosen the timing belt tensioner. Remove the V-belt from the crankshaft.

6. Remove the timing belt.

To install:

7. Check that the TDC mark on the flywheel is aligned with the reference marks.

8. Loosen the camshaft sprocket bolt ½ turn and then loosen the gear from the camshaft end by tapping it with a rubber mallet.

9. Install the timing belt and remove pin 2064 from the injection pump sprocket.

10. Tension the belt by turning the tensioner to the right. Check the belt tension as detailed later in the section.

11. Tighten the camshaft sprocket bolt to 33 ft. lbs.

12. Remove the tool from the camshaft.

13. Turn the crankshaft two turns in the direction of engine rotation (clockwise) and then strike the belt once with a rubber mallet between the camshaft sprocket and the injection pump sprocket.

14. Check the belt tension again. Check the injection pump timing.

5000 Diesels

NOTE: This procedure will require the use of a number of special tools. Due to this fact, you may wish to have the work performed by an authorized Audi service technician.

1. Remove all V-belts on the front of the engine.

2. Remove the outside half of the vacuum pump pulley and remove the V-belt.

3. Remove the front timing belt covers.

4. Remove the rear timing belt cover.

5. Remove the cylinder head cover.

6. Using the large bolt on the crankshaft sprocket, turn the engine until the No. 1 cylinder is at TDC of the compression stroke. At this point, both of the valves will be closed and the mark on the flywheel will be aligned with the pointer on the clutch housing.

7. Align the marks on the injection pump sprocket mounting plate.

8. Using special tool 2064 (a pin), lock the injection pump sprocket in place so that

it cannot move and change the valve timing.

9. Using special tool 3036, hold the remaining (inside) half of the vacuum pump pulley and the injection pump drive sprocket in place. Remove the center retaining bolt and take off the pulley half and the drive sprocket along with the timing belt.

10. Using special tool 2084 to hold the crankshaft pulley in place, attach special tool 2079 to a ratchet and *loosen* the crankshaft pulley center bolt.

11. Attach special tool 2065A to the rear of the camshaft so that it will not move and alter the valve timing.

12. Loosen the adjusting bolts (2) on the water pump and turn it counterclockwise to relieve the tension on the timing belt.

13. Unbolt and remove the crankshaft pulley and slide the timing belt off of the sprockets.

To install the front timing belt:

14. Check that the No. 1 cylinder is still at TDC and the mark on the flywheel is still aligned with the pointer on the clutch housing.

15. Loosen the camshaft sprocket bolt approximately 1 turn and lightly tap the gear loose from the camshaft with a rubber mallet.

16. Install the timing belt and check the tension (see "Tension Adjustment").

17. Tighten the camshaft sprocket bolt to 33 ft. lbs. and remove special tool 2065A.

To install the rear timing belt:

18. Install the injection pump drive sprocket along with the timing belt.

19. Check that the No. 1 cylinder is still at TDC.

20. Tighten the injection pump drive sprocket retaining bolt until it is just possible to turn the sprocket by hand.

21. Check for proper tension (see "Tension Adjustment").

22. Retighten the retaining bolt to 7 ft. lbs.

23. Attach the rear timing belt cover and the outside half of the vacuum pump pulley along with the V-belt and check for proper tension.

24. Remove special tool 2064 from the injection pump.

25. Check the injection timing, and adjust if necessary.

26. Installation of the remaining components is in the reverse order of removal.

TENSION ADJUSTMENT

4000 (4 Cylinder)

1. Holding the large bolt on the tensioner pulley, loosen the small nut and turn the tensioner clockwise to tighten and counterclockwise to loosen.

2. The belt is correctly tensioned when it can be twisted 90 degrees with the thumb and forefinger, midway between the camshaft and the intermediate shaft drive sprockets.

4000 (5 Cylinder), 5000, Turbo and Quattro

1. Loosen the water pump adjusting bolts (2) and turn the pump clockwise to tighten and counterclockwise to loosen.

2. The belt is correctly tensioned when it can be twisted 90 degrees with the thumb and forefinger, midway between the camshaft drive sprocket and the water pump.

The timing belt on all models is correctly tensioned when it can be twisted 90° with the thumb and forefinger

4000 and 5000 Diesels

NOTE: Special tool VW210 will be required for this procedure.

Tension adjustment on the front timing belt is performed in the same manner as with the other four or five cylinder engines. Deflection is also checked in the same position, but with the special tool VW210 rather than your fingers. Proper tension is achieved when the scale reads 12–13.

Tension on the rear timing belt (5 cyl. engines only) is also checked with VW210, in between the two drive sprockets. The scale should read between 12 and 13. To adjust the tension, loosen the injection pump mounting bracket bolts and move the pump toward the engine to loosen and away from the engine to tighten.

Timing Gears

REMOVAL AND INSTALLATION

4000 and 5000

All of the drive sprockets are located by keys on their respective shafts (with the exception of certain diesel engine camshaft sprockets which are a taper fit) and each is retained by a bolt. To remove any or all of the sprockets, first remove the timing belt covers and belts and then use the following procedure.

1. Remove the center retaining bolt for the particular drive sprocket.

2. Gently pry the sprocket off of the shaft.

3. If the sprocket is stubborn in coming off, use a gear puller. Don't hammer on the sprocket as you may crack it.

4. Remove the sprocket being careful not to lose the key.

5. Installation is in the reverse order of removal.

NOTE: Always check valve timing after removing the drive sprockets.

Camshaft

REMOVAL AND INSTALLATION

100

This operation requires that the engine be removed from the car and rather extensively disassembled.

1. Remove the timing chain and tensioner.

2. Remove the cylinder head.

3. Remove the tappets (valve lifters). A special tool is used to lift them out. Keep them in order so they can be replaced in their original locations.

4. Remove the distributor.

5. Remove the oil pump.

6. Unbolt and remove the camshaft locating plate.

7. Carefully guide the camshaft out of the block, being cautious not to bang the lobes into the bearings. This is a lot easier if a bolt is threaded into the front of the camshaft for use as a handle.

8. On reinstallation, oil the camshaft bearing surfaces. Insert the camshaft carefully.

9. Install the locating plate, torqueing the bolts to 18 ft. lbs.

10. Check the camshaft end-play in and out of the block, using a dial indicator. If it exceeds 0.004 in., install a new locating plate.

11. The rest of the reassembly procedure is the reverse of disassembly. Make sure to align the chain and sprockets as explained under "Timing Chain and Tensioner Removal and Installation." Check the ignition timing when the job is complete.

Fox

NOTE: The manufacturer says that the camshaft must not be removed unless a special removal tool is used. This device bolts to the cylinder head and presses down on the camshaft at two places: between the lobes for cylinder 3 and between the lobes for cylinder 2. The following alternate procedure may be used, but great caution must be exercised. THE ALTERNATE PROCEDURE IS NOT RECOMMENDED BY THE MANUFACTURER.

1. Remove the timing belt.
2. Remove the camshaft sprocket.
3. Remove the air cleaner.
4. Remove the camshaft cover.
5. Unscrew and remove the No. 1, 3, and 5 bearing caps (No. 1 is at the front).
6. Unscrew the No. 2 and 4 bearing caps, diagonally and in increments.
7. Lift the camshaft out of the cylinder head.
8. Lubricate the camshaft journals and lobes with assembly lube or gear oil before installing it in the cylinder head.
9. Replace the camshaft oil seal with a new one whenever the cam is removed.
10. Install the No. 1, 3, and 5 bearing caps and tighten the nuts to 14 ft. lbs. The caps should be installed so they read right side up from the driver's seat.
11. Install the No. 2 and 4 bearing caps and diagonally tighten the nuts to 14 ft. lbs.

NOTE: If checking end-play, install a dial indicator so that the feeler touches the camshaft snout. End-play should be no more than 0.006 in.

12. Replace the seal in the No. 1 bearing cap. If necessary, replace the end plug in the cylinder head.
13. Install the camshaft cover.
14. Install the camshaft pulley and the timing belt.
15. Check the valve clearance.

4000 (4 Cylinder)-Gasoline and Diesel Engines

1. Remove the timing belt.
2. Remove the PCV line.
3. Remove the cylinder head cover.
4. Remove the camshaft drive sprocket.
5. Unscrew and remove the Nos. 1; 3 and 5 bearing caps (No. 1 is at the front of the engine).
6. Diagonally loosen bearing caps Nos. 2 and 4.
7. Remove the camshaft from the cylinder head.
8. Remove the camshaft journals, lobes, bearing shells and the contact faces of the caps with assembly lube or gear oil before reinstallation.
9. Replace the camshaft oil seal. If necessary, replace the end plug also.
10. Install the Nos. 1, 3 and 5 bearing caps and tighten the nuts to 14 ft. lbs.

NOTE: Tighten the bearing caps diagonally. Observe off center bearing position; numbers on bearing caps are not always on the same side.

11. Install the Nos. 2 and 4 bearing caps and tighten the nuts to 14 ft. lbs.
12. Replace the seal in the No. 1 bearing cap.
13. Installation of the remaining components is in the reverse order of removal.

NOTE: Always recheck the valve clearance after the camshaft has been removed.

4000 (5 Cylinder), 5000, Turbo and Quattro

1. Remove the camshaft cover.
2. Remove the drive belt and camshaft sprocket.
3. Remove bearing caps 2 and 4.
4. Diagonally loosen bearing caps 1 and 3.
5. Lift out the camshaft.
6. When installing, lightly oil the camshaft and bearings with clean engine oil.
7. Position the caps on the same journals from which they were removed.
8. Lightly tighten the nuts of caps 2 and 4.
9. Tighten all nuts to 14 ft. lbs.
10. Install the drive belt and sprocket and the camshaft cover. The sprocket bolt is torqued to 58 ft. lbs.; the cover bolts to 7 ft. lbs.

5000 Diesels

1. Remove the front and rear timing belts.
2. Remove the cylinder head cover.
3. Remove the camshaft drive sprocket.
4. Remove the injection pump drive sprocket.
5. Set cylinder No. 1 to TDC of the compressor stroke.
6. Remove bearing caps Nos. 1 and 4.
7. Diagonally loosen bearing caps Nos. 2 and 3 and remove.
8. Remove the camshaft from the cylinder head.
9. Lubricate the camshaft journals, lobes, bearing shells and the contact faces of the caps with assembly lube or gear oil before reinstallation.
10. Replace both camshaft oil seals.

NOTE: The cam lobes for the No. 1 cylinder must face upward.

11. Install bearing caps Nos. 2 and 3, tightening alternately and diagonally.
12. Install bearing caps Nos. 1 and 4.
13. Replace the seal in the No. 1 bearing cap.
14. Installation of the remaining components is in the reverse order of removal.

NOTE: Always recheck the valve clearance after the camshaft has been removed.

Pistons and Connecting Rods

100

The connecting rods must be installed in the engine with the grooved side toward the camshaft. New connecting rod bolts must always be used. Both the pistons and the piston pins must be heated to 140°F in an oven in order to install the pins. Three oversizes of pistons are available to accommodate overbores up to 0.004 in.

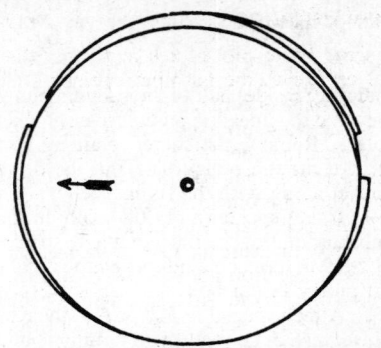

Arrow on pistons must face forward

All Other Gasoline Engines

The pistons must be installed in the block with the arrow at the edge of the crown facing to the front of the car. The connecting rod and cap alignment casting grooves must face the intermediate shaft. New connecting rod bolts must always be used. The pistons must be heated to 140°F in an oven before the piston pins can be pressed in. Three piston oversizes are available to accommodate overbores up to 0.040 in.

Align the forged marks when assembling the connecting rods and caps

Piston projection measurement on diesel engines—note spacer (arrow)

Diesel Engines

The same basic procedures apply for the diesel engine as the gasoline engine. The one important difference is that whenever new pistons are installed, the piston projection must be checked.

A spacer (Special Tool VW 385/17) and a bar with a micrometer (Special Tool VW 385/7) are necessary and should be set up as shown, to measure the maximum amount of piston projection above the top surface of the engine block. After ascertaining the projection height, select a new gasket from the following chart.

Piston Height In. (mm)	Identification Notches In Gasket	Part Number
0.026–0.031 (0.67–0.80)	1	069 103 383
0.032–0.035 (0.81–0.90)	2	069 103 383A
0.036–0.040 (0.91–1.02)	3	069 103 383B

When installing the connecting rods on the diesel engine, the forged marks on the bearing caps and on the bottom of the rods should be facing the right side of the engine.

ENGINE LUBRICATION

Oil Pan

REMOVAL AND INSTALLATION

100

1. Raise and support the car.
2. Remove the apron under the front bumper for better access.
3. Remove the radiator mounting bolts and press the radiator up out of the brackets.
4. Drain the oil.
5. Loosen and remove the Allen head bolts holding the pan. Tap it lightly with a soft hammer to break it loose. Remove the pan.
6. Clean the pan out thoroughly while it is off the engine.
7. Install new gaskets at either end of the oil pan. Apply a very thin coat of adhesive to them. Attach the pan rail gaskets to the block, using a slight amount of adhesive at both ends and in the middle. Put a tiny amount of adhesive at the extreme ends of the gaskets, adjacent to the rear main bearing cap and the timing cover. Stick

on the small gasket segment below the starter.
8. Torque the larger pan bolts to 11 ft. lbs. and the rest to 6 ft. lbs.
9. The rest of the installation is the reverse of removal. Fill the crankcase and run the engine, checking for leaks.

Fox

The front crossmember has to be lowered to remove the oil pan.

1. Raise the car, allowing the front wheels to hang down. Drain the oil.
2. Disconnect the engine vacuum line from the power brake vacuum line T fitting. Pull the vacuum line from the cylinder head on automatic transmission cars.
3. Support the rear of the engine at the cast lifting eye in the cylinder head.
4. From underneath, unbolt the lower left and right engine mounts. Carefully and evenly loosen and remove the four crossmember-to-body bolts and lower the crossmember.
5. Remove the pan bolts. Tap it lightly with a soft hammer to break it loose. Remove the pan and clean it out thoroughly while it is off the engine.
6. On installation, use a new gasket with no sealer. Torque the pan bolts in a criss-cross pattern, in steps, to 6 ft. lbs. Torque the crossmember bolts to 33 ft. lbs.

4000, 5000, Turbo and Quattro

1. Raise and support the vehicle.
2. Drain the oil.
3. Remove the oil pan bolts while supporting the pan.

NOTE: To remove the two bolts at the rear of the oil pan on the diesel engine, turn the flywheel so that the recesses are pointing down. This will afford you access to the two bolts.

4. Lower the pan from the engine. Discard the gasket.
5. Coat both sides of a new gasket with sealer and install the gasket and oil pan.
6. Torque the bolts to 7 ft. lbs. (14 ft. lbs. on 4000 Diesels).

Rear Main Bearing Oil Seal Replacement

When this seal fails, the usual result is oil leakage onto the clutch. This of course, causes clutch slippage or failure to disengage.

100

This repair requires that the engine be removed from the car and extensively disassembled.

1. Remove the engine.
2. Remove the transmission (and clutch) from the engine.
3. Remove the flywheel. Some method

of preventing the flywheel from turning will have to be devised.

NOTE: Mark the relationship between the flywheel and crankshaft to preserve balance.

4. Remove the oil pan.
5. Unbolt and remove the rear main bearing cap.
6. The circular seal may now be removed.
7. Press the new seal evenly into place with the sealing lip toward the front of the engine. This is rather difficult without special seal installing tools.
8. Torque the bearing cap to specifications.
9. The remainder of the procedure is the reverse of disassembly. Make sure to align the flywheel marks made in Step 3.

Fox

1. Remove the engine. Refer to the "Engine Removal and Installation" procedures.
2. Remove the transmission (and clutch) from the engine.
3. Remove the flywheel. Some method of preventing the flywheel from turning will have to be devised.

NOTE: Mark the relationship between the flywheel and crankshaft to preserve balance.

4. The circular seal may now be removed by placing a suitable tool under the sealing lip or behind the support ring carefully. Be very cautious not to damage the seal bearing surface.
5. Press the new seal evenly in place. This is rather difficult without special seal installing tools.
6. The remainder of the procedure is the reverse of removal. Make sure to align the flywheel marks made in Step 3.

4000 and 5000

The rear main oil seal is located at the rear of the engine block. It can be found in a housing behind the flywheel. To replace the seal it is necessary to remove the transmission.

1. Remove the transmission.
2. Unscrew the six bolts and remove the flywheel.
3. Using special tool VW2086 or a suitable tool, pry the old seal out of its housing.

Rear main oil seal (circular)—4000 and 5000

4. To install, lightly oil the replacement seal then press it into place using a canister top or other circular piece of flat metal.

—————— CAUTION ——————

Be careful not to damage the seal or score the crankshaft.

5. Install the flywheel and the transmission.

Oil Pump

REMOVAL AND INSTALLATION

100

1. Remove the distributor. Remove the oil pan.
2. Disconnect the oil line from the block and the pump.
3. Place No. 1 cylinder on TDC. This can be done by turning the engine with a finger held over the No. 1 spark plug hole. When compression is felt, turn the engine to align with 0°T mark on the crankshaft pulley with the timing pointer.
4. On replacement, turn the pump until the wide segment of the pump driveshaft faces forward. Turn the shaft 15 degrees counterclockwise and slide the oil pump shaft into the gear teeth of the camshaft.
5. Install the spacer under the pump and mounting bolt and tighten the bolt finger tight.
6. Put the oil line in place. Turn the pump or add extra gaskets at either end of the oil line to prevent any strain on the line.
7. Torque the pump mounting bolt to 18 ft. lbs. and the oil line bolts to 7 ft. lbs. Use the lock plates to hold the oil line bolts.
8. Align the distributor rotor with the No. 1 cylinder notch in the rim of the housing. Insert the distributor with the vacuum unit parallel to the engine block and pointing to the rear of the engine. When installing the distributor, wiggle the rotor back and forth to allow the shaft projections to engage the oil pump driveshaft slots. Tighten the distributor mounting bolt.

9. Replace and fill the oil pan.
10. Start the engine and watch for oil leaks. If it won't start, check the basic ignition timing. If it does start, check the final ignition timing with a timing light.

Fox

To remove the pump, remove the oil pan and the pump mounting bolts. Pull the pump straight down. Pump bolt torque is 13–16 ft. lbs.

4000

1. Drain the oil and remove the oil pan.
2. Remove the oil pump mounting bolts and pull the pump down and out of the engine.
3. Unscrew the two bolts and separate the pump halves.
4. Clean the lower half in solvent.
5. To remove the oil strainer for cleaning, bend out the metal rim of the oil strainer cover plate and remove it.
6. Examine the gears and the driveshaft for any wear or damage. Replace them if necessary.
7. Reassemble the pump halves.
8. Prime the pump with oil and install in the reverse order of removal.

5000, Turbo and Quattro

1. Loosen and remove crankshaft bolt.
2. Remove the drive belt guard.
3. Loosen the water pump bolts and turn the pump body clockwise.
4. Remove the drive belt and V-belt pulley with the drive belt sprocket.
5. Remove the dipstick and drain the engine oil.
6. Remove the front bolts on the sub frame and remove the oil pan.
7. Remove the oil suction pipe from the base of the oil pump and bracket to the engine block.
8. Remove the oil pump bolts and remove the oil pump from the front of the engine.

The slots (a) in the 100 series oil pump driveshaft and the projections (b) on the distributor driveshaft are offset. (c) indicates the wide segment of each shaft. The shafts can mate in only one way.

ENGINE COOLING

The radiator drain plug is at the bottom, adjacent to the lower hose on all models. The engine drain plug is at the front, adjacent to the alternator except on the Fox. There is a breather plug in the upper heater hose, near the firewall on 100 cars. The breather plug must be used to remove air from the system, when the engine is first started after refilling.

Radiator

REMOVAL AND INSTALLATION

100

1. Drain the coolant.
2. Remove the upper radiator hose.
3. Detach the mounting strut at the top of the radiator, and swing it forward.
4. Detach the lower radiator hose. Detach the fan thermostatic switch.
5. Unbolt the radiator mountings.
6. Lift the radiator out.
7. To install, reverse the removal procedures. Make sure that the rubber sealing strips between the radiator and radiator cowl are in place.

Fox

1. Drain the coolant. Remove the grille.
2. Remove the bolts holding the panel at the side of the radiator through the grille opening.
3. Disconnect the lower radiator hose and the radiator fan switch at the bottom of the radiator. Remove the lower radiator panel and the lower radiator mounting nuts.
4. Loosen the mounting bar and slide the upper radiator panel toward the center of the car to remove it. Unbolt the upper radiator mounts and detach the upper radiator hose.
5. Disconnect the heater and intake manifold coolant hoses at the fan shroud. Remove the radiator side mounting bolt and remove the radiator and electric fan together.

4000 (4 Cylinder)

1. Drain the cooling system.
2. If equipped with air conditioning, remove the grille and detach the condenser

Engine block coolant drain plug—100

Radiator drain plug—100

from the radiator.

3. Remove the upper and lower radiator hoses, the expansion tank supply hose and the expansion tank vent hose. Being careful not to crimp them, tie all hoses back out of the way.

NOTE: All disconnections should be done at the radiator end of the particular hose.

4. Disconnect the wiring at the temperature switch (two switches if air conditioning) and the rear of the fan motor.

5. Unscrew the fan shroud retaining bolts and remove the fan, motor and shroud as one assembly.

6. Unscrew the radiator retaining bolts and remove the radiator.

7. Installation is in the reverse order of removal.

4000 (5 Cylinder), 5000, Turbo and Quattro

1. Drain the cooling system.

2. Remove the three pieces of the radiator cowl and the fan motor assembly. Take care in removing the fan motor connectors to avoid bending them.

3. Remove the upper and lower radiator hoses and the coolant tank supply hose.

4. Disconnect the coolant temperature switch located on the lower right side of the radiator.

5. Remove the radiator mounting bolts and lift out the radiator.

6. Installation is the reverse of removal. Torque radiator mounting bolts to 14 ft. lbs. and cowl bolts to 7 ft. lbs.

The 5000 Diesel is equipped with an auxiliary radiator which must also be removed.

Correct installation of the front mounted thermostat on the 100

To remove the auxiliary radiator:

1. Remove the grille and detach the condenser (air conditioning only).

2. Remove all hoses from the auxiliary radiator.

3. Remove the radiator retaining bolts and remove the radiator.

4. Installation is in the reverse order of removal.

Water Pump

REMOVAL AND INSTALLATION

100

1. Loosen the adjustment bolt and remove the water pump drive belt.

2. Drain the coolant.

3. Remove the alternator pivot bolt at the front.

4. Loosen the clamp and pull the lower hose off the pump.

5. Remove the thermostat housing.

6. Unbolt the fan pulley. The pulley may be prevented from turning by wedging a screwdriver between the pulley hub and one of the bolts.

7. The pulley may be carefully pried off the hub with two large screwdrivers.

8. Loosen the clamp and pull the upper hose off the pump.

9. Remove the five bolts and remove the pump.

10. Reverse the procedure for installation, using new gaskets and adjusting the alternator drive belt tension. Pump mounting bolt torque is 15 ft. lbs. for the large bolts, and 9 ft. lbs. for the small ones. Thermostat housing bolt torque is 15 ft. lbs. Pulley bolt torque is 7 ft. lbs.

Fox

1. Drain the coolant.

2. Remove the alternator.

3. Remove the timing belt cover.

4. Loosen the clamps and detach the hoses from the pump.

5. Unbolt the pump, turn it slightly, and lift it out.

6. On installation, use a new pump-to-block seal and torque the pump bolts to 14 ft. lbs.

4000, 5000, Turbo and Quattro

1. Drain the cooling system.

2. Remove the V-belts, timing belt covers and timing belts as outlined earlier in this section.

3. On the 4000, unscrew the water pump pulley retaining bolts (3) and remove the pulley.

4. On the 4000, unscrew the intermediate shaft drive sprocket retaining bolt and remove the sprocket.

5. Unscrew the water pump retaining bolts and remove the pump from its housing on the 4000 or from the engine block on

all other models.

6. Always replace the old gasket with a new one.

7. Installation is in the reverse order of removal.

Thermostat

REMOVAL AND INSTALLATION

100 and Fox

1. Drain the coolant from the radiator.

2. The thermostat is inside a cast housing on the engine or the water pump, connected to the upper radiator hose. Unbolt the cover and remove the gasket and the thermostat.

3. Some thermostats have an arrow on the bar which should also point at the projection. In any case, the bar should be up. The housing bolts should be torqued to 7 ft. lbs. Always use a new gasket.

Thermostat housing—5000

4000 (4 cylinder)

The thermostat is located in the lower radiator hose neck on the bottom of the water pump housing.

1. Drain the cooling system.

2. Remove the two retaining bolts from the lower water pump neck.

NOTE: It is not necessary to disconnect the lower radiator hose.

3. Move the neck, with the hoses attached, out of the way.

4. Carefully pry the thermostat out of the water pump housing.

4000 (5 Cylinder), 5000, Turbo and Quattro

The thermostat is located in the lower radiator hose neck, on the left side of the engine block, behind the water pump housing.

Follow Steps 1–3 of the 4000 procedure.

1. Carefully pry the thermostat out of the engine block.

2. Install a new O-ring on the water pump neck.

3. Install the thermostat.

NOTE: When installing the thermostat, the spring end should be pointing toward the engine block.

4. Reposition the water pump neck and tighten the retaining bolts.

Belt Tension Adjustment

1. Loosen the two bolts holding the fan housing to the fan support arm.

2. Move the fan and housing out to tighten the belt. The belt is correctly tensioned when the longest span of belt between pulleys can be depressed about ½ in. by moderate thumb pressure.

3. Tighten the bolts.

(a) Bolts-adjusting   (d) Stop
(b) Mounting bolts   (e) Fan support
(c) Pad

Radiator fan belt tension is adjusted with bolts

EMISSION CONTROLS

Several emission control devices are used to control different sources of emissions. Engine crankcase emissions are controlled by routing them directly into the carburetor air cleaner or into the fuel vapor control system, which is connected to the air cleaner.

Fuel vapor emissions from the carburetor float bowl and the fuel tank are handled by the fuel vapor control system. The system has an activated carbon container in the engine compartment to store vapors until they can be drawn in through the air cleaner and burned.

100

The 100, 100LS, and 100GL use certain basic equipment to control exhaust emissions. The parts of the system are: a triple port intake manifold.

The triple port intake manifold has a separate intake for water, used to preheat the manifold. The preheating and the conduction of the fuel/air mixture from each stage separately leads to more complete combustion and a lower level of exhaust emissions.

The distributor uses both centrifugal and vacuum advance mechanisms.

All 100 series models are equipped with a capacitive discharge ignition system. This system reduces the normal decline in ig-

=== Exhaust and air lines

--- Vacuum control lines

········· Electrical wiring

1. Air cleaner
2. Carburetor venturi
3. Throttle valve
4. Intake manifold
5. Cylinder head intake port
6. Cylinder head exhaust port
7. Belt drive for air pump
8. Air pump
9. Air filter for air pump
10. Pressure regulating valve
11. Check valve
12. Diverter valve
13. Distributor
14. EGR filter
15. EGR valve
16. Vacuum booster
17. Vacuum reserve
18. Solenoid vacuum valve
19. Temperature switch for cooling circuit
20. Crankcase ventilation

Emission control schematic for 100 LS

nition system performance between tune-ups, keeping exhaust emissions at a minimum. It does this primarily reducing the electrical load on the breaker points and supplying very high voltage to the spark plugs.

NOTE: Some tachometers, dwell meters, and oscilloscopes will not work with this system. Some may be damaged. Check with the manufacturer of your best equipment if there is any doubt.

1976 models have the Audi continuous fuel injection system and the air injection system. California models only have a catalytic converter in the exhaust system.

Fox

The Fox uses emission control systems very similar to those on the 100 series. The fuel evaporation control system differs only in that it does not require a fuel recirculation line.

4000 and 5000

A closed, positive crankcase ventilation system (PCV) is employed on all 4000 and 5000 models. This system cycles incompletely burned fuel which works its way past the piston rings back into the intake manifold for reburning with the fuel/air

mixture. The oil filler cap is sealed and the air is drawn from the top of the crankcase into the intake manifold through a valve with a variable orifice (commonly known as a PCV valve).

The evaporative emission control system on these models includes: a sealed filler cap, a gravity vent valve, an activated charcoal canister, a charcoal canister control valve and a fuel pump check valve. All models are equipped with a dual diaphragm distributor. The purpose of the distributor is to reduce exhaust emissions during idling.

All Audis, with the exception of the Turbo, the 4000 5 cylinder and any 1979 and later car built for use in California are equipped with an EGR system to control part throttle exhaust emissions. Audi uses a vacuum operated EGR valve controlled primarily by a connection near the throttle plate where the vacuum is only present at part throttle. The EGR system also includes a temperature valve (two on cars equipped with air conditioning) which acts on engine coolant temperature, a vacuum amplifier that acts basically like a relay and a deceleration valve (found only on certain models) that aids in the fuel/air mixture adjustment on deceleration.

To aid in the reduction of exhaust emissions a catalytic converter is built into the exhaust system. There are two types of catalytic converters used: An oxidizing type and a three way type. The oxidizing type is used on the 1978 5000 (Calif.), the 1979–81 5000 (49 state) and the 1980–81 4000 (49 state). The three way type is used on the Turbo, the 4000 5 cylinder, and all 1982 and later models.

=== Exhaust and air lines
--- Vacuum control lines

1. Air cleaner
2. Carburetor venturi
3. Throttle valve
4. Intake manifold
5. Cylinder head intake port
6. Cylinder head exhaust port
7. Belt drive for air pump
8. Air pump
9. Air pump filter
10. Pressure relief valve
11. Check valve
12. Diverter valve
13. Distributor
14. EGR filter
15. EGR valve
16. Crankcase ventilation

Emission control schematic for Fox

FUEL SYSTEM

Fuel Pump

1. Fuel tank
2. Vapor expansion container
3. Engine
4. Fuel pump
5. Activated carbon container
6. Air cleaner
7. Fuel line from tank to pump
8. Breather line from neck to expansion container
9. Breather line from tank to expansion container
10. Breather line to carbon container
11. Line from carbon
11. Line from carbon container to air cleaner
12. Non-vented tank filler cap
13. Carburetor
14. Fuel return valve
15. Line from return valve to tank

Fuel vapor emission control system—typical

REMOVAL AND INSTALLATION

100

The fuel pump is on the left side of the engine, in front of the distributor.

1. Disconnect the hoses from the pump. Plug the inlet hose.

2. Remove the mounting bolts and pull out the pump.

3. When replacing the pump, use a new insulator. No other gaskets are required.

1976–77 Fox

The fuel pump is on the left side of the engine, in front of distributor.

1. Disconnect the hoses from the pump. Plug the inlet hose.

2. Remove the mounting bolts and remove the pump with the plastic insulator.

3. Reverse the procedure on installation.

1978–79 Fox

An electric pump is located on a bracket in the right rear wheel well.

1. Disconnect and plug the hoses.

2. Remove the mounting bolts and lift off the pump.

3. Installation is the reverse of removal.

4000 and 5000

An electric pump is used, mounted on a bracket near the right rear wheel well.

1. Disconnect the battery ground.

2. Clean all fuel and electrical connections.

3. Disconnect the pump wiring.

4. Disconnect the fuel lines.

5. Unbolt and dismount the pump.

6. Installation is the reverse of removal. Torque the mounting bolts to 14 ft. lbs.

Fuel Injection

For all fuel injection system repair and service procedures not detailed below, please refer to "Fuel Injection" in the Unit Repair section.

FUEL INJECTORS

Removal and Installation

1. Grasp the injector where it touches the engine block and pull firmly. It should pop right out.

2. Unscrew the injector from the fuel line.

5000 model emission control layout

100 series fuel pump. (NW) is the camshaft, (a) is the insulator, (b) is the lockwasher and (c) is the mounting bolt

Removing the injector

3. Screw the injector back into the fuel line.

4. Moisten the rubber seal with fuel and then press the injector firmly into the injector seat.

Fuel Distributor

REMOVAL AND INSTALLATION

1. Clean and remove fuel lines at distributor.

2. Remove retaining bolts and carefully lift out distributor. Take care not to drop control piston.

3. If control plunger has been removed, moisten with fuel before installing and insert small shoulder first.

4. Reinstall distributor using new O-rings.

Diesel Fuel Injection

The diesel fuel injection system is an extremely complex and sensitive system. Very few repairs or adjustments are possible by the owner. Any service other than that listed here should be referred to an authorized Audi dealer or a diesel specialist. The injection pump itself is not repairable; it can

Fuel distributor attaching screws

only be replaced.

Any work done to the diesel injection system should be done with absolute cleanliness. Even the smallest specks of dirt can have a disastrous effect on the diesel injection system.

We would advise not attempting to remove the fuel injectors. They are very delicate and must be removed with a special tool to prevent damage. The fuel in the system is also under tremendous pressure, so it's not too wise to loosen any of the lines with the engine running. Exposing your skin to the spray from the injector at working pressure can cause fuel to penetrate the skin. The only component of the injection system that we would suggest performing any sort of maintenance on are the glow plugs.

CHECKING THE GLOW PLUG CURRENT SUPPLY

1. Connect a test light between the No. 4 cylinder glow plug and a ground.

2. Turn the key to the heat position. The test light should light up.

3. If the test light doesn't light, check

the glow plug relay, the ignition switch or the fuse box relay plate.

CHECKING THE GLOW PLUGS

This check can be made only after it has first been established that there is current to the glow plugs.

1. Remove the wire and the glow plug bus bar.

2. Connect a test light between the positive battery terminal and each glow plug in turn.

3. If the test light lights, the glow plug is alright. If it does not, the glow plug is defective and will require replacement.

MANUAL TRANSMISSION

The transmission is combined with the differential in a transaxle.

REMOVAL AND INSTALLATION

100

The engine/transaxle unit must be removed from the car as explained under "Engine Removal and Installation." Then the transmission can simply be unbolted from the engine and slid back. On replacement, tighten the bolts to 54, 33, and 18 ft. lbs., respectively, for the three sizes of bolts.

Fox

The transaxle can be lowered from the car, leaving the engine in place.

1. Disconnect the battery ground cable. Raise the car on a chassis lift.

2. Detach and wire up the entire exhaust system.

3. Release the lockplates and remove the axle shaft bolts. Wire the shafts up.

4. Use pliers to unscrew the speedometer cable nut.

5. Support the transaxle. Remove the engine to transaxle bolts and the clutch guard plate.

6. Remove the lock wire and unscrew the gearshift rod coupling square headed bolt. Pull off the gearshift rod.

7. Disconnect the gearshift strut at the transmission and unbolt the small crossmember at the rear of the transmission.

8. Disconnect the backup light and seat belt system wires at the transmission.

9. Separate the transaxle from the engine and lower it. Reverse the procedure on installation. Torque the engine-to-transaxle bolts to 40 ft. lbs. and the axle shaft bolts to 28 ft. lbs.

4000

This procedure can be performed with the engine installed.

1. Disconnect the negative battery cable.

2. Unplug the two electrical connectors for the back-up lights. They can be found between the ignition coil and the fuel distributor filter.

3. Remove the upper engine/transmission bolts.

4. Using special tool 3016 or a pair of pliers, detach the speedometer cable where it attaches to the transaxle.

5. Detach the clutch cable from the clutch lever.

6. Unbolt the exhaust pipe from the exhaust manifold.

7. Unscrew the three mounting bolts and remove the center engine mount.

8. Unbolt the front exhaust pipe from the support bracket and then unbolt it from the catalytic converter (muffler on Canadian models).

9. Unscrew the six screws and remove the left halfshaft from the transaxle. Wire the halfshaft up and out of the way. Repeat the procedure for the right halfshaft.

——————— CAUTION ———————

When wiring the halfshaft, tighten the wire only enough so as to relieve any downward pressure on them.

10. Remove the cover plate.

11. Tag and disconnect all wires leading to the starter and remove the starter.

12. Remove the bolt from the shift rod coupling.

13. Pry off the linkage coupling.

14. Pull the shift rod coupling off of the shift rod.

15. Loosen the left (chassis) bolt on the rear transmission support. Remove the two bolts (some models have one) from the right (transmission) side of the support and pivot the support out of the way.

16. Remove the rubber mounting block.

17. Unscrew three bolts and remove the front transmission support.

18. Remove the lower engine/transmission bolts.

19. Carefully pry the transmission apart from the engine and remove it.

20. Installation is in the reverse order of removal. Note the following:

a. Make sure that all engine/transmission mounts are correctly aligned and free of tension.

b. Check for proper adjustment of the gear shift lever.

c. Secure the bolt on the shift rod coupling with wire.

d. Tighten the engine/transmission bolts to 40 ft. lbs.

e. Tighten the halfshaft-to-drive flange bolts to 33 ft. lbs.

f. Tighten the subframe-to-body bolts to 51 ft. lbs.

g. Tighten the front transmission support-to-transmission bolts to 18 ft. lbs.

h. Tighten the rubber mount-to-body bolts to 29 ft. lbs. (new mount, 80 ft. lbs.).

i. Tighten the rubber mount-to-transmission bolts to 40 ft. lbs.

j. Tighten the rubber mount-to-crossmember bolts to 18 ft. lbs.

5000

The manual transaxle may be remove with the engine in place.

1. Disconnect the battery ground.

2. Remove the air filter (Diesel only).

3. Remove the windshield washer bottle.

4. Remove the upper engine-transmission bolts.

5. Raise and support the car.

6. Disconnect the speedometer cable at the engine.

7. Disconnect all wires and hoses connected to the transaxle.

8. Drive out the clutch slave cylinder lockpin and remove the slave cylinder. Leave the hydraulic line connected.

9. Support the engine, either from above with a hoist or from below with a jack.

10. Remove the heat shield.

11. Remove the lower engine/transmission splash shield (Diesel only).

12. Disconnect the exhaust pipe from the manifold.

13. Remove the right side guard plate.

14. Disconnect the driveshafts from the flanges and support them out of the way with wires. On the Quattro, you must also disconnect the front/rear driveshaft at the rear output shaft on the transmission and wire it out of the way.

15. Disconnect the backup light switch.

16. Pry off the shift and adjusting rods.

17. Remove the lower engine-transmission bolts.

18. Remove the starter.

19. Remove the subframe skid plate.

20. Install a jack under the transmission and lift it slightly.

21. Remove both transmission-to-subframe bolts.

22. Remove the right side transmission bracket.

When adjusting the 100 series manual transmission floorshift linkage, the spring loaded ball should engage the slot (n) in the shift rod (33) when the transmission is in neutral. If it does not, loosen the bolts (8) and move the bracket.

23. Slide the transmission back off the locating dowels and remove it from the car.

24. When installing, place the driveshafts on top of the subframe; tighten the lower bolts first, then tighten the transmission bracket, subframe and upper bolts. Driveshaft bolts are torqued to 32 ft. lbs.; transmission bracket bolts to 29 ft. lbs.; subframe support bolts to 29 ft. lbs.; subframe to body bolts to 80 ft. lbs. and the transmission to engine bolts to 40 ft. lbs.

Install all other parts in reverse order of removal.

LINKAGE ADJUSTMENT

100

1. Slide the seats all the way back and set the handbrake.

2. Remove the six sheet metal screws which secure the console. Unscrew the shift knob and lift off the console.

3. The shift lever bracket has a spring-loaded ball which should engage the groove in the long shift rod when the transmission is in Neutral.

4. To adjust, loosen the four bolts which hold the shift lever bracket to the floor and move the bracket to the front or rear. Tighten the bolts and recheck the adjustment. There is an adjustable linkage rod above the rear of the transmission for easier adjustment.

5. If the long shift rod has a rubber damper apparatus in the middle, make sure that it is in good condition and not causing any unnecessary play.

6. Grease the moving parts lightly.

7. Replace the console and the shift knob.

Fox

1. Remove the rubber boot at the base of the shift lever.

2. Loosen the two bolts at the base of the lever and move the lever to the far right of the Neutral slot against the stop. Tighten the bolts.

3. If there is a problem with the lever sticking or jamming, loosen the two shift gate bolts from under the car and adjust the gate backward or forward. Tighten the bolts.

4000

NOTE: This procedure will require Special Tool VW 3014.

1. Place the shift lever in the Neutral position.

2. Working under the car, loosen the clamp nut on the shift rod.

3. Inside the car, remove the shift knob and the boot. It is not necessary to remove the console.

4. Align the holes in the shifter base with the holes in the bearing plate directly below it and tighten the bolts.

5. Install the Special Tool VW 3014 with the locating pin toward the front.

Loosen the clamp nut on the shift rod—4000

6. Push the shift lever to the left side of the tool cutout and tighten the lower knurled knob to secure the tool.

7. Move the top slide of the tool to the left side stop and tighten the upper knurled knot.

8. Push the shift lever into the right cutout of the slide. Align the shift rod and the shift finger under the car and tighten the clamp nut.

9. Remove the special tool.

10. Place the shift lever in the first gear position. Press the lever to the left side against the stop. Release the lever; it should spring back ¼ to ½ in. If not, move the lever housing slightly sideways to correct. Check that all gears can be engaged easily.

5000

1. Remove the gear shift boot.
2. Position the shift lever in neutral.

Front-to-rear rod clamp—5000

Shifter base plate bolts—5000

3. The seam on the plastic stop bracket should line up with the center hole in the curved stop plate. If not, proceed below:

4. Loosen the four bolts at the base of the shifter.

5. Align the holes in the shifter base with the holes in the bearing plate directly below it.

6. Tighten the bolts.

7. Loosen the clamp between the front and rear shift rods.

8. Make certain that the front shift rod is in the neutral position.

9. Clamp the shifter securely in the neutral position and tighten the shift rod clamp.

10. Release the shifter and check its operation in all gears.

11. Install the shifter boot, making sure that the top of the boot is in contact with the shift knob.

The plastic stop bracket should align with the curved stop plate—5000

CLUTCH

REMOVAL AND INSTALLATION

100

1. Remove the engine and transaxle as a unit.

2. Separate the engine and transaxle.

3. Mark the relationship of the pressure plate to the flywheel.

4. Unbolt the pressure plate from the flywheel, loosening the bolts alternately a little bit at a time to prevent warpage.

5. To install the clutch, place the driven plate on the pressure plate, making sure that it is facing the right way.

6. Hold the clutch assembly against the flywheel, aligning the marks in Step 3, and insert a dummy shaft through the pressure plate and the driven plate into the crankshaft pilot bearing.

7. Install the pressure plate bolts finger tight. Then tighten the bolts evenly, in rotation, to avoid distortion. Torque the bolts to 24–27 ft. lbs. Remove the dummy shaft.

Before removing the pressure plate bolts (a) mark the pressure plate (b) and the flywheel as shown at the arrow. The dummy shaft (d) is used to center the driven plate (clutch disc) on reinstallation.

8. The clutch release bearing in the front of the transmission housing should be checked before reassembly. It is retained by two springs.

9. Bolt the transaxle back to the engine. Bolt torque is 54, 33, and 18 ft. lbs., respectively, for the three sizes of bolts.

10. Replace the engine/transaxle unit in the car. Check the clutch adjustment.

Fox, 4000 and 5000

1. Remove the transaxle.

2. Mark the relationship of the pressure plate to the flywheel (only if it is to be reused).

3. Unbolt the pressure plate from the flywheel, loosening the bolts alternately, a little at a time, to prevent warpage.

4. To install the clutch, place the driven plate on the pressure plate, making sure that it is facing the right way.

5. Hold the clutch assembly against the flywheel, aligning the marks made in Step 2 and the three dowel pins on the flywheel with the pressure plate, and insert a dummy shaft through the pressure plate and the driven plate into the crankshaft pilot bearing.

6. Install the pressure plate bolts finger tight. Then tighten the bolts evenly, in rotation, to avoid distortion. Torque the bolts to 24 ft. lbs. Remove the dummy shaft.

7. The clutch release bearing in the front of the transaxle should be checked before reassembly. It is retained by two springs.

8. Replace the transaxle. Torque the engine-to-transaxle bolts to 40 ft. lbs. and the axle shaft to 28 ft. lbs.

PEDAL FREE-PLAY ADJUSTMENT

100 and Fox

The pedal free-play is adjusted at the clutch end of the cable. Free-play is the distance that the pedal travels from the released position to the point at which clutch spring pressure can be felt. This can be measured by placing a yardstick alongside the clutch pedal. Play should be 0.6–0.8 in.

1. On the 100, loosen the upper cable

Clutch pedal free-play adjustment nut on the 4000—100 and Fox similar

Exploded view of the 4000 clutch—Fox similar

Exploded view of the 5000 clutch

nut. Turn both nuts clockwise to reduce play, and counterclockwise to increase. After the adjustment is made, tighten the upper nut to lock the cable in place.

2. The total pedal travel on the 100 series should be at least 6.1 in. If it is not adequate, the pedal pivot can be loosened and moved up.

4000

Free-play is the distance that the pedal travels from the released position to the point at which clutch spring pressure can first be felt. This can be measured by placing a yardstick alongside the clutch pedal. Free-play should be ⅝ of an inch, measured at the pedal.

1. Locate the clutch cable bracket by the oil filter.

2. Loosen the upper cable nut.

3. Turn both nuts clockwise to reduce pedal free-play or counterclockwise to increase it.

4. When adjustment is correct, tighten the upper nut to lock the cable in position.

PEDAL HEIGHT ADJUSTMENT

5000

The clutch pedal should be at rest ⅜ inch above the brake pedal. To adjust the pedal height, remove the cotter pin holding the clutch master cylinder clevis to the pedal, loosen the locknut on the clevis shaft and turn the shaft to give the required pedal height. Tighten the locknut and install the clevis on the pedal.

Clutch Cable

REMOVAL AND INSTALLATION

1. Loosen the adjustment.

2. Disengage the cable from the clutch arm.

3. Unhook the cable from the pedal. Remove the threaded eye from the end of

the cable. Remove the adjustment nut(s).

4. Remove the C-clip which holds the outer cable at the adjustment point. Remove all the washers and bushings, first noting their locations.

5. Pull the cable out of the firewall toward the engine compartment side.

6. Install and connect the new cable. Adjust the pedal free-play.

Clutch Master Cylinder (5 Cylinder Models Only)

REMOVAL AND INSTALLATION

1. Locate the master cylinder under the instrument panel and behind the clutch pedal.

2. Remove and plug the line leading to the slave cylinder from the end of the master cylinder.

3. Remove the circlip and the pin which attaches the clevis to the clutch pedal.

4. Remove the two master cylinder mounting screws from the pedal mounting.

5. Remove and plug the remaining line which leads to the fluid reservoir and remove the master cylinder.

6. Installation is in the reverse order of removal.

7. Bleed the system.

BLEEDING THE SYSTEM

Audi recommends that the system be bled by means of a pressure bleeder. You may purchase one at an auto supply store. Follow the manufacturer's instructions for proper bleeding techniques with a pressure bleeder.

Clutch Slave Cylinder

REMOVAL AND INSTALLATION

1. Locate the slave cylinder on top of the transaxle housing.
2. Remove the retaining yoke.
3. Drive out the slave cylinder lock pin.
4. Remove and plug the fluid line (this step is necessary only if the cylinder is to be disassembled).
5. Installation is in the reverse order of removal.
6. If the fluid line was removed, bleed the system as described earlier.

AUTOMATIC TRANSMISSION

The Audi automatic transmission is a hydraulically operated three-speed unit, with a torque converter.

REMOVAL AND INSTALLATION

100

The automatic transmission can be disconnected from the engine and removed with the engine in the car.

1. Drain the transmission. Remove the grille and front apron. The engine must be mounted to the frame in some manner or suspended on a lift or jack to prevent it from falling from the mounts when the mounts are disconnected.
2. Loosen the brake pipe lines from the brake hoses and plug the ends of the brake hoses.
3. Disconnect the accelerator linkage.
4. Remove the front exhaust pipe.
5. Remove the oil filter and starter.
6. Disconnect both driveshafts and suspend them from the upper wishbones. Disconnect the stabilizer bar at both lower wishbones.
7. Unbolt the holder for the selector cable at the transmission. Remove the selector cable from the lever at the transmission. Remove the selector cable holder.
8. Disconnect the crossmember at the engine mounting and at the support. Place a jack or support under the transmission.
9. Remove the guard and disconnect the left and right engine mounts. Be careful not to alter the position of the left mount, which is fixed by means of locknuts.
10. Insert bolts (³⁄₈ in. × 8 in.) through each side in place of the engine mounts. Lower the complete power plant until the unit rests on the bolts.
11. Disconnect the transmission vacuum hose at the vacuum unit or at the T adaptor.

Insert bolts (B) through each engine mount to support the 100 series engine. Note that the starter has been removed for access to the torque converter bolts

Be sure that the projection (N) engages the groove (L) of the 100 series mount

12. Unbolt the torque converter Allen bolts by working through the hole for the starter.
13. Unbolt the engine-to-transmission connections and remove the transmission. Secure the torque converter in the transmission with a strap.
14. To install the transmission, reverse the removal procedure, noting the following: Lift the transmission and bolt it to the engine. Lift both the engine and transmission and install the selector lever holder. When installing the engine mounts, be sure that the projection engages the groove of the mount. After installing the engine and transmission assembly, check the alignment of the unit. Refer to "Engine Installation." Torque converter bolt torque is 22 ft. lbs. Transmission-to-engine bolt torque is 54, 33, and 18 ft. lbs, respectively, for the three bolt sizes. Refill the transmission.

Fox

The transaxle can be lowered from the car, leaving the engine in place.

1. Disconnect the battery ground cable.
2. Raise and support the car.
3. Remove the lockplates and remove the axle shaft bolts. Wire the shafts up.

4. Disconnect the vacuum hose. Remove the torque converter guard plate. Disconnect the kickdown switch wire.
5. Unscrew the speedometer cable nut.
6. Support the transaxle.
7. Remove the upper engine-to-transaxle bolts.
8. Remove the starter and remove the three torque converter bolts through the starter opening.
9. Unbolt the small crossmember at the rear of the transmission.
10. Lower the transaxle slightly.
11. Detach the shift linkage cable at the transmission.
12. Remove the lower engine-to-transaxle bolts.
13. Separate the transaxle from the engine and lower it. Secure the torque converter in the transmission with a strap. Reverse the procedure on installation. Torque the engine-to-transaxle bolts to 40 ft. lbs. and the torque converter bolts to 20–23 ft. lbs. New torque converter bolts and washers must be used. Torque the axle shaft bolts to 28 ft. lbs.
14. Check the shift linkage adjustment.

4000 and 5000

1. Disconnect the battery ground.
2. Remove the windshield washer bottle.
3. Drain the cooling system.
4. Remove the hoses from the transmission cooler.
5. Remove the upper end of the accelerator linkage rod.
6. Disconnect the speedometer cable at the bell housing.
7. Remove the upper engine-to-transmission bolts.
8. Raise and support the car.
9. Using a chain hoist or jack, support the engine and raise it just enough to take the weight off of the mounts.
10. Remove the skid plate from the subframe.
11. Disconnect the exhaust pipe from the transmission and the manifold.
12. Remove the right driveshaft guard plate.
13. Remove the right and left driveshafts.
14. Remove the starter.
15. Remove the selector lever cable and holder from the transmission.
16. Remove the lower accelerator linkage rod.
17. Remove the accelerator cable from the transmission support.
18. Remove the right side guard plate from the subframe.
19. Remove both transmission mounts from the subframe.
20. Rotate the torque converter and remove each bolt as it appears in the starter opening.
21. Place a jack under the transmission and raise it slightly.
22. Remove the lower engine-to-transmission bolts.

23. Remove the rear subframe mounting bolts.

24. Swing both driveshafts rearward out of the way.

25. Separate the transmission from the engine and carefully lower the transmission on the jack.

26. Installation is the reverse of removal.

— CAUTION —

Be sure that the torque converter is fully seated on the one-way clutch support. When the converter is properly seated, the distance between the converter cover nose and the end of the bell housing should be 0.393 (10 mm) inch.

27. Install the lower engine-to-transmission bolts first, then the transmission-to-subframe bolts.

28. Observe the following torques: converter bolts 22 ft. lbs.; transmission-to-engine bolts 40 ft. lbs.; starter bolts 40 ft. lbs.; subframe to body 80 ft. lbs.

29. Adjust the throttle kickdown switch.

PAN REMOVAL AND INSTALLATION

The automatic transmission fluid should be changed and the pan cleaned out every 20,000 miles. The interval should be shortened to 12,000 miles under severe use such as city driving or trailer towing.

To change the fluid:

1. Run the engine in Neutral for a minute or two.

2. Make sure that the vehicle is parked on level ground. Stop the engine.

3. Place a pan of at least four quarts capacity under the transmission.

4. Remove the plug from the transmission bottom pan, after wiping the area clean.

5. Remove the starter on the 100 series.

6. Remove and clean out the pan.

7. Replace the pan, using a new gasket. Torque the bolts to 7 ft. lbs. Wait ten minutes and retorque the bolts.

8. Clean off the plug, particularly the threads, and replace it.

9. Replace the starter on the 100 series.

10. Pour in five pints of fluid through the dipstick filler tube. The proper transmission fluid is Dexron® or Dexron® II.

11. Start the engine and shift through all the lever positions.

12. The level should reach the tip of the dipstick. Add fluid until the level reaches this point.

13. Take a short test drive. Fill the transmission until the level is between the marks on the dipstick. Retorque the bolts.

NOTE: If the transmission is overfilled, the excess must be drained.

KICKDOWN SWITCH

100 and Fox

The kickdown switch is mounted behind the accelerator pedal. With the ignition switch on, the switch should make an audible click when the pedal is pressed all the way down.

The transmission should downshift when the accelerator is depressed to the wide open throttle position at speeds between 39 and 65 mph for second gear, and 16 and 36 mph for first gear.

4000 and 5000

1. Position the accelerator pedal in the fully released position.

2. Check the distance between the pedal lower edge and the pedal stop. Clearance should be 3.0 inches.

3. If not, loosen the lockbolt which holds the cable at the pedal and place the pedal to give the three inch clearance. Tighten the lockbolt.

4. Press the pedal to the full throttle position but not into the kickdown detent. The kickdown take-up spring should not be compressed and the throttle valve should be wide open.

5. Adjust the shift linkage.

Kickdown detent linkage—4000 and 5000

NEUTRAL SAFETY SWITCH ADJUSTMENT

The neutral safety switch prevents the engine from being started with the transmission in any position other than Park or Neutral. It also activates the backup lights. The switch is at the base of the shift lever, inside the floorshift console.

To replace or adjust the switch:

1. Remove the four screws which hold the console to the floor.

2. Shift into Neutral. Remove the two screws which hold the shift position indicator plate to the console. Remove the shift knob and the console.

3. Disconnect the switch electrical leads. These are: red/black—neutral safety; black—backup lights; blue/red—backup lights. The backup light wires are at the front.

4. Remove the two switch retaining screws. Remove the switch.

5. Install the new switch so that the neutral safety switch contacts are together.

6. Install the electrical connectors. Hold the footbrake while making sure that the engine will start only in Neutral and Park. Make sure that the backup lights operate only in Reverse. If the switch does not operate properly, it may have to be moved on its slotted mounting bracket.

7. Replace the console cover.

SHIFT LINKAGE ADJUSTMENT

The function of this adjustment is to make sure that the transmission is fully engaged in each shift position. If this is not done, the transmission may be only partially engaged in a certain range position. This would result in severe damage due to slippage.

1. Place the selector lever in Park.

2. Loosen the cable clamp nut at the transmission end. On the Fox, remove the rubber cover from the bottom of the shifter (underneath the car) and loosen the cable clamp screw.

3. Press the selector lever on the transmission back to the stop.

4. Tighten the clamp nut or screw.

BAND ADJUSTMENTS

100

SECOND GEAR BAND

1. Loosen the locknut.

2. Tighten the adjusting screw to 87 in. lbs.

3. Loosen the adjusting screw and retighten to 44 in. lbs.

4. Turn the adjusting screw out 1¾–2 turns.

5. Tighten the locknut.

Automatic transmission second gear band adjusting screw and locknut (66) and (67). First gear band adjusting screw and locknut (60)

Second gear band adjustment

FIRST GEAR BAND

1. Loosen the locknut.
2. Tighten the adjusting screw to 87 in. lbs.
3. Loosen the adjusting screw and retighten to 44 in. lbs.
4. Turn the adjusting screw out 3¼–3¾ turns.
5. Tighten the locknut.

Fox

FIRST GEAR BAND

1. Loosen locknut.
2. Tighten first gear band adjusting screw to 7 ft. lbs.
3. Loosen adjusting screw and retighten to 3.5 ft. lbs.
4. Back off screw 3.25 to 3.5 turns and tighten locknut.

SECOND GEAR BAND

1. Loosen locknut.
2. Tighten adjusting screw to 7 ft. lbs.
3. Loosen screw and retighten to 3.5 ft. lbs.
4. Back off screw exactly 2.5 turns and tighten locknut.

NOTE: Transmission must be horizontal when adjusting bands or bands may jam.

4000 and 5000

SECOND GEAR BAND

1. Loosen the locknut.
2. Tighten the adjusting screw to 7 ft. lbs.
3. Loosen the adjusting screw and retighten it to 4 ft. lbs.
4. Loosen the screw exactly 2½ turns.
5. Hold the screw and tighten the locknut.

TRANSAXLE

The transmission and differential are combined in a transaxle. On models with manual transmission, the transmission and differential share a common lubricant supply. No transaxle overhaul procedures are given here due to the extensive specialized tools, knowledge, and procedures required.

REMOVAL AND INSTALLATION

100

The transaxle is removed from the car in unit with the engine. See "Engine Removal and Installation" for details. On the automatic, it is possible to remove the transaxle only, leaving the engine in place. See "Automatic Transmission Removal and Installation" for details.

Fox, 4000 and 5000

The transaxle can be removed from the car alone, leaving the engine in place. See "Transmission Removal and Installation" for details.

DRIVE AXLES

Each front wheel drive axle shaft has two Rzeppa constant velocity joints. These joints can handle lateral movement caused by suspension travel, as well as steering movements.

Halfshafts

REMOVAL AND INSTALLATION

100

NOTE: A small puller or press is required for this job.

The steering knuckles must be removed along with the shafts.

1. Support the vehicle and remove the wheels. Let the front suspension hang free.
2. Have an assistant hold the brakes. Unbolt the driveshaft from the transmission stub axle and brake disc. There should be an insulator between the driveshaft and brake disc.

The castellated nut (g) and the cotter pin must be removed before pulling out the tie rod end (h) from the 100 series steering knuckle (e). (f) indicates the steering knuckle mounting bolts.

3. Remove the cotter pin and the castellated nut from the steering tie rod end. Press out the tie rod end from the steering knuckle arm. A small puller or press is required to free the tie rod end.

4. Remove the two steering knuckle mounting bolts.
5. Remove the steering knuckle and driveshaft assembly.
6. Reverse the procedure for installation. Torques are:
7. Check the wheel alignment.

Fox

1. With the wheels on the ground, remove the front wheel spindle nut.
2. Unbolt the inner driveshaft coupling. If you are removing the right shaft, disconnect the front exhaust pipe at the manifold and the support on the transaxle. Push the inner end of the shaft up and let it rest on the transaxle.
3. Turn the steering wheel all the way in the direction of the side you are working on. Pull the driveshaft out of the steering knuckle.
4. Only the outer joint is available for replacement. If the inner joint is damaged, a new driveshaft must be installed. The outer joint can be removed by removing the snapring (inboard side) and hitting the axle end with a soft hammer.
5. On installation, torque the driveshaft coupling bolts to 25 ft. lbs.

4000

— CAUTION —
Never remove or install the axle nut with the wheel off the ground. The vehicle must be resting on the ground for these operations.

Remove the halfshafts

1. Remove the axle nut.
2. Unbolt and remove the six halfshaft retaining bolts from the drive flange.
3. Mark the position of the ball joint on the control arm, remove the two retaining nuts and remove the ball joint.

NOTE: On cars with manual transmissions, remove only the right side ball joint.

4. Pull the pivot mounting outward and remove the halfshaft.
5. Installation is the reverse of removal.

Removing the halfshaft

6. Tighten the ball joint to control arm nuts to 47 ft. lbs.

7. Always replace the self-locking axle nut with a new one and tighten to 167 ft. lbs.

8. Check for proper camber adjustment.

5000

— CAUTION —

Never remove or install the axle shaft nut with the wheel off the ground. The vehicle must be resting on the ground for these operations. A puller is required for this job.

1. Remove the axle nut.

2. Raise and support the vehicle and remove the wheels.

3. On the right side, remove the driveshaft skid plate.

4. Disconnect the axleshaft from the transmission.

5. Using a 4-armed puller mounted on the wheel hub, press the axleshaft out of the hub.

6. Guide the inside end of the shaft up over the transmission and out of the hub.

7. When installing a shaft, make certain that the splines are clean and free of grease. Apply a ⅛ inch bead of RTV silicone sealant around the leading edge of the splines. Allow it to harden at least one hour. Torque the shaft-to-transmission bolts to 32 ft. lbs. and the axleshaft nut to 203 ft. lbs.

DRIVESHAFT OVERHAUL

100

This operation requires the use of a press or puller setup. It is necessary in order to replace the rubber boots.

1. Clamp the steering knuckle in a vise.

2. Remove the cotter pin. Unscrew the castellated nut and reverse it on the threads to protect them from damage.

3. Press the driveshaft from the steering knuckle. Steps 4–8 cover steering knuckle service.

4. Press out the wheel hub from the steering knuckle.

5. Remove the spacer, Nilos ring, and ball bearing inner race.

Applying RTV sealant to the shaft splines on a 5000

(a)—Outer driveshaft with Rzeppa joint	(dl)—Clamps	(h)—Rzeppa joint with flange
(b)—Clamp	(e)—Inner driveshaft	(i)—Snap-ring
(c)—Rubber boot	(f)—Rubber boat	(k)—Pressure ring
(d)—Clamps	(g)—Clamp	(l)—Disc springs
	(Gl)—Clamp	

100 series driveshaft assembly

6. Drive the outer ball bearing race from the knuckle. Remove the internal snap-rings, using snap-ring pliers, and press out the second ball bearing outer race.

7. Replace the snap-rings. Press in the outer races. Fill the space between the races with high melting point wheel bearing grease.

8. Place the spacer and Nilos ring in the wheel hub. Press on the ball bearing inner race and install a new spacer bushing. Place the hub in the steering knuckle and press in the second ball bearing inner race.

9. Remove both rubber boot clamps and slide the boots off the joints.

10. Clamp the inner driveshaft in a vise. Spread the snap-ring in the joint and have an assistant hit the outer end of the shaft with a soft hammer. A "powerful" blow is required.

11. Drive the joint housing off the inner shaft, using the soft hammer.

12. Pull off the rubber boots.

13. Clean the joint with alcohol and air dry.

14. Install new rubber boots.

15. Place two new disc springs on the

(a)—Outer rubber boot
(b)—Disc springs
(c)—Pressure ring

Installation of the disc springs and pressure ring on the 100 series driveshaft. The Fox has only the inner disc spring.

inner shaft with their concave side out. Install a pressure ring with the convex side out.

16. Place a new snap-ring in the joint. Place the ends in the machined groove.

17. Slide the joint onto the inner shaft, so that the snap-ring begins to go into place.

Drive the joint into place, hitting the outer end of the driveshaft with a soft hammer. The snap-ring should snap into place. The outer end of the shaft may also be pounded on with a wooden block.

18. Fill each joint with 60 cc of Moly-kote grease or its equivalent.

19. Put the rubber boots in place. Install the boot clamps, making sure that the free-ends trail in the normal direction of rotation.

20. Grease and install the spacer and Ni-los ring. Press the driveshaft into the wheel hub. Adjust the hub nut so that there is 0.002–0.003 in. wheel bearing play, measured with a dial indicator at the outer edge of the wheel hub.

Fox, 4000 and 5000

NOTE: This procedure requires the use of a bench press.

CIRCLIP

CONSTANT VELOCITY JOINT, INNER

CAP
DRIVE OFF WITH DRIFT

CLAMP

DRIVESHAFT

BOOT

CIRCLIP

CONSTANT VELOCITY JOINT, OUTER

CV joint to shaft assembly sequence —5000

1. Working at the transmission end, remove the circlip.

2. Mount the assembly in a bench press and press off the inner constant velocity joint.

3. Unclamp and remove the driveshaft boot.

4. Remove the circlip from the inside of the outer constant velocity joint and drive it off the shaft with a few taps of a brass drift against the hub.

NOTE: Be careful not to lose the thrust washer or dished washer on the 4000.

5. Place the outer CV joint on a clean work surface, mark the position of the hub in relation to the cage and housing and remove the balls one at a time.

6. Turn the cage until the two rectangular slots are level with the joint edge and remove the cage and hub.

7. Turn the hub until one segment can be inserted into the rectangular hole in the cage and tilt it out.

NOTE: A cooling fin ring is installed on the left and right inner CV joint on late model 5000 cars with manual transmission. Late model 5000 series cars with automatic transmission have the cooling fin ring on the right side only.

8. Place the inner CV joint on a clean work surface and pivot the hub and cage out of the outer ring. Pull out the balls.

9. Align the grooves in the hub and cage and pull the hub from the cage.

10. When assembling the outer CV joint, never replace one or some of the balls. Always replace all of the balls as a set. Force about one ounce of EP chassis lube into each side of the joint. When assembling the inner joint, push the balls into the cage before installing cage and hub into the joint. Note that the chamfer on the inside edge of the ball hub must face the contact shoulder of the axleshaft. The cage and ball assembly must be inserted vertically into the outer ring of the joint. Make certain that a wide ball-groove in the outer ring of the joint, and a narrow groove in the hub are aligned when the hub is pivoted into the joint. When pivoting the ball hub and cage into the joint, work the hub outward until the balls are spaced to fit in the grooves. Press the cage firmly into position so that the hub can pivot back into the joint when the balls are seated. The joint is correctly assembled when the hub can be removed in and out over a full range of axial movement using only hand pressure. Force 2 ounces of EP chassis lube into the joint.

11. The outer CV joint may be tapped into place on the shaft using a brass drift. The inner CV joint must be pressed on with the bench press. Make certain that both joints are fully seated before installing the circlips.

NOTE: Don't forget the three washers when installing the CV joints on the 4000. The dished washers should have the dish side facing the joint. The thrust washer should have the side without the lip closest to the joint.

REAR SUSPENSION

Rear Axle Beam

REMOVAL AND INSTALLATION

Fox and 100

1. Remove the rear wheels. Support the axle, but don't put any load on the springs.

2. Remove the rear muffler and tailpipe.

3. Disconnect the parking brake cable at the yoke where the two cables merge into one. Detach the cable holders from the underbody.

4. Detach both rear brake lines.

5. Unbolt the control arms and the diagonal arm from the body.

6. Unbolt the bottom of the shock absorber struts from the axle.

7. Remove the axle.

8. On installation, torque the control arm-to-body bolts to 32 ft. lbs., and the diagonal arm-to-body bolts to 61 ft. lbs. Torque the lower shock absorber strut-to-axle bolts to 43 ft. lbs. Bleed the brakes.

4000

1. Raise the rear of the car and support it with jack stands.

2. Remove the wheels.

3. Unhook the exhaust system hangers located at either side of the muffler, lower the exhaust system and secure it.

4. Remove the nut on the parking brake equalizer bar.

5. Pry the parking brake cable sleeves out of their brackets.

6. Remove both parking brake cables at their retaining brackets.

7. Disconnect both brake hoses where they connect to the brake lines and plug the lines.

8. Remove the nuts from the trailing arm mounting bolts, leaving the bolts in place.

9. Disconnect the spring from the brake pressure regulator.

10. Remove the Panhard rod mounting bolt from the axle beam.

11. Remove the lower strut mounting bolts.

12. Support the axle and pull out the trailing arm mounting bolts.

13. Remove the axle while guiding the parking brake cable over the tail pipe and muffler.

To install:

14. Place the axle in position and install

both trailing arm mounting bolts and both lower strut mounting bolts. Hand tighten.

15. Install the wheels.

16. Lower the car so that the wheels are on the ground and tighten the trailing arm bolts to 72 ft. lbs. and the lower strut bolts to 51 ft. lbs.

17. Install the Panhard rod, the brake hoses, the spring for the brake pressure regulator and the parking brake cables.

18. Bleed the brakes and adjust the parking brake.

5000

NOTE: Three persons will be required for installation.

1. Loosen the wheel lugs, but do not remove the wheels. Raise and support the car. Support the rear axle with a jack.

2. Disconnect the Panhard rod at the chassis.

3. Disconnect the right brake hose at the chassis.

4. Disconnect the brake pressure regulator spring.

5. Disconnect the left brake hose at the chassis.

6. Remove the right fuel tank retaining strap.

7. Remove the parking brake from the guide on the fuel tank.

8. Loosen the left side parking brake cable bolt.

9. Loosen the parking brake compensator and disconnect the cable.

10. Remove the exhaust system from the car.

11. Disconnect the shock absorbers at the upper end.

12. Lower the axle on the jack until the springs are clear.

13. Remove the springs and the rear wheels.

14. Remove the trailing arm mounting bolt and lower the axle from the car.

15. Place the axle in position on the jack.

16. Install the trailing arm bolts lightly.

17. Install the wheels.

18. Install both rear springs at the same time while raising the axle into position.

19. Connect the shock absorbers.

20. Installation of the remaining parts is the reverse of removal.

21. Torque the shock absorber upper bolts to 14 ft. lbs., the Panhard rod-to-chassis bolt to 65 ft. lbs.; the trailing arm bolts to 51 ft. lbs.

22. Bleed the brakes.

Wheel Bearings and Stub Axles

REMOVAL AND INSTALLATION

1. Depress the brake pedal approximately 1.2 in. and hold it in that position to close the master cylinder compensating bore.

(a)—Brake drum
(b)—Rear stub axle
(c)—Cap
(d)—Cotter pin
(e)—Nut

(f)—Castellated nut
(g)—Washer
(h)—Roller bearing
(i)—Snap-ring
(k)—Roller bearing

(l)—Shaft seal
(m)—Brake assembly
(n)—Rear axle
(o)—Suspension arm
(p)—Shock absorber

Rear wheel bearing and stub axle assembly

2. Detach the brake lines on both sides and plug the lines.

3. Pry off the grease cap and remove the cotter pin, castellated nut, and washer. Remove the wheel and brake drum.

4. Remove the bearing inner race from the brake drum.

5. Carefully (the spring can fly out) pry out the brake shoe retaining spring. Remove the brake shoes complete with pressure rod and spring, bottom bracket first. Disconnect the handbrake cable.

6. Unbolt the rear stub axle and brake backing plate.

7. Pry out the shaft seal (which should be replaced) and remove the inner race of the roller bearing.

8. Drive the roller bearing outer race from the brake drum. Remove the snap-ring and drive the outer roller bearing race from the drum.

9. Replace the snap-ring and drive in the outer race of the outer roller bearing.

10. Press in the outer race of the inner roller bearing.

11. Lightly coat the inner race of the inner roller bearing with wheel bearing grease and push it into the outer race.

12. Drive a new shaft seal into position (the open side of the seal should face the roller bearing). Fill the space between the two roller bearings with approximately 10 oz. of wheel bearing grease.

13. Coat the inner race of the outer roller bearing with grease and install the inner race.

14. Replace the stub axle and brake backing plate with the groove in the stub axle facing upward. Bolt torque is 14–15 ft. lbs. for 8G bolts and 22 ft. lbs. for 10K bolts.

15. Assemble the brake shoes, connect the handbrake cable, and insert the brake shoes on the bottom bracket first, then at the wheel cylinder. Replace the retaining spring.

16. Replace the brake drum and wheel, special washer, nut, castellated nut, and a new cotter pin. Wheel bearing play should be 0.001–0.002 in. It can be measured with a dial indicator. Fill the dust cap with approximately 10 oz. of wheel bearing grease and replace it.

Struts

For all spring and shock absorber removal and installation procedures and any other strut overhaul procedures, please refer to "Strut Overhaul" in the Unit Repair section.

REMOVAL AND INSTALLATION

Fox and 100

1. On the Fox, remove the bottom cushion of the rear seat. Release the mounting tabs at the bottom of the seatback and pull it forward to detach its upper clips.

2. Support the rear of the chassis. Support the axle too, but don't put any load on the springs. Remove the rubber guard from the top of the strut, from inside the trunk.

Rear suspension—Fox and 100

3. On the Fox, peel back the insulation on the bulkhead to expose the access hole.

4. Remove the mounting nut, washer, and rubber disc.

5. Unbolt the strut from the axle and remove it.

6. You can disassemble these struts carefully without a spring compressor, but you will need a special wrench to remove the slotted nut. The springs are color coded. The stop pad inside the top of the coil is available in two sizes for slight rear end height adjustment. On reassembly, torque the slotted nut to 11 ft. lbs.

7. Reverse the procedure for installation and torque the lower strut mount bolt to 43 ft. lbs. and the upper mount nut to 23 ft. lbs.

4000

NOTE: Always remove and install the suspension struts one at a time. Do not allow the rear axle to hang in place as this may cause undue damage to the brake lines.

1. With the car at ground level, open the trunk and remove the sheet metal trim from around the shock tower.

2. Remove the rubber cap.

3. Remove the strut mounting nut.

4. Raise the rear of the car and support it with jack stands.

5. Remove the lower strut mounting bolt from the axle beam and remove the strut.

6. Installation is the reverse of removal. Torque the upper strut mounting bolt to 14 ft. lbs. and the lower strut mounting bolt to 43 ft. lbs.

5000

NOTE: The struts must be removed with the weight on the vehicle on the rear wheels. If not, a spring compressor must be used on the rear springs.

1. Remove the upper shock absorber mounting nut.

Rear suspension on the 5000—4000 similar

2. If the vehicle is not on its wheels, install the spring compressor and compress the spring.

3. Remove the lower shock absorber mounting nut.

4. Remove the shock absorber.

5. Installation is the reverse of removal. Torque the lower mounts to 40 ft. lbs. and the upper to 14 ft. lbs.

FRONT SUSPENSION

The 100 series use MacPherson strut type spring and shock absorber units with upper and lower control arms (wishbones) and have a cross-chassis stabilizer bar connecting the two lower control arms.

The Fox, 4000 and 5000 also use MacPherson struts. The strut unit, steering arm, and steering knuckle are all combined in one assembly; there is no upper control arm. The system is designed with negative roller-radius; this stabilizes the car when

different retarding forces are applied to the front wheels, as would happen if one front tire were on wet pavement and the other on dry.

NOTE: Exercise extreme caution when working with the front suspension. Coil springs and torsion bars are under great tension and can cause severe injury if released suddenly.

MacPherson Strut

For all spring and shock absorber removal and installation procedures and any other strut overhaul procedures, please refer to "Strut Overhaul" in the Unit Repair section.

REMOVAL AND INSTALLATION

100

1. Support the vehicle and remove the wheels. Let the front suspension hang free.

2. Unbolt the strut unit from the upper control arm.

1. Coil spring   5. Lower control arm
2. Upper control arm   6. Driveshaft
3. Steering knuckle   7. Caliper
4. Lower ball joint   8. Disc

100 series front suspension

1. Cotter pin
2. Tie-rod
3. Axle driveshaft
4. Circlip
5. Retainer nut
6. Brake caliper
7. Wheel bearing
8. Hub
9. Brake disc
10. Axle nut

4000 front suspension—Fox similar

3. Inside the engine compartment, remove the three nuts which hold the top of the strut unit. Do not remove the nut and locknut in the center.

4. Pull the unit down and pull the top out through the wheel opening. It may be necessary to pull the steering knuckle down a bit for clearance.

5. It is not recommended that the strut unit be disassembled unless the necessary special tools to do this safely are available. The units should be serviced in pairs to maintain equal shock absorbing qualities and ride height. Spacers are available to correct ride height. The strut unit must be disassembled to install these. The proper ride height with standard size tires is 8.2–8.7 in., measured from the floor to the 0.32 in. diameter hole in the front bearing shell of the lower control arm inner pivot.

6. When replacing the strut unit, torque the three bolts and nuts, which hold the upper end of the strut to the body, to 13–15 ft. lbs., and the lower end to 62–69 ft. lbs. The torque for the shock absorber to spring retaining nut is 18–26 ft. lbs.

7. Check the wheel alignment.

Fox

1. With the car resting on its wheels, remove the axle nut.

2. Raise the car and remove the wheels.

3. Unbolt the brake caliper, remove the brake line clip, and rest the caliper on the lower control arm.

4. Remove the bolt holding the steering knuckle to the lower control arm.

5. Detach the steering arm from the tie rod end.

6. Unbolt the stabilizer bar pivots from the lower control arm. Disconnect the lower control arm from the steering knuckle by removing the bolt at the ball joint.

7. Remove the strut mounting nuts in the engine compartment and remove the strut.

8. It is not recommended that the strut unit be disassembled unless the necessary special tools to do this safely are available. The units should be serviced in pairs to maintain equal shock qualities and ride height.

9. When replacing the strut unit, use a new nut and bolt to attach the lower control arm to the steering knuckle. Torque the strut-to-body bolts to 16 ft. lbs., the control arm-to-steering knuckle bolt to 16 ft. lbs., the brake caliper mounting bolts to 43 ft. lbs., and the stabilizer bar pivots to 7 ft. lbs.

10. Torque the axle nut to 180 ft. lbs. and check the wheel alignment.

4000 and 5000

1. With the car on the ground, remove the front axle nut and loosen the wheel bolts.

2. Raise and support the front of the car and remove the wheels.

3. Remove the brake caliper mounting bolts and the brake line bracket. Remove the brake caliper with the line still attached to it and wire it out of the way.

4. Remove the wheel bearing housing/ball joint clamp bolt.

5. Remove the retaining nut and press off the tie rod end.

6. Unscrew the retaining bolt and remove the stabilizer bar end clamps. Pivot the stabilizer bar downward. (4000 only).

7. Remove the two center stabilizer bar clamps and then unbolt it from the lower control arm. Remove the stabilizer bar (5000 only).

8. Pry the lower control arm down and remove the ball joint from the wheel hub.

9. Remove the halfshaft from the wheel hub.

10. While holding the shock absorber piston rod with an internal socket wrench, remove the retaining bolt and then remove the strut assembly (4000 only).

11. Remove the spring strut cover

2.5 MKG (18 FT LB)

SUSPENSION STRUT

DRIVESHAFT

RUBBER BUSHING

4 MKG (29 FT LB)

8.5 MKG (61 FT LB)

4.5 MKG (32 FT LB)

RUBBER BUSHING

10.5 MKG (76 FT LB)

28 MKG (203 FT LB)

11 MKG (80 FT LB)

6.5 MKG (47 FT LB)

11 MKG (80 FT LB)

2 MKG (14 FT LB)

STABILIZER BAR

RUBBER BUSHING REMOVE WITH CHISEL

5000 front suspension

(Quattro and Turbo) and remove the three strut retaining nuts, then remove the strut assembly (5000 series only).

12. Installation is in the reverse order of removal. Note the following:

a. When installing the stabilizer bar on the 4000, the positioning is correct if the clamps are difficult to install in the rubber bushings. Attach the clamps loosely, take a short test drive to bring the bushings into the correct position and then tighten to 18 ft. lbs.

b. Tighten the ball joint bolt to 36 ft. lbs. on the 4000 and 47 ft. lbs. on the 5000.

c. Tighten the axle nut to 167 ft. lbs. on the 4000, 202 ft. lbs. on the Quattro and Turbo and 203 ft. lbs. on all other 5000 models.

Upper Control Arm and Ball Joint

REMOVAL AND INSTALLATION

100

NOTE: A press is needed for ball joint installation.

1. Remove the MacPherson strut unit.
2. Remove the upper control arm-to-steering knuckle bolt.
3. Pull the control arm up so that the control arm upper joint comes loose from the steering knuckle.

Front strut upper mounting nut—5000

4. Remove the four mounting bolts and the control arm.

NOTE: Upper ball joint is a press fit and may be replaced at this time.

5. Reverse the procedure for installation.

Lower Control Arm and Ball Joint

REMOVAL AND INSTALLATION

100

1. Raise the vehicle and let the suspension hang free. Remove the wheels.
2. Remove the stabilizer bar. It may be necessary to move the exhaust pipe.
3. Support the lower control arm. Re-

move the lower control arm-to-steering knuckle bolt. Let the arm down to pull the joint loose from the steering knuckle.

4. Unbolt the bearing bolts and remove the control arm.

NOTE: To remove lower ball joint, remove retaining ring and nut and pull bad joint from joint plate.

5. Reverse the procedure for installation.

5000

1. Remove the ball joint clamp nut.
2. Pry the control arm down and out of the clamp.
3. Remove the nut on the end of the stabilizer bar.
4. Loosen the control arm-to-subframe mounting bolts and then pull the control arm off of the end of the stabilizer bar.
5. Remove the bolts and remove control arm.

NOTE: The ball joint and control arm are one unit and can only be replaced as a unit.

6. Installation is the reverse of removal.
7. Check the toe and camber adjustments.

Track Control Arm and Ball Joint

REMOVAL AND INSTALLATION

Fox

1. Remove bolts securing control arm to subframe. Before removing ball joint, mark its position on the subframe.
2. Pull ball joint retaining clamp and pull ball joint from knuckle.
3. Remove bolts securing ball joint flange to control arm.
4. To install, position new ball joint on control arm and tighten bolts to 45 ft. lbs.
5. Install control arm in reverse of above. Torque control arm-to-subframe bolts to 32 ft. lbs.

Ball Joints

REMOVAL AND INSTALLATION

4000

1. Mark the position of the ball joint flange on the lower control arm.
2. Remove the ball joint retaining clamp nut and pull the ball joint/control arm down and out of the retaining clamp.
3. Unscrew the two ball flange retaining nuts and remove the ball joint.

4. Installation is the reverse of removal. Tighten the clamp nut to 47 ft. lbs. and tighten the ball joint flange nuts to 47 ft. lbs.

Lower Control Arm

REMOVAL AND INSTALLATION

4000

1. Raise the front of the car and support it with jack stands.
2. Remove the ball joint as detailed earlier.
3. Unbolt the end of the stabilizer bar and pull it down.
4. Remove the two control arm-to-subframe bolts and remove the control arm.
5. Installation is in the reverse order of removal. Check control arm bushings for cracking or undue wear. Tighten the control arm-to-subframe bolts to 43 ft. lbs. and the stabilizer bar mounting bolts to 18 ft. lbs.

Adjustments

RIDE HEIGHT

100

The suspension strut units must be removed and be disassembled and new springs or spacers installed to adjust ride height on these models. It is not recommended that the strut unit be disassembled unless the necessary special tools to do this safely are available. The proper front ride height with standard size tires is 8.2–8.7 in., measured from the floor to the 0.32 in. diameter hole in the front bearing shell of the lower control arm inner pivot. The measurements on both sides should be alike, or different by no more than 0.3 in. The car should be bounced and settled before making the measurement. Rear ride height is not readily adjustable.

100, 100 LS, and 100 GL ride height is adjusted by inserting spacers (D) on the strut unit (A). (S) is the special strut compressor

(a)—Camber adjustment
(b)—Nut
(c)—Bolt
(d)—Locknut
(e)—Caster adjustment

100, 100 LS, and 100 GL caster and camber adjustment points

Wheel Alignment

Before checking wheel alignment, tire pressures should be brought up to specifications and the front ride height checked. The car should be bounced and settled before each alignment check or adjustment. The adjustments should be made in this order: caster, camber, toe-in.

CASTER

100

1. Loosen the large locknut at the bottom of the outer end of the lower control arm.
2. Turn the eccentric bolt, which passes through the locknut, to adjust caster.

4000, 5000 and Fox

Caster is set at the factory on these models and is not adjustable other than the replacement of damaged suspension parts.

CAMBER

Camber is checked with the wheels straight ahead.

100

1. Loosen the nut (on the top) on the bolt that passes through the outer end of the lower control arm.
2. Loosen the bolt (on the bottom) inboard of the nut loosened in Step 1.
3. Adjust camber by turning the large nut on top of the bolt loosened in Step 2.
4. Tighten the bolt and nut to 32 ft. lbs.

Fox

1. Loosen the two nuts holding the ball joint to the lower control arm.
2. Push the ball joint in or out to adjust the camber. Dealers have a special tool to lever the ball joint in or out, using the holes in the control arm.
3. Tighten the nuts to 47 ft. lbs.

4000

1. Loosen both ball joint flange mounting bolts on the control arm.
2. Using the special tool US 4490, or by just moving the ball joint with your hands, adjust the camber to specifications.

5000

1. Loosen the spring strut plate mounting bolts.
2. Attach a socket wrench to the top piston rod nut and move the assembly in the slots until the camber is correct.
3. Tighten all bolts.

Adjusting the camber on the 4000 without the special tool

To adjust the camber on the 5000, move the strut assembly in the slots of the spring strut mounting plate

TOE-IN

Toe-in is checked with the wheels straight ahead.

1. Toe-in can be determined by measuring and comparing the distance between the center of the tire tread, front and rear, or by measuring and comparing the distance between the inside edges of the wheel rims, front and rear. If the wheel rims are used as the basis of measurement, the car should be rolled forward slightly and a second set of measurements taken. This avoids any error induced by bent wheels. If at all possible, a toe-in gauge should be used; it will give a much more accurate measurement.
2. Toe-in is adjusted at the steering tie rods at either end of the steering rack on the 100 Series. Loosen the clamp. Loosen the clip for the rubber boot at the end of

the rack and slide the boot back. On the Fox, simply loosen the clamp and locknut on the adjustable left tie rod.

3. Turn both rods to lengthen or shorten them an equal amount. If the tie rods are not adjusted equally, the steering wheel will be crooked and the turning arcs of the front wheels will be changed. On the Fox, only the left tie rod is adjustable. If the steering wheel is crooked, it must be removed and repositioned.

4. Tighten the clamps and replace the boots.

STEERING

The steering is a rack and pinion type. The steering geometry is designed to give a variable ratio effect, giving faster steering response as the steering wheel is turned toward either right or left lock. The steering column and linkage is arranged so as to break away and telescope safely in an accident, rather than penetrating into the passenger compartment.

Steering Wheel

REMOVAL AND INSTALLATION

1. Center the wheel. Disconnect the battery ground cable.
2. Pry off the wheel pad (horn button).
3. Unbolt and remove the wheel. A steering wheel puller should not be necessary.
4. On installation, torque the bolt to 36 ft. lbs. (100, Fox and 5000) and 29 ft. lbs. (4000 and Turbo). Do not pound on the wheel, as the collapsible column may be damaged.

Turn Signal and Headlight Dimmer Switch Replacement

100

1. Remove the steering wheel.
2. Disconnect the battery ground cable.
3. Remove the wire from the horn contact ring. Remove the two screws and the horn contact ring.
4. Remove the screws which hold the column casing at the top and just below the instrument panel.
5. Remove the casing. Be careful to note the arrangement of any springs and washers removed from the top of the column.

6. The switch may now be disconnected, unscrewed, and removed. The wires are color coded for ease of replacement.

Fox

1. Disconnect the battery ground cable.
2. Remove the steering wheel.
3. Remove the screws in the top of the switch housing, lift off the housing and unplug the connectors, and remove the switch housing along with the wiper and turn signal levers.

4000 and 5000

1. Disconnect the negative battery cable.
2. Remove the steering wheel.
3. Remove the screws and remove the steering column cover on the 4000.

Steering column switch mounting screws—4000

To remove the switch housing on the 5000, insert a screwdriver and loosen the screw

4. Remove the steering column switches. On the 4000, remove the three screws and pull the switches off enough to unplug the electrical connectors. On the 5000, insert a screwdriver into the slot on the bottom of the switch housing, loosen the screw and pull the housing off enough to unplug the electrical connectors.

5. Installation is in the reverse of removal.

Ignition and Steering Lock Switch

REMOVAL AND INSTALLATION

100

To perform this operation, proceed with

(c)—Lower housing
(d)—Upper housing
(e)—Steering lock tang

The ignition and steering lock switch is held in place by two bolts (a) whose heads shear on installation to deter theft

Steps 1–5 of "Turn Signal and Headlight Dimmer Switch Replacement." The lock switch is clamped to the steering column with special bolts whose heads shear off on installation. These must be drilled out in order to remove the switch. When replacing the unit, make sure that the lock tang is aligned with the slot in the steering column.

4000

1. Disconnect the negative battery cable.
2. Remove the steering wheel, the steering column covers and the steering column switches.
3. Pry the lock washer off the steering column and discard it.
4. Remove the spring and pull off the contact ring.
5. Unplug the electrical connector.
6. Unscrew the retaining bolt and slide the ignition switch/steering lock assembly off of the steering column tube.
7. Installation is in the reverse order of removal. Replace the old lock washer with a new one.

Instrument panel trim pad screw, left side—5000

Fox and 5000

1. Remove the column shroud for access to the screws.
2. Drill out the special shear bolt heads.

———— CAUTION ————
These bolts also support the steering column. Support the column while removing the bolts.
————————————————

3. On installation, make sure the two

projections on the lock clamp assembly engage the two depressions in the columns. Tighten the new bolts until their heads shear off.

Steering Gear

REMOVAL AND INSTALLATION

100—Manual Steering

1. Point the front wheels straight ahead. Disconnect the steering column from the firewall.
2. Disconnect the steering shaft from the steering gear.
3. Disconnect the ends of the steering tie rods from the steering knuckles by removing the cotter pins and nuts and pressing out the tie rod ends. A small puller or press is required to free the tie rod ends.
4. Unbolt the steering gear from the firewall. Slide the unit toward the right and pull it up and out through the engine compartment.
5. On installation, center the steering gear and the steering wheel.

Fox and 5000

1. Pry off the lock plate and remove both tie rod mounting bolts from the steering rack, inside the engine compartment. Pry the tie rods out of the mounting pivot.
2. Remove the lower instrument panel trim.
3. Remove the shaft clamp bolt, pry off the clip, and drive the shaft toward the inside of the car with a brass drift.
4. Remove the steering gear mounting bolts at both ends. There is a single bolt at the right end.
5. Turn the wheels all the way to the right and remove the steering gear through the opening in the right wheel housing.
6. For installation, temporarily install the tie rod mounting pivot to the rack with both mounting bolts. Remove one bolt, install the tie rod, and replace the bolt. Do the same on the other tie rod. Make sure to install the lock plate. Torque the tie rod to 39 ft. lbs., the mounting pivot bolt to 15 ft. lbs., and the steering gear-to-body mounting bolts to 15 ft. lbs.

Power Steering Pump

REMOVAL AND INSTALLATION

1. Remove hoses from pump. Plug openings.
2. Remove belt adjusting bolt, push pump to one side and remove belt.
3. Support pump, remove mounting bolts and lift out pump.

Power steering pump adjusting bolt—5000

Steering Linkage

TIE ROD REMOVAL AND INSTALLATION

100

NOTE: A puller or press is required for this job.

1. Jack up the car and remove the wheels.
2. Disconnect the end of the steering tie rod from the steering knuckle by removing the cotter pin and nut and pressing out the tie rod end. A small puller or press is required to free the tie rod end.
3. The steering gear boots can be replaced with no further disassembly at this point.
4. Loosen the clamp and slide the rubber boot as far back as possible.
5. Turn the steering all the way to the side being worked on. Do not force it against the stops.
6. Bend open the lock plate behind the knurled cylinder on the tie rod. Unscrew the tie rod.
7. Reverse the procedure for installation. Adjust the new tie rod to the same length as the old one. Torque the tie rod to 51 ft. lbs., then set the lock plate. Tie rod outer end torque is 26 ft. lbs.

The nut (h) is loosened to remove the tie rod (i) from the 100 series steering gear

8. Check the toe-in.

Fox, 4000 and 5000

NOTE: A puller or press is required for this job.

1. Raise the car and remove the front wheels.

2. Disconnect the outer end of the steering tie rod from the steering knuckle by removing the cotter pin and nut and pressing out the tie rod end. A small puller or press is required to free the tie rod end.
3. Under the hood, pry off the lock plate and remove the mounting bolts from both tie rod inner ends. Pry the tie rod out of the mounting pivot.
4. First install the mounting pivot to the rack with both mounting bolts. Remove one bolt, install the tie rod, and replace the bolt. Do the same on the other tie rod. Make sure to install the lock plate. The inner tie rod end bolts should be torqued to 40 ft. lbs. On the Fox and 4000, 43 ft. lbs. on the 5000.
5. If you are replacing the adjustable left tie rod, adjust it to the same length as the old one. Check the toe-in when the job is done.
6. Use new cotter pins when installing the outer tie rod ends. Torque the nut to 22 ft. lbs. on the Fox and 4000 and 43 ft. lbs. on the 5000.

BRAKES

All models have dual circuit hydraulic brakes with front disc brakes and rear drum brakes. (The Turbo and Quattro utilize disc brakes at all four wheels.) All models have a brake pad lining thickness warning light. The 5000 brakes are nearly identical to those used on the Fox.

For all brake system repair and service procedures not detailed below, please refer to "Brakes" in the Unit Repair section.

Adjustment

FRONT DISC BRAKES

The front disc brakes are self-adjusting.

When adjusting the rear brakes, turn adjustin nuts (A) toward (a) to tighten and (b) to loosen

REAR DRUM BRAKES

100, Fox and 1978 5000

The rear drum brakes must be adjusted periodically, or whenever free travel is one third or more of the total pedal travel.

1. Raise the rear of the car.
2. Block the front wheels and release the parking brake. Step on the brake pedal hard to center the linings.
3. On the 100 series and Fox turn the front adjusting nut on the brake backing plate until the wheel can't be rotated forward by hand. On the 5000, remove the rubber plug and turn the adjuster with a screwdriver to lock the wheel.

Adjusting the rear drum brakes—1978 5000

4. Loosen the adjusting nut until the wheel can be turned freely without drag.
5. Repeat Steps 3 and 4 for the rear adjusting nut on the 100 and Fox.
6. Repeat Steps 3, 4, and 5 for the other rear wheel.
7. Step on the brake pedal hard and make sure the wheels still rotate without drag.

4000 and 5000 (Except 1978)

The rear drum brakes are equipped with automatic adjusters actuated by the parking brake mechanism (as are the rear disc brakes on the Turbo and Quattro). No periodic adjustment of the rear brakes is necessary if this mechanism is working properly. If the brake shoe to drum clearance is incorrect and applying the parking brake a few times does not adjust it properly, the parts will have to be disassembled for repairs.

Master Cylinder

REMOVAL AND INSTALLATION

1. Have an assistant hold the brake pedal down about 1½ in. Disconnect the brake lines nearest the firewall.
2. Hold a container under the fitting disconnected in Step 1 and have the assistant release the pedal. The contents of

1. Reservoir cap
2. Washer
3. Filter screen
4. Reservoir
5. Master cylinder plugs
6. Stop screw
7. Stop screw seal
8. Master cylinder seal
9. Residual pressure valves
10. Warning light sender unit
11. Brake master cylinder housing

4000 master cylinder—5000 similar

the reservoir will drain into the container. Discard the used fluid.

3. Disconnect the other brake line.
4. Disconnect the stoplight switch from the master cylinder.
5. Unbolt and remove the master cylinder from the power brake unit. Be careful not to lose the sealing ring between the two units.
6. Installation is the reverse of removal. Master cylinder bolt torque is 17 ft. lbs. Fill and bleed the system. There should be a pedal free-play of 0.2 in. It can be adjusted on the linkage, inside the car.

Proportioning Valve

CHECKING

1. With the wheels on the ground, depress the brake pedal firmly.
2. Release the pedal suddenly and check that the lever on the proportioning valve moves.
3. If the lever does not move, the valve will probably require replacement.

5000 brake proportioning valve; when checking, the lever (arrow) should move

NOTE: It is normal for small quantities of brake fluid to escape through the vent hole.

REMOVAL AND INSTALLATION

1. Remove and plug the four brake lines leading from the proportioning valve.
2. Disconnect the spring which is attached to the valve and the axle beam.
3. Remove the two mounting bolts and remove the valve.

NOTE: Do not disassemble the valve.

4. Installation is in the reverse order of removal.
5. Bleed the brakes.

Front Wheel Bearings

ADJUSTMENT

There is no front wheel bearing adjustment. The bearing is pressed into the steering knuckle. Axle nut torque is 180 ft. lbs. for the 100 series and Fox, 167 ft. lbs. for the 4000, 203 ft. lbs. for the 5000 and 5000 Diesel and 202 ft. lbs. for the 5000 Turbo. The axle nut should be tightened only with the wheels resting on the ground.

REMOVAL AND INSTALLATION

1. Raise the front of the car and support it with jackstands.
2. Remove the wheels.
3. Remove the caliper assembly.
4. Remove the brake disc.
5. Unscrew two retaining screws and remove the splash shield.
6. Remove the halfshaft.
7. Press off the wheel hub.
8. Remove the inner and outer circlips and press out the wheel bearing.

NOTE: The wheel bearing will be damaged upon removal and must be replaced.

9. Installation is in the reverse order of removal.

Wheel Cylinders

REMOVAL AND INSTALLATION

1. Remove the brake shoes.
2. Depress the brake pedal about 1½ in. to block the master cylinder compensating port and prevent leakage. Secure the pedal in this position.
3. Disconnect the brake line and plug the opening.
4. Remove the two mounting screws from the backing plate.
5. Remove the cylinder.
6. Reverse the procedure for installation.

(a)—Spring
(b)—Piston
(c)—Grooved cup
(d)—Cylinder
(e)—Cap
(f)—Bleeder valve
(g)—Dust cap
(h)—Brake line connection

Cross-section of a rear wheel cylinder

Parking Brake

ADJUSTMENT

100, Fox and 1978 5000

The handbrake (parking brake) must be adjusted periodically to compensate for lining wear and cable stretching. The adjuster is at the cable junction, under the center of the car.

1. Block the front wheels. Raise and support the rear of the vehicle. Do not use a jack under the rear axle tube.
2. Pull the brake up to the first notch.
3. If the wheels will not rotate freely, loosen the adjusting nut.
4. Tighten the adjusting nut until neither wheel can be turned by hand.
5. Check that there is no drag when the brake handle is fully released.

4000 and 1979 and Later 5000 (Except Turbo and Quattro)

NOTE: Because of self-adjusting rear brakes, adjustment is only necessary after replacement of any of the brake components.

1. Raise the rear of the car and support it with jack stands.
2. Release the parking brake lever.
3. Depress the brake pedal once.
4. Pull the parking brake lever onto the second tooth in the 4000 and the third tooth in the 5000.
5. Tighten the adjusting nut on the parking brake cable equalizer bar until the wheels can just be turned by hand.
6. Release the lever and check that both wheels rotate freely.
7. Turn the ignition switch on and check that the brake warning light comes on when the parking brake lever is pulled up to the first tooth and goes out when it is released.

Turbo and Quattro

NOTE: Because of the self-adjusting rear brakes, adjustment is only necessary after replacement of any of the brake components.

1. Raise the rear of the car and support it with jackstands.
2. Release the parking brake lever.
3. Check that the parking brake levers at the rear calipers stay on the stop. If not, loosen the adjusting nut.
4. Depress the brake pedal approximately 40 times and pull the parking brake lever to the third tooth.
5. Tighten the adjusting nut on the parking brake equalizer bar until the rear wheels can just be turned by hand.
6. Release the brake and check that both wheels rotate freely and that the parking brake levers at the rear calipers stay on the stops.
7. Turn the ignition switch on and check that the brake warning light comes on when the parking brake is pulled to the first tooth and goes out when it is released.

CABLE REMOVAL AND INSTALLATION

100 and Fox

1. Jack up the rear of the car.
2. Block the front wheels and release the handbrake.
3. Remove the rear brake shoes.
4. Remove the cable adjusting nut(s) and detach the cable guides from the floor pan.
5. Replace the cable and brake shoes. Check the parking brake adjustment.

4000 and 5000

1. Raise and support the rear of the car. Release the parking brake.
2. Remove the rear brake drums on all but the Turbo and Quattro.

3. Disconnect the cable from the shoe assembly by pushing the spring forward and removing the cable from the adjusting arm on all but the Turbo and Quattro.
4. Pull the parking brake cable out of its retaining clip on the caliper (Turbo and Quattro only).
5. Remove the cable compensating spring.
6. Back off the equalizer nut and guide the cable through the trailing arms and supports.
7. Installation is the reverse of removal.

NOTE: When installing the parking brake cables on the Turbo and Quattro, the long cable goes on the left side and the short one goes on the right side. The cable coupling should connect the two cables on the right side of the equalizer bar.

8. Adjust if necessary.

CHASSIS ELECTRICAL

Heater

REMOVAL AND INSTALLATION

100

To remove either the heater blower or the core, it is necessary to remove the heater unit from the car and disassemble it.

1. Drain the coolant, disconnect the battery, and remove the lower instrument panel trim and center shelf.
2. Remove the breather screw from the hose inside the engine compartment, being careful not to damage the firewall seal.
3. Detach both heater hoses.
4. Disconnect the cables that control the foot area heater flaps, the windshield flap and the heater valve.
5. Remove the plug connector from the heater controls and the lead from terminal 15 of the emergency warning light switch.
6. From the passenger compartment unbolt the heater and pull it down.
7. Installation is the reverse of removal.

NOTE: When installing the cables, place the heater levers in the Off position. Place the leg of the spring clip in the mount and install the spring clip. The cable sleeve must protrude at least 0.2 in. beyond the spring clip.

4000

1. Disconnect the negative battery cable.
2. Drain the engine coolant.

Exploded view of the 4000 heater assembly

NOTE: Save the coolant for reuse.

3. Trace the heater hoses coming from the firewall and disconnect them. One leads to the back of the cylinder head and the other leads to the heater valve located above and behind the oil filter.

4. Detach the cable for the heater valve.

5. Remove the center console.

6. Remove the left and right covers below the instrument panel.

7. Pull off the fresh air/heater control knobs.

8. Pull off the trim plate.

9. Remove the screws (2) for the controls.

10. Remove the center cover mounting screws (2 top and 2 bottom) and remove the cover.

11. Detach the right, left and center air ducts.

12. Remove the heater housing retaining spring.

13. Remove the cowl for the air plenum which is located under the hood and in front of the windshield.

14. Remove the heater housing mounting screws (4) and remove the heater housing. The mounting screws are under the hood where the air plenum was.

15. Installation is in the reverse order of

removal. Be sure to replace all sealing material.

5000

NOTE: Blower or core removal requires removal and disassembly of the entire unit.

1. Disconnect the battery ground.

2. Drain the cooling system.

——— CAUTION ———

If the vehicle is equipped with air conditioning, the A/C system must be discharged. This procedure should be left to a trained technician.

3. Discharge the air conditioning system.

4. Disconnect the:
   a. Temperature sensor connector.
   b. Evaporator/heater connector clamp.
   c. Temperature control cable.
   d. Fresh air door vacuum hose.

5. Disconnect the main harness connector.

6. Loosen the case retaining strap.

7. Remove the coolant hoses at the heater core tubes.

8. Remove the yellow, green and red vacuum hoses from the heater case.

9. Remove the air duct hoses.

10. Remove the heater case mounting screws (two in the passenger compartment, one in the engine compartment). On A/C equipped cars, remove the four evaporator housing mounting screws in the passenger compartment.

11. Support the heater/evaporator unit and pull it away from the firewall.

12. Remove the control cable grommet to facilitate case removal.

13. The case halves may be separated by removing the clips at the top and bottom with a screwdriver.

14. Installation is the reverse of removal. Replace all sealing material. Evacuate, charge and leak test the system. This last procedure should be performed by a trained technician.

Fox

The heater must be removed and disassembled to service the heater or the core.

1. Remove the windshield washer container. Remove the ignition coil.

2. Disconnect the two hoses from the heater core connections at the firewall.

3. Unplug the electrical connector.

4. Remove the heater control knobs on the dash.

5. Remove the controls from the dash complete with brackets.

6. Pull the cable connection off the electric motor.

7. Disconnect the cable from the lever on the round knob.

8. Using a screwdriver, pry the retaining clip off the fresh air housing (the front portion of the heater).

9. Remove the fresh air housing complete with the controls.

Exploded view of the 5000 heater assembly

10. Detach the left and right air hoses.

11. Lower the heater assembly.

12. Pull out the two pins and remove the heater cover. Unscrew and remove the fan motor.

13. Separate the heater halves to remove the heater core.

14. Installation is the reverse of removal.

Radio

The radio is usually a dealer installed or aftermarket unit. Thus no specific removal and installation procedures can be given. The following information applies generally to all car radios.

Care should be taken during installation to avoid reversing the ground and power leads. Reversal of these leads will cause serious damage to the radio. The power lead usually has an in-line fuse.

If the speaker needs replacement, it should be replaced with one of the same impedance, measured in ohms. Mismatched impedance can cause rapid transistor failure as well as poor radio performance. This should also be taken into consideration when adding a second speaker.

The radio should never be operated without a speaker connected or with the speaker leads shorted. This will result in transistor failure.

Wiper Motor

REMOVAL AND INSTALLATION

100

The motor can be removed from inside the engine compartment.

1. Disconnect the battery negative terminal.

2. Remove the right and left knee padding.

3. From the engine compartment, pull out the rubber grommet to give the wiring harness more play. Pull out the wiper switch and remove the leads.

4. Bend open the metal tabs holding the wiring harness and remove the harness which runs below the spray jets, together with the spray jet line.

5. Loosen the nut and pry off the lever for the linkage.

6. Remove the motor and harness.

7. Reverse the procedure for installation:

Wiper Linkage

REMOVAL AND INSTALLATION

100

The linkage can be removed from inside the engine compartment.

1. Fresh air inlet with control flap (opens with heater on)
2. Dry air flap (opens with A/C on)
3. Heater—A/C blower
4. Air outlets for ends of instrument panel
5. Heater core
6. Center air outlet
7. Floor air outlet
8. Evaporator

Fox heater system (models with A/C)

1. Remove the windshield wiper arms from the studs by prying off the cap and removing the retaining nut. Remove the lower nut, washer and seal from the recess in the body.

2. Remove the mounting screws in the engine compartment and tilt the wiper base to remove.

3. Installation of the wiper linkage and the motor is done by reversing the removal procedures. The lever connected to the wiper motor should be installed at approximately 90° to the front and rear centerline of the vehicle. The wiper arm blades have different angles. The arm with the blade at the greater angle is installed on the driver's side.

Windshield Wiper Motor and Linkage

REMOVAL AND INSTALLATION

Fox, 4000, and 5000

1. Pry off wiper arms and remove nuts from studs in cowl.

2. Remove brace-to-body screws.

3. Disconnect multiple connector at wiper motor.

4. Remove motor mounting screw, and pry off connecting rod.

5. Remove linkage followed by motor.

Instrument Cluster

REMOVAL AND INSTALLATION

100

1. Disconnect the battery ground cable.

2. Remove the screws which hold the padding on top of the instrument panel. Remove the padding.

3. Remove the nuts at the rear of the instrument cluster and remove the cover.

4. Pull the cluster out toward the driver's seat.

5. Pull off the electrical connections and unscrew the speedometer cable.

6. Remove the instrument cluster. It may be further disassembled as necessary.

Fox

1. Disconnect the battery ground cable.

2. Remove the lower instrument panel trim.

3. Disconnect the speedometer cable from the back of the speedometer. Detach the electrical plug at the back of the fuel and temperature gauge.

4. Detach the spring at either end and pull the cluster forward.

4000

1. Disconnect the negative battery cable.

2. Remove the retaining screws for the

From the top of the instrument cluster, remove the four multi-point connectors and the speedometer cable—4000

Fuse box—5000

instrument cluster cover. Remove the cover and the trim strip.

3. From the top of the instrument cluster, remove the four multi-point connectors.

4. Unscrew the speedometer cable.

5. Remove each switch panel from the side of the instrument cluster.

6. Remove the instrument cluster retaining screws and remove the cluster.

7. Installation is in the reverse order of removal.

5000

1. Disconnect the negative battery cable.

2. Remove the instrument panel trim.

3. Remove the instrument cluster cover retaining screws and remove the cover.

4. Loosen the instrument cluster retaining screws and slide it forward enough to remove the multi-point connectors and the speedometer cable.

5. Remove the cluster retaining screws and remove the cluster.

6. Installation is in the reverse order of removal.

Fuse Box Location

On the 100, the fuse box is near the clutch pedal on the left side of the car. The flasher, windshield washer, and headlight relays are mounted on the fuse box.

The fuse box for all 4000 models can be found underneath the left side of the dashboard, behind the rear panel of the package tray. The fuse box for all 5000 models is located under the hood, at the left rear of the engine compartment. The relays for both models are also plugged into the fuse box. In the cover of each fuse box (and in the Owner's Manual) is a chart which tells which circuit the fuse protects and its correct amperage. The chart also tells which circuit the relays are connected to. Each model also uses in-line fuses for certain circuits: fuel pump, battery, air conditioning and power door locks (if so equipped), 4000; air conditioning, power windows, and heated seats, 5000; glow plug, 5000 Diesel; cigar lighter, power windows and the cooling fan for the injectors, 5000 Turbo.

BMW

SERIAL NUMBER IDENTIFICATION

Manufacturer's Plate

The manufacturer's plate is located in the engine compartment on the right side inner fender panel or support, or on the right side of the firewall.

Chassis Number

The chassis number can be found in the engine compartment on the right inner fender support or facing forward on the right side of the heater bulkhead. A label is also attached to the upper steering column cover inside the vehicle.

Engine Number

The engine number is located on the left rear side of the engine, above the starter motor.

Under hood serial number location—typical

Engine serial number location

GENERAL ENGINE SPECIFICATIONS

Year	Model	Engine No. Cyl.—Displacement cu. in. (cc)	Carburetor or Injection Type	Horsepower @ rpm	Torque @ rpm (ft. lbs.)	Bore × Stroke (in.)	Compression Ratio	Oil Pressure @ rpm (psi)
'76	2002	4-121 (1990)	Solex 32/32 DIDTA	98 @ 5500	106 @ 3500	3.504 × 3.150	8.3:1	57 @ 4000
'76	3.0Si	6-182 (2985)	Bosch electronic injection	200 @ 5500	200 @ 4000	3.504 × 3.150	9.5:1	71 @ 6000
'77–'79	320i	4-121 (1990)	Bosch K-Jetronic mechanical injection	110 @ 5800	112 @ 3750	3.504 × 3.150	8.2:1	57 @ 4000

GENERAL ENGINE SPECIFICATIONS

Year	Model	Engine No. Cyl.— Displacement cu. in. (cc)	Carburetor or Injection Type	Horsepower @ rpm	Torque @ rpm (ft. lbs.)	Bore × Stroke (in.)	Compression Ratio	Oil Pressure @ rpm (psi)
'80–'81	320i	4-108 (1766)	Bosch K-Jetronic mechanical injection	101 @ 5800	100 @ 4500	3.504 × 2.795	8.8:1	57 @ 4000
'77–'79	530i 630CSi	6-182 (2985)	Bosch L-Jetronic electronic injection	176 @ 5500	185 @ 4500	3.504 × 3.150	8.1:1	71 @ 6000
'80–'81	528i	6-170 (2788)	Bosch L-Jetronic electronic injection	169 @ 5500	170 @ 4500	3.390 × 3.150	8.2:1	71 @ 4000
'82–'83	528e	6-165 (2693)	Bosch Motronic Injection	121 @ 4250	166 @ 3250	3.31 × 3.19	9.0:1	78 @ 5000
'78–'79	633CSi	6-196 (3210)	Bosch L-Jetronic electronic injection	176 @ 5500	192 @ 4000	3.504 × 3.150	8.4:1	71 @ 6000
'80–'83	633CSi	6-196 (3210)	Bosch① L-Jetronic electronic injection	174 @ 5200	184 @ 4200	3.504 × 3.386	8.0:1	71 @ 6000
'78–'79	733i	6-196 (3210)	Bosch L-Jetronic electronic injection	177 @ 5500	195 @ 4000	3.504 × 3.386	8.4:1	71 @ 6000
'80–'83	733i	6-196 (3210)	Bosch① L-Jetronic electronic injection	177 @ 5200	188 @ 4200	3.504 × 3.386	8.0:1	71 @ 6000

① 1982–83: Bosch Motronic Injection

TUNE-UP SPECIFICATIONS

Year	Model	Spark Plugs Type	Gap (in.)	Dwell (deg.)	Point Gap (in.)	Ignition Timing (deg.)③ MT	Ignition Timing (deg.)③ AT	Intake Valve Opens (deg.)	Fuel Pump Pressure (psi)	Idle Speed (rpm) MT	Idle Speed (rpm) AT	Cold Valve Clearance (in.)
'76	2002	Bosch W175T30, W200T30, WG190T30;	.026	62	.016	1600 rpm①	1600 rpm①	4B	4.3	900	900	.007
'76	3.0Si	Bosch W145T30, W175T30;	.026	38	.015	22B@ 1700	22B@ 1700	26B	30	900	900	.011

TUNE-UP SPECIFICATIONS

Year	Model	Spark Plugs Type	Gap (in.)	Distributor Dwell (deg.)	Point Gap (in.)	Ignition Timing (deg.)③ MT	AT	Intake Valve Opens (deg.)	Fuel Pump Pressure (psi)	Idle Speed (rpm) MT	AT	Cold Valve Clearance (in.)
'77–'79	320i	Bosch W125T30	.026	62	.014	25B@ 2200 (2400)	25B@ 2200 (2400)	4B	64–74	950	950	007
'80–'83	320i	Bosch WR9DS	.024	Electronic②		25B@ 2200	25B@ 2200	4B	64–74	850	900	.007
'77–'79	530i	Bosch W145T30	.026	38	.015	22B@ 1700 (2700)	22B@ 1700 (2700)	26B	35	950	950	.011
'80–'81	528i	Bosch WR9DS	.024	Electronic②		22B@ 2100	22B@ 2100	26B	35	900	900	.011
'82–'83	528e	Bosch WR9DS	.027	Electronic ②		N/A	N/A	N/A	43	④	④	.010
'77–'78	630CSi	Bosch W145T30;	.024	38	.015	22B@ 1700 (2700)	22B@ 1700 (2700)	—	36.3	950	950	.012
'78–'79	633CSi	Bosch W145T30;	.024	Electronic		22B@ 2400 (2750)	22B@ 2400 (2750)	14B	28.5	950	950	.012
'80–'83	633CSi	Bosch WR9DS	.024	Electronic②		22B@ 1650	22B@ 1650	—	35	900④	900④	.011
'78–'79	733i	Bosch W145T30;	.026	Electronic		22B@ 2400 (2750)	22B@ 2400 (2750)	26B	43	950	950	.011
'80–'81	733i	Bosch WR9DS	.024	Electronic②		22B@ 1650	22B@ 1650	26B	35	900	900	.011

①Align steel ball in flywheel with pointer on flywheel housing window at specified speed
②Air gap 0.012–0.028″
  Dwell 42° ± 10° @ 15 rpm
  52° ± 5° @ 4500 rpm

③Figures in parentheses are for California
④Idle speed controlled by computer on 1982–83 models
B Before top dead center (TDC)
N/A—Not available at time of publication

FIRING ORDERS

FRONT

1976–83
6 cylinder firing order: 1-5-3-6-2-4

FIRING ORDERS

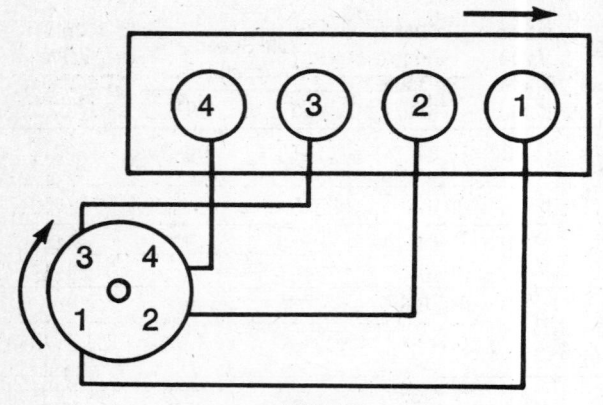

1976–79

4 cylinder firing order: 1-3-4-2

1980–83

4 cylinder firing order: 1-3-4-2

CAPACITIES

| Year | Model | Engine Crankcase (qts) | | Transmission, Refill After Draining (pts) | | Drive Axle (pts) | Gasoline Tank (gals) | Cooling System (qts) |
		With Filter Change	Without Filter Change	Manual	Automatic			
'76	2002	4.5	4.25	2.8	3.6	1.9	13.5	7.0
'76	3.0Si	5.3	5.0	2.5	3.8	3.4	16.5	12.7
'77–'79	320i	4.25	4.0	2.2	4.2	2.0	15.9	7.4
'80–'83	320i	8.5	8.0	3.2	12.0	2.0	15.3	7.4
'77–'79	530i, 630CSi	6.1	5.25	2.3	4.2	3.4	16.4	12.7
'78–'79	733i, 633CSi	6.1	5.25	2.4	4.8	4.0	22.5	12.7
'80–'83	633CSi	6.1	5.3	2.3	15.0	3.4	16.5	12.7
'80–'83	733i	6.1	5.3	2.3	15.0	4.0	22.5	12.7
'80–'81	528i	6.0	5.0	2.3	15.0	3.4	16.4	12.7
'82–'83	528e	4.46	4.2	3.4	16.8	3.8	16.6	12.7

CRANKSHAFT AND CONNECTING ROD SPECIFICATIONS
(Measurements in inches)

| Year | Model | Crankshaft | | Shaft End-Play | Thrust on No. | Journal Diameter | Connecting Rod Oil Clearance | Side Clearance |
		Main Bearing Journal Diameter	Main Bearing Oil Clearance					
'76	2002	2.1654	.0012–.0028	.003–.007	3	1.8898	.0009–.0027	.0016
'77–'83	320i	2.1653	.0012–.0027	.003–.007	3	1.8898	.0009–.0031	.0015
'77–'81	528i	2.3622	.0011–.0027	.003–.007	4	1.8897	.0009–.0027	.0016
'78–'83	733i, 633CSi	2.3622	.0012–.0027	.003–.007	4	1.8898	.0009–.0031	.0015
'76	3.0Si	2.3622	.0012–.0028	.003–.007	4	1.8898	.0013–.0027	.0016
'77–'83	530i, 630CSi	2.3622	.0011–.0027	.003–.007	4	1.8897	.0009–.0027	.0016
'82–'83	528e	2.3622	.0012–.0028	.003–.006	4	1.7717	.0012–.0028	.0016

VALVE SPECIFICATIONS

Year	Model	Seat Angle (deg.)	Face Angle (deg.)	Spring Pressure (lbs.) @ in.	Spring Free Height (in.)	Stem to Guide Clearance (in.) Intake	Stem to Guide Clearance (in.) Exhaust	Stem Diameter (in.) Intake	Stem Diameter (in.) Exhaust
'76	2002	45	45½	64@1.48	1.71	.0010–.0020	.0015–.0030	.3149	.3149
'76	3.0Si	45	45⅓	64@1.48	1.71	.0010–.0020	.0015–.0030	.3150	.3150
'77–'83	320i	45	45½	64@1.48	1.71 or 1.81①	.0010–.0020	.0015–.0030	.3149	.3149
'77–'81	528i, 530i, 630CSi	45	45⅓	64@1.48	1.71	.0010–.0021	.0015–.0027	.3149	.3149
'82–'83	528e	45	45	—	—	.006	.006	.276	.276
'78–'83	733i, 633CSi	45	45½	64@1.48	1.71 or 1.81①	.0010–.0022	.0016–.0027	.3150	.3150

— Not available at time of publication
① A dimension of 1.81 applies to some springs depending on the original manufacturer

PISTON AND RING SPECIFICATIONS
(Measurements in inches)

Year	Model	Piston to Bore Clearance	Ring Gap Top Compression	Ring Gap Bottom Compression	Ring Gap Oil Control	Ring Side Clearance Top Compression	Ring Side Clearance Bottom Compression	Ring Side Clearance Oil Control
'76	2002	.002	.012–.020	.008–.016	.010–.016	.002–.003	.001–.002	.001–.002
'76	3.0Si	.002	.012–.020	.008–.016	.010–.016	.002–.003	.001–.002	.001–.002
'77–'83	320i	.002	.012–.018	.008–.016	.010–.020	.002–.004	.002–.003	.001–.002
'77–'81	528i, 530i, 630CSi	.002	.012–.020	.008–.015	.010–.016	.002–.003	.001–.002	.001–.002
'82–'83	528e	.0004–.0015	.012–.020	.012–.020	.010–.020	.0016–.0028	.0012–.0024	.0008–.0019
'78–'83	733i, 633CSi	.002	.012–.018	.008–.016	.010–.020	.002–.004	.002–.003	.001–.002

— Not available at time of publication

TORQUE SPECIFICATIONS
(Measurements in ft. lbs.)

Year	Model	Cylinder Head Bolts	Connecting Rod Bearing Bolts	Main Bearing Bolts	Crankshaft Bolt	Flywheel Bolts	Exhaust Manifold Bolts
'76	2002	49–52	38–41	42–46	101–108	72–83	22–24
'76	3.0S, 3.0Si	53–55	38–41	42–46	174–188① 318–333	72–83	22–24
'77–'83	320i	49–52	38–41	42–45	101–108	72–83	22–24
'77–'81	528i, 530i, 630CSi	53–56	38–40	42–46	320–330	72–83	22–24

TORQUE SPECIFICATIONS
(Measurements in ft. lbs.)

Year	Model	Cylinder Head Bolts	Connecting Rod Bearing Bolts	Main Bearing Bolts	Crankshaft Bolt	Flywheel Bolts	Exhaust Manifold Bolts
'82–'83	528e	②	③	43–48	282–311	71–82	22–24④
'78–'83	733i, 633CSi	56–59	38–40	42–45	320–330	72–83	22–24

— Not available at time of publication
① Higher figure is with collar nut
② Tighten the head bolts in sequence and in three steps as follows:
   a. Torque to 22–25 ft. lbs. (30–35 Nm)
   b. Torque to 43–47 ft. lbs. (60–65 Nm)
   c. Bring the engine up to operating temperature. Use BMW angle torque tool 11 2 110 or equivalant, to turn each bolt 25° 5° in sequence.

③ Tighten in sequence as follows:
   a. Torque to 14 ft. lbs. (20 Nm)
   b. Angle torque, using BMW tool 11-2-110 or equivalent, to turn eacch bolt 70°.
④ Use loctite on upper row of exhaust bolts.

TORQUE SEQUENCES

528e—6 cylinder torque sequence

4-cylinder head torque sequence

6-cylinder head torque sequence (except 528e)

ALTERNATOR AND REGULATOR SPECIFICATIONS

Year	Model	Alternator Bosch Model or Part No.	Alternator Maximum Output (Amps)	Regulator Bosch Model or Part No.	Regulator Regulated Voltage @68°F
'76	2002	K1/14V/45/24	45	AD1/14V or ADN1/14V①	13.5–14.2
'77–83	320i	K1/14V/55A 0 120 489 608	55	0 192 052 004	13.9–14.3
'77–83	528i, 530i, 633CSi	14V/55A	55	AD1/14V	13.5–14.2
'78–83	733i, 630CSi	14V/65A 0 120 489 619	65	EE14/V3 0 192 052 006	13.5–14.2

ALTERNATOR AND REGULATOR SPECIFICATIONS

		Alternator		Regulator	
Year	Model	Bosch Model or Part No.	Maximum Output (Amps)	Bosch Model or Part No.	Regulated Voltage @68°F
'76	3.0Si	14/55A	55	ADN1/14V① or AD1/14V	13.5–14.2
'82–'83	528e	—	65	—	13.5–14.6

①With radio noise suppression

BATTERY AND STARTER SPECIFICATIONS

		Battery (12 Volt, Negative Ground) Ampere Hour Capacity	Bosch Model or Part No.	Starter No-Load Test		
Year	Model			Amps	Volts	rpm
'76	2002	44	GF(R)12V1 hp 0031 311 016	210	9.6	1300
'77–'83	320i	55	GF(R)12V1.0 hp 0 001 311 045	210	9.6	1300
'77–'83	528i, 530i, 630CSi, 533CSi	55①	GF12V1.2 hp	270	9.1	10,000
'78–'83	733i	66	GF12V1.8 hp 0 001 311 042	340	9.1	10,000
'76	3.0Si	55	GF12V1.2 hp	270	9.1	10,000
'82–83	528e	—	—	—	—	—

①633CSi—65 amp hour

BRAKE SPECIFICATIONS

(Measurements in inches)

		Lug Nut Torque (ft. lbs.)	Master Cylinder Bore	Disc		Drum		Minimum Lining Thickness	
Year	Model			Minimum Thickness	Maximum Runout (installed)	Diameter	Maximum Machined Oversize	Front	Rear
'76	2002	59–65	.813	.354	.008	9.06	9.10	.08	.12
'76	3.0Si	60–66	.874	.827F/.709R	.008	—	—	—	—
'77–'79	320i	59–65	.812	.827	.008	9.84	9.89	.12	.12
'80–'83	320i	59–65	.812	.827	.008	10.00	10.04	—	—
'77–'79	530i, 633CSi	59–65	.936	.460F/.334R	.008	—	—	—	—
'80–'81	528i	59–65	.936	.840F/.340R	.008	—	—	—	—
'82–'83	528e	72–80	—	.138F/.138R	.0020	—	—	—	—
'80–'83	633CSi	59–65	.936	.840F/.720R	.008	—	—	—	—
'78–'79	733i	60–66	.874	.827	.006	—	—	—	—
'80–'83	733i	60–66	.874	.840F/.360R	.008	—	—	—	—

WHEEL ALIGNMENT SPECIFICATIONS

Year	Model	Caster (deg.)	Front Suspension Camber (deg.)	Toe-In (in.)	Steering Axis Inclination (deg.)	Rear Suspension Camber (deg.)	Toe-In (in.)
'76	2002	4P	½P	.07	8½P	2N	.06
'76	3.0CSi	9⅔P	½P	.07	8½P	2N	.04
'77–'83	320i	8⅔P	0	.07	10½P	2N	.04
'77–'79	530i	7⅔P	½P	.07	8½P	2N	.04
'80–'81	528i	7⅔P	0	.06	8½P	2N	.04
'82–'83	528e	8⅓P	⅓N	.08	—	2N	.08
'77–'83	633CSi	7⅔P	0	.06	8P	2N	.04
'78–'83	733i	9P	0	.03	11½P	1½N	.08

TUNE-UP PROCEDURES

Spark Plugs

REMOVAL AND INSTALLATION

NOTE: Before removing spark plugs clean any dirt from the base area of the spark plugs with compressed air or a stiff brush.

— CAUTION —
Grasp the plug wire by the boot and twist slightly to loosen, before pulling on the boot (not the wire) to remove the wire from the spark plug. Bending or pulling on the wire breaks the internal conductive material.

1. Mark or tag the wires for correct reinstallation, then remove the wires from the spark plugs.

2. Using a 13/16 inch deep-well spark-plug socket and a swivel head rachet-type wrench, remove the spark plugs.

3. Inspect spark plugs for cracked and damaged insulators or threads, worn electrodes, damaged gasket and carbon or other fouling deposits.

4. If plugs are to be reused file the electrodes square.

5. Regap old spark plugs or check the gap on new spark plugs.

6. Install the spark plugs in the head and torque to 18–21 ft. lbs. (25–28 Nm).

7. Install the plug wires on the proper spark plugs.

Breaker Points and Condenser

REPLACEMENT

1. Remove the distributor cap, rotor and the point guard, if equipped.

2. Disconnect the primary wire at the inner side of the distributor body terminal.

3. Remove the point set retaining screw and lift the point set from the breaker plate.

NOTE: Some distributors have the condenser mounted on the outside of the distributor body, while others have the condenser mounted inside the housing. The condenser lead will either be attached to the distributor outside terminal or to the inside terminal. Disconnect the condenser lead wire if necessary to replace the point set or condenser.

4. To install the new point set, clean the old grease from the cam and distributor plate. Put a small amount of special cam lubricant on the distributor cam and install the point set and condenser in the reverse of the removal.

5. Align the point faces to meet squarely and ''bump'' the engine until the rubbing block is on the high point of the distributor cam.

6. Adjust the point gap by moving the point set until a feeler gauge of the specified size can be inserted in the gap.

7. Tighten the retaining screw and recheck the gap.

8. Start the engine and check the dwell.

Electronic Ignition

Breaker points and condensers are not used with the electronic ignition. The air gap between the rotating teeth and the stator teeth can be checked with a brass or plastic feeler gauge. No adjustment is possible. If the gap is not as specified, the unit should be replaced.

— CAUTION —
All repair work to the electronic ignition system should be done with the engine stopped and the ignition switch Off.

For 1982–83 the 528e, 633CSi and 733i models are equipped with a motronic engine control system. This system uses various engine sensors including an oxygen

1. Flat connector
2. Point retaining screw
3. Felt pad
4. Rubbing block

Breaker point and condensor location—typical

2. Circlip
3. Expander

Measuring rotor to stator clearance (A)

Ignition timing marks at flywheel

sensor in the exhaust to monitor engine conditions. The monitored information is fed to a Motronic (computer) unit, which in turn controls the air fuel mixture entering the engine.

Ignition Timing

The engine should be at normal operating temperature. Adjust the idle speed. Connect a timing light to the No. 1 spark plug wire and start the engine. Align the marks on the flywheel with the bell housing indicator, by rotating the distributor body. Tighten the distributor body clamp.

NOTE: The flywheel mark is either a pressed-in steel ball or a long tapered peg on the side of the starter ring gear.

Valve Clearance

All BMW engines are equipped with a chain driven, overhead camshaft, operating the intake and exhaust valves through rocker arm linkage.

NOTE: The valves must be adjusted cold.

1. Remove the rocker cover.
2. Rotate the engine until No. 1 cylinder is at TDC on compression stroke.

NOTE: Locate No. 1 cylinder firing position by the distributor rotor–to–cap position, or by observing the valve action in the opposite cylinder. Refer to following charts:

Cylinder Firing-Piston at TDC	Exhaust Valve Closing, Intake Valve Opening On Opposite Cylinder
6 CYLINDER	
1	6
5	2
3	4
6	1
2	5
4	3
4 CYLINDER	
1	4
3	2
4	1
2	3

3. Measure the valve clearance between the valve stem end and the rocker arm on the No. 1 cylinder (refer to the specifications for valve clearances).
4. Adjust the clearance by loosening the locknut on the rocker arm and turning

the eccentric with a bent rod inserted through a hole provided on the surface of the eccentric.
5. When the proper clearance is obtained, tighten the locknut and recheck the valve clearance. Complete the adjustment on both valves.
6. Rotate the engine crankshaft to the next cylinder in the firing order, adjust the valves and repeat the procedures until all the valves are adjusted.
7. Replace the rocker cover, using a new gasket.

Carburetor

IDLE SPEED AND MIXTURE ADJUSTMENT

2002

1. The engine should be at normal operating temperature.
2. Turn the idle mixture screw until the engine runs erratically.
3. Adjust the idle mixture screw until the engine reaches the highest idle speed and runs smoothly.
4. Readjust the idle speed (with the idle speed screw) to specifications as necessary.

Adjusting of engine valve clearance with bent rod after loosening the locknut (1)

Idle speed adjustment screw (1) and mixture adjustment screw (2) location—2002 and 2002A

Remove plug (3) and use special tool 13-1-060 or equivalent to adjust the CO level with the screw in the bottom of the air intake sensor—530i, 528i, 528e, 630CSi, 633CSi and 733i

Adjusting CO level with special tool. Hole plug shown—320i

Fuel Injection

IDLE SPEED AND MIXTURE ADJUSTMENT

NOTE: The idle speed and mixture can be adjusted ONLY with the aid of a CO meter. If you do not have access to this tool, do not attempt any of the following procedures; leave the work to a qualified service technician.

530i, 528i and 528e

1. Run engine to normal operating temperature.
2. Disconnect the hose from the collector to the charcoal filter. Do not plug the line.

NOTE: The hose is located between the first and second air induction tubes.

3. Disconnect the air pump hose at the air pump and plug the line.
4. Adjust the idle speed by turning the screw on the side of the throttle housing.
5. The CO level should be between 1.5–3.0% at idle speed.
6. If necessary, adjust the CO to specifications with the idle air screw located on

the air volume control, by turning the screw to the left or right.
7. Reconnect the hoses.

NOTE: The idle speed on 528e models is controlled by computer and is not adjustable. If the idle speed is not within specifications the idle speed control unit must be replaced.

NOTE: A plug in the anti-tamper cover, of the air flow sensor, must be removed in order to adjust the CO level. This should only be done if no other faults or problems are found in the ignition and injection systems and the CO% is not within specification.

320i

1. Run the engine to normal operating temperature.
2. Adjust the engine idle speed with the screw located near the throttle valve linkage.
3. Detach the exhaust check valve and plug the hose.
4. To adjust the CO, remove the plug from the fuel distributor and with a special wrench, adjust the CO level to a maximum of 2.0% for the 49 state vehicles or 3.5% for the California cars.
5. Reconnect the exhaust check valve hose and check the idle speed.

630CSi, 633CSi and 733i

1. Run the engine to normal operating temperature.
2. Disconnect the throttle housing-to-carbon filter hose. Disconnect and plug the air hose at the air pump.
3. Adjust the idle speed to specifications with the idle adjusting screw, located in the side of the throttle housing.
4. Adjust the CO to 1.5–3.0% at idle. Remove the cap from the air flow sensor and with the aid of a special tool, or short screwdriver, turn the bypass air screw located in the air flow sensor, until the CO level is as specified.
5. Reconnect the 2 hoses.

ENGINE ELECTRICAL

Distributor

REMOVAL AND INSTALLATION

All (except 528e)

1. Remove the distributor cap.
2. Disconnect the electrical wiring and vacuum hose.
3. Rotate the engine so that the rotor points to the notch on the distributor housing rim. The notch represents No. 1 cylinder.
4. Check that No. 1 piston is at TDC. The flywheel steel ball should be aligned with the indicator on the bell housing, or if the engine is equipped with a mark on the balancer, the mark should be aligned with the cast tab on the timing housing cover.
5. Remove the distributor clamp bolt and remove the distributor.
6. When the distributor is removed, the shaft and rotor will move counterclockwise. Mark the housing at this point for ease of installation.

Idle speed screw location—320i

Distance (A) rotor moves from the housing mark during the removal of the electronic distributor

Aligning rotor with the mark on the conventional distributor housing before removing the distributor

Distance (A) rotor moves from the housing mark during the removal of the conventional distributor—typical

7. Installation is the reverse of removal. Adjust the ignition timing.

NOTE: If the engine is cranked while the distributor is removed, the timing marks must be realigned and the No. 1 piston must be set at TDC, on the compression stroke.

─────── **CAUTION** ───────
Late model vehicles with electronic ignition are equipped with TDC position transmitters, which are used with the electronic test equipment. Do not damage or misalign the transmitters at the timing housing cover.

528e

─────── **CAUTION** ───────
Always turn off the ignition before working on the engine's electrical systems. Components of the computer system may be damaged by voltage surge during connecting and disconnecting procedures, if the ignition voltage is left on. Also, the extremely high voltage produced by electronic ignition could cause personal injury.

The 528e distributor rotor shaft is bolted into the front end of the overhead camshaft in front of the camshaft sprocket.

1. Remove the coil high tension wire at the distributor cap. Mark all spark plug wires for reinstallation and remove them from the distributor cap.

NOTE: A slight twist of the boot will break it loose from the cap. Pulling or twisting the wire during removal can break the internal conductive material.

2. Remove three distributor cap attaching bolts and remove the two-piece outer distributor cap, the rotor, the inner distributor cap and rubber seal.

3. Check the rotor resistance for approximately 1,000 ohms and replace the rotor if it's not within specification.

4. Transmitter and holder
5. Contact pin
6. Gauge

O/T = TDC

Electronic transmitter being gauged into position (left), and TDC mark on the balancer (right)

Alignment of the rotor with the electronic distributor housing and alignment of the balancer pulley TDC mark with the timing housing lug, before distributor removal

4. Remove the distributor guard attaching bolts and remove the guard.

NOTE: No further removal of the distributor is possible. The rotor shaft bolt also retains the camshaft sprocket onto the camshaft.

5. Install the distributor guard and rotor.

6. Install the rubber seal ring, inner cap and the two piece outer cap.

7. Install the spark plug wires and the coil wire on the proper cap terminals as marked at removal.

Alternator

REMOVAL AND INSTALLATION

1. Disconnect the battery ground cable.

2. Disconnect the wires from the rear of the alternator, marking them for later installation.

3. Loosen the adjusting and pivot bolts, and remove the alternator.

NOTE: Early model vehicles use a voltage regulator mounted on the firewall or the inner fender panel. Later model vehicles use a voltage regulator mounted on the rear of the alternator as part of the brush holder.

4. Installation is the reverse of removal. Adjust the belt tension to approximately ⅜ in., measured between the balancer and the alternator pulley.

Removal of the voltage regulator and brush holder assembly—typical

Starter

REMOVAL AND INSTALLATION

1. Disconnect the battery ground cable.

2. On fuel injection models, you may have to remove No. 6 intake tube for clearance.

3. Remove the starter solenoid wire leads, marking them for later installation.

4. Unbolt and remove the starter.

NOTE: Remove the accelerator cable holder on automatic transmission equipped vehicles.

5. Installation is the reverse of removal.

STARTER DRIVE GEAR REPLACEMENT

The starter must be disassembled to replace the starter drive. A circlip retains the drive gear on the armature shaft and must be removed before the drive gear can be replaced.

1. Remove the field coil wires from the solenoid and remove the solenoid mounting bolts.

2. Disengage the solenoid plunger from the starter drive and remove the solenoid from the starter motor.

3. Remove the small dust cap from the end of the motor.

4. Remove the C-clip, shims and gasket from the end of the starter motor shaft.

5. Remove the two long pole housing

Disassembled view of end cap, retainer clip and through-bolts of starter—typical

Removal of starter solenoid

Disassembled view of starter brush plate—typical

screws from the housing. Lift off the pole housing cap, the brushes and the brush plate.

6. Remove the intermediate bearing screws and remove the pole housing.

7. Remove the rubber seal and washer from the engaging lever housing.

8. Remove the engaging lever screw and pull the armature out of the drive bearing.

9. Push back the thrust washer on the drive pinion end of the motor shaft in order to remove the C-clip retainer.

10. Remove the starter drive pinion and bracket.

11. Install the starter pinion and bracket. Secure them on the shaft with the thrust

washer and C-clip. Lubricate the course threads, engaging ring and bearing with high temperature silicone grease.

12. Install the armature and shaft into the drive bearing, making sure that the tabs of the engaging lever are installed over the engaging ring. Lubricate the engaging lever with silicone grease.

13. Install the washer and rubber seal into the engaging lever housing, making sure the tabs on the seal and washer point toward the armature.

14. Position the pole housing so that the groove faces toward the rubber pad and install the pole housing into the drive bearing. Secure the screws with Loctite® No. 270.

15. Check the commutator bearing for looseness and then guide the field coil wires into the rubber seal.

16. Install the pole housing screws through the pole housing cap and locating slots in the brush plate. Install the brushes and pole housing cap on the starter.

17. Check armature axial play to 0.004–0.006 inches (0.1–0.15 mm) and correct any excessive play with additional shims.

18. Install end gasket, shims and C-clip on the end of the motor shaft. Install the dust cover on the end of the starter motor (over the shaft, end gasket and shims).

19. Install the solenoid on the starter and attach the field coil wires to the solenoid.

ENGINE MECHANICAL

Engine

REMOVAL AND INSTALLATION

2002

The engine can be removed with or without the transmission.

1. Scribe the hood hinge locations and remove the hood.

2. Remove the air cleaner assembly, drain the cooling system, disconnect the hoses and remove the radiator.

3. Remove the battery for safety reasons.

4. Disconnect all electric wiring and tag them for later reference.

5. Disconnect the fuel and vacuum lines. Tag the vacuum lines.

6. Disconnect the accelerator linkage.

7. Raise and support the vehicle. Remove the clutch linkage with the pushrod attached.

8. Remove the slave cylinder from the clutch housing, leaving the pressure line attached.

9. Remove the driveshaft and disconnect the exhaust pipe from the exhaust manifold.

If desired, the transmission can be removed at this point, if the engine is to be removed separately.

10. Loosen the rear transmission crossmember, disconnect the electric wires from the transmission and lower the vehicle.

11. Support the engine with a lifting device, and remove the rear crossmember.

12. Remove the engine mounts and lift the engine from the compartment with the transmission attached.

13. Installation is the reverse of removal. Connect all wiring, hoses and switches in their original positions.

3.0 Si

CARBURETED MODELS

1. Scribe the hood hinge locations and remove the hood. Disconnect and remove the battery.

2. Remove the air cleaner and hoses.

3. Drain the cooling system, disconnect the hoses and remove the radiator.

4. Remove the windshield washer reservoir and the fan.

5. Disconnect the electrical wiring from the engine components, tagging them for later installation.

6. Disconnect the accelerator linkage and unbolt the exhaust pipe from the exhaust manifold.

7. Remove the front lower apron and

loosen both engine mount retaining nuts.

8. On vehicles with power steering, remove the pump from the mounting brackets and move the pump out of the way. Do not remove the lines.

9. Raise and support the vehicle.

10. Remove the transmission refer to Transmission Removal and Installation.

11. On manual transmission cars, remove the slave cylinder from the clutch housing, leaving the pressure hose attached.

12. Lower the car and attach a lifting sling to the engine.

13. Be sure that all wires, hoses and linkages are disconnected and remove the engine.

14. Installation is the reverse of removal. Be sure all bolt and clip connections are secure and all fluids are filled before starting the engine.

FUEL INJECTION MODELS

Follow the engine removal and installation procedures for carburetor equipped models. The following procedures pertain specifically to fuel injection models.

1. Separate the electrical connection for the fuel injection wire loom by removing the 3 retaining screws.

2. Remove the wire leads from the relays, sensors, and switches. Mark the wire connections for installation.

3. Remove the transmission if equipped with an automatic transmission. If equipped with a manual transmission, the engine can be removed with the transmission attached.

NOTE: If these engines are equipped with air conditioning; detach the compressor from the engine and support it out of the way of engine removal. The refrigerant lines should be left attached to the compressor.

320i

1. Raise and support the vehicle. Remove the transmission (refer to the Transmission Removal and Installation). Remove the exhaust pipe from the exhaust manifold.

Removal and/or installation of four cylinder engine—typical

Removal and/or installation of six cylinder engine—typical

Sectional view of the 528e engine

2. Remove the hood, after scribing the hinge locations.

3. Drain the cooling system, disconnect the hoses and remove the radiator. Remove the intake air panel.

4. Disconnect and tag the lines to the injector valves.

5. Disconnect all electrical wires from the engine, marking them for installation.

6. Disconnect all fuel and vacuum lines and mark them for installation.

7. Disconnect the accelerator cable. Disconnect the battery cables and remove the battery.

8. Attach a lifting sling to the engine. Remove the retaining nuts from the left and right engine mounts and the upper engine damper, located on the left side of the engine.

9. Carefully raise and remove the engine.

10. Installation is the reverse of removal.

530i, 528i and 528e

1. Raise and support the vehicle and remove the transmission. Remove the exhaust pipe from the exhaust manifold.

2. Remove the power steering pump and place it out of the way along the inner fender panel. Leave the hoses attached.

3. Lower the vehicle, scribe the hood hinge location and remove the hood.

4. Remove the air cleaner with the duct work attached. Disconnect and remove the air volume control.

5. Disconnect and remove the battery.

6. Disconnect all electrical wires and connectors. Mark the wires and connectors for installation.

7. Disconnect all vacuum hoses, marking them for installation.

8. Drain the cooling system, disconnect the hoses and remove the radiator.

9. Disconnect the accelerator linkage.

10. Install a lifting sling on the engine.

11. Remove the left and right engine mount retaining nuts and washers.

12. Carefully lift the engine from the engine compartment.

13. Installation is the reverse of removal.

630CSi and 633CSi

1. Raise and support the vehicle and remove the transmission. Remove the exhaust pipe from the exhaust manifold and reactor.

2. Remove the power steering pump and place it out of the way. Leave the hoses attached.

3. If equipped with air conditioning, remove the compressor and place it aside. *Do not remove the hoses.*

4. Scribe the hood hinge locations and remove the hood.

5. Drain the cooling system, disconnect the hoses and remove the radiator.

6. Remove the air cleaner housing at the wheelhouse.

7. Remove the electrical wires and connectors from the engine components.

Tag the wires and connectors.

NOTE: The fuel injection control box is located either in the glove box or behind the right side kick panel. Remove the plug and thread the wire and connector through the hole in the firewall and into the engine compartment.

8. Install a lifting sling on the engine.

9. Remove the right and left engine mount retaining nuts and washers.

10. Remove the engine.

11. Installation is the reverse of removal.

733i

1. Raise and support the vehicle and remove the transmission. Remove the exhaust pipe from the exhaust manifold and reactor.

2. Remove the clutch housing from the engine.

3. Remove the power steering pump and place it out of the way. Do not disconnect the hoses.

4. If equipped with air conditioning, remove the compressor and place it out of the way. Do not disconnect the hoses.

5. Remove the damper bracket from the crankcase and lower the vehicle.

6. Scribe the hood hinge locations and remove the hood.

7. Drain the cooling system, disconnect the hoses and remove the radiator.

8. Remove the windshield washer reservoir and the air filter housing located on the inner fender panel.

9. Remove the electrical wiring from the engine components. Tag all wires.

10. Disconnect and remove the battery.

11. Remove and tag all vacuum hoses.

NOTE: Some vacuum hoses are color coded.

12. Disconnect the throttle linkage.

13. Remove the right kick panel from the passenger compartment, remove the fuel injection control unit wire connector and thread the connector and wire through the hole in the firewall.

14. Attach a lifting sling to the engine. Remove the left and right engine mount retaining nuts and washers. Lift the engine from the engine compartment.

15. Installation is the reverse of removal.

Cylinder Head

REMOVAL AND INSTALLATION

2002 and 320i

1. Remove the air cleaner and disconnect the breather tube. On the 320i remove the intake manifold.

2. Disconnect the battery ground cable and drain the cooling system.

Alignment of distributor rotor and belt pulley notch—typical

Alignment of dowel pin hole and camshaft flange notch with the cast projection of the cylinder head—four cylinder engine

3. Remove the choke cable, if equipped.

4. Disconnect the throttle linkage. Pull the torsion shaft towards the firewall until the ball is free of the torsion shaft.

5. Remove and tag the vacuum hoses.

6. Disconnect the coolant hoses from the cylinder head.

7. Disconnect the electrical wiring and connectors from the cylinder head and engine components.

8. Remove the cylinder head cover and the front upper timing case cover.

9. Rotate the engine until the distributor rotor points to the notch on the distributor body edge and the timing indicator points to the first notch on the belt pulley 320i, or second notch for the 2002 models. No. 1 piston should now be at TDC on its firing stroke.

10. Remove the timing chain tensioner piston by removing the plug in the side of the block.

——————— CAUTION ———————
The plug is under heavy spring tension.

11. Open the lockplates, remove the retaining bolts and remove the timing chain sprocket from the camshaft.

NOTE: The dowel pin hole on the camshaft flange should be in the 6 o'clock position while the notch at the top of the cam flange should be aligned with the cast projection on the cylinder head and in the 12 o'clock position for proper installation.

12. Remove the exhaust pipe from the exhaust manifold and remove the dipstick holder.

13. Unscrew the cylinder head bolts in the reverse of the tightening sequence and remove the cylinder head.

14. Installation is the reverse of removal but note the following points:

a. Tighten the cylinder head bolts in three stages, following the illustrated sequence. Adjust the valves, start the engine and bring to normal operating temperature. Stop the engine and allow it to cool to approximately 95°F (35°C). Retorque the cylinder head bolts to specifications and readjust the valves.

NOTE: The cylinder head bolts should be retorqued after 600 miles (1000 km) of driving.

b. Check the projection of the cylinder head dowel sleeve in the cylinder block mating surface. Maximum height is 0.20 in.

c. Match the cylinder head gasket to the cylinder block and head to verify coolant flow passages are correct.

d. Adjust timing and idle speed.

e. Bleed the cooling system. Set heater valve to the warm position and fill cooling system. Run the engine to normal temperature and when thermostat has opened, release the pressure cap to the first position. Squeeze the upper and lower radiator hoses in a pumping effect, to allow trapped air to escape through the radiator. Recheck coolant level and close the pressure cap to its second catch position.

3.0Si, 530i, 528i, 528e, 630CSi, 633CSi, 733i

NOTE: Small variances may be encountered among models due to model changes, difference in electrical wiring, vacuum hoses and fuel line routings, but all are basically alike.

1. Disconnect the battery ground cable.

2. Disconnect the wire connectors. Loosen the clamps and remove the air flow sensor with the air filter on the fuel injected models, or remove the air cleaner from carburetor equipped models.

3. Disconnect the rocker cover vent hose, ignition line tube and electrical wiring.

4. Remove the rocker cover.

5. Drain the cooling system and remove the coolant hoses.

NOTE: Do not interchange the heater hoses.

6. Rotate the engine so that the dis-

Timing chain tensioner plug removal or installation—typical

tributor rotor points to the notch on the distributor body edge and the timing indicator points to the notch on the belt pulley. This will place number one piston at TDC on its firing stroke.

7. Remove the upper timing housing cover after removing the distributor and thermostat housing.

8. Remove the timing chain tensioner piston.

NOTE: The 528e is equipped with a rubber drive and timing belt. To loosen belt tension, loosen the tension roller bracket pivot bolt and adjusting slot bolt. Push the roller and bracket away from the belt to release the tension.

Alignment of dowel pin (1) with the sprocket and upper bolt hole and cylinder head cast tab—six cylinder engines

---
CAUTION

The retaining plug is under heavy spring tension.

9. Open the camshaft sprocket bolt lockplates and remove the bolts. Remove the sprocket.

NOTE: For installation purposes, the sprocket dowel pin should be located at the lower left, between 7 and 8 o'clock, while the upper bolt bore must align with the threaded bore of the camshaft and the cylinder head cast tab, visable through the two bores, when at the 12 o'clock position.

NOTE: Align the timing marks when installing the timing belt. The crankshaft sprocket mark must point at the notch in the flange of the front engine cover. The camshaft sprocket arrow must point at the alignment mark on the cylinder head. Also, the No. 1 piston must be at TDC of the compression stroke.

10. Remove and tag the electrical wiring and connectors.

11. Remove and tag the vacuum lines.

12. Remove the intake tube at No. 6 cylinder (530i only).

13. Remove the wiring harness by pulling it upward through the opening in the intake neck.

14. Disconnect the fuel lines.

15. Remove the exhaust system completely (630CSi), or disconnect the exhaust line at the exhaust manifold. Remove the exhaust filter.

16. Remove the cylinder head bolts in the reverse order of the tightening sequence and install locating pins in four head bolt bores to prevent the rocker shafts from turning.

17. Remove the cylinder head.

18. Installation is the reverse of removal. Note the following points.

a. Tighten the cylinder head bolts in three stages, following the illustrated sequence. Adjust the valves, start the engine and bring it to normal operating temperature. Stop the engine and allow it to cool to approximately 95°F (35°C). Retorque the cylinder head bolts to specifications and readjust the valves.

NOTE: The cylinder head bolts (except those on the 528e) should be retorqued after 600 miles (1000 km) of driving

b. Check the projection of the cylinder head dowel sleeve in the cylinder block mating surface. Maximum height is 0.20 in. (5.0 mm).

c. Match the cylinder head gasket to the cylinder block and head to verify that the coolant flow passages are correct.

d. Adjust the timing and idle speed.

e. Bleed the cooling system. Set the heater valve in the Warm position and fill the cooling system. Start the engine and bring to normal operating temperature. A venting screw is located on the top of the thermostat housing. Run the engine at fast idle and open the venting screw until the coolant comes out free of air bubbles. Close the bleeder screw and refill the reservoir with coolant.

Installation of locating pins in the cylinder head bolt bores to prevent rocker shafts from turning—six cylinder engines

CYLINDER HEAD OVERHAUL

Refer to "Engine Rebuilding", in the Unit Repair section for overhaul procedures.

Rocker Arms and Shaft

REMOVAL AND INSTALLATION

All Models Except 528e

1. Remove the cylinder head.

2. Remove the camshaft.

3. Slide the thrust rings and rocker arms rearward and remove the circlips from the rocker arm shafts.

4. On 4-cylinder engines:

a. Remove the distributor flange from the rear of the cylinder head.

b. Using a long punch, drive the rocker arm shaft from the rear to the front of the cylinder head.

NOTE: Be sure all circlips are off the shaft before attempting to drive the shaft from the cylinder head.

Rocker arm shaft locking bolt (2) location—six cylinder engine

Circlip location on the rocker arm shaft

3. Spring   5. Rocker arm
4. Washer   6. Thrust ring

Installed position of rocker arm components

c. The intake rocker shaft is not plugged at the rear, while the exhaust rocker shaft must be plugged. Renew the plug if necessary, during the installation.

5. On 6-cylinder engines:

a. Unscrew the rocker shaft locking bolts from the cylinder head.

b. Install a threaded slide hammer into the ends of the front rocker shafts and remove the shafts from the cylinder head.

NOTE: Be sure all circlips have been removed from the rocker shafts before removal.

c. Remove the end cover from the rear of the cylinder head.

d. Install a threaded slide hammer into the ends of the rear rocker shafts and remove.

6. The rocker arms, springs, washers, thrust rings and shafts should be examined and worn parts replaced. Special attention should be given to the rocker arm cam followers. If these are loose, replace the arm assembly.

The valves can be removed, repaired or replaced, as necessary, while the shafts and rocker arms are out of the cylinder head.

7. Installation is the reverse of removal. Note the following procedures:

a. Design changes of the rocker arms and shafts have occurred with the installation of a bushing in the rocker arm and the use of two horizontal oil flow holes drilled in the rocker shaft for improved oil supply. Do not mix the previously designed parts with the later designed parts.

1. Set screw
2. Eccentric
3. Washer
4. Locking nut

Rocker arm valve adjusting mechanism

Removing the rocker arm shaft with special tool—four cylinder engine

b. When installing the rocker arms and components to the rocker shafts, install locating pins in the cylinder head bolt bores to properly align the rocker arm shafts.

c. Install sealer on the rocker arm shaft locking bolts and rear cover.

d. On the 4-cylinder engines, position the rocker shafts so that the camshaft retaining plate ends can be engaged in the slots of shafts during camshaft installation.

e. Adjust the valve clearance.

528e

The cylinder head must be removed before the rocker arm shafts can be removed.

1. Remove the cylinder head (see the "Cylinder Head—Removal and Installation" procedures).

2. Mount the head on BMW stand 11 1 060 and 00 1 490 or equivalents. Secure the head to the stand with one head bolt.

3. Remove the camshaft sprocket bolt and remove the camshaft distributor adapter and sprocket. Reinstall the adapter on the camshaft.

4. Adjust the valve play to the maximum allowable on all valves.

5. Remove the front and rear rocker shaft plugs and lift out the thrust plate.

1. Front and rear plugs
2. Rocker arm thrust plate

Removing the thrust plate from rocker shafts—528e

Removal of camshaft and rocker arm retainer plate from the cylinder head, showing the dowel pin hole on four cylinder engine

6-cylinder valve location

4-cylinder valve location

Removing spring clips from rocker arm and shaft—528e

6. Remove the spring-clips from the rocker arms by lifting them off.

7. Remove the exhaust side rocker arm shaft:

a. Set the No. 6 cylinder rocker arms at the valve overlap position (rocker arms parallel), by rotating the engine through the firing order.

b. Push in on the front cylinder rocker arm and turn the camshaft in the direction of the intake rocker shaft, using a ½ inch drive breaker bar and a deep well socket to fit over the camshaft adaptor. Rotate the camshaft until all of the rocker arms are relaxed.

c. Remove the rocker arm shaft.

8. Remove the intake side rocker arm shaft:

a. Turn the camshaft in the direction of the exhaust rocker arm.

b. Use a deep well socket and ½ drive breaker bar on the camshaft adapter to turn the camshaft until all of the rocker arms are relaxed.

Using adapter and breaker bar to rotate the camshaft on 528e during rocker shaft removal

Carburetor equipped intake manifold

c. Pull out the rocker arm shaft.

9. Installation is the reverse of removal. Installation notes:

a. The rocker arm thrust plate must be fit into the grooves in the rocker shafts.

b. The straight side of the spring-clips must be installed in the grooves in the rocker arm shafts.

c. The large oil bores in the rocker shafts must be installed down to the valve guides and the small oil bores must face inward toward the center of the head.

d. Adjust the valve clearance.

Intake Manifold

REMOVAL AND INSTALLATION

2002

1. Remove the air cleaner.

2. Remove and tag the fuel lines, vacuum lines and electrical wiring.

3. Drain the cooling system.

4. Disconnect the manual choke control cable.

5. Disconnect the accelerator linkage.

6. Disconnect the coolant lines to the manifold.

7. Disconnect the dipstick support.

8. Remove the intake manifold.

9. Installation is the reverse of removal. Use new gaskets.

NOTE: The 2 front or rear intake tubes can be removed and installed on the 2002Ti engine (four carburetors), by separating the connecting rod between the middle carburetors and removing the front or rear section as desired by using the above procedure as a guide.

3.0CSi

NOTE: Combine the next 2 operations to remove both front and rear intake manifolds.

FRONT INTAKE MANIFOLD

1. Remove the air cleaner.

2. Drain the cooling system.

3. Remove the intake air collector and the 3 front intake pipes.

4. Remove the pressure regulator and support from the intake manifold.

5. Disconnect the coolant hoses from the thermostat housing and the wiring from the coolant switches.

6. Remove the flat plugs from the injection valves by carefully pulling upward.

7. Remove the first three injection valves from the manifold.

NOTE: Leave the circular pipe connected.

8. Remove the retaining bolts from the intake manifold and remove it from the cylinder head.

9. Installation is the reverse of removal. Use new injection valve sealing rings.

Induction resonator pipe—secured with clamps

Induction system with induction tubes secured with nuts and washers

REAR INTAKE MANIFOLD

1. Disconnect the battery ground cable.
2. Remove the air cleaner.
3. Remove the intake air collector and the 3 rear intake pipes.
4. Remove the pressure regulator and support from the intake manifold.
5. Remove the flat plugs from the injection valves by carefully pulling upwards.
6. Remove the three rear injector valves.

NOTE: Leave the circular pipe connected.

7. Remove and tag the electrical flat plugs and connectors from the end of the wire loom, routed through the intake manifold.
8. Carefully pull the wire loom upward through the hole in the intake manifold.
9. Remove the intake manifold from the cylinder head.
10. Installation is the reverse of removal. Always renew the injection valve sealing rings.

320i

1. Remove the air cleaner and drain the cooling system.
2. Disconnect the accelerator cable and remove the vacuum hoses from the air collector. Tag the hoses.
3. Remove the injection line holder from No. 4 intake tube.
4. Remove the No. 3 intake tube and disconnect the vacuum and coolant lines from the throttle housing.
5. Disconnect the hoses at the EGR valve and remove the wire plugs at the temperature timing switch.
6. Remove the cold start valve from the air collector.
7. Disconnect the vacuum hose and electrical connections at the timing valve.
8. Disconnect the remaining intake tubes at the collector. Disconnect the collector brackets at the engine and remove the collector.

9. Remove the air intake tubes from the manifold and remove the injector valves.
10. Remove the intake manifold.
11. Installation is the reverse of removal.

All 6 Cylinder Models

NOTE: Slight variations may exist among models due to model changes and updating but basic removal and installation remains the same.

1. Disconnect the battery ground cable and drain the cooling system.
2. Disconnect the wire harness at the air flow sensor. Remove the air cleaner and sensor as an assembly.
3. Remove the tag and vacuum hoses and electrical plugs. Disconnect the accelerator linkage from the throttle housing.
4. Disconnect the coolant hoses from the throttle housing.
5. Working from the rear of the collector housing, disconnect the vacuum lines, and starting valve connector, fuel line and air line. Tag the hoses and lines for ease of assembly.
6. Remove the EGR valve and line.
7. Remove all intake pipes.
8. Remove the air collector housing from the engine.
9. Disconnect the plugs at the injector valves and remove the valves.
10. Disconnect the wire plugs at the coolant temperature sensor, the temperature time switch and the temperature switch.
11. Pull the wire loom upward through the opening in the intake manifold neck.
12. Remove the coolant hoses from the intake neck.

NOTE: Mark the heater hoses for proper reinstallation.

13. Remove the retaining bolts or nuts and remove either front, rear or both intake manifold necks.
14. Installation of the manifolds is the reverse of removal. Use new gaskets on the manifolds and air intake tubes.

Exhaust Manifold

REMOVAL AND INSTALLATION

2002

1. Loosen the exhaust system supports.
2. Separate the exhaust pipe from the exhaust manifold and remove the hot air guide sleeve.
3. Remove the retaining nuts and washers from the exhaust manifold studs and remove the manifold from the cylinder head.
4. Installation is the reverse of removal. Tighten the clamps holding the exhaust pipes last to avoid having an exhaust system vibration during operation.

3.0 CSi

NOTE: Each exhaust manifold can be removed separately after the exhaust pipes are disconnected.

1. Remove the air cleaner and manifold cover plate.
2. On automatic transmission equipped vehicles, detach the oil filler pipe at the rear of the cover plate.
3. Disconnect the exhaust pipe from the manifold sections.
4. Remove the retaining nuts and washers and remove the exhaust manifolds from the cylinder head.
5. Installation is the reverse of removal.

320i, 528i, 528e, 530i, 630CSi, 633CSi and 733i

The exhaust manifolds are referred to as exhaust gas recirculation reactors. Refer to the Emission Control section for operation.

The removal and installation procedures are basically the same for all models. The four cylinder manifold (used on the 320i model), is a one piece, one outlet unit, while the six cylinder manifold assembly consist of a two piece, double outlet to the exhaust

Typical timing chain arrangement—four cylinder engine illustrated

pipe. One piece can be replaced independently of the other.

1. Remove the air volume control and if necessary, air cleaner.

2. Disconnect the exhaust pipe at the reactor outlet(s).

3. Remove the guard plate from the reactor(s).

4. Disconnect the air injection pipe fitting, the EGR counterpressure line, EGR pressure line and any supports.

NOTE: An exhaust filter is used between the reactor and the EGR valve and must be disconnected. Replace the filter if found to be defective.

5. Remove the retaining bolts or nuts at the reactor and remove it from the cylinder head.

6. Installation is the reverse of removal. Use new gaskets.

Timing Chain

REMOVAL AND INSTALLATION

All Engines (Except 528e)

1. Rotate the crankshaft to set No. 1 piston at TDC, at the beginning of its compression stroke.

2. Remove the distributor (6-cylinder engines only).

3. Remove the cylinder head cover, air injection pipe and guard plate.

4. Drain the cooling system and remove the thermostat housing.

5. Remove the upper timing housing cover.

6. Remove the timing chain tensioner piston.

NOTE: The piston is under heavy spring tension.

7. Remove the drive belts and fan.

8. Remove the flywheel guard and lock the flywheel with a locking tool.

9. Remove the vibration damper assembly.

NOTE: The crankshaft Woodruff key should be in the 12 o'clock position.

10. Remove the lower timing housing cover screws and the front oil pan screws. Loosen the remaining oil pan screws.

11. Loosen the oil pan-to-timing housing cover gasket with a thin bladed tool and remove the timing housing cover.

12. Open the camshaft lockplates, remove the bolts and remove the camshaft sprocket.

13. On 4-cylinder engines:

a. Remove the bottom circlip holding the chain guide rail to the block. Loosen the upper pivot pin until the guide rail rests against the forward part of the cylinder head gasket.

b. Remove the timing chain from the sprockets and remove the guide rail by pulling downward and swinging the rail to the right.

c. Remove the chain from the guide rail and remove it from the engine.

14. On 6-cylinder engines:

a. Remove the chain from the lower sprocket, swing the chain to the right front and out of the guide rail and remove the chain from the engine.

15. Installation is the reverse of removal, but note the following:

16. Be sure that No. 1 piston remains at the top of its firing stroke and the key on the crankshaft is in the 12 o'clock position.

17. On 4-cylinder engines:

a. Position the camshaft flange so that the dowel pin bore is located at the 6 o'clock position and the notch in the top of the flange aligns with the cast tab on the cylinder head.

b. Position the chain in the chain guide rail and move the rail upward and to the left, engaging the lower locating pivot pin and threading the upper pivot pin into the block. Install the circlip on the lower guide pin.

c. Engage the chain on the crankshaft sprocket and fit the camshaft sprocket into the chain.

d. Align the gear dowel pin to the camshaft flange and bolt the sprocket into place. Use new lockplates and secure the bolt heads.

18. On 6-cylinder engines:

a. Position the camshaft flange so that the dowel pin bore is between the 7 and 8 o'clock position and the upper flange bolt hole is aligned with the cast tab on the cylinder head.

b. Position the chain on the guide rail and swing the chain inward and to the left.

c. Engage the chain on the crankshaft

Location of upper (4) and lower (3) guide rail retainers

Installation of the timing cover housing showing special sealing locations

Bleeding the chain tensioner

gear and install the camshaft sprocket into the chain.

d. Align the gear dowel pin to the camshaft flange and bolt the sprocket into place.

19. Install the chain tensioner piston, spring and cap plug, but do not tighten.

20. To bleed the chain tensioner, fill the oil pocket, located on the upper timing housing cover, with engine oil and move the tensioner back and forth with a screwdriver until oil is expelled at the cap plug. Tighten the cap plug securely.

21. Complete the assembly in the reverse order of removal. Check the ignition timing and the idle speed. Be sure the flywheel holder is removed before any attempt is made to start the engine.

Timing Belt and Front Engine Cover

REMOVAL AND INSTALLATION

528e

The 528e is equipped with a rubber drive and timing belt and the distributor guard plate is actually the upper timing belt cover.

1. Remove the distributor cap and rotor. Remove the inner distributor cover and seal.

2. Remove the two distributor guard plate attaching bolts and one nut. Remove the rubber guard and take out the guard plate (upper timing belt cover).

3. Rotate the crankshaft to set No. 1 piston at TDC of its compression stroke.

NOTE: At TDC of No. 1 piston compression stroke, the camshaft sprocket arrow should align directly with the mark on the cylinder head.

4. Remove the radiator.

5. Remove the lower splash guard and take off the alternator, power steering and air conditioning belts.

6. Remove the crankshaft pulley and vibration damper.

7. Hold the crankshaft hub from rotating with special BMW tool 11 2 150 or equivalent. Remove the crankshaft hub bolt.

8. Install the hub bolt into the crankshaft about three turns and use BMW tools 00 7 501 and 11 2 132 or a gear puller, to remove the crankshaft hub.

9. Remove the bolt from the engine end of the alternator bracket. Loosen the alternator adjusting bolt and swing the bracket out of the way.

10. Lift out the TDC transmitter and set it out of the way.

11. Remove the remaining bolt and lift off the lower timing belt cover.

12. Loosen the two tensioner pulley bolts and release the tension on the belt by pushing on the tensioner pulley bracket.

13. Mark the running direction of the timing belt and remove the belt.

14. Remove the three bolts across the front of the oil pan and loosen the remaining oil pan bolts. Try not to damage the oil pan gasket. Remove the six front engine cover bolts and remove the front engine cover.

1. Front oil pan bolts

Bolt location for front engine cover—528e

1. Tensioner adjusting slot bolt
2. Tensioner bracket pivot bolt

Releasing the tension on timing belt—528e

1. Camshaft sprocket
2. Tensioner roller
3. Crankshaft sprocket
4. Intermediate shaft sprocket
5. Timing drive belt

Location of timing belt sprockets and belt tensioner—528e

Aligning marks for timing belt installation—528e

Crankshaft sprocket timing marks aligned for installation of timing belt—528e

15. Installation is the reverse of removal. Installation notes:

   a. To tighten the timing belt, turn the engine in the direction of normal engine operation, with a ½ inch drive rachet wrench on the crankshaft bolt. When the timing belt is tight, then torque the two tensioner bolts.

   b. Align the hub centering pin through the hole in the vibration damper for proper installation.

   c. Align the timing marks when installing the timing belt. The crankshaft sprocket mark must point at the notch in the flange of the front engine cover. The camshaft sprocket arrow must point at the alignment mark on the cylinder head. Also, the No. 1 piston must be at TDC of the compression stroke.

   d. If the oil pan gasket is damaged, it must be replaced.

   e. Check and replace front cover oil seals if needed.

   f. Use BMW tools 11 2 211 (crankshaft seal aligner) and 11 2 212 (intermediate shaft seal aligner) or equivalent to install the front engine cover without damaging the oil seals.

   g. Check the engine oil level.

   h. Install engine coolant and bleed the cooling system. Bring the engine up to operating temperature and loosen the bleed screw on top of the thermostat housing. Continue to bleed until escaping coolant is free of bubbles. Add coolant to the expansion tank if needed.

Timing Housing Cover Oil Seal

REMOVAL AND INSTALLATION

All Models (Except 528e)

1. Position the No. 1 piston at TDC on the beginning of its compression stroke.
2. Remove the flywheel guard and lock the flywheel with a locking tool.
3. Remove the drive belts and the fan.
4. Remove the retaining nut and remove the vibration damper from the crankshaft.

NOTE: The Woodruff key should be at the 12 o'clock position on the crankshaft.

Position of crankshaft woodruff key (1)

5. Remove the seal from the timing housing cover.
6. Using a special seal installer or equivalent, lubricate and install the seal in the cover.

NOTE: If the balancer hub has serious scoring on the sealing surface, position the seal in the cover so that the sealing lip is in front of or behind the scored groove.

7. Lubricate the balancer hub and install it on the crankshaft, being careful not to damage the seal.
8. Complete the assembly, using the reverse of the removal procedure. Be sure to remove the flywheel locking tool before attempting to start the engine.

528e

The 528e has two oil seals on the front engine cover. One is on the crankshaft and the other is on the intermediate shaft.

1. Remove the front engine cover (see the ''Timing Belt and Front Engine Cover'', procedure).
2. Press the two radial oil seals out of the front engine cover.

3. Install the oil seals flush with the front engine cover using BMW tools 24 1 050, 33 1 180 and 005 5 500 or equivalents.
4. Install the front engine cover.

Camshaft

REMOVAL AND INSTALLATION

All Models (Except 528e)

1. Remove the oil line from the top of the cylinder head.

NOTE: Observe the location of the seals when removing the hollow oil line studs. Reinstall the seals in the same position.

2. Remove the cylinder head.
3. Adjust the valve clearance to the maximum clearance on all rocker arms.
4. Remove the fuel pump and pushrod on carbureted engines.
5. On 4-cylinder engines:

   a. Special tools (6025-1 for carbureted engines or 6025-2 for fuel injected engines) or their equivalent, are used to hold the rocker arms away from the camshaft lobes.

NOTE: The tool 6025-2 or its equivalent, must be used on fuel injection engines to avoid distorting the valve heads.

On 6-cylinder engines:

   a. A special tool (11-2-060) or its equivalent, is used to hold the rocker arms away from the camshaft lobes. When installing the tool, move the intake rocker arms of No. 2 and 4 cylinders, forward approximately ¼ in. and tighten the intake side nuts to avoid contact between the valve heads.

6. Remove the camshaft.

On 4-cylinder engines:

   a. Remove the guide plate retaining bolts and move the plate downward and out of the slots on the rocker arm shafts.

   b. Carefully remove the camshaft from the cylinder head.

On 6-cylinder engines:

   a. Rotate the camshaft so that the two cutout areas of the camshaft flange are horizontal and remove the retaining plate bolts.

   b. Carefully remove the camshaft from the cylinder head.

   c. The flange and guide plate can be removed from the camshaft by removing the lockplate and nut from the camshaft end.

7. Install the camshaft and associated components in the reverse order of removal, but observe the following:

   a. After installing the camshaft guide plate, the camshaft should turn easily. Measure and correct the camshaft end play.

   b. The camshaft flange must be properly aligned with the cylinder head before

Location of seals at hollow oil line stud

Removing camshaft thrust bearing cover— 528e

Pulling out the camshaft—528e

the sprocket is installed. Refer to the disassembly procedure.

c. Install the oil tube hollow stud washer seals properly, one above and one below the oil pipe.

d. Adjust the valves.

528e

The cylinder head and the rocker arm shafts must be removed before the camshaft can be removed.

1. Remove the cylinder head (see the "Cylinder Head—Removal and Installation" procedure).

2. Mount the head on a stand. Secure the head to the stand with one head bolt.

3. Remove the camshaft sprocket bolt and remove the camshaft distributor adapter and sprocket. Reinstall the distributor adapter on the camshaft.

4. Adjust the valve play to the maximum allowable on all valves.

5. Remove the front and rear rocker shaft plugs and lift out the thrust plate.

6. Remove the clips from the rocker arms by lifting them off.

7. Remove the exhaust side rocker arm shaft:

a. Set the No. 6 cylinder rocker arm to the valve overlap position (both rocker arms parallel).

b. Push in on the rocker arm on the front cylinder and turn the camshaft in the direction of the intake rocker shaft, using a ½ in. breaker bar and a deep well socket to fit over the camshaft adapter. Rotate the camshaft until all of the rocker arms are relaxed.

c. Remove the rocker arm shaft.

8. Remove the intake side rocker arm shaft:

a. Turn the camshaft in the direction of the exhaust valves.

b. Use a deep well socket and ½ inch drive breaker bar on the camshaft adaptor to turn the camshaft until all of the rocker arms are relaxed.

c. Pull out the rocker arm shaft.

9. Remove the camshaft thrust bearing

cover. Check the radial oil seal and round cord seal, replace them if needed.

10. Pull out the camshaft.

11. Installation is the reverse of removal. Installation notes:

a. Use BMW tool 11 2 212 or equivalent over the end of the camshaft during installation of the thrust bearing cover; This will protect the oil seals and guide the cover on.

b. The rocker arm thrust plate must be fit into the grooves in the rocker shafts.

c. The straight side of the springclip must be installed in the groove of the rocker arm shafts.

d. The large oil bores in the rocker shafts must be installed down to the valve guides and the small oil bores must face inward toward the center of the head.

e. Adjust the valve clearance.

Pistons and Connecting Rods

REMOVAL AND INSTALLATION

The pistons and connecting rods may be removed from the engine after the cylinder head, oil pan and oil pump are removed.

Location of piston in the cylinder bore with ring gaps located 180° apart

Proper piston ring installation—typical

The connecting rods and caps are marked for each cylinder with No. 1 cylinder at the sprocket end of the engine.

All reference numbers on the pistons and connecting rods must be located on the same side, with the arrow on the piston top facing the front of the engine. Measurement, ring fitting and installation procedures are outlined in the Engine Rebuilding section.

ENGINE LUBRICATION

Oil Pan

REMOVAL AND INSTALLATION

2002

1. Raise and support the vehicle. Drain the engine oil.
2. Remove the front stabilizer bar, if equipped.
3. Remove the oil pan retaining bolts and loosen the pan from the engine block.
4. Disconnect the left and right engine supports.
5. Lower the vehicle and attach a lifting sling and raise the engine slightly.
6. Rotate the crankshaft so that the No. 4 piston is at TDC.
7. Remove the oil pan toward the front.
8. Reverse the procedure to install the oil pan using a new gasket.

Removal of engine oil pan—typical

3.0 CSi, 530i and 528i

1. Raise and support the vehicle. Drain the engine oil.
2. Remove the front lower apron (3.0) and remove the stabilizer bar.
3. Loosen the alternator (remove the alternator on 530i) and remove the power steering pump, but do not disconnect the hoses.
4. Remove the lower power steering

bracket bolt and loosen the remaining bolts (remove the remaining bolts on 530i) enough to remove the oil pan retaining bolts.
5. Loosen the engine support bracket.
6. Remove the oil pan bolts and loosen the oil pan from the engine block.
7. Rotate the crankshaft until the No. 6 crankpin is above the bottom of the engine block.
8. Lower the front of the oil pan, turn the rear of the pan towards the support bracket and remove the pan.
9. Reverse the procedure to install the oil pan, using new gaskets.

320i

1. Raise and support the vehicle. Drain the engine oil.
2. Loosen the steering gear bolts and pull the steering box off the front axle carrier.
3. Remove the oil pan bolts and separate the pan from the engine block.
4. Swing the oil pan downward while rotating the crankshaft to allow the pan to clear the crankpin and remove the pan toward the front.
5. Reverse the procedure to install the oil pan, using new gaskets.

630CSi and 633 CSi

1. Raise and support the vehicle. Drain the engine oil.
2. Remove the front stabilizer bar.
3. Disconnect the wire terminal at the oil level switch.
4. Disconnect the power steering pump, but do not disconnect the hoses. Loosen all the power steering bracket bolts, and remove the bottom bolt.
5. Remove the engine oil pan bolts, separate the oil pan from the engine block and lower the front of the pan.
6. Rotate the crankshaft until the No. 6 crankpin is above the bottom of the engine block.
7. Lift the engine slightly at the clutch housing while removing the pan to the right side.
8. Reverse the procedure to install the oil pan, using new gaskets.

733i

1. Raise and support the vehicle. Drain the engine oil.
2. Remove the power steering pump, but do not disconnect the hoses.
3. Remove the lower power steering bracket bolt. Loosen the upper bracket bolts in order to move the bracket away from the oil pan.
4. Disconnect the oil level switch wire terminal.
5. Remove the oil pan bolts and separate the oil pan from the engine block.
6. Disconnect the left and right engine mounts.
7. Remove the engine vibration damper.

8. Lower the vehicle and remove the fan housing from the radiator.
9. Attach a lifting sling and raise the engine until the oil pan be removed.
10. Reverse the procedure to install the oil pan, using the new gaskets.

528e

1. Raise the vehicle and support it. Drain the engine oil.
2. Remove the front lower splash guard.
3. Disconnect the electrical terminal from the oil sending unit.
4. Remove the flywheel cover.
5. Remove the oil pan bolts and lower the oil pan. Remove the oil pump bolts and take out the oil pump and oil pan.
6. Installation is the reverse of removal. Installation notes:
   a. Clean the gasket surfaces and use a new gasket on the oil pan.
   b. Coat the joints on the ends of the front engine cover with a universal sealing compound.
   c. Install the sending unit wire and the engine oil.

Rear Main Bearing Oil Seal

REMOVAL AND INSTALLATION

The rear main bearing oil seal can be replaced after the transmission, clutch/flywheel or the converter/flywheel has been removed from the engine.

Removal and installation, after the seal is exposed, is as follows.

1. Drain the engine oil and loosen the oil pan bolts.
2. Remove the two rear oil pan bolts.
3. Remove the end cover housing from the engine block and remove the seal from the housing.
4. Install a new seal into the end cover housing with a special seal installer or equivalent.

NOTE: Fill the cavity between the sealing lips of the seal with grease before installing.

5. Using a new gasket, install the end cover on the engine block and bolt it into place.
6. Reverse the removal procedure to complete the installation.

Oil Pump

REMOVAL AND INSTALLATION

All Models (Except 528e)

1. Remove the oil pan.
2. Remove the bolts retaining the

Rear main bearing oil seal and end cover housing showing special sealing locations

Measuring clearance (A) between hub and inner rotor

Measuring outer rotor-to-pump body clearance

6. Installation is the reverse of removal. Installation notes:

a. Clean the gasket surfaces and use a new gasket on the oil pan.

b. Coat the joints on the ends of the front engine cover with a universal sealing compound.

c. Install the sending unit wire and the engine oil.

ENGINE COOLING

Bleeding the Cooling System

WITH BLEEDER SCREW ON THERMOSTAT HOUSING

Set the heater valve in the WARM position, start the engine and bring it to normal operating temperature. Run the engine at fast idle and open the venting screw on the thermostat housing until the coolant comes out free of air bubbles. Close the bleeder screw and refill the cooling system.

sprocket to the oil pump shaft and remove the sprocket.

3. On 4-cylinder engines:

a. Remove the oil pump retaining bolts and lower the oil pump from the engine block.

b. Note the location of the O-ring seal, between the housing and the pressure safety line.

c. Be sure that the oil bore in the shim is correctly positioned during the oil pump installation.

4. On 6-cylinder engines:

a. Remove the oil pump retaining bolts and lower the oil pump from the engine block.

b. Do not loosen the chain adjusting shims from the two mounting locations.

5. Install the oil pump in the reverse order of removal. On 6-cylinder engines, add or subtract shims between the oil pump body and the engine block to obtain a slight movement of the chain under light thumb pressure.

—— IMPORTANT ——
When used, the two shim thicknesses must be the same. Tighten the pump holder at the pick-up end after shimming is completed to avoid stress on the pump.

528e

1. Raise the vehicle and support it. Drain the engine oil.

2. Remove the front lower splash guard.

3. Disconnect the electrical terminal from the oil sending unit.

4. Remove the flywheel cover.

5. Remove the oil pan bolts and lower the oil pan. Remove the oil pump bolts and take out the oil pump and oil pan.

Measuring inner rotor-to-outer rotor clearance

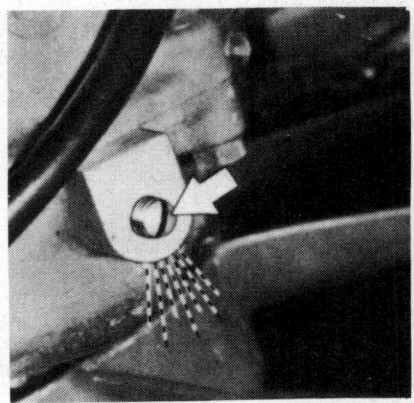

Bleeding of the cooling system with bleeder screw

WITHOUT BLEEDER SCREW

Fill the cooling system, place the heater valve in the WARM position, close the pressure cap to the second (fully closed) position. Start the engine and bring to normal operating temperature. Carefully release the pressure cap to the first position and squeeze the upper and lower radiator hoses in a pumping action to allow trapped air to escape through the radiator. Recheck the coolant level and close the pressure cap to its second position.

Radiator

REMOVAL AND INSTALLATION

The radiator can be removed after draining the cooling system, removal of the coolant hoses, disconnecting of the automatic transmission oil cooler lines, disconnecting of the temperature switch wire connectors and removing the shroud from the radiator core. Remove the radiator retaining bolts and lift the radiator from the vehicle.

NOTE: The 2002 may be equipped with an air preheater unit for the air cleaner that will have to be removed before the radiator can be taken from the vehicle.

The shroud will remain in the vehicle, resting on the fan. The radiator is installed in the reverse order of removal. Fill and bleed the cooling system.

Thermostat

REMOVAL AND INSTALLATION

The thermostat is located near the water pump, either on the cylinder head or intake manifold on some models and is located between two coolant hose sections on other models.

The removal and installation of the thermostat is accomplished in the conventional manner.

Water Pump

REMOVAL AND INSTALLATION

All Models (Except 528e)

1. Drain the cooling system and remove the radiator.
2. Remove the fan blades, loosen the drive belts and remove as necessary.
3. Remove the belt pulley from the pump flange and disconnect the coolant hoses.
4. Remove the retaining bolts and remove the water pump from the engine.

5. The installation is in the reverse of the removal procedure. Use a new gasket and bleed the cooling system.

528e

1. Drain the cooling system.
2. Remove the distributor cap and rotor. Remove the inner distributor cap and rubber sealing ring.
3. Hold the fan pulley from turning with BMW tool 11 5 030 or equivalent. Remove the fan coupling nut (left hand thread—turn clockwise to remove).
4. Remove the belt and pulley.
5. Remove the rubber guard and distributor and or upper timing belt cover.
6. Compress the timing tensioner spring and clamp pin with BMW special tool 11 5 010 or equivalent.

Compress tensioner spring with special tool during water pump removal—528e

1. Upper radiator hose
2. Lower radiator hose

Removing water pump retaining bolts— 528e

NOTE: Observe the installed position of the tensioner spring pin on the water pump housing for reinstallation purposes.

7. Remove the water hoses, remove the three water pump bolts and remove the pump.
8. Clean the gasket surfaces and use a new gasket.
9. Installation is the reverse of removal.
10. Add coolant and bleed the cooling system.

BELT TENSION ADJUSTMENT

The fan belt tension is adjusted by moving the alternator on the slack adjuster bracket. The belt tension is adjusted to a deflection of approximately ½ in. under moderate thumb pressure in the middle of its longest span.

EMISSION CONTROLS

The BMW emission controls are composed of three major systems to control engine emissions of hydrocarbons (HC), carbon monoxide (CO), and oxides of nitrogen (NOx).

The 3 systems are (1) Crankcase Emissions Control System, (2) Exhaust Emission Control System and (3) Evaporative Emission Control System.

Differences may exist between the systems used on California models or Federal models depending upon the year of production and the vehicle model.

The Emission Control Information Label attached to the vehicle should be consulted before any repairs or specification changes are made to the engine.

Measuring belt deflection

CRANKCASE EMISSION CONTROL SYSTEM

This system is considered a "sealed" system. No fresh air is allowed to enter the crankcase and the blow-by emissions are routed to the air cleaner or air collector and blended with the air/fuel mixture to be burned through normal combustion.

TESTING

The Crankcase Emission Control System is virtually maintenance free. The connecting tube from the top engine cover of the air cleaner or air collector should be inspected during the routine maintenance services and replaced if cracked, distorted or plugged.

With the engine operating and the connecting tube disconnected, a vacuum should be noted at the air cleaner or air collector side of the hose. If vacuum is not present, an air leak or plugged air induction system may be the cause.

Crankcase emission control system (with Electronic Fuel Injection)

The 528e crankcase emission control system

Crankcase emission control system (with Continuous Fuel Injection)

Air Injection System

The Air Injection system is used to add oxygen to the hot exhaust gases in the Thermal Reactor which replaces the exhaust manifold. The introduction of fresh air (oxygen) aids in more complete combustion of the air/fuel mixture lessening the hydrocarbons and the carbon monoxide emissions. A belt driven air pump is used to force air into the exhaust system, through a series of valves and tubing.

TESTING

2002 and 3.0CSi

AIR PUMP

Remove the air return pipe and hold the palm of the hand over the pressure regu-

lating valve unit while increasing the engine speed. The excess pressure valve must open between 1700 and 2000 rpm. If the valve opens early, replace the valve. If the valve opens at a higher rpm, replace the air pump.

BELT ADJUSTMENT

The air pump drive belt should have a deflection of no more than ⅜ in. measured in the middle of its longest span, when properly adjusted.

CONTROL VALVE

The control valve should be replaced if the carburetors are difficult to adjust or if the engine backfires when the throttle is released.

CHECK VALVE

The check valve should be replaced if air can be blown through the valve in both directions. Air should move towards the manifold only.

BLOW-IN PIPES

The exhaust manifold must be removed to expose the blow-in pipes. The pipes can be replaced by unscrewing them from the manifold and screwing in new ones.

320i, 530i, 630CSi, 633CSi and 733i

AIR PUMP

Disconnect the outlet hose and start the engine. The air velocity should increase as the engine speed increases. If not, the air pump drive belt could be slipping, the check valve or the air pump may be defective and would have to be adjusted or replaced.

BLOW-OFF VALVE

If backfiring occurs when releasing the accelerator or the air pump seems to be overloading, the blow-off valve may be defective.

The valve must release and blow-off during a coasting condition and the internal safety valve must open at 5 psi. The vacuum line must have suction when the engine is running and must allow the air to be blown off when reattached to the valve at idle.

ELECTRIC CONTROL VALVE– WHITE CAP

This control valve governs the blow-off valve and must be open at temperatures below

113°F (45°C) and closed above 113°F (45°C) of the coolant.

With the coolant temperatures above 113°F (45°C), the ignition switch on and the engine off, disconnect both vacuum hoses, attach a test hose to one nipple and blow air into the valve. The valve is functioning properly if air cannot flow through the valve. Turn the ignition switch off and blow into the valve again. Air should flow through the valve.

CHECK VALVE

The check valve must be replaced if air can be blown through the valves in both directions. Air should more towards the reactors only.

BLOW-IN PIPES

The air enters above the reactors, directly into the exhaust ports, behind the exhaust valves. The pipes can be replaced by removing the distribution tube assembly.

THERMAL REACTOR

The reactors have a double casing and has internally vented flame deflector plates. Spontaneous combustion, due to high temperatures, and the introduction of oxygen into the exhaust gas flow maintains the afterburning of the gases.

Triggering device with REACTOR (1) and the EGR (2) resetting buttons shown

A warning light marked "Reactor" alerts the driver to have the unit inspected for external heat damage every 25,000 miles. A triggering device, located behind the dash and operated by the speedometer cable, can be reset to open the electrical contacts and extinguish the warning light.

NOTE: Two different sized buttons are mounted side by side on the triggering device. The small button is for the reactor and the large button is for the EGR valve. Press the button to reset.

Exhaust Gas Recirculating System

The EGR valve is vacuum operated by the position of the carburetor throttle plate in the throttle bore during vehicle operation. A metered amount of exhaust gas enters the combustion chamber to be mixed with the air/fuel blend. The effect is to reduce the peak combustion temperatures, which in turn reduces the amount of nitrous oxides (Nox), formed during the combustion process.

EGR VALVE–TESTING

2002 and 3.0CSi

Remove the air filter and adjust the engine idle to 900 rpm. Remove the vacuum line from the valve and using an engine vacuum source, attach the hose to the vacuum nipple. The engine speed should drop 500-600 rpm if the valve is operating properly. If little or no change of engine speed is noted, the recirculation pipes, the cyclone filter or the EGR valve may be plugged or defective.

320i, 530i, 630CSi, 633CSi and 733i

The EGR valve is vacuum controlled from a pressure transmitter which regulates the amount of vacuum applied to the valve from signals originating at the intake manifold and from a back-pressure signal from the exhaust system.

The interior of the EGR valve consists of two diaphragms, the lower one to control the amount of exhaust gas to be recirculated and the upper one to interrupt or shut off the exhaust gas recirculation under conditions of idle, deceleration, full engine load, engine speed over 3750 rpm or coolant temperature below 113°F.

ELECTRIC CONTROL VALVE-RED CAP

The electric control valve should stop the EGR valve operation at coolant temperatures below 113°F (45°C), and speeds above 3000 rpm. Tag and disconnect both vacuum hoses at the control valve with the engine off and the coolant temperature below 113°F (45°C). Connect a test hose to one of the nipples and blow through the hose. The

1. Black   2. Red   3. Blue
Electronic control valves with attaching bolt locations

valve is functioning properly when there is air flowing through the valve with the ignition OFF and no air flow through the valve with the ignition ON.

Connect the vacuum hoses to the valve and operate the engine until the coolant is heated over 113°F (45°C). Disconnect the hoses and check for air flow through the valve. Air should now flow through the valve.

COOLANT TEMPERATURE SWITCH AND CONTROL RELAY

1. With the coolant temperature below 113°F (45°C), turn the ignition ON, but do not start the engine. Remove the wire plug at the control valve and connect a test lamp to the plug.

   a. The test lamp should light. If the test lamp does not light, connect the test lamp to ground. If the lamp now operates, the ground wire to the control valve has an open circuit.

   b. If the test lamp still does not light, disconnect the wire terminal at the coolant temperature switch and connect it to ground. If the test lamp still does not light, replace the control valve.

2. With the coolant temperature above 113°F (45°C), turn the ignition switch ON but do not start the engine. Disconnect the wire terminal plug at the control valve and connect a test lamp. The lamp should be off. If the lamp is on, the coolant temperature switch or control relay is defective.

3. With the engine running at temperatures above 113°F(45°C), connect the test light to the disconnected plug of the control valve. The test lamp should be on over an engine speed of 3000 rpm. If the test lamp does not light, the speed switch is defective.

EGR WARNING LIGHT

A warning light marked EGR is triggered at 25,000 miles, to alert the driver to service the exhaust gas recirculation system filter.

A triggering device, located under the dash and driven by the speedometer cable, can be reset to open the electrical contacts and extinguish the EGR warning light.

NOTE: Two different sized buttons are mounted side by side on the triggering device. The small button is for the reactor light and the large button is for the EGR light. Press the button to reset. See illustration in Thermal Reactor section.

Typical exhaust emission control system—four cylinder engine

Typical exhaust emission control system—six cylinder engine (black magnetic valve and high gear switch used on California and High-Altitude version with manual transmission)

Distributor Advance/ Retard Units

A vacuum advance and retard unit is attached to the distributor and is controlled by engine vacuum. The advance can be checked with a strobe light and increasing the engine speed while observing the action of the timing mark during the increase in engine speed. The retard side can be checked at idle by removing the retard vacuum line and noting the increase in engine speed of at least 300 rpm.

NOTE: Models 733i, 633CSi, 320i California and High Altitude vehicles equipped with manual transmissions, have the vacuum advance in operation only when the high gear is engaged. This is controlled by an electrical switch connected to the shifting linkage. Automatic transmission 633CSi for California and High Altitude, have the vacuum advance inoperative. Late models 530i and 630i vehicles are equipped with a vacuum retard unit only.

Electric Control Valve

TEST

Black Cap—California Equipment Only

This control valve stops the retard distributor control over speeds of 3000 rpm.

Remove the outer hose (to distributor) and start the engine. At engine rpm lower than 3000 rpm, vacuum should be present in the distributor retard unit hose and not present when the engine speed is increased above 3000 rpm.

Disconnect the wire terminal end at the control valve and have the engine operating at idle. Connect a test lamp to the terminal and check for presence of current. If current is present, the speed switch is defective.

Increase the engine speed to 3000 rpm or above, and the test lamp should light. If the test lamp does not light, the speed switch is defective.

Carburetor Dashpot

A dashpot is used to slow the carburetor throttle return while the vehicle engine is above 1800 rpm. An electrically controlled set of relays and magnetic switches are used to direct engine vacuum to release the dashpot at engine speeds under 1800 rpm.

DASHPOT TEST

Operate the engine at 2500 rpm and slowly decrease the speed to approximately 1800 rpm. The dashpot plunger should contact the throttle linkage at the 1700–1900 rpm mark (2002–1550 minimum). Adjust the dashpot plunger if necessary.

The plunger must be free of the throttle linkage under 1700 rpm minimum (2002–1550 minimum) when the engine vacuum is directed through the magnetic valve to the dashpot.

If no vacuum is present at the dashpot hose under 1700 rpm, check the engine speed relay connector. Remove the terminal end from the magnetic valve and increase the engine speed to 2000 rpm. If voltage is present at the terminal, the magnetic switch is defective and if no voltage is present, the speed sensitive relay must be replaced.

Oxygen Sensor

REMOVAL AND INSTALLATION

All Models

The oxygen sensor light on the dash will light the first time the mileage reaches 30,000. Replace the oxygen sensor and remove the light bulb from the dash. The bulb lights the first time only, however the sensor must be changed every 30,000 miles.

1. Disconnect the oxygen sensor wire connector and remove the wires from the clip.

1. Protective cover plate
2. Oxygen sensor

Removing the oxygen sensor plate and the oxygen sensor—528e

2. Pull off the sensor protective plate.
3. Unscrew the oxygen sensor.
4. Before installation coat the threads of the new sensor with CRC® copper paste.
5. Install the sensor unit.
6. Remove the call unit from the dash and remove the oxygen sensor display bulb.

Evaporative Control System

This system is designed to collect and store the raw gasoline vapors (hydrocarbons) and to direct the vapors into the engine along with the air/fuel mixture when the engine is operating.

A maintenance free vapor storage tank is located in the trunk while an activated carbon filter canister is mounted in the engine compartment.

MAINTENANCE

The only repairs or checks that can be made are to maintain the hoses and to change the canister unit if it becomes saturated with raw gasoline.

1. Three-way catalyst
2. Oxygen sensor
3. High voltage distributor
4. Fuel tank
5. Vapor storage tank
6. Activated carbon filter
7. Air flow meter
8. Air filter
9. Purge valve

Main components of the exhaust emission system—528e

FUEL SYSTEM

Fuel Pump

A diaphragm-type fuel pump is located on

Typical evaportive control system—six cylinder engine illustrated

the cylinder head and is operated by the camshaft, through a pump plunger rod. A fuel filter is located in the fuel pump while an in-line filter is located in the fuel line between the fuel pump and the carburetors.

REMOVAL AND INSTALLATION

Carburetor Equipped Models

1. Remove the air cleaner.
2. Remove and plug the fuel lines.
3. Remove the retaining bolts and separate the pump from the insulator block and cylinder head. Do not lose or shorten the pump rod.
4. Install the pump in the reverse order of removal.

Fuel Injection Models

The fuel pump is an electrical unit, delivering fuel through a pressure regulator, to a fuel distributor or a ring-line for the injection valves. The fuel pump is mounted under the vehicle, near the fuel tank, or in the engine compartment.

1. Disconnect the electrical connector.
2. Remove the fuel lines and plug the ends.
3. Remove the retaining bolts and remove the pump and expansion tank as an assembly.
4. The pump can be separated from the expansion tank after removal.
5. Installation is the reverse of removal.

Fuel Filter

REMOVAL AND INSTALLATION

The inline fuel filters on all models of BMW are easily removed.

1. Disconnect the inlet and outlet hoses. Remove the hose clamps if necessary.
2. The filters will usually be attached to a frame, floor pan or wheel well by a bracket. Loosen the bracket and remove the filter.
3. Observe the instructions on the inlet and outlet during installation.

LOCATION BY MODEL

2002

The inline filter is located in the engine compartment, next to the battery.

Electric fuel pump assembly—typical

Removal of mechanical fuel pump and plunger rod

320i, 528e and 733i

The inline filter is located directly above the final drive assembly and attached to the underside of the floor pan.

528i, 630CSi and 633CSi

The inline filter is located behind the passenger side wheel, near the frame. Above the final drive shaft.

3.0CSi and 530i

The inline filter is located above the driver's side front wheel housing and below the fuse box.

Carburetors

For carburetor overhaul procedures, refer to, "Carburetor", in the Unit Repair section.

2002

These carburetors are single-barrel downdraft units with a manually operated choke (2002 with 40PDSI) or an automatic choke (2002A vehicles with 40PDSIT).

REMOVAL AND INSTALLATION

1. Remove the air cleaner, fuel hoses, accelerator linkage and choke cable (if equipped).
2. Remove the carburetor retaining nuts and washers and remove the carburetor from the manifold.

NOTE: The cooling system will have to be partially drained on the model 2002A.

3. Using a new gasket, install the carburetor on the manifold using the reverse of the removal procedure.

THROTTLE LINKAGE ADJUSTMENT

The accelerator linkage shaft extends from the firewall, engages in the carburetor throttle lever and is fastened with a spring clip.

No linkage adjustment is provided, other than the idle speed adjustment.

FLOAT LEVEL ADJUSTMENT

1. Run the engine to normal operating temperature.
2. Remove the fuel line, carburetor top cover and gasket.
3. Using a depth gauge, measure the distance from the top of the float chamber to the top of the fuel level. The distance should be 0.70–0.75 in.

Difference in accelerator pump spray between one (A) and two (B) vacuum nipple equipped carburetors

4. If necessary, adjust the level by adding to or subtracting the seals located under the float needle valve.

ACCELERATOR PUMP ADJUSTMENT

The direction of the fuel spray is important to avoid hesitation. Carburetors with one vacuum nipple should have the fuel spray directed along the side of the main venturi. Carburetors with two vacuum nipples should have the spray directed to strike the top of the main venturi.

A special carburetor test stand is utilized to gauge the amount of fuel injected by the accelerator pump. If the test stand is not available, the desired amount of fuel can be adjusted by moving the pump rod on the pump lever. Shorten the lever to increase the amount of fuel and lengthen the lever to decrease the amount.

CHOKE ADJUSTMENT

Manual Choke (40 PDSI)

1. Pull the choke cable to stop No. 2.
2. Adjust the choke valve clearance to 0.209 ± 0.012 inch, by loosening the cable retaining screw and moving the cable.

NOTE: Be sure the choke valve will close completely when the choke cable is fully pulled. The outside cable housing may have to be readjusted.

Automatic Choke (40 PDSIT)

1. Be sure the choke valve shaft will rotate freely in its bore and that the choke cap aligning notch is aligned with the lug on the choke valve housing.
2. Depress the accelerator to allow the choke valve to close under spring tension.

NOTE: The choke valve should close if the ambient temperature is below 68°F (20°C).

3. If adjustment is needed, remove the choke cap with the water hoses attached.

4. Depress the choke rod (the vertical shaft inside choke housing) downward to its stop and check the choke valve clearance between the choke valve and the throttle bore. The gap should be 0.251–0.267 in.
5. An adjusting screw and locknut is located under the choke housing and controls the height of the choke rod. Loosen the locknut and move the screw in or out to change the choke valve gap.

Depressing the choke rod to its stop— Solex 40PDSIT

Measuring clearance (A) between choke valve and throttle bore—Solex 40PDSIT

Adjusting screw (1) location for adjustment of choke rod—Solex 40PDSIT

6. Reposition the choke cover on the carburetor. Be sure the choke arm engages the coil spring loop in the choke cover. Align the notch on the cover with the lug on the choke housing.

7. Connect the heating coil wire terminal to the housing.

NOTE: Current flow should be approximately 1 amp at 12 volts.

8. Adjust the fast idle speed to 2000–2200 rpm with the engine at normal operating temperature.

9. With the choke valve set at a gap of 0.25 inch, adjust the choke connector rod nuts to set the fast idle. Shorten the rod to reduce the rpm and lengthen the rod to increase the rpm.

Fuel Injection

For all fuel injection testing, adjustment and repair procedures not detailed below, please refer to "Fuel Injection" in the Unit Repair section.

320i

The Bosch Continuous Fuel Injection System (K-Jetronic) consists basically of mechanical type fuel injectors, a fuel distributor unit, operated by a sensor plate, and control valve. Electrical and vacuum operated regulators and switches complete the assembly. An electrical control box is not used.

3.0Si, 530i, 528i, 528e, 630CSi, 633CSi AND 733i

The Bosch L-Jetronic fuel injection system is electronically controlled to regulate the fuel supply in relation to the air flow. An air flow meter, located in the air intake chamber, converts angular movement of an air baffle plate into a voltage signal, which is sent to the control unit.

As the engine begins its revolution, twin

1. Fuel tank
2. Fuel delivery pump
3. Pressure reservoir
4. Fuel filter
5. Fuel distributor
6. System pressure regulator
7. Warm-up regulator
8. Safety switch
9. Sensor plate
10. Throttle valve
11. Idle adjusting screw
12. Auxiliary air regulator
13. Start valve
14. Thermo timing valve
15. Injection valves
16. Air inlet
17. Vacuum regulator
18. Auxiliary air valve

——— Injection press.
⬝⬝⬝⬝⬝ System pressure
▬▬▬ Return
▨▨▨ Control pressure

32013 062

Bosch K-Jetronic® Fuel Injection System

1. Control unit
2. Air flow meter
3. Throttle butterfly switch
4. Temperature sensor
5. Injection valve
6. Pre-resistance
7. Cold start valve
8. Thermo-time switch
9. Combined relay
10. Cold start relay
11. Distributor
12. Coil
13. Cable harness
14. Battery
15. Air filter

Main harness for the vehicle

Coil

Bosch L-Jetronic® Fuel Injection System

contacts, located 180 degrees apart in the base of the distributor, trigger current impulses to the control unit at one impulse per crankshaft rotation.

After computation of the signals, a command signal is sent from the control unit to the electromagnetic injector valves, which are wired in a parallel circuit, causing them to open simultaneously. To obtain smooth combustion, half the total fuel volume necessary for the engine cycle, is injected per half rotation of the camshaft, which corresponds to each rotation of the crankshaft.

Automatic cold start and warm-up devices are incorporated in the system to give better driveability and engine operation during the initial start and warm-up period, when added fuel is needed.

1. Support plate
2. Rubber ring
3. Cup flange
4. Rubber ring

Injector valve and sealing components

Air Flow Sensor

REMOVAL AND INSTALLATION

1. Disconnect the multiple terminal connector and remove the air cleaner with the air duct.
2. Separate the air flow sensor from the air duct.
3. Installation is the reverse of removal.

Throttle Valve Switch

The throttle valve switch cuts off the fuel supply to avoid engine overrunning. This is done by switch contacts, which are closed when the throttle valve is in the idling position.

When the throttle valve is moved 2°, the throttle valve switch movement opens the cut-off contacts and closes the acceleration enrichment control. Electrical impulses sent to the control unit determine the fuel quantity required for acceleration. A second switch closes the acceleration enrichment circuit only when the fuel cut-off switch is open.

REMOVAL AND INSTALLATION

1. Remove the terminal plug from the throttle valve switch.
2. Remove the switch retaining screws and remove the switch from the throttle shaft.
3. To install the switch, engage the throttle shaft into the switch orifice. Install the retaining screws and terminal plug.

Cold Start Valve

REMOVAL AND INSTALLATION

1. Remove the electrical connector and the fuel line to the valve.
2. Remove the retaining bolts and pull the valve assembly from the air collector.
3. Replace the rubber sealing ring during installation.

Injection Valves

REMOVAL AND INSTALLATION— 3.0CSi

1. Remove the electrical plug from the injection valves.
2. Loosen and remove the injection valve from the ring line.
3. Remove the retaining bolts and pull the injector from the manifold.
4. To install, replace the rubber ring and do not damage the nozzle jet during the installation.

REMOVAL AND INSTALLATION— 528i, 528e, 530i, 630CSi and 633CSi

1. With the air collector removed, disconnect the electrical connector plugs from the 6 injection valves.
2. Remove the valve retaining bolts and remove the injector tube with all the valves attached.

3. Remove the retaining clamps and remove the valves from the injector tube.
4. To install, reverse the removal procedure.

REMOVAL AND INSTALLATION— 733i

1. With the injector tube and injector valves removed from the engine, cut the metal hose clamp sleeve and remove the sleeve.
2. Heat the hose with a soldering iron and remove the injector hose from the tube.
3. To install the injector valve assembly on the tube, clean the tube adapter and coat the inside of the hose with fuel.
4. Install the fuel injector hose with the hose sleeve on the injector tube and push against the stop, with the electrical terminal facing up.
5. Complete the installation in the reverse of the removal procedure.

MOTRONIC INJECTION SYSTEM

The Motronic injection is a further development, which combines features of the L-jetronic injection and electronic ignition system. The main difference between L-jetronic and the new system is that the engine idle speed and engine firing advance are controlled by the Motronic control unit.

The Motronic system is incorporated in the 528e, 633CSi and 733i models for 1982–

Main components of the Motronic injection system—528e

83. The 528e has a redesigned engine. The 633CSi and 733i use the same engine as past years with Motronic features added.

MANUAL TRANSMISSION

For manual transmission overhaul procedures, please refer to, "Manual Transmission Overhaul", in the Unit Repair section.

REMOVAL AND INSTALLATION

1. On 4 cylinder engines remove all transmission mounting bolts which are accesible from above.
2. On 4 cylinder engines remove the exhaust pipe support bracket and separate the pipe from the exhaust manifold.
3. On all 6 cylinder engines except model 733i, remove the entire exhaust system. On model 733i disconnect the exhaust pipe from the support bracket only.
4. Disconnect the propeller shaft at the transmission. On model 733i use a special clamping tool.

Disconnecting driveshaft at transmission

5. Remove the heat guard and center bearing, then remove the propeller shaft.
6. Remove the selector lever and circlip.
7. Disconnect the back-up switch connector and the speedometer cable.
8. Remove the slave cylinder from the transmission.
9. Support the transmission and disconnect the crossmember at the body. On models 530i and 3.0 loosen the rubber bearing on the gearbox.
10. On 4 cylinder models remove the remaining transmission mounting bolts and pull out the transmission toward the rear.
11. On 6 cylinder models lower the transmission to the front axle carrier and

disconnect the transmission at the clutch housing. Remove from the rear.

NOTE: On 3.0CSi pull the gearbox out slightly and lift the spring over the spherical pin collar.

12. Installation is the reverse of removal. Install the exhaust suspension without twisting. When installing the propeller shaft, preload the center bearing by (0.078 in.) in the forward direction. Install the clutch slave cylinder with the bleed screw facing down.

CLUTCH

REMOVAL AND INSTALLATION

1. Remove the clutch housing.
2. Prevent the flywheel from turning, using a locking tool.
3. Loosen the mounting bolts one after another gradually to relieve tension from the clutch.
4. Remove the mounting bolts, clutch, and drive plate.
5. To install, reverse the removal procedure. Torque the clutch mounting bolts to 16–17 ft. lbs.

Clutch Master Cylinder

REMOVAL AND INSTALLATION

1. Remove the necessary trim panel or carpet.
2. On model 320i, disconnect the accelerator cable and pull it forward out of the engine firewall.
3. Disconnect the pushrod at the clutch pedal.
4. Remove enough brake fluid from the tank until the level drops below the refill line.
5. Disconnect the windshield washer fluid tank without removing the hoses on model 733i.
6. Disconnect the lines and retaining bolts and remove the master cylinder from the firewall.
7. Installation is the reverse of removal. Bleed the system and adjust the pedal travel with the pushrod to 6 in.

Clutch Slave Cylinder

REMOVAL AND INSTALLATION

1. Remove enough brake fluid from the reservoir until the level drops below the

refill line connection.
2. Remove the circlip or retaining bolts depending on the model.
3. Disconnect the line and remove the slave cylinder.
4. Installation is the reverse of removal. Bleed the system.

BLEEDING CLUTCH HYDRAULIC SYSTEM

1. Fill the reservoir.
2. Connect a bleeder hose from the bleeder screw to a container filled with brake fluid so that air cannot be drawn in during bleeding procedures.
3. Pump the clutch pedal about 10 times then hold it down.
4. Open the bleeder screw and tighten when no more air bubbles escape.
5. Release the clutch pedal and repeat the above procedure until no more air bubbles can be seen.

AUTOMATIC TRANSMISSION

REMOVAL AND INSTALLATION

1. Disconnect the accelerator cable.
2. On the 4 cylinder engine remove all of the transmission mounting bolts which are accessible from above.
3. Detach the oil filler neck and drain the oil.
4. On 4 cylinder engines remove the exhaust pipe support bracket and separate the pipe from the exhaust manifold.
5. On all 6 cylinder engines except model 733i, remove the entire exhaust system.
6. Detach the oil cooler lines from the transmission.

Remove the 4 torque convertor retaining bolts

TURBINE • STATOR • PUMP • A • B • C¹ • C • D • 3 • 1 • 2 • PLANETARY GEAR SET (See caption)

Typical automatic transmission cross section showing clutch identification—trans. model 3HP-12 uses Simpson planetary gear set, trans. model 3HP-22 uses Ravigineaux planetary gear set

7. Disconnect the propeller shaft at the transmission. On model 733i, use special clamping tool.

8. Disconnect the speedometer cable.

9. Remove the heat guard and center bearing and bend down and pull off the propeller shaft.

10. Remove the cover and remove the four bolts that attach the torque converter to the drive plate. Turn the engine for this procedure.

NOTE: On 1982 and later 528e, 633CSi and 733i models the speed transmitter and reference transmitter must be removed from the flywheel housing. For installation, the speed transmitter faces the gear ring. The reference transmitter has a plug with a grey ring and faces the flywheel. The engine will not start if the plugs are mixed up.

11. Support the transmission and disconnect the crossmember at the body.

12. Remove the remaining transmission mounting bolts.

13. Separate the transmission from the engine and take off the torque converter at the same time.

14. Installation is the reverse of removal. Install the exhaust suspension without twisting. When installing the propeller shaft preload the center bearing by 0.08 in.

in the forward direction. Make sure the torque converter is positioned correctly before installing.

SELECTOR LEVER ADJUSTMENT

1. Detach the selector rod (1) at the selector lever lower section (2).

P Parking
R Reverse
O Neutral
A 1st, 2nd and 3rd gear
2. 1st, and 2nd gear; 3rd gear locked out
1. 1st gear; 2nd and 3rd gear locked out

2. Move the selector lever (3) on the transmission to position 0.

3. Press the selector lever (4) against the stop (5) on the shift gate.

4. Adjust the length of the selector rod (1) until the pin (6) aligns with the bore in the selector lever lower section (2). Shorten the selector rod length by: 1 turn—320i, 630CSi, 733i; 2–2½ turns—530i; 3 turns—2002.

Selector lever adjustment—typical all models

The torque converter is installed correctly if the drive shell mounting parts are located underneath the converter housing

Accelerator linkage and accelerator cable adjustment—3.0CSi and 530i

Accelerator cable adjustment—630i, 733i

NOTE: If equipped with air conditioning on the 4 cylinder models, plates (7) must be installed between the bearing bracket and float plate and selector rod (1) must be attached in bore (K) of selector level (3).

ACCELERATOR LINKAGE ADJUSTMENT

2002

1. Remove the air cleaner.
2. Remove the accelerator cable.
3. Press the accelerator pedal down to the kick down stop into the full acceleration position. In this position the throttle valve must be fully open and not extend beyond the vertical position. When adjusting, bend the stop.
4. Adjust the length of the accelerator linkage using the eye bolt.

ACCELERATOR LINKAGE AND ACCELERATOR CABLE ADJUSTMENT

530i and 3.0CSi

1. Synchronize the idle speed with the engine at operating temperature.
2. Detach linkage (1).
3. Detach the accelerator cable at the operating lever (2).
4. Adjust linkage (1) so that the operating lever (2) rests on stop (3).

NOTE: Make sure that linkage (1) is not pulled down into the kickdown position.

5. The swivel joint (5) must align with the hole in the operating lever (2) leaving a play (0.009–0.019 in.) between nipple (4) and the end of the cable sleeve.
6. The accelerator must not sag. Press lever (6) against the acceleration stop (7) and adjust linkage (8) until the distance between nipple (4) and the end of the cable sleeve is 1.456 in. When in kickdown, the nipple (4) must be at least 1.69 in. from the end of the cable sleeve.

NOTE: If the idle speed is altered, repeat the above procedure.

ACCELERATOR CABLE ADJUSTMENT

2002

1. Remove the accelerator cable from the rotary shaft.
2. Press down the accelerator linkage to the full acceleration position.
3. Pull the accelerator cable to determine the full acceleration position. The holes in the fork head must now coincide with the hole on the rotary selector so that the bearing pin can be inserted with correct alignment.

4. Turn the fork head to adjust the cable length.

630CSi, 633CSi and 733i

1. Adjust play (S) to 0.010–0.030 in. with nuts when in Neutral.
2. Press the accelerator pedal against the stop.
3. Adjust the pressure rod (7) until the distance from the seal (3) to the end of cable (4) is 630CSi—(1.732–2.008 in.). 733i—(1.722–2.057 in.).

320i

1. Adjust the accelerator cable at nuts (1) until the accelerator cable eye (2) has a play of 0.008 in.–0.012 in.

Accelerator cable and transmission cable adjustment—320i

in. with the screw (7).

2. Depress the accelerator pedal (3) to kickdown stop; play (A) must now be 1.712–2027″. Make corrections with screw (4).

DRIVE AXLES

Final Drive

REMOVAL AND INSTALLATION

1. Disconnect the universal shaft.

NOTE: On 2002, if equipped with a joint disc, the plate remains on the shaft.

2. Disconnect the output shaft and tie it up overhead.

3. Detach the self aligning support at the final drive on 320i.

4. Disconnect the final drive from the rear axle carrier.

5. On 2002 disconnect the transverse bracket, on all other models loosen the rubber mounting screw and remove the final drive.

6. Installation is the reverse of removal.

Output Shaft (CV Type)

REMOVAL AND INSTALLATION

1. Detach the output shaft at the final drive and drive flange.

2. On 733i, support the control arm if the spring strut and shock absorber are detached.

3. On 630CSi, the spring strut serves as a retaining strap and the trailing arm must be supported if the spring strut is detached.

4. Replace the bellows as follows:
   a. Take off the sealing cover.
   b. Remove the circlip.
   c. Remove the clamp.
   d. Press the output shaft out of the joint then slide off the bellows.

5. Installation is the reverse of removal.

Output Shaft (Universal Sliding Joint Type)

REMOVAL AND INSTALLATION

2002

1. Remove the output shaft from the final drive and halfshaft.

---

2. Depress the accelerator pedal (3) to the full throttle stop screw (4).

3. There must be 0.020 in. play between the operating lever (5) and stop nut (6).

4. Adjust by the full throttle stop screw (4).

528e

1. Adjust the freeplay (s) of the cable in N position to 0.010–0.030 inches (0.25–0.75 mm). Use cable adjuster nuts (1) to adjust the freeplay.

2. In the passenger compartment, loosen the kickdown switch. Screw in the kickdown stop (2) all the way in the direction of the floor pan.

3. Press down on the accelerator pedal (4) to the transmission pressure point. Un-

screw the kickdown stop (2) until it contacts the accelerator pedal.

4. Press the accelerator to the kickdown (wide open throttle) position.

5. In kickdown position, the distance (s) must be 1.732 inches (44.0 mm). The distance (s) equals the distance from the cable seal (5) to the end of the cable sleeve (6).

TRANSMISSION CABLE ADJUSTMENT

320i

NOTE: The accelerator cable must be correctly adjusted.

1. With the transmission in the Neutral position, adjust play (A) to 0.010–0.030

1. Adjusting nuts
2. Kickdown stop
3. Locknut
4. Accelerator pedal
5. Cable seal
6. End of cable sleeve
7. Distance between 5 and 6

Automatic transmission accelerator cable adjustment—528e

Constant velocity type output shaft

Output shaft (universal sliding joint type)

2. Replace the bellows as follows:
   a. Drain the oil.
   b. Remove the hose claps.
   c. Pull off the sliding joint housing.
   d. Remove the mushroom head caps.

NOTE: Be careful not to lose the lower needle bearing pin and lift over the upper needle bearing pin.

3. To install, reverse the above.

NOTE: If the bore in the joint yoke is distorted, the complete output shaft must be replaced.

Driveshaft

REMOVAL AND INSTALLATION

1. On 530i, 630CSi, 528i, 528e remove the entire exhaust system.
2. On 2002 remove the primary muffler from the exhaust pipe.
3. On 3.0CSi remove the primary and main mufflers.
4. On 320i, detach the outer pipe at the manifold and support it at the transmission.
5. Remove the heat shield if so equipped.
6. Disconnect the propeller shaft at the transmission.

NOTE: On 733i, install a special clamping tool (BMW-261011) or equivalent around the coupling and remove the bolts.

7. Loosen the center bearing.
8. On 733i, with manual transmissions, loosen the crossmember and push the left end forward.
9. Bend the propeller shaft down and pull out.
10. Installation is the reverse of removal.
11. The propeller shaft is balanced in line and must only be renewed as a complete assembly.
12. Align the driveshaft with a gauge (BMW-21-1-000) or equivalent by moving the center bearing sideways or by placing washers underneath the center bearing.

Preload center bearing in the forward direction

13. On 733i, remove the special coupling tool only after the nuts have been tightened to prevent stress on the coupling.
14. Preload the center bearing by 0.078 in. in the forward direction.

Preload center bearing—(A)=0.08 in.

Center Bearing

REMOVAL AND INSTALLATION

3.0CSi, 528i, 528e, 530i, 630CSi, 633CSi, and 733i

1. Bend down the driveshaft and pull it out of the centering pin on the transmission (Refer to Driveshaft Removal and Installation).

Remove circlip (2) and dust guard (3)

Drive center bearing onto grooved ball bearing

1. Spring   3. Centering ring   5. Retaining ring
2. Washer   4. Ball socket   6. Sealing cap

Remove centering ring and ball socket—3.0CSi and 2002

2. Loosen the threaded bushing.

3. Mark the driveshaft position on slide with a punch mark and pull the front half of the propeller shaft out of the slide.

4. Remove the circlip and dust guard.

5. Using a standard puller remove the center bearing without the dust guard.

6. Use a puller and remove the grooved ball bearing in the center bearing.

7. Installation is the reverse of removal. Drive the center bearing onto the grooved ball bearing with tool (BMW-24-1-050) or equivalent.

320i

1. With the propeller shaft removed, mark the shafts location to the coupling.

2. Remove the circlip and pull out the propeller shaft.

3. Using a standard puller remove the center bearing without its dust cover.

4. Drive the grooved ball bearing out of the center bearing.

5. Installation is the reverse of removal.

2002

1. With the propeller shaft removed, remove the coupling nut.

2. Using a standard puller, pull off the center bearing without the dust guard.

3. Remove the grooved ball bearing with a puller.

4. Installation is the reverse of removal.

Centering Ring

REMOVAL AND INSTALLATION

3.0CSi and 2002

1. Press off the sealing cap.

2. Lift out the circlip.

3. Take out the ball cup, centering ring, disc and spring.

4. Installation is the reverse of removal. Fill the centering assembly with approximately 6g (0.2 oz.) of grease.

All Models Except 3.0CSi and 2002

1. Fill the center with grease and using a 14mm (0.551″) dia. mandrel, drive out the ring.

2. Installation is the reverse of removal.

NOTE: The shaft ring faces out.

Rear Axle Shaft, Wheel Bearings and Seals

REMOVAL AND INSTALLATION

6 Cylinder Models

1. Remove the wheel.

2. Loosen the brake caliper and leave the brake line connected.

3. Remove the brake disc.

4. Remove the driving flange as follows:

  a. Disconnect the output shaft.

  b. Remove the bookplate.

c. Loosen the collard nut and pull off the drive flange.

5. Tighten the collared nut and drive off the rear axle shaft.

6. Drive off the wheel bearings and seals toward the outside.

7. Installation is the reverse of removal.

4 Cylinder Models

1. Remove the wheel.

2. Remove the cotter pin from the castellated nut.

3. Apply the handbrake.

4. Loosen the castellated nut.

5. Release the handbrake.

6. Remove the brake drum.

7. Pull off the drive flange with a puller.

8. Disconnect the output shaft and tie it up.

9. Drive out the halfshaft with a plastic hammer using the castellated nut to protect the end of the shaft.

10. Drive out the bearing and sealing ring.

11. Take out the spacer sleeve and shim.

12. Installation is the reverse of removal.

Wheel bearing with rear axle shaft removed—6 cylinder models

Driving out rear axle shaft—4 cylinder models

Rear axle shaft seal (1), bearing (2), ring (3), spacer (4)

REAR SUSPENSION

Coil Spring, Shock Absorber, Strut Assembly

For removal of springs from struts and strut overhaul procedures refer to, "Strut Overhaul", in the Unit Repair section.

— CAUTION —

Macpherson strut springs are under tremendous pressure and any attempt to remove them without proper tools could result in serious personal injury.

REMOVAL AND INSTALLATION

All Models Except 2002

1. On model 733i remove the rear seat and back rest.

2. Jack up the car and support the control arms.

— CAUTION —

The coil spring, shock absorber assembly acts as a strap so the control arm should always be supported.

3. Disconnect the lower shock retaining bolt.

4. Disconnect the upper strut retaining nuts at the wheelbase and remove the assembly.

5. Using the appropriate spring compressor compress the coil spring far enough to remove the centering cup, then release the coil spring and separate the spring, boot and shock absorber.

Shock Absorber

REMOVAL AND INSTALLATION

2002

1. Jack up the car and support the control arm.

Rear suspension—528e

2. Remove the safety cap and remove the upper shock retaining nut.

3. Remove the lower shock retaining nut.

4. Press the shock together and remove.

5. Installation is the reverse of removal.

Coil Spring

REMOVAL AND INSTALLATION

2002

1. Remove the shock absorber.

2. Remove the rear wheel.

3. Unbolt the stabilizer from the trailing arm.

4. Disconnect the output shaft from the half-shaft and tie it up.

5. Slowly lower the supported trailing arm with the jack and take out the coil spring.

Stabilizer

REMOVAL AND INSTALLATION

All Models

1. Remove the stabilizer from the trailing arm.

2. Disconnect the stabilizer on the crossmember.

3. Check the rubber bushings for wear and replace as necessary.

Rear Control Arm

REMOVAL AND INSTALLATION

530i, 528i and 528e

1. Remove the parking brake lever.

2. Plug the front hose to prevent loss

Output shaft detached and tied up for coil spring removal—2002

Stabilizer bar—2002 shown; others similar

of brake fluid in the reservoir.

3. Support the body.

4. Disconnect the brake line at the brake hose.

5. Disconnect the driveshaft.

6. Disconnect the stabilizer and coil spring at the control arm.

7. Disconnect the control arm at the axle carrier.

8. Installation is the reverse of removal. Bleed brake system.

733i

1. Remove the rear wheel.

2. Pull up the parking brake lever and disconnect the output shaft at the drive flange.

3. Remove the parking brake lever.

4. Remove the brake fluid from the reservoir.

5. Disconnect the brake line.

6. Disconnect the control arm from the rear axle carrier.

7. Disconnect the shock absorber and remove the control arm.

8. Installation is the reverse of removal. Bleed the brake system.

Trailing Arm

REMOVAL AND INSTALLATION
2002

1. Remove the coil spring.

2. Release the handbrake cable at the handbrake lever.

3. Disconnect the stabilizer on the trailing arm.

4. Separate the brake hose from the pipe line and cap the hose to protect against dirt.

5. Disconnect both trailing arm mountings and remove the trailing arm.

6. Installation is the reverse of removal. Bleed the brake system.

3.0CSi

1. Remove the handbrake lever.

2. Remove brake fluid from the reservoir.

3. Support the body.

4. Remove the wheel.

5. Pull the handbrake cable out of the protective tube.

6. Disconnect the brake hoses.

7. Remove the output driveshaft.

8. Remove the spring strut shock absorber from the trailing arm.

9. Remove the trailing arm from the axle support.

630CSi and 633CSi

1. Remove the parking brake lever.

2. Remove the rear wheel.

3. Using vise grips clamp the front hose to prevent loss of fluid.

4. Support the body.

5. Pull the parking brake cable out of the pipe.

6. Disconnect the stabilizer and spring strut at the trailing arm.

7. Disconnect the brake line at the brake hose.

8. Disconnect the trailing arm at the rear axle support.

9. Detach the output shaft.

10. Disconnect the brake pad wear indicator wire at the right trailing arm and take the wire out of the clamps.

11. Installation is the reverse of removal. Bleed the system.

320i

1. Disconnect the parking brake cable at the parking brake lever.

2. Detach the output shaft at the rear axle shaft.

3. Remove the wheel.

4. Disconnect the coil spring/shock absorber strut at the trailing arm.

5. Support the trailing arm.

6. Disconnect the brake hose at the pipe and plug the end of the hose to prevent dirt from entering.

7. Disconnect the stabilizer at the trailing arm and remove both trailing arm mounting bolts.

8. Installation is the reverse of removal. Bleed the brake system.

FRONT SUSPENSION

Strut Assembly

For removal of springs from struts and strut overhaul procedures, refer to "Strut Overhaul" in the Unit Repair section.

— **CAUTION** —

Macpherson strut springs are under tremendous pressure and any attempt to remove them without proper tools could result in serious personal injury.

REMOVAL AND INSTALLATION
2002

1. Raise the vehicle and support safely. Remove the wheel.

2. Disconnect the angle bracket from the strut assembly.

3. Disconnect the caliper, leaving the brake line attached. Tie the caliper to the vehicle body so that the weight is not supported by the brake hose.

4. Disconnect the lower arm from the axle beam.

5. Remove the lockwire and disconnect the track rod arm from the strut assembly.

Angle bracket retaining bolt—2002

Bracket retaining bolt—320i

Front suspension—2002

1. Spacer ring　　2. Washer　　3. Wishbone

Detaching the lower arm at front axle beam

Lock wire location at strut assembly

Angle bracket location and caliper retaining nuts—3.0

Stabilizer-to-control arm attaching nut —530i, 630i

Front suspension—320i

6. Remove the three retaining nuts and detach the strut assembly at the wheel-house.

7. Installation is the reverse of removal.

320i

1. Raise the vehicle and support safely. Remove the wheel.

2. Detach the bracket at the strut assembly.

3. Disconnect and suspend the brake caliper with a wire from the vehicle body. Do not disconnect the brake line.

4. Remove the cotter pin and castle nut. Press the tie rod off the steering knuckle.

5. Remove the three retaining nuts and detach the strut assembly at the wheel house.

6. Installation is the reverse of removal.

3.0 CSi

1. Raise the vehicle and support safely. Remove the wheel.

2. Disconnect the brake caliper and suspend from the vehicle body with a wire.

Front suspension—528e

3. Disconnect the angle bracket from the strut assembly.

4. Remove the lock wire and disconnect the track rod arm from the strut assembly.

5. Remove the three retaining nuts and detach the strut assembly at the wheelhouse.

6. Installation is the reverse of removal.

530i, 528i, 528e, 630CSi and 633CSi

1. Raise the vehicle and support safely. Remove the wheel.

2. Disconnect the bracket at the strut assembly.

3. Disconnect the brake caliper and suspend from the vehicle body with wire. Do not remove the brake hose.

4. Remove the lock wire and disconnect the tie rod arm at the strut assembly.

5. Remove the three retaining nuts and detach the strut assembly at the wheelhouse.

6. Installation is the reverse of removal.

733i

1. Raise the vehicle and support safely. Remove the wheel.

2. Disconnect the vibration strut from the control arm.

Front suspension assembly—530i

Vibration strut attaching bolt—733i

3. Disconnect the bracket and clamps from the strut assembly.

4. Disconnect the wire connection and press out the wire from the clamp on the spring strut tube.

5. Remove the brake caliper and suspend it from the vehicle body with a wire. Do not remove the brake hose.

6. Disconnect the tie rod from the shock absorber.

7. Remove the three retaining nuts and disconnect the strut assembly from the wheelhouse.

8. Installation is the reverse of removal.

Control Arm

REMOVAL AND INSTALLATION

530i, 528i, 528e, 630CSi, and 633CSi

1. Raise the vehicle and support safely. Remove the wheel.

2. Disconnect the stabilizer at the control arm.

3. Remove the tension strut nut on the control arm.

Tie rod arm-to-shock absorber retaining bolts—733i

Lower control arm spacer ring in axle carrier—3.0

Front suspension—733i

4. Disconnect the control arm at the front axle support and remove it from the tension strut.

5. Remove the lock wire, remove the bolts and take the control arm off the spring strut.

6. Remove the cotter pin and nut.

7. Using special tool BMW 00-7-500 or equivalent, pull the guide joint from the tie rod arm.

8. Installation is the reverse of removal.

320i

1. Disconnect the stabilizer at the control arm.

2. Disconnect the control arm at the front axle support.

3. Remove the cotter pin and castle nut.

4. Press the control arm off the steering knuckle with special tool BMW 31-1-100 or equivalent.

5. Installation is the reverse of removal.

733i

1. Raise the vehicle and support safely.

Remove the wheel.

2. Disconnect the vibration strut from the control arm.

3. Disconnect the control arm from the axle carrier.

4. Disconnect the tie rod arm from the shock absorber.

5. Remove the cotter pin and castle nut. Press off the control arm with special tool BMW 31-1-110 or equivalent.

6. Installation is the reverse of removal.

Control Arm (Wishbone)

REMOVAL AND INSTALLATION

3.0CSi

1. Raise the vehicle and support safely. Remove the wheel.

2. Remove the lock wire and disconnect the track rod arm from the strut assembly.

3. Press the guide joint out of the track rod arm.

4. Disconnect the lower arm from the axle carrier.

5. Disconnect the trailing link from the lower arm.

6. Installation is the reverse of removal.

2002

1. Raise the vehicle and support safely. Remove the wheel.

2. Disconnect the trailing link at the lower arm.

3. Disconnect the lower arm from the front axle beam and push off at the trailing link.

4. Remove the cotter pin and castle nut. Press off the track rod at the track rod arm with special tool BMW 00-7-500 or equivalent.

5. Remove the lock wire and nuts. Remove the track rod arm with the lower arm.

6. Remove the cotter pin and nut. Press off the track rod arm from the guide joint with special tool BMW 00-7-500 or equivalent.

7. Installation is the reverse of removal.

Drilling out ball joint rivet heads

Replace rivets with nut and bolt

Trailing link retaining nut at lower arm

Slotted washers (1) should turn freely after adjustment is complete

Ball Joint

REMOVAL AND INSTALLATION

2002

1. Remove the lower control arm assembly and lock in a vise.
2. Drill out the rivet heads and drive the rivets out, using a suitable punch.
3. Replace the ball joint, using nuts and bolts.
4. Reassemble the lower control arm in the reverse of the removal.

Front Suspension Alignment

CASTER AND CAMBER

Caster and camber are not adjustable, except for replacement of bent or worn parts.

TOE-IN ADJUSTMENT

Toe-in adjusted by changing the length of the tie rod and tie rod end assembly. When adjusting the tie rod ends, adjust each by equal amount (in the opposite direction) to increase or decrease the toe-in measurement.

Front Wheel Bearing Adjustment

2002, 320i, 630CSi, 633CSi and 733i

1. Raise the vehicle and support safely. Remove the front wheels.
2. Remove the bearing cap, cotter pin and loosen the castle nut on the spindle.
3. Tighten the castle nut to 22–24 ft. lbs. (30–33 n/m), while turning the hub continuously. After the proper torque is attained, rotate the hub at least two more turns.

NOTE: This aligns the tapered bearings to the inner races.

4. Loosen the castle nut until a slight play is present on the bearings. Retighten the nut to a maximum of 2 ft. lbs. (3 n/m) and turn back to the nearest hole and insert the cotter pin.

NOTE: The slotted washer must be movable behind the castle nut without any noticeable resistance.

530i, 528i and 3.0

1. Raise the vehicle and support safely. Remove the front wheels.
2. Remove the bearing cap, cotter pin and castle nut.
3. Torque the castle nut to 7 ft. lbs. (9.5 n/m), while turning the wheel hub. This will align the taper roller bearings to the inner races.
4. Loosen the castle nut about ⅓ turn Model 530i, 528i and ¼ turn model 3.0. The slotted washer behind the castle nut, should turn freely.
5. Attach a dial indicator gauge to the wheel hub. Bearing preload should be 0.0008 to 0.0024 inch.

528e

1. Raise the vehicle and support it safely. Remove the front wheels.
2. Remove the bearing cap and the self-locking nut.

Turn signal switch adjustment

3. Install a new nut and tighten it to specified torque.
4. Lock the nut by hitting it with a round punch several times on the outer lip.
5. Install bearing cap and front wheels. Lower the vehicle.

STEERING

Steering Wheel

REMOVAL AND INSTALLATION

NOTE: Remove and install steering wheel in straight ahead position.

1. Remove steering wheel pad or BMW emblem.
2. Unscrew retaining nut and remove the wheel.
3. Installation is the reverse of removal.

Turn Signal/Dimmer Switch and Wiper Switch

REMOVAL AND INSTALLATION

All Models Except 3.0CSi

1. Disconnect negative battery terminal.
2. Remove steering wheel.
3. Remove lower steering column casing.
4. On 2002, remove upper steering column surround and leave choke cable attached.
5. Disconnect fuel relay/plate plug.
6. Installation is the reverse of removal.

NOTE: When installing turn signal switch, steering wheel is pointed in the straight ahead position, turn signal lever is in centered position and adjust play "A" to about 3 mm.

7. On 320i make sure to connect the ground strap.

3.0CSi Turn Signal and Headlight Dimmer Switch

1. Disconnect negative battery terminal.
2. Remove steering wheel.
3. Remove lower steering column casing.
4. Remove lower center left section of instrument panel housing.
5. Installation is the reverse of removal.

NOTE: When installing turn signal switch, steering wheel is pointed in the straight ahead position, turn signal lever is in the centered position and adjust play "A" to about 3 mm.

Ignition Switch

REMOVAL AND INSTALLATION

1. Disconnect negative battery terminal.

2. Remove lower steering column casing.

3. On model 3.0 remove lower center left instrument panel trim. On 320i, 630i, 633CSi, 733i, 528i and 528e models shear off the four tamperproof screws with a chisel or other tool.

4. Unscrew set screw and remove switch.

5. Disconnect central fuse/relay plate plug.

6. Installation is the reverse of removal.

NOTE: Turn ignition key all the way back and set the switch at the "O" position before installing. Marks on the switch must be opposite each other.

Manual Steering Gear

REMOVAL AND INSTALLATION

320i

1. Loosen front wheels.
2. Remove cotter pin and castle nut.
3. Press tie rods off steering knuckles.
4. Detach steering at front axle support.
5. Pull steering gear off steering spindle.

6. Installation is the reverse of removal.

NOTE: Turn steering wheel until wheels point straight ahead. Mark on dust seal must be between marks on gear box.

2002 and 3.0CSi

1. Loosen bolt connecting coupling flange to steering column, remove bolt attaching flange to steering box.

NOTE: On model 2002, do not reuse self locking nuts.

2. Remove castle nut and press off left track rod from center track rod.
3. Press the center track rod from the steering drop arm.
4. Detach and remove steering box from front axle beam.
5. Installation is the reverse of removal.

NOTE: Steering wheel must be in the straight ahead position and the markings on the steering box and the pitman shaft must align.

ADJUSTMENT

320i

1. Remove steering gear from car.
2. Clamp special tool 32-1-100, or

1. Box
2. Rack
3. Bearing bushing
4. O-rings
5. Spring
6. Pressure pad
7. O-ring
8. Spring retainer
9. Set screw
10. Cotter pin
11. Set screw
12. Cap
13. Grooved ball bearing
14. Drive pinion
15. Needle bearing
16. Washer
17. Circlip
18. O-ring
19. Set screw
20. Notched ring
21. Dust seal
22. V-ring

Steering gear—typical

Steering adjustment 320i

Adjusting friction coefficient—2002 and 3.0

Turning torque adjustment—320i

002 000   321000

Pressure pad adjustment—320i

equivalent in a vise and place steering gear assembly into the tool.

3. Unscrew nut on steering damper and slide it back.

4. Remove cap and unscrew socket head cap about ½ inch.

5. Pressure pad adjustment:

a. Remove cotter pin. Tighten set screw with special 32-1-040, or equivalent, and a torque wrench, to 4 ft. lbs. Loosen set screw by one full castle slot to align the cotter pin bore.

b. Use special tools 32-1-000 and 00-2-000 or equivalent to move rack to the left and right over the entire stroke and check for sticking and hooking. If this is the case loosen set screw by one more castle slot and insert cotter pin. Repeat test. If there is still sticking or hooking replace rack, drive pinion or the entire steering gear. Never loosen screw by 2 castle slots regardless of circumstances.

6. Turning torque adjustment:

a. Move rack to center position. Place special tools 00-2-000 and 32-1-000 or equivalent on the drive pinion, check the turning torque. If it is not between 7.8 and 11.2 ft. lbs. adjust the set screw.

b. Turn to the right to increase friction, and turn to the left to decrease friction.

c. Install cap.

2002 and 3.0CSi

1. Remove air intake filter on model 2002.

2. Position front wheels straight ahead.

3. Marking on worm shaft must be in alignment with marking on steering box.

4. Remove castle nut and press left-hand tie rod from center tie rod.

5. Remove castle nut and press center tie rod from drop arm with special tool 7009, or equivalent.

6. Remove steering wheel center and install friction gauge.

7. Turn the steering wheel one turn to the left from the straight ahead position. In this position the worm cannot be pressed one-sided into its bearing by the steering

roller shaft, which might indicate absence of play.

8. Turn adjustment screw until specified friction coefficient is reached when passing through the straight ahead position.

Power Steering

REMOVAL AND INSTALLATION

1. Turn steering to left lock.
2. Drain steering fluid.
3. Remove cotter pin and loosen castle nut.
4. Press center tie rod off steering drop arm.
5. Remove screw and slide coupling flange with steering column upward.
6. Disconnect hoses at steering gear and plug the openings.
7. Detach and remove steering gear at front axle carrier.
8. Installation is the reverse of removal.

NOTE: System must be bled and the front wheels must be in the straight ahead position. Marks on the housing and propeller shaft must align. Use new self locking nuts on all models except model 3.0CSi.

ADJUSTMENT

1. Remove steering wheel center.
2. With front wheels in straight ahead position remove cotter pin and loosen castle nut. On 630CSi models, wheels are turned to the right lock.

1. Screw
2. Hose
3. Hose

Coupling flange and steering box

Friction gauge installation

1. Locknut   2. Adjusting nut
Power steering adjustment

3. Press center tie rod off steering drop arm.

4. Turn steering wheel to the left about one turn. Install a friction gauge and turn the wheel to the right, past the point of pressure and the gauge should read 10.4 ft. lbs.

5. To adjust, turn steering wheel about one turn to the left. Loosen counter nut and turn the adjusting screw until specified friction is reached when passing over point of pressure.

Power Steering Pump

REMOVAL AND INSTALLATION

All Models Except 733i

1. Detach steering pump hoses.
2. Remove bolts from the brackets holding the front and rear of the pump.
3. Installation is the reverse of removal.

NOTE: Bleed the system and torque the hose connections to 35 ft. lbs.

733i

1. When the pump is damaged the pressure control regulator must also be replaced.
2. Discharge the hydraulic accumulator, by depressing the brake pedal with the force required for full stop breaking (about 20 times).
3. Detach hoses at pump.
4. Remove bolts from the brackets holding the pump in place.
5. Remove brake booster return hose from accumulator tank and plug the opening.
6. Installation is the reverse of removal.

NOTE: Run engine 10 minutes and turn steering wheel several times from stop to stop. Operate brake booster quickly, to obtain hard resistance, about 10 times to discard the oil leaving the return hose.

7. Stop engine, drain oil from tank and connect booster return hose on tank.

BELT ADJUSTMENT

Tighten belt so that when pressure is applied to the belt, the distance between both belt pulleys is 5 to 10 mm.

1. Drive shaft
2. Shaft seal
3. Circlip
4. Ball bearing
5. Snap rings
6. Bearing sleeve
7. Dowel pin
8. Drive end face plate
9. Rotor set
10. Cover end face plate
11. O-ring
12. O-ring
13. Spring
14. Cover
15. Hook snap ring
16. Spring
17. Valve piston assembly

Power steering pump—typical

Power steering belt adjustment

Power steering reservoir—typical

Steering linkage—all except 320i

Steering linkage—320i

SYSTEM BLEEDING

1. Fill reservoir to edge with proper fluid.
2. Start engine and add oil until oil level remains constant.
3. Turn steering wheel from lock to lock quickly until air bubbles are no longer present in the reservoir.
4. On model 733i, operate brake pedal to discharge hydraulic accumulator until oil level stops rising or noticeable resistance on brake pedal is felt.

Steering Linkage

REMOVAL AND INSTALLATION

All Models Except 320i

TIE ROD ARM

1. Remove front wheel.
2. On 2002, detach stabilizer wishbone. Detach wishbone at front axle beam. Detach trailing link from wishbone.
3. Remove cotter pin and castle nut.
4. Press outer tie rod off tie rod arm, and press stabilizer off control arm.
5. Remove lock wire and detach tie rod arm at shock absorber.
6. Press tie rod arm off control arm.
7. Installation is the reverse of removal.

OUTER TIE ROD

1. Remove cotter pin, castle nut and press outer tie rod off of center tie rod.
2. Remove cotter pin, loosen castle nut and press outer tie rod off tie rod arm.
3. Installation is the reverse of removal.
4. Align front axle.

CENTER TIE ROD

1. On 733i, remove the heat guard.
2. Remove cotter pins, loosen castle nuts and press left and right tie rods off center tie rod.

3. Press center tie rod off of steering control arm.
4. Installation is the reverse of removal.
5. Align front axle.

Model 320i

LEFT AND RIGHT TIE RODS

1. Loosen the wheel.
2. Remove cotter pin and loosen castle nut.
3. Press tie rod off steering knuckle.
4. Detach strap, slide back bellows and bend open lock plate.
5. Detach tie rod at rack.
6. Installation is the reverse of removal.

Tie rod removal—320i

BRAKE SYSTEM

For all brake system repair and service procedures not detailed below, please refer to "Brakes" in the Unit Repair section.

All BMW models incorporate dual, fluid-circuit, tandem arrangement master cylinders in their brake systems, which are similar to one another in design and function. However, even though they are similar to one another, they are not identical to one another in design or function.

By dual circuit, tandem arrangement we mean that the master cylinder is comprised of two (dual) integrally joined fluid chambers (each supplying a predetermined combination of wheel brakes) which are positioned one in front of the other (tandem).

Two variations of the standard dual circuit system are the double dual circuit system and the diagonally split, dual circuit system.

In the case of the standard dual circuit system, one chamber supplies the front brakes while the other chamber supplies the rear brakes. In the case of the double dual circuit system, one chamber supplies the

1. Steering pump
2. Oil tank
3. Pressure control regulator
4. Hudraulic accumulator
5. Steering
6. Hydraulic booster
7. Tandem master cylinder

Diagonally split, dual circuit brake system—733i

circuit to the front brakes while the other supplies a circuit to the front and rear brakes combined. In the case of the diagonally split, dual circuit system, one chamber supplies the left front and right rear brakes while the other chamber supplies the right front and left rear brakes.

A brief list of brake-system-according-to-model follows.

Model 2002: Standard dual circuit; (front) Ate four piston, fixed caliper discs with automatic pad wear compensation, (rear) internal-expanding drums with self-centering leading and trailing shoes, (park) mechanical, acting on rear wheels.

Model 320i: Standard dual circuit; (front) Ate caliper type disc brakes with automatic adjustment for pad wear, (rear). Inside shoe brakes with simplex shoes, (park) mechanical, with action on rear wheels.

Model 530i: 528i, 528e Double Dual Circuit; (front) Ate four piston with fixed caliper discs and automatic adjustment, (rear) Ate two piston, fixed caliper discs with automatic adjustment, (park) Duo servo drums.

Models 630CSi, and 633CSi; Double dual circuit brakes with brake pressure booster and governor, and brake pad wear indicator, (front) Ate four piston caliper disc brakes with automatic adjustment, (rear) Ate two piston caliper disc brakes with automatic adjustment, (park) Dual hydraulic drum brakes with cable operation on rear wheels only.

Model 733i: Diagonally split, dual circuit brake system with hydraulic brake pressure boost and mutual hydraulic pump for brakes and steering as well as pressure

accumulator for brakes including brake fluid reservoir. Equipped with an indicator for brake fluid level and brake pad wear, (front) Ate four piston caliper disc brakes with automatic adjustment, (rear) Ate two piston caliper disc brakes with automatic adjustment, (park) Dual power drum brakes with bowden cable acting on the rear wheels.

NOTE: In the hydraulically boosted power brake system, pressure developed in the booster is transferred to the standard master cylinder which is bolted to the booster unit.

The hydraulic pressure to the power booster is regulated between the power steering pump and the power booster by a pressure control regulator. The fluid is pumped through the regulator at an approximate flow rate of 7 quarts per minute, and into a fluid accumulator where it is stored (charged) at 510–810 psi, This charge is sufficient to operate the brake system several times if the power steering pump fails. When the reserve pressure is depleted the brake system will remain operational, however, considerably more force will be required to stop the vehicle.

Models 3.0Si: Double dual circuit brakes; (front) Ate four piston fixed caliper disc brakes with automatic pad wear compensation, (rear) Ate two piston fixed caliper disc brakes with automatic pad wear compensation, (park) Duo-servo drums with leading and trailing shoe drum brakes.

Master Cylinder

REMOVAL

All Models Except 320i and 733i

1. Remove the air cleaner if necessary.
2. Drain and disconnect the brake fluid reservoir from the master cylinder. The brake fluid reservoir will be mounted in one of two ways: (1) assembled directly on top of the master cylinder; it is removed by tilting the reservoir to one side and lifting it off of the master cylinder, or (2) the reservoir is mounted in the engine compartment where it is attached to the inner fender sheet metal by means of attaching bolts; carefully disconnect hoses leading to the master cylinder and allow the reservoir to drain.

— CAUTION —

Exercise extreme care in handling brake fluid near painted surface of vehicle as fluid will destroy the pain finish if allowed to come into contact with it.

3. Disconnect all brake lines from the master cylinder.
4. Remove the master cylinder to power booster attaching nuts, and remove the master cylinder.

NOTE: Observe the correct seating of the master cylinder-to-power booster seals.

INSTALLATION

1. Bench-bleed the master cylinder.

NOTE: Check for proper seating of master cylinder to power booster O-ring. Check clearance between the master cylinder piston and push rod with plastic gauge, and, if necessary, adjust to 0.002 inch by placing shims behind the head of the push rod.

2. Position master cylinder onto studs protruding from the power booster; install and tighten the attaching nuts.
3. Connect all brake lines.
4. Install the brake fluid reservoir and fill with brake fluid.

NOTE: An alternate method to bench bleeding the master cylinder is to bleed the master cylinder in the vehicle by opening (only slightly) the brake line fitting at the master cylinder, and allowing the fluid to flow from the master cylinder into a container, however, this method should be considered as an ALTERNATE METHOD ONLY as it is more difficult to control the fluid leaving the master cylinder during bleeding, thereby increasing the chance of accidentally splashing brake fluid onto the painted surface of the vehicle.

5. Bleed the brake system.

REMOVAL AND INSTALLATION

320i

1. Remove the fuel mixture control unit.
2. Disconnect the hose at the clutch connection.
3. Drain and disconnect the brake fluid reservoir.
4. Disconnect the brake lines from the master cylinder.
5. Working from the underside of the left-side inner fender panel (wheel opening area) remove the two master cylinder support bracket attaching nuts.
6. Remove the master cylinder to power booster attaching nuts, and remove the master cylinder.
7. Install in the reverse order of removal.

NOTE: **Bench bleed the master cylinder prior to installation. Refer to the aforementioned note concerning an ALTERNATE bleeding procedure.**

8. Bleed the brake system.

733i

1. Drain and disconnect the fluid reservoir.
2. Disconnect the brake lines at the master cylinder.
3. Remove the master cylinder to hydraulic booster attaching bolts, and remove the master cylinder.
4. Install in the reverse order of removal.

NOTE: **Bench bleed the master cylinder prior to installation. Refer to the aforementioned note concerning an ALTERNATE bleeding procedure.**

Vacuum Operated Power Brake Booster

REMOVAL AND INSTALLATION

2002 and 320i

1. Remove the master cylinder.
2. Disconnect the vacuum line at the power booster.
3. Remove the brake pedal apply-rod to power booster push rod pin.
4. Remove the power booster attaching nuts, and remove the power booster.
5. Install in the reverse order of removal.

NOTE: **If the original power booster unit is to reused, remove the dust boot and clean the silencer and filter. Position the slots in the silencer 180 degrees away from the slots in the filter.**

6. Adjust the extended visible length of the brake light switch head to 0.20–0.24 inch.

1. Right front
2. Left front
3. Rear wheels

Master cylinder—320i

REMOVAL AND INSTALLATION

530i, 528i, 528e, 630CSi and 633 CSi

1. Remove the coolant reservoir.
2. Remove the master cylinder.
3. Disconnect the vacuum hose at the power booster.
4. Disconnect the power booster apply rod at the brake pedal.
5. Remove the power booster attaching bolts.
6. Remove the power booster.
7. Install in the reverse order of removal.

NOTE: **If the original power booster unit is to be reused, remove the dust boot and clean the silencer and filter. Position the slots in the silencer 180 degrees away from the slots in the filter.**

8. Adjust the brake pedal distance to 9.055–9.450 inches. Adjust the stop light switch distance to 0.197–0.237 inch.

A. 9.055-9.45 inches
B. 50 mm (1.97 inches)

Brake pedal adjustment 530i, 630CSi, 528i, 528e and 633CSi

3.0CSi

1. Remove the air cleaner.
2. Remove the battery.
3. Loosen the power steering fluid reservoir, and secure it out of the way.
4. Remove the hose between the radiator and the coolant overflow reservoir.
5. Remove the master cylinder.
6. Disconnect the vacuum hose at the power booster.
7. Remove the lower left instrument panel housing, and secure it out of the way.
8. Remove the power booster apply-rod pin at the brake pedal.
9. Remove the power booster to support bracket attaching nuts, and remove the power booster.
10. Install in the reverse order of removal.

NOTE: If the original power booster unit is to be reused, remove the dust boot and clean the silencer and filter. Position the slots in the silencer 180 degrees away from the slots in the filter.

11. Adjust the power booster apply-rod length to 14.5 inches.
12. Adjust the brake pedal-to-bulk head distance to 9.65 inches.
13. Adjust the extended visible length of the brake light switch head (plunger) to 0.24–0.28 inch.

Hydraulically Operated Power Brake Booster

REMOVAL AND INSTALLATION

733i

1. Release the pressure in the hydraulic accumulator by operating the brake pedal (with the engine not running) with a force equivalent to that necessary to bring the vehicle to a full and complete stop.
2. Remove the lower left instrument panel trim.
3. Disconnect the power booster apply-rod at the brake pedal.
4. Remove the master cylinder.
5. Disconnect the fluid lines at the brake booster.
6. Remove the power booster to pedal base assembly attaching bolts, and remove the power booster.
7. Install in the reverse order of removal.
8. Adjust the distance between the brake pedal and the bulk head to 9.882–10.236 inches.
9. Adjust the extended visible length of the brake light switch head (plunger) to 0.197–0.237 inch.

A. 9.882-10.236 inches
B. 0.197-0.237 inch

Brake pedal adjustment—733i

Hydraulic Accumulator

REMOVAL AND INSTALLATION

733i

1. Release the pressure in the hydraulic accumulator by operating the brake pedal (with the engine not running) with a force equivalent to that necessary to bring the vehicle to a full and complete stop.
2. Disconnect the electrical lead at the indicator switch.
3. Disconnect the hydraulic fluid lines from the pressure control regulator:
   a. from the control regulator to the fluid reservoir.
   b. from the control regulator to the power steering gear box.
   c. from the control regulator to the power steering pump.
   d. from the control regulator to the power brake booster.
4. Fabricate a circular removing strap according to the following dimensions:
   a. 110 mm (4.33 inches)
   b. 50 mm (1.97 inches)
   c. 5 mm (0.197 inch)
5. Place the removing strap around the accumulator and clamp the ends of the strap in a vise, thereby locking the accumulator, so as to prevent the accumulator from turning when torque is applied to the pressure control regulator.
6. Install BMW special tool 34-3-200 or an equivalent removing device directly on the pressure control regulator, and turn the regulator free from the accumulator.
7. Install in the reverse order of removal.

— **CAUTION** —
When connecting the fluid lines to the pressure control regulator be certain that all lines are clean and free from dirt. The presence of foreign particles trapped in the fluid circuit can seriously impair the functioning of the pressure control regulator, thereby causing failure of power assistance to the steering and brake systems.

8. Fill the fluid reservoir with type A power steering fluid to a level approximately ⅜ inch below the top edge of the reservoir. Start the engine; and, while the engine is running, add fluid to the reservoir, if necessary, in order to maintain the level at the full mark.
9. Turn the steering wheel from stop to stop, until air bubbles stop rising in the reservoir.
10. Stop the engine.
11. Operate the brake pedal until the fluid level in the reservoir stops rising, or until there is noticeable resistance at the brake pedal.
12. Check the fluid level in the reservoir. Correct the level to approximately ⅜ inch below the top edge of the reservoir.

1. From the control regulator to the fluid reservoir
2. From the control regulator to the power steering gear box
3. From the control regulator to the power steering pump
4. From the control regulator to the power brake booster

Pressure control regulator—733i

1. Cylinder
2. Spring
3. Piston seals
4. Pistons
5. Dust caps
6. Bleeder valve
7. Dust cap

Typical wheel cylinder

1. Rubber boot
2. Locknut
3. Adjustment nut

Handbrake assembly

Rear Wheel Cylinder

REMOVAL AND INSTALLATION

2002, 3.0CSi and 320i

1. Remove the rear brake drum.
2. Loosen the wheel cylinder bleeder screw. DO NOT remove the bleeder screw.
3. Disconnect the brake line from the wheel cylinder.
4. Turn the brake shoe adjusting cams as far to the outside as possible.
5. Remove the wheel cylinder attaching bolts, and remove the wheel cylinder.
6. Install in the reverse order of removal.

Parking Brake

ADJUSTMENT

Vehicles Equipped with Rear Drum Brakes

1. Support the rear of the vehicle in a raised position.
2. Fully release the handbrake.
3. While rotating the tire and wheel assembly, turn the left hand eccentric adjustment nut counterclockwise and the right-hand eccentric adjustment nut clockwise until the brake shoes are tight against the drum and the wheel will no longer rotate.
4. Loosen the eccentric nuts by 1/8 of a turn, so that the wheel is just able to turn.
5. Push up the rubber sleeve on the handbrake lever until the locknut is visible.
6. Loosen the locknut.
7. Pull up on the handbrake lever for a distance of five notches. Measure the distance between the middle of the handle and propeller shaft tunnel. This distance should be approximately 4.5 ± 0.2 inches.
8. Tighten the adjustment nut until the wheels are locked, and retighten the locknut.
9. Release the handbrake. Make sure that the wheels turn freely when the handbrake is released.

Vehicles Equipped with Rear Disc Brakes

The procedure for adjusting the handbrake on vehicles equipped with rear disc brakes is similar to the procedure for adjusting the handbrake on vehicles equipped with rear drum brakes with one exception.

The mechanism for adjusting the brake shoes is a star-wheel type adjuster. Insert a screwdriver through the 0.6 inch hole, and turn the adjusting star-wheel until the brake disc can no longer be moved. Proceed as though adjusting the handbrake on vehicles equipped with rear drum brakes.

CHASSIS ELECTRICAL

Heater Assembly, Core and Blower

REMOVAL AND INSTALLATION

2002 (320i Similar)

1. Disconnect the battery ground.
2. Move the selector lever to the WARM position.
3. Drain the cooling system.
4. Loosen the hose clamp, and remove the heater core return hose.
5. Disconnect the heater hose between the hot water control valve and the engine.
6. Remove the package tray.
7. Remove outer tube casing.
8. Remove the lower center trim panel.
9. Remove the left side outer trim panel.
10. Remove the upper section of the steering tube casing.
11. Remove the heater control knobs.
12. Remove the heater control trim panel.
13. Remove the right side trim panel.
14. Disconnect the heater electrical lead.
15. Remove the heater housing retaining nuts.
16. Disconnect the left side distribution duct, and move the steering tube outer casing retaining bracket out of the way.
17. Remove the glove box lower trim panel.
18. Disconnect the left side distribution duct, and lift out the heater housing.
19. Remove the housing rivets.
20. Remove the housing clamps, and separate the housing halves.
21. Disconnect the bowden cable from the hot water control valve.
22. Remove the hot water control valve and hose from the water valve bracket on the heater housing.
23. Remove the rubber sleeves from the heater core inlet and outlet tubes.
24. Disconnect the electrical leads at the blower motor.
25. Disconnect the electrical leads at the blower resistor in the heater housing.
26. Open the blower motor support clamps, and remove the blower motor and fan as an assembly.
27. Install in the reverse order of removal.
28. Check operation of the heater controls. Adjust if necessary.

530i, 528i and 528e (630CSi and 633CSi Similar)

1. Remove the center tray and instrument panel trim to bottom right of tray.
2. Remove the glove box and remove heater controls at water valve and at air doors. Remove center console if equipped.

3. Disconnect the battery ground.
4. Push the selector lever to the WARM position.
5. Drain the coolant and remove the air conditioning evaporator:
   a. Drain the refrigerant slowly out of the low side Schrader® valve.
   b. Take off the no-drip tape and disconnect both refrigerent lines from the evaporator.

NOTE: Plug the refrigerant lines immediately to prevent moisture and contaminants from entering the system.

   c. Pull the temperature sensor out of the evaporator housing.
   d. Disconnect the evaporator/heater control electrical connector.
Vehicles built in September 1977 and later:
   a. Remove the right and left screw from the housing (from area where the housing meets the passenger compartment carpeting).
   b. Remove the floor pan to evaporator housing bracket. Lift the housing slightly and pull it from under the dash.
Vehicles built before September 1977:
   a. Remove the blower covers and remove seven screws from the blower case.
   b. Remove the air conditioner cover, disconnect electrical wires and pull the temperature sensor out of the evaporator housing.

--- CAUTION ---
Do not bend the temperature sensor or it will have to be replaced.
---

   c. Disconnect the blower wires and the blower resistor wire. Lift the evaporator slightly and pull the adapter and evaporator from under the dash.
6. Disconnect the heater hoses from the heater core, and remove the rubber seal.
7. Remove the lower instrument panel center trim.
8. Disconnect the heater controls at the instrument panel.
9. Disconnect the control shafts at the joints.
10. Disconnect the multiple electrical connector at the heater.
11. Remove the instrument panel center cover.
12. Working from inside the engine

compartment, remove the upper section of the fire shield.
13. Remove the heater assembly retaining nuts, and lift out the heater.
14. Open the heater housing clips, and separate the housing halves and remove the heater core.
15. Disconnect the electrical leads at the blower motor, and remove the motor.
16. Install in the reverse order of removal.

733i

1. Drain the coolant from the system.
2. Discharge the refrigerant from the air conditioner.
3. Remove the instrument trim panel.
4. Remove the cowl fresh air grille.
5. Remove the heater assembly cover attaching screws, and remove the cover.
6. Disconnect the heater hoses at the heater core.
7. Disconnect the vacuum lines at the heater.
8. Bend open the heater duct mounting clamp.
9. Disconnect the central electrical lead.
10. Pull the duct cover downward, and remove it.
11. Remove the center strut attaching bolts (4).
12. Remove the insulation from the refrigerant lines.
13. Disconnect the refrigerant lines from the evaporator.
14. Disconnect the evaporator drain tube.
15. Remove the heater assembly retaining bolts, remove the heater and the heater core.
16. Install in the reverse order of removal.

3.0CSi

1. Drain the coolant from the system.
2. Disconnect the heater hoses from the heater core, and remove the rubber seal.
3. Remove the fresh air outlet grille cover.
Coupe only:
   a. Remove the heater control cover.
   b. Disconnect the air distribution hoses from the discharge nozzles.
   c. Remove the intermediate distribution duct.

Heater assembly—530i

4. Remove the buttons from the control levers.

5. Remove the threaded knobs for the left instrument panel trim strip.

6. Remove the rear switch plate.

7. Remove the front switch plate.

8. Remove the heater retaining nuts.

9. Tilt the heater and switch plate inwards, and remove the heater.

10. Remove the heater cover plate and remove the heater core.

11. Remove the blower motor mesh grid.

12. Disconnect the electrical leads at the blower motor.

13. Remove the blower motor attaching screws, and lift out the blower motor.

14. Remove the blower motor-to-mounting retaining clips, and remove the blower motor and fan assembly.

15. Install in the reverse order of removal.

Radio

REMOVAL AND INSTALLATION

3.0CSi and 2002

1. Disconnect negative battery terminal.

2. Remove screws from both sides of the radio housing. On model 2002 remove the lower steering column shroud.

3. Detach antenna wire, ground wire, speaker wire and radio power source.

4. Installation is the reverse of removal.

530i, 528i and 528e (Others Similar)

1. Pull off the radio knobs and ornamental rings.

2. Push up on spring catches and remove them from the control shafts. Remove the radio mask.

3. Remove the bolts from supports on both sides of the radio.

4. Disconnect the automatic antenna lead, the antenna, the right and left speaker wires and the power supply.

5. Installation is the reverse of removal.

Windshield Wiper Motor

The electric wiper motor assembly is located under the engine hood, at the top of the cowl panel. A few models have covers over the wiper motor assembly, while others have the motors exposed. Link rods operate the left and right wiper pivot assemblies from a drive crank bolted to the wiper motor output shaft.

REMOVAL AND INSTALLATION

2002

1. Remove the drive crank retaining nut and washer.

2. Remove the wiper motor retaining screws.

3. Remove the electrical connector and remove the wiper motor from the vehicle.

4. The installation is in the reverse of the removal procedure.

3.0CSi

1. Remove the cover for the heater unit on the cowl panel (except coupes).

2. Remove the crank arm retaining nut and washer.

3. Remove the wiper motor retaining screws, tilt the motor downward and remove.

4. Disconnect the electrical contact plug from the wiper motor.

5. The installation is in the reverse of the removal procedure.

NOTE: The complete wiper motor, pivot assemblies and linkage can be removed as a unit, if necessary.

320i, 530i, 528i, 528e, 630CSi and 633CSi

1. Remove the cowl cover to expose the wiper motor (320i and 530i).

2. Disconnect the wiper motor crank arm from the motor output shaft.

3. Remove the motor retaining screws and disconnect the electrical connector.

4. Remove the wiper motor from the vehicle.

5. Reverse the procedure to install the motor.

733i

1. Remove the cowl fresh air intake grill and tilt rearward.

2. Remove the cover from the windshield wiper motor and remove the electrical plugs.

3. Remove the left and right wiper arms. Loosen the left and right pivot bearings.

4. Turn the rubber pad at the motor, counterclockwise and disconnect the right wiper linkage.

5. Remove the motor bracket retaining screws. Separate the spacers and remove the wiper motor assembly.

NOTE: Do not lose the shims.

6. The wiper motor can be removed from the bracket after the removal.

7. Reverse the removal procedure to install.

Windshield Wiper Switch

REMOVAL AND INSTALLATION

The wiper switch is located on the steering column and in most cases the steering wheel will have to be removed, along with the lower steering column trim panels, to gain access to the switch.

After the retaining screws and electrical connectors are removed, the switch can be lifted from the plate of the steering column.

— CAUTION —
To avoid possible electrical short-circuits, the negative battery cable should be removed before the repairs are attempted.

Windshield Wiper Motor

REMOVAL AND INSTALLATION

530i, 528i and 528e (Others Similar)

1. Lift the hood and remove the rubber gasket from the top of the engine cowl.

2. Remove the six motor and linkage screws across the top area of the engine cowl.

3. Remove the wiper motor linkage nut at the motor and remove the linkage.

4. Disconnect the wiper motor electrical plug.

5. Remove the three motor to bracket retaining screws and lift out the motor.

6. Installation is the reverse of removal.

Windshield Washer Motor

The windshield washer motor is attached to the washer reservoir and controlled from the wiper switch. A double motor is present on some models to pump the washer solution to both the windshield washers and to the headlamp cleaners.

To remove the washer pump, the reservoir should be removed from the vehicle to avoid damage to the reservoir.

A delaying relay is used on some models, to control the spraying of the washer solution for a period of five seconds, stop briefly and then recycle.

Ignition Switch

REMOVAL AND INSTALLATION

2002

1. Disconnect the negative battery cable.

2. Remove the lower center fascia trim panel.

3. Turn the ignition switch to the "HALT" (stop) position.

4. Remove the machine screws from the ignition/starter switch and disconnect the electrical leads.

5. Remove the switch from the steering column side bracket.

6. Reverse the removal procedure to install the switch. During the installation, the arrow must point to the ball with the switch in the "HALT" (stop) position and the locating lug in the slot of the steering lock.

All Others

1. Remove the negative battery cable.

2. Remove the lower steering housing cover.

3. Remove the left lower center instrument trim panel, if necessary.

4. Align the switch to housing marks, remove the switch retaining screw and pull the switch outward and away from the steering column.

5. Disconnect the electrical wiring connectors.

6. Reverse the removal procedure to install the ignition switch. Be sure the marks are aligned.

Instrument Cluster

REMOVAL AND INSTALLATION

2002

1. Disconnect the negative battery cable.

2. Remove the lower steering column trim panel.

3. Remove the lower center instrument trim panel.

4. Remove the knurled nuts from the rear of the instrument cluster.

5. Disconnect the speedometer cable from the cluster.

6. Remove the cluster from the dash and remove the wire connector plug.

7. The installation is in the reverse of the removal procedure.

3.0CSi

1. Disconnect the negative battery cable.

2. Remove the instrument panel trim cover.

3. Remove the radio speaker grill and unscrew the cluster retaining screw.

4. Remove the speedometer cable and remove the electrical wire connectors.

5. Remove the instrument cluster from the dash.

6. Reverse the removal procedure to install the cluster.

Typical instrument panel removal and installation numbers indicate screw locations

320i

1. Disconnect the negative battery cable.

2. Remove the steering wheel assembly.

3. Remove the bottom center instrument trim panel.

4. Disconnect the speedometer cable, loosen the knurled nut and pull the instrument assembly outward.

5. Remove the electrical plugs and wires.

6. Remove the instrument cluster from the dash.

7. Reverse the removal procedure to install.

530i, 528i and 528e

1. Remove the negative battery cable.

2. Remove the lower instrument trim panel.

3. Disconnect the speedometer cable.

4. Loosen the knurled nuts on the cluster back.

5. Loosen the steering column to dash screws.

6. Pull the instrument cluster outward and remove the electrical wires and connectors.

7. Remove the cluster from the dash panel.

8. Reverse the removal procedure to install the cluster.

630CSi and 633CSi

1. Disconnect the negative battery cable.

2. Remove the steering wheel assembly.

3. Remove the bottom center instrument trim panel.

4. Remove the cover from the "INQUIRY" unit.

5. Remove the three retaining screws and remove the "INQUIRY" printed circuit board.

6. Remove the light switch, leaving the wiring connected.

7. Remove the left air control knob and remove the bezel cover.

8. Remove the fog lamp switch and leave the wiring attached.

9. Remove the screws from the instrument cluster and loosen the steering column control base screws.

10. Disconnect the speedometer cable.

11. Push downward on the upper section casing and the steering column, so that the instrument cluster can be removed at an angle. Disconnect the electrical wiring and connectors.

12. Reverse the removal procedure to install the instrument cluster.

733i

1. Remove the negative battery cable from the battery post.

2. Remove the instrument panel trim section at the left bottom of the dash.

3. Remove the upper bezel retaining screws.

4. Loosen the steering column control and pull the steering housing all the way out.

5. Pull the instrument cluster outward, remove the electrical wires and plugs, after removal of the speedometer cable.

6. Turn the cluster assembly towards the right rear and pull it away from the dash.

7. The installation is in the reverse of the removal procedure.

Fuse Box Locations

The fuse box is located behind the left glove box door on the model 3.0CSi and under the engine hood on the left side, near the upper strut housing or near the battery, on the remaining models.

Various relays are also mounted on the fuse box for easy accessibility.

Capri

SERIAL NUMBER IDENTIFICATION

Engine

NOTE: Engine type can be determined by using the Vehicle Identification Plate.

Vehicle

The vehicle identification plate is located on the right-side front fender apron in the engine compartment. This plate gives details of the engine, axle, body and transmission. The vehicle identification number is also visible through the driver's side of the windshield.

ENGINE IDENTIFICATION

No. of Cylinders	Displacement (cc)	Type	Engine Model Code
4	2300	OHC	YA
6	2800	OHV	PX

A. Body Type
 ECP—three door hatchback

B. Version
 P—decor option
 D—standard
 T—Ghia

C. Vehicle number
 GAECPA19517
 G—built in Germany
 A—Cologne assembly plant
 EC—model type
 PA—assembly code
  first letter—year; second letter—month
 Sequence number—a five digit code ranging from 00001-99999

D. Drive code
 I—left hand drive

E. Engine code
 YA-2300
 PX-2800

F. Transmission code
 B—4sp.
 D—automatic

G. Rear axle code
 S—3.44:1
 R—3.22:1
 L—3.09:1

H. Paint code
 B5—White 691
 T5—Yellow 779
 J5—Orange 913
 05—Dk. red 979
 35—Silver met. 888
 45—Bronze met. 884B
 15—Med. blue met. 859
 55—Lt. green met. 924

I. Trim code
 AA—black vinyl
 LA—saddle vinyl
 KA—lt. tan vinyl
 AI—black cloth
 LI—saddle cloth
 KI—lt. tan cloth

Vehicle I.D. plate—1976–77

GENERAL ENGINE SPECIFICATIONS

Year/ Model	Engine Displacement cu. in. (cc)	Carburetor Type	Horsepower @ rpm	Torque @ rpm (ft. lbs.)	Bore x Stroke (in.)	Compression Ratio	Oil Pressure @ rpm (psi)
'76–'77 Capri II	140 (2300)	Motorcraft 2V	88 @ 5000	116 @ 2600	3.781 × 3.126	8.4:1	50 @ 2000
'76–'77 Capri II	170 (2800)	Motorcraft 2V	105 @ 4600	140 @ 3200	3.660 × 2.700	8.2:1	40 @ 1500

TUNE-UP SPECIFICATIONS

Year/ Model	Engine Displacement (cc)	Spark Plugs Type	Gap (in.)	Distributor Point Dwell (deg)	Point Gap (in.)	Ignition Timing (deg)④ MT	AT	Intake Valve Opens (deg)	Fuel Pump Pressure (psi)	Compression Press. (psi)	Idle Speed (rpm) MT	AT	Valve Clearance (in.)② In	Ex
'76–'77 Capri II	2300	③	③	Electronic		10B	10B	22B	3½–4½	①	③	③	Hydraulic	
'76–'77 Capri II	2800	③	③	Electronic		8B	10B	20B	3½–4½	①	③	③	0.014	0.016

NOTE: The underhood specifications sticker often reflects tune-up specification changes made in production. Sticker figures must be used if they disagree with those in this chart.

① Lowest 75 per cent of the highest
② Cold
③ See engine compartment sticker
④ With the vacuum lines disconnected and plugged
MT Manual transmission
AT Automatic transmission
—Not applicable

FIRING ORDER

2300 cc engine (1-3-4-2)

2800 cc engine (1-4-2-5-3-6)—circles are latch positions on 1976 models, squares are latch positions on 1977 models

CAPACITIES

Year/ Model	Engine Displacement Cu. In. (cc)	Engine Crankcase Refill After Draining (qt) With filter	Without filter	Transmission Refill After Draining (pt) Manual 4 speed	Automatic (total cap.) C3, C4	Borg Warner	Differential (pt)	Fuel Tank (gal)	Cooling (qt)
'76–'77 Capri II	140 (2300)	5	4	2.8	16	—	2.3	15	7.6
'76–'77 Capri II	170 (2800)	5	4.5	2.8	16	—	2.3	15	8.5

—Not applicable

CRANKSHAFT AND CONNECTING ROD SPECIFICATIONS

(All measurements are given in inches)

Year/ Model	Engine Displacement cu. in. (cc)	Crankshaft				Connecting Rod		
		Main Brg Journal Dia	Main Brg Oil Clearance	Shaft End-Play	Thrust on No.	Journal Diameter	Oil Clearance	Side Clearance
'76–'77 Capri II	140 (2300)	2.3982–2.3990	0.0008–0.0026	0.004–0.008	3	2.0465–2.0472	0.0008–0.0015	0.004–0.011
'76–'77 Capri II	170 (2800)	2.2433–2.2441	0.0006–0.0019	0.004–0.008	3	2.1252–2.1260	0.0006–0.0021	0.004–0.011

VALVE SPECIFICATIONS

Year/ Model	Engine Displacement cu. in. (cc)	Seat Angle (deg)	Face Angle (deg)	Spring Test Pressure (lbs @ in.)	Spring Installed Height (in.)	Stem To Guide Clearance (in.)		Stem Diameter (in.)	
						Intake	Exhaust	Intake	Exhaust
'76–'77 Capri II	140 (2300)	45	44	75 @ 1.56	1.531	0.0010–0.0027	0.0015–0.0032	0.3416–0.3423	0.3411–0.3418
'76–'77 Capri II	170 (2800)	45	44	71 @ 1.59	1.594	0.0008–0.0025	0.0018–0.0035	0.3158–0.3167	0.3149–0.3157

PISTON AND RING SPECIFICATIONS

(All measurements in inches)

Year/ Model	Engine Displacement Cu. In. (cc)	Piston Clearance	Ring Gap			Ring Side Clearance		
			Top Compression	Bottom Compression	Oil Control	Top Compression	Bottom Compression	Oil Control
'76–'77 Capri II	140 (2300)	0.001–0.002	0.010–0.020	0.010–0.020	0.015–0.055	0.0020–0.0040	0.0020–0.0040	SNUG
'76–'77 Capri II	170 (2800)	0.0011–0.0019	0.015–0.023	0.015–0.023	0.015–0.055	0.0020–0.0033	0.0020–0.0033	SNUG

TORQUE SPECIFICATIONS

(All readings in ft. lbs)

Year/ Model	Engine Displacement Cu. In. (cc)	Cylinder Head Bolts	Rod Bearing Bolts	Main Bearing Bolts	Crankshaft Bolt	Flywheel-to-Crankshaft Bolts	Manifolds	
							Intake	Exhaust
'76–'77 Capri II	140 (2300)	80–90	30–36	80–90	80–114	54–64	14–21	16–23
'76–'77 Capri II	170 (2800)	65–80	21–25	65–75	92–103②	47–52	15–18①	16–23

① Stud: 10–12
② Pulley: 18–25

CYLINDER HEAD
TORQUE SEQUENCES

2300 cc engine

2800 cc engine

BATTERY AND STARTER SPECIFICATIONS
(All cars use 12 volt, negative ground electrical systems)

Year	Model	Battery Amp Hour Capacity	Lock Test			Starter No Load Test			Brush Spring Tension (oz)	Min. Brush Length (in.)
			Amps	Volts	Torque (ft. lbs.)	Amps	Volts	rpm		
'76–'77	All	66①	Not Recommended			54	N.A.	N.A.	42	0.375

① 4 cyl. w/man. trans.: 55

BRAKE SPECIFICATIONS
(All measurements given are (in.) unless noted)

Year	Model	Lug Nut Torque (ft. lb.)	Master Cylinder Bore	Brake Disc		Brake Drum			Minimum Lining Thickness	
				Minimum Thickness	Maximum Run-Out	Diameter	Max. Machine O/S	Max. Wear Limit	Front	Rear
'76–'77	All	50–55①	0.813	0.45	0.0035	9.0	9.05	9.06	⅛	1/32 above rivets

NOTE: Minimum lining thickness is as recommended by the manufacturer. Due to variations in state inspection regulations, the minimum allowable thickness may be different than recommended by the manufacturer.

① Aluminum wheels 90–100 ft. lbs.

ALTERNATOR AND REGULATOR SPECIFICATIONS

Year	Model	Alternator			Regulator						
		Part No. or Manufacturer	Field Current @ 12v	Output (amps)	Part No. or Manufacturer	Field Relay			Regulator		
						Air Gap (in.)	Point Gap (in.)	Volts to Close	Air Gap (in.)	Point Gap (in.)	Volts @ 75°
'76–'77	All	Bosch K-1	—	35①	—	——— Not adjustable ———					13.7–14.4

① 55 Amps w/AC

WHEEL ALIGNMENT

Year	Caster (deg)	Camber (deg)	Toe-In (in)	King Pin Inclination (deg)
'76–'77	1P to 2¼P	¾P to 2¼P	0 to 9/32	7½ to 8½

N Negative
P Postive

TUNE-UP PROCEDURES

Ignition Timing

Set the dwell angle before setting the timing. Disconnect and plug the vacuum lines. Locate the timing mark on the pulley and the pointer on the engine block. Clean the pointer and the timing mark. Mark the correct timing position on the pulley with a piece of chalk or paint (see the ''Tune-up Specifications'' chart). Install a timing light and set the idle at 600 rpm. Loosen the distributor locknut at the base of the distributor. Adjust the ignition timing to the proper specifications by turning the distributor (align the pointer and the mark). Turn the distributor clockwise to advance timing. Make sure that the locknut is retightened and the vacuum lines are reconnected.

Timing marks—2800 cc engine

Timing marks 2300 cc engine

Distributor rotor position for static timing

Electronic ignition distributor

Electronic ignition system

Breakerless Ignition System—Capri II

There are no points or condenser to replace, and no adjustments to be made other than timing. An occasional check of the rotor and cap contacts for excessive burning and pitting should be performed.

Ignition timing can be performed in the same manner as with older point type systems.

Electronic ignition tachometer connections

Valve Lash Adjustment

VALVE ARRANGEMENT

2300 cc Engines

Front
E-I-E-I-E-I-E-I

2800 cc Engine

Right Bank I-E-I-E-E-I
Front
Left Bank I-E-E-I-E-I

2300 cc Engine

This engine employs hydraulic valve lifters. No periodic adjustment is necessary. To check valve lash: use the special tool available from Ford, or its equivalent and depress the cam follower until the lash adjuster is completely collapsed. Insert the proper feeler gauge (.008 int.; .010 exh) between the base circle of the cam and the follower. This should be done when the camshaft is in a position with the base circle of the lobe facing the follower. If the clearance is excessive, remove the follower and check for damage. If the follower is okay, check the spring assembled height to make sure the valve is not sticking. If the spring height is okay, check the camshaft lobe for excessive wear.

Replace damaged or worn parts as necessary.

2800 cc Engine

If some component of the valve system is replaced, the valves must be set cold before starting the engine. If the valves are set for a tune-up, adjust them hot and running. When setting the valves of the cold engine, rotate the engine so that No. 1 cylinder is

Checking hydraulic valve lash on the 2300 cc engine

Valve lash adjustment—2800 cc engine

at top dead center (TDC). Remove the valve covers. Both valves should be closed and the timing pointer and pulley mark aligned. Adjust the valves in the rest of the cylinders in firing order (1-4-2-5-3-6). This can be done by turning the crankshaft 120 degrees clockwise each time. After two full revolutions, each cylinder will have been at TDC once. To adjust the valves when the engine is hot, run the engine until it reaches operating temperature. With the engine running at idle speed, insert a feeler gauge between the valve stem and rocker arm and adjust the valve. After adjusting each valve recheck the valve clearance.

Carburetor

IDLE SPEED AND MIXTURE ADJUSTMENT

One Barrel Carburetor

Single-barrel carburetors should be adjusted in the following manner:
1. Remove the air cleaner.
2. Connect a tachometer to the engine.
3. Allow the engine to run until it reaches operating temperature.
4. Disconnect the throttle solenoid lead from the wiring harness. Make sure the idle limiter cap is against the maximum rich stop.
5. Disconnect the hose which runs from the carburetor to the decel valve and plug the decel valve fitting.

6. Turn the curb idle adjusting screw to set the engine at the lower specified idle speed (see the "Tune-Up Specifications" chart). It may be necessary to use the adjusting screw on the throttle solenoid as well as the curb idle screw to achieve the proper idle.
7. Reconnect the throttle solenoid. Set the higher specified idle speed using the solenoid plunger.
8. Move the throttle lever to allow the solenoid plunger to extend.
9. Turn the idle mixture screw to the right or left to obtain the smoothest idle.
10. Reconnect the decel valve hose and the air cleaner.

Two Barrel Carburetors

Use the following procedure for two-barrel carburetors:
1. Remove the air cleaner.
2. Connect a tachometer.
3. Allow the engine to run until it reaches operating temperature.
4. Check the ignition timing.
5. Disconnect the hose which runs from the carburetor to the decel valve and plug the decel valve fitting. Plug the vacuum line at the EGR valve. Remove the spark delay valve and connect the vacuum line to the distributor. On the 1976–77 V6, check that hot idle compensator bimetallic strip is cool and compensator plug seated. The compensator is on the rear of the carburetor.

NOTE: The factory-recommended mixture adjustment procedure for 1976–77 models requires special apparatus to temporarily enrich the mixture with propane.

6. Place the car in Drive, if the car is equipped with an automatic transmission, and in neutral if it has a manual transmission.
7. Set the idle speed to the speed listed in the "Tune-Up Specifications" chart by using the curb idle screw. This reading must be taken with the air cleaner connected. If the carburetor has a throttle solenoid, refer to the one-barrel procedure for adjustment.

Setting the curb idle—2800 cc engine

Throttle solenoid adjustment and solenoid lead disconnected

Adjust the throttle lever screw, not the solenoid, on the 2300 engine.
8. Turn the idle mixture screw to the right or left to obtain the smoothest idle. A satisfactory idle should be obtainable without removing the plastic limiter cap.

ENGINE ELECTRICAL

Distributor

REMOVAL AND INSTALLATION

The distributor is located on the left side of the 2300 cc engines, and at the rear of the V6 engine.

Before removing the distributor, match mark the distributor body and engine block with chalk or paint. Remove the distributor cap and mark the distributor body to show the direction in which the rotor is pointing. This will ensure correct distributor installation and timing.

Remove the vacuum lines and the locknut and retainer. Do not crank the engine while the distributor is removed. Install the distributor by aligning the rotor marks and the distributor marks. The cam will turn slightly to the left or right, depending on the engine. To compensate for this, determine the direction that the cam turns and align the rotor slightly before the mark, then insert the distributor. Reconnect the wires and locknut. Attach a timing light and set the ignition timing to the proper specification.

If the engine has been turned while the distributor was out, install in the following manner. Find top dead center (TDC) of the compression stroke of the number one (No. 1) cylinder. The exact location of TDC can be found by aligning the timing mark on the crankshaft pulley with the pointer on the engine block. Install the distributor so the rotor is pointing to the No. 1 spark plug wire on the distributor cap and the points are just opening. Again, use a timing light to set the timing to the proper specifications.

Alternator

ALTERNATOR PRECAUTIONS

When servicing an alternator or a circuit incorporating one, the following precautions should be observed:

1. The alternator is used on a negative ground system only.
2. When installing a battery, connect the positive cable first, then connect the negative (ground) cable.
3. Never disconnect the battery while the engine is running.
4. Remove the molded connections from the alternator when you are welding.
5. Never attempt to polarize the alternator.

REMOVAL AND INSTALLATION

2300 cc Engine

1. Disconnect the negative (ground) battery cable.
2. Remove the clip which holds the wire plug connector to the rear of the alternator, and disconnect the wiring plug.
3. Disconnect the regulator-to-alternator wiring at the alternator.

4. Disconnect the heater hose bracket from the alternator.
5. Loosen the mounting bolts.
6. Remove the mounting bolts and the alternator.
7. Position the alternator and install the mounting bolts.
8. Install the fan belt and adjust it to ½ in. free-play.
9. Connect the heater hose bracket to the alternator.
10. Connect the plug and the clip at the rear of the alternator.
11. Connect the battery.

2800 cc Engine

1. Disconnect the negative (ground) cable from the battery.
2. Remove the connectors at the rear of the alternator.
3. Remove the air cleaner and exhaust manifold heat duct.
4. Remove the adjusting bolt from the rear of the alternator.
5. Remove the mounting bolts. Slide the alternator back and away from the mounting bracket and lift it out between the battery and the exhaust manifold.
6. Position the alternator to the mounting bracket and install the mounting bolts.
7. Install the fan belt and adjust it to ½ in. free-play.
8. Connect the multiple connectors to the rear of the alternator.
9. Install the heat duct and the air cleaner.
10. Connect the battery.

FAN BELT TENSION ADJUSTMENT

The fan belt free movement should be ½ in. measured midway between the water pump pulley and the alternator. To adjust

the fan belt, loosen the front and rear lower alternator mounting bolts and the front adjusting bolt. Move the alternator to give the belt the correct tension. Retighten the adjusting bolt, then the mounting bolts.

Voltage Regulator

The regulator is located on the right fender apron. It is not adjustable and if it does not function properly it should be replaced.

REMOVAL AND INSTALLATION

1. Unplug the wiring from the alternator to the regulator.
2. Remove the regulator attaching screws and remove the regulator.
3. Position the new regulator on the fender apron and install the mounting bolts.
4. Reconnect the wiring plug to the regulator.

Starter

REMOVAL AND INSTALLATION

2300 cc Engine

1. Disconnect the battery ground cable.
2. Disconnect the wires at the solenoid.
3. Remove the attaching screws and then the starter.
4. Reverse the procedure to install the starter.

2800 cc Engine

1. Disconnect the battery ground cable.

Exploded view of the Bosch alternator

Exploded view of the Bosch starter

2. Jack up the front of the car, block the rear wheels, and support the car with jackstands.

3. Disconnect the battery cable and the two push-on wire connectors from the solenoid.

4. Remove the mounting bolts and the starter.

5. Reverse the procedures to install the starter.

STARTER DRIVE REPLACEMENT

1. Remove the starter from the engine.

2. Detach the field winding cable and remove the solenoid.

3. Remove the engaging lever guide screw.

4. Remove the end plate through bolts.

5. Remove the drive end plate.

6. Press the stop-ring toward the pinion.

7. Remove the snap-ring.

8. Remove the stop-ring and the starter drive gear.

9. Put silicone grease on the armature

Thrust ring installation

shaft thread and the starter drive gear engaging ring. Install the stop-ring and snap-ring on the armature shaft.

10. Press the snap-ring in the groove of the shaft.

11. Press on the stop-ring.

12. Install the engaging lever on the engaging ring and install the drive end plate.

13. Attach the engaging fork to the guide screw.

14. Install the steel washer, and then the rubber washer, with the tap pointing toward the armature.

15. Install the housing and rubber washer.

16. Insert the end plate bolts.

17. Hook the solenoid to the engaging fork and attach the screws.

18. Connect the field winding cable.

STARTER SOLENOID REPLACEMENT

1. Remove the starter.

2. Disconnect the field winding cable from the solenoid.

3. Unscrew the mounting bolts and remove the solenoid.

4. Link the new solenoid to the engaging lever and install the two screws.

5. Connect the field winding cable to the solenoid.

6. Seal the joints and screw heads with lacquer.

ENGINE MECHANICAL

Design

2300 cc ENGINE

The 4 cylinder 2300 cc overhead cam engine is of lightweight iron construction. The crankshaft is supported on five main bearings and the camshaft by four. Main, connecting rod, camshaft and auxiliary shaft bearings are all replaceable.

The camshaft is driven from the crankshaft by a cogged belt, which also operates the auxiliary shaft, and thusly the oil pump, fuel pump and distributor. Belt tension is maintained by a pre-loaded and locked idler pulley bearing on the outside of the belt.

Water pump and fan are separately driven from the crankshaft by a conventional V-belt which also drives the alternator.

Hydraulic adjusters are used on the valve train. These units are placed at the fulcrum point of the cam followers. Their action is similar to lifters in an OHV engine. The head is drilled to supply oil to these units.

2800 cc ENGINE

The 2800 cc engine is a V6 overhead valve design. The cylinder heads and engine block are made of cast iron. Four main bearings support the crankshaft. The distributor and the oil pump are driven by an eccentric at the front of the camshaft. The connecting rods are forged steel with replaceable copper-lead alloy insert bearings. The intake manifold is made from aluminum and has individual passages to the openings in the cylinder heads. The V6 has a full pressure lubrication system fed by a rotor-type oil pump mounted at the rear of the crankcase.

Engine Cautions

Metric and standard thread bolts are mixed throughout the engine and transmission. Since some of the metric threads are very similar to the standard threads, caution should be used when installing or removing bolts.

Metric bolts and screws will have the letters "M" or "ISOM" embossed on the head. Metric nuts will have the letter "M" on the sides.

If any repair operation requires the removal of any component of the air conditioning system, do not disconnect any of the lines of the system. If it is impossible to move the component out of the way with the lines attached, have the air conditioning system evacuated by a trained serviceman.

When installing nuts or bolts (refer to the "Torque Specifications" chart), oil the threads with lightweight engine oil. Do not oil threads that require oil-resistant or water-resistant sealers.

Engine Removal and Installation

2300 cc ENGINES

NOTE: If the engine has the thermactor air pump system, any interfering components will have to be removed.

1. Remove the hood.
2. Remove the lower splash shield from the radiator and drain the coolant.
3. Remove the air cleaner assembly.
4. Disconnect the battery.
5. Remove the upper radiator shield, disconnect the upper and lower radiator hoses, and remove the radiator.
6. Disconnect the heater hoses from the water pump and the carburetor choke fitting.
7. Disconnect the alternator wiring.
8. Disconnect the accelerator cable from the carburetor. Disconnect the automatic transmission kickdown cable.
9. Disconnect the flexible fuel line at the fuel tank line and plug the fuel tank line.
10. Disconnect the coil wires.
11. Disconnect the oil pressure and the water temperature sending unit wires at the sending units.
12. Jack up the front of the car and support it with jackstands.
13. Remove the starter motor.
14. Disconnect the muffler pipe at the exhaust manifold.
15. Remove the flywheel or converter housing lower front cover. On vehicles with automatic transmissions, disconnect the converter from the flexplate. Remove the converter housing-to-cylinder block lower attaching screws.
16. Mark the flywheel and torque converter so they can be correctly mated during installation.
17. Support the transmission.
18. Disconnect the motor mounts at the underbody bracket.
19. Lower the car to the ground.
20. Attach a chain hoist and remove the engine.
To install:
21. Place a new gasket over the exhaust inlet pipe.
22. Lower the engine into the engine compartment.
23. Line up the dowel pins on the rear face of the cylinder block with the corresponding holes in the flywheel or converter housing. Make sure that the studs in the exhaust manifold are aligned with the holes in the muffler inlet pipe. Line up the engine mount studs.
24. On a vehicle with a manual transmission, start the transmission shaft into the clutch disc. If the engine hangs up after the shaft enters, turn the crankshaft slowly until the shaft spline meshes with the clutch disc splines.
25. Install the flywheel or converter housing upper attaching screws.
26. Remove the chain hoist.
27. Remove the transmission support.
28. Jack up the front of the car and support it with jackstands.
29. Install the flywheel or converter lower attaching capscrews.
30. On a vehicle with an automatic transmission, install the converter-to-flexplate capscrews and torque them to the proper specifications.
31. Install the flywheel converter housing front cover.
32. Install the engine mounts.
33. Install the starter and wires.
34. Install the exhaust manifold-to-muffler inlet pipe retaining nuts.
35. Lower the car to the ground.
36. Connect the flexible fuel line to the fuel tank line.
37. Connect the oil pressure and temperature sending unit wires.
38. Connect the coil wires and the battery.
39. Install the bellcrank assembly to the intake manifold and connect the accelerator cable to the bellcrank assembly.
40. Connect the heater hose to the water pump and choke housing.
41. Connect the alternator wires.
42. Install the radiator and connect the hoses.
43. Fill the crankcase with oil.
44. Refill the cooling system.
45. Run the engine, check for leaks, and adjust any applicable components.
46. Install the upper and lower radiator shields.
47. Install the air cleaner assembly and hood.

2800 cc ENGINE

NOTE: If the engine has the thermactor air pump system, any interfering components will have to be removed.

1. Remove the hood.
2. Disconnect the battery and drain the cooling system.
3. Remove the air cleaner assembly and remove the radiator hoses.
4. Remove the fan shroud attaching bolts and position the shroud over the fan. Remove the radiator and shroud.
5. Remove the alternator ground wire.
6. Disconnect the fuel line from the fuel pump and plug the fuel tank line.
7. Disconnect the accelerator linkage at the carburetor and intake manifold. Disconnect the transmission downshift linkage if so equipped.
8. Disconnect the coil wires and the brake booster lines.
9. Jack up the front of the car and support it with jackstands.
10. Disconnect the muffler inlet pipes at the exhaust manifold.
11. Remove the starter.
12. Disconnect the engine from the motor mounts.
13. If equipped with an automatic transmission, remove the converter inspection cover and disconnect the flywheel from the converter. Remove the downshift rod.
14. Remove the converter housing-to-engine block bolts and the adaptor plate-to-converter housing bolt.
On vehicles equipped with manual transmissions, remove the clutch linkage and remove the bell housing-to-engine block bolts.
15. Support the transmission.
16. Install a chain hoist and remove the engine.
To install:
17. Lower the engine into the compartment.
18. Start the transmission shaft into the clutch disc. If the engine hangs up, turn the crankshaft until the gear meshes. On a vehicle with an automatic transmission, start the converter pilot into the crankshaft.
19. Install the bell housing or converter housing upper bolts, making sure that the dowel pins in the cylinder block engage the flywheel housing. Remove the transmission support.
20. Remove the hoist.
21. On vehicles with an automatic transmission, position the downshift cable on the transmission and engine.
22. Jack up the car and support it with stands.
23. On a vehicle with an automatic transmission, position the transmission linkage bracket and install the remaining converter housing bolts. Install the adaptor plate-to-converter housing bolt. Install the converter-to-flywheel nuts and install the inspection cover.
On a vehicle with a manual transmission, remove the pilot studs, and then install the lower bell housing bolts, and connect the clutch linkage to the engine block.
24. Install the starter and connect the wires.
25. Connect the muffler inlet pipes at the exhaust manifold.
26. Install the front motor mounts.
27. Lower the car to the ground.
28. Install the wires to the coil, and connect the wires to the temperature sending unit and the oil pressure sending unit. Connect the brake booster lines.
29. Install the accelerator linkage and connect the downshift rod if so equipped. Connect the vacuum lines. Connect the fuel tank line at the fuel pump.
30. Connect the ground wire at the cyl-

inder block. Install the heater hoses at the water pump and cylinder block.

31. Install the alternator and bracket. Connect the alternator ground wire to the cylinder block. Install the fan belts and adjust them to the proper specifications.

32. Position the fan shroud over the fan. Install the radiator and connect the hoses. Install the fan shroud attaching bolts.

33. Refill the cooling system. Fill the crankcase with oil. Adjust the transmission downshift linkage if so equipped.

34. Run the engine and check for leaks.

35. Install the air cleaner assembly and adjust any applicable components.

36. Install the hood.

Cylinder Head

NOTE: To prevent distortion or warping of the cylinder head, allow the engine to cool completely before removing the head bolts.

REMOVAL AND INSTALLATION

2300 cc Engines

1. Drain the cooling system.
2. Remove the air cleaner assembly.
3. Remove the valve cover.
4. Remove the exhaust manifold (see the "Exhaust Manifold Removal" procedures).
5. Remove the intake manifold, carburetor, and the decel valve as an assembly (see the "Intake Manifold Removal" procedures).
6. Remove the camshaft drive belt cover. Note the location of the belt cover attaching bolts that have rubber grommets.
7. Loosen the drive belt tensioner and remove the drive belt.
8. Remove the water outlet elbow from the cylinder head with the hose attached.
9. Using an Allen socket, remove the cylinder head bolts (this tool is available at automotive stores and parts houses).
10. Lift the cylinder head and camshaft assembly from the engine.
11. Remove all the gasket material and carbon from the top of the engine block and pistons and from the bottom of the cylinder head.
12. Place a new cylinder head gasket on the engine block and position the cylinder head on the engine.

NOTE: If you encounter difficulty in positioning the cylinder head on the engine block, it may be necessary to install guide studs in the engine block to correctly align the head on the block.

13. Tighten the head bolts in sequence, and in steps to 80–90 ft. lbs. with a torque wrench.
14. Install the camshaft drive belt (see the "Camshaft Drive Belt Installation" procedures in the following sections).

15. Install the camshaft drive belt cover with its attaching bolts. Make sure that the rubber grommets are installed on the bolts. Tighten them to 6–13 ft. lbs.
16. Install the water outlet elbow and a new gasket.
17. Install the intake and exhaust manifolds (see the "Intake and Exhaust Manifold Installation" sections).
18. Adjust the valve clearance.
19. Install the valve cover and air cleaner assembly.
20. Fill the cooling system.

2800 cc Engine

1. Remove the air cleaner assembly and disconnect the battery and accelerator linkage. Drain the cooling system.
2. Remove the distributor cap with the spark plug wires attached. Remove the distributor vacuum line and the distributor. Remove the hose from the water pump to the water outlet which is on the carburetor.
3. Remove the valve covers, fuel line and filter, carburetor, and the intake manifold.
4. Remove the rocker arm shaft (by loosening two bolts at a time, in sequence) and oil baffles. Remove the pushrods, keeping them in the proper sequence for reinstallation in their original positions.
5. Remove the exhaust manifold, referring to the appropriate procedures.
6. Remove the cylinder head retaining bolts and remove the cylinder heads and gaskets.

CAUTION
Do not lay the cylinder head flat on its surface.

---

7. Remove all gasket material and carbon from the engine block and cylinder heads.
8. Place the head gaskets on the engine block.

NOTE: The left and right gaskets are not interchangable. They are marked "front" and "top."

9. Install guide studs in the engine block. Install the cylinder head assemblies on the engine block one at a time. Tighten the cylinder head bolts in sequence, and in steps, to 65–80 ft. lbs.
10. Install the intake and exhaust manifolds.
11. Install the pushrods in the proper sequence. Install the oil baffles and the rocker arm shaft assemblies. Adjust the valve clearances.
12. Install the valve covers with new gaskets.
13. Install the distributor and set the ignition timing.
14. Install the carburetor and the distributor cap with the spark plug wires.
15. Connect the accelerator linkage, fuel line, with fuel filter installed, and distributor vacuum line to the carburetor. Fill the cooling system.

CYLINDER HEAD OVERHAUL

The procedure for the 2300 cc engine is the same as for OHV engines with this exception; if the camshaft is removed from the cylinder head, it must be installed along with the camshaft thrust plate and the camshaft drive gear and attaching bolt. The cylinder head must be removed to remove the camshaft.

For cylinder head overhaul, see the "Engine Rebuilding" section of this manual.

Rocker Shaft

DISASSEMBLY AND ASSEMBLY

2800 cc Engines Only

1. Remove the air cleaner assembly and any interfering emission control equipment.
2. Disconnect the spark plug wires and move them aside. Disconnect the throttle rod if necessary.
3. Remove the rocker arm cover and its gasket.
4. Remove the rocker arm attaching bolts (by loosening two bolts at a time, in sequence) and lift off the rocker arm assembly.
5. Remove the pin from one end of the shaft and slip off the spring washer from the shaft. The supports, springs, and rocker arms may now be removed.

NOTCH DOWNWARD FOR BOTH BANKS

Removing the rocker shaft assembly— 2800 cc engine

6. Check the shaft and its component parts for excessive wear or damage. Replace any parts that show these conditions.
7. Clean the component parts of the shaft assembly in a suitable degreasing solvent.

NOTE: Ordinarily, the rocker shaft itself is not cleaned. If there is an insufficient amount of engine oil being circulated through the rocker arm assembly, however, the inside of the shaft should be cleaned in the following manner.

Intake manifold torque sequence—2800 cc engine

Exploded view of the 2800 cc rocker shaft assembly

Remove the plugs in the rocker shaft ends by drilling a hole in one plug. Insert a long rod through the drilled hole and knock out the opposite plug. Remove the drilled plug in the same manner. Clean the shaft in a degreasing solvent and replace the plugs.

8. Assemble the rocker arm shaft. The cotter pins should be installed with their heads up.

9. Replace the rocker assembly on the cylinder head. Make sure that the notch on the end of the rocker shaft is down. Install the attaching bolts hand tight and then torque them down evenly to 43–49 ft. lbs.

10. Adjust the valve clearances (be sure to set the valves when cold and then again, when hot).

11. Clean the cylinder head and valve cover of any dirt or gasket material and replace the valve cover.

12. Replace the spark plug wires.

Intake Manifold

REMOVAL AND INSTALLATION

2300 cc Engines

1. Remove the air cleaner assembly.
2. Disconnect the fuel line from the carburetor. Remove the carburetor.
3. Disconnect the vacuum lines at the intake manifold. Disconnect the water lines at the manifold.
4. Disconnect the crankcase ventilation hose at the intake manifold.
5. Remove the intake manifold attaching bolts and remove the manifold, carburetor, and decel valve from the studs, as an assembly.

6. Clean all dirt and gasket material from the surfaces on the cylinder head and intake manifold.

7. Position a new gasket and the manifold on the studs. Torque the bolts and nuts to 14–21 ft. lbs. for the 2300 cc.

8. Connect the crankcase ventilation hose to the manifold.

9. Connect the distributor vacuum lines to the manifold.

10. Connect the fuel line to the carburetor.

11. Install the air cleaner assembly.

2800 cc Engines

1. Remove the air cleaner assembly and disconnect the battery.

2. Disconnect the throttle cables.

3. Drain the cooling system. Disconnect and remove the hose from the water outlet to the radiator and the hoses and the line from the water outlet to the water pump.

4. Remove the distributor cap and spark plug wires as an assembly. Disconnect the distributor wire and the vacuum line.

5. Mark the position of the distributor and remove it.

6. Remove the fuel line and filter between the fuel pump and the carburetor and then remove the rocker arm covers.

7. Remove the intake manifold bolts and nuts. Tap the manifold lightly with a plastic hammer to break the gasket seal; and then lift off the manifold.

8. Remove all the gasket material and dirt from the manifold and cylinder heads.

9. Apply sealing compound to the joining surfaces. Place the manifold gasket in place (make sure that the tab on the right bank of the cylinder head gasket fits into the cutout of the manifold gasket). Apply sealant to the manifold retaining bolt bosses.

10. Install the intake manifold. Tighten the attaching bolts until they are hand tight, and then torque them, in sequence, to 15–18 ft. lbs.

NOTE: Tightening one of the bolts with a torque wrench will require a "crow's foot." This tool can be obtained from an automotive supply house or parts store.

11. Install the distributor so the rotor is pointing to the mark made previously.

12. Connect the distributor wire and vacuum line.

13. Install the carburetor, fuel line, fuel filter, and the rocker arm covers.

14. Install the distributor cap and wires.

15. Install and adjust the carburetor linkage.

16. Install the air cleaner assembly and air cleaner tube to the carburetor. Connect the battery.

17. Fill the cooling system. Adjust the ignition timing.

Exhaust Manifold

REMOVAL AND INSTALLATION

2300 cc Engines

1. Remove the air cleaner.

2. Remove the two attaching nuts from the top of the exhaust manifold shroud.

3. Disconnect the two attaching nuts from the muffler inlet pipe. If engine is equipped with thermactor, disconnect the line at the check valve.

Intake manifold torque sequence—2300 cc engine

Exhaust manifold torque sequence—2300 cc engine

4. Remove the manifold attaching nuts and remove the manifold from the cylinder head.

5. This manifold does not use a gasket. When installing the manifold, smear a light coat of graphite grease on the mating surfaces of the exhaust manifold.

6. Position the manifold on the guide studs and install the attaching bolts hand tight, then torque them in sequence to 16–23 ft. lbs.

7. Install a new exhaust pipe gasket and install the two nuts.

8. Position the exhaust manifold shroud on the manifold and install the two nuts.

9. Install the air cleaner.

2800 cc Engines

1. Remove the air cleaner.

2. Remove the four attaching nuts from the exhaust manifold shroud (right side only).

3. Disconnect the attaching nuts from the muffler inlet pipe.

4. Remove the exhaust manifold attaching nuts and remove the manifold.

5. These manifolds do not use gaskets. When installing the manifold, smear a light coat of graphite grease on the mating surfaces.

6. Position the manifold on the studs and install the bolts hand tight then torque them evenly to 15–18 ft. lbs.

7. Install a new inlet pipe gasket and the attaching nuts.

8. Position the exhaust manifold shroud on the manifold and install the attaching nuts (right side).

Timing Gear Cover

NOTE: These procedures apply to the V6 engines only.

REMOVAL AND INSTALLATION

2800 cc Engine

1. Remove the oil pan as described in a following section.

2. Remove the radiator and any other necessary parts to allow clearance.

3. Remove the alternator and drive belts.

Removing the V6 cover plate

Removing the V 6 guide sleeves

Remove the water pump and water lines.

4. Remove the fan.

5. Remove the crankshaft pulley with a puller and, if necessary, remove the guide sleeves from the cylinder block.

6. Remove the front cover retaining bolts and remove the front cover. If the front cover plate gasket needs replacement, remove the two screws and the plate to replace the gasket.

7. To install, reverse the procedures, cleaning all surfaces of gasket material and installing new gaskets and sealing compound.

NOTE: If the guide sleeves were removed, install them with new seal rings but do not use sealing compound.

OIL SEAL REPLACEMENT

2800 cc Engine

Remove the front cover as previously described. Support the front cover and drive out the seal with a socket of a suitable size. To install the new seal, support the cover and drive the new seal in with a socket.

Aligning the timing marks—2800 cc engine

Timing Chain, Gears, and Tensioner

REMOVAL AND INSTALLATION

2800 cc Engine

1. Drain the cooling system.

2. Remove the timing chain cover as previously described.

3. Remove the crankshaft gear with a puller. Remove the key from the crankshaft.

4. Remove the bolt and washer which hold the camshaft gear, then pry the camshaft gear from the camshaft. Pry off the gear carefully. Do not push the camshaft toward the rear of the engine or you might knock out the oil plug at the rear of the engine. Remove the thrust plates, spacer, and key.

5. Place the spacer and thrust plate on the camshaft. Install the key in the camshaft. Align the keyway in the gear with the key and press the gear onto the shaft, making sure that it seats tight against the spacer.

6. Camshaft end-play should be 0.001–0.004 in.; it can be corrected by replacing the thrust plate. Position the crankshaft key, align the keyway and press on the gear, making sure the timing marks are aligned.

7. Install the timing chain cover and fill the cooling system.

8. Set the ignition timing.

Timing Belt Cover, Belt, and Tensioner

REMOVAL AND INSTALLATION; TENSIONER ADJUSTMENT

2300 cc Engine

1. Remove the camshaft drive belt cover.

2. Remove the distributor cap and position it out of the way.

3. Using a large socket and a breaker bar, turn the bolt on the crankshaft pulley in a clockwise direction until the following conditions exist.

a. The timing pointer on the front of the engine is aligned with the O or V mark on the pulley.

b. The pointer on the camshaft sprocket is aligned with the ball in the belt guide plate.

Incorrect fitting of the camshaft drive belt sprocket—2300 cc engine

c. The distributor rotor is aligned with the timing mark on the upper lip of the distributor housing.

NOTE: If the drive belt has slipped and is out of timing, disregard the preceding operations.

4. Loosen the drive belt tensioner bolt and move the tensioner as far to the left as possible. Tighten the tensioner adjustment bolt. This will remove the preload of the tensioner from the belt.

5. Remove the belt from the pulleys.

6. If the timing marks on the camshaft, crankshaft, and distributor were not aligned before the belt was removed, align them at this time. Turn the crankshaft (A), camshaft (B), or the auxiliary shaft (C) until the components are in the positions described in Step 3.

7. Install the belt on the three sprockets, making sure the cogs on the belt fully engage the slots in the sprockets.

8. Loosen the tensioner adjustment bolt and allow the full spring pressure of the tensioner to force the tensioner against the belt.

Timing marks—2300 cc engine

9. Using a socket and breaker bar on the crankshaft pulley bolt, turn the crankshaft two complete turns in a clockwise direction to remove all slack from the belt. Tighten the tensioner adjustment pivot bolt to 32–26 ft. lbs.

10. Continue to turn the crankshaft until the three marks described in Step 3 of the belt removal procedure are aligned. If the belt has slipped, remove the belt and repeat the installation procedure.

11. Install the distributor cap and the drive belt cover.

On vehicles where the timing belt has jumped engine timing without a known cause, e.g., foreign material, snow or ice behind the belt, or a loose tensioner, remove the camshaft sprocket from the engine. Wrap the drive belt around the sprocket

Auxilliary shaft and components—2300 cc engine

for at least 300 degrees (300°). Visually check to make sure that each cog of the belt is properly seated in the valley between the teeth on the camshaft sprocket.

Auxiliary Shaft

REMOVAL AND INSTALLATION

2300 cc Engine

1. Remove the camshaft drive belt cover.

2. Remove the drive belt and auxiliary shaft sprocket.

3. Remove the distributor and fuel pump.

4. Remove the auxiliary shaft cover and thrust plate.

5. Withdraw the auxiliary shaft from the engine block.

6. Slide the auxiliary shaft into the

housing and insert the thrust plate to hold the shaft.

7. Install a new gasket and auxiliary shaft cover.

8. Fit a new gasket to the fuel pump and install the fuel pump.

9. Insert the distributor and install the auxiliary shaft sprocket.

10. Align the timing marks and install the drive belt.

11. Install the drive belt cover.

12. Set the ignition timing.

Camshaft and/or Valve Lifters

REMOVAL AND INSTALLATION

2300 cc Engine

The camshaft is mounted on the cylinder

RECESS IN SPROCKET

KEY

SECTIONAL VIEW FOR
SPROCKET INSTALLATION

CRANKSHAFT

BELT GUIDE   CRANKSHAFT

SPROCKET

SECTIONAL VIEW FOR
CRANKSHAFT BELT GUIDE
INSTALLATION

SPROCKET   BELT GUIDE

CAMSHAFT

SECTIONAL VIEW FOR
CAMSHAFT BELT GUIDE
INSTALLATION

NOTE: If timing relationship between crankshaft, camshaft and auxiliary shaft is disturbed, check and adjust initial ignition timing and curb idle speed after reassembly.

USE A NEW BOLT OR NEW TEFLON TAPE ON BOLT THREADS WHEN INSTALLING

BELT

CRANKSHAFT 90°
TO PAN RAIL

VIEW FOR
CRANKSHAFT ALIGNMENT

TIMING BELT

WASHER

CAMSHAFT
TIMING MARK

CAMSHAFT
SPROCKET

BELT GUIDE

COVER POINTER

SPRING

ADJUSTMENT BOLT

BELT TENSIONER

CRANKSHAFT
SPROCKET

WASHER

AUXILLIARY SHAFT
SPROCKET

Camshaft drive belt assembly and components—2300 cc engine

head. The bearings are mounted in carriers that are an integral part of the cylinder head. On 2000 cc engines the bearings and their journals have a progressively larger diameter from front to rear; therefore, the cylinder head must be removed and the camshaft must be removed from the rear. The opposite is true on 2300 cc engines.

1. Remove the cylinder head.
2. Remove the rocker arms.
3. Remove the camshaft drive gear attaching bolt and washer, and remove the gear and belt guide plate.
4. Remove the camshaft thrust plate from the rear of the cylinder head.
5. Carefully slide the camshaft out of the rear of the cylinder head.

To install, reverse the procedures.

2800 cc Engine

1. Drain the cooling system.
2. Remove the radiator, fan, spacer, water pump pulley, and belt.
3. Remove the distributor cap, with the spark plug wires attached. Remove the distributor vacuum line, distributor, alternator, rocker arm covers, fuel line and filter, carburetor, and intake manifold.
4. Remove the rocker arm and shaft assemblies. Lift out the pushrods and mark them so they can be replaced in the same location.

5. Remove the oil pan.
6. Remove the timing chain cover and water pump as an assembly.
7. Remove the camshaft gear retaining bolt and slide the gear off the camshaft. Remove the camshaft thrust plate.
8. Remove the valve lifters from the engine block with a magnet. Lifters should be identified to permit installation in the same location.
9. Carefully pull the camshaft from the engine block, avoiding damage to the camshaft bearings. Remove the key and spacer ring.

10. Coat the camshaft with a cam lubricant or heavy engine oil.
11. Install the camshaft, carefully avoiding damage to the bearings.

NOTE: When installing the camshaft, do not push it hard into the engine. There is an oil plug at the rear of the engine block called the "bore plug". If the camshaft is forced into the engine, it could push this plug out, resulting in oil leaking on the clutch and pressure plate.

12. Install the spacer ring with the chamfered side toward the camshaft. Insert

BEARINGS

CAMSHAFT SPROCKET

SCREW

KEY   WASHER

CAMSHAFT REAR
BEARING BORE PLUG

CAMSHAFT

SPACER

THRUST PLATE

SCREW

BOLT

Camshaft and related parts—2800 cc engine

the camshaft key. Install the thrust plate. Camshaft end-play should be 0.001–0.004 in. The spacer ring and thrust plate are available in two sizes for adjustment.

13. Align the timing marks and install the camshaft timing gear. Install the retaining washer and bolt.

14. Install the valve lifters.

15. Install the timing cover and water pump.

16. Install the belt drive pulley and secure it with the washer and retaining bolt.

17. Install the oil pan.

18. Install the pushrods in the same locations from which they were removed. Install the intake manifold.

19. Install the oil baffles and rocker arm shaft assemblies. Adjust the valves to the cold setting.

20. Install the water pump pulley, fan spacer, fan and belt, carburetor, fuel line and filter, alternator, distributor cap, and wires.

21. Fill the cooling system.

22. Install the rocker arm covers but not permanently. Run the engine, check for leaks, and set the ignition timing.

23. Set the valves at their hot setting. Install the valve covers permanently.

Pistons and Connecting Rods

IDENTIFICATION AND POSITIONING

2300 cc Engine

Install the pistons in the same cylinders from which they were removed. The connecting rod and bearing caps are numbered on the left side from one to four, beginning at the

Piston and rod assembly—2300 cc engine

front of the engine. The numbers on the connecting rods and bearing cap must be on the same side when installed in the cylinder bore.

Install the pistons with the arrow or notch on the top facing toward the front of the engine.

2800 cc Engine

Pistons must be installed in the same cylinders from which they were removed. The connecting rod and bearing caps are num-

Piston and rod assembly—2800 cc engine

bered from one to three in the right bank and from four to six in the left bank, beginning at the front of the engine. The numbers on the connecting rod and bearing cap must be on the same side when installed in the cylinder bore.

Install the pistons with the indentation notch on the top of the piston facing toward the front of the engine.

ENGINE LUBRICATION

Oil Pan

REMOVAL AND INSTALLATION

2300 cc Engine

1. Remove the dipstick and drain the crankcase oil.

2. Disconnect the steering shaft connection from the rack and pinion.

3. Disconnect the rack and pinion from the crossmember and move it forward to provide clearance.

4. Remove the flywheel housing inspection cover.

5. Remove the oil pan attaching bolts and also remove the pan.

6. Clean the gasket mounting surfaces on the pan and block.

7. Coat the block surfaces and oil pan mounting surfaces with an oil-resistant sealer and position the pan gasket on the engine block. There is a two piece gasket.

8. Coat the oil pan front seal and the front cylinder cover with a sealer, and po-

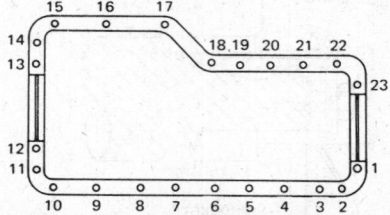

2300 cc oil pan tightening sequence

sition the seal on the front cover. Coat the rear oil pan seal with sealer and install the seal in the rear main bearing cap.

9. Position the oil pan on the engine and tighten the bolts finger tight.

10. Tighten the bolts in sequence to 7–9 ft. lbs. for M6 bolts and 11–13 ft. lbs. for M8 bolts.

11. Install the flywheel housing inspection cover.

12. Connect the rack and pinion to the crossmember, and the steering shaft to the rack and pinion.

13. Install the dipstick and fill the crankcase with oil.

14. Run the engine and check for leaks.

2800 cc Engine

1. Remove the dipstick. Remove the fan shroud and position it over the radiator. Disconnect the battery ground wire and loosen the alternator bracket and adjusting bolts.

2. Raise the vehicle and drain the oil.

3. Remove the splash pan and starter.

4. Remove the engine front support nuts. Raise the engine and place wood blocks between the engine supports and the chassis.

2800 cc oil pan tightening sequence

5. Remove the clutch or converter housing cover.

6. Remove the oil pan retaining bolts and the pan.

7. Clean the surfaces of the oil pan and the engine block. Coat the block surface and the oil pan gasket with sealer. Position the pan gasket on the engine block.

8. Position the oil pan front seal on the cylinder front cover. Position the oil pan rear seal on the rear main bearing cap.

9. Position the oil pan on the engine block and install two front and two rear bolts. Install the rest of the bolts. Torque the bolts in steps (2–4 ft. lbs., then 5–7 ft. lbs.).

10. Replace the converter housing or clutch cover.

11. Remove the wood blocks and install the support nuts.

12. Replace the starter and splash shield.

13. Lower the car. Position the alternator and tighten the bolts. Adjust the belt tension and connect the battery cable.

14. Install the fan shroud.

15. Install the dipstick. Fill the crankcase with oil. Run the engine and check for leaks.

CRANKSHAFT REAR OIL SEAL

Removal and Installation

2800 cc ENGINE

1. Remove the transmission assembly. Remove clutch pressure plate and clutch disc, if so equipped.

2. Remove flywheel, flywheel housing and rear plate.

3. Use an awl to punch two holes in the crankshaft rear oil seal. Punch the holes on opposite sides of the crankshaft and just above the bearing cap to cylinder block split line. Install a sheet metal screw in each hole. Use two large screwdrivers or small pry bars and pry against both screws at the same time to remove the crankshaft rear oil seal. It may be necessary to place small blocks of wood against the cylinder block to provide a fulcrum point for the pry bars. Use caution throughout this procedure to avoid scratching or otherwise damaging the crankshaft oil seal surface.

4. Clean the oil seal recess in the cylinder block and main bearing cap. Inspect and clean the oil seal contact surface on the crankshaft.

5. Coat the oil seal-to-cylinder block surface of the oil seal with oil. Coat the seal contact surface of the oil seal and crankshaft with Lubriplate. Start the seal in the recess and install it. Drive the seal into position until it is firmly seated.

6. Install rear plate, flywheel housing, and flywheel. Tighten flywheel bolts to specifications.

7. Install clutch disc and clutch pressure plate, if so equipped. Align clutch disc before tightening pressure plate retaining screws.

2300 cc ENGINE

1. Remove the oil pan.

2. Loosen all the main bearing cap bolts, thereby lowering the crankshaft slightly but not more than $1/32$ in.

3. Remove the rear main bearing cap, and remove the oil seal from the bearing cap and the cylinder block. Install a small sheet metal screw in one end of the cylinder block half of the seal, and pull on the screw to remove the seal.

4. Clean the seal grooves in the cap and block with a brush and solvent. Dry the area thoroughly. No solvent should come in contact with the seal.

5. Dip the seal halves in clean engine oil.

6. Carefully install the upper seal (block half) into its groove with the undercut side of the seal toward the front of the engine, by rotating it on the seal journal of the crankshaft until about $3/8$ in. protrudes below the parting surface. Be sure that no rubber has been shaved off. Wipe all oil from the mating surface of the bearing cap and cylinder block.

7. Tighten the bearing cap bolts to specifications.

8. Install the lower seal in the rear main bearing cap with the undercut side of the seal toward the front of the engine. Allow the seal to protrude about $3/8$ in. above the parting surface to mate with the upper seal when the cap is installed.

NOTE: Install the seals so that the locating tab faces the rear of the engine.

9. Apply a small amount of sealer to the mating surface of the bearing cap. No sealer compound should come in contact with the rubber seals when the bearing cap is installed and tightened.

10. Install the oil pump (if removed) and oil pan. Fill the crankcase with oil, and operate the engine, checking for leaks.

Oil Pump

REMOVAL AND INSTALLATION

2300 cc Engine

The oil pump is mounted on the bottom of the engine block and is enclosed by the oil pan. To remove the pump, remove the oil pan, the attaching bolts, and the pump. When installing, use a new gasket and fill the pump with oil to prime it.

2800 cc Engine

Remove the oil pan and remove the bolt that retains the oil pick-up screen to the main bearing cap. Remove the oil pump retaining bolts. Lift off the oil pump and pull out the oil pump driveshaft. When installing the pump, insert the driveshaft into the engine block with the pointed end facing inward. Use a new gasket and fill the pump with oil to prime it.

Exploded view of the 2300 cc oil pump

Exploded view of the 2800 cc oil pump

Checking oil pump outer race-to-housing clearance

Checking oil pump rotor end clearance

CHECKING CLEARANCES

Inspect the inside of the oil pump housing, the outer race, and the rotor, for wear or damage. Measure the outer race-to-housing clearance.

With the rotor assembly installed in the housing, place a ruler over the rotor assembly and the housing. Check the clearance between the ruler and the rotor outer race.

OIL PUMP CLEARANCE SPECIFICATIONS

Model	Outer Race-to-Housing	Rotor Assembly End Clearance
2300	0.001– 0.007	0.001– 0.004
2800	0.006– 0.012	0.001– 0.004

ENGINE COOLING

The four cylinder engines employ a pressurized cooling system with the pump fan assembly bolted to the front face of the cylinder block. Coolant is circulated from the base of the radiator up through the water pump and into the cylinder block. The coolant circulates through the engine block and cylinder head to the thermostat, located at the front of the cylinder head. It then returns to the top radiator tank, flows down the radiator tubes, and is cooled by passing air.

The V6 system has a three-stage system which uses a centrifugal-type water pump with the thermostat located in the water inlet housing at the lower left corner of the engine front cover. In the first stage, coolant flow to the radiator is blocked off to allow a quick warmup. In the second, normal temperature stage, some coolant is returned from the engine directly through a bypasss hose to the water pump. In the third, overheat stage, the bypass hose is blocked off by the thermostat so that all coolant must circulate through the radiator.

NOTE: On the V6 it may be necessary to disconnect the heater hose from the water outlet on top of the engine while filling the radiator. When water comes from both the hose and the outlet, the system is free of air.

Radiator

REMOVAL AND INSTALLATION

1. Remove the radiator upper splash shield. Unbolt the shroud and place it over the fan.
2. Place a drain pan under the radiator, remove the cap, open the drain plug, and drain the radiator.
3. Disconnect the upper and lower radiator hoses.
4. Disconnect the automatic transmission cooling lines from the radiator, if so equipped.
5. Remove the retaining screws and lift out the radiator.
6. Reverse the procedures to install.
7. Refill the cooling system with antifreeze solution.
8. Run the engine, with the cap off and heater on, to relieve any air pockets, then install the radiator cap, run the engine, and check for leaks.

Water Pump

REMOVAL AND INSTALLATION

1. Drain the cooling system.
2. Disconnect the lower radiator hose and heater hose from the water pump.
3. Remove the alternator belt. Remove the fan shroud.
4. Remove the fan attaching bolts and remove the fan, spacer, and water pump pulley. Remove the camshaft drive belt cover from OHC engines.
5. Remove the water pump attaching bolts and the water pump. Note that there are different lengths of bolts on the V6.
6. Clean all gasket material from all mounting surfaces.
7. Transfer the heater hose fitting to the new water pump.
8. Coat the new gasket with sealer and position the pump and gasket on the engine.
9. Install the pump mounting bolts. Install the camshaft drive belt cover on 4 cylinder engines.
10. Install the fan, spacer, and water pump pulley.
11. Install the alternator belt. Install the fan shroud.
12. Connect the heater and radiator hoses.
13. Fill the cooling system, run the engine, and check for leaks.

Thermostat

All thermostats installed in these engines start to open at 185–192°F.

REMOVAL AND INSTALLATION

2300 cc Engine

1. Drain the cooling system.
2. Remove the thermostat housing attaching bolts.
3. Lift the thermostat housing from the engine and remove the retaining ring, thermostat, and seal from the engine.
4. Clean all gasket material from the engine and thermostat housing.
6. Install the housing bolts and tighten them.
7. Fill the cooling system.

2800 cc Engine

1. Drain the cooling system.
2. Disconnect the radiator and heater hose from the thermostat housing cover.
3. Remove the three screws which hold the thermostat housing to the water pump. Pull the housing cover away from the water pump and remove the thermostat.
4. Clean the thermostat housing cover and water pump surfaces of all gasket material.
5. Position the thermostat in the water pump and install a new gasket and thermostat housing cover.
6. Connect the radiator and heater hoses. Fill the cooling system, run the engine, and check for leaks.

EMISSION CONTROLS

PCV Valve (Positive Crankcase Ventilation Valve)

The PCV valve is located in the oil separator on 4 cylinder engines. On the V6 engine the PCV valve is located at the left front of the intake manifold and screws out.

TESTING

With the engine running, remove the PCV valve from its mounting. Block off the end of the valve with your finger. You should feel a vacuum when the valve is blocked. Another test is to remove the valve (engine stopped) and shake it. There will be a clicking sound if the valve is free.

Dual Diaphragm Distributor

The dual diaphragm is a two-chambered housing which is mounted on the side of the distributor. The outer side of the housing is a distributor vacuum advance mechanism. The vacuum advance is connected to the carburetor by a vacuum hose. The purpose of the vacuum advance is to advance the ignition timing according to the

AMOUNT OF TRAVEL FOR RETARD DIAPHRAGM-
PLATE RESTING 0° RETARD

RETARD DIAPHRAGM AT FULL RETARD-
PLATE RESTING ON STOP

RETARD STOP

MANIFOLD VACUUM CONNECTION

ADVANCE DIAPHRAGM IN FULL ADVANCE POSITION

RETARD DIAPHRAGM

RETARD DIAPHRAGM SPRING

VACUUM ADVANCE STOP

ADVANCE TRAVEL

FULL VACUUM ADVANCE

FULL VACUUM RETARD

CARBURETOR VACUUM CONNECTION

VACUUM ADVANCE SPRING

ADVANCE DIAPHRAGM

DISTRIBUTOR BASE

VACUUM ADVANCE AND RETARD DIAPHRAGMS AT REST

Dual vacuum diaphragm

conditions under which the engine is operating.

The second side of the dual diaphragm has been added to the older type of distributor to help control engine exhaust emissions at idle and on deceleration. This inner side of the diaphragm is connected by a vacuum hose to the intake manifold. When the engine is idling, intake manifold vacuum is high and the carburetor vacuum is low. Under these conditions, intake manifold vacuum, applied to the inner side of the dual diaphragm, retards the ignition timing to promote more complete combusion of the air-fuel mixture in the engine combusion chambers.

Testing and adjustments of these distributors requires the use of an off-the-car distributor machine.

Thermactor (Air Pump) System

The Thermactor system is used on all models to reduce carbon monoxide and hydrocarbon content of exhaust gases. It does this by injecting air into the hot exhaust gases as they leave the combustion chamber. A belt-driven air pump with a centrifugal filter fan on the intake forces the air through external air passages on the 4 cylinder, and internal passages on the V6. A vacuum-operated bypass valve dumps excess air during deceleration to prevent backfiring in the exhaust manifold. A check valve in the system prevents reverse flow of exhaust gases in case of pump failure.

GAUGE ADAPTER

1/2" PIPE (2" LONG)

11/32" HOLE THROUGH PIPE PLUG

1/2" PIPE PLUG

Thermactor system test gauge adapter

TESTING

Pump Supply Test

1. The engine should be at normal operating temperature.
2. Disconnect the air supply hose at the check valve. If there are two check valves, clamp a plug in the end of one hose.
3. Clamp an adapter and pressure gauge into the air supply hose.
4. Start the engine and slowly increase its speed to 1500 rpm.
5. Air pressure should be 1 psi or more. If not, the pump must be replaced.

Check Valve Test

1. The engine should be at normal operating temperature.
2. Disconnect the air supply hose at the check valve. If there are two, disconnect them both.

3. The valve plate inside the valve body should be lightly against the seat, and away from the air or exhaust manifold.
4. Depress the valve plate with a screwdriver. It should return freely to the seat when released.
5. Leave the hose or hoses off and start the engine. Increase speed slowly to 1500 rpm.
6. Feel for exhaust gas leakage at the valve or valves. Replace any leakers.

NOTE: It is normal for the valve to flutter or vibrate at idle speed.

Bypass Valve Test

1. Disconnect the bypass-to-check valve hose at the bypass valve.
2. Start the engine and let it idle.
3. Air should be coming from the hose.
4. Pinch the vacuum line to the bypass valve shut for 5–8 seconds.
5. Air flow through the bypass valve should stop for a while when you release the vacuum hose. No time length is specified.
6. Check the bypass valve for leaks:
   a. Tee a vacuum gauge into the bypass valve vacuum hose.
   b. Plug the end of the hose.
   c. Note the gauge reading with the engine running.
   d. Remove the plug and connect the vacuum hose to the bypass valve. Check the vacuum reading after 60 seconds.
   e. If readings c. and d. differ, replace the bypass valve.

Vacuum gauge hookup for Thermactor system bypass valve test

EGR (Exhaust Gas Recirculation) System

The EGR system is used on all models to reduce combustion temperatures and production of oxides of nitrogen by introducing a small volume of exhaust gas into the combustion chamber. The vacuum operated EGR valve is mounted on a spacer plate under the carburetor. The amount of exhaust gas recirculated and when it is recirculated are controlled by engine vacuum and temperature. A venturi vacuum amplifier is used to operate the EGR valve with manifold vacuum, under the control of carburetor vacuum.

SYSTEM TEST

1. With the engine running at normal operating temperature, about 8 in. Hg, vacuum should be sufficient to open the EGR valve.
2. If the valve is operating properly, the engine should slow and idle roughly when the valve is opened at idle.
3. A rough idle may be caused by an EGR valve or gasket that isn't sealing properly.

Evaporative Emission System

This emission system is designed to limit the emission of fuel vapors into the atmosphere and prevent raw gas from escaping from the fuel tank. The system consists of four components: The fuel tank; a pressure-sensitive and vacuum-sensitive fuel tank cap; a restrictor in the vapor line; and a vapor-absorbing charcoal canister.

This system allows fuel vapors to escape but prevents liquid gasoline from escaping. The fuel vapors enter the vapor separator

outlet hose to the charcoal canister which is mounted in the engine compartment. The vapors enter the canister, pass through a charcoal filter, and then exit through a hole in the bottom. As the vapors pass through the charcoal they are cleansed of hydrocarbons so the air that passes from the canister is free of pollutants.

When the engine is running, vacuum from the carburetor draws fresh air into the charcoal canister. As the entering air passes through the charcoal in the canister, it picks up the hydrocarbons that were deposited by the gasoline vapors. This gas mixture is then carried to the carburetor where it combines with incoming air and enters the combustion chambers of the engine to be burned.

Heated Air Intake Duct

The heated air intake portion of the air cleaner consists of a thermostat and a spring-loaded temperature control door in the snorkel of the air cleaner. The temperature control door

is located between the end of the air cleaner snorkel, which draws in air from the engine compartment, and the duct that carries heated air up from the exhaust manifold. When the temperature under the hood is below 85°F (100° on the V6), the temperature control door blocks off under-hood air from entering the air cleaner and allows only heated air from the exhaust manifold to be drawn into the air cleaner. When the temperature under the hood rises above 110°F (135°F on the V6), the temperature control door blocks off heated air from the exhaust manifold and allows only under-hood air to be drawn into the air cleaner. Between 90 and 110° (135°)F, a mixture of heated and underhood air is provided. By controlling the temperature of the engine intake air this way, exhaust emissions are lowered and fuel economy increased.

TESTING

2300 cc Engine

1. With the engine cold and the temperature under the hood below 85°F, check the position of the temperature door in the air cleaner. It should be in the up (open) position, blocking off underhood air.
2. Remove the air cleaner from the car. Immerse the air cleaner duct assembly in water, raise the water temperature to 85°F, and allow the temperature to stabilize for five minutes. The flap should be open to hot air. Now raise the temperature to 110°F and stabilize. The temperature control door should be in the down position, blocking off the heated air from the exhaust manifold.

If the temperature door does not react in this manner, and the door is not binding, replace the valve and duct assembly.

2800 cc Engine

1. With the engine cold and the underhood temperature less than 100°F, the valve plate should be in the heat on position.

V6 fuel evaporative system

2. Immerse the duct assembly in water, raise the temperature to 100°F, and allow the temperature to stabilize for five minutes. The valve should still be in the heat on position.

3. Now raise the temperature to 135°F and stabilize. The valve plate should be in the heat off position. Replace the duct and valve assembly if large variations from the specified temperatures were found.

FUEL SYSTEM

Fuel Filter

REPLACEMENT

1. Remove air cleaner.
2. Loosen the clamps securing the fuel filter to the fuel line hoses.
3. Remove the fuel filter and discard the clamps.
4. Install a new filter using new clamps.
5. Crimp clamps securely, start engine and check for leaks.
6. Install air cleaner.

Fuel Pump

A single-action fuel pump is used on all models. The fuel pump is on the left side of the engine and is actuated by an eccentric on the auxiliary shaft on OHC engines or a rod driven by the camshaft (V6).

TESTING

Pressure Test

Disconnect the fuel line from the carburetor and attach a pressure tester to the line. Idle the engine and note the reading on the tester. The readings should be 3.5–5.5 psi.

Capacity Test

Disconnect the fuel line from the carburetor and insert it into a one quart container. Crank the 2300 cc engine for 35–43 seconds, and the V6 engine for 25 seconds. The bottle should be half-full (one pint).

REMOVAL AND INSTALLATION

1. Disconnect the inlet and outlet fuel lines at the fuel pump.
2. Remove the fuel pump retaining bolts and remove the pump and gasket. Discard the gasket.
3. Remove all the gasket material from the engine block and pump mounting surface. Apply oil-resistant sealer to both sides of the new gasket. Position the gasket on the fuel pump flange and hold the pump in position against the engine block.

Fuel pump pressure and capacity test

Exploded view of 5200 carburetor

NOTE: Make sure the rocker arm or rod is riding on the camshaft eccentric.

4. Press the pump tightly against the engine block, install the retaining bolts and tighten them securely.

5. Connect the fuel lines. Start the engine and check for leaks.

Carburetors

The 2300 cc engines are equipped with a model 5200 two barrel carburetor. The 2800 cc engines are equipped with a model 2150 carburetor. 1977 California 2800 cc engines use a 2700 VV (variable venturi) carburetor. On the 2bbl carburetor, the primary venturi is smaller than the secondary venturi. The two are connected by mechanical linkage and, when the primary throttle plate opens approximately 45° the secondary plate begins to open.

REMOVAL AND INSTALLATION

1. Remove the air cleaner.
2. Remove the bolt that attaches the choke water housing to the carburetor and remove the water cover with its hoses attached. Detach the electrically assisted choke wire.

3. Note the location of all fuel lines and vacuum hoses that attach to the carburetor, then disconnect them from the carburetor.

4. Disconnect the throttle linkage from the carburetor.

5. Disconnect the throttle solenoid wire at the push-on connection.

6. Remove the four nuts that attach the carburetor to the intake manifold.

7. Inspect the carburetor base gasket. If it is damaged in any way, replace it. Clean any foreign matter from the base of the carburetor.

8. Position the carburetor on the intake manifold and tighten the nuts.

9. Connect the vacuum lines and the fuel lines to the carburetor.

10. Connect the throttle linkage to the carburetor.

11. Connect the water housing to the carburetor.

12. On those models equipped with a throttle solenoid, connect the lead wire at the push-on connector.

13. Replace any coolant that was lost in the removal of the water hoses.

OVERHAUL

For overhaul procedures, please refer to "Carburetor Service" in the Unit Repair section.

CHOKE UNLOADER ADJUSTMENT

5200 Carburetor

1. Hold the carburetor throttle lever in the wide-open position.

2. Insert a 0.256 in. drill bit into the air horn of the carburetor.

3. Apply light pressure to the choke plate to remove all slack.

4. With the drill bit against the carburetor wall, the bottom of the choke plate should just contact the drill. If it does not, bend the tab on the fast idle lever where it contacts the fast idle cam to correct it.

AUTOMATIC CHOKE ADJUSTMENT

2150 and 5200 Carburetor

1. Loosen the three screws that attach the choke water housing to the choke housing.

2. Turn the choke water housing as required to align the index mark on the water housing with the specified mark on the choke housing. If the choke cap setting is index, align the notch on the water cover with the large index mark in the center of the top of the choke housing. If the choke setting is one lean, align the notch on the water cover with the first notch to the left of the large index mark on the choke housing.

CHOKE PLATE PULLDOWN ADJUSTMENT

2150 and 5200 Carburetor

1. Remove the three screws from around the choke water cover that attach the cover to the choke housing.

2. Remove the water housing with the hoses attached.

3. Position the fast idle cam so the fast idle adjusting screw is contacting the highest step on the cam.

4. Using a screwdriver, push the vacuum diaphragm stem back into the diaphragm housing until it stops. Hold the stem in this position.

5. Insert a ¼ in. (¹³⁄₆₄ in. for 1976–77 5200; ⁹⁄₆₄ in. for 1976–77 2150) drill bit into the air horn of the carburetor and apply light pressure to the choke plate to remove all slack. With the drill bit against the air horn wall, the bottom of the choke plate should just contact the drill bit.

6. If the clearance is incorrect, remove the vacuum diaphragm adjusting screw plug and insert a screwdriver into the exposed hole, then adjust the screw inward or outward as required.

Exploded view of the 2150 carburetor

Adjusting the choke linkage—5200

Dry float level adjustment—2150

Wet float level adjustment—2150

7. Install the choke water housing on the choke housing, making sure the tab on the end of the coil spring engages the slot in the choke housing shaft.

8. Install the three choke water housing attaching screws and tighten them finger-tight. Adjust the automatic choke as previously described.

FLOAT LEVEL ADJUSTMENTS

2150 Carburetor

A two stage adjustment procedure is necessary.

1. Remove and invert the air horn. With the inlet needle seated, check the distance between the top surface of the main body gasket and the top of the float. Setting should be ⅜".

2. Bend float tab, if necessary, to adjust.

3. Replace air horn and operate engine to normal operating temperature. Place vehicle on as flat a surface as possible.

4. Stop engine and remove the air horn attaching screws.

5. Start engine and remove air horn.

6. While the engine is idling, use a standard depth scale to measure the vertical distance from the top of the machined surface of the carburetor main body to the level of the fuel in the bowl. The measurement must be made at least ¼" away from any vertical surface. Setting should be ¾".

7. If adjustment is necessary, stop engine and bend tab on float to adjust.

5200 Carburetor

1. Remove the air cleaner.

2. Disconnect the fuel and decel valve hoses from the carburetor.

3. Remove the small clip that attaches the choke rod to the choke plate shaft and disconnect the rod from the shaft.

4. Remove the screws that attach the upper body of the carburetor to the main body of the carburetor and carefully lift the upper body off the main body. Be careful not to tear the upper body gasket.

5. Turn the carburetor upper body upside down and measure the clearance between the bottom of each float and the bottom of the carburetor upper body. The clearance should be 0.420 in. (0.460 for the 2300 cc).

6. If the clearance is incorrect, bend the float lever adjusting tang to correct it.

Adjusting the choke plate pull-down—2150

Float drop adjustment—5200

FLOAT

DRILL OR
GAUGE ROD

Float level adjustment—5200

NOTE: Both floats must be adjusted to the same clearance.

7. With the upper body still in the inverted position, measure the clearance between the tang on the rear of the float mounting bracket and the bumper spring on the float pivot pin. The clearance should be 0.020–0.050 in. If the clearance is incorrect, bend the float drop tang to adjust it.

8. Position the upper body and gasket of the main body of the carburetor and connect the choke rod to the choke plate lever. Install the choke rod attaching clip in the hole in the rod.

9. Install the upper body attaching screws.

10. Connect the fuel and decel valve hoses to the carburetor.

11. Install the air cleaner.

FAST IDLE CAM CLEARANCE

2150 & 5200 Carburetor

1. Place a 3/32 drill bit between the lower edge of the choke plate and the air horn wall.

2. Set the fast idle screw on the second step of the fast idle cam and measure the clearance between the choke lever tang and the arm on the fast idle cam.

3. The clearance should be about 1/8 in.

4. If the clearance is excessively large or small, bend the choke lever tang up or down. Don't bend it any more than necessary; it can break off.

FAST IDLE ADJUSTMENT

All idle and mixture adjustments are to be made with the artificial enrichment procedure. This procedure is impractical for all but Ford dealers.

2700VV CARBURETOR ADJUSTMENTS

For 1977, Ford's new 2700VV (Variable Venturi) carburetor is on California cars with the V6 engine. Since the design of this carburetor differs considerably from the other carburetors in the Ford lineup, an explanation of the differences in both theory and operation of this carburetor is presented here.

In exterior appearance, the variable venturi carburetor is similar to conventional carburetors and, like a conventional carburetor, it uses a normal float and fuel bowl

system. However, the similarity ends there. In place of a normal choke plate and fixed area venturis, the 2700VV carburetor has a pair of small oblong castings in the top of the upper carburetor body where you would normally expect to see the choke plate. These castings slide back and forth across the top of the carburetor in response to fuel/air demands. Their movement is controlled by a spring-loaded diaphragm valve regulated by a vacuum signal taken below the venturis in the throttle bores. As the throttle is opened, the strength of the vacuum signal increases, opening the venturis and allowing more air to enter the carburetor.

Fuel is admitted into the venturi area by means of tapered metering rods that fit into the main jets. These rods are attached to the venturis, and, as the venturis open or close in response to air demand, the fuel needed to maintain the proper mixture increases or decreases as the metering rods slide in the jets. In comparison to a conventional carburetor with fixed venturis and a variable air supply, this system provides much more precise control of the fuel/air supply during all modes of operation. Because of the variable venturi principle, there are fewer fuel metering systems and fuel passages. The only auxiliary fuel metering systems required are an idle trim, accelerator pump (similar to a conventional carburetor), starting enrichment, and cold running enrichment.

NOTE: Adjustment, assembly and disassembly of this carburetor require special tools for some of the operations. These tools are available from dealers or from their supplier, The Owatonna Tool Company, Owatonna, Minnesota, 55060. Do not attempt any operations on this carburetor without first checking to see if you need the special tools for that particular operation. The adjustment and repair procedures given here mention when and if you will need the special tools.

Before making any adjustments with the engine running, set the parking brake and block the wheels. Make sure the engine is

DRILL OR
GAUGE ROD

CHOKE TANG

CHECK
CLEARANCE
HERE

FAST IDLE CAM

Fast idle cam clearance—5200

FUEL FILTER

FAST IDLE
ADJUSTING SCREW

CHOKE HOUSING

Fast idle adjustment—5200

at normal operating temperature and that any power accessories are turned off.

Curb Idle Speed

Adjust the curb idle speed as you would on a conventional carburetor. Check the emission control sticker under the hood for the proper idle speed.

Internal Vent Adjustment

This adjustment must be checked whenever the curb idle speed is adjusted. After you have set the curb idle, place a .010 in. feeler gauge between the accelerator pump stem and the pump operating link.

Turn the adjusting nut until there is just a slight drag when the gauge is removed.

Cold Enrichment Metering Rod

NOTE: This procedure requires special tools.

Remove the choke cap, after noting its position so that you will be able to return it to the correct setting. Install a dial indicator with the tip of the indicator on the top of the enrichment rod and adjust the dial to zero. The cold enrichment rod is seated by installing the stator cap as a weight. After installing the cap in place of the choke cap, raise it slightly and let it drop. This should seat the cold enrichment rod. The dial indicator should still read zero. If it does not, repeat the procedure. Remove the stator cap and re-install it in the choke cap's original position. The index mark on the stator cap should be in the same relative position as the index mark on the choke cap. The dial indicator should now read 0.125 in. If it does not, turn the adjusting nut clockwise to increase or counterclockwise to decrease rod height. Reinstall the choke cap in its original position.

Control Vacuum

You will need a tachometer, a vacuum gauge and some Allen wrenches for this adjustment. With the engine at curb idle and a tachometer hooked up, turn the venturi valve diaphragm adjusting screw clockwise until the valve is completely closed. Connect a vacuum gauge to the vacuum tap on the venturi valve cover. Turn the venturi by-pass adjusting screw to reach the specified vacuum (5 in. H₂O). Then turn the venturi valve diaphragm adjusting screw counterclockwise until the vacuum drops to the specified setting. In order to get the vacuum to drop, you must rev the engine once or twice. After you get the vacuum right, check and reset the curb idle if necessary.

Fast Idle Speed

With the engine idling, EGR disconnected and the vacuum line plugged, make sure the fast idle lever is on the specified step of the fast idle cam. Turn the fast idle adjusting screw clockwise to increase speed and counterclockwise to decrease speed.

Idle Mixture Adjustment

Idle trim is adjusted with a 3/32 Allen wrench. Remove the air cleaner cover and locate the adjusting holes in the top of the carburetor. Turn the air adjusting screws clockwise to enrichen and counterclockwise to lean out.

Fuel Level Adjustment

Remove the carburetor upper body. Remove the old gasket and install a new one. Fabricate a gauge to the specified dimension of 13/64 in. Turn the upper body upside down and place the fuel level gauge on the cast surface, not on the gasket. Measure the vertical distance from the cast surface to the bottom of the float. If it needs adjustment, bend the float operating lever away from the fuel inlet needle to decrease the setting and toward the needle to increase the setting.

Float Drop Adjustment

You will need to fabricate a gauge for this adjustment, also. With the upper body in the upright position, measure the distance between the cast surface of the upper body and the bottom of the float. It should be 1 15/32 in. To adjust, bend the stop tab on the float lever away from the hinge pin to increase the setting and toward the hinge pin to decrease the setting.

Control Vacuum Regulator (CVR) Adjustment

NOTE: The cold enrichment metering rod adjustment must be set before making this adjustment.

Cycle the throttle to set the fast idle speed cam and then rotate the choke cap 180 degrees clockwise (rich). Press down on the CVR rod. If it moves downward, it is not seated and must be adjusted. To adjust, turn the rod clockwise until the adjusting nut just begins to rise. Then turn the adjusting screw clockwise in 1/4 turn increments until the rod is fully seated (no down travel). Reset the choke cap to the original setting.

High Speed Cam Positioner (H.S.C.P.) Adjustment

Holding the throttle closed, place the H.S.C.P. in the corner of the specified cam step (counting the highest step as the first). Place the fast idle lever in the corner of the H.S.C.P. Remove the diaphragm cover and turn the assembly clockwise until it just bottoms on the casting, then turn it back until the vacuum port and diaphragm hole line up. Reinstall the cover.

Fast Idle Cam Setting

1. Remove the choke cap.
2. Place the fast idle lever in the corner of the specified step of the fast idle cam (counting the highest step as the first) with the high cam speed positioner retracted.
3. Hold the throttle lightly closed with a rubber band to maintain cam position.

This step is not required if the adjustment is done on the vehicle.

4. Install the stator cap and rotate clockwise until lever contracts the adjusting screw.
5. Turn the fast idle cam adjusting screw until the index mark on the stator cap lines up with the specified notch on the choke casting.
6. Remove the stator cap and reinstall the choke cap.

MANUAL TRANSMISSION

REMOVAL AND INSTALLATION

1. Disconnect the ground cable from the battery.
2. Raise the car and support it with jackstands.
3. Disconnect the shift levers. Remove the shifter.
4. Remove the four bolts joining the driveshaft to the rear axle pinion. Also remove the two bolts securing the center bearing carrier to its bracket. Remove the driveshaft. Install a dummy yoke in the transmission to prevent oil loss if the oil has not been drained.
5. Remove the clip and the speedometer cable from the transmission.
6. Disconnect the exhaust pipe(s) from the exhaust manifold.
7. Move the clutch release lever boot and free the clutch operating cable from the lever.
8. Remove the starter motor attaching bolts and move the starter to one side.
9. Remove the bolts holding the clutch housing to the engine.
10. Remove the bolts holding the lower dust cover from the clutch housing and detach the cover.
11. Support the rear of the engine with a jack.
12. Remove the four bolts attaching the transmission crossmember to the body. Slide the transmission toward the rear of the car while supporting its weight, and remove it from the car.
13. Position the transmission assembly on the engine. Make sure that the clutch housing fully engages the dowel pins on the rear of the engine. Install the bolts attaching the clutch housing to the engine.
14. Install the four crossmember-to-body bolts and lockwashers. Remove the jack from beneath the engine.
15. Install the starter motor.
16. Replace the lower dust cover.
17. Coat the ball on the end of the clutch cable with chassis grease and install the clutch cable to the clutch release lever. Adjust the cable. (See the clutch section.) Locate the boot in the release lever opening.

18. Install the shift rods to the shifter, if so equipped.

19. Connect the exhaust pipe(s) to the exhaust manifold.

20. Install the speedometer cable and secure it with the retaining clip.

21. Install the driveshaft, aligning the mating marks. Replace the four nuts and bolts at the rear axle pinion. Locate the center bearing carrier in position and attach it to its bracket with the two bolts.

22. Refill the transmission if the oil was drained.

23. Remove the jackstands and lower the car to the ground. Check the transmission and the clutch for proper operation.

LINKAGE ADJUSTMENT

1. Make an alignment pin out of ³⁄₁₆ in. rod stock.

2. Place the gearshift lever in neutral and raise the car off the ground.

3. Remove the spring retainers and disconnect the shifter rods from the transmission shift levers.

4. Insert the alignment pin in the shift levers.

5. Place all the transmission shift levers in the neutral position.

6. Adjust the length of the shifter rods so they fit into the holes in the transmission shift levers. Install the shifter rods and the spring retainers.

7. Remove the alignment pin and lower the car to the ground. Check the transmission for proper operation.

OVERHAUL

For manual transmission overhaul procedures, please refer to "Manual Transmission Overhaul" in the Unit Repair section.

CLUTCH

REMOVAL AND INSTALLATION

1. Remove the transmission from the car.

2. Loosen each of the pressure plate-to-flywheel attaching bolts gradually to relieve the spring pressure.

3. If the same pressure plate is being used again, match-mark it with the flywheel so it may be installed in its original position.

4. Remove the clutch disc and the pressure plate from the car.

5. Position the pressure plate and the clutch disc on the flywheel and install the attaching bolts by hand, but do not tighten them with a wrench.

6. Install a clutch (dummy or pilot) shaft to the center of the clutch disc.

7. Tighten the pressure plate attaching bolts evenly to 12–15 ft. lbs.

8. Remove the dummy shaft.

9. Install the transmission.

CLUTCH ADJUSTMENT

2300 cc Engine

Pull the pedal back hard against its backstop and secure with a block of wood.

1. Raise the vehicle on a hoist and loosen the adjusting locknut. Pull the conduit forward to take up slack. While holding the cable forward, turn the adjusting nut to obtain a clearance of 3.15–3.65 mm between the adjusting nut and the clutch housing cable bushing.

2800 cc Engine

Block the clutch as above.

1. Raise the vehicle on a hoist and pull the conduit forward until the adjusting nut is pulled from its recess in the clutch housing cable bushing. Pull the cable forward just enough to take up slack in the release lever.

2. Turn the adjusting nut until it just comes in contact with the hexagon recess.

CLUTCH PEDAL STOP

2800 V-6
ADJUSTING NUT
WITH CABLE PULLED FORWARD NUT SHOULD BE FLUSH WITH BUSHING FACE
RECESSED BUSHING
CLUTCH ARM

2300 OHC
BUSHING
WITH CABLE PULLED FORWARD, ADJUST AS NECESSARY TO GIVE CORRECT PEDAL LIFT

A
B
FREE PLAY AT PEDAL

2300 OHC - 22 mm + 4 mm (0.866 + 0.157)
2800 V-6 - 27 mm + 4 mm (1.063 + 0.157 inch)

FLOORBOARD

Clutch cable adjustment

Shifter alignment pin

Release the forward pull on the cable allowing the nut to enter the recess.

3. Pedal free-play should be $2^9/_{32}$–$1^{17}/_{32}$.

AUTOMATIC TRANSMISSION

The transmission in the car can readily be identified by the vehicle identification plate.

REMOVAL AND INSTALLATION

C3 Transmission

1. Raise the vehicle on a hoist.
2. Place a drain pan under the transmission fluid pan. Starting at the rear of the pan and working toward the front, loosen the attaching bolts and allow the fluid to drain. Then remove all of the pan attaching bolts except two at the front, to allow the fluid to further drain. After all the fluid has drained, install two bolts on the rear side of the pan to temporarily hold it in place.
3. Remove the converter drain plug access cover and adapter plate bolts from the lower end of the converter housing.
4. Remove the three converter-to-flywheel attaching bolts. Crank the engine to turn the converter to gain access to the bolts, using a wrench on the crankshaft pulley attaching bolt. On belt driven overhead camshaft engines, never turn the engine backwards.
5. Crank the engine until the converter drain plug is accessible and remove the plug. Place a drain pan under the converter to catch the fluid. After all the fluid has been drained from the converter, reinstall the plug and torque to specification.
6. Remove the drive shaft and install the extension housing seal replacer tool in the extension housing.
7. Remove the speedometer cable from the extension housing.
8. Disconnect the shift rod at the transmission manual lever. Disconnect the downshift rod at the transmission downshift lever.
9. Remove the starter-to-converter housing attaching bolts and position the starter out of the way.

10. Disconnect the neutral start switch wires from the switch.
11. Remove the vacuum lines from the transmission vacuum unit.
12. Position a transmission jack under the tranmission and raise it slightly.
13. Remove the engine rear support-to-crossmember nut.
14. Remove the crossmember-to-frame side support attaching bolts and remove the crossmember.
15. Remove the inlet pipe steady rest from the inlet pipe and rear engine support; then disconnect the muffler inlet pipe at the exhaust manifold and secure it.
16. Lower the jack under the transmission and allow the transmission to hang.
17. Position a jack to the front of the engine and raise the engine to gain access to the two upper converter housing-to-engine attaching bolts.
18. Disconnect the oil cooler lines at the transmission. Plug all openings to keep out dirt.
19. Remove the lower converter housing-to-engine attaching bolts.
20. Remove the transmission filler tube.
21. Secure the transmission to the jack with a safety chain.
22. Remove the two upper converter housing-to-engine attaching bolts. Move the transmission to the rear and down to remove it from under the vehicle.
23. Torque the converter drain plug to specification if not previously done.
24. Position the converter to the transmission making sure the converter hub is fully engaged in the pump gear.
25. With the converter properly installed, place the transmission on the jack and secure with safety chain.
26. Rotate the converter so the bolt drive lugs and drain plug are in alignment with their holes in the flywheel.
27. With the transmission mounted on a transmission jack, move the converter and transmission assembly forward into position being careful not to damage the flywheel and the converter pilot.

During this move, to avoid damage, do not allow the transmission to get into a nosed down position as this will cause the converter to move forward and disengage from the pump gear. The converter must rest squarely against the flywheel. This indi-

cates that the converter pilot is not binding in the engine crankshaft.

28. Install the two upper converter housing-to-engine attaching bolts and torque them to 28–38 ft. lbs.
29. Remove the safety chain from the transmission.
30. Insert the filler tube in the stub tube and secure it to the cylinder block with the attaching bolt. Torque the bolt to 7–10 ft. lbs. If the stub tube is loosened or dislodged, it should be replaced.
31. Install the oil cooler lines in the retaining clip at the cylinder block. Connect the lines to the transmission case.
32. Remove the jack supporting the front of the engine.
33. Position the muffler inlet pipe support bracket to the converter housing and install the four lower converter housing-to-engine attaching bolts. Torque the bolts to 28–38 ft. lbs.
34. Raise the transmission. Position the crossmember to the frame side supports and install the attaching bolts. Torque the bolts to 48–52 ft. lbs.
35. Lower the transmission and install the rear engine support-to-crossmember nut. Torque the nut to 30–35 ft. lbs.
36. Remove the transmission jack.
37. Install the vacuum hose on the transmission vacuum unit. Install the vacuum line into the retaining clip.
38. Connect the neutral start switch plug to the switch.
39. Install the starter and torque the attaching bolts to 20–25 ft. lbs.
40. Install the three fylwheel-to-converter attaching bolts.

Flywheel assemblies used with C3 automatic transmissions are designed with a pilot hole to be sure of proper flywheel-to-converter alignment. Prior to installing the transmission to the engine, the flywheel must be indexed with the pilot hole, in the six o'clock position.

When assembling the flywheel to the converter, first install the attaching bolt through the pilot hole and torque to 27–37 ft. lbs. Install the remaining two bolts and torque to 30–35 ft. lbs.

If the first bolt is not installed in the pilot hole, a misalignment of the flywheel holes and the mating converter weld nuts may occur. This misalignment will cause difficulty in installing the remaining bolts, crossthreaded bolts, or interference between flywheel and bolt threads. Any of these conditions will result in improperly torqued flywheel-to-converter attaching bolts, which may contribute to transmission or flywheel failures.

41. Install the converter drain plug access cover and adapter plate bolts. Torque the bolts to 5–7 ft. lbs.
42. Connect the muffler inlet pipe to the exhaust manifold.
43. Connect the transmission shift rod to the manual lever.
44. Connect the downshift rod to the downshift lever.

45. Connect the speedometer cable to the extension housing.

46. Install the drive shaft. Torque the companion flange U-bolt attaching nuts to 17–23 ft. lbs.

47. Adjust the manual and downshift linkage as required.

48. Lower the vehicle. Fill the transmission to the proper level with the specified fluid.

Pour in five quarts of fluid; then run the engine and add fluid as required.

49. Check the transmission, converter assembly and oil cooler lines for leaks.

C4 Transmission

1. Raise the car on a lift.

2. Drain the fluid from the transmission. Place a pan under the transmission. Loosen the transmission pan attaching bolts and allow the fluid to drain. After some fluid has drained remove all the bolts and remove the pan.

3. Remove the ground cable from the battery at the engine block. Disconnect the starter cable from the starter. Remove the starter attaching bolts and remove the starter.

4. Remove the access cover from the lower part of the converter housing.

5. Remove the nuts which hold the converter to the flywheel. You must rotate the flywheel in order to gain access to the bolts. To rotate the flywheel, place a socket on the crankshaft pulley bolt and turn it.

6. Cars equipped with a V6 engine have a drain plug on the converter. Rotate the flywheel as previously described to gain access to the converter plug. Remove the plug and drain the fluid. Replace the plug after draining the fluid.

7. Mark the driveshaft for correct alignment when installing.

8. Remove the bolts which hold the driveshaft center bearing to the body.

9. Lower the driveshaft assembly and remove it from the car.

10. Remove the speedometer cable from the tailshaft.

11. Disconnect the shift cable from the lever on the transmission.

12. Remove the shift cable bracket from the converter housing.

13. Disconnect the downshift cable from the transmission downshift lever bracket.

14. Disconnect the neutral safety switch wires and the connectors from the switch.

15. Remove the vacuum line from the modulator on the transmission.

16. Support the transmission with a transmission jack and then remove the crossmember bolts and the crossmember.

17. Disconnect the transmission fluid cooler lines at the transmission.

18. Remove the transmission filler tube.

19. Secure the transmission to the jack with a chain.

20. Remove the converter housing attaching bolts. Move the transmission to the rear and down in order to remove it.

21. To install, move the transmission into position. The converter must rest squarely against the flywheel.

22. Install the converter housing to engine attaching bolts and tighten them to 23–33 ft. lbs. Remove the chain from the transmission.

23. Install the transmission filler tube.

24. Install the transmission fluid cooler lines to the transmission.

25. Position the crossmember to the frame and install the bolts.

26. Install the flywheel-to-converter nuts and tighten them to 23–28 ft. lbs.

27. Remove the transmission jack. Install the vacuum hose to the modulator.

28. Connect the neutral safety switch.

29. Connect the downshift cable to the downshift bracket. Connect the shift cable bracket to the converter housing.

30. Connect the downshift cable to the lever on the transmission.

31. Connect the speedometer cable to the tailshaft.

32. Install the driveshaft and align the marks. Install the center driveshaft bearing.

33. Install the converter housing access cover. Install the starter and the starter cable. Install the battery ground cable.

34. Lower the car to the ground and fill the transmission to the correct level with the proper fluid.

PAN REMOVAL & INSTALLATION

C4 Transmission

1. Raise the car on a hoist.

2. Place a drain pan under the transmission.

3. Starting at the rear of the pan and working toward the front, loosen the attaching bolts and allow the transmission fluid to drain.

4. Remove the bolts and the pan.

5. Remove all gasket material from the pan and the transmission mounting surface.

6. Apply gasket sealer to the oil pan and position the gasket on the pan.

7. Position the pan on the transmission and install the bolts hand-tight.

8. Torque the bolts evenly to 12–16 ft. lbs. Fill the transmission to the proper level with the specified fluid.

PAN REMOVAL AND FILTER SERVICE

C3 Transmission

1. Loosen the pan attaching bolts to drain the fluid from the transmission.

2. When the fluid has stopped draining from the transmission, remove and thoroughly clean the pan and the screen. Discard the pan gasket. Remove and clean filter screen in solvent and blow it dry.

3. Place a new gasket on the pan, and install the pan on the transmission.

4. Add three quarts of fluid to the transmission through the filler tube.

5. Run the engine at idle speed for about two minutes, and then run it at fast idle speed (about 1200 rpm) until it reaches its normal operating temperature. Do not race the engine.

6. Shift the selector lever through all the positions, place it at P, and check the fluid level. The fluid level should be above the ADD mark. If necessary, add enough fluid to the transmission to bring the level between the ADD and FULL marks on the dipstick. Do not overfill the transmission.

FILTER SERVICE

C4 Transmission

Remove the transmission pan. Remove the screws attaching the filter screen to the transmission. Wash the filter in a solvent and blow it clean of solvent with an air gun. Install the filter screen and replace the oil pan.

NOTE: Cleaning the filter screen is not a regular maintenance procedure. It should be cleaned when the oil pan has been removed for other service procedures.

FRONT BAND ADJUSTMENT

C3 Transmission

1. Remove the downshift rod from the transmission downshift lever.

2. Clean all dirt from the band adjusting screw area. Remove and discard the locknut.

3. Install a new locknut on the adjusting screw and torque to 18–23 ft. lbs.

Front band adjustment—C3

4. Back off the adjusting screw exactly one and a half turns.

5. Hold the adjusting screw from turning and torque the locknut to 23 ft. lbs.

6. Install the downshift rod on the transmission downshift lever.

INTERMEDIATE BAND ADJUSTMENT

C4 Transmission

1. Wipe the area clean around the adjusting screw on the side of the transmission.

Intermediate band adjustment—C4

2. Remove the adjusting screw locknut nd discard it.

3. Install a new locknut on the adjusting screw but do not tighten it.

4. Tighten the adjusting screw to exactly 10 ft. lbs.

5. Back off the adjusting screw exactly 1¾ turns.

6. Hold the adjusting screw so that it does not turn and tighten the locknut to 35–45 ft. lbs.

NOTE: The tools used in the illustration of band adjustment are: a torque wrench, an extension, and an Allen socket.

LOW-REVERSE BAND ADJUSTMENT

C4 Transmission

1. Wipe the area clean around the adjustment screw on the side of the transmission.

2. Remove the adjusting screw locknut and discard it.

3. Install a new locknut but do not tighten it.

4. Tighten the adjusting screw to exactly 10 ft. lbs.

Low-reverse band adjustment—C4

5. Back off the adjusting screw exactly three full turns.

6. Hold the adjusting screw so that it does not turn and tighten the locknut to 35–45 ft. lbs.

SHIFT LINKAGE ADJUSTMENT

1. Position the transmission selector lever in the Drive position.

2. Raise the car and remove the clevis pin and disconnect the cable and the bushing from the transmission.

3. Move the transmission lever to the Drive position, which is the third detent from the back of the transmission on the C4. It is the third detent from the front on the C3.

4. With the transmission selector lever and the transmission lever in the Drive positions, adjust the cable length until the clevis pin holes in the transmission lever and the end of the cable are aligned.

5. Connect the cable, lower the car, and check the operation of the transmission in each selector lever position.

Kickdown linkage adjustment—C4

DOWNSHIFT LINKAGE ADJUSTMENT

C3 Transmission

The transmission kick-down cable is adjusted by varying the position of the cable housing in its mounting bracket. To adjust:

1. Hold the accelerator pedal in full throttle position with a suitable wedge.

2. Place the transmission lever in full kick-down position.

3. Loosen the top nut and adjust bottom nut to give a 0.020 to 0.080 inch clearance between the carburetor linkage kick-down lever and the throttle operating shaft. Tighten the top nut.

4. Remove the weight from the accelerator and operate the linkage several times to be sure that wide open throttle and full transmission kick-down can be achieved.

Kickdown linkage adjustment nuts—C4

C4 Transmission

1. Press the gas pedal to the floor to completely open the throttle.

2. Position the kick-down cable so that the tang just contacts the throttle shaft.

3. If an adjustment is required, loosen the two kick-down cable adjusting nuts at the bracket and move the cable as required. Tighten the adjusting nuts.

NEUTRAL SAFETY SWITCH REMOVAL AND INSTALLATION, ADJUSTMENT

C3 Transmission

1. Raise car on hoist.

2. Disconnect cable connector from switch.

3. Use a thin wall socket to remove the neutral start switch and O-ring.

4. Install new O-ring and neutral start switch. Tighten switch to specified torque.

5. Install cable connector.

Throttle linkage adjustment—2800 cc engine

6. Check the operation of the switch in each detent position. Check to see the backup light operates in reverse only. The engine should start only with the transmission selector lever in N (neutral) and P (park).

C4 Transmission

1. Remove the downshift cable from the transmission downshift lever.

2. Remove the transmission downshift outer lever retaining nut and lever. It may be necessary to apply penetrating oil to the lever shaft and nut in order to remove the nut and lever.

3. Remove the neutral safety switch attaching bolts.

4. Disconnect the multiple wire connector. Remove the switch.

5. Install the new switch on the transmission. Install the attaching bolts.

6. With the transmission lever in neutral, rotate the switch and insert a gauge pin (No. 43 drill) into the gauge pin hole.

7. Tighten the switch attaching bolts to 4–8 ft. lbs. and remove the gauge pin.

8. Install the outer downshift lever and attaching nut, and install the downshift cable to the downshift lever.

9. Install the switch wires. Connect the multiple wire connector. Check the operation of the switch in each lever position. The engine should start only with the transmission lever in the Neutral or Park position.

DRIVE AXLE

Driveshaft and Universal Joints

The Capri uses a one-piece driveshaft with two serviceable universal joints. There is no center bearing.

Driveshaft

REMOVAL AND INSTALLATION

1. Mark the driveshaft and the rear axle pinion flange for correct realignment when installing and then remove the four attaching bolts and lockwashers.

2. Lower the driveshaft assembly and withdraw it from the transmission. A slight amount of oil may leak from the transmission.

3. Slide the front yoke into the transmission, engaging the output shaft splines, taking care not to damage the oil seal or bearing in the tail shaft.

4. Lift the rear of the driveshaft assembly, and align the marks on the driveshaft and the rear axle pinion flange. Fit the four bolts and the lockwashers, and tighten them.

5. Check the level of the transmission lubricant.

Manual linkage control

UNIVERSAL JOINT OVERHAUL

NOTE: This procedure is for service replacement. Original equipment retainers are pressed in with a preload and staked in place.

1. Remove the driveshaft.

2. Position the driveshaft assembly in a vise.

3. Remove the snap-rings which retain the bearing caps.

4. Using a suitably sized socket or an arbor press, drive one of the bearing caps in toward the center of the universal joint. This will force the opposite bearing cap out.

5. As each bearing cap is pressed or punched far enough out of the universal joint assembly so that it is accessible, grip it with a pair of pliers and pull it from the driveshaft yoke. Drive or press the spider in the opposite direction in order to make the opposite bearing cap accessible and pull it free with a pair of pliers. Use this procedure to remove all bearings from the universal joints.

6. After removing the bearings, lift the spider from the yoke.

7. Thoroughly clean the yoke areas on the driveshaft.

--- CAUTION ---
Use extreme care when installing a new bearing into position. A heavy jolt can cause one or more of the needle bearings to fall out of place which will stop the cap from sitting properly on the spider.

8. Start a new bearing into the yoke.

9. Position the spider in the yoke and press or drive the new bearing cap ¼ in. below the surface of the yoke.

10. With the bearing cap in position, install a new snap-ring.

11. Start a new bearing cap into the opposite side of the yoke.

12. Press or drive the bearing cap until the opposite bearing—which you have just installed—contacts the inner surface of the snap-ring.

13. Install a new snap-ring on the second bearing cap.

14. Position the slip yoke on the spider and install new bearings and snap-rings.

15. Check the reassembled joints for freedom of movement. Never install a driveshaft in a car if there is any binding in the universal joints.

Axle Shaft and/or Bearing Replacement

REMOVAL AND INSTALLATION

1. Jack up the rear of the car and support it with jackstands.

2. Remove the wheel, brake drum se-

curing screw, and the brake drum. Be sure that the parking brake is released.

3. Remove the bolts that secure the bearing retaining plate to the backing plate. These bolts are accessible through holes in the axle shaft flange.

4. Pull the axle and bearing assembly out of the axle housing with a slide hammer.

5. Loosen the inner retaining ring by nicking it deeply with a chisel in several places. It will then slide off easily.

6. Press off the bearing and seal assembly and install the new one by pressing it into position.

7. Press on the new retainer.

8. Assemble the shaft and the bearing in the housing.

9. Install the retaining nuts, drum, wheel, and tire.

Differential

REMOVAL

1. Jack up the car and pull the axle shafts.

2. Mark the driveshaft and pinion flanges for realignment. Remove the four bolts and washers, the ten retaining bolts, the cover, the gasket, and drain the axle.

3. Match mark and remove the differential bearing caps. Using two pry bars, remove the differential.

OVERHAUL

1. Pull off the bearings from each side of the differential assembly. Remove the shims.

2. Unscrew the ring gear retaining bolts and remove the ring gear from the differential assembly.

3. Drive out the locking pin which secures the differential pinion shaft in the differential pinions, differential side gears and adjusting shims.

4. Hold the drive pinion flange and remove the nut. Pull off the pinion flange using a puller. Remove the pinion and bearing spacer from the pinion.

5. Press off the large roller bearing from the pinion shaft, remove the spacer shim from the pinion shaft.

6. Remove the small tapered roller bearing together with the oil seal from the axle housing.

7. Drive the bearing races out from the axle housing.

8. Install the pinion bearing races, pulling them squarely into position.

9. To determine total side play of the differential case in the housing, press the taper roller bearings on the differential case without shims. Install pressure blocks into the axle tubes and install the differential into the housing. Install the bearing caps, tighten, loosen, then retighten finger tight. Mount a dial indicator gauge on the axle housing so the feeler contacts the side of

the ring gear and the dial reads zero. By moving the differential, the total side play can be measured. Record this measurement. Remove the differential and pressure blocks.

10. To determine the thickness of the pinion bearing spacer, use the trial and error method. Install the pinion with a selected spacer, small taper bearing, drive pinion flange, and the old self-locking nut. Tighten the nut to 72–87 ft. lbs. and rotate the pinion several times using an in. lbs. torque wrench. If the rotating torque required is too high, the spacer is too thin, and should be replaced with a thicker one. If the torque is too low, a thinner spacer should be used. Correct torque is 13–19 in. lbs. Remove the old nut. To check the spacer thickness, use the method described in "Pinion Mesh Markings."

11. Make sure that the new oil seal has grease between the two sealing lips and is coated with sealing compound on the other side. Install it with a new self locking nut and torque to 72–87 ft. lbs.

12. Remove the differential case bearings. Position the shims as indicated by the total side play figure, one half of the required amount on each side, on the differential case. Press the taper roller bearings on the differential case. Insert the case in the axle housing and center it. Position the bearing caps as marked. Insert the screws and torque to 43–49 ft. lbs.

DIFFERENTIAL SPECIFICATIONS

	2300 & 2800
Axle ratio	3.08:1
No. teeth in pinion	11
No. teeth in ring gear	34
Oil Capacity	2.3
Side gear play	0.004–0.006
Bearing preload	0.0012–0.0031
Backlash	0.047–0.086

13. Position the dial indicator feeler in a vertical position on one ring gear tooth and check the tooth flank backlash. If the backlash is not within 0.005–0.009 in. (0.12–0.22 mm.) the differential must be removed again. If the backlash is too large, remove the shims from the ring gear face side and transfer to ring gear back side. Reverse procedure if backlash is too small. Do not increase or decrease number of shims, but only interchange between one side and the other.

14. For proper tooth contact pattern check, see "Pinion Mesh Markings."

15. Position a new gasket and the axle

case cover on the axle case, secure with bolts and torque to 22–29 ft. lbs.

16. Install the driveshaft, axles and wheels.

Pinion Mesh Markings

The following method of determining the relative position of the ring gear and pinion, and whether or not they are in proper mesh, will prove satisfactory for all pinion and ring gears. This should be followed by a final check, even when the pinion depth has been determined by special tools. Assemble the pinion in the housing, without preload, and tighten the pinion nut until a preload of about 10 in. lbs. is developed on the bearings to insure that they are completely free of end play.

This, of course, is not the final bearing preload setting, but is a good one for checking the pinion mesh markings.

Install the differential assembly and adjust it to provide from 0.004–0.008 in. backlash of the ring gear, measured at the rim of the gear.

Paint five or six of the ring gear teeth with red lead and, while a helper brakes the ring gear with a piece of wood, slowly turn the pinion until the ring gear makes at least one full revolution. The mesh of the pinion with the ring gear will be indicated as a mark in the red lead on the ring gear teeth. Compare this mark with the accompanying illustrations. The caption on each photograph explains whether the mark indicates the pinion is too deep or too shallow, the ring gear too close or too far away.

When the marking is found to be improper, it is customary to make trial changes in increments of 0.005–0.007 in. If changing the shim 0.005–0.007 throws the marking from too deep to too shallow, the proper distance is about halfway between.

If, after changing this increment of shims, the mark still indicates that more must be changed, it is advisable to continue changing in the same increments.

While considerable time is generally required to disassemble the unit, press off the bearings, change the shims, press the bearing back on and reassemble the unit, this is still the only positive method of determining that the differential will operate quietly after it is finally installed in the car.

REAR SUSPENSION

The rear axle is suspended by two three leaf springs with a stabilizer bar. Sealed, hydraulic shock absorbers are positioned between the rear axle and the reinforced mountings on the floor pan. The shock absorbers are staggered on the axle. The righthand shock absorber axle mounting is located in front of the rear axle and the left-

STABILIZER BAR
MOUNTING CLAMP

INSULATOR

REAR STABILIZER
BAR

INSULATOR
ASS'Y.

STABILIZER END
ASS'Y.

SPRING SHACKLE

BUSHINGS

INSULATOR RETAINER

CENTER MOUNTING
INSULATOR

BUSHING

No. 1 SPRING LEAF

SPRING INSERT (4)

No. 2 SPRING LEAF

SPRING PLATE

CLAMP

CLAMP LINER

An exploded view of the rear suspension

Rear shock absorber assembly

hand shock is mounted to the rear of the axle.

Springs

REMOVAL AND INSTALLATION

1. Block each front wheel.
2. Jack up the rear of the car and support it with jackstands.
3. Position a jack under the rear axle and extend it sufficiently to support the axle.

4. Remove the rear shackle nuts and the washers and then detach the combined shackle bolt and the place assemblies. Remove the two rubber bushings.

NOTE: Skip Steps 5–10 if you are not replacing the bushings.

5. Unscrew the nut from the front mounting bracket and then withdraw the thru-bolt.
6. Remove the U-bolts and then the attaching plate.
7. Remove the spring assembly.
8. Remove the insulator sleeve and the retaining plate from the spring.
9. Pull the bushings out of the spring eyes.
10. Press in the bushings in the front and the rear eyes.
11. Position the front of the spring in its body mounting bracket. Install the thru-bolt and loosely assemble the nut and washer.
12. Position the rubber insulator sleeve around the spring and then place the retainer plate over the insulator.
13. Position the spring assembly to the axle and install the U-bolts, plate, and the

nuts. Tighten the nuts initially to about 5 ft. lbs. to compress the rubber insulators.

14. Place the spring into position and assemble the rear shackle bolt and plate assemblies. Install the nuts and washers but do not tighten them.
15. Remove the jack supporting the rear axle.
16. Lower the car to the ground.
17. Tighten the U-bolts, front hanger nuts, and the axle shackle nuts.

Shock Absorbers

REMOVAL AND INSTALLATION

1. Remove the two rear seat attaching bolts and remove the rear seat.
2. Unscrew the seat belt retaining bolt from the upper end of the B post. Remove belt.
3. Remove the B post trim.
4. Remove the upper quarter window trim.
5. Remove two screws at the rear end of the rocker panel and pull off the door weatherstrip in the side trim area.
6. Remove the side trim panel and remove the luggage compartment carpet.
7. Tilt the rear seat back rest forward and remove the rear panel trim and the side panel.
8. Remove the two nuts from the top of the shock absorber and lift off the top steel washer and the rubber bushing.
9. Raise the car on a hoist.
10. Remove the lower end of the shock absorber from the bracket on the axle by removing the nut, lockwasher and bolt. Remove the shock absorber from the car.

11. Remove the rubber bushing and steel washer from the top of the shock absorber.
12. Assemble the large steel washer and the rubber bushing to the top of the shock absorber.
13. Extend the shock absorber upward and pass it through the mounting hole in the body. Position the rubber bushing to the mounting hole in the body. Position washer and nut on the piston rod but do not tighten.
14. Position the lower end of the shock absorber in the bracket on the axle. Install the bolt, lockwasher and nut. Tighten to 40–45 ft. lbs.
15. Lower the car to the ground.
16. Tighten the shock absorber upper attaching nut to 15–20 ft. lbs. Install the lock nut and tighten securely.
17. Replace the rear panel, and side trim panel. Replace the luggage compartment carpet.
18. Replace the side trim panel, fit the door weatherstrip in place and attach the rocker panel.
19. Replace the upper quarter window and B post trim.
20. Replace the seat belt attachment at the B post and fit the rear seat.

Stabilizer Bar

REMOVAL AND INSTALLATION

1. Raise and safely support the rear of the car.
2. Disconnect the parking brake primary cable from the relay lever on the rear axle.
3. Push the stabilizer bar back for access and unbolt the clamps from the axle.
4. Remove the bar.
5. On installation, if the bushing fittings at the end of the bar have been disturbed, check that the lever arm length of the bar is correct on both sides. Adjust by screwing the bushing fittings in or out. Tighten the locknuts.
6. Locate the bar on the axle and position the bushing fittings in the frame channels. Install the bolt heads inside the frame.

262 ±2,5mm (10·24 ±01 in)

Stabilizer bar lever arm length should be adjusted to the dimension shown

Replace the plain washers and self-locking nuts loosely.

7. Hold the bar in place and start the retaining clamp bolts. Lower the car to rest on its wheels. Torque the clamp bolts to 29–37 ft. lbs. Tighten the bushing fitting pivot bolts to 33–37 ft. lbs.

FRONT SUSPENSION

This independent front suspension uses MacPherson struts. These units combine vertically mounted shock absorbers surrounded by coil springs. Side-to-side movement of each front wheel is controlled by a track control arm, and fore and aft movement is controlled by the stabilizer bar.

Downward movement of the wheel is limited by a rebound stop inside the shock absorber, and the upward movement by the spring reaching its limit of compression and by a rubber bumper around the suspension unit piston rod.

Front suspension geometry figures (i.e. camber, caster, and the kingpin inclination angles) are set when the car is manufactured

and are not adjustable. Toe-in, however, is adjustable.

Strut Assembly

REMOVAL AND INSTALLATION

1. Jack up the front of the car and support it with jackstands.
2. Remove the wheel.
3. Remove and plug the brake line.
4. Position a jack under the track control arm and jack up the suspension unit.
5. Remove the cotter pin and unscrew the castle nut holding the connecting rod end to the steering arm. Using a ball joint separator, separate the joint. Remove the jack from under the control arm.
6. Remove the cotter pin and unscrew the castle nut holding the track control arm to the base of the suspension unit and disconnect the track control arm.
7. Remove the three bolts holding the top mount assembly to the side apron panel and remove the suspension assembly from the car, complete with the disc brake caliper.
8. Lift the suspension assembly into position and secure it with the three bolts through the side apron panel, to the top mount assembly. Tighten the bolts to 15–18 ft. lbs.
9. Assemble the track control arm ball stud to the base of the suspension unit and tighten the securing nut to 30–35 ft. lbs. Install a new cotter pin.

10. Install the connecting rod end to the steering arm and tighten the castle nut to 18–22 ft. lbs. Install a new cotter pin.
11. Remove the brake line plug and install the brake line.
12. Bleed the brakes.
13. Replace the wheel and lower the car.

Disassembly and Assembly

For strut overhaul, spring, and shock absorber removal and installation procedures, please refer to "Strut Overhaul" in the Unit Repair section.

Stabilizer Bar

REMOVAL AND INSTALLATION

1. Jack up the front of the car and support it with jackstands.
2. Remove the two attachment clamps from the front of the stabilizer bar after bending back the locktabs and removing the four bolts.
3. Remove the cotter pins and unscrew the stabilizer bar nuts which hold the ends of the stabilizer bar to the track control arm. Remove the nuts and pull off the large washers.
4. Pull the stabilizer bar forward and remove it.
5. Remove the sleeve and the large washer from each end of the stabilizer bar.

Exploded view of the front suspension

Exploded view of the lower control arm and stabilizer bar

6. Remove the stabilizer bar mounting bushings.

7. Install the stabilizer bar mounting bushing by sliding them along the bar from one end until they are under the clamp bolt holes in the body bracket.

8. Assemble a large washer and a sleeve to each end of the stabilizer bar and then insert the stabilizer bar through the holes in the track control arms.

9. Assemble the large washers to the ends of the stabilizer bar and secure them with the castle nuts.

10. Remove the jackstands and lower the car to the ground. Tighten the castle nuts on the ends of the stabilizer bar to 15–45 ft. lbs. and install the cotter pins.

11. Install the stabilizer bar attachment clamps.

12. Secure the bar to the mounting points using two new lockwashers and two bolts on each clamp. With the car on the ground, tighten the bolts to 15–18 ft. lbs. Turn the tabs on the lockwashers.

Lower Control Arm

REMOVAL AND INSTALLATION

1. Jack up the front of the car and support it with jackstands.

2. Remove the cotter pin and unscrew the castle nut holding the control arm to the stabilizer bar. Pull off the large dish washer.

3. Remove the self-locking nut and the flat washer from the rear of the lower control arm pivot and release the inner end of the control arm.

4. Remove the cotter pin and unscrew the nut securing the control arm ball joint to the base of the strut unit and then separate the joint.

5. Assemble the control arm ball stud to the base of the strut unit, and tighten it to 30–35 ft. lbs. Install a new cotter pin.

6. Position the control arm so that it is in place over the stabilizer bar and then secure the inner end. Slide the pivot bolt into position from the front and install the flat washer and the self-locking nut from the rear. Tighten the nut to 22–27 ft. lbs. with the car resting on its wheels.

7. Assemble the dished washer to the end of the stabilizer bar. Install the castle nut, lower the car to the ground, and tighten the nut to 15–45 ft. lbs. Install a new cotter pin.

Front-End Alignment

Before any alignment checks are made, the following points should be checked and, if necessary, corrected.

1. Correct tire inflation.

2. Front wheel bearing adjustment.

3. Stabilizer bar brackets to body crossmember nuts for tightness.

4. Front suspension springs for proper seating.

5. Wheels for trueness.

6. Ball joints for wear.

7. The car should be unloaded.

The caster, camber, and the king pin inclination angles are not adjustable, but they should be checked and, when the readings differ from those specified, the related parts should be replaced to correct the condition.

TOE-IN ADJUSTMENT

Toe-in is the difference of the distance between the centers of the front and rear, of the front wheels. Toe-in is necessary to compensate for the tendency of the wheels to deflect toward the rear while in motion. Toe-in is adjusted by changing the length of the tie rod ends. When adjusting the tie rod ends, adjust each equal amounts (in the opposite direction) to increase or decrease the toe-in.

STEERING

Rack and pinion steering gear is used on all Capris. It is mounted in rubber insulators on brackets attached to the front crossmember.

The steering wheel is mounted on a collapsible can, so that it will collapse under a heavy impact. Movement of the steering wheel is transmitted by the steering shaft through a universal joint and a flexible coupling to the pinion. Rotation of the pinion causes the rack to move from side-to-side and the connecting rods, attached to the ends of the rack, transmit this movement to the spindle arms and cause the wheels to turn.

The steering gear holds three tenths (0.3) of a pint of SAE 90 hypoid oil. Never fill the gear completely with oil. This would result in a buildup of pressure which could burst or blow off the bellows in the gear.

Steering Wheel

REMOVAL AND INSTALLATION

1. Make sure that the front wheels are facing straight ahead. Remove the two

Exploded view of the steering column

screws holding the steering column shroud and remove the lower half. Pull off the upper shroud.

2. Pry out the steering wheel center emblem. Matchmark the steering shaft and wheel so they can be correctly realigned.

3. Remove the steering wheel retaining nut and then pull the steering wheel off the steering shaft by hand.

4. Align the steering wheel in the correct position and push it onto the shaft. Be sure that the turn signal cancelling cam is in the groove on the underside of the wheel.

5. Install the steering wheel retaining nut and tighten it to 25–30 ft. lbs.

6. Install the steering wheel center. Replace the shrouds, if removed.

Turn Signal Switch

REMOVAL AND INSTALLATION

1. Disconnect the battery ground cable.

2. Remove the steering column shroud screws and remove the lower shroud half. Pull sharply up to release the upper shroud half.

3. Remove the switch retaining screws, disconnect the electrical plug, and remove the switch.

4. On reinstallation, connect the electrical plug and screw the switch in place.

5. Replace the shroud halves.

6. Connect battery.

Ignition Switch and Lock

SWITCH REMOVAL AND INSTALLATION

1. Disconnect the negatave cable from the battery.

2. Remove the screws securing the steering column shroud. Remove the lower half of the shroud and release the shroud upper half retaining lug from its spring clip on the steering column by pulling sharply upward.

3. Be sure that the ignition key is in the O position.

4. Remove the screws holding the lower left dash trim panel. Pull the trim panel forward and down and remove the connector from the hazard warning flasher switch. Remove the trim panel from the dash.

5. Disconnect ignition wires at the connector.

6. Remove the screws securing the ignition switch to the lock and withdraw the switch.

7. Position the switch to the lock, being sure that the key remains in the O position and is correctly inserted.

8. Engage and tighten the switch retaining screws.

9. Connect ignition wires at the connection.

10. Position the lower left dash trim panel under the dash panel and connect the hazard warning flasher switch. Press the trim panel into its location and install and tighten the screws.

11. Mount the upper and lower halves of the steering column shroud and secure with screws.

12. Connect the battery negative cable and check the operation of the switch.

LOCK REMOVAL AND INSTALLATION

1. Disconnect the negative cable from the battery.

2. Remove the screws holding the steering column shroud. Remove the lower half of the shroud and release the shroud upper half retaining lug from its spring clip on the steering column by pulling sharply upward.

3. Remove the screws holding the left and right lower dash trim panels and lower the panels.

4. Remove the screws holding the turn signal switch. Move the switch out of the way.

5. Disconnect the ignition wires at the connector.

6. Remove the screws holding the steering column to the dash.

7. Turn the steering column to gain access to the headless bolts.

8. Remove lock from steering column by drilling out headless bolts or removing bolts with a screw extractor.

9. Position the new lock assembly, with the key in the lock, to the steering column.

10. Withdraw the lock to allow the pawl to enter the steering shaft.

11. Locate the loose half of the clamp to the lock, engage the shear head bolts and tighten evenly until the bolt heads shear off. While tightening the bolts, check the pawl for free operation.

12. Reconnect the ignition wires at the connector.

13. Turn the steering column in the correct position. Install the screws holding the steering column.

14. Install the turn signal switch.

15. Install the lower dash trim panel.

16. Install the upper and lower halves of the steering column shroud.

17. Connect the battery ground cable.

Steering Gear

REMOVAL AND INSTALLATION

Manual Steering

1. Set the steering wheel so the front wheels are facing straight ahead.

2. Jack up the front of the car and support it with jackstands.

3. Remove the nut and the bolt retaining the flexible coupling to the pinion splines.

4. Bend back the locktabs and remove the screws holding the steering gear to the mounting brackets on the crossmember. Remove the screws, locking plates, and the U-clamps.

5. Remove the cotter pins and slacken the castle nuts securing the connecting rod ends to the spindle arms.

6. Using a ball joint separator tool, separate the connecting rod ends from the spindle arms. Remove the castle nuts and withdraw the steering gear from the car. It may be necessary to turn one wheel to the stop to permit the steering gear assembly to be moved sideways enough to allow the other end to clear the stabilizer bar.

7. Remove the connecting rods and the locknuts. Note the number of turns required to unscrew them.

8. Replace the locknuts and the connecting rod ends; screw them in the same number of turns required to take them out.

9. Make sure the steering wheel is aligned straight ahead.

10. Set the steering gear in the straight ahead position.

11. Position the steering gear and align the mating splines on the flexible coupling and the pinion shaft.

12. Secure the steering gear assembly to its mounting brackets on the crossmember. Tighten the screws to 15–18 ft. lbs.

13. Assemble the connecting rod ends to the spindle arms. Install the castle nuts and tighten them to 18–22 ft. lbs. Install new cotter pins.

14. Tighten the flexible coupling-to-pinion shaft securing bolt to 12–15 ft. lbs.

15. Remove the jackstands and lower the car to the ground.

16. Check the front end wheel alignment. Check the position of the steering wheel.

Power Steering

1. Disconnect negative battery cable.

2. Raise car on hoist and remove engine splash shield if equipped.

3. Disconnect fluid pipes from rack and drain power steering fluid.

4. Remove steering coupling lower clamp bolt.

5. Disconnect tie rod ends from steering arm.

6. Remove the two steering rack mounting bolts and remove rack from vehicle.

7. Remove tie rod ends from track rods. Count number of turns required to disengage threads and note the number for assembly purposes.

8. Install tie rod ends on tie rods. Screw on each tie rod end the same number of turns as required to remove it.

9. Position steering rack into vehicle and locate pinion in steering coupling. En-

CONTROL
VALVE
HOUSING

PRELOAD
SPRING

FLUID LINE

COVER PLATE

PINS

SEAL

BEARING

SEAL

SHAFT

COVER

SHIMS

PEG

PINS

SPOOL
VALVE

PINS

CLIP

WASHERS

CLIP

INNER TUBE

SEAL

WASHER

TAB
WASHER

PEG

SEALS

SPRING

PINION

RACK SLIPPER

SEAL

WASHERS

RACK
BEARING

SEAL

O-RING

LOCKNUT

SPRING

WASHER

BALL SEAT

SEAL

BALL HOUSING

DUST SEAL

PIN

RACK PISTON

TIE ROD

CLAMP

BALL HOUSING

RACK

PIN

NUT

TIE ROD

BALL SEAT

WASHER

SPRING

LOCKNUT

VALVE
HOUSING

INNER
RACE

BEARING

BELLOWS

SEALS

OUTER
RACE

COVER

SHIM

LOCK
TAB

CLAMP

TIE ROD END

CLAMP

BELLOWS

CLAMP

FLUID LINES

NO. 2 CROSSMEMBER

POWER STEERING GEAR

Exploded view of power steering gear

sure bolt hole in steering coupling aligns with flat on steering pinion shaft.

10. Secure steering rack to crossmember with the two bolts.

11. Install steering coupling lower clamp bolt. Be sure coupling segments are all in same plane. Align as necessary by sliding coupling up or down on pinion shaft.

12. Connect tie rod ends to steering arms, and connect fluid lines to rack. Torque pressure lines 19–23 ft. lbs. and return lines 12–15 ft. lbs.

13. Install engine splash shield, if equipped.

Exploded view of standard steering gear

14. Check and adjust front wheel toe-in.

15. Connect negative cable battery, fill power steering reservoir, and bleed system.

16. Lower car from hoist.

Power Steering Pump

REMOVAL AND INSTALLATION

1. Open hood and disconnect negative cable from battery.

2. Raise car on hoist.

3. Remove engine splash shield, if so equipped.

4. Loosen alternator mounting bolts (2300cc) or idler pulley bolts (2800 cc) and remove drive belt.

5. Disconnect fluid lines and drain fluid.

6. On 2300 cc engines disconnect fuel pump from engine. Do not disconnect fuel pump lines, but move pump away from power steering pump mounting bolts.

7. Remove power steering pump (2300 cc). On 2800 cc equipped cars remove the pump and bracket assembly.

8. Remove pulley from pump and pump from adaptor bracket, if so equipped.

9. Secure pump properly to bracket.

10. Install pulley on pump.

11. Install pump (2300 cc) and bracket assembly.

12. Reinstall fuel pump on 2300 cc engines.

13. Connect power steering fluid lines. Torque pressure lines to 19–23 ft. lbs. and return lines to 12–15 ft. lbs.

14. Install drive belts and adjust tension.

15. Install engine splash shield, if so equipped.

16. Lower hoist and fill reservoir with power steering fluid. Bleed system.

17. Connect negative battery cable and close hood.

AIR BLEEDING

1. Open hood and check the fluid level. If the fluid is low, add power steering fluid to maximum level.

2. After adding fluid, allow fluid to stand for two minutes. Start car and run engine to 1500 rpm.

3. Slowly turn steering wheel from lock to lock. At the same time check fluid level, add fluid until lever is steady and air bubbles no longer appear.

4. Check pipe connections, bellows, valve body and pump for leaks and repair.

5. Close hood.

MANUAL STEERING GEAR ADJUSTMENTS

Support Yoke and Pinion Bearing Pre-Load

1. Carefully mount the steering gear in a vise (with protected jaws), so that the

Exploded view of power steering pump

pinion is horizontal and the rack pre-load cover plate is on top.

2. Remove the two screws attaching the rack pre-load cover plate to the housing.

3. Lift off the cover plate, shim pack and gasket. Withdraw the spring and support yoke.

4. Remove the two screws attaching the pinion bearing pre-load cover plate to the housing.

5. Lift off the cover plate, shim pack and gasket.

6. Position shim pack and pinion cover plate on bearing and install the retaining screws. The shim pack must be made up of at least three shims. One shim must be 0.093 inch thick and positioned immediately next to plate.

7. Tighten the cover retaining screws then loosen until the plate just touches shim pack.

8. Using feeler gauges, measure the gap between the cover plate and the steering gear housing. The gap should measure 0.011–0.013 inches. (To confirm that the cover plate has been pulled down evenly by the retaining screws, take feeler gauge measurements adjacent to each screw.)

9. If the gap measured exceeds 0.011–0.013 inches the shim pack must be made smaller. If the gap is smaller than specification, the shim pack must be made larger. The shim pack must still use a 0.093 inch thick shim positioned next to plate.

10. Remove the cover plate, assemble the shim pack and reinstall the cover plate. Install the attaching screws, using sealer on the threads, and tighten to 6–8 ft. lbs.

11. Set the support yoke adjustment. For the spring to exert the correct pressure on the support yoke, it is necessary for the distance between the underside of the cover plate and the top of the support yoke to be accurately set to 0.0005–0.0035 inch.

12. Assemble the support yoke to the rear of the rack and push it fully into po-sition. Using a straightedge and feeler gauges, measure the distance between the top of the support yoke and the surface of the steering gear housing at the cover plate. Note this dimension.

13. Assemble a shim pack (including two gaskets which must sandwich the shim pack), the thickness of which is 0.0005–0.0035 inch greater than the dimension obtained in the previous paragraph.

It is most important that the dimension is correctly set. If it is not, it may result in a knocking noise from the steering gear or heavy steering effort.

14. Install the spring into the recess in the support yoke.

15. Position the shim pack and gaskets and replace the cover plate.

16. Assemble the attaching screws to the cover plate, using sealer on the threads. Tighten the screws to 6–8 ft. lbs.

17. Install an in. lbs. torque wrench to the splined end of the pinion shafts.

18. Determine the torque required to start the pinion rotating. This should be 10–18 in. lbs. If the actual torque is not within the prescribed limits, the adjustment is in-correct (check the shimming) or there is some malfunction within the gear assembly (tight bearings, damaged gear teeth, lack of lubricants, etc.) which is increasing the friction level.

BRAKES

All Capris are equipped with floating cal-iper type disc brakes on the front wheels and conventional drum brakes on the rear. A twin-reservoir hydraulic system is used to operate the brakes. This provides sepa-rate hydraulic circuits for the front and rear brakes. If one circuit fails, the driver is still able to stop the car by using the other sys-tem.

All models use a floor-mounted hand-brake which is located between the front seats. This parking brake operates through a two-cable linkage and its operation causes the self-adjusting mechanism in the rear brakes to operate.

A power brake vacuum booster is in-stalled in the engine compartment. The booster operates through a rod and clevis assembly which is attached to the brake pedal at one end and the brake master cyl-inder at the other end.

For all brake system repair and service procedures not detailed below, please re-fer to "Brakes" in the Unit Repair sec-tion.

Adjustment

The front disc brakes are not adjustable. The rear drum brakes are self adjusting.

Master Cylinder

REMOVAL AND INSTALLATION

1. Siphon the fluid from the reservoir.

2. Disconnect the brake lines from the master cylinder.

3. Remove the master cylinder-to-brake booster retaining nuts.

4. Lift the master cylinder away from the brake booster, being careful not to dam-age the vacuum seal.

5. Position the master cylinder, includ-ing the fluid seal, correctly onto the pushrod and hold it in position. With the cylinder in this position, screw in all union nuts of the brake lines a few turns.

6. Connect the master cylinder to the brake booster and tighten the nuts.

7. Connect the brake lines.

Exploded view of the master cylinder

8. Fill the reservoir with heavy-duty brake fluid designated for disc brake systems. Bleed the entire brake system.

9. Check the operation of the brakes.

Pressure Differential Valve And Switch

REMOVAL AND INSTALLATION

1. Disconnect the five brake lines from the ports on the valve and the switch assembly. Plug the end of the lines from the master cylinder.

2. Disconnect the wire from the switch.

3. Unscrew the bolt securing the assembly to the rear of the engine compartment. Remove the assembly.

4. Position the assembly in place on the firewall and loosely install the attaching bolt.

5. Connect the hydraulic lines. Tighten the attaching bolt.

6. Connect the wiring to the switch.

0.10 IN. (2.54MM) 0.31 IN. (7.87 MM) 45°

Piston centralizing tool

Power Brake Booster

REMOVAL AND INSTALLATION

1. Remove the brake pushrod clevis pin from the brake pedal and remove the pin.

2. Remove the master cylinder retaining nuts and position the master cylinder assembly away from the brake booster.

3. Remove the vacuum hose from the brake booster.

4. Remove the brake booster-to-dash panel retaining screws and remove the brake booster assembly and seal.

5. Remove the retaining bracket and the gasket from the brake booster.

6. Assemble the brake booster retaining bracket with a new gasket to the brake booster.

7. Position the booster assembly and the bracket onto the bolts protruding through the dash panel. Use a new gasket. Connect the pushrod with the clevis pin to the brake pedal.

(0.039 to 0.059 INCH CLEARANCE)

B A
C
TO PARKING BRAKE HANDLE
ABUTMENT BRACKET

ROD ABUTMENT
TRANSVERSE ROD

Parking brake system details

8. Install and tighten the bracket retaining screws. Connect the vacuum hose to the booster.

9. Position the master cylinder assembly with a new seal ring on the booster and tighten the master cylinder-to-booster retaining nuts.

Wheel Bearings

REMOVAL AND INSTALLATION

1. Remove the wheel cover and dust cap.

2. Jack up the car.

3. Remove the cotter pin, nut retainer, adjusting nut, washer, and bearing.

4. Wash all parts in a solvent.

5. Hand-pack the wheel bearing with wheel bearing grease.

6. Reassemble, reversing the removal procedure.

NOTE: When installing the cotter pin it may be necessary to move the nut retainer in various positions on the nut to allow the cotter pin to go through the hole in the axle.

7. Torque the adjusting nut to 17–20 ft. lbs. while turning the disc. Back the nut off one-half turn then tighten it hand-tight or 10–15 in. lbs. Install the nut retainer and cotter pin.

Wheel Cylinders

REMOVAL AND INSTALLATION

1. Remove the wheel and drum.

2. Remove the brake shoes.

3. Disconnect, but don't pull away the brake line.

4. Remove the wheel cylinder bolts and lockwashers and remove it.

5. Position the cylinder and start the tubing connection.

6. Fasten the cylinder down.

7. Tighten the tubing connection.

8. Replace and adjust the shoes.

9. Replace the drums and bleed the brakes.

Parking Brake

CABLE REMOVAL AND INSTALLATION

1. Release the parking brake.

2. Remove the spring clip and clevis pin holding the cable to the handle.

3. Remove the spring clip and clevis pin holding the cable to the right rear brake lever.

4. Remove the clip holding the cable to transverse rod. Slide the cable clear of the rod bracket.

5. Slide the cable, adjusting nut, and

WITH WHEEL ROTATING, TORQUE ADJUSTING NUT, TO 17-25 FT. LBS.

BACK ADJUSTING NUT OFF 1/2 TURN

TIGHTEN ADJUSTING NUT TO 10-15 IN.-LBS.

INSTALL THE LOCK AND A NEW COTTER PIN

Front wheel bearing adjustment

guide clear of the abutment bracket and remove.

6. Reverse the procedure for installation. Grease the pivot points. Adjust the parking brake.

ADJUSTMENT

1. Raise and support the rear axle. Block the front wheels.

2. Check the clearance between each brake lever abutment (stop) and the backing plate. It should be 0.039–0.059 in.

3. To adjust, engage the keyed cable sleeve into the abutment slot and turn the adjuster nut to remove cable slack.

CHASSIS ELECTRICAL

Heater Assembly

REMOVAL AND INSTALLATION

Non A/C

1. Remove the lower dash trim panel and the glove box. To do this, the steering column shroud, ashtray, hazard flasher switch, and turn signal switch must be removed.

2. Remove the four-speed shift knob. Remove the screws for the center console. Pry the rear console panel up and remove the two screws. Pry up the clock panel and disconnect the electrical connections. Remove the main screw at the rear end of the area under the clock panel. Slide the plastic brace forward below the parking brake lever and remove it. Lift the console out.

3. Drain the coolant, with the heater controls on.

4. Disconnect the hoses from the heater core and detach the gasket.

5. Disconnect the right and left vent and defroster ducts from the heater assembly.

6. Disconnect the control cables from the heater and water valve.

7. Unscrew the seat belt buzzer and let it hang.

8. Disconnect the wiring harness connector from the heater blower.

9. Remove the wiper motor bracket.

10. Remove the heater assembly bolts and remove the unit.

11. On installation, replace the heater assembly and the wiper motor bracket.

12. Install the left vent and defroster ducts.

13. Connect the blower wiring.

14. Connect the control cables. Adjust the upper lever in the WARM position and the lower in the OFF position.

Heating and ventilation system (with A/C)

15. Install the right vent and defroster ducts.

16. Replace the gasket and heater hoses.

17. Fill the cooling system.

18. Replace the console, shift knob, glove box, and lower dash trim panel.

With Factory-Installed A/C

--- **CAUTION** ---

This operation requires discharging the A/C system. This should not be attempted by untrained personnel.

The assembly to be removed in this procedure is the evaporator case assembly.

1. Discharge the system.

2. Disconnect the refrigerant lines from the evaporator core and the heater hoses from the heater core in the engine compartment.

3. Remove the glove box and the lower right trim panel. Remove the control head assembly and lower instrument panel.

4. Disconnect the vacuum hoses from the evaporator case.

5. Disconnect the temperature control cable from the blend door operating lever.

6. Remove the evaporator case bolts beside the outside/recirculation air control door.

7. Remove the air conditioning and heater ducts.

8. Disconnect the blower lead plug from the blower motor resistor.

9. Remove the three evaporator attaching nuts from the engine compartment. Rotate the evaporator assembly down and away from the firewall and out from under the instrument panel.

10. Reverse the procedure for installation. Recharge the air conditioning system.

DE-ICING SWITCH • EVAPORATOR CORE • OUTSIDE/RECIRCULATING DOOR VACUUM MOTOR • HEATER CORE • UPPER CASE • OUTSIDE/RECIRCULATING DOOR • TEMPERATURE BLEND DOOR (CABLE OPERATED) • LOWER CASE • DEFROST/HEAT DOOR VACUUM MOTOR • A/C HEAT DOOR VACUUM MOTOR • BLOWER MOTOR • AIR PLENUM • DEFROST/HEAT DOOR • A/C – HEAT DOOR • BLOWER MOTOR RESISTORS • BLOWER MOTOR CASE

Evaporator case assembly (with A/C)

Heater Blower

REMOVAL AND INSTALLATION

Non A/C

1. Remove the heater assembly and separate the two halves of the heater.
2. Disconnect the two motor wires and remove the four retaining clips.
3. Remove the motor and the wheel assembly from the upper half of the heater.
4. Install the replacement assembly into the upper half of the heater and secure it with the four clips.
5. Connect the two motor wires.
6. Assemble the two halves of the heater and install it into the car.

With Factory-Installed A/C

1. Remove the glove box.
2. Remove the three screws holding the blower motor housing to the right end of the evaporator case.
3. Take the blower motor housing apart. Take off the three nuts and remove the motor.
4. Reverse the procedure for installation.

Heater Core

REMOVAL AND INSTALLATION

Non A/C

1. Remove the heater assembly, the two halves of the heater.
2. Slide the core out of the lower half of the heater.
3. Slide the replacement core into the lower half of the heater and assemble the two heater halves.

With Factory-Installed A/C

1. Remove the evaporator case assembly, covered under "Heater Assembly Removal and Installation"
2. Disconnect the vacuum motor linkage for the A/C-Heat and Defrost/Heat doors.
3. Remove the foam pad around the evaporator core inlet and outlet.
4. Remove the three screws holding the blower motor housing to the right end of the evaporator case. Remove the screws holding the air plenum to the back of the case. Disassemble the case, being careful of the moulding.
5. Carefully remove the de-icing bulb from in front of the evaporator core.
6. Remove the core mounting screws from the front of the evaporator case. Remove the evaporator and heater cores.
7. Reverse the procedure for installation.

Radio

Since the radio is usually a dealer installed or aftermarket unit, only a generalized removal procedure is given here. The following applies generally to all car radios.

Care should be taken during installation to avoid reversing the ground and power leads. Reversal of these leads would cause serious radio damage. The power lead usually has an inline fuse.

If the speaker needs replacement, it should be replaced with one of the same impedance, measured in ohms (Ω). Mismatched impedance can cause rapid transistor failure as well as low volume output. This should also be considered when adding a second speaker; it must be of the same impedance and wired in parallel with the original.

The radio should never be operated without a speaker connected or with the speaker leads shorted. This will result in transistor failure.

Removal and Installation

NOTE: This is a general procedure; it is not specific to any car.

1. Remove the package tray, if any.
2. Remove the radio knobs and unscrew the retaining nuts.
3. Remove the wire connectors from the radio and remove the brackets from the rear of the radio.
4. Remove the radio.
5. Place the radio in position and install the brackets and the wiring connectors.
6. Install the package tray.

Windshield Wiper Motor

REMOVAL AND INSTALLATION

Front Motor

1. Disconnect the negative cable from the battery.
2. Remove wiper arms and blades.
3. Remove the screws securing the steering column shroud. Remove the lower half of the shroud and release the shroud upper half retaining lug from its spring clip on the steering column by pulling sharply upward.
4. Remove retaining screws and pull lower dash panel assembly clear of dash panel.
5. Disconnect cigar lighter wiring and remove panel assembly from vehicle.
6. Remove instrument cluster bezel.
7. Remove instrument cluster.
8. Remove glovebox catch striker and glovebox assembly. Disconnect glovebox light wiring.
9. Disconnect heater control cables from heater controls.
10. Disconnect left-side defroster tube connector from heater and remove connector and tube.
11. Disconnect and remove left-side face-level vent tube.
12. Disconnect wiring at heater and wiper motor.
13. Remove left defroster vent retaining screw and remove vent.
14. Remove wiper spindle retaining nuts and motor bracket retaining screw and remove motor and linkage assembly from vehicle.
15. Separate motor from linkage.
16. Attach motor to linkage.
17. Install wiper motor and linkage assembly. Secure with spindle retaining nuts and motor bracket retaining screw.
18. Install left side defroster vent.
19. Reconnect wiper motor and heater wiring.
20. Install left side face-level vent tube.
21. Reconnect left side defroster vent tube to vent and connect defroster tube connector to heater box.

22. Connect and adjust heater control cables.

23. Install glovebox and glovebox catch striker. Reconnect glovebox light wiring.

24. Install instrument cluster.

25. Install instrument cluster bezel.

26. Reposition lower dash insulator panel and cover panel assembly. Connect cigar lighter wiring and install panel.

27. Install steering column shroud.

28. Install wiper arms and blades.

29. Connect negative battery cable and check wiper operation.

Rear Wiper Motor

1. Disconnect the negative cable from the battery.

2. Remove wiper arm and blade.

3. Open tailgate and remove tailgate trim panel.

4. Disconnect wiring at wiper motor.

5. Remove wiper spindle retaining nut, three motor bracket retaining screws and remove motor and linkage assembly from bracket.

6. Remove drive spindle nut and three retaining bolts and remove motor from bracket.

7. Remove linkage from bracket. Remove snap-ring at wiper spindle end.

8. Install linkage on bracket. Secure with snap-ring.

9. Install motor on bracket.

10. Install wiper motor and bracket on tailgate and reconnect wiper motor wiring. To avoid water leaks the position of the bracket may be altered by adjusting bracket arm and tightening nut.

11. Install wiper arm and blade.

12. Reconnect negative battery cable.

13. Check wiper operation.

14. Replace tailgate trim panel.

Instrument Cluster

REMOVAL AND INSTALLATION

Non A/C

1. Disconnect the battery ground cable.

2. Remove the steering column shroud and the ashtray.

3. Unfasten the hazard warning switch and disconnect its connector.

4. Unfasten the turn signal switch and let it hang.

5. Remove the lower trim panel screws. Pull the panel forward and down to disconnect the lighter and clock. Remove the trim panel.

6. Pull off the panel illumination control knob.

7. Remove the lower cluster bezel screws, pull the bezel down, and disconnect the seat belt warning light connector.

8. Disconnect the oil pressure line fitting.

9. Remove the cluster screws, pull the

Exploded view of the instrument cluster on V6 models

cluster forward and disconnect the speedometer cable and wiring plug. Remove the cluster.

10. On installation, connect the speedometer cable and wiring plug, and replace the cluster screws.

11. Connect the oil pressure line.

12. Connect the seat belt warning wire.

13. Hook the upper bezel retaining clips behind the tongues on the instrument panel. Push the bezel in and install the screws.

14. Replace the panel illumination control knob.

15. Put the lower trim panel in place and connect the lighter and clock. Install the panel screws.

16. Install the turn signal switch, hazard warning switch, ashtray, steering column shroud, and battery ground cable.

W/Factory A/C

1. Disconnect the negative cable from the battery.

2. Remove the screws securing the steering column shroud; remove the lower half of the shroud upper half retaining lug from its spring clip on the steering column by pulling sharply upward.

3. Withdraw the hazard flasher switch and disconnect the wiring at the cable connector.

4. Remove the screws holding the turn signal switch. Release the switch and leave it hanging in the wiring harness.

5. Pull out the instrument panel illumination control knob and radio control knobs. Remove the lower screws securing the instrument cluster bezel, release the bezel from its upper location by pulling downward, and disconnect the seat belt warning light at the connector.

6. Remove the screws securing the instrument cluster assembly to the instrument

panel, and disconnect the speedometer cable at the quick disconnect coupling by pressing the coupling off-center.

7. Disconnect the oil-pressure line coupling.

8. Disconnect the multi-plug connector from the rear of the instrument cluster. Remove the instrument cluster assembly.

9. Position the instrument cluster assembly in the instrument panel.

10. Reconnect the oil pressure line to the oil pressure gauge.

11. Reconnect the multi-plug and speedometer cable and hook the upper retaining clips on the instrument cluster bezel behind the tongues on the instrument panel. Press the bezel into its location and install the screws. Install the instrument panel illumination control knob and radio control knobs.

12. Position the right-side lower trim panel under the dash panel and connect the cigar lighter and clock cables. Press the trim panel into its location and install and tighten the screws.

13. Install the turn signal switch.

14. Position the left-side lower trim panel and connect the wiring to the hazard switch. Install the panel screws.

15. Mount the upper and lower halves of the steering column shroud and secure the lower half with screws.

16. Connect the negative battery cable and check the operation of the instruments.

Fuse Box Location

The fuse box is under the hood in front of the left hood hinge. Amp ratings for each fuse are marked on the clear plastic inner fuse box cover. There are 8 and 16 Ampere fuses.

Chrysler/ Mitsubishi

SERIAL NUMBER IDENTIFICATION

NOTE: The Colt/Champ and Sapporo/Challenger series of Chrysler cars are built by Mitsubishi. As of 1983, Mitsubishi Motor Sales of America, Inc. will also be importing, distributing and servicing their own line of cars; the Starion, Cordia and Tredia. The turbocharged 2.6 litre engine used in the Starion is similar in design and service to its normally-aspirated cousin used in the Sapporo/Challenger. Brake systems, suspensions and most transmissions are also closely related. Where product similarities exist, procedures given for the Chrysler vehicles can be used as service guidelines.

Vehicle Number

The vehicle identification plate is mounted on the instrument panel, adjacent to the lower corner of the windshield on the driver's side, and is visible through the windshield. The thirteen digit vehicle number is composed of a seven digit identification code, and a six digit sequential number.

Starting for 1981 and later, a standardized 17 digit Vehicle Identification Number (VIN) was used. The number continues to be visable from the outside of the lower driver's side winshield area.

Engine Number

The engine model number is embossed on the lower left side of the block.

Beginning 1978, the engine model number is stamped near the serial number of the upper right front side of the engine block. The serial number is stamped on a pad at the upper right front of the engine adjacent to the exhaust manifold.

Serial number location

Engine model number

Engine number location

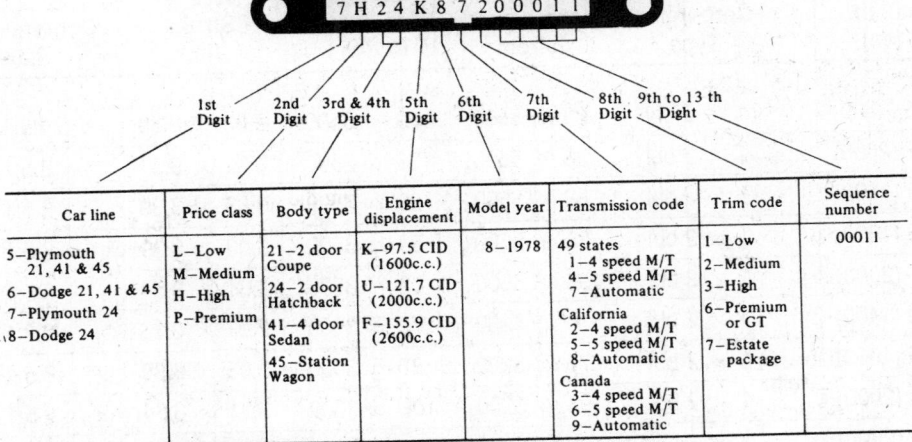

Vehicle Identification Plate

`7 H 24 K 8 7 200011`

| 1st Digit | 2nd Digit | 3rd & 4th Digit | 5th Digit | 6th Digit | 7th Digit | 8th Digit | 9th to 13th Dight |

Car line	Price class	Body type	Engine displacement	Model year	Transmission code	Trim code	Sequence number
5—Plymouth 21, 41 & 45 6—Dodge 21, 41 & 45 7—Plymouth 24 8—Dodge 24	L—Low M—Medium H—High P—Premium	21—2 door Coupe 24—2 door Hatchback 41—4 door Sedan 45—Station Wagon	K—97.5 CID (1600c.c.) U—121.7 CID (2000c.c.) F—155.9 CID (2600c.c.)	8—1978	49 states 1—4 speed M/T 4—5 speed M/T 7—Automatic California 2—4 speed M/T 5—5 speed M/T 8—Automatic Canada 3—4 speed M/T 6—5 speed M/T 9—Automatic	1—Low 2—Medium 3—High 6—Premium or GT 7—Estate package	00011

Vehicle I.D. plate—typical 1980 and earlier

```
J B 3 B E 4 4 3 9 C U 4 0 0 0 0 1
```

1st Digit	2nd Digit	3rd Digit	4th Digit	5th Digit	6th Digit	7th Digit	8th Digit	9th Digit	10th Digit	11th Digit	12th Digit	13th to 17th Digits
Manufacturing country	Sales channel	Vehicle type	Other	Vehicle line	Trim code	Body type	Engine displacement	*Check digit	Model year	Assembly plant	Transmission code	Sequence number
J—Japan	B—Dodge P—Plymouth	3—Passenger car	B—Manual seat belt	E—Colt/ Champ	2—Low 3—Medium 4—High, High (RS, LS)	4—2 door hatchback	2—1.4 litre (86.0 CID) 3—1.6 litre (97.5 CID)	1 2 . . 9 X	C—1982	U— MIZUSHIMA Plant	1—4 speed M/T Federal 2—4 speed M/T California 3—4 speed M/T Canada 4—4 x 2 speed M/T Federal 5—4 x 2 speed M/T California 6—4 x 2 speed M/T Canada 7—3 speed A/T Federal 8—3 speed A/T California 9—3 speed A/T Canada	00001 to 99999

NOTE: *"Check Digit" means a single number or letter X used to verify the accuracy of transcription of vehicle identification number.
M/T is an abbreviation for manual transaxle.
A/T is an abbreviation for automatic transaxle.
RS is an abbreviation for "Rally Sports".
LS is an abbreviation for "Luxury Sports".

Typical 1981 and later 17 digit vehicle identification number

GENERAL ENGINE SPECIFICATIONS

Year	Engine Displacement cu. in. (cc)	Carburetor Type	Horsepower @ rpm	Torque @ rpm (ft. lbs.)	Bore × Stroke (in.)	Compression Ratio	Oil Pressure (psi)
'76①	97.5 (1600)	1 × 2 bbl	83 @ 5500	89 @ 3500	3.03 × 3.39	8.5:1	57–71
	121.7 (2000)	1 × 2 bbl	96 @ 5500	109 @ 3500	3.31 × 3.54	8.5:1	50–64
'77–'78①	97.5 (1600)	1 × 2 bbl	83 @ 5500	89 @ 3500	3.03 × 3.39	8.5:1	57–71
	97.5 (1600)②	1 × 2 bbl	83 @ 5500	89 @ 3500	3.03 × 3.39	8.5:1	50–64
	121.7 (2000)②	1 × 2 bbl	96 @ 5500	109 @ 3500	3.31 × 3.54	8.5:1	50–64
'79–'82	86.0 (1400)	1 × 2 bbl	70 @ 5200	78 @ 3000	2.91 × 3.23	8.8:1	50–64
	97.5 (1600)②	1 × 2 bbl	77 @ 5200	87 @ 3000	3.03 × 3.39	8.5:1	50–64
	121.7 (2000)②	1 × 2 bbl	93 @ 5200	108 @ 3000	3.31 × 3.54	8.5:1	50–64
	155.9 (2600)②	1 × 2 bbl	105 @ 5000	139 @ 2500	3.59 × 3.86	8.2:1	50–64

GENERAL ENGINE SPECIFICATIONS

Year	Engine Displacement cu. in. (cc)	Carburetor Type	Horsepower @ rpm	Torque @ rpm (ft. lbs.)	Bore × Stroke (in.)	Compression Ratio	Oil Pressure (psi)
'83	86.0 (1400)	1 × 2 bbl	64 @ 5000	78 @ 3000	2.91 × 3.23	8.8:1	63
	97.5 (1600)②	1 × 2 bbl	72 @ 5000	85 @ 3000	3.03 × 3.39	8.5:1	63
	109.5 (1800)②③	1 × 2 bbl	82 @ 5000	73 @ 3000	3.17 × 3.46	8.5:1	63
	155.9 (2600)②	1 × 2 bbl	100 @ 5000	137 @ 2500	3.59 × 3.86	8.2:1	56
	155.9 (2600)②④	EFI	145 @ 5000	185 @ 2500	3.59 × 3.86	7.0:1	NA

① California emission:
97.5 (1600) MT: 80 @ 5500 HP
                87 @ 3500 torque
          AT: 78 @ 5500 HP
                83 @ 3500 torque
121.7 (2000) All: 93 @ 5500 HP
                  106 @ 3500 torque
② Silent shaft
③ Used only in Cordia and Tredia
④ Used only in Starion
MT—Manual transmission
AT—Automatic transmission
EFI—Electronic Fuel Injection
NA—Not available at time of publication

TUNE-UP SPECIFICATIONS
(When analyzing compression test results, look for uniformity among cylinders, rather than specific pressures.)

Year	Engine Displace. cu. in. (cc)	Spark Plugs Type	Gap (in.)	Point Dwell (deg)	Point Gap (in.)	Ignition Timing (deg) MT	AT	Intake Valve Opens (deg) BTDC	Fuel Pump Pressure (psi)	Idle Speed (rpm)	Valve Clear (in) In.	Ex.
'76	97.5 (1600)	BPR6ES	0.030	49–55	0.018–0.022	TDC	TDC	32 M 22 A	3.7–5.1	900–1000 M 800–900 A	0.006 hot	0.010 hot
	121.7 (2000)	BPR6ES	0.030	49–55	0.018–0.022	3B	3B	20	3.7–5.1	900–1000 M 800–900 A	0.006 hot	0.010 hot
'77–'78	97.5 (1600)	BPR6ES	0.030	49–55	0.018–0.022	5b ②	5B ②	24 M 19 A	3.7–5.1	①	0.006 hot	0.010 hot
	121.7 (2000)	BPR6ES	0.030	49–55	0.018–0.022	5B ②	5B ②	24	4.6–6.0	③	0.006 hot	0.010 hot
	155.9 (2600)	BPR6ES	0.039–0.043	52 ± 3	0.018–0.021	7B	7B	25	4.6–6.0	④	0.006 hot	0.010 hot⑤
'79–'82	86.0 (1400)	BPR6ES-11	0.039–0.043	52 ± 3	0.018–⑧0.021	5B	—	18	3.7–5.1	700⑨	0.006 hot	0.010 hot⑤
	97.5 (1600)	BPR6ES-11	0.039–0.043	52 ± 3	0.018–⑧0.021	5B ⑥	5B ⑥	20	3.7–5.1	650 M 700 A	0.006 hot	0.010 hot⑤

TUNE-UP SPECIFICATIONS

(When analyzing compression test results, look for uniformity among cylinders, rather than specific pressures.)

Year	Engine Displace. cu. in. (cc)	Spark Plugs Type	Spark Plugs Gap (in.)	Distributor Point Dwell (deg)	Distributor Point Gap (in.)	Ignition Timing (deg) MT	Ignition Timing (deg) AT	Intake Valve Opens (deg) BTDC	Fuel Pump Pressure (psi)	Idle Speed (rpm)	Valve Clear (in) In.	Valve Clear (in) Ex.
'79–'82	121.7 (2000)	BPR6ES	0.039–0.043	Electronic		5B	5B	25	4.6–6.0	650 M 700 A	0.006 hot	0.010 hot ⑤
	155.9 (2600)	BRP6ES	0.039–0.043	Electronic		7B ⑦	7B ⑦	25	4.6–6.0	④ ⑩	0.006 hot	0.010 hot ⑤
'83	86.0 (1400)	BUR6EA-11	0.039–0.043	ELECTRONIC		⑪	⑪	NA	2.7–3.7	⑪	⑪	⑪
	97.5 (1600)	BUR6EA-11	0.039–0.043	ELECTRONIC		⑪	⑪	NA	2.4–3.4	⑪	⑪	⑪
	155.9 (2600)	BPR5ES-11	0.039–0.043	ELECTRONIC		⑪	⑪	NA	2.8–4.3	⑪	⑪	⑪

NOTE: The underhood specifications sticker often reflects tune-up specifications changes made in production. Sticker figures must be used if they disagree with those in this chart.

① Fed: 800–900
　Alt: 900–1000
　Calif.: 900–1000 man.
　800–900 auto.
② Altitude (TDC)
　Calif.: 5A
③ Fed.: 900–1000 man.
　800–900 auto.
　Calif.: 900–1000

④ Fed.: 850 ± 50 rpm—both MT and AT
　Calif. & High Alt.: 700 ± 50 rpm—MT
　Calif.: 750 ± 50 rpm—AT
⑤ Jet valve clearance: 0.006 inch
⑥ High altitude only: 10B
⑦ Actual timing with dual diaphragm advance,
　Calif.: 3 ATDC
　High Alt.—2 BTDC
⑧ 1980 California cars and all 1981 cars:

electronic reluctor gap not adjustable
⑨ Fed.: 4 speed man. trans. (not available in California) 650 rpm
⑩ 1982–83: Man. trans., 50 states 750 rpm
　Auto. trans., 50 states 800 rpm
⑪ See underhood specification sticker
B Before top dead center
NA—Not available at time of publication

FIRING ORDERS

1400 cc and 1600 cc engines

1976 and later—2000 cc and 2600 cc engines

CAPACITIES—REAR WHEEL DRIVE CARS

Year	Model	Engine Displacement (cc)	Engine Crankcase (qts) With Filter	Engine Crankcase (qts) Without Filter	Transmission (qts) Manual 4-spd	Transmission (qts) Manual 5-spd	Transmission (qts) Automatic	Drive Axle (pts)	Gasoline Tank (gals)	Cooling System (qts) W/AC	Cooling System (qts) W/O AC
'76	All	1600	4.2	3.7	1.8	2.1	6.8	1.2	13①	7.7	7.7
		2000	4.5	4.0	—	2.4	6.8	1.2	13①	9.5	9.5
'77	All	1600	4.2	3.7	1.8	2.1	6.8	1.2	②	7.7	7.7
		2000	4.5	4.0	—	2.4	6.8	1.2	②	9.5	9.5

CAPACITIES—REAR WHEEL DRIVE CARS

Year	Model	Engine Displacement (cc)	Engine Crankcase (qts)		Transmission (qts)			Drive Axle (pts)	Gasoline Tank (gals)	Cooling System (qts)	
			With Filter	Without Filter	Manual		Automatic			W/AC	W/O AC
					4-spd	5-spd					
'78	All	1600	4.2	3.7	1.8	2.1	6.8	1.2	15.8	7.7	7.7
		2000	4.5	4.0	—	2.4	6.8	1.2	15.8	9.5	9.5
		2600	4.5	4.0		2.4	6.8	1.2	15.8	9.7	9.7
'79–'83	All	1600	4.2	3.7	—	2.1	7.2	1.2	③	7.7	7.7
		2000	4.5	4.0	—	2.4	7.2	1.2	③	9.5	9.5
		2600	4.5	4.0		2.4	7.2	1.4④	③⑤	9.5	9.5

① Station wagon: 11 gallons
② Coupe, Sedan and Hatchback: 13.2 gallons
  Hard top: 13.5 gallons
  Station wagon: 11.1 gallons
③ Colt Coupe, Sedan and Arrow: 13.2
  Challenger and Sapporo: 15.8
  Sta. Wgn.: 14.0 (1979) 13.2 (1980)
④ '81–'83: 2.7
⑤ '81–'83: 15.8

CAPACITIES—FRONT WHEEL DRIVE CARS

Year	Model	Engine Displacement (cc)	Engine Crankcase (qts)		Transaxle (qts)			Gasoline Tank (gals)	Cooling System (qts)	
			With Filter	W/O Filter	Manual		Automatic		W/AC	W/O AC
					4-spd	Twin Stick				
'79	All	1400	3.7	3.17	2.2	2.2	—	10.6	—	5.2
		1600	4.2	3.67	2.2	2.2	—	10.6	6.9	6.9
'80	All	1400	3.7	3.17	2.3	2.3	—	10.6	—	4.7
		1600	4.2	3.67	2.3	2.3	6.0	10.6	4.7	4.7
'81–'83	All	1400	3.7	3.17	2.4	2.4	—	10.6①	—	5.0
		1600	4.2	3.67	2.4	2.4	6.0	10.6①	5.0	5.0

① RS, LS: 13.2

CRANKSHAFT AND CONNECTING ROD SPECIFICATIONS
(All measurements are given in inches)

Year	Engine Displace (cu. in.)	Crankshaft				Connecting Rod		
		Main Brg. Journal Dia.	Main Brg. Oil Clearance	Shaft End-Play	Thrust on No.	Journal Diameter	Oil Clearance	Side Clearance
'76	97.5	2.2441	0.0006–0.0031	0.002–0.007	3	1.7717	0.0004–0.0028	0.004–0.010
	121.7	2.5984	0.0008–0.0028	0.002–0.007	3	2.0866	0.0006–0.0025	0.004–0.010
'77–'83	86.0	1.8898	0.0008–0.0028	0.002–0.007	3	1.6535	0.0004–0.0024	0.004–0.010
	97.5	2.2441	0.0008–0.0028	0.002–0.007	3	1.7717	0.0004–0.0028	0.014–0.010
	121.7	2.5984	0.0008–0.0028	0.002–0.007	3	2.0866	0.0008–0.0028	0.004–0.010
	155.9	2.5984	0.0008–0.0028	0.002–0.007	3	2.0866	0.0008–0.0028	0.004–0.010

VALVE SPECIFICATIONS

Year	Engine Displacement cu. in. (cc)	Seat Angle (deg)	Face Angle (deg)	Spring Test Pressure (lbs @ in.)	Spring Installed Height (in.)	Stem To Guide Clearance (in.) Intake	Stem To Guide Clearance (in.) Exhaust	Stem Diameter (in.) Intake	Stem Diameter (in.) Exhaust
'76–'83	86.0 (1400)	45	45	69 @ 1.417	1.417	0.0012–0.0024	0.0020–0.0035	0.315	0.315
	97.5 (1600)	45	45	61 @ 1.470	1.470	0.0010–0.0022	0.002–0.0033	0.315	0.315
	121.7 (2000)	45	45	61 @ 1.590	1.590	0.0010–0.0022	0.002–0.0033	0.315	0.315
	155.9 (2600)	45	45	61 @ 1.590	1.590	0.0012–0.0024	0.0020–0.0035	0.315	0.315
'78–'83	Jet valve	45	45	5.5 @ .846	.846	—	—		0.1693

PISTON AND RING SPECIFICATIONS
(All measurements in inches)

Year	Engine Displace. cu. in. (cc)	Piston Clearance	Ring Gap Top Compression	Ring Gap Bottom Compression	Ring Gap Oil Control	Ring Side Clearance Top Compression	Ring Side Clearance Bottom Compression	Ring Side Clearance Oil Control
'76–'83	86.0 (1400) 97.5 (1600)	0.0008–0.0016	0.008–0.016	0.008–0.016	0.008–0.020	0.0012–0.0028	0.0008–0.0024	—
	121.7 (2000) 155.9 (2600)	0.0008–0.0016	0.010–0.017①	0.010–0.017①	0.008–0.035	0.0024–0.0039	0.0008–0.0024	—

① '82–'83 (2600): 0.010–0.018

TORQUE SPECIFICATIONS
(All readings in ft. lbs.)

Year	Engine Displace. (cu. in.)	Cylinder Head Bolts	Rod Bearing Bolts	Main Bearing Bolts	Crankshaft Pulley Bolt	Flywheel to Crankshaft Bolts	Manifold Intake	Manifold Exhaust
'76	97.5	51–54 (cold) 58–61 (hot)	23–25	36–39	43–50	83–90	11–14	11–14
	121.7	65–72 (cold) 72–77 (hot)	33–35	54–61	80–93	83–90③	11–14	11–14
'77–'83	86.0, 97.5	51–54 (cold)	24–25	37–39	44–50①④	94–101②	11–14	11–14
	121.7	65–72 (cold)	33–34	55–61	80–94	94–101②	11–14	11–14
	155.9	65–72 (cold)	33–34	55–61	80–94	94–101②	11–14	11–14

① 1600 cc w/silent shaft—44–50 ft. lbs.
② AT drive plate—84–90 ft. lbs.
③ '76 2000 cc—94–101 ft. lbs.
④ 86.0: 37–43

CYLINDER HEAD TORQUE SEQUENCES

86.0 CID (1400 cc) and 97.5 CID (1600 cc) engines

121.7 CID (2000 cc) and 155.9 CID (2600 cc) engines

Head bolt tightening sequence

ALTERNATOR, REGULATOR AND BATTERY SPECIFICATIONS

| | | Alternator | | | Regulator③ | | | | Battery Capacity Ampere-Hour |
| | | | | No Load Adjusted Voltage | Cover Temperature | Charging Light Relay | | |
Year	Engine	Rated Output	Rotation (Viewed from Pulley)			Off Voltage	On Voltage	
'76	All	45A @ 12V	Clockwise	14.2 to 15.3V	68°F–20°C	4.2 to 5.2V	0.5 to 3.0V	60
'77	All	45A @ 12V	Clockwise	14.5 to 15.3V	68°F–20°C	4.2 to 5.2V②	0.5 to 3.0V②	60
'78–'83	1400, 1600	45A @ 12V	Clockwise	14.1 to 14.7V	68°F–20°C	4.0 to 5.8V	0.5 to 3.5V	①④
	2000, 2600	50A @ 12V⑤	Clockwise	14.1 to 14.7V	68°F–20°C	4.2 to 5.2V	0.5 to 3.0V	①④

①Coupe 1600 MT: 45 A.H.
         AT: 60 A.H.
  Sedan all models: 60 A.H.
  Hatchback 1600 MT, AT: 60 A.H.
        2000 MT: 45 A.H.
            AT: 60 A.H.
  Station wagon 1600 MT, AT: 60 A.H.
        2000, 2600 All: 65 A.H.
②1600 W/SS, off voltage: 4.0 to 5.8V
  on voltage: 0.5 to 3.5V
③All models are equipped with sealed voltage regulators which cannot be adjusted if the readings vary from the specifications.
④'82 USA: Colt/Champ—45 amp
        Challenger/Sapporo—50 amp
  '82 Canada: Colt/Champ—60 amp
          Challenger/Sapporo—55 amp
⑤'83: 55A @ 12V

STARTER SPECIFICATIONS

| | Engine (cc) and Transmission | No Load Test | | | Load Test | | | | Stall Test | | | Brush Spring Tension (lbs.) |
Year		Amp①	Volts	rpm②	Amp①	Volts	Torque②③	rpm②	Amp①	Volts	Torque③	
'76–'77	1600 MT	53	10.5	5000	150	8.6	2.53	1600	400	6.0	6.73	2.4④
	1600 AT 2000 MT	55	11.0	6500	150	9.6	2.24	2200	560	6.0	10.85	2.4④
	2000 AT	62	11.0	4500	200	9.2	3.83	1600	730	6.0	18.08	2.4④

STARTER SPECIFICATIONS

Year	Engine (cc) and Transmission	No Load Test			Load Test				Stall Test			Brush Spring Tension (lbs.)
		Amp①	Volts	rpm②	Amp①	Volts	Torque②③	rpm②	Amp①	Volts	Torque③	
'78–'83	1400,⑤ 1600 MT	53	10.5	5000	150	8.6	2.53	1600	400	6.0	6.73	3.3
	1600 AT 2000 MT	55	11.0	6500	150	9.6	2.24	2200	560	6.0	10.85	3.3
	2000 AT 2600 All	62	11.0	4500	200	9.2	3.83	1600	730	6.0	18.08	3.3

① Less than
② More than
③ Ft. lbs.
④ '77—3.3 lbs.
MT: Manual transmission

AT: Automatic transmission
Brush length, all
Max.: 669 in.
Min.: .453 in.
Pinion drive to stopper gap, all: 0 to .079 in.

⑤ '82–'83 no load test:
1600 M/T, 2000 A/T, 2600 M/T = 60 amp, 11.5 volts, 6500 rpm.
2600 A/T = 90 amp, 11.5 volts, 3,300 rpm

BRAKE SPECIFICATIONS—REAR WHEEL DRIVE CARS
(All measurements given are in. unless noted)

Year	Lug Nut Torque ft. lbs.	Master Cylinder Bore	Brake Disc Thickness			Brake Drum			Lining Thickness			
									Front		Rear	
			Max.	Min.	Runout	Diameter	Maximum	Maximum Wear	Max.	Min.⑦	Max.	Min.⑦
'76	51–58	②	0.510	0.450	0.006	9.0	9.060	9.079	0.38	0.08	0.17	0.04
'77	51–58	13/16	0.510	0.450	0.006	9.0	9.060	9.079	0.38	0.08	0.17	0.04
'78–'83	51–58 ⑪	13/16 ⑫	0.510 ③⑧⑬	0.450 ④⑨⑬	0.006⑬	9.0	9.060	9.079	0.38⑤	0.08⑥	0.157	0.04⑩

① 1600 engine equipped: 11/16 in.
2000 engine equipped: 13/16 in.
② Vehicles without power brakes: 11/16 in.
Vehicles with power brakes: 13/16 in.
③ '78–'79 Station wagon and '82 all rear drive: 0.490 in.
④ '78–'79 Station wagon and '82 all rear drive: 0.430 in.

⑤ '78–'79 Station wagon: 0.41 in.
⑥ '78–'79 Station wagon and '82 all: 0.04 in.
⑦ Due to variations in state inspection regulations, the minimum allowable lining thickness may be different from that recommended by the manufacturer.
⑧ '80–'81—0.380
⑨ '80–'81—0.08

⑩ Rear drum and disc same
⑪ Steel wheel: 51–58 ft. lbs.
Aluminum wheel: 58–72 ft. lbs.
⑫ '82–'83 vehicles: 0.875 in.
⑬ Rear brake disc:
max. 0.390–min. 0.330—runout 0.006

BRAKE SPECIFICATIONS—FRONT WHEEL DRIVE CARS
(All measurements given are in. unless noted)

Year	Lug Nut Torque ft. lbs.	Master Cylinder Bore	Brake Disc Thickness			Brake Drum			Lining Thickness			
									Front②		Rear②	
			Max.	Min.	Runout	Diameter	Maximum	Maximum Wear	Max.	Min.	Max.	Min.
'79	51–58①	13/16	0.510	0.450	0.006	7.0	7.060	7.079	0.382	0.08	0.201	0.04
'80–'83	51–58①	13/16④	0.510	0.450	0.006	7.1	7.160	7.200	0.382	0.08③	0.201	0.04

① Aluminum wheels: 58–72
② Due to variations in state inspection regulations, the minimum allowable lining thickness may be different from that recommended by the manufacturer.

③ '82–'83 minimum pad thickness: 0.04 in.
④ '83: 0.813 in.

WHEEL ALIGNMENT—REAR WHEEL DRIVE CARS

Year	Model	Caster (degrees)	Camber (degrees)	Toe-in (in.)	Steering Angle Inner Wheel (degrees)	Outer Wheel (degrees)	King Pin Angle
'76	All	1¼° ± ½°	⅚° ± ½	0.08 to 0.23	39	30½	7°
'77	Coupe Sedan Hatchback	2°05′ ± ½°	1° ± 45′	0.08 to 0.23	35	30	8°53′
	Hardtop Station Wagon	1°9′ ± ½°	51′ ± ½°	0.08 to 0.23	39	30½	9°
'78	All exc. Sta. Wgn.	2°05′ ± ½°	1° ± ½°	0.08 to 0.24	35	36	9°
	Station Wagon	2°38′ ± ½°	1°28′ ± ½°	0.08 to 0.35	39	30½	8°25′
'79	Colt Coupe & Sedan, Arrow	2°05′ ± 30′	1° ± 30′	0.08 to 0.24	35	30	9°01′
	Challenger & Sapporo	2°38′ ± 30′	1°28′ ± 30′	0.08 to 0.35	37	32	8°52′
	Colt Sta. Wagon	2°38′ ± 30′	1°28′ ± 30′	0.08 to 0.35	39	30°30′	8°52′
'80	Arrow	2°05′ ± 30′	1° ± 30′	0.08 to 0.24	35	30	9°01′
	Challenger & Sapporo	2°38′ ± 30′	1°14′ ± 30′	0.08 to 0.35	37	32	8°52′
	Colt Sta. Wagon	2°38′ ± 30′	1°14′ ± 30′	0.08 to 0.35	37	32	8°52′
'81–'83	Challenger, Sapporo	2°40′	1°10′	0 to 0.28	37	32	9°30′

WHEEL ALIGNMENT
Front Wheel Drive Cars

Year	Model	Caster (degrees)	Camber (degrees)	Toe-in (in.)	Steering Angle Inner Wheel (degrees)	Outer Wheel (degrees)	King Pin Angle (degrees)
'79–'82	All	50′ ± 20′	30′ ± 30′	0.16 in to 0.08 out	35°40′	29°17′	12°42′
'83	All	1° ± 30′	1° ± 30′	0.118 in to 0.157 out	NA	NA	12°42′

NA—Not available at time of publication

TUNE-UP PROCEDURES

NOTE: The Colt/Champ and Sapporo/Challenger series of Chrysler cars are built by Mitsubishi. As of 1983, Mitsubishi Motor Sales of America, Inc. will also be importing, distributing and servicing their own line of cars; the Starion, Cordia and Tredia. The turbocharged 2.6 litre engine used in the Starion is similar in design and service to its normally-aspirated cousin used in the Sapporo/Challenger. Brake systems, suspensions and most transmissions are also closely related. Where product similarities exist, procedures given for the Chrysler vehicles can be used as service guidelines.

All 1976–78 models use a breaker point type ignition system. In 1979 an electronic ignition system was introduced and used on various models through 1980. All 1981 and later models use electronic ignition.

Spark Plugs

REMOVAL AND INSTALLATION

NOTE: Before removing spark plugs clean any dirt from the base area of the spark plugs with compressed air or a stiff brush.

CAUTION

Grasp the plug wire by the boot and twist slightly to loosen, before pulling on the boot (not the wire) to remove the wire from the spark plug. Bending or pulling on the wire breaks the internal conductive material.

1. Mark or tag the wires for correct reinstallation, then remove the wires from the spark plugs.
2. Using a 13/16 inch deep-well spark-plug socket and a swivel head rachet type wrench, remove the spark plugs.
3. Inspect spark plugs for cracked and damaged insulators or threads, worn electrodes, damaged gasket and carbon or other fouling deposits.
4. If plugs are to be reused file the electrodes square.
5. Regap old spark plugs or check the gap on new spark plugs.
6. Install the spark plugs in the head and torque to 18–21 ft. lbs. (25–28 Nm).
7. Install the plug wires on the proper spark plug.

Breaker Points and Condenser

Snap off the two retaining clips on the distributor cap. Remove the cap and examine it for cracks, deterioration, or carbon tracking. Replace the cap, if necessary, by transferring one wire at a time from the old cap to the new one. Examine the rotor for corrosion or wear. Check the points for pitting and burning. Slight imperfections on the contact surface may be filed off with a point file (fine emery paper will also do), but it is best to replace the breaker point set when tuning. Always replace the condenser when you replace the point set.

To replace the breaker points.
1. Remove the rotor.
2. Observe which screws retain the ground and primary wires. Remove the two retaining screws and lift out the lubricator wick plate and the point set.
3. Install the new point set, making sure that the pin on the bottom engages the hole in the breaker plate.
4. Install the lubricator wick plate, primary and ground wires, and then the two retaining screws (hand-tight).
5. Turn the fan belt or crankshaft pulley until the breaker arm rubbing block is

Point gap adjustment is made by twisting a flat bladed screwdriver in slot (A)

on the high point of one of the cam lobes.
6. The correct size feeler gauge should just slip through the points. If the gap is incorrect, adjustment is made by inserting a screwdriver in the slot and pivoting it to correct the gap.
7. When the gap is correct, tighten the two retaining screws.
8. Lubricate the distributor cam wick with engine oil or silicone grease.
9. Install the rotor and distributor cap.
10. Check the dwell angle and the ignition timing as outlined in the following sections.
11. The condenser is mounted on the outside of the distributor. Undo the mounting screw and the terminal screw to replace the condenser.

Dwell Angle

The dwell angle or cam angle is the number of degrees that the distributor cam rotates while the points are closed. There is an inverse relationship between dwell angle and point gap. Increasing the point gap will decrease the dwell angle and vice versa. Checking the dwell angle with a meter is a far more accurate method of measuring point opening then the feeler gauge method.

After setting the point gap to specification with a feeler gauge check the dwell angle with a meter. Attach the dwell meter according to the manufacturer's instruction sheet. The negative lead is grounded and the positive lead is connected to the primary wire that runs from the coil to the distributor. Start the engine, let it idle and reach operating temperature, and observe the dwell on the meter. The reading should fall within the allowable range. If it does not, the gap will have to be reset.

Electronic Ignition System

This system consists of the battery, ignition switch, breaker (point-less type), electronic control unit, spark plugs and wiring. Primary circuit is switched by the electronic control unit responding to timing signals produced by a magnetic pick-up (which replaces the breaker points). Any malfunction in this system should be serviced by a qualified serviceman. The only adjustment nec-

SPARK PLUG GAP CHART

Vehicle	Spark Plug Gap	
	inches	(mm)
All USA, except vehicles using W16EPR-U10 spark plugs	.039–.043	(1.0–1.1)
Vehicles using W16EPR-U10	.035–.039	(0.9–1.0)
All Canadian vehicles	.028–.031	(0.7–0.8)

Typical electronic ignition circuit

Vacuum advance adjustment

essary is ignition timing, dwell is adjusted electronically. Plug wires, distributor cap and rotor are inspected and serviced as on breaker type distributors.

Ignition Timing

—— CAUTION ——
When performing this or any other adjustment with the engine running, be very careful of the fan belt and pulley.

Ignition timing should always be check as a part of any tune-up. Timing is checked after the points have been adjusted or replaced. An accurate stroboscopic timing light is a necessity for timing the engine.

1. Attach the timing light according to the manufacturer's instructions.
2. Locate the timing tab on the engine near the crankshaft pulley. Mark the "I" or appropriate line (according to the "Tune-Up Specifications"), and the notch in the crankshaft pulley with chalk so that they will be more visible.
3. Disconnect and plug the hose to the vacuum advance unit on the distributor if

1600 cc timing mark (1400 cc similar)

2000 cc timing mark (2600 cc similar)

it is a single unit i.e. one vacuum hose. (See paragraph below if distributor has two vacuum hoses).

4. Start the engine and allow it to reach normal operating temperature.
5. Shine the timing light at the crankshaft pulley marks. The marked line should align with pulley notch.
6. If the marks do not align, loosen the distributor mounting nut and rotate it slowly to align the timing marks.
7. Tighten the mounting nut when the ignition timing is correct.

Some of these models are equipped with vacuum advance/retard distributors. Vacuum retard functions at idle to retard the spark. Basic timing is checked by removing the rubber plug from the vacuum advance/retard unit on the distributor. Check and adjust basic timing with the vacuum advance line connected. Replace the rubber plug and check the retarded timing. Adjustment, if necessary, is made by a Phillips screw on the vacuum advance assembly. Loosen the two screws that mount the advance to the distributor. Slowly turn the Phillips screw and check the timing mark with the timing light. Tighten the mounting screws and recheck the timing.

Valve Adjustment

1976–77

Valve clearance is adjusted with the engine stopped. When adjusting the valves cold, for example after an engine rebuild, proceed as follows:

1. Adjust the valves in the firing order 1-3-4-2.
2. Turn the crankshaft pulley to bring the piston to TDC of the compression stroke on the cylinder being adjusted.
3. Loosen the two rocker adjusting screw locknuts.
4. Using a 0.003 in. feeler gauge for the intake and a 0.007 in. gauge for the exhaust, turn the adjusting screw until the clearance is correct.
5. Tighten the locknuts to 7–9 ft. lbs.

The normal valve clearance adjustment, or final adjustment after the above initial cold adjustment, is performed as follows:

1. Run the engine until it reaches normal operating temperature and then turn it off.
2. Undo the wing nut and remove the air cleaner. Pull the large crankcase ventilation hose off of the front of the air cleaner. Disconnect the two smaller hoses, one goes to the rear of the rocker arm cover and one to the intake manifold.
3. Loosen and remove the nuts and one bracket which attach the air cleaner to the rocker arm cover.
4. Lift the bottom housing of the air cleaner off of the carburetor and, with it, the hose coming up from the exhaust manifold heat stove.
5. Unsnap the spark plug wires from their clips on the rocker arm cover.
6. Loosen and remove the two rocker arm cover bolts. The rear bolt is a crankcase ventilation fitting, so you will have to use a deep socket or a box wrench.
7. Carefully lift the rocker arm cover off the cylinder head. Using a 5/16 in. Allen socket (1600cc) or regular socket (2000cc) and torque wrench, make sure that the cylinder head bolts are all tightened to 58–62 ft. lbs. on 1600 cc engines, 72–79 ft. lbs. on 2000 cc engines.
8. Valves for each cylinder are adjusted in the firing order: 1-3-4-2.

Exhaust valves

No. of cylinder

Front of engine (toward timing belt)

Intake valves

Valve adjusting sequence for all engines

Adjusting valve clearance all engines

9. Turn the crankshaft pulley to bring the piston to TDC of the compression stroke. Both valves will be closed at this point and the rocker arms will be resting on the "heel" of the camshaft lobe (the normal side, not the egg-shaped side).

10. Loosen the two rocker arm adjusting screw locknuts.

11. Using the correct thickness feeler gauge, turn the adjusting screw until the gauge just snaps through the valve stem and the rocker arm.

12. Proceed to adjust the valves of each cylinder in the firing order. Remember to bring each piston to TDC of its compression stroke.

CAUTION

The importance of correctly setting the valve clearance cannot be overemphasized. Loose valve clearances will result in excessive wear and valve train clatter; tight valve clearances will result in valve seat burning.

---

13. Apply non-hardening sealer to the rocker arm cover gasket. Replace the gasket if its condition is at all questionable.

14. Install the cover, hoses, spark plug wires, and air cleaner in the reverse order of removal. Tighten the rocker arm cover bolts to 4–5 ft. lbs.

15. Start the engine and check for leaks.

1978–83 WITH JET VALVE

A jet valve has been added to the combustion chamber (on USA models). Its adjuster is on the intake valve rocker arm. The jet valve must be adjusted *before* the intake valve.

1. Bring the selected cylinder to its firing position to TDC.

2. Back off the intake valve adjusting screw two or more turns.

3. Loosen the jet valve locknut and turn the jet adjusting screw counterclockwise to obtain 0.006 inch clearance between the jet valve and the adjusting screw.

4. Tighten the locknut and recheck the clearance.

5. Adjust the intake valve clearance. Adjust the exhaust valve clearance. Follow the procedure for non-jet valve engines.

6. The sequence of adjustment can be found by turning the engine in the normal direction of rotation and watching the exhaust valves. The following chart gives the sequence.

Exhaust Valve Closing	Adjust
No. 1 cylinder	No. 4 cylinder valves
No. 2 cylinder	No. 3 cylinder valves
No. 3 cylinder	No. 2 cylinder valves
No. 4 cylinder	No. 1 cylinder valves

Carburetor

IDLE SPEED ADJUSTMENT

1976–77 All Models

1. Warm the engine to normal operating temperature.

2. Disconnect the air shut-off solenoid electrical plug. This is located under the air control valve which is on the left-side of the engine. This equipment is part of the air injection system.

3. Adjust the idle speed to 900 rpm on manual transmission cars or 800 rpm on automatic transmission cars. Do this with

Air hose   Plug

Reed valve

Air hose removal (typical)

Adjusting screw

Jet valve clearance

Jet valve

Jet valve clearance adjustment

Air shut-off solenoid coupler

Idle speed adjusting screw

the carburetor idle speed adjusting screw (B) on manual cars. Be careful that the screw doesn't contact the thorttle arm. Use the throttle positioner screw (C) on automatic cars.

4. Connect the air shut-off solenoid.

5. On manual cars, adjust engine speed to 1000 rpm with screw B. On automatic cars, set the engine speed to 900 rpm with screw C.

6. On automatic transmission cars only, remove the rubber plug from the vacuum unit on the distributor. Adjust the idle speed to 800 rpm with screw band, reinstall the rubber plug.

7. Race the engine to about 2500 rpm a few times and observe that it returns to normal idle speed.

ENGINE IDLE SPECIFICATIONS

Engine	Transmission	Curb idle speed
97.5 CID (1600 cc)	Manual	650 ± 50 rpm
97.5 CID (1600 cc)	Automatic	700 ± 50 rpm
121.7 CID (2000 cc)	Manual	650 ± 50 rpm
121.7 CID (2000 cc)	Automatic	700 ± 50 rpm
155.9 CID (2600 cc) for California	Manual	700 ± 50 rpm
155.9 CID (2600 cc) for California	Automatic	750 ± 50 rpm
155.9 CID (2600 cc)	Manual	850 ± 50 rpm
155.9 CID (2600 cc)	Automatic	850 ± 50 rpm

1978–83 Except 1982 and Later 2600 Engines

1. Have the engine at normal operating temperature.

2. Position the manual altitude compensator knob (if equipped) with the lugs and the slot in a vertical position for altitudes over 4000 ft. and the lugs and the slot in a horizontal position for less than 4000 ft.

NOTE: Some model carburetors have a tamperproof, sealed, idle mixture screw. These cannot be adjusted except by an authorized garage.

3. Adjust the engine speed to specifications.

1982 and Later 2600 Engine

Set the idle with all accessories off and the transmission in neutral.

1. Run engine until normal operating temperature is reached.

2. Run the engine at 2,000 to 3,000 rpm for over 5 seconds, then run the engine at idle for 2 minutes.

3. Using a tachometer, set the idle to specifications.

AIR CONDITIONING IDLE ADJUSTMENT

1982 and Later 2600 Engine

Adjust the AC idle with all accessories off, the transmission in neutral and the engine warmed up.

1. Check curb idle and rest if necessary.

2. Turn air conditioning on.

3. Adjust idle-up (A/C idle) to 900 ± 50 rpm.

ENGINE ELECTRICAL

NOTE: The Colt/Champ and Sapporo/Challenger series of Chrysler cars are built by Mitsubishi. As of 1983, Mitsubishi Motor Sales of America, Inc. will also be importing, distributing and servicing their own line of cars; the Starion, Cordia and Tredia. The turbocharged 2.6 litre engine used in the Starion is similar in design and service to its normally-aspirated cousin used in the Sapporo/Challenger. Brake systems, suspensions and most transmissions are also closely related. Where product similarities exist, procedures given for the Chrysler vehicles can be used as service guidelines.

Distributor

REMOVAL AND INSTALLATION

1976–81

1. Remove the distributor cap and disconnect the primary wire.

2. Disconnect the vacuum hoses.

3. Remove the distributor mounting nuts and remove the distributor assembly.

4. Turn the crankshaft until No.1 piston is at TDC on the compression stroke, and the notch on the crankshaft pulley is aligned with the timing mark "T".

2600cc IDLE SPECIFICATION—U.S.A.

Transmission	Curb Idle rpm	
	1st 300 miles	after 300 miles
Manual	700 + 150 − 100	750 ± 100
Automatic	750 + 150 − 100	800 ± 100

1. Cap
2. Carbon
3. Rotor
4. Ground wire
5. Cam felt
6. Arm support
7. Lead wire
8. Breaker base
9. Cam
10. Locking plate
11. Vacuum control
12. Governor weight
13. Shaft
14. Housing
15. O-ring
16. Washer
17. Thrust collar
18. Gear
19. Condenser

Exploded view of the distributor

Positioning the oil pump driveshaft groove—2000 cc

1400 AND 1600 CC ENGINE (STANDARD)

a. Turn the oil pump driveshaft groove to the vertical position (1976–77).

b. Align the mating marks on the lower end of the distributor body with that of the spacer (1976), or with the mating mark on the distributor driven gear (1978–83).

c. (1978–83). Align the mating marks on the distributor attaching flange with the center of the distributor installing stud and install the distributor into the cylinder head.

1600 CC W/SILENT SHAFT, 2000 CC AND 2600 CC ENGINES

a. Align the mating marks of the distributor housing with the distributor driven gear.

b. Install the distributor into the cylinder head so that the mating marks are in an upright position.

5. Adjust the breaker points and install the distributor cap and primary wire.

6. Install the vacuum hoses and adjust the ignition timing to specifications.

Alternator

ALTERNATOR PRECAUTIONS

There are several precautions which must be strictly observed in order to avoid damaging the unit. They are:

1. Reversing the battery connections will result in damage to the diodes.

2. Booster batteries should be connected from negative to negative, and positive to positive.

3. Never use a fast charger as a booster to start the car.

4. When servicing the battery with a fast charger, always disconnect the car battery cables.

5. Never attempt to polarize an alternator.

6. Avoid long soldering times when replacing diodes or transistors. Prolonged heat is damaging to alternators.

Distributor installation 1976–77 1600cc

Distributor installation—cylinder head mounted distributors

Aligning mating marks for installation of cylinder head mounted distributors

7. Do not use test lamps of more than 12 volts (V) for checking diode continuity.

8. Do not short across or ground any of the terminals on the alternator.

9. The polarity of the batter, alternator, and regulator must be matched and considered before making any electrical connections within the system.

10. Never operate the alternator on an open circuit. Make sure that all connections within the circuit are clean and tight.

11. Disconnect the battery terminals when performing any service on the electrical system. This will eliminate the possibility of accidental reversal of polarity.

12. Disconnect the battery ground cable if arc welding is to be done on any part of the car.

REMOVAL AND INSTALLATION

1. Disconnect the battery cables and the alternator wires. Note or tag the wires so that you can reinstall them correctly.

2. Loosen and remove the top mounting bolt.

3. Loosen the elongated lower mounting nut. Slide the alternator over in its attaching bracket and remove the fan belt.

4. Remove the lower mounting nut and bolt, being sure not to lose any mounting shims.

5. Remove the alternator.

NOTE: Remember when installing the alternator that it is not necessary to polarize the system.

6. Trial fit the alternator on the engine. The shims are installed on the inside of both alternator mounting legs. Add more shims, if necessary, for a tight fit.

7. Install the lower mounting bolt and nut. Do not completely tighten it yet.

8. Fit the fan belt over the alternator and crankshaft pulleys.

9. Loosely install the top mounting bolt and pivot the alternator over until the fan belt is correctly tensioned as outlined in the next procedure.

10. Finally tighten the top and bottom bolts.

11. Connect the alternator wires and the battery cables.

BELT REPLACEMENT AND TENSIONING

1. Check the fan belt(s) for cracking, fraying, and any other deterioration. Replace it if it is at all suspect.

2. To replace the belt, loosen the mounting bolts and pivot the alternator in its bracket. Remove the old belt and slip the replacement belt over the pulleys.

3. Pry the alternator over until the belt can be deflected $\frac{9}{32}-\frac{11}{32}$ in. at its midpoint.

4. Tighten the mounting bolts.

Belt tension adjustment

Regulator

REMOVAL AND INSTALLATION

NOTE: Some late models have a regulator (solid state) built into, or mounted on the rear of the alternator.

1. Disconnect the ground cable from the battery.

2. Disconnect the electrical connector plug.

3. Loosen and remove the two mounting screws. Remove the regulator.

4. Clean the attaching area for proper grounding of the regulator.

5. Install the regulator. Do not over-

1. Stator	10. Insulator
2. Rotor	11. Brush spring
3. Ball bearing	12. Brush
4. Rear bracket assembly	13. Front bracket assembly
5. Rear bracket	14. Front bracket
6. Heat sink complete (+)	15. Ball bearing
7. Heat sink complete (−)	16. Bearing retainer
8. Brush holder assembly	17. Pulley
9. Insulator	18. Condenser

Exploded view of the alternator

IG	F	L
A	N	E

Regulator terminals

Terminal ID for testing

Up
(higher voltage)

↑

↓

Down
(lower voltage)

Adjusting the voltage

1. Lever assembly
2. Lever spring (A)
3. Lever spring (B)
4. Spring retainer
5. Electromagnetic switch
6. Through bolt
7. Front bracket
8. Front bracket bearing
9. Plate
10. Stop ring
11. Overrunning clutch
12. Armature
13. Insulating washer
14. Yoke assembly
15. Pole piece
16. Field coil
17. Brush
18. Brush holder
19. Brush spring
20. Rear bracket
21. Rear bracket bearing

Exploded view of starter

tighten the mounting screws or you will distort the case.

6. Connect the electrical plug and the battery cable.

—————— CAUTION ——————

Never operate the engine with the regulator disconnected.

VOLTAGE CHECK AND ADJUSTMENT

NOTE: Later model cars having a solid state regulator built into, or mounted on the alternator, should be serviced by a qualified serviceman.

1. Connect a voltmeter to the A and E terminals of the regulator connector plug.

NOTE: Do not disconnect the plug.

2. Disconnect one of the battery terminals while the engine is idling to unload the alternator.

3. Increase the engine speed to 2000 rpm. The voltmeter should show a value of 14.3–15.8 V at room temperature.

If the reading is not within specifications:

4. Remove the regulator cover.

5. Adjust the constant voltage relay (located on the left) by bending the end of the coil side plate up or down.

Bending the plate down reduces the voltage, bending it up increases the voltage.

6. The field relay is adjusted in the same manner as the voltage relay.

Starter

REMOVAL

1. Disconnect the battery ground cable and the starter motor wiring.

2. Loosen the two starter attaching bolts and remove the starter motor.

NOTE: With air conditioning or large steering gear box, disconnect the pitman arm from the starter motor attaching bolts and remove the starter from under the car.

INSTALLATION

1. Position the starter in the housing opening.

2. Install the attaching bolts and tighten evenly to avoid binding.

3. Install the starter wiring and connect the battery cable.

STARTER DRIVE REPLACEMENT

1. Remove the "M" terminal wire and the two solenoid mounting screws. Remove the solenoid.

2. Remove the two long starter through-

Spring retainer
Lever
Spring

Removing the starter armature and lever

Stopper
Snap ring

Removing the starter drive

Stop ring   Overrunning clutch   Stop ring

Snap ring

Installing the snap-ring stopper

bolts and separate the armature and yoke assemblies.

3. Carefully remove the armature and lever from the front bracket.

NOTE: Mark or take careful note of the direction of installation on the lever and spring as they are removed, since they must be reinstalled in the proper direction.

4. Using a piece of pipe or the equivalent, tap the stopper toward the starter drive pinion assembly, with a small hammer or mallet. The stopper must clear the snap-ring.

5. Remove the snap-ring, stopper and pinion drive assembly from the armature shaft.

6. Inspect the pinion and spline teeth for wear or damage.

NOTE: If pinion teeth are damaged always inspect the flywheel teeth for possible damage.

7. Rotate the pinion in both directions. It should turn freely in a clockwise direction and lock when turned counterclockwise.

8. Install the over–running clutch and pinion drive onto the armature shaft.

9. Install the stopper and snap-ring on the armature shaft. Push the stopper over the snap-ring. A small gear puller or arbor press may be needed to push the stopper over the snap-ring.

10. Install the small washer on the front of the armature shaft.

11. Fit the lever in the over-running clutch and install the assembly into the front bracket.

12. Install the spring and spring retainer into the front bracket.

13. Install the washer(s) onto the rear of the armature shaft.

14. Install the yoke assembly onto the front bracket and armature assembly.

15. Put the lever in the front end of the solenoid plunger and install and tighten the two solenoid attaching screws.

16. Connect the ''M'' terminal to the solenoid.

ENGINE MECHANICAL

NOTE: The Colt/Champ and Sapporo/Challenger series of Chrysler cars are built by Mitsubishi. As of 1983, Mitsubishi Motor Sales of America, Inc. will also be importing, distributing and servicing their own line of cars; the Starion, Cordia and Tredia. The turbocharged 2.6 litre engine used in the Starion is similar in design and service to its normally-aspirated cousin used in the Sapporo/Challenger. Brake systems, suspensions and most transmissions are also closely related. Where product similarities exist, procedures given for the Chrysler vehicles can be used as service guidelines.

Engine/Transmission

REMOVAL AND INSTALLATION

Except Front Wheel Drive

The engine and transmission must be removed as a unit.

1. Remove the hood. Remove the bridge panel and grille. Drain and remove the radiator. Remove the battery.

2. Disconnect the ground strap, ignition coil wiring and vacuum and fuel solenoid valves.

3. Disconnect the following: alternator, starter, transmission switch, back-up light switch, temperature gauge and oil pressure gauge.

4. Disconnect all hoses and remove the air cleaner.

5. Disconnect all carburetor linkage. Remove the heater hose.

6. Unbolt the exhaust pipe at the manifold flange and disconnect the muffler pipe bracket at the transmission.

7. Remove the hose between the fuel filter and the fuel pump return line.

8. Remove the vacuum hose from the purge control valve.

9. Disconnect the speedometer cable backup light and distributor switches.

10. Disconnect the clutch cable and shaft lever.

11. Remove the cross shaft and control rod from the bracket under the transmission. On automatic transmission, remove the tie rod.

12. Remove the leatherette cover inside the car and remove the shifter assembly.

13. Attach a hoist and remove weight from the engine mounts. Remove the attaching bolts from the engine mounts and lift the engine upward and forward.

14. Installation is the reverse of removal.

Front-Wheel Drive Models

The factory recommends that the engine and transaxle be removed as a unit.

1. Disconnect the battery cables (ground cable first) remove battery hold-down and battery. Remove the battery tray.

2. Remove the air cleaner assembly. Disconnect the purge control vacuum hose from the purge valve. Remove the purge control valve mounting bracket. Remove the windshield washer reservoir, radiator tank and carbon canister.

3. Drain the coolant from the radiator. Remove the radiator assembly with the electric cooling fan attached. Be sure to disconnect the fan wiring harness and the transmission cooler lines(if equipped with automatic trans.).

4. Disconnect the following cables, hoses and wires from the engine and transaxle: clutch, accelerator, speedometer, heater hose, fuel lines, PCV vacuum line, high-altitude compensator vacuum hose (Calif. models), bowl vent valve purge hose (U.S.A. models), inhibitor switch (auto. trans.), control cable (auto. trans.), starter, engine ground cable, alternator, ignition coil, water temperature sensor, back-up light (man. trans.) and oil pressure wires.

5. Remove the ignition coil. The next step will be to jack up the car. Before you do this, look around and make sure all wires and hoses are disconnected.

6. Jack up the front of the car after you block the rear wheels. Support the car on jack stands. Remove the splash shield (if equipped.).

7. Drain the lubricant out of the transaxle.

8. Remove the right and left driveshafts from the transaxle and support them with wire. Plug the transaxle case holes so dirt cannot enter.

— **CAUTION** —
The driveshaft retainer ring should be replaced whenever the shaft is removed.

9. Disconnect the assist rod and the control rod from the transaxle. If the car is

equipped with a range selector, disconnect the selector cable.

10. Remove the mounting bolts/bolt from the front and rear roll control rods.

11. Disconnect the exhaust pipe from the engine and secure it with wire.

12. Loosen the engine and transaxle mounting bracket nuts.

13. Lower the car.

14. Attach a lifting device and a shop crane or chain hoist to the engine. Apply slight lifting pressure to the engine. Remove the engine and transaxle mounting nuts and bolts.

15. Make sure the rear roll control rod is disconnected. Lift the engine and transaxle from the car.

— CAUTION —
Make sure the transaxle does not hit the battery bracket when the engine and transaxle are lifted.

To install:

1. Lower the engine and transaxle carefully into position and loosely install the mounting bolts. Temporarily tighten the front and rear roll control rods mounting bolts. Lower the full weight of the engine and transaxle onto the mounts and tighten the nuts and bolts. Loosen and retighten the roll control rods.

2. The rest of the engine installation is the reverse of the removal. Make sure all cables, hoses and wires are connected. Fill the radiator with coolant, the transaxle with lubricant. Adjust the clutch cable and accelerator cable. Adjust the transaxle control rod. Take another check on everything you have done. Start the engine and check for leaks.

Intake Manifold

REMOVAL AND INSTALLATION

— CAUTION —
The intake manifold is cast aluminum.

1. Remove the air cleaner.

2. Disconnect the fuel line and EGR lines on models so equipped.

3. Disconnect the throttle positioner solenoid and fuel cut-off solenoid wires.

4. Disconnect the accelerator linkage and, if equipped with automatic transmission, the shift cables at the carburetor.

5. Drain the coolant.

6. Remove the water hose from carburetor and cylinder head.

7. Remove the heater and water outlet hoses.

8. Disconnect the water temperature sending unit.

9. Remove the manifold and carburetor.

10. Clean all mounting surfaces. Before reinstalling the manifold, coat both sides with gasket sealer.

— CAUTION —
If the engine is equipped with the jet air system, take care not to get any sealer into the jet air intake passage.

11. Installation is the reverse of removal.

Exhaust Manifold

REMOVAL AND INSTALLATION

1. Remove the carburetor air cleaner assembly.

2. Remove the manifold heat stove and hose. Disconnect the EGR lines and reed valve, if equipped.

3. Disconnect the exhaust pipe bracket from the engine block.

4. Remove the exhaust pipe flange bolts (One bolt and nut may have to be removed from under the car.).

5. Remove the manifold flange stud nuts and remove the manifold from the cylinder head.

6. Installation is the reverse of removal. Port liner gaskets may be used along with the exhaust manifold gaskets on some engine models.

Cylinder Head

The timing chain and gear must be removed and hung on wire except on 1400 cc engines where only the timing belt needs to be removed. 1400 and 1600 cc engines require a 5/16 in. Allen socket; 2000 engines are hex head.

The cylinder head overhaul procedures may be found under Engine Rebuilding in the Unit Repair section of this book.

— CAUTION —
Never remove the cylinder head unless the engine is absolutely cold; the cylinder head could warp.

REMOVAL

1. Disconnect the battery ground cable, remove the air cleaner assembly, and the attached hoses.

2. Drain the coolant, remove the upper radiator hose, and the heater hoses.

3. Remove the fuel line, disconnect the accelerator linkage, distributor vacuum lines, purge valve, and water temperature gauge wire.

4. Remove the spark plug wires and the fuel pump. Remove the distributor, where necessary.

5. Disconnect the exhaust pipe from the exhaust manifold flange.

6. Remove the exhaust manifold assembly.

8a. Camshaft bearing cap
8b. No. 2, 3 and 4 caps
8c. Camshaft bearing cap (rear)
10. Cylinder head
11a. Intake valve seat ring
11b. Exhaust valve seat ring
12. Cylinder head bolt
13a. Exhaust valve guide
13b. Intake valve guide
14. Cylinder head gasket

Exploded view of the cylinder head

7. Remove the intake manifold and carburetor as a unit.

8. Turn the crankshaft to put No. 1 piston at TDC on the compression stroke.

NOTE: During the following procedures, do not turn the crankshaft after locating TDC.

1400 CC ENGINE

a. Remove the timing belt cover. Be sure that the knockout pin is at 12 o'clock and the cam sprocket mark and cylinder head pointer are aligned at 3 o'clock.

b. Loosen the timing belt tensioner mounting. Move the tensioner toward the water pump and secure it in that position. Remove the timing belt from the pulley.

c. Remove the rocker arm cover.

NOTE: The cam pulley need not be removed.

1976

1600 CC ENGINE–STANDARD

a. Remove the rocker arm cover.

b. Position the crankshaft sprocket dowel pin between 1 and 2 o'clock, with the crankshaft pulley notch aligned with the timing mark "I" at the front of the timing chain case.

c. Match-mark the timing chain and the timing mark on the camshaft sprocket with white paint. Lock the chain to the sprocket with mechanics wire.

d. Remove the sprocket from the camshaft.

1977–83

1600 CC ENGINE–WITH OR WITHOUT SILENT SHAFT

a. Align the timing mark on the upper under cover of the timing belt with that of the camshaft sprocket.

b. Match-mark the timing belt and the timing mark on the camshaft sprocket with a felt tip pen.

c. Remove the sprocket and insert a 2 inch piece of timing belt or other material between the bottom of the camshaft sprocket and the sprocket holder on the timing belt lower front cover, to hold the sprocket and belt so that the valve timing will not be changed.

d. Remove the timing belt upper under cover and the rocker arm cover.

1976–83

2000 CC AND 2600 CC ENGINES

a. Remove the rocker arm cover.

b. Position the camshaft sprocket dowel pin at the 12 o'clock position with the crankshaft pulley notch aligned with the timing mark ''T'' at the front of the timing chain case.

c. Match the timing chain with the timing mark on the camshaft sprocket.

d. Remove the camshaft sprocket bolt, distributor, gear and the sprocket from the camshaft.

9. Loosen and remove the cylinder head bolts in two or three stages to avoid cylinder head warpage.

10. Remove the cylinder head from the engine block.

INSTALLATION

1. Clean the cylinder head and block mating surfaces, and install a new cylinder head gasket.

2. Position the cylinder head on the engine block, engage the dowel pins front and rear, and install the cylinder head bolts.

3. Tighten the head bolts in three stages and then torque to specifications.

4. Install the timing belt upper under cover on the 1977–83 1600 cc engine.

5. Locate the camshaft in original position. Pull the camshaft sprocket and belt or chain upward, and install on the camshaft.

NOTE: If the dowel pin and the dowel pin hole does not line up between the sprocket and the spacer or camshaft, move the camshaft by bumping either of the two projections provided at the rear of no. 2 cylinder exhaust cam of the camshaft, with a light hammer or other tool, until the hole and pin align. Be certain the crankshaft does not turn.

6. Install the camshaft sprocket bolt and the distributor gear, and tighten. (The gear is used on 1976–83 2000 cc and 2600 cc engines).

7. Install the timing belt upper front cover and spark plug cable support.

8. Apply sealant to the intake manifold gasket on both sides. Position the gasket and install the intake manifold. Tighten the nuts to specifications.

——————— CAUTION ———————
Be sure that no sealant enters the jet air passages, when equipped.

9. Install the exhaust manifold gaskets and the manifold assembly. Tighten the nuts to specifications.

10. Connect the exhaust pipe to the exhaust manifold and install the fuel pump. Install the purge valve.

11. Install the water temperature gauge wire, heater hoses and the upper radiator hose.

12. Connect the fuel lines, accelerator linkage, vacuum hoses, and the spark plug wires.

13. Fill the cooling system and connect the battery ground cable. Install the distributor.

14. Temporarily adjust the valve clearance to the cold engine specifications.

COLD ENGINE SPECIFICATIONS

	Inch.	MM
Jet valve, if equipped	.003	.07
Intake valve	.003	.07
Exhaust valve	.007	.17

15. Install the gasket on the rocker arm cover and temporarily install the cover on the engine.

16. Start the engine and bring it to normal operating temperature. Stop the engine and remove the rocker arm cover.

17. Adjust the valves to hot engine specifications.

HOT ENGINE SPECIFICATIONS

	Inch	MM
Jet valve, if equipped	.006	.15
Intake valve	.006	.15
Exhaust valve	.010	.25

18. Reinstall the rocker arm cover and tighten securely.

19. Install the air cleaner, hoses, purge valve hose, and any other removed unit.

Typical late model rocker arm shaft assembly

Camshaft and Rocker Arm

REMOVAL AND INSTALLATION

All Except 1400 cc Engine

The camshaft and rocker arms are best removed after the cylinder head has been removed from the engine block.

1. Match-mark the rocker arm bearing caps to the cylinder head.
2. Remove the bearing cap bolts from the cylinder head, but do not remove them from the bearing caps and shafts. Lift the rocker arm assembly from the cylinder head.
3. Remove the camshaft from the bearing saddles.

NOTE: On some engines, a distributor drive gear and spacer are used on the front of the camshaft.

4. The valves, valve springs, and valve guide seals can now be removed from the cylinder head.

NOTE: Refer to the cylinder head overhaul procedures in the "Engine Rebuilding" section. Valve guides are a shrink fit, with oversize guides available. Valve seats are replaceable, with oversize seats available.

5. The rocker arm assembly can be disassembled by the removal of the bolts from the bearing caps and shafts.

NOTE: a. Keep the rocker arms and springs in proper order. The left and right springs have different tension ratings and free lengths.
b. Observe the location of the mating marks of the right and left rocker arm shaft in relation to the front bearing cap mating marks.

6. Observe the mating marks and reassemble the units in the reverse order of the removal.

1400 cc Engine

1. Remove the cylinder head rear cover.
2. Remove the camshaft thrust case tightening bolt, located on top of the rear mounting boss.

CAMSHAFT THRUST CASE TIGHTENING BOLT

Rear cam cover—1400 cc engine

3. Carefully slide the camshaft and thrust case (attached to the rear of the cam) out the rear of the cylinder head.
4. Installation is the reverse of removal. Coat all parts with clean engine oil prior to installation.

Jet Valves—1978–83

The jet valve can be removed from the cylinder head with the rocker arm either in place or removed. Care must be exercised not to twist the socket while removing or replacing the valve, so as not to break it. Torque the valve to 13.5 to 15.5 ft. lbs.

Timing Gear Cover, Chain, Counterbalance Shafts, and Tensioner

NOTE: The timing chain case is cast aluminum, so exercise caution when handling this part.

The following outlines are the recommended removal and installation procedures for the timing chain or belt. Some modifications to the procedures may be necessary due to added accessories, sheet-metal parts, or emission control units and connecting hoses.

REMOVAL—CHAIN EQUIPPED

1600 cc Engine—Standard (1976–77)

1. Drain the coolant and remove the radiator. Disconnect the battery ground cable.
2. Remove the alternator and accessory belts.
3. Rotate the crankshaft to bring No. 1 piston to TDC on the compression stroke, by aligning the notch on the crankshaft pulley with the "T" mark on the timing indicator scale.
4. Remove the crankshaft pulley and bolt.

NOTE: Do not move the crankshaft when removing the pulley. If the crankshaft is turned, return the shaft to the original position as in Step 3.

5. Remove the crankshaft pulley and bolt.
6. Remove the fan blades and the water pump assembly.
7. Remove the cylinder head assembly.
8. Raise the car and support it safely.
9. Drain the engine oil and remove the oil pan, oil pressure switch, oil filter, and oil pump.

NOTE: Undercar splash pans may have to be removed to gain access to the oil pan.

Plated link
Camshaft sprocket
Timing chain
Side guide
Tensioner lever
Tensioner plunger
Crankshaft sprocket
Plated link

1600 cc timing chain and tensioner

10. Remove the chain tension holder, spring, and plunger, on the right side of the chain cover.
11. Remove the timing chain cover from the engine block.
12. Remove the oil slinger and crankshaft gear from the crankshaft. Do not misplace the Woodruff key from the crankshaft.
13. Remove the crankshaft and camshaft sprockets with the chain attached, from the engine block.
14. If needed, remove the chain tensioner lever and side guide.

INSTALLATION

1. If removed, install the chain tensioner lever and the side guide, with the jet of the guide toward the chain and sprocket meshing point.
2. Be sure the No. 1 piston is at TDC. Using a new gasket, install the cylinder head assembly.
3. Rotate the camshaft until the dowel pin is between the 1 and 2 o'clock position.
4. Position the crankshaft sprocket and the camshaft sprocket so that the punch marks on the sprockets align with the chrome or buff plated links of the timing chain.
5. Install the Woodruff key on the crankshaft and while holding the timing chain and sprockets in position, install the sprockets onto the camshaft and the crankshaft.

Timing chain
Plated link
Camshaft sprocket
Sprocket holder
Chain guide
Chain guide
Tensioner
Crankshaft sprocket
Plated link

2000 cc timing chain and tensioner

6. If the dowel pin does not align with the hole in the camshaft sprocket, bump the camshaft on the projections provided to align the two. Install the camshaft sprocket bolt and torque to 36 to 43 ft. lbs.

NOTE: The chain must be fitted in the guide groove and against the tensioner lever.

7. Install the Woodruff key, crankshaft gear with the "F" mark toward the front. The oil slinger must be installed with its concave side facing the front of the engine.

8. Install a new gasket and seal on the front timing cover case and install the case on the engine block. Torque the bolts to 11 to 13 ft. lbs.

9. Install the tensioner lever plunger and spring into the case and torque to 29 to 36 ft. lbs.

——— CAUTION ———
Because the timing chain is supported and stretched by the tensioner lever, it is important to align the marks on the sprockets and chain.

10. Install the oil screen and oil pump.

11. Install the oil pan, oil filter, and the oil pressure gauge sender. Fill the oil pan.

12. Reinstall any splash pans and lower the car to the floor.

13. Align the oil pump shaft in a vertical position. Align the distributor marks to fire No. 1 cylinder, and install the distributor.

14. Install the crankshaft pulley and torque the bolt to 43 to 50 ft. lbs.

15. Install the water pump, fan blades, alternator and belt. Adjust the belt.

16. Install the radiator, add coolant to the system, and connect the battery ground cable.

17. Refer to the "Cylinder Head Installation" section and adjust the valves as for a cold engine. Temporarily install the rocker arm cover, start the engine, and warm it up.

18. Stop the engine and remove the rocker arm cover. Adjust the valves to the hot specifications.

REMOVAL–BELT EQUIPPED

1400 cc Engine 1981 and Later

1. Turn the engine until no. 1 piston is on TDC with the timing marks aligned.

2. Disconnect the ground (negative) battery cable.

3. Remove the fan drive belt, the fan blades, spacer and water pump pulley.

4. Remove the timing belt cover.

5. Loosen the timing belt tensioner mounting bolt and move the tensioner toward the water pump. Temporarily secure the tensioner.

6. Remove the crankshaft pulley and slide the belt off of the camshaft and crankshaft drive sprockets.

7. Inspect the drive sprockets for abnormal wear, cracks or damage and replace as necessary. Remove and inspect the ten-

sioner. Check for smooth pulley rotation, excessive play or noise. Replace tensioner if necessary.

INSTALLATION

1. Reinstall the tensioner, if it was removed, and temporarily secure it close to the water pump.

2. Make sure that the timing mark on the camshaft sprocket is aligned with the pointer on the cylinder head and that the crankshaft sprocket mark is aligned with the mark on the engine case (see illustration).

3. Install the timing belt on the crankshaft sprocket.

4. Install the belt counterclockwise over the camshaft sprocket making sure there is no play on the tension side of the belt. Adjust the belt fore and aft so that it is centered on the sprockets.

5. Loosen the tensioner from it's temporary position so that the spring pressure will allow it to contact the timing belt.

6. Rotate the crankshaft two complete turns in the normal rotation direction to remove any belt slack. Turn the crankshaft until the timing marks are lined up. If the

timing has slipped, remove the belt and repeat the procedure.

7. Tighten the tensioner mounting bolts, slotted side (right) first then the spring side.

8. Once again rotate the engine two complete revolutions until the timing marks line up. Recheck the belt tension.

NOTE: When the tension side of the timing belt and the tensioner are pushed in horizontally with a moderate force (about 11 lbs.) and the cogged side of the belt covers about a quarter of an inch of the tensioner right side mounting bolt head, (across flats) the tension is correct.

9. Reinstall the timing belt cover, the water pump pulley, spacer, fan blades and drive belt.

10. Connect the battery ground cable.

REMOVAL–BELT EQUIPPED

1600 cc Engine–Standard (1978–83)
1600 cc Engine–W/Silent Shaft (1977–83)

1. Drain the coolant and remove the radiator. Disconnect the battery cable.

Belt driven cam—1400 cc shown

2. Remove the alternator and accessory belts.

3. Rotate the crankshaft to bring No. 1 piston to TDC on the compression stroke. Align the notch on the crankshaft pulley with the "T" mark on the timing indicator scale and the timing mark on the upper under cover of the timing belt with the mark on the camshaft sprocket. Mark and remove the distributor.

4. Remove the crankshaft pulley and bolt.

5. Remove the fan blades.

6. Remove the timing belt covers, upper front and lower front.

7. Remove the crankshaft sprocket bolt.

8. Loosen the tensioner mounting nut and bolt. Move the tensioner away from the belt and retighten the nut to keep the tensioner in the off position. Remove the belt.

9. Remove the camshaft sprocket, crankshaft sprocket, flange, and tensioner.

10. Silent shaft engines:
   a. Loosen the counterbalance shaft sprocket mounting bolt.
   b. Remove the belt tensioner and remove the timing belt.
   c. Remove the crankshaft sprocket (inner) and counterbalance shaft sprocket.
   d. Remove the upper and lower under timing belt covers.

11. The water pump or cylinder head may be removed at this point, depending upon the type of repairs needed.

12. Raise the front of the car and support it safely. Remove any interfering splash pans.

13. Drain the oil pan and remove the pan from the block.

14. Remove the oil pump sprocket and cover.

NOTE: On the silent shaft engines, remove the plug at the bottom of the left side of the cylinder block and insert a screwdriver to keep the left counterbalance shaft in position while removing the sprocket nut.

15. Remove the front cover and oil pump as a unit, with the left counter shaft attached, if equipped.

16. Remove the oil pump gear and left counterbalance shaft.

NOTE: To aid in removal of the front cover, a driver groove is provided on the cover, above the oil pump housing. Avoid prying on the thinner parts of the housing flange or hammering on it to remove the case.

17. Remove the right counterbalance shaft from the engine block.

INSTALLATION

Standard Engine

1. Install a new front seal in the cover. Install a new gasket on the front of the cylinder block and using a seal protector on the front of the crankshaft, install the front cover on the engine block.

2. Tighten the front case mounting bolts to 11 to 13 ft. lbs.

3. Install the oil screen, and using a new gasket, install the oil pan. Tighten bolts to 4.5–5.5 ft. lbs.

4. If the cylinder head and/or water pump had been removed, reinstall them, using new gaskets.

5. Install the upper and lower under covers.

6. Install the spacer, flange and crankshaft sprocket and tighten the bolt to 43.5–50 ft. lbs.

7. Align the timing mark on the crankshaft sprocket with the timing mark on the front case.

8. Align the camshaft sprocket timing mark with the upper under cover timing mark.

9. Install the tensioner spring and tensioner. Temporarily tighten the nut. Install the front end of the tensioner spring (bent at right angles) on the projection of the tensioner and the other end (straight) on the water pump body.

10. Loosen the nut and move the tensioner in the direction of the water pump. Lock it by tightening the nut.

11. Ensure that the sprocket timing marks are aligned, and install the timing belt. The belt should be installed on the crankshaft sprocket, the oil pump sprocket, and then the camshaft sprocket, in that order, while keeping the belt tight.

12. Loosen the tensioner mounting bolt and nut and allow the spring tension to move the tensioner against the belt.

NOTE: Make sure the belt comes in complete mesh with the sprocket by lightly pushing the tensioner up by hand toward the mounting nut.

13. Tighten the tensioner mounting nut and bolt.

NOTE: Be sure to tighten the nut before tightening the bolt. Too much tension could result from tightening the bolt first.

14. Recheck all sprocket alignments.

15. Turn the crankshaft through a complete rotation in the normal direction.

── CAUTION ──
Do not turn in a reverse direction or shake or push the belt.

16. Loosen the tensioner bolt and nut. Retighten the nut and then the bolt.

17. Install the lower and upper front outer covers.

18. Install the crankshaft pulley and tighten the bolts to 7.5–8.5 ft. lbs.

19. Install the alternator and belt and adjust. Install the distributor.

20. Install the radiator, fill the cooling system, and inspect for leaks.

Silent Shaft Engines

1. Install a new front seal in the cover. Install the oil pump drive and driven gears in the front case, aligning the timing marks on the pump gears.

2. Install the left counterbalance shaft in the driven gear and temporarily tighten the bolt.

3. Install the right counterbalance shaft into the cylinder block.

4. Install an oil seal guide on the end of the crankshaft, and install a new gasket on the front of the engine block for the front cover.

5. Install a new front case packing, if equipped.

6. Insert the left counterbalance shaft into the engine block and at the same time, guide the front cover into place on the front of the engine block.

7. Insert a screwdriver at the bottom of the left side of the block and hold the left counterbalance shaft and tighten the bolt. Install the hole plug.

8. Install an O-ring on the oil pump cover and install it on the front cover.

9. Tighten the oil pump cover bolts and the front cover bolts to 11–13 ft. lbs.

10. Install the oil screen, and using a new gasket, install the oil pan.

11. Install the water pump and/or cylinder head, if removed previously.

12. Install the upper and lower under covers.

13. Install the spacer on the end of the right counterbalance shaft, with the chamfered edge toward the rear of the engine.

14. Install the counterbalance shaft sprocket and temporarily tighten the bolt.

15. Install the inner crankshaft sprocket and align the timing marks on the sprockets with those on the front case.

16. Install the inner tensioner (B) with the center of the pulley on the left side of the mounting bolt and with the pulley flange toward the front of the engine.

17. Lift the tensioner by hand, clockwise, to apply tension to the belt. Tighten the bolt to secure the tensioner.

18. Check that all alignment marks are in their proper places and the belt deflection is approximately ¼–½inch on the tension side.

NOTE: When the tensioner bolt is tightened, make sure the shaft of the tensioner does not turn with the bolt. If the belt is too tight there will be noise, and if the belt is too loose, the belt and sprocket may come out of mesh.

19. Tighten the counterbalance shaft sprocket bolt to 22–28.5 ft. lbs.

20. Install the flange and crankshaft sprocket. Tighten the bolt to 43.5–50.5 ft. lbs.

21. Install the camshaft spacer and sprocket. Tighten the bolt to 44–57 ft. lbs.

22. Align the camshaft sprocket timing mark with the timing mark on the upper inner cover.

23. Install the oil pump sprocket, tightening the nut to 25–28.5 ft. lbs. Align the timing mark on the sprocket with the mark on the case.

— CAUTION —

To be assured that the phasing of the oil pump sprocket and the left counterbalance shaft is correct, a screwdriver or a metal rod should be inserted in the plugged hole on the left side of the cylinder block. If it can be inserted more than 2⅜inches, the phasing is correct. If the tool can only be inserted approximately one inch, turn the oil pump sprocket through one turn and realign the timing marks. Keep the screwdriver or metal rod inserted until the installation of the timing belt is completed. Remove the tool from the hole and install the plug, before starting the engine.

24. Refer to Step 9 of the belt installation for the standard engine.

25. If the timing belt is correctly tensioned, there should be about 0.5 in. clearance between the outside of the belt and the edge of the belt cover. This is measured about halfway down the side of the belt opposite the tensioner.

26. Complete the assembly by installing the upper and lower front covers.

27. Install the crankshaft pulley, alternator, and accessory belts, and adjust to specifications.

28. Install the radiator, fill the cooling system, and start the engine.

REMOVAL–CHAIN EQUIPPED

2000 cc Engine–W/Silent Shaft (1976–83)
2600 cc Engine–W/Silent Shaft (1978–83)

1. Drain the coolant and remove the radiator. Disconnect the battery ground cable.

2. Remove the alternator and accessory belts.

3. Rotate the crankshaft to bring no. 1 piston to TDC, on the compression stroke.

4. Mark and remove the distributor.

5. Remove the crankshaft pulley.

6. Remove the water pump assembly.

7. Remove the cylinder head, if necessary.

8. Raise the front of the car and support it safely.

9. Drain the engine oil and remove the oil pan and screen.

10. Remove the timing case cover.

11. Remove the chain guides. Side (A), Top (B), Bottom (C), from the "B" chain (outer).

12. Remove the locking bolts from the "B" chain sprockets.

13. Remove the crankshaft sprocket, counterbalance shaft sprocket and the outer chain.

14. Remove the crankshaft and camshaft sprockets and the "A" (inner) chain.

15. Remove the camshaft sprocket holder and the chain guides, both left and right. Remove the tensioner spring and sleeve from the oil pump.

16. Remove the oil pump by first removing the bolt locking the oil pump driven gear and the right counterbalance shaft, and then remove the oil pump mounting bolts. Remove the counterbalance shaft from the engine block.

NOTE: If the bolt locking the oil pump driven gear and the counterbalance shaft is hard to loosen, remove the oil pump and the shaft as a unit.

17. Remove the left counterbalance shaft thrust washer and take the shaft from the engine block.

INSTALLATION

1. Install the right counterbalance shaft into the engine block.

2. Install the oil pump assembly. Do not lose the Woodruff key from the end of the counterbalance shaft. Torque the oil pump mounting bolts to 6–7 ft. lbs.

3. Tighten the counterbalance shaft and the oil pump driven gear mounting bolt.

NOTE: The counterbalance shaft and the oil pump can be installed as a unit, if necessary.

4. Install the left counterbalance shaft into the engine block.

5. Install a new O-ring on the thrust plate and install the unit into the engine block, using a pair of bolts without heads, as alignment guides.

— CAUTION —

If the thrust plate is turned to align the bolt holes, the O-ring may be damaged.

6. Remove the guide bolts and install the regular bolts into the thrust plate and tighten securely.

7. Rotate the crankshaft to bring No. 1 Piston to TDC.

8. Install the cylinder head, if removed.

9. Install the sprocket holder and the right and left chain guides.

10. Install the tensioner spring and sleeve on the oil pump body.

11. Install the camshaft and crankshaft sprockets on the timing chain, aligning the sprocket punch marks to the plated chain links.

12. While holding the sprocket and chain as a unit, install the crankshaft sprocket over the crankshaft and align it with the keyway.

13. Keeping the dowel pin hole on the camshaft in a vertical position, install the camshaft sprocket and chain on the camshaft.

NOTE: The sprocket timing mark and the plated chain link should be at the 2 to 3 o'clock position when correctly installed.

— CAUTION —

The chain must be aligned in the right and left chain guides with the tensioner pushing against the chain. The tension for the inner chain is predetermined by spring tension.

14. Install the crankshaft sprocket for the outer or "B" chain.

15. Install the two counterbalance shaft sprockets and align the punched mating marks with the plated links of the chain.

16. Holding the two shaft sprockets and chain, install the outer chain in alignment with the mark on the crankshaft sprocket. Install the shaft sprockets on the counterbalance shaft and the oil pump driver gear. Install the lock bolts and recheck the alignment of the punch marks and the plated links.

17. Temporarily install the chain guides, Side (A), Top (B), and Bottom (C).

18. Tighten Side (A) chain guide securely.

19. Tighten Bottom (B) chain guide securely.

20. Adjust the position of the Top (B) chain guide, after shaking the right and left sprockets to collect any chain slack, so that

.04 to .14 in.

Section P-P

Adjusting hole (in chain guide B)

Chain guide B

Plated link

Mating mark

Chain guide A

Mating mark

Plated link

Chain guide C

Plated link

Mating mark

Silent shaft balancing system

when the chain is moved toward the center, the clearance between the chain guide and the chain links will be approximately ⁹⁄₆₄ inch. Tighten the Top (B) chain guide bolts.

21. Install the timing chain cover using a new gasket, being careful not to damage the front seal.

22. Install the oil screen and the oil pan, using a new gasket. Torque the bolts to 4.5–5.5 ft. lbs.

23. Install the crankshaft pulley, alternator and accessory belts, and the distributor.

24. Install the oil pressure switch, if removed, and install the battery ground cable.

25. Install the fan blades, radiator, fill the system with coolant and start the engine.

Piston Installation

In preparation, check the ring gaps for staggered position. The gaps should not align with the piston pin or piston thrust directions. Also, each gap must be as far as possible from its neighboring gap.

NOTE: Installing plastic covers on the cap bolts of the piston rod will avoid damaging the cylinder bore and crank pin surface.

1. Apply engine oil all around the piston, piston rings and cylinder bore.

2. Insert the piston and connecting rod assembly into the cylinder, using a piston ring clamping tool. The cylinder mating mark should agree with the cylinder number and the arrow on the piston head should be directed to the crankshaft pulley end of the engine.

3. Install the connecting rod cap and torque the cap nuts to 24–25 ft. lbs. (32–34 Nm) on the 1400 and 1600 engines and to 33–34 ft. lbs. (45–47 Nm) on 2000 and 2600 engines.

NOTE: Make certain the match mark (cyl. no.) on the connecting rod big end and the match mark (cyl no.) on the cap are placed in the same direction or the same side.

1976 and later piston identification

Piston ring installation

Piston Identification

On 1976 and later models the pistons are stamped with a size mark.

When replacing the piston and connecting rod assembly always direct the front mark on the piston head toward the front of the engine.

Piston ring end gap position

PISTON SIZE MARKINGS

Size	Size Mark
S.T.D.	None
.010 in. O.S.	25
.020 in. O.S.	50
.030 in. O.S.	75
.039 in. O.S.	100

ENGINE LUBRICATION

NOTE: The Colt/Champ and Sapporo/Challenger series of Chrysler cars are built by Mitsubishi. As of 1983, Mitsubishi Motor Sales of America, Inc. will also be importing, distributing and servicing their own line of cars; the Starion, Cordia and Tredia. The turbocharged 2.6 litre engine used in the Starion is similar in design and service to its normally-aspirated cousin used in the Sapporo/Challenger. Brake systems, suspensions and most transmissions are also closely related. Where product similarities exist, procedures given for the Chrysler vehicles can be used as service guidelines.

Oil Pan

REMOVAL AND INSTALLATION

The engine must be raised off its mounts for the pan to clear the suspension crossmember. However, on front wheel drive models there is usually enough room without raising the engine.

1. Remove the underbody splash shield.
2. Unbolt the left and right engine mounts (except front wheel drive).
3. Jack up the engine under the bell housing (except front wheel drive).
4. Remove the oil pan.
5. Installation is the reverse of removal.

Rear Main Oil Seal

REPLACEMENT

The rear main oil seal is located in a housing on the rear of the block. To replace the seal, remove the transmission and do the work from underneath the car (except front wheel drive models) or remove the engine and do the work on the bench.

1. Remove the housing from the block.

Rear main oil seal

Exploded view of oil pump

2. Remove the separator from the housing.

3. Pry out the oil seal.

4. Lightly oil the replacement seal. The oil seal should be installed so that the seal plate fits into the inner contact surface of the seal case. Install the separator with the oil holes facing down.

Oil Pump

LOCATION

1400 cc Engine

A gear driven oil pump is mounted in the front case and driven directly by the crankshaft.

1600 cc Engine

1976–77 STANDARD–(TIMING CHAIN)

A rotor type oil pump is located in the timing chain case and driven by a crankshaft gear.

1976–83 STANDARD–(TIMING BELT)

A rotor type oil pump is located on the lower left side of the front case, driven by the timing belt.

2000 cc Engine

1976–80 W/SILENT SHAFT

A gear type oil pump is on the front of the right counterbalance shaft, driven by the timing chain.

2600 cc Engine

1978–83 W/SILENT SHAFT

A gear type oil pump is on the front of the right counterbalance shaft, driven by the timing chain.

REMOVAL AND INSTALLATION

1400 cc Engine

1. Remove the timing belt. See "Timing Belt Removal" section.

2. Remove the engine oil pan and oil screen.

3. Remove the front case assembly (seven bolts).

The oil pump is mounted in the rear of the front case. Turn the front case over and remove the oil pump cover. Service as required.

All Other Engines

To remove the rotor type pumps that are located behind the front timing cover, refer to the "Timing Gear Cover, Chain, Counterbalance Shaft and Tensioner" section and follow the procedure to remove the pump.

To remove the oil pumps that are located in the oil pan, the following procedures should be followed.

1. Place No. 1 piston at TDC on the compression stroke.

2. Loosen the left and right engine mounts and raise the engine off the mount brackets.

3. Remove the front splash shields. Drain the oil and remove the oil pan.

4. Remove the screen and the oil pump from the engine block.

5. To install, be sure that No. 1 piston is still on the compression stroke.

6. Remove the distributor cap and make sure the rotor is pointing to the No. 1 position.

TROCHOID TYPE OIL PUMP CLEARANCES
(All measurements in inches)

Measurement Point	1979–80 1400 cc Engine	1976–77 1600 cc Engine Standard—Pump in Timing Cover	1978–83 1600 cc Engine Standard—Separate Pump	1975 2000 cc Engine Standard—Separate Pump
Inner rotor to outer rotor clearance	—	.0047 or less	.0016 to .0047	.0047 or less
Rotor to cover end-play	.0016 to .0039	.0008 to .0039	.0024 to .0047	.0008 to .0079
Outer rotor to chain case clearance	.0039 to .0079	.0039 to .0063	.0039 to .0063	—
Drive shaft to cover clearance	—	—	.02 to .05	.0039 to .0063
Relief spring Free length	1.850	2.352	1.850	2.352
Tension	9.5 lbs. @ 1.575	17.2 lbs. @ 1.696	9.5 lbs. @ 1.575	17.2 lbs. @ 1.696

GEAR TYPE OIL PUMP CLEARANCES
(All measurements in inches)

Measurement Point	1981–82 1400 cc Engine	1977–81 1600 cc Engine w/Silent Shaft	1976 2000 cc Engine w/Silent Shaft	1978–80 2000 cc and 2600 cc Engine w/Silent Shaft	1981–83 2600 cc Engine
Gear end-play	.0016 to .0039	.0024 to .0047	.0024 to .0047	.0024 to .0059	.0024 to .0047
Clearance between gear shaft end and oil pump cover	.0039 to .0079	.0008 to .0019	—	—	—
Driven gear tip clearance to body	—	.0039 to .0078	.0041 to .0059	.0041 to .0059	.0043 to .0059
Drive gear tip clearance to body	—	.0059 to .0098	.0041 to .0059	.0041 to .0059	.0043 to .0059
Maximum tip clearance (both gears)	—	.0158 to .0275	—	—	—
Clearance between drive and driven gears and bearing front	②	—	.0008 to .0047①	.0008 to .0018	.0008 to .0020
Clearance between drive gear and bearing gear	③	—	.0017 to .0026	.0017 to .0026	.0016 to .0028
Relief spring Free length	1.850	1.850	1.850	1.850	1.850
Tension	9.5 lbs. @ 1.575	9.5 lbs. @ 1.575	9.5 lbs. @ 1.575	9.5 lbs. @ 1.575	9.5 lbs. @ 1.575

① 1977 Drive and Driven gears to front bearing-.0008 to .0018

② Driven gear to crescent .0087 to .0134

③ Drive gear to crescent .0083 to .0126

NOTE: This should align the distributor pawl parallel with the crankshaft center line.

7. Align the mating marks of the distributor gear and body and insert the oil pump assembly with a new gasket, into the engine block until the oil pump shaft gear is in mesh with the crankshaft gear and is engaged with the distributor pawl.

8. Using a new gasket, install the oil pan, connect the engine mounts, and install the front splash shields.

9. Install the oil, start the engine and check the ignition timing.

COOLING SYSTEM

NOTE: The Colt/Champ and Sapporo/Challenger series of Chrysler cars are built by Mitsubishi. As of 1983, Mitsubishi Motor Sales of America, Inc. will also be importing, distributing and servicing their own line of cars; the Starion, Cordia and Tredia. The turbocharged 2.6 litre engine used in the Starion is similar in design and service to its normally-aspirated cousin used in the Sapporo/Challenger. Brake systems, suspensions and most transmissions are also closely related. Where product similarities exist, procedures given for the Chrysler vehicles can be used as service guidelines.

Radiator

REMOVAL AND INSTALLATION

1. Remove the splash panel from the bottom of the car. Drain the radiator by opening the petcock. Remove the shroud on models so equipped.

2. Disconnect the radiator hoses at the engine. On automatic transmission cars, disconnect and plug the transmission lines to the bottom of the radiator.

3. Remove the two retaining bolts from either side of the radiator. Lift out the radiator. On front wheel drive models, disconnect the electric fan wiring harness. Do not remove the fan motor, blades or bracket—remove as a unit with the radiator.

4. Install the radiator in the reverse order of removal. Tighten the retaining bolts gradually in a criss-cross pattern.

Water Pump

REMOVAL

1. Drain the cooling system.

2. Remove the fan shroud and radiator if necessary for working room.

3. Remove the alternator belt and accessory belts.

4. On J and K engines:

    a. Place the piston in No. 1 cylinder at TDC of the compression stroke.

    b. Remove the crankshaft pulley, timing belt upper and lower covers, timing belt and timing belt tensioner.

    c. Remove the four water pump

1. Pump body
2. Impeller
3. Seal unit
4. Shaft assembly
5. Bracket

Cross-section of the water pump

mounting bolts and remove the water pump.

5. On U and F engines:

    a. Remove the fan blades and/or automatic hub, if equipped.

    b. Remove the water pump assembly from the timing chain case or the cylinder block.

INSTALLATION

1. Installation is the reverse of removal.

2. Fill the radiator with coolant and test for leaks.

Thermostat

REMOVAL AND INSTALLATION

The thermostat is located in the intake manifold under the upper radiator hose.

Water pump bolt length for installation on J engines

Water pump bolt length for installation on K engines

1. Drain the coolant below the level of the thermostat.

2. Remove the two retaining bolts and lift the thermostat housing off the intake manifold with the hose still attached.

NOTE: If you are careful, it is not necessary to remove the upper radiator hose.

3. Lift the thermostat out of the manifold.

4. Install the thermostat in the reverse order of removal. Use a new gasket and coat the mating surfaces with sealer.

EMISSION CONTROLS

NOTE: The Colt/Champ and Sapporo/Challenger series of Chrysler cars are built by Mitsubishi. As of 1983, Mitsubishi Motor Sales of America, Inc. will also be importing, distributing and servicing their own line of cars; the Starion, Cordia and Tredia. The turbocharged 2.6 litre engine used in the Starion is similar in design and service to its normally-aspirated cousin used in the Sapporo/Challenger. Brake systems, suspensions and most transmissions are also closely related. Where product similarities exist, procedures given for the Chrysler vehicles can be used as service guidelines.

Crankcase Emission Control System

A closed-type crankcase ventilation system is used to prevent engine blow-by gases from escaping into the atmosphere.

A hose connects the rear of the rocker arm cover and the intake manifold. A small fixed orifice is located in the intake manifold or on the rocker arm cover. Some later models have replaced the orifice with a PCV valve.

A larger hose is connected from the front of the rocker arm cover to the air cleaner assembly. Under light to medium carburetor throttle opening, the blow-by gases are drawn through the fixed orifice or PCV valve. Under heavy acceleration, both the fixed orifice or PCV valve and the large hose route the gases into the engine.

Maintenance required is to regularly check the breather hose condition, clean the orifice or PCV valve (replace if clogged) and clean the steel wool filter, in the air cleaner.

Fuel Evaporation Control System (1976–83)

This system is designed to prevent hydrocarbons from escaping into the atmosphere from the fuel tank, due to normal evaporation.

The parts of the system are as follow:

Separator Tank—Located near the gasoline tank, used to accommodate expansion, and to allow maximum condensation of the fuel vapors.

Bowl Vent System (1980–81)—Controls carburetor bowl vapors between canister and carburetor.

Carbon Element (1980–81)—Element is located in air cleaner to store vapors generated in the carburetor. Replace if clogged or dirty.

Canister—Either one or two, located in the engine compartment to trap and retain gasoline vapors while the engine is not operating. When the engine is started, fresh air is drawn into the canister, removing the stored vapors, and is directed to the air cleaner.

Vapor Check Valve (1976)—Used in the hose from the canister to the air cleaner to prevent vaporized fuel from entering the air cleaner during engine idling.

Two-Way Valve (1977–1983)—Because of different methods of tank venting and the use of a sealed gasoline tank cap, the two-way valve is used in the vapor lines. The valve relieves either pressure or vacuum in the tank.

Purge Control Valve (1977–83)— The purge control valve replaces the check valve used in previous years. During idle, the

1976 and later—typical emission controls

Late model crankcase ventilation system (typical)

valve closes off the vapor passage to the air cleaner.

Fuel Check Valve (1976–83)—This valve is used to prevent fuel leakage in case of roll over. It is installed in the vapor line between the two-way valve and the canister on the coupe, sedan, and hatchback and between the separator and the two-way valve on the station wagon.

MAINTENANCE

Be sure that all hoses are clamped and not dry-rotted or broken. Check the valves for cracks, signs of gasoline leakage, and proper operating condition.

The canister air filter (if equipped) should be inspected and changed at least every 24,000 miles.

Heated Air Intake System

All models are equipped with a temperature regulated air control valve in the air cleaner snorkel.

When the underhood air temperature is 41 degrees or lower, the air control valve allows preheated air to flow through the heat cowl of the exhaust manifold, via a flexible hose, to the air cleaner and into the carburetor.

When the underhood temperature is 108 degrees or above, the air flow is directed through the air cleaner snorkel.

At intermediate temperatures, the carburetor intake air is a blend of the direct underhood and preheated air.

MAINTENANCE

Visually check the control valve assembly when the engine is cold, to be sure that the valve is closed.

Warm up the engine and check that the control valve opens to the outside air.

Secondary Air Supply System (1976–83)

This system supplies air for the further combustion of unburned gases in the thermal reactor (if equipped) or exhaust manifold and consists of a reed valve, air hoses, and air passages built into the cylinder head.

The reed valve is operated by exhaust pulsations in the exhaust manifold. It draws fresh air through the air cleaner and supplies it to the exhaust ports.

MAINTENANCE

Check for damage to the air hoses and air pipes. Make sure the air passages are open in the head.

Pulse Air Feeder System (1981–83)

This system supplies ''secondary air'' into the exhaust system between the front and rear catalytic converters to promote oxidation of exhaust emissions in the rear converter. The system consists of a main reed valve, a subreed valve, air hoses and crankcase passages.

The main reed valve is actuated by pressures created by No. 3 piston. The sub-reed valve is actuated by exhaust pulsations. Fresh air is drawn through the air cleaner.

INSPECTION

Remove the hose connecting the ''reed valve'' at the air cleaner. Start the engine and check for vacuum in the hose. Check the hose for leaks if no vacuum is felt.

Exhaust Gas Recirculation System

The EGR system recirculates part of the exhaust gases into the combustion chambers. This dilutes the air/fuel mixture, reducing formation of oxides of nitrogen in the exhaust gases by lowering the peak combustion temperatures.

The parts of the EGR system are:

EGR Valve—Operated by vacuum drawn from a point above the carburetor throttle plate. The vacuum controls the raising and lowering of the valve pintle to allow exhaust gases to pass from the exhaust system to the intake manifold.

Thermo Valve—Used to stop EGR valve operation below approximately 131 degrees, in order to improve cold driveability and starting.

Dual EGR Control Valve (1978–83)

The EGR vacuum flow is suspended during idle and wide open throttle operation.

The primary valve controls EGR flow when the throttle valve opening is relatively narrow, while the secondary control valve operates at wider openings.

Sub-EGR Control Valve—Linked to the throttle valve to closely modulate the EGR gas flow.

EGR Maintenance Warning Light (1977–78)

A light in the speedometer assembly to alert the driver to the need for EGR system maintenance.

This device has a mileage sensor to light the visual signal at 15,000 mile intervals.

Upon completion of the required EGR system maintenance, the warning light can be turned off by resetting the switch. It is in the speedometer cable, under the instrument panel.

MAINTENANCE

1. Check all vacuum hoses for cracks, breakage and correct installation.
2. Check EGR valve operation by applying vacuum to the EGR valve vacuum nipple with the engine idling. The idle should become rough.
3. Check the passages in the cylinder head and intake manifold for clogging. Clean as necessary.
4. Cold start the engine. The EGR port nipple should be open. When the coolant is warmed to over 131 degrees, the port should be closed.

Thermal Reactor (1976–77 California and High Altitude)

This unit is used to further the combustion of the exhaust gases. It consists of a shell and a core with heat insulation material between, mounted at the exhaust manifold.

MAINTENANCE

1. Listen for any abnormal sound from the reactor.
2. Check for cracks and damage.
3. Check the thermal reactor flange on the cylinder head for warpage.

NOTE: The thermal reactor must be replaced when defective. It cannot be disassembled.

Catalytic Converter (1978–83)

This unit or units (two used in 1981–83) replaces the thermal reactor. It is filled with catalyst to oxidize hydrocarbons and carbon monoxide in the exhaust gases.

MAINTENANCE

1. Check the core for cracks and damages.
2. If the idle carbon monoxide and hydrocarbon content exceeds specifications and the ignition timing and idle mixture are correct, the converter must be replaced.

Jet Air System (1978–83)

A jet air passage is provided in the carburetor, intake manifold, and cylinder head to direct air to a jet valve, operated simultaneously with the intake valve.

On the intake stroke, jet air is forced into the combustion chamber because of the pressure difference between the ends of the air jet passage.

This jet of air produces a strong swirl in the combustion chamber scavenging the residual gases around the spark plug.

The jet air volume lessens with increased throttle opening. It is at a maximum at idle.

MAINTENANCE

NOTE: Refer to Valve Lash Adjustment for adjusting jet valve clearance.

No maintenance is required other than clearance adjustment during valve adjustment. The valve can be removed from the cylinder head for service or replacement.

Ignition Timing Control System (1976–83)

When the engine is idling or operating at low speeds under light load or deceleration, the exhaust gas temperature is low, resulting in incomplete combustion of the air/fuel mixture. To prevent this, ignition timing is retarded under these conditions to maintain high exhaust gas temperature.

The units in the Ignition Timing Control system are as follow:

Dual-diaphragm distributor—This distributor has both retard and advance mechanisms operated by vacuum.

Thermo valve—This valve is used to protect the engine from overheating. When coolant temperature reaches 203 degrees, the advance unit is allowed to operate, causing an increase in engine speed and a decrease in coolant temperature.

Single diaphragm distributor—This distributor has a single diaphragm vacuum advance unit, which advances the ignition timing as engine vacuum dictates. The single diaphragm distributor must not be interchanged with the dual diaphragm distributor. The distributor operating curves are different and would cause increased emissions. A thermo valve is *not* used with this type of distributor.

Orifice Spark Advance Control (1977)

The OSAC valve is located in the vacuum line between the distributor and the carburetor. Its function is to delay vacuum advance during medium to high speed operation, when high vacuum would be present. It is used only with the single diaphragm distributor. No maintenance is required.

Deceleration Device (1977–83)

Closing of the throttle valve on deceleration is delayed in order to burn the air/fuel mixture more thoroughly. A vacuum controlled dashpot, attached to the carburetor linkage is used.

A servo valve detects intake manifold vacuum and closes if vacuum exceeds a preset value. Since the air in the dashpot diaphragm chamber can not escape, the throttle linkage opening is temporarily retained. If the vacuum is below the preset value, the servo valve opens and the dashpot works normally.

MAINTENANCE

Inspect the hoses for breaks and damage, and the valve body for cracks.

ADJUSTMENT

1. Have the engine running, brakes locked, and a tachometer attached.
2. Push the dashpot rod, connected to the carburetor arm, upward and into the dashpot until it stops.
3. Note the rpm at the dashpot stop and adjust to the following specifications. Note the time required between suddenly releasing the dashpot rod and the return to normal curb idle.
4. The specifications are as follows:
1980
   a. 1600 cc engine—Calif. and H/Alt.
Set Speed—1900 ± 100 rpm
Required Time—3 to 6 Sec.
   b. 2000 cc engine—Calif.
Set Speed—1500 ± 100 rpm
Required time—3 to 6 Sec.
   c. 1400 cc & 1600 cc engines—49 States,
2000 cc engine—49 States
Set Speed—2000 ± 100 rpm
Required Time—3 to 6 Sec.
   d. All engines: 1981–83
Set Speed—2000 ± 100 rpm

Mixture Control Valve (1977–83)

This control valve is used to supply additional air into the intake manifold to decrease manifold vacuum during deceleration, and is activated by the intake manifold vacuum level.

Manual Altitude Compensation System (1977–83)

An off-on valve is used to increase the air supply to the carburetor to lean the mixture and decrease the EGR flow for high altitude operation.

MAINTENANCE

The required maintenance is to inspect any vacuum hoses and routing for kinks, breakage and cracks. The off-on valve should be on for high altitude and off for driving under 4000 ft.

FUEL SYSTEM

NOTE: The Colt/Champ and Sapporo/Challenger series of Chrysler cars are built by Mitsubishi. As of 1983, Mitsubishi Motor Sales of America, Inc. will also be importing, distributing and servicing their own line of cars; the Starion, Cordia and Tredia. The turbocharged 2.6 litre engine used in the Starion is similar in design and service to its normally-aspirated cousin used in the Sapporo/Challenger. Brake systems, suspensions and most transmissions are also closely related. Where product similarities exist, procedures given for the Chrysler vehicles can be used as service guidelines.

Fuel Filter

REPLACEMENT

All models use an in-line filter which should be replaced every 12,000 miles.

Mechanical Fuel Pump

REMOVAL AND INSTALLATION

1. Remove the fuel lines.
2. Unbolt the pump mounting bolts, and remove the pump, insulator, and gasket.

3. Coat both sides of a new insulator and gasket with sealer, and install the pump in the reverse order of removal.

TESTING

Disconnect the fuel line from the carburetor and attach a pressure tester to the end of the line. Crank the engine. The tester should show 3.7–5.1 psi.

Carburetors

REMOVAL AND INSTALLATION

1. Remove the solenoid valve wiring.
2. Disconnect the air cleaner breather hose, air duct and vacuum tube.

1. Throttle positioner solenoid	18. Float	34. By-pass screw
2. Compensator	19. Secondary pilot jet	35. Fuel cut solenoid
3. Stud	20. Secondary main jet	36. Intermediate lever
4. Throttle positioner	21. Primary main jet	37. Idle limiter
5. Adjusting nut	22. Pump weight	38. Pilot screw
6. Locknut	23. Steel ball	39. Accelerator pump
7. Auto-choke	24. Inner secondary venturi	40. Enrichment body assembly
8. Choke shaft	25. Inner primary venturi	41. Enrichment jet
9. Water hose	26. Primary pilot jet	42. Main body
10. Return spring	27. Choke valve	43. Insulator
11. Depression chamber	28. Throttle stop screw	44. Throttle chamber packing
12. Piston chamber	29. Abatement plate	45. Carburetor gasket
13. Float chamber cover	30. Lever	46. Throttle body
14. Float chamber packing	31. Lever spring	47. Throttle stop screw
15. Fuel joint	32. Throttle lever	
16. Filter	33. Throttle return spring	
17. Needle valve		

Exploded view of the carburetor

3. Remove the air cleaner.

4. Remove the air cleaner case.

5. Disconnect the accelerator and shift cables (automatic transmission) at the carburetor.

6. Disconnect the purge valve hose; remove the vacuum compensator, and fuel lines.

7. Drain the coolant.

8. Remove the water hose between the carburetor and the cylinder head.

9. Remove the carburetor.

10. Installation is the reverse of removal.

OVERHAUL

For all carburetor overhaul procedures, please refer to "Carburetor Service" in the Unit Repair section.

THROTTLE LINKAGE ADJUSTMENT

1976–77

Throttle linkage is adjusted at the clamp which joins the accelerator pedal rod to the carburetor rod. With the carburetor throttle valves closed, (engine at normal operating temperature), the distance between the top of the clamp and the toe-board should be about 1.4 inches. The distance between the end of the connecting rod to the toe-board should be a minimum of 0.4 inch, and the clearance between the stopper bolt and the pedal lever should be 0 to 0.8 inch.

1978–81

Adjust the stopper bolt to a distance of .75 ± 0 to 0.04 inch from the inside of the bolt holding bracket, to the contact point of the pedal lever while holding the carburetor throttle plates closed. The yoke at the carburetor end of the accelerator rod is serrated to allow the yoke to be loosened and moved so that a minimal readjustment

Throttle linkage adjustment—1978–83

Adjusting the choke on 1980 and later vehicles

of the stopper adjusting bolt is needed to give the proper throttle release and opening.

FLOAT AND FUEL LEVEL ADJUSTMENT

A sight glass is fitted at the float chamber and the fuel lever can be checked without disassembling the carburetor. Normal fuel level is within the level mark on the sight glass.

The fuel level adjustment is corrected by increasing or decreasing the number of needle valve packings. The float level may be off 0.160 inch, above or below the level mark and the operation of the engine would not be affected.

Float level adjustment

FAST IDLE ADJUSTMENT

1. Start the engine and open the throttle valve about 45 degrees. Manually close the choke valve and slowly return the throttle valve to the stop position.

2. With a tachometer, check that the fast idle speed is 2000 rpm or lower. (Not less than 1700 rpm). Adjust the speed as necessary with the fast idle speed screw.

3. Cold start the engine and check the automatic choke and fast idle operation.

AUTOMATIC CHOKE ADJUSTMENT

The choke case has five small projections. Align the center projection with the yellow punch mark of the bimetal case.

On 1980 and later models the choke is adjusted by turning the screw located on the choke spring bracket. The latest model years could have a tamper resistant cover on the screw. If choke adjustment is absolutely necessary, then the cover could be removed to make the adjustment. A new cover should be installed on the screw after the adjustment is made.

THROTTLE OPENER ADJUSTMENT

Colt/Champ—4 Speed M/T 1982 and Later—49 states

This system is not available in California. The throttle opener increases engine rpm if it drops below a specified amount. The system can be adjusted.

1. Check and adjust curb idle if needed.

2. Turn off all accessories and disconnect the electric radiator fan and hook a tachometer to the engine.

3. Warm up the engine and set the transaxle in neutral.

4. Remove the pressure on throttle opener by lifting on the unit with a finger.

— CAUTION —
Do not push up on the throttle opener lever or rod.

5. Adjust the throttle opener screw to obtain 800 to 900 rpm.

Throttle opener system in operation

MANUAL TRANSMISSION

NOTE: The Colt/Champ and Sapporo/Challenger series of Chrysler cars are built by Mitsubishi. As of 1983, Mitsubishi Motor Sales of America, Inc. will also be importing, distributing and servicing their own line of cars; the Starion, Cordia and Tredia. The turbocharged 2.6 litre engine used in the Starion is similar in design and service to its normally-aspirated cousin used in the Sapporo/Challenger. Brake systems, suspensions and most transmissions are also closely related. Where product similarities exist, procedures given for the Chrysler vehicles can be used as service guidelines.

Four and Five Speed

REMOVAL AND INSTALLATION EXCEPT FRONT WHEEL DRIVE

1. Disconnect the battery ground cable, remove the air cleaner and the starter.
2. Remove the top transmission mounting bolts from the bell housing.
3. From inside the car, raise the console assembly, if equipped, or the carpet and remove the dust cover retaining plate at the shift lever.
4. Place the four speed transmission in second gear and the five speed transmission in first gear. Remove the control lever assembly.
5. Raise the car and support it safely. Drain the transmission. Disconnect the speedometer and the backup light switch.
6. Remove the driveshaft, exhaust pipe, and the clutch cable.

7. Support the transmission and remove the engine rear support bracket.
8. Remove the bell housing cover and bolts, move the transmission rearward, and lower it carefully to the floor. Remove the transmission from under the car.
9. To install the transmission, reverse the removal procedure. Make sure the transmission is in the proper gear before installing the gear shift lever.

FRONT WHEEL DRIVE MODELS

1. Disconnect the battery ground (negative) cable.
2. Disconnect from the transaxle; the clutch cable, speedometer cable, backup light harness, starter motor and the four upper bolts connecting the engine to the transaxle.
3. Jack up the car and support on jack stands.
4. Remove the front wheels. Remove the engine splash shield.
5. Remove the shift rod and extension. It may be necessary to remove any heat shields that interfere with your progress.
6. Drain the transaxle fluid.
7. Remove the right and left driveshafts from the transaxle case.
   a. Remove center cap (front wheel hub) and nut.
   b. Remove ball joint and strut bar from lower control arm.
   c. Insert pry bar between transaxle case and double off-set joint; move bar to the right to remove the left driveshaft, left to remove the right driveshaft.

── CAUTION ──

Pry on the rib only of the transaxle. Do not insert the pry bar too deeply causing damage to the oil seal. Always replace the DOJ retainer ring each time the driveshaft is removed from the transaxle case.

   d. Use an axle shaft puller to force the driveshaft out of the front hub. Be careful not to prevent the spacer from falling out of place.

8. Disconnect the range selector cable (if equipped). Remove the engine rear cover.
9. Support the weight of the engine from above (chain hoist). Support the transaxle and remove the remaining lower mounting bolts.
10. Remove the transaxle mount insulator bolt.
11. Remove (slide away from the engine) and lower the transaxle.
12. To install reverse the removal procedure. Be sure to connect all controls and wiring. Use new retaining rings when installing the driveshafts.

OVERHAUL

For manual transmission overhaul procedures, please refer to ''Manual Transmission Overhaul'' in the Unit Repair section.

CLUTCH

Clutch Cable

REMOVAL AND INSTALLATION

1. Loosen the cable adjusting wheel inside the engine compartment.
2. Loosen the clutch pedal adjusting bolt locknut and loosen the adjusting bolt.
3. Remove the cable end from the clutch throwout lever.
4. Remove the cable end from the clutch pedal.
5. Installation is the reverse of removal.

NOTE: Lubricate the cable with engine oil and after installation, install pads isolating the cable from the intake manifold and from the rear side of the engine mount insulator on coupe, sedan, and hatchbacks only.

1. Clutch control shaft
2. Return spring
3. Clutch shift arm
4. Return clip
5. Release bearing carrier
6. Release bearing
7. Pressure plate assembly
8. Clutch disc

Exploded view of the clutch

Dimension B and C

Clutch lubrication and adjustment

2. Remove pressure plate bolts, pressure plate and clutch disc.

3. From inside the transmission bell housing, remove the return spring clip and remove the release bearing assembly.

4. If necessary, remove the release control lever and spring pin with a ³⁄₁₆ inch punch. Remove the control lever shaft assembly and clutch shift arm, two felt packings and two return springs.

5. Installation is the reverse of removal.

NOTE: Upon assembly—

a. Apply grease to the inside surface of the bushings and oil seal lips.

b. Apply grease in the clutch hub splines and main drive gear splines.

c. Apply grease to the inside of the release bearing carrier grooves.

d. Apply oil to the two felt packings.

CLUTCH DISC REPLACEMENT

1. Remove the transmission as outlined in the "Manual Transmission Removal and Installation" section.

NOTE: It is recommended that a clutch aligning tool be inserted in the clutch hub to prevent dropping of the clutch disc during disassembly.

Measure dimension A between these points

ADJUSTMENT

1. Adjust the clutch pedal height by the adjusting bolt to the distance shown in the following specifications. (Dimension A.)

2. Draw the outer cable from the cable holder on the toe-board and adjust its free-play by means of the adjusting nut. (Dimension D.)

3. Check clutch pedal free-play. (Dimension C), and the correct pedal stroke distance, (Dimension B), as outlined in the following specifications.

1. Clutch cable
2. Spring
3. Pedal support
4. Spacer
5. Bushing
6. Spring
7. Clutch pedal
8. Pedal pad
10. Silencer
11. Brake pedal

Clutch pedal components

CLUTCH ADJUSTMENT SPECIFICATIONS
Front Wheel Drive Cars

	1979–83
Pedal upper face from toe board	7.1–7.3
Pedal stroke	5.7
Clearance between adjusting nut & cable	0.20–0.24

CLUTCH AND PEDAL ADJUSTMENT SPECIFICATIONS
Rear Wheel Drive Cars

	Dimension	1976–77	1978	1979	1980	1981	1982–83
Pedal height from toe board	A	6.5–6.7 inch	6.8 inch	6.8⑤	6.8⑤	7.1	7.5
Pedal stroke	B	5.1 inch①	5.5 inch②	5.5②	5.9	5.8	6.0
Clutch pedal free-play	C	0.8–1.4 inch	0.8–1.2 inch③	0.6–0.08⑥	0.6–0.8⑥	0.6–0.8	0.6–0.8
Adjusting nut to cable holder clearance	D	0.2–0.24 inch	0.2–0.24 inch④	0.12–0.16	0.12–0.16	0.12–0.16	0.12–0.16⑦
Clearance between release bearing face and pressure plate	E	0.080 inch	0.080 inch	—	—	—	—

① 1977 Coupe, Sedan and Hatchback: 5.9 inch
② 2600 cc engine: 5.9 inch
③ Station wagon: 0.4 to 0.6 inch
④ Station wagon w/2000 cc engine: 0.14 to 0.18 inch
⑤ 2600 cc engine: 7.2
⑥ Arrow: 0.8–1.2
⑦ Measured between adjusting wheel and insulator

AUTOMATIC TRANSMISSION

NOTE: The Colt/Champ and Sapporo/Challenger series of Chrysler cars are built by Mitsubishi. As of 1983, Mitsubishi Motor Sales of America, Inc. will also be importing, distributing and servicing their own line of cars; the Starion, Cordia and Tredia. The turbocharged 2.6 litre engine used in the Starion is similar in design and service to its normally-aspirated cousin used in the Sapporo/Challenger. Brake systems, suspensions and most transmissions are also closely related. Where product similarities exist, procedures given for the Chrysler vehicles can be used as service guidelines.

1976 97.5 CID cars use a Borg-Warner aluminum case 3-speed. All others use a Chrysler Torque Flite.

Rear Wheel Drive Models

REMOVAL AND INSTALLATION

Borg-Warner

The exhaust system must be removed from the connecting pipe to the muffler.

1. Remove the air cleaner, battery with cables, starter, and the upper bolts which attach the engine to the transmission.

2. Drain the transmission. Remove the speedometer cable and driveshaft.

3. Remove the exhaust system from the connecting pipe rearward to the muffler.

4. Remove the transmission oil lines.

5. Remove the control rod.

6. Remove the bell housing cover. Rotate the torque converter and remove the four exposed bolts.

7. Place a jack under the transmission.

8. Remove the insulator attaching bolts, ground cable, and spacer. Remove the insulator.

9. Remove the torque converter housing to engine bolts and pull out the transmission.

10. To install the transmission, reverse the removal procedure.

TorqueFlite

The transmission and converter must be removed as an assembly; otherwise, the converter drive plate, pump bushing, or oil seal may be damaged. The drive plate will not support a load; therefore, none of the weight of the transmission should be allowed to rest on the plate during removal.

1. Disconnect battery ground cable, drain the transmission, and remove cooler lines at transmission.

2. Remove starter and cooler line bracket.

3. Rotate crankshaft clockwise and remove bolts attaching torque converter to drive plate.

4. Remove the driveshaft.

5. Disconnect gearshift rod and torque shaft.

6. Disconnect thorttle rod from lever at the left side of transmission. Remove linkage bellcrank from transmission if so equipped.

7. Remove the oil filler tube and speedometer cable.

8. Support the rear of the engine with jack.

9. Raise transmission slightly.

10. Remove crossmember.

11. Remove all bell housing bolts.

12. Carefully work transmission converter assembly rearward off engine block dowels and disengage converter hub from end of crankshaft. Attach a small C-clamp to edge of bell housing to hold converter in place during transmission removal.

13. Remove transmission.

14. Installation is the reverse of removal.

Front Wheel Drive Models

TRANSAXLE REMOVAL

NOTE: The transaxle and converter must be removed and installed as an assembly.

1. Disconnect the battery ground (negative) cable.

2. Disconnect the throttle control cable at the carburetor and the manual control cable at the transaxle.

3. Disconnect from the transaxle; the inhibitor switch (neutral safety) connector, fluid cooler hose and the four upper bolts connecting the engine to the transaxle.

4. Jack up the car and support on jack stands.

5. Remove the front wheels. Remove the engine splash shield.

6. Drain the transaxle fluid.

7. Remove the right and left driveshafts from the transaxle case. Refer to Step

7 in the manual transaxle removal for procedure.

8. Disconnect the speedometer cable. Remove the starter motor.

9. Remove the lower cover from the converter housing. Remove the three bolts that connect the converter to the engine drive plate.

NOTE: Never support the full weight of the transaxle on the engine drive plate.

10. Turn and force the converter back and away from the engine drive plate.

11. Support the weight of the engine from above (chain hoist). Support the transaxle and remove the remaining mounting bolts.

12. Remove the transaxle mount insulator bolt.

13. Remove (slide away from the engine) and lower the transaxle and converter as an assembly.

14. To install reverse the removal procedure. Be sure to connect all controls, wiring and hoses. Use new retaining rings when installing the drive axles.

Pan and Filter

REMOVAL AND INSTALLATION

Borg-Warner

1. Raise and support vehicle.

2. Remove pan bolts in a criss-cross fashion allowing fluid to drain at the same time.

3. Remove gasket and magnet. The magnet is used to pick up metallic foreign objects.

4. Install magnet and new gasket and attach pan, tightening bolts in a criss-cross pattern to 6–9 ft. lbs. Refill with Dexron® type fluid.

TorqueFlite

1. Raise and support vehicle.

2. Loosen the pan bolts from one end to the other allowing the fluid to drain out.

3. Unbolt the old filter from the pan.

4. Clean the pan and install a new filter. Tighten filter bolts to 35 in. lbs.

5. Install the pan and new gasket. Torque pan bolts to 6–9 ft. lbs.

6. Add four quarts of Dexron® fluid, start the engine and move the lever through all positions, pausing momentarily in each. Add enough fluid to bring the level to the full mark on the dipstick.

Front Wheel Drive Models

1. Raise and support the vehicle.

2. Loosen and remove the transmission pan drain plug and the differential drain plug.

3. Remove the pan to install a new filter. Clean the pan and reinstall with a new gasket.

4. Add four quarts of Dexron® II fluid through the dipstick after replacing the two (2) drain plugs. Start the engine and move selector lever through all positions: allow engine to run for at least two minutes.

5. Add sufficient fluid to bring level up to the lower dipstick. Recheck after transmission is at normal operating temperature.

FRONT BAND ADJUSTMENT–BORG-WARNER

1. Remove the transmission pan.

2. Loosen the locknut and move the servo lever out of the way.

3. Insert a 0.25 in. feeler gauge between the servo piston pin and the adjusting screw.

4. Torque the servo screw to 10 in. lbs.

5. Tighten the locknut and remove the feeler gauge.

REAR BAND ADJUSTMENT–BORG-WARNER

This screw is located on the right-hand outer wall of the transmission case. Loosen the

Front band adjusting screw location, Borg-Warner

Rear band adjusting screw location, Borg-Warner

locknut. Tighten the nut to 10 ft. lbs. Loosen the nut ¾ turn. Tighten down the locknut.

KICKDOWN BAND–TORQUEFLITE

The kickdown band adjusting screw is located on the left side of the transmission case.

1. Loosen locknut and back off approximately 5 turns. Test adjusting screw for free turning in the transmission case.

2. Tighten the adjusting screw to 72 in. lbs.

3. Back off adjusting screw 3 turns from Step 2. Tighten the locknut to 35 ft. lbs.

KICKDOWN BAND ADJUSTMENT–FRONT WHEEL DRIVE MODELS

1. Remove all dirt from the kickdown servo cover. Location is to right of dipstick; the large bump with a round cover.

2. Remove the snap-ring that retains the cover. Use a pair of pliers that fit into the notches of the cover and remove.

3. Loosen the locknut. Hold the kickdown servo piston from turning and tighten the adjusting screw to 7 ft. lbs., then back it off. Repeat the tightening and backing off two times. This will assure the seating of the kickdown band on the drum.

4. Tighten the adjusting screw to 3.5 ft. lbs. and back off 3.5 turns (counterclockwise).

Fluid pan removal sequence—Borg-Warner

5. Hold the adjusting screw and tighten the locknut to 12 ft. lbs.

6. Install a new cover seal ring ''D''-shaped section in the groove. Install the servo cover and snap-ring.

KICKDOWN SWITCH–BORG-WARNER

The kickdown switch is located on the carburetor and is operated when the throttle valve is opened fully by the accelerator pedal and linkage.

1. To inspect the kickdown switch, a test lamp is used to check that electrical current is flowing through the switch, with the throttle valve wide open.

2. If there is no current indication, adjust the switch. If no current is indicated with the switch plunger completely depressed, replace the switch.

3. If current flows through the switch but the kickdown is still inoperative, the internal solenoid on the valve body may be defective. A clicking noise should be heard if the solenoid is working normally.

MODULATOR VALVE ADJUSTMENT–BORG-WARNER

1. Install a vacuum gauge in the line from the engine to the transmission modulator valve.

2. Remove the pipe plug from the left rear of the transmission case and install a 0–300 psi pressure gauge.

3. Start the engine and allow it to warm up to normal operating temperature.

4. Apply the hand brake and chock the wheels. Place the selector lever in the R position.

5. With a 17.7 in. Hg reading, the oil control pressure should be 55–68 psi.

6. Increase the engine speed until the vacuum gauge reads 12 in. Hg. The pressure gauge should read 92–98 psi.

7. An engine stall vacuum reading of 2 in. Hg should result in a pressure reading of 160–195 psi.

NOTE: Do not hold the stall test longer than 10 seconds. Return the selector lever to the N position and increase the engine speed to cool both the transmission and the engine. Wait approximately two minutes between tests, if a repeat is necessary.

8. If line pressure is below the specified value, remove the modulator vacuum line and turn the adjusting screw clockwise.

9. If the line pressure is above the specified value, remove the modulator vacuum line and turn the adjusting screw counterclockwise.

NOTE:
a. One turn of the modulator screw causes a change of pressure of approximately 10 psi.

b. Do not adjust line pressure in any forward range. Use R position only.

10. Remove the vacuum and pressure gauges.

NEUTRAL START SWITCH ADJUSTMENT–BORG-WARNER

1. Place the selector lever in N position.

2. Lock the switch with a screw so that when the pin at the forward end of the rod assembly is near the crest of the pawl of the detent plate, the switch should be at the forward end of the N range.

3. Tighten the neutral start switch screw. A clearance of .059 inch should be present between the switch and the selector lever.

4. Check switch operation by attempting to start the engine in gears other than the P and N position. Make sure that the backup lights operate with the lever in the R position.

INHIBITOR SWITCH ADJUSTMENT–FRONT WHEEL DRIVE MODELS

1. Place the control lever in the ''N'' position.

2. Make sure the short end of the manual control lever covers the switch body flange. Loosen the switch mounting bolts (2) and adjust switch as necessary. Tighten the bolts.

3. Check the switch operation by attempting to start engine in gears other than the P and N positions.

LOW & REVERSE BAND–TORQUEFLITE

1. Raise vehicle, drain transmission fluid and remove the pan.

2. This transmission has an Allen socket adjustment screw at the servo end of lever.

After removing the locknut this screw is tightened to 41 in. lbs. torque then backed off 7½ turns. Tighten the locknut to 30 ft. lbs.

3. Reinstall the pan.

NEUTRAL SAFETY SWITCH–TORQUEFLITE

1. When testing the safety switch, check to see if the switch has been properly installed. Move the selector lever into N position and adjust the switch by moving it so that the pin on the forward end of the rod assembly will be in the position near the lobe of detent plate and that this position will be at the front end of the range of N connection of the switch. Temporarily tighten the attaching screws. After adjusting the selection lever clearance to 0.059 in. securely tighten the screws.

2. Test the continuity of the switch circuit by using a test light with switch connector disconnected.

SHIFT LINKAGE ADJUSTMENT–TORQUEFLITE

1. Disconnect the control cable at the transaxle (control rod on rear drive vehicles).

2. Place the selector lever in neutral and the inhibitor switch on the transaxle in neutral position (the manual control lever in neutral position on rear drive vehicles).

3. Install the control cable on the transaxle or control rod on the transmission and check for slack.

4. Turn the adjusting nut to remove any slack from the cable or rod.

5. Confirm the smoothness of lever operation and that the red indicator moves to show each gear.

6. Move the selector slowly upward until it clicks into the ''P'' position. Check to see if the starter will operate in park. After checking park move the selector toward ''N'' until the lever drops at the end of the se-

Transmission control cable adjustment on front wheel drive vehicles

Transmission rod linkage adjustment on rear wheel drive vehicles

1. Raise the cover on the throttle control cable to expose the nipple.
2. Loosen the lower cable bracket mounting bolt.
3. Move the lower cable bracket until the distance between the nipple and the cover nearest the mounting bracket is adjusted to 0.04 inches (1.0 mm).
4. Tighten the lower cable bracket mounting bolt to 9.0–15.0 ft. lbs. (12.0–14.0 Nm).
5. With the throttle lever in wide-open position (engine off), pull the cable further upward to confirm the cable has freedom of movement.

lector gate. If the starter also operates at this point, the gearshift linkage is properly adjusted.

THROTTLE ROD ADJUSTMENT—TORQUEFLITE

Warm the engine until it reaches the normal operating temperature. With the carburetor automatic choke off the fast idle cam, adjust the engine idle speed by using a tachometer. Then make the throttle rod adjustment.

1. Install each linkage. Loosen its bolts so that the rods B and C can slide properly.
2. Lightly push the rod A or the transmission throttle lever and the rod C toward the idle stopper and set the rods to idle position. In this case the carburetor automatic choke must be fully released. Tighten the bolt securely to connect the rods B and C.
3. Make sure that when the carburetor throttle valve is wide-open, the transmission throttle lever smoothly moves from idle to wide-open position (operating angle; 45°–54°) and that there is some room in the lever stroke.

NOTE: Make sure that when the throttle linkage alone is returned slowly from the fully open throttle position, that the transmission throttle lever completely returns to the idle position by spring force.

THROTTLE CONTROL CABLE ADJUSTMENT—TRANSAXLE

Warm the engine to normal operating temperature and make sure the throttle is at curb idle position. Turn engine off.

DRIVE AXLE

NOTE: The Colt/Champ and Sapporo/Challenger series of Chrysler cars are built by Mitsubishi. As of 1983, Mitsubishi Motor Sales of America, Inc. will also be importing, distributing and servicing their own line of cars; the Starion, Cordia and Tredia. The turbocharged 2.6 litre engine used in the Starion is similar in design and service to its normally-aspirated cousin used in the Sapporo/Challenger. Brake systems, suspensions and most transmissions are also closely related. Where product similarities exist, procedures given for the Chrysler vehicles can be used as service guidelines.

Driveshafts and U-Joints

The driveshaft and U-joints are of conventional design and construction. Driveshaft length differs between the manual and automatic transmission equipped vehicles.

1. Push button
2. Shift handle
3. Rod adjusting nut
4. Rod return spring
5. Selector lever assembly
6. Position indicator assembly
7. Indicator lamp socket assembly
8. Inhibitor switch
9. Shift lever rod
10. Shift lever bracket assembly
11. Lever bracket cover
12. Transmission control arm
13. Transmission control rod

Exploded view of Torqueflite automatic transmission control

1. Sleeve yoke
2. Snap-ring
3. Needle bearing
4. Dust seal
5. Universal joint journal
6. Driveshaft
7. Balance weight
8. Driveshaft flange yoke

Driveshaft components

Dynamic Damper

Transmission mounted dynamic dampers are used on all automatic transmission cars from 1976 to 1977.

Beginning 1977, dampers are installed on some models with the five speed transmission. The dynamic damper units are not interchangeable.

Driveshaft

REMOVAL AND INSTALLATION

1. Matchmark the rear flange yoke and the differential pinion flange.
2. Remove the bolts from the rear flange. Remove the driveshaft by pulling it from the rear of the transmission extension housing.

NOTE: Place a container under the transmission extension housing to collect any oil leakage when the driveshaft is removed.

3. To install the shaft, align the front sleeve yoke with the splines of the transmission output shaft, and push the driveshaft into the extension housing.

NOTE: Be careful not to damage the rear transmission seal lip upon installation.

4. Align the matchmarks on the rear yokes, install the bolts, and tighten securely.
5. Inspect the oil level of the transmission.

U/JOINT OVERHAUL

1. Remove the bearing retainer snap-rings from the flange yoke.
2. With a vise and suitable sockets, force one needle bearing cup outward from the yoke, using the cross as a ram.
3. Grasp the protruding bearing with pliers or vise grips and remove it from the yoke.
4. Reverse the sockets and again using the cross as a ram, force the opposite bearing outward from the yoke and remove it with pliers or vise grips.
5. Follow the same procedure to remove the remaining bearing in the yoke.
6. To install, place the cross in the yoke

U-joint bearing removal

Measuring the snap ring clearance

and start a bearing cup into the yoke collar, engaging the cross arm.

7. With the aid of a vise, force the bearing cup into the yoke collar until it bottoms. Install the opposite bearing cup in the same manner.

NOTE: Sockets may be used to force the bearing cup inward so that the retaining snap-rings can be installed.

8. Different thickness snap-rings are used to control the clearance between the bearing and the snap-ring.
9. Install a snap-ring and measure the clearance with a feeler gauge. Replace the snap-ring with one of the proper thickness to have a total clearance tolerance of .000 to .001 inch.

Snap-ring selection range
No color—0.0504 inch
Yellow—0.0561 inch
Blue—0.0528 inch
Purple—0.0539 inch

NOTE: When snap-rings are installed, press each bearing towards the opposite side to measure the maximum clearance.

Front Wheel Drive Models

REMOVAL AND INSTALLATION

1. Remove the hub center cap and loosen the driveshaft (axle) nut. Loosen the wheel lug nuts.
2. Lift the car and support it on jack stands. Remove the front wheels. Remove the engine splash shield.
3. Remove the lower ball joint and strut bar from the lower control arm.
4. Drain the transaxle fluid.
5. Insert a pry bar between the transaxle case (on the raised rib) and the driveshaft double off-set joint case (DOJ). Do not insert the pry bar too deeply or you will damage the oil seal. Move the bar to the right to withdraw the left driveshaft; to the left to remove the right driveshaft.
6. Plug the transaxle case with a clean rag to prevent dirt from entering the case.
7. Use a puller-driver mounted on the wheel studs to push the driveshaft from the front hub. Take care to prevent the spacer from falling out of place.
8. Assembly is the reverse of removal.

Insert the driveshaft into the hub first, then install the transaxle end.

NOTE: Always use a new DOJ retaining ring every time you remove the driveshaft.

CV-JOINT OVERHAUL

NOTE: The Birfield joint (wheel side) cannot be rebuilt. It must be replaced with the axle, however a boot kit is available.

1. Remove the boot band from double offset joint (DOJ) and slide the boot away from the joint.
2. Remove the circlip from the DOJ with a flat-blade screwdriver. Remove the driveshaft from the DOJ and wipe off the grease.
3. Remove the snap-ring that retains the inner race. Remove the inner race, cage and balls as an assembly.
4. Clean the inner race, cage and balls without disassembly.
5. Remove the Birfield joint boot, clean grease away and inspect the joint for wear; check the splines on both ends of the shaft for wear.
6. Check the DOJ for rust, damage or wear to the outer race, inner race, cage and balls. If any parts show wear, replace with the necessary kit. It is a good idea to at least replace the boots. Kits available are; Driveshaft and Birfield joint, Double offset joint, Birfield boot kit and DOJ boot kit.
7. To reassemble: Tape the ends of the splines to prevent damage to the boots when they are installed.
8. Apply gear oil to the shaft and slide the new boots on. If you are not installing a kit, apply an amount of grease equal to the amount you wiped away.
9. Installation of the old parts is the reverse of removal after you have regreased them. To install the DOJ kit, use the grease supplied with the kit and apply an amount to the inner race and cage. Install the inner race and cock slightly.
10. Apply grease to the balls and install them in the cage. Place the inner race on the driveshaft and install the snap-ring. Apply grease to the outer race and install. Install the boots and bands.
11. Install the driveshaft using a new retainer ring on the DOJ side.

Front Hub and Wheel Bearings

REMOVAL AND INSTALLATION

1. Remove driveshaft and front brake assembly.
2. Disconnect tie rod end and strut.
3. Remove hub and knuckle as an assembly.
4. Remove front hub from knuckle. It may be necessary to drive out the hub with a soft (plastic) hammer.

5. Remove disc rotor from hub.

6. The oil seal and the inner and outer bearings may now be serviced. Refer to the front wheel bearing section.

7. Assembly is the reverse of removal.

Rear Axle

REMOVAL AND INSTALLATION

Leaf Spring Type

1. Raise and support the car safely.
2. Remove the rear wheels.
3. Remove the driveshaft.
4. Disconnect all rear brake lines.
5. Remove the rear U-bolts and the shock absorbers.
6. Remove the spring shackle pin nuts and the shackle plate. With the axle housing resting on the jack, remove the rear springs.
7. To replace the axle assembly, reverse the removal procedure. Bleed the brakes.

Coil Spring Type

1. Raise the car and support it safely.
2. Remove the rear wheels and the driveshaft.
3. Disconnect the parking brake cable and the hydraulic brake hose.
4. Remove the shock absorbers from the rear housing.
5. Lower the housing and remove the coil springs.
6. Position the housing and remove the lower and upper control arms and the assist link.
7. Guide the housing from under the car with the aid of a helper.
8. Installation is the reverse order of removal.
9. Bleed the brakes thoroughly.

Rear Axle Shaft

REMOVAL AND INSTALLATION

1. Remove the rear wheels and the brake backing plate.

2. The axle shaft may be pulled out manually or with a slide hammer.
3. Installation is the reverse of removal.
4. Bleed the brakes.

Axle Shaft Bearing/Oil Seal

REMOVAL AND INSTALLATION

NOTE: Front wheel drive models use an inner and outer bearing contained in the rear brake drum hub. Refer to front wheel bearing servicing, in the brake section, for removal and installation.

Oil seal removal

1. Remove the axle shaft.
2. Grind a small notch on the inner bearing retainer and split the retainer at that point with a chisel.
3. Remove the bearing with a puller.
4. The oil seal can be removed after the axle shaft is removed.
5. Install the outer bearing retainer (raised surface facing the wheel hub), axle shaft bearing and retainer. Using packing, set the clearance between the outer bearing retainer and the bearing to 0.00–0.01 in.

Power Train

FRONT WHEEL DRIVE MODELS

The power train of the manual transaxle consists of three shafts including an input

shaft assembly, an intermediate shaft assembly, an output shaft assembly and a differential assembly.

The automatic transaxle consists of a torque converter, fully automatic three speed transmission, transfer gearing and a differential assembly.

Both the manual and automatic transaxles, combined with the four cylinder engine, make a very compact front wheel drive system.

Transaxle removal is described in a previous section. Repairs to the transaxle, other than routine maintenance, should be done by a qualified repair shop.

Differential

REMOVAL AND INSTALLATION

1. Drain the oil.
2. Remove the driveshaft.
3. Pull out both axle shafts to disengage the axle shafts from the differential gears. They need only be pulled out about 2 in.
4. Unbolt and remove the differential carrier.
5. Installation is the reverse of removal.

REAR SUSPENSION

NOTE: The Colt/Champ and Sapporo/Challenger series of Chrysler cars are built by Mitsubishi. As of 1983, Mitsubishi Motor Sales of America, Inc. will also be importing, distributing and servicing their own line of cars; the Starion, Cordia and Tredia. The turbocharged 2.6 litre engine used in the Starion is similar in design and service to its normally-aspirated cousin used in the Sapporo/Challenger. Brake systems, suspensions and most transmissions are also closely related. Where product similarities exist, procedures given for the Chrysler vehicles can be used as service guidelines.

Leaf Springs

REMOVAL AND INSTALLATION

1. Remove the hub cap or wheel cover. Loosen the lug nuts.
2. Raise the rear of the car. Install a stand at the exact point of the sill shown in

1. Wheel hub bolt
2. Rear axle shaft oil seal
3. Packing
4. Bearing retainer (inner)
5. Bearing
6. Bearing retainer (outer)
7. Bearing retainer bolt
8. Rear axle shaft

Exploded view of axle shaft

Sedan, hardtop and coupe

Station wagon

1. Carrier bumper	5. Pad bracket	9. Spring shackle assembly
2. Shock absorber	6. Pad	10. Spring pin assembly
3. Rubber cushion	7. U-bolt seat	11. Front eye bushing
4. Spring U-bolt	8. Shackle plate	12. Leaf spring assembly

Colt rear suspension (Arrow similar)

the drawing. Two dimples locate the support point on the sill flange.

> ### CAUTION
> *Damage to the unit body can result from installing a stand at any other location.*

3. Disconnect the lower mounting nut of the shock absorber.

4. Remove the four U-bolt fastening nuts from the spring seat.

NOTE: It's not necessary to remove the shock absorber, leave the top connected.

5. Place a floor jack under the rear axle and raise it just enough to remove the load from the springs. Remove the spring pad and seat.

6. Remove the two rear shackle attaching nuts and remove the rear shackle.

7. Remove the front pin retaining nut. Remove the two pin retaining bolts and take off the pin.

8. Remove the spring.

NOTE: It is a good safety practice to replace used suspension fasteners with new parts.

9. Install the front spring eye bushings from both sides of the eye with the bushing flanges facing out.

10. Insert the spring pin assembly from the body side and fasten it with the bolts. Temporarily tighten the spring pin nut.

11. Install the rear eye bushings in the same manner as the front, insert the shackle pins from the outside of the car, and tem-

porarily tighten the nut after installing the shackle plate.

12. Install the pads on both sides of the spring, aligning the pad center holes with the spring center bolt collar, and then install the spring seat with its center hole through the spring center collar.

13. Attach the assembled spring and spring seat to the axle housing with the axle housing spring center hole meeting with the

spring center bolt and install the U-bolt nuts. Tighten the nuts to 33–36 ft. lbs.

14. Tighten the lower shock absorber nut to 12–15 ft. lbs. on all models.

15. Lower the car to the floor, jounce it a few times, and then tighten the spring pin and shackle pin nuts to 36–43 ft. lbs.

Coil Springs

REMOVAL AND INSTALLATION

1. Raise and support the car safely allowing the rear axle to hang unsupported.

2. Place a jack under the rear axle, and remove the bottom bolts or nuts of the shock absorbers.

3. Lower the rear axle and remove the left and right coil springs.

4. Installation is the reverse of removal.

Shock Absorbers

REMOVAL AND INSTALLATION

1. Remove the hub cap or wheel cover. Loosen the lug nuts.

2. Raise the rear of the car. Support the car with jack stands.

NOTE: The body sill is marked with two dimples to locate the support position. Never place a stand anywhere but between these marks or you'll damage the body.

3. Remove the upper mounting bolt and nut.

Rear suspension—Mitsubishi Starion

Rear suspension—Mitsubishi Cordia and Tredia

4. While holding the bottom stud mount nut with one wrench, remove the locknut with another wrench.

5. Remove the shock absorber.

6. Check the shock for:

a. Excessive oil leakage, some minor weeping is permissable;

b. Bent center rod, damaged outer case, or other defects.

c. Pump the shock absorber several times, if it offers even resistance on full strokes it may be considered serviceable.

7. Install the upper shock mounting nut and bolt. Hand tighten the nut.

8. Install the bottom eye of the shock over the spring stud. Tighten the lower nut to 12–15 ft. lbs.

9. Finally, tighten the upper nut to 47–58 ft. lbs. on all models except station wagons, which are tightened to 12–15 ft. lbs.

Lower Control Arm— Rear Drive Vehicle

REMOVAL

1. Support the vehicle body on safety stands. Use a jack under the rear axle to raise the rear axle assembly slightly.

2. Remove the wheel and the upper control arm rod.

3. Detach the parking brake rear cable from the lower arm.

4. Remove the lower arm from the rear

Left side......L or white paint
Right side......R or no marking

Rear wheel drive lower control arm mark to identify left and right sides

Rear lower control arm removed from front wheel drive type vehicle

axle housing and from the bracket attached to the body.

INSTALLATION

1. Temporarily install the lower arm (check for marking on left side arm) and torque the bolts to 94.0–108.0 ft. lbs. (127.0–147.0 Nm). Torque the assist link bushing bolt to 47.0–58.0 ft. lbs. (64.0–78.0 Nm).

2. With the special nut assembly placed securely against the rear axle housing bracket, install the upper control arm rod to the bracket. Torque the bolt to 94.0 ft. lbs. (127.0–147.0 Nm).

———— CAUTION ————
Always use new bolts.

Lower Control Arm— Front Drive Vehicle

REMOVAL

1. Support the side frame on jack stands and remove the rear wheels. Remove the rear brake assembly.

2. Remove the muffler and jack the control arm just enough to raise it slightly.

3. Remove the shock absorber and lower the jack. Remove the coil spring and temporarily install the shock absorber to the control arm.

4. Disconnect the brake hoses at the rear suspension arms and remove the rear suspension from the body as an assembly.

INSTALLATION

1. Install the fixture to body bolts and torque to 36.0–51.0 ft. lbs. (49.0–69.0 Nm).

2. Install the coil springs and loosely install the shock absorbers. Tighten the shock absorber bolts to specification after the vehicle is lowered to the floor.

3. Install the rear brake assembly.

4. Lower the vehicle and tighten the suspension arm end nuts to 36.0–51.0 ft. lbs. (49.0–69.0 Nm). and the shock bolts to 47.0–58.0 ft. lbs. (64.0–78.0 Nm).

5. Install the brake drums and wheels.

6. Bleed the brake system and adjust the rear brake shoe clearance.

FRONT SUSPENSION

NOTE: The Colt/Champ and Sapporo/Challenger series of Chrysler cars are built by Mitsubishi. As of 1983, Mitsubishi Motor Sales of America, Inc. will also be importing, distributing and servicing their own line of cars; the Starion, Cordia and Tredia. The turbocharged 2.6 litre engine used in the Starion is similar in design and service to its normally-aspirated cousin used in the Sapporo/Challenger. Brake systems, suspensions and most transmissions are also closely related. Where product similarities exist, procedures given for the Chrysler vehicles can be used as service guidelines.

Strut

For all spring and shock absorber removal and installation procedures, and any other strut overhaul procedures, please refer to "Strut Overhaul" in the Unit Repair section.

REMOVAL AND INSTALLATION EXCEPT FRONT WHEEL DRIVE

1. Remove the front wheel and caliper. Remove the front hub with disc and dust cover.
2. Disconnect the stabilizer linkage and the lower arm. Remove the strut assembly, knuckle arm and strut insulator retaining bolts and remove the strut assembly from the wheelhouse.
3. Installation is the reverse of removal.

Front suspension—Mitsubishi Cordia and Tredia

FRONT WHEEL DRIVE MODELS

1. Jack up and support the front of the car.
2. Remove the front wheel. Remove the brake line from the strut.
3. Remove the four upper and two lower mounting nuts/bolts and remove the strut.

4. Installation is the reverse of removal. Be sure to bleed the brakes after installation.

Ball Joint
REMOVAL AND INSTALLATION

NOTE: The ball joint on front wheel drive models may be replaced by removing the mounting nut from the front hub, separating the stud from the hub and removing the two control arm mounting nuts and bolts. Installation is reverse of removal.

1. Remove the strut assembly and tie rod.
2. Remove the lower arm ball joint dust seal by prying up the dust seal ring evenly with a screwdriver.
3. Remove the snap-ring using snapring pliers.
4. Using a ball joint remover and installer tool, press off the ball joint.
5. To install the ball joint, press the ball joint properly into the burred hole, with the ball joint and lower arm mating marks aligned.

Lower Control Arm
REMOVAL AND INSTALLATION

Rear Wheel Drive

1. After disconnecting the stabilizer ring from the lower arm, remove the strut assembly.

Front suspension—Mitsubishi Starion

1. Strut insulator
2. Upper spring seat
3. Dust cover
4. Spacer
5. Bumper rubber
6. Front spring
7. Strut assembly
8. Knuckle arm
9. Lower arm bushing
10. Lower arm shaft
11. Lower arm
12. Lower ball joint
13. Strut bar bracket
14. Stabilizer
15. Stabilizer bar bushing
16. Strut bar
17. Crossmember

Arrow front suspension

2. Disconnect the steering knuckle arm and the tie rod ball joint.

3. Using the knuckle arm puller, disconnect the knuckle arm and the lower arm ball joint.

4. Remove the bolts holding the lower arm to the sub-frame, and remove the lower arm assembly.

5. Installation is the reverse of removal.

Alignment of the lower arm

NOTE: **It is not necessary to remove the ball joint from the front hub.**

2. Remove inner mounting nut and bolt and remove control arm. Installation is the reverse of removal.

Front End Alignment

CASTER AND CAMBER

Caster is preset at the factory. It requires adjustment only if the suspension and steering linkage components are damaged, in which case, repair is accomplished by replacing the damaged part. A slight caster adjustment can be made by moving the nuts on the front anchors of the strut bars.

TOE-IN

Toe-in is the difference in the distance between the front wheels, as measured at both the front and the rear of the front tires.

Toe-in is adjusted by turning the tie rod turnbuckles as necessary. The turnbuckles should always be tightened or loosened the

Front Wheel Drive Models

1. Remove lower ball joint (two bolts) and strut bar (two bolts) from the lower control arm.

1. Stabilizer
2. Lower arm shaft
3. Lower arm
4. Strut insulator
5. Spacer
6. Rubber bumper
7. Front spring
8. Strut assembly
9. Knuckle arm
10. Lower ball joint

Colt front suspension

1. Joint assembly
2. Lower arm
3. Joint cover
4. Washer
5. Bushing (front)
6. Stopper rubber
7. Stopper washer
8. Lower arm shaft
9. Spacer
10. Bushing (rear)
11. Stabilizer fixture
12. Stabilizer
13. Rubber bushing
14. Seat
15. Collar
16. Stabilizer bolt

Lower arm

same amount for both tie rods; the difference in length between the two tie rods should not exceed 0.2 in. On the Challenger and Sapporo, only the left tie rod is adjustable.

FRONT WHEEL BEARING ADJUSTMENT

1979 and Earlier

1. Remove the wheel and dust cover. Remove the cotter pin and lock cap from the nut.
2. Torque the wheel bearing nut to 14.5 ft. lbs. (19.6 Nm) and then loosen the nut. Retorque the nut to 3.6 ft. lbs. (4.9 Nm) and install the lock cap and cotter pin.
3. Install the dust cover and the wheel.

1980 and Later

1. Remove the wheel, the dust cover and the cotter pin.
2. Torque the axle shaft nut to 87.0–130.0 ft. lbs. (118.0–177.0 Nm).
3. Back off the nut to the nearest point where the slot in the nut will align with the hole in the shaft. Install the cotter pin and dust cover.
4. Install the wheel.

STEERING

NOTE: The Colt/Champ and Sapporo/Challenger series of Chrysler cars are built by Mitsubishi. As of 1983, Mitsubishi Motor Sales of America, Inc. will also be importing, distributing and serv-

icing their own line of cars; the Starion, Cordia and Tredia. The turbocharged 2.6 litre engine used in the Starion is similar in design and service to its normally-aspirated cousin used in the Sapporo/Challenger. Brake systems, suspensions and most transmissions are also closely related. Where product similarities exist, procedures given for the Chrysler vehicles can be used as service guidelines.

Steering Wheel

REMOVAL AND INSTALLATION

1. Pry off the steering wheel center foam pad.
2. Remove the steering wheel retaining nut.

Steering gear oil level check

3. Using a steering wheel puller, remove the wheel.
4. Be sure the front wheels are in a straight ahead position. Reverse the removal procedure.

Manual Steering Gear

REMOVAL AND INSTALLATION

1. Remove the clamp bolt connecting the steering shaft with the steering gear housing mainshaft. Check for or make mating marks for the assembly.
2. Using appropriate pullers, disconnect the pitman arm and the relay rod at the linkage connection.
3. Remove the gearbox from the frame by removal of the attaching bolts.
4. Remove the pitman arm from the cross shaft. Check for mating marks.
5. Installation is the reverse of removal.

ADJUSTMENT

1. Measure the mainshaft preload with an inch pound torque wrench. The allowable torque is 3–4.8 in. lbs.
2. The preload torque is corrected by reducing or increasing the number of shims under the end plate.
3. Seat the cross shaft and bearings by turning the steering mainshaft and the adjusting bolt two or three times.
4. Tighten the adjusting bolt to obtain zero free-play with the cross shaft in the center position. Tighten the locknut on the adjusting bolt.

Power Steering Gear

Beginning 1978, power steering became available with the 2600 cc engine.
The power steering consists of a belt driven pump, a separate fluid reservoir, pressure and return lines, and a steering gear assembly with an integral control valve.

REMOVAL

1. Matchmark and disconnect the steering shaft from the gearbox main shaft.
2. Disconnect the tie rod end and pitman arm from the relay rod.
3. Remove the air cleaner and disconnect the pressure and return lines from the steering gear assembly.
4. Remove any interfering splash pans from underneath the vehicle.
5. If necessary, remove the kickdown linkage splash pan shield and bolts. Move the fuel line aside to avoid damage during removal.
6. Remove the frame bolts from the gearbox and lower the unit from the vehicle.

1. Steering wheel
2. Tilt bracket
3. Steering shaft
4. Gear box
5. Tie rod assembly (right)
6. Relay rod
7. Tie rod assembly (left)
8. Idler arm

Steering system

Rack and Pinion Steering—Manual

REMOVAL

1. Jack up the car and support it on jack stands. Remove the front wheels.
2. Remove the bolt connecting the steering shaft universal joint with the steering gear. Before removing the bolt, mark its location and be sure the wheels are pointed straight.
3. Remove the tie rod ends from the hub knuckles. Disconnect mounting bolts (four) located near the inner tie rods on the crossmember.

INSTALLATION

1. Installation is the reverse of removal.
2. Fill the reservoir with Dexron® A fluid and air bleed the system. (Refer to the bleeding procedure).
3. Start the engine and inspect for leakage.

CAUTION

When installing the pressure and return hoses, be careful not to twist or strip the fittings and pipes. Route the lines so as not to interfere with adjacent parts.

ADJUSTMENT

NOTE: The steering gear must be disconnected from the steering shaft.

1. Measure the mainshaft preload with an inch pound torque wrench. The preload should be 3.5 to 6.9 in. lbs. with the cross shaft adjusting bolt backed off.

2. Adjust the valve housing top cover to obtain the proper preload. When correct, lock the top cover with the locking nut.
3. Tighten the cross shaft adjusting bolt until zero lash is present. Check the total starting torque to rotate the main shaft. The torque should be 5.2–8.7 in. lbs.
4. Adjust the cross shaft until the required starting torque is obtained and lock the adjusting bolt nut securely.

Power Steering Pump

REMOVAL

1. Remove the drive belt. If the pulley is to be removed, do so now.
2. Disconnect the pressure and return lines. Catch any leaking fluid.
3. Remove the pump attaching bolts and lift the pump from the brackets.

INSTALLATION

1. Make sure the bracket bolts are tight and install the pump to the brackets.
2. If pulley had been removed, install it and tighten the nut securely. Bend the lock tab over the nut.
3. Install the drive belt and adjust to a tension of 22 lbs. at a deflection of .28 to .39 inches at the top center of the belt. Tighten the pump bolts securely to hold the tension.
4. Connect the pressure and return lines and fill the reservoir with approved fluid. (Dexron® type A.)
5. Bleed the system. (refer to the ''Bleeding'' procedure.)

BLEEDING THE SYSTEM

1. The reservoir should be full of Dexron® A fluid.
2. Jack up the front wheels and support the vehicle safely.
3. Turn the steering wheel fully to the right and left until no air bubbles appear in the fluid. Maintain the reservoir level.
4. Lower the vehicle and with the engine idling, turn the wheels fully to the right and left. Stop the engine.
5. Install a tube from the bleeder screw on the steering gear box to the reservoir.
6. Start the engine, turn the steering wheel fully to the left and loosen the bleeder screw.
7. Repeat the procedure until no air bubbles pass through the tube.
8. Tighten the bleeder screw and remove the tube. Refill the reservoir as needed, and check that no further bubbles are present in the fluid.

CAUTION

An abrupt rise in the fluid level after stopping the engine is a sign of incomplete bleeding. This will cause noise from the pump or control valve.

Steering Linkage

The steering linkage except on cars equipped with rack and pinion steering is of the conventional type, using tie rods, tie rod ends, relay rod, and idler arm assembly. The tie rods and tie rod ends are adjustable for length, and are locked in position by locking nuts. Front wheel drive models have adjustable outer tie rod ends. On later models, heat shields are used over ball sockets located near the engine to avoid heat loss of lubricating grease.

Lubricating grease is used in the dust cover and the sealer is used to join the cover to the ball socket body.

Turn Signal Switch

REMOVAL AND INSTALLATION

1. Remove the steering wheel and have the tilt handle in the lowest position.
2. Remove the combination meter and column cover.
3. Remove the connectors from the column switch, and the column switch from the column tube.

NOTE: Early models may have the turn signal and hazard switches mounted on a base plate. Removal of the attaching screws will allow these switches to be removed without removal of the remaining switches.

4. Switch installation is the reverse of removal. Be sure that the switch is centered

in the column or self-cancelling will be affected.

Ignition Lock and Switch

REMOVAL AND INSTALLATION

1. Cut a notch in the lock bracket bolt head with a hacksaw.
2. Remove the bolt and lock.
3. Remove the column cover and unbolt and remove the ignition switch.
4. Install both lock and switch in reverse of removal.

NOTE: When installing lock, the bolt should be tightened until the head is crushed. When installing switch, install the switch bolt loosely and insert and work the key a few times to make sure everything checks out before tightening the bolt.

BRAKES

For all brake system repair and service procedures not detailed below, please refer to ''Brakes'' in the Unit Repair section.

NOTE: The Colt/Champ and Sapporo/Challenger series of Chrysler cars are built by Mitsubishi. As of 1983, Mitsubishi Motor Sales of America, Inc. will also be importing, distributing and servicing their own line of cars; the Starion, Cordia and Tredia. The turbocharged 2.6 litre engine used in the Starion is similar in design and service to its normally-aspirated cousin used in the Sapporo/Challenger. Brake systems, suspensions and most transmissions are also closely related. Where product similarities exist, procedures given for the Chrysler vehicles can be used as service guidelines.

Adjustment

The front disc brakes require no periodic adjustment. All models have self adjusting rear brakes.

Master Cylinder

REMOVAL AND INSTALLATION

1. Remove all lines connected to the master cylinder. Slowly depress the brake pedal to remove the fluid.
2. Remove the clevis pin from between the master cylinder pushrod and the pedal on non-power brakes.
3. Remove the master cylinder from the firewall and thoroughly clean it.
4. Installation is the reverse of removal. Bleed the brakes.

Combination Valve

The combination valve has three functions:
    a. rear brake pressure control
    b. warning light control
    c. differential failure control

REMOVAL AND INSTALLATION

NOTE: The valve should not be disassembled. If it is faulty, replace it.

1. Disconnect and plug brake lines at the valve.
2. Remove the valve.
3. Install the valve and tighten the attaching bolts to 6–9 ft. lbs. Tighten the brake tube nuts to 9–12 ft. lbs.

Rear Disc Brakes

The caliper support is mounted on the rear axle housing. The support consists of an antirattle spring used to keep the caliper ''floating'', and a stopper plate installed between the caliper body and the support on which the caliper body slides. The rear caliper has the parking brake mechanism, which contains an automatic adjuster to keep the parking brake stroke constant, built into the caliper.

Parking Brake

ADJUSTMENT
1976

1. Release the brake cable.

Parking brake adjustment

2. Loosen the adjusting nuts on either side of the cable.
3. Move the cable lever to each side and tighten the nuts to the tension.
4. Cable tightening should provide back plate and extension lever clearance of *less* than 0.04 in.
5. Be certain the drum does not contact the lining. Standard parking brake lever travel is 10 nothces.

1977–83 Coupe, Sedan, and Hatchback

1. Release the parking brake.
2. Adjust the extension lever to backing plate clearance to .008–.080 inch, by moving the adjustment nut on the cable.
3. Check the brake lever free stroke. Brake drag should occur at 6 to 8 notches.

1977–79 Station Wagon Challenger and Sapparo

1. Release the parking brake.
2. Adjust the extension lever to stopper clearance to 0.100 inch by loosening both cable lever attaching bolts and adjusting nut. Move the cable lever to the right. Set the left cable first and then the right.
3. Check the brake lever free stroke. Brake drag should occur at 5 to 7 notches.

1. Parking brake lever cover
2. Parking brake lever assembly
3. Parking brake cable
4. Clip
5. Bolt
6. Clip
7. Bushing
8. Clevis pin

Exploded view of parking brake linkage

CHASSIS ELECTRICAL

Heater Blower Motor

REMOVAL AND INSTALLATION

1976

The heater is located directly under the center of the dashboard.

1. Unplug the two electrical leads from the motor.

2. Remove the three retaining screws and remove the motor.

3. Install the motor in the reverse order of removal.

1977–83 Coupe, Sedan, and Hatchback

1. Remove the instrument cluster (coupe and sedan). Remove the instrument cluster and the glove box (hatchback).

2. Remove the heater control bracket assembly.

3. Remove the motor assembly and disconnect the wire connection.

4. (Coupe and sedan) Remove the motor in a horizontal position while holding the control bracket down.

1. Defroster nozzle
2. Ventilator duct assembly
3. Air duct
4. Water hose
5. Water valve assembly
6. Heater core
7. Turbo fan
8. Motor
9. DEF-VENT valve lever
10. Water valve cover
11. Air control lever
12. Heater control panel assembly
13. Duct assembly
14. Ventilator garnish

Coupe and Sedan

Hatchback

Exploded view of heater assembly—typical of coupe, sedan and hatchback vehicles

5. (Hatchback) Remove the motor through the glove box opening.

6. Installation is the reverse of removal.

1977–80 Challenger, Sapporo and Station Wagon

1. Remove the instrument cluster and the meter cluster.

2. Disconnect the wiring to the motor.

3. Remove the motor assembly.

4. Installation is reverse of removal.

1981 and Later Challenger/ Sapporo

1. Remove the lower instrument pad cover assembly from under the glove box.

2. Remove the passenger side console cover.

3. Remove the glove box to center support attaching screw.

4. Loosen the stops at either side of the glove box so that the glove box swings free.

5. Disconnect the glove box light.

6. Remove the glove compartment assembly from the instrument pad.

7. Remove the ducts, heater fan switch connector and control cables.

8. Remove three attaching bolts and lift out the blower assembly.

9. Remove the wiring bracket and the motor connector. Remove the vent tube and three motor attaching screws. Lift out the motor and remove the fan from the motor assembly.

10. Installation is the reverse of removal.

Heater Core

NOTE: The 1976 models use an air conditioner evaporator and blower unit that is not integral with the heating system. To remove the heater assembly, it may be necessary to first remove or loosen various parts of the air conditioner unit.

REMOVAL AND INSTALLATION

1976–83 Coupe, Sedan and Hatchback

1. Drain the cooling system.

2. Disconnect the battery ground cable.

3. Place the water valve in the OFF position.

4. Remove the under tray, defroster nozzle and console box.

5. Disconnect each heater control wire and connectors at the heater assembly.

6. Disconnect the water hoses, heater duct and wiring harness.

7. Remove the heater assembly.

8. Remove the heater core.

9. Installation is the reverse of removal.

1. Defroster nozzle
2. Ventilator duct assembly
3. Air duct
4. Water hose
5. Water valve assembly
6. Heater assembly
7. Turbo fan
8. Motor
9. Heater-defroster lever
10. Water valve lever
11. Air control lever
12. Valve (Hardtop)
13. Duct assembly (Hardtop)
14. Ventilator garnish (Hardtop)

Exploded view of heater assembly—typical of hardtop and station wagon vehicles

1976–80 Hardtop and Station Wagon

1. Drain the cooling system.
2. Remove the glove box, instrument cluster and console assembly.
3. Disconnect the heater control wires at the heater box.
4. Remove the heater control assembly.
5. Disconnect all heater hoses and air ducts.
6. Remove the heater assembly.
7. Remove the heater core.
8. Installation is the reverse of removal.

NOTE: Upon removal of the heater control box, the heater core is removable. Replace all gaskets and insulation in its proper place.

1981 and Later Challenger/Sapporo

1. Disconnect the negative battery terminal.
2. Remove the steering wheel horn pad attaching screws, from the back of the steering wheel. Remove the horn pad.
3. Remove the steering wheel lock nut and remove the steering wheel using a steering wheel puller tool.

— **CAUTION** —

Do not apply impact to the column or wheel with a hammer to loosen the wheel from the column. Use the steering wheel puller tool.

4. Loosen the tilt lock lever and lower the steering column fully.
5. Remove the meter (instrument cluster) hood. Remove the meter (instrument cluster) assembly and disconnect the electrical and cable connectors.
6. Remove the inner box from the console accessory box. Press on the spring catch, to remove the remote control mirror switch from the accessory box.
7. Remove the accessory box assembly and disconnect the electrical connector.
8. Pull off the heater control knob, pull out the control panel and take out the illumination harness.
9. Pull off the radio knobs and remove the radio to panel attaching nuts. Remove the radio panel.
10. Remove the cover assembly attaching screws from below the glove box and remove the cover assembly.
11. Remove the console side covers (both sides).
12. Remove the shift knob on manual transmission vehicles and remove the center console.
13. Remove the instrument pad bolt covers at both ends of the instrument pad and remove the attaching nuts.
14. Take off the hood lock release knob and remove the release cable attaching screws. Remove the hood lock release assembly from the instrument pad.
15. Remove the defroster garnish.
16. Remove the screws attaching the glove compartment to the center dash reinforcement.

17. Remove all remaining instrument pad attaching bolts.
18. Disconnect the clock, glove box, chime and dimmer control and remove the instrument pad.
19. Disconnect the defogger switch, radio, chime driver, defogger relay connectors and the antenna feeder end.
20. Remove the center reinforcement.
21. Set the heater temperature control to "WARM" position and drain the coolant from the radiator.
22. From the engine compartment, remove the heater hoses from the heater assembly.
22. From under the dash, remove the heater ducts from the heater assembly. To remove the rear seat heater duct, move the outlet control link to the "VENT" side, insert a finger into the outlet and remove the duct from inside heater.
23. Disconnect the power relay connector, remove three attaching bolts and remove the heater assembly. Remove the heater core.
24. The installation is the reverse of removal.
25. Connect the heater hoses in a fully seated position on the inlet and outlet fittings of the heater core assembly, so they will not leak.
26. Adjust the heater control cable by setting the control panel to "COOL" and heater unit lever on "COOL" and tighten the cable at that position.

NOTE: In order to fill the engine cooling and heating system completely it may be necessary to open the water valve fully, run the engine to circulate the coolant and then stop the engine and add more coolant.

Windshield Wiper Motor and Linkage

REMOVAL AND INSTALLATION

NOTE: The wiper motor may be located on either the right or left side of the front deck, depending upon the year and model. A wiper removing hole is provided to gain access to the linkage for removal purposes.

1. Remove the wiper arms. Remove the arm shaft locknuts and push in the shafts. Disconnect the electrical wiring.
2. Remove the bolts holding the motor bracket to the body and pull the wiper assembly outward and away from the body.
3. Hold the motor shaft and the linkage at right angles to each other and disconnect them. Remove the motor.
4. The linkages can be pulled from the opening in the front deck.
5. The installation is in the reverse of the removal, being sure to insert the linkage shaft bracket positioning boss positively in

Heater core

Partition

Air mix damper

By-pass damper

Center ventilator
changeover damper

Outside air

〰 - HEAT
changeover damper

Inside air

Inside/outside air
changeover damper

Blower motor assembly

Heater system on 1981 and later Challenger and Sapporo vehicles

the hole provided in the body before tightening the wiper shaft nut.

6. Locate the wiper blades in the stopped position approximately ½ to ¾ inch above the bottom moulding or sealer of the windshield.

Radio

REMOVAL AND INSTALLATION

Colt

1. Remove glove box then loosen the knobs and attaching nuts on the front of the radio.

2. Remove speaker, antenna, and power wires from the back of the radio. Remove the radio attaching bracket and take out the radio.

3. Installation is the reverse of removal.

Arrow

1. Remove the instrument cluster.

2. Remove the radio knobs from the radio panel.

3. Remove the nuts from behind the knobs, the screw from the bracket and remove the radio (AM radio). Remove the bolts from under the brackets and remove the radio (AM/FM radio).

NOTE: The AM radio circuit fuse block is located on the right rear side of the radio, the AM/FM circuit fuse block is installed in the line with the power cable.

Instrument Cluster

REMOVAL AND INSTALLATION

Colt

NOTE: Disconnect the battery ground cable before cluster removal.

1. Loosen screws at the upper and lower part of the instrument cluster. Loosen the screws holding the heater control knobs, ash tray, and cigarette lighter from their respective brackets. Remove blind cover on the right side of the glove box and remove the attaching screws on the right side of the cluster.

2. Remove the harness cover at the bottom of the instrument panel and disconnect lighting switch and the instrument panel harness.

3. Pull the instrument panel cluster a little toward you, disconnect multiple connector, antenna feeder, speaker connector, heater fan connector and meter cables and then remove instrument cluster assembly.

4. Installation is the reverse of removal.

After the instrument cluster has been installed, draw out the meter cables as long as the marking tape can be seen from the engine compartment.

Arrow

1. Remove the air intake control knob, the ash tray and heater control knobs and the radio knobs and retaining nuts.

2. Remove the three upper screws and a lower screw, a screw located behind the blind cover above the air intake control panel, and the three screws behind and in the upper inside part of the ash tray.

3. Pull the ash tray out a little and disconnect the heater, meter and speedometer connectors.

4. Remove the ground cable which is

attached to the body by a screw and remove the cluster.

5. To install reverse the removal procedure.

Challenger/Sapporo

1. Remove the battery ground cable.
2. Remove three screws from the top and three screws from the bottom of the cluster assembly.

NOTE: Two of the bottom screws are located behind the "brake warning" and "fasten seat belt" lens and the third bottom screw is located at the ash tray opening. A thin tipped screwdriver or a wire hook is required to remove the lenses to gain access to the screws.

3. Move the instrument cluster away from the dash and disconnect the meter connections, heater fan connections, speedometer cable and any other connector or ground cables.

4. Remove the cluster assembly from the dash.

5. Installation is the reverse of removal.

1978–81 Station Wagon

The instrument cluster hood is removed separately to expose the instrument cluster attaching screws. Remove the screws, attaching wires and cables, and remove the cluster from the dash. Install in the reverse of the removal procedure.

Fuse Block Location

1980–83 COLT/CHAMP

The fuse block is located up under the instrument panel on the driver's side of the steering column.

1976–83 ALL OTHER MODELS

The fuse block is located on the lower part of the driver's side front piller post.

1. Printed circuit board	5. Temperature gauge	9. Temperature gauge
2. Tachometer	6. Speedometer	10. Instrument cluster case
3. Fuel gauge	7. Chime	11. Instrument cluster panel
4. Select indicator	8. Fuel gauge	12. Instrument cluster glass

13. Instrument cluster hood
14. Speedometer cable
15. Printed circuit board (for indicator)

Instrument cluster arrangement

Datsun/ Nissan

SERIAL NUMBER IDENTIFICATION

Engine Number

The engine number is stamped on the right side top edge of the cylinder block. The engine serial number is preceded by the engine model code.

Engine serial and code number

ENGINE I.D. TABLE

Number of Cylinders	Displacement cu. in. (cc)	Type	Engine Model Code
4	119.1 (1952)	OHC	L20B
4	85.24 (1397)	OHV	A14
6	146 (2393)	OHC	L24,L24E
6	168 (2753)	OHC	L28,L28E,L28ET
6	170 (2793)	OHC	LD28
4	75.48 (1237)	OHV	A12A
4	90.80 (1488)	OHV	A15
4	90.8 (1488)	OHC	E15
4	119.1 (1952)	OHC	Z20S,Z20E
4	133.4 (2181)	OHC	Z22E
4	120.4 (1974)	OHC	CA20

Chassis Number

The chassis number is on the firewall under the hood. Late model vehicles also have the chassis number on a plate attached to the top of the instrument panel on the driver's side. The chassis serial number is preceded by the model designation.

VEHICLE IDENTIFICATION PLATE

The vehicle identification plate is attached to the hood ledge or the firewall. This plate is mounted on the left hood ledge panel at the back of the strut housing on the 280Z and on the right side of the firewall, behind the battery, on the 280ZX. The identification plate gives the vehicle model, engine displacement in cc., SAE horsepower rating, wheelbase, engine number and chassis number.

Chassis number location

Vehicle identification plate

VIN location

GENERAL ENGINE SPECIFICATIONS

Year	Model	Type (Model)	Engine Displacement cu. in. (cc)	Carburetor Type	Horsepower (SAE) @ rpm	Torque @ rpm (ft. lbs.)	Bore × Stroke (in.)	Compression Ratio	Normal Oil Pressure (psi)
'76–'78	B210	OHV 4 (A14)	85.2 (1397)	Dual throat downdraft	80 @ 6000	83 @ 3600	2.99 × 3.03	8.5:1	43–50
	F10	OHV 4 (A14)	85.2 (1397)	Dual throat downdraft	80 @ 6000	83 @ 3600	2.99 × 3.03	8.5:1	43–50
'76	610	OHC 4 (L20B)	119.1 (1952)	Dual throat downdraft	112 @ 5600	108 @ 3600	3.35 × 3.39	8.5:1	50–57
'76–'77	710	OHC 4 (L20B)	119.1 (1952)	Dual throat downdraft	110 @ 5600	112 @ 5600	3.35 × 3.39	8.5:1	50–57
'76–'78	280Z	OHC 6 (L28)	168 (2753)	EFI	170 @ 5600	177 @ 4400	3.39 × 3.11	8.3:1	50–57
'77–'78	200SX	OHC 4 (L20B)	119.1 (1952)	Dual throat downdraft	97 @ 5600	102 @ 3200	3.35 × 3.39	8.5:1	50–57
	810	OHC 6 (L24)	146 (2393)	Electronic fuel injection	154 @ 5600	155 @ 4400	3.27 × 2.90	8.6:1	50–57
'78	510	OHC 4 (L20B)	119.1 (1952)	Dual throat downdraft	97 @ 5600	102 @ 3200	3.35 × 3.39	8.5:1	50–57
'79	200SX, 510	OHC 4 (L20B)	119.1 (1952)	dual throat downdraft	92 @ 5600	107 @ 3200	3.35 × 3.39	8.5:1	50–57
	280ZX	OHC 6 (L28)	168 (2753)	EFI	135 @ 5200	144 @ 4400	3.39 × 3.11	8.3:1	50–57
'79–'80	810	OHC 6 (L24)	146 (2393)	Electronic fuel injection	120 @ 5200	125 @ 4400	3.27 × 2.90	8.9:1 ①	50–60
	310	OHV 4 (A14)	85.2 (1397)	Dual throat downdraft	65 @ 5600	75 @ 3600	2.99 × 3.03	8.9:1	43–50
'79–'82	210	OHV 4 (A12A)	75.5 (1237)	Dual throat downdraft	58 @ 5600	67 @ 3600	2.95 × 2.75	8.5:1	43–50
		OHV 4 (A14)	85.3 (1397)	Dual throat downdraft	65 @ 5600	75 @ 3600	2.99 × 3.03	8.5:1 ②	43–50
		OHV 4 (A15)	90.8 (1488)	Dual throat downdraft	67 @ 5200	80 @ 3200	2.99 × 3.23	8.9:1	43–50
'80	200SX	OHC 4 (Z20E)	119.1 (1952)	Electronic fuel injection	100 @ 5200	112 @ 3200	3.35 × 3.39	8.5:1	50–60
	510	OHC 4 (Z20S)	119.1 (1952)	Dual throat downdraft	92 @ 5200	112 @ 2800	3.35 × 3.39	8.5:1	50–60
	280ZX	OHC 6 (L28)	168 (2753)	EFI	132 @ 5200	144 @ 4000	3.39 × 3.11	8.3:1	50–57
'81	310	OHV 4 (A15)	90.8 (1488)	Dual throat downdraft	65 @ 5200	82 @ 2800	2.99 × 3.23	8.9:1	43–50
	510	OHC 4 (Z20)	119.1 (1952)	Dual throat downdraft	92 @ 5200	112 @ 2800	3.35 × 3.39	8.5:1	50–60
	200SX	OHC 6 (Z20)	119.1 (1952)	EFI	100 @ 5200	112 @ 3200	3.35 × 3.39	8.5:1	50–60

GENERAL ENGINE SPECIFICATIONS

Year	Model	Type (Model)	Engine Displacement cu. in. (cc)	Carburetor Type	Horsepower (SAE) @ rpm	Torque @ rpm (ft. lbs.)	Bore × Stroke (in.)	Compression Ratio	Normal Oil Pressure (psi)
'81–'83	810	OHC 6 (L24)	146 (2393)	EFI	120 @ 5200	134 @ 2800	3.27 × 2.90	8.9:1	50–60
	810 (Diesel)	OHC 6 (LD28)	170 (2793)	DFI	80 @ 4600	120 @ 2400	3.33 × 3.27	22.7:1	NA
	280ZX	OHC 6 (L28E)	168 (2753)	EFI	145 @ 5200	156 @ 4000	3.39 × 3.11	8.8:1	50–57
	280ZX (Turbo)	OHC 6 (L28ET)	168 (2753)	EFI	180 @ 5600	202 @ 2800	3.39 × 3.11	7.4:1	NA
'82–'83	310, Sentra	OHC 4 (E15)	90.8 (1488)	Dual throat downdraft	67 @ 5200	85 @ 3200	2.92 × 3.23	9.0:1	50–57
	200SX	OHC 4 (Z22)	133.4 (2181)	EFI	102 @ 5200	129 @ 2800	3.43 × 3.62	8.5:1	50–60
	Stanza	OHC 4 (CA20)	120.4 (1974)	Dual throat downdraft	88 @ 5200	112 @ 2800	NA	8.5:1	50–60

NA: Not available at time of publication
EFI: Electronic Fuel Injection
DFI: Diesel Fuel Injection
① 1980 Calif.: 8.6:1
② 1981–82: 8.9:1

GASOLINE ENGINE TUNE-UP SPECIFICATIONS

(When analyzing compression test results, look for uniformity among cylinders, rather than specific pressures)

		Spark Plugs		Distributor		Ignition Timing (deg)		Fuel Pump Pressure (psi)	Idle Speed (rpm)		Valve Clearance (in.)	
Year	Model	Type	Gap (in.)	Point Dwell (deg)	Point Gap (in.)	MT	AT		MT	AT	In	Ex
'76	F10	BP5ES	.031–.035	49–50①	.018–.022②	10B	—	3.8	700	—	.014	.014
'77–'78	F10	BP5ES	.039–.043	Electronic	②	10B	—	3.8	700	—	.014	.014
'76–'77	B210	BP5ES	.031–.035	49–55①	.018–.022②	10B	10B	3.8	700	650	.014	.014
'78	B210 Exc. FU	BP5ES	.039–.043	Electronic	②	10B	8B③	3.9	700	650	.014	.014
'78–'79	B210, 210 FU	BP5EQ	.043–.051	Electronic	②	5B		3.9	700	—	.014	.014
'79–'80	210 Exc. FU	BP5ES	.039–.043	Electronic	②	10B④⑤	8B④	3.9	700	650	.014	.014
'81–'82	210	BP5ES-11 BPR5ES-11	.039 .043	Electronic	②	5B⑥	5B	3.8	700	650	.014	.014
'79	310	BP5ES⑦	.039–.043	Electronic	②	10B④	—	3.8	700	—	.014	.014
'80	310	BP5ES⑦	.039–.043	Electronic	②	8B	—	3.8	750	—	.014	.014

C 205

GASOLINE ENGINE TUNE-UP SPECIFICATIONS

(When analyzing compression test results, look for uniformity among cylinders, rather than specific pressures)

Year	Model	Spark Plugs Type	Gap (in.)	Point Dwell (deg)	Point Gap (in.)	Ignition Timing (deg) MT	AT	Fuel Pump Pressure (psi)	Idle Speed (rpm) MT	AT	Valve Clearance (in.) In	Ex
'81	310	BP5ES-11⑦	.039–.043	Electronic	②	5B	—	3.8	750	—	.014	.014
'82–'83	310	BP5ES-11⑦	.039–.043	Electronic	②	2A⑨	2A⑨	3.8	750	750⑩	.011	.011
'78–'79	510	BP6ES	.039–.043 ⑪	Electronic	②	12B⑫	12B	3.8	600	600	.010	.012
'80	510	BPR6ES⑬	.031–.035	Electronic	②	12B⑭	12B⑭	3.8	600	600	.010⑮	.012
'81	510	BP6ES⑯	.031–.035	Electronic	②	6B	6B	3.8	600	600	.012	.012
'76	610, 710	BP6ES	.031–.035 ⑰	49–55①	.018–.022②	12B	12B	3.8	750	650	.010	.012
'77	710	BP6ES	.039–.043	49–55①	.018–.022②	12B	12B	3.8	750⑱	650⑲	.010	.012
'77	200SX	BP6ES	.039–.043⑳	49–55①	.018–.022②	9B㉑	12B	3.8	600⑱	600⑲	.010	.012
'78–'79	200SX	BP6ES	.039–.043⑳	Electronic	②	9B㉑	12B	3.8	600	600	.010	.012
'80	200SX	BP6ES	.031–.035	Electronic	②	8B㉒	8B㉒	37	700	700	.012	.012
'81	200SX	BP6ES⑯	.031–.035	Electronic	②	6B㉓	6B㉓	37	750	700	.012	.012
'82–'83	200SX	BPR6ES㉔	.031–.035	Electronic	②	8B	8B	37	750	700	.012	.012
'77–'83	810	BP6ES㉖	.039–.043	Electronic	②	10B㉕	10B㉕	36	700	650	.010	.012
'76	280Z	BP6ES	.028–.031	Electronic	②	㉗ 7B③	③ 7B㉗	36	800	700	.010	.012
'77–'78	280Z	BP6ES-11㉘	.039–.043㉙	Electronic	②	10B	10B	36	800	700	.010	.012
'79	280ZX	B6ES-11㉘	.039–.043	Electronic	②	10B	10B	36	800㉚	700	.010	.012
'80–'83	280ZX	BP6ES-11⑯	.039–.043	Electronic	②	10B㉛	10B㉛	36	700	700㉜	.010	.012
'81–'83	280ZX Turbo	BPR6ES-11	.039–.043	Electronic	②	20B	20B	36	650	650	.010	.012
'82–'83	Sentra	BPR5ES-11	.039–.043	Electronic	②	4A	6A	3.8	750	650	.011	.011

GASOLINE ENGINE TUNE-UP SPECIFICATIONS

(When analyzing compression test results, look for uniformity among cylinders, rather than specific pressures)

Year	Model	Spark Plugs Type	Spark Plugs Gap (in.)	Distributor Point Dwell (deg)	Distributor Point Gap (in.)	Ignition Timing (deg) MT	Ignition Timing (deg) AT	Fuel Pump Pressure (psi)	Idle Speed (rpm) MT	Idle Speed (rpm) AT	Valve Clearance (in.) In	Valve Clearance (in.) Ex
'82–'83	Stanza	㉝	.039–.043	Electronic	②	0	0	3.8	650	—	.012	.012

NOTE: Emission control requires a very precise approach to tune-up. Timing and idle speed are peculiar to the engine and its application, rather than to the engine alone. Data for the particular application is on a sticker in the engine compartment on all late models. If the sticker disagrees with this chart, use the sticker figure. The results of any adjustments or modifications should be checked with a CO meter.

● Set hot
▲ In Drive
FU: Hatchback with 5 spd. sold in US but not in Calif.
A: After Top Dead Center
B: Before Top Dead Center
① Calif. cars are equipped with electronic ignition—dwell is pre–set and non–adjustable
② Electronic ignition: Air gap .008–.016 (1976–78)
.012–.020 (1979–83)
③ Calif.: 10B
④ Calif.: 5B
⑤ 1980 A14 engine: 8B
⑥ A12A with M/T and Canada: 10B

⑦ Canada: BPR5ES-11; gap .031–.035
⑧ 1980
⑨ Canada: 4A
⑩ Canada: 650
⑪ Canada: .031–.035
⑫ 1979 Fed. cars: 11B
⑬ Z20S engine: BP6ES
⑭ Z20S engine: Fed.-8B; Calif.-6B
⑮ Z20S engine: .012
⑯ Canada and 1981 280ZX: BPR6ES-11
⑰ Calif.: .039–.043
⑱ Calif.: 600; Canada: 750
⑲ Calif.: 600; Canada: 650
⑳ Canada: .031–.035
㉑ Calif. and Canada: 12B

㉒ Calif.: 6B
㉓ Canada: 8B
㉔ Fig. for intake side; exhaust side—BPR5ES
㉕ 1978 Calif. and 1982–83 (all): 8B
㉖ 1978–79: B6ES
1980–81: BP6ES-11
1982–83: BPR6ES-11
㉗ 13B with engine cold on dual reluctor models
㉘ Canada: BR6ES
㉙ Canada: .028–.031
㉚ 700—Non–Calif. with catalytic converter
㉛ 1981–83 US: 8B
㉜ 1982–83: 650
㉝ Intake: BPR6ES-11
Exhaust: BPR5ES-11

DIESEL ENGINE TUNE-UP SPECIFICATIONS

Year Model	Engine Displacement cu. in. (cc)	Warm Valve Clearance (in.) In	Warm Valve Clearance (in.) Ex	Intake Valve Opens (deg)	Injection Pump Setting (deg)	Injection Nozzle Pressure (psi) New	Injection Nozzle Pressure (psi) Used	Idle Speed (rpm)	Compression Pressure (psi)
'81–'83 Diesel	170 (2,793)	0.010	0.012	NA	align marks	1,920–2,033	1,778–1,920	650	455

NA Not available at time of publication

FIRING ORDERS

L20B engine

L24, L28 engines

A-series engines

FIRING ORDERS

FIRING ORDER: 1–3–4–2
DISTRIBUTOR ROTATION: COUNTERCLOCKWISE
Z20 engine—1980 (49 states)

FRONT

FIRING ORDER: 1–3–4–2
DISTRIBUTOR ROTATION: COUNTERCLOCKWISE
Z20, Z22 engine—1980 (Calif.), 1981–83 (all)

CA20 engine

Firing order—1,3,4,2

E15 engine

CAPACITIES

| Year | Model | Engine Crankcase | | Transmission (pts) | | Automatic (Total Capacity) | Drive Axle (pts) | Gas Tank (gals) | Cooling System (qts) |
		With Filter	Without Filter	4-Spd	5-Spd				
'76	280Z	5.0	4.25	3.13	—	11.8	2.75	17.25	11.00
'76	610	4.5	4.0	4.25	—	11.8	1.75/2.2 (wagon)	14.5/13.75 (wagon)	7.25
'76–'77	710	4.5	4.0	4.25 ①	—	11.8	2.75	13.25/11.8 (wagon)	7.25
'76–'78	B210	3.8	3.4	2.75	3.6	11.8	1.8	11.5	6.25④
	F10	3.6	3.2	4.90	4.9	—	—	10.6/9.1 (wagon)	7.00
'77–'78	810	6.0	5.5	3.60	—	11.8	2.75/2.2 (wagon)	15.9/14.5 (wagon)	11.0

CAPACITIES

Year	Model	Engine Crankcase		Transmission (pts)		Automatic (Total Capacity)	Drive Axle (pts)	Gas Tank (gals)	Cooling System (qts)
		With Filter	Without Filter	4-Spd	5-Spd				
'77–'78	280Z	5.0	4.25	3.63	4.25	11.8	2.75	17.25	11.0
'77–'79	200SX	4.5	4.0	—	3.6	11.8	2.75	15.9	7.90
'78–'79	510	4.5	4.0	3.6	3.6	11.8	2.4	13.2	9.40
'79–'82	210	②	—	③	2.5	11.8	1.8	13.25	6.25④
'79–'81	310	3.4	2.8	4.9	4.9	—	—	13.25	6.25
'79–'80	810	5.9	5.25	3.7	4.25	11.8	2.0	15.9/14.5 (wagon)	11.00
'79–'83	280ZX	4.75⑥	4.25⑥	3.63	4.25	11.8	2.75	21.12	11.12
'80–'81	510	⑤	—	3.15	3.6	11.8	2.4	13.25	9.25
'80–'83	200SX	4.4	4.1	—	4.25	11.8	2.4	14/15.9 (hatchback)	10
'82–'83	310	4.12	3.6	4.9	5.74	12.75	—	13.25	6.50
'81	810	5.25	4.75	—	4.25	11.8	2.1	16.4/15.9 (wagon)	11.6
'82–'83	810	5.0⑦	4.5⑦	—	4.25	11.8	2.1	16.4/15.9 (wagon)	11.6⑧
'82–'83	Sentra	4.1	3.6	4.8	5.75	13.1	—	13.25	5.0
'82–'83	Stanza	4.1	3.6	—	5.75	12.75	—	14.3	7.8

① 3.6 pts., 1977
② A12A, A14 engines: 3.46 qts.
   A15 engine: 3.25 qts.
③ A12A engine: 2.5 pts.
   A14 engine: 2.75 pts.

④ Automatic transmission: 6 qts.
⑤ L20B engine: 4.5 qts.
   Z20S engine: 4.65 qts.
⑥ Turbo: 5.5 with, 5.0 without

⑦ Figures are for gasoline engine. For diesel engine: w/filter—6.5 qts., w/o filter—6.0 qts.
⑧ Figure is for gasoline engine. For diesel engine: 11.0 qts.

CRANKSHAFT AND CONNECTING ROD SPECIFICATIONS

Engine Model	Crankshaft				Connecting Rod Bearings		
	Main Brg. Journal Dia.	Main Brg. Oil Clearance	Shaft End-Play	Thrust on No.	Journal Diameter	Oil Clearance	Side Clearance
L20B	2.3599–2.360	0.0008–0.0024	0.002–0.007	3	1.9660–1.9670	0.001–0.002	0.008–0.012
L24, L24E	2.1631–2.1636	0.001–0.003	0.002–0.007	center	1.9670–1.9675 ①	0.001–0.003	0.008–0.012
L28 (1976–78)	2.1631–2.1636	0.0008–0.0028	0.002–0.007	center	1.9670–1.9675	0.0010–0.0022	0.0079–0.0118
L28 (1979–83)	2.1631–2.1636	0.0008–0.0026	0.002–0.007	center	1.9670–1.9675	0.0009–0.0026	0.0079–0.0118
A14 (1976–78)	1.966–1.967	0.0008–0.002	0.002–0.006	3	1.7701–1.7706	0.0008–0.002	0.008–0.012
A12A, A14, A15 (1979–82)	1.9666–1.9671	0.001–0.0035	0.002–0.0059	3	1.7701–1.7706	0.0012–0.0031	0.008–0.012
Z20S, Z20E, Z22E	2.1631–2.1636	0.0008–0.0024	0.002–0.0071	3	1.967–1.9675	0.001–0.0022	0.008–0.012

CRANKSHAFT AND CONNECTING ROD SPECIFICATIONS

Engine Model	Crankshaft				Connecting Rod Bearings		
	Main Brg. Journal Dia.	Main Brg. Oil Clearance	Shaft End-Play	Thrust on No.	Journal Diameter	Oil Clearance	Side Clearance
LD28	2.1631–2.1636	0.0008–0.0024	0.0020–0.0071	center	1.9670–1.9675	0.0008–0.0024	0.008–0.012
E15	1.9663–1.9671	②	0.002–0.007	3	1.5730–1.5738	0.0012–0.0024	0.004–0.0146
CA20	2.0847–2.0852	0.0016–0.0024	0.002–0.007	3	1.770l–1.7706	0.0008–0.0024	0.008–0.012

①L24E: 1.7701–1.7706
②#1 & 5: 0.0012–0.0030
　#2, 3, 4: 0.0012–0.0036

VALVE SPECIFICATIONS

Model	Seat Angle (deg)	Spring Test Pressure lbs @ in.		Spring Installed Height (in.)		Stem to Guide Clearance(in.)		Stem Diameter (in.)	
		Outer	Inner	Outer	Inner	Intake	Exhaust	Intake	Exhaust
L20B	45°	108 @ 1.16	56.2 @ 0.965	1.575	1.378	0.0008–0.0021	0.0016–0.0029	0.3136–0.3142	0.3128–0.3134
A14 (1975–78)	45°	52.9 @ 1.52	—	1.83	—	0.0006–0.0018	0.0016–0.0028	0.3138–0.3144	0.3128–0.3134
A12A, A14, A15 (1979–82)	45°30′	52.7 @ 1.19	—	1.83	—	0.0006–0.0018	0.0016–0.0028	0.3138–0.3144	0.3128–0.3134
E15	45°30′	128 @ 1.19	—	1.543	—	0.0008–0.0020	0.0018–0.0030	0.2744–0.2750	0.2734–0.2740
CA20	45°30′	NA	NA	1.575	1.378	0.0008–0.0021	0.0016–0.0029	0.2742–0.2748	0.2734–0.2740
L24	45°	108 @ 1.16②	56.2 @ 0.965⑥	1.575	1.378	0.001–0.002	0.002–0.003	0.3136–0.3142	0.3128–0.3134
L28, L28E, L28ET	45°①	108 @ 1.16	56 @ 0.965	1.575	1.378	0.0008–0.0021	0.0016–0.0029	0.3136–0.3142	0.3128–0.3134
LD28	45°	115.3 @ 1.18	—	1.575	—	0.0008–0.0021	0.0016–0.0029	0.3136–0.3142	0.3128–0.3134
Z20E, Z20S, Z22E	45°	115.3 @ 1.16	57 @ 0.98	1.575	1.378	0.0008–0.0021	0.0016–0.0029	0.3136–0.3142	0.3128–0.3134

NA Not available at time of publication
①45°30′, 1979 and later
②Figure is for Exhaust; for Intake:
　Outer 105.2 @ 1.181
　Inner 54.9 @ 0.984

PISTON AND RING SPECIFICATIONS
(All measurements in inches)

Engine Model	Piston Clearance	Ring Gap			Ring Side Clearance		
		Top Compression	Bottom Compression	Oil Control	Top Compression	Bottom Compression	Oil Control
L20B	0.001–0.002	0.010–0.016	0.012–0.020	0.012–0.035	0.002–0.003	0.001–0.003	—

PISTON AND RING SPECIFICATIONS
(All measurements in inches)

Engine Model	Piston Clearance	Ring Gap			Ring Side Clearance		
		Top Compression	Bottom Compression	Oil Control	Top Compression	Bottom Compression	Oil Control
L24, L24E	0.001–0.002	0.009–0.015	0.006–0.012	0.012–0.035	0.002–0.003	0.001–0.003	0.001–0.003
L28 (1976)	0.001–0.0018	0.0091–0.0150	0.0059–0.0118	0.0059–0.0118	0.0018–0.0031	0.0012–0.0018	0
L28 (1977–78)	0.001–0.0018	0.0098–0.0157	0.0118–0.0197	0.0118–0.0354	0.0016–0.0019	0.0012–0.0028	0
L28 (1979–80)	0.001–0.0018	0.0098–0.0157	0.0118–0.0197	0.0118–0.0354	0.0016–0.0029	0.0012–0.0025	0
L28E (1981–83)	0.001–0.0018	0.0098–0.0157	0.0059–0.0118	0.012–0.035	0.0016–0.0029	0.0012–0.0025	—
L28ET (1981–83)	0.0010–0.0018	0.0075–0.0130	0.0059–0.0118	0.012–0.035	0.0016–0.0029	0.0012–0.0025	0.0009–0.0028
LD28 (1981–83)	0.0020–0.0028	①	0.0079–0.0138	0.0118–0.0177	0.0024–0.0039	0.0016–0.0031	0.0012–0.0028
Z20E, Z20S, Z22E	0.001–0.002	0.0098–0.016	0.006–0.012	0.012–0.035	0.002–0.003	0.001–0.0025	0
A14 (1976–78)	0.0009–0.002	0.008–0.014	0.006–0.012	0.012–0.035	0.002–0.003	0.001–0.002	Combined ring
A12A, A14, A15 (1979–82)	0.001–0.002	0.008–0.014	0.006–0.012	0.012–0.035	0.002–0.003	0.001–0.002	Combined ring
E15 (1982–83)	0.001–0.002	0.0098–0.0157	0.0059–0.0018	0.0118–0.0354	0.0016–0.0029	0.0012–0.0025	Snug
CA20 (1982–83)	0.0009–0.0017	0.0079–0.0138	0.0059–0.0118	0.0118–0.0354	0.0016–0.0029	0.0012–0.0025	0.002–0.0057

①Without mark—0.0079–0.0014
With mark—0.0055–0.0087

TORQUE SPECIFICATIONS
(All readings in ft. lbs.)

Engine Model	Cylinder Head Bolts	Main Bearing Bolts	Rod Bearing Bolts	Crankshaft Pulley Bolt	Flywheel to Crankshaft Bolts	Manifolds	
						Intake	Exhaust
L20B	51–61	33–40	33–40	87–116	101–116	9–12	9–12
L24	51–61	33–40	33–40	101–116	94–108	④	④
L28, L28E, L28ET	54–61⑤	33–40	33–40	94–108②	94–108	③	③
LD28	87–94	51–61	33–40	101–116	101–116	⑥	⑥
Z20E, Z20S, Z22E	51–58	33–40	33–40	87–116	101–116	12–15	12–15
A12A, A14, A15, E15	51–54	36–43	23–27	108–145⑦	58–65①	11–14	11–14
CA20	51–58	33–40	22–27	90–98	72–80	13–16	13–17

①1976–78 A14: 54–61 ft. lbs.
②1977–78: 87–116; 1979–83: 101–116
③8 mm bolts: 10–13; 10 mm bolts: 25–36
④8 mm bolts: 11–18; 10mm bolts: 25–33;
   8 mm nut: 9–12

⑤Tighten in three steps: 1st, 30; 2nd, 44;
   3rd, 54–61
⑥Upper bolt (M10): 24–27 ft. lbs.
   Lower nut and bolt (M8): 12–18 ft. lbs.
⑦E15: 83–108

CYLINDER HEAD TORQUE SEQUENCES

L20B engine

L24 and L28 engines

A-series engines

LD28 engine

Z20, Z22 engine

E15 engine

CA20 engine

ALTERNATOR AND REGULATOR SPECIFICATIONS

Model	Year	Alternator Identification Number	Rated Output @ 5000 rpm (amps)	Output @ 2500 rpm (not less than) (volts)	Brush Length (in.)	Brush Spring Tension (oz.)	Regulated Voltage (volts)
F-10	1976–77	Lt150–26	50	37.5	0.295	9.0–12.2	14.3–15.3
	1978	LR150–36①	50	40	0.295	8.99–12.7	14.3–15.3
		LR160–46①②	60	45	0.295	8.99–12.17	14.4–15.0
B210	1976	LT150–19	50	37.5	0.295	9.0–12.2	14.3–15.3
	1977	LT150–26	50	37.5	0.295	9.0–12.2	14.3–15.3
	1978	LR150–36①	50	40	0.295	9.0–12.2	14.3–15.3
210	1979–80	LR150–36①	50	40	0.295	8.99–12.17	14.4–15.0
210	1980–82	LR150–99①④	50	40	0.28	8.99–12.17	14.4–15.0
310	1979–80	LR160–46①	60	40	0.295	8.99–12.17	14.4–15.0
310 USA	1980–83	LR160–125①	50	35	0.295	8.99–12.17	14.4–15.0
310 Canada	1980–83	LR150–99①	50	35	0.295	8.99–12.17	14.4–15.0
Sentra	1980–83	LR150–125B①	50	42	0.28	8.99–12.17	14.4–15.0
510	1978–79	LR150–35①	50	40	0.295	8.99–12.17	14.4–15.0
		LR160–47①③	60	41	0.295	8.99–12.17	14.4–15.0
	1980–81	LR150–52①⑤	50	40	0.295	8.99–12.17	14.4–15.0
Stanza	1982–83	LR160–104①	60	40	0.295	8.99–12.17	14.4–15.0
610	1976	LT150–13	50	37.5	0.310	9.0–12.2	14.3–15.3
710	1976	LT150–13	50	37.5	0.295	9.0–12.2	14.3–15.3
	1977	LT150–25	50	37.5	0.295	9.0–12.2	14.3–15.3

ALTERNATOR AND REGULATOR SPECIFICATIONS

Model	Year	Alternator Identification Number	Rated Output @ 5000 rpm (amps)	Output @ 2500 rpm (not less than) (volts)	Brush Length (in.)	Brush Spring Tension (oz.)	Regulated Voltage (volts)
810	1977	LT160–39	60	40	0.310	9.0–12.2	14.3–15.3
	1978–79	LT160–42①	60	40	0.280	8.99–12.17	14.4–15.0
	1980	LR160–42B①	60	50	0.295	8.99–12.17	14.4–15.0
	1981–83⑥	LR160–82①⑧	60	50	0.280	8.99–12.17	14.4–15.0
	1981–83⑦	LR160–97①⑨	60	52	0.240	10.79–14.60	14.4–15.0
200SX	1977–79	LR150–35①	50	40	0.295	8.99–12.17	14.4–15.0
	1980	LR160–47①	60	45	0.295	8.99–12.17	14.4–15.0
	1981	LR260–78①	60	50	0.280	8.99–12.17	14.4–15.0
	1982–83	LR160–78B①	60	50	0.280	8.99–12.17	14.4–15.0
280Z	1976–77	LT160–23	60	45	0.310	9.0–12.2	14.3–15.3
280ZX	1978	LT160–42①	60	45	0.280	8.99–12.17	14.4–15.0
	1979–80	LR160–42B①	60	50	0.276	8.99–12.17	14.4–15.0
	1981–83	LR160–82①	60	50	0.276	8.99–12.17	14.4–15.0

① Uses integral voltage regulator
② With air conditioning
③ Optional in USA; standard in Canada
④ 1982: LR150–99B
⑤ 1981: LR150–98
⑥ Gasoline
⑦ Diesel
⑧ 1982–83: LR160–82B
⑨ 1982–83: LR160–97B

BATTERY AND STARTER SPECIFICATIONS
(All cars use 12 volt, negative ground electrical systems)

Year	Model	Battery Amp Hour Capacity	Lock Test Amps	Lock Test Volts	Torque (ft. lbs.)	No Load Test Amps	No Load Test Volts	rpm	Brush Spring Tension (oz.)	Min. Brush Length (in.)
All	610, 710	50, 60	430 MT	6.0	6.3	60	12	7000	49–64	0.47
			540 AT	5.0	6.0	60	12	6000	49–64	0.47
All	F10	60	Not Recommended			60	12	7000	49–64	0.47
All	B210	60	420	6.3	6.5	60	12	7000	49–64	0.47
			Not Recommended			60	12	6000	29	0.37
			Not Recommended			100	12	4300 RG	56–70	0.43
'76–'77	280Z	65	Not Recommended			60	12	5000	56.4	0.43
'78	280Z	65	Not Recommended			100	12	4300	63.4	0.43
'77–'78	200SX	60	Not Recommended			60 MT	12	7000	49–64	0.47
			Not Recommended			60 AT	12	6000	49–64	0.47
			Not Recommended			100 RG	12	4300	56–70	0.43
'79	280ZX	60①	Not Recommended			100	12	4300	63.4	0.43
'83	280ZX	60①	Not Recommended			100	11	3900	63.4	0.43
'79–'83	510, 200SX, Stanza	60	Not Recommended			60 MT	11.5	7000	50–64	0.47
			Not Recommended			60 AT	11.5	6000	50–64	0.47
			Not Recommended			100 RG	11	3900	56–70	0.43

BATTERY AND STARTER SPECIFICATIONS

(All cars use 12 volt, negative ground electrical systems)

Year	Model	Battery Amp Hour Capacity	Starter						Brush Spring Tension (oz.)	Min. Brush Length (in.)
			Lock Test			No Load Test				
			Amps	Volts	Torque (ft. lbs.)	Amps	Volts	rpm		
All	210, 310, Sentra	60	Not Recommended			60	11.5	7000	50–64	0.47
			Not Recommended			100 RG	11	3900	56–70	0.43
'77–'79	810	60①	Not Recommended			100 RG	12	4300	56–70	0.43
'80–'83	810	60① ②	Not Recommended			100 RG	11	3900	56–70③	0.43④

① Canada and optional in USA: 70 amps
② Diesel: 80
③ Diesel: 96–117
④ Diesel: 0.35

MT: Manual Transmission
AT: Automatic Transmission
RG: Reduction Gear type starter

BRAKE SPECIFICATIONS

(All measurements given are in inches unless noted)

Model	Year	Lug Nut Torque (ft. lbs.)	Brake Disc			Drum		Minimum Lining Thickness	
			Master Cylinder Bore	Minimum Thickness	Maximum Run-Out	Diameter	Max. Wear Limit	Front	Rear
510	1978–81	58–72	0.8125	0.331	0.0047	9.000	9.060	0.080	0.059
810	1977–80	58–72	0.8125	0.413	0.0059	9.000	9.060	0.080	0.059
	1981–83	58–72	0.8125	0.630①	0.0059②	9.000	9.060	0.079	0.059
B210	1976–78	58–65	0.750	0.331	0.0047	8.000	8.051	0.063	0.059
610	1976–77	58–65	0.750	0.331	0.0048	9.000	9.055	0.079	0.059
710	1976–77	58–65	0.750	0.331	0.0047	9.000	9.055	0.079	0.059
200SX	1977–79	58–65	0.750	0.331	0.0047	9.000	9.060	0.059	0.059
	1980–83	58–72	0.8750	③	④	—	—	0.079	0.079
F-10	1977–78	58–65	0.750	0.339	0.0059	8.000	8.050	0.063	0.039
210	1979–82	58–65	0.8125	0.331	0.0047	8.000	8.050	0.063	0.059
280Z	1976	58–65	0.8748	0.413	0.0039	9.000	9.055	0.079	0.059
	1977–78	58–65	0.8750	0.413	0.0039	9.000	9.060	0.079	0.059
280ZX	1979–83	58–72	0.9375	0.709①	0.0039②	—	—	0.080	0.080
310	1979–83	58–72	0.8125	0.339	0.0047	8.000	8.050	0.079	0.059
Sentra	1982–83	58–72	0.750	0.433	0.0047	7.09	7.13	0.079	0.059
Stanza	1982–83	58–72	0.8125	0.633	0.0059	8.000	8.050	0.080	0.059

NOTE: Minimum lining thickness is as recommended by the manufacturer. Due to variation in state inspection regulations, the minimum allowable thickness may be different than recommended.
① Rear disc: 0.339
② Rear disc: 0.0059
③ Front disc: 0.413; Rear disc: 0.339
④ Front disc: 0.0047; Rear disc: 0.0059
— Not applicable

WHEEL ALIGNMENT SPECIFICATIONS

Year	Model	Caster Range (deg)	Caster Preferred Setting (deg)	Camber Range (deg)	Camber Preferred Setting (deg)	Toe-In (in.)	Steering Axis Inclination (deg)	Wheel Pivot Ratio(deg) Inner Wheel	Wheel Pivot Ratio(deg) Outer Wheel
'76–78	B210	1°00′–2°30′	1°45′	0°25′–1°55′	1°10′	0.08–0.16	7°32′–9°02′	37–39	31–33
	280Z	2°3′–3°33′	—	0°18–1°48′	—	0–0.12	11°14′–12°44′	33°54′–34°54′	32°6′–34°6′
	280Z 2 + 2	2°3′–3°33′	—	0°21′–1°51′	—	0–0.12	11°14′–12°44′	36°18′–37°18′	34°24′–36°24′
'76–'77	610, 710	1°–2°35′	1°45′	1°15′–2°45′	2°	①	6°15′–7°45′	32–33°	29°30′–31°30′
'76–'78	F10	20′–1°50′	—	0°50′–2°20′	—	②	9°15′–10°45′	36°30′–39°39′	31–34°
'77–'79	200SX	1°05′–2°35′	—	0°20′–1°50′	—	0.08–0.16	7°20′–8°20′	34°–36°	29°–31°
'77–'80	810	1°10′–2°40′	—	0°–1°30′	—	0.0–0.08	7°10′–8°40′	36°–40°	29°–33°
'81–'83	810	2°55′–4°25′	3°40′	−20′–1°10′	25′	−0.04–0.04	11°25′–12°55′	36°–40°	30°–34°
'78–'81	510 Sedan Hatchback	1°05′–2°35′	—	−15′ to 1°15′	—	0.04–0.12	8°05′–9°35′	40°–42°	32°30′–36°30′
	510 Station Wagon	55′–2°25′	—	0°5′–1°35′	—	0.04–0.12	7°45′–9°15′	40°–42°	32°30′–36°30′
'82–'83	Stanza	40′–2°10′	1°15′	−45′–45′	0	0–0.08	NA	36°–40°	30°–34°
'79–'83	210 Sedan, Hatchback	1°40′–3°10′	—	0°–1°30′	—	0.04–0.12	7°50′–9°20′	38°–42°	31°30′–35°30′
	210 Station Wagon	1°55′–3°25′	—	0°–1°30′	—	0.04–0.12	7°50′–9°20′	38°–42°	31°30′–35°30′
	310	25′–1°55′	—	0°15′–1°45′	—	0.0–0.08	11°10′–12°30′	36°30′–39°30′	29°30′–32°30′
	280ZX	4°10′–5°40′	—	−35′–+0.55′	—	0.04–0.12	8°35′–10°5′	33°30′–37°30′ ③	29°–33° ④
	Sentra	45′–2°15′	—	−35′–1°05′	—	0.12–0.20	12°10′–13°40′	40°–44′	31°–35°
'80	200SX	1°45′–3°15′	—	−40′–+50′	—	0.0–0.08	7°25′–8°55′	33°–35°	27°–29°
'80–'83	200SX	1°45′–3°15′	2°30′	−40′–50′	5′	0.0–0.08	7°25′–8°55′	33°–35°	27°–29°

① 0.16–0.24 Radial tires
　0.24–0.31 Bias tires
② 0–0.79 Radial tires
　0.20–0.28 Bias tires

③ With power steering: 32°–36°
④ With power steering: 24°30′–28°30′
— Information not applicable
NA Not available at time of publication

TUNE-UP PROCEDURES

Spark Plugs

Number the spark plug wires and clean any foreign material from around the spark plugs prior to removing them. Use a spark plug socket with a rubber insert to remove the plugs. This will prevent cracking the porcelain insulator. Each spark plug should be individually inspected and, if necessary, replaced. Refer to the "Troubleshooting" in the Unit Repair section for an analysis of plug tip conditions. Clean reusable spark plugs and file the center electrode flat. Adjust the spark plug gap, according to the "Tune-Up Specifications" chart, with a wire type feeler gauge. Lightly oil the threads and torque the spark plugs to 11–15 ft. lbs.

Breaker Points and Condenser

Either single point or dual point systems may be used. Dual points are serviced in the same manner as single points, with the exception of setting dwell, which is covered later.

1. Release the distributor cap clips and remove the cap.

2. Remove the distributor rotor by pulling straight up. Replace it if the contact tip is burned or corroded. Do not file the tip.

3. Inspect the points; if they are burned, worn, or corroded, replace them.

4. Use a magnetic screwdriver to remove the points hold-down screws. On distributors with the condenser mounted inside, the points screws also retain the condenser. Remove the points (and condenser, if inside). Loosen the screw in the side of the distributor to allow the points wire to slip out.

5. On dual point distributors and single point distributors with the condensers mounted outside the distributor, remove the condenser lead screw(s) and remove the condenser(s). On dual point models, note the locations of the condensers; they have

1. Primary lead terminal
2. Ground lead wire
3. Set screw
4. Adjuster
5. Screw

Typical single point distributor

different electrical capacities, and replacements must be installed in the same relationship.

6. Place a dab of grease on the distributor points cam and spread it around evenly. Do not use oil.

7. Install the new points and condenser(s). Tighten the condenser mounting screws, but leave the points screws slightly loose.

8. Check that the points meet squarely. The fixed point can be bent slightly if necessary.

9. Adjust the point gap. The rubbing block of the points must be on one of the high points of the distributor cam. The engine can be rotated with a wrench on the crankshaft pulley bolt (sparkplugs removed) or bumped around with the starter.

1. Lead wire terminal set screws
2. Adjuster plate
3. Primary lead wire—advanced points
4. Primary lead wire—retarded points
5. Primary lead wire set screw
6. Set screw—advanced points
7. Set screw—retarded points
8. Adjuster plate set screws
9. Breaker plate set screws

Typical dual point distributor. This view shows two screws (8) which must never be disturbed when adjusting or replacing the points

Insert a flat feeler gauge of the correct thickness (see the specifications chart) between the points. Adjust the gap until the feeler gauge slides through with a slight drag.

10. Tighten the points hold down screws and recheck the adjustment. When the gap is correct, pull a matchbook cover or business card through (between) the points to clean them. Install the rotor and cap, and set the dwell and ignition timing.

Dwell Angle

If the distributor has one set of points, proceed as follows:

1. Hook up a dwell meter according to the manufacturer's instructions. Zero the meter needle if necessary. Start the engine and read the dwell on the meter. If the dwell is correct, shut off the engine and remove the meter.

2. If the dwell requires adjustment, shut off the engine, remove the distributor cap, and adjust the point gap. Open the point gap to decrease dwell, close the gap to increase dwell.

3. Replace the cap and start the engine. Check the dwell and repeat the process as necessary.

If the distributor has two sets of points, proceed as follows:

1. Unplug the distributor from the engine wiring harness.

2. Connect the two black wires with a jumper wire. This activates the advanced set of points.

3. Check and adjust the dwell of the advanced set of points.

4. Take one end of the jumper wire from the distributor side of the plug. Connect the black wire in the engine harness to the yellow wire from the distributor. This activates the retarded set of points.

5. Check and adjust the dwell of the retarded set of points.

6. Reconnect the plug.

Electronic Ignition

AIR GAP ADJUSTMENT

Through 1978

Reluctor air gap should be checked periodically. Standard air gap is 0.008–0.016 in. for both single and dual gap distributors. If the gap is incorrect, adjustment may be made by loosening the pick-up coil screws and inserting a feeler gauge.

NOTE: The use of a non-magnetic feeler gauge such as plastic or brass, is recommended for accurate gapping.

Remove the rubber cap from the tip of the rotor shaft. Add grease if necessary. The reluctor cannot be removed. To remove the pick-up coil, take out the two pick-up coil assembly and core screws clamping the primary wire. Reverse the sequence to install.

Checking the air gap—1976–78

1979 and Later
WITH RING-TYPE PICK-UP

All models built in 1979 and later with the exception of those listed under "With Stator" use ring-type of electronic ignition system.

Adjustment of these models is made by simply loosening the pick-up coil (toothed stator ring) retaining screws and centering the ring around the reluctor until the proper gap is achieved.

Checking the air gap—1979 and later with ring-type pick-up

Checking the air gap—1979 and later with stator

WITH STATOR

Models using this type of electronic ignition system include: 1980–83 510 and 200SX (W/Z20 engine), 1982 210 (USA models only), 1982–83 310, Sentra and Stanza.

Adjustment of these models is made by simply loosening the stator mounting screws and moving the stator until the proper gap is achieved.

Ignition Timing

Timing settings for each model are given in the "Tune-Up Specifications" chart.

NOTE: Datsun does not give ignition timing adjustments for 1980 California models or for any 1981–83 models. These models are not covered in this section. If the ignition timing requires adjustment, please refer to the underhood specifications sticker for applicable procedures.

ADJUSTMENT

All Except 1976 280Z

1. Set the dwell to the proper specification.
2. Locate the timing marks on the crankshaft pulley and the front of the engine.
3. Clean off the timing marks so that you can see them.
4. Use chalk or white paint to color the mark on the crankshaft pulley and the mark on the scale which will indicate the correct timing when aligned with the notch on the crankshaft pulley.
5. Attach a tachometer to the engine.
6. Attach a timing light to the engine, according to the manufacturer's instructions.
7. Leave the vacuum line connected to the distributor vacuum diaphragm on all models except the 1979 210 wagons with automatic transmission, the A15 engine and 1980 and later A series engines; disconnect and plug the hose on those models. On 1980 810s, disconnect the throttle valve switch harness connector and plug the purge hose from the intake manifold. Plug the opening in the intake manifold. On 1980 49 States models, also disconnect the hose from the air induction pipe and cap the pipe, and disconnect and plug the vacuum advance hose at the distributor. Note that the disconnect and plug instructions for the air induction pipe and the distributor vacuum advance do not apply to 1980 models sold in Canada.
8. Check to make sure that all of the wires clear the fan and then start the engine. Allow the engine to reach normal operating temperature.

1980 and later throttle valve switch

Top mark of crank pulley

Typical timing marks

Loosen the distributor lockbolt and turn the distributor slightly to advance (upper arrow) or retard (lower arrow) the timing

9. Adjust the idle to the correct setting.
10. Aim the timing light at the timing marks. If the marks that you put on the pulley and the engine are aligned when the light flashes, the timing is correct. Turn off the engine and remove the tachometer and the timing light. If the marks are not in alignment, proceed with the following steps.
11. Turn off the engine.
12. Loosen the distributor lockbolt just enough so that the distributor can be turned with a little effort.
13. Start the engine. Keep the wires of the timing light clear of the fan.
14. With the timing light aimed at the pulley and the marks on the engine, turn the distributor in the direction or rotor rotation to retard the spark, and in the opposite direction of rotor rotation to advance the spark. Align the marks on the pulley and the engine with the flashes of the timing light. Tighten the hold-down bolt.

NOTE: See the "Emission Controls" section for adjustment of phase difference on dual point models.

1976 280Z

1. Connect a timing light and tachometer to the engine. Clean the timing scale and pulley notch; repaint the marks if necessary.
2. On all models (except California), disconnect the red temperature switch and ground the *harness* end of the wire with a jumper. Make sure that *all* wires are out of the way of the engine fan and other rotating parts.

3. Start the engine and operate it at idle speed. If the car has an automatic transmission, securely apply the parking brake and put the transmission in drive.
4. Verify that the idle speed is approximately correct as shown in the "Tune-Up" chart. If not, adjust it until it is correct as described in the carburetor adjustment section of this chapter.
5. Carefully keeping the wires away from all rotating parts, aim the light at the timing marks. Compare the indication with the specified timing.
6. If the timing is not correct, stop the engine and loosen the nut which holds the distributor clamped in position (it is on the front of the clamp).
7. Then, restart the engine (putting an automatic transmission back in drive).
8. Slowly rotate the distributor back and forth until the timing is correct.
9. Stop the engine and tighten the clamp nut, being careful not to disturb the setting.
10. Recheck the timing and readjust it as necessary.
11. Run a jumper wire across the two terminals of the connection to the temperature switch. On all models (except California), disconnect the temperature switch wire.
12. Again check the timing exactly as described above. It should be 7 degrees retarded. If the timing is incorrect, adjust the phase difference as follows:
  a. Loosen the set screws which hold the adjuster plate in position and turn the plate using the notch in the adjuster plate. Timing is retarded by turning the plate counterclockwise. The edge of the distributor is marked in graduations which equal 4 degrees of crankshaft rotation each.
  b. Recheck the ignition timing. Repeat the adjustment and check until retard timing is within specifications.
  c. Make sure to disconnect all jumper wires and securely reconnect all disturbed ignition wiring.

Valve Lash

ADJUSTMENT

B210, F10, 210, 310 and Sentra

1. Run the engine until it reaches normal operating temperature. Oil temperature, not water temperature, is critical to valve adjustment. With this in mind, make sure the engine is fully warmed up since this is the only way to make sure the parts have reached their full expansion. Generally speaking, this takes around fifteen minutes. After the engine has reached normal operating temperature, shut it off.
2. Purchase a new valve cover gasket before removing the valve cover. The new silicone gasket sealers are just as good or better if you can't find a gasket.

Valve adjustment—E-series engines (A-series engine similar)

3. Note the location of any hoses or wires which may interfere with valve cover removal, disconnect them and move them aside. Then, remove the bolts which hold the valve cover in place.

4. After the valve cover has been removed, the next step is to get the number one piston at TDC on the compression stroke. There are at least two ways to do it; you can bump the engine over with the starter or turn it over by using a wrench on the front pulley attaching bolt. The easiest way to find TDC is to turn the engine over slowly with a wrench (after first removing No. 1 plug) until the piston is at the top of its stroke and the TDC timing mark on the crankshaft pulley is in alignment with the timing mark pointer. At this point, the valves for No. 1 should be closed.

NOTE: Make sure both valves are closed with the valve springs up as high as they will go. An easy way to find the compression stroke is to remove the distributor cap and see toward which spark plug lead the rotor is pointing. If the rotor points to number one spark plug lead, number one cylinder is on its compression stroke. When the rotor points to number two spark plug lead, number two cylinder is on its compression stroke, etc.

5. With No. 1 piston at TDC of the compression stroke, check the clearance on valves No. 1, 2, 3 and 5 (counting from the front to the rear). Adjust valves No. 1, 2, 3 and 6 on 1982 and later 310 and Sentra.

6. To adjust the clearance, loosen the locknut with a wrench and turn the adjuster with a screwdriver while holding the locknut. The correct size feeler gauge should pass with a slight drag between the rocker arm and the valve stem.

7. Turn the crankshaft one full revolution to position the No. 4 piston at TDC of the compression stroke. Adjust valves No. 4, 6, 7 and 8 in the same manner as the first four. Adjust valves No. 4, 5, 7 and 8 on 1982 and later 310 and Sentra.

8. Replace the valve cover.

1976–80 510 and 200SX (49 State models only), 610 and 710

1. The valves are adjusted with the engine at normal operating temperature. Oil

temperature, and the resultant parts expansion, is much more important than water temperature. Run the engine for at least fifteen minutes to ensure that all the parts have reached their full expansion. After the engine is warmed up, shut it off.

2. Purchase either a new gasket or some silicone gasket seal before removing the camshaft cover. Note the location of any wires and hoses which may interfere with cam cover removal, disconnect them and move them aside. Then remove the bolts which hold the cam cover in place and remove the cam cover.

Checking the valve lash with a flat feeler gauge—L-series engines

Loosen the locknut and turn the pivot adjuster to change the clearance

3. Place a wrench on the crankshaft pulley bolt and turn the engine over until the valves for No. 1 cylinder are closed. When both cam lobes are pointing up, the valves are closed. If you have not done this before, it is a good idea to turn the engine over slowly several times and watch the valve action until you have a clear idea of just when the valve is closed.

4. Check the clearance of the intake and exhaust valves. You can differentiate between them by lining them up with the tubes of the intake and exhaust manifolds. The correct size feeler gauge should pass between the base circle of the cam and the rocker arm with just a slight drag. Be sure the feeler gauge is inserted *straight* and not on an angle.

5. If the valves need adjustment, loosen the locking nut and then adjust the clearance with the adjusting screw. You will probably find it necessary to hold the locking nut while you turn the adjuster. After

you have the correct clearance, tighten the locking nut and recheck the clearance. Remember, it's better to have them too loose than too tight, especially exhaust valves.

6. Repeat this procedure (Steps 3–5) until you have checked and/or adjusted all the valves. (Be sure to adjust in the firing order.) Keep in mind that all that is necessary is to have the valves closed and the camshaft lobes pointing up. It is not particularly important what stroke the engine is on.

7. Install the cam cover gasket, the cam cover and any wires and hoses which were removed.

810 and 280Z, ZX

1977 810 engines must be "overnight" cold before the valves can be adjusted. They must not be operated for about eight hours before adjustment. 1978–83 810 engines and all Z and ZX engines are adjusted hot.

NOTE: Skip Steps 7–8 if you have a 1978–83 810 or a 1976–83 280Z, ZX; complete Steps 7–8 if you have a 1977 810.

1. Note the locations of all hoses or wires that would interfere with valve cover removal, disconnect them and move them aside. Then, remove the six bolts which hold the valve cover in place.

2. Bump one end of the cover sharply to loosen the gasket and then pull the valve cover off the engine vertically.

3. Place a wrench on the crankshaft pulley bolt and turn the engine over until the first cam lobe is pointing straight up. The timing marks on the crankshaft pulley should be lined up approximately where they would be when the No. 1 spark plug fires.

NOTE: If you decide to turn the engine by "bumping" it with the starter, be sure to disconnect the high tension wire from the coil to prevent the engine from accidentally starting and spewing oil all over the engine compartment.

CAUTION
Never attempt to turn the engine by using a wrench on the camshaft sprocket bolt; this would put a tremendous strain on the timing chain.

---

4. See the illustration for primary adjustment and check the clearance for valves (1), (3), (7), (8), (9) and (11) using a flat-bladed feeler gauge. The feeler gauge should pass between the cam and the cam follower with a very slight drag. Insert the feeler gauge *straight*, not at an angle.

5. If the clearance is not within the specified limits, loosen the pivot locking nut and then insert the feeler gauge between the cam and the cam follower. Adjust the pivot screw until there is a very slight drag on the gauge, tighten the locking nut, recheck the adjustment and correct as necessary.

Primary valve adjustment, No. 1 cam lobe pointing up—810 and 280Z, ZX

Secondary valve adjustment, No. 1 cam lobe pointing down—810 and 280Z, ZX

6. Turn the engine over so that the first cam lobe is pointing straight down. See the illustration for secondary adjustment and then check the clearance on valves (2), (4), (5), (6), (10) and (12). If clearance is not within specifications, adjust as detailed in Step 5.

7. Reinstall the valve cover gasket and hoses, start the engine, and operate it until the is fully warmed up (1977 only).

8. Repeat the entire valve adjustment procedure using the gauges specified in the "Tune-Up" chart, but do not loosen the locking nuts unless the gauge indicates that adjustment is required.

9. When all valves are at hot specifications, clean all traces of old gasket material from the valve cover and the head. Install the new gasket in the valve cover with sealer and install the valve cover. Tighten the valve cover bolts evenly in several stages going around the cover to ensure a good seal. Reconnect all hoses and wires securely and operate the engine to check for leaks.

1980 and Later 510, 200SX (with Z20 and Z22 Engines) and 1982 and Later Stanza

1. The valves must be adjusted with the engine warm, so start the car and run the

engine until the needle on the temperature gauge reaches the middle of the gauge. After the engine is warm, shut it off.

2. Purchase either a new gasket or some silicone gasket sealer before removing the camshaft cover. Counting on the old gasket to be in good shape is a losing proposition; always use new gaskets. Note the location of any wires and hoses which may interfere with cam cover removal, disconnect them and move them to one side. Remove the bolts holding the cover in place and remove the cover. Remember, the engine will be hot, so be careful.

3. Place a wrench on the crankshaft pulley bolt and turn the engine over until the first cam lobe behind the camshaft timing chain sprocket is pointing straight down.

NOTE: If you decide to turn the engine by "bumping" it with the starter, be sure to disconnect the high tension wire from the coil(s) to prevent the engine from accidentally starting and spewing oil all over the engine compartment.

Primary valve adjustment, No. 1 cam lobe pointing down—Z20, Z22 and CA20 engines

Secondary valve adjustment, No. 1 cam lobe pointing up—Z20, Z22 and CA20 engines

4. See the illustration for primary adjustment and adjust valves (1), (4), (6), and (7) using a flat-bladed feeler gauge. The feeler gauge should pass between the valve stem end and the rocker arm screw with a very slight drag. Insert the feeler gauge *straight,* not an angle.

5. If the clearance is not within specified value, loosen the rocker arm lock nut and turn the rocker arm screw to obtain the proper clearance. After correct clearance is obtained, tighten the lock nut.

6. Turn the engine over so that the first cam lobe behind the camshaft timing chain sprocket is pointing straight up and adjust the valves marked (2), (3), (5), and (8) in the secondary adjustment illustration. They, too, should be adjusted to specifications as in Step 5.

7. Install the cam cover gasket, the cam cover and any wires and hoses which were removed.

Carburetor

IDLE SPEED AND MIXTURE ADJUSTMENT

NOTE: 1980 and later model Datsuns require a CO meter to adjust their mixture ratios, therefore, no procedures concerning this adjustment are given. Also, many California model Datsuns have a plug over their mixture control screw. It is suggested that in both of these cases, mixture adjustment be left to a qualified technician.

1. Start the engine and allow it to run until it reaches normal operating temperature.

2. Allow the engine idle speed to stabilize by running the engine at idle for at least one minute.

1. Throttle adjusting screw
2. Idle adjusting screw
3. Stopper
4. Idle limiter cap

Downdraft carburetor idle adjustment screw

3. If it hasn't already been done, check and adjust the ignition timing to the proper setting.

4. Shut off the engine and connect a tachometer.

5. Disconnect and plug the air hose between the three way connector and the check valve, if equipped. On 1980 and later models, disconnect the air induction hose and plug the pipe. With the transmission in Neutral, check the idle speed on the tachometer. If the reading is correct, continue onto Step 6 for 1975–79 models. For 1980 and later and certain California models, proceed to Step 8 below if the idel is correct. If not, turn the idle speed adjusting screw clockwise with a screwdriver to increase idle speed or counterclockwise to decrease it.

6. With the automatic transmission in Drive (wheels blocked and parking brake on) or the manual transmission in Neutral, turn the mixture screw out until the engine rpm starts to drop to an overly rich mixture.

7. Turn the screw in past the starting point until the rpm starts to drop due to an overly lean mixture. Turn the mixture screw in until the idle speed drops 60–70 rpm with manual transmission, or 15–25 rpm with automatic transmission (in Drive) for 1976 B 210, 610, and 710; 35–45 rpm with manual transmission or 10–20 with automatic for 1977–78 B 210; 35–45 rpm (all transmissions) for 1977–78 F 10; or 45–55 rpm for all 1977 710, and 1978–79 510, 200 SX. If the mixture limiter cap will not allow this adjustment, remove it, make the adjustment, and reinstall it. Go on to Step 8 for 1975–79 model.

8. Install the air hose. If the engine speed increases, reduce it with the idle speed screw.

Electronic Fuel Injection

IDLE SPEED ADJUSTMENT

To adjust the mixture controls on these units requires a CO meter and several special Datsun tools, therefore we will confine ourselves to idle speed adjustment.

1. Start the engine and run it until the water temperature indicator points to the middle of the temperature gauge. It might be quicker to take a short spin down the road and back.

Idle speed adjusting screw—200SX

Idle speed adjusting screw—1977–80 810

Idle speed adjusting screw—1981–83 810

2. Open the engine hood. Run the engine at about 2,000 rpm for a few minutes with the transmission in Neutral and all accessories off. If you have not already done so, check the ignition timing and make sure it is correct. Hook up a tachometer. For automatic transmission, set parking brake, block wheels and set shift selector in Drive position.

3. Run the engine at idle speed and disconnect the hose from the air induction pipe, then plug the pipe. Allow the engine to run for about a minute at idle speed.

4. Check the idle against the specifications given earlier in this section. Adjust the idle speed by turning the idle speed adjusting screw. Turn the screw clockwise for slower idle speed and counterclockwise for faster idle speed.

5. Connect hose and disconnect the tachometer. If idle speed increases, adjust it with the idle speed adjusting screw.

Diesel Fuel Injection

IDLE SPEED ADJUSTMENT

NOTE: A special diesel tachometer will be required for this procedure. A normal tachometer will not work.

1. Make sure all electrical accessories are turned off.

2. The automatic transmission (if so equipped) should be in 'D' with the parking brake on and the wheels blocked.

3. Start the engine and run it until it reaches the normal operating temperature.

4. Attach the diesel tachometer's pickup to the No. 1 injection tube.

NOTE: In order to obtain a more accurate reading of the idle speed, you may wish to remove all the clamps on the No. 1 injection tube.

Loosen the idle screw locknut while holding the control lever—diesel engine

Idle speed adjusting screw—diesel engines

5. Run the engine at about 2,000 rpm for two minutes under no-load conditions.

6. Slowly the engine down to idle speed for about 1 min. and then check the idle.

7. If the engine is not idling at the proper speed, turn it off and disconnect the accelerator wire from the injection pump control lever.

8. Move the control lever to the full acceleration side, and then loosen the idle screw lock nut while still holding the control lever.

9. Start the engine again and turn the adjusting screw until the proper idle is obtained. Stop the engine.

10. Tighten the idle adjusting screw lock nut while still holding the control level to the full acceleration side and then connect the accelerator wire.

ENGINE ELECTRICAL

Distributor

REMOVAL

1. Unfasten the retaining clips and lift the distributor cap straight up. It will be easier to install the distributor if the wiring

is not disconnected from the cap. If the wires must be removed from the cap, mark their positions to aid in installation.

2. Disconnect the distributor wiring harness.

3. Disconnect the vacuum lines.

4. Note the position of the rotor in relation to the base. Scribe a mark on the base of the distributor and on the engine block to facilitate reinstallation. Align the marks with the direction the metal tip of the rotor is pointing.

5. Remove the bolt(s) which holds the distributor to the engine.

6. Lift the distributor assembly from the engine.

INSTALLATION

1. Insert the distributor shaft and assembly into the engine. Line up the mark on the distributor and the one on the engine with the metal tip of the rotor. Make sure that the vacuum advance diaphragm is pointed in the same direction as it was pointed originally. This will be done automatically if the marks on the engine and the distributor are lined up with the rotor.

2. Install the distributor hold-down bolt and clamp. Leave the screw loose enough so that you can move the distributor with heavy hand pressure.

3. Connect the primary wire to the coil. Install the distributor cap on the distributor

housing. Secure the distributor cap with the spring clips.

4. Install the spark plug wires if removed. Make sure that the wires are pressed all the way into the top of the distributor cap and firmly onto the spark plug.

5. Adjust the point dwell and set the ignition timing.

NOTE: If the crankshaft has been turned or the engine disturbed in any manner (i.e., disassembled and rebuilt) while the distributor was removed, or if the marks were not drawn, it will be necessary to initially time the engine. Follow the procedure given below.

CAP ASSEMBLY
ROTOR HEAD
ROLL PIN
SHAFT HEAD
THRUST WASHER
SHAFT
HOUSING
THRUST WASHER
GASKET
ROLL PIN
COLLAR

Exploded view of the electronic distributor—Turbo

1. Cap assembly
2. Rotor head assembly
3. Condenser assembly
4. Earth wire assembly
5. Lead wire assembly
6. Contact set
7. Breaker plate assembly
8. Cam assembly
9. Governor spring
10. Governor weight
11. Thrust washer
12. Shaft assembly
13. Vacuum control assembly
14. Terminal assembly
15. Clamp
16. Fixing plate
17. Collar set

Typical points–type distributor

1. Cap
2. Rotor head
3. Rollpin
4. Reluctor
5. Pick-up coil
6. Contactor
7. Breaker plate assembly
8. Packing
9. Rotor shaft
10. Governor spring
11. Governor weight
12. Shaft assembly
13. Cap setter
14. Vacuum controller
15. Housing
16. Fixing plate
17. O-ring
18. Collar

Exploded view of the electronic distributor—1976–78

Exploded view of the electronic distributor—with ring-type pick-up

INSTALLATION—ENGINE DISTURBED

1. It is necessary to place the No. 1 cylinder in the firing position to correctly install the distributor. To locate this position, the ignition timing marks on the crankshaft front pulley are used.

2. Remove the No. 1 cylinder spark plug. Turn the crankshaft until the piston in the No. 1 cylinder is moving up on the compression stroke. This can be determined by placing your thumb over the spark plug hole and feeling the air being forced out of the cylinder. Stop turning the crankshaft when the timing marks that are used to time the engine are aligned.

3. Oil the distributor housing lightly where the distributor bears on the cylinder block.

4. Install the distributor so that the rotor, which is mounted on the shaft, points toward the No. 1 spark plug terminal tower position when the cap is installed. Of course you won't be able to see the direction in which the rotor is pointing if the cap is on the distributor. Lay the cap on the top of the distributor and make a mark on the side of the distributor housing just below the No. 1 spark plug terminal. Make sure that the rotor points toward that mark when you install the distributor.

5. When the distributor shaft has reached the bottom of the hole, move the rotor back and forth slightly until the driving lug on the end of the shaft enters the slots cut in the end of the oil pump shaft and the distributor assembly slides down into place.

6. When the distributor is correctly installed, the breaker points should be in such a position that they are just ready to break contact with each other; or, on engines with electronic ignition, the reluctor teeth should be aligned with the pick-up coil. This can be accomplished by rotating the distributor body after it has been installed in the engine. Once again, line up the marks that you made before the distributor was removed.

7. Install the distributor hold-down bolt.

8. Install the spark plug into the No. 1 spark plug hole and continue from Step 3 of the preceding distributor installation procedure.

Alternator

ALTERNATOR PRECAUTIONS

An alternator is used on all models. The following precautions must be observed to prevent alternator and regulator damage:

1. Be absolutely sure of correct polarity when installing a new battery, or connecting a battery charger.

2. Do not short across or ground any alternator or regulator terminals.

Exploded view of the electronic distributor—with stator

the regulator is part of the alternator, no adjustments are possible or necessary.

1. Disconnect the negative battery terminal.
2. Disconnect the electrical lead connector of the regulator.
3. Remove the two mounting screws and remove the regulator from the vehicle.
4. Install the regulator in the reverse order of removal.

VOLTAGE SPECIFICATIONS

Ambient Temperature (°F)	Regulated Voltage
14	14.6–15.6
32	14.5–15.5
50	14.3–15.3
68	14.2–15.2
86	14.0–15.0
104	13.9–14.9

ADJUSTMENT

1. Adjust the voltage regulator core gap by loosening the screw which is used to secure the contact set on the yoke, and move the contact up or down as necessary. Retighten the screw. The gap should be 0.024–0.039 in.
2. Adjust the point gap of the voltage regulator coil by loosening the screw used to secure the upper contact and move the upper contact up or down. The gap for all models is 0.014–0.018 in.

1. Contacts   3. Adjusting screw
2. Feeler gauge   4. Phillips screwdriver

Adjusting the core gap

3. The core gap and point gap on the charge relay coil is or are adjusted in the same manner as previously outlined for the voltage regulator coil. The core gap is to be set at 0.032–0.039 in. and the point gap adjusted to 0.016–0.024 in.
4. The regulated voltage is adjusted by loosening the locknut and turning the adjusting screw clockwise to increase, or

3. Disconnect the battery ground cable before replacing any electrical unit.
4. Never operate the alternator with any of the leads disconnected.
5. When steam cleaning the engine, be careful not to subject the alternator to excessive heat.
6. When charging the battery, remove it from the car or disconnect the alternator output terminal.

REMOVAL AND INSTALLATION

1. Disconnect the negative battery terminal.
2. Disconnect the two lead wires and connector from the alternator.
3. Loosen the drive belt adjusting bolt and remove the belt.
4. Unscrew the alternator attaching bolts and remove the alternator from the vehicle.
5. Installation is in the reverse order of removal.

BELT TENSION ADJUSTMENT

The correct belt tension for all alternators gives about ½ in. play on the longest span of the belt.

1. Loosen the alternator pivot and mounting bolts.
2. Pry the alternator toward or away from the engine until the tension is correct. Use a hammer or wooden prybar.
3. When the tension is correct, tighten the bolts and check the adjustment. Be careful not to overtighten the belt, which will lead to bearing failure.

Regulator

REMOVAL AND INSTALLATION

NOTE: 1978–83 models are equipped with integral regulator alternators. Since

1. Feeler gauge
2. Screw
3. Phillips screwdriver
4. Upper contact

Adjusting the point gap

1. Wrench
2. Phillips screwdriver
3. Adjusting screw
4. Locknut

Adjusting the regulator voltage

1. Magnetic switch assembly
2. Dust cover (Adjusting washer)
3. Torsion spring
4. Shift lever
5. Dust cover
6. Thrust washer
7. E-ring
8. Rear cover metal
9. Through bolt
10. Rear cover
11. Brush holder
12. Brush (−)
13. Brush spring
14. Brush (+)
15. Yoke
16. Field coil
17. Armature
18. Center bracket
19. Pinion assembly
20. Dust cover
21. Pinion stopper
22. Stopper clip
23. Gear case
24. Gear case metal

Exploded view of a non-reduction gear starter

counterclockwise to decrease the regulated voltage. The voltage should be between 14.3–15.3 volts at 68°F.

Starter

The starter is mounted at the right rear of the engine. The solenoid is mounted on top of the starter and engages the drive pinion through a pivot yoke shift lever.

1. Magnetic switch assembly
2. Dust cover (adjusting washer)
3. Torsion spring
4. Shift lever
5. Through bolt
6. Rear cover
7. "O" ring
8. Yoke
9. Field coil
10. Brush
11. Armature
12. Center bearing
13. Brush spring
14. Brush holder
15. Dust cover
16. Center housing
17. Reduction gear
18. Pinion gear
19. Packing
20. Gear case

Exploded view—reduction-type starter

REMOVAL AND INSTALLATION

1. Disconnect the negative battery cable.
2. Disconnect and label the wires from the terminals on the solenoid.
3. Remove the two bolts which secure the starter to the flywheel housing and pull the starter forward and out. To install, reverse the removal procedure.

BRUSH REPLACEMENT

Non-Reduction Gear Type

1. Remove the starter. Remove the dust cover (if so equipped), the E-ring, and the two thrust washers from the rear cover. Remove the two brush holder set screws from the rear cover.
2. On all models, remove the two through bolts and remove the rear cover.
3. Remove the brushes from their holders by lifting the brush spring away from the brush; you can use a hook fabricated from wire to do this.
4. Unsolder the brush electrical connections.
5. Remove the brushes.
To install:
6. Insert the brushes into the holder. Solder the brush electrical connections. Raise the brushes far enough to permit installing the brush holder over the commutator.
7. Install the rear cover through bolts. Replace the brush holder set screws, and replace the thrust washers, E-ring, and the dust cover.

Reduction Gear Type

1. Remove the starter. Remove the solenoid.
2. Remove the through bolts and the rear cover. The cover can be pried off with a small prybar or the like, but be careful not to damage the O-ring.
3. Remove the starter housing, arma-

ture, and brush holder from the center housing. They can be removed as an assembly.

4. Remove the positive side brush from its holder. The positive brush is insulated from the brush holder, and its lead wire is connected to the field coil.

5. Carefully lift the negative brush from the commutator and remove it from the holder.

6. Unsolder the brush electrical connections. Remove the brushes.

7. Install the new brushes and solder their wires to the connections. Install the brush holder, armature, and starter housing to the center housing. Install the rear cover and O-ring. Install the solenoid.

DRIVE REPLACEMENT

Non-Reduction Gear Type

1. Loosen the locknut and remove the connection going to the ''M'' terminal of the solenoid. Remove the securing screws and remove the solenoid.

2. Remove the dust cover, E-ring, thrust washers, and the two screws retaining the brush holder assembly. Remove the brush cover throughbolts and remove the cover assembly (all models).

3. Lift the brushes to free them from the commutator and remove the brush holder.

4. Tap the yoke assembly lightly with a wooden hammer and remove it from the field and case.

Pinion stopper removal

5. Remove the nut and bolt which serve as a pin for the shift lever, carefully retaining the associated washers.

6. Remove the armature assembly and shift lever.

7. Push the stop ring (located at the end of the armature shaft) toward the clutch and remove the snap-ring. Remove the stop ring.

8. Remove the clutch assembly from the armature shaft.

To install the drive:

1. Install the clutch assembly onto the armature shaft.

2. Put the stop ring on and hold it toward the clutch while installing the snap-ring.

3. Install the armature assembly and shift lever into the yoke.

4. Install the washers, nut and bolt which serve as a shift lever pivot pin.

5. Install the field back onto the yoke assembly.

6. Lift the brushes and install the brush holder. Install the brush cover and through-bolts.

7. Replace the brush holder set screws, the thrust washers, E-ring, and the dust cover.

8. Install the solenoid. Reconnect the wire to the ''M'' terminal of the solenoid.

Reduction Gear Type

1. Remove the starter.

2. Remove the solenoid and the shift lever.

3. Remove the bolts securing the center housing to the front cover and separate the parts.

4. Remove the gears and the starter drive.

5. Installation is the reverse.

SOLENOID REPLACEMENT

All Models

1. Loosen the locknut and remove the connection going to the ''M'' terminal of the solenoid.

2. Remove the three securing screws and remove the solenoid.

3. To install, reverse the removal procedures.

ENGINE MECHANICAL

Engine

REMOVAL AND INSTALLATION

Datsun engines are all inline, with either four or six cylinders. Some have overhead valves with a rocker arm arrangement and others have a single overhead camshaft. Refer to the Engine Identification Chart for identification of engines by model, number of cylinders, displacement, and camshaft location. Engines are referred to by model designation codes throughout this section.

Rear Wheel Drive

It is best to remove the engine and transmission as a unit.

1. Mark the location of the hinges on the hood. Unbolt and remove.

2. Disconnect the battery cable. Remove the battery on the 220E California models with air conditioning.

3. Drain the coolant and automatic transmission fluid.

4. Remove the grille on 510, 610, and 710 models. Remove the radiator after disconnecting the automatic transmission coolant tubes.

5. Remove the air cleaner.

6. Remove the fan and pulley.

7. Disconnect:
  a. water temperature gauge wire
  b. oil pressure sending unit wire
  c. ignition distributor primary wire
  d. starter motor connections
  e. fuel hose
  f. alternator leads
  g. heater hoses
  h. throttle and choke connections
  i. engine ground cable
  j. thermal transmitter wire—B210, 280Z
  k. fuel cut-off switch wire—B210
  l. vacuum cut solenoid wire—B210

NOTE: A good rule of thumb when disconnecting the rather complex engine wiring of today's cars is to put a piece of masking tape on the wire and on the connection you removed the wire from, then mark both pieces of tape 1, 2, 3, etc. When replacing wiring, simply match the pieces of tape.

——— CAUTION ———
On models with air conditioning, it is necessary to remove the compressor and the condenser from their mounts. DO NOT ATTEMPT TO UNFASTEN ANY OF THE AIR CONDITIONER HOSES.

8. Disconnect the power brake booster hose from the engine.

9. Remove the clutch operating cylinder and return spring.

10. Disconnect the speedometer cable from the transmission. Disconnect the backup light switch and any other wiring or attachments to the transmission. On cars with the L20B engine, disconnect the parking brake cable at the rear adjuster.

11. Disconnect the column shift linkage. Remove the floorshift lever. On the Z20 and B210 models, remove the boot, withdraw the lock pin, and remove the lever from inside the car.

12. Detach the exhaust pipe from the exhaust manifold. Remove the front section of the exhaust system.

13. Mark the relationship of the driveshaft flanges and remove the driveshaft.

14. Place a jack under the transmission. Remove the rear crossmember. On B210 models, remove the rear engine mounting nuts.

15. Attach a hoist to the lifting hooks on the engine (at either end of the cylinder head). Support the engine.

16. Unbolt the front engine mounts. Tilt the engine by lowering the jack under the transmission and raising the hoist.

17. Reverse the procedure to install the engine.

Front Wheel Drive

It is recommended that the engine and transmission be removed as a unit. If need be, the units may be separated after removal.

1. Mark the location of the hinges on the hood. Remove the hood by holding at both sides and unscrewing bolts. This requires two people.

2. Remove the battery and drain radiator coolant.

3. Remove the air cleaner and disconnect the accelerator wire from the carburetor.

4. Disconnect the following wires and hoses:

Engine harness connector—F–10

a. Ignition wire from the coil to the distributor.

b. Ignition coil ground wire and the engine ground cable.

c. Disconnect the block connector from the distributor.

d. Remove fusible links.

e. Unplug all engines harness connectors.

f. Remove the fuel and fuel return hoses.

g. Disconnect the upper and lower radiator hoses.

h. Detach the heater inlet and outlet.

i. Remove the Master-Vac vacuum hose.

j. Disconnect the carbon canister hoses and the air pump air cleaner hose.

5. Remove the air pump air cleaner.

6. Remove the carbon canister.

7. Remove the auxiliary fan and the washer tank.

8. Remove the grille and radiator with the fan assembly.

9. Remove the clutch cylinder from the clutch housing.

Disconnecting the front exhaust pipe—F–10

10. Remove both buffer rods (do not alter the length of the rods) and disconnect the speedometer cable.

11. Remove the spring pins from the transmission gear selection rods.

12. Attach suitable engine slingers to the block and attach chain or cable. Keep the lifting source slack at this point.

13. Disconnect the exhaust pipe at both the manifold connection and the clamp holding the pipe to the engine.

14. Disconnect the right and left side drive shafts from their side flanges and remove the bolt holding the radius link support.

15. Lower the shifter and selector rods and remove the securing bolts from the motor mounts.

    a. Remove the nuts holding the front and rear motor mounts to the frame.

16. Lift the engine up and away from the car.

Installation is the reverse of removal with the following cautions and observations.

1. When lowering the engine into the car and onto the frame, make sure to keep it as level as possible.

2. Check the clearance between the frame and clutch housing and make sure that the engine mount bolts are seated in the groove of the mounting bracket.

    a. Distance "H" should be 0.394–0.472 in. (F10 and 310).

3. After installing the motor mounts, adjust and install the buffer rods. The right side should be 8.23–8.31 in. and the left 5.39–5.47 in. (F10 and 310).

1. Link support
2. Radius link

Removing radius link support—F–10

1. Clutch housing
2. Sub-frame

Clearance between frame and clutch housing

Tightening torque
0.8 to 1.2 kg-m (5.8 to 8.7 ft-lb)

Adjusting buffer rod length

Cylinder Head

REMOVAL AND INSTALLATION

NOTE: To prevent distortion or warping of the cylinder head, allow the engine to cool completely before removing the head bolts.

A14 and A15 Overhead Valve Engines

To remove the cylinder head on OHV engines:

1. Drain the coolant.

2. Disconnect the battery ground cable.

3. Remove the upper radiator hose. Remove the water outlet elbow and the thermostat.

4. Remove the air cleaner, carburetor, rocker arm cover, and both manifolds.

5. Remove the spark plugs.

6. Disconnect the temperature gauge connection.

7. Loosen the rocker arm adjusting nuts and turn the adjusting screws out to disengage the push rods. Loosen the rocker shaft bolts evenly and remove the rocker shaft assembly. Remove the push rods, keeping them in the same order for reassembly.

8. Remove the head bolts and remove the head. Rap the head with a mallet to loosen it from the block. Remove it and discard the gasket.

To replace the cylinder head on OHV engines:

1. Make sure that head and block surfaces are clean. Check the cylinder head

Pushrod, cam and valve assemblies—A series engines

surface with a straightedge and a feeler gauge for flatness. If the head is warped more than 0.003 in., it must be trued. If this is not done, there will probably be a leak. The block surface should also be checked in the same way. If the block is warped more than 0.003 in., it must be trued (machined flat).

2. Install a new head gasket. Most gaskets have a TOP marking. Make sure that the proper head gasket is used so that no water passages are blocked off.

3. Install the head. Install the pushrods in their original locations. Install the rocker arm assembly. Loosen the rocker arm adjusting screws to prevent bending pushrods when tightening the head bolts. Tighten the head bolts finger tight. The single bolt marked T must go in the No. 1 position on the center right side of the engine.

4. Refer to the "Torque Specifications" chart for the correct head bolt torque. Tighten the bolts to one third of the specified torque in the order shown in the head bolt tightening sequence illustration. Torque the rocker arm mounting bolts to 15–18 ft. lbs.

5. Tighten the bolts to two thirds of the specified torque in sequence.

6. Tighten the bolts to the full specified torque in sequence.

7. Adjust the valves. If no cold setting is given, adjust the valves to the normal hot setting.

8. Reassemble the engine. Intake and exhaust manifold bolt torque is 11–14 ft. lbs. Fill the cooling system. Start the engine and run it until normal temperature is reached. Remove the rocker arm cover. Torque the bolts in sequence once more. Check the valve clearances.

9. Retorque the head bolts after 600 miles of driving. Check the valve clearances after torquing, as this may disturb the settings.

E15 Overhead Camshaft Engines

1. Crank the engine until the No. 1 piston is at Top Dead Center on its compression stroke and disconnect the negative battery cable. Drain the cooling system and remove the air cleaner assembly.

2. Remove the alternator.

3. Number all spark plug wires as to their respective cylinders and remove the distributor, with all wires attached.

4. Remove the EAI pipes bracket and EGR tube at the right (EGR valve) side. Disconnect the same pipes on the front (exhaust manifold) side from the manifold.

5. Remove the exhaust manifold cover and the exhaust manifold, taking note that the center manifold nut has a different diameter than the other nuts.

6. Remove the A/C compressor bracket and the power steering pump bracket (if equipped).

7. Label and disconnect the carburetor throttle linkage, fuel line, and all vacuum and electrical connections.

8. Remove the intake manifold with

carburetor.

9. Remove water pump drive belt and pulley. Remove crankshaft pulley.

10. Remove the rocker (valve) cover.

11. Remove upper and lower dust cover on the camshaft timing belt shroud.

12. With the shroud removed, the cam sprocket, crankshaft sprocket, jackshaft sprocket, tensioner pulley, and toothed rubber timing belt are in front of you.

13. Mark the relationship of the camshaft sprocket to the timing belt and the crankshaft sprocket to the timing belt with paint or a grease pencil. This will make setting everything up during reassembly much easier if the engine is disturbed during disassembly.

14. Remove the belt tensioner pulley.

15. Mark an arrow on the timing belt showing direction of engine rotation, because the belt wears a certain way and should be replaced the way it was removed. Slide the belt off the sprockets.

16. Carefully remove the cylinder head from the block, pulling the head up evenly from both ends. If the head seems stuck, DO NOT pry it off. Tap lightly around the lower perimeter of the head with a rubber mallet to help break the joint. Label all head bolts with tape or magic marker, as they must go back in their original positions.
To Install the Cylinder Head:

1. Thoroughly clean both the cylinder block and head mating surfaces. Avoid scratching either.

2. Turn the crankshaft and set No. 1 cylinder at TDC on its compression stroke. This causes the crankshaft timing sprocket mark to be aligned with the cylinder block cover mark.

3. Align the camshaft sprocket mark with the cylinder head cover mark. This causes the valves for No. 1 cylinder to position at TDC on the compression stroke.

4. Place a new gasket on the cylinder block.

5. Install the cylinder head on the block and tighten the bolts in two stages: first to 29–33 ft. lbs. on all bolts, then go around again and torque them all up to 51–54 ft. lbs. After the engine has been warmed up, check all bolts and re-torque if necessary.

6. Reassemble in the reverse order of disassembly, making sure all timing marks are in proper alignment.

L20B Overhead Camshaft Engines

1. Crank the engine until the No. 1 piston is TDC of the compression stroke and disconnect the negative battery cable, drain the cooling system and remove the air cleaner and attending hoses.

2. Remove the alternator.

3. Disconnect the carburetor throttle linkage, the fuel line and any other vacuum lines or electrical leads, and remove the carburetor.

4. Disconnect the exhaust pipe from the exhaust manifold.

5. Remove the fan and fan pulley.

6. Remove the spark plugs.

7. Remove the rocker cover.

8. Remove the water pump.

9. Remove the fuel pump.

10. Remove the fuel pump drive cam.

11. Mark the relationship of the camshaft sprocket to the timing chain with paint or chalk. If this is done, it will not be necessary to locate the factory timing marks. Before removing the camshaft sprocket, it will be necessary to wedge the chain in place so that it will not fall down into the front cover. The factory procedure is to wedge the timing chain in place with the wooden wedge shown here. The problem with this procedure is that it may allow the chain tensioner to move out far enough to cock itself against the chain. If this happens, you'll find that the chain won't go back over the sprocket after you've put the sprocket back on. In this case, you'll have to remove the front cover and push the tensioner back. After you've wedged the chain, unbolt the camshaft sprocket and remove it.

On overhead cam engines, the wedge shown by the arrow can be used to prevent the timing chain from slipping off the crankshaft sprocket.

12. Loosen and remove the cylinder head bolts. You will need a 10 mm allen wrench to remove the head bolts. Keep the bolts in order since they are different sizes. Lift the cylinder head assembly from the engine. Remove the intake and exhaust manifolds as necessary.

13. Thoroughly clean the block and head mating surfaces. Check for warpage; see the proceding A-series engine section for instructions. Install a new head gasket on the block. Do not use sealer on the gasket.

14. With the crankshaft turned so that the No. 1 piston is at TDC of the compression stroke (if not already done so as mentioned in Step 1), make sure that the camshaft sprocket timing mark and the oblong groove in the plate are aligned.

15. Place the cylinder head in position on the cylinder block, being careful not to allow any of the valves to come in contact with any of the pistons. Do not rotate the crankshaft or camshaft separately because of possible damage which might occur to the valves.

Dimensions of wooden wedge used to hold chain in place

16. Temporarily tighten the two center right and left cylinder head bolts to 14.5 ft. lbs.

17. Install the camshaft sprocket together with the timing chain to the camshaft. Make sure the marks you made earlier line up with each other. If you get into trouble, see "Timing Chain Removal and Installation" for timing procedures.

18. Install the cylinder head bolts. Note that there are two sizes of bolts used; the longer bolts are installed on the driver's side of the engine with a smaller bolt in the center position. The remaining small bolts are installed on the opposite side of the cylinder head.

19. Tighten the cylinder head bolts in three stages: first to 29 ft. lbs., second to 43 ft. lbs., and lastly to 47–62 ft. lbs.

Tighten the cylinder head bolts on all models in the proper sequence.

20. Install and assemble the remaining components of the engine in the reverse order of removal. Adjust the valves. Fill the cooling system; start the engine and run it until normal operating temperature is reached. Retorque the cylinder head bolts to specification, then readjust the valves. Retorque the head bolts again after 600 miles, and recheck the valves at that time.

L24, L26, L28 and LD28 Overhead Cam Engines

1. Crank the engine until the No. 1 piston is at TDC of the compression stroke, disconnect the battery, and drain the cooling system.

NOTE: To set the No. 1 piston at TDC of the compression stroke on the LD28

Remove the plug in the rear plate to set the No. 1 piston at TDC—diesel engines

engine, remove the blind plug from the rear plate. Rotate the crankshaft until the marks on the flywheel and rear plate are in alignment. The No. 1 piston should now be at TDC.

2. Remove the radiator hoses and the heater hoses. Unbolt the alternator mounting bracket and move the alternator to one side.

3. If the car is equipped with air-conditioning or power steering, unbolt the compressor or pump and place it to one side. *Do not disconnect the compressor lines. Severe injury could result*.

4. Remove the fan and the fan pulley.

5. Remove the water pump. Remove the spark plug leads from the spark plugs (gasoline engine only).

6. Remove the cold start valve and the fuel pipe as an assembly. Remove the throttle linkage.

7. Remove all lines and hoses from the intake manifold. Mark them first so you will know where they go.

8. Unbolt the exhaust manifold from the exhaust pipe. The cylinder head can be removed with both the intake and exhaust manifolds in place.

9. Remove the camshaft cover.

10. Mark the relationship of the camshaft sprocket to the timing marks chain with paint. There are timing marks on the chain and the sprocket which should be visible when No. 1 piston is at TDC, but the marks are quite small and not particularly useful.

11. Before removing the camshaft sprocket, it will be necessary to wedge the chain in place so that it will not fall down into the front cover. The factory procedure is to wedge the timing chain in place with the wooden wedge shown here. The problem with this procedure is that it may allow the chain tensioner to move out far enough to cock itself against the chain. If this happens, you'll find that the chain won't go back over the sprocket after you've put the sprocket back on. In this case, you'll have to remove the front cover and push the tensioner back. After you've wedged the chain, unbolt the camshaft sprocket and remove it.

12. Remove the cylinder head bolts. They

Matchmark the timing chain to the camshaft sprocket

MATING MARK

require an allen wrench type socket adapter. Keep the bolts in order as two different sizes are used.

13. Lift off the cylinder head. You may have to tap it *lightly* with a hammer.

14. Clean the block and head mating surfaces thoroughly and check for warpage according to the procedure described in the A-series engine section. Install a new head gasket on the block and lower the head into position.

15. Install a new head gasket and place the head in position on the block.

16. Install the head bolts in their original locations.

17. Torque the head bolts in three stages: first to 29 ft. lbs., then to 43 ft. lbs., then to 62 ft. lbs.

18. Reinstall the camshaft sprocket in its original location. The chain is installed at the same time as the sprocket. Make sure the marks you made earlier line up. If the chain has slipped, or the engine has been disturbed, correct the timing as described under "Timing Chain Removal and Installation."

19. Reinstall all ancillary parts, coolant, etc.

20. Adjust the valves.

21. After 600 miles of driving, retorque the head bolts and readjust the valves.

Z20E, Z20S, Z22 Overhead Camshaft Engine

1. Complete Steps 1–5 under "L24 Overhead Camshaft Engine." Observe the following note for step 5.

NOTE: The spark plug leads should be marked, however it would be wise to mark them yourself, especially the dual spark plug models.

2. Disconnect the throttle linkage, the air cleaner or its intake hose assembly (fuel injection). Disconnect the fuel line, the return fuel line and any other vacuum lines or electrical leads. On the Z20S, remove the carburetor to avoid damaging it while removing the head.

NOTE: A good rule of thumb when disconnecting the rather complex engine wiring of today's automobiles is to put a piece of masking tape on the wire or hose and on the connection you removed the wire or hose from, then mark both pieces of tape 1, 2, 3, etc. When replacing wiring, simply match the pieces of tape.

3. Remove the EGR tube from around the rear of the engine.

4. Remove the exhaust air induction tubes from around the front of the engine on Z20S engines and from the exhaust manifold on Z20E engines.

5. Unbolt the exhaust manifold from the exhaust pipe. On the Z20S, remove the fuel pump.

6. On the Z20E, remove the intake manifold supports from under the manifold. Remove the PCV valve from around the

rear of the engine if necessary.

7. Remove the spark plugs to protect them from damage. Remove the valve cover.

8. Mark the relationship of the camshaft sprocket to the timing chain with paint or chalk. If this is done, it will not be necessary to locate the factory timing marks. Before removing the camshaft sprocket, it will be necessary to wedge the chain in place so that it will not fall down into the front cover. The factory procedure is to wedge the timing chain in place with the wooden wedge shown here. The problem with this procedure is that it may allow the chain tensioner to move out far enough to cock itself against the chain. If this happens, you'll find that the chain won't go back over the sprocket after you've put the sprocket back on. In this case, you'll have to remove the front cover and push the tensioner back. After you've wedged the chain, unbolt the camshaft sprocket and remove it.

9. Working from both ends in, loosen the cylinder head bolts and remove them. Remove the bolts securing the cylinder head to the front cover assembly.

10. Lift the cylinder head off the engine block. It may be necessary to tap the head *lightly* with a copper or brass mallet to loosen it.

To install the cylinder head:

11. Thoroughly clean the cylinder block and head surfaces and check both for warpage. See "A12, etc. Overhead Valve Engines" cylinder head removal section for procedure. (Step 1 of assembly process).

12. Fit the new head gasket. Don't use sealant. Make sure that no open valves are in the way of raised pistons, and do not rotate the crankshaft or camshaft separately because of possible damage which might occur to the valves.

13. Temporarily tighten the two center right and left cylinder head bolts to 14 ft. lbs.

14. Install the camshaft sprocket together with the timing chain to the camshaft. Make sure the marks you made earlier line up with each other. If you get into trouble, see "Timing Chain Removal and Installation" for timing procedures.

15. Install the cylinder head bolts and torque them to 20 ft. lbs., then 40 ft. lbs., then 58 ft. lbs. in the order shown in the illustration.

16. Assemble the rest of the components in the reverse order of disassembly.

NOTE: It is always wise to drain the crankcase oil after the cylinder head has been installed to avoid coolant contamination.

CA20 Overhead Camshaft Engines

1. Turn the crankshaft so that the #1 cylinder is at TDC.

2. Drain the cooling system.

3. Remove the drive belts.

4. Remove the front cover.

5. Remove the water pump pulley.

6. Remove the crankshaft pulley.

7. Remove the distributor-to-canister vacuum tube.

8. Remove the alternator adjusting bracket.

9. Remove the drive belt tensioner and camshaft sprocket.

10. Remove the water pump.

11. Remove the oil pump.

12. Loosen the cylinder head bolts in the sequence shown.

13. Lift off the head.

14. Installation is the reverse of removal. When installing the bolts, tighten the two center bolts temporarily to 15 ft. lbs. Install all the head bolts loosely. After the timing belt and front cover have been installed, torque all the head bolts in the sequence shown to the specification given in the torque chart.

Rocker Shaft

REMOVAL AND INSTALLATION

NOTE: All rocker shaft removal and installation procedures other than those detailed below are given in the "Camshaft Removal and Installation" section.

A14 and A15 Engines

1. Remove rocker cover.

2. Loosen rocker adjusting bolts and push adjusting screws away from pushrods.

3. Unbolt and remove rocker shaft assembly.

4. To install, reverse the above. Tighten rocker shaft bolts to 14–18 ft. lbs. in a circular sequence. Adjust the valves.

Intake and Exhaust Manifolds

REMOVAL AND INSTALLATION

280Z and 280Z

NOTE: It is important to replace the gasket whenever either manifold is removed. Because the manifolds share a common gasket, it is necessary to remove both manifolds for access to the gasket. Be sure to get the correct replacement gasket for your car. 1979–83 models have square exhaust ports, instead of the round ports used on 1976–78 models. The gaskets are not interchangeable.

1. Disconnect the air and vacuum hoses from the air cleaner. Disconnect the hose linking the balance tube and the temperature sensor at the balance tube end, on carbureted models.

2. Remove the air cleaner.

3. On carbureted models: disconnect the coolant, air, vacuum, and fuel hoses from the intake manifold and carburetors (drain enough coolant from the bottom of the radiator to perform this without losing coolant). Remove the carburetors from the manifold. Disconnect the rear coolant inlet pipe and the exhaust gas inlet tube at the manifold. Remove the air conditioner fast idle mechanism and bracket from the manifold, if equipped. Remove the securing nut and disconnect the coolant tube from the balance tube.

4. On fuel injected models: relieve fuel line pressure as outlined in the fuel filter replacement procedure. Disconnect the fuel injection wiring harness. Disconnect the hose from the rocker cover to the throttle chamber at the rocker cover. Drain the coolant into a clean container. Disconnect the coolant hose which runs from the heater to the coolant inlet at the inlet. Remove the bolt securing the coolant pipe/fuel pipe to the cylinder head. Remove the tube connecting the heater to the thermostat housing. Disconnect the fuel lines.

5. Disconnect the vacuum hose to the EGR valve, and the EGR tube from the exhaust manifold.

6. On models with an air pump, disconnect the air injection hose from the air injection gallery on the exhaust manifold at the check valve.

7. Disconnect the exhaust pipe from the exhaust manifold or from the exhaust outlet of the turbocharger if so equipped. Remove the exhaust manifold heat shield.

8. Remove the intake and exhaust manifolds.

9. Install the manifolds in the reverse order of removal. Always use a new gasket; air leaks will cause burnt valves and misfiring. Tighten the manifold bolts from the center outwards, in two progressive steps, to the proper torque.

Intake Manifold

REMOVAL AND INSTALLATION

All Except 810 and 1980–83 200SX/510

1. Remove the air cleaner assembly together with all of the attending hoses.

2. Disconnect the throttle linkage and fuel and vacuum lines from the carburetor.

3. The carburetor can be removed from the manifold at this point or can be removed as an assembly with the intake manifold.

4. Disconnect the intake and exhaust manifold unless both are being removed on A-series engines. Loosen the intake manifold attaching nuts, working from the two ends toward the center, and then remove them.

5. Remove the intake manifold from the engine.

810 intake manifold mounting bolt locations—gasoline engines

6. Install the intake manifold in the reverse order of removal.

810

NOTE: Certain procedures may apply only to the gasoline engine.

1. Disconnect all hoses to the air cleaner and remove the air cleaner.

2. Disconnect all air, water, vacuum and fuel hoses to the intake manifold. Remove the cold start valve and fuel pipe as an assembly. Remove the throttle linkage.

3. Remove the B.P.T. valve control tube from the intake manifold. Remove the EGR hoses.

4. Disconnect all electrical wiring to the fuel injection unit. Note the location of the wires and mark them in some manner to facilitate reinstallation.

5. Make sure all wires, hoses, lines, etc. are removed. Unscrew the intake manifold bolts. Keep the bolts in order since they are of two different sizes. Remove the manifold.

6. Installation is the reverse of removal. Use a new gasket, clean both sealing surfaces, and torque the bolts in several stages, working from the center outward.

810 intake manifold—diesel engines

1980–83 200SX/510

1. Drain the coolant.
2. On the fuel injected engine, remove the air cleaner hoses. On the carbureted engine, remove the air cleaner.

3. Remove the radiator hoses from the manifold.

4. For the carbureted engine, remove the fuel, air and vacuum hoses from the carburetor. Remove the throttle linkage and remove the carburetor.

5. Remove the throttle cable and disconnect the fuel pipe and the return fuel line on fuel injection engines. Plug the fuel pipe to prevent spilling fuel.

NOTE: When unplugging wires and hoses, mark each hose and its connection with a piece of masking tape, then match-code the two pieces of tape with the numbers 1, 2, 3, etc. When assembling, simply match the pieces of tape.

6. Remove all remaining wires, tubes, the air cleaner bracket (carbureted engines) and the E.G.R. and P.C.V. tubes from the rear of the intake manifold. Remove the air induction pipe from the front of the carbureted engine. Remove the manifold supports on the fuel injected engine.

7. Unbolt and remove the intake manifold. On fuel injected engines, remove the manifold with injectors, E.G.R. valve, fuel tubes, etc., still attached.

8. Installation is the reverse of removal. Use a new intake manifold gasket.

Z20E—remove the manifold with injectors, etc., still attached

Exhaust Manifold

REMOVAL AND INSTALLATION

NOTE: You may find that removing the intake manifold will provide better access to the exhaust manifold.

1. Remove the air cleaner assembly, if necessary for access. Remove the heat shield, if present.

2. Disconnect the exhaust pipe from the exhaust manifold. Disconnect the intake manifold from the exhaust manifold (A-series engines only) unless you are removing both.

3. Remove all temperature sensors, air induction pipes and other attachments from the manifold. Disconnect the EAI and EGR tubes from their fittings on the E-series manifold.

4. Loosen and remove the exhaust manifold attaching nuts and remove the manifold from the engine.

5. Install the exhaust manifold in the reverse order of removal.

Turbocharger

The turbocharger is installed on the exhaust manifold. This system utilizes exhaust gas energy to rotate the turbine wheel which drives the compressor turbine installed on the other end of the turbine wheel shaft. The compressor supplies compressed air to the engine to increase the charging efficiency so as to improve engine output and torque.

REMOVAL AND INSTALLATION

1. Remove the heat insulator, inlet tube, air duct hose and suction air pipe.

2. Disconnect the exhaust gas sensor harness connector, front tube, oil delivery tube and oil drain pipe.

3. Loosen the nuts which attach the turbocharger unit to the exhaust manifold, then remove the turbocharger.

NOTE: The turbocharger should not be disassembled. The turbocharger is replaced as a whole unit if found to be defective.

Front Cover

REMOVAL AND INSTALLATION, OIL SEAL REPLACEMENT

A14 and A15 Overhead Valve Engines

1. Remove the radiator. Loosen the alternator adjustment and remove the belt.

EXHAUST MANIFOLD

GASKET*

GASKET*

RETAINER

Replace if necessary.

TURBOCHARGER ASSEMBLY

EXHAUST OUTLET

Turbocharger assembly

Loosen the air pump adjustment and remove the belt on engines with the air pump system.

2. Remove the fan and unbolt and remove water pump.

3. Bend back the lock tab from the crankshaft pulley nut. Remove the nut with a heavy wrench. Rap the wrench with a hammer. The nut must be unscrewed opposite normal engine rotation. Pull off the pulley.

4. It is recommended that the oil pan be removed or loosened before the front cover is removed.

5. Unbolt and remove the timing chain cover.

6. Replace the crankshaft oil seal in the cover. Most models use a felt seal.

7. Reverse the procedure to install, using new gaskets. Apply sealant to both sides of the timing cover gasket. Front cover bolt torque is 4 ft. lbs., water pump bolt torque is 7–10 ft. lbs., and oil pan bolt torque is 4 ft. lbs.

L20B, L24, L28, Z20 and Z22 Overhead Cam Engines

NOTE: It may be necessary to remove the cylinder head to perform this operation if you cannot cut the front of the head gasket cleanly as described in Step 10. If so, you will need a new head gasket.

1. Disconnect the negative battery cable from the battery, drain the cooling system, and remove the radiator together with the upper and lower radiator hoses.

2. Loosen the alternator drive belt adjusting screw and remove the drive belt. Remove the bolts which attach the alternator bracket to the engine and set the alternator aside out of the way.

3. Remove the distributor.

4. Remove the oil pump attaching screws, and take out the pump and its drive spindle.

5. Remove the cooling fan and the fan pulley together with the drive belt.

6. Remove the water pump.

7. Remove the crankshaft pulley bolt and remove the crankshaft pulley.

FRONT COVER

FRONT OIL SEAL

Front cover—gasoline engines

8. Remove the bolts holding the front cover to the front of the cylinder block, the four bolts which retain the front of the oil pan to the bottom of the front cover, and the two bolts which are screwed down through the front of the cylinder head and into the top of the front cover.

9. Carefully pry the front cover off the front of the engine.

10. Cut the exposed front section of the oil pan gasket away from the oil pan. Do the same to the gasket at the top of the front cover. Remove the two side gaskets and clean all of the mating surfaces.

11. Cut the portions needed from a new oil pan gasket and top front cover gasket.

12. Apply sealer to all of the gaskets and position them on the engine in their proper places.

13. Apply a light coating of grease to the crankshaft oil seal and carefully mount the front cover to the front of the engine and install all of the mounting bolts. Tighten the 8 mm bolts to 7–12 ft. lbs. and the 6 mm bolts to 3–6 ft. lbs. Tighten the oil pan attaching bolts to 4–7 ft. lbs.

14. Before installing the oil pump, place the gasket over the shaft and make sure that the mark on the drive spindle faces (aligned with) the oil pump hole. Install the oil pump so that the projection on the top of the shaft is located in the exact position as when it was removed or in the 11:25 o'clock position with the piston in the No. 1 cylinder

placed at TDC on the compression stroke, if the engine was disturbed since disassembly. Tighten the oil pump attaching screws to 8–10 ft. lbs. See "Oil Pump Removal and Installation".

LD28 Diesel Engine

NOTE: It may be necessary to remove the cylinder head to perform this procedure if you cannot cut the front of the head gasket cleanly as described in Step 16. If so, you will need a new head gasket.

CAUTION

This procedure requires the removal and subsequent installation of the fuel injection pump. It is a good idea to read through the "Diesel Fuel Injection" section before you continue with this procedure—you may decide that the job is better left to a qualified service technician.

---

1. Disconnect the negative battery cable. Drain the cooling system and then remove the radiator together with the upper and lower radiator hoses.

2. Remove the fan, fan coupling and fan pulley.

3. Unscrew the retaining bolts on the crankshaft damper pulley. Use a plastic mallet and lightly tap around the outer edges of the pulley, this should loosen it enough so that you can pull if off. If not, use a two armed gear puller.

4. Remove the power steering pump, bracket and idler pulley (if so equipped).

Remove the dust cover on the diesel

5. Unscrew the five mounting bolts and remove the front dust cover.

6. Remove the thermostat housing and the bottom bypass inlet with the hose.

7. Remove the engine slinger.

8. Tag and disconnect all hoses and lines running from the injection pump. Make sure to plug any hoses or lines to prevent dust or dirt from entering.

9. Drain the engine oil.

10. Remove the oil cooled and coolant hose together with the oil filter.

11. Remove the water inlet, the oil dipstick and the right side engine mounting bracket.

12. Remove the oil pump.

13. Remove the injection pump as detailed in Chapter 4.

14. Remove the water pump.

15. Loosen the mounting bolt and remove the injection pump drive crank pulley. You will need a two armed gear puller.

16. Remove the bolts holding the front cover to the front of the cylinder block, the four bolts which retain the front of the oil pan to the bottom of the front cover, and the two bolts which are screwed down through the front of the cylinder head and into the top of the front cover.

17. Carefully pry the front cover off the front of the engine.

18. Follow Steps 10–14 of the previous "L20B, etc." procedure.

19. Installation of the remaining components is in the reverse order of removal.

E15 Overhead Cam Engines

1. Disconnect the negative battery cable from the battery, drain the cooling system, and remove the radiator together with the upper and lower radiator hoses.

2. Loosen the air conditioner belt and remove.

3. Loosen the alternator adjusting bolt, and remove the alternator belt. Unbolt the alternator mounting bracket and remove the alternator.

4. Remove the power steering belt (if equipped) by loosening the steering pump adjusting bolt.

5. Remove the water pump pulley.

6. Remove crankshaft pulley.

7. Loosen and remove the eight bolts securing the timing cover and remove the cover.

8. Installation is the reverse of removal. Adjust all accessory drive belts and tighten the mounting bolts. Torque the crank pulley bolt to 83–108 ft. lbs.; the water pump pulley bolt to 2.7–3.7 ft. lbs.; and the belt cover bolts to 2.7–3.7 ft. lbs.

Timing Chain and Camshaft

REMOVAL AND INSTALLATION

A14 and A15 Overhead Valve Engines

This operation can only be performed with the engine out of the car.

1. Remove the engine.

2. Remove the rocker cover and rocker shaft assembly.

3. Remove the pushrods.

4. Invert the engine.

5. Remove the timing chain cover.

6. Remove the chain tensioner.

7. Remove the camshaft sprocket retaining bolt.

8. Remove the camshaft sprocket, crankshaft sprocket, and timing chain as an assembly. Be careful not to lose the shims (if present) and oil slinger from behind the crankshaft sprocket.

A14 and 15 sprocket and timing chain assembly

9. Remove the distributor, and distributor drive spindle. Remove the oil pump and pump driveshaft.

10. Unbolt and remove the camshaft locating plate. Remove the camshaft carefully. The engine must be inverted to prevent the lifters from falling down into the engine. If the lifters must be removed, remove the oil pan and remove them after withdrawing the camshaft. Keep the lifters in order and return them to their original positions.

11. The camshaft bearings can be pressed out and replaced. They are available in undersizes, should it be necessary to regrind the camshaft journals. The bearings must be line-bored after installation.

12. Coat the bearings and camshaft with engine oil. Reinstall the camshaft. If the locating plate has an oil hole, it should be to the right of the engine. The locating plate is marked with the word LOWER and an arrow. The engine locating plate bolt torque is 3–4 ft. lbs. Be careful to engage the drive pin in the rear end of the camshaft with the slot in the oil pump driveshaft.

13. Camshaft end-play can be measured after temporarily replacing the camshaft sprocket and securing bolt.

If end-play is excessive, replace the locating plate. They are available in several sizes.

14. If the crankshaft or camshaft has been replaced, install the sprockets temporarily and make sure that they are parallel. Adjust by shimming under the crankshaft sprocket.

15. Assemble the sprockets and chain, aligning them.

16. Turn the crankshaft until the keyway and No. 1 piston is at top dead center. Install the sprockets and chain. The oil slinger behind the crankshaft sprocket must be replaced with the concave surface to the front. If the chain and sprocket installation is correct, the sprocket marks must be aligned between the shaft centers when No. 1 piston is at top dead center. Engine camshaft sprocket retaining bolt torque is 33–36 ft. lbs.

17. The rest of the reassembly procedure is the reverse of disassembly. Engine chain tensioner bolt torque is 4–6 ft. lbs.

Timing Belt and Camshaft

REMOVAL AND INSTALLATION

E15 Overhead Cam Engines

1. Removal of the cylinder head from the engine is optional. Crank the engine until the No. 1 piston is at Top Dead Center on its compression stroke.

2. Follow the "Front Cover" removal procedure and remove the cover. Mark the relationship of the camshaft sprocket to the timing belt and the crankshaft sprocket to the timing belt with paint or a grease pencil. This will make setting everything up during reassembly much easier, if the engine is disturbed during disassembly.

3. Remove the distributor.

4. Remove the thermostat housing.

5. Remove the timing belt from the sprockets, after loosening the belt tensioner pulley.

6. Remove the rocker cover and remove the rocker shaft.

7. Loosen and remove the cam drive sprocket.

8. Remove the camshaft front retainer plate.

NOTE: Be careful not to damage the oil seal lip between the front retainer plate and the end of the camshaft.

9. Squirt a small amount of clean oil around the camshaft bearings. Carefully slide the camshaft out of the carrier in the cylinder head.

10. To install, lightly oil the camshaft bearings with clean motor oil and slowly slide the cam into place in the cylinder head.

11. Install the camshaft front retainer plate on the cylinder head.

E-series engine valve timing mark alignment

12. Reassemble the remainder of the head assembly in the reverse order of removal. Check the valve timing after all sprockets and timing belts are installed. Tighten the camshaft drive sprocket to 4.3–5.8 ft. lbs. Install a new gasket behind the thermostat housing. Adjust the valves, and adjust all drive belts.

Timing Chain and Tensioner

REMOVAL AND INSTALLATION

L20B, L24, L28, Z20 and Z22 Overhead Cam Engines

1. Before beginning any disassembly procedures, position the No. 1 piston at TDC on the compression stroke.

2. Remove the front cover as previously outlined. Remove the camshaft cover and remove the fuel pump if it runs off a cam lobe in front of the camshaft sprocket.

3. With the No. 1 piston at TDC, the timing marks on the camshaft sprocket and the timing chain should be visible. Mark both of them with paint. Also mark the relationship of the camshaft sprocket to the camshaft. At this point you will notice that there are three sets of timing marks and locating holes in the sprocket. They are for making adjustments to compensate for timing chain stretch. See the following "Timing Chain Adjustment" for more details.

4. With the timing marks on the cam sprocket clearly marked, locate and mark the timing marks on the crankshaft sprocket.

1. Fuel pump drive cam
2. Chain guide
3. Chain tensioner
4. Crankshaft sprocket
5. Camshaft sprocket
6. Chain guide

Camshaft chain installation—OHC Engines

Timing chain and sprocket alignments— Z20 engines

Also mark the chain timing mark. Of course, if the chain is not to be re-used, marking it is useless.

5. Unbolt the camshaft sprocket and remove the sprocket along with the chain. As you remove the chain, hold it where the chain tensioner contacts it. When the chain is removed, the tensioner is going to come apart. Hold on to it and you won't lose any of the parts. There is no need to remove the chain guide unless it is being replaced.

6. Using a two-armed gear puller, remove the crankshaft sprocket.

7. Install the timing chain and the camshaft sprocket together after first positioning the chain over the crankshaft sprocket. Position the sprocket so that the marks made earlier line up. This is assuming that the engine has not been disturbed. The camshaft and crankshaft keys should both be pointed upward. If a new chain and/or gear is being installed, position the sprocket so that the timing marks on the chain align with the marks on the crankshaft sprocket and the camshaft sprocket (with both keys pointing up). The marks are on the right-hand side of the sprockets as you face the engine. The L20B has 44 pins between the mating marks of the chain and sprockets when the chain is installed correctly. The 1976–78 L24 and L28 engine used in the 810 and 280Z has 42 pins between timing marks. The L24 (1979–83), L28 (1979–83), Z20 and Z22 engines do not use the pin counting method for finding correct valve

Use the No. 2 mark and hole to align the camshaft—Z20 engines

timing. Instead, position the key in the crankshaft sprocket so that it is pointing upward and install the camshaft sprocket on the camshaft with its dowel pin at the top using the No. 2 (No. 1—L24 and L28) mounting hole and timing mark. The painted links of the chain should be on the right hand side of the sprockets as you face the engine. See the illustration.

NOTE: The factory manual refers to the pins you are to count in the L-series engines as links, but in America, this is not correct. Count the pins. There are two pins per link. This is an important step. If you do not get the exact number of pins between the timing marks, valve timing will be incorrect and the engine will either not run at all, in which case you may stand the chance of bending the valves, or the engine will run very feebly.

Timing chain and sprocket alignment— 1979–83 810, gas and diesel engines (280Z and ZX similar)

8. Install the chain tensioner. Adjust the protrusion of the tensioner spindle to zero clearance. Install the remaining components in the reverse order of disassembly.

LD28 Diesel Engine

1. Follow Steps 1–6 of the preceding "L20B, etc." procedure. You need not remove the fuel pump as detailed in Step 2.

2. Install the crankshaft sprocket. Make sure that the mating marks on the sprocket face the front of the car.

Chain tensioner mounting—1979–83 810, gas and diesel engines (280Z and ZX similar)

3. Install the timing chain and the camshaft sprocket together after first positioning the chain over the crankshaft sprocket. Position the cam sprocket so that the marks made earlier line up. This is assuming that the engine has not been disturbed. The camshaft and crankshaft keys should be pointing upward. If a new chain and/or gear is being installed, position the sprocket so that the timing marks on the chain align with the marks on the crankshaft and camshaft sprockets (with both keys pointing up). The marks are on the right-hand side of the sprockets as you face the engine. Insert the camshaft dowel pin into the No. 1 hole in the camshaft sprocket. Install and tighten the camshaft sprocket bolt.

4. Install the chain guide (if removed) and the chain tensioner. Tighten the slack side (left side when facing the engine) chain guide mounting bolt so that the protrusion of the chain tensioner spindle is 0 in.

5. Installation of the remaining components is in the reverse order of removal.

TIMING CHAIN ADJUSTMENT

When the timing chain stretches excessively, the valve timing will be adversely affected. There are three sets of holes and timing marks on the camshaft sprocket.

If the stretch of the chain roller links is excessive, adjust the camshaft sprocket location by transferring the set position of the camshaft sprocket from the factory position of No. 1 or No. 2 to one of the other positions as follows:

1. Turn the crankshaft until the No. 1 piston is at TDC on the compression stroke. Examine whether the camshaft sprocket location notch is to the left of the oblong groove on the camshaft retaining plate. If the notch in the sprocket is to the left of the groove in the retaining plate, then the chain is stretched and needs adjusting.

2. Remove the camshaft sprocket together with the chain and reinstall the sprocket and chain with the locating dowel on the camshaft inserted into either the No. 2 or 3 hole of the sprocket. The timing mark on the timing chain must be aligned with the mark on the sprocket. The amount of modification is 4 degrees of crankshaft rotation for each mark.

3. Recheck the valve timing as outlined in Step 1. The notch in the sprocket should be to the right of the groove in the camshaft retaining plate.

4. If and when the notch cannot be brought to the right of the groove, the timing chain is worn beyond repair and must be replaced.

Camshaft

REMOVAL AND INSTALLATION

L20B, L24, L28 and LD28

1. Removal of the cylinder head from the engine is optional. Remove the camshaft sprocket from the camshaft together with the timing chain.

2. Loosen the valve rocker pivot locknut and remove the rocker arm by pressing down on the valve spring.

3. Remove the two retaining nuts on the camshaft retainer plate at the front of

Remove the rocker arm by pressing down on the valve spring

Carefully slide the camshaft out of the carrier

When installing the retaining plate, make sure the oblong groove is facing the front of the engine

the cylinder head and carefully slide the camshaft out of the camshaft carrier.

4. Lightly coat the camshaft bearings with clean motor oil and carefully slide the camshaft into place in the camshaft carrier.

5. Install the camshaft retainer plate with the oblong groove in the face of the plate facing toward the front of the engine.

6. Check the valve timing as outlined under "Timing Chain Removal and Installation" and install the timing sprocket on the camshaft, tightening the bolt together with the fuel pump cam (gasoline engines only) to 86–116 ft. lb.

7. Install the rocker arms by pressing down the valve springs with a screwdriver and install the valve rocker springs.

8. Install the cylinder head, if it was removed, and assemble the rest of the engine in the reverse order of removal.

Timing chain adjustment

BEFORE ADJUSTMENT   AFTER ADJUSTMENT

① TO ③: TIMING MARK
1 TO 3: LOCATION HOLE

OBLONG GROOVE
LOCATION MATCH

Z20 and Z22

1. Removal of the cylinder head from the engine is optional. Remove the camshaft sprocket from the camshaft together with the timing chain, after setting the No. 1 piston at TDC on its compression stroke.

2. Loosen the bolts holding the rocker shaft assembly in place and remove the six center bolts. Do not pull the four end bolts out of the rocker assembly because they hold the unit together.

CAUTION

When loosening the bolts, work from the ends in and loosen all of the bolts a little at a time so that you do not strain the camshaft or the rocker assembly. Remember, the camshaft is under pressure from the valve springs.

Note the difference in rocker shafts—Z20 engines

3. After removing the rocker assembly, remove the camshaft.

NOTE: Keep the disassembled parts in order.

If you need to disassemble the rocker unit, assemble as follows.

4. Install the mounting brackets, valve rockers and springs observing the following considerations.

The two rocker shafts are different. Both have punch marks in the ends that face the front of the engine. The rocker shaft that goes on the side of the intake manifold has two slits in its end just below the punch mark. The exhaust side rocker shaft does not have slits.

The rocker arm for the intake and exhaust valves are interchangeable between cylin-

Rocker shaft mounting brackets are assembled in this order—Z20 engines

ders one and three and are identified by the mark ''1''. Similarly, the rockers for cylinders two and four are interchangeable and are identified by the mark ''2''.

The rocker shaft mounting brackets are also coded for correct placement with either an ''A'' or a ''Z'' plus a number code. See the illustration for proper placement.

To install the camshaft and rocker assembly:

5. Place the camshaft on the head with its dowel pin pointing up.

6. Fit the rocker assembly on the head, making sure you mount it on its knock pin.

7. Torque the bolts to 11–18 ft. lbs., in several stages working from the middle bolts and moving outwards on both sides.

NOTE: Make sure the engine is on TDC of the compression stroke for No. 1 piston or you may damage some valves.

See the section on timing chain installation. Adjust the valves.

Pistons and Connecting Rods

REMOVAL AND INSTALLATION

All Engines

1. Remove the cylinder head.
2. Remove the oil pan.
3. Remove any carbon buildup from the cylinder wall at the top end of the piston travel with a ridge reamer tool.
4. Position the piston to be removed at the bottom of its stroke so that the connecting rod bearing cap can be reached easily from under the engine.
5. Unscrew the connecting rod bearing cap nuts and remove the cap and lower half of the bearing.
6. Push the piston and connecting rod up and out of the cylinder block with a length of wood. Use care not to scratch the cylinder wall with the connecting rod or the wooden tool.
7. Keep all of the components from each cylinder together and install them in the cylinder from which they were removed.
8. Coat the bearing face of the connecting rod and the outer face of the pistons with engine oil.
9. See the illustrations for the correct placement of the piston rings for your model and year Datsun.
10. Turn the crankshaft until the rod journal of the particular cylinder you are working on is brought to the TDC position.
11. With the piston and rings clamped in a ring compressor, the notched mark on the head of the piston toward the front of the engine, and the oil hole side of the connecting rod toward the fuel pump side of the engine, push the piston and connecting rod assembly into the cylinder bore

until the big bearing end of the connecting rod contacts and is seated on the rod journal of the crankshaft. Use care not to scratch the cylinder wall with the connecting rod.

12. Push down farther on the piston and turn the crankshaft while the connecting rod rides around on the crankshaft rod journal. Turn the crankshaft until the crankshaft rod journal is at BDC (bottom dead center).

13. Align the mark on the connecting rod bearing cap with that on the connecting rod and tighten the bearing cap bolts to the specified torque.

14. Install all of the piston/connecting rod assemblies in the manner outlined above and assemble the oil pan and cylinder head to the engine in the reverse order of removal.

IDENTIFICATION AND POSITIONING

The pistons are marked with a notch (or F) in the piston head. When installed in the engine, the notch (or F) markings are to be facing toward the front of the engine.

The connecting rods are installed in the engine with the oil hole facing toward the right side of the engine.

NOTE: It is advisable to number the pistons, connecting rods, and bearing caps in some manner so that they can be reinstalled in the same cylinder, facing the same direction, from which they are removed.

Piston and rod positioning

ENGINE LUBRICATION

Oil Pan

REMOVAL AND INSTALLATION

All Models

1. If the engine is in the vehicle, attach a lift, support the engine, and remove the engine mounting bolts as described in "Engine Removal and Installation".

2. Raise the engine just slightly, watching to make sure that no hoses or wires are damaged.

3. Drain the engine oil.

4. Remove the oil pan bolts and slide the pan out to the rear.

To install the pan:

1. Use a new gasket, coated on both sides with sealer.

2. Apply a thin bead of silicone seal to the engine block at the junction of the block and front cover, and the junction of the block and main bearing cap. Then apply a thin coat of silicone seal to the new oil pan gasket, install the gasket to the block and install the pan.

3. Tighten the pan bolts in a circular pattern from the center to the ends, to 4–7 ft. lbs. Overtightening will distort the pan lip, causing leakage.

4. Reinstall engine mounting bolts as described under ''Engine Removal and Installation,'' using the specified torque and maintaining support until all mounts are secure.

5. Refill the oil pan to the specified level.

Rear Main Oil Seal

REPLACEMENT

All Models

In order to replace the rear main oil seal, the rear main bearing cap must be removed. Removal of the rear main bearing cap requires the use of a special rear main bearing cap puller. Also, the oil seal is installed with a special crankshaft rear oil seal drift. Unless these or similar tools are available to you, it is recommended that the oil seal be replaced by a Datsun service center.

1. Remove the engine and transmission assembly from the vehicle.

2. Remove the transmission from the engine. Remove the oil pan.

3. Remove the clutch from the flywheel.

4. Remove the flywheel from the crankshaft.

5. Remove the rear main bearing cap together with the bearing cap side seals.

Oil pump, OHC Engines

1. Pump body
2. Inner rotor and shaft
3. Outer rotor
4. Pump cover
5. Pressure regulator valve
6. Valve spring
7. Washer
8. Cap
9. Gasket

Oil pump, OHC Engines

6. Remove the rear main oil seal from around the crankshaft.

7. Apply lithium grease around the sealing lip of the oil seal and install the seal around the crankshaft using a suitable tool.

8. Apply sealer to the rear main bearing cap as indicated, install the rear main bearing cap, and tighten the cap bolts to 33–40 ft. lbs.

9. Apply sealant to the rear main bearing cap side seals and install the side seals, driving the seals into place with a suitable drift.

10. Assemble the engine and install it in the vehicle in the reverse order of removal.

Oil Pump

REMOVAL AND INSTALLATION

A14 and A15 Engines

1. Drain the engine oil.

2. Remove the front stabilizer bar if it is in the way of removing the oil pump.

3. Remove the splash shield.

4. Remove the oil pump body with the drive spindle assembly.

5. Install the A-series oil pump in the reverse order of removal.

6. Fill the pump housing with engine oil, then align the punch mark on the spindle with the hole in the oil pump.

7. With a new gasket placed over the drive spindle, install the oil pump and drive spindle assembly so that the projection on the top of the drive spindle is located in the 11:25 o'clock position.

8. Install the distributor with the metal tip of the rotor pointing toward the No. 1 spark plug tower of the distributor cap.

9. Assemble the remaining components in the reverse order of removal.

E15 Engines

1. Loosen alternator lower bolts.

2. Remove alternator belt and adjusting bar bolt.

3. Move the alternator out of the way and support it safely.

4. Disconnect the oil pressure gauge harness.

5. Remove the pump assembly.

6. For installation, fill the pump with clean engine oil and rotate it several times.

7. Install the pump on the engine using a new gasket. Torque the pump mounting bolts to 7–9 ft. lbs.

CA20 Engines

1. Drain the oil and remove the oil pan.

2. Remove the water pump belt, crankshaft pulley and crankshaft damper.

3. Remove the timing belt, crankshaft sprocket and timing belt tensioner.

4. Remove the oil pump.

5. Installation is the reverse of removal. Fill the pump with clean engine oil

and rotate it several times prior to installation. After aligning its locating notches with those of the crankshaft, install the pump along the locating notch. Apply RTV sealant to the front oil seal end of the pan prior to installation.

1976–79 L20B, L24, and L28 Engines

These oil pumps are mounted at the bottom of the engine front cover.

1. Remove the distributor.

2. Drain the oil.

3. Remove the front stabilizer.

4. Remove the splash shield.

5. Unbolt and remove the oil pump.

6. Before replacing the pump, prime the pump and position No. 1 cylinder at top dead center. Install the oil pump with the spindle punch mark toward the front. The projection on top of the drive spindle must be in the 11:25 o'clock position, viewed from above. Torque the mounting bolts to 11–15 ft. lbs.

7. Install the distributor with the rotor pointing to the No. 1 spark plug lead in the cap.

8. Reverse the rest of the removal procedure.

1980 and Later L20B, L24, L28, LD28, Z20 and Z22 Engines

1. Drain the oil from the oil pan.

2. Turn the crankshaft so that the No. 1 piston is at top dead center on its compression stroke.

3. Remove the distributor cap and mark the position of the distributor rotor in relation to the distributor base with a piece of chalk.

4. Remove the front stabilizer bar, if so equipped.

5. Remove the splash shield.

6. Remove the oil pump body with the drive spindle assembly.

7. To install, fill the pump housing with engine oil, align the punch mark on the spindle with the hole in the oil pump. The No. 1 piston should be at top dead center (TDC) on its compression stroke.

8. With a new gasket placed over the drive spindle, install the oil pump and drive spindle assembly, making sure the tip of the drive spindle fits into the distributor

FRONT

Position of the distributor drive spindle— L-series gas engines

shaft notch securely. The distributor rotor should be pointing to the match mark you made earlier.

NOTE: Great care must be taken not to disturb the distributor rotor while installing the oil pump, or the ignition timing may be wrong.

9. Assemble the remaining components in the reverse order of removal.

ENGINE COOLING

Water Pump

REMOVAL AND INSTALLATION

1. Drain the engine coolant.
2. Loosen the bolts retaining the fan shroud to the radiator and remove the shroud.
3. Loosen the belt, then remove the fan and pulley from the water pump hub.
4. Remove the bolts retaining the pump and remove the pump together with the gasket from the front cover.
5. Remove all traces of gasket material and install the pump in the reverse order. Use a new gasket and sealer. Tighten the bolts uniformly.

Thermostat

REMOVAL AND INSTALLATION

The engine thermostat is housed in the water outlet casting on the cylinder head.
1. Drain the coolant.
2. Remove the upper radiator hose and unbolt the water outlet elbow.
3. The thermostat may now be removed.
4. Reverse the removal procedure to replace the thermostat. When installing be sure that the side with the spring faces into the engine. Use a new gasket. 1979 and later models use a thermostat with an air bleed hole. The thermostat should be installed with the hole facing the left side of the engine. When replacing the Thermostat, be sure the new one has a bleed hole.

THERMOSTAT SPECIFICATIONS

Engine	Opening Temperature of Thermostat (°F)	Full Opening of Thermostat (in.)
All	183	0.315 @ 203°F

Radiator

REMOVAL AND INSTALLATION

To remove the radiator:
1. Drain the coolant.
2. Disconnect the upper hose, lower hose, and expansion tank hose.
3. Disconnect the automatic transmission oil cooler lines after draining the transmission. Cap the lines to exclude dirt.
4. If the fan has a shroud, unbolt the shroud and move it back, hanging it over the fan.
5. Remove the radiator mounting bolts and radiator.
6. Reverse the procedure to replace the radiator. Fill the automatic transmission to the proper level. Fill the cooling system.

Correct thermostat installation

EMISSION CONTROLS

Various systems are used to control crankcase vapors, exhaust emissions, and fuel vapors. The accompanying chart shows the systems used with various models and engines.

Crankcase Ventilation System

The closed crankcase ventilation system is used to route the crankcase vapors to the intake manifold (carburetor equipped) or throttle chamber (fuel injected), to be mixed and burned with the air/fuel mixture.

An air intake hose is connected between the air cleaner assembly or the throttle chamber, and the valve cover. A return hose is connected between a steel net baffle on the side of the crankcase to the intake man-

EMISSION CONTROL EQUIPMENT APPLICATIONS TABLE

Year	Model	Engine	Emission Control Systems
1976–1977	610	L20B	1, 3, 4, 6, 7, 8, 9, 10, 11
1976–1977	710	L20B	1, 3, 4, 6, 7, 8, 9, 10, 11
1976–1978	B210	A14, A15	1, 3, 4, 6, 7, 8, 10, 11
	280Z	L28	1, 6, 7, 9, 11, 12
1977–1978	280Z	L28	1, 6, 7, 9, 12
1977–1978	F-10	A14	1, 3, 4, 6, 7, 8, 10, 11
1978–1980	510	L20B	1, 3, 4, 6, 7, 8, 9
1978–1980 ①	810	L24	1, 3, 6, 7, 9, 13, 17, 18
1978–1980	200SX	L20B	1, 3, 4, 6, 7, 8, 9
1979–1980	210	A12A A14 A15	1, 3, 5, 6 1, 5, 8 10, 13, 14
1979–1980	310	A14	1, 3, 5, 6, 8, 10, 14, 17
1979–1980	280ZX &	L28	1, 3, 5, 6, 8, 10, 13, 17, 18

1. Closed crankcase ventilation system
2. Not used
3. Air pump system
4. Engine modification system
5. Fuel vapor control system
6. Exhaust gas recirculation system
7. Catalytic converter California cars only
8. Early fuel evaporation system
9. Boost controlled deceleration device
10. High altitude compensator—California option
11. TCS—manual transmission exc. California
12. Floor temperature sensing device
13. Spark timing control & 280ZX
14. Air induction system—49 states
15. Catalytic converter—50 states
16. Catalytic converter—49 states
17. 3 way catalytic converter w/exhaust sensor (California only)
18. Electronic fuel injection
① 1979–80: All 810 models are equipped with catalytic converter

1. Oil level gauge
2. Baffle plate
3. Flame arrester
4. Filter
5. P.C.V. valve
6. Steel net
7. Baffle plate

⇨ FRESH AIR
➡ BLOW-BY GAS

PCV valve air flow

Air pump system

ifold or throttle chamber, with a metering positive crankcase ventilation (PCV) valve in the hose.

To test the system, allow the engine to idle. With the PCV valve removed from the hose, a hissing sound should be heard, and vacuum should be felt when you cover the engine side of the valve with your finger. The PCV valve should be replaced at regular intervals of 24,000 miles.

Air Injection Reactor System

In this system, an air injection pump, driven by the engine, compresses, distributes, and injects filtered air into the exhaust port of each cylinder. The air combines with unburned hydrocarbons and carbon monoxide to produce harmless compounds. The system includes an air cleaner, the belt driven air pump, a check valve, and an anti-backfire valve.

The air pump draws air through a hose connected to the carburetor air cleaner or to a separate air cleaner. The pump is a rotary vane unit with an integral pressure regulating value. The pump outlet pressure passes through a check valve which prevents exhaust gas from entering the pump in case of insufficient pump outlet pressure. An anti-backfire valve admits air from the air pump into the intake manifold on deceleration to prevent backfiring in the exhaust manifold.

In 1976 California models utilized a secondary system consisting of an air control valve which limits injection of secondary air and an emergency relief valve which

controls the supply of secondary air. This system protects the converter from overheating. In 1977 the function of these two valves was taken by a single combined air control (C.A.C.) valve.

All engines with the air pump system have a series of minor alterations to accommodate the system. These are:

1. Special close-tolerance carburetor. Most engines, except the L16, require a slightly rich idle mixture adjustment.
2. Distributor with special advance curve. Ignition timing is retarded about 10° at idle in most cases.
3. Cooling system changes such as larger fan, higher fan speed, and thermostatic fan clutch. This is required to offset the in-crease in temperature caused by retarded timing at idle.
4. Faster idle speed.
5. Heated air intake on some engines.

The only periodic maintenance required on the air pump system is replacement of the air filter element and adjustment of the drive belt.

AIR PUMP SYSTEM TESTS AND REPAIRS

Air Pump Test, Removal and Installation

To test air pump output pressure:
1. The engine must be at normal operating temperature.
2. Stop the engine. Disconnect the air supply hose from the check valve at the exhaust manifold. Disconnect the vacuum

1. Air pump
2. Air pump air cleaner
3. Emergency air relief valve
4. Air relief valve
5. Air cleaner
6. Check valve
7. Air gallery pipe
8. Carburetor
9. Air control valve
10. Injection nozzle
11. Exhaust manifold
12. Anti-backfire valve

Air pump system schematic—typical

hose from the air control valve (Calif. cars only).

3. Start the engine. Check the pump pressure output at 1,500 rpm. With an L24, or L28 engine, the pressure should be 0.063 in. (16 mm.) Hg or more. 1976 and later L20B, A14 and A15, Z20S, L20B engines should have at least 3.94 in. Hg pressure.

4. If air pressure is not as specified, disconnect the air hose at the anti-backfire valve. Plug the hose opening and repeat the pressure test.

5. At 1500 rpm, close the hole of the gauge with a finger. If leaking air is felt at the relief valve, replace the relief valve.

6. Replace the pump if it does not show proper pressure.

To remove and replace the air pump:

1. Disconnect the hoses from the pump.

2. Remove the bolt holding the pump to the belt adjustment arm or adjusting bracket.

3. Unbolt the pump from the mounting bracket. Remove the belt.

4. Remove the pump from the car.

5. Reverse the procedure to install, adjusting the belt to have about ½ in. play under thumb pressure at the longest span between pulleys.

Check Valve Test, Removal and Installation

To test the check valve action:

1. The engine must be at normal operating temperature.

2. Stop the engine. Disconnect the air supply hose from the check valve at the exhaust manifold.

3. The valve plate inside the valve body should be lightly positioned against the valve seat away from the air distributor manifold.

4. Insert a small screwdriver into the valve and depress the valve plate. The plate should reset freely when released.

5. Start the engine. Increase the idle speed to 1500 rpm and check for exhaust leakage. Valve pulsation or vibration at idle is a normal condition.

To remove and replace the check valve:

1. Remove the check valve from the air gallery pipe, holding the air gallery flange with a wrench.

2. On reinstallation, the proper torque is 65–76 ft. lbs.

Air Control Valve Test, Removal and Installation

1. Warm engine to normal operating temperature.

2. Check all hoses for leaks.

3. Disconnect the outlet side hose of the valve and check for air flow. If no air is felt, replace the valve.

4. Disconnect the vacuum hose from the valve. If air flow from the air hose stops, the valve is working correctly, if air flow continues, replace the valve.

5. To replace valve, disconnect hoses and remove from bracket.

Emergency Air Relief Valve Test, Removal and Installation

1. Warm engine to normal operating temperature.

2. Check all vacuum hoses for leaks.

3. Run engine at 2000 rpm and check for air flow at outlet port of valve. If no air is felt, the valve is normal.

4. Disconnect the vacuum hose from the valve. Run engine at 2000 rpm and check for air at the outlet port of the valve. If air is felt, the valve is normal.

5. To remove valve, remove hoses and disconnect valve from mounts.

Anti-Backfire Valve Test, Removal and Installation

To test the anti-backfire valve:

1. The engine must be at normal operating temperature.

2. Disconnect the air hose from the air cleaner at the anti-backfire valve. Plug the hose.

3. Open and close the throttle rapidly. Air flow should be felt at the valve for 1-2 seconds on deceleration. If no air flow is felt or flow is felt continuously for more than 2 seconds, replace the valve.

To remove the anti-backfire valve, simply disconnect the hoses.

Air Induction System

This system is used on models 210, 310 and 810 models made in USA and Canada except California, models 200SX and 510 in all of USA and model 280ZX in USA except California.

The system is designed to send fresh air into the exhause manifold without the need of an air pump, utilizing a vacuum caused by exhaust pulsation in the exhaust manifold. The fresh air promotes burning of hot HC and Co gases which otherwise would escape the combustion process.

The only periodic maintenance required is the replacement of the air induction filter, installed at the dust side of the air cleaner at 24,000 mile or 30 month intervals.

Exhaust Gas Recirculation System (EGR)

Oxides of nitrogen (NO_x) are formed in the engine under conditions of high temperature and high pressure. Elimination of one of these two conditions reduces the formation of NO_x. Exhaust gas recirculation is used to reduce combustion temperatures in the engine.

1976–78 280Z, 1979 and Later 280ZX

Only models sold in California have EGR in 1976. All 1977-79 models have EGR,

and all 1980 and later models sold in Canada and for 49 State use in the U.S. have EGR; 1980 and later models sold in California do not have the system.

1. Solenoid valve
2. EGR valve
3. EGR vacuum tube
4. Attaching nut
5. Sealing nut
6. Rear carburetor
7. Throttle valve
8. Throttle valve fully open

L24 EGR system

An EGR valve is mounted on the intake manifold. The exhaust gas is drawn from the exhaust manifold, through the EGR valve, and into the intake manifold. The EGR valve is closed when the engine is idling; exhaust gas recirculation would cause a rough idle. As the throttle is opened, vacuum is applied to the EGR valve vacuum diaphragm. When the vacuum reaches about 2 inches of mercury (in. Hg) the diaphragm moves against spring pressure and is fully open at 8 in. Hg of vacuum. As the diaphragm moves up, it pulls the EGR valve pintle from its seat, allowing exhaust gas to be pulled into the intake manifold by intake vacuum. The valve closes at full throttle, when EGR is not needed, as a means of improving fuel economy.

1976 models have an electrically operated solenoid valve mounted on the EGR valve. The vacuum signal to the EGR valve must travel through the solenoid valve. The solenoid valve prevents EGR when the engine is cold. 1976 models use a temperature switch installed in the engine coolant outlet housing; as long as engine coolant temperatures remain below approximately 122°F (50°C) the solenoid valve blocks vacuum to the EGR valve. When the temperature of the engine coolant, or the passenger compartment, reaches normal operating temperature, the solenoid is deactivated and intake manifold vacuum is allowed to act upon the EGR valve diaphragm and exhaust gas recirculation takes place.

On 1977 and later models, a thermal vacuum valve (TVV) controls the application of vacuum to the EGR valve. When the engine coolant reaches a predetermined temperature, the TVV opens and allows vacuum to be routed to the EGR valve. Below the predetermined temperature, the TVV closes and blocks vacuum to the EGR valve.

All 1977–78 models, all 1979 U.S. models, and all 1980 and later 49 State U.S. models have a back pressure transducer (BPT) valve installed between the EGR valve and the thermal vacuum valve. The BPT valve has a diaphragm raised or lowered by exhaust back pressure. The diaphragm opens or closes an air bleed, which is connected into the EGR vacuum line. High pressure results in higher levels of EGR, because the BPT diaphragm is raised, closing off the air bleed, which allows more vacuum to reach and open the EGR valve. Thus, the amount of recirculated exhaust gas varies with exhaust pressure.

1977–78 models sold in California, 1979 models with a catalytic converter, and 1980 and later 49 State models have a vacuum delay valve (VDV) installed in the line between the thermal vacuum valve and the EGR valve. The valve delays rapid drops in vacuum in the EGR signal line, thus effecting a longer EGR time.

INSPECTION

1976

Inspect the individual components as follows.

1. Remove the EGR valve from the intake manifold.
2. Apply 6.0 in. Hg of vacuum to the EGR valve vacuum connection. The valve should open. Pinch off the connection with the vacuum still applied. The valve should remain in the raised position for at least 30 seconds.
3. Inspect the EGR valve for any signs of warpage or damage, and replace as necessary.
4. Clean the EGR valve seat with a brush and compressed air.
5. Connect the solenoid to a 12 volt DC power source. The solenoid should click when power is applied. If the valve clicks, it is considered to be working properly.
6. Check the temperature switch by removing it from the engine (drain the engine coolant first) and placing it in a container of water together with a thermometer. Connect a self-powered test light to the temperature switch electrical leads. Heat the water. The switch should conduct current when the water temperature is below 122°F (50°C) on 1976 models. The switch should stop conduction somewhere between 134–145°F (57–63°C). Replace the switch if it behaves otherwise.

1977 and Later

1. Remove the EGR valve. Apply enough vacuum to the EGR valve vacuum connection to raise the diaphragm and open the valve. Pinch off the vacuum connection. The valve should remain open for at least thirty seconds. If not, the diaphragm is leaking and the valve must be replaced.
2. Check the valve for damage (warpage, cracks, etc.) and replace as necessary.
3. Clean the valve seat with a wire brush and compressed air.
4. Install the EGR valve on the engine. Start the engine and allow it to idle. With the engine idling, reach up under the EGR

valve and raise the diaphragm by pushing it upwards with your fingers. Wear a glove to protect your hand if the engine is hot. When the diaphragm is raised, the engine idle should become rough, indicating that exhaust gases are recirculating. If the roughness does not occur, the EGR passages are blocked.

5. To check the operation of the thermal vacuum valve, drain the engine coolant and remove the valve. Connect two lengths of vacuum hose to the two TVV vacuum connections. Place the valve in a container of water together with a thermostat, with the vacuum hoses above the level of the water. Do not allow water to get into the valve. When the water temperature is below 177°F (47°C), the vacuum passage should be closed. You can check this by sucking on one of the vacuum hoses.

6. Heat the water. On 1977 models, the valve should open (conduct vacuum) when the water temperature reaches 117–127°F (47–53°C). On 1978–80 models, the valve should open at about 122°F (50°C), and remain open until the water temperature reaches about 203°F (95°C). On 1978 and later models only, the valve should close again when water temperature reaches about 208°F (98°C). Replace the valve if it behaves otherwise.

7. To test the BPT valve installed on some 1977 and later models, disconnect the two vacuum hoses on the valve. Plug one of the ports. While applying pressure to the bottom of the valve, apply vacuum to the unplugged port and check for leakage. If any exists, replace the valve.

8. To check the delay valve installed on some 1977 and later models, remove the valve and blow into the side which connects to the EGR or BPT valve. Air should flow. When air is applied to the other side, air flow resistance should be greater. If not, replace the valve.

All Models Except 280Z and 280ZX

An EGR valve is mounted on the center of the intake manifold. The recycled exhaust gas is drawn into the bottom of the intake manifold riser portion through the exhaust manifold heat stove and EGR valve. A vacuum diaphragm is connected to a timed signal port at the carburetor flange.

As the throttle valve is opened, vacuum is applied to the EGR valve vacuum diaphragm. When the vacuum reaches about 2 in. Hg, the diaphragm moves against spring pressure and is in a fully up position at 8 in. Hg of vacuum. As the diaphragm moves up, it opens the exhaust gas metering valve which allows exhaust gas to be pulled into the engine intake manifold. The system does not operate when the engine is idling because the exhaust gas recirculation would cause a rough idle.

On 1976 and later models, a thermal vacuum valve inserted in the engine thermostat housing controls the application of the vac-

uum to the EGR valve. When the engine coolant reaches a predetermined temperature, the thermal vacuum valve opens and allows vacuum to be routed to the EGR valve. Below the predetermined temperature, the thermal vacuum valve closes and blocks vacuum to the EGR valve.

All 1978–79 models and the 1980 and later 210, 510 (Canadian), 200SX (Canadian), 310 and 810 have a BPT valve installed between the EGR valve and the thermal vacuum valve. The BPT valve has a diaphragm which is raised or lowered by exhaust back pressure. The diaphragm opens or closes an air bleed, which is connected into the EGR vacuum line. High pressure results in higher levels of EGR, because the diaphragm is raised, closing off the air bleed, which allows more vacuum to reach and open the EGR valve. Thus, the amount of recirculated exhaust gas varies with exhaust pressure.

The 1980 and later 510 (USA), 200SX (USA), 310 (California), and 210 (California) use a VVT valve (venturi vacuum transducer valve) instead of the BPT valve. The VVT valve monitors exhaust pressure and carburetor vacuum in order to activate the diaphragm which controls the throttle vacuum applied to the EGR control valve. This system expands the operating range of the EGR unit, as well as increasing the EGR flow rate as compared to the BPT unit.

Many 1976 and later Datsuns are equipped with an EGR warning system which signals via a light in the dashboard that the EGR system may need service. The EGR warning light should come on every time the starter is engaged as a test to make sure the bulb is not blown. The system uses a counter which works in conjunction with the odometer, and lights the warning signal after the vehicle has traveled a pre-determined number of miles.

To reset the counter, which is mounted in the engine compartment, remove the grommet installed in the side of the counter and insert the tip of a small screwdriver into the hole. Press down on the knob inside the hole. Reinstall the grommet.

TEST

1. Remove the EGR valve and apply enough vacuum to the diaphragm to open the valve.
2. The valve should remain open for over 30 seconds after the vacuum is removed.
3. Check the valve for damage, such as warpage, cracks, and excessive wear around the valve and seat.
4. Clean the seat with a brush and compressed air and remove any deposits from around the valve and port (seat).
5. To check the operation of the thermal vacuum valve, remove the valve from the engine and apply vacuum to the ports of the valve. The valve should not allow vacuum to pass.

6. Place the valve in a container of water with a thermometer and heat the water. When the temperature of the water reaches 134°–145°F, remove the valve and apply vacuum to the ports; the valve should allow vacuum to pass through it.

7. To test the BPT valve installed on 1978 and later models, disconnect the two vacuum hoses from the valve. Plug one of the ports. While applying pressure to the bottom of the valve, apply vacuum to the unplugged port and check for leakage. If any exists, replace the valve.

8. To test the check valve installed in some 1978 and later models, remove the valve and blow into the side which connects to the EGR valve. Air should flow. When air is applied to the other side, air flow resistance should be greater. If not, replace the valve.

9. To check the VVT valve which replaces the BTP valve on some 1980 and later models, disconnect the top and bottom center hoses and apply a vacuum to the top hose. Check for leaks. If a leak is present, replace the valve.

1. Ignition switch
2. Amplifier
3. Speed detecting switch Blow 10 M.P.H.: ON (For M/T)
4. Inhibitor switch "N" or "P" position: ON (For A/T)
5. Vacuum control solenoid valve
6. Adjusting nut
7. Lock spling
8. Altitude corrector
9. Vacuum control valve
10. Diaphragm I
11. Air passage
12. Diaphragm II
13. Air control valve
14. Air passage
15. Air passage
16. Throttle valve
17. Vacuum chamber I
18. Vacuum chamber II
19. Vacuum passage
20. Idle speed adjusting screw

BCDD sectional view

Early Fuel Evaporation System (E.F.E.)

The 1976–79 A-series and all L-series engines use a system much akin to the old style exhaust manifold heat riser. In this system, a control valve is welded to the valve shaft and installed on the exhaust manifold through bushing. This heat control valve is actuated by a coil spring, thermostatic spring and counterweight which are assembled on the valve shaft projecting at the rear outside of the manifold. The counterweight is secured to the shaft with a key, bolt and snap-ring. A chamber between the intake and exhaust manifolds above the manifold stove heats the air-fuel mixture by means of exhaust gases. This results in better atomization and lower HC content.

The 1980 and later carbureted engines use coolant water heat instead of exhaust gas heat to pre-warm the fuel mixture. This system should be trouble-free.

TESTING

1. Run engine and visually check for movement.
2. In cold weather, the counterweight will move counterclockwise until it reaches the stop pin. As the engine warms up the counterweight gradually moves down.
3. As engine speed increases, the flow of exhaust gases causes the counterweight to move clockwise. When the heat control valve is full open the counterweight should again be in contact with the stop pin.

Check for bent stop pin, broken heat valve key, axial clearance between heat control valve and manifold of 0.028″0.059″, and cracks or flaking at the heat control valve weld.

Boost Control Deceleration Device (BCDD)/Throttle Opener Control System (TOCS)

The Boost Control Deceleration Device (BCDD) used on the L-series and non-fuel injected Z-series engines, and the Throttle Opener Control System (TOCS) used on A-series engines (except 1980 and later California) both accomplish the same purpose: to reduce hydrocarbon emissions during coasting conditions.

High manifold vacuum during coasting prevents the complete combustion of the air/fuel mixture because of the reduced amount of air. This condition will result in a large amount of HC emission. Enriching the air/fuel mixture for a short time (during the high vacuum condition) will reduce the emission of the HC.

However, enriching the air/fuel mixture with only the mixture adjusting screw will cause poor engine idle or invite an increase in the carbon monoxide (CO) content of the exhaust gases. The BCDD consists of an independent system that kicks in when the engine is coasting and enriches the air/fuel

1. Intake manifold
2. Stove gasket
3. Manifold stove
4. Heat shield plate
5. Snap ring
6. Counterweight
7. Key
8. Stopper pin
9. Screw
10. Thermostat spring
11. Heat control valve
12. Control valve shaft
13. Exhaust manifold
14. Cap
15. Bushing
16. Coil spring

Exhaust gas flows:
⟵ valve closed
⟵ - - valve opened

Early Fuel Evaporation (EFE) system

mixture, which reduces the hydrocarbon content of the exhaust gases. This is accomplished without adversely affecting engine idle and the carbon monoxide content of the exhaust gases.

The TOCS system used on 1980 A-series non-California models achieves the same end as the BCDD system but uses a slightly different method. The system consists of a servo diaphragm, vacuum control valve, throttle opener solenoid valve, speed detecting switch and amplifier on manual transmission models. Automatic transmission models use an inhibitor and inhibitor relay in the place of the speed detecting switch and amplifier. At the moment when the manifold vacuum increases, as during deceleration, the vacuum control valve opens to transfer the manifold vacuum to the servo diaphragm chamber, and the carburetor throttle valve opens slightly. Under this condition, the proper amount of fresh air is sucked into the combustion chamber. As a result, a more thorough ignition takes place, burning much of the HC in the exhaust gases.

1980 and Later Z20E Engine (200SX)

This engine uses a simplified version of the boost control system. In place of the BCDD (see above) is a vacuum control valve which works on manifold vacuum. Service is restricted to replacing the valve.

ADJUSTMENT

Normally, the BCDD never needs adjustment. However, if the need should arise because of suspected malfunction of the system, proceed as follows:
1. Connect a tachometer to the engine.
2. Connect a quick-response vacuum gauge to the intake manifold.
3. Disconnect the solenoid valve electrical leads.
4. Start and warm up the engine until it reaches normal operating temperature.
5. Adjust the idle speed to the proper specification.
6. Raise the engine speed to 3000-3500 rpm under no-load (transmission in Neutral or Park), then allow the throttle to close quickly. Take notice as to whether or not the engine rpm returns to idle speed and if it does, how long the fall in rpm is interrupted before it reaches idle speed.

At the moment the throttle is snapped closed at high engine rpm the vacuum in the intake manifold reaches between −23 to −27.7 in. Hg and then gradually falls to about −16.5 in. Hg at idle speed. The process of the fall of the intake manifold vacuum and the engine rpm will take one of the following three forms:
   a. When the operating pressure of the BCDD is too high, the system remains inoperative and the vacuum in the intake manifold decreases without interruption just like that of an engine without a BCDD.

   b. When the operating pressure is lower than that of the case given above, but still higher than the proper set pressure, the fall of vacuum in the intake manifold is interrupted and kept constant at a certain level (operating pressure) for about one second and then gradually falls down to the normal vacuum at idle speed.
   c. When the set of operating pressure of the BCDD is lower than the intake manifold vacuum when the throttle is suddenly released, the engine speed will not lower to idle speed.

To adjust the set operating pressure of the BCDD, remove the adjusting screw cover from the BCDD mechanism mounted on the side of the carburetor. On 810 models, the BCDD system is installed under the throttle chamber.

The adjusting screw is a left-hand threaded screw. Late models may have an adjusting nut instead of a screw. Turning the screw ⅛ of a turn in either direction will change the operation pressure about 0.79 in. Hg. Turning the screw counterclockwise will increase the amount of vacuum needed to operate the mechanism. Turning the screw clockwise will decrease the amount of vacuum needed to operate the mechanism.

The operating pressure for the BCDD on most models should be between −19.9 to −22.05 in Hg. The decrease intake manifold vacuum should be interrupted at these levels for about one second when the BCDD is operating correctly.

Don't forget to install the adjusting screw cover after the system is adjusted.

ADJUSTMENT—TOCS

Adjustment procedures for TOCS are the same as those for BCDD. Observe the following pressures.

When snapping the throttle closed as described in Step 6 for BCDD, the vacuum in the intake manifold should reach −23.6 in. Hg or above and then gradually decreases to idle lever.

The operating pressure of the TOCS should be −22.05 ± 0.79 in. Hg.

Turning the adjusting screw clockwise raises the vacuum level. Turning the screw counterclockwise lowers the vacuum level.

NOTE: When adjusting the TOCS, turn the adjusting nut in or out with the lock spring in place. Always set the lock spring properly to prevent changes in the set pressure.

Evaporative Emission Control System

These systems include the positive-seal fuel tank cap and vapor vent line of the earlier system. Additionally, a carbon canister, vacuum signal line, and canister purge line are used. The canister stores fuel vapors until vacuum pressure in the vacuum signal line forces a purge control valve to open. This admits fuel vapor from the canister into the intake manifold to be burnt with the incoming charge. The only maintenance required with this system is to change the carbon canister filter, located in the bottom of the canister, once every two years, and to periodically check the lines for leaks or obstructions.

Automatic Temperature Controlled Air Cleaner

This system is used on all Datsun models, except the 810, 280Z, 280ZX and the 200SX.

The rate of fuel atomization varies with the temperature of the air that the fuel is being mixed with. The air/fuel ratio cannot be held constant for efficient fuel combustion with a wide range of air temperatures. Cold air being drawn into the engine causes a denser and richer air/fuel mixture, inefficient fuel atomization, and thus, more hydrocarbons in the exhaust gas. Hot air being drawn into the engine causes a leaner air/fuel mixture and more efficient atomization and combustion for less hydrocarbons in the exhaust gases.

The automatic temperature controlled air cleaner is designed so that the temperature of the ambient air being drawn into the engine is automatically controlled, to hold the temperature of the air and, consequently, the fuel/air ratio at a constant rate for efficient fuel combustion.

A temperature sensing vacuum switch controls vacuum applied to a vacuum motor operating a valve in the intake snorkle of the air cleaner. When the engine is cold or the air being drawn into the engine is cold, the vacuum motor opens the valve, allowing air heated by the exhaust manifold to be drawn into the engine. As the engine warms up, the temperature sensing unit shuts off the vacuum applied to the vacuum motor which allows the valve to close, shutting off the heated air and allowing cooler, outside (under hood) air to be drawn into the engine.

TESTING

When the air around the temperature sensor of the unit mounted inside the air cleaner housing reaches 100°F, the sensor should block the flow of vacuum to the air control valve vacuum motor. When the temperature around the temperature sensor is below 100°F, the sensor should allow vacuum to pass onto the air valve vacuum motor thus blocking off the air cleaner snorkle to under hood (unheated) air.

When the temperature around the sensor is above 118°F, the air control valve should be completely open to under hood air.

If the air cleaner fails to operate correctly, check for loose or broken vacuum hoses. If the hoses are not the cause, replace the vacuum motor in the air cleaner.

Dual Spark Plug Ignition System

The California model Z-series engine has two spark plugs per cylinder. This arrangement allows the engine to burn large amounts of recirculated exhaust gases without effecting performance. In fact, the system works so well it improves gas mileage under most circumstances.

Both spark plugs fire simultaneously, which substantially shortens the time required to burn the air/fuel mixture when exhaust gases (EGR) are not being recirculated. When gases are being recirculated, the dual spark plug system brings the ignition level up to that of a single plug system which is not recirculating exhaust gases.

ADJUSTMENT

The only adjustments necessary are the regular tune-up and maintenance procedures outlined in the tune-up section.

Spark Timing Control System

The spark timing control system has been used in different forms on Datsuns since 1972. The first system, Transmission Controlled Spark System (TCS) was used on most Datsuns through 1979. This system consists of a thermal vacuum valve, a vacuum switching valve, a high gear detecting switch, and a number of vacuum hoses. Basically, the system is designed to retard full spark advance except when the car is in high gear and the engine is at normal operating temperature. At all other times, the spark advance is retarded to one degree or another.

The 1980 and later Spark Timing Control System replaces the TCS system. The major difference is that it works solely from engine water temperature changes rather than a transmission-mounted switch. The system includes a thermal vacuum valve, a vacuum delay valve, and attendant hoses. It performs the same function as the earlier TCS system; to retard tull spark advance at times when high levels of pollutants would otherwise be given off.

INSPECTION AND ADJUSTMENTS

Normally the TCS and Spark Timing Control systems should be trouble-free. However, if you suspect a problem in the system, first check to make sure all wiring (if so equipped) and hoses are connected and

free from dirt. Also check to make sure the distributor vacuum advance is working properly. If everything appears all right, connect a timing light to the engine and make sure the initial timing is correct. On vehicles with the TCS system, run the engine until it reaches normal operating temperature, and then have an assistant sit in the car and shift the transmission through all the gears slowly. If the system is functioning properly, the timing will be 10 to 15 degrees advanced in high gear (compared to the other gear positions). If the system is still not operating correctly, you will have to check for continuity at all the connections with a test light.

To test the Spark Timing Control System, connect a timing light and check the ignition timing while the temperature gauge is in the "cold" position. Write down the reading. Allow the engine to run with the timing light attached until the temperature needle reaches the center of the gauge. As the engine is warming up, check with the timing light to make sure the ignition timing retards. When the temperature needle is in the middle of the gauge, the ignition timing should advance from its previous position. If the ignition timing does not change, replace the thermal vacuum valve.

Mixture Ratio Rich-Lean and EGR Large-Small Exchange System

This system controls the air-fuel mixture ratio and the amount of recirculated exhaust gas on 1980 California A series engines (manual transmission models only) in accordance with the engine coolant temperature and car speed. The system consists of a vacuum switching valve, a power valve, a speed detecting switch located in the speedometer, a speed detecting switch amplifier and a water temperature switch.

When the coolant temperature is above 122°F and the car is traveling at least 40 miles per hour, the vacuum switching valve is on and acts to lean down the fuel mixture. It also allows a small amount of EGR to be burned on manual transmission cars. When the coolant temperature is above 122°F but the vehicle is traveling less than 40 miles per hour, the vacuum switching valve is off and allows the mixture to richen. It also allows a large amount of EGR to be burned in manual transmission models. When coolant temperature is below 122°F the vacuum switching valve is always on and acts to lean down the fuel mixture.

TESTING

Warm up the engine and jack up the drive wheels of the vehicle. Support the raised end of the car on jack stands and chock the

wheels still on the ground. Start the engine and shift the transmission into TOP speed and maintain a speedometer speed higher than 50 mph. Pinch the hose running from the vacuum switching valve to the air cleaner and see if the engine speed decreases and operates erratically. Shift the transmission into 3RD speed and run the car at a speed lower than 30 mph. Disconnect the vacuum hose running between the vacuum switching valve and the power valve, by detaching it at the power valve and blocking its open end with your finger. The engine should operate erratically. If the expected engine reaction in both of these tests does not happen, check all wiring connections and hoses for breaks and blockage.

Mixture Ratio Feedback System

The need for better fuel economy coupled to increasingly strict emission control regulations dictate a more exact control of the engine air/fuel mixture. Datsun has developed a Mixture Ratio Feedback System in response to these needs. The system is installed on all 1980 and late 280ZX and 810 models sold in California.

The principle of the system is to control the air/fuel mixture exactly, so that more complete combustion can occur in the engine, and more thorough oxidation and reduction of the exhaust gases can occur in the catalytic converter. The object is to maintain a stoichiometric air/fuel mixture, which is chemically correct for theoretically complete combustion. The stoichiometric ratio is 14.7:1 (air to fuel). At that point, the converter's efficiency is greatest in oxidizing the reducing HC, CO, and NOx into CO_2, H_2O, O_2, and N_2.

Components used in the system include an oxygen sensor, installed in the exhaust manifold upstream of the converter; a three-way oxidation-reduction catalytic converter; an electronic control unit, which is part of the electronic fuel injection control unit; and the fuel injection system itself.

The oxygen sensor reads the oxygen content of the exhaust gases. It generates an electrical signal which is sent to the control unit. The control unit then decides how to adjust the mixture to keep it at the correct air/fuel ratio. For example, if the mixture is too lean, the control unit increases the fuel metering to the injectors. The monitoring process is a continual one, so that fine mixture adjustments are going on at all times.

The system has two modes of operation: open loop and closed loop. Open loop operation takes place when the engine is still cold. In this mode, the control unit ignores signals from the oxygen sensor and provides a fixed signal to the fuel injection unit. Closed loop operation takes place when the engine and catalytic converter have warmed to normal operating temperature.

In closed loop operation, the control unit uses the oxygen sensor signals to adjust the mixture; the burned mixture's oxygen content is read by the oxygen sensor, which continues to signal the control unit, and so on. Thus, the closed loop mode is an interdependent system of information feedback.

Mixture is, of course, not readily adjustable in this system. All system adjustments require the use of a CO meter; thus, they should be entrusted to a qualified dealer with access to the equipment and special training in the system's repair. The only regularly scheduled maintenance is replacement of the oxygen sensor at 30,000 mile intervals. This procedure is covered in the following section.

It should be noted that proper operation of the system is entirely dependent on the oxygen sensor. Thus, if the sensor is not replaced at the correct interval, or if the sensor fails during normal operation, the engine fuel mixture will be incorrect, resulting in poor fuel economy, starting problems, or stumbling and stalling of the engine when warm.

OXYGEN SENSOR INSPECTION AND REPLACEMENT

An exhaust gas sensor warning light will illuminate on the instrument panel when the car has reached 30,000 miles. This is a signal that the oxygen sensor must be replaced.

Note that the warning light is not part of a repeating system; that is, after the first 30,000 mile service, the warning light will not illuminate again. However, it is important to replace the oxygen sensor every 30,000 miles, to ensure proper monitoring and control of the engine air/fuel mixture.

The oxygen sensor can be inspected using the following procedure:

1. Start the engine and allow it to reach normal operating temperature.

2. Run the engine at approximately 2,000 rpm under no load. Block the front wheels and set the parking brake.

3. An inspection lamp has been provided on the bottom of the control unit, which is located in the passenger compartment on the driver's side kick panel, next to the clutch or brake pedal. If the oxygen sensor is operating correctly, the inspection lamp will go on and off more than 5 times in 10 seconds. The inspection lamp can be more easily seen with the aid of a mirror.

4. If the lamp does not go on and off as specified, the system is not operating correctly. Check the battery, ignition system, engine oil and coolant levels, all fuses, the fuel injection wiring harness connectors, all vacuum hoses, the oil filler cap and dipstick for proper seating, and the valve clearance and engine compression. If all of these parts are in good order, and the inspection lamp still does not go on and off

at least 5 times in 10 seconds, the oxygen sensor is probably faulty. However, the possibility exists that the malfunction could be in the fuel injection control unit. The system should be tested by a qualified dealer with specific training in the Mixture Ratio Feedback System.

To replace the oxygen sensor:

1. Disconnect the negative cable from the battery.

2. Disconnect the sensor electrical lead. Unscrew the sensor from the exhaust manifold.

3. Coat the threads of the replacement sensor with a nickel base anti-seize compound. Do not use other types of compounds, since they may electrically insulate the sensor. Install the sensor into the manifold. Installation torque for the sensor is 29–36 ft. lbs. (4.0–5.0 kg-m). Connect the electrical lead. Be careful handling the electrical lead; it is easily damaged.

4. Connect the negative battery cable.

After the first 30,000 mile replacement, the warning lamp harness connector should be unplugged to extinguish the lamp. The connector is located under the right side of the instrument panel; the harness wire color is green with a yellow stripe.

Catalytic Converter

All 1976 and later models sold in California, some 1979 models sold in the other 49 States of the U.S., and all 1980 and later models sold in the U.S. and Canada have a catalytic converter, which is a muffler-shaped device installed into the exhaust system. The converter is filled with a monolithic substrate coated with small amounts of platinum and palladium. Through catalytic action, a chemical change converts carbon monoxide and hydrocarbons into carbon dioxide and water. All 1980 and later 280ZX and 810 models sold in California have a three-way catalytic converter. Platinum, palladium, and rhodium are used in an oxidation-reduction process which acts on all three major constituents of exhaust pollution; HC and CO and oxidized in the usual manner into H_2O and CO_2, and oxides of nitrogen are reduced to free hydrogen and nitrogen (H_2 and N_2 respectively).

1976–78 models (all California models) have a floor temperature warning system, consisting of a temperature sensor installed onto the floor of the car above the converter; a relay, located under the passenger seat; and a light, installed on the instrument panel. The lamp illuminates when floor temperatures become abnormally high, due to converter or engine malfunction. The light also comes on when the ignition switch is turned to Start, to check its operation. 1979 and later models do not have the warning system.

1980 and later 280ZX and 810 California models have an oxygen sensor warning light on the dashboard, which illuminates at the first 30,000 mile interval, signaling the need

for oxygen sensor replacement. The oxygen sensor is part of the Mixture Ratio Feedback System, described in this section. The Feedback System uses the three-way converter as one of its major components.

No regular maintenance is required for the catalytic converter system, except for periodic replacement of the Air Induction System filter on some 1980 and later models. The Air Induction System is described earlier in this section. The Air Induction System is used to supply the catalytic converter with fresh air; oxygen present in the air is used in the oxidation process.

REMOVAL AND INSTALLATION

1. Apply the parking brake.

2. Disconnect the temperature sensor connectors (1976–78 Calif.) and pull the connectors outside of the floor.

3. Block the wheels.

4. Jack and support the car.

5. Remove the temperature sensor protector (1976–78 Calif.).

6. Remove the catalytic converter shield.

7. Unbolt and remove the catalytic converter. Handle the converter gently; it is very delicate.

8. Installation is the reverse of removal.

FLOOR TEMPERATURE WARNING SYSTEM

1976–78 California Models

This system employs temperature sensors to warn of impending catalytic converter overheating. The system consists of a floor sensor located in the luggage compartment, a floor sensor relay located under the front passenger seat and a warning lamp located on the left side of the instrument panel.

TESTING

Lamp should light when ignition is turned to ON.

To test sensor, wait until floor temperature is below 80°F. Then heat floor area around sensor to 239°F. Light should come on.

FUEL SYSTEM— GASOLINE ENGINES

Mechanical Fuel Pump

The mechanical fuel pump is driven from the engine camshaft on all engines. It is mounted on the side of the engine on OHV engines and on the side of the cylinder head

1. Screw
2. Lockwasher
3. Cover
4. Cover gasket
5. Packing
6. Valve
7. Valve retainer
8. Valve retainer screw
9. Diaphragm
10. Pull rod
11. Spring
12. Seal washer
13. Seal
14. Lockwasher
15. Nut
16. Elbow
17. Screw
18. Lockwasher
19. Connector
20. Spring
21. Rocker arm slide spacer
22. Spacer
23. Gasket
24. Rocker arm
25. Pin
26. Rocker arm slide spacer

Typical mechanical fuel pump

on OHC engines. The pump is on the right side of all engines.

REMOVAL AND INSTALLATION

1. Disconnect the inlet and outlet lines from the pump.
2. Remove the mounting bolts.
3. Remove the pump and discard the gasket.
4. Lubricate the pump rocker arm, rocker arm pin, and lever pin before reinstallation.
5. Bolt the pump into position, using a new gasket.
6. Connect the fuel lines.

FUEL PUMP TESTS

Static Pressure Test

1. Disconnect fuel line at carburetor.
2. Attach adapter and tee to fuel line and connect a pressure gauge.
3. Run engine at varying speeds. Pressure should remain constant, 3–4 psi.

Electric Fuel Pump

DESCRIPTION

1976 and Later 280Z, 280ZX

The electric pump used on 260Z models is a transistorized plunger type which force feeds the conventional mechanical fuel pump in order to minimize the chances of vapor lock or other fuel deficiency problems. The pump is located in the corner where the differential mounting member intersects the side member. The 1976 and later Z and ZX models are equipped with one electric fuel pump mounted near the fuel tank and the right rear wheel.

1977 and Later 810 and 200SX

The fuel injected 810 and 200SX use an electric fuel pump mounted near the fuel tank on the 810 and near the center of the car on the 200SX. The pump is of wet type construction. A vane pump and roller are directly coupled to a motor filled with fuel. A relief valve in the pump is designed to open when the pressure in the fuel line rises over 64 psi. Normal operating pressure is 36–43 psi. The pump is automatically activated when the ignition switch is turned to the "start" position. If the engine stalls for some reason, the fuel pump is cut off even though the ignition switch remains in the "on" position.

PRESSURE TEST

1976–78 280Z

1. Reduce the fuel line pressure to zero, following Steps 1–3 of the pump removal and installation procedure.

2. Connect a pressure gauge into the fuel line in the engine compartment between the fuel tube and the fuel filter outlet hose.
3. Disconnect the wire from the "S" terminal of the starter motor solenoid.
4. Connect the negative battery cable.
5. Turn the ignition key to Start.
6. Pressure should be approximately 36.3 psi (2.55 kg/cm^2).
7. If not, replace the pressure regulator (see the replacement procedure following) and repeat the tests. If the pressure is still not correct, check all fuel lines for kinks or blockage, and replace the pump as necessary.

1979 and Later 280ZX

1. Reduce the fuel pressure to zero. For 1979 models, follow Steps 1–3 of the 1975–79 fuel pump replacement procedure. For 1980 and later models, follow Step 1 of the 1980 fuel pump replacement procedure.
2. On 1979 models, connect the negative battery cable.
3. Connect a fuel pressure gauge into the fuel line in the engine compartment between the fuel pipe and the fuel filter outlet hose.
4. Start the engine and read the fuel pressure. It should be approximately 30 psi (2.1 kg/cm^2) at idle, and approximately 37 psi (2.6 kg/cm^2) at any speed above idle.
5. If the pressure is incorrect, replace the pressure regulator, following the replacement procedure given later in this chapter. After replacement of the regulator, repeat the pressure test. If still incorrect, check the fuel lines for kinks or blockage, and replace the pump as necessary.

1977 and Later 810 and 200SX

1. Fuel pressure must be reduced to zero.
2. Connect a fuel pressure gauge between the fuel feed pipe and the fuel filter outlet.
3. Start the engine and read the pressure. It should be 30 psi at idle, and 37 psi at the moment the accelerator pedal is fully depressed.
4. If pressure is not as specified, replace the pressure regulator and repeat the test. If the pressure is still incorrect, check for clogged or deformed fuel lines, then replace the fuel pump.

FUNCTIONAL TEST

1976–78 280Z

1. Disconnect the cable from the "S" terminal of the starter motor solenoid.
2. Unplug the cold start valve wiring harness connector.
3. Turn the ignition key to Start. You should be able to hear the fuel pump running. If not, check the wiring circuits and fuses. If the circuits and fuses are in order, replace the pump.

1979 and Later 280ZX

1. Disconnect either the wire to the alternator "L" terminal, or the oil pressure switch connector.

2. Turn the ignition key to Start. You should be able to hear the fuel pump running. If not, check the wiring circuits and fuses; if they are in order replace the fuel pump.

1977 and Later 810 and 200SX

Fuel pressure must be reduced to zero before tests are made.

On 1977–79 810's, disconnect the ground cable from the battery. Disconnect the cold start valve wiring harness at the connector. Connect two jumper wires to the terminals of the cold start valve. Touch the other ends of the jumpers to the positive and negative terminals of the battery for a few seconds to release the pressure.

For 1980 and later 810's and 200SX's, start the engine, disconnect the harness connector of fuel pump relay-2 while the engine is running. After the engine stalls, crank it over two or three times to make sure all of the fuel pressure is released.

NOTE: If the engine will not start remove the fuel pump relay-2 harness connector and crank the engine for about 5 seconds.

REMOVAL AND INSTALLATION

1976–79 280Z and 280ZX

1. Disconnect the battery ground cable.

2. Disconnect the wiring harness to the cold start valve.

3. Using two jumper wires from the battery, energize the cold start valve for two or three seconds to relieve pressure in the fuel system.

— CAUTION —
Be careful not to short the two jumpers together.

4. Jack up the rear of the car and safely support it on stands. Have a can and a rag handy to catch any spilled fuel.

5. Clamp the hose between the fuel tank and the fuel pump.

6. Loosen the hose clamps on the fuel lines at both ends of the pump and remove the lines from the pump.

7. Remove the two retaining screws and remove the fuel pump bracket.

8. Disconnect the fuel pump harness connector. On 280Z models, roll back the carpet behind the passenger seat to reach the connector. On 280Z 2 + 2 models, remove the rear seat and remove the harness cover. Disconnect the wiring. On ZX models, remove the mat in the luggage compartment, and disconnect the harness connector at the rear of the compartment.

9. Pull the harness through the rubber grommet in the floor and remove the fuel pump.

10. Install the fuel pump in the reverse order of removal.

1980 and Later 280ZX

1. Reduce the fuel line pressure to zero: start the engine and remove the fuel pump relay #2 while the engine is running. After the engine stalls, crank the engine with the starter two or three times. Turn the ignition off.

2. Disconnect the negative battery cable.

3. Remove the luggage compartment mat. Disconnect the fuel pump harness wiring at the connector at the rear of the compartment. Push the wires and grommet through the floor.

4. Raise and support the rear of the car.

5. Clamp the hose between the fuel tank and the pump.

6. Loosen the fuel line clamps and disconnect the hoses from the pump. Have a metal container ready to catch the fuel which will spill from the lines.

7. Remove the bolts which secure the pump bracket to the body and remove the pump.

8. Installation is the reverse.

1977 and Later 810 and 200SX

1. Reduce the fuel pressure to zero. See procedures under the "Testing" section, above.

2. Disconnect the electrical harness connector at the pump. The 810 pump is located near the fuel tank. The 200SX pump is located near the center of the car.

3. Clamp the hose between the fuel tank and the pump to prevent gas from spewing out from the tank.

4. Remove the inlet and outlet hoses at the pump. Unclamp the inlet hose and allow the fuel lines to drain into a suitable container.

5. Unbolt and remove the pump. The 200SX pump and fuel damper can be removed at the same time.

6. Installation is the reverse of removal. Use new clamps and be sure all hoses are properly seated on the fuel pump body.

Carburetors

The carburetor used is a two-barrel downdraft type with a low-speed (primary) side and a high-speed (secondary) side.

All models have an electrically-operated anti-dieseling solenoid. As the ignition switch is turned off, the valve is energized and shuts off the supply of fuel to the idle circuit of the carburetor.

REMOVAL AND INSTALLATION

1. Remove the air cleaner.

2. Disconnect the fuel and vacuum lines from the carburetor.

3. Remove the throttle lever.

4. Remove the four nuts and washers retaining the carburetor to the manifold.

5. Lift the carburetor from the manifold.

6. Remove and discard the gasket used between the carburetor and the manifold.

7. Install the carburetor in the reverse order of removal, using a a new carburetor base gasket.

FUEL LEVEL ADJUSTMENT

All Nihonkikaki (Nikki) carburetors have a glass float chamber side cover marked with a fuel level line. Fuel level is adjusted by bending the float seat tab with the float cover removed and inverted, and the float fully raised.

1.3 to 1.7 mm (0.0512 to 0.0669 in)

Float level adjustment

THROTTLE LINKAGE ADJUSTMENT

On all models, make sure the throttle is wide open when the accelerator pedal is floored. Some models have an adjustable accelerator pedal stop to prevent strain on the linkage.

DASHPOT ADJUSTMENT

A dashpot is used on carburetors of cars with automatic transmission as means of slowly closing the throttle valve to prevent

1. Locknut
2. Mounting arm
3. Dashpot
4. Throttle lever

Typical dashpot

stalling. It is also used in later years as an emission control device on models with either automatic or manual transmissions. The dashpot should be adjusted to contact the throttle lever on deceleration at approximately 1900–2100 rpm for manual transmissions, or 1600–1800 rpm for automatic transmission with the L series engines, or 2000–2300 rpm for all models of the A series engine, or 2,300–2,500 rpm for all E15 engines. The 1980 and later Z20S engine's dashpot contact point should be between 1400–1600 rpm for automatic transmissions.

NOTE: Before attempting to adjust the dashpot, make sure the idle speed, timing and mixture adjustments are correct.

SECONDARY THROTTLE ADJUSTMENT

On the two stage carburetors used on Datsuns, the secondary throttle plate begins to open when the primary throttle plate has opened to an angle of approximately 50° (from the fully closed position). This works out to a clearance measurement of approximately 0.28–0.32 in. between the throttle valve and the carburetor body. This can be measured with a drill bit of the correct diameter. If adjustment is required, bend the connecting link between the two linkage assemblies.

1. Connecting lever
2. Return plate
3. Adjusting plate
4. Secondary throttle chamber
5. Primary throttle valve
a. Primary throttle opening in degrees
G. Primary throttle opening in inches

Secondary throttle adjustment

AUTOMATIC CHOKE ADJUSTMENT

1. With the engine cold, make sure the choke is fully closed (press the gas pedal all the way to the floor and release).
2. Check the choke linkage for binding. The choke plate should be easily opened

and closed with your finger. If the choke sticks or binds, it can usually be freed with a liberal application of a carburetor cleaner made for the purpose. A couple of quick squirts of the right stuff normally does the trick.

If not, the carburetor will have to be disassembled for repairs.

3. The choke is correctly adjusted when the index mark on the choke housing (notch) aligns with the center mark on the carburetor body. If the setting is incorrect, loosen the three screws clamping the choke body in place and rotate the choke cover left or right until the marks align. Tighten the screws carefully to avoid cracking the housing.

1. Thermostat cover
2. Thermostat housing
3. Groove

Choke index setting

CHOKE UNLOADER ADJUSTMENT

1. Close choke valve completely.
2. Hold choke valve by stretching a rubber band between choke shaft lever and carburetor.

1. Rubber band
2. Unloader tongue
3. Choke valve

3. Pull throttle lever until it completely opens.
4. Adjust gap between the choke plate and the carburetor body to:
A-series engines:
1976–77: 0.0791 in.
1978–80: 0.0929 in. except:
1978 and later: Non-Cal. 5 speed hatchback 210, B210 and 1980 and later Canada manual trans. A12A: 0.0854 in.
L-series engines, 1980 Z20S engine:
1976–77: 0.096 in., except:
1977 710: 0.0807–0.1122 in.
1978–80: 0.0807–0.1122 in.
E-series engines:
1982–83: 0.0929 in.
CA-series engines:
1982–83: 0.0965 in.

FAST IDLE ADJUSTMENT

1. With the carburetor removed from the vehicle, place the upper side of the fast idle screw on the second step (first step for 1977–81 L and Z engines) of the fast idle cam and measure the clearance between the throttle valve and the wall of the throttle valve chamber at the center of the throttle valve. Check it against the following specifications:
1976 B210:
0.0315–0.0346 in. M/T
0.0421–0.0461 in. A/T
1976–78 F10: 0.0287–0.0343 in.
1976 610, 710:
0.040–0.048 in. M/T
0.049–0.052 in. A/T
1977–78 B210:
0.0287–0.0343 in. M/T
0.0394–0.0449 in. A/T

Typical choke unloader adjustment

1977 710, 1978–79 510, 200SX:
0.0370–0.0465 in. M/T
0.0457–0.0551 in. A/T
1979–80 310:
0.0283–0.0350 in.
1979–82 210, A12A engine:
0.0248–0.0315 in. M/T
A14 engine:
0.0283–0.0350 in. M/T
A15 engine:
0.0386–0.0461 in. A/T
1980–81 510:
0.0299–0.0354 in. M/T
0.0378–0.0433 in. M/T
1981 310:
0.0287–0.0343 in.

Fast idle adjustment—L-series carbureted engines

1982 310:
0.0287–0.0343 in. M/T
0.0393–0.0449 in. A/T
1982 Stanza:
0.0260–0.0315 in.
1982–83 Sentra:
0.0315–0.0343 in. M/T
0.0421–0.0449 in. A/T
''M/T'' means manual transmission. ''A/T'' means automatic transmission.

NOTE: The first step of the fast idle adjustment procedure is not absolutely necessary.

2. Install the carburetor on the engine.
3. Start the engine and measure the fast idle rpm with the engine at operating temperature. The cam should be at the 2nd step.

1976 B210:
M/T 2,450–2,650 rpm
A/T 2,700–2,900 rpm
1976–78 F10:
1900–2700 rpm
1976 710, 610:
M/T 1,900–2,100 rpm
A/T 2,300–2,500 rpm
1977 710, 1978–79 510, 200SX:
M/T 1,900–2,800 rpm
A/T 2,200–3,200 rpm
1977–78 B210:
M/T 1,900–2,700 rpm
A/T 2,400–3,200 rpm
1980 and later 210, A12A, A14 engines:
49 states M/T 2,400 and 3,200 rpm
California M/T 2,300–3,100 rpm
A15 engines:
A/T 2,700–3,500 rpm
M/T 2,300–3,100 rpm
1979–81 310:
49 states 2400–3200 rpm
Calif. 2300–3100 rpm
Canada 1900–2700 rpm

1982 310:
49 states 2400–3200 rpm
Calif. 2300–3100 rpm
Canada 1900–2700 M/T
2400–3200 A/T
1982–83 Sentra:
Calif. 2,300–3,100 rpm
49 States 2,400–3,200 rpm
Canada 1,900–2,700 rpm M/T
2,400–3,200 rpm A/T

4. To adjust the fast idle speed, turn the fast idle adjusting screw counterclockwise to increase the fast idle speed and clockwise to decrease the fast idle speed.

OVERHAUL

For all carburetor overhaul procedures, please refer to ''Carburetor Service'' in the Unit Repair Section.

Fuel Injection

The fuel injection system is an electronic type, using various types of sensors to convert engine operating conditions into electrical signals. The information generated is fed to a control unit, giving it the right figures to set the injector open-valve period.

——— **CAUTION** ———
The 1979 and later Electronic Control Unit must not be installed on 1978 or earlier models. Damage to the ECU will result. A special adapter harness must be used with the factory EFI analyzer when testing the 1979 and later ECU.

For all fuel injection system repair and service procedures, please refer to ''Fuel Injection'' in the Unit Repair section.

FUEL SYSTEM— DIESEL ENGINES

Injection Pump

NOTE: The diesel injection pump is located at the right front side of the engine. In case of pump failure or damage, the pump must be replaced as an assembly, except for certain simple parts on the outside of the pump.

REMOVAL AND INSTALLATION

1. Disconnect the negative battery cable.
2. Remove the air cleaner duct. Remove the engine under cover.
3. Drain the engine coolant and then remove the radiator and its shroud.

Fast idle adjustment—E-series engines

Injection tube routing—diesel engines

4. Loosen the fan pulley nuts and then remove the drive belts (air conditioning, alternator and power steering pump).

5. Disconnect the power steering oil pump and position it out of the way.

6. Tag and disconnect the accelerator wire, the overflow hose (on the spill tube side), the fuel cut solenoid connector and the fuel return hose.

7. Tag and disconnect the potentiometer, the injection timing control solenoid valve wire, the cold start device water hoses (at the 4-way connector side) and the vacuum hoses for the vacuum modulator (A/T models only).

8. Remove the crank damper pulley. Use a plastic mallet and tap lightly around the sides, if this does not loosen the pulley you will need a two-armed gear puller.

9. Remove the pulley bracket and the idler pulley (if so equipped) and then remove the front dust cover.

10. Loosen the spring set pin, set the tensioner pulley to the "free tension" position and then tighten them.

11. Slide the injection pump drive belt off its pulleys.

12. Loosen the retaining nut and remove the injection pump drive gear. You may need a two-armed gear puller.

13. Disconnect the injection tubes at the injection nozzle side.

14. Unscrew the injection pump fixing nuts and the bracket bolt.

15. Remove the injection pump assembly with the injection tubes attached.

NOTE: If you plan to measure plunger lift, remove the injection before removing the pump.

Injection pump drive gear alignment marks—diesel engines

Installation is in the reverse order of removal. Observe the following:

1. Set the No. 1 cylinder at TDC of the compression stroke. Make sure that the grooves in the rear plate and the flywheel align and that the No. 1 cam lobe on the camshaft is in the position shown.

2. Install the injection pump and temporarily tighten the mounting bolts.

3. Use the alignment marks as shown in the illustration and install the injection pump drive gear. Tighten the nut to 43–51 ft. lbs. (59–69 Nm).

NOTE: The injection pump drive shaft is tapered.

If the drive gear is difficult to install, use a plastic mallet and drive it into place.

4. Make sure that the tensioner pulley is still in the free position and slide the injection drive belt over the pulleys.

5. The drive belt should have two timing marks on it. Align one with the mark on the crank pulley and the other with the mark on the drive gear. If the timing marks on the drive belt are not clear enough to read, set the marks on the drive gear and the crank pulley so that there are 20 cogs of the drive belt between them when it is installed.

Timing mark alignment on the injection pump drive belt—diesel engines

6. Loosen the spring set pin and the tensioner so that the belt is automatically set to the "tension" position.

7. Adjust the injection timing as detailed later in this chapter.

8. Tighten the injection pump nuts to 12–15 ft. lbs. (16–21 Nm) and the bracket bolt to 22–26 ft. lbs. (30–35 Nm).

9. Reconnect the injection tubes. Connect them to the cylinders in this order: 4, 2, 6, 1, 5, 3.

10. Bleed the air from the fuel system as detailed later in this chapter.

INJECTION PUMP TIMING

1. Remove the under cover and drain the coolant as detailed in Chapter 1.

2. Remove the coolant hoses that are connected to the cold start device.

3. Remove the power steering pump as detailed in Chapter 8.

4. Set the No. 1 cylinder at TDC of its compression stroke. Make sure that the grooves in the rear plate and the drive plate are aligned with each other. Make sure that the No. 1 camshaft lobe is in the position shown in the illustration.

5. Using two wrenches, remove the fuel injection tubes as detailed later in this chapter.

6. Loosen the fork retaining screw on the cold start device. Turn the fork 90° and then set the cold start device in the free position.

— CAUTION —
Never remove the screw on the cold start device wire. If it should be removed accidentally, the pump assembly should be readjusted at a service shop specified by the manufacturer.

DIAL INDICATOR

Remove the plug bolt and attach a dial indicator—diesel engines

7. Remove the plug bolt from the rear side of the injection pump and, in its place, attach a dial indicator.

8. Loosen the injection pump mounting nuts and bracket bolt.

9. Turn the crankshaft counterclockwise 15 to 20 degrees from the No. 1 cylinder TDC position.

10. Find the dial indicator needle rest point and set the gauge to zero.

11. Turn the crankshaft clockwise two complete revolutions in order to remove the play in the camshaft mechanism. Loosen the tensioner and then retighten it.

12. Turn the crankshaft clockwise until the No. 1 cylinder is again at TDC and then read the dial indicator.

	Plunger lift mm (in) For low altitudes
M/T	0.85 ± 0.03 (0.0335 ± 0.0012)
A/T	0.81 − 0.03 (0.0319 ± 0.0012)
	For high altitudes (Non-California model only)
M/T	0.90 ± 0.03 (0.0354 ± 0.0012)
A/T	0.85 ± 0.03 (0.0335 ± 0.0012)

13. If the dial indicator is not within the above range, turn the injection pump counterclockwise to increase the reading and clockwise to decrease it.

14. Tighten the injection pump mounting nuts and bracket bolt (torque figures are given in the preceding section).

15. Remove the dial indicator and reinstall the plug bolt with a new washer. Tighten the plug bolt to 10–14 ft. lbs. (14–20 Nm).

16. Set the fork at the cold start device in its original position by pulling on the cold start device wire and then tighten the fork screw.

17. Connect the injection tubes as detailed in the preceding section.

18. Install the power steering pump, connect the cold start device water hoses, refill the pump with coolant and replace the under cover.

BLEED THE FUEL SYSTEM

NOTE: Air should be bled from the fuel system whenever the injection pump is removed or the fuel system is repaired.

1. Loosen the priming pump vent screw and pump a few times. Make sure that the fuel overflows at the vent screw.

2. Tighten the vent screw.

3. Disconnect the fuel return hose and install a suitable hose over the overflow connector. Place a small pan under the over flow hose.

4. Prime the priming pump to make sure that the fuel overflows at the open end of the hose.

5. Remove the pan and the overflow hose and then install the return hose.

Fuel Injectors

REMOVAL AND INSTALLATION

1. Remove the injection tubes at the injector and then remove the spill tube assembly.

2. Unscrew the two mounting bolts and pull out the injectors and their washers.

3. Installation is in the reverse order of removal. Tighten the injector mounting nuts to 12–15 ft. lbs. (16–21 Nm). Tighten the injection tube-to-injector nut to 16–18 ft. lbs. (22–25 Nm). Always use a new injector small washer.

NOZZLE SIDE

COMBUSTION CHAMBER SIDE

Proper positioning of the small washer—diesel engines

MANUAL TRANSMISSION

REMOVAL AND INSTALLATION

The transmission may be removed separately from under the vehicle. Transmission removal and replacement procedure for early models is generally similar.

Rear Wheel Drive

1. Raise and support the vehicle. Disconnect the battery. Disconnect the backup light switch on all models and neutral switch, if equipped.

2. On the Z and ZX, remove the exhaust system. On models with the A14, L20B, Z20 and Z22 engine, disconnect the exhaust pipe from the manifold. On the 280Z and 280ZX and the 1980 and later 810 and 200SX, disconnect the accelerator linkage. Remove the bent shield plate on the 280Z and ZX.

3. Unbolt the driveshaft at the rear and remove. If there is a center bearing, unbolt it from the crossmember. Seal the end of the transmission extension housing to prevent leakage.

4. Disconnect the speedometer drive cable from the transmission.

5. Remove the shift lever.

6. Remove.the clutch operating cylinder from the clutch housing.

7. Support the engine with a large wood block and a jack under the oil pan.

8. Unbolt the transmission from the crossmember. Support the transmission with a jack and remove the crossmember.

9. Lower the rear of the engine to allow clearance.

10. Remove the starter.

11. Unbolt the transmission. Lower and remove it to the rear.

12. Reverse the procedure for reinstallation. Check the clutch linkage adjustment.

Front Wheel Drive

You must remove the engine/transmission unit as a whole. Refer to "Engine Mechanical" for instructions.

After removal, remove the bolts holding the transmission to the engine and separate by pulling the transmission towards the clutch housing.

NOTE: The clutch assembly will remain attached to the engine.

Installation is the reverse of removal. The bolts holding the transmission should be torqued to 10–13 ft. lbs.

1. Disc
2, 3. Clutch cover assembly with pressure plate
4. Bolt
5. Lockwasher
6. Withdrawal lever
7. Retainer spring
8. Bearing sleeve
9. Release bearing
10. Bearing sleeve holder spring
11. Dust cover
12. Return spring
13. Withdrawal lever push nut
14. Locknut

Diaphragm spring clutch—510 shown

— **CAUTION** —

If the clutch has been removed, it will have to re-aligned and when connecting drive-shafts, insert O-rings between differential side flanges and drive shafts.

CLUTCH

All models in all years use diaphragm spring pressure plates.

Rear Wheel Drive

REMOVAL AND INSTALLATION

1. Remove the transmission from the engine.
2. Insert a clutch aligning bar or similar tool all the way into the clutch disc hub. This must be done so as to support the weight of the clutch disc during removal. Mark the clutch assembly-to-flywheel relationship with paint or a center punch so that the clutch assembly can be assembled in the same position from which it is removed.
3. Loosen the bolts in sequence, a turn at a time. Remove the bolts.

L24 clutch release mechanism. (1) is the withdrawal lever, (2) is the return spring and (3) is the release bearing

4. Remove the pressure plate and clutch disc.
5. Remove the release mechanism. Apply multi-purpose grease to the bearing sleeve inside groove, the contact point of the withdrawal lever and bearing sleeve, the contact surface of the lever ball pin and lever. Replace the release mechanism.
6. Inspect the pressure plate for wear, scoring, etc., and reface or replace as necessary. Inspect the release bearing and replace as necessary. Apply a small amount of grease to the transmission splines. Install the disc on the splines and slide back and forth a few times. Remove the disc and remove excess grease on hub. Be sure no grease contacts the disc or pressure plate.

7. Install the disc, aligning it with a splined dummy shaft.
8. Install the pressure plate and torque the bolts to 11–16 ft. lbs.
9. Remove the dummy shaft.
10. Replace the transmission.

Front Wheel Drive

REMOVAL AND INSTALLATION

F10 and 1979–80 310

Because of the unique configuration of the F10 and 310 transmission/drive shaft system (transaxle), the transmission is impossible to remove from the car without removing the engine.

Due to this problem, Datsun has made provisions for clutch service through an access plate (cover) on the top of the housing. The engine and transmission need not be removed to permit repair or replacement.

NOTE: The clutch cover and pressure plate are balanced as a unit. If replacement is necessary, replace both parts.

1. Disconnect the following cables, wires and hoses:
   Battery ground cable
   Fresh air duct
   Engine harness connectors on the clutch housing
   Ignition wire between the coil and the distributor
   Carbon canister hoses
2. Remove the inspection plate from the top of the clutch housing and remove the six bolts holding the clutch cover.

Removing clutch cover bolts—F-10

NOTE: In order to reach all six bolts, you are going to have to jack up the car and, as you loosen the bolts, rotate the right front wheel with the car in top gear. This will rotate the clutch cover.

— **CAUTION** —
Be sure to loosen the bolts evenly in order.

3. Rotate the steering wheel all the way to the right and remove the inspection plate inside the right wheel well.
4. Disconnect the withdrawal lever and remove the six bolts on the bearing house. Reaching through the wheel well inspection hole, pull out the primary drive gear assembly.

NOTE: To remove the withdrawal lever pin you must first remove the E-ring that holds it to the bearing housing.

5. After removing the drive gear, go back to the engine compartment and lift the clutch cover and the disc assembly out through the open section of the clutch housing. You may also remove the diaphragm at the same time.

1. Flywheel
2. Diaphragm spring
3. Pressure plate
4. Clutch disc
5. Clutch cover
6. Push rod
7. Release bearing
8. Withdrawal lever
9. Rubber cover

F–10 clutch components

6. Remove the strap holding the pressure plate to the clutch cover and remove the clutch from the center.

NOTE: This strap must be replaced in the same position it had been in before removal. Mark the relative position before removal. Installing it out of position will cause an imbalance.

Installation is the reverse of removal. But, you must observe the following:

1. Paying particular attention to the alignment marks, reassemble the disc and cover to the pressure plate. Tighten the strap bolts to 5–6 ft. lbs. (F10), 7–9 ft. lbs. (310).

2. Put the diaphragm spring and cover assembly onto the flywheel and screw the bolts in with your fingers.

NOTE: These bolts should remain loose enough to shift the assembly when installing the drive gear. There are a pair of aligning pins on the flywheel.

3. Install the drive gear assembly by aligning the disc hub with the gear spline. After alignment, tighten the cover bolts to 5–7.2 ft. lbs.

Sentra, Stanza and 1981–82 310

1. Remove the transaxle.
2. Insert a clutch disc centering tool into the clutch disc hub for support.
3. Loosen the pressure plate bolts evenly, a little at a time to prevent distortion.
4. Remove the clutch assembly.
5. Installation is the reverse of removal. Apply a light coating of chassis lube to the clutch disc splines and the input shaft. Use a centering tool to aid installation. Torque the pressure plate bolts in a crisscross pattern, a little at a time each to 12–15 ft. lbs.

Clutch Linkage

ADJUSTMENT—HYDRAULIC CLUTCH

Refer to the Clutch Specifications Chart for clutch pedal height above floor and pedal free-play.

Pedal height is usually adjusted with a stopper limiting the upward travel of the pedal. Pedal free-play is adjusted at the master cylinder pushrod. If the pushrod is nonadjustable, free-play is adjusted by placing shims between the master cylinder and the firewall. On a few models, pedal free-play can also be adjusted at the operating (slave) cylinder pushrod. Pushrods are available in three lengths for the F-10 and 310.

ADJUSTMENT— MECHANICAL CLUTCH

All 1982 and later front wheel drive models use a mechanical clutch. Check pedal height and free travel, adjust if necessary. Refer to "Clutch Specifications" chart for proper adjustment specifications.

1. Loosen the locknut and adjust the pedal height by means of the pedal stopper. Tighten the locknut.
2. Adjust withdrawal lever play at the lever tip end with the locknuts.
3. Depress and release the clutch pedal several times and then recheck the withdrawal lever play again. Readjust if necessary.
4. Measure the pedal free travel at the center of the pedal pad.

Clutch Master Cylinder

REMOVAL AND INSTALLATION

1. Disconnect the clutch pedal arm from the pushrod.
2. Disconnect the clutch hydraulic line from the master cylinder.

NOTE: Take precautions to keep brake fluid from coming in contact with any painted surfaces.

3. Remove the nuts attaching the master cylinder and remove the master cylinder and pushrod toward the engine compartment side.
4. Install the master cylinder in the reverse order of removal and bleed the clutch hydraulic system.

Clutch Slave Cylinder

REMOVAL AND INSTALLATION

1. Remove the slave cylinder attaching bolts and the pushrod from the shift fork.
2. Disconnect the flexible fluid hose from the slave cylinder and remove the unit from the vehicle.
3. Install the slave cylinder in the reverse order of removal and bleed the clutch hydraulic system.

HYDRAULIC SYSTEM BLEEDING

Bleeding is required to remove air trapped in the hydraulic system. This operation is necessary whenever the system has been leaking or dismantled. The bleed screw is usually located on the clutch operating (slave) cylinder.

1. Remove the bleed screw dust cap.
2. Attach a tube to the bleed screw, immersing the free end in a clean container of brake fluid.
3. Fill the master cylinder with fluid.
4. Open the bleed screw about ¾ turn.
5. Depress the clutch pedal quickly. Hold it down. Have an assistant tighten the bleed screw. Allow the pedal to return slowly. Bleeder screw torque: 5–6 ft. lbs.
6. Repeat steps 2 and 5 until no more air bubbles are seen in the fluid container.
7. Remove the bleed tube. Replace the dust cap. Refill the master cylinder.

AUTOMATIC TRANSMISSION

Only external transmission adjustments and repairs, and transmission removal and re-

CLUTCH PEDAL SPECIFICATIONS

Model	Pedal Height Above Floor (inches)	Pedal Free Play (inches)
B210	6.02	0.04–0.12
210 (1980)	5.75	0.04–0.20
310 (1979–81)	7.29	0.04–0.20
710	7.09	0.04–0.20
810	6.90	0.04–0.20
F-10	6.90	0.23–0.55
200SX	7.60	0.04–0.12
510	6.50	0.04–0.20
280Z (1976–79)	8.78	0.039–0.197
280ZX (1980–83)	7.99	0.04–0.20
Stanza	6.50	0.43–0.63
Sentra, 310 (1982–83)	8.00	0.43–0.83

Automatic transmission linkage adjustment—1979 and later

1. Snap-ring
2. Dust cover
3. Pushrod
4. Piston
5. Spring
6. Inlet valve spring
7. Inlet valve
8. Spring retainer
9. Shims
10. Inlet valve release pin
11. Housing
12. Fluid reservoir
13. Reservoir cap

Clutch master cylinder—B210 shown; others similar

placement, are covered in this book.

All models use a JATCO automatic transmission, model 3N71B. This transmission uses Dexron® fluid.

Shift Linkage Adjustment

1976–78 (All But 280Z)

This adjustment is only necessary on the 1976–78 B210, 1978 200SX, all 610 and 710 models, and the 1978 510.

1. Loosen the trunnion locknuts at the lower end of the control lever. Remove the selector lever knob and console.
2. Place the selector lever in Neutral.
3. Place the transmission shift lever in neutral position by pushing it all the way forward, then pulling it back two stops.
4. Check the vertical clearance between the top of the shift lever pin and transmission control bracket. The clearance ("B") should be 0.1–1.1 mm (0.020–0.059 in.). Adjust by turning the nut at the lower end of the selector lever compression rod.
5. Check the horizontal clearance of the shift lever pin and transmission control bracket ("C"). This should be 1.0 mm. Adjust with the trunnion locknuts.
6. Replace the console, making sure that the shift pointer is correctly aligned. Install the knob.

1976–78 280Z

1. Loosen the adjusting nuts ("B").

2. Set both transmission control lever and range selector lever in the "N" position.
3. Tighten the adjusting nuts so that they both just touch the trunnion ("2").
4. Tighten the nuts. Test the shifter for proper operation.

1979 and Later (All Models)

Adjustment is made at the locknuts at the base of the shifter, which control the length of the shift control rod.

1. Place the shift lever in "D".

2. Loosen the locknuts and move the shift lever until it is firmly in the "D" range, the pointer is aligned, and the transmission is in "D" range.
3. Tighten the locknuts.
4. Check the adjustment. Start the car and apply the parking brake. Shift through all the ranges, starting in "P". As the lever is moved from "P" to "1", you should be able to feel the detents in each range. If proper adjustment is not possible, the grommets are probably worn and should be replaced.

Downshift Solenoid Check

The solenoid is controlled by a downshift switch on the accelerator linkage inside the car. To test the switch and solenoid operation:

1. Turn the ignition on.
2. Push the accelerator all the way down to actuate the switch.
3. The solenoid should click when actuated. The solenoid is screwed into the outside of the case. If there is no click, check the switch, wiring, and solenoid.

1. Control lever knob
2. Pusher
3. Control lever assembly
4. Selector range lever
5. Control lever bracket
6. Joint trunnion
7. Selector rod

Automatic transmission linkage adjustment—1976–78

Downshift solenoid

To remove the solenoid, first drain 2–3 pints of fluid, then unscrew the unit.

Neutral Safety and Backup Light Switch Adjustment

The switch unit is bolted to the left side of the transmission shift lever. The switch prevents the engine from being started in any transmission position except Park or Neutral. It also controls the backup lights.

1. Remove the transmission shift lever retaining nut and the lever.
2. Remove the switch.
3. Remove the machine screw in the case under the switch.
4. Align the switch to the case by inserting a 0.059 in. diameter pin through the hole in the switch into the screw hole. Mark the switch location.
5. Remove the pin, replace the machine screw, install the switch as marked, and replace the transmission shift lever and retaining nut.
6. Make sure while holding the brakes on, that the engine will start only in Park or Neutral. Check that the backup lights go on only in reverse.

1. Neutral safety switch
2. Manual shaft
3. Washer
4. Nut
5. Manual plate
6. Nut
7. Washer
8. Neutral safety switch
9. Transmission shift lever

Neutral safety and back-up light switch —JATCO transmission

REMOVAL AND INSTALLATION

1. Disconnect the battery cable.
2. Remove the accelerator linkage.
3. Detach the shift linkage.
4. Disconnect the neutral safety switch and downshift solenoid wiring.
5. Remove the drain plug and drain the torque converter. If there is no converter drain plug, drain the transmission. If there is no transmission drain plug, remove the pan to drain. Replace the pan to keep out dirt.
6. Remove the front exhaust pipe.
7. Remove the vacuum tube and speedometer cable.
8. Disconnect the fluid cooler tubes.
9. Remove the driveshaft and starter.
10. Support the transmission with a jack under the oil pan. Support the engine also.
11. Remove the rear crossmember.
12. Mark the relationship between the torque converter and the drive plate. Remove the four bolts holding the converter to the drive plate through the hole at the front, under the engine. Unbolt the transmission from the engine.
13. Reverse the procedure for installation. Make sure the drive plate is warped no more than 0.020 in. Torque the drive plate-to-torque converter and converter housing-to-engine bolts to 29–36 ft. lbs. Drive plate-to-crankshaft bolt torque is 101–116 ft. lbs.
14. Refill the transmission and check the fluid level.

TRANSAXLE

Shift Linkage Adjustment

MANUAL TRANSMISSION

F-10 4 Speed

1. Loosen control lever adjusting nuts.
2. Measure the initial clearance between the case cover and the shift lever when the shift lever is pushed completely into the case cover.
3. Relocate the shift lever to increase the clearance by 8 mm. Move shift lever fully downward (hand lever in 4th gear).
4. Push select lever fully upward so that hand lever guide plate touches detent pin.
5. Turn upper adjusting nut until it contacts trunnion plate then back off one full turn.
6. Tighten lower adjusting nut.

F-10 5 Speed

1. Loosen all 4 locknuts and move shift lever completely into transmission case, then back out 8 mm.

2. Move shift lever down so that gears are in 3rd position.
3. Push select lever fully down so that hand lever guide plate touches detent pin.
4. Turn selector shaft upper adjusting nut until it touches the trunnion plate. Then turn it one complete turn more and tighten lower nut.
5. Place hand lever in neutral and adjust hand lever to detent gap to one to two millimeters. Tighten lock nuts.

310 4 and 5 Speed

Adjustment can be made by adjusting the select lever.

1. Loosen the adjusting nuts at each end of the control rod lever near the bottom of the linkage.
2. Set the shift control lever in the Neutral position.
3. Fully push the shift lever (transmission side) in the direction P1, as shown in the illustration. On the four speed transmission, pull the lever back about 8 mm (0.31 in.). On the five speed, pull the shift lever back 11.5 mm (0.453 in.). With the select lever held in the above position, move the shift lever in direction P2, which engages third gear on four speed transmissions and second gear on five speed transmissions.
4. Push the control rod select lever as far as it will go in direction P3, then turn the upper adjusting nut until it touches the trunnion. Turn the nut a quarter turn more, and lock the select lever with the other adjusting nut.
5. Operate the shift control lever in the car to see if it shifts smoothly through the gears.

AUTOMATIC TRANSMISSION

Of all the vehicle covered in this book, only the 1982 310, Sentra and Stanza are available with an automatic transmission. This is the RN3F01A 3-speed unit.

Throttle Wire Adjustment

The throttle wire is adjusted by means of double nuts on the carburetor side.

1. Loosen the adjusting nuts.
2. With the throttle fully opened, turn the threaded shaft inward as far as it will go and tighten the first nut against the bracket.
3. Back off the first nut ½ turn and tighten the second nut against the bracket.
4. The throttle wire stroke between the threaded shaft and the cam should be 1.079–1.236 in.

Control Cable Adjustment

1. Place the control lever in Park.
2. Connect the control cable end to the lever in the transaxle unit, and tighten the cable securing bolt.
3. Move the lever to the 1 position.

Make sure that the lever works smoothly and quietly.

4. Place the lever in Park.

5. Make sure that the lever locks in Park. Remove the cable adjusting outer nut and loosen the inner nut. Connect the control cable to the trunnion and install the outer nut.

6. Pull on the cable a couple of times, then tighten the outer nut until it just contacts the bracket. Tighten the inner nut securely. The length of the cable between the inner end of the rubber boot and the outer end of the rod should be 4.75 in.

7. Check all parts to ensure smooth working order. Check the cable spring cotter pin to make sure that it is assembled as shown.

Band Adjustment

1. Loosen the band adjuster locknut.

2. Tighten the anchor end pin locknut to 3–4 ft. lbs.

3. Back off the anchor end pin lock nut exactly 2½ turns.

4. Tighten the locknut to 12–16 ft. lbs. making absolutely certain that the anchor end pin locknut does not move.

DRIVE AXLE

Driveshaft and U-Joints

REMOVAL AND INSTALLATION

510, 610 Sedan, 710, B210, 200SX with Automatic Transmission, 280Z and ZX

These driveshafts are the one piece type with a U-joint and flange at the rear, and a U-joint and a splined sleeve yoke which fits into the rear of the transmission, at the front.

1. Front propeller shaft
2. Rear propeller shaft
3. Dust seal
4. Snap ring
5. Ball bearing
6. Cushion
7. Center bearing insulator

Two piece driveshaft with center bearing and three U-joints

The U-joints must be disassembled for lubrication at 24,000 mile intervals if no grease fittings are present. The splines are lubricated by transmission oil.

1. Release the handbrake.

2. The insulator, pipe, and muffler on the 280Z; the front pipe and the heat shield plate must come off on 280ZX models sold in California.

3. Matchmark the flanges on the driveshaft and differential so that the driveshaft can be reinstalled in its original orientation; this will help maintain driveline balance.

4. Unbolt the rear flange.

5. Pull the driveshaft down and back.

6. Plug the transmission extension housing.

7. Reverse the procedure to install, oiling the splines. Flange bolt torque is 17–24 ft. lbs., except for the Z models, which should be tightened to 25–33 ft. lbs.

610 Wagon, 200SX with Manual Transmission, 810

These models use a driveshaft with three U-joints and a center support bearing. The driveshaft is balanced as an assembly. It is not recommended that it be disassembled.

1. Mark the relationship of the driveshaft flange to the differential flange.

2. Unbolt the center bearing bracket.

3. Unbolt the driveshaft flange from the differential flange.

4. Pull the driveshaft back under the rear axle. Plug the rear of the transmission to prevent oil or fluid loss.

5. On installation, align the marks made in Step 1. Torque the flange bolts to 17–24 ft. lbs. Center bearing bracket bolt torque is 26–35 ft. lbs. on the 610.

U-JOINT OVERHAUL

Disassembly

1. Mark the relationship of all components for reassembly.

2. Remove the snap-rings. The snap-rings seat in the needle bearing races.

3. Tap the yoke with a soft hammer to release one bearing cap. Be careful not to lose the needle rollers.

4. Remove the other bearing caps. Remove the spiders from the yokes.

Inspection

1. Spline backlash should not exceed 0.0197 in.

2. Driveshaft runout should not exceed 0.015 in.

3. On units with snap-rings seated in the needle bearing races, different thicknesses of snap-rings are available for

1. Sleeve yoke
2. Propeller shaft
3. Companion flange

Single type driveshaft with two U–joints

U-joint adjustment. Play should not exceed 0.0008 in. Use snap-rings of equal thickness on each side of the U-joint to maintain balance.

4. U-joint spiders must be replaced if their bearing journals are worn more than 0.0059 in. from their original diameter.

Assembly

1. Place the needle rollers in the races and hold them in place with grease.
2. Put the spider into place in its yokes.
3. Replace all seals.
4. Tap the races into position and secure with the snap-rings.

CENTER BEARING REPLACEMENT

The center bearing is a sealed unit which must be replaced as an assembly if defective.

1. Remove the driveshaft.
2. Paint a matchmark across where the flanges behind the center yoke are joined. This is for assembly purposes. If you don't paint or somehow mark the relationship between the two shafts, they may be out of balance when you put them back together.
3. Remove the bolts and separate the shafts. Make a matchmark on the front driveshaft half which lines up with the mark you made on the flange half.
4. You must devise a way to hold the driveshaft while unbolting the companion flange from the front driveshaft. Do not place the front driveshaft tube in a vise, because the chances are it will get crushed. The best way is to grip the flange somehow while loosening the nut. It is going to require some strength to remove.
5. Press the companion flange off the front driveshaft and press the center bearing from its mount.
6. The new bearing is already lubricated. Install it into the mount, making sure that the seals and so on are facing the same way as when removed.
7. Slide the companion flange on to the front driveshaft, aligning the marks made during removal. Install the washer and lock nut. If the washer and locknut are separate pieces, tighten them to 145–175 ft. lbs. If they are a unit, tighten it to 180–217 ft. lbs. Check that the bearing rotates freely around the driveshaft. Stake the nut.
8. Connect the companion flange to the other half of the driveshaft, aligning the marks made during removal. Tighten the bolts securely.
9. Install the driveshaft.

Half Shafts

REMOVAL AND INSTALLATION

Front Wheel Drive Only

1. Jack up the car and support it with jackstands.
2. Remove the wheel and tire assembly.
3. Remove the brake caliper assembly.
4. Pry off the cotter pin from the castellated nut on the wheel hub.
5. Loosen, but do not remove, the wheel hub nut from the halfshaft while holding the wheel hub with a suitable tool.
6. Remove the tie rod ball joint. Remove the lower ball joint. Do not reuse the nut once it has been removed; install a new nut during assembly.
7. Drain the gear oil from the transaxle.

Removing driveshaft

8. Remove the bolts holding the halfshaft flange to the transaxle. Remove the halfshaft, along with the wheel hub and knuckle.
9. Insert a suitable bar, wooden dowel or similar tool into the transaxle to prevent the sidegear from dropping inside.

---CAUTION---
When removing the transaxle, be very careful not to damage the grease seal on the transaxle side.

Removing the clip and outer ring

10. Installation is the reverse of removal. Coat the transaxle-end halfshaft spline with a molybdenum-disulfide grease before insertion. Make sure the rubber gaiters on both ends of the halfshaft are in good shape; if not, replace them (use new metal bands to retain the gaiters).

Final Drive Unit— Independent Rear Suspension

REMOVAL AND INSTALLATION

280Z

1. Chock the front wheels. Raise and support the rear of the vehicle.
2. Remove the main muffler.
3. Unbolt the driveshaft.

1. Outside joint assembly (Birfield joint)
2. Band
3. Dust cover
4. Band
5. Inner ring
6. Cage
7. Ball
8. Outer ring
9. Plug
10. Inside joint assembly (Double offset joint)

Driveshaft assembly—F-10

4. Loosen the transverse link spindle inner bolts (on the front of the front differential mounting crossmember) enough to free the crossmember.

5. Unbolt the axle shafts.

6. Support the differential unit with a jack.

7. Remove the two mounting nuts from the rear of the rear differential mounting crossmember.

8. Remove the four nuts from the bottom of the front crossmember.

9. Lower the front crossmember and final drive unit together.

10. Unbolt the front crossmember from the differential unit.

11. Reverse the procedure to install. Tighten the transverse link spindle inner bolts with the vehicle lowered to the ground and with two 150 lb. passengers.

610 Sedan

1. Chock the front wheels. Raise and support the rear of the vehicle.

2. Disconnect the handbrake rear cable driveshaft, and axle shafts.

3. Support the differential unit with a jack.

4. Unbolt the differential rear mounting crossmember from body.

5. Remove the four bolts holding the differential to the rear suspension crossmember.

6. Remove the differential to the rear.

7. Support the rear suspension crossmember with stands to prevent damage to the insulators.

8. Unbolt the differential rear mounting crossmember from the differential.

9. Reverse the procedure to install. Pry the differential unit into position.

280ZX and 810 Sedan

1. Jack up the rear of the car and drain the oil from the differential.

2. Disconnect the driveshaft.

3. Disconnect the halfshafts.

4. Remove the side flange fixing bolts, and disconnect the flange yokes together with the halfshafts. Support the case with a jack.

5. Remove the four bolts retaining the case to the suspension carrier.

6. Pull the case backwards on the jack until clear of the car.

7. After the case is removed, support

the suspension on a stand to prevent damage.

8. Installation is the reverse. Tighten the rear cover-to-insulator nuts to 65–87 ft. lbs.; the case-to-suspension bolts to 43–58 ft. lbs., and the side flange and driveshaft bolts to 36–43 ft. lbs.

Axle Shaft—Solid Rear Axle Models

REMOVAL AND INSTALLATION

NOTE: Bearings must be pressed on and off the shaft with an arbor press. Unless you have access to one, it is inadvisable to attempt any repair work on the axle shaft and bearing assemblies.

1. Remove the hub cap or wheel cover. Loosen the lug nuts.

2. Raise the rear of the car and support it safely on stands.

3. Remove the rear wheel. Remove the four brake backing plate retaining nuts. Detach the parking brake linkage from the brake backing plate.

4. Attach a slide hammer to the axle shaft and remove it. Use the slide hammer and a two-pronged puller to remove the oil seal from the housing.

NOTE: If a slide hammer is not available, the axle can sometimes be pried out using pry bars on opposing sides of the hub.

If end-play is found to be excessive, the bearing should be replaced. Shimming the bearing is not recommended as this ignores end-play of the bearing itself and could result in improper seating of the bearing.

5. Using a chisel, carefully nick the bearing retainer in three or four places. The retainer does not have to be cut, only collapsed enough to allow the bearing retainer to be slid off the shaft.

6. Pull or press the old bearing off and install the new one by pressing it into position.

7. Install the outer bearing retainer with its raised surface facing the wheel hub, and then install the bearing and the inner bearing retainer in that order on the axle shaft.

8. With the smaller chamfered side of the inner bearing retainer facing the bear-

ing, press on the retainer. The edge of the retainer should fully touch the bearing.

9. Clean the oil seal seat in the rear axle housing. Apply a thin coat of chassis grease.

10. Using a seal installation tool, drive the oil seal into the rear axle housing. Wipe a thin coat of bearing grease on the lips of the seal.

11. Determine the number of retainer gaskets which will give the correct bearing-to-outer retainer clearance of 0.01 in.

12. Insert the axle shaft assembly into the axle housing, being careful not to damage the seal. Ensure that the shaft splines engage those of the differential pinion. Align the vent holes of the gasket and the outer bearing retainer. Install the retaining bolts.

13. Install the nuts on the bolts and tighten them evenly, and in a criss-cross pattern, to 20 ft. lbs.

Half Shaft— Independent Rear Suspension Models

REMOVAL AND INSTALLATION

All Except 1982 and Later 810

1. Raise and support the car.

2. Remove the U-joint yoke flange bolts at the outside. Remove the U-joint center bolt at the differential.

3. Remove the axle shaft.

4. Installation is the reverse. Torque the outside flange bolts to 36–43 ft. lbs. (5.0–6.0 kg-m). Tighten the four differential side flange bolts to 36–43 ft. lbs. (5.0–6.0 kg-m). On axle shafts retained to the differential with a single center bolt, tighten the bolt to 17–23 ft. lbs. (2.4–3.2 kg-m), 1976–77, or 23–31 ft. lbs. (3.2–4.3 kg-m), 1978–83.

1982 and Later 810

1. Raise and support the rear of the car.

2. Disconnect the half shaft on the wheel side by removing the four flange bolts.

3. Grasp the half shaft at the center and extract it from the differential carrier by prying it with a suitable pry bar.

4. Installation is in the reverse order of removal. Install the differential end first and then the wheel end. Tighten the four flange bolts to 20–27 ft. lbs. (2.3–3.8 kg).

— **CAUTION** —
Take care not to damage the oil seal or either end of the half shaft during installation.

Use a slide hammer to remove the axle shaft—solid rear axle models

Use a chisel to collapse the bearing retainer

1. Drive shaft
2. Drive shaft ball
3. Ball spacer
4. Drive shaft stopper
5. Rubber boot
6. Boot band
7. Snap ring
8. Sleeve yoke
9. Sleeve yoke plug
10. Spider journal
11. Flange yoke
12. Oil seal
13. Needle bearing
14. Snap ring

Axle driveshaft for independent rear suspension

Stub Axle and Rear Wheel Bearings— Independent Rear Suspension Models

REMOVAL AND INSTALLATION

1. Block the front wheels. Loosen the wheel nuts, raise and support the car, and remove the wheel.

2. Remove the axle shaft.

3. On cars with rear disc brakes, unbolt the caliper and move it aside. Do not disconnect the hose from the caliper. Do not allow the caliper to hang by the hose; support the caliper with a length of wire or rest it on a suspension member.

4. Remove the brake disc on models with rear disc brakes. Remove the brake drum on cars with drum brakes.

5. Remove the stub axle nut. You will have to hold the stub axle at the outside while removing the nut from the axle shaft side. The nut will require a good deal of force to remove, so be sure to hold the stub axle firmly.

6. Remove the stub axle with a slide hammer and an adapter. The outer wheel bearing will come off with the stub axle.

7. Remove the companion flange from the lower arm.

8. Remove and discard the grease seal and inner bearing from the lower arm using a drift made for the purpose or a length of pipe of the proper diameter.

The outer bearing can be removed from the stub axle with a puller. If the grease seal or the bearings are removed, new parts must be used on assembly.

9. Clean all the parts to be reused in solvent.

10. Sealed-type bearings are used. When the new bearings are installed, the sealed side must face out. Install the sealed side of the outer bearing facing the wheel, and the sealed side of the inner bearing facing the differential.

11. Press the outer bearing onto the stub axle.

12. The bearing housing is stamped with an "A", "B", or "C", through 1978. 1979 and later models have an "N", "M", or "P". Select a spacer with the same marking. Install the spacer on the stub axle.

13. Install the stub axle into the lower arm.

14. Install the new inner bearing into the lower arm with the stub axle in place. Install a new grease seal.

15. Install the companion flange onto the stub axle.

16. Install the stub axle nut. Tighten to 181–239 ft. lbs. (25–33 kg-m).

17. Install the brake disc or drum, and the caliper if removed.

18. Install the axle shaft. Install the wheel and lower the car.

REAR SUSPENSION

Springs

REMOVAL AND INSTALLATION

Leaf Spring Type

B210, 1977–79 200SX, 710, AND F-10 AND 610 WAGONS

1. Raise the rear axle until the wheels hang free. Support the car on stands. Support the rear axle with a jack.

2. Unbolt the bottom end of shock absorber.

1. Leaf spring
2. Front mounting
3. Shackle
4. Shock absorber
5. Axle housing
6. Differential carrier
7. Torque arrester
8. Handbrake cable
9. Brake hose
10. Bound bumper

Typical leaf spring rear suspension—B210 shown

3. Unbolt the axle from the spring leaves. Unbolt and remove the front spring bracket. Lower the front of the spring to the floor.

4. Unbolt and remove the spring rear shackle.

5. Before reinstallation, coat the front bracket pin, bushing, shackle pin, and shackle bushing with a soap solution.

6. Reverse the procedure to install. The front pin nut and the shock absorber mounting should be tightened after the vehicle is lowered to the floor. Make sure that the elongated flange of the rubber bumper is to the rear.

510 AND 810 STATION WAGONS

1. Raise the rear of the car and support it with jackstands.

2. Remove the wheels and tires.

3. Disconnect the lower end of the shock absorber and remove the U-bolt nuts.

4. Place a jack under the rear axle.

5. Disconnect the spring shackle bolts at the front and rear of the spring.

6. Lower the jack slowly and remove the spring.

7. Installation is in the reverse order of removal.

Coil Spring Type

Three types of coil spring suspension are used:

Trailing Arm Type—F10, 310, 610 and Sentra

Four Bar Link Type—210, 510 and 1980–83 200SX

MacPherson Strut Type—810, 280Z and ZX and Stanza

— CAUTION —

Coil springs are under considerable tension and can exert enough force to cause bodily injury. Exercise extreme caution when working with them.

1. Axle tube
2. U-bolt
3. Shock absorber
4. Bumper rubber
5. Shackle
6. Spring seat
7. Leaf spring
8. Front pin

F–10 wagon rear suspension

TRAILING ARM TYPE

1. Raise the rear of the vehicle and support it on stands.

2. Remove the wheels.

3. Disconnect the handbrake linkage and return spring.

4. Unbolt the axle drive shaft flange at the wheel end.

5. Unbolt the rubber bumper inside the bottom of the coil spring.

6. Jack up the suspension arm and unbolt the shock absorber lower mounting.

7. Lower the jack slowly and cautiously. Remove the coil spring, spring seat, and rubber bumper.

8. Reverse the procedure to install, making sure that the flat face of the spring is at the top.

FOUR BAR LINK TYPE

1. Raise the car and support it with jackstands.

2. Support the center of the differential with a jack or other suitable tool.

3. Remove the rear wheels.

4. Remove the bolts securing the lower ends of the shock absorbers.

5. Lower the jack under the differential slowly and carefully and remove the coil springs after they are fully extended.

6. Installation is in the reverse order of removal.

MACPHERSON STRUT TYPE

For all strut overhaul procedures, please refer to "Strut Overhaul" in the Unit Repair section.

1. Suspension member
2. Suspension arm
3. Member mounting insulator
4. Differential mounting insulator
5. Coil spring
6. Bumper rubber
7. Spring seat
8. Shock absorber
9. Drive shaft
10. Differential mounting member
11. Differential carrier

Trailing arm-type rear suspension—610 shown

1. Rear axle case
2. Drain plug
3. Filler plug
4. Breather cap
5. Breather
6. Rear axle case end shim
7. Bearing collar
8. Oil seal
9. Rear axle bearing
10. Bearing spacer
11. Rear axle shaft
12. Shock absorber lower end bolt
13. Shock absorber assembly
14. Special washer
15. Shock absorber mounting bushing
16. Shock absorber mounting bushing
17. Bound bumper cover
18. Bound bumper rubber
19. Shock absorber mounting insulator
20. Coil spring
21. Upper link bushing bolt
22. Upper link bushing

Four link rear suspension

1. Differential carrier
2. Differential case mount rear member
3. Differential case mount rear insulator
4. Strut assembly
5. Link mount brace
6. Rear axle shaft
7. Drive shaft
8. Transverse link
9. Differential case mount front member
10. Differential case mount front insulator

MacPherson strut-type rear suspension—Z-car shown

280Z

1. Raise and support the rear of the car with stands placed under the frame. Remove the wheels.

2. Disconnect and plug the brake hose where it connects to the tube; disconnect the parking brake cable.

3. Disconnect the stabilizer bar at the crossmember and transverse link.

4. Remove the transverse link outer spindle nuts and spindle bolt. Pull the spindle out and separate the transverse link and strut.

5. Disconnect the outer end of the half-shaft.

6. Place a jack under the lower end of the strut. Remove the upper mounting nuts of the strut inside the cargo compartment. Carefully and slowly lower the jack until all spring tension is released, and remove the strut.

7. Installation is the reverse. The spindle is installed with the shorter length (measured from the locking bolt notch) toward the front. Be certain to bleed the brakes after installation.

810, 280ZX and Stanza

The shock absorber and spring must be removed as a unit.

1. Block the front wheels. Raise the rear of the car until the suspension hangs free and support the car with stands under the frame members.

2. Remove the upper shock absorber mounting nuts (inside the trunk on the 810, or under covers in the cargo compartment in the ZX).

3. Disconnect the lower end of the shock and remove the assembly.

4. Installation is the reverse. Install the top end of the unit first.

Shock Absorber

REMOVAL AND INSTALLATION

200SX and 210, 510, 610, 710 Sedans

1. Open the trunk and remove the cover panel if necessary to expose the shock mounts. Pry off the mount covers, if so equipped. On leaf spring models, jack up the rear of the vehicle and support the rear axle on stands.

2. Remove the two nuts holding the top of the shock absorber. Unbolt the bottom of the shock absorber.

3. Remove the shock absorber.

4. Installation is the reverse of removal.

510, 610, 710, 810 Station Wagons

1. Jack up the rear of the car and support the axle on stands.

2. Remove the lower retaining nut on the shock absorber.

1. Suspension member mounting stay
2. Suspension member mounting bolt
3. Member mounting insulator
4. Member mounting upper stopper
5. Suspension mounting bolt
6. Suspension member assembly
7. Suspension arm assembly
8. Differential mounting plate
9. Differential mounting insulator
10. Differential mounting adapter plate
11. Differential mounting bracket
12. Shock absorber assembly
13. Special washer
14. Shock absorber mounting bushing A

15. Shock absorber mounting insulator
16. Spring seat rubber
17. Shock absorber mounting bushing B
18. Bound bumper cover
19. Bound bumper
20. Dust cover
21. Coil spring
22. Suspension arm bushing
23. Stabilizer bushing
24. Stabilizer collar
25. Stabilizer mounting bushing
26. Stabilizer mounting clip
27. Stabilizer mounting bracket
28. Rear stabilizer

280 ZX and 810 sedan independent rear suspension

3. Remove the upper retaining bolt(s).
4. Remove the shock from under the car.
5. On the 610, remove the retaining strap from the old shock and install it on the replacement shock.
6. Installation is the reverse of removal.

F-10, 310 and Sentra

1. Raise and support the rear of the car.
2. Remove the wheels.
3. Support the rear arm with a jack at the lower end.
4. Remove the upper and lower shock mounting nuts.
5. Slowly and carefully lower the jack and remove the shock.
6. Installation is the reverse.

810, 280Z and ZX and Stanza

For all shock absorber removal and installation procedures and all strut overhaul procedures, please refer to "Strut Overhaul" in the Unit Repair section.

Rear Wheel Bearings

ADJUSTMENT

F-10 and 310

The rear wheel bearings on the F-10 and 310 are adjusted in the same manner as front wheel bearings. Use this procedure for all F-10 and 310 models.

1. Raise and support the rear of the car.
2. Remove the wheel.
3. Remove and discard the cotter pin.
4. Tighten the wheel bearing lock nut to 18–22 ft. lbs. (F-10) 29–33 ft. lbs. (310).
5. Rotate the drum back and forth a few revolutions to snug down the bearing.
6. On the F-10, loosen the locknut, then tighten handtight.
7. On the 310, after turning the wheel, recheck the torque of the nut then loosen it 90° from its position.
8. Check the drum rotation. If it does not move freely, check for dragging brake shoes, or dirty bearings.
9. Align the cotter pin hole in the spindle with that in the locknut, and install a new cotter pin.

10. Turn the nut slightly clockwise on the F-10 to align the holes. On the 310, tighten the nut no more than 15° to align the holes.

FRONT SUSPENSION

This independent front suspension uses MacPherson struts. Each strut combines the function of coil spring and shock absorber. The spindle is mounted to the lower part of the strut which has a single ball joint. No upper suspension arm is required in this design. The spindle and lower suspension transverse link (control arm) are located fore and aft by the tension rods to the front part of the chassis on most models. Compression rods, which run rearward, are used on the 280Z. A cross-chassis sway bar is used on all models.

Strut

REMOVAL AND INSTALLATION

All Models

1. Jack up the car and support it safely. Remove the wheel.
2. Disconnect and plug the brake hose.
3. Disconnect the tension rod (compression rod on the "Z" series) and stabilizer bar from the transverse link.
4. Unbolt the steering arm.
5. Place a jack under the bottom of the strut.
6. Open the hood and remove the nuts holding the top of the strut.
7. Lower the jack slowly and cautiously until the strut assembly can be removed.
8. Reverse the procedure to install. The self locking nuts holding the top of the strut must be replaced.

OVERHAUL

For all spring and shock absorber removal and installation procedures and any other strut overhaul procedures, please refer to "Strut Overhaul" in the Unit Repair section.

Ball Joint

INSPECTION

The lower ball joint should be replaced when play becomes excessive. Datsun does not publish specifications for this, giving instead a rotational torque figure for the ball

1. Strut mounting
2. Strut mounting bearing
3. Upper spring seat
4. Bumper rubber
5. Dust cover

6. Piston rod
7. Front spring
8. Strut assembly
9. Hub assembly
10. Spindle

11. Ball joint
12. Transverse link
13. Tension rod
14. Stabilizer
15. Suspension member

B210 strut-type front suspension. On the 280Z, the tension rods are replaced by compression rods running to the rear

1. Strut mounting insulator
2. Coil spring
3. Strut assembly
4. Stabilizer
5. Suspension crossmember
6. Tension rod bracket
7. Tension rod
8. Transverse link
9. Lower ball joint

Front suspension—200SX (510 and 810 similar)

Be sure the wheel bearings are properly adjusted before making this measurement. A double check can be made; while the tire is being moved up and down, observe the ball joint. If play is seen, replace the ball joint.

REMOVAL AND INSTALLATION

Rear Wheel Drive Models

The ball joint should be greased every 30,000 miles. There is a plugged hole in the bottom of the joint for installation of a grease fitting.

1. Raise and support the car so the wheels hang free. Remove the wheel.
2. Unbolt the tension rod (compression rod on "Z" series) and stabilizer bar from transverse link.

Separate the ball joint from the knuckle

Removing the ball joint

3. Unbolt the strut from the steering arm.
4. Remove the cotter pin and ball joint stud nut. Separate the ball joint and steering arm.
5. Unbolt the ball joint from the transverse link.
6. Reverse the procedure to install a new ball joint. Grease the joint after installation.

F-10

1. Raise the car and support with safety stands. Remove the wheel and tire.
2. Remove the nut holding the ball stud to the knuckle and force out the stud with a ball joint fork, being careful not to damage the ball joint dust cover.

joint. However, this requires removal for measurement. An effective way to determine play is to jack up the car until the wheel is clear of the ground. Do not place the jack under the ball joint; it must be unloaded. Place a long bar under the tire and move the wheel up and down. Keep one hand on top of the tire while doing this. If ¼ in. or more of play exists at the top of the tire, the ball joint should be replaced.

3. Remove the ball joint bolts and ball joint.

Install the ball joint in the reverse order of removal. Tighten the ball stud attaching nut to 22–29 ft. lbs., and the ball joint to transverse link attaching bolts to 40–47 ft. lbs.

310, Sentra and Stanza

1. Jack up the car and support it on stands.
2. Remove the wheel.
3. Remove the halfshaft.
4. Separate the ball joint from the steering knuckle with a ball joint remover, being careful not to damage the ball joint dust cover if the ball joint is to be used again.
5. Remove the other ball joint from the transverse link and remove the ball joint.

Installation is the reverse of removal. Tighten the ball stud attaching nut (from ball joint to steering knuckle) to 22–29 ft. lbs., and the ball joint to transverse link bolts to 40–47 ft. lbs.

Lower Control Arm (Transverse Link) and Ball Joint

REMOVAL AND INSTALLATION

You'll need a ball joint remover for this operation.

1. Jack up the vehicle and support it with jackstands; remove the wheel.
2. Remove the splash board, if so equipped.
3. Remove the cotter pin and castle nut from the side rod (steering arm) ball joint and separate the ball joint from the side rod. You'll need either a fork type or puller type ball joint remover.
4. Separate the steering knuckle arm from the MacPherson strut.
5. Remove the tension rod and stabilizer bar from the lower arm. Front wheel drive models do not have tension rods. On Z models through 1978, remove the compression rod.
6. Remove the nuts or bolts connecting the lower control arm (transverse link) to the suspension crossmember on all models.
7. On the 810, to remove the transverse link (control arm) on the steering gear side, separate the gear arm from the sector shaft and lower steering linkage; to remove the transverse link on the idler arm side, detach the idler arm assembly from the body frame and lower steering linkage.
8. Remove the lower control arm (transverse link) with the suspension ball joint and knuckle arm still attached.

Installation is the reverse of removal with the following notes.

9. When installing the control arm, temporarily tighten the nuts and/or bolts securing the control arm to the suspension crossmember. Tighten them fully only after the car is sitting on its wheels.
10. Lubricate the ball joints after assembly.

Wheel Alignment

Caster and camber angles cannot be adjusted except by replacing worn or bent parts. Suspension height is adjusted by replacing the front springs. Various springs are available for adjustment. Toe-in is adjusted by changing the length of the steering side-rods. The length of these rods should always be equal. Steering angles are adjusted by means of a stop bolt on each steering arm.

Toe adjustment is made at the tie-rod

STEERING

Steering Wheel

REMOVAL AND INSTALLATION

1. Position the wheels in the straight-ahead direction. The steering wheel should be right-side up and level.
2. Disconnect the battery ground cable.
3. Look at the back of your steering wheel. If there are countersunk screws in the back of the spokes, remove the screws and pull off the horn pad. Some models have a horn wire running from the pad to the steering wheel. Disconnect it.

There are three other types of horn buttons or rings on Datsuns. The first simply pulls off. The second, which is usually a large, semi-triangular pad, must be pushed up, then pulled off. The third must be pushed in and turned clockwise.

4. Remove the rest of the horn switching mechanism, noting the relative location of the parts. Remove the mechanism only if it hinders subsequent wheel removal procedures.

STEERING APPLICATIONS

Model	Type
510, 610, 521, 710, B210, 210, 200SX, 810, 280ZX①	Recirculating ball
280Z F-10 280ZX② 310 Sentra Stanza	Rack and pinion

① Power steering
② Manual steering

610 horn pad removal

Horn pads on later models pull right off

5. Match-mark the top of the steering column shaft and the steering wheel flange.
6. Remove the attaching nut and remove the steering wheel with a puller.

--- **CAUTION** ---
Do not strike the shaft with a hammer, which may cause the column to collapse.

7. Install the steering wheel in the reverse order of removal, aligning the punch marks. Do not drive or hammer the wheel into place, or you may cause the collapsible steering column to collapse; in which case you'll have to buy a whole new steering column unit.

Use a puller to remove the steering wheel

8. Tighten the steering wheel nut to 14–18 ft. lbs. on the 1976–77 F-10, 22–25 ft. lbs. on the 1200, B210, 1978 F-10, 310, 1977–79 200SX and 36–51 ft. lbs. on the 1976 Z models. Tighten all other steering wheel nuts to 28–36 ft. lbs.

9. Reinstall the horn button, pad, or ring.

Turn Signal Switch

REMOVAL AND INSTALLATION

On some later model Datsuns, the turn signal switch is part of a combination switch. The whole unit is removed together.

1. Disconnect the battery ground cable.

Typical turn signal switch removal

2. Remove the steering wheel as previously outlined. Observe the "caution" on the collapsible steering column.

3. Remove the steering column covers.

4. Disconnect the electrical plugs from the switch.

5. Remove the retaining screws and remove the switch.

6. Installation is the reverse of removal. Many models have turn signal switches that have a tab which must fit into a hole in the steering shaft in order for the system to return the switch to the neutral position after the turn has been made. Be sure to align the tab and the hole when installing.

Steering Lock

The steering lock/ignition switch/warning buzzer switch assembly is attached to the

Steering lock securing screw—1977–79 200SX (others similar)

steering column by special screws whose heads shear off on installation. The screws must be drilled out to remove the assembly. The ignition switch is on the back of the assembly, and the warning switch on the side. The warning buzzer, which sounds when the driver's door is opened with the steering unlocked, is located behind the instrument panel.

Power Steering Pump

REMOVAL AND INSTALLATION

1. Disconnect and plug the hoses at the pump.

2. Disconnect the pump mounting bolts and remove the drive belt.

3. Remove the pump. Installation is the reverse. Adjust the belt tension after installation, and fill and bleed the system.

BELT TENSION ADJUSTMENT

1. Loosen the tension adjustment and mounting bolts.

2. Move the pump toward or away from the engine so that the belt deflects ¼–½ in. midway between the idler pulley and the pump pulley under moderate thumb pressure.

3. Tighten the bolts and recheck the tension adjustment.

SYSTEM BLEEDING

1. Fill the pump reservoir and allow to remain undisturbed for a few minutes.

2. Raise the car until the front wheels are clear of the ground.

3. With the engine off, quickly turn the wheels right and left several times, lightly contacting the stops.

4. Add fluid if necessary.

5. Start the engine and let it idle.

6. Repeat Steps 3 and 4 with the engine idling.

7. With the steering wheel all the way to the left, open the bleeder screw on the steering gear to allow the air to bleed. Close

the screw when fluid is expelled.

8. Stop the engine, lower the car until the wheels just touch the ground. Start the engine, allow it to idle, and turn the wheels back and forth several times. Check the fluid level and refill if necessary.

BRAKE SYSTEM

Front disc brakes are used on all current models, with drum brakes at the rear. 1979 and later 280ZX and 1980 and later 200SX models have rear disc brakes. All models have a vacuum booster system to lessen required pedal pressure. The parking brake operates the rear brakes through a cable system.

For all brake system repair and service procedures not detailed below, please refer to "Brakes" in the Unit Repair section.

Adjustment

There are four basic types of brake adjusting systems used. Only drum brakes require periodic adjustment; disc brakes are self-adjusting.

To adjust the brakes, raise the wheels, disconnect the handbrake linkage from the rear wheels, apply the brakes hard a few times to center the drums, and proceed as follows:

BOLT ADJUSTER

Turn the adjuster bolt on the backing plate until the wheel can no longer be turned, then back off until the wheel is free of drag. Repeat the procedure on the other adjuster bolt on the same wheel. Some models may have only one adjuster bolt per wheel.

BOLT ADJUSTER WITH CLICK ARRANGEMENT

The adjuster is located on the backing plate. The adjustment proceeds in clicks or notches. The wheel will often be locked temporarily as the adjuster passes over center for each click. Thus the adjuster is alternately hard and easy to turn. When the wheel is fully locked, back off 1–3 clicks.

Bolt adjuster

STAR WHEEL ADJUSTER

Remove the rubber boot from the backing plate. Insert a screwdriver through the adjusting hole to engage the toothed wheel. Turn the adjuster teeth down until the wheel is locked, then push them up about 12 notches so that the wheel is free of drag.

Loosening the "Z" series rear brake adjuster

SELF-ADJUSTING

No manual adjustment is required. The self-adjusters operate whenever the hand or foot brakes are used.

After Adjustment

After adjusting the brakes, reconnect the handbrake linkage. Make sure that there is no rear wheel drag with the handbrake released. Loosen the handbrake adjustment if necessary.

Master Cylinder

REMOVAL AND INSTALLATION

Clean the outside of the cylinder thoroughly, particularly around the cap and fluid lines. On ZX models, remove the heatshield plate. Disconnect the fluid lines and cap them to exclude dirt. On models with a fluid level gauge, disconnect the electrical connector. Remove the clevis pin connecting the pushrod to the brake pedal arm inside the vehicle. This pin need not be removed on models with the vacuum booster. Unbolt the master cylinder from the firewall and remove. If the pushrod is not adjustable, there will be shims between the cylinder and the firewall. These shims, or the adjustable pushrod, are used to adjust brake pedal free-play. After installation, bleed the system and check for pedal free-play. The 1980 and later 200SX's pushrod is not adjustable, as the rod between the brake booster and the master cylinder is secured by adhesion. After installation, bleed the system and check the pedal free-play.

1. Reservoir cap
2. Strainer
3. Stopper ring
4. Stopper screw
5. Stopper
6. Primary piston
7. Spring
8. Secondary piston
9. Spring
10. Plug
11. Check valve

Exploded view of typical master cylinder

NOTE: Ordinary brake fluid will boil and cause brake failure under the high temperatures developed in disc brake systems. Special fluid meeting DOT 3 or 4 specifications for disc brake systems must be used.

PEDAL ADJUSTMENT

Before adjusting the pedal, make sure that the wheelbrakes are correctly adjusted.

Adjust the pedal free-play by means of an adjustable pushrod or shims between the master cylinder and the firewall. Adjust the pedal height by means of the pedal arm stop pad. Free-play should be approximately 0.04–0.20 in. on all models. Pedal height (floorboard to pedal pad) should be approximately 6 in. on all B210s, 1978–80 510s and 1980 and later 200SX and 210 models; 7 in. on all 200SX, 610, 710, 810 and F-10 models; and 8 in. on all Z models.

Parking Brake

ADJUSTMENT

Handbrake adjustments are generally not needed, unless the cables have stretched.

All Models Except the "Z" Series

There is an adjusting nut on the cable under the car, usually at the end of the front cable and near the point at which the two cables from the rear wheels come together (the equalizer).

1. Adjust the rear brakes with the parking brake fully released.
2. Apply the handbrake lever so that it is approximately 3–3½ in. from its fully released position.
3. Adjust the parking brake turnbuckle, locknuts, or equalizer so that the rear brakes are locked.
4. Release the parking brake. The wheels should be free to turn. If not, loosen the parking brake adjuster until the wheels turn with no drag.

280Z

The driveshaft must be removed to gain access to the adjusting nut on the front linkage rod.

1. Release the handbrake fully and block the vehicle wheels.
2. Loosen the locknut at the rear of the front rod.
3. Measure the dimension between the wheel cylinder lever pin hole centers and their respective buffer plates.
4. Rotate the front rod to bring the dimension to 0.453–0.492 in. (11.5–12.5 mm) on both sides.
5. Tighten the locknut at the rear of the front rod.

280ZX

1. Pull up the handbrake lever, counting the number of ratchet clicks for full engagement. Full engagement should be reached in 4–6 notches.
2. Release the parking brake.
3. Adjust the lever stroke at the cable

equalizer under the car: loosen the locknut and tighten the adjusting nut to reduce the number of ratchet clicks necessary for engagement. Tighten the locknut.

4. Check the adjustment and repeat as necessary.

5. After adjustment, check to see that the rear brake levers (at the calipers) return to their full off positions when the lever is released, and that the rear cables are not slack when the lever is released.

6. To adjust the warning lamp, bend the warning lamp switch plate down so that the light comes on when the lever is engaged one notch.

CHASSIS ELECTRICAL

Heater Unit

REMOVAL AND INSTALLATION

F-10

1. Disconnect battery ground cable and drain coolant.

2. Disconnect inlet and outlet hoses and remove defroster hoses from each side of the heater unit.

3. Remove the cable retaining clamps for the heater valve, floor door and intake door.

4. Disconnect electrical connectors. Remove the four unit retaining screws and remove the heater unit.

5. Installation is the reverse of removal.

B210

1. Disconnect battery ground strap.
2. Drain engine coolant.
3. Remove the defroster hose from both sides of heater unit.
4. Disconnect electrical wires from heater unit.
5. Remove clamps and disconnect water hose from right side of heater.
6. Remove one attaching bolt from each side of the unit and one at the top center and remove unit by pulling forward and out.
7. Reverse procedure for installation.

210 and 510

1. Disconnect the ground cable at the battery. Drain the coolant.
2. Remove the console.
3. Remove the driver's side of the instrument panel. See the section following.
4. Remove the heater control assembly: remove the defroster ducts, door cables at the doors, harness connector, and control assembly.
5. Remove the radio.
6. Disconnect the heater ducts, side defrosters, and center vent duct.
7. Remove the screws attaching the defroster nozzle to the unit. Disconnect the blower wire, and the heater hoses.
8. Remove the retaining bolts and the heater unit.
9. Installation is the reverse.

310 without A/C

1. Disconnect the battery ground cable.
2. Set the temperature lever to the HOT position and drain the engine coolant.
3. Remove the instrument panel assembly. See the following section for in-

structions.

4. Disconnect the control cables and rod from the heater unit. Disconnect the heater motor harness.

310 with A/C

1. Disconnect the battery ground.
2. Set the temperature control lever to HOT and drain the cooling system.
3. Remove the instrument panel.
4. Disconnect the hoses at the core.
5. Disconnect all wiring from the unit.
6. Loosen the band seal at the joint between the cooling and heater units.
7. Unbolt and remove the heater.

Sentra

1. Set "TEMP" lever to maximum "HOT" position and drain engine coolant.
2. Disconnect heater hoses at engine compartment.
3. Remove instrument assembly.
4. Remove heater control assembly.
5. Remove heater unit assembly. Installation is the reverse of removal.

Stanza without A/C

1. Remove the instrument panel.
2. Disconnect the heater hoses and vacuum tube in the engine compartment.
3. Remove the heater control assembly.
4. Unbolt and remove the heater unit.
5. Installation is the reverse of removal.

1977–79 200SX

1. Disconnect the battery ground cable. Drain the coolant. Disconnect the heater hose clamp at the engine.

2. Inside the car, disconnect the electrical connectors at each side of the instrument panel.

3. Remove the instrument panel: Remove the steering column covers; disconnect the speedometer cable and radio antenna cable; disconnect all electrical connectors; remove the steering column clamp bolts; remove the package tray; remove the bolts attaching the panel to the side brackets; remove the right windshield pillar moulding and remove the panel bolt there; remove the panel moulding; remove the panel bolts and remove the panel.

4. Remove the defroster hoses. Remove the coolant hoses.

5. On air conditioned models, disconnect the electrical wires between the heater and a/c unit.

6. Remove the three bolts and heater.

7. Installation is the reverse.

1980 and Later 200SX

1. Set the TEMP lever to the HOT position and drain the coolant.

2. Disconnect the heater hoses from the driver's side of the heater unit.

3. At this point the manufacturer sug-

1. Connector
2. Clip
3. Heater hose (inlet)
4. Defroster nozzle (R.H.)
5. Defroster duct (R.H.)
6. Heater switch
7. Heater control
8. Heater case (R.H.)
9. Heater core
10. Heater case (L.H.)
11. Heater hose (outlet)
12. Defroster nozzle (L.H.)
13. Defroster duct (L.H.)

F–10 heater construction

gests you remove the front seats. To do this, remove the plastic covers over the ends of the seat runners, both front and back, to expose the seat mounting bolts. Remove the bolts and remove the seats.

4. Remove the console box and the floor carpets.

5. Remove the instrument panel lower covers from both the driver's and passenger's sides of the car. Remove the lower cluster lids.

6. Remove the left hand side ventilator duct.

7. Remove the radio, sound balancer and stereo cassette deck. (See below for procedures).

8. Remove the instrument panel-to-transmission tunnel stay.

9. Remove the rear heater duct from the floor of the vehicle.

10. Remove the center ventilator duct.

11. Remove the left- and right-hand side air guides from the lower heater outlets.

12. Disconnect the wire harness connections.

13. Remove the two screws at the bottom sides of the heater unit and the one screw and the top of the unit and remove the unit together with the heater control assembly.

Installation is the reverse of removal.

NOTE: You may be able to skip several of the above steps if only certain components of the heater unit need service.

610

1. Disconnect the battery ground cable.

2. Drain the coolant.

3. Detach the coolant inlet and outlet hoses.

4. Remove the center ventilator grille from the bottom of the instrument panel.

5. Remove the heater duct hose.

6. Detach the defroster hose from each side of the heater unit.

7. Disconnect the control cables.

8. Disconnect the wires at the connectors.

9. Remove the bolt at each side of the unit and the one on the top for 1973 models and two on each side for 1974–76 models.

10. Remove the unit.

11. Reverse the procedure for installation. Run the engine for a few minutes with the heater on to make sure the system is filled with coolant.

710

1. Disconnect battery ground strap.

2. Drain engine coolant. Disconnect the heater hoses at the firewall (engine compartment side).

3. Remove intake duct hose and defroster duct from both sides of heater unit. Remove console box if so equipped.

4. Disconnect electrical wires at connectors.

1. Defroster nozzle
2. Defroster hose
3. Intake box
4. Heater duct hose
5. Heater unit
6. Center grille
7. Control assembly

610 heater installation

5. Loosen retaining clamps and remove control cables.

6. Remove two bolts on each side of unit and one on top. Remove unit from vehicle.

7. Install in reverse of the above.

1977–80 810

1. Disconnect the battery ground cable.

2. Drain the engine coolant.

3. Remove the console box and the console box bracket. Remove the front floor mat.

4. Loosen the screws and remove the rear heater duct.

5. Remove the hose clamps and remove the inlet and outlet hoses.

6. Remove the heater duct and remove the defroster hoses from the assembly.

7. Remove the air intake door control cable.

8. Disconnect the wiring harness to the heater.

9. Remove the retaining bolts and remove the heater unit.

10. Installation is in the reverse order of removal.

1981–83 810

NOTE: You may be able to skip several of the following steps if only certain components of the heater assembly need service.

1. Set the TEMP lever to the HOT position and drain the coolant.

2. Disconnect the heater hoses from the driver's side of the heater unit.

3. At this point the manufacturer suggests that you remove the front seats. To do this, remove the plastic covers over the ends of the seat runners, front and back, to expose the seat mounting bolts. Remove the bolts and lift out the seats.

4. Remove the front floor carpets.

5. Remove the instrument panel lower covers from both the driver's and passenger's sides of the car.

6. Remove the left side ventilator duct.

7. Remove the instrument panel assembly as detailed later in this chapter.

8. Remove the rear heater duct from the floor of the car.

9. Tag and disconnect the wire harness connectors.

10. Remove the two screws at the bottom sides of the heater unit and the one screw from the top of the unit. Lift out the heater together with the heater control assembly.

11. Installation is in the reverse order of removal.

280Z without A/C

1. Disconnect the negative battery cable.

2. Remove the clamp at the air intake duct so as to disconnect the air intake box control cable.

3. Disconnect blower and resistor wires at the connectors.

4. Remove the retaining screws and remove the blower unit.

5. The motor and fan may be separated from the blower unit by removing the three mounting screws. Be careful to retain the washers and spacers.

6. Reassembly is accomplished in reverse order. When reassembling the control cable for the air intake door, set the AIR lever in the OFF position and position the wire in the clamp so that the door will just be closed.

280Z with A/C

1. Disconnect the battery negative cable. Disconnect the vacuum hose at the intake door actuator.

"Z" series heater installation

2. Remove the defroster duct which is located near the passenger seat.

3. Disconnect the connectors at the blower motor and at the resistor.

4. Remove the three housing mounting bolts and remove the housing.

5. The motor may be removed by removing the three bolts and pulling it out. Be careful to retain the three washers and three spacers.

6. Installation is the reverse of removal.

280ZX without A/C

1. Disconnect the negative battery cable.

2. Remove the lower instrument panel cover and the glove box.

3. Remove the floor nozzle, defroster duct, and the side defroster duct on the right side.

4. Remove the heater duct.

5. Disconnect the blower motor wiring harness.

6. Disconnect the control cable at the blower assembly by removing the clip.

7. Remove the bolts securing the blower assembly to the firewall and remove the blower assembly.

8. The motor and fan can be removed by removing the three motor retaining screws. The fan simply bolts onto the motor shaft.

9. Installation is the reverse.

The motor and fan can also be removed without removing the entire blower housing assembly:

1. Disconnect the negative battery cable.

2. Remove the lower instrument panel cover and the floor nozzle on the right side.

3. Disconnect the blower motor wiring harness.

4. Remove the three motor attaching screws and remove the motor and fan as a unit from the blower housing.

280ZX with A/C

1. Disconnect the negative battery cable.

2. Remove the instrument panel lower cover on the right side. Remove the glove box.

3. Remove the floor nozzle, the defroster duct, and the side defroster duct on the passenger's side.

4. Disconnect the blower motor electrical harness.

5. Disconnect and label the two vacuum hoses.

6. Remove the three blower assembly mounting bolts and remove the assembly.

7. Installation is the reverse.

The motor can be removed without removing the blower assembly:

1. Disconnect the negative battery cable.

2. Remove the instrument panel lower cover and the floor nozzle on the right side.

3. Disconnect the blower motor electrical harness.

4. Remove the three blower motor attaching screws and remove the motor and fan as an assembly from the blower housing.

5. Installation is the reverse.

Heater Core

REMOVAL AND INSTALLATION

610 and 710

The heater unit need not be removed to remove the heater core. It must be removed to remove the blower motor.

1. Drain the coolant.

2. Detach the coolant hoses.

3. Disconnect the control cables on the sides of the heater unit.

4. Remove the clips and the cover from the front of the heater unit. Remove the console if so equipped.

5. Pull out the core.

6. Reverse the procedure for installation. Run the engine with the heater on for a few minutes to make sure the system fills with coolant.

B210, F-10

1. Remove heater from car.

2. Remove clip and slide hose from cock.

3. Pry off five clips and separate left and right sides of heater case.

4. Lift out heater core.

280Z

1. Remove heater from car.

2. Loosen clamp on heater cock side.

3. Remove screws retaining heater cock and remove from case.

4. Loosen clamp on core side and disconnect hose.

5. Remove E-ring from floor door operating rod.

6. Remove five screws and take off side cover. Pull out heater core with the floor door open.

7. Assemble in reverse of the above.

1977–79 200SX

1. Remove the heater unit.

2. Remove the control lever assembly. Remove the knobs, disconnect the lamp wire, remove the center vent (4 screws), disconnect the fan wires, remove the clips and cables, remove the retaining screws and the unit.

3. Disconnect the hose from the heater cock.

4. Remove the connecting rod (with bracket) from the air door.

5. Remove the clips on each side of the box, split the box, and remove the core.

6. Installation is the reverse of removal.

1980 and Later 200SX

1. Remove the heater unit as described earlier.

2. Remove the hoses from the heater core and remove the core.

3. Installation is the reverse of removal.

1978 and Later 510, 210 and Sentra

1. Remove the heater unit.

2. Disconnect the inlet and outlet hoses.

3. Remove the case clips and split the case. Remove the core.

4. Installation is the reverse of removal.

810

1. Remove the heater unit.

2. Remove the center vent cover and heater control assembly, loosening the clips and screws.

3. Remove the screws securing the door shafts.

4. Remove the clips from the case and split the case. Remove the core.

5. Installation is the reverse of removal.

280ZX

1. Remove the heater unit.

2. Remove the water cock.

3. Remove the case clips and split the heater case. Remove the core.

310

1. Remove the heater unit from the vehicle.

2. Disconnect the inlet and outlet hoses from the core if you have not done so already.

3. Remove the clips securing the case halves and separate the halves.

4. Remove the heater core.

5. Installation is the reverse of removal.

Stanza

1. Remove pedal bracket mounting bolts, steering column mounting bolts, brake and clutch pedal cotter pins.

2. Move the pedal bracket and steering column to the left.

3. Disconnect the air mix door control cable and heater valve control lever, then remove the control lever.

4. Remove the core cover.

5. Disconnect the hoses at the core.

6. Installation is the reverse of removal. Be sure to bleed the system.

Windshield Wiper Motor

REMOVAL AND INSTALLATION

610, 710, 280Z, 810

The wiper motor and operating linkage is on the firewall under the hood.

1. Lift the wiper arms. Remove the securing nuts and detach the arms.

2. Remove the nuts holding the wiper pivots to the body. Remove the air intake grille for access.

3. Open the hood and unscrew the motor from the firewall.

4. Disconnect the wiring connector and remove the wiper motor with the linkage.

5. Reverse the procedure for installation.

NOTE: If the wipers do not park correctly, adjust the position of the automatic stop cover on the wiper motor.

B210 and Sentra

The wiper motor is on the firewall under the hood. The operating linkage is on the firewall inside the car.

1. Detach the motor wiring plug.

2. Inside the car, remove the nut connecting the linkage to the wiper shaft.

3. Unbolt and remove the wiper motor from the firewall.

1 Wiper motor
2 Wiper arm
3 Pivot
4 Wiper arm
5 Pivot

610 wiper installation

4. Reverse the procedure for installation.

F-10

1. Disconnect battery ground cable and remove meter cover and glove box.

2. Remove the base of the wiper arm from the pivot shaft by raising the wiper blade away from the glass and loosening the attaching nut.

3. Remove the wiper motor by removing the ball joint connecting the motor shaft to the wiper link. Remove the motor from the dash.

4. Remove the pivot bolts and remove the link assembly.

Installation is the reverse of removal. Make sure the angle is correct to obtain the right sweeping zone.

1978 and Later 510, 210, 280ZX, 1980 and Later 310, 200SX and Stanza

1. Disconnect the battery ground cable.

2. Disconnect the electrical connector.

3. Remove the motor attaching bolts.

4. Remove the nut securing the arm to the motor shaft. Remove the motor.

1977–79 200SX

1. Remove the wiper arms.

2. Disconnect the motor electrical connector.

3. Remove the cowl top grille.

4. Remove the motor retaining bolts.

5. Pull the motor out a little and disconnect the motor from the linkage.

Instrument Cluster

REMOVAL AND INSTALLATION

B210

1. Disconnect the battery negative lead.

2. Depress the wiper, light switch, and choke knobs, turning them counterclockwise to remove.

3. From the rear, disconnect the lighter wire. Turn and remove the lighter outer case.

4. Remove the radio and heater knobs.

5. Remove the shell cover from the steering column.

6. Remove the screws which hold the instrument cluster to the instrument panel. Pull out the cluster.

7. Disconnect the wiring connector. Disconnect the speedometer cable by unscrewing the nut at the back of the speedometer.

8. Individual instruments may be removed from the rear of the cluster.

610, 710

1. Disconnect the battery ground cable.

2. Remove the four screws and the steering column cover.

3. Remove the screws which attach the cluster face. Two are just above the steering column, and there is one inside each of the outer instrument recesses.

4. Pull the cluster lid forward.

5. Disconnect the multiple connector.

6. Disconnect the speedometer cable.

7. Disconnect any other wiring.

8. Remove the cluster face.

9. Remove the odometer knob if the vehicle has one.

10. Remove the six screws and the cluster.

11. Instruments may now be readily replaced.

12. Reverse the procedure for installation.

F-10

1. Disconnect the battery ground cable.

2. Disconnect the speedometer cable from the back of the speedometer.

3. Remove the package tray and disconnect the heater control cables from the heater.

4. Disconnect all wire harness connectors from the back of the instrument panel after noting their locations and tagging them.

5. Remove the choke knob and nut.

6. Remove the steering column bracket installation bolts.

1 Cluster lid
2 Meter assembly
3 Instrument mounting lower bracket
4 Instrument pad
5 Ventilation grille
6 Defogger nozzle
7 Instrument garnish
8 Radio
9 Speaker
10 Ventilation duct
11 Package tray
12 Glove box
13 Glove box lid
14 Ash tray
15 Ash tray cover

200SX instrument panel and gauges

7. Loosen the instrument panel upper attaching screws.

8. Remove the bolts securing the sides of the instrument panel.

9. Remove the bolts attaching the instrument panel to the pedal bracket.

10. Remove the instrument panel.

11. Installation is in the reverse order of removal.

210

1. Disconnect the battery ground cable.

2. Remove the steering wheel.

3. Remove the steering column cover.

4. Remove the illumination control rheostat.

5. Pull off the heater control knob and remove control panel. Remove the screw attaching the panel to the instrument panel.

6. Pull off the radio knobs; remove the nuts and washers.

7. Remove the ash tray and ash tray holder.

8. Remove the cluster lid screws.

9. Disconnect the electrical connectors.

10. Remove the cluster lid.

11. Remove the cluster gauge screws.

12. Disconnect the speedometer cable by pushing and turning the cap counterclockwise.

13. Disconnect the cluster wires and remove the instrument cluster.

1978 and Later 510

1. Disconnect the battery ground cable.

2. Remove the steering column covers. Disconnect the hazard warning switch connector.

3. Remove the wiper switch. Pull out the ash tray, remove the heater control knobs, and remove the heater control plate by inserting a screwdriver into the fan lever slit and levering the plate out.

4. Remove the finish plate to the left of the glove compartment.

5. Pull off the radio knobs and remove the nuts and washers.

6. Remove the choke and side defroster knobs.

7. Remove the cluster lid screws.

8. Disconnect the electrical connectors.

9. Remove the cluster lid.

10. Remove the instrument cluster retaining screws. Disconnect the speedometer cable by pushing and turning counterclockwise.

11. Disconnect the instrument cluster wire connectors and remove the cluster.

1977–80 810

1. Disconnect the battery ground cable.

2. Remove the knobs and nuts on the radio and the knob on the choke control wire. Remove the ash tray.

3. Remove the steering column covers.

4. Disconnect the harness connectors after noting their location and marking them.

5. Remove the retaining screws and remove the instrument panel.

6. Installation is in the reverse order of removal.

1981–83 810

1. Disconnect the negative battery cable.

2. Remove the instrument lower cover.

3. Remove the steering wheel.

4. Disconnect the speedometer cable.

5. Remove the six mounting screws and lift out the cluster lid.

6. Unscrew the mounting bolts and lift off the left side instrument pad (this is the hooded part of the dashboard that the instrument cluster sits in).

1. Trip meter reset cable	6. Oil/Temp gauge	11. Speedometer
2. Rheostat	7. Volt/Fuel gauge	12. Cigarette lighter
3. Bracket	8. Clock	13. Escutcheon
4. Cigarette lighter retaining nut	9. Trip meter knob	14. Tachometer
5. Cigarette lighter housing	10. Rheostat knob	15. Panel

280 Z instrument panel and gauges

7. Loosen the instrument cluster mounting screws, pull it out slightly and disconnect all wiring. Remove the cluster.

8. Installation is in the reverse order of removal.

1977–79 200SX

1. Disconnect the battery ground cable.
2. Remove the steering column covers.
3. Disconnect the speedometer cable and the radio antenna.
4. Disconnect all the wires from the back of the panel after noting their location and marking them.
5. Remove the bolts which secure the steering column clamp. Remove the package tray.
6. Unbolt the panel from the brackets on the left and right-hand sides.
7. Remove the right-side windshield pillar trim and remove the bolt which attaches the panel to the pillar.
8. Remove the instrument garnish.
9. Remove the retaining bolts and remove the panel.
10. Installation is in the reverse order of removal.

280ZX

1. Disconnect the battery ground cable.
2. Remove the steering wheel.
3. Remove the steering column cover.
4. Remove the instrument panel lower cover on the left side.
5. Disconnect the speedometer cable at the intermediate connection.
6. Remove the combination switch.
7. Remove the cluster retaining screws, pull out slightly and disconnect the elec-trical connectors. Remove the instrument cluster.

1980 and Later 200SX

1. Disconnect the battery ground terminal.
2. It may be necessary to remove the steering wheel and covers to remove the instrument cluster.
3. Remove the screws holding the cluster lid in place and remove the lid.
4. Remove the five bolts holding the cluster in place and pull the cluster out, then remove all connections from its back. Make sure you mark the wiring to avoid confusion during reassembly.

310 and Stanza

1. Disconnect the battery terminals.
2. Remove the steering wheel and the steering column covers.
3. Remove the instrument cluster lid by removing its screws.
4. Remove the instrument cluster screws, pull the unit out and disconnect all wiring and cables from its rear. Mark the wires to avoid confusion during assembly. Be careful not to damage the printed circuit.
5. Remove the cluster.
6. Installation is the reverse of removal.

Instruments

REMOVAL AND INSTALLATION

280Z

The speedometer and tachometer are both attached at the rear with two wingnuts. Access is from under the instrument panel. After the wingnuts are removed, the instrument can be pulled out through the instrument panel. The other three gauge units are held to brackets by slotted head hex bolts. To gain access, the center console panel must be removed.

FUSE BOX LOCATION CHART

Model	Fuse Box Location	Fusible Link Location
310	Under dash at extreme right	Right fender area of eng. comp.
610	Below hood release knob	Adjacent to battery
710	Engine compartment right rear	Relay bracket right front of engine compartment
280ZX 280Z 810	Under dash at extreme right	Right rear of engine compartment①
B210, 210	Above brake light switch	Engine compartment below voltage regulator
F-10, 510	Under dash at extreme left	Off of (+) cable on battery

①A fusing link for the fuel injection is in (+) battery cable

Fiat

SERIAL NUMBER IDENTIFICATION

Vehicle and Engine

The vehicle serial number is stamped on a metal plate located on the left front corner of the instrument panel, visible through the windshield. The serial number is also stamped on a non-removable rib or bulkhead of the body.

An identification plate, mounted on the engine compartment wall (front trunk XI/9), carries the chassis number and the spare parts ordering number. The engine number is stamped on a pad on the engine block.

From Sept. 1, 1980, federal regulations require a new format for all vehicle identification numbers. All 1981 and later vehicles have the new 17-digit V.I.N. format.

A—Chassis type and serial number
B—Identification plate
C—Engine type and serial number

X1/9 Identification locations

A—Chassis type and serial number
B—Identification plate
C—Engine type and serial number

128 and Strada typical identification locations

A—Chassis type and serial number
B—Engine type and serial number
C—Identification plate

131 and Brava identification locations

ENGINE IDENTIFICATION

Year	Model	Displacement (cc)	Engine Serial Prefix
'76	128 all types—49 states	1290	128 A1 040 6
	128 all types—California	1290	128 A1 031 6
	X1/9—49 states	1290	128 AS 031 6
	X1/9—California	1290	128 AS 031 5
	131 all types—49 states	1756	132 A1 040 5
	131 all types—California	1756	132 A1 031 5
	124 Sport Spider—49 states	1756	132 A1 040 5
	124 Sport Spider—California	1756	132 A1 031 5
'77–'78	128 all types—49 states	1290	128 A1 040 6
	128 all types—California	1290	128 A1 031 6
	X1/9—49 states	1290	128 AS 031 6
	X1/9—California	1290	128 AS 031 5
	Brava, 131—manual trans., 49 states	1756	132 A1 040 6
	Brava, 131—auto. trans., Calif.	1756	132 A1 040 5
	Brava, 131—manual trans., Calif.	1756	132 A1 031 5
	Brava, 131—auto trans., Calif.	1756	132 A1 031 5
	124 Sport Spider—49 states	1756	132 A1 040 6
	124 Sport Spider—California	1756	132 A1 031 6
'79	Strada—49 states	1498	138 AS 040
	Strada—California	1498	138 AS 031
	X1/9—49 states	1498	138 AS 040
	X1/9—California	1498	138 AS 031
	124 Spider—49 states	1995	132 C2 040
	124 Spider—California	1995	132 C2 031
	131, Brava—49 states	1995	132 C2 040
	131, Brava—California	1995	132 C2 031
'80	Strada—49 states	1498	138 AS 040
	Strada—California	1498	138 AS 031
	X1/9—49 states	1498	138 AS 040
	X1/9—California	1498	138 AS 031
	124 Spider—49 states	1995	132 C3 040
	124 Spider—California	1995	132 C3 031
	131, Brava—49 states	1995	132 C3 040
	131, Brava—California	1995	132 C3 031
'81–'83	Strada—49 states	1498	138 BS 031
	Strada—California	1498	138 BS 031
	X1/9—49 states	1498	138 BS 031
	X1/9—California	1498	138 BS 031
	124 Spider—49 states	1995	132 C3 031
	124 Spider—California	1995	132 C3 031
	131, Brava—49 states	1995	132 C3 031
	131, Brava—California	1995	132 C3 031

GENERAL ENGINE SPECIFICATIONS

Year	Model	Displacement (cc)	SAE net Horsepower @ rpm	Torque (ft. lbs.) @ rpm	Bore & Stroke (in.)	Compression ratio
'76–'77	128 all types—49 states	1290	62 @ 6000	67 @ 4000	3.39 × 2.19	8.5:1
	128 all types—California	1290	61 @ 5800	67 @ 4000	3.39 × 2.19	8.5:1
	X1/9	1290	61 @ 5800	67 @ 4000	3.39 × 2.19	8.5:1

GENERAL ENGINE SPECIFICATIONS

Year	Model	Displacement (cc)	SAE net Horsepower @ rpm	Torque (ft. lbs.) @ rpm	Bore & Stroke (in.)	Compression ratio
'76–'77	131 all types—49 states	1756	86 @ 6200	90 @ 2800	3.31 × 3.12	8.0:1
	131 all types—California	1756	86 @ 5800	89 @ 2800	3.31 × 3.12	8.0:1
	124 Spider—49 states	1756	86 @ 6200	90 @ 2800	3.31 × 3.12	8.0:1
	124 Spider—Calif.	1756	83 @ 5800	89 @ 2800	3.31 × 3.12	8.0:1
'78	128—all w/SE	1290	62 @ 6000	67 @ 4000	3.39 × 2.19	8.5:1
	w/CC	1290	61 @ 5800	67 @ 4000	3.39 × 2.19	8.5:1
	X1/9—w/SE	1290	61.5 @ 5800	67 @ 4000	3.39 × 2.19	8.5:1
	w/CC	1290	61 @ 5800	67 @ 4000	3.39 × 2.19	8.5:1
	124 Spider—w/SE	1756	86 @ 6200	90 @ 2800	3.31 × 3.12	8.0:1
	w/CC	1756	83 @ 6200	89 @ 2800	3.31 × 3.12	8.0:1
	131—all, Brava—all w/SE	1756	86 @ 6200	90 @ 2800	3.31 × 3.12	8.0:1
	w/CC	1756	83 @ 6200	89 @ 2800	3.31 × 3.12	8.0:1
'79	X1/9	1498	66 @ 5250	75.9 @ 4000	3.40 × 2.52	8.5:1
	Brava & Spider 2000	1995	80 @ 5000①	100 @ 3000②	3.31 × 3.54	8.1:1
	Strada	1498	65 @ 5100	75 @ 2900	3.40 × 2.52	8.5:1
'80	X1/9	1498	66 @ 5250	75.9 @ 4000	3.40 × 2.52	8.5:1
	Brava & Spider 2000	1995	80 @ 5000①	100 @ 3000②	3.31 × 3.54	8.1:1
	Strada	1498	65 @ 5100	75 @ 2900	3.40 × 2.52	8.5:1
'81	X1/9	1498	75 @ 5500	79.6 @ 3000	3.40 × 2.52	8.5:1
	Brava & Spider 2000	1995	102 @ 5500	110 @ 3000	3.31 × 3.54	8.1:1
	Strada	1498	75 @ 5500	79.6 @ 3000	3.40 × 2.52	8.5:1
'82–'83	X1/9	1498	75 @ 5500	79.6 @ 3000	3.40 × 2.52	8.5:1
	Strada	1498	75 @ 5500	79.6 @ 3000	3.40 × 2.52	8.5:1
	Spider Turbo	1995	120 @ 6000	130 @ 3600	3.31 × 3.54	8.2:1
	Spider 2000	1995	102 @ 5500	110 @ 3000	3.31 × 3.54	8.1:1

① W/F.I.: 102 @ 5500
② W/F.I.: 110 @ 3000
  SE—Standard exhaust
  CC—Catalytic Converter

TUNE-UP SPECIFICATIONS

Year	Model	Displacement (cc)	Spark Plug Type ⑨	Spark Plug Gap (in.)	Points Gap (in.)	Points Dwell (deg.)	Ignition Timing (deg.)	Idle Speed (rpm)	Valve Lash Intake (in.)	Valve Lash Exh. (in.)	Intake Valve Opens (deg.)	Mixture (% CO)
'76–'77	128 49 states	1290	Champion N9Y	.023	.016	55	TDC	850	.012	.016	10B	1.0 ± .05
	128 California	1290	Champion N9Y	.023	.016	55	TDC	825	.012	.016	10B	2.0 ± .05
	X 1/9	1290	Champion N9Y	.023	.016	55	TDC②	825	.012	.016	10B	2.0 ± .05
	131 49 states	1756	Champion N9Y	.023	.016DP	55	TDC	MT-850 AT-725	.018	.020	5B	MT-0.5 ± 0.2 AT-0.7 ± 0.2
	131 California	1756	Champion N9Y	.023	.016DP	55	TDC	MT-825 AT-725	.018	.020	5B	3 ± 0.5

C

TUNE-UP SPECIFICATIONS

Year	Model	Displacement (cc)	Spark Plug Type ⑨	Spark Plug Gap (in.)	Points Gap (in.)	Points Dwell (deg.)	Ignition Timing (deg.)	Idle Speed (rpm)	Valve Lash Intake (in.)	Valve Lash Exh. (in.)	Intake Valve Opens (deg.)	Mixture (% CO)
'76–'77	124 Spider— 49 states	1756	Champion N7Y ④	.023	.016DP	55	TDC	850	.018	.020	5B	0.5 ± 0.2
	124 Spider— Calif.	1756	Champion N7Y ④	.023	.016DP	55	TDC	825	.018	.020	5B	3 ± 0.5
'78	128 all	1290	⑤	.023	.015–.017	52–58	TDC⑧	800–850	.011–.014	.015–.018	10B	1.5–2.5%
	X 1/9	1290	⑥	.027–.031	.015–.017	52–58	TDC⑧	800–850	.016–.019	.018–.021	5B	1.5–2.5
	124 Spider	1756	⑤	.023–.027	.015–⑦.017	52–58	TDC⑧	800–850	.016–.019	.018–.021	5B	1.5–2.5
	131 all	1756	⑥	.027–.031	.015–⑦.017	52–58	TDC⑧	800–850	.016–.019	.018–.021	5B	1.5–2.5
	Brava all	1756	⑥	.027–.031	.015–⑦.017	52–58	TDC⑧	800–⑨850	.018	.020	5B	1.5–2.5
'79	X 1/9	1498	⑤⑥	.023 .027	Electronic		5 BTDC①	800–850	.011–.014	.015–.018	12B	1.0–2.0
	Strada	1498	⑤⑥	.023 .027	Electronic		MT-5 BTDC① AT-5 BTDC	800–850 700–750	.011–.014	.015–.018	12B	1.0–2.0
	131, Brava	1995	⑤⑥	.023 .027	Electronic		MT-10 BTDC AT-10 BTDC	800–850 700–750	.016–.019	.018–.021	5B	1.0–2.5
	Spider	1995	⑤⑥	.023 .027	Electronics		MT-10 BTDC AT-10 BTDC	800–850 700–750	.016–.019	.018–.021	5B	1.0–2.5
'80	X 1/9	1498	⑥	.027–.031	Electronic		MT-10 BTDC AT-10 BTDC	800–850 700–750	.011–.014	.015–.018	12B	.05–.09
	Strada	1498	⑥	.027–.031	Electronic		MT-10 BTDC AT-10 BTDC	800–850 700–750	.011–.014	.015–.018	12B	.05–.09
	131, Brava	1995	⑥	.027 .031	Electronic		MT-10 BTDC AT-10 BTDC	800–850 700–750	.016–.019	.018–.021	5B	.05–.09
	Spider	1995	⑥	.027–.031	Electronic		MT-10 BTDC AT-10 BTDC	800–850 700–750	.016–.019	.018–.021	5B	.05–.09
'81–'83	X 1/9	1498	⑥	.027–.031	Electronics		MT-10 BTDC AT-10 BTDC	800–850 700–750	.011–.014	.015–.018	12B	.05–.09

TUNE-UP SPECIFICATIONS

Year	Model	Displacement (cc)	Spark Plug Type ⑨	Spark Plug Gap (in.)	Points Gap (in.)	Points Dwell (deg.)	Ignition Timing (deg.)	Idle Speed (rpm)	Valve Lash Intake (in.)	Valve Lash Exh. (in.)	Intake Valve Opens (deg.)	Mixture (% CO)
'81–'83	Strada	1498	⑥	.027–.031	Electronic		AT-10 BTDC	800–850	.011–.014	.015–.018	12B	.05–.09
							AT-10 BTDC	700–750				
	131m, Brava	1995	⑥	.027–.031	Electronic		MT-10 BTDC	800–850	.016–.019	.018–.021	5B	.05–.09
							AT-10 BTDC	700–750				
	Spider	1995	⑥	.027–.031	Electronic		MT-10 BTDC③	800–850	.016–.019	.018–.021	5B	.05–.09
							AT-10 BTDC③	700–750				

NOTE: The underhood specifications sticker often reflects tune-up specification changes made in production. The sticker specifications must be used if they disagree with those in the chart.

① At 800 to 850 rpm
② 10 BTDC on 1976-77 California models
③ Spider Turbo timing is 8.5 BTDC @ 800–850 rpm
④ 1977 models—N9Y plugs or equivalent
⑤ Regular
  Bosch W175T30
  Marelli CW7LP
  Champion N9Y
  AC 42 XLS

⑥ Resistor
  Bosch W175TR30
  Marelli CW7LPR
  Champion RN9Y
  AC R42 XLS
⑦ Starting point gap—.012–.019 inch
⑧ w/auto trans—5 BTDC

⑨ Original equipment spark plugs; similar characteristic plugs of different manufacture may be used without damage to the engine
DP Dual point distributor; see text for explanation
MT Manual transmission
AT Automatic transmission

FIRING ORDERS

Firing Order 1-3-4-2

DRIVING DIRECTION

124 and 131

1-3-4-2

DRIVING DIRECTION

128 and Strada

Firing Order 1-3-4-2

DRIVING DIRECTION

X1/9

CAPACITIES

Year	Model	Engine Disp. (cc)	Crankcase (qts) With Filter	Crankcase (qts) Without Filter	Trans-axle (pts)	Transmission Manual (pts)	Transmission Automatic (pts)	Rear Axle (pts)	Fuel Tank (gals)	Cooling System (qts)
'76–'79	128 Sedan, Wagon	1290	4.5	4.5	6.6	6.6③	—	—	9.5	6.8
	128 SL, 3P	1290	4.5	4.5	6.6	6.6③	--	—	12.5	7.0
'76–'83	X1/9	1290	4.5	4.5	6.6	6.6③	—	—	12.7	11.6
		1498	4.75	4.5	7.0	7.0③	—	—	12.2	11.6

C2

CAPACITIES

Year	Model	Engine Disp. (cc)	Crankcase (qts) With Filter	Crankcase (qts) Without Filter	Trans-axle (pts)	Transmission Manual (pts)	Transmission Automatic (pts)	Rear Axle (pts)	Fuel Tank (gals)	Cooling System (qts)
'76–'79	124 Spider	1756	4.5	4.0	—	3.5	6.0②	2.8	11.4	8.0①
	131 Sedan and Wagon Brava Sedan, Wagon	1756	4.5	4.0	—	3.8	6.0②	2.8	12.2	8.0
'80–'81	Brava	1995	5.5	4.3	—	3.5	6.0②	2.8	12.2	8.5
'80–'83	Spider 2000 and Turbo	1995	5.5	4.3	—	3.5	6.0②	2.8	11.4	8.0
'79–'82	Strada	1498	4.75	3.75	7.0	7.0③	6.0②	—	12.1	7.5

NOTE: Because of the high temperatures associated with turbocharging, a superior grade oil must be used. Fiat recommends only oils with an SF/CC rating for use in the Turbo Spider, preferably straight 30 or 40.

① 1976–77 models; 8.8 qts.
② 12 pints to refill after total disassembly and rebuild
③ SAE 90 (not EP)

CRANKSHAFT AND CONNECTING ROD SPECIFICATIONS
(All measurements in inches)

Engine Displacement (cc)	Crankshaft Main Bearing Journal Dia.	Crankshaft Main Bearing Oil Clearance	Crankshaft End-Play	Crankshaft Thrust on No.	Connecting Rod Journal Dia.	Connecting Rod Oil Clearance
1290	1.9994–2.0002	0.0016–0.0033	0.0021–0.0104	5	1.7913–1.7920	0.0014–0.0034
1756	2.0860–2.0868	0.0020–0.0037	0.0021–0.0120	5	1.9997–①2.0001	0.0018–0.0032
1498	1.9990–1.9997	0.0019–0.0037	0.0021–0.0104	NA	2.1459–2.1465	0.0014–0.0034
1995	2.0860–2.0868	0.0012–0.0030	0.0021–0.0120	NA	2.2329–2.2334	0.0008–0.0025

① Class "A", 1.9997–2.0001; Class "B", 1.9993–1.9997 in.

NA: Not available at time of publication

VALVE SPECIFICATIONS

Engine Displacement (cc)	Seat Angle (deg)	Face Angle (deg)	Spring Test Pressure (lbs. @ in.) Inner	Spring Test Pressure (lbs. @ in.) Outer	Stem To Guide Clearance (in.) Intake	Stem To Guide Clearance (in.) Exhaust	Stem Diameter (in.) Intake	Stem Diameter (in.) Exhaust
1290, 1498	45	45.5	32.7 @ 1.220	75.5 @ 1.417	0.0012–0.0026	0.0012–0.0026	0.3139–0.3146	0.3139–0.3146
1756 1995	45	45.5	32.7 @ 1.220	85.5 @ 1.417	0.0012–0.0026	0.0012–0.0026	0.3139–0.3146	0.3139–0.3146

PISTON AND RING SPECIFICATIONS
(All measurements in inches)

Engine Displacement (cc)	Piston Clearance	Ring Gap			Ring Side Clearance		
		Top Compression	Top Oil Control	Bottom Oil Control	Top Compression	Top Oil Control	Bottom Oil Control
1290	0.0028–0.0035	0.0118–0.0176	0.0118–0.0176	0.0098–0.0157	0.0018–0.0030	0.0016–0.0028	0.0012–0.0024
1756	0.0016–0.0024	0.0118–0.0176	0.0079–0.0138	0.0079–0.0138	0.0018–0.0030	0.0011–0.0027	0.0011–0.0024
1498	0.0011–0.0019	0.0118–0.0177	0.0118–0.0177	0.0098–0.0157	0.0018–0.0030	0.0016–0.0028	0.0011–0.0024
1995	0.0016–0.0024	0.0118–0.0177	0.0118–0.0177	0.0098–0.0157	0.0018–0.0030	0.0011–0.0027	0.0011–0.0024

TORQUE SPECIFICATIONS
(All readings in ft. lbs.)

Displacement (cc)	Cylinder Head Bolts	Rods Bearing Bolts	Main Bearing Bolts	Crankshaft Pulley Bolt Chart	Flywheel to Crankshaft Bolts	Manifolds	
						Intake	Exhaust
1290, 1498	69	36	58	101	61	22	22
1756	61	36	83①	87	61	18	18
1995	61	54	83	181	105	18	18

① Front main bearing cap bolts—58ft. lbs.

TORQUE SEQUENCES

128, X1/9 and Strada

124 and 131

ALTERNATOR AND REGULATOR SPECIFICATIONS

Year	Model	Alternator			Regulator						
						1st Stage		2nd Stage			Armature to Core Gap (in.)
		Part No. or Manufacturer	Output Current @ 14v	Max. Output (amps)	Part No. or Manufacturer	Testing Current (amps)	Regulating Voltage (volts)	Testing Current (amps)	Regulating Voltage (volts)	Contact Gap (in.)	
'76–'79	128,	Marelli A124-14V	60	70	Marelli	40–	13.7–	10–	14.2	.018	.059③
'76–'83	X1/9	60A Variant 1 ①			RC2/12E①	45①	14.2	14			

ALTERNATOR AND REGULATOR SPECIFICATIONS

Year	Model	Alternator Part No. or Manufacturer	Output Current @ 14v	Max. Output (amps)	Regulator Part No. or Manufacturer	1st Stage Testing Current (amps)	1st Stage Regulating Voltage (volts)	2nd Stage Testing Current (amps)	2nd Stage Regulating Voltage (volts)	Contact Gap (in.)	Armature to Core Gap (in.)
'76–'79 '79–'83	124 Spider 2000	Fiat A12M 124/ 12/42M	42	53	Marelli RC2/12B	25– 35	13.5– 14.0	2– 12	14.2	.018	.059③
'76–'81	131, Brava	Marelli A-124-14V-44A②	43	53	Marelli RC2/12D②	25– 35②	13.5– 14.0	10– 14	14.2	.018	.059③
'80–'82	Strada with A/C	Bosch K1-14-V65 A21	65	65	Integral Bosch Electronic	20– 22	13.8– 14.2	20– 22	14.2	—	—
'79–'80	Strada without A/C	Marelli A125-14V55A	55	55	Integral Fimm Rtt113C Electronic	20– 22	13.8– 14.2	20– 22	14.2	—	—
		Delco-Remy 1101-039-70A	70	70	Integral Delco-Remy Electronic	20– 22	13.8– 14.2	20– 22	14.2	—	—

①X1/9 not equipped with A/C uses Marelli A124-14V-44A alternator and Marelli RC2/12D regulator with 1st stage testing current of 25-35 amps

②131 models equipped with A/C use Marelli A124-14V-60A alternator and Marelli RC2/12E regulator with 1st stage testing current of 40–45 amps

③1978–83 models use electronic non-adjustable regulators

④1979 Strada with air conditioning modified per P.I.C 129

BATTERY AND STARTER SPECIFICATIONS

(All cars use 12 volt, negative ground electrical systems)

Year	Model	Battery Amp Hour Capacity	LOCK TEST Amps	LOCK TEST Volts	LOCK TEST Torque (ft. lbs.)	NO LOAD TEST Amps	NO LOAD TEST Volts	NO LOAD TEST rpm	Brush Spring Tension (oz.)	Manufacturer or Part No.
'76-'79 '76-'83	128 X1/9,	50 60	370 370	8.3 8.3	7.9 7.9	35 35	11.7 11.7	7000 7000	40 40	Fiat E84-0.8/12 Variant 1
'76-'83	131, Brava Spider	60	530	7	12.6	28	12	5200	35	Fiat E100-1.3/12
'79-'82	Strada (Automatic)	60	370	8.5	9①	45	11.5	7000	40	Bosch 0-001-212-210
	Strada (Manual)	60	450	7.5	11①	40	11.5	6500	40	Marelli E95-0,9/12

BRAKE SPECIFICATIONS

(All measurements given are in inches unless noted)

Year	Model	Lug Nut Torque (ft. lbs.)	Master Cylinder Bore	Brake Disc Minimum Thickness	Brake Disc Maximum Run-Out	Brake Drum Diameter	Brake Drum Max. Machine O/S	Brake Drum Max. Wear Limit	Minimum Lining Thickness Front	Minimum Lining Thickness Rear
'76-'79	128	50	0.75	Regrind 0.368	0.0006	7.2929– 7.3043	7.3234– 7.3358	7.3554	0.08	0.06
'80-'82	Strada			Wear limit 0.354						

BRAKE SPECIFICATIONS

(All measurements given are in inches unless noted)

Year	Model	Lug Nut Torque (ft. lbs.)	Master Cylinder Bore	Brake Disc		Brake Drum			Minimum Lining Thickness	
				Minimum Thickness	Maximum Run-Out	Diameter	Max. Machine O/S	Max. Wear Limit	Front	Rear
'76-'78 '79-'83	124 Spider 2000 and Turbo	51	0.75	Regrind front—0.368 rear—0.371 Wear limit 0.354	0.006	①	-	-	0.08	0.08
'76-'81	131, Brava Sedan, Wagon	51	0.75	Regrind 0.368 Wear limit 0.354	0.006	8.9882–9.000	9.0182–9.0300	9.0551	0.06	0.18
'76-'83	X1/9	50	0.75	Regrind 0.368 Wear limit 0.354	0.006	①	-	-	0.08	0.08

① Disc brakes on four wheels

WHEEL ALIGNMENT SPECIFICATIONS

(Applies only to unladen vehicle)

Year	Model	Caster Front (deg)	Camber Front (deg)	Camber Rear (deg)	Toe-in Front (in.)	Toe-in Rear (in.)
'76–'81	128 Sedan, Wagon	1⅙P to 2⅙P	1⅙P to 2⅙P	⅔N to ⅓P① ⅙N to 1⅙P②	− 0.120 + 0.040	+ 0.059 + 0.217
'76–'81	128 SL, 3P	1⅙P to 2⅙P	½P to 1½P	⅔N to 1⅔N	− 0.060 + 0.100	+ 0.079 + 0.236
'79–'81	Strada	1½P to 2½P	1⅙P to 2⅙P	½P to 1½P	− 0.177 − 0.098	0 + 0.078
'76–'78 '79–'83	124 Sport Spider Spider 2000	2⅔P to 3⅔P	⅓N to ⅔P	Fixed	+ 0.160 + 0.320③	Fixed
'76–'83	X1/9	6½P to 7½P	0 to 1N	1⅙N to 2⅙N	+ 0.080 + 0.240	+ 0.360 + 0.510
'76–'78 '79–'81	131 Sedan, Wagon Brava Sedan, Wagon Brava, Super Brava	3¼P to 4¼P	¼P to 1¼P	Fixed	+ 0.236 + 0.393③	Fixed

NOTE: Toe-in = + sign Toe-out = − sign
① Sedan
② Wagon
③ 1979–81 Spider 2000 & Brava + 0.0157 to + 0.315
P Positive
N Negative

TUNE-UP PROCEDURES

Spark Plugs

NOTE: Tag all spark plug wires before removal. Tighten all plugs to 27 ft. lbs.

Spark plugs should be cleaned and re-gapped at 6000 mile intervals, and replaced every 12,000 miles.

Since all Fiat engines use aluminum alloy cylinder heads, care should be taken to avoid damage to the spark plug threads. Remove the plugs with a ¹³⁄₁₆″ socket wrench and use a feeler gauge to check the electrode gap. When reinstalling used plugs, clean and lightly oil the threads. Thread the plugs in by hand (a short piece of fuel line slipped over the porcelain will facilitate installation) and use the socket to seat the plug snugly against the head, forming a good compression seal. Torque to 27 ft. lbs. Do not overtighten.

NOTE: Use caution when threading plugs, they go in on an angle.

If cross-threaded or stripped threads are encountered, see the engine rebuilding section at the end of the book.

Electronic Ignition

All 1979 and later Fiat engines are equipped with electronic ignition. Strada, 128 and X1/9 models use a Bosch system, 131 and Spider models use a Marelli system.

Primary voltage is supplied from the battery through the ignition switch to the electronic control module and, through a resistor, to the coil. The resistor functions as a heat dissipator.

NOTE: The Marelli ignition does not use an external resistor.

The ground side of the coil primary circuit is connected to the control module. The control module has a circuit which connects with the magnetic pick-up in the distributor. Primary voltage is controlled by the electronic module to supply a regulated current to the primary windings of the ignition coil.

The control module is triggered by an impulse generated in the distributor. This turns the coil primary circuit on and off. Each time the primary circuit is broken, a high voltage is induced in the coil secondary windings. This voltage is distributed to the spark plugs through the distributor rotor and cap in the conventional manner.

ELECTRONIC IGNITION TEST

1. Set key to ON position.
2. Check that voltage at primary coil terminal equals battery voltage.
3. Repeat test at tachometer coil terminal. Voltage should be within 0.3 of battery voltage.
4. If not, check coil primary winding for open circuits.
5. Resistance across low coil terminals should be 0.8 ohms.

NOTE: Do not remove ignition cables with engine running or while attempts are made at starting. Do not ground tachometer lead.

IGNITION DISTRIBUTOR TEST

1. With key in OFF position remove connector from module.
2. Place ohmmeter leads on module connector.
3. Reading should be 700–800 ohms (890 to 1285 ohms on Bosch).
4. Remove distributor cap and check rotor arm resistance.
5. Should be about 5000 ohms.

NOTE: If above tests indicate proper results module is at fault.

Breaker Points and Condenser
REMOVAL AND INSTALLATION

Breaker points should be inspected and re-gapped at 6000 mile intervals, and replaced with the condenser(s) at 12,000 mile intervals.

128 and X1/9

NOTE: Fiat recommends servicing the points and condenser with the distributor removed. See "Distributor Removal and Installation" in the Engine Electrical section.

1. Unsnap the two distributor cap clasps and remove the cap with spark plug wires connected. On some models, the cap is retained by two screws that stay with the cap.
2. Pull straight up and remove the rotor. At this time, it is good practice to apply a few drops of light (10W) oil to the lubricating wick at the top of the distributor shaft.
3. Disconnect the breaker points lead and condenser lead at the primary connection. Remove the condenser bracket retaining screws, and replace the condenser. Remove the breaker point retaining screws (and wire clip on 1976–79 128 and X1/9 models) and remove the points. Apply a light film of silicone based grease to the distributor cam lobes. Wipe off any excess.

ELECTRONIC IGNITION TEST SPECIFICATIONS

	Bosch	Marelli
Pick up coil resistance—wires from terminal 7 and 31d of module	890 to 1285 ohms	700 to 800 ohms
Pick up insulator—wire from terminal 7 to the distributor body	∞ (Infinity)	∞ (Infinity)
Primary input—positive coil terminal to ground	6 volts or more	6 volts or more
Control module ground—negative battery terminal to module support mount	0.2 ohms or less	0.2 ohms or less
Coil primary resistance—disconnect primary coil wires	1.1 to 1.7 ohms	0.75 to 0.81 ohms
Primary resister—disconnected	0.85 to 0.95 ohms	—
Coil secondary resistance to primary	6,000 to 10,000 ohms	10,000 to 11,000 ohms
Stator pole to reluctor gap	0.3 to 0.5mm (.011 to .019 in.)	0.5 to 0.6mm (0.020 to 0.024 in.)
Control module—check only after all other components have checked out good	Disconnect the coil tower wire. Position wire 5mm—¼in. from ground. Rotate the engine manually and observe spark as each tooth passes the pick up.	Disconnect high voltage wire from distributor. Do not disconnect from coil. While holding wire 5mm from ground. Crank engine and check for spark. If no spark is seen-replace module.

NOTE: Hold all high voltage wires with insulated tool to avoid shock.

Ignition points—1976–78 128 and X1/9

1. Main breaker points
2. Auxiliary breaker points
3. Capacitor, main breaker points
4. Capacitor, auxiliary breaker points

Ignition points—1976–78 124 and 131

4. Install new breaker points and condenser. To adjust point gap, rotate the crankshaft pulley until the breaker point rubbing block rests on the high point of the distributor cam lobe. Slightly loosen the breaker points retaining screw and insert the proper sized feeler gauge between the point contacts. Move the fixed arm in or out to obtain the specified clearance. Tighten the retaining screw.

5. Connect the electrical leads for the breaker points and condenser. Install the cap and rotor.

6. Check dwell angle and ignition timing.

RUBBER BLOCK ON HIGH SIDE

.015–.017 GAP

ADJUSTMENT SCREW

1976–78 128 and X1/9 point gap adjustment

131, 1976–79 124 Sport Coupe and Spider (1756 cc)

NOTE: These models are equipped with a dual point distributor. The dual point sets do not operate simultaneously; one set is used for starting, and the other for running. The starting set provides 10 degrees of additional spark advance during starter cranking. The running set returns the spark timing to Top Dead Center. On 1976–79 models with automatic choke, the starting set is actuated by coolant temperatures of 36–46°F or less. On both systems, the starting set cuts out and the running set takes over when full cold oil pressure is reached.

1. Remove the two distributor cap retaining screws. The screws will stay with the cap. Remove the cap.

2. Pull straight up and remove the rotor. Apply a few drops of light (10W) oil to the lubricating wick atop the distributor shaft.

3. Crank the engine over, or rotate the crankshaft pulley by hand or push the car in 4th gear, until both point sets open with their rubbing blocks on the high points of the distributor cam lobes. Disconnect both breaker points leads and condensers leads at the primary connections. Remove and replace both point sets and condensers. Apply a light film of silicone based grease to the distributor cam lobes. Wipe off any excess.

4. Adjust the point gap for both breaker point sets by inserting the feeler gauge between the point contacts; set both sets for .015–.017 inch gap.

The running points are connected to the green wire and the starting points are connected to the green/black wire. If the points need adjustment, insert a screwdriver in the adjusting slot and twist it one way or the other to change the gap.

NOTE: For longer service, set the gap to the maximum specification, as the rubbing block will wear down in service and slowly close the gap.

5. Install the rotor. Install the distributor cap.

6 Check dwell angle and ignition timing.

Dwell Angle

NOTE: Dwell angle is not applicable on electronic ignition.

Dwell angle is the amount of degrees of distributor shaft rotation that the points remain closed (making contact). Increasing the point gap decreases dwell, while de-creasing the point gap increases dwell. Dwell angle may be checked with the engine running, or with the engine cranking over at starter speed. With a running engine, the dwell angle reading should be fairly constant. When the engine is being cranked over, the dwell angle reading will fluctuate between zero and the maximum figure for that angle.

Dwell angle should always be checked after adjusting or installing new points. Using a dwell meter, connect the negative lead to a good ground (such as an engine bolt) and the positive lead to the primary distributor connection at the coil (the small wire that leads from the distributor to the coil). On 18 and X1/9 models, disconnect and plug the vacuum retard signal line at the distributor.

NOTE: Leave the line connected on high altitude versions.

On all models with dual points, both sets must be checked separately. To check the running set of points, first locate the ignition mode selector relay. Trace the wires from the distributor until you locate it. Usually, it is located on the passenger's side fender well. Remove the relay from the plug and connect a jumper wire between the Power side and the Running side as shown in the illustration. Connect the dwell-meter positive lead to the green distributor lead. Crank the engine and check the dwell. If the dwell needs adjusting, remove the distributor cap and adjust the point gap. To check the dwell on the starting set of points, leave one end of the jumper wire on the power side of the relay and connect the other end to the Starting side as shown. Connect the dwell meter positive lead to the green/black lead at the distributor. Crank the engine and check the dwell.

On all other Fiat models, dwell is adjusted in the normal manner. Simply connect the dwell meter positive lead to the distributor primary wire and the negative lead to a good ground. When adjusting the dwell, remember that increasing the point gap decreases the dwell, while decreasing the point gap increases dwell.

Once you have set the dwell, the ignition timing must be checked. A 1° increase in dwell results in the ignition timing being retarded 2° and vice versa.

Ignition Timing

--- CAUTION ---
On Spider Turbo models the ignition timing must be carefully set according to specifications. Altering the timing beyond specifications could cause detonation and serious engine damage.

Fiat recommends that the ignition timing be checked at 6000 mile intervals, or whenever the breaker points, dwell angle setting, or distributor body is disturbed. All timing checks are made with the engine warmed to operating temperature, and idling in neutral (manual transmission cars) or Drive (automatic equipped cars), with the hand brake on.

NOTE: The timing marks are located on the front cover. There will be three lines, the longest is TDC, the shortest is 10° BTDC.

ELECTRONIC MODELS

Ignition timing is checked in the conventional manner, using a timing light.

1. Locate the timing marks on the front cover. Clean and highlight the marks with chalk or paint.
2. Start the engine and allow it to warm up to operating temperature. Make sure the idle speed is correct.
3. Connect the timing light according to the manufacturer's instructions.

NOTE: When using a timing light with an inductive pickup, place the pickup along the no. 1 spark plug wire at a point where it can be separated from the other wires to eliminate false signals generated by the strong firing impulses.

A = 10° (Adv.)
B = 5° (Adv.)
C = 10° (TDC)

Timing marks—124 and 131

4. Using the timing light, check the position of the timing mark on the crankshaft pulley. The mark should index with the timing pointer according to specifications. If the timing is within specs, no further adjustment is necessary.
5. If the initial timing needs adjustment, loosen the distributor hold-down locknut and turn the body of the distributor to advance or retard timing.

SINGLE POINT MODELS

1. 1976 and later 128's, Strada's, and X1/9's are equipped with two sets of timing marks—one set is in the conventional position on the front cover and the other set is located on the flywheel, visible through a small opening in the bellhousing. On 1976 and later 128's, and Strada's, remove the spare tire and you'll see the marks.

A = 0° (Adv.)
B = 5° (Adv.)
C = 10° (T.D.C.)

Timing marks on flywheel—128, Strada and X1/9

1. TDC   3. 10° BTDC
2. 5° BTDC   4. Crankshaft pulley mark

Timing marks—Strada

2. Locate the correct mark and highlight it with paint or chalk. If you're timing the engine through the bellhousing, tap the engine over with the starter or turn it over by hand until you can find the punch mark on the flywheel. Put a spot of paint or chalk on it.
3. Connect the timing light according to the manufacturer's instructions.
4. Start the engine and let it warm up. Check the idle speed and make sure it is correct before setting the timing.
5. Disconnect the vacuum line from the distributor and plug it. Remember this is a vacuum *retard*, not a vacuum advance.
6. Aim the timing light at the marks. The marks should coincide. Keep in mind that with the vacuum line disconnected, the timing should be 10° BTDC. If the timing needs adjusting, stop the engine, loosen the distributor hold-down clamp and turn the distributor in the engine.
7. Reconnect the vacuum retard line. The timing should now be TDC. You may have to mark the timing marks with different paint colors to distinguish between them.

Adjusting retard—not for high altitude versions

8. If the retard mechanism has not provided approximately 10 degrees retard, stop the engine and remove the cap and rotor. Depress the retard follower cap and rotate the eccentric star wheel to change the amount of retard. Counterclockwise equals more retard and clockwise equals less retard.

NOTE: On high altitude versions, simply leave the vacuum line connected and time the engine. There is no need to check the ignition retard.

9. After the timing is set, recheck the idle speed as it may have changed.

DUAL POINT MODELS

1. Locate the timing marks on the front cover and mark them with paint. Mark the pulley also. The longest mark is TDC and the shortest mark is 10° BTDC. The middle mark is 5° BTDC.
2. Start the engine and let it warm up. Check to make sure the idle is correct before setting the timing.

Ignition mode selector relay and terminal—1976–78 124 and 131

Timing marks aligned at TDC on the running points

Timing marks advanced 10° on the starting points

Setting timing on running points

JUMPER WIRE
RUNNING TERMINAL
POWER TERMINAL

Checking advance on starting points

JUMPER WIRE
STARTER TERMINAL
POWER TERMINAL

1. Lobe
2. Plate
3. Tappet
4. Feeler gauge

Measuring gap on overhead cam lobe to tappet plate

3. Locate the ignition mode selector relay. This is generally found on the passenger's side fender well. Remove the top of the relay and connect a jumper wire (with blade ends) between the Power and Running terminals.

4. Connect the timing light according to the manufacturer's instructions.

5. Start the engine and aim the timing light at the marks. The TDC mark on the front cover and the reference mark on the pulley should coincide. If they don't, stop the engine, loosen the distributor hold-down clamp and rotate the distributor as necessary to obtain a reading of TDC. Tighten the hold-down clamp once you get the timing right.

6. Shut the engine off and connect the Starting and Power terminals in the relay block. Start the engine and check the timing. It should now be 10° BTDC. If it isn't, adjust the amount of advance by changing the dwell angle of the starting points. If the timing is less than 10° BTDC, increase the point gap. If it's more than 10° BTDC, decrease the point gap.

7. Once you have the starting timing correct, remove the jumper wire and replace the relay.

8. Check and reset the idle speed if necessary.

Valve Clearance Adjustment

Valve clearance should be checked every 12,000 miles—sooner if the head is removed or if excessive valve train noise is noticed. On both single and double overhead cam engines (128, X1/9, 131, 124 Sport, and Strada), valve clearance is adjusted by the thickness of the Shim (plate) between the cam lobe and tappet bucket, requiring special service tools.

ALL MODELS

NOTE: Special tools required for this job include a tappet depressor tool #A60421 (128, Strada, X1/9), or #A60422 (124, 131), a pair of curved tip needle nose pliers (such as #A87001), a lever #A60443 (Twin cam only), and a compressed air source and air chuck to blow out the old adjusting shim. The engine must be cold for a valve clearance check.

1. Remove the retaining screws and remove the camshaft cover.

2. Turn the crankshaft until the lobe controlling the tappet being checked is pointing upward and is at a right angle to the tappet plate.

NOTE: To simplify crankshaft rotation on the 128, Strada, and X1/9, place the transmission in 4th gear and raise the car so that the right front wheel (right rear wheel on the X1/9) is free to rotate. Turn the free wheel to rotate the engine to the valve adjustment positions.

3. Measure the clearance between the tappet plate and the camshaft lobe with a feeler gauge.

4. If the clearance is not at the proper specification, a tappet plate of the required thickness will have to be installed.

5. To remove the old tappet plate (shim), the tappet must be depressed and held in that position. On the 128, Strada, and X1/9, this is accomplished with special tool #A60421 (see illustration). However, on the 124 and 131 twin cam engines, this is a two step process. First, depress the tappet with special lever #60443 or rotate the camshaft until the lobe depresses the tappet. Then, install the tappet clamping tool #60422 which will keep the tappet depressed. If you rotated the camshaft to depress the tappet, rotate it again to give clearance for plate removal. Finally, using compressed air through the notch in the tappet or needle nose pliers, or both, remove the old plate.

6. Install a new tappet plate after determining its thickness by comparing it to the clearance measurement taken in Step 3.

Removing or replacing shim plate

mm	in.	mm	in.
3.25	0.128	4.02	0.158
3.30	0.130	4.10	0.161
3.40	0.134	4.20	0.165
3.50	0.138	4.30	0.169
3.60	0.142	4.40	0.173
3.70	0.146	4.50	0.177
3.80	0.150	4.60	0.181
3.90	0.154	4.70	0.185
4.00	0.157	4.80	0.189

Valve shim size

Single overhead cam—cylinder and valve location

Tappet clearance adjustment plates are available in a range of thicknesses from 0.146 in. to 0.185 in. with a difference between each plate of 0.002 in.

The thickness of the plate is shown on one of the plate's flat sides. This side should be installed facing the tappet. It is recommended that the plate's thickness be checked to make sure that it is actually the thickness specified.

Double overhead cam—cylinder and valve location

1. Seal
2. Dowel
3. Plates of adjusting valve clearance
4. Tappets
5. Locks
6. Upper cups
7. Inner spring
8. Outer springs
9. Lower cups
10. Exhaust valve guide
11. Exhaust valve
12. Flat washer
13. Intake valve
14. Intake valve guide
15. Oil seal
16. Camshaft
17. Welch plug

Exploded view of single overhead cam valve mechanism—typical

1. Depress Tappet
2. Tappet retaining tool

Preparing to change shim plate—double overhead cam type

NOTCH AT 4 O'CLOCK

NOTCH AT 8 O'CLOCK

Preparing to change shim plate—single overhead cam type

VALVE SHIM SIZE

mm	in.	mm	in.
3.25	0.128	4.02	0.158
3.30	0.130	4.10	0.161
3.40	0.134	4.20	0.165
3.50	0.138	4.30	0.169
3.60	0.142	4.40	0.173
3.70	0.146	4.50	0.177
3.80	0.150	4.60	0.181
3.90	0.154	4.70	0.185
4.00	0.157	4.80	0.189

Carburetor

Often mistaken for an improperly adjusted carburetor is an incorrectly adjusted air cleaner climatic setting. This adjustment provides warmed intake air for cold climates and cool intake air for warm climates. See ''Emission Controls'' for details.

IDLE SPEED AND MIXTURE ADJUSTMENT

All models

NOTE: On models equipped with a catalytic converter, idle speed and mixture is checked with the air injection hose between the diverter valve and check valve pinched shut with locking pliers.

1. Start the engine and warm to operating temperature (176°F min.). Make sure the choke plate is open.

NOTE: If possible, make all adjustments with the air cleaner on, as removal may artificially lean out the mixture. On 1979 and later 49 State versions, remove the air cleaner lid and block the inlet to the reed valves; replace the lid.

2. Adjust the idle speed to specifications with the idle speed screw. The idle speed is set with the transmission in Neutral on manual transmission cars, and is set in Drive with the parking brake firmly applied on automatic cars.

3. Adjust the idle mixture (% CO) to specifications (see ''Tune-up'' chart) with the idle mixture metering screw.

NOTE: Fiat recommends the use of a carbon monoxide (CO) meter for setting the mixture. However, if one is not available, a satisfactory setting should be found by first screwing the mixture screw all the way in until it lightly sets, and then backing it out about 2 to 3½ turns. This will get you in the ballpark, and then you can adjust the mixture for the highest possible rpm within that range. Screw clockwise to lean (decrease CO), and counterclockwise to richen (increase CO).

4. After adjusting mixture, recheck idle speed and adjust if necessary.

1. Vacuum inlet from intake manifold for fast idle diaphragm (*).
2. Vacuum advance connection.
3. Blow-by connection.
4. Canister connection.
5. Bowl vapor vent.
6. Fuel recirculation outlet.
7. Primary throttle opening adjusting screw (*).
8. Automatic choke system water heating connections.
9. Diaphragm device for partial opening of choke valves.
10. Dashpot.
11. Idle speed adjusting screw.
12. Idle stop solenoid.
13. Idle mixture adjusting screw..
14. Throttle operating lever.
15. Choke fast idle adjustment screw.
16. Fuel inlet.
(*) Vehicle equipped with air conditioning system.

1. Idle speed
2. Idle mixture

Access holes for carburetor adjustment—X1/9 only

Adjustments and vacuum connections—typical

ENGINE ELECTRICAL

Distributor

All Fiat distributors use a centrifugal ignition advance system which advances spark timing in direct proportion to increasing engine rpm. In addition, 128 and X1/9 models with the Ducellier distributor utilize a vacuum retard system which retards the ignition timing about 10° under high vacuum situations such as idling and deceleration.

Models with electronic ignition have a vacuum advance mechanism in addition to the centrifugal advance. Turbo Spider models have an advance limiter replacing one of the springs on the centrifugal advance weights.

REMOVAL AND INSTALLATION

The quick method of distributor removal is to mark the distributor body and rotor positions relative to some stationary engine component before removal, and then put it back the way you found it. However, on the 1756 cc engines installed in the 124 and 131 (these are the ones with the distributor located at the right rear of the engine above the exhaust manifold), the distributor drive gear is helical (slanted drive). Therefore, the rotor will rotate about 30–40 degrees during removal or installation. For this reason, mark the position of the rotor before removal and just after removal. When you go to install the distributor, align the rotor with the mark you made just after removal so when the distributor is installed, the rotor will correctly align with the first mark.

1—Vacuum retard
2—Rotor toward #4 terminal
3—Primary lead facing grille
4—Condenser

Single point distributor

Dual point distributor

The Fiat approved method of distributor removal is the following:

1. Remove the spark plug wires from the distributor.
2. Remove the low tension leads and disconnect the vacuum control (if equipped).
3. Rotate the crankshaft to bring no. 1 cylinder to Top Dead Center (TDC) of compression stroke (both valves closed). Align the timing marks.
4. Remove the distributor clamp bolt at the base of the distributor and remove the distributor from the engine. To install:
5. Position the distributor rotor opposite the no. 1 contact in the cap. At this point the contact breaker points are about to open.
6. Fit the distributor into its housing and tighten the clamp bolt.
7. Replace the distributor cap and connect the spark plug wires in the correct firing order.
8. Check the ignition timing with a timing light and the point dwell with a dwell meter.

Alternator

ALTERNATOR PRECAUTIONS

Certain precautions should be observed when working on this, or any other AC charging system.

1. Never switch battery polarity.
2. When installing a battery, connect the ground cable last.
3. Never disconnect the battery while the engine is running.
4. If the molded connector is disconnected from the alternator, do not ground the hot wire.
5. Never run the alternator with the main output cable disconnected.
6. Never electric weld around the vehicle, without disconnecting the alternator.
7. Never apply any voltage, other than battery voltage, when testing.
8. Never apply more than 12 volts to jump a battery for starting purposes.

REMOVAL AND INSTALLATION

NOTE: Disconnect the battery first.

The alternator is removed by disconnecting the electrical leads and unscrewing the nut on the upper bracket and the screw which attaches the bracket to the engine. Remove the two nuts of the lower brackets, alternator and water pump belt. Installation is the reverse of removal.

1981 and later Strada and X1/9 models with air conditioning use a new drive belt system. The system consists of three V-belts and an adjustable crankshaft pulley. The alternator belt rides on the inner groove of the waterpump pulley. Adjust

V-belt configuration—Strada and X1/9

alternator belt tension to 30–45 lbs. Do not pry on the alternator case or pulley when adjusting belt tension.

NOTE: The water pump belt is adjusted by removing the crankshaft outer pulley half and removing or adding shims. A shim change of 0.5 mm (.020 in.) causes a change in belt tension of 17–22 lbs. If the waterpump pulley is removed to replace the alternator belt, reinstall the original shims and check belt tension. Proper waterpump belt tension is 60–80 lbs.

Voltage Regulator

Only the electro-mechanical regulator mounted separately from the alternator is adjustable. All later models have integral alternator and voltage regulator.

ADJUSTMENTS

Cut-out

1. Measure the air gap for the cut-out relay between the clapper and the edge of the core nearest the contacts.
2. Make the cut-in adjustment with the unit at 65–95°F.
3. Adjust by bending the spring tension arm until the points close at the proper specification.
4. Check the reverse current by connecting a two-way ammeter in series with the battery lead to the regulator.
5. Run the alternator to 4500 rpm and gradually reduce speed, noting the reverse current at the point where the contacts open. (See specifications for the proper amperage.)
6. The range between cut-in and cut-out action can be adjusted by enlarging or reducing the air gap.

Starter

REMOVAL AND INSTALLATION

124, 128 and 131

1. Jack up the car and place jack stands beneath the frame.

2. Disconnect the battery positive terminal to prevent accidental shorting.

3. Remove the exhaust manifold and muffler to provide clearance.

4. Disconnect the wires from the starter, tagging each wire to facilitate later identification.

5. Remove the mounting bolts and pull the starter from the housing.

6. Installation is the reverse of removal.

X1/9

1. Raise the car at the rear and set it on two stands at the control arms.

2. Disconnect the battery (positive) cable to prevent shorting.

3. Disconnect and remove the lower linings of the compartment.

4. If necessary, remove the exhaust manifold and muffler.

5. Disconnect the wires from the starter motor and tag each wire to facilitate later identification.

6. Remove the mounting bolts and the starter.

7. Installation is the reverse of removal.

Strada

1. Disconnect battery ground cable.

2. Disconnect and tag all electrical leads to starter.

3. On manual transmission cars, remove three bolts, lockwashers and washers to remove starter (Marelli).

4. On automatic transmission cars, remove two bolts, lockwashers and nut plate. Remove three bolts, lockwashers and washers to remove starter (Bosch).

5. Reinstall in reverse order.

STARTER DRIVE REPLACEMENT

The starter can be broken down into the following subassemblies; solenoid, commutator end head, frame, armature, drive and pinion end head.

1. To disassemble, disconnect the starter motor lead from the solenoid and remove the solenoid.

2. Remove the brush cover and disconnect the brush holder.

3. Lift the brushes slightly and retain them in their holders by arranging springs against their sides.

4. Unscrew the two self-locking nuts and take off the brush holder bracket, saving the fiber and steel thrust washers.

5. Slide the frame off the pinion end.

6. Remove the cotter pin from the linkage pivot and remove the pivot. The armature can then be taken out, along with the drive and fork lever.

7. Assembly is the reverse of removal.

1-2. Nuts
3. Flat washer
4-5. Positive clamp insulators
6. Positive diode plate
7. Screw, positive clamp
8-9. Spring washers
10. Diode terminal connector insulator
11. Spring washer
12. Screw, positive diode plate, diode terminals and stator phases ends attachment
13. Plate
14-15. Insulators
16. Flat washer
17. Nut
18. Insulated connector for charge indicator blade plug
19. Negative diode
20. Stator
21. Rotor
22. Key
23. Drive end frame
24. Spring washer
25. Pulley nut
26. Rubber seal, bearing outer race
27. Positive brush
28. Screw
29. Brush holder
30. Spring washer
31. Negative brush
32. Diode end frame
33-34-35. Rubber bushing components
36. Nut
37. Through-bolt

Fiat A12M 124/12/41M alternator—others similar

1. Split pin
2. Rubber pad
3. Lever pivot pin
4. Starter drive pinion shifter fork
5. Armature
6. Commutator end head
7. Bushing
8. Protection band screw
9. Field winding
10. Pole shoe
11. Pole shoe attaching screw
12. Grommet
13. Nut, solenoid to drive end head
14. Lock washer
15. Plain washer
16. Solenoid assembly
17. Lock washer
18. Nut, current lead clamping
19. Nut, field winding terminal
20. Lock washer
21. Plain washer
22. Nut, protection band screw
23. Commutator end head protection band
24. Screw, brush terminal clamping
25. Lock washer
26. Brush spring
27. Brush
28-29. Plain washers
30. Fibre thrust washer
31. Thru-bolt nut
32. Starter thru-bolt
33. Starter drive sleeve
34. Drive pinion
35. Stop ring
36. Snap ring
37-38. Plain washers
39. Drive end head
40. Bushing

Fiat E84-0.8/12 starter—all 128, X1/9—others similar

ENGINE MECHANICAL

Engine

REMOVAL AND INSTALLATION

All 124 and 131 Models

1. Removal of 124 and 131 engines is facilitated by removing the radiator and the transmission. Proceed as follows:

2. Jack up the car and place it on jack stands.

3. Drain the radiator, auxiliary tank, block and heater system by first moving the heater lever to far right, then opening the radiator drain cock and removing the plug on the right-hand side of the block.

4. Speed drainage by removing the radiator and auxiliary tank caps.

5. Disconnect the battery leads.

6. Then disconnect the ignition coil, alternator, starter, low oil pressure and water temperature indicator wires.

NOTE: Tag all wires to avoid confusion during reassembly.

7. Disconnect the accelerator rod, sliding it out of the lever ball joint end toward the dash.

8. Remove the air filter.

9. Detach the choke cable from the carburetor.

—————— CAUTION ——————

On Fuel Injection models, depressurize fuel system before removing any fuel lines.

10. Disconnect the line from the fuel

1. Propellor shaft yoke
2. Flexible coupling
3. Clamp
4. Transmission mount

Installation of flex coupling clamp before removal

pump and detach the exhaust pipe from the manifold.

11. Disconnect the radiator and heater hoses.

12. Remove the upper two screws that hold the radiator to the body, then remove the radiator by sliding it from the lower support bracket.

NOTE: On cars with automatic transmission, follow the procedures outlined in the transmission section for removal and installation.

13. Working from inside the car, remove the gearshift lever by pressing down the upper part of the sleeve and, with a screwdriver, releasing the spring ring from its seating in the lower part of the lever. The upper part of lever can then be slipped from the lower part.

14. Remove the transmission cover.

15. From under the car, disconnect the driveshaft spider and transmission mainshaft from the universal.

NOTE: This is facilitated by placing a 5 inch diameter hose clamp or a band, Tool A70025, on the coupling itself to compress it slightly.

16. Disconnect speedometer cable from the transmission and disconnect the flexible cable from the clutch fork.

17. Remove the flywheel cover, electrical ground cable and exhaust pipe bracket clip.

18. Remove the heat shield from the exhaust manifold and the three bolts that hold the starter to the front of the transmission.

19. Position a hydraulic jack under the transmission for support.

20. Remove the four bolts which mount the transmission to the crankcase.

21. Remove the crossmember that holds the transmission to the car floor.

22. Supporting the transmission jack, move it toward the rear of the car so as to withdraw the clutch shaft from the pilot bushing and clutch hub.

23. Lower the jack and pull the transmission from under the car.

24. Remove the starter from the engine compartment.

25. Using a chain hoist, pass the rear sling under the crankcase and the front sling under the thermostat housing.

26. Supporting the engine with a hoist, remove the front mounts and lift the engine clear. Push the car out from under the raised engine, then gently lower the hoist. Make sure the engine is stable before attempting further disassembly.

27. Installation is the reverse of removal.

—————— CAUTION ——————

Support the engine in such a manner so as not to damage the oil pan or any cast aluminum parts.

128

NOTE: The engine and transaxle are removed as a unit from below. Make sure the car can be raised high enough to allow sufficient clearance for removal.

1. Place the car on jack stands and be sure the car is in a stable position before removal.

2. Raise the hood and unhook the stay rod. Place covers on the fenders.

3. Loosen the wing nut and remove the spare tire.

4. Take off the lower guards.

5. Drain the water from the radiator, supply tank, cylinder block and passenger compartment heating system in the following way:

a. Completely lower the heater lever inside the car.

b. Open the cock at the bottom of the radiator and remove the radiator cap.

c. Open the cock at the inner side of the engine block and take the cap off the supply tank to help water drainage.

6. Disconnect the battery cables.

7. Disconnect the primary and secondary wires from the coil to the distributor.

NOTE: Tag all wires to avoid confusion during reassembly.

8. Disconnect the wires from the alternator.

9. Disconnect the wires from the starter, the oil pressure sending unit, and the water temperature sending unit.

10. Disconnect the air cleaner.

11. Disconnect the linkage and choke wire from the carburetor.

—————— CAUTION ——————

On fuel injection models, depressurize the fuel system before removing any fuel lines.

12. Disconnect the fuel inlet hose from the fuel pump.

13. Disconnect the exhaust pipe from the manifold.

14. Remove the two rubber hoses from the union with the thermostat to the radiator.

15. Disconnect the water inlet and outlet hoses from the engine to the passenger compartment heater.

16. Disconnect the speedometer drive from the transmission housing by unscrewing the retaining ring.

17. Remove the adjustable rod of the flexible cable from the clutch release lever by unscrewing the locknut and nut.

18. Detach the anti-roll bar by removing the screws which clamp the brackets and insulators to the body. Then unscrew the nuts which fasten the ends to the control arms.

19. Remove the exhaust pipe support bracket from the transmission housing.

20. Disconnect the rod from the gearshift control lever.

21. Remove the ground strap from the transmission housing.

22. Take off the left-hand wheel. Unscrew the left tie rod-to-steering nut and disconnect the ball joint.

23. Remove the shock absorber from the pillar.

24. Unscrew the constant-speed joint nuts from both front wheels.

25. From above the car, working in the engine compartment, disconnect the reaction strut.

26. Hook up the engine and put the cable under light tension. Then, working from above, unscrew the engine to body clamping bolt and, from below, detach the crossmember from the underbody.

27. Work the shaft of each constant-speed joint out of its seat in the pillars and secure the axle shafts with wire to prevent them from coming away from their seats in the differential.

28. Using a hoist, lower the engine group to remove. Lower slowly and check for any wires, hoses, or linkage that may become snagged.

29. Install in the reverse order.

X1/9

— CAUTION —

Discharge air conditioning, if installed, before attempting to remove engine assembly.

NOTE: The engine and transaxle are removed as a unit from below. Make sure the car can be raised high enough to allow sufficient clearance for removal.

1. Disconnect the battery and drain the cooling system.

2. Remove the air cleaner assembly.

3. Disconnect the air pump inlet hose and outlet hose from the pump.

4. Disconnect the heater return hose at the coupling joint and disconnect the heater hose from the pump.

5. Disconnect the wires from the alternator.

NOTE: Tag all wires to avoid confusion during reassembly.

6. Remove the two bolts retaining the louvered protection panel below the carbon trap in the rear firewall.

7. Disconnect the manual choke linkage from the carburetor. On models with automatic choke, remove water lines.

8. Disconnect all vacuum hoses from the carburetor. Disconnect the electrical leads from the solenoid and the carburetor vent hose from the carburetor.

9. Disconnect the coil wires at the distributor. Disconnect the leads from the oil pressure and water temperature sending units. Disconnect the electrical wires from the starter.

— CAUTION —

On fuel injection models, depressurize the fuel system before removing any fuel lines.

10. Remove the clamp securing the fuel lines to the firewall and disconnect the fuel supply and return lines from the firewall.

11. Remove the stopbolt from the accelerator cable, slide the seal off the cable, remove the retainer clip from the cable sheath and remove the cable from the support.

12. Remove the bolts securing the coolant expansion tank, top and bottom, and lift the tank, allowing the water to drain into the engine. Disconnect the hoses from the tank at the thermostat and remove the tank.

13. Remove the hoses from the thermostat.

14. Remove the cotter pin holding the slave cylinder pushrod to the clutch shaft. Loosen the two bolts securing the slave cylinder to the transmission. Open the bleeder screw of the slave cylinder and allow the pushrod to retract. Swing the slave cylinder out of the way.

15. From underneath the vehicle, remove the remaining bolt holding the louvered panel and remove the panel from the firewall. Remove the heat shield located behind the alternator. Remove the three panels from the bottom of the engine compartment and the panel in board of each rear wheel.

16. Drain the transmission/differential lubricant.

17. Disconnect the electrical connectors for the seatbelt interlock system and the back-up lights. Remove any clamps as necessary to allow the wires to be removed with the engine.

18. Disconnect the speedometer cable from the differential and secure the cable out of the way.

19. Remove the bolts retaining the gearshift linkage to the shifting tube. Loosen the bolt at the transmission end of the flexible link and swing the link to one side.

20. Remove the bolts holding the ground strap to the body.

21. Straighten the lock-tabs on the exhaust manifold flange. Remove the four nuts and lock-tab plates. Remove the 2 bolts from the upper bracket at the left end of the muffler. Remove the two nuts retaining the center support of the muffler to the crossmember and remove the muffler assembly. Remove the two nuts and bolt retaining the upper bracket to the differential case and remove the bracket.

22. Remove the three bolts securing the axle boots retaining ring on the right and left sides and slide the boots away from the differential, draining excess oil.

23. Remove the handbrake cable bracket at the forward end of each suspension control arm.

24. Take note of and record the number of shims at each suspension control arm mounting point.

25. Remove the four bolts and nuts plus the shims holding the control arms to the body and swing the control arms downward out of their brackets. Move the control arms away from the differential until the axles are free of the differential. Secure the axle assemblies to the control arms.

NOTE: If necessary, the entire suspension assemblies may be removed at this time by removing the wheels and brake calipers and the three nuts securing the top of the shock absorbers.

26. Straighten the lock-tabs on the two bolts on each end of the lower crossmember and loosen the bolts. Lower the vehicle until the engine is resting on a support.

— CAUTION —

Support the engine in such a manner so as not to damage the oil pan or any cast aluminum parts.

Remove the bolts from the lower crossmember.

27. From the top of the engine compartment, disconnect the engine torque rod from the bracket on the engine.

28. Remove the bolt from the engine mount, raise the car slightly and rock the engine/transmission assembly in order to clear the front engine mount.

29. Carefully raise the vehicle while supporting the engine. Watch for snags by wires, hoses or linkage.

30. Install the engine in the reverse order of removal.

Strada

NOTE: The engine and transaxle are removed as a unit from below. Make sure the car can be raised high enough to allow sufficient clearance for removal.

1. Remove hood, jack and spare tire.

2. Disconnect battery positive and negative leads, starter and ground at engine.

3. Drain the cooling system. Discharge air conditioning, if equipped.

— CAUTION —

The sudden discharge of freon from any A/C system can be extremely dangerous.

4. Remove three nuts and washers to remove air cleaner cover. Remove four self-locking nuts to remove air cleaner assembly complete with hoses to cold air box, exhaust manifold shield, oil separator, reed valve, or check valve for air pump.

5. Plug openings to prevent dirt entry.

6. Mark to identify, then remove electrical leads to engine left and right side sending units, engine bottom side sending unit, reverse gear switch, starter solenoid, intake manifold, idle stop solenoid and A/C compressor.

7. For vehicles with separate voltage regulator, disconnect alternator leads at voltage regulator, and two leads near heater box.

8. For vehicles with integral regulator, disconnect two alternator leads near heater box.

— CAUTION —

On Fuel Injection models, depressurize fuel system before attempting to remove any fuel lines.

9. Remove fuel lines and vapor canister lines from carburetor. Disconnect vapor canister hose from exhaust manifold shield.

10. Disconnect vacuum hose to brake booster at intake manifold and disconnect air hose to gulp valve.

11. On A/C cars, disconnect vacuum hose to fast idle diaphragm at carburetor.

12. Disconnect vacuum hose to vacuum manifold at T-fitting. Disconnect vacuum hose at electrovalve.

13. On manual transmission cars, disconnect return spring for carburetor. Slide lock ring off ball socket and remove ball socket from bracket.

14. On automatic transmission cars, loosen locknuts on trans linkage (kickdown).

15. Remove accelerator cable from bracket and unhook eyelet from trans kickdown lever.

16. On A/C vehicles, disconnect compressor delivery hose at condensor and compressor return hose at barometric valve.

17. Disconnect heater hoses at engine.

18. Disconnect radiator upper and lower hoses at engine.

19. Raise car on lift and support it safely.

20. Remove the front wheels, left and right splash shields from fender wells and from front center.

21. Remove the gearshift control rod, reverse lamp connector, left side reaction rod (manual trans), left side hub support, left side control arm, right side control arm and center rubber mount.

22. Disconnect the power unit support bracket.

23. Remove two nuts and bolts, each side, to separate strut assembly from hub carrier.

24. Remove the nut on each side and use Fiat tool A.47038 or equivalent to separate tie rod ball joint from hub carrier.

25. Remove six allen head capscrews and three plates, each side, to separate axles (half-shafts) from differential.

NOTE: Discard allen screws and replace with new ones for installation.

26. Make sure catalytic converter is cool, then straighten lock tabs on the mounting nuts and remove the converter.

27. On air pump equipped vehicles, remove two nuts, washers and bolts from exhaust pipe. Remove exhaust pipe.

28. Disconnect speedometer cable from trans.

29. On manual transmission cars, scribe an alignment mark on the shift rod and bracket. Remove two nuts, washers, lockwashers and bolts. Disconnect shift rod.

30. On automatic cars, place gear selector in 1. Remove E-clip and washer and slide shift cable eyelet off pin on transmission lever.

31. Remove nut from cable clamp and lay cable aside.

32. Attach lift sling to engine and transmission assembly.

33. Place a jack under center engine mount. Remove two bolts and washers to separate engine mount from body.

34. Remove two bolts, lockwashers and washers attaching right engine mount to mounting bracket.

35. Remove two upper and loosen only lower bolts, lockwasher and washer. Remove mounting bracket. Do not remove right engine mount.

36. On automatic transmission models, remove the bolt and washer from the left engine mount. Remove two bolts and lockwashers to separate sway bar from mounting bracket.

37. Remove two bolts and lockwashers to separate mounting bracket from body.

38. On manual transmission cars, remove three nuts, lockwashers and bolts to separate mounting bracket from body.

39. Slowly remove jack supporting center engine mount. Slowly lower engine out of engine compartment.

40. Install engine in reverse order of removal. Refill the cooling system and inspect all lines for tightness.

Cylinder Head

REMOVAL AND INSTALLATION

124 and 131 DOHC Engine

1. Before beginning any dismantling procedures, it's helpful to find the valve timing marks first. Turn the engine over until the timing mark on the crank pulley is aligned with the TDC mark on the front cover, and the rotor is pointing at no. 4 in the distributor cap. At this point, you should be able to see the marks on the cam housings in line with the holes in the cam gears.

2. Drain the cooling system and disconnect the upper radiator hose.

3. Remove the air cleaner.

CAUTION

On fuel injection models, depressurize the fuel system before removing any fuel lines.

4. Disconnect all linkage and hoses from the carburetor and cylinder head.

5. Remove the carburetor and intake manifold as an assembly.

1. Knob	8. Cam housing
2. Washer	9. Cam housing gasket
3. Stud	10. Cylinder head
4. Cover gasket	11. Studs
5. Cover	12. Locating dowel
6. End cover gasket	13. Head gasket
7. End cover	14. Engine block

Exploded view of dual cam cylinder head—typical

6. Disconnect the exhaust manifold from the side of the cylinder head.

7. Remove the timing belt shroud from the front of the engine.

8. Loosen the timing belt tensioner (idler) and remove the timing belt from the camshaft drive pulleys.

9. Remove the spark plug wires from the spark plugs.

10. Unscrew the cylinder head attaching bolts and carefully lift off the cylinder head. Lift the head straight up so as not to damage any of the open valves.

11. Clean the mating surfaces of all gasket material.

12. Before placing the cylinder head on the block, make sure the holes in the cam gears are aligned with the marks on the cam housings. Once the timing marks are aligned, avoid turning the camshafts until the drive belt has been installed.

13. Carefully place the cylinder head on the block. Do not allow any of the open valves to contact the block.

14. Install the cylinder head bolts and torque to specifications in the proper sequence.

15. Install the belt on the crankshaft pulley, auxiliary shaft pulley, intake camshaft pulley, exhaust cam pulley and the tensioner.

NOTE: Timing belts should never be re-used. Replace the timing belt if removed for any reason.

16. The Fiat recommended procedure for tightening the belt is to allow the tensioner to remove the play from the belt.

17. Check the belt tension after turning the crankshaft two or three times.

18. Check for proper valve timing by checking the timing marks. Refer to Timing Belt Removal and Installation if you get in trouble. Assemble the remaining components in the reverse order of removal.

128 and Strada SOHC Engine

NOTE: The aluminum cylinder head sometimes seizes on 128 and X1/9 models. To remove the head, remove all nuts and washers, then saturate the area around the studs with penetrating oil and allow to soak overnight. Before reassembly, clean all oil from the studs and housings and apply anti-seize compound.

1. Drain the cooling system. Disconnect the battery.

2. Remove the spare tire from the engine compartment.

3. Remove the air cleaner.

4. Disconnect the spark plug cables.

5. Disconnect the accelerator control linkage from the carburetor.

———— **CAUTION** ————

On fuel injection models, depressurize the fuel system before removing any fuel lines.

6. Disconnect the fuel line and the choke heater hoses from the carburetor.

1. Cover
2. Cover gasket
3. Cam housing
4. Cam housing gasket
5. Locating dowel
6. Bushing
7. Cylinder head gasket
8. Cylinder head
9. Welsh plug
10. Engine block

Exploded view of single cam cylinder head—typical

7. Disconnect the temperature sending unit electrical lead and thermoswitch leads.

8. Disconnect the heater inlet hose, the upper and lower radiator hoses, and the coolant pump delivery hose from the thermostat housing. On A/C equipped models, remove the distributor.

9. Disconnect the exhaust pipe from the manifold and remove the bracket.

10. Remove the belt guard cover, working from below the vehicle to get at the lower screw after removing a guard. 1977 and later models have a two-piece cover.

11. Loosen the belt tensioner pulley retaining nut and remove the belt from the camshaft sprocket.

NOTE: Timing belts should never be re-used. Replace the timing belt if removed for any reason.

12. Unscrew the belt guard lower screw.

13. Remove the shroud by unscrewing the set screws. Remove air pump and alternator brackets.

14. Disconnect the reaction rod from the bracket in the cylinder head.

15. Remove the cylinder head retaining screws and nuts and remove the cylinder head along with the intake and exhaust manifolds, carburetor, and the camshaft housing. Removal of these parts is best performed with the cylinder head out of the vehicle.

ALIGN CAMSHAFT TIMING MARKS WITH CAM HOUSING MARKS

PULLEY TIMING MARK IS AT 0° (TDC)

Timing mark alignment—DOHC engines

ALIGN CAMSHAFT TIMING MARK WITH BELT COVER POINTER

FLYWHEEL TIMING MARK IS AT 0° (TDC) (BELL HOUSING VIEW)

Timing mark alignment—SOHC engines

— **CAUTION** —

Do not allow the cylinder head to rest on any open valves. The proper size cap screws on each corner will ensure enough clearance during bench work.

---

16. Install the cylinder head, with the intake and exhaust manifolds, carburetor and camshaft housing assembled to it, in the reverse order of removal. Tighten the cylinder head bolts in the proper sequence in two stages; 29 ft/lbs the first time and to specifications the second time.

X1/9 SOHC Engine

See the note preceding the 128 cylinder head removal section before beginning.
1. Drain the cooling system and disconnect the battery.
2. Remove the air cleaner assembly.

— **CAUTION** —

On fuel injection models, depressurize the fuel system before removing any fuel lines.

---

3. Disconnect the fuel hoses from the carburetor and pull the two hoses out of the bracket on the camshaft cover.
4. Disconnect the accelerator linkage leading from the carburetor at the camshaft.
5. Disconnect the spark plug cables from the spark plugs.
6. Disconnect the distributor vacuum hose from the fitting in the cylinder head.
7. Remove the stop-bolt from the accelerator cable.
8. Slide the seal off of the cable and remove the clip retaining the cable to the camshaft cover. Remove the cable.
9. Disconnect the expansion tank hose, water pump inlet and outlet hoses, and the water pump-to-union hose.
10. Remove the bolt retaining the engine torque rod in its bracket and move the rod out of the way.
11. Disconnect the hose from the exhaust shroud.
12. Disconnect the electrical leads of the thermostatic switch on the carburetor.
13. Disconnect the evaporative hose from the carburetor.
14. Remove the air pump hoses.
15. Disconnect the muffler from the exhaust manifold flange.
16. Remove the bolts and washers attaching the timing cover. 1977 and later covers are two-piece. The earlier covers are often broken during removal. If so, replace with the later version.
17. Remove the lower right shield from under the engine.
18. Remove the alternator and the drive belt.
19. Remove the air pump.
20. Loosen the nut on the timing belt tensioner pulley and remove the timing belt.

NOTE: Timing belts should never be re-used. Replace the timing belt if removed for any reason.

21. Remove the lower bolt through the belt guard.
22. Remove the cylinder head attaching bolts and nuts and lift the cylinder head straight up and off of the engine. The carburetor and intake and exhaust manifolds are removed with the cylinder head as an assembly and removed from the cylinder head on the work bench.
23. Install the cylinder head in the reverse order of removal. Tighten the cylinder head bolts in the proper sequence. The valve timing is adjusted in the same manner as for the 128.

CYLINDER HEAD OVERHAUL

See Engine Rebuilding Unit Repair Section.

Intake and Exhaust Manifolds

REMOVAL AND INSTALLATION

All Models

NOTE: Depressurize fuel system on fuel injection models.

1. Remove the air cleaner.
2. Remove the fuel line, all vacuum lines, coolant lines and accelerator linkage from the carburetor.
3. The carburetor can be removed at this point or removed after the manifold is removed from the vehicle.
4. Disconnect the exhaust pipe from the manifold. This is not necessary if removing just the intake manifold on DOHC engines.
5. Remove the manifold retaining bolts from the cylinder head and remove the manifold from the engine.

6. Install the manifold(s) in the reverse order of removal, tighten the retaining bolts to specification in an alternating sequence starting at the center and working toward the ends. Torque all bolts to 20 ft. lbs.

Turbocharger

The Turbo Spider uses an I.H.I.RHB6 turbocharger unit that is calibrated to deliver a maximum boost of 6 psi. The low inertia turbine wheel is connected to a compressor wheel by a shaft. The shaft is supported by two bearings floating on a thin film of engine oil. The turbocharger unit is bolted to a modified exhaust manifold and is driven by exhaust gases that will spin the turbine wheel at up to 100,000 rpm. A wastegate, controlled by boost pressure, prevents damaging overboost by allowing some exhaust to bypass the turbocharger when the pressure exceeds 6 psi.

NOTE: The fuel injection system is modified to allow boost and load enrichment and contains an overboost fail-safe circuit that will shut off the fuel injectors should the wastegate fail and boost pressure reach 9 psi.

REMOVAL AND INSTALLATION

1. Remove the air intake and output hoses from the compressor side of the turbocharger.
2. Disconnect the oil feed and return lines.

NOTE: Use a new compression fitting when reinstalling oil lines.

3. Remove the eight allen head bolts attaching the turbocharger flanges to the exhaust system.

I.H.I. RHB6 turbocharger

Turbocharger mounting location

NOTE: Discard the allen bolts. Use new bolts for installation.

4. Disconnect the Lambda sensor.
5. Remove the allen bolts from the exhaust elbow to the support bracket.
6. Remove the bolts from the turbocharger support bracket and remove the turbocharger assembly.
7. Reinstall in reverse order, torquing all bolts to specifications.

NOTE: Turbocharger mounting and flange bolts should be torqued every 15,000 miles.

TURBOCHARGER TORQUE REFERENCE

Description	Torque (ft.lbs.)
Turbocharger to exhaust manifold	20
Exhaust manifold nuts	22
Outlet elbow to turbo-charger bolts	22
Outlet elbow to exhaust pipe nuts	22
Outlet elbow support bracket to block bolts	30
Plenum support bracket to plenum bolt	12
Lambda sensor	30
Exhaust manifold heat shield	22

NOTE: Retorque all bolts 1500 miles after reinstalling turbocharger.

Timing Gear Cover

REMOVAL AND INSTALLATION

131 and 124 DOHC

The valve mechanism drive belt cover on these engines is removed by simply removing the retaining screws and lifting the cover from the engine. Install in reverse order.

128 and X1/9

Removal of the timing belt cover on 1976 engines is quite difficult because of the lack of space, particularly on the X1/9. There are only three bolts, but reaching them is a chore. Cover breakage on the early models is quite common. 1977 and later covers are two piece for this reason.

1. On 128 models, loosen the right engine mount and jack the engine up slightly.
2. On X1/9 models, there is no room to jack the engine. Remove the bolts that retain the belt cover and work the cover loose. There is no easy way to do this.
3. On 128 models, remove the bolts and tilt the cover up and out. If the engine is jacked up far enough, the cover should come out intact.
4. Installation is the reverse of removal.

Strada

1. Remove bolts, lockwashers and washers holding timing belt covers. Remove covers.
2. Remove attaching hardware for inner shields. Remove shields.

3. Installation is the reverse of removal.

NOTE: Lower cover bolt must be removed from under car.

Timing Belt

NOTE: Fiat recommends that the timing belt not be reused. Anytime belt tension is relieved, the timing belt must be replaced. The belt should also be replaced every 25,000 miles.

REMOVAL AND INSTALLATION

124 and 131 DOHC

1. Before dismantling anything, turn the engine over by hand until no. 4 cylinder is on TDC and the timing mark on the crank pulley is aligned with the TDC mark on the timing cover. The rotor should be pointing at no. 4 in the distributor cap.
2. At this point, you should be able to see that the holes in the cam pulleys are aligned with the small cast fingers on the cam housing.
3. If the car is equipped with air-conditioning, remove the compressor drive belt.
4. Partially drain the cooling system and remove the upper radiator hose.
5. Remove the thermostat housing.
6. Remove the timing belt cover.
7. Remove the drive belt for the air pump. Remove the alternator drive belt.
8. Loosen the nut on the belt tensioner. Loosen the bolt for the spring support. Pry the tensioner away from the belt and remove the belt.

1. Valve timing pointers
2. Intake camshaft drive pulley
3. Timing belt
4. Exhaust camshaft/distributor drive pulley
5. Roller retaining nut
6. Tensioner spring
7. Tensioner roller
8. Tensioner retaining screw
9. Oil pump drive pulley
10. Crankshaft pulley

124, 131 engine cam drive

1. Exhaust camshaft sprocket
2. Intake camshaft sprocket
3. Oil dipstick tube
4. Tensioner bracket bolt
5. Spring retaining bolt
6. Hole
7. Bolt
8. Crankshaft sprocket
9. Auxiliary shaft sprocket
10. Spacer
11. Tensioner pulley
12. Belt

124 and 131 DOHC engine

9. Install a new belt. Allow the tensioner to remove the play from the belt, and tighten the tensioner and the spring support. Rotate the engine a couple of times and recheck the belt tension.

10. Loosely install the belt cover and check to make sure all the valve timing marks line up.

11. If the valve timing is correct, reinstall the timing belt cover.

12. Reinstall the remaining components in the reverse order of removal.

128 SOHC

1. Remove the timing gear cover. The lower retaining screw of the cover must be removed from under the car after removing the right side guard.

2. Check the valve timing by aligning the timing mark on the camshaft sprocket with the fixed mark on the engine and making sure that the timing mark on the crankshaft sprocket is simultaneously aligned with its fixed index mark.

3. Remove the water pump and alternator drive belt.

4. Loosen the tensioner pulley retaining nut and relieve the spring action to remove the timing belt.

5. Install the new belt, making sure the belt and sprocket teeth engage perfectly.

6. Tighten the tensioner pulley nut to 33 ft. lbs.

X1/9

1. Turn the crankshaft until no. 4 piston is at TDC of the compression stroke.

The timing mark on the front (right) crankshaft pulley should be at TDC and the camshaft timing pulley mark should be aligned with the cast finger of the support, visible through the hole in the camshaft cover.

NOTE: Throughout this entire procedure remember that if the camshaft is turned independently of the crankshaft the valves may hit the pistons causing damage.

2. Remove the bolts attaching the timing cover, remove the right guard from under the engine, remove the lower bolt retaining the timing cover and remove the cover.

3. Loosen the alternator and remove the alternator water pump drive belt.

4. Remove the drive pulley from the crankshaft.

5. Loosen the air pump and remove the drive belt.

6. Remove the camshaft cover. Check and make sure the cam lobes of no. 4 cylinder are pointing up.

7. Remove the distributor.

8. Loosen the idler pulley locknut, push it on the support and tighten the locknut. Remove the timing belt, starting at the idler pulley.

9. Install the new timing belt, starting at the crankshaft. Twist the belt gently into position around the crankshaft pulley. Do not kink the belt.

10. Slip the belt over the camshaft pulley. The camshaft pulley may have to be turned slightly to align the slots with the belt cogs.

11. Install the belt over the idler pulley last.

12. Loosen the idler pulley locknut and retighten after tension is on the belt. Turn the crankshaft of the engine one half of a turn in the direction of normal rotation by either pushing the car with it in fourth gear or bumping the starter.

13. Release the idler pulley locknut to make sure all slack is removed from the belt and then retighten the locknut.

14. Continue to turn the crankshaft of the engine in the direction of normal rotation by either method mentioned in Step 12 until no. 4 piston reaches TDC of the compression stroke (one and one-half turns).

NOTE: Never push the car backward in gear or allow the engine to rock backward while pushing the car. Slack will develop in the belt, allowing the belt to jump timing.

15. Position the belt cover on the engine and check to make sure the crankshaft timing mark is at TDC and that the camshaft mark is aligned with the pointer. Tighten the tensioner pulley nut to 32 ft. lbs.

16. Install the pulley on the crankshaft.

17. Install the drive belt on the air pump.

18. Install the drive belt for the water pump and the alternator. Adjust the belt tension.

19. Install the timing gear cover.

20. Install the lower right guard.

21. Install the camshaft cover.

22. Install the distributor. The rotor should be pointing toward no. 4 cylinder spark plug tower of the distributor cap.

1. Camshaft timing reference mark (engine on car)
2. Camshaft drive pulley
3. Toothed timing belt, driving the camshaft and pulley 8
4. Camshaft timing reference mark (engine on bench)
5. Idler pulley tensioner
6. Idler pulley support
7. Idler pulley
8. Drive pulley for oil pump and ignition distributor
9. Reference mark for pulley 10 setting
10. Crankshaft sprocket

128, X1/9 and Strada engine cam drive

Strada

1. Disconnect battery cable. Remove spark plugs.

2. Remove timing belt covers (lower bolt must be removed from under car).

3. Rotate the engine until crankshaft pulley mark is aligned with TDC indicator and cam sprocket mark is aligned with mark on belt guard.

4. Loosen alternator (and A/C compressor if equipped) mounting bolts and remove the pulley belt.

5. Loosen idler pulley nut and move pulley toward the firewall as far as possible. Secure idler pulley in place with nut.

6. Remove timing belt.

7. Install new timing belt with slack on tensioner side. Make sure the teeth are perfectly aligned with sprockets.

8. Loosen idler pulley nut and tensioner will tighten timing belt. Torque idler pulley nut to 33 ft. lbs.

9. Check that timing marks are still aligned.

10. Reinstall covers, spark plugs and battery cable.

Camshafts

REMOVAL AND INSTALLATION

128, Strada, and X1/9 SOHC

1. Remove the camshaft drive belt.

2. Remove the camshaft carrier attaching bolts and remove the camshaft carrier assembly from the engine.

3. Remove the camshaft drive sprocket.

4. Remove the camshaft thrust plate from the opposite end (opposite the belt end) of the camshaft carrier.

5. Carefully slide the camshaft out of the camshaft carrier.

6. Install the camshaft in the reverse order of removal, making sure the valve timing marks on the camshaft sprocket and the crankshaft sprocket are properly aligned before installing the timing belt. See timing belt removal and installation procedure.

1. Camshaft sprocket
2. Tensioner pulley
3. Drive pulley
4. Auxiliary shaft sprocket
5. Tensioner
6. Belt guard
7. Bracket

Removing the belt tensioner pulley nut

1. Piston pin bore class
2. Piston class
3. Matching number of connecting rod to cylinder

Piston identification marks

1. Camshaft seal
2. Exhaust camshaft dowel
3. Exhaust camshaft
4. Tappet plate
5. Exhaust valve tappet
6. Exhaust valve inner spring
7. Lower cup
8. Locks
9. Exhaust valve oil seal
10. Exhaust valve guide
11. Intake camshaft
12. Upper cup
13. Dowel
14. Exhaust valve outer spring
15. Intake valve inner spring
16. Exhaust valve
17. Lower cup
18. Intake valve
19. Intake valve guide
20. Oil seal
21. Washer
22. Intake valve outer spring
23. Upper cup
24. Intake valve tappet

124 and 131 DOHC valve mechanism—typical

1. Location of the connecting rod and bearing cap identification and cylinder number
2. Piston pin offset 0.08 in.
3. Auxiliary shaft

NOTE: Arrow shows direction of crank-shaft rotation

Piston and connecting rod installation for all engines

124 and 131 DOHC

1. Remove the timing cover and remove the camshaft drive belt.
2. Remove the camshaft housings.
3. Remove the bolts in the center of the cam pulleys. Remove the cam pulleys with a gear puller.
4. Remove the three nuts retaining the front cam covers.
5. Slide the camshafts out from the cam housings.
6. Installation is the reverse of removal. Refer to the timing belt removal and installation procedure.

PISTON AND CONNECTING ROD IDENTIFICATION AND POSITIONING

If the connecting rod and piston assemblies are going to be reinstalled in the engine, they should be clearly identified during disassembly so they can be reinstalled in their original positions.

128, Strada, and X1/9 SOHC

The piston and connecting rod assembly is installed in the cylinder block with piston identification letter toward the timing belt end of the engine and the connecting rod and cap identification numbers facing away from the auxiliary shaft.

124, 131 DOHC

The piston and connecting rod assemblies are installed with the piston identification

letter facing toward the front of the engine and the connecting rod and cap identification numbers facing away from the auxiliary shaft.

ENGINE LUBRICATION

Oil Pan

REMOVAL AND INSTALLATION

124 and 131

1. Drain the engine oil.
2. Raise the car in the air and support it securely.
3. The engine will have to be raised about six inches in the chassis in order for the oil pan to be removed. Unbolt the motor mounts and raise the engine up about six inches.
4. You will have to fabricate some way of holding the engine in the air while removing the oil pan. Remove the oil pan bolts and remove the pan.
5. Installation is the reverse of removal.

128 and X1/9

1. Raise the car in the air and support it securely. Drain the engine oil.
2. The oil pan can be removed from the bottom only if the engine is supported with a hoist or other lifting device which will allow the engine mounting crossmember and splash shields to be removed.
3. If a hoist is available, raise the engine high enough to take the strain off, and remove the crossmember and splash shields. The crossmember holds the engine up, so be careful.
4. Unbolt the oil pan and remove it.
5. Installation is in the reverse of removal.

Strada

1. Raise the car and support it safely.
2. Drain the engine oil.
3. Remove the 20 bolts and lockwashers holding the oil pan.
4. Remove the oil pan and gasket.
5. Installation is the reverse of removal. Clean oil pan and block mating surfaces, use a new gasket.

1. Blow-by gas and oil vapor hose
2. Collar
3. Flam trap
4. Breather hose
5. Bolt and washer
6. Breather
7. Collar
8. Hose
9. Seal
10. Vapor return connection
11. Stud, lockwasher, and nut
12. Breather tube
13. Bolt
14. Gear bushing
15. Retaining plate
16. Bolt and lockwasher
17. Spring washer
18. Auxiliary shaft
19. Dowel
20. Front bushing
21. Rear bushing
22. Seal
23. Oil filler cap

124 and 131 DOHC engine lubrication components

Oil Pump

REMOVAL AND INSTALLATION

All Models

1. Remove the oil pan.
2. Remove the oil pump assembly attaching bolts and remove the oil pump.
3. Install the oil pump in the reverse order of removal.

CHECKING CLEARANCES

All Models

1. Remove the oil pump from the engine.
2. Remove the pump cover to expose the oil pump gears.
3. Measure the clearance between the gear teeth and the pump housing with a feeler gauge.
4. Place a straight edge across the pump housing and measure the clearance between the straight edge and the ends of the gears with a feeler gauge.
5. Place the blade of the feeler gauge between the teeth of the two gears and measure the gear backlash.
6. Replace any worn part and reassemble the oil pump in the reverse order of disassembly.

Crankshaft Oil Seals

REPLACEMENT–REAR

All Models

The transmission must be removed in order to replace the rear main oil seal. The oil seal housing is bolted to the rear of the engine block. With the housing removed, press the old seal out of the housing and

1. Breather hose	10. Gasket
2. Flame trap	11. Oil filter connector
3. Seal	12. Dipstick seal
4. Blow-by gas and oil vapor hose	13. Oil pump
5. Oil filler cap	14. Bushing
6. Oil pressure sw	15. Oil pump drive gear
7. Breather oil return pipe	16. Oil filter
8. Crankcase breather	17. Auxiliary shaft
9. Dipstick	18. Bushings
	19. Gasket

Strada and X1/9 engine lubrication components

Measuring clearance between gear and housing of oil pump

Measuring clearance between ends of gears and straight edge

press the new seal into place. Oil the lips of the seal before installation. All engines use indexing lugs to aid the centering of the seal and housing.

REPLACEMENT—FRONT

All Models

The timing belt and cover assembly must be removed from the front of the engine to expose the front crankshaft seal housing. The seal is pressed into the housing. The housing has indexing lugs to assist the centering of the housing. Lubricate the seal lips before installation.

Auxiliary Shaft Seals

REPLACEMENT

All Models

The auxiliary shaft seal housing is exposed with the removal of the timing belt, cover assembly, and front accessories. Unbolt the housing from the engine, and remove the old seal. Press the new seal into the housing cover, center the cover over the shaft flange, and bolt it into place. Oil the lips of the seal before installation.

ENGINE COOLING

NOTE: All models use an electric cooling fan, operated by a thermoswitch.

Radiator
REMOVAL AND INSTALLATION
124, 131

1. Open the petcock at the bottom of the radiator and drain the coolant from the radiator and cylinder block.

2. Remove the hose which connects the radiator and thermostat cover.

3. Remove the hose which connects the radiator and water pump.

4. Remove the pipe which connects the radiator to the auxiliary tank.

5. When equipped with automatic transmission disconnect oil lines.

6. Unbolt and remove the radiator.

7. Installation is the reverse of removal.

128, Strada

1. Drain the radiator and the cylinder block.

2. Disconnect the thermal fan switch and the fan relay switch.

3. Disconnect the hose running from the radiator to the expansion tank.

4. Remove the hoses running from the

1. Bolt and lockwasher	8. Bolt and lockwasher
2. Auxiliary shaft cover	9. Rear cover
3. Gasket	10. Gasket
4. Cover	11. Gasket
5. Bolt	12. Bolt and lockwasher
6. Gasket	13. Drain plug
7. Oil seal	14. Oil sump

15. Stud, lockwasher, and nut
16. Bolt and lockwasher
17. Front cover
18. Oil seal
19. Bolt and lockwasher
20. Gasket
21. Oil seal

Oil pan and crankshaft seal locations—typical

thermostat union to the radiator.

5. Remove the screws that attach the top part of the radiator to the brackets fitted on the body, together with the rubber pads, washers, and spacers.

6. Slide the radiator, fan, and shroud out of the top of the engine compartment.

7. Installation is the reverse of removal.

NOTE: Do not use coolant containing sealers or rust inhibitors.

X1/9

1. Drain the cooling system.

2. Remove the three lower screws securing the grille to the crossrail.

3. Remove the four nuts retaining the guard plate to the body and remove the plate.

4. Disconnect the hoses at the radiator.

5. Disconnect the electrical connector for the fan motor and the wires from the thermostatic switch.

6. Remove the bolt and nut holding the bottom crossrail at each side and remove the crossrail.

7. Lower the radiator out from under the car, being careful of the fan. Installation is the reverse of removal.

BLEEDING

The radiator must be bled after it is refilled with coolant. The bleeder valve is on the top of the radiator (accessible through the trunk once the radiator is in place on X1/9). Start the car and check for leaks. Turn on the heater. Connect a pressure tester to the radiator and pump in no more than 11 psi of air. Open the bleeder valve and repeat the operation until all air is removed from the system.

Water Pump

REMOVAL AND INSTALLATION

124 and 131

1. If necessary, remove the radiator from the vehicle.

2. Unbolt and remove the fan from the water pump flange.

3. Remove the hose which connects the water pump and radiator.

4. Remove the water pump from the mounting.

5. Installation is the reverse of removal.

128

1. Remove the spare wheel.

2. Place protective coverings on the fenders.

3. Drain the water from the cooling system.

4. Disconnect the hot air hose and the

1. Water pump
2. Gasket
3. Gasket
4. Automatic choke to thermovalve housing hose
5. Engine to automatic choke hose
6. Water pump intake pipe
7. Thermostat to radiator hose
8. Thermovalve housing to thermostat hose
9. Thermostat to water pump hose
10. Thermostat housing
11. Radiator to thermostat hose
12. Radiator

Cooling system components—Strada and X1/9

accelerator rod from the shroud.

5. Remove the shroud.

6. Disconnect the passenger compartment heater water delivery and return hoses.

7. Slacken the nuts that hold the alternator on the two lower brackets and remove the top bracket.

8. Unscrew the nuts which attach the pump to the crankcase and slide off the pump assembly.

9. Installation is the reverse of removal.

Strada

1. Drain the cooling system.

2. If equipped with air pump, remove top half of timing belt cover.

3. Remove air pump and drive belt.

4. Remove alternator, drive belt and alternator mount.

5. If equipped with air conditioning, remove compressor, drive belt and compressor mount.

6. Remove two bolts holding water pipe to water pump and disconnect pipe.

7. Remove four bolts holding water pump to block. Remove pump and gasket.

8. Installation is reverse of removal. Install a new pump gasket.

9. Refill radiator with approved coolant, start engine and check for leaks.

10. Stop engine and bleed the cooling system.

X1/9

1. Drain the cooling system.

2. Remove the protection panels from the bottom right side of the engine.

3. Remove the alternator and drive belt.

4. Disconnect the hoses from the water pump.

5. Remove the three nuts and washers retaining the heater hose pipe to the pump.

6. Remove the bolt holding the support for the air pump to the water pump.

7. Remove the four bolts holding the water pump to the engine and remove the pump.

8. Install the pump in the reverse order of removal.

9. Bleed the cooling system.

Thermostat

REMOVAL AND INSTALLATION

124 and 131

1. Drain off part of the coolant in the radiator (to a level below the inline bypass thermostat).

2. Disconnect the 3 hoses to the inline thermostat and withdraw the thermostat.

Immerse the thermostat in the water and heat the water. When the temperature reaches 185–192°F, the thermostat valve should begin to open. The valve should be completely open when the water temperature reaches 212°F. If the thermostat does not meet specifications, it is defective and must be replaced.

3. Installation is the reverse of removal.

1. Large coolant hoses
2. Thermovalve hose
3. Mounting bolt
4. Thermostat assembly
5. Gasket

Thermostat assembly—typical

128, X1/9 and Strada

1. Drain the water from the cooling system.

2. Remove the spare wheel from the engine compartment on the 128 and Strada.

3. Disconnect the hoses from the thermostat union.

4. Unscrew the attachment screws and remove the union complete with the thermostat.

5. Unscrew the union cover and slide out the thermostat and its seal.

6. Installation is the reverse of removal.

7. Bleed the cooling system.

EMISSION CONTROLS

Application

Crankcase Ventilation System—All models

Fuel Evaporative System—All models

Engine Modification System—All models except fuel injection

Deceleration Throttle Positioner System—All models except fuel injection

Air Injection System—All models 1976–79. All California models

Air Induction System—1979 and later 49 States versions

Air Gulp System—1979 and later 49 States versions

Exhaust Gas Recirculation—All models 1976 and later except fuel injection

Catalytic Converter—All models 1977 and later, all California models

Fuel Injection—1980 Spider, Super Brava, all models 1981 and later

Turbocharging—1982 and later Spider 2000

Crankcase Ventilation System

This is a closed system in which all crankcase vapors are drawn into the engine's combustion chambers to be consumed, rather than being vented to the atmosphere.

During idle and part-throttle operation, intake vacuum draws the vapors from the crankcase and a connecting hose (with a flame trap) conveys them to the air cleaner and into the carburetor.

During full-throttle engine operation, the crankcase vapors are conveyed directly to the intake manifold downstream of the carburetor by an additional smaller diameter hose; this part of the circuit is controlled by a valve which is activated by the throttle mechanism of the carburetor.

NOTE: The crankcase ventilation system functions much the same way on fuel injection versions. On Turbo models, the crankcase vapor hose is rerouted from the throttle housing to the turbocharger compressor inlet hose.

MAINTENANCE

Every 12,000 miles, this blowby gas and oil vapor recirculation system, including the carburetor, vent valve and flame trap must be cleaned and flushed with solvent.

Evaporative Emission Control

This system is designed to prevent the escape of raw fuel vapors into the atmosphere—that is, in effect, a "sealed" fuel system.

The fuel tank is of the "limited filling" type—that is, it maintains a volume of air space which is normally slightly pressurized. The tank and filler cap are non-vented.

Fuel vapors originating in the fuel tank are conveyed to the separator; this component passes vapors but is designed to return liquid fuel to the tank. The vapors are then conveyed to a three-way valve. With the fuel tank slightly pressurized, fuel vapors are passed through this valve to the active carbon trap and become absorbed there.

As the engine is operated, intake manifold vacuum is applied to the trap. This draws warm air from a collector, normally near the exhaust manifold, into the trap and up through the carbon trap; the warm air regenerates the carbon, purifying it and releasing the fuel vapors to be drawn into the intake manifold. Turbo models have a check valve installed in the vapor line to prevent boost from pressurizing the canister.

MAINTENANCE

It is recommended that the components of the system be visually inspected periodically in order to determine that all units and hoses are intact and hose connections are secure. Replace the charcoal canister every 25,000 miles.

NOTE: 1979 and later models use a permanent charcoal canister. The new canister requires no maintenance and should last the life of the car.

Engine Modification System

This system is a catch-all for all the emission control features and components that do not fall under any of the other headings. Basically, it consists of a leaner, more carefully controlled carburetor; a recalibrated distributor that brings in the ignition advance at a higher rpm; a revised camshaft and valve timing; and a lower compression ratio.

1. Hose to exhaust manifold shield
2. Air cleaner
3. Hose to oil separator
4. Hose to reed valve or check valve
5. Hose to cold air box
6. Air cleaner cover
7. Nut and washer

Thermostatic air cleaner components

Engine Family 128

Engine Family 132

1. Emission feedback line to air cleaner
2. Flame trap
3. Air cleaner-to-control valve line
4. Control valve

4a. Control valve in engine beyond idle condition
4b. Control valve in engine idling condition
5. Intake manifold

6. Sump-to-air cleaner line
7. Cyclone liquid/vapor separator
8. Oil drain line into sump

Crankcase emission control systems—128 and 132 engine families

To help the engine burn the leaner air/fuel mixture, a climatic setting is provided on the air cleaner (all models except X1/9). In cold weather, the air cleaner can be adjusted to draw in only exhaust manifold heated intake air, providing for better fuel atomization and overall better driveability when cold. In warm climates, the air cleaner can be adjusted to draw in only cool (ambient) intake air.

NOTE: 1979 and later models with thermostatic air cleaner are self-adjusting. No seasonal maintenance is required.

An idle stop solenoid is used on the carburetor linkage to prevent dieseling or "running on" after the key is shut off. The solenoid cuts off the fuel supply to the engine, closing the throttle plate completely.

MAINTENANCE

The only maintenance item is the air cleaner climatic setting. In temperate zones, the setting is adjusted in spring and autumn. Adjust the air intake as per the following:
1. Remove the air cleaner cover bolts.
2. Lift the air cleaner cover and align the marks with the arrow on the snorkel duct according to climate.
   I—ambient temperature below 60°F
   E—ambient temperature above 60°F

Air cleaner climate settings

Deceleration Throttle Positioner System

This system, also known as the Fast Idling System, reduces emissions by holding the throttle slightly open when decelerating in third or fourth gears (manual transmission), and when decelerating in second or third gears (automatic transmission). If uncontrolled, deceleration from speed causes a high vacuum condition when the throttle plate closes with the engine in the middle to upper rpm range. This high vacuum draws in raw fuel which causes an overrich condition. With the throttle positioner holding the throttle open to the fast idle position, extra air is admitted with the fuel, leaning out the mixture and reducing emissions.

The carburetor is provided with a vacuum-sensitive diaphragm which is linked to the primary throttle plate shaft. Vacuum to operate this diaphragm is derived from the intake manifold through an electropneumatic valve. This valve is mounted on the vehicle firewall or side wall of the engine compartment, depending on car model, and is operated by applying an electrical ground to complete the activating circuit.

One switch is fitted to the transmission, and is closed (activating the circuit) when 3rd or 4th gears are engaged.

Another switch is fitted at the clutch pedal and is connected in series with the first switch. It is closed when the pedal is released and opens as the pedal is depressed. Thus, with 3rd or 4th gear engaged and the clutch pedal released, both switches are closed and the electrovalve is energized. Under such conditions, manifold vacuum is applied to the diaphragm keeping the throttle plate from returning completely to the closed or idle position. If the transmission is in a position other than 3rd or 4th gears, or the clutch pedal is depressed regardless of conditions existing in the trans-

1. Compensating intake
2. Vacuum-sensitive capsule
3. Throttle adjustment screw for fast idle speed
4. Vacuum connection on intake manifold
5. Electrovalve
6. Button switch for fast idle speed control
7. Switch closed when clutch is engaged
8. Switch closed by transmission on 3rd-4th gear
9. Fuse
10. Ignition switch
11. Battery

Deceleration throttle positioner system—typical

mission, the activating circuit is broken and the device is rendered inoperative.

In order to be able to check and/or adjust the fast idle setting, a pushbutton switch is provided to manually ground, or activate, the electrovalve. This switch is mounted on the firewall or side of the engine compartment, depending on the car model. Fast idle speed is then adjusted with the screw on the vacuum diaphragm unit on the carburetor.

NOTE: This circuitry is fused through the windshield wiper system; therefore, if that circuit is inoperative, the device will not function.

MAINTENANCE

The only adjustment on the system is the fast idle speed, which can be checked after setting normal idle speed and mixture. With the engine warm and idling in neutral, depress and hold down the fast idle electrovalve button (located inside the engine compartment on the firewall, radiator support or fender apron) while accelerating the engine to approximately 2500 rpm. This will activate the system and simulate a deceleration condition. While still depressing the button, allow the engine speed to decrease to the fast idle speed; 1600 rpm on a manual transmission car and 1300 rpm with an automatic. Adjust as necessary with the fast idling adjusting screw on the fast idle diaphragm and recheck. Finally, release the pushbutton switch and check that the engine speed returns to normal idle speed, within 1–3 seconds.

Air Injection System

Fiats are equipped with this system (also known as a thermal reactor system) to control emissions. A belt-driven air pump delivers filtered air to the exhaust ports. Here, the additional oxygen supplied by the vane type pump reacts with the uncombusted fuel mixture, promoting an afterburning effect in the hot exhaust manifold. To prevent a damaging reverse flow in the air injection manifold when exhaust gas pressure exceeds air supply pressure, a non-return check valve is used. Also, to prevent backfiring in the exhaust system during deceleration, a diverter valve is used to divert pump air to the atmosphere under these conditions. The diverter valve also serves to cutout the air pump air during cold temperature starts.

MAINTENANCE

On 128, Strada, and X1/9 models with the Bosch or Nippondenso air pump, replace the air pump filter cartridge at 12,000 mile intervals; sooner if the car is driven in dusty areas. On 124 and 131 models with the Saginaw air pump, the filter is integral with the pump and does not require servicing.

Air pump belt tension cannot be adjusted when the toothed belt is used (V-belts are adjustable). Replace belt if worn. Average belt life should be 25,000–35,000 miles.

Air Gulp System

Beginning with 1979 models, the gulp valve replaces the diverter valve to prevent an overrich situation (backfiring) during deceleration by supplying fresh air to the intake manifold on demand. A vacuum signal from the intake manifold controls the valve. When starting, the gulp valve is held closed by a vacuum signal from the electrovalve which is energized through the starting cir-

Fast idle electrovalve button—124 Spider shown

1. Primary throttle
2. Idler lever
3. Tie rod
4. Diaphragm controlling opening of primary throttle
5. Vacuum tapping line on intake manifold
6. Fast idle adjustment screw
7. Calibrated bushing
8. Air suction orifice

Cross section of fast idle adjusting screw and vacuum control

cuit. If the engine temperature is below 46°F the thermoswitch is closed, energizing the electrovalve and closing the gulp valve. Above 54°F the thermoswitch opens, de-energizing the electrovalve and allowing varying vacuum signals from the engine to control the operation of the gulp valve. The vacuum signal is strongest during deceleration.

MAINTENANCE

No maintenance is required on the air gulp system, however if a sudden backfiring condition is encountered, check the gulp valve and electrovalve for proper operation.

Air Induction System

Beginning with some 1979 models, the air induction system replaces both the air pump and diverter valve on 49 States versions. The air induction system supplies filtered air to the exhaust charge as it leaves the combustion chamber in order to complete the burning cycle and lower emissions. Fresh air is drawn in by exhaust pulses rather than pumped in under pressure. Inducted air passes through a filter on the air cleaner housing and is supplied to a delivery passage in the cylinder head that feeds all cylinders. Two reed valves mounted on the cylinder head prevent any damaging reverse flow of exhaust gases in the system.

MAINTENANCE

The only required maintenance is to replace the induction system air filter every 30,000 miles. The air filter is mounted on the air cleaner housing and also serves as a silencer for the system.

Exhaust Gas Recirculation System

All Fiat models, except fuel injection versions, are equipped with an Exhaust Gas Recirculation (EGR) System to control nitrogen oxide emissions. The system recirculates a small portion (about 10%) of the exhaust manifold into the intake mixture during past-throttle conditions. Since the exhaust gases contain little oxygen, they cannot burn when fired, thereby lowering the peak combustion chamber temperatures and reducing NOx. To ensure good drive-ability of the car, an EGR valve is used to prevent exhaust gas recirculation during periods of idling or wide open throttle, and is used to meter the degree of recirculation during part-throttle applications, depending on engine load. A thermostatic switch cuts out recirculation when the engine is cold (catalytic converter models only). Also, on 1977 and later models, recirculation is prevented when 5th gear is engaged.

1. Clamp
2. Air induction housing
3. Retainer bolts

Reed valve filter housing

1. Air filter
2. Air injection pump
3. Excess pressure valve
4. Diverter valve
5. Electrovalve (normally closed) (C.C. cars)
6. Delay valve
7. Ignition retardation capsule
8. Check valve
9. Air injection manifold
10. Electrovalve (normally closed) (C.C. cars)
11. Thermovalve
12. Diverter valve control signal intake
13. Ignition retardation capsule control signal intake
14. Automatic choke system
15. Dashpot
16. Idle stop solenoid
17. Diverter valve control thermoswitch (C.C. cars)
18. Relay
19. Gearshift lever (switch open with transmission in neutral) (C.C. cars)
20. Switch closed with 4th gear engaged (C.C. cars)
21. Control unit (C.C. cars)
22. "Slow down" signal indicator (C.C. cars)
23. Thermocouple (C.C. cars)
24. Fuse
25. Ignition switch
26. Battery.

1977 X1/9 emission control schematic

On 1976 models only, an odometer actuated EGR service reminder system is used. At 25,000 mile intervals, the system will light an "EGR" service warning lamp on the dash. Beginning with the 1977 model year, the EGR system has been recertified for 50,000 miles eliminating the need for the 25,000 mile service reminder system.

MAINTENANCE

On 1976 models, check the vacuum lines for leaks or cracks every 25,000 miles. Also check the EGR valve and exhaust gas line for deposits, particularly if a steady diet of leaded fuel is used. Clean with a bristle bore brush, or replace as necessary. 1977 and later models have no regularly scheduled EGR maintenance specified.

On 1976 models with the EGR service reminder system, the warning light is extinguished by resetting the odometer counter, located on the firewall of the engine compartment.

To reset the switch:

1. Remove the odometer counter lockwire (5) and unscrew the cap (6).
2. Rotate the screw switch to "50".
3. Replace the fuse in holder (6). Install the cap and lockwire.
4. At 50,000 mile EGR service, repeat Step 1 and rotate screw back to "25". Repeat Step 3.

Catalytic Converter System

All models manufactured for sale in California, as well as all (50 states) 1976 X1/9 models, and all 1979 and later models are equipped with a catalytic converter to further reduce emissions. The converter is located in the exhaust system, upstream from the muffler. The converter is filled with a platinum/palladium pellet substrate which rapidly oxidizes emissions of hydrocarbons and carbon monoxide into carbon dioxide and water.

On 1976 models, a catalyst protection system is used to prevent overheating of the catalyst. Whenever the throttle is released fully while the engine speed is 2650 rpm or greater (such as deceleration from speed), the carburetor idle stop solenoid will shut off the fuel supply until engine speed drops below 2650 rpm. This prevents raw fuel from being sucked into the intake during deceleration. On 1977 and later models, this system is not used.

Also on 1976 models, a catalyst temperature warning system is used. If a malfunction in the fuel system should occur, leading to an overrich condition and subsequent converter overheating, a thermo sensor in the converter will activate a dash warning light which reads "slow down." The hotter the catalyst, the faster the warning light will blink on and off. 1977 and later models do not use this system.

Also on 1976 models only is an odometer actuated catalytic converter replacement reminder system. Identical to the EGR service reminder, at 25,000 mile intervals, a dash warning light will display "catalyst", indicating that it's time to replace the converter. Beginning with the 1977 model year, the converter has been re-certified for 50,000 miles or more, with no regularly scheduled replacement intervals.

49 State version

1. Fast idle capsule
2. Continuity hole
3. Exhaust gas recirculation intake
4. EGR valve control vacuum intake
5. Fast idle valve control vacuum intake
6. EGR valve control thermovalve
7. Diverter valve control vacuum intake
8. EGR valve
9. Air injector
10. Air injection manifold
11. Check valve
12. Air pump
13. Diverter valve
14. Ignition contact matched switch

15. Fuse
16. Switch contacts closed by transmission on 3rd-4th gear
17. Fast idle control switch
18. Electrovalve
19. Battery
20. Switch closed when clutch is engaged
21. Idle stop solenoid
22. Automatic choke system
23. Electrovalve
24. Transmission switch (closed with 5th gear engaged)
25. Thermoswitch
26. Electrovalve
27. Magnetic reversing switch
28. Catalytic converter
29. Gear shift lever (switch open with transmission in neutral)

1977 124 and 131 emission control system schematic with catalytic converter

1. Catalytic converter
2. Nut
3. Lock ring
4. Spring

Catalytic converter installation—typical

MAINTENANCE

On 1976 models, replace the converter at 25,000 mile intervals, and reset the odometer switch. The switch, and resetting procedure is the same as that listed under EGR Maintenance. 1977 and later models do not require replacement of the converter in normal service.

FUEL SYSTEM

Mechanical Fuel Pump

A mechanical type fuel pump is used on 1977 and later models without fuel injection. The pump is located on the engine block and is driven by the auxiliary shaft. A pushrod (128 engine) or pump lever (132 engine) riding on the camshaft or auxiliary shaft eccentric operates the fuel pump diaphragm.

1. Actuating rod
2. Gasket
3. Adjustable gasket
4. Insulator
5. Fuel pump

Mechanical fuel pump assembly—Strada

REMOVAL AND INSTALLATION

All Models

1. Remove and plug the fuel lines leading to the fuel pump.
2. Remove the mounting nuts and care-

1. Screw
2. Lockwasher
3. Cover
4. Screw
5. Filter
6. Upper body
7. Diaphragm
8. Spacer
9. Spring
11. Lower body
12. Flat washer
13. Pivot pin
14. Operating lever
15. Spring

Mechanical fuel pump—124

fully remove the fuel pump from the block (or crankcase).

3. If the pump is equipped with a pushrod, remove the pushrod, gasket and insulator from the mounting.

4. Installation is the reverse of removal. Perform the following additional steps on the 128, Strada, and X1/9.

a. Before replacing the fuel pump, adjust the projection of the pump pushrod.

b. Fit the insulating spacer to its seat with a gasket.

NOTE: On the X1/9, Strada, and 128, the outer gasket used must be 0.012 in. In all cases, adjust pushrod projection only with the inner gasket thickness.

c. Slide in the pushrod. The projection of the pushrod should be 0.59–0.61 in. If the projection is not within specified limits, adjust the projection by replacing the inner gasket with another. Service gaskets are available in the following thicknesses: 0.012 in., 0.027 in., and 0.047 in.

SERVICE

Sludge deposited in the fuel chamber or on the filter may be removed with the pump cover off. Intake and outlet valves should be inspected and replaced if damaged. Check springs for good condition.

Control mechanism for the intake chamber diaphragm should be washed in kerosene and lightly lubricated with thin oil. Lightly coat new fuel pump seals with grease before assembly. If a new diaphragm is to be installed, soak it in kerosene for a few minutes before assembly.

Electric Fuel Pump

NOTE: All fuel injection versions use an electric fuel pump.

An electric fuel pump is used on the later Strada, 128, 131, and all 1976 124 Sport Coupe and Spider models. On the 128 and Strada the pump is located beneath the floor pan, near the fuel tank. On 124 and 131 models, the pump is located inside the luggage compartment. The fuel pump is activated by a relay located in the engine compartment. The system is also protected by an 8 amp fuse located in the fuse box.

NOTE: If the fuel pump stops, check the relay and the fuse box before attempting any repairs.

REMOVAL AND INSTALLATION

—————— **CAUTION** ——————
Depressurize fuel system on fuel injection models.

1. Jack up the rear of the car and place it on stands allowing room to work on the pump.
2. Remove the hot wire from the pump.
3. Remove the ground wire. (If applicable.)
4. Before removing the gas inlet line, find something to stop the gas from flowing. A small piece of hose with the end pinched or with a bolt in the end will do. Or pinch shut the lines.
5. Remove the gas lines.
6. Remove the fuel recirculating lines.
7. Remove the mounting screws and the pump.

NOTE: On models with the pump in the trunk, use the Steps 2–7 given above.

FUEL FILTER

The fuel filter should be replaced every 6000 miles. From '76 to '77, all Fiat models except X1/9 use a cartridge type fuel filter encased in a glass bowl. Removal is accomplished by moving the lock handle down and off the bowl, and replacing the element. On '78 and later models the filter is an in-line type, located near the carburetor or near the gas tank. Removal is accomplished by loosening the two hose clamps.

—————— **CAUTION** ——————
Do not use plastic body fuel filters in the engine compartment. Fiat recommends metal body filters for all models.

Be sure to install the new fuel filter with the arrow pointing toward the carburetor. Never operate any vehicle without a fuel filter in place.

1. Fuel filter
2. Element
3. Handle

Glass bowl fuel filter

Carburetors

All Fiat engines use Weber two-barrel downdraft carburetors with differential opening of the secondary throttle, automatic butterfly-valve choke and accelerating pump. An idle stop device comes into operation when the ignition is turned off. If the vehicle is equipped with a catalytic converter, the idle stop device also functions in case of abrupt deceleration above 2600 rpm.

The Weber carburetors are specially calibrated so that the air/fuel ratio allows the best post combustion of exhaust gases by the secondary injected air to help control emissions. The automatic choke is regulated by engine water temperature and the carburetor is provided with a vacuum-sensitive capsule which partially opens the primary barrel throttle from the idle position (fast idle).

REMOVAL AND INSTALLATION

1. Disconnect the accelerator rod, sliding it out of the lever ball joint end toward the dashboard.
2. Remove the air filter.
3. Disconnect the fuel line.
4. Disconnect all of the vacuum, electrical and water lines.
5. Remove the mounting bolts or nuts.
6. Remove the carburetor and gasket.
7. Installation is the reverse of the above procedure.

OVERHAUL

For carburetor overhaul procedures, see the Carburetor Unit Repair Section.

THROTTLE LINKAGE ADJUSTMENT

All Fiat models use cable type throttle linkage. Adjustments can be made at the carburetor by loosening the hold-down screw of the eye in which the cable slides. Proper adjustment will allow the gas pedal to be fully released from the floor boards and at the same time the carburetor will be in the fully-closed position.

NOTE: If the gas pedal suddenly becomes sloppy, before checking the adjustment be sure that the cable housing is securely mounted.

1. Carburetor cover
2. Needle valve
3. Lug
4. Valve needle
5. Return hook
6. Movable ball
7. Tang
8. Float arm
9. Float
10. Gasket

a = 0.236 in. (6mm) = distance between float and cover with gasket, in vertical position
b = 0.590 in. (15mm) = maximum distance of float from cover face with gasket
b·a = 0.354 in. (9mm) = float travel

Float level adjustment—128 engine family

CARBURETOR IDENTIFICATION

Model	Year	Carburetor Number
128	'76–'79	32 DATRA
131	'76–'78	32 ADFA
	'79–'80	28/32 ADHA[1]
Strada	'79–'80	28/30 DHTA
	'81	Fuel Injection
124 Coupe & Spider	'76–'78	32 ADFA
	'79–'80	28/32 ADHA[1]
	'81 & Later	Fuel Injection
X1/9	'76–'78	32 DATRA
	'79–'80	28/30 DHTA[1]
	'81 & Later	Fuel Injection

[1]Calif. Models Use Fuel Injection

1 Carburetor cover
2 Needle valve
3 Tab
4 Valve needle
5 Movable ball
6 Pull clip
7 Tang
8 Float arm
9 Float
10 Gasket

a = 6 mm (.236 in.) = distance between float and cover with gasket, in vertical position
b = 14 mm (.551 in.) = maximum distance of float from cover face, with gasket
b-a = 8 mm (.315 in.) = float travel

Float level adjustment—131 engine family

Mechanical and vacuum accelerator pumps—typical

1. Choke plate
2. Housing alignment mark
3. Cover alignment mark

Choke alignment marks—typical

FLOAT LEVEL ADJUSTMENT

1. Remove the air horn section of the carburetor from the rest of the carburetor assembly.

2. Check to make sure that the needle valve is screwed all the way into its seat. Make sure that the float is not dented or punctured and can turn freely on its hinge.

3. Holding the air horn assembly so that the float hangs vertically, the distance between the top side of the float and the cover with the gasket in place should be 0.236 in.

4. Holding the air horn assembly in the normal horizontal position, the float should drop so that the maximum distance between the end of the float and the cover mating surface with the gasket in place is distance "b" (see illustrations). Total float travel is b-a.

5. To adjust the float level, carefully bend the tang of the float that attaches to the needle valve.

Vacuum Accelerator Pump

1979 and Later Models

In addition to the standard accelerator pump

operated by throttle linkage, another pump is provided for enrichment of the fuel mixture during cold engine operation. The vacuum pump uses the same output circuit as the mechanical pump. Under high manifold vacuum, the diaphragm is pulled back, compressing the spring and allowing the pump cavity to fill. A drop in vacuum will allow the spring to push the diaphragm, causing a discharge of fuel through the accelerator pump nozzle.

The operation of the vacuum accelerator pump is controlled by a thermovalve which senses coolant temperature. The thermovalve is open when the engine is cold.

AUTOMATIC CHOKE ADJUSTMENT

1. Remove three screws securing choke cover to housing on carburetor.

2. Make sure the lug on the spring inside the choke cover is properly located in the fork of the choke opening lever.

3. Rotate the choke cover to align the index mark with the mark on the housing.

4. Secure the cover with three screws.

5. With the index marks aligned and the carburetor at room temperature of 77°F, check that the choke plate closes fully and

remains closed when the primary throttle is opened.

DASHPOT ADJUSTMENT

1. Obtain a 0.052 in. wire gauge drill.
2. Open the choke plate and throttle plate fully.
3. Allow the throttle plate to close on drill while holding choke plate. Release choke plate.
4. Loosen the locknut on the dashpot and turn the dashpot until there is clearance between the plunger and the tab.
5. Turn the dashpot clockwise until the plunger just touches the tab, then tighten the locknut.

FAST IDLE SPEED ADJUSTMENT

See the "Deceleration Throttle Positioner Maintenance" portion of the Emission Control section.

Fuel Injection

All Fiat engines equipped with fuel injection use the Bosch L-Jetronic system. The Bosch fuel injection system measures intake air volume and meters the proper fuel to obtain the best air/fuel ratio for emissions and performance under a wide range of driving conditions.

For all overhaul and adjustment procedures not detailed below, see the Fuel Injection Unit Repair section.

1. Tab on fast idle lever
2. Throttle plate
3. Dashpot
4. Locknut
5. Mounting bracket
6. Plunger

Dashpot adjustment—typical

RELIEVING FUEL PRESSURE

——— CAUTION ———

The fuel system pressure must be relieved before attempting to disconnect or remove any fuel lines or components. Take precautions to avoid any risk of fire while servicing any part of the fuel system.

All Models

1. Remove the vacuum hose from the fuel pressure regulator.
2. Connect a hand vacuum pump to the regulator and pump up to 20 inches.
3. Fuel pressure will be vented into the fuel tank.

NOTE: Although the pressure is relieved by this method, some fuel will remain in the lines.

ALTERNATE METHOD FOR RELIEVING FUEL PRESSURE

If a hand vacuum pump is not available, use this procedure to ensure fuel pressure release.

1. Start the engine.
2. Disconnect the connector to the fuel injection relay set while the engine is running.
3. After the engine stalls, crank it over two or three times.

Bosch L-Jetronic fuel injection schematic

Relieving fuel pressure

Relieving fuel pressure—alternate method

Fuel injector—typical

Fuel Injectors

REMOVAL AND INSTALLATION

All Models

1. Relieve fuel pressure.
2. Disconnect wire harness from injectors, remove fuel supply hose from fuel manifold, vacuum hose and fuel return hose from pressure regulator and fuel feed hose to cold start valve.
3. Remove 10 mm bolts holding fuel manifold to intake manifold. Remove four 10 mm nuts and washers holding injector retainers to intake manifold.
4. Remove fuel manifold complete with injectors and pressure regulator. Be careful

Fuel injector installation—typical

Injector-to-fuel manifold assembly

Removing the cold start valve

of rubber bushings in intake manifold, they may fall out.
5. Remove four small and four large rubber bushings and retainers from injectors. Inspect for cracks or damage.
6. Separate injector from hose to fuel manifold. Replace the hose whenever replacing an injector, making sure the hose is tight against the collars at both ends.
7. Reinstall large and small bushings on injectors along with retainers. Reinstall injectors and fuel manifold, making sure all components seat and seal properly.

Cold Start Valve

REMOVAL AND INSTALLATION

1. Relieve fuel system pressure.
2. Provide a container to catch any fuel.

Lambda (Oxygen) Sensor

NOTE: Take care to prevent dirt from entering the fuel system.

3. Disconnect electrical connector from cold start valve.
4. Remove clamp holding fuel line on valve and pull fuel hose off cold start valve.

—— CAUTION ——
Use care in removing fuel hose, valve body is plastic.

5. Using a 5 mm Allen wrench, remove the two screws holding the valve in the intake manifold and remove the valve.
6. Installation is the reverse of removal. Make sure hose clamp is tight and check for leaks.

Lambda (Oxygen) Sensor

The Lambda sensor is a probe with a ceramic body in a protective housing. It measures the oxygen concentration in the exhaust system and provides a feedback signal to the control unit. This signal allows the ECU to adjust the air/fuel mixture for the best combination of performance and exhaust emissions.

The Lambda sensor must be replaced every 30,000 miles. A warning system consisting of a switch unit, speedometer connection and the dash mounted "EX GAS SENSOR" light alerts the driver when the sensor is in need of replacement. The switch must be reset after servicing.

REMOVAL AND INSTALLATION

1. Allow the exhaust system to cool.

4. Turn the ignition off and reconnect the relay connector.

LAMBDA SENSOR
REPLACEMENT INDICATOR

"EX GAS SENSOR" warning light

Resetting Lambda service reminder switch unit

CAP
SCREW

SWITCH
UNIT

CO ADJUSTMENT
SCREW

AIR FLOW SENSOR

Setting CO level on fuel injection—typical

2. Locate the Lambda sensor in the exhaust manifold and disconnect the wire.

3. Remove the sensor from the manifold with a deep socket wrench.

4. Coat the threads of the new sensor with anti-seize, anti-rust grease.

— CAUTION —

Do not allow grease to get on the sensor surface or it will contaminate and ruin the sensor. Exercise care when coating the threads.

5. Thread the new sensor in by hand, then torque to 30–36 ft. lbs.

6. Connect the wire to the Lambda sensor and check the CO. Reset the warning switch.

NOTE: Setting the CO level on fuel injection models requires the use of an infra-red exhaust emissions analyzer with a special adaptor. No attempt should be made to adjust the CO without the proper equipment.

RESETTING THE SERVICE REMINDER

1. Locate the switch unit under the dash.

2. Remove bore screening cap screw. Remove screw.

3. Insert a small screwdriver through the housing and gently press on switch contacts. Contact will reset to a high point on the wheel.

4. Make sure the dash light is out.

NOTE: On Strada, it is necessary to lower the heater control panel to gain access to the switch unit.

IDLE CO ADJUSTMENT

CO level is pre-set at the factory on all fuel injection models and no further adjustment is necessary unless a fuel injection component is replaced. This operation requires the use of an exhaust gas analyzer.

IDLE SPEED ADJUSTMENT

1. Run the engine until it reaches normal operating temperature.

2. Connect a tachometer according to the manufacturer's instructions.

3. On cars with automatic transmission, set the parking brake, chock the front wheels and put the selector lever in DRIVE.

4. Turn the idle speed adjustment screw all the way in.

5. Loosen the locknut on the accelerator linkage stop screw. Adjust the stop screw to obtain:
Manual transmission   700–800rpm
Automatic transmission   600–700rpm

6. Back out the idle speed adjustment screw to:
Manual transmission   800–900rpm
Automatic transmission   700–800rpm

7. Hold the throttle linkage stop screw and tighten the locknut.

KICK-DOWN CABLE ADJUSTMENT

NOTE: Make sure idle speed is set correctly.

1. Depress accelerator cable until throttle lever contacts the maximum opening stop. Check that kick-down cable starts to pull.

2. Depress accelerator fully and check that kick-down cable extends 9–11 mm (3.5–4.25 in.).

3. If necessary, adjust nuts on housing to obtain correct extension of cable.

MANUAL TRANSMISSION

REMOVAL AND INSTALLATION

124 and 131 Models

1. Working from the inside of the car, remove the gear lever and cover plate.

2. Underneath the car, remove the flexible coupling from the spider on the mainshaft. Remove the drain plug and drain the transmission.

3. Remove the speedometer drive from the support on the transmission.

4. Disconnect the clutch withdrawal fork return spring.

5. Remove the locknut and unscrew the adjusting rod from the flexible clutch cable.

Idle speed and linkage adjustments on fuel injection

Adjusting kick-down linkage on fuel injection—typical

1. Gear lever return spring anchor screw
2. Flat washer
3. Lever return spring
4. Gasket
5. Socket plate
6. Gasket
7. Flat washer
8. Gear lever stop screw
9. Lower part of gear lever with ball
10. Upper socket plate
11. Dome washer
12. Spring
13. Cup washer
14. Retaining snap-ring
15. Gasket
16. Flange
17. Spring washer
18. Nut
19. Grommet
20. Spring clip
21. Rubber boot
22. Knob
23. Upper part of gear lever
24. Shoulder block
25. Rubber bushings
26. Spacer
27. Rubber bushings
28. Spring-ring

Exploded view of 124 4-speed shifter assembly

6. Remove the flywheel cover from the bellhousing.

7. Remove the bolt which secures the exhaust pipe bracket to the transmission. On the 131, remove the driveshaft protection bracket. Detach the exhaust piping.

8. Detach the exhaust piping.

9. Remove the starter motor heat shield and the starter motor. Disconnect clutch and transmission emission control switch wires.

10. Support the transmission, and disconnect the transmission mount from the underbody. Remove the 4 bolts which secure the transmission to the engine.

11. Move the transmission carefully away from the engine and lower it to the ground. Do not rest input shaft on clutch disc or release bearing.

12. To install, reverse the removal procedure.

LINKAGE ADJUSTMENT

124 and 131

The shifter linkage is integral with the transmission assembly and does not require adjustment.

OVERHAUL

For overhaul procedures, see the Manual Transmission Unit Repair section.

CLUTCH

A single, dry clutch disc and diaphragm spring pressure plate are utilized on all models. Clutch actuation is by cable, except on the X1/9, which uses a hydraulic master and slave cylinder system.

REMOVAL AND INSTALLATION

128, Strada, and X1/9

1. Jack up the car and remove the transaxle.

NOTE: It is important that the input shaft never be allowed to rest on the fingers of the pressure plate, as the fingers may be bent.

2. Mark the position of the clutch in relation to the flywheel to facilitate assembly.

3. Remove the bolts (in stages) which secure the clutch cover to the flywheel. The bolts should be removed evenly to prevent

distortion of the clutch.

4. Remove the pressure plate and clutch disc.

5. Check the condition of the pilot bushing which is pressed into the crankshaft. If necessary, replace the bushing. Installation of the clutch is the reverse of removal. Use an old input shaft or wooden dummy shaft to center the clutch disc. Tighten the clutch cover bolts diagonally, in rotation, to 11 ft. lbs.

NOTE: Be careful not to get oil or grease on the clutch disc during installation.

124 and 131

1. Jack up the car and remove the transmission.

2. Before removing the clutch, mark the position of the clutch in relation to the flywheel to facilitate reassembly (f the clutch is to be reused).

3. Remove the bolts which secure the clutch cover to the flywheel. Remove them in stages to prevent distortion.

4. Remove the pressure plate and clutch.

5. Before reinstallation, check the pilot bushing in the crankshaft for wear, replacing as necessary.

6. Install the clutch using an alignment tool or an old input shaft to center the clutch disc. A wooden dummy shaft cut to the proper size will also work.

7. With the clutch disc centered, tighten the cover bolts diagonally, in rotation, to 22 ft. lbs.

8. Install the transmission.

CLUTCH PEDAL ADJUSTMENT

NOTE: On all models check the clutch control cable grommet for damage. A damaged grommet will not allow the cable sheath to react correctly, thus causing a clutch malfunction. To correct this problem, replace the grommet. Lubricate to prevent clutch "shudder".

1. Half moon block
2. Adjusting nut
3. Lever

Clutch adjustment location

128

1. Open hood, remove the spare tire and locate the cable nut and locknut shown in the illustration.

2. Adjust the nut until the pedal has one in. of free-play. Tighten the locknut.

Strada

1. Open hood, remove the spare tire and locate the cable nut and locknut.

2. Loosen the 10 mm locknut on the clutch cable and adjust the nut next to the half-moon block until the clutch pedal is one inch below the brake pedal height.

3. Tighten the locknut and check adjustment.

NOTE: As the clutch wears, the clutch pedal will rise. When the clutch pedal is one inch above the brake pedal, the clutch may be worn enough to need replacing.

1. Adjusting nut
2. Locknut
3. Bleed nipple

Clutch adjusting location—X1/9

X1/9

1. Jack up the rear of the car.

2. Clutch pedal free-play (distance before resistance is felt when depressing pedal) should be 1.25 in.

3. If not, adjust as necessary by loosening the locknut and turning the adjusting nut on the slave cylinder pushrod where it contacts the clutch release lever. Tighten locknut.

4. Lower car and recheck adjustment. If slave cylinder does not operate at all, check for air in system and bleed circuit.

131

Clutch adjustment is not required. Automatic wear adjustment. No pedal free travel.

124

1. Jack up the front of the car.

2. Adjustment is made at the cable nut at the clutch release lever as shown in the illustration.

3. Adjust the pedal travel to 0.98 in.

Clutch Master Cylinder

REMOVAL AND INSTALLATION

X1/9 Only

NOTE: The upper steering column assembly must first be removed to gain access to the clutch master cylinder.

1. Disconnect the battery.

2. Remove the five screws retaining the steering column upper and lower trim halves.

3. Disconnect the column wiring (three connectors and one wire).

4. Remove the two nuts and two bolts retaining the upper column assembly to the

1. Lockring
2. Seal
3. Boot
4. Gasket
5. Connector
6. Lockplate
7. Cylindetr
8. Spring
9. Seal
10. Seal
11. Gasket
12. Plunger

Exploded view of clutch master cylinder—X1/9

underside of the dashboard. Support the column and steering wheel assembly and pull it straight back and out, disconnecting it from the steering box shaft. Remove the complete column and steering wheel assembly from the car.

5. Place absorbant rags over the driver's side floor carpets. Locate the master cylinder up over the clutch pedal. Disconnect and plug the fluid line to the slave cylinder.

NOTE: Use a small length of fuel line with a screw or bolt in one end, just slip it over the flared end of the hydraulic line.

6. Remove the two retaining bolts. Pull the cylinder out far enough to disconnect and plug the fluid line to the reservoir. Pull the cylinder off the pushrod. Remove from car.

7. Reverse Steps 1–6 to install. Refill the fluid reservoir and bleed the hydraulic system.

Clutch Slave Cylinder

REMOVAL AND INSTALLATION

X1/9 Only

1. Disconnect and plug the fluid line banjo connector from the rear of the slave cylinder.
2. Remove the cotter pin from the end of the slave cylinder pushrod.
3. Disconnect the release arm return spring.
4. Remove the two slave cylinder retaining bolts and remove the cylinder.
5. Reverse Steps 1–4 to install, using new copper gaskets at the fluid line banjo connector. Bleed the hydraulic system. Adjust clutch pedal free-play, if necessary.

Hydraulic System

BLEEDING

X1/9 Only

1. Connect a bleeder hose to the slave cylinder bleeder nipple. Place the other end of the hose in a container partially filled with brake fluid. Make sure the hose end is immersed in fluid.
2. Fill up the clutch fluid reservoir with clean brake fluid. Open the bleeder nipple screw.
3. Have an assistant pump the clutch pedal until all air bubbles stop coming out of the hose. Periodically check the reservoir level so that it doesn't run dry.
4. When all air is expelled, close the nipple screw and remove the hose. Discard the old clutch (brake) fluid. Refill the reservoir and check clutch operation.

1. Spring	4. Housing	7. Boot	10. Seal
2. Washer	5. Bleeding screw	8. Seal	11. Bushing
3. Lockring	6. Rod	9. Piston	

Exploded view of clutch slave cylinder—X1/9

NOTE: Hydraulic fluid will absorb moisture from the atmosphere if left standing in an open container. Any brake fluid that has been stored in anything other than a tightly sealed container should be considered contaminated and discarded.

AUTOMATIC TRANSMISSION

NOTE: Any model equipped with an automatic transmission may be towed a maximum of 30 miles @ 30 mph with the driveshaft connected. However if the transmission is damaged or if speed and distance will be greater than 30 mi. @ 30 mph, disconnect the driveshaft or lift the drive wheels.

The automatic transmission available in the 124 and 131 series is the GM/Adam Opel Trimatic. It is a three-speed unit with a variable torque multiplication ratio of between 2.4 to 1 and 1 to 1.

Automatic Transmission

REMOVAL AND INSTALLATION

124 and 131

1. Disconnect the battery.
2. Remove dipstick, remove bolts holding filler tube to engine bracket and remove filler tube.
3. Remove center console in driver's compartment, disconnect wiring for transmission switch and push connector through opening in floor.
4. Raise the car and drain the transmission fluid.

5. Remove three 13 mm bolts holding starter to transmission. Remove starter and secure out of the way.
6. Remove 10 mm bolt, nut and washers holding the clamp for the speedometer cable.
7. Disconnect speedometer cable from clamp. Remove the safety wire holding the connector for the cable.
8. Remove 10 mm bolt, nut and washers holding the clamp for the cooling lines.
9. Remove two 13 mm bolts holding the bracket for the exhaust pipe.
10. Disconnect the vacuum hose from the modulator valve. Disconnect the vacuum tube from the spring clip on the transmission.
11. Remove 13 mm bolt holding bracket for the kick-down cable.
12. Remove the bracket and disconnect the cable from the kick-down valve.
13. Remove 13 mm nut holding lever to control rod in transmission. Disconnect the lever.
14. Remove cooling lines from fittings in transmission.
15. Remove the driveshaft.
16. Support the transmission with a removal tool and a jack.
17. Remove two 13 mm bolts and washers holding support to body.
18. Remove four 10 mm bolts and washers holding flywheel cover.
19. Remove three 15 mm bolts holding flywheel to torque converter, turn flywheel to gain access to bolts.

—— CAUTION ——
Support the torque converter while removing or installing the transmission.

20. Remove four 19 mm bolts holding transmission to engine.
21. Tilt rear of transmission down and carefully slide transmission back.
22. Lower the transmission with the jack.
23. When reinstalling transmission, feed the connector for the transmission switch up through the floor before positioning transmission.

24. Position the filler tube up from the bottom.

25. Install transmission in reverse order.

26. Torque all bolts to specifications in the transmission bolt torque chart.

NOTE: After attaching transmission to engine, push the torque converter against the flywheel flange. Check that the gap between boss and attachment point is 0.008 to 0.048 in. (0.2 to 1.21 mm). Use a feeler gauge to check each point. If the clearance is not correct, replace the flywheel. Attach the flywheel to the converter with three 15 mm bolts and washers.

TRANSMISSION INSTALLATION BOLT TORQUE

Description	Torque (ft. lbs.)
Bolt, bell housing to engine	61.5
Bolt, converter to flywheel	47.0
Self-locking nut, gear selection rod lever	14.5
Bolt, starter to engine	14.5
Bolt, support plate to rear housing	36.0

PAN REMOVAL AND FILTER SERVICE

124 and 131

1. Raise the car and support it safely.
2. Drain all fluid from the oil pan.
3. Remove the oil pan and gasket. Discard the old gasket.
4. Remove the strainer assembly and strainer gasket and discard the gasket.
5. Install a new oil strainer gasket. Install a new strainer assembly.
6. Install a new gasket on the oil pan and install the pan. Tighten the attaching bolts to 7–10 ft. lbs.
7. Lower the car and add approximately three (3) pints of transmission fluid (Dexron) through the filler tube.
8. With the manual control lever in the Park position, start the engine. **DO NOT RACE THE ENGINE.** Move the manual control lever through each range.
9. Immediately check the fluid level with the selector lever in Neutral, engine running, and vehicle on a level surface. (Set the parking brake.)
10. Add additional fluid to a level between the MIN and MAX marks on the dipstick. Do not overfill.

Strada

1. Raise the car and support it safely.
2. Drain all fluid from the oil pan.
3. Remove the oil pan and gasket. Discard the old gasket.

4. Remove two capscrews holding oil filter and remove oil filter and seal. Discard old oil filter and seal.
5. Install new oil filter and seal. Torque oil filter capscrews to 2.2 ft. lbs.
6. Clean the oil pan and install using nnew gasket. Torque the oil pan capscrews to 14.5 ft. lbs.
7. Lower the car and add approximately 2½ quarts of Dexron® transmission fluid through the filler tube.
8. Place the gear selector in Park and start the engine. **DO NOT RACE THE ENGINE.** Move the shift lever through all ranges.
9. Allow engine to idle and check oil level on transmission dipstick. If oil level is below MIN, top up with Dexron until oil level is between marks.

NOTE: The difference between MIN and MAX is one pint. DO NOT OVERFILL.

10. Test drive to heat up transmission fluid and recheck fluid level.

BAND ADJUSTMENT

124 and 131

1. Drain the transmission.
2. Remove the pan and gasket.
3. Remove the servo brake band cover.
4. Loosen the locknut for the servo brake adjusting screw.
5. Tighten the adjusting screw to 40 *inch pounds*. Then, back off the adjusting screw five full turns.
6. Without disturbing the adjustment, tighten the locknut to 12–15 ft. lbs.
7. Install the servo brake band cover, using a new gasket. Tighten to 17–19 ft. lbs.
8. Install the pan and gasket. Tighten to 7–10 ft. lbs.
9. Fill the transmission with Dexron automatic transmission fluid. Follow Steps 7–10 under "Pan Removal and Filter Service."

Strada

1. Raise the car and support it safely.
2. Remove the throttle and kick-down lever nut and remove lever to gain access to band adjuster screw.
3. Loosen locknut on band adjuster screw.
4. Using 5 mm hex and socket adapter (Fiat tools A.57140/4 and A.57140/1), torque band adjuster screw to 7.23 ft. lbs. to remove all slack.
5. Loosen adjuster screw and retorque to 3.6 ft. lbs., then back off adjuster 2½ turns and tighten locknut.
6. Reinstall throttle and kick-down lever and check adjustment.

GEAR SELECTOR LINKAGE ADJUSTMENT

124 and 131

1. With the engine off, place the shift lever in Drive.
2. Jack up the front of the car and support with jack stands.
3. Disconnect the shifter tie rod at the relay lever (shift lever).
4. Move the cross shaft actuating lever (shift lever on transmission) to the Drive position, which is third detent from the front.
5. Without disturbing either of the two levers, try to insert the end of the shifter tie rod into the relay lever. If necessary, loosen the adjusting nut and rotate until the tie rod end will just slip into the eye of the relay lever. Then, tighten the adjusting nut. Connect the tie rod to the relay lever using a new circlip.
6. Remove the jack stands and lower the car. Check shifter operation.

Strada

1. Remove the shift nameplate by squeezing, then remove two screws retaining center console. Remove console.
2. Place gearshift lever in Park posi-

1. Brake band anchoring pin
2. Brake band
3. Transmission main case
4. Brake actuating rod
5. Sleeve
6. Release spring
7. Damping spring seat
8. Damping spring
9. Piston ring
10. Retainer
11. Piston
12. Circlip
13. Adjusting screw
14. Nut

15. Servobrake cover
16. Cover bolt

Band adjustment—124 and 131 automatic transmission

1. Torque wrench
2. Drive socket and hex wrench A.57140/4
3. Brake band adjusting screw
4. Adjusting screw pushrod
5. Brake band

Adjusting brake band on Strada automatic transmission

1. Upper handle	9. Relay lever	17. Speedometer drive support
2. Lower handle	10. Tie rod adjustable end	18. Bracket
3. Selector lever	11. Adjusting nut	19. Flat washer
4. Starter inhibitor switch	12. Tie rod	20. Bushing
5. Gear selector	13. Cross shaft actuating lever	21. Cotter pin
6. Bolt	14. Flat washer	22. Cotter pin
7. Support	15. Oil union	23. Gear selector bolt
8. Bracket bolt	16. Oil union	

Shift lever linkage adjustment—124 and 131 automatic

CABLE PULLED FROM STOP ABOUT 13mm (½ in.)

14mm ADJUSTING NUTS

FROM TRANSMISSION LINKAGE

Detail C—carburetor linkage

FROM ACCELERATOR PEDAL

17mm ADJUSTING BOLTS

TO CARBURETOR LINKAGE

TO GEAR SELECTOR

LINKAGE A

Detail D—transmission linkage

tion. Rock the car slightly to make sure the lock inside the transmission is engaged.

3. Remove the pin attaching the shift cable to the gearshift lever.

4. Loosen the 8 mm locknut on the shift cable. Adjust the clevis until the pin can be freely installed, then tighten the locknut.

5. Reinstall center console and shift nameplate. Check operation.

KICKDOWN LINKAGE ADJUSTMENT

Strada

1. Check accelerator pedal travel, total travel should be 4 in. (10 cm).

2. If pedal travel is incorrect, bend the pedal rod to obtain proper distance.

NOTE: Include floor mat thickness in adjustment.

3. With accelerator pedal fully depressed, including kickdown, verify that transmission linkage (A) is at full travel up.

4. If transmission linkage is not at full travel up, loosen and adjust 17 mm adjuster nuts.

5. Fully depress accelerator pedal, including kickdown, and verify that the throttle is wide open and the carburetor cable is pulled about ½ in. (13 mm) from its stop.

6. If necessary, adjust the 14 mm adjuster nuts at the cable brace near the carburetor to obtain proper linkage travel.

7. Release the accelerator pedal and verify that the throttle closes (choke plate open) without binding.

NOTE: Linkage control cables and connections should be lubricated periodically to ensure smooth operation and prevent binding.

124 and 131

1. Disconnect telescopic link from control lever on transmission.

2. Push accelerator pedal down until ball end on cable is just touching cable pin.

8. Push the pedal to floor stop and check that cable has extended 7 to 9 mm.

4. If cable travel is not correct, adjust cable nuts to obtain proper travel.

8mm LOCKNUT

SHIFT CABLE

CLEVIS

PIN AND CIRCLIP

Detail A—gear shift selector lever—Strada

5. Push accelerator pedal to floor stop. Hold transmission control lever in full throttle position, extend telescopic link and check that link can be connected to control lever. If link cannot be connected to trans control lever, loosen link nuts and adjust.

6. Release accelerator pedal until ball end is just touching cable pin. Move trans control lever to full throttle position and check that telescopic link can be connected to control lever without extending. If link cannot be connected, loosen nuts and adjust link.

NOTE: When adjusting link, make equal adjustments at each end. For correct adjustment, it is necessary for the kickdown valve to move its specified travel when accelerator pedal is fully depressed.

TRANSAXLE

REMOVAL AND INSTALLATION

128

1. Disconnect the battery.
2. Remove the spare tire.
3. Remove the speedometer drive.
4. Disconnect the flexible cable adjusting rod from the clutch release lever and unhook the return spring.
5. Unscrew the guard-to-body nut.
6. Unscrew the transmission-to-crankcase attachment screws and nuts, accessible from above.
7. Attach the engine support crosspiece.
8. Remove the hub caps from the front wheels and unscrew the constant speed joint-to-wheel hub nuts.
9. Remove the lft front wheel.
10. Disconnect the left tie rod from the steering arm.
11. Remove the stabilizer bar.
12. Unscrew the two lower left shock absorber-to-pillar attaching screws and nuts.
13. Remove the two lower guards.
14. Unscrew the nuts which fasten the

exhaust clamping bracket to the transmission.
15. Disconnect the gearshift and selection lever control rod.
16. Unscrew the starter motor-to-transmission assembly bolts.
17. Remove the engine support crossmember.

CAUTION

Make sure that the engine is properly supported from above.

18. Remove the flywheel cover.
19. Unscrew the remaining transmission-to-engine attachment screws.
20. Disconnect the ground cable from the transmission assembly.
21. Using wire, fix the axle shafts complete with constant-speed joints, to the transmission in order to prevent them from coming away from their seats in the differential.
22. Remove the transmission-differential assembly from beneath the car using a hydraulic jack.
23. Installation is the reverse of removal.

X1/9

1. Remove the air cleaner and the carburetor cooling duct.
2. Disconnect the battery cables from the battery.
3. Dsconnect the clutch slave cylinder from the clutch linkage, remove the two slave cylinder attaching bolts and move the cylinder out of the way.
4. Support the engine and remove the nuts and bolts holding the transmission to the cankcase that are accessible from above.
5. Raise the vehicle and remove the rear wheels.
6. Remove the three lower guards on the left side.
7. Mark the position of the shift tube where it is connected to the gearshift flexible link.
8. Remove the two bolts holding the flexible link to the shift tube, loosen the bolt at the transmission end of the link and swing the link out of the way.
9. Disconnect the electrical connector for the backup lights and remove the clamp securing the wires to the body.
10. Disconnect the connector for the seat belt system in the transmission. The connector is located inboard and forward of the transmission near the engine water hoses.
11. Remove the starter from the transmission.
12. Disconnect the ground strap.
13. Remove the exhaust pipe.
14. Remove the hub nuts holding the constant speed joints to the wheel hubs.
15. Remove the two bolts and nuts securing the suspension control arms to their supports. Pll the hub off the constant speed joints and attach the axle shafts to the transmission with wire to prevent them from coming out.

16. Remove the flywheel cover.
17. Remove the crosspiece supporting the engine.

CAUTION

Make sure that the engine is properly supported from above.

18. Remove the remaining nuts and bolts securing the transmission to the engine.
19. Remove the transmission/differential from below the vehicle. Use a hydraulic jack to support the assembly.
20. Install the transmission/differential in the reverse order of removal.

Strada

NOTE: On automatic models, Fiat recommends removing the engine and transaxle as a unit. See Engine Removal section.

1. Disconnect the battery.
2. Remove the spare tire.
3. Disconnect speedometer drive from transmission.
4. Remove the air cleaner.
5. Attach engine support crosspiece.
6. Raise the vehicle and support it safely.
7. Remove front shield and left side shield.
8. Disconnect ground cable from transmission.
9. Disconnect clutch operating cable at transmission end.
10. Disconnect reverse light switch connector.
11. Remove three bolts holding starter to transmission.

NOTE: Before removal of gear selector link, mark position of slots in relation to bolts so that adjustment will remain the same upon installation.

12. Remove two nuts and bolts holding gear selector link to linkage joint.
13. Remove six allen head bolts and disconnect left side half-shaft complete with constant velocity joint from flange.

NOTE: Discard allen head bolts and replace with new ones upon installation.

14. Remove six allen head bolts and disconnect right side half-shaft complete with constant velocity joint from flange.
15. Remove three bolts and disengage drive shaft from transmission.
16. Place a jack under the transmission.
17. Remove the center mount bolt.

CAUTION

Make sure the engine is supported from above.

18. Remove three nuts and support bracket.
19. Remove three bolts to flywheel guard and remove guard.
20. Remove retaining nut and three bolts holding transmission to engine.
21. Disconnect left side rubber mount and bracket by removing two bolts on rub-

1. Guide plate
2. Upper socket
3. Lower socket
4. Spring
5. Support
6. Cotter pin
7. Flat washer
8. Bushings
9. Rod
10. Screw
11. Bushing
12. Spring washer
13. Flexible rod
14. Nut
15. Plate
16. Screw
17. Knob
18. Screw
19. Lever
20. Dust boot
21. Pin
22. Guard and boot
23. Return spring
24. Guard
25. Screw and washer
26. Nut and spring washer

Gearshift mechanism for 128—X1/9 and Strada similar

ber mount and four bolts holding bracket to transmission.

22. Lower transmission with jack.
23. Installation is the reverse of removal.

NOTE: If after installation difficult shifting or jumping out of gear is encountered, adjust gearshift linkage.

1. Fork connecting rear prop shaft to drive pinion sleeve
2. Spider snap ring
3. Spider assy.
4. Snap ring
5. Spider assy.
6. Rear prop shaft

124 and 131 driveshaft rear section

SHIFT LINKAGE ADJUSTMENT—MANUAL TRANS

128, X1/9 and Strada

1. Place the transmission in Neutral.
2. Loosen the two adjustment screws at the transmission end of the shift rod.
3. Place the gear shift lever in the neutral position (centered and straight up and down) and tighten the two adjusting screws at the transmission end of the shift rod. The holes in the flexible shift rod are slotted to allow for adjustment.

DRIVE AXLE

Driveshaft and U- Joints

124 and 131

Fiat 124 and 131 driveshafts are in two parts; a splined tubular front piece connected to the transmission through a flexible spider coupling and a solid rear piece, connected to the front piece by a universal joint and to the rear axle by a universal joint.

REMOVAL AND INSTALLATION

NOTE: Special tool A.70025 or a 5 in. diameter screw type hose clamp is required to remove the sleeve of the front shaft.

1. Install the special tool or 5 in. diameter hose clamp and unscrew the 3 self-locking nuts and withdraw the bolts.
2. Remove the retaining clip of the brake hose from the rear shaft cover and disconnect the hose from the rear brake pipe.
3. Release the brake pipe from the two clips on the rear shaft cover.

4. Disconnect the rear shaft cover from the differential.
5. Disconnect the handbrake return spring from the central support.
6. Unscrew the nuts holding the central support to the body and slide the shafts toward the front to remove.
7. Install the driveshaft in the reverse order of removal.

DISASSEMBLY AND ASSEMBLY

1. Remove the spider of the universal joint.
2. Unscrew the attaching nut of the universal joint fork.
3. Remove the fork and the shield snap-ring.
4. Slide the rear shaft and bearing out of the tubular cover.
5. Remove the bearing from the end of the shaft.
6. When the cover has been removed, the sliding sleeve will come off the front.
7. To assemble, reverse the disassembly procedure using grease to lubricate the couplings.

NOTE: The universal joint fork nut must be tightened to 69 ft. lbs. and then staked with a center punch.

U-JOINT OVERHAUL

NOTE: It is best to use a small press when working with U-joints although a vise can be used in a pinch. It is very easy to crush the needle bearings during installation, so be careful during overhaul.

1. Mark the driveshaft halves so you can put them together in the same way they were taken apart.
2. See ''Driveshaft Removal and Installation'' and remove the shaft.
3. Remove the snap-rings which retain the cups.
4. Press the joint toward the center. This will make one of the cups accessible with pliers.

1. Flexible coupling
2. Bushing
3. Sleeve
4. Lubrication fitting
5. Slotted sleeve and spring
6. Seal
7. Resilient pad
8. Yoke
9. Nut
10. Disc
11. Lock ring
12. Ball bearing

13. Disc
14. Front prop shaft
15. Socket
16. Bolts securing sleeve to flexible coupling
17. Self locking nut

124 and 131 driveshaft front section

5. Remove the cup, turn the shaft over and press out the other side.

6. Press the other two cups out in the same manner and remove the joint.

7. Before installing the new joint, clean the shaft surfaces where the cups are pressed through and be sre to check the snap-ring groove for burrs as the snap-rings must seat perfectly.

8. Insert the first cup in its seat and press it through until it is flush with the shaft.

9. Remove all of the cups from the joint and insert the joint through the hole opposite the installed cup, then slide the joint into the cup making sure that the needle bearings stay in order.

10. Insert the second cup in its seat and press it halfway into the shaft.

11. Carefully move the joint from side-to-side until it reaches the point where the joint is making contact with the needle bearings in both cups, then press them together driving the second cup in far enough to insert the snap-ring.

12. Insert the ring, turn the shaft over and press the cup in and insert the other ring.

13. Use the same procedure to connect the shaft halves observing the marks made in Step 1.

14. It is best to have someone assist you in connecting the shafts together because of the weight and awkwardness of the assembly.

Axle Shafts

REMOVAL AND INSTALLATION

124

1. Jack up the rear of the car. Remove

131 rear axle and axle shaft assembly

the wheels. Remove the caliper support bracket assembly without disconnecting the brake fluid lines.

2. Remove the snap-ring which retains the bearing dust cover.

3. Using a slide hammer, remove the axle shaft, complete with snap-ring, dust cover, bearing and bearing retained collar.

4. Extract the shaft oil seal and O-ring.

NOTE: Always use a hydraulic press to remove the axle shaft bearing retaining collar.

5. Fit the oil seal and O-ring to the housing.

6. Insert the complete axle shaft and fit the snap-ring to the housing.

7. Fit the brake disc to the axle shaft hub with two centering screws.

8. Fit the caliper support bracket and caliper assembly to the axle.

1. O ring
2. Oil seal
3. Axle housing
4. Axle shaft
5. Snap-ring
6. Dust shield
7. Ball bearing
8. Bearing retaining collar

9. Fit the wheel and lower the car to the ground.

131

1. Jack up the rear of the car and block the front wheels. Release the parking brake. Remove the rear wheel.

2. Remove the two brake drum retaining bolts and pull off the drum.

3. Working through the axle shaft flange, remove the four backing plate bolts.

4. Attach a slide hammer to the axle shaft flange and pull out the axle shaft, bearing and retainer.

NOTE: Do not stretch or bend brake line.

5. Remove and replace the oil seal in the axle housing.

6. Check that the axle bearing is tight against its retainer and axle shaft shoulder. If replacement is necessary, press off the retainer with an arbor press. Never reuse the retainer. To install the new retainer, heat to 578°F and press on so that the bearing inner race is locked between the retainer and axle shaft shoulder.

7. Install the axle shaft assembly. Install the backing plate bolts, brake drum, and wheel.

128

1. Drain the transmission oil.

2. Unscrew the oil seal boot at the transmission.

3. Remove the outer clamps on the boot at the constant-speed joint and pull back both boots enough to uncover both joints.

4. Clean the grease off both joints.

5. Open the sealing ring on the constant-speed joints and remove the shaft ends from their seats in the joint.

6. Turn the car wheels to enable the shafts to be fully removed from their seats in the differential.

124 rear axle and axle shaft assembly

NOTE: Some early cars are equipped with twin type axle shafts. If it becomes necessary to replace one of these shafts it can be replaced with the later integral type shaft.

7. Installation is the reverse of the removal procedure, bearing the following in mind.

8. When each axle shaft end has been inserted into the constant-speed joint, check that the snap-ring is lying in its axle shaft groove.

CAUTION

Make sure that the axle shaft snap-ring is, in fact, lying in its groove. Move the shaft inward and outward a few times; this operation is necessary as correct ring setting is vital.

---

9. Grease the constant-speed joint sockets and the protection boot. No more than 3 oz. of grease should be used.

X1/9 (4-Speed)

1. Remove the wheel/tire assembly.
2. Remove the two bolts and nuts securing the shock absorber to the pillar.
3. Remove the nut holding the ball joint of the control arm in the pillar and remove the ball joint from the pillar.
4. Remove the nut retaining the strut ball joint to the pillar and remove the ball joint from the pillar.
5. Drain the transmission.
6. Remove the three bolts and washers retaining the oil seal boot to the differential.
7. Pull the axle shaft and wheel hub from the differential.
8. Remove the brake caliper and support bracket from the pillar.
9. Remove the bolts securing the retaining plate and brake rotor to the hub and remove the plate and rotor.
10. Remove the clamp retaining the boot to the constant-speed joint and pull the boot back to uncover the joint. Clean the grease off the joints.
11. Remove the lock-ring from the constant-speed joints, using a pair of pliers.
12. Remove the axle shaft from the constant-speed unit.
13. Install the axle shaft in the reverse order of removal. After installing the axle shaft in the constant-speed joint and installing the snap-ring in the groove of the axle shaft, mak sure the snap-ring is properly seated by moving the shaft in and out. Grease the constant-speed joint with no more than 3 oz. of grease.

Half-Shaft

REMOVAL AND INSTALLATION
Strada and X1/9 (5-Speed)

1. Jack up the car and support it safely.

1. Driveshaft flange
2. CV joint
3. Allen head bolts
4. Protective boot
5. Half-shaft
6. Protective boot
7. CV joint

Drive axle assembly—Strada

2. Remove the wheel.
3. With brakes applied, remove hub nut and washer.
4. Remove six allen head bolts holding half-shaft to driveshaft flange.

NOTE: Discard allen head bolts and replace with new ones upon installation.

5. Pull half-shaft out of hub carrier.
6. Remove large clamp holding protective boot on constant velocity (CV) joint (drive end).
7. Remove circlip retaining CV joint on half-shaft and slide CV joint off.
8. To remove CV joint from hub carrier end, remove large clamp holding protective boot and pull CV joint from half-shaft so that circlip remains in its seat.
9. Reinstall CV joints and half-shaft in reverse order. Torque new allen head bolts to 31 f. lbs.

NOTE: Wheel side constant velocity joints are graded into classes and identified by paint marks. They must always be fitted in matched pairs as shown in table.

HALF-SHAFT TO CV JOINT MATING REFERENCE

Half-Shaft		CV Joint	
Class	Color	Class	Color
A	Blue	A	Blue
B	Red	B	White
		C	Red

NOTE: Class B joints can be mated with both half-shaft classes.

Stub Axle

128

1. Raise and support the front of the car.

2. Remove the wheel.
3. Disconnect the shock absorber from the steering knucke.
4. Disconnect the brake caliper from the steering knuckle.
5. Remove the brake disc and mounting plate from the hub.
6. Disconnect the tie rod from the steering knuckle.
7. Disconnect the anti-roll bar from the control arm.

NOTE: When removing the anti-roll bar from the control arms, make sure to take note of the number of adjustment shims inserted between the ends of the bar and the control arm bushings so they can be replaced in their original positions.

8. Disconnect the control arm from the body.
9. If necessary, remove the control arm from the steering knuckle.
10. Remove the stub axle from the steering knuckle with a press.
11. Install the stub axle in the reverse order.

X1/9 (4-Speed)

1. Remove the axle shaft.
2. Remove the hub and pillar assembly from the car.
3. Remove the hub nut and washer.
4. Pull the constant-speed joint out of the hub.
5. Press the hub from the pillar.
6. Remove the ring nut securing the bearing in the pillar and remove the bearing from the pillar.
7. Install the new bearing in the pillar.
8. Screw the *new* ring nut into the pillar to hold the bearing. Tighten the nut to 43 ft. lbs. Fiat tool A.57123 is the socket used to tighten the nut.

NOTE: Whenever the bearing in the pillar is replaced, use a new ring nut. It is necessary to replace the bearing every time the hub (stub axle) is removed from the pillar.

1. Tripod joint
2. Circlip
3. Axle shaft
4. Flange
5. Oil seal boot
6. Boot
7. Snapring
8. Constant-speed joint
9. Boot clamps
10. Sealing ring
11. Bushing

The arrow indicates the shoulder with which the boot (6) should be in contact after installation

Left axle shaft assembly—128

9. Press the hub into the pillar.

10. Install the constant-speed joint into the hub.

11. Install the washer and hub nut and tighten the nut to 100 ft. lbs. Stake the nut with a punch.

Differential

REMOVAL AND INSTALLATION

124 and 131

NOTE: A case spreader is required to remove the carrier assembly.

To remove only the differential, use the following procedure.

1. Unscrew the drain plug in the lower part of the axle housing and drain the gear oil.

2. Jack the rear of the car and remove the rear wheels. Disconnect the driveshaft.

3. Withdraw the axle shafts far enough to disengage them from the side gears.

·4. Unbolt and remove the differential from the housing.

5. Installation is the reverse of removal. Tighten pinion nut to 14 to 18 in. lbs.

OVERHAUL

NOTE: The overhaul of the differential assembly requires the use of a bench press and several special tools. Fiat recommends that an authorized dealer perform the repairs.

REAR SUSPENSION

NOTE: Replacement of shock absorbers requires removal of rear suspension. On 131 station wagon only, the rear shock absorbers are replaced in the conventional manner.

REMOVAL AND INSTALLATION

128 and Strada

1. Jack up the rear of vehicle and place safety stands underneath.

2. Remove the rear wheels.

3. Plug the outlet hole of the brake fluid reservoir.

4. Detach the flexible brake fluid hose from the metal pipe.

5. Release the handbrake relay lever and detach the cable from the shoe control levers on the brake backing plate.

6. Disconnect the braking regulator torsion bar from the left control arm.

7. Place a hydraulic jack under the control arm, raise the suspension, and detach the shock absorbers inside the luggage compartment. Remove the jack.

8. Detach the rubber pads which attach the leaf spring to the control arms.

9. Unscrew the nuts that attach the swivels of the control arms to the screws which pass through the plate that mounts the suspension to the body. Keep track of any shims.

10. Attach the control arm to the body by passing the two screws through the plate. Torque the nuts to 36.2 ft. lbs.

11. Reattach the rubber pads used to anchor the leaf spring.

12. Link the braking regulator torsion bar to the left control arm.

13. Slip the bottom rubber bushing onto the top stud of the shock absorber. Apply a hydraulic jack under the suspension and lift the whole assembly to enable the top stud of the shock absorber to be inserted into the special hole provided in the luggage compartment.

14. Mount the top rubber bushings, the retainer cap, and the self-locking nut to the top stud of the shock absorber.

15. Tighten the shock absorber nuts to 18.1 ft. lbs.

16. Reattach the handbrake control cable to the lever on the brake backing plate and reconnect the brake fluid hose and metal pipe to each other.

17. Restore the brake fluid and bleed the system.

X1/9

1. Remove the wheel.

2. Disconnect the flexible brake tube from the caliper if the caliper is to be removed with the suspension assembly or, in order to save from bleeding the brake hydraulic system, remove the caliper from the

128 rear suspension components—Strada similar

suspension assembly and support with heavy gauge wire attached to the body.

3. Disconnect the parking brake cable from the caliper, depending on whether or not it is being removed from the vehicle or not.

4. Remove the exhaust pipe.

5. Note the number of shims and their position on the control arm. Remove the nut, washer, and bolt attaching the control arm to the bracket at the front of the suspension. Allow the shims to remain between the arm and bracket.

6. Remove the nut, washer, and bolt securing the arm to the bracket at the rear of the suspension. Take note to the number of shims and their position. Allow the shims to remain between the arm and bracket.

7. Remove the hub nut and washer.

8. Remove the three nuts and washers securing the top of the shock absorber.

9. Slide the suspension assembly off of the constant-speed joint shaft. Position the axle shaft so that it will not come out of the differential.

To install the suspension assembly:

10. Install the shims in their original positions and loosely attach the arm to the brackets.

11. Raise the assembly and mount the hub to the constant-speed joint.

12. Insert the upper attachment of the shock absorber in the holes in the body and install the three attaching nuts and spring washers.

13. Place the washer on the axle shaft and thread a new hub nut onto the shaft. Tighten the nut to 101 ft. lbs. and stake the nut.

NOTE: Always use a new hub nut.

14. Install the exhaust pipe.

15. Install the wheel.

16. Lower the car to the ground.

17. With the vehicle laden (two people sitting inside), tighten the control arm attaching nuts to 72 ft. lbs. Tighten the three upper shock absorber attaching nuts to 43 ft. lbs.

124 and 131

1. Jack up the rear of the car. Remove the rear wheels after placing the car on jack stands.

2. Disconnect the driveshaft.

3. Disconnect the brake lines.

4. Disconnect the handbrake cables.

5. Free the cables from their clips on the body.

6. Disconnect the shocks from inside the trunk. On 131 wagons, disconnect the shocks from their upper mounts, beneath the car.

7. Disconnect the two stabilizer bar links.

8. Disconnect the brake regulator link.

9. Support the rear axle with a hydraulic jack.

10. Disconnect the anchor rods and the sway bar.

1. Nut	6. Nut	12. Boot
2. Washer	7. Washer	13. Bushing
3. Washer	8. Washer	14. Control arm
4. Washer	9. Bolt	15. Bushing
5. Bolt	10. Pillar	

Exploded view of the rear control arm assembly for X1/9

1. Flat washer	9. Flat washer	19. Lock washer
2. Spacer	10. Rubber bushing	20. Lower bracket
3. Rubber bushing	11. Rubber bushing	21. Shock absorber, complete
4. Upper side rod	12. Spacer	22. Bolt fixing shock absorber
5. Rubber bushing	13. Flat washer	to lower bracket
6. Flat washer	14. Nut	23. Rubber bushing
7. Bolt anchoring upper side	15. Lock washer	24. Upper cup
rod to axle housing	16. Nut	25. Lock washer
8. Bolt anchoring upper side	17. Nut	26. Nut
rod to body	18. Nut	

124 rear suspension shock absorbers

11. Remove the assembly by lowering the jack.

12. Remove the stabilizer bar brackets and the bar.

13. Remove the shocks at the spring mounts, or lower attachment (131 wagon).

14. Remove the anchor rods and sway bar from the axle.

NOTE: Do not tighten any bolts during assembly unless otherwise instructed. Bolts should be tightened in sequence with the vehicle on a level surface.

15. Connect the anchor rods and the sway bar to the housing.

16. Bolt the shocks to the spring seats or lower mount (131 wagon), and tighten them.

17. Bolt up the stabilizer bar with its links, but do not tighten it completely.

18. Seat the springs with pads to the axle plates.

19. Place the jack in position.

20. Connect the axle to the body, but do not fully tighten the anchor rods to their brackets.

21. Connect the stabilizer bar links to the housing, but do not tighten fully.

22. Connect the brake regulator rod to the housing.

1. Rubber pad
2. Bolt anchoring cross rod to body
3. Lock washer
4. Nut
5. Bolt anchoring lower side rod to bracket 6
6. Bracket
7. Flat washer
8. Rubber bushing
9. Lower side rod
10. Rubber bushing

11. Spacer
12. Nut
13. Lock washer
14. Flat washer
15. Nut
16. Lock washer
17. Bolt anchoring lower side rod to axle housing
18. Lock washer
19. Nut
20. Bolt anchoring cross rod to axle housing

21. Cross rod
22. Flat washer
23. Spacer
24. Rubber bushings
25. Flat washer
26. Lock washer
27. Nut
28. Lower ring-pad
29. Coil spring
30. Upper seating ring
31. Upper rubber ring-pad
32. Rubber buffer

124 rear suspension rods and springs

23. Tighten the shocks at the luggage compartment, or upper mount (131 wagon).

24. Install the driveshaft and tighten.

25. Install brake lines and handbrake cables.

26. Bleed the brake system.

27. Install the wheels. Lower the vehicle and torque the wheels to 51 ft. lbs.

28. Tighten the nuts on the pivot bolts.

NOTE: The following bolts should be tightened in the order in which they appear. They should be gradually loaded until the specified torque is obtained.

    a. Anchor rod-to-the housing (124)—72 ft. lbs.

    b. Sway bar-to-the axle (124)—72 f. lbs.

    c. Stabilizer bar links-to-axle—25 ft. lbs.

    d. Reaction strut nuts (131)—58 ft. lbs.

    e. Transverse strut nuts (131)—58 ft. lbs.

NOTE: The above procedure prevents the rubber bushings from being unduly stressed.

ADJUSTMENTS

NOTE: Camber and toe-in adjustments on the rear suspension are done at the same time.

128 and Strada

Rear wheel camber and toe-in are adjusted at the lower control arm-to-body attaching bolts by means of shims. To increase the negative camber angle, add an equal number of shims. To decrease the negative camber angle, remove an equal number of shims. To increase toe-in, add shims to the rear bolt or remove shims from the front bolt. To decrease toe-in, add shims to the front bolt or remove shims from the rear bolt.

To adjust, proceed as follows:

1. Raise the rear of the vehicle.

1. Shock absorber
2. Coil spring
3. Transverse strut support
4. Transverse strut
5. Lower reaction strut
6. Lower reaction strut support
7. Upper reaction strut support
8. Upper reaction strut

131 rear suspension

128 and Strada rear suspension adjustment locations

REAR

ADJUST TIE ROD

X1/9 rear suspension adjustment locations

2. Compress one end of the leaf spring to shift it from the flexible guide which anchors it to the control arm.

3. Remove the guide.

4. Slowly release the spring.

5. Unscrew the nuts which attach the pivot to the body.

6. Partly remove the screw to free the adjustment shims.

7. Carry out the required variation in the number of shims.

8. Reinsert the screw.

9. Carry out this operation on both control arm-to-body screws.

10. Adjust the other wheel as necessary.

11. Reassemble the two flexible guides which anchor the leaf spring to the control arms and tighten the attachment nuts to 22 ft. lbs.

X1/9

Toe-in is adjusted by turning the reaction rod, thus lengthening or shortening the rod to the desired toe-in specification. Toe-in with the vehicle unladen should be between +0.360 and +0.510 in.

Camber should be −1°10′ to −2°10′.

Leaf Spring

REMOVAL AND INSTALLATION

128 and Strada

1. Place car on hoist or jack stands and support it safely. Rear suspension must be unladen.

2. Disconnect brake compensator torsion bar from link.

3. Remove two nuts and bolts to remove spring guide.

4. Remove four nuts and washers to remove rubber buffers.

5. Remove leaf spring. To separate leaf spring, slowly remove clamp at the center.

6. Installation is the reverse of removal. Torque buffer nuts to 22 ft. lbs. and spring guide nuts to 25 ft. lbs.

FRONT SUSPENSION

The 124 model range is equipped with parallel upper and lower control arm front suspension. A coil spring is located between the control arms, along with a shock absorber. The steering knuckles are located in ball joints. A stabilizer bar is used on all models.

The 128, 131, Strada and X1/9 are equipped with MacPherson front suspension. The suspension strut acts as shock absorber, suspension (with a concentric coil spring), and upper locating member. A control arm is located at the bottom of the steering knuckle. A stabilizer bar is used on all models.

REMOVAL AND INSTALLATION

124

1. Support the front of the car with safety stands.

2. Remove the front wheels.

3. Remove the shock.

4. Using a spring compressor, compress the spring until it no longer exerts pressure on the control arm.

CAUTION

Make sure spring compressor is properly attached.

---

5. Disconnect the stabilizer bar at the lower control arm.

6. Disconnect the brake hoses.

7. Disconnect the tie rod at the steering knuckle arm.

8. Unscrew the fixing nut and remove the pivot bolt to allow the control arm to separate from the body.

9. Remove the nuts which secure the lower control arm to the crossmember. Be sure to mark the number of shims removed and from which stud they were removed.

10. The assembly can now be removed and disassembled.

NOTE: Shims are located between the body and the pivot bar to which the control arm is mounted.

11. Install the stabilizer bar to the body.

12. Insert the shims and install the wishbone assembly, bolting the lower control arm to the crossmember.

13. Insert the spring with tool attached into its seat in the control arm.

14. Compress the spring until its height will allow you to connect the upper control arm.

15. Connect the upper control arm, but do not tighten it fully.

16. Connect the stabilizer bar to the control arm.

1. Cup	15. Cup	30. Self-locking nut fixing steering knuckle to lower control arm
2. Nut fixing upper control arm to body	16. Resilient bushing	
3. Resilient bushing	17. Flat washer	31. Spring
4. Upper control arm	18. Pivot bar	32. Spring seat
5. Buffer	19. Nut fixing lower control arm to crossmember 10	33. Rubber pad
6. Bolt	20. Spring washer	34. Self-locking nut fixing steering knuckle to upper control arm
7. Spring washer	21. Flat washer	
8. Flat washer	22. Tab strip	35. Bolt
9. Tab strip	23. Plug	36. Seal
10. Crossmember	24. Lower ball joint	37. Bolt
11. Flat washer	25. Nut	38. Spring washer
12. Spring washer	26. Spring washer	39. Nut
13. Nut	27. Bolt	40. Upper ball joint
14. Nut fixing pivot bar 18 to lower control arm	28. Seal	41. Plug
	29. Lower control arm	

Exploded view of 124 front suspension

17. Connect the tie-rod to the steering arm.

18. Connect the brake lines.

19. Bleed the brake system.

20. Seat the spring by unloading the compressor.

21. Remove the compressor and install the shock.

22. Install the tires, lower the car and torque the wheels to 50 ft. lbs.

23. With the vehicle on a level surface, gradually tighten the following bolts in the order in which they appear and to the proper specification.

    a. Nut on the pin connecting the upper control arm to the body—72 ft. lbs.

    b. Nuts retaining the lower control arm to the crossmember—43 ft. lbs.

    c. Nuts fixing the lower control arm to the pin—72 ft. lbs.

128 and Strada

1. Loosen the front wheel stud bolts.
2. Loosen the front wheel hub nuts.
3. Place the vehicle on jack stands.
4. Remove the front wheels.
5. Unscrew the nuts which attach the brake caliper to the pillar and secure the caliper to the body.

1. Shock absorber and spring
2. Screws and nuts attaching the shock absorber to the pillar
3. Pillar
4. Control arm

Left front suspension assembly on 128–131 and Strada similar

6. Unscrew the nut which attaches the tie rod ball joint to the steering arm and then remove the swivel with a puller.

7. Unscrew the nut which attaches the end of the anti-roll bar to the control arm.

8. Detach the control arm from the body.

9. Remove the hub nut.

10. Release the top attachment of the sock absorber by unscrewing the 3 mounting nuts in the engine compartment and slide the suspension assembly off the constant-speed joint shaft and support the axle shaft in such a way as to prevent it from slipping out of the differential. Remove the suspension assembly for further service.

11. Attach the anti-roll bar to the body.

12. Take up each completely reassembled control arm and mount the hub on the shaft of the constant-speed joint. At the same time, insert the upper attachment of the shock absorber into the holes provided in the body and secure it with the nuts and the spring washers.

13. Place a flat washer on the shaft of the constant-speed joint and screw up the attachment nut. Torque hub nut to 159 ft. lbs.

14. Grease the rubber bushings in the anti-roll bar-to-control arm joint.

15. Using as many shims as were present on disassembly, reattach the end of the anti-roll bar and its flexible pads to the control arm and reinstall the latter on the body.

16. Attach the tie rod to the steering arm and tighten the nut to 58 ft. lbs.

17. Remount the brake caliper onto the brake disc.

X1/9 and 131

1. Remove the wheel and tire.

2. If the brake caliper is to be removed with the suspension, disconnect the flexible brake line from the caliper and plug it. If the caliper need not be removed from the vehicle, remove it from the suspension and support it with a length of heavy gauge wire.

1. Nut	7. Washer
2. Washer	8. Spacer
3. Washer	9. Bolt
4. Rubber bushing	10. Nut
5. Control arm	11. Pillar
6. Rubber bushing	

Exploded view of front control arm assembly—X1/9

3. Disconnect the stabilizer strut (sway bar) from the suspension.

4. Remove the bolt holding the control arm to the body mount.

5. Remove the nut holding the tie rod ball joint to the steering arm and remove the ball joint.

6. Support beneath the steering knuckle. Disconnect the top of the shock absorber by removing the three nuts and washers.

7. Lower the suspension strut assembly out of the car.

8. Install the suspension assembly in the reverse order. Tighten the attaching nuts and bolts with the vehicle under a load. Tighten the knuckle-to-tie rod attaching nut to 58 ft. lbs.; the control arm-to-lower pillar attaching nut to 51 ft. lbs. (X1/9) 58 ft. lbs. (131); the control arm-to-body attaching bolt to 29 ft. lbs. (X1/9) 65 ft. lbs. (131); and the stabilizer strut bar attaching bolt to 29 ft. lbs. (X1/9) 43 ft. lbs. (131).

Ball Joint
CHECKING

1. Using a jack, raise the control arm slightly to unload the ball joint.

2. Use Fiat gauge A.96505 to check that lower lip does not touch the threaded pin on the ball joint.

3. If not as specified, the control arm/ball joint assembly must be replaced. See removal of front suspension.

Shock Absorber

REMOVAL AND INSTALLATION
124

1. Working from inside the engine compartment, disconnect the upper end of the shock holding the shank from turning with a wrench.

2. Remove the nut and bolt fixing the shock to the lower control arm.

3. Remove the shock through the lower control arm.

4. Installation is the reverse of the removal procedure to include replacing all the worn bushings and washers.

128, Strada, and X1/9

1. Detach the shock at the top by unscrewing the three nuts that attach it to the body.

2. Jack up the front of the car and support beneath the subframe with jack stands. Remove the wheel.

3. Remove the two bolts retaining the lower end of the strut to the knuckle or pillar.

4. Remove the shock and coil spring (strut assembly) as a unit.

5. Reinstall strut assembly in reverse order.

Removing front shock upper attachment—all except 124

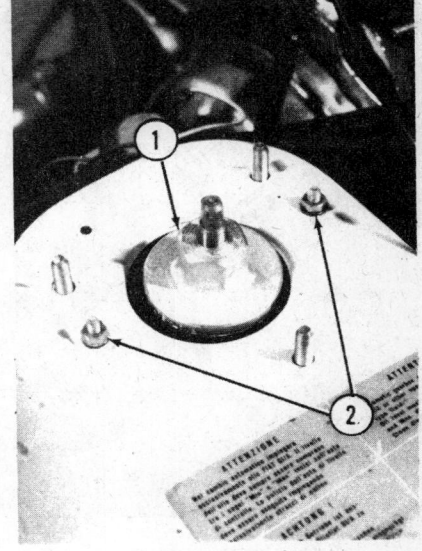

1. Tool A.74375
2. Retainer nuts

Removing shock absorber assembly

CAUTION

The replacement of MacPherson strut shock absorber inserts requires the proper use of a spring compressor to prevent serious damage or bodily injury. See the Unit Repair section for overhaul procedures and safety precautions before attempting disassembly.

131

1. With car on the ground, remove the upper nut and washer from the shock absorber shaft.

2. Remove the three nuts and washers and remove rubber mounting assembly.

3. With the car still on the ground, install and tighten tool A.74375 on shock absorber shaft. **THIS TOOL IS A MUST.**

4. Remove two nuts and washers holding shock assembly to body.

5. Jack up the car, support it safely, then remove the wheel.

6. Disconnect brake hose from tube in clip.

7. Remove nut and washer holding ball joint. Remove ball joint.

8. Remove nut and washer holding sway bar to lower support arm. Pry rubber bushing off threaded end of sway bar.

9. Remove bolt, nut and washers holding support arm to bracket on frame.

10. Remove arm from bracket. Push arm to rear to remove arm from sway bar.

11. Carefully lower suspension out of car. Install in reverse order.

NOTE: Do not attempt to disassemble the MacPherson shock absorber struts without a suitable spring compressor. See the Unit Repair section.

Front End Alignment

CAMBER ADJUSTMENT

124

Camber angle adjustments are made by changing the number of shims under the

A. Crossmember carrying lower track control arms and engine mounting
B and C. Bolts fixing crossmember to body
D. Crossmember shims
E. Upper control arm pivot bolt
F and G. Bolts fixing lower control arms to crossmember
H and I. Nuts fixing bolts of lower control arms
O. Hub cup
S. Shims to adjust camber and caster angles

124 Spider front suspension adjustments

two bolts that hold the lower control arm to the frame crossmember. Camber is increased by removing shims and reduced by adding shims. Add or remove the same number for each bolt, otherwise caster will be affected.

X1/9, 131, 128 and Strada

Camber cannot be adjusted and is built into the suspension. Replace weak, worn, or damaged springs or other suspension components to gain the proper camber measurement.

CASTER ADJUSTMENT

124

Caster angle is increased by moving these shims from the front bolts to the rear and decreased by moving them from the rear bolt to the front.

131

Caster is adjusted by adding or removing shims between the sway bar and lower support (control) arm.

1. Tie rod
2. Flats for wrench
3. Locknut
4. Tie rod end

Toe-in adjustment on 128, Strada and X1/9

FRONT

ADJUST SHIMS

ADJUST TIE ROD

Caster and toe-in adjustments—131

FRONT

ADJUST SHIMS

ADJUST TIE ROD

Caster and toe-in adjustments—128 and Strada

FRONT

ADJUST SHIMS

ADJUST TIE ROD

Caster and toe-in adjustments—X1/9

128 and Strada

If the caster angles are incorrect, the necessary corrections must be made by varying the number of shims inserted between the end of the anti-roll bar and the rubber pad of the control arm. The angle is reduced by about 15 minutes for each extra shim.

1. Raise the front of the vehicle on a pneumatic jack.
2. Remove the nut which anchors the anti-roll bar to the control arm.
3. Disconnect the control arm from the body.
4. Withdraw the end of the anti-roll bar from the control arm.
5. Add or remove as many shims as necessary to correct the caster angle.
6. Reassemble the various components. Lwer the vehicle and rock it a few times to settle down the suspension before tightening the two attachment nuts to their correct torque values.

X1/9

Caster is adjusted on the X1/9 by adding or subtracting shims between the front reaction struts and body-end supports.

TOE-IN

124

Toe-in is adjusted by loosening the clamp bolts and turning sleeves to lengthen or shorten the left and right-hand tie rods. Turn the sleeves in opposite directions and to an equal extent. After adjusting, make sure the gaps in the sleeves and clamps are on the same side and flush.

X1/9, 128 and Strada

1. Set the wheels straight ahead. Make sure the spokes on the steering wheel are positioned properly.
2. Loosen the locknut on the inboard end of the tie rod sleeve and turn the rod in or out until the proper toe-in is obtained. Do not change the position of the steering wheel spokes.
3. Tighten the locknut.

131

131 toe-in is adjusted in the same manner as the 128 and X1/9, except that the outboard locknut is loosened to rotate the tie rod.

NOTE: Lubricate the steering rod boot so it doesn't tear.

Wheel Bearings

REMOVAL AND ADJUSTMENT
128 and Strada

1. Remove the wheel, caliper, disc, and plate.
2. Remove the hub nut and discard.
3. Remove the tie rod end, shock absorber bolts, and lower ball joint spindle from the knuckle pillar.
4. Slide the knuckle pillar from the constant-speed joint.
5. Remove the bearing retainer ring or retaining nut from the pillar.
6. Press the old bearing out of the bearing cavity.

NOTE: Fiat recommends replacing the wheel bearings if removed for any reason.

7. Press the new bearing into the bearing cavity.

8. Reinstall the snap-ring or retaining nut. Torque the retaining nut to 44 ft. lbs. Stake to the knuckle pillar.

9. Complete the assembly in the reverse of removal. Torque the hub attachment nut to 100 ft. lbs. and stake the collar of the nut.

X1/9

1. Jack up the front end of the vehicle and remove the wheel.

2. Disconnect the brake calipers and support bracket from the steering pillar.

3. Remove the bolt and centering stud holding the brake rotor and plate and remove the rotor and plate.

4. Remove the nut securing the tie rod to the pillar and remove the ball joint from the pillar.

5. Remove the nut holding the control arm to the pillar and remove the control arm ball joint from the pillar.

6. Remove the two nuts and bolts holding the shock absorbers to the pillar and remove the pillar from the vehicle.

7. Remove the nut and washers holding the hub to the pillar and press the hub out of the pillar.

8. Remove the ring nut holding the bearing in the pillar and pull the bearing out of the pillar.

NOTE: The removal and installation of the bearing is facilitated by using special Fiat tools A.57123 socket to remove the bearing ring nut and 8015 bearing puller/installer to remove and install the bearing.

9. Discard the old bearing.

10. Install the new bearing.

11. Screw a *new* ring nut into the pillar. Tighten the nut to 43 ft. lbs. Always use a new ring nut.

12. Stake the ring nut with a punch.

13. Install the hub in the pillar and press it into place with a press. Install the two washers and a nut and tighten the nut to 100 ft. lbs. Stake the nut with a punch.

14. Install the steering pillar to the car in the reverse order of removal.

124 and 131

NOTE: A puller is required to remove the wheel hub.

1. Raise and support the front of the car. Remove the wheel, caliper assembly, disc and plate.

2. Remove the hub nut and discard.

3. Remove the hub from the spindle using a puller.

4. The inner and outer bearings can be driven or pressed from the hub and new or repacked ones installed. Pack the bearings and the area between the bearings with grease.

NOTE: Some replacement bearings are of the sealed type and do not require lubrication. Follow the package instructions.

5. Install the hub on the spindle and tighten the new hub nut to 15 ft. lbs. while turning the hub back and forth.

6. Back off the nut and retighten to 5 ft. lbs.

7. Back the nut off 30 degrees and check the hub end-play. It should measure between 0.001 and 0.004 inch.

8. Stake the nut to the spindle and reverse the removal process to complete assembly.

STEERING

Steering Wheel

REMOVAL AND INSTALLATION

128, X1/9 and 131

1. Disconnect the battery. Remove the screws attaching the horn button cover.

2. Remove the screws holding the steering column masking sleeves and remove the sleeves.

3. Unscrew the steering wheel attaching nut and remove the steering wheel.

4. Install in the reverse order.

124

1. Disconnect the battery. Pry off the horn button by inserting a screwdriver between the button and the wheel hub.

2. Disconnect the horn wire at the button.

3. Unscrew and remove the steering wheel attaching nut and remove the steering wheel from the shaft.

4. Install the steering wheel in the reverse order.

Strada

1. Center steering wheel and front wheels.

2. Disconnect battery.

3. Pry horn button from steering wheel.

4. Remove two horn button springs.

5. Remove nut holding wheel to shaft. Mark steering wheel and steering shaft for reinstallation. Pull wheel off shaft.

6. Reinstall in reverse order. Torque wheel retaining nut to 36 ft. lbs.

Horn/Directional/Light Switch Assembly

REMOVAL AND INSTALLATION

1. Remove horn button and steering wheel.

2. Disconnect switch wiring. Remove shroud.

1. Bolt	10. Bushing	19. Lockwasher
2. Washer	11. Steering column	20. Bolt
3. Retainer	12. Bushing	21. Shaft
4. Support	13. Cover	22. Clamp
5. Nut	14. Screw	23. Pad
6. Lockwasher	15. Pad	24. Clamp
7. Washer	16. Gasket	25. Lockwasher
8. Steering wheel	17. Steering box	26. Nut
9. Nut	18. Nut	27. Pad

Exploded view of steering column and steering gear—X1/9

3. Remove attaching clamp and slide off switch.

4. Installation is the reverse of removal.

Steering Gear

REMOVAL AND INSTALLATION

128

1. Disconnect the battery leads.
2. Rest the front of the car on stands.
3. Unscrew the stud bolts and remove the front wheels.
4. Remove the spare wheel.
5. Disconnect the drive pinion from the lower section of the steering column at the universal joint.
6. Using a puller, remove the tie rods from the steering ams.
7. Remove the screws which attach the top guard in order to facilitate removal of the steering box.
8. Unscrew the steering box from the mounting bracket and remove it from the right-side of the vehicle.
9. To install, insert the steering box (complete with tie rods and filled with oil), from the right-side of the vehicle.
10. With the steering wheel in the straight ahead position, connect the drive pinion to the steering column lower section, with the universal joints.
11. Mount the assembly on the body by means of the brackets. The rubber cushions must be inserted between the two parts.
12. Connect the tie rods to the steering arms. Torque the nuts to 58 ft. lbs.
13. Attach the top guard to the body.
14. Replace the front wheels and return the spare wheel to the engine compartment.

X1/9, 131 and Strada

1. Remove the bolt and nuts retaining the universal on the bottom of the steering column to the pinion shaft of the steering box.
2. Remove the three screws securing the gasket cover to the steering box on the floor boards.
3. Jack up the front of the vehicle and remove the two front wheels.
4. Remove the nuts securing the ball joints in both knuckles. Remove the tie rods from the knuckles.
5. Remove the four bolts securing the steering box to the body and remove the steering box from the vehicle.
6. Install the steering bx in the reverse order of removal.

Brava with Power Steering

1. Remove nut on tie rod.
2. Remove ball joint from steering knuckle.
3. Repeat for other side.
4. Remove hoses and allow box to drain.

5. Remove box and nut on steering shaft.
6. Remove bolt holding left side of box.
7. Remove 2 bolts holding right side.
8. Remove steering box from cr.
9. Install steering bx in reverse order of removal.
10. Fll with Dextron ATF fluid.

124

1. Disconnect the battery.
2. Remove the horn button and emblem cover.
3. Remove the steering wheel retaining nut and pull the steering wheel from the shaft, using a wheel puller.
4. Remove the turn signal switch half covers and unscrew the retaining collar of the turn signal switch. This is located on the bracket which fixes the steering column to the body.
5. Disconnect the steering column bracket from the ignition switch (threaded ring) and remove the retaining collar of the turn signal switch.
6. Remove the screw which clamps the steering column to the worm shaft and remove the steering column from inside the car.

1. Adjusting screw nut
2. Screw ring
3. Adjusting screw
4. Plug
5. Roller shaft
6. Ball bearings
7. Bearing retainer
8. Shims
9. Worm screw thrust cover
10. Cover screws
11. Pitman arm
12. Nut, pitman arm to roller shaft
13. Washer
14. Worm screw
15. Bearing retainer
16. Roller shaft seal
17. Steering column seal
18. Steering gear housing
19. Gasket
20. Steering housing upper cover
21. Upper cover screws
22. Oil filter plug

Exploded view of 124 steering gear

7. Unscrew the nuts which fix the left-hand steering arm and intermediate arm pins.
8. Remove the pins with an appropriate puller.
9. Remove the steering box from the body by removing the 3 mounting screws.

NOTE: Shims can be placed on the steering box bolts to ensure proper alignment.

Note the number and placement of such shims.
10. Drain the oil from the steering box.
11. Using a puller, remove the drop arm from the roller shaft.
12. Remove the roller shaft cover, complete with roller shaft adjusting screw, adjusting disc, lockwasher and locknut.
13. Remove the roller shaft assembly from the steering box.
14. Remove the worm shaft thrust cover and the front bearing adjusting shims.
15. Turn the worm shaft to withdraw the front roller bearing.
16. Use a puller and remove the outer race of the rear roller bearing.
17. Remove the worm and shaft from the steering box along with the inner race of the inner roller bearing.

ADJUSTMENTS

124

1. Measure the amount of free-play in the steering wheel by moving it back and forth until the wheels will not respond. At this point whatever movement is left in the wheel is free-play.
2. To adjust this condition, loosen the locknut and turn the adjusting screw in.
3. Gradually adjust the free-play out of the steering wheel until it becomes minimal.
4. Tighten the locknut while holding the adjustment screw in place.

NOTE: Serious damage may result from turning the adjustment screw in too far. A small amount of free-play should remain to insure against this condition.

128, X1/9, 131 and Strada

Adjustments to the steering gear are not necessary during normal service. Adjustments are performed only as part of overhaul.

Power Steering Pump

REMOVAL AND INSTALLATION

1. Remove two hoses from pump.
2. Allow system to drain.
3. Remove power steering pump tensioer bolt and mounting bolt.
4. Remove belt and power steering pump.
5. Reinstall in reverse order. Tension

1. Tensioner bolt
2. Tensioner bracket
3. Belt
4. Support bracket
5. Mounting bolt
6. Pump

Power steering pump—Brava

belt and fill system with Dexron transmission fluid.

NOTE: There is no rack adjustment on power steering models.

BRAKES

Spider and X1/9 models are equipped with four wheel disc brakes, while 128, 131 and Strada models use front disc and rear drum brakes. All models use a vacuum-hydraulic power assist booster acting on all four wheels through a dual brake circuit. A proportioning valve or brake compensator provides a pressure differential between front and rear brake systems according to load conditions and deceleration.

ADJUSTMENT

Rear Drum Brakes

The rear brakes on all models are self-centering with an automatic clearance ajustment. Periodic inspection of brake linings for wear and the wheel cylinders for leakage is the only required maintenance. No adjustment is necessary.

Master Cylinder

REMOVAL AND INSTALLATION

124 and 131

1. Remove the reservoir cover and plug the fluid outlet port.

1. Brake drum
2. Bolt
3. Wheel locating pin

Typical rear drum brake assembly

1. Brake fluid level switch
2. Reservoir cap
3. Reservoir
4. Brake line, right side
5. Nut
6. Master cylinder
7. Power brake booster
8. Brake line, left rear
9. Brake line, front

Typical master cylinder and booster assembly

1. Spring
2. Boot
3. Housing
4. Lockplate
5. Connection
6. Gasket
7. Gasket
8. Screw
9. Gasket
10. Piston
11. Spacer
12. Seal
13. Spring
14. Spring
15. Seal
16. Spacer
17. Piston
18. Spacer
19. Seal
20. Spring

Exploded view of master cylinder—X1/9

2. Disconnect the pipe between the reservoir and master cylinder.

3. Remove the 3 brake lines from the master cylinder.

4. Unbolt the master cylinder from the firewall, or power booster (124, 131).

5. Reverse the removal procedure to install the master cylinder. Bleed the system after installation.

X1/9

1. Remove the steering column as follows:

   a. Disconnect the battery.

   b. Remove the five screws holding the steering column cover halves and remove the covers.

   c. Disconnect the three electrical connectors and one wire.

   d. Remove the two nuts and washers holding the column to the top of the dashboard.

   e. Remove the two bolts and washers holding the column to the bottom of the dashboard.

   f. Slide the shaft off of the steering box shaft and remove the column from the vehicle.

2. Disconnect the hoses from the master cylinder reservoir.

3. Remove the nuts and washers holding the master cylinder to its support.

4. Pull the master cylinder off of the actuating rod. Remove the hoses from the master cylinder and switch assembly.

5. Remove the master cylinder from the vehicle and drain the fluid into an appropriate container.

6. Install the master cylinder and steering column in the reverse order of removal and bleed the brake hydraulic system.

Strada

1. Remove the jack and spare tire. Remove spare tire support.

1. Nut
2. Lockwasher
3. Vacuum hose
4. Power booster assembly
5. Clamp
6. Brake booster pushrod

Removing brake booster—typical

2. While holding brake fluid level switch, unscrew cover from reservoir.

3. Drain reservoir with syringe.

4. Using gentle side-to-side rocking motion, pull reservoir from master cylinder.

5. Disconnect three brake lines from master cylinder. Cap the lines to keep out dirt.

6. Remove the two mounting nuts and pull master cylinder away from power brake.

7. Install in reverse order, making sure all fittings and lines are clean.

8. Bleed the system.

128

1. Remove the spare wheel from the engine compartment.

2. Remove the fluid reservoir cover and plug the outlet to the master cylinder in order to keep the reservoir from draining.

3. Disconnect the reservoir-to-master cylinder tubes.

4. Disconnect the fluid delivery tubing to the front and rear brakes, removing the fastening screws.

5. Remove both nuts and spring washers which secure the master cylinder to the power booster and remove the master cylinder.

6. Installation is the reverse of removal. Bleed the system.

OVERHAUL

For overhaul procedures, see the Brake Unit Repair section.

Power Brake Booster

REMOVAL AND INSTALLATION

All Models

1. Remove reservoir and master cylinder as previously outlined.

2. Loosen clamp and disconnect vacuum hose from brake booster.

3. Remove cotter pin and washer to disconnect brake booster push rod from brake pedal.

4. Remove four nuts and lockwashers holding booster. Remove brake booster.

5. Reinstall in reverse order.

Brake Pressure Regulator

This device, located near the rear axle is used on 124, 128, Strada, and 131 models. It serves to adjust hydraulic line pressure to prevent rear wheel lock-up under hard braking. An important safety factor, the pressure regulator will apply a reduced line pressure to the rear brakes (roughly half that of the front brakes) when the rear suspension is off-loaded. A torsion bar, anchored

1. Cylinder body
2. Spring and cup
3. Rear brake fluid inlet port
4. Piston
5. Seal
6. Feed to front brakes
7. Spring and cup
8. Front brake fluid inlet port
9. Piston
10. Seal
11. Dust cover
12. Stop bolt and sealing washer
13. Spacer
14. Springs
15. Seal
16. End plug and feed to rear brakes

Sectional view of master cylinder

to the rear axle, senses suspension angle, and transmits this mechanically to the pressure regulator valve. The result is straight line stopping and more even braking effect.

ADJUSTMENT

NOTE: Car must be unladen, on a level surface.

The pressure regulator need only be adjusted upon initial installation, or if its mounting bolts become loose in service. By loosening the mounting bolts, the regulator may b pivoted to adjust the travel of the torsion bar.

124, 131, 128 and Strada

1. Raise rear of car and support on stands.
2. Disconnect regulator torsion bar (E) at axle connecting link (G).
3. Pivot axle end of the torsion bar to distance "X" from the rubber buffer resting surface.
4. Lift dust boot (C) and check that regulator piston (D) contacts other end of torsion bar.
5. If not, loosen regulator mounting screws (A + B) and pivot regulator until pston just grazes torsion bar.
6. Then tighten the mounting screws and connect the torsion bar. On the 128 and Strada, torque the bolts to 14 ft. lbs. Distance "X" is:

5.78 in.—124 Sport Coupe
2.7 in.—Strada
3.74 in.—124 Sport Spider
12.0 in.—131 Sedan
12.25 in.—131 Wagon
2.126 in.—128 All

Bleeding

ALL MODELS

For brake bleeding procedures, see the Brake Unit Repair section.

Disc Brakes

ALL MODELS

For all service and overhaul procedures, see the Brake Unit Repair section.

Rear Drum Brakes

ALL MODELS

For all service and overhaul procedures, see the Brake Unit Repair section.

1. Pressure regulator
2. Rubber buffer seat
3. Torsion bar
3B. Torsion bar end, anchor pin side
4. Torsion bar to control arm link
5. Torsion bar link to control arm link
6. Link anchor pin support
7. Control arm

Brake pressure regulator on 128—Strada similar

1. Bar
2. Anchor pin
3. Rubber cover
4. Bolt
5. Bolt
6. Piston
7. Torsion bar
8. Base of rubber bumper

Brake pressure regulator—131 models

1. Rubber buffer
2. Master cylinder tube
3. Pressure regulator
4. Rear brakes tube
5. Torsion bar
6. Lower reaction arm
7. Support
8. Nut
9. Support
10. Bolts
11. Rubber boot

Brake pressure regulator installation—131 shown

Parking Brake

CABLE ADJUSTMENT

ALL MODELS

NOTE: The 124 and 128 cable adjusters are located under the car. The 131 and Strada models have the adjuster located on the underside of the handbrake lever. The X1/9 adjuster is located on the underside of the car underneath an access plate, or on the lever similar to 131.

1. Disengage the handbrake cable, using the lever.
2. Pull the lever up three or four notches.
3. Loosen the locknut on the tensioner and turn the adjusting nut until the cable is stretched and the wheels are locked.
4. Tighten the locknut.
5. The cable is correctly tensioned when the car is held by a movement of the lever through 3 notches.
6. Release the lever and check that the wheels are free to turn. Make sure the locking spring presses against a flat side of the adjuster nut.

1. Cover
2. Lever
3. Release button
4. Adjustment nut
5. Spring

Parking brake adjustment—131 and Strada

1. Main cable
2. Threaded tensioner
3. Adjusting nut and locknut

Parking brake adjustment—128

Parking brake adjustment access window—X1/9

CHASSIS ELECTRICAL

Heater Assembly

REMOVAL AND INSTALLATION

124

1. Drain the engine cooling system and the heater radiator.
2. The lower heater lever must be moved to the right.
3. Loosen the hose clips on the flow and return pipes to the heater.
4. From the engine compartment, remove the rubber seals on the heater pipes.
5. Remove the valve cable from the clip.
6. Disconnect the yellow cable to the fan.
7. Release the spring clips and remove the fan housing.
8. Lower the radiator and remove the air intake shutter control cable.
9. Remove the eater from the car.
10. Installation is the reverse of removal. Be sure that the gasket between fan and body is psitioned correctly. Run the engine and fill the radiator.

1. Plug
2. Cover
3. Spring
4. Water control valve
5. Gasket
6. Nut
7. Washer
8. Plate
9. Heater core
10. Heater assembly
11. Hose

Heater assembly components—131

1. Upper shutter, for fresh air admission to car interior
2. Lower shutter, for air flow onto radiator (10)
3. Attaching screw, washers and nut
4. Water shield
5. Housing
6. Water drain plug
7. Valve
8. Gasket
9. Gasket
10. Radiator
11. Gasket
12. Spring clips
13. Nut, attaching impeller to motor
14. Impeller
15. Rubber pad
16. Motor
17. Fan housing

Starting from car with chassis No. 215963 a grid has been added to the heater housing

Heater assembly components—128

128

1. Completely drain the cooling system.

2. Loosen the clips which retain the inlet and outlet hoses.

3. Remove the screw and nut from the air shutter actuating rod.

4. Remove the air conveyor.

5. Slide out the radiator housing spring clips.

6. Withdraw the outside shutter actuating rod.

7. Remove the heater valve control cable.

8. Remove the heater core.

9. Remove the fan housing attaching nuts.

10. Disconnect the cables which feed the motor at the fan switch.

11. Installation is the reverse of removal.

NOTE: Be sure to check all hses and clamps and the drain cock and gaskets before reinstalling the heater core. Heater disassembly is done easily by removing or prying out the case clips. The electric fan is also mounted with clips.

X1/9

1. Drain the cooling system. Make sure you have drained it thoroughly, or there will be water left in the heater radiator.

1. Nut
2. Heater box
3. Control console
4. Screw
5. Nut
6. Control panel
7. Return hose
8. Feed hose
9. Bolt
10. Bleed valve

Heater box and control panel—Strada

1. Wiper blade
2. Wiper arm
3. Wiper motor
4. Wiper arm transmission
5. Linkage
6. Bracket, mounting

Exploded view of 124 wiper assembly

1. Bracket, mounting
2. Motor drive arm
3. Wiper motor
4. Bracket lug
5. Connecting link
6. Wiper transmission and drive arm

Exploded view of 128 wiper assembly

1. Wiper motor
2. Connecting link
3. Right Wiper transmission
4. Washer
5. Spacer
6. Nut
7. Left Wiper transmission
8. Drive link
9. Motor drive arm
10. Bracket, mounting

Exploded view of X1/9 wiper assembly

2. The heater assembly is located behind the console in the center of the car. Remove the console.

3. Remove the hoses from the heater assembly.

4. The heater assembly box is a two piece unit which is held together with clips. Remove all attached components ad remove the heater assembly.

5. Installation is the reverse of removal.

131

1. Drain the cooling system. Make sure you have drained it thoroughly or there will be water left in the heater radiator.

2. The heater assembly is located in the center of the dashboard behind the console (if equipped).

3. Remove all hoses and control cables from the heater. The heater is a two piece unit, held together with clips. Remove the heater assembly.

4. Installation is the reverse of removal.

Strada

1. Disconnect battery cable.

2. Drain cooling system.

3. Remove spare tire and air cleaner.

4. Remove four nuts and carefully pull control console down from dash.

5. Remove three screws to separate control panel from control console.

6. Loosen the two clamps to remove feed and return hoses from heater core connections.

7. Remove two nuts and one bolt holding heater box to firewall. Carefully lift heater box from its mounting until electrical lead to blower motor can be disconnected.

8. Remove heater box by slowly feeding control panel through dash and firewall.

9. Installation is everse of removal.

10. After installation and refill of cooling system, bleed heater core. Run engine at fast idle with heater knob turned to full hot position, slowly open bleed valve next tto feed hose inlet on heater box.

Windshield Wiper Motor

REMOVAL AND INSTALLATION

124

The windshield wiper motor is removed from the engine compartment side in the following manner:

1. Unscrew the left-hand spacer nut and remove the left-hand wiper blade and arm.

2. Remove the retaining nuts from the bracket and pull the motor back slightly.

3. Remove the clip connecting the right half-link to the motor and remove the motor.

4. Installation is the reverse of removal.

128

1. Remove the wiper blades and arms.
2. Back out the attaching nuts and remove the wiper blade pivot spacers.
3. Remove the spare wheel.
4. Remove the speedometer cable clip from the body.
5. Remove the screws which attach the wiper assembly to the mounting bracket.
6. Disconnect the connector block and remove the unit completely.
7. Installation is the reverse of removal.

X1/9

1. The X1/9 wiper motor is located on the driver's side under a screen on the cowling.
2. Remove the cowl screen. The wiper motor and linkage will then be visible.
3. Unbolt the wiper motor to remove it.
4. Installation is the reverse of removal.

131

1. The wiper motor is located under a plastic cover on the firewall.
2. Remove the plastic cover. The wiper motor should now be visible.
3. Unbolt and remove the motor.
4. Installation is the reverse of removal.

Strada—Front

NOTE: Wipers should be in Park position.

1. Disconnect electrical connector.
2. Remove shaft nut.
3. Remove three bolts holding motor assembly. emove motor.
4. Installation is reverse o removal.

Strada and 131 Wagon—Rear

1. Swing wiper arm up to locked position and remove it.
2. Remove nut at shaft base.
3. Remove bolt holding motor assembly.
4. Remove motor and disconnect electrical connector.
5. Installation is reverse of removal.

Instrument Cluster

REMOVAL AND INSTALLATION

124 Spider

1. Unscrew the 4 mounting screws securing the cluster.
2. Disconnect the speedometer cable.
3. Disconnect the 5 cluster connectors.

CUSTOM MODELS WITH LUXURY PACKAGES

CUSTOM MODELS

STANDARD MODEL

A. Digital Clock
B. Hazard indicator
C. Turn indicator
D. Low oil indicator
E. Coolant temp. gauge
F. Tachometer
G. Lights indicator
H. High beam indicator
I. Fasten belt indicator
J. Brake indicator
K. Low fuel indicator
L. Rear window washer/wiper switch
M. Rear window defogger switch
N. Panel light rheostat
O. Fuel gauge
P. Speedometer
Q. Trip recorder
R. Odometer
S. Rear window defogger indicator
T. Battery charge indicator
U. Hazard switch
V. Outer lighting switch
W. Quartz clock

Instrument panel arrangements

4. Remove the cluster.
5. Install the cluster in the reverse order of removal.

131

1. Remove the screws which hold the instrument cluster to the panel.
2. Pull the cluster out a short way and disconnect the electrical connections and the speedometer cable.
3. Remove the instrument cluster.
4. Installation is the reverse of removal.

128

1. Open the hood and remove the spare wheel.

2. Back out the speedometer cable retainer pate screw.
3. Remove the instrument cluster retainer screw from inside the car.
4. Withdraw the instrument cluster.
5. To install, reverse the removal procedure.

X1/9

1. Remove the five screws retaining the instrument cluster to the instrument panel.
2. Slide the cluster out enough to disconnect the three electrical connectors and the speedometer cable.
3. Remove the instrument custer from the istrument panel.
4. Install the instrument cluster in the

reverse order of removal.

Strada

1. Disconnect battery.
2. Remove jack and spare tire.
3. Rmove steering wheel.
4. From spare wheel recess area, re-move bolt on firewall holding instrument cluster.

5. Release tabs on both sides of instru-ment cluster and carefully pull cluster out of housing.

6. Dsconnect electrical connectors and speedometer cable, then remove cluster completely.

7. Installation is the reverse of re-moval.

Fuse Box Location

On all Fiat models, the fuse box will be in one of three possible locations:
1. Under the left side dash.
2. Under the right side glove box.
3. Under the hood on the right side next to the relay assembly.

Fiesta

VEHICLE IDENTIFICATION PLATE

The vehicle identification plate is riveted on the panel above the right front headlight, just under the hood.

The eleven digit number is composed of a six digit identification code and a five digit serial number.

VIN plate location

FB	---	3 Door Hatchback
G	---	Germany
C	---	Assembled at Saarlouis
T-U	---	T-1977 (Calendar Year) U-1978 (Calendar Year)
P	---	Month Code
10001	---	Numerical Sequence of Assembly

VIN plate general information

GENERAL ENGINE SPECIFICATIONS

Year	Engine Displacement Cu. In. (cc)	Carburetor No. of Bbls.	Horsepower @ rpm	Torque @ rpm (ft. lbs.)	Bore X Stroke (in.)	Compression Ratio	Oil Pressure (psi)
'78–'80	97.5 (1600)	2V	65 @ 5000	82 @ 3200	3.188 × 3.056	8.6:1	24–45 @ 2000 rpm

TUNE-UP SPECIFICATIONS

Year	Engine Displacement Cu. In (cc)	Spark Plug Type	Spark Plug Gap (in.)	Distributor Point Dwell (deg.)	Distributor Point Gap (in.)	Ignition Timing (deg.) MT	Ignition Timing (deg.) AT	Intake Valve Opens BTDC (deg.)	Fuel Pump Pressure (psi)	Valve Clearance (in.) In.	Valve Clearance (in.) Ex.	Idle Speed (rpm)
'78–'80	97.5 (1600)	AWRF-32	.050	Electronic Dura-Spark II		12° BTDC	—	29	3.5 @ 700 rpm	0.008–.010 (cold)	.021 ① (cold)	②

① 0.018 in. Hot
② See underhood sticker

FIRING ORDER

Firing order 1-2-4-3

Engine—Front

Front of car

CAPACITIES

Year	Engine Displacement Cu. In. (cc)	Engine Crankcase (qts.) With Filter	Engine Crankcase (qts.) W/Out Filter	Transaxle Assembly (pts.) MT	Transaxle Assembly (pts.) AT	Gasoline Tank (gal.)	Cooling System (qts.) W/AC	Cooling System (qts.) W/O AC
'78–'80	97.5 (1600)	3.5	3.0	5	—	10	6.6	6.6

CRANKSHAFT AND CONNECTING ROD SPECIFICATIONS

Year	Engine Displacement Cu. In. (cc)	Main Bearing Journal Diameter (in.)	Main Bearing Oil Clearance (in.)	Main Bearing Shaft End-Play (in.)	Main Bearing Thrust Taken on No.	Connecting Rod Bearing Journal Diameter (in.)	Connecting Rod Bearing Oil Clearance (in.)	Connecting Rod Bearing Side Clearance (in.)
'78–'80	97.5 (1600)	2.1253–2.1261	0.0005–② 0.0015	0.003–0.011 ①	3	1.9368–1.9376	0.0004–0.0015	0.004–0.010

① Controlled by half-circled thrust washers
② 1979–80: 0.0004–0.0015

VALVE SPECIFICATIONS

Year	Engine Displacement Cu. In. (cc)	Seat Angle (deg.)	Face Angle (deg.)	Spring Test Pressure (lbs. @ in.)	Spring Installed Height (in.)	Stem To Guide Clearance (in.)		Stem Diameter (in.)	
						Intake	Exhaust	Intake	Exhaust
'78–'80	97.5 (1600)	45	45	42 @ 1.263 104 @ .952	1¼–1⁹⁄₃₂	0.0008– 0.0027	0.0017– 0.0036	0.3098– 0.3105	0.3089– 0.3096

PISTON AND RING SPECIFICATIONS

(All measurements given in inches)

Year	Engine Displacement Cu. In. (cc)	Piston Clearance (in.)	Ring Gap (in.)			Ring Side Clearance (in.)		
			Top Compression	Bottom Compression	Oil Control	Top Compression	Bottom Compression	Oil Control
'78–'80	97.5 (1600)	0.0009– 0.0017	0.009– 0.017	0.009– 0.017	0.009– 0.014	0.0016– 0.0036	0.0016– 0.0036	0.0018– 0.0038

TORQUE SPECIFICATIONS

(All readings in ft. lbs.)

Year	Engine Displacement Cu. In. (cc)	Cylinder Head Bolts	Rod Bearing Bolts	Main Bearing Bolts	Crankshaft Pulley Bolts	Flywheel To Crankshaft Bolts	Manifold	
							Intake	Exhaust
'78–'80	97.5 (1600)	65–70①	30–35	55–60	24–28④	50–55	12–15②	9–12③

①Step 1—5 ft. lbs.
  Step 2—20–30 ft. lbs.
  Step 3—50–55 ft. lbs.
  Step 4—65–70 ft. lbs.
②Intake manifold to cylinder head nuts—12–15 ft. lbs.
  Intake manifold to cylinder head studs—9–12 ft. lbs.
③Exhaust manifold to cylinder head nuts—15–18 ft. lbs.
④1979–80: 40–44

CYLINDER HEAD TORQUE SEQUENCE

STARTER SPECIFICATIONS

Year	Engine Displacement Cu. In. (cc)	No-Load Test			Load Test			Lock Test			Brush Spring Tension (lbs.)	Brush Minimum Length (in.)
		Amps	Volts	rpm	Amps	Volts	rpm	Amps	Volts	Torque (ft. lbs.)		
'78–'80	97.5 (1600)	NOT RECOMMENDED						350	12	6.9	2.0–2.7	.39

BATTERY, ALTERNATOR AND REGULATOR SPECIFICATIONS

Year	Engine Displacement Cu. In. (cc)	Battery④ Capacity (amp. hr.)	Alternator Field Current @ 12V	Alternator Rated Output (amps.)	Brush Spring Tension (oz.)	Brush Minimum Length (in.)	Regulator Type	Regulator Voltage Setting
'78–'80	97.5 (1600)	35	—	40	—	—	Electro-mechanical	14V
		43①	29	60②	—	0.3125	Electro-mechanical	14V
			29	55③	10.6–14.1	0.200	Integral	13.7–14.4V

① Heavy duty
② With rear window defogger
③ With air conditioning
④ Located in engine compartment

BRAKE SPECIFICATIONS
(All measurements in inches unless noted)

Year	Engine Displacement Cu. In. (cc)	Wheel Lug Nut Torque (ft. lbs.)	Master Cylinder Bore	Brake Disc Max. Thickness	Brake Disc Min. Thickness	Brake Disc Max. Runout	Brake Drum Diameter	Brake Drum Max. Machine	Wear Limit	Lining Thickness Minimum Front	Lining Thickness Minimum Rear
'78–'80	97.5 (1600)	52–74	—	0.390	0.340	0.006	7.00	①	①	0.060	0.060

NOTE: Minimum lining thickness is as recommended by the manufacturer. Due to variation in state inspection regulations, the minimum allowable thickness may be different than recommended by the manufacturer.
① Refer to state inspection regulations.

WHEEL ALIGNMENT SPECIFICATIONS

Year	Engine Displacement Cu. In. (cc)	Caster① Range (deg.)	Caster Pref. Setting (deg.)	Camber① Range (deg.)	Camber Pref. Setting	Toe Adjustment (In or Out)	Steering Axis Inclination	Standard Tire Size
'78–'80	97.5 (1600)	−0°25'– +1°20'	+0°20'	+3°15'–+1°15'	+2°15'	Out 0.10 ± 0.04 in. (13/64 ± 3/64)	—	155SR12

① Maximum variation—LH side to RH side 1°15'

TUNE-UP PROCEDURES

NOTE: Refer to the Emission Control Sticker for the required specifications.

Distributor

The Fiesta uses the Dura-Spark II solid state ignition system which eliminates the conventional contact point and condenser set. The gap between the magnetic pickup assembly and the armature is preset and no attempt should be made to change it.

Spark Plug and Coil Wires

Inspect all wiring for cracks, fraying, loose connections and other damage. Measure the secondary cable resistance, which should not exceed 4100 ohms per foot of cable.

NOTE: Be sure the ignition switch is in the OFF position, because any movement of the distributor armature spoke past the pick-up coil will cause high voltage to occur in the coil secondary circuit.

NOTE: If a high tension lead was disconnected from the coil, spark plug or distributor cap, silicone grease must be applied to the boot before reconnection.

Electronic ignition tachometer connection

Ignition Coil

Inspect the ignition coil for cracks and carbon traces on both the primary and secondary sides. The primary resistance should be between 1.0 to 2.0 ohms, while the secondary resistance should be between 7700 and 9300 ohms. The primary circuit resistance (ignition switch–to–control module) should range from 1.05 to 1.15 ohms.

Spark Plugs

Remove the spark plugs and inspect them. If reusable, a sand blaster cleaner or equivalent can be used to remove the accumulated carbon. Do not prolong the cleaning operation. After cleaning, inspect the spark plugs for cracked or broken insulators, badly pitted electrodes or other signs of failure. If the spark plugs are to be reused, lift the ground electrode slightly and file both the ground and the center electrode as flat as possible without removing much metal from the contact surfaces. Using a round wire gauge, gap the spark plug, both new or used, to the correct specifications.

Ignition Timing

Use the following procedures for the adjustment of ignition timing.

STATIC

1. Place a white mark on the proper degree line on the front cover and the crankshaft damper as per the specification given on the engine sticker.
2. Align the two marks by rotating the engine crankshaft.
3. Loosen the distributor hold-down bolt and rotate the distributor so that the rotor points to the no. 1 cylinder tower of the distributor cap.
4. By moving the distributor body, align the armature squarely with the lug on the magnetic pick-up coil, and tighten the distributor hold-down bolt. Verify that the distributor body has not moved.

NOTE: An error of ½ a tooth is equal to 7¾ engine degrees timing error.

DYNAMIC

1. Place a white mark on the proper degree line on the front cover and the crankshaft damper as per the specification given on the engine sticker.
2. Disconnect and plug the distributor vacuum line.
3. Connect a timing light to the No. 1 spark plug cable.

NOTE: A special timing light may be necessary for this type system. Inductive pickup type lights may work satisfactorily if an insulated standoff, such as a piece of split vacuum hose, is placed around the spark plug wire.

4. Start the engine and adjust the idle to specifications. Inspect the timing mark location with the timing light.
5. If the timing is within ±2 degrees of specifications, do not reset, but if the timing is off more than ±2 degrees, reset by loosening the distributor hold-down bolt and moving the distributor body to correct the timing alignment and retighten the distributor hold-down bolt.
6. Recheck the ignition timing mark alignment after the hold-down bolt is tightened.

Valve Adjustment

The valves should be checked with the engine at normal operating temperature. The clearance should be checked by inserting a feeler gauge between the valve stem and the rocker arm, with the cam lobe at its lowest point.

The following chart gives the sequence for valve adjustment.

VALVE ADJUSTMENT SEQUENCE

Rotate engine to fully open these valve numbers to check valve clearance of these valves			
1 + 6	2 + 4	3 + 8	5 + 7
3 + 8	5 + 7	1 + 6	2 + 4

The adjusting screws are self-locking.

CRANKSHAFT PULLEY
Timing marks

← FRONT OF ENGINE

FRONT OF CAR ↓

Valve arrangement in cylinder head
Front of engine   1-2-3-4-5-6-7-8

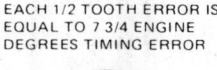

EACH 1/2 TOOTH ERROR IS EQUAL TO 7 3/4 ENGINE DEGREES TIMING ERROR

TOOTH MUST BE PERFECTLY ALIGNED WITH STATOR

ROTOR

STATOR

Distributor armature and stator lug alignment

WRENCH

ADJUSTING SCREW

FEELER GAUGE

Adjusting engine valves

Carburetor

All specifications for carburetor adjustments are on the engine emission sticker.

CURB IDLE SPEED ADJUSTMENT

1. Have the engine at normal operating temperature, apply the parking brake and chock the wheels.

2. Disconnect the engine electric fan temperature switch wires, located on the thermostat housing. Use a jumper wire and connect the two wires so that the fan will run continuously.

3. Remove the air cleaner assembly from the engine and check the throttle linkage for freedom of movement.

4. Remove the Spark Delay Valve from the vacuum advance hose, if equipped, and connect a jumper hose between the two hoses.

5. Disconnect the fuel decel valve hose, if equipped, and plug the hose.

6. If equipped with a ported vacuum switch (PVS) to control the exhaust gas recirculation valve (EGR), disconnect the EGR valve by removing and plugging the vacuum hose at the EGR-PVS. If the engine is *not* equipped with an EGR-PVS unit, *do not* disconnect the EGR valve.

7. Attach a tachometer and run the engine for 15 seconds at 2500 rpm.

8. Allow engine to return to idle and to stabilize.

9. If the curb idle speed is incorrect, adjust.

10. If you are unable to obtain the specified curb idle speed, check the dashpot, if equipped, for hanging or misadjustment.

11. Reinstall the air cleaner and recheck the curb idle speed.

NOTE: Final curb idle speed reading must be taken with the air cleaner assembly installed.

12. Stop the engine and reinstall the radiator fan temperature switch wires.

PROPANE ENRICHMENT IDLE FUEL MIXTURE ADJUSTMENT

NOTE: Ford Motor Co. recommends the use of propane gas to adjust the idle fuel mixture. The equipment necessary is not readily available to the general public. This procedure should not be attempted without the required equipment.

ENGINE ELECTRICAL

Distributor

REMOVAL

1. Rotate the engine so that the timing

A—Secondary wires
B—Cap
C—Rotor
D—Electronic pickup assembly
E—Harness multiplug

Exploded view of distributor

marks are aligned at 12 degrees BTDC with No. 1 piston on its firing stroke.

2. Remove the distributor cap, primary wire, vacuum line and distributor hold-down bolt.

3. Note the position of the rotor in relationship to the distributor body and pull the distributor up from the engine block.

INSTALLATION

1. Be certain that the engine has not moved from its previous position.

NOTE: If the engine crankshaft has been turned while the distributor is out of the engine, locate No. 1 piston on its firing stroke by removing No. 1 spark plug and holding a finger over the hole.

BOSS—LINES UP WITH

PIN—PROTRUDING THIS SIDE

Aligning distributor body to shaft before installation

Rotate the engine in its normal rotation until compression build-up can be felt; align the timing marks at 12 degrees BTDC.

2. Install a new O-ring on the distributor body. Align the projecting side of the drive gear retaining pin with the boss in the distributor body.

3. Install the distributor in the engine block so that the vacuum advance unit is parallel to the engine centerline. Install the distributor hold-down bolt loosely.

4. Align the armature lug to the lug on the pickup assembly for No. 1 cylinder (rotor pointing to the No. 1 segment in the distributor cap) and snug down the distributor body hold-down bolt.

5. Attach the primary wire, distributor cap, a timing light and tachometer.

6. Plug the vacuum hose to the advance unit.

7. Start the engine and bring it to normal operating temperature.

8. Check the engine idle speed. Check the timing with the timing light.

9. If the timing is within ±2 degrees of specifications, do not retime. If the timing is off by more than ±2 degrees, reset as necessary.

10. Tighten the distributor body hold-down bolt and recheck the timing. Reset the curb idle speed if necessary. Stop the engine and install the vacuum advance hose.

11. Remove the timing light and the tachometer.

NOTE: Obtain all specifications from the engine emission sticker attached to the engine.

Alternator

Three different alternators are used.
Motorcraft 40 amp.—used as standard equipment.
Motorcraft 60 amp.—used with rear window defogger.
Bosch 55 amp.—used with air conditioning, has an integral voltage regulator.

ALTERNATOR PRECAUTIONS

To prevent damage to the alternator and regulator, the following precautionary measures must be taken when working with the electrical system.

1. Never reverse battery connections. Always check the battery polarity visually. This is to be done before any connections are made to ensure that all of the connections correspond to the battery ground polarity of the car.

2. Booster batteries must be connected properly. Make sure the positive cable of the booster battery is connected to the positive terminal of the battery which is getting the boost.

3. Disconnect the battery cables before using a fast charger; the charger has a ten-

dency to force current through the diodes in the opposite direction for which they were designed.

4. Never use a fast charger as a booster for starting the car.

5. Never disconnect the voltage regulator while the engine is running, unless as noted for testing purposes.

6. Do not ground the alternator output terminal.

7. Do not operate the alternator on an open circuit with the field energized.

8. Do not attempt to polarize the alternator.

9. Disconnect the battery cables and remove the alternator before using an electric arc welder on the car.

10. Protect the alternator from excessive moisture. If the engine is to be steam cleaned, cover or remove the alternator.

REMOVAL AND INSTALLATION

Bosch

1. Disconnect the ground battery cable.

2. Remove the wiring connections at the rear of the alternator and retaining clips.

NOTE: A wiring connector is used on some models.

3. Disconnect the heater hose bracket from the alternator.

4. Loosen the three mounting bolts, move the alternator toward the engine and remove the drive belt.

5. Remove the mounting bolts and remove the alternator from the engine.

6. To install, reverse the removal procedure.

7. Adjust the drive belt tension to give 0.5 in. of free movement, midway along the longest belt span.

1. Fan	8. Rectifier (diode) pack
2. Spacer	9. Stator
3. Drive end housing	10. Slip rings
4. Thrust plate	11. Rotor
5. Slip ring end bearing	12. Drive end housing
6. Slip ring end housing	13. Spacer
7. Brush box and regulator	14. Pulley

Exploded view of the Bosch 55 amp alternator

Motorcraft

1. Disconnect the negative battery cable.

2. Remove the drive belt by loosening the alternator mounting bolts and moving the alternator toward the engine.

3. Remove the wiring connections at the rear or side (mark the wires for proper reinstallation).

4. Remove the mounting bolts and lift the alternator from the engine brackets.

5. To install the alternator, reverse the removal procedure.

6. Adjust the belt tension to give 0.5 inch of free movement, midway along the longest belt span.

Starter

A Bosch positive engagement–type starter is used. It has an integral solenoid on top of the starter motor. A separate starter relay is not used.

REMOVAL AND INSTALLATION

1. Disconnect the battery ground cable.

2. Raise the front of the vehicle and support safely.

3. Disconnect the solenoid wires, marking them for reinstallation.

4. Remove the two rubber insulators holding the exhaust connection to the body and engine crossmember, and the two clamp bolts holding the exhaust pipe to the manifold. Lower the exhaust pipe to gain clearance for starter removal.

5. Remove the starter motor retaining bolts and remove the starter.

6. Installation is the reverse of removal.

Exploded view of a typical Motorcraft alternator

OVERHAUL

1. Mount the starter assembly in a vise.
2. Remove the nut and washer holding the field winding cable to the solenoid.
3. Remove the three solenoid mounting screws and guide the solenoid yoke away from the drive end housing and solenoid armature. Unhook the solenoid armature from the actuating lever.
4. Remove the commutator end housing cap, seal and screws.
5. Remove the C-clip and shims from the armature end.
6. Remove two nuts and washer from the studs and remove the commutator end housing.

NOTE: Some Bosch starters use screws instead of nuts and studs.

7. Remove brushes from the brush plate assembly before the brush plate is removed.
8. Separate the drive end housing and armature assembly from the yoke by tapping with a soft hammer.
9. Remove the armature assembly from the drive end housing and uncouple the actuating arm at the same time (the actuator arm may be removed from the drive end housing by removal of the actuating arm pin).
10. Separate the thrust collar from the C-clip and remove the C-clip from its groove. Slide the thrust collar and drive pinion assembly off the armature shaft.
11. Assembly of the starter is the reverse of disassembly.

NOTE: New bushings should be completely submerged in engine oil for at least 30 minutes before being installed.

NOTE: When installing the brush plate, align the cutout openings with the loops in the field windings so that the main case through bolts fit into the cutouts.

ENGINE MECHANICAL

Engine/Transmission

REMOVAL AND INSTALLATION

1. Disconnect the battery and remove it.
2. Drain the coolant and remove the upper and lower radiator hoses. Remove the heater hoses from the side water pipe and intake manifold connector.
3. Remove the air cleaner assembly.
4. Disconnect the accelerator cable at the carburetor. Remove the cable bracket from the intake manifold. Press the cable retaining clip out of the carburetor and remove the cable.
5. Disconnect the fuel line at the carburetor and fuel pump and remove. Dis-

connect the fuel vent hose at the carburetor.
6. Tag and disconnect all emission control and servo vacuum hoses.
7. Tag and disconnect the electrical leads from the engine electrical units. Remove the engine ground strap.

Removing or installing clutch cable in the clutch release lever

8. Disconnect the speedometer at the speedometer drive gear, on the transmission.
9. Remove the clutch cable from the release lever by briefly depressing and releasing the cable, while disengaging the cable ball from the slot on the release lever.
10. Remove the exhaust manifold heat tube and the inlet pipe from the exhaust manifold.

NOTE: Wire the inlet pipe to the body.

11. Disconnect the air pump ground wire.
12. Engage 4th gear to insure proper gear shift adjustment during assembly.
13. Raise the vehicle high enough to allow the engine/transmission assembly to be removed from underneath. Support the vehicle safely.
14. Loosen the clamp bolt and remove the gear selector rod. Unhook the spring between the selector rod and the longitudinal body member.
15. Loosen the mounting nuts on the stabilizer rubber insulators and engine mounts. Loosen the stud lock nut and remove the stud from the transmission (an Allen wrench is needed to remove the stud).
16. Remove the complete exhaust system as a unit, after removing the rubber mounting brackets.
17. Remove the shifter tower from the floor pan. Rotate the gear selector rod with the stabilizer half way around. Hang it on a wire to avoid dropping the rod to the floor.
18. Disconnect the starter leads and the alternator leads.
19. Disconnect the left axle driveshaft at the coupling with the stubshaft, by removing the six Allen headed bolts.
20. Disconnect the right driveshaft at the inner constant velocity joint by removing the six allen headed bolts.
21. Support the engine/transmission as-

| 12. Brush assembly |
| 13. Main feed terminal |
| 14. Main case |
| 15. Drive gear housing |
| 16. Solenoid retaining screw |
| 17. Bearing bushing |
| 18. Pivot screw |
| 19. Engaging fork (activating arm) |
| 20. Maincasing through bolt |
| 21. Brush spring |
| 22. Brush |
| 23. Commutator |
| 24. Armature |
| 25. Drive assembly |
| 26. Thrust washer |
| 27. "C" clip |

1. Solenoid body	5. Retaining screw	9. Shim washers
2. Gasket	6. End cover	10. Bearing bushing
3. Switch contacts	7. Seal	11. Commutator end housing
4. Main terminals	8. "C" clip	

Exploded view of the Bosch starter assembly

Right–hand driveshaft connection

Left-hand driveshaft connection

sembly on a jack and remove the engine mounts:

a. Remove the right front upper engine mounting rubber insulator.

b. Remove the engine to body bracket in the engine compartment.

c. Remove the left engine mount.

d. Remove the bottom engine mounting strap.

22. If the vehicle is on a hoist, raise the hoist and lift the vehicle off the engine/transmission assembly. If the vehicle is on stands, lower the engine/transmission assembly from under the vehicle.

23. Installation of the engine/transmission assembly is the reverse of removal.

A—Lock shift lever in 4th gear. Install spacer.
B—Rotate shift shaft against stop.

Installing shift lever rod

The following precautions must be noted.

a. Be sure that the front mount rubber insulators are parallel to the engine front and do not distort when tightening the attaching nuts.

b. Be sure that the shift selector is still in the 4th gear position when installing the shift rod.

c. Use a 0.16 in. arbor to lock the shift lever in the 4th gear position in the shift tower, and a 2.76 in. spacer between the floor pan and selector rod. Rotate the shift shaft clockwise until it is stopped by the spacer. Tighten the selector rod locating bolt in this position.

d. The clutch cable need not be adjusted since the Fiesta is equipped with an automatic clutch adjuster. Refer to the clutch section for information.

e. The acclerator cable must be routed over the air cleaner spout to prevent damage and to prevent ignition interference.

Cylinder Head

REMOVAL AND INSTALLATION

1. Remove the air cleaner assembly.
2. Remove the fuel line from the fuel pump to the carburetor.
3. Drain the coolant from the radiator and the engine block.
4. Disconnect the spark plug wires and tie them out of the way. Disconnect the fan switch wires and the temperature sending switch wire.
5. Remove the heater and vacuum hoses at the intake manifold. Disconnect the hoses at the choke housing.
6. Disconnect the exhaust inlet pipe and cover the pipe opening to avoid loss of nuts or bolts.
7. Disconnect the throttle linkage and vacuum hoses at the carburetor.
8. Disconnect and remove the air pump and brackets from the cylinder head.
9. Remove the thermostat and housing.
10. Remove the rocker arm cover and the rocker arm assembly.
11. Lift the push rods out of the head, while keeping them in proper order.

12. Remove the cylinder head bolts and lift the cylinder head off the engine block.

13. Installation is the reverse order of removal. Note the following during installation:

a. Clean the gasket sealing area and measure the flatness. Warpage should not exceed 0.0015 in. in a twelve inch span.

b. Tighten the cylinder head bolts in sequence in the increments listed in the specifications.

c. Adjust the valves.

Rocker Shafts

REMOVAL AND INSTALLATION

1. Remove the air cleaner. Mark (if necessary) and then disconnect the spark plug secondary cables. Pull cables out of the clips on the rocker cover, and then tie them out of the way.

2. Remove the rocker cover attaching screws, pull the cover off, and discard the gasket.

3. Remove the rocker shaft attaching bolts, and remove the rocker shaft assembly.

4. If it is necessary to remove rockers from the shaft, remove the cotter pin from one end of the shaft, and slip the flat washer, crimped washer, and second flat washer off the shaft. Note order of disassembly and remove rockers, supports and springs as necessary.

5. When reassembling rocker shaft assembly note the following points:

a. Bolt holes in the shaft supports must face the side on which the rocker adjusting screws are located.

b. There are right hand and left hand type rockers. They must be installed with the pads inclined toward the support.

c. When springs, rockers, and supports are assembled, install washers and then insert the cotter pins with the heads upward and the legs bent over.

6. Lubricate valve stem tips, rocker arm pads, and push rod ends with Lubriplate® or equivalent.

7. Install the assembly, engaging the

push rods with the adjusting screws before installing bolts. Install bolts and torque evenly in several stages to 25–30 ft. lbs.

8. Adjust valve clearances.

9. Clean all old gasket material off the valve and cylinder head cover, and install a new gasket. Install the valve cover and tighten screws evenly.

10. Reverse the remaining removal procedures.

Intake Manifold

REMOVAL AND INSTALLATION

1. Remove the carburetor air cleaner assembly.
2. Drain the cooling system.
3. Disconnect the accelerator cable from the carburetor throttle lever.
4. Disconnect the fuel line and the vacuum line at the carburetor.
5. Disconnect the fan switch wires; remove the thermostat and housing.
6. Disconnect the water outlet hose and the crankcase ventilation hose from the manifold.
7. Remove the decel valve-to-carburetor pipe, if equipped, from the carburetor.
8. Remove the manifold attaching bolts and nuts and remove the manifold from the cylinder head.
9. Installation of the intake manifold is the reverse of removal and the following recommendations should be observed:
   a. Clean the gasket surface of all old material.
   b. Apply waterproof sealer to both sides of the manifold gaskets at the water ports.
   c. Tighten all nuts and bolts to the proper torque specifications.

Exhaust Manifold

REMOVAL AND INSTALLATION

1. Remove the air cleaner assembly if necessary.
2. Remove the bolts holding the exhaust inlet pipe and separate the joint.

NOTE: It may be necessary to remove the air pump and brackets before removing the exhaust inlet pipe.

3. Disconnect the hot air pipe from the air cleaner at the exhaust manifold.
4. Remove the bolts and nuts holding the exhaust manifold to the cylinder head. Remove the manifold and gasket.
5. Installation is the reverse of removal.

NOTE: Inspect the heat tube if the manifold is to be reinstalled. Replace if needed.

Timing Gear Cover

REMOVAL AND INSTALLATION

1. Remove the engine from the car as described above.
2. Remove the air pump, alternator, and water pump drive belts.
3. Remove the water pump.
4. Remove the crankshaft pulley with a puller.
5. Remove the front cover.
6. To install, position the front cover gasket, portions of the oil pan gasket if necessary, and the end seal on the front cover. Apply an oil resistant sealer at all seal ends. Then, position the cover on the block—the centralizing lug and pulley will ensure proper location.
7. Tighten attaching bolts evenly.
8. Position the crankshaft pulley on the crankshaft with the key and keyway aligned. Install the bolt and torque to 40–44 ft. lbs.
9. Install the water pump. Reconnect belts and adjust their tension.
10. Reinstall the engine. Run the engine and check for leaks.

TIMING COVER OIL SEAL REPLACEMENT

The oil seal can be replaced while the cover is on the car provided special tools, a seal remover and a seal installer, are used.

1. Loosen the alternator and remove the drive belt.
2. Raise the vehicle on a hoist. Remove the crankshaft damper retaining bolt and washer and remove the damper with a puller.
3. Use a seal remover to remove the seal.

Exploded view of engine block, head and oil pan assembly—external parts

Removing the front cover oil seal

4. Install the new seal with a seal installer.

5. Reverse the remaining removal procedures to install, torquing pulley and damper bolt to 40–55 ft. lbs.

Timing Chain and Tensioner

REMOVAL AND INSTALLATION

1. Remove the front cover as described above.

2. Remove the crankshaft oil slinger. Then, remove the camshaft sprocket retainer and bolts.

3. Remove the oil pan.

4. Remove the two attaching bolts and remove the timing chain tensioner and arm.

Timing chain tensioner in position

5. Unbolt the camshaft sprocket and remove it and the timing chain.

6. To install, locate the timing chain over the camshaft sprockets so the timing marks are aligned as shown when the sprocket is installed. Torque the mounting bolts and bend over the locking tabs.

7. Install the crankshaft oil slinger, camshaft sprocket retainer and bolts. Install the timing chain tensioner. Reinstall the front cover.

Camshaft

REMOVAL AND INSTALLATION

1. Remove the engine from the vehicle as described above.

2. Remove the fuel line at the fuel pump and remove the air pump drive belt, air pump, and brackets.

3. Remove the alternator drive belt and water pump pulley.

4. Remove the oil pump and the fuel pump.

5. Remove the rocker arm cover from the head.

6. Remove the distributor from the engine.

7. Remove the rocker arm retaining bolts and lift out the rocker arm assembly.

8. Lift the pushrods from the engine and keep them in order.

9. Invert the engine. Remove the oil pan and gasket, dipstick and with a puller, the crankshaft pulley. See the appropriate procedure below for oil pan removal.

10. Remove the front cover, crankshaft oil slinger, and the timing chain tensioner

assembly.

11. Remove the timing chain and the camshaft sprocket.

12. Remove the camshaft thrust plate and remove the camshaft from the engine block, being careful not to damage the cam bearings.

13. Carefully install the camshaft into the engine block so as not to damage the camshaft bearings.

14. Install the thrust plate into the camshaft groove and install the retaining bolts.

15. Measure the free play between the thrust plate and the camshaft flange. Clearance should be between 0.0025 and 0.0075 in.

16. Align the timing marks on the crankshaft and camshaft gears and install the timing chain.

17. Install the tensioner arm on the pivot pin and install the timing chain tensioner.

18. Install the crankshaft oil slinger and the front cover, using new gaskets.

19. Install the oil pan, using new gaskets and oil resistant sealer at all joints.

20. Install the dipstick.

21. Install the crankshaft pulley and tighten to specifications.

22. Install and time the distributor.

23. Install the oil pump, using a new gasket. Install a new oil filter.

24. Install the fuel pump to the engine block, using a new gasket.

25. Install the pushrods into their original positions.

26. Install the rocker arm shaft assembly.

27. Adjust the valve clearance to specifications.

28. Install the water pump pulley, vacuum lines, fuel lines, and drive belts. Ad-

Timing marks on crankshaft and camshaft sprockets

just as necessary.

29. Install the engine into the vehicle.

30. Start the engine and check for any oil or water leaks.

31. Readjust the valves to normal operating temperature specifications. Install the rocker arm cover.

Pistons and Connecting Rods

REMOVAL

1. Remove the engine from the car as described above.

2. Remove the cylinder head from the engine as described above.

3. Remove the oil pan from the engine as described below.

4. Remove the oil inlet tube and screen, and return tube. Clean the oil pan and block faces and remove the end seals.

5. Inspect the connecting rods to make sure that all rods have been numbered correctly. The numbers should be stamped on the camshaft side of the big end.

6. Remove the ring ridge at the top of each cylinder bore with a ridge reamer.

7. Partially remove the bearing cap bolts and then tap the bolt ends to release the caps. Completely remove the bearing bolts and remove caps, keeping them in the same order. Push the piston and rod upward and out of each bore.

PISTON SELECTION

Cylinder bores and pistons are graded according to size. This piston grade number is marked on the piston crown and stamped

Piston, rings and connecting rod assembly

on the pushrod side of the block adjacent to the top face.

When selecting new standard size pistons, measure each cylinder bore $2^{11}/_{32}$ in. from the top face of the block across the axis of the crankshaft. Select a standard size piston according to the grade number found on each cylinder bore so the proper clearance will result. It may be necessary to hone the bore to get the correct fit.

INSTALLATION

1. Position the bearing inserts in the connecting rods and end caps. Turn the crankshaft as necessary to fit each connecting rod big end to the crankpin.

2. Measure the bearing clearances with Plastigage® as described in "Engine Rebuilding" in the Unit Repair section.

3. After the proper bearing inserts have been fitted, remove all Plastigage® material, and install connecting rod caps, torquing rod bolts to specifications.

4. Reverse disassembly procedures for the remaining disassembled items, referring to the proper procedures for oil pan, cylinder head, and engine installation.

PISTON AND CONNECTING ROD POSITIONING

1. The "Front" markings on the connecting rod must align with the arrow on the piston crown.

2. "Front" and arrow markings must face forward when rods and pistons are assembled into the engine.

3. Position the oil ring gap to the rear of the piston and the top and second compression ring gaps at 180 degree and 90 degree angles.

NOTE: Dip the piston assembly into an oil filled container before compressing the rings. Make sure the cylinder walls and connecting rod journals are clean and oiled before installation of the piston/rod assembly.

Exploded view of engine internal parts

ENGINE LUBRICATION

Rear Main Bearing Oil Seal

REMOVAL AND INSTALLATION

1. Remove the engine from the vehicle.
2. Remove the pressure plate and clutch plate.
3. Remove the flywheel, oil pan, and gaskets.
4. Remove the rear oil seal carrier from the rear of the engine block.
5. Install the new oil seal in the carrier and using a new gasket, install the carrier on the engine block.

Rear main bearing oil seal installation

NOTE: An aligner tool should be used to align the seal to the crankshaft as the carrier is tightened.

6. Reverse the removal operation to reassemble the units to the block.
7. Install the engine, start, and inspect for leaks.

Oil Pump

REMOVAL AND INSTALLATION

1. Place a container under the oil pump.
2. Remove the pump attaching bolts and remove the oil pump with filter attached, from the engine.
3. Separate the oil filter from the pump.
4. Installation is the reverse of removal. Use a new oil filter.

Oil Pan

REMOVAL AND INSTALLATION

1. Raise the vehicle and support safely.

2. Drain the oil pan and remove the dipstick.
3. Disconnect the battery ground cable.
4. Disconnect the throttle linkage from the carburetor.
5. Disconnect the steering cable from the rack and pinion unit.
6. Remove the rack and pinion unit from the crossmember and move it forward to provide oil pan removal clearance.

Oil pan bolt tightening sequence—follow alphabetical first, then numerical

7. Remove the starter motor.
8. Remove the lower flywheel cover.
9. Remove the oil pan bolts and remove the oil pan assembly.
10. Installation is the reverse of removal. Note the following:
   a. Clean the inlet screen and tube assembly.
   b. Clean the seal retainer grooves in the front cover and the rear main bearing cap.
   c. Install the gasket to the engine block with an oil resistant sealer.
   d. Apply oil resistant sealer to the end joints of the gasket and end seals.

— CAUTION —
When installing the oil pump, prime it by filling the inlet or outlet port with engine oil and rotating the pump by hand. This will prevent damage when the engine is started.

ENGINE COOLING

Radiator

REMOVAL AND INSTALLATION

1. Drain the cooling system.
2. Remove the top and bottom hoses. Remove the expansion tank tube from the radiator filler neck.
3. Disconnect the wire loom connection from the fan motor and unclip the loom from the shroud clip.
4. Remove the two lower radiator attaching bolts from the front of the vehicle.
5. Remove the two upper radiator attaching bolts from inside the engine compartment.

Removing or installing radiator shroud/ fan assembly

6. Remove the radiator assembly with the shroud and fan attached.
7. Installation is the reverse of removal.

Water Pump

REMOVAL AND INSTALLATION

1. Disconnect the battery ground cable and drain the cooling system.
2. Loosen the three pump pulley bolts while the belts are still attached.
3. Remove the air pump belt and air pump brackets and loosen the alternator bolts.
4. Move the alternator toward the engine and remove the drive belt.
5. Remove the lower hose from the water pump, the three pump pulley bolts, and the pulley.
6. Remove the three pump body retaining bolts and the pump assembly.
7. Installation is the reverse of removal. Note the following:
   a. Clean the old gasket from the sealing surface; use a new gasket and a waterproof sealer.
   b. The air pump pivot bolt may have a nut welded to the bracket or a loose nut.

Thermostat

The thermostat housing is on the front top of the engine secured by two bolts. Two different length housings are used, short for regular duty and long for air conditioning.

EMISSION CONTROLS

The engine tune-up and emission control information is on a sticker located in the engine compartment or on the engine. This information is critical to the proper adjustment of the engine and emission system.

A—Impeller
B—Seal
C—Bearing shaft
D—Pump body
E—Pump pulley hub

Exploded view of water pump assembly

NOTE: It is suggested that the sticker information be copied and saved with the owners manual and other important papers.

Two emission control systems are used for the Fiesta engine, one for 49 states and High Altitude, and one for California.

Catalytic Converter

The catalytic converter is installed in the exhaust system to change most exhaust gases into carbon dioxide and water vapor. Unleaded fuel only is to be used with the catalytic converter. Two lengths of converters are used, short for 49 states and High Altitude, and long for California.

49 States　　　**California**

Two types of catalytic converters used on Fiesta

Exhaust Gas Recirculation System

The EGR system is used to re-introduce metered amounts of exhaust gases into the air/fuel mixture in the intake manifold to lower the peak temperature of the mixture at time of the combustion. This lowers the emission of Oxides of Nitrogen (NOx). The amount and timing of recirculation is controlled by engine vacuum and temperature.

The EGR valve is located on the intake manifold and is vacuum operated. As the valve is opened, exhaust gases are allowed to enter directly from the exhaust manifold, through a stainless steel tube, into the intake manifold.

EGR SYSTEM DIAGNOSIS

1. Apply 8 in. Hg vacuum to the EGR valve vacuum fitting. The vacuum reading should hold within 1 in. Hg for a minimum of 30 seconds.

2. With the engine at idle, apply at least 8 in. Hg vacuum to the EGR valve. The valve stem or pintle should move to the full extent of travel. The engine should run roughly, slow down, or stop completely. If nothing happens, the EGR valve or passageway is defective or blocked.

Ported vacuum switch—typical

Ported Vacuum Switch

An engine temperature controlled ported vacuum switch is used in the EGR system for California.

Vacuum to the EGR valve is controlled through one of four differently calibrated switches, ranging from 90 to 155 degrees (F).

As the switch temperature is reached, the switch ports are opened and vacuum is allowed to pass to the EGR valve.

PORTED VACUUM SWITCH DIAGNOSIS

1. Cold start the engine and check for vacuum at the EGR valve. None should be present.

FRONT OF VEHICLE

A—TVS switch (normally closed)
B—EGR valve
C—Air cleaner bimetal sensor
D—TVS switch (normally open)
E—Ported vacuum switch (PVS) (2 required)
F—Valve assembly (air bypass)
G—Air cleaner assembly
H—Oil filler cap assembly

J—Valve assembly (vacuum vent)
K—Check valve
L—Delay valve
M—Vacuum reservoir
N—Fitting (PVS valve)
P—Distributor
Q—Adapter (PVS fitting)
R—Adapter (PVS fitting)

California emission controls

EGR valve location

Labels on diagram:
- SEAL-AIR CLEANER
- CARBURETOR ASSY. -9510
- FUEL INLET
- FUEL RETURN
- CARBURETOR VENT TO EVAP. CAN
- NOTE: EXHAUST GAS ENTERS THROUGH STAINLESS STEEL TUBE FROM EXHAUST MANIFOLD
- NUT-5/16 x 21 UNF 4 PLACES TORQUE 16, 3-20, 3Nm WASHER-LOCK
- BOWL VENT AND FUEL ON/OFF SWITCH CONNECT 12V FOR HOTTEST
- GASKET
- STUD-5/16 x 18 UNC 4 PLACES TORQUE 2, 7-4, 1Nm
- STUD-5/16 x 18 UNC x M6 TORQUE 16, 3-20, 3Nm WASHER-LOCK
- BOLT-5/16 x 18 UNC TORQUE 16, 3-20, 3Nm WASHER-LOCK
- GASKET-9D476 EGR VALVE ASY.-9D425
- NUT-M6 TORQUE WASHER-LOCK

2. Allow the engine to warm up to normal operating temperature and recheck for vacuum at the EGR valve. Vacuum should be present at light to medium throttle opening.

Thermactor System

The Thermactor system injects fresh air into the stream of hot exhaust gases leaving the combustion chambers, to further burn carbon monoxide and hydrocarbons. This burning occurs in the exhaust manifold and front exhaust inlet pipe area.

The injected air is supplied by an air pump, belt driven from the engine crankshaft.

Three types of air bypass valves are used to control the timing and amount of injected air introduced into the exhaust manifold. The bypass valves are controlled by engine vacuum and internal spring tension.

Two of the bypass valves use a one nipple vacuum control port and have a normally closed internal valve. The third type uses double nippled vacuum control ports and has an internal timed air bypass valve which is normally open.

All bypass valves have a relief valve to exhaust excessive injected air when the demand from the engine is low.

BYPASS VALVE DIAGNOSIS

Normally Closed Bypass Valve

1. Remove the bypass outlet hose. Start the engine and increase the engine speed to 1500 rpm.

2. The air should be felt and heard at the bypass valve outlet.

3. Remove the vacuum hose and plug it. Again increase the engine speed to 1500 rpm.

4. There should be virtually no air flow felt or heard from the bypass valve outlet. The air should be exhausted from the end of the valve silencer cover.

Timed Bypass Valve With Vacuum Vent

1. Remove the air outlet hose from the bypass valve.

2. Cap the bypass valve vacuum vent nipple (top). Remove or circumvent any restrictions or delaying devices in the sensing vacuum hose (bottom).

3. Start the engine and increase the speed to 1500 rpm.

4. Air should be felt and heard from the bypass valve air outlet.

5. Pinch off the sensing vacuum hose to simulate the air bypass cycle. Release the pinched hose.

6. Air flow through the bypass hose should diminish or stop and then resume its normal air flow.

7. Remove the cap from the vacuum vent nipple (upper) and leave the nipple open.

8. Increase the engine speed to 1500 rpm. The air should be discharged through the exhaust port. Air should not be felt or heard at the bypass valve air outlet.

Vacuum Vent Valve

The vacuum vent valve is used to deactivate the Thermactor system after a period of idling.

Vacuum is applied to both sides of the vent valve, causing a dump valve to seat and allowing vacuum to be applied to the system.

At idle, the vacuum is stopped at one side of the valve, allowing the dump valve to leave its seat. This allows air to enter the system to reduce the vacuum applied to the retard delay valve.

VACUUM VENT VALVE DIAGNOSIS

1. Remove the valve from the air cleaner assembly, if necessary, to gain access to the vacuum ports on the valve. Disconnect the vacuum tubing or the connector block from the valve.

2. Connect a manifold vacuum source to the black or covered vacuum port.

3. Connect an external vacuum source to the white or body vacuum port.

4. Start the engine so that vacuum is applied to the black or covered port.

5. Apply 10 in. Hg vacuum from an outside source to the white port. If 10 in. Hg vacuum cannot be obtained, replace the valve.

Typical vent valve and check valve location in the emission control system

Cross section of the vacuum vent valve

6. If 10 in. Hg is held, remove manifold vacuum source from the black port. The vacuum should drop to zero. If the vacuum does not drop, replace the valve.

7. Reinstall the valve on the air cleaner. Reinstall all vacuum hoses.

Check Valve

CHECKING SEALING

1. Apply 5 in. Hg vacuum to the white side of valve.
2. After 30 seconds, the vacuum should not be less than 4 in. Hg.
3. If the vacuum reading is less, replace the valve.

Vacuum Delay Valve

1. Install a vacuum gauge to the white side of the delay valve.
2. Apply 10 in. Hg vacuum to the "Dist." side of valve (brown or green).
3. Measure the time for gauge to go from zero to 8 in. Hg.
4. The time interval in seconds should be: White and brown colored valves—Minimum–2 seconds, Maximum–5 seconds. White and green colored valves—Minimum–9 seconds, Maximum–20 seconds.

Air Pump

CHECKING AIR SUPPLY

1. Disconnect the air supply hose from the air pump to the air bypass valve.
2. Insert a Thermactor pump pressure gauge into the end of the disconnected hose and secure.
3. Start the engine and increase the speed to 1000 rpm. The air pressure gauge should register 2.25 psi minimum.
4. If the special gauge is not available, start the engine and increase the speed to

1500 and place a hand over the open hose. Air flow should be felt and heard.

Exhaust Check Valve

This valve is located between the bypass valve and the exhaust port drillings and allows the Thermactor air to enter the exhaust port drillings but prevents the reverse flow of exhaust gases in the event of a malfunction of the system.

VALVE CHECK

1. Remove the air delivery hose from the valve and by using a probe, make sure the check valve operates.
2. Push down on the check valve. When released, spring tension should return the valve to its seat.
3. If the valve does not return, replace the valve.

Oil Filler and Breather Cap

Fresh air is drawn into the engine air cleaner assembly and routed to the oil filler and breather cap, where it passes through a one-way valve, an outlet, and on to the crankcase.

The fresh air is mixed with the blow-by gases and is routed internally to the valve cover to be drawn upward into the filler and breather cap.

The gases are further routed through a metered orifice and into the intake manifold.

At times of low fresh air intake, the gas pressure closes the fresh air intake valve to avoid spilling oil laden fumes into the air cleaner assembly. A second valve is opened within the filler and breather cap, and the gases are directed into the intake manifold system through the metered orifice.

Fuel Inlet Bowl Vent System

The float bowl has a dual venting system through a solenoid valve, located on the carburetor. With the ignition on, the vapors are vented internally into the air cleaner. With the ignition off, the vapors are vented externally to be stored in the carbon canister and returned to the carburetor when the engine is again started.

Carburetor Decel Valve

A carburetor decel valve is used on some emission control systems to permit more complete combustion by the addition of a metered air/fuel mixture to the engine on deceleration.

Fuel Shut Off System

This system is utilized to close off the fuel supply to the carburetor idle system when the ignition switch is turned off. This prevents dieseling or running on.

FUEL SYSTEM

Fuel Pump

A single action mechanical fuel pump is attached to the engine block, under the intake manifold. It is operated by the engine camshaft.

If any problem is suspected with the fuel pump, both the pressure and the volume output should be tested.

The minimum volume should be a pint in 38 seconds, at an engine speed of 500 rpm. Pressure should be 3.5 lbs. at 700 rpm.

REMOVAL AND INSTALLATION

1. Disconnect the battery ground cable.
2. Disconnect the inlet and outlet hoses from the fuel pump ports.
3. Remove the two retaining bolts and remove the pump from the engine block.
4. To install the pump, clean the gasket surface and install a new gasket.
5. Position the pump on the engine block so that the pump arm contacts the camshaft.
6. Install the retaining bolts and tighten securely.
7. Connect the inlet and outlet lines to the pump ports.
8. Connect the battery cable, start the engine and check for leakage.

NOTE: If the air cleaner assembly was removed, place the accelerator cable on top of the fresh air intake tube on installation.

VALVE COLOR CODE	TIME IN SECONDS	
	MINIMUM	MAXIMUM
WHITE AND BROWN	2	5
WHITE AND GREEN	9	20

Testing vacuum delay switch

A — Thermactor idle vacuum valve (TIV)
B — Exhaust gas recirculation (EGR) valve
C — Bimetal sensor
D — TVS switch (normally open)
E — Vacuum reservoir
F — Valve assembly (air bypass)

G — Air cleaner assembly
H — Oil filter cap assembly
J — Valve assembly (vacuum vent)
K — Check valve
L — Delay valve
M — Distributor

Typical hose arrangement to check fuel pump pressure and volume

A — Air horn
B/C — Venting with ignition on
D — Vent valve with ignition off
E — Vent valve with ignition on
F — Float
G — Venting with ignition off
H — Connection for canister
J — Solenoid

Cross section of fuel inlet bowl vent valve

A — Vent solenoid
B — Vent connection (external)
C — Fuel filter

D — Electric choke
E — Choke pulldown diaphragm
F — Dash pot

G — Fuel shutoff solenoid
H — Throttle Modulator (A/C only)
J — Primary venturi

K — Secondary venturi
L — Accelerator pump

Carburetor external components

Carburetor

The carburetor is a Weber model 740, two venturi, two stage design. The primary and secondary bores are of equal size.

The primary side is operated by the accelerator linkage, while the secondary side is operated by mechanical linkage from the primary throttle linkage. The secondary is preset to start to open after the primary throttle plate has opened approximately 45 degrees.

The vacuum supply ports for the emission control units are on the primary side of the carburetor.

REMOVAL AND INSTALLATION

1. Remove the carburetor air cleaner assembly.
2. Disconnect the fuel shut off solenoid wire and the electric choke wire.
3. Disconnect the fuel line from the fuel filter.

NOTE: Have a container or shop rags to catch any leakage. Plug the hose end.

4. Disconnect the throttle linkage from the carburetor throttle arm.
5. Remove the four attaching nuts from the carburetor base and lift the carburetor from the intake manifold.

6. Installation is the reverse of removal.

ADJUSTMENTS

Choke Plate Initial Vacuum Pulldown

1. Remove the air cleaner assembly.
2. Remove the carburetor from the manifold.
3. Remove the choke retaining screws, retaining ring, choke housing, and the heat shield.
4. Set the fast idle cam on the first step and close the throttle.

NOTE: Open the throttle and close the choke plate by hand.

5. Connect a hand vacuum pump to the vacuum channel on the pump bore under the base of the carburetor. Pump to attain 17 in. Hg.
6. Check the clearance of the choke plate to the air horn. It should be between .110 to .178 in.

NOTE: Light thumb pressure may be needed to assist in closing the choke plate.

NOTE: The modulator spring should not be compressed.

7. To adjust the clearance, rotate the vacuum diaphragm adjusting screw, located under a seal on the diaphragm, in or out as required.

NOTE: A new seal should be installed after the adjustment has been made.

8. Reassemble the choke cover, reinstall the carburetor on the manifold and install the air cleaner assembly.

Fast Idle Speed

1. Warm up the engine, remove the air cleaner assembly and attach a tachometer.
2. Disconnect the electrical leads from the radiator temperature fan switch and connect the two leads with a jumper wire so that the fan will run continuously.
3. If there is a spark delay valve in the distributor advance line, disconnect it and install a jumper hose.
4. Disconnect the decel valve hose, if any, at the carburetor and plug the hose.
5. If the vehicle is equipped with the EGR-PVS system, disconnect and plug the EGR vacuum line.

NOTE: If the vehicle is not equipped with the EGR-PSV system, do not disconnect the EGR valve.

6. Turn off all accessories.
7. Remove the electric choke cap unit after noting and marking the setting and the bi-metal spring-to-choke lever relationship. Start the engine.
8. Set the choke linkage so that the fast idle screw is against the shoulder of the highest step of the cam.
9. Check the fast idle speed and correct as required.

1. Cover (assy.)
2. Choke shaft bushings
3. Choke plate
4. Choke plate screws
5. Secondary choke shaft
6. Secondary choke link

7. Choke linkage retaining clips	17. Electric choke retaining screws
8. Primary choke shaft	18. Electric choke retaining ring
9. Primary choke link dirt seal	19. Electric choke unit
10. Dirt seal retainer	20. Choke housing dirt shield
11. Primary choke link	21. Choke housing screws
12. Choke bimetal shaft bushing	22. Choke pulldown spring
13. Fast idle cam spring	23. Cover
14. Choke bimetal lever	24. Choke pulldown adjusting screw
15. Choke bimetal shaft	25. Choke pulldown adjusting screw seal
16. Choke assist spring	26. Choke pulldown diaphragm assembly

27. Choke housing (assy.)
28. Choke housing vacuum seal (O ring)
29. Choke lever
30. Choke bimetal shaft lock washer
31. Choke bimetal shaft nut
32. Cover gasket
33. Fuel bowl float
34. High speed air bleeds
35. Well tubes
36. Idle jet holder
37. Idle jet

Exploded view of the carburetor

NOTE: The fast idle speed specification will be found on the engine emission sticker.

10. Recheck the fast idle speed.
11. Reassemble the choke cover and install the air cleaner assembly.

Electric Choke Cap and Choke Linkage Check

1. With the air cleaner assembly off the carburetor and the engine at normal operating temperature, check that the choke cap is correctly set and that electric current is present to the cover terminal while the engine is running. Stop the engine.
2. Check that the choke plates are in the full open position.
3. Hold the throttle at the one-quarter open position and close the choke plates.
4. Release the choke plates. They should rotate to the full open position.
5. If the choke plates do not open properly or there is binding, the linkage or the electric heating components may be worn or damaged.

A—Inner cable grommet
B—Pedal shaft
C—Outer cable grommet
D—Outer cable
E—Engine compartment rear bulkhead

Exploded view of accelerator cable routed through firewall

A—Decal
B—Accelerator cable
C—Spout

Accelerator cable routing over air intake spout of air cleaner

Accelerator Cable

REMOVAL

1. Remove the battery ground cable and the air cleaner assembly.
2. Remove the lower insulator panel and disconnect the accelerator cable from the pedal shaft.
3. Punch out the firewall grommet to detach the cable from the firewall.

NOTE: The grommet will be broken and cannot be reused.

4. Disconnect the accelerator cable from the carburetor linkage and detach the cable.
5. Remove the retaining clip, depress the retaining pegs, and twist the cable from the bracket.

INSTALLATION

1. Route the inner cable through the firewall and connect it to the pedal shaft.
2. Install a new cable grommet into the firewall and push the cable through the grommet.
3. Install the cable into the bracket at the carburetor end.
4. Connect the cable to the carburetor linkage and adjust to give full throttle opening when the accelerator pedal is fully depressed.
5. Refit the lower insulator panel.

1. Primary throttle valve
2. Cam return spring
3. Vacuum passage
4. Bushing
5. Vacuum diaphragm device
6. Rod
7. Choke valve opening lever
8. Bi-metal spiral spring
9. Choke valve control shaft
10. Lever
11. Throttle valve rod
12. Choke throttle valve
13. Choke fast idle adjustment cam
14. Choke fast idle adjustment screw
15. Spring
16. Throttle operating lever

Exploded view of choke mechanism—typical

A—THROTTLE PLATES AT IDLE

IDLE SYSTEM   PRIMARY   SECONDARY

B—SECONDARY THROTTLE PLATE OPENING

SECONDARY SYSTEM

Carburetor flow schematic

Accelerator cable adjustment point

A—Smaller housing section
B—Larger housing section
C—Stabilizer rubber insulator
D—Stabilizer
E—Gear shift lever
F—Stabilizer to floor pan rubber mounting
G—Shift housing
H—Selector rod boot
J—Selector rod
K—Shift shaft boot

Transmission shift linkage components

6. Install the air cleaner assembly. Route the acclerator cable over the air intake spout and retain it with a clip.

7. Reinstall the battery ground cable.

MANUAL TRANSAXLE

REMOVAL

1. Disconnect the battery ground cable.

2. Install an engine support in the engine compartment to hold the engine during transmission removal.

3. Disconnect the speedometer cable at the transaxle assembly.

4. Disconnect the clutch cable from the clutch release lever by pulling the cable from the slot in the release lever.

5. Remove the four upper transmission flange bolts.

6. Jack up the vehicle and support it safely. Drain the transmission oil by removing the plunger-retainer. Do not lose the spring.

Suggested Ford type engine holding support

7. Be sure the transmission is in fourth gear. Remove the shift rod spring from the body to the rod.

8. Loosen the clamping screw and remove the shift rod from the selector shaft.

Remove the stabilizer mechanism from the transmission.

9. Loosen the locknuts and remove the stabilizer bar stud from the transmission housing with an Allen wrench.

10. Remove the six Allen head screws from the left drive shaft at the coupling of the inner constant velocity joint and stub shaft and separate the coupling.

11. Separate the right axle assembly from the inner constant velocity joint by removing the six Allen head screws.

12. Disconnect the starter cable and remove the starter motor.

13. Place a jack under the transmission assembly.

14. Remove the lower flange bolts from the transmission housing.

15. Remove the bolts from the engine mounting member and remove it from the vehicle.

16. Remove the transmission from the vehicle.

INSTALLATION

1. Lubricate the splines of the driveshaft and differential gear. Align the engine adapter plate to the engine guide bushing.

2. Install the transmission to the engine block and secure with two flange bolts, lightly tightened.

2.76 in

Use of spacer for shift linkage adjustment

3. Install the upper and lower support assembly and align with two drifts. Lower the engine/transmission assembly, but do not remove the jack.

4. Using three new self-locking bolts, attach the support assembly to the transmission and torque to 65 ft. lbs. Torque the lower flange bolts to 30 ft. lbs.

—————— CAUTION ——————
Due to the light metal construction of the transmission housing, it is essential to use new self-locking bolts and to properly torque them to specifications.

NOTE: Relieve some of the weight of the transmission/engine assembly to aid in the installation of the bolts, and then remove the jack.

5. Install the plunger retainer and spring for the control shaft.

6. Install the starter motor and cables.

7. Reconnect the right and left axles at the constant velocity joint couplers.

8. Position the shift stabilizer strut at the transmission housing. Start and thread the Allen screw into the housing until it bottoms. Thread the inner lock nut to the rubber and lock with the outer nut.

9. Check that the transmission is still in fourth gear and install the gear selector rod to the gear shift shaft.

10. Align the holes in the selector housing and the end of the gear lever. Lock it into position with a 0.160 inch pin.

11. Place a 2.76 inch spacer between the floor pan and the selector rod. Rotate the shift shaft clockwise until it stops. Push the shaft into the transmission and hold it in position.

12. Lock the selector rod clamp bolt, then remove the spacer from the shift rod and pin from the selector housing/gear lever assembly.

13. Connect the selector rod spring from the vehicle body to the rod. Check for proper shifting.

14. Fill the transmission to the indicated level. Lower the vehicle.

15. Install the top transmission flange bolts and torque to 30 ft. lbs.

Transaxle location in relation to engine and drive wheels

16. Connect the clutch cable to the clutch release lever. No adjustment is necessary.

17. Install the speedometer driven gear and connect the battery ground lead to the battery.

18. Remove the engine lifting support bar.

CLUTCH

The clutch assembly is comprised of a pressure plate, clutch disc, release bearing and automatically adjusted clutch cable. A pilot shaft bushing is not used.

REMOVAL AND INSTALLATION

1. Expose the clutch assembly by removal of the transaxle or the engine.

2. Remove the pressure plate bolts from the flywheel, loosening the bolts a few turns at a time in rotation, and remove the clutch/pressure plate assembly.

3. To install, position the clutch/pressure plate assembly on the flywheel and center the clutch plate with special tool 177F-7137A or equivalent.

NOTE: The flat side of the disc must face the flywheel side.

4. Tighten the pressure plate bolts to 13 ft. lbs. and remove the centering tool.

5. Install the engine or transaxle.

A—Automatic adjusting device toothed segment
B—Automatic adjusting device pawl
C—Release shaft
D—Pressure plate
E—Clutch disc
F—Release bearing with fork
G—Clutch cable
H—Clutch pedal
J—Toothed segment tension spring

Exploded view of clutch assembly and operating mechanism

Clutch Cable

REMOVAL

1. Disconnect the clutch cable from the clutch release lever.

2. Remove the dash left lower insulating panel from inside the car.

3. Disconnect the clutch cable from the clutch pedal. Pull the clutch pedal to the rear to release the adjusting pawl from the toothed segment. Rotate the toothed seg-

ment forward and unhook the cable from the segment. The toothed segment will swivel backward.

4. Pull the cable outward through the recess between the pedal and the automatic adjusting unit and then remove the cable assembly from the engine compartment side.

INSTALLATION

1. Insert the clutch cable through the firewall and between the pedal and the automatic adjusting device.

2. Swivel the toothed segment rearward and connect the cable to the segment.

3. Connect the cable to the release lever at the transaxle housing.

4. Operate the clutch pedal several times to make sure the automatic adjusting mechanism is operating correctly.

5. Install the insulation panel.

Automatic Self-Adjuster

The clutch pedal linkage is kept automatically adjusted by the action of a ratchet device attached to the clutch pedal pivot.

As clutch wear develops into cable slack and as the pedal is depressed, the pawl moves over the toothed segment in stages and engages the next tooth in line to maintain a predetermined tension of the clutch cable.

A—Clutch cable C—Toothed segment
B—Pawl   D—Tension spring

Operation of automatic clutch cable adjuster

DRIVE AXLES

Right and left intermediate driveshafts of equal length are used to transfer the power to the front wheels.

The right shaft assembly uses a primary

Connecting and disconnecting the clutch cable

shaft support bearing to control the rotating whipping action of the driveshafts and the constant velocity U-joint.

Left Drive Axle

REMOVAL

1. Remove the wheel center cap and remove the hub retaining nut and washer. Loosen the wheel lug bolts.

2. Raise the front of the car and support it safely. Remove the wheel and tire assembly.

3. Remove the six Allen head bolts and washers from the constant velocity joint to the stub shaft flange.

4. Remove the brake caliper retaining bolts and lift the caliper free of the support.

——— CAUTION ———
Do not allow the weight of the caliper to hang from the brake hose. Secure the caliper with a length of wire.

5. Remove the disc and hub assembly from the driveshaft.

NOTE: A puller may have to be used to pull the disc and hub from the driveshaft splines.

6. Remove the tie rod end from the steering arm.

7. Remove the lower arm to body mounting retaining bolt and remove the inner end of the arm from the mounting point.

8. Remove the ball joint to carrier clinch bolt and detach the outer end of the lower arm assembly.

——— CAUTION ———
Do not strain the tie-bar forward mounting by pushing the rear end of the bar downward.

9. Remove the driveshaft assembly from the spindle carrier and the vehicle.

INSTALLATION

1. Repack the constant velocity U-joint with grease.

2. Install the outer end of the driveshaft through the spindle carrier.

3. Loosely install the six Allen head bolts securing the constant velocity joint to the stub shaft.

4. Connect the lower arm ball joint to the spindle carrier and install the clinch bolt.

5. Position the lower arm inner end to the body mount and install the retaining bolt and nut.

6. Connect the tie rod end to the steering arm, tighten the nut, and install a new cotter pin.

7. Push the hub and disc assembly onto the splined end of the drive shaft by hand. Use the front hub installer special tool or its equivalent to pull the hub and disc onto the driveshaft to its normal position.

——— CAUTION ———
Do not attempt to drive the hub and disc onto the driveshaft; the constant velocity joint can be damaged.

8. Install a new hub retaining nut and washer and snug them on the driveshaft threads.

9. Reinstall the brake caliper and tighten the bolts securely.

10. Tighten the six Allen head bolts to 28–32 ft. lbs.

11. Install the wheel and lower the vehicle to the ground.

12. Tighten the wheel lug bolts.

13. Torque the hub retaining nut to 180 to 200 ft. lbs. and stake the nut to the slot of the driveshaft.

14. Install the wheel center cap.

Right Drive Axle

REMOVAL

1. Remove the wheel center cap and the hub retaining nut and washer. Loosen the wheel lug bolts.

DIFFERENTIAL

LEFT-HAND DRIVESHAFT

RIGHT-HAND DRIVESHAFT

A B C D E

F G H J K L M N P Q R

A—Left hand outer C.V. joint
B—Left hand intermediate driveshaft
C—Left hand inner C.V. joint
D—Left hand stubshaft
E—Right hand stubshaft
F—Universal joint

G—Primary shaft
H—Primary shaft bearing support bracket
J—Primary shaft support bearing
K—Primary shaft support bearing housing
L—Right-hand inner C.V. joint
M—Bellows

N—Right-hand intermediate driveshaft
P—Bellows
Q—Right-hand outer C.V. joint
R—Spindle shaft

Exploded view of driveshaft and differential assembly

INNER (LH)

INNER (RH)

OUTER
(LH SHOWN)

A—Outer constant-velocity joint
B—Snap ring (outer joint)
C—Snap ring (inner joint)

D—Inner constant-velocity joint
E—Oil seal
F—Inner driveshaft

G—Snap ring (inner driveshaft retaining)
H—Intermediate driveshaft
J—Support bearing

Driveshaft retaining ring locations

PRIMARY SHAFT

LINK

ALLEN HEAD BOLTS

UNIVERSAL JOINT

ALLEN HEAD BOLTS

LINK

Right side driveshaft coupling

NOTE: The hub retaining nut and washer may be removed by an alternate method with the wheels off the ground. Install two lug bolts, and while holding the brake pedal on, loosen and remove the retaining nut. Release the foot brake and remove the wheel lug bolts.

2. Raise the front of the car and support it safely. Remove the wheel.

3. Remove the six Allen head bolts from the inner constant velocity joint to the primary shaft flange.

4. Remove the bolts holding the primary shaft bearing housing to the bracket. Allow the primary shaft and bearing assembly to rest clear of its location.

5. Remove the driveshaft assembly from the spindle carrier and the vehicle.

INSTALLATION

1. Repack the constant velocity joint with grease.

2. Insert the driveshaft through the spindle carrier.

3. Loosely install the six Allen head bolts to secure the constant velocity joint to the primary shaft flange.

4. Align the primary shaft bearing housing to the support bracket and install the two bolts.

5. Loosely install a new hub retainer nut and washer on the driveshaft.

6. Torque the six Allen head bolts to 28–32 ft. lbs.

7. Install the wheel and lower the vehicle to the ground. Fully tighten the lug bolts.

8. Torque the hub retaining nut to 180 to 200 ft. lbs. and stake the nut to the slot of the driveshaft.

9. Install the center cap.

Primary Driveshaft

REMOVAL

1. Raise the front of the car and support it safely.

2. Remove the six Allen head bolts from the constant velocity joint to primary shaft flange.

CAUTION

Support the intermediate driveshaft with wire to avoid unnecessary strain on the universal joint.

3. Remove the primary shaft bearing housing bolts and guide the primary shaft and constant velocity joint from the stub shaft.

4. Loosen the bolts holding the bearing bracket to the engine.

Bellow location on right and left drive shafts

NOTE: It is necessary to loosen the bearing bracket to avoid any stress or misalignment during assembly.

INSTALLATION

1. Repack the constant velocity joint with grease.

2. Align and install the primary shaft and constant velocity joint assembly into the stub shaft.

3. Attach the bearing housing to the support bracket and install the two bolts.

4. Align the constant velocity joint to the primary shaft flange and install the six Allen head bolts. Torque the bolts to 28–32 ft. lbs.

5. Tighten the bearing support bracket at the engine and lower the vehicle to the ground.

Levering left stub axle shaft from transaxle housing

Primary Shaft Support Bearing

REMOVAL (PRIMARY SHAFT REMOVED)

1. Clamp the primary shaft in a soft jawed vise.

2. Tap the universal joint from the splined end of the primary shaft, using a soft faced hammer.

3. With a press and adapters, remove the bearing and housing from the driveshaft.

4. Support the housing and press the bearing from the housing.

INSTALLATION

1. With a press and adapters, press the bearing into the housing.

NOTE: The bearing is a sealed, factory lubricated unit with built-in colored seals. The red seal must face the transmission case while the black seal must face the right wheel, when assembled.

2. Press the bearing and housing assembly onto the driveshaft followed by the dirt shield.

NOTE: Be sure the bearing seats to the shoulder on the shaft flange.

3. Tap the universal joint in place on the splined end of the primary shaft with a soft faced hammer.

Bellows

REMOVAL

1. Separate the driveshafts as in the driveshaft removal procedure.

2. Remove the clamps from the bellows and slide the bellows on the shaft to expose the retaining ring for the constant velocity joint.

3. Remove the retaining ring and constant velocity joint, allowing the bellows to be slipped from the driveshaft.

INSTALLATION

1. Install the bellows on the shaft.

2. Install the constant velocity joint and retaining ring. Clamp the bellows in the proper position.

NOTE: Be sure the bellows clamps are crimped securely.

3. Reassemble the driveshafts as required.

Front Wheel Bearings

REMOVAL

1. Remove the center cap, hub retaining nut, and washer. Loosen the wheel lug bolts.

2. Raise the vehicle and support it safely. Remove the wheel.

3. Remove the caliper and hang it by wire from the body.

CAUTION

Do not allow the caliper weight to hang from the brake hose.

4. Remove the hub and disc assembly.

NOTE: A puller may be needed to remove the hub from the shaft.

Support bearing location on primary shaft

5. Remove the tie rod end from the steering arm.

6. Remove the lower arm-to-body mounting retaining bolt and pull down the inner end of the arm.

7. Separate the ball joint from the knuckle by removal of the ball joint clinch bolt.

8. Remove the top mount-to-apron panel retaining bolts.

9. Support the driveshaft at the outer constant velocity joint and pull the knuckle clear of the driveshaft and out of the vehicle.

10. Mount the unit in a vise or other support, and carefully remove the dust shield from the groove in the knuckle.

11. Using a slide hammer and seal remover, remove the inner and outer grease retainers and bearings.

12. Drive out the bearing cups.

INSTALLATION

1. Install new bearing cups into the knuckle. Make sure the cups are properly seated.

2. Pack the new bearings with grease and install them in their races.

3. Using a seal driver, install the grease retainers.

4. Gently tap the disc shield into position in the groove on the inner face of the knuckle.

NOTE: Align the cutout portion of the shield at the bottom, in line with the ball joint.

5. Position the knuckle assembly in the vehicle over the end of the driveshaft.

6. Install the top mount in the apron panel and install two bolts.

7. Reconnect the lower ball joint to the knuckle. Install the clinch bolt and the lower arm inner pivot bolt.

8. Reinstall the tie rod end to the steering arm. Tighten and install a new cotter pin.

9. Install the splined end of the driveshaft through the hub and disc assembly.

10. Mount the brake caliper and install the mounting bolts.

11. Install the wheel, snug the lug bolts, and lower the vehicle to the ground.

12. Securely tighten the lug bolts and torque the hub retaining nut to 180–200 ft. lbs. Stake the retaining nut to the slot in the driveshaft.

Stub Shaft

REMOVAL

1. Raise the vehicle and support it safely.

2. Remove the six Allen head bolts from the left driveshaft inner constant velocity joint to left stub shaft flange.

NOTE: Support the intermediate driveshaft with a wire to the vehicle underbody to avoid unnecessary strain to the constant velocity joint.

3. Place a container under the stub axle to be removed, and lever the stub axle out of the differential side gear.

NOTE: Tapping the lever with a hammer may be necessary to overcome the retainer ring resistance.

4. Using a seal remover tool, remove the seal from the transaxle housing.

Stub shaft seal removal

5. Disconnect the right intermediate driveshaft from the primary driveshaft by removing the six Allen head bolts.

NOTE: Support the intermediate driveshaft by wire.

6. Remove the two bolts securing the primary shaft bearing housing to the bracket and relocate the shaft from the stub shaft.

Stub shaft seal installation

7. Loosen the bearing support bracket at the engine block.

NOTE: It is necessary to loosen the bearing bracket to avoid any stress or misalignment during assembly.

8. Insert a long slender drift or other tool through the differential at the left stub shaft opening and force the right stub shaft out by firm blows.

NOTE: Do not allow the stub shaft to drop.

9. Remove the right oil seal from the transaxle housing with a seal remover tool.

INSTALLATION

1. Install new left and right oil seals in the transaxle housing.

2. Install a new retaining ring on the stub axle shafts.

3. Beginning at either side, position a stub axle into the transaxle opening. With the aid of a soft faced hammer, bump the stub axle into place. Repeat the process with the second stub axle shaft.

NOTE: The stub shaft will be felt to snap into place as the retaining ring mates with the inner face of the differential side gears.

4. Repack the constant velocity joint with grease. Align the primary shaft and universal joint assembly to the stub shaft and slide it into position.

5. Align the bearing housing to the support bracket. Install the bolts.

6. Align the inner right constant velocity joint and secure it with the six Allen head bolts. Torque to 28–32 ft. lbs.

A — Intermediate shaft
B — Snap ring
C — Grease retainer
D — Bearings
E — Grease retainer
F — Hub
G — Retaining nut
H — Washer
J — Outer driveshaft
K — Knuckle
L — Shield

Front wheel bearings and grease retainer locations

RETAINER RING

SEAL   STUBSHAFT   UNIVERSAL JOINT   PRIMARY SHAFT

Exploded view of right stub shaft, universal joint, and primary shaft

Left stub shaft retaining ring location

7. Align the left side constant velocity joint to the left side stub shaft and secure with the six Allen headed bolts. Torque to 28–32 ft. lbs.

8. Tighten the bearing support bracket to the engine block, add transmission oil as necessary, and lower the vehicle to the floor.

REAR SUSPENSION

The rear axle is of tubular construction. Coil springs, a Panhard (transverse) rod, shock absorbers, and lower control arms are used to stabilize the axle assembly to the vehicle body. A stabilizer bar is used as an option to help control the roll effect on turns.

Rear Axle and Suspension Assembly

REMOVAL

1. Loosen the rear wheel lug bolts, raise the car and support it safely both front and rear. Remove the wheels.

2. Loosen the exhaust pipe at the exhaust manifold. Release the pipe from the rear supports and lower the exhaust system.

3. Disconnect the handbrake cable from the adjuster. Remove the hydraulic lines at the axle.

4. Remove the Panhard (transverse) rod bolts from both the body and the axle. Remove the rod.

5. Position a jack under the center of the axle and remove the lower arm bolts from the body bracket.

6. Remove the two stabilizer bar to body bracket retaining nuts, if any.

7. Raise the tailgate and parcel tray, remove the plastic caps, and detach the shock absorber upper mounting nuts and washers. Note the location of the rubber insulators.

8. Lower the axle assembly and remove it from under the vehicle.

INSTALLATION

1. Position the rear assembly under the vehicle. Position the springs and insulator pads and raise the assembly to the vehicle body. Connect the lower arms to the body.

2. Connect the shock absorbers at the upper mounts and replace the plastic caps.

3. Connect the stabilizer bar-to-body brackets and install the retaining nuts.

4. Connect the Panhard (transverse) rod to the body and axle and tighten securely.

5. Connect the brake lines at the axle.

6. Connect the handbrake cable at the adjuster.

NOTE: Refer to the brake section for handbrake adjustment and hydraulic system bleeding.

7. Mount the exhaust system to the rear supports and secure the pipe at the exhaust manifold.

8. Install the wheels, lower the vehicle to the floor, tighten the lower arms and the wheel lug bolts.

Rear Springs

Rear spring removal requires the same procedures as removal of the rear axle and suspension assembly.

Installation is the reverse of removal.

NOTE: During the installation of the springs, be sure the spring tang end butts are on the axle spring seats.

Upper rear spring insulator positioned in line with spring coil end

Lower Arms

The lower arms are removed by supporting the rear axle and removing the front and rear attaching bolts. Reinstall the arms in the reverse of the removal.

A—Lower arms
B—Spring insulator pads
C—Shock absorbers
D—Stabilizer bar
E—Springs
F—Bumper rubbers
G—Axle
H—Track bar
J—Integral hub and brake drum

Rear axle and suspension assembly

Shock Absorbers

REMOVAL

1. Loosen the rear wheel lug bolts, raise the vehicle and support it safely. Remove the wheel.

2. Position a jack under the rear axle to relieve spring tension.

3. Remove the plastic cap from the inner upper fender panel and remove the nut and washer from the shock absorber upper mount. Note the positioning of the insulator for installation.

4. Remove the bolt from the lower shock mounting.

5. With the aid of a lever, remove the shock absorber arm from the locating peg. Remove the shock absorber from the vehicle.

NOTE: New bushings may be installed in the lower mount with the use of lubricant. The top insulator is in two pieces and the lower part of the insulator must be in place before the shock absorber is installed.

Location of upper shock mount—left side shown

A—Upper insulator
B—Lower insulator
C—Shock absorber top mount

Shock absorber upper mounting insulators

INSTALLATION

1. Position the shock absorber and with the aid of a flat lever, apply a steady pressure to push the bushing onto the locating peg.

2. Locate the bottom of the shock into the mount and install the bolt and nut. Tighten securely.

A—Hollow tube or socket
B—Washer
C—Rubber bushing
D—Rubber bushing housing
E—Peg base

Installing bushing over shock absorber locating peg with a flat lever and socket

3. With the top insulator properly positioned, install the upper mounting nut and washer. Reinstall the plastic cap on the inner fender panel.

4. Replace the wheel, lower the vehicle to the floor and tighten the wheel lug bolts.

FRONT SUSPENSION

The front suspension used on the Fiesta is of the MacPherson strut design. A conventional lower control arm with a bolt-on ball joint is used, attached to a spindle carrier by the ball joint spindle and retained by a clinch bolt. A rubber top mount, a coil spring mounted between two seats, and an integral shock absorber unit, which is bolted to the top of the spindle carrier, completes the suspension.

NOTE: If the two original bolts are removed from the strut-to-spindle carrier for any reason, two close-tolerance bolts must be installed in their place. The close-tolerance bolts can be identified by two knurled sections on the bolt body.

Front End Alignment

The bearings, cups, hub, and knuckle are all machined to close tolerances, allowing the bearings to be self-setting at the time of installation and to require no other adjustment. A retaining nut and washer are used. The nut is retained to the driveshaft by staking.

Refer to the Drive Axle section for bearing, cup, or seal replacement procedures.

Suspension and Spindle Carrier Assembly

REMOVAL

1. Loosen the wheel lug bolts, raise car and support safely. Remove the road wheels.

2. Disconnect the flexible brake hose and plug the end to prevent fluid loss.

3. Remove the tie bar mounting bracket from the body.

4. Remove the tie rod end cotter pin and retaining nut. Remove the tie rod end from the steering arm with the use of a special tie rod end remover tool or equivalent.

5. Remove the lower arm pivot bolt at the body and the top mount retaining bolts at the apron panel reinforcement.

6. Remove the suspension and knuckle assembly from the vehicle.

INSTALLATION

1. Position the suspension and the knuckle assembly in the vehicle and install the top mount bolts.

2. Connect the lower arm to the body bracket.

3. Connect the tie rod end to the steering arm and install the nut and new cotter pin.

4. Connect the tie bar mounting bracket to the body reinforcement.

5. Connect the brake flexible hose and bleed the affected brake.

6. Install the wheels, lower the vehicle to the floor and tighten the wheel lug bolts.

Suspension Strut

REMOVAL

1. Loosen the wheel lug bolts, raise the front of the vehicle, and support it safely. Remove the wheel.

2. Remove the suspension strut-to-spindle carrier retaining bolts.

3. Remove the two top mounted apron panel retaining bolts and remove the suspension strut assembly from the vehicle.

INSTALLATION

1. Position the suspension assembly into the vehicle and secure the top mount to the apron panel by the retaining bolts.

2. Install two close-tolerance bolts to retain the suspension strut to the spindle carrier, replacing the regular production bolts removed.

A—Front suspension strut
B—Knuckle
C—Strut to knuckle retaining nuts and bolts

Front suspension strut retaining bolt location

Close tolerance bolts

NOTE: The close-tolerance bolts can be identified by two knurled sections on the bolt body.

3. Mount the wheel, lower the vehicle to the floor, and tighten the wheel lug bolts.

NOTE: It is advisable to check the wheel toe-out setting.

OVERHAUL

For spring and shock removal, and all strut overhaul procedures, please refer to "Strut Overhaul" in the Unit Repair section.

Lower Control Arm

REMOVAL

1. Loosen the wheel lug bolts, raise the vehicle and support it safely. Remove the wheel.
2. Remove the tie bar-to-body mount bracket assembly.
3. Remove the lower ball joint clinch bolt.
4. Remove the lower arm-to-body retaining bolt and remove the arm assembly from the vehicle.

A—Lower arm
B—Lower arm bushing
C—Tie bar and ball joint to lower arm retaining bolts
D—Lower arm ball joint
E—Ball joint to knuckle clinch bolt

Lower arm components

INSTALLATION

1. Position the lower arm assembly and install the body-to-arm retaining bolt.
2. Insert the lower ball joint spindle into the spindle carrier and install the clinch bolt.
3. Install the tie bar mounting bracket to the frame and secure it with the bolts.
4. Install the wheel, lower the vehicle to the floor, and tighten the lugs.

A—Mounting bracket
B—Retaining nut
C—Tie bar

Front tie bar body mount assembly

A—Knuckle body
B—Ball joint
C—Clinch bolt and nut

Clinch bolt used on the lower ball joint

Lower Ball Joint

REPLACEMENT (VEHICLE RAISED OFF FLOOR)

The lower ball joint can be replaced by removing the clinch bolt holding the ball joint spindle to the spindle carrier and the two tie bar retaining bolts. Position the new ball joint and install the retaining bolts and the clinch bolt. The toe-out setting should be checked to complete the repairs.

STEERING

The steering system is comprised of a rack and pinion unit, mounted to the engine compartment rear firewall, with tie rods linked to the steering arms of the spindle carrier.

The steering column assembly is a two piece tubular shaft type, designed to collapse under impact. The steering column lock assembly is secured by shear-off bolts that must be drilled out if the lock assembly is to be replaced.

Steering Gear

REMOVAL

1. Center the steering wheel. Raise the front of the vehicle and support it safely. Remove the front wheels.
2. Remove the clinch bolt holding the steering gear pinion to the lower steering shaft.
3. Remove the left and right tie rod end retaining cotter pins and nuts.
4. Using a tie rod end remover tool, separate the tie rod ends from the steering arms.
5. Straighten the lock tabs on the steering gear retaining bolts and clamps and remove.
6. Carefully remove the steering gear from the vehicle. Remove the rack clamp insulators.

Lower shaft to pinion coupler

NOTE: If the tie rod ends are removed, count the number of turns necessary to disconnect them.

INSTALLATION

1. Install the tie rod ends using the same number of turns required to remove each.
2. Install the rack clamp mounting insulators.
3. Set the steering wheel and steering gear in the straight ahead position.
4. Locate the steering gear in the vehicle and engage the steering gear pinion to the steering shaft. Install the clamp and clinch bolt loosely.
5. Install the clamps over the insulators and install the retaining bolts with new lock tabs. Secure the bolts and bend the lock tabs over the bolt heads.
6. Install the tie rod ends in the steering arms and secure them with nuts and new cotter pins.
7. Secure the steering gear pinion-to-steering shaft clinch bolt.
8. Install the wheels, lower the vehicle to the floor and tighten the lug bolts.
9. Check the steering wheel position and front wheel toe-out setting.

ADJUSTMENT

NOTE: The steering gear must be out of the vehicle to perform the following rack slipper bearing adjustment.

NOTE: A dial indicator and a mounting block must be used to measure the thickness of shims needed for the adjustment.

1. Position the steering gear with the rack slipper bearing cover plate facing up.
2. Remove the cover plate, shim pack and gasket from the housing.
3. Place the dial indicator in the mounting block and zero the gauge. Remove the gauging discs and position the base of the tool against the slipper. The dial reading will indicate the thickness of the shim pack needed between the slipper and the outer cover.
4. Assemble the shim pack as per the dial indicator reading and preload by adding a 0.002–0.005 inch shim.
5. Install the cover plate, the corrected shim pack and gasket on the gear housing.
6. Using an inch pound torque wrench, rotate the steering gear pinion at approximately 4 rpm. The torque reading should be in a range of 5 to 18 in. lbs.

Steering Wheel

REMOVAL AND INSTALLATION

1. Pry out the center steering wheel insert.

A —Steering mounting brackets and insulators
B —Upper steering shaft
C —Tie rod ends
D —Tie rods
E —Rubber bellows
F —Steering gear housing
G —Upper and lower steering shaft shrouds
H —Collapsable steering shaft coupling
J —Multi-switches
K —Brace
L —Lower steering shaft
M —Pinion and rack assembly

Steering gear and shaft assemblies

Installing the dial indicator in tool

Measuring rack slipper height clearance

Use of dial indicator and mounting tool to measure rack slipper height clearance

Rack slipper cover, shims and gasket

Using torque wrench to determine steering gear pinion resistance

2. Remove the steering wheel retaining nut and lift the steering wheel from the shaft.

NOTE: Observe any match marks for alignment during installation.

3. Installation is the reverse of removal.

Combination Switch

REMOVAL AND INSTALLATION

1. Disconnect the negative battery cable.

2. Remove the steering wheel assembly and the turn signal direction indicator cam from the steering shaft.

3. Remove the steering column upper and lower shrouds.

4. Remove the attaching screws for the multi-lever switches and remove the wiring retaining clip from the column tube.

5. Disconnect the wiring at the terminal connectors.

6. Installation of the switches is the reverse of removal.

Ignition Switch

REMOVAL

1. Disconnect the battery ground cable.

2. Remove the upper and lower steering column shrouds.

3. Disconnect the ignition switch multi-wire plug.

4. Center punch and drill out the two lock retaining bolts and remove the ignition switch.

A—Shear off bolts
B—Steering column tube
C—Steering column lock assembly

Ignition switch location and shear-off bolts

INSTALLATION

1. Position the ignition switch on the steering column and install new shear bolts.

2. Tighten the shear bolts until the heads break off.

3. Attach the ignition switch multi-wire plug.

4. Install the column upper and lower shrouds.

5. Connect the battery ground cable and check the ignition switch operation.

Steering Linkage

TIE ROD END REMOVAL AND INSTALLATION

The tie rod end is removed from the steering arm by removal of the cotter pin and castellated nut from the tie rod end spindle. Use a tie rod end removal tool to separate the tie rod end from the steering arm. Install the tie rod end using the same number of turns that were necessary to remove it.

A—Ball joint   D—Castellated nut
B—Locknut   E—Cotter pin
C—Tie rod

Tie rod end assembly

TIE ROD REMOVAL AND INSTALLATION

Pins secure the tie rod ball joint housing and locknut and must be drilled out before the locknut can be loosened.

─── **CAUTION** ───

A ⁵⁄₃₂ inch diameter drill bit with a 0.400 inch depth stop must be used. Do not drill deeper than 0.400 inch. A special tool is available for use in the drilling operation.

A—4.0 mm (5/32 in) dia. locking pin hole
B—Maximum depth 9.5 mm (0.4 in) deep

Drilling lock pin from locknut/ball housing

The locknuts can be loosened and the tie rod unscrewed from the rack rod, allowing the ball seat to be removed.

Installation is as follows:

1. Assemble the tie rod ball and seat, tie rods, housing and locknuts to the rack.

NOTE: Coat the parts with lubricant before assembly.

2. Adjust the tie rod movement resistance by tightening the housing and locknuts and measuring the resistance by one of the following methods:

a. Remove the tie rod end and lock two nuts together on the tie rod threads. Tighten the ball housing until a reading of 2.6–5.1 ft. lbs. is required to turn the tie rod with a torque wrench and socket on the locked nuts. Lock the ball housing with the locknut and rotate the tie rod at least seven times. Recheck the resistance to verify that it still remains within specifications. Remove the two locknuts and reinstall the tie rod end.

b. With a piston pull gauge attached to the tie rod approximately ¼ in. from the end, measure the effort required to move the tie rod. The reading should be 5.1 lbs. Lock the ball housing with the locknut and recheck the effort.

3. Center punch and drill a hole on the housing to locknut mating faces, using a ⁵⁄₃₂ inch drill bit with a stop adjusted to 0.400 inch. Drill a new hole, even if the old hole lines up.

4. Install new retaining pins in the drilled holes and retain them by peening over the surrounding metal with a punch.

5. Install the rack bellows and retain them in position with clamps.

A—Housing   D—Rack
B—Tie-rod   E—Locking ring
C—Ball seat

Inner tie rod ball seat assembly

A—Piston pull scale or spring balance
B—Wire hook 6 mm (0.25 in) from end of tie rod
C—Tie-rod
D—Ball joint housing spanner

Checking tie rod movement effort with a scale gauge

A—Seal
B—Cover plate
C—Gasket
D—Pinion and bearing assy.
E—Bushing
F—Housing
G—Rack support bushing

H—Rack slipper
J—Spring
K—Shims
L—Gasket
M—Cover plate
N—Locking pin
P—Ball housing
Q—Locking ring
R—Ball seat
S—Rack
T—Bellows
U—Bellows clip
V—Track or tie-rod

Exploded view of steering gear assembly

BRAKE SYSTEM

The Fiesta is equipped with a dual hydraulic brake system, using disc brakes on the front wheels and drum brakes on the rear wheels.

The hydraulic system is split diagonally, so that one front and the opposite rear brake are in one circuit, while the remaining front and opposite rear brakes are in the second circuit.

Any brake imbalance created is overcome by the front suspension design.

A power brake unit is available as an option.

For all brake system repair and service procedures not detailed below, please refer to "Brakes" in the Unit Repair section.

Master Cylinder

REMOVAL

1. Disconnect the battery ground cable.

2. Remove the brake fluid from the master cylinder reservoir and detach the pressure lines from the cylinder body.

NOTE: Install plugs in the fluid line ports to avoid leakage.

3. Remove the switch wires from the brake differential pressure valve.

4. Remove the spring clip, clevis pin and bushing from the pedal and master cylinder pushrod.

5. Remove the attaching nuts and washers from the studs and remove the master cylinder from the firewall.

INSTALLATION

1. Position the master cylinder on the firewall and secure with the nuts and washers.

2. Remove the plugs from the fluid line ports. Attach the fluid lines to the cylinder body and tighten securely.

3. Install the clevis pin and bushing in the brake pedal, connect the master cylinder pushrod, and secure with the spring clip.

4. Fill the master cylinder reservoir with brake fluid and bleed the system.

5. Connect the battery ground cable and road test the vehicle.

Power Brake Servo

REMOVAL

1. Follow the procedure for removal of the master cylinder.

2. Remove the spring clip and clevis pin securing the actuating rod to the brake pedal.

3. Disconnect the vacuum hose from the vacuum valve at the servo unit.

4. Remove the four nuts and washers retaining the servo unit to the firewall studs.

INSTALLATION

1. Secure the power brake servo to the firewall studs with the retaining nuts and washers.

2. Install the vacuum hose to the vacuum valve nipple.

3. Install the clevis pin in the actuating rod and pedal. Retain the pin with the spring clip.

4. Reinstall the master cylinder to the power brake servo unit. Bleed the hydraulic system.

Rear Wheel Cylinder

REMOVAL AND INSTALLATION

1. Remove the rear brake shoes.

2. Disconnect the brake line and plug to avoid fluid leakage.

3. Remove the two capscrews holding the wheel cylinder to the carrier plate and remove the cylinder.

4. Installation is the reverse of removal.

5. Bleed the brake system.

Rear Wheel Bearings

ADJUSTMENT

1. Tighten the retaining nut to 27 ft. lbs. torque while rotating the wheel.

2. Back off the retaining nut 90 degrees

A—Reservoir
B—Master cylinder assembly
C—Rubber seals
D—Check valve
E—Master cylinder body
F—Primary return spring
G—Primary piston assembly
H—Secondary return spring
J—Secondary piston assembly
K—Boot
L—Operating rod seal
M—Snap ring

Exploded view of master cylinder

and install the nut retainer, new cotter pin, and install the dust cap.

Parking Brake

The parking brake is comprised of a floor mounted lever assembly, a primary or forward cable, left and right cables connected to an equalizer bracket assembly and to the rear wheel handbrake levers. Adjustment is made at the rear of the primary cable with an adjustment nut.

ADJUSTMENT

1. Raise the vehicle and support it safely.

2. Loosen the adjuster locknut and rotate the cable adjuster to put slack in the cable.

3. Tighten the cable until all slack is removed and the handbrake levers just begin to move off the back stops of the carrier plates.

4. Move the adjuster three complete turns and secure the locknut.

NOTE: After the adjustment is complete, the machined groove in the primary cable threaded shaft must not protrude past the locknut.

5. Be sure the rear brakes do not drag. Lower the vehicle to the floor.

CHASSIS ELECTRICAL

Heater Assembly

REMOVAL

1. Disconnect the battery ground cable.

2. Drain the cooling system and remove the heater hoses from the core tubes.

3. Remove the cover plate for the core tubes from the firewall. Plug the tubes to avoid leakage.

4. Remove the four screws holding the right and left lower dash trim panels.

5. Remove the ash tray and bracket.

6. Remove the two vent hoses from the heater assembly adapter.

7. Remove the heater assembly-to-instrument panel bracket and the two retaining nuts holding the heater assembly to the top cowl panel.

8. Pull the heater assembly rearward until the core tubes clear the firewall opening.

9. Disconnect the blower motor wires and remove the heater assembly, complete with the control panel, to the right and out of the vehicle.

INSTALLATION

1. Position the heater assembly into the vehicle from the right side. Connect the blower motor wire lead and bolt the heater assembly to the top panel. Be sure the gasket is in place.

2. Install the heater assembly-to-instrument panel bracket and control to the instrument panel.

3. Slide the vent nozzle hoses onto the outlets on the heater assembly.

4. Replace the ash tray and bracket.

5. Install the cover plate over the core tubes and secure it to the firewall.

6. Install the heater core hoses to the tubes and tighten the hose clamps.

7. Fill the cooling system and connect the battery ground cable.

8. Install the lower dash trim panels.

Blower Motor

REMOVAL-HEATER ASSEMBLY OUT

1. Cut the foam gasket on the heater assembly joint with a knife.

2. Remove the two retaining clamps from the motor mounting and separate the two housings.

3. Separate the two halves and remove the blower motor.

A—Handbrake lever
B—Primary cable
C—Cable adjuster
D—Transverse cable
E—Equalizer
F—Rear cable

Exploded view of hand brake components

Blower motor retainer clip location

Heater core location in the heater assembly

INSTALLATION

1. Insert the blower motor with the wire leads pointing to the rear of the vehicle. Fit the wire loom into the groove under the seal gasket.

2. Press the two halves of the heater assembly together and guide the control valve shafts into their respective holes.

3. Use additional retaining clamps to fasten the two halves together.

4. The heater assembly is ready for installation into the vehicle.

Heater Core

REMOVAL AND INSTALLATION–HEATER ASSEMBLY OUT

1. Remove the two retaining screws holding the core into the housing assembly.

2. Slide the core out of the heater housing assembly.

3. Installation is the reverse of removal.

4. The heater assembly is ready for installation into the vehicle.

Radio

REMOVAL AND INSTALLATION

NOTE: It is recommended that the battery ground cable be disconnected before the radio is removed.

The radio is mounted to the bottom of the instrument panel. Remove the hot wire and antenna lead from the rear of the radio. Remove the attaching screws and brackets and remove the radio.
Reverse the removal procedure to install.

A—Defroster nozzle (with center nozzle)
B—Heater assembly
C—Heater core
D—Control panel
E—Temperature control valve cable
F—Distribution valve cable
G—Vent nozzle
H—Blower motor

Heater-defroster assembly with controls

Windshield Wipers

The front windshield wiper motor is located on the right side of the cowl panel, in the engine compartment. It is electrically controlled with an interval type control available as an option.

The front windshield washer reservoir is near the front of the left inner fender panel and is powered by an electric pump. The nozzle is a single post, dual opening unit, mounted on the top of the cowl air intake panel.

A rear windshield wiper and washer are available as an option and are mounted on the rear liftgate. The rear washer reservoir is on the left rear floor panel.

Front Wiper Motor

REMOVAL

1. Disconnect the battery ground cable.

2. Disconnect the two multi-plugs from the wiper motor.

3. Remove the three mounting bolts and pull the wiper motor and bracket away from the cowl panel so that the wiper linkage is accessible.

4. Disconnect the wiper linkage from the wiper operating arm and remove the wiper motor from the vehicle.

INSTALLATION

1. Position the wiper motor and bracket to the cowl panel and install the wiper linkage to the motor operating arm.

2. Apply the sealer to the mating surfaces of the mounting bracket and the cowl panel.

3. Install the retaining bolts and tighten the motor bracket securely to the cowl panel.

4. Connect the two multi-plugs to the wiper motor and connect the battery ground cable.

A —Wiper operating arm
B —Two speed control
C —Power supply

Wiper motor connections for linkage and wiring

A —Wiper motor and bracket assembly
B —Bracket to motor retaining nut
C —Lock washer and insulating assembly
D —Wiper bracket to cowl panel retaining bolt
E —Left and right pivot shaft assemblies and connecting link
F —Wiper arm
G —Retaining washer
H —Retaining nut
I —Wiper blade assembly
J —Connecting link - motor to pivots

Exploded view of wiper components

A —Bracket
B —Seat belt warning relay
C —Heated backlight relay
D —Intermittent wiper relay
E —Ignition buzzer
F —Cooling fan relay
G —Hazard warning flasher

Flasher and relay identification

Front Wiper Linkage

To service the wiper linkage, the hood lock mounting plate must be removed. The linkage is removed or replaced through the opening.

Wiper Arms

To remove or replace the wiper arms on the pivot shaft assemblies, lift the rear cover of the arm upward to expose the nut and washer used to retain the wiper arm to the pivot shaft.

Before installing the wiper arm, make sure the wiper motor is in the park position.

Instrument Cluster

REMOVAL AND INSTALLATION

1. Remove two retaining screws from the lower instrument panel cover and remove the cover, if any.
2. Grasp the speedometer cable lock and press in on the grooved section to disconnect the cable from the rear of the instrument cluster.
3. Remove the cluster bezel by pulling outward on the bezel opening sides.
4. Remove the instrument cluster retaining screws and move the cluster toward the steering wheel.
5. Disconnect the wiring connectors from the rear of the cluster and remove the cluster.
6. Installation is the reverse of removal.

Fuse Box Location

The fuse block is located on the left side of the steering column under the edge of the instrument panel on standard models and inside the top of the instrument panel storage space on Ghia models.

The relays and flashers are located on a special frame under the instrument panel.

NOTE: The lower instrument panel would have to be removed on Ghia models to gain access to the flashers and relays.

Honda

SERIAL NUMBER IDENTIFICATION

Vehicle Identification (Chassis) Number

Honda vehicle identification numbers are mounted on the top edge of the instrument panel and are visible from the outside. In addition, there is a Vehicle/Engine Identification plate under the hood on the cowl.

Engine Serial Number

The engine serial number is stamped into the clutch casing. The first three digits indicate engine model identification. The re-

maining numbers refer to production sequence. This same number is also stamped onto the Vehicle/Engine Identification plate mounted on the hood bracket.

Serial number identification

Transmission Serial Number

The transmission serial number is stamped on the top of the transmission/clutch case.

GENERAL ENGINE SPECIFICATIONS

Year	Model	Engine Displacement (cc)	Carburetor Type	Horsepower @ rpm	Bore x Stroke (in.)	Compression Ratio	Torque @ rpm (ft. lbs.)
'76–'79	Civic Exc. CVCC	1237	Hitachi 2 bbl	N.A.	2.83 × 2.99	8.1:1	N.A.
'76–'82	Civic	1487	Keihin 3 bbl	63 @ 5000	2.91 × 3.41	7.9:1②	77 @ 3000
'76–'78	Accord	1600	Keihin 3 bbl	68 @ 5000	2.91 × 3.66	8.0:1	85 @ 3000
'79–'83	Accord, Prelude	1751	Keihin 3 bbl	72 @ 4500	3.03 × 3.70	8.0:1①	94 @ 3000
'80–'83	Civic	1335	Keihin 3 bbl	N.A.	2.83 × 3.23	7.9:1③	N.A.

① 1980 8.8:1 in Calif, '81 8.9:1 in Calif, '82–8.8:1
   N.A. Not available
② '80–9.0:1, 8.9:1 Calif, '81–8.8:1, '82–9.3:1
③ '81–8.8:1, '82 9.3:1

TUNE-UP SPECIFICATIONS

(When analyzing compression test results, look for uniformity among cylinders, rather than specific pressures.)

Year	Model	Engine Displacement (cc)	Orginal Equipment Spark Plugs Type	Gap (in.)	Distributor Point Dwell (deg)	Point Gap (in.)	Basic Ignition Timing (deg) MT	AT	Intake Valve Fully Opens (deg)	Fuel Pump Pressure (psi)	Idle Speed (rpm) MT	AT	Valve Clearance (in.) Intake (cold)	Auxiliary (cold)	Exhaust (cold)
'76	Civic	1237	BP6ES or W20EP	0.028–0.032	49–55	0.018–0.022	7B ⑧	7B ⑧	10A	2.56 ④	750–850 ⑤	700–800	0.004–0.006	—	0.004–0.006
'77	Civic	1237	BP6ES or W20EP	0.028–0.032	49–55	0.018–0.022	TDC ⑧	TDC ⑧	10A	2.56	700–800 ④	700–800 ⑤	0.004–0.006	—	0.004–0.006
'78–'79	Civic	1237	BP6ES or W20EP	0.028–0.032	49–55	0.018–0.022	2B ⑧	2B ⑧	10A	2.56	650–750 ④	650–750 ⑤	0.004–0.006	—	0.004–0.006
'76	Civic CVCC	1487	B-6ES or W20ES W20ES ②	0.028–0.032	49–55	0.018–0.022	2B ⑥⑨	2B ⑦⑨	10A	1.85–2.56	800–900 ④	700–800 ⑤	0.005–0.007	0.005–0.007	0.005–0.007
'77	Civic CVCC	1487	B6EB or W20ES-L	0.028–0.032	49–55	0.018–0.022	6B ⑩	6B ⑩⑦	10A	1.85–2.56	750–850 ④	650–750 ⑤	0.005–0.007	0.005–0.007	0.005–0.007
'78–'79	Civic CVCC	1487	B6EB or W20ES-L	0.028–0.032	49–55	0.018–0.022	6B ⑩	6B ⑩	10A	1.85–2.56	650–750 ④	600–700 ⑤	0.005–0.007	0.005–0.007	0.007–0.009
'76–'77	Accord CVCC	1600	B6ES or W20ES ①②	0.028–0.032	49–55	0.018–0.022	2B ⑨	TDC ⑨	10A	1.85–2.56	750–850 ④	630–730 ⑤	0.005–0.007	0.005–0.007	0.005–0.007
'78	Accord	1600	B6EB or W20ES-L	0.028–0.032	49–55	0.018–0.022	6B ⑨⑩	6B ⑨⑩	10A	2.13–2.84	750–850 ④	650–750 ⑤	0.005–0.007	0.005–0.007	0.007–0.009
'79	Accord	1751	B7EB	0.028–0.032	Electronic		6B ⑨⑫	4B ⑬⑪	10A	2.13–2.84	650–750 ④	650–750 ⑤	0.005–0.007	0.005–0.007	0.010–0.012
'80	Civic	1487	B7EB-11	0.42	Electronic		15B ⑭	TDC ⑮	—	2.5	700–800	700–800	0.005–0.007	0.005–0.007	0.007–0.009
	Civic	1335	W20ES-L11	0.42	Electronic		2B	TDC	10A	2.5	700–800	700–800	0.005–0.007	0.005–0.007	0.007–0.009
	Accord	1751	B7EB	0.30	Electronic		4B	TDC	—	2.5	750–850	700–800	0.005–0.007	0.005–0.007	0.010–0.012
	Prelude	1751	B7EB	0.30	Electronic		TDC	TDC	—	2.5	750–850	700–800	0.005–0.007	0.005–0.007	0.010–0.012
'81	Civic	1487	B6EB-11	0.042	Electronic		10B⑯	2A	10A	2.5	700–800	700–800	0.005–0.007	0.005–0.007	0.007–0.009
	Civic	1335	W20ES-L11	0.042	Electronic		2B	2B	10A	2.5	700–800	750–850	0.005–0.007	0.005–0.007	0.007–0.009
	Accord	1751	B6ER-L11	0.042	Electronic		TDC	TDC	10A	2.5	750–850	750–850	0.005–0.007	0.005–0.007	0.010–0.012
	Prelude	1751	B6EB-L11	0.042	Electronic		TDC	TDC	10A	2.5	750–850	750–850	0.005–0.007	0.005–0.007	0.010–0.012
'82	Civic	1487	B6REB-L11	0.042	Electronic		18B	18B	10A	2.5	650–750	650–750	0.005–0.007	0.005–0.007	0.007–0.009
	Civic	1335	W20ESR-L11	0.042	Electronic		20B	—	10A	2.5	650–750	—	0.005–0.007	0.005–0.007	0.007–0.009

TUNE-UP SPECIFICATIONS
(When analyzing compression test results, look for uniformity among cylinders, rather than specific pressures.)

Year	Model	Engine Displacement (cc)	Orginial Equipment Spark Plugs		Distributor		Basic Ignition Timing (deg)		Intake Valve Fully Opens (deg)	Fuel Pump Pressure (psi)	Idle Speed (rpm)		Valve Clearance (in.)		
			Type	Gap (in.)	Point Dwell (deg)	Point Gap (in.)	MT	AT			MT	AT	Intake (cold)	Auxiliary (cold)	Exhaust (cold)
	Accord	1751	BR6EB-L11	0.042	Electronic		16B⑰	16B	10A	2.5	750–850	750–850	0.005–0.007	0.005–0.007	0.010–0.012
	Prelude	1751	BR6EB-L11	0.042	Electronic		10B⑱	16B	10A	2.5	700–800	700–800	0.005–0.007	0.005–0.007	0.010–0.012
'83	All				SEE UNDERHOOD SPECIFICATIONS STICKER										

NOTE: The underhood specifications sticker often reflects tune-up specification changes made in production. Sticker figures must be used if they disagree with those in this chart.

① For continuous highway use over 70 mph, use cooler NGK B-7ES, Nippon Denso W-22ES or equivalent
② For continuous low-speed use under 30 mph, use hotter NKG B-5ES, Nippon Denso W-16ES or equivalent
④ In neutral, with headlights on
⑤ In drive range, with headlights on
⑥ 5-speed Sedan (Hatchback) from engine number 2500001-up—6B
⑦ Station wagon—TDC
⑧ Aim timing light at red notch on crankshaft pulley with distributor vacuum hose(s) connected at specified idle speed
⑨ Aim timing light at red mark (yellow mark, '78–'79 Accord M/T) on flywheel or torque converter drive plate distributor vacuum hose connected at specified idle speed

⑩ California (KL) and High Altitude (KH) models: 2B
⑪ Aim light at blue mark (49 states models)
⑫ California (KL) and High Altitude (KH) models: TDC (white mark)
⑬ California (KL) and High Altitude (KH) models: 2 ATDC (black mark)
⑭ 49 States Wagon 10B
⑮ California and High Altitude TDC
⑯ Wagon/Sedan—4B, Calif-2A
⑰ Calif.—12B
⑱ Calif.—16B
TDC—Top Dead Center
B—Before top dead center
A—After top dead center
—Not applicable
N.A. Not available

FIRING ORDERS

1170, 1237cc
FIRING ORDER
1 - 3 - 4 - 2

Front of car

Non–CVCC firing order

CVCC
FIRING ORDER
1 - 3 - 4 - 2

Front of car

CVCC firing order

CAPACITIES

Year	Model	Engine Displacement (cc)	Engine Crankcase (qts)②	Transmission (pts) Manual 4-sp	5-sp	Auto.③	Gasoline Tank (gals)	Cooling System (qts)
'76–78	Civic	1237	3.8	5.2	—	5.2	10.6	4.2
	Civic CVCC	1487	3.8	5.2	5.2	5.2	10.6①	4.2
	Accord	1600	3.8	5.2	5.2	5.2	13.2	4.2
'79	Civic	1237	3.8	5.2	—	5.2	10.6	4.8
	Civic	1487	3.8	5.2	5.6	5.2	10.6①	4.8
	Accord	1751	3.8	5.2	5.2	5.2	13.2	6.4
	Prelude	1751	3.8	5.2	5.2	5.2	13.2	6.0
'80–'81	Civic	1335, 1487	3.8	4.8	5.2	5.2	10.8	5.2
	Accord & Prelude	1751	3.8	5.0	5.0	5.2	13.2	6.4
'82–'83	Civic	1335, 1487	3.7	5.6	5.6	5.2	10.8	5.2
	Accord	1751	3.7	5.0	5.0	5.2	15.8	6.0
	Prelude	1751	3.7	5.0	5.0	5.2	13.2	6.0

① Sta. Wgn.: 11.0
② Includes filter
③ Does not include torque converter. Total capacity from dry is 8.8 pts.

CRANKSHAFT AND CONNECTING ROD SPECIFICATIONS

(All measurements given in in.)

Year	Engine Displacement (cc)	Crankshaft Main Brg Journal Dia	Main Brg Oil Clearance	Shaft End-Play	Thrust on No.	Connecting Rod Journal Dia	Oil Clearance	Side Clearance
'76–'79	1237	1.9685–1.9673	0.0009–0.0017	0.0039–0.0138	3	1.5736–1.5480	0.0008–0.0015	0.0079–④ 0.0177
'80–'83	1335	1.9676–⑥ 1.9685	0.0010–0.0022	0.004–0.014	3	1.6526–1.6535	0.0008–0.0015	0.006–0.012
'76–'83	1487, 1600, 1751	1.9687–⑤ 1.9697	0.0010–① 0.0021	0.0039–③ 0.0138	3	1.6525–1.6535	0.0008–0.0015	0.0059–0.0118

① 1751—.009–.0017
③ '81 with 1487, 1751—.004–.014
④ '75–'76: 0.0059–0.0118
⑤ '81 with 1487—1.9676–1.9685, '82 with 1487—1.9687–1.9803
⑥ '80—1.9687–1.9697

VALVE SPECIFICATIONS

Year	Engine Displacement (cc)	Seat Angle (deg)	Face Angle (deg)	Spring Installed Height (in.)	Stem To Guide Clearance (in.) Intake	Exhaust	Auxiliary	Stem Diameter (in.) Intake	Exhaust	Auxiliary
'76–'79	1237	45	45	Inner—1.6535 Outer—1.5728①	0.0004–0.0016 ②	0.0020–0.0031	—	0.2591–0.2594	0.2579–0.2583	—

VALVE SPECIFICATIONS

Year	Engine Displacement (cc)	Seat Angle (deg)	Face Angle (deg)	Spring Installed Height (in.)	Stem To Guide Clearance (in.)			Stem Diameter (in.)		
					Intake	Exhaust	Auxiliary	Intake	Exhaust	Auxiliary
'76–'78	1487	45	45	Inner—1.358 Outer—1.437 Auxiliary—0.906④	0.0004–0.0016	0.0020–0.0031	0.0008–0.0020	0.2592–0.2596	0.2580–0.2584	0.2162–0.2166
'76–'78	1600 CVCC	45	45	①	0.0008–0.0020	0.0020–0.0032	0.0008–0.0020	0.2591–0.2594	0.2579–0.2583	0.2157–0.2161
'79	1487	45	45	Intake inner—1.401 Intake outer—1.488 Exhaust inner—1.358 Exhaust outer—1.437 Auxiliary—0.906	0.0004–0.0016	0.0020–0.0031	0.0008–0.0021	0.2592–0.2596	0.2580–0.2584	0.2162–0.2166
'80–'83	1335, 1487	45	45	Intake inner—1.402 Intake outer—1.488 Exhaust inner—1.402 Exhaust outer—1.488 Auxiliary—0.984⑤	0.0008–0.0020	0.0024–0.0035	0.0009–0.0023	0.2591–0.2594	0.2574–0.2578	0.2587–0.2593
'79–'80	1751	45	45	Intake inner—1.000 Intake outer—1.094 Exhaust inner—1.031 Exhaust outer—1.109 Auxiliary—0.875	0.0008–0.0020	0.0024–0.0035	0.0009–0.0023	0.2748–0.2753	0.2732–0.2736	0.2587–0.2593
'81–'83	1751	45	45	Intake inner—1.402 Intake outer—1.488 Exhaust inner—1.402 Exhaust outer—1.488 Auxiliary—0.984	0.001–0.002	0.002–0.004	0.0009–0.0023	0.2748–0.2751	0.2732–0.2736	0.2587–0.2593

① Intake Inner—1.6654
  Outer—1.6649
  Exhaust Inner—1.9882
  Outer—2.1181
  Auxiliary (CVCC)—1.1457
② '78–'79: 0.0008–0.0020
④ '78 Intake Inner—1.401
  Outer—1.488
⑤ '80 1335cc—0.906

C377

PISTON AND RING SPECIFICATIONS
(All measurements are given in inches)

Year	Engine Displacement (cc)	Piston Clearance	Ring Gap			Ring Side Clearance		
			Top Compression	Bottom Compression	Oil Control	Top Compression	Bottom Compression	Oil Control
'76–'79	1237	0.0012–0.0039	0.0098–0.0157	0.0098–0.0157	0.0118–0.0394	0.0008–0.0018	0.0008–0.0018	Snug
'76–'78	1487 CVCC, 1600	0.0012–0.0039	0.0079–0.0157	0.0079–0.0157	0.0079–0.0354 ①	0.0008–0.0018	0.0008–0.0018	Snug
1979	1487 CVCC	0.0012–0.0060	0.0079–0.0157	0.0079–0.0157	0.0079–0.0354	0.0008–0.0018	0.0008–0.0018	Snug
'80–'81	1335, 1487	0.0004–0.0024	0.006–0.014	0.006–0.014	0.012–0.035	0.0008–0.0018	0.0008–0.0018	Snug
'82–'83	1335, 1487	0.0004–0.0024	0.006–0.014	0.006–0.014	0.012–0.035	0.0012–0.0024	0.0012–0.0020	Snug
'79–'83	1751 CVCC	0.0008–0.0028 ②	0.0059–0.0138	0.0059–0.0138	0.0118–0.0354	0.0008–0.0018	0.0008–0.0018	Snug

① 1600 engine oil control ring gap—0.0118–0.0354
② 0.0004–0.0024–1982
③ 1335–0.0004–0.0024

TORQUE SPECIFICATIONS
(All readings are given in ft. lbs.)

Year	Engine Displacement (cc)	Cylinder Head Bolts	Main Bearing Bolts	Rod Bearing Bolts	Crankshaft Pulley Bolts	Flywheel to Crankshaft Bolts	Manifold		Spark Plugs	Oil Pan Drain Bolt
							In	Ex		
'76–'79	1237	30–35① 37–42②	27–31	18–21	34–38	34–38	13–17	13–17③	9–12	29–36
'76–'78	1487 CVCC, 1600	40–47	30–35	18–21	34–38	15–17	15–17	15–17	11–18	29–36
'79–'83	1335, 1487	43④	29	21	61⑤	51	18	18	15⑥	33
'79–'83	1751	43④	48	23⑦	61⑧	51	18	18	15⑥	33

① To engine number EB 1-1019949
② From engine number EB 1-1019950
③ 1975–76 models w/air—22–33 ft. lbs.
④ Two step procedure—see text
⑤ '80–'82—80 ft. lbs.
⑥ '80–'82—13 ft. lbs.
⑦ '82—21 ft. lbs.
⑧ '81–83 ft. lbs, '82—195 ft. lbs.

CYLINDER HEAD TORQUE SEQUENCE

ALTERNATOR AND REGULATOR SPECIFICATIONS

		Alternator			Regulator					Regulator		
						Field Relay					Regulator	
Year	Engine Displacement (cc)	Part No. or Manufacturer	Field Current @ 12V (amps)	Output (amps) @ 5,000 rpm	Part No. or Manufacturer	Yoke Gap (in.)	Point Gap (in.)	Volts to Close	Yoke Gap (in.)	Point Gap (in.)	Volts @ 5,000 rpm
'76–81	1237	Hitachi	2.5	40① 35②	Hitachi	0.008– 0.018	0.0016– 0.0472	4.5– 5.8	0.008– 0.024	0.010– 0.018	13.5– 14.5
'76–'83	1487 CVCC	Nippon Denso	2.5	35③ 45④	Nippon Denso	N.A.	0.016– 0.047	4.5– 5.8	0.020	0.016– 0.020	13.5– 14.5
'76–'78	1600 CVCC	Nippon Denso	2.5	50	Nippon Denso	N.A.	0.016– 0.047	4.5– 5.8	0.020	0.016– 0.047	13.5– 14.5
'80–'83	1335 CVCC	Nippon Denso	2.5	45	Nippon Denso	0.008– 0.018	0.02– 0.05	N.A.	0.02	0.016– 0.047	13.5– 14.5
'79–'83	1751 CVCC	Nippon Denso	2.5	50	Nippon Denso	0.008– 0.024	0.016– 0.047	N.A.	0.020	0.016– 0.047	13.5– 14.5

① From no. 1011759
② Up to no. 1011158
③ Without A/C
④ With A/C
N.A. Not applicable

BATTERY AND STARTER SPECIFICATIONS
(All cars use 12 volt, negative ground electrical systems)

			Starter								
		Battery Amp Hour Capacity	Lock Test			No Load Test			Brush Spring Tension (oz.)	Min. Brush Length (in.)
Year	Model (cc)		Amps	Volts	Torque (ft. lbs.)	Amps	Volts	rpm		
'76–'77	(1237)	45	380 or less	4.9	5.4	less than 70	12	7000 or more	56–57	0.16
'78–'79	(1237)	45	380 (max.)	5.5	6.15	70 (max.)	11	6000	56–57	0.16
'80–'83	CVCC (1335, 1487)	47	230	8.0	4.7	90②	11.5①	3000③	N.A.	0.39
'76–'79	CVCC (1487)	47	160	9.6	N.A.	less than 80	11.5	N.A.	N.A.	0.39
'76–'78	CVCC (1600)	47	300 (max.)	2.5	5.0	90 (max.)	11.5	3000	53–67	0.35
'79–'83	CVCC (1751)	47	400 (max.)	2.4	7.9	90 (max.)	11.5	3500	N.A.	0.55

① Cal. Nippon Denso; Hitachi 11.0
② Cal. Nippon Denso; Hitachi 70
③ Cal. Nippon Denso 5000; Hitachi 6000
N.A. Not available

BRAKE SPECIFICATIONS

(All measurements given are in in. unless noted)

Year	Model	Lug Nut Torque (ft. lbs.)	Brake Disc		Brake Drum		Minimum Lining Thickness	
			Minimum Thickness	Maximum Run-Out	Inner Diameter	Max. Machine O/S	Front	Rear
'76–'83	Civic Sedan, Hatchback, (Wagon '80–'82)	51–65	0.354⑤	0.006	7.087	7.126	0.063③	0.079
'76–'79	Civic Wagon	51–65	0.449①	0.006	7.874	7.913②	0.300	0.118④
'76–'83	Accord, Prelude	51–65	0.433⑦	0.006	7.087⑧	7.126⑨	0.039⑥	0.079

①0.437—'77
②7.93—'77–'79
③0.24—'76–'77
④0.08—'77–'79
⑤'81–'82—0.394
　'80 Wagon—0.394

⑥0.063—'80–'82
⑦'80—0.4126, '81—0.4134, '82—0.60
⑧'82—7.87
⑨'82—7.91

WHEEL ALIGNMENT SPECIFICATIONS

Year	Model	Caster		Camber		Toe-Out (in.)	Steering Axis Inclination (deg)
		Range (deg)	Preferred Setting (deg)	Range (deg)	Preferred Setting (deg)		
'76–'79	Civic—all exc. Station Wagon	1¼P–2¼①	1¾P②	0–1P	½P	0.04	8.9③
'76–'79	Civic Station Wagon	½P–1½P	1P④	0–1P	½P	0.04	9.3
'80–'81	Civic—all exc. Station Wagon	¾P–2¾P	1¾P	1N–1P	0	⅞N–⅛P	12°20'
'80–'81	Civic Station Wagon	0–2P	1	1N–1P	0	⅞N–⅛P	12°20'
'83	Civic—all exc. Station Wagon	P–3P	2P	1N–1P	0	⅞N–⅛P	—
'82	Civic Station Wagon	18'P–2°18'P	1°18'P	1N–1P	0	⅞N–⅛P	—
'76–'77	Accord	1⅓P–2⅓P	1⅚P	⅙P–1¹/₁₆P	⅔P	0.04	12.2
'78	Accord	1P–3P	2P	0–1P	½P	0.04	12.2
'79–'83	Accord Prelude	—	1½P	—	0	0	12.8

①1–2P—'77
　0–1P—'78–'79
②1½—'77
　½—'78–79
③9.3—'77–'79
④½P—'78–79
P—Positive

TUNE-UP PROCEDURES

Spark Plugs

REMOVAL

1. Place a piece of masking tape around each spark plug wire and number it according to its corresponding cylinder.

2. Pull the wires from the spark plugs, grasping the wire by the end of the rubber boot and twisting off.

NOTE: Avoid spark plug removal while the engine is hot. Since the cylinder head spark plug threads are aluminum, the spark plug becomes tight due to the different coefficients of heat expansion. If a plug is too tight to be removed even while the engine is cold, apply a solvent around the plug followed with an application of oil once the solvent has penetrated the threads. Do this only when the engine is cold.

3. Loosen each spark plug with a ¹³/₁₆ in. spark plug socket. When the plug has been loosened a few turns, stop to clean any material from around the spark plug holes. Compressed air is preferred; however, if air is not available, simply use a rag to clean the area.

NOTE: In no case should foreign matter be allowed to enter the cylinders. Severe damage could result.

4. Finish unscrewing the plugs and remove them from the engine.

INSPECTION AND CLEANING

Before attempting to clean and re-gap plugs, be sure that the electrode ends aren't worn or damaged and that the insulators (the white porcelain covering) are not cracked. Replace the plug if this condition exists.

Clean reusable plugs with a plug cleaner

Always use a round wire gauge to check spark plug gap

or a wire brush. The plug gap should be checked and readjusted, if necessary, by bending the ground (side) electrode with a spark plug gapping tool.

NOTE: Plugs removed from a Honda CVCC engine may have more carbon build-up than plugs from conventional engines. This is a normal condition caused by a spark plug igniting the rich mixture supplied to the pre-combustion chamber.

NOTE: Do not use a flat gauge to check plug gap; an incorrect reading will result. Use a wire gauge only.

INSTALLATION

1. Lightly oil the spark plug threads and hand tighten them into the engine.

2. Tighten the plugs securely with a spark plug wrench (about 10–13 ft. lbs. of torque).

—————— CAUTION ——————
Do not overtighten because of the aluminum threads.

3. Reconnect the wires to the plugs, making sure that each is securely fitted.

Breaker Points and Condenser

1979 Accords and all 1980 and later models have electronic ignition, eliminating the breaker points and condenser. No routine maintenance is required.

NOTE: There are two rules that should always be followed when adjusting or replacing points. The points and condenser are a matched set; never replace one without replacing the other. If you change the point gap (or dwell) of the engine, you also change the ignition timing. Therefore, if you adjust the points, you must also adjust the timing.

INSPECTION

1. Disconnect the high-tension wire from the coil.

2. Unfasten the two retaining clips to remove the distributor cap.

3. Remove the rotor from the distributor shaft by pulling it straight up. Examine the condition of the rotor; if it is cracked or the metallic tip is excessively burned, replace it.

4. Pry the breaker points open with a screwdriver and examine the condition of the contact points. If the points are excessively worn, burned, or pitted they should be replaced.

NOTE: Contact points which have been used for several thousand miles will have a gray, rough surface, but this is not necessarily an indication that they are

malfunctioning. The roughness between the points matches so that a large contact area is maintained.

5. If the points are in good condition, polish them with a point file. If the points are to be filed, they should be removed from the distributor to keep the grit from falling into it.

NOTE: Do not use emery cloth or sandpaper as they may leave particles on the points which could cause them to arc.

After polishing the points, refer to the section following the breaker point replacement procedures for proper adjustment. If the points need replacing, refer to the following procedure.

REMOVAL AND INSTALLATION

1. Remove the small nut from the terminal screw located in the side of the distributor housing and remove the nut, screw, condenser wire, and primary wire from the terminal. Remove the terminal from the slot in the distributor housing.

2. Remove the screw(s) which attaches the condenser to the outside of the distributor housing (most models), or to the breaker plate inside the distributor (CVCC Hondamatic models), and remove the condenser.

3. Unscrew the Phillips head screw which holds the ground wire to the breaker point assembly and lift the end of the ground wire out of the way.

4. Remove the two Phillips head screws which attach the point assembly to the breaker plate and remove the point assembly.

NOTE: You should use a magnetic or locking screwdriver. Trying to locate one of these tiny screws after you've dropped it can be an excruciating affair.

Pull straight up to remove the rotor

1. Adjusting screw
2. Hold-down screws
3. Points wire
4. Ground wire

Internal components of the distributor

Rotate the crankshaft pulley with a wrench on the pulley bolt (Civic)

Point set screw removal

5. Wipe all dirt and grease from the distributor plate and cam with a lint-free cloth. Apply a small amount of heat resistant lubricant to the distributor cam. Although the lube is supplied with most breaker point kits, you can buy it at any auto parts store if necessary.

6. Properly position the new points on the breaker plate of the distributor and secure with the two point screws. Attach the ground wire, with its screw, to the breaker plate assembly. Screw the condenser to its proper position on the distributor housing, or breaker plate.

7. Fit the terminal back into its notch in the distributor housing and attach the condenser and primary wires to the terminal screw and fasten with the nut. Adjust the gap using the following procedure.

ADJUSTMENT

With a Feeler Gauge

1. Rotate the crankshaft pulley until the point gap is at its greatest (where the rubbing block is on the high point of the cam lobe). This can be accomplished by using either a remote starter switch or by rotating the crankshaft pulley by hand.

2. At this position, insert the proper sized feeler gauge between the points. A slight drag should be felt. Point gap should be 0.018–0.022 in.

3. If no drag is felt, or if the feeler gauge cannot be inserted, loosen, but do not remove the two breaker point set screws.

4. Adjust the points as follows:
Insert a screwdriver through the hole in the breaker point assembly and into the notch provided on the breaker plate. Twist the screwdriver to open or close the points. When the correct gap has been obtained, retighten the point set screws.

5. Recheck the point gap to be sure that it did not change when the breaker point attaching screws were tightened.

6. Align the rotor with the distributor shaft and push the rotor onto the shaft until it is fully seated.

7. Reinstall the distributor cap and the coil high-tension wire.
Connect a dwell/tachometer, in accordance with its manufacturer's instructions, between the distributor primary lead and a ground.

With the engine warmed up and running at the specified idle speed (see the tune-up chart), take a dwell reading.

If the point dwell is not within specifications, shut the engine off and adjust the point gap, as outlined above.

Adjust the point gap with a flat feeler gauge

Crankshaft pulley bolt access window on left front fender—CVCC models

NOTE: Increasing the point gap decreases the dwell angle and vice versa.

Install the dust cover, rotor, and cap. Check the dwell reading again and adjust it, as required.

Ignition Timing

Honda recommends that the ignition timing be checked at 15,000 mile intervals. Also, the timing should always be adjusted after installing new points or adjusting the dwell angle. On all non-CVCC engines, the timing marks are located on the crankshaft pulley, with a pointer on the timing belt cover; all visible from the driver's side of the engine compartment. On all CVCC engines, the timing marks are located on the flywheel (manual transmission) or torque converter drive plate (automatic transmission), with a pointer on the rear of the cylinder block; all visible from the front right-side of the engine compartment after removing a special rubber access plug in the timing mark window. In all cases, the timing is checked with the engine warmed to operating temperature (176°F), idling in Neutral (manual trans.) or 2nd gear (Hondamatic), and with all vacuum hoses *connected*.

1. Stop the engine, and hook up a tachometer according to the manufacturer's instructions.

CVCC timing mark window

Non-CVCC timing marks. The white notch is TDC

1. Ignition timing mark
2. TDC mark
3. Timing pointer

CVCC timing marks

NOTE: On some models you will have to pull back the rubber ignition coil cover to reveal the terminals.

2. Hook up a timing light to the engine according to the manufacturer's instructions.

3. Make sure that all wires are clear of the cooling fan and hot exhaust manifolds. Start the engine. Check that the idle speed is set to specifications with the transmission in Neutral (manual transmission) or 2nd gear (Hondamatic). If not, adjust as outlined later. At any engine speed other than the specified idle speed, the distributor advance or retard mechanisms will actuate, leading to an erroneous timing adjustment.

— CAUTION —
Make sure that the parking brake is firmly applied and the front wheels blocked to prevent the car from rolling forward when the automatic transmission is engaged.

4. Point the timing light at the timing marks. On non-CVCC cars, align the pointer with the "F" or red notch on the crankshaft pulley. On CVCC cars, align the pointer with the red notch on the flywheel or torque converter drive plate (except on cars where the timing specifications is TDC in which case the "T" or white notch is used).

NOTE: Different colors are used in different years; see the footnotes below the "Tune-up Specifications" Chart for details.

5. If necessary, adjust the timing by loosening the larger distributor hold-down (clamp) bolt and slowly rotate the distributor in the required direction while observing the timing marks.

— CAUTION —
Do not grasp the top of the distributor cap while the engine is running as you might get a nasty shock. Instead, grab the distributor housing to rotate.

After making the necessary adjustment, tighten the hold-down bolt, taking care not to disturb the adjustment.

NOTE: There are actually two bolts which may be loosened to adjust ignition timing. There is a small bolt on the underside of the distributor swivel mounting plate. This smaller bolt should not be loosened unless you cannot obtain a satisfactory adjustment using the upper bolt. Its purpose is to provide an extra range of adjustment, such as in cases where the distributor was removed and then installed one tooth off.

Valve Lash Adjustment

Honda recommends that the valve clearance be checked at 15,000 mile intervals.

NOTE: While all valve adjustments must be as accurate as possible, it is better to have the valve adjustment slightly loose than slightly tight, as burned valves may result from overly tight adjustments.

ALL NON-CVCC MODELS

1. Adjust valves when the engine is cold (100°F or less).
2. Remove the valve cover and align the TDC (Top Dead Center) mark on the crankshaft pulley with the index mark on the timing belt cover. The TDC notch is the one immediately following the red 5° BTDC notch used for setting ignition timing.
3. When No. 1 cylinder is at TDC on the compression stroke, check and adjust the following valves (numbered from the crankshaft pulley end of the engine):
   Intake—Nos. 1 and 2 cylinders
   Exhaust—Nos. 1 and 3 cylinders
   Adjust the valve as follows:
   a. Check valve clearance with a flat feeler gauge between the tip of the rocker arm and the top of the valve. There should be a slight drag on the feeler gauge;
   b. If there is no drag or if the gauge cannot be inserted, loosen the valve adjusting screw locknut;
   c. Turn the adjusting screw with a screwdriver to obtain the proper clearance;
   d. Hold the adjusting screw and tighten the locknut;
   e. Recheck the clearance.
4. Then rotate the crankshaft 360° and adjust:
   Intake—Nos. 3 and 4 cylinders
   Exhaust—Nos. 2 and 4 cylinders

On non-CVCC engines, align the marks on the cam sprocket with the top of the cylinder head.

On all CVCC engines except the 1980 and later Civic, when the camshaft sprocket is in the correct position, the word "UP" will be facing up and the small arrow will point to the sprocket mark. The marks are slightly off in this photo

CVCC MODELS

1. Make sure that the engine is cold (cylinder head temperature below 100°F).

2. Remove the valve cover. From the front of the engine, take a look at the forward face of the camshaft timing belt gear. When No. 1 cylinder is at Top Dead Center (TDC), the word "UP" will be at the top of the gear on all models except the 1980 and later Civics. On these models the cut-away in the pulley will be at the top. You can doublecheck this by distributor rotor position. Take some chalk or crayon and mark where the No. 1 spark plug wire goes into the distributor cap on the distributor body. Then, remove the cap and check that the rotor points toward that mark.

3. With the No. 1 cylinder at TDC, you can adjust the following valves (numbered from the crankshaft pulley end of the engine):

Intake—Nos. 1 and 2 cylinders
Auxiliary Intake—Nos. 1 and 2 cylinders
Exhaust—Nos. 1 and 3 cylinders
Adjust the valve as follows:

a. Check valve clearance with a flat feeler gauge between the tip of the rocker arm and the top of the valve. There should be a slight drag on the feeler gauge;

b. If there is no drag or if the gauge cannot be inserted loosen the valve adjusting screw locknut;

c. Turn the adjusting screw with a

On 1980 and later Civic engines, when the no. 1 piston is set at TDC, the cut-away in the pulley is at the top and the groove on the rear of the pulley is aligned with the top edge of the cylinder head

Valve adjustment—all models

Valve adjustment—CVCC auxiliary valve

Distributor rotor at TDC (#1 cylinder)

screwdriver to obtain the proper clearance;

d. Hold the adjusting screw and tighten the locknut;

e. Recheck the clearance.

4. To adjust the remaining valves, rotate the crankshaft to the No. 4 cylinder TDC position. To get the No. 4 cylinder to the TDC position, rotate the crankshaft 360 degrees. This will correspond to an 180 degree movement of the distributor rotor and camshaft timing gear. The rotor will not be pointing opposite the mark you made for the No. 1 cylinder. The camshaft timing gear "UP" mark or (cut-away) will now be at the bottom (6 o'clock position). At this position, you may adjust the remaining valves:

Intake—Nos. 3 and 4 cylinders

Auxiliary Intake—Nos. 3 and 4 cylinders

Exhaust—Nos. 2 and 4 cylinders

Carburetor

IDLE SPEED AND MIXTURE ADJUSTMENT

NOTE: All carburetor adjustments must be made with the engine fully warmed up to operating temperature (176°F.)

Non-CVCC (1237 cc Engine)

1. The idle speed is adjusted with the headlights on and the radiator cooling fan off. To make sure that the cooling fan stays off while you are making your adjustments, disconnect the fan leads.

NOTE: Do not leave the cooling fan leads disconnected for any longer than necessary, as the engine may overheat.

Manual transmission cars are adjusted with the transmission in Neutral. On Hondamatic cars, the idle adjustments are made with the car in gear "1." As a safety precaution, firmly apply the parking brake and block the front wheels.

2. Remove the plastic limiter cap from the idle mixture screw. Hook up a tachometer to the engine with the positive lead connected to the distributor side (terminal) of the coil and the negative lead to a good ground. On 1976 models, disconnect the breather hose from the valve cover.

3. Start the engine and adjust first the mixture screw (turn counterclockwise to richen), and then the idle speed screw for the best quality idle at 870 rpm (Hondamatic in gear).

4. Then, lean out the idle mixture (turn mixture screw clockwise), until the idle speed drops to the correct idle speed, according to the "Tune-Up Specifications" chart or the emission control decal in the engine compartment.

5. Replace the limiter cap, connect the cooling fan, and disconnect the tachometer.

CVCC with Kelhin 3-bbl

1976–79

1. The idle speed is adjusted with the headlights on and the radiator cooling fan on. With the engine warmed to operating temperature and idling, the cooling fan should come on. But, if it doesn't, you can load the engine's electrical system (for purposes of adjusting the idle speed), by turning the highspeed heater blower on instead. Do not have both the cooling fan and heater blower operating simultaneously, as this will load the engine too much and lower the idle speed abnormally. Manual transmission cars are adjusted with the transmission in Neutral. On Hondamatic cars, the idle adjustments are made with the car in gear "2" (that's right, Hi-gear). As a safety precaution, apply the parking brake and block the front wheels.

2. Remove the plastic cap from the idle mixture screw. Hook up a tachometer to the engine with the positive lead connected to the distributor side (terminal) of the coil and the negative lead to a good ground.

3. Start the engine and rotate the idle mixture screw counterclockwise (rich), until the highest rpm is achieved. Then, adjust the idle speed screw to 910 rpm (manual transmission), or 810 rpm (Hondamatic in Second gear) for the Civic. Adjust the idle to 880 rpm (manual) or 730 rpm (automatic) for the Accord and Prelude.

4. Finally, lean out the idle mixture (turn mixture screw in clockwise), until the idle speed drops to the correct idle speed, according to the "Tune-Up Specifications" chart or the emission control decal in the engine compartment.

5. Replace the limiter cap and disconnect the tachometer.

1. Idle speed screw
2. Idle mixture screw

Idle speed and mixture screws—Keihin 3 bbl carburetor

1980 AND LATER

Changes in the carburetors have made the adjustment of the idle mixture impossible without a propane enrichment system not available to the general public. The idle speed may be adjusted as follows:

1. With the engine at normal operating temperature; remove the vacuum hose from the intake air control diaphragm and clamp the hose end.

2. Connect a tachometer to the engine.

3. With the headlights, heater blower, rear window defroster, cooling fan and air conditioner off, adjust the idle speed by turning the throttle stop screw to the rpm listed in the "Tune-Up Specifications" or underhood sticker.

ENGINE ELECTRICAL

Distributor

REMOVAL AND INSTALLATION

1. Disconnect the high tension and primary lead wires that run from the distributor to the coil.

2. Unsnap the two distributor cap retaining clamps and remove the distributor cap. Position it out of the way.

3. Using chalk or paint, carefully mark the position of the distributor rotor in relation to the distributor housing, and mark the relation of the distributor housing to the engine block. When this is done, you should have a line on the distributor housing directly in line with the tip of the rotor, and another line on the engine block directly in line with the mark on the distributor housing.

NOTE: This aligning procedure is very important because the distributor must be reinstalled in the exact location from which it was removed, if correct ignition timing is to be maintained.

4. Note the position of the vacuum line(s) on the vacuum diaphragm with

Distributor—arrow points to the helical drive gear

masking tape and then disconnect the lines from the vacuum unit.

5. Remove the bolt which attaches the distributor to the engine block or distributor extension housing (CVCC), and remove the distributor from the engine.

— CAUTION —

Do not disturb the engine while the distributor is removed. If you attempt to start the engine with the distributor removed, you will have to retime the engine.

---

6. To install, place the rotor on the distributor shaft and align the tip of the rotor with the line that you made on the distributor housing.

7. With the rotor and housing aligned, insert the distributor into the engine while aligning the mark on the housing with the mark on the block, or extension housing (CVCC).

NOTE: Since the distributor pinion gear has helical teeth, the rotor will turn slightly as the gear on the distributor meshes with the gear on the camshaft. Allow for this when installing the distributor by aligning the mark on the distributor with the mark on the block, but positioning the tip of the rotor slightly to the side of the mark on the distributor.

8. When the distributors is fully seated in the engine, install and tighten the distributor retaining bolt.

9. Align and install the distributor cap and snap the retaining clamps into place.

10. Install the high-tension and primary wires onto the coil.

11. Check the ignition timing.

INSTALLATION WHEN ENGINE HAS BEEN DISTURBED

If the engine was cranked with the distributor removed it will be necessary to retime

the engine. If you have installed the distributor incorrectly and the engine will not start, remove the distributor from the engine and start from scratch.

1. Install the distributor with No. 1 cylinder at the top dead center position on the compression stroke (the "TDC" mark on the crankshaft pulley or flywheel aligned with the index mark on the timing belt cover or crankcase and both intake and exhaust valves closed).

2. Line up the metal end of the rotor head with the protrusion on the distributor housing.

3. Carefully insert the distributor into the cylinder head opening with the attaching plate bolt slot aligned with the distributor mounting hole in the cylinder head. Then secure the plate at the center of the adjusting slot. The rotor head must face No. 1 cylinder.

NOTE: Since the distributor pinion gear has helical teeth, the rotor will turn slightly as the gear on the distributor meshes with the gear on the camshaft. Allow for this when installing the distributor by positioning the tip of the rotor to the side of the protrusion.

4. Inspect and adjust the point gap and ignition timing.

Alternator

PRECAUTIONS

1. Observe the proper polarity of the battery connections by making sure that the positive (+) and negative (−) terminal connections are not reversed. Misconnection will allow current to flow in the reverse direction, resulting in damaged diodes and an overheated wire harness.

2. Never ground or short out any alternator or alternator regulator terminals.

3. Never operate the alternator with any of its or the battery's leads disconnected.

4. Always remove the battery or disconnect its output lead while charging it.

5. Always disconnect the ground cable when replacing any electrical components.

6. Never subject the alternator to excessive heat or dampness if the engine is being steam-cleaned.

7. Never use arc-welding equipment with the alternator connected.

REMOVAL AND INSTALLATION

1. Disconnect the negative (−) battery terminal.

2. Label and unplug the wires from the plugs on the rear of the alternator.

3. Loosen and remove the two alternator mounting bolts and remove the V-belt and alternator assembly.

4. To install, reverse the removal procedure. Adjust the alternator belt tension according to the "Belt Tension Adjustment" section below.

CVCC alternator wiring connections— others similar

BELT TENSION ADJUSTMENT

The initial inspection and adjustment to the alternator drive belt should be performed after the first 3,000 miles or if the alternator has been moved for any reason. Afterwards, you should inspect the belt tension every 12,000 miles. Before adjusting, inspect the belt to see that it is not cracked or worn. Be sure that its surfaces are free of grease and oil.

1. Push down on the belt halfway between pulleys with a force of about 24 lbs. The belt should deflect 0.47–0.67 in. (12–17 mm).

2. If the belt tension requires adjustment, loosen the adjusting link bolt and move the alternator with a pry bar positioned against the front of the alternator housing.

During removal and installation, the rotor will move 30 degrees. Take this into account when positioning the distributor. The illustration shows two typical installations, left is with manual transaxle; right is with automatic transaxle

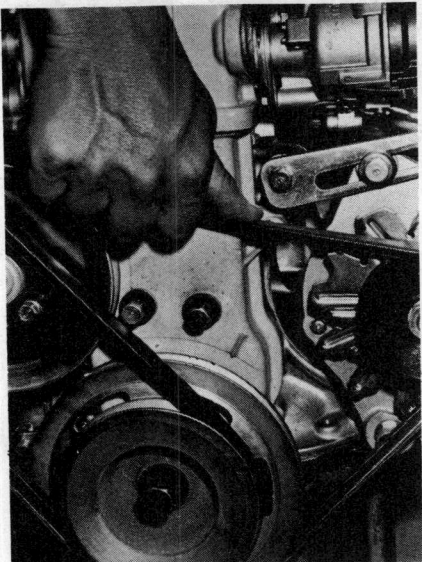

Check belt tension midway between pulleys

3. After obtaining the proper tension, tighten the adjusting link bolt.

Voltage Regulator

REMOVAL AND INSTALLATION

The regulator is inside the engine compartment, attached to the right fender wall just above the battery.

1. Disconnect the negative (−) terminal from the battery.
2. Remove the regulator terminal lead wires.

NOTE: You should label these wires to avoid confusion during installation.

3. Unscrew the two regulator retaining bolts and remove the regulator from the car.
4. To install, reverse the removal procedure.

Starter

REMOVAL AND INSTALLATION

1. Disconnect the ground cable at the battery negative (−) terminal, and the starter motor cable at the positive terminal.
2. Disconnect the starter motor cable at the motor.

Mounting bolts—non-CVCC starter

3. Remove the starter motor by loosening the two attaching bolts. On CVCC models, the bolts attach from opposing ends of the starter.
4. Reverse the removal procedure to install the motor. Be sure to tighten the attaching bolts to 29–36 ft. lbs. and make sure that all wires are securely connected.

STARTER DRIVE REPLACEMENT

All Non-CVCC Civics, and California and High Altitude CVCC Civics

1. Remove the solenoid by loosening and removing the attaching bolts.
2. Remove the two brush holder plate retaining screws from the rear cover. Also pry off the rear dust cover along with the clip and thrust washer(s).
3. Remove the two thru–bolts from the rear cover and lightly tap the rear cover with a mallet to remove it.
4. Remove the four carbon brushes from the brush holder and remove the brush holder.

Removing pinion gear from armature

5. Separate the yoke from the case. The yoke is provided with a hole for positioning, into which the gear case lock pin is inserted.
6. Pull the yoke assembly from the gear case, being sure to carefully detach the shift lever from the pinion.
7. Remove the armature unit from the yoke casing and the field coil.
8. To remove the pinion gear from the armature, first set the armature on end with the pinion end facing upward and pull the clutch stop collar downward toward the pinion. Then remove the pinion stop clip and pull the pinion stop and gears from the armature shaft as a unit.
9. To assemble and install the starter motor, reverse the disassembly and removal procedures. Be sure to install new clips, and be careful of the installation direction of the shift lever.

Reduction Gear Type

A reduction gear starter is used on the Prelude, Accord and the 49 States CVCC Civics.

1. Remove the solenoid end cover. Pull out the solenoid. There is a spring on the shaft and a steel ball at the end of the shaft.
2. Remove the through bolts retaining the end frame to the motor and solenoid housing.
3. Remove the end frame. The overrunning clutch assembly complete with drive

Exploded view of CVCC starter

Rear mounting bolt—CVCC starter

gear can be removed. The idler and motor pinion gears can be removed separately. The idler gear retains five steel roller bearings.

4. The clutch assembly is held together by a circlip. Push down on the gear against the spring inside the clutch assembly and remove the circlip with a circlip expander. Slide the stopper ring, gear, spring, and washer out of the clutch assembly.

5. Assembly is the reverse. The stopper ring is installed with the smaller end with the lip towards the clutch. Be sure that the steel ball is in place at the end of the solenoid shaft. Grease all sliding surfaces of the solenoid before reassembly.

ENGINE MECHANICAL

Engine

REMOVAL AND INSTALLATION

— **CAUTION** —

If any repair operation requires the removal of a component of the air conditioning system (on vehicles so equipped), do not disconnect the refrigerant lines. If it is impossible to move the component out of the way with the lines attached, have the air conditioning system evacuated by a trained serviceman. The air conditioning system contains freon under pressure. This gas can be very dangerous. Therefore, under no circumstances should an untrained person attempt to disconnect the air-conditioner refrigerant lines.

1237 cc Models

1. Raise the front of the car and support it with safety stands.
2. Remove the front wheels.
3. Drain the engine, transmission, and radiator.
4. Remove the front turn signal lights (through 1977) and grille.
5. Remove the hood support bolts and the hood. Remove the fan shroud, if so equipped.
6. Remove the air cleaner case, and air intake pipe at the air cleaner.
7. Disconnect the battery and engine ground cables at the battery and the valve cover.
8. Disconnect the hose from the fuel vapor storage canister at the carburetor.
9. Disconnect the fuel line at the fuel pump.

NOTE: Plug the line so that gas does not siphon from the tank.

10. Disconnect the lower coolant hose

Speedometer cable removal

at the water pump connecting tube and the upper hose at the thermostat cover.

11. Disconnect the following control cables and wires from the engine:

a. Throttle and choke cables at the carburetor;

b. Clutch cable at the release arm;

c. Ignition coil wires at the distributor;

d. Starter motor positive battery cable connection and solenoid wire;

e. Back-up light switch and T.C.S. (Transmission Control Spark) switch wires from the transmission casing;

f. Speedometer and tachometer cables;

— **CAUTION** —

When removing the speedometer cable from the transmission, it is not necessary to remove the entire cable holder. Remove the end boot (gear holder seal) and the cable retaining clip and then pull the cable out of the holder. Do not disturb the holder unless it is absolutely necessary.

The holder consists of three pieces: the holder, collar, and a dowel pin. The dowel pin indexes the holder and collar and is held in place by the bolt that retains the holder. If the bolt is removed and the holder rotated, the dowel pin can fall into the transmission case, necessitating transmission disassembly to remove the pin. To insure that this does not happen when the holder must be removed, do not rotate the holder more than 30° in either direction when removing it. Once removed, make sure that the pin is still in place. Use the same precaution when installing the holder.

g. Alternator wire and wire harness connector;

h. The wires from both water temperature thermal switches on the intake manifold;

i. Cooling fan connector and radiator thermoswitch wires;

j. Oil pressure sensor;

k. Vacuum hose to throttle opener at opener, and vacuum hose from carburetor insulator to throttle opener;

l. By-pass valve assembly and bracket.

NOTE: It would be a good idea to tag all of these wires to avoid confusion during installation.

12. Disconnect the heater hose by removing the "H" connector from the two hoses in the firewall.

13. Remove the engine torque rod from the engine and firewall.

14. Remove the starter motor.

15. Remove the radiator from the engine compartment.

16. Remove the exhaust pipe-to-manifold clamp.

17. Remove the exhaust pipe flange nuts and lower the exhaust pipe.

18. Disconnect the left and right lower control arm ball joints at the knuckle, using a ball joint remover (or special tool 07941-6340000).

Driving out gearshift rod pin

19. Hold the brake disc and pull the right and left drive shafts out of the differential case.

20a. Manual transmission only: Drive out the gearshift rod pin (8 mm) with a drift and disconnect the rod at the transmission case.

NOTE: Do not disconnect the shift lever end of the gearshift rod and extension.

20b. Hondamatic only: Disconnect shift cable at console and cooler line at transmission.

21. Disconnect the gearshift extension at the engine (man. trans. only).

22. Screw in two engine hanger bolts in the torque rod belt hole and the bolt hole just to the left of the distributor. Then, engage the lifting chain hooks to the hanger bolts and lift the engine just enough to take the load off the engine mounts.

Center mount nuts

23. After being sure that the engine is properly supported, remove the two center mount bracket nuts.

24. Remove the left engine mount.

25. Lift the engine out slowly, taking care not to allow the engine to damage other parts of the car.

26. To install, reverse the removal procedure. Pay special attention to the following points:

a. Lower the engine into position and install the left mount. Do not attach mounting bolts at this time.

b. Align the center mount studs with the beam and tighten the nuts and washer several turns (just enough to support the beam).

c. Lower the engine so it rests on the lower mount. Torque the lower mount nuts to 7–12 ft. lbs.;

d. Use a new shift rod pin;

e. After installing the driveshafts, attempt to move the inner joint housing in and out of the differential housing. If it moves easily, the driveshaft end clips should be replaced;

f. Make sure that the control cables and wires are connected properly;

g. When connecting the heater hoses, the upper hose goes to the water pump connecting pipe and the lower hose to the intake manifold;

h. Refill the engine, transmission, and radiator with their respective fluids to the proper levels;

i. On Hondamatic cars, check shift cable adjustment.

1335 and 1487 cc Civic CVCC

1. Raise the front of the car and support it with jackstands. On models through 1979, remove both front wheels.

2. Disconnect the battery and on 1980 and later models, remove the battery, hold-down equipment, tray and mount.

3. Remove the headlight rim attaching screws and the rims.

4. Open the hood. Disconnect both parking light connectors; remove the parking light retaining bolts and backing plate and remove the parking lights, through 1977 only.

5. Remove the lower grill molding and remove the six grille retaining bolts and the grille.

6. Disconnect the windshield washer hose and remove it from the underside of the hood.

7. Remove the upper torque (engine locating) arm.

8. Disconnect the vacuum hose at the power brake booster, thermosensors "A" and "B" at their wiring connectors, and the coolant temperature gauge sending unit wire.

9. Drain the radiator. After all coolant has drained, install the drain bolt finger tight.

10. Disconnect all four coolant hoses. Disconnect cooling fan motor connector and the temperature sensor. Remove the radiator hose to the overflow tank.

11. On Hondamatic cars only, remove both ATF cooler line bolts.

NOTE: Save the washers from the cooler line banjo connectors and replace if damaged.

12. Remove the radiator.

13. Label and disconnect the starter motor wires. Remove the two starters mounting bolts (one from each end of the starter), and remove the starter.

14. Label and disconnect the spark plug wires at the plug. Remove the distributor cap and scribe the position of the rotor on the side of the distributor housing. Remove the top distributor swivel bolt and remove the distributor (the rotor will rotate 30° because the drive gear is beveled).

15. On manual transmission cars, remove the C-clip retaining the clutch cable at the firewall. Then, remove the end of the clutch cable from the clutch release arm and bracket. First, pull up on the cable, and then push it out to release it from the bracket. Remove the end from the release arm.

16. Disconnect the back-up light switch wires. Disconnect the control valve vacuum hose, the air intake hose, and the preheat air intake hose. Disconnect the air bleed valve hose from the air cleaner. Label and disconnect all remaining vacuum hoses from the underside of the air cleaner. Remove the air cleaner.

17. Label and disconnect all remaining emission control vacuum hoses from the engine. Disconnect the emission box wiring connector and remove the black emission box from the firewall.

18. Remove the engine mount heat shield.

19. Disconnect the engine-to-body ground strap at the valve cover.

20. Disconnect the alternator wiring connector and oil pressure sensor leads.

21. Disconnect the vacuum hose from the start control and electrical leads to both cut-off solenoid leads.

22. Disconnect the vacuum hose from the charcoal canister and both fuel lines to the carburetor. Mark the adjustment and disconnect the choke and throttle cables at the carburetor.

23. On Hondamatic cars only, remove the center console and disconnect the gear selector control cable at the console. This may be accomplished after removing the retaining clip and pin.

24. Drain the transmission oil.

CAUTION

On cars with air conditioning, be sure to use the following procedure.

a. Disconnect the heater hose with the heater valve cable attached.

b. Remove the compressor belt cover, then loosen the adjusting nut.

c. Loosen the belt on the compressor hose bracket at the radiator.

d. Remove the compressor mounting bolt then lift the compressor out of the bracket with the hoses attached and wire it up to the firewall.

NOTE: The system does not have to be discharged.

e. Remove the compressor bracket (5 bolts).

25. Remove the fender well shield under the right fender, exposing the speedometer drive cable. Remove the set screw securing the speedometer drive holder. Then, slowly pull the cable assembly out of the transmission, taking care not to drop the pin or drive gear. Finally, remove the pin, collar, and drive gear from the cable assembly.

26. Disconnect the front suspension stabilizer bar from its mounts on both sides. Also, remove the bolt retaining the lower control arm to the subframe on both sides.

27. Remove the forward mounting nut on the radius rod on both sides. Then, pry the constant velocity joint out about ½ in. and pull the stub axle out of the transmission case. Repeat for other side.

28. Remove the six retaining bolts and remove the center beam.

29. On manual transmission cars only, drive out the pin retaining the shift linkage.

30. Disconnect the lower torque arm from the transmission.

31. On Hondamatic cars only, remove the bolt retaining the control cable stay at the transmission. Loosen the two U-bolt

nuts and pull the cable out of its housing.

32. Disconnect the exhaust pipe at the manifold. Disconnect the retaining clamp also.

33. Remove the rear engine mount nut.

34. Attach a chain pulley hoist to the engine. Honda recommends using the threaded bolt holes at the extreme right and left ends of the cylinder head (with special hardened bolts) as lifting points, as opposed to wrapping a chain around the entire block and risk damaging some components such as the carburetor, etc.

35. Raise the engine enough to place a slight tension on the chain. Remove the nut retaining the front engine mount. Then, remove the three bolts retaining the front mount. While lifting the engine, remove the mount.

36. Remove the three retaining bolts and push the left engine support into its shock mount bracket to the limit of its travel.

37. Slowly raise the engine out of the vehicle.

Accord 1600 and Accord and Prelude 1751

1. Disconnect the negative battery terminal.

2. Drain the radiator of coolant, and drain the engine and transmission oil.

3. Jack up the front of the car and remove the front wheels. Be sure to support the car with safety stands.

4. Remove the air cleaner.

5. Remove the following wires and hoses:

a. The coil wire and the ignition primary wire from the distributor.

b. The engine subharness and the starter wires. (Mark the wires before removal to ease installation.)

c. The vacuum tube from the brake booster.

d. On Hondamatic models, remove the ATF cooler hose from the transmission.

e. The engine ground cable.

f. Alternator wiring harness.

g. Carburetor solenoid valve connector.

h. Carburetor fuel line.

i. On 1981–82 models with California and high altitude disconnect the hoses at the air controller.

6. Remove the choke and throttle cables.

7. Remove the radiator and heater hoses.

Accord component removal points

Emission control box

Accord driveshaft removal

1. Temperature
2. Thermosensor A
3. Thermosensor B

CVCC sending unit locations

Accord engine removal

8. Remove the emission control "black box."

9. Remove the clutch slave cylinder with the hydraulic line attached.

10. Remove the speedometer cable. Pull the wire clip from the housing, and remove the cable from the housing. Do not, under any circumstances, remove the housing from the transmission.

11. Attach an engine hoist to the engine block, and raise the engine just enough to remove the slack from the chain.

12. Disconnect the right and left lower ball joints, and the tie rod ends. You will need a ball joint remover tool for this operation. An alternative method is to leave the ball joints connected, and remove the lower control arm inner bolts, and the radius rods from the lower control arms.

13. Remove the driveshafts from the transmission by prying the snap-ring off the groove in the end of the shaft. Then, pull the shaft out by holding the knuckle.

14. Remove the center engine mount.

15. Remove the shift rod positioner from the transmission case.

16. Drive out the pin from the shift rod using a small pin driver.

17. On Hondamatics, remove the control cable.

18. Disconnect the exhaust pipe.

19. Remove the three engine support bolts and push the left engine support into the shock mount bracket.

20. Remove the front and rear engine mounts.

21. Raise the engine carefully and remove it from the car.

22. Install the engine in the reverse order of removal, making the following checks:

   a. Make sure that the clip at the end of the driveshaft seats in the groove in the differential. *Failure to do so may lead to the wheels falling off.*

   b. Bleed the air from the cooling system.

   c. Adjust the throttle and choke cable tension.

   d. Check the clutch for the correct free play.

   e. Make sure that the transmission shifts properly.

Cylinder Head

REMOVAL AND INSTALLATION

NOTE: You will need a 12 point socket to remove and install the head bolts on the CVCC engine.

Removal Precautions

1. To prevent warping, the cylinder head should be removed when the engine is cold.

2. Remove oil, scale or carbon deposits accumulated from each part. When decarbonizing take care not to score or scratch the mating surfaces.

3. After washing the oil holes or orifices in each part, make sure they are not restricted by blowing out with compressed air.

4. If parts will not be reinstalled immediately after washing, spray parts with a rust preventive to protect from corrosion.

All Except Accord and Prelude 1751 cc

NOTE: If the engine has already been removed from the car, begin with Step 12 in the following procedure.

1. Remove the turn signals, grille, and hood (Civic through 1977 only). Disconnect the negative battery cable.

2. Drain the radiator.

3. Disconnect the upper radiator hose at the thermostat cover.

   a. On CVCC models, remove distributor cap, ignition wires and primary wire. Also, loosen the alternator bracket and remove the upper mounting bolt from the cylinder head.

   b. On CVCC models with A/C, remove the compressor drive belt cover, then loosen the drive belt adjusting nut. Remove the compressor mounting bolts and move the compressor to one side without discharging it. Remove the compressor bracket.

4. Remove the air cleaner case.

5. Disconnect the tube running between the canister and carburetor at the canister.

6. Disconnect the throttle and choke control cables. Label and disconnect all vacuum hoses.

7. Disconnect the heater hose at the intake manifold.

8. Disconnect the wires from both thermoswitches.

9. Disconnect the fuel line.

   a. On CVCC models, disconnect the temperature gauge sending unit wire, idle cut-off solenoid valve, and primary/main cut-off solenoid valve.

10. Disconnect the engine torque rod.

11. Disconnect the exhaust pipe at the exhaust manifold.

12. Remove the valve cover bolts and the valve cover.

13. Remove the two timing belt upper cover bolts and the cover.

14. Bring No. 1 piston to top dead center. Do this by aligning the notch next to the red notch you use for setting ignition timing, with the index mark on the timing belt cover (1237 cc) or rear of engine block (CVCC).

15. Loosen, but do not remove, the timing belt adjustment bolt and pivot bolt.

16. On 1237 cc models only, remove the camshaft pulley bolt. Do not let the woodruff key fall inside the timing cover. Re-

ROCKER ARM SHAFTS

EXHAUST VALVE

INTAKE VALVE

CAMSHAFT

OIL PUMP DRIVE GEAR

ENGINE BLOCK

EXHAUST MANIFOLD

INTAKE MANIFOLD

CAM SPROCKET

CYLINDER HEAD

UPPER BELT COVER

Exploded view of the 1237 cc engine

move the pulley with a pulley remover (or special tool 07935-6110000).

—— **CAUTION** ——
Use care when handling the timing belt. Do not use sharp instruments to remove the belt. Do not get oil or grease on the belt. Do not bend or twist the belt more than 90°.

17. On 1237 cc models only, remove the fuel pump and distributor.

18. On 1237 cc models only, remove the oil pump gear holder and remove the pump gear and shaft.

19. Loosen and remove the cylinder head bolts in the *reverse* order given in the head bolt tightening sequence diagram shown under the torque specifications chart. The

number one bolt is hidden underneath the oil pump. On CVCC engines, to prevent warpage, unscrew the bolts ⅓ turn each time and repeat sequence until loose.

20. Remove the cylinder head with the carburetor and manifolds attached.

21. Remove the intake and exhaust manifolds from the cylinder heads.

CVCC cylinder head components

Hidden bolt next to the oil pump gear

NOTE: After removing the cylinder head, cover the engine with a clean cloth to prevent materials from getting into the cylinders.

22. To install, reverse the removal procedure, being sure to pay attention to the following points:

a. Be sure that No. 1 cylinder is at top dead center before positioning the cylinder head in place;

b. Use a new head gasket and make sure the head, engine block, and gasket are clean.

c. The cylinder head aligning dowel pins should be in their proper place in the block before installing the cylinder head;

d. Tighten the head bolts in three progressive steps to the proper torque according to the diagram. On the 1335 and 1487 cc engine, tighten the head bolts in two steps. First to 22 ft. lbs. in sequence then to 43 ft. lbs. in the same sequence;

e. After the head bolts have been tightened, install the woodruff key and camshaft pulley (if removed), and tighten the pulley bolt according to specification. On the 1237 cc and the 1335 cc engine, align the marks on the camshaft pulley so they are parallel with the top of the head and the woodruff key or cutout is facing up; on the 1487 engine, the word "UP" or cut out should be facing upward and the mark on the cam sprocket should be aligned with the arrow on the cylinder head;

f. After installing the pulley (if removed), install the timing belt. Be careful not to disturb the timing position already set when installing the belt.

Accord and Prelude 1751 cc

— **CAUTION** —
Cylinder head temperature must be below 100°F.

1. Disconnect the battery ground cable.

Timing belt pivot and adjustment bolts

Remove the non-CVCC camshaft sprocket with the woodruff key facing up

VALVE KEYS AND RETAINER

VALVE SPRINGS

SPRING SEAT

VALVE GUIDE SEAL

VALVE GUIDE

VALVE HOLDER NUT

AUXILIARY VALVE HOLDER

AUXILIARY VALVE

CHAMBER COLLAR

CYLINDER HEAD

EXHAUST VALVE   INTAKE VALVE

CVCC cylinder head and valve train

belt. Disconnect the hoses and plug the hoses and fitting to prevent contamination. Remove the pump mounting bolt and swing the pump to the right side of the engine.

11. On cars without A/C, remove the bolt holding the alternator bracket to the head. Loosen the adjustment bolt.

12. On cars with A/C, remove the alternator and bracket from the car.

13. Disconnect the brake booster vacuum hose at the one-way valve.

14. Remove the valve cover and timing bolt upper cover.

15. Loosen the timing belt pivot and adjust bolts and slide the belt off the pulley.

16. Remove the oil pump gear cover and pull the oil pump shaft out of the head.

17. Remove the head bolts in sequence working from the ends, across the head, toward the center. This is the reverse of the tightening sequence. To prevent warpage, unscrew the bolts ⅓ turn each time and repeat the sequence until loose.

18. Carefully lift the head from the block.

19. Thoroughly clean the mating surfaces to the head and block.

20. Always use a new gasket.

21. Install the head in reverse order of the removal procedure. Make sure the head dowel pins are aligned. Make sure that the UP mark on the timing belt pulley is at the top. Torque the cylinder head bolts in two equal steps. Tighten all bolts to 22 ft. lbs. in sequence, then to 43 ft. lbs. in the final step.

Camshaft and Rocker Shafts

REMOVAL AND INSTALLATION

NOTE: To facilitate installation, make sure that No. 1 piston is at Top Dead Center before removal of camshaft.

1. Follow the "Cylinder Head" removal procedure before attempting to remove the camshaft.

2. Loosen the camshaft and rocker arm shaft holder bolts in a crisscross pattern, beginning on the outside holder.

3. Remove the rocker arms, shafts, and holders as an assembly.

2. Drain the cooling system.

3. Remove the air cleaner, tagging all hoses for installation.

4. Disconnect the wires from the thermosenser temperature gauge sending unit, idle cut-off solenoid valve, primary/main cut-off solenoid valve, and the automatic choke.

5. Disconnect the fuel lines and throttle cable from the carburetor.

6. Tag all emission hoses going to the carburetor then remove them and the carburetor.

7. Disconnect all wires and hoses from the distributor, tagging them for installation, and remove the distributor.

8. Remove all coolant hoses from the head.

9. Disconnect the hot air ducts and head pipe from the head. Loosen the exhaust

manifold-to-engine bracket bolts to ease assembly.

10. If equipped with power steering, loosen the adjustment bolt and remove the

CVCC rocker arm assembly

4. Lift out the camshaft and right head seal (or tachometer body if equipped).

5. To install, reverse the removal procedure, being sure to install the holder bolts in the reverse order of removal.

NOTE: Back off valve adjusting screws before installing rockers. Then adjust valves as outlined earlier.

Valves and Valve Guides

REMOVAL AND INSTALLATION

1. Using a valve spring compressor, remove the valve keepers, retainers, springs, and seats. Then remove the valves.

2. Remove the valve guides with a hammer and a valve guide driver. Drive the guides out from the combustion chamber side.

NOTE: On aluminum alloy heads, an application of heat (approx. 200°F) may be necessary before the valve guides will be "loose" enough to drive out.

3. Use the guide driver and a hammer to press the valve back into the head.

4. After installing a valve guide, use a valve guide reamer to obtain a proper valve stem fit. Use the reamer with an in-out motion while rotating. For the finished dimension of the valve guide, check the "Valve Specifications" chart.

NOTE: Do not forget to install valve guide seals.

Intake Manifold

REMOVAL AND INSTALLATION

Non-CVCC

1. Drain the radiator.
2. Remove the air cleaner and case.
3. Remove the carburetor from the intake manifold.
4. Remove the emission control hoses from the manifold T-joint. One hose leads to the condensation chamber and the other leads to the charcoal canister.
5. Remove the hose connected to the intake manifold directly above the T-joint and underneath the carburetor, leading to the air cleaner check valve.
6. Remove the thermo-switch wires from the switches.
7. Remove the solenoid valve located next to the thermo-switch.
8. Remove the six (6) intake manifold attaching nuts in a crisscross pattern, beginning from the center and moving out to both ends. Then remove the manifold.
9. Clean all old gasket material from the manifold and the cylinder head.

10. If the intake manifold is to be replaced, transfer all necessary components to the new manifold.

11. To install, reverse the removal procedure, being sure to observe the following points:

    a. Apply a water-resistant sealer to the new intake manifold gasket before positioning it in place;

    b. Be sure all hoses are properly connected;

    c. Tighten the manifold attaching nuts in the reverse order of removal.

Exhaust Manifold

REMOVAL AND INSTALLATION

Non-CVCC

——————— **CAUTION** ———————
Do not perform this operation on a warm or hot engine.

1. Remove the front grille.
2. Remove the three (3) exhaust pipe-to-manifold nuts and disconnect the exhaust pipe at the manifold.

    a. Disconnect the air injection tubes from the exhaust manifold and remove the air injection manifold.

3. Remove the hot air cover, held by two bolts, from the exhaust manifold.
4. Remove the eight (8) manifold attaching nuts in a crisscross pattern starting from the center, and remove the manifold.
5. To install, reverse the removal procedure. Be sure to use new gaskets and be sure to tighten the manifold bolts in the reverse order of removal to the proper tightening torque.

Intake and Exhaust Manifold

REMOVAL AND INSTALLATION

CVCC Models

1. Drain the radiator. Disconnect manifold coolant hoses.
2. Remove the air cleaner assembly.
3. Label and disconnect all emission control vacuum hoses and electrical leads.
4. Disconnect the fuel lines, throttle, and choke linkage.
5. Remove the carburetor from the intake manifold.
6. Remove the upper heat shield. Loosen, but do not remove the four bolts retaining the intake manifold to the exhaust manifold.
7. Disconnect the exhaust pipe from the exhaust manifold.
8. Remove the nuts retaining the intake and exhaust manifolds to the cylinder head.

The two manifolds are removed as a unit.

9. Reverse the above procedure to install, using new gaskets. The thick washers used beneath the cylinder head-to-manifold retaining nuts must be installed with the dished (concave), side toward the engine. Tighten in sequence shown to specifications given in the Torque Specifications chart. Readjust the choke and throttle linkage and bleed the cooling system.

When installing the CVCC combination manifold, tighten the four bolts after the manifolds have been installed to avoid cracking the manifold ears

Intake manifold torque sequence—1976–79 1487 cc, 1979 1751 cc, 1980 1751 cc (Exc. Calif.) and 1980 1335 cc engines.

Intake manifold torque sequence—1980 and later 1487 cc, 1981 and later 1335 cc and 1980 1751 cc (Calif.), 1981 all 1751 cc engines

Intake manifold torque sequence—1982 and later 1751 cc engines

Timing Gear Cover

REMOVAL AND INSTALLATION

1. Align the crankshaft pulley (1237 cc), or flywheel pointer (CVCC), at Top Dead Center (TDC).

2. Remove the two bolts which hold the timing belt upper cover and remove the cover.

3. Loosen the alternator and air pump (if so equipped), and remove the pulley belt(s).

4. Remove the three water pump pulley bolts and the water pump pulley.

5. Remove the crankshaft pulley attaching bolt. Use a two-jawed puller to remove the crankshaft pulley.

NOTE: The crankshaft bolt cannot be reused. It must be replaced whenever removed.

6. Remove the timing gear cover retaining bolts and the timing gear cover.

7. To install, reverse the removal procedure. Make sure that the timing guide plates, pulleys and front oil seal are properly installed on the crankshaft and before replacing the cover.

Timing Belt and Tensioner

REMOVAL AND INSTALLATION

1. Turn the crankshaft pulley until it is at Top Dead Center of the compression stroke. This can be determined by observing the valves (all closed) or by feeling for pressure in the sparkplug hole (with your thumb or a compression gauge) as the engine is turned.

2. Remove the pulley belt, water pump

Remove the washers behind the tensioner and adjuster bolts to allow removal of the cover without removing the bolts.

pulley, crankshaft pulley, and timing gear cover. Mark the direction of timing belt rotation.

3. Loosen, *but do not remove*, the tensioner adjusting bolt and pivot bolt.

4. Slide the timing belt off the camshaft timing sprocket and the crankshaft pulley sprocket and remove it from the engine.

5. To remove the camshaft timing sprocket, first remove the center bolt and then remove the sprocket with a pulley remover or a brass hammer. This can be accomplished by simply removing the timing belt upper cover, loosening the tensioner bolts, and sliding the timing belt off to expose the sprocket for removal.

NOTE: If you remove the timing sprocket with the timing belt cover in place, be sure not to let the woodruff key fall inside the timing cover when removing the sprocket from the camshaft.

Inspect the timing belt. Replace if over 10,000 miles old, if oil soaked (find source of oil leak also), or if worn on leading edges of belt teeth.

6. To install, reverse the removal procedure. Be sure to install the crankshaft and camshaft timing sprockets in the top dead center position. (See "Cylinder Head Removal" for further details.) On the non-CVCC engine, align the marks on the camshaft timing gear so they are parallel with the top of the cylinder head and the Woodruff key is facing up.

When installing the timing belt, do not allow oil to come in contact with the belt. Oil will cause the rubber to swell. Be careful not to bend or twist the belt unnecessarily, since it is made of fiberglass; nor should you use tools having sharp edges when installing or removing the belt. Be sure to install the belt with the arrow facing in the same direction it was facing during removal.

Belt adjustment (lower) and pivot (upper) bolts

Non CVCC engine timing bolt installation. The crankshaft key is straight up and the cam sprocket marks are parallel with the cylinder head

After installing the timing belt, adjust the belt tension by first rotating the crankshaft counterclockwise ¼ turn. Then, retighten the adjusting bolt and finally the tensioner pivot bolt.

— CAUTION —

Do not remove the adjusting or pivot bolts, only loosen them. When adjusting, do not use any force other than the adjuster spring. If the belt is too tight, it will result in a shortened belt life.

Pistons and Connecting Rods

REMOVAL AND INSTALLATION

For removal with the engine out of the car, begin with Step 8.

1. Remove the turn signals (Civic through 1977), grille, and engine hood.

2. Drain the radiator.

3. Drain the engine oil.

4. Raise the front of the car and support it with safety stands.

5. Attach a chain to the clutch cable bracket on the transmission case and raise just enough to take the load off the center mount.

NOTE: Do not remove the left engine mount.

6. Remove the center beam and engine lower mount.

7. Remove the cylinder head (see

PISTON RINGS

PISTON

PISTON PIN

CONNECTING ROD

CONNECTING ROD BEARING

CYLINDER BLOCK

CONNECTING ROD BEARING AND CAP

CVCC engine block and piston

"Cylinder Head Removal and Installation").

8. Loosen the oil pan bolts and remove the oil pan and flywheel dust shield. Loosen the oil pan bolts in a criss-cross pattern beginning with the outside bolt.

To remove the oil pan, lightly tap the corners of the oil pan with a mallet. It is

not necessary to remove the gasket unless it is damaged.

CAUTION

Do not pry the oil pan off with the tip of a screwdriver.

9. Remove the oil passage block and the oil pump assembly.

CAUTION

As soon as the oil passage block bolts are loosened, the oil in the oil line may flow out.

NOTE: Before removing the pistons, check the top of the cylinder bore for

carbon build-up or a ridge. Remove the carbon or use a ridge-reamer to remove the ridge before removing the pistons.

10. Working from the underside of the car, remove the connecting rod bearing caps. Using the wooden handle of a hammer, push the pistons and connecting rods out of the cylinders.

NOTE: Bearing caps, bearings, and pistons should be marked to indicate their location for reassembly.

11. When removing the piston rings, be sure not to apply excessive force as the rings are made of cast iron and can be easily broken.

NOTE: A hydraulic press is necessary for removing the piston pin.

12. Observe the following points when installing the piston rings:
   a. When installing the three-piece oil ring, first place the spacer and then the rails in position. The spacer and rail gaps must be staggered 0.787–1.181 in. (2–3 cm);
   b. Install the second and top rings on the piston with their markings facing upward;
   c. After installing all rings on the piston, rotate them to be sure they move smoothly without signs of binding;
   d. The ring gaps must be staggered 120° and must NOT be in the direction of the piston pin boss or at right angles to the pin. The gap of the three-piece oil ring refers to that of the middle spacer.

Mark the pistons and rods if they are not marked from the factory

NOTE: Pistons and rings are also available in four oversizes, 0.010 in. (0.25 mm), 0.020 in. (0.50 mm), 0.030 in. (0.75 mm), and 0.040 in. (1.00 mm).

13. Using a ring compressor, install the piston into the cylinder with the skirt protruding about ⅓ of the piston height below the ring compressor. Prior to installation, apply a thin coat of oil to the rings and to the cylinder wall.

NOTE: When installing the piston, the connecting rod oil jet hole or the mark on the piston crown faces the intake manifold.

14. Using the wooden handle of a hammer, slowly press the piston into the cylinder. Guide the connecting rod so it does not damage the crankshaft journals.

15. Reassemble the remaining components in the reverse order of removal. Install the connecting rod bearing caps so that the recess in the cap and the recess in the rod are on the same side. After tightening the cap bolts, move the rod back and forth on the journal to check for binding.

ENGINE LUBRICATION

Oil Pan

REMOVAL AND INSTALLATION

1. Drain the engine oil.
2. Raise the front of the car and support it with safety stands.
3. Attach a chain to a bracket on the transmission case and raise just enough to take the load off the center mount.

NOTE: Do not remove the left engine mount.

4. Remove the center beam and engine lower mount.
5. Loosen the oil bolts and remove the oil pan flywheel dust shield.

NOTE: Loosen the bolts in a criss-cross pattern beginning with the outside bolt. To remove the oil pan, lightly tap the corners of the oil pan with a mallet. It is not necessary to remove the gasket unless it is damaged.

6. To install, reverse the removal procedure. Apply a coat of sealant to the entire mating surface of the cylinder block, except the crankshaft oil seal, before fitting the oil pan. Tighten the bolts in a circular sequence, beginning in the center and working out towards the ends.

Rear Main Oil Seal

REPLACEMENT

The rear oil seal is installed in the rear main bearing cap. Replacement of the seal requires the removal of the transmission, flywheel and clutch housing, as well as the oil pan. Refer to the appropriate sections for the removal and installation of the above components. Both the front and rear main seal are installed after the crankshaft bearing caps have been torqued, if the crankshaft has been removed. Special drivers must be used.

Driving in the rear main seal

Oil Pump

REMOVAL AND INSTALLATION

To remove the oil pump, follow the procedure given for oil pan removal and installation. After the oil pan has been dropped, simply unbolt the oil passage block and oil pump assembly from the engine. Remove the oil pump screen to find the last bolt. When installing the pump, tighten the bolts to no more than 8 ft. lbs.

OVERHAUL

1. Check the rotor radial clearance on both the upper and lower rotors. Clearance is 0.006–0.008 in.
2. Check body-to-rotor clearance on both rotors. Clearance is 0.004–0.007 new, with 0.008 in. as the service limit.
3. Check the rotor end-play between the rotor face and the gasket surface, gasket installed. End-play should be 0.001–0.004 in. new, with a service limit of 0.006 in. Use a straightedge and feeler gauge for this check.
4. If rotors should require replacement, inner and outer rotors on both upper and lower halves, are installed with the punch marks aligned adjacent to one another.

Oil pump removal; there is a bolt under the screen

Oil pump retaining bolt under screen

Use a soft mallet when installing the oil pump screen

OIL PUMP SPECIFICATIONS
(In.)

Description	Non-CVCC Engine	CVCC Engine
Rotor radial clearance		
New	.0059	.002–.006
Service limit	.0079	.008
Body-to-rotor radial clearance		
New	.0039–.0071	.004–.007
Service limit	.0079	.008
Body-to rotor axial clearance		
New	.0012–.0039	.001–.004
Service limit	.0059	.006

ENGINE COOLING

Radiator

REMOVAL AND INSTALLATION

NOTE: When removing the radiator, take care not to damage the core and fins.

1. Drain the radiator.
2. Disconnect the thermo-switch wire and the fan motor wire. Remove the fan shroud, if so equipped.
3. Disconnect the upper coolant hose at the upper radiator tank and the lower hose at the water pump connecting pipe. Disconnect and plug the Hondamatic cooling lines at the bottom of the radiator, if so equipped.
4. Remove the turn signals (Civics through 1977) and front grille.
5. Detach the radiator mounting bolts and remove the radiator with the fan attached. The fan can be easily unbolted from the back of the radiator.
6. To install, reverse the removal procedure. Bleed the cooling system.

Water Pump

REMOVAL AND INSTALLATION

1. Drain the radiator.
2. On 1237 cc cars only, loosen the alternator bolts. Move the alternator toward the cylinder block and remove the drive belt.
3. Loosen the pump mounting bolts and

Cooling system bleed bolt

Thermostat housing and coolant bleed bolt, non-CVCC

Thermostat housing and coolant bleed bolt, CVCC

remove the pump together with the pulley and the seal rubber.

4. To install, reverse the removal procedure using a new gasket. Bleed the cooling system.

Thermostat

REMOVAL AND INSTALLATION

1. On 1237 cc cars, the thermostat is located on the intake manifold, under the air cleaner nozzle, so you will first have to remove the air cleaner housing. On CVCC cars, it is located at the rear of the distributor housing.
2. Unbolt and remove the thermostat cover and pull the thermostat from the housing.
3. To install, reverse the removal procedure. Always install the spring end of the thermostat toward the engine. Tighten the two cover bolts to 7 ft. lbs. Always use a new gasket. Bleed the cooling system.

EMISSION CONTROLS

Emission controls fall into three basic systems: Crankcase Emission Control System, Exhaust Emission Control System and Evaporative Emission Control System.

Crankcase ventilation system operation—1237 cc engine (CVCC similar)

Thermostat installation

1976 and later PCV orifice location

Crankcase Emission Control System

All engines are equipped with a "Dual Return System" to prevent crankcase vapor emissions. Blow-by gas is returned to the combustion chamber through the intake manifold and carburetor air cleaner. When the throttle is partially opened, blow-by gas is returned to the intake manifold through breather tubes leading into the tee orifice located on the outside of the intake manifold. When the throttle is opened wide and vacuum in the air cleaner rises, blow-by gas is returned to the intake manifold through an additional passage in the air cleaner case.

Exhaust Emission Control System

Control of exhaust emissions, hydrocarbon (HC), carbon monoxide (CO), and Oxides of nitrogen (NOx), is achieved by a combination of engine modifications and special control devices. Improvements to the combustion chamber, intake manifold, valve timing, carburetor, and distributor comprise the engine modifications. These modifications, in conjunction with the special control devices, enable the engine to produce low emission with leaner air-fuel mixtures while maintaining good driveability. The special control devices consist of the following:

   a. Intake air temperature control;
   b. Throttle opener;
   c. Transmission and temperature controlled spark advance (TCS) for the 4-speed transmission.

INTAKE AIR TEMPERATURE CONTROL

Intake air temperature control is designed to provide the most uniform carburetion possible under various ambient air temperature conditions by maintaining the intake air temperature within a narrow range. When the temperature in the air cleaner is below 100°F (approx.), the air bleed valve, which

consists of a bimetallic strip and a rubber seal, remains closed. Intake manifold vacuum is then led to a vacuum motor, located on the snorkel of the air cleaner case, which moves the air control valve door, allowing only preheated air to enter the air cleaner.

When the temperature in the air cleaner becomes higher than approx. 100°F, the air bleed valve opens and the air control valve door returns to the open position allowing only unheated air through the snorkel.

THROTTLE OPENER

When the throttle is closed suddenly at high engine speed, hydrocarbon (HC) emissions increase due to engine misfire caused by an incombustible mixture. The throttle opener is designed to prevent misfiring during deceleration by causing the throttle valve to remain slightly open, allowing better mixture control. The control valve is set to allow the passage of vacuum to the throttle opener diaphragm when the engine vacuum is equal to or greater than the control valve preset vacuum (21.6 ± 1.6 in. Hg) during acceleration.

Thermosensors: upper energizes a solenoid, giving vacuum advance (engine cold); lower is used when the engine is warm (1977 and earlier)

Under running conditions, other than fully closed throttle deceleration, the intake manifold vacuum is less than the control valve set vacuum; therefore the control valve is not actuated. The vacuum remaining in the throttle opener and control valve is returned to atmospheric pressure by the air passage at the valve center.

IGNITION TIMING RETARD UNIT

When the engine is idling, the vacuum produced in the carburetor retarder port is communicated to the spark retard unit and the ignition timing, at idle, is retarded.

TCS SYSTEM

The transmission and temperature controlled spark advance for 4-speed trans-

missions is designed to reduce NOx emissions during normal vehicle operation.

The vacuum is cut off to the spark advance unit regardless of temperature when First, Second, or Third gear is selected. Vacuum advance is restored when Fourth gear is selected.

TEMPERATURE CONTROLLED SPARK ADVANCE

Temperature controlled spark advance on cars equipped with Hondamatic transmission is designed to reduce NOx emissions by disconnecting the vacuum to the spark advance unit during normal vehicle operation.

When the coolant temperature is approximately 120° or higher, the solenoid valve is energized, cutting off vacuum to the advance unit.

Air Injection System

On 1976 and later models, an air injection system is used to control hydrocarbon and carbon monoxide emissions. With this system, a belt-driven air pump delivers filtered air under pressure to injection nozzles located at each exhaust port. Here, the additional oxygen supplied by the vane-type pump reacts with any uncombusted fuel mixture, promoting an afterburning effect in the hot exhaust manifold. To prevent a reverse flow in the air injection manifold when exhaust gas pressure exceeds air supply pressure, a non-return check valve is used. To prevent exhaust afterburning or backfiring during deceleration, an anti-afterburn valve delivers air to the intake manifold instead. When manifold vacuum rises above the preset vacuum of the air control valve and/or below that of the air by-pass valve, air pump air is returned to the air cleaner.

THROTTLE CONTROLS

This system controls the closing of the throttle during periods of gear shifting, deceleration, or anytime the gas pedal is released. In preventing the sudden closing of the throttle during these conditions, an overly rich mixture is prevented which controls excessive emissions of hydrocarbons and carbon monoxide. This system has two main parts; a dashpot system and a throttle positioner system. The dashpot diaphragm and solenoid valve act to dampen or slow down the throttle return time to 1–4 seconds. The throttle positioner part consists of a speed sensor, a solenoid valve, a control valve and an opener diaphragm which will keep the throttle open and predetermined minimum amount any time the gas pedal is released when the car is traveling 15 mph or faster, and closes it when the car slows to 10 mph.

IGNITION TIMING CONTROLS

A variety of ignition timing control systems are used on various models to reduce hydrocarbons and oxides of nitrogen emissions. These timing controls combined with centrifigal advance affect the time at which each spark plug ignites the air/fuel mixture. The ignition spark is controlled according to the engine's speed, load and coolant temperature.

HOT START CONTROL

This system is designed to prevent an over-rich mixture condition in the intake manifold due to vaporization of residual fuel when starting a hot engine. This reduces hydrocarbon and carbon monoxide emissions.

Start control solenoid valve

ANTI-AFTERBURN VALVE

Various 1979 and later models have an anti-afterburn valve. The valve lets fresh air into the intake manifold when it senses sudden increases in manifold vacuum. The valve responds only to sudden increases in vacuum and the amount of time it stays open is determined by an internal diaphragm which is acted on by the vacuum level.

CVCC ENGINE MODIFICATIONS

By far, the most important part of the CVCC engine emission control system is the Compound Vortex Controlled Combustion (CVCC) cylinder head itself. Each cylinder has three valves: a conventional intake and conventional exhaust valve, and a smaller auxiliary intake valve. There are actually *two* combustion chambers per cylinder: a precombustion or auxiliary chamber, and the main chamber. During the intake stroke, an extremely lean mixture is drawn into the main combustion chamber. Simultaneously, a very rich mixture is drawn into the smaller precombustion chamber via the auxiliary intake valve. The spark plug, located in the precombustion chamber, easily ignites the rich pre-mixture, and this combustion spreads out into the main combustion chamber where the lean mixture is ignited. Due to the fact that the volume of the auxiliary chamber is much smaller than the main chamber, the overall mixture is very lean (about 18 parts air to one part fuel). The result is low hydrocarbon emissions due to the slow, stable combustion of the lean mixture in the main chamber; low carbon monoxide emissions due to the excess oxygen available; and low oxides of nitrogen emissions due to the lowered peak combustion temperatures. An added benefit of burning the lean mixture is the excellent gas mileage.

Air Jet Controller

This is a atmospheric pressure sensing device used on 1981 and later California and High Altitude models. As altitude changes, a valve opens and closes to maintain the proper air flow to the carburetor.

Evaporative Emission Control System

This system prevents gasoline vapors from escaping into the atmosphere from the fuel tank and carburetor and consists of the components listed in the illustration.

Fuel vapor is stored in the expansion chamber, in the fuel tank, and in the vapor line up to the one-way valve. When the vapor pressure becomes higher than the set pressure of the one-way valve, the valve opens and allows vapor into the charcoal canister. While the engine is stopped or idling, the idle cut-off valve in the canister is closed and the vapor is absorbed by the charcoal.

At partially opened throttle, the idle cut-off valve is opened by manifold vacuum. The vapor that was stored in the charcoal canister and in the vapor line is purged into the intake manifold. Any excessive pressure or vacuum which might build up in the fuel tank is relieved by the two-way valve in the filler cap.

MAINTENANCE AND SERVICE

Components Pertaining To Emission Controls

The proper control of exhaust emissions depends not only on the primary components of the emission controls mentioned above, but also on such related areas as ignition timing, spark plugs, valve clearance, engine oil, cooling system, etc. Before tackling the primary emission controls, you should determine if the related components are functioning properly, and correct any deficiencies.

Crankcase Emission Control System

1. Squeeze the lower end of the drain tube and drain any oil or water which may have collected.

2. Make sure that the intake manifold T-joint is clear by passing the shank end of a No. 65 (0.035 in. dia.) drill through both ends (orifices) of the joint.

3. Check for any loose, disconnected, or deteriorated tubes and replace if necessary.

Exhaust Emission Control System

INTAKE AIR TEMPERATURE CONTROL SYSTEM (ENGINE COLD)

1. Inspect for loose, disconnected, or deteriorated vacuum hoses and replace as necessary.

2. Remove the air cleaner cover and element.

3. With the transmission in Neutral and the blue distributor disconnected, engage the starter motor for approximately two (2) seconds. Manifold vacuum to the vacuum motor should completely raise the air control valve door. Once opened, the valve door should stay open unless there is a leak in the system.

4. If the valve door does not open, check the intake manifold port by passing a No. 78 (0.016 in. dia.) drill or compressed air through the orifice in the manifold.

5. If the valve door still does not open, proceed to the following steps:

   a. Vacuum Motor Test—Disconnect the vacuum line from the vacuum motor inlet pipe. Fully open the air control valve door, block the vacuum motor inlet pipe, then release the door. If the door does not remain open, the vacuum motor is defective. Replace as necessary and repeat Steps 1–3;

   b. Air Bleed Valve Test—Unblock the inlet pipe and make sure that the valve door fully closes without sticking or binding. Reconnect the vacuum line to the vacuum motor inlet pipe. Connect a vacuum source (e.g. hand vacuum pump) to the manifold vacuum line (disconnect at the intake manifold fixed orifice) and draw enough vacuum to fully open the valve door. If the valve door closes with the manifold vacuum line plugged (by the vacuum pump), then vacuum is leaking through the air bleed valve. Replace as necessary and repeat Steps 1–3;

CAUTION

Never force the air bleed valve (bi-metal strip) on or off its valve seat. The bi-metal strip and the valve seat may be damaged.

---

c. **Check Valve Test**—Again draw a vacuum (at the manifold vacuum line) until the valve door opens. Unplug the line by disconnecting the pump from the manifold vacuum line. If the valve door closes, vacuum is leaking past the check valve. Replace as necessary and repeat Steps 1–3.

6. After completing the above steps, replace the air cleaner element and cover and fit a vacuum gauge into the line leading to the vacuum motor.

7. Start the engine and raise the idle to 1500–2000 rpm. As the engine warms, the vacuum gauge reading should drop to zero.

NOTE: Allow sufficient time for the engine to reach normal operating temperature—when the cooling fan cycles on and off.

If the reading does not drop to zero before the engine reaches normal operating temperature, the air bleed valve is defective and must be replaced. Repeat Step 3 as a final check.

TEMPERATURE AND TRANSMISSION CONTROLLED SPARK ADVANCE (ENGINE COLD)—ALL MODELS

1. Check for loose, disconnected, or deteriorated vacuum hoses and replace as necessary.

2. Check the coolant temperature sensor switch for proper operation with an ohmmeter or 12V light. The switch should normally be open (no continuity across the switch terminals) when the coolant temperature is below approximately 120°F (engine cold). If the switch is closed (continuity across the terminals), replace the switch and repeat the check.

3. On manual transmission models, check the transmission sensor switch. The switch should be open (no continuity across the connections) when Fourth gear is selected, and closed (continuity across the connections) in all other gear positions. Replace if necessary and repeat the check.

4. Remove the spark control vacuum tube, leading between the spark advance/retard unit and the solenoid valve, and connect.

Evaporative Emission Control System (Engine at Normal Operating Temperature)

CHARCOAL CANISTER

1. Check for loose, disconnected, or deteriorated vacuum hoses and replace where necessary.

2. Pull the free end of the purge air guide tube out of the body frame and plug it securely.

3. Disconnect the fuel vapor line from the charcoal canister and connect a vacuum gauge to the charcoal canister vapor inlet according to the diagram.

4. Start the engine and allow it to idle.

Since the vacuum port in the carburetor is closed off at idle, the vacuum gauge should register no vacuum. If vacuum is available, replace the charcoal canister and recheck for no vacuum. A vacuum reading indicates that the charcoal canister idle cut-off valve is broken or stuck.

5. Open the throttle to 2000 rpm and make sure that the charcoal canister idle cutoff valve is opening by watching the vacuum.

a. Disconnect the vacuum signal line and connect the vacuum gauge to the carburetor T-joint orifice formerly occupied by the signal line. The vacuum reading at 2000 rpm should be greater than 3 in. Hg. If vacuum is now available (with the throttle open), replace the charcoal canister and repeat Steps 4 & 5. If vacuum is still not available, or is below 3 in. Hg proceed to the next step.

b. If vacuum is less than 3 in. Hg (with the throttle open), the carburetor vacuum port or T-joint might be plugged. Clear the passages with compressed air. If vacuum is now available, repeat Steps 4 & 5. If vacuum is not available, or below 3 in. Hg, the carburetor vacuum port is blocked. Repair or replace as necessary and repeat Steps 4 & 5. If vacuum is *still* not available, proceed to the next step.

c. Plug the solenoid valve vacuum line (the other line to the carburetor T-joint) and recheck for vacuum. If vacuum is now available, the leak is in the advance/retard solenoid valve. Repair or replace as necessary and repeat Steps 4 & 5.

FUEL SYSTEM

All 1976–79 Civics with the 1237 cc engine use a two-barrel downdraft Hitachi carburetor. Fuel pressure is provided by a camshaft-driven mechanical fuel pump. A replaceable fuel filter is located in the engine compartment in-line between the fuel pump and carburetor.

On all other models a Keihin three-barrel carburetor is used. On this carburetor, the primary and secondary venturis deliver a lean air/fuel mixture to the main combustion chamber. Simultaneously, the third or auxiliary venturi which has a completely separate fuel metering circuit, delivers a small (in volume) but very rich air/fuel mixture to the precombustion chamber. Fuel pressure is provided by an electric fuel pump which is actuated when the ignition switch is turned to the "on" position. The electric pump is located under the rear seat beneath a special access plate on Civic sedan and hatchback models, and located under the rear of the car adjacent to the fuel tank on all other models. A replaceable in-line fuel filter located on the inlet side of the electric fuel pump is used on all models except the 1976–79 Civic with the 1237 cc engine.

Fuel filter (non-CVCC Civic)

Fuel Filter

REPLACEMENT

— CAUTION —
Before disconnecting any fuel lines, be sure to open the gas tank filler cap to relieve any pressure in the system. If this is not done, you may run the risk of being squirted with gasoline.

All models use a disposable-type fuel filter which cannot be disassembled for cleaning. The filter is replaced after the first 15,000 miles, and every 30,000 miles (through 1980) 60,000 miles (1981 and later) thereafter.

On 1976–79 Civics with the 1237 cc engine, the filter is located in the engine compartment, inline between the fuel pump and carburetor. Replacement is a simple matter of pinching the lines closed, loosening the hose clamps and discarding the old filter.

On all 1980 and later Civic Sedan models, the rear filter is located beneath a special access cover under the rear seat on the driver's side. The rear seat can be removed after removing the bolt at the rear center of the

1. Fuel pump
2. Filter

Rear fuel filter location—CVCC sedan

cushion and then pivoting the seat forward from the rear. Then, remove the four screws retaining the access cover to the floor and remove the cover. The filter, together with the electric fuel pump, are located in the recess. Pinch the lines shut, loosen the hose clamps and remove the filter.

On all Wagons and Accord and Prelude models, the rear filter is located under the car, in front of the spare tire, together with the electrical fuel pump. To replace the fuel filter, you must raise the rear of the car, support it with jackstands, and clamp off the fuel lines leading to and from the filter. Then, loosen the hose clamps and, taking note of which hose is the inlet and which is the outlet, remove the filter. Some replacement filters have an arrow embossed or printed on the filter body, in which case you want to install the new filter with the arrow pointing in the direction of fuel flow. After installing the new filter, remember to unclamp the fuel lines. Check for leaks.

All 1982 and later models are also equipped with a front in-line desposible fuel filter, located at the carburetor. Replacement is the same as the others.

Mechanical Fuel Pump

REMOVAL AND INSTALLATION

1237 cc Engine

The fuel pump in the Civic is located in back of the engine, underneath the air cleaner snorkle.

1. Remove the air cleaner and cover assembly.
2. Remove the inlet and outlet fuel lines at the pump.
3. Loosen the pump nuts and remove the pump.

NOTE: Do not disassemble the pump. Disassembly may cause fuel or oil leakage. If the pump is defective, replace it as an assembly.

Mechanical fuel pump—arrow indicates air hole

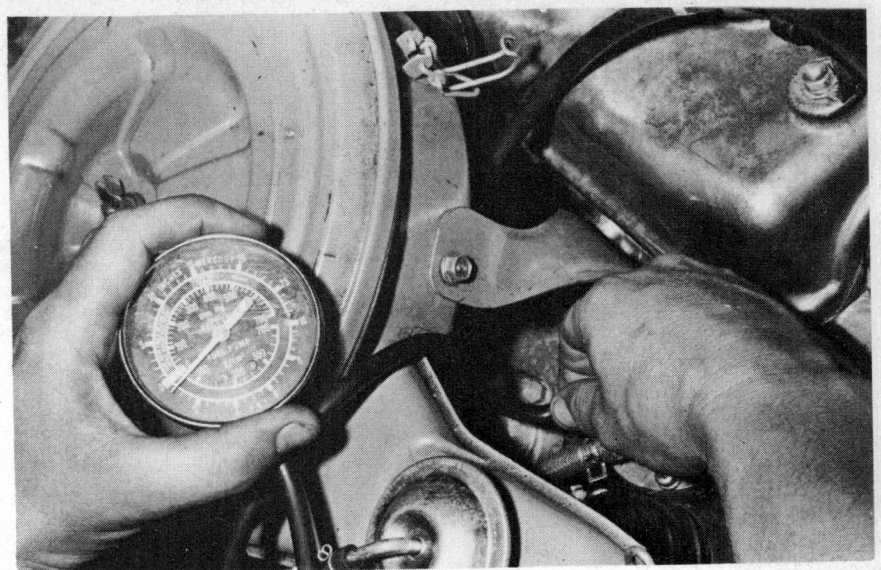

Checking fuel pump pressure

MECHANICAL FUEL PUMP SPECIFICATIONS

Engine rpm	Delivery Pressure (lb. in.²)	Vacuum (in. Hg.)	Displacement (in.³/minute)
600	2.56	17.72	27
3,000	2.56	7.87–11.81	43
6,000	2.56	7.87–11.81	46

4. To install the fuel pump, reverse the removal procedure.

INSPECTION

1. Check the following items:
   a. Looseness of the pump connector.
   b. Looseness of the upper and lower body and cover screws.
   c. Looseness of the rocker arm pin.
   d. Contamination or clogging of the air hole.
   e. Improper operation of the pump.
2. Check to see if there are signs of oil or fuel around the air hole. If so, the diaphragm is damaged and you must replace the pump.
3. To inspect the pump for operation, first disconnect the fuel line at the carburetor. Connect a fuel pressure gauge to the delivery side of the pump. Start the engine and measure the pump delivery pressure.
4. After measuring, stop the engine and check to see if the gauge drops suddenly. If the gauge drops suddenly and/or the delivery pressure is incorrect, check for a fuel or oil leak from the diaphragm or from the valves.
5. To test for volume, disconnect the fuel line from the carburetor and insert it into a one quart container. Crank the engine for 64 seconds at 600 rpm, or 40 seconds at 3000 rpm. The bottle should be half full (1 pint).

Electrical Fuel Pump

REMOVAL AND INSTALLATION

All Except 1237 cc Engine

1. Remove the gas filler cap to relieve any excess pressure in the system.
2. Obtain a pair of clothes pins or other suitable clamps to pinch shut the fuel lines to the pump.
3. Disconnect the negative battery cable.
4. Locate the fuel pump. On Civic sedan and hatchback models, you will first have to remove the rear seat by removing the bolt at the rear center of the bottom cushion and pivoting the seat forward from the rear. The pump and filter are located on the driver's side of the rear seat floor section beneath an access plate retained by four Phillips head screws.

On station wagon models and the Accord and Prelude, you will probably have to raise the rear of the car to obtain access. On Accord and Prelude models, remove the left rear wheel. In all cases, make sure, if you are crawling under the car, that the car is securely supported. *Do not venture beneath the car when it is supported only by the tire changing jack.*

5. Pinch the inlet and outlet fuel lines

shut. Loosen the hose clamps. On station wagon and Accord models, remove the filter mounting clip on the left hand side of the bracket.

6. Disconnect the positive lead wire and ground wire from the pump at their quick disconnect.

7. Remove the two fuel pump retaining bolts, taking care not to lose the two spacers and bolt collars.

8. Remove the fuel lines and fuel pump.

9. Reverse the above procedure to install. The pump cannot be disassembled and must be replaced if defective. Operating fuel pump pressure is 2–3 psi.

Carburetor

REMOVAL AND INSTALLATION

1. Disconnect and label the following:
a. Hot air tube.
b. Vacuum hose between the oneway valve and the manifold—at the manifold.
c. Breather chamber (on air cleaner case) to intake manifold at the breather chamber.
d. Hose from the air cleaner case to the valve cover.
e. Hose from the carbon canister to the carburetor—at the carburetor.
f. Throttle opener hose—at the throttle opener.

2. Disconnect the fuel line at the carburetor. Plug the end of the fuel line to prevent dust entry.

3. Disconnect the choke and throttle control cables.

4. Disconnect the fuel shut-off solenoid wires.

5. Remove the carburetor retaining bolts and the carburetor. Leave the insulator on the manifold.

NOTE: After removing the carburetor, cover the intake manifold parts to keep out foreign materials.

OVERHAUL

For all carburetor overhaul procedures, please refer to "Carburetor Service" in the Unit Repair section.

THROTTLE LINKAGE ADJUSTMENT

1237 cc Models

1. Check the gas pedal free-play (the amount of free movement before the throttle cable starts to pull the throttle valve). Adjust the free-play at the throttle cable adjusting nut (near the carburetor) so the pedal has 0.04–0.12 in. (1.0–3.0 mm) free-play.

2. Make sure that when the accelerator pedal is fully depressed, the primary and secondary throttle valves are opened fully

CVCC throttle cable adjusting location

(contact the stops). If the secondary valve does not open fully, adjust by bending the secondary throttle valve connecting rod.

1335, 1487, 1600 and 1751 cc CVCC Models

1. Remove the air cleaner assembly to provide access.

2. Check that the cable free-play (deflection) is 3/16 to 3/8 in. (4–10 mm). This is measured right before the cable enters the throttle shaft bellcrank.

3. If deflection is not to specifications, rotate the cable adjusting nuts in the required direction.

4. As a final check, have a friend press the gas pedal all the way to the floor, while you look down inside the throttle bore checking that the throttle plates reach the wide open throttle (WOT) vertical position.

5. Install the air cleaner.

FLOAT AND FUEL LEVEL ADJUSTMENT

1237 cc Models

1. Check the float level by looking at the sight glass on the right of the carburetor. Fuel level should align with the dot on the sight glass. If the level is above or below the dot, the carburetor must be disassembled and the float level set.

NOTE: Try to check float level with the dot at eye level.

2. Remove the carburetor from the engine and disconnect the air horn assembly from the carburetor body.

NOTE: When removing the air horn, do not drop the float pin.

3. Invert the air horn and raise the float.

4. Measure the distance between the float tang and the needle valve stem. The distance should be 0.051–0.067 in. (1.3–17 mm). Adjust by bending the float stop tang.

5. For 1977 and later models, remove and invert the air horn until the float arm just touches the needle valve, or there is

about 0.1 mm (0.004 in.) clearance between them. Measure the distance between the bottom of the air horn (gasket installed) and the center of the bottom of the float. The distance should measure 36.4 mm (1.39–1.47 in.). Adjust by turning the needle valve seat. Be careful not to allow the valve seat to protrude from the seat attaching boss, which would allow the valve to fall. If this is the case, bend the float arm slightly until the proper clearance can be obtained.

6. When the carburetor is installed, recheck the float level by looking into the carburetor float sight glass. Fuel level should be within the range of the dot on the glass.

1335, 1487, 1600 and 1751 cc CVCC Models

1976–81

Due to the rather unconventional manner in which the Keihin 3 bbl carburetor float level is checked and adjusted, this is one job best left to the dealer, or someone with Honda tool No. 07501-6570000 (which is a special float level gauge/fuel catch tray/drain bottle assembly not generally available to the public). This carburetor is adjusted while mounted on a running engine. After the auxiliary and the primary/secondary main jet covers are removed, the special float gauge apparatus is installed over the jet apertures. With the engine running, the float level is checked against a red index line on the gauge. If adjustment proves necessary, there are adjusting screws provided for both the auxiliary and the primary/secondary circuits atop the carburetor.

1982 AND LATER

With the car on level ground and at normal operating temperature, check the primary and secondary fuel level inspection windows. If the fuel level is not touching the dot, adjust it by turning the adjusting screws.

NOTE: Do not turn the adjusting screws more than 1/8 turn every 15 seconds.

Inspection window showing the fuel level on 1982 and later models

Float level adjustment screw—1982 and later models

FAST IDLE ADJUSTMENT

During cold engine starting and the engine warm-up period, a specially enriched fuel mixture is required. If the engine fails to run properly or if the engine over-revs with the choke knob pulled out (on models so equipped) in cold weather, the fast idle system should be checked and adjusted. This is accomplished with the carburetor installed.

1237 cc Models

1976

1. Open the primary throttle plate and insert an 0.8 mm (0.032 in.), diameter drill bit between the plate and the bore.
2. With the throttle plate opened 0.8 mm, bend the reference tab so that it is midway between the two scribed lines on the throttle control lever.

1977–79

1. With the engine running at normal operating temperature, pull the choke knob all the way out.
2. The engine speed should increase to 1400–2200 rpm. The arm of the choke lever should align with the boss on the carburetor.
3. Adjust by bending the link lever.

1487 and 1600 cc CVCC Models

1976–79

1. Run the engine until it reaches normal operating temperature.
2. Place the choke control knob in its second detent position (two clicks out from the dash). With the choke knob in this position, run the engine for 30 seconds and check that the fast idle speed is 3000 rpm plus or minus 500 rpm.
3. To adjust on all models except 1978 and later Accords, bend the slot in the fast idle adjusting link. Narrow the slot to lower the fast idle, and widen the slot to increase. Make all adjustments in small increments.
4. On 1978–79 Accord and Prelude, adjust the fast idle by means of the fast idle

CVCC fast idle adjusting location

adjusting screw, located on the throttle arm below the choke housing.

1335, 1487 (1980 AND LATER) AND 1751 cc MODELS

1. Run the engine to normal operating temperature.
2. Connect a tachometer according to the manufacturer's specifications.
3. Disconnect and plug the hose from the fast idle unloader.
4. Shut the engine off, hold the choke valve closed, and open and close the throttle to engage the fast idle cam.

5. Start the engine, run it for one minute. Fast idle speed should be 2300 to 3300 rpm for manual transmission models and 2200 to 3200 rpm for automatic transmission models.

NOTE: Underhood specifications sticker figures must be used if they differ from those above.

6. Adjust the idle by turning the fast idle screw.

CHOKE ADJUSTMENT

1237 cc Models

The choke valve should be fully open when the choke knob is pushed in, and fully closed with the choke knob pulled out. The choke valve is held in the fully closed position by spring action. Pull the choke knob to the fully closed position and open and close the choke valve by rotating the choke valve shaft. The movement should be free and unrestricted.

If adjustment is required, adjust the cable length by loosening the cable clamp bolt.

Choke adjustment—1237 cc engines

1. Stop tab
2. Relief lever adjusting tang
3. Actuator rod
4. Choke opener diaphragm

CVCC choke adjustment components

PRECISION ADJUSTMENT

1. Using a wire gauge, check the primary throttle valve opening (dimension G1) when the choke valve is fully closed. The opening should be 0.050–0.066 in. (1.28–1.68 mm).

2. If the opening is out of specification, adjust it by bending the choke rod. After installing, make sure that the highest fast idle speed is 2500–2800 rpm while the engine is warm.

NOTE: When adjusting the fast idle speed, be sure the throttle adjusting screw does not contact the stop.

1487, 1600 cc CVCC Models

1976–79

1. Push the choke actuator rod towards the diaphragm, so it does not contact the choke valve linkage.

2. Pull the choke knob out to the first detent (click) position from the dash. With the knob in this position, check the distance between the choke butterfly valve and the venturi opening with a ³⁄₁₆ in. drill (shank end).

3. Adjust as necessary by bending the relief lever adjusting tang with needle nose pliers.

4. Now, pull out the choke knob to its second detent position from the dash. Again, make sure the choke actuator rod does not contact the choke valve linkage.

5. With the choke knob in this position, check that the clearance between the butterfly valve and venturi opening is ⅛ in. using the shank end of a ⅛ in. drill.

6. Adjust as necessary by bending the stop tab for the choke butterfly linkage.

1335, 1487 (1980 and Later) and 1751 cc Models

The choke plate should close to less than 3 mm (⅛ in.) clearance when the engine is

cold (ignition on) on models with the automatic choke.

1. Remove the choke cover (3 screws) and check free movement of the linkage. Repair or replace as necessary.

2. Install the choke cover and adjust so that the index marks on the cover and thermostat body align. If the choke still does not close properly, replace the cover and retest.

CHOKE CABLE ADJUSTMENT

1976 1237 cc Models

NOTE: Perform the adjustment only after the throttle plate opening has been set.

1. Make sure that the choke cable is correctly adjusted.
   a. With the choke knob in, the choke butterfly should be completely open;
   b. Slowly pull out the choke knob and check for slack in the cable. Remove any excessive free-play and recheck for full open when the knob is pushed in.

2. Check the link rod adjustment by pulling the choke knob out to the first detent. The two scribed lines on the throttle control lever should line up on either side of the reference tab. If not, adjust by bending the choke link rod.

1977 and Later 1237 cc Models

Turn the adjusting nut until there is zero clearance between the choke lever and stay plate. The choke should be fully closed when the knob is pulled all the way out, and fully opened when the knob is pushed all the way in.

All 1487 cc CVCC Civics; 1600 cc CVCC Accords through 1977

1. Remove the air cleaner assembly.
2. Push the choke knob all the way in

at the dash. Check that the choke butterfly valve (choke plate) is fully open (vertical).

3. Next, have a friend pull out the choke knob while you observe the action of the butterfly valve. When the choke knob is pulled out to the second detent position, the butterfly valve should just close. Then, when the choke knob is pulled all the way out, the butterfly valve should remain in the closed position.

4. To adjust, loosen the choke cable locknut and rotate the adjusting nut so that with the choke knob pushed flush against the dash (open position), the butterfly valve just rests against its positioning stop tab. Tighten the locknut.

5. If the choke butterfly valve is notchy in operation, or if it does not close properly, check the butterfly valve and shaft for binding. Check also the operation of the return spring.

THROTTLE VALVE OPERATION

1976 1237 cc Models

1. Check to see if the throttle valve opens fully when the throttle lever is moved to the fully open position. See if the valve closes fully when the lever is released.

2. Measure the clearance between the primary throttle valve and the chamber wall where the connecting rod begins to open the secondary throttle valve. The clearance should be 0.221–0.237 in. (5.63–6.03 mm).

3. If the clearance is out of specification, adjust by bending the connecting rod.

NOTE: After adjusting, operate the throttle lever and check for any sign of binding.

ACCELERATOR PUMP ADJUSTMENT

1237 cc Models

Check the pump for smooth operation. See if fuel squirts out of the pump nozzle by operating the pump lever or the throttle lever. When the pump is operated slowly, fuel must squirt out until the pump comes to the end of its travel. If the pump is defective, check for clogging or a defective piston. Adjust the pump by either repositioning the end of the connecting rod arm in the pump lever, or the arm itself.

1487 and 1600 cc CVCC Models

1976–79

1. Remove the air cleaner assembly.
2. Check that the distance between the tang at the end of the accelerator pump lever and the lever stop at the edge of the throttle body is 11.0–13.3 (0.43–0.53 in.) through 1977, or 14.5–15.1 mm (0.57–0.6 in.) 1978 and later. This corresponds to effective pump lever travel.

1. Choke butterfly valve
2. Adjusting nut
3. Locknut

CVCC choke cable adjustment

CVCC accelerator pump adjustment; "a" is 0.57–0.60 in.

3. To adjust, bend the pump lever tang in the required direction.

4. Install the air cleaner.

1335, 1487 (1980 and Later) and 1751 cc Models

1. Remove the air cleaner.
2. Make sure that the pump shaft is moving freely throughout the pump stroke.
3. Check that the pump lever is in contact with the pump shaft.
4. Measure between the bottom end of the pump lever and the lever stop tang. The gap should be $\frac{9}{16}$ to $\frac{19}{32}$ inch (through 1980), $\frac{29}{64}$ to $\frac{31}{64}$ inch (1981 and later). If not, bend the tang to adjust.

Fuel Tank

REMOVAL AND INSTALLATION

1. Drain the tank by loosening the tank drain bolt.

NOTE: Catch the fuel in a clean, safe container.

2. Disconnect the fuel tubes, filler neck connecting tube and the clear viny tube.

NOTE: Disconnect the fuel tubes by removing the clips, taking care not to damage the tubes.

3. Disconnect the fuel meter unit wire at its connection.
4. Remove the fuel tank by removing its attaching bolts.
5. To install, reverse the removal procedure. Be sure that all tubes and fuel lines are securely fastened by the clips.

MANUAL TRANSAXLE

REMOVAL AND INSTALLATION

Four and Five-speed Except Prelude and Civic (1980 and Later)

1. Disconnect the battery ground cable at the battery and the transmission case. Unlock the steering column; place the transmission in neutral.
2. Drain the transmission.
3. Raise the front of the car and support it with safety stands.
4. Remove the front wheels.
5. Remove the starter motor positive battery cable and the solenoid wire. Then remove the starter.
6. Disconnect the following cables and wires:

   a. Clutch cable at the release arm (Civics);

   b. Back-up light switch wires;

   c. TCS (Transmission Controlled Spark) switch wires;

   d. Speedometer cable;

   e. Hydraulic hose at slave cylinder (Accord).

— **CAUTION** —

When removing the speedometer cable from the transmission, it is not necessary to remove the entire cable holder. Remove the end boot (gear holder seal), the cable retaining clip and then pull the cable out of the holder. In no way should you disturb the holder, unless it is absolutely necessary. For further details, see the Engine Removal section.

Exploded view of the gearshift mechanism

Driving out the gearshift rod pin

Engine center mount nuts

7. Disconnect the left and right lower ball joints at the knuckle, using a ball joint remover.

8. Pull on the brake disc and remove the left and right driveshafts from the differential case.

9. Drive out the gearshift rod pin (8 mm) with a drift and disconnect the rod at the transmission case.

10. Disconnect the gearshift extension at the clutch housing.

11. Screw in the engine hanger bolts (see the ''Engine Removal'' section) to the engine torque rod bolt hole and to the hole just to the left of the distributor. Hook a chain onto the bolts and lift the engine just enough to take the load off the engine mounts.

12. After making sure that the engine is properly supported, remove the two center beam-to-lower engine mount nuts. Next, remove the center beam, followed by the lower engine mount.

13. Reinstall the center beam (without mount) and lower the engine until it rests on the beam.

14. Place a jack under the transmission and loosen the 4 attaching bolts. Using the jack to support the transmission, slide it away from the engine and lower the jack until the transmission clears the car.

15. To install, reverse the removal procedure. Be sure to pay attention to the following points:

   a. Tighten all mounting nuts and bolts to their specified torque (see the ''Engine Removal'' section);

   b. Use a new shift rod pin;

   c. After installing the driveshafts, attempt to move the inner joint housing in and out of the differential housing. If it moves easily, the driveshaft end clips should be replaced;

   d. Make sure that the control cables and wires are properly connected;

   e. Be sure the transmission is refilled to the proper level.

Prelude and Civic (1980 and Later)

1. Disconnect the battery ground.

2. Unlock the steering and place the transmission in neutral.

3. Disconnect the following wires in the engine compartment:

   a. battery positive cable

   b. black/white wire from the solenoid

   c. temperature gauge sending unit wire

   d. ignition timing thermosensor wire

   e. backup light switch

   f. distributor wiring

4. Unclip and remove the speedometer cable at the transmission. Do not disassemble the speedometer gear holder!

5. Remove the clutch slave cylinder with the hydraulic line attached.

6. Remove the side and top starter mounting bolts.

7. Raise and support the car.

8. Drain the transmission.

9. Remove the splash shields from the underside.

10. Remove the stabilizer bar.

11. Disconnect the left and right lower ball joints and tie rod ends, using a ball joint remover.

12. Turn the right steering knuckle out as far as it will go. Place a heavy screwdriver against the inboard CV joint, pry the right axle out of the transmission about ½ inch. This will force the spring clip out of the groove inside the differential gear splines. Pull it out the rest of the way. Repeat this procedure on the other side.

13. Disconnect the shift lever torque rod from the clutch housing.

14. Remove the bolt from the shift rod clevis.

15. Raise the transmission jack securely against the transmission to take up the weight.

16. Remove the engine torque rods and brackets.

17. Remove the remaining starter mounting bolts and take out the starter.

18. Remove the remaining transmission mounting bolts and the upper bolt from the engine damper bracket.

19. Start backing the transmission away from the engine and remove the two lower damper bolts.

20. Pull the transmission clear of the engine and lower the jack.

21. To ease installation, fabricate two 14 mm diameter dowel pins and install them in the clutch housing.

22. Raise the transmission and slide it onto the dowels. Slide the transmission into position aligning the mainshaft splines with the clutch plate.

23. Attach the damper lower bolts when the positioning allows. Tighten both bolts until the clutch housing is seated against the block.

24. Install two lower mounting bolts and torque them to 33 ft. lbs.

25. Install the front and rear torque rod brackets. Torque the front torque rod bolts to 54 ft. lbs., the front bracket bolts to 33 ft. lbs., the rear torque rod bolts to 54 ft. lbs. and the rear bracket bolts to 47 ft. lbs.

26. Remove the transmission jack.

27. Install the starter and torque the mounting bolts to 33 ft. lbs.

28. Turn the right steering knuckle out far enough to fit the end into the transmission. Use new 26 mm spring clips on both axles. Repeat procedure for the other side.

— CAUTION —

Make sure that the axles bottom fully so that you feel the spring clip engage the differential.

29. Install the lower ball joints. Torque the nuts to 32 ft. lbs.

30. Install the tie rods. Torque the nuts to 32 ft. lbs.

31. Connect the shift linkage.

32. Connect the shift lever torque rod to the clutch housing and torque the bolt to 7 ft. lbs.

33. Install the stabilizer bar.

34. Install the lower shields.

35. Install the front wheels and torque the lugs to 108 ft. lbs.

36. Install the remaining starter bolts and torque to 33 ft. lbs.

37. Install the clutch slave cylinder.

38. Install the speedometer cable using a new O-ring coated with clean engine oil.

39. Connect all engine compartment wiring.

40. Fill the transmission with SAE 10W-40 engine oil.

Halfshaft (Driveshaft)

REMOVAL AND INSTALLATION

The front driveshaft assembly consists of a sub-axle shaft and a driveshaft with two universal joints.

A constant velocity ball joint is used for both universal joints, which are factory-packed with special grease and enclosed in sealed rubber boots. The outer joint cannot be disassembled except for removal of the boot.

1. Remove the hubcap from the front wheel and then remove the center cap.

2. Pull out the 4 mm cotter pin and loosen, but do not remove, the spindle nut.

3. Raise the front of the car and support it with safety stands.

4. Remove the wheel lug nuts and then the wheel.

5. Remove the spindle nut.

6. Drain the transmission.

7. Remove the lower arm ball joints at the knuckle by using a ball joint remover.

8. To remove the driveshaft, hold the knuckle and pull it toward you. Then slide the driveshaft out of the knuckle. Pry the CV joint out about ½ in. Pull the inboard joint side of the driveshaft out of the differential case.

9. To install, reverse the removal procedure. If either the inboard or outboard joint boot bands have been removed for inspection or disassembly of the joint (only the inboard joint can be disassembled), be sure to repack the joint with a sufficient amount of bearing grease.

— CAUTION —

Make sure the CV joint sub-axle bottoms so that the spring clip may hold the sub-axle securely in the transmission.

SHIFT LINKAGE ADJUSTMENT

The Honda shift linkage is non-adjustable. However, if the linkage is binding, or if there is excessive play, check the linkage bushings and pivot points. Lubricate with light oil, or replace worn bushings as necessary.

CLUTCH

All models use a single dry disc with a diaphragm spring type pressure plate. The Civic and the 1982 and later Accord clutch is cable operated. However, on the Accord (1976–'81) and Prelude, a hydraulic master and slave cylinder system is used.

REMOVAL AND INSTALLATION

1. Follow Steps 1 through 14 of the trans-axle removal procedure, previously given. Matchmark the flywheel and clutch for reassembly.

2. Hold the flywheel ring gear with a tool made for the purpose, remove the retaining bolts and remove the pressure plate and clutch disc.

NOTE: Loosen the retaining bolts two turns at a time in a circular pattern. Removing one bolt while the rest are tight may warp the diaphragm spring.

3. The flywheel can now be removed, if it needs repairing or replacing. Inspect it for scoring and wear, and reface or replace as necessary. Installation torque is 35 ft. lbs. Tighten in a criss-cross pattern.

4. To separate the pressure plate from the diaphragm spring, remove the 4 retracting clips.

5. To remove the release, or throwout bearing, first straighten the locking tab and remove the 8 mm bolt, followed by the release shaft and release arm with the bearing attached.

NOTE: It is recommended that the release bearing be removed after the release arm has been removed from the casing. Trying to remove or install the bearing with the release arm in the case will damage the retaining clip.

6. If a new release bearing is to be installed, separate the bearing from the holder, using a bearing drift.

7. To assemble and install the clutch, reverse the removal procedure. Be sure to pay attention to the following points:

a. Make sure that the flywheel and the end of the crankshaft are clean before assembling;

b. When installing the pressure plate, align the mark on the outer edge of the flywheel with the alignment mark on the pressure plate. Failure to align these marks will result in imbalance.

c. When tightening the pressure plate bolts, use a pilot shaft to center the friction disc. The pilot shaft can be bought at any large auto supply store or fabricated from a wooden dowel. After centering the disc, tighten the bolts two turns at a time, in a criss-cross pattern to avoid

Civic clutch assembly through 1979 (others similar)

warping the diaphragm springs; tighten to 7 ft. lbs.;

d. When installing the release shaft and arm, place a lock tab washer under the retaining bolt;

e. When installing the transmission, make sure that the mainshaft is properly aligned with the disc spline and the aligning pins are in place, before tightening the case bolts (17–22 ft. lbs.).

PEDAL HEIGHT ADJUSTMENT

Civic

1976–79

Check the clutch pedal height and if necessary, adjust the upper stop, so that the clutch and brake pedals rest at approximately the same height from the floor. First, be sure that the brake pedal free-play is properly adjusted.

1980 AND LATER

The pedal height should be 1³⁄₁₆ in. minimum from the floor.

Accord and Prelude

1. Pedal height should be 184 mm (7.24

in.) measured from the front of the pedal to the floorboard (mat removed).

2. Adjust by turning the pedal stop bolt in or out until height is correct. Tighten the locknut after adjustment.

FREE-PLAY ADJUSTMENT

Civic and 1982 and Later Accord

Adjust the clutch release lever so that it has 0.12–0.16 in. (3–4 mm) through 1980 or ⁷⁄₁₆–⁹⁄₁₆ in. (4.4–5.4 mm) 1981 and later for Civics; ¹⁄₅–¹⁄₄ in. (5.2–6.4 mm) for all 1982 and later Accords, of play when you move the clutch release lever at the transmission with your hand, or 15–20 mm (0.6–0.8 in.) through 1979 or 10–30 mm (³⁄₈–1³⁄₁₆ in.) 1980 and later Civics and 1982 and later Accords, at the pedal. This adjustment is made at the outer cable housing adjuster, near the release lever on all models except the 1487 cc engine (through 1979). Less than ¹⁄₈ in. of free-play may lead to clutch slippage, while more than ¹⁄₈ in. clearance may cause difficult shifting.

— CAUTION —

Make sure that the upper and lower adjusting nuts are tightened after adjustments.

On 1487 cc models through 1979 and 1982 and later Accords, the free-play adjustment is made on the cable at the firewall. Remove the C-clip and then rotate the threaded control cable housing until there is sufficient free-play at the release lever.

1976–81 Accord and Prelude

1. Free-play should measure 2.0–2.6 mm (0.08–0.1 in.) at the clutch release fork.
2. Adjust by loosening the locknut on the slave cylinder pushrod. Turn the pushrod in or out to adjust. Standard adjustment is made by turning the pushrod in until all play is removed, then backing out the pushrod 1¾–2 turns to achieve specified free-play. Tighten the locknut after adjustment.

1976–81 Accord slave cylinder locknut and adjusting nut

Clutch Master Cylinder

REMOVAL AND INSTALLATION

1976–81 Accord and Prelude

1. The clutch master cylinder is located on the firewall in the engine compartment next to the brake master cylinder. Remove the hydraulic line. Either plug the port to prevent leakage or drain the reservoir prior to removing the hydraulic line.
2. Remove the cotter pin which retains the pivot pin in the yoke of the pushrod (under the instrument panel at the clutch pedal).
3. Detach the pushrod from the clutch pedal.
4. Remove the two bolts retaining the master cylinder to the firewall. Remove the master cylinder.
5. Installation is the reverse. Bleed the system after installation.

OVERHAUL

1. Remove the snap ring which retains the stopper plate. Note the installed position of the stopper plate before removal.

2. Apply compressed air to the inlet port to remove the piston assembly. Note the order of all components.
3. Check the cylinder bore for corrosion or wear. Light scores or scratches can be removed with crocus cloth or a brake cylinder hone. The cylinder should be replaced if heavily worn.
4. Replace the piston and spring with new ones. Reassemble in correct order. Coat the inside of the cylinder and the piston with clean brake fluid before installation.
5. Install the cylinder and bleed the system.

Clutch Slave Cylinder

REMOVAL AND INSTALLATION

1976–81 Accord and Prelude

1. The slave cylinder is retained by two bolts. Disconnect and plug the hydraulic line at the slave cylinder and remove the two mounting bolts. Remove the return spring and remove the slave cylinder.
2. Installation is the reverse. Bleed system after installation.

OVERHAUL

1. Apply compressed air to the inlet port to remove the piston and seal.
2. Inspect the cylinder bore for pitting, corrosion, or wear. Replace the cylinder if worn.
3. Coat the parts with clean brake fluid and reassemble.

Clutch Hydraulic System Bleeding

1976–81 ACCORD AND PRELUDE

The hydraulic system must be bled whenever the system has been leaking or dismantled. The bleed screw is located on the slave cylinder.

1. Remove the bleed screw dust cap.
2. Attach a clear hose to the bleed screw. Immerse the other end of the hose in a clear jar half filled with brake fluid.
3. Fill the clutch master cylinder with fresh brake fluid.
4. Open the bleed screw slightly and have an assistant slowly depress the clutch pedal. Close the bleed screw when the pedal reaches the end of its travel. Allow the clutch pedal to return slowly.
5. Repeat Steps 3 and 4 until all air bubbles are expelled from the system.
6. Discard the brake fluid in the jar. Replace the dust cap. Refill the master cylinder.

AUTOMATIC TRANSAXLE

Hondamatic

REMOVAL AND INSTALLATION

Civic and Accord

The automatic transmission is removed in the same basic manner as the manual transmission (refer to "Manual Transmission Removal and Installation"). The following exceptions should be noted during automatic transmission removal and installation.

1. Remove the center console and control rod pin.
2. Remove the front floor center mat and control cable bracket nuts.
3. Jack and support the front of the car.
4. Remove the two selector lever bracket nuts at front side.
5. Loosen the bolts securing the control cable holder and support beam and disconnect the control cable.
6. Disconnect the transmission cooler lines at the transmission.
7. Remove the transmission together with the engine. Remove the engine mounts and torque converter case cover.
8. Remove the starter motor and separate the transmission from the engine.
9. Installation of the automatic transmission is the reverse of removal. Close attention should be paid to the following points.
10. Be sure that the stator hub is correctly located and moves smoothly. The stator shaft can be used for this purpose.
11. Align the stator, stator shaft, main shaft and torque converter turbine serrations.
12. After installation of the engine-transmission unit in car, make all required adjustments.

Shift Lever

INSPECTION

1. Pull up fully on the parking brake lever and run the engine at idle speed, while depressing the brake pedal.

— CAUTION —
Be sure to check continually for car movement.

2. By moving the shift selector lever slowly forward and backward from the "N" position, make sure that the distance between the "N" and the points where the D clutch is engaged for the "2" and "R" positions are the same. The D clutch engaging point is just before the slight re-

Exploded view of Hondamatic gearshift mechanism

sponse is felt. The reverse gears will make a noise when the clutch engages. If the distances are not the same, then adjustment is necessary.

ADJUSTMENT

1. Remove the center console retaining screws, and pull away the console to expose the shift control cable and turnbuckle.

2. Adjust the length of the control cable by turning the turnbuckle, located at the front bottom of the shift lever assembly. After adjustment, the cable and turnbuckle should twist toward the left (driver's) side of the car when shifted toward the ''R'' position and toward the right-side when shifted into the ''2'' position. The hole in the cable end should be perfectly aligned with the holes in the selector lever bracket (pin removed).

REAR SUSPENSION

All Civic sedan and hatchback models and the Accord and Prelude utilize an independent MacPherson strut arrangement for each rear wheel. Each suspension unit consists of a combined oil spring/shock absorber strut, a lower control arm, and a radius rod or arm. The Accord and Prelude have adjustable rear suspension.

Station wagon models use a more conventional leaf spring rear suspension with a solid rear axle. The springs are three-leaf, semi-elliptic types located longitudinally with

a pair of telescopic shock absorbers to control rebound. The solid axle and leaf springs allow for a greater load carrying capacity for the wagon.

Strut Assembly

For all spring and shock absorber removal and installation procedures and any other strut overhaul procedures, please refer to ''Strut Overhaul'' in the Unit Repair section.

REMOVAL AND INSTALLATION

1. Raise the rear of the car and support it with safety stands.

2. Remove the rear wheel.

3. Disconnect the brake line at the shock absorber. Remove the retaining clip and separate the brake hose from the shock absorber.

4. Disconnect the parking brake cable at the backing plate lever.

5. Remove the lower strut retaining bolt or pinch bolt and hub carrier pivot bolt. To

remove the pivot bolt, you first have to remove the castle nut and its cotter pin.

6. Remove the two upper strut retaining nuts and remove the strut from the car.

7. To install, reverse the removal procedure. Be sure to install the top of the strut in the body first. After installation, bleed the brake lines.

Lower Control Arm and Radius Arm

REMOVAL AND INSTALLATION

Except Station Wagon

1. Raise the rear of the car and support it with safety stands.

2. Remove the rear wheels and brake drums.

3. Disconnect the hydraulic brake line and parking brake cable.

4. Remove the backing plate assembly.

5. Remove the radius arm nuts and bolts, and remove the radius arm.

6. Remove the shock absorber pinch

MACPHERSON STRUT

LOWER CONTROL ARM

RADIUS ROD

Civic sedan and hatchback rear suspension through 1979

bolt, then separate the hub carrier from the shock absorber.

7. Remove the lower control arm retaining bolts, then remove the arm.

Rear Wheel Alignment

Caster and camber are fixed as on the front suspension. However, toe-out is adjustable by means of an eccentric adjusting bolt at the forward anchor of the radius rod.

Leaf Spring

REMOVAL AND INSTALLATION

Station Wagon Only

1. Raise the rear of the car and support it on stands placed on the frame. Remove the wheels.
2. Remove the shock absorber lower mounting bolt.
3. Remove the nuts from the U-bolt and remove the U-bolts, bump rubber, and clamp bracket.
4. Unbolt the front and rear spring

Exploded view of station wagon rear suspension

shackle bolts, remove the bolts, and remove the spring.

5. To install, first position the spring on the axle and install the front and rear shackle bolts. Apply a soapy water solution to the bushings to ease installation. Do not tighten the shackle nuts yet.

6. Install the U-bolts, spring clamp bracket and bump rubber loosely on the axle and spring.
7. Install the wheels and lower the car. Tighten the front and rear shackle bolts to 33 ft. lbs. Also tighten the U-bolt nuts to 33 ft. lbs., after the shackle bolts have been tightened.
8. Install the shock absorber to the lower mount. Tighten to 33 ft. lbs.

Shock Absorbers

REMOVAL AND INSTALLATION

Station Wagon Only

1. It is not necessary to jack the car or remove the wheels unless you require working clearance. Unbolt the upper mounting nut and lower bolt and remove the shock absorber. Note the position of the washers and lock washers upon removal.
2. Installation is the reverse. Be sure the washers and lock washers are installed correctly. Tighten the upper mount to 44 ft. lbs. and the lower mount to 33 ft. lbs.

Civic sedan rear control arm

Rear toe adjustment location—Accord

Rear toe adjustment location—Civic

FRONT SUSPENSION

All models use a MacPherson strut type front suspension. Each steering knuckle is suspended by a lower control arm at the bottom and a combined coil spring/shock absorber unit at the top. A front stabilizer bar, mounted between each lower control arm and the body, doubles as a locating rod for the suspension. Caster and camber are not adjustable and are fixed by the location of the strut assemblies in their respective sheet metal towers.

Front Strut Assembly

For all spring and shock absorber removal and installation procedures and any other strut overhaul procedures, please refer to "Strut Overhaul" in the Unit Repair section.

INSPECTION

1. Check for wear or damage to bushings and needle bearings.
2. Check for oil leaks from the struts.
3. Check all rubber parts for wear or damage.
4. Bounce the car to check shock absorber effectiveness. The car should continue to bounce for no more than two cycles.

REMOVAL AND INSTALLATION

1. Raise the front of the car and support it with safety stands. Remove the front wheels.
2. Disconnect the brake pipe at the strut and remove the brake hose retaining clip.
3. Remove the caliper and carefully hang from the undercarriage of the car with a piece of wire.
4. On Accord models, disconnect the stabilizer bar from the lower arm.
5. Loosen the bolt on the knuckle that retains the lower end of the shock absorber.

Lower strut retaining (pinch) bolt

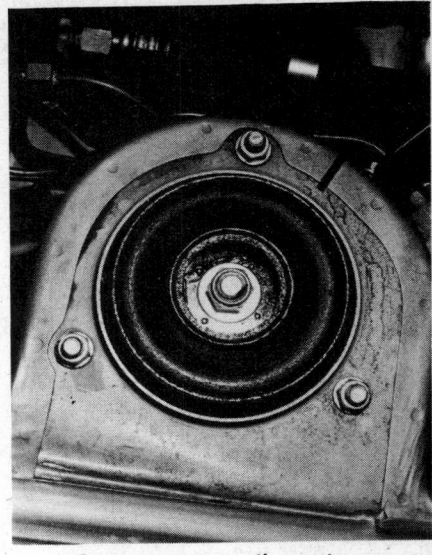

Strut upper mounting nuts

Push down firmly while tapping it with a hammer until the knuckle is free of the strut.

6. Remove the three nuts retaining the upper end of the strut and remove the strut from the car.
7. To install, reverse the removal procedure. Be sure to properly match the mating surface of the strut and the knuckle notch. Tighten the knuckle bolt to 40 ft. lbs. (43–51 ft. lbs.—Accord).

Lower Ball Joints

INSPECTION

Check ball joint play as follows:

a. Raise the front of the car and support it with safety stands.
b. Clamp a dial indicator onto the lower control arm and place the indicator tip on the knuckle, near the ball joint;

Front suspension and steering gear—typical

c. Place a pry bar between the lower control arm and the knuckle. Replace the lower control arm if the play exceeds 0.020 in.

Lower Control Arm and Stabilizer Bar

REMOVAL AND INSTALLATION

1. Raise the front of the car and support it with safety stands. Remove the front wheels.
2. Disconnect the lower arm ball joint as described above. Be careful not to damage the seal.
3. Remove the stabilizer bar retaining brackets, starting with the center brackets.
4. Remove the lower arm pivot bolt.
5. Disconnect the radius rod and remove the lower arm.
6. To install, reverse the removal procedure. Be sure to tighten the components to their proper torque. On the Civic, tighten the ball joint to 29–35 ft. lbs. and install a new cotter pin. Tighten the radius rod to arm bolts to 25–36 ft. lbs., and the stabilizer bar to radius rod bracket bolts to 5–9 ft. lbs. Tighten the lower arm pivot bolts to 25–36 ft. lbs.

On the Accord, tighten the ball joint nut to 29–35 ft. lbs. and install a new cotter pin. Tighten the radius rod to arm bolts to 36–43 ft. lbs. and the stabilizer bar to rod bracket bolts to 14–18 ft. lbs. Raise the lower arm with a jack to simulate body weight before tightening the arm pivot bolt to 25–36 ft. lbs. After tightening, bend one of the unused tabs of the lockwasher against the bolt flat. Do not re-use a bent tab during reassembly.

Steering Knuckles

REMOVAL AND INSTALLATION

1. Raise the front of the car and support it with safety stands. Remove the front wheel.
2. Remove the spindle nut cotter pin and the spindle nut.
3. Remove the two bolts retaining the brake caliper and remove the caliper from the knuckle. Do not let the caliper hang by the brake hose, support it with a length of wire.

NOTE: In case it is necessary to remove the disc, hub, bearings and/or outer dust seal, use Steps 4 and 5 given below. You will need a hydraulic press for this (see the Brakes Section). If this is unnecessary, omit Steps 4 and 5.

4. Install a hub puller attachment against the hub with the lug nuts.
5. Attach a slide hammer in the center hole of the attachment and pull out the hub, with the disc attached, from the knuckle.
6. Remove the tie-rod from the knuckle using the ball joint remover. Use care not to damage the ball joint seals.
7. Remove the lower arm from the knuckle using the ball joint remover.
8. Loosen the lockbolt which retains the strut in the knuckle. Tap the top of the knuckle with a hammer and slide it off the shock.
9. Remove the knuckle and hub, if still attached, by sliding the driveshaft out of the hub.
10. To install, reverse the removal procedure. If the hub was removed, refer to Brake Disc Removal, for procedures with the hydraulic press. Be sure to visually check the knuckle for visible signs of wear or damage and to check the condition of the inner bearing dust seals.

TORQUE SPECIFICATIONS

Part(s)	Torque (ft. lbs.)
Lower ball joint retaining nut	
Civic	22–29
Accord and Prelude	33
Lower control arm-to-body mount bolts	
Civic	25–36
Accord and Prelude	40
Front radius rod-to-knuckle bolt	40
Rear radius rod-to-carrier bolt	40–54
Rear radius rod-to-body bolt	40
Front stabilizer mount bolts	5–9
Strut center nut (front and rear)	40–50
Strut to body retaining bolts (front and rear)	16
Front strut to-knuckle retaining bolt	36–43
Rear strut-to-carrier mount bolts	26–35
Rear strut-to-control arm bolt	36–47

Front End Alignment

CASTER AND CAMBER ADJUSTMENT

Caster and camber cannot be adjusted on any Honda. If caster, camber or kingpin angle is incorrect or front end parts are damaged or worn, they must be replaced.

TOE-OUT ADJUSTMENT

Toe is the difference of the distance between the forward extremes of the front tires and the distance between the rearward extremes of the front tires. On Hondas, the fronts of the tires are further apart than the rear to counteract the pulling-together effect of front wheel drive.

Toe-out can be adjusted on all Hondas by loosening the locknuts at each end of the tie-rods. To increase toe-out, turn the right tie-rod in the direction of forward wheel rotation and turn the left tie-rod in the opposite direction. Turn both tie-rods an equal amount until toe-out becomes 0.039 in. (1 mm).

STEERING

Steering Wheel

REMOVAL AND INSTALLATION

1. Remove the steering wheel pad by lifting it off.
2. Remove the steering wheel retaining nut. Gently hit the backside of each of the steering wheel spokes with equal force from the palms of your hands.

— CAUTION —
Avoid hitting the wheel or the shaft with excessive force. Damage to the shaft could result.

Exploded view of steering wheel and related parts

3. Installation is the reverse of the removal procedure. Be sure to tighten the steering wheel nut to 22–36 ft. lbs.

Turn Signal Switch

REMOVAL AND INSTALLATION

1. Remove the steering wheel.
2. Disconnect the column wiring harness and coupler.

Loosening the turn signal cam nut screw

— CAUTION —
Be careful not to damage the steering column or shaft.

3. Remove the upper and lower column covers.
4. On models so equipped, remove the cruise control slip ring.
5. Remove the turn signal cancelling sleeve.
6. On later models, remove the switch retaining screws, then remove the switch.
7. Loosen the screw on the turn signal switch cam nut and lightly tap its head to permit the cam nut to loosen. Then remove the turn signal switch assembly and the steering shaft upper bushing.
8. To assemble and install, reverse the above procedure. When installing the turn signal switch assembly, engage the locating tab on the switch with the notch in the steering column. The steering shaft upper bushing should be installed with the flat side facing the upper side of the column. The alignment notch for the turn signal switch will be centered on the flat side of the bushing.

NOTE: On earlier models, if the cam nut has been removed, be sure to install it with the small end up.

Ignition Switch

REMOVAL AND INSTALLATION

1. Remove the steering column housing lower cover.
2. Disconnect the ignition switch wiring at the couplers.
3. The ignition switch assembly is held onto the column by two shear bolts. Remove these bolts, using a drill, to separate and remove the ignition switch.
4. To install, reverse the removal procedure. You will have to replace the shear bolts with new ones.
On 1982 and later Accords the mechanical part of the switch does not have to be removed to replace the electrical part. To remove the electrical part or base of the switch proceed as follows:
1. Remove the steering column lower cover.
2. Disconnect the electrical connector at the switch.
3. Insert the key and turn it to lock position.
4. Remove the two switch retaining screws, then remove the switch (base) from the rest of the switch.

Steering Gear

TESTING

1. Remove the dust seal bellows retaining bands and slide the dust seals off the left and right side of the gearbox housing.
2. Turn the front wheels full left and, using your hand, attempt to move the steering rack in an up-down direction.
3. Repeat with the wheel turned full right.
4. If any movement is felt, the steering gearbox must be adjusted.

Steering box and linkage

LOCKNUT

RACK GUIDE
ADJUSTING
SCREW

STEERING BOX

Steering box adjustment

Separate the air tube from the dust boot

Tie—rod lockwasher removal

ADJUSTMENT

1. Make sure that the rack is well lubricated.
2. Loosen the rack guide adjusting locknut.
3. Tighten the adjusting screw just to the point where the front wheels cannot be turned by hand.
4. Back off the adjusting screw 45 degrees and hold it in that position while adjusting the locknut.
5. Recheck the play, and then move the wheels lock-to-lock, to make sure that the rack moves freely.
6. Check the steering force by first raising the front wheels and then placing them in a straight-ahead position. Turn the steering wheel with a spring scale to check the steering force. Steering force should be no more than 3.3 lbs.

Tie-Rods

REMOVAL AND INSTALLATION

1. Raise the front of the car and support it with safety stands. Remove the front wheels.
2. Use a ball joint remover to remove the tie-rod from the knuckle.
3. Disconnect the air tube at the dust seal joint. Remove the tie-rod dust seal bellows clamps and move the rubber bellows on the tie-rod rack joints.
4. Straighten the tie-rod lockwasher tabs at the tie-rod-to-rack joint and remove the tie-rod by turning it with a wrench.
5. To install, reverse the removal procedure. Always use a new tie-rod lockwasher during reassembly. Fit the locating lugs into the slots on the rack and bend the outer edge of the washer over the flat part of the rod, after the tie-rod nut has been properly tightened.

Power Steering Pump

REMOVAL AND INSTALLATION

1. Drain the fluid from the system: Disconnect the cooler return hose from the reservoir and place the end in a large container. Start the engine and allow it to run at fast idle. Turn the steering wheel from lock to lock several times, until fluid stops running from the hose. Shut off the engine and discard the fluid. Reattach the hose.
2. Disconnect the inlet and outlet hoses at the pump.
3. Remove the drive belt.
4. Remove the bolts and remove the pump.
5. To install, install the pump on its mounts, install the belt, adjust belt tension, and install the fluid hoses.
6. Fill the reservoir with fresh fluid, to the full mark. Use only genuine Honda power steering fluid; ATF or other brands of fluid will damage the system.
7. Start the engine and allow to fast idle. Turn the steering wheel from side to side several times, lightly contacting the stops. This will bleed the system of air. Check the reservoir level and add fluid if necessary.

BELT ADJUSTMENT

1. Loosen the bolt on the adjuster arm.
2. Move the pump toward or away from the engine, until the belt can be depressed approximately 9/16 in. at the midpoint between the two pulleys under moderate thumb pressure. If the tension adjustment is being made on a new belt, the deflection should only be about 7/16 in., to allow for the initial stretching of the belt.
   There is a raised bump on the top of the adjusting arm. If the belt has stretched to the point where the adjustment bolt is at or beyond the bump, the belt should be replaced.

3. Tighten the bolt and recheck the adjustment.

STEERING TORQUE SPECIFICATIONS

Ft. Lbs.	
Tie-rod locknut	
Tie-rod ball joint nut	29.0–35.0
Bask guide locknut	29.0–36.0
Steering wheel retaining nut(s)	22.0–36.0

BRAKE SYSTEM

Honda uses a dual hydraulic system, with the brakes connected diagonally. In other words, the right front and left rear brakes are on the same hydraulic line and the left front and right rear are on the other line. This has the added advantage of front disc emergency braking, should either of the hydraulic systems fail. The diagonal rear brake serves to counteract the sway from single front disc braking.

A leading/trailing drum brake is used for the rear brakes, with disc brakes for the front. All Hondas are equipped with a brake warning light, which is activated when a defect in the brake system occurs.

For all brake system repair and service procedures not detailed below, please refer to ''Brakes'' in the Unit Repair section.

Adjustments

BRAKE PEDAL FREE-PLAY

Free-play is the distance the pedal travels from the stop (brake light switch) until the pushrod contacts the vacuum booster, which actuates the master cylinder.

To check free-play, first measure the distance (with the carpet removed) from the floor to the brake pedal. Then push down the pedal until contact is felt and again measure the distance from the floor to the brake pedal. The difference between the two measurements is the pedal free-play. The specified free-play is 0.04–0.20 in. Free-play adjustment is made by loosening the locknut on the brake light switch and rotating the switch body until the specified clearance is obtained.

FRONT DISC BRAKES

The front discs are inherently self adjusting. No adjustments are either necessary or possible.

Drum brake adjustment location

REAR DRUM BRAKES

1. Block the front wheels, release the parking brake and raise the rear of the car, supporting it with safety stands.
2. Depress the brake pedal two or three times and release.
3. The adjuster is located on the inboard side, underneath the control arm. Turn the adjuster clockwise until the wheel no longer turns.
4. Back off the adjuster two (2) clicks and turn the wheel to see if the brake shoes are dragging. If they are dragging, back off the adjuster one more click.

Master Cylinder

REMOVAL AND INSTALLATION

—————— CAUTION ——————
Before removing the master cylinder, cover the body surfaces with fender covers and rags to prevent damage to painted surfaces by brake fluid.

1. Disconnect and plug the brake lines at the master cylinder.
2. Remove the master cylinder-to-vacuum booster attaching bolts and remove the master cylinder from the car.
3. To install, reverse the removal procedure. Before operating the car, you must bleed the brake system.

Vacuum Booster

INSPECTION

A preliminary check of the vacuum booster can be made as follows:
   a. Depress the brake pedal several times using normal pressure. Make sure that the pedal height does not vary;
   b. Hold the pedal in the depressed position and start the engine. The pedal should drop slightly;
   c. Hold the pedal in the above posi-

tion and stop the engine. The pedal should stay in the depressed position for approximately 30 seconds.
   d. If the pedal does not drop when the engine is started or rises after the engine is stopped, the booster is not functioning properly.

REMOVAL AND INSTALLATION

1. Disconnect the vacuum hose at the booster.
2. Disconnect and plug the brake lines at the master cylinder.
3. Remove the brake pedal-to-booster link pin and the four nuts retaining the booster. The pushrod and nuts are located inside the car under the instrument panel.
4. Remove the booster with the master cylinder attached.
5. To install, reverse the removal procedure. Check the vacuum booster pushrod-to-master cylinder piston clearance as outlined in the master cylinder removal procedure. Don't forget to bleed the brake system before operating the car.

Front Wheel Bearings

REMOVAL AND INSTALLATION

NOTE: The following procedure for wheel bearing removal and installation necessitates the use of a hydraulic press. You will have to go to a machine or auto shop equipped with a press. Do not attempt this procedure without a press.

1. Raise the front of the car and support it with safety stands. Remove the front wheel.
2. Remove the caliper assembly from the brake disc and separate the tie-rod ball joint and lower ball joint from the knuckle.
3. Loosen the lockbolt which retains the front strut in the kunckle. Tap the top of the kunckle with a hammer and slide it off the shock. Remove the knuckle and hub by sliding the driveshaft out of the hub.
4. Remove the wheel bearing dust cover on the inboard side of the kunckle.
5. Remove the four bolts which hold the brake disc onto the hub. Remove the splashguard by removing the three retaining screws.
6. Remove the outer bearing retainer.
7. Remove the wheel bearings by supporting the knuckle in a hydraulic press, using two support plates. Make sure that the plates do not overlap the outer bearing race. Now use a proper sized driver and handle to remove the bearings.

NOTE: Whenever the wheel bearings are removed, always replace with a new set of bearings and outer dust seal.

8. Pack each bearing with grease before installing (see below).
9. To install the bearings, press them into the knuckle using the same support plates as above, plus the installing base. Use the same driver and handle you used to remove the bearing.

NOTE: The front wheel bearings are the angular contact type. It is important that they be installed with the manufacturer's markings facing inward (towards each other).

10. Use the press to install the front hub (see above).
11. The rest of installation is the reverse of the removal procedure.

CLEANING AND REPACKING

1. Clean all old grease from the driveshaft spindles on the car.
2. Remove all old grease from the hub and knuckle and thoroughly dry and wipe clean all components.
3. When fitting new bearings, you must pack them with wheel bearing grease. To do this, place a glob of grease in you left palm, then, holding one of the bearings in your right hand, drag the face of the bearing heavily through the grease. This must be done to work as much grease as possible through the ball bearings and the cage. Turn the bearing and continue to pull it through the grease, until the grease is thoroughly packed between the bearing balls and the cage, all around the bearings. Repeat this operation until all of the bearings are packed with grease.
4. Pack the inside of the rotor and knuckle hub with a moderate amount of grease. Do not overload the hub with grease.
5. Apply a small amount of grease to the spindle and to the lip of the inner seal before installing.
6. To install the bearings, check the above procedures.

CHECKING AND ADJUSTING

The front wheel bearings should be inspected and repacked (or replaced) every 30,000 miles. To check the wheel bearings for any play, jack up each wheel and shake it to check the bearings for any play. If any play is felt, tighten the castellated spindle nut to the specified torque (87–130 ft. lbs.) and reinspect. If play is still present, replace the bearing.

NOTE: Overtightening the spindle nuts will cause excessive bearing friction and will result in rough wheel rotation and eventual bearing failure.

Wheel Cylinders

REMOVAL AND INSTALLATION

1. Remove the brake drum and shoes.
2. Disconnect the parking brake cable and brake lines at the backing plate. Be sure to have a drip pan to catch the brake fluid.
3. Remove the two wheel cylinders retaining nuts on the inboard side of the backing plate and remove the wheel cylinder.
4. To install, reverse the removal procedure. When assembling, apply a thin coat of grease to the grooves of the wheel cylinder piston and the sliding surfaces of the backing plate. Bleed the brakes.

Handbrake

CABLE REMOVAL AND INSTALLATION

1. Remove the adjusting nut from the equalizer mounted on the rear axle and separate the cable from the equalizer.
2. Set the parking brake lever to a fully released position and remove the cotter pin from the side of the brake lever.
3. After removing the cotter pin, pull out the pin which connects the cable and the lever.
4. Detach the cable from the guides at the front and right side of the fuel tank and remove the cable.
5. To install, reverse the removal procedure, making sure that grease is applied to the cable and the guides.

ADJUSTMENT

Inspect the following items:
   a. Check the ratchet for wear;

Parking brake equalizer assembly

   b. Check the cables for wear or damage and the cable guide and equalizer for looseness;
   c. Check the equalizer cable where it contracts the equalizer and apply grease if necessary;
   d. Check the rear brake adjustment.

The rear wheels should be locked when the handbrake lever is pulled 1 to 5 notches on the ratchet. Adjustment is made by turning the nut located at the equalizer, between the lower control arms.

Rear Wheel Bearings

ADJUSTMENT

Rear wheel bearings are not adjustable on the 1976–79 Civic models. Tighten the castle nut to 83 ft. lbs. and install a new cotter pin whenever removed.

To adjust the bearings on all other models.
1. Tighten the castle nut to 18 ft. lbs.
2. Rotate the drum a few times.
3. Back off the castle nut about 100°.

4. Tighten the castle nut to 1.1–3.6 ft. lbs.

5. Install the lock nut with its slots as close as possible to the spindle hole. Tighten the castle nut/lock nut just enough to align the slots and the hole, and install a new cotter pin.

CHASSIS ELECTRICAL

Heater

REMOVAL AND INSTALLATION

NOTE: These procedures do not apply to cars equipped with air conditioning. On cars equipped with air conditioning, heater removal may differ from the procedures listed below. Only a trained air conditioning specialist should tamper with A/C equipped units. Air conditioning units contain pressurized Freon which can be extremely dangerous (e.g. burns and/or blindness) to the untrained.

Civic

1976–79

1. Drain the radiator.
2. Disconnect the right and left defroster hoses.
3. Disconnect the inlet and outlet water hoses at the heater assembly.

NOTE: There will be a coolant leakage when disconnecting the hoses. Catch the coolant in a container to prevent damage to the interior.

4. Disconnect the following items:
   a. Fre-Rec control cable;
   b. Temperature control rod;
   c. Room/Def. control cable;
   d. Fan motor switch connector;
   e. Upper attaching bolts;
   f. Lower attaching bolts;
   g. Lower bracket.

Exploded view of parking brake components

5. Remove the heater assembly through the passenger side.

6. To install the heater assembly, reverse the removal procedure. Pay attention to the following points:

 a. When installing the heater assembly, do not forget to connect the right side of the upper bracket;

 b. Connect the inlet and outlet water hoses SECURELY;

NOTE: The inlet hose is a straight type, and the outlet hose is an L-type.

 c. Install the defroster nozzles in the correct position;

 d. Connect the control cables securely. Operate the control valve and lever to check for proper operation.

 e. Be sure to bleed the cooling system.

1980 AND LATER

1. Drain the radiator.
2. Remove the dashboard.
3. Disconnect both heater hoses at the firewall and drain the coolant into a container.
4. Remove the heater lower mounting nut on the firewall.
5. Remove the two heater duct retaining clips.
6. Disconnect the control cables from the heater.
7. Remove the heater valve cable cover and remove the heater assembly.
8. Installation is the reverse of removal. Bleed cooling system and make sure cables are properly adjusted.

Accord

NOTE: To remove the heater core, it is necessary to first remove the entire instrument panel and heater assemblies.

1. Drain the cooling system.
2. Remove the steering column lower trim cover.
3. Remove the two nuts and two bolts retaining the column to the firewall support.
4. Remove the instrument wire harnesses from cabin wire harness couples.
5. Reach behind the instrument cluster and disconnect the speedometer cable and four wiring harness connectors at rear of cluster. Pry out the lock tabs to disconnect.
6. Disconnect radio lead and antenna wire.
7. Remove the heater fan switch knob, heater lever knobs and heater control bezel. Remove heater control center panel. Disconnect cigarette lighter and blower motor leads.
8. Disconnect clock leads.
9. Remove the seven sheet metal screws retaining the instrument panel to the firewall. There are two at each end of the dash (adjacent to windshield pillar), two beneath the radio and one adjacent to the clock.
10. Pull out the instrument panel and support. Check for any wires still connected.
11. Inside the engine compartment, dis-

connect the two heater hoses at the firewall. Remove the nut retaining the heater unit to the firewall.

12. Disconnect the three heater control cables from the heater unit. Disconnect the cable clip from the heater valve.

13. Remove the heater unit lower mounting bolt and the right and left upper mounting bolts. Separate the blower hose from the heater.

14. Lay some towels underneath to catch residual coolant leakage. Remove the heater unit.

15. To service the heater core, separate the heater housing halves.

16. Reverse the above to install. Bleed the cooling system using the bleed bolt located near the ignition distributor.

Prelude

1. Remove the blower by removing the instrument panel side cover.
2. Remove the glove box and the three blower mounting bolts.
3. Remove the blower from the heater case.
4. Drain the coolant.
5. Remove the lower dash panel.
6. Place a drain pan under the case and disconnect both heater hoses at the core tubes.
7. Remove the heater lower mount nut on the firewall.
8. Disconnect the cable at the water valve.
9. Remove the control cables from the heater case.
10. Remove the upper mount bolts and remove the heater.

Blower Motor

REMOVAL AND INSTALLATION

1. Remove the three lower retaining screws for the glovebox. Then, push down and remove the glovebox. Remove the three screws for the glovebox ceiling, and remove the ceiling.

2. Disconnect the fresh air control cable from the blower housing. Disconnect the blower leads.

3. Remove the three bolts retaining the blower housing to the firewall. Separate the heater duct hose from the blower housing, and remove the blower housing.

4. To service the blower motor, separate the blower housing halves.

5. Reverse the above to install.

Windshield Wipers

REMOVAL AND INSTALLATION

Motor and Linkage

The wiper motor on all models is connected

to the engine compartment wall, below the front windshield.

1. Remove the negative (−) cable from the battery.
2. Disconnect the motor leads at the connector.
3. Remove the motor water seal cover clamp, and the seal, from the motor.
4. Remove the special nut which holds the wiper arms to the pivot shafts and remove the arms.
5. Remove the left and right pivot nuts and push the pivots down.
6. Remove the three wiper motor mounting bolts and remove the wiper/linkage assembly from the engine compartment.
7. Pull out the motor arm cotter pin and separate the linkage from the motor.
8. Remove the three bracket bolts to remove the motor from its mounting bracket.
9. To install, reverse the removal procedure. Be sure to inspect the linkage and pivots for wear and looseness. When installing the motor, be sure it is in the "automatic stop" position.

Removing the cotter pin from the motor arm linkage

Instrument Cluster

REMOVAL AND INSTALLATION

Meter Case Assembly

1. Remove the three meter case mounting wing nuts from the rear of the instrument panel.
2. Disconnect the speedometer and tachometer drive cables at the engine.
3. Pull the meter case away from the panel. Disconnect the meter wires at the connectors.

NOTE: Be sure to label the wires to avoid confusion during reassembly.

4. Disconnect the speedometer and tachometer cables at the meter case and remove the case from the car.
5. To install, reverse the removal procedure.

Switch Panel

1. Loosen the four steering wheel column cover screws and remove the upper and lower covers.
2. Remove the four steering column bolts (remove the upper two bolts first) and rest the steering assembly on the floor.

Civic instrument panel retaining screw locations through 1979

3. Remove the four switch panel screws from the rear of the instrument panel.

4. To release the switch panel, remove the switches in the following manner:

a. Remove the light switch by prying the cover off the front of the knob. Pinch the retaining tabs together and pull off the knob;

b. Remove the wiper switch by pushing the knob in and turning counterclockwise. Then remove the retaining nut;

c. Remove the choke knob by loosening the set screw. Then remove the retaining nut.

5. To install, reverse the removal procedure.

Civic Instrument Panel Assembly (Complete)

1976–79

1. Loosen the four steering wheel column cover screws and remove the upper and lower covers.

2. Remove the four steering column bolts (remove the upper two bolts first) and rest the steering assembly on the floor.

3. Remove the screw on the outside edge of each fresh air vent and pry off the vents with a screwdriver.

4. Disconnect the instrument panel wiring harness from their cabin harnesses by removing the connectors and couplers.

5. Disconnect the speedometer and tachometer cables at the engine.

6. Disconnect the choke cable at the panel.

7. Remove the following switches:

a. Remove the light switch by prying the cover off the front of the knob. Pinch the retaining tabs together and pull off the knob;

b. Remove the wiper switch by pushing the knob in and turning counterclockwise. Then remove the retaining nut;

c. Remove the choke knob by loosening the set screw. Then remove the retaining nut.

8. Disconnect the three heater control cables.

9. Remove the heater fan motor wire connector.

10. Remove the six bolts which attach the panel.

11. Pull the panel out slightly and disconnect the speedometer and tachometer cables at the instruments. Then remove the instrument panel.

12. To install, reverse the removel procedure. Pay attention to the following points:

a. First, connect the speedometer and tachometer cables to the instruments. Then install the panel in place with the center pin in the panel locating hole;

b. Temporarily tighten the bolts which secure the upper, right, and left sides of the instrument panel. Make sure that the wiring harnesses are properly routed.

1980–83

1. On 1980–81 models remove the steering column.

2. On 1982 and later models lower the steering column.

3. On 1980–81 models remove the bulb access panel and remove the two upper mounting screws through the access panel; then the lower mounting bolt and screws.

4. On 1982 and later models, remove the four screws and trim cover.

5. Disconnect the speedometer cable and tachometer cable if so equipped.

6. Disconnect any remaining mount screws and wire connecters and remove the instrument panel.

7. Installation is the reverse of removal.

Accord and Prelude Instrument Panel Assembly (Complete)

1. Remove the instrument cluster as outlined earlier.

2. Remove the speaker grille and then remove the clock panel and take out the clock.

3. Remove the control knobs and remove the heater control panel from the instrument panel.

4. Remove the three screws which hold the inner panel. The center panel and the heater control assembly are tightened together.

5. Remove the instrument panel left and right side covers, and remove the two bolts on either side.

6. Remove the two bolts in the center of the instrument panel.

7. Remove the bolt behind the clock panel.

8. You should now be able to remove the instrument panel.

9. Installation is the reverse of removal. Remember the following points:

a. void bending the heater lever when installing the dashboard. Make sure the heater levers move freely without binding.

b. Make sure the instrument wiring harnesses aren't pinched.

Fuses and Fusible Links

All models are equipped with a fusible link connected between the starter relay and the main wiring harness of the car, located next to the battery.

The Civic fuse box is located below the glove compartment, on the right bulkhead. The rating and function of each fuse is posted inside the fuse box cap for quick reference.

The Accord and Prelude fuse box is a flip down affair, located under the left side of the instrument panel.

Accord fuse box location

Civic fuse box location

Isuzu

SERIAL NUMBER IDENTIFICATION

Vehicle

The vehicle identification number is embossed on a plate attached to the top left of the instrument panel. The number is visible through the windshield from outside the car.

Engine

The engine serial number is stamped on the top right front corner of the engine block on gasoline engines. On diesel models, the engine serial number is stamped on the left rear corner of the engine block.

Transmission

Both manual transmissions have their serial numbers on the side of the main case. The automatic location is similar.

Vehicle identification plate location

Engine serial number location—diesel

DI-0002

Engine serial number location—gasoline

GENERAL ENGINE SPECIFICATIONS

Year	Engine Displacement (cu. in.)	Carburetor Type	Horsepower (@ rpm)	Torque @ rpm (ft. lbs.)	Bore × Stroke (in.)	Compression Ratio	Oil Pressure @ rpm (psi)
'81–'83	110.8	Hitachi DCH340	80 @ 4800	95 @ 3000	3.31 × 3.23	8.5:1	57 @ 1400
	110.8	Diesel	51 @ 5000	72 @ 3000	3.31 × 3.23	22.0:1	64 @ 1400

GASOLINE ENGINE TUNE-UP SPECIFICATIONS

When analyzing compression test results, look for uniformity among cylinders, rather than specific pressures

Year	Displacement (cu. in.)	Spark Plugs Type	Gap (in.)	Distributor Point Dwell (deg)	Point Gap (in.)	Ignition Timing (deg) MT	AT	Intake Valve Opens (deg)	Fuel Pump Pressure (psi)	Idle Speed (rpm)	Valve Clear (in.) (cold) In	Ex
'81–'83	110.8	NGK-BPR6ESII	0.040	Electronic		6B	6B	21	3.6	800①	0.006	0.010

NOTE: The underhood specifications sticker often reflects tune-up specification changes made in production. Sticker figures must be used if they disagree with this chart.
① AT—900 RPM
B Before top dead center

DIESEL ENGINE TUNE-UP SPECIFICATIONS

Year	Injector Opening Pressure (psi)	Low Idle (rpm)	Valve Clearance Intake	Exhaust	Intake Valve Opens (deg.)	Injection Timing (deg.)	Firing Order
'81–'83	2133	625①	0.010	0.014	32B	18B②	1-3-4-2

①A/T: 725 rpm
②12B on 1982 and later

FIRING ORDERS

Firing order—gasoline engine

FRONT ➡

Firing order—diesel engine, 1-3-4-2

CAPACITIES

Year	Model	Engine Displacement (cu.in.)	Engine Crankcase (qts) With Filter	Without Filter	Transmission (pts) Manual 4-spd	5-spd	Automatic	Drive Axle (pts)	Gasoline Tank (gals)	Cooling System (qts) W/ AC	W/O AC
'81–'83	Gas	110.8	5.8	5.3	2.7	2.7	14①	2.7	13.7	6.4	6.4
	Diesel	110.8	5.8	5.3	2.7	2.7	14①	2.7	13.7	7.4	7.4

①26.8 pts with torque converter

CRANKSHAFT AND CONNECTING ROD SPECIFICATIONS

(All measurements are given in inches)

Year	Engine Displacement (cu.in.)	Crankshaft Main Brg. Journal Dia.	Crankshaft Main Brg. Oil Clearance	Crankshaft Shaft End-Play	Crankshaft Thrust on No.	Connecting Rod Journal Diameter	Connecting Rod Oil Clearance	Connecting Rod Side Clearance
'81–'83	110.8 (Gas)	2.2050	0.0008–0.0025	0.0117	3	1.929	0.0007–0.0030	0.0137
	110.8 (Diesel)	2.2020	0.0012–0.0027	0.0018	3	1.925	0.0016–0.0027	0.0137

VALVE SPECIFICATIONS

Year	Engine Displacement (cu.in.)	Seat Angle (deg)	Face Angle (deg)	Spring Test Pressure (lbs. @in.)	Spring Installed Height (in.)	Stem to Guide Clearance (in.) Intake	Stem to Guide Clearance (in.) Exhaust	Stem Diameter (in.) Intake	Stem Diameter (in.) Exhaust
'81–'83	110.8 (Gas)	45①	45	outer—34.5 @ 1.614 inner—20 @ 1.516	outer—1.61 inner—1.51	0.009–0.0022	0.0015–0.0031	0.315	0.315
	110.8 (Diesel)	45①	45	outer—34.6 @ 1.614 inner—20 @ 1.515	outer—1.85 inner—1.78	0.0015–0.0027	0.002–0.003	0.313	0.313

①Because of the aluminum head and valve seat inserts, cut the valve seat with 15, 45 or 75 degree cutters. Use the minimum necessary to remove dents or damage, leaving the contact width inside the 0.0472–0.063 range.

PISTON AND RING SPECIFICATIONS

(All measurements in inches)

Year	Engine Displacement (cu. in.)	Piston Clearance	Ring Gap Top Compression	Ring Gap Bottom Compression	Ring Gap Oil Control	Ring Side Clearance Top Compression	Ring Side Clearance Bottom Compression	Ring Side Clearance Oil Control
'81–'83	110.8 (Gas)	0.0018–0.0026	0.008–0.016	0.008–0.016	0.008–0.035	0.0059	0.0059	0.0059
	110.8 (Diesel)	0.0002–0.0017	0.008–0.016	0.008–0.016	0.008–0.016	0.0059	0.0059	0.0059

ALTERNATOR AND REGULATOR SPECIFICATIONS

Year	Alternator Manufacturer or Part Number	Alternator Output Amps @ rpm	Voltage Regulator Charge Indicator Relay Back Gap (in.)	Voltage Regulator Charge Indicator Relay Point Gap (in.)	Voltage Regulator Regulator Back Gap (in.)	Voltage Regulator Regulator Air Gap (in.)	Voltage Regulator Regulator Point Gap (in.)	Regulated Voltage
'81–'83	LT140-126	40	0.036	0.020	0.015	0.014	0.012	13.8–14.8
	L150-144	50	0.036	0.020	0.015	0.014	0.012	13.8–14.8
	LT150-131B	50	0.036	0.020	0.015	0.014	0.012	13.8–14.8

TORQUE SPECIFICATIONS
(All readings in ft. lbs.)

Year	Engine Displacement (cu. in.)	Cylinder Head Bolts	Rod Bearing Bolts	Main Bearing Bolts	Crankshaft Pulley Bolt	Flywheel to Crankshaft Bolts	Manifolds	
							Intake	Exhaust
'81-'83	110.8②	72①	43	72	87	69	13	15
	110.8③	90①	58	72	108	43	26	15

① Install head bolts according to pattern and tighten to one-half torque value, then torque to specifications.
② Gasoline engine
③ Diesel engine

TORQUE SEQUENCE

FRONT COVER FIXING SCREW

Cylinder head bolt torque sequence—gasoline engine

Cylinder head bolt torque sequence—diesel engine

BATTERY AND STARTER SPECIFICATIONS
(All cars use 12 volt, negative ground electrical systems)

Year	Engine Cu. in.	Battery Amp Hour Capacity	Starter						Brush Spring Tension (oz)	Min. Brush Length (in.)
			Lock Test			No Load Test				
			Amps	Volts	Torque	Amps	Volts	rpm		
'81-'83	110.8	50	NOT RECOMMENDED						56	0.472

BRAKE SPECIFICATIONS
(All measurements given are in. unless noted)

Year	Model	Lug Nut Torque (ft. lbs.)	Master Cylinder Bore	Brake Disc		Brake Drum			Minimum Lining Thickness	
				Minimum Thickness	Maximum Run-Out	Diameter	Max. Machine O/S	Max. Wear Limit	Front	Rear
'81-'83	All	50①	0.875	.339	.006②	9.00	9.04	9.06	.067	.040

① 90 ft. lbs. on aluminum wheels
② Front wheel bearings properly adjusted

WHEEL ALIGNMENT SPECIFICATIONS

(All settings at curb weight)

| Year | Model | Caster | | Camber | | Toe-In (in.) |
		Range (deg)	Preferred Setting (deg)	Range (deg)	Preferred Setting (deg)	
'81–'83	All	4P–6P	5P	½N–½P	0	⅛

Note: Caster angle is pre-set and cannot be serviced

TUNE-UP PROCEDURES

The Isuzu automobile comes equipped with a tune-up label in the engine compartment. This label has information developed during production. Should information in any way disagree with the specifications label, follow the label information for proper settings.

Spark Plugs

REMOVAL AND INSTALLATION

NOTE: Spark plugs should be replaced every 30,000 miles and inspected every 15,000 miles.

Grasp each ignition wire by the boot around the plug and pull straight out. Do not pull on the wire lead itself. Check the condition of the boot and wire and replace if necessary. Slowly back out the plug, being careful not to damage the threads in the cylinder head. Be sure to keep the socket straight on the plug to avoid breaking the ceramic insulator. If the insulator is cracked or damaged in any way, the spark plug should be replaced.

Inspect the plugs for signs of wear or abnormal combustion. Discard plugs that are fouled badly or have a damaged electrode. Clean and regap all plugs before installation. Use a wire gauge to set the correct plug gap, according to the tune-up chart. The wire should pass through the electrode gap with a slight drag. Never attempt to adjust the center electrode. Lightly oil the threads of the plug before reinstalling in the head. Start the plugs in by hand to avoid crossthreading, then tighten the plugs with the socket to 18–21 ft. lbs. If crossthreaded plug holes are encountered, see the cylinder head overhaul section. Install the ignition wires firmly on the plugs, being careful not to cross any wires.

Electronic Ignition

AIR GAP SETTING

All models of gasoline engines have electronic ignition. The only adjustment possible on this ignition system is the setting of the air gap inside the distributor.

1. Remove the distributor cap and O-ring.
2. Remove the rotor.
3. Use a feeler gauge (brass) to measure the air gap at the pick up coil projection. The gap should be 0.008–0.016 in. Adjust if necessary.
4. Loosen the screws and move the signal generator until the gap is correct. Tighten the screws and recheck the gap.

Distributor air gap adjustment

Checking resistance in signal generator with ohmmeter

NOTE: The electrical parts in this system are not repairable. If found to be defective they must be replaced.

The signal generator can be checked for proper operation by using an ohmmeter to determine its resistance. It should be 140–180 ohms. If the resistance is not correct, replace the signal generator.

Ignition Timing

ADJUSTMENT

NOTE: The timing marks are located at the front of the crankshaft pulley and consist of a graduated scale attached to the engine block and a notch in the crankshaft pulley. Check and adjust the timing every 30,000 miles.

1. Locate and clean off the timing marks. Highlight the marks with paint or chalk.
2. Connect a timing light according to the manufacturer's instructions. The spark plug connection may be made at either No. 1 or No. 4 cylinder.
3. Start the engine and allow it to reach operating temperature. Make sure the engine is idling smoothly.
4. Aim the timing light at the marks and check the position of the crankshaft pulley notch on the timing scale. If necessary, adjust the timing by loosening the distributor clamping bolt and turning the

Ignition timing marks

Adjusting valve clearance

distributor. The timing should be set at 6°BTDC @ 900 rpm for automatic transmission models, (800 rpm for manual transmission).

5. After timing is set to specifications, tighten the distributor clamping bolt and remove the timing light connections.

Valve Lash

ADJUSTMENT

All Models

1. Remove the air cleaner and rocker shaft cover.

NOTE: Engine should be cold for adjustment. Adjust the valves every 15,000 miles.

2. Check the rocker arm shaft bracket nuts for tightness before adjusting the valves. Torque bracket nuts to 16 ft. lbs.

3. Bring either No. 1 or No. 4 piston up to top dead center on the compression stroke. Align the timing mark with the pointer on the crankshaft pulley by turning the crankshaft (it's a lot easier if you take out the plugs).

4. Once the engine is set up at TDC, adjust the valves for the cylinder at TDC, then move down in order after turning the crankshaft one revolution for each cylinder.

5. Measurements should be taken at the clearance between rocker arm and valve stem. Standard valve clearances at low temperatures are:

	Diesel	Gasoline
Intake	0.25 mm (0.01 in)	0.15 mm (0.006 in)
Exhaust	0.35 mm (0.014 in)	0.25 mm (0.010 in)

Measuring valve clearances

6. To adjust the clearance, loosen the locknut and use a screwdriver to turn the adjusting stud until a slight drag is felt on the feeler gauge.

NOTE: While all valve adjustments must be made accurately, it's better to have the valve adjustment slightly loose than slightly tight. A burned valve or warped valve stem can result from overly tight adjustments.

7. Tighten the locknut and recheck the adjustment.

8. When all valves are correctly adjusted, replace the rocker arm cover using a new gasket. Check for oil leaks.

Idle Speed

ADJUSTMENT

Gasoline Engine

NOTE: Idle speed should be adjusted every 30,000 miles.

1. Set the parking brake and block the drive wheels.

2. Place the transmission in Neutral, start the engine and allow it to reach normal operating temperature.

NOTE: If the engine is idling for more

Checking rocker shaft for tightness

TDC timing mark alignment

NUT

WASHER

SPARK PLUG BRACKETS

Rocker arm cover showing attaching bolts

than five minutes, precede all adjustments with a clear-out blip for a few seconds.

3. The adjustments should be made with the choke open, air conditioner off, air cleaner installed, and distributor vacuum line, canister purge line and EGR vacuum line disconnected and plugged, and idle compensator vacuum line closed by bending rubber hose.

4. Turn throttle adjusting screw to adjust engine to 900 ± 50 rpm if the car is an automatic, and 800 ± 50 rpm if the car has a manual trans.

5. If the car has an air conditioner, turn the A/C on Max Cold and High blower. Open the throttle to approximately ⅓ and allow the throttle to close. (This allows the speed up solenoid to reach full travel) Adjust the speed up solenoid adjusting screw to set the idle at 900 ± 50 rpm.

DIESEL ENGINE

NOTE: Idle speed should be adjusted every 30,000 miles.

1. Set the parking brake and block the drive wheels.
2. Place the transmission in Neutral.
3. Start the engine and allow it to warm up to operating temperature.
4. Connect a tachometer according to the manufacturer's instructions.
5. If the idle speed deviates from the specified range, loosen the idle adjusting screw lock nut and turn the screw in or out until the idle speed is correct.

MIXTURE ADJUSTMENT

Gasoline Engine

1. Set parking brake and block the drive wheels.
2. Place the transmission in neutral and remove the carburetor assembly. (see carburetor section for R&R procedures)
3. Remove the plug for the idle mixture screw using a screwdriver which is inserted into the slit on the carburetor lower flange.
4. Reinstall the carburetor assembly.

PLUG; Idle mixture screw

Removing mixture plug

5. Make the engine idle speed adjustments with the engine at normal operating temperature, choke open, A/C off, distributor vacuum line and EGR vacuum line disconnected and plugged, and idle compensator vacuum line closed by bending the rubber hose.

NOTE: The exact fuel mixture can only be set with the use of an emissions analyzer. While these adjustments will get you in the ballpark, all adjustments must be double-checked and fine-tuned by a qualified shop with the proper test equipment.

6. Turn the idle mixture screw all the

way in and back out one turn on California models, two turns on 49 states models.

7. Check that engine idle is still at specifications. Adjust if necessary.

8. Adjust the setting of the idle mixture screw to achieve the maximum rpm, then reset idle to specs using idle adjusting screw (clockwise is lean).

9. Fine-tune mixture adjustment to achieve correct idle speed.

10. Replace the idle mixture plug.

Diesel Injection Timing

ADJUSTMENT

1. Check that the notched line on the injection pump flange is in alignment with the notched line on the injection pump front bracket.

2. Bring the piston in No. 1 cylinder to TDC on the compression stroke by turning the crankshaft as necessary.

3. With the timing pulley housing cover

Correct injection pump alignment

Correct alignment of timing marks

AIR HOSE

ECS HOSE   PCV HOSE

TCA HOSE

Air cleaner hoses

Static timing gauge J-29763

removed, check that timing belt is properly tensioned and that the timing marks are aligned. (see timing belt adjustment)

4. Disconnect the injection pipe from the injection pump and remove the distributor head screw, then install static timing gauge (special tool J-29763).

5. Use a wrench to hold the delivery holder when loosening the sleeve nuts on the injection pump side.

6. Bring the piston in No. 1 cylinder to a point 45–60 degrees before top dead center by turning the crankshaft, then calibrate the dial indicator to zero.

7. Turn the crankshaft pulley slightly in both directions and check that gauge indication is stable.

8. Turn the crankshaft in the normal direction of rotation (clockwise) and take the reading on the dial indicator when the timing mark (18° BTDC) on the crankshaft pulley is in alignment with the pointer.

NOTE: 1982 and later models do not have a cold start device. Set injection timing to 12BTDC.

9. If the reading on the dial indicator deviates from the specified range, hold the crankshaft in position 18 degrees before top dead center and loosen two nuts on the injection pump flange.

10. Move the injection pump to a point where the dial indicator gives a reading of 0.5 mm (0.020 in) then tighten the pump flange nuts to 42–52 ft. lbs.

Dial indicator (lower inset) is read when the timing mark is aligned with the pointer

FAST IDLE SPEED ADJUSTMENT

1. Start and warm up the engine.
2. Connect a tachometer according to the manufacturer's instructions.
3. Disconnect the hoses from the vacuum switch valve, then connect a pipe (4 mm diameter) in position between the hoses.
4. Loosen the adjusting nut and adjust engine idle speed. Fast idle should be around 900–950 rpm.

Glow plugs and connector locations

5. Tighten the adjusting nut and remove the tachometer.

Glow Plugs

REMOVAL AND INSTALLATION

The glow plugs are designed to preheat the combustion chambers so that the diesel engine will have sufficient temperature to fire the fuel on initial starting. They resemble spark plugs and are removed much the same way. Disconnect the wire leads and use a deep socket to remove the glow plug from the cylinder head. Care must be taken not to damage the glow plug in any way or to

Testing continuity of glow plug

strip the threads in the cylinder head. If a tight glow plug is encountered, coat the threads with some light weight oil and allow it to soak for a while. Be sure to use the correct glow plug for the car. They are not interchangeable.

TESTING

NOTE: If the glow plugs should fail to work, check the fusible link before removing the glow plugs.

1. Remove the glow plug.
2. Using a circuit tester, check for continuity across the plug terminals and the body. If no continuity exists, the glow plug should be replaced.

ENGINE ELECTRICAL

Distributor

REMOVAL AND INSTALLATION

NOTE: Every 30,000 miles, the distributor should be checked for proper operation. Check the cap and wires, rotor, air gap, vacuum advance mechanism and lubricate all working parts lightly.

1. Disconnect the battery cable.
2. Tag the wires and remove distributor cap with ignition wires attached.
3. Disconnect the coil and vacuum line.
4. Remove the distributor clamp bolt and bracket and lift out the distributor.

Glow circuit schematic

Ignition system schematic—gasoline only

Distributor cap, O-ring and rotor

— CAUTION —

Never hammer on the distributor housing to tap it loose.

5. Installation is the reverse of removal. Check the timing and adjust if necessary.

Generator

REMOVAL AND INSTALLATION

Removing the generator is simply a matter of loosening the mounting and adjustment bolts, removing the belt and lifting out the generator assembly. Diesel models have a vacuum pump mounted on the front of the generator assembly. It must be removed along with the generator for service.

1. Disconnect the battery.
2. Loosen all mounting and adjusting bolts and remove generator drive belt.
3. Remove mounting bolts and lift out generator.

NOTE: Tag all wires before removing them from the generator.

4. Installation is the reverse of removal. Proper belt deflection is 10 mm (0.4 in.)

Voltage Regulator

TESTING AND ADJUSTING

1. Perform this test with the regulator on the car and the engine running.
2. Connect a voltmeter between the condenser lead and ground with all electrical loads disconnected, including the blower relay connector.
3. The voltage regulator is working properly when the lower side points are closed while the engine is turned off, and upper points are closed when the engine is running at idle. If the points are not working normally, chances are that the regulator is out of adjustment, or the voltage coil is open.
4. Check the coil resistance and replace the regulator assembly if found to be malfunctioning. If the coil resistance is normal, adjust the regulator.
5. Start the engine and increase the engine speed gradually. Voltage should increase with engine rpm up to 1400–1850

rpm. A normal condition is indicated when the voltage is within the range of 13.8–14.8 volts. Reconnect blower relay connector.
6. Remove the regulator cover and check all internal parts for wear or damage. Be careful of all gaskets and seals.
7. Check the points for burning—file if necessary until all burrs are removed. Use an ohmmeter to check the resistance of the regulator and relay coils. The regulator coil resistance should be 102 ohms and the relay coil resistance should be 24 ohms. If an open or shorted coil is indicated, replace the regulator assembly.
8. Check the resistor resistance. It should be 10.5 ohms. If it's not, replace the resistor.
9. Connect a voltmeter between "N" terminal and ground then increase engine speed gradually. Voltmeter reading should be 4–5.8 volts when indicator light goes out. Adjust cut-in voltage by adjusting armature core gap and point gap. If voltage is too high, adjust by bending core arm "A" down. Bend up if cut-in voltage is too low.
10. If adjustment of core arm does not correct cut-in voltage, proceed with point gap adjustment.
11. Disconnect battery. Check armature core gap with armature depressed until moving point is in contact with "B" side point. Armature core gap should be 0.3 mm (0.012 in) or more. Adjust by bending point arm "B".
12. Release the armature and adjust the gap between the "B" side point and the

Regulator test connections

Generator and voltage regulator wiring

1. Vacuum pump
2. Cover
3. Brush
4. Through bolt
5. Pulley assembly
6. Pulley nut
7. Pulley

8. Fan
9. Rotor assembly
10. Spacer
11. Ball bearing
12. Rotor
13. Front cover assembly
14. Front cover

15. Ball bearing
16. Bearing retainer
17. Screw
18. Terminal bolt and nut
19. Condenser
20. Rear cover
21. Stator

22. Diode
23. Holder plate
24. Brush holder
25. IC regulator assembly
26. Lead wire

Exploded view of generator—typical

moving point by bending point arm "C". Point gap should be 0.4–1.2 mm (0.016–0.04 in.)

13. After point gap adjustment, recheck cut-in voltage. If not within 4–5.8 volts, repeat cut-in voltage adjustment.

14. If the no load regulated voltage is not within the 13.8–14.8 range, adjust the voltage regulator setting. If the voltage is too high, bend core arm "D" down. If the voltage is low, bend it up.

15. If the core arm adjustment does not correct the voltage problem, adjust the regulator point gap. Make sure the battery ground cable is disconnected.

16. Depress the armature until the moving point contacts "E" side point. Bend point arm "E" to obtain armature gap of 0.3 mm (0.012 in.)

17. Release the armature and adjust the gap between "E" side point and moving point by bending point arm "F". The gap should be 0.3–0.46 mm (0.012–0.016 in.)

18. After the gap adjustment is made, recheck no load regulated voltage and repeat core arm adjustment if necessary.

Voltage relay adjustment

Voltage regulator adjustments

Adjustment of regulator voltage

Adjustment of regulator point gap

19. Adjust the point gap by loosening 3 mm screw attaching upper contact. Move contact up or down as desired.

20. Adjust the regulated voltage with the adjusting screw. Turn clockwise to decrease it. Be sure to tighten the lock nut when adjustments are complete.

Starter

REMOVAL AND INSTALLATION

Gasoline Engines

1. Disconnect battery cables at the battery posts.

2. Disconnect the EGR pipe from the EGR valve and exhaust manifold, then remove the EGR pipe.

3. Disconnect the wiring from the starter magnetic switch.

NOTE: Tag all wires before disconnecting.

4. Remove the bolts and nuts attaching the starter to the motor.

5. Remove the starter assembly through the clearance under the intake manifold.

6. Installation is the reverse of removal.

Starter with magnetic valve removed—gasoline engine

Diesel Engines

1. Open the hood and disconnect the battery cables at the posts.

2. Disconnect magnetic switch wiring at the connector.

NOTE: Label all wires before disconnecting.

3. Remove starter motor attaching nut and bolt and remove starter motor.

4. Installation is the reverse of removal.

Typical diesel engine starter assembly showing adjustment shims

ENGINE MECHANICAL

Engine

REMOVAL AND INSTALLATION

Gasoline Engine

1. Remove the battery cables.

2. Scribe the position of the hood hinges on the underside of the hood. Remove the four attaching bolts and lift off the hood.

3. Remove the bottom shrouds and drain the crankcase and cooling system.

4. Disconnect the PCV hose from the air cleaner body. Disconnect the air hose from the air pump and remove the air duct from the air cleaner.

5. Remove the bolts attaching the air cleaner and loosen the clamp bolt.

6. Disconnect the thermostatic air cleaner (TAC) hot air hose and remove the manifold cover.

7. Tag and disconnect the generator wires at the connector.

8. Remove the two nuts connecting the exhaust pipe to the exhaust manifold and disconnect the exhaust pipe.

9. Take the tension off the clutch control cable by loosening the adjusting nut.

10. Disconnect the heater hose from the engine to the heater control valve at the engine side.

11. Disconnect the heater hose from the heater unit and joint.

12. Disconnect the control cable from the heater temperature valve and remove the control valve together with the hose.

13. Remove the engine mounting nut.

14. Support the engine with special tool J-26555 or equivalent. Attach the engine hangar using exhaust manifold stud bolts.

15. Disconnect the cable grounding the cylinder block to the frame.

16. Disconnect the fuel lines and vapor lines from the carburetor and charcoal canister.

17. Remove the high tension cable from the coil. Disconnect the vacuum hose from the rear of the intake manifold at the connector.

18. Disconnect the accelerator control cable from the carburetor.

19. Disconnect the starter motor wiring.

NOTE: Tag all wires before disconnecting.

20. Disconnect the thermo-unit, oil pressure switch and distributor wiring at the connectors.

21. Disconnect the carburetor solenoid valve and the automatic choke wiring at the connectors.

22. Disconnect the back-up light switch and transmission switch wiring at the connector on the rear part of the engine.

23. Disconnect the emission control hose from the oil pan.

24. Remove the engine mounting nut.

——— CAUTION ———
Make sure the engine is well-supported from above.

25. Remove the stopper plate.

26. Connect the engine hoist. Raise the engine slightly and disconnect the left side engine mounting stopper plate.

27. Disconnect air conditioner hoses.

——— CAUTION ———
Discharge A/C system before attempting to disconnect any hoses.

28. Disconnect the radiator upper and lower hoses. Remove the bolts attaching the fan shroud and remove the shroud.

29. Remove the radiator attaching bolts

and remove the radiator by lifting straight upward.

30. Remove the fan blades from the pulley.

31. Remove the gearshift lever assembly.

32. Disconnect the parking brake return spring and disconnect the cable.

33. Disconnect the propeller shaft from the transmission. Remove the clutch return spring.

34. Disconnect the clutch control cable from the clutch withdraw lever and remove it from engine stiffner.

35. Remove the front side exhaust pipe bracket from the transmission.

36. Disconnect the front and rear side exhaust pipes at the joint, then remove the front side exhaust pipe.

37. Disconnect the speedometer cable.

38. Remove the rear engine mounting bolts.

NOTE: Check that the engine is slightly lifted before removing rear mounting bolts.

39. Check to make certain all the parts have been removed or disconnected from the engine and that the parts are tied safely out of the way so as not to snag when the engine is being lifted clear.

40. Lift the engine and slide it toward the front of the car. Remove the transmission from the engine and set it on the floor.

41. Slowly lift the engine clear.

42. Installation is the reverse of removal. Fill the crankcase and cooling system. Check and adjust the clutch pedal free play and check the carburetor and clutch linkage for smooth operation. Start the engine and check for leaks.

Diesel Engine

1. Open the hood and remove the battery cables at the posts. Remove the battery.

2. Scribe the position of the hinges on the underside of the hood and remove the hood.

3. Remove the bottom shrouds.

4. Drain the radiator and crankcase.

5. Remove the fan shroud attaching screws and remove the shroud. Remove the radiator attaching bolts and remove the radiator after disconnecting upper and lower hoses.

6. Remove the air connecting hose.

7. Disconnect the heater hoses at the thermostat housing pipe and water inlet pipe.

8. Disconnect the quick start and silent idle (Q.S.S.I.) thermo switch, fast idle thermo switch, thermo unit wiring at the connector on the thermostat housing.

9. Tag and disconnect the generator wiring at the connector.

10. Disconnect the vacuum hose from the connector at the rear of the vacuum pump.

11. Disconnect the vacuum hose from the actuator of fast idle.

1. Starter motor assembly
2. Cooling fan
3. V-belt
4. Fan pulley
5. Damper pulley
6. Engine hanger
7. Water by-pass hose
8. Generator assembly and engine foot
9. Thermostat housing
10. Cam cover with positive crankcase ventilation valve
11. Injection pipe and clip
12. Nozzle holder assembly
13. Glow plug and connector
14. Oil pressure switch, unit and oil pipe
15. Oil cooler and oil filter
16. Oil pan
17. Tension spring
18. Dust cover

Diesel engine major components

12. Remove the two nuts connecting the exhaust pipe to the exhaust manifold and separate pipe from the manifold, then remove two nuts connecting the exhaust front pipe to exhaust mounting bracket and separate front pipe from bracket and remove the front pipe.

13. Disconnect the accelerator cable from the injection pump lever.

14. Disconnect the fuel cut colenoid valve switch wiring at connector. Disconnect tachometer pickup sensor wiring at connector (if equipped).

15. Tag and disconnect the starter motor wiring at the connector. Disconnect the oil pressure switch, oil pressure unit wiring at connector.

20. Disconnect fuel hoses at injection pump.

21. Disconnect sensing resistor wiring at connector.

22. Disconnect back-up lamp switch and top/third switch wiring at the connector on the rear of the engine.

23. Remove the return spring and disconnect the clutch control cable from the hook on the withdraw lever.

24. Disconnect the speedometer cable at the transmission side.

25. Remove the four bolts connecting the propeller shaft with the extension shaft and disconnect the propeller shaft flange yoke from the extension shaft, then pull the propeller shaft rearward. When the pro-

peller shaft has been removed, wrap a small plastic bag around the rear transmission housing to prevent any leakage of fluid.

26. Untie the strings on the console boot and remove the screws on each side of the console box. Remove the grommets between the floor carpet and floor panel.

27. Pry off the edge of the gearshift lever dust boot and remove the gearshift lever assembly upward.

NOTE: Plug the gearshift lever fitting hole to prevent entry of dust or foreign material.

28. Remove the bolts and nuts attaching the rear mounting bracket, then remove the bolts attaching the exhaust mounting bracket.

29. Using a chain, engine lifting fixtures or other suitable means, lift the engine slightly.

30. Remove the engine mount nuts and disconnect the engine damper from the frame.

31. Check to make certain all parts have been removed or disconnected and tied out of the way so as not to snag on the motor when it is lifted clear.

32. Attach the engine hoist and remove the engine assembly with the transmission attached. Slowly lift the engine clear of the chassis.

33. Installation is the reverse of removal. Fill crankcase, cooling system and check all cable adjustments.

34. Bleed the fuel system by filling the filter with diesel fuel and operating the priming pump handle several times. The force needed to operate the priming pump becomes greater as the filter fills up.

35. Start the engine and check for leaks.

Cylinder Head

REMOVAL AND INSTALLATION

Gasoline Engines

1. Remove the cam cover.
2. Remove the EGR pipe clamp bolt at the rear of the cylinder head.

3. Raise the vehicle and safely support it.

4. Disconnect the exhaust pipe at exhaust manifold.

5. Drain the cooling system.

6. Lower the car.

7. Disconnect the heater hoses at the intake manifold and at the rear of the cylinder head.

8. Disconnect accelerator linkage at the carburetor, fuel line at the carburetor, all necessary electrical connections, spark plug wires and necessary vacuum lines.

NOTE: Tag all wires and hoses before disconnecting them from the engine.

9. Rotate the camshaft until # 4 cylinder is in firing position. Remove distributor cap and mark rotor to housing relationship. This simple act will save untold grief when trying to get the distributor back in correctly.

10. Lock the timing chain adjuster by depressing and turning automatic chain adjuster slide pin 90° clockwise.

11. Remove timing sprocket to camshaft bolt and remove the sprocket from the camshaft. Keep the sprocket on the chain damper and tensioner. Do not remove the sprocket from the chain.

12. Disconnect the air pump hose and check valve at exhaust manifold.

13. Remove the cylinder head to timing cover bolts.

14. Remove cylinder head bolts using extension bar with socket. Remove bolts in progressive sequence, beginning with the outer bolts.

NOTE: Use light oil to free frozen bolts.

15. With the aid of an assistant, remove the cylinder head, intake and exhaust manifolds as an assembly.

16. Clean all gasket material from the cylinder head and block surfaces. Check for nicks or heavy scratches on the mating surfaces.

17. Installation is the reverse of removal. Cylinder bolt threads in the block and threads on the bolts must be cleaned. Dirt will affect head torque.

18. Torque all head bolts to specifica-

tions according to the sequence in the front of the chapter. Torque bolts to half normal value in sequence, then to specifications on the second pass.

CYLINDER HEAD BOLT TORQUE

First Pass	61 ft. lbs.
Second Pass	72 ft. lbs.

Diesel Engines

1. Drain the cooling system by opening the drain plug on the cylinder block.

2. Remove the camshaft.

3. Remove the sensing resistor assembly.

4. Remove the six screws attaching injection pipe clip and remove the injection pipe clip.

5. Remove eight sleeve nuts attaching injection pipes and separate the injection pipes.

6. Remove the clip attaching the fuel leak off hose and separate the hose from the return pipe.

7. Remove the two nuts connecting the exhaust manifold to the exhaust pipe and separate the pipe from the manifold.

8. Disconnect the joint bolt attaching oil feed line to head side.

9. Disconnect heater hose at thermostat housing pipe.

10. Remove the cylinder head bolts by

Diesel fuel injector showing injection pipe union

Locking the timing chain adjuster

Keep the timing sprocket attached to the chain while aligning or removing

Location of TOP mark

loosening them in sequence, then remove the cylinder head and gasket.

NOTE: Use light oil to free stubborn bolts.

11. Clean the head and block of all gasket material before reassembly.

12. Installation is the reverse of removal. Refill the cooling system. Torque all bolts in sequence given at the front of this section. Apply oil to threads and clean them thoroughly before reinstalling them in the head.

NOTE: Make sure cylinder head gasket is properly placed before lowering head. Look for "TOP" mark to assure proper placement.

CYLINDER HEAD BOLT TORQUE

First Pass	21–36 ft. lbs.
Second Pass	83–98 ft. lbs.
Reused Bolt	90–105 ft. lbs.

13. Reinstall the camshaft and rocker arm assembly. Reinstall the timing belt and adjust the valve clearance.

14. Start the engine and check for leaks.

Rocker Arms/Shaft

REMOVAL AND INSTALLATION

All Engines

1. Remove cam cover.
2. Loosen the rocker arm shaft bracket nuts a little at a time, in sequence, commencing with the outer brackets.
3. Remove the nuts from the rocker arm shaft brackets.

4. Disassemble the rocker arm shaft assembly by removing the spring from the rocker arm shaft and then removing the rocker arm brackets and arms.

5. Inspect the rocker arm shaft for runout. Support the shaft on V-blocks at each end and check runout by slowly turning it with the probe of a dial indicator. Replace the shaft with a new one if the runout exceeds 0.4 mm (0.0156 in). Runout should not exceed 0.2 mm (0.0079 in).

6. Inspect the rocker arm shaft for wear, replace the shaft if obvious signs of wear are encountered.

7. Installation is the reverse of removal. Use a liberal amount of clean engine

Rocker shaft torque sequence —diesel engine

oil to coat the shaft, rocker arms and valve stems. Install the longer shaft on the exhaust valve side, shorter shaft on the intake side, so that the aligning marks on the shafts are turned to the front of the engine.

8. Torque the rocker arm shaft bracket stud nuts to 16–22 ft. lbs. Hold the rocker arm springs with an adjustable wrench while torquing nuts to prevent damage to the springs. Torque nuts a little at a time in sequence, beginning with the center bracket and working outward.

9. Adjust valve clearances, reinstall cam cover and check for leaks.

Intake Manifold

REMOVAL AND INSTALLATION

Gasoline Engines

1. Drain the cooling system.

NOTE: Before removing the intake manifold, check to make certain the engine coolant is completely drained. If any water remains in the block it will flow into the cylinders when the intake manifold is removed.

2. Remove the air cleaner assembly.
3. Disconnect the radiator hose from the front part of the intake manifold.
4. Disconnect the fuel lines, all vacuum lines and the carburetor control cable.
5. Disconnect the heater hoses from the rear part of the manifold and from the connector under the dashboard.
6. Disconnect the distributor vacuum

Rocker arm shaft installation—gasoline engine

Rocker arm assembly—gasoline engine

Diesel rocker arms showing removal sequence

Intake manifold—gasoline engine

Exhaust manifold—gasoline engine

hose and all thermo-valve wiring. Disconnect electric choke or solenoid wires.

NOTE: Tag all wires before disconnecting them.

7. Disconnect the PCV hose from the rocker cover. Disconnect the EGR valve from the EGR pipe and disconnect the air injection vacuum hose from the three-way connector.

8. Remove the eight nuts attaching the intake manifold and lift it clear, being careful not to snag any loose lines.

9. Installation is the reverse of removal. Check the manifold for cracks or damage. The manifold head surfaces can be checked for distortion by using a straight edge and a feeler gauge. Distortion should be no more than 0.4 mm (0.0157 in), if it is beyond the limit, the distortion has to be corrected with a surface grinder.

10. Replace the gasket and torque all nuts in sequence to 25–32 ft. lbs.

Diesel Engine

1. Open the hood and disconnect the battery. Remove the air cleaner assembly.

2. Remove the connecting hose and PCV hose.

3. Remove the sensing resistor assembly.

4. Remove the six screws attaching the injection pipe clips and remove the injection pipe.

5. Remove the ten bolts attaching upper dust cover and remove the upper dust cover.

6. Remove the two bolts attaching the engine hanger and remove the engine hanger.

7. Remove two bolts attaching the stay and remove the stay. Remove the three bolts and two nuts attaching the intake manifold and lift off the manifold.

8. Installation is the reverse of removal. Use a new manifold gasket. Torque to 25–32 ft. lbs.

Exhaust Manifold

REMOVAL AND INSTALLATION

Gasoline Engines

1. Remove the bolts attaching the air cleaner and loosen the clamp bolt.

2. Lift the air cleaner slightly and remove the hot air hose.

3. Remove the three bolts attaching the manifold cover and remove the manifold cover.

4. Remove the EGR pipe clip from the upper portion of the transmission and disconnect EGR pipe from the exhaust manifold.

5. Remove the two nuts connecting the exhaust pipe with the exhaust manifold and disconnect the exhaust pipe from the manifold.

6. Remove the seven nuts mounting the exhaust manifold and remove the manifold.

7. Installation is the reverse of re-

Exhaust manifold—diesel engine

moval. Use a straight edge to check for distortion as described in the intake section. Use new gaskets and torque to 11–18 ft. lbs.

Diesel Engines

1. Open the hood and disconnect the battery.

2. Remove the oil level gauge.

3. Remove the two nuts attaching the exhaust pipe to the manifold and separate the pipe.

4. Remove the six bolts and two nuts attaching the exhaust manifold to the cylinder head. Remove the distance tube, manifold and gaskets.

5. The gasket surfaces should be cleaned and inspected for nicks or deep scratches. Use a new gasket when installing with the "TOP" mark turned to the manifold side.

6. Installation is the reverse of removal. Torque all manifold nuts and bolts to 11–18 ft. lbs.

Timing Chain

REMOVAL AND INSTALLATION

Gasoline Engines

1. Open the hood and disconnect the battery. Drain the cooling system.

2. Disconnect the radiator inlet and outlet hoses. Remove the radiator.

Intake manifold—diesel engine

Removing the timing chain

J-25031

Using a puller to remove crankshaft sprocket

3. Remove the generator and the A/C drive belts.

4. Remove the engine fan.

5. Remove the crankshaft pulley center bolt and remove pulley and hub assembly.

6. Remove the cylinder head.

7. Remove the oil pan.

8. Remove the oil pickup tube from the pump.

9. Remove the air pump belt, remove the compressor (if equipped with A/C) and lay it to one side. Remove the compressor mounting brackets.

10. Remove the distributor.

11. Remove the front cover attaching bolts and remove the front cover.

12. Remove the timing chain from the crankshaft sprocket. Check sprockets for damage or wear. If sprocket on the crankshaft must be replaced a gear puller will be necessary to remove it.

13. Inspect automatic chain adjuster for wear or damage. Replace any component that is doubtful. Make sure adjuster is freely rotating on its pins.

14. Install timing sprocket and pinion gear (groove side toward front cover). Align key grooves with key on crankshaft then drive into position with special tool J-26587 or equivalent.

15. Install the timing chain by aligning mark plate on the chain with the mark on the crankshaft timing sprocket. The side of

the chain with the mark plate is on the front side.

The side of the chain with the most links between mark plates is on the chain guide side.

16. Keep the timing chain engaged with the camshaft timing sprocket until the sprocket is installed on the camshaft. Install the sprocket so that the marked side faces foreward and so that the triangular mark aligns with the chain mark plate.

17. Install the front cover and reverse the removal instructions from 1–10.

TIMING COVER SEAL REPLACEMENT

1. Once the timing cover is exposed, the seal can be pried out with a suitable screwdriver.

2. Replace the seal using tool J-26587 or equivalent.

J-26587

Installing timing cover seal

Timing Belt

REMOVAL AND INSTALLATION

Diesel Engines

1. Open the hood and disconnect the battery. Drain the radiator system.

2. Remove the lower engine shrouds.

3. Remove the fan shroud, v-belt, cooling fan and pulley.

Dust covers on diesel engine

Locking the pump pulley

4. Remove the ten retaining bolts on the upper dust cover and remove the cover.

5. Remove the bypass hose.

6. With the piston in No. 1 cylinder at TDC, make sure the setting mark on the pump pulley is in alignment with the front plate, then lock the pulley with 8 mm 1.25 pitch bolt.

7. Remove the cam cover. Loosen the adjusting screws so that the rocker arms are held in a free state. Lock the camshaft by fitting a plate to the slit in the rear end of the camshaft.

8. Remove the damper pulley after making sure the piston in No. 1 is at top dead center.

9. Remove the lower dust cover, then remove the timing belt holder.

10. Remove the tension spring. Loosen the tension pulley and plate bolts and remove the timing belt.

11. Remove the bolt locking the camshaft pulley and remove the pulley from the camshaft. Put the pulley back on the shaft, but only tighten the bolts enough to allow the pulley to be turned by hand.

12. Install the new timing belt, making sure the cogs on the pulley and the belt are

Locking the camshaft with fixing plate

Location of timing belt holder

engaged properly. The crankshaft should not be turned.

13. Concentrate belt looseness on tension pulley, then depress the tension pulley with your fingers and install the tension spring. Semi-tighten the bolts in numerical sequence to prevent movement of the tension pulley.

14. Tighten the camshaft pulley bolts.

15. Remove the injection pump pulley lock bolt.

16. Remove the locking plate on the end of the camshaft.

17. Install damper pulley on the hub and make sure the No. 1 piston is still at TDC.

――――――― CAUTION ―――――――
Do not turn the crankshaft in an attempt to make an adjustment.

18. Make sure the injection pump pulley mark is in alignment with the mark on the plate.

19. Loosen the tensioner pulley and plate bolts. Concentrate looseness of belt on ten-

Install timing belt in numerical sequence

Tensioner pulley bolt tightening sequence

sioner, then tighten the bolts in numerical sequence. Torque the bolts to:

Bolt No.	Torque
1	11–18 ft. lbs.
2	11–18 ft. lbs.
3	47–61 ft. lbs.

20. Check valve adjustment and install cam cover.

21. Remove the damper pulley and install the belt holder in position away from the timing belt.

22. Install the bypass hose and dust covers.

23. Install the damper pulley and reverse removal steps 1–5.

24. Refill the cooling system.

Camshaft

REMOVAL AND INSTALLATION

Gasoline Engines

1. Remove cam cover.

2. Rotate camshaft until No. 4 cylinder is in firing position. Remove the distributor cap and mark rotor to housing position.

3. Lock the timing chain adjuster by depressing and turning the automatic adjuster slide pin 90° in a clockwise direction. After locking the chain adjuster, check that the chain is loose.

Locking the timing chain adjuster

4. Remove the timing sprocket to camshaft bolt and remove the sprocket on the chain damper and tensioner without removing the chain from the sprocket.

5. Remove the rocker arm, shaft and the bracket assembly.

6. Remove the camshaft.

7. Installation is the reverse of removal. Use a liberal amount of clean oil to coat the camshaft before installing. Check that the mark on the No. 1 rocker arms shaft bracket is in alignment with the mark on the camshaft and that the crankshaft pulley groove is aligned with the TDC mark ("O" mark) on the front cover.

8. Assemble the timing sprocket to the camshaft by aligning it with the pin on the camshaft. Use care not to remove the chain from the sprocket.

Half-moon seal

Removing camshaft pulley with gear puller

9. Install the sprocket retaining bolt. Remove the half-moon seal in the front end of the head, insert torque wrench and torque bolt to 58 ft. lbs. Replace half-moon seal in head.

10. Set the automatic adjuster by turning the adjuster slide pin 90° counterclockwise with a screwdriver.

11. Check valve timing and rotor mark alignment on distributor. Reinstall distributor cap.

Diesel Engines

1. Remove the cam cover.

2. Remove the timing belt.

3. Remove the rear plug and hold the shaft by attaching the fixing plate (J-29761 or equivalent) into the slit at the rear of the camshaft.

4. Remove the camshaft pulley bolt, then remove the pulley with a gear puller.

5. Remove the rocker arm and shaft.

6. Remove the bolts attaching the front head plate and remove the plate.

7. Remove the bolts attaching the camshaft bearing caps. Remove the caps and bearings.

8. Remove the camshaft oil seal, then remove the camshaft.

9. Installation is the reverse of removal. Use a liberal amount of clean oil to

Bolt loosening sequence for removing rocker arm assembly

coat the camshaft and journals during assembly.

10. Install a new oil seal and apply Permatex® or equivalent gasket compound to the cylinder head fitting face of the No. 1 camshaft bearing cap.

11. Torque rocker arm shafts and camshaft bearing caps to specifications.

Piston and Connecting Rod

All Engines

It is not advisable to remove the piston from the connecting rod unless part replacement is necessary. Whenever a piston is removed, the piston pin should be replaced. When examining a piston, look for scuffs, cracking or wear. The rings should be removed with a ring expander and should be kept separately to avoid interchanging parts. All clearances should be checked with a micrometer or comparable precision gauge. Assemble the piston rings to the piston so that the NPR or TOP marks are turned up. Every piston has a mark to designate proper installation, this "Front Mark" is located on the top edge, in line with the piston pin bore. In addition, the cylinder number that the piston came from is stamped on the connecting rod and the bearing cap.

Piston correctly installed

Cylinder identification on connecting rod and bearing cap

ENGINE LUBRICATION

Oil Pan

REMOVAL AND INSTALLATION

All Engines

NOTE: Isuzu recommends removing the engine (or at least raising it up) to service the oil pan. There isn't sufficient clearance to remove the pan with the engine bolted down.

1. Remove or raise the engine to allow sufficient room to clear the oil pan.

2. Remove the bolts and nuts attaching the oil pan to the engine block. Remove the oil pan and gasket.

3. Clean the oil pan and engine block gasket surface carefully to remove all traces of the old gasket.

4. Install in reverse order of removal, using a thin coat of Permatex® #2 or equivalent to hold the gasket in place while installing the bolts and to prevent any oil leaks.

5. Torque the oil pan bolts evenly to 4 ft. lbs. Check the edges of the gasket to ensure that it is seated properly. If the gasket projects unevenly around the oil pan plange, remove the gasket and reinstall carefully.

NOTE: Do not overtighten the oil pan bolts. Bolts that are too tight cause as many leaks as bolts that are too loose.

Oil pan and gasket—gasoline engine

Oil pan and gasket—diesel engine

6. Start the engine and check for leaks.

Rear Main Bearing Oil Seal

REMOVAL AND INSTALLATION

1. Remove the transmission and oil pan.

2. On manual transmission models, remove the clutch cover and pressure plate assembly.

3. Remove the starter and lay to one side or wire to the frame.

NOTE: Disconnect the battery before removing starter.

4. Remove the six flywheel bolts and the flywheel assembly.

5. Remove the four rear crankshaft seal retainer bolts and remove retainer seal assembly.

6. Pry the old seal out of the retainer and discard.

7. Place new seal in position in retainer. Fill clearance between lips of seal with grease and lubricate the seal lip with engine oil.

8. Place the retainer on a flat surface and drive the seal into place using installer tool J-22354 or equivalent.

9. Installation is the reverse of removal steps 1–6. When installing the flywheel, install washer and bolts and torque to 69 ft. lbs.

10. Start engine and check for leaks.

Installing crankshaft rear seal with special tool

Flywheel torque sequence

Removing flywheel assembly

SEAL

REAR PLATE

OIL SEAL RETAINER

Rear main oil seal assembly

NOTE: Diesel engines use a different number seal installing tool (J-29818), and the seal is installed on the No. 5 crankshaft bearing cap. Other than that, the removal and replacement procedures are identical for all engines.

PICKUP TUBE

OIL PUMP

Oil pump assembly (engine upside down)

Oil Pump

REMOVAL AND INSTALLATION

Gasoline Engine

NOTE: The oil pump can be serviced with the engine in or out of the vehicle. The procedure below is for the engine in the car.

1. Remove the cam cover.
2. Remove the distributor assembly.
3. Remove the engine oil pan.

4. Remove the bolt attaching the oil pickup tube to the block and remove the tube from the oil pump.
5. Remove the oil pump mounting bolts and remove the pump assembly.
6. Remove the rubber hose and relief valve from the oil pump.
7. Installation is in reverse order of re-

1. Oil pump body
2. Drive shaft
3. Drive rotor
4. Rotor pin
5. Drive gear
6. Gear pin
7. Driven rotor
8. Cover assembly
9. Relief valve
10. Spring
11. Fitting
12. Dowel pin

moval. Align the mark on the camshaft with the mark on the No. 1 rocker arm shaft bracket. Align the notch on the crankshaft pulley with the "O" mark on the front cover. When the two sets of marks are aligned, the No. 4 cylinder is at top dead center on the compression stroke.

8. Install the driven rotor so that the alignment mark lines up with the mark on the drive rotor.

9. Install the oil pump assembly by engaging the oil pump drive gear with the pinion gear on the crankshaft, so that the alignment mark on the drive gear is turned rearward and is away from the crankshaft by approximately 20° in a clockwise direction.

10. When the oil pump is installed, check to assure that the mark on the oil pump drive gear is turned to the rear side as viewed from the clearance between the front cover and the cylinder block and that the slit at the end of the oil pump drive shaft is in parallel with the front face of the cylinder block and is off-set foreward as viewed through the distributor fitting hole.

11. Check for leaks after assembly. Measure the oil pressure by attaching a pressure gauge to the hole for the oil pressure switch. Correct oil pump pressure is 56–71 psi.

Diesel Engine

1. Remove the timing belt.
2. Remove the Allen bolts attaching the oil pump and remove the pump together with the pulley.

Exploded view of oil pump

Oil pump alignment

Checking oil pump alignment

View through distributor fitting hole

NOTE: The special tool for the Allen bolts is J-29767.

3. Disassemble the oil pump on the workbench. A gear puller may be necessary to remove the pulley.

4. Installation is the reverse of removal. Apply generous amounts of clean engine oil to all components before installation. Install the vane with the taper side toward the cylinder body.

5. Install a new O-ring into the groove in the housing. Lubricate with oil. Install the rotor and then the pump body together with the pulley. Torque the Allen bolts to 11–18 ft. lbs.

Using special tool to remove Allen bolts on oil pump

4. Key
5. Pin
6. Rotor
7. Shaft
8. Housing
9. Oil seal

1. Nut
2. Oil pump pulley
3. Vane

Exploded view of diesel oil pump and pulley assembly

Install vane with taper side toward the cylinder body

ENGINE COOLING

Radiator

REMOVAL AND INSTALLATION

All Models

1. Open the hood and disconnect the battery.

2. Remove the radiator cap and drain the cooling system.

— **CAUTION** —
The engine should be cold for removal procedures.

3. Loosen the top and bottom hose clamps and remove the radiator hoses.

4. Remove the fan shroud.

5. Remove the bolts and nuts attaching the radiator and remove the radiator assembly.

6. Installation is the reverse of removal. Fill the cooling system with water and the proper proportion of anti-freeze solution. Start the engine and check for leaks.

Radiator with shroud attached

Water Pump

REMOVAL AND INSTALLATION

Gasoline Engines

1. Open the hood and disconnect the battery. Remove the lower engine cover.

2. Drain the cooling system.

3. On cars without A/C, remove the fan.

Water pump on gasoline engines

4. On cars with A/C, remove the air pump and generator mounting bolts, then remove the fan and air pump drive belt (pivot the generator and air pump in toward the engine). Remove the fan and pulley with set plate. Remove the hoses to the pump.

5. Remove the six bolts attaching the water pump and remove the water pump assembly. Clean all gasket surfaces carefully.

6. Installation is the reverse of removal. Fill the cooling system with the correct anti-freeze and water solution and adjust all drive belts. Use a new gasket.

7. Start the engine and check for leaks.

Diesel Engines

1. Open the hood and disconnect the battery. Remove the radiator cap.

2. Drain the cooling system and remove the hoses from the pump.

3. Remove the fan and pulley.

4. Remove the four attaching bolts holding the damper pulley. Remove the damper pulley.

5. Remove the engine dust covers.

6. Remove the bypass hose.

7. Remove the five bolts attaching the water pump and remove the pump and gasket.

8. Clean all gasket surfaces carefully and inspect for nicks, cracks or deep scratches.

9. Installation is the reverse of removal. Use a new gasket. Torque all water pump mounting bolts to 11–18 ft. lbs.

Thermostat

REMOVAL AND INSTALLATION

All Models

NOTE: Engine should be cold for this procedure.

1. Drain the cooling system and remove the air cleaner.

2. Remove the two attaching bolts holding the thermostat housing.

3. Lift the housing and remove the thermostat.

4. Remove all traces of old gasket.

5. Reinstall in reverse order using a new gasket. Permatex® is a good idea to avoid leaks. Make sure the thermostat is installed properly (it doesn't work upside-down).

Water pump attaching bolts

Jiggle valve

Thermostat—typical for all models

Testing thermostat operation in hot water

EMISSION CONTROLS

GENERAL INFORMATION

Gasoline Engine

There are two versions of the Isuzu gasoline engine, the 49 State (Federal) version and the California version. The CO and HC settings are different, so it is wise to check the underhood specifications sticker to verify any settings before adjustment. An exhaust gas analyzer is required to properly adjust emission levels to comply with Federal or Local standards. The adjustment of carbon monoxide and hydrocarbon levels should be left to a qualified repair shop with the proper equipment. All other emission control maintenance can be done by the owner.

EQUIPMENT USED

Positive Crankcase Ventilation System—all models
Evaporative Control System—all models
Thermostatic Air Cleaner—all models
Over Temperature Control System—all models
Coasting Richer System—all models
Air Injection Reactor (Air Pump)—California models only
Exhaust Gas Recirculation System—all models
Oxidizing Catalytic Converter System—all models

Crankcase Emission Control System (PCV)

COMPONENTS AND OPERATION

NOTE: The PCV system is the only emission control device used on the diesel engine.

The Positive Crankcase Ventilation System is designed to force blow-by gases generated in the engine crankcase back into the intake manifold, then deliver them, together with the fuel mixture, to the combustion chambers. This system is a closed type and consists of a baffle plate in the rocker arm cover for separating oil particles from blow-by gases; an orifice in the intake manifold for controlling suction of blow-by gases; a hose connecting these parts and another hose from the air cleaner to allow fresh air into the system. Under normal operating conditions, blow-by gases passing between piston rings and cylinder walls and fuel vapor from the fuel tank air mixed with ambient air supplied from the air cleaner. This mixture of gases is then drawn through the regulating orifice into the intake manifold for burning. When the engine is running with the throttle wide open, part of the blow-by generated is drawn directly into

PCV system—gasoline engine

Intake pipe

P.C.V. valve

Baffle plate

Cam cover

Intake manifold

Oil pan

← Blow-by gas
←-- Fresh air
⇐ Blow-by gas + fresh air

PCV system—diesel engine

the air cleaner via the rear end of the rocker arm cover.

MAINTENANCE

Clean internal parts of hoses and regulating orifice with solvent and blow out any obstructions with compressed air. Check hoses for cracks, fatigue and swelling; replace if defective. Make sure all connections are tight.

Evaporative Emission Control System

COMPONENTS AND OPERATION

The evaporative system is designed to lead the fuel vapors from the tank into the crankcase and the vapors from the carburetor float bowl into the carbon canister. The fuel evaporative system consists of the vapor separator tank, check and relief valve, charcoal (carbon) canister, vent switching valve, ventilation valve and the hoses that connect it all together. The vapors drawn into the engine crankcase are mixed with blow-by gases and drawn into the intake manifold for combustion when the engine is running. The charcoal canister stores the vapors when the engine is off. The stored fuel vapor is purged when the engine is started and the vapors are drawn into the intake manifold. The purge rate is controlled by the manifold

pressure and the orifice in the purge control valve.

MAINTENANCE

Aside from checking the hoses and connections for leaks and deterioration no maintenance is required. Should the charcoal canister become saturated with fuel, it must be replaced.

CAUTION

Never use compressed air to clear a blockage in the evaporative control system. Fuel vapors in the charcoal canister could be ignited by the friction of the pressurized air.

Thermostatic Air Cleaner

COMPONENTS AND OPERATION

The automatic temperature-controlled air cleaner is designed so that the temperature of ambient air is automatically controlled to hold the fuel/air ratio constant for efficient combustion. The system consists principally of the thermo-sensor, vacuum motor, hot air control valve and hot idle compensator. These components are mounted to the air cleaner body and snorkel. The hot air control valve is fully open when the engine is cold, allowing only air heated by the manifold heat stove into the engine. As the engine heats up, the thermosensor bleeds off vacuum and gradually closes the hot air control valve. Under conditions of hard acceleration when cold, the vacuum drops low enough to allow the diaphragm spring to open the snorkel passage and allow more air into the engine as required. Under conditions of hot operation (idling, climbing a long grade, etc.) excessive fuel vapors cause an over-rich situation, so the car is equipped with a hot idle compensator mounted in the air cleaner. The idle compensator allows ambient air into the intake manifold to lean out the temporarily rich mixture.

THERMO SENSOR

IDLE COMPENSATOR

Hot air controls mounted in air cleaner

1. Air cleaner assembly
2. Body assembly
3. Cover assembly
4. Vacuum control
5. Sensor assembly—thermo
6. Nut
7. Grommet
8. Clamp
9. Element
10. Idle compensator
11. Gasket
12. Gasket
13. Hose
14. Hose
15. Duct—air intake
16. Cover
17. Protector
18. Hose
19. Cap
20. Clip
21. Clip

Exploded view of thermostatic air cleaner system

Evaporative control system—typical

Typical air cleaner hose connections

MAINTENANCE

Periodically check the function of the thermostatic air cleaner system by observing component operation when cold through the warm-up cycle. Check all connections for leaks and deterioration. No other maintenance is required.

Over Temperature Control System

COMPONENTS AND OPERATION

When the engine is coasting, the coasting fuel cut device prevents catalytic converter overheating caused by poor combustion. When the catalyst reaches a temperature of 730°C (1350°F) due to high speed and high load driving, the secondary air diverted to the atmosphere to reduce the chemical reaction in the catalyst, lowering the temperature and preventing damage to the converter. A thermo-sensor is installed in the front side of the catalytic converter and monitors the catalyst temperature. The thermo-sensor provides the signal to the vacuum switching valve.

Air Injection Reactor System

COMPONENTS AND OPERATION

The AIR system is designed to lower exhaust emissions by injecting ambient air into the exhaust charge from the engine, causing an "afterburner" effect that consumes the unburned fuel in the exhaust manifold (postcombustion). Ambient air is pressurized by the air pump and delivered via a diverter valve and check valve to the injector nozzles mounted in the exhaust manifold. Pump pressure is limited by a relief valve pressed into the pump housing. The check valve mounted on the air injection manifold allows air to pass in one direction and prevents exhaust gas from backing up into the air lines and damaging the system. The diverter valve (mixture control valve) prevents backfiring during deceleration by venting pump air to the atmosphere whenever the intake manifold vacuum increases rapidly.

MAINTENANCE

The air pump drive belt can be adjusted by loosening the mounting bolts and moving the pump and adjusting plate. Proper belt tension can be checked by pressing on the belt at a point mid way between pulleys. A belt deflection of 10 mm (0.4 in) indicates proper tension. The air pump itself is non-servicable and must be replaced if found to be defective.

NOTE: Air pumps are normally a little noisy in operation. Before replacing a noisy pump, first try tightening the mounting bolts. A loose belt or worn bushings can also cause pump noise.

The AIR system should be periodically checked for proper operation and any leaks or deterioration in the lines. The air pump output can be checked by removing the delivery hose from the back of the pump and making sure that the air volume increases with engine rpm. The check valve on the

OVER TEMPERATURE CONTROL SYSTEM

* MANUAL TRANS. ONLY
** NEUTRAL SWITCH (MANUAL TRANS.)
   INHIBITOR SWITCH (AUTOMATIC TRANS.)

ACCEL SW.   ** TRANSMISSION SW.

* CLUTCH SW.

ANTI-DIESELING SOLENOID & COASTING FUEL CUT SOLENOID

RELAY

TO ATMOSPHERE

TO AIR MANIFOLD VIA CHECK VALVE

VACUUM SWITCHING VALVE

AIR SWITCHING VALVE

IGN. COIL

IGN. SWITCH

FROM AIR PUMP

TO INTAKE MANIFOLD

DISTRIBUTOR

THERMO CONTROLLER

THERMO SENSOR

ENGINE SPEED SENSOR

TO SILENCER

FROM ENGINE

CATALYTIC CONVERTER

Over temperature control system

AIR CLEANER

AIR SWITCHING VALVE

RELIEF VALVE

AIR PUMP

CHECK VALVE
AIR MANIFOLD
AIR INJECTION NOZZLE
EXHAUST VALVE

EXHAUST MANIFOLD

CATALYTIC CONVERTER

INTAKE MANIFOLD

MIXTURE CONTROL VALVE

→ NORMAL PASSAGE
--→ AT DECELERATION

Air injection reactor system

air manifold should be removed and blown through to verify one-way operation. The diverter (mixture control) valve may be checked by removing the rubber hose connecting the valve with the intake manifold, then plugging the intake manifold side. If the secondary air continues to blow out from the valve for a few seconds when the accelerator pedal is depressed fully and quickly released, the valve is operating properly. If the air continues to blow out of the valve for more than five seconds, replace the valve.

Exhaust Gas Recirculation (EGR) System

COMPONENTS AND OPERATION

The EGR system is used to lower the peak combustion temperatures by recirculating non-combustible exhaust gases through the intake manifold, thereby lowering the level of oxides of nitrogen in the exhaust. Exhaust gas is drawn into the intake manifold through a steel pipe and EGR valve mounted on the exhaust manifold. The vacuum diaphragm of the EGR valve is attached to a signal port at the carburetor flange through a Back Pressure Transducer responsive to exhaust pressure. This transducer modulates the vacuum signal and a thermal vacuum valve which operates the EGR cold override. As the carburetor throttle is opened, vacuum is applied to the diaphragm of the EGR valve which allows exhaust gas to be metered into the intake manifold. The faster the engine runs, the more EGR. The thermal vacuum valve cuts out the EGR system

Vacuum circuits—gasoline engine

when the engine temperature is below 54°C (129°F) to improve cold response and driveability.

NOTE: The Back Pressure Transducer is not used on California versions.

MAINTENANCE

The operation of the EGR valve should be checked periodically by applying an outside vacuum source (hand vacuum pump) to the vacuum supply tube at the top of the diaphragm chamber. The diaphragm should not "leak down" and should move to the full up position at about 125 mm (5 in.) of mercury. In addition, the EGR valve should be removed and all carbon deposits sandblasted using a plug cleaning machine. Once the valve is clean, remove any grit with compressed air blown through the valve chamber. If heavy carbon deposits are noted

EGR system

EGR valve

in the intake manifold ports, the manifold must be removed for proper cleaning.

NOTE: Never try to remove carbon deposits with the intake manifold installed on the engine. Clean all metal lines with solvent and a bristle bore brush.

FUEL SYSTEM

Fuel Pump

OPERATION—GASOLINE ENGINES

The fuel pump is a lightweight, motor-driven centrifugal type mounted near the bottom of the fuel tank. The pump will shut off immediately if the generator belt breaks, if there is a loss of voltage signal from the generator, or if the fusible link is open. At idle, the shut down is immediate; at fast idle or if the accelerator is partially depressed, the shut down is delayed 30–45 seconds to use up the fuel in the carburetor float bowl.

TESTING DELIVERY PRESSURE

1. Disconnect the main fuel hose at the carburetor side and connect a fuel pump pressure gauge using a T-fitting.

Fuel pump—gasoline engine

Fuel pump location

Fuel system schematic

2. Start the engine and note the pressure reading on the gauge.
3. Delivery pressure at 900–4800 rpm is 2.4–3.3 psi.
4. If the measured value is different from specifications, replace the fuel pump.

— **CAUTION** —
Do not operate the fuel pump under no-load conditions and perform all tests with the filter installed.

REMOVAL AND INSTALLATION

1. Disconnect the fuel return hose from the pipe and drain fuel.

— **CAUTION** —
Fire hazard. Take precautions to avoid igniting any spilled fuel. Be particularly careful when using a work light around the fuel system.

2. Remove the fuel tank cover.
3. Remove the two screws holding the fuel pipe cover and remove the cover.
4. Disconnect the fuel hose from the fuel pipe.

5. Disconnect the fuel pump wiring.
6. Remove the nine screws attaching the fuel pump and remove the fuel pump assembly from the fuel tank.
7. Installation is the reverse of removal. Check for leaks and cracked hoses.

Fuel Filter

REMOVAL AND INSTALLATION

The fuel system has a cartridge type, in-line filter installed on the left side panel in the luggage compartment.

1. Remove the bolts attaching the cover on the side of the fuel tank in the luggage compartment, then remove the cover.
2. Disconnect the hoses from the filter.
3. Remove the fuel filter from the clip.
4. Installation is the reverse of removal.

Carburetor

The carburetor is a two barrel down draft type composed of a low-speed side (primary) and a high-speed side (secondary) which are integrated into a single unit.

REMOVAL AND INSTALLATION

1. Disconnect the PCV hose from the cylinder head cover.
2. Disconnect the ECS hose from the air cleaner body.
3. Disconnect the AIR hose from the air pump.
4. Remove the bolts attaching the air cleaner and loosen the clamp bolts.
5. Lift the air cleaner slightly and disconnect the TCA vacuum hose and air duct, then remove the air cleaner.

Cross section of carburetor—typical

1. Float
2. Needle valve
3. Coasting richer solenoid
4. Coasting jet
5. Coasting air bleed
6. Locknut
7. Slow Jet
8. Secondary-Slow air bleed
9. Secondary-Main air bleed
10. Air vent

11. Secondary-Main nozzle
12. Secondary-Small venturi
13. Choke valve
14. Primary-Small venturi
15. Air vent
16. Vacuum jet
17. Primary-Main air bleed
18. Economizer bleed
19. Primary-Slow jet
20. Primary-Slow air bleed

21. Weight
22. Plug
23. Accel pump piston
24. Vacuum piston
25. Diaphragm spring
26. Diaphragm
27. Plug
28. Secondary-Main jet
29. Secondary-Throttle valve
30. Accel pump nozzle

31. Primary-Throttle valve
32. Primary-Main nozzle
33. Idle mixture adjusting screw
34. Primary-main jet
35. Plug
36. Anti-dieseling solenoid
37. Power valve
38. Idle hole
39. EGR signal port
40. Check ball

6. Disconnect the vacuum signal hose from the EGR valve.

7. Disconnect the electrical leads connector.

8. Disconnect the accelerator cable.

9. Disconnect the fuel line at the carburetor.

——————— CAUTION ———————

Fire hazard. Use rags to catch any fuel and be careful with work lights. A broken light bulb landing on raw fuel can be quite spectacular.

10. Disconnect the ECS hose from the carburetor.

11. Remove the four nuts and lockwashers securing the carburetor to the intake manifold and remove the carburetor.

12. Installation is the reverse of removal. Clean all gasket surfaces before installation and always use a new gasket.

13. Start engine and adjust the carburetor. Any time the carburetor is removed for

inspection or overhaul, the emissions levels must be reset using an exhaust gas analyzer. Unless you happen to own an expensive exhaust gas analyzer, see your local dealer or qualified repair shop.

LINKAGE ADJUSTMENTS

When the primary throttle valve is opened to an angle of 47° (about half way) the adjust plate, which is interlocked with the primary throttle valve, is brought into contact with the kick lever. When the primary throttle valve is opened further, the return plate is pulled apart from the stopper, allowing the secondary throttle valve to open. To measure just when the secondary is opening:

1. Measure the clearance between the primary throttle valve and the wall of the throttle chamber at the center of the throttle valve when the adjust plate is brought into contact with the kick lever.

2. Standard clearance is 6.1–7.6 mm

(0.24–0.30 in). If necessary, make adjustments by bending the kick lever.

PRIMARY THROTTLE VALVE OPENING ADJUSTMENT

Check and make necessary adjustment so that the primary throttle valve is opened, by means of the fast idle adjusting screw, to an angle of 16°MT or 17°AT when the choke valve is completely closed. To check the opening angle of the primary throttle valve:

1. Close the choke valve completely and measure the clearance between the throttle valve and the wall of the throttle valve chamber at the center part of the valve.

2. Standard clearance is 1.28–1.51 mm (0.050–0.059 in) for manual and 1.40–1.63 mm (.055–.064 in.) for automatic transmissions. If necessary, adjust by bending the kick lever.

C447

FLOAT LEVEL ADJUSTMENT

The fuel level is normal if it is within the marks on the window glass of the float chamber when the engine is off. If fuel level is outside of the lines, make adjustment by bending the float seat. The needle valve should have an effective stroke of about 1.5 mm (0.59 in).

The needle valve is adjusted by bending the float stopper, but accomplishing that simple task requires the removal and disassembly of the carburetor. See the Unit Repair Section.

Checking float level

Adjusting float level

AUTOMATIC CHOKE ADJUSTMENT (FAST IDLE)

──── CAUTION ────

The automatic choke fast idle is adjusted by opening angle of the throttle valve on the carburetor, NOT by engine speed.

The adjusted throttle valve opening at the first step of the fast idle cam is 16° ± 1°(MT) and 17° ± 1°(AT). The engine fast idle speed becomes approximately 3200 rpm after the engine is warmed up, or if the vacuum line to the distributor, idle compensator and EGR valve is plugged.

OVERHAUL

For carburetor overhaul instructions, see the Unit Repair Section.

Choke components

Diesel Injection System

For additional information on diesel maintenance, etc., please refer to "Diesel Maintenance" in the Unit Repair section.

DIESEL INJECTION PUMP

NOTE: The diesel injection pump is an extremely complicated device, built to tolerences of millionths of an inch. Servicing should be left to a qualified diesel specialist. Never use cold water to clean a hot engine or the diesel injection pump may seize.

REMOVAL AND INSTALLATION

1. Remove the timing belt as previously described.
2. Remove the nut attaching the injection pump pulley.
3. Remove the pulley using a suitable puller and remove the lock bolt.

4. Disconnect the fuel cut-off solenoid valve switch wiring and tachometer sensor wiring, if equipped.
5. Disconnect accelerator cable from the pump lever. (A/T models only)
6. Disconnect the vacuum hose from the actuator of the fast idle device.
7. Disconnect the fuel hoses at the injection pump.
8. Remove the six screws attaching the injection pipe clips and remove clips.
9. Remove eight sleeve nuts attaching injection pipes and remove pipes.
10. Remove the four bolts attaching the

Removing nut on injection pump pulley

Cross section of diesel injection pump

Using a puller to remove injection pump pulley

Diesel injection pipes showing routing

pump rear bracket and remove the rear bracket. Disconnect the spring of the control lever.

11. Remove the two nuts attaching the injection pump flange and remove the injection pump together with the fast idle device.

12. Install the injection pump together with the fast idle device by aligning notched line on the flange with the line on the front plate.

13. Tighten the bolts in sequence. No clearance should be between the rear bracket and injection pump bracket.

14. Install the injection pump pulley by aligning it with the key groove. Align the

Removing pump flange nuts

Aligning marks on injection pump and front plate

mark on the pulley with the mark on the front plate, then tighten the nut using the lock bolt to prevent pulley turning.

15. Reinstall the timing belt as previously described and set injection timing.

16. Install injection pipes, clips and vacuum hose for actuator. Connect all control cables and wiring.

17. Fill the filter with fuel by operating the priming handle several times. Adjust the idle speed.

Bolt tightening sequence for injection pump mount

Timing mark alignment for injection pump pulley

Securing injection pump pulley

Diesel fuel filter with priming pump (arrows)

Injection Timing

Follow directions outlined under removal and installation of timing belt for proper injection timing procedure.

MANUAL TRANSMISSION

REMOVAL AND INSTALLATION (4 AND 5 SPEED)

1. Disconnect the battery ground cable.

2. Remove the shift lever assembly from inside the car.

3. Loosen the clutch cable adjusting nuts at the left side of the engine compartment.

4. Remove the upper starter mounting nut and disconnect the starter wiring.

5. Raise the car and safely support it.

6. Remove the driveshaft.

7. Disconnect the speedometer cable.

8. Remove the clutch cable.

9. Remove the starter lower bolt and remove the starter.

10. Disconnect the exhaust pipe from the manifold.

11. Remove exhaust pipe bracket.

12. Remove flywheel inspection cover.

13. Remove rear transmission support mounting bolt.

14. Support transmission under case and remove rear transmission support from frame.

15. Lower transmission approximately four inches. Disconnect back-up light and coasting fuel cut-off switch (gasoline models only) wires.

16. Remove transmission housing to engine block bolts.

—— **CAUTION** ——
Make sure transmission is supported by a suitable jack.

Removing manual shifter assembly from inside car—typical

17. Move the transmission slowly back and lower it clear of the car.

18. Installation is the reverse of removal. Lubricate the drive gear shaft spline with a light coat of grease before installing.

19. Adjust the clutch as described in the clutch section. Fill the transmission with SAE 30 engine oil (yes, that's right) until it begins to run out the filler hole.

LINKAGE ADJUSTMENT

The shift lever is mounted on top of the transmission extension housing and requires no adjustment. For further details, see the Unit Repair Section.

CLUTCH

REMOVAL AND INSTALLATION

1. Remove transmission as previously described.

2. Mark the clutch assembly position on the flywheel with paint or a scribe.

3. Install clutch aligning tool J-24547 or equivalent and remove the six retaining bolts. Remove clutch assembly.

4. Remove the release bearing to yoke retaining springs, and remove release bearing with support.

5. Remove release yoke from transmission ball stud.

6. Wash all metal parts of the clutch assembly, except the release bearing and friction plate in suitable cleaning solution.

— CAUTION —

Soaking the release bearing in cleaning solution will ruin the bearing, soaking the clutch plate in cleaning solution will damage the facings.

7. Inspect all parts for wear or deep scoring. Replace any parts that show excessive wear.

8. Installation is the reverse of removal. Lubricate the ball stud when installing the release yoke. Align clutch with scribe marks and use aligning tool to assure proper positioning of clutch.

Clutch Cable

REMOVAL AND INSTALLATION

1. Loosen clutch lock and adjusting nuts.

2. Raise the car and support it safely with jackstands.

3. From under the car, remove the clutch cable from the release yoke and slide it foreward through the retaining bracket.

4. Disconnect the cable from the pedal and remove.

5. Installation is the reverse of removal.

Location of clutch cable under car —typical

CLUTCH CABLE ADJUSTMENT

1. Loosen the lock and adjusting nuts on the clutch cable.

2. Pull the cable foreward toward the front of the car to take up slack.

3. Turn the adjusting nut inward until the clutch pedal free travel is 16 mm (5/8 in.)

4. Tighten the locknut and check the adjustment.

NOTE: Correct pedal height from the floor is 157.5 mm (6.2 in.), adjust the clutch switch to obtain, then lock the switch in position with the lock nut.

Exploded view of clutch components

Clutch cable adjustment location

AUTOMATIC TRANSMISSION

REMOVAL AND INSTALLATION

1. Disconnect the battery cables and raise the vehicle. Make sure it is supported safely.

2. Remove the transmission dipstick. Drain the fluid into a suitable container and discard.

3. Remove the starter toward the front of the vehicle.

4. Disconnect the propeller shaft from the central joint, then slide the propeller shaft rearward and remove it.

5. Disconnect the shift control rod from the shift lever.

6. Disconnect the speedometer cable.

7. Remove the exhaust pipe bracket.

8. Disconnect the oil cooler lines by loosening the joint nuts at the transmission.

NOTE: Secure the cooler lines closer to the body to avoid damage during transmission removal.

9. Remove the four bolts attaching the converter housing lower cover and remove the cover.

10. Remove the lower cover on the front part of the engine to permit turning of the engine and torque converter.

11. Remove the six bolts fastening the torque converter and drive plate by turning the crankshaft pulley.

12. Remove the bolt on the center part of the rear mounting frame bracket.

13. Raise the engine and transmission using a suitable jack and support the rear end of the engine to hold it in position when the transmission is removed.

14. Remove the four bolts or nuts securing the rear mounting frame bracket, then remove the bracket.

15. Lower the transmission slightly, then remove the bolts and nuts fixing the converter housing, then remove the transmission toward the rear.

Removing torque converter bolts

1. Shift lever
2. Shift lever rod
3. Selector pin
4. Return spring
5. Knob with push button
6. Spring
7. Set screw
8. Shift lever bracket
9. Bushing
10. Control shaft
11. Washer
12. Nut
13. Rubber boot
14. Neutral start switch
15. Screw
16. Indicator upper cover
17. Indicator lower cover
18. Slider
19. Indicator lens
20. Washer
21. Screw
22. Indicator light
23. Indicator light bulb

Exploded view of shifter assembly

Throttle valve cable adjustment—gasoline engine

Throttle valve cable adjustment—diesel engine

— CAUTION —
When removing the transmission, exercise care so as not to let the torque converter slide out.

16. Installation is the reverse of removal. Refill the transmission with fluid according to the capacities chart. Adjust the throttle valve control cable.

DRIVE AXLE

Driveshaft and U-Joint

REMOVAL AND INSTALLATION

1. Raise the rear of the car and support it safely on jack stands at the rear jack brackets.
2. Disconnect the parking brake return spring from the rod.
3. Mark the mating parts of the U-joint and the drive pinion extension shaft flange.
4. Remove the bolts and nuts connecting the U-joint and the extension shaft flange.
5. Work the propeller shaft slightly foreward, lower the rear end of the shaft and slide the assembly rearward. Remove the thrust spring from the front of the shaft.
6. Install a plug (or wrap a small plastic bag) on the transmission extension housing to prevent the loss of oil.

— CAUTION —
When replacing any fasteners or attaching bolts, be sure to use the proper grade bolt. Substitution of lesser quality hardware could cause failure and serious damage.

1. Torque tube
2. Rubber support cushion
3. Support bracket
4. Bearing Assembly
5. Rubber cushion
6. Retainer
7. Rubber cushion ring

8. Drive pinion extension shaft
9. Bearing shield
10. Bumper rubber
11. Washer
12. Extension shaft flange
13. Spacer ring
14. Washer
15. Flange nut
16. Bushing
17. Damper weight

Exploded view of central joint

7. Installation is the reverse of removal. Make certain transmission rear seal is not damaged. Align all marks and torque bolts to 18 ft. lbs.
8. Connect the parking brake return spring.

Central Joint

REMOVAL AND INSTALLATION

1. Raise and support the rear of the car safely under the axle tubes.
2. Disconnect the parking brake return spring from the brake rod.
3. Unhook the exhaust system bracket from the central joint support bracket.
4. Mark the universal joint and flange, then disconnect the propeller shaft from the flange and support it out of the way.
5. Support the torque tube with a floor jack using minimum pressure.
6. Remove the central joint support bracket to underbody attaching bolts.
7. Allow the floor jack to lower the torque tube.
8. Disconnect the torque tube from the differential carrier by removing the attaching bolts.
9. Installation is the reverse of removal. Align all marks, torque all bolts to specifications.

BOLT TORQUE SPECIFICATIONS

Location	Torque (ft. lbs.)
Extension shaft flange nut	87
Extension shaft flange to universal joint	18
Central joint support bracket to under body	30
Torque tube to carrier	20
Central joint support bracket to support cushion	15
Rubber cushion retainer to central joint support	10

Rear Axle

REMOVAL AND INSTALLATION

1. Raise the rear of the car and support it safely with jackstands positioned under jack brackets on each side of the car. Loosen the lug nuts and remove the rear wheels.
2. Disconnect the parking brake cable equalizer and the return spring from the brake rod.
3. Remove the clamps securing the rear stabilizer bar to the body and loosen bolts

REAR U-JOINT

FRONT U-JOINT

COIL SPRING

Propeller shaft

and nuts connecting the stabilizer bar and axle bracket.

4. Disconnect shock absorbers at lower end.

5. Disconnect lateral rod at left end.

6. Unhook the exhaust system brackets.

7. Disconnect the universal joint from the companion flange and support or tie propeller shaft out of the way after marking mating areas. If the propeller shaft is removed, plug the rear of the transmission to prevent fluid loss.

8. Disconnect the brake hose from the brake line at the differential and remove the retainer clip.

9. Lower the rear axle assembly far enough to remove coil springs.

10. Remove the central joint support bracket to underbody retaining nuts and bolts.

11. Disconnect the lower control arms at the rear axle assembly bracket and roll the assembly from under the car.

12. Installation is the reverse of removal.

NOTE: If any attaching nuts or bolts must be replaced, be sure to use the proper grade of nut or bolt. Failure to use the proper grade fastener may result in component failure and serious damage.

13. Torque central joint support bolts to 30 ft. lbs. Torque universal joint bolts to 18 ft. lbs.

14. Torque lower control arm to axle housing bolts to 29 ft. lbs. Torque lateral rod to rear axle attaching nut to 54 ft. lbs. Torque shock absorber nuts to 29 ft. lbs. Tighten the stabilizer nuts as tightly as possible.

Axle Shaft

REMOVAL AND INSTALLATION

1. Raise the car and support it safely with jackstands at the jack brackets.

2. Remove the wheel and brake drum assembly.

3. Working through the access holes in the axle shaft flange, remove the four nuts and washers that retain the axle shaft and bearing retainer.

4. Install an axle shaft puller (slaphammer) and remove the axle shaft.

5. To replace the bearing parts, first remove the retaining ring by cutting it off with a chisel. The bearing must be pressed off with a suitable bench press.

1. Rear axle housing assembly
2. Rear axle case
3. Bolt—axle housing to lateral rod
4. Nut
5. Washer
6. Bolt—bearing cap to axle case
7. Rear axle breather assembly
8. Pinion bearing shim
9. Pinion rear bearing
10. Collapsible distance spacer
11. Shim—distance piece
12. Pinion front bearing
13. Oil deflector plate
14. Sliding sleeve oil seal
15. Barrel spline sleeve
16. Drive pinion washer
17. Pinion nut
18. Pressure cap
19. Differential case
20. Ring gear and pinion
21. Ring gear setting bolt
22. Side gears
23. Pinion gears
24. Side gear thrust washer
25. Rear axle pinion shaft
26. Lock pin
27. Side bearing
28. Side gear shim
29. Differential cover
30. Differential cover gasket
31. Brake pipe union bracket
32. Union bracket bolt
33. Wheel nut
34. Oil filler plug
35. Oil filler gasket
36. Rear axle shaft
37. Axle shaft bearing retainer
38. Axle shaft bearing
39. Axle shaft bearing retaining ring
40. Wheel pin
41. Axle shaft shim
42. Bolt—bearing retainer to axle case
43. Spring washer
44. Nut
45. Rear brake drum

Exploded view of rear axle assembly

J-8805-01

J-2619-01

Removing axle shaft with slide hammer and adaptor

6. Installation is the reverse of removal. Press the new bearing on to the axle shaft with a suitable press.

7. Check the axle shaft end play by using a depth gauge to measure the depth of the rear axle bearing seat in the axle housing with the backing plate in place.

8. Measure the width of the bearing outer race. The difference between the two measurements indicates the required thickness of the shims. If necessary to increase end-play, add shims. To decrease end-play, remove shims. Standard end play is 0–0.2 mm (0–0.008 in.). Shims are only available in 0.15 mm (0.006 in.) thickness.

9. Coat all rear axle components with gear oil before installation. Torque lock washers and nuts to 28 ft. lbs.

Differential
REMOVAL AND INSTALLATION

1. Raise the car and support it safely at the rear axle.

2. Remove the rear axle cover bolts and drain the lubricant into a suitable container.

3. Disconnect the left end of the lateral rod and wire it to the left shock absorber. Remove the rear wheels.

4. Working through the access holes in the axle shaft flange, remove the four nuts and washers retaining the axle shafts on each side. Loosen the brake backing plate to the axle housing.

5. Using a suitable puller, remove the axle shafts, taking care not to damage the oil seals.

6. Remove the differential cover and discard the gasket.

7. Mark the rear axle side bearing caps and carrier so that the caps can be re-installed in their original positions.

8. Remove the rear axle side bearing cap bolts and caps.

9. Using two wooden hammer handles or similar devices, pry the differential case assembly from the carrier.

—— **CAUTION** ——
Do not drop or interchange differential side bearing outer races.

10. Installation is the reverse of removal.

OVERHAUL

The successful overhaul of a differential assembly requires the use of several special tools and many precise adjustments. Any overhaul procedures should be left to an experienced service technician. Isuzu recommends you see your local dealer.

1. Control arm
2. Bushing
3. Bushing
4. Lateral rod
5. Bushing
6. Bushing
7. Sleeve
8. Spring
9. Insulator
10. Insulator
11. Shock Absorber assembly
12. Rear stabilizer bar
13. Bushing
14. Clamp
15. Bracket
16. Bushing
17. Sleeve

REAR SUSPENSION

Shock Absorbers

REMOVAL AND INSTALLATION

1. Raise the car and support it safely under the axle housing.

NOTE: Backing the car onto a set of car ramps and chocking the front wheels is the easiest way to do it.

2. Disconnect the lower end of the shock absorber from the axle.

3. Remove the fuel tank cover from inside the trunk and disconnect the upper end of the shock absorber.

4. Working from under the car, remove the shock absorber.

5. Installation is the reverse of removal. Use lock nuts at each end. Torque all shock absorber nuts to 29 ft. lbs.

Exploded view of rear suspension system

Rear Coil Springs

REMOVAL AND INSTALLATION

1. Raise the rear of the car on the axle housing and support it at the jack side brackets with jackstands.
2. Position a hydraulic jack under the differential housing, but use a light contact pressure.

NOTE: A hydraulic floor type jack is recommended for this procedure. Using a hydraulic bottle type jack is asking for trouble.

3. Disconnect the shock absorbers lower mounting bolts.
4. Slowly lower or separate the axle assembly from the car body to the point where the spring becomes loose enough to allow removal.

―――― CAUTION ――――
Do not stress the brake hoses when lowering the axle.

5. Installation is the reverse of removal. Position the spring correctly. Make sure that the insulator is in position on top of the spring.
6. Torque the shock absorber lower bolts to 29 ft. lbs.

Rear Control Arm

REMOVAL AND INSTALLATION

1. Raise the car and support it safely.
2. Remove the bolt connecting the control arm to the axle case.
3. Remove the bolt connecting the control arm to the body.
4. Remove the control arm assembly.
5. Installation is the reverse of removal. Torque the bolts to 29 ft. lbs.

NOTE: When reinstalling the control arm assembly, leave the bolts semi-tight. Lower the car before torquing any nuts. The vehicle weight should be on all suspension components when torquing nuts.

Installing rear control arm

FRONT SUSPENSION

Front Wheel Bearings

ADJUSTMENT AND REPACKING

1. Raise the car and safely support it with jackstands. Remove the front wheel.
2. Remove the grease cap. Remove and discard the cotter pin, then remove the spindle nut and washer.
3. Wiggle the hub and the wheel bearing will pop out enough to grab it. Wipe any dirt or old grease off of the spindle.

NOTE: If the rear wheel bearing is to be inspected, the hub will have to be removed. Remove and tie up the brake caliper as outlined in the brake section and the hub will be free to be removed.

4. Inspect the wheel bearing for signs of wear, nicks or obvious damage. Clean the bearings in solvent and blow dry with compressed air.

―――― CAUTION ――――
Do not give in to the impulse of spinning the clean bearing with the air nozzle. Running a dry bearing at high rpm while holding it in your hand can damage the bearing.

5. Carefully repack the front wheel bearings with new high temperature wheel bearing grease. Put a glob of grease in your palm and force it into the bearing with a scraping motion until the grease comes out the top. Coat the packed bearing with a covering of grease and install taper side in.
6. Clean and install the washer and spindle nut. Torque the spindle nut to 22 ft. lbs. while rotating the hub. This will seat the bearing.
7. Back off the spindle nut completely, then turn it back all the way using only your fingers. Once the spindle nut is snug, insert a new cotter pin.

Removing spindle nut on front hub

NOTE: If the holes on the spindle nut and spindle do not align, tighten the nut only enough to align. A properly adjusted wheel bearing has a small amount of end-play and a slightly loose nut when adjusted in this manner.

Shock Absorbers

REMOVAL AND INSTALLATION

1. Raise the car and support it safely. Remove the front wheel.
2. Disconnect the shock absorber from the upper control arm using two wrenches.
3. Remove the shock absorber nuts from the engine compartment.
4. Remove the shock absorber. Installation is the reverse of removal. Torque control arm nut to 29 ft. lbs. Tighten the top nut to the end of the threads on the rod. Use lock nuts.

Coil Springs

REMOVAL AND INSTALLATION

1. Raise the car and safely support it with jackstands. Remove the wheel.
2. Remove tie rod end cotter pin and castle nut. Discard cotter pin.

WASHER
CUSHION RUBBER
WASHER
CUSHION RUBBER
WASHER

Shock absorber installation in engine compartment

1. Cross member assembly
2. Lower control arm assembly
3. Lower ball joint assembly
4. Boot
5. Clamp ring
6. Clamp ring
7. Upper control arm assembly
8. Upper ball joint
9. Boot
10. Clamp ring
11. Clamp ring
12. Washer
13. Washer
14. Washer
15. Through-bolt
16. Spring washer
17. Nut
18. Steering knuckle
19. Nut
20. Nut
21. Front coil spring
22. Damper rubber
23. Bumper rubber
24. Shock absorber
25. Stabilizer bar
26. Rubber bushing
27. Clamp
28. Bolt
29. Retainer
30. Grommet
31. Nut
32. Distance tube
33. Under cover

Exploded view of front suspension system

Disconnecting shock absorber from upper control arm

Lifting control arm with hydraulic jack

Disconnecting lower ball joint with special tool

Brake caliper attaching bolts

3. Use a suspension fork to separate the tie rod end from the steering knuckle.

4. Remove the lower shock absorber bolt and push the shock up as far as possible.

5. Remove the stabilizer bar bolt and grommet assembly from the lower control arm.

6. Remove the upper brake caliper bolt and slide the hose retaining clip back about ½ in.

7. Place the lifting pad of a hydraulic floor jack under the outer extreme of the control arm and raise the lower control arm until it is level.

CAUTION

Secure a safety chain through one coil near the top of the spring and attach it to the upper control arm to prevent the spring from coming out unexpectedly. The coil spring will come out with a lethal force, so don't take any chances.

8. Loosen the lower ball joint lock nut until the top of the nut is flush with the top of the ball joint. Using tool J-26407 or equivalent, disconnect the lower ball joint from the steering knuckle.

9. Remove the hub assembly and steering knuckle from the lower ball joint and support with a wire or rope out of the way.

10. Pry the lower control arm down, using extreme caution so as not to injure yourself. Remove the spring.

11. Installation is the reverse of removal. Properly seat the spring and use the safety chain. Use the hydraulic jack to compress the new spring until the control arm is level.

12. Torque the ball joint lock nut to 58 ft. lbs. Torque shock absorber lower mounting nuts and all other attaching hardware according to the specifications chart at the end of the section.

Ball Joints

NOTE: The lower ball joint is splined to the lower control arm. The upper ball joints are off-set to allow for camber setting.

REMOVAL AND INSTALLATION

Upper Ball Joint

1. Raise the car and support it safely. Remove the wheel.

2. Remove the upper brake caliper bolt and slide the hose retaining clip back about ½ in.

3. Remove the lower shock absorber nut and bolt and push the shock absorber up.

4. Place a hydraulic jack under the outer extreme of the lower control arm and raise until level.

5. Loosen the upper ball joint nut until the top of the nut is flush with the top of the ball joint.

6. Using special tool J-26407 or equivalent, disconnect the upper ball joint from the steering knuckle.

7. Remove the two bolts connecting the upper ball joint to the upper control arm. Remove the ball joint.

8. Installation is the reverse of removal. Install the new ball joint in the control arm so that the cut-off portion is facing outward. Torque the ball joint lock nut to 40 ft. lbs. Torque all attaching nuts and bolts. For specifications, see the torque chart at the end of the section.

NOTE: The car should be aligned

Installing upper ball joint in control arm

whenever any suspension components are replaced.

Lower Ball Joint

1. Raise the car and support it safely. Remove the front wheel.

2. Remove the tie rod end cotter pin and castle nut. Discard the pin and separate the tie rod end with a suspension fork. Remove the tie rod from the steering knuckle.

3. Remove the stabilizer bar bolt and grommet assembly from the lower control arm.

4. Rmove the upper brake caliper bolt and slide the brake hose retaining clip back about ½ in.

Removing ball joint from steering knuckle

Removing lower ball joint from steering knuckle

Removing lower ball joint from control arm

5. Remove the shock absorber lower bolt and push the shock up.

——————— **CAUTION** ———————

Secure a safety chain through the upper and lower control arms to prevent the possibility of the spring coming out and causing serious damage or injury. Allow enough room to get the ball joint out.

6. Place a hydraulic jack under the outer extremity of the lower control arm and raise it until level.

7. Loosen the ball joint lock nut until the top of the nut is flush with the top of the ball joint.

8. Using special tool J-26407 or equivalent, disconnect the lower ball joint from the steering knuckle.

9. Remove the hub assembly and steering knuckle from lower ball joint and support with a wire or rope.

10. Remove the lower ball joint from the control arm using tool J-9519-03 or equivalent.

11. Installation is the reverse of removal. Do not strike the ball joint bottom. Torque the ball joint nut to 50 ft. lbs.

12. Torque all bolts to specifications as listed in the chart at the end of the section.

Control Arms

REMOVAL AND INSTALLATION

Upper Control Arm

1. Raise the car and support it safely. Remove the front wheel.

2. Remove the upper brake caliper bolt and slide the brake hose retainer clip back about ½ in.

3. Remove the lower shock bolt and push the shock absorber up.

4. Place a hydraulic jack under the control arm on the outer extreme and raise the control arm until it is level.

5. Loosen the upper ball joint lock nut until the top of the nut is flush with the top of the ball joint. Disconnect the upper ball joint from the steering knuckle using tool J-26407 or equivalent.

6. Disconnect and remove the through bolt connecting the upper control arm to the crossmember. Remove the upper control arm.

7. Installation is the reverse of removal. On installation, make sure the smaller washer is on the inner face of the front arm and the larger washer is on the inner face of the rear arm.

8. Torque all attaching hardware to the specifications in the chart at the end of the section. Align the front end.

Removing lower control arm

Removing upper control arm from crossmember

Installation of upper control arm

NOTE: Always check the camber when working around the upper control arm area.

Lower Control Arm

1. Follow steps 1–10 for removal of coil springs.
2. Remove the bolts connecting the lower control arm to the crossmember and the body.
3. Installation is the reverse of removal. Torque all bolts and nuts to specifications.

NOTE: When reinstalling front end components, it's best to snug all the bolts and nuts first, then lower the car so that there is weight on the suspension when final torque adjustments are made.

Front End Alignment

NOTE: Steering problems are not always the result of improper alignment. Before aligning car, check all suspension components for damage or excessive wear.

BALL JOINT CHECK

The maximum permissible axial play in the ball joints is 0.2 mm (0.008 in.) Replace any joint that exceeds this value.

CAMBER ADJUSTMENT

Camber angle can be increased approximately one (1) degree by removing the upper ball joint, rotating it ½ turn and reinstalling it with the cut-off portion of the upper flange on the inboard side of the control arm.

Camber adjustment

CASTER ADJUSTMENT

The caster angle is pre-set at the factory and cannot be adjusted.

TOE-IN ANGLE ADJUSTMENT

Toe-in is controlled by adjusting the tie rod.

Toe-in adjustment

To adjust the toe-in setting loosen the nuts at the steering knuckle end of the tie rod. Rotate the rod as required to adjust the toe-in. Retighten the cover and locknuts, check that the rubber bellows is not twisted. For all specifications, see the Alignment Specs in the front of the chapter.

BOLT TORQUE SPECIFICATIONS

Location of Fastener	Torque (ft. lbs.)
Wheel nuts (steel wheel)	50
Wheel nuts (aluminum wheel)	90
Lower ball joint to knuckle	58
Lower control arm to crossmember	47
Lower control arm to body	47
Upper ball joint to knuckle	47
Upper ball joint to control arm	29
Upper control arm to crossmember	47
Shock absorber to upper arm	29
Brake backing plate to steering knuckle	4
Brake caliper to knuckle	36
Brake disc to front wheel hub	36

NOTE: Use a reliable torque wrench to tighten all parts. These specifications are for clean threads, lightly oiled. Dirty threads produce different torque values by increasing friction and giving a false reading.

STEERING

Steering Wheel

REMOVAL AND INSTALLATION

1. Raise the hood and disconnect the battery ground cable.
2. On models with the 2-spoke wheel, remove the two screws retaining the horn shroud and disconnect the horn contact.
3. On models with the 3-spoke wheel, remove the medallion cover from the center of the wheel by prying lightly around the edge with a small screwdriver.
4. Remove the steering wheel nut and washer. Mark the steering wheel and shaft to assure proper positioning later.
5. Using a steering wheel puller, remove the steering wheel. Installation is the reverse of removal. Align the marks you made earlier.
6. Torque the steering wheel nut to 22 ft. lbs.

Combination Switch (Wiper/Washer, Lights, etc.)

REMOVAL AND INSTALLATION

1. Remove the steering wheel as previously described.
2. Remove the steering column covers and disconnect the electrical connectors to the switches.
3. Remove the washer/wiper switch by removing the two retaining screws.
4. Remove the turn signal/headlight switch and hazard switch by removing the four retaining screws.

Removing emblem cover

3-SPOKE STEERING WHEEL
MEDALLION COVER
SHROUD
UPPER COLUMN COVER
STEERING SHAFT
STEERING COLUMN
2-SPOKE STEERING WHEEL
LOWER COLUMN COVER
LOCK CYLINDER HOUSING

Exploded view of steering column assembly

3. Remove both tie rod ends cotter pin and castle nut. Discard the pins and use tool J-21687-02 or equivalent to disconnect the tie rod ends from the steering knuckles.

4. Disconnect the rack retaining bolts from the crossmember. Expand the steering shaft coupling and remove the assembly.

5. Installation is the reverse of removal. Before installing the rack assembly, set the steering gear to the high point by positioning the front wheels straight ahead with the steering wheel centered.

6. Torque the crossmember retaining bolts to 14 ft. lbs. Torque steering shaft coupling bolt to 19 ft. lbs.

STEERING GEAR ADJUSTMENTS

Adjustment of the steering gear assembly is accomplished by turning the adjusting screw in or out.

1. Set steering to high point by positioning the front wheels straight ahead with the steering wheel centered.

2. Thread the adjusting screw into the steering gear housing and torque the adjusting screw to 11 ft. lbs.

3. Back off the adjusting screw slightly, then torque the locknut to 58 ft. lbs.

5. Installation is the reverse of removal. Make sure the connectors are tight and properly connected.

Steering Gear—Rack and Pinion

REMOVAL AND INSTALLATION

1. Raise the car and safely support it with jackstands. Remove the lower engine shrouds.

2. Remove the steering shaft coupling bolt.

Removing tie-rod end from steering knuckle

BRAKES

General Information

The Isuzu brake system on all models consists of a dual master cylinder operating front disc and rear drum brakes. The front brakes are self-adjusting due to the design of the disc brake system. The rear brakes are self-adjusting by virtue of a lever-type mechanism that automatically adjusts the rear brakes whenever the parking brake is applied. The brakes are power-assisted by a power brake unit that operates off of engine vacuum. A combination valve serves both as the failure indicator and pressure control valve (proportioning valve). It is

WINDSHIELD WIPER SWITCH ATTACHING SCREW
COMBINATION SWITCH ATTACHING SCREW

Removing combination switches

RETAINING BOLTS

Removing steering rack from crossmember

Exploded view of steering gear

fluid on any painted surface. You'll know if you do and fail to clean it off.

5. Installation is the reverse of removal. For information on bleeding the master cylinder and brake system, see the Unit Repair Section on brakes.

Power Brake Unit

REMOVAL AND INSTALLATION

1. Wipe the master cylinder, power unit and lines clean with a clean rag. Use rags to catch any leaking fluid.
2. Disconnect the hydraulic lines at the master cylinder, and cover the lines with a clean, lint-free material to prevent dirt from contaminating the system.
3. Remove the master cylinder bracket bolts to the cylinder and fender skirt and remove the bracket.
4. Remove the bolts securing the fluid reservoir bracket.
5. Remove the vacuum hose clip and the hose from the check valve.
6. Remove the clevis pin from the brake pedal and separate the clevis and pedal.
7. Remove the power unit retaining nuts holding it to the dash panel and lift out the power unit and master cylinder/reservoir as an assembly.
8. Installation is the reverse of removal. Bleed the brake system and top up the fluid level.

mounted on the left side of the engine compartment. Hydraulic brake fluid with a DOT-3 rating is recommended for normal use.

For all brake system repair and service not detailed below, please refer to "Brakes" in the Unit Repair section.

Master Cylinder

REMOVAL AND INSTALLATION

1. Set the parking brake and chock the wheels to prevent the car from rolling.
2. Open the hood and disconnect the front and rear brake lines from the master cylinder.
3. Remove the nuts securing the master cylinder to the power brake unit and the support bracket.
4. Remove the nuts securing the fluid reservoir bracket and remove the master cylinder and fluid reservoir as an assembly. (remove the rubber hoses, too)

NOTE: Be careful not to spill brake

1. Tandem master cylinder assembly
2. Cylinder body
3. Primary piston assembly
4. Secondary piston assembly
5. Primary piston spring
6. Secondary piston spring
7. Check valve
8. Connector
9. Check valve spring
10. Washer
11. Gasket
12. Stop—bolt
13. Gasket
14. Snap-ring
15. Connector
16. Clip

17. Gasket
18. Bracket
19. Bolt
20. Washer
21. Fluid reservoir assembly
22. Body
23. Filter
24. Cover
25. Bracket
26. Screw
27. Washer
28. Bolt
29. Washer
30. Front rubber hose
31. Rear rubber hose
32. Clip
33. Nut
34. Washer

Exploded view of master cylinder

Exploded view of power brake unit

Parking brake adjustment

Parking Brake

ADJUSTMENT

NOTE: Adjustment of the parking brake is necessary every time the rear brake cables are disconnected for any reason.

1. Fully release the parking brake lever and check the cable for free movement.
2. Remove the cable play by turning the brake lever rod adjusting nut.
3. When adjustment is complete, check that the travel of the parking brake lever is within 8–10 notches from full off to full on. If the travel is incorrect, readjust to specifications.

CHASSIS ELECTRICAL

Heater Blower

REMOVAL AND INSTALLATION

1. Disconnect the battery cables.
2. Disconnect the wiring at the blower motor.
3. Remove the retaining screws and pull out the blower motor and squirrel cage.

4. Remove the retaining clip holding the squirrel cage to the motor and separate the two.
5. Installation is the reverse of removal.

Heater Core

REMOVAL AND INSTALLATION

1. Disconnect the battery cables.

2. Drain the radiator.

— **CAUTION** —

This operation should only be carried out on a cold engine.

3. Disconnect the heater hoses at the core connections and plug the core tubes to prevent the spillage of coolant when removing the core inside the car.
4. Remove the outer blower unit case cover and disconnect the fresh air door control cable.
5. Disconnect the temperature cable at the water valve.
6. Remove the steering wheel as previously described.
7. Remove the instrument cluster as described.
8. Disconnect the wiring for the console gauges, remove the console retaining screws, untie the shift lever leather boot and remove the console.
9. Remove the heater control and radio face plate.
10. Remove the glovebox.
11. Remove the radio as described.
12. Disconnect the selector mode cable from the driver's side of the heater assembly.
13. Carefully pull the temperature and fresh air door cables through the cowl and

Heater installation

Heater system components

remove the control panel through the cluster opening.

14. Remove the instrument panel assembly as described.

15. Remove the heater unit assembly through-bolt located at the rear and bottom of the heater.

16. Remove the four attaching nuts holding the heater unit and blower unit together and remove the heater unit assembly.

17. Remove the bolts holding the heater unit case halves together and remove the heater core.

18. Installation is the reverse of removal. Refill and bleed the cooling system.

Radio

REMOVAL AND INSTALLATION

1. Remove the battery cables.
2. Remove the ash tray and ash tray support.
3. Remove the radio knobs and heater control knobs by pulling them straight back.
4. Remove the radio shaft nuts and trim panel.
5. Remove the radio retainer screws from under the dash board.
6. Disconnect the electrical and speaker connections and antenna cable.
7. Remove the radio down through the back of the dash.
8. Installation is the reverse of removal.

Wiper system components

Wiper Motor

REMOVAL AND INSTALLATION

1. Disconnect the battery cables.
2. Working under the instrument panel, remove the nut and crank-arm from motor.
3. Disconnect the wiring connector.
4. Remove the three nuts securing the wiper motor and remove the motor.

5. Installation is the reverse of removal.

Instrument Cluster

REMOVAL AND INSTALLATION

1. Disconnect the battery.
2. Remove the steering wheel as previously described.

Exploded view of wiper components

PRINTED CIRCUIT

HOUSING

TEMPERATURE GAUGE

FUEL GAUGE

SPEEDOMETER

BULB SOCKET

BULB

CLOCK

TACHOMETER

BEZEL

Exploded view of instrument cluster

3. Disconnect the speedometer cable from the speedometer and remove wing nut.

4. Remove the instrument cluster attaching screws and remove the cluster assembly outward.

5. Disconnect the connectors and clock harness (if equipped). Disconnect the harness connecting to the speedometer reed switch on diesel models.

6. Installation is the reverse of removal.

Fuse Box Location

The fuse box is located on the left kick panel, just under the dash.

Mazda

SERIAL NUMBER IDENTIFICATION

Vehicle

The serial number is on a plate located on the driver's side windshield pillar and is visible through the glass.

A vehicle identification number (VIN) plate, bearing the serial number and other data, is attached to the cowl.

Engine

The engine number is located on a plate which is attached to the engine housing, just behind the distributor or on a machined pad at the right front side of the engine block.

The engine number consists of an iden-

tification number followed by a six-digit production number.

GENERAL ENGINE SPECIFICATIONS—PISTON ENGINE

Year	Model	Engine Displacement cu. in. (cc)	Carb Type	Net Horsepower (@ rpm)	Net Torque @ rpm (ft. lbs.)	Bore × Stroke (in.)	Compression Ratio	Oil Pressure (@ rpm)
'76–'78	808	96.8 (1586)	2V	70 @ 5000	82 @ 3400	3.07 × 3.27	8.6:1	50–64 @ 3000
'76–'78	808	77.6 (1272)	2V	52 @ 5000	64 @ 3000	2.87 × 2.99	9.2:1	50–64 @ 3000
'79–'82	626	120.2 (1970)	2V	75 @ 4500	105 @ 2500	3.15 × 3.86	8.6:1	50–64 @ 3000
'77–'78	GLC	77.6 (1272)	2V	52 @ 5000	65 @ 3000	2.87 × 2.99	9.2:1	50–64 @ 3000
'79–'80	GLC	86.4 (1415)	2V	77 @ 4300	109 @ 2400	3.03 × 2.99	9.0:1	50–64 @ 3000
'81–'83	GLC	90.9 (1490)	2V	68 @ 5000	82 @ 3000	3.03 × 3.15	9.0:1	43–64 @ 3000

GENERAL ENGINE SPECIFICATIONS—ROTARY ENGINE

Model	Engine Displacement cu. in. (cc)	Carburetor Type	Net Horsepower @ rpm	Net Torque @ rpm	Rotor Displacement (cu. in.)	Compression Ratio	Oil Pressure @ rpm (psi)
RX-7	70 (1146)	4-bbl	100 @ 6000	105 @ 4000	35	9.4:1	71.1 @ 3000
RX-3SP	70 (1146)	4-bbl	95 @ 6000	100 @ 4000	35	9.4:1	71.1 @ 3000
RX-3	70 (1146)	4-bbl	90 @ 6000	96 @ 4000	35	9.4:1	71.1 @ 3000
RX-4 Cosmo	80 (1308)	4-bbl	110 @ 6000	120 @ 4000	40	9.2:1	71.1 @ 3000

TUNE-UP SPECIFICATIONS—PISTON ENGINE

(When analyzing compression test results, look for uniformity among cylinders, rather than specific pressures)

Year	Engine Displacement (cu. in.)	Spark Plugs Type	Gap (in.)	Distributor Point Dwell (deg)	Point Gap (in.)	Ignition Timing (deg) MT	AT	Intake Valve Opens (deg)	Fuel Pump Pressure (psi)	Idle Speed (rpm)	Valve Clearance (in.) In	Ex
'76–'78	96.8	BP6ES	.031	49–55	.020	5B②	5B②	13	2.8–3.6	800–850③	.012	.012
	77.6	BP6ES	.031	49–55	.020	7B④	11B	13	2.84–3.84	700–750⑤	.010	.012
'79	86.4	BP5ES, BPR5ES	.031	49–55	.020	7B⑥	7B⑦	15	2.8–3.8	700–750 ⑨⑩	.010	.012
	120.2	BP5ES, BPR5ES	.031	Electronic		8B	8B	10	2.8–3.6	650–700	.012	.012
'80	86.4	BP5ES, BPR5ES	.031	Electronic		5B	5B	15	2.8–3.8	700–750⑨	.010	.012
'80–'82	120.2	BP5ES, BPR5ES	⑬	Electronic		5B⑧	5B⑧	10	2.8–3.6	750–700	.012	.012
'81–'83	90.9	BPR5ES, BPR6ES	⑫	Electronic		8B	8B	15	2.8–3.8	850⑪	.010	.012

NOTE: The underhood specifications sticker often reflects tune-up specification changes made in production. Sticker figures must be used if they disagree with those in this chart.

② California: 8B
③ Automatic: 650–700 in Drive
④ California: 11B
⑤ Automatic: 600–650 in Drive
⑥ California: 5B
  Canada: 8A
⑦ California: 5B
  Canada: 8B
⑧ Canada: 8B
⑨ Federal:
  Automatic: 600–650
⑩ Canada:
  Manual: 800–850
  Automatic: 700–750
⑪ Automatic 750 in Drive
⑫ BPR5ES—.080, BPR6ES—.031
⑬ '80—.031, '81–'82 BP5ES, BPR5ES—.080,
  BP6ES, BPR6ES—.031
N.A. Information not available

TUNE-UP SPECIFICATIONS—ROTARY ENGINE

(When analyzing compression test results, look for uniformity among cylinders, rather than specific pressures)

Year	Engine Displacement (cu. in.)	Spark Plugs Type	Gap (in.)	Distributors Point Dwell (deg)	Point Gap (in.)	Ignition Timing (deg) Leading Normal	Retarded	Trailing Normal	Idle Speed (rpm) MT	AT
'76	70	RN278B	0.039–0.043	58 ± 3 ②	.018	TDC	15A	20A	700–750	700–750①
'76	80	RN278B	0.039–0.043	58 ± 3 ②	.018	5A	20A	20A	700–750	700–750①

TUNE-UP SPECIFICATIONS—ROTARY ENGINE

(When analyzing compression test results, look for uniformity among cylinders, rather than specific pressures)

Year	Engine Displacement (cu. in.)	Spark Plugs Type	Gap (in.)	Distributors Point Dwell (deg)	Point Gap (in.)	Ignition Timing (deg) Leading Normal	Leading Retarded	Trailing Normal	Idle Speed (rpm) MT	AT
'77	70.80	RN278B	0.039–0.043	58 ± 3	.018	5A	—	25A	725–775	725–775 ①
'78	70 ③	RN278B	0.039–0.043	58 ± 3	.018	0	—	20A	725–775	725–775 ①
'78	80	RN278B	0.039–0.043	58 ± 3	.018	5A	—	25A	725–775	725–775 ①
'79	70	RN280B	0.039–0.043	58 ± 3	.018	0	—	20A	725–775	725–775 ①
'80	70	RN280B	0.039–0.043	Electronic		0	—	20A	725–775	725–775 ①
'81–'83	70	④	0.053–0.057	Electronic		0	—	20A	750	750 ①

NOTE: The underhood specifications sticker often reflects tune-up specification changes made in production. Sticker figures must be used if they disagree with those in this chart.
① Transmission in Drive
② Leading retarded dwell angle is 53 ± 3
③ Used in RX-3SP only
④ NGK-BR7EQ14, BR8EQ14, BR9EQ14
    NIPPON DENSO-W22EDR14,
    W25EDR14, W27EDR14
TDC—Top dead center
A—After top dead center
B—Before top dead center
MT—Manual transmission
AT—Automatic transmission
deg—degrees

FIRING ORDERS

1976 and later rotary engine (© Toyo Kogyo Co. Ltd.)

All except 1490 cc engine with front wheel drive
Note: Distributor cap wire locations vary depending on model. Always verify #1 wire position (© Toyo Kogyo Co. Ltd.)

1490 cc engine—GLC front wheel drive
(© Toyo Kogyo Co. Ltd.)

C-467

CAPACITIES

Year	Model	Engine Displacement cu. in. (cc)	Engine Crankcase (qts)		Transmission (pts)			Drive Axle (pts)	Gasoline Tank (gals)	Cooling System (qts)
			With Filter	Without Filter	Manual 4-spd	Manual 5-spd	Automatic			
'76	RX-3	70 (1146)	5.5	4.4	3.6	4.6	13.2	3.0	15.6 ⑤	9.8
	RX-4	80 (1308)	—	3.8	3.2	4.6	13.2	2.8	16.9 ④	10.0
'76–'78	808 (1600)	96.8 (1586)	3.8	—	3.2	3.6	11.6	3.0	11.9 ②	7.9
	808 (1300)	77.6 (1272)	3.2	—	2.8	—	—	2.2	11.7 ②	5.8
'77–'78	RX-4, RX-3SP	80 (1308)	6.8	5.3	3.6	4.6	13.2	2.8	16.9 ④	10.0
	Cosmo	80 (1308)	6.8	5.3	—	3.6	13.2	2.6	17.2	10.0
	GLC	77.6 (1272) ⑥	—	3.2	2.8	3.6	12.0	1.6	10.0	6.8
'79–'80	GLC	86.4 (1415)	—	3.2	2.8	3.6	12.0	2.2	10.6 ⑦	5.8
'79–'82	626	120.2 (1970)	—	4.1 ⑧	3.0	3.6	13.2	2.6	14.5	7.9
'79	RX-7	70 (1146)	5.5	4.4	3.6	3.6	13.2	2.6	14.5	7.6
'80–'83	RX-7	70 (1146)	5.5	4.4	3.6	3.6	13.2	2.6	14.5 ⑨	10.0
'81–'83	GLC	90.9 (1490)	—	3.9	6.8	6.8	12	—	11.1	5.8

② Station wagon: 10.4
④ Station wagon: 17.4
⑤ Station wagon: 14.3
⑥ Also available with 60.1 cu. in./985 cc engine: same oil capacity
⑦ Station wagon: 11.9
⑧ '82—3.8
⑨ '81–'83—16.4

ECCENTRIC SHAFT SPECIFICATIONS—ROTARY ENGINE
(All measurements are given in inches)

Model	Journal Diameter		Oil Clearance		Eccentric Shaft End-Play		Min. Shaft Run-Out
	Main Bearing	Rotor Bearing	Main Bearing	Rotor Bearing	Normal	Limit	
All	1.6929	2.9134	0.0016–0.0028	0.0016–0.0031	0.0016–0.0028	0.0035	0.0008

ROTOR AND HOUSING SPECIFICATIONS—ROTARY ENGINE
(All measurements are given in inches)

Model	Rotor			Housings					
				Front and Rear		Rotor		Intermediate	
	Side Clearance	Standard Protrusion of Land	Limit of Protrusion of Land	Distortion Limit	Wear Limit	Width	Distortion Limit	Distortion Limit	Wear Limit
RX-3 RX-3SP	0.0051–0.0067	0.004–0.006	0.003	0.002	0.004	2.7539	0.002	0.002	0.004
RX-7	0.0047–0.0071	—	—	0.0016	0.0039	2.7559	0.0024	0.0016	0.0039
RX-4 Cosmo	0.0039–0.0083	—	—	0.0016	0.0039	3.150	0.0024	0.0016	0.0039

CRANKSHAFT AND CONNECTING ROD SPECIFICATIONS—PISTON ENGINE
(All measurements are given in inches)

| Year | Engine Displacement cu. in.(cc) | Crankshaft | | | | Connecting Rod | | |
		Main Brg. Journal Dia.	Main Brg. Oil Clearance	Shaft End-Play	Thrust on No.	Journal Dia.	Oil Clearance	Side Clearance
'76–'78	96.8 (1586)	2.4804	0.001–0.002	0.003–0.009	5	2.0866	0.001–0.003	0.004–0.008
'76–'78	77.6 (1272)	2.4804	0.0012–0.0024	0.003–0.009	5	1.7717	0.0011–0.0029	0.004–0.008
'79–'80	86.4 (1415)	1.9685	0.0009–0.0017	0.004–0.006	5	1.5748	0.0009–0.0019	0.004–0.008
'79–'82	120.2 (1970)	2.4804	0.0012–0.0020	0.003–0.009	5	2.0866	0.001–0.003	0.004–0.008
'81–'83	90.9 (1490)	1.9664	0.0009–0.0017	0.004–0.006	5	1.5729	0.0009–0.0019	0.004–0.010

SEAL CLEARANCES—ROTARY ENGINE
(All measurements are given in inches)

| Model | Apex Seals | | | | Corner Seal | | Side Seal | | | |
| | To Side Housing | | To Rotor Groove | | To Rotor Groove | | To Rotor Groove | | To Corner Seal | |
	Normal	Limit	Normal	Limit	Normal	Limit	Normal	Limit	Normal	Limit
RX-3, RX-3SP	0.0020–0.0028 ①	0.0039	0.0014–0.0029	0.0039	0.0008–0.0019	0.0031	0.0016–0.0028	0.0039	0.002–0.006	0.016
RX-4, Cosmo	0.0051–0.0067	0.0118	0.0020–0.0035	0.006	0.0008–0.0019	0.0031	0.0016–0.0028	0.0040	0.0020–0.0059	0.0157
RX-7	0.0051–0.0075	—	0.0020–0.0035	0.0059	—	—	0.0012–0.0031	0.0030	0.0020–0.0059	0.0157

① Arctic specifications—0.0004–0.0020

SEAL SPECIFICATIONS—ROTARY ENGINE
(All measurements are given in inches)

| Model | Apex Seal | | Corner Seal Width (OD) | Side Seal | | Oil Seal Contact Width of Lip | |
	Normal Height	Height Limit		Thickness	Height	Normal	Limit
RX-3, RX-3SP	0.03937	0.03150	0.2756	0.0394	0.1378	0.008	0.031
RX-4, Cosmo	0.33500	0.27600	0.4331	0.0394	0.1378	0.008	0.031
RX-7	0.3347	0.2756	0.4331	0.0394	0.1378	0.0197	—

VALVE SPECIFICATIONS—PISTON ENGINE

Year	Engine Displacement cu. in. (cc)	Seat Angle (deg)	Face Angle (deg)	Spring Test Pressure (lbs.@in.)	Spring Installed Height (in.)	Stem-to-Guide Clearance(in.) Intake	Stem-to-Guide Clearance(in.) Exhaust	Stem Diameter(in.) Intake	Stem Diameter(in.) Exhaust
'76–'77	96.8 (1586)	45	45	①	②	0.0007–0.0021	0.0007–0.0023	0.3150	0.3150
'76–'78	77.6 (1272)	45	45	③	④	0.0007–0.0021	0.0007–0.0023	0.3150	0.3150
'77–'78	109.6 (1796)	45	45	⑤	②	0.0007–0.0021	0.0007–0.0023	0.3150	0.3150
'79–'80	86.4 (1415)	45	45	⑥	④	0.0007–0.0021	0.0007–0.0021	0.3150	0.3150
'79–'82	120.2 (1970)	45	45	⑦	②	0.0007–0.0021	0.0007–0.0021	0.3150	0.3150
'81–'83	90.0 (1490)	45	45	N.A.	N.A.	0.0007–0.0021	0.0007–0.0021	0.3164	0.3163

① Outer: 31.4 @ 1.339
Inner: 20.9 @ 1.260
② Outer: 1.339
Inner: 1.260
③ Outer: 43.7 @ 1.319
Inner: 20.9@1.260
④ Outer: 1.319
Inner: 1.260

⑤ Outer: 31.4 @ 1.339
Inner: 20.9 @ 1.260
⑥ Outer: 36.6 @ 1.319
Inner: 17.9 @ 1.260
⑦ Outer: 31.4 @ 1.339
Inner: 17.9 @ 1.260
N.A. Not available

PISTON AND RING SPECIFICATIONS
(All measurements are given in inches)

Year	Engine Displacement cu. in. (cc)	Piston Clearance	Ring Side Clearance Top Compression	Ring Side Clearance Bottom Compression	Ring Side Clearance Oil Control	Ring Gap Top Compression	Ring Gap Bottom Compression	Ring Gap Oil Control
'76–'79	96.8 (1586)	0.0022–0.0028	0.0014–0.0028	0.0012–0.0025	0.008–0.016	0.008–0.016	0.008–0.016	0.008–0.016
'76–'78	77.6 (1272)	0.0021–0.0026	0.0014–0.0028	0.0012–0.0025	0.008–0.016	0.008–0.016	0.008–0.016	0.008–0.016
'79–'80	86.4 (1415)	0.0021–0.0026	0.0012–0.0025	0.0012–0.0025	0.008–0.016	0.008–0.016	0.008–0.016	0.012–0.035
'79–'82	120.2 (1970)	0.0014–0.0030①	0.0012–0.0028	0.0012–0.0025	0.008–0.016	0.008–0.016	0.008–0.016	0.012–0.035
'81–'83	90.9 (1490)	0.0010–0.0026	0.0012–0.0028	0.0012–0.0028	0.008–0.016	0.008–0.016	0.008–0.016	0.012–0.035

① '82-0.0019–0.0025

TORQUE SPECIFICATIONS—PISTON ENGINE
(All figures in ft. lbs.)

Year	Engine Displacement (cc)	Cylinder Head Bolts (cold)	Rod Bearing Bolts	Main Bearing Bolts	Crankshaft Pulley Bolt	Flywheel to Crankshaft Bolts	Manifolds Intake	Manifolds Exhaust
'76–'78	1600	56–60	36–40	61–65	101–108	112–118	14–19	16–21
'76	1300	56–60	36–40	61–65	101–108	112–118	14–19	16–21
'77–'78	1300	47–51	29–33	43–47	80–87	60–65	14–19	12–17

TORQUE SPECIFICATIONS—PISTON ENGINE
(All figures in ft. lbs.)

Year	Engine Displacement (cc)	Cylinder Head Bolts (cold)	Rod Bearing Bolts	Main Bearing Bolts	Crankshaft Pulley Bolt	Flywheel to Crankshaft Bolts	Manifolds	
							Intake	Exhaust
'79–'80	1415	47–51	22–25	43–47	80–87	60–65	14–19	12–17
'79–'82	1970	59–64①	29–33	61–65	101–108	112–118	14–19	16–21
'81–'83	1490	56–59	22–25	48–51	80–87	60–65	14–19	14–17

①'82—65–69

TORQUE SPECIFICATIONS—ROTARY ENGINE
(All figures in ft. lbs.)

Engine Displacement cu. in. (cc)	Front Cover	Bearing Housing	Rear Stationary Gear	Eccentric Shaft Pulley Bolt	Flywheel to Eccentric Shaft Nut	Manifolds		Oil Pan	Tension Bolts
						Intake	Exhaust		
70 (1146)	15	15	15	45	325	15	30②	7	20③
80 (1308)	—	—	—	54–69①	289–362	15	32–43	5–7	23–27

①1977–78—72–87
②RX-7: 35
③RX-7: 25

TORQUE SEQUENCES

Tension bolt loosening sequence (© Toyo Kogyo Co. Ltd.)

Tension bolt tightening sequence (© Toyo Kogyo Co. Ltd.)

Piston engine cylinder head torque sequence

ALTERNATOR AND REGULATOR SPECIFICATIONS

Year	Model	Alternator		Regulator							
				Field Relay			Regulator				
		Field Current @14v	Output (amps)	Air Gap (in.)	Point Gap (in.)	Back Gap (in.)	Air Gap (in.)	Point Gap (in.)	Back Gap (in.)	Volts @75°
'76	RX-3, RX-4	—	56	0.035–0.055	0.028–0.043	0.028–0.059	0.028–0.051	0.012–0.018	0.028–0.059	14–15
'76–'78	808	—	40	0.035–0.055	0.028–0.043	0.028–0.059	0.028–0.051	0.012–0.018	0.028–0.059	14–15
'77–'78	All Rotary	—	63	0.035–0.055	0.028–0.043	0.028–0.049	0.028–0.051	0.012–0.018	0.028–0.059	14
'77–'80	GLC, 626	—	30	0.039–0.059	0.020–0.035	0.028–0.059	0.028–0.051	0.012–0.018	0.028–0.059	14–15
'79–'80	RX-7	—	40	0.035–0.055	0.028–0.043	0.028–0.059	0.028–0.051	0.012–0.018	0.028–0.059	14–15
'81–'83	All	—	50	Not Adjustable						

BATTERY AND STARTER SPECIFICATIONS
(All cars use 12 volt, negative ground electrical systems)

Year	Model	Battery Amp Hour Capacity	Starter							Brush Spring Tension (oz)	Min. Brush Length (in.)
			Lock Test			No Lead Test					
			Amps	Volts	Torque (ft. lbs.)	Amps	Volts	rpm			
'76–'78	RX-4 w/MT	70	780	5	7.97	75	11.5	4900		56	.45
	RX-4 w/AT	70①	1100	5	17.36	100	11.5	7800		56	.45
'76–'77	808	60	400	6	6.7	53	10.5	5000		56	.45
'76	RX-3 w/MT	60	780	5	8.0	75	11.5	4900		56	.45
	RX-3 w/AT	60	1100	5	17.4	100	11.5	7800		56	.45
'77–'78	Cosmo w/MT	45	600	5	6.9	50	11.5	5600		56	.45
	Cosmo w/AT	70	1050	5	15.9	100	11.5	6600		56	.45
'77–'80	GLC	45②	310	5	5.4	53	11.5	6800		56	.45
'79–'80	626	45	310	5	5.4	53	11.5	6800		56	.45
'79–'80	RX-7	55	600	5	6.9	50	11.5	5600		56	.45
'81–'82	626 w/MT	45	310	5	5.4	53	11.5	6800		56	.45
	626 w/AT	45	500	5	8.3	60	11.5	6600		56	.45
'81–'82	RX-7 w/MT	④	600	5	6.9	50	11.5	5600		71	.45
	RX-7 w/AT	④	1100	4	22.4	100	11.5	3500		71	.45
'81–'82	GLC	⑤	310	5	5.4	53	11.5	6800		—	.45

① 60 amp w/MT
② '77 Canada: 45 amp
    Exc Calif.: 60 amp
    Calif.: 35 amp
  '78 Calif.: 35 amp
  '79–'80 Calif.: 33 amp

③ Calif.: 35
④ Calif.: 45
  MT Exc Calif.: 55 amp optional
⑤ 33, 45 or 60
MT—Manual transmission
AT—Automatic transmission

WHEEL ALIGNMENT SPECIFICATIONS

Year	Model	Camber Range (deg)	Camber Preferred Setting (deg)	Caster Range (deg)	Caster Preferred Setting (deg)	Toe-In (in.)	Steering Axis Inclination (deg)
'76	808 (1600)	①	②	③ →2P	½P	0–0.24	8½P
'76–'77	808 (1300)	④	⑤	½N–1½P	½P	0–0.24	8⅔P
'76–'78	RX-3, RX-3SP	③	⑥	½N–1½P	½P	0–0.24	8⅔P
	RX-4	1P–2P	1½P	⑦	⑧	0–0.24	9⅔P⑨
'77	Cosmo	1½P–3P⑩	2¼P⑪	0–2P	1P	0–0.24	9¾P
'77–'78	808 (1600)	⑫	⑬	⑭	⑮	0–0.24	⑯
	GLC	—	⅔P	⅝P–2⅓P	1³⁵⁄₆₀	0–0.24	8½P
'78	Cosmo	0P–2P	1P	1½P–3P⑰	2¼⑱	o–0.24	9¾P
'79–'80	GLC	15'–1°15'⑲	45'⑳	15'–2°25'㉑	1°45'㉒	0–0.24	8°45'
'79–'80	626	45'–1°45'	1°15'	㉓	㉔	0–0.24	10°40'
'79–'80	RX-7	40'P–1°40'P	1°10'	㉕	㉖	0–0.24	10°44'
'81–'83	GLC (exc.wagon)	25'–2°25'	50'P	1°10'–2°40'	1°55'	0.12 out–0.12 in	12°10'
'81–'83	RX-7	30'–1°30'	1P	㉗	㉘	0–0.24	10°40'
'81	GLC(wagon)	43'–1°–43'	1°13'	47'–2°17'	1°32'	0–0.24	8°17'
'82–'83	GLC(wagon)	17'–1°17'	47'	51'–2°21'	1°36'	0–0.24	8°43'
'81–'82	626	44'–1°44'	1°14'	2°42'–4°12'	3°27'	0–0.24	10°36'

① Sedan: ⅝P–2⅓P
  coupe: 1P–2½P
  wagon: 1P–2⅓P
② Sedan: 1½P
  coupe: 1⅝P
  wagon: 1⅔P
③ Sedan & wagon: ⅝N–1⅕P
  coupe: 1¹⁄₁₂P–2P
④ Sedan: ⅔P–2⅙P
  coupe wagon: 1P–2⅓P
⑤ Sedan: 1⅓P
  coupe wagon: 1⅔P
⑥ Sedan & wagon: 1⅔P
  coupe: 1½P
⑦ Sedan & hardtop: 0–2P
  wagon: ⅓P–1⅓P
⑧ Sedan & hardtop: 1P
  wagon: ½P
⑨ Wagon: 9⅓P
⑩ Manual: 1P–2P
⑪ Manual: 1½P
⑫ Sedan & wagon: 1P–1½P
  coupe: 1⅓P–2⅚P
⑬ Sedan & wagon: 1⅚P
  coupe: 2¹⁄₁₂P
⑭ Sedan & coupe: ¹⁄₁₂P–2½P
  wagon: ¼P–2¼P
⑮ Sedan & coupe: 1¹⁄₁₂P
  wagon: 1¼P
⑯ Sedan & coupe: 8⁵⁄₁₂P
  wagon: 8¼P
⑰ Manual: 1⁵⁄₆₀–2³⁵⁄₆₀
⑱ Manual: 1⅝
⑲ Station wagon: 30'–1°30'

⑳ Station wagon: 1°
㉑ Station wagon: 1°–2°30'
㉒ Station wagon: 1°45'
㉓ Right side: 2°55'–4°25'
  Left side: 2°25'–3°55'
㉔ Right side: 3°45'
  Left side: 3°10'
㉕ Right side: 4°P–5°P
  Left side: 3°30'P–4°30'P
㉖ Right side: 4°30'P
  Left side: 4°P
㉗ Right side: 3°40'–4°40'
  Left side: 3°10'–4°10'
㉘ Right side: 4°10'
  Left side: 3°40'

BRAKE SPECIFICATIONS
(All measurements given are in. unless noted)

Model	Lug Nut Torque (ft. lbs.)	Master Cylinder Bore	Brake Disc		Brake Drum			Minimum Lining Thickness	
			Minimum Thickness	Maximum Run-Out	Diameter	Max. Machine O/S	Max. Wear Limit	Front	Rear
RX-3	65	0.875	0.394	0.003	7.874	7.90	7.9135	0.276	0.039
RX-4	65–72	0.875	0.433	0.004	9.0	9.025	9.0395	0.276	0.039
808	65–72	0.8125	0.394	0.004	7.874	7.90	7.9135	0.256	0.039
Cosmo	65–72	0.875	0.6693①	0.0024②	—	—	—	0.276	0.276
GLC	65–72④	¹³⁄₁₆	0.4724⑤	0.0024⑥	7.874⑦	③	7.9135⑧	0.276⑨	0.039⑩
626	65–80	⅞	0.4724	0.004	7.874⑪	③	7.9135⑫	0.256⑬	0.039
RX-7	65–80	0.8125	0.6693	0.0039	7.8741	③	7.9135	0.236	0.039

NOTE: Minimum lining thickness is as recommended by the manufacturer. Due to variations in state inspection regulations, the minimum allowable thickness may be different than recommended by the manufacturer.
① Rear: 0.354
② Rear: 0.004
③ No matching maximum given—remove minimum amount which smooths surface, then ensure drum inner diameter meets specification.
④ 65–80—'79–'83
⑤ 0.43—'81–'83
⑥ 0.004—'81–'83
⑦ 7.09—'81–'83
⑧ 7.13—'81–'83
⑨ 0.04—'81–'83
⑩ 0.04—'81–'83
⑪ 9.0001—'81–'82
⑫ 9.0395—'81–'82
⑬ 0.04—'81–'82

TUNE-UP PROCEDURES

Compression

ROTARY ENGINE

Because of the unusual shape of the combustion chamber, the lack of valves and because there are three chambers for each rotor, a normal gauge is useless for the measurement of rotary engine compression.

Mazda makes a special recording compression tester which produces a separate graph for each of the three chambers.

This is an expensive piece of equipment and not one that most mechanics are likely to have. If low compression is suspected, check with your local Mazda dealer.

PISTON ENGINE

The compression is checked in the conventional manner.

Compression pressures are considered normal if lowest reading is within 75% of the highest.

Breaker Points and Condenser

ALL MODELS

1976 and later rotary engines have a single distributor with either dual or triple point sets. Most piston engines are equipped with breaker point distributors through 1979. GLC models from 1977 use a breakerless dis-

Adjusting the dual point distributor (© Toyo Kogyo Co. Ltd.)

tributor except those built for California and Canadian models. The 1979 and later 626 models are equipped with breakerless ignition. On the breakerless distributors there are no points or condenser to replace.

Electronic Ignition

ROTARY ENGINE

1. Spark plugs—rotary engine type with 3 electrodes.

0.3 ~ 0.35mm (0.012 ~ 0.014in)

Checking the air gap in the electronic ignition distributor (© Toyo Kogyo Co. Ltd.)

2. Distributor—breakerless type.
   a. Signal rotor—timing teeth
   b. Vacuum and centrifugal advance—standard.
   c. Pick-up coils—1 leading and 1 trailing; generates the signals to the igniter (control unit).

3. Igniter—receives signals from the pick-up coils and switches the primary ignition current off and on.

4. Ignition coils—1 leading and 1 trailing coil; not to be exchanged with standard ignition coils.

PISTON ENGINES

In 1979 the 626 and GLC models were equipped with electronic ignition. Unlike the rotary engines the piston engines have a single coil ignition system. As of 1980, all Mazda vehicles sold in the USA, were equipped with electronic ignition.

Ignition Timing

ROTARY ENGINE

1976

1. Run the engine at normal operating temperature.
2. Connect a tachometer.
3. Connect a timing light to the leading spark plug of the front rotor housing.
4. Run engine at idle speed.
5. If the timing is not correct, rotate the distributor housing until the timing mark on the pulley aligns with the indicator pin.
6. Recheck the leading timing.
7. Connect the timing light to the trailing spark plug of the front rotor housing.
8. Check the trailing timing.
9. If the trailing timing is not correct, note the amount of error and stop the engine.
10. Remove the distributor cap and rotor.
11. Disconnect the primary wire from the leading retard point set.

1976—1586 cc (Except Calif.) (© Toyo Kogyo Co. Ltd.)

1976—1586 cc (Calif.) (© Toyo Kogyo Co. Ltd.)

1977 and later 1586 cc, exc Calif.

1977 and later 1586 cc, Calif.

1976 and later 1272 cc

1977 and later 1796 cc

1976—1146 cc engine (© Toyo Kogyo Co. Ltd.)

1977 and later 1146 cc

1976—1308 cc (© Toyo Kogyo Co. Ltd.)

1977 and later 1308 cc

12. Remove the breaker base plate and external lever for leading set.
13. Slightly loosen the breaker base set screws of the trailing side and turn the base plate as required. Install the leading breaker base assembly, rotor and cap.
14. Check the trailing and leading timing. If they are not correct, repeat the above steps.
15. Leave timing light connected to trailing plug of the front rotor housing.
16. Connect a jumper between both terminals in the coupler of the primary lead wires.
17. Check the leading retard timing. Adjust by moving the external adjusting lever.

1977–78

1. Have the engine at normal operating temperature.
2. Connect a timing light to the leading spark plug wire and a tachometer to the engine.
3. Operate the engine at the specified idle speed. On automatic transmission equipped vehicles, place the selector in DRIVE and block the wheels.
4. Check the timing on the crankshaft pulley and if the leading timing is not correct, loosen the distributor body locknut and rotate the distributor housing to correct the timing. Tighten the locknut and recheck the timing.
5. Install the timing light on the trailing spark plug and check the trailing timing.

Adjusting the ignition timing: 1976–77 rotary (© Toyo Kogyo Co. Ltd.)

Ignition timing adjustment: 1977-79 RX-4 and Cosmo (© Toyo Kogyo Co. Ltd.)

(Insert the screwdriver here and rotate the breaker base)

DISTRIBUTOR LOCK NUT
● Loosen this nut and turn the distributor housing.

Retard / Advance

LEADING BREAKER BASE ASSEMBLY
● Slighly loosen two screws (shown with ▷) and turn the breaker base

(Timing marks on pulley)

25° (ATDC)
5 (ATDC)L—yellow

5° ATDC (Leading)
20° ATDC (Trailing and leading retard)

Timing marks, 1976 RX-4 (© Toyo Kogyo Co. Ltd.)

6. If the trailing timing is not correct, loosen the vacuum unit for the trailing points and move the unit in or out until the correct timing is obtained.

7. Tighten the trailing vacuum unit and recheck the trailing timing.

1979 and Later Except 1979 Automatic Transmission After Chassis No. 522504

1. Warm the engine up until it reaches operating temperature. Connect a tachom-

0° TDC (Leading)
15° ATDC (Trailing)
20° ATDC (Leading retard)

Ignition timing marks, 1976 RX-3

eter (or use the tachometer on the dash). On automatic transmission cars, securely apply the handbrake, block the wheels, and put the car in Drive. Reading the tach as for a conventional four cylinder engine, verify that the engine is running at its normal idle speed. If not, adjust idle speed to specification.

2. Stop the engine and connect a timing light to the leading (lower) spark plug on the front rotor. Then, restart the engine. Aim the timing light at the pin on the front housing cover, and observe timing. If the timing pointer does not line up with the first (yellow) notch on the pulley, loosen the distributor locknut and rotate the distributor either way until timing is correct. Tighten the locknut and check that timing is still correct.

3. Stop the engine and connect the timing light to the trailing (upper) spark plug on the front rotor. Start the engine (putting automatic transmission cars in Drive), and check the trailing timing. The timing pointer

Except for RX-3SP with automatic transmission

Vacuum unit attaching screws

(Trailing)
Retard / Advance

Advance

(Leading)

Retard

Distributor lock nut

Trailing timing adjustment for 1978-79 rotary engines (© Toyo Kogyo Co. Ltd.)

should line up with the second (red) notch in the pulley.

4. If the trailing timing is not correct, loosen the vacuum unit attaching screws (manual transmission) or the adjusting lever attaching screws (automatic transmission) and move the vacuum unit (manual transmission) or adjusting lever (automatic transmission) in or out until the timing pointer lines up with the second mark on the pulley, then tighten the screws and recheck the timing.

1979 Automatic Transmission After Chassis No. 522504

Complete Steps 1–3 under "1979 Models—Automatic Transmission Up To . . . etc."

To adjust the trailing timing, stop the engine and remove the distributor cap and rotor. Slightly loosen the breaker base attaching screws, then reinstall the rotor and distributor cap. Start the engine. Set the selector lever in Drive and run the engine at idle speed. Loosen the external adjusting lever attaching screws and move the adjusting lever in or out until the timing pointer lines up with the second (red) mark on the pulley, then tighten the adjusting lever attaching screws. Stop the engine, remove the distributor cap and rotor and tighten the two breaker base attaching screws. Refit the rotor and distributor and recheck the trailing timing.

PISTON ENGINE

NOTE: Some 1977 and most 1978 and later models require the ignition timing adjusted with the vacuum line connected to the distributor. Refer to the emission sticker (under the hood) to determine if the vacuum line is to be connected or disconnected and plugged.

1. If required, disconnect and plug the distributor vacuum line.

Typical piston engine timing marks except 1490 cc engine (front wheel drive) (© Toyo Kogyo Co. Ltd.)

2. Set the parking brake and block the front wheels. Start and run the engine until it reaches the normal operating temperature. Shut off the engine and connect a tachometer. Restart and check engine idle speed. Adjust if necessary. Shut off engine.

NOTE: Prior to starting the engine, clean off any grease or oil that will prevent seeing the timing marks on the crankshaft pulley. Mark the pulley notches with chalk or paint.

3. Connect a timing light to the engine following the manufacturer's instructions. Start the engine and observe the timing by pointing the light at the timing marks on the crankshaft pulley.

NOTE: If the car is equipped with an automatic transmission put the lever in "D"; check emission sticker or tune-up "specs" for requirement.

4. If the timing is not correct, loosen the distributor mounting bolt and rotate the distributor as necessary to produce the correct timing mark alignment. Recheck the timing after tightening the lock bolt. Readjust if necessary. Check idle speed.

5. On 1978 non-California cars with manual transmissions, the advance timing may be checked by disconnecting the leads to the switch which is operated by the accelerator pedal. If the advance setting is not at 11° BTDC, check the dwell angles of both sets of points. If the advance setting is not correct, it indicates unequal dwell angles, or, more rarely, faulty parts in one or both

Connecting the distributor coupler with jumper—rotary engine (© Toyo Kogyo Co. Ltd.)

contact sets or a worn distributor shaft or cam.

NOTE: Some Canadian models require the bullet connectors at the water temperature connector disconnected before timing the ignition; check the emission sticker for requirements.

6. Reconnect the vacuum line, accelerator switch or bullet connectors if disconnected. Recheck idle speed, readjust if necessary.

Dwell Angle

ROTARY ENGINES

1976

1. Run the engine until it is warm.
2. Connect the dwell meter in accordance with the manufacturer's instructions. The dwell meter must be connected to the coil which fires the leading plugs to test the leading contact points, and to the coil which fires the trailing plugs to test the trailing contact points.
3. Run the engine at idle speed and observe the meter reading. It should be within the range specified in the tune-up chart.
4. If dwell is not within the specified range, adjust the contact gap as described above. If dwell angle is too high, the point gap is too small; if dwell angle is too low, the point gap is too wide.
5. After setting dwell of leading and trailing contact points, stop the engine and disconnect the connector in the wiring harness which leads to the distributor. Then, run two jumper wires exactly as shown in the illustration. This will cause the *leading* ignition coil to be operated through the leading-retard contact points, and enable you to read the dwell for those contacts. Dwell for this set of contacts is 53 degrees.
6. Be sure to recheck dwell after tightening the adjusting screw, because the point gap (and dwell) sometimes changes when this is done. If dwell cannot be brought to specification, check for a bent contact arm, worn rubbing block, or worn distributor cam or shaft.

1977 and Later

The method of dwell angle adjustment described here requires that some of the high tension wiring be re-routed to permit the engine to run with the distributor cap and rotor off. While this re-routing process requires some extra time, the dwell adjustment may be made with the engine running, which will save considerable time and make it possible for the dwell to be brought to specification on the first adjustment.

1. Run the engine until it is hot and stop it.
2. Note their locations, and then disconnect high tension leads at leading and trailing ignition coils.
3. Note its location in the distributor

cap, and then disconnect the leading spark plug wire for the front rotor at the cap. Connect it to the tower of the leading ignition coil.
4. Note its location in the distributor cap, and then disconnect the leading spark plug wire for the rear rotor at the cap. Connect it to the tower of the trailing ignition coil.
5. Remove the distributor cap and rotor.
6. Check the high tension wiring with the illustration. The plug wires for the top two plugs will still be connected to the rotor, but the bottom two plugs must be wired as shown.
7. Connect the dwell angle tester to the trailing ignition coil. Then, start the engine and read the dwell. If the dwell is incorrect, loosen the set screw for the trailing contact set *only slightly* (or the engine will stop). Then, very gradually move the stationary contact back and forth until dwell is within the specified range (55–61 degrees).
8. When dwell is correct, tighten the set screw and recheck dwell. Readjust it as necessary.

On 1977 and later rotary engines to set dwell with engine running, re-route high tension wiring as shown (© Toyo Kogyo Co. Ltd.)

9. Connect the dwell meter to the leading ignition coil and repeat Steps 7 and 8 for the leading contacts.
10. Reconnect all wiring and reinstall the cap and rotor.

PISTON ENGINE

1. Start the engine and run until it is hot and running at normal idle speed.
2. Connect a dwell meter to the ignition coil as described in the manufacturer's instructions. Read the dwell and compare the reading to the specification shown in the "Tune-Up Chart."
3. If dwell is incorrect, stop engine, remove distributor cap and rotor and adjust point gap as described above. If dwell is very far from the specified range, simply set contacts to the specified gap. If dwell is just a little too high, open the contact

gap just slightly; if dwell reading is too low, close the point gap just slightly.

4. After contact adjustment, replace cap and rotor, start engine, and read dwell again. Readjust if necessary.

Valve Lash

PISTON ENGINE ONLY

Adjust the valves in the firing order 1-3-4-2.

1. Rotate the crankshaft so that the No. 1 cylinder (front) is in the firing position.
2. The clearance can be checked at the camshaft or at the valve.
3. If the valve clearance is incorrect, loosen the adjusting screw locknut and adjust the clearance.
4. Rotate the crankshaft (in the normal direction of rotation), adjusting the valves for each cylinder at TDC of the compression stroke.

Carburetor

NOTE: For further carburetor adjustments see the "Fuel System."

IDLE SPEED AND MIXTURE

Adjustment of the idle mixture requires the use of an exhaust gas analyzer, a piece of equipment the amateur mechanic does not usually own. The mixture adjustment procedure is given here for those who have access to an exhaust gas analyzer.

Piston Engine

1. Thoroughly warm the engine.
2. Make sure that the choke valve is fully open.
3. Connect a tachometer.
4. Adjust the idle speed screw to specifications.
5. The mixture should be checked by a CO meter. The carbon monoxide percentage at idle should be 0.1%–2.0%.
6. Disconnect the tachometer.

Idle and Throttle Screw Adjustment

If for some reason the idle and throttle screws need adjustment, use the following procedure.

HC/CO Analyzer

1. Adjust the throttle angle opening to specifications. Make the adjustment from the fully closed position.
2. Adjust the idle speed.
3. Using the gas analyzer, check the HC (hydrocarbon) and CO (carbon monoxide) readings. If the HC is less than 200 ppm (parts per million) and the CO is between 0.1–2.0%, no further adjustment is needed.
4. If the HC and CO are not within specifications, adjust the CO reading to as close to 0.1% as possible, keeping the HC reading below 200 ppm. Use the idle fuel screw to make this adjustment.
5. Recheck the idle speed.

1976–80 Rotary Engine

Idle speed changes with air temperature. It is suggested by Mazda that the idle adjustment be made indoors with a floor fan blowing through the radiator to assist in cooling. Whenever operating an engine indoors, make certain that provision is made for removal of exhaust gases. Idle speed should be adjusted with the engine at normal operating temperature, all accessories off and fuel tank cap removed.

1. Disconnect the idle compensator tube at the air cleaner and plug the end of the tube.
2. Run the engine at normal operating temperature and make sure that the choke is wide open.
3. Check the float level.
4. Connect an exhaust gas analyzer and tachometer.
5. With engine at idle, check the CO density.
6. Adjust the idle speed to specification with the idle adjusting screw.
7. Turn the mixture adjusting screw clockwise until the engine lopes severely.
8. Turn the screw slowly counterclockwise until the CO density reaches 0.1%, then turn it an additional one quarter turn in the same direction.

Adjusting the idle speed, 1976-79 rotary; (1) air adjust screw, (2) mixture screw

1981 and Later Rotary Engine

When adjusting the idle speed and mixture on the 1981 and later rotary engines, take the following steps.

1. Start with a cold engine.
2. Set the parking brake and block the wheels.
3. Remove the fuel filler cap.
4. Switch off all accessories.
5. Disconnect the vacuum line at the idle compensator in the air cleaner and plug the line.
6. Check the dash pot rod and the air conditioner throttle opener. Make certain these devices are not stopping the throttle linkage from returning to a fully seated idle stop position.
7. Connect a tachometer to the negative terminal of the leading coil and a good ground. The leading coil is the rear coil on the driver's side fender well.
8. Bring the engine up to operating temperature.
9. Set vehicles equipped with automatic transmissions in the drive selector position. Adjust the idle stop screw to obtain 750 rpm in drive. Adjust manual transmission equipped vehicles to 750 rpm in neutral.
10. Adjust the idle mixture by removing the mixture screw limiter cap. Richen the idle mixture to obtain the highest rpm before it starts to drop. Reset the idle speed to specification. Repeat these procedures until both the highest rpm and the idle speed are correct. Install a replacement limiter cap on the idle mixture screw.

ENGINE ELECTRICAL

Distributor

REMOVAL AND INSTALLATION

Rotary Engines

1. Rotate the engine in normal direction of rotation until the first ("TDC" or

Idle speed (1) and mixture (2) screws —piston engine

Idle adjustments—rotary engine (© Toyo Kogyo Co. Ltd.)

"Leading") timing mark aligns with the pin on the front cover. Matchmark the body of the distributor and the engine rotor housing.

2. The easiest way to clear the high tension wires out of the way is to simply remove the cap and set it aside with the wires still attached. However, if you wish to keep the cap with the distributor, pull the wires out of the cap, observing markings.

3. Disconnect vacuum advance and, if so equipped, retard hoses. Disconnect the primary electrical connector.

4. Remove the distributor adjusting bolt. Pull the distributor vertically out of the engine.

5. To install the distributor, first make sure the engine has not been disturbed. If it has been moved, again turn the crankshaft until the first timing mark lines up with the pin on the front cover. Then align the dimple in the distributor gear with the notch or line cast into the body of the distributor.

6. Insert the distributor carefully and slowly into the engine with distributor body and rotor housing matchmarks aligned. Avoid allowing the shaft to turn and be careful not to damage the housing when inserting the gear into it.

7. Install the adjusting bolt, but do not tighten. Turn the distributor until the leading points just start to open, and then tighten the locking bolt.

8. Install vacuum hoses, electrical connectors, and high tension wires in reverse of the removal procedure.

9. If ignition points have been disturbed or replaced, set the dwell as described previously. Set ignition timing.

Piston Engines

1. Unfasten the clips which hold the distributor cap to the top of the distributor, and remove the cap. Note the location of the wire going to No. 1 (the front) cylinder where it enters the cap.

2. Rotate the engine with the starter or by using a socket wrench on the bolt which retains the front pulley until the timing mark on the pulley is aligned with the pin on the front cover. Check to see if the contact on the rotor is pointing toward the No. 1 spark plug wire. If the rotor is half a turn away from the No. 1 plug wire, turn the crankshaft ahead one full turn until the timing mark is again aligned with the pin. Match mark the distributor body with the cylinder head.

3. Disconnect the vacuum advance line at the advance unit and disconnect the primary wire at the connector near the distributor.

4. Remove the adjusting bolt, and pull the distributor out of the engine.

5. To install the distributor, first align the dimple on the distributor drive gear with the mark cast into the base of the distributor body by rotating the shaft. Then, being careful not to rotate the shaft, insert the

When installing the distributor on the 1490 cc engine front wheel drive, make sure the distributor shaft fits into the groove in the camshaft (© Toyo Kogyo Co. Ltd.)

distributor back into the cylinder head with distributor body and cylinder head match marks aligned and seat it.

6. Install the mounting bolt, but do not tighten it. Rotate the distributor until the points are just opening, and tighten the mounting bolt.

7. Install the distributor cap, and reconnect the vacuum advance line and the primary connector.

8. If the ignition points have been disturbed, set the dwell as described in the previous chapter. Set timing.

NOTE: If the engine has been rotated while the distributor was out, it will be necessary to turn the crankshaft until the point where No. 1 cylinder is just about to fire. To do this, remove No. 1 spark plug and rotate the engine until you can

feel compression pressure building (with your finger over the spark plug hole) as the engine is turned forward. Then, turn the engine until the timing mark on the front pulley is aligned with the pin on the front cover, and proceed with Step 5.

Alternator

REMOVAL AND INSTALLATION

Disconnect all of the leads. Remove the alternator adjusting link bolt. Do not remove the adjusting link. Remove the drivebelt and remove the alternator.

1. Pulley	6. Front bearing
2. Fan	7. Bearing retainer
3. Spacer	8. Rotor
4. Slinger	9. Rear bearing
5. Front housing	10. Stator

11. Terminal bolt
12. Diode plate (rectifiers)
13. Brush holder
14. Rear housing
15. Condenser

Exploded view of typical alternator (© Toyo Kogyo Co. Ltd.)

NOTE: The alternator is removed from under the vehicle on 1981 and later GLC models. If necessary to raise the vehicle make sure it is safely supported with jack stands.

Installation is the reverse order of removal. Adjust the drivebelt.

BELT TENSION ADJUSTMENT

Check tension by applying thumb pressure to the belt, midway between the eccentric shaft and alternator pulleys. The belt should deflect about ½ in.

Regulator

REMOVAL AND INSTALLATION

Externally Mounted

Disconnect the wiring and remove the regulator mounting screws. Remove the regulator.

Installation is the reverse of removal.

VOLTAGE ADJUSTMENTS

Models With Ammeters Only

1. Remove the cover.
2. Check the air gap, the point gap, and the back gap with a feeler gauge.
3. Adjust the gaps by bending the stationary contact bracket.
4. Connect a voltmeter between the "A" and "E" terminal of the regulator.
5. Run the engine at 2000 rpm. The voltmeter reading should be 13.5–14.5 V.
6. Stop the engine.
7. Bend the upper plate *down* to decrease the voltage setting or *up* to increase the setting, as required.
8. If the regulator cannot be brought within specifications, replace it.

Regulator mechanical adjustments (© Toyo Kogyo Co. Ltd.)

Testing the voltage regulator (© Toyo Kogyo Co. Ltd.)

REGULATOR TEST

Models With Warning Light

CONSTANT VOLTAGE RELAY

1. Use an almost fully charged battery and connect a voltmeter between the "A" and "E" terminals of the regulator.
2. Run the engine at 2000 rpm and read the voltmeter. It should read from 14–15 volts.
3. If not, adjust the voltage relay.

PILOT LAMP RELAY

1. Using a voltmeter and variable resistor, construct a circuit as shown.
2. Light the pilot lamp.
3. Gradually increase voltage.
4. Read the voltage between the "N" and "E" terminals of the regulator. If the voltage is 3.7–5.7 volts, it is operating properly.
5. Decrease the voltage. Note the point on the voltmeter where the light will light again. If the reading is less than 3.5 volts, the unit is working properly.

CONSTANT VOLTAGE RELAY

Air gap 0.028–0.043 in.
Point gap 0.012–0.016 in.

Back gap 0.028–0.043 in.

PILOT LAMP RELAY

Air gap 0.035–0.047 in.
Point gap 0.028–0.043 in.
Back gap 0.028–0.043 in.

Internally Mounted

Late model alternators have the voltage regulator mounted within the unit as part of the brush holder assembly. No adjustments can be made to the regulator assembly and the alternator must be removed and disassembled to replace the voltage regulator.

Starter

REMOVAL AND INSTALLATION

Rotary Engine

The starter is removed in the conventional manner. If the car is equipped with the lower mounted starter, remove the gravel shield from underneath the engine.

Installation is the reverse of the above.

Piston Engine

The air cleaner/air intake tube must be removed. Remove the starter out below the emission system hoses.

STARTER DRIVE REPLACEMENT

Unless disassembly of the starter is desired, do not remove the thru-bolts.

1. Remove the solenoid.
2. Remove the plunger from the drive engagement fork.
3. Remove the nuts from the thru-bolts.

1. Front housing
2. Overrunning clutch
3. Engagement fork
4. Center frame
5. Solenoid
6. Stop
7. Idler gear
8. Armature
9. Field coil
10. Brush holder
11. End frame

Typical starter components (© Toyo Kogyo Co. Ltd.)

4. Remove the drive housing.

5. Remove the engagement fork, spring and spring seat.

6. Withdraw the over-running clutch from the armature shaft.

Assembly is the reverse order of disassembly. Check the clearance between the pinion and the stop collar with the solenoid closed. It should be 0.001–0.006 in.

ENGINE MECHANICAL

Rotary Engine

NOTE: Because of the unique design of the Mazda rotary engine, some procedures require the use of special factory tools. The text notes where these tools are necessary. If the tools are not available, the job should not be undertaken.

DESIGN

The Mazda rotary engine replaces conventional pistons with three-cornered rotors which have rounded sides. The rotors are mounted on a shaft which has eccentrics rather than crank throws.

The chamber which the rotor travels in is roughly oval-shaped, but with the sides of the oval bowed in slightly. The technical name for this shape is a two-lobe epitrochoid.

As the rotor travels its path in the chamber, it performs the same four functions as the piston in a traditional piston engine.

1. Intake
2. Compression
3. Ignition
4. Exhaust

But all four functions in a rotary engine are happening concurrently, rather than in four separate stages.

Ignition of the compressed fuel/air mixture occurs each time a side of the rotor passes the spark plugs. Since the rotor has three sides, there are three complete power impulses for each complete revolution of the rotor.

As it moves, the rotor exerts pressure on the cam of the eccentric shaft, causing the shaft to turn.

Because there are three power pulses for every revolution of the rotor, the eccentric shaft must make three complete revolutions for every one of the rotor. To maintain this ratio, the rotor has an internal gear that meshes with a fixed gear in a three-to-one ratio. If it were not for this gear arrangement, the rotor would spin freely and timing would be lost.

The Mazda rotary engine has two rotors mounted 60 degrees out of phase. This produces six power impulses for each complete revolution of both rotors and two power impulses for each revolution of the eccentric shaft.

Because of the number of power impulses for each revolution of the rotor, and because all four functions are concurrent, the rotary engine is able to produce a much greater amount of power for its size and weight than a comparable reciprocating piston engine.

Instead of using valves to control the intake and exhaust operations, the rotor uncovers and covers ports on the wall of the chamber as it turns. Thus, a complex valve train is unnecessary. The resulting elimination of parts further reduces the size and weight of the engine, as well as eliminating a major source of mechanical problems.

Spring-loaded carbon seals are used to prevent loss of compression around the rotor apexes and cast iron seals are used to prevent loss of compression around the side faces of the rotor. These seals are equivalent to compression rings on a conventional piston but must be more durable because of the high rotor rpm to which they are exposed.

Oil is controlled by means of circular seals mounted in two grooves on the side face of the rotor. These oil seals function to keep oil out of the crankcase, in a similar manner to the oil control ring on a piston.

The rotor housing is made of aluminum and the surfaces of the chamber are chrome plated for durability and the prevention of wear damage.

REMOVAL AND INSTALLATION

All Except RX-7

Be sure that the engine has completely cooled before attempting to remove it.

1. Scribe matchmarks on the hood and hinges. Remove the hood from the hinges.

2. Working from underneath the car, remove the gravel shield then drain the cooling system and the engine oil.

3. Disconnect the cable from the negative (−) battery terminal.

4. Remove the air cleaner, its bracket, and its attendant hoses.

5. Detach the accelerator cable, choke cable, and fuel lines from the carburetor.

6. Remove the nuts which secure the thermostat housing. Disconnect the ground cable from the housing and install the housing again after the cable is removed.

7. Disconnect the power brake vacuum line from the intake manifold.

8. Remove the fan shroud securing bolts and then the shroud itself.

9. Remove the bolts which secure the fan clutch to the eccentric shaft pulley. Withdraw the fan and clutch as a single unit.

— CAUTION —

Keep the fan clutch in an upright position so that its fluid does not leak out.

10. Unfasten the clamps and remove both radiator hoses.

11. Note their respective positions and remove the spark plug cables. Disconnect the primary leads from the distributors and remove both distributor caps.

12. Detach all of the leads from the alternator, the water temperature sender, the oil pressure sender, and the starter motor.

13. Disconnect all of the wiring from the emission control system components.

14. Detach the heater hoses at the engine.

15. Detach the oil lines from the front and the rear of the engine.

16. Disconnect the battery cable from the positive (+) battery terminal and from the engine.

17. Unfasten the clutch slave cylinder retaining nuts from the clutch housing and tie the cylinder up and out of the way.

NOTE: Do not remove the hydraulic line from the slave cylinder.

18. Remove the exhaust pipe and the thermal reactor.

— CAUTION —

Be sure that the thermal reactor has completely cooled; severe burns could result if it has not.

19. Remove the nuts and bolts, evenly and in two or three stages, which secure the clutch housing to the engine.

20. Support the transmission by a jack placed underneath it.

21. Remove the nuts from each of the engine mounts.

22. Attach a lifting sling to the lifting bracket on the rear of the engine housing.

23. Use a hoist to take up the slack on the sling.

— CAUTION —

Be sure that the hoist is secure to prevent personal injury or damage to the engine.

24. Pull the engine forward until it clears the transmission input shaft. Lift the engine straight up and out of the car.

— CAUTION —

Be careful not to damage any of the components remaining in the car.

25. Remove the heat stove from the exhaust manifold.

26. Remove the thermal reactor as outlined below.

27. Mount the engine on a workstand.

NOTE: A special three part workstand, designed for the rotary engine, is available from Mazda.

Engine installation is performed in the reverse order of removal. Remember to refill all fluids according to specifications and to adjust the ignition after installation.

RX-7

CAUTION
Be sure that the engine has completely cooled before attempting to remove it.

1. Scribe matchmarks on the hood and hinges and remove the hood. The matchmarks are made so that you can align the hood on its hinges when installing it.

2. Working from underneath the car, remove the gravel shield then drain the cooling system and the engine oil.

3. Disconnect the negative (−) battery cable and disconnect the high tension wires from the center towers of the ignition coils.

NOTE: A good rule of thumb when disconnecting the engine wiring and vacuum hoses is to put a piece of masking tape on the wire or hose and on the connection you remove the wire or hose from, then mark both pieces of tape, 1, 2, 3, etc. When replacing wiring and hoses, simply match the pieces of tape.

4. Disconnect the distributor wiring, the oil level sensor lead, the water temperature lead and, on all except California models, the coupler from the oil thermo sensor.

5. On all California models and 1980 and later automatic transmission models, disconnect the vacuum sensing tube for the vacuum switch. Disconnect the evaporative hose.

6. Disconnect the hoses from the oil cooler, located beneath the radiator. Disconnect the radiator coolant level sensor lead from the top of the radiator and disconnect the coolant reservoir hose.

7. Remove the bolts holding the coolant fan and drive unit to the drive pulley and remove. Remove the air cleaner.

CAUTION
On models with air conditioning it will be necessary to remove the compressor and the condensor from their mounts. DO NOT ATTEMPT TO UNFASTEN ANY OF THE AIR CONDITIONER HOSES.

8. On 1980 and later models except those made in California and Canada, disconnect the connectors from the No. 2 water temperature sensor, located on the radiator next to the radiator cap.

9. Remove the lower and upper radiator hoses. Disconnect the transmission fluid pipes from the radiator (automatic transmission only).

10. Remove the radiator and shroud assembly.

11. Remove the vacuum hose for the brake booster. Disconnect the heat exchanger pipe from the rear of the intake manifold.

12. Disconnect the coupler from the power valve solenoid on 1979 automatic transmission and California manual transmission models and on all 1980 models except Canadian manual transmission.

13. Disconnect the coasting enrichment connector from manual transmission models. Disconnect the leads from the choke heater and the anti-afterburn solenoid. Disconnect the idle switch coupler on manual transmission models.

14. On 1980 and later models except California and Canada, disconnect the lead from the choke return solenoid valve.

15. Remove the two upper transmission to engine bolts. Remove the rear cover from the exhaust manifold, if equipped. Disconnect the accelerator, choke and hot start assist cables.

16. Disconnect the fuel lines from the carburetor and plug the fuel intake line to prevent leaks.

17. Disconnect the sub-zero start assist hose, if equipped, and disconnect the wiring from the alternator.

18. Disconnect the wiring from the water temperature switch and the air vent solenoid. Disconnect the heater hose from the left side of the engine.

19. From underneath the car, disconnect and remove the starter. Remove the lower engine to transmission bolts.

20. On automatic transmission models, remove the converter housing lower cover, matchmark the drive plate in relation to the torque converter, then remove the torque converter to drive plate bolts. You will have to turn the engine to remove all of the bolts.

21. Disconnect all interfering exhaust system components. The thermal reactor (1979–80) or the catalysts (1981 and later) may be very hot if the engine is still warm, so use caution.

22. Support the front of the transmission with a floor jack, then remove the left and right side engine mount bolts.

23. Attach a suitable sling to the engine hanger brackets and raise the engine with a hoist slightly.

24. Pull the engine forward until it clears the clutch shaft or torque converter, then lift it out of the car.

25. Mount the engine on a stand.

NOTE: A special hanger and work stand are available from Mazda (engine stand tool number 49 0107 680A, hanger tool number 49 1114 005).

Engine installation is performed in the reverse order of removal. Be sure to refill the engine with all fluids and check the engine timing.

DISASSEMBLY

All Models

NOTE: Because of the design of the rotary engine, it is not practical to attempt component removal and installation. It is best to disassemble and assemble the entire engine, or, go as far as necessary with the disassembly procedure. Refer to the specification charts for measurements of the components.

1. Mount the engine on a stand.

2. Remove the oil hose support bracket from the front housing.

3. Disconnect the vacuum hoses, air hoses and remove the decel valve.

4. Remove the air pump and drive belt. Remove the air pump adjusting bar.

5. Remove the alternator and drive belt.

6. Disconnect the metering oil pump connecting rod, oil tubes and vacuum sensing tube from the carburetor.

7. Remove the carburetor and intake manifold as an assembly.

8. Remove the gasket and two rubber rings.

9. Remove the thermal reactor and gaskets.

10. Remove the distributor.

11. Remove the water pump.

12. Invert the engine.

13. Remove the oil pan.

14. Remove the oil pump.

15. Identify the front and rear rotor housings with a felt tip pen. These are common parts and must be identified to be reassembled in their respective locations.

16. Turn the engine on the stand so that the top of the engine is up.

17. Remove the engine mounting bracket from the front cover.

18. Remove the eccentric shaft pulley.

19. Turn the engine on a stand so that the front end of the engine is up.

20. Remove the front cover.

21. Remove the O-ring from the oil passage on the front housing.

22. Remove the oil slinger and distributor drive gear from the shaft.

23. Unbolt and remove the chain adjuster.

24. Remove the locknut and washer from the oil pump driven sprocket.

25. Slide the oil pump drive sprocket and driven sprocket together with the drive chain off the eccentric shaft and oil pump simultaneously.

26. Remove the keys from the eccentric and oil pump shafts.

27. Slide the balance weight, thrust washer and needle bearing from the shaft.

28. Unbolt the bearing housing and slide the bearing housing, needle bearing, spacer and thrust plate off the shaft.

Mark the front and rear rotor housings to prevent confusion during assembly (© Toyo Kogyo Co. Ltd.)

Remove any side seals adhering to the front housing surfaces (© Toyo Kogyo Co. Ltd.)

29. Turn the engine on the stand so that the top of the engine is up.

30. If equipped with a manual transmission, remove the clutch pressure plate and clutch disc. Remove the flywheel with a puller.

31. If equipped with an automatic transmission, remove the drive plate. Remove the counterweight.

32. Working at the rear of the engine, loosen the tension bolts.

NOTE: Do not loosen the tension bolts one at a time. Loosen the bolts evenly in small stages to prevent distortion. Mark tension bolts to replace in original holes during reassembly.

33. Lift the rear housing off the shaft.

34. Remove any seals that are stuck to the rotor sliding surface of the rear housing and reinstall them in their original locations.

35. Remove all the corner seals, corner seal springs, side seal and side seal springs from the rear side of the rotor. Mazda has a special tray which holds all the seals and keeps them segregated to prevent mistakes during reassembly. Each seal groove is marked to prevent confusion.

36. Remove the two rubber seals and two O-rings from the rear rotor housing.

Use a felt-tipped pen to mark the bottom of each apex seal (© Toyo Kogyo Co. Ltd.)

37. Remove the dowels from the rear rotor housing.

38. Lift the rear rotor housing away from the rear rotor, being very careful not to drop the apex seals on the rear rotor.

39. Remove each apex seal, side piece and spring from the rear rotor and segregate them.

40. Remove the rear rotor from the eccentric shaft and place it upside down on a clean rag.

41. Remove each seal and spring from the other side of the rotor and segregate these.

42. If some of the seals fall off the rotor, be careful not to change the original position of each seal.

43. Identify the rear rotor with a felt tip pen.

44. Remove the oil seals and the springs. Do not exert heavy pressure at only one place on the seal, since it could be deformed. Replace the O-rings in the oil seal when the engine is overhauled.

45. Hold the intermediate housing down and remove the dowels from it.

46. Lift off the intermediate housing being careful not to damage the eccentric shaft. It should be removed by sliding it beyond the rear rotor journal on the eccentric shaft while holding the intermediate housing up and, at the same time, pushing the eccentric shaft up.

47. Lift out the eccentric shaft.

48. Repeat the above procedures to remove the front rotor housing and front rotor.

INSPECTION AND REPLACEMENT

Front, Intermediate and Rear Housings

1. Check the housing for signs of gas or water leakage.

2. Remove the carbon deposits from the front housing with extra fine emery cloth.

3. Remove any of the old sealer which

The front rotor is marked with an "F" on its internal gear side; The rear rotor is marked with an "R" in a similar manner. (© Toyo Kogyo Co. Ltd.)

Measure the housing distortion along the axes indicated (© Toyo Kogyo Co. Ltd.)

Measuring housing wear with a dial indicator

Most of the front and rear housing wear occurs at the end of the minor axis as shown. (© Toyo Kogyo Co. Ltd.)

Position the O-ring in the groove on the stationary gear (arrow)

is adhering to the housing, using a brush or a cloth soaked in Ke-tone.

4. Check for distortion by placing a straightedge on the surface of the housing. Measure the clearance between the straightedge and the housing with a feeler gauge. If the clearance is greater than 0.002 in. at any point, replace the housing.

5. Use a dial indicator to check for wear on the rotor contact surfaces of the housing. If the wear is greater than 0.004 in., replace the housing.

NOTE: The wear at either end of the minor axis is greater than at any other point on the housing. However, this is normal and should be no cause for concern.

Front Stationary Gear and Main Bearing

1. Examine the teeth of the stationary gear for wear or damage.

2. Be sure that the main bearing shows no signs of excessive wear, scoring, or flaking.

3. Check the main bearing-to-eccentric journal clearance by measuring the journal with a vernier caliper and the bearing with a pair of inside calipers.

Main Bearing Replacement

1. Unfasten the securing bolts, if used. Drive the stationary gear and main bearing assembly out of the housing with a brass drift.

2. Press the main bearing out of the stationary gear.

3. Press a new main bearing into the stationary gear so that it is in the same position that the old bearing was.

4. Align the slot in the stationary gear flange with the dowel pin in the housing and press the gear into place. Install the securing bolts, if required.

NOTE: To aid in stationary gear and main bearing removal and installation, Mazda manufactures a special tool, part number 49 0813 235.

Rear Stationary Gear and Main Bearing

Inspect the rear stationary gear and main bearing in a similar manner to the front. In addition, examine the O-ring, which is located in the stationary gear, for signs of wear or damage. Replace the O-ring, if necessary.

To replace the stationary gear, use the following procedure.

1. Remove the rear stationary gear securing bolts.

2. Drive the stationary gear out of the rear housing with a brass drift.

3. Apply a light coating of grease to a new O-ring and fit it into the groove on the stationary gear.

4. Apply sealer to the flange of the stationary gear.

5. Install the stationary gear on the housing so that the slot on its flange aligns with the pin on the rear housing.

--------- CAUTION ---------
Use care not to damage the O-ring during installation.

6. Tighten the stationary gear bolts evenly, and in several stages, to 15 ft. lbs.

Measure the rotor housing distortion along the axes indicated (© Toyo Kogyo Co. Ltd.)

Check the rotor housing width at eight points near the trochoid surface (© Toyo Kogyo Co. Ltd.)

Rotor Housings

1. Examine the inner margin of both housings for signs of gas or water leakage.

2. Wipe the inner surface of each housing with a clean cloth to remove the carbon deposits.

NOTE: If the carbon deposits are stubborn, soak the cloth in a solution of Ke-tone. Do not scrape or sand the chrome plated surfaces of the rotor chamber.

3. Clean all of the rust deposits out of the cooling passages of each rotor housing.

4. Remove the old sealer with a cloth soaked in Ke-tone.

5. Examine the chromium plated inner surfaces for scoring, flaking, or other signs of damage. If any are present, the housing must be replaced.

6. Check the rotor housings for distortion by placing a straightedge on the axes.

7. If distortion exceeds 0.002 in., replace the rotor housing.

8. Check the widths of both rotor housings, at a minimum of eight points near the trochoid surfaces of each housing, using a vernier caliper.

If the difference between the maximum and minimum values obtained is greater than 0.0031 in. (RX-3) or 0.0024 in. (RX-4, RX-7), replace the housing. A housing in this condition will be prone to gas and coolant leakage.

Rotors

1. Check the rotor for signs of blow-by around the side and corner seal areas.

2. The color of the carbon deposits on the rotor should be brown, just as in a piston engine.

NOTE: Usually the carbon deposits on the leading side of the rotor are brown, while those on the trailing side tend toward black, as viewed from the direction of rotation.

3. Remove the carbon on the rotor with a scraper or extra fine emery paper. Use the scraper carefully, when doing the seal grooves, so that no damage is done to them.

4. Wash the rotor in solvent and blow it dry with compressed air.

5. Examine the internal gear for cracks or damaged teeth.

Measure the rotor width at the point indicated

Weight classification letter placement (arrow)

NOTE: If the internal gear is damaged, the rotor and gear must be replaced as a single assembly.

6. With the oil seal removed, check the land protrusions by placing a straightedge over the lands. Measure the gap between the rotor surface and the straightedge with a feeler gauge.

7. Check the gaps between the housings and the rotor on both of its sides.

   a. Measure the rotor width with a vernier caliper.

   b. Compare the rotor width against the width of the rotor housing which was measured above.

   c. Replace the rotor, if the difference between the two measurements is not within 0.0051–0.0067 in.

8. Check the rotor bearing for flaking, wearing, or scoring and proceed as indicated in the next section, if any of these are present.

The rotors are classified into five lettered grades, according to their weight. A letter between A and E is stamped on the internal gear side of the rotor. If it becomes necessary to replace a rotor, use one marked with a "C" because this is the standard replacement rotor, and it can be used in most balancing combinations.

Rotor Bearing Replacement
— CAUTION —
The use of the special service tools, as indicated in the text, is mandatory, if damage to the rotor is to be avoided.

Insert the special bearing expander into the rotor

Check the clearance between the rotor bearing and the rotor journal on the eccentric shaft. Measure the inner diameter of the rotor bearing and the outer diameter of the journal. The wear limit is 0.0039 in.; replace the bearing if it exceeds this.

1. Install the bearing expander (Mazda part number 49 0813 245) in the rotor bearing. If the expander is not used, bearing deformation will result when the holes are drilled.

2. Drill a 0.14 in. diameter hole, roughly 0.028 in. deep, into each of the lockscrews which secure the bearings to the rotor. Use a #28 drill.

3. Remove the bearing expander.

4. Support the rotor with the internal gear facing upward.

5. Using the rotor bearing remover (Mazda part number 49 0813 240), less the adaptor ring, press the bearing out of the rotor.

— CAUTION —
Be extremely careful not to damage the internal gear. It cannot be replaced separately from the rotor.

6. If the bore in which the bearing is installed is damaged, dress it with emory paper and blow it clean with compressed air.

Installing a new rotor bearing

7. With the rotor internal gear facing upward, press-fit a new bearing into the bore. Use the bearing replacer with the adaptor screws removed.

NOTE: Be sure that the oil hole in the bearing is aligned with the hole in the apex side of the rotor. Once the bearing is installed, it should be flush with the rotor boss.

8. Insert the rotor bearing expander into the new bearing, as in Step 1.

9. Drill 0.14 in. holes, about 0.28 in. deep, within 0.28 in. of the original lockscrew holes (either to the left or right of them) with a #28 drill. The center of the holes must be 0.02 in. from the rotor bore.

NOTE: The new holes should all be in the same direction from the original holes; e.g., if the first hole is drilled to the left

Oil seal protrusion (© Toyo Kogyo Co. Ltd.)

of the original hole, drill the remaining holes to the left of the other lockscrew holes.

10. Thread the holes with an M4, P-0.70 mm metric tap.

11. Install the bearing lockscrews and stake them with a punch so that they cannot work loose.

12. Wash the rotor and blow it dry with compressed air.

Oil Seal Inspection

NOTE: Inspect the oil seal while it is mounted in the rotor.

1. Examine the oil seal.

2. If the width of the oil seal lip is greater than 0.031 in., replace the oil seal.

3. If the protrusion of the oil seal is greater than 0.020 in., replace the seal.

Oil Seal Replacement

NOTE: Replace the rubber O-ring in the oil seal as a normal part of engine overhaul.

1. Pry the seal out by inserting a screwdriver into the slots on the rotor.

— CAUTION —
Be careful not to deform the lip of the oil seal if it is to be reinstalled.

2. Fit both of the oil seal springs into their respective grooves so that their ends

Position the oil seal spring gaps at arrows

Eccentric shaft blind plug assembly (© Toyo Kogyo Co. Ltd.)

are facing upward and their gaps are opposite each other on the rotor.

3. Insert a new O-ring into each of the oil seals.

NOTE: Before installing the O-rings into the oil seals, fit each of the seals into its proper groove on the rotor. Check to see that all of the seals move smoothly and freely.

4. Coat the oil seal groove and the oil seal with engine oil.

5. Gently press the oil seal into the groove with your fingers. Be careful not to distort the seal.

NOTE: Be sure that the white mark is on the bottom side of each seal when it is installed.

6. Repeat the installation procedure for the oil seals on both sides of each rotor.

Check the gap between the apex seal and groove with a feeler gauge

Apex seal-to-side housing gap (© Toyo Kogyo Co. Ltd.)

Apex Seals

— **CAUTION** —

Although the apex seals are extremely durable when in service, they are easily broken when they are being handled. Be careful never to drop them.

1. Remove the carbon deposits from the apex seals and their springs. Do not use emory cloth on the seals as it will damage their finish.

2. Wash the seals and the springs in cleaning solution.

3. Check the apex seals for cracks.

4. Test the seal springs for weakness.

5. Use a micrometer to check the seal height. Refer to specifications chart.

6. With a feeler gauge, check the side clearance between the apex seal and the groove in the rotor. Insert the gauge until its tip contacts the bottom of the groove. If the gap is greater than 0.005 in., replace the seal.

7. Check the gap between the apex seals and the side housing in the following manner:

a. Use a vernier caliper to measure the length of each apex seal.

b. Compare this measurement to the *minimum* figure obtained when the rotor housing width was being measured.

c. If the seal is too long, sand the ends of the seal with emory cloth until the proper length is reached.

— **CAUTION** —

Do not use the emory cloth on the faces of the seal.

Side Seals

1. Remove the carbon deposits from the side seals and their springs.

2. Check the side seals for cracks.

3. Check the clearance between the side seals and their grooves with a feeler gauge. Replace any side seals with a clearance of more than 0.0039 in.

4. Check the clearance between the side seals and the corner seals with both installed in the rotor.

a. Insert a feeler gauge between the end of the side seal and the corner seal.

NOTE: Insert the gauge against the direction of the rotor's rotation.

Check the clearance of the seals at the points indicated (© Toyo Kogyo Co. Ltd.)

Clearance-Apex Seal, Groove
Clearance-Corner Seal, Side Seal Outer
Clearance-Side Seal, Groove
Clearance-Corner Seal, Side Seal Inner
Clearance-Corner Seal, Groove

Reaming the corner seal groove

b. Replace the side seal if the clearance is greater than 0.016 in.

5. If the side seal is replaced, adjust the clearance between it and the corner seal as follows:

a. File the side seal on its reverse side, in the same rotational direction of the rotor, along the outline made by the corner seal.

b. The clearance obtained should be 0.002–0.006 in. If it exceeds this, the performance of the seals will deteriorate.

— **CAUTION** —

There are four different types of side seals, depending upon location. Do not mix the seals up and be sure to use the proper type of seal for replacement.

Corner Seals

1. Clean the carbon deposits.

2. Examine each of the seals.

3. Measure the clearance between the corner seal and its groove. The clearance should be 0.008–0.0019 in. The wear limit of the gap is 0.0031 in.

4. If the wear between the corner seal and the groove is uneven, check the clearance with the special "bar limit gauge" (Mazda part number 49 0839 165). The gauge has a "go" end and a "no go" end.

a. If neither end of the gauge goes into the groove, the clearance is within specifications.

Corner seal installation

Needle bearing components (© Toyo Kogyo Co. Ltd.)

Position the dial indicator as shown to measure shaft run-out

b. If the "go" end of the gauge fits into the groove, but the "no go" end does not, replace the corner seal with one that is 0.0012 in. oversize.

c. If both ends of the gauge fit into the groove, then the groove must be reamed out. Replace the corner seal with one which is 0.0072 in. oversize, after reaming.

NOTE: Take the measurement of the groove in the direction of maximum wear, i.e., that of rotation.

Seal Springs

Check the seal springs for damage or weakness. Be exceptionally careful when checking the spring areas which contact either the rotor or the seal.

Eccentric Shaft

1. Wash the eccentric shaft in solvent and blow the oil passages dry with compressed air.

2. Check the shaft for wear, cracks, or other signs of damage. Make sure that none of the oil passages are clogged.

3. Measure the shaft journals.
Replace the shaft if any of its journals shows excessive wear.

4. Check eccentric shaft runout. Rotate the shaft slowly and note the dial indicator reading. If runout is more than specifications, replace the eccentric shaft.

5. Check the blind plug at the end of the shaft. If it is loose or leaking, remove it with an Allen wrench and replace the O-ring.

6. Check the operation of the needle roller bearing for smoothness by inserting a mainshaft into the bearing and rotating it. Examine the bearing for signs of wear or damage.

7. Replace the bearings, if necessary, with the special bearing replacer (Mazda part numbers 49 0823 073 and 49 0823 072).

ASSEMBLY

All Models

1. Place the rotor on a rubber pad or cloth.

2. Install the oil seal rings in their respective grooves in the rotors with the edge of the spring in the stopper hole. The oil seal springs are painted cream or blue in color. The cream colored springs must be installed on the front faces of both rotors.

The rear rotor must be positioned as shown during engine assembly

The blue colored springs must be installed on the rear faces of both rotors. When installing each oil seal spring, the painted side (square side) of the spring must face upward (toward the oil seal).

3. Install a new O-ring in each groove. Place each oil seal in the groove so that the square edge of the spring fits in the stopper hole of the oil seal. Push the head of the oil seal slowly with the fingers, being careful that the seal is not deformed. Be sure that the oil seal moves smoothly in the groove before installing the O-ring.

4. Lubricate each oil seal and groove with engine oil and check the movement of the seal. It should move freely when the head of the seal is pressed.

5. Check the oil seal protrusion and install the seals on the other side of each rotor.

6. Install the apex seals without springs and side pieces into their respective grooves so that each side piece positions on the side of each rotor.

7. Install the corner seal springs and corner seals into their respective grooves.

8. Install the side seal springs and side seals into their respective grooves.

9. Apply engine oil to each spring and check each spring for smooth movement.

10. Check each seal protrusion.

11. Invert the rotor being careful that the seals do not fall out, and install the oil seals on the other side in the same manner.

12. Mount the front housing on a workstand so that the top of the housing is up.

Apply sealer to the grey shadowed areas of the rotor housing (© Toyo Kogyo Co. Ltd.)

13. Lubricate the internal gear of the rotor with engine oil.

14. Hold the apex seals with used O-rings to keep the apex seals installed and place the rotor on the front housing. Be careful not to drop the seals. Turn the front housing so that the sliding surface faces upward.

15. Mesh the internal and stationary gears so that one of the rotor apexes is at any one of the four places shown and remove the old O-ring which is holding the apex seals in position.

16. Lubricate the front rotor journal of the eccentric shaft with engine oil and lubricate the eccentric shaft main journal.

17. Insert the eccentric shaft. Be careful that you do not damage the rotor bearing and main bearing.

18. Apply sealing agent to the front side of the front rotor housing.

19. Apply a light coat of petroleum jelly onto new O-rings and rubber seals (to prevent them from coming off) and install the O-rings and rubber seals on the front side of the rotor housing.

NOTE: The inner rubber seal is of the square type. The wider white line of the rubber seal should face the combustion chamber and the seam of the rubber seal should be positioned as shown. Do not stretch the rubber seal.

20. If the engine is being overhauled, install the seal protector to only the inner rubber seal to improve durability.

21. Invert the front rotor housing, being careful not to let the rubber seals and O-rings fall from their grooves, and mount it on the front housing.

22. Lubricate the dowels with engine oil and insert them through the front rotor housing holes and into the front housing.

23. Apply sealer to the front side of the rotor housing.

24. Install new O-rings and rubber seals on the front rotor housing in the same manner as for the other side.

25. Insert each apex spring seal, making sure that the seal is installed in the proper direction.

26. Install each side piece in its original position and be sure that the springs seat on the side piece.

27. Lubricate the side pieces with engine oil. Make sure that the front rotor housing is free of foreign matter and lubricate the sliding surface of the front housing with engine oil.

Intermediate housing installation

1. Flywheel
2. Oil seal
3. Main bearing
4. Locknut
5. Washer
6. Rear stationary gear
7. O-ring
8. Oil seal O-ring
9. Oil seal
10. Oil seal
11. Oil seal spring
12. Eccentric shaft
13. Rotor bearing
14. Grease seal
15. Needle bearing
16. O-ring
17. Blind plug
18. Front rotor
19. Side seal spring
20. Side seal
21. Corner seal and spring
22. Apex seal and spring
23. Ball
24. Spring
25. Oil nozzle
26. Rear rotor
27. Rotor bearing
28. Front stationary gear
29. Thrust washer
30. Thrust bearing
31. Spacer
32. Bearing housing
33. Needle bearing
34. Washer
35. Thrust plate
36. Balance weight
37. Oil pump drive sprocket
38. Distributor drive gear
39. Spacer
40. Oil slinger
41. Eccentric shaft pulley
42. Washer
43. Pulley bolt

Rotor and eccentric shaft components (© Toyo Kogyo Co. Ltd.)

28. Turn the front housing assembly with the rotor, so that the top of the housing is up. Pull the eccentric shaft about 1 in.

29. Position the eccentric portion of the eccentric shaft diagonally, to the upper right.

30. Install the intermediate housing over the eccentric shaft onto the front rotor housing. Turn the engine so that the rear of the engine is up.

31. Install the rear rotor and rear rotor housing following the same steps as for the front rotor and the front housing.

32. Turn the engine so that the rear of the engine is up.

33. Lubricate the stationary gear and main bearing.

34. Install the rear housing onto the rear rotor housing. If necessary, turn the rear rotor slightly to mesh the rear housing stationary gear with the rear rotor internal gear.

35. Install a new washer on each tension bolt, and lubricate each bolt with engine oil.

36. Install the tension bolts and tighten

them evenly, in several stages following the sequence shown. The specified torque is 23–27 ft. lbs.

NOTE: Be sure bolts are installed in their original positions. Longer bolts are used in later engines and are not interchangeable.

37. After tightening the bolts, turn the eccentric shaft to be sure that the shaft and rotors turn smoothly and easily.

38. Lubricate the oil seal in the rear housing.

39. On vehicles with manual transmission, install the flywheel on the rear of the eccentric shaft so that the keyway of the flywheel fits the key on the shaft.

40. Apply sealer to both sides of the flywheel lockwasher and install the lockwasher.

41. Install the flywheel locknut. Hold the flywheel SECURELY and tighten the nut to THREE HUNDRED AND FIFTY FT. LBS. (350 ft. lbs.) of torque.

NOTE: 350 ft. lbs. is a great deal of torque. In actual practice, it is practically impossible to accurately measure that much torque on the nut. At least a 3 ft. bar will be required to generate sufficient torque. Tighten it as tight as possible, with no longer than 3 ft. of leverage. Be sure the engine is held SECURELY.

42. On vehicles with automatic transmission, install the key, counterweight, lockwasher and nut. Tighten the nut to 350 ft. lbs. SEE STEP 41 AND THE NOTE FOLLOWING STEP 41. Install the drive plate on the counterweight and tighten the attaching nuts.

43. Turn the engine so that the front faces up.

44. Install the thrust plate with the tapered face down, and install the needle bearing on the eccentric shaft. Lubricate with engine oil.

45. Install the bearing housing on the front housing. Tighten the bolts and bend up the lockwasher tabs.

The spacer should be installed so that the center of the needle bearing comes to the

Align the slot in the stationary gear flange with the pin in the housing (arrow)

Installing oil pump

Position the slots in the distributor drive as shown (© Toyo Kogyo Co. Ltd.)

center of the eccentric shaft and the spacer should be seated on the thrust plate.

46. Install the needle bearing on the shaft and lubricate it with engine oil.

47. Install the balancer and thrust washer on the eccentric shaft.

48. Install the oil pump drive chain over both of the sprockets. Install the sprocket and chain assembly over the eccentric shaft and oil pump shafts simultaneously. Install the key on the eccentric shaft.

NOTE: Be sure that both of the sprockets are engaged with the chain before installing them over the shafts.

49. Install the distributor drive gear onto the eccentric shaft with the "F" mark on the gear facing the front of the engine. Slide the spacer and oil slinger onto the eccentric shaft.

50. Align the keyway and install the eccentric shaft pulley. Tighten the pulley bolt to 60 ft. lbs.

51. Turn the engine until the top of the engine faces up.

52. Check eccentric shaft end-play in the following manner:

   a. Attach a dial indicator to the flywheel. Move the flywheel forward and backward.

   b. Note the reading on the dial indicator; it should be 0.0016–0.0028 in.

   c. If the end-play is not within specifications, adjust it by replacing the front spacer. Spacers come in four sizes, ranging from 0.3150–0.3181 in. If necessary, a spacer can be ground on a surface plate with emory paper.

   d. Check the end-play again and, if it is now within specifications, proceed with the next step.

53. Remove the pulley from the front of the eccentric shaft. Tighten the oil pump drive sprocket nut and bend the locktabs on the lockwasher.

54. Fit a new O-ring over the front cover oil passage.

55. Install the chain tensioner and tighten its securing bolts.

56. Position the front cover gasket and the front cover on the front housing, then secure the front cover with its attachment bolts.

57. Install the eccentric shaft pulley again. Tighten its bolt to 60 ft. lbs.

58. Turn the engine so that the bottom faces up.

59. Cut off the excess gasket on the front cover along the mounting surface of the oil pan.

60. Install the oil strainer gasket and strainer on the front housing and tighten the attaching bolts.

61. Apply sealer to the joint surfaces of each housing.

62. Install the oil pan.

63. Turn the engine so that the top is up.

64. Install the water pump.

65. Rotate the eccentric shaft until the yellow mark (leading side mark) aligns with the pointer on the front cover.

66. Align the marks on the distributor gear and housing and install the distributor so that the lockbolt is in the center of the slot.

67. Rotate the distributor until the leading points start to separate and tighten the distributor locknut.

68. Install the gaskets and thermal reactor.

69. Install the hot air duct.

70. Install the carburetor and intake manifold assembly.

71. Connect the oil tubes, vacuum tube and metering oil pump connecting rod to the carburetor.

Use a dial indicator attached to the flywheel to measure eccentric shaft end-play

72. Install the decel valve and connect the vacuum lines, air hoses and wires.

73. Install the alternator bracket, alternator and bolt and check the clearance. If the clearance is more than 0.006 in., adjust the clearance using a shim. Shims are available in three sizes: 0.0059 in., 0.0118 in., and 0.0197 in.

ECCENTRIC SHAFT SPACER THICKNESS CHART

Mark-ing	Thickness	
	mm	in.
X	8.08 ± 0.01	0.3181 ± 0.0004
Y	8.04 ± 0.01	0.3165 ± 0.0004
V	8.02 ± 0.01	0.3158 ± 0.0004
Z	8.00 ± 0.01	0.3150 ± 0.0004

74. Install the alternator drive belt.

75. Install the air pump.

76. Install the engine hanger bracket.

77. Remove the engine from the stand.

78. Install the engine in the vehicle.

Intake Manifold

REMOVAL AND INSTALLATION

To remove the intake manifold and carburetor assembly with the engine remaining in the automobile, proceed in the following manner:

1. Perform Steps 2–7 "Engine Removal and Installation." Do not remove the engine. Do not drain the engine oil; merely remove the metering oil pump hose from the carburetor.

2. Perform Steps 1–4 of "Engine Disassembly."

Install the intake manifold and carburetor assembly in the reverse order of removal.

Thermal Reactor

REMOVAL AND INSTALLATION

1978–80

— **CAUTION** —

The thermal reactor operates at extremely high temperatures. Allow the engine to cool completely before attempting to remove it.

To remove the thermal reactor, which replaced the exhaust manifold:

NOTE: The bottom nut is difficult to reach. Mazda makes a special wrench (part number 49 213 001) to remove it. If the wrench is unavailable, a flexible drive metric socket wrench may be substituted.

1. Remove the air cleaner.
2. Unbolt and remove the air injection pump.
3. Remove the intake manifold complete with carburetor.
4. Remove the heat stove from the thermal reactor.
5. Unfasten the thermal reactor securing nuts, including those on the exhaust pipe flange.
6. Remove the thermal reactor.
7. Installation is the reverse of removal.

1981 and Later

On 1981 and later models, the thermal reactor/heat exchanger system is replaced by two catalytic converters and a special reactive exhaust manifold. See Emission Control section for explanation.

ENGINE LUBRICATION— ROTARY

A conventional oil pump, which is chain driven, circulates oil through the rotary engine. A full-flow filter is mounted on the top of the rear housing and an oil cooler is used to reduce the temperature of the engine oil.

An unusual feature of the rotary engine lubrication system is a metering oil pump which injects oil into the float chamber of the carburetor. Once there, it is mixed with the fuel which is to be burned, thus providing extra lubrication for the seals. The metering oil pump is designed to work only when the engine is working under a load.

Oil Pan

REMOVAL AND INSTALLATION

NOTE: The only component(s) that can be serviced by removing the oil pan are the oil strainer and the oil pressure control valve.

1. Drain the engine oil.
2. Disconnect the oil level sensor and the oil thermo unit, if equipped.
3. Remove the pan bolts and lower the pan.
4. To install, clean all of the old gasket material off the pan and engine mating surfaces, then apply a continuous bead of sealer (part no. 8527 77 739) to the pan surface. The bead should be from 0.16–0.24 in. (4–6 mm) wide and should overlap at the end.
5. Fit the gasket on the pan, then apply an identical bead of sealer on top of the gasket.

6. Fit the gasket and torque the bolts to 6–8 ft. lbs. (0.8–1.1 m-kg).
7. Fill the crankcase with oil.

Oil Pump

REMOVAL AND INSTALLATION

Oil pump removal and installation is contained in the engine overhaul section above. Perform only those steps needed to remove the oil pump.

Checking Clearances

1. Separate the halves of the oil pump.
2. The clearance between the lobes of the rotors should be 0.0004–0.0035 in. Replace both of the rotors if the clearance exceeds 0.006 in.
3. The clearance between the outer rotor and the housing should be 0.008–0.010 in. If the clearance is greater than 0.012 in., replace both of the rotors.
4. Place a straightedge across the pump housing. Measure the gap between the straightedge and the housing with a feeler gauge. The gap should be 0.001–0.005 in. If the gap exceeds 0.012 in., replace the rotors or the pump housing.

Metering Oil Pump

OPERATION

A metering oil pump, mounted on the top of the engine, is used to provide additional

Measure the clearance between the rotors with a feeler gauge

Measure the gap between the straightedge and the housing

lubrication to the engine when it is operating under a load. The pump provides oil to the carburetor, where it is mixed in the float chamber to be burned.

The metering pump is a plunger type and is controlled by throttle opening. A cam arrangement, connected to the carburetor throttle lever, operates a plunger. The plunger, in turn, acts as a differential plunger, the stroke of which determines the amount of oil flow.

When the throttle opening is small, the amount of the plunger stroke is small; as the throttle opening increases, so does the amount of the plunger stroke.

TESTING

1. At the carburetor, disconnect the oil lines which run from the metering oil pump to the carburetor.
2. Use a container which has a scale calibrated in cubic centimeters (cc) on its side to catch the pump discharge from the oil lines.
3. Run the engine at 2,000 r.p.m. for six minutes.
4. At the end of this time, 2.4–2.9 cc should be collected in the container. If not, adjust the pump.

ADJUSTMENTS

Rotate the adjusting screw on the metering oil pump to obtain the proper oil flow. Clockwise rotation of the screw *increases* the flow; counterclockwise rotation *decreases* the oil flow.

Arrow (right) indicates the metering oil pump adjusting screw. The 3 arrows (left) indicate the connecting rod adjusting holes

① : 248cc / 6,000rpm / Hr
② : 174cc / 6,000rpm / Hr
③ : 104cc / 6,000rpm / Hr

Connecting rod adjusting holes
(ⓒ Toyo Kogyo Co. Ltd.)

Cooling system (© Toyo Kogyo Co. Ltd.)

If necessary, the oil discharge rate may be further adjusted by changing the position of the cam in the pump connecting rod. The shorter the rod throw, the more oil will be pumped. Adjust the throw by means of the three holes provided.

Oil Cooler

REMOVAL AND INSTALLATION

The oil cooler is easily removed after removing the gravel shield and disconnecting the lines. Unbolt the cooler from the radiator.

Installation is the reverse of removal.

ENGINE COOLING— ROTARY

Radiator

REMOVAL AND INSTALLATION

1. Drain the engine coolant.
2. Remove the shroud.
3. Remove the upper, lower, and expansion tank hoses.
4. Remove the oil cooler.
5. Withdraw the radiator.
6. Install in the reverse order of removal.

Water Pump

REMOVAL AND INSTALLATION

All Except RX-7

1. Drain the cooling system and remove the air cleaner.
2. Disconnect the water temperature sending unit.
3. Remove alternator and air pump and their belts.
4. Disconnect the upper radiator hose at the thermostat housing. Remove the upper fan shroud.
5. Remove the attaching bolts, and remove the fan and fan drive as an assembly.
6. Installation is in reverse order. Coat a new water pump gasket with sealer on both sides, and torque water pump attaching bolts, a little at a time, in the order shown to 13–20 ft. lbs.

RX-7

1. Remove the air cleaner and disconnect the water temperature switch wiring from the radiator.
2. Remove the air conditioner, air pump and alternator drive belts.
3. Remove the cooling fan and drive assembly.
4. Remove the drive pulley for the air conditioner compressor from in front of the alternator/air pump drive pulleys (the pulley on the eccentric shaft, not the one on the front of the compressor).
5. Place a pan under the lower radiator hose then disconnect the hose and allow the coolant to drain out of the system.
6. Remove the upper radiator hose.
7. Remove the attaching bolts and remove the water pump.
8. When installing, clean the old gas-

ket from the mating surfaces, and install a new gasket with sealer. Torque the attaching bolts evenly and in the order shown to 13–20 ft. lbs. (1.8–2.7 m-kg). Remaining installation is the reverse of removal.

Thermostat

REMOVAL AND INSTALLATION

------ **CAUTION** ------
The thermostat is equipped with a plunger which covers and uncovers a by-pass hole at its bottom. Because of this unusual construction, only the specified Mazda thermostat should be used for replacement. A standard thermostat will cause the engine to overheat.

Thermostat installation and by-pass circuit (© Toyo Kogyo Co. Ltd.)

1. Drain the engine coolant.
2. Remove the thermostat housing and the thermostat.
3. Installation is the reverse of removal.

ENGINE MECHANICAL

Piston Engine

The Mazda piston engines are four cylinder, chain driven single overhead camshaft operating double rocker arm assemblies. The engines are water cooled and lubricated by a chain driven oil pump. Five main bearings support the crankshaft. Varied displacement engines are used in the Mazda models.

1. 96.8 cu. in.—1586 cc
2. 77.6 cu. in.—1272 cc
3. 120.2 cu. in.—1970 cc
4. 86.4 cu. in.—1415 cc
5. 90.9 cu. in.—1490 cc

The varied engines are constructed basically the same, but with many external differences, such as distributor and fuel pump locations, carburetor usages and Emission Control components. Many differences exist internally and the manufacturer sources must be consulted before any attempt is made to interchange internal parts.

REMOVAL AND INSTALLATION

Rear Wheel Drive

The engine is removed separately, leaving the transmission in place.

1. Remove the hood.
2. Remove the engine splash shield.
3. Drain the coolant.
4. Drain the engine oil.
5. Disconnect all electrical wires and leads. Remove battery.
6. Disconnect all fluid lines and hoses.
7. Remove the air cleaner.
8. Unbolt and remove the radiator and cowling.
9. Disconnect the throttle cable from the carburetor and remove the throttle linkage from the rocker cover.
10. Disconnect the choke cable.
11. Remove the starter.
12. Disconnect the exhaust pipe.
13. Remove the clutch cover plate. Support the transmission.
14. Unbolt the right and left engine mounts.
15. Attach a lifting sling to the engine and pull the engine forward until it clears the clutch shaft.
16. Lift the engine from the vehicle.
17. Installation is the reverse of removal.

GLC—Front Wheel Drive

NOTE: The factory recommends that the engine and transaxle be removed from the car as a unit.

1. Mark the outline of the hood hinges for reinstallation alignment. Remove the hood.
2. Disconnect the battery cables from the battery; negative cable first. Remove the battery.
3. Loosen the front wheels lugs. Jack up the car and safely support it on jackstands.
4. Remove the two front wheels. Remove the bottom and side splash shields. Drain the coolant, engine oil and transaxle fluid.
5. Remove the air cleaner assembly. Remove the radiator hoses and the radiator shroud and electric fan assembly.
6. Connect an engine lifting sling to the engine. Connect a chain hoist or portable engine crane to the lifting sling and apply slight upward pressure to the engine and transaxle assembly.
7. Remove the mounting bolts from the engine crossmember. Remove the crossmember.
8. Disconnect the lower ball joints. Dismount the steering knuckles and drive axles.

9. Cars equipped with manual transaxles: Disconnect the shifting rod and extension bar. Cars equipped with an automatic transaxle: Disconnect the selector rod and counter rod.
10. Remove the front and rear transaxle mounting bushings. Disconnect the exhaust pipe from the converter. Remove the transaxle crossmember.
11. Disconnect all wires and hoses from under the engine and transaxle. Label them for identification.
12. Disconnect all wires, heater hoses and vacuum hoses from the upper side of the engine and transaxle. Label them for correct installation.
13. Disconnect the accelerator cable, speedometer cable, clutch cable, power brake booster line and fuel lines.
14. Check to be sure all remaining hoses and wiring are disconnected. Remove the evaporative canister. Remove the right side upper engine mount through bolt.
15. Lift the engine and transaxle assembly from the car. Take care not to allow the assembly to swing forward into the radiator.
16. If the car must be moved from underneath the engine: remount the steering knuckles, secure the drive axles so that they can still turn, mount the front wheels and lower the car from the jackstands.
17. Installation is in the reverse order of removal.

Cylinder Head

REMOVAL AND INSTALLATION

Be sure that the cylinder head is cold before removal. This will prevent warpage. Do not remove the cam gear from the timing chain. The relationship between the chain and gear teeth should not be disturbed.

1. Drain the cooling system.
2. Remove the air cleaner.
3. Disconnect all applicable electrical wires and leads.
4. Rotate the crankshaft to put the No. 1 cylinder at TDC on the compression stroke.
5. Remove the distributor.
6. Remove the rocker arm cover.
7. Raise and support the vehicle. Disconnect the exhaust pipe from the manifold.
8. Remove the accelerator linkage.
9. Remove the nut, washer and the distributor gear from the camshaft.
10. Remove the nut, washer and camshaft gear.
11. Remove the cylinder head bolts and cylinder head-to-front cover bolt.
12. Remove the rocker arm assembly.
13. Remove the camshaft from the camshaft gear.
14. Lift off the cylinder head.
15. Installation is the reverse of removal. Adjust the chain tension, and valves.

Valve Guide

REMOVAL AND INSTALLATION

Consult the "Engine Rebuilding" section for general procedures that will apply.

Rocker Shafts

REMOVAL AND INSTALLATION

This operation should only be performed on a cold engine; the bolts which hold the rocker shafts in place also hold the cylinder head to the block.

1. Disconnect the choke cable.
2. If equipped, disconnect the air by-pass valve cable.
3. Remove the rocker cover.
4. Remove the rocker arm shaft attaching bolts.
5. Installation is the reverse of removal. Install the rocker arm assemblies on the cylinder head. Temporarily tighten the cylinder head bolts to specifications and offset each rocker arm support 0.04 in. from the valve stem center.

Intake Manifold

REMOVAL AND INSTALLATION

1. Drain the cooling system.
2. Remove the air cleaner.
3. Remove the accelerator linkage.
4. Disconnect the choke cable and fuel line.
5. Disconnect the PCV valve hose.
6. Disconnect the heater return hose and by-pass hose.
7. Remove the intake manifold-to-cylinder head attaching nuts.
8. Remove the manifold and carburetor as an assembly.
9. Installation is the reverse of removal.

Exhaust Manifold

REMOVAL AND INSTALLATION

1. Remove the two attaching nuts from the exhaust pipe at the manifold.
2. Remove the retaining nuts and remove the manifold.
3. Installation is the reverse of removal.

Front Cover, Timing Chain and Tensioner

REMOVAL AND INSTALLATION

NOTE: On front wheel drive GLC models, the engine must be removed from the car. Start procedure at Step 5.

1. Bring number one piston to TDC (timing marks aligned). Drain the cooling system. Remove the radiator hoses, thermostat housing, thermostat, fan, water pump and radiator.

2. Remove all lower and side splash or skid shields. Remove the crankshaft pulley and any driven units (alternator, air pump, etc.) that will interfere with front cover removal.

3. Remove the blind cover (small plate retained by two or three bolts that covers the chain adjuster). Install the special clamping tool or make a simple device to prevent the slipper head of the chain adjuster from popping out.

4. Remove the cylinder head, oil pan and timing chain front cover.

5. On GLC front wheel drive models: Remove the chain tensioner (located on the left upper corner of the timing cover) before removing the cylinder head. Remove the crankshaft pulley and proceed as follows.

6. Remove the oil slinger from the crankshaft. Depending on engine, remove the oil pump pulley and chain or the timing chain with sprockets first, the remaining sprockets and chain second. Loosen the timing chain guide strip and remove the chain tensioner if necessary.

7. Installation is in the reverse order of removal.

8. When installing the oil pump sprocket and chain check for excessive slack. Re-

place the chain if necessary. On the 626 models slack should be 0.015 in. Adjusting shims (between the oil pump and mounting) are available in thicknesses of 0.006 in.

9. Inspect the slipper head of the chain adjuster, the chain guide strip and the vibration damper for wear or damage. Check the adjuster spring for loss of tension. Replace parts as necessary.

10. Place the camshaft sprocket into the timing chain as shown on the appropriate illustration. Wire the sprocket and chain in position.

11. Install the timing chain onto the crankshaft sprocket as illustrated. Tighten the chain guide. Install the timing chain tensioner (except GLC—front wheel drive).

Timing chain installation—1490 cc engine (front wheel drive). Match the ring plate mark (shiny white) of the timing chain with the timing mark of the crankcase sprocket (© Toyo Kogyo Co. Ltd.)

Alignment of the timing chain and timing gear marks—1979–80 1415 cc engine, 1978 1300 cc engine and 1981–82 GLC wagon 1490 cc engine (© Toyo Kogyo Co. Ltd.)

Align the bright links and the marks, 1586 cc piston engine

Timing chain installation—1970 cc piston engine, 1979 and later (© Toyo Kogyo Co. Ltd.)

Timing chain installation—1272 cc piston engine, 1976–77 (© Toyo Kogyo Co. Ltd.)

49 1975 260

CHAIN ADJUSTER

Special clamping tool used to compress timing chain tensioner on—1300, 1415, 1490 (GLC wagon) and 1970 cc engine (© Toyo Kogyo Co. Ltd.)

Make sure the snubber spring is fully compressed. Install clamping tool.

12. Install a new timing cover oil seal. Install the timing chain front cover, oil pan and cylinder head. When installing the front cover be sure tension is applied to the timing chain to prevent it from coming off of the crankshaft sprocket. If the chain comes off of the sprocket, incorrect timing and engine damage will occur.

13. Install the sprocket and timing chain on the camshaft. Refer to illustrations. Adjust the timing chain tension.

14. Further installation is the reverse of removal.

Timing Chain Tensioner

REMOVAL, INSTALLATION AND ADJUSTMENT

All Except GLC-Front Wheel Drive

FRONT COVER INSTALLED

1. Remove the water pump. (Early engines).

2. Remove the tensioner cover.

3. Remove the attaching bolts from the tensioner. Remove the tensioner.

To install the tensioner:

4. Fully compress the snubber spring. Insert a screwdriver into the tensioner release mechanism.

5. Without removing the screwdriver, insert the tensioner and align the bolt holes. Install and torque the bolts.

6. Adjust the chain tension as follows:

a. Remove the two blind plugs and aluminum washers from the front cover.

b. Loosen the guide strip attaching screws.

c. Press the top of the chain guide

Push the sleeve into the body completely and lock it with pin—1490 cc engine (front wheel drive) (© Toyo Kogyo Co. Ltd.)

strip through the adjusting hole in the cylinder head.

d. Tighten the guide strip attaching screws.

e. Remove the screwdriver from the tensioner and let the snubber take up the slack in the chain.

f. Install the blind plugs and aluminum washers.

g. Install the tensioner cover and gasket.

h. Install a new gasket and water pump, if removed. Install the crankshaft pulley and drive belt and adjust the tension. Check the cooling system level.

GLC—Front Wheel Drive

The chain tensioner is located on the left upper side of the timing case cover, it is operated by spring plus hydraulic pressure. The tensioner has a one-way locking system and an automatic release device. After assembly, it will automatically adjust when the engine is rotated one or two times. No disassembly of the tensioner is required.

1. The tensioner is retained by two bolts. Remove the bolts and the tensioner.

2. Check the number of teeth showing on the sleeve of the tensioner. If thirteen or more notches are showing the timing chain is stretched and must be replaced.

3. To install the tensioner, push the sleeve back into the body and lock it with the swivel catch on the tensioner body. In-

Sleeve

Pin

After the adjuster is installed on the 1490 cc engine (front wheel drive), the pin is removed by the action of the timing chain and the sleeve projects automatically, completing the adjustment (© Toyo Kogyo Co. Ltd.)

stall the tensioner into the timing cover. After installation the catch is released by the action of the timing chain when the engine is rotated one to two revolutions. The sleeve projects automatically providing the proper chain adjustment.

Front Cover Oil Seal

REMOVAL AND INSTALLATION

The front cover oil seal can be replaced, in most cases, without removing the front cover.

Installing the chain adjuster—1490 cc engine (front wheel drive) (© Toyo Kogyo Co. Ltd.)

1. Drain the cooling system (except GLC front wheel drive).
2. Remove the radiator (except GLC front wheel drive).
3. Remove the drive belts and crankshaft pulley.
4. Pry the front oil seal carefully from the timing case cover.
5. Install the new oil seal. The rest of the installation is in the reverse order of removal.

Camshaft

REMOVAL AND INSTALLATION

Perform this operation on a cold engine only. Do not remove the camshaft gear from the timing chain. Be sure that the gear teeth and chain relationship is not disturbed. Wire the chain and cam gear to a place so that they will not fall into the front cover.
1. Remove the water pump if necessary.
2. Rotate the crankshaft to place the No. 1 cylinder on TDC of the compression stroke.
3. Remove the distributor.
4. Remove the valve cover.
5. Release the tension on the timing chain.
6. Remove the cylinder head bolts.
7. Remove the rocker arm assembly.
8. Remove the nut, washer and distributor gear from the camshaft.
9. Remove the nut and washer holding the camshaft gear.
10. Remove the camshaft.
11. Installation is the reverse of removal. End-play should be 0.001–0.007 in.

Piston and Connecting Rod Positioning

REMOVAL AND INSTALLATION

Refer to the ''Engine Rebuilding'' section for general engine service.

The "F" marks (arrow) face the front of the engine

ENGINE LUBRICATION— PISTON ENGINE

Oil Pan

REMOVAL AND INSTALLATION

1. Jack up the front of the car and safely support on jackstands. Disconnect negative battery cable. Remove the engine splash shield or skid plate.
2. Remove the clutch slave cylinder, if equipped. Do not disconnect the hydraulic line, let the cylinder hang.
3. Remove the engine rear brace attaching bolts and loosen the bolts on the left side, if equipped.
4. Disconnect the emission line from the oil pan, if equipped.
5. Loosen the front motor mounts, raise the front of the engine and block up to gain clearance if necessary (except GLC—front wheel drive).
6. Remove the oil pan and allow it to rest on the crossmember. Remove the oil pump pickup tube, if necessary, to remove the oil pan.
7. Install in the reverse order of removal.

Rear Main Oil Seal

REPLACEMENT

If the rear main oil seal is being replaced independently of any other parts, it can be done with the engine in place. If the rear main oil seal and the rear main bearing are being replaced, together, the engine must be removed.
1. Remove the transmission.
2. Remove the clutch disc, pressure plate and flywheel.
3. Punch two holes in the crankshaft rear oil seal. They should be punched on opposite sides of the crankshaft, just above the bearing cap-to-cylinder block split line.
4. Install a sheet metal screw in each hole. Pry against both screws at the same time to remove the oil seal.
5. Clean the oil recess in the cylinder block and bearing cap. Clean the oil seal surface on the crankshaft.
6. Coat the oil seal surfaces with oil. Coat the oil surface and the seal surface on the crankshaft with Lubriplate. Install the new oil seal and make sure that it is not cocked. Be sure that the seal surface was not damaged.
7. Install the flywheel. Coat the threads of the flywheel attaching bolts with oil-resistant sealer.
8. Install the clutch, pressure plate and transmission.

Oil Pump

CHECKING OIL PUMP

1. Measure the clearance between the lobes of the rotors. If the clearance exceeds 0.010 in., replace both rotors.
2. Check the clearance between the outer rotor and the pump body. Clearance should be 0.006–0.010 in. If it exceeds 0.012 in., replace the pump.
3. Place a straight-edge across the pump body and measure the clearance between the rotor and the straight-edge. Place a straight-edge across the pump cover and measure the clearance between the straight-edge and the cover. The combined clearances is the rotor end-play. If it is 0.006 in. or more, correct it by grinding the cover. End-play should be 0.002–0.004 in.

REMOVAL AND INSTALLATION

Remove the oil pan. Remove the oil pump gear attaching nut. Remove the bolts attaching the oil pump to the block. Loosen the gear on the pump. Remove the oil pump and gear.

Installation is the reverse of removal.

ENGINE COOLING— PISTON ENGINE

Radiator

REMOVAL AND INSTALLATION

1. Drain the coolant from the radiator.
2. Remove the fan blades and shroud or disconnect the electric harness from the electric fan motor and remove the fan and cowling mount.
3. Remove the upper and lower hoses. Disconnect the transmission cooler lines, if equipped.
4. Remove the radiator mounting bolts and remove the radiator.
5. Install the radiator by reversing the removal procedure.

Water Pump

REMOVAL AND INSTALLATION

1. Drain the coolant from the radiator.
2. On GLC front wheel drive models, jack up the front of the car and safely sup-

Thermodetector Control unit

Idle switch Heat hazard warning light

Heat hazard sensor

Air cleaner

Charcoal canister Altitude compensator

Distributor

Thermosensor

Deceleration control valve

Ignition coil

L

T

Ignition switch

Air control valve

Battery

Air pump

Check valve
Condense tank

Thermal reactor

Fuel tank

Air injection nozzle

⇨ Fresh air
⟾ Secondary air
⟾ Additional air
➡ Blow-by gas
⟾ Exhaust gas
⟾ Air/Fuel mixture
⟾ Ventilation air, fuel vapor and blow-by gas
➡ Vacuum
→ Fuel vapor
--- Ventilation air

Typical rotary engine emission control system (© Toyo Kogyo Co. Ltd.)

port it on jackstands. Remove the splash shield. Remove the drive belt, lower hose and by-pass pipe with O-ring. Remove the water pump.

3. On other models, remove the air pump if interfering. Remove the fan from the fan pulley if not equipped with electric fan assembly. Loosen and remove the fan drive belt. Remove the radiator hose.

4. Loosen and remove the water pump mounting bolts, remove the water pump.

5. Clean all gasket surfaces. Mount the new water pump and gasket. Tighten the mounting bolts evenly in several stages. The rest of the installation is in the reverse order of removal.

Thermostat

REMOVAL AND INSTALLATION

1. Drain several quarts of coolant from the radiator so that the coolant level is below the thermostat.

2. Disconnect the radiator hose from the thermostat housing.

3. Remove the thermostat housing mounting bolts, housing, gasket and thermostat.

4. Clean all gasket surfaces. Install the new thermostat with the temperature sensing pellet downwards. Use a new mounting gasket and install the housing.

5. The rest of the installation is in the reverse order of removal.

EMISSION CONTROLS

The Emission Control System is separated into three different categories.

1. Crankcase emission control system
2. Evaporative emission control system
3. Engine exhaust gas emission control system

The three sub-systems vary in application on the vehicle models, depending upon the areas in which the vehicle is to be operated, such as Federal, California, High Altitude or Canada. The engine/transmission applications will vary the requirements needed to comply with the Federal or State regulations.

Crankcase Emission Control System

The crankcase emission control system is a closed system, maintaining a specific ventilation in the crankcase and positively prevents vapors from being emitted to the atmosphere by being recirculated to the combustion chamber for burning with the air/fuel mixture.

Vacuum gauge

Ventilation valve

Testing the PCV valve (© Toyo Kogyo Co. Ltd.)

ROTARY ENGINE

The fresh air enters the air cleaner and is routed through the inlet hose and into the engine air space. The fresh air then mixes with the blow-by gases and any other vapors in the engine air space. The blow-by gases then pass through the outlet hose and ventilation valve, to be routed to the intake manifold and to be mixed with the air/fuel mixture and be burned.

NOTE: Evaporated fuel from the fuel tank is also held in the crankcase.

PISTON ENGINE

The fresh air enters the air cleaner and is routed through the inlet hose to the rocker arm cover and into the crankcase. There the fresh air mixes with the vapors and blow-by gases. The blow-by gases then pass through the outlet hose and ventilation valve, into the intake manifold to be mixed with the air/fuel mixture and be burned. It should be noted that the ventilation valve can be at valve cover area or at the intake manifold area.

NOTE: When the volume of blow-by gases is very high, such as operating the engine under heavy loads, the gases and vapors may back into the inlet hose and air cleaner.

Evaporative Emission Control System

The evaporative emission control system is designed to control the gasoline vapors from the carburetor and fuel tank areas, from entering the atmosphere. The vapors are stored in a canister containing activated carbon (charcoal) while the engine is stopped and are drawn into the intake manifold to be burned with the air/fuel mixture, when the engine is operating. Numerous hoses, check valves, and condenser tanks are used in the systems. Size and locations vary with the vehicle models.

The major differences between the evaporative emission control system used with the piston engines and the rotary engines are the locations of the canisters, the use of an air vent on the rotary engines, while not used on the piston engines, the routing of fuel vapors to the crankcase on the rotary engines as a storage point, while not used on the piston engines.

ROTARY ENGINE

An air vent valve is used with the rotary engines and is located on the carburetor float chamber. Its purpose is to control the passage of vapors from the carburetor float chamber, into the canister or air horn. When the engine is stopped, an electrical solenoid is opened, allowing the vapors to pass from the float chamber to the canister in the air

cleaner. When the engine is started, the passage is closed and the vapors are directed to the carburetor air horn. The gasoline in the fuel tank that evaporates when the engine is not operating, is held in the tank and lines until a preset pressure is reached. This preset pressure operates the check valve in the ventilation and check valve assembly, allowing the excess gasoline vapors to be routed to the crankcase and to the canister, where it is held until the engine is started and then burned with the air/fuel mixture.

A check and cut valve is used in the vapor line and has three functions. When the pressure in the fuel tank becomes high, the check valve opens to the atmosphere and releases the excess pressure. When the negative pressure in the tank becomes high, the check valve again opens and allows atmosphere pressure to enter and equalize the inner and outer pressures. The third function of the valve is to prevent fuel from flowing out, should the vehicle overturn.

PISTON ENGINES

The system for the piston engines consists of either condensing tanks or spaces for the fuel vapors to be collected and be condensed back into fuel and returned to the fuel tank. The vapors that are not condensed are routed through a check valve and into a canister containing activated charcoal which absorbs the vapors. When the engine is started, the vapors are drawn into the intake manifold, mixed with the air/fuel mixture and burned. The check valve is used to prevent negative pressure in the tank and to open at a specific point to allow atmosphere pressure to flow into the tank. When positive pressures build up in the tank and the canister and lines can accept no more vapors, the check valve will open at a specific pressure and allow a controlled release of the pressure from the tank to avoid tank damage.

Engine Exhaust Emission Control System

AIR INJECTION AND THERMAL REACTOR SYSTEM

Rotary Engines

1976–80

This system is designed to direct fresh air (secondary air) into the hot exhaust gases, just released from the combustion chambers and into the thermal reactor, through the exhaust ports. The purpose of the addition of fresh air to the exhaust is to completely burn the HC and CO contained in the exhaust gases. The fresh air is supplied by an

Testing the air control valve (© Toyo Kogyo Co. Ltd.)

air pump, driven by the engine. The air is directed through lines and a check valve, to the thermal reactor. The thermal reactor is a chamber to maintain the temperature of hot gases as high as possible to facilitate reaction between the hot gases and the fresh or secondary air. The check valve also performs the function of preventing the exhaust gases from backflowing into the air pump and causing damage.

The check valve or air control valve, contains three valves. A Number one relief valve, a Number two relief valve and an anti-afterburn valve. The Number one and two relief valves control the air from the air pump according to engine needs, determined by engine speed and load.

Number One Relief Valve Operation

Excessive high heat can cause the thermal reactor to deteriorate rapidly, because of the high temperatures, needed to burn the unburned elements in the exhaust gases. The function of the Number one relief valve is to aid in the cooling of the outer jacket of the thermal reactor when air pressure in the system becomes higher than specified. The operation of the Number one relief valve is the same for vehicles, so equipped.

Number Two Relief Valve Operation

FEDERAL AND CANADA

The number two relief valve is closed when the engine rpm is below 1500. When the engine speed is increased to over 1500 rpm, the relief valve is opened by intake manifold vacuum, controlled by the engine load. As the relief valve is opened, the air from the air pump is directed to the air cleaner, rather than to the thermal reactor.

CALIFORNIA

The relief valve remains closed under the following conditions.
   1. When the engine is below 1500 rpm.
   2. When the choke knob is fully pulled.
   3. When accelerating in any gears except 4th and 5th within 130 seconds after engine starting with the choke pulled.
   4. When accelerating in any gears except 4th and 5th, after the 130 seconds, with the engine rpm below 3000.

Under any other conditions than those listed above, the valve opens and releases part of the air from the air pump into the air cleaner, according to the vacuum signal to the valve, which is controlled by the load applied to the engine. The result is a balanced air-exhaust gas mixture required for the reburning of the exhaust gases in the thermal reactor.

SPLIT-AIR SYSTEM
Rotary Engines
1981 AND LATER

A new system, using the air injection principle and major components, eliminates the thermal reactor, but uses two catalytic converters in its place. A reactive exhaust manifold is bolted to the engine and acts as a chamber to combust the unburned Hydrocarbons (HC) and Carbon Monoxide (CO) by the addition of fresh or secondary air. The exhaust gases then pass through the first of the two catalysts, a monolith type, and then through the second, which is a two bed, pellet type. The air pump is driven by the engine with the air flow controlled by an air control valve, which directs the fresh air to either the exhaust port, the pellet catalyst or to the engine air cleaner assembly, as required by the engine speed and/or load.

During the operation of the engine at low speeds, when the HC and the CO pollutants are produced in larger amounts, the air is directed to the engine exhaust port to begin the oxidation of the HC and CO in the exhaust port and to continue in the 1st and 2nd catalytic converters.

With the engine operating at mid-range speeds, the air control valve directs the fresh air to the pellet or second converter. The air from the air pump is injected through a nozzle located between the two pellet beds and stopped from entering the exhaust port manifold. The front pellet bed acts as a three way catalyst, primarily taking care of the oxides of nitrogen (NO_x), while the rear bed with the split air continues to oxidize HC and CO pollutants.

The function of the 1st or monolith catalyst, consisting of a small capacity platinum and rhodium base three-way catalyst, is as a back-up unit, for the reactive exhaust manifold to oxidize the increased amounts of HC and CO pollutants. It is also used to heat up the exhaust gases, shorten the warm-up time of the pellet catalyst so that it will reach full operating capacity in a shorter period of time.

Low inherent NO_x emissions are experienced with the rotary engine. With this air injected system used, there is no need for the exhaust gas recirculation (EGR) valve, normally used to control the NO_x.

Piston Engines

The air injection system is used to inject fresh or secondary air into the exhaust manifold for the purpose of reburning the unburned elements in the exhaust gases. The system consists of the air pump, air injection manifold, air injection nozzles (one for each cylinder), port liners, air control valve, control unit and heat hazard sensor.

Certain vehicles do not use the control unit or the sensors, but rely upon the vacuum signal from the engine intake manifold to the control valve, to direct the fresh or secondary air to the injection nozzles or to the air cleaner assembly. A second type of air injection system is used. This system does not use the air pump, but relies upon the pulse of the exhaust gases to draw fresh air into the exhaust manifold through a one-way reed valve.

AIR INJECTION SYSTEM WITH CONTROL UNIT

The air pump is supplied fresh air from the air cleaner and directs the air, under pressure, to the air control valve. The control valve has two valves, Number one relief valve which controls the exhausting of the compressed air to the atmosphere when the engine speed is over 4000 rpm or when the floor temperature reaches 302°F. The Number two relief valve controls the injection of fresh or secondary air into the exhaust manifold by the intake manifold vacuum signals, dependent upon the speed and the load of the engine.

The electric control switch (engine speed switch) sends the electrical signal to the solenoid valve of the air control valve to release the fresh or secondary air and to prevent heat damage to the exhaust system when the engine speed is over 4000 rpm. The heat hazard switch sends an electrical signal to the solenoid valve of the air control valve, to release the fresh or secondary air to the atmosphere to prevent heat damage to the floor when the floor temperature reaches 302°F from the exhaust system burning of the unburned elements in the exhaust gases.

Two check valves are used. The check valve on the injection pipes is used to prevent the backflow of exhaust gases into the air pump, while the check valve for the Number one relief valve controls the intake manifold vacuum to the Number one relief valve of the air control valve, accordingly to the engine load and speed.

AIR INJECTION AND CATALYTIC CONVERTER SYSTEM

Reed Valve Operation

This system inducts fresh or secondary air into hot gases, flowing into the exhaust system from the cylinder head exhaust ports, for the purpose of reburning the unburned elements of the exhaust gases. A catalytic converter is used to convert the hydrocarbons (HC) and the carbon monoxide (CO), contained in the exhaust gases, into harmless water (H_2O) and carbon dioxide (CO_2).

The system consists of a reed valve, air distribution manifold, air injection nozzles, air silencer and catalytic converter.

The reed valve is operated by the exhaust gas pulsations to induct the fresh or secondary air into the exhaust ports from the air cleaner assembly. A silencer is used in the air cleaner to insulate the noise of the reed valve during its operation. The air manifold divides and distributes the inducted air to the injection nozzles, one for each cylinder, and placed to direct the injected fresh air into the hot gases discharged from the cylinder head exhaust ports. As the exhaust gases are directed through the exhaust system, the gases enter the catalytic converter. The inducted air continues the combustion of the unburned elements in the exhaust gases and the catalytic converter converts the remaining hydrocarbons (HC) and carbon monoxide (CO) into harmless water (H_2O) and carbon dioxide (CO_2).

Air Pump Operation

The operation of the air injection and catalytic converter system, using an air pump is virtually the same as the air injected system, with the exception of the addition of a catalytic converter to the exhaust system. The air pump is used in place of the reed valve to inject a more positive force of fresh air into the exhaust gases. The electric control box may or may not be used in this type of system, along with the floor heat hazard warning system.

Testing the thermodetector (© Toyo Kogyo Co. Ltd.)

HEAT HAZARD WARNING SYSTEM

The heat hazard warning system is used to prevent potential heat hazard to the vehicle due to the excessive heat radiated from the exhaust system and the catalytic converter. A test system for the warning light is provided to warn the vehicle operator should the warning lamp circuit not operate. When the warning lamp is operating properly, it will come on when the ignition switch is

Thermal reactor cooling circuit (© Toyo Kogyo Co. Ltd.)

turned on and go out when the engine is started. The warning temperature setting varies with vehicle models, but ranges from 212° to 302°F. Should the temperature rise and cause the heat hazard warning system to operate, the fresh or secondary air is directed from the exhaust system to deny the exhaust gases the fresh air to continue the combustion of the unburned elements in the exhaust system and the catalytic converter, which in turn, lowers the heat from the exhaust system.

CATALYTIC CONVERTERS

Various catalytic converter configurations are used from the monolithic (block type) to the pellet type, each containing, but not limited to, platinum, palladium and rhodium as the catalyst. The construction of the various converters differ, depending upon the vehicle model usage, but the main purposes of the units are to reduce the oxides of nitrogens (NO_x) and to oxidize the hydrocarbons (HC) and carbon monoxide (CO) into harmless water H_2O) and carbon dioxide (CO_2).

Catalytic Converter Precautions

1. Unleaded fuel must be used to avoid contaminating the converter catalyst.

2. Do not park the vehicle over inflammable materials.

3. Do not operate the engine with the spark plug wires disconnected.

4. Do not coast the vehicle with the ignition switch turned off and the engine internal parts rotating.

5. Avoid driving with the choke control knob (manual) pulled out with the engine warmed up.

Deceleration Control System

ROTARY ENGINES

The deceleration control system is designed to maintain a balanced air/fuel mixture and to prevent excessive afterburn in the exhaust system. The system uses a deceleration control valve, idle switch and control unit. The deceleration control valve contains two valves: one, the anti-afterburn valve which prevents the fuel detonation and two, the coasting valve which compensates for the insufficient air/fuel mixtures. Both valves will allow fresh air to enter the intake manifold to prevent the exhaust afterburn, when the ignition switch is turned off. At the beginning of sudden deceleration, rich air/fuel mixture is present in the intake manifold and is supplied to the cylinders. This excessively rich mixture does not completely burn in the combustion chambers and when this unburned rich mixture is discharged into the exhaust manifold and the injected fresh air is mixed with it, an un-

Combination anti-afterburn and coasting valve connections (© Toyo Kogyo Co. Ltd.)

desirable combustion type explosion occurs in the exhaust system. To prevent this occurence in the exhaust system, the anti-afterburn valve permits fresh air to enter the intake manifold upon sudden increase of the manifold vacuum and the fresh air mixes with the over-rich mixture of air and fuel, reducing the mixture to a combustible mixture so that it can be burned normally in the engine combustion chambers.

The system consists of the following.

1. Anti-afterburn valve—allows fresh air to enter the intake manifold.

2. Coasting valve—allows fresh air to enter the intake manifold.

3. Solenoids—when energized, close the air passages for the anti-afterburn and coasting valves air chambers.

4. Idle switch—detects decelerating conditions and cuts the electric current from the ignition switch to the coasting valve, through the control unit.

5. Control unit—detects the operational mode condition and sends the signals to the solenoids.

The afterburn and coasting valves operate under the following conditions.

1. Immediately after the ignition switch is turned off. When the ignition switch is turned off, the solenoids for the two valves are turned off, which allows the air chambers to open. Atmospheric pressure acts on the diaphragms to open the valves. As a result, fresh air is allowed to enter the intake manifold for a brief period of time.

NOTE: On California and Federal models with automatic transmissions, the coasting valve is closed and cannot operate.

2. Immediately after deceleration—anti-afterburn valve. Immediately after deceleration, the anti-afterburn valve is opened by a difference of pressures between the air chamber and the vacuum chamber. The solenoid on the valve is not off, but is turned on by the ignition switch being in the "ON" position. As the intake manifold pressure is increased, the diaphragm is pulled down and the valve is opened to supply fresh air to the intake manifold, momentarily. The metering orifice controls the time of valve

operation (open) as the vacuum equalizes through the top of the diaphragm.

3. Immediately after deceleration—coasting valve. During deceleration over 1150 rpm of engine speed, the coasting valve is opened by the difference of pressure between the atmospheric pressure in the air chamber and the vacuum pressure in the vacuum chamber. The electrical signals from the idle switch and the control unit are not sent to the coasting valve solenoid, which allows the air passage to be opened to the air chamber of the coasting valve diaphragm. As a result, the coasting valve is opened by the pressure difference between the air chamber and the vacuum chamber, which in turn, allows air to enter the intake manifold.

When the engine speed decreases below 1150 rpm during the deceleration, the electrical signals from the idle switch and control unit are sent to the solenoid on the coasting valve, closing the air passage and not allowing fresh air to enter the intake manifold.

Shutter Valve (1981 and Later)

To eliminate misfirings and the accompanying emissions of raw hydrocarbons (HC), which is a common characteristic of the early rotary engines, a shutter valve is installed in the primary intake passage for the rear rotor chamber and is closed by vacuum during deceleration and diverts the total air/fuel mixture through a bypass port and into the front rotor chamber. The front chamber continues to run with sufficient air/fuel mixture to eliminate engine misfiring. To avoid an abnormally high manifold vacuum from the rear chamber, a coasting valve, linked to the shutter valve, is opened as the shutter valve closes, allowing fresh air to enter the rear chamber and reducing the vacuum.

PISTON ENGINES

The deceleration control system used on the piston engines is designed to balance the air/fuel mixture during deceleration. The system utilizes an anti-afterburn valve to

Arrow indicates the position of the anti-afterburn valve

prevent afterburning of the rich mixture in the exhaust system and coasting richer valve to compensate for lean (insufficient) air/fuel mixtures in automatic equipped vehicles.

At the beginning of sudden deceleration, the engine air/fuel mixture is extremely rich and will not burn completely in the combustion chamber. This overrich mixture is discharged into the exhaust system and when mixed with the fresh air supplied by the air injection system, abnormal combustion and explosions occur within the exhaust system. To prevent this condition, the anti-afterburn valve allows fresh air to be routed to the intake manifold, diluting the overly rich mixture and allowing the mixture to be burned properly in the combustion chambers before entering the exhaust system.

Coasting Richer Valve (Automatic Transmission Equipped Only)

The coasting richer valve is attached to the carburetor and begins to operate during the deceleration and after the anti-afterburn valve has started its operation. The air/fuel mixture is extremely rich before the anti-afterburn valve operates, and after the valve has opened its passage and allowed fresh air to enter the manifold, the mixture becomes too lean. Should this occur, the mixture would not complete its combustion to burn the elements from the exhaust gases and the mixture being too lean, the air injected into the exhaust manifold would be of no value. To avoid this condition, a coasting richer valve, attached to the carburetor, opens and allows fuel passage to the secondary stage of the carburetor to supply an additional amount of fuel, to prevent the mixture from becoming too lean, so that the

Arrow indicates the position of the coasting valve

Limiter cap

Stopper pin

Adjusting the idle switch (© Toyo Kogyo Co. Ltd.)

Idle switch position

complete combustion of the mixture can take place in the combustion chambers and the emissions of hydrocarbons (HC) and carbon monoxide (CO) are reduced.

The operation of the coasting richer valve is controlled by the accelerator switch and the vehicle speed switch, and operates only for a duration while both switches are in the circuit for the coasting richer valve. The accelerator switch is mounted on the accelerator linkage and depressing the accelerator pedal opens the circuit. The speed switch is mounted on the speedometer and

operates when the speed is 16 ± 1.5 m.p.h. and over.

Throttle Opener System

ROTARY ENGINE

Dash Pot

The dash pot is used to slow the throttle valve return upon the release of the accelerator pedal. By slowing the throttle valve, a balanced air/fuel mixture is maintained to prevent engine misfire.

NOTE: Vehicles with automatic transmissions are not equipped with the dash pot or coasting valve, although an anti-afterburn valve is used.

Coasting Valve

The coasting valve allows additional air to enter the intake manifold to prevent misfiring during the deceleration of the engine at speeds over 1150 rpm.

PISTON ENGINES

The throttle opener system is in operation during the deceleration of the engine at times of high engine vacuum, sensed by a vacuum control valve to open a passage so that engine vacuum can react on the servo-diaphragm to open the primary throttle valve slightly, to provide the additional richness to the lean air/fuel mixture. The diaphragm return spring of the vacuum control valve is set to start operating when the intake manifold vacuum exceeds 22.4 in. Hg. Under this vacuum setting, the throttle opener system does not operate, therefore controlling the system only on deceleration. An

Typical piston engine emission control system (© Toyo Kogyo Co. Ltd.)

GLC servo diaphragm check; "F" is the vacuum sensing tube. If the idle speed increases to 1400 rpm, the system is ok. (© Toyo Kogyo Co. Ltd.)

altitude corrector (bellows) in the vacuum control valve prevents varied responses due to the differences in atmospheric pressure at the different levels of altitude, by adjusting the diaphragm return spring to the proper tension.

NOTE: Canadian vehicles equipped with the throttle opener system operate above 22.0 in. Hg and do not have the altitude correction bellows included in the vacuum control valve.

Dash Pot

The dash pot is used to maintain a balanced air/fuel mixture during gearshifting to prevent excessive hydrocarbons (HC), to accumulate during the deceleration of the engine when the accelerator is released, and to allow the throttle valve to gradually return to normal idle.

A combination of spring pressure and air pressure is used to operate the dash pot. A metered orifice with a check valve connects the two chambers of the dash pot diaphragm with a spring operated assist against the

Servo diaphragm

diaphragm and stem during acceleration, to move the stem towards the throttle lever of the carburetor. When the throttle lever is released by the release of the accelerator pedal and the tension of the throttle return spring overcomes the diaphragm return spring pressure, the stem and diaphragm are moved into the dash pot. The metered air orifice connecting the two chambers in the dash pot diaphragm, controls the rate of movement of the stem. The duration of the rod movement of 0.18 inch with a 2.4 lb. load on the stem, is 0.8 seconds, approximately.

Exhaust Gas Recirculation (EGR) System

The increase of exhaust temperatures also increases the emissions of oxides of nitrogen (NO_x) from the exhaust gases. The EGR system is used to dilute the air/fuel mixture in the intake manifold with a small percentage of exhaust gas. The exhaust gas does not burn, but absorbs some of the combustion heat to lower the emissions of NO_x.

The EGR system consists of the EGR control valve, three way solenoid valve and water temperature switch. The EGR valve is a cone type valve and meters the exhaust gases into the intake manifold in response to the varying vacuum signals of the engine. The three way solenoid valve closes the vacuum line leading to the EGR valve when the coolant temperature is lower than approximately 131°F to provide good driveability of the vehicle when cold. The system operates only on acceleration.

2. EGR relay is used to open or close the electrical current from the Number one vacuum switch to the EGR solenoid, accordingly to the signals of the water temperature switch or control unit.

3. The EGR solenoid opens the vacuum sensing passage to the EGR valve when the electrical current is directed from the Number one vacuum switch through the EGR relay.

4. The Number one vacuum switch and number one delay valve detect the condition of acceleration by using intake manifold vacuum.

5. The control unit sends the electrical signal to the EGR relay, from the choke switch, according to driving conditions.

Federal Models With Automatic Transmission

The EGR relay is controlled by the water temperature switch. When the temperature of the coolant is higher than 140°F, the relay is allowed to be turned on.

California Models With Automatic Transmission

The EGR relay is controlled by the water temperature switch and control unit so that

the relay turns on to close the circuit from the number one vacuum switch to the EGR solenoid, when the engine coolant temperature is more than 140°F or after 130 seconds from starting the engine with the choke knob pulled out.

EGR WARNING SYSTEM

This system is used to alert the operator to either perform or have performed, the EGR maintenance service on the system. A warning lamp on the dashboard will illuminate every 12,500 miles of operation.

To reset the EGR maintenance interval detector, located under the left side of the dash panel, simply reverse the connector to the detector terminals.

Piston Engines

The EGR system used on the piston engines consists of the EGR valve, three way solenoid valve and a coolant temperature switch. The EGR control valve is used to modulate the exhaust gas flow into the intake manifold in response to the varying vacuum signal of the intake manifold when the vehicle is in the acceleration mode. The system is not in operation when the coolant temperature is less than 131°F. When the coolant temperature is lower than 131°F, the three-way solenoid valve is energized to close the vacuum passage between the three-way valve and the EGR valve. When the coolant temperature is over 131°F, the three-way switch is de-energized and the passage from the three-way solenoid valve to the EGR valve is opened so that vacuum from the carburetor acts on the EGR valve diaphragm to open the EGR valve stem, to allow the exhaust gas to enter the intake manifold.

NOTE: At engine idle and full throttle, the exhaust gas is not mixed with the air/fuel mixture, so that full power and a smooth idle can be obtained.

A vacuum amplifier is used on certain vehicles used in the state of California. The purpose of the vacuum amplifier is to increase or amplify the weak vacuum signal from the carburetor venturi and to give a more positive vacuum signal to the EGR valve.

Automatic Choke Release System

ROTARY ENGINE

Type 1

The automatic choke release system controls the opening and the closing of the choke valve in the air horn of the carburetor, to provide the correct air/fuel mixture at the time of engine start-up. The choke valve is operated manually to restrict the air flow through the carburetor and remains closed while the engine is cranking. As soon as the engine has started, the choke valve opens slightly to allow more air to enter the air horn so as to correct the air/fuel mixture. The choke valve is opened slightly by a vacuum diaphragm and the force of a bi-metal spring. The tension of the bi-metal spring is weakened by the electrical circuit flowing through the choke switch to the choke heater, when the choke lever is pulled.

It should be noted that when the engine is being cranked the intake manifold vacuum is so low that the vacuum diaphragm does not operate. When the engine starts a high intake manifold vacuum is created and is routed to the vacuum diaphragm to open the choke valve in a preset manner. As the carburetor heater for the choke bi-metal spring is heated, the choke valve is gradually opened. This prevents an overly rich mixture during start-ups or while driving with the choke knob pulled out.

Type 2

FEDERAL

To avoid excessively high temperatures in the thermal reactor from an overly rich air/fuel mixture during the engine warm-up period, the manually operated choke control pull rod is held in place by an electrical magnet, when the coolant temperature is below a specified degree and is released automatically when the coolant temperature rises above the specified degree, governed by a coolant temperature switch.

The choke operation is basically the same as the choke mechanism used on many piston engines, but with wiring differences. The type two rotary engine choke magnet is grounded through the choke switch case or from a case connector lead to ground, while the piston engine choke magnet is grounded through the coolant temperature switch.

CALIFORNIA

To more closely control the automatically returned choke valve to the vertical position, to avoid excessive high temperatures to be developed in the thermal reactor due to an overly rich air/fuel mixture, in addition to the controls of the federal vehicle choke assembly, the following components are required in the state of California.

1. The full choke magnet switch which controls the electric current to the choke magnet according to the Number two vacuum switch operation.

2. Number two vacuum switch which stops the electric current to the full choke switch.

3. Number two delay valve which controls the Number two vacuum switch operating time.

With the choke knob is pulled half way out, the operation is the same as the Federal choke operation. With the control knob pulled all the way out and the ignition switch turned on, the electric current flows to the choke magnet and holds the control rod in

the full closed position. After approximately 30 seconds from engine starting, the vacuum switch cuts or stops the current between the ignition switch and the choke magnet according to the intake manifold vacuum and the choke knob is forcibly returned to the "OFF" position.

PISTON ENGINES

To avoid having the choke valve on for a long period of time and causing an overly rich air/fuel mixture, the choke control pull rod is held in place by an electrical magnet, wired in series with a coolant temperature switch, with the electrical current controlled by the ignition switch. The choke control pull rod can be controlled manually by the vehicle operator, when the magnet is in use.

With the coolant temperature below 131°F, the coolant switch is on and current is allowed to move from the ignition switch, to the magnet and to the temperature switch, energizing the magnet and holding the choke control pull rod in the "ON" position, as set by the operator. As the coolant temperature rises over 131°F the coolant temperature switch contacts open and the flow of electrical current is interrupted, causing the magnetic field to collapse and release the choke control pull rod. Internal linkage forces the rod to move to the "OFF" position and allows the choke valve to open, thereby allowing more air to enter the carburetor and preventing the air/fuel mixture from becoming too rich.

Intake Air Temperature Control System

ROTARY ENGINES

This system is designed to keep the temperature of the air drawn into the carburetor as even as possible, regardless of the ambient temperature.

When the temperature of the intake air is more than 45°F, the bimetal strip connected to the air duct valve begins to operate. It closes the cold air intake from the engine compartment area and opens the hot air intake from the thermal reactor area.

When the temperature is more than 115°F, the bimetal strip connected to the air duct valve again begins to operate. The hot air duct from the thermal reactor is closed and the duct from the engine compartment is opened to allow the colder air to enter the air cleaner assembly and carburetor.

PISTON ENGINES

Both a thermostat type and a vacuum operated type flapper valve arrangement is used on the piston engine carburetors to control the temperature of the induction air.

The vacuum operated valve has a me-

tered amount of vacuum to operate the flapper valve when cold and a thermostatic valve to overcome the metered vacuum pressure to open the flapper valve when warm.

The fully thermostatic operated flapper valve is controlled by the temperature of the inducted air flowing through the intake tube, to either close or open the air ducts.

Fuel Enrichment System

ROTARY ENGINES

Richer Solenoid

This system is used in two different modes of operation, depending upon the area and the transmission equipment. The richer solenoid is used on Federal and California vehicles, equipped with manual transmissions. The purpose of the system is to supply additional fuel to the intake manifold to prevent engine misfire during the deceleration mode, with engine speeds greater than 1150 rpm. This additional fuel maintains a balanced air/fuel mixture during the deceleration.

During the deceleration over 1150 rpm, the electric signal from the control unit is sent to the richer solenoid through the idle switch, causing the richer solenoid to open and supply the additional fuel to the intake manifold.

As the engine speed decreases to below 1150 rpm during deceleration, the electrical signal is stopped by the low speed switch in the control unit, and the additional fuel is cut off from entering the intake manifold.

Power Valve Solenoid

This system is used on Federal vehicles using automatic transmissions and on California vehicles using manual or automatic transmissions. The power valve solenoid for California vehicles differs in its function and operation, from that used on the Federal and Canada vehicles. The solenoid appearance is the same, but the timing of the opening and closing of the valve differs.

CALIFORNIA

The power valve solenoid closes the vacuum passage to the power valve so that the additional fuel can be supplied from the power valve to the intake manifold at the following times.

1. When accelerating in any gear except 4th and 5th at any engine speed of 1150 to 3000 rpm.

2. When accelerating over 4600 rpm and when the engine is 1150 to 4600 rpm within 130 seconds from the initial engine starting with the choke used.

FEDERAL AND CANADA

The power valve closes the vacuum passage leading to the power valve during acceleration so that the additional fuel is supplied by the power valve to the intake manifold.

Idle Compensation System

ROTARY ENGINES

The need to stabilize the engine idle under various operating conditions are required and an idle compensator and throttle opener are used.

Idle Compensator

The idle compensator is used to supply a small amount of air into the intake manifold under extremely hot conditions, through an opening of a bimetal valve, located in the carburetor air cleaner, with the air routed to the intake manifold by a tube or hose. The compensator valve opens when the inlet air temperature reaches and exceeds 149°F.

Throttle Opener

The throttle opener system is used to improve the idle stability of an engine in an air condition equipped vehicle with the air conditioning turned on and the engine speed under 1150 rpm.

The system consists of a control unit, housing a low speed switch, an air conditioning relay, an air conditioning solenoid valve and a throttle opener.

When the idle speed is below 1150 rpm and the air conditioning is turned on, current is routed through the low speed switch and the air conditioning relay, to the air conditioning solenoid. As the solenoid is energized, the vacuum passage between the throttle opener and the intake manifold is opened, allowing vacuum to act upon the diaphragm inside the throttle opener. The movement of the diaphragm is controlled and the linkage connecting the diaphragm stem to the throttle valve is moved, causing the primary throttle valve to open slightly more than at idle, causing an increase in the engine rpm and preventing stalling out of the engine.

Kickdown Control System

ROTARY ENGINE

The purpose of the kickdown system is to increase the engine speed when the choke knob is pulled out, by having the automatic transmission in a reduction gear.

When the choke valve is pulled out, the choke switch allows electrical current to flow to the kickdown relay and operates the kickdown valve in the transmission. When the choke knob is released, the transmission is allowed to up-shift into the higher gear ratios.

NOTE: This system is related to the shifting operation of the transmission and not to any other emission control system or device.

Ignition Control System

ROTARY ENGINES

California Models

The ignition control system is used to warm-up the thermal reactor quickly by controlling the operation of the leading and trailing ignition systems.

The methods of ignition controls are as follows.

1. The leading spark plug ignition only (normal and retarded modes).
2. Both leading or trailing spark plug ignition.

The system consists of the following.

1. Trailing ignition relay—controls the trailing ignition circuit.
2. Retard relay—selects the flow of electrical current sent from the leading or trailing coil when the choke knob is pulled out. Usually the leading coil will be connected to the trailing contact points and the trailing coil will be disconnected from the circuit.
3. Idle, choke and overdrive switch—detects the specific conditions such as, deceleration, cold starting or cruising in overdrive. Each electrical signal is sent to the control unit separately.
4. Vacuum control valve—closes the vacuum sensing tube to the trailing vacuum diaphragm, so that under a cold condition, no vacuum advance will occur at the trailing contact points.
5. Control unit—sends the electrical signal to the trailing ignition relay and retard relay.

RETARDED LEADING IGNITION

The following conditions must occur simultaneously to retard the leading ignition timing. When this happens, there is no trailing ignition.

1. Within 130 seconds after the engine starting, with the choke knob pulled out, except during engine deceleration (choke switch and timer are "ON" and idle switch is "OFF".
2. Engine speed is over 1150 rpm and under 4600 rpm.

NOTE: If the choke knob is pushed back in during the 130 seconds, the engine idle speed should be over 1150 and under 4000 rpm.

NORMAL LEADING IGNITION CALIFORNIA MODELS WITH AUTOMATIC TRANSMISSIONS

To have normal leading ignition, the following conditions must occur simultaneously.

1. Engine speed is over 1150 and under 2500 rpm, except while in a deceleration condition.

2. The time span should be more than 130 seconds when the choke knob is pulled out (timer "OFF").

CALIFORNIA MODELS WITH MANUAL TRANSMISSION

To have normal leading ignition, the following conditions must occur simultaneously.

1. Engine speed over 1150 and under 3000 rpm, except while in a deceleration mode.
2. The time span should be more than 130 seconds when the choke knob is pulled out (timer "OFF").

BOTH LEADING AND TRAILING SPARK PLUG IGNITION

The leading and trailing spark plugs will ignite when the trailing ignition relay is "ON", the retard relay is deactivated and the following conditions are occurring.

1. When the engine speed is lower than 1150 rpm and the timer is "OFF".
2. During deceleration.
3. When the engine speed is more than 3000 rpm (manual transmission) or 2500 rpm (automatic transmission) after 130 seconds from starting with the choke knob pulled out or in cases of starting without the choke.
4. During operation of the engine while the transmission is in overdrive gear (5th—manual transmission).
5. When starting the engine with the choke knob pulled out during the 130 seconds and the engine speed is over 4600 rpm.

NOTE: Should the choke knob be pushed back in within the 130 seconds, the engine speed will be altered to 4000 rpm.

PISTON ENGINES

Federal With Electronic Ignition and Manual Transmission

The ignition control system retards or advances the ignition timing as required, with the engine operating under certain conditions. The system consists of a top switch, accelerator switch and the transistorized ignition system. The timing advances normally when the accelerator and top switches are in the "OFF" position and retards when the switches are in the "ON" position.

The accelerator switch is "ON" when the accelerator pedal is depressed to ¾ of its travel, while the top switch is on when the transmission is in the 1st, 2nd, 3rd or reverse gear positions.

Federal and Canada With Dual Point Distributors

The system consists of a dual point distributor, containing a retard and an advance (normal) set of ignition points, a vehicle speed switch (Federal) or a water temperature switch (Canada) to control the retard or advanced sets of ignition points during the operation.

The operating conditions are as follows.

1. The advanced set of ignition points operate when the vehicle speed is higher than 42 mph (Federal) or when the coolant temperature is more than 112–140°F (Canada).

2. The retard set of ignition points operate when the vehicle speed is lower than 42 mph (Federal) or when the coolant temperature is lower than 122–140°F (Canada).

FUEL SYSTEM

Electric Fuel Pump— All Except GLC

The electric fuel pump is located in the luggage compartment of all models except the RX-7, 626 and station wagons. On station wagons, it is located behind the left-hand trim panel in the luggage compartment. On the 626 and RX-7 it is located under the rear of the vehicle near the fuel tank.

REMOVAL AND INSTALLATION

All Except 626, RX-7, and Station Wagons

1. Remove the rear inside trim panel.
2. Disconnect the wiring and the fuel lines.
3. Remove the pump.
4. Installation is the reverse of removal.

Station Wagons

1. Remove the left-hand cargo compartment trim panel.
2. Disconnect the wiring and fuel lines.
3. Remove the pump.
4. Installation is the reverse of removal.

626

1. Disconnect the negative battery cable at the battery.
2. Disconnect the fuel pump lead wire in the luggage compartment.
3. Raise the vehicle and support with jack stands.
4. Disconnect the fuel pump bracket.
5. Disconnect the fuel inlet and outlet hoses and remove the fuel pump.
6. Installation is the reverse of removal.

RX-7

1. Remove the rear floor mat and floor plate.

2. Disconnect the fuel pump electrical connection under the floor plate.
3. Raise the car and support it on jack stands.
4. Remove the fuel pump protecting cover, then block the fuel lines and then remove the pump from the cover.

Installation is the reverse of removal.

Mechanical Fuel Pump—GLC

The mechanical fuel pump is mounted on the right front side of the engine block.

NOTE: The 1981 and later GLC fuel pump is mounted on the left side of the intake manifold.

REMOVAL AND INSTALLATION

1. Slide the two fuel line clips from the pump inlet and outlet hoses. Remove the hoses.
2. Remove the fuel pump mounting bolts and remove the pump, gasket and spacer.
3. The installation is the reverse of the removal procedure.

Fuel Filter

REMOVAL AND INSTALLATION

All Except 626 and RX-7

The fuel filter on all 1976–77 coupes and sedans except the GLC is located behind the trim panel in the luggage compartment. On all wagons except the GLC it is inside the left rear quarter panel. On the 1977–80 GLC and the 1977 and later GLC wagon it is located on the right side of the engine compartment. On the 1981 and later GLC it is located on the left side of the engine compartment.

1. Remove the trim panel by unfastening its two securing screws. On those models so equipped.
2. Detach both hoses from the filter.
3. Unfasten the filter from its mounting bracket.

Install the new filter in the reverse order of removal.

626 and RX-7

The fuel filter is located under the rear of the car just in front of the fuel tank.

1. Raise the rear of the car and support it on jackstands. Locate the filter: use the illustration as a guide to its shape.
2. Loosen the clips at both ends of the filter and place a collection pan beneath it to catch any of the fuel that is in the lines.
3. Disconnect the fuel filter lines and remove the filter from its retainer.

4. Install the new filter, paying close attention to the direction of the filter in relation to the direction of fuel flow. See the illustration for correct positioning.
5. Turn the starter to ON to activate the fuel pump and check the fuel filter connections for leaks.

NOTE: If the filter is held by spring tension clamps, it would be wise to replace them with new clamps when the filter is changed.

Carburetor

REMOVAL AND INSTALLATION

Rotary Engine

1. Remove the air cleaner.
2. Detach the choke and accelerator cables.
3. Label and disconnect the fuel and vacuum lines and plug the main fuel line to prevent leakage.
4. Remove the oil line.
5. Remove all electrical wiring from carburetor.
6. Remove the carburetor.
7. Installation is the reverse of removal.

Piston Engine

1. Remove the air cleaner and duct.
2. Disconnect the accelerator shaft.
3. Disconnect the fuel supply and fuel return lines.
4. Disconnect the leads from the throttle solenoid and deceleration valve at the quick-disconnects.
5. Disconnect the throttle return spring.
6. Disconnect the choke cable.
7. Remove the carburetor.
8. Installation is the reverse of removal.

ACCELERATOR LINKAGE ADJUSTMENT

RX-4, Cosmo, RX-3, RX-3SP, RX-7 and 1976–79 808

1. Check the pedal position. The accelerator pedal should be lower than the brake pedal by 2.3 in.—rotary pickup, 1.0 in.—808, 2.2 in.—Cosmo, 1.6 in.—RX-3, RX-4 and GLC, 1.7 ± 0.2 in.—RX-7.

Float level adjustment, float bowl inverted and gasket installed (© Toyo Kogyo Co. Ltd.)

2. If necessary, adjust the nut on the linkage above the pedal to obtain the proper height.

3. Check the free-play of the cable at the carburetor. It should be 0.04–0.12 in. If not, adjust by turning the clevis nut.

FLOAT AND FUEL LEVEL ADJUSTMENTS

RX-3 and RX-3SP

1. Bend the float stop to adjust the fuel amount through the needle valve. Distance between lowest part of the float and lower air horn face should be 2.1–2.2 in.

2. Invert the air horn (float seat lip contacting needle valve).

3. The distance between float and the surface of the air horn gasket should be 0.47 in.

4. Bend the float seat lip in order to adjust the float setting.

1976 and Later RX-4 and Cosmo

1. With the engine running, check the fuel level in the sight glass, using a mirror.

2. If the fuel levels are not within the specified marks on the sight glass, remove the air horn with the floats.

3. Invert the air horn and let the float hang so that it just contacts the needle valve.

4. Measure the clearance between the float and the air horn gasket, which should be 0.100 in. for 1976 and later models. Bend the float seat lip to adjust the clearance if necessary.

FUEL LEVEL MARK

Fuel level mark on sight glass: piston engine

1300, 1415, 1490 and 1970 cc Engine (808, GLC, 626)

1. Remove the carburetor air horn assembly.

2. Invert the air horn and allow the float to hang so that the needle valve contacts the seat.

3. Measure the clearance between float and the air horn without the air horn gasket in place. The clearance should be 0.433 inches.

4. The clearance should be 0.433 inches.

5. Adjust by bending the float seat lip.

6. Reassemble and recheck idle.

6.5±0.5mm (0.256±0.020 in.)

1.2–0.1mm (0.047–0.004 in.)

Piston engine float adjustment: bend tab "A" to adjust float drop and bend tab "B" to adjust float level (© Toyo Kogyo Co. Ltd.)

Fast idle adjustments: measure the angle "A" and clearance "B"—rotary engines (© Toyo Kogyo Co. Ltd.)

808 (1600)

1. With the engine running, observe the fuel level in the fuel bowl sight glass.

2. If the adjustment is necessary, stop the engine and remove the carburetor assembly.

3. Remove the fuel bowl sight glass and invert the carburetor.

4. Measure the clearance between the float and the top of the bowl (now inverted).

5. The clearance should be 0.256 inches.

6. Adjust the float by bending the float seat lip.

RX-7

1. Remove the carburetor air horn assembly.

2. Invert the air horn to a position with the float facing upward. The air horn gasket surface must be level. Place the air horn on a carburetor work stand, if available, in order to insure a level position.

3. The distance between the float and the air horn gasket should be 0.63 ± 0.02 in., measured at the top of the float.

4. Install the air horn assembly.

FLOAT DROP

1976 and Later RX-4, Cosmo and RX-3, RX-3SP

1. Remove the air horn with the floats and allow the floats to hang free.

2. Measure the clearance between the bottom of the float and the air horn gasket. The clearance should be 2.05 in. (2.13 RX-3).

3. If not, adjust the distance by bending the float stop.

808 and GLC with 1300, 1415, 1490 cc Engine

1. With the air horn inverted, lift the float and measure the clearance between the float seat lip and the needle valve.

2. The clearance should be 0.051 to 0.067 inch.

3. Adjust the clearance by bending the float stopper.

808 (1600)

1. Have the carburetor upright and the fuel bowl sight glass removed.

2. Measure the bottom of the float to the bottom of the bowl.

3. The clearance should be 0.047 inch.

4. Adjust the clearance by bending the float stopper.

5. Reinstall the float bowl and install the carburetor on the engine.

1979–80 626 w/1970 cc Engine

1. With the engine running, check fuel level in the fuel bowl sight glass.

2. When the fuel level is not at the specified level on the sight glass, remove the carburetor from the vehicle.

3. Remove the fuel bowl sight glass.

4. Invert the carburetor on a stand and allow the float to lower by its own weight.

5. Measure the clearance from the float to the bowl.

6. Bend the float seat lip until a clearance of 8.5 mm (0.335 in.) is obtained.

7. Turn the carburetor to its normal position and the float should drop by its own weight.

8. Set the clearance between the bottom of the float and the bowl at 1.0 mm (0.039 in.).

9. Install the sight glass on the carburetor.

10. Install the carburetor on the engine.

11. Operate the engine and check for the specified level of fuel at the sight glass.

1981 and Later 626 w/1970 cc Engine

1. Measure the distance between the bottom of the float and the air horn bowl. The distance should be 1.811 in. Bend the float stopper to adjust.

2. Turn the air horn to the normal position and allow the float to lower by its own weight.

RX-7

1. Remove the carburetor air horn assembly.

2. Position the air horn in the normal installed position. The air horn gasket surface should be level.

Fast idle cam adjustment showing cam lever in the first position (see text)—1415, and 1490 cc engine (© Toyo Kogyo Co. Ltd.)

3. The float should be in a fully dropped position. Measure the distance between the lowest part of the float and the air horn gasket.

4. The measured distance should be 2.0 ± 0.02 in. If the distance is not correct, bend the tab on the float to obtain the correct distance.

5. Install the air horn.

FAST IDLE CAM ADJUSTMENT

All Except 1415, 1490 and 1970 cc Engine

1. Remove the carburetor from the engine.

2. With the choke valve fully closed, adjust the clearance between the primary throttle valve and the wall of the throttle bore by bending the connecting rod between the choke valve and the throttle valve to the following specifications:

1415, 1490 and 1970 cc Engines

1. On the 1415 cc engine, remove the bi-metal cover.

2. Using your fingers, close the choke valve fully.

3. Make sure the fast idle cam is on the first position. (Third position-GLC with 1490 cc engine).

4. Check the clearance at the throttle valve opening and adjust by turning the adjustment screw.

Fast idle cam adjustment—1970 cc engine (© Toyo Kogyo Co. Ltd.)

Year/Model	Clearances
808 (1300)	0.052 inch
808 (1600), RX-3 RX-3 SP	MT-0.079 ± 0.008 inch AT-0.079 ± 0.008 inch (Calif. AT 0.087 ± 0.008 inch)
1976 RX-4	0.073 ± 0.006 inch
1977–78 RX-4	0.043 ± 0.004 inch (Calif. 0.056 ± 0.056 ± 0.004 inch)
1976–77 Cosmo	0.041 ± 0.004 inch (Calif. 0.054 ± 0.004 inch)
1978 Cosmo	0.043 ± 0.004 inch (Calif. 0.056 ± 0.004 inch)
1977–79 GLC	0.054 ± 0.006 inch
1980 GLC 1981 GLC 1982 GLC 1979–80 626	0.043 inch 0.048–0.060 inch 0.067 inch 0.019–0.026 inch (U.S.A.) 0.035–0.049 inch (Canada)
1981 626	0.019–0.026 inch
1982 626	0.018–0.030 inch
1979 RX-7	0.051–0.059 inch (Calif.) 0.035–0.040 inch (49 states and Canada)
1980 RX-7	0.051–0.059 inch (U.S.A.) 0.035–0.040 inch (Canada)
1981–82 RX-7	0.031–0.039 inch

MANUAL TRANSMISSION

REMOVAL AND INSTALLATION

All Except GLC (Rear Wheel Drive) and 626

1. Remove the console over the shift lever.

2. Remove the floor mat.

3. Remove shift lever.

4. Tie the clutch release cylinder up out of the way. Do not disconnect the hydraulic line from the clutch release cylinder. On RX-4, RX-7 models, remove the starter motor and loosen the 3 upper engine-to-transmission bolts.

5. Detach the back-up light switch multiconnector which is located near the clutch release cylinder. On RX-4s, RX-7s, remove the brake booster vacuum line bracket from the clutch housing.

6. Drain the oil. Remove the driveshaft.

7. Detach the exhaust pipe from the thermal reactor flange. On RX-4 models, remove the heat insulators first. Remove the converter cover, brackets and lower exhaust pipe (rear) and the pellet converter assembly on the RX-7 models.

8. Unfasten the speedometer cable.

9. Remove the starter.

10. Support the transmission.

11. Unbolt the transmission support.

12. Remove the bolts which retain the bell housing.

13. Carefully slide the transmission rearward until the input shaft has cleared the clutch disc.

14. Lower the transmission.

15. Transmission installation is the reverse of removal. Align the clutch plate with an arbor or an old input shaft. Adjust the clutch and shift linkage as detailed elsewhere. Refill the transmission with gear oil.

GLC (Rear Wheel Drive)

1. Disconnect the (−) battery cable.

2. Put the transmission in neutral and remove the shift lever.

3. Remove the two upper bolts from the clutch housing.

4. Raise the vehicle and support it securely on axle stands or a lift.

5. Drain the transmission oil and replace the plug.

6. Remove the driveshaft, and plug or cover the hole in the extension housing.

7. Disconnect the speedometer cable and back-up light switch wires.

8. Disconnect the exhaust pipe hanger from the bracket on the clutch housing.

9. Remove the exhaust pipe support bracket from the clutch housing. Disconnect the clutch cable at the release lever.

10. Remove the lower clutch housing cover.

11. Remove the starter electrical connections, remove the bolts, and remove the starter.

12. Disconnect the exhaust pipe hanger at the extension housing.

13. Place a jack under the engine, using a block of wood to protect the oil pan. Make sure the jack can securely support the weight of the engine.

14. Disconnect the transmission support member at the transmission.

15. Remove transmission-to-engine attaching bolts.

16. Carefully slide the transmission rearward until the input shaft has cleared the clutch disc, and lower it out of the car.

17. In installation, reverse above procedures, aligning the clutch plate with an arbor or old input shaft. Adjust clutch and shift linkage. Refill the transmission with the proper grade of gear oil.

626

1. Remove the gearshift lever knob.
2. Remove the console box.
3. Remove the gearshift lever boot and the gearshift lever.
4. Disconnect the negative battery cable.
5. Raise the vehicle and support it with jack stands.
6. Drain the transmission lubricant.
7. Disconnect the propeller shaft.
8. Disconnect the exhaust pipe hanger.
9. Remove the starter motor.
10. Disconnect the back-up switch wire.
11. Disconnect the speedometer cable.
12. Place a jack under the engine, protecting the oil pan with a block of wood.
13. Remove the transmission attaching bolts and remove the transmission.
14. Transmission installation is performed in the reverse order of removal. Align the clutch plate with an old arbor or an old input shaft. Add lubricant until the level reaches the bottom of the filler plug hole.

SHIFT LEVER ADJUSTMENT

The shift lever may be adjusted during transmission installation by means of the adjusting shims on the three bolts between the cover plate and the packing. The force required to move the shift knob should be 4.4–8.8 lbs.

MANUAL TRANSAXLE

REMOVAL AND INSTALLATION

1. Raise the vehicle on a hoist and support it safely. Disconnect the negative battery cable.
2. Disconnect all electrical wiring and connections, control linkages from the transaxle. Mark these units to aid in reassembling.
3. Remove the front wheels. Disconnect the lower ball joints from the steering knuckles. Pull the driveshafts from the differential gears.

NOTE: A circlip is positioned on the driveshaft ends and engages in a groove, machined in the differential side gears. The driveshafts may have to be forced from the differential housing to release the clip from the groove.

— CAUTION —

Do not allow the driveshafts to drop. Damage may occur to the ball and socket joints and to the rubber boots. Wire the shafts to the vehicle body when released from the differential.

4. Support the engine with a jack. Remove the mounting bolts retaining the transaxle in place. Remove the unit from the vehicle.
5. Installation is the reverse of removal.

— CAUTION —

Be sure the rubber mounts are not twisted or distorted and not in contact with the body.

6. To properly install the driveshafts in the differential side gears, position the open end of the circlip in the up position, and with the driveshaft in a horizontal position, push the driveshafts into the side gears. To be sure the circlip engages the groove, a sound may be heard or attempt to pull the driveshaft from the differential. Reconnect the ball joints at the lower arms.

CLUTCH AND FLYWHEEL

REMOVAL AND INSTALLATION

The flywheel nut on rotary engine models is tightened to 350 ft. lbs. with no more than a 3 foot extension on the wrench.

1. Clutch disc
2. Bolt
3. Clutch cover and pressure plate assembly
4. Service hole cover
5. Release fork
6. Oil seal

1. Remove the transmission.
2. Remove the clutch cover.
3. Remove the clutch disc.
4. Remove the flywheel.

From the Clutch Housing:

5. Unhook the return spring from the throwout bearing and remove the bearing.
6. Pull out the release fork until the retaining spring frees itself from the ball stud.
7. Installation is the reverse of removal.

Apply Loctite® (RX-3 only) on the eccentric shaft threads.

Apply sealer to both sides of the flywheel lockwasher and position the lockwasher on the eccentric shaft.

Install the flywheel locknut(s) and tighten it to 350 ft. lbs. (Rotary), (112–118 ft. lbs.—Piston); then bend the tabs of the lockwasher up around it.

PEDAL HEIGHT ADJUSTMENT

Loosen the locknut on the adjusting bolt. Turn the adjusting bolt until the clearance between the pedal pad and the floormat is 7.28 in. (7.50—RX-7, 7.48—'77–'80 GLC, 9.05—'81–'83 GLC, 7.60—626). Carefully tighten the locknut.

PEDAL FREE-PLAY ADJUSTMENT

1976 and Later RX-3, RX-4, Cosmo, 1976 and Later 808

The free-play of the clutch pedal before the pushrod contacts the piston in the master cylinder should be 0.02–0.12 in.

7. Dust boot
8. Reamer bolt
9. Release bearing
10. Spring
11. Clutch housing

Clutch components (© Toyo Kogyo Co. Ltd.)

1. Master cylinder
2. Rod
3. Locknut
4. Adjusting bolt
5. Locknut
6. Clutch pedal

Clutch pedal height adjustment (© Toyo Kogyo Co. Ltd.)

1.5~2.25mm (0.06~0.09in)

GLC clutch cable adjustment (© Toyo Kogyo Co. Ltd.)

Release fork free-play is measured at arrows (© Toyo Kogyo Co. Ltd.)

To adjust the free-play, loosen the locknut and turn the pushrod until the proper adjustment is obtained. Tighten the locknut after the adjustment is complete.

GLC

Loosen the locknut and pull the outer cable away from the engine side of the firewall. Turn the adjusting nut on the cable to obtain a 0.060 to 0.090 inch clearance between the adjusting nut and the firewall. Tighten the locknut. Adjust the 1981 and later GLC cable to obtain free play of 0.43–0.67 in.

1979 and Later RX-7 and 626

Loosen the locknut on the clutch master cylinder pushrod. Turn the pushrod to ob-tain 0.02–0.12 in. free play between the pedal and the pushrod. Tighten the locknut on the pushrod.

Clutch Master Cylinder

REMOVAL AND INSTALLATION

Unfasten the hydraulic line from the master cylinder outlet. Remove the master cylinder.

Installation is the reverse of removal. Bleed the hydraulic system.

Clutch Release Cylinder

REMOVAL AND INSTALLATION

1. Unscrew the hydraulic line.
2. Unhook the release fork return spring from the cylinder.
3. Remove the release cylinder.

Installation is the reverse of removal. Bleed the hydraulic system. Adjust the release fork free-play.

Bleeding the Clutch Hydraulic System

1. Remove the rubber cap from the bleeder screw on the release cylinder.
2. Place a bleeder tube over the end of the bleeder screw.
3. Submerge the other end of the tube in a jar half-filled with hydraulic (brake) fluid.
4. Depress the clutch pedal fully and allow it to return slowly.
5. Keep repeating Step 4, while watching the hydraulic fluid in the jar. As soon as the air bubbles disappear, close the bleeder screw.

NOTE: During the bleeding procedure the reservoir must be kept at least ¾ full.

AUTOMATIC TRANSMISSION

REMOVAL AND INSTALLATION

RX-3 and RX3-SP

The automatic transmission is filled with Type F fluid.

1. Remove the heat shroud. Remove the exhaust pipe bracket from the torque converter housing.
2. Detach the exhaust pipe.

— CAUTION —
The exhaust system on rotary engine-equipped Mazda's gets considerably hotter than a conventional system; be sure to allow enough time for it to cool.

3. Remove the driveshaft.
4. Detach the speedometer cable.
5. Remove the control rod.
6. Unfasten the vacuum lines from the vacuum modulator.
7. Unfasten the multiconnector from the downshift solenoid and the neutral safety switch.
8. Disconnect the oil cooler lines.
9. Remove the starter.
10. Matchmark the torque converter and the flex-plate.
11. Working through the starter motor mounting hole, remove the four bolts which secure the torque converter to the flex-plate.

Loosening the torque converter bolts

12. Support the transmission.
13. Remove the crossmember.
14. Remove the bolts which secure the torque converter housing to the top of the engine.
15. Raise the transmission so that it is level.
16. Use a screwdriver to carefully apply pressure between the torque converter and the flex-plate.
17. Slide the transmission rearward and lower it from the car.

— CAUTION —
Do not rest the weight of the transmission on the torque converter splines.

18. Automatic transmission installation is the reverse of removal. There are several points which should be noted, however:
19. Before installing the transmission, use a dial indicator to measure flex-plate runout. If runout exceeds 0.020 in., the flex-plate must be replaced.
20. Hand-tighten the four torque converter installation bolts and then lock the flex-plate with a brake. Next, tighten the four bolts evenly, and in several stages, to 29–36 ft. lbs.

Check the fluid level again and road test the car.

RX-4, RX-7 and Cosmo

The transmission is filled with Type F fluid.

1. Remove the converter access hole cover. Lock the flex-plate by holding the drive pulley lockbolt with a wrench.

2. Matchmark the converter and flex-plate. Unfasten the four converter-to-flex-plate securing bolts.

3. Remove the exhaust pipe.

4. Remove the driveshaft.

5. Remove speedometer cable.

6. Remove all vacuum lines and electrical leads from the transmission.

7. Remove the starter.

8. Remove the bottom cover from the converter housing.

9. Support the transmission and remove the crossmember.

10. Disconnect the oil cooler.

11. Unbolt the converter housing, raise the transmission to a level place and separate it from the flex-plate.

12. Automatic transmission installation is the reverse of removal. There are several points which should be noted, however.

Before installing the transmission, use a dial indicator to measure flex-plate runout. Runout should be around 0.012 in. If runout exceeds 0.020 in., the flex-plate must be replaced.

Tighten the converter to drive plate attaching bolts to 25–36 ft. lbs.

After completing transmission installation, rotate the eccentric shaft to be sure that there is no interference in the transmission.

808, 1977–80 GLC and 626

Use only Type F transmission fluid.

1. Drain the transmission.

2. Remove the heat insulator.

3. Disconnect the exhaust pipe.

4. Disconnect the driveshaft at the rear axle flange.

5. Remove the driveshaft.

6. Disconnect the speedometer cable.

7. Disconnect the shift rod.

8. Remove all vacuum hoses.

9. Disconnect all wiring.

10. Disconnect the oil cooler lines.

11. Remove the access cover from the lower end of the converter housing.

12. Matchmark the drive plate and torque converter for realignment and remove the converter bolts.

13. Support the transmission with a jack and remove the crossmember.

14. Remove the converter housing-to-engine bolts.

15. Remove the filler tube.

16. Separate the flex-plate and the converter.

17. Remove the transmission and converter as an assembly.

18. To install the transmission, reverse the removal procedure.

Transmission linkage adjustment (© Toyo Kogyo Co. Ltd.)

SHIFT LINKAGE ADJUSTMENT

1976 and Later All Models Except RX-7

1. Place the transmission selector lever in Neutral.

2. Disconnect the clevis from the lower end of the selector arm.

3. Move the manual lever to the N position.

NOTE: The N position is the third detent from the back.

4. Loosen the two clevis retaining nuts and adjust the clevis so that it freely enters the lever hole.

5. Tighten the retaining nuts.

6. Connect the clevis to the lever and secure with the spring washer, flat washer and retaining clip.

NEUTRAL SAFETY SWITCH ADJUSTMENT

RX3-SP, RX-3 and RX-7

1. Check the shift linkage.

2. Remove the nut from the gear selector lever and the neutral safety switch attaching bolts.

3. Unfasten the screw underneath the switch body.

4. Place the selector shaft in Neutral by using the gear selector lever.

Align the neutral safety switch by inserting a drill through the holes on it. (© Toyo Kogyo Co. Ltd.)

Adjusting the neutral safety switch—RX-4 and Cosmo (© Toyo Kogyo Co. Ltd.)

NOTE: If the linkage is adjusted properly, the slot in the selector shaft should be vertical.

5. Move the switch body so that the screw hole in the case aligns with the hole in the internal rotor.

6. Check the alignment by inserting an 0.009 in. diameter pin or a No. 53 drill through the holes.

7. Once the proper alignment is obtained, tighten the switch mounting bolts.

8. If it still is not operating properly, i.e., the car starts in position other than P (Park) or N (Neutral) or the back-up lights come on in gears other than R (Reverse), replace the switch.

RX-4, Cosmo and 808

1. Remove the housing from the shift lever.

2. Adjust the shift lever so that there is 0–0.012 in. clearance between the pin and the guide plate, when the lever is in Neutral.

3. Adjust the neutral safety switch so that the pin hole in the switch body is aligned with the pin hole of the sliding plate when the shift lever is in Neutral.

4. Check the adjustment by trying to start the engine in all gears. It should only start in Park or Neutral.

5. Reinstall the housing on the shift lever.

1977–80 GLC

1. Place the manual lever in N. N is the third detent from the back.

2. Remove the manual lever.

3. Loosen the neutral switch attaching bolts and remove the screw from the alignment hole at the bottom of the switch.

4. Rotate the switch so that the hole in the switch aligns with the hole in the internal rotor. The 0.078 in. diameter pin should be inserted while tightening switch.

5. Install the alignment hole screw and manual lever.

626

1. Place the transmission selector lever in the neutral position.

2. Loosen the neutral switch attaching screws.

3. Position the manual shift lever shaft in the neutral position by adjusting the range select lever. The proper neutral position is where the slot of the manual shaft is positioned vertically and the detent positions in the shaft correctly with a click sound.

4. Move the neutral switch so that the identification marks on the switch body and the sliding plate are aligned.

5. Tighten the neutral switch adjusting screws.

6. Check the adjustment by trying to start the engine in all gears. It should only start in Park and Neutral.

KICKDOWN SWITCH AND DOWNSHIFT SOLENOID ADJUSTMENT

All Except 626

1. Check the accelerator linkage for smooth operation.

2. Turn the ignition on but do not start the engine.

3. Depress the accelerator pedal fully to the floor. As the pedal nears the end of its travel, a light "click" should be heard from the downshift solenoid.

Kickdown switch the downshift solenoid circuit (© Toyo Kogyo Co. Ltd.)

4. If the kickdown switch operates too soon, loosen the locknut on the switch shaft. Adjust the shaft so that the accelerator linkage makes contact with it when the pedal is depressed 7/8-15/16 of the way to the floor. Tighten the locknut.

5. If no noise comes from the solenoid at all, then check the wiring for the solenoid and the switch.

6. If the wiring is in good condition, remove the wire from the solenoid and connect it to a 12V power source. If the solenoid does not click when connected, it is defective and should be replaced.

NOTE: When the solenoid is removed, about two pints of transmission fluid will leak out.

626

1. Disconnect the wiring connectors from the kickdown switch.

2. Screw out the kick-down switch a few turns.

3. Fully depress the accelerator pedal.

4. Gradually screw in the kick-down switch until you hear a clicking sound then screw it in ½ turn more.

5. Tighten the locknut and connect the wiring connectors.

BAND ADJUSTMENT

JATCO Model 3N71B

1. Raise the vehicle and support safely.

2. Drain the transmission fluid and remove the transmission pan.

3. Loosen the locknut and torque the servo adjusting bolt to 9–11 ft. lbs.

4. Back off the servo bolt two full turns and tighten the locknut.

5. Install the pan assembly and fill with fluid.

JATCO Model R3A

1. Raise the vehicle and support safely.

2. Locate the servo cover and remove from the right side of the transmission case.

3. Loosen locknut and tighten the servo adjusting bolt to 9–11 ft. lbs. torque.

4. Loosen the servo bolt two full turns and tighten the locknut.

5. Install the servo cover and lower vehicle.

AUTOMATIC TRANSAXLE

REMOVAL AND INSTALLATION

1. Raise the vehicle on a hoist and support it safely. Disconnect the negative battery cable.

NOTE: When removing or installing the transaxle assembly the rear end of the power plant (engine) must be lifted with the aid of a chain.

2. Disconnect all electrical wiring and connections, control linkages from the transaxle. Mark these units to aid in reassembling.

3. Remove the front wheels. Disconnect the lower ball joints from the steering knuckles. Pull the driveshafts from the differential gears.

NOTE: A circlip is positioned on the driveshaft ends and engages in a groove, machined in the differential side gears. The driveshafts may have to be forced from the differential housing to release the clip from the groove.

— **CAUTION** —

Do not allow the driveshafts to drop. Damage may occur to the ball and socket joints and to the rubber boots. Wire the shafts to the vehicle body when released from the differential.

---

4. Support the engine with a jack. Remove the mounting bolts retaining the transaxle in place. Remove the unit from the vehicle.

5. Installation is the reverse of removal.

— **CAUTION** —

Be sure the rubber mounts are not twisted or distorted and not in contact with the body.

---

6. To properly install the driveshafts in the differential side gears, position the open end of the circlip in the up position, and with the driveshaft in a horizontal position, push the driveshafts into the side gears. To be sure the circlip engages the groove, a sound may be heard or attempt to pull the driveshaft from the differential. Reconnect the ball joints at the lower arms.

SHIFT LEVER ADJUSTMENT

The shift lever adjustment should be performed by the forward and backward of the shift lever with the shift lever setting at the "P" range.

VACUUM DIAPHRAGM SWITCH

Intake manifold vacuum controls the vacuum line pressure and the diaphragm varies the position of the throttle valve through the interconnecting rod. No adjustment can be made to the vacuum modulator, the unit must be replaced if it is found to be defective.

DOWNSHIFT SOLENOID

When the accelerator pedal is fully depressed, the kickdown switch becomes active and the downshift solenoid gets power. The downshift valve in the control valve is pushed up to kickdown position 3-to-2 and position 2-to-1 at a given speed.

NEUTRAL SAFETY/ REVERSE LAMP SWITCH

The switch contacts should operate when the switch plunger is moved into its respective operating positions. The switch operates from closed (starter solenoid on) to the neutral (or "off") position and then to the reverse light ("on" position). The switch plunger must operate smoothly otherwise the gear selector will be affected.

DRIVELINE

Driveshaft and U-Joints

REMOVAL AND INSTALLATION

1977–80 GLC, RX-3, RX-3SP, RX-7 and 808 Models

Do not remove the oil seals from models with center bearing, unless they are defective.

1. Matchmark the flanges on the driveshaft and pinion so that they may be installed in their original position.
2. Lower the back end of the driveshaft and slide the front end out of the transmission.
3. Plug up the hole in the transmission to prevent it from leaking.
4. Driveshaft installation is the reverse of removal.

1. Roller bearing (cup)   4. Yoke
2. Spider   5. Driveshaft
3. Oil seal   6. Snap-ring

Components of the U-joint

RX-4, 626 and Cosmo Models

Perform this operation only when the exhaust system is *cold*.

1. Remove the front heat insulator.
2. Remove the nuts which secure the downpipe to the thermal reactor flange.

1. Rear axle shaft   4. Shim   7. Bearing collar
2. Bearing retainer   5. Spacer   8. Oil seal
3. Gasket   6. Bearing

Components of the axle shaft assembly (© Toyo Kogyo Co. Ltd.)

3. Remove the downpipe from the main muffler flange.
4. Matchmark the pinion and driveshaft flange bolts.
5. Unfasten the center bearing.
6. Remove the driveshaft.
7. Driveshaft installation is the reverse of removal. Tighten the yoke-to-front driveshaft locknut to 116–130 ft. lbs.

REAR AXLE

Axle Shafts

REMOVAL, INSTALLATION AND ADJUSTMENT

Rear Wheel Drive Only

1. Remove the wheel.
2. Remove the brake shoes.
3. Remove the brake backing plate and the bearing retainer.
4. Withdraw the axle shaft with a puller.
5. Apply grease to the oil seal lips and then insert the oil seal into the axle housing.
6. Check the axle shaft end-play.
   a. Temporarily install the brake backing plate on the axle shaft.

1. Yoke
2. Spider and bearing cup assembly
3. Snap ring
4. Shaft
5. Yoke

Components of the RX-3 driveshaft (© Toyo Kogyo Co. Ltd.)

b. Measure the depth of the bearing seat and then measure the width of the bearing outer race.
c. The difference between the two measurements is equal to the overall thickness of the adjusting shims required. Shims are available in thicknesses of 0.004 and 0.016 in.

NOTE: The maximum permissible end-play is 0.004 in.

7. Remove the backing plate, apply sealer to the rear axle surfaces and install the backing plate.
8. Install the rear axle shaft, bearing retainer, gasket, and shims. Coat the shims with sealer.
9. Install the brake shoes.

Axle Shaft Bearing and Seal

REPLACEMENT

Rear Wheel Drive Only

1. Install the retainer and spacer on the shaft.
Position the bearing on the shaft with the sealed side toward the shaft flange. Press it on until the spacer comes in contact with the shoulder of the shaft.
Press the bearing retaining collar onto the shaft until it contacts the bearing inner race.

NOTE: If the bearing retaining collar can be press fitted with a force less than 2.5 tons, replace the collar.

2. Remove the rear axle shaft.
3. Press the axle shaft out of the collar and bearing.

NOTE: If the pressure needed to press out the shaft exceeds 10 tons, grind off part of the bearing retaining collar and cut it with a cold chisel.

4. Remove the bearing retainer.

Differential

REMOVAL AND INSTALLATION

Rear Wheel Drive Only

1. Drain the lubricant.

2. Remove the driveshaft.

3. Remove both of the axle shafts.

4. Remove the differential carrier.

5. Installation is the reverse of removal.

DRIVEAXLES

Front Wheel Drive Only

INSPECTION

1. Loosen the front wheel lugs, raise the car and safely support it on jackstands. Remove the wheels and tires.

2. Check the driveaxle inner and outer boots for cracks or damage, for leaking grease or loose bands. Replace or repair if necessary.

3. Turn the driveaxle by hand, if the splines or joints are excessively loose, replace or repair as necessary.

4. Examine the driveaxle for cracks or twist. Replace if necessary.

REMOVAL AND INSTALLATION

1. See Step 1 of Inspection. Drain the transaxle fluid after removing the splash shields.

2. Loosen the driveaxle locknut at the center of the disc brake hub after raising the lock tab. Apply brake pressure while loosening.

3. Remove the lower ball joint from the steering knuckle.

4. Remove the driveaxle from the transaxle case by pulling the brake caliper outward with increasing force. While applying outward force, hit the driveaxle shaft with a brass hammer, if necessary, to help in removal.

5. Remove the locknut and pull the driveaxle from the steering knuckle. Remove the driveaxle and plug the transaxle case with a clean rag to prevent dirt from entering.

6. Installation is in the reverse order of removal. Before installing the driveaxle into the transaxle case, check the oil seals for cuts or damage. Replace the oil seals if necessary. Insert the axle into the transaxle case by pushing on the wheel hub assembly. Always install a new clip on the driveaxle.

JOINT OVERHAUL

NOTE: The joint on the wheel side of the driveaxle is non-rebuildable. If worn, the joint and axle must be replaced. The boot may be changed if necessary. Do

not interfere with the balancer found on the right axle unless necessary for wheel/joint boot replacement. If balancer is removed it must be reinstalled in the same position 14.45 ins. from the front of the wheel joint.

1. Remove the boot band by raising the locking clip and band with a pair of pliers.

2. Remove the lock clip from the inner edge of the ball joint casting. Remove the casting.

3. Remove the snap-ring from the end of the splines and remove the cage and bearings.

4. Carefully pry the balls from the bearing cage. After the balls are removed turn the cage slightly and remove it from the inner ring.

5. Wash all of the parts in a safe solvent and inspect for wear.

6. A joint kit for the transaxle end and boot kits for both ends are available. The kits are installed in the reverse order of disassembly. Always use the grease supplied with the kits. Tape the spline ends of the shaft when installing the rubber boots.

REAR SUSPENSION

Springs

REMOVAL AND INSTALLATION

RX-3, RX-4 and 808 Models

1. Remove the wheel.

2. Support the rear axle housing.

3. On RX-4 and 808 models, disconnect the lower part of the shock from the spring clamp. On all models, remove the U-bolt seat, rubber pad, plate, and the U-bolt itself.

4. Unfasten the two bolts and the nut that secure the spring pin to the front end of the rear spring.

5. Pry the spring pin out with a large, flat prybar inserted between the spring pin and its body bracket.

1. Bushing
2. Bushing
3. Bound stopper
4. U-bolt seat
5. U-bolt
6. Plate
7. Rubber pad
8. Rear spring
9. Bushing

10. Shackle hanger
11. Bushing
12. Shackle plate
13. Bushing
14. Bushing
15. Spring pin
16. Rubber pad
17. Bushing
18. Bushing
19. Spring clamp
20. Damper stopper
21. Shackle
22. Washer
23. Holder
24. Damper stopper casing
25. Rear shock absorber

RX-3 sedan and coupe rear suspension—wagon and RX-4 similar (© Toyo Kogyo Co. Ltd.)

6. Unfasten the nuts and the bolts which attach the rear shackle to the body.

7. Withdraw the rear spring assembly, complete with its shackle.

8. Remove the shackle assembly from the end of the spring.

9. Pull the rubber bushings out from both ends of the spring.

10. Rear spring installation is the reverse of removal. When installing the rubber bushings, do not lubricate them.

Cosmo

1. Remove the rear wheels.
2. Support the lower arms with a jack.
3. Remove the pivot bolt and nut which secures the rear end of the lower arm to the axle housing.
4. Lower the jack to relieve the spring pressure on the lower arm and remove the spring.
5. If replacing one spring only, a suitable adjusting plate will be necessary to give equal road clearance on each side.
6. Install spring in reverse order of removal, but do not tighten bolts while car is on stands.

1977–80 GLC

1. Raise the rear end of the vehicle and place jack stands under the frame side rails.
2. Remove the rear wheel.
3. Remove the upper and lower shock absorber bolts and nuts and remove the shock absorber.
4. Place a jack under the lower arm to support it.
5. Remove the pivot bolt and nut that secures the rear end of the lower arm to the axle housing.
6. Slowly lower the jack to relieve the spring pressure on the lower arm, then remove the spring.
7. Install the spring in the reverse order of removal.

RX-7

1. Raise the rear of the vehicle and support it safely.
2. Remove the rear wheel.
3. Disconnect the shock absorber lower end and the lower link bolt (just to the front of the lower shock bolt). Remove the rear bolt from the upper link.

NOTE: These trailing control arm links run parallel from the front to rear on the vehicle, with the smaller watt links running side to side on the vehicle.

4. Disconnect the front ends of the stabilizer bar (if equipped).
5. Remove the right and left watt links at the rear axle housing.
6. Carefully lower the rear axle housing and remove the coil spring and the rubber seat.
7. The installation is the reverse of the removal.

Arrow shows the location of the upper rear shock nut on RX-3 coupes and sedans

Shock Absorbers

REMOVAL AND INSTALLATION

RX-3, RX-4, 808, RX-3 SP, RX-7 Coupes and Sedans and Cosmo

On 808 models, tighten the upper nuts until ¼ in. exists between the top of the shock absorber rod and the top of the top nut.

Remove the trim panel from the rear of the luggage compartment. On RX-4 models it will be necessary to remove the rear seat first.

1. Unfasten the nuts, then remove the washers and rubber bushings from the upper shock absorber mounts.
2. Unfasten the nut and bolt which secure the end of the rear shock to the axle housing.
3. Remove the shock.
4. Installation is the reverse of removal.

Removing the rear shock upper mounting bracket on RX-3 wagons

RX-3, RX-4, 808 Wagons

On 808 models tighten the upper nuts until ¼ in. exists between the bottom of the shock absorber rod and the bottom of the nut.

1. Remove the locknuts, washers, and rubber bushings from the bottom shock absorber mount.
2. Compress the shock. Unfasten the bolts which secure the upper shock absorber mount.
3. Withdraw the shock.
4. Shock absorber installation is the reverse of removal.

1. Crossmember
2. Rear stabilizer bar
3. Lateral link
4. Mounting block
5. Spring upper seat
6. Rubber seat
7. Dust cover
8. Coil spring
9. Shock absorber
10. Rear hub spindle
11. Trailing link

Rear suspension assembly—GLC front wheel drive (© Toyo Kogyo Co. Ltd.)

1977–80 GLC

1. Raise the rear end of the vehicle and place jack stands under the frame side rails.

2. Remove the rear wheel.

3. Remove the upper and lower shock absorber bolts and nuts and remove the shock absorber.

4. Install the shock absorber in the reverse order of removal.

NOTE: The 1981 and later GLC shock absorber is part of the strut assembly.

Strut Assembly

REMOVAL AND INSTALLATION

GLC—Front Wheel Drive

1. Remove the side trim panels from inside the "trunk." Loosen and remove the top mounting nuts from the shock absorber assembly.

2. Loosen the rear wheel lugs, raise the car and safely support it on jackstands.

3. Remove the rear wheels. Disconnect the flexible brake hose from the strut.

4. Disconnect the trailing arm from the lower side of the strut: Separate the lateral link and strut by removing the bolt assembly.

5. Remove the strut from the lower unit by removing the two through nuts and bolts.

6. Remove the strut and brake assembly.

Clamp the strut assembly in a vise and loosen the nut at the top of the shock absorber.

— **CAUTION** —
Do not remove the nut at this time.

OVERHAUL

For all strut overhaul procedures, please refer to "Strut Overhaul" in the Unit Repair section.

FRONT SUSPENSION

MacPherson Struts

REMOVAL AND INSTALLATION

1. Remove the wheel cover and loosen the lug nuts.

2. Raise the front of the vehicle and support it with jackstands. Do not jack it or support it by any of the front suspension members. Remove the wheel.

1. Front side bushing
2. Spindle
3. Lower arm
4. Ball joint
5. Mounting block
6. Spring upper seat
7. Rubber seat
8. Dust cover
9. Coil spring
10. Shock absorber
11. Knuckle

Front suspension assembly—GLC front wheel drive (© Toyo Kogyo Co. Ltd.)

— **CAUTION** —
Be sure that the car is securely supported. Remember, you will be working underneath it.

3. Remove the brake caliper and disc on all models except the GLC with front wheel drive.

4. Unfasten the nuts which secure the upper shock mount to the top of the wheel arch.

5. Unfasten the two bolts that secure the lower end of the shock to the steering knuckle arm.

6. Remove the shock and coil spring as a complete assembly.

7. Installation is in the reverse order.

OVERHAUL

For all spring removal and installation procedures and any other strut overhaul procedures, please refer to "Strut Overhaul" in the Unit Repair section.

Control Arm

REMOVAL AND INSTALLATION

All Except GLC (Front Wheel Drive)

Remove the control arm and steering knuckle as an assembly.

1. Remove the wheel.

2. Remove the cotter pin and nut, which secure the tie rod end, from the knuckle arm; then use a puller to separate them.

3. Unbolt the lower end of the shock absorber.

4. Remove the nut, then withdraw the

1. Cap
2. Rubber mounting
3. Bearing
4. Seal
5. Spring seat (upper)
6. Rubber seat (upper)
7. Adjusting plate
8. Dust seal ring
9. Boot
10. Rubber seat (lower)
11. Coil springs
12. Front shock absorber assembly
13. Knuckle arm
14. Rubber bushing
15. Dust seal
16. Setring
17. Ball joint
18. Plug
19. Arm

GLC (Front Wheel Drive)

1. Loosen the wheel lugs, raise the car and safely support it on jackstands. Remove the front wheel.

2. Remove the thru–bolt connecting the lower arm to the steering knuckle.

3. Remove the bolts and nuts mounting the control arm to the body (two inner and three outer).

4. Remove the lower control arm. The ball joint can be serviced at this time if necessary.

5. Installation is in the reverse order of removal.

Mounting Torque;

Ball Joint-to-Steering Knuckle: 32–40 ft. lbs.

Outer Bolts: 43–54 ft. lbs.

Inner Bolts: 69–86 ft. lbs.

Front Hub and Steering Knuckle

REMOVAL AND INSTALLATION

GLC—Front Wheel Drive

1. Loosen the lug nuts, raise the front of the car and safely support it on jackstands. Remove the tire and wheel.

2. Raise the staked tab from the hub center nut, remove the nut from the axle. Apply the brake to help hold the rotor while loosening the nut.

3. Remove the tie-rod end from the steering knuckle. Disconnect the horseshoe clip that retains the brake line to the strut.

4. Remove the mounting bolts that hold the caliper assembly to the knuckle. Wire

Typical MacPherson strut front suspension—except GLC (© Toyo Kogyo Co. Ltd.)

Removing the control arm except GLC front wheel drive (© Toyo Kogyo Co. Ltd.)

rubber bushing and washer which secure the stabilizer bar to the control arm.

5. Unfasten the nut and bolt which secure the control arm to the frame member.

6. Push outward on the strut assembly while removing the end of the control arm from the frame member.

7. Remove the control arm and steering knuckle arm as an assembly.

8. Separate the knuckle arm from the control arm with a puller.

9. Installation of the control arm is the reverse of removal.

1. Wheel hub
2. Disc plate
3. Spacer
4. Bearing inner race
5. Oil seal, outer
6. Oil seal, inner
7. Bearing inner race
8. Bearing outer race
9. Dust cover

Front hub and knuckle assembly—GLC front wheel drive (© Toyo Kogyo Co. Ltd.)

the caliper out of the way, do not allow the caliper to be supported by the brake hose.

5. Remove the thru–bolt and nut that retains the lower ball joint to the steering knuckle and disconnect the ball joint.

6. Remove the two bolts and nuts retaining the strut to the steering knuckle. Separate the steering knuckle and hub from the strut and drive axle.

7. The hub is pressed through the wheel bearings into the knuckle. Replacement of the wheel bearings or hub removal requires a special puller and access to a bench press, your dealer or local automotive machine shop can handle the job for you.

8. Remove the inner oil seal and bearing. Remove the wheel hub from the knuckle with a wheel hub puller (Mazda tool 49 F001 726). Remove the outer bearing using a press and Mazda tools 49 F401 368 and 49 F401 365. Drive the outer and inner race from the knuckle with a brass drift and hammer.

9. Install new inner and outer races. Pack the inner and outer bearing and install in knuckle. Use Mazda tool 49 B001 727 to tighten the tool nut and measure the preload with a scale connected to the caliper mounting hole on the knuckle. Various spacers are available to increase or decrease the preload. Preload should be 1.7–6.9 ft. lbs.

10. Install the inner and outer grease seals. Press fit the hub through the bearings into the knuckle.

11. Installation of the knuckle and hub is in the reverse order of removal. Always use a new axle locknut and tighten it to 116–174 ft. lbs. Stake the locknut after tightening. Knuckle to strut mounting; 58–86 ft. lbs. Knuckle to ball joint; 33–40 ft. lbs. Knuckle to tie rod end; 22–33 ft. lbs.

Ball Joints

INSPECTION

All Exc. GLC

1. Perform Steps 1–5 of the control arm removal procedure.

Checking the ball stud rotational torque with a spring scale (© Toyo Kogyo Co. Ltd.)

GLC rear wheel drive—strut and lower control arm (© Toyo Kogyo Co. Ltd.)

① 3.0~4.5m-kg (22~33ft-lb) Use a new pin
② Disconnect Use puller
⑫ 4.0~5.5m-kg (29~40ft-lb)
Use a new pin
7.8~9.8m-kg (56~71ft-lb)
⑩ Disengage
④ Disengage
③ 6.4~9.5m-kg (46~69ft-lb)

1. Castle nut and cotter pin
2. Tie-rod end
3. Strut to lower arm bolts
4. Strut and wheel spindle
5. Cap nut
6. Cotter pin
7. Castle nut
8. Washer
9. Bushing
10. Anti-roll bar and bushing
11. Nut and washer
12. Suspension arm bolt
13. Suspension arm

2. Check the ball joint dust boot.

3. Check the amount of pressure required to turn the ball stud, by hooking a pull scale into the tie rod hole in the knuckle arm. Pull the spring scale until the arm just begins to turn; this should require 13–24 ft. lbs.—RX-3, 27–40 ft. lbs.—1977 and earlier RX-4 and Cosmo, 17.6–30 ft. lbs.—808, or 4.4–8.8 ft. lbs.—1978–79 Cosmo and RX-4 or 4.6–9.2 ft. lbs.—RX-3SP.

If the reading is lower than 14 oz. on the RX-7, replace the ball joint and the suspension arm as a unit.

GLC (1977 and Later)

1. Check the dust boot for wear.

2. Raise the wheels off the ground and grip the tire at the top and bottom and alternately push and pull to check ball joint end-play. Wear limit is .04 in. If necessary, replace the ball joint and control arm assembly.

REMOVAL AND INSTALLATION

All Exc. GLC

Remove the control arm.

1. Remove the set-ring and the dust boot.

2. Press the ball joint out of the control arm.

3. Clean the ball joint mounting bore and coat it with kerosene.

4. Press the ball joint into the control arm.

NOTE: If the pressure required to press the new ball joint into place is less than 3,300 lbs., the bore is worn and the control arm must be replaced.

GLC (1977 and Later)

The ball joint and control arm assembly is replaced as a unit on models through 1980. On 1981 and later models it may be removed during lower control arm removal. See Control Arm removal and installation. Torque the ball joint nut to 43–51 ft. lbs.—(1977–80), check the revolving torque of the ball joint on 1981 and later models (63–109 ft. lbs).

Front End Alignment

CASTER AND CAMBER

Caster and camber are preset by the manufacturer. They require adjustment only if the suspension and steering linkage components are damaged. In this case, adjustment is accomplished by replacing the damaged part, except for the RX-4, Cosmo and GLC (FWD).

On these models, the caster and camber may be changed by rotating the shock absorber support. If they can't be brought to within specifications, replace or repair suspension parts as necessary.

Caster and camber adjustment—RX-4 (© Toyo Kogyo Co. Ltd.)

TOE-IN ADJUSTMENT

To adjust the toe-in, loosen the tie rod locknuts and turn both tie rods an equal amount, until the proper specification is obtained.

STEERING

Steering Wheel

REMOVAL AND INSTALLATION

1. Remove the crash pad/horn button assembly. On four-spoke steering wheels, pull the center cap toward the wheel top.
2. Punch matchmarks on the steering wheel and steering shaft.
3. Remove the wheel.
4. Installation is the reverse of removal.

Combination (Turn Signal) Switch

REPLACEMENT

808, RX-3, RX-3SP and RX-7

1. Remove the steering wheel.
2. Remove the left-hand column shroud.
3. Remove the retaining ring (screw on 808) from the combination (turn signal) switch.
4. Withdraw the switch over the steering column.
5. Installation is the reverse of removal.

RX-4, Cosmo and 626

1. Remove the steering wheel.
2. Loosen the nut which secures the

vent knob (left side) and allow the knob assembly to drop away from its mounting bracket.
3. Remove choke knob. Remove the choke retaining nut and separate the choke from the panel.
4. Remove the upper column cover.
5. Disconnect the panel light dimmer switch wiring.
6. Disconnect the exhaust temperature warning light wiring.
7. Loosen, but don't remove the screws at either end of the lower panel cover.

NOTE: The left-hand screw is located in the hole which was covered by the upper column cover and the right-hand screw is above the ashtray opening (ashtray removed).

8. Pull the upper column cover away from the instrument panel.
9. Disconnect the combination switch connector.
10. Remove the retaining ring from the steering column.
11. Unfasten the combination switch retaining screw and remove the switch.
12. Installation is the reverse of removal.

Cut slots in the switch securing bolts and remove them with a screwdriver (© Toyo Kogyo Co. Ltd.)

GLC

1. Disconnect the negative battery cable.
2. Remove the horn cap and steering wheel.
3. Remove the steering column covers.
4. Disconnect the wire connectors.
5. Remove the stop ring from the shaft.
6. Remove the attaching screw and remove the combination switch.
7. To install reverse the removal procedure.

Ignition Lock/Switch Assembly

REMOVAL AND INSTALLATION

RX-3, RX-3SP, RX-7 and 808

NOTE: For 808 models, follow procedure for removing combination switch, then skip to Step 5.

1. Remove the light switch knob.
2. Remove the left and right steering column shrouds.
3. Disconnect the multiconnector from the switch assembly.
4. Use a file or a hacksaw to make slots in the switch securing bolts. Remove the bolts with a screwdriver.
5. Withdraw the switch assembly.
6. To install the switch, reverse the removal procedure. After tightening the switch securing bolts, break their heads off, in order to make the switch difficult for a thief to remove.

RX-4, GLC, Cosmo and 626

1. Follow steps under "Combination Switch Replacement".
2. Remove the instrument frame brace.
3. Disconnect the switch wires.
4. Remove the switch.
5. Installation is the reverse of removal.

Steering Linkage

REMOVAL AND INSTALLATION

All Exc GLC (Front Wheel Drive)

The front wheels should point straight ahead. Align the marks on the pitman arm and the sector shaft to ensure proper steering linkage alignment.

1. Remove the cotter pins and the castellated nuts which secure the ends of the tie rods to the center link and the steering knuckle.
2. Remove the tie rods.
3. Remove the idler arm.
4. Remove the pitman arm. Remove the center link. On RX-4 models, remove steering damper first.

5. Unfasten the nut which secures the pitman arm to the sector shaft and use a puller to separate them.

6. Installation is the reverse of removal.

NOTE: See "Steering Gear and Linkage" for 1981 and later GLC with front wheel drive.

Idler Arm

REPLACEMENT

All exc. 1977–80 GLC

1. Remove the front wheels.
2. Disconnect the center link from the idler arm.
3. Unbolt the idler arm bracket from the frame.
4. Hold the assembly in a vise and remove the arm from the bracket by turning the arm counterclockwise.
5. Check all parts for wear and replace as necessary.
6. Insert the spring into the bracket and screw the idler arm into the bracket until the distance between the lip edge on the idler arm and the leading edge of the bracket is 0.157–0.236 in.
7. Check the revolving torque of the arm with a spring scale. If the torque is less than 0.2 lbs., screw in the arm until the correct reading is obtained. If the torque is greater than 6.6 lbs., unscrew the arm until the correct torque is obtained.
8. If the correct torque cannot be obtained, replace the spring.
9. Grease the assembly through a nipple replacing the plug in the end of the bracket.
10. Attach the idler arm and bracket assembly to the frame.
11. Connect the idler arm to the center link.

1. Castle nut and cotter pin
2. Tie-rod end
3. Castle nut and cotter pin
4. Tie-rod end
5. Castle nut and cotter pin
6. Steering arm
7. Castle nut and cotter pin
8. Idler arm
9. Center link

1977–80 GLC center link removal; other models similar (© Toyo Kogyo Co. Ltd.)

1977–80 GLC

1. Remove the front wheels.
2. Disconnect the center link from the idler arm by removing the nut and split pin and using a puller.
3. Unbolt the idler arm bracket from the frame.
4. Remove the split pin and nut from the idler arm at the frame bracket and remove the arm from the bracket.
5. To install reverse the removal procedure. Torque the bracket to frame bolt and nut to 32–40 ft. lbs. and the center link to idler arm nut to 18–25 ft. lbs.

Pitman Arm

REMOVAL AND INSTALLATION

1. Remove the wheels.
2. Disconnect the center link at the pitman arm.

1. Castle nut and cotter pin
2. Tie-rod end
3. Castle nut and cotter pin
4. Tie-rod end
5. Tie-rod

1977–80 GLC tie-rod removal; other models similar (© Toyo Kogyo Co. Ltd.)

3. Remove the pitman arm.
4. Install the pitman arm onto the sector shaft, aligning the identification marks. Tighten the nut to 94–123 ft. lbs. (1975–76), 108–130 ft. lbs. (1977–1979 exc GLC), 58–87 ft. lbs. (GLC).
5. Connect the center link to the pitman arm.

Tie Rod

REMOVAL AND INSTALLATION

1. Disconnect the tie rod from the center link and knuckle arm. A puller will be necessary.
2. Install the tie rod to the center link and knuckle arm. Tighten the nuts to 22–32 ft. lbs. and install new cotter pins.

Steering Gear

REMOVAL AND INSTALLATION

RX-3, RX-3SP and RX-7

1. Remove the steering wheel.
2. Remove the column covers.
3. Remove the combination switch assembly.
4. Remove the steering lock and ignition switch assembly.
5. Remove the steering column support bracket.
6. Raise and support the front end.
7. Remove the front wheel.
8. Remove the cotter pin and nut and disconnect the center link from the pitman arm using a ball joint puller.
9. Unbolt the steering gear from the frame, taking note of the presence of any shim for realigning the gear with the shaft.
10. Remove the steering column dust cover and remove the gear housing, column jacket and aligning shim.

11. Reverse the removal for installation. Place the shim in its original position for realignment. Gear housing-to-frame bolt torque is 32–40 ft. lbs.

RX-4, Cosmo and 626 Manual Steering

1. Remove the front wheel.
2. Remove the nut and cotter pin and disconnect the center link from the pitman arm with a ball joint puller.
3. Unbolt the flexible coupling from the worm shaft.
4. Unclip the speedometer cable from the gear housing and the power brake unit.
5. Unbolt and remove the gear housing.
6. Install in reverse of the above.

RX-4 and Cosmo Power Steering

1. Remove the oil filter cartridge.
2. Mark and disconnect the pressure and return lines from the gear. Plug the lines.
3. Raise and support the vehicle.
4. Disconnect the center link at the pitman arm.
5. Remove the gear housing-to-frame bolts.
6. Remove the clamp that holds the flexible coupling to the steering gear and slide the gear off the coupling.
7. Install in reverse of removal. Fill and bleed the system.

1976–81 808, 1977–80 GLC

1. Remove the steering wheel.
2. Remove the column covers.
3. Remove the combination switch assembly.
4. Remove the steering lock and ignition switch assembly.
5. Remove the steering column support bracket.
6. Raise and support the front end.
7. Disconnect the center link from the pitman arm using a ball joint puller.
8. Remove the steering gear retaining bolts and check for the existence of a shim. Note its position for realignment.
9. Remove the steering column dust cover.
10. Remove the gear housing, column jacket and aligning shim.
11. Installation is the reverse of removal.
12. Place shim in its original position.

Steering Gear and Linkage

REMOVAL AND INSTALLATION

GLC (Front Wheel Drive)

1. Raise the front of the vehicle and support it with safety stands.

Adjusting backlash

2. Remove the wheels.
3. Disconnect the tie-rod ends from the knuckles.
4. Remove the boot band and attaching bolts and remove the gear and linkage from the engine compartment through the tie-rod hole.
5. Installation is the reverse of removal. Make sure the steering wheel is straight forward and tighten to the following torques: Mounting bracket bolts: 23–34 ft. lbs.; tie rod end and knuckle bolts: 21–35 ft. lbs.; Intermediate shaft and pinion connecting bolt: 13–19.5 ft. lbs.

STEERING GEAR ADJUSTMENT

Worm Bearing Preload

1. Remove the gear.
2. Rotate the worm shaft with a torque wrench and check the torque. Rotating torque should be 7.8–13 in. lbs. for RX-3; 8–10 in. lbs. for RX-4; 0.44–1.1 in. lbs. for RX-7; 5–11 in. lbs. for Cosmo; 8–13 in. lbs. for 808; 5–7 in. lbs. for GLC. If not, adjust as follows:
3. Remove the end cover and shims.
4. If the preload was too light, remove shims; if too heavy, add shims.
5. Install the end cover.

Backlash

The sector shaft adjusting screw, located in the cover, raises or lowers the sector shaft to provide proper mesh with the sector gear and rack. Adjust as follows:
1. Turn the wormshaft gently and stop it at the center position.
2. Loosen the locknut and turn the adjusting screw in or out. The standard backlash is 0–0.0039 in.
3. Tighten the adjusting screw.

Power Steering Pump

REMOVAL AND INSTALLATION

1. Disconnect the fluid hoses from the pump.

2. Loosen the pump belt adjusting bolt, slide the pump to one side and remove the belt.
3. Support the pump, remove the mounting bolts and lift out the pump.
4. Installation is the reverse of removal. Adjust belt to give a ½ in. deflection at the mid-point of its longest stretch. Fill the reservoir and bleed the system.

BRAKE SYSTEM

For all brake system repair and service procedures not detailed below, please refer to "Brakes" in the Unit Repair section.

Adjustments

FRONT DISC BRAKES

Disc brakes are self-adjusting by design. As the brake pads and disc wear, fluid pressure compensates for the amount of wear. Because this action causes the fluid level to go down, the level should be checked periodically and replenished as necessary.

REAR DRUM BRAKE

All Exc. 1977–80 GLC

1. Release the parking brake completely.
2. Remove the adjusting hole plugs.
3. Engage the adjuster with a brake spoon. Turn the adjuster in the direction of the arrow stamped on the backing plate until the brake shoes are locked.
4. Pump the brake pedal several times to be sure that the brake shoe contacts the drum evenly.

NOTE: If the wheel turns after you remove your foot from the brake pedal, continue turning the adjuster until the wheel will no longer rotate.

5. Back off on the adjuster, about five notches (2–3 notches—RX-4). The wheel should rotate freely, without dragging.

FRONT

TURNING DIRECTION

↻ —Anchor pin (to expand brake shoe)

↻ —Lock nut (to tighten)

1977–80 GLC rear brake adjustment
(© Toyo Kogyo Co. Ltd.)

1. Return spring
2. Stop lamp switch
3. Locknut
4. Locknut
5. Brake pedal
6. Push rod
7. Power brake unit

Free travel:
5~15mm
(0.2~0.6")

Brake pedal component (© Toyo Kogyo Co. Ltd.)

NOTE: The RX-7 has rear disc brakes as an option. No adjustment is needed.

1977–80 GLC

1. Release the parking brake.
2. Loosen the locknut that secures the anchor pin.
3. Hold the locknut and turn the anchor pin counterclockwise until the wheel is locked. See illustration.
4. Then release the anchor pin until the wheel just turns freely.

5. Hold the anchor pin in position and tighten the locknut.
6. Repeat the above adjustment for each brake shoe.

NOTE: 1981 and later GLC has self-adjusting brakes.

BRAKE PEDAL

1. Detach the wiring from the brake light switch terminals.

2. Loosen the locknut on the switch.
3. Turn the switch until the distance between the pedal and the floor is 7.3 in.
4. Tighten the locknut on switch.
5. Loosen the locknut located on the push rod.
6. Rotate the pushrod, until a pedal free travel of 0.2–0.6 in. is obtained.
7. Tighten the pushrod locknut.

Master Cylinder

REMOVAL AND INSTALLATION

NOTE: On models which have a fluid reservoir located separately from the master cylinder, remove the lines which run between the two and plug the lines to prevent leakage.

Detach and plug the lines. Unbolt and remove the master cylinder.
Installation is the reverse of removal.

Brake Failure Warning Valve

CENTRALIZING

1. Turn the ignition switch to the ON position.
2. Make sure that the fluid level in the master cylinder is at the ¾ mark.
3. Depress the brake pedal and the piston will center itself causing the light to go off.
4. Turn the switch to OFF and check the fluid level. Check for a firm pedal.

Wheel Bearings— Front Discs

REMOVAL AND INSTALLATION

All Except GLC w/Front Wheel Drive

1. Remove the brake disc/hub.
2. Drive the seal out and remove the inner bearing.
3. Drive the outer bearing races out.
4. Installation is the reverse of removal. Repack the bearings and the hub cavity with lithium grease. Adjust the bearing.

ADJUSTMENT

NOTE: This operation is performed with the wheel, grease cap, nut lock, and cotter pin removed.

1. To seat the bearings, back off on the adjusting nut three turns and then rotate the

1. Cap assembly
2. Screw
3. Reservoir
4. Grommet
5. Front brake fitting
6. Rear brake fitting
7. Boot
8. Snap ring
9. Washer
10. Primary piston and cup
11. Primary spring
12. Secondary piston stop bolt and washer
13. Secondary piston and cup
14. Secondary spring

1977–80 GLC brake master cylinder; others similar (© Toyo Kogyo Co. Ltd.)

hub/disc assembly while tightening the adjusting nut.

2. Back off on the adjusting nut about ⅙ of a turn.

3. Hook a spring scale in one of the bolt holes on the hub.

4. Pull the spring scale squarely, until the hub just begins to rotate. The scale reading should be 0.9–2.2 lbs.—all passenger cars exc. GLC, 626 and RX-7. GLC: 0.33–1.32 lbs.; 626: 0.77–1.92 lbs.; RX-7: 0.99–1.43 lbs. Tighten the adjusting nut until the proper spring scale reading is obtained.

5. Place the castellated nut lock over the adjusting nut. Align one of the slots on the nut-lock with the hole in the spindle and fit the cotter pin into place.

GLC W/Front Wheel Drive

NOTE: On these models refer to the "Front Hub and Steering Knuckle" removal and installation procedure in the Front Suspension section.

Wheel Cylinder

REMOVAL AND INSTALLATION

1. Remove the wheel.
2. Remove the brake drum and brake shoes.
3. Disconnect and plug the brake line.
4. Remove the stud nuts and bolt attaching the wheel cylinder to the backing plate and remove the wheel cylinder.
5. Installation is the reverse of removal.

1. Boot
2. Piston
3. Cylinder body
4. Piston cup
5. Return spring
6. Steel ball
7. Bleeder screw
8. Bleeder screw cap
9. Hydraulic line seat
10. Push rod

Rear wheel cylinder components (© Toyo Kogyo Co. Ltd.)

Parking Brake

ADJUSTMENT

1. Adjust the rear brake shoes.
2. Adjust the front cable with the nut

1. Boot
2. Release rod
3. Spacer
4. Button
5. Cap
6. Parking brake lever
7. Plate
8. Return spring
9. Parking lamp switch
10. Sector
11. Parking lamp switch wire
12. Front cable
13. Adjusting nut
14. Clip
15. Clip
16. Rear cable
17. Cable clip

RX-3 parking brake components—RX-2 and RX-4 similar (© Toyo Kogyo Co. Ltd.)

located at the rear of the parking brake handle. The handle should require 3–7 notches for RX-3, RX-4, GLC (1977–80) and Cosmo models, 3–4 notches for 808, 6–8 notches for RX-7, 5–7 for the 626 and 5–9 for the GLC (1981–1983) to apply the parking brake.

3. Operate the parking brake several times; check to see that the rear wheels do not drag when it is fully released.

Parking Brake Shoes

REPLACEMENT

Cosmo Only

1. Remove the brake disc.
2. Remove the brake shoe return springs.
3. Remove the secondary brake shoe retaining spring and guide pin.
4. Remove the brake shoe.

5. Installation is the reverse of removal.

CHASSIS ELECTRICAL

Wiper Motor

REPLACEMENT

1. Remove the wiper arms.
2. Remove the cowl plate screws, move the cowl plate up at the front and disconnect the washer hose. Remove the cowl plate.
3. Disconnect the wires from the wiper motor.
4. Unbolt and remove the motor.
5. Installation is the reverse of removal.

PRESS HERE

SPEEDOMETER CABLE   SPEEDOMETER

Speedometer cable removal, all models
(© Toyo Kogyo Co. Ltd.)

Instrument Cluster

REMOVAL AND INSTALLATION

RX-3, RX-3 SP and RX-7

1. Pull the knob off of the steering column-mounted headlight switch. Remove the halves of the steering column shroud.
2. Open the left-hand (driver's side) door, to gain access to the screw located on the side of the instrument cluster.
3. Remove the three retaining screws which are located underneath the instrument cluster.
4. Tip the top of the cluster toward the steering wheel.
5. Disconnect the wiring and the speedometer cable from the back of the instrument cluster.
6. Remove the cluster.
7. Installation is the reverse of removal.

808, RX-4, Cosmo, and 626

1. Remove the steering wheel.
2. Loosen the nut which secures the vent knob (left side) and allow the knob assembly to drop away from its mounting bracket.
3. Remove choke knob. Remove the choke retaining nut and separate the choke from the panel.
4. Remove the upper column cover.
5. Disconnect the panel light dimmer switch wiring.
6. Disconnect the exhaust temperature warning light wiring.
7. Loosen, but don't remove the screws at either end of the lower panel cover.

NOTE: The left-hand screw is located in the hole which was covered by the upper column cover and the right-hand screw is above the ashtray opening (ashtray removed).

8. Pull the upper column cover away from the instrument panel.
9. Remove the instrument cluster surround.
10. Unfasten the instrument cluster wiring harness(es).
11. Disconnect the speedometer cable.
12. Tilt the top of the cluster forward, and lift the cluster out.
13. Installation is the reverse of removal.

GLC (Standard Dash) Through 1980

1. Disconnect the negative battery cable.
2. Remove the screw above each meter and remove the instrument cluster outside cover.
3. Remove the woodgrain center panel cover by removing the screw from the left side and unclipping the panel from the right side.
4. Remove the instrument panel pad by removing the three screws located under the front edge of the pad.
5. Disconnect the speedometer cable.
6. Remove the three instrument cluster retaining screws and pull the cluster out of the dash.
7. To install reverse the removal procedure.

GLC (Sport Dash) Through 1980

1. Disconnect the negative battery cable.
2. Remove the tripmeter knob and the cluster cover retaining screws and clips.
3. Remove the woodgrain center panel cover by removing the screw from the left

1. Seaming welt
2. Garnish
3. Defroster nozzle
4. Cloth cover
5. Instrument panel pad
6. Defroster nozzle bracket
7. Louver
8. Instrument panel lower
9. Glove box switch
10. Instrument panel lower
11. Glove box lamp
12. Glove tray
13. Instrument panel center bracket
14. Stopper
15. Spring
16. Striker
17. Spring plate
18. Cushion
19. Gasket
20. Ventilator
21. Control wire
22. Duct
23. Glove box lid

Cosmo instrument panel (© Toyo Kogyo Co. Ltd.)

GLC meter cover retaining screws (© Toyo Kogyo Co. Ltd.)

GLC meter retaining screws (© Toyo Kogyo Co. Ltd.)

side and unclipping the panel from the right side.

4. Remove the instrument panel pad by removing the three screws located under the front edge of the pad.

5. Remove the three screws and remove the instrument cluster outward.

6. Disconnect the electrical connectors and the speedometer cable.

7. To install reverse the removal procedure.

GLC (1981 and Later)

1. Disconnect the negative battery cable.

2. Remove the steering wheel.

3. Remove the meter hood by removing the four screws.

4. Disconnect the speedometer cable and electrical coupler.

5. Installation is the reverse of removal.

Heater Core

REMOVAL AND INSTALLATION

All Models

NOTE: On models equipped with air conditioning access to the heater core will be more difficult.

— CAUTION —

Do not attempt to discharge the air conditioning system unless you are thoroughly familiar with the system. Escaping refrigerant will freeze any surface it contacts. If you do not have the proper training, have the system discharged and recharged by a professional.

1. Disconnect the negative battery cable. Drain the coolant from the radiator.

2. Disconnect the heater hoses at the engine firewall.

3. Disconnect the duct which runs between the heater box and the blower motor

or, depending on the model, remove the crash pad and instrument panel pad from the dash. See preceding section for pad and panel removal.

4. Disconnect the defroster hose(s) if necessary, set the control to the DEF and HOT position and disconnect the control wires if they are in the way.

5. Unfasten the retaining screws that secure the halves of the heater box together or remove the heater unit and separate the heater box for access to the heater core.

6. Detach the hoses if not already disconnected. Remove the mounting clips and the heater core. Reverse the removal procedure for installation.

Blower Motor

REMOVAL AND INSTALLATION

All Models

1. Disconnect the negative battery cable.

2. Remove the dash undercover if equipped. Disconnect the multiconnector to the blower motor.

3. Remove the right side defroster hose for clearance if necessary.

4. If equipped with sliding heater controls, move the control to the HOT position

PLASTIC HOUSING

FUSIBLE METAL

The new style plug-in fuse used on 1980 and later cars (© Toyo Kogyo Co. Ltd.)

and disconnect the control wire if in the way.

5. Remove the mounting screws and dismount the blower motor.

6. Installation is the reverse of removal.

Fuse Box Location

RX-3, COSMO

On the RX-3 models, the box is located just above the lower parcel shelf, and uses a back-hinged cover.

The cover has the location, amperage, and the circuit protected by each individual fuse stamped on it.

The cable running from the positive side of the battery is equipped with a fusible link.

RX-4, 808

The main fuse and secondary fuse block are located next to the battery in the engine compartment. An additional fuse box is located beneath the glove compartment. The amperage of each fuse is printed on the fuse box lids.

RX-3 SP, RX-7, GLC AND 626

The main fuse block is mounted under the dash near the driver's side kick panel.

Fusible Links

On all rotary engine cars and the 808, these are located in either one or two boxes next to the battery in the engine compartment. If these links blow, they may be replaced with the specified parts by disconnecting the battery, disconnecting wiring to each link requiring replacement, removing the attaching screws and the link, and installing the new link or links in the reverse of the removal procedure.

On the GLC, there is a connector block located on the radiator panel on the right side of the radiator inside the engine compartment. Two links connected there are color coded red and green and may simply be unplugged to remove them, and replaced by plugging in replacement parts. Make sure to disconnect the battery before replacing them.

Fusible links in the engine compartment—RX–7 (© Toyo Kogyo Co., Ltd.)

Fusible links in the steering column—RX–7 (© Toyo Kogyo Co., Ltd.)

Mercedes-Benz

ENGINE/VEHICLE IDENTIFICATION

Model	Chassis Type	Engine Model	No. of Cyls.	Engine Type	Engine Description (Fuel, Fuel Delivery, Valve Gear, Displacement)	Years
240D	115.117	OM616	4	616.916	Diesel (2404 cc)	1976
240D	123.123	OM616	4	616.912	Diesel (2404 cc)	1977–83
300D	115.114	OM617	5	617.910	Diesel (3005 cc)	1976
300D	123.130	OM617	5	617.912	Diesel (3005 cc)	1977–81
300D	123.133	OM617	5	617.952	Diesel, Turbocharged (3005 cc)	1982–83
300CD	123.150	OM617	5	617.912	Diesel (3005 cc)	1978–81
300CD	123.153	OM617	5	617.952	Diesel, Turbocharged (3005 cc)	1982–83
300SD	116.120	OM617	5	617.950	Diesel, Turbocharged (3005 cc)	1978–80
300SD	126.120	OM617	5	617.951	Diesel, Turbocharged (3005 cc)	1981–83
300TD	123.190	OM617	5	617.912	Diesel (3005 cc)	1979–80
300TD Turbo	123.193	OM617	5	617.952	Diesel, Turbocharged (3005 cc)	1981–83
230	115.017	M115	4	115.951	Gas, Carb., OHC (2307 cc)	1976
230	123.023	M115	4	115.954	Gas, Carb., OHC (2307 cc)	1977–80
280	114.060	M110	6	110.921	Gas, Carb., DOHC (2746 cc)	1976
280C	114.073	M110	6	110.921	Gas, Carb., DOHC (2746 cc)	1976
280S	116.020	M110	6	110.922	Gas, Carb., DOHC (2746 cc)	1976
280E	123.033	M110	6	110.984	Gas, Fuel Inj., OHC (2746 cc)	1977–81
280CE	123.053	M110	6	110.984	Gas, Fuel Inj., DOHC (2746 cc)	1978–81
280SE	116.024	M110	6	110.985	Gas, Fuel Inj., OHC (2746 cc)	1977–80
380SEL	126.033	M116	8	116.961	Gas, Fuel Inj., OHC (3839 cc)	1981–83
380SL	107.045	M116	8	116.960	Gas, Fuel Inj., OHC (3839 cc)	1981–83
380SLC	107.025	M116	8	116.960	Gas, Fuel Inj., OHC (3839 cc)	1981–81
380SEC	126.043	M116	8	116.963	Gas, Fuel Inj., OHC (3839 cc)	1982–83
450SE	116.032	M117	8	117.986	Gas, Fuel Inj., OHC (4520 cc)	1976
450SEL	116.033	M117	8	117.986(5)	Gas, Fuel Inj., OHC (4520 cc)	1976–80
450SL	107.044	M117	8	117.985	Gas, Fuel Inj., OHC (4520 cc)	1976–80
450SLC	107.024	M117	8	117.985	Gas, Fuel Inj., OHC (4520 cc)	1976–80
6.9	116.036	M100	8	100.985	Gas, Fuel Inj., OHC (6836 cc)	1978–79

NOTE: 1976–83 models are covered in this section. The years given are not necessarily production years.

SERIAL NUMBER IDENTIFICATION

1. Certification tag (left door pillar)
2. Identification tag (left window post)
3. Chassis no.
4. Body no. and paintwork no.
5. Engine no.

Location of important information—230, 240D, 280, 280C, 300D models through 1976

1. Catalyst and certification tag (left door pillar)
2. Identification tag (left window post)
3. Chassis no.
4. Body no. and paintwork no.
5. Engine no. on rear engine block
6. Emission control information

Location of important information—450SL, 450SLC, 380SL, 380SLC

1. Certification tag (left door pillar)
2. Identification tag (left window post)
3. Chassis no.
4. Body no. and paintwork no.
5. Engine no.
6. Emission control tag
7. Emission control tag catalyst information

Location of important information—300SD, 300TD, 380SEL, 380SEC

1. Certification tag (left door pillar)
2. Identification tag (left window post)
3. Chassis no.
4. Body no. and paintwork no.
5. Engine no. on engine block, rear
6. Emission control information

Location of important information—1977 and later models except 300SD, 300TD, 450SL, 450SLC, 380SL, 380SEC, 380SEL

Example: Engine Family 80.22.45.30

| 80 | 22 | 4 | 5 | 30 |

Model Year

Emission System Version
20 = Federal and California
21 = Federal
22 = California

Combustion Version
1 = Carburetor   3 = Diesel
2 = Injection, Gasoline   4 = Diesel, Turbo

Number of Cylinders

Piston Displacement
3000 cm³ / 183.0 in³

The key to 1980 Vehicle Identification is an 8 digit number

Example: Engine Family B MB 3.8 V 6 F B 4

| | B | MB | 3.8 | V | 6 | F | B | 4 |

Model year
A = 1980, B = 1981 etc.

Manufacturer's code
MB = Mercedes Benz

Piston displacement
here 3800 cc

Vehicles class
D = passenger car with diesel engine
V = passenger car with gasoline engine

Type of fuel feed
6 = mechanical injection
9 = mechanical injection with turbocharger

Type of catalyst
F = 3-way catalyst in combination with lambda control
J = no catalyst (diesel)

For free use of manufacturer

Check digit

The key to 1981 and later engine identification is a 10 digit number.

TRANSMISSION APPLICATIONS

Model	Automatic Transmission	Manual Transmission
230	W4B 025	—
240D (thru '80)	W4B 025	G-76/18C(4-spd.)
240D ('81 and later)	W4B 025	GL68/20A (4-spd.)
280, 280C	W4B 025	—
280E, 280CE	W4B 025	—
280S, 280SE	W4B 025	—
300D, 300CD, 300TD	W4B 025	—
300TD Turbo 1981–83	W4A 040	—
300SD 1978–80	W4B 025	—
300SD 1981–83	W4A 040	—
380SL, 380SLC, 380SEL, 380SEC	W4A 040	—
450SE, 450SEL, 450SL, 450SLC	W3A 040	—
6.9	W3B 050	—

Transmission Identification

Mercedes-Benz cars for the U.S. market have been equipped with either a 4-speed manual transmission or with a fully automatic 3 or 4-speed unit. The automatic transmissions are equipped with a torque converter.

Serial numbers on the manual transmission are located on a pad on the side cover of the transmission (left side).

Automatic transmission serial numbers are located on a metal plate which is attached to the driver's side of the transmission.

Transmission identification number

GENERAL GASOLINE ENGINE SPECIFICATIONS

Year/Model	Engine Model	Engine Displacement (cc)	Carburetor Type	Horsepower @ rpm (SAE)	Torque @ rpm (ft. lbs.) (SAE)	Bore x Stroke (mm)	Compression Ratio	Firing Order
230	M115	2307	Stromberg 175 CDT	95 @ 4800 ①	128 @ 2500 ②	93.75 × 83.6	8.0:1	1 3 4 2
280S ('76)	M110	2746	Solex 4-bbl	120 @ 4800	143 @ 2800	86.00 × 78.80	8.0:1	1 5 3 6 2 4
280, 280C ('76)	M110	2746	Solex 4-bbl	120 @ 4800	143 @ 2800	86.00 × 78.80	8.0:1	1 5 3 6 2 4
280E, 280CE ('77–'81) 280SE ('77–'80)	M110	2746	Fuel Injection	142 @ 5750 ③	149 @ 4600 ④	86.00 × 78.80	8.0:1	1 5 3 6 2 4
380SL 380SLC 380SEL 380SEC ('81–'83)	M116	3839	Fuel Injection	155 @ 4750	196 @ 2750	88.0 × 78.9	8.3:1	1 5 4 8 6 3 7 2
450SE 450SEL 450SL 450SLC ('76–'80)	M117	4520	Fuel Injection	180 @ 4750	220 @ 3000	92.00 × 85.00	8.0:1	1 5 4 8 6 3 7 2
6.9	M100	6836	Fuel Injection	250 @ 4000	360 @ 2500	107.0 × 95.0	8.0:1	1 5 4 8 6 3 7 2

NOTE: Horsepower may vary depending on year of application.
① 1975 California—85@4500
② 1975–79 California—122@2500
③ 1977 and later California—137@5750
④ 1977 and later California—142@4600

GENERAL DIESEL ENGINE SPECIFICATIONS

Car Model	Engine Model	Engine Displacement (cc)	Fuel Delivery	Horsepower @ rpm (SAE)	Torque @ rpm (ft. lbs.) (SAE)	Bore x Stroke (mm)	Compression Ratio	Firing Order
240D	OM616	2404	Fuel Injection	62–67 @ 4000	97 @ 2400	91.0 × 92.4	21:1	1 3 4 2
300D ('77–'81) 300CD ('78–'81) 300TD ('79–'80)	OM617	3005	Fuel Injection	77–83 @ 4000	115–120 @ 2400	91.0 × 92.4	21:1	1 2 4 5 3
300TD Turbo ('81–'83) 300D('82–'83) 300CD ('82–'83)	OM617	3005	Fuel Inj. Turbocharged	120 @ 4350	170 @ 2400	91.0 × 92.4	21:1	1 2 4 5 3
300SD	OM617	3005	Fuel Inj. Turbocharged	110–120 @ 4200	168–170 @ 2400	91.0 × 92.4	21:1	1 2 4 5 3

NOTE: Horsepower may vary depending on year and application.

GASOLINE ENGINE TUNE-UP SPECIFICATIONS
(When analyzing compression test results, look for uniformity among cylinders, rather than specific pressures)

Year	Model	Spark Plugs Type	Gap (in.)	Distributor Point Dwell (deg)	Ignition Timing (deg)	Intake Valve Opens (deg)	Fuel Pump Pressure (psi) Idle●	▲ Idle Speed (rpm)	Valve Clearance* (in.) In (cold)	Ex (cold)
'76	230	N9Y	0.024	47–53	10B w/vacuum	14B	2–3	800–900	0.004	0.008
	280, 280C, 280S	N9Y	0.024	34–40	7B w/o vacuum	7B	3.5–5.0	800–900	0.004	0.010
	450SE, 450SEL	N9Y	0.024	Elec.	TDC w/vacuum	③	75–84 ①	700–800	Hyd.	Hyd.
	450SL, 450SLC	N9Y	0.024	Elec.	TDC w/vacuum	③	75–84 ①	700–800	Hyd.	Hyd.
'77	230	N10Y	0.028	46–53	10B w/vacuum	14B	2–3	850	0.004	0.008
	280E	N10Y	0.028	Elec.	TDC w/vacuum	7B	75–84 ①	800	0.004	0.010
	280SE	N10Y	0.028	Elec.	TDC w/vacuum	7B	75–84 ①	800	0.004	0.010
	450SE, 450SEL	N10Y	0.028	Elec.	TDC w/vacuum	③	75–84 ①	750	Hyd.	Hyd.
	450SL, 450SLC	N10Y	0.028	Elec.	TDC w/vacuum	③	75–84 ①	750	Hyd.	Hyd.
'78–'79	230	N10Y	0.032	Elec.	10B w/vacuum	14B	2–3	850	0.004	0.008
	280E, 280CE, 280SE	N10Y	0.032	Elec.	TDC w/vacuum	7B	75–84 ①	800	0.004	0.010
	450SEL	N10Y	0.032	Elec.	TDC w/vacuum	③	75–84 ①	750	Hyd.	Hyd.
	450SL, 450SLC	N10Y	0.032	Elec.	TDC w/vacuum	③	75–84 ①	750	Hyd.	Hyd.
	6.9	N10Y	0.032	Elec.	TDC w/vacuum	④	75–84 ①	600	Hyd.	Hyd.
'80	280E, 280CE, 280SE	N10Y	0.032	Elec.	10B	7B	⑤	700–800	0.004	0.010
	450SEL	N10Y	0.032	Elec.	5B	⑥	⑤	600–700	Hyd.	Hyd.
	450SL, 450SLC	N10Y	0.032	Elec.	5B	⑥	⑤	600–700	Hyd.	Hyd.
'81	280E, 280CE	N10Y	0.032	Elec.	10B	7B	⑤	700–800	0.004	0.010
	380SEL	N10Y	0.032	Elec.	5B	24A	⑤	500	Hyd.	Hyd.
	380SL, 380SLC	N10Y	0.032	Elec.	5B	24A	⑤	500	Hyd.	Hyd.

GASOLINE ENGINE TUNE-UP SPECIFICATIONS
(When analyzing compression test results, look for uniformity among cylinders, rather than specific pressures)

Year	Model	Spark Plugs Type	Gap (in.)	Distributor Point Dwell (deg)	Ignition Timing (deg)	Intake Valve Opens (deg)	Fuel Pump Pressure (psi) Idle●	▲ Idle Speed (rpm)	Valve Clearance* (in.) In (cold)	Ex (cold)
'82–'83	380SL	N10Y	0.032	Elec.	5B	24A	⑤	500–600	Hyd.	Hyd.
	380SEL	N10Y	0.032	Elec.	5B	24A	⑤	500–600	Hyd.	Hyd.
	380SEC	N10Y	0.032	Elec.	5B	24A	⑤	500–600	Hyd.	Hyd

CAUTION: If the specifications listed above differ from those on the tune-up decal in the engine compartment, use those listed on the tune-up decal.

NOTES: 1. On transistor ignitions, only a transistorized dwell meter can be used. Transistor ignitions are recognizable by the "8lue" ignition coil, 2 series resistors and the transistor switchgear.

2. To counteract wear of the fiber contact block, adjust the dwell to the lower end of the range.

① Injection pump pressure
② Right side camshaft—3° ATDC
   Left side camshaft—5° ATDC
③ Right side camshaft—4.5° ATDC
   Left side camshaft—6.5° ATDC
④ Right side camshaft—12° ATDC
   Left side camshaft—10° ATDC
⑤ Approximately 1 quart in 30 seconds
⑥ Left side—22° ATDC
   Right side—20° ATDC
A After Top Dead Center
B Before Top Dead Center
w/vacuum—vacuum advance connected
w/o vacuum—vacuum advance disconnected
* Below 0°F; increase valve clearance by 0.002 in.
—Not Available
▲ In Drive
● Timing for test measurements @ 2mm valve lift

DIESEL ENGINE TUNE-UP SPECIFICATIONS

Model	Valve Clearnace (cold)① Intake (in.)	Exhaust (in.)	Intake Valve Opens (deg)	Injection Pump Setting (deg)	Injection Nozzle Pressure (psi) New	Used	Idle Speed (rpm) ②	Cranking Compression Pressure (psi)
240D (4-cylinder) '76–'81	0.004	0.016	13.5B	24B	1564–1706	1422–1706	750–800	284–327
240D 4-cylinder '82–'83	0.004	0.016	13.5B	24B	1564–1706	1422–1706	700–800	284–327
300D, 300CD, 300TD (5-cylinder, non-turbo)	0.004	0.012	13.5B ④	24B	1635–1750 ③	1422	700–800	284–327
300SD, 300TD (5-cylinder, turbo) '76–'81	0.004	0.014	13.5B ④	24B	1958–2074	1740	650–850	284–327

DIESEL ENGINE TUNE-UP SPECIFICATIONS

| Model | Valve Clearance (cold) ① | | Intake Valve Opens (deg) | Injection Pump Setting (deg) | Injection Nozzle Pressure (psi) | | Idle Speed (rpm) ② | Cranking Compression Pressure (psi) |
	Intake (in.)	Exhaust (in.)			New	Used		
300D 300CD 300SD 300TD (5-cylinder, turbo) '82–'83	0.004	0.014	13.5B ④	24B	1958–2074	1740	650–850	284–327

① In cold weather (below 5°F.), increase valve clearance 0.002 in.
② Manual transmission in Neutral; Automatic in Drive.
③ Difference in opening pressure on injection nozzles should not exceed 71 psi.
④ The injection pump is in start of delivery position when the mark on the pump camshaft is aligned with the mark on the injection pump flange.
B Before Top Dead Center

FIRING ORDERS

4-cylinder gas engine

6-cylinder gas engine

V-8

NOTE: The position of No. 1 tower on the distributor cap may vary. To avoid confusion when replacing wires, always replace wires one at a time. The notch cut into the rim of the distributor body always indicates No. 1 cylinder.

CAPACITIES

Year	Model	Cooling System (qts)	Engine Crankcase (qts) ▲ With Filter	Engine Crankcase (qts) ▲ Without Filter	Transmission (pts) Manual (4-spd)	Transmission (pts) Automatic	Drive Axle (pts)	Steering Gear (pts) Power	Steering Gear (pts) Manual	Level Control (qts)
'76–'80	230	10.5	5.8	5.3	—	11.5	②	3.0	⅝	—
'76	240D	10.5	6.3	5.3	3.4	11.5	②	3.0	⅝	—
'77–'83	240D	10.5	6.3	5.3	3.4	11.5	②	3.0	⅝	—
'76	280, 280C	11.5	6.3	5.8	—	12.3	②	3.0	—	—
'77–'81	280E, 280CE	11.5	6.3	5.8	—	12.3	2.1	3.0	—	—
'76	280S	11.5	6.3	5.8	—	12.3	2.1	3.0	—	—
'77–'80	280SE	11.5	6.3	5.8	—	12.3	2.1	3.0	—	—
'76	300D	11.7	6.8	5.8	—	11.5	③	3.0	—	—
'77–'81	300D, 300CD	⑤	6.8	5.3	—	11.5	③	3.0	—	—
'82	300D Turbo 300CD Turbo	13.2	8.0	7.5	—	13.0	2.1	3.0	—	—
'78–'80	300SD, 300TD	12.7⑤	6.8	5.3	—	11.5	2.1	3.0	—	6.2④
'81	300SD, 300TD Turbo	13.2	8.0	7.5	—	13.0	⑥	2.5	—	—
'82	300SD	13.2	8.0	7.5	—	13.0	2.1	2.5	—	—
'81	380SL, SLC 380SEL	13.7	8.5	8.0	—	13.0	2.7	⑦	—	—
'82	380SL	13.2	8.5	8.0	—	13.0	2.7	3.0	—	—
'82	380SEL 380SEC	13.2	8.5	8.0	—	13.0	2.7	2.5	—	—
'76–'80	450SE, 450SEL, 450SL, 450SLC	16.0	8.5	8.0	—	16.5	①	3.0	—	—
'78–'79	6.9	16.0	11.5	10.5	—	16.5	2.7	3.0	—	6.2④

① 450SL, 450SLC—2.7 pts
450SE, 450SEL—3.0 pts
② See text:1st version—2.4 pts
2nd version—2.1 pts
③ 1975–76—1st version—2.4 pts
2nd version—2.1 pts   See Text
④ Approximately 1 qt between dipstick maximum and minimum marks

⑤ 300D—11.7 qts; 300SD—13.0 qts
⑥ 300SD—2.7
300TD—2.1
⑦ 380SEL—2.5
380SL, SLC—3.0
▲ Add approximately ½ quart if equipped with additional oil cooler
— Not Applicable

CRANKSHAFT AND CONNECTING ROD SPECIFICATIONS
(All measurements are given in millimeters)

Car Model	Engine Displace (cc)	Engine Model	Crankshaft Main Brg. Journal Dia.	Crankshaft Main Brg. Oil Clearance	Crankshaft Shaft End-Play	Crankshaft Thrust on No.	Connecting Rod Journal Diameter	Connecting Rod Oil Clearance	Connecting Rod Side Clearance
240D	2404	OM616	69.955–69.965	0.045–0.065	0.100–0.240	①	51.955–51.965	0.035–0.055	0.110–0.260
300D, 300CD, 300TD, 300SD	3005	OM617	69.955–69.965	0.045–0.065	0.100–0.240	①	51.955–51.965	0.035–0.055	0.110–0.260

CRANKSHAFT AND CONNECTING ROD SPECIFICATIONS

(All measurements are given in millimeters)

Car Model	Engine Displace (cc)	Engine Model	Crankshaft				Connecting Rod		
			Main Brg. Journal Dia.	Main Brg. Oil Clearance	Shaft End-Play	Thrust on No.	Journal Diameter	Oil Clearance	Side Clearance
230	2307	M115	69.955–69.965	0.045–0.065	0.100–0.240	①	51.955–51.965	0.035–0.055	0.110–0.260
450SL 450SLC 450SE 450SEL	4520	M117	63.955–63.965	0.035–0.075	0.100–0.240	①	51.955–51.965	0.035–0.065	0.220–0.380
280 280C 280S 280E 280CE 280SE	2746	M110	59.96–59.95	0.03–0.07	0.10–0.24	①	47.95–47.96	0.15–0.50	0.11–0.23
6.9	6836	M100	69.945–69.965	0.045–0.065	0.100–0.240	①	54.940–54.600–	0.045–0.065–	0.220–0.359–
380SEL 380SL 380SLC 380SEC	3839	M116	N.A.	0.045–0.065	0.100–0.240	①	N.A.	0.045–0.065	0.220–0.359

①Center main on 5 main bearing engines; rear main on 7 main bearing engines; 3rd from front on 300D (5-cylinder)
N.A. Not Available

VALVE TIMING SPECIFICATIONS

Model	Camshaft Code Number	Intake Valve		Exhaust Valve	
		Opens ATDC	Closes ABDC	Opens BBDC	Closes ATDC
240D	02	13.5	15.5	19	17
300D, 300CD, 300TD, 300SD	00	13.5	15.5	19	17
230	05	14	20	22	12
450SE ('76)③ 450SEL ('76–'77)③ 450SL ('76–'77)③ 450SLC ('76–'77)③	56/57③ 54/55③	5	21	25	5
450SE, 450SL, 450SEL, 450SLC ('77–'80)	00/01	L-6.5 R-4.5	L-18.5 R-16.5	L-23 R-25	L-8 R-10
280, 280C, 280S, 280E, 280SE ('76–'80)	67/71	7	21	30	12
6.9	36/37	L-12 R-10	L-25 R-23	L-32 R-34	L-19 R-21
380SL, 380SLC, 380 SEL, 380SEC	62/63 L R	24	7.5	4	12.5

①Camshafts with identification number 46, 48, or 52 are for the left bank of cylinders (5–8). Camshafts with identification code number 47, 49, or 53 are for the right bank of cylinders (1–4).
②Code number 30 for exhaust camshaft Code number 33 for intake camshaft

③New engine with new timing chain
L Left
R Right
BTDC Before Top Dead Center
ABDC After Bottom Dead Center
BBDC Before Bottom Dead Center

VALVE SPECIFICATIONS

Car Model	Engine Displacement (cc)	Seat Angle (deg)	Spring Test Pressure (mm@KP)	Spring Installed Height (mm)	STEM DIAMETER (mm)	
					Intake	Exhaust
240D	2404	30 + 15′	38.4 @ 23–26.4	29.9	9.920–9.905	9.918–9.940
300D, 300CD, 300TD, 300SD	3005	30 + 15′	38.4 @ 23–26.4	29.9	9.920–9.905	9.918–9.940
230	2307	45 + 15′	39 @ 36 ①	30.0 ①	8.948–8.970	10.918–10.940
450SL 450SLC 450SE 450SEL	4520	45 + 15′	42 @ 29.5–32.5 ①	30.5 ①	8.955–8.970	10.928–10.950
280 280C 280CE 280S 280E 280SE	2746	45 + 15′	84–92 @ 30.5	N.A.	N.A.	0.431 (thru 1979) 0.353 (1980 and later)
6.9	6834	45 + 15′	44.5 2.3	35.4	8.948–8.970	11.932–11.950
380SL 380SLC 380SEL 380SEC	3839	N.A.	N.A.	N.A.	8.955–8.970	9.0

① Outer spring—the spring should be installed so that the close coils are in contact with the cylinder head

TORQUE SPECIFICATIONS
(All readings in ft. lbs.)

Car Model	Engine Model	Cylinder Head Bolts ②	Rod Bearing Bolts	Main Bearing Bolts	Crankshaft Pulley Bolt	Flywheel To Crankshaft Bolts	Cam Sprocket Bolt(s)	Exhaust Manifold Bolts
240D	OM616	65	①	65	151–158	①	18	18–21
300D, 300CD 300TD, 300SD	OM617	65	①	65	195–240	①	18	18–21
230	M115	58	①	58 ③	151–158	①	18	18–21
450SL 450SLC 450SE 450SEL	M117	36	①	④	180–194	①	36	18–21
280 280C 280S 280E 280CE 280SE	M110	58	①	58	206–226	①	58	N.A.

TORQUE SPECIFICATIONS
(All readings in ft. lbs.)

Car Model	Engine Model	Cylinder Head Bolts ②	Rod Bearing Bolts	Main Bearing Bolts	Crankshaft Pulley Bolt	Flywheel To Crankshaft Bolts	Cam Sprocket Bolt(s)	Exhaust Manifold Bolts
6.9	M100	65	①	⑤	289	①	72	N.A.
380SL 380SEL 380SLC 380SEC	M116	⑥	30– 37 ①	⑤	289	①	74	N.A.

① See text
② With cold engine; cylinder head bolts should be tightened in at least 3 stages
③ 65 on M115 engines
④ M 10 bolts—37 ft. lbs.
  M 12 bolts—72 ft. lbs.
⑤ M 10 bolts—43 ft. lbs.
  M 12 bolts—58 ft. lbs.
⑥ Tighten to 22 ft. lbs. then to 45 ft. lbs. in proper sequence. After 10 mins. loosen and tighten again to 45 ft. lbs.
N.A. Not Available

TORQUE SEQUENCES

4-cylinder gas engine

4-cylinder diesel engine

Main bearing cap—4.5 V8

V8 cylinder head

5-cylinder diesel bolts marked "a" are tightened with a hex socket bit

● Tighten ○ Concealed, cannot be tightened

6-cylinder gasoline cylinder head and camshaft housing

TORQUE SEQUENCES

Main bearing cap torque sequence—3.8 liter V-8's

Main bearing cap—3.8 V8

BATTERY AND STARTER SPECIFICATIONS

(All cars use 12 volt, negative ground electrical systems)

Engine Model	Starter						Brush Spring Tension (oz)	Min. Brush Length (in.)
	Lock Test			No Load Test				
	Amps	Volts	Torque (ft. lbs.)	Amps	Volts	rpm		
All w/Diesel Engine	650–750	9.0	1000–1200	80–95	12	7500–8500	N.A.	N.A.
All w/Gas Engine	290–300	9.0	1600–1800	50–70	12	9000–11000	N.A.	0.5

N.A. Not specified by manufacturer

BRAKE SPECIFICATIONS

(All measurements given are in inches unless noted. See following summary of Brake Pad Application)

Model	Lug Nut Torque (ft. lbs.)	Master Cylinder Bore	Brake Disc		Brake Drum			Minimum Lining Thickness	
			Minimum Thickness	Maximum Run-Out	Diameter	Max. Machine O/S	Max. Wear Limit	Front ▲	Rear ▲
240D 300D 300CD 300TD 230 280 280C 280E 280CE	75	15/16	0.44	0.0047 (max.)	—	—	—	0.08 ③	0.08 ③
450SL 450SLC 380SL	75	15/16	0.36	0.0047 (max.)	—	—	—	0.08 ③	0.08 ③

BRAKE SPECIFICATIONS

(All measurements given are in inches unless noted. See following summary of Brake Pad Application)

Model	Lug Nut Torque (ft. lbs.)	Master Cylinder Bore	Brake Disc		Brake Drum			Minimum Lining Thickness	
			Minimum Thickness	Maximum Run-Out	Diameter	Max. Machine O/S	Max. Wear Limit	Front ▲	Rear ▲
450SE 450SEL 280S 280SE 300SD 380SEL 380SEC 6.9	75	¹⁵⁄₁₆	0.79	0.0047 (max.)	—	—	—	0.08 ③	0.08 ③

NOTE: Minimum lining thickness is as recommended by the manufacturer. Due to variations in state inspection regulations, the minimum allowable thickness may be different than recommended by the manufacturer.

① Caliper w/57 mm piston diameter—0.81 in.
　Caliper w/60 mm piston diameter—0.79 in.
② Caliper w/57 mm piston diameter—0.44 in.
　Caliper w/60 mm piston diameter—0.42 in.
▲ New thickness of brake lining and backing plate—0.59 in.
　New thickness of backing plate—0.20 in.
　New thickness of brake lining—0.39 in.
— Not Applicable

SUMMARY OF BRAKE PAD APPLICATION

Model	Arrangement mm/in.	Thickness of Pad mm/in.	Brake Pad Repair Set Part No.	Color Code	Remarks
107 1st version 114.010,015,023 115 except 115.114	Front axle Caliper with 57/2.244 dia. piston	15/0.591	001 586 19 42 001 586 31 42	gn-yl-gn-gn gn-gn-gn-gn-bu	—
Without brake pad sensor 107 2nd version 114.060, 073 116 1st version	Front axle Caliper with 60/2.362 dia. piston	15/0.591	001 586 18 42 001 586 32 42	gn-yl-gn-gn gn-gn-gn-gn-bu	—
With brake pad sensor 107 3rd version 116 2nd version 123 1st version	Front axle Caliper with 60/2.362 dia. piston	15/0.591	001 586 33 42 001 586 36 42	gn-yl-gn-gn gn-gn-gn-gn-bu	—
With brake pad sensor 116 123 Beginning '80	Front axle Caliper with 60/2.362 dia. piston	17.5/0.689	002 586 45 42 002 586 46 42	gn-gn-gn-gn-bu gn-yl-gn-gn	These linings must only be combined with the rear axle linings 002 586 47 42 or 002 586 48 42
107 All except 116 '80 models 123	Rear axle Caliper with 38/1.496 dia. piston	15/0.591	000 586 76 42	gn-gn-bu-bu	—
116 123 Beginning '80	Rear axle Caliper with 38/1.496 dia. piston	15.0/0.610	002 586 47 42 002 586 48 42	gn-gn-bu-gn-bu gn-yl-yl-gn-yl	These linings must only be combined with the front axle linings 002 586 45 42 or 002 586 46 42

SUMMARY OF BRAKE PAD APPLICATION

Model	Arrangement mm/in.	Thickness of Pad mm/in.	Brake Pad Repair Set Part No.	Color Code	Remarks
123.190 All	Rear axle Caliper 2ith 42/1.654 dia. piston	15/0.591	001 586 64 42	gn-gn-bu-bu-bu	—

gn—green
yl—yellow
bu—blue

WHEEL ALIGNMENT SPECIFICATIONS

Car Model	Front Wheels			Rear Wheels	
	Camber (deg)	Caster (deg) Power Steering	Toe-in (in.)	Camber (deg)	Toe-In (mm)
230 ('76) 240D ('76) 300D ('76)	0°15' + 10' − 20'	3°40' ± 20'	0.08– 0.16	See Chart 1	See Chart 2
240D ('77–'81) 300D ('77–'81) 300CD ('77–'81) 300TD ('79–'80) 280E ('77–'80) 280CE ('77–'80) 230 ('77–'80)	0° ± 10'	8°45' ± 30'	0.08– 0.16	See Chart 3	See Chart 4
280 ('75–'76) 280C ('75–'76)	0°15' + 10' − 20'	3°40' ± 15'	0.04– 0.12	See Chart 1	0 ± 2
280S ('75–'76)	20'N①	9°30'–10°30'	0.08– 0.16	See Chart 5	See Chart 4
450SL 450SLC	0° + 10' − 20'	3°40' ± 20'	0.04– 0.12	See Chart 1	See Chart 2
450SE 450SEL 280SE 300SD (thru '80) 6.9	20'N	9°30'–10°30'	0.08– 0.16	See Chart 5	See Chart 4
380SL 380SLC	0° + 10' − 20'	3°40' ± 20'	0.04– 0.12	0°10' to 0°40' See Chart 6	0–35
380SEL 300SD ('81 and later) 380SEC	0° ± 10'	9°15'–10°15'	0.13 0.21	See Chart 7	②

① A 0°10' change in a positive or negative direction yields a 0°10' change in caster in the corresponding direction
② If trailing arm position is
   0–35 mm toe-in .06–.18
   35–50 mm toe-in is .08–.19
   50–60 mm toe-in is .10–.21
N Negative

WHEEL ALIGNMENT CHART 1

Control Arm Position mm (in.)	Corresponds to Rear Wheel Camber On:	
	230, 240D, 300D, 280, 280C	450SL, 450SLC
+80(3.17")	+2°30'±30'	—
+75(2.98")	+2°15'±30'	—
+70(2.78")	+2° ±30'	—
+65(2.58")	+1°45'±30'	—
+60(2.38")	+1°30'±30'	—
+55(2.18")	+1°15'±30'	—
+50(1.99")	+1° ±30'	+0°50'±30'
+45(1.79")	+0°45'±30'	+0°35'±30'
+40(1.59")	+0°30'±30'	+0°20'±30'
+35(1.39")	+0°15'±30'	+0°05'±30'
+30(1.12")	0° ±30'	−0°10'±30'
+25(0.99")	−0°15'±30'	−0°25'±30'
+20(0.79")	−0°30'±30'	−0°40'±30'
+15(0.60")	−0°45'±30'	−0°55'±30'
+10(0.40")	−1° ±30'	−1°10'±30'
+5(0.20")	−1°15'±30'	−1°25'±30'
0	−1°30'±30'	−1°40'±30'
−5(0.20")	−1°45'±30'	−1°55'±30'
−10(0.40")	−2° ±30'	−2°10'±30'
−15(0.60")	−2°15'±30'	−2°25'±30'
+20(0.79")	−2°30'±30'	−2°40'±30'

WHEEL ALIGNMENT CHART 2
('76, 230, 240D, 300D)

Rear Wheel Control Arm Position mm (in.)	Corresponds to Rear Wheel Toe-In of:
0 to +35 mm (0–1.39")	$1 {}^{+2}_{-1}$ mm or $0°10' {}^{+20'}_{-10'}$
+35 to +50 mm (1.39"–1.99")	$1.5 {}^{+2}_{-1}$ mm or $0°15' {}^{+20'}_{-10'}$
+50 to +60 mm (1.99"–2.38")	$2 {}^{+2}_{-1}$ mm or $0°20' {}^{+20'}_{-10'}$
+60 to +70 mm (2.38"–2.78")	$2.5 {}^{+2}_{-1}$ mm or $0°25' {}^{+20'}_{-10'}$
+70 to +80 mm (2.78"–3.17")	$3.0 {}^{+2}_{-1}$ mm or $0°30' {}^{+20'}_{-10'}$

WHEEL ALIGNMENT CHART 4
(All models except '76 230, 240D, 300D)

Rear Wheel Control Arm Position	Corresponds to Rear Wheel Toe-In of:
0 to +35 mm (0 to +1.38")	$0°10' {}^{+20'}_{-10'}$ or $1 {}^{+2}_{-1}$ mm $(0.04'' {}^{+0.08''}_{-0.04''})$
+35 to +50 mm (+1.38" to +1.97")	$0°15' {}^{+20'}_{-10'}$ or $1.5 {}^{+2}_{-1}$ mm $(0.06'' {}^{+0.08''}_{-0.04''})$
+50 to +60 mm (+1.97" to +2.36")	$0°20' {}^{+20'}_{-10'}$ or $2 {}^{+2}_{-1}$ mm $(0.08'' {}^{+0.08''}_{-0.04''})$
+60 to +70 mm (+2.36" to +2.76")	$0°25' {}^{+20'}_{-10'}$ or $2.5 {}^{+2}_{-1}$ mm $(0.10'' {}^{+0.08''}_{-0.04''})$
+70 to +80 mm (+2.76" to +3.15")	$0°30' {}^{+20'}_{-10'}$ or $3 {}^{+2}_{-1}$ mm $(0.12'' {}^{+0.08''}_{-0.04''})$

REAR WHEEL CAMBER CHART 3
('77–'79 230, 240D, 280E, 280CE, 300D, 300CD, 300TD)

Semi-trailing Arm Position mm (inches)	Corresponds to Rear Wheel Camber
+70(+2.76)	+1°45'±30'
+65(+2.56)	+1°30'±30'
+60(+2.36)	+1°15'±30'
+55(+2.17)	+1° ±30'
+50(+1.97)	+0°45'±30'
+45(+1.77)	+0°30'±30'
+40(+1.58)	+0°15'±30'
+35(+1.37)	−0° ±30'
+30(+1.18)	−0°15'±30'
+25(+0.98)	−0°30'±30'
+20(+0.79)	−0°45'±30'
+15(+0.59)	−1° ±30'
+10(+0.39)	−1°15'±30'
+5(+0.20)	−1°30'±30'
0(0)	−1°45'±30'
−5(−0.20)	−2° ±30'
−10(−0.39)	−2°15'±30'
−15(−0.59)	−2°30'±30'

REAR WHEEL CAMBER CHART 5
(450SE, 450SEL, 300SD, 280S, 280SE, 6.9)

Semi-trailing Arm Position mm (inches)	Corresponds to Rear Wheel Camber
+ 65(2.58″)	+ 1°45′ ± 30′
+ 60(2.38″)	+ 1°30′ ± 30′
+ 55(2.18″)	+ 1°15′ ± 30′
+ 50(1.99″)	+ 1° ± 30′
+ 45(1.79″)	+ 0°45′ ± 30′
+ 40(1.59″)	+ 0°30′ ± 30′
+ 35(1.39″)	+ 0°15′ ± 30′
+ 30(1.12″)	0° ± 30′
+ 25(0.99″)	− 0°15′ ± 30′
+ 20(0.79″)	− 0°30′ ± 30′
+ 15(0.60″)	− 0°45′ ± 30′
+ 10(0.40″)	− 1° ± 30′
+ 5(0.20″)	− 1°15′ ± 30′
0	− 1°30′ ± 30′
− 5(0.20″)	− 1°45′ ± 30′
− 10(0.40″)	− 2° ± 30′
− 15(0.60″)	− 2°15′ ± 30′
− 20(0.79″)	− 2°30′ ± 30′

WHEEL ALIGNMENT CHART 7
('81 and Later 300SD, 380SEL, 380SEC)

Semi-trailing Arm Position mm	Corresponds to Rear Wheel Camber
+ 65	+ 1°30′ ± 30′
+ 60	+ 1°15′ ± 30′
+ 55	+ 1° ± 30′
+ 50	+ 0°45′ ± 30′
+ 45	+ 0°30′ ± 30′
+ 40	+ 0°15′ ± 30′
+ 35	0° ± 30′
+ 30	− 0°15′ ± 30′
+ 25	− 0°30′ ± 30′
+ 20	− 0°45′ ± 30′
+ 15	− 1° ± 30′
+ 10	− 1°15′ ± 30′
+ 5	− 1°30′ ± 30′
0	− 1°45′ ± 30′
− 5	− 2° ± 30′
− 10	− 2°15′ ± 30′
− 15	− 2°30′ ± 30′
− 20	− 2°45′ ± 30′

REAR WHEEL ALIGNMENT CHART 6
(380SL, 380SLC)

Semi-trailing Arm Position mm	Corresponds to Rear Wheel Camber
35	0° ± 30′
30	− 0°15′ ± 30′
25	− 0°30′ ± 30′
20	− 0°45′ ± 30′
15	− 1° ± 30′
10	− 1°15′ ± 30′

REAR WHEEL ALIGNMENT CHART 6
(380SL, 380SLC)

Semi-trailing Arm Position mm	Corresponds to Rear Wheel Camber
5	− 1°30′ ± 30′
0	− 1°45′ ± 30′
− 5	− 2° ± 30′
− 10	− 2°15′ ± 30′
− 15	− 2°30′ ± 30′
− 20	− 2°45′ ± 30′

TUNE-UP

Ignition System Precautions

Mercedes-Benz has determined that some transistorized switching units have been damaged due to improper handling during service and maintenance work. The following precautions should be observed when working with transistorized switching units.

1. Do not shut off a running engine by shorting terminal 15 (terminal 1 or 15 on 1981 6-cylinder engines) of the ignition coil to ground or the transistorized switching unit will be destroyed.

2. Do not steam clean or apply water pressure to transistorized switching units, fuel injection control units, or ignition components, since water may enter these and short them.

3. Do not assume that transistor switching units are defective without checking the plug terminals. The plug terminals are frequently corroded because the rubber boot was not properly seated. In addition, the terminals can become corroded even if the rubber boot is properly seated. Mercedes-Benz recommends that all contacts be cleaned before assuming that a transistorized switching unit is defective.

4. Do not test for spark by holding a spark plug wire at a distance from the plug or pull off a spark plug wire with the engine running.

5. Disconnect test instruments with the engine off.

6. Do not operate the ignition without the harness connected.

7. Do not connect lights or noise suppression devices to terminal 1 of the ignition coil.

8. Do not install adapters (for timing lights, etc.) in series with ignition wires.

Spark Plugs

NOTE: Spark plugs should be removed and inspected one at a time to avoid confusion. On most models, the plug wires are numbered at the cap and on the wire with small yellow rings.

To gap the spark plugs, remove each one in turn and measure the gap with a round feeler gauge of the appropriate thickness. Prior to removing the plugs, blow dirt away with compressed air. This is especially necessary on 6 cylinder DOHC engines. Insert the round feeler gauge between the center and side electrode. To adjust the gap, bend the side electrode with the tool on the end of the feeler gauge until the specified gap is obtained.

Reinstall and tighten the spark plugs to 18–21 ft. lbs. and install the spark plug wires on their respective plugs.

Check the spark plug wires and replace any that are cracked or brittle. Bend the wires into a loop to check for cracks.

Breaker Points and Condenser

NOTE: 1976 V8, 1977 and later 6-cylinder and 1978 and later 4-cylinder engines are equipped with electronic ignition and have no points. Some 6-cylinder engines may be equipped with a flyweight in the distributor rotor to limit maximum rpm. 1981 6-cylinder engines are equipped with a new style electronic ignition identified by a ''Danger! High Voltage'' plate on the air cleaner. Components of various ignition systems cannot be interchanged.

REPLACEMENT

NOTE: Transistor ignitions prior to 1977 (6-cylinder) or 1978 (4-cylinder) can be recognized by the blue ignition coil, 2 series resistors and transistor switchgear.

1. Remove the rubber or plastic cover from the distributor (if equipped).
2. Release the clips on the side of the distributor cap and remove the cap. Lay it aside.
3. Remove the rotor and dust shield from the distributor shaft. Some distributors have a protective cover installed over the points.
4. Remove the distributor contact holder by removing the screw or screws. Some

1. Condenser
2. Point set
3. Point set attaching screw
4. Vacuum advance unit
5. Adjusting lugs and notch in breaker plate
6. Point gap (must be on the high point of the distributor cam to measure)
7. Notch in distributor rim indicating no. 1 cylinder

Internal view of breaker point type distributor

models also have a snap-ring on the bearing contact lever, which must also be removed. Pry the wire from the connecting terminal or loosen the screw at the terminal and remove the wire from the connecting terminal.

5. Disconnect the condenser wire and remove the condenser from its bracket.
6. Before installing new points, clean the contact surfaces by squeezing them against a clean matchbook cover. This will remove any film or condensate.
7. Lightly coat the slide piece of the contact breaker with high temperature multipurpose grease. It isn't necessary to lubricate the felt pad.
8. Check to be sure that the contacts are parallel and at the same level with each other when closed. Misalignment can be corrected by bending the fixed contact support. Never bend the movable contact support.
9. Install a new condenser and connect the wire.
10. Install a new contact set or sets into the distributor. If equipped, install the protective cover over the points.
11. Install the hold-down screw(s) and/or the snap-rings on the bearing pins of the contact plate.
12. Connect the wire to the terminal and tighten the nut, if necessary.
13. Install the plate and rotor on the shaft.
14. Install the cap.

15. Check the dwell angle and ignition timing. Adjust if necessary.

Dwell Angle

ADJUSTMENT

A dwell meter virtually eliminates errors in point gap caused by distributor cam lobes being unequally worn, or human error. In any case, point dwell should be checked as soon as possible after setting with a feeler gauge, because it is a far more accurate check of point operation under normal operating conditions.

Because the fiber block wears down gradually in service, it is good practice to set the dwell on the low side of any dwell range (smaller number of degrees) given in specifications. As the block wears, the dwell becomes greater (toward the center of the range) and point life is increased between adjustments.

All Engines Without Electronic Ignition

1. The dwell angle should be measured at idle speed.
2. Raise the hood and connect a dwell meter and tachometer.
3. Start the engine and allow it to reach

The condenser attaching screw is located on the outside of the distributor housing

normal idle speed. Read the dwell angle from the meter on the appropriate scale.

4. If the dwell varies by 5 or more degrees from the specifications, the points should be replaced.

5. If the dwell angle is not according to specifications, remove the distributor cap and adjust the dwell angle. Reduce the point gap if the dwell angle is too small, or increase the contact point gap if the dwell angle is too large.

6. To actually adjust the point gap, loosen the hold-down screw and insert a screwdriver between the lugs on the breaker plate and move the plate to the desired location. Tighten the hold-down screw. On some models the point gap is adjusted with the eccentric screw in the breaker plate.

7. Recheck the dwell angle and adjust the gap again if it is still not satisfactory. Repeat the process until the dwell angle is as specified.

All Engines With Electronic Ignition

It is not possible to adjust the dwell angle on Mercedes-Benz electronic ignitions.

Ignition Timing

ADJUSTMENT

Before setting the ignition timing, be sure that the point gap (dwell angle) is set to the proper specifications since this will influence the timing, while timing will have no influence on the dwell angle.

Before attempting to set the timing, read the ''Ignition Timing Specifications'' chart carefully and determine at what speed the timing should be set and whether the vacuum should be connected or disconnected.

NOTE: It is a good idea to paint the appropriate timing mark with dayglow or white paint to make it quickly and easily visible.

On engines with transistorized coil ignition, the timing light may or may not work depending on the construction of the light. If in doubt, consult a Mercedes-Benz dealer or the manufacturer of the timing light.

All Gas Engines

The diesel uses no distributor, so requires no ignition timing adjustment.

1. Raise the hood and connect a tachometer.

Vacuum connections—280, 280C, 280S (1976)

If 2 timing scales are used, the TDC scale is the one with the pin (arrow)

2. Connect a timing light as specified by the manufacturer.

3. On carbureted 280, 280C and 280S engines, disconnect and plug both vacuum lines.

4. Run the engine at the specified speed and read the firing point on the balancing plate or vibration damper while shining the light on it.

NOTE: The balancer on some engines has 2 timing scales. If in doubt as to which scale to use, rotate the crankshaft (in the direction of rotation only) until the distributor rotor is aligned with the notch on the distributor housing (No. 1 cylinder). In this position, the timing pointer should be at TDC on the proper timing scale.

5. Adjust the ignition timing by loosening the distributor clamp bolt and rotating the distributor. To advance the timing, rotate the distributor in the opposite direction of normal rotation. To retard the timing, rotate the distributor in the direction of normal rotation.

6. Once the timing has been adjusted, recheck the timing once more to be sure that it has not been disturbed.

7. Remove the timing light and tachometer and connect any wires that were removed.

Valve Clearance

ADJUSTMENT

The valve clearance of all gasoline engines can be checked and, if necessary, adjusted when the engine is hot or cold. Consult the valve location illustrations. The valve clearance on intake and exhaust valves is different, but all valves should be set slightly loose, rather than too tight.

4 and 6-Cylinder Gasoline Engines

NOTE: Prior to rotating 6-cylinder engine manually, disconnect the transmit-

1. Tension spring 3. Threaded bushing
2. Adjusting screw 4. Pressure piece

Check the valve clearance between the sliding surface of the rocker arm and the heel of the camshaft lobe on DOHC—6-cylinder engines

ter-ignition distributor plug (green cable) from the switching unit.

The valve clearance is measured between the sliding surface of the rocker arm and the heel of the camshaft lobe. The highest point of the camshaft lobe should be at a 90° angle to the sliding surface of the rocker arm.

1. Remove the air vent hose and air cleaner from the valve cover. Remove the spark plugs.

2. Remove the valve cover and gasket.

3. Note the position of the intake and exhaust valves.

4. Rotate the crankshaft, using a socket wrench on the crankshaft pulley bolt, until the heel of the camshaft lobe is perpendicular to the sliding surface of the rocker arm.

1. Threaded bushing
2. Adjusting screw
3. Pressure piece

Measure the valve clearance between the sliding surface of the rocker arm and the heel of the camshaft lobe on 4-cylinder engines

Valve location—4-cylinder engines

Valve location—DOHC 6-cylinder engine

NOTE: Do not rotate the engine using the camshaft sprocket bolt. The strain will distort the timing chain tensioner rail. Always rotate the engine in the direction of normal rotation only.

5. Some models have holes in the vibration damper plate to assist in crankshaft rotation. In this case, a large drift can be used to carefully rotate the crankshaft.

6. To measure the valve clearance, insert a feeler blade of the specified thickness between the heel of the camshaft lobe and the sliding surface of the rocker arm. The clearance is correct if the blade can be inserted and withdrawn with a very slight drag.

7. If adjustment is necessary, it can be done by turning the ball pin head at the hex collar. If the clearance is too small, increase it by turning the ball pin head in. If the clearance is too large, decrease it by turning the ball pin head out. If the adjuster turns too easily or the proper clearance can't be obtained, check the torque of the adjuster.

NOTE: This adjustment is ideally made with a special adapter and a torque wrench. By using it, the torque wrench can be directly aligned with the ball pin head.

8. When the ball pin head is turned, the adjusting torque should be 14–25 ft. lbs. If the torque is less than 14 ft. lbs., the ball pin head will vibrate and the clearance will not remain as set. If the valve clearance is too small, and the ball pin head

(a)—Spark plug holes 1, 3 and 5
(b)—Spark plug holes 2 and 4

Two versions of rubber gaskets

cannot be screwed in far enough to correct it, a thinner pressure piece should be installed in the spring retainer. To replace the pressure piece, the rocker arm must be removed.

9. After all the valves have been checked and adjusted in the manner described above, install the valve cover. Be sure that the gasket is seated properly. It is best to use a new gasket whenever the valve cover is removed.

NOTE: Two types of triangular rubber gaskets are used on 6-cylinder engines, but only the later type with 3 notches are supplied for service.

10. Install the spark plugs.
11. Reconnect the air vent line to the valve cover and install the air cleaner, if removed.
12. Run the engine and check for leaks at the rocker arm cover.

V8 Engines

NOTE: 1976 and later V8 engines use hydraulic valve lifters and require no periodic adjustment.

The valve clearance is measured between the sliding surface of the rocker arm and the heel of the camshaft lobe. The highest

1. Threaded bushing   3. Spring
2. Adjuster   4. Pressure piece

Valve clearance measurement—V8 engines

V8 (except 6.9) valve location

point of the camshaft lobe should be at a 90° angle to the sliding surface of the rocker arm.

1. Loosen the venting line and remove the regulating linkage. Remove the valve cover.

2. Disconnect the cable from the ignition coil.

3. Identify all of the valves, as intake or exhaust.

4. Beginning with No. 1 cylinder, crank the engine with the starter to position the heel of the camshaft approximately over the sliding surface of the rocker arm.

5. Rotate the crankshaft by means of a socket wrench on the crankshaft pulley bolt until the heel of the camshaft lobe is perpendicular to the sliding surface of the rocker arm.

NOTE: Do not rotate the engine using the camshaft sprocket bolt. The strain will distort the timing chain tensioner rail. Always rotate the engine in the direction of normal rotation only.

6. Some models have holes in the vibration damper plate to assist in crankshaft rotation. In this case, a screwdriver can be used to carefully rotate the crankshaft.

7. To measure the valve clearance, insert a feeler blade of the specified thickness between the heel of the camshaft lobe and the sliding surface of the rocker arm. The clearance is correct if the blade can be inserted and withdrawn with a very slight drag.

8. If adjustment is necessary, it can be done by turning the ball pin head at the hex collar. If the clearance is too small, increase it by turning the ball pin head in. If the clearance is too large, turn the ball pin head out.

NOTE: If the adjuster turns very easily, or if the proper clearance can't be obtained, check the torque on the adjuster using a special adapter ("crow's foot").

9. When the ball pin head is turned, the adjusting torque should be 14–29 ft. lbs. If the torque is lower, either the adjusting screw, the threaded bolt, or both will have to be replaced. If the valve clear-

Valve locations—6.9 V8

A valve adjusting wrench (crow's foot) is required to accurately measure torque on all models

ance is too small, and the ball pin head cannot be screwed in far enough to correct it, a thinner pressure piece should be installed in the spring retainer. To replace the pressure piece, the rocker arm must be removed. (See the "Engine Mechanical" section.)

10. Install the regulating linkage, valve cover gasket, and valve cover. Be sure the gasket is seated prperly.

11. Connect the cable to the coil and the venting line. Run the engine and check for leaks at the valve cover.

Diesel Engines

1. Remove the valve cover and note the position of the intake and exhaust valves.

2. Turn the engine with a socket and breaker bar on the crankshaft pulley or by using a remote starter, hooked to the battery (+) terminal and the large, uppermost starter solenoid terminal. Due to the extremely high compression pressures in the diesel engine, it will be considerably easier to use a remote starter. If a remote starter is not available,

Valve arrangement—4-cylinder diesels

Valve arrangement—5-cylinder diesels

Measure valve clearance on diesel engines at arrow

7. Capnut	14. Holding wrench
8. Locknut	16. Adjusting wrench

Adjusting valve clearance on diesel engine

the engine can be bumped into position with the normal starter.

NOTE: Do not turn the engine backwards or use the camshaft sprocket bolt to rotate the engine.

3. Measure the valve clearance when the heel of the camshaft lobe is directly over the sliding surface of the rocker arm. The lobe of the camshaft should be vertical to the surface of the rocker arm. The clearance is correct when the specified feeler gauge can be pulled out with a very slight drag.

4. To adjust the clearance, loosen the cap nut while holding the hex nut. Adjust the valve clearance by turning the hex nut.

5. After adjustment hold the cap nut and lock it in place with the hex nut. Recheck the clearance.

6. Check the gasket and install the rocker arm cover.

Idle Speed

CATALYTIC CONVERTER PRECAUTIONS

With the exception of diesels and the 1976 230, all Mercedes-Benz cars are equipped with catalysts. The following points should be adhered to:

1. Use only unleaded gas.
2. Maintain the engine at the specified intervals.
3. Avoid running the engine with an excessively rich mixture. Do not run the engine excessively on fast idle.
4. Prolonged warm-up after a cold start should be avoided.
5. Do not check exhaust emissions over a long period of time without air injection.
6. Do not alter the emission control system in any way.

CARBURETORS

Stromberg 175 CDT

1. Turn off the heater and A/C and run the vehicle to normal operating temperature.
2. Check the throttle valve for ease of operation.

Idle speed adjusting screw (8)—1976 230

Idle speed adjusting screw (8)—1977 and later 230

Adjust the idle by turning the idle shut-off valve on 1976 230

CO adjustment—1977 and later 230

3. Connect a tachometer and adjust the idle speed to specifications with the idle speed adjusting screw.

4. See whether the idle speed stop is resting against the throttle valve lever and not against the vacuum governor. Set the vacuum governor back if required.

5. If an exhaust gas analyzer (CO meter) is available, check the exhaust gas for percentage of CO. On '76 models, check CO without air injection. Disconnect and plug the center line from the blue switch-over valve. On 1977 models, be sure the wheel for altitude compensation is set correctly.

6. If required, adjust the CO by means of the fuel mixture screw or idle shut-off valve on the '76 230. Loosen the locknut while simultaneously holding the nozzle screw and turning the fuel shut-off valve. Accelerate a brief instant after each adjustment of the idle speed and fuel control screw, to stabilize the mixture.

7. Check the idle speed again and adjust with the idle speed adjusting screw, if required.

8. Adjust the control linkage as follows:

Run the engine at idle speed. Set the control rod so that it can be attached with no binding.

Solex 4 A 1

1. The idle speed adjustment on this carburetor is made with the air cleaner installed and the crankcase breather connected. If equipped with cruise control, be sure the cable is connected to the regulating lever without binding.

2. Warm the engine to normal operating temperature. Do not adjust the idle after the engine has been driven very far because the engine will be too hot.

3. On '76 280, 280C and 280S models with catalytic converter, disconnect the blue/purple vacuum line, to prevent air injection.

4. Check the throttle valve shaft for binding.

5. Adjust the idle speed to specifications with the idle speed adjusting screw. This should be done with a tachometer installed. Be sure that the idle speed stop is on the throttle valve lever and not on the vacuum governor. Loosen the spring of the vacuum governor, if necessary, by altering the setting of the adjusting nut.

6. Check the CO content of the exhaust gas. Follow the manufacturer's directions. If necessary, turn both mixture control screws to the right against the stop. Turn both screws simultaneously to the left until the CO percentage is within specifications. Turning the screws out will give a richer mixture and turning the screws in will give a leaner mixture.

7. Check the idle speed once again un-

61. Adjusting nut
68. Idling speed adjusting screw
130. Regulating rod

Solex 4A 1 idle speed adjustment

Mixture adjusting screws—carbureted 6-cylinder engines

Adjust the idle speed on 1976-79 V-8's at the idle air screw (arrow)

Adjust the CO with a special wrench on 1976 and later V8 fuel injection

Regulating lever adjustment—1976 and later V8's

til both the idle speed and CO percentage of the exhaust gas are as specified.

8. On '76 280, 280C and 280S, reconnect the blue/purple vacuum line.

FUEL INJECTION

1976–79

The mechanical fuel injection is the air flow controlled type known as Bosch K-Jetronic®. The idle speed should be adjusted with the air conditioner off and the transmission in Park.

1. Connect a tachometer.

2. Be sure the cruise control cable is connected to the regulating lever with no binding or kinking.

3. Run the engine to normal operating temperature.

4. Be sure the throttle valve rests against the idle speed stop.

5. Set the idle speed to specifications with the idle air screw.

6. If possible, check the CO level.

All 1976 engines—Check CO without air injection. Disconnect the blue/purple

Idle speed adjusting screw—1980 and later 6-cylinder

Idle speed adjusting screw—1980 and later V8

vacuum line at the blue thermal valve and plug the opening at the thermal valve to stop air injection.

1977–79 models—Disconnect the hose at the exhaust back pressure line and connect the CO tester to the line. On Federal V8 engines, check CO with air injection connected. On all others, disconnect the blue/purple vacuum line from the blue thermal valve and plug the thermo valve to cancel air injection.

7. Adjust the CO valve by unscrewing the plug and inserting the special adjusting tool (Allen wrench). Turn the screw in to richen the mixture and out to lean the mixture.

8. Accelerate briefly and check the speed and CO again.

9. Reconnect the vacuum lines and check the CO value again. It should be below the specified value.

10. Adjust the regulating lever so that the roller rests in the gate lever without binding. Put the transmission in Drive and turn on the A/C. Turn the wheels to full lock and adjust the idle speed so the engine runs smoothly.

1980 6-Cylinder and V8

1. Connect a tachometer and remote oil temperature gauge.

2. Run the engine to approximately 176° F oil temperature.

3. The automatic transmission should be in Park and the A/C off.

4. Be sure the throttle valve lever rests against the idle stop.

5. Adjust the Bowden cable with the adjusting screw so there is no tension against the throttle valve lever.

6. Check idle speed. If necessary, adjust with idle air adjustment screw.

1981 6-Cylinder

1. Run the engine to normal operating temperature (167°–185° oil temperature) and connect a tachometer.

2. The automatic transmission should be in Park and A/C off.

Adjusting nut for dashboard idle speed knob

CO tap on 1976 and later V8's

3. Be sure the throttle valve lever rests against the idle speed stop.

4. Be sure the cruise control actuating rod rests against the idle speed stop. Disconnect the connecting rod and push the lever of the actuating lever clockwise to the idle speed position.

5. Reconnect the connecting rod; make sure that the actuating element is approximately .04 in. from the idle speed stop. Adjust this clearance with the pull rod.

6. Check and adjust the idle speed. Idle speed is adjusted at the idle speed air screw.

1981–83 V8

These engines have electronically controlled idle speed, using a solenoid connected to terminals 1 and 5 of the control unit.

DIESEL ENGINES

1976–80 Except 1980 300SD

Since the diesel engine has no ignition distributor or ignition coil there is no way to connect an conventional external tachometer to measure idle speed. Using the built-in tachometer on the dash is not the most accurate way to set idle speed. See the "Diesel Services" unit repair section for more accurate methods of measuring idle speed.

1. On models before 1977, turn the knob on the instrument panel completely clockwise. Turn it again counterclockwise. The travel before the idle speed is raised should not exceed about ½ turn. If required, adjust the travel with the nut.

2. On 1977 and later models, turn the knob on the instrument panel completely clockwise and check the distance between the adjusting ring and the specially shaped spring. It should be approximately .04 in.

3. With the engine stopped, depress the accelerator pedal while turning the idle knob counterclockwise.

4. Start the engine. The idle should be 1000–1100 rpm. Adjust this with the adjusting screw, but do not exceed 1100 rpm.

5. On 1977 and later models, be sure the special spring is installed correctly.

1. Main fuel filter
2. Vent screw
3. Hollow screw with throttle screw
4. Fuel return line
5. Overflow line
6. Injection nozzle leakage line
7. Injection pump
8. Pressure line from injection pump to injection nozzle
9. Angular lever for auxiliary mechanical control
10. Injection nozzle
11. Venturi control unit
12. Vacuum line with throttle screw
13. Linkage and lever for accelerator pedal control
14. Fuel tank
15. Fuel prefilter
16. Fuel feed pump with hand pump
17. Adjusting lever
18. Accelerator pedal
19. Lever for auxiliary mechanical control
20. Heater plug starting switch with starting and stopping cable

Schematic diagram of diesel fuel system

1. Cable
2. Spring
3. Adjusting barrel
4. Lever

Be sure the specially shaped spring is installed as shown

Diesel engine idle speed adjustment—4-cylinder

6. Run the engine to operating temperature.

7. Turn the idle adjusting know on the dash fully to the right.

8. Disconnect the regulating rod and adjust the idle speed with the idle speed adjusting screw. 1977 and later models have a locknut on the idle speed adjusting screw.

9. Reconnect the regulating rod.

1980 300SD and 1981–83 Diesels Except 1982–83 240D

1. Run the engine to normal operating temperature.

2. On normally aspirated engines, turn the idle speed adjuster on the dash completely to the right.

3. Disconnect the pushrod at the angle lever.

4. Check the idle speed. Adjust by loosening the locknut and adjusting the idle speed screw. Tighten the locknut.

5. On all except Turbodiesels, adjust the pushrod so that a clearance of approximately .2 in. exists between the cam on the lever and the actuator on the switchover valve. The lever on the fuel injection pump must rest against the idle stop.

6. On all models except the 1981 Tur-

Diesel engine idle speed adjustment (4)—300D and 300CD

Clearance between cam and actuator on switch-over valve—1980 and later except turbodiesel

Diesel engine idle speed adjustment—1976 and later

1. Adjusting screw 2. Bowden cable, cruise control
Bowden cable adjustment—1980 and later diesels

Idle speed adjustment (3) on 1982–83 240D

bodiesel, depress the stop lever as far as possible. The cruise control Bowden cable should be free of tension against the angle lever. Use the adjusting screw to alter the tension. Let go of the stop lever. The Bowden cable should have a slight amount of play.

7. On Turbodiesels, adjust the pushrod so that the roller in the guide lever rests free of tension against the stop.

8. Put the automatic transmission in Drive, and turn the steering wheel to full lock. The engine should run smoothly. If not, adjust the idle speed. Disconnect the cruise control connecting rod, and push the lever clockwise to the idle stop. Attach the connecting rod, making sure the lever is about 0.04 in. from the idle speed stop.

CAUTION
If the engine speed is adjusted higher, it will be above the controlled idle speed range of the governor and the engine can increase in speed to maximum rpm.

1982–83 240D

1. Run the engine to normal operating temperature.

2. Turn the idle speed adjuster knob on the dashboard completely to the right.

20. Temperature switch 42°C/107°F coolant
21. Control unit electronic idle speed regulation
23. Idle speed adjuster
29. Voltage supply relay
30. Excess voltage protection unit
a. To control unit lambda control, term. 8
b. To relay air injection
c. To control unit lambda control, term. 6

Electronic idle control system

3. Disconnect the pushrod at the operating lever.

4. Move the guide lever to the idle speed position. Set the edge of the guide lever at the mark (arrow) on the cap.

5. Check, and if necessary, adjust the idle speed. Use the idle speed adjusting screw.

6. Attach the pushrod to the injection pump lever so that the rod is free of tension when the lever is against the idle speed stop.

7. Check to be sure the cruise control rods are free of tension.

8. Move the automatic transmission into Drive. Turn on the A/C and turn the wheels to full lock. The engine should run smoothly. Adjust the idle speed if necessary.

ENGINE ELECTRICAL

Distributor

REMOVAL AND INSTALLATION

The removal and installation procedures for all distributors on Mercedes-Benz vehicles are basically similar. However, certain minor differences may exist from model to model.

1. The distributor is usually located on the front of the engine.

2. Remove the dust cover, distributor cap, cable plug connections, and vacuum line.

3. Rotating the engine in the normal direction, crank it around until the distributor rotor points to the mark on the rim of the distributor housing. This indicates No. 1 cylinder.

4. The engine can be cranked with a socket wrench on the balancer bolt or with a screwdriver inserted in the balancer.

5. Matchmark the distributor body and the engine so that the distributor can be returned to its original position. White paint can be used for this purpose.

6. Remove the distributor hold-down bolt and withdraw the distributor from the engine.

NOTE: Do not crank the engine while the distributor is removed.

7. To install the distributor, reverse the removal instructions. Insert the distributor so that the matchmarks on the distributor and engine are aligned.

8. Tighten the clamp bolt and check the dwell angle and ignition timing.

Electronic Ignition

TESTING

All Except 1981 6-Cylinder

1. Check the screw type plug terminals and the plug wires.

2. With the ignition ON, a primary current of about 8 amps will flow continuously through the system.

3. Check the input voltage at the terminal block. Terminal 15 should show 4.5 volts and terminal 1 should show 0.5–2.0 volts. If the voltage at terminal 1 is excessive, replace the switching unit.

4. If there is no spark but terminal 1 voltage is OK, check the armature resis-

Testing armature resistance—electronic ignition prior to 1980

Testing pick-up coil resistance—electronic ignition prior to 1980

tance (terminal 7 and 31 d). Resistance should be 450–750 ohms.

5. Test the pick-up coil resistance. There should be infinite resistance between terminal 7 and ground.

6. Check the armature and pick-up coil for mechanical damage. An air gap should exist between them.

7. Check the dwell angle. Even though it cannot be adjusted, it should be 25–39° at 1400–1500 rpm.

8. If the armature and pick-up coil are functioning, replace the switching unit. If the armature and pick-up coil indicate no damage, replace the switching unit. If the armature or pick-up coil are defective, replace the distributor.

1981 6-Cylinder

This engine uses a new breakerless transistorized ignition system with no preresistance and no current flow unless the engine is running. The new system consists of ignition coil, distributor, harness and switching unit. Do not replace the coil with a previously used coil. Also, see the ignition system precautions given previously.

1. Test the voltage between bushing 5 of the diagnosis plug and ground with the ignition ON. Nominal battery voltage should be indicated. If not, test the voltage via the ignition switch. If voltage is correct, go to Step 2.

2. Test the voltage between bushing 4 and 5 of the diagnosis plug socket. Zero voltage should be indicated. If voltage is more than 0.1 volt, switch off the ignition immediately. Renew the switching unit. Check the pressure relief plug in the ignition coil and the ohmic value of the ignition coil between terminals 1 and 15. If the pressure relief plug has poppsed out or the resistance is not .7Ω, replace the ignition coil.

3. Test the dwell angle. It should be 7–25°. If more than 25°, replace the switching unit. If no reading or the reading is correct, go to Step 4.

4. Disconnect the green control line from the switching unit and test the resistance between terminals 3 and 7. Resistance should be 500–700 ohms. If the resistance is wrong, pull the green cable from the distributor and see if there are 500–700 ohms present at the connector plugs. If so, replace the green cable. If not, replace the distributor.

5. Remove the green cable from the control unit. There should be 200 kΩ between terminals 3 or 7 and ground. If not, disconnect the green cable from the distributor and test the resistance between any of the plugs and ground. If 200 kΩ are not present, replace the distributor.

Alternator

All Mercedes-Benz cars covered in this book use 12 volt electrical systems with alternators, in conjunction with the transistor or electronic ignition system.

1. Distributor cap
2. Rotor
3. Dust cover
4. Armature and pick-up assembly
5. Distributor housing with pick-up connection

Breakerless ignition distributor—1975-80

ALTERNATOR PRECAUTIONS

Some precautions that should be taken into consideration when working on this, or any other, AC charging system are as follows:

1. Never switch battery polarity.

2. When installing a battery, always connect the grounded terminal first.

3. Never disconnect the battery while the engine is running.

4. If the molded connector is disconnected from the alternator, do not ground the hot wire.

5. Never run the alternator with the main output cable disconnected.

6. Never electric weld around the car without disconnecting the alternator.

7. Never apply any voltage in excess of battery voltage during testing.

8. Never "jump" a battery for starting purposes with more than 12 volts.

REMOVAL AND INSTALLATION

Viewing the engine from the front, the alternator is located on the left or right-hand side, usually down low. Because of the location, it is sometimes easier to remove the alternator from below the vehicle. The following is a general procedure for all models.

1. Locate the alternator and disconnect and tag all wires.

2. Loosen the adjusting (pivot) bolt or the adjusting mechanism and swing the alternator in toward the engine.

3. Remove the drive belt from the alternator pulley.

4. The alternator can now be removed from its mounting bracket or the bracket and alternator can be removed from the engine.

5. Installation is the reverse of removal.

6. Tighten all of the drive belts that were loosened.

Belt Tension Adjustment

All alternator drive belts should be tensioned to approximately ½ in. deflection under thumb pressure at the middle of the longest span.

Starter

All Mercedes-Benz passenger cars are equipped with 12-volt Bosch electric starters of various rated outputs. The starter is actuated and the pinion engaged by an electric solenoid mounted on top of the starter motor.

When removing the starter, note the exact position of all wires and washers since they should be installed in their original locations. Also, on some models it may be necessary to position the front wheels to the left or right to provide working clearance.

REMOVAL AND INSTALLATION

1. Remove all wires from the starter and tag them for location.

2. Disconnect the battery cable.

3. Unbolt the starter from the bellhousing and remove the ground cable.

4. Remove the starter from underneath the car.

5. Installation is the reverse of removal. Be sure to replace all wires and washers in their original locations.

Battery

The battery is located in the engine compartment and can be easily removed by disconnecting the battery cables and removing the hold-down clamp.

NOTE: If installing an aftermarket battery, be sure to get one of sufficient rated power for diesel models. Also, check the physical dimensions.

ENGINE MECHANICAL

All engines have an overhead cam design, operating the valve through individual rocker arms. The smallest of the engines is the 2307 cc gasoline engine installed in the 230. A 4-cylinder diesel engine of 2404 cc displacement is also available in the 240D. Six-cylinder, OHC cam engines are available in displacements from 2746 to 2778 cc's. The exception to the six-cylinder engine family is the DOHC engine installed in the 280, 280C, 280E, 280S, 280SE, and 280CE. All larger sedans use either a 3.8, 4.5 or 6.9 liter V8. The 6.9 liter engine is used exclusively in the 6.9 model. In 1981 a 3.8 liter V8 was introduced for the 380SEL, 380SEC and 380SL models. All V8's are OHC models with one camshaft per head.

NOTE: Care should be taken when working on Mercedes-Benz engines, since there are many aluminum parts which can be damaged if carelessly handled.

Engine

REMOVAL AND INSTALLATION

NOTE: In all cases, Mercedes-Benz engines and transmissions are removed as a unit.

——— **CAUTION** ———
Air conditioner lines should not be indiscriminately disconnected without taking proper precautions. It is best to swing the compressor out of the way while still connected to its hoses. Never do any welding around the compressor—heat may cause an explosion. Also, the refrigerant, while inert at normal room temperature, breaks down under high temperature into hydrogen fluoride and phosgene (among other products), which are highly poisonous.

230, 240D, 300D, 300CD, 300TD, 300SD

1. First, remove the hood, then drain the cooling system and disconnect the battery. While not strictly necessary, it is better to remove the battery completely to prevent breakage by the engine as it is lifted out.

2. Remove the fan shroud, radiator, and disconnect all heater hoses and oil cooler lines.

3. Remove the air cleaner and all fuel, vacuum and oil hoses (e.g., power steering

Engine removal—6-cylinder gas engine. Inset shows lift attaching points.

and power brakes). Plug all openings to keep out dirt.

4. Remove the viscous coupling and fan and, on applicable engines, disconnect the carburetor choke cable.

5. On diesel engines, disconnect the idle control starting cables. On the 300SD, loosen the oil filter cover slightly; siphon off the power steering fluid and disconnect the hoses.

6. On all engines, disconnect the accelerator linkage.

7. Disconnect all ground straps and electrical connections. It is a good idea to tag each wire for easy reassembly.

8. Detach the gearshift linkage and the exhaust pipes from the manifolds.

9. Loosen the steering relay arm and pull it down out of the way, along with the center steering rod and hydraulic steering damper.

10. The hydraulic engine shock absorber should be removed.

11. Remove the hydraulic line from the clutch housing and the oil line connectors from the automatic transmission.

12. Unbolt the clutch slave cylinder from the bellhousing after removing the return spring.

13. Remove the exhaust pipe bracket attached to the transmission and place a wood-padded jack under the bellhousing, or place a cable sling under the oil pan, to support the engine. On turbocharged models, disconnect the exhaust pipes at the turbo charger.

14. Mark the position of the rear engine support and unbolt the two outer bolts, then remove the top bolt at the transmission and pull the support out.

15. Disconnect the speedometer cable and the front driveshaft U-joint. Push the driveshaft back and wire it out of the way.

16. Unbolt the engine mounts on both sides and, on four-cylinder engines, the front limit stop.

17. Unbolt the power steering fluid reservoir and swing it out of the way; then, using a chain hoist and cable, lift the engine and transmission upward and outward. An angle of about 45° will allow the car to be pushed backward while the engine is coming up.

18. Reverse the procedure to install, making sure to bleed the hydraulic clutch, power steering, power brakes and fuel system.

V8 Engines

NOTE: Removal of a V8 engine equipped with air conditioning requires disconnecting the air conditioning system. This should only be done by an air conditioning specialist. Take the car to an air conditioning specialist to have the system discharged prior to engine removal.

1. Remove the hood. On the 380SEC, the hood can be tilted back 90° and does not have to be removed.

1. U-Joint flange
2. Front driveshaft
3. Hex bolt
4. U-Joint plate
5. Wooden block

Supporting the transmission—V8's

2. Drain the cooling system.

3. Remove the radiator and fan shroud.

4. Remove the cable plug from the temperature switch.

5. Remove the battery, battery frame and air filter.

6. Drain the power steering reservoir and windshield washer reservoir.

7. Disconnect and plug the high pressure and return lines on the power steering pump.

8. Detach the fuel lines from the fuel filter, pressure regulator, and pressure sensor.

9. If equipped, loosen the line to the supply and anti-freeze tanks. On the 6.9, disconnect the lines to the hydro-pneumatic suspension.

10. Disconnect the cables from the ignition coil and transistor ignition switch-box.

11. Disconnect the brake vacuum lines.

12. Detach the cable connections for the following:
   a. venturi control unit
   b. temperature sensor
   c. distributor
   d. temperature switch
   e. cold starting valve
   f. speedometer inductance transmitter (3.8 only)

13. Remove the regulating shaft by pushing it in the direction of the firewall.

14. Disconnect the thrust and pullrods.

15. Disconnect the heater lines.

16. Detach the lines to the oil pressure and temperature gauges.

17. Remove the ground strap from the vehicle.

18. Detach the cables from the alternator, terminal bridge, and battery. Remove the battery.

19. On the 6.9, remove the oil line shield and disconnect the oil lines between the oil pan and oil reservoir.

20. Position a lifting sling on the engine and take up the slack in the chain.

21. Remove the left-hand engine mount

and loosen the hex nut on the right-hand mount.

22. Remove the exhaust system. Remove the connecting rod chain on the rear level control valve and loosen the torsion bar slightly. Raise the vehicle slightly at the rear and remove the exhaust system in a rearward direction.

23. Disconnect the handbrake cable.

24. Remove the shield plate from the transmission tunnel.

25. Place a block of wood between the transmission and cross yoke so the engine will not sag, when the rear mount is removed.

26. Loosen the driveshaft intermediate bearing and the driveshaft slide.

27. Support the transmission with a jack.

28. Mark the installation of the crossmember and remove the crossmember. Remove the rear engine carrier with the engine mount.

29. Unbolt the front U-joint flange on the transmission and push it back. Do not loosen the clamp nut on the intermediate bearing. Support the driveshaft.

30. Disconnect the speedometer shaft, shift rod, control pressure rod, regulating linkage (on automatic transmissions), kick-down switch cable, starter lockout switch cable, and the cable for the back-up light switch.

31. Remove the front engine mounting bolt and remove the engine at approximately a 45° angle.

32. Installation is the reverse of removal. Lower the engine until it is behind the front axle carrier. Place a jack under the transmission and lower the engine into its compartment. While lowering the engine, install the right-hand shock mount.

Fill the engine with all required fluids and start the engine. Check for leaks.

280, 280C, 280E, 280CE, 280SE, 280S

1. Scribe alignment marks on the hood hinges and remove the hood. Drain the coolant from the radiator and block.

2. Remove the radiator.

3. Disconnect the lines from the vacuum pump.

4. On vehicles with air conditioning, remove the compressor and place it aside.

CAUTION

Do not remove the refrigerant lines from the compressor. Physical harm could result.

---

5. Disconnect and tag all electrical connections from the engine.

6. Disconnect all coolant and vacuum lines from the engine.

7. Disconnect and plug the pressure oil lines from the power steering pump, after draining the pump reservoir.

8. Remove the accelerator linkage control rod by pulling off the lockring and pushing the shaft in the direction of the firewall.

9. Loosen and remove the exhaust pipes from the manifold and transmission supports.

10. Disconnect the transmission linkage and all other connections.

11. Loosen the front right (driving direction) shock absorber from the front axle carrier.

12. Remove the left-hand engine shock absorber from the engine mount.

13. Attach a lifting device to the engine and tension the cables.

14. Unbolt the engine and transmission mounts and remove the engine at a 45° angle.

15. Installation is the reverse of removal. Be sure to check all fluids and fill or top up as necessary. Check all adjustments on the engine.

Studs (arrows) on the 5-cylinder engine are for attaching the rocker cover.

Cylinder Head

REMOVAL AND INSTALLATION

4 and 5-Cylinder Engines

In order to perform a valve job or to inspect cylinder bores for wear, the head must be removed. While this may seem fairly straightforward, some caution must be observed to ensure that valve timing is not disturbed.

1. Drain the radiator and remove all hoses and wires.

2. Remove the camshaft cover and associated throttle linkage, then press out the spring clamp from the notch in the rocker arm.

3. Push the clamp outward over the ball cap of the rocker, then depress the valve with a large screwdriver and lift the rocker arm out of the ball pin head.

4. Remove the rocker arm supports and the camshaft sprocket nut.

5. On diesels, the rockers and their supports must be removed together.

6. Using a suitable puller, remove the camshaft sprocket, after having first marked the chain, sprocket and cam reassembly.

7. Remove the sprocket and chain and wire it out of the way.

——— CAUTION ———

Make sure the chain is securely wired so that it will not slide down into the engine.

8. Unbolt the manifolds and exhaust header pipe and push them out of the way.

9. Loosen the cylinder head holddown bolts in the reverse order of that shown in torque diagrams for each model. It is good practice to loosen each bolt a little at a time, working around the head, until all are free. This prevents unequal stresses in the metal.

10. Reach into the engine compartment and gradually work the head loose from each end by rocking it. Never, under any circumstances, use a screwdriver between

4-cylinder diesel engine cylinder head (5-cylinder is similar)

4-cylinder head

the head and block to pry, as the head will be scarred badly and may be ruined.

11. Installation is the reverse of removal.

V8 Engines

Before removing the cylinder head from a

V8, be sure you have the 4 special tools necessary to torque the head bolts; without them it will be impossible. Do not confuse the left and right-hand head gaskets—the left side has 2 attaching holes in the timing chain cover, the right side has only 1 hole.

Cylinder heads on 3.8 and 4.5 liter V8's are not interchangeable.

You need these tools to remove or install the V8 cylinder head. Without them it is practically impossible.

Be careful removing the cylinder head bolts on a V8. The inner row of cam bolts are the only bolts NOT holding the head on. Note the angle of the bolts.

NOTE: Cylinder heads can only be removed with the engine cold.

1. Drain the cooling system.
2. Remove the battery.
3. Remove the air cleaner. Remove the fan and fan shroud.
4. Pull the cable plug from the temperature sensor.
5. On the 6.9, to remove the right-hand head, remove the alternator (with bracket), windshield washer reservoir and bracket and automatic transmission dipstick tube.
6. Detach the vacuum hose from the venturi control unit.
7. Remove the following electrical connections:
    a. injection valves
    b. distributor
    c. venturi control unit
    d. temperature sensor and temperature switch
    e. starting valve
    f. temperature switch for the auxiliary fan.
8. Loosen the ring line on the fuel distributor.
9. Loosen the screws on the injection valves and pressure regulator or mixture regulator. Remove the ring line with the injection valves and pressure regulator.
10. Plug the holes for the injection valves in the cylinder head.
11. Remove the regulating shaft by disconnecting the pull rod and the thrust rod.
12. Remove the ignition cable plug.
13. Loosen the vacuum connection on the intake manifold.
14. Loosen the vacuum connection for the central lock at the transmission.
15. Remove the oil filler tube from the right-hand cylinder head and remove the temperature connector.
16. Remove the oil pressure gauge line from the left-hand cylinder head.
17. Loosen the coolant connection on the intake manifold.
18. Remove the intake manifold. This

DOHC camshafts and related parts

Cylinder head right 1-14

1. Filler plug
2. Sealing ring
3. Cylinder head cover
4. Sealing ring
5. Holder for cable to injection valves
6. Connection
7. Valve cover gasket
8. Connection to temperature sensor
9. Sealing ring
10. Cylinder head
11. Cylinder head gasket
12. Cable holder
13. 5 Washers
14. Hollow dowel pins

Cylinder head left 20-34

20. Connection
21. Sealing ring
22. Cylinder head cover
23. 8 Screws
24. 8 Sealing rings
25. Cylinder head cover gasket
26. 36 Washers
27. Sealing ring
28. Screw connection oil pressure gauge
29. 3 Studs
30. 13 Studs
31. Cylinder head
32. Valve seat ring—intake
33. Valve seat ring—exhaust
34. Cylinder head gasket

Cylinder head bolts

(a)—10 M 10 x 50chrauben)

(camshaft bearing fastening bolts)
(b)—10 M 10 x 155
(c)—18 M 10 x 80
(d)—8 M 10 x 55
(e)—4 M 8 x 30
(f)—1 M 8 x 70

Valve arrangement 40-55

40. Tensioning spring
41. Rocker arm
42. Adjusting screw
43. Threaded bushing
44. Thrust piece
45. Valve cone piece
46. Valve spring retainer
47. Outer valve spring
48. Inner valve spring
49. Rotator
50. Intake valve seal
51. Exhaust valve guide
52. Intake valve
53. Exhaust valve seal
54. Exhaust valve guide
55. Exhaust valve

Engine timing 60-100

60. Camshaft-right
61. Oil pipe (external lubrication)
62. Connecting piece
63. Connecting piece
64. Camshaft bearing-flywheel end
65. Camshaft bearing 4

Oil pipe to camshaft bearing

66. Camshaft bearing 2 and 3
67. Camshaft bearing-cranking end
68. 5 Hollow dowel pins
69. Spring washer
70. Camshaft-left
71. Compensating washer
72. Camshaft gear
73. Washer-camshaft gear
74. Spring washer
75. Bolt
76. 3 Slide rails
77. 6 Bearing bolts
78. Drive gear ignition distributor
79. Guide rail
80. Lockwasher
81. Spring—chain tensioner, oil pump
82. Washer
83. Screw
84. Clamp
85. Single roller chain (oil pump drive)
86. Crankshaft gear
87. Slide rail
88. 4 Screws
89. 4 Spring washers
90. Plug
91. Sealing ring
92. Bearing bolt
93. Tensioning lever
94. 2 Bolts
95. 2 Spring washers
96. Chain tensioner
97. Gasket
98. Double roller chain
99. Spacer ring
100. Idler gear

V-8 engine cylinder head

is not necessary on 3.8 liter V8's although the intake manifold bolts must be removed.

19. Loosen the alternator belt and remove the alternator and mounting bracket.

20. Remove the electrical connections from the distributor and electronic ignition switch-gear.

21. Drain some fluid from the power steering reservoir and disconnect and plug the return hose and high pressure supply line.

22. Disconnect the exhaust system. On 3.8 liter V8's, remove the exhaust manifolds.

23. Loosen the right-hand holder for the engine damper.

24. Remove the right-hand chain tensioner.

25. Matchmark the camshaft, camshaft sprocket, and chain. Remove the camshaft sprocket and chain after removing the cylinder head cover. Be sure to hang the chain and sprocket to prevent it from falling into the timing chain case.

26. Remove the upper slide rail. On 3.8 liter V8's, remove the distributor and remove the inner slide rail on the left cylinder head. Remove the rail after the camshaft sprocket.

27. Unscrew the cylinder head bolts. This should be done with a cold engine. Unscrew the bolts in the reverse order of the illustrated torque sequences. Unscrew all the bolts a little at a time and proceed in this manner until all the bolts have been removed. On the 6.9, you'll need to raise the engine to remove No. 12 and 18 bolts on the left-side head. To do this, place the level adjusting switch at "S" (first notch).

NOTE: Cylinder head bolts on 3.8 liter V8's are nickel plated and 10 mm longer than those for previous engines.

28. Remove the cylinder head. Do not pry on the cylinder head.

29. Remove the cylinder head gasket.

30. Clean the cylinder head and cylinder block joint faces.

31. To install, position the cylinder head gasket.

32. Do not confuse the cylinder head

gaskets. The left-hand head has two attaching holes in the timing chain cover while the right-hand has three.

33. Install the cylinder head and torque the bolts according to the illustrated torque sequence.

34. Further installation is the reverse of removal. On 3.8 liter V8's, insert the rear cam bearing cylinder head bolt before positioning the cylinder head. Also, install the exhaust manifolds only after the cylinder head bolts have been tightened. The camshaft sprocket should be installed so that the flange faces the camshaft. Check the valve clearance and fill the engine with oil. Top up the power steering tank and bleed the power steering system.

35. Run the engine and check for leaks.

6-Cylinder DOHC Engine

NOTE: Two people are best for this job. The head must be removed STRAIGHT up. The 2 bolts in the chain case are removed with a magnet.

To install use 2 pieces of wood ½ in. × 1½ in. × 9 in. to support the head while aligning the bolt holes. The exhaust camshaft gear bolt is 0.2 in. shorter.

1. Completely drain the cooling system.

2. Remove the air filter.

3. Remove the radiator.

4. Remove the rocker arm cover.

5. Remove the battery. Remove the idler pulley and the holding bracket for the compressor.

6. Remove the compressor and bracket and lay it aside without disconnecting any of the lines.

CAUTION
Disconnecting any of the refrigerant lines could result in physical harm.
---

7. Unbolt the cover from the camshaft housing.

8. Disconnect the heating water line from the carburetor, the vacuum line on the starter housing, and the distributor vacuum line.

9. Disconnect all electrical connec-

tions, water lines, fuel lines, and vacuum lines which are connected to the cylinder head. Tag these for reassembly.

10. Remove the regulating linkage shaft.

11. Remove the EGR line between the exhaust return valve and the exhaust pipe.

12. Disconnect and plug the oil return line at the cylinder head.

13. At the thermostat housing, loosen the hose which passes between the thermostat housing and the water pump. Unscrew the bypass line on the water pump.

14. Loosen the oil dipstick tube from the clamp and bend it slightly sidewards.

15. Unbolt the exhaust pipes from the exhaust manifolds and bracket on the transmission.

16. Force the tension springs out of the rocker arm with a screwdriver.

17. Remove all of the rocker arms.

18. Crank the engine to TDC. This can be done with a socket wrench on the crankshaft pulley bolt. The marks on the camshaft sprockets and bearing housings must be aligned.

19. Hold the camshafts and remove the bolt which holds each camshaft gear to the camshaft.

20. Remove the upper slide rail. Knock out the bearing bolts with a puller.

21. Remove the chain tensioner.

22. Push both camshafts toward the rear and remove the camshafts' sprockets.

23. Remove the spacer sleeves on both camshafts. The sleeves are located in front of the camshaft bearings.

24. Remove the guide wheel by unscrewing the plug and removing the bearing bolt.

25. Lift off the timing chain and suspend the chain from the hood with a piece of wire. Pull out the guide gear.

26. Remove the slide rail in the cylinder head by removing the bearing pin with a puller.

27. Loosen the cylinder head bolts in small increments, using the reverse order of the tightening sequence. This should be done on a cold engine to prevent the possibility of head warpage.

28. Pull out the two bolts in the chain

Fabricated tools for installing the cylinder head on DOHC 6-cylinder engines

The marks on the camshaft and bearing housing must align on DOHC 6-cylinder engines when the engine is at TDC

While the head is removed from a 6-cylinder engine, always replace this rubber hose, whether it needs it or not; it is impossible to replace with the cylinder head installed.

Replacing valve guides

case with a magnet. Be careful not to drop the washers.

29. Pull up on the timing chain and force the tensioning rail toward the center of the engine.

30. Lift the cylinder head up in a vertical direction.

NOTE: Mercedes-Benz recommends two people for this job.

31. Remove the cylinder head gasket and clean the joint faces of the block and head.

32. To install, cut two pieces of wood ½ in. × 1½ in. × 9½ in. Lay one piece upright between cylinders 1 and 2; lay the other flat between cylinders 5 and 6.

33. Install the cylinder head in an inclined position so that the timing chain and tensioning rail can be inserted.

34. Lift the cylinder head at the front and remove the front piece of wood toward the exhaust side. Carefully lower the cylinder head until the bolt holes align.

35. Lift the head at the rear so that the board can be removed toward the exhaust side. Carefully lower the cylinder head until all the bolt holes align.

36. Tighten the cylinder head bolts in gradual steps until they are fully tightened. Follow the torque sequence illustrated.

37. Check to be sure that both camshafts rotate freely after the bolts are tight.

38. The remainder of installation is the reverse of removal. Be sure that the spacer for the camshaft gear with the engaging lugs for the vacuum pump drive gear is installed on the exhaust side. Also, the washers for the bolts attaching the camshaft gears to the camshafts must be installed with the domed side against the head of the bolt.

39. Note that the attaching bolt for the exhaust camshaft gear is 0.2 in. shorter.

40. Be sure to adjust the valve clearance and fill the cooling system. Run the engine and check for leaks.

OVERHAUL

Overhaul procedures for cylinder heads are contained in "Engine Rebuilding" in the Unit Repair section of this book. Consult this section for detailed overhaul procedures.

Valve Guides

REMOVAL AND INSTALLATION

See "Engine Rebuilding" in the Unit Repair section also.

1. Remove the cylinder head.

2. Clean the valve guide with a brush, knocking away all loose carbon and oil deposits.

3. Knock out the old valve guide with a drift.

4. Check the bore in the cylinder head and clean up any rough spots. Use a reamer for this purpose. If necessary, the valve guide bore can be reamed for oversize valve guides.

5. Clean the basic bores for the valve guides.

6. Heat the cylinder head in water to approximately 176–194°F.

7. If possible cool the valve guides slightly.

8. Drive the valve guides into the bores with a drift. Coat the bores in the cylinder head with wax prior to installation and be sure that the circlip rests against the cylinder head.

9. Let the head cool and try to knock the valve guide out with light hammer blows and a plastic drift. If the guide can be knocked out, try another guide with a tighter fit.

10. Install the cylinder head.

Rocker Arms

REMOVAL AND INSTALLATION

Diesel Engines

Rocker arms on diesel engines can only be removed as a unit with the respective rocker arm blocks.

1. Detach the connecting rod for the venturi control unit from the bearing bracket lever and remove the bearing bracket from the rocker arm cover.

2. Remove the air vent line from the rocker arm cover and remove the rocker arm cover.

3. Remove the stretchbolts from the rocker arm blocks and remove the blocks with the rocker arms. Turn the crankshaft in each case so that the camshaft does not put any load on the rocker arms.

NOTE: Turn the crankshaft with a socket wrench on the crankshaft pulley bolt. Do not rotate the engine by turning the camshaft sprocket.

4. Before installing the rocker arms, check the sliding surfaces of the ball cup and rocker arms. Replace any defective parts.

5. To install, assemble the rocker arm blocks and insert new stretchbolts.

6. Tighten the stretchbolts. In each case, position the camshaft so that there is no load on the rocker arms. See the previous NOTE.

7. Check to be sure that the tension clamps have engaged with the notches of the rocker arm blocks.

8. Adjust the valve clearance.

9. Reinstall the rocker arm cover, air vent line, and bearing bracket for the reverse lever. Attach the connecting rod for the venturi control unit to the reversing lever.

10. Make sure that during acceleration, the control cable can move freely without binding.

11. Start the engine and check the rocker arm cover for leaks.

Hydraulic Valve Lifters

V8 ENGINES

Hydraulic valve lifters are used with overhead cams on 1976 and later V8 engines. The rocker arm is always in contact with the cam, reducing noise and eliminating operating clearance.

Checking Base Setting

The base setting is the clearance between the upper edge of the cylindrical part of the plunger and the lower edge of the retaining cap (dimension A) when the cam lobe is vertical.

NOTE: A dial indicator with an extension and a measuring thrust piece (MBNA #100 589 16 63 00, 0.187 in. thick are necessary to perform this adjustment.

1. Turn the cam lobe to a vertical position, relative to the rocker arm.

2. Attach a dial indicator and tip extension and insert the extension through the bore in the rocker arm onto the head plunger. Preload the dial indicator by 0.08 in. and zero the instrument.

3. Depress the valve with a valve spring compressor. The lift on the dial indicator should be 0.028–0.075 in.

4. If the lift is excessive, the base setting can be changed by installing a new thrust piece.

5. Remove the dial indicator.

6. Remove the rocker arm.

7. Remove the thrust piece and insert the measuring disc.

8. Install the rocker arm and repeat Steps 1–3.

9. Select a thrust piece according to the table. If the measured valve was 0–0.002 in. and the 0.2146 in. thrust piece will not give the proper base setting, use the 0.2283 in. thrust piece.

10. Remove the dial indicator and the rocker arm. Install the selected thrust piece.

11. Reinstall the rocker arm and dial indicator and repeat Steps 1–3.

1. Camshaft
2. Rocker arm
3. Hydraulic valve clearance compensating element
4. Cylinder head
5. Valve guide
6. Exhaust valve
7. Valve seat ring
8. Thrust piece
9. Valve spring retainer
10. Valve keeper
11. Outer valve spring
12. Inner valve spring
13. Valve stem seal
14. Rotocap

Valve train on 3.8 V8

SELECTIVE THRUST PIECES

Measured Value (in.)	Thrust Piece Thickness(s) (in.)
0–0.002	0.2146/0.2283
0.002–0.034	0.2008
0.035–0.066	0.1870
0.067–0.099	0.1732
0.099–0.131	0.1594
above 0.131	0.1457

Thrust piece thickness

Cutaway view of hydraulic valve lifter

15. Valve connection
16. Nut
17. Washer
18. Gasket
19. Idle speed air line
20. Screw connection
21. Sealing ring
22. Upper Intake manifold
23. Holder
24. Hex bolt
25. Connection
26. Sealing ring

27. Gasket
28. Screw connection
29. Sealing ring
30. Screw connection
31. Sealing ring
32. Bottom intake manifold
33. Rubber connecting piece
35. Hex bolt
34. Hex bolt
36. Sealing ring
37. Plug
38. Hose

V8 intake manifold

9. Remove the intake manifold. If a portion of the manifold must be replaced, disassemble the intake manifold. Replace the rubber connections during reassembly.

10. Intake manifold installation is the reverse of removal. Replace all seals and gaskets. Adjust the linkage and idle speed.

Exhaust Manifold

REMOVAL AND INSTALLATION

V8 Engine

1. Unbolt the exhaust pipes from the manifolds.
2. Disconnect the rubber mounting ring from the exhaust system.
3. Loosen the shield plate on the exhaust manifold.
4. When removing the left-hand exhaust manifold, remove the shield plate for the engine mount together with the engine damper.
5. Unbolt the manifold from the engine.
6. Pull the manifolds off of the mounting.
7. Installation is the reverse of removal.

Timing Chain Tensioner

REMOVAL AND INSTALLATION

4 and 5-Cylinder Engines

There are 2 kinds of timing chain tensioners. One uses an O-ring seal and the other

Removal and Installation

Temporarily removed valve lifters must be reinstalled in their original locations. When replacing worn rocker arms, the camshaft must also be replaced. If the rocker arm, or hydraulic lifter is replaced, check the base setting.

Remove the rocker arm and unscrew the valve lifter with a 24 mm socket.

Intake Manifold

REMOVAL AND INSTALLATION

V8 Engine

1. Partially drain the coolant.
2. Remove the air cleaner.
3. Disconnect the regulating linkage and remove the longitudinal regulating shaft.
4. Pull off all cable plug connections.
5. Disconnect and plug the fuel lines

on the pressure regulator and starting valve.
6. Unscrew the nuts on the injection valves and set the injection valves aside.
7. Remove the 16 attaching bolts from the intake manifold.
8. Loosen the hose clip on the thermostat housing hose and disconnect the hose.

Replace the rubber connecting pieces on the intake manifold, anytime the manifold is removed.

The inside bolt (arrow) on the V8 chain tensioner can only be reached by inserting a long, straight allen key underneath the exhaust manifold.

13. Closing plug
14. Sealing ring
15. Threaded ring
16. Chain tensioner
17. Tension rail
18. Cylinder head

6-cylinder timing chain tensioner

Remove the plug with a 17 mm allen key

a flat gasket. Do not install a flat gasket on a tensioner meant to be used with an O-ring.

Chain tensioners should be replaced as a unit if defective.

1. Drain the coolant. If the car has air conditioning, disconnect the compressor and mounting bracket and lay it aside. Do not disconnect the refrigerant lines.

On diesel engines, drain the coolant from the block.

2. Remove the thermostat housing.

3. Loosen and remove the chain tensioner. Be careful of loose O-ring.

4. Check the O-rings or gasket and replace if necessary.

5. To fill the chain tensioner, place the tensioner (pressure bolt down) in a container of SAE 10 engine oil, at least up to the flat flange. Using a drill press, depress the pressure bolt slowly, about 7–10 times. Be sure this is done slowly and uniformly.

Remove the threaded plug.

Remove the chain tensioner with a 10 mm allen key

Install the chain tensioner

6. Install the chain tensioner. Tighten the bolts evenly.

V8 Engines

The chain tensioner is connected to the engine oil circuit. Bleeding occurs once oil pressure has been established and the tensioner is filling with oil.

Since December of 1974, a venting hole

Tighten the tensioner until it "clicks"

has been installed in the tensioner to prevent oil foaming. If you have a lot of timing chain noise, use this type of tensioner, which is identified by a white paint dot on the cap.

Service procedures for tensioners and rails on the 3.8 liter V8 are the same as for the 4.5 liter V8. Arrangement and shape and size of parts however, is slightly different.

1. On California models, disconnect the line from the tensioner.

2. Remove the attaching bolts and remove the tensioner. The inside bolts will probably require a long, straight 6 mm Allen key to bypass the exhaust manifold. It is a tight fit.

3. Place the tensioner vertically in a container of engine oil. Operate the pressure bolt to fill the tensioner. After filling, it should permit compression very slowly under considerable force. If not, replace the tensioner with a new unit.

4. Install the tensioner and tighten the bolts evenly.

6-Cylinder Engines

1. On A/C vehicles, remove the battery. Unbolt the refrigerant compressor and lay it aside. Do not disconnect the refrigerant lines.

2. Remove the plug with a 17 mm Allen key.

3. Tighten the threaded ring and loosen the ball seat ring.

4. Remove the threaded ring.

Attachment for tensioning rails for 3.8 V8 (left) and 4.5 V8 (right)

2 different tensioning rails are used. (1) is used on 3.8 V8's and is 133mm (a). (2) is used on 4.5 V8's and is 161.5mm (b). (3) is the lining for the 3.8 V8 rail.

5. Remove the chain tensioner with a 10 mm Allen key.

6. Be sure the tight side of the chain is tight.

7. Compress the tensioner and install the chain tensioner with a 10 mm Allen key. Do not bump the Allen key or the tensioner will release.

8. Screw in the threaded ring and tighten it to 44 ft. lbs.

9. Tighten the ball seat ring to 18 ft. lbs. The pressure bolt should jump forward with an audible click. If it does not, the assembly must be removed and the installation repeated until it does click.

10. Install the plug.

11. Reinstall the A/C compressor, battery and air cleaner.

Timing Chain

REPLACEMENT

All Models

An endless timing chain is used on production engines, but a split chain with a connecting link is used for service. The endless chain can be separated with a "chainbreaker." Only one master link (connecting link) should be used on a chain.

1. Remove the spark plugs.

2. Remove the valve cover(s).

3. Clamp the chain to the cam gear and cover the opening of the timing chain case

Clamp the chain to the gear and cover the opening with rags

Remove the link with a chain breaker

Crank the engine by hand until the new chain has come all the way through the engine. Be sure to keep tension on chain.

Clamp the chain again, cover the opening and remove the old chain from the master link. Connect both ends of the new chain.

with rags. On 6-cylinder and V8 engines, remove the rocker arms from the right-hand camshaft.

4. Separate the chain with a chain breaker.

5. Attach a new timing chain to the old chain with a master link.

6. Using a socket wrench on the crankshaft, slowly rotate the engine in the direction of normal rotation. Simultaneously, pull the old chain through until the master link is uppermost on the camshaft sprocket. Be sure to keep tension on the chain throughout this procedure.

7. Disconnect the old timing chain and connect the ends of the new chain with the master link. Insert the new connecting link from the rear, so that the lockwashers can be seen from the front.

8. Rotate the engine until the timing marks align. Check the valve timing. Once the new chain is assembled, rotate the engine (by hand) through at least one complete revolution to be sure everything is OK. See valve timing for illustrations.

Camshaft

REMOVAL AND INSTALLATION

4 and 5-Cylinder Engines

When the camshaft is replaced, be sure the rocker arms are also replaced.

1. Remove the valve cover.

2. Remove the chain tensioner.

3. Remove the rocker arms.

4. Set the crankshaft at TDC for No. 1 cylinder and be sure that the camshaft timing marks are aligned.

5. Hold the camshaft and loosen the cam gear bolt. Remove the cam gear and wire it securely so that the chain does not loose tension nor slip down into the chain case.

6. Remove the camshaft.

7. Installation is the reverse of removal. Be sure to check that the valve timing marks align when No. 1 cylinder is at TDC. Check the valve clearance.

6-Cylinder Engines

With the engine installed in the car, the camshafts can only be removed together with the camshaft housing. If a new camshaft is installed, be sure to use new rocker arms.

Remove the vacuum pump and camshaft cover.

Loosen the camshaft bolts.

Bolts to be removed during the camshaft housing removal

○ Unscrew M 8 bolts

① Unscrew cylinder head bolts in reverse order

● Do not loosen bolts

Remove the rocker arm springs, rocker arms and thrust pieces.

1. Remove the refrigerant compressor but do not disconnect the refrigerant lines.
2. Remove the battery.
3. Remove the vacuum pump from the right-hand cylinder head.
4. Drain the coolant and remove the water hoses.
5. Remove the rocker arm cover.
6. Remove the cover from the front of the camshaft housing.
7. Remove the rocker arm springs.
8. Remove the rocker arms.
9. Crank the engine around in the normal direction of rotation (using the crankshaft bolt) until No. 1 piston is at TDC, the pointer aligns with the TDC mark on the crankshaft pulley and the camshaft timing marks are aligned.
10. Hold the camshaft(s) and loosen the camshaft bolts.

NOTE: Wire the camshaft gears up so that tension is applied to the chain. The chain must not be allowed to slip off the camshaft or crankshaft gears.

11. Remove the chain tensioner.
12. Remove the slide rail from the camshaft housing. You'll need a small puller for this.
13. Loosen the cover at the right-hand rear side of the camshaft housing and push the right-hand camshaft toward the rear. Remove the camshaft gear.
14. Loosen the camshaft housing retaining bolts. Do not loosen the 5 lower cylinder head bolts or the 2 M8 bolts.
15. Remove the camshaft housing with the camshafts.
16. Remove the rear covers from the camshaft housing.
17. Hold the left-hand camshaft and loosen the attaching bolt.
18. Push the camshaft rearward and remove the camshaft gear. Remove the spacer from the intake camshaft.

19. Remove both camshafts from the housing.
20. Oil the bearings and install the intake camshaft (left-hand) with cam gear and spacer. Use retaining bolt and washer (not springs).
21. Install the exhaust (right-hand) camshaft. Do not install the gear until the housing is installed.
22. Install the rear camshaft covers. Do not tighten the one on the right-hand side.
23. Install the camshaft housing.
24. Lubricate the bolts and tighten them in 3 stages:
- Starting with Bolt #2, tighten to 30 ft. lbs.
- Starting with Bolt #2, tighten to 44 ft. lbs.
- Starting with Bolt #1, tighten to 67 ft. lbs. First, slightly loosen the 5 lower cylinder head bolts.
25. When you are finished torquing the camshaft housing bolts, torque the cylinder head bolts. When all bolts have finally been tightened, the camshafts should rotate easily and freely.
26. Install the righthand camshaft gear. Be sure the cam timing is accurate and the engine is set at TDC on No. 1 cylinder.

--- **CAUTION** ---
Some engines have a scale for BDC as well as one for TDC. The TDC mark is next to the pin in the balancer.

27. Install the timing chain rail.
28. Install the rockers and tension springs. Adjust the valve.
29. Crank the engine by hand and check the valve timing.
30. Tighten the camshaft gear bolts to 59 ft. lbs.
31. Install the chain tensioner.
32. Install the camshaft rear housing

covers (if not already done) and the vacuum pump.
33. Install the rocker covers.

V8 Engines
Experience shows that the right-hand camshaft is always the first one to require replacement. When the V8 camshaft is removed, keep the pedestals with the camshaft. In particular, make sure that the 2 left-hand rear cam pedestals are not swapped. The result will be no oil pressure. Always replace the oil gallery pipe with the camshaft.

NOTE: Arrangement of parts on the 3.8 liter V8 is slightly different compared to the 4.5 liter V8. Service procedures are the same.

1. Remove the valve cover.
2. Remove the tensioning springs and rocker arms.
3. Using a wrench on the crankshaft pulley, crank the engine around until No. 1 piston is at TDC on compression. Using some stiff wire, hang the camshaft gear so that the chain will not slip off the gears.
4. Remove the camshaft gear.
5. Unbolt the camshaft, camshaft bearing pedestals and the oil pipe. Note the angle of the bolts holding the cam bearing pedestals to the engine. The inner row of bolts are the only bolts that do not hold the head to the block.
6. Install the bearing pedestals and camshaft. On the left-hand camshaft, the outer bolt on the rear bearing must be inserted prior to installing the bearings or it will not clear the power brake unit. Tighten the bolts from the inside out. When finished tightening, the camshaft should rotate freely.
7. Check the oil pipes for obstructions and replace if necessary.
8. When installing the oil pipes, also check the 3 inner connecting pipes.

Using a puller, remove the pins from the slide rails and remove the slide rails.

The camshaft flange (arrow) on 3.8 liter V-8's faces rearward

9. Install the compensating washer so that the keyway below the notch slides over the Woodruff key of the camshaft.

10. Install the rocker arms and tensioning springs.

11. Adjust the valve clearance and check the valve timing. See valve timing for illustrations.

Engine Overhaul

DISASSEMBLY

NOTE: This procedure is general and intended to apply to all Mercedes-Benz engines. It is suggested, however, that you be entirely familiar with Mercedes-Benz engines and be equipped with the numerous special tools before attempting an engine rebuild. If at all in doubt concerning any procedure, refer the job to a qualified dealer. While this may be more expensive, it will probably produce better results in the end. If you attempt the rebuild yourself, refer often to the "Engine Rebuilding" section, and read the procedure carefully before beginning.

1. Remove the engine and support it on an engine stand or other suitable support.

2. Set the engine at TDC and matchmark the timing chain and timing gear(s). Remove the cylinder head(s) and gasket(s).

3. Remove the oil pan bolts and the pan and, on most models, the lower crankcase section.

4. Remove the oil pump.

5. Matchmark the connecting rod bearing caps to identify the proper cylinder for reassembly. Matchmark the sides of the connecting rod and side of the bearing cap for proper alignment. Pistons should bear an arrow indicating the front. If not, mark the front of the piston with an arrow using a magic marker. Also identify pistons as to cylinder so they may be replaced in their original location.

6. Remove the connecting rod nuts, bearing caps, and lower bearing shells.

7. Place small pieces of plastic tubing on the rod bolts to prevent crankshaft damage.

8. Inspect the crankshaft journals for nicks and roughness and measure diameters.

1. Screw
2. Cup washers
3. Screw
4. Pulley
6. Vibration damper
7. Hub
8. Crankshaft sprocket
9. Crankshaft
10. Woodruff key
11. Crankshaft bearing shell in cylinder crankcase
12. Crankshaft bearing shell in bearing cap

13. Fitted bearing shell in cylinder crankcase
14. Fitted bearing shell in bearing cap
15. Connecting rod bearing shells
16. Discs
17. Flex plate 1.5 mm thick, 296 mm dia.
18. Flex plate 1 mm thick, 287 mm dia.
19. Stretch bolt for driven plates
20. Ring gear with welded-on steel ring
21. Fitted screws
22. Spring washer
23. Nut

Exploded view of 3.8 liter V-8 crankshaft and related parts

Check the oil pipes (arrow) on a V8 engine.

Match mark the connecting rod bearing caps.

9. Turn the engine and ream the ridge from the top of the cylinders to remove all carbon deposits.

10. Using a hammer handle or other piece of hardwood, gently tap the pistons and rods out from the bottom.

11. The cylinder bores can be inspected at this time for taper and general wear. See the Engine Rebuilding section.

12. Check the pistons for proper size and inspect the ring grooves. If any rings are cracked, it is almost certain that the grooves are no longer true, because broken rings work up and down. It is best to replace any such worn pistons.

4-cylinder diesel engine cylinder block components (5-cylinder 300D is similar)

4-cylinder gasoline engine cylinder block components

6-cylinder engine block components

V-8 engine block and crankshaft components

Piston and connecting rod 1-8

1. Piston
2. Circlip
3. Connecting rod bearing
4. Connecting rod bolt
5. Nut
6. Connecting rod
7. Wrist pin
8. Piston rings

Timing housing cover 20-42

20. Timing housing cover
21. Threaded bolts for adjusting lever of ignition distributor
22. Bearing bushing (guidewheel bearing)
23. 2 O-rings
24. Bearing bushing (intermediate gear shaft)
25. Bolt
26. Spring plate
27. Crankshaft sealing ring (front)
28. Washer
29. Screw
30. Washer
31. Screw
32. 4 Screws
33. 4 Washers
34. End cover
35. Gasket
36. Screw connection
37. Sealing ring
38. Plug
39. Sealing ring
40. Holder-engine damper
41. 6 Screws
42. 6 Washers

Cylinder crankcase 50-66

50. Cylinder block

51. 4 Hollow dowel pins
52. 3 Plugs (oil duct)
53. Plug (rear main oil duct)
54. 2 Supporting angle pieces
55. 2 Washers
56. 2 Screws
57. 2 Sealing rings
58. 2 Plugs
59. Sealing ring
60. Screw connection
61. Bearing bushing intermediate gear shaft rear
62. Plug (front main oil duct)
63. Sealing ring
64. Plug
65. 2 Cyl. pins
66. Idler gear bearing

Intermediate flange 70-82

70. Intermediate flange
71. 4 Spring washers
72. 4 Screws
73. Cover (crankcase sealing ring, rear)
74. 8 Washers
75. 3 Screws
76. Crankshaft sealing ring (rear)
77. 2 Cyl. pins
78. 2 Set pins
79. Cover
80. Sealing strip
81. Cover plate
82. 3 Screws

Crankshaft 90-113

90. Crankshaft
91. Main bearing shell (top)
92. Fitted bearing shell (top)
93. Connecting rod bearing shell (top)
94. Connecting rod bearing shell (bottom)
95. Fitted bearing shell (bottom)

96. Main bearing shell (bottom)
97. Crankshaft bearing cap (fitted bearing)
98. 10 Washers
99. 10 Washers
100. 10 Hex bolts
101. 10 Hex socket bolts
102. Crankshaft bearing cap (main bearing)
103. Key
104. Crankshaft gear
105. Vibration damper pulley
106. Plate springs
107. Bolt
108. Indicating needle
109. Vibration damper
110. Pulley
111. 6 Circlips
112. 6 Screws
113. Pulley cover

Flywheel and driven plate 120-125

120. Flywheel
121. Ball bearing 6202
122. Closing ring
123. 8 bolts
124. Driven plate
125. Spacers

Oil pan 130-138

130. Oil pan
131. Oil drain plug
132. Sealing ring
133. Guide tube (oil dipstick)
134. Oil dipstick
135. Stop-ring (oil dipstick)
136. Oil pan gasket
137. 30 washers
138. 30 Screws

V8 engine cylinder block and crankshaft components

13. The pistons, pins and connecting rods are marked with a color dot assembly code. Only parts having the same color may be used together.

14. If the cylinders are bored, make sure the machinist has the pistons beforehand—cylinder bore sizes are nominal, and the pistons must be individually fitted to the block. Maximum piston weight deviation in any one engine is 4 grams.

15. The flywheel and crankshaft are balanced together as a unit. Matchmark the location of the flywheel relative to the crankshaft, then remove the flywheel. Stretch bolts are used on some newer flywheels and can be identified by their "hourglass" shape.

Once used, they should be discarded and replaced at assembly.

16. Remove the water pump, alternator, and fuel pump, if not done previously.

17. Unbolt and remove the vibration damper and crankshaft pulley. On certain models, it is necessary to clamp the vibration damper with C-clamps before remov-

Pistons normally are marked with an arrow (a) indicating front and a weight or size marking (b).

Before removing the flywheel, mark its position. It should be returned to its original position

Piston marking on 3.8 V8

On V8 models, dress the inside of the vibration damper hub before reinstalling. This will allow you to "feel" the key when installing. On early models, the key extends only ⅓ of the length of the keyway; on later models, ½ the length of the keyway.

ing the bolts. Otherwise, the vibration damper will come apart.

18. Remove the timing chain tensioner and chain cover.

19. Matchmark the position of the timing chain on the timing gear of the crankshaft.

20. Matchmark the main bearing caps for number and position in the block. It is important that they are installed in their original positions. Most bearing caps are numbered for position. Remove the bearing caps.

21. Lift the crankshaft out of the block in a forward direction.

22. With the block completely disassembled, inspect the water passages and bearing webs for cracks. If the water passages are plugged with rust, they can be cleaned out by boiling the block at a radiator shop.

——— CAUTION ———
Aluminum parts must not be boiled out. They will be eroded by chemicals.

Preferred tools for torqueing by angle rotation. A torque wrench is also needed.

ASSEMBLY

1. Assemble the engine using all new gaskets and seals and make sure all parts are properly lubricated. Bearing shells and cylinder walls must be lubricated with engine oil before assembly. Make sure no metal chips remain in the cylinder bores or crankcase.

2. To install pistons and rods, turn the engine right side up and insert the rods into the cylinders. Clamp the rings to the piston, with their gaps equally spaced around the circumference, using a piston ring compressor. Gently tap the piston into the bore, using a hammer handle or similar hard wood, making sure the rings clear the edge.

NOTE: Pistons on the 3.8 liter V–8 are installed with the arrow facing in the driving direction.

3. Torque the rod and main caps to specification and try to turn the crankshaft by hand. It should turn with moderate resistance, not spin freely or be locked up. Stretchbolts are used for the connecting rods. These bolts are tightened by angle of rotation rather than by use of a torque wrench. Make sure the stretch section diameter is greater than 0.35 in. (−0.003 in.). Remove the bolt from the rod and measure the diameter at the point normally covered by the rod; it should be at least 0.31 in. For reasons of standardization, the angle of rotation for all the screw connections tightened according to angle of rotation has been set to 90° + 10°. Initially the bolts should be torqued to 22–35 ft. lbs., then an additional 90°.

4. Disassemble the oil pump and check

Unbolt and remove the crankshaft pulley (V8 shown,

Check the connecting rod bolts

the gear backlash. Place a straightedge on the cover and check for warpage. Deep scoring on the cover usually indicates that metal or dirt particles have been circulating through the oil system. Covers can be machined, but it is best to replace them if damaged.

5. Install the oil pump.

6. Install the oil pan and lower crankcase and tighten the bolts evenly all around, then turn the engine right side up and install the cylinder head gasket and head. Make sure the gasket surfaces are clean before installation; a small dirt particle could cause gasket failure. Tighten the cylinder head bolts in sequence, in stages, to insure against distortion. Don't forget the small bolts at the front of the head.

7. Install the engine into the vehicle.

NOTE: It is a good practice to use a good break-in oil after an engine overhaul. Be sure that all fluids have been replaced and perform a general tuneup. Check the valve timing.

Valve Timing

Ideally, this operation should be performed by a dealer who is equipped with the necessary tools and knowledge to do the job properly.

Checking valve timing is too inaccurate at the standard tappet clearance, therefore timing values are given for an assumed tappet clearance of 0.4 mm. The engines are not measured at 0.4 mm but rather at 2 mm.

1. To check the timing, remove the rocker arm cover and spark plugs. Remove the tensioning springs. On the 6-cylinder engine install the testing thrust pieces. Eliminate all valve clearance.

2. Install a degree wheel.

NOTE: If the degree wheel is attached to the camshaft as shown, values read from it must be doubled.

3. A pointer must be made out of a bent section of 3/16 in. brazing rod or coathanger wire, and attached to the engine.

4-cylinder diesel engine components (5-cylinder is similar).

6-cylinder crankshaft and components (4-cylinder engine is similar)

The V8 timing marks on the left-hand cam

On 6 cylinder engines, always replace the thrust piece (arrow) if the front seal is replaced. If you don't it will almost always leak. If a new thrust piece is not available, at least remove it and turn it around. This provides a new surface for the seal because the seal does not ride on the centerline of the thrust piece.

The valve timing marks must align (6-cylinder shown)

Note that the timing marks on the right-hand cam do not exactly align. This is because the timing chain travels farther on the right side than on the left.

4. With a 22 mm wrench on the crankshaft pulley, turn the engine, in the direction of rotation, until the TDC mark on the vibration damper registers with the pointer and the distributor rotor points to the No. 1 cylinder mark on the housing.

The camshaft timing marks should align at this point.

NOTE: Due to the design of the chain tensioner on V8 engines, the right side of the chain travels slightly farther than the left side. This means the right-side cam will be almost 7° retarded compared to the left side, and both marks will not simultaneously align.

5. Turn the loosened degree wheel until the pointer lines up with the 0° (OT) mark, then tighten it in this position.

6. Continue turning the crankshaft in the direction of rotation until the camshaft lobe of the associated valve is vertical (e.g., points away from the rocker arm surface). To take up tappet clearance, insert a feeler gauge (thick enough to raise the valve slightly from its seat) between the rocker arm cone and the pressure piece.

7. Attach the indicator to the cylinder head so that the feeler rests against the valve spring retainer of No. 1 cylinder intake valve. Preload the indicator at least 0.008 in. then set to zero, making sure the feeler is exactly perpendicular on the valve spring retainer. It may be necessary to bleed down the chain tensioner at this time to facilitate readings.

8. Turn the crankshaft in the normal direction of rotation, again using a wrench on the crankshaft pulley, until the indicator reads 0.016 in. less than zero reading.

9. Note the reading of the degree wheel at this time, remembering to double the reading if the wheel is mounted to the camshaft sprocket.

10. Again turn the crankshaft until the valve is closing and the indicator again reads 0.016 in. less than zero reading. Make sure, at this time, that preload has remained constant, then note the reading of the degree wheel. The difference between the two degree wheel readings is the timing angle (number of degrees the valve is open) for that valve.

11. The other valves may be checked in the same manner, comparing them against each other and the opening values given in "Tune-Up Specifications." It must be remembered that turning the crankshaft contrary to the normal direction of rotation results in inaccurate readings and damage to the engine.

12. If valve timing is not to specification, the easiest way of bringing it in line is to install an offset Woodruff key in the camshaft sprocket. This is far simpler than replacing the entire timing chain and it is the factory-recommended way of changing valve timing provided the timing chain is not stretched too far or worn out. Offset keys are available in the following sizes:

VALVE TIMING OFFSET KEYS

Offset	Part No.	For a Correction at Crankshaft of
2° (0.7)	621 991 04 67	4°
3°20′ (0.9)	621 991 02 67	6½°
4° (1.1)	621 991 01 67	8°
5° (1.3)	621 991 00 67	10°

13. The Woodruff key must be installed with the offset toward the "right", in the normal direction of rotation, to effect advanced valve opening; toward the "left" to retard.

14. Advancing the intake valve opening too much can result in piston and/or valve damage (the valve will hit the piston). To check the clearance between the valve head and the piston, the crankshaft must be positioned at 5° ATDC (on intake stroke). The procedure is essentially the same as for measuring valve timing.

15. As before, the dial indicator is set to zero after being preloaded, then the valve is depressed until it touches the top of the piston. As the normal valve head-to-piston clearance is approximately 0.035 in., you can see that the dial indicator must be preloaded at least 0.042 in. so there will be enough movement for the feeler.

Offset woodruff keys for V8 engine

With installation position "A" opening begins earlier

With installation position "B" opening begins later

Offset woodruff keys for 6-cylinder engine

If the clearance is much less than 0.035 in., the cylinder head must be removed and checked for carbon deposits. If none exist, the valve seat must be cut deeper into the head. Always set the ignition timing after installing an offset key.

ENGINE COOLING

Mercedes-Benz passenger car engines are all equipped with closed, pressurized, water cooling systems. Care should be exercised when dealing with the cooling system. Always turn the radiator cap to the first notch and allow the pressure to decrease before completely removing the cap.

Radiator

REMOVAL AND INSTALLATION

1. Remove the radiator cap.
2. Unscrew the radiator drain plug and drain the coolant from the radiator. If all of the coolant in the system is to be drained, move the heater controls to WARM and open the drain cocks on the engine block.
3. If the car is equipped with an oil cooler, drain the oil from the cooler.
4. If equipped, loosen the radiator shell.
5. Loosen the hose clips on the top and bottom radiator hoses and remove the hoses from the connections on the radiator.
6. Unscrew and plug the bottom line on the oil cooler.
7. If the car is equipped with an automatic transmission, unscrew and plug the lines on the transmission cooler.
8. Disconnect the right-hand and left-hand rubber loops and pull the radiator up and out of the body. On 450SL and SLC and 280S models, push the retaining springs toward the fenders to remove the radiator from the shell.
9. Inspect and replace any hoses which have become hardened or spongy.
10. Install the radiator shell and radiator (if the shell was removed) from the top and connect the top and bottom hoses to the radiator. Bolt the shell to the radiator.
11. Attach the rubber loops or position the retaining springs, as applicable.
12. Attach the lines to the oil cooler.
13. Position the hose clips on the top and bottom hoses.
14. Attach the lines to the oil cooler.
15. On cars with automatic transmissions, connect the lines to the transmission cooler.
16. Move the heater levers to the WARM position and slowly add coolant, allowing air to escape.
17. Check the oil level and fill if necessary. Run the engine for about one minute at idle with the filler neck open.
18. Add coolant to the specified level. Install the radiator cap and turn it until it seats in the second notch. Run the engine and check for leaks.

Water Pump

REMOVAL AND INSTALLATION

All Except V8

1. Drain the water from the radiator.
2. Loosen the radiator shell and remove the radiator.
3. Remove the fan with the coupling and set it aside in an upright position.
4. Loosen the belt around the water pump pulley and remove the belt.
5. Remove the bolts from the harmonic balancer and remove the balancer and pulley.
6. Unbolt and remove the water pump.
7. Installation is the reverse of removal. Tighten the belt and fill the cooling system.

V8 Models

NOTE: The water pump on 3.8 liter V8's cannot be used on 4.5 liter V8's.

1. Drain the water from the radiator and block.
2. Remove the air cleaner.
3. Loosen and remove the drive belt.
4. Disconnect the upper water hose from the radiator and thermostat housing.
5. Remove the fan and coupling.
6. Remove the hose from the intake (top) connection of the water pump.
7. Set the engine at TDC. Matchmark the distributor and engine and remove the distributor. Crank the engine with a socket wrench on the crankshaft pulley bolt or with a screwdriver inserted in the balancer. Crank in the normal direction of rotation only.
8. Turn the balancer so that the recesses provide access to the mounting bolts. Remove the mounting bolts. Rotate the engine in the normal direction of rotation only.
9. Remove the water pump.
10. Clean the mounting surfaces of the water pump and block.
11. Installation is the reverse of removal. Always use a new gasket. Set the engine at TDC and install the distributor so that the distributor rotor points to the notch on the distributor housing. Fill the cooling system and check and adjust the ignition timing.

Thermostat

REMOVAL AND INSTALLATION

4 and 5-Cylinder Engines

The thermostat housing is a light metal casting attached directly to the cylinder head.

1. Open the radiator cap and depressurize the system.
2. Open the radiator drain cock and partially drain the coolant. Drain enough coolant to bring the coolant level below the level of the thermostat housing.
3. Remove the four bolts on the thermostat housing cover and remove the cover.
4. Note the installation position of the thermostat and remove it.
5. Installation is the reverse of removal. Be sure that the thermostat is positioned with the ball valve at the highest point and that the 4 bolts are tightened evenly against the seal.
6. Refill the cooling system and check for leaks.

6-Cylinder Engines

1. Drain the coolant from the radiator.
2. Remove the vacuum pump and put the pump aside.
3. Remove the three bolts on the thermostat housing.
4. Remove the cover and the thermostat.
5. Installation is the reverse of removal. Install the thermostat so that the ball valve is at the highest point. Refill the cooling system.

V8 Engines

1. Drain the coolant from the radiator and block.
2. Remove the air cleaner.
3. Disconnect the battery and remove the alternator. Usually this need not be done on 450 SL, 450SLC, 450SE, 450SEL, 380SL, 380SLC, 380SEL or 380SEC.
4. Unscrew the housing cover on the side of the water pump and remove the thermostat. Note that the thermostat used on 4.5 liter V8 models differs from the one used on other models due to a different positioning of the ball valve.
5. If a new thermostat is to be installed, always install a new sealing ring.
6. Installation is the reverse of removal. Be sure to tighten the screws on the housing cover evenly to prevent leaks. Refill the cooling system and check for leaks.

EMISSION CONTROLS

1976

The 1976 emission control system is close to the system used in 1975. Catalytic converters are used on all engines, but the 450 series cars have the catalysts installed on the exhaust manifold. Due to Federal regulations, the routing of the fuel evaporation lines has been changed.

The 230 (California only) and all other gas-

2. Distributor
9. Switchover valve, ignition (red)
10. Switchover valve, throttle lift (grey)
12. Switchover valve, EGR (brown)
14. 77° F temperature switch
31. EGR valve
33. Switchover valve, air injection (blue)
45. Muffler (air filter for noise suppression)
51. Vacuum control, throttle lift

1975-76 230 emission control component location

5. Relay box	39. Charcoal canister
7. 62° F temperature switch	46. Resistor, automatic
8. 212° F temperature switch	choke cover
12. Switchover valve, EGR (brown)	54. Vacuum booster
31. EGR valve	60. Venturi connection
32. 149° F temperature switch	
33. Switchover valve, air injection (blue)	
37. Switchover valve, fuel evaporation	
control system (green)	

1975-76 280 and 280C emission control component location

oline engines are equipped with catalysts. These models must be operated only with unleaded gasoline.

All of the following tests should be made in the specified sequence with the engine at operating temperature.

The base color of vacuum lines for emission control is white. Lines originating at a vacuum source have only one color stripe. These lines are connected to the center con-

nection of the switchover valve of the same color. Lines terminating at a vacuum operated device have 2 color stripes. Purple is always the second color. The lines are connected to the outer connection of the switchover valve of the same color.

Switchover valve filter caps are color coded as follows:
RED—Valve for ignition advance.
GREY—Valve for throttle lift.

Brown—Valve for EGR.
Blue— Valve for air injection.

230

Testing the System

77°F. TEMPERATURE SWITCH

1. Disconnect the temperature switch plug and ground the switch. The engine rpm should increase.

2. If not, check the vacuum line connections.

3. Unplug the relay box and connect terminals 7 and 1; an audible click should be heard. If not, replace the relay box.

4. Disconnect and ground the temperature switch. Place your hand over the air pump muffler. A light air flow should be present.

5. If no air flow is present, check the vacuum line connections.

6. Disconnect the plug from the relay box and connect terminals 6 and 7. The blue switchover valve should click. If not, replace the switchover valve. If the valve does click, the relay is defective.

RPM SWITCH

1. Increase engine speed to about 2500 rpm and remove the red/purple vacuum line from the distributor. The engine speed should drop slightly. Below about 2000 rpm, there should be 13 volts at the switch. If there is less than 11 volts, temporarily replace the rpm relay or relay box and repeat the test.

EGR SWITCHOVER VALVE

1. Disconnect the brown vacuum line at the carburetor and brown/purple vacuum line at the carburetor. Blow into the brown vacuum line and simultaneously increase the rpm to about 3600. At idle, air can be blown through the line, while above 3600, no air should pass.

5. Relay box
7. 62° F temperature switch
8. 212° F temperature switch
12. Switchover valve, EGR (brown)
31. EGR valve
32. 149° F temperature switch
33. Switchover valve, air injection (blue)
37. Switchover valve, fuel evaporation
    control system (green)
39. Charcoal canister
46. Resistor, automatic choke cover
54. Vacuum booster
60. Venturi connection

1975-76 280S emission control component location

EGR VALVE

1. Connect the EGR valve to intake manifold vacuum. Disconnect the red line at the carburetor and the brown/purple line at the carburetor. Connect both lines together. The engine should run poorly or stall. If not be sure that the valve stem is moving and if not, replace the valve. If the valve works, clean the EGR valve with a 10 mm drill.

VACUUM GOVERNOR

1. Increase the engine speed to about 2500 rpm and release the throttle slowly. At the same time watch the vacuum control on the carburetor. It should pop out about 2000 rpm and retract below 1800 rpm. If not, remove the plug from the relay box and connect terminals 2 and 7. With the ignition ON, the valve should click audibly. If it does, replace the relay box.

280, 280C, 280S

The system remains basically unchanged except for different color coding of vacuum lines and addition of a catalytic converter in all states.

Testing the System

EGR

1. Remove the brown/purple vacuum line from the EGR valve and turn the ignition ON. Blow air into the line. Place the gear selector in a driving position (not N or P). The line should be closed.

2. Remove the brown vacuum line on the carburetor and the green line on the carburetor. Connect the brown line in place of the green line. Start the engine and place the gear selector in a driving position (not N or P).

3. The engine should run roughly or stall. If not, either the vacuum booster or the EGR valve is at fault.

AIR INJECTION

1. Remove the air injection hose at the air filter (center hose) and run the engine at idle. There should be no air flow present. If air is discharged at idle, replace the diverter valve.

62°F TEMPERATURE SWITCH

1. Disconnect the plug from the switch in the oil filter housing and ground the switch. Air flow in the injection line should cease. If it does not, disconnect the plug from the blue switchover valve and connect a voltmeter. Disconnect and ground the temperature switch. Turn the ignition ON; the voltmeter should read about 12 volts. If no voltage is present, replace the relay box.

AUTOMATIC CHOKE RESISTOR

1. Connect a voltmeter to the resistor outlet (top connection) and to ground. Disconnect the plug of the 62°F temperature switch and connect it to ground. Disconnect

the plug of the 149°F temperature switch and turn the ignition ON. With the 62° switch grounded the voltmeter should read about 7-8 volts. If the ground is interrupted, it should read about 12 volts.

2. If the voltage is not as specified, check the relay box. Connect a voltmeter to the input of the resistor (lower connection) and to ground. Ground the plug of the 62° temperature switch and the voltmeter should read about 12 volts. If not, replace the relay box.

FLOAT CHAMBER VENT VALVE

1. Connect a vacuum gauge to the green/purple vacuum line to the float chamber vent valve. Start the engine and briefly accelerate. The vacuum should build up and remain constant. With the ignition OFF, the vacuum should drop to zero.

2. If no vacuum is present, connect a voltmeter to the switchover valve. About 13 volts should be present, and the valve should click audibly.

If vacuum does not remain constant, unscrew the float chamber vent valve. With the vacuum line connected run the engine at idle. The valve rod should move. If necessary, replace the valve vacuum diaphragm.

CHARCOAL CANISTER PURGE VALVE

1. Remove the thin center hose from the charcoal canister and close the end of

the hose with your finger. Increase engine speed to more than 2000 rpm. At idle, slight vacuum should be felt, increasing with engine speed. If not, the purge valve should be replaced, or there is a restriction in the line.

450SE, 450SEL, 450SL, 450SLC

These cars with the M117 engine use one emission system for the entire U.S. market, including California.

The base color of the vacuum lines is opaque (white). Lines originating at a vacuum source have only one color stripe; lines terminating at a vacuum source have 2-color stripes. Purple is always the second color.

Thermo vacuum valves are used to control the ignition changeover, EGR and air injection. They are color coded.

   Black—104°F valve.
   Blue—63°F valve.

The retard side of the vacuum control unit is only activated when the coolant is below 212°F, during deceleration with the A/C off. The advance side of the vacuum control unit is activated when temperatures at the thermovalve are 104°F or above and the advance is determined by the position of the throttle plate.

The EGR valve works in 2 stages. The first stage (small amount) takes place with coolant temperature above 104°F. There is

2. Distributor	56. Vacuum control switch
8. 212°F temperature switch	60. 104°F thermo-vacuum valve (black)
9. Switch-over valve, ignition retard (yellow)	61. 63°F thermo-vacuum valve (blue)
31. EGR valve	
39. Charcoal canister	

1976 450SE, 450SEL, 450SL and 450SLC emission control component location

no EGR with coolant temperature below 86°F.

The second (larger) stage of EGR occurs during acceleration with coolant temperature above 140°F and vacuum less than 7.9 in. Hg. Air injection takes place above 62°F and is cancelled below 50°F (coolant temperature).

Testing the System

IGNITION CHANGEOVER SIWTCH

Unplug and ground the temperature switch. The engine rpm should increase and the auxiliary fan should operate.

If the engine speed does not increase, check the vacuum lines. The yellow line from the throttle valve housing should go to the center of the yellow switchover valve. The yellow/purple line goes to the outer connection of the siwtchover valve to the inner chamber of the vacuum unit (retard). Disconnect the plug from the relay and bridge terminals 3 and 4. With the ignition ON, the switchover valve should click. If not, replace the relay. If the switchover valve does not function, replace the valve.

Check the auxiliary fan. Disconnect the relay and bridge terminals 1 and 3. With ignition ON, the fan should run. If not, replace the fan.

Check the relay. Remove the plug and bridge terminals 1 and 3. With the ignition ON, the fan should run. If so, replace the relay.

IGNITION RETARD RELAY

Switch on the A/C. The engine rpm should increase slightly. If not, check that the A/C is operating. If the A/C is operating, replace the relay.

IGNITION ADVANCE

Remove the yellow/purple and red/purple vacuum lines from the distributor. The engine speed should increase slightly. Connect the yellow/purple vacuum line to the upper connection at the vacuum diaphragm. The engine speed should increase.

If not, replace the 2-way vacuum diaphragm.

EGR SWITCHOVER VALVE

Remove the red/purple vacuum line at the EGR valve. Connect a vacuum gauge to the red/purple line and run the engine at idle. Increase speed to 2500 rpm. At idle, the gauge should show no vacuum; at 2500 rpm, vacuum should be present.

If no vacuum is indicated, check the line connections. The red line from the red connection at the throttle valve housing should go to the angular connection of the thermo-vacuum valve. The red/purple line should be attached to the vertical connection at the thermo-vacuum valve, to the red connection of the vacuum control switch and red connection of the EGR valve.

Check the 104°F thermo-vacuum valve. It should open if the surrounding temperature is above 104°F. It should close below 86°F. If the valve is not functioning properly, check the bore of the throttle housing vacuum connection.

VACUUM CONTROL SWITCH

Remove the brown/purple vacuum line from the EGR valve. Connect a vacuum gauge between the line and the bottom of the EGR valve. Increase engine speed to 2500 rpm. At idle vacuum should not be present. During acceleration, vacuum should be present briefly until the rpm stabilizes. If no vacuum is present, check the vacuum lines. The red/purple line should be connected to the red connection at the vacuum control switch, the white line to the center of the vacuum control switch and the red/purple line to the brown control switch connection. If vacuum still is not present, replace the control switch.

EGR VALVE

Disconnect the yellow/purple line from the distributor diaphragm. Disconnect both vacuum lines at the EGR valve. Connect the yellow/purple line with the upper, then the lower connection of the EGR valve. The engine should run rough or stall in both cases. If not, replace the EGR valve.

DIVERTER VALVE

Run the engine at idle. Connect a CO tester. Note the reading. Remove the blue/purple vacuum line from the blue thermovalve and note reading again. It should change noticeably.

If not, check the vacuum lines. The blue line runs to the angular connection on the blue thermo-vacuum valve. The blue/purple line goes to the vertical connection of the same valve.

Check the diverter valve. Remove the muffler on the valve. Disconnect the blue/purple vacuum line at the blue thermovacuum valve. Air should flow from the diverter valve. If there is no air flow, replace the diverter valve. If necessary, check the drive belt tension.

CHARCOAL CANISTER

Remove the thin hose from the charcoal canister. Cover the hose opening with finger or connect vacuum gauge. Slowly increase rpm to 2500. At idle a small amount of vacuum should be present, and vacuum should increase with engine speed.

If no vacuum is present at idle, check the purge line to the intake manifold. Disconnect the charcoal canister hose at the purge valve and clean it by blowing through with compressed air in the direction of the intake manifold. Replace the purge valve if necessary.

If vacuum does not increase at idle, check the vacuum at the purge valve. Disconnect the white vacuum line at the purge valve. Connect a vacuum gauge or close the line with a finger. Increase engine speed. At idle, there should be no vacuum. With increasing engine speed, vacuum should increase. If vacuum is present replace the purge valve. If no vacuum is present, blow through the line towards the throttle valve housing.

1977

The following tests should be performed in the order given with the engine at normal operating temperature.

2. Distributor
31. EGR valve
39. Charcoal canister
41. Diverter valve
51. Vacuum governor
61. 62° F thermo-vacuum valve (blue); for EGR, located at front of engine next to distributor
61. 62° F thermo-vacuum valve (blue), for air
73. 122° F thermo-vacuum valve (black with green dot)
161. Float chamber vent valve

1977-79 230 emission control component location

230

Testing the System

EGR

1. Run the engine at idle speed.

2. Remove the brown vacuum line at the carburetor and the gray vacuum line at the intake manifold. Connect the brown line at the intake manifold.

3. The engine should run roughly or stall. If the rpm does not change, check the vacuum line connections. Check for leaks and blow through the vacuum connection on the carburetor.

4. Check the thermo-vacuum valve (blue plastic portion and "50AB5" stamped in metal housing). Remove the brown/purple vacuum line and race the engine. Vacuum must be present at the open connection when accelerating.

5. Check the EGR valve. Remove the EGR valve. Connect the brown/purple vacuum line to the EGR valve and slowly increase engine rpm. Cover the bores in the intake manifold. The valve stem should lift from its seat; if not replace the EGR valve with a new one.

AIR INJECTION

1. Connect a CO tester to the test connection and remove the vacuum hose from the vertical connection of the thermo-vacuum valve. The air injection thermo-vacuum valve has "50AA" stamped in the metal housing. Plug the connection on the valve. The CO reading should drop noticeably.

2. If the CO does not drop, and vacuum IS indicated, replace the thermo-valve. If the CO does not drop and vacuum is NOT indicated, clean the vacuum line to the intake manifold with compressed air.

3. Check the connection of the vacuum lines.

4. Check the vertical connection of the thermal-vacuum valve for vacuum. If vacuum is present, replace the diverter valve. If no vacuum is present, remove the blue vacuum line from the thermo-vacuum valve and check for vacuum at the line.

5. If the CO still does not decrease, check that the thermo-valve is open; if not, replace the valve.

NOTE: Below approximately 120°F, the valve should be open; above that, it should be closed.

THROTTLE VALVE LIFT

1. Remove the vacuum hose from the vacuum governor on the carburetor. The idle speed should increase. Reconnect the hose. The idle speed should decrease.

2. If the rpm does not increase, check the connection of the hose. Check the hose for leaks.

3. Run the engine at idle. Remove the vacuum line on the carburetor; the idle speed should increase. If not, replace the vacuum governor.

1. Carburetor
2. Distributor
31. EGR valve
39. Charcoal canister
40. Air pump
41. Diverter valve
42. Check valve
61. 62° F thermo-vacuum valve (blue), for EGR, located at front of engine next to distributor
61. 62° F thermo-vacuum valve (blue), for air injection, located at rear of engine
73. Thermo-vacuum valve 50° C/122° F
74. Pressure relief valve
78. Air filter for noise suppression

A To cylinder head
B To catalyst
C Air conditioning
D Central locking system
E Fuel tank ventilation connection
F To air filter

rt = red
gr = gray
bl = blue
br = brown
vi = purple

1977 230 emission control schematic

1. Mixture regulator assembly
2. Ignition distributor
9. Ignition switch-over valve
31. EGR valve
35. Check valve
39. Charcoal canister
40. Air pump
41. Diverter valve
42. Check valve
45. Muffler (air filter)
60. 104° F thermo-vacuum valve
61. 62° F thermo-vacuum valve
74. Pressure relief valve
75. Exhaust pressure transducer
78. Muffler (air filter)

A. Air injection line
B. Connection, fuel tank vent

1977 280E, 280SE Federal emission control schematic

2. Distributor
31. EGR valve
39. Charcoal canister

60. 104° F thermo-vacuum valve
61. 62° F thermo-vacuum valve

1977-79 280E, 280CE, 280SE Federal emission control component location

2. Distributor
31. EGR valve
39. Charcoal canister

60. 104° F thermo-vacuum valve
61. 62° F thermo-vacuum valve
73. 122°F thermo-vacuum valve

1977-79 280E, 280CE, 280SE California emission control component location

A. Air injection line, cylinder head
B. Air injection line, between catalysts
C. Connection, fuel tank vent

1. Mixture regulator assembly
2. Ignition distributor
9. Switch-over valve, ignition
31. EGR valve
39. Charcoal canister

40. Air pump
41. Diverter valve
42. Check valve
60. 104° F thermo-vacuum valve
61. 62° F thermo-vacuum valve

73. 122° F thermo-vacuum valve
74. Pressure relief valve
75. Exhaust pressure transducer
78. Muffler (air filter)

1977 280E, 280SE California emission control schematic

2. Distributor
31. EGR valve
39. Charcoal canister

60. 104° F thermo-vacuum valve (black)
80. Suction hose to aspirator/check valve

1977-79 4.5 V8 Federal emission control location

FUEL EVAPORATION CONTROL SYSTEM

1. Remove the solenoid plug from the float chamber vent valve. Reconnect the solenoid; it should click audibly.

2. If the solenoid does not click, turn on the ignition and connect a test lamp to the plug. The test lamp should light with the ignition ON. If not, check the proper fuse. If the lamp still does not light, replace the solenoid.

3. Remove the middle purge hose to the carburetor from the charcoal canister and cover the hose opening with your finger. Slowly increase engine speed to over 2000 rpm. At idle no vacuum should be present. As engine speed increases, vacuum should increase. If no vacuum is present as the engine speed increases, check the connection of the purge hose. Check the hose for leaks and clean it out with compressed air.

4. On 1978–79 models, remove the hose from the purge valve and repeat the test. If vacuum is present, replace the purge valve.

280E AND 280SE (FEDERAL)

Testing the System

The following tests should be performed with the engine at idle speed, at operating temperature and in the order listed.

EGR

1. Remove the brown vacuum line from the EGR valve and slowly increase engine rpm. At about 1200 rpm, the engine should run roughly or stall.

2. If it does not run roughly or stall, check the vacuum line connections. The connections at the exhaust pressure transducer are marked with colored rings and must be connected to the same color code.

3. Disconnect the vacuum line from the vertical connection of the thermo-vacuum valve marked "50AA4" in the metal housing. Run the engine and increase rpm. Vacuum should be present at the connection.

4. Run the engine at idle and disconnect the brown line between the EGR valve and exhaust pressure transducer. Cover the line with your finger; vacuum must be present at idle. If not, replace the exhaust pressure transducer.

5. Run the engine at idle and remove both vacuum lines from the EGR valve. Connect the brown line to the connection on the red/purple line on the EGR valve. The engine should run roughly or stall. If not, replace the EGR valve.

AIR INJECTION

1. Connect a CO tester to the exhaust back pressure line. Remove and plug the vacuum hose from the vertical connection at the thermo-vacuum valve. The CO should increase.

2. If not, check the vacuum line connections. The (large) cap end connection of the check valve must face the intake manifold (Federal only).

3. Remove the blue vacuum line from the thermo-vacuum valve and cover it with your finger. Vacuum must be present at idle; if not, check for leaks and clean the line with compressed air.

4. If vacuum is present, check the thermo-vacuum valve and replace if necessary.

5. Disconnect the blue/purple line from the thermo-vacuum valve marked "50AB5" on the metal housing. Run the engine. Vacuum should be present at the vertical connection. If not, replace the diverter valve.

FUEL EVAPORATION CONTROL SYSTEM

1. Remove the black purge line from the charcoal canister. Cover the opening with your finger and increase rpm to over 2000 rpm. No vacuum should be present at idle and vacuum should increase with engine speed. If not, check the vacuum line

1. Mixture regulator assembly
2. Distributor
9. Ignition switch-over valve
31. EGR valve
39. Charcoal canister
60. 104° F thermo-vacuum valve
75. Exhaust pressure transducer

B. Connection, fuel tank vent

1977 4.5 V8 Federal emission control schematic

connections, check for leaks and clean the line with compressed air.

If vacuum is still not present, remove the purge line from the front of the purge valve. If vacuum is present, replace the purge valve.

280E AND 280SE (CALIFORNIA)

Testing the System

EGR

See 280E and 280SE (Federal).

AIR INJECTION

1. Connect a CO tester to the exhaust pressure transducer. Remove the vacuum line from the vertical connection of the 122°F thermo-vacuum valve and connect it to the

vertical connection of the 62°F thermo-vacuum valve. The CO should drop.

2. If not, check the vacuum line connections.

3. Run the engine at idle and check for vacuum at the vertical connection of the 62°F thermo-vacuum valve. If vacuum is present, replace the diverter valve.

If no vacuum is present, remove the blue line from the 62°F thermo-vacuum valve and check for vacuum at the valve. If vacuum is present, replace the thermo-vacuum valve. If no vacuum is present, remove the line from the intake manifold and clean it with compressed air.

4. If the CO still does not drop, check the 122°F thermo-vacuum valve. It will have "50AA13" stamped in the metal housing. Above 122°F, the valve is closed and no vacuum should be present at the vertical

2. Distributor
31. EGR valve
39. Charcoal canister
60. 104° F thermo-vacuum valve (black)
61. 62° F thermo-vacuum valve (blue)

1977-79 V8 California emission control component locations

2. Distributor
31. EGR valve
39. Charcoal canister
60. 104° F thermo-vacuum valve
61. 62° F thermo-vacuum valve

1977 6.9 emission control component location

1. Mixture regulator assembly
2. Distributor
9. Ignition switch-over valve
31. EGR valve
35. Vacuum check valve
39. Charcoal canister
40. Air pump
41. Diverter valve
42. Check valve
60. 104° F thermo-vacuum valve
61. 62° F thermo-vacuum valve
75. Exhaust pressure transducer

A. Air injection line to cylinder head
B. Fuel tank vent connection

1977 4.5 V8 California emission control schematic

connection. Below 122°F, vacuum should be present at the vertical connection. If these conditions are not met, replace the valve.

FUEL EVAPORATION CONTROL SYSTEM

See 280E and 280SE (Federal).

450SL, 450SLC, 450SEL (FEDERAL)

Testing the System

The following tests should be performed with the engine running at normal operating temperature in the order given.

EGR

1. Remove the brown line at the EGR valve and slowly increase engine speed. Above 1200 rpm, the engine should run roughly or stall. If not check the vacuum line connections.

2. Check the thermo-vacuum valve with "50AA4" stamped in the metal housing (104° F valve). Remove the red/purple line from the vertical connection, run the engine and accelerate briefly. Vacuum should be present at the vertical connection.

3. Run the engine at idle and remove the brown vacuum line at the EGR valve. If no vacuum is present at idle, replace the exhaust pressure transducer.

4. Run the engine at idle and remove both lines from the EGR valve. Connect the brown line to the connection for the red/purple line. The engine should run roughly or stall. If not, replace the EGR valve.

AIR INJECTION

1. Remove the suction hose from the aspirator/check valve in the air cleaner and cover with your finger. Vacuum should be present and a suction noise should be audible. If no vacuum is present, replace the aspirator/check valve.

FUEL EVAPORATION CONTROL SYSTEM

See this test under 280E and 280SE(Federal).

450SL, 450SLC, 450SEL (CALIFORNIA) AND 6.9

Testing the System

EGR

See 450SL, 450SLC, 450SEL (Federal).

IAR INJECTION

1. Connect a CO tester to the exhaust gas back pressure line and remove the blue/purple vacuum line from the vertical connection of the 62°F thermo-vacuum valve. Plug the connection. The CO should increase.

2. If not, check the vacuum line connections. The check valve must be installed

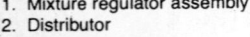

1. Mixture regulator assembly
2. Distributor
5. Purge valve
9. Ignition switch-over valve
31. EGR valve
39. Charcoal canister
60. 104° F thermo-vacuum valve
75. Exhaust pressure transducer
80. Auxiliary air valve
81. Shaped hose

B. Fuel tank vent connection

bl = blue
br = brown
ge = yellow
gr = gray
or = orange
rt = red
vi = purple
ws = white

1978-79 4.5 V8 Federal emission control schematic component. Location same as 1977

1. Carburetor
2. Distributor
5. Fuel evaporation control system purge valve
31. EGR valve
39. Charcoal canister
40. Air pump
41. Diverter valve
42. Check valve
61. 62° F thermo-vacuum valve (blue), for EGR, located at front of engine next to distributor
61. 62° F thermo-vacuum valve (blue), for air injection, located at rear of engine
73. 122° F thermo-vacuum valve
74. Pressure relief valve
78. Air filter for noise suppression
A. To cylinder head
B. To catalyst
C. Air conditioning
D. Central locking system
E. Fuel tank ventilation connection
F. To air filter
    bl = blue
    br = brown
    gr = gray
    rt = red
    vi = purple

1978-79 230 Emission control schematic component. Location same as 1977

with the larger (cap) end toward the intake manifold.

3. Remove the vacuum line from the angular connection of the 62°F thermo-vacuum valve and cover the valve with your finger. If no vacuum is present at idle, check the lines for leaks and clean the vacuum pick-up bore with compressed air.

4. If vacuum is present, check the thermo-vacuum valve and replace if necessary.

5. The thermo-vacuum valve can be identified by the "50AB5" stamped in the metal body. Remove the blue/purple vacuum line, run the engine at idle and accelerate briefly. Vacuum should be present at the vertical connection; if not, replace the diverter valve.

FUEL EVAPORATION CONTROL SYSTEM

See this test under 280E and 280SE (Federal).

1978–79

The emission control system for 1978–79 models is very similar in components and operation to the 1977 version.

230

Perform the following tests in the order given with the engine at idle at normal operating temperature.

Testing the System

See the 1977 230 procedures for "Testing the System."

280E, 280CE, 280SE (FEDERAL)

Perform the following tests in the order given with the engine at normal operating temperature and idling.

Testing the System

See the 1977 280E and 280SE (Federal) procedures for "Testing the System."

1. Mixture regulator assembly
2. Ignition distributor
5. Purge valve
9. Ignition switch over valve
31. EGR valve
39. Charcoal canister
40. Air pump
41. Diverter valve
42. Check valve
60. 104° F thermo-vacuum valve
61. 62° F thermo-vacuum valve
73. 122° F thermo-vacuum valve
74. Pressure relief valve
75. Exhaust pressure transducer
78. Muffler (air filter)
80. Auxiliary air valve
81. Shaped hose

A. Air injection line, cylinder head
B. Fuel tank vent connection

1978-79 280E, 280CE, 280SE Federal emission control schematic component. Location same as 1977.

1. Mixture regulator assembly
2. Ignition distributor
5. Purge valve
9. Ignition switch-over valve
31. EGR valve
39. Charcoal canister
40. Air pump
41. Diverter valve
42. Check valve
60. 104° F thermo-vacuum valve
61. 62° F therm74. Pressure relief valve
75. Exhaust pressure transducer
78. Muffler (air filter)
80. Auxiliary air valve
81. Shaped hose

A. Air injection line, cylinder head
B. Air injection line, between catalysts
C. Fuel tank vent connection

bl = blue
br = brown
ge = yellow
gr = gray
or = orange
rt = red
vi = purple
ws = white

1978-79 280E, 280CE, 280SE California emission control schematic component. Location same as 1977

280E, 280CE, 280SE (CALIFORNIA)

Perform the following tests in the order given with the engine at idle and normal operating temperature.

Testing the System

See the procedures under "Testing the System" for 1977 280E and 280SE California models.

450SL, 450SLC, 450SEL (FEDERAL)

Perform the following tests in the order given

with the engine idling at normal operating temperature.

Testing the System

See the procedures for "Testing the System" under 1977 450SL, 450SLC, 450SEL (Federal) models.

450SL, 450SLC, 450SEL (CALIFORNIA) AND 6.9

Perform the following tests in the order given with the engine idling at normal operating temperature.

Testing the System

See the procedures for "Testing the System" under 1977, 450SL, 450SLC, 450SEL (California) and 6.9 models.

Catalyst Replacement Warning Indicator

A warning light in the instrument cluster comes on at 37,500 mile intervals, indicating that the catalyst should be replaced. The catalyst mileage counter is located under the dash and is driven by the speedometer cable. To reset the mileage counter, push the reset pin on the counter.

1. Mixture regulator assembly
2. Distributor
5. Purge valve
9. Ignition switch-over valve
31. EGR valve
35. Vacuum check valve
39. Charcoal canister
40. Air pump
41. Diverter valve
42. Check valve
60. 104° F thermo-vacuum valve
61. 62°F thermo-vacuum valve
73. 122°F thermo-vacuum valve
74. Pressure relief valve
75. Exhaust pressure transducer
80. Auxiliary valve
81. Shaped hose

A. Air injection line to cylinder head
B. Fuel tank vent connection

bl = blue   or = orange
br = brown   rt = red
ge = yellow   vi = purple
gr = gray   ws = white

1978-79 V8 Federal emission control schematic component. Location same as 1977

Catalyst elapsed mileage indicator reset button (arrow)

1980

6-CYLINDER ENGINES

The base color of the emission control vacuum lines is white. Colored stripes identify various functions:

Advanced timing = red
Retarded timing = yellow/purple
Air injection = blue

A Lambda oxygen sensor control system ensures a constant air fuel ratio of approximately 14.5:1. The oxygen sensor is screwed into the front part of the exhaust pipe to constantly monitor the oxygen content of the exhaust gases. An electronic control unit, located behind the kick panel, receives input from a throttle valve switch and oil temperature switch to maintain an ideal fuel mixture in conjunction with the 3-way catalyst. The oxygen sensor must be replaced every 30,000 miles (light on the dash warns driver).

An air injection system is used, the components of which are very similar to those used in 1979.

Testing the System

A special test adaptor that connects to the electronic control unit plug and a special test meter that connects to the adaptor are necessary to properly test the emission system. Do not attempt to try and test electrical components of the system with an ordinary volt-ohmmeter.

The only tests that can be performed without special equipment are as follows:

Color Code
bk = black
bl = blue
gr = green
ye = yellow
re = red
pu = purple
wh = white

1. Intake manifold	16. Oxygen sensor	31. Exhaust manifold
2. Throttle valve housing	17. Frequency valve	32. Cylinder head
3. Air duct housing	18. Throttle valve switch	33. Primary catalyst
4. Air flow sensor	19. Temperature switch, oil 60° F	36. Thermo-vacuum valve 63° F
5. Fuel distributor	25. Air pump	37. Thermo-vacuum valve 122° F
6. Warm-up enrichment compensator	26. Pressure relief valve	50. Fuel tank
7. Pressure damper	27. Diverter valve	51. Vent valve
8. Ignition distributor	28. Muffler (air filter)	52. Charcoal canister
9. Restricting orifice	29. Check valve	53. Purge valve
15. Electronic control unit	30. Air injection line	a. Leak-off connection

Emission control schematic—1980 6-cylinder engines

AIR INJECTION VACUUM TEST

1. Pull the Y-fitting from the angled connections at the thermo-vacuum valves and check for vacuum at the Y-fitting. If no vacuum is present, clean the connection at the intake manifold with compressed air.

2. Be sure the fitting and connecting lines are not plugged. If vacuum is present, the thermo-vacuum valves should be open. If the valves are open, replace the diverter valve.

FUEL EVAPORATION CONTROL SYSTEM

1. Remove the purge line from the charcoal canister (connected to the throttle valve housing) and block it with your finger. Slowly increase the engine speed to more than 2000 rpm.

2. There should be no vacuum at idle, but vacuum should increase with rpm.

3. If vacuum does not increase with rpm, test the purge line connection and purge

valve. The purge line must be connected to the throttle valve housing, and must not leak. Clean out the throttle valve housing with compressed air. If vacuum is still not present, remove the purge line from the front of the purge valve. If vacuum is present, replace the purge valve.

V8 ENGINES

Color coding of the vacuum lines is identical to the 6-cylinder engines and operation of the Lambda oxygen sensor control system is the same as 6-cylinder engines.

Air injection uses a shut-off valve in a special shaped hose between the air filter and the aspirator valve, which is in the air injection line leading to the cylinder head.

Primary, underfloor and catalyst/muffler combination catalytic converters are used, depending on application.

The fuel evaporation control system is identical to the 1979 system.

Testing the System

A special test adapter that connects to the electronic control unit plug and a special test meter that connects to the adapter are necessary to properly test the emission control system. Do not attempt to try and test electrical components of the system with an ordinary volt-ohmmeter.

The only tests that can be performed without special equipment are as follows:

FREQUENCY VALVE

1. With the engine idling at normal operating temperature, place your hand on the frequency valve.

2. Operation of the frequency valve can be felt. If not replace the valve.

AIR INJECTION

1. Idle the engine and remove the specially shaped hose from the air shut-off valve. A suction sound should be audible.

2. If there is no suction sound, check

Color Code
bk = black
bl = blue
gr = green
ye = yellow
re = red
wh = white
pu = purple

1. Intake manifold	17. Frequency valve	33. Primary catalyst
2. Throttle valve housing	18. Throttle valve switch	36. Thermo valve 63° F
3. Air duct housing	19. Temperature switch, oil 60° F	37. Thermo valve 122° F
4. Air flow sensor	25. Air pump	37a. Thermo valve 122° F
5. Fuel distributor	26. Pressure relief valve	50. Fuel tank
6. Warm-up compensator	27. Diverter valve	51. Vent valve
7. Silencer (damper)	28. Silencer	52. Charcoal canister
8. Ignition distributor	29. Check valve	53. Purge valve
9. Orifice	30. Air injection line	
15. Control unit	31. Exhaust manifold	a. Leak-off connection
16. Oxygen sensor	32. Cylinder head	b. from the air cleaner

Emission control schematic 1981–83 6-cylinder engines

1. Intake manifold	16a. O₂ sensor 380 SEC	37. Thermo-vacuum valve 50°C	53. Purge valve
2. Throttle valve housing	17. Frequency valve	37a. Thermo-vacuum valve 50°C	a. Leak-off connection
3. Air guide housing	18. Throttle valve switch	38. Air cleaner	b. To exhaust manifold
4. Air flow sensor	19. Temperature switch (oil)	40. Air injection shutoff valve	**Color code**
5. Fuel distributor	25. Air pump	43. Switchover valve	bk = black
6. Warm-up compensator	29. Check valve (air injection)	44. Check valve (vacuum)	bl = blue
7. Damper	30. Suction line, air pump	46. Timing chain housing cover	gr = green
8. Ignition distributor	32. Cylinder head	50. Fuel tank	pu = purple
9. Orifice	33. Primary catalyst 380 SL	51. Vent valve	re = red
15. Lambda control unit	33a. Primary catalyst 380 SEC	52. Charcoal canister	wh = white
16. O₂ sensor 380 SL			

1982–83 3.8 V8 emission control system

the vacuum lines and vacuum supply. Check the blue line connected to the air shut-off valve. Disconnect the line at the air shut-off valve. If vacuum is not present, clean out the vacuum connection at the throttle valve housing.

3. If vacuum is present at the air shut-off valve, remove the valve. If the suction sound is still audible, replace the air shut-off valve. If no suction sound could be heard at the air shut-off valve, replace the aspirator valve.

1981–83

6-CYLINDER ENGINES

The emission control system is the same as 1980, with two exceptions. The air pump intake is connected to the clean side of the air cleaner. A rubber scoop inside the air cleaner facilitates air intake. The second change is that the fuel evaporation control purge system is controlled by a thermo valve and is effective only at temperatures above 122°F.

Color coding of the vacuum lines is as follows:

Device	Color of line originating at a vacuum source	Color of line terminating at a vacuum operated device
Ignition advance	Red	
Ignition retard	Yellow	
Air injection	Blue	Blue/purple
Fuel evaporation thermo valve	Black	Black/purple

Lines originating at a vacuum source have only one color stripe; lines terminating at a vacuum operated device have 2 color stripes and purple is always the second color.

Testing the System

See "Testing the System" under 1980.

V8 ENGINES

Color coding of the vacuum lines is identical to the 6-cylinder engines. Operation of the Lambda oxygen sensor control system is the same as 1980. Only the oxygen sensor itself has been modified for production reasons. The air pump is a maintenance-free vane type pump, similar in operation to the 1980 system. Three-way-catalysts have been slightly modified dimensionally, but operate the same as those in 1980. The fuel evaporation control system is the same as 1980, except that the purge system is controlled by a thermo valve that allows purge only at coolant temperatures below approximately 122°F.

Testing the System

See "Testing the System" under 1980.

ELECTRONIC IDLE SPEED CONTROL

1. The engine should be at operating temperature with the ignition ON.
2. Pull the plug from the idle speed adjuster and check the voltage. If 12 volts are present, go to Step 4.

3. If there is no voltage, pull the plug from the control unit and check the voltage between terminals 2 and 4 (arrows). There should be approximately 12 volts. If there is no voltage, check the voltage supply and replace any defective parts. If 12 volts are present, check the wires from the plug of the idle speed adjuster and the control unit plug (black/yellow wire to terminal 5 of the control unit and the black wire to terminal 1 of the control unit). If there are infinite ohms, replace the wire. If there are 0 ohms, connect the coupling to the control unit and measure the voltage at the idle speed adjuster. If there are 0 volts, replace the control unit.

4. Check the control unit. With the engine idling at operating temperature, connect the plug to the idle speed adjuster so that you can check voltage at the plug. If there are 4–6 volts, go to Step 5. If there are no volts, replace the control unit.

5. Check the idle speed adjuster. Idle the engine and pull the plug from the coolant temperature switch. Bridge the terminals. The idle speed should increase. If not, apply battery voltage to the idle speed adjuster (for no more than 5 seconds). If the speed drops or the engine stops, replace the control unit. If the idle speed does not drop, replace the idle speed adjuster.

FUEL SYSTEM

Fuel Filter

6-CYLINDER CARBURETED ENGINES

The fuel filter is located in the carburetor housing. Put some rags under the fuel return valve to absorb the inevitable gasoline spillage.

1. Unscrew the fuel return valve and plug it at the carburetor.
2. Remove the fuel filter.
3. Renew the gasket at the seal plug.
4. Install a new filter. Check for leaks.

6-CYLINDER (FUEL INJECTED) AND V8

Two types of filter are used, one on the electronically controlled fuel injection and the other on the CIS fuel injection. Both are located between the rear axle and the fuel tank.

1. Unscrew the cover box.
2. Remove the pressure hoses.
3. Loosen the attaching screws and remove the filter. Remove the connecting plug from the old filter and install it on a new filter using a new gasket.
4. Install a new filter in the direction of flow.
5. Replace the attaching screws.

6. Install the pressure hoses.
7. Install the fuel filter in the holder by positioning it in the center of the transparent holder. Be sure the plastic sleeve between the fuel filter and fuel pump is installed. Galvanic corrosion may occur in cases of direct contact between these components.
8. Replace the cover box and check for proper sealing.

4-CYLINDER CARBURETED ENGINE

1. Loosen the hose clips.
2. Remove the fuel filter.
3. Install a new filter in the direction of flow (arrow) along with new fuel hoses.

Remove the main diesel fuel filter after removing the center attaching bolt. The bleed screw is (2).

Some diesel injection pumps have a manually operated delivery pump (1)

Diesel engines use a pre-filter in addition to the main fuel filter. The arrow indicates the hard operated delivery pump

4. Replace the hose clips.
5. Check for proper sealing.

DIESEL ENGINES

Main fuel Filter

1976 240D, 300D

1. Drain the fuel from the housing.
2. Remove the center bolt and remove the filter housing and filter.
3. Wash the filter housing in clean diesel fuel and install a new filter element.
4. Use a new gasket in the filter cap and reassemble the filter and housing.
5. Bleed the fuel filter. Loosen the bleed bolt on the fuel filter housing and release the manually operated delivery pump. Operate the delivery pump until the fuel emerges free of bubbles at the bleed screw. Close the bleed bolt and operate the pump until the overflow valve on the injection pump opens (a buzzing noise will be heard). Close the manual pump before starting the engine. To bleed the injection pump on 4-cylinder diesels, loosen the bleed screw on the injection pump and keep pumping the hand pump until fuel emerges free of bubbles.

1977 AND LATER DIESELS

Loosen the center attaching bolt and remove the filter cartridge downward. Lubricate the new filter gasket with clean diesel fuel and install a new filter cartridge.

To bleed the fuel filter, see Step 5 preceding.

Diesel Prefilter

Diesel engines use a prefilter in addition to the main fuel filter, since even the minutest particle of dirt will clog the injection system. The prefilter is located in the line just before it enters the injection pump.

To replace it, simply unscrew the clamps on each end and remove the old filter. Install a new filter and bleed the system (see Main Fuel Filter).

Fuel Pump Strainer (Carbureted Engines)

Plunger type fuel pumps on carbureted engines use a strainer located behind the cover.

1. Disconnect and plug the fuel line at the pump.
2. Remove the center screw and remove the cover. A small amount of fuel will run out.
3. Replace the strainer, gasket, screw and aluminum washer, all of which are part of the replacement kit.
4. Replace the cover. There are assembly marks on the cover and fuel pump body.
5. Reconnect the fuel line. Start the engine and check for leaks.

Mechanical Fuel Pump

All Mercedes-Benz carbureted engines are a diaphragm type fuel pump, which is mounted on the side of the block. It is operated by a gear driven eccentric shaft through a rocker arm on the fuel pump.

REMOVAL AND INSTALLATION

1. Clean the joint around the fuel pump base and cylinder block.
2. One at a time, remove and plug the intake and outlet lines from the fuel pump.
2. Unbolt the retaining bolts and remove the fuel pump and gasket from the cylinder block.
4. Clean the mating surfaces of the engine and cylinder block.
5. Install a new gasket.
6. Insert the fuel pump into the block and install the retaining bolts. Be sure that the bolts are tightened evenly.
7. Reconnect the intake and outlet lines to the fuel pump.
8. Run the engine and check for leaks.

TESTING DELIVERY PRESSURE

1. Remove the wire from the coil to prevent starting.
2. Connect a pressure gauge into the output line of the fuel pump.
3. Crank the engine and read the delivery pressure on the pressure gauge. The pressure should be a constant 1.5–2.5 psi.
4. If the pressure is not within specifications or is erratic, remove the pump for service or for replacement with a new or rebuilt unit. No adjustment is provided.

Testing fuel pump pressure, 1976 and later

Electric Fuel Pump

NOTE: Do not confuse the electric fuel pump with the injection pump.

All Mercedes-Benz fuel injected engines are equipped with electric fuel pumps. The electric fuel pump is located underneath the rear floor panel. The fuel return line was also eliminated and a check ball installed in its place. Beginning in 1980, the fuel pump uses a replaceable check valve on the outside of the pump which can be replaced separately.

Two types of fuel pumps have been used. One, the large pump, has been replaced with a new small design which has a bypass system to prevent vapor lock.

REMOVAL AND INSTALLATION

1. Jack the left rear of the car and support it on jack stands. This will provide sufficient working clearance.
2. Remove and plug the intake, outlet and bypass lines from the pump.
3. Disconnect the electrical leads.
4. Unbolt and remove the fuel pump and vibration pads.
5. Install the fuel pump in the reverse order of removal. Be sure that the electrical leads are connected to the proper terminals. The negative wire (brown) is connected to the negative terminal (brown plastic plate) and the positive wire (black/red) is connected to the positive terminal (red plastic plate). If the terminals are reversed, the pump will operate in the reverse direction of normal rotation and will deliver no fuel.

TESTING FUEL PUMP DELIVERY PRESSURE

Remove the fuel return hose from the fuel distributor. Connect a fuel line and hold the end in the measuring cup. Disconnect the plug from the safety switch on the mixture regulator and turn on the ignition for 30 seconds. If the delivery rate is less than 1 liter in 30 seconds, check the voltage at the fuel pump (11.5) and the fuel lines for kinks. Disconnect the leak off line between the fuel accumulator and the suction damper. Check the delivery rate again. If it is low replace the accumulator.

Replace the fuel filter and test again. If still low, replace the fuel pump.

Carburetors

REMOVAL AND INSTALLATION

Stromberg 175CDT (1976–78 230)

1. Remove the air cleaner.
2. Remove and plug the fuel lines.

----- **CAUTION** -----
Do not pull off the fuel lines. They should be pried off along with the securing discs.
----

3. Disconnect the control linkage.
4. Remove the vacuum lines.
5. Disconnect the water hoses for the automatic choke.
6. Disconnect the leads for the automatic choke and fuel shut-off valve.
7. Remove the carburetor retaining nuts and remove the carburetor.
8. Installation is the reverse of removal. Adjust the carburetor. See "Tune-Up".

1. Carburetor attachment screw
2. Gasket
3. Rubber flange fastening screw
4. Rubber flange
5. Insulating flange
6. Gasket
7. Shielding plate
8. Intake pipe

Stromberg 175 CDT carburetor gaskets

New style gasket on Solex 4A1 beginning 1974. The top is shown on the left and the bottom on the right

Solex 4 A 1 (280, 280C and 280S)

1. Remove the air filter.
2. Remove the electric cable from the starter cover and cut-off valves.
3. Remove the vacuum lines.
4. To prevent corrosion from leaked coolant, cover the starter housing with a rag. Release the pressure in the cooling system by cracking the radiator cap until pressure has escaped. Install and tighten the radiator cap. Remove and plug the coolant water hoses from the carburetor.
5. Remove and plug the fuel lines.
6. Remove the retaining nuts and remove the carburetor from the manifold.
7. Installation is the reverse of removal. Install the insulating flange on the intake manifold as shown. The paper side of the insulating flange must face UP. These models use a new style insulating flange begun with 1974 models.
8. Install the retaining nuts and tighten evenly, torquing the nuts in a crossing pattern. Torque the nuts to 7–11 ft. lbs.
9. Be sure to adjust the idle speed. See "Tune-Up".

OVERHAUL

For all carburetor overhaul procedures, please refer to "Carburetor Overhaul" in the Unit Repair Section.

Install the gasket on a Solex 4A1 carburetor with the mark as shown (lower left corner)

Home-made gauge for measuring Stromberg 175 CDT float level (dimensions in mm)

ADJUSTMENTS

Stromberg 175CDT

DAMPER FLUID LEVEL

1. Unscrew the top of the damper and check the fluid level.
2. If necessary, top up the reservoir with engine oil, or in cold weather, automatic transmission fluid (ATF). 1976–78 models use only ATF.
3. The fluid level should be to the top edge of the piston ring or on 1976–77 models, to the lower edge of the filler plug threads.
4. Replace the top on the reservoir.

FLOAT ADJUSTMENT

1. Remove the carburetor.
2. Remove the float chamber cover and idling speed cut-off valve.
3. Do not loosen the lock screw from the needle, or the needle will have to be recentered.
4. Remove the fuel nozzle and compensating element.
5. Push the float down until the float needle valve ball is fully pushed in.
6. Check the float level with a home-made gauge.
7. To correct the float level, bend the float arm at the tang over the needle valve. The float arm must always remain perpendicular to the needle valve. Also, check the sealing ring under the needle valve for specified thickness (1.5 mm) and replace if necessary.
8. Replace the float chamber cover and install the carburetor.
9. Adjust the idle.

1. Connecting rod
2. Hex nut
3. Threaded bolt
4. Hex nut
5. Actuating lever
6. Venting valve

Stromberg 175CDT automatic choke adjustment

AUTOMATIC CHOKE

1. The idle should be set and the engine should be at normal operating temperature.
2. On vehicles with air conditioning, remove the air cleaner and air intake.
3. Check the adjustment of the choke cover. The index marks should be aligned.
4. Raise the throttle linkage slightly and insert a screwdriver through the slot of the starter housing on the carburetor. Push the screwdriver against the engaging lever in the direction of the engine. Release the throttle linkage and engaging lever. This will set the engine at fast idle.
5. The fast idle speed should be 3300–3600 rpm. If the speed requires adjustment, loosen both locknuts on the connecting rod and turn the threaded bolt. ½ turn of the bolt will change the engine rpm by about 200–300 rpm. Decreasing the length of the bolt will decrease rpm and increasing the length will increase rpm.

FAST IDLE (1976–78 ONLY)

The fast idle adjustment is done with the cam on the second step.

1. Run the engine to normal operating temperature.
2. With the engine idling, raise the throttle linkage slightly.
3. At the same time, push the engaging lever with a small screwdriver, through the slot of the choke housing in the direction of the engine, against the stop on the pull down diaphragm rod. Do not force it past the stop.
4. Raise the throttle linkage, while holding the engaging lever against the stop.
5. Check the CO and fast idle.
6. Adjust the fast idle speed with the upper adjusting screw to 1600–1800 rpm.
7. Adjust the CO with the mixture adjusting screw to 5–8%. To check the CO, the center vacuum line for the air injection switchover valve must be disconnected and plugged.

FULL THROTTLE STOP (1976–78 CALIFORNIA ONLY)

1. With the accelerator pedal fully depressed, adjust the full throttle stop screw

Fast idle adjusting screw (114) on Stromberg 175CDT—1979 and prior years

8. Idle adjusting screw
114. Fast adjusting screw (cold start).

Access slot (arrow) on Stromberg 175CDT—1979 and prior years

so that a clearance of .02 in. exists between the throttle valve lever and carburetor housing.

THERMO AIR VALVE

1. Disconnect the hoses from the thermo-air valve and blow into one hose. If the valve is cold, no air can pass through the valve. If the valve is warm (slightly above room temperature) air should pass through the valve.

Solex 4A1

FUEL LEVEL

1. There is no provision for measuring the fuel level, other than with the special Mercedes-Benz tool. It is a measuring rod which is inserted through the bore of the carburetor cover, and can be purchased from a dealer or fabricated.
2. Run the engine briefly at fast idle and shut off the ignition.
3. Insert the measuring gauge through the bore of the carburetor cover as far as it will go.
4. Remove the gauge and read the fuel level. The reading should be within the tolerance range marked on the stick.
5. To adjust the level, remove the carburetor cover and adjust the float by bending it on the hinge.
6. Reinstall the cover and test the level again.

115. Throttle valve lever
116. Full throttle adjusting screw
Full throttle stop adjusting screw

Measurements in mm.

Fabricated tool for measuring fuel level on Solex 4A1 carburetor

Measuring fuel level on Solex 4A1 carburetor

FLOAT LEVEL

1. Remove the carburetor cover. The carburetor does not have to be removed.
2. With the float needle valve installed, push the connecting web of the float arms down until a noticeable stop. Be sure to push at the web. If not, the float shaft will lift from the bottom and result in an incorrect measurement.
3. Using a T-gauge or a homemade gauge, measure the level of the float below the carburetor housing without the gasket installed.
4. If the float level is not correct, remove the float in the desired direction.
5. Reinstall the carburetor cover.

Bend the float at the arrow to adjust the float level on Solex 4A1 carburetor

Fabricated tool for measuring float level on Solex 4A1 carburetor

VACUUM GOVERNOR

1. Set the idle speed and make sure that the engine is at normal operating temperature.
2. Run the engine at idle and pull the vacuum hose from the governor.
3. Set the engine speed to approximately 1200–1400 rpm. Loosen the locknut and adjust the rpm with the adjusting screw. Hold the diaphragm rod and turn the adjusting nut.
4. Adjust the compression spring with the transmission in gear.
5. The speed should be 600–700 rpm. If necessary, adjust the compression spring with the adjusting nut.
6. Turn on the air conditioning, and turn the wheels to full lock. The engine should keep running. If it does not, adjust the speed with the adjusting nut again. See Step 3.

AUTOMATIC CHOKE

1. Check the choke for ease of operation.
2. Switch on the ignition and check to be sure that the choke opens after a minute or so.
3. Check the adjustment on the choke cover. The markings on the housing and cover should be aligned.

CHOKE GAP

1. Run the engine at idle until the diaphragm in the vacuum unit has been pulled completely against the stop.

3. Throttle valve lever
60. Spring
61. Adjusting nut
62. Counternut
63. Adjusting screw
Vacuum governor adjustment—Solex 4A1

Automatic choke adjustment—Solex 4A1. If the choke gap is too large, push the bend apart; if the choke gap is too small, push the bend together

2. Then clamp the hose to block all vacuum.

3. Be sure that the diaphragm is still against the stop and slightly raise the throttle valve lever. Position the stepped disc upward against the top stop. Release the throttle valve lever.

4. Push the lever of the bi-metallic spring until the stop is felt. The connecting rod will now by against the stop in the slot of the lever.

5. Measure the choke gap with a drill (0.060 in.—1973–74 Federal; 0.010 in.—1973–74 California; 0.108–0.120 in.—1975–76) between the choke plate and the wall of the air horn.

6. To adjust the gap, remove the coolant hose from the choke housing. Cover the choke housing with a rag and release the pressure in the radiator. Tighten the radiator cap again. Remove the coolant hose and clamp it shut.

7. Hold the connecting rod with a screwdriver. Bend the connecting rod with a second screwdriver. On later models, the adjustment is made by turning the adjusting

On later models, adjust the choke gap with the adjusting screw (211) located in the housing (210)

Solex 4A1 fast idle adjustment

screw in the choke housing cover in (decrease gap) or out (increase gap).

8. While making the adjustment, be sure that the diaphragm in the vacuum unit is still against its stop.

FAST IDLE

1. Adjust the idle speed and be sure that the engine is at normal operating temperature.

2. Run the engine at idle speed.

3. Raise the throttle valve lever slightly and position the stepped disc completely upward against the top stop.

4. Release the throttle valve lever.

5. Connect a tachometer and measure the engine speed. It should be 2400–2600. If required, adjust the fast idle with the fast idle speed adjusting screw.

ACCELERATOR PUMP

1. Move the throttle valve lever several times. A strong jet of fuel should be forced out of the fuel outlets.

2. If not, remove the accelerator pump cover and check the diaphragm. Blow out the ducts with compressed air.

3. Install the accelerator pump cover.

4. If there still is no fuel from the injection tube, remove the carburetor cover.

5. Actuate the accelerator pump. If fuel emerges from the ball valves, blow out the injection holes in the carburetor cover with compressed air.

6. Install the carburetor cover. Tighten the screws evenly to 11 ft. lbs.

Solex 4A1 accelerator pump adjustment

FUEL RETURN VALVE

1. Pull the fuel return hose from the connection to the return line below the fuel pump.

2. Hold the return hose in a container and check whether a strong fuel jet comes from the line with the automatic transmission in Drive and the air conditioning on.

Fuel Injection

Mercedes-Benz uses the Bosch K–Jetronic (CIS) fuel injection system.

Minor running changes and improvements are made during production, but essential operation and service of the system remains alike on all vehicles equipped with the CIS injection.

For all fuel injection system service and repair procedures not detailed below, please refer to ''Fuel Injection'' in the Unit Repair section.

--- CAUTION ---

Even a seemingly minor adjustment, such as idle speed, can necessitate adjustments to other portions of the fuel injection system. Be extremely careful when adjusting the idle. If any difficulty at all is experienced, immediately refer the vehicle to a Mercedes-Benz dealer. Further attempts at adjustment will only upset the balance of an already delicate system.

TESTING

Delivery Capacity

See ''Testing Fuel Pump Output'' under Fuel Pump earlier in this section.

Cold Start Valve

1. Disconnect the plugs from the safety switch and mixture control regulator.

2. Remove the cold start valve with fuel line connected.

3. Hold the cold start valve in a container.

4. Turn on the ignition. Connect the valve to battery voltage. It should emit a cone shaped spray.

5. Dry the nozzle off. No fuel should leak out.

Hot Start System

Perform the test at coolant temperature 104°–122°F.

1. Remove the coil wire.

2. Connect a voltmeter to hot start terminal 3 and ground.

3. Actuate the starter. In approximately 3–4 seconds, the voltmeter should read about 11 volts for 3–4 seconds.

4. If 11 volts are not indicated, check fuse 10. Connect the plug of the 104°F temperature switch and ground and repeat the test. If 11 volts are now indicated, replace the temperature switch. If 11 volts are not

380SEL control pressure adjustment. The clamp screw is (6) and the ball socket (19)

1981 300SD control pressure adjustment. Adjust the ball socket (19) at the adjusting screw (15)

indicated, or if the time periods are wrong, replace the hot start relay.

Fuel Pump Safety Circuit

The pump will only run if the starter motor is actuated or if the engine is running.
1. Remove the air filter.
2. Turn on the ignition and briefly depress the sensor plate.
3. Remove the coil wire from the distributor.
4. Connect a voltmeter to the positive fuel pump terminal and ground.
5. Actuate the starter. Voltmeter should indicate 11 volts.
6. If the fuel pump runs only when the sensor plate is depressed or only when the engine is cranked, replace the fuel pump relay. If the pump is already running when the ignition is turned ON, replace the safety switch.

ADJUSTMENTS

1976–79

CONTROL LINKAGE

1. Check the control linkage for ease of operation.
2. Disconnect the control rod. The throttle valve should rest against the idle stop. Reconnect the control rod.
3. Adjust the control rod so that the roller rests tension free in the gate slot.

FULL THROTTLE STOP

1. With the engine stopped, press the accelerator pedal until it rests against the kickdown switch.
2. The throttle valve lever should rest against the full throttle stop. If necessary, adjust the throttle valve lever.
3. If the full throttle stop is not reached, adjust the control rod (bell crank lever to

accelerator pedal) to 4.8 in. (from center to center of ball sockets).
4. Adjust the accelerator pedal linkage if necessary with the fastening screw.
5. Adjust the control pressure rod (at idle) by compressing the adjusting clip, and moving the rod completely to the rear against the stop.

1980–81

THROTTLE VALVE SWITCH

1. Set an ohmmeter to 0-infinity.
2. Check the idle speed stop. Push the throttle valve against the idle speed stop. Connect the ohmmeter across terminals 1 and 2. Rotate the throttle valve switch until the ohmmeter reads 0.
3. Advance the throttle valve slightly. The ohmmeter should read 0-infinite ohms.
4. Check the full throttle stop. Push the throttle valve against the full throttle stop and connect an ohmmeter across terminals 2 and 3. The reading should be 0 ohms.
5. Turn the throttle valve back slightly. A reading of infinite ohms should result.

Turbocharger— Turbodiesels Only

NOTE: There is no particular maintenance associated with the turbocharger. It should also be noted that a turbocharger cannot be installed on an engine that was not meant for one, without incuring serious engine damage.

The exhaust gas turbocharger is a Garret Model TA 0301. It uses the aerodynamic energy of the exhaust gases to drive a centrifugal compressor which in turn delivers high pressure air to the cylinders of the diesel engine. The turbine wheel and the compressor wheel are mounted on a common shaft. The turbocharger is mounted between the exhaust manifold and the exhaust pipe. For lubrication and cooling, the turbocharger is connected directly to the engine lubrication system.

A boost pressure control valve (waste-

1. Mixture regulator assembly
2. Airflow sensor
20. Fuel distributor
50. Hot-start solenoid
70. Warm-up/full-load enrichment compensator
80. Injection nozzles
85. Fuel accumulator
86. Fuel filter
87. Fuel pump
95. Suction damper
96. Auxiliary air valve
98. Cold-start valve

Air Flow Controlled injection system components

AIR OUTLET

COMPRESSOR

TURBINE

AIR INLET

EXHAUST OUTLET

TO TURBINE

TO WASTEGATE

EXHAUST INLET

WASTEGATE BOOST CONTROL

Garret TA0301 turbocharger operation

1. Mounting bracket
2. Intermediate flange
3. Turbocharger

Remove the mounting nuts (arrow) to remove the turbocharger

fill a new turbocharger with ¼ pint of engine oil through the engine oil supply bore before operating.

gate valve) is attached to the turbine housing to insure that a certain boost pressure is not esceeded. Should the boost pressure control valve malfunction, an engine overload protection system will prevent a failure of the engine.

For further information on turbochargers, please refer to "Turbocharging" in the Unit Repair Section.

OPERATION

Turbocharger

The exhaust gases of the engine are routed via the exhaust manifold directly into the turbine housing (6) and to the turbine wheel (7). The velocity of the exhaust gases causes the turbine wheel (7) to turn. This turns the compressor wheel (2) which is directly connected to the turbine wheel via the shaft (5). The turbocharger can obtain a maximum of approximately 100,000 rpm; the fresh air drawn in by the compressor wheel is compressed and delivered to the pistons of the engine.

At idle speed, the engine operates as a naturally aspirated engine. With increasing load and engine rpm, (increasing velocity of the exhaust gases), the turbine wheel (7) accelerates and boost pressure is produced by the compressor wheel (2). The boost pressure is routed via the intake manifold to the individual cylinders.

The exhaust gases produced by the combustion are routed into the turbine housing and from there into the exhaust pipe.

Boost Pressure Control Valve

In order not to exceed the designed boost pressure, a boost pressure control valve (8) is installed on the turbine housing (6). The boost pressure is picked up at the compressor housing (1) and connected to the boost pressure control valve (8) via a connecting hose (9). If the maximum permissible boost pressure is obtained, the boost pressure control valve (8) starts to open the bypass canal (c) for the exhaust gas around the turbine wheel (7). A part of the exhaust gas flows now directly into the exhaust pipe. This keeps the boost pressure constant and prevents it from increasing beyond its designed limits.

REMOVAL AND INSTALLATION

1. Remove the air filter.
2. Disconnect the electrical cable from the temperature switch.
3. Loosen the lower hose clamp on the air duct that connects the air filter with the compressor housing.
4. Remove the vacuum line and crankcase breather pipe.
5. Remove the air filter and air intake duct.
6. Disconnect the oil line at the turbocharger.
7. Remove the air filter mounting bracket.
8. Disconnect the turbocharger at the exhaust flange.
9. Disconnect and remove the pipe bracket on the automatic transmission.
10. Push the exhaust pipe rearward.
11. Remove the mounting bracket at the intermediate flange.
12. Unbolt and remove the turbocharger.
13. Remove the intermediate flange and oil return line at the turbocharger.
14. Installation is the reverse of removal. Before installing the turbocharger, install the oil return line and intermediate flange. Install the flange gasket between the turbocharger and exhaust manifold with the reinforcing bead toward the exhaust manifold.

Use only heat proof nuts and bolts and

TROUBLESHOOTING

To properly evaluate the turbocharger, the full throttle stop, maximum no-load engine rpm, start of delivery and opening pressure of the injection nozzles must be within specifications.

Complaint: Poor engine performance
Probable cause: Boost pressure too low
Remedy:

1. Clean air filter and check air intake shroud and duct for obstructions.
2. Check turbocharger for leaks at following points:
Between exhaust manifold and turbine housing; tighten nuts.
Between compressor housing discharge and intake manifold.
Between intake or exhaust manifold and cylinder head.
3. Check pressure line between intake manifold and aneroid compensator.
4. Check fuse No. 4 or the black/red wire at the switchover valve for breaks or loose connection.
5. The boost pressure control valve (waste-gate) on the turbocharger should close. If not, replace the turbocharger.

Complaint: Engine surges at full load.
Probable cause: Boost pressure control valve does not open.
Remedy: Check the connecting hose between the compressor housing and wastegate. If the hose is leaking or has a kink, replace the hose. If the hose is OK, replace the turbocharger.

MANUAL TRANSMISSION

The 240D is the only model currently imported into the U.S. that uses a manual transmission. A 4-speed, side cover, model G76/18 4-speed is used on 1976–81 models,

Clutch housing (1) and clutch housing attaching bolts (2) which can only be reached from inside the clutch housing

Exploded view of clutch

1. Plate spring clutch
2. Driven plate
3. Throwout
6. Thowout rocker
8. Slave cylinder
12. Shim
13. Clutch housing

with certain minor running modifications, and a GL68/20A is used on 1982 and later models. Both are very similar in design, operation and service. See the Manual Transmission Overhaul Unit Repair section for service.

The transmission should only be removed with the engine as a unit, since the transmission-to-clutchhousing bolts can only be reached from the inside. Once the engine/transmission unit has been removed from the vehicle, the transmission and bellhousing must be separated from the engine, as follows:

REMOVAL AND INSTALLATION (WITH ENGINE)

See the "Engine" section to remove the engine/transmission.

1. After removing the engine/transmission unit, unbolt the bellhousing from the engine. The bolts which hold the transmission to the bellhousing cannot be reached except from inside the bellhousing.

2. Remove the starter from its mounting position and pull the transmission and bellhousing from the engine.

3. The bolts which secure the bellhousing to the transmission are now visible and can be removed to separate the bellhousing and transmission.

4. To install, connect the engine, bellhousing, and transmission, after coating the splines of the mainshaft with grease.

5. Install the starter.

6. Further installation is the reverse of removal.

LINKAGE ADJUSTMENT

The only type of shifter used is a floor mounted type.

——————— **CAUTION** ———————
On all types of transmissions, never hammer or force a new shift knob on with the shift lever installed, as the plastic bushing connected to the lever will be destroyed and cause hard shifting.

Proper adjustment of the shift linkage is dependent on both the position of the levers

at the transmission and the length of the shift rods. The shift levers and bearing block are under the floor tunnel which may have to be removed, from underneath the car.

1. Check the positioning of the shift levers at the transmission (see illustration) and correct by loosening the clamp bolts. The diagram shows the levers in Neutral.

2. Lock the three levers by inserting a 0.2156 in. rod (a No. 3 drill will do or other tool of approximately the same diameter) through the levers and the hole in the bearing block.

3. With the shift levers at the lower steering column locked and the levers at the transmission adjusted, try hooking the shift rods into their respective levers. If they are too long or short, adjust their length by loosening the locknuts and turning the ball socket ends. Remove the locking rod and try shifting through the gears. Very slight further adjustments may clear up any binding.

CLUTCH

REMOVAL AND INSTALLATION

1. To remove the clutch, first remove the transmission and bell housing.

2. Loosen the clutch pressure plate holddown bolts evenly, 1–1½ turns at a time, until tension is relieved. Never remove one bolt at a time, as damage to the pressure plate is possible.

3. Examine the flywheel surface for blue heat marks, scoring, or cracks. If the flywheel is to be machined, always machine both sides.

4. To reinstall, coat the splines with high temperature grease and place the clutch disc against the flywheel, centering it with a clutch pilot shaft. A wooden shaft, available at automative jobbers, is satisfactory, but an old transmission mainshaft works best.

5. Tighten the pressure plate hold-down bolts evenly 1–1½ turns at a time until tight, then remove the pilot shaft.

4-speed transmission linkage Arrow at top shows locating pin installed prior to adjustment

Wear limit has been reached

─── CAUTION ───

Most clutch plates have the flywheel side marked as such (Kupplungsseite). Do not assume that the pressure springs always face the transmission.

CHECKING CLUTCH PLATE WEAR

A spring plate clutch that automatically compensates for wear is used, so no periodic adjustments are required. Apart from the usual slippage which accompanies severe wear of the clutch plate or disc, Mercedes-Benz has a simple tool, which

1. Clutch slave cylinder
2. Plastic shim
3. Thrust rod
4. Measuring gauge
   (Part No. 115 589 07 23 00)
(a)—Direction of measuring on lefthand drive vehicle with steering wheel and center shift, as well as on righthand drive vehicles with center shift
(b)—Direction of measuring on righthand drive vehicles with steering wheel shift

Wear limit has not been reached

can be purchased from a dealer that measures the amount of wear on the clutch plate. Actually, it is a simple "go-no go" gauge.

1. A plastic shim is installed between the slave cylinder and the bell housing.

2. The shim is provided with two flat grooves running diagonally from bottom to center. When the shim is installed, these grooves appear as slots. Use groove (a) for left-hand drive vehicles and groove (b) for right-hand drive vehicles.

3. The clutch slave cylinder pushrod has two different diameters. The width of the slot in the test gauge corresponds to the smaller diameter of the pushrod. If the notches on the test gauge disappear when the test gauge is inserted as far as it will go, the clutch plate is still operational.

4. If however, the notches on the test gauge remain visible, this is an indication that the clutch plate is worn severely and should be replaced.

Clutch Slave Cylinder

REMOVAL AND INSTALLATION

1. Detach and plug the pressure line from the slave cylinder.
2. Remove the attaching screws from the slave cylinder.
3. Remove the slave cylinder, pushrod, and spacer.
4. To install, place the grooved side of the spacer in contact with the housing and hold it in position.
5. Install the slave cylinder and pushrod into the housing. Be sure that the dust cap is properly seated.
6. Install the attaching screws.
7. Connect the pressure line to the slave cylinder.
8. Bleed the slave cylinder.

BLEEDING THE SLAVE CYLINDER

The same principle is used as in bleeding the brakes.

1. Check the brake fluid level in the compensating tank and fill to maximum level.
2. Put a hose on the bleeder screw of the right front caliper and open the bleeder screw.
3. Have a helper depress the brake pedal until the hose is full and there are no air bubbles. Be sure that the bleeder screw is closed each time the pedal is released.
4. Put the free end of the hose on the bleeder screw of the slave cylinder and open the bleeder screw.
5. Keep stepping on the brake pedal. Close the bleeder screw on the caliper and release the brake pedal. Open the bleeder screw and repeat the process until no air bubbles show up at the mouth of the inlet line of the compensating tank.

Between operations, check and, if necessary, refill the compensating tank.
6. Close the bleeder screws on the caliper and slave cylinder and remove the hose.
7. Check the clutch operation and the fluid level.

AUTOMATIC TRANSMISSION

REMOVAL AND INSTALLATION

Mercedes-Benz automatic transmissions are removed as a unit with the engine. Consult the "Engine Mechanical" section for removal and installation procedures concerning a given engine.

PAN AND FILTER REPLACEMENT

1. Drain the transmission of all fluid by loosening the dipstick tube.
2. Remove the transmission pan.
3. Remove the bolt or bolts which retain the filter to the transmission.
4. Remove the filter and replace it with a new one.
5. Install the transmission pan, using a new gasket.
6. Refill the transmission to the proper level with the specified brand of fluid.

Bottom view of automatic transmission showing dipstick tube (1), converter drain plug (2) and pan (3)

SELECTOR ROD LINKAGE ADJUSTMENT

NOTE: Before performing this adjustment on any Mercedes-Benz vehicle, be sure that the vehicle is resting on its wheels. No part of the vehicle may be jacked for this adjustment.

COLUMN MOUNTED LINKAGE

See the "Transmission Application" chart in the specifications for Transmission Application.

W3A 040

1. Loosen the counternut on the ball socket.

2. Disconnect the selector rod from the shift lever bracket.

3. Set the transmission selector lever and the selector rod in Neutral.

4. Adjust the length of the selector rod until the ball socket aligns with the end of the ball on the intermediate lever.

5. Attach the ball socket to the intermediate lever, making sure that the play in the selector lever in position Three (D) and Four (S) is about equal.

6. Tighten the counternut on the ball socket.

W3A 040 (380SEL, 450SE and 450SEL Only), W4B 025 and W4A 040

1. Loosen the counternut on the rear selector rod while holding both recesses of the front selector rod with an open end wrench.

2. Disconnect the selector rod from the selector lever.

3. Set the selector lever on the transmission and on the column to Neutral.

4. Adjust the selector rod until the bearing pin is aligned with the bearing bushing in the selector lever.

5. Connect the rear selector lever to the selector rod and secure it with the lock. Be sure that the clearance of the selector lever in D and S is equal.

6. Tighten the locknut on the rear selector rod while holding the front selector rod as in Step 1.

FLOOR MOUNTED LINKAGE

NOTE: The vehicle must be standing with the weight normally distributed on all four wheels. No jacks may be used.

1. Disconnect the selector rod from the selector lever.

2. Set the selector lever in Neutral and make sure that there is approximately 1 mm clearance between the selector lever and the N stop of the selector gate.

3. Adjust the length of the selector rod so that it can be attached free of tension.

4. Retighten the counternut.

STARTER LOCKOUT AND BACK-UP LIGHT SWITCH ADJUSTMENT

1. Disconnect the selector rod and move the selector lever on the transmission to position Neutral.

2. Tighten the clamping screw prior to making adjustments.

3. Loosen the adjusting screw and insert the locating pin through the driver into the locating hole in the shift housing.

1. Selector rod
2. Ball socket
3. Intermediate lever
4. Connecting link
7. Range selector lever

Column mounted selector rod linkage—W3A 040

5. Bearing bracket
6. Starter and backup light switch
7. Selector lever
8. Rear selector rod

1. Front selector rod
2. Counternut
3. Intermediate lever
4. Elastic intermediate piece

Selector rod linkage on W3A 040 (380SEL, 450SE, 450SEL only) and W4B 025

1. Selector range lever
2. Washer
3. Adjusting screw
4. Shaft
5. Locating pin
6. Clamping screw

(a)—Column shift for left-hand and right-hand drive vehicles 220/8, 220 D/8, 230/8, 280 S/8, 280 SE/8 and 300 SEL/8.

(b)—Steering wheel shift for left-hand drive vehicles (220/8, 220 D/8, 230/8, 250/8)

(c)—Steering wheel shift for right-hand drive vehicles (220/8, 220 D/8, 230/8, 250/8)

(d)—Steering wheel shift for left-hand drive vehicles (280S/8, 280 SE/8, 300 SEL/8, 280 SE 3.5 and 300 SEL 3.5)

Starter lockout and backup light switch adjustment

4. Tighten the adjusting screw and remove the locating pin.

5. Move the selector lever to position N and connect the selector rod so that there is no tension.

6. Check to be sure that the engine cannot be started in Neutral or Park.

KICKDOWN SWITCH

1. The kickdown position of the solenoid valve is controlled by the accelerator pedal.

2. Push the accelerator pedal against the kickdown limit stop. In this position the

9. Accelerator pedal
10. Kickdown switch
11. Return lever

A. Idling position
B. Full throttle position
C. Kickdown position

Kickdown switch adjustment

1. Control pressure rod
2. Bellcrank
3. Screw
4. Bellcrank

Control pressure rod adjustment—1979 and prior 230

throttle lever should rest against the full load stop of the venturi control unit.

3. Adjustments are made by loosening the clamping screw on the return lever on the accelerator pedal shaft and turning the shaft. Tighten the clamping screw again.

CONTROL PRESSURE ROD (1975–83 EXCEPT 1981–83 300SD, 300TD, 300D, 300CD, 380SL, 380SLC, 380SEL and 380SEC)

230

1. Remove the vacuum control unit from the carburetor.

2. Disconnect the automatic choke connecting rod so the throttle valve rests against the idle stop.

3. Loosen the screw and turn the levers against each other so the control rod rests against the idle stop.

4. Tighten the screw and depress the accelerator to the kickdown position. The throttle valve must rest against the full throttle stop. If necessary adjust the full throttle stop (see Fuel System).

5. Install the vacuum control unit on the distributor and connect the automatic choke rod.

Diesel Engines

The control pressure rod can only be adjusted with a special gauge available only from Mercedes-Benz dealers.

6-Cylinder Engines

1. Disconnect the control pressure rod.
2. Push the angle lever in the direction of the arrow.
3. Push the control pressure rod rear-

ward against the stop and adjust its length so there is no binding.

4. Tighten the counternut after adjustment.

V8 Engines

1. Remove the air filter and disconnect the control pressure linkage.
2. The throttle valve should rest against the idle speed stop.

1. Selector lever
4. Counternut
5. Selector rod
6. Gear selector lever

Floor mounted selector rod linkage

57.	Control pressure rod	120.	Angle lever
58.	Ball socket	144.	Connecting rod
59.	Counternut		

Control pressure rod adjustment—6-cylinder engine

3. Push the regulating lever and angle lever to the idle position.

4. Push the control pressure rod completely rearward against the stop and adjust the length of the rod so there is no tension.

5. When checking the rod for length, hold it to the left of the socket, not above to compensate for rotary motion of the linkage.

CONTROL PRESSURE WIRE (1981–83)

380SEL, 380SEC, 380SL, 380SLC

1. Remove the air cleaner.
2. Loosen the clamping screw.
3. Push the ball socket back, then carefully forward until a slight resistance is felt. At this point, tighten the clamp screw.
4. Install the air cleaner.

Turbodiesels

1. Pry off the ball socket.
2. Push the ball socket back, then pull carefully forward until a slight resistance is felt.
3. Hold the ball socket above the ball

7.	Roller	18.	Stop pin
11.	Connecting rod	19.	Gate lever
12.	Bearing bracket	20.	Angle lever
13.	Control pressure rod	31.	Connecting rod
17.	Regulating lever		

Control pressure rod adjustment—V8 engine

head. The drag lever should rest against the stop.

4. Adjust the cable at the adjusting screw so that the ball socket can be attached with no strain.

DRIVE AXLE

Mercedes-Benz automobiles use either two or three piece driveshafts to connect the transmission to a hypoid independent rear axle. All models covered in this book use independent rear suspension with open or enclosed driveshafts to the rear wheels.

Driveshaft and U-Joints

REMOVAL AND INSTALLATION

240D, 300D, 300CD, 300TD, 230, 280, 280C, 280E, 280CE

Matchmark all driveshaft connections prior to removal.

1. Remove the equalizer and disconnect the parking brake cables.

2. Remove the bolts which secure the two brackets to the chassis at the front and rear and remove the brackets. It may be necessary to lower the exhaust system slightly to allow access to the left-hand bolts on the rear bracket.

3. Loosen the nut on the driveshaft about 2 turns without pushing the rubber sleeve back (it slides along). On a two-piece shaft, only loosen the front clamp nut.

4. Remove the nuts which secure the attaching plate to the transmission flange and rear axle.

NOTE: A new coupling flange is used on 1981–83, 280E and 280CE models. The new coupling flange uses a thinner washer in place of the previous self-locking hex nut and thicker washers. Do not mix the two types.

16.	Rear axle carrier
17.	Cheesehead bolts

Rear driveshaft mounting flange

1981 driveshafts use a new design coupling flange with thinner washers

5. Remove the bolts which secure the intermediate bearing(s) to the chassis. Push the driveshaft together and slightly down, and remove the driveshaft from the vehicle.

NOTE: If possible, do not separate the parts of the driveshaft since each driveshaft is balanced at the factory. If separation is necessary, all parts must be marked and reassembled in the same relative positions to assure that the driveshafts will remain reasonably well balanced.

6. Installation is the reverse of removal.

7. Pack the cavities of the two centering sleeves with special Mercedes-Benz grease.

8. Install the driveshaft and attach the intermediate bearing(s) to the chassis.

9. Rock the car backward and forward several times to be sure that the driveshaft is properly centered without forcing.

10. Prior to tightening the clamp nuts on a three piece driveshaft, be sure that the intermediate shaft does not contact either the front or rear intermediate bearing. The clearance between the intermediate shaft and the bearing should be the same at both ends.

All Other Models

NOTE: Steps 1–3 apply to V8 models. Matchmark all driveshaft connections prior to removal.

1. Fold the torsion bar down after disconnecting the level control linkage (if equipped).

2. Remove the exhaust system.

3. Remove the heat shield from the frame.

4. Support the transmission with a jack and completely remove the rear engine mount crossmember.

5. Without sliding the rubber sleeve back, loosen the clamp nut approximately two turns (the rubber sleeve will slide along).

NOTE: On 3 piece driveshafts, only the front clamp nut need be loosened.

6. Unscrew the U-joint mounting flange from the U-joint plate.

NOTE: The 1981 and later 380SEL and 380SEC uses a new design coupling flange with thinner washers under a new hex nut. The previous design used thicker washers. Do not mix the two types.

7. Bend back the locktabs and remove the bolts that attach the driveshaft to the rear axle pinion yoke.

8. Remove the bolts which attach the intermediate bearing(s) to the frame. Push the driveshaft together slightly and remove it from the vehicle.

9. Try not to separate the driveshafts. If it is absolutely necessary, matchmark all components so that they can be reassembled in the same order.

10. Installation is the reverse of removal. Always use new self-locking nuts. After the driveshaft is installed, rock the car back and forth several times to settle the driveshaft. Make sure that neither intermediate shaft is binding aginst either intermediate bearing, and that the clearance between the intermediate bearing and the driveshaft is the same at both ends.

Axle Shaft

NOTE: The rubber covered joints are filled with special oil. If they are disassembled for any reason, they must be refilled with special oil.

REMOVAL AND INSTALLATION

Models Without Torque Compensator (Torsion Bar)

NOTE: On the 280, 280C and 280E only, axle shafts identified with a yellow paint dot or part No. 107 350 07 10 (left) or Part No. 107 350 0810 (right) can be installed.

Most models do not use a torque compensator (torsion bar) which is actually a steel bar used to locate the rear axle under acceleration. In general, only the large sedans use a torque compensator, but it is wise to check for one prior to servicing the axle shaft. The illustrations apply to either type.

1. Jack up the rear of the car and remove the wheel and center axle hold-down bolt (in hub).

2. Remove the brake caliper and suspend it from a hook.

3. Drain the differential oil and place a jack under the differential housing.

4. Unbolt the rubber mount from the chassis and the differential housing, then remove the differential housing cover to expose the ring and pinion gears.

5. Press the shaft from the axle flange. If necessary, loosen the shock absorber.

Most models do not use a torque compensator (arrow)

Removing the lock-ring (26) from the axle shaft with pliers (1) or a screwdriver

Axle shaft markings (r)

6. Using a screwdriver, remove the axle lock ring inside the differential case.

7. Pull the axle from the housing by pulling the splined end from the side gears, with the spacer.

NOTE: Axle shafts are stamped R and L for right and left units. Always use new lockrings.

8. Installation is the reverse of removal. Fill the rear axle. New radial seal

rings are used on 1980 and later models. Lubricate the outside diameter of rubber covered radial sealing rings with hypoid gear lubricant prior to installation.

—————— **CAUTION** ——————
Check end-play of the lockring in the groove. If necessary, install a thicker lockring or spacer to eliminate all end-play, while still allowing the lockring to rotate. Do not allow the joints in the axle shaft to hang free or the joint bearing may be damaged and leak.

Models with Torque Compensator (Torsion Bar)

1. Drain the oil from the rear axle.
2. Disconnect and plug the brake lines.
3. Loosen the connecting rod and unscrew the torsion bar bearing bracket. Lower the exhaust system slightly and remove the torsion bar.
4. Loosen the shock absorber.
5. Remove the bolt which attaches the rear axle shaft to the rear axle shaft flange.
6. Disconnect the brake cable control. Remove the bracket from the wheel carrier, remove the rubber sleeve, and push back the cover.
7. Force the rear axle shaft out of the flange with a suitable tool.
8. Support the rear axle with a jack.
9. Remove the rubber mount.
10. Clean the axle housing and remove the cover fan from the housing.

NOTE: The axle shafts are the floating type and can be compressed in the constant velocity joints.

11. Remove the locking ring from the end of the axle shafts which engage the side gears in the differential.

12. Disengage the axle shaft from the side gear and remove the axle shaft together with the spacer.

—————— **CAUTION** ——————
Do not hand the outer constant velocity joint in a free position (without any support) as the shaft may be damaged and the constant velocity joint housing may leak.

13. Installation is the reverse of removal.

14. If either axle shaft is replaced, be sure that the proper replacement shaft is installed. Axle shafts are marked L and R for left and right.

15. Check the end-play between the lockring on the axle shaft and the side gear. There should be no noticeable end-play, but the lock-ring should be able to turn in the groove.

16. Be sure to bleed the brakes and fill the rear axle with the proper quantity and type of lubricant. New radial seal rings are used on 1980 and later models. Lubricate the outside diameter of rubber covered radial seal rings with hypoid gear lubricant prior to installation.

Differential

REMOVAL AND INSTALLATION

All Models

1. Drain the oil from the rear axle.
2. On cars without torque compensation, remove the brake caliper and suspend it on a hook.
3. On cars with torque compensation, disconnect the brake cable control, unbolt the holding bracket on the wheel carrier, remove the rubber sleeve and push the cover back.
4. Remove the bolt from both sides that holds the rear axle shaft to the flange.
5. Press the rear axle shaft out of the flange.
6. If required, loosen the right-hand rear shock absorber and lower it to the stop.
7. Remove the exhaust system, if necessary.
8. On sedans remove the heat shield, if equipped.
9. Loosen the clamp nut and remove the intermediate bearing from the floor pan. On 3 piece driveshafts, only remove the front nut.
10. Unbolt the driveshaft and remove it.
11. Support the rear axle housing.
12. Unbolt the rear rubber mount from the frame floor.
13. On the 450 and 380 series and 300SD, lower the jack until the self-locking nuts are accessible.
14. Unbolt the rear axle center housing from the rear axle carrier.
15. On all other models, remove the bolt from the rubber mount on the cover of the rear axle housing. Fold back the rubber mat in the trunk and remove the rubber plugs; unbolt the rear axle center housing from the rear axle carrier.
16. Lower the rear axle center housing and remove it with the axle shaft. Do not allow the axle shafts to hang free, or the seals will be damaged, resulting in leaks.
17. Installation is the reverse of removal. Install new self-locking nuts, adjust the parking brake and fill the rear axle with the correct fluid.

REAR SUSPENSION

Springs

REMOVAL AND INSTALLATION

240D, 230, 280, 280C, 280CE, 300D, 300TD, 300CD, 450SL, 450SLC, 380SL, 380SLC

1. Jack up the rear of the car.

5. Spring strut
16. Dome on frame floor
17. Rubber mount
18. Rear spring
19. Semi-trailing arm

Rear spring—230, 240D, 280, 280C, 280E, 280CE, 300D, 300TD, 300CD, 450SL, 450SLC, 380SL, 380SLC

2. Remove the rear shock absorber.
3. With a floor jack, raise the control arm to approximately a horizontal position. Install a spring compressor to aid in this operation.
4. Carefully lower the jack until the control arm contacts the stop on the rear axle support.
5. Remove the spring and spring compressor with great care.
6. Installation is the reverse of removal. For ease of installation, attach the rubber seats to the springs with masking tape.

280S, 280SE, 300SD, 450SE, 450SEL, 6.9, 380SEL, 380SEC

1. Jack and support the rear of the car and the trailing arm.
2. Remove the rear shock absorber.
3. Be sure that the upper shock absorber attachment is released first.
4. Compress the spring with a spring compressor.
5. Remove the rear spring with the rubber mount.
6. Installation is the reverse of removal. When installing the shock absorber, tighten the lower mount first.

72. Semi-trailing arm
73. Rear spring
74. Rubber mounting
75. Shock absorber or spring strut
76. Dome on frame floor

Rear spring—450SE, 450SEL, 280SE, 300SD, 6.9, 380SEL, 280S, 280SE, 380SEC

Shock Absorber

REMOVAL AND INSTALLATION

230, 240D, 280, 280C, 280CE, 280E, 300D, 300CD, 300TD, 450SL, 450SLC, 380SL and 380SLC

1. Jack up the rear of the car and support the control arm.
2. From inside the trunk (sedans), remove the rubber cap, locknut, and hex nut from the upper mount of the shock absorber. On 450SL, 450SLC, 380SL and 380SLC the upper mount of the rear shock absorber is accessible after removing the top, top flap, rear seat, backrest and lining.
3. Unbolt the mounting for the rear shock absorber at the bottom and remove the shock absorber.
4. Installation is the reverse of removal.

280S, 280SE, 300SD, 450SE, 450SEL, 6.9, 380SEL, 380SEC

1. Remove the rear seat and backrest.
2. Remove the cover from the rear wall.
3. Jack and support the car and the trailing arm.
4. Loosen the nuts on the upper mount. Remove the washer and rubber ring.

1. Front axle carrier
3. Lower control arm
4. Upper control arm
10. Front spring
11. Front shock absorber
12. Torsion bar
29. Rubber mounting
31. Rubber mounting for front spring

Rear wheel camber measurement of 1976 230, 240D, 280, 280C and 300D and all 450, 450SLC models. Control arm position (difference in height between the axis of the rear control arm mount (A) and the lower edge of the cup on the outer constant velocity joint (B)

5. Loosen the lower mount and remove the shock absorber downward.

6. Installation is the reverse of removal. Tighten the upper mounting nut to the end of the threads.

Independent Rear Suspension Adjustments

Suspension adjustments should only be checked when the vehicle is resting on a level surface and is carrying the required fluids (full tank of gas, engine oil, etc.).

CAMBER

All Models

Rear wheel camber is determined by the position of the control arm. The difference in height (a) between the axis of the control arm mounting point on the rear axle subframe and lower edge of the cup on the constant velocity joint is directly translated in degrees of camber.

TOE-IN

Toe-in, on the rear wheels, is dependent on the camber of the rear wheels.

Front spring removal—1976 230, 240D, 280, 280C, 300D models 450SL, 450SLC, 380SL and 380SLC

7. Installation is the reverse of removal.

8. For ease of installation, tape the rubber mounts to the springs.

9. If the eccentric adjusters were not matchmarked, install the eccentric bolts as illustrated under "Front End Alignment".

All Other Models

1. Jack and support the front of the car and support the lower control arm.

Rear wheel camber measurement—all models except 1976 230, 240D, 280, 280C, 300D and all 450SL, 450SLC, 380SL, 380SLC

FRONT SUSPENSION

Springs

REMOVAL AND INSTALLATION

1976 230, 240D, 280C, 300D Models and All 450SL, 450SLC

NOTE: Be extremely careful when attempting to remove the front springs are compressed and under considerable load.

1. Jack up the front of the up jack stands and remove the front wheels.

2. Remove the front shock absorber and disconnect the sway bar.

3. First punchmark the position of the eccentric adjusters, then loosen the hex bolts.

4. Support the lower control arm with a jack.

5. Then knock out the eccentric pins and gradually lower the arm until spring tension is relieved.

6. The spring can now be removed.

NOTE: Check caster and camber after installing a new spring.

4. Lower control arm
11. Front shock absorber
12. Front spring
13. Rubber mount for front spring
14. Retainer for front spring
38. Front end

Front spring—all models except 1976 230, 240D, 280, 280C, 300D and all 450SL, 450SLC, 380SL, 380SLC

2. Remove the wheel. Unbolt the upper shock absorber mount.

3. Install a spring compressor and compress the spring.

4. Remove the front spring with the lower mount.

5. Installation is the reverse of removal. Tighten the upper shock absorber suspension.

Shock Absorbers

REMOVAL AND INSTALLATION

1976 230, 240D, 280, 280C, 300D Models and All 450SL, 450SLC, 380SL, 380SLC

Shock absorbers are normally replaced only if leaking excessively (oil visible on outside cover) or if worn internally to a point where the car no longer rides smoothly and rebounds after hitting a bump. A good general test of shock absorber condition is made by bouncing the front of the car. If the car rebounds more than two or three times it can be assumed that the shock absorbers need replacement.

1. For removal and installation of shock absorbers, it is best to jack up the front of the car until the weight is off of the wheels and support the car securely on jack stands.

2. When removing the shock absorbers, it is also wise to draw a simple diagram of the location of parts such as lockrings, rubber stops, locknuts and steel plates, since many shock absorbers require their own peculiar installation of these parts.

3. Raise the hood and locate the upper shock absorber mount.

4. Support the lower control arm with a jack.

5. Unbolt the mount for the shock absorber at the top. On 450SL, 450SLC, 380SL and 380SLC, remove the coolant expansion tank to allow access to the right front shock absorber.

6. Remove the nuts which secure the shock absorber to the lower control arm.

7. Push the shock absorber piston rod in, install the stirrup, and remove the shock absorber.

8. Remove the stirrup, since this must be installed on replacement shock absorbers.

9. Installation is the reverse of removal. Always use new bushings when installing replacement shock absorbers.

All Other Models

1. Jack and support the car. Support the lower control arm.

2. Loosen the nuts on the upper shock absorber mount. Remove the plate and ring.

3. Place the shock absorber vertical to the lower control arm and remove the lower mounting bolts.

4. Remove the shock absorber.

3. Lower control arm
4. Upper control arm
5. Steering knuckle
6. Guide joint
7. Supporting joint
8. Front wheel hub
9. Brake disc
24. Steering knuckle arm
32. Cover plate
35. Wheel

Steering knuckle and ball joints

4. Lower control arm
5. Steering knuckle
6. Upper control arm
7. Support joint
8. Guide joint
9. Front wheel hub
29. Steering knuckle arm
34. Brake disc
43. Wheel

Steering knuckle—450SE, 450SEL, 380SEL, 380SEC, 280S, 280SE, and 1977 and later 230, 240D, 300D, 280E, 280CE, 300 CD

5. Installation is the reverse of removal. On Bilstein shocks, do not confuse the upper and lower plates.

NOTE: The 1981 380SEL shock absorber uses a protective plastic sleeve that must be installed between the lower retainer and lower rubber ring. Also, a slot is provided for holding the piston rod, in place of the 2 flats used previously.

NOTE: 380SEC Shock absorbers have the same part number regardless of manufacturer. However, the shock absorbers on these cars has a larger diameter and narrower lower mounting eye than other models.

Steering Knuckle and Ball Joints

CHECKING BALL JOINTS

1. To check the steering knuckles or ball joints, jack up the car, placing a jack directly under the front spring plate. This unloads the front suspension to allow the maximum play to be observed.

2. Late model ball joints need to be replaced only if dried out with plainly visible wear and/or play.

REMOVAL AND INSTALLATION

1976 230, 240D, 280, 280C, 300D, and All 450SL, 450SLC, 380SL and 380SLC.

1. Jack and support the car. For safety, it's a good idea to install some type of clamp on the front spring. Position jack stands at the outside front against the lower control arms.

2. Remove the wheel.

3. Remove the steering knuckle arm from the steering knuckle.

4. Remove and suspend the brake caliper.

5. Remove the front wheel hub.

6. Loosen the brake hose holder on the cover plate.

7. Loosen the nut on the guide joint and remove the joint from the steering knuckle.

8. Loosen the nut on the support joint.

9. Swivel the steering knuckle outward and force the ball joint from the lower control arm.

10. Remove the steering knuckle.

11. If necessary, remove the cover plate from the steering knuckle.

12. Installation is the reverse of removal. Use self-locking nuts and adjust the wheel bearings.

All Other Models

1. This should only be done with the front shock absorber installed. If, however,

1. Upper control arm
2. Threaded bolt
3. Cam bolt
4. Dust cap
5. Thrust washer (top)
6. Thrust washer (bottom)
7. Dust sleeve
8. Upper bearing bushing
9. Kingpin
10. Steering knuckle
11. Bottom bearing bushing
12. Compensating washer
13. Lockwasher
14. Hex nut
15. Steering knuckle carrier with threaded bolt
16. Lower control arm
17. Pin

Cross-section of steering knuckle and kingpin

the front shock absorber has been removed, the lower control arm should be supported with a jack and the spring should be clamped with a spring tensioner. In this case, the hex nut on the guide joint should not be loosened without the spring tensioner installed.

2. Jack up the front of the car and support it on jack stands.

3. Remove the wheel.

4. Remove the brake caliper.

5. Unbolt the steering relay lever from the steering knuckle. For safety, install spring clamps on the front springs.

1. Upper control arm
2. Pivot pin
3. Rubber sealing ring
4. Threaded bushing

Upper control arm and pivot shaft

6. Remove the hex nuts from the upper and lower ball joints.

7. Remove the ball joints from the steering knuckle with the aid of a puller.

8. Remove the steering knuckle.

9. Installation is the reverse of removal. Be sure that the seats for the pins of the ball joints are free of grease.

10. Bleed the brakes.

Upper Control Arm

REMOVAL AND INSTALLATION

All Models Except 1976 230, 240D, 280, 280C, 300D Models and All 450SL, 450SLC, 380SL, 380SLC

1. Jack and support the car. Position jack stands at the outside front against the lower control arms.

2. Remove the wheel.

3. Loosen the nut on the guide joint.

4. Remove the guide joint from the steering knuckle.

5. Secure the steering knuckle with a hook on the upper control arm stop to prevent it from tilting.

6. Loosen the clamp screw and separate the upper control arm from the torsion bar.

7. Loosen the upper control arm bearing at the front and remove the upper control arm.

8. Installation is the reverse of removal. Use new self-locking nuts and check the front wheel alignment.

1976 230, 240D, 280, 280C, 300D Models and All 450SL, 450SLC, 380SL, 380SLC

1. The front shock absorbers should remain installed. Never loosen the hex nuts of the ball joints with the shock absorber removed, unless a spring clamp is installed.

2. Jack the front of the car and remove the wheel.

3. Support the front end on jack stands.

4. Remove the steering arm from the steering knuckle.

5. Separate the brake line and brake hose from each other and plug the openings.

6. Support the lower control arm and unscrew the nuts from the ball joints.

7. Remove the ball joints from the steering knuckle.

8. Loosen the bolts on the upper control arm and remove the upper control arm.

9. Installation is the reverse of removal.

— **CAUTION** —

Mount the front hex bolt from the rear in a forward direction, and the rear hex bolt from the front in a rearward direction.

10. Bleed the brakes.

Lower Control Arm

REMOVAL AND INSTALLATION

All Models Except 1976 230, 240D, 280, 280C, 300D and All 450SL, 450SLC, 380SL, 380SLC

The lower control arm is the same as the front axle half. For safety install a spring compressor on the coil spring.

1. Jack and support the front of the car and remove the wheels.

2. Remove the front shock absorber. Loosen the top mount first.

3. Remove the front springs.

4. Separate and plug the brake lines.

5. Remove the track rod from the steering knuckle arm.

6. Matchmark the position of the eccentric bolts on the bearing of the lower control arm in relation to the from crossmember.

7. Remove the shield from the cross yoke.

8. Support the front axle half.

9. Loosen the eccentric bolt on the front and rear bearing of the lower control arm and knock them out.

10. Remove the bolt from the cross yoke bearing.

11. Loosen the screw at the opposite end of the cross yoke bearing.

12. Pull the cross yoke bearing down slightly.

13. Loosen the support of the upper control arm on the torsion bar. Remove the clamp screw from the clamp.

14. Remove the upper control arm bearing on the front end.

15. Remove the front axle half.

16. Installation is the reverse of removal. Tighten the eccentric bolts of the lower control arm bearing with the car resting on the wheels. Bleed the brakes and check the front end alignment.

1976 230, 240D, 280, 280C, 300D and All 450SL, 450SLC, 380SL, 380SLC

1. Since the front shock absorber acts as a deflection stop for the front wheels, the lower shock absorber attaching point should not be loosened unless the vehicle is resting on the wheels or unless the lower control arm is supported.

2. Jack up the front of the vehicle and support it on jack stands.

3. Support the lower control arm.

4. Loosen the lower shock absorber attachment.

5. Unscrew the steering arm from the steering knuckle.

6. Separate the brake line and brake hose and plug the openings.

7. Remove the front spring.

8. Unscrew the hex nuts on the ball joints.

1.	Front axle carrier
2.	Rubber mount for suspension of front axle
2a.	Stop buffer for inward deflection
2b.	Stop plate
2c.	Stop buffer for outward deflections
2d.	Hex. bolt with snap-ring
2e.	Fastening nut
2f.	Nut holder
3.	Lower control arm
4.	Upper control arm
5.	Steering knuckle
6.	Guide joint
6d.	Circlip

6f.	Sleeve
6h.	Clamping ring
7.	Supporting joint
7d.	Circlip
7f.	Sleeve
7h.	Clamping ring
8.	Front wheel hub
8a.	Radial sealing ring
8b.	Inside tapered roller bearing
8c.	Outside tapered roller bearing
8d.	Washer
8e.	Clamp nut
8f.	Wheel cap

8g.	Contact spring
9.	Brake disc
18.	Brake caliper
18a.	Lockwasher
24.	Steering knuckle arm
28.	Rubber slide bearing
29.	Rubber bearing (torsion bearing)
30.	Cam bolt
30a.	Cam washer
32.	Cover plate
33.	Holder for brake hose
38.	Protective cap for steering lock

Lower control arm and pivot shaft

9. Remove the lower ball joint and remove the lower control arm.

10. Installation is the reverse of removal. Bleed the brakes and check the front end alignment.

Front End Alignment

Caster and camber are critical to proper handling and tire wear. Neither adjustment should be attempted without the specialized equipment to accurately measure the geometry of the front end.

CASTER/CAMBER ADJUSTMENT

All Models Except 1976 230, 240D, 280, 280C, 300D and All 450SL, 450SLC, 380SL, 380SLC

The front axle provides for caster and camber adjustment, but both wheel adjustments

1.	Frame side member
2.	Frame cross member for front axle
4.	Lower control arm
5.	Steering knuckle
6.	Upper control arm
7.	Supporting joint
8.	Guide joint
10.	Torsion bar
19.	Eccentric bolt (camber adjustment)
21.	Torsion bar mounting on front end
48.	Supporting joint
48a.	Ball pin (caster adjustment)
49.	Supporting tube

Camber and caster adjustment points on 1977 and later 230, 240D, 280CE, 300D, 300CD and 300TD

1. Front axle carrier
3. Lower control arm
4. Upper control arm
5. Steering knuckle
30a. Cam bolt front (caster)
30b. Cam bolt rear (camber)

Caster and camber adjustment points on 1976 230, 240D, 280, 280C, 300D models and all 450SL and 450SLC models

Camber eccentric (Rear seating)

inwards   inwards

Caster eccentric (front seating)
Mechanical steering

inwards   inwards

Caster eccentric (front seating)
Power steering

outwards   outwards

Basic caster and camber settings on 1976 240D, 280, 280C, 300D

can only be made together. Adjustments are made with cam bolts on the lower control arm bearings.

The front bearing cam bolt is used to set caster, while the rear bearing cam bolt is used for camber.

1976 230, 240D, 280, 280C, 300D and All 450SL, 450SLC, 380SL, 380SLC

Caster and camber are dependent upon each other and cannot be adjusted indepen-

outwards   outwards

Basic caster and camber setting on 450SL, 450SLC, 380SL and 380SLC

1. Eccentric bolt for camber adjustment
2. Hex screw with lockwasher
3. Locking plate
4. Adjusting washer for caster adjustment
5. Rubber sealing ring
6. Kingpin
7. Threaded bolt
8. Eccentric bushing with drive pin
10. Upper control arm

Caster and camber adjustment points— 280 and 300 series (except 280, 280C, 280E, 280S and 280SE 1977 and later and 300D)

dently. They can only be adjusted simultaneously.

Caster is adjusted by turning the lower control arm around the front mounting, using the eccentric bolt.

Camber is adjusted by turning the lower control arm about the rear mounting, using the eccentric bolt. Bear in mind that caster will be changed accordingly.

When camber is adjusted in a positive direction, caster is changed in a negative

direction, and vice versa. Adjustment of camber by 0°15′ results in a caster change of approximately 0°20′. Adjustment of caster by 1° results in a camber change of approximately 0°7′.

TOE-IN ADJUSTMENT

Toe-in is the difference of the distance between the front edges of the wheel rims and the rear edges of the wheel rims.

To measure toe-in, the steering should be in the straight ahead position and the marks on the pitman arm and pitman shaft should be aligned.

Toe-in is adjusted by changing the length of the two tie rods or track rods with the wheels in the straight ahead position. Some older models have a hex nut locking arrangement rather than the newer clamp, but adjustment is the same.

NOTE: Install new tie rods so that the left-handed thread points toward the left-hand side of the car.

STEERING

Steering Wheel

REMOVAL AND INSTALLATION

450SL, 450SLC, 380SL, 380SLC

1. Pry the three-pointed star trademark from the center padding.
2. Unscrew the hex nut from the steering shaft and remove the spring washer and the steering wheel.

NOTE: 1980 and later models use an Allen screw in place of a hex nut. The Allen screw must be renewed if removed.

3. Installation is the reverse of removal. Be sure that the alignment mark on the steering shaft is pointing upward and be sure that the slightly curved spoke of the steering wheel is down.

All Models Except 450SL, 450SLC, 380SL, 380SLC

NOTE: 380SEC uses a bolt and spring that pushes the power piston into the teeth of the Pitman shaft when the steering is in the center position. Any backlash (play at the steering wheel) is taken up.

1. Remove the padded plate. Pull at one corner near the wheel spokes.
2. Unscrew the hex nut from the steering shaft and remove the spring washer and the steering wheel.

NOTE: 1980 and later models use an Allen screw in place of the hex nut. The Allen screw must be replaced if removed.

3. Installation is the reverse of removal. Be sure that the alignment mark on the steering shaft is pointing upward and be sure that the slightly curved spoke of the steering wheel is down.

Power Steering Gear

REMOVAL AND INSTALLATION

1. Suck the oil from the power steering reservoir using a syringe.
2. Detach the high-pressure hose and oil return hose from the steering assembly.
3. Cap both lines to prevent entry of dirt, then remove the clamp screw from the lower part of the coupling flange.
4. Remove the rubber plug from the cover plate and remove the U-joint socket screw. On LS90 power steering units, remove the steering spindle. Pull the steering spindle up only until the coupling is no longer engaged with the worn gear.
5. The tailpipe and left side exhaust pipe may have to be removed for access.
6. Detach the tie rod and center tie rod (or drag link and track rod) from the pitman arm, using pullers or a tie rod splitter.
7. Remove the hex-head bolts that hold the gearbox to the frame, then press the worm shaft stub from the steering coupling and remove the gearbox from underneath the car.
8. To install, first install the pitman arm (if it has been removed) aligning the matchmarks. Tighten the pitman arm nut to 110 ft/lbs and install the cotter pin. Use new self-locking nuts to attach the gear to the frame.
9. Remove the screw plug from the steering box. Turn the wormshaft until the center of the power piston is directly below the bore in the housing. Check dimension (a) which can be altered by changing the position of the pitman arm on its shaft.
10. Center the steering wheel.
11. Press the worm shaft stub into the steering shaft coupling, making sure not to damage the serrations.

NOTE: Install assembly pin as for manual steering.

12. Install and tighten the hex-head screws that hold the gearbox to the chassis, then install and tighten the coupling clamp screw.
13. Install the plug in the gearbox, using a new gasket; attach the tie rods to the pitman arm and make sure that the steering knuckle arms rest against their stops at full left and right lock.
14. Check toe-in and correct if necessary. Remove the dust covers from the fluid lines, then reconnect the high- and low-pressure lines.
15. Fill the reservoir and connect a hose between the bleed screw on the steering and the reservoir.

16. Open the bleed screw and, with engine running, bleed the system and top up.

Power Steering Pump

REMOVAL AND INSTALLATION

Many types of power steering pumps are used on Mercedes-Benz vehicles. Use only the instructions that apply to your vehicle.

1976 230, 240D, 300D

1. Remove the wing nut on the reservoir and remove the cover, spring, and damping plate.
2. Suck the fluid from the reservoir with a syringe.
3. Loosen the hose on the pump and plug both pump and hose.
4. On pumps with the reservoir attached, loosen the return hose and plug it.
5. On other types, loosen the connecting hose from the reservoir to the pump.
6. Remove the radiator.
7. Remove the nut from the pulley shaft. On pumps with cylindrical shafts, remove the pulley.
8. On pumps with tapered shafts, pull the pulley from the shaft with a jaw type puller.
9. Unscrew both front mounting bolts.
10. Remove the rear mounting bolt with spacer.
11. Remove the pump from the mounting bracket.
12. On all 4 cylinder models, remove the screws between the pump housing and the bracket. Remove the pump and pulley.
13. Installation, in all cases, is the reverse of removal.

All Models Except 1976 230, 240D, 300D

1. Remove the nut from the supply tank.
2. Remove the spring and damping plate.
3. Drain the oil from the tank with a syringe.
4. Loosen and remove the expanding and return hoses from the pump. Plug all connections and pump openings.
5. If necessary for clearance, loosen the radiator shell. Loosen the mounting bolts, and move the pump toward the engine by using the toothed wheel. Remove the belt. Remove the pulley, and then remove the pump.
6. Loosen the nut on the attaching plate and the bolt on the support.
7. Push the pump toward the engine and remove the belts from the pulley.
8. Unscrew the mounting bolts and remove the pump and carrier.
9. Installation is the reverse of removal.

Bottom view of steering linkage showing track rod and drag link

Steering Linkage

REMOVAL AND INSTALLATION

All Models

TRACK ROD

1. Remove the cotter pins and castellated nuts from the track rod joints.
2. Remove the track rod from the steering arms with a puller.
3. Check the track rod ends. The rods use 22 mm ball joints and should be replaced if either ball joint is defective.
4. Check the rubber sleeves. The ball joint should be replaced if the sleeve is defective.
5. Installation is the reverse of removal. Install the track rods so that the end with the left-hand threads is on the left side.

DRAG LINK

1. Remove the castle nuts from the drag link joints.
2. Unbolt the steering damper and force it from the bracket.
3. Remove the drag link with a puller.
4. Installation is the reverse of removal.
5. Check the front wheel alignment.

BRAKES

All Mercedes-Benz cars imported into the U.S. are equipped with 4-wheel disc brakes. The disc brakes are basically similar on all models, though there may be slight differences in design from model to model. The caliper bore sizes, for instance, differ depending upon application. The bore size (in mm) is usually stamped on the outside of the caliper, but occasionally, a code is used. For instance, the 14 on a Teves (ATE) caliper is really a 57 mm bore (obviously, it isn't a 14 mm bore).

Three different manufacturers make calipers for Mercedes-Benz production—Teves (ATE), Bendix or Girling—but calipers of the same manufacturer are installed on the same axle. For service, install calipers of the same manufacturer on the front axle; on the rear axle, calipers of any manufacturer can be installed.

Most models are equipped with brake pad wear indicators to indicate when the pad lining requires replacement. Beginning in 1976, a new design, step-type master cylinder is used which eliminates the need for the vacuum pump previously used on 230, 280, 280C and 280S. The brake circuits are reversed from 1975 models; the front brakes are connected to the primary side of the master cylinder and the rear brakes to the secondary side. A pressure differential warning indicator is also used, which will immediately indicate the total loss of one part of the braking system by lighting the brake warning light on the dash. Once the warning light has come on, it will remain on until the system is repaired and the switch on the master cylinder reset. The warning light will only go out after pushing the reset pin in the switch.

Beginning with 1978 models, the pressure differential warning indicator has been eliminated from models with the step-type master cylinder. The master cylinder reservoir has 2 chambers with 2 sets of electrical contacts. Loss of brake fluid in either reservoir will light the warning light on the dash.

For all brake system service and repair procedures not detailed below, please refer to "Brakes" in the Unit Repair section.

Adjustment

Since disc brakes are used at all four wheels, no adjustments are necessary. Disc brakes are inherently self-adjusting. The only adjustment possible is to the handbrake, which is covered at the end of this section.

Master Cylinder

The dual master cylinder has a safety feature which the single unit lacks—if a leak develops in one brake circuit (rear wheels, for example), the other circuit will still operate.

Failure of one system is immediately obvious—the pedal travel increases appreciably and a warning light is activated. When the fluid falls below a certain level, a switch activates the circuit.

Reset pin (arrow) on master cylinder with pressure warning differential

REMOVAL AND INSTALLATION

1. To remove the master cylinder, first open a bleed screw at one front, and one rear, wheel.

2. Pump the pedal to empty the reservoir completely. Make sure both reservoirs are completely drained.

3. Disconnect the switch connectors using a small screwdriver. Disconnect the brake lines at the master cylinder. Plug the ends with bleed screw caps or the equivalent.

4. Unbolt the master cylinder from the power brake unit and remove. Be careful you do not lose the O-ring in the flange groove of the master cylinder.

5. Installation is the reverse of removal. Be sure to replace the O-ring between the master cylinder and the power brake unit, since this must be absolutely tight. Torque the nuts to 12–15 ft. lbs. Be sure that both chambers are completely filled with brake fluid and bleed the brakes.

5. Steering knuckle
7. Supporting joint
9. Front wheel hub
9a. Radial sealing ring
9b. Tapered roller bearing, inside
9c. Tapered roller bearing, outside
9d. Clamping nut
9e. Wheel cap
9f. Contact spring
34. Brake disc
35. Cover plate

Wheel bearing cut away—all except 1976 230, 240D, 280, 280C, 300D and all 450SL, 450SLC, 380SL, 380SLC

5. Steering knuckle
8. Wheel hub
8a. Radial sealing ring
8b. Tapered roller bearing, outside
8c. Tapered roller bearing, inside
8d. Washer
8e. Clamping nut
8f. Wheel cap
9. Brake disc
17. Brake hose
18. Brake caliper
32. Cover plate

Wheel bearing cut away—1976 230, 240D, 280, 280C, 300D and all 450SL, 450SLC, 380SL, 380SLC

Wheel Bearings

REMOVAL AND INSTALLATION

If the wheel bearing play is being checked for correct setting only, it is not necessary to remove the caliper. It is only necessary to remove the brake pads.

1. Remove the brake caliper.

2. Pull the cap from the hub with a pair of channel-lock pliers. Remove the radio suppression spring, if equipped.

3. Loosen the socket screw of the clamp nut on the wheel spindle. Remove the clamp nut and washer.

4. Remove the front wheel hub and brake disc.

5. Remove the inner race with the roller cage of the outer bearing.

6. Using a brass or aluminum drift, carefully tap the outer race of the inner bearing until it can be removed with the inner race, bearing cage, and seal.

7. In the same manner, tap the outer race of the bearing out of the hub.

8. Separate the front hub from the brake disc.

9. To assemble, press the outer races into the front wheel hub.

10. Pack the bearing cage with bearing grease and insert the inner race with the bearing into the wheel hub.

11. Coat the sealing ring with sealant and press it into the hub.

12. Pack the front wheel hub with 45–

Dial indicator set-up for checking wheel bearing play

55 grams of wheel bearing grease. The races of the tapered bearing should be well packed and also apply grease to the front faces of the rollers. Pack the front bearings with the specified amount of grease. Too much grease will cause overheating of the lubricant and it may lose its lubricity. Too little grease will not lubricate properly.

13. Coat the contact surface of the sealing ring on the wheel spindle with Molykote® paste.

14. Press the wheel hub onto the wheel spindle.

15. Install the inner race and cage of the outer bearing.

16. Install the steel washer and the clamp nut.

ADJUSTMENT

1. Tighten the clamp nut until the hub can just be turned.

2. Slacken the clamp nut and seat the bearings on the spindle by rapping the spindle sharply with a hammer.

3. Attach a dial indicator, with the pointer indexed, onto the wheel hub.

4. Check the end-play of the hub by pushing and pulling on the flange. The end-play should be approximately 0.0004–0.0008 in.

5. Make an additional check by rotating the washer between the inner race of the outer bearing and the clamp nut. It should be able to be turned by hand.

6. Check the position of the suppressor pin in the wheel spindle and the contact spring in the dust cap.

7. Pack the dust cap with 20–25 grams of wheel bearing grease and install the cap.

8. Install the brake caliper and bleed the brakes.

Handbrake

FRONT CABLE

Removal and Installation

230, 240D, 300D, 300CD, 300TD, 280, 280C, 280CE

1. Remove the spring from the equalizer.

2. Back off the adjusting screw completely.

3. Detach the relay lever from the bracket on the frame and from the adjusting shackle.

4. Detach the cable from the relay lever by pulling the cotter pin out of the bolt.

5. Remove the clip from the cable guide. Remove the clips from the chassis.

6. Detach the brake cable from the parking brake link. Remove the clip from the cable guide and detach the brake cable from the parkbrake.

7. Pull the cable downward from the chassis.

8. Installation is the reverse of removal.

450SL, 450SLC, 380SL, 380SLC

1. Remove the exhaust system.

2. Disconnect the return spring.

3. Remove the bolts which attach the guide to the intermediate lever and pull the cotter pin from the flange bolt. Remove the flange bolt.

4. Remove the spring clamp from the cable guide and remove the cable control from the bracket.

7. Remove the tunnel cover.

8. Disconnect the brake control from the parking brake and remove the spring clamp from the cable guide. Remove the cable control from the parking brake.

9. Remove the brake control cable out of the frame toward the rear.

10. Installation is the reverse of removal.

280S, 280SE, 300SD, 380SEL, 380SEC 450SE, 450SEL, 6.9

1. Remove the floor mat.

2. Remove the legroom cover (upper and lower).

3. Remove the air duct.

4. Disconnect the 4 rubber rings and lower and support the exhaust system.

5. Remove the shield above the exhaust pipes.

6. Disconnect the return spring from the bracket.

7. Back off the adjusting screw on the bracket.

8. Disconnect the intermediate lever from the adjusting bracket.

9. Loosen the brake cable controls on the intermediate lever while pulling the cotter pin from the flange bolt. Remove the flange bolt.

10. Remove the spring clip from the cable guide on the floor pan.

11. Disconnect the brake cable control from the parking brake bracket.

12. Remove the spring clip from the cable and remove the cable control from the parking brake.

13. Pull the cable away upward.

14. Installation is the reverse of removal. Adjust the parking brake.

REAR BRAKE CABLE

Removal and Installation

230, 240D, 280, 280C, 280CE, 280E, 300D, 300CD, 300TD

1. Remove the parking brake shoes after removing the wheel.

2. Remove the screws from the wheel support and detach the brake cable.

3. Back off the adjusting screw from the adjusting shackle.

4. Remove the spring clips, detach the cable, and remove the equalizer.

5. Installation is the reverse of removal.

450SL, 450SLC, 380SL, 380SLC

1. Remove the parking brake shoes.

2. Remove the bolt from the wheel carrier and remove the cable.

3. Remove the exhaust system. On some models the exhaust system can be lowered and supported after removing the rubber rings. If equipped, remove the heat shield from above the exhaust pipes.

4. Disconnect the draw spring from the holder.

5. Detach the guide from the intermediate lever.

6. Remove the adjusting screw from the bracket.

7. Disconnect the intermediate lever on the bearing and remove it from the adjusting bracket.

8. Remove the holder, compensating lever, cable control plates, and intermediate lever from the tunnel.

9. Remove the spring clamps and disconnect the cable from the plate.

10. Installation is the reverse of removal.

Adjustment

ALL MODELS

1. If the floor pedal can be depressed more than two notches before actuating the brakes, adjust by jacking up the rear of the car, then removing one lug bolt and adjusting the star wheel with a screwdriver.

2. Move the screwdriver upward on the left (driver's) side, downward on the right (passenger's) side to tighten the shoes.

3. When the wheel is locked, back off about 2–4 clicks.

Cut-away view of rear brake shoe adjustment

4. With this type system, the adjusting bolt on the cable relay lever only serves to equalize cable length; therefore, do not attempt to adjust the brakes by turning this bolt.

CHASSIS ELECTRICAL

Heater Blower

REMOVAL AND INSTALLATION

240D (thru 1976), 300D, 230 (thru 1976), 280, 280C, 300D (thru 1976)

1. Remove the heater box.
2. Back out the three retaining screws.
3. Slightly pull out the blower and remove the electrical plug and the blower.
4. Installation is the reverse of removal. To prevent leaks, install the three screws with three new special washers exactly like those removed.

450SL, 450SLC, 380SL, 380SLC

1. Remove the panel which covers the heater blower.
2. Loosen the blower retaining nuts.
3. Pull the plug from the series resistance that is located on the firewall.
4. Remove the series resistance.
5. Lift the cable and remove the blower.
6. Installation is the reverse of removal. Be sure that the sealing frame is not damaged.

230 (1977 and later), 240D (1977 and later), 280E, 280CE, 300D (1977 and later), 300CD, 300TD, 280S, 280SE, 300SD, 450SE, 450SEL, 6.9, 380SEL

1. Unplug the resistor on the firewall, located just above the automatic transmission and dipstick.
2. Unscrew the resistor.
3. Remove the air intake grille.
4. Remove the glove compartment.
5. Remove the cover under the right-hand instrument panel.
6. Remove the hose between the center air duct and right-hand outlet.
7. Remove the clip and disconnect the wire control from the lever.
8. Unbolt and remove the blower.
9. Installation is the reverse of removal.

Instrument panel removal showing rubber retaining strip

Instrument Cluster

REMOVAL AND INSTALLATION

230 (thru 1976), 240D (thru 1976), 280, 280C, 300D (thru 1976)

1. Remove the cover plate from the left side underneath the dashboard.
2. On vehicles with automatic transmission, disconnect the Bowden cable for the gear selector lever, after engaging Park.
3. Remove the bracket holding the handbrake.
4. Unscrew the knurled nut and pull the instrument cluster slightly forward.
5. Disconnect the tachometer drive.
6. Cover the steering column to prevent scratches.
7. If only bulb replacement is desired, this is sufficient. To remove the entire cluster, continue with the remaining steps.
8. Disconnect the oil pressure line.
9. Remove the electrical plug connections.
10. Release the excess pressure in the cooling system and install the cap afterward.
11. Remove the temperature sensor from the cylinder head and plug the hole.
12. Carefully remove the instrument cluster with the capillary tube and temperature sensor.

——————— CAUTION ———————
Do not bend the capillary tube.

13. Installation is the reverse of removal.

280S, 280SE, 300SD (thru 1980), 450SE, 450SEL, 380SL, 380SLC, 450SL, 450SLC, 6.9

1. Remove the padding from the steering wheel.
2. Remove the steering wheel.
3. The instrument cluster is held in place by a rubber ring which fits into a groove. Remove the ring and pull the instrument cluster slightly forward.
4. Loosen and disconnect the speed-

Remove the instrument cluster with a small screwdriver

ometer shaft, the electrical plug connections, and the oil pressure line.
5. Completely remove the instrument cluster.

——————— CAUTION ———————
Do not bend the oil pressure line.

6. Installation is the reverse of removal. Be sure that the speedometer is not bent excessively or it will vibrate when running.

1977 and Later 230, 240D, 280E, 280CE, 300D, 300CD, 300TD, 1981 and later 300SD, 380SEL, 380SEC

1. Remove the instrument cluster

Fabricated tool for removing the instrument cluster

Recess slot in the instrument cluster

slightly by hand. Don't pull on the edge of the glass.

2. A removal hook can be fabricated and inserted between the instrument cluster and the dashboard.

3. Guide the removal hook up to the right to the recess (arrow) and pull the instrument cluster out.

NOTE: The 1981 380SEL, 380SEC and 300SD models use 5 clips to hold the instrument cluster in place.

4. Pull it out as far as possible and disconnect the speedometer cable, electrical connections and oil pressure line.

5. To install, reconnect the electrical connections, oil pressure line and speedometer cable. To avoid speedometer cable noise, guide it into the largest radius possible.

6. Push the instrument cluster firmly into the dashboard.

Ignition Switch

REMOVAL AND INSTALLATION

All Models with Ignition Switch in Dashboard

1. Remove the instrument cluster.
2. Remove the right-hand cover plate under the dashboard.
3. Remove the plug connection from the ignition switch.
4. Remove the screws which hold the ignition switch to the rear of the lock cylinder and remove the ignition switch.
5. To install the ignition switch, attach the plug connection, after fastening the switch to the steering lock.
6. Install the instrument cluster.
7. Check the switch for proper function and install the lower cover.

Lock Cylinder (Key Can be Removed in Position 1)

REMOVAL AND INSTALLATION

1. Turn the key to position 1 and remove the key.
2. Pry the cover sleeve from the lock cylinder with a small screwdriver.
3. Using a bent paper clip, hook onto the cover sleeve and remove the sleeve. Be sure that you do not remove the rosette in the dashboard also.
4. Insert the paper clip between the rosette and the steering lock and push in the

1. Steering lock 4. Steel wire (paper clip)
3. Rosette 5. Locking cylinder

Ignition lock cylinder removal from the instrument panel (both types)

lock pin. Remove the lock cylinder slightly with the key.

5. Insert the paper clip into the locking hole and pull the lock cylinder completely out.

6. Installation is the reverse of removal. Turn the lock cylinder to position 1 and insert it into the steering lock, making sure that the lock pin engages. Push the cover sleeve into position 1.

7. Make sure that the cylinder operates properly.

Lock Cylinder (Key Cannot Be Removed in Position 1)

REMOVAL AND INSTALLATION

Because of legal requirements, the lock was changed from the previous version, so that the key can only be removed in position 0.

1. Turn the key to position 1.
2. Lift the cover sleeve to the edge of the key and turn the key to position 0.
3. Remove the key and cover sleeve.
4. Insert the key into the lock cylinder and turn to position 1 (90° to the right), push in the lock pin and remove the lock cylinder.
5. To install the lock cylinder, turn the lock cylinder to position 1 and insert the lock cylinder, making sure that the locking pin engages.
6. Turn the key to position 0 and remove the key.
7. Place the cover sleeve on the steering lock, insert and turn the key, and push in the cover sleeve at position 1.
8. Check the locking cylinder for proper function.

Steering Lock

REMOVAL AND INSTALLATION

1. Disconnect the ground cable from the battery.
2. Remove the instrument cluster.
3. Remove the plug connection from the ignition switch behind the dashboard.
4. Pull the ignition key to position 1.
5. Loosen the attaching screw for the steering lock.
6. Remove the cover sleeve from the steering lock.
7. On vehicles with the latest version of the steering lock, pull the connection for the warning buzzer.
8. Push in the lock pin with a small punch.
9. Turn the steering lock and remove it from the holder in the column jacket. Be sure that the rosette is not damaged.

CAUTION
The lock pin can only be pushed in when the cylinder is in position 1.

---

10. To install the steering lock, connect the warning buzzer if so equipped.
11. Place the steering lock in position 1 and insert the lock into the steering column while pushing the lock pin in. Be sure that the lock pin engages.
12. Tighten the attaching clamp screw.
13. Attach the plug connection to the ignition switch.
14. Push the cover sleeve onto the lock in position 1.
15. Install the instrument cluster.
16. Check to be sure that the steering lock works properly.

Headlights

REMOVAL AND INSTALLATION

230 (1976), 280, 280C, 240D (1976)

1. Loosen the screw on the lower portion of the unit.
2. Remove the trim ring together with the lower part of the unit.
3. Push the retaining ring in and, at the same time, turn the ring left to the stop.
4. Remove the ring, selaed beam lamp, and disconnect the plug.
5. Installation is the reverse of removal. If installing a Mercedes-Benz replacement sealed beam, be sure that the number "2" is at the top in the center. Be sure to have the headlights adjusted.

1981 and later 300SD, 380SEL, 380SEC

1. Open the hood and unscrew the 5 plastic knurled nuts.

2. Remove the assembly from the front of the car. Unplug the electrical connector.

3. Remove the headlight attaching screws.

4. Disconnect the electrical connector and remove the headlight.

5. Installation is the reverse of removal.

All Other Models

1. Loosen the attaching screws and remove the cover.

2. Remove the headlight attaching screws and remove the retaining ring and light as a unit.

NOTE: Do not disturb the headlight aiming screws.

3. Pull the retaining ring and light slightly forward and disconnect the plug.

4. Remove the headlight and retaining ring.

5. Installation is the reverse of removal. Be sure that the plug and socket on the rear of the light are tight.

Fuses

A listing of the protected equipment and the amperage of the fuse if printed in the lid of the fuse box. Spare fuses and a tool for removing and installing fuses are contained in the vehicle tool kit.

Fuses cannot be repaired—they must be replaced. Always determine the cause of the blown fuse before replacing it with a new one.

FUSE BOX LOCATION

230, 240D, 300D, 300TD, 280, 280C, 280E, 280CE, 300CD

On early models, the fuse box may be found in the kick panel on the driver's side. On later models the fuse box is located in the engine compartment on the driver's side, next to the brake master cylinder. Some models have separate fuse boxes or inline fuses for additional equipment. The radio is usually fused with a separate inline glass fuse behind the radio and the ignition is unfused.

280S, 280SE, 300SD, 450SE, 450SEL, 6.9, 380SEL, 380SEC

The fuse box is located in the engine compartment, on the driver's side, next to the brake master cylinder. Some models may have separate fuse boxes or inline fuses in the engine compartment for additional equipment. The radio is usually fused with a separate inline glass fuse behind the radio and the ignition is unfused. The fuse box also contains various relays.

450SL, 450SLC, 380SL, 380SLC

The fuse box is located in the right-hand (passenger's side) kick panel, behind a cover plate. There may also be separate fuse boxes or inline fuses in the engine compartment for additional equipment. The radio is usually fused with a separate inline glass fuse behind the radio and the ignition is unfused. The kick panel area also contains various relays and switches.

MG

SERIAL NUMBER IDENTIFICATION

Vehicle

The vehicle serial number can be found stamped on a plate located on the inner fender panel of the engine compartment. Late model cars have the plate located on the top of the dashboard, visible through the windshield.

Engine

The engine serial number is located on a plate riveted to the engine block on the distributor side.

VEHICLE IDENTIFICATION—MIDGET
(Serial number prefix codes)

The car number prefix comprises a series of letters and numbers, presenting in code the make, the engine type, the body type, the series, and, where applicable, left-hand drive.

1st PREFIX LETTER—Name G—MG	2nd PREFIX LETTER—Engine type A
3rd PREFIX LETTER—Body type N—2-seater Tourer	

4th PREFIX—Series of model 6—6th series, MG	5th PREFIX (used to denote car if different to standard right-hand drive) L—Left-hand drive U-USA	6th PREFIX (Model Year)—USA and CANADA F—1975 G—1976 H—1977 J—1978

CODE EXAMPLE

G — A N 6 — 25788

25788—Serial number
6—6th Series
N—2-seater Tourer
A—'A' type Engine
G—MG

VEHICLE IDENTIFICATION—MG

(Serial number prefix codes)

The car number prefix comprises a series of letters and numbers presenting in code the make, engine type, body type and the series.

1st PREFIX LETTER—NAME G—MG	2nd PREFIX LETTER—Engine type H	3rd PREFIX LETTER—Body type N—2 seater tourer D—Coupe or GT
4th PREFIX 5—5th series	5th PREFIX L—LHD U—USA	6th PREFIX—Model Year G—1976 H—1977 J—1978

CODE EXAMPLE

G — H D 5 —————— Serial number
        5—5th Series
        D—GT
        H—'B' type Engine
        G—MG

G — H N 5 U G —————— Serial number
        G—1976
        U—USA
        5—5th Series
        N—Tourer
        H—'B' type Engine
        G—MG

ENGINE IDENTIFICATION—MIDGET

Year	Engine Code	No. of Cylinders	Displacement (cc)
'76–'79	PE94J	4	1493

ENGINE IDENTIFICATION—MGB

Year	Engine Code	No. of Cylinders	Displacement (cc)
'76–'80	18V	4	1798

GENERAL ENGINE SPECIFICATIONS

Model	Year	Engine Code	Displacement (cc)	Carburetor Type	Advertised Horsepower @ rpm	Advertised Torque @ rpm	Bore × Stroke (in.)	Comp. Ratio	Oil Pressure
Midget	'76–'79	PE94J	1493	CD4 (1)	50 @ 5000	67 @ 2500	2.90 × 3.44	7.5:1	40–60
MGB	'76–'80	18V	1798	CD5T (1)	62.5 @ 4600	105 @ 2500	3.16 × 3.50	8:1	50–80

TUNE-UP SPECIFICATIONS

Model	Year	Engine Code	Spark Plugs Orig. Equip.	Spark Plugs Gap (in.)	Distributor Dwell (deg)	Distributor Gap (in.)	Timing (deg)	Compression pressure (psi)	Valves Clearance (in.) Intake	Valves Clearance (in.) Exhaust	Intake Opens (deg)	Idle Speed (rpm)	Fuel Pump Pressure (psi)
Midget	'76	PE94J	N12Y	0.025	①	.014–.016②	2A	120	0.010C	0.010C	18B	800	2.5–3.0
	'77–'79	PE94J	N12Y	0.025	①	.014–.016②	10B③	120	0.010C	0.010C	18B	800	—
MGB	'76–'77	18V	N9Y	0.025	①	.010–.017②	10B④	130	0.013H	0.013H	16B	850	2.5–3.0
	'78–'80	18V	N9Y	0.035	①	.010–.017②	10B②	130	0.013H	0.013H	8B	850	—

NOTE: The underhood specifications sticker often reflects tune-up specification changes made in production. Sticker figures should be used if they disagree with this chart.

① Factory installed electronic ignition with fixed dwell.
② Electronic ignition: figure is for pick-up air gap.
③ Calif. models: 2A

④ 1976 w/o catalytic converter: 13B
B Before top dead center
H Engine hot
C Engine cold

FIRING ORDERS

MGB

Midget

CAPACITIES

Model	Engine	Crankcase (qts.) With Filter	Crankcase (qts.) Without Filter	4-Speed Transmission (pts.)	Drive Axle (pts.)	Fuel Tank (gals.)	Coolant with Heater (qts.)
Midget	PE94J	4.8	4.2	3.0	2.1	7.2①	6.3②
MGB	18V	3.8	3.0	6.0	2.0	12.0③	6.0④

① 1978–79: 7.5 ③ 1978–80: 13
② 1978–79: 5.7 ④ 1978–80: 7.25

CRANKSHAFT AND CONNECTING ROD SPECIFICATIONS

Model	Engine	Main Bearing Journals (in.) Journal Diameter New	Main Bearing Journals (in.) Journal Diameter Minimum	Oil Clearance	Shaft End-Play	Thrust on No.	Connecting Rod Bearing Journals (in.) Journal Diameter New	Connecting Rod Bearing Journals (in.) Journal Diameter Minimum	Oil Clearance	Side Clearance
Midget	PE94J	2.3115–2.3120	−0.010	0.0005–0.0025	0.006–0.014	5	1.8750–1.8755	−0.030	0.001–0.003	N.A.
MGB	18V	2.1262–2.1270	−0.040	0.001–0.0027	0.004–0.005	3	1.8759–1.8764	−0.040	0.001–0.0027	0.008–0.012

N.A. Not available

VALVE SPECIFICTIONS

Model	Engine	Face Angle (deg)	Seat Angle (deg)	Valve Spring Free Lenth (in.)		Spring Pressure (lbs.)		Stem Diameter (in.)		Stem to Guide Clearance (in.)		Guide Height Above Head (in.)
				Inner	Outer	Intake	Exhaust	Intake	Exhaust	Intake	Exhaust	
Midget	PE94J	45	45.5	—	1.52	123	123	0.3107–0.3113	0.3100–0.3105	0.0007–0.0023	0.0015–0.0030	.750
MGB	18V	44.5	45.5	—	1.92	142	142	0.3429–0.3434	0.3423–0.3428	0.0007–0.0019	0.0013–0.0025	①

① Intake 0.750 exhaust 0.625

PISTON AND RING SPECIFICATIONS

All measurements in inches

Model	Engine	Piston Clearance	Ring Gap			Ring Side Clearance		
			Top Compression	Bottom Compression	Oil Control	Top Compression	Bottom Compression	Oil Control
Midget	PE94J	0.0002–0.0016	0.012–0.022	0.012–0.022	0.015–0.055	0.0015–0.0035	0.0015–0.0035	0.0015–0.0035
MGB	18V	0.0006–0.0012	0.012–0.022	0.012–0.022	0.015–0.045	0.0015–0.0035	0.0015–0.0035	0.0015–①0.0036

① 1976–77: 0.0016–0.0036

TORQUE SPECIFICATIONS

(ft. lbs.)

Model	Engine	Cylinder Head Bolts	Main Bearing Bolts	Rod Bearing Bolts	Crankshaft Damper Bolt(s)①	Flywheel to Crankshaft Bolt(s)	Manifold Nuts	
							Intake	Exhaust
Midget	PE94J	50	65	40–45	150	②	14	25
MGB	18V	45–50	70	31–33	70	40	15③	15③

① Torque figure given applies to crankshaft pulley on cars not equipped with damper
② Cadmium plated: 40
   Others: 45
③ 1978–80: 16

TORQUE SEQUENCES

Midget

MGB

ALTERNATOR AND REGULATOR SPECIFICATIONS

Model	Engine	Type	Output Volts	Output Amps	Field Current Draw (amps @ 12V)	Brush Tension (oz.)	Type	Air Gap (in.)	Point Gap (in.)	Point Close (volts)	Air Gap (in.)	Volts @ 125 deg
Midget	PE94J	16ACR	12–15	34①	3	9–13	8TR 11TR		Integral with alternator, transistor type—no adjustment			14.0–14.4
MGB	18V	18ACR	12–15	34②	3	9–13	8TR 11TR		Integral with alternator, transistor type—no adjustment			14.0–14.4

① 34 amps at 6000 alternator rpm (3000 engine rpm) @ 14 volts
② 43 amps at 6000 alternator rpm (3000 engine rpm) @ 14 volts

BATTERY AND STARTER SPECIFICATIONS
(All cars use 12 volt, negative ground electrical systems)

Model	Engine	Capacity (amp hrs.)	Type	Amps	Volts	Torque (ft. lbs.)	Amps	Volts	rpm	Brush Spring Tension (oz.)
Midget	PE94J	①	①	350–375	7	7.0	65	11.5	8000–10000	28
MGB	18V	66	CP11	463	7	14.4	40	11.5	6000	36

① Lucas A9/AZ9: 40 amp hr. All/AZ11: 50 amp hr.

WHEEL ALIGNMENT SPECIFICATIONS

Model	Engine	Caster Range	Caster Ideal	Camber Range	Camber Ideal	Toe-In (in.)	Kingpin Inclination (deg)	Wheel Pivot Ratio Inner	Wheel Pivot Ratio Outer
Midget	PE94J	—	3P	—	¾P	⅛	6¾	20	19¾
MGB	18V	5P–7¼P	7P	1¼N–1¼P	1P	1¹⁄₁₆	8	20	19

P Positive
N Negative

OIL PUMP SPECIFICATIONS

Oil Pump Clearances Locations	PE94J	18V
Inner and outer rotor end-play	0.0004 in. (0.1 mm)	0.005 in. (0.127 mm)
Outer rotor to pump body clearance	0.008 in. (0.2 mm)	0.010 in. (0.254 mm)
Rotor lobe clearance	0.010 in. (0.25 mm)	0.006 in. (0.152 mm)

BRAKE SPECIFICATIONS
(All measurements given are in inches unless noted)

Model	Engine	Lug Nut Torque (ft. lbs.)	Master Cylinder Bore	Brake Disc		Brake Drum			Minimum Lining Thickness	
				Minimum Thickness	Maximum Run-Out	Diameter	Max. Machine O/S	Max. Wear Limit	Front	Rear
Midget	PE94J	45	¾	0.29	0.006	7.0	0.015	0.030	⅟₁₆	40%②
MGB	18V	60–65	¾①	.340–.350	0.003③	10.75	0.015	0.030	⅟₁₆	40%②

NOTE: Minimum lining thickness is as recommended by the manufacturer. Due to variations in state inspection regulations, the minimum allowable thickness may be different than recommended by the manufacturer.

① 1¹³⁄₁₆ in. from vehicle number G-HD3/138, 401 (GT only)
② If riveted; 25% if bonded
③ 1978–80—0.006

TUNE-UP PROCEDURES

Spark Plugs

Number each spark plug wire by placing a piece of tape on the wire indicating the cylinder number. Grasp each spark plug wire by the rubber boot on the end of the wire and remove the wire from the plug.

Using a socket and a ratchet remove the spark plug. Before installing new plugs, gap each plug according to specification in the ''Tune-Up Specification'' chart. Install the new plugs by hand then tighten them snugly with the wrench.

Electronic Ignition

All 1976 and later MGs are equipped with an electronic ignition system, adjusting the pick-up air gap is the only routine service necessary.

1. Pick-up retaining screws
2. Air gap

Air gap and pickup retaining screw locations

PICK-UP AIR GAP ADJUSTMENT

1. Disconnect the battery and remove the air cleaner.
2. Remove the distributor cap, rotor and anti-static shield.
3. Insert a feeler gauge (see ''Tune-Up Specifications'' chart for proper thickness) between the pickup and the cam; it should pull through easily with a slight drag.
4. If the gap is incorrect, loosen the two retaining screws and move the pickup assembly on the pivot screw to adjust.
5. When adjusted properly, tighten retaining screws and recheck gap.
6. Reinstall the rest of the components and reconnect the battery cable.

Timing marks—Midget

Ignition Timing

Dynamic (engine running) timing is done with a timing light. Connect the light as per manufacturer's instructions. Mark the notch in the crankshaft pulley with a bright

Timing marks—MGB

color that will be easily visible (such as yellow chalk). Disconnect and plug the vacuum advance line from the intake manifold.

The engine should be warm and running steadily at the correct idle speed when the timing check is made. If the timing is no more than 5 degrees off, correction can usually be made with the vernier adjustment knob on the vacuum advance unit of the distributor (most models). Otherwise, the distributor clamp pinch-bolt will have to be loosened and the distributor rotated to the correct position. Check the timing once again after the pinch-bolt has been tightened, and reconnect the vacuum advance line after final adjustment is made to check operation of the vacuum advance unit.

Valve Adjustment

Valve clearances for the different MG models can be found in ''Tune-Up Specifications.'' Adjustment procedures for all models are the same. Valve adjustment should be carried out at every engine tune-up or whenever excessive valve train noise is noticed. Loose valve clearance will generally only cause a metallic thrashing sound, while overtight adjustment can cause rough running and burnt valves.

To adjust the valves, remove the rocker cover and provide a means of turning the engine over slowly. Although the engine may be turned over by hand or with the ignition switch, the best method is connecting an auxiliary starter wire to the solenoid. An auxiliary starter wire can be either a two-position switch with one lead connected to the battery cable terminal at the solenoid and the other lead connected to the small gauge wire at the separate solenoid terminal, or simply a short length of wire connected momentarily in the above manner to turn the engine over.

VALVE ADJUSTMENT CHART①

With this Valve Open	Adjust this Valve
1	8
2	7
3	6
4	5
5	4
6	3
7	2
8	1

①Valve rocker clearance adjusting

------ **CAUTION** ------

Make sure that the transmission is in Neutral before turning the engine over while outside the vehicle.

In order to adjust an individual valve, it must be in a certain relationship to the camshaft; i.e., it must be on the low side of the camshaft lobe. Because the relationship of one valve to the action of another is known (through camshaft configuration), it is possible to position one of the valves in its fully opened position (valve spring compressed) and thus know that another valve is correctly positioned for adjustment. If a line is drawn at the midpoint of the head separating the valves into two equal groups, then this relationship is symmetrical. In other words, if one of the end valves is open,

Valves No. 4 and 7 open, valves No. 5 and 2 positioned for adjustment

then the valve at the opposite end can be adjusted; if the second valve in from one end is open, the second valve in from the other end can be adjusted, etc.

When a valve is correctly positioned for adjustment, check the clearance between the valve stem and the rocker arm. If clearance is incorrect, loosen the adjusting screw locknut and turn the screw (clockwise to decrease clearance, counterclockwise to increase clearance) until the feeler gauge blade slides in and out with some resistance. To double check adjustment, try inserting the next size thinner and next size thicker feeler blade. If, for example, desired clearance is 0.010 in., the 0.009 in. blade should fit quite easily, while the 0.011 or 0.012 in. blade should be too thick to fit. When correct clearance has been obtained, hold the adjusting screw from turning and tighten the locknut. Recheck clearance in case the adjustment screw turned slightly when the locknut was tightened.

When all valves have been adjusted, reinstall the rocker cover. Make sure that the cover gasket is in good condition or an oil leak will develop. Breather hose connections at the rocker cover (if any) should be tight.

Carburetors

Midgets from 1976 on are equipped with a Zenith-Stromberg 150 CD4. MGBs from 1976 and later are equipped with a Zenith 175 CD5T.

IDLE SPEED AND MIXTURE ADJUSTMENTS

Prior to adjusting the carburetors, the following checks should be made to ensure that accurate adjustment is possible. Start the engine and spray or squirt a safe solvent (e.g., Gumout⑩) on the carburetor bodies

at the throttle shaft pivots. If engine speed changes, an air leak is indicated and adjustment of the carburetors will prove impossible. To alleviate the situation, the carburetors must be rebuilt and the throttle shaft bushings and/or shafts replaced.

Check the carburetor pistons for sticking by lifting them all the way and letting them fall. Their descent should be steady and a metallic click should be heard when they hit bottom. If there is evidence of sticking, remove and clean the pistons in solvent. Do not lubricate any part of the piston except the rod. Check that the piston damper chambers have the proper amount of oil. On carburetors with vented damper caps the level should be ½ in. above the piston rod, and with non-vented caps the level should be ½ in. below the rod.

The carburetor bodies and throttle linkage should be cleaned before adjustments are made. Check the manifold and carburetor nuts for looseness which could cause an air leak.

Measuring valve lash

Oil level ½ inch below the tube

Idle adjusting screw (inset)—CD4 and CD5 carburetors

The only adjustment that can be made on 1976 and later cars is that for normal idle speed. A carbon-monoxide meter is required for mixture adjustment under all circumstances. You can, however, take the car to a diagnostic center for checking of CO (carbon-monoxide) emmissions. If you are experiencing rough idle and poor running at low speeds, a CO reading well off specification would confirm the need for carburetor adjustment or repair by a qualified shop with the proper equipment. See the engine compartment sticker for CO specifications.

Make the idle speed adjustment with the engine hot as after a drive of several miles, using an accurate tachometer. On the Midget, first make sure the fast idle screw is not touching the fast idle cam. On the MGB, first disconnect the air manifold hose at the air pump and plug it, disconnect the float chamber vent pipe at the carburetor, and then run the engine at 2500 rpm for 30 seconds. Then, make the adjustment immediately.

ENGINE ELECTRICAL

Distributor

REMOVAL AND INSTALLATION

The electronic ignition distributor on the Midget uses vacuum retard. The unit used on the MGB has a vacuum advance unit that is not connected.

To remove and install the electronic ignition distributor:

1. Disconnect the battery. On the Midget, disconnect the heater air intake hose at the heater air intake, and move it aside.

2. Remove the distributor cap and leads, and set aside.

3. On the Midget, disconnect the three low tension leads. On the MGB, disconnect the multi-connector plug.

4. On the Midget, disconnect the vacuum line at the vacuum retard unit.

5. Turn the crankshaft until the timing notches on the crankshaft pulley are aligned with the 10 degree BTDC mark on Midgets, and the 0 degree mark on MGBs. Check that the distributor rotor arm is in position to fire the No. 1 spark plug. If not, turn the crankshaft exactly 360 degrees, so that the timing marks are aligned as described above.

6. Loosen the clamp bolt nut, and remove the unit.

7. To replace the distributor, position it so the rotor arm points to the firing po-

Correct rotor angle for distributor installation in a Midget

sition for the No. 1 spark plug, and install it into the block. Tighten the clamp bolt.

8. Reverse the procedures in Steps 1–4. Adjust ignition timing.

1. Rotor
2. Shield
3. Circlip
4. Washer
5. O-ring
6. Pick-up
7. Timing rotor
8. Base plate
9. Felt pad
10. Spindle
11. Return spring
12. Spring clip
13. Shim
14. Pin
15. Amplifier module
16. Vacuum unit
17. Pin
18. O-ring
19. Thrust washer
20. Driving dog

Exploded view of the distributor

Alternator

ALTERNATOR PRECAUTIONS

1. Do not run the engine with the batteries out of the circuit or any of the charging circuit wires disconnected (except as given in test procedures). All charging circuit electrical connections must be clean and tight, and the drive belt properly adjusted.

2. Correct battery and alternator polarity (negative ground) must be maintained or the alternator will be destroyed. If arc welding equipment is used on the car the alternator and regulator leads must be disconnected.

REMOVAL AND INSTALLATION

Midget

1. Disconnect the battery. Disconnect the wiring connector at the alternator.

2. Remove the adjusting bolt, nut, and washer.

3. Remove the nuts, washers, and one bolt that fasten the alternator guard to the adjusting bracket and the air pump mounting bracket, and remove the guard.

4. Slide the fan belt off the alternator pulley, and loosen the bolts holding the air pump to the air pump mounting bracket, and the air pump mounting bracket to the engine front mounting plate.

5. Remove the bolt that attaches the alternator to the air pump mounting bracket, and remove the alternator.

6. Replace the alternator in reverse of the above, tightening the bolt holding the alternator to the air pump mounting bracket, and the adjusting bolt, just slightly. Install the fan belt, adjust fan belt tension, and tighten bolts securely.

MGB

1. Remove the air pump adjusting link bolt, and air pump mounting bolt, and move the air pump to one side. Remove the air pump drive belt.

MGB alternator mounting

1. End cover
2. Rectifier pack
3. Through-bolt
4. End bracket
5. Stator
6. Slip-rings
7. Slip-ring bearing
8. Rotor
9. Field windings
10. Drive end bearing
11. Circlip
12. Oil sealing ring
13. Drive end-bracket
14. Shaft nut
15. Brush holder box
16. Brush assembly

Exploded view of the typical alternator (16ACR shown)

2. Disconnect the alternator wiring connector (4).

3. Remove the alternator adjusting nut (5).

4. Remove the alternator mounting bolts (6) and remove the alternator.

5. In installation, reverse Steps 1–4, leaving the adjusting nut (5) loose. Place the fan belt over the alternator pulley, tension the belt, and tighten the adjusting nut.

Regulator

REMOVAL AND INSTALLATION

The 8TR and 11TR regulators are used interchangeably with the 16ACR alternator. The regulator unit is located *inside the alternator*. To replace it the alternator must be removed from the car. When the plastic alternator end-cover is removed the regulator is accessible. Note the positions of the regulator leads and remove them. Remove the lower mounting screw and the regulator will be free.

To remove the regulator from the 18ACR alternator used on 1976 and later MGBs, first remove the alternator then remove the two end cover bolts, and remove the end cover. On 1976 and 1977 cars, unplug the connector from the terminal blade between the inner and outer rectifier plates. Also, on these models, remove the two upper screws from the brush assemblies, and disconnect the two connectors. Then, on all models, remove the screw which fastens the regulator to the brush holder, and remove the regulator. On 1978 and later models, note the location of the connector and spacer for easy reassembly.

NOTE: Never attempt to polarize an alternator or alternator regulator.

Starter

REMOVAL AND INSTALLATION

1. Disconnect the battery. Remove the distributor or, if necessary, the fuel pump.

2. On the Midget, remove the skid plate. Remove the top starter bolt.

3. Disconnect and tag the starter wires.

4. Remove the lower starter bolt and remove the starter.

5. Installation is the reverse of removal.

STARTER DRIVE REPLACEMENT

1. Disconnect the cable from the terminal on the solenoid marked "STA".

2. Remove the solenoid attaching nuts.

3. Remove the solenoid from the starter case and disengage it from the drive lever.

4. Remove the brush cover and remove the brushes.

5. Remove the thru-bolts from the end bracket.

6. Remove the lever pivot pin from the drive gear.

7. Separate the drive end bracket from the yoke and remove the drive gear engagement lever.

8. Remove the armature and separate the commutator plate from the yoke.

9. Remove the thrust washers from the shaft.

10. Remove the drive gear. Reverse the procedure to install.

ENGINE MECHANICAL

Engine

REMOVAL AND INSTALLATION

Midget

The engine of the Midget can be removed with or without the transmission. Either way, the preliminary steps are:

1. Drain the crankcase.
2. Disconnect the battery.
3. Remove the hood.
4. Disconnect the radiator and heater hoses and oil cooler lines (late models only), and remove the radiator.
5. Disconnect the choke and throttle cables and tachometer cable.
6. Disconnect the oil pressure gauge pipe from the engine.
7. Disconnect and tag all electrical connections to the engine.
8. Disconnect the high tension wires from the coil and spark plugs, and remove the distributor cap.
9. Unbolt the exhaust header pipe from the manifold and tie the pipe out of the way.
10. Remove the air cleaners and disconnect the fuel line.

At this point, the engine can be removed either with or without the transmission. If it is desired to remove only the engine:

1. Remove the starter motor.
2. Remove the fuel filter bowl (only).
3. Support the transmission with a jack, and remove the bell housing bolts.
4. Connect a hoist to the engine and unbolt the right-side engine mount from the chassis bracket.
5. Disconnect the left-side engine mount from the front engine plate and lift the engine from the vehicle, taking care not to damage the transmission mainshaft.

If it is desired to remove the engine and the transmission as a unit:

1. Drain the transmission oil and disconnect the back-up light switch lead (later models only).
2. Remove the gearshift lever cover, and remove the spring cap, spring and plunger.
3. Unbolt the shift lever retaining plate and lift out the lever.
4. With the carpet turned back, remove the rear transmission mount bolts.
5. From underneath the car, unscrew the speedometer cable from the transmission housing and release the cable support bracket from the bell housing.
6. Unbolt the clutch slave cylinder from the bell housing.
7. Unbolt the driveshaft from the differential flange and slide it out. Be sure to

1. Pole shoe retaining screws (4)
2. Housing
3. Field winding
4. Brushes—field winding
5. Commutator
6. Brush springs
7. Brushes—terminal connector
8. Commutator end bracket
9. Bearing bush
10. Plate
11. Felt seals
12. Screw (2)
13. Thrust washer
14. Armature
15. Bearing bushing
16. Drive-end bracket
17. Screw (2)
18. Pinion and barrel
19. Spring
20. Spiral gear
21. Main spring
22. Drive assy.

Exploded view of the starter—Midget

1. Armature end cap
2. Retaining ring
3. Bearing bush
4. Commutator end cover
5. Through-bolts
6. Brushes—field winding
7. Seal
8. Rivet—field winding connection
9. Armature
10. Field winding and pole-shoe screw
11. Brushes—terminal connector
12. Bearing bush
13. Screw and spring washer
14. Drive-end bracket
15. Sealing block
16. Pivot pin—engagement lever
17. Seal—drive end bracket
18. Drive assembly
19. Jump ring
20. Thrust collar
21. Roller clutch and pinion
22. Engagement lever and thrust washers
23. Spring ring
24. Cover and contacts
25. Solenoid unit
26. Spring, seat and dust excluder
27. Plunger and return spring

Exploded view of the starter—MGB

mark the flanges so that the driveshaft can be reinstalled correctly.

8. Connect a hoist to the engine and remove the remaining transmission mounting bolts.

9. Unbolt the right-side engine mount from the chassis bracket and disconnect the left-side mount from the front engine plate.

10. Lift the engine/transmission unit from the vehicle.

11. Installation of the engine or engine/transmission unit is in reverse order of removal. Be sure to refill the engine, transmission, and radiator.

MGB

1. Disconnect the battery and remove the hood.

2. Drain engine and transmission oil.

3. Drain the cooling system. On 1978 and later models, remove the screw, nuts, and washers, and remove the acoustic insulator.

4. Disconnect the oil cooler pipes and oil pressure gauge at the engine.

5. Disconnect top and bottom radiator hoses at the engine. Remove oil cooler mounting bolts, and remove the radiator assembly (radiator, oil cooler, and shroud).

6. Tag and disconnect wiring at alternator, distributor, and spark plugs. Remove the distributor cap.

7. Disconnect the heater hoses and, if so equipped, heater control cable.

8. On 1978 and later models, remove the heater water valve from the engine, and move it to one side. Disconnect the water temperature sending unit and intake manifold heater at the engine.

9. On 1978 and later models, remove the air cleaner, and then disconnect the fuel line and throttle cable at the carburetor.

10. On 1976–77 models, remove the cover and disconnect the starter wiring. Then, disconnect the fuel line and throttle cable at the carburetor and remove the air cleaner.

11. Disconnect: the purge PCV line from the top of the rocker cover; the adsorption canister line at the carburetor and rocker cover; power brake vacuum line at the manifold; running-on control valve vacuum line at the valve.

12. Remove the gearshift lever escutcheon. Raise the rubber boot, unscrew the lever retaining bolts, and remove the gearshift lever.

13. On 1978–80 models, disconnect starter wiring from under the car.

14. Disconnect wiring from back-up light switch and overdrive isolation switch, and remove the wiring harness clip from the gearbox and starter motor flange.

15. Disconnect the clutch slave cylinder at the gearbox, and move it out of the way.

16. Disconnect the speedometer cable.

17. Attach a hoist to the engine and support the weight of the engine with it.

18. Disconnect exhaust pipe(s) from the manifold. On 1978–80 models, remove the

seals from the ends of the exhaust pipes and disconnect the pipes at the front support.

19. Matchmark and remove the driveshaft.

20. On 1976–77 models, remove the mount-to-frame nuts from the front engine mounts.

21. Loosen the engine restraining rod front nut. Remove the rear nuts and pull out the rear plate and rubber insulator. Remove the nut and bolt which hold the restraining rod to the gearbox mounting bracket, and pull the rod out of the bracket on the crossmember.

22. Remove the four bolts which hold the rear crossmember to the frame. On 1976–77 cars, remove the two bolts which hold the lower tie bracket to the crossmember.

23. Lower the gearbox so that it rests on the crossmember that is not removable. Then, on 1978–80 models, remove the two bolts which hold the lower tie bracket to the removable crossmember.

24. Remove the nuts which hold the rear mounts to the removable crossmembers and remove the crossmember.

25. On 1978–80 models, remove the nuts which secure the front engine mounts to the frame.

26. Ease the assembly forward until the gearbox is clear of the crossmember, tilt it, and lift the assembly from the car.

27. Installation is in the reverse order. When installing the engine restraint rod, tighten the rear nut first, and then the front nut. Driveshaft nuts are torqued to 30–35 ft. lbs.

Cylinder Head

REMOVAL AND INSTALLATION

The cylinder head nuts should be loosened, gradually in the same order as they are tightened, to prevent the head from warping (see "Tightening Sequences"). For the same reason, the head should be removed only when the engine is cold. When the cylinder head nuts and all accessories have been unbolted from the head, it may be necessary to tap each side of the head with a rubber mallet to break the head gasket seal. When the head is free, lift it evenly over the studs. If any water has found its way into the cylinders it should be immediately removed and the cylinder walls coated with oil. If the head is not to be installed for a day or more, it is a good idea to stuff towels into the cylinders to protect them.

The cylinder head removal procedure for all models is as follows:

1. Drain the radiator.

2. Disconnect the radiator and heater hoses from the cylinder head.

3. Remove the heater control valve and unbolt the top radiator bracket.

4. Remove the carburetor and air cleaners, and unbolt the manifolds and pull them back out of the way.

5. Remove the rocker cover and remove the cylinder head nuts in the proper order (see "Tightening Sequences").

6. Lift the rocker shaft assembly off and remove the pushrods, keeping them in order.

7. Remove the spark plugs and disconnect the water temperature sending unit from the head.

8. Disconnect the air supply hose from the check valve (if so equipped).

9. Unbolt the air pump from its mounting point on the head (if so equipped).

10. Lift the head from the cylinder block.

Installation is in reverse order of removal. Thoroughly clean the mating surfaces of the cylinder block and head, and always use a new gasket. The gasket is marked Top and Front to facilitate correct installation. Gasket sealing compound is not necessary, but may be used. Cylinder head nuts should be tightened gradually, in the correct sequence (see "Tightening sequences"), and to the proper torque value (see "Torque Specifications"). When the head has been tightened the valves must be adjusted (see "Valve Adjustment"). After running the engine for between 200 and 500 miles, the head should be retorqued and the valves readjusted. When retorquing the head, simply back off each nut slightly and retighten to specification, one at a time and in the proper sequence.

VALVE GUIDE REMOVAL AND INSTALLATION

1. Lay the cylinder head machined side down on a clean surface and drive the valve guide downward with a proper size punch. The sizes for MGs are as follows:

MGB: 9/16 in. diameter; 4 in. long with 5/16 in. opening in tip extending one inch into tool.

Midget: 7/16 in. diameter; 4 in. long with 9/32 in. opening in tip extending one inch into tool.

2. Insert the new valve guides from the top with the end having the most chamfer being on the top.

3. Drive them in until they are the specified height above the machined surface of the valve spring seating (See "Valve Specifications" chart).

VALVE SEAT GRINDING

Pitted or uneven valve seats must be renewed using a grinder or cutter, being careful to remove only the metal necessary to restore the seat.

When grinding, the valve seat should be lightly coated with a fine or medium grade carborundum paste. Avoid the use of too much paste and make sure that it remains only in the area that is being ground.

A light coil spring placed under the valve head will help the grinding process. Grind the valve to its seat with a semi-rotary motion occasionally allowing it to rise from

A. Exhaust
B. Intake
C. 1.437–1.438 in.
D. .186–.188 in.
E. Maximum radius—.015 in.
F. 1.330–1.350 in.
G. 1.218–1.228 in.
H. Throat diameter—1.146–1.66 in.
I. 45 degrees
J. Blend from seating to throat diameter
K. 1.592–1.593 in.
L. 1.552–1.572 in.
M. 1.427–1.447 in.
N. Throat diameter 1.302–1.322 in.

Valve seat insert dimensions

the pressure of the spring. This will aid in the spreading of the paste.

When finished the entire assembly should be cleaned in a suitable solvent such as kerosene and then when dry, blown out with compressed air.

VALVE SEAT INSERTS

MGB

If the valve seats cannot be corrected using the cutting procedures, valve seat inserts may be installed. Machine the head to the dimensions shown in the illustration, press in the inserts, and then cut them to the specifications shown.

OVERHAUL

See ''Engine Rebuilding Section.''

Rocker Shafts

REMOVAL AND INSTALLATION

1. Drain the cooling system, remove all connections from the rocker cover and remove it.

2. Loosen the rocker arm retaining nuts gradually a turn at a time. The external cylinder head bolts should also be released in order to avoid cylinder head warpage.

3. Remove the rocker arm retaining bolts and lift off the rockershaft assembly.

4. Remove the pushrods, keeping them in order so they may be replaced in the same positions later.

5. To dismantle the rocker shaft, remove the rocker shaft locating screw at the front mounting bracket.

6. Remove the cotter pins, washer and spring from the end of the shaft, and slide the rockers, brackets and springs from the shaft.

7. Remove the plug from one end of the shaft and clean out the inside of the shaft. (The screwed-shaft end plug faces the front of the engine).

8. Installation is the reverse of removal, but make sure to torque the nuts according to the applicable cylinder head removal and installation procedure.

Intake/Exhaust Manifold

REMOVAL AND INSTALLATION

Midget

1. Drain the cooling system and remove the carburetor from the intake manifold.

2. Disconnect all water hoses, vacuum lines, and the EGR line from the intake manifold. Remove the EGR line from the EGR valve. Remove the running-on control valve vacuum pipe adapter.

3. Remove the three nuts, bolts, and washers, and disconnect the exhaust pipe. Remove and discard the gasket.

4. Remove the nut and washer connecting intake and exhaust manifolds. Remove the flame trap bracket and the water return pipe bracket.

5. Remove the six nuts and washers that hold the manifolds onto the cylinder head. Pull the manifolds out slightly from the head, and remove the intake manifold and spacer. Then, remove the exhaust manifold and gasket.

6. In installation, install a new gasket, and then position the exhaust manifold onto the cylinder head studs. Install the two larger clamps and their washers to the two lower studs. Start the two longer nuts onto the two inner, lower studs.

7. Position the intake manifold and spacer onto the exhaust manifold, locate it properly on the cylinder head dowels with

the clamps properly positioned, and then push the manifolds into position as an assembly. Reverse the remaining procedures.

MGB 1976–77

1. Remove the air cleaner and carburetor.

2. Disconnect the distributor vacuum line, brake booster vacuum line, and running-on control valve at the manifold.

3. Remove the EGR and gulp valves.

4. Remove the hot air duct. Remove the two attaching screws, and remove the heat shield from the water line.

5. Disconnect the exhaust pipe. Remove the six nuts and washers, and remove the two manifolds. Note that the four center nuts use larger washers and hold both intake and exhaust manifolds in position, while the nuts at the ends, using smaller washers hold only the exhaust manifold in place.

6. In installation, use a new gasket, reverse the above procedures, and be sure to torque to specification.

MGB 1978 and Later

1. Drain the cooling system.

2. Remove the air cleaner. Disconnect: the vapor return hose from the carburetor; the heater pipe at the lower radiator hose; the wire at the induction heater.

3. Remove carburetor attaching nuts, and remove the carburetor, intake heater, bracket, and heat shield.

4. Disconnect the brake vacuum hose at the manifold, the running-on control valve hose at the manifold, and the small gulp valve hose at the manifold.

5. Loosen the clamp for the large gulp valve hose, and then remove the bolt which attaches the gulp valve to the intake manifold. Be careful not to lose the copper washers. Pull the gulp valve off the manifold, disconnecting the large hose.

6. Remove the hot air shroud.

7. Jack up the car and remove the bolt which holds the exhaust pipe to the front bracket. Disconnect the exhaust pipe going to the rear of the car from the catalytic converter, retaining the seal.

8. Remove the two bolts, three nuts, and flat washers attaching the manifold to the head, and pull off the manifold and hot air shroud base plate.

9. In installation, use a new manifold gasket and replace other exhaust seals wherever they are damaged. Tighten the connection between exhaust pipe and catalytic converter before connecting the exhaust pipe to the front bracket.

Timing Gear Cover

REMOVAL AND INSTALLATION

Midget

1. Remove the drive belt.

Exploded view of the rocker shaft assembly—Midget

2. Remove the bolts which retain the fan to the water pump pulley and remove the fan.

3. Remove the crankshaft damper nut (accessible from below).

NOTE: It may be necessary to block the flywheel to stop the crankshaft from turning.

Replace the nut loosely, and pull off the damper with a gear puller.

4. Remove the screws, bolts, and nuts which retain the timing gear cover to the engine. Remove the bottom air pump bolt and spacer. Lift off the cover with the gasket, taking care not to damage the seal.

5. To install, reverse the above procedure, taking care to install a new cover gasket on the cover dowels. To ease installation of the cover, hold the chain tensioner back with a bent length of rod (9b) until the tensioner clears the chain. When installing the pulley, take care to position the drive key between the pulley and the crankshaft spindle and tighten the nut to specifications. Readjust the drive belt tension.

Hold the chain tensioner back with a bent piece of wire—Midget

MGB through 1977

1. Remove the radiator.

2. Loosen the generator adjustment bolts and remove the fan belt.

NOTE: It is necessary to unbolt the engine mounts and exhaust pipe in order to raise the front of the engine to provide clearance for removal of the pulley.

3. Bend the locktab back and unscrew the crankshaft pulley nut.

4. Carefully pry the pulley from the crankshaft.

5. Unbolt and remove the timing gear cover.

6. Lubricate the hub of the pulley and insert it into the oil seal, turning the pulley in a clockwise direction to avoid damaging the seal.

7. Align the pulley keyway with the crankshaft key and push the pulley (with the cover and cover gasket) onto the crankshaft.

8. Replace the cover bolts and tighten them evenly.

9. Tighten and lock the crankshaft pulley nut.

10. Reinstall the fan belt, and replace and fill the radiator.

MGB 1978 and Later

1. Remove the acoustic insulating board. Remove the radiator.

2. Loosen adjusting and attaching bolts on the air pump and alternator, and remove belts.

3. Remove the crankshaft pulley retaining bolt, and remove the pulley with a wheel puller.

4. Remove the screws and washers, and remove the timing cover.

5. Reverse the procedure to install, using a new gasket and a new lockwasher on the crankshaft pulley.

OIL SEAL REPLACEMENT

1. Pry the old seal out of the cover.

2. Lubricate the new seal and install it evenly into the cover in the same position as the old one, taking care not to damage it.

3. If the seal is made of rubber, fill the groove between the seal lips with grease. Felt seals do not need to be lubricated in this manner.

4. Make sure that the oil thower behind the crankshaft pulley is installed with the concave side (early engines) or the face marked F (later engines) away from the engine.

5. Make sure that the seal is centered in the timing cover. A special centering tool is made for this purpose and can be used to hold the seal in a centered position while installing and tightening the cover.

Timing Gear and Chain

REMOVAL AND INSTALLATION

The camshafts in all MG engines are driven by a chain from the crankshaft. The MGB has an endless, duplex chain and a chain tensioner. Chain tensioner removal and service procedures can be found under "Timing Chain Tensioner Service—MGB."

The crankshaft and camshaft timing gears and the timing chain usually do not require service or replacement, due to high mileage or improper lubrication, gear tooth wear is noticeable. If wear is evident, replace all three components. Worn gears or chain stretch as isolated problems almost never occur.

MGB

1. To remove the chain and gears, first remove the timing gear cover (see preceding section). On the MGB, remove the chain tensioner or retract and lock the rubbing block by removing the plug from the tensioner body and turning the adjusting bolt clockwise (see following section).

Timing gear marks—MGB

2. Bend the locktab back and remove the camshaft timing gear nut. The camshaft and crankshaft timing gears may now be removed together with the chain by easing the gears off the shafts simultaneously, using a puller or suitable levers.

3. When replacing the timing chain and gears, set the crankshaft with its keyway at twelve o'clock and the camshaft with its keyway at one o'clock as seen from the front. The washers behind the crankshaft gear are spacers to align the two gears properly.

4. When reassembling, the same number of washers should be installed as were removed *unless* any of the following components have been replaced: crankshaft, crankshaft main bearings and thrust washers, crankshaft timing gear, camshaft, camshaft timing gear, or camshaft locating plate. If any of the above components have been replaced, timing gear alignment can be checked and adjusted by placing a straightedge across the gear sides and adding or subtracting washers to eliminate any gaps between the gear side surfaces and the straightedge (after the gears have been installed).

5. To install the timing gears and chain, assemble the chain onto the gears with the

Gear alignment can be checked using a straight-edge and feeler gauge

gear marks facing each other so that a line drawn through them would pass through the camshaft and crankshaft axes. Keeping the gears in this position, start the crankshaft gear onto the crankshaft (with the gear keyway and crankshaft key aligned).

6. Install the camshaft gear onto the camshaft, turning the camshaft to align the key with the keyways if necessary.

7. Make a final check of alignment of the timing gears and gear marks, and install the camshaft gear lockwasher and nut. Replace the timing cover.

Midget

1. Remove the timing gear cover as outlined in the applicable ''Timing Gear Cover Removal and Installation'' procedure.

2. Remove the oil thrower.

3. Check timing chain wear by placing a straightedge along the slack length of chain. If the free-play between the straightedge and the chain at a point midway between the two sprockets exceeds 0.4 in., the chain must be discarded and replaced.

4. Rotate the crankshaft until the crankshaft key is at 12 o'clock and the sprocket dots align.

5. Pry back the locking tabs and remove the bolts which retain the camshaft sprocket to the camshaft.

6. Taking care not to disturb the crankshaft or camshaft, remove both sprockets with the timing chain.

7. To check alignment of the sprockets, remove the crankshaft drive key and temporarily install both sprockets. Place a straightedge across the teeth of both sprockets. Correct any misalignment by placing shims behind the crankshaft sprocket.

2. Camshaft gear to camshaft mark alignment
3. Crankshaft
4. Crankshaft and camshaft gear markings and alignment
7. Crankshaft keyway
15. Measuring for allowable timing chain free play—0.40 inch or less

Timing gear alignment and timing chain looseness inspection—Midget

Timing gear marks—Midget

8. After checking the alignment, remove the sprockets, install the crankshaft drive key, and place the sprocket and chain assembly into position, aligned dot to dot, and install the camshaft sprocket retaining bolts using a new lockplate.

9. Install the oil thrower.

10. Install the timing gear cover as outlined in the applicable ''Timing Gear Cover Removal and Installation'' procedure.

Timing Chain Tensioner

REMOVAL AND INSTALLATION

MGB

On models built in 1978 and later, no adjusting bolt is used. The tensioner must be removed cautiously because of the spring pressure on the rubbing block.

1. To remove the tensioner (after the timing gear cover has been removed), first unscrew the plug from the tensioner body. Using a 1/8 in. Allen wrench, turn the tension adjusting bolt clockwise until the rubbing block is fully retracted and locked behind the limit peg.

2. Unbolt and remove the tensioner and its backing plate.

3. Withdraw the rubbing block and plunger from the tensioner body, and turn the tension adjusting bolt clockwise until the piston and spring are released.

4. Clean the components in solvent and blow out the oil passages with compressed air.

5. Check the bore of the tensioner body for ovality. If the diameter of the bore at or near the mouth varies more than 0.003 in., the complete tensioner unit should be replaced. If within the limit given, it is acceptable to replace just the rubbing block.

6. To reassemble the tensioner, insert the spring and piston into the bore and compress the spring.

7. Turn the piston clockwise until the

1. Gasket
2. Backplate
3. Spacer to prevent disengagement
4. Tensioner body
5. Inner cylinder
6. Spring
7. Peg
8. Slipper head

Exploded view of the typical timing chain tensioner

inner end is below the peg. Install the rubbing block plunger into the bore.

CAUTION
Do not attempt to turn the tension adjusting bolt counterclockwise.

---

8. Bolt the backing plate and tensioner onto the cylinder block and lock the mounting bolts with the locktab.

9. Release the rubbing block for operation by turning the adjusting bolt clockwise until the block contacts the chain under spring pressure.

10. Check the rubbing block for freedom of movement and make sure that it does not bind against the backing plate.

11. Replace and lock the plug in the tensioner body.

ADJUSTMENT

MGB

The timing chain tensioner utilized on the MGB is self-adjusting, and no manual adjustment is provided.

Midget

The tensioner is non-adjustable. If the chain cannot be tensioned properly and the chain itself is not stretched, then the tensioner should be replaced. To remove the tensioner, first remove the timing chain cover as previously described, spread apart the tensioner blades, and then slide the tensioner off its anchor pin. Reverse the removal procedure to install, making sure that the convex surface of the tensioner faces the timing chain.

Camshaft

REMOVAL

Removal of the camshaft from the Midget or the MGB can be accomplished without removing the engine from the chassis. The following procedure can, however, be used whether the engine is in or out of the car.

1. Drain the crankcase and remove the oil pan from the engine.

2. Remove the rocker cover from the head and unbolt and remove the rocker shaft assembly and pushrods, keeping the pushrods in order.

3. Remove the intake and exhaust manifolds.

4. Remove the lifter covers from the side of the cylinder block.

5. Remove the lifters, and, as with the pushrods, keep them in order.

6. Remove the timing cover and gears.

7. Remove the oil pump.

8. Remove the distributor.

9. Remove the camshaft locating plate.

10. Pull the camshaft from the front of the engine rotating it slowly to assist removal.

NOTE: Removal procedures for individual units such as the oil pump, timing gear cover, etc. can be found under appropriate subheads in the ''Engine'' section.

INSTALLATION

Camshaft installation in all cases is in the reverse order of removal. Camshaft bearings, except in cases of insufficient lubrication, almost never need replacement. Clearance can be checked with a feeler gauge. Replacement of bearings requires special pullers and machine tools (for alignboring) and should be left to a machine shop.

Camshaft end-play can be checked before installation by assembling the locating plate and timing gear onto the camshaft and measuring fore and aft play. If it exceeds specification, the locating plate should be replaced.

CAMSHAFT SPECIFICATIONS
(in.)

Model	End-Play	Oil Clearance
Midget	0.0045–0.0085	0.0016–0.0036
MGB	0.003–0.007	0.001–0.002

NOTE: Valve lift for the different engine models can be found under VALVE SPECIFICATIONS. Intake valve opening timing (deg. BTDC) can be found under TUNE-UP SPECIFICATIONS.

Pistons and Connecting Rods

NOTE: On engines with floating or press-fit type wrist pins, the pistons are select-fitted to the bores, and the piston crowns and cylinders are marked with identification numbers.

1. Piston ring—parallel
2. Piston ring—taper
3. Piston ring—taper
4. Piston ring—scraper
5. Piston
6. Piston pin lubricating hole
7. Piston pin
8. Connecting rod
9. Clamping screw and washer
10. Cylinder wall lubricating jet
11. Connecting rod bearings
12. Connecting rod cap
13. Lock washer
14. Bolts
15. Connecting rod and cap marking

Piston and connecting rod—Midget

1. Piston
2. Oil ring
3. Compression rings—taper
4. Compression ring—parallel
5. Wrist pin bushing
6. Wrist pin
7. Circlip
8. Wrist pin lubrication hole
9. Connecting rod
10. Cylinder wall lubrication jet
11. Connecting rod bearing cap
12. Locktab
13. Rod bolts
14. Rod bearings
15. Connecting rod and cap assembly marks

Piston and connecting rod—MGB

Oversize piston markings

Piston and connecting rod installation position for all models is indicated in the accompanying illustrations. Unmarked pistons must be identified with regard to cylinder and installation position prior to removal so that they may be reinstalled in the same position. Select-fitted pistons are identified by a number enclosed in a diamond stamped on the piston crown and block. Oversize dimensions are stamped on the piston crown, enclosed in some cases in an ellipse.

All later pistons are marked with the word "Front", or a triangular indentation which must face the front of the engine.

ENGINE LUBRICATION

Oil Pan

REMOVAL AND INSTALLATION

Midget

1. Drain the oil and unbolt and lower the oil pan.
2. Always replace the two pan gaskets and the two main bearing cork seals when the pan has been removed. It may be necessary to soak the cork seals in hot water to keep them from breaking when installing them.

Typical rear main bearing oil seal components

MGB

1. Drain the oil. Drain the radiator and disconnect the hoses.
2. Unbolt the engine mounts and lift the front of the engine enough to gain access to the front oil pan bolts.
3. Unbolt and lower the pan.
4. Clean the cylinder block and oil pan mating surfaces and replace the pan gasket to preclude the possibility of an oil leak.

Oil pump rotor position

Oil Pump

REMOVAL AND INSTALLATION

Midget

1. Remove the oil pan.
2. Remove the three bolts and withdraw the oil pump assembly.
3. Installation is in reverse order of removal. Be careful when installing the paper gasket, that the intake and delivery ports are not obstructed. Use a new gasket if the old one is damaged in any way, and use new locktabs.

MGB

1. Remove the oil pan.

2. Oil pump drive shaft and gear
3. Outer pump body and cover
4. Inner and outer rotors

Exploded view of the oil pump—MGB

2. Remove the three nuts that secure the pump to the crankcase and withdraw the pump assembly.
3. Installation is in reverse order of removal. Use a new gasket when the pump is reinstalled.

OIL PUMP CLEARANCES

Midget

Concentric Engineering pump:
The concentric pump is replaceable as a unit only; parts are not available.

Burman pump:
1. Remove the pump cover and withdraw the rotor and vane assembly. Remove the sleeve from the end of the rotor and remove the vanes.
2. Replace any worn or damaged parts.
3. Coat all parts with motor oil before assembly.

Holbourn-Eaton pump:
4. Remove the pump cover and lift out the inner and outer rotors.

2. Oil pump cover 3. Inner rotor 4. Outer rotor
Exploded view of the oil pump—Midget

5. Check clearance between the outer rotor and the pump body. If the clearance exceeds 0.010 in., the complete pump assembly should be renewed.
6. Check clearance between the rotor lobes.

Checking rotor end play

7. Rotor end play measurement
8. Outer rotor to pump body clearance
9. Inner rotor lobe to outer rotor clearance

Measurement position for oil pump component clearances

7. Replace the rotors if clearance exceeds 0.006 in.

8. Check the rotor end float. If the clearance exceeds 0.005 in., remove the dowels from the pump body mating surface and mill or lap the surface until clearance is within specification.

9. Coat all parts with fresh motor oil before assembling. Install the outer rotor in the pump body with the beveled end at the drive end of the pump body.

10. Check the pump for freedom of movement after assembly.

MGB

MGB oil pump service procedures are identical to those of the Holbourn-Eaton pump on the Midget (see "Oil Pump Specifications" chart).

ENGINE COOLING

Radiator

REMOVAL AND INSTALLATION

Midget

1. Disconnect the bottom hose at the radiator and drain the coolant into a container.

2. Disconnect the expansion tank hose at the radiator, and the top hose at the thermostat housing. Disconnect the heater air intake hose bracket at the body, and carefully ease the hose rearward and out of the way.

3. Remove the two screws which hold the radiator cowl to the hood support panel, remove the four radiator cowl bolts and nuts, and remove the cowl and radiator as an assembly.

4. Transfer the thermostat housing hose, fan guard and radiator cowl to the new radiator if the unit is being replaced, and install in reverse of the installation procedure.

MGB

1. Drain the cooling system by disconnecting the lower hose at the radiator. Disconnect the upper hose at the radiator. Disconnect the expansion tank hose at the radiator.

2. Disconnect the wiring going to the thermostatic switch. Remove the screws holding the radiator to the mounting bracket.

3. Loosen the screws that hold the radiator mounting bracket straps to the hood latch platform and pull the straps to one side.

4. Ease the radiator toward the front of the car and remove it.

5. Install in exact reverse order.

Water Pump

REMOVAL

Midget

1. Remove the radiator.

2. Remove the fan retaining bolts and remove the fan.

3. Loosen the air pump mounting bolts, remove the adjusting strut bolt, remove the belt and swivel and pump up out of the way (Emission Control models only).

4. Loosen the generator mounting bolts, remove the belt, remove the top mounting bolts and lower the generator out of the way.

5. Disconnect the by-pass hose and lower radiator hose from the water pump.

6. Remove the water pump mounting bolts and remove the pump.

MGB 1976–77

1. Remove the radiator. Unbolt and remove the fan and drive pulley.

2. Remove the air pump adjusting link screws. Remove the top mounting bolt, nut, and washer from the alternator.

3. Disconnect the water pump lower hose. Remove water pump retaining bolts and remove the pump.

4. Install in reverse order, using new gaskets, and making sure that gasket surfaces are clean.

MGB 1978 and Later

1. Drain the cooling system. Remove the screw which holds the air pump adjusting link in place.

2. Loosen the air pump mounting bolt, remove the air pump drive belt and pivot the pump upwards to get it out of the way.

3. Remove the alternator adjusting link nut and mounting bolts, remove the drive belt, and put the alternator aside.

4. Disconnect the lower hose from the water pump.

5. Remove screws and lockwashers holding the drive belt pulley and spacer in place, and remove the pulley and spacer.

6. Remove the water pump mounting

bolts. Remove the air pump adjusting link brackets. Remove the water pump.

7. Replace the water pump in reverse order, using a new gasket and tightening to 17 ft. lbs.

INSTALLATION

Installation in all cases is a reversal of removal procedures. Make sure that the mating surface of the cylinder block is cleaned of pieces of the old gasket that may remain. Always use a new gasket, and torque the mounting bolts evenly.

Thermostat

REMOVAL AND INSTALLATION

The thermostat on all MGs is located in the aluminum housing, bolted to the cylinder head, that connects to the upper radiator hose.

1. Replacement involves simply unbolting the housing and lifting out the thermostat.

2. Before unbolting the housing, drain (and save) about half of the coolant from the radiator to prevent loss when the housing is removed. Thermostats of three different opening temperatures are available: 160°F, 180°F, and 190°F. The 180° thermostat is suitable for all around use in most climates, while the 160° and 190° thermostats can be used in very hot or cold weather, respectively.

3. The thermostat should always be installed with the bellows or spring facing downward toward the block.

4. Use a new gasket between the thermostat housing and the cylinder head. If the gasket is made of cork, as some replacements are, be careful not to overtighten the housing nuts or the cork will be completely crushed out and will not seal.

NOTE: Never remove the thermostat in an attempt to cure overheating, as this may cause a blown head gasket, burnt valves, etc. due to localizing overheating. Instead, install a restricting washer or a gutted thermostat body.

EMISSION CONTROLS

Emission Control Applications

The Emission Control Systems reduce the emissions of Oxide of Nitrogen (NOx), Hydrocarbons (HC), and Carbon Monoxide (CO), generated by combustion.

Three systems are used:

    a. Crankcase Emission Control and Components

    b. Exhaust Emission Control and Components

    c. Evaporative Loss Control and Components

Crankcase Emission Control

The engine breather outlet is connected by hoses to the controlled depression chamber; the chamber between the piston and the throttle disc valve, of the carburetor. Engine fumes and blow-by gases are drawn from the crankcase by the depression in this chamber, through an oil separator flame trap incorporated into the top of the valve rocker cover, and from there to the depression chamber on the Midget; or through an oil separator incorporated in the engine outlet connection, and from there to the intake manifold on the MGB. Air for engine breathing is drawn through the filtered absorption canister of the evaporative loss control system into the valve rocker cover on the MGB; on the Midget, it joins the engine fumes and blow-by gases drawn from the crankcase. A restricter in the absorption canister connection (Midget) or in the rocker cover connection (MGB) reduces the air flow to ensure crankcase depression under all conditions.

Exhaust Emission Control

EXHAUST AIR INJECTION

The EAI system consists of a belt driven air pump that forces air into the exhaust port of each cylinder, causing a reburning of exhaust gases in order to reduce the number of harmful emissions.

Air is drawn into the pump through a replaceable paper filter.

A relief valve in the pump vents excessive air pressure, created by high rpm operation, to the atmosphere.

A check valve, located in the pump output line to the injection manifold, protects the pump from exhaust gas backflow.

A gulp valve, located in the pump output

EAI system components—MGB

1. Relief valve
2. Intake chamber
3. Rotor
4. Output chamber
5. Spring
6. Carbons
7. Vane assemblies
8. Rotor bearing support plate
9. Output port
10. End-cover
11. Intake port

Exploded view of a typical air pump

line to the intake manifold, leans out the rich fuel/air mixture that develops when the engine is decelerating (engine overrun). A line between the intake manifold and the gulp valve allows the valve to be activated by changes in manifold vacuum. On some engines a restrictor is located in the output line between the pump and valve to prevent engine surge when the valve is operating.

In addition to the air pump and its attendant equipment, all vehicles with emission control systems are equipped with the distributor and carburetors modified to meet emission standards. These units are covered separately in the ''Engine Electrical'' and ''Fuel System'' sections, as well as in the ''Specifications'' section.

The efficient and trouble-free operation of the emission control system depends to a large extent upon the engine being correctly tuned. Proper tuning specifications given for a particular engine should be strictly adhered to (see ''Tune-Up Specifications'').

Maintenance

At the time of an engine tune-up (6,000 miles recommended), the entire exhaust air injection system should be inspected. Clean or replace the air pump air filter element. Check the air hoses and connections for any evidence of leaking. (This is very important, because an air leak can cause overheating, resulting in burnt valves, a blown head gasket, etc.) Check the air pump drive belt tension and adjust it if necessary. Properly adjusted, the belt should have a total deflection of ½ inch midway between the pulleys. Adjustment is made by loosening the mounting bolt and adjusting strut bolts, in the same manner as generator adjustment.

Component Testing

1. Disconnect the air supply hose that runs between the diverter valve and air pump at the air pump.

2. Connect a vacuum gauge via a Tee

to the disconnected end of the diverter valve hose. Then, start the engine and idle it.

3. Seal the open end of the Tee and watch the gauge for 15 seconds. The gauge should indicate zero vacuum. Otherwise, replace the diverter valve.

4. Holding the Tee open end shut, open and close the the throttle rapidly. Unseal the open end of the Tee to restore air pressure to the gauge, then reseal it and repeat the test. Verify that vacuum is produced each time the test is repeated. If no vacuum is created, replace the diverter valve.

5. Test the check valve by removing it and blowing through both ends. Air should pass through in one direction only, or the valve requires replacement. Do not use compressed air to test the check valve.

Removal and Installation

AIR PUMP

1. Disconnect the air hoses from the pump connections and remove the air pump filter assembly. On Midget, remove the oil filter.

2. Loosen the retaining and adjusting bolts and remove the drive belt from the pump pulley.

3. Remove the top adjusting bolt and remove the nut securing the pump mounting bolt.

4. While supporting the pump, remove the mounting bolt and lift the pump from the engine.

RELIEF VALVE

1. Remove the air pump, and pump pulley.

2. Slide a ½ in. diameter drill bit through the exhaust connection and tap out the relief valve with it.

3. Place a new copper seating washer on the new relief valve and place the valve into the pump assembly.

4. Force the valve into the pump until the copper seating washer is held firmly. This is done with a five inch piece of pipe with an inside diameter of 1 inch.

1. Air pump
2. Air pump air cleaner
3. Check valve
4. Air manifold
5. Gulp valve
6. Sensing pipe
7. Oil separator/flame trap
8. Breather pipe
9. Restricted connection
10. Purge line
11. Air vent pipe
12. Sealed oil filter cap
13. Primary charcoal absorption canister
14. Vapour lines
15. Canister inter-connecting pipe
16. Sealing cap
17. Secondary charcoal absorption canister
18. Running-on control valve
19. Running-on control hose
20. Running-on control pipe
21. Fuel filter
22. Exhaust gas recirculation (E.G.R.) valve
23. E.G.R. valve hose
24. Air temperature control valve
25. Fuel cut-off valve

Typical emission control components—1978 MGB shown

CHECK VALVE

1. Unscrew the air supply hose from the check valve connection.
2. Hold the air manifold connection to prevent its twisting and unscrew the check valve.
3. Installation is the reverse of removal.

GULP VALVE

Disconnect the air hoses, unscrew the mounting screw and remove the gulp valve.

Exhaust Gas Recirculation System

The EGR valve is mounted on the engine manifold and controls the introduction of exhaust gas into the intake manifold. A spring-loaded diaphragm, connected to the valve pintle shaft, is controlled by engine vacuum and regulates the amount of exhaust gas to be mixed with the air/fuel mixture and is governed by engine speed.

SERVICE

The EGR system requires service every 25,000 miles. A warning light in the dash comes on after the car has been driven that many miles. After servicing is accomplished, reset the service interval indicator as described in the last step of the procedure below.

1. Run the engine until it reaches operating temperature.
2. Disconnect the vacuum hose at the EGR valve. Disconnect the hose running between the intake manifold and the diverter valve at the manifold.
3. Connect a piece of rubber tubing between the open fittings on intake manifold and EGR valve. Then, start and run the engine while watching the EGR valve stem. The stem should move upward when the engine is started and as the engine is accelerated, it should move up farther.
4. Disconnect the vacuum hose at the EGR valve. The valve stem should drop.

Insert the key in the service indicator as shown

5. Remove the extra piece of vacuum hose, and reconnect the diverter valve hose to the manifold.
6. Remove the EGR valve as described below. Check that the valve is closed. If it is not seated, replace it. Clean all gasket material off both the valve and manifold surfaces.
7. Clean all carbon deposits from the valve restrictor, ports in the manifold, and the ports within the valve body. Make sure no deposits fall into the manifold. Do not touch the valve spindle or attempt to clean the valve disc or seat.
8. Install the new or serviced EGR valve and reconnect the hose, using a new gasket. Check valve operation as described in steps 1–5.
9. Using the special key provided with the Emissions Parts Pack, reset the interval indicator located on the left fire wall under the hood. To do this, remove the grommet from the unit, insert the key in the reset button, and turn it clockwise, watching the odometer, until the odometer reads zero. Remove the key and replace the grommet.

REMOVAL AND INSTALLATION

1. Pull off the top two vacuum lines and lay them aside.
2. Unscrew the two pipe connections and remove the EGR valve.
3. Installation is the reverse of removal.

Running-On Control Valve

This valve is used to prevent engine overrunning (dieseling) when the ignition is turned off. It stops the air flow into the manifold at the absorption canister.

TESTING

1. Check the control valve line fuse.
2. Disconnect the control valve electrical lead at the oil pressure switch.
3. Ground the disconnected lead and if the valve and circuits are normal, the valve will be heard to operate.

Air Temperature Control Valve

An air temperature control valve is used in the carburetor air induction system to direct air, warmed by the exhaust manifold, to the carburetor during the warm-up period and during cold weather. As the engine compartment and the air passing over the valve warms, the valve will automatically move to allow a blend of cool and warm air to enter the carburetor.

TESTING

1. The engine and air cleaner should be cold.
2. The valve plate should be resting against the cold air intake and blocking the passage.
3. Run the engine to normal operating temperature.
4. Observe the valve plate action. The plate should move towards the cool air position to allow the cool and hot air to blend.
5. The valve assembly must be replaced as a unit.

Catalytic Converters

Catalytic converters are used on various models to assist in the reduction of exhaust emissions.

Evaporative Loss Control System

The system is designed to collect fuel vapor from the fuel tank and carburetor float chambers. The vapor is stored in the absorption canister while the engine is stopped, and when the engine is restarted it passes through the crankcase ventilation system and into the combustion chambers. Vapors are drawn into the engine directly when the engine is running. An air bleed chamber is located in the fuel tank to prevent overfilling, and a small separation tank, between the fuel tank and absorption canister, prevents liquid fuel from being drawn into the canister.

The only component of the system that needs servicing is the absorption canister. The filter pad should be replaced at 12,000 mile intervals, and the canister unit should be replaced at 50,000 miles. If the canister becomes saturated with fuel, it must be replaced sooner. Do not attempt to clear the canister with compressed air.

1. To remove the canister, disconnect the lines and loosen the clamp screw, and lift it out.
2. To replace the filter pad, unscrew the lower end cap of the canister.
3. Remove the filter, clean the cap, install a new filter, and replace the end cap.
4. To pressure check the fuel system for leaks, first make sure that there is fuel in the tank and that the fuel system is primed.
5. Disconnect the fuel tank ventilation line from the absorption canister.
6. Connect a low scale pressure gauge between the fuel tank ventilation line and a low pressure air supply (such as a tire pump). Pressurize the system to 1 psi. Do not exceed this pressure at any time. The pressure should not fall below ½ psi over a period of ten seconds. If there is evidence of a leak, check all fuel system components and connections beginning with the fuel filler cap. The cap is not vented and should not

Evaporative loss control system

1. Charcoal adsorption canister
2. Vapor lines
3. Purge lines
4. Restricted connection
5. Sealed oil cap
6. Oil flame trap
7. Fuel pipe
8. Fuel pump
9. Break in control valve
10. Running-on control pipe
11. Running-on control hose
12. Air vent pipe
13. Fuel tank
14. Sealed filler cap
15. Vapor line
16. Vapor tube
17. Capacity limiting tank
18. Separation tank

allow any pressure loss. When the test is completed, remove the fuel filler cap and check that the gauge returns to zero. **Reconnect the fuel tank ventilation line to the canister.**

NOx Control System

The regulation of nitrogen oxide (NOx) emissions is accomplished through slight modifications to engine components, and no special service is necessary. To ensure that the engine is within emission standards, particular attention should be paid to tune-up specifications and procedures.

FUEL EXPANSION

An air chamber is provided within the fuel tank to provide space for fuel expansion during periods of high temperature operation.

FUEL CUT-OFF VALVE

A fuel cut-off valve is fitted in the main fuel line between the fuel filter and the carburetor. Should the vehicle receive an impact or overturn, the valve automatically cuts off the fuel supply to the carburetor. To reset the valve, depress the valve plunger.

FUEL SYSTEM

Mechanical Fuel Pump (Midget)

REMOVAL AND INSTALLATION

All Midgets are equipped with an AC me-

chanical diaphragm type fuel pump on the left side of the engine.

To remove the fuel pump, disconnect fuel inlet and outlet lines.

NOTE: Gasoline will spill on the engine unless precautions are taken.

Unscrew the attaching nuts. The pump will now be free and can be removed.

When installing, make sure that the pump lever (rocker arm) is positioned correctly above its lobe on the cam.

DISASSEMBLY

When removing the diaphragm assembly, turn the assembly 90° counterclockwise before lifting it out of engagement with the link lever. When replacing the inlet and outlet valve assemblies, be sure that the valves are pointed in the proper directions. Fuel pump delivery pressure should be 1½– 2½ pounds per square inch (psi).

——— **CAUTION** ———
Be certain that the fuel lines are snug to the pump, but do not overtighten them.

CLEANING

Every 12,000 miles the fuel pump should be serviced. This may be accomplished by:
1. Removing the top bolt and domed cover.
2. Removing the gauze filter and thoroughly washing it in a safe solvent.
3. Cleaning out the sediment in the fuel bowl with a small screwdriver. The preferred method for removing loosened sediment is compressed air. Wipe out the interior of the fuel bowl with a soft, clean rag.

1. Cover screw
2. Gasket
3. Filter cover
4. Filter cover gasket
5. Filter
6. Upper casting
7. Screw
8. Lockwasher
9. Valve gasket
10. Valve assembly
11. Valve retainer
12. Screw
13. Diaphragm
14. Spring
15. Metal washer
16. Fiber washer
17. Pump body
18. Rocker arm
19. Rocker arm link
20. Rocker arm spring
21. Rocker arm pin
23. Clip
24. Priming lever
25. Spring
26. Gasket

Exploded view of the Midget fuel pump

--- CAUTION ---
The interior of the fuel bowl must be absolutely free of grease or lint.

4. Renew the cork gasket if it is cracked or brittle. Fuel pump parts are delicate; use caution. When reassembling, be sure that the filter gauze is facing down.

TESTING AND ADJUSTMENT

No adjustments may be made to the fuel pump. Before removing and overhauling the old fuel pump, the following test may be made while the pump is still installed on the engine.

--- CAUTION ---
To avoid accidental ignition of fuel during the test, remove the coil high-tension wire from the distributor and the coil.

1. If a fuel pressure gauge is available, connect the gauge to the engine and operate engine until the pressure stops rising. Stop the engine and take the reading. If the reading is within the specifications given in the "Tune-up Specifications" chart, the malfunction is not in the fuel pump. Also check the pressure drop after the engine is stopped.

A large pressure drop below the minimum specification indicates leaky valves. If the pump proves to be satisfactory, check the tank and inlet line.

2. If a fuel pressure gauge is not available, disconnect the fuel line at the pump outlet, place a vessel beneath the pump outlet, and crank the engine. A good pump will force the fuel out of the outlet in steady spurts. A worn diaphragm spring may not provide proper pumping action.

3. As a further test, disconnect and plug the fuel line from the tank at the pump, and hold your thumb over the pump inlet. If the pump is functioning properly, a suction should be felt on your thumb. No suction indicates that the pump diaphragm is leaking, or that the diaphragm linkage is worn.

4. Check the crankcase for gasoline. A ruptured diaphragm may leak fuel into the engine.

Electric Fuel Pump (MGB)

REMOVAL AND INSTALLATION

1. Disconnect the electrical supply and ground wires from the pump, and insulate the supply wire against grounding.

2. Disconnect the fuel lines and the breather pipe (later cars) from the pump and cap the fuel lines.

3. Remove the pump bracket bolts and remove the pump.

4. When installing the pump, make sure that the ground wire makes a good connection and that the breather pipe is correctly routed.

On 1978 and later models, make sure the pump connections are angled as shown in the illustration.

Install fuel pump connections at the angle shown on 1978 and later models

TESTING THE FUEL PUMP ON THE VEHICLE

S.U. electric fuel pumps maintain a low, constant pressure, thus making fuel delivery more even and easing the load on the temperamental carburetor needle and seat units. When fuel pressure drops below a predetermined level the pump will operate (audible as a series of clicks), and when pressure is built up again it will shut itself off.

1. To check pump operation, disconnect the fuel line at the carburetors and switch the ignition on.

2. The pump should be heard to operate and fuel should flow readily from the line.

If it does not, disconnect the output line at the pump and switch the ignition on again. If the pump now operates, the fuel line to the carburetors is blocked and should be cleared with compressed air. If the pump does not operate, disconnect the fuel intake line from the pump and check for a free flow of gasoline from the tank.

3. The line may be cleared, if necessary, with compressed air by pressurizing the gas tank through the tank filler tube.

--- CAUTION ---
Never blow compressed air through the fuel pump, and on vehicles equipped with Evaporative Loss Control systems the fuel lines must never be pressurized unless the absorption canister is disconnected.

If the fuel lines are clear and the pump will not operate, the electrical connections at the pump should be checked.

4. Switch on the ignition and connect a test light between the supply (battery) wire and ground. If it does not light, the pump is not being supplied with electricity. If it does light, check the ground wire con-

* Early pumps
† Delivery air bottle (later pumps)

1. Coil housing
2. Armature spring
3. Impact washer
4. Armature centralizing roller
5. Diaphragm and spindle assembly
6. Set screw
7. Spring washer
8. Ground connector
9. Set screw
10. Rocker mechanism
11. Rocker pivot pin
12. Terminal tag
13. Terminal tag
14. Ground tag
15. Terminal stud
16. Pedestal
17. Spring washer
18. Lead washer
19. Terminal nut
20. End cover seal washer
21. Contact blade
22. Washer
23. Contact blade screw
24. Condenser
25. Condenser clip

26. Spring washer
27. Pedestal screw
28. End cover
29. Shakeproof washer
30. Lucar connector
31. Nut
32. Insulating sleeve
33. Sealing band
34. Vent valve
35. Gasket
36. Pump body
37. Fiber washer
38. Outlet connection
39. Sealing washer
*40. Diaphragm plate
41. Plastic diaphragm barrier   AUF
*42. Rubber diaphragm   300
43. Rubber "O" ring   type
*44. Spring end cap
*45. Diaphragm spring
†46. Delivery flow smoothing
     device cover
47. Set screw
48. Gasket
49. Inlet air bottle cover
50. Dished washer

51. Spring washer ⎫
52. Set screw   ⎪
53. Outlet valve ⎪
54. Valve cap   AUF
55. Filter   300
56. Sealing washer type
57. Inlet valve   ⎪
58. Valve cap   ⎪
59. Clamp plate   ⎪
60. Set screw   ⎭
61. Pump body
62. Fiber washer
63. Outlet connection
64. Filter
65. Washer
66. Plug
67. Inlet valve   ⎫
68. Thin fiber washer   ⎪ HP
69. Outlet valve cage   ⎪ type
70. Outlet valve   ⎬
71. Spring clip   ⎪
72. Medium fiber washer ⎪
73. Outlet connection   ⎭
74. Gasket
75. Sandwich plate

Exploded view of the MGB fuel pump

tinuity by connecting a jumper wire between the ground terminal on the pump and a good chassis ground.

5. If the pump still does not operate, the fault lies in the pump unit itself. Refer to the following section.

SERVICING THE FUEL PUMP

If the pump unit is not operating correctly, remove it from the vehicle.

1. Remove the intake and outlet line fittings from the pump body and remove the small fuel filter (if fitted).

2. Examine the ports for any foreign matter that may be lodged inside.

3. Clean the ports, if necessary, and clean and replace the filter and line fittings.

4. Remove the plastic end-cover by removing the electrical terminal retaining nut and the rubber or tape joint seal.

5. Examine the contact points for burning, and check the contact rotor assembly

movement. If the end-cover was not sealed properly, the contact and rocker assemblies will have been exposed to water and dirt and should be thoroughly cleaned or replaced.

If the contacts are not badly burnt, they may be smoothed with fine sandpaper and cleaned with a non-oily solvent such as an aerosol-type carburetor cleaner.

6. When adjusting the points, make sure that when the outer rocker is pressed onto the pump housing, the contact blade rests

1. Insulator sleeve, retaining nut, connector and washer
2. Joint seal and end-cover
3. Contact blade and retaining screw
4. Contact points should be centered and blade should rest on rib

S.U. electric fuel pump contact points cover and contact blade

1. Pedestal
2. Contact blade
3. Outer rocker
4. Inner rocker
5. Trunnion
6. Housing
A—0.035 in.
B—0.070 in.

Contact points and rocker assembly

on the narrow rib of the pedestal. The contact blade may be bent slightly if necessary.

7. Proper sealing of the plastic end-cover is very important.

8. Check that there are no cracks in it, and, after the cover is installed on the pump, wrap electrical tape around the mating surface of the pump housing and cover.

9. Pump operation should be checked by temporarily connecting the electrical wires and fuel lines to it and switching on the ignition.

10. Allow a few seconds for the pump to prime itself, and check fuel flow at the carburetors.

11. At this point, if the pump is still not operating correctly, the pump unit will have to be replaced. Do not discard the pump, as most MG dealers carry factory rebuilt S.U. fuel pumps instead of new ones (at a considerable savings), and will allow some trade-in on the old unit.

Fuel Filter

On vehicles equipped with the Evaporative Loss Control system an inline filter is located on the fuel feed line to the carburetors. The filter element requires no maintenance, but should be replaced at 12,000 mile intervals.

Carburetors

REMOVAL AND INSTALLATION

150CD4T

1. Remove the air cleaner. Remove the two mounting bolts, and remove the air cleaner cover, gasket, and heat shield.

2. Disconnect: the purge line; the EGR valve flame trap line; the distributor vacuum line flame trap elbow (at the vacuum line coming from the distributor); the distributor vacuum line at the carburetor; the fuel delivery and vapor lines; the two water hoses at the automatic choke; the throttle linkage rod at the carburetor link rod ball joint.

3. Remove the two carburetor securing nuts, and remove the carburetor and insulating gasket.

4. Reverse the removal procedure to install.

175CD5T

1. Disconnect the fuel line at the car-

1. Air valve and diaphragm assembly
2. Damper cap
3. Air valve piston
4. Bottom float chamber plug
6. "O" ring
7. Float chamber to body screws (6)
8. Float chamber and gasket
9. Float and float hinge
10. Inlet needle valve and seat with washer
11. Top cover screws (4)
12. Top cover
13. Piston spring
14. Outer locating tab of air valve diaphragm
15. Diaphragm retaining screws
16. Inner locating tab of air valve diaphragm
17. Needle valve retaining screw (grubscrew)
18. Special tool S-353 for idle air/fuel adjustment
19. Needle valve
20. Idle air regulator cover
21. Idle air regulator retaining screw
22. Idle air regulator and gasket
23. Retaining nut and washer
24. Throttle quadrant and locating plate
25. Choke operating lever retaining nut and washer
26. Choke linkage outer lever, bushing and spring
27. Choke inner lever and spring
28. Choke housing retaining screws
29. Choke housing assembly and gasket
30. Choke water jacket retaining screws
31. Choke water jacket and sealing ring
32. Choke cover retaining screws
33. Choke bi-metal spring assembly
34. Vacuum kick piston cover and gasket
40. Float measurement location

Exploded view of the 175CD5T carburetor (150CD4T similar)

buretor, and the return springs at the throttle cam.

2. Remove the air cleaner and temperature control assembly.

3. Disconnect: the adsorption canister pipe at the carburetor; the PCV line at the carburetor; the EGR valve line at the carburetor; the upper water hose leading to the choke. Loosen the clamp on the lower choke water hose.

4. Remove the mounting nut and washer, and remove the throttle cam.

5. Remove the four nuts and washers securing the carburetor to the manifold, and remove it, disconnecting the lower choke water hose after it is free of the manifold studs.

6. Installation is in reverse order. Install the rear/lower mounting nut and washer first. Refill the cooling system to replace coolant lost from the choke water lines.

THROTTLE LINKAGE ADJUSTMENT

1. Make sure the throttle moves freely.
2. With the accelerator pedal fully depressed, adjust the throttle linkage, if necessary, to open the throttle valve completely.

FLOAT LEVEL ADJUSTMENT

1. Remove the carburetor from the engine and separate the float chamber from the carburetor body.

2. Invert the float body so that the needle valve is held closed by the weight of the float.

3. Measure the distance between the float chamber face and the highest point on the floats. Adjust the top of the floats to 0.625–0.672 inch from the chamber face.

4. Adjust the floats by bending the float tabs or by installing washers under the needle valve and seat assembly.

5. Reassemble the carburetor.

Checking the float level

1. Water jacket
2. Heat mass
3. Insulator
4. Rod-vacuum kick piston
A—$3/32$ in (2.4 mm)
5. Fast idle cam
6. Idle speed screw
7. Throttle stop screw
8. Fast idle pin
B—0.025 in (0.64 mm)

Adjustment of automatic choke and fast idle linkage—175CD5T (150CD4T similar)

AUTOMATIC CHOKE ADJUSTMENT

1. Remove the carburetor. Open the throttle butterfly and wedge it in the open position.

2. Disconnect the choke water lines. Remove the bolt and washer which retain the choke water jacket, and remove the water jacket and sealing ring.

3. Remove the three screws and washers that retain the heat sink, and remove the heat sink and insulator.

4. Rotate the operating arm and:
   a. Check that the vacuum kick piston and rod move freely throughout their normal travel.
   b. Check that the fast idle cam and level move freely.
   c. Move the cam away from the lever and make sure it returns under spring pressure to the lever and remains there when the lever is rotated.

5. Remove the wedge from the throttle. Set the gap between choke and throttle levers to $3/32$ in. with the adjusting screw.

6. Adjust the throttle stop screw located on top of the choke housing, to obtain a clearance of .035 on 150CD4T carburetors, and .025 in. on 175CD5T carburetors,

as measured between the end of the fast idle pin and the cam. Tighten the throttle stop screw locknut.

7. Reinstall the heat sink and choke water jacket. Make sure the thermostatic spring engages the choke arm. Align the marks on the heat sink and choke body, and then tighten the clamp plate screws to 8–10 in. lbs.

8. Install the choke water lines, and then tighten the center bolt to 65–75 in. lbs.

9. Reinstall the carburetor.

OVERHAUL

For overhaul procedures, please refer to "Carburetor Service" in the Unit Repair section.

MANUAL TRANSMISSION

REMOVAL AND INSTALLATION

On all models the engine and transmission are removed as a unit (see "Engine Removal and Installation"). On the Midget, MGB, the transmission can be unbolted from the engine by simply removing the bell housing bolts.

Installation in all cases is in reverse order of removal. On the Midget, MGB, the clutch disc will have to be centered if the clutch assembly has been removed (see "Clutch Removal and Installation").

OVERHAUL

For overhaul procedures, please refer to "Manual Transmission Overhaul" in the Unit Repair section.

CLUTCH

REMOVAL AND INSTALLATION

All Models

1. Remove the engine from the car, and, if the engine and transmission are removed as a unit, separate them. On the Midget, remove the starter motor.

2. Loosen the clutch pressure plate bolts gradually until the spring pressure is released, and remove the pressure plate and disc from the flywheel.

3. Examine the flywheel surface for scoring and signs of overheating. If scored at all, the flywheel should be turned down on a lathe or replaced. If it appears to have

1. Pressure plate
  assembly
2. Spring
3. Release fork retainer
4. Eyebolt
5. Eyebolt nut
6. Release fork pin
7. Strut
8. Release fork
9. Thrust plate
10. Pressure plate
11. Anti-rattle spring
12. Release bearing
13. Retainer
14. Disc
15. Pressure plate
  mounting bolt
16. Lockwasher

Exploded view of the Midget clutch assembly

been overheated (blue discoloration), the surface should be checked for warpage and turned down if necessary. If disc wear is evident, the pressure plate and release bearing, as well as the disc, should be replaced. The pilot bushing in the end of the crankshaft should be checked for wear and replaced if galled or elongated. Lubricate the bushing with a graphite base grease or white grease such as *Molykote*.

4. Upon reinstallation of the disc and pressure plate, the disc must be centered so that the transmission mainshaft will engage the pilot bushing as well as the disc splines. To accomplish this, install the disc and pressure plate on the flywheel with the bolts only finger tight so that the disc can be moved.

5. At this point a dummy transmission mainshaft or clutch aligning tool (available from most tool manufacturers and from MG dealers) should be inserted through the disc hub and into the pilot bushing to hold the disc in position while the pressure plate bolts are tightened.

6. Tighten the bolts gradually and evenly, and remove the centering tool. If a new coil type pressure plate is used, be sure to remove the small U-shaped tabs that keep the spring slightly compressed. The tabs are

used to prevent distortion of the plate, due to its unloaded condition, during storage and shipping.

7. Bolt the transmission back onto the engine if they were removed as a unit; on Midget, install the starter motor, and reinstall the engine in the chassis.

NOTE: If a clutch centering tool is not available it is possible to center the disc by eye, if it is done very carefully. If trouble is experienced in mating the engine and transmission, the indication is that the disc is not centered properly and it should be rechecked.

Clutch Hydraulic System

ADJUSTMENTS

No adjustments to the master or slave cylinder should be attempted.

Master Cylinder

REMOVAL AND INSTALLATION

Midget

To remove the clutch master cylinder, remove the screws securing the mounting bracket cover plate and lift the cover off. Disconnect the pushrod from the clutch pedal. Disconnect the hydraulic line from the clutch master cylinder and cap it. Remove the cylinder mounting bolts and lift the cylinder out.

Installation is in the reverse order of removal. When the hydraulic line has been reconnected, the clutch hydraulic system must be bled.

MGB 1976–77

1. Remove the cover screws and remove the brake/clutch master cylinder cover.

2. Attach a rubber tube to the bleed screw in the slave cylinder. Bleed the system by opening the bleed screw one full turn and depressing the clutch pedal fully and holding. Then close the bleed screw and release the clutch pedal. Repeat the operation until the system is drained.

3. Remove the cotter pin, washer, and clevis pin from the pushrod, and disconnect the clutch pedal lever.

4. Clean the hydraulic pipe connection, disconnect the pipe, and plug the open fitting in the cylinder.

5. Unscrew the mounting bolts and remove the master cylinder from the mounting bracket.

6. Installation is in reverse order. The

1. Pressure plate
  assembly
2. Cover with driving
  struts and springs
3. Pressure plate
4. Strut bolt
5. Clip
6. Locktab
7. Disc
8. Release bearing
9. Bearing retainer clip
10. Pressure plate
  mounting bolt
11. Lockwasher

Exploded view of the MGB clutch assembly

longer bolt goes through the mounting bracket where it is braced. Bleed the system.

MGB 1978 and Later

1. Install a bleed line onto the bleed screw on the clutch slave cylinder, and open the bleed screw.

2. Pump the clutch pedal with the master cylinder cap removed to drain fluid out of the master cylinder.

3. Remove the left hand lower dash panel.

4. Remove the access plug from the firewall.

5. Remove the eight screws, and remove the cover plate and seal from the pedal box.

6. Remove the clevis pin which secures the pushrod to the clutch pedal.

7. Loosen the hydraulic line banjo bolt, unscrew the union, and pull the hydraulic line off the master cylinder.

8. Unscrew the mounting bolts and nuts, and remove the master cylinder from the pedal box. Access to one bolt is from inside the car through the access hole in the dash.

9. To install, reverse the removal procedure and bleed the system.

Slave Cylinder

REMOVAL AND INSTALLATION

On all models, to remove the slave cylinder simply disconnect and cap the hydraulic line, disconnect the pushrod from the clutch release lever, and unbolt and remove the cylinder.

Installation is in reverse order of removal. When the hydraulic line has been reconnected, the clutch hydraulic system must be bled.

MASTER AND SLAVE CYLINDER REBUILDING

Rebuilding kits are available, and usually contain the rubber seals and metal washers. Pistons and springs are available as individual pieces.

When the piston assembly has been re-

Exploded view of the MGB clutch master cylinder

1. Filler cap
2. Reservoir
3. Body
4. Spring
5. Spring retainer
6. Main cup
7. Piston washer
8. Piston
9. Secondary cup
10. Dished washer
11. Circlips
12. Rubber boot
13. Pushrod

Cross-section of the Midget clutch master cylinder

moved from the cylinder, examine the bore. If it is pitted or scored the entire cylinder assembly should be replaced. If bore damage is light it may be honed, but in most cases the repair will not be lasting and the cylinder may begin to leak again after a short time. When honing a cylinder, occasionally dip the hone in clean brake fluid for lubrication.

Whenever a cylinder is disassembled for inspection or rebuilding, the rubber seals should be replaced as a matter of course. Before installing the seals lubricate them thoroughly with brake fluid or the special lubricant that is included in some rebuilding kits. All internal components of the cylinder, especially the bore, must be completely free of dirt and grit or the cylinder may leak or fail to operate properly. When installing the piston and seals into the bore make sure that the seal lips are not turned back as they enter the cylinder. Once the cylinder has been installed on the car the clutch hydraulic system must be bled.

BLEEDING THE CLUTCH HYDRAULIC SYSTEM

The purpose of bleeding the hydraulic system is to expel air that is trapped in the cylinders and lines. Air in the system is what gives the pedal a spongy feel, because air can be compressed while a liquid, for all practical purposes, cannot be. Bleeding is accomplished in the following manner:

1. Fill the master cylinder with brake fluid. (Recheck the fluid level often during bleeding.)

2. Attach a rubber tube to the slave cylinder bleed valve and immerse the other end of the tube in a jar or can containing a small amount of clean brake fluid.

3. With a helper in the car pump the clutch pedal several times until some resistance can be felt, hold the pedal down, and open the bleed valve about ½ turn.

4. With the bleed valve still open, pump the pedal slowly through its full travel several times. Close the bleed valve and check

the pedal for firmness and proper free-play (about 0.5–1.0 in. free-play before the release bearing contacts the pressure plate).

5. If sponginess or excessive free-play indicates that some air is still in the system, it may be necessary to repeat Step 3 until the fluid running from the bleed valve is clear and free of air bubbles.

DRIVE AXLE

Driveshaft

REMOVAL AND INSTALLATION

To remove the driveshaft on the Midget, MGB, mark the U-joint flanges and the transmission and differential flanges (for assembly purposes). Remove the nuts and bolts from the flanges and lower the driveshaft assembly. When reinstalling the driveshaft make sure that the alignment marks on the flanges are positioned correctly.

Universal Joint

REMOVAL, INSTALLATION AND OVERHAUL

NOTE: If only the rear U-joint is to be replaced, unbolt the differential flange from the driveshaft flange and pull the driveshaft out toward the rear of the car to separate the driveshaft at the spline.

After the driveshaft has been removed and the outside surfaces of the U-joints have been cleaned:

1. Remove all four snap-rings retaining the bearing cups. If the ring does not come out, tap the bearing cup lightly to relieve pressure on the ring.

Exploded view of the MGB U-joint

2. Flange yoke
3. Sleeve assembly—yoke
4. Lubricator
8. Journal assembly
9. Bearing assembly —needle
10. Circlip
11. Gasket
12. Retainer—gasket
13. Lubricator journal
14. Bolt—shaft to pinion flange
15. Nut for bolt
16. Spring washer

Exploded view of the Midget U-joint

2. Tap the flange and driveshaft yokes with a hammer until one of the bearings begins to come out. If difficulty is experienced, use a small screwdriver to tap the bearings out from the inside. Repeat this operation until all four bearing cups and their rollers have been removed.

3. Thoroughly clean the flange and driveshaft yokes.

4. Fill the reservoir holes in the spider journals with grease (sealed joints without grease fittings).

5. Fill the bearing cups to a depth of

⅛ in. with grease and install the needle rollers in the cups.

6. Install the seals on the spider journals (sealed joints).

7. Position the spider inside the flange yoke and install the bearings and snap-rings. Place the spider inside the driveshaft yoke and install the remaining two bearings and snap-rings.

NOTE: Make sure that the grease fittings on joints so equipped face away from the flanges, toward the center of the driveshaft.

8. Lubricate the joint with a grease gun (early type with grease fitting).

9. Check the joint for freedom of movement. If it binds, tap it lightly with a soft-metal or wooden hammer to relieve pressure from the bearing cups on the ends of the journals.

10. Remove any surplus grease from the joint and replace the driveshaft.

1. Case assembly
2. Gear carrier stud
3. Bearing retaining nut
4. Gear carrier to axle case nut
5. Spring washer
6. Washer

7. Breather assembly
8. Drain plug
9. Gear carrier joint
10. Carrier assembly
11. Bearing cap stud
12. Plain washer
13. Spring washer
14. Nut
15. Filler plug
16. Differential bearing
17. Bearing packing washer
18. Differential cage
19. Differential gear
20. Thrust washer
21. Differential pinion
22. Thrust washer
23. Pinion pin
24. Pinion peg
25. Ring gear and pinion
26. Bolt
27. Lockwasher
28. Pinion thrust washer
29. Inner pinion bearing
30. Bearing spacer
31. Pinion outer bearing
32. Oil seal
33. Dust cover
34. Universal joint flange
35. Pinion nut
36. Spring washer
37. Hub assembly
38. Wheel stud
39. Nut
40. Oil seal
41. Hub bearing
42. Oil seal ring
43. Hub shaft joint
44. Axle shaft
45. Screw
46. Bumper
47. Axle shaft
48. Hub assembly Wire
49. Wheel stud   wheels
50. Hub extension only
51. Welch plug

Exploded view of the Midget rear axle

Axle Shaft

REMOVAL AND INSTALLATION

Midget

1. Raise the rear of the vehicle and support it under the springs.
2. Release the parking brake and back off the brake adjusters if the wheel does not spin freely.
3. Remove the brake drum retaining screws and remove the drum.

If wire wheels:

1. Remove the nuts which secure the axle hub to the splined wheel hub.
2. Remove this splined wheel hub, and withdraw the axle shaft, gasket, and O-ring.

If disc wheels:

1. Remove the axle shaft retaining screws and withdraw the axle and gasket.
2. Installation is in reverse order of removal. Always use a new gasket and O-ring (wire wheels). Adjust the brakes if necessary after the wheels have been installed.

MGB Tube-type Axle 1976–77

The tube-type axle has been used on the MGB since 1967, and on the MGB-GT since its introduction. The tube-type axle is semi-floating, with hypoid ring and pinion gearset. The axle shafts and the pinion oil seal can be removed with the drive axle in place.

NOTE: The GT uses stronger springs which should not be used on the convertible except in axle pairs.

1. Raise the rear of the car and remove the wheel.
2. Back off the brake adjuster if the brake drum will not spin freely, and remove the drum.
3. Remove the cotter pin and unscrew the axle shaft nut. Remove the wheel hub.
4. Disconnect the parking brake cable and hydraulic line, and remove the backing plate. Plug the hydraulic line.
5. Remove the oil seal collar, bearing cap, and oil seal from the axle shaft.
6. Attach a slide hammer to the hub and remove it. Remove the axle shaft.
7. Installation is the reverse of removal. The oil seal should be replaced at this time; also the brakes should be bled and adjusted after the drums have been installed.

MGB Tube-type 1978–80

1. Support the car securely just in front of the rear spring front shackle.
2. Remove the wheel. Remove the cotter pin, nut, and collar (3) which retain the brake drum.
3. Remove the brake drum (4) and drive flange with a special hub remover.
4. Remove the cotter pin, and remove the pin (5) securing the handbrake cable to the lever on the backing plate.

Exploded view of the 1978–80 MGB axle shaft

5. Disconnect and plug the hydraulic line (6) from the brake cylinder.
6. Unscrew the four bolts and nuts (7), and remove the backing plate.
7. Remove the bearing cap (8) and oil seal (9).
8. Remove the axle shaft (10) with an impact tool.
9. If the axle shaft bearing (11) is to be replaced, it must be pressed on via the center of the bearing and packed with an approved wheel bearing lubricant.
10. In installation:
   a. Coat joining surfaces of the bearing cap and axle housing with a locking compound.
   b. Tighten axle shaft nut to 150 ft. lbs.
   c. Bleed brakes and check rear axle fluid level.

Differential

REMOVAL AND INSTALLATION

MGB

The removal of the differential unit requires a special tool to stretch the axle case and even with this tool it is very easy to permanently damage the case while using the tool. For these reasons, removal and installation of the differential should be left to an MG dealer.

Midget

1. Drain the drive axle.
2. Remove the axle shafts as previously described.
3. Mark the flanges and disconnect the driveshaft from the differential.
4. Remove the nuts securing the differential assembly to the drive axle and withdraw the complete assembly.
5. Installation is in reverse order of removal. Always use a new gasket, and make sure that the differential and drive axle mating surfaces are clean.

DISASSEMBLY

1. Mark and remove the housing caps, and withdraw the differential cage.
2. Remove the bearings and shims from the cage.
3. Bend back the locktabs, remove the ring gear bolts, and remove the ring gear.
4. Drive out the dowel pin which locates the pinion shaft. The pin is 1/8 in. in diameter, and it must be driven out from the ring gear side of the differential cage.
5. Remove the pinions and thrust washers. Remove the pinion nut, drive flange, and end-cover.
6. Drive the pinion shaft toward the rear through the carrier. It will carry with it the inner race and rollers of the rear bearing.
7. Remove the inner race of the front bearing and the oil seal.
8. Remove the bearing outer races using a puller.
9. Slide off the pinion sleeve and shims.
10. Remove the rear bearing inner race, the spacer, and the bearing outer race.

ASSEMBLY

If no components other than the oil seal have been replaced, assembly is in reverse order of disassembly. Note that the thrust face of the differential bearings are marked with the word THRUST.

If any gears or bearings have been replaced see "Differential Gear Adjustment."

ADJUSTMENTS

Pinion Depth Adjustment

Pinion depth adjustment is an adjustment of the pinion mounting distance D. In the absence of special factory tools for measuring this distance the pinion can be accurately positioned by taking note of the markings on the original and replacement pinions and using suitable shims behind the pinion head. A number with a plus or minus sign is etched into the pinion head C, which is the deviation (in thousandths of an inch) of pinion head thickness from nominal. If there is not an etched number on the pinion head the pinion is of nominal thickness. If, for example, the old pinion is marked -2 and the new pinion is marked -2, the same shims may be used behind the pinion head. If, however, the new pinion is marked -5 a shim or combination of shims 0.003 in. thick must be added as compensation. Therefore, if the new pinion is undersized as compared to the old one, shims must be added, and if the new pinion is oversized shim thickness must be decreased proportionately.

Pinion Bearing Preload

Preload adjustment is automatically made by the collapsible spacer when the differential drive flange nut is tightened. *It is of extreme importance that the nut is not overtightened.* See "Pinion Oil Seal Replacement" under the applicable model section for tightening procedures and torque values. The collapsible spacer should be replaced whenever the differential is disassembled.

Preload and ring gear mesh adjustment

Differential Bearing Preload and Ring Gear Mesh Adjustment

Bearing preload and mesh adjustment can be made simultaneously by first measuring total differential end-play, using a dial indicator to determine shim thickness needed. Either the ring or pinion must be removed to accurately measure end-play. To this measurement must be added 0.004 in., which is the amount of pinch needed to properly preload the bearings (all models).

1. With both gears in position, shift the differential assembly to one side so that the gap at Y is reduced to zero, and measure ring gear backlash with a dial indicator.
2. From the measurement obtained,

Checking ring gear backlash

subtract the correct backlash figure, which is etched into the rear face of the ring gear. This will give the shim thickness required at Y. Subtract this figure from A $+0.004$ in., and the remainder will be shim thickness required.

If the above calculations have been done correctly, backlash should be within specification and the ring gear should be meshing properly with the pinion gear.

3. Gear mesh can be checked by painting the ring gear teeth with red lead or machinist's blue dye and rotating the gear to obtain a mesh pattern. If correction is necessary do not alter the total number of shims (total thickness), but increase or decrease thickness as needed.

REAR SUSPENSION

Springs

REMOVAL AND INSTALLATION

Midget

1. Raise and support the car as above.
2. Remove the wheels.
3. From inside the car remove the bolts which secure the spring anchor bracket to the body.
4. From beneath the car remove the two front bracket bolts.
5. Remove the four U-bolt nuts and the shock absorber anchor plate.
6. Remove the rear shackle nuts, pins, and plates, and remove the spring.
7. Installation is in reverse order of removal. The axle limit strap may be removed to facilitate U-bolt installation.

1. Main leaf assembly	10. Plate	19. Pad	28. Washer
2. Bushing	11. Plate	20. Bracket	29. Bolt
3. Second leaf	12. Bushing	21. Bolt	30. Nut
4. Locating bolt	13. Nut	22. Nut	31. Washer
5. Spacer	14. Washer	23. Washer	32. Bumper
6. Nut	15. Clip	24. Strap	33. Clip
7. Locknut	16. Nut	25. Spacer	34. Pad
8. Clip	17. Pedestal	26. Nut	35. Strip
9. Clip	18. Plate	27. Washer	

Exploded view of the rear suspension—typical of all models

Tighten the spring bolt fully after the car is lowered and the spring is loaded.

MGB

1. Remove the wheel adjacent to the spring that is to be removed.

2. Raise and support the body and support the axle with a hydraulic jack to enable the axle to be lowered to relieve tension in the spring.

3. Disconnect the shock absorber link from its bracket and the rebound strap from the rebound spindle.

4. Remove the nuts and spring washers from the eyebolt and shackle plate pins and take off the outer shackle plate.

5. Using a small prybar, tap each shackle plate pin alternately until the plate and pins are free of the spring and mounting bracket.

6. Remove the eyebolt from the front of the spring.

7. Remove the locknuts and nuts from the two U-bolts. Remove the shock absorber bracket, locating plate, and pad which will fall from the under side of the spring.

8. Remove the spring, the upper locating plate pad, pedestal, and U-bolts.

9. Installation is the reverse of removal.

Shock Absorber

REMOVAL AND INSTALLATION

1. To remove a rear shock absorber simply disconnect the connecting link arm from the shock lever and unbolt the unit. Shock absorbers should be replaced in axle sets (pairs).

2. If a new shock absorber appears to operate erratically, allow the hydraulic fluid a few minutes to become deaerated.

FRONT SUSPENSION

Springs

REMOVAL AND INSTALLATION

1. Removal of a front spring requires a spring compressor. Once the spring is slightly compressed the spring seat can be unbolted and the spring withdrawn. If a spring compressor is not available, remove two of the spring seat mounting bolts as shown and substitute two long slave bolts that will allow the spring to expand slowly when unbolted evenly (Midget only).

2. If the car is equipped with an anti-sway bar, before removing the spring, the sway bar must be unbolted from the side linkage.

3. Installation is in reverse order of removal.

Shock Absorbers

REMOVAL AND INSTALLATION

1. Place a jack under the lower wishbone and raise the wheel.

2. Remove the top kingpin pivot bolt and swing the wheel down, taking care not to strain the brake line.

Spring removal

NOTE: The clamp bolt must be removed before the pivot bolt can be withdrawn.

3. Unbolt and remove the shock absorber unit.

4. Installation is in reverse order of removal.

Kingpin

REMOVAL AND INSTALLATION

1. Place a jack under the lower wishbone and raise and remove the wheel.

2. Disconnect the tie rod from the steering arm.

3. Unbolt the brake caliper and support it clear of the hub.

4. Remove the hub and brake disc.

5. Remove the top kingpin pivot bolt and swing the stub axle down.

6. On the Midget, remove the nut from the lower pivot locating pin and drive the pin completely out. Unscrew the pivot end plug (core plug on later models) and unscrew the pivot using a screwdriver.

7. On the MGB, unscrew the nut from the lower pivot bolt and remove the bolt.

8. Withdraw the stub axle and kingpin assembly from the lower control arm.

9. Unscrew the nut from the top of the stub axle and kingpin assembly and remove the kingpin, washers, and seals.

10. Press the bushings out from the bottom of the axle.

11. Install the new bushings, taking care that the open end of the oil groove enters first and that the hole in the bushing is in line with the lubrication channel in the axle.

12. On the MGB the bushings must be line-bored after installation (most machine shops can perform this operation).

The bushings should be machined to these dimensions:

MGB—top bushing: 0.7815–0.7820 in.; bottom bushing: 0.9075–0.9080 in.

13. On the Midget the kingpin bushings do not require reaming. However, the kingpin should be lubricated and installed to check the fit. If it takes excessive effort to rotate the kingpin, the bushing surfaces may be refinished using a brake cylinder hone.

14. Install the kingpin in the axle body along with the washers and seals, as removed, and tighten the nut.

15. Lubricate the bushings via the grease fittings using a high pressure grease gun, and check the resistance of the kingpin to rotation. If it is excessively stiff, remove the nut and substitute a thinner floating thrust washer (MGB) or a thicker adjustment washer (Midget).

From this point on, installation is in reverse order of removal.

Upper Control Arm

REMOVAL AND INSTALLATION

The upper wishbone is formed by the shock absorber lever. See ''Shock Absorber Removal and Installation.''

Lower Control Arm

REMOVAL AND INSTALLATION

1. Raise the front of the car and remove the wheel.

2. Remove the spring.

3. Disconnect the tie rod from the steering arm.

4. Remove the lower kingpin pivot. On the Midget it is necessary to remove the locating pin and pivot bolt end cap before the pivot can be unscrewed.

5. Swivel the stub axle and hub assembly up slightly and support it.

6. Unbolt the wishbone pivot bracket and remove the wishbone.

Rear half of the control arm

Exploded view of the MGB front suspension

1. Crossmember
2. Bolt
3. Pad
4. Pad
5. Plate
6. Nut
7. Washer
8. Shock absorber
9. Bolt
10. Lockwasher
11. Pivot bolt
12. Bushing
13. Nut
14. Spring
15. Plate
16. Bolt
17. Nut
18. Lockwasher
19. Spring pan assembly
20. Wishbone assembly

21. Bolt
22. Bolt
23. Nut
24. Lockwasher
25. Spacer
26. Thrust washer
27. Seal
28. Support
29. Nut
30. Bolt
31. Nut
32. Lockwasher
33. Pivot bracket
34. Bolt
35. Nut
36. Lockwasher
37. Bushing
38. Washer
39. Nut
40. Buffer

41. Spacer
42. Bolt
43. Bolt
44. Lockwasher
45. Nut
46. Kingpin
47. Bushing
48. Setscrew
49. Stub axle assembly
50. Bushing
51. Bushing
52. Grease fitting
53. Seal
54. Spacer
55. Spring
56. Spacer
57. Thrust washer
58. Floating thrust washer—.052 to .057 in.
59. Trunnion—suspension link.

60. Nut
61. Grease fitting
62. Steering arm
63. Bolt
64. Hub assembly
65. Stud
66. Nut
67. Hub assembly
68. Collar
69. Oil seal
70. Bearing
71. Spacer
72. Shim—.003 in.
73. Bearing
74. Washer
75. Nut
76. Grease cap
77. Collar

Adjustments

Front suspension geometry is preset and nonadjustable.

STEERING

Steering Wheel

REMOVAL AND INSTALLATION

Cars With Plastic Steering Wheel Rims (Except Below)

1. Pry off the steering wheel hub emblem housing. On some models the horn button is released after three small set-screws in the steering wheel hub are loosened.

2. Remove the wheel retaining nut.

3. Mark the steering shaft and hub to facilitate correct installation and remove the wheel. It may be necessary to use a puller if the wheel does not come off easily.

4. Installation is in reverse order of removal. Make sure that the steering wheel is centered when the front wheels are straight ahead. The steering wheel nut in all cases should be tightened to 40 ft. lbs.

Cars With Leather Covered or Wood Steering Wheel Rims (Except Below)

1. Pry off the steering wheel hub emblem housing.

2. Bend back the locktabs, remove the wheel retaining bolts, and remove the wheel.

3. Installation is in reverse order of re-moval. The retaining bolts should be tightened to 12–17 ft. lbs.

1978–80 MGB

1. Put the steering wheel in the straight ahead position and remove the hub cover.

2. Remove the wheel retaining nut. Match mark the hub of the wheel and the inner column so the wheel may be reinstalled in the same position.

3. Using a wheel puller, pull the wheel off the column.

NOTE: Do not tap on the wheel or column to remove the wheel—this can damage the collapsible column.

4. With the wheels still in the straight ahead position, set the cancelling cam so the ridge faces the direction signal lever.

5. Install the steering wheel, making sure the tabs engage the slots in the cancelling cam.

6. Torque the steering wheel nut to 28 ft. lbs. Install the hub cover.

Turn Signal Switch

REPLACEMENT

Midget and MGB through 1977

Unfasten the screws that hold the halves of the steering column shroud together. Remove both halves, except on the late MGB models, on which it is necessary only to remove the left (turn signal side) of the shroud.

Disconnect the snap connector (underneath the instrument panel) and remove the screws that mount the switch. Withdraw the switch assembly.

Installation is the reverse of removal.

MGB 1978 and Later

1. Loosen the three bolts which hold the steering column in place at the firewall.

NOTE: In the next step, the bolts holding the column to the underside of the dash must be removed. Column alignment is obtained through use of various numbers of washers used on these bolts. When removing the bolts, do not allow bolts and washers to be separated, or, alternatively, count and record the number of washers attached to each bolt. If washers are not replaced in original position, column misalignment and steering problems will result.

2. Support the column and remove column-to-dash mounting bolts.

3. Unscrew the bolts holding the halves

1. Rack housing	23. Ball housing (male)	45. Setscrew	67. Draught excluder
2. Rack	24. Ball socket assembly	46. Setscrew	68. Steering wheel
3. Damper pad	25. Boot	47. Plain washer	69. Nut
4. Damper pad spring	26. Clip	48. Spring washer	70. Lockwasher
5. Damper pad housing	27. Ring	49. Outer column	71. Steering column lock
6. Shim	28. Plain washer	50. Inner column tube	72. Shear bolt
7. Secondary damper pad	29. Nut	51. Felt bearing (top)	73. Locating screw
8. Secondary damper spring	30. Locknut	52. Felt bearing (bottom)	74. Lock key
9. Secondary damper housing	31. Lock washer	53. Felt bearing (bottom)	75. Steering wheel
10. Housing washer	32. Seal	54. Clip	76. Steering wheel nut
11. Pinion	33. Clip (inner)	55. Bolt	77. Badge
12. Pinion tail bearing	34. Clip (outer)	56. Nut	78. Nut
13. Shim	35. Lubricator	57. Bracket	79. Set screw
14. Setscrew	36. Lubricator	58. Bracket cap	80. Locking ring
15. Spring washer	37. Dished washer	59. Shim	81. Slip-ring
16. Pinion thrust washer (top)	38. Fiber washer	60. Setscrew	82. Steering wheel boss
17. Pinion thrust washer (bottom)	39. Retainer	61. Plain washer	83. Steering wheel
18. Pinion seal	40. Bracket and cap assembly	62. Spring washer	84. Horn contact
19. Tie-rod	41. Setscrew	63. Seating	85. Lock-ring
20. Ball housing (female)	42. Spring washer	64. Setscrew	86. Horn push
21. Ball seat	43. Seating	65. Plain washer	
22. Shim	44. Packing	66. Spring washer	

77. Badge — Midget Mk. III (GAN5)
83. Steering wheel — From car number Midget Mk. III (GAN5) 89515

Midget steering gear components

of the column cover together. Remove the attaching screw for the left-hand cowl and remove the cowl. Remove the indicator/wiper switch.

4. Installation is the reverse of removal, but make sure steering column-to-dash bolts are shimmed as discussed in the note above and torqued to 15 ft. lbs.

Steering Gear

REMOVAL AND INSTALLATION

Midget

1. Remove the radiator and turn the steering wheel to the straight ahead position with the slot of the column clamp uppermost. Remove the wheels.

2. Remove the nuts from the tie rod assemblies and detach the tie rod assemblies from the steering levers.

3. Remove the steering column "U" bolt and the three toe plate bolts.

4. Loosen the three steering column upper retaining bolts and pull the column back enough to disengage the sleeve from the pinion.

5. Mark the steering rack housing in relation to the mounting bracket to assist when replacing.

6. Remove the clamps and bolts from the mounting brackets and withdraw the steering rack assembly.

To install:

7. Position the rack on the mounting brackets and install the clamps, but do not tighten the clamp bolts.

8. Make sure that the rack is in the straight ahead position with the pinch bolt flat on the top of the pinion shaft.

9. Check that the column is in the straight ahead position with the slot of the clamp at the top.

10. Slide the column over the pinion shaft

MGB steering gear components

1. Housing assembly	23. Ball seat	45. Circlip
2. Bushing	24. Thrust spring	46. Bolt
3. Seal	25. Housing	47. Nut
4. Rack	26. Locknut	48. Lockwasher
5. Yoke	27. Seal	49. Column assembly—inner
6. Damper	28. Clip	50. Column assembly—inner—R.H.D.
7. Spring	29. Clip	51. Column tube
8. Shim	30. Socket assembly	52. Column tube—R.H.D.
9. Gasket	31. Boot	53. Bearing
10. Cover plate	32. Retainer	54. Bearing
11. Bolt	33. Spring	55. Bushing (felt)
12. Lockwasher	34. Washer	56. Clip
13. Pinion	35. Nut	57. Steering wheel
14. Grease fitting	36. Locknut	58. Nut
15. Pinion bearing	37. Bolt	59. Clamp
16. Nut	38. Nut	60. Spacer
17. Lockwasher	39. Lockwasher	61. Bolt
18. End cover	40. Steering column U-joint	62. Washer
19. Gasket	41. Yoke	63. Lockwasher
20. Bolt	42. Journal assembly	64. Nut
21. Lockwasher	43. Seal	65. Bracket
22. Tie-rod	44. Retainer	66. Plate

67. Nut
68. Lockwasher
69. Boot
70. Lock assembly—steering and ignition
71. Key
72. Shim
73. Rivet
74. Bushing locating screw
75. Bushing
76. Wheel hub
77. Steering wheel
78. Ring
79. Bolt
80. Nut
81. Emblem housing
82. Wheel hub
83. Steering wheel
84. Ring
85. Bolt
86. Horn push contact
87. Horn push
When steering lock is fitted.
1970 and later cars.

as far as it will go; then tighten the three toe plate bolts.

11. Turn the steering wheel one complete turn to the left and right; check that the marks made in the removal section, Step 5, are aligned, and tighten the clamp bolts.

12. Tighten the steering column "U" bolt to 9–12 ft. lbs.

13. Reverse the procedure in Steps 1 and 2.

MGB

1. Disconnect the batteries and take the air cleaners off the carburetors.

2. Turn the steering wheel so that the wheels point straight ahead.

3. Mark the inner steering column and the universal joint to ensure correct alignment when reinstalling.

4. Remove the pinch bolt and nut securing the universal joint to the steering column.

5. Disconnect the multi-connector block; disconnect the wiring from the ignition switch.

6. Remove the bolts retaining the steering column upper and lower support clamp brackets; note the location, quantity, and thickness of the packing washers between the column upper fixing flanges and the body brackets. Remove the washers.

NOTE: If the packing washers are mislaid or their installed positions not recorded, the steering must be aligned when the column is refitted.

7. Remove the steering column complete with outer tube, steering wheel, direction indicator and ignition/steering lock switch.

Installation is the reverse of removal but note the following:

8. Check that the steering rack is in the straight ahead position.

9. Check that the steering column is in the straight ahead position.

10. Note that in Steps 1 and 4–8, the outer tube is installed to the steering column with the gaitered end towards the floor board. In Step 3, ensure that the marks align when installing the inner column to the universal joint.

To align the steering column:

11. Remove the three bolts from the steering column retaining plate near the firewall.

12. Install the rack assembly with the shims that were originally removed and check, by pushing and pulling, that the column slides reasonably freely over the steering rack pinion shaft. If the column is stiff, shims may be added or removed from behind the rack or the steering column support bracket.

ADJUSTMENTS

No adjustments are possible.

Steering/Ignition Lock Switch

REMOVAL AND INSTALLATION

Midget and MGB through 1977

1. Remove the steering column, along with the steering wheel and center hub.

2. Remove the combined turn signal-high beam switch.

3. Remove the turn signal lever from the inner column.

4. Loosen the top lock bracket and slide it off the steering column, turn the key to the unlocked position.

5. Drill out the retaining shear bolts, remove the positioning screw, and remove the lock.

6. Installation is the reverse of removal.

1978 and Later MGB

1. Lower the steering column as described in Steps 1 and 2 of the "Direction Signal Switch Removal and Installation" procedure above. Unscrew and remove right hand switch cover.

2. Disconnect the ignition switch connector and remove the tape holding the cable onto the column.

3. Drill the shear bolts out of the clamp plate.

4. Remove the lock and clamp plate. Remove the screw which holds the switch in the lock, and remove the switch.

5. Position the lock body over the slot in the outer steering column and install the clamp plate, tightening the shear bolts *only* hand-tight.

6. Reconnect ignition switch connector, and then test ignition lock and switch *thoroughly* to ensure they function correctly in every way.

7. Tighten shear bolts until heads break off.

8. Reinstall cowl right-hand cover, and reinstall steering column as described in the last step of the "Direction Signal Switch Removal and Installation" procedure above.

BRAKE SYSTEMS

For all brake system repair and service procedures not detailed below, please refer to "Brakes" in the Unit Repair section.

Adjustment

While turning wheel, rotate adjuster clockwise until shoes lock the drum, then turn back slightly until wheel rotates freely.

Master Cylinder

REMOVAL AND INSTALLATION

Midget

1. Disconnect H.T. wire from ignition coil. Disconnect white/blue lead from the connector.

2. Remove the four cover plate mounting screws, and remove the plate and coil.

3. Remove cotter pin, and washer, and disconnect linkage at clevis pin.

4. Unscrew all hydraulic connections and plug master cylinder and pipe connections.

1. Filler cap	7. Main cup	13. Pinion washer	19. Stop washer
2. Plastic reservoir	8. Spring	14. Circlip	20. Washer
3. Reservoir seals	9. Piston link	15. Cup	21. Spacer
4. Main cup	10. Pin	16. Circlip	22. Spring
5. Piston washer	11. Pin retainer	17. Piston	23. Pushrod
6. Piston	12. Main cup	18. Spring retainer	24. Retainer ring

Cross-section of the dual master cylinder

5. Unbolt the master cylinder from the pedal box, being careful to retain all bolts, nuts, and washers.

6. Install in reverse order, and completely bleed the system.

MGB

1. Siphon the fluid from the reservoir or pump the fluid out the front brake bleed screw by opening the front brake bleed and pumping the brake pedal.

2. Disconnect warning light wiring.

3. Disconnect the secondary feed pipe, which enters the cylinder at an angle from below on the left side.

4. Disconnect the primary lines, which enter the cylinder on the left side horizontally. Plug both secondary lines and both secondary cylinder ports.

5. Remove the two nuts and lockwashers, and remove the master cylinder from the brake booster.

6. Reverse the removal procedure to install and bleed the system.

Power Brakes Booster

REMOVAL AND INSTALLATION

British Leyland recommends that the brake booster is to be replaced as a unit if trouble is experienced. A Lockheed Type 6 booster is used on the MGB.

To remove the booster, first disconnect the hydraulic line(s) from the master cylinder and disconnect the vacuum line from the booster. Then simply unbolt and remove the booster and master cylinder as an assembly. Upon reinstallation the brakes must be bled.

Wheel Bearings

REMOVAL, INSTALLATION AND ADJUSTMENT

Midget

1. Raise and support the front of the car.

2. Remove the wheel.

3. Remove the brake pads.

4. Remove and support the caliper out of the way.

5. Remove the grease cap, cotter pin and hub nut.

6. Cars using pressed (solid) wheels, remove the hub with tool 18G304 and adapters. Cars with wire wheels, use tool 18G1032.

7. Remove the outer bearing from the hub and hammer out the race with a drift. Remove the inner bearing and race in a like manner.

8. Pack the new bearings with grease so that the grease protrudes from the bearings.

9. Drive the races into place and install the bearings and grease seal.

10. Pack the hub recess with grease and install the hub on the spindle.

11. Tighten the hub bolt to 46 ft. lbs. and align the cotter pin hole by tightening, if necessary, the nut.

12. Assemble remaining parts in reverse of removal.

MGB

1. Raise and support the front of the car.

2. Remove and support the caliper out of the way.

3. Remove the grease cap, cotter pin and nut.

4. On cars with solid wheels, remove the hub with tool 18G304 and adapters. On cars with wire wheels, use tool 18G363.

5. From the hub, remove the bearing retaining washer, outer bearing, shims, spacer, inner bearing, oil seal collar and oil seal.

6. If necessary, the races may be hammered out with a drift.

7. Install new races, if necessary.

8. Pack each bearing with grease until it squeezes out.

9. Fill the cavity between the bearing and the oil seal with grease and lightly grease the spacer.

10. Assemble hub parts, minus the shims, and install hub on spindle.

11. Install the retaining washer and nut and tighten the nut until the bearings bind.

12. Remove the nut and hub and pull the outer race.

13. Install enough shims to produce excessive end-play with a dial gauge. Reduce the number of shims to give an end-play of 0.002–0.004''.

14. When desired end-play is attained, tighten the nut to 40–70 ft. lbs., aligning the cotter pin hole.

15. Install a new cotter pin. Install remaining parts.

Parking Brake Cable

ADJUSTMENT

Adjustment can be made at the brake balance lever where the main parking brake cable splits into separate cables for each rear wheel, underneath the car near the axle. Adjust the cable so that the brake is fully applied when the lever is pulled up four or five notches. Some cars have grease fittings on the cables and balance lever pivot, and these points must be lubricated regularly to prevent brake drag.

REMOVAL AND INSTALLATION

Midget

1. Raise and support the rear of the car at the axle.

2. Disconnect the battery ground.

3. Remove the driver's seat.

4. Unbolt the handbrake lever from the mounting plate.

5. Remove the warning switch wires.

6. Unbolt the mounting plate from the tunnel and rotate it 180°.

7. Pull the handbrake lever away from the tunnel and remove the cotter pin and clevis.

8. Remove and separate the handbrake lever and mounting plate.

9. Remove the cotter pin, washer and clevis pin from the equalizer lever.

10. Free the cable rear adjustment nut and slide it along the cable.

11. Remove the threaded sleeve and cable from the equalizer.

12. Remove the cable front locknut and remove the cable from the front bracket and tunnel.

13. Installation is the reverse of removal. Use new cotter pins.

MGB

1. Raise and support the car.

2. Remove the adjusting nut and remove the cable end from the lower end of the lever.

3. Remove the nut securing the lever to the spindle and remove the spring washer, forked lever and plain washer. Remove the lever.

4. Remove the right side seat.

5. Disconnect the brake switch wiring.

6. Unbolt the ratchet plate from the tunnel.

7. Remove the nut and spring washer securing the outer to the bracket.

8. Remove the clips securing the cable assembly to the body axle.

9. Remove the bolt, nut and spring washer securing the two halves of the compensating lever.

10. Completely loosen the self-locking nut securing the lever to the axle bracket and release the cable bracket trunnion from the lever.

11. Remove the cotter pins and clevis pins to release the cable yokes from the levers on the backing plates.

12. Replacement is the reverse of removal.

CHASSIS ELECTRICAL

Heater Blower

REMOVAL AND INSTALLATION

Midget

1. Remove the battery. Remove the battery tray.

2. Disconnect the bottom radiator hose to drain the cooling system.

3. Disconnect fan motor wires at the connectors.

4. Disconnect the control cable by removing the bolt holding it to the air intake tube. Loosen the bolt on the air intake flap lever and pull the inner cable out of the clamp on the lever.

5. Pull the air intake hose off the tube on the heating unit.

6. Disconnect the two heater hoses at the core.

7. Remove the six screws that fasten the unit to the firewall. Pull the clip that holds the water temperature capillary tube in place aside.

8. Remove the heater unit from the car.

9. Turn the unit so as to drain the heater core.

10. Remove the five spring clips and pull the heater cover off the unit, being careful not to damage the seal. Pull the heater core out of the heater unit.

11. Remove the three screws which hold the fan and motor to the heater unit, and remove the fan and motor.

12. Note the position of the fan on the motor spindle. Then, remove the retaining clip, and gently tap the motor spindle out of the fan.

13. Install in reverse order, applying sealer to the heater cover seal.

MGB

The heater blower is part of the heater assembly, mounted in the rear of the engine compartment, adjacent to the firewall. To remove the blower, disconnect the batteries, separate the leads at the snap connectors, and remove the three blower mounting bolts.

Install in the reverse order of removal.

Heater Core

REMOVAL AND INSTALLATION

Midget

Follow steps 1–10 of the blower removal and installation procedure.

MGB

The heater core is located in the heater box, in the rear of the engine compartment, adjacent to the firewall.

1. To remove the heater core, it is necessary to remove the heater assembly as follows:

2. Disconnect the heater valve control cable (if the valve is mounted on the heater box).

3. Separate the blower motor leads at the snap connectors.

4. Drain the cooling system, and remove the water hoses from the heater unit.

5. Remove the screws which retain the heater box in the engine compartment.

6. Remove the center console (speaker panel).

7. Remove the defroster hose plate and pull the defroster tubes out of the heater box.

8. Remove the heater trim panel and loosen the clip which retains the air control cable.

9. Remove the heater air control from the dash panel, disconnect the control cable from it, and lift out the heater assembly.

10. To remove the core from the heater box, pry off the spring clips which retain the front panel to the assembly.

11. Assemble and install in the reverse order of disassembly and removal. Following installation, bleed the heater in the same manner as described for the Midget.

Radio

The radios used in MGs are dealer installed or aftermarket units. It is therefore impossible to give specific procedures for these radios. The following information applies generally to all radios installed in MGs.

Care should be exercised during installation to prevent reversing the ground and power leads. Reversal of the leads will result in serious damage to the radio. The power lead may be identified by an in-line fuse holder. The ground lead is not fused.

Should the speaker require replacement, it must be replaced with one of the same impedance. A speaker of the proper impedance must also be used during initial radio installation (consult the radio manual). Failure to observe proper impedance can result in rapid transistor failure.

— **CAUTION** —
Never operate a radio without load (no speaker), or with the speaker leads shorted together. This will result in transistor failure.

Windshield Wiper Motor

REMOVAL AND INSTALLATION

Midget

1. Disconnect the battery. Remove the wiper arms and blades.

2. Unscrew the nut which holds the drive tube onto the motor assembly. Pull off the wiring connector.

3. Remove the two bolts and washers which hold the motor mounting band to the wheel well, and remove the mounting band.

4. Remove the motor.

5. Reverse the procedure to install, lubricating the inner cable with a multipurpose grease.

MGB 1976–77

1. Disconnect the battery. Remove the wiper arms.

2. Remove the dash left hand lower panel cover.

3. Disconnect wiring at the motor terminals.

4. Unscrew the outer cable retaining nut at the motor housing.

5. Remove the two motor mounting bolts, and withdraw the motor, gearbox, and inner drive cable as an assembly.

6. To install, reverse the removal procedure, making sure the inner drive cable meshes with the wheelbox gear teeth.

MGB 1978–80

1. Remove the wiper arms. Remove the glovebox.

2. Disconnect the wiring connector at the motor.

3. Unscrew the cable retaining nut at the motor ferrule.

4. Remove the motor retaining strap mounting screws. Remove the retaining strap, mounting pad, and mounting plate.

5. Disconnect the ground lead at the motor. Pull the motor and cable rack off the mounting.

6. To install, reverse the removal procedures, greasing the cable rack, and ensuring that it engages the wheel box gear teeth.

Instrument Cluster

REMOVAL AND INSTALLATION

Instruments are mounted individually in the panel and are removed by unbolting the panel and releasing the instrument brackets.

Fuse Box Location

The fuse box is located in the engine compartment, on the right inner fender wall.

1. Four-way fuse block.
2. Current rated 17-amp. (35-amp. blow rated) fuses.
3. Spare fuses.
4. Starter solenoid.

Fuse block—MGB

Peugeot

SERIAL NUMBER IDENTIFICATION

Vehicles

504 and 505 MODELS

The vehicle serial number is stamped on the left hand engine mounting lug. The same number is stamped on the right front fender well. The manufacturer's identification plate is located on the right fender well. On later models, the VIN may also be located on a plate attached to the frivers side of the dashboard, visible through the windshield.

604 MODELS

The serial number is stamped on the right front fender well and the manufacturer's plate is located on the right front fender well. On later models, the VIN may also be located on a plate attached to the drivers side of the dashboard, visible through the windshield.

1. Serial number
2. Serial number
3. Engine number

The 504 and 505 serial number is located on the right fender well. The engine number is located on the camshaft tunnel

1. Engine serial number
2. Engine letter code

The last digit of the 504 and 505 engine number is a letter code that is keyed to the engine type

Engine

The engine number is stamped on the camshaft tunnel of the engine. The number consists of a letter followed by 5 digits, and a final identification letter.

GENERAL ENGINE SPECIFICATIONS

Year	Model	Engine Displacement cu. in. (cc)	Fuel Delivery	Horsepower @ rpm	Torque @ rpm (ft. lbs.)	Bore × Stroke (in.)	Compression Ratio	Oil Pressure (psi)
'76–'79	504	120.3 (1971)	2–1 bbl	87 @ 5500	119 @ 3000	3.46 × 3.19	7.6:1	27–50
'80–'83	505	120.3 (1971)	F.I.	96 @ 4900	116 @ 3300	3.46 × 3.19	8.35:1	27
'76–'83	504D 505D	140.6 (2304)	D.F.I.	71 @ 4500	99 @ 2500	3.70 × 3.26	23.0:1	NA
'81–'83	505TD	140.6 (2304)	Turbo D.F.I.	80 @ 4150	136 @ 2000	3.70 × 3.26	21.0:1	NA
'77–'80	604	163 (2664)	1–2 bbl	133 @ 5750	150 @ 3500	3.47 × 2.87	8.2:1	28
'82–'83	604TD	140.6 (2304)	Turbo D.F.I.	80 @ 4150	136 @ 2000	3.70 × 3.26	21.0:1	NA

F.I. Fuel Injection   D.F.I. Diesel Fuel Injection   NA Not available at time of publication

1. Serial number
2. Engine type
3. Engine serial number
4. Peugeot code number
5. Regulations code number

604 model Engine and vehicle serial number location

GASOLINE ENGINE TUNE-UP SPECIFICATIONS

Year	Model	Engine Displacement cu. in. (cc)	Spark Plugs Type	Spark Plugs Gap (in.)	Distributor Point Dwell (deg)	Distributor Point Gap (in.)	Ignition Timing④ MT (deg)	Ignition Timing④ AT (deg)	Idle Speed MT (rpm)	Idle Speed AT (rpm)	Valve Clearance① Intake (in.)	Valve Clearance① Exhaust (in.)
'76–'79	504	120.3 (1971)	44 XL	.024	55–59	.016	5	5	800–850	800–850	.004	.010
'80–'83	505	120.3 (1971)	WR 7 DS	.024	ELECTRONIC		8	8	900–950	900–950	.004	.010
'77–'80	604	163 (2664)	BN 9Y	.024	ELECTRONIC②③		12⑤	12⑤	900–950	900–950	.004	.010

NOTE: The underhood specifications sticker often reflects tune-up specification changes made in production. Sticker figures must be used if they disagree with those in this chart.

① Valves must be adjusted in proper sequence
② Conventional ignition is used in Canada (.016 in gap or 76° dwell)
③ Air gap on Schlumberger ignition system: .021 in.
④ All timing degrees BTDC
⑤ Schlumberger ignition system: 10°
BTDC Before top dead center

DIESEL ENGINE TUNE-UP SPECIFICATIONS

Year	Model	Valve Clearance (cold)		Intake Valve Opens (deg)	Injection Pump Setting (deg)	Injection Nozzle Pressure (psi)		Idle Speed (rpm)	Compression Pressure (psi)
		Intake (in.)	Exhaust (in.)			New	Used		
'76–'83	504D, 505D	.010	.010	12.5B	13B	1740–1813	1668–1813	780–830①	261
'81–'83	505TD, 604TD	.006	.010	NA	.016②③	NA	NA	650–850④	NA

NA Not available at time of publication
① With A/C: 830–860
② Figure is for in. BTDC
③ Canada: .031
④ With A/C: 700–800

FIRING ORDERS

V-6 firing order—conventional ignition

V-6 firing order—electronic ignition

V-6 firing order—Schlumberger electronic ignition

FIRING ORDER 1-3-4-2

4 cylinder firing order

PEUGEOT
504, 505, 604

CAPACITIES

Year	Model	Engine Crankcase (qts) With filter	Transmission (pts) Man	Transmission (pts) Auto	Drive Axle (pts)	Gasoline Tank (gals)	Cooling System (qts)
'76–'79	504	4.3	2.1	3.5	2.8	14.8	8.5
	504SW	4.3	2.1	3.5	2.8	15.8	8.5
'80–'83	505	4.3	③	3.4	2.8	18.0	7.5①
'77–'80	604	6.3	2.8	3.2	3.2	18.5	11.0
'76–'83	504D, 505D	5.3	③	3.4	2.8	18.0②	10.6
'81–'83	505TD, 604TD	5.3	③	3.4	2.8	17.4	10.6

① 7.7 with AT
② Station wagon: 15.8
③ BA 7: 2.4
   BA 105: 3.4

CRANKSHAFT AND CONNECTING ROD SPECIFICATIONS
(All measurements in inches)

Year	Model	Engine Displacement cu. in. (cc)	Crankshaft Main Bearing Journal Dia.	Crankshaft Main Bearing Oil Clearance	Crankshaft End-Play	Connecting Rod Journal Diameter	Connecting Rod Oil Clearance	Connecting Rod Side Clearance
'76–'79	504	120.3 (1971)	①	0.045–0.065	0.0031–0.0079	1.9079–1.9685	NA	NA
'80–'83	505	120.3 (1971)	①	0.045–0.065	0.0031–0.0079	1.9079–1.9685	NA	NA
'76–'83	504D, 505D	140.6 (2304)	2.3606–2.3602	0.030–0.070	0.0031–0.0114	1.9689–1.9678	NA	0.0015–0.0036
'77–'80	604	163 (2664)	2.7576–2.7583	0.035–0.075	0.0028–0.0106	2.0578–2.0585	NA	NA
'81–'83	505TD, 604TD	140.6 (2304)	2.1661–2.1651	0.030–0.070	0.0031–0.0114	1.9689–1.9678	NA	0.0015–0.0036

NA Not available at time of publication
① Rear journal 2.1616–2.1646
  Rear interm. 2.2102–2.2073
  Center 2.2509–2.2515
  Front interm. 2.3050–2.3060
  Front journal 2.3386–2.3392

VALVE SPECIFICATIONS

Year	Model	Seat Angle (deg)	Spring Test Pressure (lbs. @ in.)	Stem-to-Guide Clearance (in.) Intake	Stem-to-Guide Clearance (in.) Exhaust	Stem Diameter (in.) Intake	Stem Diameter (in.) Exhaust
'76–'83	504, 505	44.5	181.5 @ 1.18	0.0012–0.0024	0.0024–0.0035	0.3132–0.3135	0.3120–0.3126
'76–'83	504D, 505D	①	②	NA		0.3344–0.3338	0.3336–0.3331
'77–'80	604	44.5	170 @ 1.06	NA		.3096	.3475
'81–'83	505TD, 604TD	90	②	NA		0.3344–0.3338	0.3336–0.3331

NA Not available at time of publication
① Intake: 120
  Exhaust: 90
② Inner: 34.8 @ 0.866
  Outer: 101.4 @ 1.02

PISTON AND RING SPECIFICATIONS
(All measurements in inches)

Year	Model	Piston Clearance	Ring Gap			Ring Side Clearance		
			Top Compression	Bottom Compression	Oil Control	Top Compression	Bottom Compression	Oil Control
'76–'83	504, 505 604	SPECIFICATIONS NOT AVAILABLE AT TIME OF PUBLICATION						
'76–'83	504D, 505D, TD 604TD	0.0010	0.0137–0.0236	0.0137–0.0236	0.0059–0.0118	0.0012–0.0035	0.0019–0.0032	0.0011–0.0024

TORQUE SPECIFICATIONS
(All readings in ft. lbs.)

Year	Vehicle Model	Cylinder Head Bolts	Rod Bearing Bolts	Main Bearing Bolts	Crankshaft Pulley Bolt	Flywheel to Crankshaft Bolts
'76–'83	504, 505	①	29	55	123.5	49
'77–'80	604	②	34	NA	119.0	31.5
'76–'83	504D, 505D, TD 604TD	③	42④	80	40	56

NA Not available at time of publication
① Torque the head bolts in sequence to 36.0 ft. lbs. (51.4 Nm). Loosen the head bolts and retorque to 15 ft. lbs. (20.3 Nm). Match-mark the bolt head to the cylinder head and tighten ¼ of a turn more on the head bolts (90 degrees).

② Torque the head bolts in sequence to 43.2 ft. lbs. (58.8 Nm). Fully loosen the head bolts and then retorque them in sequence to 14.4 ft. lbs. (19.6 Nm). Match-mark the head bolts to the cylinder head and tighten ¼ of a turn more on the head bolts (90 degrees).

③ Torque the head bolts in sequence to 22 ft. lbs. Retorque all bolts in the same sequence to 47 ft. lbs. (51 ft. lbs. on Turbo-Diesels). Loosen the head bolts ¼ turn in the same sequence and then retorque them to 47 ft. lbs. again (51 ft. lbs. on Turbo-Diesels)
④ Turbo-Diesels: 44 ft. lbs.

TORQUE SEQUENCES

V-6 cylinder head torque sequence

504 and 505 cylinder head torque sequence

BRAKE SPECIFICATIONS
(All measurements in inches)

Year	Vehicle Model	Lug Nut Torque (ft. lbs.)	Master Cyl. Bore (in.)	Front Disc Minimum Thickness	Front Disc Maximum Run-Out	Rear Disc③ Minimum Thickness	Rear Disc③ Maximum Run-Out	Minimum Lining Thickness Front	Minimum Lining Thickness Rear
'76–'83	504	43.5	①	0.43	0.0028	0.42②	0.0028	0.10	0.10
'77–'83	604	61.2	0.86	N.A.	N.A.	N.A.	N.A.	0.10	0.10
'80–'83	505	43.5	N.A.	0.44	0.0028	0.43	0.0028	0.10	0.10

① There are seven different type master cylinders on 504 models. The bore could be 0.824 in. or 0.76 in. depending on the type master cylinder in the vehicle.

② Some earlier type rear discs have minimum thickness of 0.34 in. (Girling type AH12MK1)

③ Models equipped with rear drum brakes have a maximum drum oversize of 11.3 in. except Saloon L models which have a maximum oversize of 10.3 inches.

N.A. Not available at time of publication

WHEEL ALIGNMENT SPECIFICATIONS

Year	Model	Caster Range (deg)	Caster Pref. Setting (deg)	Camber Range (deg)	Camber Pref. Setting (deg)	Toe-In (in.)	King Pin Inclination (deg)
'76–'83	504	2°40′ ± 30′	2°40′	0°38′ ± 30′	0°38′	1/32–5/32②	8°54′ ± 30′
'77–'83	604①	3°30′ ± 30′	3°30′	0°30′ ± 45′	0°30′	1/32–5/32②	10° ± 30′
'80–'83	505	3°30′ ± 30′	3°30′	0°42′ ± 45′	0°42′	1/32–5/32②	9°05′ ± 30′

① Rear wheels Camber Range 1° to 2°
                Pref. 1°30′
  Toe-in Range 1/32 to 5/32 inch
        Pref. 5/64 inch

② Preferred setting is 5/64 inch

TUNE-UP PROCEDURES

Spark Plugs

The average life of a spark plug is approximately 12,000 miles. This is, however, dependent on the mechanical condition of the engine, the type of fuel that is used, and the type of driving conditions under which the car is used. For some people, spark plugs will last 5,000 miles and for others, 15,000 or 20,000 miles.

The electrode end of the spark plug (the end that goes into the cylinder) is also a very good indicator of the mechanical condition of your engine. If a spark plug should foul and begin to misfire, you will have to find the condition that caused the plug to foul and correct it. It is also a good idea to occasionally give all the plugs the once-over to get an idea how the inside of your engine is doing. A small amount of deposit on a spark plug, after it has been in use for any period of time, should be considered normal. But a black liquid deposit on the plugs indicates oil fouling.

REMOVAL

1. Place a piece of masking tape around each plug wire and number it according to its corresponding cylinder.
2. Pull the wires from the spark plugs, grasping the wire by the end of the rubber boot and twisting it off.
3. Loosen each spark plug with a spark plug socket. On the 504 you will need a socket extension attached to the socket in order to reach the plug through the plug tube. When the plug has been loosened a few turns, stop to clean any material from around the spark plug holes. Compressed air is preferable; however, if air is not available, simply use a rag to clean the area.

NOTE: In no case should foreign matter be allowed to enter the cylinders. Severe damage could result.

4. Finish unscrewing the plugs and remove them from the engine.

INSPECTION

It should be remembered that any type of deposit will decrease the efficiency of the plug. If the plugs are not to be replaced, they should be thoroughly cleaned before installation. If the electrode ends of the plugs are not worn or damaged and if they are to be reused, wipe off the porcelain insulator on each plug and check for cracks or breaks. If either condition exists, the plug must be replaced.

If the plugs are judged reusable, have them cleaned on a plug cleaning machine (found in most service stations) or remove the deposits with a stiff wire brush. Check the plug gap on both new and used plugs before installing them in the engine. The ground electrode must be parallel to the center electrode and the specified size wire gauge should pass through the opening with a slight drag. If the center or ground electrode has worn unevenly, level them off with a file. If the air gap between the two electrodes is not correct, open or close the ground electrode, with the proper tool, to bring it to specifications. Such a tool is usually provided with a gap gauge.

INSTALLATION

1. Lightly oil the spark plug threads and hand-tighten them into the engine.
2. Tighten the plugs securely with a spark plug wrench (only about 10 ft. lbs. of torque is necessary). In any case, avoid overtightening the plugs.
3. Reconnect the wires to the plugs making sure that each is securely fitted.

Breaker Points and Condenser

REMOVAL AND INSTALLATION

Early 504 models and certain 604 models made in Canada are equipped with conventional ignition systems. To replace the points and condenser, follow the procedure outlined below:

1. Remove the distributor cap, and inspect it for carbon tracks and cracks.

NOTE: The procedure for the 604 dual point is the same as outlined below, the only difference is that it must be performed for both sets of points.

2. Disconnect the condenser, primary and breaker point ground wires from the terminal located in the side of the distributor housing.
3. Remove the screw which attaches the condenser to the outside of the distributor housing and remove the condenser.

Breaker point gap—typical

4. Remove the breaker point set screw using a magnetic or locking screwdriver. Remove the breaker points from the distributor.

5. Wipe all dirt and grease from the distributor plate and cam with a lint-free cloth. Apply a small amount of heat-resistant lubricant to the distributor cam. Although the lube is supplied with most breaker point kits, you can buy it in any auto parts store if necessary. On those distributors with a felt lubricating pad, simply add a small amount of lubricant to the pad.
6. Properly position the new points on the breaker plate and secure with the set screw, if you have a locking screwdriver. If not, install the breaker point attaching screw in the slot in the points and install the points in the distributor. Do not allow the screw to fall into the hole in the breaker plate in the distributor.
7. Fit the terminal back into the housing in the distributor body and attach the breaker point ground wire, the condenser wire and primary wire.
8. Adjust the breaker point gap with a feeler gauge or dwell meter, as outlined below.

ADJUSTMENT

1. If the two contact points of the breaker point assembly are not parallel, bend the stationary contact slightly to correct.

NOTE: Bend only the bracket portion of the points, do not bend the other side.

2. Turn the engine until the point gap is at its greatest (where the rubbing block is on one of the four high points or corners of the distributor cam). This can be accomplished either by having an assistant quickly turn the ignition switch to the ''start'' position and release it, or by placing the proper size wrench on the bolt in the center of the lower pulley. If you choose the wrench method, *be sure to always turn the engine in the direction of normal rotation.*
3. Insert the correct size feeler gauge between the points. To determine the correct feeler gauge size, see the point gap column in the ''Tune-Up Specifications'' chart in the front of this section. The gauge should fit between the contacts with just a slight amount of drag. Always insert the gauge so that it is parallel with the contacts on the points.
4. If the point gap is too large or too small, slightly loosen the point set screw and insert a screwdriver blade into the notch in the points. Twist the screwdriver to open or close the points as required. Tighten the breaker point attaching screw when the correct gap is obtained.
5. Recheck the point gap to make sure that it did not change when the breaker point set screw was tightened. Since this is a common occurrence, you may have to compensate for the change when you are tightening the set screw.
6. Align the rotor with the distributor shaft and push the rotor onto the shaft until it is fully seated.
7. Reinstall the distributor cap and the coil high-tension wire.

Dwell Angle

ADJUSTMENT

1. Adjust the points with a feeler as described above.

2. Connect a dwell meter to the engine in accordance with the manufacturer's instructions, between the distributor primary lead and a ground.

3. With the engine warmed up and running at the specified idle speed (see the "Tune-Up Specifications" chart at the beginning of this section, observe the reading on the dwell meter.

----- CAUTION -----

When working on a vehicle with the engine running, the following precautions must be observed. Work only in a well-ventilated area. Be certain that the transmission is in Neutral and that the parking brake is firmly applied. Always keep your hands, clothing and tools clear of the moving radiator fan.

If your dwell meter does not have a scale for four-cylinder engines, multiply the eight-cylinder reading by two. If the reading is within the specified range, turn the engine off and disconnect the meter.

4. If the reading is above the specified range, the breaker point gap is too small. If the reading is below the specified range, the gap is too large. In either case, turn off the engine and close or open the point gap as required. Start the engine and recheck the dwell reading. When correct, turn off the engine and disconnect the meter.

5. Check and adjust the ignition timing as required.

NOTE: On vehicles equipped with electronic ignition, this setting is made at the factory, and no adjustment is required.

Electronic Ignition

Electronic ignition is used on all 504, USA 50 states, starting in 1978. In the United States, 604 models use electronic ignition. All 505 models use the electronic ignition.

Electronic ignition uses transistorized switching triggered by magnetic pulse signals to eliminate breaker points.

The type of electronic ignition used in Peugeot ignition systems has no provision for setting the air gap (with the exception of the schlumberger ignition system). The reluctor is a stationary piece. The only serviceable part in the distributor is the pick-up coil. To remove the coil, Take out the two pick-up piece retaining screws and noting their position, remove the two wires leading from the coil.

OPERATION

When the polarity wheel teeth come in alignment with the pickup coil magnet core, a magnetic field is built up around the pick-up coil. This magnetic field collapses when the timer tooth moves away from the pick-up coil core. This movement induces a small current in the pick-up coil windings. This current is amplified in the amplifier module and triggers a transistor to stop the primary current to the ignition coil. The resulting collapse of the primary coil field through the secondary coil windings induces the secondary current to fire the spark plug.

MAJOR COMPONENTS

1. Magnetic pulse generator:
   a. Polarity wheel (reluctor): Timer teeth that rotate with distributor shaft. The system has one tooth for each cylinder.
   b. Electro-magnet coil (pick-up coil): generates the pulse signal to the amplifier module as each timing tooth passes by the core of the pick-up coil.

2. Ignition coil: A special high energy type coil is used and cannot be interchanged with conventional type coils.

3. Amplifier module: The module receives pick-up impulses, amplifies them to signal the transistor and shuts off the primary current flowing through the ignition coil.

TESTING

By following a certain sequence of tests the correct diagnosis can be made.

Test For Spark

1. Remove the distributor cap.

2. Position the polarity wheel (reluctor) so that two teeth are on either side of the pick-up core (teeth not aligned with the core).

3. Remove the high tension lead from the distributor cap.

4. Turn the ignition key on.

5. Position the high tension lead ½ inch away from ground.

NOTE: Choose a ground point as far away from the coil and module as possible.

6. Pass a screwdriver over the pick-up coil core. A spark should occur with each pass of the screwdriver.

7. If there is no spark:
   a. Check the primary voltage at the ignition coil
   b. Check the pick-up coil
   c. Test the ignition coil
   d. Test the amplifier module

Primary Voltage Test at the Ignition Coil

1. Connect a test lamp from the coil positive terminal to ground. If the test lamp lights, continue with the electronic ignition test procedures. If the test lamp does not

1. Reluctor tooth
2. Pick-up core

To test for spark, position the timing teeth on either side of the pick-up core

Position the high tension lead from the coil, ½ in. from ground, to test for spark

1. Pick-up core
2. Screwdriver

Pass a screwdriver over the pick-up core and a spark should occur

Check for voltage at the electronic control module

light, check for a primary ignition wiring problem or faulty ignition switch.

Test the Pick-Up Coil

1. Turn the ignition off and disconnect the pick-up coil connector from the module.
2. Attach an ohmmeter between the pick-up coil terminals.
3. Check the pick-up coil resistance for 900–110 ohms.
4. Remove the vacuum line from the vacuum advance unit and attach an outside vacuum source to the advance unit.
5. While observing the ohmmeter, apply slowly and steadily, up to 20 inches of vacuum to the advance unit.

Check the pick-up coil for insulation to ground

6. If the ohm values move out of the 900–1100 range by more than 50 ohms, replace the pick-up coil.
7. Check pick-up coil insulation by attaching the ohmmeter between one of the coil terminals and ground.
8. If a less than infinite reading is obtained, replace the pick-up coil.

Testing the Ignition Coil

1. Remove the coil connector from the coil terminals and using an ohmmeter, check:
   a. The primary coil windings for 0.48–0.61 ohms.
   b. The secondary coil windings for 9000–11,000 ohms.
   c. Check the leads connecting the control module to the ignition coil for continuity (0) ohms.
2. Replace the ignition coil if not within specifications.

Check the pick-up coil for resistance

Color codes on the distributor-to-coil high tension wires

Testing the Amplifier Module

1. Remove the distributor connector from the module and the high tension wire from the distributor cap.
2. Position the high tension wire ½ inch from ground and as far from the module and coil as possible.
3. Turn on the ignition.
4. Using a jumper wire from the positive battery terminal, make and break contact with the G terminal of the module.
5. At each impulse, a spark should occur. If there is no spark, repeat the test using a new amplifier module.

R1. Primary coil resistance
R2. Secondary coil resistance

Checking the electronic ignition coil

AIR GAP ADJUSTMENT— SCHULMBERGER IGNITION

1. Position the engine so the mark on the timing sprocket is opposite the sensor port, and the notch in the pulley is approximately 30° in front of the 0 graduation on the timing plate.

The mark on the timing sprocket (1) should be opposite the sensor port before tightening the screw (2)

Fit the sensor (3) into the holder. Set the gap by tightening the screw (4)

2. Fit the sensor bolder in place using new seals, and lightly tighten the screw.

3. Pivot the holder as far as it will go in a clockwise direction (maximum retard).

4. Position the sensor towards the slot in its holder.

5. Insert an 0.55 mm thick feeler gauge between the end of the sensor and the sprocket web.

6. Tighten the sensor into the holder until a slight drag is felt on the feeler gauge.

7. Find the No. 1 cylinder advance point.

8. The mark on the distributor arm should be located between the marks on the casing and the pulley notch opposite the 10° graduation in the timing plate.

9. Pivot the sensor holder in a counterclockwise direction (maximum advance).

10. Repeat Steps 4–6 above.

Ignition Timing

504 AND 505

1. Loosen the distributor clamp bolt.

2. Disconnect the vacuum line from the advance unit and plug the line.

3. Connect a timing light to No. 1 spark plug wire and a tachometer to the negative coil terminal. Ground the tachometer.

4. While checking and adjusting initial timing, do not exceed an idle of 850 rpm.

5. Loosen the distributor clamp bolt.

6. Adjust the distributor so that the timing mark is at 5° BTDC on the timing plate. Adjustment is made by turning the distributor until the timing marks are properly aligned.

7. Tighten the distributor clamp and recheck the timing with the timing light.

504 timing mark and hole location

604 MODELS WITH CONVENTIONAL IGNITION

The 604 conventional type ignition has dual points and dual coils. The distributor cam has three lobes and each set of ignition points fires just three cylinders. For this reason, the timing light must be attached to the No. 1 spark plug wire and then to the No. 6 spark plug wire, when adjusting the timing.

The factory high tension coil leads are color coded. The color code on the front coil (4, 5, and 6 cylinders) is grey and the back coil (1, 2, and 3 cylinders) is black.

1. To adjust the timing, loosen the distributor clamp bolt.

2. Disconnect and plug the vacuum advance line.

3. Connect a timing light to the No. 1 spark plug wire.

4. Attach a tachometer to the negative post of the rear coil and ground the other tachometer lead.

5. Check the timing on Number one cylinder and adjust it to 0° BTDC. To adjust the No. 1 cylinder timing; rotate tbe distributor.

6. Check the timing on the No. 6 spark plug wire and adjust it to 0° BTDC. To adjust the No. 6 cylinder timing; turn the screw located on the outside of the distributor body.

604 MODELS WITH SCHLUMBERGER® ELECTRONIC IGNITION

1. Remove the vacuum advance line and plug it.

2. Attach a tachometer to the negative coil post and ground the other tachometer lead.

604 timing mark location

3. Connect a timing light to the No. 1 spark plug wire.

4. Start the engine and idle it at a maximum of 950 rpm.

5. If the timing is out of specifications, loosen the timing sensor (at the front of the left cylinder head) and rotate the sensor counterclockwise to increase advance and clockwise to decrease advance.

6. Tighten the sensor and recheck the timing.

604 MODELS WITH BOSCH® ELECTRONIC IGNITION

1. Remove the vacuum advance line and plug it.

2. Attach the timing light to the No. 6 spark plug wire. Connect a tachometer to the negative coil post and ground.

3. Start the engine and idle it a maximum of 900 rpm.

4. Set the timing to a specification of 12° BTDC. If the timing is out of specification adjust it by rotating the distributor until the timing light shows the pulley mark lining up with 12° BTDC on the timing plate.

5. Stop the engine, reconnect the vacuum advance hose and remove the tachometer and timing light.

6. If necessary adjust the idle speed to 900 rpm.

Valve Lash

ADJUSTMENT

504 and 505

1. Remove the air cleaner (carburetor models), the spark plug wires, the spark plugs and any hoses, vacuum lines or wires in the way of the valve cover.

2. Adjust the valves with the engine cold.

3. Place a wrench on the lower crankshaft pulley bolt and turn the wrench in the direction of engine rotation until the No. 1 exhaust valve is fully open.

Set fully open	to adjust	
E_1	A_3	E_4
E_3	A_4	E_2
E_4	A_2	E_1
E_2	A_1	E_3

E = Exhaust — A = Inlet

504 and 505 valve clearance adjusting sequence

4. Using a feeler gauge, check the clearance between the rocker arm and the camshaft lobe of the No. 3 intake and the No. 4 exhaust valves. If the clearance does not correspond to the value given in the chart, loosen the locknut with a screwdriver to increase or decrease the clearance. When the setting is correct, tighten the locknut, making sure that you do not disturb the setting.

5. Repeat Steps 3–4 for the rest of the valves in sequence.

ROCKER ARM ADJUSTMENT SEQUENCE

No. 1 Piston on TDC		Rocker Arms To Be Adjusted
Firing stroke	A1①	E1②
	A2①	E3②
	A4①	E6②
End of exhaust	A3①	E2②
Commencement of inlet	A5①	E4①
stroke	A6①	E5②

① Inlet: 0.10 mm
② Exhaust: 0.25 mm

1. Position of the rotor with #1 cylinder on TDC of the compression stroke
2. Mark on rotor
3. Mark on distributor
4. Position of the rotor with #1 cylinder on the end of the exhaust stroke and the beginning of the intake stroke
5. Intake valve
6. Exhaust valve

Valve lash sequence for V6 engines

604

1. Using a remote starter switch, bring the No. 1 piston to TOP DEAD CENTER (TDC) on the compression stroke.
2. Remove the distributor cap and check the position of the rotor. The arm should be directly in line with the marks on the distributor housing.
3. Check the location of the notch on the belt pulley, it should be aligned with the "O" notch on the timing plate.
4. With the engine in this position, adjust the No. 1, 2, and 4 intake valves and the No. 1, 3, and 6 exhaust valves.
5. Again using the starter switch, bring the piston to the end of the exhaust stroke and to the beginning of the intake stroke.
6. The rotor arm should be pointing 180° away from the markings on the distributor housing.
7. The notch of the belt pulley should again be aligned with the "O" notch on the timing plate.
8. With the engine in this position, adjust the No. 3, 5, and 6 intake valves and the No. 2, 4, and 6 exhaust valves.
9. Using new gaskets, install the valve covers, distributor cap and vacuum lines.

Carburetors

IDLE SPEED AND MIXTURE

General

1. Select Park on an automatic transmission or Neutral on a manual transmission.
2. Set the parking brake.
3. Turn off the air conditioning and all electrical accessories.

4. Route the pressure from the air injector pump, away from the manifolds by connecting a jumper wire across the electro-valve control switch terminals.

Without CO Analyzer

1. Adjust the engine idle speed to 950–100 rpm.
2. Adjust the idle mixture screw to obtain the highest rpm.
3. Adjust the idle speed back to 950–1000 rpm.
4. Repeat these procedures until the 950–1000 rpm is obtained as the highest idel mixture rpm.
5. Adjust the idle speed to 900–950 rpm.
6. Remove the jumper wire from the electro-valve and adjust the idle to 900–950 rpm.

With a CO Analyzer

1. Connect the CO analyzer according to the manufacturers instructions.

NOTE: The exhaust system and test equipment must be free of leaks to prevent erroneous readings.

2. Turn the mixture screw to obtain a CO level of 1.5–2.5%.
3. Adjust the idle speed to 900–950 rpm again.
4. Repeat the procedures until a 1.5–2.5% CO reading is obtained at 900–950 rpm. The 604 models, should be adjusted to 800–850 rpm and 3.0–4.0% CO.
5. Remove the electro-valve jumper wire and adjust the engine idle to 900–950 rpm.

1. Richness adjusting screw
2. Idle speed adjusting screw
3. Primary carburetor
4. Secondary carburetor
5. Secondary adjustment

Do not adjust secondary—preset at factory

Adjusting the 504 twin single barrel carburetors

1. Primary carburetor   3. Idle speed screw
2. Secondary carburetor   4. Idle mixture screw

Adjusting the 604 carburetors

CAUTION

Never adjust the secondary carburetor (the side that does not have the deceleration valve attached) on 504 models.

NOTE: During adjustments if the engine idles for more than three minutes at a time, increase the engine speed to 2000 rpm for one minute to clear the engine of a rich idle mixture.

Fuel Injection

IDLE SPEED AND MIXTURE

Several Peugeot special tools or their equivalent will be needed to adjust the idle speed and fuel mixture on Peugeot K-Jetronic® fuel injection. The tools are: a mixture adjusting tool, an idle speed adjusting tool and a CO sampling connecting tube.

In addition, a good tachometer and an infra-red HC/CO analyzer will be needed. If any of these special tools are not readily available, we suggest that the work be done by an authorized service technician.

1. Connect the tachometer and using the idle adjustment tool, adjust the air bleed to obtain an idle speed of 900–950 rpm.

2. Disconnect the wire 47c from the air slide valve thermo-contact and connect it to ground number five (5) on the shock tower.

3. Disconnect and plug the vacuum supply hose at the canister purge valve.

4. Remove the air injection hose at the intake port of the diverter valve and plug it with a 0.9 in. (23 mm) plug.

5. Attach the CO sampling tube to the front of the catalytic converter. Connect the CO analyzer.

6. Locate the CO mixture regulator and remove the access plug to the CO mixture screw.

Location of the fuel mixture adjusting screw on the mixture regulator

1. Wire (47C)
2. Air slide valve thermo-contact
3. Vacuum supply hose to canister purge valve
4. Air injection hose
5. Diverter valve intake port
6. Fire wall
7. Right side shock tower

The location of wires and hoses to be altered and disconnected during fuel injection adjustment

Adjusting the idle speed on Peugeot K-Jetronic® fuel injection system

7. Start the engine and set the idle at 900 rpm.

8. Using the CO mixture adjusting tool or equivalent, adjust the CO reading to 0.5–1.5%.

NOTE: Do not push down on the adjusting tool as it will change the CO reading.

9. Repeat the procedure until both the idle and the CO % are correct.

10. Install the mixture plug.

11. Connect the wire 47c to the thermocontact, the vacuum hose to the canister purge valve, the air injection hose on the diverter valve and remove the sampling tube from the catalytic converter. Install the cap nut on the converter tap.

ENGINE ELECTRICAL

Distributor

REMOVAL AND INSTALLATION

1. Remove the common intake manifold on 505 models only.

2. Bring the No. 1 piston to TDC of the compression stroke. Match mark the position of the rotor to the distributor body.

3. Remove the distributor clamp bolt and lift out the distributor. Do not rotate engine crankshaft.

4. Install the distributor in the same position it was when it was removed.

5. Install the common intake manifold on the 505 models.

6. Check and adjust the timing.

INSTALLATION WITH ENGINE DISTURBED

If the engine was cranked with the distributor removed, it will be necessary to retime the engine. If you have installed the distributor incorrectly and the engine will not start, remove the distributor from the engine and start from scratch.

1. Hold the distributor close to the engine and install the cap on the distributor in its normal position.

2. Locate the No. 1 spark plug wire tower on the distributor cap.

3. Scribe a mark on the body of the distributor directly below the No. 1 spark plug wire tower on the distributor cap.

4. Remove the distributor cap from the distributor and move the distributor and cap out of the way.

5. Remove the No. 1 spark plug and crank the engine over until the No. 1 cylinder is on the compression stroke. To accomplish this, place a wrench on the lower

CAP

ROTOR

CAM

CENTRIFUGAL ADVANCE

DUAL POINT BREAKER PLATE

CONDENSERS

SHAFT

ADVANCE UNIT

BODY

Exploded view of the 604 conventional ignition distributor

DISTRIBUTOR CAP

ROTOR

CONTACT POINT CARRIER

FELT LUBRICATION PAD

VACUUM ADVANCE

BREAKER CAM

CENTRIFUGAL ADVANCE MECHANISM

DISTRIBUTOR SHAFT

DISTRIBUTOR BODY

CAPACITOR (CONDENSER)

Exploded view of the 504 conventional ignition distributor

engine pulley and turn the engine slowly in the direction of normal engine rotation.

— **CAUTION** —
Never turn the engine against its normal rotational direction.

When the No. 1 piston is on the compression stroke, air will be forced out of the No. 1 spark plug hole. When the No. 1 cylinder is on the compression stroke, continue to turn the engine over until the ignition timing marks are properly aligned on the scale and pulley. The proper timing mark

is the ignition timing figure given in the "Tune-Up Specifications" chart.

6. With the timing mark aligned, align the distributor rotor with the mark which was scribed on the distributor housing in Step 3.

7. Install the distributor in the engine keeping the rotor aligned with the mark. While inserting the distributor into the collar, be sure to properly engage the end of the distributor driveshaft into the oil pump drive slot. Install and hand-tighten the collar nut.

8. Turn the distributor in the engine until the points just start to open. Tighten the distributor collar nut.

9. Install the distributor cap and wires. Plug the vacuum line(s) to the distributor.

10. Attach a timing light and check and adjust the ignition timing.

11. After checking and correcting the timing, reconnect the distributor vacuum line(s).

Alternator

ALTERNATOR PRECAUTIONS

1. Observe the proper polarity of the battery connections by making sure that the positive (+) and negative (−) terminal connections are not reversed. Misconnection will allow current to flow in the reverse direction, resulting in damaged diodes and an overheated wire harness.

2. Never ground or short out any alternator or alternator regulator terminals.

3. Never operate the alternator with any of its or the battery's leads disconnected.

4. Always remove the battery or disconnect its output lead while charging it.

5. Always disconnect the ground cable when replacing any electrical components.

6. Never subject the alternator to excessive heat or dampness if the engine is being steam-cleaned.

7. Never use arc-welding equipment with the alternator connected.

REMOVAL AND INSTALLATION

1. Disconnect the negative battery cable from the battery.

2. Tag and disconnect the wires leading from the alternator.

3. Loosen the alternator mounting bolts and remove the belt.

4. Remove the alternator mounting bolts and remove the alternator. On the Diesel, remove the lug support on the cylinder block.

5. On the Diesel, to install, first check the clearance between the support lug and the two fastening bosses on the cylinder block. Should the clearance be in excess of 0.004 in., insert adjusting washers to bring the clearance within proper specifications.

6. On all models, be sure to adjust the alternator belt tension and to complete all installation procedures (in the reverse order of removal) before connecting the negative battery cable.

CAP

ROTOR ARM

ROTOR

PICK-UP COIL

RELUCTOR

PLATE

CENTRIFUGAL ADVANCE

ADVANCE

BODY

DRIVE PINION

Exploded view of the Bosch® electronic ignition distributor used on 604 models

| 1. Alternator | 3. Solenoid | 5. Ignition switch |
| 2. Regulator | 4. Starter motor | 6. Battery |

Typical starter and charging circuit

Regulator

ADJUSTMENT

The regulator should be set to produce between 13.6 and 14.8 volts at 3000 rpm. There is a switch on the regulator that can be set to heavy or light electrical load. Position number one (1) is for high electrical load and position number two (2) is for light electrical load.

REMOVAL AND INSTALLATION

1. Disconnect the negative cable from the battery.
2. Disconnect the wiring harness from the regulator.
3. Remove the regulator attaching screws and the regulator.
4. To install, reverse the removal procedures

Starter

REMOVAL AND INSTALLATION

The positive engagement starter is connected to the battery (when the ignition key is turned to the ''start'' position) by a starter relay. When current is received from the battery, the starter drive engages the starter with the flywheel and turns the engine.

REMOVAL AND INSTALLATION

1. Disconnect the starter cable from the starter. On the 504 and Diesel, this may be facilitated by first removing the battery and battery support.
2. Remove the starter attaching bolts (including the fastening screw on the Diesel cylinder block and, if necessary, the angle iron support), and the starter.
3. To install, reverse the removal procedures. Tighten the clutch housing bolts to 14.5 ft. lbs.

STARTER DRIVE DISASSEMBLY

1. Remove the starter from the engine.
2. Remove the brush cover band.
3. Remove the thru-bolts and solenoid cover housing bolts just enough to allow removal of the rear drive end housing and the plunger lever.
4. Remove the pivot pin which attaches the starter drive plunger lever to the starter end housing frame.
5. Remove the stop ring retainer and stop ring from the armature shaft.
6. Remove the starter driver from the armature shaft.

Cross section of a typical starter motor

7. Inspect the teeth on the starter drive. If they are excessively worn, inspect the teeth on the ring gear of the flywheel. If the teeth on the flywheel are excessively worn, the flywheel should be replaced.
8. To install, first apply a thin coat of white grease to the armature shaft in the area in which the starter drive operates.
9. Install the starter drive on the armature shaft and install a new stop ring.
10. Fill the drive end housing bearing bore ¼ full with grease.
11. Position the plunger lever in the end housing and install the pivot pin with a new stop ring.
12. Fit the drive end housing, with plunger lever attached, to the starter frame. *Make sure that the plunger lever is properly engaged with the starter drive.*
13. Tighten the starter thru-bolts and install the brush cover band on the starter.
14. Install the starter.

Battery

The battery is located on the driver's side front of the engine compartment of all models. There are no special problems to gaining access to the battery.

ENGINE MECHANICAL

Engine

REMOVAL AND INSTALLATION

504

On vehicles with automatic transmissions, drain the fluid.

1. Remove the battery and the tray.
2. Remove the hood and the radiator.
3. Remove the ignition coil and the starter.

4. Disconnect the heater hoses and the carburetor fuel line.
5. Noting their exact position, remove the carburetor linkages.
6. Remove the air filter bracket and the air filter.
7. Turn the steering wheel to the left and lower the steering rack.
8. Remove the exhaust pipe from the exhaust manifold.
9. Remove the flywheel protector plates and the clutch housing bolts.
10. Noting their positions, remove the main vacuum line and all electrical wires that interfere with removal of the engine.
11. Using Peugeot tool 8 0102x engine hoist or equivalent, attach the hoist hooks to the holes marked ''404'' and raise the engine until it is under a slight load.
12. Remove the four securing bolts from the crossmember.
13. Raise the engine until the transmission touches the tunnel.

NOTE: Make sure that the left brake line is tight against the crossmember.

14. On vehicles with automatic transmissions, remove the torque converter–to–flywheel bolts and disconnect the converter.
15. Seperate the engine from the transmission without changing the position of the engine hoist.
16. Installation is the reverse of removal. Torque the automatic transmission converter bolts to 16 ft.lbs. (22.1 Nm). Other installation torques are:
Clutch housing to engine   40 ft.lbs. (53.9 Nm)
Starter bolts   14.5 ft.lbs.(19.6 Nm)
Crossmember bolts   7.2 ft.lbs.(9.8 Nm)

———— CAUTION ————
Make sure to check the engine oil and water levels before attempting to start.

505

The removal and installation is basically the same as in the 504 models. The following extra steps must be taken for the fuel injection.

1. Remove the fuel hoses from the fuel distributor and the cold start injector.

2. Remove the air mixture regulator and the air filter.

3. If equipped with air conditioning, move the compressor to the side and move the condenser and receiver-dryer to the left. Secure these air conditioning components out of the way while leaving all freon hoses connected.

NOTE: It is recommended that a thread locking compound be used on the converter bolts at assembly.

604

1. Remove the hood. Drain the automatic transmission if equipped.

2. Remove the air mixer and air filter.

3. Drain the cooling system.

4. Disconnect the electrical connectors at the electric fan, the oil pressure switch, the air conditioning compressor and the thermostat.

5. Remove the electric fan.

6. Remove the radiator supports and battery on air conditioned cars.

7. Remove the top and bottom radiator hoses and transmission cooler lines if equipped.

8. Separate the condenser and receiver dryer from the radiator.

9. Remove the fan shroud and the radiator.

10. Remove the air conditioning compressor and set it on the right fender, leaving the freon lines attached.

11. Disconnect the battery ground cable, the temperature sending unit, the vacuum line to the brake booster and the fuel pump lines.

12. Remove the carburetor controls and the primary and secondary coil leads.

13. On air conditioned vehicles, disconnect the electro-valve wire and the lead to the carburetor idle cut out switch.

14. Remove the heater hoses and plug the ends.

15. Disconnect the starter and alternator harness connectors.

16. Remove the top bolts from the clutch housing or the torque converter if automatic transmission.

17. Disconnect the filter tube on automatic transmission vehicles.

18. Remove the exhaust pipe clamp bolts and the engine mounting bolts.

19. Remove the exhaust pipes, heat deflector and brackets.

20. Remove the starter and the clutch/converter cover.

21. Remove the power steering pump, support and power steering belt.

22. Support the weight of the engine on the hoist, using Peugeot tool number 80135 or equivalent. When the gearbox makes contact with the transmission tunnel, then lower it .04 in. (1 cm).

23. Remove the power steering pump and set it to one side without disconnecting the lines.

24. Retract the front seats and remove the inner securing bolts.

25. Raise and safely support vehicle. Using the threaded rods supplied with Peugeot tool number 8.1511, install the tool (drive shaft support bar) under the floor of the vehicle. Use the threaded rods in the seat bolt holes under the floor.

26. Remove the upper flex coupling bolt from the steering shaft.

27. Temporarily install the two rear main crossmember bolts in place.

28. Remove the front crossmember securing bolts and loosen the rear crossmember bolts enought to lower the crossmember ⅛in. (3 mm).

29. On automatic transmissions remove the torque converter-to-ring gear bolts.

30. Remove the two lower clutch housing or torque converter housing bolts.

31. Move the engine forward in order to separate from transmission. Hold the torque converter in place on automatic transmission equipped vehicles.

32. Installation is the reverse of removal except for the following adjustments.

33. Adjust the automatic transmission kick down cable. Set the accelerator pedal stop at 2 inches (51 mm). Place a 0.3 inch (7 mm) spacer between the stop and the accelerator pedal.

34. Hold the carburetor control quadrant in the fully open position. Unclip the linkage return springs. Secure the accelerator cable in place, pull on the cable lightly to tension it, but do not compress the compensator spring. The accelerator cable goes through a hole in the quadrant and is secured ⅞ of the way around the quadrant at the accelerator holding tab.

35. Clip the kickdown cable into the control quadrant. Put tension on the kickdown cable by pulling on it lightly.

36. Set the cable stop into the cable bracket and tighten the nuts on both sides of the bracket.

37. One nut will tighten against the lug. Adjust the other nut to obtain 0.04 inches (1 mm) clearance between the nut and the bracket.

38. Remove the spacer at the accelerator pedal and check for proper carburetor operation.

39. When the engine is hot, the clearance on the accelerator cable should be 0.08 in. (2 mm).

Use the following torque specifications when installing the 604 engine:

Flywheel to starter ring 34.2 ft. lbs.

Crossmember to frame 30.6 ft. lbs.

Steering column clamp 10.8 ft. lbs.

Gearbox to engine 28.8 ft. lbs.
Compressor mounting 12.6 ft.

Compressor pulley 9.0 ft. lbs.

Diesel

1. Drain the cooling system and the crankcase.

2. Remove the hood and its supports.

3. Remove the battery and its tray, the coolant expansion tank, and the air filter.

4. Disconnect the intake pipe on the vacuum pump.

5. Disconnect the upper and lower water hoses and radiator mounts.

6. Disconnect the self-disengaging fan cut-off switch and remove the fan and radiator.

7. Disconnect the injection pump controls and the fuel lines.

8. Remove the heater return line and disconnect the starter, oil pressure switch, pre-heating circuit, and thermistor.

9. Remove the wastegate attaching bolts on the turbo–diesel.

10. Disconnect the alternator and cooling hose from the cylinder head.

11. Disconnect the exhaust pipe from the manifold.

12. Remove the retaining nut from the right-hand engine support block.

13. Remove the clutch housing sealing plates and the upper housing bolts.

14. Remove the retaining nut from the left-hand engine support block.

15. Remove the bolt securing the exhaust pipe bracket to the gearbox and remove the right-hand clutch housing cover plate.

16. Insert lifting hooks into the holes provided at the front and rear of the engine block and raise the engine until the gearbox comes into contact with the driveshaft tunnel.

18. Remove the two lower clutch housing bolts.

19. Pull the engine forward to release the transmission input shaft and hoist the engine from the compartment.

20. Installation is the reverse of the removal procedure. However, be sure to pay attention to the following points:

 a. When the engine comes in contact with the clutch housing, first insert the upper housing bolt and then the two lower bolts. Tighten the three bolts to 43.5 ft lbs;

 b. Bleed the fuel system after replacing all fluids and completing all connections;

 c. Adjust the injection delay mechanism on the injection pump.

Cylinder Head

Removal and Installation

504

1. Drain the coolant from the block.

2. Remove the air cleaner, carburetor, ignition distributor, spark plugs, upper radiator hose and water pump belt.

3. Remove the spark plug tube seals and cups.

4. Separate the exhaust pipe from the manifold.

5. Remove the head bolts and install the cylinder head guide pins.

6. Remove the rocker shaft assembly and pushrods.

7. Remove the guide pin from the front end of the engine.

8. Pivot the head to separate it from the block and lift off the head. Remove the gasket and second cylinder head guide.

9. Lock the cylinder liners with the Peugeot tool 8.0104D or equivalent retaining screws.

10. Installation is the reverse of removal.

11. Torque the head bolts in sequence to 36 ft. lbs. (49 Nm). Loosen the head bolts , and retorque to 15 ft. lbs. (20.3 Nm). Then match mark the bolt head to the cyliner head. Then tighten exactly 90° (¼ turn) more. Do this to all head bolts, in sequence.

505

1. Drain the cooling system and remove the Lambda® sensor (if equipped) from the exhaust header pipe.

2. Remove the header pipe from the exhaust manifold connector.

3. Remove the mounting brackets from the intake/exhaust manifold.

4. Disconnect the battery ground cable.

5. Separate the intake manifold.

6. Remove the distributor cap.

7. Remove the fuel injectors. Remove the diagnostic plug bracket.

8. Tag and remove the following electrical wires:

   a. Primary ignition at the coil.

   b. Secondary ignition at the coil.

   c. Temperature sending unit at the engine.

   d. Thermo-time switch at the engine.

   e. Thermocontact sender unit in the heater hose.

   f. Temperature sending units at the water pump.

   g. Spark plug wires at the spark plugs.

9. Remove and tag the following air and vacuum hoses:

   a. All injection pump hoses and the auxiliary air device.

   b. Two vacuum hoses on the fuel distributor.

   c. Vacuum hoses at the three vacuum regulators on the fender well (manifold side of engine). All other vacuum lines on the manifold side.

10. Remove the upper radiator hose and the water pump ends of the lower radiator hose and heater hose.

11. Remove the power steering pump reservoir bracket from the head.

12. Remove the radiator fan shroud.

13. Remove the fan baldes. Remove only the 3 nuts that are lined up with the recesses in the fan hub.

14. Remove the water pump belt.

15. Remove the vacuum hoses, electrical wire and coolant hoses from the air slide

valve. Remove the air slide valve bracket.

16. Remove the remaining air injection hoses and the air injection assembly.

17. Remove the rocker arm oil feed pipe (sometimes referred to as ''banjo fittings'').

18. Remove the valve cover, declutchable fan brush holder and spark plug tube sealing rings.

19. Remove the rocker arm assembly, pushrods and cylinder head bolts.

20. Using Peugeot tools number 0.0149 or equivalent, break the cylinder head loose.

21. Install Peugeot tools 8.0132A1Z or equivalent retainers to keep the cylinder sleeves from moving in the engine block.

22. Installation of the head is the reverse of removal. Follow the specified torque sequence on head bolts and torque the bolts to 36 ft. lbs. (49 Nm). Loosen the head bolts, and retorque to 15 ft. lbs. (20.3 Nm). Then match mark the head bolt to the cylinder head. Then tighten exactly 90° (¼ turn) more. Do this to all head bolts, in sequence. Torque the rocker arm nuts to 10.9 ft. lbs. (14.7 Nm).

23. Adjust the valve clearances.

604

1. Drain the cooling system.

2. Remove the hood, air mixer chamber casing, air filter and battery.

3. Remove the intake manifold.

4. Remove the plate fitted under the intake manifold.

5. Remove the clips between the cylinder head and the water pump.

6. When removing the head from under the power brake booster, the engine crossmember must be lowered.

7. The accessories on the head opposite the brake booster do not have to be removed.

8. Remove all hoses and vacuum lines.

9. On the left hand cylinder head:

   a. Remove the fuel pump leaving the line connected.

   b. Remove the hot air duct.

   c. Loosen the positive battery lead and remove the negative battery lead.

10. On the right hand cylinder head:

   a. Remove the distributor and the front ignition coil.

   b. Remove the automatic transmission fill tube if equipped.

11. Remove the front exhaust silencer mounting bracket.

12. Remove the exhaust pipe from the exhaust manifold.

13. On the left side, remove the bolt from the steering flex coupling upper end.

14. Using Peugeot tool 8.1511C or equivalent; lower the crossmember 0.12 inch or (3 mm).

15. Remove the rocker arm cover and camshaft rear cover plate.

16. Remove the camshaft sprocket bolt access plug from both heads.

17. Position both sprockets with the drive studs (timing marks) at the top.

18. Hold the crankshaft from turning with a 35 mm box wrench. Loosen the camshaft

sprocket with Peugeot tool ST 10 or equivalent Allen type socket wrench tool.

19. Place the Peugeot tool 8.0134M or equivalent camshaft sprocket supports on the timing gear casing. Secure the support fingers tight with two bolts. Torque the bolts to 10.8 ft. lbs. (14.7 Nm).

20. Unscrew 8 bolts on each cylinder head and remove all but the two bolts under the power brake booster. Raise the two bolts as far as they will go and secure them with a rubber band.

21. Loosen the camshaft thrust flange bolt and remove the thrust flange.

22. Remove the camshaft. Make sure the cams do not foul the rocker arm pads while unscrewing the sprocket bolt.

23. On the left hand cylinder, lift the rocker arm to clear the camshaft.

24. Remove the timing gear case-to-cylinder head bolts from both the left and right heads.

25. Insert the two levers, Peugeot tool 0.0149 into two head bolts holes. Break the cylinder head loose by prying on the levers.

26. Remove the rocker arm assembly.

27. Clean the head gasket surface and retain the cylinder liners with special retainers, Peugeot tool 8.0132A or equivalent.

28. Remove the cylinder head locating dowels using Peugeot tool 8.0134L (extractor) or equivalent.

29. Install the Peugeot temporary camshaft bearing tools 8.0134N or equivalent on both heads.

30. Shims may be required under the bearing bracket, on the head surface.

31. Installation is the reverse of removal.

------ **CAUTION** ------

Do not release the timing chain tension or disturb the chain position while removing and installing heads.

------

32. Torque the camshaft flange bolts to 9.4 ft. lbs. (12.7 Nm). Torque the camshaft sprocket bolts to 54.0 ft. lbs. (73.5 Nm).

33. Torque the head in sequence and to 36 ft. lbs. (49 Nm). Loosen the head bolts, and retorque to 15 ft. lbs. (20.3 Nm). Then match mark the head bolt to the cylinder head. Then tighten exactly 90° (¼ turn) more. Do this to all head bolts, in sequence.

34. Adjust the valve clearances.

35. Install the rocker covers and follow the reverse of Steps 1–13 for completing the re-installation. Install coolant and check the system by running the engine.

Rocker Arms and Shafts

REMOVAL AND INSTALLATION

504 and 505

1. Remove the rocker arm cover.

2. Remove the five rocker stand nuts and ten head bolts. Lift off the rocker shaft.

3. Install in the reverse order of removal. Torque the head bolts in sequence to 36 ft. lbs. (12.7 Nm). Loosen the head bolts, and retorque to 15 ft. lbs. (20.3 Nm). Then match mark the head bolt to cylinder head. Then tighten exactly 90° (¼ turn) more. Do this to all head bolts, in sequence.

4. Adjust the valve clearances.

----- CAUTION -----
With the head bolts removed, the cylinder head can be broken loose from the block. Do not jar the cylinder head or rotate the crankshaft.

604

1. Remove the air filter, heater air inlet, battery ground cable and rocker arm covers.

2. Remove the rocker shaft retaining bolts from the left rear and right front support bosses.

3. Remove all head bolts from both banks. The two left rear head bolts under the brake booster may be hard to remove. If necessary, move the engine slightly so they will clear the brake booster.

----- CAUTION -----
With the head bolts removed, the cylinder head can be broken loose from the block. Do not jar the cylinder head or rotate the crankshaft.

4. Installation is the reverse of removal.

5. Torque the head bolts in sequence to 36 ft. lbs. (12.7 Nm). Loosen the head bolts, and retorque to 15 ft. lbs. (20.3 Nm). Then match mark the head bolt to cylinder head. Then tighten exactly 90° (¼ turn) more. Do this to all head bolts, in sequence.

Intake Manifold

REMOVAL AND INSTALLATION

504

1. Remove the air intake tubing and any wires or vacuum lines in the way of manifold removal.

2. Remove the air cleaner and carburetor.

3. Remove the intake manifold bolts. Lift out the manifold.

505

1. Remove the air intake boot and electrical and vacuum connections from the throttle plate housing.

2. Remove the intake manifold mounting brackets and slide the intake manifold back and out.

604

1. Drain the cooling system.
2. Remove the air mixer casing and intake tube.
3. Remove the air filter and disconnect the negative battery cable.
4. Remove the intake manifold.
5. Installation is the reverse of removal.

Exhaust Manifold

REMOVAL AND INSTALLATION

504

1. Remove the nuts and the clamp holding the exhaust pipe to the exhaust manifold.
2. Using caution, move the exhaust pipe out of the way.
3. Remove the eight retaining bolts and remove the manifold.
4. Installation is the reverse of removal.

505

1. Remove the Lambda® sensor wire and the three nuts holding the header pipe to the exhaust manifold.
2. Remove the exhaust manifold retaining nuts and lift out the manifold.
3. Installation is the reverse of removal.

604

1. Remove the right and left side exhaust pipes from the manifolds.
2. Remove six manifold-to-head bolts on the right and left sides of the engine.
3. Lift out the manifolds.
4. Installation is the reverse of removal.

Turbocharger

REMOVAL AND INSTALLATION

1. Remove the air filter.
2. Disconnect the electrical connection from the temperature switch.
3. Loosen the lower hose on the air duct that connects the air filter with the compressor housing.
4. Remove the vacuum line and the crankcase breather pipe.
5. Remove the air filter and the air intake duct.
6. Disconnect the oil line at the turbocharger.
7. Remove the air filter mounting bracket.
8. Disconnect the turbocharger at the exhaust flange.

9. Disconnect and remove the pipe bracket on automatic transmission models.
10. Push the exhaust pipe toward the rear.
11. Remove the mounting bracket at the intermediate flange.
12. Unbolt and remove the turbocharger.
13. Remove the intermediate flange and the oil line at the turbocharger.
14. Installation is the reverse of removal. Before installing the turbocharger, install the oil return line and the intermediate flange.

Timing Chain Cover

REMOVAL AND INSTALLATION

504 and 505

1. Drain the coolant.
2. Remove the radiator, fan belt, spark plugs and the crankshaft pulley.

NOTE: To hold the crankshaft from turning in manual transmission equipped vehicles, apply the handbrake and engage 4th gear. On vehicles with automatic transmissions, remove the torque converter cover and hold the flywheel.

3. Remove the timing housing.
4. Installation is the reverse of removal.

604

1. Drain the engine oil.
2. Disconnect the negative battery cable.
3. Remove the air filter and the air mixer casing and the hot air duct.
4. Drain the cooling system.
5. Remove the radiator struts, radiator hoses and separate the fan casing from the radiator.
6. Remove the fan and the fan casing.
7. Remove the power steering belt and the alternator belt.
8. Remove the power steering pump and hang it to the fender well with wire.
9. Remove the clutch or converter housing cover plate.
10. Use Peugeot tool 8.01234 or equivalent to lock the flywheel in place.
11. Remove the crankshaft pulley.
12. Remove the power steering pump bracket, the hot air duct and the rocker arm covers.
13. Remove the timing gear casing bolts and lift the timing gear casing from the engine.
14. Installation is the reverse of removal. Torque the crankshaft pulley nut to 123 ft.lbs. (166 Nm).

Diesel

1. Remove the radiator from the engine compartment and unbolt the fan from the injection pump pulley.

2. Remove the fan belt and crankshaft pulley belt.

3. Remove the injection pump pulley nut and crankshaft pulley nut. Then remove both pulleys.

NOTE: Be sure that the handbrake is applied and the transmission is in 4th gear while the pulleys are being removed.

4. Remove the timing gear housing bolts, the housing, and the oil slinger.

5. Before installing the cover, refit the oil slinger cup and a new timing housing gasket.

6. Refit the cover and tighten the cover bolts to 8 ft.lbs.

7. Refit the woodruff key(s) and the pulley(s). Tighten the crankshaft pulley bolt to 123 ft.lbs.

Timing Chain Cover Oil Seal

REPLACEMENT

504 and 505 Gasoline Engine Models

The 504 (XN1 engine) uses an oil slinger on the front end of the crankshaft. This means that some leakage can occur when parking on steep grades. There is no oil seal to be replaced.

Diesel Engine Models

1. Remove the crankshaft pulley and the oil seal.

2. Install the seal and the woodruff key.

3. Install the crankshaft pulley. Torque the nut to 123 ft.lbs. (166 Nm).

Timing Chain and Tensioner (Valve Timing)

REMOVAL AND INSTALLATION

504 and 505

1. Remove the timing chain cover.
2. Loosen the tensioner spring.

RENOLD® TENSIONER

a. Remove the tensioner adjuster plug.

b. Using a .12 inch (3mm) Allen wrench, turn the adjuster key clockwise to release the tension on the timing chain.

SEDIS® TENSIONER

a. Turn the rachet clockwise with a screwdriver to release the tension on the timing chain.

3. Remove the tensioner and tension plate.

4. Remove the filter from the block.

Reynholds® timing chain tensioner used in some 504 models

5. Before removing the timing chain, position the crankshaft Woodruff key slot to the left and the two white timing chain links to the right, while facing the front of the engine. An imaginary line through the Woodruff key slot and the middle of the two white links should be parallel to the leading edge of the oil pan.

— CAUTION —
If either the crankshaft or camshaft are rotated with the timing chain removed, valve damage might occur. Never rotate the crankshaft and always position the crankshaft as described in Step 5 before rotating the camshaft, when the timing chain is removed.

6. Take the tensioner apart and clean it.

— CAUTION —
On the Sedis® tensioner, do not remove the rachet screw (tension adjusting screw). Once removed it is impossible to put it back.

7. Witbout altering the position of the crankshaft, install the Woodruff key and the sprocket.

8. Keep the two white timing chain links at the camshaft sprocket mark and the one white link at the crankshaft sprocket mark with the centers of the crankshaft and camshaft, forming a straight line through the white chain links and the reference marks on the sprockets.

9. Install the new tab washers on the camshaft sprocket and torque the camshaft sprocket bolts to 16 ft.lbs. (20 Nm).

10. Lock the bolts by bending the tabs around tbe bolt heads.

11. Install the filter.

12. Using Peugeot tool 0.0137 or equivalent to hold the tensioner together, install the tensioner.

13. On the Renold® tensioner, load the tensioner by turning the Allen key clockwise. Install a new tab washer and install the plug. Bend the tab to lock the plug.

14. Remove the retaining tool.

— CAUTION —
Never assist the tensioner action.

15. Load the Sedis® tensioner by turning the screw clockwise.

NOTE: The Sedis® and Renold® tensioners are interchangeable as a unit.

16. Install the thrust washer if needed and the oil thrower cup.

NOTE: The 505 uses an oil seal. Always install a new seal during reassembly.

17. Use a new housing gasket and center the timing housing with Peugeot tool 0.0128 or equivalent.

18. Install the Woodruff key and the crankshaft pulley. Torque the pulley nut to 123 ft.lbs. (166 Nm).

19. Bend the tab around the nut.

20. Install remaining components in the reverse order of removal.

21. Fill the engine with oil and the radiator with coolant.

22. Check the timing.

Diesel

1. Remove the timing gear cover.

2. Unload the chain tensioner by first removing the sealing plug from the tensioner body and then engaging a 3 mm allen wrench through the hole in the tensioner piston recess. Turn the allen wrench clockwise to release the tensioner shoe.

3. Loosen the eccentric rod gear fastening nut. Then move the pinion to its slackest position.

1. Ratchet screw in locked position
2. Rack
3. Pad
4. Spring
5. Ratchet screw in unlocked position

Sedis timing chain tensioner used in some 504 models

4. Remove the following:
   a. The injection pump pinion and the chain;
   b. The injection pump pinion hub and bearing;
   c. The rod gear with its eccentric;
   d. The guide shoe and the chain;
   e. The crankshaft pinion;
   f. The chain tensioner;
   g. The housing gasket.
5. To install, reassemble the components in the reverse order of removal, paying attention to the following points:
   a. To facilitate installation of the chain, adjust the eccentric in the position for maximum slack;
   b. With the crankshaft pinion reference mark facing down, simultaneously install the injection pump pinion and the chain, conforming to the reference marks. The copper link should be opposite the crankshaft pinion mark; the links marked by a line should be opposite the camshaft pinion mark and the injection pump bearing mark. Then install the pump bearing pinion and the pin;
   c. After installing the chain, adjust the idler pinion eccentric, rotating it in the direction opposite to that of engine rotation so that the play between the tensioner pad and its support is from 0.02–0.04 in. Then tighten the eccentric fastening nut to 36 ft.lbs. Load the tensioner by turning the allen wrench to the right and stop turning when the pad is pushed onto the chain. Be sure to screw in and lock the tensioner plug bolt;
   d. Place a straightedge on the chain connecting the camshaft pinions and the injection pump. Be sure that the guide shoe is flush against the chain, readjusting if necessary;
   e. Be sure to recheck the timing.

604
TIMING CHAIN

1. Remove the timing chain cover.
2. Check the timing chain tensioner projection. If the projection is greater than 0.38 in. (9.5 mm) replace the timing chains.
3. Rotate both the tensioner adjusters counterclockwise to release the timing chain tension.
4. Remove the oil pump drive chain and sprockets. Also remove the oil pump crankshaft spacer and Woodruff key.
5. Remove the oil pump.
6. Bring the No. 1 piston up to TDC on the compression stroke and mark the position of the crankshaft sprocket reference line. Also, mark the position of both of the camshaft sprocket reference lines.
7. Secure the crankshaft from rotating by installing Peugeot tool 8.01311 or equivalent on the flywheel.
8. Remove the camshaft sprocket bolts.
9. Remove the right hand camshaft sprocket and timing chain and then the left side camshaft sprocket and timing chain.
10. Remove both tensioners and the small oil filter in the block behind each tensioner.
11. Install the left bank chain and sprocket along with the crankshaft sprocket and Woodruff key. The camshaft sprocket reference mark should be centered between the two white marks on the timing chain. The crankshaft sprocket reference should be directly in line with the single white mark on the timing chain. This means that there is no slack in the lower half of the chain and all of the slack is on the upper side (tensioner side). The match marks should be exactly where they were marked before the chain was removed.
12. Install the right bank chain and camshaft sprocket. Position the camshaft sprocket reference mark between the two white marks on the timing chain. The single white mark on the chain should be directly opposite the crankshaft sprocket reference mark. This means that all of the slack is on the tensioner side of the timing chain. The match marks should be exactly where they were marked before the timing chain was removed.
13. Install the tensioners and filters. Torque the tensioner bolts to 5.5 ft.lbs. (7.8 Nm).
14. Place the two chains under tension by turning the tensioner adjusters clockwise.

15. Install the spacer, Woodruff key and sprocket for the oil pump chain drive.
16. Install the oil pump, using new lock washers on the four bolts. Torque the oil pump bolts to 9 ft.lbs. (13 Nm).
17. Place the chain over both sprockets and install the three sprocket to oil pump bolts. Use new lock washers on the bolts and torque them to 4.0 ft.lbs. (5.9 Nm).
18. Install new timing chain cover gaskets and secure the cover with twenty five bolts. Torque the bolts to 9 ft.lbs. (13 Nm).
19. Lubricate and install a new crankshaft pulley seal. Use Peugeot special tool 8.0134 or equivalent and tap the seal in with a mallet.
20. Install the crankshaft pulley and bolt. Coat the bolt threads with a medium duty locking compound. Torque the bolts to 123 ft.lbs. (166 Nm).
21. Reinstall all components removed during the removal procedure of the timing chain cover.
22. Install engine oil and coolant.
23. Remove the special tool holding flywheel in place and install the clutch or converter housing cover plate.

VALVE TIMING
If the timing is not marked while the piston of the No. 1 cylinder is on the compression stroke or the marks are lost, then use the following valve timing procedure.

1. Rotate the crankshaft clockwise so that the Woodruff key slot is straight up in a vertical position.
2. On the left hand cylinder head, place the camshaft so that the rocker arms on Number one cylinder are in balance. The camshaft slot will be aligned with the edge of the camshaft thrust flange. The slot and sprocket reference mark will be in a vertical position with head installed on the block.
3. Rotate the crankshaft clockwise until the crankshaft Woodruff key slot is aimed at the center line of the left bank camshaft.
4. Install the timing chain over the left camshaft sprocket with the reference mark centered between the two white marks on the timing chain.
5. Install the timing chain over the crankshaft sprocket with the reference mark lined up with the single white mark on the timing chain.
6. Fasten the camshaft sprocket with the sprocket bolt and torque the bolt to 51 ft.lbs. (73 Nm).
7. Rotate the right side camshaft to a position where the No. 4 cylinder rocker arms are balanced. The slot in the camshaft will be pointing to an imaginary line through the center of the camshaft and parallel to the lower surface of the head.
8. Turn the crankshaft clockwise until the crankshaft sprocket reference mark lines up with the center of the lowest oil pump bolt hole.

9. Install the timing chain over the right side camshaft sprocket with the reference mark between the two white marks on the timing chain.

10. Install the timing chain on the outer crankshaft sprocket with the single white mark on the chain lined up with the reference mark on the crankshaft sprocket.

11. Install the bolt and the camshaft sprocket on the camshaft and torque the bolt to 51 ft.lbs. (73 Nm).

12. Install the timing chain tensioners and filters. Torque the tensioner bolts to 5.5 ft.lbs. (7.8 Nm).

13. Place the timing chains under tension by turning the tensioner adjusters clockwise.

— CAUTION —

Never attempt to assist the tensioning action of the tensioners.

14. Install the timing gear cover, using new gaskets.

15. Install a new timing cover oil seal.

16. Install the crankshaft pulley and install the bolt to a torque of 123 ft.lbs. (166 Nm).

17. Install the power steering pump brackets and the power steering pump.

18. Install the rocker arm covers and the hot air duct.

19. Install the power steering and water pump belts.

20. Install the fan casing and fan.

21. Install the radiator hoses and radiator struts.

22. Install the engine coolant and engine oil.

23. Install the air mixer, hot air duct and air filter. Connect the negative battery cable.

Camshaft

REMOVAL AND INSTALLATION

504 and 505

1. Drain the engine oil, the coolant and disconnect the battery ground cable.

2. Remove the air cleaner assembly, spark plugs, distributor, carburetor, rocker arm cover, fan belt, radiator and various wire and hose connections.

NOTE: On 505 fuel injected vehicles, remove the Lambda® sensor wire at the exhaust pipe, fuel injectors at the intake manifold, all electrical wires, air hoses, water hoses, power steering, thermoslide valve connections, air induction hoses and rocker arm oil feed line.

3. Remove the spark plug tubes from the head and the exhaust pipe from the exhaust manifold.

4. Remove the head bolts and install Peugeot head guide tools 8.0115Y or equivalent.

1. Crankshaft
2. Timing chain tensioner
3. Camshaft
4. Timing chain
5. Rocker arm
6. Rocker arm shaft
7. Distributor
8. Fuel pump

Cutaway view of the 604 engine timing and valve train

5. Remove the rocker shaft and the push rods.

6. Remove the front head guide and pivot the head on the back head guide to break it loose from the block and lift off the head.

7. Lock the cylinder liners with special retainer tools, Peugeot number 8.0104D or equivalent.

8. Remove the valve lifters (cam followers).

9. Remove the crankshaft pulley nut.

NOTE: On vehicles with manual transmissions, apply the parking brake and engage 4th gear to hold the crankshaft from rotating while removing the crankshaft pulley and camshaft sprocket. To remove the crankshaft pulley and camshaft sprocket on automatic transmission vehicles, remove the converter cover and use a flywheel tool to hold the engine.

10. Remove the timing chain cover.

11. If the engine is equipped with a Renold® tensioner, remove the plug and turn the adjuster clockwise with an Allen wrench to release the timing chain tension.

12. If the engine is equipped with a Sedis® tensioner, turn the rachet adjuster counterclockwise with a screwdriver to release the timing chain tension.

13. Remove the chain tensioner and the filter behind it.

14. Remove the camshaft sprocket, crankshaft sprocket, Woodruff key and the timing chain.

15. Remove the camshaft thrust flange and withdraw the camshaft.

16. Installation is the reverse of removal.

17. Install a new filter behind the tensioner and use Peugeot special tool 0.0137 or equivalent to hold the tensioner together while installing it.

604

1. Drain the engine oil and engine coolant.

2. Disconnect the ground cable from the battery.

3. Remove the air filter, the air mixer casing and the hot air duct.

4. Remove the radiator struts, disconnect the hoses and separate the fan casing from the radiator.

5. Remove the fan and the fan casing.

6. Remove the power steering belt and the alternator drive belt.

7. Remove the power steering pump and hang it to the side, without removing the hoses.

8. Remove the clutch/converter housing cover plate.

9. Install the flywheel locking tool Peugeot number 0.0134C or equivalent

10. Remove the crankshaft pulley.

11. Remove the hot air duct from the exhaust manifold and the rocker arm covers.

12. Remove the power steering pump support bracket.

13. Remove the timing chain cover.

14. Remove both oil pump drive sprockets, the oil pump chain, the spacer and the Woodruff key.

15. Remove the oil pump.

16. Release the two tensioners.

17. Match mark the camshaft drive sprockets to the head.

18. Remove the right camshaft sprocket and timing chain and then remove the left camshaft sprocket and timing chain.

19. Remove both chain tensioners and the filters behind them.

20. Remove the camshaft sprocket and Woodruff key.

21. Remove the right and the left side rocker arm assemblies. Mark the rocker arms right and left for reinstallation.

22. Remove the camshaft thrust flange

from the front of the head, the bearing cover plate and gasket.

23. Remove the camshaft from the rear of the head.

24. Installation is the reverse of removal.

NOTE: The left hand camshaft has the fuel pump cam on it and the right hand camshaft has the distributor drive pinion on it.

25. Torque the rear cover plates to 4.3 ft.lbs. (5.8 Nm).

26. Torque the thrust flange bolts to 9.4 ft.lbs. (12.7 Nm).

Diesel

1. Remove the engine and follow Steps 1—4 of the 504 timing gear section.

2. After removing the timing housing gasket, remove the valve cover, rocker arm shaft, tappet inspection holes, pushrods and tappets.

3. Using a two-jawed puller, remove the camshaft pinion and its thrust plate and woodruff key.

4. Gently withdraw the camshaft from the engine being careful to avoid scoring the bearings.

5. To reassemble, first heat the camshaft pinion in well-heated oil.

6. Install the thrust plate, woodruff key and pinion onto the camshaft, pressing the pinion onto the shaft until there is a clearance of 0.002–0.006 in. between the sprocket hub and the shaft flange.

7. Lubricate the cam lobes and journals and insert the camshaft, with the pinion attached, into the block.

8. Reassemble the remaining components in the reverse order of removal.

Pistons and Connecting Rods

REMOVAL AND INSTALLATION

504 and 505

1. Remove the cylinder head.

2. Remove the lifters, the distributor support and the distributor driveshaft.

3. Remove the oil pan and oil pump.

4. Mark the pistons and rods, 1—4, rear to front. The No. 1 cylinder is at the clutch end of the engine.

5. Remove the end caps from the connecting rods. Push the piston and liner assembly from the block. Keep the end caps with the proper piston and liner as it is removed.

6. Set the liners in position in the block without the seals and check them for distortion with a flat surface and a dial indicator.

Checking the liner protrusion above the block on the 504 and 505

1. Dial indicator
2. Adaptor
3. Piston liner protrusion, above the engine block, with no gasket under the liner

PISTON AND LINER MATCHING CHART②

Mark On Piston	Matching Mark On The Liner①
A	1 mark
B	2 marks
C	3 marks

① Machined lines mark the upper edge of the liner.

② Piston ring gap and clearance specifications are not given. It is recommended by the manufacturer that pistons, rings and liners be replaced as complete new set for all cylinders.

7. Take a dial indicator reading at four points around the liner. The difference between the four measurements should be less than 0.0028 in. (0.07 mm).

NOTE: The 505 procedure is the same except that the protrusion specification is 0.0055 in. (0.14 mm) and the maximum difference between liners is 0.0016 in. (0.04 mm).

NOTE: The distance being measured is the amount of protrusion of the cylinder liners above the cylinder block.

8. Select the proper size liner seal by subtracting the measured distance with no seal from the maximum allowable liner protrusion. Pick the seal size nearest to and not exceeding the subtracted difference.

9. Install the liners in the same positions as match marked before removal.

10. Install special Peugeot tools 8.0128 or equivalent to compress the cylinder liner gaskets, on the XN1 engines.

11. Check the dial indicator readings on each liner and if they are from zero to 0.0055 in. (0.14 mm), install the liner retainer bolts, Peugeot number 8.0104D or equivalent.

1. Inner tabs fit into grooves in the liner
2. Reference tab position at right angle to the flat spot
3. Flat spot

Installing the piston liner seals with the tab in the proper position in the 504 and 505 models

Remove the Peugeot liner compressor tool number 8.0128 or equivalent.

12. Using a ring expander tool, install the rings on the pistons. Install the pistons into the liners from the top side, follow the match marks made on removal.

13. Install the rod bearing caps and nuts. Torque the rod bearing cap nuts to 29 ft.lbs. (39 Nm).

14. Install the cylinder head, the wires, the vacuum lines and air cleaner assembly.

GASKET TO BE FITTED

Highest Point on the Liner (Without Gasket)	Reference	Thickness
0.0015 to 0.0018 in. (0.039 to 0.045 mm)		0.0028 to 0.0041 in. (0.070 to 0.105 mm)
0.0007 to 0.0015 in. (0.019 to 0.038 mm)		0.0033 to 0.0047 in. (0.085 to 0.120 mm)
−0.0002 to +0.0007 in. (−0.006 to +0.018 mm)		0.0041 to 0.0055 in. (0.105 to 0.140 mm)
−0.0037 to −0.0003 in. (−0.095 to −0.007 mm)		0.0051 to 0.0065 in. (0.130 to 0.165 mm)

1. Liner compressing tool
2. Piston liner protrusion

Measuring liner protrusion with the gasket installed on 504 models with compressed type liners

604

1. Remove the air cleaner, wires, vacuum lines and the cylinder heads.

2. Use Peugeot tool 8.0134N and M or equivalents on both head surfaces to secure the camshaft sprockets. Shims are available in selective thicknesses to install under the camshaft sprocket holding tools. The shims may be needed to ensure the tightness of the timing chains while working on the pistons.

———— CAUTION ————

If slack is allowed in the timing chains or the special tools are not available the timing chains will have to be removed and the valve timing reset.

3. Use the special tools, cylinder liner retainers, Peugeot number 8.0132A or equivalent, to secure the cylinder liners in the block.

4. Remove the lower oil pan, the oil strainer, the anti-emulsion baffle, the sump securing bolts, the main bearing securing nuts and remove the oil sump.

604 MODEL SELECTIVE CYLINDER LINER SEALS

Color	Thickness
Blue	0.0034 in. (0.087 mm)
White	0.0040 in. (0.102 mm)
Red	0.0048 in. (0.122 mm)
Yellow	0.0058 in. (0.147 mm)

5. Remove the connecting rod cap nuts.

6. Matchmark the cylinder liners to the block and the connecting rod caps to the connecting rods. Normally, the pistons have arrows on them to mark the direction of installation. If the pistons have the arrows, note the direction before removal and reinstall in the same direction. If no arrows are on the pistons, mark them with a felt tip pen for future reference.

7. Remove the pistons, piston rods and cylinder liners at the same time. Keep matching parts together.

8. If the liner is distorted beyond specification, install a new liner set.

NOTE: Pistons, rings, and liners are available in sets only. This helps retain engine balance.

9. The piston liners must project above the cylinder block gasket face between

COLOR CODED TABS

Correct position of the tabs on the 604 model piston liners, when correctly installed

0.0064 in. (0.16 mm) and 0.0092 in. (0.23mm).

10. Cylinder liner seals are to be installed between the liner and the lower flange of the block.

11. Cylinder liner seals are available in the following thicknesses.:

12. Measure the cylinder liner projection above the engine block with no seal under it. Subtract this measurement from 0.0092 in. (0.23 mm) and select a seal that will provide a maximum cylinder liner projection of 0.0092 in. (0.23 mm), or as close to it as possible without exceeding the maximum. For example:

Maximum allowable projection 0.0092 in.

Largest measurement—no seal 0.0040 in.

Difference to be taken up by the selected seal 0.0052 in.
The seal selected will be red 0.0488 in. (0.122 mm).

13. Install the seals with their color code facing the top of the engine.

14. Install the liners and seals in a position so that the color tabs are visible and will not be squeezed under the adjacent liner.

15. Check the final liner projection above the block for each cylinder liner. Mark the position of the liners on the straight edge of the block.

16. Install a piston ring tool around the piston crown and compress the rings. Oil the liner and install the piston. Match the marks on the liner and the piston.

17. When installing pistons and liners, always match the letter on the piston crown to the number of machine marks on the liner.

18. Install the piston and liner assemblies into the block.

19. Install the rod bearings and rod caps. Torque the rod bearing cap nuts to 34 ft.lbs. (46 Nm).

20. Install the cylinder heads and all related wires, vacuum lines and the air cleaner assembly.

ENGINE LUBRICATION

Oil Pan

REMOVAL AND INSTALLATION

504 and 505

The Peugeot four cylinder engines have a separate oil sump pan on the bottom of the crankcase pan.

1. To remove the oil sump, bolts and the sump pan.

2. To remove the entire crankcase pan, the engine will have to be raised for working clearances.

3. Installation is the reverse of removal.

4. On the diesel, be sure to position the pump so that the feed tube is engaged in the hole in the strainer and that the thrush washer is under a light spring tension.

604

The 6 cylinder engines have a front lower oil sump that is removable with the engine in the vehicle. If the entire crankcase must be removed, the engine must be removed from the vehicle.

NOTE: If the entire crankcase must be removed, refer to the ''engine removal and installation'' section.

1. Drain the engine oil.

2. Remove the sump pan bolts and take off the sump pan.

3. Clean off the gasket surfaces and install a new gasket.

4. Install the sump pan and torque the bolts to 9.4 ft.lbs. (12.7 Nm).

5. Torque the drain plug to 27 ft.lbs. (36 Nm).

6. Fill the engine with 6.3 quarts (6.0 liters) of engine oil.

Rear Main Oil Seal

REMOVAL AND INSTALLATION

504 and 505

Seals are not used on the rear of the crankshaft. An oil slinger arrangement is used to direct the oil back into the reservoir. The crankshaft may need new thrust washers, if end play is excessive. Side seals are used on the rear main bearing cap.

1. Check the end float of the crankshaft. The end float (end-play) must be between 0.003 in. (0.08 mm) and 0.008 in. (0.20 mm).

2. If there is too much end float (end-play), oversize thrust washers are available

in thicknesses of: 0.096 in. (2.4 mm), 0.098 in. (2.45 mm), and 0.10 in. (2.5 mm).

3. Install the new rear bearing cap side seals and torque the bearing cap bolts to 55 ft.lbs. (73.5 Nm).

604

The transmission and the flywheel must be removed on 604 models in order to work on the rear main seal. See "Transmission Removal and Installation" in this section for procedures.

1. Check the crankshaft end play for between 0.0028 in. (0.07 mm) and 0.0108 in. (0.27 mm).

2. If needed, install oversized thrust washers selected from available sizes of: 0.092 in. (2.3 mm), 0.096 in. (2.4 mm), 0.098 in. (2.45 mm) and 0.10 in. (2.5 mm).

3. Remove the seal and fit a new seal by hand.

4. Install the flywheel and transmission.

Oil Pump

REMOVAL AND INSTALLATION

504 and 505

NOTE: The oil pump procedures for the diesel are the same. The only difference in the pumps is that the diesel pump is larger and has a greater volume.

1. Drain the oil.

2. Remove the oil sump and oil pump. Do not lose the two oil pump locating dowels.

3. Install a new O-ring on the bottom of the oil pump.

4. Be certain that the locating dowels are in place.

5. Be certain that the oil pump drive blade engages the oil pump drive rod.

6. Torque the bolts to 7 ft.lbs. (9.8 Nm).

7. Use a new gasket and install the oil sump.

8. Torque the sump bolts to 7 ft.lbs. (9.8 Nm).

9. Install the drain plug and fill the engine with oil.

——————— CAUTION ———————
Oil sumps made of either pressed steel or aluminum which do not have an oil return passage, must not be installed on XM engines with a rear main bearing cap which incorporates an oil return hole.

——————— CAUTION ———————
A special oil pan gasket of rubber/asbestos must be used on USA models with a metal alloy sump.

604

1. Drain the engine oil and remove the timing chain cover.

2. Remove the oil pump drive sprockets, drive chain and Woodruff key.

3. Remove the oil pump.

4. Installation is the reverse of removal.

5. Torque the oil pump sprocket bolts to 4 ft.lbs. (5.0 Nm).

6. Torque the oil pump bolts to 9 ft.lbs. (12.7 Nm).

Diesel

The Diesel oil pump is fitted in the right-side (when looking toward the front) of the engine block and, due to the lack of ignition components, is driven by a pinion gear off the camshaft. The pump is held in place through external bolts on the block.

1. To remove the oil pump, first drain the oil and remove the oil pan. Remove the external bolt and thrust plug and pull the pump down through the oil pan opening.

2. To install the pump, first position it correctly in the cylinder block with the tapered hole on the pump body facing the threaded hole. Be sure that the gear teeth mesh properly with the camshaft pinion teeth.

3. Fit the tapered end screw and tighten the locknut with its copper washer.

4. Install the thrust plug temporarily without its washer, and moderately tighten the plug.

5. Using a feeler gauge, check the clearance between the bearing surfaces of the plug and the cylinder block, through the cutout provided for this purpose.

6. Install a washer of a thickness in excess of 0.002 in. (0.05 mm) to 0.004 in. (0.1 mm) to obtain the appropriate operating clearance. Washers are available in four sizes: 0.1 mm, 0.2 mm, 0.5 mm, and 1 mm.

7. Reinstall the remaining components in the reverse order of removal.

ENGINE COOLING

Radiator

REMOVAL AND INSTALLATION

504 and 505

1. Drain the coolant.

2. Remove the fan shroud retaining bolts.

3. Remove the upper and lower radiator hose.

4. Remove the lower radiator bolts.

5. Remove the radiator.

6. Installation is the reverse of removal.

604

1. Drain the cooling system.

2. On air conditioned vehicles:

a. Remove the electric fan lead,

b. Remove the oil pressure switch wires,

c. Remove the compressor wire,

d. Remove the temperature sending wire,

e. Remove the three electric fan bolts,

f. Remove the radiator stays,

g. Remove the battery.

3. Remove the overflow hose from the left side of the radiator.

4. Remove the top and the bottom radiator hoses.

5. On vehicles with an automatic transmission, remove the transmission cooler lines.

6. On air conditioned vehicles, disconnect the condenser receiver/dryer assembly from the radiator.

7. Remove the fan cowl and the radiator.

8. Installation is the reverse of removal.

9. Refill the cooling system.

Water Pump

REMOVAL AND INSTALLATION

504 and 505

1. Drain the coolant.

2. Remove the top radiator hose and the heater hose from the water pump.

3. Remove the fan belt.

4. Remove the water pump bolts and remove the water pump.

5. Clean the gasket surfaces.

6. Replace the gasket and install the pump in the reverse order or removal.

7. Install coolant in the engine.

604

1. Drain the cooling system.

2. Remove the air mixer casing and duct, the hot air duct and the air filter.

3. Remove the intake manifold and the insulating plate under the manifold.

4. Remove the water pump belt and the alternator drive belt.

5. Separate the fan casing from the radiator.

6. Remove the heater and radiator hoses at the water pump.

7. Remove the wire lead from the temperature sending unit.

8. Loosen the hose clamps on the two rubber hoses at the heads.

9. Remove the bolts securing the water casings to the block.

10. Remove the two heater hoses from the back of the water pump.

11. Remove the water pump bolts.

12. Remove the water pump and casing as an assembly.

13. Installation is the reverse of removal.

NOTE: Install new O-rings where the casing fits to the block.

14. Torque the water casing bolts to 9.4 ft.lbs. (12.7 Nm).

15. Torque the water pump bolts to 14.6 ft.lbs. (17.2 Nm).

Diesel

1. Drain the radiator.

2. Remove the radiator, the top hose, and then the fan belt.

3. Disconnect the heater hose from the pump.

4. Disconnect the self-disengaging fan brush holder.

5. Remove the pump attaching bolts and the pump.

6. Clean the mating surfaces of the pump and cylinder head.

7. Apply Permatex® No. 2 on both sides of a new gasket and install the pump in the reverse order of removal.

8. Adjust the fan belt, install the radiator, connect the hoses and refill the cooling system.

Radiator Fan

REMOVAL AND INSTALLATION

504

1. Remove the water pump.

2. Using a pulley holder tool mounted in a vise, remove the pump hub nut.

3. Tap on the end of the shaft to disengage the pump body from the pulley. Remove the Woodruff key from the slot in the shaft.

4. Installation is the reverse of removal.

5. Torque the pump hub nut to 25 ft.lbs. (34.2 Nm).

505 and 604

1. Remove the fan casing from the radiator.

2. Remove the four fan-to-thermostatic fan clutch bolts.

3. Lift off the fan.

4. Installation is the reverse of removal.

Belt Tension Adjustment

Peugeot recommends that all of their belts be adjusted by measuring reference marks on the belts, except on the model 505 air pump-alternator belt the adjustment is made by loosening the idler pulley bolts and torqueing idler bracket nut to 58.0 ft.lbs. (78.4 Nm). For all other belts:

1. Loosen the belt adjusting bracket bolts.

2. With no tension on it, mark two ref-

erence lines on the belt, 4 inches (100 mm) apart.

3. Stretch the belt when tightening it so that the reference marks will be 4.12 inches (103 mm) apart.

EMISSION CONTROLS

The Peugeot emission controls are composed of three major systems: crankcase emissions control, evaporative emissions control and exhaust emissions control. Differences may occur between California and Federal vehicles. Therefore, the emission control information label on the vehicle should be consulted before repairs are made.

Crankcase Emission Control System

The system is considered a closed system with the crankcase breathing from the air cleaner air intake. The PCV valve vents measured amounts of crankcase gases and vapors into the intake manifold to be burned with the air/fuel mixture.

1. PCV recirculating tube
2. Intake manifold
3. Filter
4. Calibrated jet
5. Calibrated hole in air cleaner
6. Air intake
7. Air cleaner assembly

604 crankcase emission system

Evaporative Emission Control System

In order to control the evaporation of fuel into the atmosphere from the fuel tank and the carburetor when the engine is shut off, both are vented into a charcoal canister. A calibrated valve in the fuel tank line meters the flow of vapors into the charcoal canister to an amount that the canister can handle.

1. Charcoal canister
2. Canister to carburetor vapor hose
3. Vapor-liquid separator (wagon only)
4. Separator return hose (wagon only)
5. Filler neck to separator hose (wagon only)
6. Fuel tank to canister hose
7. Calibrated jet

Evaporative emission system used on all models

The station wagons have an additional vapor-liquid separator located near the fuel tank. When the engine is started, the system pulls the vapors out of the charcoal canister and into the intake manifold, thereby purging the canister of fuel vapors.

Exhaust Emission Control Systems

AIR INJECTION

The air injection system adds oxygen into the exhaust manifold, allowing unburned hydrocarbons (HC) in the hot exhaust gases to be burned more completely. The system consists of a belt driven rotary vane air pump, a diverter valve, and an electro-valve, an intake manifold injection valve and non-return valves.

Air Pump

Some precautions should be taken when working on the air pump.

1. Do not operate the engine with the pump removed or drive belt disconnected.
2. Do not lubricate the pump.
3. If the filter is contaminated, replace it. Do not attempt to clean it.
4. When adjusting the drive belt, never pry on the pump body.

1. Vacuum port
2. Vacuum port
3. Electronic control unit
4. Throttle plate
5. Delay valve
6. Delay valve
7. Vacuum switch
8. Vacuum switch
9. Thermo-contact wire
10. Air slide valve

Model 505 emission control components located in the engine compartment

504 air injection pump

5. Never clamp the pump body in a vise.

6. The internal parts of the air pump are not serviceable. Replace the pump as an assembly.

7. The following external parts may be replaced on the pump: drive pulley, filter and pressure relief valve.

8. Do not hand rotate the pulley on a new pump and never rotate the pulley in the direction opposite to the normal direction.

EGR VALVE

In order to reduce the nitrogen oxide (NO_x) in the exhaust, a controlled amount of exhaust gas is recirculated into the intake manifold. The main component of the system is the valve, which opens between the exhaust and intake manifolds. The valve opening is controlled by vacuum, according to engine conditions, by a vacuum control electro-valve and a vacuum amplifier. California engines have an additional vacuum switch.

ELECTRO-VALVE

During engine start up and warm up, the electro-valve stops the flow of vacuum to the EGR valve, to prevent the EGR valve from opening when the choke is operating.

VACUUM AMPLIFIER

This valve controls the amount of vacuum to the EGR valve according to engine conditions.

504 deceleration valve

VACUUM SWITCH

This switch reacts to close the EGR valve during high intake manifold vacuum situations. The valve is only used on California vehicles.

CATALYTIC CONVERTER

The catalytic converter reduces hydrocarbons (HC) and carbon monoxide (C) by converting them to carbon dioxide and water.

FLOW OF OUTSIDE AIR
CRANKCASE EMISSIONS — PRIMARY CIRCUIT
CRANKCASE EMISSIONS — SECONDARY CIRCUIT

1. Crankcase breather
2. Air filter inlet
3. Air filter
4. Calibrated tube
5. Carburetor throttle plates
6. Intake manifold
7. Calibrated orifice

504 and 505 crankcase emission system

504 catalytic converter

Lambda® Sensor

The 505 fuel injected models use the Lambda® oxygen sensor system to check the exhaust gases for unburned hydro-carbons. The sensor sends signals from the exhaust pipe to the control unit. Under certain conditions, the signals will cause the control unit to alter the fuel ratio to bring it into specifications. If the engine has not reached operating temperature the signals will be overridden and the enrichment system will operate.

FUEL SYSTEM

Fuel Filter

REMOVAL AND INSTALLATION

6-Cylinder Engines

1. Unscrew the fuel return valve and plug it at the carburetor.
2. Remove the fuel filter.
3. Replace the gasket at the seal plug.

4. Install the new filter and check for leaks.

6-Cylinder Engines (Fuel Injected)

1. Unscrew the cover box.
2. Remove the pressure hoses.
3. Loosen the attaching screws and remove the filter. Remove the connecting plug from the old filter and install it on the new filter with a new gasket.
4. Install the new filter.
5. Replace the attaching screws.
6. Install the pressure hoses.
7. Replace the cover box and check for leaks.

4-Cylinder Engines

1. Loosen the hose clips.
2. Remove the fuel filter.
3. Install a new filter along with new hoses.
4. Replace the hose clips.
5. Check for leaks.

Fuel Pump

REMOVAL AND INSTALLATION

All Models

The fuel pump is located on the drivers side of the engine. Disconnect the fuel inlet and outlet lines. Remove the attaching bolts and the pump.

When installing, make sure the fuel pump rocker arm is positioned correctly on the cam.

Carburetors

REMOVAL AND INSTALLATION

1. Remove the accelerator cable.
2. Remove the downshift cable on vehicles equipped with automatic transmissions.
3. Remove all fuel and vacuum lines.
4. Remove the carburetor mounting bolts and lift off the carburetor.
5. Installation is the reverse of removal.

OVERHAUL

For all carburetor overhaul procedures, please refer to "Carburetor Service" in the Unit Repair section.

THROTTLE LINKAGE ADJUSTMENT

504

Adjust the throttle linkage to 0.08 in. (2 mm) of clearance, with the engine warm.

604

1. Check the height of the accelerator pedal stop. The pedal stop height should be 2.04 in. (51 mm).

1. Throttle cable
2. Snap ring
3. Common intake manifold
4. 0.08 in. (2 mm)

504 throttle cable adjustment

Positioning the accelerator before adjusting the throttle cable on 604 models

1. Throttle drum
2. Stop washer
3. Throttle rod
4. Fixed stop
5. Moveable stop

VIEW A

VIEW B

1.7mm (0.067 in.)

604 throttle linkage adjustment

2mm

Adjusting the throttle cable at the retaining bracket on 504 and 604 models

2. Place a 0.28 in. (7 mm) spacer between the accelerator pedal and the pedal stop.
3. Hold the accelerator pedal and the spacer in a fully depressed position.
4. Remove the two linkage return springs.
5. Hold the carburetor control quadrant in the fully open position.
6. Secure the accelerator cable in place on the control quadrant, pulling on the cable just enough to tension it. Do not compress the compensator spring on the cable when tensioning it.
7. Install the two linkage return springs.
8. Remove the spacer from under the accelerator pedal.
9. When the engine is hot, the clearance on the accelerator cable to holding bracket should be 0.08 in. (2 mm).

FLOAT LEVEL ADJUSTMENT

504

1. Remove the air cleaner, connecting linkages and fuel lines from the float bowl cover of the carburetor.
2. Remove the float bowl cover from the carburetor.
3. With the needle valve completely closed, check the float level, by measuring the distance from the float bowl cover mating surface to the small diameter of the float.
4. If the float level does not measure 1.4 in. (35.5 mm) adjust it by bending the pivot arm on the float.

604

1. Remove the air cleaner, linkages and fuel line.
2. Remove the float chamber cover.
3. Drain the fuel and clean out the float chamber.
4. Hold the float chamber cover in a vertical position with the fuel inlet pointing up.
5. With float chamber gasket in position, check the float level from the mating surface of the cover to the bottom of the float.
6. If the float level does not check to

Checking the float level on 34TBIA Solex® carburetors used on 604 models

Checking the float level on the 35CEEI Venturi injection carb used on some models

1.6 in. (40 mm), adjust the float level by bending the tab on the float.

7. Invert the air horn so that the float is at its lowest point. Check the float for 0.5 in. (12.5 mm) of drop. Adjust by bending the float drop tab.

AUTOMATIC CHOKE ADJUSTMENT

504

1. Pull out the manual choke control.
2. Push in the vacuum pull-off rod to obtain the initial choke opening.
3. Measure the opening between the venturi and the choke butterfly at the notch in the lower end of the butterfly.
4. If the gap is not between 0.08 in. (2 mm) and 0.12 in. (3mm), adjust by bending the tab on the linkage.

604

1. Start the engine and bring it up to operating temperature.

1. 0.295 in. (7 mm) drill or gauge rod
2. Locknut
3. Adjusting screw
4. Choke gauge tool (8.0143)
5. Choke housing

604 choke adjustment

— CAUTION —
Make sure the gearshift is in Neutral or Park and the handbrake is set.

---

2. Always check the idle speed and mixture for correct setting before adjusting the choke.
3. Remove the air and choke housing cover plate.
4. Install the Peugeot choke gauge tool 8.0143 or equivalent to engage the choke mechanism pivoting roller onto the tool. Rock the tool back and forth slightly until it contacts the choke housing.
5. Increase the engine speed to obtain the total choke opening after start (COAS). The pull-off opening should be 0.295 in. (7.5 mm) from the choke plate to the wall of the choke bore.
6. If the choke plate clearance is incorrect, loosen the adjusting locknut and turn the screw to obtain the proper clearance. Tighten the locknut.
7. Remove the gauge tool.
8. Install the choke housing cover and the air cleaner assembly.

Fuel Injection

For all fuel injection system service and repair procedures not detailed below, please refer to "Fuel Injection" in the Unit Repair section.

INJECTOR

Removal and Installation

1. Remove the fuel line from the injector.
2. Pull the injector out of the rubber seal.

— CAUTION —
Do not pull on the fuel line when removing the injector. Pull directly on the injector body.

---

3. Always use a new rubber seal when reinstalling an injector.

NOTE: Moisten the new rubber seal with fuel before installing the injector.

4. Press in the injector until it is fully seated.

Testing

1. Use injector test stand, Peugeot number 8.0141A and adaptors 8.0141B, 8.0141C and 8.0141H or equivalents.
2. Close the test stand valve.
3. Install adaptors 8.0141B and 8.0141C or equivalents on the test stand.
4. Install test adaptor 8.0141H or equivalent on the injector and install the assembly onto the test stand. Do not tighten the assembly.
5. Before tightening the nut on the test stand pipe, activiate the tester several times to bleed the pipe.
6. Tighten the nut on the pipe to adaptor fitting.
7. Activate the tester several times until the injector is bled.
8. Open the test stand valve one turn.
9. Pump the test stand lever one stroke every two seconds until the injector sprays.
10. The injector opening pressure should be from 43.6 to 59.5 psi (3 to 4.1 bar).
11. If the opening pressure is not within specifications, replace the injector.

NOTE: The injectors can be replaced individually.

12. Loosen the test stand valve and increase the pressure to 7.0 lbs (0.5 bar) below the opening injector pressure. Maintain this pressure for 15 seconds. No leakage should occur. If an injector leaks, replace it.
13. During spray testing, the injector should make a groaning noise and have a spray span of 35°. If an injector is not operating properly, replace it.

FUEL FILTER

Removal and Installation

1. Remove the negative cable from the battery.

2. Remove the fuel filter mounting screw.

3. Remove the fuel filter from its mounting.

4. Loosen the fuel lines to relieve the pressure, then remove the fuel lines. Remove the filter.

5. Install new sealing rings on the filter fittings and torque the inlet and outlet nuts to 24.5 ft.lbs. (32.3 Nm). Torque the outlet banjo bolt to 18.0 ft.lbs. (23.8 Nm.)

Diesel Injection Pump

REMOVAL AND INSTALLATION

1. Disconnect the battery.

2. Disconnect the stop, fast idle and acceleration linkages from the pump.

3. Disconnect the injector return hose and the fuel inlet and outlet couplings.

4. Remove the injector pipe assembly and leave the couplings on the pump and the injector holder.

5. Plug all couplings.

6. Remove the pump rear support from the cylinder head.

7. Remove the injection pump.

8. Installation is the reverse of removal.

MANUAL TRANSMISSION

REMOVAL AND INSTALLATION

504 and 505

1. Disconnect the negative battery cable.

2. Drain the gear oil.

3. Remove the ignition coil, the upper radiator mounting and both bolts from the lower radiator mounting on the front crossmember.

NOTE: Draining the cooling system will not be necessary.

4. Remove the starter motor and starter motor dust cover plate.

5. Remove the air cleaner.

6. Remove the nuts securing the exhaust pipe to the exhaust manifold.

7. Remove the nut on the hanger holding the exhaust pipe at the front silencer.

8. Remove the hanger on the exhaust pipe near the rear end of the transmission extension housing.

9. Remove the rear tail pipe hanger.

10. Turn the steering wheel to a clockwise position, so that the front exhaust pipe can be disengaged.

11. Allow the exhaust system to rest on the rear crossmember.

12. Remove the heat dissipation plate.

13. Install the gearbox support tool, Peugeot number 8.0125 or equivalent. Line the slot in the bolt adaptor with the notch in the forward flange of the clutch housing.

14. If the special gearbox support tool is not available, use a jack stand to support the clutch housing.

15. Using an 8 mm Allen type socket, remove the three bolts from the differential to gearbox connecting tube (at the gearbox). Loosen the fourth bolt with an 8 mm shouldered Allen key.

16. Remove the two differential to crossmember Allen bolts.

17. Separate the connecting tube and the driveshaft from the gearbox. Install the driveshaft holding plate, Peugeot number 8.0403S or equivalent.

18. Remove the clutch slave cylinder without disconnecting the hydraulic line.

19. Remove the shift lever and shift rods.

20. Remove the back-up light switch leads, gearbox ground strap and speedometer cable.

21. Remove the lower steering shaft pinch clamp bolt, (remove 2 steering knuckle bolts on 505 models).

22. Remove the steering gear housing bolts.

23. Lower the steering gear housing without removing any more bolts.

24. Remove the clutch housing cover plates.

25. Remove the clutch housing support, Peugeot number 8.0125 or the jack stand.

26. Remove the three allen bolts holding the clutch housing to the engine.

27. Install the engine hoisting brackets on the engine.

28. Using an engine crane–type lift or equivalent, lift the engine to rotate it on its rubber mounting blocks in order to remove the gearbox from the engine.

29. Install a block of wood between the radiator and the hoisting bracket to avoid damage to the radiator hoses.

30. Rotate the gearbox a quarter turn counterclockwise and remove the gearbox by pulling it back.

31. Remove the clutch release ball bearing.

32. Installation is the reverse of removal.

33. Torque the bolts as follows:

Item	Ft.lbs. (Nm)
Connecting tube to gearbox	43.5 ft.lbs. (58.8 Nm)
Gearbox drain plug	20.0 ft.lbs. (22.0 Nm)
Starter motor bolts	14.5 ft.lbs. (19.6 Nm)

NOTE: Use grease on the release bearing guide and the engine driveshaft before installing them.

34. Adjust the gear shift linkage and check the clutch pedal for proper operation.

604

On the 604 models, the engine and transmission must be removed as a unit.

1. Drain the gearbox oil.

2. Remove the hood, the air mixer housing and the air filter.

3. Drain the cooling system.

4. Remove the radiator support struts and the battery.

5. Disconnect the radiator hoses at the radiator.

6. Remove the radiator and the fan casing.

7. Remove the ground cable at the engine, the temperature sending unit, the power brake booster vacuum hose and the fuel pump hoses.

8. Remove the carburetor controls, primary coil leads and high tension coil-to-distributor wire.

9. Remove the plug and heater hoses.

10. Remove the starter and alternator harness connection.

11. Remove the exhaust pipe-to-manifold flange bolts and separate the pipe from the manifold.

12. Remove the engine mounting bolts.

13. Remove the exhaust mounting brackets at the silencers, the center exhaust mounting and the heat baffle.

14. Remove the clutch housing lower cover plate.

15. Remove the starter harness retaining clip.

16. Remove the power steering pump and the power steering belt.

17. Raise the engine with engine lift tool Peugeot number 8.0135Z or equivalent, until the gearbox contacts the floor tunnel. Lower the engine until the gearbox clears the tunnel by 0.4 in. (10.16 mm).

18. Push back the front seats and remove the front seat securing bolts.

19. Install studs Peugeot number 8.1511B or equivalent, under the vehicle in the seat bolts holes.

20. Install flat washers and nuts on the studs on the inside of the vehicle. Tighten the nuts.

21. Install the driveshaft support tool Peugeot number 8.1511A or equivalent and adjust the support tool to contact the driveshaft tube.

22. Remove the bolt from the steering shaft pinch clamp at the flexible coupling flange.

23. Remove the two rear main crossmember bolts and replace them with longer bolts, Peugeot number 8.1511C or equivalent.

24. Remove the two front crossmember bolts and lower the longer bolts so that the crossmember drops 1.2 in. (30.5 mm).

25. Remove the clutch cylinder snap-ring

and push the cylinder back 0.12 in. (3 mm).

26. Remove the clutch cylinder bolts and wire the cylinder to the side of the vehicle.

27. Remove the back-up light switch leads, the gearshift control and the speedometer drive fitting.

28. Remove the driveshaft tube-to-gearbox bolts.

29. Separate the driveshaft and driveshaft tube from the gearbox and install the driveshaft retaining plate Peugeot number 8.0403SZ or equivalent on the driveshaft.

30. Remove the engine and gearbox together by tilting them up in the front and raising the assembly out of the vehicle.

—————— CAUTION ——————

Do not damage the power steering hoses.

31. Lower the assembly onto an engine stand.

32. Remove the clutch housing cover plate, the starter casing and the clutch housing-to-engine bolts.

33. Separate the gearbox from the engine.

34. Installation is the reverse of removal.

35. Follow these torque specifications:

Item	ft. lbs.	(Nm)
Clutch housing to engine	12.6	(17.1)
Driveshaft tube to gearbox	39.6	(53.9)
Steering shaft pinch-clamp	12.8	(17.1)

NOTE: The clearance between the steering wheel and the steering column casing should be 0.08 in. (2 mm).

LINKAGE ADJUSTMENT

1. To adjust linkage, first raise the front of the car and support it with safety stands.

2. Remove the return spring and the two control links. Clean the plastic ball joint sockets and make sure they have not been damaged during dismantling. Replace any defective parts and grease the ball joints prior to installation.

3. Check and adjust the socket center-to-socket center distances of the two link rods before refitting. Their lengths are 287 and 89 millimeters respectively (see the illustrations).

4. Place the bottom selector lever in the Neutral position. Fit the lower link rod on its gear shifter and bottom lever socket balls, positioning the ball sockets for fit. Then tighten the locknut on the link rod shaft.

5. Make sure that the gear selector lever is in Neutral and connect the fixed ball socket on the selector link to the selector jack lever.

6. Push the link upward as far as possible and check the alignment of the ball joint with the lever on the gearbox.

7. Correctly position the link bottom ball joint socket on the gear selector lever and tighten the locknut on the link shaft.

8. Install the return spring.

OVERHAUL

For all manual transmission overhaul procedures, please refer to "Manual Transmission Overhaul" in the Unit Repair section.

CLUTCH

REMOVAL AND INSTALLATION

504

1. Remove the transmission. Refer to the "Transmission Removal and Installation" procedures.

2. Matchmark the clutch assembly in

1. Clutch housing
2. Flywheel
3. Clutch disc
4. Clutch pressure plate
5. Cover
6. Diaphragm
7. Guided thrust bearing
8. Bushing
9. Clutch fork
10. Pivot
11. Release cylinder
12. Release cylinder housing
13. Bleed screw
14. Driveshaft
15. Crankshaft

Cross section of the 504 clutch assembly

relation to the flywheel, if the unit is to be reused.

3. Remove the clutch assembly retaining bolts and separate the assembly from the flywheel.

4. Check the bearing surface of the disc on the flywheel. If needed, remove the flywheel and true up the surface on a lathe. Always take the same cut from the disc surface and the bolt attaching surface in order to maintain the same clutch diaphragm tension and height.

5. Place the clutch disc correctly with the flexible hub facing the gearbox. Center the disc on the flywheel using a centering tool.

6. Align the matchmarks (on a re-installed unit), and install the clutch assembly to the flywheel with the attaching bolts. Torque the bolts to 10 ft. lbs. (15 Nm).

7. Re-install the transmission and complete the assembly.

505

1. The clutch may be removed without removing the engine. Disconnect the battery, drain the cooling system, and remove the radiator.

2. Remove the fan belt and move the belt tensioner aside.

3. Remove the alternator and regulator after disconnecting the battery wire.

4. Disconnect the clutch return spring.

5. Loosen, but do not remove, the two left front tie-rod studs.

6. Remove the two bolts attaching the left front tie-rod fork to the alternator support.

7. Position the tie-rod and fork assembly to one side.

8. Disconnect the heater hose from the water pump.

9. Rotate the engine until the tab lock for the pulley attachment screw faces downward.

10. Loosen the pulley screw using a large offset screwdriver.

11. Remove the air cleaner.

12. While holding the crankshaft pulley, loosen the attaching bolt further.

13. Remove the crankshaft pulley and backing spring, if so equipped.

14. Remove the clutch housing cover and throwout bearing.

15. Align the pressure plate notch with the 8 mm pin hole in the clutch housing.

16. Remove the clutch using a puller.

17. Before installation, clean the shaft and splined drive gear and lubricate with a moly spray.

—————— CAUTION ——————

Do not spray lubricant on the drive gear oil seal surface.

18. Make sure that the crankshaft reference hole is aligned with the top of the cylinder.

19. Position the clutch assembly on the crankshaft so that the notch on the clutch

cover aligns with the hole in the clutch housing.

20. Rotate the clutch back and forth so as to engage the clutch disc over the gear.

NOTE: The six clutch assembly bolts must not be tightened in order to allow centering of the clutch disc.

21. Temporarily install the crankshaft pulley and tighten the attachment screw slightly to fully engage the clutch.

22. Tighten the six clutch assembly bolts to 18 ft. lbs. and then remove the crank pulley.

23. Pack the clutch hub groove with grease.

24. Install the throwout bearing and, if so equipped, the thrust bearing.

25. Install the clutch housing cover, making sure that the flat side of the clutch fork is facing toward the throwout bearing.

26. Tighten the clutch housing cover bolts to 7 ft. lbs. and refit the crankshaft pulley, making sure that it engages the locking ball on the clutch hub.

27. Install the attaching bolt with a new tab and tighten to 47 ft. lbs. while holding the pulley. Bend the tab and lock after tightening.

28. Install components in reverse order of removal and adjust fan belt and clutch free travel.

604

1. Remove the engine and transmission as a unit before separating the transmission.

2. Remove the clutch housing cover plate.

3. Remove the two starter-to-clutch housing bolts. Remove the four clutch housing-to-engine bolts.

4. Matchmark the clutch assembly in relation to the flywheel, (if the unit is to be re-used).

5. Remove the clutch assembly retaining bolts and separate the assembly from the flywheel.

6. Check the bearing surface of the disc on the flywheel. If needed, remove the flywheel and true up the surface on a lathe. Always take the same cut from the disc surface and the bolt attaching surface in order to maintain the same clutch diaphragm tension and height.

7. Place the clutch disc correctly with the flexible hub facing the gearbox. Center the disc on the flywheel using a centering tool.

8. Align the matchmarks (on a re-installed unit), and install the clutch assembly to the flywheel with the attaching bolts. Torque the bolts to 15 ft. lbs. (20 Nm).

9. Install the gearbox on the engine and torque the bolts to 12 ft. lbs. (17 Nm).

10. Install the engine and transmission assembly into the vehicle.

PEDAL ADJUSTMENT AND FREE-PLAY

Because of the hydraulic operation of Peugeot clutches, the clutch is largely self-adjusting. Should excessive play or slackness become evident at the clutch pedal, then fluid is somehow draining out of the clutch hydraulic system and must be investigated and corrected at once.

A minimal adjustment can be made on the 304 by adjusting the screw locknut on the slave cylinder pushrod. The free travel at the clutch fork stop should be 0.10 in. (2 mm). This should correspond to a free pedal travel of 1.2 to 1.4 in. If you are unable to obtain the correct free travel after adjusting the screw to the above specifications, check, and if necessary, bleed the hydraulic system.

Clutch Slave Cylinder

REMOVAL AND INSTALLATION

1. Remove the hydraulic line and plug it.

2. Remove the cylinder.

3. Install the cylinder and the hydraulic line.

4. Fill the clutch master cylinder reservoir and bleed the system.

BLEED THE SYSTEM

Peugeot recommends using a pressure bleed tank to bleed the clutch slave cylinder. However, if a pressure tank is not available, the system can be bled manually by depressing the clutch and opening the bleeder screw momentaily, to allow air to escape.

1. Attach a pressure bleeding tank to the bleed screw on the slave cylinder.

2. Adjust the pressure to approximately 25 psi.

3. Open the bleed screw one full turn.

4. Check the rise of fluid in the reservoir.

5. Stop the bleeding when the level in the reservoir is correct.

6. Check the hydraulic control operation.

NOTE: Use Lockheed© 55 or equivalent fluid.

AUTOMATIC TRANSMISSION

REMOVAL AND INSTALLATION

504 and 505

1. Remove the exhaust hanger at the intermediate exhaust pipe, the middle exhaust hanger and the exhaust hanger near the front end of the differential.

2. Remove the two differential side mounting bolts.

3. Place the driveshaft connecting tube on the rear crossmember.

4. Remove the two steering shaft flange bolts on 505 models.

   a. Conventional Steering Gearbox   Remove the two steering box bolts and lower the steering gearbox without disconnecting the steering linkage.

   b. Power Steering Gearbox   Replace the rear bolts on the front crossmember with Peugeot tool number 8.1511C or equivalent and remove the two forward crossmember bolts. Lower the crossmember 2.0 in. (50.8 mm) by turning the special tool bolts.

5. Remove the steering shaft pinch clamp bolt on 504 models and the steering gear housing bolts. Lower the steering, without disconnecting the steering linkage.

6. Drain the transmission fluid.

7. Remove the oil cooler lines at the transmission and plug them.

8. Remove the two starter-to-torque converter housing bolts.

9. Remove the transmission fill tube.

10. Remove the passenger side converter housing cover plate.

11. Remove the sensor plate cover and the sensor from the front driver's side of the transmission converter housing on 505 models, if so equipped.

NOTE: Take care not to alter the adjustment of the sensor.

12. Remove the converter-to-flexplate bolts and lock the ring gear with Peugeot tool number 8.0144B, 8.0110J or equivalents.

13. Secure the torque converter with Peugeot tool number 8.0135A or equivalent.

14. Place a transmission jack under the transmission and raise the jack to support the weight of the transmission.

15. Remove the four driveshaft connecting tube-to-extension housing bolts. Separate the connecting tube and driveshaft from the extension housing.

16. Install Peugeot tool 8.0403SZ or equivalent, driveshaft retaining plate on the driveshaft.

17. Remove the gearshift linkage, transmission wiring harness and speedometer drive fitting.

18. Drop the transmission as far down as it will go by lowering the transmission jack. Remove the converter/flexplate bolts.

19. Install engine lifting bracket, Peugeot number 8.0102X or equivalent.

20. Move the engine as far as it will go with the engine mounts still in place, to clear the transmission under the floor tunnel.

21. Remove the torque converter housing-to-engine bolts and separate the converter from the flexplate.

22. Lower the transmission on the transmission jack.

23. Installation is the reverse of removal.

24. Use the following torque specifications:

Item	ft. lbs.	(Nm)
Starter	18.0	(24.5)
Torque converter	39.6	(53.9)
Flywheel	21.6	(29.4)
Driveshaft tube	39.6	(53.9)
505 steering coupling	12.6	(17.1)
504 steering pinch bolt	12.6	(17.1)

604

1. Remove the hood.
2. Remove the air filter and assembly.
3. Drain the cooling system.
4. Remove the radiator hoses and upper radiator struts.
5. Remove the battery, the fan motor wires and the transmission cooler lines.
6. Remove the radiator and the fan casing.
7. Remove the ground cable at the engine and the temperature sending unit.
8. Remove the brake booster vacuum hose and the fuel pump lines.
9. Remove the carburetor controls and the primary coil leads. Remove the high tension coil wire.
10. Remove the heater hoses and plug the ends.
11. Remove the starter and alternator harness connectors.
12. Remove the exhaust pipe-to-exhaust manifold bolts and the engine mounting bolts.
13. Remove the front and center exhaust hangers.
14. Remove the heat baffle.
15. Remove the lower torque converter housing cover plate.
16. Remove the starter harness retainer clip.
17. Remove the power assisted steering pump and power steering belt.
18. Secure the power steering pump assembly to the fender well.
19. Lift the engine with a hoist until the transmission makes contact with the tunnel, then lower it approximately 0.4 in. (10.16 mm).
20. Push back the front seats and remove the seat securing bolts.
21. Raise the vehicle. Install threaded rods, Peugeot number 8.1511B or equivalent, into the seat bolts holes.
22. Lower the vehicle. Install flat washers and nuts on the ends of the threaded rods and tighten them.
23. Install the driveshaft support tool, Peugeot number 8.1511 or equivalent, onto threaded rods. Adjust the tool to support the driveshaft tube.

24. Remove the bolt from the pinch clamp on the steering shaft.

25. Remove the two rear main crossmember bolts and install tool, Peugeot number 8.1511C or equivalent. Remove the two front main crossmember bolts. Lower the main crossmember 1.2 in. (30.5 mm), by turning the special bolts.

26. Remove the cooler lines and the electrical connector at the transmission.

27. Remove the driveshaft tube-to-extension housing bolts.

28. Separate the driveshaft and driveshaft tube from the extension housing.

29. Install the driveshaft retaining plate tool, Peugeot number 8.0403SZ or equivalent, onto the driveshaft.

30. Move the back of the engine/transmission assembly out of the vehicle.

─── **CAUTION** ───

Do not damage the power steering hoses or the transmission cooler lines.

31. Separate the transmission from the engine. Leave the converter with the transmission. Installation is the reverse of removal.

32. Use the following torque specifications during reassembly and installation.

Item	ft. lbs.	(Nm)
Driveshaft tube	43.5	(58.8)
Starter motor	14.5	(19.6)
Converter to ring gear	34.7	(46.6)
Converter housing	28.8	(39.2)
Steering flange	10.8	(14.9)

33. Adjust the kickdown cable.
34. Fill the transmission with fluid.

NEUTRAL SAFETY SWITCH ADJUSTMENTS

ZF Transmissions

Two types of neutral start switches are used on the ZF automatic transmissions.

TYPE 1

The type 1 switch is attached to the side of the transmission case and is operated by a connecting rod attached to the transmission manual lever. The adjustment of the switch must be checked after the manual linkage has been adjusted.

1. Locate the selector lever in the Neutral position.
2. Loosen the switch retaining screw and the switch lever nut. Adjust the switch so that the engine will start only in the Neutral or Park positions.
3. Tighten the switch retaining screw and the lever nut.

TYPE 2

The type 2 switch is located with the selector lever assembly and cannot be ad-

justed. To replace the switch assembly, the console assembly must be removed. Remove the shift lever assembly from the floor. Remove the switch retaining screw and install the new switch. The switch pins must be engaged in the holes in the shift gate.

GM Transmission

1. Place the gear shift selector lever in Neutral.
2. Loosen the retaining nuts on the switch retaining bracket.
3. Align the mark on the switch body with the mark on the pivot housing.
4. Tighten the retaining nuts.
5. Check for starting in Neutral and Park. Check for not starting in Reverse, 3, 2, and 1. In the reverse position, the backup lights should operate.

1. Mark on the switch body
2. Pivot housing

Adjusting alignment marks on the GM transmission neutral safety switch

SHIFT LINKAGE AND ADJUSTMENT

1. Disconnect the rod at the transmission lever.
2. Set the gear shift selector lever in the Neutral position.
3. Set the transmission lever in Neutral. The position is provided by the ball lock inside the transmission.
4. If the rod will not fit into the transmission lever without moving the lever, adjust the rod length so that it will fit into the transmission lever.
5. Install the rod on the transmission lever.

SHIFT SELECTOR LEVER

CONNECTING ROD

TRANSMISSION LEVER

Adjusting the shift linkage on automatic transmissions for all models

BAND ADJUSTMENT

GM Transmission Only

The GM Transmissions have no external band adjustment. The servo apply pins are available in different lengths. Selection the proper length pin is equivalent to adjusting the bands. This can only be done with the transmission disassembled.

DRIVE AXLES

Driveshaft (Enclosed Type)

REMOVAL AND INSTALLATION

504 and 505

1. Remove the exhaust system from the exhaust manifold and remove all exhaust hangers. Let the system rest on the front and rear crossmembers.
2. Remove the heat dissipation plate.
3. Remove the two differential bolts. Let the rear part of the driveshaft tube rest on the rear crossmember.
4. Place a jack under the left side crossmember support.
5. Remove the rear seat cushion. Loosen all three left side crossmember nuts. Raise the tab lock and remove the plastic plug from the guide hole. Screw the threaded end of the guide rod, Peugeot number 8.0906K1 or equivalent, through the guide hole and into the crossmember. Insert a pin into the guide rod.
6. Remove the crossmember securing nuts.
7. Lower the jack until the pin rests on the floor. Repeat these operations on the right hand crossmember support.
8. Remove the driveshaft tube from the differential.
9. Move the differential back and support it on a wooden block.
10. Remove the small spring from the end of the driveshaft.

NOTE: If the vehicle is to be moved from one work area to another, secure the differential to the rear crossmember with two Peugeot number 204 cylinder head bolts or equivalent.

11. Remove the driveshaft tube at the transmission.
12. Install driveshaft holding plate, Peugeot tool number 8.0403S or equivalent.
13. Lower the exhaust pipe at the front end.
14. Angle the driveshaft and driveshaft tube and remove them toward the front of the vehicle.
15. Installation is the reverse of removal.

16. Use the following torque specifications:

Item	ft. lbs.	(Nm)
Driveshaft tube bolts	43.5	(58.8)
Differential attaching bolts	27.0	(36.8)

17. Install the rear seat cushion and lubricate the driveshaft center bearing.

604

1. Remove the console shifter trim.
2. Pull back the bellows and remove the two shift lever bolts.
3. Remove the heat baffle and the center exhaust pipe hanger.
4. From under the vehicle, remove the front gearshift lever nut.
5. Using a jack stand or other safe method, take the weight off the extension housing of the transmission.
6. Remove the four driveshaft tube-to-extension housing bolts.
7. Remove the four driveshaft tube-to-differential bolts.
8. Remove the driveshaft and driveshaft tube toward the rear of the vehicle.
9. Install the driveshaft and tube onto the differential and transmission. Torque the bolts to 43.2 ft. lbs. (58.8 Nm).
10. Install the front nut on the shift lever, from under the vehicle.
11. Set the exhaust baffles over the muffler.
12. Install the exhaust pipe hangers on the exhaust pipe.
13. Bolt on the heat baffles.
14. Install the two gear shift lever bolts, the bellows and the trim.

OVERHAUL

The tube and/or the shaft will have to be replaced if either is out of balance or damaged.

Axleshafts
REMOVAL AND INSTALLATION

1. Raise the rear of the vehicle and place jack stands under the suspension arms.

2. Remove the wheel and install holding tool, Peugeot number 8.0521 A or equivalent, on the hub.
3. Loosen the hub nut without removing it and remove the holding tool.
4. Remove the brake thrust spring, pad returning fork and brake pads.
5. Loosen the brake line retaining clamp on the rear control arm.
6. Remove the caliper and hang it on the body without distorting the brake line.
7. Remove the hub-to-disc retaining screw. Mark the location of the retaining screw on the disc.
8. Remove the disc.
9. Remove the bolts holding the spindle hub to the suspension arm.
10. Install special bolts, Peugeot numbers 8.0521 B1 and B2 or equivalents, into the back of the hub assembly. Install the thrust plate, Peugeot number 8.0521 B3 or equivalent onto the hub.
11. To remove the hub assembly, alternately tighten bolts B1 and B2 against plate B3.
12. Remove the disc brake backing plate, if equipped.
13. Remove the hub nut washer.
14. Remove the final driveshaft from the hub knuckle. Use an arbor press, if necessary.
15. Installation is the reverse of removal.

— CAUTION —
Use a new final driveshaft nut on every re-installation. Stake the new nut to hold it.

16. Use the following torque specifications:

	ft. lbs.	(Nm)
Brake pad holding fork	31.0	(40.9 Nm)
Final driveshaft nut	181.0	(245 Nm)
Wheel lug nuts	43.5	(58.8 Nm)

NOTE: The station wagon has axle housings attached to the differential and the axle shafts are enclosed.

Rear Wheel Bearings
REMOVAL AND INSTALLATION

1. Remove the final drive axleshaft from the vehicle.

1. Rear axle knuckle assembly
2. Rear axle retaining washer
3. Rear axle retaining nut

Rear axle hub assembly

2. Separate the hub and knuckle assembly from the final drive axleshaft. Use an arbor press if necessary.

3. Clamp the hub assembly in a soft jawed vise.

4. Remove the hub assembly nut.

5. Press the hub from the knuckle assembly.

6. Press out the bearing assembly from the knuckle.

7. Turn the knuckle over in the vise and remove the outer oil seal.

8. Install a new outer oil seal.

9. Install a new inner oil seal.

10. Press in a new bearing assembly.

11. Install the knuckle nut and torque it to 181 ft. lbs. (245 Nm).

12. Install the hub onto the knuckle assembly.

13. Install the final drive axleshaft into the hub and knuckle assembly.

14. Complete the installation on the vehicle.

15. Torque the final drive axleshaft nut to 181 ft. lbs. (245 Nm).

—————— CAUTION ——————
Use a new final drive axleshaft on every re-installation. Stake the new nut to hold it.

REAR SUSPENSION

Shock Absorbers

REMOVAL AND INSTALLATION

1. If a frame contact lift is used, support the control arms before removing the shock absorber bolts.

2. Open the trunk lid and use an open end wrench to hold the shock while removing the shock nut from the shock bolt.

3. Remove the rubber washer and the sheet metal cup from the upper shock bolt.

4. Remove the lower shock bolt from the control arm.

5. Remove the shock by pulling it through the hole in the control arm.

6. Always replace the rubber washer,

1. Rear crossmember
2. Vibration damper
3. Lower crossmember mounting
4. Trailing suspension arm
5. Hub spindle
6. Trailing arm bushing
7. Stabilizer bar link
8. Upper suspension crossmember
9. Stabilizer bar
10. Upper crossmember mounting
11. Shock absorber and suspension spring
12. Rubber blocks
13. Housing
14. Inner support

604 rear suspension

upper sheet metal cup and upper self locking nut, every time the shock is installed.

7. Fully extend the shock absorber rod and install the thrust cup, rod protector, centering cup, rubber washer and nylon spacer.

8. Use new lock washers and install the lower shock bolt on the control arm.

9. Place the new rubber washer and metal cup on the shock and secure it with a new locknut.

Rear Control Arm and Coil Springs

REMOVAL AND INSTALLATION

1. Remove the final driveshafts from both sides.

2. Support the rear control arms and remove the rear shocks.

3. Remove the stabilizer bar links at the control arms.

4. Slowly lower the rear control arms to release the tension on the coil springs. Remove the coil springs.

5. Remove the four control arm-to-crossmember bolts and lower out the control arms.

6. Installation is the reverse of removal.

FRONT SUSPENSION

The front suspension is of the MacPherson strut type.

MacPherson Strut

For all spring and shock absorber removal and installation procedures and any other strut overhaul procedures, please refer to "Strut Overhaul" in the Unit Repair section.

REMOVAL AND INSTALLATION

1. Raise the vehicle and support both sides of the front crossmember.

2. Remove the front wheel.

3. Remove the brake caliper and suspend it from the frame.

4. Remove the steering rod end from the knuckle.

5. Remove the connecting link from the rear bar of the triangular suspension arm.

6. Remove the strut from the knuckle.

7. Remove the locking nut securing the front arm to the rear arm.

8. Place a jack under the wheel hub.

9. Remove the three bolts securing the

504 rear suspension

1. Front crossmember
2. Stabilizer bar
3. A-frame front arm
4. A-frame rear arm
5. Strut
6. Main crossmember
7. Knuckle
8. Brake caliper
9. Steering rod end (tie rod)
10. Connecting link

504 and 505 front suspension

1. Front crossmember
2. Stabilizer bar
3. A-frame front arm
4. A-frame rear arm
5. Strut
6. Main crossmember
7. Knuckle
8. Brake caliper
9. Steering rod end (tie rod)
10. Connecting link

604 front suspension

upper spring holder to the inner fender well.

10. Lower the jack and remove the strut assembly from the vehicle.

Ball Joint

INSPECTION

Check ball joint play as follows:

a. Raise the front of the car and support it with safety stands.

b. Clamp a dial indicator onto the lower control arm and place the indicator tip on the knuckle, near the ball joint.

c. Place a pry bar between the lower control arm and the knuckle. Replace the ball joint if the play exceeds 0.1 in. vertical motion or 0.25 in. horizontal motion.

REMOVAL AND INSTALLATION

1. Raise the front of the car and support with safety stands under the front cross-member.

2. Unlock the lower ball joint locknut using special socket No. 8.0906 C or D.

3. Remove the ball joint retaining nut with the castled socket No. 8.0906 F.

4. Use the extractor No. 8.0906 B to remove the arm from the steering knuckle. Remove the extractor, the rubber dust cover

and its spring clip, the lower cup, ball joint, and upper cup.

5. Before reassembling, the following parts must be replaced:

a. Rubber dust cover:
b. Cover spring clip;
c. Upper ball joint cup;
d. Ball joint head (if necessary);
e. Lower cup;
f. Locknut (with grease nipple).

6. Grease the ball joint housing and then place the arm on the steering knuckle ball joint cone.

Wheel Alignment

CASTER AND CAMBER ADJUSTMENT

Caster and camber are preset at the factory and cannot be adjusted on any Peugeot. If caster, camber or kingpin angle is incorrect, or front end parts are damaged or worn, they must be replaced.

TOE-IN ADJUSTMENT

Toe-in (or toe-out) is the difference of the distance the forward extremes of the front tires and the distance between the rearward extremes of the front tires. Toe-in is adjustable on all Peugeots.

1. Make sure that tbe car is in its correct riding position and that the front wheels are pointed straight-ahead.

2. Slacken the two clamp nuts on the adjustable tie-rod.

3. Hold the tie-rod ball joint with its two flats *horizontal* using a 14 mm open end wrench.

4. Screw or unscrew the tie-rod to obtain the specified toe-in.

NOTE: One turn of the tie-rod is equivalent to 0.177 in. at the wheel rim.

5. Hold the tie-rod in the newly corrected position and tighten the two clamp bolts to 9 ft. lbs. while ensuring that the ball joint remains on a horizontal plane.

1. Inner seal
2. Knuckle
3. Outer seal
4. Wheel stud
5. Knuckle nut
6. Bearing assembly
7. Washer
8. Outer seal
9. Control arm to knuckle attaching bolt
10. Washer
11. Final drive shaft nut
12. Hub

Exploded view of the front wheel bearing assembly

Front Wheel Bearing Adjustment

Torque the hub nut to 28.0 ft. lbs. (39.0 Nm), then loosen the nut and re-torque it to 7.0 ft. lbs. (9.8 Nm). Lock the hub nut in place.

STEERING

Steering Wheel

REMOVAL AND INSTALLATION

1. Remove the negative battery cable.
2. Place the wheels in a straight ahead position.
3. Remove the horn cover pad and horn contact assembly.
4. Remove the steering wheel nut.
5. Matchmark the steering wheel and the steering shaft.
6. Use a steering wheel puller tool to remove the steering wheel.
7. Installation is the reverse of removal.

Combination Switch

The horn and turn signal switches are combined as a unit.

REMOVAL AND INSTALLATION

1. Remove the steering wheel.
2. Remove the horn assembly and column cover.
3. Disconnect all wiring to the switch.
4. Remove the switch.
5. Installation is the reverse of removal.

Ignition Switch

REMOVAL AND INSTALLATION

The steering wheel does not have to be removed.
1. Remove the negative battery cable.
2. Remove the steering column and ignition switch cover to expose the ignition switch.
3. Remove the wiring from the switch connections.
4. Remove the switch–to–column attaching bolts and remove the switch. Installation is the reverse of the removal procedure.

Manual Steering Gear

REMOVAL AND INSTALLATION

1. Remove the tie rod ends from the steering arm knuckles.

1. Tie rod end
2. Tie rod
3. Steering column knuckle
4. Crossmember
5. Housing
6. Power steering pump
7. Power steering hoses

504 and 505 power steering assembly

2. Remove the steering gear bolts and the lower shaft flange bolt.
3. Insert a 0.24 in. (6 mm) diameter punch in the flange bolt hole.
4. Disengage the gearbox by rocking it with the punch. Remove the gearbox assembly.
5. When installing, position the steering wheel bars vertically.
6. Place the passenger side front wheel in the straight ahead position.
7. Place the driver's side wheel to a turned-in position.
8. Center the rack in relation to the rack housing.
9. Temporarily connect the tie rod end on the passenger side.
10. Rotate the flange ¼ turn to align the flange collar with the splined end of the steering shaft.
11. Rock the flange slightly to install it on the splined shaft.
12. Install the steering gear to crossmember bolts. Torque the bolts to 22.7 ft. lbs. (31.8 Nm).
13. Install the bolt and a new locknut on the flange-to-column collar. Torque the nut to 10.8 ft. lbs. (14.7 Nm).
14. Install the tie rod ends on the steering arm knuckles.
15. If the tie rod end has a cotter pin hole in the stud, position the hole parallel to the length of the tie rod, tighten the nut and install the cotter pin.
16. Without the cotter pin, use a new locking nut and torque the nut to 30.6 ft. lbs. (41.7 Nm).
17. Adjust the front wheel toe-in.

Power Steering Gear

REMOVAL AND INSTALLATION

The removal and installation of the power type gearbox is basically the same procedure as the manual type gearbox. The system must be drained of hydraulic fluid and the hydraulic liners disconnected from the pump.

Power Steering Pump

REMOVAL AND INSTALLATION

1. Remove the high pressure hose and drain the system. Move steering wheel back and forth to insure complete drainage. Do not start engine.
2. Remove the belt adjusting nut, remove the belt and the pump attaching bolts.
3. Remove the pump.
4. Installation is the reverse of removal.

BELT ADJUSTMENT

1. Make two marks on the belt to be installed 4 in. (100 mm) apart.
2. On a used belt tighten the belt so that the marks are 4.06 in. (101.5 mm) apart.
3. On a new belt, tighten the belt so that the marks are 4.1 in. (102.5 mm) apart.

SYSTEM BLEEDING

The power steering system is automatically bled by turning the steering gear to its full stop in both directions, several times.

BRAKE SYSTEM

All Peugeot models are equipped with disc brakes on the front. The 504 models are equipped with drum brakes on the rear, while the remaining models are equipped with rear disc brakes.
For all brake system repair and service procedures not detailed below, please refer to "Brakes" in the Unit Repair section.

Drum Brake Adjustment

ALL MODELS

1. Remove the plug on the adjustment hole located in the rear of the drum brake housing.
2. Using a spoon, turn the drum slowly while adjusting the brakes until the drum cannot be turned.
3. Back the adjustment wheel off until a slight drag is felt when the drum is turned.

Master Cylinder

REMOVAL AND INSTALLATION

The master cylinder may have a single or a dual type reservoir.

—————— CAUTION ——————
Care should be taken to insure that the correct parts are used for replacement.

1. Drain the reservoir.
2. Remove the brake lines.
3. Remove the master cylinder retaining bolts and carefully remove the master cylinder.

—————— CAUTION ——————
Do not pull the thrust rod from the booster unit.

4. Installation is the reverse of removal.

Power Brake Unit

REMOVAL AND INSTALLATION

Remove the brake pedal linkage. Drain the brake fluid. Remove the brake lines from the master cylinder and remove the bolts at the firewall. Remove the power brake unit.

Rear Wheel Cylinders

REMOVAL AND INSTALLATION

504

1. Remove the road wheels and drums.
2. Remove the brake lining return spring and release the shoes from the wheel cylinder.
3. Remove the brake fluid line from the back of the wheel cylinder.
4. Remove the wheel cylinder bolts and the wheel cylinder.
5. Installation is the reverse of removal.

Parking Brake Adjustment

FLOOR MOUNTED LEVER

1. Raise the vehicle and remove the rear wheels.
2. Loosen the cable adjusting nuts so that no tension exists on the cable.
3. If the vehicle is equipped with drum brakes adjust them.
4. Apply the parking brake four clicks and adjust the cable.
5. Release the handbrake and make sure the rotors or drums can rotate freely.
6. Install the wheels and lower the vehicle.

CHASSIS ELECTRICAL

Heater Blower/Core

REMOVAL AND INSTALLATION

504

The heater blower unit is located underneath the dashboard. To remove the unit, first drain the cooling system and then remove the center console. Remove the radio and, on cars so equipped, the air conditioning vent unit screwed on underneath the dash. Pull the knobs off the heating control levers. Loosen and remove the two screws which hold the subdash unit containing the heater controls. Loosen the clamps and pull the two water hoses off the heater unit, being careful to catch any spilling coolant. Three screws on each side at the top hold the blower unit to the car. Remove the six screws and pull the unit out of the car. The heater core is housed within the blower unit and can be reached by disengaging the assembling clips or, on older models, by pulling out the pop-rivits (be sure that you know how to reinstall these before disassembling). Reassembly and installation of the heater unit is the reverse of the removal procedure. Be sure that all lines are properly secured and that the correct amount of coolant is added.

505 and 604

The blower motor for these models is located on the passenger side fire-wall.
1. Remove the box which contains the heater blower.
2. Loosen the blower retaining nuts.
3. Pull the plug from the series resistance cable that is located on the firewall.
4. Remove the cable.

5. Remove the blower.
6. Installation is the reverse of removal. Make sure that the sealing frame is not damaged.

Radio

REMOVAL AND INSTALLATION

To remove the radio, first disconnect the antenna lead and then pull off the front knobs. Remove the front control shaft nuts and template and disconnect the power and speaker leads to the rear of the radio. Disconnect the rear support and pull the radio out from under the dash. To install, reverse the removal procedure, making sure that all wires are properly connected or damage to the radio and/or speaker could result.

Windshield Wiper/ Washer Motor

REMOVAL AND INSTALLATION

1. Disconnect the battery ground cable.
2. Remove the air grill from the area under and in front of the windshield.
3. Disconnect the wires to the motor.
4. Remove the instrument cluster from the dash.
5. Reach into the dash area and remove the spindle drive nut and the three nuts securing the wiper motor to the firewall.
6. Remove the motor from the grill area.
7. Installation is the reverse of the removal procedure.

Instrument Cluster

REMOVAL AND INSTALLATION

1. Remove all screws retaining the instrument cluster panel to the main dash.
2. Lift the panel out and disconnect all wiring from the back of the instrument cluster.
3. Remove the speedometer cable.
4. Lift out the instrument panel.
5. Installation is the reverse of removal.

Fuse Box Location

504 and 604

The fuse box is located under the driver's side of the dash, to the left of the steering column.

505

The fuse box is located on the top of the left inner front fender.

Porsche
911, 912, 914, 930

SERIAL NUMBER IDENTIFICATION

Chassis

The chassis number on all models is located on the driver's side windshield post and is visible from the outside of the car. The chassis number on 911 and 912E models is also found in the luggage compartment under the rug and on the identification plate near the front hood lock catch. The 914 chassis number is stamped on the right front wheel well and on the identification plate on the right headlight housing inside the luggage compartment.

The 911 and 912E series chassis identification number breaks down in the following manner:

911 chassis serial number location

911 SERIES

	Serial Number Example— 911-6-2-1-0001
Series Type	911, 911S or or 930 (Turbo)
Model Year	5 = 1975
	6 = 1976
	7 = 1977
	8 = 1978
	9 = 1979
	0 = 1980
	1 = 1981
Engine Type	1 = T
	2 = E or 2.7S
	3 = S
	4 = Carrera
	8 = Turbo

Body Type	0 = Coupe
	1 = Targa

Four Digit Serial Number—Sequential.

911 identification plate location

914 identification plate location (bottom) and chassis serial number location (top)

912 SERIES

	Serial Number Example— 912-6-0-0-0001
Vehicle Type	912 = Model
Model Year	6 = 1976
Motor	0 = 912E/2 ltr.
Body	0 = Coupe

Serial Number 0001-9999 (Sequential)

The 914 series chassis identification number is broken down as follows:

914 SERIES

47.5-29-00001

Series Type	47 = 914 series
Model Year	5 = 1975
	6 = 1976

Factory Number 29
Five digit sequential serial number—00001-99999

914 2.0 liter engine serial number

914 1.8 liter engine serial number

Engine

The engine number for the 911 model is located on the right side of the crankcase adjacent to the blower. The 1.8 liter, 914 engine number is stamped on the upper right of the crankcase, below the air intake runners. The 2.0 liter, 914 engine number is stamped on the upper part of the crankcase between the oil filler and the blower housing.

The 912E engine number is stamped in the crankcase on the left side near mount for the air pump.

911 engine numbers are divided as follows:

911 SERIES

Engine Number Example—
6-3-6-0001

Engine Type 6 = cylinder

Engine
Model

1 = T—Japan—3.01 ltr.
2 = E—USA—3.01 ltr.
3 = S—Rest of
World—3.01 ltr.
4 = Carrera
5 = Calif.—3.01 ltr.
8 = Turbo—3.31 ltr.

Model Year

5 = 1975
6 = 1976
7 = 1977
8 = 1978
9 = 1979
0 = 1980
1 = 1981
2 = 1982

Four digit sequential number—0001

914 SERIES

Engine Number Example—
GA-0-000-001

Engine Type   GA = 2.0 liter 4 cyl.
                  EC = 1.8 liter 4 cyl.

Seven digit sequential engine number

NOTE: Small "a" after engine reference letter(s) indicate engine usage in USA except California. Small "b" after engine reference letter(s) indicate engine usage in California.

912E MODEL

One engine was used in this model, a four cylinder, two liter unit. The identification is included in the chassis VIN number.

GENERAL ENGINE SPECIFICATIONS

Year	Model	Engine Displacement cc	(cu. in.)	Carburetor Type	Horsepower @ rpm	Torque @ rpm	Bore × Stroke (in.)	Compression Ratio
'76	911S	2687	(164)	Fuel inj.	157 @ 5800①	166 @ 4000	3.54 × 2.77	8.5:1
	930 Turbo.	2994	(183)	Fuel inj.	234 @ 5500	245 @ 4000	3.74 × 2.77	6.5:1
	912E	1971	(120.3)	Fuel inj.	86 @ 4900	98 @ 4000	3.70 × 2.79	7.6:1
	914 (1.8)	1795	(109.5)	Fuel inj.	72.5 @ 4900	89 @ 4000	3.66 × 2.60	7.3:1
	914 (2.0)	1971	(120.3)	Fuel inj.	84 @ 4900	97 @ 4000	3.70 × 2.79	7.6:1
'77	911S	2687	(164)	Fuel inj.	157 @ 5800	168 @ 4000	3.54 × 2.77	8.5:1
	930 Turbo.	2994	(183)	Fuel inj.	234 @ 5500	245 @ 4000	3.70 × 2.77	6.5:1
'78–'83	911	2994	(182.7)	Fuel inj.	172 @ 5500	175 @ 4200	3.74 × 2.77	8.5:1
	930 Turbo.	3299	(201.3)	Fuel inj.	261 @ 5500	291 @ 4000	3.82 × 2.93	7.0:1

NOTE: The underhood specifications sticker often reflects tune-up specification changes made in production. Sticker information must be used if it disagrees with the information in this chart.
① California: 152 @ 5800

TUNE-UP SPECIFICATIONS

Year	Model	Engine Displacement cc (cu. in.)	Spark Plugs Type ②	Spark Plugs Gap (in.)	Distributor Point Dwell (deg)	Distributor Point Gap (in.)	Ignition Timing (deg) Basic	Ignition Timing (deg) Dynamic @ rpm	Intake Valve Opens (deg)	Compres. Press (psi)	Idle Speed (rpm)	Valve Clearance (in.) In	Valve Clearance (in.) Ex
'76	911S	2687 (164)	W235-P21	0.022	38 ± 3 ②	0.016	5A	—	6A	①	850–950	0.004	0.004
	Turbo (930)	2994 (183)	W280–P21	0.024	Electronic		7A	29B @ 4000	3A	①	950–1050	0.004	0.004
	912E	1971 (120.3)	W175–M3	0.028	47 ± 3	0.016	—	27B @ 3500	12B	①	925	0.006	0.008

TUNE-UP SPECIFICATIONS

Year	Model	Engine Displacement cc (cu. in.)	Spark Plugs Type ②	Spark Plugs Gap (in.)	Distributor Point Dwell (deg)	Distributor Point Gap (in.)	Ignition Timing (deg) Basic	Ignition Timing (deg) Dynamic @ rpm	Intake Valve Opens (deg)	Compres. Press (psi)	Idle Speed (rpm)	Valve Clearance (in.) In	Valve Clearance (in.) Ex
'76	914 1.8	1795 (102.5)	W175–M3	0.028	47 ± 3	0.016	7½B	—	12B	①	850–950	0.006	0.006
	914 2.0	1971 (120.3)	W175–M3	0.028	47 ± 3	0.016	—	27B @ 3500	12B	①	850–950	0.006	0.008
'77	911S	2687 (164)	W235–P21	0.024	38 ± 3 ②	0.016	TDC ③	—	6A	①	900–1000	0.004	0.004
	Turbo (930)	2994 (183)	W280–P21	0.024	Electronic		7A	29B @ 4000	3A	①	950–1050	0.004	0.004
'78–'83	911SC	2994 (183)	W225–T30	0.028	Electronic		TDC @ 950 ⑤	—	6A	① ④	900–1000	0.004	0.004
'78–'79	Turbo (930)	3299 (201.3)	W280–P21	0.024	Electronic		7 ± 2° ATDC @ 950	—	1B	① ④	900–1000	0.004	0.004

① All cylinders should be within 22 psi of the highest reading. Compression test to be performed with engine warmer than 140°F
② Bosch spark plugs
② With Bosch distributor; 37° ± 3° with Marelli distributor
③ California: 15ATDC
④ With valve clearance of 1 mm (.0394 in.)
⑤ California 1978–79 15 ± 2° ATDC @ 1000
B Before top dead center
A After top dead center

FIRING ORDERS

NOTE: The position of No. 1 tower on the distributor cap may vary. To avoid confusion when replacing wires, always replace wires one at a time. The notch cut into the rim of the distributor body always indicates No. 1 cylinder.

FIRING ORDER: 1-4-3-2

914 firing order

FIRING ORDER: 1-4-3-2

912E firing order

FIRING ORDER: 1-6-2-4-3-5

1976–77 911 firing order (ex. 1977 Turbo)

FIRING ORDER: 1-6-2-4-3-5

1978–83 911 firing order (inc. 1977 Turbo)

CAPACITIES

Year	Model	Engine Displacement cc (cu. in.)	Engine Crankcase (qts)	Transaxle (qts)	Gasoline Tank① (gals)
'76	911S	2687 (164)	11.6⑤⑥	3.17	21.13③
	Turbo (930)	2994 (183)	13	3.91	21.13③
	912E	1971 (120.3)	3.7④	3.17	21.13
	914	All	3.7④	2.6	16.4
'77	911S	2687 (164)	13⑦	3.17	21.13③
	Turbo (930)	2994 (183)	13	3.91	21.13③
'78–'83	911SC	2994 (182.7)	②	3.2	21③
	Turbo (930)	3299 (201.3)	②	4.0	21③

①Including 1.6 gal reserve
②Initial filling including oil cooler is 13.7 qts
  10.6 qts for refill
③1976–'83 911 series—2.1 reserve
  1976–'79 Turbo series—2.0 reserve
④With filter, 3.2 qts refill without filter
⑤Total capacity with Sportomatic is 13.6 qts;
  however, only 10.4 qts are added when
  refilling

⑥Total capacity of 14.2 qts with optional oil
  cooler.
  Capacity with oil cooler and Sportomatic is
  16.9 qts.
  Normal refill for all models is 10.4 qts.
⑦15 qts with Sportomatic

CRANKSHAFT AND CONNECTING ROD SPECIFICATIONS
(All measurements in inches)

Model	Engine Displacement		Crankshaft				Connecting Rod		
	cc	(cu. in.)	Main Brg. Journal Dia.①	Main Brg. Oil Clearance	Shaft End-Play	Thrust on No.	Journal Diameter①	Oil Clearance	Side Clearance
911, Turbo (930)	All		2.2429–2.2437	0.0004–0.0028	0.0004–0.0077	1	2.0461–2.0468	0.0012–0.0035	0.0079–0.0158
914	1795	(109.5)	2.3615–2.3623	0.0197–0.0039	0.0028–0.0051	1	1.5742–1.5748	0.0008–0.0028	0.0039–0.0158
914, 912E	1971 1991	(120.3) (121.5)	2.3615–2.3623	0.0197–0.0039	0.0028–0.0051	1	1.9678–1.9683	0.0008–0.0028	0.0039–0.0158

①Undersize bearings available in 0.0098, 0.0197, 0.0295 inch sizes

VALVE SPECIFICATIONS

Model	Engine Displacement cc (cu. in.)	Face Angle (deg)	Spring Test Pressure (lbs. @ in.)	Spring Installed Height (in.)	Stem to Guide Clearance (in.)		Stem Diameter (in.)	
					Intake	Exhaust	Intake	Exhaust
911	All	45	176.4 @ 1.21①	1.3779③④	0.030–0.057	0.050–0.077	0.3531	0.3523
914/912E	All	45②	168–186 @ 1.14	1.1811	0.45	0.45	0.3125	0.3507

①Intake: 165.3 @ 1.25 for exhaust
②30° for intake valves on 1.8 engines
③1.3976 in. for exhaust
④1.5197 in. for exhaust (911SE)

PISTON AND RING SPECIFICATIONS
(All measurements in inches)

Model	Engine Displacement		Piston Clearance	Ring Gap			Ring Side Clearance		
	cc	(cu. in.)		Top Compression	Bottom Compression	Oil Control	Top Compression	Bottom Compression	Oil Control
911	2341	(142.8)	0.0008–0.002	0.004–0.008	0.004–0.008	0.0158–0.055	0.0028–0.004	0.002–0.003	0.0008–0.002
911	2687	(164)	0.0008–0.002	0.0039–0.0079	0.0059–0.0018	0.0158–0.055	0.0028–0.004	0.0015–0.0029	0.0008–0.002
911 Turbo (930)	2994	(182.7)	0.006	0.004–0.008	0.004–0.008	0.006–0.012	0.003–0.004	0.002–0.003	0.001–0.002
Turbo (930)	3299	(201.3)	0.006	0.004–0.008	0.004–0.008	0.006–0.012	0.003–0.004	0.002–0.003	0.001–0.002
912E, 914	1971	(120.3)	0.0008–0.002	0.014–0.022	0.014–0.022	0.010–0.016	0.0015–0.0028	0.0015–0.0028	0.0008–0.020
914	1795	(109.5)	0.0023	0.014–0.021	0.012–0.022	0.016	0.0023–0.0035	0.0016–0.0027	0.0008–0.0019

TORQUE SPECIFICATIONS
(All readings in ft. lbs.)

Model	Engine Displacement cc (cu. in.)	Cylinder Head Bolts	Rod Bearing Bolts	Main Bearing Bolts	Crankshaft Pulley Bolt	Flywheel To Crankshaft Bolts
914/912E	All	23	24	24	43	80
911, Turbo (930)	All	24	36	25	58	109

TORQUE SEQUENCES

Four cylinder engine cylinder head torque sequence

BATTERY AND STARTER SPECIFICATIONS
(All cars use 12 volt, negative ground electrical systems)

Model	Battery Amp Hour Capacity	Starter						Brush Spring Tension (oz)	Min. Brush Length (in.)
		Lock Test			No Load Test				
		Amps	Volts	Torque (ft. lbs.)	Amps	Volts	rpm		
911/912E	(2) 36①	160–200	9	1100–1400	33–50	11.5	6400–7900	42.3	0.5
914	45	170–205	9	900–1300	35–45	12	7400–9100	42	N.A.

① 1978–'82: (1) 66

ALTERNATOR AND REGULATOR SPECIFICATIONS

Model	Alternator		Regulator						
	Part No. or Manufacturer	Output (amps.)	Part No. or Manufacturer	Field Relay			Regulator		
				Air Gap (in.)	Point Gap (in.)	Volts to Close	Air Gap (in.)	Point Gap (in.)	Volts @ 75°
911/912E	Bosch	55①	Bosch	————————Not adjustable————————					13.5–14.5
914	Bosch	50	Bosch	————————Not adjustable————————					13.5–14.5

① 1978–'81: 70
1982–'83: 75

BRAKE SPECIFICATIONS
(All measurements given are in inches unless noted)

Year	Model	Lug Nut Torque (ft. lbs.)	Master Cylinder Bore	Brake Disc Minimum Thickness	Brake Disc Maximum Run-Out	Minimum Lining Thickness Front	Minimum Lining Thickness Rear
'76–'83	911/912E①	94	0.75	③	0.008	0.08	0.08
'76	914	94	0.687	0.35②	0.008	0.08	0.08

NOTE: Minimum lining thickness is as recommended by the manufacturer. Due to variations in state inspection regulations, the minimum allowable thickness may be different than recommended by the manufacturer.
① Solid discs on 912E; ventilated on all 911 models
② Wear limit—0.335 in.
③ 912E (front)—0.45 in.
912E (rear)—0.37 in. (wear limit) 0.35 in.
911 (front/rear)—0.725 (refinish limit) or 0.70 (wear limit) (in.)

WHEEL ALIGNMENT

Year	Model	Caster Range (deg)	Caster Pref Setting (deg)	Camber Range (deg)	Camber Pref Setting (deg)	Toe-In (deg)
'76–'77	911/912E	5°50'–6°20'	6°5'	−50'–(+)10'	0°①	0°②
'76	914	5°30'–6°30'	6°	−40'–(+)20'	0°③	+20' ± 10'④
'77–'83	911, 911SC	6°5' ± 15'	6°5'	+30'–(±)10'	+30'	0°⑤

① Rear wheels: −1 ± 10'
② Rear wheels: 0° ± 20'
③ Rear wheels: −30' ± 20'
④ Rear wheels: 0° ± 15'
⑤ Rear wheels: +10' ± 10'

TUNE-UP

Spark Plugs

In addition to performing their basic function of igniting the air-fuel mixture, spark plugs can also serve as very useful diagnostic tools. Once removed, compare your spark plugs with the samples in the "Troubleshooting" section. Typical plug conditions are illustrated along with their causes and remedies. Plugs which exhibit only normal wear and deposits can be cleaned, gapped, and reinstalled.

Before removing the spark plug leads, number the towers on the distributor cap with tape. Grasp each spark plug boot and pull it straight out. Check the condition of the rubber boot and/or shroud seals and replace them if necessary. Install the spark plug socket on the plug's hex and remove it. If removal is difficult, loosen the plug only slightly and drip some light oil onto the threads. Allow the oil to penetrate and then unscrew the spark plug. Proceeding this way will prevent damaging the threads in the cylinder head. Be sure to keep the socket straight to avoid breaking the ce-

Checking the spark plug gap

Bending the side electrode

ramic insulator. Most spark plug sockets are lined with rubber for this reason. Inspect the plugs using the "Troubleshooting" section illustrations and then clean or discard them according to their condition. Recommended spark plug gap is given in the "Tune-Up Specifications" chart. Use a spark plug wire gauge for checking the gap. The wire should pass through the electrodes with just a slight drag. Using the electrode bending tool on the end of the gauge, bend the side electrode to adjust the gap. Never attempt to adjust the center electrode. Lightly oil the threads of the replacement plug and install it hand-tight. The spark plugs in all engines should be tightened to a torque of 18–21 ft. lbs. Install the ignition wire boots firmly on the spark plugs. On the 914 models, be sure that the cooling shroud seals are snug or cooling efficiency will be lost.

Breaker Points and Condenser

Snap the two retaining clips off the distributor cap. Remove the cap and examine it for cracks, deterioration, or carbon tracks. Replace the cap, if necessary, by transferring one wire at a time from the old cap to the new one. Some 911 models have a dust cover which must be removed to service the points. Examine the rotor for corrosion or wear and replace it if necessary.

NOTE: Marelli rotors are retained by a screw.

Check the points for pitting and burning. Slight imperfections on the contact surface may be filed off with a point file (fine emery paper will also do), but it is usually wise to replace the breaker point set when tuning. Replace the cap, if necessary, by transferring point set. All Porsches are equipped with externally mounted condensers mounted

1. Retaining screw
2. Breaker plate
3. Primary connection
4. Distributor shaft felt
5. Breaker arm pivot (place a few drops of oil on 4 and 5)
914 distributor

1. Rotor
2. Stator
3. Transmitter coil
4. Stator plate
5. Rotor bushing
6. Stator bushing
7. Outer clearance
8. Magnet
9. Inner clearance
10. Carrier plate and bushing (fixed)
Internal view of electronic distributor

on the body of the distributor. To replace the condenser, disconnect its lead from the distributor primary terminal and unscrew it from the mounting on the body. Reverse the removal procedure to install a replacement condenser.

REMOVAL AND INSTALLATION

911

NOTE: Porsche recommends removing the distributor to replace the breaker points on these models. The problem is one of access and working space. Some mechanics find they are able to remove the points with the distributor in the car; however it is much easier to do it out of the car. Follow the directions in the "Engine Electrical" section to remove the distributor and then remove the points as outlined below.

The Turbo is equipped with pointless, electronic ignition and requires only distributor cap and wire condition checks.

1. Undo the retaining screw(s), if so equipped, and remove the rotor.
2. Remove the breaker point retaining screw(s), disconnect the primary lead from the terminal, and lift out the breaker point set.

NOTE: When removing the points in the car, it is best to use a magnetic screwdriver to prevent dropping the screws.

3. Install the replacement point set, but leave the adjustment screw hand-tight.
4. Turn the engine until the rubbing block of the breaker arm rests on the highest point of a cam lobe.
5. Insert a 0.016 in. feeler gauge be-

tween the two contact points. The gauge should pull through the points with just a slight drag.

6. When the gap is adjusted, tighten the retaining screw. Lightly lubricate the cam with silicone grease.
7. Install the rotor.
8. Install the distributor cap. Check the dwell angle and ignition timing as outlined in the following sections.

914 and 912E

The 914, in addition to resistor spark plugs, is equipped with a resistor rotor. The rotor may be checked with an ohmmeter. If a resistance greater than 10k ohms is indicated, the rotor should be replaced.

1. Remove the breaker point retaining screw.
2. Unclip the wire lead and remove the point set.
3. Install the replacement point set, tightening the retaining screw only hand-tight.
4. Turn the engine (with a remote starter switch or by having an assistant "bump" the starter) until the rubbing block of the point set is on the high point of a cam lobe.
5. Using 0.016 in. feeler gauge, adjust the point gap and then tighten the retaining screw.
6. Place a few drops of engine oil on the pivot bearing of the breaker arm and the felt in the center of the distributor shaft.
7. Install the rotor and distributor cap.
8. Check the dwell angle and ignition timing as outlined in the following sections.

1. Ground connection
2. Primary connection
911 dwell meter hook-up

Dwell Angle

The dwell angle or cam angle is the number of degrees that the distributor cam rotates while the points are closed. There is an inverse relationship between dwell angle and point gap. Increasing the point gap will decrease the dwell angle and vice versa. Checking the dwell angle with a meter is a far more accurate method of measuring point opening than the feeler gauge method.

After setting the point gap to specification with a feeler gauge, check the dwell angle with a meter. Hook-up the dwell me-

911 distributor showing breaker point retaining screws

ter according to the manufacturer's instructions. The negative lead is grounded and the positive lead connected to the primary wire (terminal No. 1 on 911 models) that runs from the coil to the distributor. Start the engine, let it idle and reach operating temperature, and observe the dwell. The reading should fall within the allowable range. If it does not, the gap will have to be reset or the breaker points will have to be replaced.

Electronic Ignition

Turbocharged engines were equipped with electronic ignition starting in 1976 and the 911 models in 1978.

MAJOR COMPONENTS

1. Rotor (reluctor)—timing teeth build a magnetic field at each pick-up coil triggering projection.

2. Pick-up coil—sends a small inducted current signal to the control unit each time a tooth in the rotor passes a pick-up coil triggering projection.

3. Control unit—receives signals from the pick-up coil. These signals switch the primary current at the ignition coil off and on. This collapses the primary field and generates the secondary voltage necessary to fire the spark plug.

4. Ignition coil—electronic coils cannot be interchanged with standard ignition coils.

5. Spark advance and retard—conventional type operation.

Electronic ignition replaces breaker points with an inductive signal system. When the timing teeth of the rotor come in alignment with the triggering projections on the pick-up coil, a magnetic field builds around the pick-up coil. When the timing teeth leave the area of the triggering projection, the magnetic field collapses around the pick-up coil and generates a small current pulse.

Using a transistor in the control unit, this small current pulse switches the primary voltage to the ignition coil on and off. The secondary voltage produced by the coil fires the spark plug. Dwell is controlled by the electronic system. However, timing is set in the normal way.

TESTING

Always check for spark. If no spark is available, then check for primary voltage at the ignition coil. If no voltage is available at the coil, check the primary resistors and electrical connectors for looseness or corrosion.

If voltage is available at the coil, check all of the components of the electronic ignition system as listed in the Testing Specifications Chart. If voltage is available at the control unit and all other components check out good, replace the control unit.

If the engine is missing or breaking down under load, check the secondary ignition and wires. Check the pick-up coil ohms while applying vacuum to the vacuum advance from an outside source. Check for dwell variation at 1500 r.p.m. and 5000 r.p.m.

Electronic Ignition Testing Specifications

Component Tested	Specification (ohms)
Rotor resistance	5000
Pick-up coil	890–1285
Ignition coil (primary)	0.95–1.40
Ignition coil (secondary)	5500–8000
High tension coil lead	Less than 5000

Ignition Timing

—— CAUTION ——
When performing this or any other adjustment with the engine running, be very careful of the fan belt and pulley.

Ignition timing should always be checked as part of any tune-up. Timing is checked after the points have been adjusted or replaced. A stroboscopic timing light is a necessity for timing any Porsche and, in addition, a static 12 V timing light is necessary for the 911 and the 914.

1976–79 911

These models are equipped with a vacuum retard unit which retards the ignition to 5° ATDC at idle. Ignition timing is checked both at idle and at 6000 rpm with a stroboscopic timing light. Leave the vacuum hose on. The crankshaft pulley has a TDC notch ("Z1"), a 5° ATDC notch directly to the left of the "Z1" notch, a 30° BTDC notch, and a 35° notch. The retaining nut is loosened and the distributor swivels on the mounting stud to make timing changes.

1. Start the engine and allow it to reach normal operating temperature.

1976 series timing mark

1977 and later 911 series timing marks

Diagram of Porsche electronic ignition system

————— Primary current
– – – – – Control current

T— Transistor
R₁—Resistor
R₂—Resistor
R₃—Resistor

1. Positive connection
2. Ground connection
3. No. 1 terminal

911 timing light hook-up

2. Stop the engine and attach a timing light to No. 1 spark plug according to the manufacturer's instructions.

3. Restart the engine. Make sure that the idle speed is according to specifications and that the vacuum advance hose is connected.

4. When the timing light flashes, the 5° ATDC notch in the pulley should be aligned with the reference notch in the blower housing.

5. If the notches do not align, loosen the retaining nut and slowly rotate the distributor as necessary until they line up. Ignition timing is now correct at idle.

6. Dynamic timing is checked at this point. Total advance at 6000 rpm should be between 32° and 38°.

7. While you stand at the rear with the timing light aimed at the timing notches on the crankshaft pulley, have an assistant accelerate the engine to 6000 rpm for an instant.

── CAUTION ──
Do not hold the engine at this high speed for an extended period.

8. The pulley has a 30° and 35° notch, so 32–38° would start to the right of the 30° notch and end just to the right of the 35° notch. The blower housing reference notch should be aligned with the desired timing area on the crankshaft pulley when the light flashes.

9. If the timing is incorrect, loosen the nut and slowly rotate the distributor to adjust it.

10. Stop the engine and remove the timing light.

1977– 83 911S, SC and Turbo

Ignition timing is done with the vacuum hose on. Use the same basic procedure given for the earlier models. Timing for the 49 states 911S is TDC at normal idle (Z1 notch). California 911S models get 15° ATDC at idle speed (15° notch to the left of Z1). The

5° BTDC (Black Notch)   27° BTDC (Red Notch)

914 engine timing marks

7½° BTDC

1976 914 series timing marks

centrifugal advance timing check is no longer performed on these models. Basic timing for the Turbo is 7° ATDC at idle. Full centrifugal advance should be 29° BTDC and come in at 4000 rpm.

1976 914

1. Hook up the timing light.
2. Disconnect the distributor vacuum hose(s).
3. Unscrew the inspection hole cover from the cooling shroud.
4. Start the engine and bring it to normal operating temperature.
5. Advance should be 7.5° BTDC at idle speed on 1.8 engine models.
6. On 2.0 models, accelerate the engine to 3500 rpm. Timing should be at 27° BTDC (red notch aligned with V-shaped notch in blower housing).
7. If the timing is off specifications, loosen and turn the distributor until it is correct.
8. Shut the engine off and connect the vacuum hose(s).

1976 912E

The engine is essentially the same as the 2.0 liter engine used in the 914. Timing is checked in the same manner as for the 2.0 914. The only difference is in the location of the timing marks. The air injection pump

VOR 40 36 32 28 24 20 16

1976 912E Series timing marks

made it necessary to move the timing marks. The TDC marker is located on the fanbelt pulley. The timing scale is on a bracket attached to the intake housing.

Valve Lash

ADJUSTMENT

1. The engine must be cold when adjusting the valves on any Porsche. Remove the rocker arm covers, two per head in the case of the 911.

2. The valves of each cyliner are adjusted with that piston at the top of its compression stroke. Both the intake and exhaust valves will be closed at this point. Turn the engine to align the TDC mark ("Z1" for the 911 and the black notch on 914 models) with the reference mark.

3. Using a feeler gauge (thickness equal to a figure given in the "Valve Clearance" column of the "Tune-Up Specifications" chart, check the clearance between the valve stem and the rocker arm. The feeler gauge should just slip through: if it has to be forced the clearance will be incorrect.

4. If the clearance is not within specifications, loosen the locknut with a box wrench and, using a screwdriver, turn the rocker arm adjusting screw while holding the locknut. A tool to simplify this procedure is available from automotive suppliers. It has a screwdriver bit which can be turned while the locknut is held with a socket.

5. Tighten the locknut while holding the adjusting screw. Recheck the valve clearance to ensure that it wasn't changed when the locknut was tightened. Repeat this procedure on the other valve of No. 1 cylinder.

6. Proceed to adjust the valves of the remaining cylinders in an order of 1-2-3-4 for four-cylinder engines or 1-6-2-4-3-5 for six-cylinder engines. The piston of the cylinder on which the valves are being adjusted must be at TDC. Turn the engine until both valves of the cylinder being adjusted are closed. Six-cylinder engines have TDC marks for each cylinder on the crank-

914 valve clearance adjustment (special adjusting tool shown)

911 valve clearance adjustment

shaft pulley. Adjust the valves in the same manner as No. 1 cylinder.

7. Install the rocker arm or camshaft housing covers with new gaskets. Start the engine and check for leaks.

Fuel Injection

IDLE SPEED

911

The idle speed adjustment on the CIS system used on all later models is done with the bypass screw on the throttle valve housing. The engine should be at normal operating temperature.

1976 2.0

1. Remove the air filter and connect a tachometer to the engine.
2. Start the engine and set the idle speed to specifications. Turning the adjustment screw clockwise increases the idle speed. Turning the screw counterclockwise decreases the idle speed.

1976 914 1.8 and 912E

1. Make sure all hoses are tight. Connect a tachometer to the engine.
2. Start the engine and bring it to normal operating temperature.
3. The idle speed adjustment screw is located on the throttle housing. Do not touch the idle mixture screw which is covered with a plastic plug.

914 idle speed screw

ENGINE ELECTRICAL

Distributor

REMOVAL AND INSTALLATION

911

1. Remove the heated air intake duct.
2. Unsnap and remove the distributor cap. Position it out of the way.
3. Mark the direction in which the rotor is pointing on the body of the distributor.

NOTE: Some models have a scribe mark indicating the correct rotor positioning for No. 1 cylinder. On these models it will be more convenient to turn the engine so that the rotor points to this mark before removing the distributor.

1. Rotor
2. Stator

Electronic distributor disassembled in major components

4. Detach the distributor leads. Remove the vacuum line.
5. Loosen and remove the retaining nut from the base of the distributor. Pull the distributor straight out of the engine. Check and, if necessary, replace the sealing ring on the distributor housing.
6. Insert the distributor into the engine. Swivel the rotor back and forth to engage the distributor and crankshaft gears. If the engine has been turned while the distributor was out, bring No. 1 cylinder to TDC as described before under "Ignition Timing."
7. Adjust the static and dynamic timing.

914 and 912E

1. Remove the air cleaner.
2. Loosen the clamp on the right-hand

914 distributor drive gear positioning

heater hose and pull it from the heater. Position the hose out of the way.
3. Screw the inspection hole cover out of the cooling shroud.
4. Turn the engine until the black notch in the crankshaft pulley aligns with V-shaped notch in the blower housing.
5. Remove the distributor cap and check that the rotor is, indeed, pointing towards the No. 1 cylinder position.
6. Detach the two electrical leads and vacuum hoses from the distributor.
7. Loosen the retaining nut on the base of the distributor and pull it out of the engine.

To install the distributor with the engine undisturbed.

8. Ensure that the spring is in place in the center bore of the drive gear. A length of wire may be used to install the spring if it has been removed.

9. Insert the distributor, making sure that the dog on the distributor engages the slot in the drive gear. Turning the rotor a few times will ease installation.
10. Push the distributor in firmly. Tighten the clamp nut.
11. Install the distributor leads and vacuum hoses. Install the distributor cap.

12. Check the ignition timing. Install the inspection cover, heater hose, and air cleaner.

Install the distributor in the following manner if the engine has been disturbed:

13. Turn the engine to bring No. 1 cylinder up to TDC. At this point, the black notch in the crankshaft pulley should be aligned with the V-shaped notch in the blower housing and the slot in the distributor drive gear should be at approximately a 12° angle to the engine centerline. The slot should be pointing toward the rear retaining screw of the air filter support and the smaller side of the gear should be facing the center of the engine.
14. Install the distributor using Steps 8–12.

Alternator

ALTERNATOR PRECAUTIONS

A few precautions should be observed when servicing an electrical system that uses an alternator. Failure to do so can result in serious damage to the charging system. The negative terminal(s) of the battery(ies) is (are) always grounded. Always connect the correct battery terminals when attaching a battery charger or replacing a battery. Never operate the alternator on an open, uncontrolled circuit. Never ground or short across any regulator or alternator terminals. Never attempt to polarize the alternator. Remove the battery cables from the terminals when charging the battery in the car.

REMOVAL AND INSTALLATION

911

The alternator is located in the blower housing.

1. Disconnect the battery ground straps.
2. Remove the air cleaner assembly.
3. Remove the upper shroud retaining bolts.
4. Hold the alternator pulley and remove the pulley nut.
5. Remove the drive belt.

911 alternator pulley nut removal

911 alternator removal

6. Remove the blower housing strap retaining bolts.
7. Pull the blower housing/alternator towards the rear until there is enough clearance to disconnect the wiring.
8. Remove the alternator.
9. Install the alternator in the reverse order of removal. Be sure that the blower housing is seated on the dowel in the crankcase.
10. Tighten the pulley nut to 29 ft. lbs.

912E, 914

Remove the alternator cover plate and the surrounding sheet metal to expose the alternator for removal and installation.

BELT TENSION ADJUSTMENT

911

A correctly tensioned belt can be deflected ½–¾ in. by light hand pressure. If the tension is not within specifications; follow the steps below to adjust or replace the belt.

1. Remove the pulley nut as outlined above in "Alternator Removal and Installation."
2. Remove the outside half of the pulley.
3. Remove the adjustment spacers to increase belt tension. Add spacers to decrease belt tension.
4. When the correct spacer grouping is achieved, install the belt, pulley half, spacers, and nut.
5. Tighten the nut to 29 ft. lbs.

911 fan belt pulley adjustment spacers

NOTE: If you have removed spacers, install the extra spacers on the outside of the pulley so they won't become lost or misplaced.

6. Recheck the belt tension after about 60 miles of driving.

914, 912E

A correctly tensioned belt will be able to be deflected approximately ½ in. by light hand pressure. If the tension is not within specification, follow the steps below to adjust or replace the belt.

1. Remove the small cover plate from the alternator cover.
2. Loosen the socket screw and slide the alternator left or right as necessary.
3. Tighten the screw and replace the cover.

Regulator

REMOVAL AND INSTALLATION

911, 912E and 914

1. Disconnect the ground cable from the battery.
2. Disconnect the wiring from the regulator.
3. Remove the mounting screws and remove the regulator.
4. Install the regulator. Do not overtighten the screws. An alternator system requires no polarization.

911 voltage regulator wiring schematic

Starter

REMOVAL AND INSTALLATION

911

1. Disconnect the battery ground strap.
2. Jack up the rear of the car and support it with jack stands.
3. Note their locations (tag to be sure) and then remove the starter electrical connections.
4. Loosen the retaining bolts, support the starter, remove the bolts, and then pull out the starter.
5. Install the starter using the reverse order of the removal procedure. Ensure that the terminal connections are correctly installed and tight.
6. Lower the car and connect the battery ground strap.

914 and 912E

1. Open the engine compartment lid. Disconnect the battery ground cable.
2. The top retaining bolt is accessible from within the engine compartment. Remove the nut.
3. Jack up the starter side of the car and support it with jack stands.

4. Remove the bottom bolt and pull out the starter.

5. Install the starter into the transaxle housing and the long top bolt into the mounting bracket hole. Install and tighten the bottom bolt.

6. Connect the electrical leads to the correct terminals.

7. Install and tighten the nut on the top bolt.

8. Seal the mounting bracket and transaxle housing with a suitable self-adhesive sealer.

9. Lower the car and connect the battery cable.

OVERRUN CLUTCH AND DRIVE

Replacement

1. Remove the starter.
2. Press clutch operating shaft by turning slightly.
3. Pull both off shaft by turning slightly.
4. Hold armature in vise and push pinion and sleeve on shaft until detent locks.

ENGINE MECHANICAL

Engine

REMOVAL AND INSTALLATION

All Porsche engines are removed and installed with the transaxle attached. The recommended method for removal is to raise the rear of the car high enough for working clearance and then support it on jack stands. A hydraulic transmission/differential jack or service jack of at least 800 lbs. capacity is required for lowering the engine/transaxle and raising it back into the chassis. Have an assistant steady the engine/transaxle during removal. Strap the engine to the jack so that it doesn't slide off. Proceed slowly and carefully as the engine/transaxle combination is both heavy and delicate.

911 and 912E

1. Disconnect the battery. Drain the engine and transaxle oil.

2. Open the engine compartment lid and detach the hot air ducts from the air gates and exhaust manifold heat exchangers.

3. Detach the two heater control cables.

4. Remove the hot air ducts from the T-union between the air cleaners and then remove the T-union from the blower housing.

5. Remove the tops of the air cleaners.

6. Tag for installation and then remove

911 and 912 rear engine-to-body mounts

911 and 912 transaxle crossmember mounting

the electrical cables from the generator and blower housing.

7. Tag for installation and remove the wires from the coil.

8. Remove the connections from the oil temperature and pressure sending units.

9. Remove the fuel line from the fuel pump and detach its clip from the engine shield.

10. Remove the Allen bolts retaining the axle shaft flange to the transaxle. Free the axle shafts from the transaxle and drop them out of the way.

11. Remove the starter electrical leads.

12. Disconnect the clutch cable from the control lever.

13. Remove the ground strap.

14. Detach the back-up light lead.

15. Disconnect the throttle linkage from the cross-shaft at the transaxle.

16. Remove the cover in the center of the rear floor.

17. Detach the rubber shift lever cover from the flange on the body and pull it forward on the control lever.

18. Remove the safety wire from the square-headed joint. Loosen the screw and slide the shift rod off its base.

19. Position the jack, including the flat support plate, under the engine/transaxle. The jack should be under the point of balance of the powertrain.

20. Raise the jack a slight amount.

21. Remove the body mounting bolts on either side of the engine compartment.

22. Remove the body mounting bolts from the short transaxle crossmember. The engine is removed with this crossmember attached.

Releasing throwout bearing tension

23. Very carefully lower the engine, while your assistants help balance it.

24. Roll the engine/transaxle out from under the car.

Follow Steps 25–30 for engine and transaxle separation.

Remove the starter. Release the throwout fork tension by disconnecting the return spring if one is used.

After releasing throwout bearing tension it is necessary to slide the throwout fork past the bearing. To do this, insert a screwdriver in the opening in the transaxle and turn the bearing 90°. Slide the fork past the bearing. The transaxle may not be separated from the engine.

25. Remove the engine-to-transaxle bolts and nuts. Carefully pull the transaxle away from the engine. Be sure that the full weight of the transaxle is supported, so as not to damage the pilot bushing, throwout bearing, clutch disc, or pressure plate.

26. Whichever component you are repairing, rebuilding, or replacing may now be moved to a suitable workbench, dolly, or engine stand.

27. Before reinstalling the transaxle, fill the pilot bushing in the gland nut with a small amount of graphite grease (no more than 3 cc, or $\frac{1}{10}$ oz.).

Sliding the fork past the throwout bearing

28. Lightly grease the transmission input shaft splines, starter shaft bushing, and the starter and flywheel gear teeth.

29. Carefully attach the transaxle to the engine. Remember the transmission input shaft will be passing through the throwout bearing, pressure plate, clutch disc, and pilot bushing, so give it ample support during the attachment procedure.

NOTE: If the clutch disc splines and the input shaft splines don't line up, as they so often won't, have an assistant turn the crankshaft pulley until they do.

30. Push the transaxle home so that the mounting flanges are flush. Align the bottom holes and install the bolts. Install the top bolts, and then tighten all of the retaining bolts evenly.

31. The engine/transaxle is installed by following the removal steps in reverse order.

32. After the engine is installed, check the clutch adjustment as described below.

33. Refill the engine and transaxle with the correct lubricant. Lower the car.

34. Start the engine and check for leaks.

914

1. Scribe the hinge positioning, and then remove the engine compartment lid.

2. Disconnect the battery cables.

3. Remove the air cleaner and attendant hoses.

4. Tag each of the eleven cables for the fuel injection (for correct reinstallation) and then disconnect them. Tape the cables to the engine compartment sides so that they are out of harm's way.

914 shift rod container

5. Disconnect the throttle cable and push it through the front engine firewall.

6. Open the fuel line retaining clip. Disconnect and plug the fuel lines near the pressure regulator.

7. Remove the top retaining nut for the starter (accessible from the engine compartment).

8. Jack up the car and support it safely with stands.

9. Remove the muffler shrouding. Drain the engine and transaxle.

10. Remove the lower heater components.

11. Detach the dust cover and then unscrew the shift rod retainer.

12. Remove the protective cover, unscrew the retaining nuts, and remove the rear shift rod.

13. Remove the heater box, hoses, and control cables.

14. Loosen the cable pulley adjusting nut and retaining nut. Bend the retaining bracket and pull the clutch cable towards the front.

15. Loosen the speedometer cable and pull it forward.

16. Remove the starter. Detach the ground strap from underbody.

17. Detach the axle driveshafts from the transaxle as described below. Wire the driveshafts out of the way.

18. Position the jack and plate under the engine/transaxle and raise it slightly.

19. Unscrew the four transaxle support retaining nuts. Remove the two Allen bolts on the front engine mount.

20. Lower the engine/transmission down and out of the car.

21. Engine/transaxle separation is similar to that given for the 912 and 911, with exception of Step 25.

22. Installation is essentially a reverse of the removal procedure, with the addition of the following Steps.

a. Be especially careful that the injection valve fuel lines aren't squashed when repositioning the engine. The parking brake cables go above the engine mount.

b. Torque the engine mount Allen bolts to 22 ft. lbs. The transmission mount nuts are tightened to 15 ft. lbs. Tighten the axle driveshaft bolts to 33 ft. lbs.

c. Adjust the clutch as described later.

d. Adjust the throttle cable.

e. Refill the engine and transaxle with lubricant.

f. Lower the car. Start the engine and check for leaks.

Cylinder Head

For removal and installation, see the ''Engine Disassembly and Assembly'' section.

Rocker Shafts

REMOVAL AND INSTALLATION

911

Each rocker arm has an individual shaft on this single overhead camshaft engine. One or all of the shafts and rocker arms may be removed with the engine in the chassis.

1. Remove the camshaft housing cover nuts and spring washers. Remove the covers.

2. Scribe the rocker arms being removed so that they can be returned to the same position.

3. Unscrew the Allen bolt in the rocker shaft. Push the shaft out of its bore and remove it along with the rocker arm.

NOTE: If the rocker is under pressure, you won't be able to push the shaft

1. Voltage supply relay
   4-pole
2. Two injection valves
   left 2-pole
3. One throttle valve
   switch 4-pole
4. Temperature feeler
   1-pole
5. Mass connections
   3-pole
6. Cold starting valve
   2-pole

7. Thermal switch
   1-pole
8. Ignition distributor
   release contact
   3-pole
9. Temperature feeler
   1-pole
10. Two injection valves
    right 2-pole
11. Pressure feeler
    4-pole

914 fuel injection connections

911 rocker arm removal

1. Allen nut cone
2. Shaft
3. Bushing cone
4. Allen bolt

911 rocker arm shaft assembly

out. Turn the crankshaft until the rocker rests on the heel of the cam lobe.

4. Check the rocker arm and shaft for excessive wear or damage. Replace any suspect piece.

NOTE: End rockers are installed with the Allen screw heads facing towards cylinders No. 2 and 5 respectively.

5. Place the rocker arm on its shaft.
6. The rocker arm shaft should be centered in its bore so that each groove is recessed 0.059 in. (1.15 mm).
  a. Insert a 0.06 in. feeler gauge in the groove on one side of the shaft. Push the shaft in until the feeler gauge is held tight against the edge.
  b. Carefully remove the gauge and push the shaft in approximately 0.06 in. more, using the feeler gauge to judge the distance.
7. Tighten the Allen bolt to 156 in. lbs.
8. Install the camshaft cover.

914 and 912E

Each cylinder head mounts two rocker assemblies, each one consisting of a shaft and two rocker arms. Each shaft is mounted in

Correct rocker arm shaft positioning

two bearings which are positioned on studs and retained by nuts. The rocker arm shaft assemblies can be removed with the engine in the car.

1. Remove the rocker arm cover.
2. Unscrew the retaining nuts and lift the rocker arm assemblies off the cylinder head.
3. When installing the rocker arm assemblies, the open slots of the bearings must face down.
4. With the rocker assemblies mounted on the head, tighten the retaining nuts to 120 in. lbs.

Exhaust Pipe and Muffler

REMOVAL AND INSTALLATION

911 and 912E

1. Remove the flange nuts and bolts.
2. Loosen the retaining clamps and detach the muffler from its support.
3. Position the muffler on its support and then fit the clamps.
4. Install new gaskets between the muffler and exhaust manifold/heat exchanger.
5. Install and alternately tighten the flange nuts and bolts.
To remove only the exhaust pipe:
1. Remove the two tailpipe-to-muffler retaining bolts.
2. Pull the tailpipe out of the muffler.
3. Install the tailpipe using two new gasket rings. Tighten the two retaining bolts.

To remove the tailpipe and muffler:
1. Remove the three flange nuts on each side.
2. Pry the muffler loose and remove it.
3. Use new flange gaskets when installing the muffler. Tighten the six flange retaining nuts alternately.

Exhaust Manifold/Heat Exchanger

REMOVAL AND INSTALLATION

911, 912E and 914

1. Remove the muffler as previously outlined. Detach and remove the connecting hose from the heat exchanger to the heater valve chamber.
2. Detach the heater hose from the heat exchanger.
3. Remove the three sunken bolts from the bottom of the heat exchanger.
4. Remove the six cylinder head-to-heat exchanger nuts using a universal socket setup.

NOTE: For 914 models, skip Steps 3 and 4 and loosen the four retaining clamps.

5. Remove the heat exchanger.
6. Examine the heat exchanger for damaged flanges or cracks. Replace it, if necessary.
7. Install the heat exchanger in the reverse order of removal. Use new flange gaskets and tighten the retaining nuts and bolts alternately.

1. Nut
2. Seal
3. Muffler
4. Bolt
5. Spring washer
6. Washer
7. Bolt
8. Washer
9. Cone seal
10. Seal ring
11. Exhaust pipe
12. Bolt
13. Heater duct
14. Screw
15. Washer
16. Clip
17. Bolt
18. Warm air cover
19. Warm air duct
20. Nut
21. Heat exchanger
22. Seal ring

914 exhaust system

1. Nut
2. Aluminum washer
3. Cover
4. Gasket
5. Cover
6. Gasket
7. Bolt
8. Bushing
9. Nut
10. Rocker arm shaft
11. Rocker arm
12. Nut
13. Adjusting screw
14. Rocker arm assembly
15. Camshaft
16. Cover
17. Housing

Six cylinder camshaft housing assembly

Engine Disassembly and Assembly

Further component removal and installation requires engine removal and disassembly. Follow the steps of engine disassembly and then assembly for the part being replaced. A general engine rebuilding section is included at the end of the book.

911

Follow the disassembly procedure for four cylinder Porsche engines up to the rocker carriers and the cylinder heads. Further disassembly of the 911 engine is as follows:

Removal of the cylinder heads on the 911 involves removing the overhead camshafts. All three cylinder heads on each bank can be removed as a unit complete with the camshaft and rockers or each cylinder head can be removed individually. For access to the cylinder heads and valves, the camshaft housing must be disassembled and removed.

Rockers: Scribe a mark on the rockers for later installation. Remove the 5mm Allen retaining screws in the rocker shafts, holding the cone-nut that is released on the other end of the shaft. Push out the shafts and lift away the rockers. *Position the camshaft so that the cam lobe does not press against the rocker being removed.*

Camshaft: Remove the timing chain cover at each camshaft. Unbolt the chain tensioner and the intermediate wheel, using tools P 202 and P 203. Withdraw the dowel pin from the camshaft wheel with tool P212. Remove the sliding wedges and withdraw the wheel and flange. Take the key from the camshaft, unscrew the three sealing ring screws, and remove the sealing ring together with the O-ring and the gasket. Withdraw the camshaft toward the rear. Note that both camshafts turn in the same direction and therefore require that the cam lobes be positioned differently.

Cam housing: Unscrew the hex nuts and the three Allen screws to lift off the camshaft housing. Each housing fits either cylinder bank.

Cylinder head: Loosen the cylinder head securing nuts (using tool P 119) and remove the cylinder head. Cylinders are numbered from the crankshaft pulley on the left bank as 1, 2 and 3 (left when facing the front of the car), and on the right bank as 4, 5 and 6.

1. Head gasket
2. Cylinder
3. Base seal
4. Lock ring
5. Piston pin
6. Piston
7. Top compression ring
8. Bottom compression ring
9. Oil control ring

911 cylinder and piston assembly

Removing the camshaft housing and cylinder heads as a unit

The upper and lower sealing surfaces of the cylinder head (between the head and the camshaft and between the head and the cylinder) should not be machined. Permitted distortion at the cylinder seating surface must not exceed 0.15 mm (0.0059 in.). Examine the mating surfaces to ensure that they are in good condition.

When installing the cylinder heads, use new cylinder head gaskets with the perforations set toward the cylinder. Carefully position each head, insert the washers and tighten the hex nuts lightly.

The camshaft housing is sealed to the cylinder heads only with sealing compound. Assemble the camshaft housing and oil return pipes on the cylinder heads, but only hand-tighten.

The Porsche factory workshop manual suggests that at this point in reassembly, the cylinder head be torqued down first and then the camshaft housing. Some mechanics prefer to torque the camshaft housing first for more accurate tensioning. Either way, the camshaft must be checked frequently for free turning. If tightening one side binds the crankshaft, tightening the opposite side must free it again. If not, the housing must be loosened and tightening steps must be made in a different sequence.

Tighten the cylinder head to 21.6–23.8 ft. lbs. (3.0–3.3 mkg). Tighten the camshaft housing to 15.9–18.1 ft. lbs. (2.2–2.5 mkg).

From this point, further disassembly of the 911 engine is the same as the four cylinder procedure. Valve timing is outlined below.

Valve timing adjustment for the 911:
Turn the crankshaft until the mark Z1 on the crankshaft pulley lines up exactly with the crankcase joint. Taking care that the valves and pistons do not collide with each other, turn both camshafts (tool P 202) to bring the punch marks, stamped on the face of the camshafts, exactly above the shaft vertical center. Back off a little if the slightest resistance is felt during the turn. Then turn the free shaft to bring the valves and pistons into proper harmony before continuing with the first shaft.

With the crankshaft timing marks aligned and the camshaft punch marks exactly on the top, the engine is timed at the firing point in cylinder No. 1 with overlapping in cylinder No. 4. Find which hole in the camshaft sprocket lines up with a corresponding hole in the sprocket flange and insert the aligning dowel pin.

Slip on the washer and tighten the retaining nut to 101 ft. lbs. (14.7 mkg).

Adjust cylinder No. 1 intake valve clearance to 0.10 mm (0.004 in.) and attach a dial gauge. The gauge sensor must be positioned exactly on the edge of the valve spring retaining collar. Adjust the gauge to a preload of 10 mm (0.39 in.) to provide for sensor travel when the cam lobe depresses the valve. Depress the chain tensioner with a screwdriver to tighten the chain (on the side to be measured) and turn the crankshaft one complete turn until the timing marks are aligned again. The dial gauge should read between 4.2 and 4.6 mm (0.165–0.181 in.). A preferred range is 4.25 to 4.45 mm.

If the gauge shows a lower or higher reading, the camshaft has to be readjusted as follows:

1. Remove the sprocket retaining nut, spring washer and aligning dowel pin.

Six cylinder valve timing position

2. Make sure that the crankshaft pulley mark is still aligned with the crankcase joint.

3. Depress the tensioner to tighten the chain and turn the camshaft until the dial gauge indicates 4.4 to 4.45 mm (0.173–0.175 in.).

4. Find the hole in the camshaft sprocket which lines up with the sprocket flange and insert the dowel pin. Replace the spring washer and nut and tighten.

5. Turn the crankshaft two complete turns to the right and read the dial gauge. If the specified value is still not obtained, repeat the steps above.

When the valves overlap in cylinder No. 1, cylinder No. 4 is at firing point (TDC). Repeat the procedure for cylinder No. 4 valve timing adjustment.

1. Cylinder head
2. Keys
3. Valve spring retainer
4. Outer valve spring
5. Inner valve spring
6. Spring seat
7. Valve seal
8. Washer
9. Exhaust valve
10. Intake valve
11. Intake valve seat
12. Exhaust valve seat
13. Valve guide
14. Retaining nut
15. Washer
16. Threaded insert
17. Nut
18. Washer
19. Intake seal
20. Nut
21. Nut
22. Exhaust seal

911 cylinder head components

1. Crankcase half
2. Crankshaft assembly
3. No. 8 bearing
4. Bearing shell
5. Thrust bearing shell
6. Seal
7. Nut

8. Lock washer
9. Intermediate shaft
10. Oil pump assembly
11. Connecting shaft
12. Seal
13. Seal
14. Camshaft chain

15. Intermediate shaft
   thrust bearing
16. Intermediate shaft
   bearing
17. Oil strainer
18. pin
19. bushing

Six cylinder crankcase assembly

914 AND 912E

Mount the engine on a stand. Drain the engine oil and remove the muffler and heat exchanger. Remove the rear engine cover plate. Remove the intake distributor and intake pipe with the injection valves (on fuel injection engines). Remove the ignition distributor and the front engine cover plate. Remove the cooling blower impeller. Remove the cooling blower housing with the alternator attached. Remove the engine mount. Remove the front and rear cylinder jackets with the warm air guides. Remove the oil cooler, oil filter and oil pump. Remove the rocker arm shafts with the protective tubes, pushrods, and tappets. Remove the cylinder heads, cylinders and pistons. Remove the clutch and flywheel. Disassemble the crankcase, being careful not to score any of the mating surfaces by

1. Bolt
2. Washer
3. Flywheel
4. Pin
5. Bushing
6. Seal
7. Bolt
8. Spring washer
9. Pulley
10. Pin
11. Seal
12. Nut
13. Washer
14. Cover
15. Seal
16. Nut
17. Spring washer
18. Washer
19. Cover
20. Seal
21. Oil strainer
22. seal
23. Nut
24. Washer
25. Breather cover
26. Seal
27. Slide rail bolt
28. Seal
29. Slide rail
30. Nut
31. Washer
32. Nut
33. Washer
34. Seal
35. Crankcase bolt
36. Washer
37. Seal
38. Nut
39. Washer
40. Seal
41. Nut
42. Spring washer
43. Thermostat
44. Seal
45. Oil pressure switch

Six cylinder crankcase assembly

trying to pry the halves apart. Remove the camshaft and crankshaft with the connecting rods.

Assembly is the reverse of disassembly, noting the following procedures. Check the riveting of the camshaft gear and the camshaft. Check the camshaft for out-of-true using V-blocks. The maximum allowable wear is 0.0016 in. Check the end-play of the guide bearing which should be 0.0016–0.0051 in. The oil holes in the crankshaft bearing journals and bearings should have no sharp edges. Carefully remove any metallic foreign substances. Install the crankshaft and connecting rods. Install the cam-

Four cylinder engine timing marks

shaft and gear so that the tooth marked with a 0 is located between the two teeth of the crankshaft gear which are identified with a punch mark. Coat the mating surfaces of the housing halves with a thin coat of sealing compound. Be sure that no sealing compound enters the oil ducts. Assemble the crankcase halves and lightly tighten the screw for the oil intake pipe. Screw on the sealing nuts with the sealing ring on the outside and tighten to the specified torque. Rotate the crankshaft to ensure free rotation. Grease the needle bearing in the flywheel with a

1. Camshaft
2. Crankshaft assembly
3. No. 1 bearing
4. No. 4 bearing
5. Camshaft plug
6. Camshaft bearing
7. Camshaft bearing
8. Camshaft bearing
9. Pin
10. Crankshaft bearing
11. Crankshaft half

Four cylinder engine crankcase and crankshaft assembly

small amount of multipurpose grease. Moisten the felt ring with engine oil, wiping off any excess. Install the flywheel and adjust the axial play of the crankshaft. Measure the axial play by installing the flywheel with two spacing washers but without the sealing rings. Using a dial gauge, measure the play by rotating the flywheel. The thickness of the third spacer can be computed by subtracting 0.0039 in. from the measured result. Remove the flywheel and install the sealing ring, felt ring, and three spacers. Three spacers must always be installed for the required thickness. Spacers are available in the following sizes: 0.0094, 0.0118, 0.0126, 0.0134, 0.0142 and 0.0150 in. Each spacer is marked for proper identification. The axial play of the crankshaft, measured with the engine assembled and the flywheel screwed on, should be 0.0028–0.0051 in. Clean the contact surface of the clutch disc and flywheel. Check the splining of the input shaft and coat lightly with molybdenum disulphide powder, applied with a brush. The clutch disc should slide easily. Check the throwout bearing. Do not wash in any solvent but wipe it clean. Replace bearings which are contaminated or noisy. Grease the guide bushing lightly with molybdenum disulphide paste. Center the clutch disc and clutch on the flywheel using an input shaft. When a new clutch is installed, the balancing marks should be 180° apart. A white paint stripe on the outside edge of the flywheel indicates the heavy end, and a white paint stripe indicates the

1. Rocker arm cover
2. Gasket
3. Nut
4. Spring washer
5. Rocker arm bearing
6. Exhaust rocker arm
7. Thrust washer
8. Spring
9. Intake rocker arm
10. Valve adjusting screw
11. Nut
12. Rocker arm shaft
13. Rocker arm cover retainer
14. Pushrod
15. Pushrod tube seal (white)
16. Pushrod tube seal (black)
17. Pushrod tube
18. Valve lifter
19. Nut
20. Washer
21. Cylinder head
22. Bolt
23. Washer
24. Bolt
25. Washer
26. Baffle plate
27. Valve keys
28. Valve spring retainer
29. Valve spring
30. Valve stem seal
31. Intake valve
32. Exhaust valve
33. Intake valve guide
34. Exhaust valve guide

Four cylinder engine cylinder head components

heavy end of the clutch. Tighten the bolts to 14.5 ft. lbs. Clean all pistons and check for wear. Check the marking of the pistons according to the following designations:

The letter next to the arrow is the index of the spare parts number.

The punched in arrow indicates that the piston must be installed with the arrow facing the flywheel.

The color dot (blue, pink or green) indicates the paired size of the piston.

A statement of weight class (+ or −) is punched in or printed.

The weight class is indicated by a color dot (brown equals (−) weight and grey equals (+) weight).

Number indicates the piston size in mm. Fit the compression and oil scraper rings. The designation TOP should face up. Insert the locking rings of pistons 1 and 2 on the side facing the flywheel. The locking rings of pistons 3 and 4 should be fitted on the impeller side. Fit the piston pin. The piston pin may slide in easily by hand, which is normal. Should the pin not fit easily, heat the piston to approximately 176°F and slide in the piston pin without bottoming the pin on the locking ring. Seat the second locking ring. Lubricate the piston and piston pin. Compress the piston rings. Lubricate the cylinder bore and fit the cylinder bore. The sealing ring must also be fitted. The studs of the crankcase may not touch the cooling fins of the cylinder. Check the cylinder head for cracks and the spark plug threads for damage. Replace the sealing ring and the cylinder head. Pre-tighten the cylinder head nuts slightly and finally tighten according to sequence. Replace the baffle plate. Insert the tappets with engine oil. Slide the protective tubes with new sealing rings up to the stop, taking care not to damage the sealing rings. Slide the bearing pieces on the rocker arm shafts so that the slots face downward and the broken edges outward when settling on the studs. The clip which secures the protective tubes should enter the slots of the bearing pieces and rest against the bottom edges of the protective tubes. Lubricate the gear wheel and driveshaft and insert into the oil pump housing. Install the oil pump cover with the lubricated rubber

sealing ring. Check the gear wheels for proper running. Install the oil pump, with a new seal, into the crankcase. The journal of the driveshaft should be in alignment with the slot in the camshaft gear. Center the oil pump by two crankshaft revolutions and tighten the nuts. Clean the sealing surface on the flange for the oil filter. Lubricate the rubber seal slightly and screw the filter in until the filter is seated. Tighten the oil filter. Replace the oil cooler after checking for leaks and tighten1ng all welded seats. Replace the front and rear cylinder jackets and warm air guides. Replace the engine mount. Replace the cooling blower housing with the alternator and adjust the V-belt tension. Replace the cooling blower impeller and the front engine cover plate. Replace the ignition distributor. Bring cylinder No. 1 to the firing point. The black notch should be in alignment with the reference mark. The center offset slot in the head of the ignition distributor driveshaft should be at an angle of approximately 12° in relation to the longitudinal axis of the engine. Turn the distributor rotor to the mark for cylinder No. 1 on the distributor housing. Insert the ignition distributor. Replace the oil filler neck with the oil vent. Replace the intake distributor with the intake pipes and injection valves. Mount the rear engine cover plate. Replace the exhaust muffler and heat exchanger. Fill the engine with oil and replace the engine in the car. Adjust the ignition timing.

EMISSION CONTROLS

Crankcase Ventilation System

All models are equipped with a crankcase ventilation systems. The purpose of the

crankcase ventilation system is two-fold. It keeps harmful vapors from escaping into the atmosphere and prevents the buildup of pressures within the crankcase which could cause oil leaks.

The 911 system carries vapors from the crankcase to the oil tank and then to the air cleaner. The crankcase emissions are then burned along with the air/fuel mixture. The ventilation system on 914 models supplies fresh air from the air cleaner to the rocker arm covers, where it mixes with crankcase vapors and continues through the pushrod tubes and into the crankcase. The mixture of fresh air and crankcase vapors is then released through the oil breather and a regulator valve into the intake air distributor to be burned with the air/fuel mixture. The only maintenance required on the crankcase ventilation system is a periodic check. At every tune-up, examine the hoses for clogging or deterioration. Clean or replace the hoses as required.

Evaporative Emission Control System

The systems used on the 911, 912E and 914 are basically similar and consist of an expansion chamber, evaporation chamber, and an activated charcoal filter. Fuel vapors which reach the filter deposit hydrocarbons on the surface of the charcoal element. The engine fan forces fresh air into the charcoal filter when the engine is running. The air purges the filter and the hydrocarbons are sent into the air cleaner where they become part of the air/fuel mixture and are burned.

Maintenance on this system consists of checking the condition of the various connecting lines and the charcoal filter at 10,000 mile intervals. The charcoal filter, which is located in the front luggage compartment on all models, should be replaced at 50,000 mile intervals.

Four cylinder engine piston positioning

911 crankcase ventilation schematic

911 evaporative emission control system

914 evaporative emission control system

Dual Diaphragm Distributors

The purpose of the dual diaphragm distributor is to improve exhaust emissions during idling. The distributor has a vacuum retard diaphragm, in addition to a vacuum advance diaphragm.

TESTING

1. Connect a timing light to the engine. Check the ignition timing.
2. Remove the retard hose from the distributor and plug it. Increase the engine speed. The ignition timing should advance. If it doesn't, then the vacuum unit is faulty and must be replaced.

Exhaust Gas Recirculation

California 914 models, all 912E models and some 911 models are equipped with EGR. This system directs a portion of the exhaust gases back into the intake where they combine with the incoming mixture. This diluting of the mixture lowers peak combustion temperatures and reduces NO_x.

Thermal Reactor

A thermal reactor is used on certain 911 models and the 912E. The thermal reactor is used to reduce HC and CO emissions by supplying an improved location for exhaust combustion. 911s with the thermal reactor are equipped with an additional heater blower.

Catalytic Converter

California delivered 914 models are equipped with a catalytic converter in the exhaust system. When the hot exhaust gases mix with air in the presence of the catalyst, HC, CO, and NO_x are reduced to harmless gases.

FUEL SYSTEM

Electric Fuel Pump

REMOVAL AND INSTALLATION

All models are electric fuel pumps. The Turbo is equipped with two electric pumps. One is mounted at the front crossmember near the fuel tank, the second at the rear near the engine. All 911 and 912E model fuel pumps are located at the front near the

911 fuel pump removal

tank. The 914 fuel pump is located behind a small access panel in the front luggage compartment near the fuel tank.

911, 912E

1. Remove the cap nuts.
2. Withdraw the pump with its mounting bracket.
3. Loosen the hose clamp and remove the pump from the bracket.
4. Loosen the hose clamps and remove the three fuel lines from the pump.
5. Install the pump using a reverse of the removal procedure. Coat both electrical terminals with grease and make sure that the rubber boot is firmly seated.

914

1. Pinch the fuel hoses to prevent spillage and remove the cable plug.
2. Cut the hose clamps and pull the hoses from the pump, catching any fuel with a rag.
3. Raise the fuel pressure hose to prevent draining any fuel.
4. Unscrew the retaining nuts and remove the pump.
5. Fit the hoses to the pump. Use new hose clamps.
6. Mount the pump on its supports and remove the clamps used to pinch the hoses.
7. Replace the cable plug, ensuring that the protective cap is correctly installed.

Fuel Injection

For all fuel injection system repair and service procedures, please refer to "Fuel Injection" in the Unit Repair section.

TRANSAXLE

Transaxle separation is covered in the "Engine Removal" procedure.

SHIFT LINKAGE ADJUSTMENT

911, 912E

1. Position the shift lever in Neutral. Remove the rear tunnel cover in front of the rear seat.
2. Pull the rubber dust cover forward on the shift rod.
3. Loosen the clamp bolt on the shift rod.
4. Move the transmission selector shaft all the way to its left stop, keeping it in Neutral.
5. With the transmission still in Neutral, move the gearshift rod to the right to its stop.
6. Tighten the clamp bolt to 18 ft. lbs.
7. Test the shift lever. Play should be the same in all gears in all directions.

911 and 912 linkage adjustment

Clutch disc centering

911 and 912 pedal travel adjustment

1976 914

1. Loosen the shift linkage retaining bolt on the shift mount.

2. Place the shift lever in Neutral and to the right (toward the Fourth and Fifth gear side).

3. Remove the rear tunnel cover in the passenger compartment.

4. Rotate the shift rod clockwise (fac1ng toward the front of the car).

5. Tighten the mounting screw hand-tight.

6. Shift lever travel must be the same for Second, Third, Fourth, and Fifth gears. Make sure that First and Reverse are easily engaged.

7. Finally tighten the mounting bolt to 18 ft. lbs.

CLUTCH

REMOVAL AND INSTALLATION

Each Porsche covered in this section is equipped with single dry disc clutch and diaphragm pressure plate. Clutch actuation is controlled by a cable.

1. Separate the engine/transaxle.

2. Gradually loosen the pressure plate bolts one or two turns at a time in a criss-cross pattern to prevent distortion.

3. Remove the pressure plate and clutch disc.

4. Check the clutch disc for uneven or excessive lining wear. Examine the pressure plate for cracking, scorching, or scoring. Replace any questionable components.

5. On 912 and 911 models, fill the pilot bearing with about 2 cc of grease.

6. Install the clutch disc and pressure plate. Use a pilot shaft or an old transaxle input shaft to keep the disc centered.

7. Gradually tighten the pressure plate-to-flywheel bolts in a criss-cross pattern. Torque the bolts to 25 ft. lbs. on the 912 models. Tighten the bolts on the 914 to 15 ft. lbs. On 911S, tighten the bolts to 18 ft. lbs.

8. Install the throwout bearing.

9. Install the transaxle on the engine.

FREE PLAY ADJUSTMENT

1976 911 and 912E

This adjustment is made at the throwout arm on the transaxle. Free-play should be between ¾ in. and 1 in.

1. Jack up the rear of the car and support it on stands.

2. On older models, loosen the locknut on the clevis and turn the adjusting nut as necessary to obtain the correct free-play.

3. A threaded cable extension is provided on later models. While holding the flats on the cable end to prevent it from turning, screw the self-locking nut in or out for the correct free-play.

Free-play adjustment

1977–83 911 and Turbo

These models are equipped with an auxiliary spring to reduce pedal effort. Free-play is no longer checked at the Pedal. Play is checked by measuring the distance between the adjusting belt and the positioning lever. The distance should be 1 mm (0.04 in.).

1. Release the cable.

2. Adjust clutch play to 1.2 mm (0.047 in.).

3. Tighten the cable at the holder until play is reduced to 1 mm. (0.04 in.).

4. Adjust the stop on the pedal floor plate so that the release travel is 25 mm (0.984 in.) for the S or 27 mm (1.063 in.) when the clutch pedal is depressed.

914

1. Raise the rear of the car and support it on jackstands.

2. Hold the threaded cable end with

pliers and turn the self-locking adjustment nut in or out until the free-play is ½ in. to ¾ in.

PEDAL TRAVEL ADJUSTMENT

1. Pull the front carpeting back.

2. Loosen the two retaining bolts on the pedal stop.

3. Move the pedal up or down until reverse can be engaged with only a slight amount of gear clash.

4. Tighten the pedal stop bolts.

5. Double check the adjustment by shifting into reverse several times. Reinstall the floor carpeting.

DRIVE AXLES

Axle Driveshaft

REMOVAL AND INSTALLATION

911 and 912E

1. Jack up the rear of the car and support it on stands.

2. Remove the wheels. Remove the brake caliper and disc.

3. Raise the trailing arm with a hydraulic jack.

4. Remove the lower shock absorber mounting.

Hub nut removal (Porsche tool P36b shown)

5. Install a fixture similar to Porsche tool P36b to hold the hub.

6. Remove the cotter pin and using a long ratchet handle extension, remove the hub nut.

7. Remove the Allen bolts at the axle driveshaft/transaxle flange.

8. Use a flat chisel to pry the flanges apart.

— CAUTION —
Don't damage the flanges when separating them.

9. Check the axle driveshaft joints for excessive play and replace them if necessary.

10. Use a new gasket on the transaxle flange. Ensure that the flanges are clean and free from burrs.

11. Pack the joints with a moly grease.

12. Install the axle driveshaft using a reverse of the removal procedure.

13. Tighten the flange bolts to 60 ft. lbs. The hollow side of the lock washer should face the spacer slate.

14. Using a long extension handle wrench, tighten the castellated nut to 217–253 ft. lbs. and install a new cotter pin.

NOTE: Be prepared to apply considerable force on this unit.

15. Tighten the shock absorber bolt to 54 ft. lbs.

16. Install the brake caliper and disc.

17. Install the wheels and lower the car.

914

1. Raise the rear of the car and support it on jackstands.

2. Remove the wheels.

3. Remove the brake caliper and disc.

4. Using a ratchet handle with a long extension (a pipe will provide more leverage), remove the castellated hub nut.

5. Remove the heat exchangers.

6. Unscrew the Allen bolts at the transaxle/driveshaft flange.

7. Using a chisel or flat-edged screwdriver, pry the flanges apart and separate the driveshaft.

8. Pull the driveshaft from the hub and

Disconnecting inner driveshaft joint at transaxle

down out of the case. Be careful not to damage the flange surfaces.

9. Clean the flanges and install a new gasket.

10. Install the axle driveshaft and tighten the flange bolts to 31 ft. lbs. Use new lock washers and install them so that their hollow ends are against the spacer plate.

11. Tighten the hub nut to 217–253 ft. lbs., using a long extension on the wrench handle and plenty of muscle.

12. Install the brake disc and caliper.

13. Install the wheels and lower the car.

REAR SUSPENSION

All models covered in this section have independent rear suspension. The 911 and 912E rear suspension is a semi-trailing arm design. Springing is provided by transverse torsion bars located forward of each trailing arm. Telescopic shock absorbers at each wheel provide dampening. A rear stabilizer bar is standard equipment on the 911S Turbo and Carrera and optional on the other two 911 models.

The 914 is also equipped with trailing arms, but they are one piece arms as opposed to the two piece arms on the 911. Telescopic strut/shocks with concentric coil springs support the weight of the car. A rear stabilizer bar is optionally available on later models.

911 and 912 rear suspension

Torsion Bars

REMOVAL AND INSTALLATION

911 and 912E

1. Jack up the rear of the car and support it safely with stands.

2. Remove the wheel on the side where the torsion bar is being removed.

3. Fabricate a fixture similar to the one shown. The fixture is necessary to hold the trailing arm while it is raised and lowered.

Raising the trailing arm

The special Porsche tool for this purpose is number P 289.

4. Using a hydraulic jack under the holding fixture, raise the trailing arm.

5. Remove the lower shock absorber bolt.

6. Remove the trailing arm retaining bolts. Remove the toe and chamber adjusting bolts.

7. Remove the four retaining bolts from the trailing arm cover. Withdraw the spacer.

8. Using two screwdrivers, pry off the trailing arm cover.

9. Remove the holding fixture.

10. Knock out the round body plug and remove the trailing arm.

11. Paint a reference mark on the torsion bar support, matching the location of the "L" or "R" side identification letter, so that the torsion bar may be installed in the same position.

NOTE: The torsion bars are splined to allow adjustment of the rear riding height.

12. Remove the torsion bar. Do not scratch the protective paint on the torsion bar, or it will corrode and possibly develop fatigue cracks.

NOTE: If you are removing a broken torsion bar, the inner end can be knocked from its seat by removing the opposite torsion bar and tapping through with a steel rod. Torsion bars are not interchangeable from side-to-side and are marked "L" and "R" for identification.

13. Check the torsion bar splines for

Installing the trailing arm cover

damage and replace it if necessary. If any corrosion is present on the bar, replace it.

14. Coat the torsion bar lightly with a multi-purpose grease. Carefully grease the splines.

15. Apply glycerine or another rubber preservative to the torsion bar support.

16. Install the torsion bar, matching the ''L'' or ''R'' with the paint mark you made before removal.

17. Install the trailing arm cover into position and start the three accessible bolts.

18. Raise the trailing arm into place with the holding fixture (or special tool P 289) until the spacer and the fourth bolt can be installed.

19. Assemble the remaining components in a reverse order of their removal.

20. Tighten the trailing arm cover bolts to 34 ft. lbs. Tighten the trailing arm retaining bolts to 65 ft. lbs.

21. Tighten the camber adjusting bolt to 43 ft. lbs. and the toe-in adjusting bolt to 36 ft. lbs. Tighten the shock absorber bolt to 45 ft. lbs.

22. Adjust the rear wheel camber and toe-in.

Spring Strut

REMOVAL AND INSTALLATION

914

1. Jack up the rear of the car and support it safely with stands.

2. Support the wheel on the side where the spring strut is being removed.

3. Loosen and remove the bottom through-bolt and nut from the trailing arm.

4. Loosen and remove the nut at the top of the strut. Hold the strut shaft while loosening the nut.

5. Remove the strut by pulling it down and out of the car.

6. When reinstalling the strut, use a new nut at the top. Install the bottom nut and bolt.

7. Tighten the top nut to 36–43 ft. lbs. Torque the bottom bolt to 72–87 ft. lbs.

DISASSEMBLY

For all strut disassembly and overhaul procedures, please refer to ''Strut Overhaul'' in the Unit Repair section.

Shock Absorbers

REMOVAL AND INSTALLATION

911 and 912E

1. Leave the car standing on the ground, so that the shock absorber is not tensioned.

2. Open the engine compartment lid and

Top shock absorber mounting

Bottom shock absorber mounting

remove the rubber cover from the top of the shock absorber.

3. Hold the shock absorber shaft and remove the nut.

4. On the bottom, remove the retaining nut and bolt.

5. Remove the shock absorber.

6. If the shock exhibits excessive free travel or is leaking, replace it.

7. Install the shock up through the body and screw the nut on hand-tight.

8. Align the shock absorber eye with the hole in the trailing arm and install the nut and bolt.

9. Tighten the top nut and install the rubber cover.

10. Tighten the bottom retaining bolt to 54 ft. lbs.

Stabilizer

REMOVAL AND INSTALLATION

911 and 912E

1. Jack the rear of the car and safely support it with stands.

2. Using a large screwdriver, pry the upper eyes of the stabilizer bar off the studs in the trailing arm.

3. Remove the body mounting brackets.

1. Camber
2. Toe-in

911 and 912 rear wheel alignment adjustment points

4. Remove the stabilizer.

5. Check the rubber bushings for wear or damage and, if necessary, replace them.

6. Install the stabilizer bar using a reverse of the removal steps.

Adjustments

CAMBER ADJUSTMENT

911 and 912E

The rearmost of the two Allen bolts on the trailing arm provides camber adjustment. Tighten the bolt to 43 ft. lbs. after the camber is adjusted to specifications.

914

Camber is adjusted by removal or insertion of shims under the trailing arm bearing plate. Scribe the plate's position, so the toe-in setting isn't lost, and then remove the center bolt and loosen the two end bolts. Each 1 mm shim results in a 10′ change in camber. Tighten the bolts to 18 ft. lbs. after the correct camber is reached.

TOE-IN ADJUSTMENT

911 and 912E

The front Allen bolt on the trailing arm adjusts the toe-in. Tighten the bolt to 36 ft. lbs. after toe-in is adjusted to specification.

914 rear wheel alignment adjustment point

914

Loosen all three bolts on the trailing arm bearing plate and push the arm forward or backward as necessary to correct the toe-in. Tighten the bolts to 18 ft. lbs. when the adjustment is complete.

FRONT SUSPENSION

Front suspension is similar in design on all models; but parts are not interchangeable from one type to the other. Springing is provided by a longitudinal torsion bar at each wheel. A triangular lower arm links the torsion bar to the shock absorber strut and steering knuckle. A permanently lubricated ball joint is located at the bottom of the strut.

Torsion Bars

REMOVAL AND INSTALLATION

911 and 912E

1. Jack up the front of the car and support it safely with stands.
2. Remove the torsion bar adjusting screw.
3. Take the adjusting lever off the torsion bar and withdraw the seal.

Loosening torsion bar adjusting screw

4. Unscrew the retaining bolts from the front mount cover bracket and remove the bracket.
5. Using a drift, carefully drive the torsion bar out of the front of the arm.
6. Check the torsion bar for spline damage and rust. If necessary, replace the bar.
7. Give the torsion bar a light coating of grease before installing it.

NOTE: Torsion bars are marked "L" or "R" to identify them and are not interchangeable.

8. Insert the end cap of the torsion bar, protruding side out, into the control arm. Drive the torsion bar into position with a drift. Carefully.
9. Tighten the retaining bolts on the front mount to 34 ft. lbs.
10. Slide the seal onto the torsion bar from the open side of the crossmember.
11. Using a tire iron, or other suitable lever, pry the control arm down as far as possible. While holding the control arm, slide the adjusting lever onto the splines of the torsion bar. There should only be a slight amount of clearance at the lever adjusting point.
12. Grease the adjusting screw threads with a moly grease and hand tighten the screw.
13. Check that the end cap is properly seated in the control arm.
14. Install the rubber mount cover bracket. Tighten the retaining bolts to 34 ft. lbs.
15. Lower the car.
16. Check the front wheel alignment.

914

1. Jack up the front of the car and support it safely with stands.

1. Strut
2. Brake disc
3. Intermediate
4. Universal joint
5. Stabilizer bar
6. Tie-rod
7. Adjusting screw
8. Bellows
9. Control arm
10. Steering column
11. Steering gear
12. Crossmember
13. Bearing support

911 and 912 front suspension and steering

1. Strut
2. Strut support bracket
3. Steering shaft
4. Dust boot
5. Steering gear
6. Brake caliper
7. Control arm
8. Crossmember
9. Ball joint

914 front wheel suspension and steering

2. Unscrew the torsion bar adjusting screw.

3. Pull the adjusting lever off the torsion bar and remove the seal.

4. Loosen the cheesehead screw for the front mount cover and remove the cover.

5. Carefully drive the torsion bar out of the rear of the control arm with a drift.

6. Check the torsion bar for spline damage and rust. If necessary, replace the bar.

7. Give the torsion bar a light coating of grease before installing it.

NOTE: Torsion bars are marked "L" or "R" for identification and are not interchangeable from side-to-side.

8. Slide the seal onto the torsion bar.

9. Using a tire iron, or other suitable lever, pry the control arm down as far as possible against the stop in the shock absorber strut. Push the adjusting lever onto the torsion bar as closely as possible against the stop.

10. Grease the adjusting screw threads and then install it hand-tight.

11. Make sure that the cover in the control arm is correctly seated. Improper assembly of the adjusting lever may force the torsion bar out of the control arm splines at the front.

12. Screw on the front mount cover.

13. Lower the car.

14. Check the front wheel alignment.

Shock Absorbers

REMOVAL AND INSTALLATION

911 and 912E

1. Jack up the front of the car and support it safely on stands. Remove the wheels.

2. Remove the brake line from the clip on the suspension strut. A small amount of brake fluid will run out of the line, plug it so that dirt cannot enter the system.

3. Unscrew the retaining bolts and remove the caliper.

4. Using a soft mallet, tap the hub cap to loosen it.

5. Pry the hub cap off with a screwdriver.

6. Loosen the Allen screw in the wheel bearing clamp. Unscrew the clamp nut and remove the nut and washer.

7. Remove the wheel hub along with the brake disc and wheel bearing.

8. Remove the backing plate retaining bolts and remove the plate.

9. Withdraw the cotter pin from the castellated nut on the steering tie rod end and remove the nut. Using a suitable puller, remove the tie rod joint from the strut.

10. Remove the control arm-to-strut ball joint retaining bolt and pull the ball joint

Loosening ball joint retaining bolt

out of the strut by pulling down on the lower control arm.

NOTE: The torsion bar adjusting screw will have to be loosened and the adjusting arm removed.

11. Remove the keeper for the nut on the top of the strut. Unscrew the nut and remove it, the keeper plate, and washer.

12. Remove the strut from the bottom. It will be necessary to loosen and pull the side of the luggage compartment out for clearance.

13. Check the shock absorber strut for excessive free travel and leaking. Replace the shock absorber if it is at all suspect.

14. Install the strut in a reverse order of the removal.

15. Tighten the top nut to 58 ft. lbs. Use a new keeper plate and ensure that the peg on the plate is pointing up.

16. Tighten the ball joint bolt to 47 ft. lbs.

NOTE: Remember to install the washer between the ball joint seal and strut.

17. Install the torsion bar adjusting lever as described in "Torsion Bar Removal and Installation."

18. Tighten the tie rod nut to 33 ft. lbs. and install a new cotter pin.

19. Torque the backing plate bolts to 18 ft. lbs.

20. Install and adjust the wheel bearings.

21. Tighten the caliper retaining bolts to 50 ft. lbs.

22. Bleed the brakes.

23. Install the wheels and lower the car.

24. Check the wheel alignment.

914

1. Jack up the front of the car and support it safely with stands. Remove the wheels.

2. Remove the brake line from its retainer on the shock absorber strut.

3. Remove the retaining bolts and detach the caliper.

4. Carefully pry the hub cap off.

5. Loosen the screw in the wheel bearing clamp nut. Unscrew the clamp nut and remove the washer.

6. Remove the brake disc and the wheel bearings.

7. Remove the retaining bolt and remove the splash shield.

8. Remove the cotter pin and nut and remove the tie rod joint from the strut with a suitable puller.

9. Loosen the torsion bar adjusting screw and remove the adjusting lever.

10. Loosen the ball joint retaining bolt on the strut. Pull the control arm down to free the strut from the ball joint.

11. Open the front luggage compartment lid. Remove the strut retaining nut, lock washer, and tab washer.

12. Pull the strut down and out of the car.

13. Check the shock absorber strut for

Top mounting nut removal

excessive free travel and leaking and replace it, if necessary.

14. Installation of the strut is essentially a reverse order of the removal. Remember to install the washer on the ball joint before attaching the strut.

15. Tighten the top nut to 58 ft. lbs. Use a new lock washer and ensure that its tab points up. Torque the ball joint bolt in the strut to 47 ft. lbs.

16. Reinstall the torsion bar adjusting lever as outlined in "Torsion Bar Removal and Installation."

17. Tighten the tie rod end nut to 33 ft. lbs. and install a new cotter pin. Torque the three splash shield bolts to 18 ft. lbs.

18. Install and adjust the wheel bearings.

19. Install new lock washers on the caliper retaining bolts. Tighten both bolts to 51 ft. lbs.

20. Bleed the brake system.

21. Install the wheels and lower the car.

22. Check the wheel alignment.

CONTROL ARM AND BALL JOINT

914

REMOVAL

1. Remove torsion bar adjusting screw and pull adjusting lever from torsion bar. Remove seal.

2. Loosen ball joint hex bolt, push control arm downward and pull ball joint from shock absorber strut.

3. Remove control arm and auxiliary carrier hex bolt.

4. Unbolt and remove front control arm bearing protective cap.

5. Remove control arm bearing bolts.

6. Push control arm together with torsion bar out of auxiliary carrier and remove.

NOTE: If both control arms are to be removed, first remove one arm and tighten the control arm and carrier hex bolt so that the carrier is supported.

7. Clamp the control arm in a softjawed

vise and unlock the bolt joint nut, removing the ball joint.

INSTALLATION

1. Position ball joint in control arm and tighten nut to 108 ft. lbs.

2. Coat torsion bar lightly with lithium grease, paying attention to the serrations, and insert torsion bar into control arm.

3. Position control arm and torsion in carrier.

NOTE: Torsion bars are not interchangeable. They are marked R and L for identification.

4. Torque control arm bolts (front) to 34 ft. lbs.

5. Torque hex bolt for ball joint to 34 ft. lbs.

6. Slide seal across torsion bar and push control arm, with shock absorber connected, down against stop in strut. Slide the adjusting lever as closely as possible against the stop of the auxiliary carrier for the adjusting screw on the torsion bar.

7. Grease the threads of the adjusting screw with molybdenum di-sulfide grease and slightly tighten the adjusting screw.

8. Check the closing cover in the control arm for a good seal.

9. Attach the control arm protective cap.

10. Check front end height.

Stabilizer Bar

REMOVAL AND INSTALLATION

911 and 912E

1. Jack up the front of the car and safely support it on stands.

2. Loosen the stabilizer clamp bolts and pry the lever ends off their mounts.

3. Remove the stabilizer bar along with the levers.

4. Check the rubber bushings for deterioration and, if necessary, replace them. Lubricate the bushings with glycerine or some other rubber preservative.

5. Install the stabilizer bar in a reverse order of the removal.

6. The square end of the stabilizer should protrude slightly above the clamp. Tighten the clamp nuts to 18 ft. lbs.

Adjustments

CAMBER ADJUSTMENT

Camber is adjusted at the top of the strut. Pull back the luggage compartment rug to expose the three mounting bolts. Scrape the undercoating from the bolts and plates. Scribe the positions of the two plates under the bolts. Loosen the bolts and move the strut in or out as necessary to correct the camber angle.

Caster and camber adjustment location

CASTER ADJUSTMENT

Caster is adjusted in the same manner as camber, except that the strut is moved forward or backward to change the caster angle.

TOE-IN ADJUSTMENT

Toe-in is set with the front wheels straight ahead. Tie rod length is adjusted by loosening the tie rod clamps and moving them an equal amount in or out to obtain the correct toe-in.

STEERING

All models are equipped with rack and pinion type steering gear. No maintenance is required on the steering system. It is filled with a special lubricant at the time of manufacture and does not require checking or filling.

Steering Wheel

REMOVAL AND INSTALLATION

1. Disconnect the battery(ies). Place the wheels in a straight ahead position.

Steering wheel center cover removal

2. Twist the center cover to the left and remove it.

3. Remove the horn contact pin.

4. Remove the steering wheel nut.

5. Mark the steering wheel and the shaft so that it can be reinstalled in the same position.

6. Remove the steering wheel. Catch the bearing support ring and spring.

7. Install the spring and bearing support ring on the wheel hub.

8. Lightly grease the horn contact ring.

9. Install the wheel. Make sure that you align the match marks before removal.

10. Tighten the steering wheel nut to 58 ft. lbs. on 911 models and 36–43 ft. lbs. on 914s.

11. Twist the center cover back on to the right to snap it into place.

Turn Signal/Headlight Flasher Switch

REMOVAL AND INSTALLATION

911 and 912E

The combination turn signal, headlight dimmer, and flasher switch is located in the steering column housing. The wiper/washer switch removal and installation procedure is identical.

1. Remove the steering wheel as outlined above.

2. Reach under the instrument panel and disconnect all wiring to the switch.

3. Remove the two horn contact ring screws, disconnect the wire, and remove the ring.

4. Remove the two upper housing retaining nuts. Pull the entire assembly off the column, leading the switch wires through the hole in the housing.

5. Remove the three retaining screws and remove the switch.

6. Reverse the removal steps to reinstall the switch.

914

Both the turn signal/headlight dimmer and wiper/washer switches are located within the steering column cover halves.

1. Remove the steering wheel as previously outlined.

2. Unscrew and remove the horn contact ring.

3. Remove the screw retaining the horn ground wire and remove the wire.

4. Remove the retaining screw from the top and bottom covers. Detach the covers.

5. Remove the switch attaching screws and remove the switch.

6. Installation is a reverse of the removal procedure. Make sure that the turn signal switch is in Neutral, or the cancelling cams will be damaged.

Disconnecting steering coupling

Ignition Switch/ Steering Lock

REMOVAL AND INSTALLATION

911 and 912E

1. Remove the ignition switch cover.

2. Drill out the two shear bolts which retain the switch.

3. Remove the steering lock and spacer.

4. Disconnect the electrical wiring and remove the switch.

5. Place the steering lock into position.

6. Insert the protective plate.

7. Install and evenly tighten the new shear bolts until their heads break off.

Steering Gear

REMOVAL AND INSTALLATION

911 and 912E

1. Remove the front luggage compartment carpeting. Jack up the front of the car and support it safely with stands.

2. Remove the auxiliary heater duct from the steering post and position it to one side.

3. Open the access door and the intermediate steering shaft cover by prying the spring clips off with a screwdriver.

4. Remove the three heater fuel pump retaining bolts and position the pump to one side.

5. Remove the cotter pin from the lower universal joint bolt and loosen the castellated nut. Pull the universal joint off the steering shaft.

6. Remove the Allen bolts from the steering shaft bushing bracket. Remove the bracket and pull the bushing and dust cover.

7. Loosen and remove the steering coupling bolts.

8. Remove the retaining bolts and remove the bottom shield.

9. Remove the cotter pins and nuts, and then pull the tie rod ends out of the suspension struts with a suitable puller.

10. Remove the two rack and pinion housing retaining bolts.

Removing tie rod ends

Rack and pinion retaining bolts

11. Remove the right side crossmember brace.

12. Pull the steering assembly out the right side of the car.

13. Remove the retaining bolts from the tie rod yokes.

14. Installation is the reverse of the removal procedure.

15. Tighten the yoke bolts to 34 ft. lbs.

16. Make sure that the crossmember brace mounts without binding. Tighten the nuts to 47 ft. lbs. and the bolts to 34 ft. lbs.

17. Install the steering housing bolts with new lockwashers and tighten to 34 ft. lbs.

18. Tighten the tie rod end nuts to 33 ft. lbs. and install new cotter pins.

19. Tighten the steering bushing bracket Allen bolts to 18 ft. lbs.

20. Install new washers on the steering coupling bolts and tighten them to 18 ft. lbs.

21. Lower the car.

914

1. Raise the front of the car and support it safely on stands.

2. Remove the nut and bolt from the bottom universal joint.

3. Remove the cotter pins and castellated nuts from the tie rod ends. Using a suitable puller, remove the tie rod ends from the struts.

4. Remove the front shield.

5. Loosen the crossmember retaining bolts for the steering gear.

6. Loosen the torsion bar adjusting screws.

914 brake system

911 and 912 brake system

7. Remove the adjusting levers and seals from the torsion bars.

8. Remove the crossmember and control arm retaining bolts and remove the crossmember.

9. Remove the steering gear and tie rods.

10. Detach the tie rods from the steering gear by removing the yoke bolts.

11. Installation is essentially a reverse of the removal procedure. Reinstall the torsion bar adjusting levers as described in "Torsion Bar Removal and Installation."

12. The tie rod yoke bolts are tightened to 34 ft. lbs., the steering housing mounting bolts to 34 ft. lbs., and the crossmember mounting bolts to 65 ft. lbs.

13. Torque the tie rod end nuts to 33 ft. lbs. Tighten the steering coupling bolts and universal shaft nut to 18 ft. lbs.

BRAKE SYSTEM

All models are equipped with four wheel disc brakes. Fixed, two-piston calipers are utilized on each system. The discs on the 914 and 912E are solid. 911s are equipped with internally vented discs at each wheel. Disc brakes on all of these models are self-adjusting and require no periodic adjustment.

Each car has a tandem master cylinder, remote reservoir (mounted in the front luggage compartment for convenience), and separate hydraulic circuits for the front and rear brakes. The 914 rear circuit includes a pressure regulator which maintains maximum rear brake pressure at a predetermined level to prevent rear wheel lockup under hard braking. The 1977–83 911 models are equipped with power brakes. A vacuum booster is mounted in tandem with the master cylinder. It is located under the luggage compartment carpet.

For all brake system repair and service procedures not detailed below, please refer to "Brakes" in the Unit Repair section.

Master Cylinder

REMOVAL AND INSTALLATION

1. Pull the accelerator back and out of its pushrod. Pull back the driver's side carpeting.

2. Unscrew the floorboard retainer(s) under the brake and clutch pedals.

3. Remove the master cylinder dust cover.

4. Jack the front of the car up and support it with stands.

5. Siphon the brake fluid out of the reservoir. Discard the fluid, don't save it for reuse.

6. Unbolt the front splash shield.

7. Remove the brake lines from the master cylinder. Disconnect the brake failure warning light sending unit wire.

8. Remove the two master cylinder mounting nuts.

9. Disconnect the reservoir lines and remove the master cylinder.

10. Before installing the master cylinder, apply body sealer around the mounting flange.

11. Install the cylinder, making sure that the piston pushrod is correctly positioned. Torque the mounting nuts to 18 ft. lbs.

12. The piston pushrod should have 0.04 in. (1 mm) clearance between it and the

Master cylinder removal

Correct piston pushrod clearance

piston. Loosen the piston rod nut and turn the rod to adjust the clearance.

13. Refill the system with new brake fluid. Bleed the brakes as outlined below.

14. Tighten the splash shield bolts to 34 ft. lbs. (larger bolt) and 18 ft. lbs. (smaller bolt).

15. Test the brake failure warning light.

a. Switch on the ignition. The handbrake warning light will go on. If it doesn't, replace the bulb.

b. Start the engine. While you depress the brake pedal, have an assistant open a bleeder valve on one of the wheels to simulate a brake failure. The light should go on.

c. When your assistant closes the valve, the light should go out.

d. Repeat the test on the other brake circuit.

If the light fails to light during one of the tests, check the circuit failure sender which screws into the master cylinder.

Pressure Regulator Valve

REMOVAL AND INSTALLATION

914

1. Have an assistant slightly depress the brake pedal to prevent the fluid in the reservoir from running out.

2. Disconnect the brake lines at the brake pressure regulator.

3. Remove the retaining bolts and remove the valve.

4. Install the regulator valve.

5. Bleed the brakes.

914 brake pressure regulator

CHECKING AND ADJUSTMENT

914

The brake pressure regulator is not repairable and must be replaced if defective. To check if the valve is operating, have an assistant depress the brake pedal while you hold your hand on the valve. When your assistant releases the brake pedal, you should feel a slight knock in the regulator. High pressure gauges are required to thoroughly check and adjust the valve. If you suspect the valve, replace it.

Wheel Bearings

REMOVAL AND INSTALLATION

911 and 912E

NOTE: The inner bearing, seal, and outer bearing may be removed and lubricated once the hub/disc assembly is off the car. If after cleaning, the bearings are noticeably worn or damaged they should be replaced along with their races. If the bearings are satisfactory, skip the race removal steps.

1. Remove the brake disc/hub assembly.

2. Match mark the hub and disc for correct reassembly, remove the five assembly bolts, and separate the hub and disc.

3. Pry the inner seal out of the hub. Remove the inner bearing and outer bearing.

4. Wash the bearings in solvent and blow them dry. Examine the bearings for pitting, scoring, or other damage. Replace the bearing and race as a unit if there is any question as to their condition.

5. Heat the wheel hub to 250°–300°F.

6. Press the inner bearing race out of the hub on a press table, using suitable spacers to prevent damaging the hub.

7. Press out the outer bearing race, using suitable spacers and a support fabricated from the accompanying drawing.

8. Press a new inner bearing race into the hub and then press in a new outer bearing race.

9. Pack the bearings with a lithium multipurpose grease.

10. Align the match marks and install the hub on the disc. Insert the assembly bolts from the inside out and tighten them to 17 ft. lbs.

11. Lightly coat the spindle with grease. Fill the hub with about 2 oz of grease. Lubricate and install the bearings.

12. Grease the sealing edges of a new inner oil seal and carefully tap it into place. The oil seal must be flush with the hub.

13. Install the hub/disc assembly on the car.

14. Adjust the wheel bearings.

914

Wheel bearing procedures are similar to those for the above models, except that the hub and disc are one piece and the bearing races can be driven out with a brass or copper drift.

ADJUSTMENT

Check and adjust the front wheel bearings after the car has not been run for a few hours. The bearings will be cold then.

1. The front wheel bearings are correctly adjusted when the thrust washer can be moved slightly sideways under light pressure from a screwdriver, but no bearing play is evident when the wheel hub is shaken axially.

2. Jack up the front of the car, support it on stands, and remove the wheels. Turn the hub several times to seat the bearings.

3. Pry the hub cap off with a screwdriver and perform the check described in Step 1.

NOTE: Don't press the screwdriver against the hub. Hold it lightly in your hand so you get a better feel.

4. If the bearings require an adjust-

Checking wheel bearing play

Final tightening of the wheel clamp nut—check play again before installing hub cap

ment, loosen the Allen screw and turn the clamp nut in or out as necessary.

5. Tighten the clamp nut Allen screw to 11 ft. lbs. without altering the adjusted position of the clamp nut.

6. Double check the adjustment and readjust, if necessary.

7. Give the clamp nut and thrust washer a light coating of lithium grease. Tap the hub cap into place with a plastic or rubber mallet.

8. Install the wheels and lower the car.

Handbrake

The 911 and 912E models are equipped with a separate handbrake system. The center, pull-up lever mechanically operates a pair of brake shoes inside each rear disc, which act as drums through a pot-shaped center section.

The 914 handbrake mechanically applies the rear service brakes. The rear calipers are equipped with automatic adjusting mechanisms.

CABLE

Adjustment

911 AND 912E

1. Jack up the rear of the car and support it on stands. Remove the wheels.

2. Release the handbrake lever.

3. Push the brake pads away from the disc so that it can be turned by hand.

4. Loosen the cable adjusting nuts to release tension.

5. Insert a screwdriver into the disc access hole and rotate the handbrake star wheel until the disc can no longer be turned by hand.

6. Repeat this operation on the other side.

7. Readjust the cable nuts to take up the slack.

8. Pull up the center tunnel cover and

Adjusting the handbrake

handbrake lever boot at the rear. By looking through the two inspection holes, see if the cable equalizer is exactly perpendicular to the car's centerline.

9. If the equalizer positioning is off, correct it by loosening or tightening the cable adjusting nuts. Tighten the locknuts after the adjustment is correct.

10. Back off each brake star wheel by four or five teeth until the disc can be turned by hand.

11. Check the handbrake lever clearance. There should be a slight clearance at the lever. The handbrake should be set when the lever is pulled up.

12. After completing the handbrake adjustment, depress the brake pedal several times to reposition the rear caliper pistons. Check the fluid level in the reservoir and top it up, if necessary.

Removal and Installation

1. Jack up the rear of the car and support it on stands. Remove the wheels.

2. Remove the center tunnel cover and handbrake lever boot.

3. Remove the heater control knob.

4. Undo the handbrake support housing bolts.

5. Unscrew the heater control lever nut. Remove the cup spring, discs, and the lever.

6. Slightly raise the handbrake support housing. Snap off the retaining clip and pull out the cable equalizing stud.

7. Disconnect the handbrake light switch wire.

Hand brake star wheel adjustment

8. Remove the handbrake support housing.

9. Detach the cables from the cable equalizer.

10. Remove the rear brake calipers.

11. Remove the rear brake discs and spacer rings.

12. Remove the cotter pin, castellated nut, and disc from each cable. Pull the cable toward the center of the car.

13. Pull the cables out from the center tunnel in the passenger compartment.

14. Lubricate the replacement cables with multipurpose grease and then feed them into the tube.

15. Place a washer between the spacer sleeve and the brake expander. Place another washer under the castellated nut.

16. Tighten the nut until a new cotter pin can be inserted. Make sure that the brake expander is correctly seated.

17. Install the brake disc and calipers.

18. Connect the handbrake light wire to the switch.

19. Insert the heater control lever into the handbrake support housing.

20. Install and clip the equalizer stud. Ensure that the handbrake cables are correctly seated.

21. Torque the handbrake support housing bolts to 18 ft. lbs.

22. Install a friction disc, the heater control lever, another friction disc, pressure disc, cup spring, and the nut.

23. Tighten the nut so that the lever doesn't slip back when the heater is on full, and yet isn't too tight to operate.

24. Bleed the brakes.

25. Check the handbrake adjustment.

26. Install the wheels and lower the car.

PARKING BRAKE SHOES

Removal and Installation
911 AND 912E

1. Jack up the rear of the car and support it on stands. Remove the wheels.

2. Remove the brake calipers.

3. Detach the brake discs.

4. Remove the cotter pin, castellated nut, and washer from the brake cable.

Star wheel assembly removal

Correct handbrake lining and spring installation

5. Pull the cable out toward the center of the car.

6. Remove the expander and spring.

7. Depress the upper spring and twist the holddown cup to remove it and the spring.

8. Pull the brake shoe outward and remove the pin through the rear.

9. Using a screwdriver, raise the upper brake shoe and remove the star wheel assembly. Unhook the spring.

10. Repeat Steps 7 and 8 for the bottom shoe.

11. Unhook the front return spring and remove both shoes.

NOTE: Complete the brake shoe removal and installation one side at a time, so the opposite side can be used as a reference.

12. Clean all metal parts in alcohol. Contaminated or worn brake shoes should be replaced.

13. Insert the brake cable from the back and slide the inner part of the expander onto the cable. Don't forget to install a washer between the spacer tube and the expander.

14. Install the front return spring (two coils) so that the coils point towards the center of the axle.

15. Install the upper and lower brake shoes.

16. Install the pins, springs, and holddown cups.

17. Insert the inner expander into the seats in the brake shoes.

18. Raise the upper brake shoe with a screwdriver and install the star wheel assembly so that the adjusting sprocket is on both brake shoes.

19. Install the outer brake return spring.

20. Turn the cable adjusting nut in the tube all the way back.

21. Install the spring, second expander half, washer, and castellated nut. Tighten the nut until a new cotter pin can be installed.

22. Install the brake discs and calipers.

23. Bleed the hydraulic system.

24. Adjust the handbrake.
25. Install the wheels and lower the car.

CHASSIS ELECTRICAL

Heater

The primary heating system in all models uses fresh air drawn in by the engine cooling fan, directs it to heat exchangers around the exhaust pipes, through a muffler, and distributes warm air into the passenger compartment via a system of ducts. A variable speed blower, located in the front luggage compartment on all models, speeds the circulation of heated and/or fresh air. 914 models are equipped with a blower motor in the engine compartment. An auxiliary, gasfired heater is an option on 911 models.

Blower

REMOVAL AND INSTALLATION

911 and 912E

1. Disconnect the battery cables.
2. Remove the front luggage compartment carpeting.
3. Open the blower compartment lid. Remove the steering shaft cover.
4. Disconnect the electrical wiring.
5. Loosen the hose clamps and disconnect the hoses from the blower.
6. Pull the blower off the air intake stack and remove it from the car.
7. Install the blower on the intake stack. Make sure that the sealing ring is correctly seated.
8. Fasten the hoses on the blower and tighten the hose clamps.
9. Connect the electrical wiring.
10. Install the steering shaft cover and close the blower compartment lid.

Correct blower cable installation

11. Cement the carpeting to the right front side panel.
12. Connect the battery cables.

914

1. Remove the front luggage compartment lid.
2. Remove the fuel tank.
3. Unscrew the mounting bolt on each end of the fresh air intake box.
4. Loosen the hose clamps on the two air hoses and pull them from the blower.
5. Squeeze the corbin clamps on the two water drain hoses and pull them from the fresh air box.
6. Loosen the cable clamp nut and detach the cable from the blower by pushing the retaining clip off. Be careful not to bend the cable.
7. Disconnect the electrical wiring.
8. Remove the fresh air box and blower as an assembly.
9. Unscrew the attaching bolts and separate the fresh air box and blower.
10. Install the blower in the fresh air box.
11. Install the cable on the blower. The cable casing should protrude from the retaining clip by about ¼ in.
12. Install the fresh air box/blower assembly in a reverse manner of removal. Adjust the cable, if necessary.

Auxiliary Heater

The 911 auxiliary heater assembly is mounted in the front luggage compartment in the place of the standard blower.

REMOVAL AND INSTALLATION

1. Jack up the front of the car and support it on stands.
2. Disconnect the battery cables.
3. Remove the luggage compartment lid.
4. Open the heater compartment lid.
5. Loosen the clamp on the hot air hose and pull the hose off the heater unit.
6. Remove the three mixture pump retaining bolts and remove them from the bracket.
7. Disconnect the fuel lines and wiring from the pump.
8. Working under the car, loosen the front muffler clamp. Disconnect the exhaust pipe and bend it down and out of the way.
9. Remove the muffler clamp and slide the white collar onto the heater unit.
10. Disconnect all wiring to the heater and carefully lift it out of the car.
11. Installation is the reverse of the removal procedure. Ensure that the wiring is correctly reinstalled.

Windshield Wiper Motor and Linkage

REMOVAL AND INSTALLATION

911 and 912E

The windshield wiper motor and linkage are located in front of the instrument panel.

1. Pull back the front luggage compartment carpeting. Disconnect the battery cables.
2. Remove the retaining clip and air duct. Remove the fresh air box.
3. Disconnect the blower motor wires.
4. Remove the wiper arms. Remove the rubber bushings under the arms and unscrew the shaft retaining nuts.
5. Pull the motor and linkage down as a unit. Separate the motor and linkage.
6. Installation is the reverse of the removal procedure.

914

The windshield wiper motor and linkage are mounted on a common frame.

1. Disconnect the battery.
2. Unscrew the retaining nut on each wiper arm.
3. Remove the rubber bearing cap.
4. Unscrew the retaining nut and remove the washers and seals.
5. Remove the fuel tank.
6. Remove the evaporative emission charcoal canister.
7. Remove the fresh air box and blower as previously described.
8. Remove the anti-vibration bearing retaining nut from under the instrument panel. Make sure that the bearing isn't twisted.
9. Pull the windshield wiper assembly down and out.
10. Disconnect the electrical wires.
11. To separate the motor and linkage:
    a. Remove the wiper motor shaft nut and washer.
    b. Using a puller, remove the linkage drive crank from the motor shaft.
    c. Remove the three retaining bolts and remove the motor.
12. To install the motor onto the linkage:
    a. The motor must be in the park position. Ground the motor and connect terminals 53 and 53a to a positive battery wire.
    b. Run the motor for a few seconds and then disconnect terminal 53. The motor will be parked.
    c. Position the drive crank parallel to the drive rod.
    d. Attach the motor with a washer and nut. Install the three retaining bolts.
13. Connect the electrical wiring.
14. Install the wiper arms in a reverse order of removal. Ensure that they are in the parked positon.
15. Install the fresh air box/blower assembly.

1 2 1 1 3 4 3 1 5 6 7 8 1 9

(31) (31) (15) (1) (31) (9) (+)

1. Instrument lights
2. Side marker indicating light (green)
3. Turn signal indicating light (green)
4. High beam indicating light (blue)
5. Charging control light (red)
6. Warning light, fuel reserve (red)
7. Oil temperature warning light (red); 914/6 only
8. Hand brake warning light (red)
9. Oil pressure indicating light (green)
The numbers in parenthesis are terminal designations.

914 instrument panel connections

16. Connect the battery.

911 Rear Window Wiper

1. Pull the wiper arm from the rear window.
2. Open the engine compartment lid.
3. Disconnect the wiper motor electrical wiring.
4. Disconnect the wiper arm linkage at the bellcrank.
5. Remove the three wiper motor bracket bolts and remove the motor/linkage assembly.
6. Install the wiper motor/linkage assembly in a reverse order of removal.
7. Adjust the linkage at the bellcrank for correct wiper operation.

Instrument Panel

REMOVAL AND INSTALLATION

911 and 912E

The gauges are mounted in individual rubber rings.
1. Pry the gauge out until you can grip

911 and 912 instrument removal

it firmly, and then pull it out of the instrument panel.
2. Disconnect the wiring and/or cable and remove the gauge.
3. Connect the wiring or cable and position the gauge in its opening.

4. Align the gauge and then push it into place.

914

1. Disconnect the battery.
2. Remove the steering wheel as outlined in the "Steering" section.
3. Remove the four Phillips retaining screws.
4. Disconnect the speedometer cable and the trip odometer cable.
5. Pull the instrument panel out.
6. Individual gauges are retained by rubber rings. Push the gauge out towards the front to remove it.
7. Be sure that the wires are correctly reinstalled on the gauge.
8. Install the instrument panel in a reverse order of removal.

Fuse Box Location

The 911 and 912E fuse box is located in the left front of the luggage compartment. The 914 fuse box is located under the instrument panel to the left of the steering column.

Porsche
924, 928, 944

SERIAL NUMBER IDENTIFICATION

Vehicle

The chassis serial number is located on the left windshield post and can be viewed from the outside. The vehicle identification plate is in the engine compartment near the battery.

Engine

The engine serial number is stamped on the left of the crankcase near the clutch housing.

924 Serial number

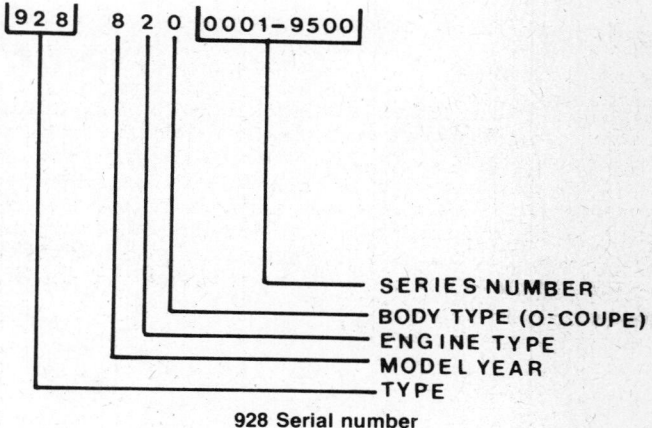

928 Serial number

GENERAL ENGINE SPECIFICATIONS

Year	Model	Engine Displacement cc	(cu. in.)	Fuel System	Horsepower @ rpm (SAE)	Torque @ rpm (SAE)	Bore × Stroke (in.)	Compression Ratio	Oil Pressure @ rpm (psi)
'76–'77	924	1984	(121)	Fuel inj.	95.4 @ 5500	109.2 @ 3000	3.41 × 3.32	8.0:1	71–100 @ 5000
'78–'82	924	1984	(121)	Fuel inj.	110 @ 5750	111.3 @ 3500	3.41 × 3.32	8.5:1	71–100 @ 5000
'79–'80	924 Turbo	1984	(121)	Fuel inj.	143 @ 5500	147 @ 3000	3.41 × 3.32	7.5:1	70 @ 5500
'81–'82	924 Turbo	1984	(121)	Fuel inj.	154 @ 5750	154.8 @ 3500	3.41 × 3.32	8.0:1	70 @ 5500
'78–'79	928	4474	(273)	Fuel inj.	219 @ 5250	245 @ 3600	3.74 × 3.11	8.5:1	70 @ 5500
'80–'83	928	4474	(273)	Fuel inj.	220 @ 5500	265 @ 4000	3.74 × 3.11	9.0:1	70 @ 5500
'83	944	2479	(151)	Fuel inj.	143 @ 5500	137 @ 3000	3.94 × 3.11	9.5:1	50–70 @ 5500

TUNE-UP SPECIFICATIONS

Year	Model	Engine Displacement cc	(cu. in.)	Spark Plugs Type	Gap (in.)	Ignition Timing① (rpm)	Intake Valve Opens (deg)	Idle Speed (rpm)	Valve Clearance (cold) (in.) Intake	Exhaust
'76–'81	924	1984	(121)	W200-T30	.028–.032	10°ATDC @ 925	5°BTDC	850–1000	0.004	0.016
'79–'81	924 Turbo.	1984	(121)	WR7DS	.024	20°BTDC @ 2000	—	900–1000	0.004	0.016
'82	924	1984	(121(	WR6DS	.028	0° ± 1° @ 750–800③	—	850–1000	0.006	0.016
'82	924 Turbo	1984	(121)	WR6DS	.028④	6°–10°BTDC @ 900⑤	—	900–1000	0.006	0.016
'78–'79	928	4474	(273)	W145-T30	.028–.032	31°BTDC @ 3000	8°ATDC②	800	Hyd.	Hyd.
'80–'81	928	4474	(273)	WR8DS	.028	23°BTDC @ 3000	12°ATDC	700–800	Hyd.	Hyd.
'82–'83	928	4474	(273)	WR8DS	.028–.032	23°BTDC @ 3000	—	700–800	Hyd.	Hyd.
'83	944	2479	(151)	WR8DS	.028	3°–7°BTDC @ 900⑤	1°ATDC	850–950	Hyd.	Hyd.

NA—Not Available
① With vacuum hose disconnected, if so equipped.
② .0393 in., zero valve clearance
③ With connector above idle stabilizer in front of the left wheel arch disconnected.
④ If Champion N7GY is used, gap should be .024 in.
⑤ Checking specification only.

FIRING ORDERS

Firing order—924 and 944 engines

Firing order—928 engine

CRANKSHAFT AND CONNECTING ROD SPECIFICATIONS

(All measurements given in inches)

Year	Model	Engine Displacement (cu. in.)	Crankshaft				Connecting Rod		
			Main Brg. Journal Diameter	Main Brg. Oil Clearance	Shaft End-Play	Thrust on No.	Journal Diameter	Oil Clearance	Side Clearance
'76–'82	924	(121)	2.40	0.0020–0.0040	0.0040	3	1.90	0.0008–0.0032	0.0040–0.0092
'79–'82	924 Turbo.	(121)	2.50	0.0008–0.0030	0.0040	3	1.89–1.97	0.0008–0.0030	0.0020–0.0120
'78–'83	928	(273)	2.80	0.0008–0.0039	0.0044–0.0124	3	2.08	0.0008–0.0028	—
'83	944	(151)	2.80	0.0008–0.0039	0.0044–0.0124	3	2.08	0.0008–0.0028	—

CAPACITIES

Year	Model	Engine Displacement		Engine Crankcase (qts.)		Transaxle (qts.)		Gasoline Tank (gal.)	Cooling System (qts.)
		cc	(cu. in.)	With Filter	Without Filter	Manual	Auto.		
'76–'82	924	1984	(121)	5.30	4.75	2.75①	3.17②	16.4④	8.5
'79–'82	924 Turbo.	1984	(121)	5.30	4.75	2.6	5.5	18.6④	8.5
'78–'79	928	4474	(273)	7.90	6.40	4.0③	5.8	22.7	16.2
'80–'83	928	4474	(273)	8.50	8.00	4.0⑤	5.8	23	16.8
'83	944	2479	(151)	5.80	—	2.75④	3.0⑦	17.4	8.2

NA—Not available.
① SAE 80 or 80W gear oil
② At oil change ATF Dexron®, differential
   1.06 qt. SAE 90 gear oil
③ Mid-1978 model year—change manual
   gear oil usage to Dexron® ATF
④ 1982 and later—17.4
⑤ Use SAE 75w-90 oil, meeting API/GL5
   specifications.
⑥ Use SAE 80 oil, meeting API/GL4
   specifications.
⑦ Dry refill capacity—6.9 qts. Use Dexron®
   transmission fluid.

VALVE SPECIFICATIONS

Year	Model	Engine Displacement		Seat Angle (deg)	Face Angle (deg)	Stem-to-Guide Clearance (Maximum)		Stem Diameter (Minimum)	
		cc	(cu. in.)			Intake (in.)	Exhaust (in.)	Intake (in.)	Exhaust (in.)
'76–'82	924, 924 Turbo.	1984	(121)	45	45¼	0.0196	0.0196	0.352	0.352
'78–'83	928	4474	(273)	45	45	0.0196	0.0196	0.352	0.352
'83	944	2479	(151)	45	45	0.0196	0.0196	0.352	0.352

PISTON AND RING SPECIFICATIONS
(All measurements given in inches)

Year	Model	Engine Displacement		Piston Clearance	Ring Gap (Limit)			Ring Side Clearance (Limit)		
		cc	(cu. in.)		Top Compression	Bottom Compression	Oil Control	Top Compression	Bottom Compression	Oil Control
'76–'82	924, 924 Turbo.	1984	(121)	0.0011–0.0031	0.0120–0.0200	0.0120–0.0200	0.0120–0.0200	0.0016–0.0028	0.0016–0.0028	0.0016–0.0028
'78–'83	928	4474	(273)	0.0031①	0.0078–0.0157	0.0078–0.0157	0.0157–0.5510	0.0019–0.0032	0.0019–0.0032	0.0009–0.0053
'83	944	2479	(151)	0.0031①	0.0078–0.0157	0.0078–0.0157	0.0157–0.5510	0.0019–0.0032	0.0019–0.0032	0.0009–0.0053

①Maximum clearance

TORQUE SPECIFICATIONS
(All readings in ft. lbs.)

Year	Model	Engine Displacement		Cylinder Head Bolts	Rod Bearing Bolts	Main Bearing Bolts	Crankshaft Pulley Bolt	Flywheel to Crankshaft Bolts	Manifold	
		cc	(cu. in.)						Intake	Exhaust
'76–'81	924	1984	(121)	56①	34–42	58②	181	65	15	15
	924 Turbo.	1984	(121)	72	47	58②	181	65	15	15
	928	4474	(273)	58③	42	29④	181	69	N.A.	N.A.
'82–'83	924	1984	(121)	47⑤	34–42	58②	181	65	15	15
	924 Turbo.	1984	(121)	⑥	47	58②	181	72	15	15
	928	4474	(273)	⑦	44.5	⑧	181	69	N.A.	15
	944	2479	(151)	⑦	44.5	⑧	181	65	N.A.	15

① 63 ft. lbs. warm

② Allen head bolts on cap #5 are torqued to 47 ft. lbs.

③ Tighten in three steps: 1st—14 ft. lbs.; 2nd—36 ft. lbs.; 3rd—61 ft. lbs. Thirty minutes later, loosen each bolt ¼ turn, then retorque each bolt (in order) to 58 ft. lbs.

④ Tighten in two steps: 1st—14 ft. lbs.; 2nd—29 ft. lbs.

⑤ Tighten all head bolts in order to 47 ft. lbs., then (in order) tighten each bolt ½ turn further.

⑥ Tighten in three steps (in order each time): 1st—29 ft. lbs.; 2nd—58 ft. lbs; 3rd—80 ft. lbs. (engine warm). One hour later, loosen each bolt 30° then repeat tightening sequence. Run the engine to 176°F. (coolant temp.), loosen each bolt 30°, then repeat the tightening sequence again.

⑦ Tighten in three steps (in order each time): 1st—14 ft. lbs.; 2nd—36 ft. lbs.; 3rd—61 ft. lbs. Thirty minutes later, loosen each bolt ¼ turn then repeat the tightening sequence.

⑧ M10 bolts: 1st step—14.5 ft. lbs.; 2nd step—33.5 ft. lbs.
M12 bolts: 1st step—14.5 ft. lbs.; 2nd step—30.0 ft. lbs.; 3rd step—48 ft. lbs.

N.A.—Not available

TORQUE SEQUENCES

Cylinder head bolt torque sequence—924 engine

Cylinder head bolt torque sequence—944 engine

TORQUE SEQUENCES

Cylinder head bolt torque sequence—928 engine

ALTERNATOR AND REGULATOR SPECIFICATIONS

Year	Model	Alternator Manufacturer	Alternator Output (amps)	Regulator Manufacturer	Field Relay Air Gap (in.)	Field Relay Point Gap (in.)	Field Relay Volts to Close	Regulator Air Gap (in.)	Regulator Point Gap (in.)	Volts @ 75 degrees
'76–'82	924	Bosch	75	Bosch	—Sealed unit not adjustable—					13.5–14.5
'79–'82	924 Turbo.	Bosch	68	Bosch	—Sealed unit not adjustable—					13.5–14.5
'78–'83	928, 944	Bosch	90	Bosch	—Sealed unit not adjustable—					13.5–14.8

BATTERY AND STARTER SPECIFICATIONS

(All cars use 12 volt, negative ground electrical systems)

Year	Model	Battery Amp Hour Capacity	Lock Test Amps	Lock Test Volts	Lock Test Torque (ft. lbs.)	No Load Test Amps	No Load Test Volts	No Load Test RPM	Brush Spring Tension (oz)	Min. Brush Length (in.)
76–83	924,944	63	250–300	7	N.A.	N.A.	N.A.	N.A.	N.A.	0.47
	928	88	N.A.	N.A.	N.A.	N.A.	N.A.	N.A.	N.A.	N.A.

BRAKE SPECIFICATIONS

(All specifications given in inches, unless noted)

Year	Model	Lug Nut Torque (ft. lbs.)	Master Cylinder Bore	Brake Disc Minimum Thickness	Brake Disc Maximum Run-Out	Brake Drum Diameter	Brake Drum Maximum Machine (O/S)	Brake Drum Maximum Wear Limit	Minimum Lining Thickness Front	Minimum Lining Thickness Rear
'76–'81	924	80①	0.81	0.410	N.A.	9.06	0.30	N.A.	0.07	0.09
	924 Turbo.	80①	0.83	0.480	N.A.	9.20	0.30	N.A.	0.07	0.09
	928	80①	0.95	0.720	N.A.	N.A.	N.A.	N.A.	0.08	0.08
'82–'83	924	80①	0.81	0.472	N.A.	N.A.	N.A.	9.094	0.08	0.09
	924 Turbo. 944	94	0.83	0.752②	N.A.	—			0.08	0.08
	928	94	0.95	1.228②	N.A.	—	—	7.125	0.08	0.08

① Alloy wheel 94 ft. lbs. torque
② 0.756 for rear discs.
N.A.—Not available

WHEEL ALIGNMENT SPECIFICATIONS

Year	Model	Caster Range	Caster Preferred Setting	Camber Front Range	Camber Front Preferred Setting	Camber Rear Range	Camber Rear Preferred Setting	Toe Front①	Toe Rear②
'76–'83	924	2°15′P–3°P	2°30′P	20′N ± 15′	20′N	1°N ± 20′	1°N	15′A–5′B	0° ± 5′
	928	3°P–3°30′P	3°P	30′N ± 10′	30′N	40′N ± 10′	40′N	0° ± 5′	10′B ± 5′
	944	2°15′P–3°P	2°30′P	20′N ± 15′	20′N	1°N ± 20′	1°N	15′A–5′B	0° ± 5′

N—Negative
P—Positive
A—In
B—Out
① Wheels pressed
② Per wheel

TUNE-UP PROCEDURES

Spark Plugs

Because Porsche engines use aluminum cylinder heads, always apply a small amount of graphite or anti-seize compound to the threads of the plug prior to installation. Be very careful when threading the plug into the head. NEVER use a wrench to ''start'' the plug, finally tighten the plugs to 18–22 ft. lbs.

Electronic Ignition

—CAUTION—

The engine should be turned off or the battery cable disconnected when ignition system parts are replaced or engine test equipment is connected to the ignition system, because of the dangerous current that can be present in the primary and secondary circuits. Personal injury could occur.

Distributor cap and distributor cap mount of the 944. Note how the distributor cap screw clips are to engage (arrows)

Three fully electronic ignition systems have been used since 1976. All 928 models and 1976–80 924 have used a Bosch transistorized ignition coil system. 1981 and later non-turbocharged 924 models use a Hall effect electronic system, while the 1981 and later 924 Turbo and the 944 use a Digital Ignition Timing Control (DITC) ignition system.

Tune-up maintenance is limited to checking the ignition wires, distributor cap and rotor condition. Except for ignition timing (where applicable), adjustments to any of the electronic ignition systems is not necessary.

Timing mark—1976–77½ 924 models

Ignition Timing

924, 924 Turbo Through 1980

—CAUTION—

The engine should be turned off or the battery cable disconnected when ignition system parts are replaced or engine test equipment is connected to the ignition system, because of the dangerous current that can be present in the primary and secondary circuits.

1. Run the engine to normal operating temperature.
2. Leave the vacuum hoses on the distributor and connect a timing light according to the light manufacturer's instructions.

Timing mark—1977½–80 924 and 924 Turbo models

3. The timing marks are not on the crankshaft pulley, but are on the flywheel, visible through a small access hole in the clutch housing.
4. With the engine at the correct idle speed, focus the timing light on the timing slot.
5. If the timing is not correct, loosen the distributor holddown bolt and turn the distributor as necessary. Retighten the bolt when the timing is correct.

924—1981 and Later

1. Run the engine to normal operating temperature.
2. By-pass the idle stabilizer by disconnecting the connector plugs from each other. The plugs are located on the wiring harness on the driver's front wheel well inside the engine compartment.

Timing mark—1981 and later 924 models

3. Set the engine idle speed to 800 rpm.

4. Connect a timing light to number one cylinder spark plug lead according to the timing light manufacturer's instructions.

5. With the engine idling, focus the timing light on the timing port. The timing marks are located on the flywheel.

6. If timing is off, loosen the distributor holddown clamp and turn the distributor until the timing is correct. Retighten the holddown bolt.

7. After adjusting, reconnect the idle stabilizer leads and rev the engine a few times.

8. Check the idle speed.

924 Turbo and 944—1981 and Later

Due to the DITC fully electronic transistor ignition system, ignition timing adjustments are not necessary.

928

——————— CAUTION ———————
See "CAUTION" under "924 through 1980", above.

1. Run the engine to normal operating temperature.

2. Connect a timing light to the engine. A positive terminal for connecting the timing light is located in the engine compartment. Connect a tachometer or use the one in the dashboard.

3. With the timing light connected to the ignition cable for cylinder number 1, detach both vacuum hoses at the distributor.

——————— CAUTION ———————
When connecting test equipment to the ignition system, the ignition key must be off or the battery disconnected.

4. The timing marks are located on the crankshaft pulley and are colored for identification (TDC and 31° or 23° BTDC). With the engine at 3000 rpm, focus the timing light on the timing marks. Timing should be 31° BTDC through 1979, 23° BTDC for later models.

The timing marks of the 928 are on the vibration damper at the front of the engine

5. If the timing is incorrect, loosen the distributor holddown bolt and turn the distributor as necessary. Tighten the holddown bolt when the timing is correct.

Valve Lash

924 (Including Turbo)
——————— CAUTION ———————
When turning the engine for valve adjustment, do not turn it with the camshaft pulley. Use the crankshaft pulley or bump the starter. The timing belt can be damaged by turning the camshaft pulley.

924 and 924 Turbo valve lash adjustment. One full turn of the wedge screw changes the valve clearance 0.002 in.

Adjustment is made by means of a wedge type adjustment screw which is flat on one side. The flat side rides directly on the valve stem. Five different diameter adjustment screws are available to compensate for wear. Adjustment is made by inserting an Allen wrench through the hole in the cam follower. Adjustment is made in full turns. If more than several turns are necessary to correct the clearance, the adjustment screw will probably have to be replaced with the next larger size. Always start with the smallest adjustment screws (white) after a valve job.

NOTE: One turn of the screw changes the valve clearance 0.002 in.

1. Remove the camshaft cover.

2. Turn the crankshaft pulley until No. 1 cylinder is at TDC of the compression stroke (both cam lobes pointing up).

3. Insert the correct feeler gauge be-

Intake (I) and exhaust (E) valve arrangement of the 924 and 924 Turbo

tween the cam follower and the camshaft heel.

4. If adjustment is necessary, insert an Allen wrench and turn the adjustment screw until clearance is correct.

5. Proceed to adjust the valve clearance for each cylinder in the same way.

NOTE: Early engine models had paint colors as identifying marks on the adjusting screws. Later engine models use notches, ground on the screw end, opposite the adjusting tool hole, as the identity marks. The higher number of notches indicates the increased thickness of the adjusting screw.

Valve adjusting screw identification # 2
White—6.6 mm—Replaced by "no notch" screw
Blue—6.9 mm—Replaced by "one notch" screw
Red—7.2 mm—Replaced by "two notch" screw
No color—new—"three notch" screw
Yellow—7.5 mm—Replaced by "four notch" screw

928, 944

The overhead cams operate bucket-type hydraulic valve lifters, located directly over the valve stems and therefore, no valve adjustment is necessary.

Idle Speed and Mixture Adjustments

The idle speed may be adjusted on 1976–81 models without the use of emissions testing equipment. Idle mixture on all models, and idle speed on 1982 and later models cannot be properly adjusted without the use of a CO meter. If necessary, refer these adjustments to a professional shop.

IDLE SPEED

924 and 924 Turbo Through 1980

The engine must be in perfect running condition and the ignition timing must be set correctly before adjusting the idle speed.

1. Run the engine to normal operating temperature.

2. Idle speed is adjusted at the bypass screw located on the throttle housing. Turn the screw in or out as necessary to obtain the proper idle speed.

NOTE: Any special instructions for idle speed adjustments concerning individual engines may be found on the underhood specifications sticker.

1981 924

Idle speed adjustments are performed in the same manner as on the 924 through 1980, except for one procedure. The idle stabilizer must be disconnected and bridged before the idle can be adjusted or the stabilizer will attempt to offset any adjustment by

Idle adjustment screw location on the 924 (arrow)

Idle adjustment screw location on the 924 Turbo (arrow)

advancing or retarding the ignition timing. To by-pass the idle stabilizer, disconnect its connector, located on the wiring harness on the driver's side front fender well inside the engine compartment. Disconnect the two plugs from each other.

1981 924 Turbo

The timing control unit stabilizes the idle speed by varying the ignition timing at idle. As a result, basic idle speed adjustment must be made using an ignition timing light.

To eliminate the influence of the intake air temperature sensor, it must be removed during the idle adjustment procedure.

1. Unscrew the temperature air sensor from the intake manifold and place it in the fresh air tray behind the engine fire wall, leaving the wire connected (sensor temperature must be below 120°F). A suitable

Before adjusting the idle speed on the 1981 924 Turbo, the fresh air sensor (arrow) must be removed and its hole plugged

plug (M 14 × 1.5) must be screwed in the opening in the intake manifold during adjustment procedures.

2. Run the engine to normal operating temperature.

3. Connect a timing light according to the light manufacturer's instructions to the ignition wire for number 1 cylinder.

4. While pointing the timing light at the timing marks, turn the idle control screw (by-pass air screw) until the ignition timing mark (dot) is fully visible at the reference edge and jumps partially below the mark.

5. The idle speed should not be below 900 rpm (timing will vary slightly because the ignition timing is being regulated).

928 Through 1981

Idle speed is adjusted at the idle speed screw on the throttle housing. The engine must be at normal operating temperature and in perfect running order. In addition, a separate tachometer must be used; do not ad-

Idle adjustment screw location on the 928 (arrow)

just the idle speed using the tachometer in the instrument panel. Consult the underhood specifications sticker for any special information concerning individual engines.

ENGINE ELECTRICAL

Distributor

REMOVAL AND INSTALLATION

All Models Except 1981 and Later 924 Turbo

1. Disconnect the negative battery cable.

2. Unsnap the two retaining clips and remove the distributor cap.

3. Set number 1 cylinder on top dead center (TDC). Number 1 cylinder is at top dead center when the TDC mark on the flywheel or crank pulley aligns with the timing pointer and the distributor rotor points toward the distributor cap tower for number one cylinder spark plug wire. Turn the engine over by hand until these signs are evident.

4. Disconnect the vacuum hose(s) from the distributor, then disconnect the electrical connections at the distributor.

5. Loosen and remove the distributor holddown bolt and clamp, then remove the distributor.

6. If the engine has not been turned over since the distributor was removed, align the rotor on the distributor with the number 1 cylinder distributor cap tower. There is a notch in the distributor body which the rotor

924 and 924 Turbo distributor holddown bolt location (arrow)

will point to when in this position. Install the distributor.

7. If the engine was turned while the distributor was removed, it will be necessary to relocate number 1 cylinder TDC. To do this, remove number 1 cylinder spark plug, then turn the engine over in the normal direction of rotation while holding your thumb over the number 1 cylinder spark plug hole. When the piston starts blowing air out of the hole, the number 1 cylinder is on its compression stroke. When this happens, continue turning the engine until the timing mark for TDC on the flywheel or crank pulley aligns with the timing pointer. Install the distributor as described in step 6.

8. Install the vacuum hoses, electrical connections and distributor cap. Adjust the ignition timing.

1981 and Later 924 Turbo

1. Disconnect the negative battery cable.

2. Remove the distributor cap and place it out of the way. Do not disconnect the spark plug leads from the cap.

3. Set number 1 cylinder on TDC. In this position, the Z1 mark on the flywheel will align with the timing pointer edge and the mark on the camshaft will be opposite the notch at the top rear of the timing belt cover.

4. Remove the primary wiring from the distributor.

5. Loosen and remove the holddown bolt and clamp, then remove the distributor.

6. If the engine was not turned while the distributor was removed, install the distributor so that the tab for the distributor cap faces the flywheel and the distributor cap mounting clips face in the direction of the car's longitudinal axis. In addition, the distributor rotor must be mounted so that it faces the notch on the distributor body for cylinder number 1 and aligns with the number 1 cylinder distributor cap tower.

7. If the engine was moved while the distributor was removed, find number 1 cylinder TDC as described in step 2 of this procedure, then install the distributor as described in step 5.

8. When the distributor is installed, reconnect the electrical connections and install the distributor cap.

Alternator

REMOVAL AND INSTALLATION

924, 924 Turbo

The alternator and voltage regulator are combined in one housing. No voltage adjustment can be made with this unit. The regulator can be replaced without removing and disassembling the alternator, just unbolt it from the rear.

1. Disconnect the battery cables.

2. Remove the cooling shroud and scoop from the alternator. The scoop is retained by a snap clip.

3. Remove the oil filter.

4. Disconnect the multi-connector from the rear of the alternator.

5. Loosen and remove the two Allen head retaining bolts.

6. Remove the fan belt. Remove the alternator.

7. Installation is the reverse of removal. Properly tension the fan belt. Deflection of the belt midway between the pulleys should be about ⅜ in.

928, 944

The voltage regulator is bolted to the rear of the alternator. Remove the alternator before attempting to remove the voltage regulator.

The alternator is removed from the bottom of the vehicle.

1. Remove the battery ground cable.

2. Raise the vehicle and support safely.

3. Remove the engine splash shield and the alternator cooling vent cover and tube.

4. Loosen the belt tension lock bolt, move the alternator inward and remove the belt from the pulley.

The alternator on the 924 and 924 Turbo (black arrow) is located on the passenger side of the engine. The air intake hose (white arrow) supplies fresh air to the alternator to keep it cool

1. Pulley
2. Fan
3. Drive end housing
4. Stator
5. Diode plate
6. Drive end bearing
7. Rotor
8. Commutator bearing

Exploded view of a typical alternator

To loosen the alternator and air conditioning compressor drive belt of the 944: Loosen the tensioner end bolts (outer arrow); loosen the locknuts; then turn the tensioner tube (circular arrow) as required. When tightening the belt, the end bolts are to be tightened last

1. Solenoid
2. Bushing
3. Starter drive housing
4. Field coil
5. Brush holder
6. Brush
7. Bushing
8. Lock ring
9. Alternate bushing
10. Starter drive
11. Armature

Exploded view of the starter

NOTE: On the 944, first loosen the end bolts of the tensioner, then loosen the locknuts of the tensioner and rotate the tensioner tube as necessary.

5. Remove the wire connections from the rear of the alternator.

6. Remove the alternator pivot bolt and remove the alternator from the engine.

7. Installation is the reverse of removal.

Starter

REMOVAL AND INSTALLATION

1. Disconnect the battery ground cable.

2. Jack up the right front of the car and support it with a stand.

3. Disconnect the two small wires from the starter solenoid. One wire connects to the ignition coil and the second to the ignition switch through the wiring harness.

4. Disconnect the large cable, which is the positive battery cable, from the solenoid.

5. Remove the two starter retaining bolts.

6. Pull the starter straight out and to the front, then lower it out of the car.

7. Installation is the reverse of removal.

OVERHAUL

Use the following procedure to replace brushes or starter drive.

1. Remove the solenoid.

2. Remove the end bearing cap.

3. Loosen both of the long housing screws.

4. Remove the lockwasher and spacer washers.

5. Remove the long housing screws and remove the end cover.

6. Pull the two field coil brushes out of the brush housing.

7. Remove the brush housing assembly.

8. Loosen the nut on the solenoid housing, remove the sealing disc, and remove the solenoid operating lever.

9. Loosen the large screws on the side of the starter body and remove the field coil along with the brushes.

NOTE: If the brushes require replacement, the field coil and brushes and/or the brush housing and its brushes must be replaced as a unit. Have the armature "turned" on a lathe if it is out-of-round, scored, or grooved.

10. If the starter drive is being replaced, push the stop-ring down and remove the circlip on the end of the shaft. Remove the stop-ring and remove the drive.

11. Assembly of the starter is the reverse of disassembly. Use a gear puller to install

the stop-ring in its groove. Use a new circlip on the shaft.

SOLENOID REPLACEMENT

1. Remove the starter.
2. Remove the nut which secures the connector strip on the end of the solenoid.
3. Take out the two retaining screws on the mounting bracket and withdraw the solenoid after it has been unhooked from the operating lever.
4. Installation is the reverse of removal. In order to facilitate engagement of the lever, the pinion should be pulled as far as possible when inserting the solenoid.

ENGINE MECHANICAL

The 924 engine is based on an Audi cylinder block. It is a watercooled, inline four with a belt driven overhead cam. The engine is inclined 40° to the right.

A V8 engine with an overhead cam mounted on each head and driven by a toothed belt from the crankshaft, is used in the 928 models. The two piece engine block and cylinder heads are of cast aluminum. The cylinder walls are impregnated with a silicone compound, making cylinder liners unnecessary.

The 944 inline four cylinder engine, derived from the 928 V-8, is an overhead camshaft (belt-driven) water cooled design. The engine employs twin, belt driven balance shafts which cancel the vibration inherent with most large-displacement four cylinder engines. Both the cylinder head and engine block are aluminum, with the block having linerless, silicone-impregnated cylinder walls.

Engine

REMOVAL AND INSTALLATION

924, 924 Turbo, 944

NOTE: On the 924 Turbo, some turbocharger components may have to be removed during engine removal. Wastegate and turbocharger services can be found following Exhaust Manifold Removal and Installation.

1. Disconnect the battery cables. Raise the car and support it on jack stands.
2. Support the engine. Use an overhead hoist. If using a jack under the engine be careful not to damage the aluminum oil pan. Use a wooden block between the jack and pan.
3. Remove the splash panel. Remove

the windshield washer tank and bracket and place it behind the right headlight.
4. On models so equipped, disconnect the clutch cable. Remove the bottom clutch adjustment locknut and detach the cable from the lever.
5. Remove the access plate from the bottom of the clutch housing.
6. Have an assistant turn the engine with the crankshaft pulley. Remove the pressure plate bolts gradually until all pressure is released.
7. Remove the exhaust pipe flange bolts.
8. Remove the bracket at the rear of the transaxle.
9. Remove the entire exhaust system.
10. Remove the back up light switch from the transaxle.
11. Disconnect the axle driveshafts at the transaxle and let them hang down out of the way.

NOTE: If the car is going to be moved around with the engine out of the car, wire the driveshafts up so that they don't become damaged.

12. Remove the clutch housing-to-engine bolts.
13. Place a wooden block under the front tunnel reinforcement to support the transaxle tube.
14. Remove the transaxle mounting bolts and slide the transaxle toward the rear.
15. Remove the air cleaner. Disconnect the brake booster vacuum line.
16. Disconnect the plug the fuel line.
17. Disconnect the accelerator cable.
18. Drain the cooling system.
19. Disconnect the radiator hoses. Remove the electric cooling fan.
20. Remove the hood. Detach the air conditioning compressor and place it out of the way. Do not disconnect the lines.
21. Remove the radiator and expansion tank. Disconnect the heater hoses from the engine.
22. Disconnect the starter wiring.
23. Attach the engine lift chains to the hoist points on the engine. Disconnect the steering at the rack universal joint.
24. Disconnect the two side mounts on the engine block. Remove the left side mount from the car.
25. Lift the engine from the car.
26. Installation is basically the reverse of removal. Tighten the pressure plate bolts to 24 ft. lbs., the clutch housing bolts to 60 ft. lbs. (12 mm bolt), 36 ft. lbs. (10 mm bolt) and 20 ft. lbs. (8 mm bolt).

928

1. Disconnect the battery ground cable.
2. Remove the engine compartment cross brace.

NOTE: The vehicle must be on its wheels when the cross brace is removed or replaced.

3. Disconnect wiring and hoses to the

under side of the hood, loosen hood bolts and supports, and remove the hood.
4. Remove the air intake hoses and the air cleaner assembly.
5. Raise the vehicle and support safely.
6. Remove the bottom splash pan and drain the coolant from the radiator.
7. Drain the engine block of coolant by removing the drain plugs on the right and left sides of the crankcase.
8. Drain the engine oil.
9. Remove the lower body brace.
10. Disconnect the exhaust pipes at the exhaust manifolds and the right and left side heat shields.
11. Disconnect the body ground cable from the engine.
12. Remove the clutch slave cylinder at the clutch housing. Do not disconnect the hydraulic line.
13. Disconnect the starter wires and remove the starter along with the clutch housing cover.
14. Disconnect the clutch release lever at the ball pin by depressing the release lever in the direction of the clutch.
15. Remove the starter wires from the clamps on the steering crossmember.
16. Remove the bolts from the clamping sleeve on the driveshaft and slide the sleeve rearward.
17. Unscrew the throwout bearing sleeve mounting bolts and push the sleeve towards the clutch.
18. Disconnect the left and right engine shock absorber at the control arms and remove with the right and left upper shock mounts.
19. On vehicles with air conditioning:
   a. Disconnect the temperature switch wires on the radiator.
   b. Disconnect the power lead to the compressor.
   c. Loosen the compressor, remove the belt and remove the compressor from the mounting brackets. Do not remove the hoses.
   d. Suspend the compressor from the frame with a wire.
20. Remove the air pump filter housing and disconnect the alternator cooling hose.
21. Remove the lower fan shroud from the radiator, remove the cooling hoses and the oil cooler line from the radiator bottom.
22. By lifting the engine one side at a time, remove the engine mounts and carefully set the engine on the front crossmember.
23. Remove the clutch housing to engine bolts and lower the vehicle to the floor.
24. Remove the upper coolant hose and the vent from the radiator and thermostat housing.
25. Remove the upper oil cooler line from the upper part of the radiator.
26. Loosen the top mountings of the radiator and remove the assembly carefully.
27. Remove the heater hoses and electrical connections from the engine.
28. Remove the electronic control unit and loosen the ignition coil and set aside.

C 725

29. Disconnect the feed and return fuel lines.

30. Disconnect the lines at the power steering pump.

31. Disconnect the vacuum line to the power brake cylinder at the manifold.

32. Disconnect the accelerator cable by removing the holder and clamp.

NOTE: On air conditioned vehicles, cover the condenser with a wood board to prevent damage during the engine removal.

33. Attach a lifting cable to lifting device and to the engine.

34. Raise the assembly slightly and remove the engine block-to-clutch housing upper mounting bolts.

35. Pull the engine forward and remove the short driveshaft with the guide tube.

36. Lift the engine carefully from the engine compartment.

37. Installation is the reverse of removal.

Cylinder Head

REMOVAL AND INSTALLATION

924, 924 Turbo

1. Disconnect the battery cables.
2. Drain the cooling system.
3. Remove the air cleaner.
4. Disconnect the radiator and heater hoses.
5. Disconnect all electrical wires from the cylinder head.
6. Detach the spark plug wires. Remove the distributor.
7. Disconnect the exhaust manifold from the exhaust pipe.
8. Disconnect the EGR line. Remove the exhaust manifold.
9. Remove the fuel injection lines from the cylinder head.
10. Remove the throttle valve housing and intake manifold as a unit.
11. Disconnect the air pump lines on models so equipped.
12. Remove the timing belt cover. Loosen the tensioner and remove the belt.
13. Loosen the cylinder head bolts in the reverse of the tightening sequence and remove the bolts.
14. Carefully lift off the cylinder head.
15. Installation is the reverse of removal. Be sure to correctly position the new cylinder head gasket. Align the timing marks and install the timing belt and properly tension it. This procedure is under Timing Belt. Tighten the cylinder head bolts in the proper order and to the correct value. Refer to the Torque Specifications at the beginning of this section. Follow the information with the chart EXACTLY.

928

NOTE: The cylinder heads can be removed with the engine in the vehicle.

924 cylinder head and related components (924 Turbo similar)

1. Drain the cooling system; both radiator and engine block.

— CAUTION —
Because of the use of aluminum, do not allow the anti-freeze coolant mixture to enter the cylinders. Severe engine damage could result after engine start-up.

2. Remove the upper timing belt cover assembly.

3. Remove the upper coolant hoses and heater hoses from the thermostat housing area.

4. Remove the air intake tube and the air cleaner assembly.

5. Remove all connecting linkages, wires and hoses from the intake manifold and injector system.

6. Rotate the engine to bring the crankshaft pulley mark to TDC, and, if working with the left cylinder head, mark and remove the distributor assembly.

7. Remove the intake manifold and injector system from the cylinder head and engine block.

8. From the lower right side of the engine block, loosen the timing belt tensioner bolt and remove the timing belt from the sprockets.

NOTE: Accessory drive belts may have to be either loosened or removed.

9. Remove the rubber plugs from the upper portion of the camshaft housing and remove the Allen head screws from the holes.

10. Remove the exposed Allen head screws from the lower portion of the camshaft housing and remove the housing from the cylinder head.

NOTE: The camshaft housing must be removed and replaced as an assembly.

11. Remove the exhaust manifold from the cylinder head. Remove the inner right and left belt housing, as necessary.

12. Remove the cylinder head nuts and washers by starting from the center and alternating toward each end.

13. Remove the cylinder head from the engine block studs, being careful not to mark or scratch the cylinder head sealing surface.

14. Remove the head gasket from the studs and clean both the head and the block.

15. Installation is the reverse of removal.

16. During the installation, attention should be given to the following:

   a. Left and right cylinder head gaskets

42 46 41 33 45 34 37 27 31 30 3248 25 16
43 44 47 40 39 35 38 26 36 28 32 19 18 17

6a 1 2 3 5 6 8 9 10 12 14 4 15 21 20 24 23 22
         11 13 7   29

1. Bolt	13. Seal	26. Hydraulic valve lifter	39. Spring retainer
2. Washer	14. O-ring	27. Lifter sleeve	40. Valve spring
3. Camshaft sprocket	15. Woodruff key	28. Gasket	41. Shim
4. Woodruff key	16. Bolt	29. Left camshaft	42. Valve stem seal
5. Camshaft oil seal	17. Washer	30. Bolt	43. Intake valve
6. Spacer	18. End cover	31. Washer	44. Exhaust valve
6a. Spacer	19. Gasket	32. Lifting eye	45. Valve guide
7. O-ring	20. Plug	33. Spark plug	46. Plug
8. Distributor drive gear	21. Bolt with washers	34. Nut	47. Seal
9. Spacer	22. Bolt	35. Washer	48. Dowel pin
10. Bolt	23. Washer	36. Cylinder head	
11. Washer	24. Camshaft housing	37. Left gasket	
12. Bearing carrier	25. Gasket	38. Valve keeper	

928 cylinder head and related components (944 similar)

are different. TOP/OBEN faces up and the arrow faces forward.

b. Turn both camshafts until the notches on the sprockets align with the marks on the camshaft housings. Be sure the crankshaft pulley is at TDC (# 1 piston on compression). Install the toothed belt and the belt tensioner.

Tighten the cylinder head bolts in the proper order and to the correct valve. Refer to the Torque Specifications at the beginning of this section. Follow the information with the chart EXACTLY.

944

NOTE: It is not necessary to remove the engine in order to remove the cylinder head.

1. Disconnect the negative (ground) battery cable and remove the cap from the coolant expansion tank.

2. Remove the engine splash guard.

Remove the radiator drain plug and allow the coolant to drain into a clean container.

3. Remove the drive belt for the alternator and air conditioning compressor from the front of the engine.

4. Remove the timing belt cover.

5. Rotate the engine as necessary to position the No. 1 piston on TDC—compression. Align the marks of both the camshaft sprocket and the flywheel according to the accompanying illustrations.

6. Remove the distributor cap. Unscrew the distributor arm and remove the plastic cap.

Alignment of the camshaft sprocket and distributor cap mount timing marks—944

Alignment of the flywheel and clutch housing timing marks—944

During removal of the 944 cylinder head, disconnect the fuel lines where indicated (arrows).

7. Remove the distributor cap mount.

8. Release the tension of the camshaft drive belt and pull the belt off of the camshaft sprocket.

9. Remove the two rear drive belt cover mounting bolts.

10. Detach the fuel lines from the locations shown in the accompanying illustration.

11. Remove the plastic cover from the fuel collection tube. Detach the wiring from the fuel injectors and lay the wiring harness aside.

12. Remove the aluminum plugs from the camshaft housing and detach the coolant line from the camshaft housing. Remove the camshaft housing from the cylinder head.

NOTE: Use care to keep the hydraulic valve tappets in place.

13. Remove the air cleaner assembly. Remove the bolt of the air intake brace.

14. Remove the intake manifold by disconnecting the following items:
   a. Oil dipstick tube bracket
   b. Brake booster hose
   c. Intake manifold hose
   d. Accelerator cable retaining clamp

15. Remove the intake manifold mounting bolts then remove the manifold.

16. Remove the bolts from the exhaust manifold/convertor pipe flange.

17. Remove the hose clamp from the heater regulating valve and the two screws from the valve neck.

18. Remove the cylinder head mounting bolts in the reverse order of the installation torque sequence.

19. Remove the cylinder head.

20. Installation is performed in the reverse order of the previous steps. After installing the head, tighten the bolts to the correct value and in the proper order. Refer to the Torque Specifications at the beginning of this section. Torque the camshaft housing mounting bolts to 14 ft. lbs. and the aluminum plugs to 29 ft. lbs. Install and adjust the camshaft drive (timing) belt as outlined later in the Engine section (Timing Belt Removal and Installation procedure). Adjust the alternator and air conditioning compressor drive belt tension.

OVERHAUL

Refer to Engine Rebuilding in the Unit Repair Section for overhaul information.

Intake Manifold

REMOVAL AND INSTALLATION

924, 924 Turbo

The intake manifold and throttle valve housing are removed as one unit.

1. Remove the air cleaner on the 924.

2. Disconnect the accelerator cable.

3. Disconnect the EGR connections.

4. Detach all electrical leads.

5. On the 924 Turbo, remove the pressure duct, being careful not to drop anything into the turbocharger housing. Cap the turbocharger opening after removing the duct.

6. Disconnect the auxiliary air regulator hose.

7. Remove all vacuum hoses attached to the intake manifold.

8. Remove the eight retaining nuts and remove the throttle valve housing and intake manifold as a unit.

9. Installation is the reverse of removal. Tighten the nuts to 15 ft. lbs.

Exhaust Manifold

REMOVAL AND INSTALLATION

NOTE: Always purchase new gaskets before removing the exhaust manifold.

1. On the 924 Turbo, remove the turbocharger and wastegate as outlined later.

2. Disconnect the EGR line from the manifold.

3. On models so equipped, remove the air pump connections.

4. Disconnect the exhaust pipe(s) from the manifold(s).

5. Remove the retaining nuts and remove the manifold(s)

6. Clean the cylinder head(s) and manifold mating surfaces.

7. Using new gaskets, install the exhaust manifold(s).

8. Tighten the nuts to 15 ft. lbs. Work from the inside out.

9. Install the remaining components in the reverse order of removal. Use a new manifold flange gasket if the old one is deteriorated.

Turbocharging System

The exhaust gas turbocharger is mounted at the right side of the engine under the exhaust manifold. The turbocharger wastegate is located near the right side of the bell housing. A boost pressure safety switch is located in the pressure duct between the turbocharger and the throttle valve housing. When the boost pressure increases to about 1.1–1.4 bar, the safety switch will turn off the two fuel pumps until pressure recedes. In operation, the exhaust gases flow into the turbocharger, and from there through the 3-way catalyst and rear muffler. The connection for the wastegate is integrated in the manifold. The pipe from the wastegate is attached to the catalytic converter housing.

Turbocharger component configuration

For additional information on turbocharger maintenance, please refer to "Turbocharging" in the Unit Repair Section.

WASTEGATE REMOVAL AND INSTALLATION

1. Jack up the vehicle and support it on stands.
2. Pull off the rubber cap from plug terminal for oxygen sensor and plug.
3. Remove the starter. Remove the bypass line between the exhaust manifold and wastegate.
4. Remove the nuts between the turbine housing and the exhaust pipe.
5. Unscrew the mounting bolts on the flange of the primary muffler/final muffler.
6. Loosen the final muffler bracket and strap, then remove the final muffler.
7. Loosen the heat shields over bypass line II, then loosen the pipe clamp at bypass line II.
8. Detach the holder and control line at the wastegate, then remove the entire line with the wastegate.

— CAUTION —
Do not damage the oxygen sensor.

NOTE: Some of the first cars produced have a vent line for the wastegate. The vent line connector will be accessible only after lowering the exhaust pipe.

9. Installation is the reverse of removal. Use new gaskets where applicable.

TURBOCHARGER REMOVAL AND INSTALLATION

1. Disconnect the negative battery cable.
2. Raise the vehicle and support it on jack stands. Remove the engine splash shield.
3. Remove the wastegate as previously outlined.
4. Disconnect the oil lines leading to the engine oil cooler, then disconnect the oil feed line for the turbocharger at the oil filter flange. Plug all oil lines.
5. Disconnect and remove the oil filter flange. Have a pan ready to catch escaping oil.
6. Loosen oil line clamps and pull out the oil lines toward the front.
7. Disconnect the oil return line.
8. Disconnect the pressure duct and remove.
9. Take off the air cleaner duct and remove.
9. Take off the air cleaner upper and lower sections.
10. Remove the three mounting nuts from the bottom of the fuel distributor.
11. Loosen the hose clamps on the dust cover and move the fuel distributor to one side.
12. Unscrew the mounting bolt on the pressure duct and take off the pressure duct.

13. Remove the nuts holding the exhaust manifold/turbocharger. Unscrew the allen head bolts at the base of the unit, then loosen the hose clamp at the bottom of the turbocharger.
14. Disconnect both sides of the stabilizer, then disconnect the steering gear from the control arm.
15. Disconnect the turbocharger base and remove the turbocharger with console toward the front.
16. Pull off the hose for the wastegate connection.

Installation is the reverse of removal with the following notes:
a. When placing the turbocharger on the engine, the allen bolts loosened in step 13 must still be loose.
b. Push the hose on at the bottom of the turbocharger while installing the unit. There is not enough clearance to install the hose after the turbocharger is installed.
c. First tighten the mounting nuts of the exhaust manifold/turbocharger, then tighten the turbocharger base bolts.
d. Always use new seals on oil lines.
e. Make sure that the round seal fits properly on the pressure duct.
f. First install both pressure ducts, then tighten the bolt(s).
g. Tighten the steering gear bolts to 14 ft. lbs.
h. Before starting the engine for the first time, lubricating oil for the turbocharger has to be primed for 15 seconds. To do this, pull off the plugs from the manifold pressure limiting switch and operate the starter.

Timing Belt Cover

REMOVAL AND INSTALLATION

924, 924 Turbo

1. Loosen the alternator mounting bolts, pivot the alternator over, and slip the drive belt off the pulleys.
2. Unscrew the cover retaining bolts and remove the cover. Keep the washers and spacers together.
3. Reposition the spacers and then install the washers and bolts.
4. Install the alternator belt and adjust the tension.

928

The timing cover consists of an outer right upper, an outer left upper and an outer bottom cover. Left and right inner belt guide covers are also used. The outer upper covers can be removed without the removal of the drive belts.

944

1. Disconnect the negative (ground) battery cable.

2. Loosen the alternator and compressor drive belt tensioner and remove the belt.
3. Remove the timing belt cover.
4. Installation is performed in the reverse of the previous steps.

Timing Belts

REMOVAL, INSTALLATION AND TENSIONING

924, 924 Turbo

1. Remove the timing belt cover.
2. While holding the larger hex on the tensioner pulley, loosen the pulley locknut.
3. Release the tensioner from the timing belt.
4. Slide the belt off the two toothed pulleys and remove it.
5. Using the large center bolt on the crankshaft pulley, turn the engine until the No. 1 cylinder is at TDC of the compression stroke. At this point, both valves will be closed and the timing marks at the flywheel will be aligned.
6. Check that the timing dot on the rear face of the camshaft pulley is aligned with the camshaft cover as shown in the illustration. If not, turn the pulley so that it does.

Timing belt installation on the 924 and 924 Turbo: The dot on the camshaft sprocket should align as shown

7. Check that the V-notch in the crankshaft pulley aligns with the adjusting lug on the oil pump housing as shown. If they don't align, turn the crankshaft until they do.

Timing belt installation on the 924 and 924 Turbo: The V-notch on the crankshaft pulley should align with the adjusting lug on the oil pump housing as shown

— CAUTION —

If the timing marks are not correctly aligned with the No. 1 piston at TDC of the compression stroke and the belt is installed, valve timing will be incorrect. Poor performance and possible engine damage can result from improper valve timing.

Timing belt tensioner bolt of the 924 and 924 Turbo

8. Install the belt on the pulleys.

9. Adjust the tensioner by turning the large hex on the pulley to the left until the belt can be twisted 90° with the thumb and forefinger at the midpoint between the camshaft pulley and the crankshaft pulley. Tighten the locknut to 30 ft. lbs.

10. Install the timing belt cover and check the ignition timing.

928

1. Loosen and remove the drive belts for the proper steering pump, fan and air pump, alternator and air conditioning compressor.

2. Remove the fan assembly and bracket for clearance.

NOTE: Do not lay the fan assembly flat. The silicone oil filler will leak out and the fan will become inoperative.

3. Remove any hoses or lines that may interfere with the cover or belt removal.

4. Remove the upper right, upper left and the bottom cover from the front of the engine.

5. Rotate the engine to TDC with number one piston on the compression stroke and the distributor rotor pointing to number one cylinder spark plug wire terminal of distributor cap.

Timing belt tensioner of the 928 as viewed from beneath the vehicle

Right hand camshaft alignment of the 928

6. Loosen the belt tensioner bolt and remove the belt from the sprockets.

7. Align the camshaft notches with the marks on the cam housings and install a new toothed belt, being sure the crankshaft marks remain aligned at TDC.

NOTE: The water pump pulley is turned by the back of the toothed belt.

Left hand camshaft alignment of the 928

8. Tighten the belt tensioner bolt until the belt can be twisted only 90° between the tension roller and the right camshaft sprocket.

9. Install the covers, hoses or lines, fan and bracket assembly, and the drive belts. Adjust the drive belts to have a deflection of ½ inch between pulleys.

10. Check and adjust the ignition timing as necessary.

944

1. Disconnect the negative (ground) battery cable.

2. Remove the engine splash guard.

3. Remove the drive belt for the alternator and air conditioning compressor from the front of the engine.

4. Remove the timing belt cover.

5. Rotate the engine as necessary to position the No. 1 piston on TDC—compression. Align the marks of both the camshaft pulley and the flywheel according to the illustrations given with Cylinder Head Removal and Installation.

6. Remove the distributor cap. Unscrew the distributor arm and remove the plastic cap.

7. Remove the distributor cap mount.

8. Release the tension of the camshaft

Timing belt tensioner of the 944—turn the large hex as required to tighten or loosen the belt

drive (timing) belt and carefully remove the belt from the sprockets.

— CAUTION —

DO NOT rotate any of the sprockets while the belt is removed.

9. After making sure that all timing marks are still properly aligned, the new belt may be installed in the following manner:

a. Install the belt on the crankshaft sprocket first, then to the tensioning roller, water pump pulley, and the camshaft sprocket. Preload the belt slightly by hand each time it is routed around the components, so that it can be pushed onto the camshaft sprocket.

b. Again, make sure all timing marks have remained aligned.

c. Carefully turn the crankshaft about 10 crankshaft degrees counterclockwise, which is equal to 1½ teeth to the mark on the camshaft sprocket.

NOTE: Porsche special tool #9201 is needed to complete the remainder of the procedure.

d. Pull the lockpin out of the special tool. Completely push out the gauge pin which is opposite the lock pin.

e. Zero the telltale needle of the special tool and slide the special tool onto the belt.

NOTE: The slides of the special tool must rest flat with the full surface of the belt.

— CAUTION —

DO NOT turn or move the belt while testing the belt tension.

f. Push the measuring needle of the tool inward slowly until you hear the lockpin engage. Read the value on the dial gauge of the special tool. The value should read as follows:
New belt—2.0 ± 0.3
Old belt—1.6 ± 0.3

g. If necessary, adjust the belt tension according to the above specifications.

h. Remove the special tool from the belt and install /attach remaining components in the reverse of steps 1–8.

Balance Shaft Drive Belt

REMOVAL AND INSTALLATION

944

1. Disconnect the negative (ground) battery cable.

2. Remove the engine splash guard.

3. Remove the alternator and air conditioning drive belt.

4. Remove the camshaft drive (timing) belt cover.

5. Loosen the balance shaft idler pulley so that the pulley does not touch the balance shaft drive belt.

6. Rotate the crankshaft clockwise as necessary to position the No. 1 cylinder at TDC—compression (refer to the timing mark illustrations which accompany the Cylinder Head Removal and Installation procedure).

NOTE: At this point, the marks on the balance shaft sprockets should be aligned with the marks on the rear belt cover.

7. Turn the tensioner nut counterclockwise to loosen the balance shaft drive belt. Carefully remove the old belt from the sprockets.

—————— **CAUTION** ——————

DO NOT move any sprocket while the belt is removed, or while installing the new belt.

8. Carefully route the new belt around the sprockets, making sure that the color coded tooth of the belt faces away from the sprockets.

9. Adjust the belt tension in the same manner as the camshaft drive (timing) belt, according to the appropriate steps of the Timing Belt Removal and Installation procedure. Turn the tensioner nut (same one

Prior to removing or installing the balance shaft drive belt, the balance shaft sprocket marks should be aligned with the marks on the rear cover as shown

Prior to installation of the 944 timing belt, the camshaft sprocket and the rear timing belt cover should be aligned as shown

1. Crankshaft sprocket
2. Tensioning roller
3. Water pump pulley
4. Camshaft sprocket

The 944 timing belt should be installed on each sprocket/pulley in the numerical order shown

Special timing belt tension tool shown installed on the 944 timing belt. Note that the tool is installed in the same manner on the balance shaft drive belt. Measuring needle (arrow) to be pushed in when "setting-up" the tool

Balance shaft idler pulley of the 944. During removal of the balance shaft drive belt, the pulley should be adjusted so that it does not touch the belt

used during step 7) to tighten the belt to the proper value (2.7 0.3 dial reading).

10. Adjust the idler pulley so that there is 0.5 mm clearance between the pulley and the portion of the belt below the pulley. Tighten the pulley nut in this position.

NOTE: If the correct clearance cannot be obtained, rotate the pulley 180° and repeat step 10.

11. The remaining components are installed in the reverse order of removal.

Timing Sprockets

REMOVAL AND INSTALLATION

The camshaft and crankshaft sprockets are located by keys on their respective shafts and each is retained by a bolt. To remove either or both of the sprockets, first remove the timing belt cover and belt and then use the following procedure.

NOTE: When removing the crankshaft sprocket on the 924, don't remove the four bolts which retain the outer belt pulley to the timing belt sprocket.

1. Remove the center bolt.
2. Gently pry the sprocket off the shaft.

The balance shaft tensioner nut of the 944. Turn the nut counterclockwise to loosen the belt; clockwise to tighten

If the sprocket is stubborn, use a gear puller. Don't hammer on the sprocket.

3. Remove the sprocket and the key.
4. Install the sprocket in the reverse order of removal.
5. Tighten the center bolt on the crankshaft sprocket to 58 ft. lbs. Tighten the camshaft sprocket retaining bolt to 15 ft. lbs.
6. Install the timing belt, check valve timing, tension belt, and install the cover.

Camshaft

REMOVAL AND INSTALLATION

924, 924 Turbo

1. Remove the timing belt.
2. Remove the camshaft sprocket.
3. Remove the air cleaner.
4. Remove the camshaft cover.
5. Remove the distributor and mounting housing.
6. Remove the oil injection tube and then reinstall the retaining nuts hand tight.
7. Unscrew and remove the Nos. 1, 3 and 5 bearing caps (No. 1 is at the front of the engine).

8. Unscrew the Nos. 2 and 4 bearing caps, diagonally and in increments.
9. Lift the camshaft out of the cylinder head.
10. Lubricate the camshaft journals and lobes with assembly lube or gear oil before installing it in the cylinder head. Bolts are tightened to 8 ft. lbs. and nuts to 20 ft. lbs.
11. Tighten bearing caps Nos. 2 and 4 carefully in a diagonal pattern.
12. Install bearing caps Nos. 1, 3 and 5.
13. Install the oil injection tube. You will have to loosen the nuts on Nos. 2 and 4 again.
14. Install the camshaft cover using new gaskets and seals.
15. Install the camshaft pulley and the timing belt.
16. Check the valve clearance.

928, 944

Refer to the cylinder head removal and installation section for the removal of the cam housing as a unit.

1. Remove the hydraulic lifters, lifter sleeves and gaskets from the cam housing.
2. Remove the rear housing end plate and gasket.
3. On the 928, remove the camshaft sprocket, the front bearing carrier on the right head and the distributor and bearing carrier on the left cam housing. On the 944, remove the camshaft sprocket and the bearing carriers.
4. Pull the camshaft to the rear and out of the cam housing.
5. The distributor gear and spacer can be removed from the camshaft at this time.
6. Installation is the reverse or removal.

NOTE: The front camshaft seals can be replaced while the front bearing carriers are off the cam housings or when the timing sprocket is removed from the camshaft.

Pistons and Connecting Rods

REMOVAL AND INSTALLATION

924, 924 Turbo

Pistons and connecting rods are removed after the cylinder head and oil pan have been removed. Connecting rod and piston assemblies must be marked on disassembly. The projections on the connecting rods must face toward the front of the engine when installed. The arrow or notch in the piston crown must face toward the front of the engine.

928, 944

The pistons and connecting rods may be removed after the cylinder head and the pan have been removed. The connecting rod ends are offset. On the 928, make sure that the narrow side with the small chamfer faces the neighboring connecting rod, while the wide side with the large chamfer faces the crankshaft web. The pistons must be installed with the valve pockets facing toward the exhaust manifold. The wrist pin is pressed out of the piston after the snap rings are removed.

ENGINE LUBRICATION

The 924 full pressure lubrication system consists of a wet sump, crankshaft driven oil pump, oil temperature gauge with sender in the oil pan, and a disposable type oil filter on the passenger side of the block.

The 928 and 944 oil sump lower section is divided into four chambers to maintain a constant oil supply for the suction pipe during periods of high speed driving and sharp turns. A thermostatically controlled oil cooler is located in the radiator and the oil pump is mounted on the front of the engine and is driven by the toothed belt. The oil filler tube and oil level sending unit are threaded into the top of the oil pan front. A full pressure lubrication system is used.

Oil Pan

REMOVAL AND INSTALLATION

924, 924 Turbo

1. Drain the oil. Remove the engine splash shield.
2. Disconnect the temperature sending unit wire.
3. Disconnect the side engine mounts and raise the engine for pan removal clearance.
4. Remove the pan retaining bolts and lower the pan from the car.
5. Install the pan using the reverse of the removal procedure. Use new gaskets and seals.

928, 944

1. Raise the vehicle and support safely.
2. Remove the bottom protective engine plate.
3. Drain the engine oil and unscrew the oil fill pipe from the pan. Disconnect the oil level indicator wire.
4. Remove the oil pan retaining bolts and maneuver the oil pan downward so that the oil pump suction tube is not twisted or damaged.
5. Using a new gasket, install the oil pan in the reverse order of removal.

Cylinder block and related components of the 924 and 924 Turbo

Rear Main Seal

REPLACEMENT

924, 924 Turbo

The rear main oil seal is located in the back of the cylinder block and so replacement involves disconnecting the torque tube and pulling the transaxle back, removing the clutch housing, and then removing the flywheel.

1. Carefully pry the seal out with a screwdriver.
2. Lightly oil the replacement seal with engine oil and carefully tap it into place.

Do not damage the seal or score the flywheel.

3. Install the flywheel, clutch housing and torque tube and transaxle. Tighten the flywheel-to-crankshaft bolts to 65 ft. lbs.

928, 944

The rear main oil seal can be replaced by separating the clutch housing from the engine and removing the flywheel. Remove the seal from the engine block with a sharp edged tool, being careful not to mark the crankshaft surface. Using a special centering tool, install the seal into the engine block with the lubricated lip towards the crankshaft. Reassemble in the reverse order of disassembly.

7. Seal
8. Bolt
9. Washer
10. Oil pump
11. Gasket

1. Bolt
2. Washer
3. Pulley bolt
4. Washer
5. Pulley
6. Oil pump gear

Exploded view of the 924 and 924 Turbo oil pump

Oil Pump

REMOVAL AND INSTALLATION

924, 924 *Turbo*

The oil pump is driven directly from the crankshaft.
1. Remove the oil pan.
2. Remove the timing belt cover.
3. Remove the timing belt.
4. Remove the crankshaft pulley.
5. Unbolt and remove the oil pump. Remove the oil pickup.
6. Clean and then install the oil pickup to the replacement oil pump.
7. Install the oil pump. Tighten the pump-to-crankcase bolts to 8 ft. lbs.
8. Install the remaining components in reverse order of removal.

928, 944

The oil pump is located on the front of the engine block and is driven by the toothed timing belt.
1. Remove the toothed timing belt. (Refer to the timing belt removal and installation section).
2. Remove the oil pump sprocket and the oil pump retaining bolts.
3. Remove the oil pump from the engine block.
4. Installation is the reverse of removal. Install a new O-ring seal on the pump body.

NOTE: An oil pump shaft seal is used and can be replaced after removal of the sprocket and woodruff key.

ENGINE COOLING

The 924 and 944 cooling system consists of a radiator, belt driven water pump, expansion tank, electric thermostatically controlled fan, and a conventional thermostat.

The 928 cooling system includes a radiator, belt driven water pump located on the upper front of the engine block, thermostat and a temperature controlled fan assembly. An expansion tank and coolant level sending unit is located in the right rear of the engine compartment.

Radiator

REMOVAL AND INSTALLATION

1. Drain the cooling system.
2. Remove the fan and radiator shroud.
3. Remove the radiator hoses.

1. Coolant neck
2. Thermostat
3. Lower thermostat housing
4. Gasket
5. Water pump
6. Pulley
7. Radiator
8. Fan shroud
9. Fan
10. Bolt
11. Expansion tank
12. Cap

Exploded view of the 924 cooling system (924 Turbo and 944 similar)

4. Disconnect the expansion tank (924 and 944) and move it out of the way.
5. Unbolt the radiator and remove it.
6. Installation is the reverse of removal. Refill the cooling system as follows: set the heater on the hot position, remove the vent plug on the radiator hose, fill the cooling system, start the engine and run it for one minute at fast idle, replace the vent plug when no more air bubbles appear at the plug opening.

Water Pump

REMOVAL AND INSTALLATION

924, 924 *Turbo*

1. Drain the cooling system.
2. Remove the timing belt cover.
3. Remove the fan belt.
4. Disconnect the radiator hoses from the pump.
5. Unbolt and remove the water pump.
6. Clean the crankcase and pump mating surfaces.
7. Install the water pump using a new gasket.

8. Install the remaining components in the reverse order of removal. Refill the cooling system. See ''Radiator Removal and Installation.''

928, 944

1. Drain the cooling system.
2. Rotate the engine to TDC, with the Number one piston on the firing stroke and the distributor rotor pointing to Number one terminal of the distributor cap.
3. On the 944, remove the timing belt cover assembly as previously outlined. On the 928, remove the upper right and left timing belt covers and remove the fan and bracket.

NOTE: Maintain upright position of the fan assembly so that the silicone fluid does not drain out (928).

4. Loosen and remove the toothed belt from the water pump pulley. (Refer to the timing belt removal and installation section).
5. Remove the bolts and water pump from the engine block.
6. Using a new gasket, install the water pump in the reverse order of removal.

Thermostat

REMOVAL AND INSTALLATION

The thermostat is located in the upper radiator hose neck on the engine.

1. Drain the cooling system.
2. Don't disconnect the radiator hose, unbolt the neck and lift out the thermostat.
3. Clean the mating surfaces and install the new thermostat (spring down) using a new gasket.
4. Refill the cooling system. See "Radiator Removal and Installation."

EMISSION CONTROLS

Positive Crankcase Ventilation (PCV)

The 924 uses a conventional crankcase ventilation system. A PCV valve, located on the driver's side of the engine, meters blow-by gases into the air intake.

The 928 and 944 crankcase ventilation system utilizes an oil separator, which is also used as an oil filler tube. The crankcase fumes are routed through the separator pipe, where the liquid oil can settle and flow back into the crankcase. The fumes continue through a hose to the lower section of the air cleaner, where a flame arrestor is located. A coolant preheat line is placed along a portion of the vent hose to warm the crankcase fumes before entering the air cleaner.

SERVICE

The PCV valve should be replaced at the recommended intervals. Check hoses for plugging and cracking and replace as necessary.

Exhaust Gas Recirculation (EGR)

All models are equipped with this system which lowers NOx emissions. Metered amounts of cooling exhaust gases are added to the air/fuel mixture. The recirculated gas lowers the peak flame temperature during combustion to cut the output of oxides of nitrogen. Exhaust gas from the exhaust pipe passes through a filter where it is cleaned. The vacuum operated EGR valve controls the amount of exhaust gas which enters the intake.

TESTING

1. Disconnect the vacuum line from the EGR valve.

2. Disconnect the vacuum hose from the distributor vacuum unit and extend the hose.

3. Start the engine and allow it to idle.

924 PCV location

The EGR vacuum amplifier is located on the right side inner fender panel—model 924

The 924 EGR filter is located on the driver's side of the engine

1. EGR valve
2. Vacuum amplifier
3. Vacuum reservoir
4. EGR filter

EGR system—typical

4. Connect the distributor vacuum hose to the EGR valve. The engine should stumble or stall.

5. If the idle speed stays even, the EGR line is clogged or the EGR valve is defective.

SERVICE

The only required maintenance is that the EGR filter be replaced at the recommended intervals. The filter is located on the right side of the engine block under the intake housing.

1. Disconnect the line fittings at each end of the filter.

2. Unbolt the bracket retaining screws and remove the filter.

3. Install the bracket replacement filter using the reverse order of removal.

EGR VALVE REMOVAL AND INSTALLATION

The EGR valve is located on the rear of the intake housing.

1. Disconnect the vacuum line from the EGR valve.

The 924 EGR valve is located on the rear of the intake housing

2. Unbolt the EGR line fitting on the opposite side of the valve.

3. Remove the two retaining bolts and lift the EGR valve from the intake housing.

4. Install the EGR valve in the reverse order of removal. Use a new gasket.

Air Injection

This system is used on 1977 924 models for use in the 49 states and the 1977 ½–79 924 models in California only. All 928 models are equipped with the air system.

This system, used on 49 state 924s only, reduces exhaust emissions by pumping fresh air into the exhaust port. There it combines with the hot exhaust gas to burn away excess hydrocarbons and reduce carbon monoxide. The system consists of a belt driven pump, air filter, diverter valve and check valve.

1. Air pump
2. Check valve
3. Air filter

Air injection system—typical

TESTING

Diverter Valve

The diverter valve is located between the air pump and the check valve on the intake housing. The diverter valve also houses a relief valve, so that it serves two functions. The valve diverts air during deceleration to

The filter for the 924 air injection system is located under the coolant expansion tank

prevent backfiring and relieves excess pressure during high rpm to prevent damage to the hoses and air pump.

To test the valve:

1. Pinch the vacuum line closed and wait a few seconds for the vacuum to stabilize on either side of the diaphragm.

2. When you release the line, the sudden surge of vacuum will make the valve work. If it's operating properly, you should be able to hear it open and exhaust air.

Check Valve

The check valve is located on the intake housing. It keeps hot exhaust gases from flowing back into the pump and hoses and destroying them.

To test the valve:

1. With the engine off and cool enough so that there is no danger of being burned, disconnect the hose and use mouth pressure to blow through it.

2. You should be able to easily blow through the valve towards the intake housing but the valves should seal tightly when you draw back. Replace the valve if it doesn't seal.

Typical 924 exhaust system showing the catalytic convertor (arrow)

Air Pump

1. Disconnect a hose at the diverter valve.

2. With the engine idling, check the flow of air by feeling at the hose with your hand.

3. Increase the engine speed to about 1500 rpm and again check the air flow. If it increases as the engine is accelerated, the pump output is sufficient.

4. Inspect the filter element in the air cleaner for blockage and replace it if necessary before assuming the pump to be deficient.

Catalytic Converter

Catalytic converters were used on the 1977 924 models for California only, but were made standard on all 1977½ and later 924, 928 and 944 models. This device contains noble metals which act as catalysts to cause a reaction to convert hydrocarbons and carbon monoxide into harmless water and carbon dioxide. Service on the converter consists of replacing it when it malfunctions.

Evaportive Emission Control System

This system prevents the escape of raw fuel vapors into the atmosphere. The system consists of a charcoal canister and an expansion chamber. Vapors from the fuel tank are trapped in the canister. When the engine is running, fresh air is drawn in through the charcoal filter. The fresh air cleans the canister and routes the unburned hydrocarbons through the air cleaner to be burned during combustion. The fuel tank is vented to an expansion chamber which prevents fuel vapors from entering the atmosphere.

FUEL SYSTEM

Fuel Filter

REPLACEMENT

924, 924 Turbo, 944

On all models except the 944, the fuel filter is located in the fuel line on the driver's side of the engine compartment. The fuel filter of the 944 at the right rear of the vehicle above the axle halfshaft.

1. Place a shop rag under the filter.

2. Using a line wrench, unscrew both line connections from the filter.

3. Loosen the filter clamp and remove the filter.

4. Install the replacement filter in the line and tighten both fittings. Tighten the filter clamp, if so equipped.

Fuel filter location—model 924

928

The fuel filter and fuel accumulator are located behind a cover, in front of the right rear wheel well.

Electric Fuel Pump

The fuel pump(s) is electrical on all models. 1980 and later 924 and 924 Turbo models and 1978–79 928 models are equipped with dual fuel pumps, the feed pump is located in the fuel tank, while the main pump is located in the right rear wheel well. On the 928 with dual pumps, one fuel pump is located under a plate on the rear of the fuel tank and the second is mounted inside the tank. Two pumps were used on these models to prevent the occurance of vapor lock in the fuel system. 1977–79 924 and 1983 944 models are equipped with one fuel pump located near the fuel tank behind the right rear wheel. 1980 and later 928 models have one fuel pump mounted on a console with the fuel filter, on top of the fuel tank.

Cars equipped with C.I.S. fuel injection require a fuel pressure accumulator (some models have two) which improves warm engine start ups by trapping a pressurized amount of fuel in the system when the engine is stopped. This trapped fuel is released when the engine is first turned over and is the initial fuel charge used to start the car. Because of the fuel accumulator, the warm engine may be started instantly, with no time wasted waiting for the fuel pump to build up pressure. The fuel pressure accumulator also helps smooth out pressure pulses in the fuel system and helps prevent vapor lock. The accumulator(s) is usually located side by side with the main fuel pump or the fuel filter.

REMOVAL AND INSTALLATION

1977–79 924 and 1983 944

The fuel pump is located near the fuel tank behind the right rear wheel.

1. Raise the rear of the car and support it on jack stands. Disconnect the negative battery cable.

2. Locate the fuel pump. There will be pressurized fuel in the lines. Allow the engine to cool, then wrap a rag around one of the fuel pump fittings and crack it open with a wrench to bleed off the fuel.

———— **CAUTION** ————
Do not allow fuel to splash on hot exhaust components.

3. Unplug the electrical connections at the pump, taking note of their positions.

4. Disconnect the fuel lines and plug them.

5. Unscrew the retaining clamp and remove the pump.

6. Install the new pump. Clean the electrical connections to ensure continuity.

1980 and Later 924, 924 Turbo

Two fuel pumps are used. One is located in the fuel tank and the second is located in the right rear wheel well.

IN-TANK PUMP

1. Disconnect the negative battery cable.

2. Raise the rear of the vehicle.

3. Drain the fuel tank.

———— **CAUTION** ————
Be very careful around raw fuel. Do not smoke.

Fuel filter on the 944. Loosen the line fittings first (outer arrows) then the filter mounting clamp (inner arrow) to remove the filter

4. Disconnect the electrical connections from the fuel pump.

5. Disconnect the fuel line, having a container ready to catch any residual fuel left in the system.

6. Unscrew the pump from the bottom of the fuel tank.

7. When installing a new pump, make sure the gasket for the pump is in place. After installation, fill the tank with a few gallons of fuel and check for leaks.

EXTERNAL PUMP

1. Disconnect the negative battery cable. Drain the fuel tank.

2. Raise the rear of the vehicle and support it with jack stands.

3. Locate the fuel pump. Quickly remove and plug the fuel lines from the pump. Have a container ready to catch the fuel.

—— CAUTION ——
Be very careful. Do not smoke.

4. Loosen the strap and remove the fuel pump.

5. Install a new pump in the reverse order of the removal procedure.

928 Through 1979

Two fuel pumps are used, one located under a plate on the rear of the fuel tank and the second mounted in the fuel tank. See the in-tank fuel pump removal procedure for the 1980 and later 924, 924 Turbo for removal and installation procedures for the in-tank fuel pump. To remove the external pump, remove the guard plate on the rear of the fuel tank, pinch shut the hose running from the pump to the fuel tank with a suitable clamp, then disconnect and remove the pump. Have a container ready to catch the

fuel that will be present in the fuel lines and DO NOT SMOKE! Installation is the reverse of removal.

1980 and later 928

A single fuel pump is located with the fuel filter on a mutual console underneath a plastic hood on the fuel tank.

1. Disconnect the negative battery cable.

2. Raise the rear of the vehicle and support it on jack stands. Expose the fuel pump.

3. Pinch shut the hose running from the fuel tank to the fuel pump with a suitable clamp.

4. Disconnect the pump wiring, disconnect both fittings from the pump, undo its retaining strap and remove the pump.

—— CAUTION ——
Some fuel will be present in the lines. Have a container ready to catch it and do not smoke.

5. Install a new pump in the reverse order of pump removal.

TESTING AND ADJUSTMENT

No adjustments may be made to the fuel pump. If the pump is not functioning properly, it must be discarded and replaced. To check the function of the fuel pump, the pump should be connected to a pressure gauge. Be careful not to switch the electrical leads. If the pump fails to pump its normal capacity, or if it cannot pump that

capacity at its specified rate of current consumption, it must be replaced. Because of the highly technical nature of this operation, it is best to refer this job to a qualified technician.

Fuel Injection

924 and 924 Turbo models are equipped with the Bosch continuous flow injection system (CIS). Prior to 1980, the 928 also used CIS, but changed to the Bosch L-Jetronic in 1980. The 928 L-Jetronic system is used up to and including the current model year. The 944 uses a new Bosch Digital Motor Electronic (DME) fuel injection system.

Due to the complexity of these fuel injection systems, diagnosis and repair should be referred to a professional service shop.

For all fuel injection system repair and service procedures please refer to "Fuel Injection" in the Unit Repair section.

CLUTCH

REMOVAL AND INSTALLATION

924 (All), 924 Turbo (79–80)

To gain access to the clutch disc and pressure plate assembly the transaxle, torque tube and clutch housing must be dismounted and pulled back out of the way.

1. Disconnect the battery ground cable. Raise the car and support it on jack stands.

2. Support the engine with an overhead hoist or a jack and cradle under the engine.

3. Remove the engine splash shield.

4. Disconnect the clutch cable.

5. Remove the bottom clutch adjustment lock nut and detach the cable from the lever.

6. On the four-speed, remove the access plate from the bottom of the clutch housing. Have an assistant turn the engine with the crankshaft pulley. Remove the pressure plate bolts gradually until all pressure is released.

7. Remove the exhaust pipe flange bolts.

8. Remove the bracket at the rear of the transaxle and any other attachment which will hinder the transaxle's rearward movement.

9. Remove the entire exhaust system.

10. Remove the back-up light switch from the transaxle.

11. Disconnect the axle driveshafts at the transaxle and let them hang down out of the way.

12. On the 4-speed, remove the clutch housing-to-engine bolts. On the 5-speed, disconnect the center tube from the clutch housing.

13. Place a wooden block under the front

1. Cable
2. Disc
3. Pressure plate
4. Throwout bearing
5. Guide sleeve
6. Clutch housing

Clutch components of the 924 (except 924 Turbo)

tunnel reinforcement to support the transaxle tube.

14. Remove the transaxle mounting bolts and slide the transaxle toward the rear. Support the transaxle on a jack.

15. On the five speed, remove the clutch housing bolts, the clutch housing and the clutch assembly.

16. On the 4-speed, remove the pressure plate and clutch disc.

17. On the 4-speed install the pressure plate and clutch disc onto the driveshaft in the clutch housing. On the 5-speed install the clutch using a centering pilot. The word "Schwungradseite" on the clutch disc faces the flywheel.

18. Push the transaxle, torque tube, and clutch housing assembly forward to the engine.

19. Install the clutch housing-to-engine bolts. Tighten the 12mm bolts to 60 ft. lbs., the 10mm bolts to 36 ft. lbs. and the 8mm bolts to 24 ft. lbs. in a gradual diagonal pattern.

20. Install the remaining components in the reverse order of removal. Adjust the clutch.

924 Turbo (1981 and Later), 944

As specific procedures have not yet been published concerning Clutch Removal and Installation in these models, it is best to refer this service to a professional shop. The flywheel sensing components used in these models for the digital ignition system are very delicate and easily damaged.

1. Bolt
2. Washer
3. Guide sleeve
4. Driveshaft
5. Bolt
6. Washer
7. Pressure plate
8. Clutch disc (spring loaded)
9. Starter ring
10. Clutch disc (not spring loaded)
11. Snap-ring
12. Thrust washer
13. Release bearing
14. Release lever
15. Preload washer
16. Ball socket bushing
17. Intermediate plate

Dowel pin centered 928 clutch assembly

928

1. Disconnect the battery ground strap.
2. Raise the vehicle and support safely.
3. Remove the lower body brace.
4. Remove the clutch slave cylinder and keep hydraulic lines attached.
5. Remove the starter and clutch housing cover as a unit and attach to the stabilizer bar with a wire. If applicable, remove the catalytic converter.
6. Remove the coupling screws and push the coupler rearward on the drive shaft.
7. Remove the release bearing sleeve bolts and move the sleeve towards the flywheel.
8. Matchmark the clutch components and loosen all pressure plate mounting bolts evenly until all the pressure is removed from the plate.

9. Remove the mounting bolts and press down on the release lever (towards the flywheel) and disconnect the release lever at the ball stud.

10. Push the complete clutch assembly rearward and move the assembly downward and out of the clutch housing.

NOTE: The clutch assembly consists of the pressure plate, front and rear clutch discs, release lever, release bearing sleeve and short driveshaft.

Installation is the reverse of removal.

NOTE: The clutch discs are different.
a. The clutch disc with the rigid center is installed between the flywheel and the intermediate plate.
b. The clutch disc with the spring center is installed between the intermediate plate and the pressure plate.

1. Intermediate ring
2. Intermediate plate
3. Stop bracket
4. Stop
5. Distance 0.7 to 1.0 mm
6. Position of intermediate plate
A. Release bearing side
S. Flywheel side

To prevent clutch drag on the 928, move the three clutch stop brackets toward the pressure plate until the correct gap (5) exists

1. Bolt
2. Washer
3. Guide sleeve
4. Driveshaft
5. Bolt
6. Washer
7. Pressure plate
8. Clutch disc (spring loaded)
9. Intermediate plate
10. Clutch disc (not spring loaded)
11. Snap-ring
12. Thrust washer
13. Release bearing
14. Release lever
15. Preload washer
16. Snap-ring
16A. Ball socket bushing
17. Bolt
18. Washer
19. Starter ring
20. Bolt
21. Flywheel with centering collar

Diameter centered 928 clutch assembly

1. Clutch lever
2. Hex nut
3. Servo spring
4. Knife-edge bearing
5. Master cylinder
6. Throw-out lever
7. Rubber plug
8. Slave cylinder
9. Pedal stop

Hydraulic clutch actuation system of the 924 Turbo and 944. Clutch wear may be checked after removing the rubber plug (7)

1. Clutch pedal
2. Pedal stop
3. Wing nut
4. Over-center spring
5. Knife-edge bearing
6. Pushrod
7. Clutch slave cylinder
8. Slave cylinder piston
9. Spring
10. Front disc
11. Intermediate plate

12. Rear disc
13. Pressure plate
14. Diaphragm spring
15. Release bearing
16. Clutch release lever
17. Inspection plug
18. Pushrod
19. Piston in slave cylinder
20. Flexible mount for intermediate plate

Hydraulic clutch actuation system of the 928. Clutch wear may be checked after removing the rubber plug (17)

Clutch cable adjusting nut location of the 924 (except 924 Turbo)

CAUTION

To prevent clutch drag, move the three stop brackets towards the pressure plate until a gap of 0.0275 to 0.0394 inch exists between the intermediate plate and the stop bracket.

FREE-PLAY ADJUSTMENT

924

Clutch pedal free-play should be ¾–1 in. (20–25 mm).

Adjust the clutch pedal free-play by loosening the two nuts on the cable near the intake housing. After obtaining the correct free-play at the pedal, tighten the adjusting nuts.

924 Turbo, 944

The clutch linkage is self-adjusting. Clutch wear can be checked by removing the rubber plug located on the starter side of the bell housing. The throwout lever gradually moves backwards as the clutch wears. On a new clutch, there should be 18 mm clearance between the lever and the front of the hole. On a worn clutch the replace distance is 34 mm.

928

Clutch adjustment is not necessary because of the automatic adjustment of the slave cylinder. The only clearance check should be a ³⁄₃₂ inch free play between the push rod and the clutch master cylinder piston, which should give a ³⁄₁₆ inch pedal free play.

The clutch wear limit is reached when, upon removal of a rubber plug on the slave cylinder side of the clutch housing, the front edge of the release lever can just be seen.

Clutch Master Cylinder

REMOVAL AND INSTALLATION

924 Turbo, 928, 944

The clutch master cylinder is located beside the brake master cylinder in the engine compartment and shares the brake master cylinder's fluid reservoir. Access is limited, and, depending on model year and options, several other components may have to be relocated before the clutch master cylinder can be removed.

1. Drain the clutch section of the fluid reservoir. Remove and plug the line leading to the clutch master cylinder from the brakes master cylinder fluid reservoir.

───── CAUTION ─────

Be very careful not to let any brake fluid drip onto painted surfaces, as it will permanently discolor them.

2. From inside the car, disconnect the clutch master cylinder pushrod.

3. Disconnect the fluid tube which runs to the clutch slave cylinder from the master cylinder and plug it. Before loosening the tube's fitting, wrap a rag around it so that brake fluid is not spilled.

4. Disconnect and remove the master cylinder from the vehicle.

5. Installation is the reverse of removal. Bleed the system at the slave cylinder. For information, see the slave cylinder removal procedure.

Clutch Slave Cylinder

REMOVAL AND INSTALLATION

924 Turbo, 928, 944

1. Drain the clutch section of the brake fluid reservoir.

2. Jack up the vehicle and support it on stands. Locate the slave cylinder—it is at the bottom of the bell housing.

3. Disconnect the clutch fluid line from the slave cylinder.

4. Remove the retaining bolts and remove the slave cylinder.

5. Installation is the reverse of removal. Prime the cylinder with clean brake fluid before installing.

When the slave cylinder is installed, the system must be bled. To bleed the system, fill the clutch portion of the fluid reservoir with clean brake fluid, then attach a hose to the bleed nipple on the slave cylinder and position the other end of the hose so that it is submerged in a partially filled container of brake fluid. Have an assistant pump up the clutch pedal several times, then open the bleed nipple with a wrench. Air bubbles will appear at the side of the hose submerged in the brake fluid. When the bubbles stop, with your assistant's foot still pressing on the clutch pedal close the bleed nipple. Have your assistant pump up the pedal again and repeat the process until no bubbles appear in the container, then close the bleed nipple and test the pedal. If the pedal feels spongy or "not right," there is probably still some air in the system. Repeat the bleeding procedure.

NOTE: During the bleeding process, make sure the fluid in the clutch section of the reservoir does not completely disappear or you'll be pumping the system up with air rather than fluid.

MANUAL TRANSAXLE

REMOVAL AND INSTALLATION

924, 924 Turbo, 944

4-SPEED

Transaxle removal and installation are outlined with the Clutch Removal and Installation procedure. Disconnect the torque tube from the transaxle for servicing.

5-SPEED

1. Jack up the vehicle and support it on stands.

2. Remove the entire exhaust system from behind the catalytic converter.

3. Disconnect the wires from the backup light switch.

4. Remove the reinforcement strut at the front of the transaxle to facilitate work procedures.

5. Engage 5th gear. Remove the rubber cap from the front transmission cover. Position the socket head screw for removal by turning a rear wheel (hold the other wheel). Unscrew the screw from the coupling using a long reach extension and a 6 mm socket. Keep the transaxle in 5th gear.

6. Detach the axle half-shafts from the transaxle and suspend them on wire to prevent damage.

7. Unscrew the self-locking nuts from the transmission mounts (the rubber/metal mounts).

8. Position a jack underneath the transmission and secure the transaxle to it using a strap.

9. Unscrew the bolts from the rubber/metal mounts, lift the transaxle slightly with the jack and remove the mounts. Do not lift the unit too far, as the brake line for the left rear wheel may become damaged.

10. Disconnect the shift linkage.

11. Remove the bolts between the drive shaft tube and the transaxle. Remove or disconnect any other interfering components, then carefully remove the transaxle unit, moving rearward and down.

12. Installation is the reverse of removal.

928

1. Remove the nuts from the spring struts bolts, extending into the trunk compartment.

2. Remove the battery and loosen the rear wheels.

3. Place the transmission in fifth gear.

4. Raise the vehicle and remove the rubber plug from underneath the front of the transmission. Looking into the hole, position the coupling bolt head between the drive and input shafts, so that it can be removed.

NOTE: During removal of the bolt, do not allow the shaft to turn and jam the socket or bolt in the transmission housing.

5. Place the transmission in neutral, remove the rear wheels and remove the brake calipers, wire them to the frame.

6. Remove the exhaust system, from the catalytic converter rearward.

7. Remove the exhaust heat shield and the battery box.

8. Disconnect the back-up light switch wires and loosen the pulse transmitter for the speedometer. Remove the wires from the clip.

9. Move the dust cover from the shift rod coupling and remove the locking set screw. Remove the shift rod from the main rod.

10. Disconnect the axle shafts at the transmission end. Suspend the axles from the cross member.

11. Disconnect the stabilizer bar at the lower control arm.

12. With the use of a strap, chain or heavy wire, support the transaxle assembly from the stabilizer bar.

13. Remove the transmission-to-rear axle cross member bolts and the bolts between the rear axle cross member and frame.

14. Mark the position of the rear axle cross member and place a jack under member. Remove the bolts and tilt the rear axle so that the spring struts and control arms do not twist. Support the rear axle in the tilted position to keep the weight off the lower control arm link pins.

15. Place jack under the transmission assembly and remove the bolts between the drive shaft tube and the transmission. Remove the holding strap, pull the unit rearward and lower.

16. Installation is the reverse of removal.

LINKAGE ADJUSTMENT

Linkage adjustments are not normally required and should be attempted only if the mechanic is familiar with direct-distant shift mechanisms.

924 Four Speed

1. Place the transaxle in neutral.

2. Raise the rear of the vehicle, support it on stands and block the front wheels.

3. Make sure the intermediate lever on the selector shaft leans toward the back of the car approximately 5°. If not, loosen the lever's pinch bolt and adjust it to this position.

4. Move the intermediate lever to the middle of the neutral travel.

5. Loosen the link piece retaining bolt at the rear of the selector shaft and move the bolt in its slot until the link piece is vertical. Tighten the bolt.

6. Adjust the shift plate at the bottom of the shift lever in the passenger compartment until the lever is at an 82° angle (rearward) with the propeller shaft tunnel.

All Five Speeds

These transaxles usually require adjustment only when the unit has been overhauled. Adjustments should be performed by a qualified technician.

OVERHAUL

Refer to the Unit Repair Section for overhaul procedures.

Axle Halfshafts

Power is transferred to the rear wheels by independent axle halfshafts. Each shaft is equipped with both an inner and an outer constant velocity joint.

REMOVAL AND INSTALLATION

1. Jack the rear of the car up and support it on jack stands.

2. Remove the six star bolts on the inside joint at the transaxle.

3. Remove the six star bolts at the stub axle. Use a wide, flat bladed prybar to pry the flanges apart.

4. Drop the axle driveshaft down and out of the 924 and 924 Turbo. On the 928, remove the axle from the upper left side of the hub assembly.

5. Pack the constant velocity joints with grease before installation.

6. Installation is the reverse of removal. Tighten the bolts to 30 ft. lbs.

AUTOMATIC TRANSAXLE

REMOVAL AND INSTALLATION

Removal and installation of the automatic transaxle is performed in the same manner as the previous Manual Transmission Removal and Installation. Be sure to mark all linkage, etc. to facilitate the installation of the unit.

NOTE: Adjustments not listed here should be referred to a professional shop.

SHIFT LINKAGE ADJUSTMENT

924

1. Raise the vehicle and support it on jack stands.

2. Move the selector lever into the Park position.

3. Loosen the clamping bolt at the transmission lever.

4. Pull the transmission lever against the stop.

5. Tighten the clamping bolt with the lever in this position.

NOTE: When tightening the clamping bolt, make sure that the cable does not twist and that the transmission lever does not bend. The in-car selector lever must not touch the selector gate in either the "P" or the "1" positions.

6. Run the engine at idle and move the selector lever from "P" to "R", from "N" to "R" and from "N" to "D". In each case the gear should engage within one second after the selector is moved. The clearance between the selector and the front of the selector gate in position "P" should be the same as the clearance between the selector and the back of the gate in position "1".

NEUTRAL SAFETY SWITCH ADJUSTMENT

924

The neutral safety switch prevents the engine from being started in any position except "P" and "N". To test it, position the selector lever in every position of its quadrant and attempt to start the engine. If the engine starts in any position besides "P" or "N", the neutral safety switch is out of adjustment. To adjust it, remove the selector gate for the selector lever, loosen the neutral safety switch mounting bolts and adjust its position, then retighten the bolts.

THROTTLE CABLE AND TRANSMISSION CABLE ADJUSTMENTS

924 Through 1978 Model

1. With the accelerator pedal against its idle stop and the throttle valve lever closed, make sure the transmission lever is in the rest position. Also make sure that the safety yoke is flat against the bracket on the upper accelerator pedal.

2. At the safety yoke, adjust both cables so that they can be attached without tension. Adjust the cable to the throttle housing at its mount on the intake manifold. Adjust the transmission lever cable at the mounting bracket on the side of the transmission.

3. To test the kickdown position adjustment, make sure no obstructions, such

as optional floor mats, are under the accelerator pedal kickdown stop. Just before the accelerator pedal is fully depressed, there should be a slight movement (about 2mm) of the transmission lever. If not, or if the movement is too great, readjust the cable at the transmission bracket.

4. To test the full throttle adjustment, depress the accelerator pedal to the first noticeable pressure point (beginning of the kickdown detent). In this position the throttle valve lever should be fully open. If not, adjust at the cable.

924 1979 and Later Models

1. Screw in the cable sleeve mounting nut on the transmission bracket completely and tighten.

2. Loosen the bolts on the roller holder bracket, push the roller holder in its slot forward (as seen from the driving direction) as far as possible and tighten the bolts.

3. Completely loosen the short cable at the firewall and the long cable on the roller holder.

4. Turn the roller so that the operating lever faces forward at an angle of 29° (in this position the opening for the cable locator will face the reinforcement rib of the holder).

A. Reinforcement rib

On the 1979 and later 924, turn the roller so that the operating lever faces forward at an angle of 29°

To adjust the throttle cable of the 1979 and later 924, screw in the cable sleeve mounting nut as far as possible on the bracket then tighten (lower arrow)

5. Hold the roller in this position and mount the throttle valve push rod without tension on the rod.

6. Place the cable around the roller in the correct position and adjust the long cable sleeve until the cable locator just rests in the opening without tension.

7. Adjust the cable going to the accelerator pedal so that it does not have tension at the adjuster.

When the cable has been adjusted correctly, the accelerator pedal will be in its neutral position (11°30' inclination), the throttle valve will be closed and the lever on the transmission will be on its bottom stop.

8. To check the full throttle position adjustment, depress the accelerator pedal to the first noticeable pressure point and check whether the throttle valve is fully open.

9. To check the kickdown adjustment, depress the pedal past the full throttle pressure point until it comes against its stop and check to make sure the roller stop has lifted off the operating lever by about ¼ in. In this position the lever on the transmission should be resting on the final stop or at most about 1° away.

BAND ADJUSTMENTS

924

The second gear band is adjustable.

NOTE: Only adjust the band with the transmission positioned horizontally, or the band could jam.

1. Locate the second gear band adjuster. It is on the driver's side of the case next to the selector levers.

2. Loosen the locknut and tighten the adjusting screw to about 7 ft. lbs.

3. Loosen the screw and tighten it to 4 ft. lbs.

4. From this position, loosen the screw exactly 2½ turns and secure with the locknut.

928

Band adjustments are not normally required on the 928 automatic transmission.

REAR SUSPENSION

Torsion Bars

REMOVAL AND INSTALLATION

924, 924 Turbo, 944

NOTE: This procedure requires that the rear wheel camber and toe-in be checked and adjusted as the final step.

1. Allen head bolt	8. Lockwasher
2. Plate	9. Bolt
3. Axle shaft	10. Washer
4. Nut	11. Shock absorber
5. Lockwasher	12. Nut
6. Bolt	13. Washer
7. Nut	14. Plain washer
15. Bolt	22. Bolt
16. Plain washer	23. Lockwasher
17. Nut, self-locking	24. Cover
18. Plain washer	25. Rubber mount, outer
19. Bolt	26. Torsion plate
20. Plain washer	27. Rubber mount, inner
21. Trailing arm	28. Torsion bar

Rear suspension of the 924 and 924 Turbo (944 similar)

1. Shock absorber mounting	12. Control arm	17. Bushings
2. Shock absorber	13. Torsion bar cover	18. Bolt
3. Driveshaft	14. Bearing	19. Torsion bar housing
4. Boot	15. Trailing arm (spring plate)	20. Torsion bar
5. CV joint	16. Stabilizer mounting	21. Stabilizer bar
6. Stub axle		
7. Seal		
8. Inner wheel bearing		
9. Bumper		
10. Outer wheel bearing		
11. Seal		

Rear control arm and related components of the 924 and 924 Turbo (944 similar)

1. Jack up the rear of the car and support it on stands.

2. Remove the wheel on the side where the torsion bar is being removed.

3. Using a hydraulic jack and a block of wood with a slot cut in it, raise the trailing arm.

4. Remove the lower shock absorber bolt.

5. Remove the trailing arm retaining bolts. Remove the toe and camber adjusting bolts.

6. Remove the four retaining bolts from the trailing arm cover.

7. Using two screwdrivers, pry off the trailing arm cover.

8. Lower the jack.

9. Remove the round body plug and remove the trailing arm.

10. Paint a reference mark on the torsion bar support, matching the location of the L or R side identification letter, so that the torsion bar may be installed in the same position.

NOTE: The torsion bars are splined to allow adjustment of the rear riding height.

11. Remove the torsion bar. Do not scratch the protective paint on the torsion bar, or it will corrode and possibly develop fatique cracks.

NOTE: If you are removing a broken torsion bar, the inner end can be knocked from its seat by removing the opposite torsion bar and tapping it through with a steel bar. Torsion bars are not interchangeable from side to side and are marked L and R for identification.

12. Check the torsion bar splines for damage and replace the bar if necessary. If there is any corrosion on the bar, replace it.

13. Coat the torsion bar lightly with grease. Carefully grease the splines.

14. Apply glycerine or another rubber preservative to the torsion bar support.

15. Install the torsion bar, matching the L or R with the paint mark you made before removal.

16. Install the trailing arm cover into position and start the three accessible bolts.

17. Raise the trailing arm into place with a jack and wooden block until the spacer and the fourth bolt can be installed.

18. Assemble the remaining components in the reverse order of their removal.

19. Tighten the trailing arm cover bolts to 25 ft. lbs. Tighten the shock absorber bolt to 50 ft. lbs.

20. Adjust rear wheel camber and toe-in.

Upper Control Arm

REMOVAL AND INSTALLATION

928

1. Raise the vehicle and support it safely. Remove the rear wheels and support the lower arm assembly with a jack.

2. Loosen and remove the inner and outer bolts from the upper arm ends.

3. Remove the upper arm from the rear crossmember and from the rear flexible mount.

NOTE: The bushings are replaceable.

Installation is the reverse of removal.

Lower Control Arm

REMOVAL AND INSTALLATION

928

1. Raise the vehicle and support safely. Remove the rear wheels.

2. Support the hub assembly and the spring strut with a jack.

3. Remove the outer pivot pin nuts and washers. Disconnect the stabilizer bar link.

4. Remove the inner pivot bolts from the arm and pull the front pivot pin from the hub assembly and the spring strut.

NOTE: The bushings are replaceable.

5. Installation is the reverse of removal.

Shock Absorbers

REMOVAL AND INSTALLATION

924, 924 Turbo, 944

1. Raise the car on a drive-on hoist or

1. Rear axle crossmember	8. Lower control arm outer bushing	17. Shock bumper
2. Upper strut	9. Cone washer	18. Lower spring seat
3. Upper strut bushings	10. Pivot pin	19. Suspension height adjuster
4. Lower control arm	11. Wheel bearing carrier	20. Flange
5. Lower control arm inner bushing	12. Upper shock mount	21. Shock absorber
6. Lower control arm rocker mount	13. Shock mount retainer	22. Stabilizer bar mount
7. Lower control eccentric	14. Lower shock mount	23. Stabilizer bar
	15. Upper spring mount	24. Link
	16. Coil spring	

Exploded view of the 928 rear suspension

support the wheels on stands for this procedure.

2. Remove the bottom retaining bolt and nut.

3. Remove the top bolt.

4. Remove the shock absorber.

5. Install the replacement shock in the reverse order of removal. Tighten the retaining bolts to 50 ft. lbs.

928

1. Remove the locking nuts from the spring strut, located within the trunk area.

2. Raise the vehicle, support safely and remove the wheel.

3. Remove the front nut on the outer pivot pin rod and remove the pivot rod from the rubber bushings.

4. Disconnect the stablizer bar link from the lower control arm.

5. Remove the spring strut from the vehicle.

6. Installation is the reverse of removal.

NOTE: The spring can be removed from the shock unit with the use of a spring clamping tool. An adjusting nut and sleeve is used to control the vehicle rear height.

NOTE: Please refer to "Strut Overhaul" in the Unit Repair section for spring removal procedures.

Rear wheel alignment points of the 924 and 924 Turbo. Loosen the fasteners (arrows) to alter the camber and toe-in

Rear Wheel Alignment

CAMBER ADJUSTMENT

Rear wheel camber is adjusted by changing the trailing arm spring plate setting. To increase positive camber, loosen the spring plate-to-trailing arm bolts (with the wheels

1. Strut
2. Shock absorber
3. Bearing
4. Seat
5. Buffer
6. Clamp nut
7. Outer wheel bearing
8. Inner wheel bearing
9. Seal
10. Steering knuckle
11. Ball joint
12. Control arm
13. Stabilizer bushing
14. Stabilizer bar
15. Bushing
16. Crossmember

Front suspension of the 924, 924 Turbo, and 944

on the ground). To increase negative camber, do so with car on hoist. Tighten bolts after adjustment.

TOE-IN ADJUSTMENT

Rear wheel toe-in is adjusted by moving the control arm in the slots of the spring plates.

FRONT SUSPENSION

924, 924 Turbo, 944

The 924 front suspension is a MacPherson strut design. The strut consists of the strut housing, a shock absorber insert in the housing, and a concentric coil spring. The steering knuckle is bolted to the strut as-

sembly. A lower control arm locates the strut at the bottom. A ball joint is riveted to the control arm and bolted to the steering knuckle.

928

The 928 front suspension is an independent type with upper and lower control arms, coil springs mounted on the shock absorbers and upper and lower ball joints. Provisions for front end alignment are provided by eccentrics located at the bottom of the lower ball joint mounting plate.

MacPherson Strut

REMOVAL AND INSTALLATION

For all strut overhaul procedures, please refer to "Strut Overhaul" in the Unit Repair section.

Rear camber adjustment on the 944

Rear toe-in adjustment on the 944

1. Upper control arm
2. Lower control arm support
3. Lower control arm
4. Lower shock mount
5. Lower ball joint
6. Caster eccentric (outer), camber eccentric (inner)
7. Stabilizer bar
8. Bushing
9. Link
10. Steering knuckle
11. Inner front wheel seal
12. Inner front wheel bearing
13. Outer front wheel bearing
14. Upper shock mount
15. Upper spring seat
16. Spring
17. Suspension stop
18. Lower spring seat
19. Shock absorber

Exploded view of the 928 front suspension

924, 924 Turbo, 944

1. Jack up the front of the car and support it on stands.
2. Remove the brake line from the bracket on the strut.
3. Remove the two through bolts that retain the strut to the steering knuckle.
4. Remove the four retaining nuts from the inner fender in the engine compartment.
5. Pry the lower control arm down and remove the strut from the car.
6. To replace either the spring or shock absorber, place the strut in a spring compressor and remove the large retaining nut at the top.

7. Installation is the reverse of removal. Front wheel alignment must be reset after a strut is removed.

928

1. Remove the self-locking nuts on the upper strut mount, located on the inner fender panel.
2. Remove the front wheel. Remove the flange locknut and press the upper ball joint from the spindle carrier.
3. Remove the inner pivot shaft nuts from the upper control arm.
4. Remove the shock absorber mounting bolts and remove the shock and upper arm as an assembly.

Lower Control Arm

REMOVAL AND INSTALLATION

924, 924 Turbo, 944

1. Jack up the front of the car and support it on stands.
2. Remove the through-bolt at the front that retains the control arm to the suspension crossmember.
3. Detach the stabilizer bar from the control arm.
4. Remove the two bolts that retain the control arm bracket at the rear.
5. Remove the ball joint pinch bolt at the steering knuckle.
6. Pry the control arm down and remove it from the car.
7. Installation is the reverse of removal. Caster must be reset after the control arm has been removed.

928

1. Raise and support the vehicle then remove the wheel.
2. Mark the alignment eccentrics on the lower arm for approximate installation location, if the ball joint is to be removed.
3. Remove the strut bottom link bracket and stabilizer link bolt.
4. Remove the lower ball joint stud nut and press the stud from the spindle. Move the spindle and upper arm upward and block it to gain working clearance.
5. Remove the bolts from the tie-down bracket and control arm bracket. Lower the control arm from the vehicle.
6. The lower ball joint can be replaced, if necessary, while the lower arm is out of the vehicle.
7. Installation is the reverse of removal.

NOTE: The front end suspension must be aligned upon completion of the installation.

Ball Joint

REMOVAL AND INSTALLATION

924, 924 Turbo, 944

1. Remove the lower control arm.
2. Drill out the three rivets retaining the ball joint to the control arm.
3. Install the replacement ball joint using the bolts and nuts supplied in the kit.
4. Reinstall the control arm and align the wheels.

928

The upper ball joint is replaced as a unit with the upper arm assembly. Refer to the Strut Removal and Installation Section.

The lower ball joint may be replaced by

removing the nut from the ball joint stud and pressing the stud from the spindle. The alignment eccentric bolts are removable and the ball joint can be removed from the lower arm assembly.

NOTE: The front suspension must be realigned after the suspension work is done.

Front Wheel Bearings

ADJUSTMENT

The front wheel bearings are correctly adjusted when the thrust washer can be moved slightly sideways under light pressure from a screwdriver, but no bearing play is evident when the wheel hub is shaken axially.

1. Remove the wheels.
2. Pry the hub cap off with a screwdriver and perform the check as described above. Don't press the screwdriver against the hub.
3. If the bearings require an adjustment, loosen the Allen screw and turn the clamp nut. Proper adjustment is achieved when the flat washer can just be moved by finger pressure on a screwdriver.
4. Tighten the clamp nut Allen screw to 11 ft. lbs. without altering the adjusted position of the clamp nut.

Front End Alignment

CAMBER ADJUSTMENT

924, 924 Turbo, 944

Camber is adjusted at the upper strut-to-steering knuckle retaining bolt.

928

Camber is adjusted by turning the cam bolts on the inner arm bushings.

Camber is adjusted at the upper strut eccentric on the 924, 924 Turbo, and 944

CASTER ADJUSTMENT

Caster is adjusted by loosening the two control arms to crossmember bolts and moving the control arm laterally.

Front suspension caster (e) and camber (d) adjustment eccentrics of the 928

Caster is adjusted at the lower control arm mounting on the 924, 924 Turbo, and 944

TOE-IN ADJUSTMENT

924, 924 Turbo, 944

Toe-in is set by loosening the locknuts on the tie rod ends and turning them in or out as necessary.

928

Toe-in adjustments are made by turning cam bolts, located at the front of the rear control arms.

STEERING

Steering Wheel

REMOVAL AND INSTALLATION

1. Disconnect the negative battery cable.
2. Remove horn pad and straighten the front wheels.
3. If necessary, disconnect the horn wiring. Matchmark the steering wheel to the steering shaft.
4. Remove retaining nut and washer.
5. Using a steering wheel puller, remove the wheel.

— CAUTION —
Do NOT strike the steering wheel!

6. Installation is the reverse of above. Make sure the wheels are straight ahead and

Tie-rod ends are adjustable for toe (924 shown)

steering wheel is centered. Torque steering wheel nut to 33 ft. lbs.

Turn Signal Switch

REMOVAL AND INSTALLATION

1. Disconnect the negative battery cable.
2. Remove steering wheel.
3. Disconnect electrical connector at switch.
4. Remove four screws holding switch.
5. To install, reverse the above.

Ignition Lock and Switch

REMOVAL AND INSTALLATION

1. Disconnect the negative battery cable.
2. Remove steering wheel.
3. Drill out casing tube shear bolts, disconnect electrical connectors, and pull column and casing out of car.
4. Remove the casing from steering column.
5. Remove pinch bolt holding switch housing to column.
6. Remove retaining screw and pull ignition switch from rear of casing.
7. Depress lock cylinder retainer with an ice pick or similar tool and remove lock cylinder.
8. Installation is the reverse of removal.

Make sure the wheels are straight ahead and steering wheel is centered when installing. Torque steering wheel nut to 33 ft. lbs. Torque shear bolts to 23 ft. lbs.

Steering Gear

REMOVAL AND INSTALLATION

1. Remove bolt connecting gear box to steering column driveshaft.

1. Steering rack
2. Steering shaft attachment
3. Boot
4. Lock
5. Tie-rod attachment
6. Tie-rod
7. Tie-rod end

Steering rack of the 924, 924 Turbo, and 944

2. Press out tie rod ends.
3. Remove steering gear and tie rods from car.
4. Remove tie rods from steering gear.
5. To install, reverse the above. Center steering gear with Porsche special tool 9116 or its equivalent. Be sure that both tie rod lengths are equal (68–68.5 mm). Tighten tie rod counter nuts to 29 ft. lbs. and gear box to driveshaft bolt to 23 ft. lbs.

Steering column and steering gear assembly—model 928

ADJUSTMENT

1. Tighten adjusting screw (on front of gear box) until it just touches the washer.
2. Hold adjusting screw tightly and tighten locknut.

Tie-Rod End

REPLACEMENT

1. Loosen the jam nut which connects the tie-rod end to the knuckle. Mark the tie-rod position on the threads of the rod.
2. Using a ball joint separator, remove the tie-rod end from the knuckle, counting how many complete turns it takes to remove it.
3. Install a new tie-rod end in reverse order of removal. Install the new tie-rod end the same number of turns as counted in step 2. Have the wheel alignment checked as soon as possible.

BRAKES

All 924 models including the Turbo use front disc brakes and rear drum brakes (European models have four-wheel discs). The 928 and the 944 both use disc brakes all around.

A vacuum brake booster is used on all models to decrease brake pedal apply effort. The hydraulic system of all models is of the split/diagonal design, which allows one front brake and one rear brake (opposite sides) to stop the car in the event of hydraulic failure in the other half of the system.

The cable-operated parking brake acts on the rear drum brakes, expanding the brake shoes against the drums (924 & 924 Turbo), or expanding small brake shoes within drums cut into the rear brake discs (928 & 944).

For all brake system repair and service procedures not detailed below, please refer to "Brakes" in the Unit Repair section.

ADJUSTMENT

The front disc brakes require no adjustment, as disc brakes automatically adjust themselves to compensate for pad wear. The rear drum brakes must be periodically adjusted, or whenever free travel is one third or more of the total pedal travel.

1. Raise the rear of the car.

Dual hydraulic circuit

Split/diagonal hydraulic brake system. If half of the hydraulic circuit fails, one front and one rear brake will remain operational to stop the vehicle

2. Block the front wheels and release the parking brake. Step on the brake pedal hard to center the linings.

3. Remove the rubber plugs from the rear of the backing plate on each wheel.

4. Insert a brake adjusting tool or wide-blade screwdriver and turn the adjuster wheel until the brakes drag as you turn the tire/wheel.

5. Turn the adjuster in the opposite direction until you just pass the point of drag.

6. Repeat on the other wheel.

7. Lower the car and road-test. Readjust, if necessary.

Master Cylinder

REMOVAL AND INSTALLATION

1. To prevent brake fluid from spilling out and damaging the paint, place a protective cover over the fender.

2. Disconnect the plug and brake lines.

3. Disconnect the electrical plug from the sending unit for the brake failure switch.

4. Remove the two master cylinder mounting nuts.

5. Lift the master cylinder and reservoir out of the engine compartment being careful not to spill any fluid on the fender. Empty out and discard the brake fluid.

———— **CAUTION** ————
Do not depress the brake pedal while the master cylinder is removed.

6. Position the master cylinder and reservoir assembly onto the studs for the booster and install the washers and nuts. Tighten the nuts to no more than 10 ft. lbs.

7. Remove the plugs and connect the brake lines.

8. Bleed the entire brake system as explained further on in this chapter.

Parking Brake

ADJUSTMENT

924, 924 Turbo

1. Raise the rear wheels and support on stands. Adjust the brakes.

2. Remove the parking brake handle boot.

3. Pull the lever up two teeth.

4. Tighten the parking brake adjusting nut until both wheels can just barely be turned by hand.

928, 944

1. Raise the vehicle and remove the rear wheels.

2. Release the parking brake lever and move the disc brake pads so that the rotor can be easily moved.

3. Loosen the cable adjusting nuts so that no tension exists on the cable.

4. Insert a screwdriver through the hole in the brake rotor and turn the brake adjuster until the rotor cannot be moved.

5. Turn the adjuster in the opposite direction just until the rotor is free to rotate.

6. Pull the brake lever up two notches and adjust the cable so that the rotors can just be turned.

NOTE: At four notches of the lever, the rotors should be tight and be unable to turn.

7. Release the handbrake and make sure the rotors turn freely. Install the wheels and lower the vehicle.

CHASSIS ELECTRICAL

Heater Assembly

REMOVAL AND INSTALLATION

The heater core and blower are contained in the heater assembly which is removed and disassembled to service either component. The heater assembly is located under the center of the instrument panel.

1. Disconnect the battery ground cable.

2. Drain the cooling system.

3. Disconnect the two hoses from the heater core connections at the firewall.

4. Unplug the heater electrical connector.

5. Detach the center console and the right side of the instrument panel.

6. Remove the heater control knobs from the instrument panel.

7. Remove the two retaining screws and remove the controls from the instrument panel.

8. Disconnect the heater control cables.

9. Using a screwdriver, pry the retaining clip off the heater housing. Detach the left and right hoses.

10. Remove the heater-to-instrument panel mounting screws and lower the heater.

11. Pull out the two pins and remove the heater top cover. Pry the retaining clips off and separate the two heater halves.

12. Remove the heater core and/or blower.

13. Installation is the reverse of removal. Refill the cooling system. See ''Radiator Removal and Installation.''

Radio

REMOVAL AND INSTALLATION

NOTE: Many radios are dealer installed options, therefore this procedure may differ from unit to unit. The following is a general removal and installation procedure.

1. Disconnect the battery ground cable.

2. Remove the radio knobs.

3. Release the radio bezel by pressing

924 and 924 Turbo rear drum brakes—remove the rubber plugs (arrows) in order to gain access to the brake adjusters

the springs in the shaft openings outward to their stops.

4. Remove the bezel.

5. Remove the nuts on the shafts.

6. Loosen the brackets and pull the radio out.

7. Disconnect the fuse, ground, speaker, and antenna wires. Remove the radio.

8. Installation is performed in the reverse of the previous steps.

Windshield Wiper Motor

REMOVAL AND INSTALLATION

The windshield wiper motor is located on the driver's side of the cowl under a plastic cover.

1. Remove the cover.

2. Disconnect the battery ground cable.

3. Unscrew the wiper linkage, disconnect the electrical plugs, unscrew the motor, remove the mounting screw on the frame, lift frame slightly, and remove motor.

4. Installation is the reverse of removal. Note the following during installation:

a. Connect the plug and turn on the ignition before fastening the linkage.

b. Move the wiper arms to the off position and mount the linkage.

Instrument Cluster

REMOVAL AND INSTALLATION

928

1. Disconnect the negative battery cable.

2. Remove the steering wheel.

3. Remove the steering column switch.

4. Remove the instrument cover mounting screws.

5. Remove the rear window wiper and defogger switch.

6. Disconnect the two 12-pin multiplugs at the instrument cluster.

7. Lift the instrument cluster carefully and tilt it to the rear. Unscrew the mounting bolt and remove the instrument cluster.

Center Console Instruments

REMOVAL AND INSTALLATION

924, 924 Turbo, 944

1. Disconnect the negative battery cable.

2. Remove the two screws at the top of the instrument panel and pull out the panel while lifting the bottom slightly.

3. Remove the knurled knobs and brackets to remove individual instruments. Disconnect wiring.

Installation is the reverse of removal.

Speedometer, Tachometer, Combination Meter

REMOVAL AND INSTALLATION

924, 924 Turbo, 944

1. Disconnect the negative battery cable.

2. The individual instruments are pressed out of the instrument panel toward the driver's seat from behind the instrument panel. Remove the tachometer and combination meter first.

1. Defroster vents
2. Central vents
3. Side vents
4. Lower vents
5. Cover

Heater duct layout of the 924, 924 Turbo, and 944

3. To remove the speedometer, it is better to remove the other two instruments first, then press out the speedometer. It may be necessary to insert an appropriate tool (angled flat iron bar, large socket wrench, etc.) behind the speedometer housing to press out the speedometer.

4. Press in the instruments to install. Do not apply force to the instrument glass when installing.

Fuse and Relay Panel Location

The fuse panel on the 924, 924 Turbo, and 944 is located underneath the dashboard on the driver's side of the vehicle. The relays are arranged above the fuses. On some models, an additional line of fuses is located above the main fuse/relay panel.

The fuse panel on the 928 is located beneath a hinged wooden panel at the front of the passenger's floor area. Pull back the carpet to expose the cover. The relays are arranged below the fuse line.

On all models, fuse amperage ratings and applications are given in the owner's manual.

1. Air distributor
2. Air distributor
3. Gasket
4. Right air guide
5. Left air guide
6. Cover
7. Heat exchanger
8. Bearing clip
9. Clip
10. Clip
11. Right housing half
12. Blower
13. Control flap
14. Shut-off flap
15. Shut-off flap lever
16. Shut-off flap shaft
17. Left housing half

Heater unit of the 924, 924 Turbo, and 944

Renault

SERIAL NUMBER IDENTIFICATION

Engine Number and Identification

LE CAR

The engine registration plate is located at the rear of the engine block above the clutch housing. The engine type number of 1979 and earlier models is 810-28; the engine number for 1980 and later models is 847-25. Both engines are of the same basic design, though the bore, stroke, compression and camshaft profiles differ between engines.

18i AND FUEGO

The engine plate is located above the starter unit, and fastened to the engine block.

Vehicle Identification Plate

1979 AND EARLIER LE CAR—MODEL R1228

These vehicles use two identification plates: one diamond shaped and one oval shaped, both of which are located in the engine compartment.

1980 AND LATER LE CAR—MODEL R1229

These vehicles use one rectangular plate located on the fender apron.

18i—MODELS R1348 & R1358 AND FUEGO

A vehicle identification plate is found on the upper left corner of the instrument panel visible through the windshield. A VIN number plate is found on the driver's door center pillar, and an oval manufacturer's plate is found on the right front inner fender liner.

GORDINI   LE CAR

Diamond shaped identification plate—typical of Le Car

1. Engine type number
2. Engine fabrication number

Engine identification plate—typical of 18i and Fuego

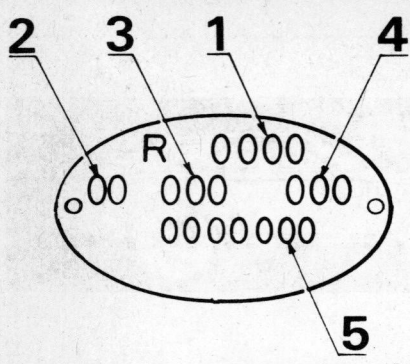

1. The model number of the vehicle
2. The first number indicates manual or automatic transmission the second number indicates any special feature (basic appearance)
3. Basic equipment, according to country (see table)
4. Additional optional factory equipment (sunroof, tinted glass, etc.)
5. The fabrication number

Oval Identification plate—typical of 18i and Fuego

Location of transaxle identification plate— typical of 18i and Fuego

10. The model number
11. The serial number
12. The maximum allowable load for the vehicle
13. The maximum allowable load for the front and rear axles
14. The date of manufacture (month-year)
15. The vehicle class

Rectangular identification plate—typical of 18i and Fuego

LE CAR

A. Vehicle type
B. Equipment number
C. Manufacturing number
D. Version number

Oval identification plate—typical of Le Car

GENERAL ENGINE SPECIFICATIONS

Year	Model	Engine Displacement (cu. in.)	Horsepower @ rpm (SAE)	Torque @ rpm (ft. lbs.)	Bore × Stroke (inches)	Firing Order
'76–'79	Le Car	78.7	60@6000	70@3500	2.874 × 3.031	1-3-4-2
'80–'83	Le Car	85.2	N/A	N/A	2.992 × 3.031	1-3-4-2
'81–'83	18i	100.5	82@5500	86@2500	3.110 × 3.307	1-3-4-2
'82–'83	Fuego	97.6①	82@5500②	86@2500③	3.110 × 3.307④	1-3-4-2

① W/Turbo 95.5 cu. in.
② W/Turbo 107@5500
③ W/Turbo 120@2500
④ W/Turbo 3.035 × 3.307
N/A—Not available

TUNE-UP SPECIFICATIONS

Year	Model	Engine Displacement (cu. in.)	Spark Plugs Type①	Gap (in.)	Distributor Point Dwell (deg)	Ignition Timing ⑤	Idle Speed (rpm)	Valve Clearance (cold) (in.) Intake	Exhaust
'76–'79	Le Car	78.7	W7B②	.025–.028	57③	TDC	850	.006	.008
'80–'83	Le Car	85.2	WR9DS	.025–.028	Electronic	3B ± 2°	750	.006	.008
'81–'83	18i	100.5	WR7DS	.022–.026	Electronic	10B	⑥	.008	.010
'82–'83	Fuego	97.6	—	.026	Electronic	10B	800④	.008	.010

NOTE: The underhood sticker often reflects tune-up specification changes made in production. Sticker figures must be used if they disagree with those in this chart.

① Listings for spark plugs are Bosch, although no brand name is recommended in particular.
② 1977–79 Federal uses W8B spark plug.
③ Some 1979 models may be equipped with electronic ignition.
④ Auto trans.—650 rpm in drive
⑤ Check the timing with the vacuum advance disconnected.
⑥ Manual trans.—850 rpm, Auto. trans.— 650 rpm in "Drive"

FIRING ORDERS

Spark plug wiring schematic—18i and Fuego

Spark plug wiring schematic—Le Car

CAPACITIES

Year	Model	Engine Displacement (cu. in.)	Crankcase With Filter (qts.)	Transmission (pts.)		Gasoline Tank (gals.)	Cooling System (qts.)
				Manual	Automatic		
'76–'83	Le Car	All	3.5	4.0	6.6	10.0	6.5
'81–'83	18i	100.5	4.5	4.0①	②	14.0③	8.0
'82–'83	Fuego	97.6	4.25	4.2	10.5	14.8	6.2

①Both the four and five-speed transmissions have the same capacity.
②Oil change—2⅔quarts
Converter—2 quarts
Transmission total (excluding converter)—
5¼quarts
③15 gallon—station wagon

CRANKSHAFT AND CONNECTING ROD SPECIFICATIONS

(All measurements in inches)

Year	Model	Engine Displacement (cu. in.)	Crankshaft			Connecting Rod		
			Main brg. Journal dia.	Main brg. Oil clearance	Shaft End-Play	Journal Diameter	Oil Clearance	Side Clear
'76–'79	Le Car	78.7	2.157	0.0004–0.0014	0.002–0.009	1.731	0.0010–0.0026	0.012–0.023
'80–'83	Le Car	85.2	2.158	0.0004–0.0014	0.002–0.009	1.732	0.0010–0.0026	0.012–0.023
'81–'83	18i	100.5	2.158	0.0006–0.0015	0.002–0.009	1.890	N/A	0.012–0.022
'82–'83	Fuego	97.6	N/A	N/A	N/A	N/A	N/A	N/A

N/A Not available at time of publication

VALVE SPECIFICATIONS

Year	Model	Engine Displacement (cu. in.)	Seat Angle (deg)	Face Angle (deg)	Stem to Guide Clearance (in.)		Stem Diameter(in.)	
					Intake	Exhaust	Intake	Exhaust
'76–'79	Le Car	78.5	45	45	0.006	0.006	0.276	0.276
'80–'83	Le Car	85.2	45	45	0.006	0.006	0.276	0.276
'81–'83	18i	100.5	45	45	0.0008	0.0008	0.315	0.315
'82–'83	Fuego	97.6	45	45	0.0008	0.0008	0.315	0.315

TORQUE SPECIFICATIONS

(All readings in ft. lbs.)

Year	Model	Engine Displacement (cu. in.)	Cylinder Head Bolts	Rod Bearing Bolts	Main Bearing Bolts	Crankshaft Pulley Bolt	Flywheel to Crankshaft Bolts	Manifold Intake	Manifold Exhaust
'76–'79	Le Car	78.7	40	35	50	N/A	40	10	10
'80–'83	Le Car	85.2	45	35	50	N/A	40	10	10
'81–'83	18i	100.5	55–60	30	45	N/A	35	25	25
'82–'83	Fuego	97.6	N/A	N/A	N/A	N/A	N/A	N/A	N/A

N/A Not available at time of publication

TORQUE SEQUENCES

Cylinder head bolt torque sequence—18i and Fuego

Cylinder head bolt torque sequence—Le Car

ALTERNATOR AND REGULATOR SPECIFICATIONS

Alternator Part No.	Alternator Output (amps.)	Regulator Part No.	Regulator Volts
A13R154	50①	AYB218	13.4–14.4
A13R243	50①	Integral	13.5–15.0

① Air conditioning—60 amp

BATTERY AND STARTER SPECIFICATIONS

(12 volt negative ground)

Starter Part No.	Battery Amps	Starter Lock Test Amps	Starter Lock Test Volt	Starter Lock Test Torque (ft. lbs.)	Min. Brush Length (in.)
D8E121	45	400	N/A	9	5/16
D10E54	45	400	N/A	13	N/A

N/A Not available

BRAKES SPECIFICATIONS

Year	Model	Lug Nut Torque (ft. lbs.)	Master Cylinder Bore	Brake Disc		Brake Drum			Minimum Lining Thickness	
				Minimum Thickness	Maximum Run-Out	Diameter	Max. Machine O/S	Max. Wear Limit	Front	Rear
'76–'83	Le Car	40–45	0.811	0.354	0.008	7.096	①	7.136	.280	N/A
'81–'83	18i	45–60	0.748	0.354	0.007	8.996	①	9.035	.276	N/A

① The manufacturer does not recommend machining of the brake drums
N/A Not available

WHEEL ALIGNMENT SPECIFICATIONS

Year	Model	Caster		Camber		Toe Setting (inches)
		Range (deg)	Pref. Setting (deg)	Range (deg)	Pref. Setting (deg)	
'76–'77	Le Car	+12 to +13	+12	—	+1°30′	+0.047″ to +.188″
'78–'79 ③	Le Car	+12 to +13	+12	0 to 1	½	+0.093″ to +.188″
'79–'83 ③	Le Car	—	+6	—	+1°30′	−³⁄₆₃″ to −³⁄₁₆″
'81–'83	18i	②	②	0 ± 30′	0	0 to +¹⁄₁₆″
'82–'83	Fuego	Not available at time of publication				

①
② W/power steering: +1°30′ to +3°
w/manual steering: 0°30′ to +2°
③ Some early 1979 models may be equipped with the 12° caster suspension. The 6° caster suspension (late 1979) is identified by steering arms with adjustment provisions at the ball socket end of the steering arm. See the text for further information.

TUNE-UP

The Renault Le Car used a conventional point/condenser ignition system in vehicles made prior to September 1979, at which point the current transistorized breakerless ignition system began production. The 18i and Fuego also use electronic ignition.

The electronic (transisotrized breakerless) ignition uses an "impulse generator" which consist of a rotating trigger plate with one arm per cylinder, magnetic impulse senders and an impulse sender coil. Two impulse senders are used, the main impulse sender and the secondary impulse sender. At times when the engine oil temperature is below 60°F (15°C), an oil temperature switch triggers a relay which activates the secondary impulse sender, the secondary impulse sender then advances the spark 3° (6° flywheel). Dwell in the electronic ignition distributor cannot be adjusted, although the trigger plate gap and the ignition timing are adjustable.

Spark Plugs

When replacing spark plugs, mark or tag the ignition cables to avoid placing them on the wrong spark plug during reassembly. When replacing the spark plug cables, remove and replace one at a time to avoid cross-firing when the engine is started.

Breaker Points and Condenser

REMOVAL AND INSTALLATION

Le Car

1. Release the two spring steel clamps which retain the distributor cap and move the cap aside (with the plug wires connected).
2. Remove the rotor and disconnect the wiring at the point set.
3. Loosen the condenser bracket mounting screw and remove the condenser.
4. Remove the point set. Installation is the reverse of the removal procedure. Adjust the dwell after the new points have been installed.

Dwell Angle—Point Type Ignition

ADJUSTMENT

1. Connect a dwell meter to the engine as per the manufacturer's instructions, start the engine, and read the dwell meter.
2. Set the dwell to specifications: On Le Car models, turn off the engine and manually move the contact point set.

Electronic Ignition

ADJUSTMENTS

Although it is possible to adjust certain components of the distributor, these ad-

1. Vacuum advance capsule
2. Trigger plate
3. Adjustment screws for the secondary impulse sender-to-trigger plate clearance
4. Main impulse sender
5. Secondary impulse sender
6. Adjustment screws for the main impulse sender-to-trigger plate clearance

Electronic distributor ignition parts identification

A. Top dead center
B. 4 degrees advanced

Ignition timing—Le Car

justments are not normally required at each tune-up.

Trigger Plate Gap

1. Loosen the impulse sender retaining screws slightly.

2. Measure the distance between an impulse sender stud and one of the arms of the trigger plate. The gap must be 0.012–0.24 in. (0.3–0.6 mm).

3. Move the impulse sender(s) as required and tighten the retaining screws. Check the gap for all four arms of the trigger wheel and adjust as necessary.

NOTE: If the trigger wheel gap for certain arms of the trigger wheel cannot be correctly adjusted, replace the distributor.

Secondary Impulse Sender Timing

NOTE: This adjustment must be performed after every trigger plate gap adjustment.

1. Loosen the screws (A) as illustrated in the accompanying diagram.

2. Align one arm of the trigger plate with the primary impulse sender stud (B).

3. Move the secondary impulse sender so that the center of the secondary impulse sender stud (C) is located opposite the edge of the trigger plate arm which is aligned with the primary impulse sender stud.

4. Tighten the screws which were loosened in Step 1.

A. Screws to be loosened for adjustment of the secondary impulse sender
B. Primary impulse sender stud
C. Secondary impulse sender stud

Secondary impulse sender timing adjustment

Ignition Timing

ADJUSTMENT

Le Car

NOTE: The dwell should be correctly adjusted before setting the ignition timing, if required.

1. Using the proper distributor wrench, loosen the distributor clamp.

2. Connect a timing light to the number one spark plug wire and the battery.

3. Disconnect the vacuum line to the distributor vacuum advance.

4. Start the engine and allow the engine to idle.

5. Rotate the distributor to align the clutch housing mark with the timing mark on the flywheel.

6. Tighten the distributor hold-down clamp and recheck the timing setting.

Identification of initial timing—typical

Timing location when equipped with manual transmission—18i and Fuego

18i and Fuego

NOTE: The timing initial advance must be adjusted at an idle speed of 800 rpm. The identification clip attached to the input wire of the ignition coil shows the ignition timing value that is to be used (may be located on spark plug wire for later engines).

1. Loosen the distributor clamp using a bent leverage wrench.

2. Connect a timing light to No. 1 spark plug wire, start the engine and run at 800 rpm.

3. The timing is at top dead center when; Automatic transmission: The hole in the converter lines up with the 0 mark on the graduated plate of the converter housing. Manual transmission: The slot in the flywheel lines up with the 0 mark on the bell housing graduated section of the flywheel housing.

4. Adjust the ignition initial timing to specifications. Tighten the distributor clamp and remove the timing light.

Valve Clearance

ADJUSTMENT

NOTE: Valve adjustment should be done through manual maintenance or when the cylinder head bolts are retorqued.

Exh. valve fully open on cyl. no.	Adj. int. valve on cyl. no.	Adj. exh. valve on cyl. no.
1	3	4
3	4	2
4	2	1
2	1	3

Valve adjustment sequence—Le Car

1. Rotate the engine in correct rotation until the exhaust valve for the No. 1 cylinder is fully open.

2. Adjust the rocker arms of the intake valve for the No. 3 cylinder and the exhaust valve for the No. 4 four cylinder.

3. Rotate the engine in correct rotation until the No. 3 cylinder exhaust valve is fully open. Adjust the rocker arms of the intake valve for No. 4 cylinder and the exhaust valve for the No. 2 cylinder.

4. Rotate the engine in correct rotation until the No. 4 cylinder exhaust valve is fully open. Adjust the rocker arms of the intake valve for the No. 2 cylinder and the exhaust valve for the No. 1 cylinder.

5. Rotate the engine in correct rotation until the No. 2 cylinder exhaust valve is fully open. Adjust the rocker arms of the

Valve arrangement—Le Car

DISTRIBUTOR SIDE OF ENGINE
Valve arrangement—18i

intake valve for the No. 1 cylinder and the exhaust valve for the No. 3 cylinder.

6. Rotate the engine in the correct rotation, and recheck the rocker arm adjustments for proper specification clearances.

VALVE ADJUSTING SEQUENCE—18i AND FUEGO

Valve Position	Cylinder Number
Exhaust valve fully open on	
Adjust exhaust valve on	
Intake valve fully open on	
Adjust intake valve on	

Carburetor

IDLE SPEED AND MIXTURE ADJUSTMENT

NOTE: 1977 California models and all 1978–81 models must be adjusted with the use of a CO meter to obtain the cor-

Timing location when equipped with automatic transmission—18i and Fuego

rect emissions reading and idle speed. It is advised that these procedures be performed only by a qualified service person. Previous models may be adjusted by the lean drop method.

Without a CO Meter (1977 and Earlier Except California)

1. Clamp off the air injection hose between the diverter valve and the engine, using the appropriate special tool.
2. Turn the throttle plate screw so that the engine speed is 775 rpm.
3. Turn the idle mixture screw to obtain the highest possible idle speed.
4. Lower the engine speed 20–25 rpm by turning the idle mixture screw clockwise. Remove the air injection hose block-off clamp and check the idle speed which should be 850 ± 50 rpm. If the idle speed is incorrect, turn the throttle plate screw to adjust.

Carburetor adjustment screws —Le Car

With a CO Meter

1. Clamp off the air injection hose between the diverter valve and the engine using the appropriate special tool.
2. Turn the throttle plate screw so that the engine speed is 775 rpm.
3. Turn the idle mixture screw to obtain the following readings:

1976–79   2.5% + .5% − 2%

1980 Federal   2.0% + .5% − 2%

4. Remove the air injection hose block-off clamp and recheck the idle speed. Idle speeds should read as follows:

Year	RPM
1976	800 ± 50
1977	850 ± 50
1978	800 ± 50
1979	850 ± 50
1980	750 ± 50
1981 and Later	850 ± 50 MT
	650 ± 50 AT

5. Repeat Steps 2–4 if necessary.

WITH A VACUUM GAUGE

1. Tee a vacuum gauge into the line which runs from the vacuum solenoid regulator to the carburetor. The amount of vacuum applied to the carburetor actuators will be measured.
2. Adjust the fuel metering screw to obtain an idle speed of 750 ± 50 rpm.
3. Adjust the mixture screw to obtain a vacuum reading of 1.5 ± 1.2 Hg.
4. Readjust the fuel metering screw to correct the idle speed.

NOTE: To obtain the correct idle speed, only the fuel metering screw should be adjusted.

Fuel Injection

IDLE SPEED AND MIXTURE ADJUSTMENT

With a CO Meter

1. Bring the engine to normal operating temperature.
2. Clamp off the air injection hose between the diverter valve and the engine using the appropriate special tool.
3. Rotate the throttle plate housing screw as necessary to obtain an idle speed of 800 rpm.
4. Turn the airflow meter bypass screw until a CO meter reading of 2 ± 1% is obtained.
5. Remove the air injection hose block-off clamp and readjust the idle speed to specifications with screw.

Without a CO Meter

1. Bring the engine to normal operating temperature.
2. Clamp off the air injection hose between the diverter valve and the engine using the appropriate special tool.
3. Turn the flowmeter bypass screw completely inward.
4. Turn the throttle housing screw as necessary to obtain an idle speed of 850 rpm.
5. Turn the flowmeter bypass screw outward slowly to lower the idle speed to 800 rpm.
6. Remove the air injection hose block-off clamp and set the idle speed to specifications with the throttle housing screw.

ENGINE ELECTRICAL

Distributor

REMOVAL AND INSTALLATION

Le Car

1. Rotate the engine in order to position the No. 1 cylinder at top dead center. Remove the distributor cap.

1. Distributor cap	7. Vacuum advance unit
2. Contact	8. Condenser
3. Rotor	9. Mainshaft
4. Dust cover	10. Cap retaining clip
5. Point set	11. Body
6. Breaker plate	12. Drive flange

Exploded view of the point type distributor

2. Mark the relationship between the distributor body and the engine, and the firing point of the rotor and the distributor body (point one).

3. Remove the hold-down clamp and remove the distributor. Mark the position of the rotor on the distributor body after removal (point two).

4. Installation is the reverse of the removal procedure. Do not turn the engine while the distributor is removed. Position the rotor at the mark made during Step 3 (point two). The distributor drive (camshaft) and driven gears are helical cut, causing the rotor to rotate towards the removal marking (point one) during installation.

5. Adjust the ignition timing.

18i and Fuego

1. Remove distributor cap and wire assembly.

2. Rotate the engine until the No. 1 cylinder is in its firing position, with the rotor end tab pointing to the No. 1 spark plug wire terminal in the distributor cap.

3. The hole in the converter should line up with the "O" mark on the graduated plate of the converter housing, if equipped with an automatic transmission, or if equipped with a standard transmission, the slot in the flywheel should line up with the "O" mark on the bell housing graduated section.

4. With the flywheel or converter marks lined up and the distributor rotor end tab pointing towards the No. 1 spark plug wire terminal in the distributor cap, the firing position of No. 1 cylinder is verified.

5. Remove the distributor hold down clamp, the vacuum hose to the vacuum ad-

Exploded view of alternator—18i and Fuego

vance and the electrical wire connectors. Remove the distributor from the engine.

6. Observe the position of the off-set lug at the bottom of the distributor shaft and the location of the matching lug in the distributor drive gear bore.

7. Do not rotate the engine crankshaft while the distributor is out of the engine.

8. The installation of the distributor is the reverse of the removal procedure. Be sure the distributor bore drive lug is positioned in the same place as it was when the distributor was removed.

9. Connect the electrical and vacuum connections and reinstall the distributor cap and wire assembly.

10. Time the distributor to the engine as required.

Alternator

REMOVAL AND INSTALLATION

1. Disconnect the negative battery cable at the battery.

2. Mark and disconnect the alternator wiring.

3. Remove the belt tension adjusting bolt and the drive belt.

4. Remove the remaining alternator attaching bolt and remove the alternator. Installation is the reverse of the removal procedure. Adjust the belt to a maximum of ½" total deflection.

1. Front housing
2. Front bearing
3. Rotor
4. Stator
5. Rear bearing
6. Rear housing
7. Diode carrier
8. Shield
9. Pulley
10. Fan
11. Front bearing retainer
12. Brush holder

Exploded view of alternator—Le Car

Regulator

REMOVAL AND INSTALLATION

NOTE: 18i and Fuego regulators are part of the alternator assembly. The alternators must be disassembled for regulator removal.

The regulator is mounted on the fender panel and is retained by two screws. Disconnect the wiring connectors and remove the retaining screws to exchange regulator. Reverse the removal procedure to install the regulator.

Starter

REMOVAL AND INSTALLATION

Le Car

1. Remove the air cleaner assembly.
2. Drain the cooling system, disconnect the hoses and linkage.
3. Disconnect the negative battery cable.
4. Remove the flange coupling at the exhaust manifold and remove the manifold.
5. Disconnect the positive battery cable at the starter.

Exploded view of starter—Le Car

Exploded view of starter—Paris Rhone type D10E79—18i and Fuego (USA)

Exploded view of starter—Paris Rhone type D10E63—18i and Fuego (Canada)

6. Disconnect the starter solenoid feed line.
7. Remove the starter attaching bolts and remove the starter. Installation is the reverse of the removal procedure.

18i and Fuego

1. Disconnect the negative battery cable.
2. Disconnect the positive battery cable at the starter.
3. Disconnect the ignition switch-to-solenoid feed wire.
4. Remove the starter heat shield fasteners.
5. Remove the starter retaining bolts, slide the starter towards the rear, then sideways and remove the starter. Installation is the reverse of the removal procedure.

STARTER DRIVE

Removal and Installation

1. To replace the starter drive unit, the starter must be completely disassembled.
2. Remove the circlip from the end of the armature shaft. Remove the stopcollar and starter drive from the shaft.
3. To install the starter drive, slide the drive and stopcollar in place on the armature shaft and install the shaft circlip.
4. Reassemble the starter components.

ENGINE MECHANICAL

Engine

REMOVAL AND INSTALLATION

NOTE: The engine/transmission assembly can be removed as a unit, if so desired on all models.

Le Car

1. Disconnect and remove the battery.
2. Drain the cooling system.
3. Drain the lubricating fluids from both the engine and the transaxle.
4. Remove the following items:
   a. Grille
   b. Hood
   c. Inner fender support braces (2)
5. Disconnect all wiring, water and vacuum hoses, and cables. Mark for identification during reconnection.
6. Loosen the windshield washer bottle and place it on its side.
7. Remove the transaxle cover.
8. Remove the air filter support rod.

9. Disconnect the exhaust pipe at the manifold flange.

10. Remove the radiator assembly.

11. Remove the flex coupling bolts from the steering shaft.

12. Remove the front wheels and the brake calipers—do not disconnect the brake lines.

13. Disconnect the steering arms at the end of the rack.

14. Disconnect the upper ball joints and tilt the spindles outward.

15. Mark the steering box shims to identify the right and left sides, and remove the steering box.

16. Remove the air injection filter, pump, and pump bracket.

17. Remove the two top transaxle bolts and position a lifting hook (Renault tool #Mot. 498 or its equivalent) onto the transaxle. Install two 1⅜" long bolts in place of the transaxle bolts to secure the lifting tool to the transaxle.

NOTE: The tool securing bolts must be 1⅜" long to distribute the lifting stress over a sufficient number of threads.

18. Remove the engine mount bolts and the right side reinforcement bolts.

19. Remove the transmission shift rod support bolts.

20. Free the clutch cable from the clutch fork and push the sleeve retainer back from the support tab.

21. Attach a suitable engine hoist to the lifting tool.

22. Remove the front transaxle mount.

23. Push the transaxle side-to-side and free the driveshaft ends from the transaxle.

24. Remove the engine/transaxle assembly.

25. Installation is the reverse of the removal procedure. Take note of the following:

    a. Lightly lubricate the clutch shaft and driveshaft splines.

    b. When reinstalling the driveshafts, pay special attention so as not to damage the oil seal lips for the differential adjusting ring nut.

    c. Be sure to reinstall the rubber bushing between the flex coupling and the intermediate shaft flange.

    d. After the tie rod inner pins have been reinstalled, make sure that they are positioned horizontally (applicable to 1979 and earlier Le Car).

    e. Adjust the clutch, accelerator cable and the choke cable.

18i and Fuego

1. Disconnect the battery.

2. Remove the under pan from beneath the engine.

3. Drain the cooling system at the radiator and at the engine block.

4. Drain the engine oil from the crankcase.

5. Remove the radiator grille, the upper crossmember of the grille and the radiator along with the cooling fan.

6. If equipped with air conditioning, remove the cooling fans, disconnect the condenser from the radiator and place it on the bumper so that the freon will not have to be discharged.

7. Remove the battery, the starter, the exhaust heat shields, the catalytic converter and the air intake hose.

8. Remove the clutch cable and its brackets, if equipped with a clutch.

9. Remove the alternator assembly.

10. If equipped with power steering, remove the power steering pump and lines. Place it on the frame rails.

11. If equipped with air conditioning, remove the compressor and place it on the frame rail. Do not disconnect the system.

12. Disconnect the heater hoses, the vacuum hoses and emission control hoses. Mark their positions for easier installation.

13. Remove the accelerator cable and if equipped with speed control, remove the electrical leads and control cables.

14. If equipped with automatic transmission, remove the cable swivel and governor cable, using a special wrench.

15. Remove the fuel lines and use a special tool to pinch the fuel line to prevent leakage of fuel.

16. Remove the sending units from the cylinder head.

17. If equipped with automatic transmission:

    a. remove the heat shield

    b. the converter holding bolts.

18. Remove the upper transmission/engine bolts.

19. Remove the engine flywheel protective shield.

20. Remove the lower transmission/engine bolts and the side engine bolts.

21. Place a lifting tool on the engine and raise until the transmission touches the steering crossmember and secure the transmission in this position.

22. Pull the engine forward to disengage the clutch shaft or the converter centering and remove the engine from the vehicle through the top.

NOTE: On vehicles with automatic tramissions, be careful that the converter is not pulled from the transmission as the engine is removed. Install a converter retaining plate to the housing.

23. The installation is the reverse of the removal procedure.

24. For vehicles equipped with automatic transmissions:

    a. Lubricate the converter centering housing in the crankshaft.

    b. In order to line up the mark located on the converter with the distributor timing mark on the housing, the painted mark on the converter must face the part of the driving plate blade that has the sharp edges.

    c. The bolts that attach the driving plate to the converter must be replaced with new bolts.

    d. Connect and adjust the governor cable.

25. For vehicles equipped with a speed control:

    a. Connect the control cable.

26. For all vehicles:

    a. Adjust the accelerator cable travel distance.

    b. Adjust the belt tension.

    c. Fill and bleed the cooling system.

    d. Adjust the upper crossmember of the grille to allow the hood to close properly.

Cylinder Head

REMOVAL AND INSTALLATION

Le Car

1. Disconnect the battery cables at the battery.

2. Drain the cooling system.

3. Remove the air cleaner assembly.

4. Disconnect all wiring, water and vacuum hoses, and cables. Mark for identification during reconnection.

5. Remove the air injection pump drive belt.

6. Disconnect the exhaust pipe at the manifold.

7. Remove the valve cover.

8. Remove all of the cylinder head bolts except the bolt next to the distributor, which should be loosened slightly.

9. Tap lightly on the ends of the cylinder head with a soft-faced (preferably plastic) hammer to break the cylinder head loose from the block. Remove the remaining cylinder head bolt.

10. Mark and remove the pushrods. Remove the cylinder head.

NOTE: Turn the cylinder head on the block to break it loose from the cylinder liners (rotating motion) before lifting the head; if this is not done, the lower liner seals may break.

11. Installation is the reverse of the removal procedure.

NOTE: The cylinder liners must be securely retained to avoid breaking the cylinder liner-to-block seals.

Retention of the cylinder liners after head removal —typical

18i and Fuego

1. Disconnect the battery cables at the battery.

2. Drain the cooling system.

3. Remove the air cleaner assembly.

4. Remove the following items:
   a. Catalytic converter
   b. Alternator (w/drive belt)
   c. Water pump drive belt
   d. Valve cover
   e. Distributor
   f. Diagnostic socket
   g. Fuel lines (clamp to prevent leakage).

5. Disconnect the exhaust pipe at the manifold and remove the manifold.

6. Unscrew the rocker arm adjusting screws.

7. Mark and remove the pushrods.

8. Remove the six inner cylinder head bolts, while putting a rubber band or string around the four end bolts to clamp the rocker arm assemblies in place.

9. Tap lightly on the ends of the cylinder head with a soft-faced (preferably plastic) hammer to break the cylinder head loose from the block.

10. Remove the cylinder head.

NOTE: Turn the cylinder head on the block to break it loose from the cylinder liners (rotating motion) before lifting the head; if this is not done, the lower liner seals may break.

11. Installation is the reverse of the removal procedure.

NOTE: The cylinder liners must be securely retained to avoid breaking the cylinder liner-to-block seals.

1. Camshaft pulley	10. Cylinder liner	19. Crankshaft thrust bearings
2. Camshaft	11. Cylinder liner-to-block seal	20. Crankshaft
3. Camshaft flange	12. Camshaft oil seal	21. Crankshaft key
4. Timing chain	13. Camshaft bearing	22. Crankshaft sprocket
5. Camshaft sprocket	14. Connecting rod bearing	23. Pilot bearing
6. Timing chain tensioner	15. Connecting rod	24. Main bearings
7. Timing cover	16. Crankshaft oil seal	25. Main caps
8. Piston ring set	17. Cylinder block	26. Oil pump
9. Piston	18. Flywheel	27. Oil pan

Exploded view of cylinder block and component parts—Le Car

Holding the four cylinder head bolts with a rubber band

Valve Guides

REMOVAL AND INSTALLATION

The valve guides are replaceable and are available in three sizes (original and two oversizes). The outside diameter of the guides are 0.004 inch larger than the bore in the cylinder head, in order to remain tight during normal engine operations.

The valve guides are driven from the cylinder head with special driving tools. Any one unfamiliar with valve guide installation procedures should not attempt the operation. Remove the guides from the valve seat side to the top of the cylinder head. The installation is from the seat to the top of the cylinder head.

--- CAUTION ---

Verify the distance from the top of the valve seat to the end of the guide before removal. Distance is 31 mm for the intake and 40 mm for the exhaust guides.

Exploded view of cylinder head and manifolds—Le Car

1. Rocker arm cover
2. Rocker arm cover gasket
3. Rocker arm shaft
4. Rocker arm
5. Rocker arm shaft pedestal
6. Rocker arm adjuster
7. Pushrod
8. Valve locks
9. Valve spring retainers
10. Valve springs
11. Valve spring seats
12. Valves
13. Cylinder head studs
14. End plate gasket
15. End plate
16. Cylinder head
17. Cylinder head gasket
18. Manifold-to-head gasket
19. Intake/exhaust manifolds
20. Exhaust manifold-to-exhaust pipe connector

Exploded view of cylinder head and manifolds—Le Car

Exploded view of cylinder head assembly—18i and Fuego (USA)

Exploded view of cylinder head assembly—18i and Fuego (Canada)

Rocker Arms

REMOVAL AND INSTALLATION

1. Remove the cylinder head cover and necessary components to expose the rocker arm assembly.
2. Drain the cooling system.
3. Unscrew the rocker arm adjusting screws and remove the push rods, keeping them in proper order.
4. Remove the cylinder head bolts retaining the rocker arm assembly to the cylinder head.
5. Lift the assembly from the cylinder head.
6. Remove the retaining roll pins, mark the components and disassemble.

——— CAUTION ———

Do not remove the cup plugs from the ends of the rocker shafts.

NOTE: The rocker supports are the same for Nos. 1 and 4, which contain lubrication holes and locating dowels. Nos. 2, 3 and 5 are identical but have no lubricating holes.

7. The assembly and installation is the reverse of the removal procedure.
8. The cylinder head bolts must be retorqued and valves adjusted as previously outlined.

NOTE: The intake and exhaust valve rocker arms are different from each other. Do not interchange.

Rocker arm assembly. Note lubrication holes—18i and Fuego

Intake/Exhaust Manifold

REMOVAL AND INSTALLATION

Le Car

1. Disconnect the battery cables at the battery.
2. Remove the air cleaner intake hose.
3. Drain the cooling system.
4. Remove the following items:
   a. Carburetor heating hoses from the carburetor
   b. Accelerator rod
   c. Fuel line
   d. Vacuum lines (mark them with ad-

Exploded view of cylinder block assembly—18i and Fuego

Removing the crankshaft sprocket and location of the camshaft flange (retaining) screws—Le Car

gine Removal and Installation'' procedure in the beginning of this section.

2. Remove the timing cover and clean all of the gasket surfaces.

3. If the timing chain is to be replaced, secure the shoe of the tensioner (component that actually contacts the chain) to the body of the tensioner with a piece of wire.

4. Remove the chain tensioner assembly.

NOTE: If the timing chain tensioner must be serviced, refer to the next section.

5. Remove the camshaft sprocket bolt and install a suitable puller. Tighten the puller to draw the camshaft sprocket and chain off of the camshaft.

Aligning the timing marks—Le Car

1. Shoe
2. Spring
3. Piston
4. Body

Exploded view of the timing chain tensioner—Le Car

hesive tape to identify them for installation)

5. Remove the carburetor assembly.

6. Disconnect the exhaust pipe at the manifold.

7. Remove the manifold-to-cylinder head fasteners and remove the manifold along with the starter heat shield.

NOTE: If the manifold is excessively difficult to remove, disconnect the left engine mount and tilt the engine slightly to the right to provide extra clearance for manifold removal.

8. Installation is the reverse of the removal procedure.

18i and Fuego

The intake manifold assembly is part of the Bosch L-Jetronic Fuel Injection system and is disassembled in sequence with its components.

The exhaust manifold is removed after

the tri-functional catalytic converter is removed. The oxygen sensor can be removed with the manifold or separately.

For proper functioning of both the induction and exhaust system, all necessary gaskets must be replaced when the components are assembled.

Timing Chain and Related Components

DISASSEMBLY: TIMING COVER, TIMING CHAIN TENSIONER, TIMING COVER GASKET AND SEAL

Le Car

1. Remove the engine/transaxle assembly from the vehicle according to the ''En-

6. If the crankshaft gear is to be replaced, draw the gear off of the crankshaft with a suitable puller.

ASSEMBLY

Le Car

1. Press the crankshaft sprocket onto the crankshaft using a suitable tool.
2. Temporarily install the camshaft sprocket (marking facing outward) without the timing chain and align the timing marks.

———— **CAUTION** ————
Do not rotate either the camshaft or the crankshaft once the timing marks are aligned.

3. Remove the camshaft sprocket.
4. Position the timing chain onto the camshaft sprocket and reinstall the camshaft sprocket/timing chain assembly, making sure that the timing marks are aligned properly.
5. Install the camshaft sprocket retaining bolt and torque the bolt to 20 ft. lbs.
6. Install the timing chain tensioner.
7. Using a new gasket and cover-to-oil pan seal, install the timing cover.
8. Install the engine/transaxle assembly according to the ''Engine Removal and Installation'' procedure in the beginning of this section.

Timing Chain Tensioner

The timing chain tensioner is an automatic wear take-up mechanism which eliminates the necessity of manual timing chain adjustments.

Locking the timing chain tensioner—Le Car

LE CAR

Disassembly

1. Release the wire which was installed around the tensioner shoe and body in Step 3 of ''Timing Chain and Related Components—Disassembly''.
2. Separate the tensioner shoe from the tensioner body.
3. Inspect the shoe, spring, piston and tensioner body for damage.

Assembly

1. Lock the piston into the shoe using a 3 mm Allen wrench.
2. Insert the shoe into the body and place a 2 mm thick shim between the shoe

and the body to prevent inadvertent take-up.
3. Install the tensioner and the timing chain.
4. Remove the shim and press on the shoe until the piston bottoms in the body. Release the shoe without assisting the spring action.

Timing Cover and Chain

18i AND FUEGO

Removal

1. Disconnect the battery cables at the battery.
2. Remove the cylinder head, distributor and distributor drive gear.
3. Remove the radiator.
4. Remove the crankshaft pulley retaining bolt. Using a suitable puller, remove the crankshaft pulley.
5. Remove the timing cover; raise the engine if necessary to gain working clearance.
6. Remove the timing chain guide shoes and chain tensioner.
7. Remove the two camshaft retaining bolts.
8. Using a suitable puller, remove the crankshaft sprocket and key along with the timing chain.

Location of timing chain and sprocket retaining bolts—18i and Fuego

Timing chain alignment–18i

Installation

1. Position the timing chain onto the camshaft sprocket. Position the camshaft sprocket timing mark so that the mark points toward the crankshaft centerline.
2. Install the crankshaft key and rotate the crankshaft so that the key faces up.
3. Place the crankshaft sprocket inside the timing chain to simulate installation. Make sure that the timing marks align properly.
4. After the marks have been aligned as necessary, install the crankshaft sprocket and timing chain.
5. Install the following items:
   a. Camshaft retaining bolts
   b. Timing chain tensioner
   c. Timing chain guide shoes—push the chain guides against Renault gauge Mot. 420 (or its equivalent) and tighten the guide bolts.
   d. Timing cover, using a new gasket and seal
   e. Radiator
   f. Crankshaft pulley
   g. Cylinder head, distributor drive gear and distributor. Time engine.
6. Reconnect the battery cable.

A. Camshaft flange bolts
B. Chain tensioner bolts
C. Unlocking the chain tensioner

Timing chain assembly—18i

Piston/Liner Assembly

REMOVAL AND INSTALLATION

With the cylinder head and the oil pan removed from the cylinder block, the connecting rod bearing cap is removed and the piston, connecting rod and liner assembly is removed from the engine block. Number and mark each component.

When new piston and liners are required, the pistons and liners are supplied in a kit of four with each piston marked and matched to a specific liner. The letters ''A'' to ''D'' are used to identify each piston/liner assembly.

Liner, piston and ring assembly in kit form. Note markings

Liner seated in engine block on "O" ring. "X" represents liner protrusion

Sealing "O" rings are used between the bottom of the cylinder liner and the engine block. Liner protrusion is most important in the successful sealing of the cylinder head–to–gasket–to–cylinder liners. To check the cylinder liner protrusion, proceed as follows:

1. Place a cylinder liner into the engine block, without its "O" ring in place.
2. The protrusion should be 0.004 to 0.007 inch ((0.10 to 0.17 mm).
3. If the correct protrusion cannot be obtained, check with another set of new cylinder liners to ascertain if the defect is in the cylinder block or the set of liners.
4. The difference in protrusion between two adjacent liners should be no greater than 0.002 inch (0.04 mm). Reposition the liners as necessary.
5. If required, stepped down cylinder liner protrusion çan be made, from the No. 1 cylinder to the No. 4 cylinder.

Checking liner protrusion with dial indicator

Piston Pins

REMOVAL AND INSTALLATION

Because of a pressing requirement, the piston pin removal and installation should be done in a shop that is equipped with the required equipment.

NOTE: The connecting rod must be heated to a temperature of 482° F. (250° C.) before the new piston pin is installed.

Connecting Rod Bearing, Main Bearings

REMOVAL AND INSTALLATION

Refer to the engine rebuilding section for complete information on bearing installation and fitting to the crankshaft journals.

Piston Rings

The piston rings are pre-gapped at the time of manufacture. The gaps should be located approximately 120 degrees apart, when installed on the pistons.

Camshaft

REMOVAL AND INSTALLATION

1. Remove the timing cover, camshaft sprocket and timing chain as previously outlined.
2. Remove the valve cover (and the pushrods where applicable).
3. Remove the cylinder head as previously outlined.
4. Remove the air injection pump sprocket where applicable.
5. Remove the camshaft flange screws.
6. Temporarily reinstall the camshaft sprocket (to assist in removal as a handle) and carefully withdraw the camshaft from the engine.
7. Remove the camshaft oil seal.
8. Installation is the reverse of the removal procedure. Take note of the following:

   a. On Le Car models, check the clearance between the camshaft and the flange with a feeler gauge. The clearance should be between 0.002–0.005 in. If the clearance is excessive, the flange should be replaced.

   b. Use the proper seal installation tool to install a new camshaft oil seal.

   c. Install the camshaft from the timing chain end of the engine.

Camshaft and related components—Le Car

Checking the camshaft flange clearance—Le Car

LUBRICATION

Oil Pan

REMOVAL AND INSTALLATION

No prescribed method is suggested by the manufacturer to remove the oil pan from the engine while mounted in the vehicle. Because of the type of repairs necessary when the oil pan is removed, the recommended procedure is to remove the engine from the vehicle for this operation. Should it be deemed necessary, by removing covering pans and draining the oil from the crankcase, the oil pan can be removed.

Rear Main Bearing Oil Seal

The engine/transmission assembly must be separated for this operation and either the flywheel or converter must be removed to gain access to the seal. The engine oil pan must also be removed.

1. With the No. 1 cap in place, pry the oil seal from its seat in the cap and block.

Oil pump location—18i and Fuego

─── CAUTION ───
Do not mar the sealing surface on the cap and block.

2. With the use of a special seal installer, lubricate and install the seal by tapping the tool lightly on its driving end, until the tool makes contact with the crankshaft.

3. Should the No. 1 main bearing cap be removed, the side seals, when installed, must project approximately 0.2 mm or 1/32 inch above the cap and block.

4. Complete the assembly of the engine/transmission unit.

Oil Pump

REMOVAL AND INSTALLATION

The oil pump is located with-in the oil pan and is bolted to the engine block bottom.

Measuring clearance of rotors—clearance from 0.002 to 0.011 inch (A clearance)

Measuring clearance of rotors—clearance from 0.001 to 0.006 inch (B clearance)

The oil pump is driven by the crankshaft, through a connecting drive shaft. The oil pan must be removed before the oil pump can be serviced.

The oil pump is removed by the removal of attaching bolts. Remove the two rotors with the pump. Prime the oil pump with oil before installation.

ENGINE COOLING

Radiator

REMOVAL AND INSTALLATION

1. Drain the cooling system. Disconnect the battery.

NOTE: The manufacturer recommends clamping off the top, bottom and hose to the expansion bottle so as to keep the coolant in the engine area.

2. Remove the upper grille crossmember and the grille.

3. Disconnect the hoses at the radiator.

4. If equipped with air conditioning, remove the radiator cooling fans and disconnect the condenser from the radiator, placing it on the bumper to avoid discharging the system.

5. Remove the radiator along with the cooling fan.

6. If the radiator is to be replaced, separate the cooling fan and thermostat from the radiator and install on the new radiator.

• 7. The installation is in the reverse of the removal procedure. Fill the radiator before the clamps are removed from the hoses and then bleed the cooling system.

Water Pump

REMOVAL AND INSTALLATION

1. Disconnect the battery and drain the cooling system.

2. Remove the upper grille crossmember and the grille.

3. Remove the radiator and the cooling fan.

4. Remove the water pump drive belt.

5. Remove the water pump retaining bolts and remove the water pump from the engine block.

6. To install the water pump, reverse the removal procedure. Clean the gasket surface properly before water pump installation.

7. Fill and bleed the cooling system as the system comes to normal operating temperature.

Exploded view of water pump assembly— 18i and Fuego

NOTE: Bleed screws are located on the heater return hose and on the upper radiator hose.

Thermostat

REMOVAL AND INSTALLATION

The thermostat is located in the bottom of the upper hose at the water pump outlet. Drain the cooling system and remove the hose clamps. Install the new thermostat and re-install the hose clamps. Tighten the clamps, fill the cooling system and bleed as required.

EMISSION CONTROLS

Most vehicles are equipped with the following systems:

Air Injection

A belt-driven pump delivers fresh, compressed air to the exhaust ports of the engine. The presence of oxygen will lengthen the combustion process, which reduces the amount of unburned gases in the exhaust. A relief valve and a diverter valve control the amount of air delivered to the exhaust ports. Depending upon whether the engine is accelerating/cruising or decelerating, the diverter valve either delivers the air to the exhaust ports, or closes off the air passage to the exhaust ports, respectively. A check valve is provided in the system which will prevent damage to the air injection pump should the engine backfire.

Accelerated Idle System

This system is intended to reduce the amount of hydrocarbon emissions during deceler-

Air Injection Reactor system (A.I.R.)—typical

VEHICLE EMISSION CONTROL INFORMATION
ENGINE FAMILY: BRE1.6V5FZ9 ENGINE C10: 100.5
EXHAUST EMISSION CONTROL TYPE: EE1 CL CAT.
EVAPORATIVE FAMILY: ECS 4

THIS VEHICLE CONFORMS TO U.S. E.P.A. AND STATE OF CALIFORNIA REGULATIONS APPLICABLE TO 1981 NEW MOTOR VEHICLES PROVIDED THAT THIS VEHICLE IS ONLY INTRODUCED INTO COMMERCE FOR SALE IN THE STATE OF CALIFORNIA

CATALYST

ITEM	SPECIFICATION		INSTRUCTIONS
	MANUAL TRANS.	AUTO. TRANS.	
1 TIMING SETTING (DEGREES AT RPM)	10°±1° BTDC AT 800±50 RPM	10°±1° BTDC AT 650±50 RPM	VACUUM ADVANCE DISCONNECTED
2 IDLE SPEED (RPM)	800±50 RPM	650±50 RPM	SET BY TURNING AIR BY PASS THROTTLE PLATE HOUSING
3 IDLE MIXTURE	NOT ADJUSTABLE	NOT ADJUSTABLE	IDLE MIXTURE IS PRESET AT FACTORY AND NOT ADJUSTED DURING SCHEDULED MAINTENANCE.

CHOKE SETTING: COLD START INJECTOR — VALVE LASH: INTAKE: 0.008 in EXHAUST: 0.010 in — SPARK PLUG TYPE: BOSCHWR 7DS SPARK PLUG GAP: 0.024 TO 0.028 in

REGIE NATIONALE DES USINES RENAULT

Emission control label—typical (18i shown)

ENGINE FAMILY BRE1.6V5FZ9

Vacuum line diagram—typical (18i shown)

ation. The primary throttle plate is opened slightly during deceleration, between speeds of 15–20 miles per hour.

Evaporative Emission Control System

The main component is a canister containing charcoal and a filter. When the engine is off, gasoline vapor settles in the charcoal instead of being vented to the atmosphere. When the engine is started, intake manifold vacuum pulls fresh air in from beneath the charcoal (filtered) and carries the unburned gases to the intake manifold to be burned in the combustion chambers. The vacuum will continue to draw a small amount of vapor from the tank (through a calibrated orifice) even while the engine is running. The process will cycle in this manner, beginning at the time the engine is turned off.

Three way catalytic converter—typical

Oxygen sensor—typical

1. Air pump
2. Air pump filter
3. Relief and divertor valve assembly
4. Check valve
5. Air injection manifold
6. Delay valve
7. Carburetor
8. Intake manifold
9. Exhaust manifold
10. Air filter pre-heated air take-off
11. Air filter pre-heated air intake duct
12. Thermostatic air cleaner
13. Thermovalve activating sensor
14. Electronic tachometer switch
15. Throttle plate opener
16. Distributor
17. Throttle plate opening solenoid
18. Throttle plate plunger
19. Electro-vacuum switch
20. Choke control switch
21. EGR valve
22. Vacuum amplifier
23. Thermovalve
24. Catalytic converter
25. Choke knob
26. Solenoid valve
27. Transmission switch
28. Calibrated orifice
29. Calibrated orifice
30. Air shut-off valve
B. Blue side of delay valve
X. Calibrated orifice

Emission control diagram—1979 Le Car (California)

1. Air pump
2. Air pump filter
3. Relief and divertor valve assembly
4. Check valve
5. Air injection manifold
6. Distributor
7. Carburetor
8. Intake manifold
9. Exhaust manifold
10. Thermostatic air cleaner
11. Thermovalve activating sensor
12. Coolant temperature switch
13. Air shut-off valve
14. EGR solenoid valve
15. EGR valve
16. Catalytic converter
17. Throttle plate opener
18. Oil thermoswitch
19. Delay valve
20. Choke control switch
21. Choke control cable
22. Transmission switch
23. Air intake system pre-heated air stove
24. Calibrated orifice
25. Calibrated orifice
26. Solenoid valve (vacuum advance)
27. Calibrated orifice
B. White side of vacuum delay valve

Emission control diagram—1980 Le Car (Federal)

Ignition Timing Advance Control System

A contact switch which works in conjunction with the choke cable (on Le Car models) closes and activates a solenoid which admits full vacuum to the distributor vacuum advance unit for improved emissions and driveability when the choke valve is closed. Some models use a coolant temperature sensing switch to activate the solenoid.

Carburetor Air Intake Pre-Heating System

A thermostatically controlled air cleaner mixes heated and ambient incoming air to the carburetor, thereby improving fuel vaporization which assists in improving emissions and driveability during cold engine operation.

P.C.V. (Positive Crankcase Ventilation) System

Crankcase vapors are routed to the induction system to be burned in the combustion chambers instead of merely being vented to the atmosphere.

Catalytic Converter

The catalytic converter chemically alters the exhaust gases before the gases reach the atmosphere. A "two-way" catalyst uses either pellets or screens coated with platinum and palladium. The chemical content of the precious metals oxidizes (neutralizes) controlled amounts of carbon monoxide and hydrocarbons. A "three-way" catalyst uses platinum, palladium, and rhodium, which acts on oxides of nitrogen emissions. Some "three-way" converters also are ported to accept fresh air (from an injection pump) which further reduces oxides of nitrogen emissions.

1. Protective sleeve
2. Ceramic sensor
3. Base
4. Contact cover
5. Protective cover
6. Contact spring
7. Air opening
8. Electrical connection
9. Exhaust gas

Cross section of oxygen sensor—typical

E.G.R. (Exhaust Gas Recirculation) System

The E.G.R. valve admits varying amounts of exhaust gases into the combustion chambers, thereby diluting the incoming air/fuel mixture to reduce oxides of nitrogen. The introduction of "pre-burned" gases into the combustion chambers also lowers combustion chamber temperature. If detonation is a problem, check the E.G.R. system for proper operation.

FUEL INJECTION

Refer to the Unit Repair Section for complete Fuel Injection coverage.

Both the Fuego and the 18i use the Bosch design "L-Jetronic" fuel injection system. The two systems are nearly identical. The systems offer more precise metering of the fuel under varying conditions by using the Lambda oxygen sensor system. Basic operation of the components is as follows:

1. **Control Unit:** Receives data from the engine sensors and varies the injection valve opening time accordingly.

2. **Injection Valve:** Atomizes and in-

1. Airflow meter
2. Electronic control unit
3. Injector
4. Cold start injector
5. Coolant temperature sensor
6. Thermo-coolant time switch
7. Auxiliary air regulator
8. Relay
9. Ignition distributor
10. Intake manifold chamber
11. Throttle plate assembly
12. Throttle position switch
13. Fuel filter
14. Fuel pump
15. Fuel tank
16. Exhaust manifold
17. Oxygen manifold
18. Trifunctional catalytic converter
19. Fuel pressure regulator
20. Throttle plate bypass screw
21. Airflow meter bypass screw
22. Air temperature sensor

Typical Schematic of fuel injection system—18i and Fuego

jects fuel in front of the intake valve according to the input from the control unit.

3. **Air Flow Meter:** Measures the amount and the velocity of the incoming (intake) air and sends data to the control unit to compensate accordingly.

4. **Temperature Sensor II:** Sends engine temperature information to the control unit.

5. **Thermo-Time Switch:** The thermotime switch controls the operation of the cold start valve through sensing of the engine temperature.

6. **Cold Start Valve:** Injects extra fuel to the intake tract to richen the mixture during cold engine operation.

7. **Fuel Pump:** Pressurizes fuel from the tank and supplies this fuel to the engine.

8. **Fuel Filter:** Self explanatory.

9. **Pressure Regulator:** Self explanatory.

10. **Auxiliary Air Valve:** Supplies extra air to the engine during warm-up.

11. **Throttle Valve Switch:** Sends throttle position information to the control unit.

Fuel injection wiring connector numbers on the control unit

12. **Ignition Distributor:** Sends engine speed and timing information to the control unit.

13. **Temperature Sensor:** Sends air intake temperature information to the control unit.

14. **Relay Set:** Controls the power at the fuel pump and the control unit.

The injection system requires special tools and training for any adjustment or repair other than idle speed.

For all fuel injection system service procedures not detailed below, please refer to "Fuel Injection" in the Unit Repair section.

Fuel Injector

REMOVAL AND INSTALLATION

1. Remove the injector clamping bolts, disconnect the fuel lines and the electrical connectors.

2. Pull the injectors from the ramp assembly.

3. To remove the injector hose, use a heat gun to cut through the hose. Clean the surfaces, lubricate and install the new hose.

4. Reinstall the injector, connecting the fuel and electrical lines.

5. Install the clamping bolts.

1. Airflow meter
3. Injector
4. Cold start injector
5. Coolant temperature sensor
6. Thermo-coolant time switch
7. Auxiliary air regulator
9. Ignition distributor
10. Intake manifold chamber
11. Throttle plate assembly
16. Exhaust manifold

17. Oxygen sensor
18. Trifunctional catalytic converter
19. Fuel pressure regulator
20. Throttle valve bypass screw
21. Airflow sensor bypass screw
23. Charcoal canister
35. Carbon monoxide socket plug
C. Oil condenser
D. Oxygen sensor maintenance indicator

Fuel injection component location—typical of 18i and Fuego

MANUAL TRANSMISSION (TRANSAXLE)

Le Car

REMOVAL

1. Disconnect the battery leads and the transaxle ground wire.
2. Disconnect the speedometer cable.
3. Remove the water pump drive belt.
4. Remove the camshaft pulley, the air pump filter, the air pump and the mounting bracket.
5. Remove the two upper bolts on the starter.
6. Remove the clutch housing bolts which are on the engine.
7. Remove the wheels and the brake calipers without disconnecting the brake hoses.
8. Disconnect the steering arms at the steering rack end.
9. Disconnect the upper ball joints from the upper suspension.
10. Remove the drive shafts from the side gears by tilting the stub axle carriers downward.

— CAUTION —
Do not damage the oil seal lips on the differential adjusting nuts while removing the drive shafts.

11. Remove the two mounting bolts from the support on the transaxle.
12. Disconnect the clutch cable at the lever and push the sleeve retainer to free it from the supporting tab.
13. Remove the top bolt and then the tubular crossmember, in the direction of the arrow.
14. Replace the top bolt in the frame hole and then remove the bottom bolts from the crossmember.
15. Tap the crossmember towards the rear of the vehicle and remove it.
16. Replace the bottom bolt in the frame hole.
17. Support the front end of the transaxle with a jack and remove the front mounting pad with its bracket.
18. Remove the starter bottom bolt and then the starter.
19. Remove the side reinforcement mounting bolts and the clutch cover.
20. Special holding tools should be used to hold the engine while the transaxle is removed from the vehicle body. Remove the transaxle assembly.

INSTALLATION

The installation of the transaxle is the reverse of the removal procedure. The clutch

Exploded view of shift lever assembly—18i and Fuego (model 395)

free-play at the end of the clutch lever should be adjusted to within ⅛ to 5/32 inch.

18i and Fuego

REMOVAL

Models 352 and 395 Transmissions

The transmissions may be removed with the engine from the top of the vehicle or separately from the bottom of the vehicle. The procedure given is the removal of the transmission separately from the bottom of the vehicle.

NOTE: It is not necessary to drain the lubrication from the transmission since the side gears are sealed.

1. Disconnect the battery, the positive cable to the starter and the power lead to the solenoid.
2. Remove the three starter attaching bolts from the bell housing.
3. Remove the rear attaching bolt of the starter.
4. Loosen the bolt of the engine mount on the starter side and swing the rear fixing bracket into a horizontal position.
5. Pull the starter back the length of its nose. On the 352 model transmissions, turn the starter 90 degrees and remove the starter (both transmission models).
6. Disconnect the clutch cable at the fork lever.
7. Place the special transmission removal tool support plates between the lower

shock absorber fixing pins and the lower suspension arm shafts, if using the tool.
8. Loosen the front wheel bolts.
9. Raise the vehicle on a hoist or by other means.
10. Remove the front wheels.
11. Remove the brake calipers from both front wheel assemblies.
12. Punch out the roll pins on the sides of the gear/axle shafts.
13. Remove the steering tie rod ball joint nut and loosen the tie rod ball joint.
14. Loosen the upper suspension ball joint stud after removing the retaining nut.
15. Tilt the stub axle carrier, disengaging the drive axle shaft from the side gear shaft. Remove the opposite axle shaft in the same manner.
16. Disconnect the speedometer cable and the wiring to the back-up lights and emission control switches.

Location of pin in drive axle flange—typical

Exploded view of differential assembly—18i and Fuego

17. Disconnect the gear shift linkage.

CAUTION

Do not remove the gear shift linkage ball joints from their housings.

18. Remove the clutch protective shield.
19. If using the transmission remover jack assembly, place it under the transmission and lift the transmission slightly. Remove the left and right transmission mounts.
20. Remove the transmission attaching bolts and pull the assembly to the rear, being careful not to damage the pressure plate. Lower the transmission to the floor.

INSTALLATION

1. Lightly lubricate the splines of the clutch shaft and raise the transmission in line with the engine/flywheel assembly.
2. Push the transmission assembly forward into the position with the engine, while engaging the clutch shaft into the clutch plate.
3. Install the left and right transmission supports and remove the installing jack.
4. Install the clutch protective cover and be sure the top dead center sensor is positioned 1.0 mm (0.039 inch) from the engine flywheel.
5. Reconnect the speedometer cable, the back-up light wires, the emission control switch wires and the gear shift linkage.
6. Lightly lubricate the splines of the differential side gears and position the drive axle shaft next to the side gear (either side).
7. Tilt the stub axle while engaging the drive axle shaft in the side gear. Line the holes in the drive shaft and stub axle and install the roll pin. Do the same procedure on the opposite side. Be sure the roll pin is installed.
8. Engage the stub axle carrier in the upper suspension ball joint and lock the cone. Tighten the nut to the proper torque.
9. Engage the tie rod ball joints. Tighten the nuts to the proper torque.
10. Install the front calipers on the front suspension.
11. Install the front wheels and lower the vehicle. Tighten the wheel lugs.
12. Connect the clutch cable to the fork.
13. Place the starter in its housing, pull

Typical cross section of clutch assembly

the support bracket into position and tighten the bracket bolt.
14. Tighten the starter attaching bolts.
15. Check the gear shift lever adjustment and the clutch cable adjustment.

NOTE: The release bearing must be in constant contact with the pressure plate diaphragm.

16. Complete the assembly of disconnected components.
17. Connect the battery and road test the vehicle.

LINKAGE ADJUSTMENT

1. Place the transmission in neutral. Loosen the tightening nut of the yoke so that the shift linkage can turn freely.
2. Put the lever at the transmission against the 3rd/4th gear line.
3. Place a shim, 2.0 mm (0.079 inch) for the 352 models and 10.0 mm (0.394 inch) for the 395 models, between the end piece of the shift linkage and the surface of the transmission housing.
4. Tighten the yoke clamping nut and be sure the clearance is the same as the shim thickness when the shim is removed from between the shift linkage and the surface of the housing.

NOTE: Refer to the Unit Repair section for overhaul procedures.

CLUTCH

REMOVAL AND INSTALLATION

Upon removal of the transaxle assembly, the clutch pressure plate, clutch plate assembly is exposed. Removal of the pressure plate retaining bolts will allow the assembly to be removed from the flywheel.

Upon installation, the clutch plate must be centered on the flywheel and in proper alignment with the transaxle drive shaft, with the use of a clutch aligning tool.

The clutch release bearing is attached to

the clutch fork shaft, on the transaxle housing.

CLUTCH CABLE ADJUSTMENT

Le Car

From underneath the vehicle, unlock the locknut and screw the adjusting nut in or out to obtain a clearance of ⅛ to 5⁄32 inch at the end of the lever. After verifying the clearance, lock the nut.

18i and Fuego

1. Keep the release bearing tight against the pressure plate diaphragm by pulling the release lever towards the clutch pedal.
2. Screw the adjusting nut in or out, so that when the cable is pulled towards the flywheel, a clearance of 3⁄32 inch is present between the clutch cable journal and the operating lever seat.

AUTOMATIC TRANSMISSION

18i and Fuego

REMOVAL

1. Disconnect the battery and drain the transmission assembly.
2. Disconnect the vacuum control hose and the wiring connectors. Remove the support.
3. Special spacers should be placed between the lower shock absorber base and the lower suspension arm pivot shaft.
4. Place the vehicle on jack stands and drive out the roll pins from the drive shafts.
5. Separate the steering ball joints and the upper suspension ball joints.
6. Tilt the stub axle carriers to free the drive shafts from the side gears.
7. Disconnect the selector linkage while the lever is in the neutral position.

Exploded view of shift lever assembly— 18i and Fuego (model 352)

8. Remove the transmission dipstick and the converter protector plate.

9. Remove the three converter bolts and the exhaust pipe bracket nut which is attached to the transmission.

10. Place a jack assembly under the vehicle and remove the two transmission supports.

11. Lower the transmission enough to disconnect the speedometer and the governor cables.

12. Remove the engine/transmission bolts and lower the transmission from the vehicle.

NOTE: Do not allow the converter to slip out of bell housing.

INSTALLATION

Installation is the reverse of the removal procedure. Note the following steps:

1. When installing the converter, place the boss that is located opposite the timing hole in line with the sharp cornered edge on the converter drive plate, which is marked by a dab of paint.

2. Lightly lubricate the side gear splines and position the drive shafts in line with the side gears.

3. If the vehicle is equipped with a TDC sensor, the sensor must be positioned approximately 0.039 inch (1.0 mm) from the engine flywheel.

4. Adjust the gear selector lever and the governor cable.

5. Be sure the computer and governor connections are made and the transmission ground wire is connected.

Governor-Computer

The governor is a small, low wattage alternator which supplies alternating current to the computer. The current varies with the speed of the vehicle and the position of the accelerator pedal, corresponding to engine load. The computer then sends electrical impulses to the solenoid ball valves, according to the gear selector lever position and the current supplied by the governor.

The removal and installation of this unit should be accomplished by technicians skilled in automatic transmission repairs.

Kick-down Switch

The kick-down switch is activated by the accelerator pedal at the end of its travel. The adjustments are made with the accelerator cable.

ADJUSTMENT

With the accelerator cable completely depressed, approximately 1/16 inch (3.0 to 4.0 mm) clearance should exist to allow movement by the stop sleeve.

Neutral/Start Switch

The neutral/start switch is operated by the transmission internal shifting lever and is mounted on the transmission case. No adjustments are possible, but the switch should be inspected to be sure the engine will only start in the "P" or "N" positions. Replace the switch, if necessary.

Drive Shaft

REMOVAL

1. Lift the vehicle on the side to be repaired, by a hoist or jack. Remove the wheel assembly.

2. Remove the stub axle nut.

3. Loosen the upper ball joint nut and the steering arm nut, but do not remove them.

4. Loosen the ball joint cones with special tools.

5. Remove the two caliper retaining bolts and lift the caliper assembly from the rotor. Do not disconnect the brake hose.

6. Remove the ball joint and steering arm nuts and tilt the stub axle carrier in order to disengage the drive shaft.

7. Drive the roll pins from the drive shaft coupling on the gear box side of the drive shaft.

8. Remove the drive shaft.

9. Installation is the reverse of removal.

Boot Replacement

1. Remove the collar from the stub axle.

2. Remove as much grease as possible from the assembly.

3. Remove the bell-shaped stub axle from the drive shaft by raising the arms of the retaining starplate, one by one.

─────── **CAUTION** ───────
Do not twist the arms of the starplate.

4. Remove the boot. Save the thrust ball and the spring.

INSTALLATION

NOTE: A special boot replacing tool should be used to install the boot to avoid damage.

1. Place the drive shaft in a vise with the shaft yoke up. Fully engage the installing tool on the shaft yoke.

2. Lubricate the inside of the boot with clean engine oil.

3. Pull the boot over the end of the special tool with the small end first.

4. Bring the boot as close as possible to the cylindrical part of the tool and let it return halfway back. Do this several times in order to soften the rubber of the boot. Relubricate the arms of the tool and the boot as required during the installation.

1. Bell-shaped stub axle
2. Retaining starplate
3. Spider
4. Shaft yoke
5. Retaining collar
6. Rubber boot
7. Retaining O-ring

Cross section of drive axle—typical

5. Place the spring and the thrust ball joint in the spider.

6. Move the roller cages towards the center and position the retaining star plate. Each arm should be the bisector of the angles formed by the spider.

7. Install the collar and secure.

Axle Spicer or Yoke Replacement

1. Place a piece of adhesive tape or a protective end piece on the seal surface of the differential adjuster nuts.

2. Cut the retaining collar and the boot along their whole length. Remove as much of the grease as possible.

3. Remove the three tabs of the locking plate and remove the yoke.

NOTE: Do not remove the rollers from their respective journals. The roller cages and needle bearings are matched and must never be separated. To prevent the separating of the unit during this operation, mount the plastic collar that is furnished with new spiders. Tape the collar as a safeguard to prevent the collar from coming off.

4. Using a press, remove the spider assembly.

5. To replace the spider or a boot:

a. Lubricate the drive shaft and slide on the new retaining collar and boot.

b. Push the spider back on the splined shaft.

c. Make three crimps with 120° spacing by stamping the metal splines on the drive shaft.

d. Take off the plastic collar and/or tape. Engage the spider in the yoke and insert a shim (special tool) between the locking plate and the yoke.

e. Carefully put the locking tabs of the plate back into their original positions and then remove the special tool shim.

f. Put approximately 5¼ oz. of grease into the boot and yoke. Position the lips of the boot in the grooves of the drive shaft and on the metal housing.

g. Install the retaining spring on the boot. Insert a smooth round-ended rod between the boot and the yoke to relieve the air trapped in the boot.

h. Lengthen or shorten the joint until

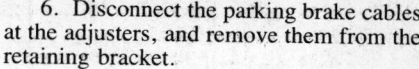
a measurement of 6.378 ± 0.039 inch (162.0 ± 1.0 mm) is obtained between the end of the boot and the largest diameter machined face of the yoke. When the joint has been adjusted correctly, remove the air release rod.

i. Place the retaining spring on the boot with a flexible wire.

— CAUTION —

The spring must not be stretched and the coils must still be touching after assembly.

6. If the yoke must be replaced:

a. Lubricate the drive shaft and slide on the retaining collar and the new boot.

b. Engage the yoke's metal housing on the shaft and the spider on the splines of the shaft.

c. Make three crimps with 120° spacing by stamping the metal splines on the drive shaft.

d. Fit the two bosses of the metal housing facing a perforation on the yoke, supplied with its new "O" ring and fit the parts one inside the other.

e. The crimping of the housing is on the yoke and is done on a press, by a hammer and a crimping tool.

INSTALLATION

1. Coat the splines of the shaft with lubricant and engage the drive shaft into the side gear. Check the positioning of the drive shaft retaining pin holes.

2. Install the retaining roll pins.

3. Engage the drive shaft into the hub. Install the washer and stub axle nut on the axle.

4. Reconnect the upper ball joint and steering arm joint and install the nuts. Tighten as required.

5. Torque the stub axle nut to 185 ft. lbs.

6. Reinstall the brake caliper and the wheel assembly. Operate the brakes several times to re-seat the disc pads to the rotor.

Differential

The differential is part of the transmission assembly and must be removed and replaced with the unit. Refer to the Unit Repair section.

REAR SUSPENSION

Rear Axle Assembly

REMOVAL AND INSTALLATION

18i and Fuego

1. Position the vehicle on a hoist or on jack stands.

2. Remove the wheels and the lower mountings on the shock absorbers. Push the shock absorbers upward as far as possible.

3. Remove the flexible brake lines from the limiter.

4. Pull downward on the rear axle to remove the springs.

5. Remove the two side arm nuts on the chassis side and remove the two bolts.

6. Disconnect the parking brake cables at the adjusters, and remove them from the retaining bracket.

7. Place a jack under the rear axle assembly.

8. Disconnect the brake limiter valve.

9. Remove the two center arm bolts and remove the rear axle assembly.

The installation is the reverse of the removal procedure. With the components in place and tightened correctly, place the vehicle back on its wheels.

1. Check the brake limiter valve adjustment.

2. Bleed the brake system.

3. Adjust the parking brake.

4. With the weight of the vehicle on the rear suspension, retighten all bolts as required.

Center Arm

REMOVAL AND INSTALLATION

18i and Fuego

1. Place the vehicle on a lift and disconnect the brake limiter control rod.

2. Remove the nuts from the front and rear attaching bolts.

3. Remove the clamp and the center arm retaining bolts.

4. Remove the center arm. The bushings must be pressed in and out of the arm.

Installation is in the reverse of the removal procedure. Torque the bolts as required and check the adjustment of the limiter valve. Refer to the Brake Unit section.

Side Arms/Stabilizer Assembly

REMOVAL AND INSTALLATION

18i and Fuego

1. Place the vehicle on a lift and disconnect the two parking brake cables.

2. Remove the arm retaining nuts front and rear.

3. Drive the bolts from the arms and remove the arm stabilizer assembly. The bushings must be pressed from and into the arm.

The installation is the reverse of the removal procedure. Torque the bolts to their proper tightness.

Le Car

The rear suspension of the Le Car model is an individual torque arm type unit and each side is removed and replaced separately.

1. Support the rear of the vehicle with jack stands.

Exploded view of rear suspension—18i and Fuego

Cross section of rear axle assembly—Le Car

30 ft-lbs (4 N-m)

55 ft-lbs (7.5 N-m)

60 ft-lbs (8 N-m)

30 ft-lbs (4 N-m)

45 ft-lbs (6 N-m)

Releasing automatic adjuster on rear brakes—18i and Fuego

2. Remove the sway bar and the shock absorber.

3. Disconnect the flexible brake line and set the torsion bars to zero position by their adjusting cams.

4. Assemble the special torsion bar removal tool in place of the shock absorber and tighten the tool until the adjusting lever lifts off the cam. Remove the torsion bar from both sides.

5. Remove the two other mounting bolts and the three inner mounting bolts. Remove the arm.

Installation is the reverse of the removal procedure. Be sure to bleed the brake system, check the limiter cut-off pressure and check the rear wheels for proper tracking.

BUSHING REPLACEMENT

Le Car

1. Both the inner and outer arm bushings are pressed into the arm tube. Bend back the crimped lugs with a chisel and remove the outer case.

2. Remove the rubber bushing outer sleeve using a three jawed puller. This operation will tear the rubber.

3. Saw through the rubber bushing inner sleeve, being careful not to mar the tube.

4. Press the new bushings in place with a press, crimping the lugs while the arms are in the press.

Rear Axle Bearings

REMOVAL AND INSTALLATION

18i and Fuego

1. Raise the rear of the vehicle and remove the rear wheels.

2. Remove the rear brake drum;

a. Release the parking brake.

b. Slacken the secondary cables of the parking brake so that the lever may be pulled back.

c. Remove the dust plug in the backing plate so that the automatic adjusting system may be disengaged.

d. Insert a screwdriver type tool into the hole in the backing plate, through a companion hole in the brake shoe, to the parking brake lever.

e. Push in with the tool to disengage the catch from the brake shoe. Push the lever to the rear with the tool.

f. Remove the dust cover, the retaining lock nut/cotter pin, the stub axle nut and washer.

g. Remove the drum, the outer bearing and seal as an assembly.

3. With the use of special pulling tools, the inner bearing is removed from the stub axle, along with the deflector.

INSTALLATION

1. Install the inner deflector, making sure it is mounted correctly.

2. Install the inner bearing on the stub axle by carefully driving it to its seat.

3. Install any of the bearing cups as required. Add lubricant to the bearings and cups.

4. Install the drum assembly in the reverse of its removal procedure.

5. Check the bearing end play, which should be between 0.000 and 0.001 inch (0.00 and 0.03 mm).

6. Adjust the foot brake by repeatedly pushing down on the brake pedal.

7. Adjust the parking brake. Install the plug in the rear of the backing plate.

Le Car

1. Raise the vehicle and support safely.

2. Remove the rear wheel(s) and the brake drum.

3. Remove the outer bearing and the oil seal.

4. Remove the bearing races as required.

5. With a special puller, remove the inner bearing from the rear axle spindle.

NOTE: Some inner bearings will have a thrust washer that must be removed

with the bearing assembly. **A different type bearing puller is then used.**

There are two methods of bearing replacement, hot or cold. The hot method is preferred and consists of pre-heating the washer so that it can be assembled to the stub axle without the use of tools. The cold method utilizes the special tools to press the components in place. The components should be heated to approximately 200–250 degrees F.

CAUTION

Do not use an open flame to pre-heat the components.

ADJUSTMENT

An end play of between 0.004 and 0.002 inch (0.01 to 0.05 mm) should exist between the brake drum and the stub axle. Rotate the stub axle nut in or out to obtain this required adjustment. Install the lockplate, nut and cotter pin. Add ⅓ oz. of grease in the dust cover and install.

Rear Shock Absorber

LE CAR

Removal

1. Remove the upper nuts from the shock top, located in the trunk area.
2. Raise the vehicle and remove the bottom nuts.
3. Remove the shock absorber.

Installation

1. Install the top mounted nut first and then attach the lower nut. Complete the installation and lower the vehicle to the ground.

18i and FUEGO

Removal

1. Open the trunk and remove the gas tank protection shield.
2. Remove the upper fastener (nut).
3. Raise the vehicle and remove the wheel(s).
4. Remove the lower fastening nut and compress the shock absorber by hand.
5. Remove the retaining clips of the brake hoses from the rear axle.
6. Push the axle assembly downward and remove the shock absorber with the spring. Remove the spacers and the rubber bushings.

Installation

Before installing a new shock absorber, pump it up and down manually several times while in an upright position.
1. Place the rubber insulators on the shock absorbers as required on both the top and bottom.
2. Push down on the rear axle assembly

and engage the shock absorber with the spring, positioning the spring so that its lower end is placed in the stop of the lower cup.
3. Attach the upper half of the shock absorber with the retaining nut. Be sure to replace the bushings and cups as they were removed.
4. Extend the shock absorber and install its lower retaining nut. Again, be sure to replace the bushings and cups as they were removed.
5. Install the retaining clips of the brake hose to the rear axle.
6. Install the wheels and lower the vehicle to the ground.

Rear Spring

REMOVAL AND INSTALLATION

18i and Fuego

To remove the rear spring, it is necessary to remove the bottom shock absorber retaining nut and loosen the rear axle assembly as was outlined in "Rear Axle Removal and Installation." Refer to the appropriate section.

FRONT SUSPENSION

Upper Control Arm

LE CAR

Removal

1. Remove the cooling system expansion bottle and the ignition coil. Raise the front end.

2. Disconnect the upper ball joint using the removal tool.
3. Screw on and tighten a lock nut on the front end of the arm hinge pin (bolt). Remove the rear lock nut.
4. Remove the pin and lock nut assembly towards the front.
5. Remove the upper arm from the chassis.

Installation

To install the upper arm, reverse the removal procedure. Tighten the nuts up to the end of the threads of the hinge pin (bolt).

18I AND FUEGO

Removal

1. Raise the front of the vehicle and remove the wheel on the side to be repaired.
2. Loosen the shock absorber lower lock nut.
3. Disconnect the caster link at the suspension arm side. Disconnect the suspension upper ball joint with the removal tool.
4. Remove the retaining bolt from the suspension arm on the chassis. Raise the arm and unscrew the shock absorber pillar.
5. Remove the suspension arm from the vehicle.

Installation

The installation is the reverse of the removal procedure. When the vehicle is returned to the ground, torque the upper arm bolt, the shock absorber pillar bolt and the caster link nut.

Lower Control Arm

REMOVAL AND INSTALLATION

Le Car

1. Raise the vehicle and remove the necessary wheel.

65 ft-lbs (9 N-m)

40 ft-lbs (5.5 N-m)

25 ft-lbs (3.5 N-m)

75 ft-lbs (10 N-m)

35 ft-lbs (4.5 N-m)

30 ft-lbs (4 N-m)

40 ft-lbs (5 N-m)

90 ft-lbs (12 N-m)

Cross section of front suspension with torque applications—Le Car

30 ft-lbs.

30 ft-lbs.

59 ft-lbs.

64 ft-lbs.

59 ft-lbs.

ft-lbs.)

11 ft-lbs.

11 ft-lbs.

59 ft-lbs.

64 ft-lbs.

48 ft-lbs.

48 ft-lbs.

Cross section of front suspension with torque applications—18i and Fuego

2. Remove the stub axle nut.

3. Disconnect the anti-sway bar and the bottom mounting of the shock absorber. Remove the bottom pin.

4. Disconnect the steering arm ball joint and the lower suspension arm ball joint with the removal tool.

5. Unscrew the two bushing tightening nuts and the nut on the arm hinge pin and free it from the side frame member.

6. Insert a spacer between the thrust screw and the drive shaft.

7. Push in the drive shaft to free the bottom ball joint from the stub axle carrier. Do not remove the shaft completely.

8. The joint is removed by turning the right hand half axle to the left and the left hand half axle to the right.

9. Remove the lower arm from the assembly.

To install:

The installation is the reverse of the removal procedure. Be sure to properly tighten the suspension retaining nuts.

18i and Fuego

1. Raise the vehicle and support safely. Remove the required wheel(s).

2. Loosen the ball joint nut and unscrew it until it comes in contact with the C.V. joint. Continue the pressure with the nut and force the ball joint stud to be removed from its seat.

NOTE: The nut will have to be replaced with a new one.

3. Remove the bolt on the inner part of the arm and remove the arm from the chassis.

The installation is in the reverse of the removal procedure. Torque the new nut to specifications.

Upper Control Arm Joint

REMOVAL AND INSTALLATION

Le Car

1. Raise the vehicle and support safely. Remove the required wheel(s).

2. Remove the upper ball joint stud from its seat and drill the rivet heads.

3. Remove the rivets and remove the old joint.

4. Install the new ball joint and secure with the supplied bolts. Reinstall the ball joint stud in its seat and tighten the retaining nut to specifications.

5. After lowering the vehicle, the caster, wheel track and steering box height setting should be checked.

18i and Fuego

1. Raise the vehicle and support safely. Remove the required wheels.

2. Disconnect the suspension upper ball joint and the caster link.

3. Remove the ball joint bolts and remove the ball joint.

To install:

1. Install the ball joint in the upper arm and install the retaining bolts.

2. Reconnect the caster link and the ball joint stud. Tighten the nut to specifications.

3. Lower the vehicle.

4. Adjust the caster, camber and toe-out as required.

Lower Control Arm Joint

REMOVAL AND INSTALLATION

Le Car

1. Raise the vehicle and support safely. Remove the wheels.

2. Remove the retaining rivets and remove the ball joint, then the retaining nut.

3. Remove the ball joint from the lower arm.

To install:

1. The installation is the reverse of the removal procedure.

2. Check the caster angle, the steering box height setting and the wheel track as required.

18i and Fuego

The lower arm must be removed to replace the lower ball joint. Drill the rivet heads and remove the rivets and the ball joint. Install the new ball joint with the bolts supplied in the ball joint kit. Adjust the front alignment as required.

Struts

REMOVAL AND INSTALLATION

Le Car

1. The front shock absorbers are removed by the removal of the upper retaining nuts and washers. Remove the bottom through bolt and compress the shock absorber.

2. Withdraw the shock absorber from the suspension.

3. Install the new shock absorber into position and install the top retaining nuts and washers.

Caster shim placement—Le Car

4. Install the bottom through bolt and tighten to specifications.

18i and Fuego

1. The upper spring lower seat rests on a projection of the front shock absorber. Remove the front upper arm as previously instructed.

2. With a special tool, compress the spring and remove the upper shock absorber retaining nuts and washers.

3. Carefully lower the spring until the tension is relieved. Pull the shock absorber from the spring assembly.

4. To install the new shock absorber, reverse the removal procedure.

OVERHAUL

For all strut overhaul procedures, please refer to "Strut Overhaul" in the Unit Repair section.

Front End Alignment

LE CAR

During the 1979 model year, Renault changed the design of the Le Car front suspension. The early design is referred to as the 12° caster suspension, the later design

Horizontal positioning of the rod pin—first design suspension of Le Car

is the 6° caster suspension. The 1979 model year includes both designs; make sure to identify the suspension before an alignment is performed. Suspension components are *not interchangeable* between the early and late designs, unless the front axle (complete), steering box and steering arms are changed to the desired design. Service parts are available for both suspension designs.

Caster and camber are adjustable on the Le Car models.

18i AND FUEGO

Front alignment is not adjustable. Toe-out can be adjusted by rotation of the steering link sleeves.

STEERING

Steering Wheel

REMOVAL AND INSTALLATION

Remove the snap cap and the steering wheel retaining nut from the steering shaft. Use a protective puller and remove the steering wheel from the steering shaft.

NOTE: Depending upon the type puller used, the steering column top and bottom bezel may have to be removed to gain access.

Combination Lighting– Directional Signal Switch

REMOVAL AND INSTALLATION

Le Car

1. Disconnect the battery.
2. Remove the instrument panel housing screws.
3. Remove the switch bottom shell.
4. Remove the switch screws and disconnect the junction blocks.
5. Remove the switch.

The installation is the reverse of the removal procedure.

18i and Fuego

1. Disconnect the battery.
2. Remove the steering wheel and the two half housings.
3. Remove the retaining bolt and the retaining screw. Remove the junction block.
4. Remove the switch assembly by pulling it upward.

The installation is the reverse of the removal procedure.

Ignition Switch

REMOVAL AND INSTALLATION

Le Car

1. Disconnect the battery and remove the combination switch shell assembly.
2. Disconnect the ignition switch connector.
3. Turn the key to the "garage" position and remove the key.
4. Remove the retaining screw from the side of the switch housing.
5. Press the retaining catch with the top of a scriber and push the switch out from behind to withdraw it.

To install the switch, reverse the removal procedure, using a new switch assembly.

Combination switch—typical of 18i and Fuego

18i and Fuego

1. Disconnect the battery.
2. Remove the steering wheel and the two half housings around the steering column.
3. Disconnect the ignition switch connector.
4. Place the key in the park position and remove the key.
5. Remove the retaining screw and push in on the retaining pin and push behind the switch to remove it from the housing.

The installation is the reverse of the removal procedure.

Steering Gear

LE CAR, 18i AND FUEGO

The steering gear is of the rack and pinion design, both for manual and power steering. The disassembly and adjustments require the use of special tools and should not be attempted by unskilled personnel.

Steering Linkage

LE CAR, 18i AND FUEGO

The tie rods are of a sleeve design and the tie rod end is screwed into it. To adjust the tie rod, loosen the lock nut and screw the tie rod in or out to obtain the desired distance.

1. Hydraulic pump
2. Rotating valve (drive element)
3. Double acting power cylinder (power element)
4. Fluid reservoir
5. Pump feed (low-pressure)
6. Valve feed (high-pressure)
7. Power cylinder feed (high-pressure)
8. Reservoir return (low-pressure)

Component parts of the power steering assembly—18i and Fuego

BRAKES

For all brake system repair and service procedures not detailed below, please refer to "Brakes" in the Unit Repair section.

Adjustment

FRONT BRAKES

The front brakes on the Le Car, 18i and the Fuego are of the disc brake design and require no adjustments.

REAR BRAKES

Le Car

The rear brakes are of the conventional shoe design and require adjustments at regular intervals. To adjust, raise the wheels and turn the adjuster lug of the front shoe, in a downward movement to the front. Lock the drum and then release the adjuster until the wheel turns freely. Adjust the rear lug in the same manner, only to the rear in a downward movement.

————— CAUTION —————
Be certain the rear drums are not dragging as the wheels are rotated in checking for freeness of the brakes.

18i and Fuego

The rear brakes are of the conventional shoe design, but have automatic adjusters. To initially set the adjusters, a clearance of approximately 0.039 inch (1.0 mm) should be present between the link and the primary brake shoe, with the parking brake lever resting against the brake shoe. If this dimension can not be obtained, it is necessary to replace the link tension spring as well as the two brake shoe return springs. After the initial adjustment, install the drums and op- erate the foot brake pedal to further adjust the shoe-to-lining clearance.

Master Cylinder

REMOVAL AND INSTALLATION

Le Car

NOTE: The master cylinder is not repairable.

1. Drain the brake fluid reservoir with a syringe.
2. Disconnect the brake lines and disconnect the warning light switch wire.
3. Withdraw the master cylinder pushrod.
4. Remove the two retaining bolts and remove the master cylinder.
5. The installation is in the reverse of the removal procedure. Be sure to do the following during the installation:
   a. Seal the master cylinder sealing surface to firewall.
   b. Adjust the pedal clearance to $^{13}/_{64}$ inch at the pedal pad (free play).
   c. Bleed the main brake system and then the by-pass system.

18i and Fuego

1. Empty the brake fluid reservoir with a syringe.
2. Remove the reservoir with the seals.
3. Unscrew the four brake lines and mark them for reinstallation.
4. Remove the two retaining nuts and then the master cylinder.
5. The installation is the reverse of the removal procedure. The brake lines must be in their correct positions when reattached to the master cylinder.
6. Bleed the brake system.

NOTE: The piston rod projection from the power unit should be 0.354 inch from the mating surface of the power unit, to the end of the piston rod.

Power Booster

REMOVAL AND INSTALLATION

18i and Fuego

1. Remove the master cylinder.
2. Remove the brake pedal pushrod adjuster link pin.
3. Remove the brake booster retaining nuts on the firewall.
4. Remove the brake booster from the vehicle.

NOTE: Save the spacer plate for reinstallation.

5. The installation is in the reverse of the removal procedure. Bleed the brake system before vehicle operation.

Parking Brake

ADJUSTMENT

Le Car

1. Release the handbrake and loosen the locknut on the handbrake rod.
2. Tighten the adjusting nut until the lining just touches the drum.
3. Check that the hand brake lever travel is approximately six notches.
4. Tighten the locknut. Be sure the brakes do not drag.

18i and Fuego

For the self-adjusting rear brakes to operate properly, the cable tension must be adjusted as follows.

NOTE: The parking brake should only be adjusted after the rear brakes have been worked on or the parking brake cable has been replaced, never at any other time.

1. Raise the vehicle and support safely. Have the parking brake handle in the released position.
2. Tighten the adjusting cable nut until the deflection between the secondary cable and the vehicle chasis measures approximately ¾ inch.
3. Check the parking brake lever handle travel. The minimum it should move is 12 notches.

CHASSIS ELECTRICAL

Heater Blower

NOTE: The motor brushes are the only blower motor components that are serviceable. The blower motor assembly must

be replaced if a fault exists in any other blower motor component.

REMOVAL AND INSTALLATION

Le Car

1. Disconnect the negative battery cable.
2. Disconnect the blend door lever control cable and remove the cable from the clip.
3. Disconnect the motor electrical connector.
4. Remove the accelerator cable and the bleed screw hose from their respective clips.
5. Remove the two blower case assembly fastening bolts and remove the blower case assembly.
6. Separate the two blower case halves by removing the clips.
7. Remove the blend door support panel by removing the two clips on the air inlet side of the case.
8. Remove the blower motor retaining screws (3) from the upper blower case. Retain the rubber vibration dampers.
9. Remove the fan-to-motor retaining sleeve and take the fan off of the motor. Installation is the reverse of the removal procedure.

18i and Fuego

NOTE: The motor cannot be repaired and the fans cannot be disassembled.

1. Disconnect the battery.
2. Either clamp the heater hoses or drain the cooling system.
3. Disconnect the hoses and the connectors for the heater blower motor and the wiper motor.
4. Remove the clip from the airflow flap cable sleeve and disengage the end of the cable.
5. Remove the retaining screws and the nuts.

NOTE: The nuts are located under the dashboard.

6. Remove the heating/ventilating assembly and the seal.
7. Remove the clips on the housing and

Heater core removal and installation—Le Car

remove the center bolt from the heating/ventilating assembly.
8. Separate the two half shells and remove the motor.
9. To install the motor, proceed in the reverse of the removal procedure. Seal the mating surfaces of the housings.

Heater Core

REMOVAL AND INSTALLATION

Le Car

1. Remove the blower case assembly as outlined in the previous procedure.
2. Drain the cooling system.
3. Remove the bottom heater hose, the heater control valve, and the bleed screw hose.
4. Remove the heater core mounting bolts and withdraw the heater core. Installation is the reverse of the removal procedure.

18i and Fuego

The heater core is removed in the same manner as the blower motor. The heater core is a part of the heating/ventilating assembly that must be removed and separated.

Radio

REMOVAL AND INSTALLATION

Because of the many types of radio assemblies that are available for the vehicles, no procedure is recommended, but must rely upon the radio manufacturer for specific instructions. Above all, before attempting any removal or installation of electrical components, disconnect the battery cables to avoid damage to the unit.

Windshield Wiper Motor

REMOVAL AND INSTALLATION

Le Car

1. Remove the drive arm nut from the motor shaft.
2. Remove the motor mounting screws. Disconnect the electrical connector.
3. Remove the motor from the assembly.
4. The installation is the reverse of the removal procedure.

Wiper motor assembly—Le Car: A—drive link, B—driven link

18i and Fuego

1. Remove the wiper arms and the outer retaining post nuts.
2. Disconnect the electrical connector and the ground wire.
3. Remove the plate retaining bolt and push inward to free the two spindles and then pull the assembly to the right, as viewed from the front of the vehicle, and withdraw the wiper assembly.
4. Remove the drive link retaining nut and remove the three motor retaining bolts.
5. Remove the motor.
6. The installation is in the reverse of the removal procedure. When installing the assembly, be sure the drive links are in line, with the motor in the park position.

Wiper motor assembly—18i and Fuego: A—drive link, B—driven link

Instrument Cluster

REMOVAL AND INSTALLATION

Le Car

1. Disconnect the battery cables.
2. Disconnect the speedometer cable in the engine compartment.
3. Unclip the instrument panel cowl.
4. The instrument panel is held securely to the support plate by side clips. Press in on the side clips until they clear the support plate and pull the instrument panel from the plate.
5. Unscrew the speedometer cable and disconnect the two electrical connectors.
6. The installation is in the reverse of the removal procedure.

18i Custom Models

1. Disconnect the battery cables.

2. Remove the two half housings around the steering column.

3. Remove the two screws that hold the panel to the dash.

4. Disconnect the speedometer cable and the three junction blocks.

5. Tilt the panel outward by inserting a small prybar while pushing the bottom in.

NOTE: The panel pivots on two hinge pins, one on each side of the opening.

6. The installation is the reverse of the removal procedure.

18i Deluxe Models

1. Disconnect the battery cables.

2. Remove the covers on the left and right sides of the panel.

3. Unscrew the two retaining screws.

4. Remove the bezel from the switch panel and disconnect the switches and remove the panel.

5. Squeeze the instrument panel clips and pull the instrument panel out in such a manner as to unclip the speedometer cable.

6. Remove the electrical junction blocks.

7. The installation is the reverse of the removal procedure.

Fuse Panels

The fuse panels are located on the left side of the steering column, under the dash or covered by a panel that must be removed, in the same location.

SAAB

SERIAL NUMBER IDENTIFICATION

Vehicle

The vehicle serial number is located in two places on all SAAB models: the serial number is stamped on a plate at the lower left hand corner of the windshield, and the serial number is punched in the car body under the left side of the rear seat cushion.

Beginning with the 1981 and later models, the vehicle serial number is located on the right side of the rear cross beam in the luggage compartment.

Chassis Number Up To and Including 1980

Example—

$$\underline{90}\ \underline{79}\ \underline{2}\ \underline{000001}$$
$$(1)\ \ (2)\ (3)\ \ \ (4)$$

(1) Model:
   90 = 900
   99 = 99
(2) Year:
   76 = 1976
   77 = 1977
   78 = 1978
   79 = 1979
   80 = 1980
(3) Assembly Plant:
   1 = Trollhättan
   2 =
   3 = Nystäd
(4) Serial number:
   000001

Chassis Number Beginning With 1981 and Later

Example—

$$\underline{YS3}\ \underline{A}\ \underline{G}\ \underline{3}\ \underline{1}\ \underline{S}\ \underline{X}\ \underline{B}\ \underline{1}\ \underline{000001}$$
$$(1)\ \ (2)\ (3)\ (4)\ (5)\ (6)\ (7)\ (8)\ (9)\ \ \ (10)$$

(1) Manufacturer:
   YS3 = Sweden
   YK1 = Finland

(2) Production line:
   A = 900
(3) Series:
   G = 900
   S = 900S
   E = 900S
   T = Turbo 900
(4) Body Type:
   3 = Two side doors and one tailgate
   4 = Four side doors
   5 = Four side doors and one tailgate
(5) Engine:
   1 = B20C
   2 = B20T
   3 = B20I
   4 = B20S
(6) Safety equipment:
   A = Air bags
   P = Passive safety belts
   S = Active safety belts
(7) Check digit:
   0–9 or X
(8) Model Year:
   B = 1981
   C = 1982
   D = 1983
   E = 1984
(9) Assembly Plant:
   1 = Trollhättan—Line one
   2 = Trollhättan—Line two
   3 = Arlov
   4 = Finland
(10) Serial Number:
   000001

Engine Number Up To and Including 1980

Example—

$$\underline{BT}\ \underline{20}\ \underline{P01}\ \underline{000001}$$
$$(1)\ \ (2)\ \ (3)\ \ \ (4)$$

(1) BT = Gasoline engine, twin carburetor
   BI = Gasoline engine, mechanical injection
   BSI = Gasoline engine, Turbo and mechanical injection

(2) Cylinder volume in deciliter (dl). (deciliter equals 1/10 of liter)
(3) Variant designation, such as engine/transmission combination and geographic location
(4) Serial number in six digits

Engine Number From 1981 and Later

Example—

$$\underline{B}\ \underline{20}\ \underline{S}\ \underline{M}\ \underline{UC}\ \underline{01}\ \underline{B}\ \underline{000001}$$
$$(1)\ (2)\ (3)\ (4)\ (5)\ \ (6)\ (7)\ \ \ (8)$$

(1) B = Gasoline engine
(2) Cylinder volume in deciliter (dl) (deciliter equal 1/10 of liter)
(3) Model:
   C = Single carburetor
   T = Twin carburetor
   I = Fuel injection
   S = Turbo
(4) Transmission type:
   M = Manual
   A = Automatic
(5) Exhaust emission control level:
   UC = USA
   SW = Sweden
   EU = Europe
(6) Equipment variants, such as engine/transmission combinations and geographic locations
(7) Year designations:
   B = 1981
   C = 1982
   D = 1983
   E = 1984
(8) Serial number in six digits

Engine

On the 1985 cc engine the number is stamped on a plate which is secured to the upper portion of the engine directly forward of the fuel injection unit.

SAAB-SCANIA TROLLHATTAN - SWEDEN

Chassi Nr	Vehicle No.			
Fahrgest Nr	No de chassis			
Till. Totalvikt	G V W R		Max. tågvikt	Max. train W
Zul. Gesamtgew.	P. max. Adm.		Ges. Zuggew.	P. M A. train
Till. Axeltryck f.	GAWR front		Till. Axeltryck b.	GAWR rear
Zul. Achslast v.	P. max. l'ess. AV.		Zul. Achslast h.	P. max. l'ess. AR.

S 6789

Chassis number sign

BODY COLOUR
148 B

S 6879

Color code sign

VEHICLE EMISSION CONTROL INFORMATION
MANUFACTURER: SAAB-SCANIA AB, SWEDEN   ENGINE SIZE: 121.1 CU IN.
MODELS: SAAB 2.0 IM (MANUAL)   ENGINE FAMILY: BI 20 P
SAAB 2.0 IA (AUTOMATIC)
EXHAUST EMISSION CONTROL TYPE:
MANUAL TRANS.: FUEL INJECTION, VACUUM IGNITION ADVANCE DELAY VALVE,
DECELERATION VALVE.
AUTOMATIC TRANS.: FUEL INJECTION, E.G.R. AND DECELERATION VALVE.
IDLE SPEED: 875 ±50 RPM
CO LEVEL AT IDLE: 1.5% ± 0.5 (EVAP. CANISTER PURGE LINE DISCONNECTED).
IGNITION TIMING AT 2000 RPM (DISCONNECTED VACUUM LINE, TRANSMISSION
IN NEUTRAL) MODEL IM: 20° B.T.D.C. MODEL IA: 23° B.T.D.C.
DECEL. VALVE SETTING: COAST DOWN FROM 3000 RPM TO IDLE IN 5 ± 1 SEC.
VALVE CLEARANCE: INLET 0.006 — 0.012 IN. EXHAUST 0.014—0.020" IN.
DWELL ANGLE: 50° ± 3°
SPARK PLUG GAP: 0.024 - 0.028 IN.
THIS VEHICLE CONFORMS TO CANADIAN EXHAUST EMISSION CONTROL
REGULATIONS APPLICABLE TO 1979 NEW MOTOR VEHICLES.
SAAB-SCANIA   9323965

Directions for exhaust emission
control

Gearbox number, automatic transmission

Gearbox number, manual transmission

Engine number

SPECIFICATIONS

Chassis number punched in car body,
3-door model (Placed under back
seat cushion)

Chassis number punched in car body,
5-door model (Placed under back
seat cushion)

Component identification number locations

GENERAL ENGINE SPECIFICATIONS

Year	Engine Displacement cc (cu. in.)	Fuel Delivery Type	Horsepower @ rpm	Torque @ rpm	Bore × Stroke (in.)	Compression Ratio	Maximum Oil Pressure (psi)
'76–'83	1985 (121.0)	Bosch C.I. Fuel injection	②	③	3.543 × 3.071	①	57–71

① Federal Model—1976   8.7:1
           1977–83   9.25:1
  California—1976–79   8.7:1
        1980–83   9.25:1
  Canada—1976–83   9.25:1
  Turbo—1979–83   7.2:1
② 1976–78—115 @ 5500 Federal
        110 @ 5500 California
        118 @ 5500 Canada
  1979–80—100 @ 5200 w/single carburetor
        108 @ 5200 w/twin carburetor
        118 @ 5500 w/fuel injection
        145 @ 5000 Turbo
  1981–83—110 @ 5500 w/catalyst equipped, except Turbo
        115 @ 5500 non-catalyst
        135 @ 4800 Turbo
        118 @ 4800 Canada
③ 1976–78—123 @ 3500 Federal and Canada
        119 @ 3500 California
  1979–80—115 @ 3500 w/single carburetor
        127 @ 3300 w/twin carburetor
        123 @ 3700 w/fuel injection
        174 @ 3000 Turbo
  1981–83—119 @ 3500 w/catalyst equipped engine except Turbo
        160 @ 3500 Turbo
        123 @ 3500 Canada and non-catalyst Federal engine

TUNE-UP SPECIFICATIONS

Year	Engine Displacement cc	Spark Plugs Type	Spark Plugs Gap	Distributor Point Dwell (deg)	Distributor Reluctor Gap (in.)	Basic Ignition Timing (deg)	Intake Valve Opens (deg)	Fuel Pump Pressure psi	Idle Speed rpm	Valve Clearance Intake	Valve Clearance Exhaust
'76–'83	1985	NGK BP6ES ③	0.024–0.028	Electronic	0.010	②⑥	10 BTDC⑤	①	875	0.008–0.010	0.016–⑤ 0.018

NOTE: If these specifications differ from those on the engine compartment stickers, use the sticker specifications.
① Fuel injected engines (all models): Fuel line pressure before the control pressure regulator is 66.9–69.7 (setting valve), and 48.5–54.0 psi (warm engine) after the control pressure regulator (located in fuel distributor).
② '76 Federal—14° BTDC @ 800 rpm
  '76 California—12° BTDC @ 800 rpm
  '76–'83—20° @ 2000 rpm
  '76–'83 Canada, manual transmission—20° BTDC @ 2000 rpm
  '76–'83 Canada, automatic transmission—23° BTDC @ 2000 rpm
③ Turbo—NGK-BP7ES
④ Turbo—.018–.020
⑤ Turbo—12° BTDC
⑥ With vacuum hose disconnected

FIRING ORDERS

Firing order and ignition cable positioning to 1980

Firing order and ignition cable positioning—1981 and later

CAPACITIES

Year	Engine Displacement (cc)	Engine Crankcase (qts.)		Transmission (pts.)		Drive Axle (pts.)	Fuel Tank (gals.)	Cooling System (qts.) w/o AC
		With Filter	Without Filter	Manual	Automatic			
'76–'83	1985	3.7	3.2	4.4①	17	1.3	14.5③	8.5②

① 5.3—5 speed trans. & 4 speed w/o dipstick
② '79–'80—10.5, '81–'83—10.8 qts
③ '80–'83—16.6 U.S. gals.

CRANKSHAFT AND CONNECTING ROD SPECIFICATIONS

		Crankshaft				Connecting Rod	
Year	Engine Displacement (cc)	Main Bearing Journal Diameter (in.)	Main Bearing Oil Clearance (in.)	Shaft End-Play (in.)	Thrust on No.	Journal Diameter (in.)	Oil Clearance (in.)
'76–'83	1985	2.283–2.284	0.0008–0.0025	0.003–0.011	3	2.0465–2.0472	0.0010–0.0025

VALVE SPECIFICATIONS

Year	Engine Displacement (cc)	Valve Seat Angle (deg)	Valve Face Angle (deg)	Spring Test Pressure (lbs. @ in.)	Installed Spring Height (in.)	Stem To Guide Clearance (in.)		Stem Diameter (in.)	
						Intake	Exhaust	Intake	Exhaust
'76–'83	1985	45	44.5	178–198 @ 1.16	1.56	0.020①	0.020①	0.3134–0.3139	0.3132–0.3142

① Maximum clearance measured with valve face pulled 3 mm (0.12 in.) from valve seat

PISTON AND RING SPECIFICATIONS

			Ring Gap (in.)			Ring Side Clearance (in groove) (in.)	
Year	Engine Displacement (cc)	Piston Diameter (in.)	Top Compression	Bottom Compression	Oil Control	Top Compression	Bottom Compression
'76–'83	1985	3.5425–3.5428	0.014–0.022	0.012–0.018	0.015–0.055	0.002–0.003	0.002–0.003

TORQUE SPECIFICATIONS
(ft. lbs.)

Year	Engine Displacement (cc)	Cylinder Head Bolts	Rod Bearing Bolts	Main Bearing Bolts	Crankshaft Pulley or Gear Bolt	Flywheel to Crankshaft Bolts	Camshaft Gear Bolt	Intake Manifold	Exhaust Manifold
'76–'83	1985	①②	40	79	137	43	14	13	18

① 1976–81—with 17mm screw head: 69 ft. lbs.
with 15mm screw head: 1st stage—44 ft. lbs.
2nd stage—65 ft. lbs.—Run engine to warm.
Allow 30 minutes cool time—Retighten to 65 ft. lbs.

② 1982 and later—1st stage—43 ft. lbs.
2nd stage—72 ft. lbs.—Run engine to warm.
Allow 30 minutes cool time—Retighten to 72 ft. lbs.

TORQUE SEQUENCES

Cylinder head bolt torque sequence to 1980

Cylinder head bolt torque sequence, 1981 and later

ALTERNATOR AND REGULATOR SPECIFICATIONS

Year	Engine Displacement (cc)	Model	Rated Voltage (volts @ rpm)	Alternator Maximum Continuous Load (amps. @ rpm)	Minimum Brush Length (in.)	Brush Spring Pressure (oz.)	Regulating Voltage
'76–'80	1985	99	14 @ 2000	55 @ 5000	0.34	10.5–14	13.5–14.2
'76–'83	1985	900	14 @ 2000	55 @ 5000	①	10.5–14	13.5–14.2
'76–'83	1985	900	14 @ 2100	65 @ 5000	①	10.5–14	13.5–14.2
'76–'83	1985	900	14 @ 2100	70 @ 5000	①	10.5–14	13.5–14.2

① 0.020 inch protruding from opening of brushnut assembly

BATTERY AND STARTER SPECIFICATIONS

Year	Engine Displacement (cc)	Battery Ampere Hour Capacity	Battery Volts	Battery Terminal Ground	Starter Load Test Amps.	Starter Load Test Volts	Starter Load Test @ rpm	Starter No Load Test Amps.	Starter No Load Test Volts	Starter No Load Test @ rpm	Brush Spring Tension (oz.)
'76–'83	1985	60	12	Neg.	205–235	9	1000–1300	35–55	11.5	6500–8500	41–46

BRAKE SPECIFICATIONS

Year	Wheel Lug Nut Torque (ft. lbs.)	Master Cylinder Bore	Brake Disc (in.) Minimum Thickness	Brake Disc (in.) Maximum Axial Run-Out	Pad Thickness (in.) Front	Pad Thickness (in.) Rear
'76–'83	65–80	⅞	0.461 Front 0.374 Rear	0.004	0.425	0.335

WHEEL ALIGNMENT

Year	Caster	Camber	Toe-In (in.)①	King Pin Angle	Wheel Angle During Turns (deg)	
					Inner Wheel	Outer Wheel
'76–'83	1° ± ½°②	½° ± ½°	0.08 ± 0.04″	11½° ± 1°	20¾° ± ½°③	20°

① Measured at the rims
② 2° ± ½°—vehicles equipped with power steering
③ 20½° ± 1°—SAAB 99 series

TUNE UP

Spark Plugs

The spark plugs are replaced in the conventional manner. Anyone unfamiliar with the spark plug firing order, should remove and replace only one spark plug wire and spark plug at a time or tag each wire and number them, starting at the rear of the engine at number one cylinder and working towards the front, to avoid mismatching the spark plug wires to the proper spark plugs.

Distributor

1976–80

All vehicles that are sold in the United States are equipped with a breakerless ignition system with an electromagnetic pulse generator in the distributor and an electronic control unit which performs the task of the conventional point system.

1981 and later

An electronic ignition system using a semiconductor impulse transmitter (Hall transmitter) in the distributor with a control unit incorporating an electronic breaker, is used on all models destined for the United States and is also used on all Turbo engines. The ignition coil used with this system is capable of producing approximately 15% more voltage than the earlier breakerless ignition system and should not be interchanged. The ignition coil is provided with a safety fuse, should the coil become overheated.

Ignition Timing

Ignition timing is set in the conventional manner, using the marks that are located on the flywheel.

However, the engine is also equipped for checking the timing using an ignition service instrument.

The equipment in the vehicle comprises a pin in the engine flywheel and a service socket in the clutch cover. The ignition service instrument is connected to the clutch cover by means of a special connector and to the plug lead No. 1 cylinder by means of a terminal. The ignition service instrument is also connected to the ignition service socket at the fuse box and by means of an impulse transmitter at the plug lead for No. 1 cylinder.

NOTE: The SAAB ignition service instrument consists of a tachometer, cam angle meter, stroboscope lamp and switch for operating the starter.

Valve Lash

1. Remove the valve cover (1981 and later models, the pistons of cylinders numbers one and four must be at TDC before distributor and valve cover can be removed).
2. Using an appropriate special tool (Saab #8392185 or its equivalent), rotate the crankshaft as necessary to position the high point of the camshaft lobe 180° away from the valve depressor face (base circle of the cam lobe must contact the valve depressor) on the valve which the clearance is to be checked.

NOTE: The special crankshaft turning wrench fits the center screw of the crankshaft belt pulley at the dash panel.

3. Try the maximum and minimum clearances with a feeler gauge. The minimum feeler should slip in, but the maximum feeler should not.
4. Measure and record the clearance of all the valves in the same manner. Adjust the clearance of any valves that do not lie within the following limits.
   Intake valves: 0.008–0.010 inch
   Exhaust valves (except turbo.): 0.016–0.018 inch.
   Exhaust valves (turbo):0.018–0.020 inch.
5. To adjust the valves, remove the camshaft, tappets and adjusting pallets (shims) of any valves that need to be adjusted.

NOTE: See the proper procedure for camshaft removal and installation which is located in this section of this manual.

6. Using a micrometer, measure and record the thickness of the pallet (shim). This thickness plus the valve clearance adds up to the total distance between the valve and the cam.
7. The choice of the adjusting pallet(shim) is determined by the measured total distance between the valve depressor (tappet) and the cam, less the specified valve clearance for an intake or exhaust valve as the case may be.
8. Insert the new adjusting pallet (shim) and the valve depressor (tappet) and reinstall the camshaft.
9. Repeat the measurement procedure to insure that the clearances are correct.
10. Install the valve cover using a new valve cover gasket.

Checking valve clearance with feeler gauge

Valve Adjustment Table

Valve clearance measured with dial indicator (mm) — at left; column headings are the measured pallet (shim) thickness (mm).

Clearance (mm)	2,89	2,84	2,79	2,74	2,69	2,64	2,59	2,54	2,48	2,43	2,38	2,33	2,28	2,23	2,18	2,13	2,08	2,03	1,98	1,93	1,88	1,82	1,77					
0,00	2,64	2,59	2,54	2,48	2,43	2,38	2,33	2,28	2,23	2,18	2,13	2,08	2,03	1,98	1,93	1,88	1,82	1,77										
0,02	2,69	2,64	2,59	2,54	2,48	2,43	2,38	2,33	2,28	2,23	2,18	2,13	2,08	2,03	1,98	1,93	1,88	1,82	1,77									
0,05	2,69	2,64	2,59	2,54	2,48	2,43	2,38	2,33	2,28	2,23	2,18	2,13	2,08	2,03	1,98	1,93	1,88	1,82	1,77									
0,07	2,74	2,69	2,64	2,59	2,54	2,48	2,43	2,38	2,33	2,28	2,23	2,18	2,13	2,08	2,03	1,98	1,93	1,88	1,82	1,77								
0,10	2,74	2,69	2,64	2,59	2,54	2,48	2,43	2,38	2,33	2,28	2,23	2,18	2,13	2,08	2,03	1,98	1,93	1,88	1,82	1,77								
0,12	2,79	2,74	2,69	2,64	2,59	2,54	2,48	2,43	2,38	2,33	2,28	2,23	2,18	2,13	2,08	2,03	1,98	1,93	1,88	1,82	1,77							
0,15	2,79	2,74	2,69	2,64	2,59	2,54	2,48	2,43	2,38	2,33	2,28	2,23	2,18	2,13	2,08	2,03	1,98	1,93	1,88	1,82	1,77							
0,17	2,84	2,79	2,74	2,69	2,64	2,59	2,54	2,48	2,43	2,38	2,33	2,28	2,23	2,18	2,13	2,08	2,03	1,98	1,93	1,88	1,82	1,77						
0,20	2,84	2,79	2,74	2,69	2,64	2,59	2,54	2,48	2,43	2,38	2,33	2,28	2,23	2,18	2,13	2,08	2,03	1,98	1,93	1,88	1,82	1,77						
0,22	2,89	2,84	2,79	2,74	2,69	2,64	2,59	2,54	2,48	2,43	2,38	2,33	2,28	2,23	2,18	2,13	2,08	2,03	1,98	1,93	1,88	1,82	1,77					
0,25	2,89	2,84	2,79	2,74	2,69	2,64	2,59	2,54	2,48	2,43	2,38	2,33	2,28	2,23	2,18	2,13	2,08	2,03	1,98	1,93	1,88	1,82	1,77					
0,27		2,89	2,84	2,79	2,74	2,69	2,64	2,59	2,54	2,48	2,43	2,38	2,33	2,28	2,23	2,18	2,13	2,08	2,03	1,98	1,93	1,88	1,82	1,77				
0,30		2,89	2,84	2,79	2,74	2,69	2,64	2,59	2,54	2,48	2,43	2,38	2,33	2,28	2,23	2,18	2,13	2,08	2,03	1,98	1,93	1,88	1,82	1,77				
0,32			2,89	2,84	2,79	2,74	2,69	2,64	2,59	2,54	2,48	2,43	2,38	2,33	2,28	2,23	2,18	2,13	2,08	2,03	1,98	1,93	1,88	1,82	1,77			
0,35			2,89	2,84	2,79	2,74	2,69	2,64	2,59	2,54	2,48	2,43	2,38	2,33	2,28	2,23	2,18	2,13	2,08	2,03	1,98	1,93	1,88	1,82	1,77			
0,37				2,89	2,84	2,79	2,74	2,69	2,64	2,59	2,54	2,48	2,43	2,38	2,33	2,28	2,23	2,18	2,13	2,08	2,03	1,98	1,93	1,88	1,82	1,77		
0,40				2,89	2,84	2,79	2,74	2,69	2,64	2,59	2,54	2,48	2,43	2,38	2,33	2,28	2,23	2,18	2,13	2,08	2,03	1,98	1,93	1,88	1,82	1,77		
0,42					2,89	2,84	2,79	2,74	2,69	2,64	2,59	2,54	2,48	2,43	2,38	2,33	2,28	2,23	2,18	2,13	2,08	2,03	1,98	1,93	1,88	1,82	1,77	
0,45					2,89	2,84	2,79	2,74	2,69	2,64	2,59	2,54	2,48	2,43	2,38	2,33	2,28	2,23	2,18	2,13	2,08	2,03	1,98	1,93	1,88	1,82	1,77	
0,47						2,89	2,84	2,79	2,74	2,69	2,64	2,59	2,54	2,48	2,43	2,38	2,33	2,28	2,23	2,18	2,13	2,08	2,03	1,98	1,93	1,88	1,82	1,77
0,50						2,89	2,84	2,79	2,74	2,69	2,64	2,59	2,54	2,48	2,43	2,38	2,33	2,28	2,23	2,18	2,13	2,08	2,03	1,98	1,93	1,88	1,82	1,77
0,52							2,89	2,84	2,79	2,74	2,69	2,64	2,59	2,54	2,48	2,43	2,38	2,33	2,28	2,23	2,18	2,13	2,08	2,03	1,98	1,93	1,88	1,82
0,55							2,89	2,84	2,79	2,74	2,69	2,64	2,59	2,54	2,48	2,43	2,38	2,33	2,28	2,23	2,18	2,13	2,08	2,03	1,98	1,93	1,88	1,82
0,57								2,89	2,84	2,79	2,74	2,69	2,64	2,59	2,54	2,48	2,43	2,38	2,33	2,28	2,23	2,18	2,13	2,08	2,03	1,98	1,93	1,88
0,60								2,89	2,84	2,79	2,74	2,69	2,64	2,59	2,54	2,48	2,43	2,38	2,33	2,28	2,23	2,18	2,13	2,08	2,03	1,98	1,93	1,88
0,62									2,89	2,84	2,79	2,74	2,69	2,64	2,59	2,54	2,48	2,43	2,38	2,33	2,28	2,23	2,18	2,13	2,08	2,03	1,98	1,93
0,65									2,89	2,84	2,79	2,74	2,69	2,64	2,59	2,54	2,48	2,43	2,38	2,33	2,28	2,23	2,18	2,13	2,08	2,03	1,98	1,93
0,68										2,89	2,84	2,79	2,74	2,69	2,64	2,59	2,54	2,48	2,43	2,38	2,33	2,28	2,23	2,18	2,13	2,08	2,03	1,98
0,70										2,89	2,84	2,79	2,74	2,69	2,64	2,59	2,54	2,48	2,43	2,38	2,33	2,28	2,23	2,18	2,13	2,08	2,03	1,98
0,72											2,89	2,84	2,79	2,74	2,69	2,64	2,59	2,54	2,48	2,43	2,38	2,33	2,28	2,23	2,18	2,13	2,08	2,03

Pallet thickness measured

Inlet, mm	2,89	2,84	2,79	2,74	2,69	2,64	2,59	2,54	2,48	2,43	2,38	2,33	2,28	2,23	2,18	2,13	2,08	2,03	1,98	1,93	1,88	1,82	1,77
Exhaust (standard) mm	2,89	2,84	2,79	2,74	2,69	2,64	2,59	2,54	2,48	2,43	2,38	2,33	2,28	2,23	2,18	2,13	2,08	2,03	1,98	1,93	1,88	1,82	1,77
Exhaust (Turbo) mm	2,89	2,84	2,79	2,74	2,69	2,64	2,59	2,54	2,48	2,43	2,38	2,33	2,28	2,23	2,18	2,13	2,08	2,03	1,98	1,93	1,88	1,82	1,77

HOW TO USE THE VALVE ADJUSTMENT TABLE

The following example illustrates how the table is used: The inlet valve clearance is 0.13 mm and therefore needs adjustment. The measured thickness of the adjusting pallet (shim) for this valve is 2.54 mm. Starting from 0.12 mm, which is the closest figure in the table to the measured clearance, go horizontally across the table to the column above the inlet pallet thickness of 2.54 mm. The correct pallet thickness, 2.43 mm, can be read from the table at the intersection of the horizontal line from 0.12 mm and the vertical column from inlet 2.54 mm.

Fuel Injection

IDLE SPEED AND MIXTURE

1. Run the engine until it reaches operating temperature.

2. Adjust the idle speed to 875 ± 50 rpm.

3. If the vehicle is not equipped with a catalytic converter, remove the pulse-air hose and plug the air intake to the non-return valves. On 1979 vehicles sold in the United States and Canada, remove the large bore hose from the charcoal canister. Connect the CO meter sensor to the exhaust pipe.

4. On 1979 vehicles equipped with a catalytic converter, remove the large bore hose at the charcoal canister. Connect the CO meter sensor to the exhaust pipe. Remove the oxygen sensor wire.

5. On 1980 and later vehicles equipped with a catalytic converter, remove and plug the front exhaust pipe and connect the CO meter sensor to the pipe with the aid of a connecting piece. Remove the oxygen sensor wire.

6. Read and adjust the idle speed and CO valve as required. Before each reading, increase the engine speed and allow it to return to idle. Wait 30 seconds before taking the next CO reading.

7. Adjust the idle speed by turning the idle adjusting screw on the throttle valve housing.

8. Adjust the CO by turning the adjusting screw located on the fuel distributor (clockwise = richer mixture; counterclockwise = leaner mixture).

NOTE: These adjustments effect each other, therefore the adjustments should be carried out in steps.

Adjusting the idle speed

9. On 1980 and later catalyst equipped vehicles: Connect the oxygen sensor wire and remove the CO meter probe from the front exhaust pipe connection. Install the plug in the front exhaust pipe. Insert the probe at the rear of the tailpipe. The CO meter reading should be less than 0.4% (less than 0.3%, 1982 and later) with the engine at idle, and the engine and converter at normal operating temperature.

Adjusting the CO value

PERMISSIBLE CO CONTENT OF EXHAUST GASES

Non-catalyst equipped, up to and including 1978 models ① ②	1.25 ± 0.75%
Non-catalyst equipped, from 1980 models ① ②	0.75 ± 0.25%
Catalyst equipped, up to and including 1979 models ② ③	0.75 + 0.25 or − 0.5% ⑤
Catalyst equipped, from 1980 models ③ ④	1.0 ± 0.25% ⑥
Canada, except Turbo ②	1.5 ± 0.5%

① Pulse air disconnected and plugged
② Charcoal canister disconnected
③ Check value with sensor connected, after catalyst. Maximum 0.4 to 1981 models. Maximum 0.3% 1982 and later.
④ 1982 models and later, probe in front of catalyst—0.5 to 1.2% CO. Probe behind catalyst—less than 0.3% CO.

⑤ Sensor disconnected, test probe after catalyst.
⑥ Sensor disconnected, test probe before catalyst.

ENGINE ELECTRICAL

Distributor

REMOVAL AND INSTALLATION

To 1980 models

1. Release the distributor cap hold-down clips, and lift the cap off of the distributor and out of the way. On some models, it may be necessary to remove the cap from the vehicle completely due to space limitations.
2. Disconnect the low voltage wire from the ignition coil. Pull off the vacuum hose.
3. Crank the engine until the flywheel marking is at the ignition position on No. 1 cylinder.
4. Remove the distributor retaining screw and remove the distributor from the engine.
5. Installation is the reverse of removal.

1. Battery
2. Ignition switch
3. Electronic control unit
4. Compensating resistor
5. Distributor
6. Ignition coil
7. Screened cable
8. To fuel pump relay, tachometer and TSI socket
9. To relay terminal 87a (connected at start)

Breakerless ignition system schematic, less Hall effect

1. Rotor
2. Stator
3. Induction coil
4. Stator plate
5. Rotor sleeve
6. Stator sleeve
7. Outer gap
8. Magnet
9. Inner gap
10. Retaining plate and sleeve

Cross section of electronic distributor—to 1981

1981 and Later

1. Remove the distributor cap after marking the location of number one spark plug wire on the distributor housing.

NOTE: Number one cylinder is at the rear of the engine.

2. Disconnect the primary wire connector from the distributor and hose from the vacuum advance unit.

3. Crank the engine until the flywheel

Distributor location—1981 and later

marking is at TDC (0°) and the distributor rotor is pointing to the indicating or reference mark on the distributor housing for the number one cylinder.

4. Match mark the distributor housing to the valve cover housing. Remove the distributor retaining bolts and pull the distributor forward from the end of the valve cover housing. Note the position of the distributor drive lugs.

CAUTION

Do not rotate the engine crankshaft when the distributor is removed from the engine.

5. Installation is the reverse of the removal procedure. Be sure to align the distributor rotor to the number one spark plug wire reference mark on the distributor housing, while aligning the match marks on the valve cover housing and distributor housing.

1. Slotted rotor
2. Hall transmitter

Distributor assembly with Hall effect pickup

1. Battery
2. Ignition lock
3. Control unit
4. Distributor
5. Ignition coil
6. Insulated wires.

Breakerless ignition system with Hall transmitter schematic

ELECTRONIC IGNITION DIAGNOSIS—EXCEPT HALL EFFECT
Engine Completely Dead, Fires Without Starting or Is Difficult to Start

Check	Reading	Condition of the system Probable fault	Check and remedy as necessary
1. Turn the engine over on the starter and check the length of the spark between the high tension lead from the coil and ground	More than 12 mm	Starter circuit and starter relay probably working	Check 0.4 mm compensating resistor by means of ohmmeter. Check the ignition setting. Check for flashover in coil isolator, distributor cap, rotor, ignition leads and plugs. Check the fuel system.
	Less than 12 mm or no spark		Check that current flows from the starter relay circuit to the connection on the compensating resistor. When the starter is running, the voltage between the common connection and the + on the battery should be 0. If not, check the relay and wiring. Proceed to step 2.
2. Switch on the ignition. Before proceeding, check that the battery charge is at least 11 V	Less than 11 V		Charge the battery; readings taken with insufficient battery voltage will give faulty values.
	More than 11 V		Proceed to step 3.
3. Measure the voltage between terminal 15 on the coil and ground	0 V	Break in compensating resistor or leakage from terminal 15 on ignition switch	Check compensating resistor by means of ohmmeter. Check that voltage from the ignition switch is present at the single terminal on the 0.4 ohm resistor. If not, check ignition switch and wiring.
	Less than 6 V	Short-circuit in primary winding of coil	Check resistance of primary winding (0.95–1.4 ohm)
	6–8 V	Primary coil winding and compensating resistor sound.	Proceed to step 4.
	8–12 V	Bad ground connection	Check using ohmmeter that contact pin 31 on the control unit connector has good ground connection.
	12 V	Break in primary coil winding	Check using ohmmeter (0.95–1.4 ohm)
		Control unit not conducting	Check for battery voltage at contact pin 15, using voltmeter
4. Measure the voltage between terminal 1 on coil and ground	0 V	Short-circuit in control unit	Exchange control unit
	0.5–2 V	Power transistor in control unit sound	Proceed to step 5.
	12 V	Control unit not conducing	Change control unit. Check for faulty insulation on cables to terminal 16 on the control unit.
5. Measure resistance in the coil winding	Should be 5, 5–8 k ohm		
	Appreciable deviation	Defective secondary winding in coil	Change the coil Proceed to step 6

ELECTRONIC IGNITION DIAGNOSIS—EXCEPT HALL EFFECT
Engine Completely Dead, Fires Without Starting or Is Difficult to Start

Check	Reading	Condition of the system Probable fault	Check and remedy as necessary
6. Connect a dwell meter Check dwell angle	60–80° (65–90%)	Control unit and impulse transmitter probably without fault.	
	Maximum reading on scale	Dwell meter range insufficient (many dwell meters have maximum reading of 70°) and consequently no information is obtained	Connect a voltmeter across pins 7 and 31d of control unit cable connector. At starting speed (100 rev/min), a minimum reading of 1 V a.c. should be obtained. This indicates that impulses of sufficient strength are being generated. If there is no voltage or the voltage is too low, check the screened impulse cable. Thereafter, check the impulse transmitter in the distributor using an ohmmeter (895–1285 ohm). Check the air gap between the rotor and the stator and, if necessary, adjust to 0.25 mm using a non-magnetic feeler gauge. If the fault persists, change the impulse transmitter.
		The control unit does not react to impulses from the impulse transmitter	Change the control unit

NOTE: Poor running of the engine is unlikely to be caused by faulty electronics. Check the following items first:
1. Good connections throughout ignition system.
2. Ignition setting and centrifugal and vacuum advance.
3. General condition of spark plugs.

1. Plastic cover
2. Power transistor
3. Printed circuit board
4. Base plate

Electronic Control Unit for the Breakerless Ignition system

ELECTRONIC IGNITION DIAGNOSIS—WITH HALL EFFECT

Conditions for Testing

Fully-carged battery, fuel in tank, engine and ambient temperature 32–104°F (0–40°C). Temperature has a considerable effect on values recorded.

Starter motor turns, engine does not fire or starts and runs roughly

↓ Yes

Check breaker gap is 12 mm. Ignition spark at 12 mm?
— No → Adjust ignition.

↓ Yes

Check ignition setting. Is ignition setting correct?
— No → Adjust ignition.

↓ Yes

Check fuel system. Is the engine receiving sufficient fuel?
— No → Repair fuel system.

↓ Yes

Remove the control unit which should be rotated round the earthed bolt so that the fuse is visible from the side. Pull back the rubber cover from the fuse (the fuse should not be removed). Connect a voltmeter between terminals 4 and 2, turn on the ignition and measure the voltage which should be the same as that of the battery. Correct voltage reading?
— No → Check the wiring from the ignition lock to the control unit. Rectify fault.

↓ Yes

Check the ignition coil. Ignition coil primary winding (15 and 1) 0.52–0.76 ohm. Ignition coil secondary winding (4 and 1) 7–9 kOhm. Correct resistance readings?
— No → Replace the ignition coil.

↓ Yes

Remove the wire from the distributor. Connect a voltmeter terminals 15 and 1 on the ignition coil. Turn on the ignition. The voltmeter should drop from 6 V approx. to 0 V within 1 - 2 seconds. Correct voltage reading?
— No → Replace the control unit.

↓ Yes

The engine should now start.

Check HT part of ignition system. Spark plugs, distributor arm, distributor cap, HT cables and connections. Ignition spark at 12 mm?
— No → Check the wiring from the ignition lock to the control unit. Rectify fault.

↓ Yes

Detach the control unit, pull back the rubber collar from the fuse (the fuse should not be removed). Connect a voltmeter between terminals 4 and 2 and measure the voltage which should be the same as that of the battery. Correct voltage reading?
— No → First inverstigate if the wiring between the control unit and the distributor is satisfactory. If so replace the control unit.

↓ Yes

Disconnect the wire from the distributor. Measure the voltage between the + and - connections which should have the same voltage as the battery. Correct voltage reading?
— No → Hall transmitter faulty. Must be replaced.

↓ Yes

Connect a voltmeter between terminals 6 and 3 on the control unit (the fuse should not be removed). Remove the distributor cap and dust cover. Turn the starter motor over momentarily so that the aperture of the slotted rotor is in the gap of the Hall transmitter. Leave the ignition on. The voltage reading sould be 0.4 V or less. Correct voltage reading?
— No → Hall transmitter faulty. Must be replaced.

↓ Yes

Repeat the above until the slotted rotor blocks the gap in the Hall transmitter. The voltage should now read 1.0 V or more. Correct voltage reading?

Alternator

REMOVAL AND INSTALLATION

1. Disconnect the negative battery cable.

2. Remove the alternator wiring connections, retaining screw and the adjusting screw.

3. Remove the alternator belt.

4. Remove the alternator from the vehicle.

5. Installation is the reverse of removal.

BELT TENSION ADJUSTMENT

Adjust the alternator belt tension so that the belt can be depressed about ½inch at the mid-point of its longest straight run.

1. Drive bearing assembly
2. Stator
3. Slip ring end bracket
4. Rotor
5. Rectifier unit
6. Voltage regulator and carbon brush holder

Exploded view of alternator—typical

Bosch-type alternator wiring schematic

Motorola-type alternator wiring schematic

To current-consuming units

Ignition lock

Battery

Indicator light

D+

B+

Voltage regulator

EXC

Rectifiers

Stator winding

Exciter winding

Rectifiers

Regulator

REMOVAL AND INSTALLATION

NOTE: **On 900 series, the voltage regulator is incorporated into the back of the alternator.**

1. Disconnect the negative battery cable.
2. Remove the voltage regulator connecting wires.
3. Remove the hold-down screws and remove the unit from the vehicle.
4. Installation is the reverse of removal.

Starter

REMOVAL AND INSTALLATION

All Except Turbo

1. Disconnect the battery. On the 99 series, disconnect the pre-heater hose.
2. Remove the flywheel cover. Remove the gearbox dipstick if the vehicle is equipped with manual transmission.
3. Remove the starter motor heat shield and the rear mounting bolts.
4. Disconnect the starter motor wires. Remove the front mounting bolts.
5. Carefully remove the starter from the vehicle.
6. Installation is the reverse of removal.

Turbo

1. Disconnect the battery. On the 99 series, remove the battery and the battery tray.

1. Screws, bearing housing
2. Solenoid
3. Drive housing
4. Bushing, drive side
5. Capsule bracket
6. U-washer
7. Shim
8. Rubber gasket
9. Bushing, commutator side
10. Commutator bearing housing
11. Brush plate
12. Field winding
13. Starter housing
14. Rotor
15. Rubber washer
16. Steel washer
17. Engaging lever arm
18. Pinon
19. Bushing, pinion
20. Stop ring
21. Lock ring

Exploded view of starter assembly—typical

2. Remove the turbocharger suction pipe, pre-heater hose and the flywheel cover.

3. On the 900 series, remove the gearbox dipstick (manual transmission only). Remove the bracket and bolts between the turbocharger and the gearbox.

4. Disconnect the starter motor wires. On the 99 series, remove the front starter mounting bolts.

5. Loosen the oil return pipe on the turbocharger enough to allow it to be bent outwards somewhat. On the 99 series, remove the oil return pipe.

6. Remove the starter motor heat shield and the rear mounting bolts.

7. On the 900 series, remove the front starter mounting bolts.

8. Carefully remove the starter from the vehicle.

9. To install, reverse the removal procedure. Be careful to fit a new gasket on the oil return pipe connecting flange on the turbocharger.

ENGINE MECHANICAL

Engine

REMOVAL AND INSTALLATION

99 Series

NOTE: The engine and transmission should be removed from the vehicle as a unit.

1. Remove the hood.
2. Disconnect the battery cables. Remove the battery.
3. Remove the servo cylinder vacuum hose from the inlet manifold and remove the rubber bellows from between the air flow sensor and the inlet manifold.
4. Remove the connections on the fuel distributor and detach the lines. Disconnect the electrical connection on the air flow sensor.
5. On vehicles sold in California, detach the EGR system vacuum hoses from the venturi tap at the air cleaner and from the EGR valve at the throttle valve housing. Remove the clamps at the rubber bellows.
6. Remove the air cleaner and the mixture control unit.
7. Remove the cable connections from the ignition coil, temperature transmitter, radiator fan, thermostat contact, headlights and the switch on the transmission (automatic transmission only).
8. Disconnect the cables from the injection system at the warm-up regulator, auxiliary air valve, cold start valve and the thermo-time switch.
9. Detach the throttle control cable from the bracket on the throttle valve housing.

10. Detach the hoses at the connections to the thermostat housing, radiator, inlet manifold and water pump.

11. Remove the grille. Remove the hood lock operating cable from its position at the dash panel and wheel housing. Remove the two front sheet metal screws and nuts, and the four sheet metal screws holding the headlights to the body. Remove the complete front assembly by lifting forward and upward.

12. If the vehicle is equipped with manual transmission, disconnect the clutch hose from the slave cylinder. Plug the hose and the hole in the slave cylinder.

13. If the vehicle is equipped with automatic transmission, remove the protective cover from the exhaust manifold.

14. Disconnect the exhaust pipe at the exhaust manifold.

15. Disconnect the ground cable from the transmission. On some vehicles it may be necessary to remove the alternator, depending on the type of engine lifting crane that is being used for the removal procedure.

16. On California vehicles, remove the air pump.

17. Raise the vehicle on a hoist and support it safely.

18. If the vehicle is equipped with manual transmission, put the gear lever in Neutral. Tap out the front taper pin from the gear shift rod joint and pull the rubber bellows free of the groove in the gear selector rod. Separate the gear selector rod from the gear selector joint.

NOTE: The rubber bellows has been discontinued (1977) and need not be installed in older vehicles when repair is being made.

19. If the vehicle is equipped with automatic transmission, remove the gear selector cable retaining screw from the transmission and position the gear selector lever in "P".

NOTE: On early models, detach the spring which holds the cable to the gear selector by inserting a pliers in the end of the spring. Rotate it slightly and then pull out the cable. On later models, push back the spring-loaded sleeve on the gear selector lever and release the end of the cable.

20. Remove the speedometer cable from the transmission. Remove the engine brackets.

21. Remove the large clips from around the rubber bellows on the inner universal joints.

22. Install the engine lifting hoist to the two engine lifting lugs.

23. Remove the lower end piece from the control arm on the right side and turn the steering wheel to the left.

24. Raise the engine and transmission from the rear engine cushions and withdraw the left universal joint, by moving the assembly to the right. Move the assembly to

the left and withdraw the right universal joint.

25. Lift the unit and disconnect the starter wires and cables.

26. Carefully remove the unit from the vehicle. Install protective caps over the inner drivers and rubber bellows.

27. Installation is the reverse of removal.

900 Series

NOTE: The engine and transmission should be removed as a unit.

1. Disconnect the positive battery cable. Drain the radiator.
2. Disconnect the windshield washer hose, unbolt the hood hinge links and remove the hood from the vehicle.
3. If the vehicle is equipped with power steering, disconnect the lines at the servo pump.
4. Disconnect the positive battery lead at the starter. Remove the radiator hoses. Remove the engine ground wire. Disconnect the temperature transmitter cable. Remove the coil.
5. Disconnect the cable harness from the clutch cover. If the vehicle is equipped with manual transmission, disconnect the hydraulic line from the clutch slave cylinder and plug the lines.
6. Disconnect the CI system electrical connections from the warm-up regulator, thermo-time switch cold start valve and the auxiliary air valve. On catalytic converter equipped vehicles, also disconnect the oxygen sensor and the throttle switch cables.
7. Disconnect the oil pressure transmitter cable. Loosen the fuel line connections at the fuel distributor. Remove the air filter along with the mixture control unit.
8. Disconnect the throttle cable. Disconnect the hose at the expansion tank. Disconnect the heater hoses at the heater. Disconnect the brake vacuum hose.
9. Remove the clips and remove the bellows from the inner drivers.
10. Place the spacer (Saab tool no. 83-93-209) or equivalent between the upper control arm underside and the car body.

NOTE: Insert the tool from the engine compartment side. The spacer makes the front suspension unloaded when the vehicle is raised.

11. Lift the front end of the vehicle and support it safely.
12. Remove the lower end piece from the control arm. Pull out the steering knuckle assembly and support the end piece against the control arm outer end.
13. If the vehicle is equipped with manual transmission put the gear lever in Neutral. Remove the nut and tap out the taper pin in the gear shift rod joint. Separate the joint from the gear shift rod.
14. If the vehicle is equipped with automatic transmission, remove the retaining screw from the gear selector cable at the transmission. Withdraw the cable with the

gear selector rod in its extreme forward position ''P''. Slide back the spring-loaded sleeve on the gear shift rod and unhook the end of the cable.

15. Separate the exhaust pipe from the exhaust manifold. Disconnect the speedometer cable from the transmission.

16. Remove the rear engine mounting bolts. Slacken the front engine mounting nut so that the mounting can be lifted out of the bracket.

17. Attach the hoist to the two lugs on the engine and raise the assembly slightly. Move the assembly to one side and free the two universal joints.

18. Carefully remove the unit from the vehicle.

19. Installation is the reverse of removal.

Cylinder Head

REMOVAL AND INSTALLATION

NOTE: It may be necessary to remove certain components of the turbocharging system on vehicles so equipped. Turbocharger removal and installation procedures are outlined following the Engine Repair Section.

1. Disconnect the battery cables. Drain the radiator.

2. Remove the rubber bellows from between the air flow sensor and the throttle valve housing and disconnect the throttle cable from the throttle valve housing.

3. Disconnect the cable from the temperature transmitter. Remove the vacuum hose of the power brake booster from the intake manifold.

4. Disconnect the fuel lines from the fuel distributor to the injection valves. Tape the ends of the lines to prevent dirt from entering the system. Remove the bracket from the throttle valve housing mounting.

5. Remove the hose clamps at the connections to the thermostat housing, water pump and intake manifold.

6. Unbolt the exhaust pipe from the exhaust manifold.

7. Remove the distributor cap and ignition wires. Remove the valve cover. 1981 and later, rotate the engine until cylinders one or four are at TDC, before lifting the valve cover from the engine. The design of the distributor driving dog only allows the valve cover/distributor assembly to be removed with the engine in this position.

8. Remove the camshaft sprocket as follows: 1976–1980 models—bolt the mounting plate to the center of the camshaft sprocket, using one of the camshaft sprocket retaining screws. Tighten the nut (screw) securely to immobilize the center stud. Otherwise the chain tensioner will tighten the chain and lock in a new position so that the sprocket cannot be refitted. The chain ten-

sioner cannot be reset without lifting the engine out of the car.

1981 and later, remove the sprocket bolts. Keep chain on sprocket and place sprocket/chain assembly between chain guide and tensioner. A center bolt is not used on the sprocket.

9. 1976–1980 models—Remove the retaining screws from the camshaft sprocket. Separate the wheel from the camshaft plate until it hangs free in the mounting plate by the center stud. 1981 and later—Remove the two bolts from the timing cover under the front of the head.

10. Remove the cylinder head bolts. Mount two guide pins in two of the cylinder head bolt holes (1976–1981 models).

11. Raise the vehicle on the hoist and support it safely. Place a support under the rear end of the engine. Remove the engine mounting bolt in the cylinder head.

12. Remove the screws in the transmission cover. Remove the cylinder head from the vehicle.

13. Installation is the reverse of removal with the following additions: Be sure to use a new cylinder head gasket. Torque the bolts first to 44 ft. lbs. and then to 70 ft. lbs.

14. Make sure that the markings on the camshaft and the bearing cap are in line with one another.

15. Check that the flywheel mark is in line with the mark on the cylinder block and that the engine is set on No. 1 cylinder.

16. 1976–80 models—When mounting the camshaft sprocket, the nut (screw) on the camshaft sprocket center must not be unscrewed before the sprocket is tightly screwed to the camshaft.

17. 1981 and later—Refit the two screws in the timing cover on the front of the cylinder head. Refit the timing chain and sprocket as follows:

 a. Remove the tension from the chain tensioner with special tool 83 93 357 or equivalent. Hook the tool into the catch of the tensioner and pull upwards.

 b. Place the timing sprocket on the camshaft so that the mark on the sprocket

and the screw holes coincide. If necessary, move the chain to position.

 c. Install the three retaining bolts in the sprocket and cam shaft.

 d. If the distributor is mounted to the valve cover, the rotor should be facing the line on the edge of the distributor housing.

Valves

REMOVAL

(Cylinder head removed from the block)

1. Remove the camshaft bearing caps.

2. Lift the camshaft from the cylinder head.

3. Using a magnetic probe, remove the valve depressers.

4. Remove the adjusting pallets, keeping them in their proper order.

5. Remove the camshaft bearing assembly. Install a valve spring depressing tool.

6. Depress the valve spring and remove the valve lock clips. Release the spring tension and remove the valve spring tool.

7. Remove the top valve retainer, valve spring and guide sleeve. Withdraw the valve from the guide.

INSTALLATION

1. Oil the valve stem and install the valve into the valve guide.

2. Install the valve guide sleeve, the spring and the spring retainer.

3. Using a valve spring depressing tool, depress the valve spring and install the valve lock clips.

4. Mount the camshaft bearing assembly to the cylinder head.

5. Install the adjusting pallets by replacing them in their original position.

6. Install the valve depressers and lubricate the bearing surface with oil.

7. Install the camshaft and the bearing caps.

1. Valve
2. Valve spring seat
3. Valve spring
4. Retainer
5. Lock
6. Adjusting pallet
7. Valve depressor
8. Camshaft

Valve mechanism components

Exploded view of engine components, 1981 and later

Preparing sodium filled valves for discard

---— CAUTION ——---

Do not turn or tip the cylinder head after inserting the valve depressers. The depressers and the adjusting pallets will fall out of position and be randomized.

NOTE: Never discard sodium filled valves before they have been properly treated by drilling into the center of the valve head to the sodium content. Drill or cut the stem approximately one inch from the bottom. Throw the valve in a bucket of water to neutralize the sodium. A safe distance from the bucket is no closer than three feet.

---— CAUTION ——---

Keep the valve and sodium compound well away from the water when drilling or cutting the valve. Exposing the sodium to water or other compounds will cause an explosion.

Valve Guides

CHECKING

1. Pull the valve out from its seat approximately 0.120 inch and check the radial play by rocking the valve head. If radial play exceeds 0.020 inch, the valve guide must be replaced.

REPLACING THE VALVE GUIDE

1. Heat the cylinder head and withdraw the valve guide from the camshaft side, using a special pull rod and washers.
2. To replace the guide, heat the cylinder head and press the valve guide into place with SAAB special installing tool or equivalent.
3. After the guide is pressed into position, the valve seat must be reground to 45 degrees.

Intake Manifold

REMOVAL AND INSTALLATION

NOTE: It may be necessary to remove certain components of the turbocharging system on vehicles so equipped. Turbocharger removal and installation procedures are outlined following the Engine Repair Section.

1. Disconnect all hoses, wires and connectors that would inhibit the intake manifold from being removed.

NOTE: It may be necessary to remove the distributor cap and the ignition wires to gain clearance.

2. Remove the throttle valve housing.
3. Remove the manifold bolts and remove the manifold from the vehicle together with the engine lifting lug.
4. Installation is the reverse of removal.

NOTE: Be sure the proper gasket is used. A coolant leakage could occur if the wrong one is used.

Exhaust Manifold

REMOVAL AND INSTALLATION

NOTE: It may be necessary to remove certain components of the turbocharging system on vehicles so equipped. Turbocharger removal and installation procedures are outlined following the Engine Repair Section.

1. Disconnect all necessary hoses, wires, and connectors that would inhibit the exhaust manifold from being removed.
2. Unbolt the exhaust pipe at the connecting flange.
3. If the vehicle is equipped with a heat shield, remove it.
4. Remove the manifold bolts and remove the exhaust manifold from the vehicle.
5. Installation is the reverse of removal.

Timing Chain

REMOVAL AND INSTALLATION

1976–1980

NOTE: In order to accomplish the following procedure the engine will have to be removed from the vehicle.

1. Remove the engine from the vehicle.
2. Remove the cylinder head. See the

Timing mark locations on cam gear and flywheel—1981 and later (1980 and earlier similar)

Idler shaft timing marks—1980 and earlier models

Timing chain assembly—1980 and earlier models

proper procedure in this section of the repair manual.

3. Remove the belt pulley bolt and the pulley, using the necessary puller.

4. Remove the timing chain cover. Remove the timing chain tensioner.

5. Remove the chain guides and the mounting plate with the camshaft sprocket and the timing chain.

6. Remove the crankshaft sprocket using a suitable gear puller, if necessary.

7. Remove the idler shaft sprocket, if it is going to be replaced.

8. Installation is the reverse of removal. Note the following.

9. If it was removed, install the idler shaft. The marking (the bulge in the hold on the idler shaft chainwheel) should line up with the small hole in the keeper plate.

10. Assemble the camshaft sprocket and mounting plate if they have been disassembled. Fit the chain over the camshaft sprocket. Lower the timing chain and mounting plate past the camshaft flange until the center stud of the sprocket is lined up with the camshaft.

11. Rotate the camshaft sprocket until the screw holes match the threaded holes in the camshaft flange.

12. Install the timing chain over the other sprockets so that it hangs straight from the camshaft to the crankshaft.

NOTE: The shaft settings must not be altered.

13. Guide the center stud of the camshaft sprocket into the camshaft. Install the retaining bolts.

14. Mount the curved chain guide plate together with the mounting plate (the chain guide plate nearest the block) with its mounting bolts and stretch the chain as required.

15. Check the camshaft-crankshaft-idler shaft setting.

16. Install the timing chain tensioner.

NOTE: Different versions of the chain tensioner exist and the assembly procedures are different.

REYNHOLDS VERSION

Before installation, remove the tensioner neck. Tension the spring, by turning the ratchet sleeve (actuated by the spring)

Timing chain assembly—1981 and later

clockwise and at the same time pushing it until it locks in its innermost position. Fit the tensioner neck and a spacer piece, so that the tensioner neck will not bottom in the chain tensioner housing and release the self-adjuster.

JWIS VERSION

Place the lock washer with the spiral rod in the chain tensioner housing. Install the spring with the small diameter against the lock washer. Fit the tensioner neck into the housing by simultaneously pressing and turning it into its inner position. The ten-

sioner neck must be held depressed while the chain tensioner is being fitted, right until the chain has been tensioned.

17. Mount the chain tensioner with the guide plate on the engine block.

18. Press the curved chain guide against the chain to stretch it and push the tensioner neck against the spacer piece. Remove the spacer piece while the chain is kept tensioned. Then adjust to leave a clearance of 0.02″ between the housing and the tensioner neck.

Tighten the chain guides.

19. Rotate the crankshaft one full turn in its normal sense and check the chain tension. The movement of the tensioner neck from its butted position must be at least 0.02″ and not more than 0.06″.

20. Remove the bolt from the camshaft sprocket center. Install the timing chain cover using a new gasket.

1981 and Later

1. Remove the engine from the vehicle, following the prescribed outline.

2. Support the engine safely and rotate the crankshaft until the number one cylinder is on its firing stroke and the "0" mark on the flywheel lines up with the line on the rear engine plate.

3. The mark on the rotor should line up with the line on the distributor housing.

NOTE: If no line is found on the distributor housing, mark the housing in line with the rotor point.

4. Remove the valve cover assembly as previously outlined.

5. Remove the sprocket from the camshaft and rest it on the chain tensioner and the chain guide.

6. Remove the cylinder head as previously outlined.

Jwis timing chain tensioner

Reynholds timing chain tensioner

7. Remove the crankshaft pulley and oil pump assembly.

8. Remove the water pump and pulley assembly.

9. Remove the timing chain cover.

10. Remove the timing chain and chain wheel (sprocket) from the engine.

11. Remove the chain tensioner, if required.

12. To install the chain assembly, have the number one piston at TDC and the camshaft in position for number one cylinder-firing position to be in its firing mode, before the cylinder head is installed.

NOTE: Do not rotate either the camshaft or the crankshaft without the chain in place. Damage to the valves or pistons can occur, after the cylinder head is installed.

13. Replace the chain tensioner, if removed.

14. Place the camshaft sprocket to the chain and suspend it from the crankshaft sprocket. Position the chain between the chain guide and the tensioner.

15. Install the timing chain cover assembly while pulling up the chain to avoid being caught under the cover.

16. Install the water pump assembly and install the cylinder head. Torque the head bolts to specifications.

17. Using the tensioner release tool, disengage the tensioner and refit the cam sprocket and chain to the camshaft. Align the marks on the sprocket and the camshaft bearing.

18. Install the sprocket retaining bolts. Release the tensioner assembly.

19. Install the oil pump assembly, seal and pulley.

20. Complete the assembly as required.

—————— **CAUTION** ——————
Do not use an early type inlet manifold gasket. Coolant leakage could occur within the engine.

Timing Chain Oil Seal

The timing chain oil seal can be removed without removing the engine from the vehicle.

1. Disconnect the negative battery cable. Remove the alternator belt. If the vehicle is equipped with power steering or air conditioning, remove the required belts.

2. Remove the clutch cover (torque converter cover) and lock the crankshaft using Saab tool #83-92-987 or equivalent by locking the tool to the ring gear.

3. From beneath the vehicle, remove the pulley retaining bolt using Saab tool #83-92-961 or equivalent. Pull the pulley from the vehicle.

4. Pull off the old seal ring using a suitable tool.

5. Installation is the reverse of removal. Torque the retaining bolt to 137 ft. lbs.

Crankshaft locking procedure

CHECKING TIMING CHAIN TENSION

1976–80

In order to prevent damage caused by the chain tensioner running out too far, the position of the chain tensioner can be checked with the engine mounted in the car.

1. Remove the valve cover.

2. Insert a steel ruler down against the rubber neck on the chain tensioner and measure the distance to the level of the cylinder head cover.

3. The distance should be more than 11.8″. If the distance is less than 11.8″, the engine should be removed as soon as possible for correction. For completely tight chain tensioners (newly adjusted chains), the distance should be about 12.3″.

Camshaft

REMOVAL AND INSTALLATION

1976–80

1. Remove the valve cover.

2. Remove the camshaft sprocket as follows. Bolt the mounting plate to the center of the camshaft sprocket using one of the camshaft sprocket retaining screws.

NOTE: Tighten the nut (screw) securely to immobilize the center stud. Otherwise the chain tensioner will tighten the chain and lock in a new position so that the sprocket cannot be refitted. The chain tensioner cannot be reset without lifting the engine out of the car.

3. Undo the retaining screws from the camshaft sprocket. Separate the wheel from the camshaft plate until it hangs free in the mounting plate by the center stud.

4. Remove the camshaft bearing cups.

5. Remove the camshaft from the vehicle.

6. Installation is the reverse of removal with the following notations.

7. Make sure that the markings on the camshaft and the bearing caps are in line with one another.

8. Check that the flywheel mark is in line with the mark on the No. 1 cylinder block and that the ignition is set on No. 1 cylinder.

9. The screw on the camshaft sprocket center must not be unscrewed before the sprocket is tightly screwed to the camshaft.

1981 and Later

1. Rotate the flywheel until the ''0'' mark indexes with the line on the bell housing. Number one cylinder should be on its firing mode.

2. Remove the valve cover assembly as previously outlined.

3. Be sure both the crankshaft and camshaft are at the number one cylinder firing mode and the indexing lines still are aligned.

4. Remove the camshaft sprocket, keeping the chain on the sprocket. Place the sprocket between the chain guide and tensioner.

5. Remove the camshaft bearing caps and lift the camshaft from the bearing assembly housing. The bearing assembly housing can then be removed, if necessary.

6. To install, reverse the removal procedure. Be certain the timing marks are properly aligned.

Pistons and Connecting Rods

REMOVAL AND INSTALLATION

1. Remove the engine from the vehicle and separate the unit from the transmission.

2. Inspect the connecting rods to make sure that all rods have been numbered correctly.

3. Remove the ring ridge at the top of the cylinder bore, if present, to avoid ring and piston damage, upon removal of the pistons.

4. Loosen the connecting rod cap bolts

Piston and connecting rod assembly

and lightly tap the caps to loosen. Remove the caps and push the connecting rod and piston assembly upward and out of the cylinder bore.

5. Upon installation of the piston rings, place the lower compression ring with the side marked "TOP" uppermost.

6. Rotate the compression rings so that the gaps in alternate rings will be at 180 degrees to each other, positioned alternately over the two ends of the piston pins.

7. Make sure that the spring gaps of the top and bottom rings in the three-piece scraper ring are staggered.

NOTE: Oil the piston rings before assembly.

8. Contine the installation in the reverse of the removal procedure.

ENGINE LUBRICATION

Rear Main Oil Seal

REMOVAL AND INSTALLATION

This seal is otherwise known as the crankshaft seal at the flywheel end. The seal can be changed with the engine in the vehicle, but the clutch and flywheel must first be removed.

1. Remove the clutch and the flywheel from the vehicle.

2. Remove the old seal ring using the proper tool.

3. Install the new seal with the spring ring turned inwards toward the crankshaft using the proper seal installation tool.

4. Continue the installation in the reverse order of the removal.

Oil Pump

REMOVAL AND INSTALLATION

1976–80

1. Remove the four retaining screws from the oil pump body.

2. Remove the oil pump and the sealing ring between the pump and the intermediate plate from the vehicle.

3. Installation is the reverse of removal.

1981 and Later

The oil pump is a gear-type pump and is driven by the crankshaft. It is poistioned between the timing cover and crankshaft pulley. The pump assembly can be removed with the engine in the vehicle.

1. Remove the crankshaft pulley.

2. Lock the crankshaft in place by using a flywheel locking bracket.

3. Remove the oil pump retaining bolts. Remove the oil pump from the timing cover.

4. Before installation, prime the pump assembly and be sure the mark on the outer gear is visible.

5. Install a new gasket and refit the pump

1. O-ring
2. Pump housing
3. O-ring
4. Rotors
5. Cover
6. Valve piston
7. Spring
8. Plug
9. O-ring
10. Locking pin

Exploded view of oil pump—1976–80

and the timing cover. Complete the assembly as required.

6. Before starting the engine, remove the oil filter base and fill the passage way on the pressure side with oil. Replace the filter base.

CHECKING CLEARANCES

1976–80

1. Remove the screws holding the pump cover and the pump housing together and separate the two.

2. Remove the rotors and the O-ring from the pump housing.

3. Remove the pressure reducing valve located in the cover by pulling out the locking pin and then removing the plug, the O-ring, the spring and the valve piston.

4. Check the axial clearance of the inner and outer rotors to the rotor housing with a rule and feeler gauge. The clearance should be 0.00197–0.00354″.

5. If the clearance must be adjusted, grind the sealing surface of the housing or the sides of the rotor with fine emery cloth on a flat surface.

6. Check the evenness to the cover with a ruler. All deformities, scratches and pits should be removed by grinding.

7. Assemble the pump in the reverse order of the removal.

NOTE: The chamfered edge of the outer rotor faces inwards in the pump housing (toward the driveshaft).

NOTE: Published data on oil pump clearance for 1981 and later engines is not available.

ENGINE COOLING

Radiator

REMOVAL AND INSTALLATION

99 Series

1. Drain the radiator.

2. Remove the hose clamps at the radiator and disconnect the hoses.

3. Disconnect the wiring terminals for the radiator fan and the thermoswitch.

4. Remove the grill. Remove the hood lock operating cable from its fastenings at the dash panel and wheel housing.

5. Remove the two front sheet retaining screws and nuts, and the four screws holding the headlights to the body.

6. Remove the front sheet metal complete with the radiator assembly, lifting forward and upward.

7. Installation is the reverse of removal.

900 Series

1. Drain the radiator.
2. Remove the hose clamps on the radiator hoses and disconnect the hoses from the radiator.
3. Disconnect the leads to the radiator fan and the auxiliary fan, if equipped.
4. Disconnect the lead to the thermal switch. Remove the ignition coil.
5. Remove the two bolts in the upper radiator support, and lift the radiator out of the vehicle, pulling the top of the radiator slightly backwards.
6. Installation is the reverse of removal.

Water Pump

REMOVAL

1976–80

NOTE: The water pump is available in three different types which require different removal and installation procedures. Types one and two are used on the 99 series from 1976 through 1977, type three is used on all Saabs from 1977. Type 1: Impeller retained by means of a bolt (cylindrical fitting on the shaft). Type 2: Impeller retained by a nut (conical fitting on the shaft). Type 3: Impeller pressed on the shaft. The thread on the end of the shaft is only provided for dismantling purposes. No nut is required.

1. Drain the radiator. Remove the battery ground cable. Disconnect the intake manifold.
2. Remove the alternator and the alternator bracket.
3. On 99 series vehicles, unbolt both

1. Pump cover
2. Gasket
3. Impeller
4. Water pump seal
5. Sealing ring
6. Ball bearing lock ring
7. Ball bearing
8. Pump shaft

Exploded view of Type 3 water pump

1. Pump cover
2. Gasket
3. Impeller
4. Water pump seal
5. Thrower
6. Seal ring
7. Ball bearing lock ring
8. Ball bearing
9. Oil thrower ring
10. Bearing housing
11. O-rings
12. Seal ring
13. Pump shaft

Exploded view of Type 1 water pump

rear engine mounts. Place a jack under the rear of the engine and raise the engine high enough to remove the upper bolt holding the alternator bracket to the transmission cover. Slacken the lower retaining screw and turn the bracket so that it is as far from the engine as possible.

4. Remove the retaining bolts from the water pump cover and remove the cover.

NOTE: Tapping-out hammers or equivalent must not be used during the removal or installation process on types two and three water pumps.

TYPE 1

1. Remove the center bolt from the impeller. Hold the impeller with a pair of pliers and unscrew it clockwise (left-handed thread). Save the washer.
2. Using the tapping-out hammer with adapter Saab tool #83-92-136 or equivalent on the water pump shaft, carefully withdraw the pump unit.

NOTE: The bearing housing may be left behind in the cylinder block. If so, extract the bearing housing with a tapping-out hammer fitted with a nut and flat washer, external diameter 1.0″.

TYPE 2

1. Position Saab tool #83-92-441 or equivalent over the water pump. Install the two bolts without tightening. Turn the tool counterclockwise so that the peg on the tool engages the fins of the impeller. Tighten the two bolts.

2. Loosen the impeller center nut (left-handed thread). Remove the water pump using Saab tool #83-92-649 or 83-92-490 or equivalent.

NOTE: The bearing housing may be left behind in the cylinder block. If so, extract the bearing housing by means of a tapping-out hammer fitted with a nut and flat washer with an external diameter of 1.0″.

TYPE 3

Remove the water pump using Saab tool #83-92-649 or 83-92-490 or equivalent. The tool fits into the threaded end of the shaft.

NOTE: With regard to all three types of water pump removal, if the impeller is not immobilized while the center bolt is unscrewed, the gear teeth on the pump shaft and idler shaft are liable to be damaged. Up to and including model 1976 (Types 1 and 2), the pump bearing and seals are mounted in a separate bearing housing, which in turn is mounted in the engine block. From model 1977 (Type 3), the pump bearing and seals are mounted directly in the engine block. On most 1976 models, the bottom end of the pump shaft is seated in a bush. In later engines, the shaft end is seated directly in the engine block.

INSTALLATION

Installation is the reverse of removal with the exception of the following notations.

TYPE 1

1. Mount the pump in the engine block.

1. Pump cover
2. Gasket
3. Impeller
4. Water pump seal
5. Seal ring
6. Ball bearing lock ring
7. Ball bearing
8. Bearing housing
9. O-rings
10. Pump shaft

Exploded view of Type 2 water pump

Check that the pump gear engages the gear on the idler shaft.

2. Seat the bearing housing using Saab tool #83-90-536 or equivalent. Make certain that the flange on the bearing housing butts against the plane of the engine block.

3. Install the impeller with the washer and bolt. Torque the bolt to 18 ft. lbs.

TYPE 2

1. Mount the pump in the engine block. Check that the pump gear engages the gear on the jackshaft.

2. Seat the bearing housing using Saab tool #83-92-649 or 83-92-490 or equivalent and Saab tool #83-90-536 or equivalent.

3. Mount the impeller and the nut. Position Saab tool #83-92-441 or equivalent over the pump with the two screws. Do not tighten the screws. Then turn the tool clockwise so that the peg on the tool engages one of the wings on the impeller. Tighten the two screws to 10.8 ft. lbs.

TYPE 3

1. Mount the pump shaft with the bearing and the circlip in the engine block using Saab tool #83-90-551 and 82-92-490 or equivalent. Check to insure that the pump gear engages to the gear on the idler shaft before pressing into position.

2. Install the lower and upper seal using Saab tool #83-0551 and 83-90-536 or equivalent. Press on the impeller shaft. Turn the tightening bolt ¼ turn at a time, unscrew it and then tighten down ¼ turn again until the impeller is finally in position.

1981 and Later

The water pump is located on the engine front and is driven by a "V" belt from the crankshaft pulley. The pump removal is accomplished by removing the "V" belt, pulley and pump retaining bolt. Installation is the reverse of the removal procedure.

Radiator Fan

REMOVAL AND INSTALLATION

1. Disconnect the negative battery cable.

2. On some models, it may be necessary to remove the battery.

3. Disconnect the wires and cables from the ignition coil and the fan motor.

4. Disconnect the cable harness from the fan housing.

5. Remove the fan housing and remove the fan motor from the vehicle.

6. Installation is the reverse of removal.

EMISSION CONTROLS

Crankcase Emission Controls

The crankcase ventilation system is completely enclosed. The system is comprised of a three-way nipple in the valve cover, from which a small hose is routed to the inlet manifold, and a thicker hose routed to the air cleaner assembly. The sizes of the hoses are designed to efficiently regulate the removal of the crankcase gases and to route them into the engine to be mixed with the air/fuel mixture for combustion. The normal routing of the gases are to the inlet manifold, but at times of full acceleration, the gases are routed directly to the air cleaner assembly and mixed with the air as it is drawn into the inlet manifold.

Exhaust Emission Control System

ELECTRIC DECELERATION DEVICE

This device consists of an electronic speed

EMISSION CONTROL EQUIPMENT

System	'76 Federal	'76 Calif.	'77 w/o Catalytic Converter	'77–'79 with Catalytic Converter	'78–'79 w/o Catalytic Converter	'80 and Later with Catalytic Converter	Turbo. '79	Turbo. '80 and Later
Deceleration device electric							X	
Deceleration device vacuum	X	X	X	X	X	X		X
Deceleration device dashpot						X		X
Delay valve			X		X			
EGR on-off	X①							X
EGR proportional		X	X					
EGR two port					X	X		
Air injection		X						
Pulse air			X		X			
Oxygen sensor & catalytic converter				X		X	X	X
Compression 7.2:1							X	X
Compression 8.7:1	X	X		X				
Compression 9.25:1			X		X	X		
ELCD system	X	X	X	X	X	X	X	X

① Automatic transmission only

transmitter which is located below the instrument panel. This transmitter is actuated by electric pulses from the speedometer and the solenoid at the throttel bousing. The solenoid serves as a variable idling stop. During engine overrun the idle speed is increased if the speed of the vehicle exceeds 10 mph.

VACUUM DECELERATION DEVICE

This system consists of a vacuum controlled spring-loaded valve cone which is actuated by the vacuum in the intake manifold.

DASHPOT DECELERATION DEVICE

This device is installed on the throttle housing and acts to mechanically dampen the throttle valve when it shuts. The retardation time can be altered by loosening the locknut and screwing it in away from the throttle stop, which causes shorter deceleration time or toward the throttle stop, which causes longer deceleration time.

DELAY VALVE

A delay valve is mounted in the vacuum passage between the throttle valve housing and the vacuum control unit of the distributor. The valve delays the formation of a vacuum by around 6 seconds. The ignition advance is therefore also delayed during acceleration and the emission of nitric oxide (NO_x) is reduced.

The white end of the delay valve should be towards the vacuum control unit of the distributor. It is also important that the valve is fitted with the shorter hose running between the valve and the vacuum control unit of the distributor.

When the suction line is to be disconnected (e.g. in conjunction with checking of ignition timing), always disconnect the hose at the throttle housing. Otherwise there will be a risk of dirt entering and clogging the delay valve.

ON-OFF EGR

When this type of EGR valve opens, a small quantity of exhaust gases flows via the metering orifice from the exhaust manifold, through the EGR crosspipe and the EGR valve to the inlet manifold. The EGR valve is controlled by means of a vacuum from the throttle valve housing. The vacuum hole is located relative to the throttle valve so that a vacuum signal is obtained when the engine speed is about 1.900 rev/min. or somewhat higher. Even during conditions of small loads, a sufficiently strong vacuum is obtained to open the valve completely. At full throttle and slightly below, the vacuum is so weak that the valve does not open.

The PVS valve senses the temperature of the coolant and cuts out the vacuum at temperatures lower than approximately 100° F (38°C) which means that improved driveability is obtained immediately after starting with a cold engine.

PROPORTIONAL EGR

The EGR valve is controlled by means of a vacuum regulator. When the valve opens, a small quantity of the exhaust gases is recirculated through the EGR crosspipe and the EGR valve to the inlet manifold. When the induction air passes through the venturi, a venturi signal which is proportional to the total air flow is obtained. The signal is transmitted to the EGR vacuum amplifier which amplifies the signal 14 times by means of the manifold vacuum reservoir.

The manifold vacuum reservoir is connected to the amplifier. The amplified signal then goes via the vacuum signal switch and the PVS valve to the EGR valve. The vacuum signal switch cuts out the EGR signal at engine speed below 2.500 ± 500 rev/min. This has been arranged by means of a hole drilled through the throttle valve housing (during the running-in of the engine, the cut-off speed can be somewhat lower). The PVS valve senses the temperature of the coolant and cuts off the EGR signal at temperatures lower than approx. 100°F, which results in improved driveability immediately after cold engine starting. At wide open throttle, the vacuum in the manifold reservoir disappears after a few seconds and the EGR valve closes.

TWO-PORT EGR

In the two-port EGR system, the opening of the EGR valve is regulated by two adjacent vacuum ports in the throttle valve housing, a holding valve, a release valve and a PVS valve. When the EGR valve opens, a small proportion of the exhaust gases are recirculated to the inlet manifold.

As the throttle valve is opened slightly and the valve passes the two vacuum ports, a gradual increase in the vacuum is obtained and, consequently, a gradual opening of the EGR valve.

When the throttle valve is opened wide and the vacuum in the ports diminishes, the earlier vacuum at the EGR valve is maintained for about six seconds by means of the holding valve.

When the throttle valve is closed, the EGR valve must also be closed to prevent rough idling of the engine. A release valve is fitted for this purpose and the valve is regulated by an additional port located inside the throttle valve housing. Thus, the vacuum maintained by the holding valve is released.

When the temperature of the engine is below approx. 104°F (40°C), the PVS valve shuts off the vacuum between the throttle valve and the EGR valve to improve the

running of the engine during the warming-up period.

AIR INJECTION SYSTEM

The function of the air injection system is to create afterburning in the exhaust pipes and the exhaust manifold. The air pump is driven by a belt from the crankshaft pulley. The air is drawn into the pump via a labyrinth seal at the pulley and is pumped out to the air hose and the distributor pipe. A relief valve opens if the pressure in the distributor becomes too great.

1. Air pump
2. Air inlet hose
3. Check valve
4. Air distribution pipe with injection tubes

Air injection system—typical

The function of the check valve is to prevent exhaust gases from entering the air pump if the belt should break. The air distribution pipe connects the check valve with the four injection tubes. The ends of injection tubes are located at the hottest part of the exhaust passage in order to achieve a maximum afterburning effect.

The pump noise is partly absorbed by the labyrinth seal and partly by a small silencer located above the relief valve. In addition insulation is glued to the dash panel behind the pump.

PULSE AIR SYSTEM

Federal cars are equipped with a pulse air system. In common with the air injection system, the purpose of the pulse air system is to supply air to the exhaust gases from the engine to bring about continued oxi-

1. Check valves
2. Distribution pipes
3. Inlet pipes

Pulse air system—typical

dation of the hydrocarbons and carbon monoxide in the exhaust system.

The system is composed of two check valves which are connected to the exhaust manifold by means of dual inlet pipes. The pipes open into the exhaust valves where the exhaust gases are hot, which is important in achieving efficient oxidation in the exhaust system.

The check valves are grouped so that one goes to No. 1 and No. 4 cylinders, and the other to no. 2 and no. 3 cylinders. Air is supplied to the valves by means of a hose from the air cleaner.

The function of the pulse air system is based on the vacuum occurring in the exhaust system during the pulses. For a brief moment immediately prior to the closing of the exhaust valve (at the start of the suction stroke), a vacuum is produced in the exhaust manifold whereupon the check valve opens and a small amount of air is drawn into the exhaust manifold.

Inspection Service

Remove the hose between the air cleaner and the check valve and check that it is free from dents or cracks. Run the engine at idling speed and check that air is drawn through the check valves. Suction should be felt with the thumbs placed over the openings.

CATALYTIC CONVERTER

The catalytic converter is located in the exhaust system between the engine and muffler. The unit is composed of a ceramic material insert of honeycomb design. Prior to the use of the Lambda oxygen sensor in conjunction with the special continuous injection system, the cars were equipped with a dual-type catalytic converter, but with the use of the oxygen sensor and CIS system, a new three-way converter is now employed. This new three-way converter is capable of reducing the content of the exhaust gases of hydrocarbons, carbon monoxide and oxides of nitrogen, down to the prescribed Federal and State emission levels, on the conditions that the accurate regulation of the air/fuel ratio is maintained under all driving conditions.

Platinum and palladium are used in the dual type converter, while platinum, palladium and rhodium are used as the catalyst in the three-way converters.

Evaporative Emission Control System

EVAPORATIVE LOSS CONTROL DEVICE (ELCD)

The ELCD device is a charcoal filter, which absorbs the vapor from the fuel tank. The charcoal canister is placed in the engine compartment. It is connected to the vent hose of the fuel tank and with a hose to the air cleaner. When the engine is running, fresh air is drawn through the charcoal filter and to the engine inlet system. The filter will then be cleaned of vapors. The vehicles are equipped with a roll-over valve. The valve is connected to the ventilation hose between the filler tube and the charcoal canister. In the event of the car rolling over or ending up on its side, a pendulum will actuate the valve which will shut off the ventilation hose thereby preventing the escape of fuel.

OXYGEN-SENSOR REGULATED CI-SYSTEM

All 1980 and later vehicles are equipped with a special continuous injection system combined with an electronic control system which is regulated by an oxygen sensor that is located in the exhaust manifold. These vehicles are also equipped with a three-way catalytic converter which is located between the exhaust manifold and the muffler in the exhaust system. The sensor-regulated injection system ensures that the air/fuel mixture is continually kept within the required limits for vehicle operation and emission controls.

FUEL SYSTEM

Fuel Pump

REMOVAL AND INSTALLATION

1976–79

1. Disconnect the negative battery cable.

1. Control unit
2. Throttle valve switch, full-load enrichment
3. Oxygen sensor
4. Catalytic converter
5. Modulating valve

Oxygen-sensor regulated CI system

2. On all vehicles except SAAB 900 series and the 99 Combi Coupe, roll back the carpet in the trunk.

3. On the 900 series and the 99 Combi Coupe, remove the rear floor cover and the floor panel in the luggage compartment.

4. Remove the circular cover plate on top of the pump mounting.

5. Remove the rubber cover from the fuel pump, if equipped. Disconnect the electric terminals at the fuel pump.

6. Disconnect the fuel line from the fuel pump.

NOTE: Hold the fuel pump with an open-end spanner wrench when loosening the connection.

7. Using the proper tool, turn the fuel pump mounting counterclockwise to the nearest groove to unlock the bayonet socket.

8. Lift the fuel pump out carefully. Save the O-ring for installation.

NOTE: The fuel pump can only be removed in one position, as one of the bayonet tongues is wider than the others.

1. Fuel tank
2. Fuel pump
3. Fuel accumulator
4. Fuel filter
5. Fuel distributor
6. Warm-up regulator
7. Cold start valve
8. Injection valves
9. Line pressure regulator

Fuel injection system

9. Installation is the reverse of removal.

1980 and later

NOTE: Beginning in 1980, all models are equipped with a plastic gas tank. Care should be exercised when removing the fuel pump from the plastic gas tank.

1. Disconnect the negative battery cable.

2. Remove the rear floor panel in the luggage compartment. Remove the valve cover from above the fuel pump.

3. Disconnect the electrical connections from the fuel pump.

4. Disconnect the fuel pipes from the pump.

NOTE: Use an open-ended spanner wrench to hold the pump steady while loosening the connections.

5. Remove the fuel pump mounting clamp. Lift the fuel pump from the vehicle.

6. Installation is the reverse order of removal.

FUEL PUMP DELIVERY CHECK

Voltage Check

1. Remove the round cover plate from the top of the fuel pump.

2. Measure the voltage between the positive and negative terminals when the fuel pump is operating.

3. The lowest permissible voltage is 11.5 volts.

Capacity Check

NOTE: Be sure that the fuel filter is not clogged and that the battery is fully charged.

1. Disconnect the return fuel pipe from the fuel distributor.

2. Connect the test pipe to the fuel distributor and place the other end in a suitable container.

3. On vehicles with the safety switch on the air flow sensor, remove the switch connector from the air flow sensor.

4. On vehicles with the fuel pump relay and the pulse sensor, remove the pump relay. Connect a jumper lead between terminals 15 and 87 on 99 series and terminals 30 and 87 on 900 series vehicles.

5. Switch on the ignition and allow the pump to run for 30 seconds. Measure the quantity of fuel. The proper specification should be 750 cm^3/30 sec. up to and including 1979 models and 900 cm^3/30 sec. for 1980 and later models, measured in the return line.

Fuel Injection

All Saab vehicles sold in the U.S. are equipped with a Bosch CI (continuous injection) injection system.

1. Thermo time switch
2. Start valve
3. Starter motor
4. Pressure impulse contact
5. Lambda sond
6. Control unit, lambda
7. Throttle switch
8. Pulse relation valve
9. Pulse relay
10. Electronic control unit, ignition system
11. Lambda relay
12. Pulse relay, warm start
13. R.p.m. regulation relay
14. Time relay
15. Interchange relay, start valve
16. Fuel pump relay
17. Test outlet
18. Line pressure valve
19. Auxilliary air valve

Wiring schematic—1976–81 Lambda system

1. Ignition coil
2. Test outlet
3. Hot start pulse relay
4. Engine speed relay (Turbos) 3,800 rpm
5. Deceleration system relay (cars with manual transmission)
6. Acceleration enrichment time relay
7. Cold/Hot start ground relay
8. Acceleration enrichment pulse relay
9. Control unit, Lambda
10. Throttle switch 65°C (149°F) only turbo
11. Throttle switch 0°C (32°F)
12. Fuel shut-off system solenoid (cars with manual transmission)
13. Temperature contact, 49°C (120°F)
14. Thermo time switch
15. Start valve
16. Vacuum switch
17. Starter motor
18. Fuel pump relay
19. Pulse relation valve
20. Fuel pump
21. Auxiliary air valve
22. Pilot pressure valve
23. Lambda sensor

Wiring schematic—1982 and later Lambda system

Injector

REMOVAL AND INSTALLATION

1. Thoroughly clean the area around the injection nozzle and its connection.

2. Disconnect the fuel line from the injector. Hold the injector with an open end wrench to prevent it from turning.

3. Loosen the bolt and remove the injector retaining plate.

4. Lift out the injector and remove the rubber seal.

5. Installation is in the reverse order of removal.

TESTING

1. Remove the rubber bellows from the air flow sensor.

An electric fuel pump which is mounted inside the gas tank provides fuel at a constant pressure to the mixture control unit. The latter consists of an air flow sensor which measures the flow of air to the engine and which acts mechanically on the fuel distributor. The fuel distributor provides the injection valves with the correct amount of fuel. The fuel is injected continuously into the intake manifold immediately upstream of the inlet valve. 1980 and later vehicles are equipped with a special CI system which is composed of an electronic control unit that is regualted by an oxygen sensor located in the exhaust manifold.

For all repair and adjustment procedures not detailed below involving the SAAB fuel injection system, please refer to "Fuel Injection" in the Unit Repair section.

2. Remove the injection valves from the intake manifold. Place the valves in a suitable container.

NOTE: The fuel lines should be left connected.

3. Turn on the ignition and remove the safety circuit plug from the air flow sensor. On 1977 and later 99 series vehicles, connect a jumper lead between the terminals 15 and 87 and between terminals 30 and 87 on 1979 and later 900 series in the relay holder. This will enable the fuel pump to operate.

4. For fuel atomization, lift the lever in the air flow sensor and check the spray pattern that is being emitted at the injection valves. If atomization is poor, correct as necessary.

5. For valve tightness, turn off the ignition to obtain the rest pressure. Wipe the

Injection valve cross section

area dry around the injection nozzles. Lift the lever and check for leakage. It should not take less than 15 seconds for a drop to form. Correct as required.

Fuel Distributor

REMOVAL AND INSTALLATION

1. Clean and remove fuel lines at distributor.
2. Remove retaining bolts and carefully lift out distributor. Take care not to drop control piston.
3. If control plunger has been removed, moisten with fuel before installing and insert small shoulder first.
4. Reinstall distributor using new O-rings.

NOTE: The fuel distributor must not be disassembled, but should be replaced when faulty.

Fuel Filter

REMOVAL AND INSTALLATION

The fuel filter is bolted in-line and must be uncoupled for replacement. Filter is installed with arrows pointing in direction of flow.

Fuel Accumulator

REMOVAL AND INSTALLATION

1. Clean the area around the fuel accumulator connections.

1. Bellows pipe
2. Valve
3. Regulator housing
4. Gasket
5. Bearing housing
6. Gasket
7. Heat shield
8. Gasket
9. Diaphragm housing
10. Flat washer
11. Inner diaphragm washer
12. Diaphragm
13. Outer diaphragm washer
14. Diaphragm nut
15. Inner spring seating (Model 1979 six holes, model 1980 four holes)
16. Spring
17. Inner spring seating
18. Lock nut
19. Diaphragm housing cover
20. Cooling air pipe

Charge pressure regulator disassembled

1. Turbo-compressor
2. Charge pressure regulator
3. Pressure switch
4. Turbo instrument
5. Suction pipe
6. Pressure pipe
7. Bellows pipe
8. Exhaust pipe
9. Oil supply line
10. Oil return line
11. Cooling air pipe
12. Exhaust pressure line

Typical turbocharger system—to 1980

2. Disconnect the connections and remove the fuel accumulator from the vehicle.

3. Installation is the reverse of removal.

Air Cleaner Element

REPLACEMENT

1. Remove the rubber bellows from between the air flow sensor and the throttle valve housing.

2. Remove the retaining bolts holding the lower section of the air flow meter to the air cleaner.

3. Raise the mixture control slightly and remove the cleaner element. Do not damage the fuel line.

4. Remove the element holder from the bottom of the cleaner assembly and clean the air cleaner casing.

5. Install the new air cleaner element and reassemble in the reverse order of the removal procedure.

Turbocharger

Turbocharing is achieved by means of a turbo-compressor which utilizes the exhaust gases from the engine to drive the turbine. The exhaust gases are routed to an exhaust gas turbine, causing the wheel to rotate. The turbine wheel is mounted on the same shaft as a compressor impeller which rotates at the same speed. The compressor is located in the induction system where it effects an increase in the charging pressure in the combustion chamber.

The Saab Turbo has been designed to start operating at relatively low engine speeds, in order to provide increased torque at engine speeds typical of normal driving conditions.

To prevent engine overspeeding, the pump relay cuts off the fuel pump at engine rpm above 6000. While at excessive charging pressures, an overpressure switch cuts off the current to the fuel pump.

1. Turbocharger
2. Wastegate boost control
3. Diaphragm capsule
4. Over-pressure guard
5. Turbo gauge
6. Hose, air cleaner to turbocharger
7. Hose, turbocharger to inlet manifold
8. Exhaust outlet pipe
9. Oil supply line
10. Oil return line

Turbocharger system—1981 and later

REMOVAL AND INSTALLATION

1. Remove the charge pressure regulator and block off the exhaust pipe. Remove the battery as required.

2. Disconnect the hose between the compressor and the throttle housing.

3. Disconnect the oil supply line and the oil return line at the turbo unit.

4. Remove the retaining bolts securing the turbo to the exhaust manifold. Remove the turbo unit from the vehicle. Plug the holes in the turbo unit to prevent dirt from entering.

5. Installation is the reverse of removal with the following exceptions.

6. Fill the lubricating inflow of the turbo unit with engine oil before connecting the oil return line at the turbo.

7. Crank the engine for about 30 seconds with terminal 15 on the ignition coil disconnected. This will fill the lubricating system of the turbo before the engine is started.

TURBOCHARGER TROUBLE DIAGNOSIS

Problem	Cause	Solution
Noise or vibration from the turbo compressor	a) Poor lubrication of the turbo shaft bearing	a) Check the oil pressure and flow to the turbo. If the fault should persist after remedial action (permanent bearing damage) exchange the turbo compressor)
	b) Leakage in the induction or exhaust system	b) Tighten leaking connections and replace defective seals and gaskets
	c) Unbalanced turbo shaft owing to damage	c) Exchange the turbo compressor

TURBOCHARGER TROUBLE DIAGNOSIS

Problem	Cause	Solution
Insufficient charging pressure	a) Leakage between the compressor and cylinder head or between the cylinder head and turbine b) Correct setting of charging pressure c) Valve in charge pressure regulator sticks in open position d) Partially clogged exhaust system e) Clogged air cleaner f) Binding turbo shaft	a) Tighten leaking connections and replace defective seals and gaskets b) Adjust the charge pressure regulator c) Overhaul the charge pressure regulator d) Clean or replace exhaust system e) Change cartridge f) Exchange turbo compressor
Excessive charging pressure	a) Leakage at exhaust pressure line connections b) Clogged exhaust pressure line c) Damaged diaphragm in charge pressure regulator d) Valve in charge pressure regulator sticks in closed position e) Ice formation in exhaust pressure line. (Excessive pressure occurs 1–2 min after cold start when temperature below freezing) f) Incorrect setting of charging pressure	a) Tighten; if necessary, replace nipples b) Remove and clean c) Replace diaphragm d) Overhaul the charge pressure regulator e) Avoid heavy loading of engine immediately after cold starting f) Adjust charge pressure regulator
Metallic noise from charge pressure regulator	a) Play in regulator valve b) Spring insufficiently offset in charge pressure regulator	a) Overhaul the charge pressure regulator b) Adjust position of spring (replace as necessary)
Engine knocking	a) Excessive charging pressure b) Unsuitable fuel (octane too low) c) Ignition setting too far advanced	a) Adjust charging pressure b) Change fuel c) Adjust timing

Oil leakage at turbo shaft seals (oil fumes in exhaust)	a) Poor return flow from turbo:
	  Clogged return line
	  Excessive crankcase pressure
	  Air cleaner clogged oil coating on compressor seals
	b) Turbo unit seals damaged
		a) Check:
		  Return line
		  Crankcase ventilation
		  Change air cleaner
		
		b) Exchange turbo compressor

MANUAL TRANSAXLE

REMOVAL AND INSTALLATION

1. Remove the engine transmission as a unit from the vehicle.
2. Drain the engine oil. Remove the clutch cover. Remove the starter.
3. Withdraw the clutch shaft using a tapping-out tool or equivalent.
4. Remove the three bolts for the slave cylinder.
5. Remove the screws in the mating flanges of the engine and transmission.
6. Carefully separate the engine from the transmission. At the same time, remove the release bearing guide sleeve.
7. Installation is the reverse of removal.

NOTE: When fitting the engine and transmission together, make sure that the mating surfaces are clean. Check that the two guide sleeves are fitted in the transmission. Install a new gasket on the transmission flange.

OVERHAUL

For transmission overhaul procedures, refer to the Unit Repair Section.

CLUTCH

REMOVAL AND INSTALLATION

99 Series

1. Drain the radiator. Remove the hood. Disconnect the negative battery cable.
2. Disconnect the cable harness from the fan housing. Disconnect the cables to the ignition coil, oil pressure switch, temperature transmitter, headlamp wiper motor and the fan thermal switch on the radiator.
3. Disconnect the hoses from the ra-

Pressure plate and related components

diator. Remove the grille. Remove the radiator assembly.

4. Remove the clutch cover bolts, then remove the clutch cover.

5. Mount spacer (Saab part #8390023) between the clutch cover and the diaphragm spring. When installing the spacer, make sure that the clutch pedal is fully depressed.

NOTE: A different clutch housing was used on some 1976 vehicles, therefore a special spacer (Saab part #8790826) must be used to remove the housing. This spacer is deeper than the standard spacer.

6. Remove the retaining clip (lock-ring on 1976–77 vehicles) and the seal cap from the clutch shaft. Remove the plastic propeller (O-ring on 1976–77 vehicles) from the clutch shaft.

7. Remove the clutch shaft using a tapping-out hammer or equivalent.

8. Remove the retaining bolts that secure the slave cylinder (guide sleeve) to the primary gear housing.

9. Remove the clutch retaining screws, the clutch, clutch disc, slave cylinder (guide sleeve) and the release bearing. It is not necessary to disconnect the hydraulic hose on the slave cylinder (guide sleeve).

NOTE: Be sure that the diaphragm spring does not damage the slave cylinder.

10. Installation is the reverse of removal.

900 Series

1. Remove the clutch housing cover.
2. Install the spacer (Saab part #8390023) between the clutch fork and the diaphragm spring. Keep the clutch pedal depressed when the ring is being installed.
3. Unhook the spring clip and remove the cover located in front of the clutch shaft. Remove the clutch shaft plastic propeller.
4. Remove the clutch shaft by means of an M8 bolt installed in the shaft end and Saab tool no. 83-93-175. Withdraw the shaft as far as possible.
5. Remove the clutch slave cylinder retaining bolts.
6. Remove the clutch retaining bolts and remove the clutch, clutch disc and the slave cylinder complete with the clutch release bearing.

NOTE: Make sure that the slave cylinder sleeve is not damaged by the clutch during the removal procedure.

7. Installation is the reverse of removal.

CHECKING CLUTCH WEAR

Early Design Slave Cylinder

1. Remove the inspection hole cover on the clutch housing.
2. Disengage the clutch and then release the pedal. The release bearing will then be in contact with the fingers on the pressure plate.

1. Housing
2. Spring with seat
3. Sealing
4. Washer
5. Piston and rear seal
6. Push rod assembly

Exploded view of clutch master cylinder

3. Looking through the inspection hole, check that the sliding lock ring on the piston in the slave cylinder is in contact with the cylinder walls.

4. Check the distance between the sliding lock ring and the lock ring behind the release bearing.

5. If distance is 0 to 1.0 mm, the clutch must be replaced. The distance on a new clutch disc would be 6.0 mm.

Later Design Slave Cylinder

1. Remove the inspection hole cover and look through the inspection hole.

2. When the distance between the plastic sleeve front edge and the front edge of the turned surface is less than 2.0 mm the clutch disc must be replaced.

Clutch Master Cylinder

REMOVAL AND INSTALLATION

1. Remove the clamp holding the pipe from the cylinder at the body and remove the pipe at the cylinder.

2. Remove the left-hand screen under the instrument panel.

3. Remove the pin holding the push rod to the clutch pedal.

4. Remove the bolts inside the dash panel. Remove the clutch cylinder from inside the engine compartment.

5. Remove the hose from the fluid container and hang it out of the way so that the fluid does not come out.

6. Installation is the reverse of removal.

BLEEDING

1. Connect a hose to the slave cylinder bleeder valve. Place the other end of the hose in a suitable jar partially filled with brake fluid.

2. Fill the master cylinder with brake fluid.

3. Open the bleeder valve on the slave cylinder a half turn.

4. Place a cooling system tester gauge over the opening of the master cylinder.

5. Pump the tester until all air has been expelled from the system.

6. Close the slave cylinder bleeder valve.

7. Check that all air has been removed from the system by depressing the clutch pedal.

Clutch Slave Cylinder

In order to remove the clutch slave cylinder, the clutch must first be removed. Refer to the clutch removal procedure in this section for the proper information.

AUTOMATIC TRANSAXLE

REMOVAL AND INSTALLATION

1. Remove the engine transmission as a unit from the vehicle.

2. Drain the engine oil. Remove the flywheel cover. Remove the starter.

1. Slave cylinder housing
2. Sleeve
3. Piston
4. Lip seal
5. O-ring
6. Release bearing
7. O-ring
8. Lock ring
9. Lock ring

Cross section of slave cylinder

3. Disconnect the throttle wire from the throttle valve housing.

4. Remove all bolts from the mating surfaces of the engine and transmission.

5. Remove the four bolts securing the flywheel ring gear to the torque converter.

NOTE: These bolts can be reached from above the oil pump mounting.

6. Turn the flywheel so that the two plate angles will be horizontal. Carefully lift the engine off of the transmission.

7. Installation is the reverse of removal.

NOTE: When fitting the engine and transmission together, make sure that the mating surfaces are clean. Check that the two guide sleeves are fitted into the transmission.

NEUTRAL SAFETY SWITCH ADJUSTMENT

1. Disconnect the wires from the switch.

NOTE: The wide terminals are for back-up lights and the narrow ones are for the starter motor.

2. Loosen the locknut using an $^{11}/_{16}$ inch crows foot and unscrew the switch two turns.

3. With the selector in Drive, connect a test light between the narrow terminals. The light should light up.

4. Screw in the switch until the light goes out. Mark that position on both the transmission and the switch.

5. Move the test lamp, the wide terminals and screw switch in until the light goes out again. Count the number between the two lights going out.

6. Turn the switch to a point halfway between the two lights–out points.

7. Secure the locknut to 4–6 ft. lbs. torque.

NOTE: If the safety switch is locked too tight, it may be damaged.

SHIFT LINKAGE

Checking

1. Move the selector lever to "N". Check the clearance from the selection lever pin to the neutral detent.

2. Move the selector lever to "D".

Manual linkage clearance, equal in "N" and "D"

Check the clearance from the selector lever pin to the drive detent. The clearance at the "N" and the "D" position should be equal. If they are not equal adjust the cable.

3. Check for proper selector lever pin position in the "P", "R", "2" and "1" ranges.

Adjusting

1. Remove the gear selector lever cover.

2. Slack off the gear selector lever housing nuts with tool no. 839123 or equivalent.

3. Lift the gear selector lever housing and turn it so that the adjustment nuts of the cable will be reachable.

4. Adjust the cable longer or shorter to bring the "N" and "D" clearance into equality.

5. Assemble the gear selector housing and check the clearance in "N" and "D".

6. A fine setting of the selector cable can be accomplished by adding or removing shims at the transmission case end of the cable. A maximum of three shims may be used.

BAND ADJUSTMENT

Type 35 Transmission

FRONT BAND (INSIDE TRANSMISSION)

1. Place tool no. 8790073 or equivalent, ¼ inch thickness gauge between the adjusting screw and the boss on the piston.

2. Loosen the lock nut.

3. Tighten the adjusting screw to 10 in. lbs. of torque and tighten the lock nut.

NOTE: On transmissions with self-adjusting mechanism, check the gap between the self-adjusting spring and the lever. It should be 1.5 to 2.0 thread flights.

REAR BAND

The rear band adjusting screw is located outside the transmission case on the driver's side.

1. Loosen the lock nut a few turns.

2. Tighten the adjusting screw to 10 ft lbs. and then back off ¾ turn.

3. Hold the adjusting screw and torque the lock nut to 30–40 ft. lbs.

Type 37 Transmission

FRONT BAND (INSIDE TRANSMISSION)

Up to serial numbers 001-1700, 002-2800

1. Loosen the locknut and position tool number 87-90-073 or equivalent ¼ inch thick, between the adjusting screw and the piston pin.

2. Tighten the adjusting screw to 9 ft. lbs. and then loosen one turn.

3. Hold the adjusting screw and tighten the locknut to 24–28 ft. lbs.

After serial numbers 001-1710, 002-2801

1. Loosen the locknut and position tool

number 87-90-030 or equivalent, $^{11}/_{32}$ inch thick, between the screw and the piston pin.

2. Tighten the adjusting screw to 9 ft. lbs. *Do not* loosen the adjusting screw.

3. Hold the adjusting screw and tighten the locknut to 24–28 ft. lbs.

REAR BAND

The rear band adjusting screw is located on the outside of the transmission on the left side.

1. Loosen the locknut a few turns.

2. Tighten the adjusting screw to 10 ft. lbs. with tool number 87-90-115 or equivalent. Back off the adjusting screw ¾ turn.

3. Hold the adjusting screw and tighten the locknut to 24–28 ft. lbs.

DRIVE AXLES

Driveshaft

REMOVAL AND INSTALLATION

NOTE: The entire front axle assembly must be removed in order to remove the driveshaft from the vehicle.

1. On 900 series vehicles, remove the upper bolt of the shock absorber before jacking up the vehicle.

Inner universal joint

2. Raise the vehicle on a hoist and support it safely. Remove the wheel.

3. Remove the brake housing and hang it on the wheel housing to avoid damage to the brake hose. Remove the brake disc and parking brake assembly with the cable.

4. Remove the large clamp from the rubber bellows on the inner universal joint.

NOTE: To separate the inner universal joint, install the cover (Saab part #7323736) in the rubber bellows to stop the needle bearings from falling out and to keep dirt from entering. Install the protective cap (Saab part #7838469) on the inner driver.

1. Lock nut
2. Washer
3. Wheel hub
4. Outer drive shaft
5. Bearing with seals
6. Outer drive shaft joint

Outer universal joint

5. Disconnect the tie rod from the steering arm using the proper tool. Remove the nut on the upper ball joint. Remove the bolts from the lower control arm bracket.

6. Remove the driveshaft through the wheel housing and remove the entire front axle assembly.

7. If the differential bearing cap is to be removed, remove the retaining bolts and remove the cap and the inner drive using the proper removal tools.

8. Installation is the reverse of removal.

OVERHAUL

1. Mount the steering knuckle housing in a press and press out the outer driveshaft.

2. Remove the intermediate driveshaft from the outer universal joint by loosening the rubber bellows on the outer universal joint and sliding it along the shaft.

3. Mount the shaft in a press and press together the two conical washers so that the circlip inside the hub can move in its groove.

4. Open the circlip using pliers to remove the pressure.

5. Withdraw the intermediate shaft from the hub together with the spherical shaped washer, the two conical washers and the shaft locking ring. The circlip on the hub remains in the groove.

6. Installation is the reverse of removal.

1. Hub
2. Wheel bolt
3. Wheel bearings
4. Seal

Rear wheel hub and bearings—typical

REAR AXLE

REMOVAL AND INSTALLATION

1. Jack up the rear of the vehicle and support it safely.

--- **CAUTION** ---

Do not place jack under rear axle to lift vehicle. Damage to the rear axle could occur.

1. Rear axle
2. End piece
3. Stub axle
4. Spring links
5. Rear links
6. Cross bar
7. Spring seat
8. Coil spring
9. Spring insulator
10. Rubber buffer
11. Stop
12. Shock absorber

Rear suspension assembly

2. Disconnect the brake hoses in front of the rear axle. Disconnect the lower shock absorber bolts and the cross bar.

3. Lower the axle and remove the rear springs.

4. Remove the bolts of the spring link rear bushings and lift away the rear axle assembly.

5. Installation is the reverse of removal. Bleed the hydraulic brake system.

NOTE: The rubber bearings must be mounted in such a way that no strain occurs when the weight of the vehicle is supported by the wheels. They must be drawn tight only when the vehicle is standing empty on its four wheels.

Rear Wheel Bearings

REMOVAL AND INSTALLATION

NOTE: Each rear wheel hub has two tapered roller bearings. From 1976 until 1978, these two bearings were the same size. Beginning with the 1979 models, the inner bearing has a larger diameter than the outer bearing.

1. Raise the vehicle on a hoist and support it safely.

NOTE: Do not place the jack under the rear axle, as this is likely to deform the axle.

2. Remove the wheel. Remove the brake housing and the brake disc. Support the brake housing to avoid damage to the brake pipe.

3. Remove the dust cap. Remove the locknut and the washer. Pull off the hub. If necessary, use a suitable puller.

4. Break out the seal ring with a suitable tool (it cannot be removed intact). Remove the inner rings of both bearings.

5. Place a suitable drift in the milled recesses of the hub and drive out the outer bearing rings.

NOTE: It is advisable to place a wooden board under the hub to avoid deforming the end faces.

6. Installation is the reverse of removal. Torque the locknut to 36 ft. lbs., than slacken the nut completely and torque it to 2.9 ft. lbs.

REAR SUSPENSION

Shock Absorbers

REMOVAL AND INSTALLATION

Pneumatic Shock

NOTE: Pneumatic shock absorbers are gas filled which can cause injury if not handled properly. In order to avoid the risk of injury the shock absorbers should be emptied of the gas before being scrapped. This is accomplished by drilling a 2 mm hole in the pressure chamber 10–15 mm from the edge of the shock housing.

1. Raise the vehicle on a hoist and support it safely.

2. Place an additional jack stand under the rear axle to prevent it from dropping and stretching the brake lines.

3. Insert a jack at the rear of the spring-link. Remove the shock absorber retaining nuts.

4. Remove the bolts in the spring-link mounting on the rear axle.

5. Using the jack, lower the spring-link so that the shock absorber can be removed from the vehicle.

6. Installation is the reverse of removal.

Springs

REMOVAL AND INSTALLATION

1. Raise the vehicle on a hoist and support it safely.

2. Remove the hub cap, tire wheel assembly. Install a jack under the spring-link and disconnect the lower end of the shock absorber.

3. From underneath of the vehicle, remove the two locknuts that secure the front spring-link bearing to the body of the vehicle.

4. Place a jack stand under the rear axle to prevent the brake lines from being damaged by the weight of the rear axle.

5. Lower the spring-link so that the spring can be removed from the vehicle together with the upper spring support and the rubber spacer at the lower spring seating which is retained by the spring tension.

6. Installation is the reverse of removal.

FRONT SUSPENSION

Shock Absorbers

Some vehicles are equipped with pneumatic shocks.

NOTE: Pneumatic shock absorbers are gas-filled which can cause injury if not

1. Upper control arm
2. Lower spring support
3. Coil spring
4. Rubber buffer
5. Shock absorber

Front suspension assembly

handled properly. In order to avoid the risk of injury, the shock absorbers should be emptied of the gas before being scrapped. This is accomplished by drilling a 2 mm hole in the pressure chamber 10–15 mm from the edge of the shock housing.

REMOVAL AND INSTALLATION

1. On 900 series vehicles, remove the upper shock absorber nut before raising the vehicle.

2. Raise the vehicle and support it safely. Remove the wheels.

3. Remove the shock absorber retaining bolts and remove the shock from the vehicle. Save all washers and rubber parts.

4. Installation is the reverse of removal.

Ball Joints

REMOVAL AND INSTALLATION

1. Raise the vehicle and support it safely. Remove the wheel.

2. Remove the brake housing and hang it out of the way so that the brake hose will not be damaged.

3. Remove the nut that holds the ball joint ball bolt to the steering knuckle housing. Remove the bolt using the proper removal tool.

4. Remove the ball joint from the control arm assembly.

5. Installation is the reverse of removal.

Springs

REMOVAL AND INSTALLATION

1. On 900 series remove the upper shock absorber nuts before raising the vehicle.

2. Raise the vehicle on a hoist and support it safely. Remove the wheel.

3. Install a spring compression tool or equivalent, engaging the upper shanks directly in the spring at the second free turn from the top of the lower shanks around the spring cups.

NOTE: These are located on the last turn of the spring with the color-coded cup right beside the end of the coil.

4. Compress the spring at the top end, approximately 1½ inch. If the upper spring attachement of the steel cone is left behind in the wheel housing, remove it.

5. Remove the spring and the steel cone from the vehicle.

6. Installation is the reverse of removal.

Upper Control Arm

REMOVAL AND INSTALLATION

NOTE: To remove the left upper control arm, the engine must first be removed from the vehicle. See the engine removal procedure in this section of this manual.

1. Raise the vehicle on a hoist and support it safely.

2. Remove the wheel. Remove the shock absorber. Compress the coil spring, using a spring compression tool.

3. Back-off and remove the two bolts attaching the upper ball joint and lower spring seat to the upper control arm.

1. Upper control arm   4. Bearing
3. Rubber bushing   5. Spacers

Upper control arm assembly

4. Remove the bolts from both upper control arm bearing brackets.

5. Remove the coil spring from the vehicle.

6. Remove the control arm and bearings from the vehicle.

NOTE: Save the spacers under the bearings and record the number of spacers used under each bearing.

7. Remove both of the bearing nuts. Now the bearings and bushings can be removed from the control arm.

8. Installation is the reverse of removal.

NOTE: When mounting the bearings to the control arm, the angle between the control arm and the bearing should be 52 ± 2° when both nuts are tightened.

Lower Control Arm

REMOVAL AND INSTALLATION

1. Raise the vehicle on the hoist and support it safely. Remove the wheel.

Checking the angle between the upper control arm and bearing

2. Disconnect the lower end of the shock absorber.

3. Back-off and remove the two bolts that attach the ball joint to the control arm.

4. Remove the lower control arm attaching bolts from under the engine compartment floor.

5. Remove the control arm and its attaching brackets from the vehicle.

6. Remove the control arm bearing nuts and remove the bearings from the control arm.

7. Installation is the reverse of removal.

NOTE: When mounting the bearings to the control arm, the angle between the control arm and the bearing should be $18 \pm 2°$ when both nuts are tightened.

2. Lower control arm
3. Rubber bushing
4. Bearing

Lower control arm assembly

Checking the angle between the lower control arm and bearing

Front End Alignment

TOE-IN

1. Roll the car straight forward on a level floor and stop it without using brakes. It must not be moved backward after this.

2. Take a reading of measurement A with the toe-in gauge between the front wheel rims level with the axles. Mark the measurement points with chalk. Roll the car forward until the chalk marks are level with but behind the axles, and take a reading of B. Any necessary adjustment is made by altering the length of the tie rod.

3. Remove the nut on the outer end of the tie rod and the outer clip on the steering gear rubber bellows.

4. Use a suitable pair of grippers to twist the tie rod right or left; adjust until the toe-in is right. Hold the bellows during the twisting.

CASTER

The caster is the angle by which the steering knuckle axis departs from the vertical when viewed from the side and the measurement is generally expressed in degrees. If the caster needs adjusting, spacers are inserted under the bearing brackets of the upper control arms.

To increase the caster, transfer spacers from the front bracket to the rear bracket. To reduce the caster, transfer spacers from the rear bracket to the front bracket. In either case, the total spacer thickness removed from one bracket must be added to the other one.

CAMBER

Camber is the angle by which the center-lines of the wheels lean from the vertical. The camber is positive (+) if the wheels lean outward, and negative (−) if they lean inward.

The camber, and with it the "king pin" angle, can be adjusted with spacers placed under the two bearing brackets of the upper control arms. The desired result can thus be obtained by increasing or reducing the number of spacers used. To increase or reduce camber, use the same number of spacers under both brackets.

Front Wheel Bearings

REMOVAL AND INSTALLATION

NOTE: The entire front axle assembly must be removed from the vehicle when removing the wheel bearings.

1. On 900 series vehicles, remove the upper bolt of the shock absorber before jacking up the vehicle.

2. Raise the vehicle on a hoist and support it safely. Remove the wheel.

3. Remove the brake housing and hang it by the wheel housing to avoid damage to

Toe-in adjustment

the brake hose. Remove the brake disc and parking brake assembly with the cable.

4. Remove the large clamp from the rubber bellows on the inner universal joint.

NOTE: To separate the inner universal joint, install the cover (Saab part #7323736) in the rubber bellows to stop the needle bearings from falling out and to keep dirt from entering. Install the protective cap (Saab part #7838469) on the inner drive.

5. Disconnect the tie rod from the steering arm using the proper tool. Remove the nut on the upper ball joint. Remove the bolts from the lower control arm bracket.

6. Remove the driveshaft through the wheel housing and remove the entire front axle assembly.

7. Place the steering knuckle housing in a press and press out the driveshaft.

8. Remove the lock-ring and press out the bearing using a suitable drift.

9. Installation is the reverse of removal.

1. Steering wheel
2. Plastic sleeve
3. Slip ring
4. Driver
5. Bushing
6. Rubber bushing
7. Steering column

8. Steering column tube
9. Rubber bushing
10. Bushing
11. Rubber washer
12. Intermediate shaft
13. Rubber bellows
14. Joint half
15. Double joint

Typical steering column assembly

STEERING

Steering Wheel

REMOVAL AND INSTALLATION

1. Disconnect the negative battery cable.
2. On early models, remove the bottom cover of the steering wheel bearing.
3. Remove the steering wheel safety pad. 1981 models, remove the steering wheel emblem by lifting with a small screwdriver. Remove the horn contact. Remove the steering wheel holding nut and washer.
4. Remove the steering wheel using the proper steering wheel removal tool.
5. Installation is the reverse of removal.

Combination Switch

REMOVAL AND INSTALLATION

NOTE: From 1981 models, the turn-signal arm return actuator is removable.

1. Disconnect the negative battery cable.
2. Remove the steering wheel.
3. Remove the cover beneath the bearing support.
4. Remove the combination switch retaining bolts and electrical connections.
5. Remove the switch from the vehicle.
6. Installation is the reverse of removal.

Manual Steering Gear

REMOVAL AND INSTALLATION

1. Remove the left screen under the instrument panel and loosen the rubber bellows at the body lead-through for the steering gear intermediate shaft, if required.
2. Raise the vehicle and remove the bolt holding the joint to the steering gear pinion or intermediate shaft.
3. Loosen the steering column tube from the body and separate the steering column joint from the pinion.

NOTE: Hang up the steering column so that the wiring harness is not damaged.

4. Remove the front wheels from the vehicle.
5. Remove the tie rod ends at the steering arms with the proper removal tool.
6. Remove the two steering gear clamps.
7. Move the rack to the right as far as possible.
8. Lift the steering gear to the right so

that the tie rod can be bent down in the opening of the engine compartment floor.
9. Pull the rack (maximal stroke) to the left and lift the steering gear down through the opening in the engine compartment floor.
10. Installation is the reverse of removal.

ADJUSTMENT

Radial Play

1. Fit the plunger without the spring and screw on the cap without the gasket by hand until it butts against the plunger. Do not use a wrench, as you will damage the cap.
2. Measure the clearance between the cap and the housing with a feeler gauge.

1. Clearance to be measured with feeler gauge
2. Cap
3. Plunger

Radial-play adjustment

3. Add 0.002–0.006″ to the measured clearance to allow for the play to be left between the plunger and cap after assembly. Measure the thickness of the gasket and shims with a micrometer. Shims are available in thickness of 0.005″, 0.0075″, 0.010″, 0.015″ and 0.020″.

Power Steering Gear

REMOVAL AND INSTALLATION

99 Series

1. Drain the fluid from the power steering reservoir.
2. Loosen the power steering pump and remove it from its mounting so that the double joint and the servo valve are accessible.
3. Raise the vehicle and remove the left engine mounting.
4. Turn the steering wheel to the full left position and remove the clamp screw which holds the double joint on the intermediate shaft to the steering gear.
5. Remove the pipe clamps at the front suspension panel.
6. Raise the vehicle on a hoist and support it safely. Remove the wheels.
7. Remove the tie rod ends at the steering arm using the proper removal tool. Unscrew the left tie rod end.
8. Disconnect the speedometer cable from the gear box. Disconnect the left

handbrake cable at the brake yoke and wheel housing. Remove the right handbrake cable clamp on the steering gear.
9. Remove the steering gear mountings from the body. On the left side, remove the two retaining bolts and remove the intermediate piece. On the right side, remove the yoke and the intermediate piece.
10. Disconnect the hoses from the servo valve.
11. Release the intermediate shaft by pulling the steering gear downward and slightly to the right.
12. Move the steering gear to the right until the left tie rod can be bent down through the opening in the body. At the same time, twist the valve housing backwards.
13. Remove the steering gear from the vehicle by guiding it down and to the left.
14. Installation is the reverse of removal.

900 Series

Other than the removal and installation of the fluid lines, the power steering unit is removed and re-installed in the vehicle following the procedures for the manual steering gear removal and installation.

ADJUSTMENT

Radial Play

1. Screw in the adjusting screw all the way until the resistance of the twisting steering gear is felt.
2. Back off the adjusting screw 1/12 turn.
3. Check that the steering gear can be turned from lock to lock in both directions without jamming.
4. Tighten the lock nut with a torque of 50–60 ft. lbs.

Power Steering Pump

REMOVAL AND INSTALLATION

1. Drain the fluid from the power steering pump.
2. Drain the coolant from the drain cock on the engine block and disconnect the hose from between the expansion tank and the water pump.
3. Disconnect the power steering pump hoses.

NOTE: Grip the heaxagonal nipple on the pump when removing the delivery line.

4. Unbolt the pump unit from the bracket and the engine mounting. Lift off the power steering belt and remove the pump unit complete with its mounting.
5. Installation is the reverse of removal.

BELT ADJUSTMENT

Tighten the belt so that when pressure is

applied to the belt at a given point the distance between both belt pulleys is 5–10 mm.

SYSTEM BLEEDING

1. Fill the power steering pump with the proper fluid.
2. Start the engine and top-off the level of fluid to .4 inch above the bottom of the filter.
3. Turn the steering wheel from left to right several times to expel air from the system.
4. Refill the pump as needed.

Steering Linkage

REMOVAL AND INSTALLATION

Tie Rod Ends

1. Raise the vehicle on the hoist and support it safely.
2. Remove the wheel. Remove the nut.
3. Disconnect the ball bolt from the steering arm using the proper removal tool.

NOTE: Do not knock the ball bolt out, as this could cause damage to the ball bolt and other related parts.

4. Back off the nut that locks the end assembly to the tie rod.
5. Unscrew the end assembly from the tie rod.
6. Installation is the reverse of removal. Check and adjust the toe-in as required.

BRAKE SYSTEM

NOTE: For replacement and repair procedures on all major brake components not detailed below, please refer to "Brakes" in the Unit Repair section.

Master Cylinder

REMOVAL AND INSTALLATION

1. Disconnect the electrical connection to the brake warning switch.
2. Disconnect the hose from the clutch master cylinder to the fluid reservoir. Insert a plastic stopper in the nipple of the reservoir.
3. Disconnect the brake lines to the master cylinder.
4. Remove the nuts that hold the master cylinder to the power brake booster. Remove the master cylinder from the vehicle.
5. Installation is the reverse of removal. Bleed the system as required.

1. Cap
2. Fluid level contact
3. Float
4. Sealing ring
5. Brake fluid container
6. Pin
7. Sealing ring
8. Stop pin
9. Cylinder housing
10. Spring, secondary piston
11. Secondary piston
12. Sleeve
13. Spring, primary piston
14. Primary piston
15. Lock ring

Typical brake master cylinder

Vacuum Booster

REMOVAL AND INSTALLATION

1. Remove the steering column bearing cover, ash tray and safety padding screw. Remove the upper circlip on the brake pedal push rod, if equipped.
2. Remove the two electrical connections on the brake light switch. Remove the safety padding screws in the engine compartment.
3. Remove the vacuum hose from the non-return valve which is located on the vacuum booster.
4. Disconnect the brake lines and the electrical connections for the brake warning switch from the master cylinder. Disconnect the line to the clutch master cylinder from the fluid reservoir. Insert stoppers in the lines to prevent loss of the brake fluid.
5. Remove the cotter pin from the servo unit push rod at the brake pedal.
6. Remove the vacuum booster together with the master cylinder and the bracket.

NOTE: The bracket is mounted on the dash panel with four bolts and nuts. Three of these bolts are accessible from underneath in the passenger compartment after removal of the screen section and parts of the dash panel insulation felt below the instrument panel. The fourth nut is accessible from the engine compartment by the bracket.

7. Separate the master cylinder and bracket from the vacuum booster.

Parking brake adjustment procedure

8. Installation is the reverse of removal. Bleed the system as required.

Parking Brake

ADJUSTMENT

Check the adjustment of the handbrake cable. Check the distance between the handbrake lever and the yoke: the clearance should be a maximum 0.019 in. (0.50 mm) and should be equal on both sides. Adjust as necessary using the adjustment nut on the handbrake lever.

Note that the cables cross over, therefore the right-hand adjustment nut should be used to adjust the left-hand brake mechanism and vice versa.

CHASSIS ELECTRICAL

Heater Blower Motor

99 Series

1. Remove the windhsield wiper motor assembly.
2. Disconnect the blower motor cables.
3. Remove the three blower motor retaining screws and pull the motor along with the impeller out of the housing carefully.
4. Separate the motor from the impeller at the rubber coupling. Remove the motor first, then the impeller.
5. Remove the plate with the fan bearing on the opposite side of the fan casing.
6. Installation is the reverse of removal.

900 Series

1. Disconnect the positive battery cable.
2. Remove the switch panel and the upper section of the instrument panel.
3. Disconnect the electrical leads to the fan motor.

4. Remove the retaining screws for the right hand defroster valve housing.

5. Remove the fan retaining screws and lift the fan from its housing.

6. The installation is in the reverse of the removal procedure.

Heater Core

REMOVAL AND INSTALLATION

99 Series

1. Drain the radiator. Remove the alternator and radiator fan relay.

2. Remove the front part of the fan casing. Unscrew the heater core retaining plate.

3. Remove the water valve cap, remove the control wire and the water valve retaining screws.

4. Loosen the hose clamps on the heater core and the water valve. Disconnect the hoses.

5. Disconnect the thermostat coil from the heater core and remove the water valve with its coil.

6. Remove the heater core from the thermostat housing.

7. Installation is the reverse of removal.

900 Series

When removing the heater core and/or the coolant shut off valve, remove as a unit.

1. Remove the cover under the switches on the steering column and the lower section of the instrument panel.

2. Remove the air diffuser and retaining screws.

3. Remove the left defroster and speaker grill.

4. Remove the control rod from between the coolant shut off valve and the control rod by sliding the rod as far forward as it will go to free it from the knob, then pull it rearward to free it from the shut off valve.

NOTE: The plastic joint at the control knob is accessible from underneath once the switches below the heater controls have been pressed backwards.

5. Remove the lower section of the heater housing.

6. Drain the coolant and disconnect the hoses. Plug the ends of the hoses to prevent coolant from leaking into the compartment.

7. Separate the heater core from the housing and guide it backward and downward. It will be necessary to disconnect the brake pedal return spring and depress the brake pedal slightly.

8. The water valve and the heater core can be separated after their removal. Do not kink or break the capillary tube.

9. Install the assembly in the reverse order of the removal procedure.

Radio

The radios used in Saab vehicles are dealer-installed or aftermarket units. It is therefore impossible to give specific procedures for removal and installation of these units. Care should be exercised when servicing a vehicle that has a radio problem.

Windshield Wiper Motor

REMOVAL AND INSTALLATION

99 Series

1. Remove the wiper arms from the wiper spindles.

2. Remove the nut that holds the steel tube to the wiper motor.

3. Release the wiper motor and remove the motor and the flexible cable (pull the cable out of the tube).

4. Installation is the reverse of removal.

900 Series

1. Remove the wiper arms from the vehicle. Remove the rubber grommets.

2. Remove the four screws and disconnect the lead. Remove the wiper unit from the vehicle.

3. Separate the wiper motor from the wiper assembly.

4. Installation is the reverse of removal.

Instrument Cluster

REMOVAL AND INSTALLATION

99 Series

1. Disconnect the negative battery cable. Remove the safety padding.

2. Remove the four screws that secure the panel.

3. Disconnect the speedometer wire and the electric wiring to the clock and combination instrument panel. Remove the instrument panel illumination bulb holder.

4. Carefully lift the instrument panel from the vehicle.

5. Installation is the reverse of removal.

900 Series

1. Disconnect the positive battery cable. Remove the steering wheel.

2. Remove the four screws in the switch panel and tilt the panel back. Watch the length of the screws as they are not interchangeable.

3. Remove the left speaker/defroster grille. Pull apart the instrument panel connectors. Disconnect the speedometer cable.

4. Remove the instrument panel retaining screws. Carefully remove the unit from the vehicle.

5. Installation is the reverse of removal.

Ignition Switch

REMOVAL AND INSTALLATION

1. Disconnect the negative battery cable.

2. Remove the center console.

3. Disconnect the electrical connections from the switch.

4. Remove the assembly from the vehicle.

5. Installation is the reverse of removal.

Fuse Box Location

The fuse panel is located under the hood of the vehicle. It is on the left-hand side for the 900 series and on the right hand side for the 99 series.

Windshield wiper/washer wiring schematic—900 series

Subaru

SERIAL NUMBER IDENTIFICATION

The Vehicle Identification Number is stamped on a tab located on the top of the dashboard on the driver's side, visible through the windshield. The Vehicle Iden- tification Plate is on the bulkhead in the engine compartment. The engine number is stamped on the crankcase, behind the distributor.

VEHICLE IDENTIFICATION

Year	Model	Body Type	Transmission Type		Serial Number		
'76	1400 STD	2-dr sedan	4-speed	A22L	924001	and	after
	1400 DL	2-dr sedan	4-speed	A22L	924001	and	after
		4-dr sedan	4-speed	A22L	819501	and	after
		2-dr coupe	5-speed	A22L	404001	and	after
		station wagon	4-speed	A62L	735501	and	after
	1400 GF	hardtop	5-speed	A22L	005001	and	after
	1400 4WD	station wagon	4-wheel drive	A64L	806001	and	after
	1600 DL	2-dr sedan	automatic	A26L	106001	to	730000
		4-dr sedan	automatic	A26L	605001	to	610000
		station wagon	automatic	A66L	604001	to	609000
	1600 GF	hardtop	automatic	A26L	305001	to	309000
'77	1600 STD	2-dr sedan	4-speed	A26L	205001	to	209000
	1600 DL	2-dr sedan	4-speed	A26L	405001	to	409000
			automatic	A26L	730001	to	732000
		4-dr sedan	4-speed	A26L	505001	to	507000
			automatic	A26L	610001	to	612000
		2-dr coupe	5-speed	A26L	905001	to	909000
		station wagon	4-speed	A66L	705001	to	710000
			automatic	A66L	609001	to	612000
	1600 GF	hardtop	5-speed	A26L	805001	to	808000
			automatic	A26L	309001	to	310000
	1600 4WD	station wagon	4-wheel drive	A67L	002001	to	010000

VEHICLE IDENTIFICATION

Year	Model	Body Type	Transmission Type		Serial Number		
'78	1600 STD	2-dr sedan	4-speed	A26L	209001	to	215000
	1600 DL	2-dr sedan	4-speed	A26L	409001	to	419000
			automatic	A26L	732001	to	739000
		4-dr sedan	4-speed	A26L	507001	to	511000
			5-speed	A26L	662001	to	670000
			automatic	A26L	612001	to	618500
		2-dr coupe	5-speed	A26L	909001	to	915500
		station wagon	4-speed	A66L	710001	to	716500
			5-speed	A66L	302001	to	313000
			automatic	A66L	612001	to	619000
	1600 GF	hardtop	5-speed	A26L	808001	to	816500
			automatic	A26L	310001	to	314500
	1600 4WD	station wagon	4-wheel drive	A67L	010001	to	047000
'79	1600 STD	2-dr sedan	4-speed	A26L	215001	and	after
	1600 DL	2-dr sedan	4-speed	A26L	419001	and	after
			automatic	A26L	739001	and	after
		4-dr sedan	4-speed	A26L	511001	and	after
			5-speed	A26L	670001	and	after
			automatic	A26L	618501	and	after
		2-dr coupe	5-speed	A26L	915501	and	after
		station wagon	4-speed	A66L	71650l	and	after
			5-speed	A66L	313001	and	after
			automatic	A66L	619001	and	after
			4-wheel drive	A67L	047000	and	after
		BRAT (M.P.V.)	4-wheel drive	A69L	026001	and	after
	1600 FE	2-dr coupe	5-speed	A26L	670001	and	after
	1600 GF	hardtop	5-speed	A26L	816501	and	after
			automatic	A26L	314501	and	after
	1600 GL	station wagon	4-wheel drive	A67L	502001	and	after
		BRAT (M.P.V.)	4-wheel drive	A69L	502001	and	after
'80	1600 STD	2-dr sedan	4-speed	AF21FAG	002001	and	after
		2-dr sedan with converter	4-speed	AF21FAG	802001	and	after
		2-dr sedan	4-wheel drive	AF31FAG	702001	and	after
	1600 DL	hardtop	5-speed	AW21FAG	502001	and	after
		hardtop with converter	5-speed	AW21FAG	402001	and	after
		2-dr sedan	5-speed	AF21FAG	202001	and	after
		2-dr sedan with converter	5-speed	AF21FAG	402001	and	after
		2-dr sedan	4-wheel drive	AF31FAG	702001	and	after
		4-dr sedan	4-speed	AB21FAG	002001	and	after
		4-dr sedan with converter	4-speed	AB21FAG	802001	and	after
		station wagon	4-speed	AM21AG	002001	and	after
		station wagon	4-wheel drive	AM31FAG	702001	and	after
		BRAT (M.P.V.)	4-wheel drive	A69L	041001	and	after
	1600 GL	4-dr sedan	4-wheel drive	AB21FAG	202001	and	after
		station wagon	5-speed	AM21FAG	202001	and	after
		station wagon	4-wheel drive	AM31FAG	702001	and	after
		BRAT(M.P.V.)	4-wheel drive	A69L	515001	and	after

VEHICLE IDENTIFICATION

Year	Model	Body Type	Transmission Type	Serial Number			
'80	1600 GLF	hardtop	5-speed	AW21FAG	202001	and	after
	1800 DL	2-dr sedan	automatic	AF41FAG	502001	and	after
	1800 GL	4-dr sedan	automatic	AB41FAG	502001	and	after
		station wagon	automatic	AM41FAG	502001	and	after
	1800 GLF	hardtop	automatic	AW41FAG	502001	and	after
'81	1600 STD	2 door	4-speed	AF21BBA	100001	and	after
	1600 DL	2 door	5-speed	AF22BBB	100001	and	after
		4 door	4-speed	AB22BBA	200001	and	after
		4 door	5-speed	AB22BBB	200001	and	after
		hardtop	4-speed	AW22BBA	300001	and	after
		hardtop	5-speed	AW22BBB	300001	and	after
	1800 STD	2 door	4-wheel drive	AF51BBD	100001	and	after
	1800 DL	2 door	4-wheel drive	AF52BBD	100001	and	after
		station wagon	4-speed	AM42BBA	400001	and	after
		station wagon	5-speed	AM42BBB	400001	and	after
		station wagon	4-wheel drive	AM52BBD	400001	and	after
		BRAT (M.P.V.)	4-wheel drive	AR52BBD	500001	and	after
	1800 GL	2 door	5-speed	AF43BBB	100001	and	after
		2 door	automatic	AF43BBC	100001	and	after
		2 door	4-wheel drive dual range	AF53BBE	100001	and	after
		4 door	5-speed	AB43BBB	200001	and	after
		4 door	automatic	AB43BBC	200001	and	after
		station wagon	5-speed	AM43BBB	400001	and	after
		station wagon	automatic	AM43BBC	400001	and	after
		station wagon	4-wheel drive dual range	AM53BBE	400001	and	after
		BRAT (M.P.V.)	4-wheel drive dual range	AR53BBE	500001	and	after
	1800 GLF	hardtop	5-speed	AW44BBB	300001	and	after
		hardtop	automatic	AW44BBC	300001	and	after
'82	1600 STD	hatchback	4-speed	AF21BXA	100001	and	after
	1600 DL	hatchback	5-speed	AF22BXB	100001	and	after
		4 door	4-speed	AB22BXA	200001	and	after
		4 door	5-speed	AB22BXB	200001	and	after
		hardtop	4-speed	AW22BXA	300001	and	after
		hardtop	5-speed	AW22BXB	300001	and	after
	1800 STD	hatchback	4-wheel drive	AF51BXD	100001	and	after
	1800 DL	hatchback	4-wheel drive	AF52BXD	100001	and	after
		station wagon	4-speed	AM42BXA	400001	and	after
		station wagon	5-speed	AM42BXB	400001	and	after
		station wagon	4-wheel drive	AM52BXD	400001	and	after
		BRAT (M.P.V.	4-wheel drive dual range	AT53BXE	500001	and	after
	1800 GL	hatchback	5-speed	AF43BXB	100001	and	after
		hatchback	automatic	AF43BXC	100001	and	after
		hatchback	4-wheel drive dual range	AF53BX	100001	and	after
		4 door	5-speed	AB43BXB	200001	and	after
		4 door	automatic	AB43BXC	200001	and	after
		station wagon	5-speed	AM43BXB	400001	and	after

VEHICLE IDENTIFICATION

Year	Model	Body Type	Transmission Type		Serial Number		
'82	1800 GL	station wagon	automatic	AM43BXC	400001	and	after
		station wagon	4-wheel drive dual range	AM53BXE	400001	and	after
		BRAT (M.P.V.)	4-wheel drive dual range	AT53BXE	500001	and	after
	1800 GLF	hardtop	5-speed	AW44BXB	300001	and	after
		hardtop	automatic	AW44BXC	300001	and	after

ENGINE CODES

Year	Displacement (cm³/cu. in.)	Transmission Type	Code
'76	1361/83.2	4-speed	EA63AFA, FB①
		5-speed	EA63AP5, P6①
		4-wheel drive	EA63EF4, F5①
	1590/97	automatic	EA71AT, T2①
'77	1590/97	4-speed	EA71AF, F3, F2①
		5-speed	EA71AP, P3, P2①
		4-wheel drive	EA71EF, F3, F2①
		automatic	EA71AT4, T6, T5①
'78	1590/97	4-speed	EA71AA, AH, AK, AC①
		5-speed	EA71GA, GH, GK, GC①
		4-wheel drive	EA71WA, WH, WK, WC①
		automatic	EA71TA, TH, TK, TC①
'79	1595/97	4-speed	E71AA2, AK2, AC2①
		5-speed	E71AA2, AK2, AC2①
		5-speed (FE)	E71GA2A, GK2A
		4-wheel drive	E71WA2, WK2, WC2①
		automatic	E71TA2, TK2, TC2①
'80	1595/97	4-speed	E71AA3, GA3A, GK3A, AC3①
		5-speed	E71AA3, GA3A, GK3A, AK3, E71AC3①
		4-wheel drive	E71WA3, WA4, WK3, WK4, E71WC3, WC4①
	1800/109	automatic	E81TA, TK, TC①
'81–'82	1595/97	4-speed	EA71AA4, AK4
		5-speed	EA71GA4, GK4
	1781/109	4-speed	EA81AA, AK
		5-speed	EA81GA, GK, EA81GA1P, GK1P, GA1J, GK1J, EA1D, GK1D
		automatic	EA81TA2P, TK2P, TA2D, TK2D, EA81MA2P, MK2P, MA2D, MK2D
		4-wheel drive	EA81WA, WK, EA81JA, JK
		4-wheel drive dual range	EA81KA, KK, KA81PA1L, PK1L

①California vehicles only

GENERAL ENGINE SPECIFICATIONS

Year	Type	Displacement cu. in. (cc)	Carburetor	Horsepower @ rpm (SAE)	Torque @ rpm (SAE)	Bore and Stroke (in.)	Comp. Ratio	Normal Oil Pressure (psi)
'76	4 cylinder horizontally opposed	83.2 (1400)	2bbl	58 @ 5200 ①	68 @ 2400 ②	3.35 × 2.36	8.5:1	36–57
	4 cylinder horizontally opposed	97 (1600)	2 bbl	67 @ 5200 ③	81 @ 2400 ④	3.62 × 2.36	8.5:1	36–57
'77–'83	4 cylinder horizontally opposed	97 (1600)	2 bbl	67 @ 5200	81 @ 2400	3.62 × 2.36	8.5:1	36–57
'80–'83	4 cylinder horizontally opposed	109 (1800)	2 bbl ⑥	72 @ 4800 ⑤	92 @ 2400	3.62 × 2.64	8.7:1	50–57

① 4WD:56 @ 5200
② 4WD:67 @ 2400
③ 4WD:65 @ 5200
④ 4WD:80 @ 2400
⑤ 4WD:71 @ 4200
⑥ 1 bbl with feedback system

TUNE-UP SPECIFICATIONS

(When analyzing compression test results, look for uniformity among cylinders, rather than specific pressures)

Year	Engine Displacement (cu. in.)	Spark Plugs ⑤ Type	Gap (in.)	Distributor Point Dwell (deg)	Point Gap (in.)	Ignition Timing (deg)	Intake Valve Opens (deg)	Fuel Pump Pressure (psi)	Idle Speed (rpm)	Valve Clearance (in.) In	Ex
'76	EA63 (1400)	BP6ES	.032	49–55	0.018	8B @ 900	24B	1.8–2.6	900	0.011	0.015
	EA71 (1600)	BP6ES	.032	49–55	0.018	8B @ 900	24B	1.8–2.6	900	0.011	0.015
'77–'79	EA71 (1600)	BP6ES	.032	49–55②	0.018②	8B @ 850	24B	2.6	850①	0.010	0.014
'80	(1600)	BP6ES	.032	Electronic		8B @ 850	24B	2.6	850①	0.009	0.013
	(1800)	BP6ES	.032	Electronic		8B @ 850	24B	2.6	850①	0.009	0.013
'81–'82	(1600)	BPES-11	.040	Electronic		8B @ 700	20B	1.3–2.0	700	0.010	0.014
	(1800)	BPES-11	.040	Electronic		8B @ 700③	20B	1.3–2.0	700④	0.010	0.014
'83	(1600)	(See Underhood Specifications Sticker)									
	(1800)	(See Underhood Specifications Sticker)									

NOTE: The underhood specifications sticker often reflects tune-up specification changes made in production. Sticker figures must be used if they disagree with those in this chart.
① California 900
② California—Electronic ignition
③ Auto trans; 8B @ 800
④ 800 rpm w/Auto trans.
⑤ OEM spark plugs or NGK.
B—Before top dead center
M—Manual transmission
A—Automatic transmission

FIRING ORDERS

FRONT

Firing order is 1-3-2-4

CAPACITIES

Year	Model	Engine Displacement (CC)	Engine Crankcase (Qts) With Filter	Engine Crankcase (Qts) Without Filter	Transmission (Pts) 4-spd	Transmission (Pts) 5-spd	Auto	4WD	Gasoline Tank (Gals)	Cooling System (Qts)
'76	1400 series	1400	3.8	3.5	5.2	5.8	—	6.34①	13.2②	6.3
'76	1600 series	1600	3.8	3.5	—	—	12.5④	—	13.2	6.3
'77–'79	1600 series	1600	3.8	3.5	5.2	5.8	12.5	6.34	13.2	6.3
'80–'83	1600 series	1600	3.8	3.5	5.8	5.8	12.5⑤	6.34①	13.2③	5.6
'80–'83	1800 series	1800	3.8	3.5	5.8	5.8	12.5⑤	6.34①	13.2③	5.8

① 4WD rear differential; 1.7 pts
② Station wagon and 4WD; 11.9 gal
③ 4WD vehicles; 11.9 gal
④ Refill is 6.4 pts—level with top mark on dipstick when warm.
⑤ Automatic transmission differential; 2.5 pts

CRANKSHAFT AND CONNECTING ROD SPECIFICATIONS

(All measurements are given in inches)

Year	Engine	Crankshaft Main Brg. Journal Dia.	Crankshaft Main Brg. Oil Clearance	Crankshaft Shaft End-Play	Crankshaft Thrust On. No.	Connecting Rod Journal Diameter	Connecting Rod Oil Clearance	Connecting Rod Side Clearance
'76	1400, 1600	1.9667–① 1.9673	0.0004–② 0.0020	0.0016– 0.0054	2	1.7715– 1.7720	0.0012– 0.0029	0.0028– 0.0130
'77–'83	1600	1.9667–① 1.9673	0.0004–③ 0.0016	0.0016– 0.0054	2	1.7715– 1.7720	0.0008– 0.0028	0.0028– 0.0130
'80–'83	1800	2.1636– 2.1642	0.0004–④ 0.0012	0.0016–⑤ 0.0054	2	1.7715– 1.7720	0.0008– 0.0028	0.0028– 0.0130

① Center: 1.9673–1.9677 inch
② Center: 0.0000–0.0014 inch
③ 1977–79 center: 0–0.0018
   1980–83: 0.0004–0.0014 with the center: 0.0004–0.0010
④ Center: 0.0004–0.0010
⑤ 1982–83: 0.0004–0.0037

VALVE SPECIFICATIONS

Year	Engine Year	Seat Angle (deg)	Face Angle (deg)	Spring Test Pressure (lbs.)		Spring Compressed Height (in.)		Stem-to-Guide Clearance (in.) ▲		Stem Diameter (in.)	
				Inner	Outer	Inner	Outer	Intake	Exhaust	Intake	Exhaust
'76	1400	45	45	40–47 @ 1.16	91–105 @ 1.25	1.01	1.16	.0014–.0026	.0020–.0032	.3130–.3136	.3124–.3130
'76	1600	45	45	39–45 @ 1.16	88–101 @ 1.25	1.16	1.25	.0014–.0026	.0020–.0032	.3130–.3136	.3124–.3130
'77–'79	1600	45	45	43–50 @ 1.10	91–105 @ 1.22	1.008	1.16	.0015–.0026	.0016–.0028	.3130–.3136	.3128–.3134
'80–'83	1600	45	45	42–48 @ 1.22	112–127 @ 1.201	—	1.20	.0014–.0026	.0016–.0028	.3130–.3136	.3128–.3134
'80–'83	1800	45	45	42–48 @ 1.22	112–127 @ 1.201	—	1.20	.0014–.0026	.0016–.0028	.3130–.3136	.3128–.3134

▲ Valve guides are removable

PISTON AND RING SPECIFICATIONS

Year	Engine	Piston Clearance	Ring Gap			Ring Side Clearance		
			Top Compression	Bottom Compression	Oil Control	Top Compression	Bottom Compression	Oil Control
'76–'79	1400, 1600	.001–.002	.012–.020	.012–.020	.012–.035	.001–.003	.001–.003	None
'80–'83	1600	.001–.002	.008–.013	.008–.013	.008–.035	.001–.003	.001–.003	None
'80–'83	1800	.001–.002	.008–.013	.008–.013	.008–.035	.001–.003	.001–.003	None

TORQUE SPECIFICATIONS
(All readings in ft. lbs.)

Year	Engine	Cylinder Head Bolts	Rod Bearing Bolts	Crankcase Halves	Crankshaft Pulley Bolt	Flywheel To Crankshaft Bolt	Manifold	
							Intake	Exhaust
'76–'83	1400, 1600, 1800	37–43①	29–31	10 mm bolts 29–35 8 mm bolts 17–19 6 mm bolts 3–4	39–42	30–33	13–16	12-15

① 1976–78; 1600 cc (1st step) 14 ft. lbs.
          (2nd step) 25–29 ft. lbs.
          (3rd step) 37–43 ft. lbs.
  1979–83; 1600 cc (1st step) 22 ft. lbs.
  1980–83; 1800 cc (2nd step) 43 ft. lbs.
          (3rd step) 47 ft. lbs.

TORQUE SEQUENCES

Tighten head from center outward; loosen in reverse order

ALTERNATOR AND REGULATOR SPECIFICATIONS

Year	Model	Alternator Output (amps) @ 12 Volts	Regulator							
			Charge Relay				Voltage Regulator			
			Yoke Gap (in.)	Core Gap (in.)	Point Gap (in.)	Volts to Open	Yoke Gap (in.)	Core Gap (in.)	Point Gap (in.)	Volts @ 1200 & 75°
'76	all models	50	.035	.032–.039	.016–.024	8–10	.035	.024–.039	.012–.016	14.0
'77–'79	all models	50	.035	.032–.039	.016–.024	8–10	.035	.024–.039	.014–.018	14.0
'80–'81	all models	50①	.035	.032–.039	.016–.024	8–10	.035	.024–.039	.014–.018	14.0
'82–'83	all models	55	—	—	—	—	solid state internally mounted			

① 1980 station wagon 4WD GL: 55A

BATTERY AND STARTER SPECIFICATIONS

Year	Model	Battery			Lock Test			No Load Test			Brush Spring Tension (oz.)
		Amp-Hour Capacity	Volts	Terminal Grounded	Amps	Volts	Torque (ft. lbs.)	Amps	Volts	rpm	
'76	all models	50	12	Neg	700①	7.7②	9.4③	50	11	5000	35–54
'77–'79	all models	50	12	Neg	600	7.7②	9.4③	50④	11	5000	37–47.6
'80–'83	all models	60⑤	12	Neg	600⑥	7.7⑦	9–13⑧	50⑨	11	5000⑩	37–47.6

① Automatic transmission vehicles except California—600
② Automatic transmission vehicles except California—7.0
③ Automatic transmission vehicles except California—13.0
④ Automatic transmission vehicles except California—60

⑤ Optional—65A
⑥ Gear reduction—400A
⑦ Gear reduction—2.4V
⑧ Gear reduction—8 ft. lbs. (5 ft. lbs. if manual transmission)
⑨ Gear reduction—90A
⑩ Gear reduction—4100 rpm (3000 rpm if manual transmission)

BRAKE SPECIFICATIONS

(All measurements given are (in.) unless noted)

Year	Model	Lug Nut Torque (ft. lbs.)	Master Cylinder Bore	Brake Disc		Diameter	Brake Drum		Minimum Lining Thickness	
				Minimum Thickness	Maximum Run-Out		Maximum Machine O/S	Maximum Wear Limit	Front	Rear
'76–'79	all models	58–72	.75	.33	.006	7.09	7.17	7.17	.06	.06
'80–'81	all models	58–72	.8125	.394	.0039	7.09	7.17	7.17	.295①	.06
'82–'83	all models	58–72	.8125	.394	.0039	7.24	7.17	7.17	.295①	.059

NOTE: Minimum lining thickness is as recommended by the manufacturer. Because of variations in state inspection regulations, the minimum allowable thickness may be different than recommended by the manufacturer.
① Includes back metal

REAR END ALIGNMENT

Year	Model	Body Type	Ride Height① (in.)	Camber (deg)	Toe-In (in.)	Tracking (in.)②
'76	DL, GL, GF	Sedan, Coupe, H.T.	11.3–11.9	15'–1°30'	.04–.20	− .12– + .12
	DL	Wagon	12.2–12.8	1°–2°	.08–.24	− .12– + .12
	4WD	Wagon	14.2–14.8	1°30'–2°15'	.08–.24	0– + .16
'77–'79	DL, GL, GF	Sedan, Coupe, H.T.	11.2–12.0	− 15'–1°	.04–.20	− .12– + .12
	DL	Wagon	12.2–13.0	15'–2°	.08—.24	− .12– + .12
	4WD	Wagon	13.6–14.4	30'–2°	.08–.24	0– + .16
'80–'81	exc. 4WD	Sedan, H.T.	10.2–11.0	− 45'–45'	—	− .20– + .20
	exc. 4WD	Station Wagon	11.0–11.8	− 45'–45'	—	− .20– + .20
	4WD	Sedan	12.6–13.4	− 45'–45'	—	− .20– + .20
	4WD	exc. Sedan	13.1–13.9	− 20'–1°	—	− .20– + .20
'82–'83	exc. 4WD	Hatchback, Sedan and Hardtop	10.3–11.1	− 45'–45'	− 0.12–0.12	− .20– + .20
	exc. 4WD	Station Wagon	11.1–11.9	− 45'–45'	− 0.12–0.12	− .20– + .20
	4WD	Hatchback	12.6–13.4	− 45'–45'	− 0.12–0.12	− .20– + .20
	4WD	Exc. Hatchback	13.2–14.0	− 25'–1°05'	− 0.12–.012	− .20– + .20

① Measured from outer center of torsion bar
② Measured with one passenger aboard

FRONT WHEEL ALIGNMENT

Year	Model	Caster①		Camber①		Toe-In (in.)
		Range (deg)	Pref. Setting (deg)	Range (deg)	Pref. Setting (deg)	
'76	Sedan, Coupe, H.T.	0–1°30'	45'	1°–2°	1°30'	.08–0.32
	Station Wagon	0–1°30'	45'	1°–2°	1°30'	.08–0.32
	4WD	0–1°30'	45'	2°–3°	2°30'	.24–0.47

FRONT WHEEL ALIGNMENT

Year	Model	Caster ① Range (deg)	Caster ① Pref. Setting (deg)	Camber ① Range (deg)	Camber ① Pref. Setting (deg)	Toe-In (in.)
'77–'79	Sedan, Coupe, H.T.	−5°––1°30′	−3°15′	45′–2°15′	1°30′	.08–0.32
	Station Wagon	−1°–30′	15′	1°–2°30′	1°	.08–0.32
	4WD	−5°––1°30′	−3°15′	1°30′–3°	2°15′	.24–0.47
'80–'81	Sedan and H.T.	−1°10′–20′	—	45′–2°15′	—	.08–0.31
	Station Wagon	−50′–40′	—	1°–2°30′	—	.08–0.31
	Sedan 4WD	−1°15′–15′	—	1°50′–3°20′	—	.24–0.47
	4WD	−1°20′–5′	—	1°50′–3°20′	—	.24–0.47
'82–'83	exc. 4WD and Station Wagon	−1°10′–20°	—	45′–2°30′	—	.04 ± .04
	exc. 4WD Station Wagon	−50′–40′	—	1°–2°30′	—	.04 ± .04
	4WD Hatchback	−1°15′–15′	—	1°50′–3°20′	—	.08 ± .04
	4WD exc. Hatchback	−1°25′–05′	—	1°50′–3°20′	—	.08 ± .04

① Not adjustable—MacPherson Strut

TUNE-UP PROCEDURES

Spark Plugs

NOTE: Number the spark plug wires before removing them.

1. Using a spark plug wrench, remove all of the spark plugs.
2. Check them for damage or wear and clean or replace them.
3. Set the gap between the two electrodes, using a spark plug gap gauge.
4. Install the spark plugs in the engine, tightening to 13–17 ft. lbs.

Breaker Points and Condenser

1. To replace the points, remove the hold-down screws, the ground lead and the condenser lead.
2. Lift out the point assembly and insert the new assembly.

NOTE: Always replace the condenser when replacing the points.

3. Install the hold-down screws and the leads in their proper positions. Do not tighten the attaching screws, just leave them snug so the point gap can be adjusted.
4. Adjust the gap by placing the proper size feeler gauge between the contacts and

Checking the breaker point gap

Ignition circuit of a typical breakerless ignition system

turning the adjusting eccentric with a screwdriver.

5. The breaker point arm must be on a high point of the cam. Turn the eccentric screw until there is a slight drag when the gauge is drawn through the gap.

6. Lubricate the cam surface with cam lube.

7. Replace the distributor cap, making sure that the spark plug wires are installed tightly in the top of the cap.

Dwell Angle

1. Hook up a dwell meter according to the manufacturer's instructions. Start the engine and read the meter. If the dwell is correct, then shut off the engine and remove the dwell meter.

2. If the dwell must be adjusted, shut off the engine, remove the distributor cap and adjust the point gap.

3. Open the points to decrease the dwell, close them to increase the dwell.

4. Replace the cap and start the engine. Check the dwell. If it is correct, shut off the engine and remove the dwell meter. If the dwell is not correct, repeat the above steps.

Components of a breaker point distributor plate

Breakerless Distributor

1977 through 1979 California engines and all engines from 1980 have a breakerless distributor. The centrifugal advance, vacuum advance, and retard units are the same as with the conventional distributor.

AIR GAP ADJUSTMENT

1. The distributor cap is held on by two clips. Release them with a screwdriver and lift the cap straight up and off, with the wires attached. Inspect the cap for cracks, carbon tracks, or a worn center contact. Replace it if necessary, transferring the wires one at a time from the old cap to the new.

2. Pull the ignition rotor (not the spoked reluctor) straight up to remove. Replace it if its contacts are worn, burned, or pitted. Do not file the contacts. To replace, press

Adjusting air gap on a typical breakerless ignition

it firmly onto the shaft. It only goes on one way, so be sure it is fully seated.

3. Before replacing the ignition rotor, check the reluctor air gap. *Use a non-magnet feeler gauge.* Rotate the engine until a reluctor spoke is aligned with the pick-up coil (either bump the engine around with the starter, or turn it with a wrench on the crankshaft pulley bolt).

Air Gap Adjustment

1977–79	
Calif; Manual Trans.	.008–.016
Calif; Auto Trans.	.012–.016
1980	
Exc. 4-WD;	.008–.016
4-WD;	.012–.016
1981–82	
Exc. 4-WD;	.008–.016
4-WD;	.012–.020

Adjustment, if necessary, is made by loosening the pick-up coil mounting screws and shifting its position on the "breaker plate" either closer to, or farther from, the reluctor. Tighten the screws and recheck the gap.

4. Inspect the ignition wires for cracks or brittleness. Replace them one at a time to prevent crosswiring, carefully pressing the replacement wires into place. The cores of wires used with electronic ignition are more susceptible to breakage than those of standard wires, so treat them gently.

Ignition timing marks

Ignition Timing

The ignition timing marks are located on the edge of the flywheel, graduated in 2° increments from 0° to 16°. The marks are visible through a port in the flywheel housing, just behind the dipstick. There is usually a plastic cap in the opening. Set the timing with the engine at normal operating temperature.

NOTE: If your vehicle is equipped with electronic ignition, an inductive timing light is recommended because it is not susceptible to crossfiring or false triggering due to the greater voltage.

1. After cleaning the timing marks, connect a timing light to the ignition following the manufacturer's instruction. Disconnect and plug the distributor vacuum line(s).

2. Start the engine and aim the timing light at the timing marks on the flywheel.

3. Adjust the ignition timing by loosening the bolt on the distributor retaining plate, and rotating the distributor clockwise to advance or counterclockwise to retard the timing.

Valve Lash

VALVE LASH ADJUSTMENT

Before adjusting the valves, make sure the cylinder head nuts/bolts are torqued (tightened) to the proper specifications. To torque the head and intake manifold nuts/bolts, use the following procedure.

1. Make sure the engine is cold.

2. Remove the valve covers from both sides of the engine.

3. Loosen the three bolts holding the intake manifold on the right (#1–#3) side cylinder head (as viewed from the driver's seat). These bolts should be loosened no more than 60 degrees. Do not loosen the left side (#2–#4) intake manifold bolts.

4. Refer to the "Tightening Sequence" chart for the correct pattern to use while checking and retorquing the cylinder head.

NOTE: It is important to follow the Tightening Sequence Chart when checking the head nuts/bolts. Warpage of the cylinder or water leaks could occur if the proper tightening pattern is not followed.

5. Loosen the center cylinder head nut/bolt no more than 60 degrees. If loosened too much, coolant leaks may occur. Lubricate the nut/bolt with engine oil, tighten and loosen it several times. Retighten the nut/bolt to the specified torque.

6. Move on to the next nut/bolt as indicated on the sequence chart an perform the same steps as before, proceed until all of the nuts/bolts have been tightened.

7. Go back to number one nut/bolt and recheck the torque, tighten if necessary. Recheck the rest of the nuts/bolts following the specified order.

8. After rechecking all the head nuts/bolts tighten the intake manifold bolts on the right side (#1–#3) cylinder head.

9. Rotate the engine so that the No. 1 piston is at top dead center (TDC) of its compression stroke. To determine TDC, remove the distributor cap and the plastic flywheel housing dust cover. The No. 1 piston is at top dead center when the distributor rotor is pointing to No. 1 spark plug lead terminal (as though the distributor cap were in place) and the "O" mark on the flywheel is opposite the pointer on the housing.

10. Check the clearance of both the intake and exhaust valves of the No. 1 cylinder by inserting a feeler gauge between each valve stem an rocker arm. See the "Tune-Up Specifications" chart for the proper stem-to-rocker arm clearance.

11. If the clearance is not within specifications, loosen the locknut with the proper size metric box wrench and turn the adjusting stud either in or out until the valve clearance is correct.

12. Tighten the locknut and recheck the valve stem-to-rocker arm clearance.

13. The rest of the valves are adjusted in the same way; bring each piston to TDC of its compression stroke, then check and adjust the valves for that cylinder. The proper valve adjustment sequence is 1-3-2-4, which is the firing order.

14. To bring the No. 3 piston to TDC

Idle speed adjustment

of its compression stroke, rotate the crankshaft 180° and make sure that the distributor rotor is pointing to the No. 3 spark plug terminal. Rotate the crankshaft 180° after each valve adjustment before going on to the next adjustment.

15. When the valve adjustment is complete, install the distributor cap, the valve covers, and the dust cover on the flywheel housing port.

Carburetor

IDLE SPEED AND MIXTURE ADJUSTMENT

1. Run the engine and allow it to reach normal operating temperature.

2. Stop the engine and connect a tachometer in accordance with the manufacturer's instructions.

3. Disconnect and plug the hose that runs to the distributor vacuum retard unit.

4. Remove the air cleaner by disconnecting the emission control system hoses from it, unfastening the wing nut(s) and removing the screws which secure it to its mounting brackets.

5. Check proper idle speed in the "Tune-Up Specifications" chart and adjust to that setting by turning the throttle adjusting screw.

6. Continue adjusting the idle, this time by means of the throttle adjusting screw and the idle mixture adjusting screw, until a reading of 50 rpm above the proper idle setting is attained.

Idle mixture adjustment

NOTE: The idle mixture adjusting screw should have a plastic limiter cap on it| adjustments must be made within the range of this cap or exhaust emissions will be increased. Do not remove the cap.

7. Then turn the idle mixture adjusting screw *clockwise* until the idle speed drops to the figure given in the "Tune-Up Specifications" chart.

NOTE: Following this procedure should keep the carbon monoxide (CO) emission level within pollution law standards. However, it is a good idea to have the CO level checked by a qualified garage with an exhaust analyzer whenever a tune-up is performed.

Throttle adjuster and idle adjuster screw locations

8. Disconnect the tachometer. Reconnect the hoses to the air injection manifold (if equipped). Install the air cleaner.

ENGINE ELECTRICAL

Distributor

REMOVAL AND INSTALLATION

1. Remove the air cleaner assembly, taking note of the hose locations.

2. On models equipped with conventional ignition system, disconnect the primary wire at the coil. On models equipped with breakerless ignition, disconnect the distributor wiring connector from the vehicle wiring harness.

3. Note the positions of the vacuum line(s) on the distributor diaphragm, disconnect the lines at the diaphragm. Unsnap the two distributor cap retaining clamps and remove the cap. Position the cap and ignition wires to one side.

NOTE: If it is necessary to remove the ignition wires from the cap to get enough room to remove the distributor, make sure to label each wire and the cap for easy and accurate reinstallation.

4. Use chalk or paint to carefully mark the position of the distributor rotor in relationship to the distributor housing and mark the position of the distributor housing in relationship to the engine block. When this is done, you should have a line on the distributor housing directly in line with the tip of the rotor and another line on the engine block directly in line with the mark on the distributor housing. This is very important because the distributor must be reinstalled in the exact same position from which it was removed, if correct ignition timing is to be maintained.

5. Remove the distributor hold-down bolt.

6. Remove the distributor from the engine, taking care not to damage or lose the O-ring.

1. Cam
2. Screw
3. Governor spring
4. Governor weight
5. Shaft
6. Washer
7. Screw
8. Condenser
9. Bolt
10. Gear
11. Plate
12. Vacuum unit
13. Housing
14. Breaker plate
15. Clamp
16. Screw
17. Breaker points
18. Breaker point set screw

19. Rotor
20. Boot
21. Cap
22. Ground wire
23. Clamp
24. Lead wire
25. Terminal
26. Carbon brush
27. Pointer

Exploded view of a point-type distributor

NOTE: Do not disturb the engine while the distributor is removed. If you crank or rotate the engine while the distributor is removed you will have to retime the engine.

7. If the engine was not disturbed while the distributor was removed, position the distributor in the block (make sure the O-ring is in place) have the rotor aligned with the mark previously scribed on the distributor body and the marks on the distributor body and engine in alignment. Install the octane selector, if so equipped, and tighten the hold-down bolt finger tight.

8. Reinstall the distributor rotor, cap and wires, if removed. Reconnect the primary wire to the coil or reconnect the wiring harness. Install the air cleaner.

9. Plug the vacuum line(s) to the distributor and recheck the timing using a timing light.

INSTALLATION—TIMING LOST

If the engine has been cranked, disassembled or the timing otherwise lost, proceed as follows.

1. Remove the plastic dust cover from the timing port on the flywheel housing.

2. Remove the No. 1 spark plug. (No. 1 spark plug is the front plug on the right side of the engine). Use a wrench on the crankshaft pulley bolt (on manual transmission cars place transmission in Neutral) and slowly rotate the engine until the TDC "O" mark on the flywheel aligns with the pointer. While turning the engine place your finger over the No. 1 spark plug hole, when you feel air escaping past your finger the piston is on the compression stroke and when the marks align the piston is at TDC (top dead center).

2a. If Step 2 is impractical, for any reason, the following method can be used to get No. 1 piston on TDC. Remove the two bolts that hold the right (passenger's side) valve cover and remove the cover to expose the valves on No. 1 cylinder. Rotate the engine so that the valves in No. 1 cylinder are closed and the TDC "O" mark on the flywheel lines up with the pointer.

3. Align the small depression on the distributor drive pinion with the mark on the distributor body; this will align the rotor with the No. 1 spark plug terminal on the distributor cap. On models with the octane selector, set the pointer midway between the "A" and "R". Make sure the O-ring is located in the proper position.

4. Align the matchmarks you have made on the distributor body with those on the engine block and install the distributor in the engine. Make sure the drive is engaged. Install the hold-down bolt fingertight. Time the engine with a timing light.

Alternator

ALTERNATOR PRECAUTIONS

1. Pay particular attention to the polarity connections of the battery when connecting the battery cables. Make sure that you connect the correct cable to the corresponding terminal.

2. If a jumper battery is used to start the vehicle, make sure that the cables leading from the jumper battery are matched with the terminals on the battery being jumped, positive to positive and negative to a good chassis ground.

3. When testing or adjusting the alternator, install a condenser between the alternator output terminal and the ground. This is to prevent the diode from becoming damaged by a spark which occurs due to testing equipment with a defective connection.

4. Do not operate the alternator with the output terminals disconnected. The diode would be damaged by the high voltage generated.

5. When recharging the battery by a quick charge or any other charging apparatus, disconnect the alternator output terminal before hooking up the charging leads.

6. When installing a battery, always connect the grounded terminal last.

7. Never disconnect the battery while the engine is running.

8. Never electric weld on the car without disconnecting the alternator.

9. Never apply any voltage in excess of the battery voltage during testing.

10. Never jump a battery for starting purposes with more than the battery voltage.

1. Pulley nut set
2. Alternator pulley set
3. Alternator front cover
4. Pan head screw
5. Packing
6. Packing retainer
7. Ball bearing
8. Alternator bearing retainer

9. Alternator rotor ass'y
10. Ball bearing
11. Alternator stator ass'y
12. Alternator rear cover ass'y
13. Diode ass'y
14. Diode cover
15. Pan head screw
16. Alternator brush ass'y
17. Brush cover
18. Pan head screw
19. Terminal bolt set
20. Bolt
21. Through bolt
22. Through bolt

Exploded view of a typical alternator

REMOVAL AND INSTALLATION

1. To remove the alternator from the vehicle, first disconnect the negative battery terminal.

2. Tag and disconnect the wiring to the alternator.

3. Remove the alternator attaching bolts and nuts.

4. Remove the drive belt and take out the alternator.

5. Install in the reverse order of removal.

BELT TENSION ADJUSTMENT

1. To adjust the belt tension, first loosen

the adjusting bolt on the right of the alternator (looking from the rear).

2. Lift up on the alternator to increase the tension on the belt. When it takes moderate thumb pressure to move the longest span of belt ½ in., the tension adjustment is correct.

3. Tighten the adjusting bolt so that the alternator will not move in the adjusting bracket.

Regulator

NOTE: Late models have a solid state regulator built into the alternator. This regulator is non-adjustable and is serviced, when necessary, by replacement.

REMOVAL AND INSTALLATION

1. Disconnect the cable from the negative (−) battery terminal.

2. Disconnect the multi-wire connector and automatic choke lead (1975 and later models) from the regulator.

3. Remove the two regulator mounting screws and remove the regulator from the fender panel.

Installation is the reverse of the removal procedures.

VOLTAGE ADJUSTMENTS— ON THE CAR

This test should be made after the engine compartment and the regulator have had a chance to cool down. The test should never be done on a "hot engine".

1. Make sure all electrical equipment on the car is turned off or disconnected.

2. Using an ammeter rated at 10 amps, a 30-volt voltmeter, and a resistor rated at .25 ohms, connect up a test circuit as shown in the illustration.

3. BEFORE STARTING THE ENGINE, connect a jumper wire from the far terminal of the .25 ohm resister to the neg-

Voltage adjustment test schematic

ative (−) terminal of the ammeter. See illustration. After the engine is started, disconnect the jumper but be sure to reconnect it each time the engine is restarted.

4. Start the engine and gradually increase the speed from idle to about 2000 rpm. 2000 engine rpm is equal to about 1200 alternator rpm.

5. The voltage reading shown should compare with that on the spec chart, allowing for the temperature around the regulator.

Adjustment points of the voltage regulator

NOTE: The ammeter reading should be below 5 amps. Recharge or substitute the battery with a charged one if the reading is not below 5 amps.

6. If the voltage is not within the specified range, adjust as follows;

a. Remove the screws and take off the regulator cover. Loosen the locknut and turn the adjusting screw until the voltage falls within specifications.

b. If the voltage cannot be brought within specs, proceed with a mechanical adjustment.

c. If the voltage is now within the required specs: shut off the engine, remove the test equipment, replace the regulator cover and reconnect any electrical system components or accessories you disconnected at the beginning of the test.

VOLTAGE ADJUSTMENTS—OFF THE CAR

Charge Relay Adjustment

NOTE: The opening voltage of the charge relay is 8–10 volts at alternator terminal "A". However, the coil on the charge relay operates at half of this voltage (i.e., 4–5 volts).

Charge relay test circuit

1. Remove the regulator from the car.

2. Hook up the test circuit illustrated with a car battery, 0–150 ohm rheostat, voltmeter, heavy-duty switch, and a test light.

3. Close the switch with the rheostat set at 150 ohms (maximum).

4. Gradually decrease the resistance.

5. When the test light goes out, the voltmeter should read 4–5 volts.

6. If the light doesn't go out at the specified setting, remove the regulator cover and make the following adjustments. Loosen the locknut on the charge relay, and turn the adjusting screw until the voltage is within specifications. Tighten the locknut.

7. If the charge relay voltage cannot be brought within specifications, perform the "Mechanical Adjustments" outlines next.

8. If the charge relay is working properly, put the cover on the regulator and install it in the car.

Mechanical Adjustments

—— **CAUTION** ——

All mechanical adjustments must be performed with the regulator removed from the car to prevent battery and charging system damage.

1. Remove the voltage regulator from the car and remove the regulator cover.

2. Inspect both sets of points. If they are rough or dirty, polish them with #500 or #600 emery paper.

NOTE: If the points are so badly damaged that polishing them doesn't help, replace the regulator.

3. Measure and adjust the gaps of both the voltage regulator and the charge relay in the same manner. Use the specifications given in the "Alternator and Regulator Specifications" chart, Adjust both sets of gaps in the following sequence:

NOTE: It is not necessary to adjust the yoke gap.

a. Core gap—measure the clearance for both the regulator and charge relay between their armatures and coil cores. Adjust each, as necessary, by loosening the 4 mm screw which secures the con-

1. Thickness gauge
2. Contact set
3. Screw

Adjusting the core gap

1. Upper contact
2. Screw
3. Thickness gauge

Adjusting the point gap

tact set to the yoke and moving the set up or down. Tighten the screw.

b. Point gap—measure the distances between the points for both the voltage regulator and charge relay. Adjust each, as necessary, by loosening the 3 mm screw which secures the upper contact and mving the contact up or down. Tighten the screw.

4. Reinstall the regulator and test its operation as outlined above. If the voltage still cannot be brought within specifications, replace the regulator. If the voltage is still incorrect, the fault probably lies in the alternator.

Starter

Two types of starter motor are used, the direct drive motor and the gear reduction motor.

The direct drive motor uses a drive mounted on the end of the armature to engage the engine flywheel.

The gear reduction motor uses an idler gear driven by the end of the armature to turn the starter drive. The rotation speed of the starter drive is reduced approximately ⅓ of the armature speed.

REMOVAL AND INSTALLATION—ALL STARTERS

1. Remove the spare tire from the engine compartment.

2. Disconnect the cable from the negative (ground) battery terminal.

3. Disconnect the wiring harness at the starter located on top of the transaxle at the rear of the engine.

4. Remove the two nuts which secure the starter to the transaxle and pull the starter out.

5. Starter installation is the reverse of removal.

SOLENOID REPLACEMENT—DIRECT DRIVE STARTER

1. With the starter removed from the car, remove the nut underneath the solenoid

1. Brush holder plate assembly
2. Spring type brush holder
3. Brush
4. Commutator frame assembly
5. Bushing
6. Thru-bolt
7. Rubber parts
8. Spring
9. Washer
10. Lock plate
11. End frame cap
12. Snap ring
13. Pinion stop collar
14. Over running clutch assembly
15. Armature assembly
16. Yoke assembly
17. Pole core screw
18. Field coil assembly
19. Brush
20. Housing assembly
21. Housing bushing
22. Screw
23. Lever set bolt
24. Drive lever assembly
25. Plate
26. Rubber parts
27. Magnet switch assembly

Exploded view of the direct drive starter motor

terminal and disconnect the wires from the starter.

2. Remove the two screws which hold the solenoid to the starter.

NOTE: It may be necessary to use an impact driver to remove the two screws.

3. Lift the solenoid up and then pull it toward the rear in order to separate it from the starter.

4. Installation is performed in the reverse order of removal. Be sure to engage the hook on the end of the solenoid with the starter drive lever before installing the solenoid securing screws.

STARTER OVERHAUL— DIRECT DRIVE STARTER

Starter Drive Replacement

1. Remove the starter from engine. Remove the two thru-bolts.

2. Remove solenoid as outlined above.

3. Slide the pinion housing off the end of the starter. (It may be necessary to tap the pinion housing lightly with a hammer to remove it.)

4. Using a length of pipe the same diameter as the armature shaft, tap the pinion stop collar down toward the starter drive so that it is off the snap-ring. Use a pair of snap-ring pliers to remove the snap-ring from the armature shaft. Slide off the pinion stop collar.

5. Remove the starter drive from the threaded spline, taking care not to damage the spline.

6. To install the starter drive, slip the starter drive onto the armature shaft and install the snap-ring into position. Drive the pinion stop collar down onto the snap-ring. Assemble and install the starter in reverse order of removal and disassembly.

Brush Replacement–Direct Drive Starter

1. Remove the starter from engine. Remove the two thru-bolts.

2. Remove the two small mounting screws which hold the end frame cap. Remove the cap, lock plate, spring and rubber seal.

3. Slide the end frame off the starter assembly.

4. Remove the starter brushes from their holders by moving each brush holder spring aside.

5. Lift off the brush holder plate. The yoke may now be separated from the housing by sliding them apart.

6. If the brushes are worn to less than 0.043 in. they should be replaced by soldering in new ones.

----- CAUTION -----

When soldering in new positive brushes (those attached to the field coil) be careful not to get excess solder or dirt on the field coil.

---

7. Assemble and install the starter in reverse order of removal and disassembly.

GEAR REDUCTION STARTER REPAIRS

NOTE: The starter must be removed from the car to perform any of these operations.

1. Disconnect the lead wire between the solenoid and the starter body. Never loosen the terminal bolt.

2. Remove the two screws that secure the solenoid to the housing.

3. Remove the two bolts that attach the housing to the solenoid.

4. Separate the housing ad the solenoid.

5. Remove the starter drive unit. Take care ot to lose the spring or the ball.

6. Remove the two field brushes from the brush holder and remove the holder. Be careful ot to scratch the armature.

7. Remove the idler gear and starter

1. Through bolt
2. Brush holder
3. Brush spring
4. Felt washer
5. Ball bearing
6. Armature
7. Yoke
8. Rubber packing
9. Magnet switch
10. Drive gear
11. Idler gear
12. Roller
13. Retainer
14. Coil spring
15. Steel ball
16. Clutch
17. Housing

Exploded view of the gear reduction starter motor

drive from the solenoid. Be careful not to lose the five rollers.

8. Inspect the component parts for wear. If the solenoid is faulty, replace it as a uit. Check the gears for clips or worn teeth. If the brushes are worn, replace the assembly. Take care when soldering in the field brushes, do not get excessive solder or dirt on the field coils.

9. Assembly of the starter motor is the reverse of the disassembly. Grease the ball, rollers and gears with high temperature grease. If you have removed the armature be sure to reinstall the felt washer.

10. Reinstall the starter motor in the engine. Make sure all connections are tight.

ENGINE MECHANICAL

Engine

REMOVAL AND INSTALLATION

NOTE: On these models, the engine is removed separately from the transaxle.

1. Open the hood as far as possible and secure it with the stay.

2. Disconnect the ground cable from the negative (−) battery terminal.

3. Remove the 8 mm bolt which secures the ground cable at the intake manifold and disconnect the cable. It is unnecessary to remove the cable fully; leave it routed along the side of the body.

4. Remove the spare tire from the engine compartment.

5. Remove the emission control system hoses from the air cleaner. Remove the air cleaner brackets, remove the wing nut, and lift the air cleaner assembly off the carburetor.

6. Place a suitable container under the fuel line union to catch the gasoline. Disconnect the hoses at the union by removing the clip and pulling the hose off. Drain the engine oil.

7. Drain the coolant and disconnect the radiator hoses.

   a. Place a clean container, large enough to hold the contents of the cooling system, beneath the radiator drain plug so that the coolant may be rused.

   b. Loosen the drain plug on the radiator and turn it so that its slot faces downward.

   c. Disconnect both of the hoses at the radiator, leaving them connected to the engine.

   d. Disconnect the heater hoses from the pipe at the side of the engine.

   e. On automatic transmission models,

disconnect the oil cooler inlet and outlet hoses at the radiator.

8. Disconnect the following electrical wiring.

   a. Alternator multi-connector

   b. Oil pressure sender connection

   c. Three engine cooling fan connectors

   d. Temperature sender connection

   e. Primary distributor lead

   f. Secondary ignition leads (ignition side)

   g. Sarter wiring harness

   h. Anti-dieseling solenoid lad

   i. Automatic choke lead

   j. EGR vacuum solenoid

   k. EGR coolant temperature switch

   l. On automatic transmission models, disconnect the neutral safety switch harness and downshift solenoid harness.

9. Loosen the two radiator securing bolts, remove the ground lead from the upper side of the radiator, and lift the radiator out.

NOTE: On 4WD models, remove the engine fan from the pulley.

10. Remove the horizontal damper in the following order.

   a. Remove the front nut from the damper.

   b. Remove the nut on the body bracket and withdraw the damper.

   c. Pull the damper rearward away from the engine lifting hook. Be careful not to lose any of the damper parts.

11. Remove the starter assembly, as outlined above under "Engine Electrical".

12. Disconnect the following cables, hoses and linkages.

   a. Loosen, but don't remove, the screw in the carburetor throttle lever. Remove the outer end of the accelerator cable and withdraw it.

   b. Remove vacuum hose and purge hose from vapor canister.

   c. On standard transmission models, remove the clutch return spring from the release lever and intake manifold, and remove the clutch cable from the lever.

   d. On automatic transmssion models, disconnect the vacuum hose attached to the transmission.

   e. Disconnect the vacuum hose from the power brake unit (if so equipped).

13. On 4WD models, remove the under guard by unscrewing the attaching bolts.

14. Remove the Y-shaped exhaust pipe. (Be careful not to lose the insulators and gaskets.)

   a. Loosen the clamp fastening the air intake hose to the air stove on the exhaust pipe, and remove the hose.

   b. Remove the air stove and remove the four nuts attaching the exhaust pipe to the cylinder heads.

   c. Remove the two bolts and nuts connecting the exhaust pipe to the pre-muffler.

   d. While supporting the exhaust pipe by hand, remove the two bolts attaching the exhaust pipe to the transmission bracket. Lower the exhaust pipe.

NOTE: As the exhaust pipe is heavy, it is a good idea to have help supporting and lowering it.

15. On automatic transmission models, remove the torque converter bolts.

  a. Remove the timing hole cover from the torque converter housing.

  b. Remove the four bolts connecting the torque converter to the drive plate through the timing hole.

NOTE: Be careful that the bolts do not fall into the torque converter housing.

16. Set up a chain hoist on the engine, with hooks at the front and rear engine hangers. Adjust the hoist so that the weight of the engine is supported, but do not raise the engine.

NOTE: The purpose of supporting the engine at this point is to prevent the unstable movement of the engine and protect the people working underneath the vehicle.

17. Position a suitable jack under the transaxle to support its weight when the engine is removed.

18. Remove the four nuts (four each on top and bottom) connecting the engine and transmission.

19. Remove the nuts holding the front engine mounts (rubber) to the crossmember.

20. Before going on to the next step, be sure that all of the above steps have been completed.

21. Using the hoist, raise the engine slightly (about 1″). Keeping it level, move the engine forward, off the transaxle input shaft.

Engine mount alignment

Long hole

Projection

Cushion

Crossmember bracket

——— **CAUTION** ———

Do not raise the engine more than one inch prior to removing it from the input shaft or damage may occur to the drive-shaft double offset joints. On standard transmission models, be sure that the input shaft does not interfere with the clutch spring assembly. On automatic transmission models, leave the torque converter on the transaxle input shaft.

22. Hoist the engine carefully until it is completely out of the car, and place it on a suitable stand or workbench.

Engine installation is performed in the reverse order of removal. However, be sure to observe the following.

1. Use the following torque specifications when installing the engine.
Transmission to engine: 34–40 ft. lbs.
Torque converter to drive plate: 17–20 ft. lbs.
Engine mount to cross member: 14–24 ft. lbs.

Horizontal damper nut: 7–10 ft. lbs.
Exhaust pipe to engine:
  12–14 ft. lbs. (pre-1977 models)
  19–22 ft. lbs. (1977 and later models)
Exhaust pipe to pre-muffler: 31–38 ft. lbs.
Radiator mounting bolt: 6–10 ft. lbs.

2. Use care not to damage the input shaft splines or the clutch spring while lowering the engine in place.

3. When installing the exhaust pipe and/or converter always use new gaskets.

4. Perform the following adjustment to the horizontal damper:

  a. Tighten the body bracket nut.

  b. Turn the front nut until the clearance between the front washer and rubber cushion is zero.

  c. Insert the bushing and tighten the front nut to specifications (Step 1).

5. Make all of the clutch and accelator linkage adjustments, as detailed elsewhere in the book.

6. Replenish the engine oil and coolant supplies.

Cylinder head installation spacer

1. Cylinder head
2. Valve guide
3. Oil seal
4. Cylinder head gasket
5. Bolt
6. Crankcase hanger
7. Nut
8. Oil level gauge
9. O-ring
10. Timing hole plug
11. Bolt
12. Hanger washer
13. Crankcase hanger
14. Washer
15. Distributor wire loom
16. Nut
17. Battery cable support
18. Stud
19. Flywheel housing
20. Oil seal
21. Bolt
22. Washer
23. Bolt
24. Washer
25. Nut
26. Gasket
27. Crankcase plug
28. Oil seal
29. Oil pressure switch
30. Stud bolt
31. Plug
32. Gasket

Exploded view of a typical engine

Cylinder Head

REMOVAL AND INSTALLATION

The engine must be removed from the vehicle to remove the cylinder heads. Although it is physically possible (on some models) to remove the cylinder heads with the engine installed, head gasket failure will result upon installation, due to misalignment of the cylinders. The cylinder heads should be removed with the engine cold to prevent warpage.

1. Remove the engine from the vehicle.

2. Unbolt and remove the intake manifold together with the carburetor and the various pollution control devices. (The pipe attached to the exhaust manifold port in the cylinder head should have been removed before the engine was taken out.) On 1977 and later models, remove the EGR pipe from the intake manifold and cylinder head.

NOTE: Move or disconnect any engine wiring that might impair intake manifold removal.

3. Remove the spark plugs.

4. Disconnect the crankcase ventilation hose(s) and remove the valve covers.

5. Loosen the alternator adjusting bolts, and unbolt the alternator bracket from the cylinder head.

6. Remove the air injection distributor tubes from the cylinder heads by unscrewing the fittings.

7. Remove the valve covers. Loosen the valve rocker locknuts and adjusting screws. Loosen the rocker shaft mounting nuts, and remove the rocker arm assembly and pushrods.

NOTE: If the pushrods are to be reused, keep them in order so that they are installed in the original positions.

8. Gradually loosen the head bolts or nuts in the reverse of the tightening sequence, and remove the cylinder heads and pushrods.

9. Install the heads in the reverse order of removal.

The cylinder heads must be installed with the cylinders vertical, to avoid misalignment, and to permit the head gasket to crush evenly around the cylinder. Prior to installation of the heads, cylinder liner projection must be checked on the 1400 engine. It must be 0.003–0.004 in. Liner projection is adjusted by varying the size of the liner gaskets.

NOTE: Liner projection must be checked whenever a 1400 engine head gasket has failed.

Torque in the specified sequence, in stages, using a spacer in place of the rocker shaft support. After the head is torqued to specifications, remove the rocker shaft bolts

Valve guide installed height

Valve arrangement in cylinder head

(or nuts) and the spacers, and install the rocker shafts.

SERVICE

Using a straightedge, check the cylinder heads for warpage. Should warpage exceed 0.002 in., the cylinder head must be resurfaced (grinding limit 0.016 in.). Should the valve sink exceed approximately 0.040 in., the seats must be replaced. The valve guides are pressed in, and should be replaced if clearance exceeds specifications. The intake valve guide should extend 0.71 and the exhaust 0.91 in. from the spring seat.

Rocker Shafts

With the engine removed from the vehicle, remove the rocker arm covers and gaskets from the cylinder heads. Unscrew the nuts which hold the rocker arm assemblies from the engine. Identify the pushrods so they can be replaced in their original positions. Install in the reverse order of removal.

Intake Manifold

REMOVAL AND INSTALLATION

1. Remove the EGR pipe from the manifold.

2. Remove the water by-pass hose from the intake manifold.

3. Disconnect the wiring harness lead from the oil pressure switch.

4. Disengage the harness from the clip on the water pipe.

5. Remove the six bolts and remove the intake manifold.

6. To install reverse the removal procedure.

Exhaust Manifolds

An exhaust manifold, as a separate item, is not found on these models. Instead, the Y-shaped exhaust pipe bolts directly to a flange on each cylinder head. Removal procedures for this exhaust pipe can be found in the "Engine Removal and Installation" section.

1. Screw
2. Spring washer
3. Accelerator cable clamp
4. Bolt
5. Spring washer
6. Accelerator cable bracket
7. Washer
8. Thermostat cover
9. Thermostat cover gasket
10. Thermostat
11. Hose clamp
12. Water bypass hose
13. Water bypass connector
14. Gasket
15. Water bypass connector
16. Bolt
17. Bolt
18. Intake manifold gasket
19. Intake manifold
20. Stud
21. Plug
22. Temperature sending unit
23. Carburetor gasket
24. Spring washer
25. Nut

Exploded view of a 1400 intake manifold

1. Nut
2. Spring washer
3. Carburetor gasket
4. Washer
5. Bolt (8 x 26 x 23)
6. Bolt
7. Thermostat case cover
8. Thermostat case cover gasket
9. Thermostat
10. Thermometer
11. Bolt
12. Bolt

13. Spring washer
14. Intake manifold gasket
15. Intake manifold
16. Stud bolt (8 x 36 x 12)
17. Stud bolt
18. Spark plug cord stay 2
19. Spark plug cord supporter

Exploded view of a typical 1600 intake manifold (1800 similar)

Removing or installing crankcase plugs

Timing Gear Cover

REMOVAL AND INSTALLATON

The flywheel housing covers the timing gears. In order to remove it, the engine has to be removed from the vehicle.

1. Separate the engine from the transmission. Remove the torque converter with the automatic transmission.

2. Remove the clutch cover and the clutch disc from the flywheel. Remove the flywheel or automatic transmission converter drive plate.

3. Remove the flywheel housing bolts and work the housing from the two aligning dowels.

4. Install the cover in the reverse of removal.

TIMING GEAR COVER (FLYWHEEL HOUSING) OIL SEAL REPLACEMENT

The housing cover oil seal is pressed in.

1. Remove the engine from the vehicle, separating the transmission from the engine.

2. Remove the flywheel and clutch assembly or converter drive plate from the engine.

3. Remove the housing from the engine and remove the oil seal from the housing.

4. Install the new oil seal, pressing it into place.

5. Reassemble the engine and install it in the reverse order of disassembly and removal.

Remove the crankcase access plugs

Camshaft

REMOVAL AND INSTALLATION

The camshaft turns on journals that are machined directly into the crankcase. To remove the camshaft, the engine must be removed from the vehicle disassembled and the crankcase separated.

1. Remove the engine from the vehicle, separating the transmission from the engine.

2. Remove the clutch and flywheel assembly or converter drive plate.

3. Remove the flywheel housing.

4. Straighten the lockwashers and remove the bolts that hold the camshaft retaining plate to the crankcase. The lockwashers are straightened and the bolts removed through the access holes in the camshaft gear.

5. Remove the intake manifold and separate the two halves of the crankcase and remove the camshaft.

6. Before installing the camshaft, measure the end-play of the camshaft, using a feeler gauge. The end-play should be 0.012 in. or less. Install the camshaft in the reverse order of removal.

7. Assemble the engine and reinstall it in the vehicle in the reverse order of disassembly and removal.

NOTE: One of the bolt holes in the crankshaft gear has a larger chamber than the others.

Position the crankshaft so that the punch mark on the cam gear tooth can be seen through this bolt hole.

This should position the Woodruff key slot of the camshaft at an 11:30 o'clock position, and the crankshaft Woodruff key slot at 7 o'clock.

Removing or installing the piston pin circlip through the crankcase holes

Pistons and Connecting Rods

REMOVAL AND INSTALLATION

To remove the pistons and connecting rods, it is necessary that the engine be removed from the vehicle.

Only the 1400 engine has removable cylinder liners.

1. Separate the engine and the transmission.

2. Remove the intake manifold, oil pan, flywheel and clutch assembly, flywheel housing, cylinder heads and gaskets.

3. Unscrew and remove the two bolts and lockwashers that hold the camshaft retaining plate in place. The bolts and lockwashers are removed through two access holes in the camshaft gear.

4. Remove the crankcase plugs from the crankcase by using an Allen wrench.

5. Remove the cylinder liners on the 1400 engine by using a cylinder liner puller.

6. Remove the cylinder liner gaskets, keeping the cylinder liners and the gaskets of each cylinder together. The flanges of the liner should be marked so that they can be reinstalled in the correct positions.

7. Remove the circlips that hold the wrist pins in the pistons by inserting the piston circlip pliers through the crankcase plug holes.

8. Remove the wrist pins by inserting the wrist pin remover through the crankcase plug holes. Keep the pistons and the wrist pins together for each cylinder so that they do not become mixed. Make marks on the pistons and the liners so as not to change the direction in which they are installed.

Position each connecting rod with the side mark facing forward. Each connecting rod has its own mating cap with a matching number

Installation of the piston rings. The top and second rings are provided with an "R" or "N" mark. Install the rings with the mark facing upward.

9. Separate the crankcase halves. Remove the oil seal. Be sure to replace it with a new one when reassembling the engine.

10. Remove the crankshaft together with the connecting rod and the distributor gear as an assembly.

11. Mark the connecting rods for identification purposes so they can be installed in the same position from which they were removed.

12. Install and reassemble the engine in the reverse order of removal.

Piston ring gap position

Installation of piston and pin when cylinder liners are used

1. Bolt
2. Valve rocker cover seal washer
3. Valve rocker cover
4. Valve rocker cover gasket
5. Exhaust valve
6. Valve spring retainer key
7. Valve spring retainer
8. Valve spring (outer)
9. Valve spring (inner)
10. Intake valve
11. Snap-ring
12. Washer
13. Nut
14. Valve rocker arm
15. Valve rocker screw
16. Rocker shaft spring washer
17. Rocker shaft supporter
18. Valve rocker arm
19. Rocker shaft spacer
20. Valve rocker shaft
21. Valve rocker arm
22. Valve rocker arm
23. Bolt
24. Lockwasher
25. Camshaft gear
26. Camshaft plate
27. Camshaft
28. Woodruff key
29. Valve lifter
30. Valve push rod
31. Valve rocker bushing

Typical camshaft and rocker arm assembly

1. Bolt
2. Washer
3. Crankshaft pulley
4. Drive belt
5. Distributor drive gear
6. Woodruff key
7. Crankshaft
8. Woodruff key
9. Needle bearing
10. Oil seal
11. Crankshaft gear
12. Flywheel (MT)
13. Starter ring gear
14. Bolt
15. Bolt
16. Drive plate (AT)
17. Connecting rod
18. Nut
19. Connecting rod bolt
20. Connecting rod bearing
21. Piston rings
22. Piston
23. Piston pin
24. Circlip

Typical crankshaft, piston and connecting rod assembly

ENGINE LUBRICATION

Oil Pan

REMOVAL AND INSTALLATION

1. To remove the oil pan, it is not necessary that the engine be removed from the vehicle.

2. Remove the attaching bolts that hold the oil pan to the bottom of the crankcase, and remove the oil pan.

3. Remove the oil pan gasket and clean the mating surfaces of the oil pan and the crankcase.

4. Install in the reverse order of removal.

Measuring the tip clearance

REAR MAIN OIL SEAL REPLACEMENT

The rear main oil seal is located in the flywheel housing (timing gear cover). See "Timing Gear Cover Removal and Installation" for the rear main oil seal replacement procedures.

Oil Pump

REMOVAL AND INSTALLATION

The oil pump can be removed with the engine in the vehicle. The oil pump and the oil filter can be removed as a unit. Remove

1. Oil filter	8. Relief valve spring	15. Oil pump holder
2. Oil pump body	9. Washer (6 mm)	16. Screw
3. Bolt (6X54 mm)	10. Washer	17. O ring
4. Bolt (6X32 mm)	11. Plug	18. Bypass valve spring
5. Spring washer	12. O ring	19. Ball
6. Washer	13. Rotor	20. O ring
7. Oil relief valve	14. Gear	21. Gasket

Exploded view of the oil pump

Measuring the side clearance

Measuring the clearance between the outside rotor and the pump body

the four attaching bolts, and remove the oil pump from the engine along with the gasket. The oil pump is driven directly by the camshaft. The oil pump shaft fits into a slot in the end of the camshaft. When the oil pump is reinstalled, make sure that the oil pump shaft fits into the slot in the end of the camshaft and that the mating surfaces are flush. Install in the reverse order of removal.

CHECKING CLEARANCES

1. Remove the oil pump from the engine.
2. Remove the oil filter from the oil pump.
3. Remove the screws that hold the oil pump body in place and remove body.
4. With a feeler gauge, measure the tip clearance between the inner and outer rotor, when one of the lobes of the inner rotor is on the very top of one of the lobes of the outer rotor. The tip clearance should be between 0.001 in. and 0.005 in. If the clearance is more than this, the oil pump should be replaced.
5. Measure the side clearance by placing a straightedge across the top of th pump body and the inner and outer rotors and measuring the gap between the straightedge and the rotors. The clearance should be between 0.002 in. and 0.005 in. If the clearance is more than allowed, either the rotors or the pump housing must be replaced.
6. Measure the radial clearance between the outer rotor and the pump housing

with a feeler gauge. The clearance should be between 0.006 in. and 0.008 in.

ENGINE COOLING

Radiators

REMOVAL AND INSTALLATION

1. Drain the cooling system by removing the drain plug in the bottom of the radiator. After loosening the drain plug, remove the radiator cap, which will allow the coolant to drain faster.
2. Loosen the hose clamps and remove the inlet (upper) and outlet (lower) hoses from the radiator.
3. Remove the two radiator mounting bolts.
4. Before removing the radiator from the vehicle, disconnect the wiring harness of the following items: thermostat and thermoswitch wiring, oil pressure switch wiring, fan motor wiring, and secondary terminal of the distributor.
5. Remove the fan and motor assembly from the radiator by removing the four bolts which hold the assembly to the radiator. 4WD models also have an engine driven fan.
6. Install the radiator in the reverse order of removal.

Water Pump

REMOVAL AND INSTALLATION

A centrifugal water pump, mounted on the front of the engine, is utilized. To remove,

drain the coolant, and remove the radiator hose from the pump. Remove the drive belt, unbolt and lift out the pump.

Install in the reverse order of removal.

Thermostat

REMOVAL AND INSTALLATION

A wax pellet type thermostat is used. It is removed by removing the air cleaner assembly and the thermostat cover, which is adjacent to the carburetor.

Install in the reverse order of removal.

NOTE: It is essential to the proper operation of the cooling system that the thermostat be installed in the proper direction.

Diagram of the crankcase emission control system

1. Pump assembly
2. Screw
3. Cover plate
4. Gasket
5. Impeller
6. Clip
7. Pulley

Exploded view of the water pump

EMISSION CONTROLS

Crankcase Emission Control System

EA63 Engines and EA71 Engines Through 1978

The closed crankcase ventilation system used on these engines is a closed system consisting of a sealed oil filler cap, hoses and an oil separator integral with the air cleaner. Blow-by gases from the crankcase are routed to the air cleaner via the two hoses, where they are pulled into the carburetor and burned with the air/fuel mixture.

The oil, which is trapped by the oil separator in the air cleaner, returns through the crankcase ventilation system hoses to the valve covers, where it is mixed with the oil used to lubricate the valve train.

EA71 and EA81 Engines 1979 and Later

These engines use a sealed crankcase emission system, which prevents blow-by gases from being emitted from the air. The system consists of a sealed oil filler cap, valve covers with an emission outlet and a fresh air inlet, connecting hoses, a PCV (positive crankcase ventilation) valve and an air cleaner.

Strong intake vacuum at part throttle sucks blow-by gases from the crankcase, through

Air suction system

a connecting hose (from #2 and #4 valve cover) and into the intake manifold via the PCV valve. However, at wide open throttle, the increase in volume of blow-by and the decrease in manifold vacuum make the

flow through the PCV valve inadequate. Under these conditions excess vapors are drawn into the air cleaner (via a connecting hose fom #1 and #3 valve cover) and pass through the carburetor into the engine.

Evaporative Emission Control System

1976

Evaporative gas from the fuel tank is not discharged into the atmosphere but conducted to the air cleaner unit and then burned in the combustion chamber. No absorbent is used.

The system consists of a sealed fuel tank and filler cap, two reservoir tanks on the station wagon, an air breather valve or a restriction, breather hoses, breather pipe and the air cleaner.

While the engine is running, evaporative gas is absorbed into the intake manifold due to the suction pressure of the manifold, and never discharged directly into the atmosphere. While the engine is stopped, the gases collect on the inner wall of the element of the air cleaner.

There is an air breather valve located at the filler cap. When the flap (door) is opened, a spring exerts pressure on the rubber breather hose and pinches it shut.

The vacuum relief valve filler cap relieves any vacuum condition that might arise in the gas tank.

Routing of crankcase emissions

1977 and Later

On 1977 and later models, the EEC system was revised to include a vapor canister which collects the fuel vapor before it reaches the carburetor. Once in the canister, the fuel vapor is absorbed on a supply of activated charcoal particles. These particles hold the vapor until the engine idle speed increases to a point where the carburetor vacuum is sufficient to open the purge valve on the canister. With the valve open the fuel vapor is sucked out of the charcoal particles and into the intake manifold; fresh air is drawn through a filter at the bottom of the canister to displace the escaping fuel vapor.

The system also incorporates two orifices located on the line between the fuel tank and vapor canister, these prevent fuel spillage in the event of impact. On station wagons (1977–79), two small reserve tanks on both sides of the fuel tank are employed to prevent liquid fuel from flowing into the air cleaner in case of an abrupt stop, etc. California models (1977–79) have a check valve on the line between the canister and the intake manifold to prevent a build-up of vapor in the manifold when the engine is stopped. 1980 and later California models have a carburetor vapor line connecting the float chamber and canister, as well as a tank vapor line. The (1977–79) 4 state (high altitude) models employ a two-way valve between the fuel tank and canister. It functions to control the flow of fuel vapor to the canister according to pressure in the fuel tank.

SERVICE

Keep all of the lines in good repair and free from cracks and blockage. The system should be relatively air tight. On 1977 through 1979 models replace the canister filter every 25,000 miles.

Air Suction System

The system utilizes vacuum created by exhaust gas pulsation and normal intake manifold vacuum. Each exhaust port is connected to the air suction valve by air suction manifolds. When a vacuum is created in the exhaust ports a reed in the suction valve opens allowing fresh air to be sucked through the air cleaner and silencer (pre-1980 models) or the secondary air cleaner (1980 and later models) and into the exhaust ports. When there is pressure rather than vacuum in the exhaust ports, the reed in the air suction valve closes, preventing the flow of exhaust gases.

The fresh air sucked through the air suction valve is used for oxidation of HC and CO in the exhaust passages and partly for combustion in the cylinders.

MAINTENANCE

1. Check the air suction hose and manifolds for cracks, damage, looseness or leakage.
2. Check the reed valve for cracks or abnormal projections. Check the rubber seat for cracks.

Port Liner

On certain models, an exhaust port liner made from stainless steel plate is built into the cylinder head as one unit.

The port liner has a built in air layer which decreases heat transfer to the cylinder head while keeping the exhaust port at a higher temperature. This insulation of the exhaust port helps oxidation of residual HC and CO with the help of the remaining air in the exhaust gases.

Anti-Afterburning Valve

The anti-afterburning valve prevents afterburning that occurs on cold starts. Below about 50 degrees centigrade the temperature valve has an open passage connecting the afterburning valve with the intake manifold via a vacuum line. The vacuum line remains opened and the afterburning valve in operation until the coolant temperature becomes hot enough to shut off the vacuum and override the afterburning system.

Coasting Bypass System

To control the HC emissions while the vehicle is in the coasting or decelerating mode, a controlled amount of air/fuel mixture is channelled through the coasting bypass passage in the carburetor.

The high engine vacuum reacts on a bypass valve diaphragm, opening a vacuum passage to the servo valve on the carburetor, which in turn opens a metered passage from the carburetor air horn to the section of the throttle bore below the secondary throttle plate.

As engine vacuum drops on acceleration, the bypass valve closes the passage to the servo valve and the carburetor returns to its normal function.

Engine Modification System

The principle of this system is not only to obtain correct air/fuel mixture while the vehicle is decelerating, but also to promote complete combustion by retarding the ignition timing, thus reducing the amount of emissions released into the atmosphere.

While the vehicle is decelerating, the primary throttle valve is closed, causing a high vacuum in the intake manifold. This vac-

Choke cap with bi-metal spring and heating element

uum is conducted through a vacuum control valve and on to the carburetor where a bypass jet is opened and extra mixture is allowed to enter the venturi below the throttle plates. This enriches the mixture and promotes cleaner combustion.

The vacuum is also routed to the distributor vacuum retard unit.

There is an anti-dieseling solenoid mounted opposite the float bowl on the carburetor. This switch prevents the engine from dieseling when the ignition switch is turned off. When the ignition switch is turned off, an electromagnet in the switch is also cut off. A spring inside the housing forces a plunger into position, blocking the fuel passages leading to the opening below the throttle plates. When the ignition switch is turned on, it energizes the electromagnet in the switch and pulls the plunger out of the fuel passage, allowing fuel to reach the opening below the throttle plates.

Electrically Assisted Automatic Choke

The vacuum automatic choke uses a choke cap containing a heating element to speed up choke valve opening and reduce CO emissions during warm-up. The heating element gets its power from a special tap on the voltage regulator, when the ignition is on and the engine running.

TESTING

1. Disconnect the choke lead from the voltage regulator.
2. Connect an ohmmeter between the lead that you just disconnected and a good ground. The ohmmeter should read about 9 ohms.
3. Replace the choke cap if the reading shows an opened (no resistance) or shorted (infinite resistance) heating coil.

Carburetor Dashpot

ADJUSTMENT

1. Be sure that the throttle valve is in the idle (closed) position.
2. The dashpot stem should be able to move about 0.16 in. beyond the throttle lever's idle position.

Exhaust gas recirculation system

3. If the stem does not move the correct distance, adjust the dashpot, by loosening its locknut and rotating the dashpot until the correct amount of movement is obtained.

4. Tighten the locknut and recheck dashpot stem movement.

Exhaust Gas Recirculation (EGR) System

An exhaust gas recirculation (EGR) system is used to reduce NO_x (oxides of nitrogen) emissions by lowering peak flame temperature during combustion. A small portion of the exhaust gases are routed into the intake manifold via a vacuum-operated EGR control valve.

TESTING

EGR System

1. Start the engine and allow it to reach normal operating temperature.

2. Increase the engine speed to 3000–3500 rpm (no load). The valve shaft should move upward.

3. Decrease the engine speed to idle, the valve shaft should go down.

4. If the valve shaft fails to raise in Step 2, check the vacuum lines, connections, and the carburetor throttle vacuum port. Replace any clogged or damaged hoses, and clean the throttle port if it is clogged.

5. Connect the EGR valve vacuum hose directly to the throttle port on th carburetor. Speed the engine up and return it to idle as in Step 2 and 3. If the valve works, the fault lies in the vacuum solenoid valve or the temperature switch.

6. If the EGR valve doesn't work, perform the following EGR valve checks:

a. Remove the EGR valve from the intake manifold.

b. Plug the vacuum inlet on the top of the valve diaphragm.

c. Depress and release the pintle (valve plunger) several times.

d. The pintle should remain depressed as long as the vacuum inlet is plugged. If it doesn't, the diaphragm is leaking and the valve assembly must be replaced.

e. If the valve stem appears to be stuck, clean the pintle with a wire brush or spark plug cleaning machine.

f. Install the valve and retest it.

Vacuum Solenoid Valve and Coolant Temperature Switch

1. Disconnect the vacuum solenoid leads.

2. Connect the solenoid directly to a 12-volt power source. The solenoid should click.

3. If the solenoid is working properly and everything else in the system is in proper operating order, replace the coolant temperature switch.

Hot Air Control System

The hot air control system consists of the air cleaner, the air stove on the exhaust pipe and the air intake hose connecting the air cleaner and air stove. The air cleaner is

Cross section of reed valve assembly

Hot air control system

equipped with an air control valve which maintains the temperature of the air being drawn into the carburetor at 100°–127° F to reduce HC emission when the underhood temperature is below 100° F. This system should be inspected every 12,000 miles.

TEMPERATURE SENSOR

Removal and Installation

1. Using pliers, flatten the clip securing the vacuum hose to the sensor vacuum pipe.

2. Disconnect the hose from the sensor.

3. Remove the clip from the sensor vacuum pipe and remove the sensor body from the air cleaner.

NOTE: The gasket is glued to the air cleaner and should not be removed.

4. To install reverse the removal procedure.

VACUUM MOTOR

Removal and Installation

1. Remove the screws securing the vacuum motor to the air cleaner.

2. Disconnect the valve shaft, attached to the vacuum motor diaphragm, at the air control valve, and remove the vacuum motor from the air cleaner.

3. To install reverse the removal procedure.

ECC System

An electronically controlled carburetor (ECC) is used on late models in conjunction with a three–way catalyst, exhaust gas recirculation, air injection, an ignition control system and (in some cases) a high altitude kit.

The three-way catalyst reduces HC, CO and NOx in exhaust gases and permits simultaneous oxidation. The concentration of exhaust gas pollutants varies with the air/fuel mixture (ratio).

The air/fuel ratio needs to be controlled to a value within a very narrow range to purify the exhaust gas components. The ECC system is employed to control the air/fuel ratio.

The system includes: an oxygen sensor, an electronic control module (ECM), a duty solenoid and a carburetor. The components provide a feedback system to control the air/fuel ratio during operation by supplying a measured amount of air into the carburetor air bleeders. To avoid feedback during certain driving conditions, vacuum switches, a thermosensor and an engine speed sensing circuit are provided.

ECC COMPONENT FUNCTIONS

Oxygen (O₂) Sensor

The oxygen sensor is installed on the ex-

1. Vacuum hose
2. Vacuum diaphragm assembly
3. Nipple (fuel inlet)
4. Stopper
5. Washer
6. Nipple guide
7. Pump cover
8. Choke chamber
9. Washer
10. Cotter pin
11. Filter
12. Primary slow air bleed (#200)
13. Piston
14. Needle valve
15. Pump lever spring
16. Spring washer
17. Washer
18. Pump lever
19. Shaft (pump lever)
20. Connecting rod (accelerator pump)
21. Washer
22. Secondary slow air bleed (#70)
23. Spring washer
24. Screw
25. Boot
26. Heater cord
27. Bimetal cover
28. Cam connecting rod
29. Washer
30. Gasket (float chamber)
31. Shaft (float)
32. Float
33. Piston return spring
34. Weight (injector)
35. Primary slow jet (#43)
36. Ball (5/32")
37. Primary main air bleed (#60)
38. Primary emulsion tube
39. Washer
40. Solenoid valve
41. Primary main jet (#95, #93)
42. Drain plug (primary)
43. Washer
44. Drain plug (secondary)
45. Secondary main jet (#155)
46. Idle limiter cap
47. Idle adjust screw
48. Spring (idle adjust screw)
49. Throttle adjusting screw
50. Spring (throttle adjusting screw)
51. Washer
52. Screw
53. Connecting lever
54. Spring
55. Nut
56. Spring washer
57. Throttle return spring
58. Throttle lever
59. Sleeve
60. Fast idle adjust screw
61. Lever A (fast idle)
62. Sleeve
63. Spring (throttle adjusting screw)
64. Lever B (fast idle)
65. Plate
66. Connecting rod
67. Throttle chamber
68. Gasket (throttle chamber)
69. Insulator
70. Gasket (throttle chamber)
71. O-ring
72. Servo diaphragm
73. Air bleed (coasting)
74. Secondary slow jet (#60)
75. Slow jet (coasting) (#50)
76. Washer
77. Power valve (#45)
78. Secondary emulsion tube
79. Secondary main air bleed (#90)

Exploded view of a typical carburetor

haust manifold and provides information to the Electronic Control Module (ECM) that pertains to the amount of pollutants in the exhaust gases caused by an over-rich or lean air/fuel ratio.

Electronic Control Module (ECM)

Upon receiving information from the O_2 sensor (value of the air/fuel mixture) the ECM signals the duty solenoid to allow either more or less air into the carburetor to maintain the correct air/fuel mixture.

Duty Solenoid

The duty solenoid(s) is (are) controlled by the ECM. At a given signal, the duty solenoid will admit more or less air to the carburetor; maintaining the proper air/fuel ratio.

NOTE: On late models equipped with an Hitachi carburetor, two duty solenoids are installed on the exhaust manifold. Models equipped with a C-W carburetor have the duty solenoid mounted on the carburetor.

Vacuum Switches and Thermosensor

Vacuum switches, thermosensors (and speed sensing circuits) furnish information to the ECM to help determine the air/fuel ratio.

Service

To insure proper performance of the ECC system, make sure all vacuum and air hoses are connected tightly. Check the air lines and hoses to make sure no cracks, splits or hardening exists. Replace any vacuum line or hose that is suspect. Check all electrical connects for tightness. Check all electrical wiring for cuts or burns. Repair as necessary.

FUEL SYSTEM

Fuel Filter
REPLACEMENT

All Subarus use a cartridge fuel filter, located in the fuel pump-to-carburetor fuel line. The filter is the disposable type which cannot be cleaned.

To replace the filter cartridge:

1. Loosen, but do not remove, the nuts which secure the two hose clamps located at either end of the filter.
2. Work the hoses off the filter necks.
3. Snap the filter out of its mounting bracket, if so equipped.
4. Throw the old filter away.

NOTE: When removing the old filter, be careful not to allow any fuel to drip onto hot engine components. Installation is the reverse of removal. Be sure that the hose clamps are tightened securely.

Fuel Pump

The electric fuel pump is located in the engine compartment, mounted on the right side. It is to be replaced as an assembly if defective.

REMOVAL AND INSTALLATION

1. Remove the fuel delivery hoses from the fuel pump.
2. Tag and disconnect the fuel pump wiring.
3. Loosen the fuel pump mounting nuts and remove the fuel pump from the vehicle.
4. Install in the reverse order of removal.

TESTING

Check all hoses for leaks and tightness. Make sure all wiring connections are tight. Disconnect the fuel line (filter to pump) from the filter and place a finger over the hose to check for suction.

Carburetor

REMOVAL AND INSTALLATION

1. Remove the air cleaner emission control system hoses, mounting bracket screws, wing nut, and lift the air cleaner assembly off the carburetor.
2. Disconnect the fuel lines from the carburetor.
3. Unfasten the vacuum hoses from the servo diaphragm, automatic choke diaphragms, distributor, and the EGR port (if so equipped).
4. Disconnect the anti-dieseling switch and automatic choke heater electrical leads.
5. Remove the accelerator cable from the throttle lever.
6. Unfasten the 4 nuts which secure the carburetor and take it off the intake manifold. Cover the hole in the intake manifold, to prevent anything from falling in.

Installation is the reverse of removal.

OVERHAUL

Refer to the carburetor section under Unit Repairs.

NOTE: The following adjustments pertain to all models except the C-W carburetor used on feedback systems.

PRIMARY/SECONDARY THROTTLE LINKAGE ADJUSTMENT

1. With the carburetor removed from the engine, operate the linkage so that the connecting rod contacts the groove on the end of the secondary actuating lever.
2. Measure the clearance between the lower end of the primary throttle valve and

$G_2 = 6.0mm$ when primary throttle valve opening is 49° from full close. (EA63A)

Throttle linkage adjustment

its bore. It should be about 0.24 in. for all models.

3. Adjust the clearance by bending the connecting rod.

4. Check that the linkage operates smoothly.

FLOAT AND FUEL LEVEL ADJUSTMENT

On models with a sight glass on the carburetor float bowl, the fuel should be level (within ⅟₁₆ in.) with the dot on the glass when the engine is running.

The float level may be adjusted with the carburetor installed on the engine:

1. Disconnect the accelerator pump actuating rod from the pump lever.

2. Remove the throttle return spring.

3. Disconnect the choke cable from the choke lever, and remove it from the spring hanger.

4. Remove the spring hanger, the choke bellcrank, and the remaining air horn retaining screws.

5. Lift the air horn slightly, disconnect the choke connecting rod, and remove the air horn.

6. Invert the air horn (float up), and measure the distance between the surface of the air horn and the float.

7. Bend the float arm until the clearance is approximately 0.41 in.

8. Invert the air horn to its installed position and measure the distance between the float arm and the needle valve stem. This dimension should be 0.050–0.065 in., and is adjusted by bending the float stops.

Float adjustment

FAST IDLE ADJUSTMENT

1. With the carburetor removed from the engine, set the fast idle cam adjusting lever on the fourth step of the fast idle cam.

2. Check to be sure that the choke valve is fully closed.

3. Measure the clearance between the lower edge of the primary throttle valve and its bore. The clearance should be as specified in the "Fast Idle" chart, above.

4. If the clearance is incorrect, turn the

R-2 = Choke plate opening
G = Throttle plate opening and angle

Fast idle adjustment

fast idle adjusting screw to bring it within specifications. Turning the screw *in* increases the throttle clearance and vice versa.

Model	Primary Throttle-to-Bore Clearance
1976	0.056 in.
1977–79	0.047 in. ①
Auto. trans.	0.060 in.
Man. trans.	0.050 in. ②

①California models and 49 state high altitude models—0.060 in.
②HB-STD, HB-DL, SD-DL, and HT-DL use 0.041 in.

AUTOMATIC CHOKE ADJUSTMENT

1. Adjust the fast idle as detailed above, and perform the adjustments which follow, in the sequence given.

2. Pull the main choke diaphragm lever as far as it will go to the left and measure the clearance between the upper end of the choke valve and its bore with a wire gauge. The clearance should be 0.046–0.055 in. Adjust, as necessary, by bending the diaphragm-to-choke connecting rod.

3. Apply 8–9 in. Hg of vacuum to the main diaphragm, it should operate the choke valve. If it does not, replace the diaphragm with a new one.

4. Place the fast idle cam adjusting lever on the *third* step of the fast idle cam. Measure the clearance between the upper end of the choke valve and its bore. The clearance should be 0.063–0.074 in. for

1976 cars; 0.026–0.037 in. for 1977–80 cars and 0.039–0.052 for later models. Carefully bend (turn) the fast idle cam to obtain the correct clearance, as necessary. To obtain the clearance, bend the cam clockwise; to decrease it, bend the cam counterclockwise.

5. Loosen the 3 choke cap securing screws, and match the line on it up with the longest line on the choke coil housing. Tighten the retaining screws.

——— CAUTION ———
Do not loosen the screw which secures the choke lever.

6. Fit the tang on the bimetal lever, which is connected to the auxiliary diaphragm, against the stop in the choke coil housing. Pull the setting piston of the auxiliary diaphragm back and, with the piston in this position, tighten the compensator adjusting screw so that it contacts the tang on the bimetal lever; the gap should be 0.197 in. on 1976 cars, and 0.34 in. on later models.

7. Apply vacuum from an outside source to the auxiliary diaphragm. It should take 9.5–11.8 in. Hg of vacuum to operate the diaphragm on 1976 cars; and 6.9–9.2 in. Hg of vacuum on 1977 and later models. To adjust the vacuum setting, bend the diaphragm rod. Vacuum is reduced when the rod is bent to shorten it and increasd when the rod is bent to lengthen it.

NOTE: When the setting piston is released, there should be no clearance between the tang on the bimetal lever and the stop on the coil housing. If they don't contact, the bimetal lever has been bent too much.

Bi-metal compensation adjustment

Automatic choke fast idle adjusting lever on the third step of the fast idle cam

TRANSAXLE

REMOVAL AND INSTALLATION

NOTE: The transaxle can be removed separately from the car.

1. Open the hood and secure it.
2. Remove the spare wheel from engine compartment, if installed.
3. Disconnect the battery cable from the negative (−) terminal.
4. Remove the spare wheel supporter.
5. On MT (manual transaxle), disengage the clutch cable as follows:
   a. Remove the clutch cable return spring.

   b. Remove both the lock nut and adjusting nut from the clutch cable.
   c. Unfasten the clip which retains the outer cable.
   d. Detach the rubber boot.
6. On AT (automatic transaxle), disconnect the diaphragm vacuum hose.
7. Disconnect the speedometer cable from the transmission. Unfasten the clip on the speedometer cable.
8. Disconnect the following wiring connections.
   a. Back-up lamp switch connector
   b. Ground cable (on the car body)
   c. Starter harness (Black and white)
9. On AT, remove the four bolts connecting the torque converter to the drive plate through the timing hole.

NOTE: Be careful that the bolts do not fall into the converter housing.

10. On AT, disconnect the oil cooler hose from the transmission. Plug the lines.
11. Remove the starter with the battery cable, and put the starter on the bulkhead.
12. Remove the upper bolts which secure the engine to the transmission; loosen the lwer nuts.
13. Loosen the nut which retains the pitching stopper to the transmission side, and tighten the nut by an equal amount on the engine side. Slightly tilt the engine backward in order to facilitate removal of the transmission.

NOTE: Do not loosen or tighten the nut; more than 10 mm.

14. On the 4WD model, separate both the 4WD selector system and gearshift system from transmission as follows.
   a. Remove hand brake tray cover, and then hand brake cover.
   b. Remove rod cover.
   c. Set the drive selector lever at "4WD" position.
   d. Remove the nut connecting the two rods.

   e. Remove the two nuts to separate the rod and drive selector lever from the plate.
   f. Remove the boot installing screws.
   g. Remove nut connecting gearshift lever with lever, and pull up gearshift lever with boot.
15. Disconnect O₂ sensor harness and unclamp it, if equipped.
16. Raise the front end of the car and support with jackstands.
17. Remove the front exhaust pipe assembly as follows:
   a. Disconnect the hot air intake hose.
   b. Loosen the nuts which secure the exhaust pipe assembly to the exhaust port of the engine.
   c. Remove the bolts which secure the front exhaust pipe to the rear exhaust pipe.
   d. Remove the bolts which secure the front exhaust pipe to the bracket on the car body.
   e. Supporting the front exhaust pipe assembly, remove the nuts from the exhaust port of the engine. The exhaust pipe assembly can now be removed.

NOTE: Be careful not to strike the oxygen sensor against any adjacent parts during removal, if equipped.

18. On AT, drain out the automatic transmission fluid and then disconnect the oil supply pipe. Take care not to damage the O-ring. Drain the MT transmission fluid.
19. On the 4WD models remove the transmission shield.
20. On the 4WD model, remove the bolts which secure the propeller shaft to the rear differential gear, and detach the propeller shaft.

NOTE: When disconnecting the propeller shaft, plug the open end of the drive shaft with a cap to prevent the oil from running out of the drive shaft. Be careful not to damage the oil seal located at the end of the propeller shaft.

21. Remove the exhaust cover, if so equipped.
22. On MT, remove the bolts which secure the gearshift system to free it from the transmission. (All manual transmission models except 4WD).
23. On AT, move the select lever to the "P" position, and at this point, mark the location of the connector nut and separate the manual lever from the linkage rod.
24. Remove the stabilizer.
25. Remove the bolts which secure the left and right transverse links to the front crossmember, and lower the transverse links.
26. Drive both the left and right spring pins out of the axle shaft.

NOTE: Discard and do not re-use the spring pins.

27. Push the wheels toward the outer side, separate the axle shaft from the drive shaft.
28. On MT, unfasten the clamp on the

left side of the hand brake cable, in order to facilitate the removal of the center crossmember. On the automatic transmission model, remove the right hand brake cover, in order to facilitate the removal of the rear crossmember.

29. On MT, remove the nuts which secure the left and right transmission mount rubber cushions.

30. On AT, remove the mount retaining nut from the rear crossmember.

31. Securely support the transmission by placing a jack under it.

32. Remove the crossmember.

33. Remove the two nuts which secure the engine to the tranmission, and move the transmission away from the engine just enough so that the transmission mainshaft does not interfere with the engine.

Lower the jack and remove the transmission.

34. Installation is in the reverse order of removal!

NOTE: Apply a slight coat of grease on the transmission mainshaft before installation. If the mainshaft is hard to align, turn the left and right shafts until the mainshaft engages.

1. Flywheel
2. Starter ring gear
3. Clutch disc
4. Clutch cover
5. Spring washer
6. Bolt
7. Clutch release bearing
8. Release bearing holder
9. Release bearing holder spring
10. Clutch release fork
11. Clutch release fork sealing
12. Release fork spring

Exploded view of the typical clutch assembly

TORQUE SPECIFICATIONS

(ft. lbs.)

Transverse link to front crossmember	50
Stabilizer to leading rod and rear crossmember	15
Rear crossmember to vehicle body	60
Front crossmember to vehicle body	40
Front engine mount to crossmember	20
Rear engine mount to crossmember	20
Propeller shaft to rear differential (4WD)	15

CLUTCH

REMOVAL AND INSTALLATION

1. To remove the clutch, the transaxle must be removed from the vehicle.

2. Gradually unscrew the six bolts which hold the pressure plate assembly on the flywheel. Loosen the bolts only one turn at a time, working around the pressure plate.

Do not unscrew all the bolts on one side at one time.

3. When all of the bolts have been removed, remove the clutch plate and disc.

——— CAUTION ———
Do not get oil or grease on the clutch facing.

4. Unfasten the two retaining springs and remove the throwout bearing and the release fork.

Do not disassemble either the clutch cover or disc. Inspect the parts for wear or damage and replace any parts as necessary. Replace the clutch disc if there is any oil or grease on the facing.

Do not wash or attempt to lubricate the throwout bearing. If it requires replacement, the bearing may be pressed out and a new one pressed into the holder.

Installation is as follows:

1. Fit the release fork boot on the front of the transmission housing; Install the release fork.

2. Insert the throwout bearing assembly and secure it with the two springs. Coat the inside diameter of the bearing holder and the fork-to-holder contact points with grease.

3. Insert a pilot shaft through the clutch cover and disc, then insert the end of the pilot into the needle bearing.

4. Gradually tighten the pressure plate retaining bolts one turn at a time, working around the cover, to 7–9 ft. lbs.

NOTE: When installing the clutch pressure plate assembly, make sure that the O marks on the flywheel and the clutch pressure plate assembly are at least 120° apart. This is for purposes of balance.

Clutch linkage free-play adjustment at the release fork

Also, make sure that the clutch disc is installed properly, noting the FRONT and REAR markings.

5. After installation, adjust the pedal free-play and height.

Clutch Cable

REMOVAL AND INSTALLATION

The clutch cable is connected to the clutch pedal at one end and to the clutch release lever on the other end.

The cable conduit is retained by a bolt and clamp on the clutch pedal bracket and by a clip type clamp on a bracket mounted on the flywheel housing.

To replace the cable assembly, disconnect both the cable and conduit and remove the assembly from under the vehicle.

Install the replacement cable assembly and secure both the cable and conduit.

ADJUSTMENT

Remove the clutch release fork return spring, loosen the cable locknut, and adjust the spherical nut so that there is 0.142 to 0.181 in. play between the spherical nut and the release fork seat. Tighten the locknut and reconnect the release spring.

The pedal free-play should be 0.94 to 1.18 in. with a full stroke of 5.12 in. The pedal stroke is adjustable at the pedal bracket.

Automatic Transaxle

BRAKE BAND ADJUSTMENT

This adjustment can be performed on the outside of the transmission.

1. Park the car on a level surface or support it on jackstands, engine off.
2. Locate the adjusting screw above the pan on the left side of the transmission.
3. Loosen the locknut.
4. **1976–81:** Torque the adjusting screw to 6.5 ft. lbs., then turn it back exactly two full turns.

From 1981: Torque the adjusting screw to 18 ft. lbs., then turn it back exactly ¾ turn.

5. Tighten the lock nut.

Following the above procedure will adjust the transmission brake band to the factory specified setting. However, if any of the following conditions are detected the adjusting screw can be moved ¼ turn in either direction after Step 4:

Turn ¼ turn clockwise if transmission:
—jolts when shifting from 1st to 2nd;
—engine speed abruptly rises from 2nd to 3rd; or,
—shift delays in kickdown from 3rd to

① Adjusting nut [Tightening torque: (5.78 to 8.68 ft-lb)
② Linkage
③ Indicator (selector dial)
④ Selector dial fitting screw
⑤ Spring pin
o Adjust the linkage so that the position "N" of the detent of the manual valve and the spring pin of selector lever will come in alignment with the position "N" of the guide plate.

Details for automatic shift linkage adjustment

2nd.

Turn ¼ turn counterclockwise if
—car slips from 1st to 2nd; or
—there is braking action at shift from 2nd to 3rd.

NEUTRAL SAFETY SWITCH ADJUSTMENT

This switch is mounted on the transmission shift lever shaft, bolted to the transmission. It also operates the backup lights.

1. Remove the shift lever shaft nut.
2. Remove the shift lever from the shaft.
3. Make sure that the slot in the shaft is vertical (Neutral position).

4. Remove the switch mounting bolts, but leave the switch in place.
5. Remove the setscrew from the lower face of the switch.
6. Insert a 0.059 in. drill bit through the setscrew hole. Turn the switch slightly so that the bit passes through into the back part of the switch.
7. Bolt the switch down.
8. Remove the bit and replace the setscrew.
9. Replace the lever and tighten the shaft nut.
10. Check that the engine can start only in Park or Neutral, and that the backup lights go on in Reverse.

SHIFT LINKAGE ADJUSTMENT

1. Loosen the clamp nuts on the shifting rod at the bottom of the shift lever on the transmission.
2. Put the selector lever in Neutral and hold it forward against the detent.
3. Check that the transmission shift lever is in the Neutral position (pull it all the way back into Park and push it forward two positions).
4. Tighten the clamp nuts.

KICKDOWN SOLENOID

An audible click should be heard from the solenoid on the right side of the transmission, when the accelerator pedal is pushed down all the way with the engine off and the ignition switch on. The switch is operated by the upper part of the accelerator

Second gear band adjustment mechanism

Automatic transmission kickdown system

axle shaft to the driveshaft, by lightly tapping with a hammer. Throw the old pin away; do not reuse it.

6. Remove the self-locking nuts which attach the ends of the control arm to the stabilizer bar and the crossmember inner pivot.

7. Separate the control arm from the crossmember pivot by prying it rearward with a suitable lever.

8. To disconnect the control arm from the stabilizer bar, swing the link forward.

9. Pull the axle shaft out of the drive-shaft (double-offset joint side) by pushing outward on the front suspension assembly.

10. Pull the other end of the drive axle out of the housing, while holding the shaft so that it doesn't drop.

Installation is as follows:

1. Thread a metric bolt which is long enough to fit through the axle housing, into the end of the stub axle.

2. Fit the bolt through the axle housing, using care not to damage the oil seal, splines, or bearing. Draw the drive axle

lever inside the car. The position of the switch can be varied to give quicker or slower kickdown response.

DRIVE AXLE

The drive axle consists of a double-offset joint (DOJ) at the inner end, an axle shaft, a constant velocity joint at the outer end, and a stub axle.

Disassembled double-offset joint

Axle Shaft

REMOVAL AND INSTALLATION

1. Engage the parking brake. Remove the wheel cover (sedans and wagon), and loosen the lug nuts. Loosen the hub nut. Later models have the hub nut staked in place; unstake it with a thin chisel or a punch.

2. Raise the car the support it with jackstands.

3. Remove the lug nuts, wheel and tire. Remove the hub nut.

4. Remove the drum brake or disc brake assembly.

5. Drive out the spring (roll) pin, which fastens the double-offset joint end of the

1. Spring pin
2. Axle shaft
3. Oil seal
4. Bearing
5. Housing
6. Castle nut
7. Cotter pin
8. Transverse link
9. Dust seal (Ball joint)
10. Circlip
11. Spacer
12. Disc cover
13. Spring washer
14. Bolt
15. Disc
16. Hub bolt
17. Disc hub
18. Spring washer
19. Bolt
20. Center piece
21. Lock washer
22. Lock plate
23. Nut

Exploded view of a typical front axle assembly

A. ◯ Axial direction view

Installing the axle nut

LINK NUT

WRENCH (SPECIAL TOOL)

Removing the link nut using a special tool

assembly into place by grasping the end of the bolt with a puller.

3. Install the brake disc and hub.

4. Install the spacer, conical spring washer and the hub nut. Tighten the nut to 160–180 ft./lbs. (174 ft./lbs. preferred). Secure the hub nut to the axle shaft by using a punch to stake the flange on the nut to the groove in the end of the axle shaft.

5. Connect the double-offset joint side of the axle shaft to the driveshaft and secure them with a new spring pin.

6. Fit the washer and bushing over the end of the stabilizer bar and then connect the transverse link to the end of the stabilizer.

Install the remaining washer and bushing and temporarily secure them with a new self-locking nut.

7. Install the control arm to the crossmember pivot. Temporarily secure them with another new self-locking nut.

8. Install the dust cover, caliper, and parking brake cable.

9. Install the wheel and remove the jackstands.

10. Tighten the new self-locking nuts used at each end of the transverse link to 72–87 ft./lbs. with the car resting on its wheels.

U-JOINT OVERHAUL

1. Remove the bands from the boots at both the constant velocity and double-offset joints, and slide the boots away from the joints.

2. Pry the circlip out of the double-offset joint, and slide the outer race of the joint off the shaft.

3. Remove the balls from the cage, ro-

tate the cage slightly, and slide the cage inward on the axle shaft.

4. Using snap-ring pliers, remove the outer snap-ring which retains the inner race to the shaft.

5. Slide the inner race, cage, and boot off the axle shaft.

NOTE: Exercise care to avoid damaging the boot on the inner snap-ring.

6. Pull back the constant velocity joint boot and pivot the stub axle around the joint far enough to expose a ball.

7. Remove the exposed ball, and continue this procedure until all balls are removed, at which time the outer race (stub axle) may be removed from the axle shaft.

8. Remove the retaining snap-ring, and slide the inner race off the shaft.

9. Inspect the parts of both joints for wear, damage, or corrosion, and replace if necessary. Examine the axle shaft for bending or distortion, and replace if evident. Should the boots be dried out, cracked, or distorted, they must be replaced.

10. Install the constant velocity joint inner race on the axle shaft, and retain with a snap-ring.

11. Assemble the joint in the opposite order of disassembly.

12. Slide the double-offset joint cage onto the shaft, with the counterbore toward the end of the shaft.

13. Install the inner race on the shaft, and install the retaining snap-ring.

14. Position the cage over the inner race, and fill the cage pockets with grease.

15. Insert the balls into the cage.

16. Fill the well in the outer race with approximately 1 oz. grease, and slide the outer race onto the axle shaft.

17. Install the retaining circlip, and add 1 oz. more grease to the interior of the joint. Fill the boot with approximately 1 oz. grease, and slide it into position over the double-off-set joint.

18. Fill the constant velocity joint boot with 3 oz. grease, and install the boot over the joint.

19. Band the boots on both joints tightly enough that they cannot be turned by hand.

NOTE: Use only grease specified for use in constant vlocity joints.

Rear Axle Shaft Four Wheel Drive

REMOVAL AND INSTALLATION

Early Models

1. Jack up the rear of the body and support with jack stands.

2. Turn the rear wheel to position the driveshaft and remove the driveshaft retaining bolts on the wheel side and the differential gear side.

1. Differential assembly
2. Driveshaft assembly
3. Propeller shaft assembly
4. Mounting member
5. Mounting bracket
6. Bracket
7. Stoppper
8. Bushing
9. Breather cap

Rear drive assembly—4WD vehicles

3. Remove the driveshaft assembly.

4. To disassemble the ball spline hold the driveshaft in a vise and remove the rubber band, snap-ring and stopper.

5. To disassemble the U-joint remove the snap-ring and needle bearing.

6. To reassemble and install, reverse the above procedure.

7. Selective snap-rings are used to obtain a clearance of 0.0008 inch between the bearing cap and driveshaft yoke.

8. Snap-ring thicknesses are as follow:
0.0587 in.
0.0598 in.
0.0610 in.
0.0622 in.
0.0457 in.
0.0646 in.
0.0657 in.

Late Models

1. Drain the differential oil.

2. Raise the rear wheels and support the car on jackstands.

3. Remove the rear wheels. Drive out the spring pins from the inner and outer DOJs (double offset joints).

4. Detach the outer DOJ from the spindle, lower it and disconnect from the differential spindle.

5. Installation is in the reverse order of removal. Use new spring pins on installation.

Driveshaft
(Four Wheel Drive)

REMOVAL AND INSTALLATION

1. Drain the transmission oil.

2. Jack up the rear of the body, and support with jack stands.

3. Remove the bolts connecting the driveshaft yoke to the rear differential companion flange.

4. Gently pull the driveshaft rearward to remove.

5. To install reverse the removal procedure.

OVERHAUL

Selective snap-rings are used to provide proper clearance of the bearing cap to yoke. The clearance should be 0.0008 inch and the opposing snap-rings must be of the same thickness.

SELECTIVE SNAP-RINGS

Thickness	Paint Color
0.0787 in.	White
0.0795 in.	Yellow
0.0803 in.	Red
0.0811 in.	Green
0.0819 in.	Blue
0.0827 in.	Light Brown
0.0835 in.	No paint
0.0843 in.	Pink

Rear Axle Spindle, Bearing and Seals
(Four Wheel Drive)

REMOVAL AND INSTALLATION

1. Jack up the car and remove the wheel.

2. Loosen the axle nut.

3. Disconnect the axle shaft from the rear axle companion flange.

4. Remove the nut retaining the com-

1. Side gear
2. Pinion mate gear
3. Drive gear
4. Differential case
5. Drive pinion
6. Pinion height adjusting washer
7. Rear bearing
8. Preload adjusting spacer
9. Preload adjusting washer
10. Front bearing
11. Spacer
12. Pilot bearing
13. Oil seal
14. Companion flange
15. Pinion nut
16. Side bearing
17. Side bearing retainer

Exploded view of the 4WD rear differential

1. Snap-ring
2. Stopper
3. Ball
4. Ball spacer
5. Rubber boot
6. Boot band
7. Yoke
8. Bolt
9. Spring washer
10. Snap-ring
11. Stopper

12. Sleeve yoke
13. Plug
14. O-ring
15. Snap-ring
16. Spider
17. Bearing race
18. Oil seal
19. Snap-ring
20. Dust cover (oil seal)
21. Bolt
22. Spring washer
23. Washer
24. O-ring
25. Side yoke

Exploded view of 4WD rear axle shaft

1. Shim
2. Bushing
3. Trailing arm
4. Shock absorber
5. Rubber bushing
6. Cushion rubber
7. Washer
8. Bushing
9. Bracket
10. Torsion bar
11. Bolt
12. Nut
13. Spring washer
14. Washer
15. Brake pipe

Exploded view of the typical rear suspension

panion flange to the spindle and remove the companion flange.

5. Pull the brake drum and spindle to the outer side, and take the outer oil seal off with the spindle.

6. Remove the axle nut from the spindle, disconnect the brake drum and pull out the outer oil seal.

7. Unlock the link nut and remove the nut with a wrench (special tool).

8. Remove the inner seal.

9. New seals may be pressed into place at this time or if the bearing is to be replaced proceed as follows:

10. Dismount the rear suspension including the rear brake back plate.

11. Use a press and remove the bearing.

12. When replacing the inner and outer seals place the inner and outer side of the housing on a V-block and press the seals into place.

13. Hold the trailing arm in a vise and lightly tighten the link nut in the housing with the special wrench. Torque the nut to 130–166 ft. lbs.

14. Lock the link nut.

15. Install the rear trailing arm to the body.

16. Fit the back plate (22–35 ft. lbs.) and connect the brake pipe (11–14 ft. lbs.).

17. Temporarily fit the brake drum to the spindle.

18. Bleed brake system.

19. Position the companion flange to the spindle inner end and tighten the locknut to 145–181 ft. lbs.

NOTE: When tightening, apply the foot brake to produce reaction force.

20. Make sure the bearing rotates smoothly and stake the locknut.

21. Fit the center piece, conical spring washer and retaining nut onto the axle shaft and tighten the retaining nut to 174 ft. lbs.

NOTE: Punch the flange portion of the retaining nut toward the groove of the axle after tightening.

22. Connect the axle shaft and companion flange and tighten the retaining nuts to 29–36 ft. lbs.

23. Install the spindle and wheel assembly. Tighten the wheel nuts to 58–72 ft. lbs.

REAR SUSPENSION

Semi-trailing arms mounted to torque tubes, which act on an internal torsion bar are used. Shock absorbers are mounted to the trailing arm, close to the stub axle.

Torsion Bars

REMOVAL AND INSTALLATION

1. Raise the vehicle and remove the rear wheels.

2. Remove the shock absorber from the trailing arm and the brake tube from the brake hose.

3. Remove the inner bushing retaining bolts.

4. Loosen the locking bolt of the outer bracket and remove the rear suspension from the body.

5. Pull the outer bracket out of the outer bushing after removing the locking bolt.

6. Pull the torsion bar out of the trailing arm.

7. The inner and outer bushings can be replaced by using a press.

NOTE: The torsion bars are marked L and R and are to be installed on the proper side. Premature breakage of the bars can result if they are installed on the wrong-side.

------ CAUTION ------
When inserting the torsion bar, align the marks on the end of the torsion bar to that of the outer bracket and inner bushing.

8. Adjust the ride height and rear wheel alignment prior to tightening the inner bushing retaining bolts.

9. Tighten the outer bushing retaining bolts when the vehicle is on the floor and unloaded.

Shock Absorbers

REMOVAL AND INSTALLATION

1. Remove the wheel cover and loosen the lug nuts. Raise the rear of the car and support it with jackstands, after setting the parking brake and blocking the front wheels.

2. Remove the lug nuts and the rear wheels.

3. Loosen the two upper shock absorber mounting nuts. Remove the washer and the bushing, being sure to note their correct assembly sequence for installation.

4. Unfasten the nut on the trailing arm pin and remove the shock absorber. Note the installing positions of the washers.

Installation is the reverse of removal. Do not fully tighten the upper mounting nuts until the lower shock nut has been installed with the washer and the pin shoulder contacting each other. Tighten the upper nuts to 22–32 ft. lbs. Adjust the ride height bolt.

Ride Height

Vehicle height can be adjusted by turning the outer and inner end of the torsion bar

1. Damper strut	10. Bracket	19. Cross member
2. Helper	11. Stabilizer	20. Bolt
3. Coil spring	12. Rubber bushing	21. Self lock nut
4. Cap	13. Transverse link	22. Nut
5. Strut mount	14. Ball joint	23. Spring washer
6. Oil seal	15. Bracket	24. Washer
7. Spring seat	16. Plate	25. Thrust washer
8. Rubber seat	17. Bushing	
9. Stabilizer bushing	18. Pipe	

Exploded view of the typical front suspension

by the same number of serration teeth in the opposite direction to the arrow mark on the outer end surface of the torsion bar.

Turning the torsion bar in the direction of the arrow lowers the vehicle height, and changes the height 0.20 in. per tooth shifted.

The torsion bar must be removed from the inner and outer brackets to make the adjustment. 4-wheel drive vehicles have a unique adjusting device that will alter the

ride height (in addition to adjusting the torsion bars). See the following procedure.

ADJUSTMENT OF REAR ROAD CLEARANCE

1980 and Later 4 Wheel Drive Vehicles

1. Measure the height of the vehicle

from the lowest point of the rear axle cross-member to the ground.

2. To adjust the rear height remove the access cover from the service hole in the vehicles floor above the rear axle. Turn the adjusting bolt, clockwise to increase the height; counter clockwise to lower it.

FRONT SUSPENSION

MacPherson Strut Assembly

REMOVAL AND INSTALLATION

NOTE: For strut overhaul refer to the Unit Repair Section.

1. Raise and support the vehicle. Remove the battery cable from the negative terminal of the battery.

2. Remove the hub caps, loosen the lug nuts, jack up the vehicle until the tire clears the ground and remove the lug nuts and the wheel/tire assembly. Place the jackstands under the vehicle and remove the jack. Perform this operation on the opposite side if the suspension is to be removed from both sides of the vehicle.

3. Remove the handbrake cable bracket and the handbrake cable hanger from the transverse link and the tie rod end. Remove the handbrake cable end.

4. Remove the axle nut, lockplate, washer, and center piece and remove the front brake drums by using a puller.

5. Disconnect the brake hoses from the brake fluid pipes.

6. With front disc brakes, remove the handbrake cable end from the caliper lever. Remove the outer cable clip from the cable-end support bracket at the caliper. Remove the handbrake cable bracket from the housing mount by loosening the nuts.

7. Drive out the spring pins of the double offset joint by using a drift pin and a hammer. The double offset side of the axle is the side closest to the transaxle.

8. Remove the lower control arm by loosening the self-locking nut which holds it to the inner pivot shaft of the crossmember. Loosen and remove the nuts which clamp the control arm to the stabilizer. Remove the stabilizer rearward from the crossmember by using a lever and pulling the control arm out from the end of the stabilizer.

9. Remove the cotter pin from the castle nut and remove the nuts and ball stud from the knuckle arm of the tie rod end ball joint housing. Take care not to bend the housing.

10. Remove the nuts which hold the strut mount to the body (suspension assembly upper mounting nut-top of the shock absorber tower).

11. Pull the double offset joint out of the driveshaft and then remove the suspension assembly from the body.

Install the suspension assembly in the reverse order of removal. Bleed the brakes after installation.

Shock Absorbers & Coil Spring

REMOVAL AND INSTALLATION

NOTE: See Unit Repair Section for Strut Repair

Ball Joints

REMOVAL AND INSTALLATION

1. Jack up the front of the car and remove the wheel.

2. Disconnect the ball stud from the housing by removing the cotter pin and castle nut.

3. Remove the bolt attaching the ball nut to the transverse link and remove the ball joint.

4. To install reverse the removal procedure. Torque the castle nut to 35–40 ft. lbs., ball joint to transverse link nut to 80–94 ft. lbs.

20. Spring washer
21. Packing
22. Spring (sleeve)
23. Plate (sleeve)
24. Sleeve
25. Pinion
26. Bolt
27. Rubber coupling

1. Dust seal
2. Snap ring
3. Tie rod end
4. Lock nut
5. Boot
6. Snap ring (boot)
7. Ball joint ass'y
8. Lockwasher
9. Rack
10. Gear box unit
11. Bushing-A
12. Clip
13. Adapter-A
14. Adapter-B
15. Air vent tube
16. Cap (steering gear box)
17. Adjusting screw
18. Lock nut
19. Bolt
28. Cotter pin
29. Castle nut
30. Torque rod

Exploded view of the steering gear

Lower Control Arm

REMOVAL AND INSTALLATION

1. Remove the wheel cover and loosen the lug nuts.
2. Jack up the car and support it with jackstands. Block the rear wheels.
3. Remove the lug nuts and the wheel.
4. Remove the parking brake cable clamp from the control arm by unfastening its nut.
5. Unfasten the self-locking nut which attaches the control arm to the crossmember. Be sure to note the installation sequence of the washers.
6. Unfasten the self-locking nut which secures the stabilizer bar to the control arm. Again, note the installation sequence of the washers.
7. Pry the control arm off the crossmember.
8. Push the control arm forward and detach it from the end of the stabilizer bar.
9. Remove the cotter pin from the castellated nut. Unfasten the nut and remove the ball joint from the axle housing with a puller.
10. Remove the control arm from under the car.

Installation is the reverse of removal. Do not grease the upper ball joint stud which fits into the axle housing. Tighten the castellated nut to 30–40 ft. lbs. Use new self-locking nuts on the crossmember and stabilizer bar mounts. Tighten the new self-locking nuts to 73–87 ft. lbs. with the vehicle resting on the wheels.

Front End Alignment

CASTER AND CAMBER

Caster and camber are not adjustable on these models. If either of these specifications is not within the factory recommended range, this would indicate bent or damaged parts that must be replaced.

TOE-IN

Toe-in is adjusted by loosening the locknuts on the tie rods, and turning the tie rods.

NOTE: Before performing the toe-in adjustment, be sure that the steering gear is centered by aligning the marks on it, and that the wheels are straightahead.

Tighten the locknuts after the toe-in adjustment is completed.

STEERING

Steering Wheel

REMOVAL AND INSTALLATION

1. Disconnect the negative battery cable.
2. Unfasten the horn lead from the wiring harness beneath the instrument panel.
3. Working from behind the steering wheel remove the horn assembly retaining screws. It may be necessary to lower the column from the dash by removing the mounting screws.
4. Lift the crash pad assembly off the front of the wheel.
5. Matchmark the steering wheel and the column for installation.

1. Washer
2. Spring washer
3. Bolt
4. Bushing (steering column)
5. Bolt
6. Universal joint
7. Cotter pin
8. Castle nut
9. Gearbox bracket
10. Lock plate
11. Washer
12. Bolt
13. Steering gearbox
14. Nut

Typical steering system

6. Remove the steering wheel retaining nut and pull the wheel from the column with a puller.

Installation is the reverse of removal. Index the matchmarks and tighten the retaining nut to 20–29 ft. lbs.

— CAUTION —
Do not hammer on the steering wheel or the steering column; damage to the collapsible column could result.

Turn Signal Switch

REMOVAL AND INSTALLATION

1. Remove the steering wheel.
2. Separate the steering column wiring connectors underneath the instrument panel.
3. Remove the turn signal switch securing screws and unscrew the hazard warning switch knob.
4. Remove the contact plate, cancelling cam, and switch assembly from the steering column housing.

Installation is the reverse of removal.

Ignition Switch

REMOVAL AND INSTALLATION

The ignition switch is mounted to the steering column using shear bolts. These bolts are constructed so that the head is sheared off when the bolt is tightened. For this reason removal of the ignition switch is rather complicated.

1. Remove the steering wheel as outlined above.
2. Disconnect the steering shaft from the universal joint (located near the steering gear box) by loosening the locking bolt.
3. Remove the steering shaft installing bolt from the instrument panel.
4. Pull the steering shaft assembly from the hole in the floor board and remove the assembly from the car.
5. Loosen the screws holding the column cover to the steering column and hazard knob, and pull the steering shaft out of the column cover.
6. Drill into the shaft of the shear bolts and extract them with an E-Z Out®. Remove the switch.

Installation is the reverse of removal. Be sure to use new shear bolts to install the ignition switch.

Manual Steering Gear

All Subaru models are equipped with rack and pinion steering. No maintenance is required.

REMOVAL AND INSTALLATION

1. Jack up the front of the vehicle and remove the front wheels.
2. Remove the cotter pin and loosen the castle nut. Remove the tie rod end from the knuckle arm of the housing.
3. Remove the handbrake cable hanger from the tie rod.
4. Pull out the cotter pins and remove the rubber coupling connecting bolts and disconnect the pinion with the gearbox from the steering shaft.
5. Straighten the lockplate and remove the bolts which hold the gearbox bracket to the crossmember.
6. On DL, GF, and GL models, loosen the front engine mounting bolts and lift up the engine by about 0.2 in. to avoid touching the gearbox with the engine. Remove the gearbox from the vehicle.

NOTE: On 4WD models remove the fan protector on top of the radiator and remove the pitching stopper before lifting the engine.

Installation is the reverse of removal. Tighten the rack and pinion assembly securing bolts to 33–40 ft. lbs. Tighten the rubber coupling castellated nut to 4–5 ft. lbs. Tighten the tie rod end castellated nuts to 18–22 ft. lbs. Adjust the toe-in after completing installation.

NOTE: Check the collapsible steering shaft for straightness or looseness and always replace with a new one if found damaged.

ADJUSTMENT

Tighten the backlash adjuster fully to bottom, back off the screw ⅛ turn, and lock the locknut. A clearance of 0.006 inch is provided between the screw tip and the sleeve plate.

Power Steering

The power steering gearbox is a rack and pinion type integral system. The power cylinder is built in the gearbox, using the rack shaft as a piston. The control valve is arranged around the pinion shaft.

Steering Pump

REMOVAL AND INSTALLATION

1. Remove the battery ground cable from the battery.
2. Remove the spare tire from the engine compartment.
3. Jack up the front of the vehicle and safely support it on jackstands.
4. Drain the fluid from the system by removing the line flare nuts from the center of the power steering gearbox and turning the steering wheel from left to right.
5. Loosen and remove the drive belt. See belt procedure that follows.
6. Disconnect the hoses connected to the air cleaner and remove the air cleaner assembly. Remove the engine oil dipstick. Remove any other interference that will prevent pump removal.
7. Disconnect the fluid hoses from the back of the pump.
8. Remove the pump mounting bolts/nuts and remove the pump.
9. Installation is in the reverse order of removal.
10. Fill the pump with fluid before starting the engine.

DRIVE BELT ADJUSTMENT

1. Remove the idler cover cap by turning and pulling. Adjustable jawed pliers with a piece of rag between the jaws can be used.
2. Turn the adjusting bolt until the correct belt tension is obtained. If removing the belt, loosen the adjusting bolt until the drive belt can be removed.
3. After a new belt is installed and the correct tension obtained, replace the idler cap cover by pushing in and turning.

Tie Rod Ends

REMOVAL AND INSTALLATION

1. Raise the front end of the car and support it on jack stands.
2. Remove the front wheels.
3. Remove the cotter pin and castle nut from the tie rod end stud. Detach the tie rod end using a suitable puller or extracting tool.

Installation is the reverse of removal. Torque the castle nut to 20 ft. lbs.

BRAKES

Since 1976, all models were equipped with front disc brakes. This system employs piston pressure to force two pads against both surfaces of a disc, or rotor. The advantages of disc brakes are in over all braking effect, road stability during braking effect, road stability during braking and service life of the brakes. All models are equipped with a tandem master cylinder, which employs a dual hydraulic circuit with each circuit supplying pressure to diagonally opposed wheels. This is a safety feature which allows for at least 50% braking action on the event of a fluid leak at any one wheel.

Brake Service

Refer to the Unit Repair Section for servicing the brake system.

Adjustment

FRONT DISC BRAKES

The front disc brakes require no adjustment, as hydraulic pressure maintains the proper brake pad-to-disc contact at all times.

NOTE: The brake fluid level in the master cylinder should be checked regularly.

REAR BRAKES-ALL MODELS

Perform rear brake adjustment every 6 months/6,000 miles, whichever occurs first. Adjust the rear brakes by turning the wedge, which is located on the bottom of the backing plate.

1. Chock the front wheels and set the parking brake.
2. Raise the rear of the car and support it with jackstands.

1. Cylinder
2. Primary piston ass'y
3. Secondary piston ass'y
4. Washer (piston stop)
5. Ring (piston stop)
6. Stopper
7. Gasket
8. Band (reservoir)
9. Brake fluid (reservoir)
10. Cap (reservoir)
11. Check valve spring
12. Check valve
13. Tube seat
14. Check valve cap

Cross section of dual master cylinder

CAUTION

Be sure that the car is securely supported.

3. Loosen the locknut on the wedge.
4. While rotating the wheel, turn the wedge clockwise until the brakes lock.
5. Turn the wedge back 180° (½-turn) from the locked position.
6. Tighten the locknut and perform the adjustment on the other rear drum.

Master Cylinder

REMOVAL AND INSTALLATION

CAUTION

Avoid spilling brake fluid on painted surfaces.

1. Remove the brake lines from the master cylinder.
2. Remove the nuts which connect the master cylinder to the pedal bracket or power booster.
3. Pull the master cylinder assembly forward and out.
4. Install in the reverse order of removal.

Power Brake Booster

The power brake booster uses engine manifold vacuum against a diaphragm to assist in the application of the brakes. The vacuum is regulated to be proportional to the pressure placed on the pedal.

REMOVAL AND INSTALLATION

1. Disconnect the pushrod from the brake pedal by pulling the cotter pn out and removing the pivot pin.
2. Loosen the master cylinder nuts and disconnect the vacuum hose from the (vacuum booster).
3. Remove the bracket nuts from the passenger compartment side.
4. Remove the master cylinder nut, and remove the booster.
5. Installation is the reverse of removal. Make sure that the arrow marking on the check valve is facing toward the engine. Check fr fluid leakage after the master cylinder has been installed and the brake pedal is fully depressed for 10 seconds, three or four times.

Parking Brake Cable

REMOVAL AND INSTALLATION

1. Jack up the vehicle and remove the wheel and tire.
2. Remove the brake drum (drum brake type).
3. Remove the hand brake cover and console.
4. Loosen the cable adjusting nt.
5. Remove the cable end from the equalizer.

1. Rear shell
2. Valve rod and plunger
3. Diaphragm
4. Diaphragm plate (power piston)
5. Reaction disc
6. Push rod
7. Diaphragm return spring
8. Front shell
9. Flange
10. Check valve

Exploded view of the power brake booster

6. Remove the cable end tightening clip.

7. Remove the service hole cover on the tunnel.

8. Remove the cable clamp from the crossmember.

9. Remove the cable installing bracket from the control arm.

10. Remove the handbrake cable hanger from the tie rod end.

11. Remove the handbrake cable end from the handbrake lever by removing the secondary shoe.

12. Remove the cable end nut, washer, and spring washer from the inside of the backing plate and pull the handbrake cable out from the backing plate (drum brakes).

13. Pull the brake hose clamp out and remove the handbrake cable end from the lever and spindle assembly (disc brakes).

14. Pull the handbrake cable assembly from the engine compartment and remove it from the body together with the grommet.

15. Installation is the reverse order of removal.

ADJUSTMENT

1. Pull the parking brake lever up forcefully. Release it and repeat several times.

2. It should take 7–8 notches to apply the parking brake.

3. Loosen the locknut on the turnbuckle and adjust the length of the cable, so that the parking brake is applied within specifications.

4. Tighten the locknut and recheck operation of the parking brake lever.

Hill-Holder

The hill-holder was introduced on late model cars. It is a device that prevents the car from drifting backwards when starting up an incline from a stop. The hill-holder holds the brake on temporarily until the clutch pedal is released and the car is in forward motion.

CHASSIS ELECTRICAL

Heater Unit

REMOVAL AND INSTALLATION

1976–79 Without Air Conditioning

The heater unit contains the core and blower. The entire assembly must be removed from the car before either the blower or core can be serviced. To remove the heater unit:

1. Hand brake lever assembly
2. Hand brake lever button
3. Hand brake lever grip
4. Hand brake lever spring
5. Pan head screw
6. Spring washer
7. Washer
8. Hand brake switch
9. Bolt
10. Spring washer
11. Clevis pin
12. Hand brake rod assembly
13. Cotter pin
14. Hand brake cable clip
15. Hand brake pin
16. Washer
17. Equalizer
18. Hand brake pin
19. Hand brake spring
20. Hand brake adjuster
21. Nut
22. Hand brake cable assembly
23. Clamp B
24. Bracket (Side frame)
25. Grommet
26. Clamp (rear crossmember)
27. Clamp (rear crossmember, added for AT only)
28. Hand brake cable clip
29. Nut
30. Spring washer
31. Bolt (6 mm)
32. Spring washer
33. Bolt (6 mm)
34. Washer
35. Nut (6 mm)

Exploded view of typical parking brake

1. Disconnect the ground cable from the battery.

2. Remove the console, luggage shelf, meter and visor assembly, and center ventilation grill.

3. Drain the coolant and disconnect the two heater hoses in the engine compartment.

4. Disconnect the heater control cable, fan motor harness, and the control rod connecting the air flow fan switch control lever on the instrument panel to the heater unit, on the right side.

Remove the two mounting bolts and remove the heater unit.

5. To install reverse the removal procedure.

6. To reconnect the control rod push up the link provided at the side of the heater unit to its full stroke, set the air/fan switch control lever to vent and then connect the rod to the link.

7. To reconnect the heater control cable set the temperature control lever to cold, the heater control lever on the heater unit to off then connect the cock cable.

1980 and later—without Air Conditioning

On various models the heater unit contains the core and blower. The entire assembly must be removed from the car before either the blower or core can be serviced. To remove the heater unit, use the following procedure. If, however, the blower motor is exposed on the passengers kickpanel, refer to next section.

1. Disconnect the ground cable (−) from the negative terminal of the battery.

2. Drain the engine coolant through the radiator drain plug.

3. Disconnect the heater hoses in the engine compartment.

4. Remove the rubber grommet that the heater hoses run through on the kick panel inside the car. The location is slightly above and to the right of the accelerator pedal.

5. Remove the radio box or console.

6. Remove the instrument panel.

7. Disconnect the heater control cables and fan motor harness.

8. Disconnect the duct between the heater unit and blower assembly. Remove the right and left defroster nozzles.

9. Remove the two mounting bolts at the top sides of the heater unit.

10. Lift up and out on the heater unit.

11. Installation is the reverse of removal.

Blower Motor and Heater Core

WITHOUT AIR CONDITIONING

After the heater unit has been removed the case is separated by removing the retaining

1. Wiper blade	8. Bolt	15. Cap
2. Clip	9. Spring washer	16. Spring washer
3. Wiper arm	10. Bracket	17. Flange bolt
4. Special nut	11. Nut	18. Packing
5. Nut	12. Spring washer	19. Washer
6. Spring washer	13. Link assembly	20. Clip
7. Washer	14. Wiper motor	A—Link adjuster

Exploded view of a typical wiper assembly

springs and any necessary service can be carried out.

If the car has an exposed blower,

1. Disconnect the ground cable from the battery.

2. Remove the luggage shelf and glove box.

3. Detach the heater duct from the blower assembly.

4. Set the mode control to the CIRC position and disconnect the vacuum hose.

5. Disconnect the wiring harness to the blower motor.

6. Remove the actuator from the blower assembly.

7. Remove the blower motor assembly from the heater body.

8. Separate the blower case.

9. Installation is in the reverse order of removal.

Radio

REMOVAL AND INSTALLATION

1. Disconnect the negative battery cable.

2. Use a phillips screwdriver with a short shank to remove the screws holding the speaker grille down. Remove the grille.

3. Disconnect the speaker lead from the radio connector.

4. Remove the instrument cluster bezel screws at the radio end.

5. Unfasten its screws and lift out the console.

6. Pull the knob off the fresh air lever, unfasten the two securing screws at either end, and remove the center outlet grille.

7. Pull both knobs off the radio shafts.

8. Remove the ash tray. Pull the knobs off the heater controls.

9. Remove the nuts from the radio control shafts.

10. Unfasten the screws which secure the radio surround panel. Remove the panel.

11. Unfasten the radio bracket screws.

12. Disconnect the radio leads and pull the radio out of the dash.

Installation is the reverse of removal.

Windshield Wiper Motor

REMOVAL AND INSTALLATION

1976–79

1. Disconnect the negative battery cable.

2. Remove the windshield washer reservoir.

3. Unfasten the 3 screws which secure the motor to the firewall.

4. Remove the wiper arms and cowl by unfastening their respective securing nuts (2) and screws (6).

5. Disconnect the wiper motor wiring.

6. Unfasten the clip which attaches the motor to the link, and remove the motor.

Installation is the reverse of removal.

1980 and Later

1. Disconnect the negative (−) battery cable.

2. Remove the wiper blades from the wiper arms by pulling the retaining lever up and sliding the blade away from the arm.

3. Slide the covering boot up the wiper arm.

4. Remove the retaining nuts that hold the wiper arms to the linkage and remove the arms.

5. Disconnect the electric wires to the wiper motor.

6. Remove the screws holding the cowl to the body. Remove the cowl.

7. Remove the plastic clip that attaches the linkage to the wiper motor.

8. Remove the bolts that mount the wiper motor to the firewall. Remove the motor.

9. Installation is the reverse of removal.

Instrument Cluster

REMOVAL AND INSTALLATION

1976

1. Disconnect the negative (−) battery cable.

2. Detach the driver's side fresh air vent duct by loosening its securing clamp.

3. On GL Coupe models, perform the following, working from underneath the dash:

    a. Disconnect the rear window defogger switch leads.

    b. Disconnect the tachometer lead.

    c. Loosen the trip odometer reset knob setscrew and pull the knob off.

4. On all models, reach up underneath the dash and disconnect the speedometer cable and the junction block.

5. Remove the screws which secure the instrument cluster bezel.

6. On GL Coupes, pull the cluster/bezel assembly out just far enough to disconnect the following electrical leads:

    a. Clock

    b. Brake warning lamp

    c. Seat belt warning lamp

7. Pull the cluster/bezel assembly out, away from the dash and lift it out of the car. Separate the cluster from the bezel by removing its attaching screws.

Installation is performed in the reverse order of removal.

1977–78

1. Disconnect the cable from the negative terminal of the battery.

2. Remove the instrument cluster bezel, with rear window defogger switch, by removing the mounting screws.

3. Remove the four screws mounting the instrument cluster.

4. Disconnect the speedometer cable and wiring harness from the back of the instrument cluster.

5. Remove the instrument cluster. Installation is the reverse of removal.

1979 and Later

1. Disconnect the negative cable.

2. Remove the bolts securing the steering column and pull it down.

3. Disconnect the electrical wiring connectors then remove the screws securing the meter visor and remove the visor.

4. On the GL and GLF models remove the center ventilator control lever by pulling it.

5. On the station wagon 4WD GL, remove the passing lamp switch.

6. Remove the screws securing the combination meter then pull the meter out far enough to disconnect the speedometer cable and electrical connectors from behind and remove the combination meter.

7. Installation is the reverse of removal.

Toyota

SERIAL NUMBER IDENTIFICATION

Vehicle

All models have the vehicle identification number (VIN) stamped on a plate which is attached to the left side of the instrument panel. This plate is visible through the windshield.

The serial number consists of a series identification number followed by a six-digit production number.

Engine

Bascially, 1976–83 Toyota vehicles have used five types of engines: The "A" series (1A-C, 3A, 3A-C); "K" series (3K-C, 4K-C); "M" series (4M, 4M-E, 5M-E, 5M-GE); "R" series (20R, 22R); and the "T" series (2T-C, 3T-C). Engines within each series are similar, as the cylinder block designs are the same. Variances within each series may be due to ignition types (point or electronic), displacements (bore × stroke), cylinder head design (single or double-overhead camshafts) and fuel system type (carburetor or fuel injection). Refer to the accompanying engine I.D. chart.

When ordering engine parts, it may be necessary to obtain the engine serial number. Serial numbers of the engines may be found on the following locations:

"A" series engines—stamped vertically on the left side rear of the engine block.

"K" series engine—stamped on the right side of the engine, below the spark plugs.

"M" series engines—stamped horizontally on the passenger side of the engine block, behind the alternator.

"R" series engine—stamped horizontally on the driver's side of the engine block, behind the alternator.

"T" series engines—stamped horizontally on the driver's side of the engine block, just above the alternator.

CHASSIS IDENTIFICATION

Model	Year	Chassis Designation
Corolla 1200	'77–'79	KE
Corolla 1600	'76–'79	TE
Corolla 1800	'80–'83	TE
Corona	'76–'82	RT
Celica (exc. Supra)	'76–'83	RA
Celica Supra	'79–'83	MA
Cressida	'78–'83	MX32, MX36, MX62
Mark II	'76	MX13, MX29
Starlet	'81–'83	KP
Tercel	'80–'83	AL

ENGINE IDENTIFICATION

Model	Year	Engine Displacement Cu. in.(cc)	Engine Series Identification	No. of Cylinders	Engine Type
Celica (exc. Supra)	'76–'80	133.6 (2189)	20R	4	SOHC
	'81–'83	144.4 (2367)	22R	4	SOHC
Celica Supra	'79½–'80	156.4 (2563)	4M-E	6	SOHC
	'81	168.4 (2759)	5M-E	6	SOHC
	'82–'83	168.4 (2759)	5M-GE	6	DOHC
Corolla (exc. Tercel)	'77–'79	71.2 (1166)	3K-C	4	OHV
	'76–'79	96.9 (1588)	2T-C	4	OHV
	'80–'83	108.0 (1800)	3T-C	4	OHV
Corolla Tercel	'80–'83	88.6 (1452)	1A-C, 3A, 3A-C	4	SOHC
Corona	'76–'80	133.6 (2189)	20R	4	SOHC
	'81–'82	144.4 (2367)	22R	4	SOHC
Cressida	'78–'79	156.4 (2563)	4M	6	SOHC
	'80	156.4 (2563)	4M-E	6	SOHC
	'81–'83	168.4 (2759)	5M-E	6	SOHC
Mark II	'76	156.4 (2563)	4M	6	SOHC
Starlet	'81–'83	78.7 (1290)	4K-C	4	OHV

DOHC—Double-overhead camshaft
OHV—Overhead valves
SOHC—Single-overhead camshaft

GENERAL ENGINE SPECIFICATIONS

Engine Type	Year	Engine Displacement cu. in. (cc)	Carburetor Type	Horsepower @ rpm①	Torque @ rpm (ft. lbs.)①	Bore × Stroke (in.)	Compression Ratio
1A-C, 3A	'80–'82	88.6 (1452)	2 bbl.	60 @ 4800	72 @ 2800	3.05 × 3.03	8.7:1
2T-C	'76–'79	96.9 (1588)	2 bbl.	75 @ 5800	83 @ 3800	3.35 × 2.76	9.0:1
3K-C	'76–'77	71.8 (1166)	2 bbl.	65 @ 6000	67 @ 3800	2.95 × 2.60	9.0:1
	'78–'79	71.8 (1166)	2 bbl.	58 @ 5800	63 @ 3800	2.95 × 2.60	9.0:1
3A-C	'81	88.6 (1452)	2 bbl.	62 @ 4800	75 @ 2800	3.05 × 3.03	9.0:1
	'82–'83	88.6 (1452)	2 bbl.	62 @ 5200	75 @ 2800	3.05 × 3.03	9.0:1
3T-C	'80–'81	108.0 (1800)	2 bbl.	75 @ 5000②	95 @ 2600②	3.35 × 3.07	9.0:1
	'82–'83	108.0 (1800)	2 bbl.	70 @ 4600	93 @ 2400	3.35 × 3.07	9.0:1
4K-C	'81–'83	78.7 (1290)	2 bbl.	58 @ 5200	67 @ 3600	2.95 × 2.87	9.0:1
4M	'76–'77	156.4 (2563)	2 bbl.	108 @ 5000	130 @ 2800	3.15 × 3.35	8.5:1
	'78–'79	156.4 (2563)	2 bbl.	108 @ 5000	134 @ 2800	3.15 × 3.35	8.5:1

GENERAL ENGINE SPECIFICATIONS

Engine Type	Year	Engine Displacement cu. in. (cc)	Carburetor Type	Horsepower @ rpm[1]	Torque @ rpm (ft. lbs.)[1]	Bore × Stroke (in.)	Compression Ratio
4M-E	'80	156.4 (2563)	EFI[3]	110 @ 4800	136 @ 2400	3.15 × 3.35	8.5:1
5M-E	'81–'83	168.4 (2759)	EFI[3]	116 @ 4800	145 @ 3600	3.27 × 3.35	8.8:1
5M-GE	'82–'83	168.4 (2759)	EFI[3]	145 @ 5200	155 @ 4800	3.27 × 3.35	8.8:1
20R	'76–'77	133.6 (2189)	2 bbl.	96 @ 4800	120 @ 2800	3.48 × 3.50	8.4:1
	'78–'79	133.6 (2189)	2 bbl.	95 @ 4800	122 @ 2400	3.48 × 3.50	8.4:1
	'80	133.6 (2189)	2 bbl.	90 @ 4800	122 @ 2400	3.48 × 3.50	8.4:1
22R	'81–'83	144.4 (2367)	2 bbl.	96 @ 4800	129 @ 2800	3.62 × 3.50	9.0:1

[1] Horsepower and torque ratings are given in SAE net figures

[2] Calif. — 73 hp @ 5000 rpm; 90 ft. lbs. @ 2600 rpm

[3] Electronic Fuel Injection

TUNE-UP SPECIFICATIONS

Year	Engine Type	Spark Plugs Type (NGK)	Spark Plugs Gap (in.)	Distributor Point Dwell (deg)	Distributor Point Gap (in.)	Ignition Timing (deg)[5] MT	Ignition Timing (deg)[5] AT	Compression Press.	Fuel Pump Press.	Idle Speed (rpm) MT	Idle Speed (rpm) AT	Valve Clearance (in.) (hot) Intake	Valve Clearance (in.) (hot) Exhaust
'76–'77	2T-C	BP6ES	0.030	52[3]	0.018	10B[7]	10B[7]	171	2.8–4.3[8]	850	850	0.008	0.013
	20R	BP6ES	0.030	52	0.018[9]	8B	8B	156	2.2–4.2	850	850	0.008	0.012
	4M[1]	BP6ES	0.030	41	0.018	10B	10B	156	4.2–5.4	800	750	0.007	0.010
	4M[2]	BP6ES	0.030	41	0.018	5B	5B	156	4.2–5.4	800	750	0.007	0.010
	3K-C	BP5ES-L	0.031	52	0.018	5B	—	156	2.8–4.3	750	—	0.008	0.012
'78–'79	3K-C	BPR5EA-L	0.031	Electronic		8B	8B	156	3.0–4.5	750	750	0.008	0.012
	2T-C	BP5EA-L	0.031	Electronic[4]		10B[10]	10B[10]	171	3.0–4.5	850	850	0.008	0.013
	4M	BPR5EA-L	0.031	Electronic[4]		10B[10]	10B[10]	156	4.2–5.4	750	750	0.011	0.014
	20R	BP5EA-L[11]	0.031	Electronic[4]		8B	8B	156	2.2–4.2	800	850	0.008	0.012
'80–'81	1A-C	BP6EK-A	0.039	Electronic[4]		5B	—	177	—	650	800	0.008	0.012
	3A	BPR5EA-L	0.031	52	0.018	5B	5B	177	—	650	800[13]	0.008	0.012
	3A-C	BPR5EA-11[14]	0.043	Electronic[4]		5B	5B[5]	177	—	550[13][15]	800[13]	0.008	0.012
	3T-C	BPR5EA	0.043	Electronic[4]		10B	10B	163	—	850[6]	850[6]	0.008	0.013
	4K-C	BPR5EA-11[19]	0.043[19]	Electronic[4]		8B	8B	156	2.8–4.2	650[13][20]	650[13][20]	0.008	0.012
	4M-E	BPR5EA-L	0.031	Electronic[4]		—	12B	156	33–38	—	800	0.011	0.014
	5M-E	BPR5EA-L	0.031	Electronic[4]		—	8B	156	33–38	—	800	0.011	0.014
	20R, 22R	BPR5EA-L	0.031	Electronic[4]		8B	8B	156	2.2–4.3	800[12]	850	0.008	0.012

TUNE-UP SPECIFICATIONS

Year	Engine Type	Spark Plugs		Distributor		Ignition Timing (deg)[5]		Com-pres-sion Press.	Fuel Pump Press.	Idle Speed (rpm)		Valve Clearance (in.) (hot)	
		Type (NGK)	Gap (in.)	Point Dwell (deg)	Point Gap (in.)	MT	AT			MT	AT	Intake	Exhaust
'82–'83	3A	BPR5EA-L	0.031	52	0.018	5B	5B	177	—	650	800[13]	0.008	0.012
	3A-C	BPR5EA-11[14]	0.043	Electronic[4]		5B[5]	5B[5]	177	—	550[13][15]	800[13]	0.008	0.012
	3T-C	BPR5EA-11[16]	0.043[16]	Electronic[4]		7B[5][17]	7B[5][17]	163	—	[18]	[18]	0.008	0.013
	4K-C	BPR5EA-11[19]	0.043[19]	Electronic[4]		8B	8B	156	2.8–4.2	650[13][20]	650[13][20]	0.008	0.012
	5M-E	BPR5EA-L	0.031	Electronic[4]		—	8B	156	33–38	—	800	0.011	0.014
	5M-GE	BPR5EY	0.031	Electronic[4]		8B[13]	8B[13]	164	35–38	800	800	[21]	[21]
	22R	BPR5EA-L	0.031	Electronic[4]		8B[13]	8B[13]	171	—	700[22]	750[22]	0.008	0.012

NOTE: If the information given in this chart disagrees with the information on the emission control specification decal, use the specifications on the decal.

① Except California
② California only
③ Dual points—main 57°, sub. 52°
④ Air gap 0.008–0.016 inch
⑤ With vacuum advance disconnected
⑥ M/T without power steering—700 rpm
  A/T without power steering—750 rpm
⑦ Dual points—main 12B, sub. 19–25B (degrees)
⑧ Electric pump (California)—2.4 to 3.8 psi
⑨ California model Celica GT equipped with transistorized ignition
⑩ California—8B
⑪ Celica—BPR5EA-L
⑫ Four-speed manual—700 rpm
⑬ With cooling fan OFF; trans. in Neutral
⑭ California models use BPR5EA-L11
⑮ For 4-speed transmission. 5-speed—650 rpm
⑯ Canada models use BPR5ES, gapped at 0.031 in.
⑰ Canada models—10°BTDC
⑱ Without power steering:
  U.S., M.T.—650 rpm
  U.S., A.T.—750 rpm
  Canada, M.T.—700 rpm
  Canada, A.T.—750 rpm
  With power steering: 850 rpm
⑲ California models use BPR5EA-L, gapped at 0.031
⑳ California models—700 rpm w/cooling fan OFF, trans. in Neutral
㉑ Self-adusting lash adjusters are used—no adjustment necessary
㉒ Canadian models—850 rpm
MT Manual transmission
AT Automatic transmission
TDC Top dead center
B Before top dead center

FIRING ORDERS

Firing order—all four cylinder engines except the 20R and 22R

Firing order—all "M" series engines

LEFT SIDE

Firing order—20R and 22R engines

CAPACITIES

Model	Year	Crankcase (qt)		Transmission (qt)		Drive Axle (pt)	Fuel Tank (gal)	Cooling System w/Heater (qt)
		W/Filter	W/O Filter	Manual	Automatic			
Corolla								
1200	'76–'79	3.7	2.9	①	—	2.2	12.0	5.1
1600	'76–'79	4.6	3.7	1.6	2.5	2.4	13.2	8.8
1800	'80–'83	4.0	3.5	1.8	2.5	2.2	13.2	8.5
Tercel	'80–'83	3.7	3.2	3.4	2.3	2.0	11.9	5.4
Corona								
2200	'76–'80	4.8	4.1	2.9②	2.3③	⑤	14.5④	7.4⑥
2400	'81–'82	4.8	4.1	2.9②	2.3③	⑤	16.1	8.5
Celica								
2200	'76–'80	4.9	4.0	2.9②	2.3③	⑤	13.0⑦	8.5⑧
2400	'81–'83	4.9	4.0	2.5	2.5	⑤	16.1	8.5
Mark II								
2600	'76	6.2	5.2	2.9	3.0	2.6	15.⑨	12.3

CAPACITIES

Model	Year	Crankcase (qt)		Transmission (qt)		Drive Axle (pt)	Fuel Tank (gal)	Cooling System w/Heater (qt)
		W/Filter	W/O Filter	Manual	Automatic			
Cressida								
2600	'78–'80	4.9⑩	4.3⑩	—	2.5⑪	3.0	17.2⑫	11.6
2800	'81–'83	4.7	4.0	—	2.5	⑬	17.2⑫	9.5
Supra								
2600	'79½–'80	4.9	4.3	2.8	2.5	3.2	16.1	9.5
2800	'81	4.9	4.3	2.7	2.5	3.2	16.1	9.5
2800	'82–'83	5.4	4.9	2.6	2.5	2.6	16.1	8.5
Starlet	'81–'83	3.7	3.2	2.6	—	2.2	10.6	6.0

① 4 sp: 1.8
  5 sp: 2.6
② 5 speed: 2.8
③ '78–'80: 2.5
④ 1978–79: 15.5; 1980: 16.1
⑤ Unitized type: 2.6
  Banjo type: 2.8
⑥ '79–'80: 8.5
⑦ '77: 14.5; '78–'79: 15.5; '80: 16.1

⑧ 1978–80: 8.9
⑨ Sta. Wag.: 14.5
⑩ 1978: 5.7, 4.7
⑪ 1978: 2.3
⑫ Sta. wag.: 16.2
⑬ With 7.5 in. ring gear—3.6; With 8.0 in.
  ring gear—3.8
N.A. Information not available at press time

VALVE SPECIFICATIONS

Engine Type	Seat Angle (deg)	Face Angle (deg)	Spring Test Pressure (lbs)		Spring Installed Height (in.)		Stem-To-Guide Clearance (in.)		Stem Diameter (in.)	
			Inner	Outer	Inner	Outer	Intake	Exhaust	Intake	Exhaust
3K-C	45	44.5	—	70.1	—	1.512	0.0010–0.0020③	0.0020–0.0030④	0.3140	0.3140
2T-C	45	44.5	—	58.4⑤	—	1.484	0.0012–0.0020	0.0012–0.0024	0.3140	0.3140
20R	45	44.5	—	60.0⑥	—	1.594	0.0006–0.0024	0.0012–0.0026	0.3141	0.3140
4M	45	44.5	25.7⑦	63.1①	1.504	1.642②	0.0006–0.0018	0.0010–0.0024	0.3146	0.3140
1A-C, 3A, 3A-C	45	44.5	—	52.0	—	1.520	0.0010–0.0024	0.0012–0.0026	0.2747	0.2745
4M-E	45	44.5	15.6	41.6	1.49	1.630	0.0010–0.0024	0.0014–0.0028	0.3141	0.3137
3T-C	45	44.5	—	57.9	—	1.484	0.0010–0.0024	0.0012–0.0026	0.3139	0.3139
4K-C	45	44.5	—	70.1	—	1.512	0.0012–0.0026⑧	0.0014–0.0028⑨	0.3136–0.3142	0.3134–0.3140
22R	45	44.5	—	55.1	—	1.594	0.0008–0.0024⑧	0.0012–0.0026⑨	0.3188⑩	0.3136⑪

VALVE SPECIFICATIONS

Engine Type	Seat Angle (deg)	Face Angle (deg)	Spring Test Pressure (lbs)		Spring Installed Height (in.)		Stem-To-Guide Clearance (in.)		Stem Diameter (in.)	
			Inner	Outer	Inner	Outer	Intake	Exhaust	Intake	Exhaust
5M-E	45	44.5	14.1–17.2	37.3–46.5	1.492	1.630	0.0010–0.0024⑨	0.0014–0.0028⑫	0.3138–0.3144	0.3134–0.3140
5M-GE	45	44.5	—	69.0–76.0	—	1.575	0.0010–0.0024⑧	0.0012–0.0026⑨	0.3138–0.3144	0.3136–0.3142

① Exhaust valve spring test pressure: inner—24.6 lbs; outer—59.4 lbs; 1978–79 intake and exhaust: 41.9
② Exhaust valve installed height: inner—1.520 in.; outer—1.657 in.
③ 1978 and later: 0.0012–0.0026
④ 1978 and later: 0.0014–0.0028
⑤ 1978 and later: 57.9
⑥ 1978 and later: 55.1
⑦ 1978 and later: 15.5
⑧ 0.0031 maximum
⑨ 0.0039 maximum
⑩ 0.3145 minimum
⑪ 0.3142 minimum
⑫ 0.0051 maximum

CRANKSHAFT AND CONNECTING ROD SPECIFICATIONS

(All measurements in inches)

Engine Type	Crankshaft				Connecting Rod		
	Main Brg. Journal Dia.	Main Brg. Oil Clearance	Shaft End-Play	Thrust on No.	Journal Diameter	Oil Clearance	Side Clearance
3K-C	1.9675–1.9685	0.0005–0.0015	0.0020–0.0090①	3	1.6525–1.6535	0.0006–0.0015②	0.0040–0.0080③
2-TC	2.2827–2.2834	0.0012–0.0024②	0.0030–0.0070④	3	1.8889–1.8897	0.0008–0.0020	0.0063–0.0102
20R	2.3614–2.3622	0.0010–0.0022	0.0008–0.0079⑤	3	2.0862–2.0866	0.0010–0.0022	0.0063–0.0102
4M	2.3617–2.3627	0.0012–0.0021	0.0020–0.0100	4	2.0463–2.0472	0.0008–0.0021	0.0020–0.0100⑥
1A-C, 3A, 3A-C	1.8892–1.8898	0.0005–0.0019	0.0008–0.0073	3	1.5742–1.5748	0.0008–0.0020	0.0059–0.0098
4M-E	2.3617–2.3627	0.0013–0.0023	0.0020–0.0100	4	2.0463–2.0472	0.0008–0.0021	0.0063–0.0117
3T-C	2.2825–2.2835	0.0009–0.0019	0.0008–0.0087	3	1.8889–1.8897	0.0009–0.0019	0.0063–0.0012
4K-C	1.9676–1.9685	0.0006–0.0016	0.0016–0.0095	3	1.6526–1.6535	0.0006–0.0016	0.0079–0.0150
22R	2.3614–2.3622	0.0006–0.0020	0.0008–0.0081	3	2.0862–2.0866	0.0008–0.0020	0.0063–0.0102
5M-E, 5M-GE	2.3617–2.3627	0.0013–0.0023	0.0020–0.0098	4	2.0463–2.0472	0.0008–0.0021	0.0063–0.0017

① 1978 and later: 0.0016–0.0087
② 1978 and later: 0.0009–0.0019
③ 1978 and later: 0.0043–0.0084
④ 1978 and later: 0.0010–0.0090
⑤ 1978 and later: 0.0010–0.0080
⑥ 1978 and later: 0.0063–0.0117

PISTON AND RING SPECIFICATIONS
(All measurements in inches)

Engine Type	Piston Clearance	Ring Gap			Ring Side Clearance		
		Top Compression	Bottom Compression	Oil Control	Top Compression	Bottom Compression	Oil Control
3K-C	0.0010–0.0020	0.0006–0.0014①	0.0006–0.0014①	0.0006–0.0014②	0.0011–0.0027	0.0007–0.0023③	0.0006–0.0023
2T-C	0.0024–0.0031	0.0008–0.0016④	0.0004–0.0012⑤	0.0004–0.0012⑥	0.0008–0.0024	0.0008–0.0024⑦	0.0008–0.0024⑧
20R	0.0012–0.0020	0.0004–0.0012	0.0004–0.0012	Snug	0.0008	0.0008	Snug
4M	0.0010–0.0020⑨	0.0006–0.0014⑩	0.0006–0.0014⑪	0.0008–0.0020	0.0012–0.0028⑬	0.0008–0.0024⑫	Snug
1A-C, 3A	0.0039–0.0047	0.0079–0.0157	0.0059–0.0138	0.0039–0.0236	0.0016–0.0031	0.0012–0.0028	N.A.
4M-E	0.0020–0.0028	0.0039–0.0110	0.0039–0.0110	0.0079–0.0200	0.0012–0.0028	0.0008–0.0024	N.A.
3T-C	0.0020–0.0028	0.0039–0.0098	0.0059–0.0118	0.0079–0.0276	0.0008–0.0024	0.0006–0.0022	N.A.
4K-C	0.0012–0.0020	0.0039–0.0110	0.0039–0.0118	0.0080–0.0350	0.0012–0.0028	0.0008–0.0024	Snug
22R	0.0020–0.0028	0.0094–0.0142	0.0071–0.0154	Snug	0.0080 max.	0.0080 max.	Snug
5M-E	0.0020–0.0028	0.0039–0.0110	0.0039–0.0110	0.0079–0.0200	0.0012–0.0028	0.0008–0.0024	Snug
5M-GE	0.0020–0.0028	0.0083–0.0146	0.0067–0.0209	0.0079–0.0276	0.0012–0.0028	0.0008–0.0024	Snug

① 1978 and later: 0.004–0.011 inch
② 1978 and later: 0.008–0.035 inch
③ 1978 and later: 0.001–0.003 inch
④ 1978 and later: 0.006–0.011 inch
⑤ 1978 and later: 0.008–0.013 inch
⑥ 1978 and later: 0.008–0.028 inch
⑦ 1978 and later: 0.0006–0.0022 inch
⑧ 1978–79: 0.008–0.035
⑨ 1978–79: 0.0020–0.0030 inch
⑩ 1978–79: 0.0039–0.0110 inch
⑪ 1978–79: 0.0059–0.0110 inch
⑫ 1978–79: 0.0008–0.0035 inch
⑬ 1978–79: 0.001–0.003
N.A. Not available

TORQUE SPECIFICATIONS
(All readings in ft. lbs.)

Engine Type	Cylinder Head Bolts	Rod Bearing Bolts	Main Bearing Bolts	Crankshaft Pulley Bolt	Flywheel to Crankshaft Bolts	Manifold	
						Intake	Exhaust
3K-C	39.0–47.7	28.9–37.6	39.0–47.7	29–43⑪	39–48	14–22①	
2T-C	52.0–63.5⑫	28.9–36.1	52.0–63.5	28.9–43.3⑧	41.9–47.7⑨	7.2–11.6⑬	7.2–11.6⑭
4M	55–61⑥	30–36	72–78	69–76 ⑩⑰	41–46 ⑦⑱	17–21④	12–17 ⑤⑲
20R	52–64	39–48	69–83	80–94⑮	62–68⑯	11–15	29–36

TORQUE SPECIFICATIONS

(All readings in ft. lbs.)

Engine Type	Cylinder Head Bolts	Rod Bearing Bolts	Main Bearing Bolts	Crankshaft Pulley Bolt	Flywheel to Crankshaft Bolts	Manifold	
						Intake	Exhaust
1A-C, 3A, 3A-C	40–47	26–32	40–47	55–61 [21]	55–61	15–21	15–21
3T-C	62–68	29–36	53–63	47–61 [20]	42–47	14–18	22–32
4M-E	55–61 [6]	31–34	72–78	98–119	51–57	10–15	13–16
4K-C	40–47	29–37	40–47	55–75	40–47	14–21 [1]	
22R	53–63	40–47	69–83	102–130	73–86	13–19	29–36
5M-E	55–61	31–34	72–78	98–119	51–57	10–15	13–16
5M-GE	55–61	31–34	72–78	98–119	51–57	15–17	26–32

[1] Intake and exhaust manifolds combined
[2] 8 mm bolts: 11–14 ft. lbs.
  13 mm bolts: 54–61 ft. lbs.
[3] Flex-plate (automatic): 14–22 ft. lbs.
[4] Intake manifold stud bolt: 14–18 ft. lbs.
[5] Exhaust manifold stud bolt: 6–7 ft. lbs.
[6] 8 mm bolts: 7–12 ft. lbs.
[7] 10 mm bolts: 54–61 ft. lbs.
[8] 1976: 116–145 ft. lbs.
[9] 1976: 58–64 ft. lbs.
[10] 1976: 51–58 ft. lbs.

[11] 1977: 32.5–39.8
[12] 1977–79: 61.5–68.7
[13] 1978–79: 14–18
[14] 1978–79: 22–32
[15] 1978–79: 102–130
[16] 1978–79: 73–79
[17] 1978–79: 98–119
[18] 1978–79: 51–57
[19] 1978–79: 10–15
[20] 1981 and later: 55–75
[21] 1981 and later: 80–94

TORQUE SEQUENCE

Cylinder head bolt installation torque sequence—"K" series engines

Cylinder head bolt installation torque sequence—"R" series engines

Cylinder head bolt installation torque sequence—"T" series engines

Cylinder head bolt installation torque sequence—4M and 4M-E engines

Cylinder head bolt installation torque sequence—5M-E engines

FRONT

Cylinder head bolt installation torque sequence—5M-GE engines

Cylinder head bolt installation torque sequence—"A" series engines

ALTERNATOR AND REGULATOR SPECIFICATIONS

Engine Type	Alternator Manufacturer	Alternator Output (amps)	Regulator — Field Relay Manufacturer	Regulator — Field Relay Contact Spring Deflection (in.)	Regulator — Field Relay Point Gap (in.)	Regulator — Field Relay Volts to Close	Regulator Air Gap (in.)	Regulator Point Gap (in.)	Regulator Volts
3K-C, 4K-C[8]	Nippon Denso	25[1]	Nippon Denso	0.008–0.024	0.016–0.047	4.5–5.8	0.012	0.010–0.018	3.8–14.8[2][9]
2TC, 20R, 22R[5]	Nippon Denso	40[3]	Nippon Denso	0.008–0.024	0.016–0.047[4]	4.5–5.8	0.012	0.010–0.018	13.8–14.8[2]
3T-C	Nippon Denso	50	Nippon Denso	Not adjustable					13.4–14.8[7]
4M	Nippon Denso	55	Nippon Denso	0.008–0.024	0.016–0.047	4.5–5.8	0.012	0.008–0.024	3.8–14.8
4M-E, 5M-E, 5M-GE	Nippon Denso	55	Nippon Denso	Not adjustable					14.0–14.7[6]
1A-C & 3A, 3A-C	Nippon Denso	30, 40 50 & 55	Nippon Denso	Not adjustable					13.8–14.8[7]

[1] 1976–79: 50 and 55; 1980 and later 4K-C: 45 amp
[2] W/55 amp alt.: 14.0–14.7
[3] Optional: 55 & 60 on 20R and 22R engines
[4] 1976–79: 0.0118–0.0177
[5] 1980 and later has non-adjustable regulator
[6] 1980 and later: 14.3–14.9
[7] W/55 amp: 14.0–14.7
[8] Some models use non-adjustable regulator, see text
[9] 4K-C with non-adjustable regulator—13.8–14.4V

BRAKE SPECIFICATIONS
(All measurements in inches, unless noted)

Model	Lug Nut Torque (ft. lbs.)	Master Cylinder Bore	Brake Disc Minimum Thickness	Brake Disc Maximum Runout	Maximum Brake Drum Diameter	Minimum Lining Thickness Front	Minimum Lining Thickness Rear
Corolla 1200	65–86	0.626	0.350	0.006	7.953	0.040	0.040
1600	65–86	0.813	0.350	0.006	9.079	0.040	0.040
1800	65–86	[2]	0.453	0.006	9.079	0.040	0.040

BRAKE SPECIFICATIONS
(All measurements in inches, unless noted)

Model	Lug Nut Torque (ft. lbs.)	Master Cylinder Bore	Brake Disc Minimum Thickness	Brake Disc Maximum Runout	Maximum Brake Drum Diameter	Minimum Lining Thickness Front	Minimum Lining Thickness Rear
Celica (exc. Supra)							
'76–'77	65–86	0.813	0.350	0.006	9.079	0.040	0.040
'78–'79	65–86	②	0.450	0.006	9.079	0.040	0.040
'80	65–86	②	0.453	0.006	9.079	0.040	0.040
'81	65–86	②	0.453	0.006	9.079	0.118	0.040
'82–'83	65–86	②	0.750	0.006	9.079	0.118	0.040
Celica Supra							
'79–'80	65–86	②	0.453①	0.006	—	0.040	0.040
'81	65–86	②	0.453	0.006	—	0.118	0.040
'82–'83	65–86	②	0.750③	0.006	—	0.118	0.118
Corona							
'76–'82	65–86	0.876	0.453	0.006	9.079	0.040	0.040
Cressida, Mark II④							
'76–'80	65–86	②	0.453	0.006	9.079	0.040	0.040
'81–'83	65–86	②	0.669	0.006	9.079	0.040	0.040
Starlet	65–86	②	0.354	0.006	7.950	0.040	0.040
Tercel	65–86	②	0.354	0.006	7.126	0.040	0.040

① 0.354 for the rear disc
② Not specified by the manufacturer
③ 0.669 for the rear disc
④ 1976 only for the Mark II

WHEEL ALIGNMENT SPECIFICATIONS

Model	Caster Range (deg.)	Caster Pref. Setting (deg.)	Camber Range (deg.)	Camber Pref. Setting (deg.)	Toe-In (in.)	Steering Axis Inclination (deg.)	Wheel Pivot Ratio (deg.) Inner Wheel	Wheel Pivot Ratio (deg.) Outer Wheel
Corolla 1200								
'76–'77	1½P–2⅓P	—	½P–1½P	1½P	0.04–0.20	7½–8½P	38½–41½	30–36
'78	1°20'P–2°20'P	—	1P ± 30'	1P	0.08–0.16⑤	7°15'P–8°15'P	37–39	29°25'–33°25'
'79	1°50'P ± 30'	—	1P ± 30'	1P	0.08–0.16⑤	7°50'P ± 30'	37–39	29°25'–33°25'
Corolla 1600								
'76–'77	1¼P–1½P	2P	½P–1½P	1P	0.08–0.16⑥	7½P–8½P	37–39	29°25'–33°25'
'78–'79	1°50'P ± 30'	—	1P ± 30'	1P	0.08–0.16⑤	7°50'P ± 30'	37–39	29°25'–33°25'
Corolla 1800								
'80–'81 exc wgn	1°46'P ± 30'	—	1°3'P ± 30'	—	0.12 ± 0.04①	8°25'P ± 30'	38–40	29–33

WHEEL ALIGNMENT SPECIFICATIONS

Model	Caster Range (deg.)	Caster Pref. Setting (deg.)	Camber Range (deg.)	Camber Pref. Setting (deg.)	Toe-In (in.)	Steering Axis Inclination (deg.)	Wheel Pivot Ratio (deg.) Inner Wheel	Wheel Pivot Ratio (deg.) Outer Wheel
'80–'81 wagon	1°34'P ± 30'	—	1°05'P ± 30'	—	0.12 ± 0.04①	8°20'P ± 30'	38–40	29–33
'82–'83 exc wgn	1°45'P ± 30'	—	1°05'P ± 30'	—	0.04–0.16	8°25'P ± 5'	38–40	29–33
'82–'83 wagon	1°35'P ± 30'	—	1°05'P ± 30'	—	0.04–0.16	8°20'P ± 5'	38–40	29–33
Celica (exc Supra)								
'76–'77 exc GT, ST	1¼P–2¾P	1¾P	½P–1½P	1P	0.00–0.08	7¼P–8¼P	36–38	28½–32½
'76–'77 GT	1¼P–2½P	2P	¼P–1¼P	1P	0.04–0.12	7P–8P	36–38	28–32
'76–'77 ST	½N–1½P	1P	½N–1½P	1P	0.04–0.12	7P–8P	36–38	28–32
'78–'81	1°40'P ± 30'	—	1P ± 30'	1P	0.00–0.08②	7°35'P ± 30'	36–38	28–32
'82–'83	3°20'P ± 30'	—	55' ± 30'	—	0.16–0.24③	9°20'P ± 30'	33–37	32
Celica Supra								
'79–'81	1°45'P ± 30'	—	50' ± 30'	—	0.00 ± 0.004	7°40'P ± 30'	35–37	28–32
'82–'83	4°10'P ± 30'	—	50' ± 30'	—	0.08–0.16	10°30' ± 30'	35½–39½	30°45'
Corona								
'76	½P–1½P	1P	0–1P	½P	0.04–0.12	7P	36½–38½	31
'77	⅓P–1⅓P	1P	0–1P	½P	0.04–0.12	7P	36½–38½	31
'78–'79	⅓P–1⅓P	⅘P	1/12P–1 1/16 P	⅗P	0.04–0.12	7P	37½	31
'80	1°15'P–2°15'P	1°45'P	30'P–1°30'P	1P	0.00–0.08	7°20'P–8°20'P	36–38	28–32
'81–'82	1°45' ± 30'④	—	1° ± 30'	1P	0.00–0.08	7°50'P ± 30'	36–38	28–32
Cressida								
'76–'77	44'P–1°44'P	—	20'P–1°20'P	50'P	0.08–0.16 (out)	7°10'P–8°10'P	35–39	32
'78–'80	1°P ± 30'	—	50'P ± 30'	—	0.08–0.16 (out)	7°30' ± 30'	36–39	32
'81–'83	1°30'P ± 30'	—	50'P ± 30'	—	0.08–0.16 (out)	9° ± 30'	35–39	31
Mark II ('76)	1½P–2½P	2P	½P–1½P	1P	0.16–0.24	7P	36½–38½	31
Tercel ('80–'83)	2°10'P ± 30'	—	0–1P	—	0.04–0.12	11°20'P ± 30'	34–36	33
Starlet ('81–'83)								
Sedan	1°40'P–2°20'P	2P	20'P–1°P	40'P	NA	9¾P	36°50'	34
Wagon	1°25'P–2°5'P	1°45'P	15'P–55'P	35'P	NA	9°50'P	36°50'	33°55'

① With radial tires—0.04 ± 0.04 in.
② With power steering—0.120–0.200
③ Without power steering—0.120–0.200
④ Wagon—1°30'P ± 30'
⑤ 1978–79:
  with bias ply tires—0.079 in.
  with radial ply tires—0.039 in.
⑥ 1976–77 with radial tires—0.00–0.08 in.
N—Negative
P—Positive

TUNE-UP PROCEDURES

NOTE: The procedures outlined below are the specific procedures for Toyota vehicles; general tune-up procedures may be found in the section at the end of this book.

Spark Plugs

Check, clean, and adjust the spark plugs every 6000 miles. Replace them every 12,000 miles. 1980 and later vehicles require plug changes at 15,000 miles.

Clean any foreign material from around the spark plugs before removing them. Use the spark plug wrench supplied in the tool kit.

Clean any plugs which appear to be dirty and file their electrodes flat. Adjust the gap to the figure given in the ''Tune-up Specifications'' chart, above, using a wire feeler gauge.

NOTE: Do not use a flat gauge; an inaccurate reading will result.

Inspect the spark plug hole threads for rust and, if necessary, use a 14 mm plug tap to clean them.

Examine the condition of the spark plugs and check them against the diagnosis guide at the end of the book.

Lightly oil the threads and torque the plugs to 11–14 ft. lbs. Use caution when tightening the plugs, as most Toyota models use aluminum heads.

Breaker Points and Condenser

Loosen the clips which attach the distributor cap to the distributor body and lift the cap straight up. Leave the leads connected to the cap. Remove the rotor and dust cover.

Clean the distributor cap and rotor with alcohol. Inspect them for cracks and other signs of wear or damage. Polish the points with a point file.

NOTE: Do not use emery cloth or sandpaper; these may leave particles on the points, causing them to arc.

If the points are badly pitted or worn, replace them as follows:

1. Unfasten the point lead connector.
2. Remove the point retaining clip and remove the point hold-down screw.
3. Remove the point set.
4. Installation is the reverse of removal.

After replacing the points, or as routine maintenance, adjust the points to the specifications given in the tune-up chart at the beginning of this section as follows:

1. Rotate the engine by hand or by us-

Point gap : 0.018 inch

Adjusting breaker point gap

ing a remote starter switch, so that the rubbing block is on the high point of the cam lobe.

2. Insert a 0.018 in. feeler gauge between the points; a slight drag should be felt.

3. If no drag is felt or if the feeler gauge cannot be inserted at all, loosen, but do not remove, the point hold-down screw.

4. Insert a screwdriver into the adjustment slot. Rotate the screwdriver until the proper point gap is attained. The point gap is increased by rotating the screwdriver counterclockwise and decreased by rotating it clockwise.

5. Tighten the point hold-down screw. Lubricate the cam lobes, breaker arm, rubbing block, arm pivot, and distributor shaft with a small amount of special high-temperature distributor grease.

Check the operation of the centrifugal advance mechanism by moving the rotor clockwise. Release the rotor; it should return to its original position. If it does not, check it for binding.

Check the vacuum advance unit by removing the cap and pressing in on the octane selector. Release the octane selector. It should snap back to its original position. Check for binding if it fails to do so.

Replace the condenser if it is suspect or as routine maintenance during the point replacement operation, in the following manner:

1. Remove the nut and washer from the condenser lead terminal.

2. Remove the condenser mounting screw and withdraw the condenser.

3. Installation is the reverse of removal.

NOTE: The condenser is mounted on the outside of the distributor body on all models.

Install the dust cover, rotor, and the distributor cap on the distributor. Adjust the dwell and timing, as outlined below.

Dwell Angle

Connect a dwell/tachometer, in accordance with its manufacturer's instructions, between the distributor primary lead and a ground.

With the engine warmed up and running at the specified idle speed (see the tune-up chart), take a dwell reading.

If the point dwell is not within specifications, shut the engine off and adjust the point gap, as outlined above.

NOTE: Increasing the point gap decreases the dwell angle and vice versa.

Install the dust cover, rotor, and cap. Check the dwell reading again.

Electronic Ignition

Most 1976–77 and all 1978 and later models are equipped with fully transistorized electronic ignition except Tercel with the 3A engine. The 3A engine uses a breaker point-type ignition. The system uses an ignition signal generating system in place of the breaker points. It consists of a rotor, a magnetic element and a pickup coil all mounted inside the distributor. The system needs no routine maintenance. Repair is limited to replacement of defective parts and adjustment of the air gap. Other services should be left to a qualified service person.

AIR GAP ADJUSTMENT

1. Remove the distributor cap, rotor, and the dust shield.

2. Turn the crankshaft, using a socket wrench on the crankshaft pulley bolt, until a tooth of the signal rotor aligns with the projection of the pick-up coil.

3. Using a non-magnetic feeler gauge, measure the distance between the signal rotor tooth and the pick-up coil projection. The gap should be 0.008–0.016 in.

Check and adjustment of the distributor air gap—electronic ignition (typical)

— CAUTION —

Do not use an ordinary metal feeler gauge.

---

4. If the gap is incorrect, loosen the two pick-up coil-to-distributor mounting screws. Using a screwdriver in the notch of the pick-up coil mounting, turn the pick-up until the gap is correct.

5. Tighten the pick-up coil mounting screws and recheck the gap.

6. Install the distributor cap and the rotor.

Ignition Timing

EXCEPT DUAL POINT SYSTEMS

1. Warm up the engine. Connect a tachometer and check the engine idle speed to see that it is within specifications. Adjust it as outlined below if it is not.

— CAUTION —

On models with electronic ignition, hook the dwell meter or tachometer to the negative (−) side of the coil, not to the distributor primary lead; damage to the ignition control unit will result.

If the timing mark is difficult to see, use chalk or a dab of paint to make it more visible.

"M" series engines, timing marks—typical

"R" series engines, timing marks—typical

"A" series engines, timing marks—typical

"K" series engines, timing marks—typical

"T" series engines, timing marks—typical

2. Connect a timing light to the engine, as outlined in the instructions supplied by the manufacturer of the light.

3. Disconnect the vacuum line from the distributor vacuum unit and plug the line. If a vacuum advance/retard distributor is used, disconnect and plug both vacuum lines from the distributor.

4. Allow the engine to run at the specified idle speed with the gear shift in Neutral for cars with manual transmissions, and in Drive (D) for cars with automatic transmissions.

— CAUTION —

Be sure that the parking brake is firmly set and that the wheels are chocked.

---

5. Point the timing light at the timing marks as indicated in the accompanying illustrations. With the engine at idle, timing should be at the specification given in the tune-up chart at the beginning of this section. If it is not, loosen the pinch bolt at the base and rotate the distributor to advance or retard the timing, as required.

6. Stop the engine and tighten the pinch bolt. Start the engine and recheck the timing.

7. Stop the engine and disconnect the timing light and the tachometer. Connect the vacuum line(s) to the vacuum advance unit.

DUAL POINT DISTRIBUTOR

A dual point distributor is offered as an option on some Corolla models, sold outside of California.

To adjust the dual point system, proceed as follows:

1. Adjust the timing for the main set of points as outlined in the "Single Point" section above.

2. Use a jumper wire to ground the terminal on the thermoswitch connector after removing the connector from the thermoswitch. The thermoswitch is threaded into the intake manifold and is connected to the dual point system relay. Be careful not to confuse it with any of the emission control system switches which are connected to the computer.

3. Check the timing with a light as described above, the timing should be 22° before top dead center (BTDC).

4. If the timing is off, connect a dwell meter to the *negative* side of the coil, and adjust the sub-points so that the dwell angle is 52°. The sub-points are adjusted in the same manner as the main points.

5. Remove the test equipment, and reconnect the thermoswitch.

Octane Selector

The octane selector is used as a fine adjustment to match the vehicle's ignition timing to the grade of gasoline being used. It is located near the distributor vacuum unit, beneath a plastic dust cover. The octane selector system is used mainly on point-type ignition systems. Normally the octane selector should not require adjustment, however, if necessary, adjustment is as follows:

1. Align the setting line with the threaded end of the housing and then align the center line with the setting mark on the housing.

2. Drive the car to the speed specified on the chart below, in high gear, on a level road.

3. Depress the accelerator pedal all the way to the floor. A slight "pinging" sound should be heard. As the car accelerates, the sound should gradually go away.

4. If the pinging sound is loud or if it fails to disappear as the vehicle speed increases, retard the timing by turning the knurled knob toward "R" (Retard).

5. If there is no pinging sound at all, advance the timing by turning the knob toward "A" (Advance).

6. When the adjustment is completed, replace the plastic dust cover.

Octane selector

NOTE: One graduation of the octane selector is equal to about ten degrees of crankshaft angle.

OCTANE SELECTOR TEST SPEEDS

Engine Type	Test Speed (mph)
3K-C	19–21
2T-C, 20R	16–22
4M	25

Valve Lash

3K-C AND 2T-C ENGINES

1. Start the engine and allow it to reach normal operating temperature (165–185°F).
2. Stop the engine. Remove the air cleaner assembly, its hoses, and its bracket. Remove any other hoses, cables, etc. attached to the valve cover. Remove the valve cover.
3. On 3K-C engines tighten the cylinder head bolts, in the proper sequence to the following values:
3K-C—35–48 ft. lbs.
4. Next, on the 3K-C engines, tighten the valve rocker support bolts to 13–17 ft. lbs.

--- CAUTION ---

Tighten all of the above bolts in the proper sequence and in three stages.

5. Install a suitable oil tray on the 3K-C engine, to prevent hot engine oil from being splashed out.

NOTE: The tray may be ordered from a dealer or fabricated from sheet metal. (See illustration.)

Special oil splash tray for 3K-C engine

6. Start the engine. Check the clearance between the rocker arm and the valve stem with a feeler gauge, for each valve. The clearance specifications are given in the Tune-Up Chart at the beginning of this section.
7. If the valves require adjustment, loosen the locknut and turn the adjustment screw to obtain the proper clearance.
8. Tighten the locknut. Check the valve clearance to be sure that it was not disturbed when the locknut was tightened.
9. When the valve inspection and ad-

justment are completed, replace the valve cover and all of the other components which were removed.

3T-C AND 4K-C ENGINES

1. Start the engine and allow it to reach normal operating temperature.
2. Stop the engine. Remove the air cleaner assembly and the related hoses, brackets, etc. Remove any other hoses, brackets, cables, etc., which are attached to the valve cover and remove the valve cover.
3. On 4K-C engines only, torque the cylinder head bolts (in the proper sequence) to 40–47 ft. lbs.; and the rocker support bolts to 14–17 ft. lbs.
4. Using a wrench on the center crankshaft pulley bolt, rotate the crankshaft to align the pulley mark (notch) with the "0" mark on the timing mark scale. Check that the rocker arms of the No. 1 cylinder are loose; if not, rotate the crankshaft 360°.
5. Adjust the valves referred to as the "first set" in the accompanying illustration. Loosen the locknut and turn the adjusting screw of each rocker arm until the proper clearance is obtained (refer to the "Tune-Up Specifications" chart). Tighten the locknut.
6. Rotate the crankshaft 360°, again aligning the notch with the "0" mark.
7. Repeat Step 5 for the valves referred to as the "second set" in the accompanying illustration.
8. Reinstall the valve cover, air cleaner,

Valve lash adjustment of the 4K-C engine. First, adjust the valves indicated at the top of the illustration. Rotate the crankshaft 360° from no. 1 TDC compression, then adjust the valves indicated in the lower portion of the illustration

3T-C engines, valve lash adjustment. Adjust this set of valves first

3T-C engines, valve lash adjustment. Adjust this set of valves second

and other components which were previously removed.

20R AND 22R ENGINES

1. Start the engine and allow it to reach normal operating temperature (above 180°F).
2. Stop the engine. Remove the air cleaner assembly, its hoses, and bracket. Remove any other cables, hoses, wires, etc., which are attached to the valve cover. Remove the valve cover.
3. Set the no. 1 cylinder at top dead center (TDC) of its compression stroke, with the TDC notch aligned with the pointer.
4. Measure the clearance between the valve stem and the rocker arm with a feeler gauge for the valves shown in the first illustration. See the "Tune-Up" chart for the correct clearance.
5. To adjust the valve clearance, loosen the locknut and turn the adjusting screw until the proper clearance is obtained. Tighten the locknut and check the clearance again.
6. Crank the engine *one* revolution (360°) and perform Steps 4 and 5 for the set of valves shown in the second illustration.
7. Install the spark plug in the No. 1 cylinder and reconnect the coil lead. Install the valve cover, air cleaner assembly and any other components that were removed.

ALL "M" SERIES ENGINES–EXCEPT 5M-GE

1. Allow the engine to reach normal operating temperature. Stop the engine.
2. Remove the air cleaner assembly,

INTAKE: .008" (.2MM)
FIRST
EXHAUST: .012" (.3MM)

"R" series engines, valve lash adjustment. Adjust the set of valves indicated while the engine is at TDC compression (no. 1 cylinder)

INTAKE: .008" (.2MM)
SECOND
EXHAUST: .012" (.3MM)
SECOND

"R" series engines, valve lash adjustment. Adjust the set of valves indicated after having turned the engine 360° from the first setting

air cleaner bracket, spark plug cable guides, and any other components attached to the valve cover. Remove the valve cover.

3. Crank the engine until the No. 1 cylinder is at TDC of its compression stroke. To determine this, remove the spark plug from the No. 1 cylinder and place a screwdriver over the spark plug hole. Crank the engine until pressure is felt against the screwdriver and the slot in the crankshaft pulley aligns with the "0" (TDC) on the timing scale.

4. Check and adjust the clearance of the intake valves on 1, 2 and 4 cylinders and of the exhaust valves on 1, 3 and 5 cylinders.

5. Measure the clearance between the valve stem and the adjusting screw with a feeler gauge of the proper size. (See the "Tune-Up Specification" Chart at the beginning of this section.)

6. If the valves require adjustment, loosen the locknut and turn the adjusting

screw until the proper clearance is obtained. Tighten the locknut. Check the clearance again.

7. Crank the engine one revolution (360°) and repeat Steps 5 and 6 for the remaining valves.

8. Install the cylinder head cover, spark plug cable guides, air cleaner bracket, air cleaner assembly and any other components removed. Replace the No. 1 spark plug as well.

5M-GE ENGINES

This engine uses self-adjusting lash mechanisms. Periodic valve lash adjustments are not required.

1A-C, 3A, AND 3A-C ENGINES

1. Run the engine to normal operating temperature.
2. Stop the engine. Remove the air cleaner and any other components that are in the way.
3. Turn the crankshaft to align the timing marks at TDC. Check that the rocker arms on No. 1 cylinder are loose and those on No. 4 are tight. If not, turn the crankshaft 1 complete revolution.
4. Adjust No. 1 int. and exh.; No. 3 exh.

First
Front
IN. EX. IN. EX.

"A" series engines, valve lash adjustment. Adjust this set of valves first

5. Check the clearance between the rocker arm and the valve stem. This measurement is listed in the tune-up chart.
6. If the clearance is not correct loosen the nut and turn the adjusting screw to the correct gap.

Second
Front
EX. IN. EX. IN.

"A" series engines, valve lash adjustment. Adjust this set of valves second

NOTE: For this measurement you will need a set of feeler gauges.

7. Once you have the proper clearance tighten the nut, and at the same time hold onto the adjusting screw. This is accomplished by using a box type wrench and a screwdriver.
8. Turn the crankshaft 1 complete revolution and adjust the remaining valves.
9. Reinstall the valve cover.

NOTE: Make sure that you install a new valve cover gasket.

Idle Speed and Mixture

ADJUSTMENT

1976–83 Carbureted Engines

The idle speed and mixture should be adjusted under the following conditions: the air cleaner must be installed, the choke fully opened, the transmission should be in Neutral (N), all accessories (incl. the electric engine cooling fan, if so equipped) should be turned off, all vacuum lines should be connected, and the ignition timing should be set to specification.

1. Start the engine and allow it to reach normal operating temperature.
2. Check the float setting; the fuel level should be just about even with the spot on the sight glass. If the fuel level is too high or low, adjust the float level as outlined in the Fuel System section.
3. Connect a tachometer in accordance with its manufacturer's instructions. However, connect the tachometer positive (+) lead to the coil Negative (−) terminal. Do NOT hook it up to the distributor side; dam-

"M" series engines (except 5M-GE), valve lash adjustment. Adjust this set of valves first

"M" series engines (except 5M-GE), valve lash adjustment. Adjust this set of valves second

age to the transistorized ignition could result.

NOTE: On 1980 and later models, all of which have tamper-proof idle mixture screws, merely turn the idle speed adjusting screw until the proper idle speed is obtained (refer to the "Tune-Up Specifications" chart). Disregard the following steps. Disconnect the tachometer after the adjustment is complete.

4. Turn the idle speed adjusting screw to obtain one of the following initial idle speeds:

3K-C, 2T-C—930 rpm
20R—900 rpm
4M—820 rpm
1A-C, 2A-3A—750 rpm

5. Turn the idle mixture adjusting screw to increase the idle speed as much as is possible to increase the idle speed as much as is possible.

6. Next, turn the idle speed screw to again obtain the same idle speed figure given in Step 4.

7. If possible, turn the idle mixture screw to increase the idle speed again.

8. Keep repeating Steps 6 and 7 until the idle mixture adjusting screw will no longer increase the idle speed above the figure specified in Step 4.

9. Slowly turn the idle mixture screw *clockwise*, until the idle speed specified in the "Tune-Up Specifications" chart is reached. (This makes the mixture leaner.)

10. Disconnect the tachometer.

1980–83 Fuel Injected Engines

Idle speed and mixture on 4M-E, 5M-E, and 5M-GE engines must be adjusted only by a professional service technician, as specialized equipment and knowledge are required to properly perform these adjustments.

Carburetor adjustment points for the 4M engine

Carburetor adjustment points for the 4K-C engine

Carburetor adjustment points for the 3T-C engine

Carburetor adjustment points for the "A" series engines—typical

Carburetor adjustment points for the 2T-C engine

ENGINE ELECTRICAL

Distributor

REMOVAL

1. Unfasten the cables from the spark plugs, after marking the wiring order. Remove the high tension cable from the coil.

2. Remove the primary wire and the vacuum line from the distributor. Remove the distributor cap.

3. Matchmark the distributor housing and the engine block; mark the rotor position in the distributor as well. This will aid in correct positioning of the distributor during installation.

4. Remove the clamp from the distributor. Withdraw the distributor from the block.

NOTE: It is easier to install the distributor if the engine timing is not disturbed while it is removed. If the timing has been lost, see "Installation—Timing Disturbed" below.

INSTALLATION—TIMING NOT DISTURBED

1. Insert the distributor in the block and align the matchmarks made during removal.

2. Engage the distributor drive with the oil pump driveshaft.

3. Install the distributor clamp, cap, high tension wire, primary wire, and vacuum line.

4. Install the wires on the spark plugs.

5. Start the engine. Check the timing and adjust the octane selector, if so equipped.

INSTALLATION—TIMING DISTURBED

If the engine has been cranked, dismantled, or the timing otherwise lost, proceed as follows:

1. Determine top dead center (TDC) of the number one (No. 1) cylinder's compression stroke by removing the spark plug from the No. 1 cylinder and placing a finger or a compression gauge over the spark plug hole.

Crank the engine until compression pressure starts to build up. Continue cranking the engine until the timing marks indicate TDC (or 0°).

2. Next, align the timing marks to the specifications given in the "Ignition Timing" column of the tune-up chart at the beginning of this section.

3. Temporarily install the rotor in the distributor shaft so that the rotor is pointing toward the No. 1 terminal in the distributor cap. The points should just be about to open.

4. Use a small screwdriver to align the slot on the distributor drive (oil pump driveshaft) with the key on the bottom of the distributor shaft.

5. Install the distributor in the block by

1. Cam	11. Snap ring	21. Distributor cap
2. Governor spring	12. Vacuum advance unit	22. Spring
3. Governor weight	13. Octane selector assembly	23. Rotor
4. Governor spring	14. Rubber washer	24. Dust cover
5. Distributor shaft	15. Cap spring clip	25. Breaker point assembly
6. Metal washer	16. Distributor housing	26. Movable plate
7. Bakelite washer	17. O-ring	27. Stationary plate
8. Condenser	18. Distributor clamp	28. Adjusting washer
9. Insulator	19. Spiral gear	29. Wave washer
10. Cap spring clip	20. Pin	30. Snap ring

An exploded view of the breaker point-type distributor—typical

1. Cam grease stopper
2. Signal rotor
3. Governor spring
4. Governor weight
5. Governor shaft
6. Plate washer
7. Compression coil spring
8. Thrust bearing
9. Washer
10. Dustproof packing
11. Steel plate washer
12. Rubber washer
13. Octane selector cap
14. Housing
15. O-ring
16. Sprial gear
17. Pin
18. Vacuum advance
19. Cord clamp
20. Breaker plate
21. Signal generator
22. Dustproof cover
23. Distributor rotor
24. Distributor cap
25. Rubber cap

Exploded view of a fully electronic ignition distributor—typical

rotating it slightly (no more than one gear tooth in either direction) until the driven gear meshes with the drive.

NOTE: Oil the distributor spiral gear and the oil pump driveshaft end before distributor installation.

6. Rotate the distributor, once it is installed, so that the points are just about to open. Temporarily tighten the pinch bolt.

7. Remove the rotor and install the dust cover. Replace the rotor and the distributor cap.

8. Install the primary wire and the vacuum line.

9. Install the No. 1 cylinder spark plug. Connect the cables to the spark plugs in the proper order by using the marks made during removal. Install the high tension wire on the coil.

10. Start the engine. Adjust the ignition timing and the octane selector (if so equipped), as outlined above.

Alternator

ALTERNATOR PRECAUTIONS

1. Always observe proper polarity of the battery connections; be especially careful when jump-starting the car.

2. Never ground or short out any alternator or alternator regulator terminals.

3. Never operate the alternator with any of its or the battery's leads disconnected.

4. Always remove the battery or disconnect its output lead while charging it.

5. Always disconnect the ground cable when replacing any electrical components.

6. Never subject the alternator to excessive heat or dampness if the engine is being steam-cleaned.

7. Never use arc-welding equipment with the alternator connected.

REMOVAL AND INSTALLATION

NOTE: On some models the alternator is mounted very low on the engine. On these models it may be necessary to remove the gravel shield and work from underneath the car in order to gain access to the alternator.

1. Disconnect the battery cables at the battery.

2. Remove the air cleaner, if necessary, to gain access to the alternator.

3. Unfasten the bolts which attach the adjusting link to the alternator. Remove the alternator drive belt.

4. Unfasten and tag the alternator attaching bolt and then withdraw the alternator from its bracket.

6. Installation is the reverse order of removal. After installing the alternator, adjust the belt tension.

BELT TENSION ADJUSTMENT

Inspection and adjustment to the alternator drive belt should be performed every 3,000 miles or if the alternator has been removed.

1. Inspect the drive belt to see that it is not cracked or worn. Be sure that its surfaces are free of grease or oil.

2. Push down on the belt halfway between the fan and the alternator pulleys (or crankshaft pulley) with thumb pressure. Belt deflection should be 3/8–1/2 in.

3. If the belt tension requires adjustment, loosen the adjusting link bolt and move the alternator until the proper belt tension is obtained.

— CAUTION —
Do not overtighten the belt; damage to the alternator bearings could result.

4. Tighten the adjusting link bolt.

External Regulator

REMOVAL AND INSTALLATION

1. Disconnect the battery cables at the battery.

2. Disconnect the wiring harness connector from the regulator.

3. Remove the regulator securing bolts. Remove the regulator, complete with its condenser.

4. Installation is the reverse order of removal.

VOLTAGE ADJUSTMENT

1. Connect a voltmeter to the battery terminals.

2. Start the engine and gradually increase its speed to about 1500 rpm.

3. At this speed, the voltage reading should fall within the range specified in the chart above.

4. If the voltage does not fall within the specifications, remove the cover from the regulator and adjust it by bending the adjusting arm.

5. Repeat Steps 2 and 3; if the voltage cannot be brought to specifications, proceed with the mechanical adjustments, outlined below.

MECHANICAL ADJUSTMENTS

NOTE: Perform the preceding voltage adjustment before beginning the mechanical adjustments.

Field Relay

1. Remove the cover from the regulator assembly.

2. Use a feeler gauge to check the amount that the contact spring is deflected while the armature is being depressed.

3. If the measurement is not within specifications, adjust the regulator by bending point holder P (see illustration).

6. Clean off the points with emery cloth if they are dirty and wash them with solvent.

Adjusting Arm — Contact Spring Deflection

Point Holder (P₁) — Point Holder (P₂)

Point Gap

Field relay components

Voltage Regulator

1. Use a feeler gauge to measure the air (armature) gap. If it is not within the specifications, adjust it by bending the *low*-speed point holder (see illustration).

2. Check the point gap with a feeler gauge. If it is not within specifications, adjust it by bending the *high*-speed point holder (see illustration). Clean the points with emery cloth and wash them off with solvent.

3. Check the amount of contact spring deflection while depressing the armature. The specification should be the same as that for the contact spring on the field relay. If

Armature Gap — Armature Gap

Adjusting Arm — Contact Spring Deflection

Low Speed Point Holder (PL₁) — High Speed Point Holder (PL₂)

PointGap

Voltage regulator components

the amount of deflection is not within specification, replace, do not adjust, the voltage regulator.

Go back and perform the steps outlined under "Voltage Adjustment," above. If the voltage cannot be brought within specifications after regulator replacement, the alternator is probably defective and should be replaced.

NOTE: On all vehicles with the "IC" type regulator there are no adjustments necessary. If found to be defective, it must be replaced.

Internal (IC) Regulator

The IC regulator is mounted on the alternator housing, is transistorized, and is non-adjustable.

REMOVAL AND INSTALLATION

1. Disconnect the battery cables at the battery.

2. Remove the end cover of the regulator.

3. Remove the three screws that go through the terminals.

4. Remove the (two) top mounting screws that mount the regulator to the alternator. Remove the regulator.

5. To install the new IC regulator. Place the regulator in position on the alternator. Install and secure the (two) top mounting screws. Install the (three) terminal screws. Install the end cover.

6. Reconnect the battery ground cable.

Starter

REMOVAL AND INSTALLATION

1. Disconnect the cable which runs from the starter to the battery, at the battery end.

2. Remove the air cleaner assembly, if necessary, to gain access to the starter.

NOTE: On some models with automatic transmissions, it may be necessary to disconnect the throttle linkage connecting rod.

3. On Corolla 1200 models, perform the following:

a. Disconnect the manual choke cable and the accelerator cable from the carburetor.

b. Unbolt the front exhaust pipe flange from the manifold and then remove the complete manifold assembly. (See the appropriate section(s) for details.)

4. Disconnect all of the wiring at the starter.

5. Remove the starter toward the front of the car.

6. Installation is in the reverse order of removal.

STARTER DRIVE REPLACEMENT

Direct Drive Starter

1. Disconnect the wiring and remove the starter from engine.

2. Remove the solenoid from the starter.

3. Remove the through bolts and take off the end plate.

4. Slide the armature shaft far enough out to disengage the clutch forks.

5. Remove the retaining clip and washer from shaft.

6. Slide the starter drive assembly from the shaft.

7. Install in reverse of removal. Always use a new retaining clip.

Reduction Gear Starter

Remove the starter as previously outlined, then follow Steps 1–4 of the starter solenoid procedure for the reduction gear starter which follows. Also note the assembly information at the end of the same procedure.

STARTER SOLENOID AND BRUSH REPLACEMENT

Direct Drive Starter

NOTE: The starter must be removed from the car in order to perform this operation.

1. Remove the field coil lead from the solenoid terminal.

2. Unfasten the solenoid retaining screws. Remove the solenoid by tilting it upward and withdrawing it.

3. Remove the end frame bearing cover screws and remove the cover.

4. Remove the thru-bolts. Remove the commutator end-frame.

5. Withdraw the brushes from their holder if they are to be replaced.

6. Minimum brush length should be 0.40 in. Replace the brushes with new ones if required.

7. Dress the new brushes with emery cloth so that they will make proper contact.

8. Use a spring scale to check the brush spring tension against the specification in the chart. Replace the springs if they do not meet specification.

Assembly is the reverse of disassembly.

An exploded view of a typical direct drive starter

Pack the end bearing cover with multipurpose grease before installing it.

Reduction Gear Starter

NOTE: The starter must be removed from the car, in order to perform this operation.

1. Disconnect the solenoid lead.
2. Loosen the two bolts on the starter housing and separate the field frame from the solenoid. Remove the O-ring and felt dust seal.
3. Remove the two screws and separate the starter drive from the solenoid.
4. Withdraw the clutch and gears. Remove the ball from the clutch shaft bore or solenoid.
5. Minimum brush length should be 0.40 in. Replace the brushes if they are too short.

An exploded view of a typical reduction gear starter

7. Check the gears for wear or damage. Replace as required.

Assembly is the reverse of disassembly. Lubricate all bearings and gears with high temperature grease. Grease the ball before inserting in the clutch shaft bore. Align the tab on the brush holder with the notch on the field frame. Check the positive (+) brush leads to see that they aren't grounded. Align the mark on the solenoid with the bolt anchors on the field frame.

ENGINE MECHANICAL

Engine

REMOVAL AND INSTALLATION

——————— CAUTION ———————
Be sure that the car is supported securely, during engine removal.
————————————————————

3K-C and 4K-C Engines

1. Drain the entire cooling system.
2. Unfasten the cable which runs from the battery to the starter at the battery terminal.
3. Scribe marks on the hood and hinges to aid in hood alignment during assembly. Remove the hood.
4. Unfasten the headlight bezel retaining screws and remove the bezels. Remove the five radiator grille attachment screws and remove the grille.
5. Remove the hood lock assembly after detaching the release cable.
6. Unfasten the nuts from the horn retainers and disconnect the wiring. Remove the horn assembly.
7. Remove the air cleaner from its bracket after unfastening the hoses from it.
8. Remove the windshield washer tank from its bracket but first drain its contents into a clean container.
9. Remove both the upper and lower radiator hoses from the engine after loosening the hose clamps.

NOTE: On models with automatic transmissions, disconnect the oil lines from the oil cooler.

10. Detach the radiator mounting bolts and remove the radiator.
11. Remove the accelerator cable from its support on the cylinder head cover. Unfasten the cable at the carburetor throttle arm. Disconnect the choke cable from the carburetor.
12. Detach the water hose retainer from the cylinder head.
13. Disconnect the bypass and heater hoses at the water pump. Disconnect the

other end of the heater hose from the water valve. Remove the heater control cable from the water valve.

14. Disconnect the wiring harness multiconnectors.

15. Detach the downpipe from the exhaust manifold.

16. Detach the wires from the water temperature and oil pressure sending units.

17. Remove the nut from the front left-hand engine mount.

18. Remove the fuel line from the fuel pump.

19. Detach the battery ground cable from the cylinder block.

20. Remove the nut from the front right-hand engine mount.

21. Remove the clip and detach the cable from the clutch release lever.

22. Remove the primary and high-tension wires from the coil.

23. Detach the back-up light switch wire at its connector on the right side of the extension housing.

The following steps apply to Corolla models with manual transmissions and Starlet:

24. Remove the carpet from the transmission tunnel. Remove the boots from the shift lever.

25. Remove the snap-ring from the gearshift selector lever base. Withdraw the selector lever assembly.

The following steps apply to Corolla models with automatic transmissions:

26. Disconnect the accelerator linkage torque rod at the carburetor.

27. Disconnect the throttle linkage connecting rod from the bellcrank lever.

28. Drain the oil from the transmission oil pan.

29. Detach the transmission gear selector shift rod from the control shaft.

The following steps apply to Corollas with both manual and automatic transmissions and Starlet:

30. Raise the rear wheels of the car. Support the car with jack stands.

31. Disconnect the driveshaft from the transmission.

NOTE: Drain the oil from the manual transmission transmission, first, to prevent it from leaking out.

32. Detach the exhaust pipe support bracket from the extension housing.

33. Remove the insulator bolt from the rear engine mount.

34. Place a jack under the transmission and remove the four bolts from the rear (engine support) crossmember.

35. Install lifting hooks on the engine lifting brackets. Attach a suitable hoist.

36. Lift the engine slightly; then move it toward the front of the car. Bring the engine the rest of the way out at an angle. Engine installation is the reverse order of removal. Adjust all transmission and carburetor linkages, as detailed in the appropriate section. Install and adjust the hood.

Refill the engine, radiator, and transmission to capacity.

2T-C and 3T-C Engines

1. Drain the radiator, cooling system, transmission, and engine oil.

2. Disconnect the battery-to-starter cable at the positive battery terminal.

3. Scribe marks on the hood and its hinges to aid in alignment during installation.

4. Remove the hood supports from the body. Remove the hood.

NOTE: Do not remove the supports from the hood.

5. On Corolla models, perform Steps 4–6 as detailed in the 3K-C "Engine Removal" section above.

6. Detach both the upper and lower hoses from the radiator. On cars with automatic transmission, disconnect the lines from the oil cooler. Remove the radiator.

7. Unfasten the clamps and remove the heater and bypass hoses from the engine. Remove the heater control cable from the water valve.

8. Remove the wiring from the coolant temperature and oil pressure sending units.

9. Remove the air cleaner from its bracket, complete with its attendant hoses.

10. Unfasten the accelerator torque rod from the carburetor. On models equipped with automatic transmissions, remove the transmission linkage as well.

11. Remove the emission control system hoses and wiring, as necessary.

12. Remove the clutch hydraulic line support bracket.

13. Unfasten the high-tension and primary wires from the coil.

14. Mark the spark plug cables and remove them from the distributor.

15. Detach the right-hand front engine mount.

16. Remove the fuel line at the pump.

17. Detach the downpipe from the exhaust manifold.

18. Detach the left-hand front engine mount.

19. Disconnect all of the wiring harness multiconnectors.

20. On cars equipped with manual transmissions, remove the shift lever boot and the shift lever cap boot.

21. Unfasten the four gear selector lever cap retaining screws, remove the gasket and withdraw the gear selector lever assembly from the top of the transmission.

NOTE: On Corolla five-speed models, the floor console must be removed first.

22. Lift the rear wheels of the car off the ground and support the car with jack stands.

23. On cars equipped with automatic transmissions, disconnect the gear selector control rod.

24. Detach the exhaust pipe support bracket.

25. Disconnect the driveshaft from the rear of the transmission.

26. Unfasten the speedometer cable from the transmission. Disconnect the wiring from the back-up light switch and the neutral safety switch (automatic only).

27. Detach the clutch release cylinder assembly, complete with hydraulic lines. Do not disconnect the lines.

28. Unbolt the rear support member mounting insulators.

29. Support the transmission and detach the rear support member retaining bolts. Withdraw the support member from under the car.

30. Install lifting hooks on the engine lifting brackets. Attach a suitable hoist to the engine.

31. Remove the jack from under the transmission.

32. Raise the engine and move it toward the front of the car. Use care to avoid damaging the components which remain on the car.

33. Support the engine on a workstand. Install the engine in the reverse order of removal. Adjust all of the linkages as detailed in the appropriate section. Install the hood and adjust it. Replenish the fluid levels in the engine, radiator, and transmission.

20R and 22R Engines

EXCEPT 1982–83 CELICA

1. Perform Steps 1–4 of the 2T-C and 3T-C "Engine Removal" procedure.

2. Remove the headlight bezel and the radiator grille.

3. Remove the fan shroud, the hood lock base and the base support.

4. Perform Steps 8–19 of the 2T-C and 3T-C "Engine Removal" procedure.

Perform the following steps on models with manual transmissions:

5. Remove the center console if so equipped.

6. Remove the shift lever boot(s).

7. Unfasten the four shift lever cap retaining screws. Remove the cap and withdraw the shift lever assembly.

Perform the following steps on models equipped with automatic transmissions:

8. Remove the transmission selector linkages:

   a. On models equipped with a floor-mounted selector, disconnect the control rod from the transmission.

   b. On column-mounted gear selector models, remove the shifter rod.

9. Disconnect the neutral safety switch wiring connector.

Perform the following steps on all models:

10. Raise the rear of the vehicle with jacks and support it on jack stands.

11. Remove the retaining screws and remove the parking brake equalizer support bracket. Disconnect the cable which runs between the lever and the equalizer.

12. Remove the speedometer cable from

the transmission. Disconnect the back-up light wiring.

13. Detach the driveshaft from the rear of the transmission.

NOTE: If oil runs out of the transmission, an old U-joint yoke sleeve makes an excellent plug.

14. Perform Steps 27–33 of the 2T-C and 3T-C "Engine Removal" procedure.

Installation of the engine is the reverse order of removal. Refer to the appropriate chapters for transmission and carburetor adjustments. Refill the engine oil, coolant, and transmission oil to the proper levels.

1982–83 CELICA

1. Disconnect the battery cables at the battery.

2. Mark the hood to indicate the relationship beween the hood and the hood hinges. Unbolt and remove the hood.

3. Drain the coolant from both the radiator and the engine block.

4. Remove the air cleaner assembly (mark any disconnected hoses for reassembly purposes).

5. Disconnect the accelerator linkage from the carburetor.

6. Disconnect the transmission cable from the carburetor on automatic transmission equipped models.

7. Mark and disconnect all wiring and hoses from the engine. Label each item so that it may be reattached correctly during assembly.

8. Remove the radiator grille.

9. Remove the hood lock brace, radiator upper baffle, and the hood lock.

10. Remove the radiator and the fan shroud.

11. If the vehicle is equipped with air conditioning, have the refrigerant discharged from the system by a professional service technician. Remove the air conditioning condenser from the vehicle.

12. If equipped with air conditioning, loosen the air conditioning compressor mounting bolts, remove the drive belt, remove the mounting bolts, and lay the compressor aside.

NOTE: It is not necessary to disconnect the refrigerant hoses from the compressor.

13. If the vehicle is equipped with power steering:

    a. Loosen the idler pulley bolts.

    b. Remove the power steering pump drive belt.

    c. Remove the power steering pump mounting bolts.

    d. Move the pump out of the way. It is not necessary to disconnect the hydraulic lines from the pump.

14. Disconnect the upper side of the engine shock absorber from the left engine mount.

15. Remove the engine mount bolts from each side of the engine.

16. Remove the console box to gain ac-

cess to the shift lever on vehicles with manual transmissions. Also, remove the shift lever on these models.

17. Raise the vehicle and support it safely with jackstands.

18. Remove the engine undercover and drain the engine oil.

19. Remove the exhaust pipe clamp from the transmission housing, disconnect the exhaust pipe from the manifold, and allow the pipe to hang downward.

20. On vehicles with manual transmissions, remove the clutch release cylinder.

21. Disconnect the speedometer cable from the transmission and tie the cable out of the way.

22. On vehicles with automatic transmissions, disconnect the shift linkage from the shift lever.

23. Disconnect the wiring from the following items:

    a. Back-up light switch

    b. Neutral start switch (auto. trans. only)

    c. Overdrive solenoid (auto. trans. only)

    d. Oil pressure sending unit

    e. Starter motor

24. Place a jack under the transmission, with a block of wood between the jack and the transmission. Raise the jack just enough to support the transmission and remove the transmission crossmember.

25. Detach the driveshaft from the rear of the transmission and plug the transmission.

26. Attach the engine lifting equipment to the engine. CAREFULLY lift the engine and transmission assembly out of the vehicle.

27. Installation of the engine is performed in the reverse of the previous steps. Refer to the appropriate sections for linkage adjustments. Replenish all fluid levels and check for leaks after the engine has been started.

All "M" Series Engines

1. Disconnect the battery cables and remove the battery.

2. Scribe aligning marks on the hood and hinges to aid in their assembly. Remove the hood.

3. Remove the fan shroud and drain the cooling system.

4. Disconnect both the upper and lower radiator hoses. Disconnect and plug the oil lines from the oil cooler on cars with automatic transmissions.

5. Detach the hose which runs to the thermal expansion tank at the tank. Remove the expansion tank from its mounting bracket.

6. Remove the radiator.

7. Disconnect the heater and bypass hoses from the engine.

8. Disconnect the oil pressure light sender wiring, the alternator multiconnector, and the back-up light switch wiring.

9. Disconnect the power brake unit vacuum lines.

10. Disconnect the engine oil cooler hoses at the oil filter, if so equipped.

11. Disconnect the power steering fluid cooler hose, if so equipped.

12. Remove the air cleaner assembly from its bracket, complete with hoses.

13. Detach the emission control system wires and hoses, as required.

14. Unfasten the distributor primary wire and the high tension wire from the coil.

15. Disconnect the wiring from the starter and temperature gauge sender.

16. Remove the fuel line from the fuel pump.

17. Disconnect the heater control cable from the water valve. Unfasten the heater control vacuum hose.

18. Remove the accelerator linkage from the carburetor. On fuel injected models, disconnect the accelerator linkage from the throttle body. Tag and disconnect any remaining hoses, lines, or wires which may still be attached to the engine.

19. Detach the clutch hydraulic line from its master cylinder connections (manual transmission only). Install a cap on the master cylinder fitting to keep the hydraulic fluid from running out.

20. Detach the pressure-feed lines from the steering gear housing on models equipped with power steering.

21. Raise both the front and the rear of the car with jacks. Support the car with jack stands.

22. Detach the exhaust pipe from the downpipe and remove the exhaust pipe hangers.

23. Disconnect the speedometer cable from the right side of the transmission.

24. On models with manual transmissions:

    a. Remove the center console securing screws, the gearshift knob, the gearshift boot, and then unfasten the console wiring multiconnector. Lift the console over the gearshift lever.

    b. Remove the four screws which attach the shift lever retainer to the shift tower and withdraw the shift lever assembly.

25. On models equipped with an automatic transmission, unfasten the connecting rod swivel nut and detach the control rod from the gear selector lever.

26. Disconnect the parking brake lever rod, return spring, intermediate rod, and the cable from the equalizer.

27. Disconnect the driveshaft from the end of the transmission.

NOTE: If oil runs out from the transmission, an old U-joint yoke makes a good plug.

28. Remove the left-hand gravel shield and then the front engine mounts.

29. Support the transmission with a jack.

30. Remove the rear engine mounts and the rear crossmember.

31. Attach a hoist to the engine and lift it up and forward, so that it clears the car.

32. Installation is in the reverse order of removal. Adjust the transmission and carburetor linkages, as detailed in the appropriate sections. Bleed the clutch as outlined below. Install the hood and adjust it. Replenish the fluid levels.

1A-C, 3A, and 3A-C Engines

1. Disconnect the negative battery terminal.

2. Remove the hood.

3. Remove the air cleaner and all necessary lines attached to it.

4. Drain the radiator.

5. Cover both driveshaft boots with a shop towel.

6. Remove the solenoid valve connector, water temperature switch connector, and the electric fan connector.

7. Remove the exhaust support plate bolts, and the exhaust pipe.

8. Remove the top radiator support.

9. Remove the top and bottom radiator hoses and remove the radiator with the fan.

NOTE: On cars equipped with automatic transmissions remove the cooling lines before removing the radiator.

10. Remove the windshield washer tank.

11. Remove the heater hoses and the lines to the fuel pump.

NOTE: Plug the gas line to prevent gas from leaking out.

12. Remove the accelerator cable, choke cable, and the ground strap.

13. Remove the brake booster vacuum line.

14. Remove the coil wire and unplug the alternator.

15. Remove the clutch release cable.

16. Remove the wires on the starter.

17. Remove the temperature sending and oil pressure switch connectors.

18. Remove the battery ground strap from the block.

19. Jack up your vehicle and support it with jack stands.

20. Remove the engine mounting bolts and the engine shock absorbers.

21. Support the differential with a jack.

22. Remove the transaxle mounting bolts.

NOTE: It is probably easier to remove these bolts from underneath the car.

23. Remove the engine.

24. Tie the bell housing to the cowl to keep support on the transaxle.

NOTE: The grill may be removed if necessary to give better leverage when removing the engine.

25. Installation is the reverse of removal.

Adjust all linkages as covered in the appropriate section. Refill all fluids to the proper levels. Tighten the transaxle bolts 37–57 ft. lbs.

On cars with automatic transmissions, the following procedures are necessary.

1. Remove the starter.

2. Remove the cooling lines from the transmission.

3. Support the transmission with a jack.

4. Remove the transaxle mounting bolts.

5. Remove the torque converter bolts (4).

NOTE: In order to turn the converter, place a wrench on the crankshaft pulley and turn it until you see a bolt appear in the area where the starter was.

6. While the engine is suspended from your hoist, pull it forward about 2 in.

7. Insert a pry bar in this opening and gently separate the torque converter from the engine.

8. Installation is the reverse of removal.

The following are necessary before the cylinder head can be installed. Confirm that the converter contact surface is 1.02 in. from the housing. Install a guide bolt in one of the mounting bolt holes. Remove the engine mounting insulator (left side) and the mounting bracket (right side). To secure the transaxle to the engine temporarily install the top two mounting bolts. This will facilitate easier engine installation.

Cylinder Head

---- CAUTION ----

Do not perform this operation on a warm engine. Remove the head bolts in the sequence and in several steps. Loosen the head bolts evenly, not one at a time. Keep the pushrods in their original order. Do not attempt to slide the cylinder head off of the block, as it is located with dowel pins. Lift the head straight up and off the block.

REMOVAL AND INSTALLATION

3K-C and 4K-C Engines

1. Disconnect the battery and drain the cooling system.

2. Remove the air cleaner assembly from its bracket, complete with its attendant hoses.

3. Disconnect the hoses from the air injection system or the vacuum switching valve lines.

4. Detach the accelerator cable from its support on the cylinder head cover and also from the carburetor throttle arm.

5. Remove the choke cable and fuel lines from the carburetor.

6. Remove the water hose bracket from the cylinder head cover.

7. Unfasten the water hose clamps and remove the hoses from the water pump and the water valve. Detach the heater temperature control cable from the water valve.

8. Disconnect the PCV line from the cylinder head cover.

9. Unbolt and remove the valve cover.

10. Remove the valve rocker support securing bolts and nuts. Lift out the valve rocker assembly.

11. Withdraw the pushrods from their bores.

12. Unfasten the hose clamps and remove the upper radiator hose from the water outlet.

13. Remove the wires from the spark plugs.

14. Disconnect the wiring and the fluid line from the windshield washer assembly. Remove the assembly.

NOTE: Use a clean container to catch the fluid from the windshield washer reservoir when disconnecting its fluid line.

15. Unfasten the exhaust pipe flange from the exhaust manifold.

16. Remove the head assembly retaining bolts and remove the head from the engine.

17. Place the cylinder head on *wooden* blocks to prevent damage to it.

Installation is essentially the reverse order of removal. Clean both the cylinder head and block gasket mounting surfaces. Always use a new head gasket.

NOTE: Be sure that the top side of the gasket is facing upward.

When installing the head on the block, be sure to tighten the bolts in the sequence shown (see "Torque Sequences"), in several stages, to the specified torque.

The valve rocker assembly nuts and bolts should be tightened to 13–16 ft. lbs.

NOTE: The valve clearance should be adjusted to specification with each piston at top dead center (TDC) of its compression stroke.

2T-C and 3T-C Engines

1. Perform Steps 1–2 of 3K-C and 4K-C head removal procedure.

2. Disconnect the vacuum lines which run from the vacuum switching valve to the various emission control devices mounted on the cylinder head.

3. Disconnect the mixture control valve hose which runs to the intake manifold and remove the valve from its mounting bracket.

4. Perform Step 7 of the 3K-C and 4K-C head removal procedure.

5. Detach the water temperature sender wiring.

6. Remove the choke stove pipe and its intake pipe.

7. Remove the PCV hose from the intake manifold.

8. Disconnect the fuel and vacuum lines from the carburetor.

9. Remove the clutch hydraulic line bracket from the cylinder head.

10. Raise the car and support it with jack stands. Unfasten the exhaust pipe clamp. Remove the exhaust manifold from the cylinder head.

1. Oil filler cap
2. Valve cover
3. Valve cover gasket
4. Valve guide (intake)
5. Cylinder head
6. Cylinder head gasket
7. Nut
8. Screw plug
9. Cylinder head rear cover
10. Stud
11. Valve rocker support
12. Valve rocker support
13. Valve rocker arm
14. Washer
15. Valve rocker support
16. Bolt
17. Retainer spring
18. Pushrod
19. Valve lifter
20. Intake valve
21. Compression spring
22. Valve rocker arm
23. Valve rocker shaft
24. Pushrod
25. Lock spring
26. O-ring
27. Valve spring retainer
28. Oil splash shield
29. Compression spring
30. Plate washer
31. Exhaust valve

"T" series engine—cylinder head and related components

11. Remove the valve cover.
12. Remove the cylinder head bolts in the sequence illustrated under "Torque Sequences."
13. Perform Steps 10–11 of the 3K-C and 4K-C "Cylinder Head Removal" procedure.
14. Remove the cylinder head, complete with the intake manifold.
15. Separate the intake manifold from the cylinder head.

Install the cylinder head in the following order:

1. Clean the gasket mounting surfaces of the cylinder head and the block completely.

NOTE: Remove oil from the cylinder head bolt holes if present.

2. Place a *new* gasket on the block and install the head assembly.

3. Install the pushrods and the valve rocker assembly.
4. Tighten the cylinder head bolts *evenly*, in stages, as illustrated in the "Torque Sequence" diagrams. See the "Torque Specifications" chart for the proper tightening torque.
5. Install the intake manifold, using a new gasket and tighten it to specifications.
6. The rest of the installation procedure is the reverse of removal. Adjust the valve clearances.

20R and 22R Engines

1. Disconnect the battery.
2. Remove the three exhaust pipe flange nuts and separate the pipe from the manifold.
3. Drain the engine oil.
4. Drain the cooling system (both ra-

diator and block). Save the coolant to be reused.
5. Remove the air cleaner, complete with hoses, from the carburetor.

NOTE: Cover the carburetor with a clean rag so that nothing can fall into it.

6. Mark all vacuum hoses to aid installation, and disconnect them. Remove all linkages, fuel lines, etc. from the carburetor, cylinder head, and manifolds. Remove the wire supports.
7. Mark the spark plug leads and disconnect them from the plugs.
8. If so equipped, disconnect and move the air injection system hoses. Mark the hose locations so that they may be properly reinstalled.
9. If equipped with air conditioning, remove the upper compressor mounting bracket.
10. If equipped with power steering, dismount the power steering pump and move it out of the way, WITHOUT disconnecting the hydraulic lines.
11. Matchmark the distributor housing and block. Disconnect the primary lead and remove the distributor. Installation will be easier if you leave the cap leads in place.
12. Remove the valve cover.
13. Using a wrench on the crankshaft pulley, rotate the crankshaft until the No. 1 cylinder is at TDC on its compression stroke (both valves of the No. 1 cylinder—closed).
14. Place matchmarks on both the camshaft sprocket and the timing chain to indicate the relationship between these items.
15. Remove the rubber camshaft seals. Use a 19 mm wrench to remove cam sprocket bolt. Slide the distributor drive gear off of the cam and wire the cam sprocket in place.
16. Remove the timing chain cover 14 mm bolt at the front of the head. This must be done before the head bolts are removed.
17. Remove the cylinder head bolts in the order shown under "Torque Sequences." Improper removal could cause head damage.
18. Using pry bars applied evenly at the front and the rear of the valve rocker assembly, pry the assembly off of its mounting dowels.
19. Lift the head off of its dowels. DO NOT pry it off. Support the head on a workbench.
20. Drain the engine oil from the crankcase *after* the head has been removed, because the oil will become contaminated with coolant while the head is being removed.

Installation is in the following order:

1. Apply liquid sealer to the front corners of the block and install the head gasket.
2. Lower the head over the locating dowels. Do not attempt to slide it into place.
3. Install the rocker arm assembly over its positioning dowels.
4. Tighten the cylinder head bolts evenly, in three stages, and in order to 52–63 ft. lbs.

5. Install the timing chain cover bolt and tighten it to 7–11 ft. lbs.

6. Remove the wire and install the sprocket over the camshaft dowel. If the chain won't allow the sprocket to reach, rotate the crankshaft bolt to 51–65 ft. lbs.

8. Set the no. 1 piston at TDC of its compression stroke and adjust the valves.

9. After completing valve adjustment, rotate the crankshaft one turn, so that 8°-BTDC mark on the pulley aligns with the pointer.

10. Install the distributor, as previously outlined.

11. Install the spark plugs and leads.

12. Make sure that the oil drain plug is installed. Fill the engine with oil after installing the rubber cam seals. Pour the oil over the distributor drive gear and the valve rockers.

13. Install the rocker cover and tighten the bolts to 8–11 ft. lbs.

14. Connect all the vacuum hoses and electrical leads that were removed during disassembly. Install the spark plug lead supports. Fill the cooling system. Install the air cleaner.

15. Tighten the exhaust pipe to manifold flange bolts to 25–33 ft. lbs.

16. Mount and/or reattach the air injection, air conditioning, and power steering items, as equipped.

17. Reconnect the battery. Start the engine and allow it to reach normal operating temperature. Check and adjust the timing and valve clearance. Adjust the idle speed and mixture. Road test the vehicle.

4M, 4M-E, and 5M-E Engines

NOTE: The engine must be cold before performing this operation.

CARBURETED ENGINES

1. Disconnect the battery cables from the battery.

2. Remove the air cleaner assembly and mounting brackets, complete with attached hoses. Mark the hoses so that they may be correctly attached during installation.

3. Mark and disconnect the hoses from the air injection system and the vacuum switching valve, if so equipped.

4. Disconnect the following items:

a. Accelerator cable—from both the support on the cylinder head and the throttle arm. If so equipped, also disconnect the automatic transmission linkage connected to the carburetor and the intake manifold.

b. Water hoses—upper and lower from the engine, and from the heater control valve.

c. Control cable—heater valve control.

d. PCV valve—hose to the cylinder head cover.

e. Fuel lines—to the carburetor.

f. Choke lines—lines and/or hoses to the choke.

g. Other—disconnect all other vac-

uum lines, hoses, and electrical connectors that are attached to the intake manifold. Mark the items for proper reconnection during assembly.

5. Loosen the intake manifold mounting fasteners, working from the outer fasteners, towards the center. Remove the intake manifold and carburetor as an assembly.

FUEL INJECTED ENGINES

6. Disconnect the battery cables at the battery and drain the entire cooling system. Remove the radiator and heater hoses attached to the cylinder head or manifolds.

7. Using the accompanying illustration as a guide, disconnect or remove the parts in the numerical order shown.

── CAUTION ──
The fuel system is under pressure.

8. Remove the intake air chamber (manifold) fasteners, working from the outer fasteners towards the center. Remove the chamber and injector as a unit.

ALL ENGINES

9. Remove the spark plug wires from their supports on the cylinder head cover and from the spark plugs themselves.

10. Remove the distributor assembly.

11. Remove the exhaust manifold and the oil pressure light sender.

12. Unfasten the retaining bolts and remove the valve cover assembly.

NOTE: Place a cloth over the timing gear to prevent anything from falling into the timing gear cover.

13. Turn the engine so that the No. 1 piston is at TDC on its compression stroke (both valves closed).

14. Remove the timing chain tensioner.

NOTE: The matchmarks on the timing chain and gear should now be aligned.

15. Straighten out the lockplate and unfasten the timing gear retaining bolt (left-hand thread). Withdraw the timing gear from the camshaft.

16. Loosen and remove the rocker arm shaft mounting bolts. Loosen the bolt in two or three stages. Remove the rocker arm shaft assembly.

17. Remove the camshaft bearing caps (keep them in order) and lift the camshaft off of the head.

18. In two or three stages, loosen then remove the cylinder head bolts in the reverse order of the installation torque sequence. Lift the cylinder head off of the engine block.

1. Hose	10. Hose	18. Throttle wire for A/T
2. Hose	11. Water hose	19. Ground wire
3. Hose (for PCV)	12. Water hose	20. Hose
4. Hose	13. Hose	21. Air intake chamber
5. Hose	14. Intake air connector	
6. Hose (for Idle-up)	15. Cold start injector w/ gasket	
7. Wiring	16. EGR pipe	
8. Hose	17. Throttle link	
9. Hose		

Before removing the cylinder head from 4M-E and 5M-E engines, remove the hoses in the order indicated

Installation is performed in the following manner: Prior to installation, thoroughly clean the cylinder block and head mating surfaces. Refer to the Unit Repair section for details on checking the head and block for flatness, and other services which may be necessary.

1. If compressed air is available, blow out the cylinder head mounting bolt holes. If compressed air is not available, make sure that the holes are clean and free of water.

2. Use a liquid sealer around the oil and water holes of both the head and the block, and on the timing cover upper surfaces. *Be careful not to get sealer in the passages or in the mounting holes.*

3. Place a new head gasket on the engine block and lower the cylinder head into position.

4. Using the proper sequence, tighten the cylinder head bolts in two or three stages to specifications (refer to the ''Torque Specifications'' chart).

5. Install the lower camshaft bearing halves, if previously removed. Install the camshaft and the bearing caps. Tighten the bearing cap fasteners to 12–17 ft. lbs.

NOTE: Camshaft bearing oil clearance may be checked in the same manner as the crankshaft and connecting rod oil clearance. Refer to the Unit Repair section for information concerning the use of Plastigage®.

6. Install the rocker arm shaft assembly. Tighten the mounting bolts to 12–17 ft. lbs., in sequence and in two or three stages.

7. Make sure the engine has not been turned from no. 1 (cylinder) TDC. The crankshaft pulley should have its ''V'' notch aligned with the zero mark on the timing cover scale.

8. Align the ''V'' notch on the camshaft pulley with the 5/32 in. hole on the no. 1 camshaft bearing cap; or align the pin on the camshaft flange with the embossed pointer on the no. 1 rocker shaft support.

9. Install the timing chain (marked link UP) on the camshaft gear (mark on gear aligned with marked link). Then attach the gear and chain unit to the front of the camshaft.

10. Install the timing gear-to-camshaft bolt (left hand thread) with the locking tab. Tighten the bolt to 47–54 ft. lbs.

11. Install the timing chain tensioner. Tighten to 22–29 ft. lbs.

12. Turn the crankshaft two complete revolutions. If, at the end of the two revolutions, the timing marks do not align, repeat Steps 7 through 11. If they still will not align, see Step 14.

13. Adjust the timing chain tensioner. Turn the crankshaft in the regular direction until there is a maximum amount of slack in the chain. Loosen the locknut on the tensioner and turn the screw clockwise until resistance is felt. Loosen the screw two turns and tighten the locknut.

NOTE: If the timing marks do not align after once again turning the engine two complete revolutions the chain could be stretched. Toyota has provided other pin holes in the cam gear to correct this problem.

14. If the crankshaft pulley notch will not align with the zero mark while the cam gear and chain are aligned with the rocker arm support. Remove and reposition the cam gear to the second pin hole position. Recheck crankshaft timing marks.

15. Adjust the valve clearance to the following cold specifications:
Intake—0.006 in.
Exhaust—0.008 in.

16. The rest of the cylinder head installation is in the reverse order of removal.

NOTE: Before starting the engine, change the motor oil. The old oil could be contaminated from coolant.

5M-GE Engines

1. Disconnect the battery cables at the battery.

2. Drain the cooling system.

3. Disconnect the following hoses:
   a. Air valve hose—from the air intake connector.
   b. Air valve hose—from the air intake chamber.
   c. Water bypass hoses—from the throttle body.
   d. PCV hoses (2)—from the cylinder head covers.
   e. Fuel hose—from the fuel hose support.
   f. Other—Mark (for installation) and disconnect any emission control hoses from the throttle body and air intake chamber to gain access to the cylinder head (and the throttle body hose).

4. Disconnect the air intake connector from the throttle body.

5. Disconnect the line routing brackets from the air intake chamber.

6. Remove the vacuum pipe assembly from beneath the air intake chamber.

7. Remove the ignition distributor as previously outlined.

8. Remove the spark plugs from the cylinder head.

9. Loosen the nut of the EGR pipe and remove the EGR cooler and gasket (six bolts).

10. Disconnect the following wiring:
   a. Cold start injector
   b. Water temperature sensor
   c. Start injection time switch
   d. Water temperature sending unit
   e. Throttle position sensor

11. Disconnect the cold start fuel hose from the delivery pipe.

12. Remove the air intake chamber and gasket from the intake manifold (five bolts and two nuts).

13. Remove the pulsation damper and the no. 1 fuel pipe.

14. Remove the coolant outlet housing (two bolts).

15. Remove the intake manifold and gasket (eight bolts and two nuts).

16. Loosen the power steering pump mounting bolts and remove the drive belt. Remove the pump mounting bolts. Dismount the pump and move it out of the way, WITHOUT disconnecting the hydraulic lines.

17. Remove the two exhaust manifold heat insulators (five nuts). Remove the exhaust manifold (seven nuts).

18. Rotate the crankshaft to set the no. 1 cylinder at top dead center at its compression stroke.

19. Remove the upper front timing belt cover and gasket (five bolts).

20. Loosen the timing belt idler pulley bolt and lever the pulley towards the alternator side, to relieve the tension on the timing belt. Finger-tighten the idler pulley bolt.

25. Remove the timing belt from the camshaft timing pulleys.

26. Remove the camshaft timing pulleys as follows:
   a. Hold the pulleys stationary with a spanner wrench.
   b. Remove the center pulley bolt.

— CAUTION —

DO NOT attempt to use timing belt tension as a tool to remove the center pulley bolts, as the belt could become damaged.

NOTE: Do not interchange the intake and exhaust timing pulleys, as they differ for use with each camshaft.

27. Remove the oil pressure regulator and gasket (located behind the upper, inner timing belt cover).

28. Remove the upper, inner timing belt cover and gasket (three bolts and two nuts).

29. In two or three stages, remove the cylinder head mounting bolts in the reverse order of the installation torque sequence.

30. CAREFULLY remove the cylinder head assembly from the block. If the cylinder head sticks to the block, gently pry between the head and the block to break it loose. After removal, set the cylinder head on wooden blocks (one at each end of the head).

— CAUTION —

Be careful not to nick, scratch, or otherwise damage the cylinder head mating surfaces. To remove each camshaft housing (with camshaft), remove the housing bolts in the reverse order shown in the accompanying torque sequence.

31. Installation is performed in the reverse of the previous steps. Be sure to follow the cylinder head bolt tightening sequence after installing the head bolts.

1A-C, 3A and 3A-C

1. Disconnect the negative battery terminal.

Head Cover (EX Side)

Camshaft Housing (EX Side)

Oil Seal

Gasket

Oil Seal

Head Cover (IN Side)

Camshaft Housing (IN Side)

Gasket

Lash Adjuster

Rocker Arm

Valve Keeper

Valve Spring

Valve Stem Oil Seal

Valve Spring Seat

Valve

Camshaft (EX Side)

Camshaft (IN Side)

Head Bolt

Cylinder Head

Head Gasket

Cylinder head and related components—5M-GE engine

5M-GE engines—camshaft housing bolt torque sequence

2. Remove the exhaust pipe from the manifold.

3. Drain the cooling system. Save the coolant as it can be reused.

4. Remove the air cleaner and all necessary hoses.

5. Mark all vacuum lines for easy installation and then remove them.

6. Remove all linkage from the carburetor, fuel lines, etc. from the head and manifold.

7. Remove the fuel pump.

NOTE: Before removing the carburetor cover it with a clean rag to prevent dirt from entering it.

8. Remove the carburetor.

9. Remove the manifold.

10. Remove the valve cover.

11. Note the position of the spark plug wires and remove them.

12. Remove the spark plugs.

13. Set the engine on No. 1 cylinder—top dead center. This is accomplished by removing the No. 1 spark plug, placing your finger over the hole and then turning the crankshaft pulley until you feel pressure exerted against your finger.

───── **CAUTION** ─────
Do not put your finger into the spark plug hole.

14. Remove the crankshaft pulley with an appropriate puller.

15. Remove the water pump pulley.

16. Remove the top and bottom timing chain cover.

17. Matchmark the camshaft pulley and timing belt for reassembly.

18. Loosen the belt tensioner.

19. Remove the water pump.

20. Remove the timing belt. Do not bend, twist, or turn the belt inside out.

NOTE: Check the belt for wear, cracks, or glazing. Once the belt is removed it is a good idea to replace it with a new one even though it is not necessary.

21. Remove the rocker arm bolts and remove the rocker arms.

22. Remove the camshaft pulley by holding the camshaft with a pair of channel lock pliers and removing the belt in the pulley end of the shaft.

NOTE: Do not hold the cam on the lobes, as damage will result.

23. Remove the camshaft seal.

24. Remove the camshaft bearing caps and set them down in the order they appear on the engine.

25. Remove the camshaft.

26. Loosen the head bolts in the proper order to prevent warping of the head.

27. Lift the head directly up. Do not attempt to slide it off.

28. Installation is the reverse of removal.

NOTE: When replacing the head always use a new gasket. Also replace the camshaft seal, making sure to grease the lip before installation.

The following torques are needed for installation: cam bearing caps 8–10 ft. lbs., cam sprocket 29–39 ft. lbs., crankshaft pulley 55–61 ft. lbs., manifold bolts 15–21 ft.

lbs., rocker arm bolts 17–19 ft. lbs., timing gear idler bolt 22–32 ft. lbs., belt tension 0.24–0.28 in. Adjust the valves to the proper clearances.

OVERHAUL

NOTE: General cylinder head overhaul procedures are given in the "Engine Rebuilding" section.

Rocker Arm Shafts

REMOVAL AND INSTALLATION

3K-C and 4K-C Engines

1. Remove air cleaner.
2. Remove PCV valve.
3. Remove spark plug wires.
4. Remove valve cover.
5. Loosen rocker shaft bolts, alternating front to rear.
6. Remove shaft assembly and oil tube.
7. Install in reverse of removal. Torque bolts in alternating, front to rear sequence, to 14–16 ft. lbs. Torque oil pipe bolts to 14 ft. lbs. Check valve clearance.

4M, 4M-E, and 5M-E Engines

1. Remove the air cleaner assembly.
2. Remove the choke stove outlet and inlet hose.
3. Remove the valve cover.
4. Remove the two front clamp bolts.
5. Loosen the rocker arm shaft bolts in a rotating order starting at the ends and working toward the center.
6. Remove bolts and lift off rocker shaft assemblies.
7. Install in reverse of removal. Tighten rocker shaft bolts, in a rotating order from the center to the ends, to 25 ft. lbs. Torque the front end clamp bolts to 9 ft. lbs. Check valve clearance.

2T-C and 3T-C Engines

1. Remove the air cleaner.
2. Remove the PCV valve.
3. Remove the spark plug wires.
4. Disconnect the fuel inlet from the carburetor.
5. Remove the valve cover.

NOTE: The cylinder head bolts also serve as the rocker arm shaft bolts. Remove these a little at a time in circular rotation from the ends toward the center.

6. Lift off the shaft assemblies.
7. Install the reverse of removal. Install and tighten the cylinder head bolts in a circular rotation from the center toward the ends. Torque to 63 ft. lbs. Check valve clearance.

20R and 22R Engines

1. Remove the air cleaner.

2. Disconnect all hoses and linkage clipped to the valve cover.
3. Remove the spark plug wires.
4. Remove the carburetor.
5. Remove the valve cover.
6. Remove the distributor.
7. Set the No. 1 piston at TDC of the compression stroke.
8. Paint mating marks on the timing chain and sprocket, and drive gear.
9. Remove the distributor drive gear, leaving the chain and sprocket in position.
10. Remove the one 14 mm chain cover bolt in the front of the head. This must be done before the head bolts, which also serve as rocker shaft bolts, are removed.
11. Remove the head bolts in a diagonal pattern. Start at the front carburetor side. This must be done to prevent head warpage.
12. Remove the shaft assemblies from the head. It may be necessary to use a pry bar to evenly lift the assemblies from the dowels.
13. Install in reverse of removal. Torque the head bolts in a diagonal pattern, starting at the center. Tighten in three equal stages to 64 ft. lbs. Torque the chain cover bolt to 12 ft. lbs. Torque drive gear bolt to 65 ft. lbs.

1A-C, 3A, 3A-C

1. Disconnect the negative battery terminal.
2. Remove the air cleaner and all necessary hoses.
3. Remove all the linkage from the carburetor.
4. Remove the valve cover and gasket.
5. Remove the rocker arm bolts.
6. Installation is the reverse of removal.

NOTE: Remember to install a new valve cover gasket before replacing the valve cover.

7. Tighten the rocker arm bolt 17–19 ft. lbs.

Intake Manifold

REMOVAL AND INSTALLATION

2T-C and 3T-C Engines

1. Drain the cooling system.
2. Remove the air cleaner assembly, complete with hoses, from its bracket.
3. Remove the choke stove hoses, fuel lines, and vacuum lines from the carburetor. Unfasten the emission control system hoses and the accelerator linkage from it.
4. Unfasten the four nuts which secure the carburetor to the manifold and remove the carburetor.
5. Disconnect the PCV hose.
6. Disconnect the water bypass hose from the intake manifold.
7. Unbolt and remove the manifold.

Installation is performed in the reverse order of removal. Remember to use *new* gaskets. Tighten the intake manifold bolts to specifications.

NOTE: Tighten the bolts, in several stages, working from the inside out.

20R and 22R Engines

1. Disconnect the battery.
2. Drain the cooling system.
3. Remove the air cleaner, complete with hoses, from the carburetor.
4. Disconnect the vacuum lines from the EGR valve and carburetor. Mark them first, to aid in installation.
5. Remove the fuel lines, electrical leads, accelerator linkage, and water hose from the carburetor.
6. Remove the water by-pass hose from the manifold.

1. Choke stove intake hose	4. Intake manifold	7. Choke stove outlet
2. Elbow	5. Gasket	8. Plug
3. Choke stove intake	6. Water by-pass outlet	9. Intake manifold gasket

Intake manifold of the "T" series engine—typical

1. Vacuum hose fitting
2. Intake manifold
3. Gasket (to head)
4. Gasket (bottom)
5. Bottom cover

Intake manifold of the "R" series engine—typical

7. Unbolt and remove the intake manifold, complete with carburetor and EGR valve.

8. Cover the cylinder head ports with clean rags to keep anything from falling into the cylinder head or block.

Installation is the reverse of removal. Replace the gasket with a new one. Torque the mounting bolts to specifications. Tighten the bolts in several stages working from the inside bolts outward. Refill the cooling system.

4M Engines

1. Drain the cooling system.
2. Remove the air cleaner assembly, complete with hoses, from its mounting bracket.
3. Remove the distributor cap.
4. Remove the upper radiator hose from the elbow.
5. Remove the wiring from the temperature gauge sending unit.
6. Remove the following from the carburetor: fuel lines; vacuum line; choke stove hoses; emission control system hoses; accelerator torque rod; and automatic transmission linkage (if so equipped).
7. Remove the emission control system lines and wiring from the manifold when equipped with a vacuum switching valve. Remove the EGR pipe from the intake manifold.
8. Remove the water bypass hose from the manifold.
9. Unbolt and remove the manifold, complete with the carburetor.
10. Installation is in the reverse order of removal. Remember to replace the gaskets with new ones. Torque the mounting bolts to specifications.

NOTE: Tighten the bolts, in stages, working from the inside out.

4M-E, 5M-E and 5M-GE Engines

AIR INTAKE CHAMBER

1. Disconnect the battery cables at the battery.
2. Drain the engine coolant from the radiator.
3. Refer to the numbered illustration with the "Cylinder Head Removal and Installation" procedure (for these engines) and remove/disconnect parts in the same order. Mark the items so that they may be properly reinstalled.

4. Unbolt and remove the air intake chamber.

5. Installation is performed in the reverse of the previous steps. During installation, torque the air intake chamber fasteners to 16–20 ft. lbs.

AIR INTAKE MANIFOLD

1. Remove the air intake chamber as previously outlined.
2. Disconnect and move the wiring away from the fuel delivery and injector pipe.
3. Remove the fuel injector and delivery pipe (four bolts).

—————— CAUTION ——————
Place a container under the pipe—a large amount of fuel will be released as the pipe is removed.

4. Remove the fuel pressure regulator (mounted on the center of the intake manifold).
5. Remove the EGR valve from the rear of the manifold.
6. Mark and disconnect the radiator hoses, heater hoses, and vacuum lines from the intake manifold.
7. Unlatch the distributor cap and move it out of the way.
8. Unbolt and remove the intake manifold and gasket.
9. Installation is performed in the reverse of the previous steps. During installation, torque the manifold fasteners to 10–15 ft. lbs.

NOTE: ALWAYS use a new gasket when installing the manifold assembly.

1. Automatic choke stove intake pipe
2. Automatic choke stove intake hose
3. Automatic choke stove outlet pipe
4. Carburetor heat insulator
5. Exhaust manifold
6. Water by-pass line
7. Water by-pass hose
8. Water hose joint
9. Exhaust manifold gasket
10. Intake manifold gasket (1)
11. Intake manifold gasket (2)
12. Intake manifold
13. Gasket
14. Water by-pass outlet

Intake and exhaust manifolds of the 4M engine

1. Fuel hose
2. Fuel return hose
3. Fuel pipe
4. Delivery pipe and injector
5. Pressure regulator
6. Intake manifold
7. Throttle body
8. Cold start injector
9. Air intake chamber

Fuel injected models—air intake chamber, manifold and related parts (typical)

Exhaust Manifold

REMOVAL AND INSTALLATION

> **CAUTION**
> *Do not perform this operation on a warm or hot engine.*

2T-C and 3T-C Engines

1. Detach the manifold heat stove intake pipe.
2. Unfasten the nut on the stove outlet pipe union.
3. Remove the wiring from the emission control system thermosensor.
4. Unfasten the U-bolt from the downpipe bracket.
5. Unfasten the downpipe flange from the manifold.
6. In order to remove the manifold, unfasten the manifold retaining bolts.

> **CAUTION**
> *Remove the bolts in two or three stages, working from the inside out.*

7. Installation of the manifold is performed in the reverse order of removal. Remember to use a *new* gasket.

20R and 22R Engine

1. Remove the three exhaust pipe flange bolts and disconnect the exhaust pipe from the manifold.
2. Disconnect the spark plug leads.
3. Matchmark the distributor rotor, housing and the engine block. Remove the distributor.

4. Remove the air cleaner tube from the heat stove. Remove the outer part of the heat stove.
5. Remove the manifold (14 mm nuts), complete with air injection tubes and the inner portion of the heat stove.
6. Separate the inner portion of the heat stove from the manifold.
7. Installation is the reverse of removal. Tighten the retaining nuts to 29–36 ft. lbs. working from the inside out. Install the distributor and set the timing. Tighten the exhaust pipe flange nuts to 25–32 ft. lbs.

"M" Series Engines

1. Raise the front and the rear of the car and support it with jack stands.
2. Remove the right-hand gravel shield from beneath the engine.
3. Remove the downpipe support bracket.
4. Unfasten the bolts from the flange and detach the downpipe from the manifold.
5. Remove the automatic choke and air cleaner stove hoses from the exhaust manifold. Remove the EGR valve, if so equipped.
6. Remove, or move aside, any of the air injection system components which may be in the way when removing the manifold.
7. In order to remove the manifold, unfasten the manifold retaining bolts.

> **CAUTION**
> *Remove and tighten the bolts in two or three stages, starting from the inside, working out.*

8. Installation is performed in the reverse order of removal. Always use a new gasket. Tighten the retaining bolts to specifications in two or three stages.

1. Heat insulator
2. Exhaust manifold
3. Gasket
4. Gasket
5. Manifold heat stove

Exhaust manifold of the "R" series engine—typical

Combination Manifold

REMOVAL AND INSTALLATION

———— **CAUTION** ————

Do not perform this procedure on a warm engine.

3K-C and 4K-C Engines

1. Remove the air cleaner assembly, complete with hoses.
2. Disconnect the accelerator and choke linkages from the carburetor, as well as the fuel and vacuum lines.
3. Remove, or move aside, any of the emission control system components which are in the way.
4. Unfasten the retaining bolts and remove the carburetor from the manifold.
5. Loosen the manifold retaining nuts, working from the inside out, in two or three stages.
6. Remove the intake/exhaust manifold assembly from the cylinder head as a complete unit.
7. Installation is performed in the reverse order of removal. Always use *new* gaskets. Tighten the bolts, working from the inside out.

NOTE: Tighten the bolts in two or three stages.

1A-C, 3A, and 3A-C Engines

1. Disconnect the negative battery terminal.
2. Remove the air cleaner and all necessary hoses.
3. Remove all the carburetor linkages.
4. Remove the carburetor.

NOTE: Cover the carburetor with a clean towel to prevent dirt from entering it.

5. Remove the exhaust manifold pipe.
6. Remove the exhaust manifold.
7. Installation is the reverse of removal. Tighten the manifold bolts to 15–21 ft. lbs.

Timing Cover

REMOVAL AND INSTALLATION

"K" and "T" Series Engines

1. Drain the cooling system and the crankcase.
2. Disconnect the battery.
3. Remove the air cleaner assembly, complete with hoses, from its bracket.
4. Remove the hood latch as well as its brace and support.
5. Remove the headlight bezels and grille assembly.
6. Unfasten the upper and lower radia-

tor hose clamps and remove both of the hoses from the engine.
7. Unfasten the radiator securing bolts and remove the radiator.

NOTE: Take off the shroud first, if so equipped.

8. Loosen the drive belt adjusting link and remove the drive belt. Unfasten the alternator multiconnector, withdraw the retaining bolts, and remove the alternator.
9. Perform Step 8 to the air injection pump, if so equipped. Disconnect the hoses from the pump before removing it.
10. Remove the fan and water pump as an assembly.
11. Unfasten the crankshaft pulley retaining bolt. Remove the crankshaft pulley with a gear puller.
12. Remove the gravel shield from underneath the engine.
13. The following steps apply to "K" engines only:
    a. Remove the nuts and washers from both the right and left front engine mounts.
    b. Detach the exhaust pipe flange from the exhaust manifold.
    c. Slightly raise the front of the engine.
14. On "T" engines, remove the right-hand brace plate.
15. Remove the front oil pan bolts, to gain access to the bottom of the timing chain cover.

NOTE: It may be necessary to insert a thin knife between the pan and the gasket in order to break the pan loose. Use care not to damage the gasket.

Installation is basically the reverse order of removal. There are, however, several points to remember:
1. Apply sealer to the two front corners of the "T" engine's oil pan gasket.
2. Tighten the crankshaft pulley to specifications.
3. Adjust the drive belts.

"R" and "M" Series Engines

EXCEPT 5M-GE ENGINE

1. Perform the cylinder head removal procedure as detailed in the appropriate section.
2. Remove the radiator.
3. Remove the alternator.
4. On engines equipped with air pumps, unfasten the adjusting link bolts and the drive belt. Remove the hoses from the pump; remove the pump and bracket from the engine.

NOTE: If the car is equipped with power steering see the appropriate section for its pump removal procedure.

5. Remove the fan and water pump as a complete assembly.

———— **CAUTION** ————

To prevent the fluid from running out from the fan coupling, do not tip the assembly over on its side.

6. Unfasten the crankshaft pulley securing bolts and remove the pulley with a gear puller.

———— **CAUTION** ————

Do not remove the 10 mm bolt from its hole, if installed, as it is used for balancing.

7. Loosen the bolts which secure the front of the oil pan, after draining the engine oil. Lower the front of the oil pan.
8. Remove the bolts which secure the timing chain cover. Withdraw the cover.

Installation is performed in the reverse order of removal. Apply sealer to the gaskets for both the timing chain cover and the oil pan.

NOTE: "M" engines use two gaskets on the timing chain cover.

Tighten the timing chain cover bolts to the specifications below:
"R" series engines:
All bolts—8–11 ft. lbs.
"M" series engines:
8 mm bolts—7–12 ft. lbs.
10 mm bolts—14–22 ft. lbs.

5M-GE ENGINES

The 5M-GE engine uses three timing belt covers: front upper, front lower, and rear upper. To gain access to the timing belt, only the front covers need to be removed. Refer to the following "Timing Belt Removal and Installation" procedure to remove these covers.

1A-C, 3A, and 3A-C Engines

1. Disconnect the negative battery terminal.
2. Remove all the drive belts.
3. Bring the engine to the top dead center timing position. See the "Cylinder Head Removal" section.
4. Remove the crankshaft pulley with a suitable puller.
5. Remove the water pump pulley.
6. Remove the upper and lower timing case covers.
7. Installation is the reverse of removal.
Tighten the timing belt cover to 61–99 in. lbs.

Timing Cover Oil Seal Replacement

All Engines (Except 1A-C, 3A, and 3A-C)

1. Remove the timing cover, as detailed in the appropriate section above.
2. Inspect the oil seal for signs of wear, leakage, or damage.
3. If worn, pry the old oil seal out, using a large flat-bladed screwdriver. Remove it toward the *front* of the cover.

NOTE: Once the oil seal has been removed, it must be replaced.

4. Use a socket, pipe, or block of wood and a hammer to drive the oil seal into place. Work from the *front* of the cover.

——— CAUTION ———
Be extremely careful not to damage the seal.

5. Install the timing cover as outlined above.

Timing Chain (or Belt) and Tensioner

REMOVAL AND INSTALLATION

1A-C, 3A, and 3A-C Engines

1. Remove the crankshaft and water pump pulleys.
2. Remove the top and bottom timing covers.
3. Remove the belt tensioner.
4. Matchmark the belt and camshaft gear for easy reinstallation.
5. Remove the timing belt.

"A" series engines—timing marks aligned for proper installation

NOTE: Do not bend, twist, or turn the belt inside out. Do not allow grease or water to come in contact with it.

6. Check for damaged teeth, cracks, or excessive wear. If the belt shows any of the problems it should be replaced.
7. Installation is the reverse of removal.
The following torque specifications are needed: crankshaft pulley 55–61 ft. lbs., camshaft pulley 29–39 ft. lbs., timing belt tension 0.24–0.28 in.

3K-C and 4K-C Engines

1. Remove the timing cover.
2. Unbolt and remove the chain tensioners.
3. Remove the camshaft chain sprocket and then the chain itself.
4. Check the timing chain for wear, cracks, or loose links.
5. Secure one end of the chain to a

fixed hook and pull on the other end with a spring scale. When the scale indicates 11 lbs., the chains should be no longer than 10.7 in. Replace the chain if it exceeds this specification.

"K" and "T" series engines—measure the timing chain stretch between the arrows as indicated

Installation is in the following order:
1. Install the crankshaft chain sprocket. Align the sprocket 0-mark with the straight pin on the crankshaft.
2. Fit the timing chain on the crankshaft sprocket.
3. Align the mating marks on the timing chain with the 0-marks on both sprockets, as illustrated.
4. Align the camshaft sprocket 0-mark with the one on the crankshaft.
5. Tighten the camshaft timing sprocket securing bolt to 16–22 ft. lbs.
6. Install the chain tensioner assembly and chain vibration damper. Tighten their bolts to 4–6 ft. lbs.
7. Install the timing chain cover as detailed above.

2T-C and 3T-C Engine

1. Perform Steps 1–3 of the 3K-C and 4K-C timing chain removal procedure.
2. Perform Steps 4–5 of the 3K-C and 4K-C timing chain removal procedure (chain inspection). The chain should stretch no more than 11.47 in. at 11 lbs. on the spring scale.

Installation is performed in the following order:
1. Rotate the crankshaft so its key points straight up.

NOTE: The No. 1 and No. 4 pistons should be at TDC.

2. Rotate the camshaft so its key is aligned with the timing mark on the thrust plate.
3. Install the chain on the camshaft and crankshaft timing sprockets so the marks on the timing chain align with the "Toyota" trademarks on each of the sprockets.

NOTE: The above step is performed with the sprockets off the engine.

4. Being careful to keep all the parts

Proper alignment of the "T" series engine timing marks

1. Timing chain cover	7. Camshaft
2. Timing chain cover gasket	8. Bolt
3. Bolt	9. Crankshaft pulley
4. Plate washer	10. Front oil seal
5. Bolt	11. Woodruff key
6. Plate	12. Camshaft sprocket
13. Woodruff key	
14. Crankshaft sprocket	
15. Timing chain	
16. Chain tensioner	
17. Chain vibration damper	

Timing chain and related components—"T" series engines

in proper alignment, install the timing chain/sprocket assembly to the engine. When assembled, the marks should align as in the illustration.

5. Torque the camshaft timing gear bolt to 50–79 ft. lbs.

6. Fill the chain tensioner with engine oil and install it. Install the chain damper.

7. Install the timing cover as outlined above.

20R and 22R Engines

1. Remove the cylinder head and timing cover as outlined above.

2. Separate the chain from the damper, and remove the chain, complete with the camshaft sprocket.

3. Remove the crankshaft sprocket and the oil pump drive with a puller.

4. Inspect the chain for wear or damage. Replace it, if necessary.

5. Inspect the chain tensioner for wear. If it measures less than 0.43 in., replace it.

6. Check the dampers for wear. If they are below specification replace them:

Upper damper—0.20 in.
Lower damper—0.18 in.

Installation is performed in the following order:

1. Rotate the crankshaft until its key is at TDC. Slide the sprocket in place over the key.

2. Place the chain over the sprocket so that its *single* bright link aligns with the mark on the crank sprocket.

"R" series engines—align the timing marks between the two bright links of the timing chain

3. Install the cam sprocket so that the timing mark falls between the *two* bright links on the chain.

4. Fit the oil pump drive spline over the crankshaft key.

5. Install the timing cover gasket on the front of the block.

6. Rotate the camshaft sprocket counterclockwise to remove the slack from the chain.

7. Install the timing chain cover and cylinder head, as outlined above.

4M, 4M-E, and 5M-E Engines

1. Remove the cylinder head and timing cover, as outlined above.

2. Remove the chain tensioner assembly (arm and gear).

1. Valve timing mark (5/32 in. hole)
2. V-notch—camshaft flange
3. V-notch—crankshaft pulley

"M" series engines (except 5M-GE)—correct alignment of the crankshaft and camshaft timing marks

4M and 4M-E timing mark alignment (except the camshaft sprocket)

3. Unfasten the bolts which retain the chain damper and damper guide and withdraw the damper and guide.

4. Remove the oil slinger from the crankshaft.

5. Withdraw the timing chain.

6. Inspect the chain for wear or damage. Replace it if necessary.

Installation is performed in the following manner:

1. Position the No. 1 cylinder at TDC.

2. Position the crankshaft sprocket 0-mark downward, facing the oil pan.

3. Align the ''Toyota'' trademarks on the sprockets as illustrated.

4. Fit the tensioner gear assembly on the block.

NOTE: Its dowel pin should be positioned 1.5 in. from the surface of the block.

5. Install the chain over the two gears while maintaining tension.

6. Install both of the vibration dampers and the damper guide.

7. Fit the oil slinger to the crankshaft.

8. Tie the chain to the upper vibration damper, to keep it from falling into the chain cover, once the cover is installed.

9. Install the timing cover, as detailed above.

10. Perform the cylinder head installation procedure as detailed above.

NOTE: If proper valve timing cannot be obtained, it is possible to adjust it by placing the camshaft slotted pin in the second or third hole on the camshaft timing gear, as required. If the timing is out by more than 15°, replace the chain and both of the sprockets.

5M-E engines—proper alignment of the timing chain and gear markings

4M and 4M-E timing mark alignment—timing chain and camshaft sprocket

1. Timing chain tensioner gear
2. Timing chain tensioner arm
3. Damper guide
4. Vibration damper
5. Vibration damper
6. Crankshaft oil slinger

Removing the timing chain from "M" series engines (except 5M-GE)

5M-GE Engines

1. Disconnect the battery cables at the battery.

2. Loosen the mounting bolts of each of the crankshaft-driven components (alternator, etc.) at the front of the engine and remove the drive belts.

3. Using a wrench on the center crankshaft pulley bolt, rotate the crankshaft in order to set the no. 1 cylinder to TDC of its compression stroke (both valves of the no. 1 cylinder closed, and TDC marks aligned).

4. Remove the upper, front (no. 3) timing belt cover and gasket (five bolts).

5. Loosen the idler pulley bolt and lever the idler pulley towards the alternator side of the engine in order to relieve the tension on the timing belt. Hand-tighten the idler pulley bolt.

6. Remove the timing belt from the camshaft pulleys.

5M-GE engines—Paint a mark on the timing belt prior to belt removal to indicate the belts direction of normal rotation. Point the mark in the same direction if the belt is to be reinstalled

5M-GE engines—Use a spanner wrench (SST) as shown, to hold the camshaft sprocket while loosening the camshaft sprocket bolt. DO NOT attempt to use belt tension to hold the sprocket in place while removing the camshaft sprocket bolt

7. Remove the camshaft timing pulleys as follows:

    a. Hold the pulleys stationary with a spanner wrench.

    b. Remove the center pulley bolt.

—————— **CAUTION** ——————

DO NOT attempt to use timing belt tension as a tool to remove the center pulley bolts, as the belt could become damaged.

NOTE: Do not interchange the intake and exhaust timing pulleys, as they differ for use with each camshaft.

8. Remove the center crankshaft pulley bolt. Using a puller, remove the crankshaft pulley.

9. Using chalk or a crayon, mark the timing belt to indicate its direction of rotation. This mark must face the same direction during installation of the belt.

10. Remove the lower timing belt cover, then the belt.

11. If damaged, the crankshaft pulley can be removed using a puller; the oil pump drive shaft pulley can be removed in the same manner as the camshaft pulleys.

12. Inspect the timing belt for damage, such as cuts, cracks, missing teeth, abrasions, nicks, etc.

    a. If the belt teeth are damaged, check that the camshafts rotate freely and correct as necessary.

    b. Should damage be evident on the belt face, check the idler pulley belt surface for damage.

    c. If damage is present on one side of the belt only, check the belt guide and the alignment of each pulley.

    d. If the belt teeth are excessively worn, check the timing belt cover gasket for damage and/or proper installation.

13. Check the idler pulley for damage and smoothness of rotation. Also check the free length of the tension spring, which should be 2.776 in., measured between the inside of each end "clip". Replace the spring if the length exceeds this limit.

Install the timing belt as follows:

1. Install the crankshaft and oil pump drive shaft if these items were removed previously. Torque the oil pump drive shaft pulley center bolt to 14–18 ft. lbs. The crankshaft pulley must be evenly driven into place.

2. Install the idler pulley and the tension spring. Lever the pulley towards the alternator side of the engine and tighten bolt.

3. Check the mark made during Step 9 of removal and temporarily install the timing belt on the crankshaft pulley. The mark must face in the same direction as it did originally.

Timing chain, covers and related components—5M-GE engines

4. Install the lower timing belt cover.

5. Install the crankshaft pulley and torque the center pulley bolt to 98–119 ft. lbs.

6. Remove the oil filler cap of the intake camshaft cover, and the complete camshaft cover on the exhaust side.

7. Check that the match holes of both no. 2 camshaft journals are visible through the camshaft housing match holes. If necessary, temporarily intall the camshaft pulley and guide pin, and rotate the camshaft(s) until the holes are aligned.

5M-GE engines—Proper alignment of the camshaft matchmarks with the match holes of the camshaft housings (IN—intake; EX—exhaust)

8. Install the timing pulleys. Note that the belt guide of the exhaust camshaft pulley should be positioned towards the engine; the belt guide of the intake camshaft pulley should be positioned away from the engine. DO NOT yet install the pulley retaining bolts.

5M-GE engines—When installing the camshaft sprockets, be sure that the guides are positioned as shown. (IN—intake camshaft sprocket; EX—exhaust camshaft sprocket)

9. Align the following marks:

a. Each camshaft pulley mark must be aligned with its respective mark on the rear, upper (no. 2) timing belt cover.

b. Align the crankshaft pulley notch with the TDC (0) mark of the timing tab.

NOTE: The No. 1 cylinder MUST be positioned at TDC on its compression stroke.

10. Install the timing belt.

11. Loosen the idler pulley bolt and ten-

5M-GE engines—Alignment of the camshaft sprocket marks with the no. 2 timing cover marks. Note the position of the crankshaft pulley (TDC)

sion the timing belt. The timing belt tension must be the same between the exhaust camshaft pulley and the crankshaft pulley, as it is between the intake camshaft pulley and the oil pump drive shaft pulley.

5M-GE engines—When adjusting the timing belt tension, be sure the tension at "A" is the same as that at "B"

12. There are five pin holes on each camshaft and each timing pulley. On the exhaust side: Install the match pin into the one hole of the pulley which is aligned with one of the camshaft pin holes. Repeat this on the intake side. Only one of the holes of each side should be aligned to allow insertion of the match pins.

5M-GE engines—Locating the overlapped holes of the camshaft and the camshaft sprocket. Install the match pin into the aligned set of holes (typical of either the intake or exhaust camshaft)

13. Using a spanner wrench to hold the camshaft pulleys, install and tighten the camshaft pulley bolts. These bolts should be torqued to 48–54 ft. lbs.

14. Install the exhaust camshaft cover, using a new gasket. Install the oil filler cap.

15. Install the timing belt cover and gasket.

16. Install and adjust the drive belts at the front of the engine. Reconnect the battery cables.

Timing Gears

REMOVAL AND INSTALLATION

1A-C, 3A, and 3A-C Engines

1. Remove the air cleaner.

2. Remove the throttle linkage.

3. Remove the valve cover.

4. Remove the crankshaft and water pump pulleys.

5. Remove the top and bottom timing belt cover.

6. Remove the belt tensioner.

7. Matchmark the belt and camshaft gear for easy reinstallation.

8. Remove the timing belt.

9. Remove the bolt from the camshaft gear and remove the gear.

NOTE: In order to remove this gear use a pair of channelock pliers to hold the cam from turning. Do not hold the cam by the lobes as damage may result.

10. Installation is the reverse of removal.

Camshaft

REMOVAL AND INSTALLATION

3K-C and 4K-C Engines

1. Perform the timing cover and timing chain removal procedure, above.

2. Perform Steps 1–11 of the 3K-C and 4K-C engine cylinder head removal procedure.

NOTE: It is unnecessary to remove the cylinder head.

3. Unfasten the spark plug wires and remove the spark plugs.

4. Remove the valve lifters in sequence.

NOTE: Keep the valve lifters in their proper sequence so that they go back into their original bores.

5. If you have not already done so, disconnect the vacuum line and the primary wire from the distributor, loosen its clamping bolt, and remove it.

6. Detach the fuel lines from the fuel pump and remove the pump.

7. Remove the bolts which secure the camshaft thrust plate and then remove the thrust plate, itself.

8. Carefully remove the camshaft from the cylinder block.

—————— CAUTION ——————

Use care not to damage the camshaft lobes, journals, or bearings.

9. Installation of the camshaft is performed in the reverse order of removal. Coat the camshaft bearings and journals lightly with engine oil. The camshaft thrust plate attaching bolt should be tightened to 4–6 ft. lbs.

2T-C and 3T-C Engines

1. Perform the cylinder head, timing cover, and timing chain removal procedures.

2. Unfasten the primary wire and vacuum lines from the distributor. Loosen its clamping bolt and withdraw it from the engine block.

3. Unfasten the lines from the fuel pump and remove the pump.

4. Remove the gear shifter shaft lever.

5. Use a jack to *lightly* support the transmission.

6. Remove the engine rear supporting crossmember.

7. Carefully lower the jack from beneath the transmission.

8. Unbolt and remove the camshaft thrust plate.

9. Ease out the camshaft, being careful not to damage the camshaft lobes or bearings.

10. Installation is performed in the reverse order of removal. Lubricate the camshaft journals and bearings lightly with engine oil prior to camshaft installation. Tighten the camshaft thrust plate attaching bolts to 7–11 ft. lbs.

"R" and "M" Series Engines

All of these engines utilize an overhead camshaft (OHC). Therefore, the procedure for removing the camshaft is given as part of the cylinder head removal procedure. Consult the appropriate section, above, for details.

NOTE: It will not be necessary to completely remove the cylinder head in order to remove the camshaft. Therefore, proceed only as far as is necessary, to remove the camshaft, with the cylinder head removal procedure.

1A-C, 3A, and 3A-C Engines

1. Perform the timing gear removal from the previous section.

2. Pry out the camshaft seal with a screwdriver.

3. Remove the camshaft bearing caps. Keep them in the order in which they were removed.

4. Remove the camshaft.

5. Installation is the reverse of removal.

NOTE: When reinstalling the camshaft seal place some multipurpose grease on the lip of the seal before installation.

Torque the cam to its proper specifications.

"M" series engines (except 5M-GE)—camshaft sprocket installation for 3–9° valve timing retard

"M" series engines (except 5M-GE)—camshaft sprocket installation for 9–15° valve timing retard

"M" series engines (except 5M-GE)—camshaft sprocket installation for normal valve timing

Pistons and Connecting Rods

REMOVAL AND INSTALLATION

All Engines

See the procedure in "Engine Rebuilding" in the Unit Repair section.

Piston ring gap positioning—"A" series engines

Piston ring gap positioning—"K" series engines

Piston ring gap positioning—"M" series engines

Piston ring gap positioning—"R" series engines

Piston ring gap positioning—"T" series engines

ENGINE LUBRICATION

Oil Pan

REMOVAL AND INSTALLATION

Corolla, Corona, and Starlet

1. Open the engine compartment hood.
2. Raise the front end of the car and support it with jack stands.
3. Remove the splash shield from underneath the engine.
4. Place a jack under the transmission to support it.
5. Unfasten the bolts which secure the engine rear supporting crossmember to the chassis.
6. Raise the jack under the transmission, *slightly*.
7. Unbolt the oil pan and work it out from underneath the engine.

NOTE: If the oil pan does not come out easily, it may be necessary to unbolt the rear engine mounts from the crossmember.

Installation is performed in the reverse order of removal. On Corolla models equipped with the 2T-C and 3T-C engines and Corona models, apply liquid sealer to the four corners of the oil pan. Tighten the oil pan securing bolts to the following specifications:

3K-C engine: 2–3 ft. lbs.
2T-C and 3T-C engines: 4–6 ft. lbs.
20R and 22R engines: 3–6 ft. lbs.

Application of sealer to the "R" and "T" series engine oil pan

Celica and Supra (1976–81), Cressida, Mark II

1. Drain the oil.
2. Raise the front end of the car with jacks and support it with jack stands.

— CAUTION —
Be sure that the car is supported securely. Remember, you will be working underneath it.

3. Detach the steering relay rod and the tie rods from the idler arm, pitman arm, and steering knuckles, as detailed below.
4. Remove the engine stiffening plates.
5. Remove the splash shields from underneath the engine.
6. Support the front of the engine with a jack and remove the front engine mount attaching bolts.
7. Raise the front of the engine *slightly* with the jack.
8. Unbolt and withdraw the oil pan.
Installation is performed in the reverse order of removal. Apply liquid sealer to the four corners of the oil pan gasket used on 2T-C and 3T-C engines. Torque the oil pan securing bolts to 4–6 ft. lbs.

Celica and Supra (1982 and Later)

22R ENGINE

1. Disconnect the battery cables at the battery.
2. Raise the front of the vehicle and support it with jackstands.
3. Remove the engine undercover.
4. Drain the engine oil.
5. Remove the engine shock absorber.
6. Remove the motor mount bolts.
7. Place a jack under the transmission and raise the engine about one inch.
8. Remove the oil pan fasteners, the oil pan, and the gasket.
9. Installation is performed in the reverse of the previous steps. Use a new oil pan gasket during installation. Torque the oil pan fasteners to 35–69 in. lbs.

5M-GE ENGINE

1. Disconnect the battery cables at the battery.
2. Raise the front of the vehicle and support it safely with jackstands.
3. Drain the engine oil.
4. Drain the cooling system.
5. Remove the air cleaner assembly. Mark any disconnected lines and/or hoses for easy reassembly.
6. Remove the oil level gauge.
7. Disconnect the upper radiator hose at the radiator.
8. Loosen all of the drive belts for the crankshaft-driven accessories (alternator, power steering pump, etc.).
9. Remove the four fan shroud bolts.
10. Remove the four fluid coupling flange attaching nuts, then remove the fluid coupling along with the fan and the fan shroud.
11. Remove the engine undercover.
12. Remove the exhaust pipe clamp bolt from the exhaust pipe stay.
13. Remove the two stiffener plates from the exhaust pipe.
14. Remove the clutch housing undercover.
15. Remove the four engine mount bolts from each side of the engine.
16. Place a jack under the transmission and raise the engine about 1¾ in.

17. Remove the oil pan mounting bolts and remove the oil pan from the engine.

NOTE: If difficulty is encountered while removing the pan, rotate the crankshaft a small amount to gain extra clearance.

18. Installation is the reverse of the previous steps. Use a new oil pan gasket during installation. Apply a small amount of sealer to the oil pan gasket at each of the four corners of the oil pan. Torque the oil pan fasteners to 57–82 in. lbs. Adjust the drive belts and replenish the engine with oil and the cooling system with the proper type and quantity of coolant. Check for leaks after the engine is started.

Tercel

1. Disconnect the negative battery terminal.
2. Jack up the vehicle and support it with jack stands.
3. Drain the oil.
4. Remove the sway bar and any other necessary steering linkage parts.
5. Disconnect the exhaust pipe from the manifold.
6. Jack up the engine enough to take the weight off it.
7. Remove the engine mounts and engine shock absorber.
8. Continue to jack up the engine enough to remove the pan.
9. Remove the pan bolts and remove the pan.
10. Installation is the reverse of removal.
Always use a new pan gasket when reinstalling the pan.

Rear Main Oil Seal

REPLACEMENT

All Engines

NOTE: On the 1A-C, 3A, and 3A-C engines, they must be removed before this procedure can be attempted.

1. Remove the transmission.
2. Remove the clutch cover assembly and flywheel.
3. Remove the oil seal retaining plate, complete with the oil seal.
4. Use a screwdriver to pry the old seal from the retaining plate. Be careful not to damage the plate.
5. Install the new seal, carefully, by using a block of wood to drift it into place.

— CAUTION —
Do not damage the seal; a leak will result.

6. Lubricate the lips of the seal with multipurpose grease.
Installation is the reverse of removal.

OIL PUMP CLEARANCE SPECIFICATIONS
(All measurements are given in inches unless noted)

Engine	Tip Clearance (Driven)	Side Clearance	Body Clearance	Relief Valve Spring Installed Length
3K-C, 4K-C	0.0016–0.0063	0.0012–0.0035	0.0039–0.0063	1.45
2T-C, 3T-C	0.0016–0.0063	0.0012–0.0035	0.0039–0.0063	1.45
4M, 4M-E, 5M-E, 5M-GE	0.0200–0.0240③	0.0012–0.0035	0.0012–0.0024	1.89②
20R, 22R	0.0059–0.0083④	0.0012–0.0035	0.0035–0.0059	—
1A-C, 3A, 3A-C	0.0023–0.0122①	0.0014–0.0033⑤	0.0039–0.0075	—

① Drive—0.0040–0.0100 inch
② 1980–81 opening pressure 71–85 psi
③ Gear backlash specification
④ Driven gear-to-crescent. The drive gear-to-crescent clearance should be 0.0087–0.0098 in.
⑤ 3A & 3A-C engines—0.0010–0.0030 in.

Oil Pump

REMOVAL AND INSTALLATION

All Engines (Except 20R and 22R)

1. Remove the oil pan, as outlined previously.
2. Unbolt the oil pump securing bolts and remove it as an assembly.
3. Installation is the reverse of removal.

20R and 22R Engines

1. Remove the oil pan.
2. Remove the three bolts which secure the oil strainer.
3. Remove the drive belts, the pulley bolt, and the crankshaft pulley.
4. Unfasten the bolts which secure the oil pump housing and remove the pump assembly.
5. Remove the oil pump drive spline and the rubber O-ring.
6. Installation is the reverse of removal. Apply sealer to the top oil pump housing bolt. Use a new oil strainer gasket.

CHECKING CLEARANCE

Wash the pump thoroughly and allow to air dry. Check for shiny spots which indicate wear and scuffling. Check backlash of gears and measure free length of relief valve spring, then check play between gears and housing, gears and pump cover and between gears themselves. See specification chart for tolerances.

ENGINE COOLING

Radiator

REMOVAL AND INSTALLATION

All Models

1. Drain the cooling system.
2. Unfasten the clamps and remove the radiator upper and lower hoses. If equipped with an automatic transmission, remove the oil cooler lines.
3. Detach the hood lock cable and remove the hood lock from the radiator upper support.

NOTE: It may be necessary to remove the grille in order to gain access to the hood lock/radiator support assembly.

4. Remove the fan shroud, if so equipped.
5. On models equipped with the closed cooling system, disconnect the hose from the thermal expansion tank and remove the tank from its bracket.
6. Unbolt and remove the radiator upper support.
7. Unfasten the bolts and remove the radiator.
8. Installation is performed in the reverse order of removal. Remember to check the transmission fluid level on cars with automatic transmissions. Fill the radiator to the specified level.

Water Pump

REMOVAL AND INSTALLATION

All Engines Except 1A-C, 2A and 3A-C

1. Drain the cooling system.
2. Unfasten the fan shroud securing bolts and remove the fan shroud, if so equipped.
3. Loosen the alternator adjusting link bolt and remove the drive belt.
4. Repeat Step 3 for the air pump, air conditioning compressor, or power steering pump drive belts, if so equipped.

NOTE: On some models, it may be necessary to remove the air cleaner assembly. On all 5M-GE engines, remove the air cleaner case.

5. Detach the bypass and radiator hoses from the water pump.
6. Unfasten the water pump retaining bolts and remove the water pump and fan assembly, using care not to damage the radiator with the fan.

—— CAUTION ——
If the fan is equipped with a fluid coupling, do not tip the fan/pump assembly on its side, as the fluid will run out.

Installation is the reverse of removal. Always use a new gasket between the pump body and its mounting. Check for leaks after installation is completed.

1A-C, 3A and 3A-C Only

1. Drain the radiator. Save the coolant as it can be reused.
2. Loosen all necessary drive belts.
3. Remove the top timing belt cover.

4. Remove the bottom radiator hose from the water pump.

5. Remove the pump bolts and remove the pump.

NOTE: Always use a new gasket when replacing the pump.

6. Installation is the reverse of removal.

Thermostat

REMOVAL AND INSTALLATION

All Engines

1. Drain the cooling system.
2. Unfasten the clamp and remove the upper radiator hose from the water outlet elbow.
3. Unbolt and remove the water outlet (thermostat housing).
4. Withdraw the thermostat.
5. Installation is performed in the reverse order of removal procedure. Use a new gasket on the water outlet.

— **CAUTION** —
Be sure that the thermostat is installed with the spring pointing down.

EMISSION CONTROLS

NOTE: Due to the complexity of most late models, only the major systems and basic services will be covered. Detailed servicing of any emission system should be referred to a professional technician having the proper testing equipment.

Positive Crankcase Ventilation (PCV) System

A positive crankcase ventilation (PCV) system is used on all Toyotas sold in the United States. Blow-by gases are routed from the crankcase to the carburetor, where they are combined with the fuel/air mixture and burned during combustion.

A (PCV) valve is used in the line to prevent the gases in the crankcase from being ignited in case of a backfire. The amount of blow-by gases entering the mixture is also regulated by the PCV valve, which is spring-loaded and has a variable orifice.

The valve is either mounted on the valve cover or in the line which runs from the intake manifold to the crankcase.

REMOVAL AND INSTALLATION

Remove the PCV valve from the cylinder head cover on "K" and "A" series engines. Remove the hose from the valve.

On the remainder of the engines, remove the valve from the manifold-to-crankcase hose.

Installation is the reverse of removal.

TESTING

Check the PCV system hoses and connections, to see that there are no leaks; then replace or tighten, as necessary.

To check the valve, remove it and blow through both of its ends. When blowing from the side which goes toward the intake manifold, very little air should pass through it. When blowing from the crankcase (valve cover) side, air should pass through freely.

Replace the valve with a new one, if the valve fails to function as outlined.

NOTE: Do not attempt to clean or adjust the valve; replace it with a new one.

Air Injection System

A belt-driven air pump supplies air to an injection manifold which has nozzles in each exhaust port. Injection of air at this point causes combustion of unburned hydrocarbons in the exhaust manifold rather than allowing them to escape into the atmosphere. An antibackfire valve controls the flow of air from the pump to prevent backfiring which results from an overly rich mixture under closed throttle conditions.

A check valve prevents hot exhaust gas backflow into the pump and hoses, in case of a pump failure, or when the antibackfire valve is working.

In addition newer engines have an air switching valve. On engines without catalytic converters, the ASV is used to stop air injection under a constant heavy engine load.

On engines with catalytic converters the ASV is used to protect the catalyst from overheating, by blocking the air necessary for the reaction.

On all engines, the relief valve is built into the ASV.

REMOVAL AND INSTALLATION

Air Pump

1. Disconnect the air hoses from the pump.
2. Loosen the bolt on the adjusting link and remove the drive belt.
3. Remove the pump.

— **CAUTION** —
Do not pry on the pump housing; it may be distorted.

4. Installation is in the reverse order of removal. Adjust the drive belt tension to ½–¾ in. under thumb pressure.

Antibackfire Valve and Air Switching Valve.

1. Detach the air hoses from the valve.
2. Remove the valve securing bolt.
3. Withdraw the valve.
4. Installation is performed in the reverse order of removal.

Check Valve

1. Detach the intake hose from the valve.
2. Use an open-end wrench to remove the valve from its mounting.
3. Installation is the reverse of removal.

Relief Valve

1. Remove the air pump from the car.
2. Support the pump so that it cannot rotate.

— **CAUTION** —
Never clamp the pump in a vise; the aluminum case will become distorted.

Schematic of a typical air injection system

Removing the relief valve from the air pump

3. Use a jaw-type puller to remove the relief valve from the top of the pump.

4. Position the new relief valve over the opening in the pump.

NOTE: The air outlet should be pointing toward the left.

5. Gently tap the relief valve into place, using a block of wood and a hammer.

6. Install the pump on the engine, as outlined above.

Air Injection Manifold

1. Remove the check valve, as outlined above.

2. Loosen the air injection manifold attachment nuts and withdraw the manifold.

NOTE: On "R" and "M" series engines, it will first be necessary to remove the exhaust manifold.

3. Installation is in the reverse of removal.

Air Injection Nozzles

1. Remove the air injection manifold as outlined above.

2. Remove the cylinder head, as detailed in the appropriate section, above.

3. Place a new nozzle on the cylinder head.

4. Install the air injection manifold over it.

5. Install the cylinder head on the engine block.

TESTING

Air Pump

─────── **CAUTION** ───────

Do not hammer, pry, or bend the pump housing while tightening the drive belt or testing the pump.

BELT TENSION AND AIR LEAKS

1. Before proceeding with the tests, check the pump drive belt tension to see if it is within specifications.

2. Turn the pump by hand. If it has

seized, the belt will slip, making a noise. Disregard any chirping, squealing, or rolling sounds from inside the pump; these are normal when it is turned by hand.

3. Check the hoses and connections for leaks. Hissing or a blast of air is indicative of a leak. Soapy water, applied lightly around the area in question, is a good method for detecting leaks.

AIR OUTPUT

1. Disconnect the air supply hose at the antibackfire valve.

2. Connect a pressure gauge, using a suitable adaptor, to the air supply hose.

NOTE: If there are two hoses, plug the second one.

3. With the engine at normal operating temperature, increase the idle speed to 1000–1500 rpm (1950 rpm-2T-C and 3T-C) and watch the vacuum gauge.

4. The air flow from the pump should be steady and fall between 2 and 6 psi. If it is unsteady or falls below this, the pump is defective and must be replaced.

Checking the air pump output

PUMP NOISE DIAGNOSIS

The air pump is normally noisy; as engine speed increases, the noise of the pump will rise in pitch. The rolling sound the pump bearings make is normal. But if this sound becomes objectionable at certain speeds, the pump is defective and will have to be replaced.

A continual hissing sound from the air pump pressure relief valve at idle, indicates a defective valve. Replace the relief valve.

If the pump rear bearing fails, a continual knocking sound will be heard.

Antibackfire Valve Testing

1. Detach the hose, which runs from the bypass valve to the check valve, at the bypass valve hose connection.

2. Connect a tachometer to the engine. With the engine running at normal idle speed, check to see that air is flowing from the bypass valve hose connection.

3. Speed up the engine so it is running at 1500–2000 rpm. Allow the throttle to snap shut. The flow of air from the bypass valve at the check valve hose connection should stop momentarily and air should then

flow from the exhaust port on the valve body or the silencer assembly.

4. Repeat Step 3 several times. If the flow of air is not diverted into the atmosphere from the valve exhaust port or if it fails to stop flowing from the hose connection, check the vacuum lines and connections. If these are tight, the valve is defective and requires replacement.

5. A leaking diaphragm will cause the air to flow out both the hose connection and the exhaust port at the tame time. If this happens, replace the valve.

Air Switching Valve (ASV) Tests

"T" AND "R" SERIES ENGINES

1. Start the engine and allow it to reach normal operating temperature.

2. At curb idle, the air from the bypass valve should be discharged through the hose which runs to the ASV.

3. When the vacuum line to the ASV is disconnected, the air from the bypass valve should be diverted out through the ASV-to-air cleaner hose. Reconnect the vacuum line.

4. Disconnect the ASV-to-check valve hose and connect a pressure gauge to it.

5. Increase the engine speed. The relief valve should open when the pressure gauge registers 2.7–6.5 psi.

6. If the ASV fails any of the above tests, replace it. Reconnect all hoses.

"M" SERIES ENGINES

1. Start the engine and allow it to reach normal operating temperature.

2. At curb idle, air from the pump should be discharged through the hose which runs to the check valve.

3. Race the engine and allow the throttle valve to snap shut. The air from the pump should be discharged into the air cleaner.

4. Disconnect the ASV-to-check valve hose and connect a pressure gauge to it.

5. Increase the engine speed gradually. The relief valve should open when the gauge registers 3.7–7.7 psi. Reconnect the check valve hose.

6. Unfasten the wiring connector and the hoses from the solenoid valve, which is attached to the ASV. Air should pass through the solenoid valve when either the top or bottom port is blown into.

7. Connect a 12V power source to the terminals on the valve. No air should flow through the valve when either port is blown into.

8. If the solenoid valve or the ASV fail any of the above tests, replace either or both of them, as necessary.

Vacuum Delay Valve Test

"T" AND "R" SERIES ENGINES

The vacuum delay valve is located in the line which runs from the intake manifold to either the vacuum surge tank ("R" engines) or to the ASV (''T'' engines). To check it, proceed as follows:

1. Remove the vacuum delay valve from the vacuum line. Be sure to note which end points toward the intake manifold.

2. When air is blown in from the ASV (surge tank) side, it should pass through the valve freely.

3. When air is blown in from the intake manifold side, a resistance should be felt.

4. Replace the valve if it fails either of the above tests.

5. Install the valve in the vacuum line, being careful not to install it backwards.

Check Valve Test

1. Before starting the test, check all of the hoses and connections for leaks.

2. Detach the air supply hose from the check valve.

3. Insert a suitable probe into the check valve and depress the plate. Release it; the plate should return to its original position against the valve seat. If binding is evident, replace the valve.

4. With the engine running at normal operating temperature, gradually increase its speed to 1500 rpm. Check for exhaust gas leakage. If any is present, replace the valve assembly.

NOTE: Vibration and flutter of the check valve at idle speed is a normal condition and does not mean that the valve should be replaced.

Evaporative Emission Control System

To prevent hydrocarbon emissions from entering the atmosphere, Toyota vehicles use evaporative emission control (EEC) systems. All models use a ''charcoal canister'' storage system.

The charcoal canister storage system stores fuel vapors in a canister filled with activated charcoal. All models use a vacuum switch-ing valve to purge the system. The air filter is an integral part of the charcoal canister.

REMOVAL AND INSTALLATION

Removal and installation of the various evaporative emission control system components consists of disconnecting hoses, loosening securing screws, and removing the part which is to be replaced from its mounting bracket. Installation is the reverse of removal.

NOTE: When replacing any EEC system hoses, always use hoses that are fuel-resistant or are marked ''EVAP.''

TESTING

EEC System Troubleshooting

There are several things which may be checked if a malfunction of the evaporative emission control system is suspected.

1. Leaks may be traced by using a hydrocarbon tester. Run the test probe along the lines and connections. The meter will indicate the presence of a leak by a high hydrocarbon (HC) reading. This method is much more accurate than visual inspection which would only indicate the presence of leaks large enough to pass liquid.

2. Leaks may be caused by any of the following:

   a. Defective or worn hoses;
   b. Disconnected or pinched hoses;
   c. Improperly routed hoses;
   d. A defective filler cap or safety valve (sealed cap system).

NOTE: If it becomes necessary to replace any of the hoses used in the evaporative emission control system, use only hoses which are fuel-resistant or are marked ''EVAP.''

3. If the fuel tank, storage case, or thermal expansion tank collapse, it may be the fault of clogged or pinched vent lines, a defective vapor separator, or a plugged or incorrect filler cap.

4. To test the filler cap (if it is the safety valve type), clean it and place it against your mouth. Blow into the relief valve housing. If the cap passes pressure with light blowing or if it fails to release with hard blowing, it is defective and must be replaced.

NOTE: Use the proper cap for the type of system used; either a sealed cap or safety valve cap, as required.

Check Valve

Rough idling when the gas tank is full is probably caused by a defective check valve. To test it, proceed as follows:

1. Run the engine at idle.

2. Clamp the hose between the vacuum switching valve or carburetor (4M-Calif) and the charcoal canister.

3. If the engine idle becomes smooth, replace the check valve.

Throttle Positioner

On Toyotas with an engine modification system, a throttle positioner is included to reduce exhaust emissions during deceleration. The positioner prevents the throttle from closing completely. Vacuum is reduced under the throttle valve which, in turn, acts on the retard chamber of the distributor vacuum unit (if so equipped). This compensates for the loss of engine braking caused by the partially open throttle.

Once the vehicle drops below a predetermined speed, the vacuum switching valve provides vacuum to the throttle positioner diaphragm; the throttle positioner retracts allowing the throttle valve to close completely. The distributor also is returned to normal operation.

ADJUSTMENT

1. Start the engine and allow it to reach normal operating temperature.

2. Adjust the idle speed.

NOTE: Leave the tachometer connected after completing the idle adjustments, as it will be needed in Step 5, below.

3. Detach the vacuum line from the positioner diaphragm unit and plug the line.

4. Accelerate the engine slightly to set the throttle positioner.

5. Check the engine speed with a tachometer when the throttle positioner is set.

6. If necessary, adjust the engine speed, with the throttle positioner adjusting screw, to the specifications.

7. Connect the vacuum hose to the positioner diaphragm.

8. The throttle lever should be freed from the positioner as soon as the vacuum hose is connected. Engine idle should return to normal.

Intake Manifold

← Fuel Vapor
←--- Fresh Air

Thermal Expansion Tank

Hydrocarbon absorbed. sucked into the charcoal.

Safety Type Cap

Fuel Tank

Vacuum Switching Valve (Closed)

Charcoal Canister

Charcoal

Fuel Vapor (Evaporated Hydrocarbon)

Schematic of a typical evaporative emission control system

Components of a typical throttle positioner system

9. If the throttle positioner fails to function properly, check its linkage, and vacuum diaphragm. If there are no defects in either of these, the fault probably lies in the vacuum switching valve or the speed marker unit.

NOTE: Due to the complexity of these two components they require special test equipment.

Dual-Diaphragm Distributor

Some Toyota models are equipped with a dual-diaphragm distributor unit. This distributor has a retard diaphragm, as well as a diaphragm for advance. Retarding the timing helps to reduce exhaust emissions, as well as making up for the lack of engine braking on models equipped with a throttle positioner.

TESTING

1. Connect a timing light to the engine. Check the ignition timing.

NOTE: Before proceeding with the tests, disconnect any spark control devices, distributor vacuum valves, etc. If these are left connected, inaccurate results may be obtained.

2. Remove the retard hose from the distributor and plug it. Increase the engine speed. The timing should advance. If it fails to do so, then the vacuum unit is faulty and must be replaced.

3. Check the timing with the engine at normal idle speed. Unplug the retard hose and connect it to the vacuum unit. The timing should instantly be retarded from 4 to 10 degrees. I; this does not occur, the retard diaphragm has a leak and the vacuum unit must be replaced.

Engine Modifications System

Toyota uses an assortment of engine modifications to regulate exhaust emissions. Most of these devices fall into the category of engine vacuum controls. There are three principal components used on the engine modifications system, as well as a number of smaller parts. The three major components are: a speed sensor; a computer (speed marker); and a vacuum switching valve.

The vacuum switching valve and computer circuit operates most of the emission control components. Depending upon year and engine usage, the vacuum switching valve and computer may operate the purge control for the evaporative emission control system; the transmission controlled spark (TCS) or speed controlled spark (SCS); the dual-diaphragm distributor; and the throttle positioner systems.

The functions of the evaporative emission control system, the throttle positioner, and the dual-diaphragm distributor are described in detail in the sections above. However, a word is necessary about the functions of the TCS and SCS systems before discussing the operation of the vacuum switching valve/computer circuit.

The major difference between the transmission controlled spark and speed controlled spark systems is in the manner in which systems operation is determined.

Below a predetermined speed, or any gear other than fourth, the vacuum advance unit on the distributor is rendered inoperative. By changing the distributor advance curve in this manner, it is possible to reduce emissions of oxides of nitrogen (NOx).

NOTE: Some engines are equipped with

THROTTLE POSITIONER SETTINGS
(rpm)

Year	Engine	Engine rpm (Positioner Set)
'76–'77①	2T-C	1500 MT 1400 AT①
	20R	1400 MT 1050 AT
	4M	1200 AT
	3K-C	1500 (Canada)
'78–'83	2T-C	1400 MT 1200 AT
	3T-C	1600 MT 1300 AT②
	20R, 22R	1050
	4M	950
	1A-C, 3A, 3A-C	N.A.

① 1977: 1200   AT Automatic transmission
② Calif: 1400   MT Manual transmission

Engine modification system

a thermo-sensor so that the TDS or SCS system only operates when the coolant temperature is 140°–212°F.

Aside from determining the conditions outlined above, the vacuum switching valve computer circuit operates other devices in the emission control system.

The computer acts as a speed marker; at certain speeds it sends a signal to the vacuum switching valve which acts as a gate, opening and closing the emission control system vacuum circuits.

SYSTEM CHECKS

Due to the complexity of the components involved, about the only engine modification system checks which can be made without the use of special test equipment, are the following:

1. Examine the vacuum lines to see that they are not clogged, pinched, or loose.

2. Check the electrical connections for tightness and corrosion.

3. Be sure that the vacuum sources for the vacuum switching valve are not plugged.

4. On models equipped with speed controlled spark, a broken speedometer cable could also render the system inoperative.

5. Test the thermo-sensor in the following manner:

   a. Remove the lead from its center terminal.

   b. Touch one test prod of an ohmmeter to the sensor housing.

   c. Connect the other test prod in series with a 10 ohm resistor to the center terminal of the sensor.

   d. If the engine temperature is between about 140°–212°F, the meter should show no continuity.

   e. If the engine is above or below these temperatures, the meter should show continuity.

   f. Replace the thermo-sensor if it isn't working properly.

6. If everything else is in good working order, the faul probably lies in the vacuum switching valve or the computer (speed marker). About the only way to test these, without using special equipment, is by substitution of new units.

NOTE: A faulty vacuum switching valve or computer could cause more than one of the emission control systems to fail. Therefore, if several systems are out, these two units (and the speedometer cable) would be the first things to check.

Exhaust Gas Recirculation (EGR)

In all cases, the EGR valve is controlled by the same computer and vacuum switching valve which is used to operate other emission control system components. Vacuum from the carburetor vacuum ad-

vance port flows through the vacuum switching valve to an EGR vacuum control valve. The vacuum from the advance port opens the vacuum control valve which then allows venturi vacuum to act on the chamber *above* the EGR valve diaphragm, causing the EGR valve to open. When exhaust gas recirculation is not required, the vacuum switching valve stops sending the advance port vacuum signal to the EGR vacuum control valve which closes, sending intake manifold vacuum to the chamber *below* the EGR valve diaphragm. This closes the EGR valve, blocking the flow of exhaust gases to the intake manifold.

On all engines there are several conditions, determined by the computer and vacuum switching valve, which permit exhaust gas recirculation to take place:
1. Vehicle speed
2. Engine coolant temperature

EGR VALVE CHECKS

All Except "M" Series Engines

1. Allow the engine to warm up and remove the top from the air cleaner.

NOTE: Do not remove the entire air cleaner assembly.

2. Disconnect the hose (white tape coded), which runs from the vacuum switching valve to the EGR valve, at its EGR valve end.

3. Remove the intake manifold hose (red coded) from the vacuum switching valve and connect it to the EGR valve. When the engine is at idle, a "hollow" sound should be heard coming from the air cleaner.

4. Disconnect the hose from the EGR valve; the hollow sound should disappear.

5. If the sound doesn't vary, the EGR valve is defective and must be replaced.

6. Reconnect the vacuum hoses as they were originally found. Install the top on the air cleaner.

Typical EGR valve testing—except "M" series engines

"M" Series Engines

1. Warm up the engine and allow it to idle.

2. Disconnect the vacuum sensing line from the *upper* vacuum chamber of the EGR valve.

3. Disconnect the sensing line from the *lower* chamber of the EGR valve.

4. Now, take the hose which was disconnected from the *lower* chamber and connect it to the upper EGR valve chamber.

NOTE: Leave the lower chamber vented to the atmosphere.

5. The engine idle should become rough or the engine should stall with the hoses connected in this manner. If the engine runs normally, check the EGR vacuum control valve (see below). If the vacuum control valve is in good working order, then replace the EGR valve.

6. Reconnect the vacuum sensing lines as they were originally found.

Checking the EGR valve on the 4M engine

EGR VACUUM CONTROL VALVE TESTING

1. Connect the EGR vacuum control valve hoses up, so that carburetor advance port vacuum operates directly on its diaphragm (top hose connection).

2. Disconnect the two hoses from the EGR vacuum control valve which run to the upper and lower diaphragm chambers of the EGR valve.

3. Take two vacuum gauges and connect one to each of the ports from which you removed a hose in Step 2.

4. Race the engine; the vacuum gauges should indicate the following:
Upper chamber port—Venturi vacuum
Lower chamber port—Atmospheric pressure

5. Disconnect the sensing hose from the carburetor advance port.

6. The vacuum gauges should now show the following:
Upper chamber port—Atmospheric pressure
Lower chamber port—Intake manifold vacuum

NOTE: The atmospheric pressure reading should be nearly equal to that obtained in Step 4.

7. Replace the EGR vacuum control valve if the readings on the vacuum gauges are incorrect.

8. Hook up the vacuum lines as they were originally found.

SYSTEM CHECKS

If, after having completed the above tests,

the EGR system still doesn't work right and everything else checks out OK, the fault probably lies in the computer or the vacuum switching valve systems. Proceed with the tests outlined under "System Checks" in the Engine Modification section above.

NOTE: A good indication that the fault doesn't lie in the EGR system, but rather in the vacuum supply system, would be if several emission control systems were not working properly.

Catalytic Converters

Starting in 1975 all Toyota passenger cars sold in California and all Mark IIs sold in the U.S. are equipped with catalytic converters. In 1977, all Toyota vehicles sold in this country were equipped with converters. The converters are used to oxidize hydrocarbons (HC) and carbon monoxide (CO). The converters are necessary because of the stricter emission level standards for the 1975 models.

The catalysts are made of noble metals (platinum and palladium) which are bonded to individual pellets. These catalysts cause the HC and CO to break down into water and carbon dioxide (CO_2) without taking part in the reaction; hence, a catalyst life of 50,000 miles may be expected under normal conditions.

On the 4M-E engines, there are two catalytic converters. The first one is designed to reduce the NOx to dinitrogen. The second one operates the same as the vehicles equipped with only one converter. Most late model (1980 and later) engines use a single, three-way catalytic convertor which reduces HC, CO, AND NOx emission levels.

An air pump is used to supply air to the exhaust system to aid in the reaction. A thermosensor, inserted into the converter, shuts off the air supply if the catalyst temperature becomes excessive.

The same sensor circuit also causes a dash warning light labeled "EXH TEMP" to come on when the catalyst temperature gets too high.

NOTE: It is normal for the light to come on temporarily if the car is being driven downhill for long periods of time (such as descending a mountain).

The light will come on and stay on if the air injection system is malfunctioning or if the engine is misfiring.

Precautions:
1. Use only unleaded fuel.
2. Avoid prolonged idling; the engine should run no longer than 20 minutes at curb idle, nor longer than 10 minutes at fast idle.
3. Reduce the fast idle speed, by quickly depressing and releasing the accelerator pedal, as soon as the coolant temperature reaches 120°F.
4. Do not disconnect any spark plug leads while the engine is running.
5. Make engine compression checks as quickly as possible.
6. Do not dispose of the catalyst in a place where anything coated with grease, gas, or oil is present; spontaneous combustion could result.

WARNING LIGHT CHECKS

NOTE: The warning light comes on while the engine is being cranked, to test its operation, just like any of the other warning lights.

1. If the warning light comes on and stays on, check the components of the air injection system, as outlined above. If these are not defective, check the ignition system for faulty leads, plugs, points, or control box.
2. If no problems can be found in Step 1, check the wiring for the light for shorts or opened circuits.
3. If nothing else can be found wrong in Steps 1 and 2 above, check the operation of the emission control system computer, either by substitution of a new unit, or by taking it to a service facility which has Toyota's special emission control system checker.

CONVERTER REMOVAL AND INSTALLATION

— CAUTION —

Do not perform the operation on a hot (or even warm) engine. Catalyst temperatures may go as high as 1700°F, so that any contact with the catalyst could cause severe burns.

1. Disconnect the lead from the converter thermosensor.
2. Remove the wiring shield.
3. Unfasten the pipe clamp securing bolts at either end of the converter. Remove the clamps.

4. Push the tailpipe rearward and remove the converter, complete with thermosensor.
5. Carry the converter with the thermosensor upward to prevent the catalyst from falling out.
6. Unfasten the screws and withdraw the thermosensor and gasket.

Installation is performed in the following order:
1. Place a new gasket on the thermosensor. Push the thermosensor into the converter and secure it with its two bolts. Be careful not to drop the thermosensor.

NOTE: Service replacement converters are provided with a plastic thermosensor guide. Slide the sensor into the guide to install it. Do not remove the guide.

2. Install new gaskets on the converter mounting flanges.
3. Secure the converter with its mounting clamps.
4. If the converter is attached to the body with rubber O-rings, install the O-rings over the body and converter mounting hooks.
5. Install the wire protector and connect the lead to the thermosensor.

FUEL SYSTEM

Fuel Filter

REPLACEMENT

Carbureted Engines

All engines employ a disposable, inline filter; when dirty, or at recommended intervals, remove from line and replace.

Fuel Injected Engines

1. Unbolt the retaining screws and remove the protective shield for the fuel filter.
2. Place a pan under the delivery pipe (large connection) to catch the dripping fuel and SLOWLY loosen the union bolt to bleed off the fuel pressure.
3. Remove the union bolt and drain the remaining fuel.
4. Disconnect and plug the inlet line.
5. Unbolt and remove the fuel filter.

NOTE: When tightening the fuel line bolts to the fuel filter, you must use a torque wrench. The tightening torque is very important, as under over tightening may cause fuel leakage. Insure that there is no fuel line interference and that there is sufficient clearance between it and any other parts.

6. Coat the flare nut, union nut and bolt threads with engine oil.

Typical catalytic converter system

7. Hand tighten the inlet line to the fuel filter.

8. Install the fuel filter and then tighten the inlet bolt to 23–33 ft. lbs.

9. Reconnect the delivery pipe using new gaskets and then tighten the union bolt to 18–25 ft. lbs.

10. Run the engine for a few minutes and check for any fuel leaks.

11. Install the protective shield.

Mechanical Fuel Pump

All 1A-C, 3A, and 3A-C engines use a mechanical type fuel pump. It is located on the right rear of the cylinder head. 1980 and later 20R and 22R engines also use a mechanical type fuel pump. It is located on the right front of the cylinder head.

REMOVAL AND INSTALLATION

1. Disconnect the fuel lines to the pump.
2. Remove the bolts which hold the pump to the cylinder head.
3. Remove the pump assembly.
4. Installation is the reverse of removal. Always use a new gasket when installing a fuel pump.

TESTING

1. Remove the line which runs from the fuel pump to the carburetor.
2. Attach a pressure gauge to the outlet side of the pump.
3. Run the engine and check the pressure.
4. Check the pressure against the specifications.
5. If the pressure is below the specifications replace the pump.
6. Reconnect the carburetor line.

Electric Fuel Pump

From 1976–83, all models (except those mentioned previously) use an electric fuel pump.

On models with carbureted engines, the electric fuel pump is located inside of the

Typical electric fuel pump (except EFI equipped models)

fuel tank. On fuel injected engines, the fuel pump is mounted at the rear of the vehicle, outside of the fuel tank.

Either type of fuel pump cannot be repaired if defective—it must be replaced.

REMOVAL AND INSTALLATION

Carbureted Engines

1. Disconnect the negative (−) cable from the battery.

2a. On sedans and hardtops, remove the trim panel from inside the trunk.

b. On station wagons, raise the rear of the vehicle, in order to gain access to the pump.

3. Remove the screws which secure the pump access plate to the tank. Withdraw the plate, gasket, and pump assembly.

4. Disconnect the leads and hoses from the pump.

5. Installation is performed in the reverse order of removal. Use a new gasket on the pump access plate.

Fuel Injected Engines

The pump used on these models is removed by simply disconnecting the fuel lines and electrical connector from the pump and dismounting the pump.

TESTING

CAUTION
Do not operate the fuel pump unless it is immersed in gasoline and connected to its resistor.

Carbureted Engines

1. Disconnect the lead from the oil pressure warning light sender.

2. Unfasten the line from the outlet side of the fuel filter.

3. Connect a pressure gauge to the filter outlet with a length of rubber hose.

4. Turn the ignition switch to the "ON" position, but do not start the engine.

5. Check the pressure gauge reading against the figure given in the "Tune-Up Specifications" chart.

6. Check for a clogged filter or pinched lines if the pressure is not up to specification.

7. If there is nothing wrong with the filter or lines, replace the fuel pump.

8. Turn the ignition off and reconnect the fuel line to the filter. Connect the lead to the oil pressure sender.

Fuel Return Cut Valve

Carbureted Engines Only

The fuel return cut valve controls the amount of fuel returned to the gas tank according to engine load. This prevents percolation when the engine is hot and the load light.

INSPECTION

Attach a long tube to the return pipe of the valve. Put a container under it to catch the fuel. With the engine at idle, fuel should go into the container.

Pinch-off the vacuum line. If valve is operating correctly, the fuel flow should stop.

Fuel Cut-Off Valve

Carbureted Engines Only

In case of an accident, a fuel cut-off valve was added to all systems in 1976. The valve,

"R" series engines—typical fuel pump styles (mechanical pump)

TYPE I

w/gasket

TYPE II

installed between the fuel filter and the carburetor, consists of two check balls that clog the fuel line if the automobile is in other than the normal wheels down position.

Combined with a check on the carburetor and specially designed fuel lines, the fuel cut-off system virtually eliminates the chance of spilled fuel during an accident.

Carburetors

The carburetors used on Toyota models are conventional two-barrel, down-draft types similar to domestic carburetors.

The main circuits are: *primary*, for normal operational requirements; *secondary*, to supply high-speed fuel needs; *float*, to supply fuel to the primary and secondary circuits; *accelerator*, to supply fuel for quick and safe acceleration; *choke*, for reliable starting in cold weather; and *power valve*, for fuel economy and increased high rpm/ high load performance. Although slight differences in appearance may be noted, these carburetors are basically alike. Of course, different jets and settings are demanded by the different engines to which they are fitted.

REMOVAL AND INSTALLATION

NOTE: During carburetor removal, be sure to mark all hoses, lines, electrical connectors, etc., so that these items may be properly reconnected during installation.

1. Remove the air cleaner housing, disconnect all air hoses from the air cleaner base, and disconnect the battery ground cable.

NOTE: On 20R and 22R engines, drain the coolant to prevent it from running into the intake manifold when the carburetor is removed.

2. Disconnect the fuel line, choke pipe,

and distributor vacuum line. On 20R and 22R engines disconnect the choke coolant hose.

3. Remove the accelerator linkage. (With an automatic transmission, also remove the throttle rod to the transmission.)

4. Disconnect any remaining hoses, etc., from the carburetor.

5. Remove the four nuts that secure the carburetor to the manifold and lift off the carburetor and gasket.

6. Cover the open manifold with a clean rag to prevent small objects from dropping into the engine.

7. Installation is performed in the reverse order of removal. After the engine is started, check for fuel leaks and float level settings.

OVERHAUL

For all carburetor overhaul procedures, please refer to "Carburetor Service" in the Unit Repair section.

FLOAT LEVEL ADJUSTMENT

Float level adjustments are unnecessary on models equipped with a carburetor sight glass, if the fuel level falls within the lines or aligns with the dot when the engine is running.

"A" and "T" series engines—measure the raised float level as shown

"A" and "T" series engines—adjust the raised float level at (A)

There are two float level adjustments which may be made on Toyota carburetors. One is with the air horn inverted, so that the float is in a fully *raised* position; the other is with the air horn in an upright position, so that the float falls to the bottom of its travel.

The float level is either measured with a special carburetor float level gauge, which comes with a rebuilding kit, or with a standard wire gauge.

NOTE: Gap specifications are also given so that a float level gauge may be fabricated.

Adjust the float level by bending the tabs on the float levers, either upper or lower, as required.

"A" and "T" series engines—measure the lowered float level as shown

FLOAT LEVEL ADJUSTMENTS

Engine	Gauge Type	Float Raised, Measure Distance Between	Gap (in.)	Gauge Type	Float Lowered Measure Distance Between	Gap (in.)
3K-C, 4K-C	Special	Float end and air horn	0.260④	Special	Lowest point of float and upper side of gauge	1.89③
2T-C, 3T-C⑨	Block	Float tip and air horn	0.200⑤	Wire	Needle valve bushing pin and float lip	0.047
1A-C & 3A and 3A-C⑧	Special	Float tip and air horn	0.0158	Special	Needle valve plunger and float tip	0.047
20R '78–'80	Special	Float end and air horn	0.197⑥	Special	Needle valve bushing pin and float tab	0.039
'76–'77	Special	Float end and air horn	0.370①	Special	Float end and air horn	0.910②
22R '81–'83	Special	Float top and air horn	0.386	Special	Needle valve plunger and float lip	1.890

① 1976: 0.394
② 1976: 0.039
③ 1976–77: float lip gap 0.035
    1978–79: float lip gap 0.024

④ 1978–79: 0.30
⑤ 1978–79: 0.256
⑥ 1978–79: 0.276

⑦ 1980 and later: 1A-C93A check to middle of sight glass
⑧ 1980 and later: 3T-C check to level of dot in sight glass

"A" and "T" series engines—adjust the lowered float level at (B)

"K" series engines—measure the raised float level as indicated

"K" series engines—adjust the raised float level at (A)

"K" series engines—measure the lowered float level as indicated

"K" series engines—adjust the lowered float level at (B)

4M engines—adjusting the lowered float level. Measure as indicated and bend to adjust as shown in the inset

4M engines—adjusting the raised float level. Measure as indicated and bend to adjust as shown in the inset

"R" series engines—measure as indicated and bend at (A) to adjust

"R" series engines—measure as indicated and bend at (B) to adjust

FAST IDLE ADJUSTMENT

Off Vehicle—All Years

The fast idle adjustment is performed with the choke valve fully *closed*, except on the 2T-C and 3T-C engines which should have the choke valve fully *opened*.

Adjust the gap between the throttle valve edge and bore to the specifications, where given, in the ''Fast Idle Specifications'' chart. Use a wire gauge to determine the gap.

The chart below also gives the proper primary throttle valve opening angle, where necessary, and the proper means of fast idle adjustment.

NOTE: The throttle valve opening angle is measured with a gauge supplied in the carburetor rebuilding kit. It is also possible to make one out of cardboard by using a protractor to obtain the correct angle.

On Vehicle—1976–83

NOTE: Disconnect the EGR valve vacuum line on 20R and 22R engines.

1. Adjust the idle speed/mixture. Leave the tachometer connected.
2. Remove the top of the air cleaner.
3. Open the throttle valve slightly and close the choke valve. Hold the choke valve with your finger and close the throttle valve. The choke valve is now fully closed.
4. Without depressing the accelerator pedal, start the engine.
5. Check the engine fast idle speed against the chart below.
6. If the reading on the tachometer is not within specifications, adjust the fast idle speed by turning the fast idle screw.
7. Disconnect the tachometer, install the air cleaner cover, and connect the EGR valve vacuum line if it was disconnected.

FAST IDLE SPEED—1976–83

2T-C (US)—3000 rpm (1977–79—3400)
2T-C (Calif.)—2700 rpm (1977–79—3000)
3T-C (man. trans.)—3200 rpm
3T-C (auto. trans.)—3000 rpm
20R, 22R—2400 rpm (1981–83—2600)
4M (US)—2600 rpm
4M (Calif.)—2400 rpm
1A-C and 3A-C—3600 rpm
3A—3000 rpm

AUTOMATIC CHOKE ADJUSTMENT

NOTE: The automatic choke should be adjusted with the carburetor installed and the engine running. On 20R and 22R engines, do not loosen the center bolt; the coolant will leak out.

1. Check to see that the choke valve will close from fully opened when the coil housing is turned counterclockwise (4M engines—clockwise).

FAST IDLE ADJUSTMENT

Engine	Throttle Valve to Bore Clearance (in.)	Primary Throttle Angle (deg)	To Adjust Fast Idle
3K-C, 4K-C	0.040①	9②	Bend the fast idle lever
2T-C	0.032③	7	Turn the fast idle adjusting screw
3T-C	0.032	—	Turn the fast idle adjusting screw
20R, 22R	0.047	24	Turn the fast idle screw
4M	—	16—from closed④	Turn the fast idle adjusting screw
1A-C	—	22	3600 rpm (E.G.R. off)
3A, 3A-C (MT)	—	24	4000 rpm
3A, 3A-C (AT)	—	21	3000 rpm

① 0.051 in 1976; 0.056 in 1977; 0.037 in 1978–83

② 20° open
③ 1976–79: 0.043

④ 1977–79: 9°
—Not applicable

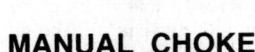

Align the marks on the choke housing

2. Align the mark on the coil housing with the center line on the thermostat case. In this position, the choke valve should be fully closed when the ambient temperature is 77°F.

3. If necessary, adjust the mixture by turning the coil housing. If the mixture is too *rich*, rotate the housing *clockwise*; if too *lean*, rotate the housing *counterclockwise*. On models equipped with the 4M engine, rotate the housing in exactly the reverse direction of the above.

NOTE: Each graduation on the thermostat case is equivalent to 9°F.

MANUAL CHOKE ADJUSTMENT

1. Close the choke by turning the choke shaft lever.

2. Check the 1st throttle valve opening angle with the tool supplied in the rebuild kit.

3. Adjust by turning the fast idle adjusting screw.

CHOKE BREAK ADJUSTMENT

20R and 22R Engines

1. Push the rod which comes out of the upper (choke break) diaphragm so that the choke valve opens.

2. Measure the choke valve opening angle. It should be 38°.

3. Adjust the angle, if necessary, by bending the relief lever link.

INITIAL IDLE MIXTURE SCREW ADJUSTMENT

When assembling the carburetor, turn the idle mixture screw the number of turns specified below. After the carburetor is installed, perform the appropriate idle speed/ mixture adjustment as outlined above.

- 3K-C (1976)—2 turns from seating
- 3K-C (1977)—1¾ turns from seating
- 3K-C, 4K-C (1978 and later)—1½ turns from seating
- 1A-C—2¼ turns from seating
- 3A, 3A-C—2¾ turns from seating
- 20R, 22R—1¾ turns from seating
- 4M—1½ turns from seating

--- CAUTION ---
Seat the idle mixture screw lightly; over-tightening will damage its tip.

UNLOADER ADJUSTMENT

Make the unloader adjustment with the primary valve fully opened. The total angle of choke valve opening, in the chart, is measured with either a special gauge, supplied in the carburetor rebuilding kit, or a guage of the proper angle fabricated from cardboard.

CHOKE UNLOADER ADJUSTMENT

Engine	Throttle Valve Fully Closed (deg)	Choke Valve Angle (deg) From Closed to Fully Open (deg)	Throttle Valve Open (Total) (deg)	Bend to Adjust
3K-C, 4K-C	9	20	90	Fast idle cam follower or choke shaft tab
2T-C	7	38	90	Fast idle lever, follower or choke shaft tab
20R, 22R	—	50①	90	Fast idle lever, follower or choke shaft tab
3T-C, 1A, 3A, 3A-C	20	—	47	Fast idle lever
4M	20	15	90	Fast idle lever

NA—Not applcable
① 45° for 22R engines

Electronic Fuel Injection

For all fuel injection system repair and adjustments not detailed below, please refer to "Fuel Injection" in the Unit Repair section.

FUEL SYSTEM

An electronic fuel pump supplies sufficient fuel, under constant pressure, to the injectors. These injectors meter the fuel into the intake manifold in accordance with signals from the EFI computer. Each injector injects, at the same time, one half of the fuel required for ideal combustion with each engine revolution.

Fuel Injector Replacement

1. Disconnect the negative battery cable.
2. Place a suitable container under the intake manifold to catch any dripping fuel.
3. Remove the air intake chamber as previously described.
4. Unplug the wiring connectors from the tops of the fuel injectors and remove the two plastic clamps that hold the wiring harness to the fuel delivery pipe.
5. Unscrew the four mounting bolts and remove the delivery pipe with the injectors attached.
6. Pull the injectors out of the delivery pipe. To install:

7. Insert six new insulators into the injector holes on the intake manifold.
8. Install the grommet and a new O-ring to the delivery pipe end of each injector.
9. Apply a thin coat of gasoline to the O-ring on each injector and then press them into the delivery pipe.
10. Install the injectors together with the delivery pipe to the intake manifold. Tighten the mounting bolts to 11–15 ft. lbs.
11. Installation of the remaining components is in the reverse order of removal.
12. Start the engine and check for any fuel leaks.

AIR INDUCTION SYSTEM

This system provides sufficient air for proper engine operation. It consists of the air cleaner, air flow meter, air valve, and air intake chamber. These are also controlled by the computer.

EFI COMPUTER

The most important part of the system is the EFI computer. It receives signals indicating a change in operating conditions such as: Air intake volume, air intake temperature, coolant temperature, engine load, acceleration/deceleration, exhaust oxygen content. These signals help the computer determine the injection duration necessary for an optimum air-fuel ratio.

MANUAL TRANSMISSION

REMOVAL AND INSTALLATION

Corolla and Starlet

Working from inside of the car, perform the following:

1. Place the gear selector in Neutral. Remove the center console, if so equipped.
2. Remove the trim boot at the base of the shift lever and the boot underneath it on the shift tower.
3. On Corolla 1200 and Starlet models only:
   a. Unfasten the snap-ring from the base of the shift lever.
   b. Withdraw the conical spring and the shift lever itself.
4. On Corolla 1600 models only:
   a. Remove the four shift lever plate retaining screws.
   b. Remove the shift lever assembly.
   c. Remove the gasket.

NOTE: Cover the hole with a clean cloth to prevent anything from falling into the transmission case.

Working from inside of the car, perform the following:

5. Drain the cooling system and disconnect the cable from the positive side of the battery.
6. Remove the radiator hoses.
7. On Corolla 1200 models only:
   a. Disconnect the backup lamp switch connector.
   b. Remove the engine fan.
8. On Corolla 1600 models only:
   a. Remove the air cleaner, complete with hoses.
   b. Unfasten the accelerator torque rod at the carburetor.
   c. Remove the clutch hydraulic line support bracket.
   d. Remove the starter assembly from the left side of the engine.
   e. Remove the upper left-hand clutch housing bolt, from the flat at the top of the clutch housing.
9. On Starlet models:
   a. Remove the upper radiator hose.
   b. Remove the air cleaner assembly.
   c. Disconnect the accelerator pump lever.
   d. Disconnect the wiring harness connector.
   e. Wrap the steering rack boot with a rag.
   f. Remove the starter assembly as previously outlined.
10. Raise the vehicle and support it safely with jackstands.
11. Drain the transmission oil.
12. Detach the exhaust pipe from the

Electronic fuel injection system

manifold and remove the exhaust pipe support bracket.

13. Remove the driveshaft.

NOTE: It will be necessary to plug the opening in the end of the transmission with an old yoke or, if none is available, cover it with a plastic bag secured by a rubber band.

14. Unfasten the speedometer cable from the right side of the transmission.

15. On Corolla 1600 models, only:

a. Remove the clutch release cylinder assembly from the transmission and tie it aside, so that it is out of the way.

b. Unplug the back-up lamp switch connector.

16. Support the front of the transmission with a jack.

17. Unbolt the engine rear mounts. Remove the rear crossmember.

18. Remove the jack from under the transmission.

19. On Corolla 1600 models, unbolt the clutch housing from the engine and withdraw the transmission assembly.

NOTE: Remove the brace, if so equipped.

20. Perform the following on Corolla 1200 and Starlet models, before removing the transmission:

a. Remove the cotter pin from the clutch release linkage.

b. Remove the clutch release cable.

c. Remove the stiffener plate, if so equipped.

d. Unbolt the clutch housing from the engine by removing the bolts in the order illustrated.

Installation is the reverse of removal, but observe the following.

Apply a light coating of multipurpose grease to the input shaft end, input shaft spline, clutch release bearing, and driveshaft end. On Corolla 1200 and Starlet models, apply multipurpose grease to the ball on the end of the gearshift lever assembly; and to the clutch release cable end.

On Corolla 1200 and Starlet models, install the clutch housing-to-engine bolts in two or three stages, and in the order shown.

After installation:

1. Fill the transmission and cooling system.

2. Adjust the clutch as detailed below.

3. Check to see that the back-up lamps function when Reverse is selected.

Corona

1. Disconnect the negative battery cable and then the positive battery-to-starter cable, complete with fusible link.

2. Drain the coolant from the radiator into a suitable clean container for re-use. Unfasten the upper radiator hose.

3. Detach the accelerator rod and link at the firewall side.

4. Raise both ends of the car and support them with jack stands.

5. Working underneath the car, remove the exhaust pipe clamp and clutch release cylinder (don't disconnect its hydraulic line; set the cylinder out of the way). Next, disconnect the back-up light switch lead and speedometer cable.

6. Remove the driveshaft from the transmission, after matchmarking it and the companion flange for assembly.

NOTE: To prevent oil from draining out of the transmission, install a spare U-joint or if none is available, cover the opening with a plastic bag secured with a rubber band.

7. Place a block of wood on the lift pad of a jack to protect the transmission, and support the transmission with it.

8. Cover the back end of the valve cover with cloths, remove the rear crossmember (see ''Engine Removal''), and lower the jack.

9. Unfasten the bolts which secure the shift lever, and remove the shift lever.

10. Remove the starter motor from the clutch housing.

11. Remove the bolts which secure the clutch housing to the engine block.

12. Move the transmission and jack rearward, until the input shaft has cleared the clutch cover. Remove the transmission from underneath the car.

13. Installation is the reverse of removal. Be sure to apply a thin coating of grease to the input shaft splines. The clutch housing-to-cylinder block bolts should be tightened to 37–58 ft. lbs. Adjust the clutch and fill the transmission with API GL-4 SAE 90 gear oil. Grease the shift lever spring seat and shift lever tip. Use the matchmarks to install the driveshaft.

Celica and Supra (1976–81), Cressida, Mark II

Perform the removal procedures as outlined for the Corolla 1600. In addition, perform the following:

1. Remove the accelerator connecting rod from the linkage.

2. With the car jacked up and supported:

a. Remove the left-hand, rear stone shield before removing the clutch release cylinder.

b. Remove the flywheel housing lower cover and its braces.

Installation is the reverse of removal.

NOTE: Use a clutch guide tool, during installation, to locate the clutch disc.

Celica and Supra (1982–83)

1. Disconnect the battery cables at the battery.

2. Drain the coolant from the radiator and engine.

3. Remove the upper radiator hose.

4. Remove the console box and the shift lever from inside the vehicle.

5. Raise the vehicle and support it safely with jackstands.

6. Drain the transmission fluid.

7. Remove the driveshaft assembly from the vehicle. Mark the driveshaft and flange so that the assembly may be installed in its original position.

8. Remove the bolt from the exhaust pipe stiffener plate.

9. Disconnect the speedometer cable and the back-up lamp switch connector from the transmission.

10. Unbolt the clutch release cylinder and tie it out of the way. It IS NOT necessary to disconnect the hydraulic line from the cylinder.

11. Remove the starter assembly as previously outlined.

12. Using a jack, raise the transmission just enough to take the weight of the transmission off of the support crossmember.

13. Remove the transmission support crossmember.

NOTE: It may be wise to enlist the aid of an assistant to remove the transmission.

14. Remove the transmission mounting bolts. Carefully, pull the transmission rearward, down, and out of the vehicle.

15. Installation is the reverse of the previous steps. Note the following points during installation:

a. Observe the following bolt torques:
Transmission mounting bolts—37–57 ft. lbs.
Transmission crossmember bolts—14–22 ft. lbs.
Exhaust pipe stiffener plate bolt—22–32 ft. lbs.
Starter mounting bolts—37–57 ft. lbs.
U-joint strap bolts—22–32 ft. lbs.

b. Use 2.5 quarts of API service GL-4 or GL-5 SAE 70W-90 or 80W-90 to refill the transmission.

Tercel

1. Disconnect the negative battery cable.

2. Drain the coolant from the radiator tank and remove the top radiator hose.

3. Remove the air cleaner intake duct.

4. Remove the intermediate steering shaft.

5. Drain the gear oil from the transmission.

NOTE: Remove all three drain plugs.

6. Remove the exhaust pipe.

7. Remove the no. 1 gear shift rod and shift lever housing rod.

8. Remove the speedometer cable and back up light switch connector.

9. Remove the rear engine support crossmember.

NOTE: Support the transaxle with a jack and a block of wood.

10. Remove the nine transmission bolts.

11. Install 4 bolts on the transaxle side to an equal depth.

12. Separate the transmission by tightening the bolts a little at a time on the transmission side.

13. Remove the transmission.

14. Installation is the reverse of removal. Tighten the transmission bolts 8–11 ft. lbs. Fill the transmission with 6.5 pints of gear oil.

Floor Shifter Adjustment

All Toyota models equipped with a floor shifter have internally-mounted shift linkages. On older models, the linkage is contained in the side cover which is bolted on the transmission case. Newer cars have the shift linkage mounted in the top of the transmission case itself.

No external adjustment is needed or possible.

CLUTCH

The clutch is a single-plate, dry disc type. Later models use a diaphragm-spring pressure plate. Clutch release bearings are sealed ball bearing units which need no lubrication and should never be washed in any kind of solvent. All clutches, except those on the Tercel are hydraulically operated.

REMOVAL AND INSTALLATION

— CAUTION —
Do not allow grease or oil to get on any of the disc, pressure plate, or flywheel surfaces.

All Models Except Tercel

1. Remove the transmission from the car as detailed above.

2. Remove the clutch cover and disc from the bellhousing.

3. Unfasten the release fork bearing clips. Withdraw the release bearing hub, complete with the release bearing.

4. Remove the tension spring from the clutch linkage.

5. Remove the release fork and support.

6. Punch matchmarks on the clutch cover and the pressure plate so the pressure plate can be returned to its original position during installation.

7. Slowly unfasten the screws which attach the retracting springs.

NOTE: If the screws are released too fast, the clutch assembly will fly apart, causing possible injury or loss of parts.

8. Separate the pressure plate from the clutch cover/spring assembly.

Inspect the parts for wear or deterioation. Replace parts as required.

Installation is performed in the reverse order of removal. Several points should be noted, however:

1. Be sure to align the matchmarks on the clutch cover and pressure plate which were made during disassembly.

2. Apply a thin coating of multipurpose grease to the release bearing hub and release fork contact points. Also, pack the groove inside the clutch hub with multipurpose grease.

3. Center the clutch disc by using a clutch pilot tool or an old input shaft. Insert the pilot into the end of the input shaft front bearing and bolt the clutch to the flywheel.

NOTE: Bolt the clutch assembly to the flywheel in two or three stages.

4. Adjust the clutch as outlined following.

Tercel

In order to replace the clutch, the engine must be removed. See the engine removal section.

1. After the engine has been removed tie the bell housing to the cowl.

2. Place matchmarks on the clutch cover and flywheel.

3. Remove the clutch cover.

NOTE: Loosen each bolt gradually to prevent distortion of the cover.

4. Remove the disc.

5. Installation is the reverse of removal.

NOTE: Do not allow grease to get on the disc lining, flywheel, or cover. When reinstalling the clutch be sure to use a spline alignment tool or an old input shaft to properly align the clutch. Tighten the cover bolts to 11–15 ft. lbs.

FREE-PLAY ADJUSTMENT

All Except Tercel

1. Adjust the clearance between the master cylinder piston and the pushrod to the specifications given in the chart below. Loosen the pushrod locknut and rotate the pushrod while depressing the clutch pedal lightly with your finger.

2. Tighten the locknut when finished the adjustment.

3. Adjust the release cylinder free-play by loosening the release cylinder pushrod locknut and rotating the pushrod until the specification in the chart is obtained.

4. Measure the clutch pedal free-play after performing the above adjustments. If it fails to fall within specifications, repeat Steps 1–3 until it does.

CLUTCH PEDAL FREE-PLAY ADJUSTMENTS

Model	Master Cylinder piston-to-pushrod clearance (in.)	Release cylinder-to-release fork free-play (in.)	Pedal free-play (in.)
Corolla 1200	0.02	1.00–1.40	1.00–1.80①
1600	0.02	0.08–0.14②	0.79–1.58
1800	Not adj.	Not adj.	0.51–0.91
Corona '76–'77	Not adj.	0.08–0.12	0.04–0.28
Corona '78–'82	Not adj.	Not adj.	0.51–0.91
Mark II	0.02–0.12	0.08–0.12	1.20–1.80
Celica '76–'77	0.04–0.12	0.08–0.14	1.00–1.75
Celica '78–'83	Not adj.	Not adj.	0.51–0.91
Supra	Not adj.	Not adj.	0.20–0.59
Starlet, Tercel	Not adj.	Not adj.	0.08–1.18③

①1978–79: 0.8–1.4　③Starlet only
②1978–79: Not adjustable

PEDAL HEIGHT SPECIFICATIONS

Model/Year	Height (in.)	Measure Between
Corolla 1200 '76–'77	2.2①	Pedal pad and floor mat
Corolla 1200 '78–'79	6.7	Pedal pad and floor mat
Tercel '80–'83	6.65	Pedal pad and floor mat
Corolla 1600 '75–'83	6.5	Pedal pad and floor mat
Corolla 1800	6.89–7.28	
Corona '76–'82	6.5–6.9	Pedal pad and floor mat
Mark II/6 '76	6.2–6.6	Pedal pad and asphalt seat
Celica '76–'77	6.3	
'78–'79	6.67	Pedal pad and floor mat
'80–81	6.48–4.87	
'82–'83	6.06–6.46	
Celica Supra '80–'81	6.48–6.87	Pedal and floor mat
Cressida '76–'83	6.1–6.5	From floor mat
Station Wagon (all)	9.6	Pedal pad and firewall
Starlet	6.93	Pedal pad and floor mat

① Pedal depressed

Tercel

The Tercel needs no clutch adjustment as it has the self adjusting type.

Clutch Master Cylinder

REMOVAL AND INSTALLATION

—————— CAUTION ——————
Do not spill fluid on the painted surfaces of the vehicle.

1. Remove the clevis pin.
2. Detach the hydraulic line from the tube.
3. Unfasten the bolts which secure the master cylinder to the firewall. Withdraw the assembly.
4. Installation is performed in the reverse order of removal. Bleed the system as detailed below. Adjust the clutch pedal height and free-play.

OVERHAUL

1. Remove master cylinder.

2. Remove the reservoir.
3. Disengage the snap-ring and take out the pushrod and piston.
4. Inspect all parts for pitting and wear and replace as necessary.
5. Apply a grease compatible with rubber to the piston seals.
6. Install the pushrod and piston and secure with a snap-ring and washer.
7. Install the reservoir. Torque to 22 ft. lbs.
8. Install master cylinder.
9. Bleed the system.

Clutch Release Cylinder

REMOVAL AND INSTALLATION

1. Plug the master cylinder cap to prevent fluid leakage.
2. Raise the front of the vehicle and support it with jack stands.
3. Remove the gravel shield, if necessary, to gain access to the release cylinder.
4. Unfasten the clutch fork return spring at the fork.
5. Detach the hydraulic line from the release cylinder.
6. Screw the release cylinder pushrod in.
7. Loosen and remove the securing nuts from the release cylinder. Remove the cylinder.
8. Installation is performed in the reverse order of removal. Adjust the release fork-to-release cylinder free-play and bleed the hydraulic system, after installation is completed.

OVERHAUL

1. Remove the release cylinder.
2. Remove the pushrod, boot, piston and cup.
3. Inspect all parts for pitting and wear. Replace as necessary.
4. Coat piston seal and cup with a grease compatible with rubber.
5. Install all parts.
6. Install cylinder.
7. Bleed the system.

Automatic Transmission

REMOVAL AND INSTALLATION

Tercel

1. Disconnect the negative battery cable.
2. Drain the coolant from the radiator tank and remove the top hose.

3. Remove the air cleaner inlet duct.
4. Remove the intermediate steering shaft.
5. Drain the fluid from the transmission.
6. Remove the exhaust pipe.
7. Remove the shift lever rod.
8. Remove the speedometer cable, back-up light connector and any throttle linkage.
9. Remove the cooling lines from the transmission.
10. Support the transaxle with a jack.
11. Remove the rear crossmember.
12. Separate the transmission from the transaxle.
13. Remove the transmission.
14. Installation is the reverse of removal.

3-Speed Toyoglide

1976 MARK II ONLY

1. Disconnect the battery.
2. Remove the air cleaner and disconnect the accelerator torque link or the cable.
3. Disconnect the throttle link rod at the carburetor side, then disconnect the backup light wiring at the firewall (on early models).
4. Jack up the car and support it on stands, then drain the transmission. (Use a clean receptacle so that the fluid can be checked for color, smell and foreign matter.)
5. Disconnect all shift linkage.
6. On early models, remove the cross shaft from the frame.
7. Disconnect the throttle link rod at the transmission side and remove the speedometer cable, cooler lines and parking brake equalizer bracket.
8. Loosen the exhaust flange nuts and remove the exhaust pipe clamp and bracket.
9. Remove the driveshaft and the rear mounting bracket, then lower the rear end of the transmission carefully.
10. Unbolt the torque converter from the drive plate. Support the engine with a suitable jack stand and remove the seven bolts that hold the transmission to the engine.

Reverse the order of the removal procedures with the following precautions.

1. Install the drive plate and ring gear, tighten the attaching bolts to 37–43 ft. lbs.
2. After assembling the torque converter to the transmission, check the clearance, it should be about 0.59 in.
3. Before installing the transmission, install the oil pump locator pin on the torque converter to facilitate installation.
4. While rotating the crankshaft, tighten the converter attaching bolts, a little at a time.
5. After installing the throttle connecting second rod, make sure the throttle valve lever indicator aligns with the mark on the transmission with the carburetor throttle valve fully opened. If required, adjust the rod.
6. To install the transmission control

rod correctly, move the transmission lever to N (Neutral), and the selector lever to Neutral. Fill the transmission with automatic transmission fluid (Type F only), then start the engine. Run the engine at idle speed and apply the brakes while moving the selector lever through all positions, then return it to Neutral.

7. After warming the engine, move the selector lever through all positions, then back to Neutral, and check the fluid level. Fill as necessary.

8. Adjust the engine idle to 550–650 rpm with the selector lever at Drive. Road test the vehicle.

9. With the selector lever at 2 or Drive, check the point at which the transmission shifts. Check for shock, noise and slipping with the selector lever in all positions. Check for leaks from the transmission.

A-40, A-40D, and A-43D

To remove and install the transmission, proceed in the following manner:

1. Perform Steps 1 through 3 of the three-speed Toyoglide removal procedure.

2. Remove the upper starter mounting nuts using a socket wrench with a long extension.

3. Raise the car and support it securely with jack stands. Drain the transmission.

4. Remove the lower starter mounting bolt and lay the starter along side of the engine. Don't let it hang by the wires.

5. Unbolt the parking brake equalizer support.

6. Matchmark the driveshaft and the companion flange, to ensure correct installation. Remove the bolts securing the driveshaft to the companion flange.

7. Slide the driveshaft straight back and out of the transmission. Use a spare U-joint yoke or tie a plastic bag over the end of the transmission to keep any fluid from dripping out.

8. Remove the bolts from the crossshaft body bracket, the cotter pin from the manual lever, and the cross-shaft socket from the transmission.

9. Remove the exhaust pipe bracket from the torque converter bell housing.

10. Disconnect the oil cooler lines from the transmission and remove the line bracket from the bell housing.

11. Disconnect the speedometer cable from the transmission.

12. Unbolt both support braces from the bell housing.

13. Use a transmission jack to raise the transmission slightly.

14. Unbolt the rear crossmember and lower the transmission about 3 in.

15. Pry the two rubber torque converter access plugs out of their holes at the back of the engine.

16. Remove the six torque converter mounting bolts through the access hole. Rotate the engine with the crankshaft pulley.

17. Cut the head off a bolt to make a

guide pin for the torque converter. Install the pin on the converter.

18. Remove the converter bell housing-to-engine bolts.

19. Push on the end of the guide pin in order to remove the converter with the transmission. Remove the transmission rearward and then bring it out from under the car.

--- CAUTION ---

Don't catch the throttle cable during removal.

Installation is the reverse of removal. Be sure to note the following, however:

1. Install the two long bolts on the upper converter housing and tighten them to 36–58 ft. lbs.

2. Tighten the converter-to-flex-plate bolts finger-tight, and then tighten them with a torque wrench to 11–16 ft. lbs.

3. When installing the speedometer cable, make sure that the felt dust protector and washer are on the cable end.

4. Tighten the cooling line and exhaust pipe bracket mounting bolts to 37–58 ft. lbs. Tighten the cooling lines to 14–22 ft. lbs.

5. Align the matchmarks made on the driveshaft and the companion flange during removal. Tighten the driveshaft mounting bolts to 11–16 ft. lbs.

6. Be sure to install the oil pan drain plug. Tighten it to 11–14 ft. lbs.

7. Adjust the throttle cable.

8. Fill the transmission to the proper capacity. Use only type ''F'' (ATF) fluid. Start the engine, run the selector through all gear ranges and place it in Park (P). Check the level on the dipstick and add type F fluid, as necessary.

9. Road test the car and check for leaks.

PAN REMOVAL

1. Remove the plug and drain the fluid from the transmission.

2. Unfasten the pan securing bolts.

3. Remove the pan.

4. Installation is the reverse of removal. Torque the pan securing bolts to 4–6 ft. lbs. Refill the transmission with fluid.

BAND ADJUSTMENTS

Front Band

NOTE: Band adjustments are not possible on A-40, A-40D, or A-43D transmissions. Also note that the 3-Speed Toyoglide (A-30) is only used in 1976 Mark II's.

3 SPEED TOYOGLIDE

1. Remove the pan as outlined above.

2. Pry the band engagement lever toward the band with a screwdriver.

3. The gap between the end of the piston rod and the engagement bolt should be 0.138 in.

1. Master cylinder push rod
2. Push rod locknut
3. Clevis
4. Pedal stop (bolt)

Clutch pedal adjustments

4. If the gap does not meet the specifications, adjust it by turning the engagement bolt.

5. Install the pan and refill the transmission as outlined above.

Rear Band

3 SPEED TOYOGLIDE

The rear band adjusting bolt is located on the outside of the case, so it is not necessary to remove the pan in order to adjust the band.

1. Loosen the adjusting bolt locknut and fully screw in the adjusting bolt.

2. Loosen the adjusting bolt one turn.

3. Tighten the locknut while holding the bolt so that it cannot turn.

NEUTRAL SAFETY SWITCH ADJUSTMENT

3-Speed Toyoglide

Models with a console-mounted selector have the neutral safety switch on the linkage located beneath the console. To adjust it, proceed in the following manner:

1. Remove the screws which secure the center console.

2. Unfasten the console multiconnec-

Adjusting the three-speed Toyoglide front band

tor, if so equipped, and completely remove the console.

3. Adjust the switch in the manner outlined in the column selector section, above.

4. Install the console in the reverse order of removal after completion of the switch adjustment.

The neutral safety switch/reverse lamp switch on the Toyoglide transmission with a column-mounted selector is located under the hood on the shift linkage. If the switch is not functioning properly, adjust as follows:

1. Loosen the switch securing bolt.

2. Move the switch so that its arm just contacts the control shaft lever when the gear selector is in Drive position.

3. Tighten the switch securing bolt.

4. Check the operation of the switch; the car should start only in Park or Neutral and the back-up lamps should come on only when Reverse is selected.

5. If the switch cannot be adjusted so that it functions properly, replace it. Perform the adjustment as outlined.

Adjusting the neutral safety switch on models with the three speed Toyoglide and floor mounted shift

Adjusting the neutral safety switch on models with the three speed Toyoglide and a column-mounted shift

All Transmissions Except 3-Speed Toyoglide

If the engine will start in any range except Neutral or Park, the neutral safety switch will require adjustment.

1. Locate the neutral safety switch on the right side of the transmission and loosen the switch bolt.

2. Move the gear selector to the Neutral position.

3. Aligh the groove on the safety switch

Neutral safety switch adjustment

shaft with the basic line which is scribed on the housing.

4. Tighten the switch bolt.

5. Using an ohmmeter, check the continuity between the switch terminals as shown in the accompanying illustration. If a continuity problem is found, replace the switch.

	B	N	RB	RL
P	O─	─O		
R			O──	──O
N	O─	─O		

Checking the neutral safety switch for continuity between the connectors

SHIFT LINKAGE ADJUSTMENT

3-Speed Toyoglide

1. Check all of the shift linkage bushings for wear. Replace any worn bushings.

2. Loosen the connecting rod swivel locknut.

3. Move the selector lever and check movement of the pointer in the shift quadrant.

4. When the control shaft is set in the neutral position the quadrant pointer should indicate "N" (Neutral), as well.

Steps 5–7 apply only to cars equipped with column-mounted shift levers.

5. If the pointer does not indicate Neutral, then check the drive cord adjustment.

6. Remove the steering column shroud.

Adjusting the column shift indicator drive cord

7. Turn the drive cord adjuster with a Phillips screwdriver until the pointer indicates Neutral.

Steps 8–10 apply to both column-mounted and floor-mounted selectors:

8. Position the manual valve lever on the transmission so that it is in the Neutral position.

9. Lock the connecting rod swivel with the locknut so that the pointer, selector, and manual valve lever are all positioned in Neutral.

10. Check the operation of the gear selector by moving it through all ranges.

All Transmissions Except 3-Speed Toyoglide

1. Check the linkage for freedom of movement.

2. Push the manual valve lever toward the front of the car, as far as it will go.

3. Bring the lever back to its third notch (Neutral).

4. Have someone hold the shift lever in Neutral, while you tighten the linkage so that it can't slip.

THROTTLE LINKAGE ADJUSTMENT

3-Speed Toyoglide

1. Loosen the locknut at each end of the linkage adjusting turnbuckle.

2. Detach the throttle linkage connecting rod from the carburetor.

3. Align the pointer on the throttle valve lever with the mark stamped on the transmission case.

4. Rotate the turnbuckle so that the end of the throttle linkage rod and the carburetor throttle lever are aligned.

NOTE: The carburetor throttle valve must be fully opened during this adjustment.

Toyoglide throttle linkage aligning marks

Toyoglide throttle linkage components

5. Tighten the turnbuckle locknuts and reconnect the throttle rod to the carburetor.

6. Open the throttle valve and check the pointer alignment with the mark on the transmission case.

7. Road-test the car. If the transmission "hunts," i.e., keeps shifting rapidly back and forth between gears at certain speeds or if it fails to downshift properly when going up hills, repeat the throttle linkage adjustment.

All Transmissions Except 3-Speed Toyoglide

1. Remove the air cleaner.

2. Confirm that the accelerator linkage opens the throttle fully. Adjust the link as necessary.

3. Peel the rubber dust book back from the throttle cable.

4. Loosen the adjustment nuts on the throttle cable bracket (rocker cover) just enough to allow cable housing movement.

5. Have someone depress the accelerator pedal fully.

6. Adjust the cable housing so that the distance between its end and the cable stop collar is 2.05 in. (0.4 in.—1980 and later).

7. Tighten the adjustment nuts. Make sure that the adjustment hasn't changed. Install the dust boot and the air cleaner.

Throttle linkage adjustment—1979 and earlier models

Throttle linkage adjustment—1980 and later models

DRIVE AXLE

Driveshaft and U-Joints

REMOVAL AND INSTALLATION

Except Tercel

1. Raise the rear of the car with jacks and support the rear axle housing with jack stands.

2. Matchmark the driveshaft and companion flange. Unfasten the bolts which attach the driveshaft universal joint yoke flange to the mounting flange on the differential drive pinion.

3. On models equipped with three universal joints, perform the following:

a. Remove the driveshaft subassembly from the U-joint sleeve yoke.

b. Remove the center support bearing from its bracket.

4. Remove the driveshaft end from the transmission.

5. Install an old U-joint yoke in the transmission or, if none is available, use a plastic bag secured with a rubber band over the hole to keep the transmission oil from running out.

NOTE: On 1982 and later Supra models, the exhaust pipe assembly must be removed in order to remove the driveshaft assembly.

6. Remove the driveshaft from beneath the vehicle.

Installation is performed in the following order:

1. Apply multipurpose grease on the section of the U-joint sleeve which is to be inserted into the transmission.

2. Insert the driveshaft sleeve into the transmission.

— CAUTION —

Be careful not to damage any of the seals.

3. For models equipped with three U-joints and center bearings, perform the following:

a. Adjust the center bearing clearance with no load placed on the driveline components; the top of the rubber center cushions should be 0.04 in. *behind* the center of the elongated bolt hole.

b. Install the center bearing assembly.

1. Transmission end of driveshaft
2. U-joint yoke and sleeve
3. U-joint spider
4. Snap ring
5. U-joint spider bearing
6. Balancing weight
7. Driveshaft
8. U-joint yoke flange
9. Intermediate driveshaft assembly
10. Center bearing support
11. U-joint flange assembly
12. Driveshaft

Two-piece driveshaft only

Driveshaft components—the upper illustration shows a single piece driveshaft

NOTE: Use the same number of washers on the center bearing bracket as were removed.

c. Match the arrow marks on the driveshaft and grease fittings.

4. Align the matchmarks. Secure the U-joint flange to the differential pinion flange with the mounting bolts.

———— CAUTION ————

Be sure that the bolts are of the same type as those removed and that they are tightened securely.

5. Remove the jack stands and lower the vehicle.

Center bearing adjustment

U-JOINT OVERHAUL

Except Tercel

1. Mark the flange yoke and shaft for reassembly.
2. Remove the snap-rings and, using a hammer and drift, drive one bearing cap most of the way out. Remove it with pliers.
3. Drive the opposite cap out.
4. Repeat this procedure for the other two caps.
5. Remove the spider.
6. Install a new spider in the yoke.
7. Press bearing caps over spider using a vise.
8. Install snap-rings.
9. Assemble driveshaft and check for smoothness of operation.

Front Drive Axle

REMOVAL AND INSTALLATION

Tercel

1. Jack up your vehicle and support it with jack stands.
2. Remove the front wheel.
3. Remove the brake caliper and tie it out of the way.
4. Remove the cotter pin, locknut and adjusting nut, from the hub.
5. Remove the bottom nut from the shock absorber.
6. Pull down on the hub to separate it from the shock.

7. Using a suitable puller pull the axle hub from the driveshaft.
8. Remove the transaxle support bracket.
9. Remove the driveshaft from the transaxle using special tool #09648-16010 available from your Toyota dealer.

NOTE: Be careful not to damage the rubber boots on the driveshaft.

10. Installation is the reverse of removal.

TRIPOD REMOVAL AND INSTALLATION

Inner Only—Tercel

1. Remove the snap-ring and boot clamp.
2. Matchmark the driveshaft and the in-board joint shaft.
3. Remove the inner boot.
4. Place matchmarks on the tripod and the shaft.

NOTE: When making these matchmarks be sure to use paint, or chalk. Do not punch mark any of these parts.

5. Drive the tripod off with a drift pin.

NOTE: Do not tap on the roller portion of the tripod.

6. Check for worn or damaged parts.
7. When reinstalling the tripod fill the boot with a lithium base grease.
8. Installation is the reverse of removal.

The manufacturer recommends that the outboard shaft be serviced as a complete unit only.

Front Drive Axle Hub

REMOVAL AND INSTALLATION

Tercel

1. Jack up your vehicle and support it with jack stands.
2. Remove the front wheel.
3. Remove the brake caliper and tie it out of the way.
4. Remove the stabilizer bar end.
5. Remove the strut bar end.
6. Remove the tie rod end, with a suitable puller.
7. Support the lower control arm with a jack.
8. Remove the lower control arm bolt.
9. Remove the bolt at the ball joint.
10. Lower the jack and remove the control arm.
11. Remove the bottom shock bolt.
12. Pull the hub from the driveshaft with a suitable puller.
13. Remove the steering knuckle from the shock absorber.
14. Installation is the reverse of removal.

The following torque specifications are needed: bottom shock bolt 40–52 ft. lbs., ball joint bolt 40–52 ft. lbs., stabilizer bar 11–15 ft. lbs., tie rod end 37–50 ft. lbs., lower control arm 51–65 ft. lbs., strut bar 29–39 ft. lbs., brake caliper 33–39 ft. lbs.

1. Wheel
2. Bearing locknut
3. Disc brake caliper
4. Stablizer bar end
5. Bolt
6. Stiffener plate
7. Driveshaft

Tercel front drive axle components

Rear Axle Shafts

REMOVAL AND INSTALLATION

Except Supra (1982 and Later)

1. Raise the rear of the car and support it securely by using jack stands.
2. Drain the oil from the axle housing.
3. Remove the wheel disc, unfasten the lug nuts, and remove the wheel.
4. Punch matchmarks on the brake drum and the axle shaft to maintain rotational balance.
5. Remove the brake drum and related components, as detailed below.
6. Remove the rear bearing retaining nut.
7. Remove the backing plate attachment nuts through the access holes in the rear axle shaft flange.
8. Use a slide hammer with a suitable adapter to withdraw the axle shaft from its housing.

—— CAUTION ——

Use care not to damage the oil seal when removing the axle shaft.

9. Repeat the procedure for the axle shaft on the opposite side.

—— CAUTION ——

Be careful not to mix the components of the two sides.

Installation is performed in the reverse order of removal. Coat the lips of the rear housing oil seal with multipurpose grease prior to installation of the rear axle shaft. Torque the bearing retaining nut to the specifications.

NOTE: Always use new nuts, as they are the self-locking type.

AXLE BEARING RETAINING NUT SPECIFICATIONS

Model	Torque range (ft. lbs.)
Corolla 1200	15–22
Corolla 1600	26–38
Corolla 1800	19–23
Corona	29–36
Mark II/6	43–52
Tercel	22
Celica	19–23
Supra①	19–23
Cressida	22

①Except 1982 and later—See text

Supra (1982 and Later)

Remove the axle shaft in the following manner:

1. Raise the rear of the vehicle and support it safely with jackstands.
2. Disconnect the axle drive shaft from the axle flange and lower the axle drive shaft out of the way.
3. Apply the parking brake completely (pulled up as far as possible).
4. Remove the axle flange nut.

NOTE: The axle flange nut is staked in place. It will be necessary to loosen the staked part of the nut with a hammer and chisel, prior to loosening the nut.

5. Using Toyota special service tool #SST 09557-22022 (or its equivalent), disconnect the axle flange from the axle shaft. Be careful not to lose the plate washer from the bearing side of the flange.
6. Remove the parking brake shoes.

7. Using Toyota special service tool #SST 09520-00031 (or its equivalent), pull out the rear axle shaft, along with the oil seal and outer bearing.

Inspect the components:

8. Clean and inspect the bearings, races, and seal. If these parts are in good condition, repack the bearings with MP grease no. 2 and proceed to Step 15 to install the axle shaft.

To replace the bearings and seals:

9. Using a hammer and chisel, increase the clearance between the axle shaft hub and the outer bearing.
10. Using a puller installed with the jaws in the gap made in Step 9, pull the outer bearing from the axle shaft and remove the oil seal.
11. Drive the outer bearing race out of the hub with a brass drift and a hammer.

NOTE: Bearing and races must be replaced in matched sets. NEVER use a new bearing with an old race, or vice-versa.

12. Drive the new outer bearing race into the axle shaft hub until it is completely seated.

NOTE: The inner bearing race is replaced in the same manner as Steps 11 and 12.

13. Repack and install both bearings into the hub, being careful not to mix the bearings.

NOTE: The bearings should be packed with no. 2 multipurpose grease.

14. Drive the seals into place. The inner seal should be driven to a depth of 1.22 in.; the outer to 0.217 in.

To install the rear axle shaft:

15. Apply a thin coat of grease to the axle shaft flange. Install the rear axle shaft into the housing and install the flange with the plate washer.
16. Using Toyota special service tool #SST 09557-22022 (or its equivalent), draw the axle shaft into the flange.
17. Remove the special service tool and install a new axle shaft flange nut. Torque the nut to 22–36 ft. lbs. There should be no horizontal play evident at the axle shaft.
18. Turn the axle shaft back and forth and retorque the nut to 58 ft. lbs.
19. Using a torque wrench, check the amount of torque required to turn the axle shaft. The correct rotational torque is 0.9–3.5 in. lbs.

NOTE: The shaft should be turned at a rate of 6 seconds per turn to attain a true rotational torque reading.

20. If the rotational torque is less than specified, tighten the nut 5–10 degrees at a time until the proper rotational torque is reached. DO NOT tighten the nut to more than 145 ft. lbs.
21. If the rotational torque is greater than specified, replace the bearing spacer and repeat Steps 18–20 (if necessary).

1. Backing plate set bolt
2. Rear axle housing
3. Rear axle shaft
4. Axle bearing inner retainer
5. Oil seal
6. Bearing
7. Spacer
8. Axle housing end gasket
9. Bearing retainer gasket
10. Axle bearing inner retainer
11. Hub bolt
12. Brake drum assembly
13. Wheel
14. Hub nut

Typical rear axle shaft and related components (except Supra—1982 and later)

CAUTION

If the maximum torque is exceeded while retightening the nut, replace the bearing spacer and repeat Steps 18–20. DO NOT back off the axle shaft nut to reduce the rotational torque.

---

22. After the proper rotational torque is reached, restake the nut into position.
23. Install the parking brake shoes.
24. Connect the axle drive shaft to the flange and torque the nuts to 44–57 ft. lbs.
25. Install the rear wheel and lower the vehicle.

Rear Axle Drive Shaft

REPLACEMENT

NOTE: The following procedure applies only to 1982 and later Supra models.

1. Disconnect the drive shaft from the differential flange.
2. Disconnect the drive shaft from the axle flange.
3. Lift either drive shaft flange over the flange studs and remove the drive shaft.
4. Installation is performed in the reverse of the previous steps.

OVERHAUL

Because the use of a hydraulic press is required to disassemble and assemble this type of drive shaft, it is recommended that overhaul be performed only by a professional automotive repair facility.

Differential

REMOVAL AND INSTALLATION

NOTE: Rear axle servicing is a complex operation. Repair should not be attempted unless the special tools and knowledge required are readily available.

Removable Rear Carrier

ALL MODELS EXCEPT TERCEL AND SUPRA (1982 AND LATER)

1. Remove the axle shaft.
2. Disconnect the driveshaft from the pinion shaft flange.
3. Unfasten the carrier securing nuts and remove the carrier assembly.

Installation is performed in the reverse order of removal. Be sure to apply liquid sealer to both the carrier gasket and the lower carrier securing nuts.

TERCEL

1. Disconnect the negative battery terminal.

Rear axle shaft—1982 and later Supra

Rear axle drive shafts—1982 and later Supra

2. Drain the water from the radiator tank.

3. Remove the top radiator hose from the engine.

4. Remove the clutch cable if so equipped.

5. Remove the starter.

NOTE: On cars equipped with automatic transmissions you must remove the torque converter bolts via the starter inset. Also remember to disconnect the oil cooling lines.

6. Remove the intermediate steering shaft.

7. Remove the bottom bolt on the engine shock absorber.

8. Remove the front driveshafts. See the section relating to this procedure.

9. Remove the exhaust pipe.

10. Remove the shifting linkage.

11. Remove the back-up light connector and the speedometer.

NOTE: On cars with automatic transmissions remove any necessary throttle linkage if so equipped.

12. Drain the oil from the transaxle and the transmission.

NOTE: Remove all three drain plugs on manual transmission cars.

13. Support the rear of the engine with a jack.

14. Remove the rear crossmember.

15. Place a jack under the transaxle.

16. Separate the transmission from the transaxle and remove the transmission.

17. Remove the bellhousing bolts and remove the transaxle.

18. Installation is the reverse of removal.

Because of the many specialized tools required to work on the differential, it is recommended that this work be performed by your dealer or a professional mechanic qualified to handle this type of work.

SUPRA (1982 AND LATER)

1. Raise the rear of the vehicle and support it safely with jackstands.

2. Remove the differential drain plug and allow the differential oil to drain.

3. Disconnect the axle drive shafts from the differential flanges.

4. Disconnect the propeller shaft flange from the differential companion flange.

5. Remove the no. 1 differential support member mounting bolt.

6. Place a jack under the differential and raise the jack in order to support the differential.

7. Remove the eight differential-to-carrier mounting bolts.

8. CAREFULLY lower the differential from the vehicle.

9. Installation is performed in the reverse of the previous steps. Observe the following fastener torques during installation:

Differential-to-carrier mounting bolts—51–72 ft. lbs.

No. 1 support member mounting bolt—51–72 ft. lbs.

Rear axle drive shaft fasteners—44–57 ft. lbs.

NOTE: The differential oil capacity is 1.3 qts. Use SAE 90 oil if ambient temperature is above 0°F; SAE 80W or 80W-90 if temperature is below 0°F. In limited-slip differentials, use oil which is specified only for this purpose.

REAR SUSPENSION

Springs

REMOVAL AND INSTALLATION

Passenger Cars with Rear Leaf Springs

1. Loosen the rear wheel lug nuts.

2. Raise the rear of the vehicle. Support the frame and rear axle housing with stands.

3. Remove the lug nuts and the wheel.

4. Remove the cotter pin, nut, and washer from the lower end of the shock absorber.

5. Detach the shock absorber from the spring seat pivot pin.

6. Remove the parking brake cable clamp.

NOTE: Remove the parking brake equalizer, if necessary.

7. Unfasten the U-bolt nuts and remove the spring seat assemblies.

8. Adjust the height of the rear axle housing so that the weight of the rear axle is removed from the rear springs.

9. Unfasten the spring shackle retaining nuts. Withdraw the spring shackle inner plate. Carefully pry out the spring shackle with a bar.

10. Remove the spring bracket pin from the front end of the spring hanger and remove the rubber bushings.

11. Remove the spring.

— CAUTION —
Use care not to damage the hydraulic brake line or the parking brake cable.

Installation is performed in the following order:

1. Install the rubber bushings in the eye of the spring.

2. Align the eye of the spring with the spring hanger bracket and drive the pin through the bracket holes and rubber bushings.

NOTE: Use soapy water as lubricant,

No.1 Mounting Bolt

Differential Carrier with Suspension Member

Differential Support Member

Bolt

Nut

Propeller Shaft

Drive Shaft

Drain Plug

Differential mounting—1982 and later Supra

1. Rear spring
2. Rear shock absorber
3. Cotter pin
4. Castle nut
5. Shock absorber cushion washer
6. Bushing
7. Shock absorber cushion washer
8. Spring bracket
9. Rear spring bumper
10. Spring washer
11. Bolt
12. Rear spring shackle
13. Nut
14. Spring washer
15. Bushing
16. Spring bracket
17. Rear spring hanger pin
18. Spring washer
19. Bolt
20. Rear spring leaf
21. Nut
22. Nut
23. Rear spring clip bolt
24. Clip bolt
25. Rear spring clip
26. Round rivet
27. Rear spring leaf
28. Rear spring leaf
29. Rear spring center bolt
30. U-bolt seat
31. U-bolt
32. Spring washer
33. Nut
34. Rear spring leaf
35. Rear spring clip
36. Round rivet
37. Rear spring leaf
38. Rear spring leaf

Typical leaf spring rear suspension

if necessary, to aid in pin installation. Never use oil or grease.

3. Finger-tighten the spring hanger nuts and/or bolts.

4. Install the rubber bushings in the spring eye at the opposite end of the spring.

5. Raise the free end of the spring. Install the spring shackle through the bushings and the bracket.

6. Install the shackle inner plate and finger-tighten the retaining nuts.

7. Center the bolt head in the hole which is provided in the spring seat on the axle housing.

8. Fit the U-bolts over the axle housing. Install the lower spring seat.

9. Tighten the U-bolt nuts.

NOTE: Some models have two sets of nuts, while others have a nut and lock-washer.

10. Install the parking brake cable clamp. Install the equalizer, if it was removed.

11. On passenger cars:

a. Install the shock absorber end at the spring seat. Tighten the nuts.

b. Install the wheel and lug nuts. Lower the car to the ground.

c. Bounce the car several times.

d. Tighten the spring bracket pins and shackles.

Passenger Cars with Rear Coil Springs

1. Remove the hubcap and loosen the lug nuts.

2. Jack up the rear axle housing and support the frame with jack stands. Leave the jack in place under the rear axle housing.

3. Remove the lug nuts and wheel.

4. If so equipped, disconnect the rear stabilizer bar from the axle housing (or suspension arm, on 1982 and later Supra models).

5. Unfasten the lower shock absorber end.

NOTE: On 1982 and later Supra models, remove the rear axle drive shaft(s) as previously outlined.

6. Slowly lower the jack under the rear axle housing until the axle is at the bottom of its travel.

7. Withdraw the coil spring, complete with its insulator.

8. Inspect the coil spring and insulator for wear, cracks, or weakness; replace either or both, as necessary.

9. Installation is performed in the reverse order of removal.

Rear Shock Absorbers

REMOVAL AND INSTALLATION

1. Jack up the rear end of the vehicle.

2. Support the rear axle housing with jack stands.

3. Unfasten the upper shock absorber retaining nuts and/or bolts from the upper frame member.

4. Depending upon the type of rear

Rear suspension—1982 and later Supra

1. Bumper
2. Spring insulator
3. Coil spring
4. Lower control arm
5. Bushing
6. Upper control arm
7. Bushing
8. Bushing
9. Lateral control rod
10. Bushing
11. Retainer
12. Cushion
13. Retainer
14. Shock absorber
15. Washer
16. Bushing
17. Washer

Mark II rear suspension

springs used, either disconnect the lower end of the shock absorber from the spring seat, or the rear axle housing, by removing its cotter pins, nuts, and/or bolts.

5. Remove the shock absorber.

6. Inspect the shock for wear, leaks, or other signs of damage. Test it as outlined in the front suspension shock absorber section.

7. Installation is performed in the reverse order from removal.

FRONT SUSPENSION

MacPherson Struts

REMOVAL AND INSTALLATION

For all spring and shock absorber re-

moval and installation procedures, and all strut overhaul procedures, please refer to "Strut Overhaul" in the Unit Repair section.

All Models Except Tercel

1. Remove the hubcap and loosen the lug nuts.

2. Raise the front of the car and support it on the chassis jacking plates provided, with jack stands.

—————— CAUTION ——————

Do not support the weight of the car on the suspension arm; the arm will deform under its weight.

3. Unfasten the lug nuts and remove the wheel.

4. Detach the front brake line from its clamp.

5. Remove the brake drum, or the caliper and wire it out of the way.

6. Unfasten the three nuts which secure the upper shock absorber mounting plate to the top of the wheel arch.

7. Remove the two bolts which attach the shock absorber lower end to the steering knuckle lower arm.

NOTE: Press down on the suspension lower arm, in order to remove the strut aseembly. This must be done to clear the collars on the steering knuckle arm bolt holes when removing the shock/spring assembly.

Installation is performed in the reverse order of removal. Be sure to note the following, however:

1. Align the hole in the upper suspension support with the shock absorber piston rod end, so that they fit properly.

2. Always use a *new* nut and nylon washer on the shock absorber piston rod end when securing it to the upper suspension support. Torque the nut to 29–40 ft. lbs.

—————— CAUTION ——————

Do not use an impact wrench to tighten the nut.

3. Coat the suspension support bearing with multipurpose grease prior to installation. Pack the space in the upper support with multipurpose grease, also, after installation.

4. Tighten the suspension support-to-wheel arch bolts to the following specification:

Corolla—11–16 ft. lbs.
Celica—14–23 ft. lbs.

5. Tighten the shock absorber-to-steering knuckle arm bolts to the following specifications:

Corolla—50–65 ft. lbs.
Celica—58–87 ft. lbs.

6. Adjust the front wheel bearing preload as outlined below.

7. Bleed the brake system.

1. Nut
2. Washer
3. Lateral control rod
4. Bushing
5. Bolt
6. Bushing
7. Upper control arm
8. Lower control arm
9. Spring insulator
10. Spring bumper
11. Coil spring
12. Washer
13. Bushing
14. Washer
15. Nut
16. Nut
17. Washer
18. Bushing
19. Shock absorber
20. Bushing

Solid, coil-sprung rear suspension—typical of all models which use rear coil springs (except the Mark II and the 1982 and later Supra)

Tercel

1. Jack up your vehicle and support it with jack stands.

2. Remove the front wheel.

3. Remove the brake caliper and tie it out of the way.

4. Remove the stabilizer bar end.

5. Remove the bottom strut bolt.

6. Push down on the steering knuckle to free the bottom of the strut.

7. Remove the top strut bolts.

8. Remove the strut.

9. Installation is in the reverse order of removal. Observe the following bolt torques:
   Shock seat bolt—29–39 ft. lbs.
   Top shock bolts—15–21 ft. lbs.
   Bottom shock bolts—40–52 ft. lbs.

Springs

REMOVAL AND INSTALLATION

----WARNING----

The coil springs are retained under considerable pressure. They can exert enough force to cause serious injury. Exercise extreme caution when servicing.

Corona and Cressida

1. Remove the hubcap (if so equipped) and loosen the nuts.

2. Raise the front of the car and support it by using jack stands.

3. Remove the lug nuts and the wheel.

4. Remove the shock absorber as detailed in the appropriate section below. Remove the stabilizer bar from the lower control arm (if so equipped).

5. Install a coil spring compressor and compress the spring until there is no load on it.

NOTE: Place a jack under the lower control arm spring seat, as a safety precaution.

6. Unfasten the lower ball joint retaining bolts and withdraw the ball joint, complete with the steering knuckle, from the lower control arm.

7. Slowly loosen the spring compressor and remove the spring. Lower the jack.

Inspect the spring, ball joint, and related components for wear or damage. Replace any parts necessary.

Installation is performed in the reverse order of removal.

NOTE: The coil springs are not interchangeable from the right side to the left side.

The ball joint/steering knuckle assembly securing bolts should be tightened to the following specifications:
   12 mm bolts—58–83 ft. lbs.
   88 bolts—11–16 ft. lbs.

After completing installation of the coil spring, check to see that it is properly seated

Components of a typical MacPherson strut front suspension

1. Steering knuckle arm
2. Retainer
3. Cushion
4. Collar
5. Dust cover
6. Retainer
7. Lower control arm
8. Bushing
9. Bushing
10. Bracket
11. Stabilizer bar
12. Strut
13. Retainer
14. Cushion
15. Collar

in the lower suspension arm. Check front end alignment.

Mark II

1. Perform Steps 1–3 of the previous Corona coil spring removal and installation procedure.

2. Unfasten the stabilizer bar.

3. Measure the distance between the serrated bolt holes on the front side of the torque strut and the attachment nut on the rear side to aid in installation. Remove the strut.

4. Remove the shock absorber.

5. Install the coil spring compressor on the third coil from the bottom. Tighten the compressor until the load is removed from the spring.

6. Remove the lower ball joint with a ball joint puller.

Specified Length: 348mm (18.7")

(A)

Measure distance A before removing the strut

Brake Hose

Brake Hose

Shock Absorber

Steering Arm Knuckle

Typical MacPherson strut shock absorber and spring combination

1. Washer
2. Cushion
3. Retainer
4. Insulator
5. Spacer
6. Coil spring
7. Dust cover
8. Shock absorber
9. Retainer
10. Cushion
11. Stabilizer bar
12. Bracket
13. Bushing
14. Collar
15. Retainer
16. Retainer
17. Cushion
18. Collar
19. Strut
20. Bumper
21. Retainer
22. Bushing
23. Shaft
24. Upper control arm
25. Camber adjusting shim
26. Plug
27. Upper ball joint
28. Bushing
29. Lower control arm
30. Lower ball joint
31. Steering knuckle
32. Brake disc
33. Oil seal
34. Roller bearing
35. Hub bolt
36. Axle hub
37. Roller bearing
38. Washer
39. Wheel adjusting nut
40. Hub cap

Mark II front suspension components

7. Unbolt and remove the lower control arm.

8. Carefully and slowly remove the spring compressor and withdraw the spring.

Inspect the components of the suspension which were removed for signs of wear or damage. Replace parts as required.

Installation is performed in the following order:

1. Install the lower control arm but do not fully tighten the mounting bolts.

2. Compress the spring with the spring compressor and install the spring.

NOTE: Keep the spring compressed after installation.

3. Install the lower ball joint on the steering knuckle and tighten it.

4. Install the strut on the lower control arm and temporarily install the other end on the frame.

　a. The distance between the serrations and the nut should be the same as that measured during removal.

　b. If a new strut is used, check for the proper installation distance.

　c. Carefully install the rear side of the strut to the control arm and tighten the mounting nut to the specifications.

5. Slowly remove the spring compressor from the coil spring.

6. Install the shock absorber.

7. Install the stabilizer bar bracket and the bar.

NOTE: Be sure to assemble the parts of the bracket in the order in which they were removed.

8. Install the wheel, remove the jack stands, and lower the car.

9. Tighten the lower control arm and strut front mount.

NOTE: These parts should be tightened with the equivalent of passenger weight in the car.

10. Check the wheel alignment, after completing installation.

Shock Absorber

REMOVAL AND INSTALLATION

Corona, Cressida and Mark II

1. Remove the hubcap and loosen the lug nuts.

2. Raise the front of the car and support it with jack stands.

3. Remove the lug nuts and the wheel.

4. Unfasten the double nuts at the top end of the shock absorber. Remove the cushions and cushion retainers.

5. Remove the two bolts which secure the lower end of the shock absorber to the lower control arm.

6. Remove the shock absorber.

Inspect and test the shock as detailed below.

Installation of the shock is performed in the reverse order of removal. Tighten the securing nuts and bolts to the following specifications:

　Upper securing nuts—14–22 ft. lbs.
　Lower mounting bolts—11–16 ft. lbs.

Lower Ball Joints

INSPECTION

Except Tercel and Celica/Supra (1982 and Later)

Jack up the lower suspension arm (except Corolla, Celica and Cressida). Check the front wheel play. Replace the lower ball joint if the play at the wheel rim exceeds 0.1 in. vertical motion or 0.25 in. horizontal motion. Be sure that the dust covers are not torn and that they are securely glued to the ball joints.

——————— CAUTION ———————
Do not jack up the control arm on Corolla, Celica or Cressida models; damage to the arm will result.

Tercel and Celica/Supra (1982 and Later)

1. Jack up the vehicle and place wooden

blocks under the front wheels. The block height should be 7.09–7.87 inches.

2. Use jack stands for additional safety.

3. Make sure the front wheels are in a straight forward position.

4. Chock the wheels.

5. Lower the jack until there is approximately half a load on the front springs.

6. Move the lower control arm up and down to check that there is no ball joint play.

REMOVAL AND INSTALLATION

NOTE: On models equipped with both upper and lower ball joints—if both ball joints are to be removed, always remove the lower and then the upper ball joint.

Except Tercel, Celica/Supra (1982 and Later), Corona, and Mark II

The ball joint and control arm cannot be separated from each other. If one fails, then both must be replaced as an assembly, in the following manner:

1. Perform Steps 1–7 of the first "Front Spring Removal and Installation" procedure. Skip Step 6.

2. Remove the stabilizer bar securing bolts.

3. Unfasten the torque strut mounting bolts.

4. Remove the control arm mounting bolt and detach the arm from the front suspension member.

5. Remove the steering knuckle arm from the control arm with a ball joint puller.

Inspect the suspension components, which were removed for wear or damage. Replace any parts, as required.

Installation is the reverse of removal. Note the following, however:

1. When installing the control arm on the suspension member, tighten the bolts partially at first.

2. Complete the assembly procedure and lower the car to the ground.

3. Bounce the front of the car several times. Allow the suspension to settle, then tighten the lower control arm bolts to 51–65 ft. lbs.

—— CAUTION ——
Use only the bolt which was designed to fit the lower control arm. If a replacement is necessary, see an authorized dealer for the proper part.

4. Remember to lubricate the ball joint. Check front-end alignment.

Tercel and Celica/Supra (1982 and Later)

1. Jack up your vehicle and support it with jack stands.

—— CAUTION ——
Do not jack up your car on the lower control arms.

2. Remove the front wheels.

3. Remove the tie rod end.

4. Remove the stabilizer bar end.

5. Remove the strut bar end.

6. Place a jack under the lower control arm for support.

7. Remove the bolt from the bottom of the steering knuckle.

8. Remove the bolt from the lower control arm.

9. Remove the control arm.

NOTE: The lower ball joint cannot be separated from the lower control arm. It must be replaced as a complete unit.

10. The following torques are required: Bottom steering knuckle nut 40–52 ft. lbs.; stabilizer bar 11–15 ft. lbs.; tie rod end 37–50 ft. lbs.; strut bar 29–39 ft. lbs.; lower control arm 51–65 ft. lbs.

Corona

1. Remove the hubcap and loosen the lug nuts.

2. Jack up your vehicle and support it with jack stands.

3. Remove the lug nuts and the wheel.

4. Compress the coil spring by placing a jack underneath the control arm and raising it.

5. Remove the cotter pin and the castelated nut from the ball joint.

6. Use a ball joint puller to detach the lower ball joint from the steering knuckle.

7. Wire the steering knuckle out of the way.

8. Remove the bolt and remove the ball joint.

Installation is the reverse of removal. Tighten the stud nut 51–65 ft. lbs.

Mark II

Perform Steps 1–7 of the Mark II coil spring removal procedure. Skip Step 3.

Installation is performed by starting with Step 3 of the Mark II coil spring installation procedure. When Step 3 is completed, go on to Steps 5–10. Lubricate the ball joints and check alignment.

Upper Ball Joint

INSPECTION

Disconnect the ball joint from the steering knuckle and check free-play by hand. Replace the ball joint, if it is noticeably loose.

REMOVAL AND INSTALLATION

NOTE: On models equipped with both upper and lower ball joints—if both are

to be removed, always remove the lower one first.

Corona

1. Perform Steps 1–5 of the Corona lower ball joint removal procedure.

2. Suspend the steering knuckle with a wire.

3. Use an open-end wrench to remove the upper ball joint.

Installation is performed in the reverse order from removal. Note the following:

1. Install the upper ball joint dust cover with the escape valve toward the rear.

2. Use sealer on the dust cover before installing it.

3. Tighten the upper ball joint-to-steering knuckle bolt to 40–50 ft. lbs.

Mark II

1. Remove the wheel cover and loosen the lug nut.

2. Raise the front of the car and support it with jack stands.

3. Remove the lug nuts and the wheel.

4. Place a jack beneath the lower control arm spring seat. Raise the jack until the spring bumper separates from the frame.

5. Detach the flexible hose from the dust cover.

6. Using a ball joint puller, remove the upper ball joint from the steering knuckle.

7. Use an open-end wrench to remove the ball joint from the upper control arm.

Installation is performed in the reverse order of removal. Tighten the components to the specifications. Lubricate the ball joint. Check front wheel alignment. (See below.) Remember to bleed the air from the flexible hose.

Lower Control Arm

REMOVAL AND INSTALLATION

Except Corona, Mark II, Tercel, and Celica/Supra (1982 and Later)

1. Raise and support the front end.

2. Remove the wheel.

3. Disconnect the steering knuckle from the control arm.

4. Disconnect the tie rod, stabilizer bar and strut bar from the control arm.

5. Remove the control arm mounting bolts, and remove the arm.

6. Install in reverse of above. Tighten, but do not torque fasteners until car is on ground.

7. Lower car to ground, rock it from side-to-side several times and torque control arm mounting bolts to 51–65 ft. lbs., stabilizer bar to 16 ft. lbs., strut bar to 40 ft. lbs., and shock absorber to 65 ft. lbs.

Corona

1. Raise and support the vehicle.

2. Remove the front wheel.

3. Remove the shock absorber and disconnect the stabilizer from the lower arm.

4. Install a spring compressor and fully tighten it.

5. Place a jack under the lower arm seat.

6. Disconnect the lower ball joint from the knuckle and lower the jack.

7. Remove the ball joint from the arm, remove the cam plates and bolts and take off the arm.

8. Install in reverse of above. Tighten all fasteners, but do not torque them to specification until vehicle is on ground.

9. Lower vehicle and rock it from side-to-side several times.

10. With no load in vehicle, torque the lower arm mounting bolts to 94–130 ft. lbs.

Mark II

1. Remove the stabilizer bar.

2. Measure the length of the strut bar from the bolt hole (front side) to the outer edge of the securing nut at the other and.

3. Remove the shock absorber.

4. Compress the front spring with a spring compressor.

NOTE: It is recommended that the compressor be installed at the third coil from the bottom.

5. Remove the lower ball joint with a puller.

6. Remove the lower arm.

7. Install the lower arm to the frame.

8. Install the ball joint and tighten the nut to 50–65 ft. lbs.

9. Install the strut bar onto the lower arm and temporarily install the front side onto the frame.

10. Set the strut bar to the length noted before removal. If a new lower arm or strut bar is used, the measurement should be 14.16".

11. Torque the strut bar rear end to 50–65 ft. lbs.

12. Remove the spring compressor and install the shock absorber.

13. Install the stabilizer bar.

14. Lower the vehicle and torque the lower arm to 65–80 ft. lbs. Torque the strut bar front end to 44–54 ft. lbs.

Tercel and Celica/Supra (1982 and Later)

See the lower ball joint removal section.

Upper Control Arm

REMOVAL AND INSTALLATION

Corona

1. Remove the upper arm mounting nuts from inside the engine compartment, but do not remove the bolts.

2. Raise the vehicle, support the lower arm and remove the wheel.

3. On vehicles equipped with a ball joint wear sensor, remove the wiring from the clamp on the arm.

4. Remove the upper ball joint.

5. Remove the control arm mounting bolts.

6. Pry out the arm with a pry bar.

7. Install in reverse of removal. Do not tighten fasteners until vehicle is on ground.

8. Lower vehicle and torque the control arm mounting bolts to 95–130 ft. lbs.

Mark II

1. Raise and support the vehicle at the frame.

2. Remove the flexible hose from the dust cover.

3. Jack up the lower arm and separate the ball joint from the steering knuckle with a ball joint remover.

4. Unbolt and remove the upper arm, taking note of the size and number of aligning shims.

5. Install in reverse of removal. Tighten, but do not torque, the fasteners until the car is on the ground.

6. Lower the car and torque the upper arm mounting bolts to 50–65 ft. lbs.; the ball joint nut to 40–54 ft. lbs.

Front-End Alignment

Front-end alignment measurements require the use of special equipment. Before measuring alignment or attempting to adjust it, always check the following points:

1. Be sure that the tires are properly inflated.

2. See that the wheels are properly balanced.

3. Check the ball joints to determine if they are worn or loose.

4. Check front wheel bearing adjustment.

5. Be sure that the car is on a level surface.

6. Check all suspension parts for tightness.

CASTER AND CAMBER ADJUSTMENTS

Except Corona

All models with the MacPherson front suspension can be adjusted for caster only. This is accomplished by adjusting the nuts on the strut bar. There is no adjustment on the camber. These parts must be inspected for wear and replaced if the adjustments are not within the specified tolerances.

Measure the caster and camber angles. If they are not within specifications, adjust them by adding or subtracting the shims on the mounting bolts between the upper control arm and the suspension member:

1. To *increase* camber, *remove* shims

Corona front end alignment adjusting cams

equally from both of the control shaft mounting bolts. Do the reverse to decrease camber.

2. To *increase* caster, add camber adjusting shims to the *rear* mounting bolt, or remove them from the front mounting bolt. Do the reverse to decrease caster.

NOTE: Caster and camber adjustments should always be performed in a single operation.

Corona

Caster and camber angles are measured in the same way and with the same equipment as all the other models above.

However, the method of adjustment is different:

1. Measure the camber and adjust it with the *rear* adjusting cam.

2. Measure the caster and adjust it with the *front* adjusting cam.

3. Check the caster and camber again.

4. Tighten the lower control arm mounting bolts to 94–132 ft. lbs.

NOTE: There should be not more than six graduations difference between the front and rear cams; inspect for damaged suspension parts if there is.

TOE-IN ADJUSTMENT

Measure the toe-in. Adjust it, if necessary, by loosening the tie rod end clamping bolts and rotating the tie rod adjusting tubes. Tighten the clamping bolts when finished.

NOTE: Both tie rod ends should be the same length. If they are not, perform the adjustment until the toe-in is within specifications and the tie rod ends are equal in length.

STEERING

Steering Wheel

REMOVAL AND INSTALLATION

Three-Spoke

_____ CAUTION _____

Do not attempt to remove or install the steering wheel by hammering on it. Damage to the energy-absorbing steering column could result.

1. Unfasten the horn and turn signal multiconnector(s) at the base of the steering column shroud.
2. Loosen the trim pad retaining screws from the back side of the steering wheel.
3. Lift the trim pad and horn button assembly(ies) from the wheel.
4. Remove the steering wheel hub retaining nut.
5. Scratch matchmarks on the hub and shaft to aid in correct installation.
6. Use a steering wheel puller to remove the steering wheel.

Installation is the reverse of removal. Tighten the wheel retaining nut to 15–22 ft. lbs., except for the Mark II, which should be tightened to 22–29 ft. lbs.

Two-Spoke

The two-spoke steering wheel is removed in the same manner as the three-spoke, except that the trim pad should be pried off with a screwdriver. Remove the pad by lifting it toward the top of the wheel.

Four-Spoke

_____ CAUTION _____

Do not attempt to remove or install the steering wheel by hammering on it. Damage to the energy absorbing steering column could result.

1. Unfasten the horn and turn signal connectors at the base of the steering column shroud, underneath the instrument panel.
2. Gently pry the center emblem off the front of the steering wheel.
3. Insert a wrench through the hole and remove the steering wheel retaining nut.
4. Scratch matchmarks on the hub and shaft to aid installation.
5. Use a steering wheel puller to remove the steering wheel.

Installation is the reverse of removal. Tighten the steering wheel retaining nut to 15–22 ft. lbs.

TURN SIGNAL SWITCH REPLACEMENT

1. Disconnect the negative (−) battery cable.
2. Remove the steering wheel, as outlined in the appropriate section above.
3. Unfasten the screws which secure the upper and lower steering column shroud halves. On 1976 Corona models, remove the lower instrument panel garnish first.
4. Unfasten the screws which retain the turn signal switch and remove the switch from the column. On Corona and Corolla models, the hazard warning and windshield wiper switches are part of the assembly, and will be removed as well.

Installation is performed in the reverse order of removal.

Ignition Lock/Switch

REMOVAL AND INSTALLATION

1. Disconnect the negative (−) battery cable.
2. Unfasten the ignition switch connector underneath the instrument panel.
3. Remove the screws which secure the upper and lower halves of the steering column cover. Remove the lower instrument panel garnish on Corona models first.
4. Turn the lock cylinder to the "ACC" position with the ignition key.
5. Push the lock cylinder stop in with a small, round object (cotter pin, punch, etc.).

NOTE: On some models it may be necessary to remove the steering wheel and turn signal switch first.

6. Withdraw the lock cylinder from the lock housing while depressing the stop tab.
7. To remove the ignition switch, unfasten its securing screws and withdraw the switch from the lock housing.

Installation is performed in the following order:

1. Align the locking cam with the hole in the ignition switch and insert the switch in the lock housing.
2. Secure the switch with its screw(s).
3. Make sure that both the lock cylinder and the column lock are in the "ACC" position. Slide the cylinder into the lock housing until the stop tab engages the hole in the lock.

Instrument Cluster Finish Panel (For Sedan and Wagon)

Instrument Cluster Finish Panel (For Hardtop, Coupe and Liftback)

Upper Steering Column Cover

Combination Switch

Steering Wheel Pad Mark

Steering Wheel

Lower Steering Column Cover

Lower Finish Garnish (For Sedan and Wagon)

Typical combination switch mounting

Turn Signal and Hazard Switch

Headlight Dimmer Switch

Light Control Switch

Wiper Switch

Horn Contact

Exploded view of a typical combination switch

4. The rest of installation is performed in the reverse order of removal.

Manual Steering Gear

REMOVAL AND INSTALLATION

Corolla and Corona (1976–82)

1. Remove the bolt attaching the coupling yoke to the steering worm.
2. Disconnect the relay rod from the pitman arm.
3. Remove the steering gear housing down and to the left.
4. Install in reverse of removal. Torque the housing-to-frame bolts to 25–36 ft. lbs.; the coupling yoke bolt to 15–20 ft. lbs.; the relay rod to 36–50 ft. lbs.

Celica, Cressida and Mark II

1. Remove the Pitman arm from the sector shaft with a puller.
2. Loosen the flexible coupling-to-worm-shaft bolt.
3. Unbolt and remove the steering gear housing.
4. Install in reverse of removal. Torque the housing bolts to 37–52 ft. lbs. on the Mark II, 36–41 ft. lbs. on the Cressida and 25–36 on the others; the Pitman arm to 36–41 ft. lbs. on the Cressida, and 72–101 ft. lbs. on the others; the coupling yoke bolts to 15–20 ft. lbs.

Tercel and Starlet

1. Jack up the vehicle and support it with jack stands.
2. Remove both front wheels.
3. Remove the intermediate shaft from the worm gear shaft.
4. Remove both tie rod ends.
5. Remove the lower suspension crossmember.
6. Remove the rack housing bracket mounting bolts and brackets.

NOTE: Be careful not to damage the rubber boots.

7. Remove the steering linkage.
8. Installation is the reverse of removal.

ADJUSTMENTS

Adjustments to the manual steering gear are not necessary during normal service. Adjustments are performed only as part of overhaul.

Power Steering Pump

REMOVAL AND INSTALLATION

1. Remove the fan shroud.
2. Unfasten the nut from the center of the pump pulley.

NOTE: Use the drive belt as a brake to keep the pulley from rotating.

3. Withdraw the drive belt.
4. Remove the pulley and the Woodruff key from the pump shaft.
5. Detach the intake and outlet hoses from the pump reservoir.

NOTE: Tie the hose ends up high so the fluid cannot flow out of them. Drain or plug the pump to prevent fluid leakage.

6. Remove the bolt from the rear mounting brace.
7. Remove the front bracket bolts and withdraw the pump.

Installation is performed in the reverse order of removal. Note the following, however:

1. Tighten the pump pulley mounting bolt to 25–39 ft. lbs.
2. Adjust the pump drive belt tension. The belt should deflect 0.13–0.93 in. under thumb pressure applied midway between the air pump and the power steering pump.
3. Fill the reservoir with Dexron® automatic transmission fluid. Bleed the air from the system.

BLEEDING

1. Raise the front of the car and support it securely with jack stands.
2. Fill the pump reservoir with Dextron® automatic transmission fluid.
3. Rotate the steering wheel from lock to lock several times. Add fluid as necessary.
4. With the steering wheel turned fully

to one lock, crank the starter while watching the fluid level in the reservoir.

NOTE: Do not start the engine. Operate the starter with a remote starter switch or have an assistant do it from inside of the car. Do not run the starter for prolonged periods.

5. Repeat Step 4 with the steering wheel turned to the opposite lock.

6. Start the engine. With the engine idling, turn the steering wheel from lock to lock two or three times.

7. Lower the front of the car and repeat Step 6.

8. Center the wheel at the midpoint of its travel. Stop the engine.

9. The fluid level should not have risen more than 0.2 in. If it does, repeat Step 7.

10. Check for fluid leakage.

Steering Linkage

REMOVAL AND INSTALLATION

1. Raise the front of the vehicle and support it with jack stands.

— CAUTION —

Be sure that the vehicle is securely supported. Do not support it by the lower control arms.

---

2. Remove the gravel shields if they prevent access to the steering linkage.

3. Unfasten the nut and, using a puller, disconnect the pitman arm from the sector shaft.

4. Unfasten the idler arm support securing bolts and remove the support from the frame.

5. Detach the tie rod ends with a puller after removing the cotter pins and castellated nuts.

NOTE: On Mark II models, it is necessary to remove the disc brake caliper in order to gain access to the tie rod ends.

6. Remove the steering linkage as an assembly.

Installation is performed in the reverse order of removal. Note the following, however:

1. Tighten the linkage parts to the torque figures given in the chart below.

2. Align the marks on the pitman arm and sector shaft before installing the pitman arm.

3. The self-locking nut used on some models, on the idler arm, may be reused if it cannot be turned by hand when fitted to the bolt.

4. Adjust the toe-in to specifications.

5. Disconnect the end of the steering damper from its bracket on the front crossmember.

6. Remove the center arm attaching nut and use a puller to remove the arm, complete with the damper.

1. Steering knuckle arm—right-hand
2. Dust seal
3. Clip
4. Tie rod end
5. Tie rod end clamp
6. Tie rod adjusting tube
7. Steering relay rod
8. Dust seal
9. Lock ring
10. Steering idler arm
11. Idler arm support
12. Steering knukle arm—left-hand

(a)—Idler arm assembly
(b)—Tie rod end assembly
(c)—Tie rod adjusting tube

Steering linkage components—except those models with rack-and-pinion steering

1. Tie rod end
2. Clip
3. Clamp
4. Rack boot
5. Rack end & claw washer
6. Lock nut
7. Rack guide spring cap
8. Spring
9. Rack guide
10. Dust cover
11. Lock nut
12. Pinion bearing adjusting screw
13. Pinion & Bearing
14. Rack
15. Rack housing

Typical parts of a rack-and-pinion steering arrangement

7. Remove the skid plate and then remove the center arm bracket from the frame.

Installation is performed in the reverse order of removal. Note the following, however:

1. Align the matchmarks, which were made during removal, on the pitman arm and the sector shaft. Tighten the mounting bolt to 120–140 ft. lbs.

2. Lubricate all of the rod ends and damper ends with multipurpose grease.

3. After the linkage is installed, adjust toe-in to the proper specifications.

BRAKES

For all brake system repair and service procedures not detailed below, please refer to ''Brakes'' in the Unit Repair section.

Front Disc Brakes

ADJUSTMENTS

Front disc brakes are self-adjusting; no adjustments are possible.

Master Cylinder

REMOVAL AND INSTALLATION

──────── **CAUTION** ────────
Be careful not to spill brake fluid on the painted surfaces of the vehicle; it will damage the paint.

1. Unfasten the hydraulic lines from the master cylinder.
2. Detach the hydraulic fluid pressure differential switch wiring connectors.
3. Loosen the master cylinder reservoir mounting bolt.
4. Then do one of the following:
   a. On models with manual brakes, remove the master cylinder securing bolts and the clevis pin from the brake pedal. Remove the master cylinder.
   b. On other models with power brakes, unfasten the nuts and remove the master cylinder assembly from the power brake unit.

Installation is performed in the reverse order of removal. Note the following, however:

1. Before tightening the master cylinder mounting nuts or bolts, screw the hydraulic line into the cylinder body, a few turns.
2. After installation is completed, bleed the master cylinder and the brake system.

Proportioning Valve

A proportioning valve is used on all models to reduce the hydraulic pressure to the rear brakes because of weight transfer during high speed stops. This helps to keep the rear brakes from locking up by improving front to rear brake balance.

REMOVAL AND INSTALLATION

1. Disconnect the brake lines from the valve unions.
2. Remove the valve mounting bolt, if used, and remove the valve.

NOTE: If the proportioning valve is defective, it must be replaced as an assembly; it cannot be rebuilt.

Installation is the reverse of removal. Bleed the brake system after it is completed.

Front Wheel Bearings

NOTE: For information concerning rear wheel bearings/adjustment on 1982 and later Supra models, refer to the ''Axle Shaft Removal and Installation'' procedure for that model.

REMOVAL AND INSTALLATION

1. Remove the disc/hub assembly, as detailed above.
2. If either the disc or the entire hub assembly is to be replaced, unbolt the hub from the disc.

NOTE: If only the bearings are to be replaced, do not separate the disc and hub.

3. Using a brass rod as a drift, tap the inner bearings cone out. Remove the oil seal and the inner bearing.

NOTE: Throw the old oil seal away.

4. Drive out the inner bearing cup.
5. Drive out the outer bearing cup.

Inspect the bearings and the hub for signs of wear or damage. Replace components, as necessary.

Installation is performed in the following order:

1. Install the inner bearing cup and then the outer bearing cup, by driving them into place.

──────── **CAUTION** ────────
Use care not to cock the bearing cups in the hub.

2. Pack the bearings, hub inner well and grease cap with multipurpose grease.
3. Install the inner bearing into the hub.
4. Carefully install a new oil seal with a soft drift.

5. Install the hub on the spindle. Be sure to install all of the washers and nuts which were removed.
6. Adjust the bearing preload.
7. Install the caliper assembly.

PRELOAD ADJUSTMENT

1. With the front hub/disc assembly installed, tighten the castellated nut to the torque figure specified.
2. Rotate the disc back and forth, two or three times, to allow the bearing to seat properly.
3. Loosen the castellated nut until it is only finger-tight.
4. Tighten the nut firmly, using a box wrench.
5. Measure the bearing preload with a spring scale attached to a wheel mounting stud. Check it against the specifications.
6. Install the cotter pin.

NOTE: If the hole does not align with the nut (or cap) holes, tighten the nut slightly until it does.

7. Finish installing the brake components and the wheel.

Measuring wheel bearing pre-load with a spring scale

PRELOAD SPECIFICATIONS

Model/Year	Initial Torque Setting (ft. lbs.)	Preload (oz.)
Tercel '80–'83	22	13–30
Corolla		
'76–'77	19–23	10–24
'78–'83	19–23	11–25
Celica		
'76–77	19–24	10–24
'78–'83	19–26	11–25
Corona		
'76–'77	19–26	10–22
'78–'82	19–26	12–31
Mark II '76	19–23	11–24
Supra ①	19–23	11–24
Cressida	22	37–56

① Except 1982 and later—see text

Wheel Cylinders

REMOVAL AND INSTALLATION

1. Plug the master cylinder inlet to prevent hydraulic fluid from leaking.

2. Remove the brake drums and shoes as detailed in the appropriate section above.

3. Working from behind the backing plate, disconnect the hydraulic line from the wheel cylinder.

4. Unfasten the screws retaining the wheel cylinder and withdraw the cylinder.

Installation is performed in the reverse order of removal. However, once the hydraulic line has been disconnected from the wheel cylinder, the union seat must be replaced. To replace the seat, proceed in the following manner:

1. Use a screw extractor with a diameter of 0.1 in. and having reverse threads, to remove the union seat from the wheel cylinder.

2. Drive in the new union seat with a 5/16 in. bar, used as a drift.

Remember to bleed the brake system after completing wheel cylinder, brake shoe and drum installation.

Parking Brake

ADJUSTMENTS

Floor-Mounted Lever

NOTE: The rear brake components should be in good condition and be properly adjusted before performing this adjustment.

1. Slowly pull the parking brake lever upward, without depressing the button on the end of it, and while counting the number of notches required until the parking brake is applied.

NOTE: Two "clicks" are equal to one notch.

2. Check the number of notches against specifications.

3. If the brake requires adjustment, loosen the cable adjusting nut cap which is located at the rear of the parking brake lever. Hold the cap with an open-end wrench.

NOTE: On some models, the adjustment and lock nuts are located under the vehicle, beneath the lever assembly.

4. Take up the slack in the parking brake cable by rotating the adjusting nut with another open-end wrench.

    a. If the number of notches is *less* than specified, turn the nut *counterclockwise*.

    b. If the number of notches is *more* than specified, turn the nut *clockwise*.

5. Tighten the adjusting cap, using care not to disturb the setting of the adjusting nut.

6. Check the rotation of the rear wheels to be sure that the brakes are not dragging.

Dash-Mounted Lever

1. Loosen the parking brake warning light switch bracket.

2. Push the parking brake lever in until it is stopped by the pawl.

3. Move the switch so that it will be "off" at this position but "on" when the handle is pulled out.

4. Tighten the switch bracket and push the brake lever in again.

5. Working from underneath the vehicle, loosen the locknut on the parking brake cable equalizer.

6. Screw the adjusting nut *in*, just enough so that the brake cables have no slack.

7. Hold the adjusting nut in this position while tightening the locknut.

8. Check the rotation of the rear wheels to make sure that the brakes are not dragging.

9. Pull out on the parking brake lever, and count the number of notches needed to

Wire adjusting nut

On models with a dash-mounted parking brake lever, adjust the rod length where indicated

apply the parking brake. Check the number against the figures given in the chart.

PARKING BRAKE SHOE REPLACEMENT

Supra (1982 and Later)

1. Raise and safely support the rear of the vehicle.

2. Remove the rear wheels.

3. Disconnect the brake line from the brake cylinder (caliper).

4. Remove the brake cylinder attaching bolts and remove the brake cylinder assembly.

5. Remove the torque plate.

6. With the parking brake lever fully released, remove the brake disc attaching screw(s) and remove the brake disc.

NOTE: If the brake disc sticks, preventing removal, it will be necessary to back-off the self adjusters. This is done through the access hole in the brake disc as shown in the accompanying illustration.

Contract

SST

1982 and later Supra parking brake adjustment—the arrow indicates the direction for loosening the parking brake shoes

Shoe Strut and Spring   Rear Shoe with Lever   Shoe Return

Pin

Pin

Spring

Front Shoe

Shoe Adjusting Screw Set   Shoe Hold-Down Spring

Exploded view of the 1982 and later Supra rear parking brake

7. Remove the brake shoe return springs. Conventional return spring removal tools may be used, though Toyota special service tool #SST 09717-20010 is recommended for this purpose.

8. Remove the brake shoe hold-down springs. Again, conventional tools may be used, but #SST 09718-00010 is recommended.

9. Remove the front brake shoe, strut, and self-adjuster assembly.

10. Disconnect the parking brake cable from the parking brake shoe lever and remove the rear parking brake shoe.

11. Inspect all parts for excessive wear and/or damage.

Note the following for inspection purposes:

Minimum brake shoe lining thickness— 0.039 in.

Maximum brake disc inner diameter— 6.61 in.

If out of round or scored, the parking brake surface of the disc may be machined, as long as the maximum diameter is not greater than the above specification.

12. If the shoes are to be replaced, remove the lever from the rear brake shoe by prying the C-washer apart and removing the washer. When installing the lever on the new shoe, first install the shim over the pin, then close the C-washer into the pin slot. A new C-washer should be used. Check the clearance between the shim and the lever; the clearance should not exceed 0.013 in. If the clearance is excessive, thicker shims are available through Toyota.

13. Apply a small amount of high-temperature grease to each of the backing plate contact pads.

14. Disassemble and clean the self-adjusters. During assembly of the adjusters, apply high-temperature to the parts as shown in the accompanying illustration.

1982 and later Supra parking brake—before assembly, lubricate the adjuster parts as indicated

15. Further installation of the shoes is performed in the reverse order of the removal steps.

16. Adjust the parking brake shoe clearance as follows:

a. Temporarily install the disc assembly, with two of the lug nuts hand-tightened on the studs. The lug nuts should be installed with the flat sides towards the disc.

b. Using a star wheel adjusting tool, turn the star wheel until the disc locks.

c. Return the adjuster (star wheel) 8 notches.

17. Install the torque plate, brake cylinder, and brake line. Bleed the brake system as previously outlined. Install the wheels, lower the vehicle, and adjust the parking brake lever travel as previously outlined. Road test the vehicle.

PARKING BRAKE ADJUSTMENT

Model/Year	Range of Adjustment (notches)
Corolla 1200	7–8 ①
Corolla 1600 ('76–'77)	2–6
Corolla 1600 ('78–'79)	4–12
Corolla 1800 and Starlet	4–7
Tercel	2–5
Celica ②	3–7
Corona	3–6
Corona	
Console	3–6
Pedal	4–8
Cressida, Supra ②	5–8
Mark II '76	8–12

① 1978–'79: 4–12
② 1982 and later Celica/Supra: 4–7

CHASSIS ELECTRICAL

Heater Blower

NOTE: On some models the air conditioner, if so equipped, is integral with the heater, and therefore, heater removal may differ from the procedures detailed below.

REMOVAL AND INSTALLATION

Tercel

1. Disconnect the negative battery terminal.

2. Remove the under tray (if so equipped).

3. Remove the blower duct and air duct.

NOTE: Before removing the air duct remember to remove the two attaching clamps.

4. Remove the glove box.

5. Remove the control cable.

6. Disconnect the electrical connector on the blower motor.

7. Remove the blower motor bolts and remove the motor.

8. Installation is the reverse of removal.

Corolla and Starlet

1. Disconnect the blower wiring harness.

2. Remove the right-hand defroster hose.

3. Remove the three screws which secure the blower motor and lift out the motor.

4. Separate the fan from the motor. Installation is the reverse of removal.

Celica, Supra and Cressida

1. Working from under the instrument panel, unfasten the defroster hoses from the heater box.

2. Unplug the multiconnector.

3. Loosen the mounting screws and withdraw the blower assembly.

4. Installation is the reverse of removal.

Mark II

1. Remove the center console, after removing the shift knob (manual), unfastening the wiring, connector, and undoing the console securing screws.

2. Unfasten the heater blower wiring connector.

3. Remove the three bolts which secure the blower motor, complete with fan, from the box.

4. Installation is the reverse order of removal.

Corona

1. Remove the package tray.

2. Remove the trim panel.

3. Disconnect the heater blower motor wiring harness.

4. Loosen the three screws which secure the motor to the housing and remove the motor/blower assembly.

5. Installation is the reverse of removal.

Heater Core

REMOVAL AND INSTALLATION

Tercel

1. Disconnect the negative battery terminal.

2. Drain the radiator.

3. Remove the ash tray and retainer.

4. Remove the rear heater duct (optional).

5. Remove the left and right side defroster ducts.

6. Remove the under tray (optional).

7. Remove the glove box.

8. Remove the main air duct.

9. Disconnect the radio and remove it.

10. Disconnect the heater control cables and remove them.

11. Disconnect the heater hoses.

12. Remove the front and rear air ducts.

13. Remove the electrical connector.

14. Remove the heater bolts and remove the heater.

NOTE: Slide the heater to the right side of car to remove it.

15. Remove the heater core.

16. Installation is the reverse of removal.

Corolla and Starlet

1. Disconnect the negative battery cable and drain the cooling system.

2. Disconnect the heater hose from the engine compartment side.

3. Remove the knobs from the heater and fan controls.

4. Remove the two securing screws, and take the heater control panel off.

5. Remove the heater control, complete with cables.

6. Disconnect the wiring harness.

7. Remove the three heater assembly securing bolts and remove the assembly.

8. Separate the core from the heater assembly.

9. Installation is the reverse of removal.

Celica, Supra, Cressida and Mark II

1. Drain the cooling system.

2. Remove the console, if so equipped, by removing the shift knob (manual), wiring connector, and console attaching screws.

3. Remove the carpeting from the tunnel.

4. If necessary, remove the cigarette lighter and ash tray.

5. Remove the package tray, if it makes access to the heater core difficult.

6. Remove the securing screws and remove the center air outlet on the Mark II/6.

7. Remove the bottom cover/intake assembly screws and withdraw the assembly.

8. Remove the cover from the water valve.

9. Remove the water valve.

10. Remove the hose clamps and remove the hoses from the core.

11. Remove the core.

12. Installation is the reverse of removal.

Corona

1. Disconnect the negative battery cable.

2. Drain the cooling system.

3. Disconnect the heater hoses from the engine.

4. Remove the center console, if so equipped.

5. Remove the package tray and disconnect the heater air duct.

6. Unfasten the screws and take the glove compartment out of the dash.

7. Working through the glove compartment opening, remove the rear duct.

8. Detach the ventilation duct.

9. Remove the instrument cluster, as detailed below.

10. Remove the radio, if installed.

11. Remove the heater control assembly.

12. Take the defroster duct assembly out.

13. Tilt the heater assembly to the right and withdraw it from the package tray side.

14. Remove the water valve and outlet hose from the heater assembly.

15. Take off the retaining band and remove the bolt.

16. Take out the core.

17. Installation is the reverse of removal.

Radio

—— CAUTION ——
Never operate the radio without a speaker; severe damage to the output transistors will result. If the speaker must be replaced, use a speaker of the correct impedance (ohms) or else the output transistors will be damaged and require replacement.

REMOVAL AND INSTALLATION

Celica and Cressida

1. Remove the knobs from the radio.

2. Remove the nuts from the radio control shafts.

3. Detach the antenna lead from the jack on the radio case.

4. Remove the cowl air intake duct.

5. Detach the power and speaker leads.

6. Remove the radio support nuts and bolts.

7. Remove the radio from beneath the dashboard.

8. Remove the nuts which secure the speaker through the service hole in the top of the glove box.

9. Remove remainder of the speaker securing nuts from above the radio mounting location.

10. Remove the speaker.

11. Installation is the reverse of removal.

Corolla and Starlet

1. Remove the two screws from the top of the dashboard center trim panel.

2. Lift the center panel out far enough to gain access to the cigarette lighter wiring and disconnect the wiring. Remove the trim panel.

3. Unfasten the screws which secure the radio to the instrument panel braces.

4. Lift out the radio and disconnect the leads from it. Remove the radio.

5. Installation is the reverse of removal.

Tercel

1. Disconnect the negative battery terminal.

2. Disconnect the antenna.

3. Disconnect the electrical connector.

4. Remove the radio knobs and remove the face plate.

5. Remove the radio.

6. Installation is the reverse of removal.

Corona

1976–82

INSTRUMENT PANEL–MOUNTED

1. Remove the two screws securing the instrument cluster surround and remove the surround.

2. Remove the knobs from the heater controls and remove the heater control face.

3. Remove the four screws which secure the center trim panel (two are behind the heater control opening).

4. Remove the radio knobs and remove the center trim panel.

5. Remove the four screws which secure the radio bracket.

6. Pull the radio far enough out to remove the antenna, power, and speaker leads.

7. Remove the radio.

8. Installation is the reverse of removal.

CONSOLE–MOUNTED

1. Remove the screws which secure the console and remove the console, by lowering the armrest rearward and lifting up on the center of the console.

2. Unplug the radio and disconnect the antenna lead.

3. Remove the radio knobs.

4. Remove the radio bracket and then remove the radio.

5. Installation is the reverse of removal.

Mark II

1. Remove the instrument cluster housing as detailed in the appropriate section below.

2. Remove the heater control panel assembly.

3. Unfasten the two radio securing bolts.

4. Detach all of the radio leads.

5. Withdraw the radio.

6. Installation is the reverse of removal.

Windshield Wiper Motor

REMOVAL AND INSTALLATION

Tercel

1. Disconnect the negative battery terminal.
2. Insert a screwdriver between the linkage and the motor.
3. Pry up to separate the linkage from the motor.
4. Disconnect the electrical connector from the motor.
5. Remove the mounting bolts and remove the motor.
6. Installation is the reverse of removal.

Corolla, Corona, and Starlet

1. Disconnect the wiper motor connector.
2. Remove the service cover and loosen the wiper motor bolts.

3. Use a screwdriver to separate the wiper link-to-motor connection.

──── CAUTION ────
Be careful not to bend the linkage.

4. Withdraw the wiper motor assembly.
5. Installation is the reverse of removal.

Celica, Supra and Cressida

1. Remove the access hole cover.
2. Separate the wiper and motor by prying gently with a screwdriver.
3. Remove the left and right cowl ventilators.
4. Remove the wiper arms and the linkage mounting nuts. Push the linkage pivot ports into the ventilators.
5. Loosen the wiper link connectors at their ends and with the linkage from the cowl ventilator.
6. Start the wiper motor and turn the ignition key off when the crank is at the position illustrated.

NOTE: The wiper motor is difficult to remove when it is in the parked position. If the motor is turned off at the wiper switch, it will automatically return to this position.

7. Unplug the connector.
8. Loosen the motor bolts and withdraw the motor.
9. Installation is the reverse of removal. Be sure to install the wiper motor with it in the park position by connecting the multiconnector and operating the wiper control switch. Assemble the crank.

Mark II

1. Remove the cover from the service hole.
2. Set the wiper crank at 180° from park, by turning the wiper switch on and then turning the ignition switch off, once the desired position is reached.
3. Separate the link from the motor crank with a screwdriver.
4. Disconnect the wiper motor connector.

WIPER ARM AND BLADE

VENTILATOR LOUVER

HOLE COVERS

WIPER LINKAGE

WIPER MOTOR

Typical wiper motor and linkage assembly (1980 Celica shown, others similar)

SEAT BELT WARNING RELAY

EMISSION CONTROL COMPUTER

TURN SIGNAL & HAZARD FLASHER

WIPER CONTROL RELAY

LIGHT CONTROL RELAY (HEADLIGHT)

LIGHT CONTROL RELAY (TAIL LIGHT)

DEFOGGER RELAY

ROOM LIGHT CONTROL RELAY

Typical relay and flasher location for late model Celicas

5. Unfasten the wiper motor bolts and withdraw the motor.

6. Installation is the reverse of removal.

Instrument Cluster

REMOVAL AND INSTALLATION

Corolla and Starlet

1. Disconnect the negative battery cable.

2. Remove the instrument cluster surround.

3. Remove the center trim panel. Disconnect the cigarette lighter wiring before completely removing the panel.

4. Remove the speedometer cable and disconnect it.

5. Pull the instrument cluster out just far enough so that its wiring harness may be disconnected.

6. Remove the cluster.

7. Installation is the reverse of removal.

Corona

1. Disconnect the negative (−) battery cable.

2. Remove the two instrument cluster surround.

3. Remove the side air outlet control knob and the clock setting knob.

4. Lift off the panel.

5. Unfasten the five screws which secure the cluster to the instrument panel support.

6. Disconnect the speedometer cable and the instrument cluster wiring harness.

7. Lift out the cluster assembly.

8. Installation is the reverse of removal.

Mark II

1. Remove the housing from the steering column.

2. Remove the control knobs from the heater and radio.

3. Loosen the heater control floodlight and pull it out slightly.

4. Remove the nine screws which attach the cluster surround.

5. Push the upper crash pad away from the surround and slightly pull out the surround.

6. Remove the heater control floodlight from the surround.

7. Remove the panel toward the right.

8. Remove the instrument panel lower garnish moldings. Remove the ash tray.

9. Remove the heater control assembly.

10. Unfasten the dash side ventilator mounting screws.

11. Remove the radio and tape deck, if so equipped.

12. Remove the heater control bracket.

13. Remove the six cluster securing bolts and lift it out slightly.

14. Detach the speedometer cable and all of the wiring harnesses. Remove the cluster.

15. Installation is the reverse of removal.

NOTE: Have the heater control floodlight installed in the cluster surround prior to its installation.

Celica (1976–77) and Cressida

1. Disconnect the battery.
2. Detach the heater control cables at the heater box.
3. Loosen the steering column clamping nuts and lower the column.

—————— CAUTION ——————
Be careful when handling the column; it is the collapsible type. Cover the column shroud with a cloth to protect it.

4. Loosen the instrument panel screws and tilt the panel forward.
5. Detach the speedometer cable and wiring connectors. Remove the entire panel assembly.

6. Remove the instruments from the panel as required.

7. Installation is the reverse of removal.

Tercel

1. Disconnect the negative battery terminal.
2. Remove the steering column cover.

NOTE: Be careful not to damage the collapsible steering column mechanism.

3. Remove the screws from the instrument panel.
4. Gently pull the panel out approximately half way.
5. Disconnect the speedometer and any other electrical connections that are necessary.
6. Remove the panel at this time.
7. Installation is the reverse of removal.

Celica and Supra (1978 and Later)

1. Disconnect the negative battery cable at the battery.
2. Remove the fuse box cover from under the left side of the instrument panel.
3. Remove the heater control knobs.
4. Using a screwdriver, carefully pry off the heater control panel.
5. Unscrew the cluster finish panel retaining screws and pull out the bottom of the panel.
6. Unplug the two electrical connectors and unhook the speedometer cable.

7. Remove the instrument cluster.
8. Installation is performed in the reverse of the previous steps.

Fuses and Fusible Links

Except Celica and Supra

The fuse box is located on the left-hand side, underneath the dashboard, on all models. All models are equipped with fusible links on the battery cables running from the positive (+) battery terminal.

Celica and Supra

1976–77

The fuse block of these models is located under the left side of the instrument panel, near the hood release lever.

1978–79

The fuse block is located behind a panel on the far left side of the instrument panel. The cover panel is next to the steering column and below the warning light display.

1980–81

These models have two fuse blocks; one is located behind a panel in the dash (same as 1978–79), while the other can be found on the left front fender apron.

1982–83

A single fuse block unit is located under the hood (driver's side) on these models.

Triumph

SERIAL NUMBER IDENTIFICATION

All Triumphs have the chassis number (commission number) stamped on a plate adjacent to the driver's door striker plate and on another small plate visible through the windshield.

ENGINE NUMBER

The engine number is stamped on the left side of the engine block on all models.

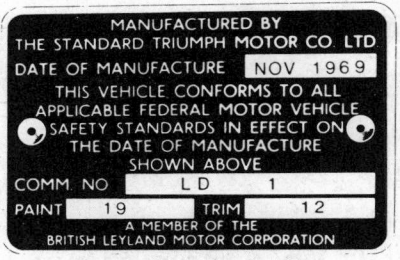

Chassis number plate

TRANSMISSION NUMBER

The transmission number is stamped on the left side of the clutch housing (TR models), or on the top right side of the transmission case (Spitfire models).

Rear axle number location—Spitfire shown, TR series similar

REAR AXLE NUMBER

The rear axle number is stamped on the housing flange on all models.

Engine number location—OHC engine

Transmission number location

Engine number location—OHV engines

Chassis number plate location

GENERAL ENGINE SPECIFICATIONS

Year	Model	Engine Displacement cu. in. (cc)	Carburetor Type	Horsepower @ rpm	Torque @ rpm (ft. lbs.)	Bore x Stroke (in.)	Compression Ratio	Oil Pressure @ rpm (psi)
'76–'77	Spitfire 1500	91.0 (1493)	Single horizontal Zenith-Stromberg 150 CDSE(V)	57 @ 5000	71 @ 3000	2.90 × 3.440	7.5:1	40–60
'78–'81	Spitfire 1500	91.0 (1493)	Single horizontal Zenith-Stromberg 150 CD4T	52.5 @ 5000	58.65 @ 2500	2.90 × 3.440	7.5:1	40–60
'76	TR-6	152.0 (2498)	Twin horizontal Zenith-Stromberg 175 CDSE(V)	106 @ 4900	133 @ 3000	2.940 × 3.740	7.75:1	70
'76–'77	TR-7	122.0 (1998)	Twin horizontal① Zenith-Stromberg 175 CDSE(V)	90 @ 5000	105 @ 3000	3.56 × 3.07	8.0:1	60
'78–'81	TR-7	122.0 (1998)	Twin horizontal Zenith-Stromberg 175 CDFEVX	85.5 @ 5500	102.5 @ 3250	3.56 × 3.07	8.0:1	60
'80–'81	TR-8	215 (3528)	Twin horizontal② Zenith-Stromberg 175 CD Set	133 @ 5000③	174 @ 3000	3.50 × 2.80	8.1:1	35

① California: single Zenith-Stromberg 175 CD4TV
② 1980 California and 1981 All: Electronic fuel injection
③ California: 148 @ 5000 rpm

TUNE-UP SPECIFICATIONS

(When analyzing compression test results, look for uniformity among cylinders, rather than specific pressures)

Year	Model	Engine Displacement (cc)	Spark Plugs Type	Gap (in.)	Point Dwell (deg)	Point Gap (in.)	Ignition Timing (deg)● MT	Ignition Timing (deg)● AT	Intake Valve Opens (deg)●	Fuel Pump Pressure (psi)	Idle Speed (rpm)	Valve Clear (in.) In	Valve Clear (in.) Ex
'76–'77	Spitfire	1493	N12Y	0.025	Electronic		10		18	1.5–2.5	800	0.010	0.010
'78–'81	Spitfire	1493	N12Y	0.025	Electronic		10②		18	2.5–3.5	800	0.010	0.010
'76	TR-6	2498	N9Y	0.025	32–38	0.014–0.016	10		18	1.5–2.5	800	0.010	0.010
'76–'77	TR-7	1998	N12Y③	0.025	Electronic		10		16	2.5–3.5	800	0.008	0.018
'78–'81	TR-7	1998	N12Y	0.025	Electronic		10②		16	2.5–3.5	800	0.008	0.018
'80–'81	TR-8	3528	N12Y	0.035④	Electronic		TDC⑤	TDC⑤	30	—	750–900	Hyd.	Hyd.

NOTE: The underhood specifications sticker often reflects tune-up specification changes made in production. Sticker figures must be used if they disagree with those in this chart.

● Figure given is before Top Dead Center unless otherwise noted.
② 2ATDC: Calif.
③ 1977: N-11Y
④ Carbureted engines: 0.030
⑤ Carbureted engines: 7B—Static; 5A—Dynamic

FIRING ORDERS

Spitfire

TR-6

TR-7

TR-8

CAPACITIES

Year	Model	Engine Displacement (cc)	Engine Crankcase (qts) With Filter	Without Filter	Transmission (pts) 4-Speed	With Overdrive	Drive Axis (pts)	Gasoline Tank (gals)	Cooling System (qts) W/AC	W/O AC
'76–'79	Spitfire	1493	4.8	4.2	1.8	3.0	1.2	8.7	—	4.8
'76	TR-6	2498	5.4	4.8	2.4	4.2	2.7	11.7	—	6.6
'76–'81	TR-7	1998	4.75	4.25	2.5①③	—	2.75②	14.4	7.75	7.75
'80–'81	TR-8	3528	6.2	5.7	3.3④	—	2.0	16.8	—	11.7

① 5-speed: 2.7 pts. ② 5-speed option: 1.6 pts. ③ Auto. trans.: 9.5 pts. ④ Auto. trans.: 14.9 pts.

VALVE SPECIFICATIONS

Year	Engine Displacement (cc)	Seat Angle (deg)	Face Angle (deg)	Spring Test Pressure (lbs. @ in.)	Spring (in.) Free Length	Stem to Guide Clearance (in.) Intake	Exhaust	Stem Diameter (in.) Intake	Exhaust
'76–'81	1493	44.5	45	27–30 @ 1.36	1.61①	0.0008–0.0023	0.0015–0.0030	0.3107–0.3112	0.3100–0.3105
'76	2498	44.5	46	—	1.14 inner 1.52 outer	0.0013–0.0017	0.0020–0.0024	0.3107–0.3112	0.3101–0.3106
'76–'81	1998	44.5	45	—	1.60	0.0017–0.0023	0.0014–0.0030	0.3107–0.3113	0.3100–0.3106

VALVE SPECIFICATIONS

Year	Engine Displacement (cc)	Seat Angle (deg)	Face Angle (deg)	Spring Test Pressure (lbs. @ in.)	Spring (in.) Free Length	Stem to Guide Clearance (in.)		Stem Diameter (in.)	
						Intake	Exhaust	Intake	Exhaust
'80–'81	3528	46	45	—	②	0.0010–0.0030	0.0050–0.0035	0.3402–0.3412	0.3402–0.3412

① 1976–79: 1.52 ② 1.577 in. at 154.35 lbs. —Not available at time of publication

CRANKSHAFT AND CONNECTING ROD SPECIFICATIONS
(All measurements are given in inches)

Year	Engine Displacement cu. in. (cc)	Crankshaft				Connecting Rod		
		Main Brg. Journal Dia.	Main Brg. Oil Clearance	Shaft End-Play	Thrust on No.	Journal Diameter	Oil Clearance	Side Clearance
'76–'79	91.0 (1493)	2.3115–2.3120	—	0.004–0.008	3	1.8750–1.8755	—	—
'76	152.0 (2498)	2.3110–2.3115	0.0015–0.0025	0.006–0.008	4	1.8750–1.8755	0.0010–0.0027	0.0070–0.0140
'76–'81	122.0 (1998)	2.1260–2.1265	0.0012–0.0022	0.003–0.011	3	1.7500–1.7505	0.0008–0.0023	0.006–0.013
'80–'81	215 (3528)	—	0.0006–0.0022	0.004–0.008	4		0.0006–0.0022	0.006–0.014

—Not available at time of publication.

PISTON AND RING SPECIFICATIONS
(All measurements in inches)

Year	Engine Displacement (cc)	Piston Clearance		Ring Gap			Ring Side Clearance		
		Crown	Skirt	Top Compression	Bottom Compression	Oil Control	Top Compression	Bottom Compression	Oil Control
'76–'81	1493	①	0.0020–0.0030	0.012–0.022	0.012–0.022	(ends butt)	0.0020–0.0025	0.0020–0.0025	0.0028–0.0038
'76	2498	0.0038–0.0045	0.0021–0.0028	0.012–0.017	0.008–0.013	②	0.0010–0.0030	0.0010–0.0030	0.0010–0.0030
'76–'81	1998	0.0296–0.0350	0.0005–0.0015	0.015–0.025	0.015–0.025	②	0.0019–0.0039	0.0015–0.0025	
'80–'81	3528	0.0296–0.0350	0.0007–0.0013③	0.017–0.022	0.017–0.022	0.015–0.055	—	—	—

① Grade F: 0.020–0.024 ② Plain oil rings: 0.015–0.055 ③ Skirt bottom
Grade G: 0.0205–0.0260 Scraper oil ring (ends butt) — Not available at time of publication

TORQUE SPECIFICATIONS
(All readings in ft. lbs.)

Year	Engine Displacement (cc)	Cylinder Head Bolts	Rod Bearing Bolts	Main Bearing Bolts	Crankshaft Pulley Bolt	Flywheel To Crankshaft Bolts	Manifold		Spark Plug
							Intake	Exhaust	
'76–'81	1493	42–46	38–42	50–55	90–110	35–40	20–25	20–25	14–20
'76	2498	65–70	38–42	55–60	90–100	55–60	①	①	14–16
'76–'81	1998	45–55	40–45	50–65	90–120	40–45	15–20	15–20	14–20
'80–'81	3528	②	30–35	65–70	210	60	15	15	12

① TR-6: outer (2)—12–14 ft. lbs., ② Nos. 1–10—70; Nos. 11–14—50
inner—16–18 ft. lbs.

TORQUE SEQUENCES

Spitfire cylinder head

TR-7 cylinder head

TR-6 cylinder head

TR-8 cylinder head (both the same)

ALTERNATOR AND REGULATOR SPECIFICATIONS

Year	Model	Alternator Part No. or Manufacturer	Field Current @ 12V	Output (amps)	Regulator Part No. or Manufacturer	Field Relay Air Gap (in.)	Field Relay Point Gap (in.)	Field Relay Volts to Close	Regulator Air Gap (in.)	Regulator Point Gap (in.)	Volts @ 75
'76–'81	Spitfire	Lucas 16 ACR	NA	34	NA		Integral regulator				14
'76	TR-6	Lucas 18 ACR	NA	43	NA		Integral regulator				14
'76–'81	TR-7	Lucas 20 ACR	NA	66	14TR		Integral regulator				14
'80–'81	TR-8	Lucas 23 ACR	NA	55	14TR		Integral regulator				14

NA Not available at time of publication.

BATTERY AND STARTER SPECIFICATIONS

(All cars use 12 volt, negative ground electrical systems)

Year	Model	Battery cAmp Hour Capacity	Starter Lock Test Amps	Lock Test Volts	Lock Test Torque (ft. lbs.)	No Load Test Amps	No Load Test Volts	No Load Test rpm	Brush Spring Tension (oz.)	Min. Brush Length (in.)
'76–'81	Spitfire	40	350–375	—	7.0	65	12	8000–10000	28	0.500
'76	TR-6	57	463	—	14.4	40	12	6000	36	0.710
'76–'81	TR-7	50	463	—	14.4	40	12	6000	36	0.710
'80–'81	TR-8	66	463	—	14.4	40	12	6000	36	0.710

— Not available

BRAKE SPECIFICATIONS

(All measurements given are in. unless noted)

Year	Model	Lug Nut Torque (ft. lb.)	Brake Disc Minimum Thickness	Brake Disc Maximum Run-Out	Diameter	Brake Drum Max. Machine O/S	Max. Wear Limit	Minimum Lining Thickness Front	Minimum Lining Thickness Rear
'76–'81	Spitfire	48	NA	0.007	7.0	7.03	7.05	⅛	¹⁄₁₆
'76	TR-6	70	NA	0.007	9.0	9.03	9.05	⅛	¹⁄₁₆
'76–'81	TR-7	72	0.375	0.007	8.0	8.03	8.05	⅛	¹⁄₁₆
'80–'81	TR-8	72	—	—	—	—	—	—	—

NOTE: Minimum lining thickness is as recommended by the manufacturer. Due to variations in state inspection laws, the minimum allowable thickness may be different than recommended by the manufacturer.
— Not available at time of publication.

WHEEL ALIGNMENT SPECIFICATIONS

Year	Model	Caster Preferred Setting (deg)	Camber Preferred Setting (deg)	Toe-in (in.)	Steering Axis Inclination (deg)
'76–'81	Spitfire	4.0P	2.0P	¹⁄₁₆	6.75
'76	TR-6	2.75P	0.25P	¹⁄₁₆	9.25
'76–'81	TR-7	3.5P	0.25N	¹⁄₁₆–⅛	11.25
'80–'81	TR-8	3.5P	0.25N	¹⁄₁₆–⅛	11.25

P Positive
N Negative

TUNE-UP PROCEDURES

Spark Plugs

REMOVAL AND INSTALLATION

Every six months or 6,000 miles, the spark plugs should be removed for inspection. At this time they should be cleaned and re-gapped. At 12 months or 12,000 mile intervals, the plugs should be replaced.

Prior to removal, number each spark plug with a piece of masking tape bearing the cylinder number. Remove each spark plug wire by grasping its rubber boot and twisting slightly to free the wire from the plug. Using a ¹³⁄₁₆ in. spark plug socket, turn the plugs counterclockwise to remove them. Do not allow any foreign matter to enter the cylinder through the spark plug holes.

If the plugs are to be reused, check the porcelain insulator for cracks and the electrodes for excessive wear. Replace the entire set if one plug is damaged. Clean the reusable plugs with a stiff wire brush, or in a sandblasting machine. Uneven wear of the center of ground electrode may be corrected by leveling off the unevenly worn section with a file. The gap must be checked with a feeler gauge.

With the ground electrode positioned parallel to the center electrode, a 0.025 in. wire gauge must pass through the opening with a slight drag. If the air gap between the two electrodes is not correct, the ground electrode must be bent to bring it to specifications.

After the plugs are gapped correctly, they may be inserted into their holes and hand tightened. Be careful not to crossthread the plugs. Torque the plugs to their proper specification. Install each numbered plug wire onto its respective plug.

Breaker Points and Condenser

REMOVAL AND INSTALLATION

Remove the distributor cap and rotor, noting their position. Inspect the contacts and replace the points if the contacts are blackened, pitted or worn excessively, if the breaker arm has lost its tension, or if the fiber rubbing block has become worn or loose. Points that appear light gray in color may be cleaned with a point file.

To replace the points and condenser, disconnect the electrical leads at the primary connection, remove the lock screw for the points and lift them straight up. Loosen the condenser retaining bracket and slide out the condenser. While the points are out, lubricate

the breaker cam with a very light coating of silicone based grease. Clean the distributor base plate with alcohol to free it of any oil film that might impede completion of the ground circuit. Also clean the contact point surfaces with the solvent. Install the new points and condenser and tighten their retaining screws. Connect the electrical leads for both at the primary connection. If the point contacts are not aligned, bend the stationary arm.

To gap the contact points, turn the engine until the rubbing block on the point assembly is resting on the high point of the cam lobe. Loosen the point holddown screw slightly and

Adjustment of ignition points—typical

insert a feeler gauge of the specified thickness (0.014-0.016 in.) between the point contacts. Fine adjustment is made either by inserting a screwdriver into the eccentric adjusting slot on the stationary arm (late distributors) or by turning the eccentric adjusting screw on the stationary arm (early distributors). When the feeler gauge passes between the point contacts with a slight drag, tighten the holddown screw without disturbing the setting.

If a dwell meter is available, proceed to "Dwell Angle Setting". If the meter is not available, install the rotor and cap, and proceed to "Ignition Timing Adjustment".

Dwell Angle Setting

The dwell angle is the number of degrees of distributor cam rotation through which the breaker points remain fully closed (conducting electricity). Increasing the point gap decreases dwell, while decreasing the point gap increases dwell.

Connect the positive wire of the meter to the distributor primary wire connection on the distributor side of the coil, and the negative wire of the meter to a good ground on the engine (e.g. thermostat housing nut).

The dwell angle may be checked either with the engine running or with the cap and rotor removed and the engine cranking at starter speed. The meter gives a constant reading with the engine running. With the engine cranking, the reading will fluctuate between zero degrees dwell and the maximum figure for that angle. While cranking, the maximum figure is the correct one. Never attempt to change dwell angle while the ignition is on, as touching the point contacts or the primary wire connection with a metal screwdriver may result in a 12 volt shock.

To change dwell angle, loosen the point holddown screw slightly and make the approximate correction. Tighten the holddown screw and test the dwell with the engine cranking. If the dwell appears to be correct, install the rotor and distributor cap and test the dwell with the engine running. Take the engine through its entire rpm range and observe the dwell meter. The dwell should remain within specifications at all times. Great fluctuation of dwell at different engine speeds indicates worn distributor parts.

Following the dwell angle adjustment, the ignition timing must be checked. A 1° increase in dwell results in the ignition timing being retarded 2° and vice-versa.

Ignition Timing

IGNITION TIMING PRELIMINARY ADJUSTMENT—ALL EXCEPT ELECTRONIC IGNITION

This procedure is used to obtain a rough initial timing setting when the distributor has been removed and the timing disturbed.

1. Adjust the gap of the breaker points as outlined under "Breaker Points Removal and Installation."

2. If the distributor was removed, install it in the engine, making sure that the drive

Timing mark—TR-6

gears are engaged. Tighten the clamp bracket.

3. Disconnect the distributor low tension lead at the coil. Hook up a 12 V test light directly to the disconnected distributor lead and to the positive terminal of the battery.

4. Rotate the engine (crankshaft) manually in the normal direction of rotation (clockwise) until the timing marks nearly coincide with the static timing figure given in the "Tune-Up Specifications" table. The test light should now be illuminated.

——— CAUTION ———
Do not rotate the engine counterclockwise.

5. Slowly rotate the crankshaft further in a clockwise direction until the test light just goes out. At this point, the No. 1 piston should be in its compression stroke and the rotor should be pointing at the distributor cap contact for the No. 1 spark plug wire.

6. If the timing is correct, the marks will be aligned at the static timing figure. If the timing proves to be incorrect and the marks do not properly align, loosen the distributor pinch bolt and turn the distributor until the points just open and the test light goes out. Rotate the engine one complete revolution again by hand and make sure that the light goes out at the static timing figure.

7. Disconnect the test light. Reconnect the distributor lead at the coil. Install the distributor cap, if removed.

8. Proceed to final (dynamic) timing adjustment.

Timing marks—Spitfire, 1500; TR-7 similar

IGNITION TIMING ADJUSTMENT

Clean the crankshaft damper and pointer on the water pump housing. Disconnect the vacuum line(s) from the intake manifold at the distributor and plug the line(s). On breakerless systems, the retard unit pipe should be connected.

Attach a tachometer to the engine and set the idle speed to specifications. Set timing to specifications. As a final check, start the engine once more to make sure that the timing marks do align.

Unplug and reconnect all disconnected hoses. Remove the timing light and tachometer from the engine.

Electronic Ignition

The only adjustment that can be made within the distributor is the pick-up air gap. This adjustment is initially made during assembly and does not have to be changed during the vehicle's accumulated mileage, unless distributor internal problems arise. A brass or plastic feeler gauge should be used when checking the air gap. The clearance should be 0.014 to 0.016 inch.

The ignition timing is adjusted in the conventional manner by rotating the distributor housing in the desired direction.

Adjusting valve lash—overhead valve engines

Valve Lash Adjustment
ALL EXCEPT TR-7 AND TR-8

Valve clearances should be as specified with the engine cold. For the four-cylinder engines, adjust the valves as follows: turn the crankshaft until the valve to be adjusted is fully open, then rotate the crankshaft one more revolution to be sure that the valve will be fully closed. Loosen the locking nut and adjust the screw until the specified feeler gauge will just fit between the valve stem and the rocker arm. Tighten the locking nut and recheck the clearance to see that it has not changed.

For the six-cylinder engines, the following sequence of valve clearance adjustments is recommended. Turn the engine clockwise and adjust as follows:

Adjust These Valves	When These Are Fully Open
1 and 3	10 and .2
8 and 11	2 and 5
4 and 6	7 and 9
10 and 12	1 and 3
2 and 5	8 and 11
7 and 9	4 and 6

TR-7

1. Rotate the engine. Check and record each valve clearance. Clearance should be checked with the cam heel facing the tappet.

2. To adjust, remove the camshaft. Remove the shim on each valve which requires adjustment. Keep them in sequence.

3. Using a micrometer, measure and record the thickness of each shim. To determine the thickness required, use the following example and install new shims where necessary.

Valve clearance measurement location—TR-7

Carburetor

IDLE SPEED AND MIXTURE ADJUSTMENT

W/Zenith–Stromberg 150 CDSE

Make the following adjustments:
1. Idle speed—screw adjustment.
2. Idle emission—to be used only with a fuel/air ratio meter.

3. Fast idle—simple screw adjustment. Settings are as follows:

1975-79 Spitfire Idle CO level: 0.5-2.5% (warm engine) Equivalent air/fuel ratio: 14.4:1-13.6:1.

1975-76 TR-6 and 1975-79 TR-7 with Twin Carburetors Zenith-Stromberg 175 CDSEV

NOTE: The following procedure requires the use of an air flow meter and a CO analyzer. Since this equipment is expensive and not readily available to the general public, it is suggested that the adjustments be made by a qualified technician.

Air flow balance adjustment

1. Check that the fast idle cam is against its stop on each carburetor, and that the fast idle screw is clear of the fast idle cam.

2. Run engine to normal operating temperature.

3. Using an air flow meter check flow on both carburetors.

4. If air flow is not equal, loosen one of the clamping nuts on one of the throttle interconnecting links and loosen the throttle adjusting screws enough to allow the throttles to close, then turn both screws so that they just touch their stops plus ½ turn.

5. Turn both adjusting screws just enough to achieve air flow balance.

Throttle adjusting screw

6. Tighten the clamping nut on the interconnecting link.

7. If necessary, turn the adjusting screws equally to achieve 800 rpm.

8. Where applicable, disconnect the air pump outlet hose and plug the hose end. Insert the analyzer probe and check the CO reading against the underhood decal.

NOTE: Do not allow the engine to idle for more than 3 minutes without a 1 minute clear-out period at 2000 rpm.

9. If the CO level is above limits, adjust the mixture as follows:

10. Remove the piston dampers and insert a mixture adjusting tool into the dashpot. The tool must be fully engaged and held correctly to prevent tearing the diaphragm.

11. Back out to richen and turn in to lean both carburetors equally until CO is within acceptable limits. Add oil to the dampers if necessary.

1. Fast idle screws
2. Cam pivots
3. Idling screws
4. Choke cable trunnion
5. Idle trimming screw

Idle speed and mixture adjusting locations—Zenith Stromberg 150 CDE(V) and 175 CDE(V) carburetors

Adjusting the mixture

FAST-IDLE ADJUSTMENT SCREW

FAST-IDLE CAM

Fast idle speed adjustment

1975-79 TR-7 (California) W/Zenith-Stromberg 175 CD4TV

NOTE: When making adjustments, do not let the engine idle for more than 3 minutes without a 1 minute clear-out period at 2000 rpm.

1. Run engine at normal operating temperature.
2. Set idle to 800 rpm.
3. Disconnect the air pump outlet hose and plug hose end.
4. Insert infrared analyzer probe and check CO readings against the underhood decal.
5. If CO readings are not within specifications, remove damper and insert mixture adjusting tool into dashpot. Tool must be inserted and held properly to avoid tearing the diaphragm.
6. Back off to enrichen and turn in to lean the mixture as required. Add oil, if necessary, to the damper.

IDLE SPEED

1980 and Later TR-8 with Zenith Stromburg 175 CDSET

NOTE: The following procedure requires the use of an air flow meter to balance the carburetors.

1. Run the engine until it reaches normal operating temperature.
2. Remove the air cleaners.
3. Disconnect the throttle linkage so that each carburetor operates independently.
4. Check the air flow through both carburetors using an air flow meter. If the air flows are not equal, rotate the throttle adjusting screw to give equal balance with an idle speed of 750 to 950 rpm.
5. Connect the link between the carburetors. The near side carburetor should then go out of balance.
6. Adjust the anti-rattle screw until the balance is returned. The idle speed should return to the previous setting.
7. Connect the throttle link rod.
8. Adjust the idle speed screws equally on both carburetors.

9. Replace the air cleaners.

MIXTURE ADJUSTMENT

1980 and Later TR-8 with Zenith Stromburg 175 CDSET

NOTE: The following procedure requires the use of an exhaust gas analyzer and a special mixture adjusting tool.

1. Disconnect the air pump diverter valve outlet hose from the valve and plug the hose.
2. Make sure the engine is at the normal operating temperature and that the idle speed is correct.
3. Insert the gas analyzer as far as possible into the exhaust pipe and check the CO reading.

NOTE: The setting must always be checked by means of a non-dispersive infrared exhaust gas analyzer.

4. To adjust the mixture, remove the piston damper from both carburetors.
5. Carefully insert the special adjusting tool into the dashpot until the outer part of the tool engages the air valve and the inner part of the tool engages the hexagon in the needle adjusting plug.
6. Holding the outer tool, turn the inner tool clockwise to enrich the mixture and counterclockwise to weaken it.
7. Adjust both the carburetors the same way.

Fuel Injection
IDLE SPEED ADJUSTMENT

1. Run the engine until it reaches normal operating temperature for at least two minutes.
2. Make sure that the engine timing is correct.
3. Connect a tachometer to the engine according to the manufacturers instructions. The tachometer that comes with the car can be used if necessary.
4. To adjust the idle speed, loosen the locknut and turn the idle adjustment bolt clockwise to decrease the idle speed and counterclockwise to increase the idle speed. After making the adjustment, retighten the locknut.

ENGINE ELECTRICAL

Distributor

REMOVAL AND INSTALLATION
All Except TR-8

1. Detach the spring clips and remove the

1. Rotor
2. Rotor contact
3. Mounting plate lead
4. Side screw
5. Cap
6. Oil retaining felt
7. Cam
8. Cam spindle
9. Upper thrust washer
10. Short side screw
11. Housing
12. Oil retaining felt
13. Upper sintered iron bearing
14. Side screw
15. Vernier adjustment knob
16. Vacuum advance mechanism
17. Clamp bolt
18. Coupling
19. Coupling pin
20. Lower thrust washer
21. Rubber O-ring
22. Staked plug
23. Tachometer drive gear
24. Thrust washer
25. Shaft and centrifugal advance mechanism unit
26. Weight
27. Control spring
28. Mounting plate
29. Condenser
30. Eccentric screw
31. Fixed contact
32. Terminal stud inner nut
33. Moving contact
34. Terminal stud
35. Lock screw
36. Low tension wire

Delco-Remy distributor disassembled—Spitfire

distributor cap, low tension wire, and vacuum connection. Remove the tachometer drive.

2. Release the clamping plate and withdraw the distributor assembly.

NOTE: Do not loosen the pinch bolt unless the ignition timing is to be reset, and note the position of the rotor prior to removal of the assembly.

3. If the pinch bolt has not been loosened, replace the distributor by reversing the installation procedure, and rotate the distributor rotor until it properly engages the driving shaft, then secure the clamping plate.

TR-8

1. Disconnect the negative battery cable.

2. Disconnect all electrical connections and the vacuum advance hose.

3. Remove the distributor cap and rotor.

4. Remove the plastic antiflash cover.

5. Temporarily push on the rotor.

6. Rotate the engine crankshaft so that the rotor is at the No. 1 firing position and the timing pointer is aligned with TDC on the crankshaft pulley scale.

7. Remove the one bolt and the clamp bracket.

8. Remove the distributor assembly.

9. Before installing the distributor, rotate the oil pump shaft with an appropriate tool so that it is in position to accept the slotted end of the distributor shaft.

10. Before installing the distributor, position the body as illustrated and the rotor vertical relative to the engine.

11. Insert the distributor, locating the slotted adapter of the distributor shaft to the oil pump shaft.

12. With the distributor flange against the timing gear cover, the rotor should be pointing as illustrated relative to the engine.

13. Install the retaining clamp and bolt and reconnect all electrical connections and vacuum advance hose.

Alternator

REMOVAL AND INSTALLATION

1. Disconnect the electrical leads.

2. Loosen the main mounting bolt and the adjustment bracket bolts.

3. Remove the drive belt.

4. Remove the outer adjustment bracket bolt and the main mounting bolt and spacer.

5. Installation is the reverse of removal. Adjust the belt tension.

ALTERNATOR PRECAUTIONS

Several precautions must be observed when performing work on alternator equipment.

1. If the battery is removed for any reason, make sure that it is reconnected with the correct polarity. Reversing the battery connections may result in damage to the one-way rectifiers.

2. Never operate the alternator with the main circuit broken. Make sure that the battery, alternator, and regulator leads are not disconnected while the engine is running.

3. Never attempt to polarize an alternator.

4. When charging a battery that is installed

1. Rotor
2. Lock screw
3. Nut
4. Insulation piece
5. Moving contact
6. Small insulation washer
7. Fixed contact
8. Moving plate
9. Side screw
10. Moving plate ground lead
11. Cam spindle screw
12. Cam
13. Cam spindle
14. Control spring
15. Weight
16. Shaft and action plate
17. Body
18. Spacer collar
19. Spring
20. Vacuum advance unit
21. Tachometer drive gear
22. Gasket
23. Cover
24. Driving dog pin
25. Driving dog
26. Thrust washer
27. Rubber O-ring
28. Clamp bolt
29. Retaining spring
30. Retard unit
31. High tension carbon brush
32. Cover
33. Condenser
34. Large insulation washer
35. Terminal block

Lucas conventional diaphragm distributor for the TR-6

Lucas electronic ignition schematic

in the vehicle, disconnect the negative battery cable.

5. When utilizing a booster battery as a starting aid, always connect it in parallel; negative to negative, and positive to positive.

6. When arc welding is to be performed on any part of the vehicle, disconnect the negative battery cable, disconnect the alternator leads, and unplug the voltage regulator.

DRIVE BELT ADJUSTMENT

Check the drive belt for cracks and wear. Replace it if its condition is questionable. The belt should be adjusted so that it is possible to depress the belt approximately ¾ in. (all except TR-8), ¼ in. (TR-8), between the pulleys of the longest run. To adjust, loosen the adjusting bolt and alternator mounting bolt, then pivot the alternator until the belt has the correct amount of free movement. Tighten the bolts in this position.

NOTE: Do not use a metal pry bar against the aluminum alternator housing to tension the belt.

Voltage Regulator

The AC voltage regulators are nonadjustable and must be replaced as a unit.

Starter
REMOVAL AND INSTALLATION

1. Removal of the starter requires disconnecting the negative battery cable, all terminal connections and removing bolts and starter.

2. To install the starter, measure the distance between the flywheel ring gear (pinion side) and the starter mounting face.

Lucas electronic (breakerless) distributor disassembled

1. Molded cover
2. Rubber O-ring
3. Slip ring end bracket
4. Through bolt
5. Stator windings
6. Field winding
7. Key
8. Bearing retaining plate
9. Pressure ring
10. Felt ring
11. Drive end bracket
12. Nut
13. Spring washer
14. Pulley
15. Fan
16. Spacer
17. Pressure ring and felt ring retaining plate
18. Drive end bearing
19. Circlip
20. Rotor
21. Slip ring end bearing
22. Slip ring moulding
23. Nut
24. Rectifier pack
25. Brushbox assembly
26. Regulator unit

Exploded view—Lucas alternator—typical

1. Moulded cover
2. Rubber O-ring
3. Slip ring end bracket
4. Through bolt
5. Stator windings
6. Field winding
7. Key
8. Bearing retaining plate
9. Pressure ring
10. Felt ring
11. Drive end bracket
12. Nut
13. Spring washer
14. Pulley
15. Fan
16. Spacer
17. Pressure ring and felt ring retaining plate
18. Drive end bearing
19. Circlip
20. Rotor
21. Slip ring end bearing
22. Slip ring moulding
23. Nut
24. Rectifier pack
25. Brushbox assembly
26. Regulator unit

1. Jump ring
2. Shaft collar
3. Main spring
4. Buffer washer
5. Screwed sleeve

6. Pinion and barrel
7. Drive end bracket

Starter drive components—M35J

Lucas 15ACR alternator

3. In addition, measure the distance from the starter face to the pinion end. End clearance from the starter pinion to the flywheel ring gear should be $3/32$ to $5/32$ in. (shims are available).

4. Connect all electrical leads.

STARTER DRIVE REPLACEMENT

M35J

1. Remove the starter.

2. Remove the two drive end bracket bolts and lockwashers.

3. Pull the drive end bracket, armature, and inertia drive assembly from the yoke.

4. Remove the four retaining bolts and lay aside the commutator end bracket.

5. Lift out the two field winding brushes and remove the commutator end bracket from the yoke.

6. Compress the main spring and ease the snap-ring from the shaft. Remove the starter drive components.

7. Installation is the reverse of removal. Lubricate the drive end bracket bushing with 10W engine oil.

M-100

The starter drive is not replaceable.

M418G and 2M 100PE

1. Remove the starter.

2. Disconnect the lead from the "STA" terminal.

3. Remove the solenoid, leaving the plunger attached to the engaging lever.

4. Remove the plunger return spring and plunger, from the engaging lever.

5. Loosen the locknut and remove the eccentric pin.

6. Remove the cover band and the brushes.

7. Remove the through bolts. Lightly rap the mounting bracket lugs.

8. Separate the commutator end bracket from the yoke.

9. Remove both the steel and fabric thrust washers. Note their placement.

10. Remove the rubber molding. Remove the armature and starter drive assembly.

11. Remove the engaging lever and thrust washer.

12. Using a $5/8$ in. I.D. tube, over the shaft end, force the thrust collar of the snap-ring toward the starter drive.

13. Remove the snap-ring.

14. Remove the thrust collar and the starter drive. Replace the entire drive assembly if the roller clutch is defective.

CAUTION
Use a solvent moistened cloth to clean the drive, carefully avoiding the roller clutch.

15. Assembly is the reverse of disassembly. Lubricate the drive sleeve splines and pinion bearing.

1. Terminal post nuts and washers
2. Commutator end bracket
3. Commutator end bracket bearing bushing
4. Cover band
5. Commutator
6. Terminal post
7. Yoke
8. Pole shoe screw
9. Pole shoe
10. Field winding
11. Shaft
12. Drive end bracket
13. Drive end bracket bearing bushing
14. Ring
15. Shaft collar
16. Main spring
17. Buffer washer
18. Screwed sleeve
19. Pinion and barrel
20. Field winding brush
21. Armature
22. Through bolts
23. Ground brush

Lucas M35G starter; the M35J is similar

Lucas M-100 starter

ENGINE MECHANICAL

Engine Removal and Installation

Spitfire

1. Remove all electrical wires, coolant lines and vacuum hoses.
2. Remove the hood.
3. Disconnect and plug the fuel intake line.
4. Remove the following:
   a. air cleaners
   b. choke controls
   c. carburetor linkage
   d. exhaust pipe at manifold
   e. radiator
   f. front seats and carpeting
   g. transmission cover
   h. speedometer cable
   i. clutch slave cylinder
   j. overdrive solenoid wires
   k. driveshaft
   l. gearshift extension.
5. Attach a hoist to the lifting eyes, disconnect all mounts and lift the engine and transmission assembly from the car.
6. Installation is the reverse of the removal.

TR-6

1. Remove the battery and hood. Drain the cooling system.
2. Disconnect the choke control, throttle linkage and fuel line.
3. Disconnect all coolant lines, vacuum hoses and electrical wires connected to the engine.
4. Disconnect the crankcase oil pressure pipe, tachometer drive and brake servo pipe, and breather pipe.
5. Remove the following:
   a. radiator and deflector
   b. crossmember from beneath the radiator
   c. air cleaner
   d. exhaust pipe from manifold
   e. seats, console, carpeting
   f. transmission cover
   g. backup light and overdrive connections
   h. driveshaft
   i. clutch slave cylinder
   j. rear mounts
   k. speedometer cable and transmission cover.
6. Attach a hoist to the lifting eyes and disconnect remaining mounts. Lift engine from car.
7. Installation is the reverse of the removal.

TR-7

Remove the engine and transmission as a unit.
1. Remove the hood.
2. Disconnect all coolant lines and electrical wires from engine.
3. Disconnect the following:
   a. brake servo hose at intake manifold
   b. vacuum hoses at intake manifold

c. fuel line
d. throttle linkage
e. gear lever assembly
f. driveshaft
g. exhaust pipe
h. speedometer cable
i. clutch slave cylinder
j. engine stabilizer
k. battery ground
l. hood lock

1. Fiber washer
2. Plain washer
3. Nyloc nut
4. Filler cap
5. Copper/asbestos washer
6. Spark plug
7. Nut
8. Adaptor
9. Gasket
10. Rear engine plate
11. Bolt
12. Rear oil seal
13. Bolt
14. Gasket
15. Oil pump drive shaft bushing
16. Oil pressure switch
17. Crankshaft thrust washer
18. Rear bearing shell
19. Rear bearing cap
20. Relief valve
21. Spring
22. Copper washer
23. Cap nut
24. Oil pump body
25. Oil pump end plate
26. Center bearing shell
27. Center main bearing cap
28. Drain plug
29. Oil pan
30. Oil pan gasket
31. Front bearing shell
32. Front main bearing cap
33. Sealing wedges
34. Sump bolt
35. Slotted screw
36. Front sealing block
37. Front engine mounting
38. Gasket
39. Front engine plate
40. Oil seal
41. Gasket
42. Front timing cover
43. Slotted setscrew
44. Bolt
45. Plain washer
46. Cotter pin
47. Chain tensioner
48. Pivot pin
49. Bolt
50. Generator pedestal
51. Dipstick
52. Bracket
53. Nyloc nut
54. Bolt
55. Nyloc nut
56. Breather pipe
57. Cylinder block
58. Cylinder head gasket
59. Cylinder head
60. Generator adjusting link
61. Rocker cover gasket
62. Rocker cover

Stationary components of four cylinder Spitfire engine

m. clutch hydraulic pipe.

4. Discharge the A/C system, if equipped.

5. Raise the rear of the car.

6. Attach a hoist to the lifting eyes, support the engine weight and disconnect the front and rear supports. Lift out the engine and transmission assembly.

7. Installation is the reverse of removal.

TR-8

NOTE: The engine and transmission are removed as a unit from the bottom on these models. Since the removal procedure requires the use of special tools, having this done by a qualified dealer is advisable.

Cylinder Head

REMOVAL AND INSTALLATION

All Models
(Except TR-7 and TR-8)

1. Disconnect the battery and drain the cooling system.

2. Remove the air cleaner(s) and the intake and exhaust manifold.

3. Remove the drive belt. Remove the water pump.

4. Remove the rocker arm cover, the rocker assembly, and the pushrods. Be sure that all electrical and hose connections to the cylinder head have been disconnected. Remove the spark plugs.

5. Loosen and remove the cylinder head nuts in reverse order of the tightening sequence. Remove the cylinder head.

NOTE: If the cylinder head does not lift readily, tap each side with a hammer, using a short piece of wood to help absorb the shock. Another method is to reinsert the spark plugs and crank the engine with the starter, using the engine's own compression pressure to supply the force needed to break the seal.

6. Before replacing the cylinder head, be sure that the gasket surfaces of the head and block are perfectly clean and smooth. If any dirt is present, the gasket may leak when the head is installed. Check for the presence of dirt or carbon particles in the stud passages in the head. Also, inspect the valves and guides for wear and damage. Check valve stems for wear and distortion. Any valve with a head thickness less than $1/32$ in. (0.8 mm) at the seat edge should be replaced. Valve guide wear may be checked by inserting a new valve into the guide, lifting it $1/8$ in. from its seat, and moving it sideways. If the movement of the valve head across the seat exceeds 0.020 in. the guide should be replaced. Valve guides must protrude above the top face of the cylinder head as follows:

Spitfire: 0.749-0.751 in.

TR-6: 0.63 in.

7. To replace the head gasket, note its markings and position it accordingly. Tighten the cylinder head nuts finger tight, then gradually tighten them in the proper order.

8. Replace the valve rocker arm assembly and reverse the cylinder head removal procedure. Check the valve clearances before running the engine, then again after a brief running period when normal temperature is reached. Make a third check after a few hundred miles and at this time check the cylinder head nuts for tightness and tighten them to the specified torque. Although tightening down the cylinder head nuts will affect valve clearances slightly, the differences will not usually be enough to warrant resetting the valves. However, the clearances should be checked.

TR-7

1. Disconnect the following:
   a. air cleaner and duct
   b. intake manifold and carburetors
   c. camshaft cover
   d. distributor cap.

2. Turn the crankshaft until the camshaft sprocket bottom bolt is accessible. Remove the bolt.

3. Anchor the sprocket to the support bracket and turn the camshaft so that the flange is in line with the groove on the front bearing cap, and the distributor arm points toward the manifold rear attachment bolt.

4. Remove the camshaft sprocket top bolt.

5. Disconnect the following:
   a. pipe from the check valve
   b. pipe from the water transfer housing
   c. exhaust pipe.

70. Piston	93. Lock tab	114. Camshaft
71. Oil control ring	94. Bolt	115. Bolt and locktab
72. Taper compression ring	95. Flywheel	116. Con-rod cap
73. Plain compression ring	96. Bush	117. Con-rod bearing shell—lower
74. Rocker assembly	97. Dowel	118. Con-rod bearing shell—upper
80. Spring—outer	98. Inner rotor and spindle	119. Dowels
81. Spring—inner	99. Outer rotor	120. Con-rod
82. Pushrod	100. Crankshaft	121. Circlip
83. Pushrod	101. Key	122. Piston pin
86. Spring seats	102. Sprocket	123. Piston pin bushing
87. Spring seats	103. Slinger	124. Nut
88. Tappet	105. Crankshaft pulley	125. Retainer and keeper
89. Tappet	109. Timing chain	126. Retainer and keeper
90. Exhaust valve	110. Bolts and lock tab	
91. Intake valve	111. Camshaft sprocket	
92. Distributor and oil pump drive gear	112. Bolt	
	113. Keeper plate	

Moving components of four cylinder Spitfire engine

77. Split keepers
78. Collar retainer
79. Spring—outer
80. Spring—inner
81. Spring seats
82. Intake valve
83. Tappet
84. Pushrod
85. Split keepers
86. Inner retainer (exhaust)
87. Outer retainer (exhaust)
88. Spring—outer
89. Spring—inner
90. Spring seats
91. Exhaust valve)
92. Pushrod
93. Tappet
94. Distributor and oil pump drive gear
95. Bolts
96. Flywheel
97. Bushing
98. Dowel
99. Inner rotor and spindle
100. Outer rotor
101. Crankshaft
102. Sprocket
102A. Shim
103. Oil slinger
104. Seal extension
105. Crankshaft pulley
106. Dowels
107. Fan boss
108. Bolt
109. Key
110. Timing chain
111. Bolts and lock plate
112. Camshaft sprocket
113. Bolt
114. Keeper plate
115. Camshaft
116. Bolt
117. Con-rod cap
118. Con-rod bearing shell—lower
119. Con-rod bearing shell—upper
120. Con-rod
121. Dowels
122. Circlip
123. Piston pin
124. Piston pin bushing
125. Circlip

65. Bolts and lock tabs
66. Balance weight
67. Washer
68. Rubber bushing
69. Fan assembly
70. Steel bushing
71. Rubber bushing
72. Piston
73. Oil control ring
74. Tapered compression ring
75. Plain compression ring
76. Rocker shaft assembly

Moving components of six cylinder—TR-6 engine

6. Remove the timing cover from the cylinder head.

7. Unbolt and remove the cylinder head.

8. Installation is the reverse of removal.

TR-8

1. Drain the cooling system.

2. Remove the air cleaner assembly.

3. Remove the intake manifold.

4. Remove the rocker covers.

5. Remove the rocker shaft assemblies.

6. Disconnect the front exhaust pipes from the manifold flanges.

7. Remove the dipstick tube on the left cylinder head on cars equipped with automatic transmission.

8. Remove the engine oil dipstick tube from the left cylinder head.

9. Loosen the alternator link pivot and clamp bolts. Remove the two pivot bolts and nuts securing the alternator to its bracket.

10. Loosen the cylinder head bolts by reversing the tightening sequence.

11. Lift off the cylinder head including the exhaust manifold and separate if needed.

12. Installation is the reverse of removal. Using the bolt tightening sequence illustration, insert the bolts into their correct holes as follows: long bolts—3.820 in.—numbers 1, 3 and 5; medium bolts—2.620 in.—numbers 2, 4, 6, 7, 8, 9 and 10; short bolts—2.160 in.—numbers 11, 12, 13 and 14.

13. Tighten the bolts evenly a little at a time in the sequence shown in the illustration to the following torque figures:

Bolt numbers 1 thru 10—65-70 ft/lbs.
Bolt numbers 11 thru 14—40-50 ft/lbs.

CYLINDER HEAD OVERHAUL

See "Engine Rebuilding" section.

Rocker Shaft

REMOVAL AND INSTALLATION

All Models
(Except TR-7 and TR-8)

1. Disconnect any PCV hoses and retaining clips for vacuum hoses from the rocker cover.

2. Remove the rocker cover and gasket.

3. Loosen the 4 nuts (four cylinder) or 6 nuts (six cylinder) which secure the rocker shaft pedestals to the cylinder head, and lift off the rocker shaft assembly.

4. Prior to installation, loosen the locknuts and back off the tappet adjusting nuts a few turns to avoid bending the pushrods when tightening the rocker shaft nuts.

5. Install the rocker shaft assembly on the cylinder head, making sure that the pushrods seat correctly on their balls and that the adjusting screws are located correctly. Hand tighten the rocker assembly nuts a few turns.

6. Evenly tighten the rocker shaft pedestal nuts in an order (from the front) of 3-2-4-1 to a torque of 26-32 ft/lbs for 4-cylinder Spitfire engines, and in an order of 4-3-5-2-6-1 to 24-26 ft/lbs for 6-cylinder TR-6 engines.

TR-8

1. Drain the cooling system.

2. Remove the air cleaner and air temperature control.

3. Remove the intake manifold.

4. Remove the rocker covers.

5. Remove the rocker shaft assemblies.

6. Remove the pushrods and tappets and retain in the sequence removed.

NOTE: If a tappet cannot be withdrawn, remove the camshaft and withdraw the tappet from the bottom.

7. Remove the split pin from the one end of the rocker shaft then remove the plain washer, a wave washer, rocker arms, brackets and springs and retain them in the proper sequence for reassembly.

8. Installation is the reverse of removal.

Intake Manifold

REMOVAL AND INSTALLATION

All Except TR-8

1. Drain the cooling system.

2. Remove the air cleaner. Disconnect the throttle linkage spring and the choke cable(s).

3. Disconnect the vacuum lines, the fuel lines, and the water hoses from the induction assembly.

4. Remove the clamps which retain the manifold to the cylinder head and to the exhaust manifold (if so equipped). Remove the manifold.

NOTE: If the intake manifold gasket is in need of replacement, the exhaust manifold must be removed first.

6. Installation is the reverse oif removal. Torque the nuts to specifications.

TR-8

1. Disconnect the negative battery cable.

2. Drain the cooling system.

3. Remove the air cleaner and temperature control assembly.

4. Remove the engine breather pipes.

5. Disconnect the main feed fuel pipe to the carburetors.

6. Disconnect the throttle cable and the mixture control cable.

7. On cars equipped with automatic transmission, remove the kickdown cable bracket.

8. Pull off the carburetor vent pipes.

9. Disconnect the inlet and outlet hoses to the heater.

10. Disconnect the coolant temperature wire.

11. Disconnect the heater return pipe, that connects to the pump, at the manifold connection.

12. Disconnect the thermostat bypass hose at the manifold connection.

13. Disconnect the brake servo hose from the manifold. Disconnect the distributor vacuum hose.

14. Disconnect the vent pipe to the radiator.

15. Disconnect the spark wires and remove the distributor cap.

16. Remove the twelve manifold retaining bolts while noting the location of the different lengths.

17. Lift off the manifold and remove the two gasket clamps.

18. Installation is the reverse of removal. Coat all the retaining bolt threads with a lu-

bricant sealant. Tighten all bolts a little at a time, evenly and alternating sides, working from the center to each end. Torque to 25-30 ft/lbs.

Exhaust Manifold

REMOVAL AND INSTALLATION

All Except TR-8

1. Remove the intake manifold (exc. TR-7).

2. Unbolt the exhaust manifold from the exhaust pipe.

3. Remove the manifold and discard the gasket.

4. Installation is the reverse of removal. Torque nuts to specifications.

TR-8–Without Fuel Injection–L.H.

1. Bend back the locking tabs on the eight manifold retaining bolts.

2. Raise and safely support the front of the car.

3. Remove the three nuts securing the down-pipe to the manifold flange.

4. Lower the car and remove the eight manifold bolts and lock washers.

5. Remove the manifold and discard the two copper O-rings.

6. When installing, use new copper O-rings on the pipe flange and tighten the bolts evenly. Lock the tabs.

TR-8–Without Fuel Injection–R.H.

1. Remove the hot air intake hose.

2. Remove the heat chamber cover.

3. Remove the heat chamber back plate by removing the four bolts.

4. Bend back the locking tabs on the eight manifold retaining bolts.

5. Raise and safely support the front of the car.

6. Remove the three nuts securing the exhaust pipe to the manifold flange.

7. Lower the vehicle and remove the eight manifold bolts and lock washers.

8. Remove the manifold and discard the two copper O-rings.

9. When installing, use new copper O-rings and tighten the eight manifold bolts evenly.

TR-8–With Fuel Injection–L.H.

1. Slacken the air-flow meter to plenum chamber clips.

2. Disconnect one end of the plenum chamber hose and remove the hose.

3. Remove the E.G.R. valve pipe to manifold bolts and remove the pipe.

4. Disconnect the vacuum pipe from the E.G.R. valve.

5. Remove the bolts and strap from the air conditioning compressor.

6. Disconnect the spark plug wires.

7. Remove the exhaust flange nuts.

8. Bend back the locking tabs on the exhaust manifold bolts then remove the bolts.

9. Remove the exhaust manifold.

10. Installation is the reverse of removal.

TR-8–With Fuel Injection–R.H.

1. Remove the windshield washer bottle.

2. Disconnect the spark plug wires.

3. Remove the starter motor heat shield.

4. Remove the exhaust flange nuts.

5. Bend back the lock tabs on the exhaust manifold bolts and remove the bolts.

6. Remove the exhaust manifold.

7. Installation is the reverse of removal.

Installing the timing chain cover while holding the tensioner back with a bent rod

Timing Gear Cover

REMOVAL AND INSTALLATION

Spitfire

1. Remove the drive belt.

2. Remove the fan.

3. Remove the crankshaft damper nut (accessible from below), and the damper.

NOTE: It may be necessary to block the flywheel to stop the crankshaft from turning. Replace the nut loosely and pull off the damper with a gear puller.

4. Remove the five screws, six bolts, and one nut which retain the timing gear cover to the engine. Lift off the cover with its gasket, taking care not to damage the seal.

5. Installation is the reverse of removal. To ease installation, hold the chain tensioner back with a bent length of rod until the tensioner clears the chain. When installing the pulley, take care to position the drive key between the pulley and the crankshaft spindle. Tighten the damper nut to specifications. Readjust the drive belt tension.

TR-6

1. Drain the cooling system. Drain the engine oil. Disconnect the overflow pipe and tank, if so equipped.

2. Remove the radiator support(s), radiator valance(s), and radiator.

3. Remove the fan, cross tube and drive belt.

4. On the TR-6, remove the U-bolts from the steering rack and ease the rack forward.

5. Remove the fan adaptor. Using a gear puller, remove the crankshaft pulley.

6. Remove the timing cover, gasket, and spacer.

7. Installation is the reverse of removal. To ease installation, hold the chain tensioner back with a bent length of rod until the tensioner clears the chain. Readjust the drive belt tension.

TR-7

1. Remove the following:
    a. hood
    b. battery ground
    c. alternator and bracket
    d. air pump, diverter and relief valve and bracket
    e. A/C compressor brackets
    f. timing cover-to-head bolts
    g. timing cover center and lower left bolts
    h. fan assembly.
2. Remove the timing cover.
3. Installation is the reverse of removal.

TR-8

1. Disconnect the battery.
2. Remove the hood.
3. Remove the radiator.
4. Remove the alternator drive belt.
5. Remove the fan blade.
6. Remove the crankcase pulley retaining bolt.
7. Turn the crankshaft to TDC number one cylinder firing.
8. Loosen the timing pointer retaining bolts and move the pointer away from the crankshaft pulley assembly.
9. Disconnect the spark plug wires and remove the distributor cap.
10. Remove the crankshaft pulley.
11. Disconnect the vacuum pipe from the distributor.
12. Remove the lower R.H. (viewing from the front of the engine) timing cover bolt and move the transducer to one side.
13. Remove the upper bolt which also releases the power steering pump and vent pipe clip.
14. Remove the power steering pump drive belt and remove the pump to one side.
15. Disconnect the brown wire, at the connector, to the transducer.
16. Disconnect the coolant temperature wire.
17. Remove the timing cover bolts securing the diagnostic socket and move to one side.
18. Disconnect the diagnostic socket leads from the coil.
19. Disconnect the electronic ignition leads from the distributor and coil and remove the plug from the heat-sink.
20. Remove the thermostat bypass and the heater return hoses from the water pump.
21. Disconnect the leads from the oil pressure switch and the oil pressure indicator.

Oil seal installation

22. Remove the two bolts securing the timing cover to the oil pan.
23. Remove the remaining five bolts, one nut and the timing cover from the cylinder block.

NOTE: The timing cover is removed complete with the distributor, oil pump, oil pressure switch, oil pressure indicator transmitter, oil filter and water pump and pulley assembly.

24. To install, clean all gasket contact surfaces.
25. Set the distributor rotor arm approximately 30 degrees before the final position (TDC number one cylinder firing).
26. Position the timing cover and secure with the five bolts and one nut. Install the two sump pump bolts.
27. The rest of the installation is the reverse of removal. When installing the crankshaft pulley assembly, tighten the retaining bolt to 140-160 ft/lbs.

Installation of front oil seal—TR-7

Oil Seal Replacement

All Models
(Except TR-7 and TR-8)

1. Remove the timing gear cover.
2. Tap out the old seal.
3. Smear the new seal with engine oil and, making sure that the cavity face of the seal faces the engine, install it into the cover using a drift or wooden block.
4. Install the timing gear cover.

TR-7

1. Remove the pulleys.
2. Pry out old seal.
3. Dip new seal in engine oil and install.

TR-8

1. Remove the crankshaft pulley.
2. Remove the old seal, taking care not to damage the cover.
3. Before installing the new seal, lubricate the outside diameter and position the seal in the housing with the lip facing toward the engine.
4. Using a suitable drift, fit the seal until the back of the seal is flush with the outer face of the seal housing.

5. Install the crankshaft pulley.

Timing Chain

REMOVAL AND INSTALLATION

All Models (Except TR-7 and TR-8)

1. Remove the timing gear cover.
2. Remove the oil thrower.
3. Check timing chain wear by placing a straight edge along the slack length of chain. If the free-play between the straight edge and the chain, at a point midway between the two sprockets, exceeds 0.4 in., the chain must be replaced.
4. Rotate the crankshaft until the crankshaft key is at 12 o'clock and the sprocket dots align.
5. Pry back the locking tabs and remove the bolts which retain the camshaft sprocket to the camshaft.
6. Taking care not to disturb the crankshaft or camshaft, remove both sprockets with the timing chain.
7. To check alignment of the sprockets, remove the crankshaft drive key and temporarily install both sprockets. Place a straight

Checking timing chain slack

edge across the teeth of both sprockets. Correct any misalignment by placing shims behind the crankshaft sprocket.

8. After checking the alignment, remove the sprockets, install the crankshaft drive key, and place the sprocket and chain assembly into position—aligned dot to dot, or line to line. Install the camshaft sprocket retaining bolts using a new lockplate.
9. Install the oil thrower.
10. Install the timing gear cover.

TR-7

1. Remove the timing chain cover, camshaft cover and distributor cap.
2. Turn the crankshaft so that the camshaft timing mark is at the bottom.
3. Remove the exposed camshaft retaining bolt and turn the crankshaft until the mark

A. Scribed alignment marks
B. Punch mark opposite camshaft groove

Relative position of timing marks on sprockets

is in line with the groove in the front bearing cap.

4. Secure the camshaft sprocket to the support bracket, and remove the last sprocket bolt.

5. Remove the hydraulic tensioner and guide plate as well as the locking bolt from the adjustable chain guide.

6. Remove the common bolt between the adjustable guide and the support and remove the guide.

7. Remove the fixed guide, chain and sprocket.

8. Install the chain over the sprockets and on the engine.

9. Loosely install the fixed guide and support bracket.

10. Loosely install the adjustable guide.

11. Install a guide bolt in the timing cover center bolt hole.

12. Install the camshaft sprocket with one bolt and turn the idler shaft sprocket so that the scribed line is halfway between the guide bolt and the lower adjustable guide bolt.

13. Install and tighten the hydraulic chain tensioner.

14. Remove the nut securing the camshaft sprocket to the support bracket and install the remaining sprocket bolt.

15. Install the distributor cap, camshaft cover and timing cover.

Checking sprocket alignment (right), correcting alignment with shims (A) (left)

C958

Intermediate shaft and timing chain gear—TR-7

TR-8

1. Set the engine number one piston at TDC.
2. Remove the timing chain cover.
3. Make sure the number one piston is at TDC.
4. Remove the distributor drive gear and the spacer.
5. Remove the gears complete with the chain.

CAUTION

Do not rotate the engine while the rocker shafts are installed, otherwise the valve gear and pistons will be damaged.

Timing chain and gear location—TR-7

NOTE: If the engine crankshaft and/or camshaft have not been rotated, proceed to step 11. If it is necessary to rotate them, proceed to step 6.

6. Remove the rocker shaft assemblies.
7. Set the engine number one piston at TDC.
8. Temporarily intall the camshaft pulley with the marking "Front" outward.
9. Turn the camshaft until the mark on the camshaft pulley is at the six o'clock posi-

tion, then remove the pulley without disturbing the camshaft.

10. Locate the pulleys to the chain with the timing marks aligned.

11. Engage the pulleys and chain assembly on the camshaft and crankshaft key locations. Check that the camshaft key is parallel to the shaft axis to ensure adequate lubrication of the distributor drive gear.

12. Make sure the timing marks line up.

13. Install the spacer with the flange to the front.

14. Install the distributor drive gear making sure the annular grooved side is fitted to the rear or towards the spacer.

15. Install the drive gear washer and bolt and tighten to 40-45 ft/lbs.

16. Install the timing chain cover.

17. Install the rocker shaft assemblies.

TIMING CHAIN TENSIONER ADJUSTMENT

The tensioner is non-adjustable. The TR-7 uses a hydraulic tensioner, the others use a spring type. If the chain is not tensioned properly and is not stretched, the tensioner must be replaced. To remove the spring type tensioner, remove the timing chain cover. Spread the tensioner blades apart and slide the tensioner off the anchor pin. The hydraulic type is a simple bolt-on unit.

Installation is the reverse of removal. Make sure that the convex surface of the tensioner faces the timing chain.

Camshaft

REMOVAL AND INSTALLATION

All Models (Except TR-7 and TR-8)

1. Drain the cooling system. Remove the radiator valence(s) and the radiator.

On TR-6 models, remove the radiator grille.

2. Remove the timing cover.

3. Remove the timing chain and camshaft sprocket. Remove the fuel pump, the distributor driveshaft, and gear.

Camshaft timing marks (6)

4. Remove the cylinder head. Remove the pushrods and lifters, keeping them in order.

5. Remove the camshaft keeper plate and slide the camshaft out.

6. Installation is the reverse of removal. Keep the camshaft end play to 0.004-0.008 in. Adjust the valve timing.

TR-7

1. Remove the cover and turn the camshaft so that the timing mark is 180° from the groove in the front bearing cap.

2. Anchor the sprocket to the support bracket and remove the exposed bolt.

3. Align the timing mark and the groove and remove the remaining bolt.

4. Number the bearing caps and remove them. Loosen the nuts evenly.

5. Remove the camshaft.

6. Install in reverse of the above.

NOTE: When installing shaft, make sure that the mark and groove are in alignment. Torque bearing cap nuts to 3-5 ft/lb.

TR-8

1. Remove the timing chain cover as described earlier in this section.

2. Remove the intake manifold complete with carburetors. See Intake Manifold removal and installation.

3. Remove the L.H. and R.H. rocker covers.

4. Remove the eight bolts (four per shaft) and remove the rocker shafts. Identify for reassembly.

5. Remove the eight push rods and identify for reassembly.

6. Remove the camshaft pulley retaining bolt and washer.

7. Remove the camshaft and crankshaft pulleys complete with the chain.

8. Remove the distributor drive gear and spacer.

9. Remove the eight hydraulic lifters and identify for reassembly.

10. Carefully remove the camshaft.

TR-7 piston assembly. The first raised part is installed on the right; the numbered side of the rod (15) goes on the left

TR-6, Spitfire, GT6 piston and connecting rod

11. Installation is the reverse of removal. Lubricate the five camshaft journals before installing the camshaft.

Piston and Connecting Rod Identification

SPITFIRE AND TR-6

Pistons and connecting rods are installed with the open end of the bearing facing the non-thrust (driver's side) side of the engine and the arrow on the piston crown facing forward.

TR-7

Two types of pistons are used with this

TR-7 connecting rod (7) and bearing caps (8)

model. One is installed with the flat raised part of the piston on the right side of the engine; the other with the arrow on the piston crown facing forward.

ENGINE LUBRICATION

Oil Pan

REMOVAL AND INSTALLATION

Spitfire

1. Drain the engine oil.

2. Unbolt the oil pan and rest it on the crossmember.

3. Raise the engine. If necessary, rotate the crankshaft. Remove the pan.

4. Installation is the reverse of removal. The long bolts go at the rear of the pan.

TR-6

1. Disconnect the negative battery cable.

2. Drain the engine oil. Remove the dipstick.

3. Remove the oil pan bolts and lower out the pan.

4. Using a new gasket and non-drying sealing compound, position the oil pan to the engine and install the retaining bolts. Torque the bolts to specifications.

5. Fill the crankcase to capacity with the proper grade of oil. Install the dipstick.

6. Connect the negative battery cable.

TR-7

1. Remove the air duct, fan guard, coupling plate bolts, and engine stabilizer.

2. Make up a support bracket from angle iron.

3. Remove the alternator support and timing cover lower bolt.

4. Attach the support bracket to the timing cover using these holes.

5. Support the engine under the bracket with a jack.

6. Remove the right engine mount and the left mount-to-frame bolts.

7. Remove the pan bolts and raise the engine far enough to remove the pan, along with the left mount.

8. Installation is the reverse of removal.

TR-8

1. Disconnect the negative battery cable.

2. Raise the car and safely support with jack stands.

3. Drain the engine oil.

4. Remove the underneath panel so that access can be gained to the crankshaft pulley assembly.

5. Place a jack under the crankshaft pulley damper.

6. Remove the two engine L.H. front mounting bolts and washers.

7. Raise the engine until a dimension of 1.5 in. exists between the center of the inboard mounting hole and the corresponding subframe mounting hole.

8. Remove the power steering hose clamp bolt.

9. Remove the fourteen oil pan retaining bolts from both sides and the front.

10. Remove the two rear oil pan retaining bolts together with the reinforcing plate.

11. Remove the two coupling plate bolts and remove the oil pan.

12. Installation is the reverse of removal.

REAR MAIN OIL SEAL REPLACEMENT
All Models (Except TR-7 and TR-8)

1. Remove the transmission.

2. Remove the flywheel. Remove the engine rear transmission adapter plate.

3. On the GT6, lift the engine sufficiently to provide access to the rear main seal bolts.

4. Remove the oil seal housing with gasket. Press out the old seal.

Rear main oil seal correctly positioned in housing

5. Smear the outside diameter of the new oil seal with grease and press it into the housing, lip toward the crankshaft.

6. Coat the crankcase face with sealing compound and smear the crankshaft with oil.

7. Using a new gasket, install the seal housing and hand-tighten the retaining bolts.

8. Position the housing to the crankcase face using a centering sleeve. After the housing is centered, tighten the bolts.

9. Further installation is the reverse of removal.

TR-7

1. Remove the transmission, clutch and flywheel.

2. Remove the two rear pan bolts and loosen the left rear pan bolt.

3. Remove the oil seal housing and pry out the seal.

4. Installation is the reverse of removal.

TR-8

1. On cars equipped with manual transmissions, remove the transmission, clutch and flywheel. On cars equipped with automatic transmissions, remove the transmission, torque converter and drive plate.

2. Remove the oil pan, strainer and baffle plate.

3. Remove the rear main bearing cap and bearing lower half.

4. Remove and discard the rear main bearing cap side seals.

5. Remove and discard the crankshaft rear oil seal.

6. To install, fit the side seals to the grooves each side of the rear main bearing cap.

NOTE: Do not cut the side seals to length. They must protrude approximately 1/16 inch above the bearing cap parting face.

7. Apply a sealing compound to the rear-most half of the rear main bearing cap parting face or to the equivalent area on the cylinder block.

8. Lubricate the bearing half and bearing cap side seals with clean engine oil.

9. Position the bearing cap to the engine and make sure it seats squarely on the cylinder block.

10. Tighten the cap bolts approximately one quarter turn, then back off one complete turn.

11. Position a seal guide, special tool number RO. 1014, on the crankshaft flange.

12. Make sure the oil seal guide and the crankshaft journal are clean. Then coat the seal guide and oil seal journal with clean engine oil.

NOTE: Make sure that the seal guide outer surface is completely coated with lubricant so that the oil seal lip is not turned back during reassembly.

13. Position the oil seal, lipped side towards the engine, on to the seal guide. The seal outside diameter must be clean and dry.

14. Push the oil seal fully by hand into the recess formed in the cap and block until it abuts against the machined step in the recess.

15. Remove the seal guide.

16. Tighten the rear main bearing cap evenly to 65-70 ft/lbs.

17. Install the oil pan, strainer and baffle plate.

18. Install the transmission and other related parts.

Oil Pump

REMOVAL AND INSTALLATION
All Models (Except TR-7 and TR-8)

1. Remove the dipstick, drain the oil pan, remove the oil pan and remove the oil pump from the crankcase.

2. With the oil pump assembled except for the top cover, measure the clearances between the inner and outer rotors, the outer rotor and the pump housing, and the inner rotor and the face of the pump housing. Clearances should fall within the specifications.

OIL PUMP CLEARANCES

Model	Inner Rotor to Outer Rotor (in. max.)	Outer Rotor to Pump Housing (in. max.)	Inner Rotor to Housing Face (in. max.)
Spitfire	0.010	0.0075	0.0035 ②
TR-6	0.004 ①	0.0075	0.0040
TR-7	0.004 ①	0.0080	0.0040
TR-8	0.008	0.0070	0.0030

① Min. —0.001 in.
② Min. —0.0015 in.

3. Replace worn components and install the inner rotor in the pump housing, followed by the outer rotor, with its chamfered face leading.

4. Installation is the reverse of removal.

TR-7

1. Remove the clutch slave cylinder, bell-housing nut and bolt, oil pump retaining bolts and pump.

2. Install in reverse of the above using a new O-ring.

Measuring oil pump outer rotor to pump housing clearance

TR-7 support bracket

Measuring oil pump rotor end clearance

TR-8

1. Remove the oil filter assembly.
2. Disconnect the electrical lead from the oil pressure switch.
3. Remove the bolts from the oil pump cover and remove the cover and gasket.
4. Remove the oil pump gears.
5. Before installation, pack the oil pump gear housing with petroleum jelly so that the pump will prime itself when the engine is started.
6. Install the oil pump gears and make sure the petroleum jelly is forced into every cavity between the teeth of the gears.
7. Replace the oil pump cover using a new gasket. Tighten the retaining bolts alternately and evenly to 9 ft/lbs.
8. Install the oil filter and the electrical lead to the oil pressure switch.

Measuring oil pump inner rotor to outer rotor clearance

ENGINE COOLING

Radiator

REMOVAL AND INSTALLATION

1. On TR-8 models with air conditioning, disconnect and remove the condenser.
2. Drain the cooling system by opening the engine block drain cock and the radiator drain cock or by disconnecting the lower radiator hose.
3. On TR-6 models, remove the radiator valance and position the stay rods to one side.

Disconnect the remaining radiator hoses. Disconnect the overflow hose to the expansion tank.

4. On TR-8 models with automatic transmission, remove and clamp the top and bottom fluid hose connections.
5. Remove the radiator retaining bolts and lift out the radiator.
6. Reverse the above procedure to install, making sure that the cooling system is filled to the proper level with a 50% ethylene glycol solution.

Water Pump

REMOVAL AND INSTALLATION

All Models (Except TR-7 and TR-8)

1. Drain the cooling system, and remove the fan belt.
2. Disconnect the radiator and water hoses at the thermostat housing and water pump, and disconnect the fuel supply line at the carburetors and fuel pump.
3. Remove the temperature transmitter connection.
4. Remove the water pump.
5. Installation is the reverse of removal.

TR-7

1. Remove the intake manifold with carburetors.
2. Remove the connecting tube from the water pump cover and the bottom hose from the pump.
3. Remove the pump from the block.
4. Installation is the reverse of removal.

TR-8

1. Disconnect the negative battery cable.
2. Drain the cooling system.
3. Remove the radiator.
4. Remove the fan assembly.
5. Remove the water pump pulley.
6. Remove the alternator belt.
7. Disconnect the diagnostic socket lead at the connector.
8. Remove the two bolts common to the timing cover and water pump and move the diagnostic socket and bracket aside.
9. Remove the two remaining common timing cover and water pump bolts and note that the upper one is longer.
10. Remove the five water pump bolts and remove the water pump and pulley assembly.
11. Use a new gasket and install in reverse of removal.

Thermostat

All thermostats are pre-set by the manufacturer; no adjustment is necessary. Servicing is by replacement only. If a thermostat malfunction is suspected, it may be tested by placing the thermostat in water of specific temperature and watching to see if unit functions at the temperature marked on the thermostat flange.

REMOVAL AND INSTALLATION

1. Drain the radiator.
2. On all models except the TR-8, remove

the two bolts securing the elbow to the thermostat housing and lift off the elbow with the top hose attached.

3. On the TR-8, disconnect the radiator top hose from the thermostat housing. Then remove the thermostat housing from the manifold.
4. Remove the thermostat.
5. Installation is the reverse of removal.

EMISSION CONTROLS

Positive Crankcase Ventilation System

Two different systems have been used on TR-6, TR-7 and Spitfire models. Both systems are closed ones, so named because they are sealed from the atmosphere.

1975 TR-6, 1975 and later TR-7, and all Spitfire models use a PCV system that draws the crankcase vapors through a combination oil strainer/flame trap in the valve cover through a metering orifice on each carburetor (Zenith-Stromberg CDSE, CD4VT or CDSE (V)) and then into the air/fuel mixture.

On the TR-8 models with carburetors, clean air is drawn from the rear of the air cleaner and passes through a hose and a filter into the crankcase. The crankcase fumes rise through the pushrod tubes to the right-hand rocker cover and pass up through a flame trap to hoses connected to the depression side of the carburetors. The fumes are finally drawn into the combustion chambers and burned.

To ensure that blow-by gases do not escape from the crankcase to the atmosphere, depression is maintained in the crankcase under all operating conditions on the TR-8 models with fuel injection. This is achieved by connecting the crankcase breathing housing to a point between the air meter flap and the throttle plate. Air is drawn in on the left hand rocker cover through an air filter and restrictor and drawn off from the engine on the right-hand rocker cover. A flame trap is fitted in the draw off housing.

COMPONENT SERVICE

The PCV system is serviced every 12 months or 12,000 miles.

Clean the crankcase breather hoses by running a solvent soaked rag on a coat hanger through them. Remove the oil filler cap and clean it with gasoline. If the cap is gummed up, chances are that the wire screen (flame guard) at the breather hose outlet on the inside of the valve cover is also dirty. Remove the valve cover and clean the screen with solvent. Replace the valve cover gasket, if necessary.

Fuel Evaporative Control System

All 1975 and later model Triumphs have

1. Crankcase purge line
2. Canister purge line
3. Canister
4. Vapor feed line
5. Fuel tank (limited fill)
6. Sealed fuel filler cap
7. Vapor separator
8. Anti run-on valve

Spitfire evaporative control system

1. Crankcase breather pipe
2. Vent valve connecting pipe(s)
3. Canister purge pipe
4. Evaporative control canister
5. Canister to fuel tank pipe
6. Run-on control valve
7. Vacuum control pipe
8. Solenoid connections
9. Canister to run-on control valve pipe
10. Flame arrestor
A. 1/32 in. restrictor
B. 3/32 in. restrictor
C. 3/16 in. restrictor

Spitfire crankcase and evaporative control emission

been equipped with an evaporative control system to prevent unburned fuel vapors in the fuel tank and carburetor float chambers from escaping into the atmosphere. The gas filler cap is sealed from the atmosphere.

All 1975 and later models use a gas filler neck that extends down into the tank, thus preventing complete filling of the tank. This eliminates the need for an expansion tank that would take up much needed trunk space. A small vapor separator, located above the tank, is used instead. The vapor separator contains a restrictor valve which prevents fuel surges from reaching the carbon canister. Those vapors which do not condense and return to the fuel tank are displaced and drawn into an activated charcoal canister located in the engine compartment. The excess fuel vapors in the

carburetor float chambers are also vented to the charcoal canister.

A solenoid actuated anti-run on (antidieseling) valve is incorporated into the evaporative control system. When the ignition is switched off, the solenoid is activated, operating a valve that seals off the atmospheric vent at the bottom of the carbon canister. With the vent sealed, the connection to the intake manifold applies a partial vacuum to the canister and subsequently to the float chambers.

The canister is a sealed unit, and must be replaced at 24 month or 24,000 mile intervals.

1. Crankcase purge line
2. Carburetor float chamber vent pipe
3. Canister purge line
4. Charcoal canister
5. Fuel tank vent pipe
6. Anti dieseling valve
7. Manifold vacuum line
8. Electrical connections for Anti dieseling valve
9. Purge air to canister
10. Flame arrestor
A. 3/16 in. restrictor
B. 5/16 in. restrictor

Crankcase and evaporative control purge system—TR-7 (Calif.)

1. Crankcase purge line
2. Carburetor float chamber vent pipe
3. Canister purge line
4. Charcoal canister
5. Fuel tank vent pipe
6. Anti dieseling valve
7. Manifold vacuum line
8. Electrical connections for anti dieseling valve
9. Purge air to canister
10. Flame arrestor
A. 3/16 in. restrictor
B. 5/16 in. restrictor

Crankcase and evaporative control purge system—TR-7 (49 states)

1. Carbon canister
2. Filter gauze
3. Base cap

Evaporation control system carbon canister

1. Crankcase breather pipe
2. Vent valve connecting pipes
3. Canister purge pipe
4. Evaporative control canister
5. Canister to fuel tank pipe
6. Run-on control valve
7. Vacuum control pipe
8. Solenoid connections
9. Canister to run-on control valve pipe
10. Flame arrestor
A. 1/32 in. restrictor
B. 3/32 in. restrictor
C. 5/16 in. restrictors

TR-6 crankcase and evaporative control emission system details showing antirun on valve

Exhaust Gas Recirculation System

Beginning in 1974, U.S.A. TR-6 and Spitfire 1500 models are equipped with an (EGR) system. All TR-7 and TR-8 models are equipped with EGR.

The EGR valve is mounted on the exhaust manifold on TR-7 and TR-8 models and Spitfires and located on the cylinder head on TR-6 models. The valve is controlled by a vacuum signal taken from a throttle edge tapping in the carburetor.

At 12 month or 12,500 mile intervals (1975 and later models), the components of the EGR system must be removed for cleaning. Most common EGR valve failures stem from exhaust deposits or a cracked diaphragm. The base of the valve may be cleaned with a wire brush. Clean the valve seat and metering valve with a sand blaster or spark plug cleaning machine. On 1975 and later models, reset the EGR service reminder light (odometer actuated) using the special British Leyland Key at 12,500 mile intervals.

Exhaust Emission Control

AIR INJECTION SYSTEM

All TR-7, TR-8 and Spitfire 1500 models are equipped with an air pump system. A belt driven air pump delivers filtered air under pressure to the exhaust ports. Here, the additional oxygen, supplied by the air pump, reacts with any uncombusted fuel mixture promoting an afterburning effect. To prevent a reverse flow in the air injection manifold when exhaust gas pressure exceeds air supply pressure, a non-return check valve is used. A

Exhaust system with catalytic converter—TR-7 (California)

EGR/Catalytic converter service reminder mechanism

Air injection reactor system—TR-7 (50 states)

TR-6 EGR system

1. Thermostatic vacuum switch
2. Vapor trap
3. Carburetor
4. E.G.R. Valve

Spitfire EGR system

1. E.G.R. valve
2. Inlet manifold
3. Exhaust port
4. Gas trap
5. Vacuum source — throttle edge tapping

Exhaust gas recirculation system—TR-7 (California)

1. E.G.R. valve
2. Inlet manifold
3. Exhaust port
4. Choke cam
5. E.G.R. cut-out valve
6. Gas trap
7. Vacuum source — throttle edge tapping

Exhaust gas recirculation system—TR-7 (49 states)

combination diverter/relief valve is installed to divert air to the atmosphere upon deceleration to prevent backfiring in the system. The diverter/relief valve also vents pump air at high speeds to prevent pump damage.

CATALYTIC CONVERTER

All TR-7 and Spitfire models manufactured for sale in the state of California are equipped with a catalytic converter. The converter is installed in the exhaust system, ahead of the muffler.

ENGINE MODIFICATIONS

Various measures have been taken to limit exhaust emissions resulting from the incom-

plete combustion of gasoline. Generally speaking, these measures have been designed to provide more efficient combustion of a "leaner" air/fuel mixture. The fuel delivery system has received the most attention in this respect with the use of the Zenith-Stromberg CDSE, CD4VT, and CDSE(V) series carburetors. Features of these carburetors include: a sealed and wired cover to discourage tampering; fixed, non-adjustable fuel jets; a biased metering needle to ensure a consistent air/fuel ratio; free-play built into the throttle linkage permitting a fast idle without disturbing the otherwise closed throttle; a temperature compensator assembly which varies the air supplied to the venturi area to correct the mixture and maintain even running with changing engine temperature; and a throttle bypass valve which is set to open at a predetermined manifold depression to admit air during deceleration.

An intake air temperature control system is used on TR-7 models to maintain the air entering the carburetor(s) at a constant temperature. By blending the engine compartment source air with the exhaust manifold heated air, the intake air is kept at roughly 99° F under all operating conditions. The system is controlled by a temperature sensitive bi-metal strip, which switches intake air sources via a flap valve.

A further reduction of exhaust emissions is gained by the use of ignition distributors that retard the spark during idling and deceleration, on all models. All models utilize distributors with centrifugal advance and vacuum retard.

Other measures taken to reduce the level of exhaust emissions include a modified camshaft that reduces overlap at low engine speeds and a modified cylinder head to promote cleaner burning. Stellite faced exhaust valves are used to maintain effective valve seating over a longer period of time. All models are modified to achieve a lower compression ratio so that regular octane fuels may be used.

Component Testing and Adjustment Temperature Compensator

If the idle speed drops off sharply during extended periods of idling, especially during warm weather, the temperature compensator may be in need of replacement.

Intake air temperature control system TR-7 (California)

Intake air temperature control system—TR-7 (49 states)

the rear air valve, the bypass valve must be replaced.

Anti-Run On Valve

If the engine continues to diesel or run on after the ignition switch is turned off, the anti-run on valve may be faulty. Check the continuity of the wiring leading to the solenoid and make sure that the electrical connections at the solenoid are tight. Then apply 12V to the solenoid with the engine running. If working properly, this will shut off the fuel supply to the engine. If not working properly, the valve must be replaced.

Air Injection Pump Components

NOTE: The air pump drive belt must be maintained at the proper tension to ensure correct air pump operation. Adjustment is correct when light thumb pressure deflects the belt ¾ to 1 in. at the mid-point of its longest run.

Air Pump and Relief/Diverter Valve

To check the air pump and relief valve install a pressure gauge between the pump and relief valve. With the engine running, air must be relieved at 8.2 to 10.5 psi or the valve is in need of replacement. If the 8.2 psi figure cannot be reached, the pump is defective and must be replaced.

Disconnect the air outlet pipe at the diverter. Make sure that air is dumped on deceleration by opening and closing the throttle quickly while feeling the valve.

Air Pump Removal and Replacement

1. Remove air hose from pump.
2. Loosen the mounting bolts and remove the belt.
3. Take the weight off the pump and remove the mounting bolts.
4. Remove the pump from the engine.
5. Installation is the reversal of removal.
6. Check and adjust belt tension.

Relief Valve Check

1. The relief valve allows excessive air pressure at high engine speed to discharge into the atmosphere.
2. Run the engine at high speeds and check the valve operation.
3. This valve cannot be repaired or adjusted. It must be replaced.

Air Manifold Removal and Installation

1. Remove the air cleaners.
2. Unbolt the manifold from the check valve.
3. Remove the manifold from the cylinder head.

NOTE: It may be easier to remove the center branches at the manifold junction.

4. Remove the manifold.
5. Installation is the reversal of removal.
6. Run engine and check for air leaks.

Check Valve

Remove the valve and blow through it orally. Air should pass from pump to manifold

1. Remove the plastic cover from the compensator.
2. With the ambient temperature at or above 85° F, the valve should be able to be pressed inward with light finger pressure and then returned to its position without jamming. If the valve jams and is still in operation, the temperature compensator should be replaced.
3. If properly adjusted, the valve will begin to open at 70–77° F, and be fully open at 85°F.
4. Replace the cover and check its operation during idling.

Bypass Valve

If the engine does not return to idle speed soon after the throttle is released, and the throttle control linkage is properly adjusted, the bypass valve may be faulty.

1. If the engine still refuses to return to idle speed when the throttle is released, turn the bypass adjusting screw on the front carburetor to the left and manually lower the idle.
2. Run the engine briefly to approximately 2000 rpm, then release the throttle. If the engine returns to idle speed, turn the screw ½ turn further to the left. If the engine does not return to idle, replace the bypass valve as a unit.
3. Remove the air cleaner and observe the air valves. Briefly race the engine and then release the throttle. The air valve of the front carburetor should normally go down to the bridge slower than the air valve of the rear carburetor. Turn the bypass adjusting screw to the right until this function is obtained. If the valve cannot be adjusted so that the front air valve goes down to the bridge slower than

end, but not from the manifold to pump end. Make sure the hose is free of blockage.

Check Valve Removal, Test and Installation

1. Disconnect the air hose from the check valve.

2. Use two open end wrenches to remove the check valve from the air manifold.

NOTE: Do not put excessive force on the air manifold.

3. Blow through the valve orally.

4. Air should pass only through the hose connection end. Should air pass through the valve at the manifold end replace the valve.

5. Installation is the reversal of removal.

EGR Valve

If a sudden loss of idle and full throttle power is noticed when it is known that the ignition, valve and fuel delivery systems are operating properly, the problem may lie in a faulty EGR valve. Warm the engine to operating temperature and make sure that the choke control is fully off. With the engine idling, modulate the throttle and place a finger beneath the EGR valve diaphragm. As the engine rpm changes, you should feel the valve diaphragm moving in conjunction with the changing engine speed. If a vacuum tester is available, make sure that the EGR valve diaphragm retains a vacuum when open. The valve should close immediately when the throttle is closed.

Emission control vacuum circuit—TR-6

COMPONENT REPLACEMENT

Temperature Compensator

1. Remove the compensator.

2. Discard the old rubber seals and replace them with new ones.

3. Install the compensator on the side of the carburetor.

4. Check the operation of the compensator during idle.

Bypass Valve

1. Remove the bypass valve.

2. Discard the old bypass valve-to-carburetor housing gasket.

3. Install a new gasket and bypass valve on the carburetor.

4. Check the operation of the bypass valve.

Anti-Run On Valve

1. Disconnect the electrical connections at the solenoid.

2. Disconnect and plug the evaporative piping from the valve.

3. Lift out the old valve and install the new unit. Connect the vacuum and electrical connections.

FUEL SYSTEM

Fuel Pump

All models are equipped with an AC mechanical diaphragm type fuel pump, located on the left side of the engine, except the TR-8 fuel injected and carburetor model engine.

1. Retaining screw	13. Spring
2. Washer	14. Washer
3. Cover	15. Washer
4. Joint	16. Retainer
5. Gauze	17. Spindle
6. Screw	18. Operating lever
7. Body	19. Return spring
8. Screws	20. Operating fork
9. Retainer	21. Distance washer
10. Valves	22. Priming lever
11. Upper retainer	assembly
12. Diaphragm	23. Lower body
assembly	

Spitfire fuel pump assembly

The carbureted engine fuel pump/fuel gauge unit is located in the fuel tank. The fuel injected model is located underneath the car directly in front of the rear.

REMOVAL AND INSTALLATION

Except TR-8

To remove the fuel pump, disconnect the fuel inlet and outlet lines.

Unscrew the attaching nuts and remove the pump.

When installing, make sure that the pump lever (rocker arm) is positioned correctly above its lobe on the cam.

FUEL PUMP CLEANING

Every 12,000 miles the fuel pump should be serviced. This may be accomplished by:

1. Removing the top bolt and domed cover.

2. Removing the gauze filter and thoroughly washing in a safe solvent (denatured alcohol).

3. Cleaning the sediment in the fuel bowl with a small screwdriver. The preferred method for removing loosened sediment is compressed air. Wipe out the interior of the fuel bowl with a soft, clean rag.

— CAUTION —
The interior of the fuel bowl must be absolutely free of grease or lint.

4. Renewing the cork gasket if cracked or brittle. Fuel pump parts are delicate; use caution. When reassembling, be sure the filter gauze is facing down.

TR-8 Carbureted Engine

1. Disconnect the battery.

2. Fold down the back of the rear seat.

3. Roll luggage compartment carpet toward rear of the car.

4. Roll the left-hand felt strip back.

5. Remove rubber grommet in the floor.

6. Disconnect the electrical plug.

7. Unscrew the pump outlet union.

8. Remove the six screws securing the pump to the tank.

9. Remove the complete assembly.

10. Remove the gasket.

11. Release the pump from the retaining clip.

12. Release the spring clip and pull the pump from the rubber elbow.

13. Remove the terminal cover and disconnect the electrical leads.

14. Installation is the reverse of removal.

NOTE: Electricity is supplied to the fuel pump via the starter solenoid and oil pressure switch. It will only operate when the engine is being started or when there is sufficient oil pressure.

TR-8 Fuel Injected Engine

NOTE: Depressurize the fuel system.

1. Remove the fuel pump ground.

2. Crank the engine for a few seconds.

3. Turn the ignition off and connect the ground.

NOTE: The fuel cut-off inertia switch may be used to disconnect the fuel pump before cranking the engine.

4. Locate the fuel pump beneath the floor in front of the rear axle.

5. Remove the two bolts and nuts on the fuel pump cover. Remove the cover.

6. Remove the fuel line and plug with a ⅜″ bolt.

7. Remove the input line and plug with a ⅜″ bolt.

8. Remove electrical leads.

9. Remove pump mounting bolts and remove pump from the car.

10. Installation is the reverse of removal.

Electronic Fuel Injection

The electronic fuel injection system is comprised of two parts, a fuel injection system and an electronic control for the fuel system.

Fuel Injection System Components

Fuel is drawn from the tank and pressurized to 2.5 kgf/cm² (361bf/in²) by an electric fuel pump located under the floor. The pump operates only when the ignition and/or the starter is energized. The fuel passes through the filters to a pressure regulator, the spring chamber of which is connected to the intake manifold. This results in the fuel pressure and manifold pressure being held constant, with excess fuel being returned to the tank via an anti-surge pot. A fuel line links the regulator with the injectors. The injectors are programmed to open in banks of four, in unison, twice per cycle. On eight cylinder engines, the two banks operate alternately. The time the injectors are open regulates the amount of fuel to the engine. To assist in cold starts, a cold start injector sprays fuel in the plenum chamber before the fuel is added by the main injectors. The fuel pump is energized independently of the electronic control unit. It is designed not to operate unless the starter motor is energized. The heart of the electronic fuel injection system is the electronic control unit. This unit is sealed, and requires no maintenance. It should not be opened or tampered with. The air flow meter is designed to smooth out air flow fluctuations. The throttle switch provides the electronic control unit with throttle operating conditions. It is located on the plenum chamber. The coolant temperature sensor is located between the cylinder heads. An extra air valve is located in the water passage and registers coolant temperature. Its purpose is to provide additional air to maintain satisfactory idle speed until the engine reaches normal operating temperature. The over-run valve allows air into the manifold via the plenum chamber when vacuum is high and thus maintains combustion during deceleration. This system also has two Lambda sensors in the exhaust system located in front of the catalytic converters. These are designed to pick up the amount of oxygen in the exhaust and thereby regulate the fuel mixture.

For all fuel injection system repair and service procedures not detailed below, please refer to "Fuel Injection" in the Unit Repair section.

FUEL PRESSURE REGULATOR REMOVAL AND INSTALLATION

1. Depressurize the fuel system.

NOTE: See fuel pump removal and installation.

2. Disconnect the battery ground.

3. Remove the bolt in the regulator bracket and pull the regulator and bracket up.

NOTE: Check direction of regulator in the bracket.

4. Clamp inlet and outlet lines on regulator.

5. Remove hose clamps and pull the lines from the regulator.

6. Remove the regulator from the bracket.

7. Installation is the reverse of removal.

Carburetors

REMOVAL AND INSTALLATION

Single Zenith-Stromberg 175 CD4TV

1. Remove the air cleaner.

2. Disconnect the fuel feed line, the distributor vacuum hose, the PCV hose, and the throttle return spring.

3. Remove the cotter pin, clevis pin, and washers. Disconnect the throttle cable.

4. Disconnect choke cable.

5. Remove the flange nuts and lift off the carburetor.

6. Installation is the reverse of removal.

Twin Zenith-Stromberg 175 CDSE(V), 175 CDFEVX and 175 CDSET

1. Remove the air cleaner.

2. Disconnect the vacuum valve lines at each carburetor and from both sides of the

1. Spring coupling clamp bolts
2. Throttle stop
3. Relay lever
4. Vacuum valve plunger
5. Vacuum valve securing screws

vacuum valve. Disconnect the distributor vacuum hose, both fuel feed lines, the accelerator control rod (from the firewall side of the rear carburetor), and both choke cables.

3. Remove the vacuum valve bracket and the carburetor flange nuts. Remove the twin carburetor and linkage assembly.

4. Installation is the reverse of removal.

THROTTLE LINKAGE ADJUSTMENT

Single Zenith-Stromberg 175 CD4TV

1. Remove the air cleaner.

2. Loosen the throttle cable nuts. Loosen the fast idle screw to obtain maximum cam clearance. Fully close the throttle. Open the throttle by turning the screw 1½ turns clockwise.

3. Loosen the locknut and set the linkage adjusting screw until the clevis pin is moved to the engine side of the slots in the linkage straps; tighten the locknut.

NOTE: It is necessary to have free-play in the linkage to allow for a fast idle setting without interfering with the closed position of the throttle.

4. Tighten the cable nuts so that the cable has no play and is not taut.

5. Install the air cleaner.

Twin Zenith-Stromberg 175 CDSE(V), 175 CDFEVX and 175 CDSET

1. Loosen the bolts on the spring couplings (both carburetor ends).

2. Adjust both idle screws to the fully closed position. Rotate the screws open exactly 1½ turns. Make sure the fast idle adjustment screw is clear of the linkage cam. Be sure the choke linkage is fully closed.

3. Start and warm the engine to operating temperature. Adjust the idle screw to set both carburetors to the specified idle speed. Stop the engine.

4. Place a ³/₃₂ in. drill bit in the space

Zenith-Stromberg 175 CDSE(V) throttle linkage

1. Spring coupling clamp
   bolts
2. Throttle stop
3. Relay lever
4. Vacuum valve plunger
5. Vacuum valve
   securing screws

Zenith-Stromberg 150 CDSE(V) throttle linkage

Fast idle adjustment—single Zenith-Stromberg 150 CDSE(V)

between the lever tongue and the lever slot edge. With the bit in position put pressure on the stop cam and tighten the spring bolts. Remove the bit.

5. Place the relay lever against the stop screw. Loosen the vacuum valve screws. Adjust the valve to 0.030 in. clearance (between the valve and the lever).

6. Move the linkage until the tongue rests in the lever slot. The valve should be fully closed (throttle should be at the point of opening).

Float level adjustment—Zenith-Stromberg 150 CDSE(V) 175 CDSE(V)

Float Level Adjustment

ZENITH-STROMBERG 175 CDSE(V), CD4TV, 175 CDFEVX AND 175 CDSET

1. Remove the carburetor(s) from the manifold.

2. Unscrew the cap(s) and drain the oil from the damping cylinder(s). Drain the fuel from the float chamber(s).

3. With the carburetor inverted and the float chamber cover removed, make sure that the distance between the highest point of the floats and the carburetor body is 0.625-0.672 in.

4. To adjust, bend the float tang which contacts the needle of the valve assembly. To lower the fuel level, a thin washer may be inserted beneath the needle valve assembly.

5. Install the float chamber cover with a

1. Idling screw
2. Starter box
3. Fast-idle screw
4. Locknut
5. Cable trunnion
6. Cam lever

Fast idle adjustment—twin Zenith-Stromberg 150 CDSE(V), 175 CDSE(V)

new gasket. Fill the damping cylinder(s) to ¼ in. from the top with Type A automatic transmission fluid and install the cap(s).

6. Install the carburetor(s).

FAST IDLE AND CHOKE ADJUSTMENT

Twin Zenith-Stromberg 175 CDSE

Make sure that with the choke control knob pushed fully in, the choke lever on each carburetor is against its stop. Adjust the tension of the choke cables as necessary. Pull out the choke control knob until the cable pivot aligns with the center of the fast idle screw and the center of the cam pivot point. Loosen the locknuts and unscrew both idle screws until

each is just contacting the cam. Start the engine and, while it is cold (68-86° F), adjust the fast idle screws an equal amount to 1100 rpm. Tighten the locknuts and recheck the fast idle speed.

AUTOMATIC CHOKE

The carburetor models 150 CD4, 175 CDFEVX and 175 CDSET are equipped with automatic chokes to comply with emission control standards. The choke assembly is to be replaced as a unit and the choke mounted carburetor must be removed to accomplish it.

NOTE: The choke assembly is mounted on the front carburetor when dual carburetors are used.

Adjustment

1. Remove the choke cover to expose the fast idle cam.

2. Rotate the fast idle cam high step to position it opposite the fast idle pin.

3. Adjust the fast idle screw until the clearance between the cam step and the fast idle pin is 0.020 inch.

4. Install the choke cover and align the scribed mark of the cover with the scribed mark on the choke housing and tighten the housing/cover screws.

Centering the Jet

The air valve should move freely by raising and allowing the valve to fall. Slow action may indicate the need for cleaning by removing and cleaning both the bore and the air valve with solvent.

If the jet is not centered it may be corrected as follows:

1. Raise the air valve and tighten the jet bushing screw. Tighten the orifice adjusting screw until it is just above the bridge.

2. Loosen the jet bushing screw to release the orifice bushing. Permit the air valve to

drop. This will align the bushing. Tighten the bushing screw to secure the bushing and re-check. Repeat until the piston falls freely.

3. Move the adjusting screw until it barely touches the air valve underside when resting on the bridge. Three turns from this position (loose) gives a reasonable figure to use when synchronizing dual carburetors.

MANUAL TRANSMISSION

REMOVAL AND INSTALLATION

Spitfire

1. Raise the vehicle and remove the gear shift knob, overdrive switch and leads, transmission cover, and driveshaft cover plate.

2. Disconnect the driveshaft and speedometer cable.

3. Remove the clutch slave cylinder and drain the transmission.

4. Support the engine, disconnect the exhaust pipe from the support on the transmission and remove the transmission rear mount nuts and washers.

5. Remove the engine restraint cable, bell housing bolts, starter, back-up light, overdrive and seat belt warning leads.

6. Remove the transmission crossmember, remaining bell housing bolts and remove the transmission.

7. Installation is the reverse of removal.

TR-6

The transmission is removed, with the engine remaining in position.

1. Disconnect the battery, drain the transmission, and remove the seat cushions and carpets.

2. Disconnect the cables from the heater control switch, the control cable from the heater unit, and the lower left control cable from the center control panel. Remove the dashboard support. Remove the headlight dimmer switch, leaving the electrical connections attached.

3. Remove the center floor cover.

4. Remove the driveshaft.

5. Remove the clutch slave cylinder, allowing it to hang by its flexible hose. Remove the clutch cover plate from the lower part of the clutch housing. Disconnect the speedometer cable and the overdrive connections (if installed).

6. With the block of wood protecting the oil pan, use a jack to support the weight of the engine and transmission. The jack should be placed as far as possible toward the rear of the oil pan.

7. Remove the exhaust pipe bracket next to the hand brake, then detach the rear mounting from the transmission and crossmember.

8. Raise the engine and transmission. Remove the crossmember by sliding it forward.

9. Unbolt the clutch housing flange from the engine.

13. Mainshaft bearing circlip
14. Mainshaft bearing snap-ring
16. Mainshaft bearing
18. Countergear cluster
19. Reverse shift fork

Spitfire and TR-7 transmission

10. Remove the transmission rearward.

11. Installation is the reverse of removal.

TR-7 and TR-8

1. Remove the shift lever, driveshaft, exhaust pipe-to-bell housing bracket, exhaust pipe-to-rear axle supports, speedometer cable, reverse switch leads, restraint cable, transmission-to-crossmember tie-bar, and support the transmission on a jack.

2. Loosen the engine stabilizer-to-frame nut (lower), and remove the stabilizer from the engine support bracket.

3. Remove the transmission rear mount.

4. Lower the transmission and engine assembly just enough to remove the bell housing top bolts.

5. Remove the starter.

6. Disconnect the wiring harness and slave cylinder pipe from the bell housing.

7. Unbolt and remove the transmission/bell housing assembly.

8. Installation is the reverse of removal. Adjust the restraint cable as follows:

a. Fully slack off the front nut at the rear end of the cable.

b. Tighten the rear nut.

c. Slack off the rear nut, hold the cable by hand and position the rear nut so that a $1/32 - 1/16''$ clearance exists between the nut and the cable bracket.

d. Tighten the front nut.

CLUTCH

REMOVAL AND INSTALLATION

1. Remove the transmission.

2. In rotation, progressively loosen the bolts which retain the clutch assembly to the flywheel.

3. Lift off the clutch cover assembly (cover, diaphragm, driving plate, and pressure plate) and pull off the driven plate.

4. Installation is the reverse of removal.

1. Driven plate
2. Pressure plate
3. Inner cover
4. Spring clips
5. Diaphragm spring
6. Circlip
7. Outer cover

Laycock clutch disassembled

1. Driven plate
2. Pressure plate
3. Fulcrum ring
4. Diaphragm spring
5. Cover pressing
6. Retractor clip
7. Rivet
8. Setscrew
9. Rivet
10. Balance weight
11. Rivet

Borg and Beck clutch disassembled

BLEEDING CLUTCH HYDRAULIC SYSTEM

If the clutch does not disengage fully, air may have entered the hydraulic system through a break in the system or because the level in the reservoir has fallen too low. Bleed the system to remove the air.

Top up the clutch fluid reservoir to within ¼ in. of the FULL level. Clean the bleed nipple on the slave cylinder and attach to it a short length of tubing. Allow the tubing to hang so that its end is below the fluid level in a clean glass container partially filled with hydraulic fluid. Unscrew the bleed nipple one complete turn.

Centering the clutch with a dummy shaft

NOTE: During the bleeding operation, the level of fluid in the reservoir will fall quickly. Constantly add new fluid to ensure that the reservoir is always at least half filled with fluid. If the reservoir should empty during the bleeding operation, air will be drawn into the system and the entire procedure will have to be repeated.

Depress the clutch pedal fully and allow it to return normally. Repeat this operation, allowing a slight pause between each depres-sion of the pedal. Note the appearance of the fluid being discharged into the glass container. When no bubbles are observed hold the clutch pedal down on the following depression. While the pedal is held down, tighten the bleed screw and remove the tubing from the nipple. Top up the master cylinder reservoir with hydraulic fluid.

Clutch hydraulic system bleeding—Spitfire shown

Clutch Master Cylinder

REMOVAL AND INSTALLATION

1. Drain the fluid from the master cylinder or pump the fluid from the bleeder nipple on the slave cylinder.
2. Disconnect the fluid pipe from the master cylinder outlet and plug the ends.
3. Pull back the protective dust cover and remove the cotter pin, washer, and clevis pin which retain the master cylinder pushrod to the top of the pedal.
4. Remove the master cylinder from the firewall.
5. Installation is the reverse of removal. Bleed the system.

OVERHAUL

1. Remove the master cylinder as outlined under "Clutch Master Cylinder Removal and Installation."

2. Pull back the rubber dust cover. Lightly press in the pushrod and, with a pair of needle pliers, remove the circlip and withdraw the pushrod and washer.
3. Connect a compressed air line to the outlet connection and, using light pressure, force out the internal parts.
4. Lift the leaf on the spring retainer and pull it free of the plunger.
5. Compress the return spring and slide the valve stem sideways through the larger offset hole of the retainer. Remove the spring, spacer, and spring washer from the valve shank.
6. Using fingers only, remove the two rubber seals and discard them. Replace with new seals. Clean all parts in methylated alcohol or in clean hydraulic fluid meeting SAE 70 R3 specifications. Lay all metal parts out to dry on a clean sheet of paper. Check the cylinder bore for pitting or scoring.
7. Reverse the above procedure to install, taking care to dip each internal part in hydraulic fluid prior to installation. Make sure that the rubber seals are installed with the lips facing the bore.

Clutch Slave Cylinder

REMOVAL AND INSTALLATION

1. Drain the clutch hydraulic system by opening the slave cylinder bleeder nipple ½ turn and pumping on the clutch pedal.
2. Disconnect the hydraulic pipe.
3. Remove the nuts and bolts which retain the cylinder to its bracket on the bellhousing.
4. Remove the dust cover and pull the cylinder forward to clear it from the pushrod. Leave the pushrod attached to the operating shaft lever.
5. Installation is the reverse of removal. Bleed the system.

OVERHAUL

1. Remove the slave cylinder as outlined under "Slave Cylinder Removal and Installation".
2. Remove the rubber dust cover. Depress the piston and, using a pair of needle nose pliers, remove the circlip from the bore.
3. If the internal parts cannot be shaken out, use low pressure compressed air injected into the inlet port to force them out.
4. Remove and discard the rubber seal. Remove the return spring.
5. Clean all metal parts in methylated alcohol or in clean hydraulic fluid meeting SAE 70 R3 specifications. Lay out the parts to dry on a clean sheet of paper. Replace the cylinder body if its bore is pitted or scored. Lubricate the bore and dip each internal part in clean hydraulic fluid.
6. To assemble, insert the internal parts into the cylinder bore, using a new rubber seal. Be careful not to bend back the lips of the seal when installing in the bore. Retain the parts in the bore with the circlip.
7. Install the cylinder as outlined under "Slave Cylinder Removal and Installation".

AUTOMATIC TRANSMISSION

A Borg-Warner, three speed automatic transmission is used in the TR-7 models as an option. A torque converter is used to couple the transmission to the engine.

REMOVAL AND INSTALLATION

1. Place the selector lever in the neutral position.
2. Disconnect the downshift cable from the accelerator linkage.
3. Raise the vehicle and support safely.
4. Remove the front exhaust pipe.
5. Disconnect the transmission dipstick tube from the oil pan and drain the transmission fluid.
6. Disconnect the selector lever breather hose, neutral start switch wire connections and disconnect the speedometer cable.
7. Disconnect the oil cooler lines at the transmission.
8. Remove the driveshaft.
9. Remove the torque converter-to-engine drive plate bolts.
10. Support the engine and transmission with a jack.
11. Remove the rear engine mount center bolt, sway bar, rear cross member, heat shield, radiator lower mounting and the exhaust support bracket.
12. Lower the engine/transmission unit and remove the bellhousing and starter bolts.

Downshift cable adjustment—Automatic Transmission

13. While supporting the engine, move the transmission rearward and down.

NOTE: While lowering the transmission, clear all wires and pipes from the downward path.

14. Installation is the reverse of removal.

ADJUSTMENTS
Downshift Cable

1. Adjust the idle speed to 750 rpm.
2. Loosen the cable locknut at the carburetor linkage.
3. Adjust the outer cable to $1/16$ inch from the stop.
4. Remove the transmission oil pan.
5. Be sure the downshift cam is in the idle mode position.
6. With the aid of a helper, fully depress the throttle cable and be sure that the downshift cam is in the kickdown position.
7. If necessary, adjust the outer cable until the idling and kickdown position can be obtained on the downshift cam.
8. Install the transmission oil pan and install the proper level of fluid.

Control Pressure

1. Raise the vehicle and support safely.
2. Remove the pressure line plug from the rear of the transmission and connect a 0-300 psi oil pressure gauge to the pressure line outlet.
3. Lower the vehicle, lock the brakes (both hand and foot), chock the wheels, start the engine and place the selector lever in the "D" position.
4. With the engine idling at 750 rpm, observe the pressure gauge reading.
5. The following is an acceptable reading: 750 rpm—60 to 75 psi 1000 rpm—Pressure increase of 15 to 20 psi.
6. If the pressure increase is less than 15 psi, increase the length of the throttle cable.
7. If the pressure increase is more than 20 psi, decrease the length of the throttle cable.
8. Repeat the operation until the pressure readings are correct.
9. Raise the vehicle, remove the pressure gauge, lower the vehicle and road test. Caution: Stop the engine before adjusting the throttle cable.

Manual Linkage

1. Place the selector lever in "N" position.
2. Raise the vehicle and support safely.
3. Loosen the locknut and remove the retaining clip from the selector lever.
4. Disconnect the selector rod from the selector lever and be sure the lever is in the "N" position.
5. Lengthen or shorten the rod until the rod end will fit into the selector lever with a free fit.
6. Tighten the locknut and install the retaining clip. Lower the vehicle.

Front transmission band adjusting screw

Front and Rear Bands

1. Raise the vehicle and support safely.
2. Loosen the adjusting screw locknuts.
3. Tighten the adjusting screws to 36 in/lbs and back off exactly ¾ turn.
4. Tighten the locknut to 22 ft/lbs and lower the vehicle.

Stall Test

The stall test is used to determine the satisfactory operation of the torque converter, transmission and/or engine.

1. Check the condition of the engine. Tune if necessary. Bring the engine-transmission to normal operating temperature.
2. Apply the brakes, chock the wheels, install a tachometer on the engine and place the instrument in a place where it can be seen by the operator.
3. Place the selector lever in "1" or "R"

Rear transmission band adjusting screw

Neutral start/back-up lamp switch

position and depress the accelerator to the kickdown position.
4. Note the rpm reading on the tachometer which should be at 2200 rpm.
5. If the reading is below 1400 rpm, the converter stator is possibly slipping.
6. If the reading is down to 1600 rpm, the engine is not developing full power.
7. If the reading is over 2400 rpm, internal transmission slippage is indicated.

─── **CAUTION** ───

Do not hold the stall test for a longer period than 10 seconds. Place the transmission selector in the neutral position and increase the engine speed to assist in cooling the transmission fluid.

Neutral Start Switch

The neutral start switch is located on the transmission gear selector shaft and is bolted to the transmission case with no adjustment provisions provided. The switch must be replaced if a malfunction occurs.

DRIVE AXLE

Driveshaft and U-Joints

REMOVAL AND INSTALLATION

1. Remove the dashboard supports and transmission cover.
2. Remove the attaching nuts. Gently angle the transmission/engine forward to remove the driveshaft. Remove the driveshaft. Models with sliding splines do not require movement of the engine/transmission assembly.
3. Installation is the reverse of removal.

U-JOINT OVERHAUL

Disassembly

1. Remove the snap-ring from the forked end of the shaft. Tap the lug until the bearing cup is seen to protrude. Remove the cup with pliers.
2. Repeat the operation on the reverse side.
3. Remove the flange.
4. Remove all remaining snap-rings. Rest the shaft on a block and gently tap out the remaining components.

Assembly

1. Place sealing compound on the shoulders of the new spider journals.
2. Fit oil seal retainers over the trunnions with a tubular drift. Fit the oil seals.
3. Place the trunnion into the bearing holes and fit the bearing caps and snap-rings. Make sure they are properly seated.
4. Fit the spider with the lubrication nipple around the driveshaft. Place the other trunnion through the bearing holes in the forked end of the driveshaft and fit the cups and snap-rings.

5. Repeat the procedure on the second universal joint.

— CAUTION —
Do not disassemble the sliding yoke for any reason.

Outer Axle Shaft and Hub Assembly

REMOVAL AND INSTALLATION

All Models (Except TR-7 and TR-8)

1. Remove the wheel and backing plate. Remove the brake hose, attaching bracket, and brake line. Disconnect the handbrake from the attaching lever.
2. Relieve the shock absorber of load.
3. Release the radius arm.
4. Remove the universal joint coupling bolts.
5. Remove the shock absorber and jack.
6. Remove the spring eye nuts. The hub and axle shafts are now free.
7. Reinstall the vertical link to the spring attaching eye; leave the nut loose.
8. Install the shock absorber and radius arm.
9. Connect the inner and outer axle shafts. Place a load of 300 lbs in the front seats. Tighten the securing nut to the vertical link.
10. Further installation is the reverse of removal.

Inner Axle Shaft

REMOVAL AND INSTALLATION

All Models (Except TR-7 and TR-8)

1. Remove the outer axle shaft.
2. Drain the rear axle.
3. Using a ³/₁₆ in. Allen wrench, remove the Allen screws from the differential housing and remove the inner axle shaft.
4. Installation is the reverse of removal.

Removing the inner axle shaft

Halfshaft

REMOVAL AND INSTALLATION

TR-7 and TR-8

1. Remove the hub-to-halfshaft nut, brake drum, handbrake cable, brake halfshaft and bearing.
2. Installation is the reverse of removal. Torque the hub nut to 100-110 ft/lbs.

DIFFERENTIAL

REMOVAL AND INSTALLATION

All Models (Except TR-7)

1. Drain the rear axle. Remove the wheels and backing plate.

Luggage compartment floor panel removed showing rear leaf spring mounting bolts—Spitfire

2. Support the vertical links and remove the shock absorbers.
3. Remove the resonator and tailpipe.
4. Disconnect the driveshaft.
5. Remove the luggage compartment floor panel; remove the spring access plate. Remove the rear spring attachments.
6. Support the weight of the differential and cautiously release the front mounts.
7. Installation is the reverse of removal.

1. Sliding yoke
2. Circlips
3. Bearing cups
4. Seals
5. Retainers
6. Spider
7. Flange

Universal joint disassembled

TR-7 and TR-8

1. Remove the wheels, hub-to-halfshaft nuts, brake drums, handbrake cables, brake pipes, back plate bolts, and halfshafts.

2. Disconnect the driveshaft from the pinion flange.

3. Remove the differential-to-axle nuts and spring washers.

4. Ease the differential out of the axles.

5. Reverse the above to install. Torque the hub nuts to 100-110 ft/lbs.

OVERHAUL

NOTE: Unless one has the experience and the special factory tools, especially the special spreader tool used by Triumph to spread the differential housing sufficiently to free the differential components, the overhaul of the differential assembly should not be attempted. The following specifications, torque figures, and tooth contact conditions are included for reference purposes.

1. Shims	26. Rubber sealing ring
2. Differential side bearing	27. Nylon bushing
3. Thrust washer	28. Shim
4. Cross-shaft locking pin	29. Stud
5. Sun gear	30. Hub
6. Planet gear	31. Nyloc nut
7. Thrust washer	32. Grease trap
8. Gasket	33. Outer seal housing
9. Rear mounting bolt	34. Seal
10. Bushing	35. Ballrace
11. Hypoid rear casing	36. Gasket
12. Circlip	37. Trunnion housing
13. Nyloc nut	38. Spacer tube
14. Seal housing plate	39. Grease plug
15. Oil seal	40. Needle roller bearing
16. Hexagon socket screw	41. Inner oil seal
17. Ball race	42. Key
18. Differential carrier	43. Outer axle shaft
19. Differential side bearing	44. Grease flinger
20. Shims	45. Universal joint assembly
21. Inner axle shaft	46. Circlip
22. Nyloc nut	47. Bearing cap
23. Bolt	48. Tubular dowel
24. Bolt	49. Bolt
25. Shim	50. Mounting rubber

51. Nyloc nut
52. Plain washer
53. Rubber pad
54. Bolt
55. Cotter pin
56. Slotted nut
57. Coupling flange
58. Oil seal
59. Pinion tail bearing
60. Shims
61. Spacer
62. Mounting plate
63. Bolt
64. Hypoid nose piece casing
65. Pinion head bearing
66. Spacer
67. Pinion
68. Ring gear
69. Cross-shaft
70. Bolt
71. Lockplate
72. Brake backplate
73. Bolt
74. Nyloc nut
75. Vertical link

Spitfire, GT6 and TR-7 rear axle

DIFFERENTIAL OVERHAUL

Spitfire and TR-7

1. Remove the differential.

2. Clamp the differential in a vise. Mark and remove the bearing caps. Remove the differential from the housing.

3. Press off the bearings and unbolt and remove the ring gear.

4. Drive out the pinion pin. Remove the side gears.

5. Remove the pinion flange cap and while holding the flange, remove the pinion shaft nut. Remove the flange.

6. Tap out the pinion assembly, and drive out the outer bearing and oil seal.

7. Drive out both bearing races.

8. Install the carrier bearings in the differential with the tapered ends toward the shafts.

9. Lubricate the bearings and install the carrier in the case.

10. Rotate the unit to seat the bearings and push the differential to one side of the case.

11. Install a dial indicator on the ring gear mounting flange and check and run-out. It should not exceed 0.003".

12. Slide the differential sideways to butt the bearing seats in either direction. Measure the lateral free-play.

13. Remove the differential and bearings. Lubricate and install the side gears.

14. Install the pinion pin. Check and record end-play.

15. Remove the pinion pin, rotate the sun gears to bring the planet gears clear of the case.

16. Lubricate the selected planet thrust washers and slide the thrust washers and planets into position. Install the pinion pin and again check end-play. Zero backlash is required.

17. Install the ring gear assembly. Apply Loctite, or its equivalent, to the ring gear bolts.

18. Install the pinion inner bearing, spacer, washer and nut.

19. Tighten the nut gradually to obtain a 15-18 in/lbs pre-load.

20. Using a dial indicator, check the measurements on the two bearing bores; add the measurements and divide by two. Twenty-two pinion head washers are available in sizes from 0.075-0.096 in.

21. Install the inner bearing. Install the pinion, spacer and bearing in the case.

22. Install a new spacer, oil seal, flange, washer and nut.

23. Gradually tighten the nut checking the bearing preload. Rotate the flange to seat the bearings and check the rotating torque. Tighten the nut to obtain a 13-20 in/lbs reading.

24. Install the ring gear assembly into the case. Mesh the ring and pinion assembly. Move the ring and pinion fully in the opposite direction and check the measurement on the gauge. Check the mesh clearance.

25. To set the backlash, subtract the required backlash (0.005) from the recorded mesh clearance above. To this, add the required bearing preload divided by two.

26. To determine the shims required for ring gear side carrier bearing, subtract the result of Step 25 from the figure recorded in Step 12. To that, add the carrier bearing preload divided by two.

27. Install the necessary carrier bearing shims.

28. Install a spreading tool in the case and carefully stretch the case enough to permit the differential assembly to be installed.

29. Remove the spreader, install the bearing caps, bolts and spring washers.

TR-6

1. Remove ring gear and differential from case.

2. Remove the ring gear.

3. Install the differential in the case and check the flange run-out. This should not exceed 0.003 in.

4. Remove the differential from the case, and press off the bearings.

Exploded view of rear axle assembly—TR-7

5. Remove the cross-shaft locking pin and the cross-shaft.

6. Remove the planet and sun gears.

7. Remove the pinion shaft nut and the flange.

8. Remove the front mounting bracket and drive out the pinion shaft, inner bearing, spacer and shim pack.

9. Drive out the outer bearing and seal.

10. Remove the bearing races.

11. Install the bearing races.

12. Install the outer bearing and seal.

13. Install the inner bearing, collar, flange, washer and nut.

14. Tighten the nut to obtain a preload of 15-18 in/lbs of preload.

15. Install a pinion gauge and dummy bearing in the case. Check the free-play to determine necessary shim thickness.

16. Install the mounting flange.

17. Install the pinion shaft and necessary shims.

18. Install the spacer flange washer and nut. Carefully tighten the nut while checking the preload. Torque the nut to 90-120 ft/lbs to obtain a preload of 15-18 in/lbs.

19. Install the sun gears, planet gears and thrust washers in the housing. Insert the planet gear across shaft and install thrust washers to obtain zero backlash.

20. Install the lock pin and secure by peening.

21. Install the inner carrier bearings, and install the case spreader.

22. Install the outer bearings to the differential and fit the differential in the case. Install a dial indicator and check the axial play of the ring gear flange.

23. Add to this measurement 0.003 in. preload. This figure is the necessary shim total.

24. Remove the differential and install the ring gear.

25. Install the differential.

26. Check the axial movement with a dial gauge.

27. Subtract the correct backlash (0.004-0.006 in.) from this reading.

28. Install the necessary shim pack.

29. Release the spreader, install and tighten the bearing caps. Check the backlash at several points on the ring gear. An average reading of 0.004-0.006 in. should be indicated.

30. Install the rear cover and gasket.

Backlash between pinion and ring gears:
All: 0.004-0.006 in. (0.10-0.15 mm)
Pinion bearing preload, without oil seal:
TR-6: 15-18 in/lbs.
GT6 and Spitfire: 12-16 in/lbs.
Differential bearing preload, measured over both bearings:
All: 0.003 in. (0.076 mm)
Maximum run-out of the ring gear, when bolted to differential carrier:
All: 0.003 in. (0.076 mm)

DIFFERENTIAL TORQUE FIGURES

TR-6, TR-7 and TR-8

Ring gear to differential case: 40-45 ft/lbs
Inner driving flange to inner axle: 100-110 ft/lbs
Driveshaft flange to pinion: TR-6: 90-100 ft/lbs

Spitfire

Hypoid pinion flange attachment:
(GT6) 90-100 ft/lbs
(Spitfire) 70-85 ft/lbs
Rear hub to axle shaft: 100-110 ft/lbs

DIFFERENTIAL TOOTH CONTACT CONDITIONS

By painting about ten teeth of the ring gear with special paint, then moving the pinion into mesh with the painted teeth, it is possible to obtain a good impression of how the teeth are making contact. The following tooth contact conditions, along with the remedies, are keyed to the accompanying diagrams:

Ideal Contact (A)

The area of contact is distributed evenly over the tooth profile, and is closer to the toe than to the heel.

High Tooth Contact (B)

The area of contact is heavy on the top of the tooth profile of the drive gear. The pinion must be moved into deeper mesh with the drive gear.

Low Tooth Contact (C)

The contact area is heavy in the root of the drive gear tooth profile, and the pinion gear is meshed too deeply with the drive gear. The pinion must be moved away.

Toe Contact (D)

The contact area is concentrated at the small end of the driven tooth. To correct, the ring gear must be moved out of mesh by increasing the backlash.

Heel Contact (E)

The contact area is concentrated at the large end of the driven tooth. To correct, the ring gear must be moved into closer mesh with the pinion by decreasing the backlash.

--- **CAUTION** ---
When decreasing the backlash, be sure to maintain the minimum backlash of 0.004 in. (0.10 mm).

REAR SUSPENSION

Transverse Leaf Spring

REMOVAL AND INSTALLATION

1. Disconnect the brake lines. Disconnect the chassis bracket. Disconnect the handbrake.

2. Jack up the suspension vertical link. Disconnect the axle shaft and couplings.

3. Support the vertical link, and remove the eye bolt from the spring eye. Remove the luggage floor plate and slide the spring from the vehicle.

4. To replace the spring: align the spring in the recess in the differential casing. Make sure the bolt is in the correct hole. (The spring is marked Front to indicate the proper position.)

5. Replace the studs in the casing. Make sure the shorter threaded end is down. Replace the spring clamp plate and fasten down. Install the luggage floor plate.

6. Connect the vertical link to the spring eyes. Do not tighten the spring eye nut. (Refit the radius arms at this point, if required.)

7. Raise the vertical link and install the shock absorber. Install the axle shaft. Install the handbrake brake lines.

8. Tighten the spring eye nuts with the car on the ground.

1. Heel
2. Coasting side
3. Toe
4. Drive side

Gear tooth markings

1. Spring eye bushing	22. Brake backplate
2. Spring	23. Seal housing
3. Spring clamp plate	24. Bearing
4. Nut	25. Gasket
5. Washer	26. Trunnion housing
6. Rubber bushing	27. Nylon bushing
7. Washer	28. Nut
8. Nut	29. Steel bushing
9. Shock absorber	30. Dust seal
10. Vertical link	31. Bolt
11. Nut	32. Radius arm
12. Washer	33. Bolt
13. Nut	34. Radius arm bracket
14. Washer	35. Shim
15. Bolt	36. Washer
16. Key	37. Nut
17. Nut	38. Washer
18. Washer	39. Washer
19. Hub	40. Nut
20. Locktab	41. Rubber bushing
21. Grease retainer	42. Stud
	43. Bolt
	44. Bolt
	45. Axle shaft coupling
	46. Bolt
	47. Nut
	48. Flinger
	49. Seal
	50. Bolt
	51. Washer
	52. Washer
	53. Nut
	54. Dust seal
	55. Rubber ring

Spitfire rear suspension

Coil Spring

REMOVAL AND INSTALLATION

1. Support the differential with a jack. Jack up the suspension arm.

2. Remove the wheel, disconnect the driveshaft, remove the shock absorber.

3. Being careful to avoid placing stress on the brake line, lower the suspension arm until the spring is free.

4. Installation is the reverse of removal.

Rear Shock Absorber

REMOVAL AND INSTALLATION

Spitfire

1. Block the front wheels. Jack the rear of the car and support the chassis.

2. Remove the wheel. Jack the vertical link to unload the shock absorber.

3. Release the lower end of the shock absorber and remove it.

4. Installation is the reverse of removal.

TR-6

1. Disconnect the shock absorber link to the suspension arm.

2. Lift the shock absorber arm and remove the link from the suspension arm, taking care not to misplace the two rubber buffers and buffer backing plates. Remove the absorber and link.

3. Clean away any dirt from the filler plug hole. Keeping the shock vertical, unscrew the filler plug and check the level of the fluid.

1. Suspension arm	10. Nyloc nut	21. Shock absorber link
2. Rubber plug	11. Bolt	22. Nut
3. Rubber plug	12. Plain washer	23. Washer
4. Stud	13. Nyloc nut	24. Rubber buffer
5. Metalastik bushing	14. Shim	25. Backing plate
6. Fulcrum bracket, inner	15. Road spring	26. Backing plate
7. Fulcrum bracket, outer	16. Rubber insulator	27. Nut
8. Bolt	17. Rubber insulator	28. Locknut
9. Plain washer	18. Shock absorber arm	29. Bump stop
	19. Bolt	30. Rebound rubber
	20. Washer	

TR-6 independent coil spring rear suspension

Top-up to the bottom of the filler plug hole with the recommended shock absorber fluid.

———— CAUTION ————

Do not overfill the shock as the air space above the fluid is required for the proper operation of the unit. Move the shock absorber arm (lever) up and down a few times to force trapped air to the top of the unit. Recheck the fluid level. Replace the filler plug. Keeping the unit vertical, pump it several times. Discard the unit if it offers pockets of no resistance or if it becomes extremely difficult to move.

4. Installation is the reverse of removal. Transfer the link to the new shock.

TR-7 and TR-8 Right Side

1. Support the car, remove the wheel, gas cap and filler neck.

2. Unbolt and remove the shock absorber.

TR-7 and TR-8 Left Side

1. Support the car, remove the wheel, access plate in the trunk, and unbolt and remove shock absorber.

2. Installation for both left and right side is the reverse of the removal procedure.

Rear Suspension Adjustments

Because special equipment is required to properly adjust the rear suspension alignment, it is not advised that the operation be attempted. The following information is included for reference purposes.

CAMBER

Rear suspension camber angle is nonadjustable. If the camber angle is not within the specifications this indicates a weak or incor-

rectly set spring or excessive wear in the vertical link bushings (Spitfire), or in the suspension arm bushings (TR-6).

TOE-IN/TOE-OUT

Rear wheel toe-in/toe-out is adjustable by means of shims. Toe-in/toe-out dimensions are influenced by vehicle load, rear spring rate, and wear factors in the vertical link linkage (Spitfire), or in the suspension arm linkage (TR-6). Unlike the front wheels, each rear wheel may be adjusted independently. Adding shims increases toe-out while removing shims decreases toe-out.

FRONT SUSPENSION

Front Spring and Shock Absorber

REMOVAL AND INSTALLATION

Spitfire

1. Loosen the bolt and nut which retain the steering trunnion to the lower control arm.

2. Unbolt the shock lower end.

3. Unbolt the front spring pad from its bracket.

4. Remove the spring and shock absorber assembly.

5. Installation is the reverse of removal. Tighten the shock with the weight of the car on the wheels.

For all spring removal and installation procedures and all strut overhaul procedures, please refer to "Strut Overhaul" in the Unit Repair section.

Front Shock Absorber

REMOVAL AND INSTALLATION

TR-7 and TR-8

1. Remove the spring.

2. Using a ⅛ in. drill, remove the indentation securing the strut tube to the cap nut.

3. Remove the cap nut and lift out the cartridge.

4. Drill a ¼ in. hole to a depth of 1/16 in. at 90° to the existing notch in the cap nut.

5. Insert the cartridge and tighten the cap nut.

6. Peen the strut at a point locking the cap nut notch.

TR-6

1. Unbolt the shock absorber from the lower attachment plate and remove the plate.

2. Remove the locknut from the top of the shock absorber and remove the shock.

3. Remove the rubber bushing and the inner washer from the top of the shock. Re-

1. Nut	24. Washer	47. Outer track
2. Nut	25. Nut	48. Bolt
3. Washer	26. Spacer	49. Brake disc
4. Mounting rubber	27. Plug	50. Hub
5. Nut	28. Steering arm	51. Outer track
6. Washer	29. Bracket	52. Inner race
7. Upper spring pan	30. Caliper bracket	53. Washer
8. Road spring	31. Dust shield	54. Nut
9. Shock absorber	32. Bolt	55. Cotter pin
10. Top control arm	33. Bolt	56. Grease cap
11. Fulcrum bolt	34. Bolt	57. Brake caliper
12. Top control arm	35. Spindle	58. Trunnion bolt
13. Fulcrum bushing	36. Dust seal	59. Shock absorber bolt
14. Bolt	37. Rubber ring	60. Lower control arm
15. Ball joint	38. Nylon bushing	61. Fulcrum bushing
16. Retainer	39. Dust seal	62. Bolt
17. Rubber seal	40. Rubber seal	63. Front fulcrum bracket
18. Vertical link	41. Trunnion	64. Rear fulcrum bracket
19. Rubber seal	42. Bushing	65. Shim
20. Bolt	43. Fulcrum bushing	66. Nut
21. Washer	44. Felt seal	67. Keeper
22. Nut	45. Seal holder	68. Lower spring pan
23. Nut	46. Inner race	

Front suspension assembly—Spitfire

move the bolts which retain the lower attaching points to the bottom of the shock.

4. Installation is the reverse of removal.

For all spring removal and installation procedures and all strut overhaul procedures, please refer to "Strut Overhaul" in the Unit Repair section.

Ball Joint

REMOVAL AND INSTALLATION

All Models (Except TR-7 and TR-8)

1. Remove the ball joint stud washer and nut. Separate the ball joint from the vertical link.

2. Unbolt the ball joint from the lower control arm. Support the hub assembly.

3. Installation is the reverse of removal.

TR-7 and TR-8

1. Remove the bottom link, plastic boot, circlip and press out the ball joint housing.

2. Press a new ball joint and housing squarely into the bottom link. Do not apply pressure to the center of the housing end cap.

3. Install the circlip and plastic boot.

Upper Control Arm

REMOVAL AND INSTALLATION

Spitfire

1. Support car, remove wheel; remove spring and shock absorber.

2. Unbolt and remove upper control arm.

3. Installation is the reverse of removal. Do not tighten control arm inner fulcrum bolts until the car is resting on the suspension.

TR-6

1. Support the car, remove the wheel, locate a jack under the lower control arm spring pad to take tension off the upper control arm, and remove the ball joint and vertical link.

2. Unbolt and remove the fulcrum bracket and upper control arm.

3. Installation is the reverse of removal.

Lower Control Arm

REMOVAL AND INSTALLATION

Spitfire

1. Support the car, remove the wheel and disconnect the sway bar from the lower control arm.

2. Unbolt the shock absorber at the bottom.

3. Unbolt and remove the control arm.

4. Installation is the reverse of removal.

TR-6

1. Support the car, remove the front wheel and spring.

2. Unbolt and remove the control arm.

3. Installation is the reverse of removal.

1. Upper inner fulcrum	26. Thrust washer	51. Spring washer
2. Rubber bushing	27. Bolt	52. Nut
3. Upper control arm— rear	28. Rebound rubber	53. Nyloc nut
4. Rubber bushing	29. Bracket	54. Fulcrum bracket
5. Washer	30. Bolt	55. Rubber seal
6. Cotter pin	31. Spring washer	56. Thrust washer
7. Slotted nut	32. Nyloc nut	57. Steel sleeve
8. Bolt	33. Plain washer	58. Nylon bushing
9. Nyloc nut	34. Nyloc nut	59. Lower control arm— front
10. Plain washer	35. Grease nipple	60. Thrust washer
11. Grease nipple	36. Bushing—nylon	61. Rubber seal
12. Upper ball joint	37. Thrust washer	62. Bolt
13. Rubber seal	38. Bolt	63. Shock absorber
14. Plain washer	39. Tab washer	64. Washer
15. Nyloc nut	40. Rubber bushing	65. Rubber bushing
16. Caliper bracket and vertical link	41. Cotter pin	66. Sleeve
17. Bump rubber	42. Rubber seal	67. Rubber bushing
18. Rubber seal	43. Nyloc nut	68. Washer
19. Bolt	44. Stud	69. Nut
20. Spring washer	45. Spring pan	71. Locknut
21. Lock stop collar	46. Serrated washer	72. Rubber collar
22. Lower control arm —rear	47. Slotted nut	73. Upper control arm— front
23. Lower trunnion bracket	48. Shock absorber attachment bracket —rear	74. Spring
24. Grease nipple	49. Shock absorber attachment bracket —front	75. Rubber collar
25. Rubber seal	50. Bolt	76. Spacer
		77. Bolt
		78. Bolt

Front suspension assembly—TR-6

Front End Alignment

TOE-IN

With the steering centralized, measure the toe-in. If adjustment is required, loosen the tie rod end locknuts and the outer clip of the rubber seals. Rotate the tie rod ends until the correct alignment is obtained. Note the reading and move the vehicle forward until the wheels rotate one-half turn, then take a second reading. This procedure allows for wheel rim run-out. Adjust the tie rods to the mean of the two readings for greater accuracy. After adjustment, tighten the tie rod locknut and rubber seal clips.

NOTE: When checking toe-in or other suspension geometry, the vehicle should be static laden, on a smooth and level surface, and should have the tires inflated to the correct pressure.

CASTER AND CAMBER

All Models (Except TR-7 and TR-8)

Adjust the caster and camber angles of the TR-6, GT6 and Spitfire front suspension by altering the number of shims positioned between the chassis and the lower inner fulcrum brackets. When adjusting these angles, raise the vehicle, loosen the lower control arm mounting nuts, increase or decrease the number of shims as required, then retighten the nuts. The addition and subtraction of shims will have the following effects:

Caster Angle—increase by adding shims to the front bracket or removing shims from the rear.

Caster Angle—decrease by removing shims from the front bracket and adding shims to the rear.

Camber Angle—increase by adding an equal number of shims to both brackets.

Camber Angle—decrease by subtracting an equal number of shims from both brackets.

CASTER AND CAMBER

TR-7 and TR-8

Caster and camber angles are not adjustable. If angles are incorrect, damaged parts must be replaced.

STEERING

Steering Wheel

REMOVAL AND INSTALLATION

Spitfire

1. Pry off the steering wheel crash pad and the horn button.
2. Remove the horn brush connection.
3. Remove the steering wheel nut and washer.
4. Scribe alignment marks on the steering wheel and column.

Exploded view of steering column and components—TR-7

5. Being careful not to jar the collapsible column, install a steering wheel puller and remove the wheel.

CAUTION
The use of a knock-off type puller may damage the column.

TR-6

1. Pry off the steering wheel crash pad and the horn button.
2. Remove the six bolts which retain the steering wheel to its support boss.
3. With the front wheels pointing straight ahead, scribe alignment marks on the support boss and steering column.
4. Remove the column nut and carefully pull the support boss from the upper inner steering column.
5. Installation is the reverse of removal.

TR-7 and TR-8

1. Remove the three screws on the underside of the spoke and lift off the pad.
2. Turn the wheels to a straight ahead position and remove the steering wheel nut and washer.
3. Remove the steering wheel.
4. Installation is the reverse of removal.

TURN SIGNAL SWITCH REPLACEMENT

Except TR-7 and TR-8

1. Remove the two screws and the switch fairings.
2. Remove the steering column clamp and harness cover.
3. Disconnect the three snap connectors.
4. Remove the two screws and spring washers.
5. Lift out the switch with its electrical leads.
6. Installation is the reverse of removal.

TR-7 and TR-8

1. Remove the upper and lower switch cover halves.

2. Remove the steering wheel.
3. Remove the wiring harness clip, disconnect the harness plugs and loosen the switch clamp screw.
4. Remove the switch and harness.
5. Installation is the reverse of removal. The arrow on the turn signal handle must align with the center of the column.

Steering Column Ignition Lock Switch

Spitfire and TR-6

1. Remove the steering column.
2. Remove the steering lock shroud and steering column tie-bar.
3. Either unscrew the shear-off bolts with a small chisel, or drill into the bolt heads and remove the bolts with an easy-out.
4. Remove the lock switch.
5. To install, position the lock switch to the column so that the switch dowel locates in the column drilling.
6. Install the steering lock shroud using two new shear-off bolts.
7. Evenly tighten the bolts until the heads shear.
8. Install the steering column.

TR-7 and TR-8

1. Disconnect the battery and remove the upper and lower switch cover halves.
2. Remove the wiring harness clip and disconnect the harness plug.
3. On vehicles with a key warning system, disconnect the single pin harness plug and the correct from below the steering column lock assembly.
4. Unbolt and remove the switch assembly.
5. Installation is the reverse of removal.

Manual Steering Gear

ADJUSTMENT

Adjust the end clearance of the pinion shaft.

This should be as little as possible with the pinion still able to rotate freely. There are shims available in thicknesses of 0.004 in. and 0.010 in. to obtain minimal end clearance with free rotation. The second adjustment involves the damper cap. With the pressure pad and cap nut installed to the rack tube, tighten the cap nut to eliminate all end clearance. Measure the clearance between the nut and the housing. Put together a shim package that is equal to the clearance between the cap nut

Measuring clearance between cap nut and housing

and the housing plus 0.004 in. (i.e., pack-clearance + 0.004 in.). Pack the unit with grease and install the cap nut, shim pack, spring, and pressure pad to the housing and tighten the cap nut. When the cap nut is correctly adjusted, a force of 2 lbs on a radius of 8 in. is required to rotate the pinion shaft. Check the unit and readjust if necessary by adding or subtracting shims from beneath the cap nut.

REMOVAL AND INSTALLATION
All Except TR-7 and TR-8

1. Place the vehicle on jack stands and remove the front wheels. Empty the cooling

Measuring load required to turn pinion

system and remove the bottom radiator hose.

2. Loosen and remove the bolt from the steering shaft coupling. Remove the steering rod end nuts. Pull the ball joints from the tie rod lever.

3. Remove nuts, U-bolts, and shims. Pull the steering unit forward. Remove the unit by pulling it through the wheel-well.

4. Count the number of pinion shaft turns required to move the gear from lock to lock. Return the shaft to the central position and move the steering wheel to straight ahead. Install the steering unit by placing the splined pinion shaft into the splined coupling.

5. Place the aluminum packing pieces behind the rack and the two front aluminum packing blocks into the dowels. These fit into holes in the rack tube.

6. Replace the U-bolts and nuts. Replace the unit in the car.

7. Place the taper pins of the tie rod ball joints into the steering levers and insert the steering washers and nuts. Replace the bolt and nut.

— CAUTION —
Check the front end alignment.

TR-7 and TR-8

1. Raise vehicle and set wheels to straight ahead position.

2. Scribe the pinion shaft and lower steering coupling.

3. Disconnect the rack tie rod outer ball joints from the steering arms.

4. Remove the pinch bolt securing the lower steering coupling to the rack pinion.

5. Remove the two bolts, spring washers and plain washers securing the pinion end of the rack to the sub-frame.

6. Remove the two nyloc nuts and washers and remaining bolts securing the rack to the sub-frame.

7. Disconnect the lower coupling from the pinion shaft, and remove the rack from the driver's side.

8. Installation is the reverse of removal.

BRAKE SYSTEM

For all brake system repair and service procedures not detailed below, please refer to "Brakes in the Unit Repair section.

Adjustment

Disc brakes are inherently self-adjusting and therefore require no adjustments between pad changes. To adjust the rear drum brakes:

1. Block the front wheels. Release the

Rear drum brake adjuster (2) Spitfire, GT6 shown; TR-6 similar

handbrake. Raise the rear of the car so that both rear wheels clear the ground.

2. Turn the square-ended adjuster on the rear of the backing plate clockwise until the wheel is locked.

3. Back-off the adjuster a notch at a time until the wheel may spin freely when turned with one hand.

NOTE: The TR-7 has self adjusting rear brakes.

Master Cylinder

REMOVAL AND INSTALLATION

1. Remove both brake lines. Be careful not to let fluid drip out.

2. Pull out the rubber dust cover. Remove the clevis pin. (This is secured by a cotter pin.)

3. Remove the master cylinder.

4. Installation is the reverse of removal. Bleed the brakes.

Piston Warning Light Centering

If, by mistake, the brake warning light piston has been pushed off center, causing the brake warning light to glow, the following procedure will have to be followed to recentralize the piston: Attach a rubber tube to a bleed nipple at the opposite end of the car to that which was being bled when the piston was actuated. Open the bleed screw and turn the ignition to the ON position without starting the engine. The brake warning light will glow, but the oil pressure warning light will be out. Push steadily on the brake pedal until the brake light dims and the oil light glows. As the piston returns to mid-position, a click will be felt on the pedal.

NOTE: If the pedal is pushed too hard, the piston will move over to the other side, necessitating the repeat of the preceding operations at the other end of the car.

Tighten the bleed screw.

WHEEL BEARING ADJUSTMENT

The end-play of the front wheel bearing should be 0.003-0.005 in. and may be checked by a suitable dial gauge. The front wheel hub nut is provided with slots to accompany a securing cotter pin. In the event that a gauge is not available, rotate the hub, tighten the nut only sufficiently to remove looseness (5 ft/lbs), then loosen the nut by one flat and secure it with a new cotter pin.

Removal and Installation

To remove the bearings, remove hub and outer bearing. Reach inside hub and pull out inner bearing and oil seal.

Rear Wheel Cylinder
REMOVAL AND INSTALLATION

1. Remove the brake shoes as outlined under "Brake Shoes Removal and Installation."

2. Disconnect and plug the flexible brake hose.

3. Remove the protective rubber shield for the wheel cylinder from the rear of the back-

ing plate and remove the horseshoe clip and spring plate which retain the cylinder.

4. Remove the wheel cylinder and hand-brake lever assembly.

5. Reverse the above procedure to install, making sure to bleed the brakes.

Parking Brake
CABLE ADJUSTMENT

Lift the rear wheels from the ground. Lock the brake drums by screwing each adjuster in to its fullest extent. Remove the spring and clevis pin. Adjust the clevis at each cable end by equal amounts to reduce play in the cable. The cable is overly tightened when the clevis pin cannot be inserted without straining the cables. Secure the clevis pin, hook up spring and adjust the cable brackets to give slight spring tension.

Parking Brake Cable
REMOVAL AND INSTALLATION
Spitfire (Front)

1. Remove the handbrake lever and disconnect the cable fork.

2. Disconnect the cable from the relay lever and pull the cable from the car.

3. Installation is the reverse of removal.

Spitfire (Rear)

1. Disconnect the compensator from the relay lever.

2. Unhook the cable return springs and forks from the backplate lever.

3. Remove the cable from the car.

4. Installation is the reverse of removal.

TR-6

1. Remove the clevis pins securing the cable forks to the backplate levers and remove the brake cable supports from the trailing arms.

2. Release the cables from the compensator.

3. Remove the cables.

4. Installation is the reverse of removal.

TR-7 and TR-8

1. Raise the body to allow access to the transmission tunnel.

2. Pull back the rubber boot and release the cable locknut.

3. Unscrew the cable from the operating rod.

4. Back off the nut to release the cable from the bracket and remove the cotter pin, washer and clevis pin retaining the cable to each operating lever.

5. Remove the trunnion nut and bolt, back off the nuts on the compensating levers and remove the cables.

6. Installation is the reverse of removal.

CHASSIS ELECTRICAL

Heater Assembly
REMOVAL AND INSTALLATION

1. Disconnect the battery and empty the cooling system.

2. Remove the heater hoses. Remove the screws which hold the water valve mounting bracket to the dash shelf. Push the bracket and valve assembly away from the dash.

3. Inside the car, remove the dashboard support bracket. Remove the passenger and driver's side parcel shelf. Remove the bracket which holds the choke and heater cable.

4. Disconnect the tachometer and speedometer cables from the back of the gauges. Pull the cables into the engine compartment. Be careful not to damage the cables or the grommet.

5. Remove the bolts which attach the heater box to the dash. Plug the heater lines. Lift out the heater.

6. Installation is the reverse of removal.

Blower Motor
REMOVAL AND INSTALLATION

1. Remove the heater.

2. Remove the screws which secure the inner and outer heater assembly.

3. Loosen the large nut in the center of the impeller. Remove the impeller from the shaft. Remove the exposed nut and lift out the motor.

4. Installation is the reverse of removal.

Windshield Wipers
REMOVAL AND INSTALLATION

1. Remove all electrical connections.

2. Make a mark on the domed cover and gearbox cover. Remove the four hold down screws. Move the gearbox and cover clear. Remove the exposed spring clip by pulling it sideways.

3. Take off the moving contact limiting switch. Remove the connecting rod.

4. Take the mounting bracket from the firewall. Move the unit to allow the vacuum

1. Defroster nozzle	12. Flap knob	22. Water control valve
2. Air hose	13. Sponge packing	23. Adapter—cylinder head
3. Hose clip	14. Sealing ring	24. Adapter—water pump
4. Heater unit	15. Water hose	25. Sealing ring
5. Heat control assembly	16. Hose clip	26. Nut
6. Bezel	17. Mounting bracket	27. Water return pipe
7. Control knob	18. Hose clip	28. Water hose
8. Blower switch	19. Drain flap (from April 1964)	29. Water hose
9. Bezel	20. Water valve lever	30. Bolt—heater attachment
10. Demister finisher	21. Drain elbow (up to April 1964)	
11. Screw		

Typical Spitfire heater assembly

assembly to be released. Remove the mounting bracket.

5. Installation is the reverse of removal.

ADJUSTING WIPER STOP (PARK POSITION)

Loosen the four holding screws and rotate the domed cover. Rotate the cover either way until the desired stop position is achieved. Replace the cover and tighten down.

Radio
REMOVAL AND INSTALLATION

Radios used in Triumphs are dealer installed or after-market units, therefore, a common procedure is not possible.

Instruments
REMOVAL AND INSTALLATION

All instruments may be replaced individually from the back of the panel. On some models it may be necessary to loosen the panel screws to get at the intrument. Take care when working behind the panel since in most cases it is a tight fit and wires can be pulled loose without knowing it.

Fuses

A fuse that is burned out may be suspected when all electrical components in the particular circuit refuse to operate. A blown fuse may be identified by merely looking at the glass enclosed metal strip. If it is separated or burned, it must be replaced.

NOTE: It is imperative that a fuse be replaced by one of the same amperage.

If a fuse is replaced and immediately fails, the source of the trouble should be found before the vehicle is operated. Otherwise, serious and costly damage may result.

TR-6

The fusebox is located on the left side of the inner fender panel at the rear of the engine compartment. It contains three 35 amp operating fuses, one fuse for a possible accessory circuit, and two spares.

Fuse one (brown leads) protects the headlamp flasher, dash warning lights, and horn. Fuse two (red/green leads) protects the tail lights, front parking and marker lamp circuits, rear marker, dash board, and license plate lamps. Fuse three (white leads) protects all other electrical components.

Spitfire

The fuse box for all Spitfire models is located under the dashboard on the left side. The unit contains two 35 amp fuses.

Volkswagen

Rear Wheel Drive

SERIAL NUMBER IDENTIFICATION

Vehicle (Chassis) Number

The first two numbers are the first two digits of the car's model number and the third digit stands for the car's model year. For example a 0 as the third digit means that the car was produced during the 1980 model year, a 1 would signify 1981, and so forth.

The chassis number is on the frame tunnel under the back seat in the Type 1. In the Type 2, the chassis number is on the right engine cover plate in the engine compartment and behind the front passenger's seat. All models also have an identification plate bearing the chassis number on the top of the instrument panel at the driver's side. This plate is easily visible through the windshield and aids in rapid identification.

Another identification plate bearing the vehicle's serial number and paint, body, and assembly codes, is found in the luggage compartment of Types 1.

Identification plate in luggage compartment

Chassis number location on dashboard

Chassis number location under rear seat

Engine Number

On Type 1 which has the upright engine cooling fan housing, the engine numbers is on the crankcase flange for the generator support. The number can readily be seen by looking through the center of the fan belt.

On Type 2 models with the suitcase engine, the number is stamped on the crankcase near the ignition coil and below the crankcase breather. The engine can be identified by the letter or pair of letters preceding the serial number. Engine specifications are listed according to the letters and model year.

Engine number location on upright fan engine

Engine number location on the suitcase engine

Transmission Identification

Transmission identification marks are stamped into the bell housing or on the final drive housing.

ENGINE IDENTIFICATION CHART

Engine Code Letter	Vehicle Type	First Production Year	Last Production Year	Engine Type	Common Designation
AJ	1	1975	1979	Fan driven by generator	1600
GD	2	1976	1978	Fan driven by crankshaft	2000
GE	2	1979	1980	Fan driven by crankshaft	2000

ENGINE IDENTIFICATION CHART

Engine Code Letter	Vehicle Type	First Production Year	Last Production Year	Engine Type	Common Designation
CV	2	1980	1983	Fan driven by crankshaft	2000
CS	2	1982	1983	Inline diesel	1600

GENERAL ENGINE SPECIFICATIONS

Year	Engine Code	Displacement cc	Horsepower @ rpm	Torque @ rpm (ft. lbs.)	Bore × Stroke (in.)	Compression Ratio	Oil Pressure @ rpm (psi)
'76–'79	AJ	1584	48 @ 4200	73.1 @ 2800	3.37 × 2.72	7.3:1	42
'76–'83	GD, GE, CV	1970	67 @ 4200	101 @ 3000	3.70 × 2.80	7.3:1	42
'82–'83	CS	1588	49 @ 4200	72 @ 2000	3.01 × 3.40	23.0:1	28

GASOLINE ENGINE TUNE-UP SPECIFICATIONS

Year	Code	Type	Common Designation	Spark Plugs Type	Gap (in.)	Distributor Point Dwell (deg)	Point Gap (in.)	Ignition Timing (deg)① MT	AT	Fuel Pump Pressure (psi) @ 4000 rpm	Compression Pressure (psi)	Idle Speed (rpm) MT	AT	Valve Clearance (in. cold) In	Ex
'76	AJ	1	1600	Bosch W145M1 Champ L288	.024	44–50	.016	5ATDC	TDC	28	85–135	875	925	.006	.006
	GD	2	2000	Bosch W145M2 Champ N288	.028	44–50	.016	7½BTDC	7½BTDC	28	85–135	900	950	.006	.006
'77	AJ	1	1600	Bosch M145M1 Champ N288	.028	44–50	.016	5ATDC	5ATDC	28	85–135	800–950	800–950	.006	.006
	GD	2	2000	Bosch M145M2 Champ N288	.028	44–50	.016	7½BTDC	7½BTDC	28	85–135	800–950	850–1000	.006	.006
'78	AJ	1	1600	Bosch W145M1 .028 Champ L288	.028	44–50	.016	5ATDC	5ATDC	28	85–135	800–950	800–950	.006	.006
	GE	2	2000	Bosch W145M2 .028 Champ N288	.028	44–50	.016	7½BTDC	7½BTDC	28	85–135	800–950	900–1000	Hyd.	Hyd.
'79	AJ	1	1600	Bosch W145M1 .028 Champ L288	.028	44–50	.016	5ATDC	5ATDC	28	85–135	800–950	800–950	.006	.006
'79–'83	GE, CV	2	2000	Bosch W145M2 .028 Champ N288	.028	44–50⑤	⑤	7½BTDC ②	7½BTDC ②	28	85–135	800–950③	850–1000④	Hyd.	Hyd.

① 1976–77: Carbon canister hose at air cleaner disconnected; at idle; vacuum hose(s) on
② 5ATDC, Calif.—idle stabilizer must be bypassed (plugs connected together)
③ Calif.: 850–950
④ Calif.: 850–950
⑤ 1980–83 Vanagon (Calif.)—electronic ignition; point gap and dwell preset and non-adjustable

DIESEL ENGINE TUNE-UP SPECIFICATIONS

Model	Valve Clearance Intake (in.)	Exhaust ① (in.)	Intake Valve Opens (deg)	Injection Pump Setting (deg)	Injection Nozzle Pressure (psi) New	Used	Idle Speed (rpm)	Cranking Compression Pressure (psi)
Diesel	.008–.012	.016–.020	NA	Align marks	1885–2001	1740–1885	770–870	406–493

NA Not available at time of publication
① Valve clearance need not be adjusted unless it varies more than .002 in. from specification

FIRING ORDER

DISTRIBUTOR
FIRING ORDER
1-4-3-2

NO. 1 CYLINDER MARK

ROTOR

FRONT OF CAR

ENGINE
FROM TOP

CYLINDER NUMBERING

CAPACITIES

Year	Type	Engine Displacement (cc)	Engine Crankcase (qts.) With Filter	Without Filter	Transaxle (pts.) Manual	Automatic Conv.	Final Drive	Gasoline Tank (gal.)
'76–'79	1	1600	—	2.5	6.3	7.6	6.3①	10.6③
'76–'83	2	1800, 2000	3.7④	3.2⑤	7.4	12.8②	2.6	15.9

① 5.3 when changed
② 6.3 when changed
③ Convertible (11.1)
④ Diesel: 4.2
⑤ Diesel: 3.7
Conv. = torque converter

VALVE SPECIFICATIONS

Year	Type	Seat Angle (deg) Intake	Exhaust	Face Angle (deg) Intake	Exhaust	Valve Seat Width (in.) Intake	Exhaust	Spring Test Pressure (lbs. @ in.)	Valve Guide Inside Dia (in.) Intake	Exhaust	Stem to Guide Clearance (in.) Intake	Exhaust	Stem Diameter (in.) Intake	Exhaust
'76–'79	1	45	45	45	45	0.05–0.10	0.05–0.10	117.7–134.8 @ 1.22	0.3150–0.3157	0.353–0.354	0.009–0.010	0.009–0.010	0.3125–0.3129	0.350–0.351
'76–'83	2	30	45	30	45	0.07–0.08	0.078–0.098	168–186 @ 1.14	0.3150–0.3157	0.3534–0.3538	0.018	0.014	0.3125–0.3129	0.3507–0.3511
'82–'83	2 (diesel)	45	45	45	45	0.078	0.096	96–106 @ 0.92	0.039 Max	0.051	NA	NA	0.314	0.313

CRANKSHAFT AND CONNECTING ROD SPECIFICATIONS

(All measurements are given in inches)

| Year | Engine | Crankshaft | | | | | | | Connecting Rods | | |
| | | Main Bearing Journal Diameter | | Main Bearing Oil Clearance | | | | | | | |
		No. 1, 2, 3	No. 4	No. 1, 3	No. 2	No. 4	Crankshaft End-Play	Thrust on No.	Journal Diameter	Oil Clearance	End-Play
'76–'79	1600	2.1640–2.1648	1.5739–1.5748	.0016–.004	.001–.003	.002–.004	.0027–.005	1 at flywheel	2.1644–2.1653	.0008–.0027	.004–.016
'76–'83	1800, 2000	2.3609–2.3617	1.5739–1.5748	.002–.004	.0012–.0035	.002–.004	.0027–.005	1 at flywheel	2.1644–2.1653①	.0008–.0027	.004–.016
'82–'83	Diesel	2.1244–2.1252	2.1244–2.1252	.001–.003	.001–.003	.001–.003	.003–.007	3	1.8803–1.8811	.0011–.0034	.014②

①On 1977–79 2000 models, connecting rod journal diameter is 1.968 in.   ②Wear limit

PISTON AND RING SPECIFICATIONS

(All measurements in inches)

| Year | Engine Displacement | Piston Clearance | Ring Gap | | | Ring Side Clearance | | |
			Top Compression	Bottom Compression	Oil Control	Top Compression	Bottom Compression	Oil Control
'76–'79	1600	0.0016–0.0023	0.012–0.018	0.012–0.018	0.010–0.016	0.0027–0.0039	0.002–0.0027	0.0011–0.0019
'76–'80	1800, 2000	0.0016–0.0023	0.014–0.021	0.012–0.022	0.010–0.016	0.0023–0.0035	0.0016–0.0027	0.0008–0.0019
'80–'83	2000	0.0016–0.0023	0.016–0.021	0.016–0.021	0.010–0.016	0.002–0.003	0.002–0.003	0.001–0.002
'82–'83	Diesel	0.001–0.003	0.012–0.020	0.012–0.020	0.010–0.016	0.002–0.004	0.002–0.003	0.001–0.002

GASOLINE ENGINE TORQUE SPECIFICATIONS

(All readings in ft. lbs.)

Year	Type Vehicle	Cylinder Head Nuts	Rod Bearing Bolts	Generator Pulley	Crankshaft Pulley Bolt	Flywheel to Crankshaft Bolts	Fan to Hub	Hub to Crankshaft	Crankcase Half Nuts Sealing Nuts	Crankcase Half Nuts Non-Sealing Nuts	Drive Plate to Crankshaft	Spark Plugs	Oil Strainer Cover
'76–'79	1	23	22–25	40–47	29–36	253	—	—	18	14	—	25	5
'76–'81	2	23	24	—	—	80①	14	23	23	14	61	22	7–9

①Automatic transmission drive plate—65 ft. lbs. (1980 and later Vanagon)

DIESEL ENGINE TORQUE SPECIFICATIONS

(All readings in ft. lbs.)

Year	Model	Cylinder Head Bolts	Rod Bearing Bolts②	Main Bearing Bolts	Crankshaft Pulley Bolt	Flywheel To Crankshaft Bolts	Manifold Intake	Manifold Exhaust
'82–'83	Diesel	65②④	33	47	56	54①	18	18

①Pressure plate to crankshaft bolts
②Cold, 69 ft. lbs. warm
③Always use new bolts

④'82 uses 12mm, 12 pt. cyl. head bolts. Bolts must always be replaced during repairs to head.

TORQUE SEQUENCES

Cylinder head torque sequence—Type 2

For 1600 cc engines, the cylinder head nuts should initially be tightened to 7 ft. lbs. in order I, then tightened to the recommended torque in order II.

Cylinder head torque sequence—diesel engine

ALTERNATOR AND REGULATOR SPECIFICATIONS

Year	Type	Alternator			Regulator	
		Maximum Output (amps)	Stator Winding Resistance (ohms)	Exciter Winding Resistance (ohms)	Load Current (amps)	Regulating Voltage Under Load (volts)
'76–'79	1	50	.13 ± .13	4.0 ± .4	25–30	13.8–14.9 ①
'75–'83	2	55 ②	.13 ± .13	4.0 ± .4	25–30	13.8–14.9 ①

① @ 2000 engine rpm's   ② 1982 and later: 65

BRAKE SPECIFICATIONS

(All measurements are given in inches)

Year	Type	Lug Nut Torque (ft. lbs.)	Master Cylinder Bore	Brake Disc		Brake Drum			Minimum Lining Thickness	
				Minimum Thickness	Maximum Run-Out	Diameter	Max. Machine O/S	Max. Wear Limit	Front	Rear
'76–'77	Type 1 (Beetle)	87–94	0.750	—	—	9.059	9.10	9.114	0.100	0.100
'76–'79	Type 1 (Super Beetle)	87–94	0.750	—	—	9.768 (fr) 9.059 (rr)	9.80 (fr) 9.10 (rr)	9.823 (fr) 9.114 (rr)	0.100	0.100
'76–'83	Type 2 (Bus)	87–94	0.938	0.472 ①	0.0008 ②	9.920	9.97 ③	9.98	0.079	0.100

NOTE: Minimum lining thickness is as recommended by the manufacturer. Due to variations in state inspection regulations, the minimum allowable thickness may be different than recommended by the manufacturer.
① 1980 and later: 0.453
② 1980 and later: 0.004
③ 1980 and later: 9.96

(fr)—front
(rr)—rear
—not applicable

STARTER SPECIFICATIONS

Starter Number	Lock Test		No Load Test			Brush Spring Tension (oz)
	Amps	Volts	Amps	Volts	rpm	
111 911 023A	270–290	6	25–40	12	6700–7800	42
311 911 023B	250–300	6	35–45	12	7400–8100	42
003 911 023A	250–300	6	35–50	12	6400–7900	42

WHEEL ALIGNMENT SPECIFICATIONS

Year	Model	Front Axle					Rear Axle		
		Caster		Camber			Camber		
		Range (deg)	Pref Setting (deg)	Range (deg)	Pref Setting (deg)	Toe-In (in.)	Range (deg)	Pref Setting (deg)	Toe-In (deg)
'76–'77	Type 1	±1°	+3°20'	±20'	+30'	+0.071–+0.213	±40'	−1°	0' ± 15'
'76–'79	Type 1①	±35'	+2°	+20'−40'	+1°	+0.071–+0.231	±40'	−1°	0' ± 15'
'76–'79	Type 2	±40'	+3°	±20'	+40'	0	±30'	−50'	+10' ± 20'
'80	Type 2	±15'	+7°15'	±30'	+40'	−0.058–+0.218	±30'	−50'	0 ± 10'
'81–'83	Type 2	±15'	+7°15'	±30'	0	−0.058–+0.218	±30'	−50'	0 ± 10'

① Super Beetle

TUNE-UP PROCEDURES

This section gives specific procedures on how to tune-up your Volkswagen and is intended to be as complete and basic as possible.

—— CAUTION ——

When working with a running engine, make sure that the transmission is in Neutral (unless otherwise specified) and the parking brake is fully applied. When the ignition is turned on and the engine running, do not grasp the ignition wires, distributor cap, or coil wire, as a shock in excess of 20,000 volts may result. Whenever working near the distributor, even if the engine is not running, make sure that the ignition is switched off. Always keep hands, clothing, jewelry, and long hair clear of the cooling fan and pulleys. Also, stay clear of the hot exhaust manifolds and catalytic converter (if so equipped).

Spark Plugs

Before attempting any work on the cylinder head, it is very important to note that the cylinder head is cast aluminum alloy. It is extremely easy to damage threads in the cylinder head. Care must be taken not to cross-thread the spark plugs or any bolts or studs. Never overtighten the spark plugs, bolts, or studs.

—— CAUTION ——

Always lubricate the spark plug threads with anti-seize compound prior to installation.

To avoid cross-threading the spark plugs, always start the plugs in their threads with your fingers. Never force the plugs into the cylinder head. Do not use a wrench until you are certain that the plug is correctly threaded.

VW spark plugs should be cleaned and regapped every 6000 miles and replaced every 12,000.

REMOVAL AND INSTALLATION

To install the spark plugs, remove the spark plug wire from the plug. Grasp the plug connector and, while removing, do not pull on the wire. Using a ¹³⁄₁₆ in. spark plug socket, remove the old spark plugs. Examine the threads of the old plugs; if one or more of the plugs have aluminum clogged threads, it will be necessary to rethread the spark plug hole. See the following section for the necessary information.

Obtain the proper heat range and type of new plug. Set the gap by bending the side electrode only. Do not bend the center electrode to adjust the gap. The proper gap is listed in the "Tune-Up Specifications" chart. Lubricate the plug threads.

Start each new plug in its hole using your fingers. Tighten the plug several turns by hand to assure that the plug is not cross-threaded. Using a wrench, tighten the plug just enough to compress the gasket. Do not overtighten the plug.

RETHREADING SPARK PLUG HOLE

It is possible to repair light damage to spark plug hole threads by using a spark plug hole tap of the proper diameter and thread. Plenty of grease should be used on the tap to catch any metal chips. Exercise caution when using the tap as it is possible to cut a second set of threads instead of straightening the old ones.

If the old threads are beyond repair, then the hole must be drilled and tapped to accept a steel bushing of Heli-Coil. It is not always necessary to remove the cylinder head to re-thread the spark plug holes. Bushing kits, Heli-Coil kits, and spark plug hole taps are available at most auto parts stores. Heli-Coil information is contained in the "Engine Rebuilding" section of this book.

Breaker Points and Condenser

REMOVAL AND INSTALLATION

NOTE: 1979–83 California Type 2 vehicles are equipped with an electronic ignition system.

1. Release the spring clips which secure the distributor cap and lift the cap from the distributor. Pull the rotor from the distributor shaft.

NOTE: Vehicles with a radio may be equipped with a static shield. Unscrew the ground strap and remove the shield before removing the cap.

2. Disconnect the points wire from the condenser snap connection inside the distributor.

3. Remove the locking screw from the stationary breaker point.

4. To remove the condenser which is located on the outside of the distributor, remove the screw which secures the condenser bracket and condenser connection to the distributor.

Breaker point removal is accomplished by disconnecting the snap connection (1) and removing the attaching screw (2)

Checking the point gap with a feeler gauge

5. Disconnect the condenser wire from the coil.

6. With a clean rag, wipe the excess oil from the breaker plate.

NOTE: Make sure that the new point contacts are clean and oil free.

7. Installation of the points and condenser is the reverse of the above; however, it will be necessary to adjust the point gap, (or dwell), and check the timing. Lubricate the point cam with a small amount of lithium or white grease. Set the dwell, or gap, before the ignition timing.

ADJUSTMENT

1. Remove the distributor cap and rotor.

2. Turn the engine by hand until the fiber rubbing block on the movable breaker point rests on a high point of the cam lobe. The point gap is the maximum distance between the points and must be set at the top of a cam lobe.

3. Using a screwdriver, loosen the locking screw of the stationary breaker point.

4. Move the stationary point plate so that the gap is set as specified and then tighten the screw. Make sure that the feeler gauge is clean. After tightening the screw, recheck the gap.

CONTACT AREA CENTERED

CORRECT ALIGNMENT

CONTACT AREA NOT CENTERED

MISALIGNMENT OF CENTERS

CONTACT AREA NOT CENTERED

MISALIGNMENT OF POINT FACES

Breaker point alignment guide

Adjusting point gap by moving stationary arm with a screwdriver

Dwell Angle

ADJUSTMENT

NOTE: The dwell angle on all cars with the electronic ignition system is set at the factory and not adjustable.

1. Setting the dwell angle with a dwell meter achieves the same effect as setting the point gap but offers better accuracy.

NOTE: The dwell must be set before setting the timing. Setting the dwell will alter the timing, but when the timing is set, the dwell will not change.

2. Attach the positive lead of the dwell meter to the coil terminal which has a wire leading to the distributor. The negative lead should be attached to a good ground.

3. Remove the distributor cap and rotor. Turn the ignition ON and turn the engine over using a starter or a starter button. Read the dwell from the meter and open or close the points to adjust the dwell.

NOTE: Increasing the gap decreases the dwell and decreasing the gap increases the dwell.

Dwell specifications are listed in the "Tune-Up Specifications" chart.

4. Reinstall the cap and rotor and start the engine. Check the dwell and reset it if necessary.

Electronic Ignition

All 1979–83 Type 2 vehicles which were made for use in California are equipped with a breakerless, transistorized ignition system. This system consists of a distributor with a "Hall" sender unit, an idle stabilizer, a stronger ignition coil and an electronic control unit to monitor the whole system.

The factory states that there are no adjustments or services to be performed on this system. Any problems which are believed to be originating in the electronic ignition system should be referred to an authorized service technician with access to workshop test equipment.

PRECAUTIONS

1. DO NOT disconnect or connect any wires with the ignition switched "ON".

2. When cranking the engine, without wanting it to start (such as when performing a compression test), always disconnect the high tension wire on the distributor and then connect it to ground.

3. DO NOT install any standard ignition coil (always note the Part no. of the old one).

4. DO NOT connect a condenser to the negative terminal of the ignition coil.

5. DO NOT connect a quick charger (for boost starting) for any longer than 1 minute.

Ignition Timing

TYPE 1 AND 2 (EXCEPT 1979–83 TYPE 2 CALIF. MODELS)

Dwell or point gap must be set before the timing is set. Also, the idle speed must be set to specifications.

NOTE: The engine must be warmed up before the timing is set (oil temperature of 122–158°F).

1. Remove the No. 1 spark plug wire from the distributor cap and attach the timing light lead. Disconnect the vacuum hose if so advised by the "Tune-Up Specifications" chart (and readjust the idle speed if necessary).

Timing marks—fuel injected Type 1 with Automatic Stick Shift

Timing marks—Type 2 except 1979–83 California models

2. Start the engine and run it at the specified rpm. Aim the timing light at the crankshaft pulley on upright fan engines and at the engine cooling fan on the suitcase engines. The rubber plug in the fan housing will have to be removed before the timing marks on the suitcase engine can be seen.

3. Read the timing and rotate the distributor accordingly.

NOTE: Rotate the distributor in the opposite direction of normal rotor rotation to advance the timing. Retard the timing by turning the distributor in the normal direction of rotor rotation.

4. It is necessary to loosen the clamp at the base of the distributor before the distributor can be rotated. It may also be necessary to put a small amount of white paint or chalk on the timing marks to make them more visible.

1979–83 TYPE 2 CALIF. MODELS

1. Run the engine until it reaches normal operating temperature and then turn it off.

2. Bypass the idle stabilizer by pulling the two leads from the unit and connecting them together.

Timing marks—1979–83 California models (Type 2)

Bypass the idle stabilizer unit (electronic ignition only) by unplugging the two leads and connecting them together

3. Hook up a dwell/tachometer as per the manufacturer's instructions, start the engine and check that the idle is between 850 and 950 rpm.

4. Turn off the engine and follow Steps 1–4 of the previous procedure.

5. Be sure to hook the idle stabilizer back up after the timing has been set.

Valve Lash

ADJUSTMENT

Gasoline Engines

NOTE: 1978–83 Type 2 vehicles are equipped with hydraulic valve lifters. No valve adjustment is possible or necessary.

NOTE: The engine must be as cool as possible before adjusting the valves. Adjust the valves as follows:

1. Remove the distributor cap and turn the engine until the rotor points to the No. One spark plug wire post in the distributor cap. To bring the piston to exactly top dead center (TDC) on the compression stroke, align the crankshaft timing marks on TDC.

2. Remove the rocker arm covers. At TDC, the pushrods should be down and there should be clearance between the rocker arms and valve stems of both valves of the subject cylinder.

3. With the proper feeler gauge, check the clearance between the adjusting screw and the valve stem of both valves for the No. 1 cylinder. If the feeler gauge slides in snugly without being forced, the clearance is correct. It is better that the clearance is a little loose then a little tight.

4. If the clearance is incorrect, the locknut must be loosened and the adjusting screw turned until the proper clearance is obtained. After tightening down the locknut, it is then advisable to recheck the clearance. It is possible to alter the adjustment when tightening the locknut.

5. The valves are adjusted in a 1-2-3-4 sequence. To adjust cylinders 2 through 4, the distributor rotor must be pointed at the appropriate distributor cap post 90° apart from each other. Align the crankshaft timing marks for each cylinder, remembering

No. 1 piston at Top Dead Center—Type 1

Checking valve clearance with a feeler gauge

that the piston must be at TDC on the compression stroke when the valves are adjusted.

NOTE: Always use new valve cover gaskets.

Diesel Engines

Check the valve clearance every 20,000 miles in firing order, with the engine at normal operating temperature.

1. Remove the camshaft cover.
2. Set the engine at TDC on No. 1 cylinder by aligning the 0°T mark on the flywheel with the pointer.

NOTE: When adjusting clearances on a diesel, the pistons must not be at TDC. Turn the crankshaft ¼ turn past TDC, so that the valves do not contact the pistons when the tappets are depressed.

3. The valve clearances of cylinder No. 1 should be checked when the valves of No. 4 cylinder overlap, i.e., when both No. 4 cylinder valves move in opposite directions simultaneously. It may be necessary to turn the crankshaft slightly to find this position. When this happens, the exhaust valve is closing and the intake opening. Check and note the clearance of both the intake and exhaust valves for No. 1 cylinder.

4. Turn the crankshaft 180° in the normal direction of rotation. Check and note the valve clearances of cylinder No. 3 at the overlap position of cylinder No. 2.

5. Turn the crankshaft 180°. Check and note the valve clearances of cylinder No. 4 at the overlap position of cylinder No. 1.

6. Turn the crankshaft 180°. Check and note the valve clearances of cylinder No. 2 at the overlap position of cylinder No. 3.

7. Compare the noted clearances with those listed in the "Tune-Up Specifications" chart. Adjustment is made by replacing the tappet clearance shim in the top of each tappet. These are available in 26 sizes ranging from 3.0 mm (0.119 in.) to 4.25 mm (0.166 in.) in increments of 0.05 mm (0.002 in.). The thickness of each shim is marked on the bottom. (These shims are available from VW dealers.)

NOTE: If a valve clearance deviates 0.002 in. or less from the specified clearance, it need not be adjusted.

8. To remove a tappet clearance shim, turn the cylinder to TDC and press down the tappet so that the shim can be lifted out.

A special tool is available from VW for this operation. Once the shim is removed, check its size and determine what size will be needed to produce the required adjustment.

9. Install the required shim. When all the clearances have been corrected, recheck valve clearances.

Fuel System Adjustments

IDLE SPEED AND MIXTURE

Gasoline Engines

IDLE MIXTURE

Volkswagen states that the idle mixture should not require adjustment during a tune-up or routine maintenance. The only time that it will require an adjustment is after replacement of the intake air sensor or after extensive engine rebuilding. Due to the requirement of an infrared exhaust gas analyzer to perform this adjustment, we suggest that if in fact the adjustment is needed, the work should be performed by an authorized service facility.

Idle speed regulator adjustment—Type 2 with automatic transmission

IDLE SPEED

1. Thoroughly warm up the engine so that the oil will be hot and the auxiliary air regulator will be fully closed.

NOTE: On 1979–83 Type 2 Calif. models the idle stabilizer must be bypassed. Pull the two leads from the stabilizer and connect them together.

2. Turn off the engine and hook up a dwell/tachometer as per the manufacturer's instructions.

NOTE: Don't forget to set the meter to the four cylinder scale.

3. Start the engine, speed it up and then allow it to return to idle. The idle speed for cars with manual transmissions is 850–950 rpm. The idle speed for cars with automatic transmissions should be 900–1000 rpm. If the idle speed is not within the limits, it will require adjustment.

4. To adjust the idle, use a screwdriver to turn the bypass screw in the throttle valve housing. Turn the screw clockwise to decrease the idle and counterclockwise to increase it.

NOTE: Make sure you reconnect the idle stabilizer if your car is so equipped.

All Type 2 vehicles with an automatic transmission require one further adjustment. When the idle speed has been set properly, set the parking brake, block the front wheels and then put the car in "Drive." The idle should drop between 150–200 rpm. If it drops more than this you will have to adjust the idle speed regulator. To adjust:

1. With the engine idling, place the transmission in "Park" and use a feeler gauge to check the clearance between the end of the plunger and the lever on the throttle valve shaft. It should be between 0.020–0.040 in.

2. If the gap is not within specifications, loosen the locknut on the plunger and screw the plunger in or out until the clearance is correct.

Fuel injection idle speed (by-pass screw) adjustment—Type 1

Fuel injection idle speed (by-pass screw) adjustment—Type 2

2. Distributor cap
3. Rotor
6. Points
8. Vacuum unit
9. Condenser
10. Holding spring
16. Ball retaining spring
17. Ball
18. Breaker plate
22. Return spring
23. Distributor cam
25. Flyweight

27. Circlip for drive dog
28. Pin for drive dog
29. Drive dog
30. 0.1 mm compensating washer
32. Distributor shaft
33. Distributor housing
34. Rubber sealing ring
35. Fuel injection trigger contacts

Fuel injection distributor

Diesel Engines

IDLE SPEED/MAXIMUM SPEED ADJUSTMENTS

Volkswagen diesel engines have both an idle speed and a maximum speed adjustment. The maximum engine speed adjustment prevents the engine from over-revving and self-destructing. The adjusters are located side by side on top of the injection pump. The screw closest to the engine is the idle speed adjuster, while the outer screw is the maximum speed adjuster.

The idle and maximum speed must be adjusted with the engine warm (normal operating temperature). Because the diesel engine has no conventional ignition, you will need a special adaptor (VW 1324) to connect your tachometer, or use the tachometer in the instrument panel, if equipped. You should check with the manufacturer of your tachometer to see if it will work with diesel engines. Adjust all engines to 800–850 rpm.

When adjustment is correct, lock the locknut on the screw and apply non-hardening thread sealer (Loctite® or similar) to prevent the screw from vibrating loose.

The maximum speed for all engines is between 5300–5400 rpm. If it is not in this range, loosen the screw and correct the speed (turning the screw clockwise decreases rpm). Lock the nut on the adjusting screw and apply a dab of thread sealer in the same manner as you did on the idle screw.

— **CAUTION** —
Do not attempt to squeeze more power out of your engine by raising the maximum speed (rpm). If you do, you'll probably be in for a major overhaul in the not too distant future.

ENGINE ELECTRICAL

Distributor

REMOVAL AND INSTALLATION

1. Take off the vacuum hose(s) at the distributor.
2. Disconnect the coil wire and remove the distributor cap.
3. Tag and disconnect any additional wires leading from the distributor.
4. Bring No. 1 cylinder to top dead center (TDC) on the compression stroke by rotating the engine so that the rotor points to the No. 1 spark plug wire tower on the distributor cap and the timing marks are aligned at 0°. Mark the rotor-to-distributor relationship. Also, matchmark the distributor housing-to-crankcase relationship.

5. Unscrew the distributor retaining screw on the crankcase and lift the distributor out.

6. If the engine has been rotated since the distributor was removed, bring the No. 1 cylinder to TDC on the compression stroke and align the timing marks on 0°. Align the matchmarks and insert the distributor into the crankcase. If the matchmarks are gone, have the rotor pointing to the No. 1 spark plug wire tower upon insertion.

7. Replace the distributor retaining screw and reconnect the condenser and coil wires. Reinstall the distributor cap.

8. Retime the engine.

Distributor Driveshaft

REMOVAL AND INSTALLATION

1. Bring the engine to TDC on the compression stroke of No. 1 cylinder. Align the timing marks at 0°.

2. Remove the distributor.

3. Remove the spacer spring from the driveshaft.

4. Grasp the shaft and turn it slowly to the left while withdrawing it from its bore.

5. Remove the washer found under the shaft.

— CAUTION —
Make sure that this washer does not fall down into the engine.

Type 1 distributor driveshaft alignment

Type 2 distributor driveshaft alignment

STATIC SHIELD

GROUND STRAP

DISTRIBUTOR CAP

CARBON BRUSH/SPRING

ROTOR

RETAINERS

TO IDLE STABILIZER

PIN

PLUG FOR HALL PICKUP

TRIGGER WHEEL

WASHERS

CONNECTING SOCKET

RETAINER

HALL SENDER

VACUUM ADVANCE CONNECTION

VACUUM UNIT

BASE PLATE

VACUUM RETARD CONNECTION

DISTRIBUTOR

GASKET

CLAMP

Electronic ignition distributor

6. To install, make sure that the engine is at TDC on the compression stroke for No. 1 cylinder with the timing marks aligned at 0°.

7. Replace the washer and insert the shaft into its bore.

NOTE: Due to the slant of the teeth on the drive gears, the shaft must be rotated slightly to the left when it is inserted into the crankcase.

8. When the shaft is properly inserted, the offset slot in the driveshaft of Type 1

engines will be perpendicular to the crank-case joint and the slot offset will be facing the crankshaft pulley. On Type 2/1800 and 2/2000 engines, the slot should be about 12° out of parallel with the center line of the engine and the slot offset should be facing outside the engine.

9. Reinstall the spacer spring.

10. Reinstall the distributor and fuel pump, if removed.

11. Retime the engine.

Alternator

ALTERNATOR PRECAUTIONS

1. Battery polarity should be checked before any connections, such as jumper cables or battery charge leads, are made. Reversing the battery connections will damage the diodes in the alternator. It is recommended that the battery cables be disconnected before connecting a battery charger.

2. The battery must never be disconnected while the alternator is running.

3. Always disconnect the battery ground lead before working on the charging system, especially when replacing an alternator.

4. Do not short across or ground any alternator or regulator terminals.

5. If electric arc welding has to be done to the car, first disconnect the battery and alternator cables. Never start the car with the welding unit attached.

REMOVAL AND INSTALLATION

Type 1

1. Disconnect the battery.

2. Remove the fan belt.

3. Remove the air cleaner and the intake air sensor.

4. Pull out the accelerator cable guide tube.

5. Remove the alternator retaining strap.

6. Disconnect the ignition cables and any hoses, air ducts and wires that might prevent the fan housing from being lifted upward.

7. Loosen and remove the mounting screws at each end of the fan housing.

8. Unbolt and remove the thermostat.

9. Raise the fan housing slightly and unscrew the four alternator mounting bolts.

10. Remove the alternator and the fan from the fan housing.

11. Remove the fan from the alternator by unscrewing the special nut and pulling the fan off the keyed alternator shaft. Note the position of any shims, as these are used to maintain a gap of 0.08 in. between the fan and the fan cover.

12. Installation is in the reverse order of removal.

1. Motorola alternator	13. Diode carrier	25. Diode carrier screw
2. Bosch alternator	14. Diode carrier	26. Retaining plate screw
3. Housing	15. Diode carrier retainer	27. Brush holder cover screw
4. Claw-pole rotor	16. B+ terminal nut	28. End plate screw
5. Claw-pole rotor	17. B+ terminal insulating washer	29. Voltage regulator
6. End plate ball bearing	18. B+ terminal insulating bushing	30. Voltage regulator
7. Ball bearing	19. Brush holder	31. Boot
8. Fan end spacer ring	20. Carbon brush holder plate	32. Terminal sleeve housing
9. Drive end spacer ring	21. End plate	33. Terminal pin housing
10. Rotor locating plate	22. O-ring	34. Spring washer
11. Stator winding	23. Retaining plate	35. Screw
12. Stator winding	24. Fan cover bolt	

Exploded view of the 50 amp alternator used in Type 1 models

Type 2/1800, 2/2000 (Fuel Injected)

1. Disconnect the negative battery cable.

2. Disconnect the alternator wiring harness at the voltage regulator and starter.

3. Pull out the dipstick and remove the oil filler neck.

4. Loosen the alternator adjusting bolt and remove the drive belt.

5. Remove the right rear engine cover plate and the alternator cover plate.

6. Disconnect the warm air duct at the right side, and remove the heat exchanger bracket and connecting pipe from the blower.

7. Disconnect the cool air intake elbow at the alternator. Remove the attaching bolt and lift out the alternator from above.

8. Reverse the above procedure to install, taking care to ensure that the rubber grommet on the intake cover for the wiring harness is installed correctly. After installation, adjust the drive belt so that moderate thumb pressure midway on the belt depresses the belt about ½ in.

ALTERNATOR BELT ADJUSTMENT

Alternator belt tension adjustment

1. Remove the insert in the cover plate and loosen the bolt in the slotted hole.

2. Move the alternator left or right to adjust the tension and then tighten the bolt. Tension is correct if the bolt can be deflected no more than ½ in. at the midpoint of the pulleys.

Voltage Regulator

REMOVAL AND INSTALLATION

Type 1

The regulator is located under the rear seat on the left side. It is secured to the frame by two screws. Take careful note of the wiring connections before removing the wiring from the regulator. Disconnect the battery before removing the regulator.

1. Elbow
2. Screw for hose clip
3. Threaded portion for hose clip
4. Cable hose clamp
5. Rubber grommet
6. Alternator wiring harness
7. Intake cover for alternator
8. Hex nut
9. Lockwasher
10. Rubber grommet for intake cover
11. B+ connection hex nut
12. Washer
13. Washer
14. Star washer
15. Contact disc
16. Three pin plug
17. Intake cover gasket
18. Positive diode carrier
19. Positive diodes
20. Screw
21. Stator winding connection screw
22. Exciter diode carrier
23. Exciter diodes
24. Seal
25. Negative diodes
26. Positive diode carrier pin
27. Brush holder screw
28. Washer
29. Spring washer
30. Alternator housing
31. Carbon brush
32. Brush retaining spring
33. Brush holder
34. Stator
35. Spring washer
36. Slip ring ball bearings
37. Claw pole rotor
38. End plate
39. Bearing end plate
40. Screw
41. Drive end ball bearing
42. Intermediate ring
43. Pulley
44. Housing bolt
45. Washer
46. Washer
47. Nut

Exploded view of the 55 amp alternator used in Type 2 models

1. Nut and lockwasher
2. Connecting strip
3. Nut and lockwasher
4. Solenoid
5. Insulating disc
6. Seal
7. Insulating plate
8. Cap
9. Circlip
10. Steel washer
11. Bronze washer
12. Brush inspection cover
13. Commutator end plate
14. Brush holder
15. Screw and lockwasher
16. Housing screws
17. Dished washer
18. Steel washer
19. Housing and field windings
20. Spring clip
21. Pin
22. Solenoid core
23. Linkage
24. Bushing
25. Spring
26. Washer
27. Drive pinion
28. Dished washer
29. Armature
30. Mounting bracket

Exploded view of VW 111 911 023A starter

— **CAUTION** —

Interchanging the connections on the regulator will destroy the regulator and generator.

Type 2

Disconnect the battery. The regulator is located in the engine compartment and is secured in place by two screws. Take careful note of the wiring connections before removing the wiring from the regulator.

VOLTAGE ADJUSTMENT

Volkswagen voltage regulators are sealed and cannot be adjusted. A malfunctioning regulator must be replaced as a unit.

Starter

REMOVAL AND INSTALLATION

1. Disconnect the battery.
2. Disconnect the wiring from the starter.
3. The starter is held in place by two bolts. Remove the upper bolt through the engine compartment. Remove the lower bolt from underneath the car.
4. Remove the starter from the car.
5. Before installing the starter, lubricate the outboard bushing with grease. Apply sealing compound to the mating surfaces between the starter and the transmission.
6. Place the long starter bolt in its hole in the starter and locate the starter on the transmission housing. Install the other bolt.
7. Connect the starter wiring and battery cables.

9 10 11 15 12 13 14 16 18 17 19 20 1 2 21 22 6 29 23 26 24 25 4 5 3 27 28 7 8

1. Nut
2. Lockwasher
3. Screw
4. Rubber seal
5. Disc
6. Solenoid switch
7. Stop-ring
8. Circlip
9. Screw
10. Washer

11. End cap
12. C-washer
13. Shim
14. Sealing ring
15. Housing screw
16. End plate
17. Spring
18. Brush holder
19. Rubber grommet
20. Housing

21. Insulating washer
22. Thrust washer
23. Pin
24. Nut
25. Lockwasher
26. Operating lever
27. Drive end plate
28. Drive pinion
29. Armature

Exploded view of Bosch 311 911 023B starter

SOLENOID REPLACEMENT

1. Remove the starter.
2. Remove the nut which secures the connector strip at the end of the solenoid.
3. Take out the two retaining screws on the mounting bracket and withdraw the solenoid after it has been unhooked from its actuating lever.
4. When replacing a defective solenoid with a new one, care should be taken to see that the distance (a) in the accompanying diagram is 19 mm when the magnet is drawn inside the solenoid.
5. Installation is the reverse of removal. In order to facilitate engagement of the actuating rod, the pinion should be pulled out as far as possible when inserting the solenoid.

Solenoid adjustment

Diesel Engine

GLOW PLUG SYSTEM CHECK

NOTE: The 1982 and later diesels have a new type quick-glow system. Nominal glow time is seven seconds. Although the wiring for this system is the same as the earlier system, the glow plugs and relay cannot be paired or interchanged with earlier parts or vice versa.

1. Connect a test light between No. 4 cylinder glow plug and ground. The glow plugs are connected by a flat, coated busbar (located near the bottom of the cylinder head).
2. Turn the ignition key to the heating (pre-glow) position. The test light should light.
3. If not, possible problems include the glow plug relay, the ignition switch and the fuse box relay plate and the glow plug fuse or a break in the wire to the relay terminal.

INDIVIDUAL GLOW PLUG TEST

1. Remove the wire and busbar from the glow plugs.
2. Connect a test light to the battery positive terminal.
3. Touch the test light probe to each glow plug in turn.
   If the test light lights, the plug is good. If the light does not light, replace the glow plug(s).

Removing the upper engine mounting bolts

ENGINE MECHANICAL— GASOLINE ENGINES

Engine

REMOVAL AND INSTALLATION

The Volkswagen engine is mounted on the transmission, which in turn is attached to the frame. In the Type 1 and 2 models, there are two bolts and two studs attaching the engine to the transmission.

When removing the engine from the car, it is recommended that the rear of the car be about 3 ft. off the ground. Remove the engine by bringing it out from underneath the car. Proceed with the following steps to remove the engine.

1. Disconnect the battery ground cable.
2. Disconnect the generator wiring.
3. Remove the air cleaner. On Type 1 engines, remove the rear engine cover plate.
4. Disconnect the throttle cable and remove the electrical connections to the automatic choke, coil, electromagnetic cutoff jet, and the oil pressure sending unit.
5. Disconnect the fuel hose at the front engine cover plate and seal it to prevent leakage.
6. Raise the car and support it with jack stands.
7. Remove the flexible air hoses between the engine and heat exchangers, dis-

connect the heater flap cables, unscrew the two lower engine mounting nuts, and slide a jack under the engine. On Type 2 engines, remove the two bolts from the rubber engine mounts located next to the muffler.

8. On Type 1 Automatic Stick Shift models, disconnect the control valve cable and the manifold vacuum hoses. Disconnect the ATF suction line and plug it.

9. On all Automatic Stick Shift and fully automatic models, remove the four bolts from the converter drive plate through the holes in the transmission case. After the engine is removed, hold the torque converter on the transmission input shaft by using a strap bolted to the bellhousing.

10. Raise the jack until it just contacts the engine and have an assistant hold the two upper mounting bolts so that the nuts can be removed from the bottom.

11. When the engine mounts are disconnected and there are no remaining cables or wires left to be disconnected, move the engine toward the back of the car so that the clutch or converter plate disengages from the transmission.

12. Lower the engine out of the car.

13. Installation is the reverse of the above. When the engine is lifted into position, it should be rotated using the generator pulley so that the clutch plate hub will engage the transmission shaft splines. Tighten the upper mounting bolts first. Check the clutch, pressure plate, throwout bearing, and pilot bearing for wear.

Cylinder Head

REMOVAL AND INSTALLATION

In order to remove the cylinder head from either pair of cylinders, it is necessary to lower the engine.

1. Remove the valve cover and gasket. Remove the rocker arm assembly. Unbolt the intake manifold from the cylinder head. The cylinder head is held in place by eight studs. Since the cylinder head also holds the cylinders in place in the VW engine,

Removing the lower engine mounting bolts

1. Cylinder head cover
2. Gasket
3. Nut
4. Spring washer
5. Rocker shaft
6. Clip
7. Thrust washer
8. Spring washer
9. Rocker arm
10. Adjusting screw
11. Nut
12. Support
13. Stud seal
14. Nut
15. Washer

16a. Type 1, Type 2/1600 cylinder head
16b. Type 3 cylinder head
17. Thermostat link
18. Valve cotter
19. Spring cap
20. Valve spring
21. Oil deflector ring
22. Intake valve
23. Exhaust valve
24. Intake valve guide
25. Exhaust valve guide
26. Pushrod tube
27. Sealing ring
28. Pushrod

Exploded view of the cylinder head—Type 1

and the cylinders are not going to be removed it will be necessary to hold the cylinders in place after the head is removed.

2. After the rocker arm cover, rocker arm retaining nuts, and rocker arm assembly have been removed, the cylinder head nuts can be removed and the cylinder head lifted off.

3. When reinstalling the cylinder head, the head should be checked for cracks both in the combustion chamber and in the intake and exhaust ports. Cracked heads must be replaced.

4. Spark plug threads should be checked. New seals should be used on the pushrod tube ends and they should be checked for proper seating.

5. The pushrod tubes should be turned so that the seam faces upward. In order to ensure perfect sealing, used tubes should be stretched slightly before they are reinstalled.

6. Install the cylinder head. Using new rocker shaft stud seals, install the pushrods and rocker shaft assembly.

NOTE: Pay careful attention to the orientation of the shaft as described in the "Rocker Shaft" section.

7. Torque the cylinder head in three stages. Adjust the valve clearance. Using a new gasket, install the rocker cover. It may be necessary to readjust the valves after the engine has been run a few minutes and allowed to cool.

VALVE SEATS

On all air-cooled VW engines, the valve seats are shrunk-fit into the cylinder head. This usually involves freezing the seat with liquid nitrogen or some other refrigerant to about 200°F below zero, and heating up the cylinder head to approximately 400°F. Due to the extreme temperatures required to shrink-fit these items, and because of the extra care needed when working with metals at these extreme temperatures, it is advised that this operation be referred to an experienced repair shop.

CYLINDER HEAD OVERHAUL AND VALVE GUIDE REPLACEMENT

See the "Engine Rebuilding" section at the end of this book.

Rocker Shafts

REMOVAL AND INSTALLATION

1. Before the valve rocker assembly can be reached, it is necessary to lever off the clip that retains the valve cover and then remove the valve cover.

2. Remove the rocker arm retaining nuts,

On Type 1 models, install the rocker shaft with the chamfer out and the slot up

On Type 2/1800 models, install the rocker shaft with the chamfer out and the slots down

the rocker arm shaft, and the rocker arms. Remove the stud seals.

3. Before installing the rocker arm mechanism, be sure that the parts are as clean as possible.

4. Install new stud seals. On Type 1, install the rocker shaft assembly with the chamfered edges of the rocker shaft supports pointing outward and the slots pointing upward. On Type 2/1800, 2/2000 models, the chamfered edges must point outward and the slots must face downward, and the pushrod tube retaining wire must engage the slots in the rocker arm shaft supports as well as the grooves in the pushrod tubes.

5. Tighten the retaining nuts to the proper torque. Use only the copper colored nuts that were supplied with the engine.

6. Make sure that the ball ends of the pushrods are centered in the sockets of the rocker arms.

7. Adjust the valve clearance. Install the valve cover using a new gasket.

Intake Manifold

REMOVAL AND INSTALLATION

1. Remove the air cleaner.

2. Remove the pressure switch which is mounted under the right pair of intake manifold pipes. Disconnect the injector wiring.

3. Remove the fuel injectors by removing the two nuts which secure them in place. See Step 7 for proper injector installation.

4. After removing the intake manifold outer cover plate, remove the two screws which secure the manifold inner cover plate.

5. The manifold may be removed by removing the two nuts and washers which hold the manifold flange to the cylinder head.

6. Installation is the reverse of the above. The inner manifold cover should be installed first, but leave the cover loose until the outer cover and manifold are in place. Always use new gaskets.

7. Connect the fuel hoses to the injectors, if removed, after assembling the injector retainer plate in place. Make sure that the sleeves are in place on the injector securing studs. Carefully slip the injectors into the manifold and install the securing nuts. Never force the injectors in or out of the manifold. Reconnect the injector wiring.

Intake Air Distributor

REMOVAL AND INSTALLATION

The intake air distributor is located at the center of the engine at the junction of the intake manifold pipes.

NOTE: It is not necessary to remove the distributor if only the manifold pipes are to be removed.

1. Remove the air cleaner and pressure switch which are located under the right pair of manifold pipes.

2. Push the four rubber hoses onto the intake manifold pipes.

3. Remove the accelerator cable and the throttle valve switch.

4. Disconnect the accelerator cable.

5. Disconnect the vacuum hoses leading to the ignition distributor and the pressure sensor and disconnect the hose running to the auxiliary air regulator.

6. Remove those bolts under the air distributor which secure the air distributor to the crankcase and remove the air distributor.

7. Installation is the reverse of removal.

Mufflers, Tailpipes, Heat Exchangers

REMOVAL AND INSTALLATION

Muffler, Type 1

1. Working under the hood, disconnect the pre-heater hoses.

2. Remove the pre-heater pipe protection plate on each side of the engine. The plates are secured by three screws.

3. Remove the crankshaft pulley cover plate.

4. Remove the rear engine cover plate from the engine compartment. It is held in place by screws at the center, right, and left sides.

5. Remove the four intake manifold preheat pipe bolts. There are two bolts on each side of the engine.

6. Disconnect the warm air channel clamps at the left and right side of the engine.

7. Disconnect the heat exchanger clamps at the left and right side of the engine.

8. Remove the muffler from the engine.

9. Installation is the reverse of above. Always use new gaskets to install the muffler.

Muffler, Type 2/1800, 2/2000

The muffler is secured to the left and right heat exchangers by three bolts. There is a bracket at the left end of the muffler. Always use new gaskets when installing a new muffler.

Heat Exchangers, Type 1

1. Disconnect the air tube at the outlet end of the exchanger.

2. Remove the clamp which secures the muffler to the exchanger.

3. Loosen the clamp which secures the exchanger to the heater hose connection at the muffler.

4. Remove the two nuts which secure the exchanger to the forward end of the cylinder head.

5. Remove the heater flap control wire.

6. Reverse the above to install. Always use new gaskets.

Heat Exchangers, Type 2/1800, 2/2000

1. Disconnect the air hose at the outlet of each exchanger.

2. Disconnect the warm air tube at the outside end of the exchanger.

3. Disconnect the three bolts which secure each exchanger to the muffler.

4. Remove the four nuts, two at each exhaust port, which secure the exchanger to the cylinder head.

Installation is the reverse of the above. Always use new gaskets.

Tailpipes, Type 1

Loosen the clamps on the tailpipes and apply penetrating oil. Work the pipe side-to-side while trying to pull the tailpipe out of the muffler.

1. Tail pipe	19. Bolt
2. Retaining ring	20. Pin
3. Seal	21. Circlip
4. Nut	22. Link
5. Clapm	23. Pin
6. Bolt	24. Pin
7. Muffler	25. Heater flap lever
8. Seal	26. Return spring
9. Heater hose	27. Damper pipe
10. Hose clamp	28. Bolt
11. Rubber grommet	29. Washer
12. Connecting pipe	30. Lockwasher
13. Gasket	31. Bolt
14. Gasket	32. Damper pipe bracket
15. Gasket	33. Bracket clamp
16. Self-locking nut	34. Bolt
17. Clamp	35. Clamp
18. Heat exchanger	36. Tailpipe

Exhaust system—Type 1

After burner pipe

Exhaust pipe

Connection for heater

Heat exchanger

Connection for warm air fan

Clamp

Pipe
from Chass. No. 226 2 077 584 without preheating for intake air

Muffler

Tail pipe

Exhaust manifold

Catalytic converter (California only)

Exhaust system—Type 2 gasoline engine

NOTE: It is often difficult to remove the tailpipes without damaging them.

Tailpipes, Type 2/1800, 2/2000

Remove the bolt which secures the pipe to the muffler. Remove the bolt which secures the pipe to the body and remove the pipe.

Pistons and Cylinders

Pistons and cylinders are matched according to their size. When replacing pistons and cylinders, make sure that they are properly sized.

NOTE: See the "Engine Rebuilding" section for cylinder refinishing.

CYLINDER REMOVAL AND INSTALLATION

1. Remove the engine. Remove the cylinder head, pushrod tubes, and the deflector plate.

2. Slide the cylinder out of its groove in the crankcase and off the piston. Match-mark the cylinders for reassembly. The cylinders must be returned to their original bore in the crankcase. If a cylinder is to be replaced, it must be replaced with a matching piston.

3. Cylinders should be checked for wear and, if necessary, replaced with another matched cylinder and piston assembly of the same size.

4. Check the cylinder seating surface on the crankcase, cylinder shoulder, and gasket, for cleanliness and deep scores. When reinstalling the cylinders, a new gasket, if required, should be used between each cylinder and the crankcase.

5. The piston, as well as the piston rings and pin must be oiled before reassembly.

6. Be sure that the ring gaps are of the correct dimension. Stagger the ring gaps around the piston, but make sure that the oil ring gap is positioned up when the pistons are in position on the connecting rods.

7. Compress the rings with a ring compressor, oil the cylinder wall, and slide the cylinder onto the piston. Make sure that the cylinder base gasket is in place.

Installing a cylinder

8. Install the deflector plates.

9. Install the pushrod tubes using new gaskets. Install the pushrods. Make sure that the seam in the pushrod tube is facing upward.

10. Install the cylinder head.

PISTON REMOVAL AND INSTALLATION

1. Remove the engine. Remove the cylinder head and, after matchmarking the cylinders, remove the cylinders.

2. Matchmark the pistons to indicate the cylinder number and which side points toward the clutch.

3. Remove the circlips which retain the piston pin.

4. Heat the piston to 176° F. To heat the piston, boil a clean rag in water and wrap it around the piston. Remove the piston pin after the piston has been heated.

Checking piston ring end gap

5. Remove the piston from the connecting rod.

6. Before installing the pistons, they should first be cleaned and checked for wear. Remove the old rings. Clean the ring grooves using a groove cleaner or a broken piece of ring. Clean the piston with solvent but do not use a wire brush or sandpaper. Check for any cracks or scuff marks. Check the piston diameter with a micrometer and compare the readings to the specifications. If the running clearance between the piston and cylinder wall is 0.008 in. (0.2 mm) or greater, the cylinder and piston should be replaced by a set of the same size grading. If the cylinder shows no sign of excessive wear or damage, it is permissable to install a new piston and rings of the appropriate size.

7. Place each ring in turn in its cylinder bore and check the piston ring end-gap. If the gap is too large, replace the ring. If the gap is too narrow, file the end of the ring until the proper gap is obtained.

Checking piston ring side clearance

8. Insert the rings on the piston and check the ring side clearance. If the clearance is too large, replace the piston. Install the rings with the marking "Open" or "Top" pointing upward.

9. If new rings are installed in a used piston, the ring ridge at the top of the cylinder bore must be removed with a ridge reamer.

10. Install the piston and piston pin on the connecting rod from which it originally came. Make sure that the piston is facing the proper direction.

11. Install the cylinders and the cylinder heads.

Crankcase

DISASSEMBLY AND ASSEMBLY

1. Remove the engine.

2. Remove the cylinder heads, cylinders, and pistons.

3. Remove the oil strainer, oil pressure switch, and the crankcase nuts. Remove the flywheel and oil pump. Matchmark the flywheel so that it can be replaced in the same position.

4. Keep the cam followers in the right crankcase half in position by using a retaining spring.

5. Use a rubber hammer to break the seal between the crankcase halves.

— CAUTION —
Never insert sharp metal tools, wedges, or any prying device between the crankcase halves. This will ruin the gasket surface and cause serious oil leakage.

6. After the seal between the crankcase halves is broken, remove the right-hand crankcase half, the crankshaft oil seal and the camshaft can now be lifted out of the crankcase half.

7. Remove the cam followers, bearing shells, and the oil pressure relief valve.

8. Before starting reassembly, check the crankcase for any damage or cracks.

9. Flush and blow out all ducts and oil passages. Check the studs for tightness. If the tapped holes are worn install a Heli-Coil.

10. Install the crankshaft bearing dowel pins and bearing shells for the crankshaft

Check the dowel pins for tightness

Tighten the 8 mm nut located next to the 12 mm stud of the No. 1 crankcase bearing first on the Type 1

and camshaft. Make sure that the bearing shells with thrust flanges are installed in the proper journal.

11. Install the crankshaft and camshaft after the bearings have been well lubricated. When installing the camshaft and crankshaft, make sure that the timing marks on the timing gears are aligned.

12. Install the oil pressure relief valve.

13. Oil and install the cam followers.

14. Install the camshaft end plug using sealing compound.

15. Install the thrust washers and crankshaft oil seal. The oil seal must rest squarely on the bottom of its recess in the crankcase. The thrust washers at the flywheel end of the crankshaft are shims used to set the crankshaft end-play.

16. Spread a thin film of sealing compound on the crankcase joining faces and place the two halves together. Torque the nuts in several stages. Tighten the 8 mm nut located next to the 12 mm stud of the No. 1 crankshaft bearing first. As the crankcase halves are being torqued, continually check the crankshaft for ease of rotation.

17. Crankshaft end-play is checked when the flywheel is installed. It is adjusted by varying the number and thickness of the shims located behind the flywheel. Measure the end-play with a dial indicator mounted against the flywheel, and attached firmly to the crankcase.

1. Camshaft
2. Crankshaft and connecting rod assembly
3. Main bearing No. 1
4. Main bearing No. 4
5. End cap for camshaft bore
6. Camshaft No. 1 bearing shell
7. No. 2 camshaft bearing
8. No. 3 camshaft bearing with shoulder for thrust
9. Crankshaft bearing dowel pin
10. No. 2 crankshaft bearing half
11. Left crankcase half

Crankcase half assembly—Type 2 gasoline engine

Camshaft and Timing Gears

REMOVAL AND INSTALLATION

1. Removal of the camshaft requires splitting the crankcase. See "Crankcase Disassembly". The camshaft and its bearing shells are then removed from the crankcase halves.

2. Before reinstalling the camshaft, it should be checked for wear on the lobe surfaces and on the bearing surfaces. In addition, the riveted joint between the camshaft timing gear and the camshaft should be checked for tightness.

3. The camshaft should be checked for the correct tooth contact and for wear.

5. If the camshaft bearing shells are worn or damaged, new shells should be fitted. The camshaft bearing shells should be installed with the tabs engaging the notches in the crankcase. It is usually a good idea to replace the bearing shells under any circumstances. Before installing the

Aligning valve timing marks on gears

camshaft, the bearing journals and cam lobes should be generously coated with oil.

6. When the camshaft is installed, care should be taken to ensure that the timing gear tooth marked (0) is located between the two teeth of the crankshaft timing gear marked with a center punch.

7. The camshaft end-play is measured at the No. 3 bearing. End-play is 0.0015–0.005 in. (0.04–0.12 mm) and the wear limit is 0.006 in. (0.16 mm).

Crankshaft

CRANKSHAFT PULLEY REMOVAL AND INSTALLATION

On the Type 1, the crankshaft pulley can be removed while the engine is still in the car. However, in this instance it is necessary for the rear cover plate of the engine

Type 2/1800 engine fan bolts

to be removed. Remove the cover plate after taking out the screws in the cover plate below the crankshaft pulley. Remove the fan belt and the crankshaft pulley securing screw. Using a puller, remove the crankshaft pulley. The crankshaft pulley should be checked for proper seating and belt contact. The oil return thread should be cleaned and lubricated with oil. The crankshaft pulley should be installed in the reverse sequence. Check for oil leaks after installing the pulley.

On the Type 2, the crankshaft pulley can be removed only when the engine is out of the car and the muffler, alternator and cooling air intake housing are removed. After these parts have been removed, take out the plastic cap in the pulley. Unscrew the three socket head screws and the self-locking nut and then remove the pulley.

Installation for Type 2/1800, 2/2000 engines is the reverse of removal. When installing, use a new paper gasket between the fan and the crankshaft pulley. If shims are used, do not forget them. Don't use more than two shims. When inserting the pulley, make sure that the pin engages the hole in the fan. Ensure that the clearance between the generator belt and the intake housing is at least 4 mm and the belt is parallel to the housing.

FLYWHEEL REMOVAL AND INSTALLATION

NOTE: In order to remove the flywheel, the crankshaft will have to be prevented from turning. This may be accomplished on Type 1 models by using a 3 or 4 foot length of angle iron or thick

stock sheet steel, such as an old fence post. **Drill out two holes in the metal bar that correspond to two of the pressure plate retaining bolt holes. The metal bar is installed as per the accompanying illustration.**

Type 1

1. The flywheel is attached to the crankshaft with a gland nut and is located by four dowel pins. An oil seal is recessed in the crankcase casting at No. 1 main bearing. A needle bearing, which supports the main driveshaft, is located in the gland nut. Prior to removing the flywheel, it is necessary to remove the clutch pressure plate and the clutch disc.

2. Loosen the gland nut and remove it, using a 36 mm wrench.

3. Before removing the flywheel, matchmark the flywheel and the crankshaft.

4. Installation is the reverse of removal. Before installing the flywheel, check the flywheel teeth for any wear or damage. Check the dowel pins for correct fit in the crankshaft and in the flywheel.

5. Adjust the crankshaft end-play and check the needle bearing in the gland nut for wear.

Type 2

Removal and installation is similar to the Type 1 except that the flywheel is secured to the crankshaft by five socket head screws.

CRANKSHAFT OIL SEAL (FLYWHEEL END)

Replacement

The seal is removed after removing the flywheel. After the flywheel is removed, inspect the surface on the flywheel joining flange where the seal makes contact. If there is a deep groove or any other damage, the flywheel must be replaced. Remove the oil seal by prying it out of its bore. Before installing a new seal, clean the crankcase oil seal recess and coat it thinly with a sealing compound. Be sure that the seal rests squarely on the bottom of its recess. Make sure that the correct side of the seal is facing outward, that is, the lip of the seal should be facing the inside of the crankcase. Reinstall the flywheel after coating the oil seal contact surface with oil.

NOTE: Be careful not to damage the seal when sliding the flywheel into place.

CRANKSHAFT REMOVAL AND INSTALLATION

NOTE: See the "Engine Rebuilding" section for crankshaft refinishing procedures.

1. Removal of the crankshaft requires splitting the crankcase. See "Crankcase Disassembly."

2. After the crankcase is opened, the

Removing or installing the flywheel on 1600 cc engines using the special bar

crankshaft can then be lifted out.

3. The crankshaft bearings are held in place by dowel pins. These pins must be checked for tightness.

4. When installing the bearings, make sure that the oil holes in the shells are properly aligned. Be sure that the bearing shells are properly aligned. Be sure that the bearing shells are seated properly on their dowel pins. Bearing shells are available in three undersizes. Measure the crankshaft bearing journals to determine the proper bearing size. Place one half of the No. 2 crankshaft bearing in the crankcase. Slide the No. 1 bearing on the crankshaft so that the dowel pin hole is toward the flywheel and the oil groove faces toward the flywheel and the oil groove faces toward the fan. The No. 3 bearing is installed with the dowel pin hole facing toward the crankshaft web.

5. To remove the No. 3 main bearing, remove the distributor gear circlip and the distributor drive gear. Mild heat (176° F) must be applied to remove the gear. Next slide the spacer off the crankshaft.

6. The crankshaft timing gear should now be pressed off the crankshaft after mild heating.

7. When the timing gear is reinstalled, the chamfer must face towards the No. 3 bearing. The No. 3 bearing can then be replaced. When removing and installing the gears on the crankshaft, be careful not to damage the No. 4 bearing journal.

8. When all of the crankshaft bearings are in place, lift the crankshaft and the connecting rod assembly into the crankcase and align the valve timing marks.

9. Install the crankcase half and reassemble the engine.

Connecting Rods

REMOVAL AND INSTALLATION

NOTE: See the ''Engine Rebuilding'' section for additional information.

1. After splitting the crankcase (See ''Crankcase Disassembly''), remove the crankshaft and the connecting rod assembly.

2. Remove the connecting rods, clamping bolts, and the connecting rod caps.

3. Inspect the piston pin bushing. With a new bushing, the correct clearance is indicated by a light finger push fit of the pin at room temperature.

4. Reinsert the new connecting rod bearings after all parts have been thoroughly cleaned.

5. Assemble the connecting rods on the crankshaft, making sure that the rods are oriented properly on the crankshaft. The identification numbers stamped on the connecting rods and connecting rod caps must be on the same side. Note that the marks on the connecting rods are pointing upward, while the rods are pointing toward their

Forge marks on connecting rods must face up

Rapping the connecting rod to relieve pre-tension

Staking the connecting rod bolt

respective cylinders. Lubricate the bearing shells before installing them.

6. Tighten the connecting rod bolts to the specified torque. A slight pre-tension between the bearing halves, which is likely to occur when tightening the connecting rod bolts, can be eliminated by gently striking the side of the bearing cap with a hammer.

7. Do not install the connecting rod in the engine unless it swings freely on its journal.

8. Using a peening chisel, secure the connecting rod bolts in place.

Measuring the connecting rod side clearance

9. Failure to swing freely on the journal may be caused by improper side clearance, improper bearing clearance, or failure to lubricate the rod before assembly.

ENGINE MECHANICAL— DIESEL ENGINES

Engine

REMOVAL AND INSTALLATION

1. Disconnect the negative battery cable.

2. Remove the top of the air cleaner. Remove the lower engine cover.

3. Open the coolant expansion tank. Disconnect the lower hose from the water pump at the connecting pipe to the radiator. Disconnect the center hose from the water pump. Disconnect the hose from the cylinder head and oil cooler and move it out of the way.

4. Remove the vacuum hose from the vacuum pump.

5. Disconnect and tag the wiring from:
   a. Oil pressure switch
   b. Two temperature sensors
   c. Glow plugs

6. Remove the coolant hose.

7. Remove the fuel supply and return lines from the injection pump.

8. Disconnect the accelerator cable from the pump lever and then remove the retaining clip at the bracket and position it to one side.

9. Disconnect the cold start cable at the lockscrew.

10. Disconnect the fuel shut-off solenoid.

11. Remove the coolant reservoir and the oil filler cap and dipstick.

12. Remove the nuts from the rear engine mounts but leave the bolts in place.

13. Remove all (7) engine/transmission mounting bolts.

14. Remove the bolts and remove the support member.

15. Support the engine.

16. Remove the nuts from the front engine mounts and then remove the front and rear engine mount bolts.

17. Lower the engine/transmission assembly until the engine can be separated from the transmission.

18. Support the transmission, remove the engine from the transmission and then lower it from the vehicle.

To install:

1. Installation is in the reverse order of removal, please note the following:

   a. Do not interchange the fuel supply and fuel return pipe union screws. For identification, the return pipe union screw is marked with OUT on the hex. The return line also has a smaller diameter then the supply line.

   b. Adjust the cold start cable and refill the cooling system.

   c. Pertinent tightening torques are:

engine-to-transmission—

   (M10 bolts) 33 ft. lbs.

   (M12 bolts) 58 ft. lbs.

engine mounts—61 ft. lbs.

support member—33 ft. lbs.

fuel line union screws—18 ft. lbs.

Cylinder Head

REMOVAL AND INSTALLATION

The head is retained by Allen bolts. The engine should be cold when the head is removed to avoid chances of warpage. The word TOP or OBEN on the new gasket should face up.

1. Disconnect the battery ground cable.

2. Drain the cooling system.

3. Remove the air cleaner.

4. Disconnect the fuel lines. Disconnect and tag all electrical wires and leads.

5. Separate the exhaust manifold from the pipe. Disconnect the radiator and heater hoses.

6. Remove the timing cover and belt (See "Timing Belt Replacement").

7. Loosen the cylinder head bolts in the reverse order of the tightening sequence.

8. Remove the head. *Do not lay the head on the gasket surface with the injectors installed.* Support it at the ends on strips of wood.

9. Install the cylinder head with a *new* gasket. Be sure the new gasket has the same number of notches and the same identifying number as the old one, unless the pistons were also repeated.

Install bolts 8 and 10 first and torque the bolts to the specification in the proper sequence. After 1000 miles, loosen all bolts ⅓ turn and retorque the bolts.

OVERHAUL

Valve guides are a shrink fit. Always install new valve seals when doing a valve job. Valve seats are not replaceable; the cylinder head should be replaced if the seat width and face angle cannot be maintained.

Refer to general information section under Engine Overhaul.

Intake Manifold

REMOVAL AND INSTALLATION

1. Disconnect the air duct from the throttle valve body. Drain the cooling system.

2. Disconnect the accelerator cable.

3. Remove the injectors and disconnect the line from the cold start valve.

4. Disconnect all coolant hoses.

5. Disconnect all vacuum and emission control hoses (label all hoses for installation).

6. Remove the auxiliary air regulator.

7. Disconnect all electrical lines (label all wires for installation).

8. Disconnect the EGR line from the exhaust manifold.

9. Loosen and remove the retaining bolts and lift off the manifold.

10. Install a new gasket. Install the manifold and tighten the bolts to 18 ft. lbs.

11. Install the remaining components in the reverse order of removal.

Exhaust Manifold

REMOVAL AND INSTALLATION

1. Disconnect the EGR tube from the exhaust manifold.

2. Remove the interfering air pump components if so equipped.

3. Remove the air cleaner hose from the exhaust manifold.

4. Disconnect the intake manifold support.

5. Separate the exhaust pipe from the manifold.

Exploded view of the diesel engine cylinder head

6. Remove the retaining nuts and remove the manifold.

7. Clean the cylinder head and manifold mating surfaces.

8. Install the exhaust manifold using a new gasket.

9. Tighten the nuts to 18 ft./lbs. Work from the inside out.

10. Install the remaining components in the reverse order of removal. Use a new manifold flange gasket.

Timing Belt Cover

REMOVAL AND INSTALLATION

1. Loosen the alternator mounting bolts.

2. Pivot the alternator and slip the drive belt off the sprockets.

3. Unscrew the cover retaining nuts and remove the cover.

4. Reposition the spacers on the studs and then install the washers and nuts.

5. Install the alternator belt and adjust its tension.

Timing Belt

NOTE: The timing belt is designed to last for more than 60,000 miles and does not normally require tension adjustments. If the belt is removed or replaced, the basic valve timing must be checked and the belt retensioned.

REMOVAL AND INSTALLATION

NOTE: This procedure will require a number of special tools and a certain expertise with diesel engines. You may wish to have the work performed by an authorized VW service technician.

1. Remove the timing belt cover. Remove the cylinder head cover.

2. Turn the engine so that No. 1 cylinder is at TDC and fix the camshaft in

Timing belt installation—diesel engine

(Labels: BELT COVER, INJECTION PUMP, TENSIONER, 2.5 MKG (18 FT LB), 4.5 MKG (32 FT LB), DRIVE BELT, 2.5 MKG (18 FT LB), INJECTION PUMP SPROCKET, INTERMEDIATE SHAFT PULLEY, V-BELT PULLEY, 4.5 MKG (32 FT LB), 8.0 MKG (56 FT LB), 2.0 MKG (14 FT LB))

Use the special tool to fix the camshaft in position

position with tool 2065A. Align the tool as follows:

—turn the camshaft until one end of the tool touches the cylinder head

—measure the gap at the other end of the tool with a feeler gauge

—take half of the measurement and insert a feeler gauge of this thickness between the tool and the cylinder head; turn the camshaft so that the tool rests on the feeler gauge

—insert a second feeler gauge of the same thickness between the other end of the tool and the cylinder head.

3. Lock the injection pump sprocket in position with pin 2064.

4. Check that the marks on the sprocket, bracket and pump body are in alignment (engine at TDC).

5. Loosen the timing belt tensioner. Remove the V-belt from the crankshaft.

6. Remove the timing belt.

Lock the injection pump in position with the special pin—diesel engine

To install:

7. Check that the TDC mark on the flywheel is aligned with the reference marks.

8. Loosen the camshaft sprocket bolt ½ turn and then loosen the gear from the camshaft end by tapping it with a rubber mallet.

9. Install the timing belt and remove pin 2064 from the injection pump sprocket.

10. Tension the belt by turning the tensioner to the right. Check the belt tension as detailed later in the section.

11. Tighten the camshaft sprocket bolt to 33 ft. lbs.

12. Remove the tool from the camshaft.

13. Turn the crankshaft two turns in the direction of engine rotation (clockwise) and then strike the belt once with a rubber mallet between the camshaft sprocket and the injection pump sprocket.

14. Check the belt tension again. Check the injection pump timing.

TENSION ADJUSTMENT

NOTE: Special tool VW210 will be required for this procedure.

Tension adjustment on the front timing belt is performed in the same manner as with the other engines. Deflection is also checked in the same position, but with the special tool VW210 rather than your fingers. Proper tension is achieved when the scale reads 12–13.

Timing Sprockets

REMOVAL AND INSTALLATION

The intermediate shaft and crankshaft sprockets are located by keys on their respective shafts and each is retained by a bolt. The camshaft sprocket is a taper–fit and has no key. To remove any or all of the pulleys, first remove the timing belt cover and belt.

NOTE: When removing the crankshaft pulley, don't remove the four Allen head bolts which hold the outer belt pulley to the timing belt sprocket.

1. Remove the center bolt or nut.
2. Gently pry the sprocket off the shaft. If the gear does not come off easily, use a gear puller. Don't hammer on the sprocket.
3. Remove the sprocket and key (if used).
4. Install in the reverse order or removal.
5. Coat the center bolt with Loctite® or similar locking compound, and tighten to 33 ft. lbs. on the top two sprockets and 108 ft. lbs. on the crankshaft sprocket.
6. Install the timing belt, check the valve timing, tension the belt, and install the cover.

Camshaft

REMOVAL AND INSTALLATION

1. Remove the timing belt (refer to proper section for correct details).
2. Remove the camshaft sprocket.
3. Remove the air cleaner.
4. Remove the camshaft cover.
5. Unscrew and remove the No. 1, 3, and 5 bearing caps (No. 1 is at the rear).
6. Unscrew the No. 2 and 4 bearing caps, diagonally and in increments.
7. Lift the camshaft out of the cylinder head.
8. Lubricate the camshaft journals and lobes with assembly lube or gear oil before installing it in the cylinder head.
9. Replace the camshaft oil seal with a new one whenever the cam is removed.
10. Install the No. 1, 3, and 5 bearing caps and tighten the nuts to 14 ft. lbs. Note that the bores are offset, and the numbers are not always on the same side.
11. Install the No. 2 and 4 bearing caps and diagonally tighten the nuts to 14 ft. lbs.

NOTE: If checking end play, install a dial indicator so that the feeler touches the camshaft snout. End-play should be no more than 0.006 in. (0.15 mm).

Piston and Connecting Rods

The pistons must be installed in the block with the arrow at the edge of the crown facing to the rear of the car. The connecting rod and cap alignment casting grooves must face the intermediate shaft. New connecting rod bolts must always be used. The pistons must be heated to 140°F in an oven before the piston pins can be pressed in. Three piston oversizes are available to accommodate overbores up to 0.040 in.

There is a piston size code stamped on the cylinder block above the water pump.

Whenever new pistons or a short block are installed, the piston projection must be checked.

A spacer (VW 385/17) and bar with a micrometer are necessary, and must be set up to measure the maximum amount of piston projection above the deck height. The following chart should be used to select a head gasket of the correct thickness to match piston projection.

Piston Projection (mm)	Gasket Identification No. of Notches	Part Number
0.43–0.63	2	0.68 103 383
0.63–0.82	3	068 103 383C
0.82–0.92	4	068 103 383G
0.92–1.02	5	068 103 383H

ENGINE LUBRICATION— GASOLINE ENGINE

Oil Strainer

REMOVAL AND INSTALLATION

The oil strainer can be easily removed by removing the retaining nuts, washers, oil strainer plate, strainer, and gaskets. The Type 2/1800 and 2/2000 strainer is secured by a single bolt at the center of the strainer. Once taken out, the strainer must be thoroughly cleaned and all traces of oil gaskets removed prior to installing new ones. The suction pipe should be checked for tightness and proper position. When the strainer is installed, be sure that the suction pipe is correctly seated in the strainer. If necessary, the strainer may be bent slightly. The measurement from the strainer flange to the tip of the suction pipe should be 10 mm.

The measurement from the flange to the bottom of the strainer should be 6 mm. The cap nuts on Type 1 engines must not be overtightened. The Type 2/1800 and 2/2000 have a spin-off replaceable oil filter as well as the strainer in the crankcase. The oil filter is located at the left rear corner of the engine.

Oil Cooler

REMOVAL AND INSTALLATION

The Type 1 oil cooler is located under the engine cooling fan housing at the left side of the engine. The Type 2/1800 and 2/2000 coolers are mounted near the oil filter, at the left corner of the engine.

The oil cooler may be removed without taking the engine out of the car. On Type 1 models, the engine fan housing must be removed. The Type 2/1800 and 2/2000 cooler is accessible through the left side engine cowling, working either in the engine compartment or from underneath the car.

The oil cooler can be removed after the three retaining nuts have been taken off. The gaskets should be removed along with the cooler and replaced with new gaskets. If the cooler is leaking, check the oil pressure relief valve. The studs and bracket on the cooler should be checked for tightness.

Oil cooler spacers on suitcase engines

Removing the oil pump housing—Type 1

1. Oil filter cover
2. Oil filter
3. Nut
4. Spring washer
5. Oil filter seal
6. Oil vent
7. Seal
8. Oil dipstick
9. Dipstick
10. Bellows
11. Nut
12. Spring washer
13. Oil filler
14. Gasket
15. Nut
16. Spring washer
17. Oil pump housing
18. Pump housing seal
19. Locknut
20. Spring washer
21. Oil pump cover
22. Pump cover sealing ring
23. Oil pump gear
24. Driveshaft
25. Oil pressure switch
26. Screw
27. Sealing ring
28. Spring
29. Piston for oil relief valve
30. Screw
31. Sealing ring
32. Spring
33. Piston for oil pressure control valve
34. Nut
35. Sealing ring
36. Oil strainer closing cover
37. Seal
38. Oil strainer
39. Closing screw
40. Sealing ring
41. Nut
42. Spring washer
43. Washer
44. Oil cooler
45. Oil cooler sealing ring
46. Oil filter
47. Nut
48. Spring washer
49. Oil filter intermediate flange
50. Seal

Type 2 (gasoline engine) lubrication system

Make certain that the hollow ribs of the cooler do not touch one another. The cooler must not be clogged with dirt. Clean the contact surfaces on the crankcase, install new gaskets, and attach the oil cooler. Types 2/1800 and 2/2000 have a spacer ring between the crankcase and the cooler at each securing screw. If these rings are omitted, the seals may be squeezed too tightly, resulting in oil stoppage and resultant engine damage. Use double retaining nuts and locking compound on the cooler studs.

Oil Pump

REMOVAL AND INSTALLATION

1. On Type 1, the pump can be removed while the engine is in the car, but it is first necessary to remove the cover plate, the crankshaft pulley, and the cover plate under the pulley.

2. On Types 2/1800 and 2/2000 the oil pump can be taken out only after the engine is removed from the car and the air intake housing, the belt pulley fan housing, and fan are dismantled.

3. On the Automatic Stick Shift models, the torque converter oil pump is driven by the engine oil pump.

4. On Type 1, remove the nuts from the oil pump cover and then remove the cover and its gasket. Remove the gears and take out the pump with a special extractor that pulls the body out of the crankcase. Care should be taken so as not to damage the inside of the pump housing.

5. On Type 2/1800 and 2/2000 engines, remove the four pump securing nuts and, prying on either side of the pump, pry the pump assembly out of the crankcase.

6. To disassemble the pump, the pump cover must be pressed apart.

7. Prior to assembly, check the oil pump body for wear, especially the gear seating surface. If the pump body is worn, the result will be loss of oil pressure. Check the driven gear shaft for tightness and, if necessary, peen it tightly into place or replace the pump housing. The gears should be checked for excessive wear, backlash, and end-play. Maximum end-play without a gasket is 1 mm (0.004 in.). The end-play can be checked using a T-square and a feeler gauge. Check the mating surface of the pump body and the crankcase for damage and cleanliness. Install the pump into the crankcase with a new gasket. Do not use any sealing compound.

8. Turn the camshaft several revolutions in order to center the pump body opposite the slot in the camshaft.

Disassembling the Type 2 (gasoline engine) oil pump

Checking oil pump end play

1. Sealing nut
2. Oil pump cover
3. Pump cover gasket
4. Driveshaft
5. Oil pump gear
6. Oil pump housing
7. Housing gasket
8. Plug
9. Seal
10. Spring
11. Relief valve piston
12. Cap nut
13. Seal
14. Oil drain plug
15. Seal
16. Oil strainer cover
17. Gasket
18. Oil strainer
19. Nut
20. Lockwasher
21. Oil cooler seal
22. Oil cooler
23. Oil filler neck cap
24. Breather gland nut
25. Oil filler and breather assembly
26. Seal
27. Grommet
28. Breather rubber valve
29. Dipstick
30. Oil pressure switch

Type 1 lubrication system

ENGINE LUBRICATION— DIESEL ENGINES

The lubrication system is a conventional wet-sump design. The gear-type oil pump is driven by the intermediate shaft. A pressure relief valve limits pressure and prevents extreme pressure from developing in the system. All oil is filtered by a full flow replaceable filter. A bypass valve assures lubrication in the event the filter becomes plugged. The oil pressure switch is located at the end of the cylinder head gallery (the end of the system) to assure accurate pressure readings.

Oil Pan

REMOVAL AND INSTALLATION

1. Drain the oil pan.
2. Support and slightly raise the engine with an overhead hoist.
3. Gradually loosen the engine cross-member mounting bolts. Remove the front and rear side engine mounts.
4. Lower the crossmember very carefully.
5. Loosen and remove the oil pan retaining bolts.
6. Lower the pan from the car.
7. Install the pan using a new gasket and sealer.
8. Tighten the retaining bolts in a crosswise pattern. Tighten hex head bolts to 14 ft. lbs., or Allen head bolts to 7 ft. lbs.
9. Raise the crossmember. Tighten the crossmember bolts to 42 ft. lbs. and the engine mounting bolts to 32 ft. lbs.
10. Refill the engine with oil. Start the engine and check for leaks.

Rear Main Oil Seal

REPLACEMENT

The rear main oil seal is located in a housing on the rear of the cylinder block. To replace the seal, it is necessary to remove the transmission and perform the work from underneath the car or remove the engine and perform the work on an engine stand or work bench. See "Transmission Removal and Installation."

1. Remove the transmission and flywheel.
2. Using a screwdriver, very carefully pry the old seal out of the support ring.
3. Remove the seal.
4. Lightly oil the replacement seal and

9. On Type 1, the cover may now be installed.
10. On Type 2/1800 and 2/2000 models, the pump was installed complete.
11. Tighten the securing nuts.

Oil Pressure Relief Valve

REMOVAL AND INSTALLATION

The oil pressure relief valve is removed by unscrewing the end plug and removing the gasket ring, spring, and plunger. If the plunger sticks in its bore, it can be removed by screwing a 10 mm tap into it.

On 1600 cc engines, the valve is located to the left of the oil pump. On Automatic Stick Shift models, it is located in the oil pump housing. On 1800 and 2000 engines, the valve is located beside the oil filter.

Before installing the valve, check the plunger for any signs of seizure. If necessary, the plunger should be replaced. If there is any doubt about the condition of the spring, it should also be replaced. When installing the relief valve, be careful that you do not scratch the bore. Reinstall the plug with a new gasket.

Type 2/1800 and 2/2000 engines, have a second oil pressure relief valve located just to the right of, and below the oil filter.

then press it into place using a circular piece of flat metal. Be careful not to damage the seal or score the crankshaft.

5. Install the flywheel and transmission. Flywheel-to-engine bolts are tightened to 36 ft. lbs.

Oil Pump

REMOVAL AND INSTALLATION

1. Remove the oil pan.
2. Remove the two mounting bolts.
3. Pull the oil pump down and out of the engine.
4. Unscrew the two bolts and separate the pump halves.
5. Remove the driveshaft and gear from the upper body.
6. Clean the bottom half in solvent. Pry up the metal edges to remove the filter screen for cleaning.

7. Examine the gear and driveshaft for wear or damage. Replace them if necessary.

8. Reassemble the pump halves.

9. Prime the pump with oil and install in the reverse order of removal.

ENGINE COOLING

Fan Housing
REMOVAL AND INSTALLATION

Type 1

1. Remove the two heater hoses and the generator strap.

2. Pull out the lead wire from the coil. Remove the distributor cap and take off the spark plug connectors.

3. Remove the retaining screws that are located on both sides of the fan housing. Remove the rear hood.

4. Remove the outer half of the alternator pulley and remove the fan belt.

5. Remove the thermostat securing screw and take out the thermostat.

6. Remove the lower part of the carburetor pre-heater duct.

7. The fan housing can now be removed with the alternator. After removal, check the fan housing for damage and for loose air deflector plates.

8. Installation is the reverse of the above.

9. Make sure that the thermostat connecting rod is inserted into its hole in the cylinder head. The fan housing should be fitted properly on the cylinder cover plates so that there is no loss of cooling air.

1. Pulley bolt	16. Lockwasher	31. Spring
2. Dished washer	17. Outer fan cover	32. Washer
3. Crankshaft pulley	18. Reinforcement flange	33. Left cooling air regulator
4. Pulley nut	19. Inner fan cover	34. Right cooling air regulator
5. Special washer	20. Lockwasher	35. Cooling air regulator connecting rod
6. Rear pulley half	21. Nut	36. Washer
7. Spacer washer	22. Fan hub	37. Cheese head screw
8. V-belt	23. Shim	38. Lockwasher
9. Front pulley half	24. Fan	39. Washer
10. Woodruff key	25. Lockwasher	40. Connecting rod
11. Generator	26. Special nut	41. Thermostat bracket
12. Nut	27. Cheese head screw	42. Thermostat
13. Strap	28. Washer	43. Lockwasher
14. Bolt	29. Cheese head screw	44. Bolt
15. Bolt	30. Return spring	

Type 1 cooling system

1. Cover plate insert	19. Screw	37. Washer
2. Socket head capscrew	20. Spring washer	38. Nut
3. Spring washer	21. Alternator cover plate	39. Screw
4. Nut	22. Alternator	40. Spring washer
5. Belt	23. Alternator sealing ring	41. Shaft retaining spring
6. Socket head capscrew	24. Alternator elbow	42. Right flap and shaft
7. Spring washer	25. Nut	43. Bearing
8. Flat washer	26. Spring washer	44. Flap link
9. Cap	27. Fan housing—rear half	45. Left flap
10. Crankshaft pulley	28. Fan housing—front half	46. Plug
11. Fan	29. Bolt	47. Bolt
12. Nut	30. Spring washer	48. Cooling air control cable roller
13. Spring nut	31. Screw	49. Sealing washer
14. Socket head capscrew	32. Spring washer	50. Cooling air control cable
15. Spacer	33. Air non-return flap	51. Bolt
16. Bolt	34. Inspection hole cover	52. Washer
17. Spring washer	35. Plug	53. Thermostat washer
18. Nut	36. Bolt	54. Thermostat
		55. Thermostat bracket

Type 2 (gasoline engine) cooling system

Fan

REMOVAL AND INSTALLATION

Type 1

1. Remove the alternator and fan assembly as described in the "Alternator Removal and Installation" section.
2. While holding the fan, unscrew the fan retaining nut and take off the fan, spacer washers, and the hub.
3. To install, place the hub on the alternator shaft, making sure that the woodruff key is securely positioned.
4. Insert the spacer washers. The clearance between the fan and the fan cover is 0.06–0.07 in. Place the fan into position and tighten its retaining nut. Correct the spacing by inserting the proper number of spacer washers. Place any extra washers between the lockwasher and the fan.
5. Reinstall the alternator and the fan assembly.

Fan Housing and Fan

REMOVAL AND INSTALLATION

Type 2/1800 and 2/2000

1. Pry out the alternator cover insert, and, using a 12 point Allen wrench, loosen the alternator adjusting bolt. Remove the alternator drive belt, the ignition timing scale and the grille over the fan. Remove the three socket head screws attaching the fan and crankshaft assembly to the crankshaft and remove the fan and pulley.
2. Disconnect the cooling air control cable at the flap control shaft.
3. On models so equipped, pull out the rubber elbow for the alternator from the front half of the fan housing.
4. Remove the four nuts retaining the fan housing to the engine crankcase. The assembled fan housing may then be removed by pulling it to the rear and off the engine. It is not necessary to separate the fan housing halves or remove the alternator to remove the fan housing.
5. Reverse the above procedure to install.

Air Flap and Thermostat

ADJUSTMENT

Type 1

1. Loosen the thermostat bracket securing nut and disconnect the thermostat from the bracket.
2. Push the thermostat upwards to fully open the air flaps.

Type 2 (gasoline engine) air flap cable control

Engine cooling air thermostat

3. Reposition the thermostat bracket so that the thermostat contacts the bracket at the upper stop, and then tighten the bracket nut.
4. Reconnect the thermostat to the bracket.

Type 2/1800 and 2/2000

1. Loosen the cable control.
2. Push the air flaps completely closed.
3. Tighten the cable control.

ENGINE COOLING— DIESEL ENGINES

The cooling system consists of a belt driven, external water pump, thermostat, radiator, and thermostatically controlled electric cooling fan. When the engine is cold the thermostat is closed and blocks the water from the radiator so the coolant is circulated only through the engine. When the engine warms up, the thermostat opens and the radiator is included in the coolant circuit. The thermostatic switch is in the bottom of the radiator and turns the electrical fan on at 199°F, off at 186°F. This reduces power loss and engine noise.

Radiator and Fan

REMOVAL AND INSTALLATION

1. Drain the cooling system.
2. Remove the inner shroud mounting bolts.
3. Disconnect the lower radiator hose.
4. Disconnect the thermostatic switch lead.
5. Remove the lower radiator shroud.
6. Remove the lower radiator mounting units.
7. Disconnect the upper radiator hose.
8. Detach the upper radiator shroud.
9. Remove the side mounting bolts and lift the radiator and fan out as an assembly.
10. Installation is the reverse of removal.

Thermostat

REMOVAL AND INSTALLATION

The thermostat is located in the bottom radiator hose neck on the water pump.
1. Drain the cooling system.
2. Remove the two retaining bolts from the lower water pump neck.

NOTE: It isn't necessary to disconnect the hose.

3. Move the neck, with the hoses attached, out of the way.
4. Remove the thermostat.
5. Install a new seal on the water pump neck.
6. Install the thermostat with the spring end up.
7. Replace the water pump neck and tighten the two retaining bolts.

Water Pump

REMOVAL AND INSTALLATION

1. Drain the cooling system.
2. Remove the alternator and drive belt.
3. Remove the timing belt cover.
4. Disconnect the lower radiator hose, engine hose, and heater hose from the water pump.
5. Remove the pump retaining bolts. Notice where the different length bolts are located.
6. Turn the pump slightly and lift it out of the engine block.
7. Installation is the reverse of removal. Use a new seal on the mating surface with the engine. Check O-ring condition and replace if necessary.

EMISSION CONTROLS

Crankcase Ventilation System

All models are equipped with a crankcase ventilation system. The purpose of the crankcase ventilation system is two-fold. It keeps harmful vapors from escaping into the atmosphere and prevents the buildup of crankcase pressure. Prior to the 1960s, most cars employed a vented oil filler cap and road draft tube to dispose of crankcase vapor. The crankcase ventilation systems now in use are improvements over the old method and, when functioning properly, will not reduce engine efficiency.

Type 1 and 2 crankcase vapors are recirculated from the oil breather through a rubber hose to the air cleaner. The vapors then join the air/fuel mixture and are burned in the engine. Fuel injected cars mix crankcase vapors into the air/fuel mixture to be burned in the combustion chambers. Fresh air is forced through the engine to evacuate vapors and recirculate them into the oil breather, intake air distributor, and then to be burned.

The only maintenance required on the crankcase ventilation system is a periodic check. At every tune-up, examine the hoses for clogging or deterioration. Clean or replace the hoses as required.

Crankcase ventilation system—Type 1

Crankcase ventilation system—Type 2

Typical evaporative emission control system

Evaporative Emission Control System

Required by law since 1971, this system prevents raw fuel vapors from entering the atmosphere. The various systems for different models are similar. They consist of an expansion chamber, activated charcoal filter, and connecting lines. Fuel vapors are vented to the charcoal filter where hydrocarbons are deposited on the element. The engine fan forces fresh air into the filter when the engine is running. The air purges the filter and the hydrocarbons are forced into the air cleaner to become part of the air/fuel mixture and burned.

Maintenance of this system consists of checking the condition of the various connecting lines and the charcoal filter at 10,000 mile intervals. The charcoal filter, which is located under the engine compartment, should be replaced at 48,000 mile intervals.

Exhaust Gas Recirculation System

In order to control exhaust emissions of oxides of nitrogen (NO_x), an exhaust gas recirculation (EGR) system is employed on all and later Type 2 models, and on all 1974 and later Type 1 models. The system lowers peak flame temperature during combustion by introducing a small (about 10%) percentage of relatively inert exhaust gas into the intake charge. Since the exhaust gas contains little or no oxygen, it cannot react with nor influence the air/fuel mixture. However, the exhaust gas does (by volume) take up space in the combustion chambers (space that would otherwise be occupied by a heat-producing, explosive air/fuel mixture), and does serve to lower peak combustion chamber temperature. The amount of exhaust gas directed to the combustion chambers is infinitely variable by means of a vacuum operated EGR valve. For system specifics, see the vehicle type breakdown under "General Description."

GENERAL DESCRIPTION

Type 1

EGR is installed on all 1976 and later models. All applications use the element type filter and single stage EGR valve. Recirculations occurs during part throttle applications as before. The system is controlled by a throttle valve switch which measures throttle position, and an intake air sensor which reacts to engine vacuum. Beginning in 1976, an odometer actuated EGR reminder light (on the dashboard) is used to inform the driver that it is time to service the EGR system. The reminder light measures elapsed mileage and lights at 15,000 mile intervals. A reset button is located behind the switch.

NOTE: On 1977 and later Calif. models, the EGR valve is operated mechanically by a rod attached to the throttle valve lever.

Type 2

All 1975 and later Type 2 models utilize an EGR system. A single stage EGR valve and element type filter are used on all applications. Recirculation occurs during part throttle openings, and is controlled by throttle position, engine vacuum, and engine compartment temperature. When the ambient temperature exceeds 54° F, a sensor switch (located above the battery) opens, permitting EGR during part throttle applications. At 15,000 mile intervals, a dash mounted EGR service reminder light is activated to warn the driver that EGR service is now due. A reset button is located behind the switch.

EGR VALVE CHECKING

Type 1 and 2 (except 1977 and later Type 1 Calif. cars)

1. With the engine idling, pull the plug off the EGR valve's vacuum unit. The engine should slow down noticeably or stall, indicating that the EGR gases are being recirculated.

Testing the EGR valve; arrow indicates the location of the plug on the vacuum unit

Temperature switch
checking: opens at temperature
above 12°C (54° F)

EGR valve
vacuum controlled)

Charcoal filter

Throttle valve switch

Type 2 EGR system

2. If there is no change when the plug is pulled, stop the engine. Turn the ignition key to the running (2) position without starting the engine.

3. Connect a test lamp as shown in the illustration. Now operate the throttle valve by hand, moving the throttle valve shaft from the idle position into the mid-speed range.

4. If the test light goes off when the throttle is moved off the idle position and lights at idle and at or near full throttle, the EGR valve is faulty and should be replaced.

1977 and Later Type 1 Calif. Cars

1. Remove the E-clip that holds the operating rod to the EGR valve.

2. With the engine idling, hand open the EGR valve.

3. The engine should slow down or stall, indicating that the exhaust gases are being recirculated. If not, the EGR valve or the EGR pipe is clogged and will require replacement or cleaning.

Catalytic Converter System

All 1976 Type 1 and 2 models sold in Cal-

1977 and later Type 1 Calif. EGR linkage; arrow indicates hex-with-pin that is turned to adjust the valve

ifornia and all 1977 and later models are equipped with a catalytic converter. The converter is installed in the exhaust system, upstream and adjacent to the muffler.

Catalytic converters change noxious emissions of hydrocarbons (HC) and carbon monoxide (CO) into harmless carbon dioxide and water vapor. The reaction takes

place inside the converter at great heat using platinum and palladium metals as the catalyst. If the engine is operated on lead-free fuel, they are designed to last 50,000 miles before replacement.

Starting in 1980, all Type 2 models made for Calif. utilize a three-way catalytic converter. The three-way converter not only reduces HC and CO emissions but it can also reduce oxides of nitrogen (NO).

However, the three-way converter can only achieve this reduction of harmful pollutants with the aid of the Lambda Control System. This system is designed to maintain close control of the air/fuel mixture under all operating conditions.

Lambda Control System

All 1980–83 Type 2 models made for use in Calif. are equipped with the Lambda Control System. Basically, the Lambda Control System is an oxygen sensor which is installed in the exhaust manifold. This oxygen sensor makes it possible to maintain the precise air/fuel mixture required by the three-way catalytic converter. The oxygen sensor continuously senses the oxygen content of the exhaust and signals the information to an electronic control unit. The control unit corrects the fuel injector operating time, so that the engine always receives an accurately metered air/fuel mixture.

The oxygen sensor system is monitored by an indicator light in the instrument panel which will light up every 30,000 miles. This is your signal to take the car to a service facility and get the Lambda Control System checked out.

Deceleration Control

All Type 2 models, as well as those Type 1 models equipped with manual transmission, are equipped with deceleration control to prevent an overly rich fuel mixture from reaching the exhaust. During deceleration, a vacuum valve (manual transmission) or electrical transmission switch (automatic transmission) opens, bypassing the closed throttle plate and allowing air to enter the combustion chambers.

FUEL SYSTEM

Electric Fuel Pump

All gasoline engine models have an electric pump. The fuel pump is located near the front axle.

REMOVAL AND INSTALLATION

1. Disconnect the fuel pump wiring. Pull the plug from the pump but do not pull on the wiring.
2. Disconnect the fuel hoses and plug them to prevent any leakage.
3. Remove the two nuts which secure the pump and then remove the pump.
4. Reconnect the fuel pump hoses and wiring and install the pump on the vehicle.

ADJUSTMENTS

Electric fuel pump pressure is 28 psi. Fuel pump pressure is determined by a pressure regulator which diverts part of the fuel pump output to the gas tank when 28 psi is reached. The regulator, located on the engine firewall, has a screw and locknut on its end. Loosen the locknut and adjust the screw to adjust the pressure. Do not force the screw in or out if it does not turn.

Fuel Injection— Gasoline Engines

All gasoline engined models, are equipped with an improved system known as the Air Flow Controlled Electronic Fuel Injection System. With this system, some of the electronic sensors and wiring are eliminated, and the control box is smaller. Fuel is metered according to intake air flow.

Type 2 fuel pump location (1) and filter (2)

Fuel pressure regulator with locknut and adjusting screw at left end

Exploded view of the Type 2 airflow controlled electronic fuel injection system

1. Intake air distributor (right side) assembly
2. Stud
3. Stud
4. Stud
5. Throttle valve housing assembly
6. Stud
7. Washer
8. Spring washer
9. Nut
10. Gasket
11. Gasket
12. Spring washer
13. Nut
14. Intake air distributor (left side) assembly
15. Stud
16. Spring washer
17. Bypass air screw
18. Connecting hose
19. Bypass air screw
20. Washer
21. Gasket
22. Intake manifold
23. Gasket
24. Spring washer
25. Nut
26. Connecting hose
27. Tee
28. Bellcrank assembly
29. Spring washer
30. Nut
31. Spring washer
32. Nut
33. Connecting rod
34. Pin
35. Circlip
36. Spring
37. Tee
38. Auxiliary air regulator
39. Spring washer
40. Screw
41. Hose
42. Throttle valve switch
43. Spring washer
44. Screw
45. Cold start valve
46. Spring washer
47. Screw
48.-52. Hoses
53. Pipe
54. Flat connector plug (two prong)
55. Boot
56. Boot
57. Flat connector plug (five prong)

Exploded view of the Type 1 airflow controlled electronic fuel injection system

1. Intake manifolds with injector seats
2. Injector inner locating sealing bushings
3. Sleeves
4. Injector plate
5. Injector outer locating bushings
6. Electromagnetic fuel injector
7. Hose connection with clamp
8. Injector retainer
9. Lock washer
10. Nut

Paired fuel injectors

1. Intake manifold
2. Intake manifold gasket
3. Lock washer
5. Inner sealing bushing
6. Outer sealing bushing
7. Retainer
8. Lock washer
9. Nut
10. Fuel injector
11. Hose connection with clamp

Individually mounted fuel injectors

Cold start valve location

The system consists of the following components;

Intake air sensor—measures intake air volume and temperature and sends voltage signals to the control unit (brain box). It also controls the electric fuel pump by shutting it off when intake air stops. It is located between the air cleaner and the intake air distributor.

Ignition contact breaker points—these are the regular points inside the distributor. When the points open, all four injectors are triggered. The points also send engine speed signals to the control unit. No separate triggering contacts are used.

Throttle valve switch—provides only for full load enrichment. This switch is not adjustable.

Temperature sensor I—senses intake temperature as before. It is now located in the intake air sensor.

Temperature sensor II—senses cylinder head temperature as before.

Control unit (brain box)—contains only 80 components compared to the old system's 300.

Pressure regulator—is connected by a vacuum hose to the intake air distributor and is no longer adjustable. It adjusts fuel pressure according to manifold vacuum.

Auxiliary air regulator—provides more air during cold warmup.

NOTE: For all fuel injection system service and repair procedures not detailed below, please refer to ''Fuel Injection'' in the Unit Repair section.

FUEL INJECTORS

There are two types of injectors. One type is secured in place by a ring that holds a single injector. The second type of injector is secured to the intake manifold in pairs by a common bracket.

Removal and Installation

SINGLE INJECTORS

1. Remove the nut which secures the injector bracket to the manifold.

2. If the injector is not going to be replaced, do not disconnect the fuel line. Disconnect the injector wiring.

3. Gently slide the injector bracket up the injector and pull the injector from the intake manifold. Be careful not to damage the inner and outer rubber sealing rings. These sealing rings are used to seal the injector to the manifold and must be replaced if they show any sign of deterioration.

4. Installation is the reverse of removal. Be careful not to damage the injector tip or contaminate the injector with dirt.

PAIRED INJECTORS

1. Disconnect the injector wiring.

2. Remove the two nuts which secure the injector bracket to the manifold. Slide the bracket up the injector. Do not disconnect the fuel lines if the injector is not going to be replaced.

3. Gently slide the pair of injectors out of their bores along with the rubber sealing rings, injector plate, and the inner and outer injector locating bushings. It may be necessary to remove the inner bushings from the intake manifold after the injectors are removed since they sometimes lodge within the manifold.

NOTE: There are two sleeves that fit over the injector bracket studs. Be careful not lose them.

4. Upon installation, place the injector bracket, the outer bushings, the injector plate, and the inner locating bushings on the pair of injectors in that order.

5. Gently slip the injector assembly into the manifold and install the bracket nuts. Be careful not to damage the injector tips or contaminate the injectors with dirt.

6. Reconnect the injector wiring.

THROTTLE VALVE SWITCH

Removal and Installation

1. Remove the air filter.

2. The switch is located on the throttle valve housing. Disconnect the throttle valve return spring.

3. Remove the throttle valve assembly but do not disconnect the bowden wire for the throttle valve or the connecting hoses to the ignition distributor.

4. Remove the throttle valve, switch securing screws and remove the switch.

5. Reverse the above steps to install. It will be necessary to adjust the switch after installation.

COLD START VALVE

Removal and Installation

The cold start valve is located near the thermo-switch and is secured to the air intake distributor by two screws. This valve sometimes jams open and causes excessive consumption, rough idle, and low power output.

FUEL PRESSURE REGULATOR

Removal and Installation

Disconnect the hoses from the regulator and remove the regulator from its bracket. The fuel pump pressure is adjustable; however, lack of fuel pressure is usually due to other defects in the system and the regulator should be adjusted only as a last resort.

Diesel Fuel Injection

The diesel fuel system is an extremely complex and sensitive system. Very few repairs or adjustments are possible by the owner. Any service other than that listed here should be referred to an authorized VW dealer or diesel specialist. The injection pump itself is not repairable; it can only be replaced.

Any work done to the diesel fuel injection should be done with absolute cleanliness. Even the smallest specks of dirt will have a disastrous effect on the injection system.

Do not attempt to remove the fuel injectors. They are very delicate and must be removed with a special tool to prevent damage. The fuel in the system is also under tremendous pressure (1700–1850 psi), so it's not wise to loosen any lines with the engine running. Exposing your skin to the spray from the injector at working pressure can cause fuel to penetrate the skin.

CHECKING INJECTION PUMP TIMING

Checking the injection pump timing also involves checking the valve timing. To alter the injection pump timing, the camshaft gear must be removed and repositioned. This also changes the valve timing. Special tool (VW 210) is necessary to properly tension the injection pump drive belt on the diesel engine.

1. Set the engine at TDC on No. 1 cylinder. In this position, the TDC mark on the flywheel should be aligned with boss on the bell housing and both valves of No. 1 cylinder should be closed.

2. The marks on the pump and mounting plate should also be aligned.

3. If the valve timing is incorrect, set the valve timing as detailed in the engine section.

ACCELERATOR CABLE ADJUSTMENT

The ball pin on the pump lever should be pointing up and be aligned with the mark in the slot. The accelerator cable should be attached at the upper hole in the bracket. With the pedal in the full throttle position, adjust the cable so that the pump lever contacts the stop with no binding or strain.

COLD START CABLE ADJUSTMENT

When the cold start knob on the dash is pulled out, the fuel injection pump timing is advanced 2.5°. This improves cold starting and running until the engine warms up.

1. Insert the washer on the cable.

2. Insert the cable in the bracket with the rubber housing. Install the cable in the pin.

3. Install the lockwasher.

4. Move the lever to the zero position (direction of arrow). Pull the inner cable tight and tighten the clamp screw.

CLUTCH

The clutch used in all models is a single dry disc mounted on the flywheel with a diaphragm spring type pressure plate. The release bearing is the ball bearing type and does not require lubrication. On Types 1 and 2 the clutch is engaged mechanically via a cable which attaches to the clutch pedal. The Vanagon, although a Type 2, utilizes a hydraulically engaged clutch. It features a clutch pedal operated master cylinder and a bell housing mounted slave cylinder.

REMOVAL AND INSTALLATION

Manual Transmission

1. Remove the engine.

4. Clutch pedal pad	37. Clutch cross shaft
5. Clutch pedal	40. Bushing—operating shaft
6. Clutch pedal shaft	41. Clutch operating lever
7. Bushings for pedal cluster	45. Clutch release bearing
12. Clutch cable	50. Clutch
13. Clutch cable sleeve	52. Pressure plate
16. Angle plate for clutch cable	54. Clutch release plate
35. Clutch return spring	56. Clutch disc

Type 1 clutch components

2. Remove the pressure plate securing bolts one turn at a time until all spring pressure is released.

3. Remove the bolts and remove the clutch assembly.

NOTE: Notice which side of the clutch disc faces the flywheel and install the new disc in the same direction.

4. Before installing the new clutch, check the condition of the flywheel. It should not have excessive heat cracks and the friction surface should not be scored or warped. Check the condition of the throw out bearing. If the bearing is worn, replace it.

5. Lubricate the pilot bearing in the end of the crankshaft with grease.

6. Insert a pilot shaft, used for centering the clutch disc, through the clutch disc and place the disc against the flywheel. The pilot shaft will hold the disc in place.

7. Place the pressure plate over the disc and loosely install the bolts.

NOTE: Make sure the correct side of the clutch disc is facing outward. The disc will rub the flywheel if it is incorrectly positioned.

8. After making sure that the pressure plate aligning dowels will fit into the pressure plate, gradually tighten the bolts.

9. Remove the pilot shaft and reinstall the engine.

10. Adjust the clutch pedal free-play.

11. Bleed the clutch (Vanagon only).

Automatic Stick Shift

1. Disconnect the negative battery cable.

2. Remove the engine.

3. Remove the transaxle.

4. Remove the torque converter by sliding it off the input shaft. Seal off the hub opening.

5. Mount the transaxle in a repair stand or on a suitable bench.

6. Loosen the clamp screw and pull off clutch operating lever. Remove the transmission cover.

7. Remove the hex nuts between the clutch housing and the transmission case.

NOTE: Two nuts are located inside the differential housing.

8. The oil need not be drained if the clutch is removed with the cover opening up and the gearshift housing breather blocked.

9. Pull the transmission from the clutch housing studs.

10. Turn the clutch lever shaft to disengage the release bearing.

11. Remove both lower engine mounting bolts.

12. Loosen the clutch retaining bolts gradually and alternately to prevent distortion. Remove the bolts, pressure plate, clutch plate, and release bearing.

13. Do not wash the release bearing. Wipe it dry only.

14. Check the clutch plate, pressure plate, and release bearing for wear and damage. Check the clutch carrier plate, needle bearing, and seat for wear. Replace the necessary parts.

15. If the clutch is wet with ATF, replace the clutch carrier plate seal and the clutch disc. If the clutch is wet with transmission oil, replace the transmission case seal and clutch disc.

16. Coat the release bearing guide on the transmission case neck and both lugs on the release bearing with grease. Insert the bearing into the clutch.

17. Grease the carrier plate needle bearing. Install the clutch disc and pressure plate using a pilot shaft to center the disc on the flywheel.

18. Tighten the pressure plate retaining bolts evenly and alternately. Make sure that the release bearing is correctly located in the diaphragm spring.

19. Insert the lower engine mounting bolts from the front. Replace the sealing rings if necessary. Some units have aluminum sealing rings and cap nuts.

20. Push the transmission onto the converter housing studs. Insert the clutch lever shaft behind the release bearing lugs. Push the release bearing onto the transmission case neck. Tighten the bolts which hold the clutch housing to the transmission case.

21. Install the clutch operating lever.

22. It is necessary to adjust the basic clutch setting. The clutch operating lever should contact the clutch housing. Tighten the lever clamp screw slightly.

23. First adjust dimension (a) to 0.335 in. Adjust dimension (b) to 3.03 in. Finally adjust dimension (c) to 1.6 in. by repositioning the clutch lever on the clutch shaft. Tighten the lever clamp screw.

24. Push the torque converter onto the support tube. Insert it into the turbine shaft by turning the converter.

25. Check the clutch play after installing the transaxle and engine.

CLUTCH CABLE ADJUSTMENT

Manual Transmission—Types 1 and 2

1. Check the clutch pedal travel by measuring the distance the pedal travels to-

1. Torque converter	8. Spring washer	15. Diaphragm clutch pressure plate
2. One-way clutch support	9. Socket head screw	16. Spring washer
3. Gasket	10. Seal	17. Socket head screw
4. Circlip for carrier plate	11. Clutch carrier plate	18. Release bearing
5. Ball bearing	12. Needle bearing	19. Seal/converter
6. O-ring for stud	13. Seal/carrier plate	20. O-ring/one-way clutch support
7. Converter housing	14. Clutch plate	

Automatic Stick Shift clutch assembly

ward the floor until pressure is exerted against the clutch. The distance is 3/8 to 3/4 in.

2. To adjust the clutch, jack up the rear of the car and support it on jackstands.

3. Remove the left rear wheel.

4. Adjust the cable tension by turning the wing nut on the end of the clutch cable. Turning the wing nut counterclockwise decreases pedal free-play, turning it clockwise increases free-play.

5. When the adjustment is completed, the wings of the wing nut must be horizontal so that the lugs on the nut engage the recesses in the clutch lever.

6. Push on the clutch pedal several times and check the pedal free-play.

7. Install the wheel and lower the car.

Automatic Stick Shift—Type 1

The adjustment is made on the linkage between the clutch arm and the vacuum servo unit. To check the clutch play:

1. Disconnect the servo vacuum hose.

2. Measure the clearance between the upper edge of the servo unit mounting bracket and the lower edge of the adjusting turnbuckle. If the clearance (e) is 0.16 in. or more, the clutch needs adjustment.

3. Reconnect the vacuum hose.

To adjust the clutch:

1. Disconnect the servo vacuum hose.

2. Loosen the turnbuckle locknut and back it off completely to the lever arm. Then turn the servo turnbuckle against the locknut. Now back off the turnbuckle 5–5½ turns. The distance between the locknut and the turnbuckle should be 0.25 in.

Wing nut for clutch cable adjustment

3. Tighten the locknut against the adjusting sleeve.

4. Reconnect the vacuum hose and road test the vehicle. The clutch is properly adjusted when Reverse gear can be engaged silently and the clutch does not slip on acceleration. If the clutch arm contacts the clutch housing, there is no more adjustment possible and the clutch plate must be replaced.

The speed of engagement of the Automatic Stick Shift clutch is regulated by the vacuum operated valve rather than by the driver's foot. The adjusting screw is on top of the valve under a small protective cap. Adjust the valve as follows:

1. Remove the cap.

2. To slow the engagement, turn the adjusting screw ¼–½ turn clockwise. To speed engagement, turn the screw counterclockwise.

3. Replace the cap.

4. Test operation by shifting from Second to First at 44 mph without depressing the accelerator. The shift should take exactly one second to occur.

CLUTCH CABLE REPLACEMENT

Types 1 and 2

1. Jack up the car and remove the left rear wheel.

2. Disconnect the cable from the clutch operating lever.

3. Remove the rubber boot from the end of the guide tube and off the end of the cable.

4. On Type 1, unbolt the pedal cluster and remove it from the car. It will also be necessary to disconnect the brake master cylinder push rod and throttle cable from the pedal cluster. On Type 2, remove the cover under the pedal cluster, then remove the pin from the clevis on the end of the clutch cable.

5. Pull the cable out of its guide tube from the pedal cluster end.

6. Installation is the reverse of the above.

NOTE: Grease the cable before installing it and readjust the clutch pedal freeplay.

Checking the clutch adjustment on the Automatic Stick Shift

Adjusting the Automatic Stick Shift clutch; (d) is 0.25 in., measured between the locknut and the turnbuckle

Adjusting screw for speed of engagement

Automatic Stick Shift basic clutch adjusting dimensions

For smooth clutch action, dimension B should be 1.0-1.7 in. Adjust the cable to provide slight sag at point B by installing spacer washers at point A.

Components of the Vanagon hydraulic clutch system

Adjusting the clutch pedal free play on the Vanagon

Adjusting the clutch pedal stop screw on the Vanagon

Clutch Master Cylinder

REMOVAL AND INSTALLATION
Vanagon

1. Siphon the hydraulic fluid from the master cylinder (clutch) reservoir.
2. Pull back the carpeting from the pedal area and lay down some absorbent rags.
3. Pull the elbow connection from the top of the master cylinder.
4. Disconnect and plug the pressure line from the rear of the master cylinder.
5. Remove the master cylinder mounting bolts and remove the cylinder to the rear.
6. Reverse the above procedure to install, taking care to bleed the system and adjust pedal free-play.

Clutch Slave Cylinder

REMOVAL AND INSTALLATION
Vanagon

1. Locate the slave cylinder on the bell housing.

2. Disconnect and plug the pressure line from the slave cylinder.
3. Disconnect the return spring from the pushrod.
4. Remove the retaining circlip from the boot and remove the boot.
5. Remove the circlip and slide the slave cylinder rearwards from its mount.
6. Remove the spring clip from the mount.
7. Reverse the above procedure to install, taking care to bleed the system and adjust pedal free-play.

CLUTCH SYSTEM BLEEDING AND ADJUSTMENT
Vanagon

Whenever air enters the clutch hydraulic system due to leakage, or if any part of the system is removed for service, the system must be bled. The hydraulic system uses high quality brake fluid meeting SAE J1703 or DOT3 or DOT4 specifications. Brake fluid is highly corrosive to plant finishes and care should be exercised that no spillage occurs. The procedure is as follows:

1. Top up the clutch fluid reservoir and make sure the cap vent is open.
2. Locate the slave cylinder bleed nipple and remove all dirt and grease from the valve. Attach a hose to the nipple and submerge the other end of the hose in a jar containing a few inches of clean brake fluid.
3. Find a friend to operate the clutch pedal. When your friend depresses the clutch pedal slowly to the floor, open the bleeder valve about one turn. Have your friend keep the pedal on the floor until you close the bleeder valve. Repeat this operation several times until no air bubbles are emitted from the tube.

NOTE: Keep a close check on the fluid level in the fluid reservoir. Never let the level fall below the ½ full mark.

4. After bleeding discard the old fluid and top up the reservoir.
5. The clutch pedal should have a free-play of 0.20–0.28 in., and a 7 in. total travel. If either of the above are not to specifications, adjust the master cylinder as follows.
6. Loosen the master cylinder pushrod locknut and shorten the pushrod length slightly.
7. Loosen the master cylinder bolts and push the cylinder as far forward as it will

go. Retighten the bolts.

8. Remove the rubber cap from the clutch pedal stop screw and adjust distance to 0.89 in. Install the rubber cap.

9. Then lengthen the pushrod as necessary to obtain a pedal free-play of 0.20–0.28 in. Tighten the pushrod locknut.

10. Road-test the car.

TRANSAXLE

Manual Transaxle

REMOVAL AND INSTALLATION

1. Disconnect the negative battery cable.

2. Remove the engine.

3. Remove the socket head screws which secure the driveshafts to the transmission. Remove the bolts from the transmission end first and then remove the shafts.

NOTE: It is not necessary to remove the driveshafts entirely from the car if the car does not have to be moved while the transaxle is out.

4. Disconnect the clutch cable from the clutch lever and remove the clutch cable and its guide tube from the transaxle. Loosen the square head bolt at the shift linkage coupling located near the rear of the transaxle. Slide the coupling off the inner shaft lever. There is an access plate under the rear seat to reach the coupling on Type 1. It is necessary to work under the car to reach the coupling on Type 2 models.

5. Disconnect the starter wiring.

6. Disconnect the back-up light switch wiring.

7. Remove the front transaxle mounting bolts.

8. Support the transaxle with a jack and remove the transaxle from the car.

10. To install, jack the transaxle into position and loosely install the bolts.

11. Tighten the transmission carrier bolts first, then tighten the front mounting nuts.

12. Install the driveshaft bolts with new

Transaxle front mounting bolts

a. Socket head screws
b. Lock washer
c. Spacer
d. Protective cap

Drive axle bolt and washer positioning

lockwashers. The lockwashers should be positioned on the bolt with the convex side toward the screw head.

13. Reconnect the wiring, the clutch cable, and the shift linkage.

NOTE: It may be necessary to align the transmission so that the driveshaft joints do not rub the frame.

14. Install the engine.

Automatic Stick Shift Transaxle

REMOVAL AND INSTALLATION

1. Disconnect the negative battery cable.

2. Remove the engine.

3. Make a bracket to hold the torque converter in place. If a bracket is not used, the converter will slide off the transmission input shaft.

4. Detach the gearshaft rod coupling.

5. Disconnect the driveshafts at the transmission end. If the driveshafts are not going to be repaired, it is not necessary to detach the wheel end.

6. Disconnect the ATF hoses from the transmission. Seal the open ends. Disconnect the temperature switch, neutral safety switch, and the back-up light switch.

7. Pull off the vacuum servo hose.

8. Disconnect the starter wiring.

9. Remove the front transaxle mounting nuts.

10. Loosen the rear transaxle mounting bolts. Support the transaxle and remove the bolts.

11. Lower the axle and remove it from the car.

12. With the torque converter bracket still in place, raise the axle into the car.

13. Tighten the nuts for the front transmission mounting. Insert the rear mounting bolts but do not tighten them at this time.

14. Replace the vacuum servo hose.

15. Connect the ATF hoses, using new washers. The washers are seals.

16. Connect the temperature switch and starter cables.

17. Install the driveshafts, using new washers. Turn the convex sides of the washers toward the screw head.

18. Align the transaxle so that the inner driveshaft joints do not rub on the frame fork and then tighten the rear mounting bolts.

19. Insert the shift rod coupling, tighten the screw, and secure it with wire.

20. Remove the torque converter bracket, and install the engine.

21. After installing the engine, bleed the ATF lines if return flow has not started after 2–3 minutes.

SHIFT LINKAGE ADJUSTMENT

1. The Volkswagen shift linkage is not adjustable. When shifting becomes difficult or there is an excessive amount of play in the linkage, check the shifting mechanism for worn parts. Make sure the shift linkage coupling is tightly connected to the inner shaft lever located at the rear of the transaxle under the rear seat. Worn parts may be found in the shift lever mechanism and the supports for the linkage rod sometimes wear out.

Shift linkage coupling

2. The gear shift lever can be removed after the front floor mat has been lifted.

3. After the two retaining screws have been removed from the gear shift lever ball housing, the gear shift lever, ball housing, rubber boot, and spring are removed as a unit.

— **CAUTION** —
Carefully mark the position of the stop plate and note the position of the turned up ramp at the side of the stop plate. Normally the ramp is turned up and on the right hand side of the hole.

4. Installation is the reverse of removal.

5. Lubricate all moving parts with grease.

6. Test the gear shift pattern. If there is difficulty in shifting, adjust the stop plate back and forth in its slotted holes.

Driveshaft and Constant Velocity U-Joint

REMOVAL AND INSTALLATION

1. Remove the bolts which secure the joints at each end of the shaft, tilt the shaft down, and remove the shaft.

2. Loosen the clamps which secure the rubber boot to the axle and slide the boot back on the axle.

3. Drive the stamped steel cover off the joint with a drift.

NOTE: After the cover is removed, do not tilt the ball hub as the balls will fall out of the hub.

4. Remove the circlip from the end of the axle and press the axle out of the joint.

5. Reverse the above steps to install. The position of the dished washer is dependent on the type of transmission. On automatic transmissions, it is placed between the ball hub and the circlip. On manual transmissions, it is placed between the ball hub and the shoulder on the shaft. Be sure to pack the joint with grease.

NOTE: The chamfer on the splined inside diameter of the ball hub faces the shoulder on the driveshaft.

AUTOMATIC TRANSMISSION

REMOVAL AND INSTALLATION

NOTE: The engine and transmission must be removed as an assembly on the Type 2/1800 and 2/2000.

1. Remove the battery ground cable.

2. On the sedan, remove the cooling air intake duct with the heating fan and hoses. Remove the cooling air intake connection and bellows, then detach the hoses to the air cleaner.

3. On the station wagons, remove the warm air hoses and air cleaner. Remove the boot between the dipstick tube and the body and the boot between the oil filler neck and the body. Disconnect the cooling air bellows at the body.

4. Disconnect the wires at the regulator and the alternator wires at the snap connector located by the regulator. Disconnect the auxiliary air regulator and the oil pressure switch at the snap connectors located by the distributor.

5. Disconnect the accelerator cable.

6. Disconnect the right fuel return line.

Engine carrier bolts positioned at the top of their elongated holes

a. 5.095 in.
b. 0.472 in.
c. 0.590 in.
d. 0.393, 0.433, and 0.472 in.

Buffer alignment gauge

7. Raise the car.

8. Disconnect the hoses from the heat exchangers.

9. Disconnect the starter wires and push the engine wiring harness through the engine cover plate.

10. Disconnect the fuel supply line and plug it.

11. Remove the heater booster exhaust pipe.

12. Remove the rear axles and cover the ends to protect them from dirt.

13. Remove the selector cable by unscrewing the cable sleeve.

14. Remove the wire from the kickdown switch.

15. Remove the bolts from the rubber transmission mountings, taking careful note of the position, number, and thickness of the spacers that are present.

— CAUTION —

These spacers must be reinstalled exactly as they were removed. Do not detach the transmission carrier from the body.

Measuring procedure for centering the buffer

16. Support the engine and transmission assembly in such a way that it may be lowered and moved rearward at the same time.

17. Remove the engine carrier bolts and the engine and transmission assembly from the car.

18. Matchmark the flywheel and the torque converter and remove the three attaching bolts.

19. Remove the engine-to-transmission bolts and separate the engine and transmission.

— CAUTION —

Exercise care when separating the engine and transmission as the torque converter will easily slip off the input shaft if the transmission is tilted downward.

20. Installation is as follows. Install and tighten the engine-to-transmission bolts after aligning the match marks on the flywheel and converter.

21. Making sure the matchmarks are aligned, install the converter-to-flywheel bolts.

22. Make sure the rubber buffer is in place and the two securing studs do not project more than 0.7 in. from the transmission case.

23. Tie a cord to the slot in the engine compartment seal. This will make positioning the seal easier.

24. Lift the assembly far enough to allow the accelerator cable to be pushed through the front engine cover.

25. Continue lifting the assembly into place. Slide the rubber buffer into the locating tube in the rear axle carrier.

26. Insert the engine carrier bolts and raise the engine until the bolts are at the top of their elongated slots. Tighten the bolts.

NOTE: A set of three gauges must be obtained to check the alignment of the rubber buffer in its locating tube. The dimensions are given in the illustration as is the measuring technique. The rubber buffer is centered horizontally where the 11 mm gauge can be inserted on both sides. The buffer is located vertically when

Checking the position of the engine carrier

the 10 mm gauge can be inserted on the bottom side and the 12 mm gauge can be inserted on the top side. See Steps 27 and 28 for adjustment.

27. Install the rubber transmission mount bolts with spacers of the correct thickness. The purpose of the spacers is to center the rubber buffer vertically in its support tube. The buffer is not supposed to carry any weight; it absorbs torsional forces only.

28. To locate the buffer horizontally in its locating tube, the engine carrier must be vertical and parallel to the fan housing. It is adjusted by moving the engine carrier bolts in elongated slots. Further travel may be obtained by moving the brackets attached to the body. It may be necessary to adjust the two rear suspension wishbones with the center of the transmission after the rubber buffer is horizontally centered. Take the car to a dealer or alignment specialist to align the rear suspension.

29. Adjust the selector lever cable.

30. Connect the wire to the kickdown switch.

31. Install the rear axles. Make sure the lockwashers are placed with the convex side out.

32. Reconnect the fuel hoses and heat exchanger hoses. Install the pipe for the heater booster.

33. Lower the car and pull the engine compartment seal into place with the cord.

34. Reconnect the fuel injection and engine wiring. Push the starter wires through the engine cover plate and connect the wires to the starter.

35. Install the intake duct with the fan and hoses, also the cooling air intake.

PAN REMOVAL AND INSTALLATION

1. Some models have a drain plug in the pan. Remove the plug and drain the transmission. On models without the plug, loosen the pan bolts 2–3 turns and lower one corner of the pan to drain.

2. Remove the pan bolts and remove the pan from the transmission.

NOTE: It may be necessary to tap the pan with a rubber hammer to loosen it.

3. Use a new gasket and install the pan. Tighten the bolts loosely until the pan is properly in place, then tighten the bolts fully, moving in a diagonal pattern.

NOTE: Do not overtighten the bolts.

4. Refill the transmission with ATF.

5. At 5 minute intervals, retighten the pan bolts two or three times.

FILTER SERVICE

The Volkswagen automatic transmission has a filter screen secured by a screw to the bottom of the valve body. Remove the pan and remove the filter screen from the valve body.

CAUTION

Never use a cloth that will leave the slightest bit of lint in the transmission when cleaning transmission parts. The lint will expand when exposed to transmission fluid and clog the valve body and filter.

Clean the filter screen with compressed air.

FRONT (SECOND) BAND ADJUSTMENT

Tighten the front band adjusting screw to 7 ft. lbs. Then loosen the screw and tighten it to 3.5 ft. lbs. From this position, loosen the screw exactly 1¾ to 2 turns and tighten the locknut.

REAR (FIRST) BAND ADJUSTMENT

Tighten the rear band adjusting screw to 7 ft. lbs. Then loosen the screw and retighten it to 3.5 ft. lbs. From this position, loosen the screw exactly 3¼ to 3½ turns and tighten the locknut.

SHIFT LINKAGE ADJUSTMENT

Make sure the shifting cable is not kinked or bent and that the linkage and cable are properly lubricated.

Front band assembly adjustment screw at top

1. Move the gear shift lever to the Park position.

2. Loosen the clamp which holds the front and rear halves of the shifting rod together. Loosen the clamping bolts on the transmission lever.

3. Press the lever on the transmission rearward as far as possible. Spring pressure will be felt. The manual valve must be on the stop in the valve body.

4. Holding the transmission lever against its stop, tighten the clamping bolt.

5. Holding the rear shifting rod half, push the front half forward to take up any clearance and tighten the clamp bolt.

6. Test the shift pattern.

Rear band assembly adjustment screw at top

REAR SUSPENSION

Diagonal Arm Suspension—Types 1 and 2 (Except Vanagon)

DIAGONAL ARM REMOVAL AND INSTALLATION

1. Remove the wheel shaft nuts.

CAUTION

Do not raise the car to remove the nuts. They can be safely removed only if the weight on the car is on its wheels.

---

2. Disconnect the driveshaft of the side to be removed.

3. Remove the lower shock absorber mount. Raise the car and remove the wheel and tire.

Matchmark the torsion bar and diagonal arm with a cold chisel

Proper positioning of the diagonal arm pivot bolt with both spacer washers on the outside

4. Remove the brake drum, disconnect the brake lines and emergency brake cable, and remove the backing plate.

5. Matchmark the torsion bar plate and the diagonal arm with a cold chisel.

6. Remove the four bolts and nuts which secure the plate to the diagonal arm.

7. Remove the pivot bolts for the diagonal arm and remove the arm from the car.

NOTE: Take careful note of the washers at the pivot bolts. These washers are used to determine alignment and they must be put back in the same place.

1. Frame or sub-frame
2. Diagonal arm (complete)
3. Double spring plate
4. Torsion bar
5. Rubber bushing, inner left
6. Rubber bushing, outer
7. Cover for spring plate hub
8. Bolt
9. Lock washer
10. Fitted bolt
11. Spacer
12. Bolt
13. Washer
14. Lock washer
15. Bolt
16. Nut
17. Shock absorber
18. Rubber stop
19. Bolt
20. Bolt
21. Lock washer
22. Nut

Diagonal arm rear suspension—Type 1 and 2 (except Vanagon)

8. Remove the spring plate hub cover.

9. Using a steel bar, lift the spring plate off the lower suspension stop.

10. On Type 1, remove the five bolts at the front of the fender. On all others, remove the cover in the side of the fender.

11. Remove the spring plate and pull the torsion bar out of its housing.

NOTE: There are left and right torsion bars designated by an (L) or (R) on the end face. (Coat any rubber bushings with talcum powder upon installation. Do not use graphite, silicon, or grease.

12. To install, insert the torsion bar, outer bushing, and spring plate. The torsion bar is properly adjusted when the spring plate, with no load, is the specified number of degrees below a horizontal position.

13. Using two bolts, loosely secure the spring plate hub cover. Place a thick nut between the leaves of the spring plate.

14. Lift the spring plate up to the lower suspension stop and install the remaining bolts into the hub cover. Tighten the hub cover bolts.

15. Install the diagonal arm pivot bolt and washers and peen it with a chisel. There must always be at least one washer on the outside end of the bolt.

16. Align the chisel marks and attach the diagonal arm to the spring plate.

17. Install the backing plate, parking brake cable, and brake lines.

18. Reconnect the shock absorber. Install the brake drum and wheel shaft nuts.

19. Reconnect the drive shaft. Bleed the brakes.

20. Install the wheel and tire.

21. Check the suspension alignment.

Exploded view of the Vanagon rear suspension

Trailing Arm Suspension—Vanagon

TRAILING ARM REMOVAL AND INSTALLATION

1. Raise the rear of the car and support it with jack stands.

2. Remove the wheel and then disconnect the brake line from the wheel cylinder.

3. Unbolt the driveshaft at the transaxle side.

4. Unscrew the four wheel hub mounting bolts and remove it along with the driveshaft.

NOTE: Removal of the brake drum may provide better access to the wheel hub mounting bolts.

5. Place a floor jack under the trailing arm to hold its position and then remove the upper and lower shock absorber retaining bolts and remove the shock absorber.

6. Lower the trailing arm until you can remove the coil spring. Note the positioning of the upper spring plate and the lower spring seat.

7. Unscrew the two trailing arm mounting bolts and then remove the trailing arm.

8. Installation is in the reverse order of removal. When installing the coil spring, be sure that the contours for the end of the spring in the seat and the trailing arm are aligned. Also, turn the spring plate so that the end of the spring fits into the depression on the plate.

9. Adjust the camber and toe.

Shock Absorber

REMOVAL AND INSTALLATION
Diagonal Arm Suspension

The shock absorber is secured at the top and bottom by a through bolt. Raise the car and remove the bolts. Remove the shock absorber from the car.

Trailing Arm Suspension

Procedures for removing the shock absorbers are detailed in the "Trailing Arm Removal and Installation" section.

Coil Spring

REMOVAL AND INSTALLATION

Vanagon Only

Procedures for removing the coil spring are detailed in the "Trailing Arm Removal and Installation" section.

REAR SUSPENSION ADJUSTMENTS

Type 1, Diagonal Arm Suspension

The only adjustment is the toe-in adjustment. The adjustment is performed by varying the number of washers at the diagonal arm pivot. There must always be one washer located on the outboard side of the pivot.

Type 2, Diagonal Arm Suspension

The transmission and engine assembly position in the vehicle is adjustable. It is necessary that the assembly be correctly centered before the suspension is aligned. It may be adjusted by moving the engine and transmission brackets in their elongated slots.

The distance between the diagonal arms may be adjusted by moving the washers at the A-arm pivots. The washers may be positioned only two ways. Either both washers on the outboard side of the pivot or a single washer on each side of the pivot. To adjust the distance, position the diagonal arms and move the washers in the same manner at both pivots.

The wheel track angle may be adjusted by moving the diagonal arm flange in the elongated slot in the spring plate.

The toe-in may be adjusted by positioning the washers and the diagonal arm pivot.

Type 2—Trailing Arm Suspension

On vehicles with the trailing arm suspension, it is possible to adjust the camber and the toe. To adjust the toe, loosen the INSIDE mounting bolt on the trailing arm and slide it forward or backward in the horizontal slot until the proper toe is achieved. To adjust the camber, loosen the OUTSIDE mounting bolt on the trailing arm and slide it up or down until the proper camber is achieved. Being careful not to move the bolts, tighten them both to 65 ft. lbs. after adjustment.

FRONT SUSPENSION

Torsion Bar Suspension—Types 1 and 2 (Except Super Beetle and Beetle Convertible)

TORSION BAR REMOVAL AND INSTALLATION

1. Jack up the car and remove both wheels and brake drums.
2. Remove the ball joint nuts and remove the left and right steering knuckles. A forked ball joint removing tool is available at an auto parts store.

—————— CAUTION ——————
Never strike the ball joint stud.

3. Remove those arms attached to the torsion bars on one side only. To remove the arms, loosen and remove the arm setscrew and pull the arm off the end of the torsion bar.

Align the square notch in the ball joint with the notch in the torsion bar upon installation

A notched ball joint on a car with a torsion bar suspension indicates that it is oversized

4. Loosen and remove the setscrew which secures the torsion bar to the torsion bar housing.
5. Pull the torsion bar out of its housing.
6. To install, carefully note the number of leaves and the position of the countersink marks for the torsion bar and the torsion arm.
7. Align the countersink mark in the center of the bar with the hole for the setscrew and insert the torsion bar into its housing. Install the torsion arm.
8. Reverse Steps 1–3 to complete.

TORSION ARM REMOVAL AND INSTALLATION

1. Jack up the car and remove the wheel and tire.
2. Remove the brake drum and the steering knuckle.
3. If the lower torsion arm is being removed, disconnect the stabilizer bar. To remove the stabilizer bar clamp, tap the wedge shaped keeper toward the outside of the car or in the direction the narrow end of the keeper is pointing.
4. On Type 1 and 2, back off on the setscrew locknut and remove the setscrew.
5. Slide the torsion arm off the end of the torsion bar.
6. Reverse the above steps to install. Check the camber and toe-in settings.

Strut Suspension— Type 1 Super Beetle, Beetle Convertible

SUSPENSION STRUT REMOVAL AND INSTALLATION

NOTE: For all strut overhaul procedures, please refer to "Strut Overall" in the Unit Repair section.

1. Jack up the car and remove the wheel and tire.

2. If the left strut is to be removed, remove the speedometer cable from the steering knuckle.
3. Disconnect the brake line from the bracket on the strut.
4. At the base of the strut, bend down the locking tabs for the three bolts and remove the bolts.
5. Push down on the steering knuckle and pull the strut out of the knuckle.
6. Remove the three nuts which secure the top of the strut to the body. Before removing the last nut, support the strut so that it does not fall out of the car.
7. Reverse the above steps to install the strut. Always use new nuts and locking tabs during installation.

TRACK CONTROL ARM REMOVAL AND INSTALLATION

1. Remove the ball joint stud nut and remove the stud from the control arm.
2. Disconnect the stabilizer bar from the control arm.
3. Remove the nut and eccentric bolt at the frame. This is the pivot bolt for the control arm and is used to adjust camber.
4. Pull the arm downward and remove it from the vehicle.
5. Reverse the above steps to install. Make sure the groove in the stabilizer bar bushing is horizontal.
6. Realign the front end.

Coil Spring Suspension—Vanagon

The front suspension consists of upper and lower control arms, a separate upper coil spring/shock absorber mount, steering knuckle and attaching ball joints and a strut arm mounted on the lower control arm for stability.

STRUT REMOVAL AND INSTALLATION

NOTE: For all strut overhaul procedures, please refer to "Strut Overhaul" in the Unit Repair section.

1. Nut
2. Spring washer
3. Washer
4. Bolt
5. Nut
6. Spring washer
7. Bolt
8. Support for axle
9. Bolt
10. Spring washer
11. Plate
12. Rubber packing, upper
13. Rubber packing, lower
14. Bolt
15. Spring washer
16. Lock washer
17. Dust cap
18. Clamp nut for wheel bearing
19. Socket hd. screw for clamp nut
20. Thrust washer
21. Outer tapered roller bearing
22. Brake drum
23. Oil seal
24. Inner tapered roller bearing
25. Bolt
26. Spring washer
27. Front wheel brake and backing plate
28. Steering knuckle
29. Retainer, small
30. Retainer, large
31. Clip, small
32. Clip, large
33. Plate, small
34. Plate, large
35. Rubber mounting, small
36. Rubber mounting, large
37. Stabilizer bar
38. Self-locking nut
39. Washer, small
40. Washer, large
41. Eccentric bushing for camber adjustment
42. Upper ball joint
43. Lower ball joint
44. Ring for rubber boot
45. Boot for lower joint
46. Boot for upper joint
47. Ring for rubber boot
48. Plug
49. Locknut
50. Setscrew for torsion bar
51. Torsion arm, upper
52. Torsion arm, lower
53. Pin
54. Pin for shock absorber
55. Nut
56. Lock washer
57. Lock washer
58. Nut
59. Plate for damper bushing
60. Damper bushing
61. Pin for buffer
62. Buffer
63. Tube
64. Shock absorber
65. Sleeve for rubber bushing
66. Rubber bushing
67. Torsion bar—10 leaf
68. Seal for upper torsion arm
69. Seal for lower torsion arm
70. Needle bearing, upper
71. Needle bearing, lower
72. Grease fitting
74. Axle
75. Bolt

Types 1 and 2 torsion bar front suspension

1. Lockplate
2. Bolt
3. Caliper
4. Hub cap
5. Wheel bearing locknut
6. Allen screw for locknut
7. Thrust washer
8. Outer taper roller bearing
9. Brake disc
10. Inner taper roller bearing
11. Oil seal
12. Bolt
13. Spring washer
14. Splash shield for disc
15. Nut
16. Spring washer
17. Washer

18. Bolt
19. Clamp for stabilizer bar
20. Nut
21. Spring washer
22. Stabilizer mounting for control arm
23. Rubber bushing for clamp
24. Stabilizer bar
25. Self-locking nut
26. Self-locking nut
27. Washer
28. Self-locking nut
29. Washer, small
30. Suspension strut bearing
31. Sealing plate
32. Spacer ring
33. Spring plate

34. Rubber stop for shock absorber
35. Retaining ring for protective tube
36. Protective tube for shock absorber
37. Coil spring
38. Damping ring, coil spring
39. Shock absorber
40. Bolt
41. Lock washer
42. Steering knuckle
43. Ball joint
44. Bolt
45. Lock washer
46. Bolt
47. Lock washer

48. Seat for damping ring
49. Damping ring for front axle carrier
50. Spacer sleeve
51. Bolt
52. Spring washer
53. Plate for damping ring
54. Damping ring for radius rod
55. Locating ring for radius rod
56. Nut
57. Spring washer
58. Bolt
59. Bushing for track control arm
60. Track control arm
61. Front axle carrier

Strut type front suspension—Type 1 Super Beetle and Beetle Convertible

1. Jack up the front of the vehicle and remove the front wheel.

2. Loosen and remove the single retaining nut at the top of the coil spring/shock absorber upper mount.

3. Remove the through bolt which retains the bottom of the shock absorber to the lower control arm and pull the shock absorber out through the bottom of the lower control arm.

4. Reverse the procedure to install.

UPPER CONTROL ARM REMOVAL AND INSTALLATION

1. Jack up the vehicle and remove the front wheel.

2. Place a jack under the lower control arm and raise to put a slight load on the coil spring.

3. Free the upper ball joint from the steering knuckle.

4. Remove the upper control arm to frame mounting bolt and remove the control arm.

5. Reverse procedure to install. Check and adjust wheel alignment.

LOWER CONTROL ARM REMOVAL AND INSTALLATION

1. Jack up the vehicle and remove the wheel.

2. Remove the coil spring.

3. Remove the lower control arm to frame mounting bolt and remove the control arm.

4. Reverse procedure to install.

Shock Absorber

REMOVAL AND INSTALLATION

Torsion Bar Suspension (Types 1 and 2)

1. Remove the wheel and tire.

2. Remove the nut from the torsion arm

stud and slide the lower end of the shock off the stud.

3. Remove the nut from the shock absorber shaft at the upper mounting and remove the shock from the vehicle.

4. The shock is tested by operating it by hand. As the shock is extended and compressed, it should operate smoothly over its entire stroke with an even pressure. Its damping action should be clearly felt at the end of each stroke. If the shock is leaking slightly, the shock need not be replaced. A shock that has had an excessive loss of fluid will have flat spots in the stroke as the shock is compressed and extended. That is, the pressure will feel as through it has been suddenly released for a short distance during the stroke.

5. Installation is the reverse of Steps 1–3.

Ball Joint

REMOVAL AND INSTALLATION

Vehicles with strut suspension have only one ball joint on each side located at the base of the strut in the track control arm. Vehicles with torsion bar suspension have two ball joints on each side located at the end of each torsion arm.

Vehicles with coil spring suspension have two ball joints on each side located at the ends of the upper and lower control arms.

Torsion Bar Suspension

1. Jack up the car and remove the wheel and tire.

2. Remove the brake drum and disconnect the brake line from the backing plate.

3. Remove the nut from each ball joint stud and remove the ball joint stud from the steering knuckle. Remove the steering knuckle from the car. A ball joint removal tool is available at an auto parts store. Do not strike the ball joint stud.

4. Remove the torsion arm from the torsion bar.

5. Remove the ball joint from the torsion arm by pressing it out.

6. Press a new ball joint in, making sure that the square notch in the joint is in line with the notch in the torsion arm eye.

NOTE: Ball joints are supplied in different sizes designated by V-notches in the ring around the side of the joint. When replacing a ball joint, make sure that the new part has the same number of V-notches. If it has no notches, the replacement joint should have no notches.

7. Reverse Steps 1–4 to complete the installation.

Strut Suspension

1. Jack up the car and remove the wheel and tire.

Exploded view of the Vanagon front suspension

2. Remove the nut from the ball joint stud and remove the stud from the track control arm.

3. Bend back the locking tab and remove the three ball joint securing screws.

4. Pull the track control arm downward and remove the ball joint from the strut.

5. Reverse the above steps to install.

Coil Spring Suspension

UPPER BALL JOINT

1. Raise the vehicle and support it on jack stands, then remove the wheel.

2. Place a jack under the lower control arm as close to the steering knuckle as possible and jack up just enough to put a slight load on the coil spring.

3. Loosen the steering knuckle-to-ball joint nut but do not remove completely.

4. Free the ball joint from the steering knuckle using a ball joint removal tool. Then remove the nut.

5. Remove the two upper ball joint to upper control arm bolts and remove the ball joint.

6. Reverse procedure to install. Check wheel alignment.

LOWER BALL JOINT

1. Jack up the front of the vehicle and support it on stands, then remove the wheel.

2. Place a jack under the lower control arm as close to steering knuckle as possible and put a slight load on the coil spring by jacking up the jack.

3. Disconnect the brake caliper hose form the caliper, and remove the brake caliper and rotor if they are in the way.

4. Loosen the upper ball joint to steering knuckle to ball joint nut, but do not remove it. Free the upper ball joint from the steering knuckle and remove the nut.

5. Remove the lower ball joint to lower control arm nut and free the ball joint from the control arm using a ball joint removal tool. Remove the steering knuckle.

6. Press the ball joint off the steering knuckle.

7. Press a new ball joint in place on knuckle, observing any alignment marks on the ball joint and the knuckle.

8. Reverse the procedure to install. Bleed the brakes.

INSPECTION

Torsion Bar Suspension

1. A quick initial inspection can be made with the vehicle on the ground.

2. Grasp the top of the tire and vigorously pull the top of the tire in and out. Test both sides in this manner.

3. If the ball joints are excessively worn, there will be an audible tap as the ball moves around in its socket. Excess play can sometimes be felt through the tire.

4. A more rigorous test may be performed by jacking the car under the lower torsion arm and inserting a lever under the tire.

5. Lift up gently on the lever so as to pry the tire upward.

6. If the ball joints are worn, the tire will move upward 1/8–1/4 in. or more.

7. If the tire displays excessive movement, have an assistant inspect each joint, as the tire is pried upward, to determine which ball joint is defective.

Strut Suspension

1. Raise the car and support it under the frame. The wheel must be clear of the ground.

2. With a lever, apply upward pressure to the track control arm.

3. Apply the pressure gently and slowly; it is important that only enough pressure be exerted to check the play in the ball joint and not compress the suspension.

4. Using a vernier caliper, measure the distance between the control arm and the lower edge of the ball joint flange. Record the reading.

5. Release the pressure on the track control arm and again measure the distance between the control arm and the lower edge of the ball joint flange.

6. Record the reading.

7. Subtract the higher reading from the lower reading. If the difference is more than 0.10 in., the ball joint should be replaced.

NOTE: Remember that even in a new joint there will be measureable play because the ball in the ball joint is spring loaded.

Front End Alignment

CASTER ADJUSTMENT

Caster is the forward or backward tilt of the spindle. Forward tilt is negative caster and backward tilt is positive caster. Caster is not adjustable on either the torsion bar or the strut suspensions.

Caster on the coil spring suspension is adjusted by moving the strut bar. Loosen the locknut and then turn the adjusting nut clockwise to increase the caster and counterclockwise to decrease the caster.

CAMBER ADJUSTMENT

Camber is the tilt of the top of the wheel, inward or outward, from true vertical. Outward tilt is positive, inward tilt is negative.

Torsion Bar Suspension

The upper ball joint on each side is mounted in an eccentric bushing. The bushing has a hex head and it may be rotated in either direction using a wrench.

Strut Suspension

The track control arm pivots on an eccentric bolt. Camber is adjusted by loosening the nut and rotating the bolt.

Coil Spring Suspension

The upper control arm pivots on an eccentric bolt. To adjust the camber, loosen the retaining nut and rotate the bolt.

TOE-IN ADJUSTMENT

Toe-in is the adjustment made to make the front wheels point slightly into the front. Toe-in is adjusted on all types of front suspensions by adjusting the length of the tie rod sleeves.

STEERING

Steering Wheel

REMOVAL AND INSTALLATION

1. Disconnect the negative battery cable.

2. Remove the center emblem. This emblem will gently pry off the wheel, or is attached by screws from the back of the steering wheel.

3. Remove the nut from the steering shaft. This is a right-hand thread.

NOTE: Mark the steering shaft and steering wheel so that the wheel may be installed in the same position on the shaft.

4. Using a steering wheel puller, remove the wheel from the splined steering shaft. Do not strike the end of the steering shaft.

Correct gap (a) between the steering wheel and column

5. Reverse the above steps to install. Make sure to align the matchmarks made on the steering wheel and steering shaft. The gap between the turn signal switch housing and the back of the wheel is 0.08–0.12 in. (0.08–0.159 for Vanagon). Install the switch with the lever on the central position.

Turn Signal Switch

REMOVAL AND INSTALLATION

1. Disconnect the negative battery cable.

2. Remove the steering wheel.

3. Remove the four turn signal switch securing screws.

4. Disconnect the turn signal switch wiring plug under the steering column.

5. Pull the switch and wiring guide rail up and out of the steering column.

6. Reverse the above steps to install. Make sure the spacers located behind the switch, if installed originally, are in position. The distance between the steering wheel and the steering column housing is 0.08-0.12 in. (0.08-0.159 for Vanagon). Install the switch with the lever on the central position.

Turn signal switch retaining screws

Ignition Switch

REMOVAL AND INSTALLATION

Type 1 and 2 (Except Vanagon)

Disconnect the steering column wiring at the block located behind the instrument panel and pull the column wiring harness into the passenger compartment.

1. Remove the steering wheel.

2. Remove the circlip on the steering shaft.

3. Insert the key and turn the switch to the ON position.

4. Remove the three securing screws and slide the switch assembly from the steering column tube.

5. After removing the wiring retainer, press the ignition switch wiring block upward and out of the housing and disconnect the wiring.

6. Remove the lock cylinder and the steering lock mechanism.

7. Remove the ignition switch screw and pull the ignition switch rearward.

8. Reverse the above steps to install. When reinstalling the turn signal switch, make sure the lever is in the center position.

Vanagon

1. Disconnect the negative battery terminal.

2. Remove the steering wheel.

3. Loosen the mounting screws and then remove the upper and lower steering column trim.

4. Unscrew the four retaining bolts and then pull off the steering column switch.

5. Loosen the steering lock housing clamp bolt and pull the assembly up and out slightly.

6. Disconnect the wiring and remove the steering lock housing.

7. Unscrew the ignition switch screw and pull out the switch.

8. Installation is in the reverse order of removal.

Ignition Lock Cylinder

REMOVAL AND INSTALLATION

1. Remove the ignition switch.

Access hole for depressing lock cylinder retaining pin

2. With the key in the cylinder and turned to the ON position, pull the lock cylinder out far enough so the securing pin can be depressed through a hole in the side of the lock cylinder housing.

3. As the pin is depressed, gently push the cylinder into its housing. Make sure the pin engages correctly and that the retainer fits easily in place. Do not force any parts together; when they are correctly aligned, they will fit easily together.

Steering Linkage

REMOVAL AND INSTALLATION

1. All tie-ends are secured by a nut which holds the tapered tie rod end stud into a matching tapered hole. There are several ways to remove the tapered stud from its hole after the nut has been removed.

2. First, there are several types of removal tools available from auto parts stores. These tools include directions for their use. One of the most commonly available tool is the fork shaped tool which is a wedge that is forced under the tie rod end. This tool should be used with caution because instead of removing the tie rod end from its hole it may pull the ball out of its socket, ruining the tie rod end.

3. It is also possible to remove the tie rod end by holding a heavy hammer on one side of the tapered hole and striking the opposite side of the hole sharply with another hammer. The stud will pop out of its hole, usually.

————— CAUTION —————
Never strike the end of the tie rod end stud. It is impossible to remove the tie rod end in this manner.

4. Once the tie rod end stud has been removed, turn the tie rod end out of the adjustment sleeve.

5. On the pieces of the steering linkage that are not used to adjust the toe-in, the tie rod end is welded in place and it will be necessary to replace the whole assembly.

6. When reassembling the steering linkage, never put lubricant in the tapered hole.

1. Trim upper	5. Shear bolt	11. Spring
2. Spacer sleeve	6. Retaining clip	12. Boot retainer
3. Ring	7. Plastic ring	13. Gasket
3a. Upper column	8. Column bracket	14. Clip
4. Column tube	9. Ball bearing	15. Boot
	10. Spreader ring	16. Lower column
		17. Flange
		18. Trim lower
		19. Steering lock housing
		20. Steering column switch
		21. Screw
		22. Cap

Exploded view of the Vanagon steering column assembly

MANUAL STEERING GEAR ADJUSTMENT

There are two types of steering gear boxes. The first type is the roller type, identified by the square housing cover secured by four screws, one at each corner. The second type is the rack and pinion type used on 1976 Super Beetles, Beetle Convertibles and the Vanagon.

Worm and Roller Type—Type 1 and 2

Disconnect the steering linkage from the pitman arm and make sure the gearbox mounting bolts are tight. Have an assistant rotate the steering wheel so that the pitman arm move alternately 10° to the left and then 10° to the right of the straight ahead position. Turn the adjusting screw in until no further play can be felt while moving the pitman arm. Tighten the adjusting screw locknut and recheck the adjustment.

Rack and Pinion Type—1976 Type 1 Super Beetle and Convertible

The steering gear requires adjustment if it begins to rattle noticeably. First, remove the access cover in the spare tire well. Then, with the car standing on all four wheels, turn the adjusting screw in by hand until it contacts the thrust washer. While holding the screws in this position, tighten the locknut.

The adjustment is correct when there is no binding and the steering self-centers properly.

Rack and Pinion Type—Vanagon

The steering gear on the Vanagon is not adjustable. If problems develop, the gear must be replaced.

BRAKES

NOTE: For all brake system repair and service procedures not detailed below, please refer to "Brakes" in the Unit Repair section.

Brake Adjustment

Disc brakes are self adjusting and cannot be adjusted by hand. As the pads wear, they will automatically compensate for the wear by moving closer to the disc, maintaining the proper operating clearance.

Drum brakes, however, must be manually adjusted to take up excess clearance as the shoes wear.

1. To adjust drum brakes, both front and rear, it is necessary to jack up the car and support it on a jack stand. The wheel

Adjusting drum brakes through the access hole in the backing plate; rear brakes shown

must spin freely.

2. On the backing plate there are four inspection holes with a rubber plug in each hole. Two of the holes are for checking the thickness of the brake lining and the other two are used for adjustment.

NOTE: There is an adjustment for each brake shoe. That means that on each wheel it is necessary to make two adjustments, one for each shoe on that wheel.

3. Remove the adjustment hole plugs and, using a screwdriver or brake adjusting tool, insert the tool into the hole.

4. Turn the star wheel until a slight drag is noticed as the wheel is rotated by hand.

5. Back off on the star wheel 3–4 notches so that the wheel turns freely.

6. Perform the same adjustment on the other shoe.

NOTE: One of the star wheels in each wheel has left-hand threads and the other star wheel has right-hand threads.

7. Repeat the above procedure on each wheel with drum brakes.

Master Cylinder

NOTE: The master cylinder fluid reservoirs on Volkswagens are found in a number of different places. The reservoirs on all Type 1 models can be found in the front luggage compartment. On Type 2 models (except the Vanagon), the reservoir is located underneath the driver's seat, while on the Vanagon, it is underneath the raised portion of the instrument panel.

With the exception of the Vanagon, all Type 2 models, in addition to the refill reservoir mentioned above, also have a twin-chamber reservoir attached directly to the master cylinder.

REMOVAL AND INSTALLATION

Type 1 and 2 (except Vanagon)

1. Drain the brake fluid from the master cylinder reservoir.

— **CAUTION** —
Do not get any brake fluid on the paint, as it will dissolve the paint.

2. Pull the plastic elbows out of the rubber sealing rings on the top of the master cylinder.

3. Remove the two bolts which secure the master cylinder to the frame and remove the cylinder. Note the spacers on the Type 1 between the frame and the master cylinder.

4. To install, bolt the master cylinder to the frame. Do not forget the spacers on the Type 1.

5. Lubricate the elbows with brake fluid and insert them into the rubber seals.

6. If necessary, adjust the brake pedal free travel. On Type 1, adjust the length of the master cylinder pushrod so that there is 5–7 mm of brake pedal free-play before the pushrod contacts the master cylinder piston. On Type 2, the free-play is properly adjusted when the length of the pushrod, measured between the ball end and the center of the clevis pin hole, is 4.17 in.

7. Refill the master cylinder reservoir and bleed the brakes.

Vanagon

1. Grasp the two recesses provided on the back of the instrument cluster frame and pull it forward.

2. Tag and disconnect any wiring leading to the back of the instrument cluster and then remove it.

Front Wheel Bearings

REMOVAL AND INSTALLATION

1. Jack up the car and remove the wheel and tire.

2. Remove the caliper and disc (if equipped with disc brakes) or brake drum.

3. To remove the inside wheel bearing, pry the dust seal out of the hub with a screwdriver. Lift out the bearing and its inner race.

4. To remove the outer race for either the inner or outer wheel bearing, insert a long punch into the hub opposite the end from which the race is to be removed. The race rests against a shoulder in the hub. The shoulder has two notches cut into it so that it is possible to place the end of the punch directly against the back side of the race and drive it out of the hub.

5. Carefully clean the hub.

1. Speedometer cable circlip
2. Hub cap dust cover
3. Clamp nut allen screw
4. Wheel bearing clamp nut
5. Thrust washer
6. Outer taper roller bearing
7. Brake drum
8. Drum seal (grease)
9. Inner taper roller bearing
10. Bolt
11. Spring washer
12. Front brake unit
13. Steering knuckle

Exploded view of the Type 1 front wheel bearings

6. Install new races in the hub. Drive them in with a soft faced hammer or a large piece of pipe of the proper diameter. Lubricate the races with a light coating of wheel bearing grease.

7. Force wheel bearing grease into the sides of the tapered roller bearings so that all the spaces are filled.

8. Place a small amount of grease inside the hub.

9. Place the inner wheel bearing into its race in the hub and tap a new seal into the hub. Lubricate the sealing surface of the seal with grease.

10. Install the hub on the spindle and install the outer wheel bearing.

11. Adjust the wheel bearing and install the dust cover.

12. Install the caliper (if equipped with disc brakes).

ADJUSTMENT

The bearing may be adjusted by feel or by a dial indicator.

To adjust the bearing by feel, tighten the adjusting nut so that all the play is taken up in the bearing. There will be a slight amount of drag on the wheel if it is hand spun. Back off fully on the adjusting nut and retighten very lightly. There should be no drag when the wheel is hand spun and there should be no perceptible play in the bearing when the wheel is grasped and wiggled from side to side.

To use a dial indicator, remove the dust cover and mount a dial indicator against the hub. Grasp the wheel at the side and pull the wheel in and out along the axis of the spindle. Read the axial play on the dial indicator. Screw the adjusting nut in or out to obtain 0.001–0.005 in. of axial play. Secure the adjusting nut and recheck the axial play.

Wheel Cylinder—Front Drum Brakes

REMOVAL AND INSTALLATION

1. Remove the brake shoes.
2. Disconnect the brake line from the rear of the cylinder.
3. Remove the bolts which secure the cylinder to the backing plate and remove the cylinder from the vehicle.
4. Reverse the above steps to install and bleed the brakes.

1. Boot
2. Piston
3. Cup
4. Cup expander
5. Spring
6. Housing
7. Bleeder valve
8. Dust cap
9. Adjusting nut
10. Adjusting screw

Front wheel cylinders disassembled: Type 1 (left), Type 2 (right)

Wheel Cylinder—Rear Drum Brakes

REMOVAL AND INSTALLATION

Remove the brake drum and brake shoes. Disconnect the brake line from the cylinder and remove the bolts which secure the cylinder to the backing plate. Remove the cylinder from the vehicle.

Parking Brake

CABLE ADJUSTMENT

Brake cable adjustment is performed at the handbrake lever in the passenger compartment. There is a cable for each rear wheel and there are two adjusting nuts at the lever.

To adjust the cable, loosen the locknut. Jack up the rear wheel to be adjusted so that it can be hand spun. Turn the adjusting nut until a very slight drag is felt as the wheel is spun. Then back off on the adjusting nut until the lever can be pulled up three notches.

— CAUTION —
Never pull up on the handbrake lever with the cables disconnected.

CABLE

Removal and Installation

1. Disconnect the cables at the handbrake lever by removing the two nuts which secure the cables to the lever. Pull the cables rearward to remove that end from the lever bracket.
2. Remove the brake drum and detach the cable end from the lever attached to the rear brake shoe.
3. Remove the brake cable bracket from the backing plate and remove the cable from the vehicle.
4. Reverse the above steps to install and adjust the cable.

1. Hand brake lever
2. Pawl rod
3. Ratchet segment
4. Lever pin
5. Cable compensator
6. Brake cable
7. Frame
8. Pawl pin
9. Pawl
10. Cable guide tube

Parking brake hand lever and cable end assembly

Parking brake cable adjusting nuts

1. Pin
2. Spring washer
3. Lever
4. Shoe
5. Clip

Parking brake hand lever and cable end assembly

CHASSIS ELECTRICAL

Heater

The Volkswagen heating system has no electrical blower. The engine cooling fan

---

● Boot

● Cup
coat with paste

● Dust cap

Bleeder screw

Spring

Wheel cylinder housing
Renew complete cylinder if scored or rusty

Piston
coat with paste

● = in repair kit

Type 2 rear wheel cylinder

blows air over the engine and out through the cooling ducts. If the heater flaps are opened, then a portion of the heated air from the engine is diverted to the passenger compartment. An auxiliary gas heater is optional on Types 1 and 2, and standard on the Vanagon.

Cable for Heater Outlet

REMOVAL AND INSTALLATION

Types 1 and 2

1. Remove the rear air outlet, hose, and heater pipe as an assembly.
2. Remove the hose from the outlet and from the pipe.
3. Remove the pin which attaches the cable to the flap in the heater pipe.

NOTE: The pin is push-fit.

4. Remove the heater pipe from the outlet.
5. Bend up the tabs which secure the cable shielding to the outlet.
6. Disconnect the opposite end from the heater controls and remove the cable.
7. Reverse the above steps to install.

Windshield Wipers

MOTOR REMOVAL AND INSTALLATION

Type 1

1. Disconnect the battery ground cable.
2. Loosen the clamp screws and remove the wiper arms.

3. Remove the wiper bearing nuts as well as the washers. Take off the outer bearing seals.
4. Remove the back of the instrument panel from the luggage compartment.
5. Disconnect the cable from the wiper motor.
6. Remove the glove compartment box.
7. Remove the screw which secures the wiper frame to the body.
8. Remove the frame and motor with the linkage.

NOTE: The ball joints at the ends of the linkage may be slipped apart by gently popping the ball and socket apart with a screwdriver. Always lubricate the joints upon reassembly.

9. Remove the lock and spring washers from the motor driveshaft and remove the connecting rod. Matchmark the motor and frame to ensure proper realignment when the motor is reinstalled.
10. Remove the nut located at the base of the motor driveshaft, and the nut at the side of the driveshaft, and remove the motor from the frame.
11. To install, reverse the above steps and heed the following reminders.
12. The pressed lug on the wiper frame must engage the groove in the wiper bearing. Make sure that the wiper spindles are perpendicular to the plane of the windshield.
13. Check the linkage bushings for wear.
14. The hollow side of the links must face toward the frame with the angled end of the driving link toward the right bearing.
15. The inner bearing seal should be placed so that the shoulder of the rubber molding faces the wiper arm.

1. Wiper shaft with crank
2. Spring washer
3. Brass nut
4. Washer
5. Inner bearing seal
6. Outer bearing seal
7. Nut
8. Wiper shaft seal
9. Bracket and arm
10. Windshield wiper blade

Type 1 wiper motor linkage

Type 2

1. Disconnect the ground wire from the battery.
2. Remove both wiper arms.
3. Remove the bearing cover and nut.
4. Remove the heater branch connections under the instrument panel.
5. Disconnect the wiper motor wiring.
6. Remove the wiper motor securing screw and remove the motor.
7. Reverse the above steps to install.

LINKAGE REMOVAL AND INSTALLATION

The windshield wiper linkage is secured at the ends by a ball and socket type joint. The ball and joint may be gently pryed apart with the aid of a screwdriver. Always lubricate the joints with grease before reassembly.

Wiper Arm Shaft

1. Remove the wiper arm.
2. Remove the bearing cover or the shaft seal depending on the type.
3. Remove the large wiper shaft bearing securing nut and remove the accompanying washer and rubber seal.
4. Disconnect the wiper linkage from the wiper arm shaft.
5. Working from inside the car, slide the shaft out of its bearing.

NOTE: It may be necessary to lightly tap the shaft out of its bearing. Use a soft face hammer.

6. Reverse the above steps to install.

Instrument Cluster

NOTE: To remove the instrument cluster on the Vanagon, grasp the two recesses provided at the back of the cluster and pull it forward.

All instruments (speedometer, clock, fuel gauge, etc.) are removed from the back. Unhook any wiring leading from the particular gauge and then remove the retaining screws. Pull the gauge out from the rear of the cluster. Installation is in the reverse order of removal.

SPEEDOMETER

Removal and Installation

1. Disconnect the negative battery cable.
2. Disconnect the speedometer light bulb wires.
3. Unscrew the knurled nut which secures the speedometer cable to the back of the speedometer. Pull the cable from the back of the speedometer.
4. Using a 4 mm Allen wrench, remove the two knurled nuts which secure the speedometer brackets. Remove the brackets.

5. Remove the speedometer from the dashboard by sliding it out toward the steering wheel.

6. Reverse the above steps to install. Before fully tightening the nuts for the speedometer brackets, make sure the speedometer is correctly positioned in the dash.

FUEL GAUGE AND CLOCK ASSEMBLY

Removal and Installation

1. Disconnect the negative battery cable.

2. Disconnect the wiring from the back of the assembly.

3. Remove the knurled nuts and brackets which secure the assembly in the dash. Use a 4 mm Allen wrench.

4. Remove the assembly by gently sliding it toward the steering wheel and out of the dash.

5. The fuel gauge is secured into the base of the clock by two screws. Remove the screws and slip the fuel gauge out of the clock.

8 amp.   16 amp.

Typical fuse box layout

6. Reverse the above steps to install. Make sure the clock and fuel gauge assembly is properly centered in the dash before fully tightening the nuts.

Fuse Box Location

All major circuits are protected from overloading or short circuiting by fuses. A 12 position fusebox is located beneath the dashboard near the steering column, or located in the luggage compartment on some air conditioned models.

When a fuse blows, the cause should be investigated. Never install a fuse of a larger capacity than specified and never use foil or a bolt or nail in place of a fuse. However, always carry a few spares in case of emergency. There are 10 8 amp (white) fuses and two 16 amp (red) fuses in the VW fusebox. Circuits number 9 and 10 use the 16 amp fuses. To replace a fuse, pry off the clear plastic cover at either end of the subject fuse.

Volkswagen

Front Wheel Drive

SERIAL NUMBER IDENTIFICATION

Vehicle Identification Plate

On the Rabbit, Jetta, Scirocco and Quantum, the vehicle identification plate is on top of the body crossmember above the grille. The same plate on the Dasher is riveted to the inner right fender. The date of manufacture and the chassis number are stamped on the plate.

Chassis Number

The chassis number plate is located on the driver's side windshield pillar on the Scirocco and Dasher, and on the left front corner of the dashboard on the Rabbit, Jetta and Quantum (visible through the windshield). The Dasher and Quantum chassis numbers are also stamped on the firewall over the windshield washer reservoir. The Rabbit, Jetta and Scirocco chassis number is also found on top of the right front suspension strut pillar. It also appears on the vehicle identification plate.

Engine Number

The engine number is stamped on a flat boss on the left side (front on the Rabbit, Jetta, Scirocco and Quantum) of the engine block, just below the cylinder head between the fuel pump and distributor.

Dasher and Scirocco chassis number

Rabbit, Jetta chassis number

Identification plate

Engine number location

Rabbit, Jetta, Quantum chassis number

Vehicle Identification Label

This label is located in the luggage compartment beside the spare wheel on Rabbit, Jetta and Scirocco, under the floor covering on Quantum, and on the left side of the cross panel behind the rear bench seat on Rabbit Convertible. The label is marked with the Vehicle Identification Number, Vehicle Code, Engine and Transmission Code, Paint and Interior code (needed for matching paint colors) and Option codes.

Safety Compliance Sticker

This sticker assures you that your VW complies with all applicable Federal Motor Vehicle Safety Standards which were in effect at the time the car was built. You can find this sticker on either the front crossmember under the hood (just above the grille) or on the left door jamb, depending on years and models.

ENGINE CODES

Model	Year	Engine Capacity	Engine Code
Rabbit, Scirocco	'76–'78	1.5 liter	FC, FG CK (diesel)
		1.6 liter	FN, EF EE
Dasher	'76–'78	1.6 liter	YK, YH YG
	'79–'80	1.6 liter	YK, YH YG
		1.5 liter	CK (diesel)
Rabbit, Scirocco, Jetta	'79–'80	1.5 liter	EH, CK (diesel) FX
		1.6 liter	EJ
Rabbit, Scirocco, Jetta, Quantum, Dasher	'81–'82	1.6 liter	EJ, EH, FX CR (diesel)
		1.7 liter	WT, EN

GENERAL ENGINE SPECIFICATIONS

Year/Model	Engine Displacement cu. in. (cc)	Fuel Delivery	Horsepower @ rpm	Torque @ rpm ft. lbs.	Bore × Stroke (in.)	Compression Ratio	Oil Pressure @ rpm (psi)
'76–'77 Dasher	97.0 (1588)	CIS Fuel inj.	81 @ 5800	90 @ 3300	3.13 × 3.15	8.0:1	40 @ 2500
'76 Rabbit, Scirocco	97.0 (1588)	2-bbl Zenith	71 @ 5600	82 @ 3300	3.13 × 3.15	8.2:1	40 @ 2500
'77 Rabbit, Scirocco	97.0 (1588)	CIS Fuel inj.	81 @ 5800	90 @ 3300	3.13 × 3.15	8.0:1	40 @ 2500
'77–'80 Rabbit (Diesel)	89.7 (1471)	Fuel inj.	48 @ 5000	56.5 @ 3000	3.01 × 3.15	23.5:1	27 @ 2000
'78–'80 Dasher	97.0 (1588)	Fuel inj.	78 @ 5500①	84 @ 3200②	3.13 × 3.15	8.0:1	28 @ 2000
'79–'80 Dasher (Diesel)	89.7 (1471)	Fuel inj.	48 @ 5000	56.5 @ 3000	3.01 × 3.15	23.5:1	28 @ 2000
'78–'80 Rabbit	88.9 (1457)	Fuel⑤ inj.	71 @ 5800③	73 @ 3500④	3.13 × 2.89	8.0:1	28 @ 2000
'80–'81 Jetta	97.0 (1588)	Fuel inj.	78 @ 5500	84 @ 3200	3.13 × 3.15	8.0:1	28 @ 2000
'78 Scirocco	88.9 (1457)	Fuel inj.	73 @ 5800	73 @ 3500④	3.13 × 2.89	8.0:1	28 @ 2000
'79–'80 Scirocco	97.0 (1588)	Fuel inj.	78 @ 5500①	84 @ 3200②	3.13 × 3.15	8.0:1	28 @ 2000
'81 Jetta, Scirocco, Rabbit	105.0 (1715)	Fuel inj.	74 @ 5000⑥	90 @ 3000⑦	3.13 × 3.40	8.2:1	28 @ 2000
'81 Dasher Rabbit (Diesel)	97.0 (1588)	Fuel inj.	52 @ 4800	72 @ 3000	3.01 × 3.40	23.0:1	28 @ 2000

GENERAL ENGINE SPECIFICATIONS

Year/Model	Engine Displacement cu. in. (cc)	Fuel Delivery	Horsepower @ rpm	Torque @ rpm ft. lbs.	Bore × Stroke (in.)	Compression Ratio	Oil Pressure @ rpm (psi)
'82 Jetta, Rabbit, Scirocco, Quantum	105.0 (1715)	CIS⑤ Fuel inj.	74 @ 5000⑥	90 @ 3000⑦	3.13 × 3.40	8.2:1	28 @ 2000
'82 Diesels	97.0 (1588)	Fuel inj.	52 @ 4800	72 @ 2000	3.01 × 3.40	23.0:1	28 @ 2000

① 76 @ 5000—Calif.
② 83 @ 3200—Calif.
③ 70 @ 5800—Calif.
④ 72 @ 3500—Calif.
⑤ Some '78, '80 and '82 Rabbits are equipped with a 1 bbl. carburetor; '82 w/ oxygen sensor
⑥ Canada: 76 hp
⑦ Canada: 92 ft. lbs.

DIESEL TUNE-UP SPECIFICATIONS

Model	Valve Clearance (cold)① Intake (in.)	Exhaust (in.)	Intake Valve Opens (deg)	Injection Pump Setting (deg)	Injection Nozzle Pressure (psi) New	Used	Idle Speed (rpm)	Cranking Compression Pressure (psi)
Diesel (All models)	0.008–0.012	0.016–0.020	N.A.	Align marks	1885	1706	800–850②	406 minimum

①Warm clearance given—Cold clearance:
Intake   0.006–0.010
Exhaust   0.014–0.018
②Volkswagen has lowered the idle speed on early models to this specification.

Valve clearance need not be adjusted unless it varies more than 0.002 in. from specification.
N.A. Not Available

GASOLINE ENGINE TUNE-UP SPECIFICATIONS

Year Model	Spark Plugs Type	Gap (in.)	Distributor Point Dwell (deg)	Point Gap (in.)	Ignition Timing (deg)	Intake Valve Opens (deg)	Compression Pressure (psi)	Idle Speed (rpm)	Valve Clearance (in.) In⑤	Ex⑤
'76–'79 Dasher	W215 T30 N7Y	0.024–0.028	44–50	0.016	3 ATDC @ Idle	4 BTDC	142–184	850–1000	0.008–0.012	0.016–0.020
'76 Rabbit, Scirocco	W200 T30 N8Y	0.024–0.028	44–50	0.016	3 ATDC @ Idle	4 BTDC	142–184	850–1000	0.008–0.012	0.016–0.020
'77 Rabbit, Scirocco	W215 T30 N7Y	0.024–0.028	44–50	0.016	3 ATDC @ Idle	4 BTDC	142–184	850–1000	0.008–0.012	0.016–0.020
'78 Rabbit, Scirocco	W175 T30 N8Y	0.024–0.028	44–50	0.016	②	4 BTDC	142–184	850–1000	0.008–0.012	0.016–0.020
'79 Rabbit	W175 T30 N8Y	0.024–0.032	44–50	0.016	3 ATDC @ Idle	4 BTDC	142–184	850–1000	0.008–0.012	0.016–0.020
'79 Scirocco	W175 T30 N8Y	0.024–0.032	44–50	0.016	3 ATDC @ Idle	4 BTDC	142–184	850–1000	0.008–0.012	0.016–0.020

GASOLINE ENGINE TUNE-UP SPECIFICATIONS

Year Model	Spark Plugs Type	Gap (in.)	Distributor Point Dwell (deg)	Point Gap (in.)	Ignition Timing (deg)	Intake Valve Opens (deg)	Compression Pressure (psi)	Idle Speed (rpm)	Valve Clearance (in.) In⑤	Valve Clearance (in.) Ex⑤
'80–'81 Dasher (49 states)	W175 T30 N8Y	0.024–0.032	44–50⑥	0.016⑥	3 ATDC @ Idle	4 BTDC	142–184	850–1000④	0.008–0.012	0.016–0.020
'80–'81 Dasher (California)	WR7DS N8GY	0.024–0.028	Electronic		3 ATDC @ Idle	4 BTDC	142–184	880–1000	0.008–0.012	0.016–0.020
'80–'83 Rabbit, Jetta, Scirocco, Quantum (49 states)	W175 T30	0.024–0.032	44–50⑥	0.016⑥	3 ATDC @ Idle③	4 BTDC	142–184⑦	850–1000④	0.008–0.012	0.016–0.020
'80–'83 Rabbit, Jetta, Scirocco, Quantum (California)	WR7DS N8GY	0.024–0.028	Electronic		3 ATDC @ Idle	4 BTDC	142–184⑦	880–1000	0.008–0.012	0.016–0.020

NOTE: The underhood specifications sticker often reflects tune-up specification changes made in production. Sticker figures must be used if they disagree with those in this chart.

① 47°–53° California

② 3 ATDC @ Idle with CIS fuel injection; 7½ BTDC @ Idle with 34 PICT-5 Carburetor

③ Non-California Rabbit w/1 barrel carburetor; timing 7½ BTDC @ Idle

④ W/o Idle stabilizer

⑤ Valve clearance need not be adjusted unless it varies more than 0.002 in. from specifications.

⑥ 1981–82 have Electronic Ignition

⑦ '82 compression pressure 131–174 psi.

FIRING ORDERS

Firing order: 1-3-4-2; all engines including diesel

CAPACITIES

Year	Model	Engine Crankcase (qts) With Filter	Engine Crankcase (qts) Without Filter	Transmission (pts) Manual	Transmission (pts) Automatic	Drive Axle (pts)	Gasoline Tank (gals)	Cooling System (pts)
'76	Dasher	3.7	3.2	3.4	12.8②	3.0	12.1	12.8
'76	Rabbit, Scirocco	3.7	3.2	2.6	12.8②	3.0	12.1	13.8
'77–'80	Dasher	3.2	2.6	3.4	12.4②	1.6	12.1	12.6
'77	Rabbit, Scirocco	3.7	3.2	2.6	12.8②	1.6	12.1	9.8

CAPACITIES

Year	Model	Engine Crankcase (qts) With Filter	Engine Crankcase (qts) Without Filter	Transmission (pts) Manual	Transmission (pts) Automatic	Drive Axle (pts)	Gasoline Tank (gals)	Cooling System (pts)
'77–'80	Rabbit (Diesel)	3.7	3.2	2.6	—	1.6	10.9	12.6
'78–'80	Rabbit	3.7	3.2	2.6④	12.8②	1.6	10.6	9.8
'78	Scirocco	3.7	3.2	3.2④	12.8	1.6	10.6	9.8
'79–'80	Scirocco	3.7	3.2	3.2④	12.8	1.6	10.6	9.8
	Dasher (Diesel)	3.7	3.2	3.2④	—	1.6	11.9	9.8
'80	Jetta	3.7	3.2	3.2④	12.8	1.6	10.5	10.2
'81	Scirocco, Rabbit, Jetta	4.5	4.0	3.2④	12.8	1.6	10.0⑤	9.8
'81	Dasher, Rabbit Jetta (Diesel)	3.7	3.2	3.2④	—	1.6	10.0⑤	14.3⑥
'82–'83	Rabbit, Jetta, Scirocco, Quantum	4.7	4.2	3.2④	12.8	1.6	⑦	14.3
	Rabbit, Jetta Quantum (Diesel)	3.7	3.2	3.2④	12.8	1.6	⑦	14.3

① At change, initial amount 4.2 pts
② Dry refill; normal refill is 6.4 pts
③ Doesn't include 1.3 gal reserve
④ 5-speed—4.2
⑤ Dasher: 12.0

⑥ Dasher: 12.2
⑦ 10.0 Rabbit; 10.6 Jetta, Convertible, Scirocco; 15.8 Quantum
— Not applicable

CRANKSHAFT AND CONNECTING ROD SPECIFICATIONS

(All measurements are given in inches)

Year/Model	Crankshaft Main Brg. Journal Dia.	Crankshaft Main Brg. Oil Clearance	Crankshaft Shaft End/Play	Crankshaft Thrust on. No.	Connecting Rod Journal Diameter	Connecting Rod Oil Clearance	Connecting Rod Side Clearance (max.)
'76–'83 All	2.126	0.001–0.003	0.003–0.007	3	1.811	0.001–0.003	0.015

NOTE: Main and connecting rod bearings are available in three undersizes

VALVE SPECIFICATIONS

Year/Model	Seat Angle (deg)	Spring Test Pressure (lbs.@in.)	Stem to Guide Clearance (in.) Intake	Stem to Guide Clearance (in.) Exhaust	Stem Diameter (in.) Intake	Stem Diameter (in.) Exhaust
'76–'83 All	45	96–106① @0.92 in.	0.039 max②	0.051 max.	0.314	0.313

NOTE: Exhaust valves must be ground by hand.
① Outer spring, inner spring test pressure is 46–51 lbs.@0.72 in.

② 1976–78 Rabbit and all Dasher Diesels: 0.051 max.

TORQUE SPECIFICATIONS
(All readings in ft. lbs.)

Year/Model	Cylinder Head Bolts	Rod Bearing Bolts④	Main Bearing Bolts	Crankshaft Pulley Bolt	Flywheel To Crankshaft Bolts	Manifold	
						Intake	Exhaust
'76–'81 Dasher	54①	33	47	58	54	18	18
'76–'83 Rabbit, Scirocco, Jetta	54①⑤	33	47	58	54②	18	18
'77–'83 Diesel Rabbit, Dasher, Jetta, Quantum	65③⑤	33	47	56	54②	18	18

① Cold; 61 ft. lbs warm—1978–79 54 ft. lbs. plus ¼ turn (6-point bolts)
② Pressure plate to crankshaft bolts
③ Cold, 69 ft. lbs. warm
④ Always use new bolts
⑤ '82 uses 12mm, 12 pt. cyl. head bolts. Bolts must always be replaced during repairs to head.

CYLINDER HEAD TORQUE SEQUENCES

Cylinder head; all engines including diesel

BRAKE SPECIFICATIONS
(All measurements in inches unless noted)

Year	Model	Lug Nut Torque (ft. lbs.)	Master Cylinder Bore	Brake Disc		Diameter	Brake Drum		Minimum Brake Lining Thickness	
				Minimum Thickness	Maximum Run-Out		Maximum Machine o/s	Maximum Wear Limit	Front	Rear
'76–'81	Dasher	65	0.82	0.41	0.004	7.87	7.90	7.97	0.250	0.098
'76–'83	Rabbit, Jetta, Scirocco Quantum	65	0.82	0.41	0.004	7.08①	7.10②	7.12③⑤	0.250④	0.098

*NOTE: Minimum lining thickness is as recommended by manufacturer. Due to variations in state inspection regulations, the minimum thickness may be different than that recommended by the manufacturer.
① Rabbit front brake drums—9.05–9.06 in.
② Rabbit front brake drums—9.087 in.
③ Rabbit front brake drums—9.106 in.
④ Rabbit front brake drums—0.039 in.
⑤ 7.91 in Quantum

BATTERY AND STARTER SPECIFICATIONS

(All models use 12 volt, negative ground system)

Year	Model	Battery Amp Hour Capacity	Lock Test Amps	Lock Test Volts	Lock Test Torque (ft. lbs.)	No Load Test Amps	No Load Test Volts	No Load Test rpm	Brush Spring Tension (oz.)	Minimum Brush Length (in.)
'76–'83	All	45/54①②	280–370	7.5	2.42	33–55	11.5	6000–8000	35.5	0.5

① With air conditioning and '81–'82 Rabbit gas engine
② 63 Ah with diesel, and Canadian gasoline engines

PISTON AND RING SPECIFICATIONS

(All measurements in inches)

Year/Model	Piston Clearance	Ring Gap Top Compression	Ring Gap Bottom Compression	Ring Gap Oil Control	Ring Side Clearance Top Compression	Ring Side Clearance Bottom Compression	Ring Side Clearance Oil Control
'76–'83 All Gasoline Engines	0.001–0.003	0.012–0.018	0.012–0.018	0.010–0.016	0.001–0.002	0.001–0.002	0.001–0.002
'77–'83 All Diesel Engines	0.001–0.003	0.012–0.020	0.012–0.020	0.010–0.016	0.002–0.004	0.002–0.003	0.001–0.002

NOTE: Three piston sizes are available to accommodate over-bores up to 0.040 in.

WHEEL ALIGNMENT

Year	Model	Caster① Range (deg)	Caster① Pref Setting (deg)	Camber② Range (deg)	Camber② Pref Setting (deg)	Toe-In③ (in.)	Steering Axis Inclination① (deg)
All	Dasher	0°–1°	0°30′	0–1°	0°30′	0.08	10°30′
All	Rabbit, Scirocco Jetta	+1°20′–2°20′	+1°50′	−10′–+50′	+20′	0.08	10°30′
'82–'83	Quantum	+30′ ± 30′	+30′	−40′ ± 30′	−40′	N.A.	N.A.

① Not adjustable
② Rear wheel camber (not adjustable)
  Rabbit (to Ch. No. 176 3 241 690)—1°N ± 30′
  Rabbit (from Ch. No. 176 3 261 691)—1¼°N ± 30′
  Scirocco (all)—1°N ± 30′
  Dasher (all)—½°N ± 30′
  Quantum 1982—1°40′ ± 20′
  Jetta—1¼°N ± 30′

③ Rear wheel toe-in (not adjustable)
  Rabbit—0° ± 15′
  Scirocco (to Ch. No. 536 2 031 722)—10′P ± 30′
  Scirocco (from Ch. No. 536 2 031 723)—20′P ± 30′
  Quantum +25′ ± 15′
  Jetta −0° ± 15′

TUNE-UP PROCEDURES

VW recommends a tune-up, including new points and plugs, at 12,000 mile intervals for all gasoline engines. The only procedure required for diesel engines in this section is the valve lash adjustment and minimum/maximum engine speed checking and adjustment.

Spark Plugs

The firing order is 1-3-4-2, with no. 1 cylinder at the front (right on the Rabbit, Jetta and Scirocco) of the engine.

1. Grasp the spark plug boot and pull it straight out. Don't pull on the wire. Either number the wires or remove them one at a time to avoid mixups.
2. Place the spark plug socket squarely on the plug and screw the spark plug out.

NOTE: The cylinder head is aluminum alloy, which is easily stripped of threads. Remove the plugs only when the engine is cold.

If removal is difficult, loosen the plug only slightly and drip penetrating oil onto the threads.

3. For the price of a set of new spark plugs, it usually isn't worth cleaning the old plugs. Purchase a new set of plugs, and set the gaps as they come out of the box(es).

The recommended spark plug gap is listed in the "Tune Up Specifications" chart. Use a round wire feeler gauge to check the gap between the plug electrodes. If the gap is incorrect, gently bend the side electrode to correct. Do not bend the center electrode.

4. Torque the new spark plugs to 22 ft/lbs. Install the ignition wire boots firmly.

Breaker Points and Condenser

Snap off the two retaining clips on the distributor cap. Unfasten ground strap at suppressor leads on 1979 and later distributors.

Points must be correctly aligned

Remove the cap and examine it for cracks, deterioration, or carbon tracking. Replace the cap, if necessary, by transferring one wire at a time from the old cap to the new one. Replace the rotor at every other tune-up. Remove the dust shield. Check the points for pitting and burning. Slight imperfections on the contact surface may be filed off with a point file. It is best to replace the breaker point set. Always replace the condenser when you replace the point set.

To replace the breaker points:
1. Remove the distributor cap.
2. Remove the rotor.
3. Unsnap the point connector from the terminal at the side of the distributor. Remore the retaining screw, and lift out the point set.
4. Install the new point set, making sure that the pin on the bottom engages the hole in the breaker plate.
5. Install the wire connector and the retaining screws (hand-tight).

Adjusting point gap

6. Turn the engine with a wrench on the crankshaft pulley until the breaker arm rubbing block on the points set is on the high point of one of the cam lobes. Turn the engine only in the direction of normal rotation to avoid damage to the timing belt.

7. A 0.016 in. feeler gauge should just slip through the points with a slight drag. If the gap is incorrect, pivot a screwdriver in the point set notch and the two projections on the breaker plate to bring it within specifications.

8. When the gap is correct, tighten the retaining screw. Recheck the adjustment.

9. Lubricate the distributor cam with silicone grease (some points sets come with a grease capsule).

Breaker points and condenser. Lubricate at (1) with a drop of engine oil and at (2) with high melting point grease.

10. Install the dust cover, rotor and distributor cap.
11. Check the dwell angle and the ignition timing.
12. The condenser is mounted on the outside of the distributor. Undo the mounting screw and the terminal block to replace.

Dwell Angle (Breaker-Point Gasoline Engines Only)

The dwell angle or cam angle is the number of degrees that the distributor cam rotates while the points are closed. There is an inverse relationship between dwell angle and point gap. Increasing the point gap will decrease the dwell angle and vice versa. Checking the dwell angle with a meter is a far more accurate method of measuring point opening than the feeler gauge method.

After setting the point gap to specification with a feeler gauge, check the dwell angle. Attach the dwell meter. The negative lead is grounded and the positive lead is connected to the primary wire, Terminal No. 1 that runs from the coil to the distributor. Start the engine, let it idle and reach operating temperature, and observe the dwell on the meter. The reading should fall within the allowable range. If it does not, the gap will have to be reset. Dwell can also be checked with the engine crank-

ing. In this case, dwell will vary between 0° and the dwell figure for that setting.

Hall Effect Electronic Ignition System

The 1980–81 Dasher, Jetta and Scirocco destined for California, the 1980 Rabbit 1.6 liter (California) and 1.5 liter (49 states) and 1981 and later Rabbits, Sciroccos and Quantums are equipped with the Hall effect electronic ignition system.

The distributor contains the Hall Effect pickup assembly which replaces the breaker points assembly in conventional systems.

The "Hall Effect" is a shift in magnetic field caused when one of the rotors on the distributor shaft passes the sensors mounted in the distributor. This shift performs the same function as breaker points, which is to allow the current (coil field) stored in the coil to collapse, causing a spark to run from the coil to the distributor and down to the spark plugs, which make the current jump a gap between the two spark plug electrodes, causing a spark which ignites the air-fuel mixture in the combustion chamber. Since there are no breaker points and condenser to replace, the system should be maintenance free, except for rotor replacement at regular intervals.

ELECTRONIC IGNITION PRECAUTIONS

When working on the Hall ignition, observe

trigger wheel

Hall sender

Hall effect electronic ignition distributor

the following precautions to prevent damage to the ignition system.

1. Connect and disconnect test equipment only when the ignition switch is OFF.

2. On the carbureted Rabbit, if you use a conventional tachometer, you will have to rig up an adapter. See below for instructions.

3. Do not crank the engine with the starter for compression tests, etc., until the high tension coil wire (terminal 4) is grounded.

4. Do not replace the original equipment coil (Part No. 211 905 115 B) with a conventional coil.

5. Do not install any kind of condenser to coil terminal 1.

6. Do not use a battery booster for longer than 1 (one) minute.

7. On the fuel injected models, do not tow cars with defective ignition systems without disconnecting the plugs on the idle stabilizer at the ignition control unit.

TACHOMETER ADAPTATION (CARBURETED RABBITS)

An adapter must be used when connecting a conventional tachometer to the Hall Effect ignition system to prevent damage to the ignition components. Use the illustration as a guide. All components will be available to you locally. Connect the positive wire of the tachometer to the adapter and the negative wire to the ground.

IGNITION COIL TEST

A defective Hall ignition coil cannot be checked with standard coil testing equipment. If there is no high tension current and all other components of the ignition system check out, see if you're getting a spark from the coil wire to the distributor cap by unplugging the coil wire at the distributor, holding the end of it with insulated pliers about ½ in. from ground (engine block, etc.) and turning over the engine. If a weak or no spark is obtained, replace the coil.

HALL PICKUP UNIT TEST

1. Check for voltage on terminal 15 (+) of the ignition coil. There should be voltage with the ignition ON.

2. Ground a high tension coil wire.

3. Connect a test light (4 to 24 volts) between terminal 15 (+) and terminal 1 (−).

Adapter for attaching a tachometer to 1980 and later carbureted Rabbit with electronic ignition

4. Crank the engine with the starter for approximately 5 seconds. The test light should flicker. If not, replace the ignition distributor.

IGNITION CONTROL UNIT TEST

1. On fuel injected models, disconnect the plugs at the control unit and connect the plugs to each other. Ground high tension coil wire on carbureted Rabbit.

2. Turn the ignition switch on and make sure there is current at terminal 15 (−) of the ignition coil. Turn the ignition OFF.

3. Disconnect the high tension wire be-

Checking ignition coil primary resistance

Checking ignition coil secondary resistance

ELECTRONIC IGNITION TESTING SPECIFICATIONS①

Component Tested	Specification
Rotor resistance②	1000 ohm; rotor must be marked R1
Ignition Timing: CIS	3° ± 2° ATDC when checking
	3° ± 1° ATDC when adjusting
Carburetor	7½° BTDC
Vacuum hoses during testing	Connected (CIS)
	Vacuum retard hose disconnected and plugged (carburetor)
Ignition coil primary resistance:② Resistance between positive and negative terminals	0.52–0.76 ohms
Ignition coil secondary resistance:② Resistance between negative terminal and coil tower	2400–3500 ohms

①All USA, California, and Canada models with electronic ignition   ②See illustration tween the ignition coil and the distributor at the distributor on fuel injected models.

4. Disconnect the wire (plug) between the control unit and the distributor at the distributor.

5. Connect the positive (+) terminal of the voltmeter 1 of the ignition coil and the negative (−) terminal to ground.

6. Turn the ignition ON. There must be a voltage reading of at least 12 volts. If voltage drops below 12 volts in one second, turn off the ignition. The control unit is defective and will have to be replaced.

7. Disconnect the green wire where it connects to the distributor and ground the wire. Turn the ignition switch ON. The voltmeter should read about 12 volts. Disconnect the ground wire. The voltage should drop to 6 volts. If not, replace the control unit. Turn off the ignition.

8. On fuel injected models, connect the terminals of the voltmeter to the outer connector of the control unit. Connect the positive (+) lead to the red wire and the negative (−) lead to the brown wire. Switch on the ignition. The voltmeter should read about 10 volts. If not, replace the control unit.

Disconnect the plugs on the idle stabilizer at the control unit and plug them together

Checking rotor resistance

IDLE STABILIZER

The idle stabilizer is located on top of the ignition control unit. The idle stabilizer controls idle speed by either advancing or retarding the distributor timing in accordance with engine load (air conditioner on, lights on, etc.) If idle speed is erratic or if the engine fails to start, try bypassing the idle stabilizer by disconnecting the two plugs at the idle stabilizer and plugging them together. If idle improves, the idle stabilizer should probably be replaced.

Ignition Timing

BREAKER-POINT IGNITION SYSTEMS

1. Attach the timing light as outlined above or according to the manufacturer's instructions. Hook-up a dwell/tachometer since you'll need an rpm indication for correct timing.

2. Locate the timing mark opening in the clutch or torque converter housing at the rear of the engine directly behind the distributor. The OT mark stands for TDC or 0° advance. The other mark designates the correct timing position. Mark them with chalk so that they will be more visible. Don't disconnect the vacuum line.

NOTE: Some models do not have an OT mark.

3. Start the engine and allow it to reach the normal operating temperature. The engine should be running at normal idle speed.

4. Shine the timing light at the marks.

5. The light should now be flashing when the timing mark and the V-shaped pointer are aligned.

6. If not, loosen the distributor holddown bolt and rotate the distributor very slowly to align the marks.

7. Tighten the mounting nut when the ignition timing is correct.

8. Recheck the timing when the distributor is secured.

With ignition timing correctly adjusted, the spark plugs will fire just before the piston hits the top of the compression stroke, thus providing maximum power and economy.

ELECTRONIC IGNITION SYSTEMS

1. Run the engine to normal operating temperature. Connect tachometer. See "Electronic Ignition Precautions," above.

2. Stop the engine. Disconnect the plugs on the idle stabilizer at the control unit and plug them together (see illustration). On the carbureted Rabbit, disconnect the vacuum retard hose and plug it. The engine speed should increase as the hose is unplugged.

3. Check the idle speed. It should be between 800 and 1000 rpm.

Dasher and Quantum timing marks aligned at 3° ATDC

Rabbit, Jetta, Scirocco timing marks (all except 1978, 1980 and later carbureted Rabbit). Manual transmission shown

Timing mark for 1978, '80 and '82 carbureted Rabbits (7½° BTDC)

1980 electronic ignition Dashers and 1982 and later Quantums have only one mark for correct timing (3° ATDC)

4. With your timing light attached according to manufacturer's instructions, shine the light on the timing hole. The pointer in the hole must line up with the notch in the flywheel. To adjust the timing, loosen the distribution at its base and turn it until timing marks line up.

5. On the carbureted Rabbit, reinstall the vacuum retard hose. Idle speed should drop to 600–750 rpm.

6. Stop the engine and reconnect the plugs at the control unit. On the carbureted Rabbit, start the engine and rev it a few times to activate the idle stabilizer. On the carbureted Rabbit, the idle speed should now be 850–950 rpm.

Valve Lash

Check the valve clearance every 20,000 miles in firing order, with the engine at normal operating temperature.

1. Remove the camshaft cover and the distributor cap.

2. Set the engine at TDC on No. 1 cylinder by aligning the 0°T mark on the flywheel with the pointer and aligning the distributor rotor with the No. 1 cylinder mark on the rim of the distributor body.

Check the valve clearance with a feeler gauge. The camshaft lobe should not be putting pressure on the valve shim

NOTE: Always turn the crankshaft in the normal direction of rotation. There is a hole in the body behind the front license plate through which a wrench can be used on the crankshaft on the Dasher. Do not turn the engine by means of the timing belt (or camshaft bolt), because the belt will stretch or lose teeth.

3. The valve clearances of cylinder no. 1 should be checked when the valves of no. 4 cylinder overlap, i.e., when both no. 4 cylinder valves move in opposite directions simultaneously. It may be necessary to turn the crankshaft slightly to find this position. When this happens, the exhaust valve is closing and the intake opening. Check and note the clearance of both the intake and exhaust valves for no. 1 cylinder.

Using tappet tool to depress tappet and remove shim.

4. Turn the crankshaft 180° (90° at the distributor rotor) in the normal direction of rotation. Check and note the valve clearances of cylinder no. 3 at the overlap position of cylinder no. 2.

5. Turn the crankshaft 180°. Check and note the valve clearances of cylinder no. 4 at the overlap position of cylinder no. 1.

6. Turn the crankshaft 180°. Check and note the valve clearances of cylinder no. 2 at the overlap position of cylinder no. 3.

7. Compare the noted clearances with those listed in the ''Tune-Up Specifications'' chart. Adjustment is made by replacing the tappet clearance shim in the top of each tappet. These are available in 26 sizes ranging from 3.0 mm (0.119 in.) to 4.25 mm (0.166 in.) in increments of 0.05 mm (0.002 in.). The thickness of each shim is marked on the bottom. (These shims are available from VW dealers).

NOTE: If a valve clearance deviates 0.002 in. or less from the specified clearance, it need not be adjusted.

8. To remove a tappet clearance shim, turn the cylinder to TDC and press down the tappet so that the shim can be lifted out.

NOTE: When adjusting clearances on a diesel, the pistons must not be at TDC. Turn the crankshaft ¼ turn past TDC, so that the valves do not contact the pistons when the tappets are depressed.

A special tool is available from VW for this operation. Once the shim is removed, check its size and determine what size will be needed to produce the required adjustment.

9. Install the required shim. When all the clearances have been corrected, recheck valve clearances.

Carburetor

The 1976 Rabbit and Scirocco use a Zenith 32/32-2B2 two barrel carburetor with a vacuum operated secondary barrel and dual floats. Some 1978, 1980 and 1982 Rabbits are equipped with a single barrel carburetor.

Idle speed adjustment screw—all carbureted models except 1978, 1980 and 1982 Rabbit

IDLE SPEED ADJUSTMENT

Solex 32/35 DIDTA Carburetor, Zenith 2B2 Carburetor

1. Start the engine and run it until normal operating temperature is reached.

2. Hook-up a tachometer to the engine and observe the idle speed.-3.

If the idle speed is not as specified, turn the curb idle screw to correct it. Make sure that you are turning the correct screw. Do not mistake the idle mixture screw for the curb idle screw.

Solex 34 PICT-5 Carburetor

1978 RABBIT

The choke must be fully open and the engine at normal operating temperature.

1. Remove the hose from the charcoal filter at the air intake elbow. Plug the hose.

2. Remove the air injection hose at the air cleaner. Plug the hose.

3. Make sure no electrical equipment is ON. In particular the cooling fan must be OFF.

4. Connect a tachometer. Adjust the idle speed to specifications at the idle speed adjusting screw (A). The CO content can be adjusted at screw (B) if a CO meter is available.

5. Disconnect the tachometer and reconnect the hoses.

1980 RABBIT

1. The engine must be at operating temperature and the choke must be fully open.

2. Remove the two hoses from the carburetor air intake elbow and plug the two hose inlets in the elbow. The air intake elbow sits right on top of the carburetor.

3. Remove both of the air injection hoses at the air injection valves, located side by side in the front middle of the engine. Plug the air injection valves.

4. Shut off all electrical equipment, including the air conditioner (if installed).

5. Connect a tachometer, timing light and CO meter (if available) to the engine.

Idle speed screw (A) and idle mixture screw (B)—1978 and 1980 carbureted Rabbit

6. Start the engine. Rev the engine a few times to start the idle stabilizer.

7. Check the idle; it should be 850–950 rpm. If the idle is not correct, disconnect the plugs at the control unit and plug them together (see electronic ignition system, above).

8. Remove the vacuum advance and retard hoses, then plug the hoses.

9. Adjust the idle speed to 800–1000 rpm at the idle adjustment screw. Check the timing, see above section for procedures.

10. If the timing was off, recheck the idle speed.

11. Reconnect the advance and retard hoses. Adjust the CO lever at the CO adjusting screw to 0.5–1.1%.

12. Reconnect the plugs at the control unit.

13. Rev the engine to reactivate idle stabilizer and check the idle speed and CO. Idle speed should be 850–950 rpm, CO should be 0.5–1.5%.

14. If the idle speed is still not correct, replace the control unit or the idle stabilizer.

Carter TYF
1982 RABBIT

NOTE: This procedure requires a special duty cycle meter which is not commonly available to the backyard mechanic. Unless you have access to this meter it is suggested that the procedure be performed by an authorized service technician.

1. Run engine up to operating temperature. Make sure choke is fully open and not sticking. Remove PCV valve from side of valve cover. Shut off all electrical equipment including air conditioner (if so equipped). Radiator fan must not be running for idle adjustment. Check timing with a timing light and adjust to 7½° BTDC ± 1° if necessary (set pointer to mark on flywheel by turning distributor).

2. Connect a tachometer to the engine according to the manufacturer's instructions.

3. Connect a duty cycle meter to the test connector on the left strut tower.

4. Start the engine, and run at 2000 rpm for 5 seconds. Check idle speed—it should be 850–1000 rpm. Duty cycle should be fluctuating between 20% and 50%.

5. To adjust idle speed, disconnect both plugs at the idle stabilizer and connect the plugs together.

6. Remove the vacuum advance and retard hoses at the distributor. Plug the hoses with golf tees or pencils.

7. Adjust idle speed to 820–900 rpm by turning idle screw ("A" in illustration). Duty cycle should still be fluctuating between 20% and 50%. If duty cycle reading is incorrect, the car should be adjusted to correct the reading by a professional, as a tamper-proof plug must be removed from the carburetor body to make this adjustment.

NOTE: On air conditioned cars, turn the air conditioner "on" and set the control to max. "cold" and "fast" fan speed before setting idle speed to 820–900 rpm.

IDLE MIXTURE ADJUSTMENT

This adjustment should only be performed with a CO meter.

Rabbit, Scirocco and Dasher

1. Run the engine until it reaches normal operating temperature.

2. Check the ignition timing and idle speed as specified.

3. Adjust the CO level with the idle mixture screw.

1978 and 1980 Rabbit

Mixture adjustment is contained in the idle speed adjustment procedure, above.

CIS Fuel Injection
IDLE AND CO ADJUSTMENT

All Except 1980 California And 1981 and Later Models

The following adjustments can be made *only* with a CO meter and the CO adjusting tool (VW-P377).

1. Run the engine until it reaches normal operating temperature.

2. Adjust the ignition timing to specification with the vacuum hoses connected and the engine at idle.

3. Adjust the idle speed to specification.

Idle mixture adjustment screw—all except 1978, 1980 and later carbureted Rabbit

4. Remove the charcoal filter hose from the air cleaner except on Canadian models.

5. Turn on the headlight high beams.

6. Remove the plug from the CO adjusting hole and insert adjustment tool VW-P377. Turn the adjustment screw clockwise to raise the percentage of CO and counterclockwise to lower the percentage of CO.

7. Remove the tool after each adjustment and accelerate the engine briefly before reading the percentage of CO. The correct CO values are as follows:

Idle speed adjustment screw (A)—1982 Rabbit

Idle speed adjustment screw—fuel injected Rabbit, Jetta, Scirocco

Idle speed adjustment screw—fuel injected Dasher

49 States:1976–78 1.5% M/T; 1.0% A/T
1979–80 0.6 + 0.4%
California:1976: 0.5%
1977–78: 0.3%
1979: 0.5 + 0.4%

1980 California, 1981 and Later Models

1. The engine must be at operating temperature.
2. Disconnect crankcase breather hose at the cylinder head and plug the hose.
3. Disconnect the two plugs on the idle stabilizer at the control unit and plug them together.
4. Do not have any electrical accessories (air conditioner, lights, etc.) on.
5. Connect a tachometer and timing light. Check the timing. Adjust if necessary.
6. Check the idle speed against the specifications chart or your underhood sticker. Adjust the idle at the idle adjustment screw on the throttle chamber (880–1000 rpm).

NOTE: Only adjust the idle when the radiator fan is not on.

The CO adjustment on these engines is sealed to prevent unauthorized adjustment. The only way CO levels can be adjusted on these models is with special dealer tools (frequency counter, CO tester, etc.) which are usually not available to the general public.

CO adjusting tool installed—CIS fuel injection (Rabbit, Jetta, Scirocco shown)

Diesel Fuel Injection

IDLE SPEED/MAXIMUM SPEED ADJUSTMENTS

Volkswagen diesel engines have both an idle speed and a maximum speed adjustment. The maximum engine speed adjustment prevents the engine from over-revving and self-destructing. The adjusters are located side by side on top of the injection pump. The screw closest to the engine is the idle speed adjuster, while the outer screw is the maximum speed adjuster.

The idle and maximum speed must be adjusted with the engine warm (normal operating temperature). Because the diesel engine has no conventional ignition, you will need a special adaptor (VW 1324) to connect your tachometer, or use the tachometer in the instrument panel, if equipped. You should check with the manufacturer of your tachometer to see if it will work with diesel engines. Adjust all engines to 770–870 rpm (through 1980) or 800–850 rpm (1981 and later).

NOTE: The sticker on your pre-1978 Rabbit may indicate an idle range of 850–950 rpm. This has been altered by Volkswagen to 770–870 rpm.

When adjustment is correct, lock the locknut on the screw and apply non-hardening thread sealer (Loctite® or similar) to prevent the screw from vibrating loose.

The maximum speed for all engines is between 5500 and 5600 rpm (through 1980) or 5300–5400 rpm (1981 and later). If it is not in this range, loosen the screw and correct the speed (turning the screw clockwise decreases rpm). Lock the nut on the adjusting screw and apply a dab of thread sealer in the same manner as you did on the idle screw.

—————— CAUTION ——————

Do not attempt to squeeze more power out of your engine by raising the maximum speed (rpm). If you do, you'll probably be in for a major overhaul in the not too distant future.

Special adapter VW 1324 is necessary to use an external tachometer on diesel engines

Diesel engine idle speed (upper) and maximum speed (lower) adjustment screws

ENGINE ELECTRICAL

Distributor

The distributor is a single breaker point unit on all 1976–79 models, and some 1980 models. Electronic ignition is used on all 1981 and later models and some 1980 models. It has both centrifugal and vacuum advance mechanisms. A vacuum retard system works only at idle.

The distributor is gear driven by an intermediate shaft which also drives the fuel pump. The distributor shaft also turns the oil pump.

REMOVAL AND INSTALLATION

1. Disconnect the coil high tension wire.
2. Detach the primary wire.

CAP

ROTOR

SPRING

HOUSING

CONTACT POINT ASSEMBLY

CONDENSER

VACUUM CONTROL

Exploded view of the points-type distributor

Rotor alignment with the notch for No. 1 cylinder

The oil pump drive should be parallel to the crankshaft

3. Remove the distributor cap.-4.-Turn the engine until the rotor aligns with the index mark on the outer edge of the distributor. This is the no. 1 position. Mark the bottom of the distributor housing and its mounting flange on the engine.

5. Remove the bolt and lift off the retaining flange. Lift the distributor straight out of the engine.

If the engine has not been disturbed while the distributor was out i.e., the crankshaft was not turned, then reinstall the distributor in the reverse order of removal. Carefully align the marks.

If the engine has been rotated while the distributor was out, then proceed as follows:

1. Turn the crankshaft so that No. 1 piston is on its compression stroke and the 0°T timing mark is aligned with the V-shaped pointer.

2. Turn the distributor so that the rotor points approximately 15° before the No. 1 cylinder position on the distributor.

3. Insert the distributor into the engine block. If the oil pump drive doesn't engage, remove the distributor and, using a long screwdriver, turn the pump shaft so that it is parallel to the centerline of the crankshaft.

4. Install the distributor, aligning the marks. Tighten the retaining nut.

5. Install the cap. Adjust the ignition timing.

Alternator

ALTERNATOR PRECAUTIONS

An alternating current (AC) generator (alternator) is used. Unlike the direct current (DC) generators used in many older cars, there are several precautions which must be strictly observed in order to avoid damaging the unit.

1. Reversing the battery connections will result in damage to the diodes.

2. Booster batteries should be connected from *negative to negative, and positive to positive*.

3. Never use a fast charger as a booster to start cars with AC circuits; use a "trickle charger."

4. When servicing the battery with a charger, always disconnect the car battery cables.

5. Never attempt to polarize an AC generator.

6. Avoid long soldering times when replacing diodes or transistors. Prolonged heat is damaging to AC generators.

7. Do not use test lamps of more than 12 volts (V) for checking diode continuity.

8. Do not short across or ground any of the terminals on the AC generator.

9. The polarity of the battery, generator, and regulator must be matched and considered before making any electrical connections within the system.

10. Never operate the AC generator on an open circuit. Make sure that all connections within the circuit are clean and tight.

11. Disconnect the battery terminals when performing any service on the electrical system. This will eliminate the possibility of accidental reversal of polarity.

12. Disconnect the battery ground cable if arc welding is to be done on any part of the car.

REMOVAL AND INSTALLATION

The alternator and 'voltage regulator are combined in one housing. No voltage adjustment can be made with this unit. The regulator can be replaced without removing

Removing the lower alternator bolt through the timing cover

the alternator. Unbolt the regulator and remove from the rear.

1. Disconnect the battery cables.

2. Remove the multi-connector retaining bracket and unplug the connector from the rear of the alternator.

3. Loosen and remove the top mounting nut and bolt.

4. Using a socket inserted through the timing belt cover (it is not necessary to remove the cover), loosen the lower mounting bolt.

5. Swing the alternator over and remove the alternator belt.

6. Remove the lower nut and bolt.

7. Remove the alternator.

8. Install the alternator with the lower bolt. *Do not* tighten it at this point.

9. Install the alternator belt over the pulleys.

10. Loosely install the top mounting bolt and pivot the alternator until the belt is correctly tensioned.

11. Tighten the top and bottom bolts to 14 ft. lbs.

12. Connect the alternator and battery wires.

BELT REPLACEMENT AND TENSIONING

1. Loosen the top alternator mounting bolt.

2. Using a socket inserted through the timing belt cover loosen the lower mounting bolt.

3. Use a wooden hammer handle or a broomstick to lever the alternator over and remove the belt.

4. Slip the new belt over the pulleys.

5. Pry the alternator over until the belt deflection midway between the crankshaft pulley and the alternator pulley is 3/8–9/16 in. (10–15 mm).

6. Securely tighten the mounting bolts.

Starter

Volkswagen has used two different types of starters on their water-cooled cars since 1974. All models covered in this book, with the exception of the Jetta equipped with automatic transmission, use the new post-1975 starter. This starter does not utilize a rear support bracket, as does the old-type (Jetta automatic) starter.

REMOVAL AND INSTALLATION

All Models Except Dasher and Quantum Diesel

1. Disconnect the battery ground cable.

2. Raise the front of the car.

3. Mark with tape and then disconnect the wires from the starter solenoid.

4. Disconnect the large cable.

1. Mounting bracket	9. Solenoid
2. End cap screws	10. Disc
3. Housing screws	11. Mounting housing
4. Cupped washer	12. Drive pinion
5. End plate bushing	13. Stop ring
6. Brushes	14. Solenoid bolt
7. Field coil housing	15. Starter bolt and nut
8. Armature	16. Circlip

Exploded view of the typcial starter

Dasher starter electrical connections: (A) solenoid, (B) coil, (C) positive battery cable

Quantum and Dasher starter removal— remove the engine mount and carrier on the starter side (arrows)

5. Remove the starter retaining nuts.

6. Unscrew the bolt. Remove the starter.

7. Installation of the starter is carried out in reverse order of removal.

Dasher and Quantum Diesel

1. Disconnect the battery ground cable.

2. Support the weight of the engine with either Volkswagen Special Tool 10-222 or use a jack with a block of wood under the oil pan. Don't jack the engine too high, just take the weight off the motor mounts. *Be careful not to bend the oil pan.*

3. Remove the engine/transmission cover plate.

4. Unbolt and remove the starter side motor mount and carrier.

5. Disconnect and mark the starter wiring.

6. Remove the bolts holding the starter and remove the starter.

7. Install the starter and tighten the nuts and bolts to 14 ft. lbs.

8. Install the engine mount and carrier.

9. Install and attach remaining components. Don't forget to reconnect the battery cable.

OVERHAUL

Use the following procedure to replace brushes or starter drive.

1. Remove the solenoid.

2. Remove the end bearing cap.

3. Loosen both of the long housing screws.

4. Remove the lockwasher and spacer washers.

5. Remove the long housing screws and remove the end cover.

6. Pull the two field coil brushes out of the brush housing.

7. Remove the brush housing assembly.

8. Loosen the nut on the solenoid housing, remove the sealing disc, and remove the solenoid operating lever.

9. Loosen the large screws on the side of the starter body and remove the field coil along with the brushes.

NOTE: If the brushes require replacement, the field coil and brushes and/or the brush housing and its brushes must be replaced as a unit.

10. If the starter drive is being replaced push the stop-ring down and remove the circlip on the end of the shaft. Remove the stop-ring and remove the drive.

11. Assembly of the starter is carried out in the reverse order of disassembly. Use a gear puller to install the stop-ring in its groove (on models so equipped). Use a new circlip on the shaft.

SOLENOID REPLACEMENT

1. Remove the starter

2. Remove the nut which secures the connector strip on the end of the solenoid.

3. Take out the two retaining screws on the mounting bracket and pull out the solenoid after it has been unhooked from the operating lever.

4. Installation is the reverse of removal. In order to facilitate engagement of the lever, the pinion should be pulled out as far as possible when inserting the solenoid.

Diesel Engine

GLOW PLUG SYSTEM CHECK

NOTE: The 1982 and later diesels have a new type quick-glow system. Nominal glow time is seven seconds. Although the wiring for this system is the same as the earlier system, the glow plugs and relay cannot be paired or interchanged with earlier parts or vice versa.

1. Connect a test light between No. 4 cylinder (rear cylinder on Dasher and Quantum and the cylinder closest to the driver's side on the Rabbit and Jetta) glow plug and ground. The glow plugs are connected by a flat, coated busbar (located near the bottom of the cylinder head).

2. Turn the ignition key to the heating (pre-glow) position. The test light should light.

3. If not, possible problems include the glow plug relay, the ignition switch and the fuse box relay plate and the glow plug fuse or a break in the wire to the relay terminal.

INDIVIDUAL GLOW PLUG TEST

1. Remove the wire and busbar from the glow plugs.

2. Connect a test light to the battery positive terminal.

3. Touch the test light probe to each glow plug in turn.

If the test light lights, the plug is good. If the light does not light, replace the glow plug(s).

ENGINE MECHANICAL

Engine

REMOVAL AND INSTALLATION

NOTE: A good rule to follow when removing engines from all models is to label all hoses, electrical wires, and linkages and their connections with tape.

Number each tape tag and the place it connects; this should help eliminate the hassles of "Where does this go?" during installation.

Dasher and Quantum

GASOLINE ENGINES

1. Disconnect the battery cables.

2. Remove the exhaust manifold heater hose and breather hose from the air cleaner.

3. Remove the air cleaner assembly.

4. On carbureted models, pull the clip off the accelerator cable and detach the cable. On fuel injected models, disconnect the electrical connector for the fuel injection, cold start valve, oxygen sensor and frequency valve (if equipped), and detach the control pressure regulator lines.

5. Loosen the upper adjustment nut on the clutch cable and detach it. (On Quantum, remove clip on clutch cable and unhook cable).

6. On carbureted models only, disconnect the fuel line from the fuel pump, plug it, and place it out of the way. On fuel injected models, disconnect the air duct. Remove the cold start valve. Remove the fuel injectors from the head (protect the ends with caps) and the accelerator cable. Remove the air flow sensor with the fuel distributor and place out of the way.

7. Detach emission control hoses. Remove power steering pump and V-belts, if equipped.

8. Disconnect the wiring from the alternator.

9. Detach the clip and remove the heater cable.

CAUTION
Do not disconnect refrigerant lines on cars equipped with air conditioning.

---

10. On cars with air conditioning:

a. Remove the horn, compressor and condenser assemblies.

b. Move the compressor and condensers out of the way, without disconnecting the refrigerant lines.

c. Disconnect the vacuum hoses and brake booster hose, if equipped.

11. Disconnect the front engine mount and remove the mount bracket.

12. Drain the coolant from the radiator. The plug is located near the lower hose, or

Quantum, Dasher engine side mounts

Lifting the Quantum and Dasher engine out of the car. Note that it must be turned for removal

remove the hose on models without the drain plug. Drain the cylinder block at the plug near the starter.

13. Disconnect the electrical wire from the coil and distributor, oil pressure and temperature sending units, fan and the thermal switch on the radiator.

14. Disconnect the radiator and heater hoses from the engine. Detach the heater valve cable.

15. Loosen the radiator shroud retainers. Remove the mounting bolts and nuts and lift out the radiator and fan.

16. Raise the front of the car and safely support it.

17. Remove the starter.

18. Disconnect the exhaust pipe from the manifold.

19. Detach the engine side mounts.

20. Loosen the upper engine-to-transmission bolts. Remove the lower bolts. If the car is equipped with an automatic transmission, remove the three torque converter-to-flywheel bolts by working through the starter hole. Use a bar to hold the flywheel. Also disconnect the automatic transmission vacuum hose.

21. Support the transmission with a floor jack.

22. Lower the car until the wheels are on the ground.

23. Attach the hoist to the engine lift points.

24. Raise the engine/transmission until the transmission touches the steering rack.

25. Adjust your jack or support so that the transmission is held firmly.

On automatic transmissions, remove three torque converter-to-flywheel bolts through the starter hole (Quantum and Dasher)

Remove the lower engine/transmission bolts and flywheel cover (arrows)

26. Remove the upper engine-to-transmission bolts.

27. Pry the engine and transmission apart and remove the intermediate plate. Install a bar or cable to the torque converter housing on automatic cars to prevent the converter from falling out.

28. Remove the engine by slowly lifting and turning simultaneously.

— CAUTION —

Do this very carefully to avoid damaging the halfshafts or transmission.

29. Installation is the reverse of removal. Be careful not to damage the input shaft of the transmission during installation. Install new torque converter mounting bolts. Tighten the torque converter bolts to 25 ft. lbs., engine to transaxle bolts to 40 ft. lbs., and the engine mount bolts to 32 ft. lbs.

DIESEL ENGINES

1. Remove the negative battery cable.

2. Set the heat control to hot. Remove the lower radiator hose and remove the thermostat to drain the coolant. Remove the thermoswitch electrical connector and the radiator brace at the bottom of the radiator, remove the top radiator shroud, upper hose, radiator mounting bolts, and remove the radiator and fan.

3. Remove the supply and return lines from the injection pump. Disconnect the throttle cable from the pump and remove the cable mounting bracket. Disconnect the cold start cable at the pin, and remove the electrical connector from the fuel shut-off solenoid.

4. Disconnect the electrical connectors from the oil pressure switch, coolant temperature sensor and glow plugs. Remove the radiator hose from the head and the vacuum hose from the vacuum pump.

5. Loosen the adjusting nuts and unhook the clutch cable from the lever.

6. Remove the hose from the water pump.

7. On Quantum, unbolt the rear of the turbocharger (if equipped) from the exhaust system.

8. Loosen the right engine mount.

9. Remove the alternator after tagging the wires for installation.

10. Remove the front engine mounts.

11. Disconnect the exhaust pipe from the manifold, and the pipe bracket from the transmission.

12. Loosen the left engine mount.

13. Remove the starter.

14. Remove the engine-to-transmission bolts, and the flywheel cover bolts.

15. Attach a lifting chain to the engine and raise the engine until the transmission touches the steering rack. Remove the left engine mount.

16. Support the transmission with a jack and raise and turn the engine at the same time to remove.

17. Installation is the reverse. Tighten the engine-to-transmission bolts to 40 ft. lbs. and the engine mount bolts to 29 ft. lbs. After installation adjust the throttle and cold starting cables.

Rabbit, Jetta and Scirocco with Manual Transmission

GASOLINE ENGINES

The engine and transmission are removed as an assembly.

1. Disconnect the battery ground cable.

2. Drain the coolant by unbolting the lower water pump flange or by removing the hoses.

— CAUTION —

Do not disconnect or loosen any refrigerant hose connections during engine removal on cars equipped with air conditioning.

3. On cars equipped with air conditioning:

   a. Loosen the compressor support bolts and remove the compressor.

   b. Remove the radiator cooling fan, air ducts and radiator.

   c. Remove the condenser.

Aligning flywheel for manual transmission and engine separation—Rabbit, Jetta, Scirocco

d. Place the air conditioning compressor and condenser out of the way without disconnecting any refrigerant lines.

4. Remove the radiator with the air ducts and fan.

5. Detach and label all the electrical wires connecting the engine to the body.

6. Disconnect and plug the fuel line at the fuel pump. Detach the coolant hoses at the left end of the engine. Disconnect the accelerator cable and remove the air cleaner.

7. Disconnect the speedometer cable from the transmission. Detach the clutch cable.

8. Remove the engine support to the right of the starter.

9. Remove the headlight caps inside the engine compartment.

10. Unbolt the driveshafts from the transmission and wire them up. up.

11. Unbolt the exhaust pipe from the manifold and unbolt the exhaust pipe brace.

12. Unbolt the transmission rear mount from the body (alongside the tunnel).

13. Detach the ground strap from the transmission and body.

14. Remove the shift linkage.

15. Attach a chain sling to the alternator bracket and the lifting eye at the left end of the engine. Lift the engine and transmission slightly.

16. Detach the engine carrier from the body and remove the left transmission carrier.

17. Lift the engine/transmission assembly carefully out of the car.

18. To separate the engine and transmission, turn the flywheel to align the lug on the flywheel (to the left of TDC) with the pointer in the opening. The engine and transmission can only be separated in this position. Remove the cover plate over the driveshaft flange and remove the engine to transmission bolts and the transmission housing cover plate.

To install the engine:

19. To attach the transmission to the engine, the recess in the flywheel edge must be at 3:00 o'clock (facing the left end of the engine). Torque the engine to transmission bolts to 40 ft./lbs. Lift the engine/transmission assembly into place. Loosen the bolts for the engine and transmission mounts. Move the engine assembly from side to side until the rear transmission mount is straight. Center the left and right transmission mounts and tighten all transmission bolts. Push the front mount upward to center the rubber cone, then tighten the mount. Loosen the exhaust pipe clamps, release any strain, then tighten the clamps. Torque the 10 mm bolts to 29 ft. lbs. Torque the driveshaft flange bolts to 32 ft. lbs. Refill the cooling system.

Rabbit, Jetta and Scirocco with Automatic Transmission

GASOLINE ENGINES

The engine and transmission are removed as an assembly.

1. Shift the transmission into "Park." Disconnect both battery cables.

2. Drain the coolant by unbolting the lower water pump flange or by removing the hoses.

─────── CAUTION ───────

Do not disconnect or loosen any refrigerant hose connections during engine removal on cars equipped with air conditioning.

3. On cars equipped with air conditioning proceed as follows:

a. Loosen the compressor support bolts and remove the compressor.

b. Remove the radiator cooling fan, air ducts, and radiator.

c. Remove the condenser.

d. Place the air conditioning components out of the way without disconnecting any refrigerant lines.

4. Remove the radiator with the air ducts and fan.

5. Remove the air cleaner.

6. Detach the speedometer cable from the transmission.

7. Detach and label all electrical wires connecting the engine to the body. Detach and label all heater and coolant hoses.

8. Remove the screws holding the accelerator cable bracket to the carburetor float bowl (do not disassemble linkage), detach the end of the gearshift selector cable from the transmission, detach the accelerator cable and pedal cable at the transmission, and remove the two bracket bolts behind this linkage on the transmission.

9. Unbolt the exhaust pipe from the manifold.

10. Remove the rear transmission mount. Unbolt the driveshafts and wire them up and out of the way.

11. Remove the converter cover plate and remove the three torque converter to drive plate bolts.

12. Attach a chain sling to the alternator bracket and the lifting eye at the left end of the engine. It may be necessary to remove the alternator. Lift the engine and transmission slightly.

13. Detach the engine front mounting support; remove the left transmission carrier and the right engine carrier.

14. Lift the engine/transmission assembly carefully out of the car.

15. The transmission can now be detached from the engine.

To install the engine:

16. The engine to transmission bolts should be torqued to 40 ft. lbs. Lift the engine/transmission assembly into place and install the left transmission carrier, tightening first the body, then the transmission bolts. Lower the assembly to attach the engine carrier to the body, tightening the bolts to 40 ft. lbs. Install the engine mounting

support. Check that all mounts and clamps are free of strain. Torque converter bolts should be torqued to 21 ft. lbs. and driveshaft bolts to 32 ft. lbs. Refill the cooling system. Check the adjustment of transmission and carburetor linkages.

DIESEL ENGINES

The diesel engine is removed with the transmission attached.

1. Disconnect the battery.

2. Disconnect the radiator hoses and drain the coolant. It can be saved for reuse, if it's not too old.

3. Remove the radiator complete with fan.

4. Remove the alternator.

5. Disconnect the fuel filter and set it aside near the windshield washer reservoir.

6. Detach the supply and return lines from the injection pump.

7. Disconnect the accelerator cable from the lever on the injection pump and remove the injection pump complete with bracket.

8. Disconnect the cold start cable from the pump.

9. Disconnect and label all electrical wires and leads.

10. Remove the front transmission mount.

11. Disconnect the clutch cable.

12. Remove the relay rod and connecting rod from the transmission and turn the relay lever shaft to the rear.

13. Disconnect the selector rod.

14. Unbolt the driveshafts and wire them up out of the way. Remove the rear support.

15. Disconnect the exhaust pipe at the manifold and remove the rear transmission mount.

16. Attach a lifting sling to the engine and take the weight from the engine mounts. Remove the left and right transmission mounts.

17. Carefully guide the engine out of the car while turning it slightly.

18. To separate the engine from the transmission, unscrew the plug from the TDC sensor opening and turn the flywheel to align the mark on the flywheel with the pointer. The engine/transmission can only be separated in this position.

19. Remove the cover plate over the driveshaft flange and remove the engine-to-transmission bolts.

20. Press the engine off the transmission.

21. Installation is the reverse of removal. Turn the flywheel so that the recess in the flywheel is level with the driveshaft flange. Lower the engine into the car and attach the left transmission mount to the transmission first. Align the rear transmission mount, center the engine/transmission and center the front transmission mount. Adjust the accelerator and cold start cables and bleed the injection system.

Cylinder Head

REMOVAL AND INSTALLATION

The engine should be cold before the cylinder head can be removed. The head is retained by 10 socket head (Allen) bolts. It can be removed without removing the intake and exhaust manifolds.

> **CAUTION**
>
> *Beginning approximately July 1977, 12 point socket head bolts were used in place of 6 point older version. These should be used in complete sets only and need not be retorqued after the mileage interval.*

Carbureted Engines

1. Disconnect the battery ground cable.
2. Drain the cooling system.
3. Remove the air cleaner. Disconnect the fuel line.
4. Disconnect the radiator, heater, and choke hoses.
5. Disconnect all electrical wires. Remove the spark plug wires.
6. Separate the exhaust manifold from the exhaust pipe.
7. Disconnect the EGR line from the exhaust manifold. Remove the EGR valve and filter from the intake manifold.
8. Remove the carburetor.
9. Disconnect the air pump fittings.
10. Remove the timing belt cover and belt.
11. Loosen the cylinder head bolts in the reverse of the tightening sequence.
12. Remove the bolts and lift the head straight off.
13. Install the *new* cylinder head gasket with the word TOP or OBEN up.
14. Install bolts no. 10 and 8 first; these holes are smaller and will properly locate the gasket and cylinder head.
15. Install the remaining bolts. Tighten them in three stages in the sequence shown. Cylinder head bolt torque (cold) is 55 ft. lbs., 12 point bolts should be tightened to 55 ft. lbs. then tightened ¼ turn more.

NOTE: After approximately 1000 miles, retighten the cylinder head bolts. Torque them hot to 61 ft. lbs. (six point bolts only).

16. Install the remaining components in the reverse order of removal.

Fuel Injected Engines

1. Disconnect the battery ground cable.
2. Drain the cooling system.
3. Disconnect the air duct from the throttle valve assembly.
4. Disconnect the throttle valve assembly.
5. Remove the injectors and disconnect the line from the cold start valve.

Exploded view of the diesel engine cylinder head showing the valve train components—gasoline engines similar

6. Disconnect the radiator and heater hoses.
7. Disconnect the vacuum and PCV lines (label lines for installation).
8. Remove the auxiliary air regulator from the intake manifold.
9. Disconnect all electrical lines and remove the spark plugs (label all lines and wires for installation).
10. Separate the exhaust manifold from the exhaust pipe.
11. Remove the EGR line from the exhaust manifold.
12. Remove the intake manifold.
13. Remove the timing belt cover and belt.
14. Loosen the cylinder head bolts in the reverse of the tightening sequence.
15. Remove the bolts and lift the head straight off.
16. Check the flatness of the cylinder block in both width ano length, then diagonally from each corner.
17. Install the *new* cylinder head gasket with the word TOP or OBEN facing upward.
18. Install bolts No. 10 and 8 first; these holes are smaller and will properly locate the gasket and cylinder head.

19. Install the reamining bolts. Tighten them in three stages using the sequence shown in the illustration. Cylinder head bolts must be torqued cold to 55 ft. lbs. 12 point bolts should be tightened to 55 ft. lbs., then tightened ¼ turn more.

NOTE: After 1000 miles, retighten the cylinder head bolts to 61 ft. lbs. hot (six point bolts only).

20. Install the remaining components in the reverse order of removal.

Diesel Engines

The head is retained by Allen bolts. The engine should be cold when the head is removed to avoid chances of warpage. The word TOP or OBEN on the new gasket should face up.

1. Disconnect the battery ground cable.
2. Drain the cooling system.
3. Remove the air cleaner.
4. Disconnect the fuel lines. Disconnect and tag all electrical wires and leads.
5. Separate the exhaust manifold from the pipe. Disconnect the radiator and heater hoses.

6. Remove the timing cover and belt (See "Timing Belt Replacement").

7. Loosen the cylinder head bolts in the reverse order of the tightening sequence.

8. Remove the head. *Do not lay the head on the gasket surface with the injectors installed.* Support it at the ends on strips of wood.

9. Install the cylinder head with a *new* gasket. Be sure the new gasket has the same number of notches and the same identifying number as the old one, unless the pistons were also repeated.

Install bolts 8 and 10 first and torque the bolts to the specification in the proper sequence. After 1000 miles, loosen all bolts ⅓ turn and retorque the bolts.

OVERHAUL

Valve guides are a shrink fit. Always install new valve seals when doing a valve job. Valve seats are not replaceable; the cylinder head should be replaced if the seat width and face angle cannot be maintained.

Refer to general information section under Engine Overhaul.

Intake Manifold

REMOVAL AND INSTALLATION

Carbureted Models

1. Remove the air cleaner. Drain the cooling system.

2. Disconnect the accelerator cable.

3. Disconnect the EGR valve connections.

4. Detach all electrical leads.

5. Disconnect the coolant hoses.

6. Disconnect the fuel line from the carburetor.

7. Remove the vacuum hoses from the carburetor.

8. Loosen and remove the retaining bolts and lift off the manifold.

9. Install a new gasket. Install the manifold and tighten the bolts from the inside out. Tightening torque is 18 ft. lbs.

10. Install the remaining components in the reverse order of removal. Refill the cooling system.

Fuel Injected Models

1. Disconnect the air duct from the throttle valve body. Drain the cooling system.

2. Disconnect the accelerator cable.

3. Remove the injectors and disconnect the line from the cold start valve.

4. Disconnect all coolant hoses.

5. Disconnect all vacuum and emission control hoses (label all hoses for installation).

6. Remove the auxiliary air regulator.

7. Disconnect all electrical lines (label all wires for installation).

8. Disconnect the EGR line from the exhaust manifold.

9. Loosen and remove the retaining bolts and lift off the manifold.

10. Install a new gasket. Install the manifold and tighten the bolts to 18 ft. lbs.

11. Install the remaining components in the reverse order of removal.

Exhaust Manifold

REMOVAL AND INSTALLATION

1. Disconnect the EGR tube from the exhaust manifold.

2. Remove the interfering air pump components if so equipped.

3. Remove the air cleaner hose from the exhaust manifold.

4. Disconnect the intake manifold support.

5. Separate the exhaust pipe from the manifold.

6. Remove the retaining nuts and remove the manifold.

7. Clean the cylinder head and manifold mating surfaces.

8. Install the exhaust manifold using a new gasket.

9. Tighten the nuts to 18 ft./lbs. Work from the inside out.

10. Install the remaining components in the reverse order of removal. Use a new manifold flange gasket.

Time Belt Cover

REMOVAL AND INSTALLATION

1. Loosen the alternator mounting bolts.

2. Pivot the alternator and slip the drive belt off the sprockets.

3. Unscrew the cover retaining nuts and remove the cover.

4. Reposition the spacers on the studs and then install the washers and nuts.

5. Install the alternator belt and adjust its tension.

Timing Belt

NOTE: The timing belt is designed to last for more than 60,000 miles and does not normally require tension adjustments. If the belt is removed or replaced, the basic valve timing must be checked and the belt retensioned.

REMOVAL, INSTALLATION, AND TENSIONING

Gasoline Engines

Timing belt installation will be easier if the engine is set to TDC prior to belt removal.

The 0°T mark will be aligned with the pointer on the bell housing, and the mark on the rear face of the camshaft pulley will align with the camshaft cover gasket on the left. Also, the V-notch in the camshaft pulley should align with the dot mark on the intermediate shaft, and the distributor rotor should be pointing toward the mark on the rim of the housing.

If the belt has broken and timing is off, remove the belt cover and belt, then set the engine to TDC before installing the belt, as outlined in Steps 5, 6, and 7.

1. Remove the timing belt cover.

2. While holding the large hex on the tension sprocket, loosen the pulley locknut.

3. Release the tensioner from the timing belt.

4. Slide the belt off the three toothed sprockets and remove it.

5. Turn the crankshaft until no. 1 cylinder is at TDC. At this point, the 0°T mark will be aligned with the pointer on the bell housing.

6. Align the timing mark on the rear face of the camshaft pulley with the camshaft cover gasket on the left.

7. Align the V-notch in the crankshaft pulley with the dot mark on the intermediate shaft. The distributor rotor should be pointing to the no. 1 cylinder mark on the rim of the distributor.

Camshaft sprocket alignment

Crankshaft pulley and intermediate shaft sprocket alignment

CAUTION

If the timing marks are not correctly aligned, valve timing will be incorrect. Poor performance and serious engine damage can result from improper valve timing. Steps 5, 6, and 7 should not be necessary if the engine was in time and set to TDC prior to belt removal.

0° T or TDC mark on the flywheel

8. Install the belt on the sprockets.

9. Adjust the tensioner by turning the large tensioner hex to the right. Tension is correct when you can just twist the belt 90° with two fingers at the midpoint. Tighten the locknut to 32 ft. lbs.

10. Install the timing belt cover and check the ignition timing.

Diesel Engine

NOTE: This procedure will require a number of special tools and a certain expertise with diesel engines. You may wish to have the work performed by an authorized VW service technician.

1. Remove the timing belt cover. Remove the cylinder head cover.

2. Turn the engine so that No. 1 cylinder is at TDC and fix the camshaft in posotion with tool 2065A. Align the tool as follows:

   a. Turn the camshaft until one end of the tool touches the cylinder head.

   b. Measure the gap at the other end of the tool with a feeler gauge.

   c. Take half of the measurement and insert a feeler gauge of this thickness between the tool and the cylinder head; turn the camshaft so that the tool rests on the feeler gauge.

   d. Insert a second feeler gauge of the same thickness between the other end of the tool and the cylinder head.

3. Lock the injection pump sprocket in position with pin 2064.

4. Check that the marks on the sprocket, bracket and pump body are in alignment (engine at TDC).

5. Loosen the timing belt tensioner. Remove the V-belt from the crankshaft.

6. Remove the timing belt.

To install:

7. Check that the TDC mark on the flywheel is aligned with the reference marks.

8. Loosen the camshaft sprocket bolt ½ turn and then loosen the gear from the camshaft end by tapping it with a rubber mallet.

9. Install the timing belt and remove pin 2064 from the injection pump sprocket.

10. Tension the belt by turning the tensioner to the right. Check the belt tension as detailed later in this section.

11. Tighten the camshaft sprocket bolt to 33 ft. lbs.

1. Alternator belt
2. Belt pulleys
3. Timing gear cover
4. Crankshaft sprocket
5. Intermediate sprocket
6. Drive belt
7. Tensioner
8. Camshaft sprocket

Exploded view of camshaft drive arrangement

12. Remove the tool from the camshaft.

13. Turn the crankshaft two turns in the direction of engine rotation (clockwise) and then strike the belt once with a rubber mallet between the camshaft sprocket and the injection pump sprocket.

14. Check the belt tension again. Check the injection pump timing.

Timing Sprockets

REMOVAL AND INSTALLATION

The camshaft, intermediate shaft, and crankshaft sprockets are located by keys on their respective shafts (Diesel engine camshaft sprockets are a taper-fit; no keys are used) and each is retained by a bolt. To remove any or all of the pulleys, first remove the timing belt cover and belt.

NOTE: When removing the crankshaft pulley, don't remove the four Allen head bolts which hold the outer belt pulley to the timing belt sprocket.

Turn the tensioner (3) toward (1) to tighten belt and toward (2) to loosen. Check tension at (4)

1. Remove the center bolt.
2. Gently pry the sprocket off the shaft. If the gear does not come off easily, use a gear puller. Don't hammer on the sprocket.
3. Remove the sprocket and key (gasoline engine only).
4. Install in the reverse order of removal.
5. Coat the center bolt with Loctite® or similar locking compound, and tighten to 58 ft. lbs. (all gas engines and 1.5 liter diesel) and 108 ft. lbs. (1.6 liter diesel).
6. Install the timing belt, check the valve timing, tension the belt, and install the cover.

Camshaft

REMOVAL AND INSTALLATION

1. Remove the timing belt.
2. Remove the camshaft sprocket.
3. Remove the air cleaner.
4. Remove the camshaft cover.
5. Unscrew and remove the no. 1, 3, and 5 bearing caps (no. 1 is at the front).
6. Unscrew the no. 2 and 4 bearing caps, diagonally and in increments.
7. Lift the camshaft out of the cylinder head.
8. Lubricate the camshaft journals and lobes with assembly lube or gear oil before installing it in the cylinder head.
9. Replace the camshaft oil seal with a new one whenever the cam is removed.

10. Install the no. 1, 3, and 5 bearing caps and tighten the nuts to 14 ft. lbs. Note that the bores are offset, and the numbers are not always on the same side.
11. Install the no. 2 and 4 bearing caps and diagonally tighten the nuts to 14 ft. lbs.

NOTE: If checking end play, install a dial indicator so that the feeler touches the camshaft snout. End-play should be no more than 0.006 in. (0.15 mm).

12. Replace the seal in the No. 1 bearing cap. If necessary, replace the end plug in the cylinder head.
13. Install the camshaft cover.
14. Install the camshaft pulley and the timing belt.
15. Check the valve clearance.

Piston and Connecting Rods

GASOLINE ENGINES

The pistons must be installed in the block with the arrow at the edge of the crown facing to the front of the car on Dashers and Quantums and toward the right front wheel on Rabbits, Sciroccos and Jettas. The connecting rod and cap alignment casting grooves must face the intermediate shaft. New connecting rod bolts must always be used. The pistons must be heated to 140°F

The arrow on the piston must face the camshaft drive belt

in an oven before the piston pins can be pressed in. Three piston oversizes are available to accommodate overbores up to 0.040 in.

There is a piston size code stamped on the cylinder block above the water pump.

NOTE: 1978 and later models have different pistons from 1976–77 models. The parts are not interchangeable.

DIESEL ENGINES

The same installation procedures apply to the diesel as to the gas engine. However, whenever new pistons or a short block are installed, the piston projection must be checked.

A spacer (VW 385/17) and bar with a micrometer are necessary, and must be set up to measure the maximum amount of piston projection above the deck height. The following chart should be used to select a head gasket of the correct thickness to match piston projection.

Piston Projection (mm)	Gasket Identification No. of Notches	Part Number
0.43–0.63	2	068 103 383
0.63–0.82	3	068 103 383C
0.82–0.92	4	068 103 383G
0.92–1.02	5	068 103 383H

The connecting rod and cap alignment casting grooves must face the intermediate shaft

1. Camshaft bearing caps
2. Camshaft cover
3. Gasket
4. Valve adjusting disc
5. Oil seal
6. Cam follower
7. End plug
8. Camshaft

Exploded view of the camshaft assembly—gasoline engines (diesel similar)

Beginning with Sept., 1977, production, the piston height (A) on diesel engines was increased from 1.759 in. to 1.768 in.

New diesel pistons (since Sept., 1977) are identified by a number "9" next to the arrow denoting installation direction

NOTE: 1978 and later models (beginning with engine CK 024 944) have pistons with a new piston height and a thicker cylinder head gasket. These pistons are marked with a "9" next to installation direction arrow. New pistons can be used in earlier cars, but only in sets of 4.

ENGINE LUBRICATION

The lubrication system is a conventional wet-sump design. The gear–type oil pump is driven by the intermediate shaft. A pressure relief valve limits pressure and prevents extreme pressure from developing in the system. All oil is filtered by a full flow replaceable filter. A bypass valve assures lubrication in the event the filter becomes plugged. The oil pressure switch is located at the end of the cylinder head gallery (the end of the system) to assure accurate pressure readings.

Oil Pan

REMOVAL AND INSTALLATION

Dasher and Quantum

1. Drain the oil pan.
2. Support and slightly raise the engine with an overhead hoist.
3. Gradually loosen the engine crossmember mounting bolts. Remove the left and right side engine mounts.
4. Lower the crossmember very carefully.
5. Loosen and remove the oil pan retaining bolts.
6. Lower the pan from the car.
7. Install the pan using a new gasket and sealer.
8. Tighten the retaining bolts in a crosswise pattern. Tighten hex head bolts to 14 ft./lbs., or Allen head bolts to 7 ft. lbs.
9. Raise the crossmember. Tighten the crossmember bolts to 42 ft. lbs. and the engine mounting bolts to 32 ft. lbs.
10. Refill the engine with oil. Start the engine and check for leaks.

Rabbit, Jetta and Scirocco

1. Drain the engine oil.
2. Loosen and remove the bolts retaining the oil pan.
3. Lower the pan from the car.
4. Install the pan using a new oil pan gasket.
5. Tighten the retaining bolts in a crisscross pattern. Tighten hex head bolts to 14 ft. lbs., or Allen head bolts to 7 ft. lbs.
6. Refill the engine with oil. Start the engine and examine the pan for leaks.

1. Oil filler cap seal
2. Oil dipstick
3. Oil pressure switch
4. Oil filter
5. Oil pump gears
6. Oil pan gasket
7. Oil pan
8. Oil drain plug

Lubrication system components

Rear Main Oil Seal

REPLACEMENT

The rear main oil seal is located in a housing on the rear of the cylinder block. To replace the seal on the Dasher and Quantum, it is necessary to remove the transmission and perform the work from underneath the car or remove the engine and perform the work on an engine stand or work bench. See "Transmission Removal and Installation."

On the Rabbit, Jetta and Scirocco, the engine should be removed from the car.

1. Remove the transmission and flywheel.
2. Using a screwdriver, very carefully pry the old seal out of the support ring.
3. Remove the seal.
4. Lightly oil the replacement seal and then press it into place using a circular piece of flat metal. Be careful not to damage the seal or score the crankshaft.
5. Install the flywheel and transmission. Flywheel-to-engine bolts are tightened to 36 ft./lbs.

Oil Pump

REMOVAL AND INSTALLATION

1. Remove the oil pan.
2. Remove the two mounting bolts.
3. Pull the oil pump down and out of the engine.
4. Unscrew the two bolts and separate the pump halves.
5. Remove the driveshaft and gear from the upper body.
6. Clean the bottom half in solvent. Pry up the metal edges to remove the filter screen for cleaning.
7. Examine the gears and driveshaft for wear or damage. Replace them if necessary.
8. Reassemble the pump halves.
9. Prime the pump with oil and install in the reverse order of removal.

ENGINE COOLING

The cooling system consists of a belt driven, external water pump, thermostat, radiator, and thermostatically controlled electric cooling fan. When the engine is cold the thermostat is closed and blocks the water from the radiator so the coolant is circulated only through the engine. When the engine warms up, the thermostat opens and the radiator is included in the coolant circuit. The thermostatic switch is in the bottom of the radiator and turns the electrical fan on

1. Oil seal
2. Flywheel

Rear main oil seal assembly

at 199°F, off at 186°F. This reduces power loss and engine noise.

Radiator and Fan

REMOVAL AND INSTALLATION

1. Drain the cooling system.
2. Remove the inner shroud mounting bolts.
3. Disconnect the lower radiator hose.
4. Disconnect the thermostatic switch lead.
5. Remove the lower radiator shroud.
6. Remove the lower radiator mounting units.
7. Disconnect the upper radiator hose.
8. Detach the upper radiator shroud.
9. Disconnect the heater and intake manifold hoses.
10. Remove the side mounting bolts and lift the radiator and fan out as an assembly.
11. Installation is the reverse of removal.

Thermostat

REMOVAL AND INSTALLATION

The thermostat is located in the bottom radiator hose neck on the water pump.
1. Drain the cooling system.
2. Remove the two retaining bolts from the lower water pump neck.

NOTE: It isn't necessary to disconnect the hose.

3. Move the neck, with the hoses attached, out of the way.
4. Remove the thermostat.
5. Install a new seal on the water pump neck.
6. Install the thermostat with the spring end up.

7. Replace the water pump neck and tighten the two retaining bolts.

Water Pump

REMOVAL AND INSTALLATION

1. Drain the cooling system.
2. Remove the alternator and drive belt.
3. Remove the timing belt cover.
4. Disconnect the lower radiator hose, engine hose, and heater hose from the water pump.
5. Remove the four pump retaining bolts. Notice where the different length bolts are located.
6. Turn the pump slightly and lift it out of the engine block.
7. Installation is the reverse of removal. Use a new seal on the mating surface with the engine. Check O-ring condition and replace if necessary.

Check the condition of the O-ring before installing the water pump

EMISSION CONTROLS

Crankcase Ventilation

The crankcase ventilation system keeps harmful vapor by–products of combustion from escaping into the atmosphere and prevents the building of crankcase pressure which can lead to oil leaking. Crankcase vapors are recirculated from the camshaft cover through a hose to the air cleaner. Here they are mixed with the air/fuel mixture and burned in the combustion chamber.

SERVICE

The only maintenance required on the crankcase ventilation system is a periodic check. At every tune–up, examine the hoses for clogging or deterioration. Clean or replace the hoses as necessary.

Evaporation Emission Control System

This system prevents the escape of raw fuel vapors (unburned hydrocarbons or HC) into the atmosphere. The system consists of a sealed carburetor, unvented fuel tank filler cap, fuel tank expansion chamber, an activated charcoal filter canister and connector hoses. Fuel vapors which reach the filter

deposit hydrocarbons on the surface of the charcoal filter element. Fresh air enters the filter when the engine is running and forces the hydrocarbons to the air cleaner where they join the air/fuel mixture and are burned.

Many 1979 and later models are equipped with a charcoal filter valve which prevents vapors from escaping from the canister when the engine is not running.

SERVICE

Maintenance of the system requires checking the condition of the various connector hoses and the charcoal filter at 10,000 mile intervals. The charcoal filter should be replaced at 50,000 mile intervals.

Dual Diaphragm Distributors

The purpose of the dual diaphragm distributor is to improve exhaust emissions during one of the engine's dirtier operating modes—idling. The distributor has a vacuum retard diaphragm, in addition to a vacuum advance diaphragm. A temperature valve shuts off vacuum from the carburetor when coolant temperatures are below 130°F.

TESTING

Advance Diaphragm

1. Connect a timing light to the engine. Check the ignition timing.
2. Remove the retard hose from the distributor and plug it. Increase the engine speed. The ignition timing should advance. If it doesn't then the vacuum unit is faulty and must be replaced.

Temperature Valve

1. Remove the temperature valve and place the threaded portion in hot water.
2. Create a vacuum by sucking on the angled connection.
3. The valve must be open above approximately 130°F.

Exhaust Gas Recirculation (EGR)

To reduce NOx (oxides of nitrogen) emissions, metered amounts of exhaust gases are added to the air/fuel mixture. The recirculated exhaust gas lowers the peak flame temperature during combustion. Exhaust gas from the manifold passes through a filter where it is cleaned. The vacuum operated EGR valve controls the volume of this exhaust gas which is allowed into the intake manifold. There is no EGR at idle, partial at slight throttle and full EGR at mid-throttle.

EGR system schematic

1. Air cleaner
2. Carburetor venturi
3. Throttle valve
4. Intake manifold
5. Cylinder head intake port
6. Cylinder head exhaust port
7. Belt drive for air pump
8. Air pump
9. Air pump filter
10. Pressure relief valve
11. Check valve
12. Diverter valve
13. Distributor
14. EGR filter
15. EGR valve
16. Crankcase ventilation

Carbureted Dasher emission control system. Arrows indicate flow

1. Air cleaner	8. Air pump air filter	15. Temperature valve
2. Carburetor	9. Diverter valve	16. Catalytic converter
3. Intake manifold	10. Pressure valve	17. Muffler
4. Intake port	11. Anti-backfire valve	18. Converter temperature light
5. Exhaust port	12. Distributor	19. EGR system indicator light
6. Air pump belt	13. EGR filter	20. Converter indicator light
7. Air pump	14. EGR valve	21. Crankcase ventilation line

Typical carbureted Rabbit, Scirocco emission control system

1976 Models

The EGR filter was discontinued on 1976 models but the 2-stage EGR valve was retained. On Federal vehicles, only the first stage is connected; California vehicles use both stages.

First stage EGR is controlled by engine vacuum and coolant temperature. The EGR valve is open above approximately 120°F coolant temperature and below approximately 80°F. At idle and during full throttle acceleration (engine hot), there is no EGR since the engine vacuum is too low to open the valve.

The second stage is controlled by temperature, engine vacuum and microswitch on the carburetor throttle valve. Vacuum is always present at the second stage and the valve is opened at about 120°F coolant temperature. When the throttle valve opens between 25° and 67°, the micro-switch activates the 2-way valve and allows engine vacuum to reach the second stage.

1977 and Later Models

The EGR valve on fuel injected models is controlled by a temperature valve and a vacuum amplifier. The valve is located at the front of the intake manifold.

TESTING

EGR Valve (1976) Carbureted Engines), Checking the First Stage

1. Disconnect the vacuum line from the EGR valve.
2. Disconnect the vacuum hose from the distributor unit and extend hose.
3. Start the engine and allow it to idle.
4. Connect the line from the anti-backfire valve to the EGR valve. The engine should stumble or stall.
5. If the idle stays even, the EGR line is clogged or the EGR valve is defective, or the filter is clogged.

EGR Valve (1976 Carbureted Engines), Checking the Second Stage

The EGR valve second stage is on 1976 California Rabbits and Sciroccos only. The system includes a micro-switch located on the side of the carburetor near the throttle valve. To check the system, manually operate the switch with the engine at idle. If the engine speed drops or the engine stalls, the switch is operating correctly. If not, check the microswitch, the EGR filter and the EGR return lines for blockage.

EGR Valve—Fuel Injected Models

Be sure the vacuum lines are not leaking. Replace any that are leaking or cracked.
1. Warm the engine to normal operating temperature.
2. Run the engine at idle.
3. Remove the vacuum hose from the

1. Temperature valve for EGR 2nd stage
2. To micro switch on throttle valve
3. Vacuum hose to brake booster
4. Two-way valve

Two stage EGR operation—1976 and later

Resetting the EGR elapsed mileage odometer

EGR valve.
4. Connect the line from the brake booster to the EGR valve (this can be done by installing a Tee in the vacuum line to the retard side of the distributor diaphragm and running a separate hose from there to the EGR valve).
5. If the engine speed does not change, the EGR valve is clogged or damaged.

EGR Temperature Valve (1976)

1. Remove the temperature valve and place the threaded portion in hot water.
2. Create a vacuum by sucking on the angled connection. The valve should be closed below approximately 120°F.

EGR Temperature Valve (1977 and Later)

Warm the engine to normal operating temperature.
1. With the engine at idle, attach a vacuum gauge between the EGR temperature control valve and the EGR valve. The valve should be replaced if the gauge shows less than 2 in. Hg.

EGR Deceleration Valve (1976 and Later)

NOTE: 1976 USA except California manual transmission Dashers are equipped with deceleration valves. No automatic transmission Volkswagens have deceleration valves. Rabbits and Sciroccos first received deceleration valves in 1977.

1. Remove the hose from the deceleration valve. Plug the hose.
2. Run the engine for a few seconds at 3000 rpm.
3. Snap the throttle valve closed.
4. With your finger, check for suction at the hose connection.
5. Remove the hose from the connector.
6. Run the engine at about 3000 rpm. No suction should be felt.

EGR Vacuum Amplifier (1976 and Later)

NOTE: 1976 Dashers are equipped with EGR Vacuum Amplifiers, while Rabbits and Sciroccos first received them in 1977.

1. Run the engine at idle.
2. Connect a vacuum gauge between the vacuum amplifier and the throttle valve port.
3. The gauge should read 0.2–0.3 in./Hg. If not, check the throttle plate for correct position or check the port for obstruction.
4. Connect a vacuum gauge between the vacuum amplifier and the temperature valve.
5. Replace the vacuum amplifier if the gauge reads less than 2 in./Hg.

MAINTENANCE

The only maintenance is to reset the EGR elapsed mileage switch.

Resetting the Elapsed Mileage Switch

The EGR reminder light in the speedometer

should light up every 15,000 miles as a reminder for maintenance.

To reset the light in the speedometer should light up every 15,000 miles as a reminder for maintenance.

To resent the light switch, press the white button. The speedometer light should go out.

Filter Replacement

1. Disconnect the filter EGR line fittings.
2. Remove the filter and discard.
3. Install the new filter into the EGR lines and securely tighten fittings.

REMOVAL AND INSTALLATION

EGR Valve

1. Disconnect the vacuum hose from the EGR valve.
2. Unbolt the EGR line fitting on the opposite side of the valve.
3. Remove the two remaining bolts and lift the EGR valve from the intake manifold.
4. Install the EGR valve in the reverse order of removal. Use a new gasket at the intake manifold.

Air Injection

The air injection system used on most carbureted engines, except the 1978 and 1980 Rabbit with 34 PICT-5 carburetor and the 1982 Rabbit with the TYF carburetor, includes a belt driven air pump, filter, check valve, anti-backfire valve or gulp valve, and connecting hoses and air lines. The system reduces exhaust emissions by pumping fresh air to the exhaust manifold or directly behind the exhaust valves where it combines with the hot exhaust gas to burn away excess hydrocarbons and reduce carbon monoxide.

The air injection systems on the 1978, 1980 and 1982 Rabbits with carburetors do not have air pumps. Instead, air is drawn from the air cleaner through a silencer to two check valves. The valves turn blue when overheated. If the valves are blue, replace them.

MAINTENANCE

Required maintenance on the air pump involves visually checking the pump, control valves, hoses and lines every 10,000 miles. Clean the air pump filter element at this interval. The filter element should be replaced every 20,00 miles or two years.

TESTING AND SERVICE

Air Pump System

1. Remove and clean the air manifold.

Emission control hoses—1979 and later CIS except California manual transmission (US models only)

Air injection system schematic. The arrows indicate air flow

2. Blow compressed air into the anti-backfire valve in the direction of the air flow.
3. Clean or replace the air pump filter.
4. Start the engine.
5. Exhaust eas should flow equally from each air inlet.
6. With the engine idling block the relief valve air outlet—only a slight pressure should be felt if the system is operating properly.

Air injection check valves on the 1978 and 1980 Rabbit (carbureted). If the valves turn blue, replace them

Anti-Backfire Valve

1. Disconnect the air pump filter line from the anti-backfire valve.
2. Briefly disconnect the anti-backfire valve vacuum line with the engine running. There should be a noticeable vacuum.

3. Replace the anti-backfire valve if the engine backfires.

Catalytic Converter

MAINTENANCE

Required maintenance on the catalytic converter involves checking the condition of the ceramic insert every 30,000 miles. As this interval is reached, an indicator light on the dash will glow. Once service to the converter is performed, the odometer must be reset.

Checking catalytic converter arrow indicates the temperature sensor

TESTING AND SERVICE

—— CAUTION ——

Do not drop or strike the converter assembly or damage to the ceramic insert will result.

Damage and overheating of the catalytic converter, indicated by the flickering of the "CAT" warning light, can be caused by the following:

1. Engine misfire caused by faulty spark plug, ignition wires and so on.
2. Improper ignition timing.
3. CO valve set too high.
4. Faulty air pump diverter valve.
5. Faulty temperature sensor.
6. Engine under strain caused by trailer hauling, high speed driving in hot weather, etc.

A faulty converter is indicated by one of the following symptoms:

1. Poor engine performance.
2. The engine stalls.
3. Rattling in the exhaust system.
4. A CO reading greater than 0.4% at the tail pipe.

Check or replace the converter as follows:

1. Disconnect the temperature sensor.
2. Loosen and remove the bolts holding the converter to the exhaust system and the chassis.
3. Remove the converter.

Oxygen sensor/catalytic converter reset button

4. Hold the converter up to a strong light and look through both ends, checking for blockages. If the converter is blocked, replace it.
5. Install the converter in the reverse order of removal.
6. Reset the elapsed mileage odometer by pushing the white button marked "CAT".

Oxygen Sensor System (1980 California and All 1981 and Later Models)

Many 1980 fuel injected California and all 1981 and later models are equipped with an oxygen sensor system which lowers toxic exhaust emissions while increasing fuel economy. In effect, the sensor system monitors the oxygen content in the exhaust system and, through a control unit and frequency valve, makes adjustments to the air/fuel mixture to achieve maximum fuel efficiency over a wide range of operating conditions. The system consists of the following.

Oxygen Sensor: located in the exhaust manifold. Unscrew to replace.
Control Unit: located behind the glove compartment cover.
Frequency Valve: located next to the fuel distributor .
Thermoswitch: located in the coolant system.
Oxygen Sensor System Relay: white colored relay located in the fuse/relay panel.
Elapsed Mileage Switch: located on the firewall.
Warning Light: marked OXS and located in the instrument panel. Comes on when the oxygen sensor must be replaced (every 30,000 miles).

RESETTING THE ELAPSED MILEAGE SWITCH

After replacing the oxygen sensor, reset the elapsed mileage switch by pushing the white button on the front of the switch.

FUEL SYSTEM

Mechanical Fuel Pump—Carbureted Engines

CLEANING

NOTE: The mechanical fuel pump found on carbureted Rabbits is mounted on the side of the engine block.

The filter screen can be removed from the pump and cleaned.

1. Remove the center cover screw.
2. Remove the screen and gasket. Clean the screen in solvent.
3. Replace the screen.
4. Install a new gasket and replace the cover.

NOTE: Make sure the depression in the pump cover engages the projection on the body of the pump.

A72/570a

1. Screen
2. Gasket
3. Cover
4. Plastic flange
5. Flange seal

Exploded view of mechanical fuel pump

REMOVAL AND INSTALLATION

The pump cannot be repaired and must be replaced when defective.

1. Disconnect and plug both fuel lines.
2. Remove the two Allen head retaining bolts.
3. Remove the fuel pump and its plastic flange.
4. Replace the pump in the reverse order of removal. Use a new flange seal.

Electric Fuel Pump– CIS Engines (Fuel Injection)

TESTING-ELECTRICAL

NOTE: Volkswagen uses a continuous injection system (CIS) in its fuel injected gasoline engines. The system includes an electric fuel pump mounted in front of the right rear axle on Rabbits and Sciroccos, and mounted below the fuel accumulator near the rear wheel on Dashers. The Jetta fuel pump is on the passenger's side in front of the rear wheel (accessible through a cover plate). The Quantum fuel pump is mounted inside the top of the car's plastic fuel tank (accessible through the rear cargo area, underneath the carpet).

1. Have an assistant operate the starter. Listen at the rear wheel to determine if the pump is running.
2. If the pump is not running, check the fuse on the front of the fuel pump relay.
3. If the fuse is good, replace the fuel pump relay.
4. If the fuel pump still does not operate, the fuel pump is faulty and must be replaced.

TESTING–FUEL PUMP DELIVERY

1. Check the condition of the fuel filter, make sure it is clean.
2. Connect a jumper wire between the #1 terminal on the ignition coil and ground.
3. Disconnect the return fuel line and hold it in a measuring container with a capacity of 1 quart or 1000 cc.
4. Have an assistant run the starter for 30 seconds while watching the quantity of fuel delivered.

The minimum allowable flow for the 1976–78 Rabbit and Scirocco is 750 cc ¾ of a quart) in 30 seconds; 900 cc (⁹/₁₀ of a quart) in 30 seconds for 1979 and later Rabbits, Jettas and Sciroccos.

For Dashers with the type A fuel pump, identified by the fuel inlet and outlet ports being at opposite ends of the pump, the pump must deliver 1000 cc (1 quart) of fuel in 32 seconds. For Dashers with the type B fuel pump, identified by the inlet and outlet ports forming a 90° angle through the center of the pump, the pump must deliver 1000 cc (1 quart) of fuel in 40 seconds. Quantum fuel pump must deliver 700 cc of

fuel in 30 seconds.

NOTE: For the above test, the battery must be fully charged. Also, make sure you have plenty of fuel in the tank.

If the pump fails its specific test, check for a dirty fuel filter, blocked lines or blocked fuel tank strainer (if so equipped). If all of these are in good condition, replace the pump.

REMOVAL AND INSTALLATION

All Models Except Quantum

1. Raise the vehicle and support it on jack stands. Disconnect the battery ground cable.
2. Remove the right rear wheel on all cars.
3. Remove the gas tank filler cap to release the fuel pressure.
4. Clamp off the line between the fuel pump and the fuel tank with a pair of soft jawed vise grips or other suitable lock pliers. Don't clamp the line too tightly or you may damage it.
5. Disconnect the clamped line from the fuel pump. There's bound to be a little gas in the line, so be careful.
6. If your vehicle has an accumulator mounted next to the fuel pump, disconnect the fuel lines from the accumulator. Disconnect the wiring from the fuel pump and remove all other lines after marking them for assembly.
7. Loosen and remove the retaining nuts and remove the fuel pump on Dashers and pre-79 Rabbits and Sciroccos. On 1979 and later Rabbits, Jettas and Sciroccos, remove the nuts on the lower bracket, loosen the nut on the upper slotted bracket where it connects to the body and slide the pump out.
8. Install the new fuel pump in the reverse order of removal. Make sure that the new seal washers are installed on the fuel discharge line.

Quantum

1. Pull up carpet under rear cargo area, revealing fuel pump access.
2. Remove cover over sending unit.
3. Detach fuel return hose, fuel supply hose, and vent hose from top of fuel pump.
4. Disconnect electrical wire from sending unit and fuel pump.
5. Loosen fuel pump attaching screws and pull fuel pump out in one motion.
6. Installation is the reverse of removal.

Carburetor

REMOVAL AND INSTALLATION

1. Remove the air cleaner.

2. Disconnect the fuel line.
3. Drain some of the coolant and then disconnect the choke hoses.
4. Disconnect the distributor and EGR valve vacuum lines.
5. Disconnect the electrical lead for the idle cut-off valve. For 1982, also disconnect the feedback solenoid, anti-diesel connector and the bowl vent connector.
6. Remove the clip which secures the throttle linkage to the carburetor. Detach the linkage, being careful not to lose any washers or bushings.
7. Unbolt the carburetor from the manifold and remove it.
8. Use a new gasket when replacing the carburetor. Don't overtighten the nuts.

AUTOMATIC CHOKE ADJUSTMENT

The standard adjustment on all versions of the automatic choke is with the two notches aligned with the notch on the housing. To adjust, loosen the three clamping screws and move the outer part of the choke unit.

Dasher automatic choke is correctly adjusted when (1) the choke cover, (2) the adjusting ring, and (3) the mark on the carburetor housing are aligned

INTERNAL CHOKE ADJUSTMENT

Dasher

If after performing the automatic choke adjustment, the choke doesn't operate correctly, use the following procedure.

1. Remove the choke cover with the coolant hoses attached and place it out of the way.
2. The control notch should be 180° opposite the adjusting notch. If not turn it with a screwdriver.
3. Reassemble the choke cover and adjust the choke.

THROTTLE GAP ADJUSTMENT

All Models Except 1978, 1980 and 1981 Rabbit

To adjust first stage throttle gap:

Dasher internal choke adjustment—(1) the adjusting notch, and (2) the control notch

Throttle gap adjusting screw, Rabbit and Scirocco with two barrel carburetor

1. The choke must be open and the first stage (primary) throttle closed.
2. Turn the first stage throttle valve stop screw until there is a gap between it and the lever it moves.
3. Turn the screw in until it just touches the lever.
4. Turn screw in ¼ turn more.
5. Adjust the idle speed and CO level. To adjust the second stage (secondary) throttle gap, proceed as follows.
6. The choke must be open and the first stage throttle must be closed.
7. Turn the second stage (secondary) adjusting screw until there is no clearance in the lever it is mounted on.
8. From this position, turn the screw out ¼ turn. There should be noticeable clearance at the lever.

1978 Rabbit

You need a vacuum gauge to set the throttle valve. The stop screw (1) is set at the factory, and should not be moved. If the screw is accidentally turned, proceed as follows. Make no adjustment at screw (2).
1. Run the engine at idle.
2. Remove the vacuum advance hose at the carburetor and connect a vacuum gauge.
3. Remove the plastic screw cap and turn the stop screw in until the gauge indicates vacuum.
4. Turn the stop screw out until the gauge indicates no vacuum. Turn the screw an additional ¼ turn and install the plastic cap.

5. Adjust the idle and CO.

1980 and 1982 Rabbit

Throttle gap is set at the factory and should not be tampered with.

FAST IDLE ADJUSTMENT

Dasher, Scirocco

It will be necessary to remove the carburetor from the engine to perform this procedure.

1978 Rabbit throttle gap adjustment (basic)

First stage throttle gap adjustment (basic)—all except 1978 and 1980 carbureted Rabbit

Second stage throttle gap adjustment—all except 1978 and 1980 carbureted Rabbit

1. Turn the carburetor upside down and drain the fuel from it.
2. With the carburetor upside down, close the choke tightly and measure the gap between the lower edge of the throttle valve and the housing wall with a drill. The measurement should be: 0.018–0.020 in. (0.45–0.50 mm).
3. Adjust the gap at the adjusting screw (beside the first stage valve) which is facing up when the carburetor is upside down.

1976 Rabbit, Scirocco

On these models it is not necessary to remove the carburetor. The engine must be at normal operating temperature.
1. Set the ignition timing.
2. Disconnect and plug the hose from the choke pull-down unit.
3. Open the throttle valve slightly and close the choke valve.
4. Close the throttle valve; the choke valve should be fully open again.
5. Set the stop screw of the fast idle cam on the highest step. Start the engine.
6. Adjust the speed with the screw to: 3150–3250 rpm manual transmission or 3350–3450 rpm automatic transmission.

1978, 1980 Rabbit

1. Run the engine up to operating temperature and make sure the ignition setting and the idle adjustment are correct.
2. Run the engine at idle and set the adjusting screw on its third notch on the choke valve lever.
3. Open the choke valve fully by hand using the choke valve lever.
4. Connect a tachometer and check the rpm, or use the tachometer in the car, if equipped.

--- **CAUTION** ---
See "Electronic Ignition Precaution," above, for warning about connecting tachometers to electronic ignition systems.

5. The fast idle speed should be between 2350–2450 rpm. If not, adjust with fast idle adjustment screw. Lock screw with safety cap after adjustment.
6. On 1978 models, stop the engine, open the choke valve fully and check the gap between the adjusting screw and fast idle cam. It should be 0.008 in.

1982 Rabbit

1. Run the engine until it reaches normal operating temperature. Make sure that the timing and idle speed are set to specifications.
2. Run the engine at idle and set the fast idle adjustment screw to the second step of the fast idle cam.
3. Disconnect the purge valve. Disconnect and plug the vacuum hose at the EGR valve.
4. Connect a tachometer as per the manufacturer's instructions and check that the engine speed is 2800–3200 rpm. If not,

turn the fast idle screw until it is.

5. Reconnect the purge valve and the vacuum hose at the EGR valve.

CHOKE GAP ADJUSTMENT

1976 Rabbit, Scirocco

1. Remove the automatic choke cover.
2. Close the choke valve and push the choke rod to the stop.

Adjusting the fast idle—1982 Rabbit

3. Hold the choke in position with a rubber band.
4. Push the choke lever down slightly to equalize the clearances.
5. Check the choke gap between the edge of the carburetor wall and the edge of the valve with a drill. It should be:

   1976—0.14 in. primary activated
      —0.20 in. secondary activated

6. Adjust the gap by turning the screw on the choke vacuum unit in to decrease the gap or out to increase the gap.

1978 Rabbit

1. Remove the cover from the automatic choke and fully close the choke.
2. Push the choke rod in the direction of the arrow and check the gap between the choke valve and the air horn wall. It should be 0.11–0.13 in.
3. Adjust the gap with the adjusting screw in the end of the vacuum unit at the side of the choke unit.
4. Reassemble the choke cover. There is an index mark on the choke housing and another on the choke cover.

1980 and 1982 Rabbit

1. Set the cold idle speed adjuster screw in its upper notch.
2. Connect a manually operated vacuum pump to the connection on the pull-down unit and build up vacuum.
3. Close the choke valve by hand with the lever and check the choke valve gap with a drill. The gap should be 3.3–3.7 mm. (3.9 mm for 1982).
4. Adjust the gap using the adjusting

Adjusting the choke gap. (1) indicates vacuum unit which houses the choke valve gap adjusting screw (not shown)

screw in the end of the vacuum unit at the side of the choke unit. After adjusting, lock the screw with sealant.

FUEL LEVEL ADJUSTMENT

Dasher, 1976 Rabbit, Scirocco

Remove the top of the carburetor. You should not have to remove the entire carburetor from the engine to perform this operation.

1. With the carburetor top upside down and canted at a 45° angle to prevent the damping ball in the needle valve from settling too deeply due to the weight of the float, measure from the highest tip of the first stage float to the carburetor surface (minus the gasket). The distance for the first stage float should be 1.10 in. ± 0.02 in. (28 mm ± 0.5 mm).
2. Adjust the float level by bending the float bracket.
3. Adjust the second stage float in the same manner. The distance for the second stage float should be 1.20 ± 0.02 in. (30 mm ± 0.5 mm).
4. Adjust the float level by bending the float bracket.

—————— CAUTION ——————
Do not scratch the float skin or the float may absorb fuel and sink.
————————————————————

If float height must be adjusted, remove the float from the carburetor to prevent damage to the needle valve.

THROTTLE LINKAGE ADJUSTMENT

All Models (Carburetor Equipped)

Throttle linkage adjustments are not normally required. However, it is a good idea to make sure that the throttle valve(s) in the carburetor open all the way when the accelerator pedal is held in the wide-open position. Only the primary (first stage) throttle valve will open when the pedal is pushed with the engine off: the secondary throttle on Volkswagen two-barrel carburetors is vacuum-operated.

Float adjustment—1976 Rabbit, Scirocco

Make note of the following:

   a. Always be careful not to kink or twist the cables during installation or adjustment—this can cause rapid wear and binding.

   b. On the Rabbits and Sciroccos, the accelerator cable will only bend one way—make sure you install it with the bends in the right positions.

NOTE: When installing new cables, all bends should be as wide as possible, and fittings between which the inner cable is exposed must be aligned.

OVERHAUL

For all carburetor overhaul procedures, please refer to "Carburetor Service" in the Unit Repair Section.

CIS Fuel Injection

For all fuel injection repair and service procedures not detailed below, please refer to "Fuel Injection" in the Unit Repair section.

Fuel Injectors

REMOVAL AND INSTALLATION

1. Grasp injector body (see illustration). DO NOT grasp and pull on fuel line.

Removing fuel injector (gasoline engine). Pull on metal area near arrow, NOT on fuel line

Pull injector straight out of manifold.

2. Protect injector tip—it is a very precision instrument and is easily damaged. Proceed to next injector and so on.

3. Moisten a *new* rubber seal with gasoline before reinstalling injectors.

4. Press each injector in fully until seated.

TESTING

1. Remove the injector but leave it connected to the fuel line.

2. Point the injector into a measuring container.

3. Remove the fuel pump relay and bridge the relay plate terminals #L13 and L14 with a fused (8 amp) jumper wire.

4. Remove the air duct from the air flow sensor.

5. Have an assistant turn the ignition switch on.

6. Lift the air flow sensor plate with a magnet and observe the injector nozzle spray pattern. The spray pattern must be cone shaped and even; if not, replace the injector.

7. Turn the ignition off and hold the injector horizontally. It should not drip.

NOTE: One or more injectors may be checked at the same time.

8. Moisten the rubber seals on the injectors with fuel before installing.

9. Press the injectors firmly into place.

Diesel Fuel Injection

The diesel fuel system is an extremely complex and sensitive system. Very few repairs or adjustments are possible by the owner. Any service other than that listed here should be referred to an authorized VW dealer or diesel specialist. The injection pump itself is not repairable; it can only be replaced.

Any work done to the diesel fuel injection should be done with absolute cleanliness. Even the smallest specks of dirt will have a disastrous effect on the injection system.

Do not attempt to remove the fuel injectors. They are very delicate and must be removed with a special tool to prevent damage. The fuel in the system is also under tremendous pressure (1700–1850 psi), so it's not wise to loosen any lines with the engine running. Exposing your skin to the spray from the injector at working pressure can cause fuel to penetrate the skin.

CHECKING INJECTION PUMP TIMING

Checking the injection pump timing also involves checking the valve timing. To alter the injection pump timing, the camshaft gear must be removed and repositioned. This also changes the valve timing. Special tool (VW 210) is necessary to properly tension the injection pump drive belt on the diesel engine.

1. Set the engine at TDC on no. 1 cylinder. In this position, the TDC mark on the flywheel should be aligned with boss on the bell housing and both valves of no. 1 cylinder should be closed.

2. The marks on the pump and mounting plate should also be aligned.

3. If the valve timing is incorrect, set the valve timing as detailed in the engine section.

ACCELERATOR CABLE ADJUSTMENT

The ball pin on the pump lever should be pointing up and be aligned with the mark in the slot. The accelerator cable should be attached at the upper hole in the bracket. With the pedal in the full throttle position, adjust the cable so that the pump lever contacts the stop with no binding or strain.

COLD START CABLE ADJUSTMENT

When the cold start knob on the dash is pulled out, the fuel injection pump timing is advanced 2.5°. This improves cold starting and running until the engine warms up.

1. Insert the washer on the cable.

2. Insert the cable in the bracket with the rubber housing. Install the cable in the pin.

3. Install the lockwasher.

4. Move the lever to the zero position (direction of arrow). Pull the inner cable tight and tighten the clamp screw.

CHECKING GLOW PLUGS CURRENT SUPPLY

1. Connect a test light between no. 4 cylinder glow plug and ground.

2. Turn the key to the heat position. The test light should light up.

3. If not, check the glow plug relay, ignition switch, or fuse box relay plate.

CHECKING GLOW PLUGS

Make this check after establishing that there is current to the glow plugs.

1. Remove the wire and glow plugs bus bar.

2. Connect the test light between the battery positive terminal and each glow plug in turn.

3. If the light lights, the glow plug is OK. If not, the glow plug is defective and must be replaced.

MANUAL TRANSMISSION

TRANSAXLE REMOVAL AND INSTALLATION

Dasher

1. Disconnect the battery ground cable.

2. Disconnect the exhaust pipe from the manifold and its bracket on the transaxle.

3. Remove the square-headed bolt on the shift linkage. Later models have a hex lead bolt.

4. Press the shift linkage coupling off.

5. Disconnect the clutch cable.

6. Disconnect the speedometer cable.

7. Detach the axle shafts from the transaxle.

8. Remove the starter.

9. Remove the inspection plate.

10. Remove the engine-to-transaxle bolts.

11. Remove the transaxle crossmember.

12. Support the transaxle with a jack.

13. Pry the transaxle out from the engine.

14. Lift the transaxle out of the car with an assistant.

15. Installation is the reverse of removal. Observe the following when installing the transaxle.

    a. When installing the transaxle crossmember, do not fully tighten the bolts until the transaxle is aligned and fully installed in the vehicle.

    b. Tighten the engine-to-transaxle bolts to 40 ft. lbs.

    c. Tighten the axle shaft bolts to 33 ft. lbs.

    d. On models with the rubber core rear transaxle mount, the rubber core must be centered in its housing.

    e. Make sure there is a ⅜ in. clearance between the header pipe and the floor of the vehicle.

    f. Adjust the clutch (see below).

Quantum

1. Disconnect battery ground strap.

2. Disconnect exhaust pipe from the manifold and its bracket.

3. Unhook the clutch cable.

4. Detach speedometer cable.

5. Remove upper engine/transmission bolts.

6. Remove engine support bolts on both sides of engine block (front).

7. Remove front muffler and exhaust pipe.

8. Unbolt both driveshafts (halfshafts) at the transmission.

9. Disconnect back-up light wiring.

10. Remove the inspection plate on bottom of transmission case.

11. Remove starter bolt.

12. Remove shift rod coupling bolt; pry off shift rod coupling ball with a prybar.

13. Pull off shift rod coupling from shift rod.

14. Place a jack under the transmission and lift slightly.

15. Remove transmission support bolts, and transmission rubber mounts.

16. Remove front transmission support bolts, lower transmission/engine support bolts.

17. Slowly pry transmission from engine.

18. Lower transmission out of the car.

When installing transmission in reverse order of removal, make sure main-shaft splines are clean and lubricated with a molybdenum-disulfide grease. Make sure inspection plate is properly seated, and that all engine/transmission mounting bolts are aligned and free of tension (holes lined up) before tightening everything. Readjust shift mechanism if necessary.

    a. Tighten transmission/engine bolts to 40 ft. lbs.

    b. Tighten driveshaft/drive flange bolts to 33 ft. lbs.

    c. Front transmission support-to-transmission is tightened to 18 ft. lbs.

    d. Transmission-to-body bolts are tightened to 80 ft. lbs.

Rabbit, Scirocco, Jetta

The engine and transaxle may be removed together as explained under "Engine Removal and Installation" or the transaxle may be removed alone, as explained here.

1. Disconnect the battery ground cable.

2. Support the left end of the engine at the lifting eye.

3. Remove the left transmission mount (between the transmission and the firewall).

4. Turn the engine until the lug on the flywheel (to the left of the TDC mark) aligns with the flywheel timing pointer.

5. Detach the speedometer drive cable, backup light wire, and clutch cable.

6. Remove the engine to transmission bolts.

7. Disconnect the shift linkage.

8. Detach the transmission ground strap.

9. Remove the starter.

10. Remove the engine mounting support near the starter.

11. Remove the rear transmission mount.

12. Unbolt and wire up the driveshafts.

13. From underneath, remove the bolts for the large cover plate, but don't remove it. Unbolt the small cover plate on the firewall side of the engine. Remove the engine to transmission nut immediately below the small plate.

14. Press the transmission off the dowels and remove it from below the car.

To install the transaxle:

15. The recess in the flywheel edge must be at 3:00 o'clock. Tighten the engine to transmission bolts to 47 ft. lbs. Tighten the engine mounting support bolts to 47 ft. lbs. Tighten the driveshaft bolts to 32 ft. lbs.

16. Check the adjustment of the shift linkage.

SHIFT LINKAGE ADJUSTMENT

Dasher To Chassis No. 3-5 2 044 764

1. Shift to Neutral.

2. Remove the round floor cover.

3. Loosen the nuts and move the bearing house so that the shift lever inclines approximately 5° to the rear.

4. Tighten the nuts.

5. Shift into second gear.

6. Loosen the stop plate bolts.

7. Adjust the plate so that the shift lever has 3/8–5/8 in. lateral movement at the shift knob.

NOTE: Moving the plate to the right increases play; moving the plate to the left decreases play.

8. Tighten the bolts. Check the shift pattern and make sure that reverse engages easily.

Dasher From Chassis No. 3-5 2 044 765 and Quantum

An adjusting tool, VW 3014, (VW 3057 for Quantum) must be used on these models.

1. Place the lever in Neutral.

2. Working under the car, loosen the clamp nut.

3. Inside the car, remove the gear lever knob and the shift boot. It is not necessary to remove the console. Align the centering holes of the lever housing and the lever bearing housing.

4. Install the tool with the locating pin toward the front. Push the lever to the left side of the tool cutout. Tighten the lower knurled knob to secure the tool.

5. Move the top slide of the tool to the left stop and tighten the upper knurled knob.

6. Push the shift lever to the right side of the cutout. Align the shift rod and shift finger under the car, and tighten the clamp nut. Remove the tool.

Quantum and Dasher transmission neutral shift lever adjustment

7. Place the lever in first. Press the lever to the left side against the stop. Release the lever; it should spring back 1/4 to 1/2 in. If not, move the lever housing slightly sideways to correct. Check that all gears can be engaged easily, particularly reverse.

Rabbit, Scirocco, Jetta

1976 MODELS WITH NONADJUSTABLE LINKAGE

1. Make the lower part of the floorshift lever vertical (in the side to side plane) in the first gear position by loosening the bearing plate that supports the end of the long shift rod that connects to the bottom of the floorshift lever. Tighten the mounting nuts when the lever is vertical.

2. Make the lower part of the floorshift lever vertical (in the fore and aft plane) in the Neutral position by pulling up the boot and loosening the two lever plate bolts. Move the plate until the lever is vertical.

1977 AND LATER MODELS

This category includes some late 1976 models; it is for Rabbits from chassis No. 176 3 000 001, and Sciroccos from chassis No. 536 2 000 001.

1. Align the holes of the lever housing plate with the holes of the lever bearing plate.

Quantum and Dasher manual transmission second gear shift lever adjustment

The short angled rod on the Rabbit and Scirocco shift linkage is to be adjusted to a length (a) of 1.18—1.25 in.

The long rod on the Rabbit and Scirocco shift linkage is to be adjusted to a length (b) of 6.42-6.50 in.

2. Loosen the shift rod clamp. Pull the boot off the lever housing and push it out of the way. It may be necessary to loosen the screws in the cover plate to free the boot.

3. Check that the shift finger is in the center of the stopping plate.

4. Adjust the shift rod end so that it is ¾ in. (⁹⁄₃₂ in. for five speed transmissions) from the right side of the lever housing. Tighten the shift rod clamp and check the shifter operation.

SELECTOR SHAFT LOCKBOLT ADJUSTMENT

Make this adjustment on Rabbits, Jettas and Sciroccos after linkage adjustment, if the linkage still feels spongy or jams.

1. Disconnect the shift linkage and put the transmission in Neutral.

2. Loosen the locknut and turn the adjusting sleeve in until the lockring lifts off the sleeve.

3. Turn the adjusting sleeve back until the lockring just contacts the sleeve. Tighten the locknut.

4. Turn the shaft slightly. The lockring should lift as soon as the shaft is turned.

5. Reconnect the linkage.

FIFTH GEAR LOCKBOLT ADJUSTMENT

Rabbit, Scirocco, Jetta Only

This adjustment is made with the transmission in neutral. The fifth gear lockbolt is located on top of the transmission next to the selector shaft lockbolt. It has a large protective cap over it.

1. Remove the protective cap.

2. Loosen the locknut and tighten the adjusting sleeve until the detent plunger in the center of the sleeve just begins to move up.

3. Loosen the adjusting sleeve ⅓ of a turn and tighten the locknut. Make sure the transmission shifts in and out of fifth gear easily. Replace the protective cap.

On Rabbit, Jetta and Scirocco, loosen the locknut and turn the adjusting sleeve

CLUTCH

PEDAL FREE PLAY ADJUSTMENT

Clutch pedal free-play should be ⅝ in. for all Dashers and pre-1979 Rabbits and Sciroccos. 1979 and later Rabbits, Jettas Sciroccos and Quantums should have ⁹⁄₁₆ in. free-play at the pedal. Pedal free-play is the distance the pedal can be depressed before the linkage starts to act on the throwout bearing.

1. Adjust the clutch pedal free-play by loosening the two nuts on the cable bracket near the oil filter on the Dasher and Quantum. On the Rabbit, Jetta and Scirocco, the cable adjustment point is on the front of the transmission.

2. After obtaining the correct free-play, tighten the adjusting nuts.

REMOVAL AND INSTALLATION

Dasher and Quantum

1. Remove the transaxle.

2. Match mark the flywheel and pressure plate if the pressure plate is being reused.

3. Gradually loosen the pressure plate bolts one or two turns at a time in a crisscross pattern to prevent distortion.

4. Remove the pressure plate and disc.

5. Check the clutch disc for uneven or excessive lining wear. Examine the pressure plate for cracking, scorching, or scoring. Replace any questionable components.

6. Install the clutch disc and pressure plate. Use a dummy shaft to keep the disc centered.

7. Gradually tighten the pressure-plate-to-flywheel bolts in a crisscross pattern. Tighten the bolts to 18 ft. lbs.

8. Install the throwout bearing.

9. Install the transaxle on the engine.

10. Replace the transaxle.

Rabbit, Scirocco, Jetta

1. Remove the transmission.

2. Attach a toothed flywheel holder and gradually loosen the flywheel to pressure plate bolts one or two turns at a time in a crisscross pattern to prevent distortion.

3. Remove the flywheel and the clutch disc.

4. Use a screwdriver to remove the release plate retaining ring. Remove the release plate.

5. Lock the pressure plate in place and unbolt it from the crankshaft. Loosen the bolts one or two turns at a time in a crisscross pattern to prevent distortion.

6. On installation, use new bolts to attach the pressure plate to the crankshaft. Use a thread locking compound and torque the bolts in a diagonal pattern to 54 ft. lbs.

7. Lubricate the clutch disc splines with multi-purpose grease. Lubricate the release plate contact surface and pushrod socket with multi-purpose grease. Install the release plate, retaining ring, and clutch disc.

8. Install a dummy shaft to align the clutch disc.

9. Install the flywheel, tightening the bolts one or two turns at a time in a crisscross pattern to prevent distortion. Torque the bolts to 14 ft. lbs.

10. Replace the transmission.

Quantum and Dasher clutch components; the adjusting sleeve and nuts are adjacent to the oil filter in the engine compartment

The Rabbit, Jetta and Scirocco clutch; the pressure plate is bolted to the crankshaft and the clutch is actuated by a pushrod working on the release plate

AUTOMATIC TRANSMISSION

TRANSAXLE REMOVAL AND INSTALLATION

Dasher and Quantum

The following procedures are for both types of Dasher automatic transmissions, the 003 and the 089. The type numbers are visible on the top of the automatic transmission unit (as opposed to the differential unit) of the transaxle. Another way to tell the type 003 transmission from the 089 is the type 003 has a vacuum modulator hose coming from the driver's side front of the trans-

mission above the pan. The type 089 does not. Don't confuse the ATF filler pipe with the above mentioned hose. Quantum transmission is the 089 model.

1. Disconnect the battery ground strap.
2. Raise the car and place the support stands so that you will have free access to the transaxle and axle shafts.
3. Disconnect the speedometer cable.
4. On the 089, remove the accelerator cable from the throttle valve housing.
5. Remove two of the upper engine/transaxle bolts. On the 089 transmission, support the engine with either special tool 10-222 or an appropriate jack.
6. Disconnect the exhaust pipe.
7. Remove the torque converter cover plate. On the 003 transmission, remove the vacuum modulator hose.

8. Remove the circlip holding the selector lever cable to the lever and remove the cable.
9. Remove the starter.
10. On the 003 disconnect the kickdown switch wires.
11. The torque converter is mounted to the flywheel by three bolts. The bolts are accesible through the starter hole. You'll have to turn the engine over by hand to remove all three.
12. Remove the axle shaft-to-transaxle socket head bolts.
13. Matchmark the position of the ball joint on the left control arm and remove the ball joint from the arm. Hold the wheel assembly out away from the arm to provide clearance between the axle shaft and the transmission.
14. Remove the exhaust pipe from the transaxle bracket.
15. Disconnect the remaining transmission controls. Those you cannot reach can be removed when the transaxle is lowered a little.
16. Unbolt the transaxle crossmember and remove it from the transaxle.
17. Support the transaxle on a jack and loosen the lower engine/transaxle bolts.
18. On the 089 transmission, remove all engine/transaxle bolts. Have an assistant pull the left wheel out as far as it will go and slowly lower the transmission, making sure the torque converter does not fall off.
19. On the 003 transmission, loosen the union nut on the ATF filler pipe so that the pipe can be swivelled. Remove the engine/transaxle bolts and lower the unit. You may have to pull the left wheel out a little so that the axle shaft clears the transaxle case. Make sure the torque converter does not fall off.
20. Installation is the reverse of removal with the following notes.
On both transaxles, the torque converter nipple must be about 1 3/16 in. from the bell housing face surface. If it sticks out further than this, the oil pump shaft has probably pulled out. You'll have to manipulate the converter and shaft until it goes in again.
Tighten the engine/transaxle bolts to 40 ft. lbs. and the torque converter bolts to 20–23 ft. lbs. New torque converter bolts should be used. Torque the axle shaft bolts to 33 ft. lbs., and the ball joint to control arm bolts to 45 ft. lbs.
Check the shift linkage adjustment.

Rabbit, Scirocco, Jetta

The engine and transaxle may be removed together as explained under Engine Removal and Installation or the transaxle may be removed alone, as explained here.
1. Disconnect both battery cables.
2. Disconnect the speedometer cable at the transmission.
3. Support the left end of the engine at the lifting eye. Attach a hoist to the transaxle.
4. Unbolt the rear transmission carrier

Dasher automatic transaxle linkage adjustment—before chassis no. 3-5 2 044 957

Rabbit, Jetta, Scirocco automatic transmission cable arrangement—fuel injected

from the body then from the transaxle. Unbolt the left side carrier from the body.

5. Unbolt the driveshafts and wire them up.

6. Remove the starter.

7. Remove the three converter to-drive plate bolts.

8. Shift into P and disconnect the floorshift linkage at the transmission.

9. Remove the accelerator and carburetor cable bracket at the transmission.

10. Unbolt the left side transmission carrier from the transmission.

11. Unbolt the front transmission mount from the transmission.

12. Unbolt the bottom of the engine from the transmission. Lift the transaxle slightly, remove the rest of the bolts, pull the transmission off the mounting dowels, and lower the transaxle out of the car. Secure the converter so it doesn't fall out.

— **CAUTION** —
Don't tilt the torque converter.

To install:

13. Be sure the torque converter is fully seated on the one-way clutch support. Push the transmission onto the mounting dowels and install two bolts. Lift the unit until the left driveshaft can be installed and install the rest of the bolts. Torque them to 39 ft. lbs.

14. Tighten the front transmission mount bolts to 39 ft. lbs. Install the left side transmission carrier to the transmission.

15. Connect the accelerator and carburetor cable bracket. Connect the floorshift linkage.

16. Tighten the torque converter to drive plate bolts to 22 ft. lbs. Torque the driveshaft bolts to 32 ft. lbs.

17. Install the rear transmission carrier

and make sure that the left side carrier is aligned in the center of the body mount. Bolt the left side carrier to the body.

18. Connect the speedometer cable and the battery cables.

PAN REMOVAL AND INSTALLATION, STRAINER SERVICE

Dasher and Quantum

VW recommends that the automatic transmission fluid be replaced every 30,000 miles, or 20,000 miles if used for trailer towing, mountain driving, or other severe service.

1. Four (4) quarts of automatic transmission fluid (Type A or Dexron) and a pan gasket are required.

2. Slide a drain pan under the transmission. Jack up the front of the car and support it.

3. Remove the drain plug and allow all the fluid to drain.

NOTE: Some models are not equipped with pan drain plugs. In this case, empty the pan by loosening the pan bolts and allowing the fluid to drain out.

4. Remove the pan retaining bolts and drop the pan.

5. Discard the old gasket and clean the pan with solvent.

6. Unscrew and clean the circular strainer. If it is dirty, it should be replaced.

7. Install the strainer, but don't tighten the bolt too much—specified torque is only 4 ft. lbs.

8. Refill the transmission with about 2¾ qts. or fluid. Check the level with the dipstick. Run the car for a few minutes and check again.

Rabbit, Scirocco, Jetta

NOTE: As of transmission No 09096 a new, cleanable oil filter is used which requires a deeper oil pan. Also beginning with transmission number EQ-15 106, the drain plug was no longer installed in the oil pan.

1. Remove the drain plug and let the fluid drain into a pan. If the pan has no drain plug, loosen the pan bolts until a corner of the pan can be lowered to drain the fluid.

2. Remove the pan bolts and take off the pan.

3. Discard the old gasket and clean the pan out. Be very careful not to get any threads or lint from rags into the pan.

4. The filter needn't be replaced unless the fluid is dirty or smells burnt. The specified torque for the strainer screws is 2 ft. lbs.

NOTE: Beginning with Transmission number 13 03 8, there is an additional strainer under the valve body. When installing it, be sure it fits into the locating lug of the transfer plate.

5. Replace the pan with a new gasket and tighten the bolts, in a crisscross pattern, to 14 ft. lbs.

6. Using a long-necked funnel, pour in 2½ qts. of Dexron® automatic transmission fluid through the dipstick tube. Start the engine and shift through all the transmission ranges with the car stationary. Check the level on the dipstick with the lever in Neutral. It should be up to the lower end of the dipstick. Drive the car until it is warmed up and recheck the level.

STRAINER
when installing, make sure strainer fits into locating lug of transfer plate

Beginning with transaxle 13 03 8, an additional strainer is used beneath the valve body. It cannot be installed on earlier models

LINKAGE ADJUSTMENT

Check the cable adjustment as follows:

1. Run the engine at 1000–1200 rpm with the parking brake on.
2. Select Reverse—a drop in engine speed should be noticed.
3. Select Park—engine speed should increase. Pull the shift lever against Reverse, the engine speed shouldn't drop (because reverse gear has not been engaged).
4. Move the shift lever to engage Reverse—engine speed should drop as the gear engages.
5. Move the shift lever to Neutral—an increase in engine speed should be noticed.
6. Shift the lever into Drive—a noticeable drop in engine speed should result.
7. Shift into 1—the lever must engage without having to overcome any resistance.
8. To adjust the cable—shift into Park. On Dashers before chassis no. 3-5 2 044 957, remove the cover from the bottom of the shift lever case under the car and loosen the cable clamp. Using pliers, press the lever on the transmission to the rear (against

spring tension) until it hits the stop and tighten the clamp.

On Dashers from chassis no. 3-5 2 044 957 and later, and Quantum, the shift cable clamp is loosened from inside the passenger's compartment. Have an assistant under the car press the transmission lever toward the Park position and tighten the clamp.

On the Rabbit, Jetta and Scirocco, shift into Park, loosen the cable clamp at the transmission end of the cable, press the transmission lever all the way to the left and tighten the cable clamp.

Dasher type 003 transaxle band adjustment—front band (first gear) being adjusted, arrow locates second gear band adjustment screw

TRANSMISSION CABLE ADJUSTMENT

NOTE: Early Dashers with the type 003 automatic transmission (identified by the modulator hose attached to the driver's side front of the transmission above the pan) have a kickdown switch rather than a throttle cable. See below for switch test.

Make sure the throttle is closed, and the choke and fast idle cam are off (carbureted models).

1. Detach the cable end at the transmission.
2. Press the lever at the transmission into its closed throttle position.
3. You should be able to attach the cable end onto the transmission lever without moving the lever.
4. Adjust the cable length to the correct setting.

KICKDOWN SWITCH CHECK

Dasher

NOTE: Early Dashers with the type 003 automatic transmission (identified by the modulator hose attached to the driver's side front of the transmission above the pan) are the only VWs equipped with kickdown switches. All other models have throttle cable kickdowns (see above).

1. Turn the ignition switch ON.
2. Floor the accelerator—you should hear a click from the solenoid on the transmission.
3. Replace the solenoid if no sound is heard. The solenoid is housed in the valve body and is accessible only be removing this unit from the transmission: a job you should depend on a qualified mechanic to perform.

FIRST AND SECOND GEAR (FRONT AND REAR) BAND ADJUSTMENTS

Dasher W/Type 003 Transmission Only

The type 003 transmission is identified by the modulator hose attached to the driver's side front of the transmission above the pan.

NOTE: The transmission must be horizontal when the band adjustments are performed.

The adjustment screws are located at the top of the transmission housing with the first gear band being closest to the front of the unit on the passenger's side of the car. The second gear band adjustment screw is located toward the rear of the unit on the driver's side of the vehicle.

1. To adjust the first gear band, loosen the locknut and tighten the adjusting screw to 7 ft. lbs.
2. Loosen the screw and retighten it to 3.5 ft. lbs.
3. Turn the screw out 3¼–3½ turns and then tighten the locknut.
4. To adjust the second gear band, repeat Steps 1 and 2 on the second gear band adjusting screw, then turn the screw out exactly 2½ turns and tighten the locknut.

SECOND GEAR (REAR) BAND ADJUSTMENT

Dasher and Quantum W/Type 089 Transmission, Rabbit, Jetta, Scirocco

NOTE: The transmission must be horizontal when band adjustments are performed.

1. Loosen the locknut on the adjusting screw, which is located on the front of the Rabbit and Scirocco transmission and the driver's side on the Dasher.
2. Tighten the adjusting screw to 7 ft. lbs.
3. Loosen the screw and tighten it again to 4 ft. lbs.
4. Turn the screw out exactly 2½ turns and then tighten the locknut.

NEUTRAL START/BACKUP LIGHT SWITCH

The combination neutral start and backup

Circlip
always replace

Constant velocity joint, inner

Dished washer

Cap
check for wear,
replace if replace if necessary

Boot
check for wear,
replace if necessary

Socket head bolt
3.5 mkg (25 ft lb)

Drive shaft
differ in length,

Clamp
always replace

Boot
check for wear,
replace if necessary

Clamp
always replace

Dished washer

Thrust washer

Circlip
always replace

Constant velocity joint, outer

Axle shaft

Axle nut
25–30 mkg (180–216 ft lb)

Dasher axle shaft (Quantum similar)

light switch is mounted inside the shifter housing. The starter should operate in Park or Neutral only. Adjust the switch by moving it on its mounts. The backup lights should only come on when the shift selector is in the Reverse position.

Pulling the Dasher axle shaft from the steering knuckle

DRIVE AXLES

HALFSHAFT REMOVAL AND INSTALLATION

Dasher and Quantum

NOTE: When removing the right side axle shaft, you must detach the exhaust pipe from the manifold and the transaxle bracket. Be sure to buy a new exhaust flange gasket.

1. With the car on the ground, remove the front axle nut.

NOTE: Use a longer breaker bar with an extension (length of pipe).

2. Raise and support the front of the vehicle.

3. Remove the socket head bolts retaining the axle shaft to the transaxle.

NOTE: When removing the left side axle shaft on automatic transmission models, matchmark the ball joint (left side) mounting position in relation to the lower control arm. Remove the two ball joint retaining nuts and remove the ball joint from the control arm to create room to remove the axle shaft.

4. Pull the transaxle side of the driveshaft out and up and place it on top of the transaxle.

5. Pull the axle shaft from the steering knuckle.

6. Installation is the reverse of removal. Tighten the transaxle bolts to 25–33 ft. lbs. The axle nut should be tightened to 145 ft. lbs. (M 18 nut), or 175 ft. lbs. (M 20 nut).

NOTE: Be aware that the axle shafts are two different lengths on automatic transmission models, with the left side axle shaft being slightly longer than the

Remove ball joint from knuckle to remove axle shaft—Rabbit, Jetta, Scirocco

KNUCKLE LEG

BALL JOINT STUD

Remove the socket head (Allen) bolts holding the axle shaft to the transaxle

right. Manual transmission and automatic transmission axle shafts are of different lengths and should not be interchanged.

Rabbit, Scirocco, Jetta

1. Complete Steps 1 through 3 under Dasher in this section. Disregard the first NOTE.

2. Remove the bolt holding the ball joint to the steering knuckle and separate the knuckle from the ball joint.

3. Removing the ball joint from the knuckle should give enough clearance to remove the axle shaft. It pulls right out of the steering hub.

4. Installation is the reverse of removal. Tighten the axle shaft to transaxle bolts to 32 ft. lbs., the ball joint bolt to 21 ft. lbs. and the axle nut to 173 ft. lbs. Be sure to check the alignment after work is completed.

Circlip
always replace

Dished washer

Gasket
note correct position
otherwise socket head bolts
become loose.

Protective cap

4.5 mkg (32 ft lb)

Gasket
Insert in joint flange before
installing axle shaft.
note correct position
otherwise socket head bolts
become loose.

Constant velocity joint, inner

Boot
check for wear
replace if necessary

Drive shaft
differ in length and material

Note
If velocity joint was disassembled for checking of wear, pump 45 grams of MOS_2 grease into each side of joint when assembling.

Clamp
always replace

Boot
check for wear
replace if necessary

Clamp
always replace

Dished washer

Thrust washer

Circlip
always replace

Constant velocity joint, outer

installing: drive onto shaft
until circlip engages in
shaft groove.

Axle nut
24 mkg (173 ft lb)

Rabbit, Jetta and Scirocco axle shaft

REAR SUSPENSION

The Dasher rear suspension has a rear axle beam containing a full length torsion bar. A trailing arm is welded to the axle beam tube on each side. The trailing arms mount to the unit body in rubber bushings. A coil spring provides the suspension at each wheel. A Panhard rod locates the axle against side forces.

The Rabbit, Jetta and Scirocco rear suspension includes a torsion beam which connects the two trailing arms. On these models, the coil spring and the shock absorber are combined into a strut. The Quantum rear axle assembly is similar to this type, but uses different axle bushings.

Coil Springs

REMOVAL AND INSTALLATION

Dasher Only

1. Raise the car on a lift.
2. Support the axle.
3. Install spring compressor on the coil spring, and remove.

Damping ring
different for left and right, note part No.

Coil spring

Note
in production springs with 1, 2 or 3 paint marks are installed, spare parts with 2 paint marks are available only, when replacing it is not necessary to replace both

Shock absorber
when checking, must not have flat spots over full stroke

6 mkg (43 ft lb)
install before lower bolt

check for wear, replace if necessary

6 mkg (43 ft lb)

remove before upper bolt

Axle beam

4.5 mkg (32 ft lb)

8.5 mkg (61 ft lb)

Rubber bushing and sleeve

Diagonal arm
check for distortion

Rubber bushing and sleeve

Rubber bushing and sleeve

8.5 mkg (61 ft lb)

Caution
if rear axle beam was removed, readjusting of the brakes and bleeding of the brake system is always necessary

Dasher rear suspension

4. Installation is the reverse of removal.

NOTE: It is not necessary to replace both springs if only one is damaged.

Shock Absorbers

REMOVAL AND INSTALLATION

Dasher

NOTE: Only remove one shock absorber at a time. Do not allow the rear axle to hang by its body mounts only, as it may damage the brake lines.

This operation requires the use of either special tool VW 655/3 or a suitable spring compressor and floor jack.

1. Raise the car and support it on jack stands. Do not place the jack stands under the axle beam.
2. Remove the wheel.
3. Attach special tool VW 655/3 between the axle beam and a prefabricated hook hung on the body frame above the beam. Jack the tool until you can see the shock absorber compressing. If you are using a spring compressor and a floor jack, compress the spring a little and, placing the floor jack under the beam below the spring, jack it up until you see the shock absorber compress.
4. Unbolt and remove the shock absorber.
5. Installation is the reverse of removal. Tighten the shock absorber bolts to 43 ft. lbs.

NOTE: There are two types of shock absorbers for the Dasher and they have different mounts. Make sure you get the correct type for your vehicle.

Strut Assembly

REMOVAL AND INSTALLATION

Rabbit, Jetta, Scirocco

1. Raise the car on a lift.
2. Support the axle, but do not put any load on the springs.
3. Remove the rubber guard from inside the car.
4. Remove the nut, washer and mounting disc.
5. Unbolt the strut assembly from rear axle and remove it.
6. Installation is the reverse of removal.

Quantum

1. Remove shock strut cover inside car.
2. Unscrew strut from body.
3. Slowly lift vehicle until wheels are slightly off ground.

Exploded view of the Rabbit, Jetta and Scirocco rear suspension (Quantum similar)

- 3.5 mkg (25 ft lb)
- Slotted nut 2 mkg (14 ft lb)
- Coil spring
- Mount
- rubber bushing can be replace with rear axle installed
- Concaved washer
- Parking brake cable holder
- Flat washer
- 6 mkg (43 ft lb)
- Rear axle
- Nut 4.5 mkg (32 ft lb)
- Shock absorber
- 4.5 mkg (32 ft lb)

4. Unscrew strut from axle.
5. Take strut out of lower mounting. Press whell down slightly when removing strut.

—— CAUTION ——
Do not remove both suspension struts at the same time as this will overload the axle beam bushings.

6. Guide strut out carefully between wheel and wheel housing. Do not damage paint on spring and wheel housing.
7. Installation is the reverse of removal.

VW STRUT TOOL 3017A

Strut self-locking nut, removal/installation

OVERHAUL

For all spring and shock absorber removal and installation procedures, and all overhaul procedures, please refer to "Strut Overhaul" in the Unit Repair section.

FRONT SUSPENSION

The front suspensions on the Rabbit, Quantum, Dasher, Jetta and Scirocco are fundamentally identical from model to model. It is a simple strut design consisting of a lower control arm, ball joint and suspension strut. In this type of design, known as a MacPherson strut, the shock absorber strut acts as a locating member for the suspension as well as a damper. The shock absorber itself is part of the strut and cannot be removed except on Dashers up to chassis No. 3-5 2 117 398, which have a removable cartridge.

In addition, all Dashers are equipped with a stabilizer bar to reduce front body roll.

Ball Joint

REMOVAL AND INSTALLATION

1. Jack up the front of the car and support it on stands.
2. Matchmark the ball joint-to-control arm position on the Dasher.
3. Remove the retaining bolt and nut from the hub (wheel bearing housing).
4. Pry the lower control arm and ball joint down and out of the strut.
5. Remove the two ball joint-to-lower control arm retaining nuts and bolts on the Dasher. Drill out the rivets on the Rabbit, Jetta and Scirocco; enlarge the holes to $^{21}/_{64}$ in.

Pulling the Dasher ball joint into alignment on installation

Ball bearing
Maintenance free
■ *Less friction, easier steering*

Spring code
for various models

Shock absorber
in strut tube

Pinch bolt
for ball joint

Ball joint
Maintenance free

A pinch bolt holds the ball joint to the combination strut and steering knuckle

6. Remove the ball joint assembly.
7. Install the Dasher ball joint in the reverse order of removal. If no parts were installed other than the ball joint, align the matchmarks made in Step 2. No camber adjustment is necessary if this is done. Pull the ball joint into alignment with pliers. Tighten the two control arm-to-ball joint bolts to 47 ft. lbs. and the strut-to-ball joint bolt to 25 ft. lbs. (M8 bolt) or 36 ft. lbs. (M10 bolt).
8. On the Rabbit, Jetta and Scirocco, bolt the new ball joint in place. Torque the bolts to 18 ft. lbs. Tighten the retaining bolt for the ball joint stud to 21 ft. lbs.

Strut

REMOVAL AND INSTALLATION

Dasher and Quantum

1. With the car on the ground, remove the front axle nut. Loosen the wheel bolts.
2. Raise and support the front of the car. Remove the wheels.
3. Remove the brake caliper from the strut and hang it with wire. Detach the brake line clips from the strut.

4. At the tie rod end, remove the cotter pin, back off the castellated nut, and pull the end off the strut with a puller.
5. Loosen the stabilizer bar bushings and detach the end from the strut being removed.
6. Remove the ball joint from the strut.
7. Pull the axle driveshaft from the strut.
8. Remove the upper strut-to-fender retaining nuts.
9. Pull the strut assembly down and out of the car.
10. Installation is the reverse of removal. The axle nut is tightened to 145 ft. lbs. (M 18 nut) or 175 ft. lbs. (M 20 nut). Tighten the ball joint-to-strut nut to 25 ft. lbs. (M8 nut) or 36 ft. lbs. (M10 nut), the caliper-to strut bolts to 44 ft. lbs. and the stabilizer-to-control arm bolts to 7 ft. lbs.

Rabbit, Jetta and Scirocco

1. Remove the brake hose from the strut clip.
2. Mark the position of the camber adjustment bolts before removing them from the hub (wheel bearing housing).
3. Remove the upper mounting nuts and remove the strut from the car.
4. Installation is the reverse of removal. The upper nuts are tightened to 14 ft. lbs. and the adjusting bolt (upper) to hub to 58 ft. lbs. Tighten the lower adjusting bolt-to-hub to 43 ft. lbs. Use new washers on the lower bolts. If the shock absorber was replaced, camber will have to be adjusted. See procedures in this chapter.

STRUT OVERHAUL

For all spring and shock absorber removal and installation procedures, and all overhaul procedures, please refer to "Strut Overhaul" in the Unit Repair section.

Lower Control Arm (Wishbone)

REMOVAL AND INSTALLATION

Volkswagen refers to the lower control arm as the wishbone.

NOTE: When removing the left side (driver's side) control arm on the Rabbit, Jetta and Scirocco equipped with an automatic transmission, remove the front left engine mounting, remove the nut for the rear mounting, remove the engine mounting support and raise the engine to expose the front control arm bolt.

1. Raise the vehicle and support it on jack stands. Remove the road wheel.
2. Remove the nut and bolt attaching the ball joint to the hub (wheel bearing housing) and pry the joint down and out of the hub.

3. Unfasten the stabilizer bar on the Dasher.

4. Unbolt and remove the control arm-to-subframe (crossmember) mounting bolts on the Dasher. On the Rabbit, Jetta and Scirocco remove the control arm mounting bolts from the frame.

5. Remove the control arm. See procedures above for ball joint removal and installation.

6. Installation is the reverse of removal. Tighten the Dasher control arm-to-subframe bolts to 50 ft. lbs., and the Rabbit, Jetta and Scirocco control arm-to-frame front bolt to 43 ft. lbs., rear bolts to 32 ft. lbs. Tighten the ball joint to hub bolt to 21 ft. lbs. on the Rabbit, Jetta and Scirocco, and to 25 ft. lbs. (M 8 nut) or 36 ft. lbs. (M 10 nut).

Front Wheel Bearings

The front wheel bearings are non-adjustable on all models and are sealed, so they should be maintenance-free. Removing the front wheel bearings requires a stand press and a myriad of special Volkswagen tools, so the procedure is not given here.

Front End Alignment

CAMBER ADJUSTMENT

Dasher and Quantum

Camber is adjusted by loosening the two ball joint-to-lower control arm bolts, and moving the ball joint in or out as necessary.

Rabbit, Scirocco, Jetta

Camber is adjusted by loosening the nuts of the two bolts holding the top of the wheel bearing housing to the bottom of the strut, and turning the top eccentric bolt. The range of adjustment is 2°.

CASTER

Other than the replacement of damaged suspension components, caster is not adjustable on any model.

TOE-IN ADJUSTMENT

Dasher and Quantum

Toe-in is checked with the wheels straight ahead. The left tie rod is adjustable. Loosen the nuts and clamps and adjust the length of the tie rod for correct toe-out. If the steering wheel is crooked, remove and align it.

Dasher front suspension; Quantum similar

Rabbit, Scirocco, Jetta

Toe-in is checked with the wheels straight ahead. Only the right tie rod is adjustable, but replacement left tie rods are adjustable. Replacement left tie rods should be set to the same length as the original. Toe-in should be adjusted only with the right tie rod. If the steering wheel is crooked, remove and align it.

STEERING

The Dasher has rack and pinion steering gear with center-mounted tie rods. This allows very little toe-in change during suspension travel. A steering damper reduces road shock transmittal to the steering wheel.

The Rabbit, Jetta and Scirocco have rack and pinion steering with end-mounted tie

Top eccentric bolt provides camber adjustment on Rabbit, Scirocco and Jetta

rods. No periodic maintenance is required on either rack and pinion steering system.

The Quantum is equipped with standard power steering (rack and pinion). The only periodic maintenance reqired is a check of the power steering fluid reservoir, and a check when underneath the car (oil change time is convenient) for steering system leaks. Replace fluid reservoir filter when changing fluid or when replacing steering system components.

Steering Wheel

REMOVAL AND INSTALLATION

1. Grasp the center cover pad and pull it from the wheel (cover varies depending

Axle nut 24 mkg (173 ft lb) always replace

Brake caliper when removing, do not detach brake hose, hang caliper up on frame with wire

Hub

Circlip check for proper seating

Wheel bearing

Suspension strut

8 mkg (58 ft lb)

Eccentric washer for adjusting camber

Eccentric bolt before removing mark position

6 mkg (43 ft lb)

Wheel bearing housing

Circlip check for proper seating

3 mkg (21 ft lb)

Ball joint

3 mkg (21 ft lb) replace cotter pin

Bonded rubber bushing

Wishbone

Bonded rubber bushing

6 mkg (43 ft lb)

4.5 mkg (32 ft lb)

4.5 mkg (32 ft lb)

Exploded view of the Rabbit, Jetta and Scirocco front suspension

on model).

2. Loosen and remove the steering shaft nut.

3. Pull the wheel off the shaft. A puller isn't normally needed.

4. Disconnect the horn wire.

5. Replace the wheel in the reverse order of removal. On the Rabbit, Jetta and Scirocco, install the steering wheel with the road wheels straight ahead and the cancelling lug pointing to the left. On the Dasher and Quantum, with the road wheels straight ahead, the cancelling lug on the steering wheel must point to the right and the turn signal lever must be in the neutral position. Tighten the steering shaft nut to 36 ft. lbs.

Turn Signal and Headlight Dimmer Switch Replacement

1. Disconnect the battery ground cable.
2. Remove the steering wheel.
3. Remove the switch retaining screws.
4. Pry the switch housing off the column.
5. Disconnect the electrical plugs at the back of the switch.
6. Remove the switch housing.
7. Replace in the reverse order of removal.

Ignition Switch

REMOVAL AND INSTALLATION

The ignition switch is located at the bottom of the ignition key cylinder body. To remove the ignition switch, remove the steering lock body, see below for procedures. On all models except Dashers made before 1978, remove the switch by removing the screw at the bottom of the switch and pulling the switch out. On Dasher made before 1978, the screw is located in the side of the cylinder body.

Installation is the reverse of removal.

Steering Lock

REMOVAL AND INSTALLATION

On some models, the hole in the lock body for removing the steering lock cylinder was not drilled by Volkswagen. To make the hole, use the following measurements in conjunction with the illustrations. Drill the hole where "a" and "b" intersect on the lock body. The hole should be drilled 1/8 in. deep.

1976–77 Dasher
a = = 11.5 mm (0.453 in.)

Dimensions for drilling ignition lock cylinder hole (if not equipped)—1976 Rabbit, Scirocco

Dimensions for drilling ignition lock cylinder hole (if not equipped)—1977 and later Rabbit, Jetta, Scirocco and 1978 and later Dasher and Quantum

b = 8.0 mm (0.315 in.)
1976 Rabbit, Scirocco
a = 11 mm (7/16 in.)
b = 11 mm (7/16 in.)
1977–82 Rabbit, Jetta, Scirocco, 1978–82 Dasher, Quantum
a = 12 mm (0.472 in.)
b = 10 mm (0.393 in.)

NOTE: Measurements are given in metric form first because this unit of measurement will be easier to make.

Remove the lock cylinder by pushing a small drill bit or piece of wire into the hole and pulling the cylinder out. It might be easier to insert the ignition key, turn it to the right a little and pull on it.

NOTE: On 1976 Rabbits and Sciroccos, the lock cylinder can also be removed by removing the steering and windshield wiper components and removing the locking plate holding the cylinder with a pair of pliers. When installing the plate, peen it slightly to hold it in place.

To remove the lock body, proceed as follows:

1. Remove the steering wheel and turn signal switch. See above for procedures. Remove the steering column shaft covers.

2. The lock is clamped to the steering column with special bolts whose heads shear off on installation. These must be drilled out in order to remove the switch.

3. On replacement, make sure that the lock tang is aligned with the slot in the steering column.

Steering Gear

REMOVAL AND INSTALLATION

Dasher and Quantum

1. Pry off the lock plate and remove both tie rod mounting bolts from the steering rack, inside the engine compartment. Pry the tie rods out of the mounting pivot.

2. Remove the lower instrument panel trim.

3. Remove the shaft clamp bolt, pry off the clip, and drive the shaft toward the inside of the car with a brass drift.

4. Remove the steering gear mounting bolts.

5. Turn the wheels all the way to the right and remove the steering gear through the opening in the right wheelhousing.

6. For installation, temporarily install the tie rod mounting pivot to the rack with both mounting bolts. Remove one bolt, install the tie rod, and replace the bolt. Do the same on the other tie rod. Make sure to install a new lockplate. Torque the tie rod bolts to 39 ft. lbs., the mounting pivot bolt to 15 ft. lbs., and the steering gear to body mounting bolts to 15 ft. lbs.

Rabbit, Jetta and Scirocco

1. Disconnect the steering shaft universal joint and wire up out of the way.

2. Disconnect the tie rods at the steering rack and wire up and out of the way.

3. Remove the steering rack and drive.

4. Install the steering rack and drive and torque the attaching hardware to 14 ft. lbs.

5. Set the steering rack with equal distances between the housing on the right side and left side.

6. Install the tie rods and screw both sides to the measurements shown in the illustration.

7. Tighten the steering gear adjusting screw until it touches the thrust washer. Tighten the locknut.

8. Install the steering shaft.

9. Check the front end alignment.

Steering Linkage

TIE ROD REMOVAL AND INSTALLATION

Dasher and Quantum

1. Raise the car and remove the front wheels.

2. Disconnect the outer end of the steering tie rod from the steering knuckle by removing the cotter pin and nut and pressing out the tie rod end. A small puller or press is required to free the tie rod end.

3. Under the hood, pry off the lockplate and remove the mounting bolts from both tie rod inner ends. Pry the tie rod out of the mounting pivot.

4. First install the mounting pivot to the rack with both mounting bolts. Remove one bolt, install the tie rod, and replace the bolt. Do the same on the other tie rod. Be sure to install a new lockplate. The inner tie rod end bolts should be torqued to 40 ft. lbs.

5. If you are replacing the adjustable left tie rod, adjust it to the same length as the old one. Check the toe-in when the job is done.

6. Use new cotter pins when installing the outer tie rod ends. Torque the nut to 22 ft. lbs.

Note
In production a non-adjustable tie rod is installed in left side. Adjust toe on right side tie rod only.
For replacement an adjustable tie rod is available

Universal joint shaft when removing detach steering drive from body. Disconnect shift linkage from steering drive. Pull steering drive off studs

2.5 mkg (18 ft lb)

3 mkg (21 ft lb)

When installing steering drive, insert pinion in universal joint first

Steering drive

steering drive is not repairable, if defective replace

3 nuts
2 mkg (14 ft lb)

Steering gear adjusting screw

Lock nut

Rabbit, Jetta, Scirocco steering gear

4 mkg (29 ft lb)

3.0 mkg (21 ft lb)

B

A

Adjusting Rabbit and Scirocco tie-rod position. b=2.64 in.

Rabbit, Jetta and Scirocco

1. Center the steering rack.
2. Remove the cotter pin and nut from the tie rod end.
3. Disconnect the tie rod from the steering rack.
4. If the left side tie rod is being replaced, adjust it to 14.92 in. (379 mm).
5. Adjust the steering rack and tie rods as outlined in Steps 5 and 6 of the Rabbit and Scirocco ''Steering Gear Removal and Installation.''
6. Tighten the tie rod end retaining nut to 21 ft. lbs. and install a new cotter pin.

BRAKES

The base model 1976–78 Rabbit is equipped with front and rear drum brakes. The optional 1976–78 Rabbit, all 1979–82 Rabbits, and all Quantums, Dashers, Jettas and Sciroccos are equipped with front disc brakes and rear drum brakes.

The hydraulic system is a dual circuit type that has the advantage of retaining 50% braking effectiveness in the event of failure in one system. The circuits are arranged so that you always have one front and one rear brake for a more controlled emergency stop. The right front and left rear are in one circuit; the left front and right rear are in the second circuit.

There is also a brake failure switch and a proportioning valve.

The brake failure unit is a hydraulic valve/electrical switch which warns of brake problems by the warning light on the instrument panel. A piston inside the switch is kept centered by one brake system pressure on one side and the other system pressure on the opposite side. Should a failure occur in one system, the piston would go to the ''failed'' side and complete an electrical circuit to the warning lamp. This switch also functions as a parking brake reminder light and will go out when the parking brake is released. The proportioning valve, actually two separate valves on manual transmission Dasher sedans, provides balanced front-to-rear braking during hard stops.

Extreme brake line pressure will overcome the spring pressure on the piston within the valve causing it to proportionately restrict pressure to the rear brakes. In this manner, the rear brakes are kept from locking. The proportioner doesn't operate under normal braking conditions.

For all brake system repair and service procedures not detailed below, please refer to ''Brakes'' in the Unit Repair section.

Adjustment

The front disc brakes require no adjustment, as disc brakes automatically adjust themselves to compensate for pad wear.

The drum brakes must be adjusted whenever free travel is one third or more of the total pedal travel. All 1979 and later Dashers, Jettas, Quantums, and many 1979 and later Rabbits and Sciroccos have self-adjusting rear brakes.

FRONT DRUM BRAKES

Rabbit Only

1. Raise and support the front of the car. Block the rear wheels.
2. Remove the rubber plugs covering the adjusters.
3. Insert a screwdriver through the hole and turn the adjuster clockwise until the brake locks.
4. Back off the adjuster until the wheel can be turned. The shoes should drag lightly.
5. Back off the adjuster two notches. The wheel should spin without brake drag. Replace the rubber plugs.

REAR DRUM BRAKES

All Models

NOTE: On all models except manual transmission Dasher sedans, it is necessary to push the brake proportioning lever toward the rear axle to relieve the pressure in the right rear brake line.

1. Raise the rear of the car. Place the jack under the center of the Dasher torsion bar/axle. The jack pad should be at least 4 in. square, otherwise you may damage the axle. Raise the Rabbit, Scirocco and Jetta on a chassis lift.

Typical drum brake adjustment

Relieving pressure at the proportioning valve. Push lever (arrow) toward rear axle

2. Block the front wheels and release the parking brake. Step on the brake pedal hard to center the linings.
3. Remove the rubber plug from the rear of the backing plate on each wheel.
4. Insert a brake adjusting tool or wide-bladed screwdriver and turn the adjuster wheel clockwise until the brakes drag as you turn the wheel in the forward direction.
5. Turn the adjuster in the opposite direction until you just pass the point of drag.
6. Repeat on the other wheel.
7. Lower the car and road test. Readjust, if necessary.

Master Cylinder

REMOVAL AND INSTALLATION

1. Disconnect and plug the brake lines.
2. Disconnect the electrical plug from the sending unit for the brake failure switch.
3. Remove the two master cylinder mounting nuts.

1. Reservoir cap
2. Washer
3. Filter screen
4. Reservoir
5. Master cylinder plugs
6. Stop screw
7. Stop screw seal
8. Master cylinder seal
9. Residual pressure valves
10. Warning light sender unit
11. Brake master cylinder housing

Master cylinder assembly for Rabbit, Jetta and Scirocco (typical)—Dasher and Quantum similar

4. Lift the master cylinder and reservoir out of the engine compartment being careful not to spill any fluid on the fender. Empty out and discard the brake fluid.

— CAUTION —
Do not depress the brake pedal while the master cylinder, front brake discs, or drum brake shoes are removed.

5. Position the master cylinder and reservoir assembly onto the studs for the booster and install the washers and nuts. Tighten the nuts to no more than 9 ft. lbs.
6. Remove the plugs and connect the brake lines.
7. Bleed the entire brake system.

Front Wheel Bearings

There is no front wheel bearing adjustment. The bearing is pressed into the steering knuckle. Axle nut torque is 175 ft. lbs. The axle nut should be tightened only with the wheels resting on the ground.

Wheel Cylinders

REMOVAL AND INSTALLATION

1. Remove the brake shoes.
2. Loosen the brake line on the rear of the cylinder, but do not pull the line away from the cylinder or it may bend.
3. Remove the bolts and lockwashers that attach the wheel cylinder to the backing plate and remove the cylinder.
4. Position the new wheel cylinder on the backing plate and install the cylinder attaching bolts and lockwashers.
5. Attach the brake line.
6. Install the brakes and bleed the system.

Parking Brake

ADJUSTMENT

Dasher and Quantum parking brake adjustment is made at the cable compensator, which is attached to the lever pushrod underneath the car. On the 1976–78 Rabbit and Scirocco, adjustment is made at the cable end nuts on the top of the handbrake lever. On 1979 and later Rabbits, Sciroccos and Jettas, the position of the cable end nuts has been changed from the top of the handbrake lever to below the front of the lever. Adjustment is performed in the same manner as on 1976–78 Rabbits and Sciroccos.
1. Block the front wheels. Raise the rear of the car.
2. Apply the parking brake so that the lever is on the second notch.
3. The Dasher and Quantum adjustment is made directly under the passenger compartment.

1. Retaining pin
2. Parking brake adjusting nut
3. Cable compensator

Dasher parking brake linkage and adjusting point (Quantum similar)

4. Tighten the compensator nut or adjusting nuts until both rear wheels can just be turned by hand. On models with self-adjusting rear brakes, you shouldn't be able to turn them at all.
5. Release the parking brake lever and check that both wheels can be easily turned.
6. Lubricate the Dasher and Quantum compensator with chassis grease.

CHASSIS ELECTRICAL

Heater

The heater core and blower on all models are contained in the heater box (fresh air housing located in the center of the passenger compartment under the dashboard. On air conditioned Rabbits, Jettas and Sciroccos, the evaporator is located in the heater box. On air conditioned Dashers and Quantums, the evaporator is located under the hood separate from the heater box.

The blower fan on non-air conditioned models before 1977 is open bladed, much like an airplane propeller. The blower fan on all air conditioned models and non-air conditioned models after 1977 is of the turbine-type.

— CAUTION —
When working on air conditioning components, use extreme caution.

REMOVAL AND INSTALLATION

1. Disconnect the battery ground cable.
2. Drain the cooling system.
3. Remove the windshield washer container from its mounts and remove the ignition coil only if they restrict your access to the heater components under the hood.
4. Disconnect the two hoses from the

heater core connections at the firewall.
5. Unplug the blower fan electrical connections. Some models are equipped with an external series resistor mounted on the heater box. Do not try to remove the wires from the resistor.
6. Remove the heater control knobs on the dash.
7. Remove the two retaining screws and remove the controls from the dash complete with brackets.
8. Some model Dashers have a cable attached to a lever which is operated by a round knob on the dashboard. Remove the cable from the lever.
9. Remove either the clips or the screws holding the heater box in place and remove the heater box with the heater controls.
10. Installation is the reverse of removal. Be sure to refill the cooling system.

Heater Blower

REMOVAL AND INSTALLATION

Pre-1977 Models

1. Remove the heater box. See procedure above.
2. On Rabbits and Scirocco, remove the screws holding the heater cover in place and remove the heater cover. Remove the circular cutoff flap by unhooking it from its hinge. On Dashers, remove the heater cover by pulling out its pins.
3. On the Rabbit and Scirocco, the heater blower should pull right out of the assembly.
4. On Dashers, remove the clips holding the heater box halves together and separate the halves. The fan should just pull out.

Installation is the reverse of removal.

NOTE: On the Dasher, when installing the fan in the heater box halves, make sure the wiring connections on the fan face the wiring harness on the heater box. Also, when jointing the housing halves,

make sure there is no side to side play in the blower motor.

1977 and Later Models

1. Remove the heater unit from the vehicle. See above for procedures.

2. Remove the screws holding the cover on the heater box and remove the cover. Remove the blower motor cover, if so equipped.

3. Remove the electrical connections from the blower motor after matchmarking them to insure that you assemble them in the correct order.

4. Remove the clamp or screws holding the motor in place and remove the motor.

Installation is the reverse of removal.

Heater Core

REMOVAL AND INSTALLATION

NOTE: On some 1977 and later models, it is possible to remove the heater core without removing the heater box. Proceed as follows:

    a. Drain the cooling system.

    b. Locate and remove the heater core cover in the side of the heater box.

    c. Disconnect the heater hoses from the core and pull the core out.

1. Remove the heater box from the vehicle.

2. If the unit has a core cover in its side, remove the screws or unclip the cover and remove it. The core should pull out.

3. On other models, remove the heater box clips that hold the two halves of the heater box together, separate the halves after removing any components that are in the way, and remove the heater core.

Windshield Wiper Motor

REMOVAL AND INSTALLATION

Dasher

1. Unplug the multi-connector from the wiper motor.

2. Remove the three motor-to-linkage bracket retaining screws.

3. Carefully pry the motor crank out of the two linkage arms.

4. Remove the motor from the car.

5. Install the motor in the reverse order of removal. The crank arm should be at a right angle to the motor.

Rabbit, Scirocco, Jetta

When removing the wiper motor, leave the mounting frame in place. On all models with two front wiper arms, do not remove

the wiper drive crank from the motor shaft.

On Sciroccos with one front wiper arm, matchmark the drive crank and motor arm and then remove the arm.

NOTE: If, for any reason you must remove the wiper drive crank from the motor shaft on two wiper arm models, matchmark both parts for reassembly.

1. Access is with the hood open. Disconnect the battery ground cable.

2. Detach the connecting rods from the motor crank arm.

3. Pull off the wiring plug.

4. Remove the 4 mounting bolts. You may have to energize the motor for access to the top bolt.

Early Rabbit, Scirocco heater

5. Remove the motor. Reverse the procedure for installation.

Instrument Cluster

REMOVAL AND INSTALLATION

1976–78 Dasher

1. Disconnect the battery ground cable.

2. Unscrew the speedometer cable from the rear of the cluster.

3. Using needle nosed pliers, detach the retaining springs on either side of the cluster.

4. Pivot the instrument cluster out of the dash.

5. Disconnect the multi-connector plug at the rear of the cluster.

6. Remove the cluster from the dash.

7. Installation is the reverse of removal.

1978 and Later Dasher

1. Remove the radio or shelf.

2. Pull the knobs off the fresh air control and fan switch.

3. Remove the six instrument cluster to dashboard retaining screws.

4. Snap out the light, emergency flasher and rear window defogger switches.

5. Disconnect the air fan switch electrical connector.

6. Remove the instrument cluster and disconnect the speedometer cable and the multi-point connector from the back of the cluster.

Scirocco 1976–81, Rabbit and Jetta

1. Disconnect the battery ground cable.

2. Remove the fresh air controls trim plate.

3. Remove the radio or glove box.

4. Unscrew the speedometer drive cable from the back of the speedometer. Detach the electrical plug.

5. Remove the attaching screw inside the radio/glove box opening.

6. Remove the instrument cluster. Reverse the procedure for installation.

1982 and Later Scirocco

1. Disconnect battery ground cable.

2. Remove the two Phillips head screws on the inner top surface of the instrument compartment (see illustration).

3. Start to pull down on the instrument compartment. Inside the top center of the compartment you will see another Phillips screw (as you pull the compartment out). Remove the screws.

4. Tip out the top of the instrument cluster.

5. Remove the speedometer cable by twisting the tabs of the plastic fixture around the end of the cable.

6. Disconnect the multi-point connector and remove instrument cluster.

1982 and Later Quantum

1. Disconnect battery ground strap.

2. Carefully pry off switch trim below instruments.

3. Pull heater control knobs off and press out heater control trim.

4. Remove two Phillips head screws holding heater control trim to panel.

5. Remove 7 Phillips screws around perimeter of instrument cluster.

6. Disconnect all wiring to switches and warning lamps. Remove all trim panels.

7. The remainder of the procedure can be completed by following the Scirocco procedure beginning at Step 3.

Fuses and Relays

The fuse/relay panel on all models is located in the lower left side of the dashboard. Use VW ceramic fuses. VW recommends that relays be replaced by your dealer.

Instrument cluster removal—Scirocco (Quantum similar)

Tip down cluster panel, revealing inside Phillips screw

1. Heater cover	7. Control flap cable
2. Main heater assembly	8. Heater valve cable
3. Heater valve	9. Heater controls
4. Heater hoses	10. Cutoff flap cable
5. Vent for side windows	11. Fresh air housing
6. Double grommet	12. Vent for side windows

Early Dasher heater assembly

Volvo

SERIAL NUMBER IDENTIFICATION

Vehicle Type Designation And Chassis Number

Important identification labels appear at several locations on every Volvo, depending on year and model. On 1976–79 models, the type designation (242, 262, etc.) and the chassis number appears on a metal plate riveted to the engine side of the firewall. They also appear on the VIN plate, located at the foot of the left door post, and are stamped into the sheet metal of the right front door pillar.

For 1980–83, the model designations are DL-GL-GT-GLT (formerly 242-244-245), GLE (formerly 264-265), Coupe (formerly 262C), and Diesel. The VIN plate on these cars is located on the top left surface of the dash, and is also stamped on the right hand door pillar. Emission control information is on a label located on the left hand shock tower under the hood. There is also a model plate on the right hand shock tower that includes the VIN number, engine type, emission equipment, vehicle weights and color codes.

Model designation and engine availability are related in the following way: from 1976 until 1979, all four cylinder Volvos are in the 240 series—242, 244 and 245. Six cylinder cars are 260 series—262, 264, 265. Starting in 1980, the 240 series became the DL, GL and GLT series. The 260 series evolved into the GLE cars.

Engine, Transmission, And Final Drive Identification

The engine type designation, part number, and serial number are given on the left side of the block (4). The last figures of the part number are stamped on a tab and are followed by the serial number stamped on the block.

The transmission type designation, serial number, and part number appear on a metal plate (5) riveted to the underside of the transmission. The final drive reduction ratio, part number, and serial number are found on a metal plate (6) riveted to the left-hand side of the differential.

Last three digits of Engine Identification Number printed on label on timing belt cover.

B21 series engine number locations

B27F and B28F engine number locations

Component Identification

A component data plate is used to specify the manufacturer of major serviceable components such as the brakes, fuel pump, clutch, alternator, and steering gear. The plate is located on the right front door pillar on some models. Each component manufacturer is assigned a code.

CHASSIS NUMBER CHART

Year	Model	Starting Chassis No.
'76	242	53865
	244	82980
	245	54710
	262	1
	264	9675
	265	5
'77	242	99680
	244	174910
	245	115350
	262	2430
	264	34470
	265	8115
'78	242	122895
	244	274965
	245	163835
	262	2660
	264	46515
	265	10920
'79	242	142125
	244	364650
	245	211325
	262	4330
	264	62105
	265	15735
'80	DL, GT (2 dr.)	165570
	DL, GL (4 dr.)	482505
	Coupe	6450
	GLE	83055
	4 cyl. wgn.	264755
	6 cyl. wgn.	21755
'81	DL, GL, GLT (2 dr.)	189180
	DL, GL (4 dr.)	592110
	Coupe	8375
	GLE	107610
	4 cyl. wgn.	317940
	6 cyl. wgn.	28320
'82	DL, GL, GLT (2 dr.)	306780
	DL, GL (4 dr.)	686100
	GLE	125110
	4 cyl. wgn.	368310

GENERAL ENGINE SPECIFICATIONS

Year and Engine Model	Engine Type	Engine Displacement cu. in. (cc)	Fuel Delivery Type	Horsepower @ rpm	Torque @ rpm (ft. lbs.)	Bore × Stroke (in.)	Compression Ratio	Oil Pressure @ rpm (psi)
'76–'78 B21F	OHC-4	130 (2127)	Bosch continuous injection	102 @ 5200 ①	114 @ 2500 ②	3.78 × 3.15	8.5:1	35–85 @ 2000
'79–'83 B21F	OHC-4	130 (2127)	Bosch continuous injection	107 @ 5500 ③	114 @ 2500	3.78 × 3.15	9.3:1	35–85 @ 2000
'82–'83 B21FLH	OHC-4	130 (2127)	Bosch LH-Jetronic	105 @ 5400	119 @ 3000	3.78 × 3.15	9.3:1	35–85 @ 2000
'81–'83 B21FT④	OHC-4	130 (2127)	Bosch continuous injection	127 @ 5400	150 @ 3750	3.78 × 3.15	7.5:1	35–85 @ 2000
'81–'83 B21A⑦	OHC-4	130 (2127)	Zenith or SU 1-bbl carburetor	100 @ 5250 ⑧	122 @ 2500 ⑨	3.78 × 3.15	9.3:1	35–85 @ 2000
'76–'78 B27F	OHC-V6	162 (2660)	Bosch continuous injection	125 @ 5500 ⑤	150 @ 2750 ⑥	3.46 × 2.87	8.2:1	58 @ 3000
'79–'80 B27F	OHC-V6	162 (2660)	Bosch continuous injection	127 @ 5500	146 @ 2750	3.46 × 2.87	8.8:1	58 @ 3000
'80–'83 B28F	OHC-V6	174 (2849)	Bosch continuous injection	130 @ 5500	153 @ 2750	3.58 × 2.86	8.8:1	60 @ 3000
'80–'83 D24	OHC-6	145 (2383)	Diesel	78 @ 4800	102 @ 3000	3.01 × 3.40	23.0:1	28 @ 2000

NOTE: OHC is Overhead Camshaft
① 99 @ 5200 in Calif.
② 114 @ 2500 in Calif.
③ 98 @ 5000, '82 and later
④ Turbocharged
⑤ 121 @ 5500 in Calif.
⑥ 148 @ 2750 in Calif.
⑦ Canada only
⑧ 96 @ 5250 in 1981
⑨ 121 @ 2500 in 1981

GASOLINE ENGINE TUNE-UP SPECIFICATIONS

(When analyzing compression test results, look for uniformity among cylinders, rather than specific pressures)

Year	Engine Model and Displacement cu. in.	Spark Plugs Type	Spark Plugs Gap (in.)	Distributor Point Dwell (deg)	Distributor Point Gap (in.)	Ignition Timing (deg) MT	Ignition Timing (deg) AT	Intake Valve Opens (deg)	Fuel Pump Pressure (psi)	Idle Speed (rpm) MT	Idle Speed (rpm) AT	Valve Clearance (cold) (in.) In	Valve Clearance (cold) (in.) Ex
'76	B 21 F 130	Bosch W175T30	0.030	Electronic		15B ①	15B ①	15B	64–75	900	800	0.014–0.016	0.014–0.016
	B 27 F 162	Bosch WA200T30 Champ BN9Y	0.026	Electronic		10B ①	10B ①	②	64–75	900	900	0.004–0.006	0.010–0.012

GASOLINE ENGINE TUNE-UP SPECIFICATIONS

(When analyzing compression test results, look for uniformity among cylinders, rather than specific pressures)

Year	Engine Model and Displacement cu. in.	Spark Plugs Type	Gap (in.)	Distributor Point Dwell (deg)	Point Gap (in.)	Ignition Timing (deg) MT	AT	Intake Valve Opens (deg)	Fuel Pump Pressure (psi)	Idle Speed (rpm) MT	AT	Valve Clearance (cold) (in.) In	Ex
'77	B 21 F 130	Bosch WA175T30	0.030	Electronic		12B ①	12B ①	—	64–75	900	900	0.014–0.016	0.014–0.016
	B 27 F 162	Bosch WA200T30	0.026	Electronic		10B ①	10B ①	—	64–75	900	900	0.004–0.006	0.010–0.012
'78	B 21 F 130	Bosch WA175T30	0.030	Electronic		12B ①	12B ①	—	64–75	900	900	0.014–0.016	0.014–0.016
'78–'79	B 27 F 162	Bosch WA200T30	0.030	Electronic		10B ①	10B ①	—	64–75	900	900	0.004–0.006	0.010–0.012
'79	B 21 F 130	Bosch W6DC	0.030	Electronic		10B ①③	10B ①③	—	64–75	900	900	0.014–0.016	0.014–0.016
'80–'83	B 21 F ⑤ 130	Bosch WR7DS	0.030	Electronic		8B ⑥⑨	8B ⑥⑨	—	64–75	900	900	0.014–0.016	0.014–0.016
'81–'83	B 21 FT 130	Bosch WR7DS	0.030	Electronic		12B ⑦	12B ⑦	—	64–75	900	900	0.014–0.016	0.014–0.016
'81–'83	B 21 A 130	Bosch W7DC	0.030	62	0.016 0.018	12B ⑥⑧	12B ⑥⑧	—	64–75	900	900	0.014–0.016	0.014–0.016
'80–'83	B 28 F 174	Bosch HR6DS	0.030	Electronic		10B ⑦④	10B ⑦④	—	64–75	900	900	0.008–0.010	0.012–0.014

NOTE: Some models are equipped with the Constant Idle Speed system (CIS) and cannot be adjusted
① @ 700 rpm
② 9B–left side; 7B–right side
③ Calif: 8B
④ Vacuum advance disconnected, A/C turned off
⑤ Includes Calif. and L–Jetronic models
⑥ @ 750 rpm
⑦ @ 900 rpm
⑧ 7° '82 and later
⑨ 12° '82 and later

DIESEL ENGINE TUNE-UP SPECIFICATIONS

Year	Model	Valve Clearance① Intake (in.)	Exhaust (in.)	Injection Pump Setting (in.)	Injector Nozzle Opening Pressure (psi)	Idle Speed (rpm)	Compression Pressure (psi)
'80–'83	D24	0.006–0.010	0.014–0.018	0.0265–② 0.0295	1700–1845③	720–④ 880	340 (min.)– 455 (max.)

NOTE: When setting injection timing, distributor plunger stroke must be at Top Dead Center
① Cold
② See text. Acceptable range when checking 0.0287–0.0315 in.
③ Acceptable range. When servicing set to 1775–1920 psi
④ Maximum safe speed: 5100–5200 rpm

FIRING ORDERS

FIRING ORDER
1-6-3-5-2-4

FIRING ORDER 1-3-4-2

FRONT

FRONT

B27F, B28

B21F

FIRING ORDER
1-5-3-6-4-2

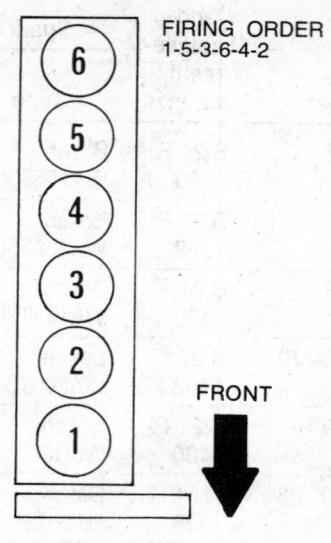

FRONT

D24 Diesel

CAPACITIES

Year	Model	Engine Displacement cu. in. (cc)	Engine Crankcase (qt)		Transmission (pts)		Drive Axle (pt)	Gasoline Tank (gal)	Cooling System (qt)
			With Filter	Without Filter	Manual 4-Spd③	Automatic			
'76–'77	242, 244, 245	130 (2127)	4.0	3.5	1.6 (4.8)	13.8	3.4	15.8	10.0①
	262, 264, 265	162 (2660)	7.4	6.8	1.6 (4.8)	13.8	3.4	15.8	12.0
'78	242, 244, 245	130 (2127)	4.0	3.5	1.6 (3.8)	14.0	3.4	15.8	10.0
	262, 264, 265	162 (2660)	6.8	6.3	1.6 (4.8)	14.0	3.4	15.8	11.5
'79	242, 244, 245	130 (2127)	4.0	3.5	1.6 (3.8)	14.0②	3.4	15.8	10.0
	262, 264, 265	162 (2660)	6.8	6.3	1.6 (4.8)	14.0②	3.4	15.8	11.5
'80–'83	DL, GL, GT	130 (2127)	4.0	3.5	1.6 (4.8)	14.6④	3.4	15.8	10.0
'80–'83	GLE, Coupe	174 (2849)	6.8	6.3	1.6 (4.8)	14.6④	3.4	15.8	11.5
'80–'83	Diesel	145 (2383)	7.4	6.6	1.6 (4.8)	14.6④	3.4	15.8	10.0

① 9.8 qts w/auto trans.
② With extra capacity fluid pan: 14.6
③ Figures in parentheses are for overdrive transmission
④ Fluid capacity for AW70 and AW71 (1982 and later) automatics is 15.6 pts.

CRANKSHAFT AND CONNECTING ROD SPECIFICATIONS

(All measurements are given in inches)

Engine Model	Engine Displacement cu. in. (cc)	Crankshaft			Thrust on No.	Connecting Rod		
		Main Brg. Journal Dia.	Main Brg. Oil Clearance	Shaft End-Play		Journal Diameter	Oil Clearance	Side Clearance
B 21	130 (2127)	2.4981– 2.4986	0.0011– 0.0033	0.0015– 0.0058	5	2.1255– 2.1260	0.0009– 0.0028	0.006– 0.014
B 27 F	162 (2660)	2.7576–	0.0015–	0.0028–	4	2.0578–	0.0012–	0.008–
B 28 F	174 (2849)	2.7583	0.0035	0.0106		2.0585	0.0031	0.015

VALVE SPECIFICATIONS

Year	Engine and Displacement cu. in. (cc)	Cylinder Head Seat Angle (deg)	Valve Face Angle (deg)	Seat Width (in.)	Spring Test Pressure (lbs. @ in.)	Spring Installed Height (in.)	Stem To Guide Clearance (in.)		Stem Diameter (in.)	
							Intake	Exhaust	Intake	Exhaust
'76–'83	B 21 130 (2127)	44.75	45.5	0.08	170 @ 1.06	1.77	0.0012– 0.0024	0.0024– 0.0035	0.3132– 0.3135	0.3128– 0.3126
'76–'79	B 27 F 162 (2660) B 28 F 174 (2849)	29.5 int 30 exh	29.5 int 30 exh	①	124.3 @ 1.27	1.86	②	②	0.3136– 0.3142 to 0.3140– 0.3146	0.3128– 0.3134 to 0.3136– 0.3142
'80–'83	B 28 F	29.5 int 30 exh	29.5 int 30 exh	①	143 @ 1.181	1.85	②	②	0.3136– 0.3142 to 0.3140– 0.3146	0.3128– 0.3134 to 0.3136– 0.3142

① 0.067–0.083 intake; 0.079–0.094 exhaust
② Tapered; valve guide ID is 0.3150–0.3158

PISTON AND RING SPECIFICATIONS

Year	Engine Displacement cu. in. (cc)	Piston Clearance	Ring Gap			Ring Side Clearance		
			Top Compression	Bottom Compression	Oil Control	Top Compression	Bottom Compression	Oil Control
'76–'83	B 21 130 (2127)	0.0004– 0.0012	0.0138– 0.0217	0.0138– 0.0217	0.010– 0.016	0.0016– 0.0028	0.0016– 0.0028	0.0016– 0.0028
'76–'79 and '80–'83	B 27 F 162 (2660) B 28 F 174 (2849)	0.0008– 0.0016	0.016– 0.022	0.016– 0.022	0.015– 0.055	0.0018– 0.0029	0.0010– 0.0021	0.0004– 0.0092

BATTERY AND STARTER SPECIFICATIONS

(All cars use 12 volt, negative ground electrical systems)

| Model | Battery Amp Hour Capacity | Starter | | | | | | Brush Spring Tension (oz.) | Min. Brush Length (in.) |
| | | Lock Test | | | No Load Test | | | | |
		Amps	Volts	Torque (ft. lbs.)	Amps	Volts	rpm		
All	60① ②	400–490	7	—	30–50	11.5	5800–7800	3.10–3.50	0.52

① 260 series: 70 amp hour battery
② Diesel: 88 or 90 ah

TORQUE SEQUENCES

Cylinder head bolt tightening sequence—B21

Diesel head bolt torque sequence. Loosen bolts in reverse order starting at 14

Cylinder head bolt tightening sequence, B27, B28

Main bearing nut tightening sequence, B27, B28

TORQUE SPECIFICATIONS

(All readings in ft. lbs.)

Year	Engine	Cyl. Head Bolts	Rod Bearing Bolts	Main Bearing Bolts	Crankshaft Pulley Bolt	Flywheel-To-Crankshaft Bolts	Manifold Bolts Intake	Manifold Bolts Exhaust	Camshaft Nut	Spark Plug	Oil Pan
'76–'83	B 21 F	76–83①	43–48	85–91	107–128	47–54	15	15	32–38	25–29	8
'76–'79 '80–'83	B 27 F B 28 F	②	33–37	③	118–132④	33–37	7–11	7–11	51–59	13–15	7–11
'80–'83	D24	65⑤	N.A.	N.A.	330⑥	55	18	18	⑧	⑦	N.A.

NOTE: From late 1980 new type cylinder head bolts are used on the diesel. They are longer and 1 mm wider. Torquing these bolts is a six-step procedure:
1. Torque to 30 ft. lbs.
2. Torque to 44 ft. lbs.
3. Torque to 55 ft. lbs.
4. Tighten 180°, in one movement, without stopping.
5. Run engine until oil temperature is minimum 50°C–120°F.
6. Tighten 90°, in one movement, without stopping.

① Torque head bolts in two stages; first, tighten in sequence to 43 ft. lbs., then to 76–83 ft. lbs.
② Torque heads bolts in sequence to 7 ft. lbs., then 22 ft. lbs., then 44 ft. lbs. Wait 10–15 minutes and slacken the bolts ½ turn. Then torque to 11–14 ft. lbs. and then protractor torque to 116–120° (⅓ of a turn). Finally run to operating temperature, shut off and allow

to cool for 30 min. Following the sequence, slacken, torque to 11–14 ft. lbs., and protractor torque to 113–117° each bolt.
③ Torque main bearing nuts to 22 ft. lbs., in sequence. Then slacken 1st nut ½ turn, tighten to 22–26 ft. lbs., and protractor torque to 73–77°. Repeat for remaining nuts following the sequence.
④ 1978–81: 175–200
⑤ Torque in two stages: 30 ft. lbs. then 65 ft. lbs. After 1000 miles torque to 62 ft. lbs. (warm)
⑥ Using regular torque wrench. If Volvo tool 5188 is used, torque to 255 ft. lbs.
⑦ Injector: 50 ft. lbs.
⑧ Front camshaft bolt: 33; Rear: 73

ALTERNATOR AND REGULATOR SPECIFICATIONS

Year	Vehicle Model	Alternator Part No. and Manufacturer	Alternator Output (amps.)	Min. Brush Length (in.)	Regulator Part No. and Manufacturer	Volts @ Alternator rpm (cold)
'75–'83	240 series DL, GL, GT	14V 55A20	55③	0.20	—	13.5–14.1 @ 4000①
'76–'83	260 series GLE Coupe	S.E.V. Marchal A14/55A 7160410	55②③	0.20	S.E.V. Marchal 72710502	13.5–14.1 @ 4000①

① After driving 10 minutes
② 1979 and later—70
③ B21F Turbo rated output 770W; max. current 55A

BRAKE SPECIFICATIONS

(All measurements given are in. unless noted)

Year	Model	Lug Nut Torque (ft. lbs.)	Master Cylinder Bore	Brake Disc Minimum Thickness	Brake Disc Maximum Run-Out	Minimum Lining Thickness Front	Minimum Lining Thickness Rear
'76–'83	240 series, DL, GL, GT	70–100	0.877	0.557 front 0.331 rear	0.004 front 0.006 rear	0.125	0.125
	260 series, GLE Coupe, Diesel	70–100	0.877	0.900 front 0.331 rear	0.004 front 0.006 rear	0.125	0.125

C 1095

WHEEL ALIGNMENT

Year	Model	Caster Range (deg)	Camber Range (deg)	Toe-in (in.)	Steering Axis Inclination (at 0° camber)	Wheel Pivot Ratio (deg) Inner Wheel	Wheel Pivot Ratio (deg) Outer Wheel
'76–'77	240 series, 260 series	2P-3P	1P-1½P	0.18–0.030①	12	20	20.8
'78	240, 260 series	2P-3P	1P-1½P	0.12–0.24②	12	20	20.8
'79–'81	All Models	2P-3P③	0–1N	0.12–0.24②	12	20	20.8
'82–'83	All Models except GLT	2P-3P③	1P to 1½P	0.18–0.24④	12	20	20.8
'82–'83	GLT	2P-3P③	¼P to ¾P	0.18–0.24④	12	20	20.8

NOTE: Toe-in specifications measured from tire outer diameter. Vehicle should not be loaded for these measurements.
① w/manual steering: ⅛ in. to ¼ in.
w/power steering: ¹⁄₁₆ in. to ³⁄₁₆ in.
② Power steering: 0.06–0.18
③ Power steering: 3P-4P
④ Power steering: 0.12–0.18 in.

TUNE-UP PROCEDURES

CAUTION

When working with a running engine, make sure that there is proper ventilation. Also make sure that the transmission is in neutral, and the parking brake is firmly applied. Always keep hands, clothing, and tools well clear of the radiator fan.

Spark Plug

REMOVAL AND INSTALLATION

Every six months or 6000 miles, the spark plugs should be removed for inspection. At this time they should be cleaned and regapped. At 12-month or 15,000 mile intervals the plugs should be replaced.

Clean the area around each sprak plug prior to plug removal, to avoid getting dirt into the engine once the plug is removed. Compressed air is excellent, if available.

Remove each spark plug wire by grasping its rubber boot on the end and twisting slightly to free the wire from the plug. Using a ¹³⁄₁₆ in. spark plug socket, turn the plugs counterclockwise to remove them. Do not allow any foreign matter to enter the cylinders through the spark plug holes.

The gap must be checked with a feeler gauge before installing the plug in the engine. With the ground electrode positioned parallel to the center electrode, the specified wire gauge must pass through the opening with a slight drag. If the air gap between the two electrodes is not correct, the ground electrode must be bent to bring it to specifications.

After the plugs are gapped correctly, they may be inserted into their holes and hand-tightened. Be careful not to crossthread the plugs. Install each spark plug wire on its respective plug, making sure that each spark plug end is making good metal-to-metal contact in its wire socket.

Breaker Points

ADJUSTING BREAKER POINTS WITH A DWELL METER

Adjusting the B21A breaker points with a dwell meter (if available) is a more precise method of adjustment than the feeler gauge method. Calibrate the dwell meter to the four-cylinder position, and connect it between the distributor primary terminal and a ground. Remove the distributor cap and rotor. Loosen the breaker point set screw about ⅛ of a turn. Observing the dwell meter, reset the screw of the stationary contact to obtain the proper (62°) dwell angle. Tighten the set screw and recheck the dwell. Install the rotor and cap, start the engine, and make a final dwell check.

ADJUSTING BREAKER POINTS WITH A FEELER GAUGE

The Canadian B21A models (carburetor-equipped) are also equipped with a conventional breaker points type ignition system. We recommend that for the cost of a new set of breaker points and condenser, it really isn't worth adjusting an old set of points. Replace old points with a new set and condenser.

To replace and adjust a new set of points, remove the distributor cap and rotor. Disconnect the wire leads from both points and condenser. Remove the points hold-down screw, condenser attaching screw, and remove the points assembly and condenser. Lightly grease the distributor cam lobe on the surface that makes contact with the points set. Install the new points assembly and condenser, attach the wire leads of both and tighten the condenser attaching screw. Do not fully tighten the points hold-down screw.

Turn the crankshaft bottom pulley (by placing a socket on the pulley bolt) until the cam lobe on the distributor shaft has fully raised the breaker arm. The points should now be up on the peak of the shaft eccentric, and should be at their most wide open point. Insert a 0.017 in. feeler gauge in between both contacts, and loosen the breaker plate hold down screw. There will be a slight drag on the feeler gauge when the gap is properly set. Tighten the hold-down screw when you are satisfied, rotate the engine once and recheck the gap. Make sure all leads are securely attached, replace the rotor and distributor cap.

Electronic Ignition

There are two major differences from the point type systems: First the points and condenser are replaced by an induction type impulse sender. Second, an electronic module has been added to amplify the electrical impulses between the distributor and coil. The impulse sender is located inside the distributor where the points are normally located on a points-type system. Instead of opening and closing an electrical circuit, the sender opens and closes a magnetic circuit. This induces impulses in a magnetic pick-up. The sender consists of a stator, pickup, rotor, and permanent magnet. The stator and armature each have the same number of teeth as there are cylinders. The permanent magnet creates a magnetic field which goes through the stator. The circuit is closed when the teeth are opposite each other. This means that the rotor opens and closes the magnetic field while rotating. This generates current pulses in the magnetic pick-up.

The electronic module is a solid state design which is fully transistorized. It amplifies the impulses from the sender and controls the dwell angle.

REPLACING THE IMPULSE SENDER

1. Unsnap the lock clasps.
2. Remove the cap, rotor and dust cover.

Contact screw removal

Impulse sender plate removal

Snap ring and shim removal

Impulse sender removal

Impulse sender-to-plate installation

3. Remove the vacuum advance unit and the cap hold-down clips.
4. Remove the screw securing the contact and pull the contact straight out.
5. Remove the impulse sender plate screws.
6. Remove the snap-ring and shims and pull the rotor straight off along with the small lock pin.
7. Remove the snap-ring retaining the sender and lift off the sender and plate.
8. Installation is the reverse of removal. Note that the screws for the vacuum unit and the hold-down clips are different lengths. When attaching the new sender to the plate, the connector pins should be directly opposite and above the attachment ear on the plate. When installation is completed, rotate the shaft several times to make sure there is no noise or binding.

Ignition Timing

ADJUSTMENT

Volvo recommends that the ignition timing be checked at 15,000 mile intervals on 1976–81 models.

Clean the crankshaft damper and pointer on the water pump housing with a solvent-soaked rag so that the marks can be seen. Connect a timing light according to the manufacturer's instructions. Scribe a mark on the crankshaft damper and on the marker with chalk or luminescent (day-glo) pain to highlight the correct timing setting. Disconnect and plug the distributor vacuum line and also disconnect the hose between the air cleaner and the inlet duct at the duct. Disconnect and plug the vacuum hose at the EGR valve.

Attach a tachometer to the engine and set the idle speed to specifications. With the engine running, aim the timing light at the pointer and the marks on the damper. If the marks do not coincide, stop the engine, loosen the distributor pinch bolt, and start the engine again. While observing the timing light flashes on the markers, grasp the distributor vacuum regulator and rotate the distributor until the marks do coincide. Stop the engine and tighten the distributor pinch bolt, taking care not to disturb the setting.

Reconnect all disconnected hoses and remove the timing light and tachometer from the engine.

NOTE: Refer to the fuel pump section for timing of the D-24 Diesel engine.

Valve Lash

ADJUSTMENT

B21 Engine

Valve clearance is checked every 15,000 miles, If it is necessary to adjust valve clearance, you will need three special tools: first, a valve tappet depressor tool used to push down the tappet sufficiently to remove the adjusting disc (shim) (Volvo tool #999 5022); second, a specially shaped pliers to actually remove and install the valve adjusting disc (Volvo tool #999 5026); and third, a set of varying thickness valve adjusting discs to make the necessary adjustments. We've included pictures of these special tools so that you might be able to find a suitable substitute. Otherwise, don't attempt the job.

The procedure for checking, and, if necessary, adjusting the valves is as follows:

1. Remove the valve cover. Scribe chalkmarks on the distributor body indicating each of the four spark plug wire leads in the cap. Remove the distributor cap.
2. Crank over the engine with a remote starter switch, or with a wrench on the crankshaft pulley center bolt (22 mm hex)

Adjusting valve clearance

5026

5022

B21 valve adjusting tools

10 2

B21 camshaft lobes at "10 and 2 o'clock" positions indicating that subject cylinder is in firing position and valves can be adjusted

until the engine is in the firing position for No. 1 cylinder. At this point, the 0 degree or TDC mark on the crankshaft pulley is aligned with the timing pointer, the rotor is pointing at the No. 1 spark plug wire cap position, and the camshaft lobes for No. 1 cylinder are pointing at the 10 o'clock and 2 o'clock positions. At this point, the clearance between the rocker arm and valve depressor (tappet) may be checked for the intake and exhaust valves of cylinder No.1, using a feeler guage. When checking clearance, the wear limit is 0.012–0.018 in. for a cold engine, and 0.012–0.020 in. for a hot one (176°F).

3. Repeat Step 2 for cylinders 3, 4, and 2 (in that order). Each time, rotate the crankshaft pulley 180° so that the rotor is pointing to the spark plug wire cap position for that cylinder, and the cam lobes are pointing at the 10 and 2 o'clock positions for the valves of that cylinder.

4. If any of the valve clearance measurements are outside the wear limit, you will have to remove the old valve adjusting disc and install a new one to bring the clearance within specifications. First, rotate the valve depressors (tappets) until their notches are at a right angle to the engine center line. Attach valve depressor tool 999 5022 or equivalent to the camshaft and screw down the tool spindle until the depressor (tappet) groove is just above the edge of its bore and still accessible with the special pliers (tool No. 999 5026).

5. Remove the valve adjusting disc and measure with a micrometer. Once you've gone to all this trouble, the valve clearance should be set to these tolerances; 0.014–0.016 in. for a cold engine, and 0.016–0.018 for a hot one. So, if the measured clearance had been 0.019 in. and the desired clearance 0.016 in. (for a net difference of 0.003 in.), then the new valve adjusting disc should be 0.003 in. thicker than the old one to take up the clearance. Valve adjusting discs are available from Volvo in sizes from 0.130 to 0.180 in. (in 0.002 in. increments). Always oil the new disc and install it with the marks facing down.

6. Remove the valve tappet depressor tool. Rotate the engine a few times and recheck clearance. Install the valve cover with a new gasket.

B27 Engine and B28F

Valve clearance is checked every 15,000 miles. No special tools are required.

1. In order to gain access to the valve covers, disconnect or remove the following:

a. Air conditioning compressor from bracket (do not disconnect refrigerant hoses)
b. EGR valve and hoses
c. A/C compressor bracket
d. Fuel injection control pressure regulator
e. Air pump
f. Vacuum pump
g. Hoses and wires from solenoid valve (Calif. only)

2. Using a 36 mm hex socket on the crankshaft pulley bolt, rotate the crankshaft to the No. 1 cylinder TDC position. At this point the "O" mark on the timing plate aligns with the crankshaft pulley notch, the distributor rotor is pointing to the No. 1 cylinder spark plug wire cap position, and both valves for No. 1 cylinder have clearance. At this position, adjust the intake valves of cylinders No. 1, 2 and 4, and the exhaust valves of cylinders No. 1, 3, and 6. Insert a feeler gauge between the rocker arm and valve stem. Loosen the locknut and turn

Positioning a new valve adjustment shim in the head. Shim must be oiled

On B27 and 28 with no. 1 cylinder at TDC, adjust these valves (arrows)

On B27 and 28, rotate the crankshaft 360 degrees and adjust the remaining valves (arrow)

the adjusting screw in the required direction. Tighten the locknut and recheck clearance. Clearance is 0.004–0.006 in. intake and 0.010–0.012 in. exhaust for a cold engine and 0.006–0.008 in. intake and 0.012–0.014 in. exhaust for a hot engine. The B28F cold intake valve adjustment 0.008–0.010 in.; cold exhaust valve adjustment 0.012–0.014 in.

3. Rotate the crankshaft pulley one full 360° turn to adjust the remaining valves. At this point, the "O" mark will again align with the pulley notch, the rotor is

pointing 180° opposite its former position, and the No. 1 cylinder rockers contact the ramps of the camshaft. At this position (see illustration), adjust the intake valves of cylinders No. 3, 5, and 6, and the exhaust valves of cylinders No. 2, 4, and 5.

4. Install the valve covers with new gaskets. Connect all disconnected equipment.

D-24 Diesel Engine

1. Remove the valve cover.

2. Use a 1¹⁄₁₆″ socket on the crankshaft pulley. Turn the pulley until the engine is ready to fire on the No. 1 cylinder. The flywheel timing mark should be at zero.

NOTE: The piston should not be at top dead center when setting the valve clearance.

Valve adjustment D24 engine

3. Line up the valve depressors.

4. Turn them so that the notches point slightly upward.

NOTE: Use tool #5196 or equivalent to depress the valve depressors. This tool is available from your Volvo dealer.

5. The depressor groves must be above the face so that the disc can be gripped with pliers. These pliers are available from your Volvo dealer under part #5195.

6. Remove the disc.

Cam disc removal D24 engine

7. Calculate the disc thickness, using a micrometer. The discs are available in thicknesses of 0.1299–0.1673 in. with increments of 0.002 in.

8. Cold engine 0.008-intake, 0.016 exhaust. Warm engine 0.010-intake, 0.018 exhaust.

NOTE: Always use new discs when performing this procedure.

9. Oil the new disc and install it with the marked side down.

10. Check the remaining valve clearances.

11. Use the following sequence 1, 5, 3, 6, 2, 4.

NOTE: Always check the valve clearances with the cylinder at top dead center. Turn the engine ¼ turn after top dead center, to set.

12. Recheck the valve clearance for all cylinders.

13. Rotate the engine several times, and recheck the clearance.

14. Install the valve cover with a new gasket.

Fuel Injection

IDLE SPEED AND MIXTURE ADJUSTMENT

Adjustment of the idle mixture on both of these systems requires a CO meter and special training. However, the idle speed adjustment may be set using a tachometer (follow the manufacturer's instructions for hook-up).

B21F Series

1. Disconnect and plug the air injection pump output hose and the EGR vacuum hose.

2. With the engine warmed to operat-

B27, 28 idle balance (nos. 1 and 2), and air adjusting screws (no. 3)

Adjusting idle speed (900 rpm)—Canadian B21A with carburetor

ing temperature (176°F), check that the idle speed is 900 rpm (manual trans) or 800 rpm (automatic) with the car idling in neutral. Adjust as necessary by rotating the air adjusting screw (knob) located beneath the air intake box.

B24F and B28F

1. Remove the air cleaner and housing.

Continuous injection idle speed adjustment—B21F

Disconnect the air pump outlet hose (large hose on rear of pump) and plug it with a large diameter screwdriver shaft. Disconnect and plug the vacuum hose at the EGR valve.

2. Set the idle balance screws (#1 and #2 in the illustration) to their basic setting by screwing them in clockwise until they bottom out, and then backing them off counterclockwise 4 full turns each.

3. Start the engine and allow it to reach operating temperature (176°F). Using the idle air adjusting screw (#3), set the idle speed to 900 rpm.

ENGINE ELECTRICAL

Distributor

REMOVAL AND INSTALLATION

1. Unsnap the distributor cap clasps and remove the cap.

2. Crank the engine until No. 1 cylinder is at Top Dead Center (TDC). At this point, the rotor should point to the spark plug wire socket for No. 1 cylinder, and the 0° timing mark on the crankshaft damper should be aligned with the pointer. For ease of assembly, scribe a chalkmark on the distributor housing to note the position of the rotor.

3. Disconnect the primary lead from the coil at its terminal on the distributor housing. On electronic fuel-injected models, disconnect the plug for the triggering contacts, On all models except Canadian B21A, remove the retaining screw for the primary voltage wire connector and pull it from the distributor housing.

4. Remove the vacuum hose(s) from the regulator. Take care not to damage the bakelite connection during removal.

5. On B21 and B27 engines, remove the distributor attaching screw and lift out the distributor.

6. When ready to install the distributor, if the engine has been disturbed (cranked), find TDC for No. 1 cylinder as outlined under ''Valve Lash Adjustment''. If the engine has not been disturbed, install the distributor with the rotor pointing to the No. 1 cylinder spark plug wire socket, or the chalkmark made prior to removal. On B21, B27 and B28F engines, the distributor drive gear teeth are bevelled, which will cause the rotor to turn counterclockwise as the distributor is installed. For this reason, it is necessary to back off the rotor clockwise (about 60° and on the B21, and 40° on the B27 and B28F) to compensate for this. What is necessary is that the rotor aligns with the

Electronic ignition distributor–240 series

mark made prior to removal after the distributor is bolted down.

7. Connect the primary lead to its terminal on the distributor housing. On electronic fuel-injected models, connect the plug for the triggering contacts. Push the primary voltage wire connector into its slot in the distributor housing and tighten the retaining screw.

8. Connect the vacuum hose(s) to the bakelite connection(s) on the vacuum regulator, (if so equipped).

9. If the distributor was disassembled, or if the contact point setting was disturbed, proceed to set the point gap and/or dwell angle on B21A (Canadian) engines.

10. Install the distributor cap and secure the clasps. Proceed to set the ignition timing. Tighten the distributor attaching screw.

Disconnecting primary lead from electronic ignition distributor

CAP

ROTOR

CONDENSATE SHIELD

ARMATURE

COIL

IMPULSE SENDER

VACUUM UNIT

Distributor assembly—B21F

Incorrect belt tension is corrected by moving the driven accessory (alternator, air pump, power steering pump or air conditioning compressor) away from or toward the driving pulley. Loosen the mounting and adjusting bolts on the respective accessory and tighten them, once the belt tension is correct. *Never* position a *metal* pry bar on the rear end of the alternator, air pump or power steering pump housing; they can be deformed easily.

REMOVAL AND INSTALLATION

1. Disconnect the negative battery cable.

1. Rod brush (carbon)
2. Distributor cap
3. Distributor arm
4. Protective cover
5. Condenser
6. Ignition contact breaker
7. Breaker plate
8. Lubricating felt
9. Circlip
10. Washer
11. Breaker cam
12. Centrifugal weight
13. Cam for triggering contacts
14. Primary terminal
15. Distributor body
16. Rubber seal
17. Washers
18. Driving collar
19. Resilient ring
20. Lock pin
21. Contact device
22. Lock clamp for distr. cap
23. Vacuum regulator
24. Centrifugal governor spring

Distributor assembly—Canadian B21A engines

Alternator

ALTERNATOR PRECAUTIONS

Several precautions must be observed when performing work on alternator equipment.

1. If the battery is removed for any reason, make sure that it is reconnected with the correct polarity. Reversing the battery connections may result in damage to the one-way rectifiers.

2. Never operate the alternator with the main circuit broken. Make sure that the battery, alternator, and regulator leads are not disconnected while the engine is running.

3. Never attempt to polarize an alternator.

4. When charging a battery that is installed in the vehicle, disconnect the negative battery cable. *This is very important.*

5. When utilizing a booster battery as a starting aid, always connect it in parallel; negative to negative, and positive to positive.

6. When arc welding is to be performed on any part of the vehicle, disconnect the negative battery cable, disconnect the alternator leads, and unplug the voltage regulator.

DRIVE BELT ADJUSTMENT

Accessory drive belt tension is checked every six months or 6000 miles. On 1980 and later models, no belt adjustment is recommended until 30,000 miles. Loose belts can cause poor engine cooling and diminish alternator output. A belt that is too tight places a severe strain on the water pump, alternator, air injection pumps, or power steering pump bearings.

Accessory drive belt tension is correct when the deflection made with light finger pressure on the belt at a midway point is about ½ in. Any belt that is glazed, frayed, or stretched so that it cannot be tightened sufficiently must be replaced.

2. Disconnect the electrical leads to the alternator.

3. Remove the adjusting arm-to-alternator bolt and the adjusting arm-to-engine bolt.

4. Remove the alternator mounting bolt.

5. Remove the fan belt and lift the alternator forward and out.

6. Reverse the above procedure to install, taking care to properly tension the fan (drive) belt.

Voltage Regulator

REMOVAL AND INSTALLATION

1. Disconnect the negative battery cable.

2. Disconnect the leads or plug socket from the old regulator taking note of their (its) location.

3. Remove the hold-down screws from the old regulator and install the new one.

4. Connect the leads or plug socket and reconnect the negative battery cable.

VOLTAGE ADJUSTMENT

Motorola (S.E.V. Marchal) Regulator

If the Motorola A.C. regulator is found to be defective, it must be replaced. No adjustments can be made on this unit.

The following test may be performed on the Motorola regulator to see if it is functioning properly. An ammeter, tachometer, and voltmeter are required.

1. Connect the alternator and regulator as shown in the illustration.

2. Run the engine at 25000 rpm (5000 alternator rpm) for 15 seconds. With no load on the alternator, and the regulator ambient temperature at 77°F, the reading on the voltmeter should be 13.1–14.4 V.

A. Alternator
B. Battery 60 Ah
C. Voltmeter 0—20 amps.
D. Ammeter 0—50 amps.
E. Voltage regulator
F. Warning lamp 12 volts. 2 watts

Wiring diagram for testing Motorola regulator

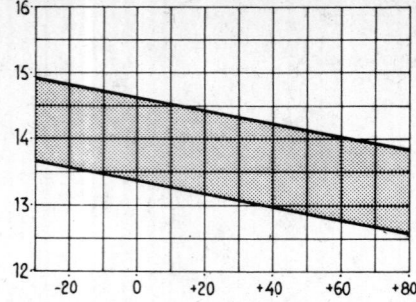

Voltage-temperature diagram for cold regulator—Motorola

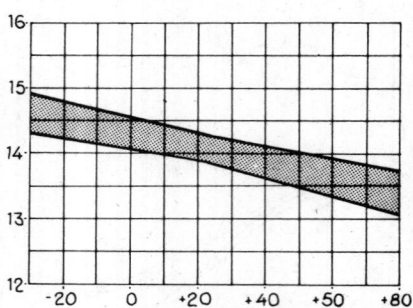

Voltage-temperature diagram for warm regulator—Motorola

For regulator ambient temperatures other than 77°F, consult the voltage-temperature diagram for cold regulator.

3. Load the alternator with 10–15 amps (high-beam headlights) while the engine is running at 2500 rpm. The voltmeter reading should again be 13.1–14.4 V. Replace the regulator if it does not fall within these limits.

4. For a more accurate indication of the regulator's performance, drive the vehicle for about 45 minutes at a minimum speed of 30 mph. The regulator will be at the correct working temperature immediately after this drive.

5. With the engine running at 2500 rpm, and the regulator ambient temperature at 77°F, the voltmeter reading should be 13.85–14.25 V. For regulator ambient temperatures other than 77°F, consult the Voltage-temperature diagram for warm regulator.

Bosch A.C. Regulator (35, 55 and 70 Amp)

The Bosch A.C. regulator is fully adjustable. To determine which adjustments are necessary—if any—perform the following test. (An ammeter, 12 V control lamp, tachometer, and voltmeter are required for this test)

NOTE: Where the numerical values differ for the 35 amp voltage regulator and the 55 amp unit, the figures for the 55 amp regulator will be given in parentheses.

1. Connect the alternator and regulator as shown in the illustration.

NOTE: The first reading must be taken within 30 seconds of beginning of test.

2. While running the engine at 2000 rpm, load the alternator with 28–30 amps (44–46 for 55 amp alternator).

3. Rapidly lower the engine to idle speed or 500 rpm, and then return it to 2000 rpm. With a load of 28–30 amps (44–46 for 55 amp alternator), the voltmeter reading should be 14.0–15.0 V (13.9–14.8 V for 55 amp alternator). The regulator should be regulated on the left (lower) contact.

4. Reduce the alternator load to 3–8 amps. The voltmeter reading should not decrease more than 0.3 (0.4 for 44 amp, alternator) V. The regulator should be regulated on the right (upper) contact.

5. Adjustment is made by bending the stop bracket for the bimetal spring. Bending the stop bracket down lowers the regulating voltage; bending it up raises the voltage. If

A. Alternator
B. Voltage lamp 12 volts
C. Control lamp 12 volts, 2 watts
D. Voltmeter 0-20 volts
F. Regulator resistance
G. Battery 60 amperehours
H. Load resistance
E. Ammeter 0-50 amps

Wiring diagram for testing Bosch A.C. regulator

1. Regulator contact for lower control range (lower contact)
2. Regulator contact for upper control range (upper contact)
3. Spring tensioner
4. Spring upper section: Steel spring Lower section: Bimetal spring

Bosch A.C. voltage adjustments

the voltmeter reading for the low amp alternator load decreased more than 0.3 (0.4 for 55 amp alternator), V, compared to the reading for the high amp alternator load, adjust the regulator by bending the holder for the left (lower) contact and simultaneously adjust the gap between the right (upper) contact and the movable contact. The gap should be adjusted to 0.010–0.015 in. (0. 25–0.40 mm). If the holder is bent toward the right (upper) contact, the regulating voltage under high amp alternator load will be lowered.

To avoid faulty adjustments due to residual magnetism in the regulator core, it may be necessary to rapidly lower the engine rpm to idle after each adjustment, then raise it to 2000 rpm to take a new reading.

NOTE: Warm regulators may be cooled to ambient temperature by directing a stream of compressed air on them. Final readings should be made with the regulator at ambient temperature.

Starter

REMOVAL AND INSTALLATION

1. Disconnect the negative battery cable at the battery.
2. Disconnect the leads from the starter motor.
3. Remove the bolts retaining the starter motor brace to the cylinder block (B21 only) and the bolts retaining the starter motor to the flywheel housing and lift it off.
4. Position the starter motor to the flywheel housing and install the retaining bolts finger-tight. Torque the bolts to approximately 25 ft. lbs., and apply locking compound to the threads.
5. Connect the starter motor leads and the negative battery cable.

STARTER DRIVE REPLACEMENT

In order to remove the starter pinion drive, it is necessary to disassemble the starter. The procedure for disassembling the starter is as follows:

1. Remove the starter from the car as outlined in "Starter Removal and Installation."
2. Unscrew the two screws and remove the small cover from the front end of the starter shaft.
3. Unsnap the lockwasher and remove the adjusting washers from the front end of the shaft.
4. Unscrew the two screws retaining the commutator bearing shield and remove the shield.
5. Lift up the brushes and retainers and remove the brush bridge from the rotor shaft. The negative brushes are removed with the bridge while the positive brushes remain in

Exploded view of a typical starter motor

the field winding. Do not remove the steel washer and the fiber washer at this time.
6. Unscrew the nut retaining the field terminal connection to the control solenoid.
7. Unscrew the two solenoid-to-starter housing retaining screws and remove the solenoid.
8. Remove the drive end shield and rotor from the stator.
9. Remove the rubber and metal sealing washers from the housing.
10. Unscrew the nut and remove the screw on which the engaging arm pivots.
11. Remove the rotor, with the pinion and engaging arm attached, from the drive end shield.
12. Push back the stop washer and remove the snap-ring from the rotor shaft.
13. Remove the stop washer and pull off the starter pinion with a gear puller.

While the starter is disassembled, a few quick checks may be performed. Check the rotor shaft, commutator, and windings. If the rotor shaft is bent or worn, it must be replaced. Maximum rotor shaft radial throw is 0.003 in. If the commutator is scored or worn unevenly, it should be turned. Minimum commutator diameter is 1.3 in. Check the end shield which houses the brushes, for excessive wear. Maximum bearing clearance is 0.005 in.

14. Lubricate the starter.
15. Press the starter pinion onto the rotor shaft. Install the stop washer and secure it with a new snap-ring.
16. Position the engaging arm on the pinion. Install the rotor into the drive end frame.
17. Install the screw and nut for the engaging arm pivot.
18. Install the rubber and metal sealing washers into the drive end housing.
19. Install the stator onto the rotor and drive end shield.
20. Position the solenoid so that the eyelet on the end of the solenoid plunger fits onto the engaging arm (shift lever). Tighten the solenoid retaining screws.
21. Place the metal and fiber washers on the rotor shaft.
22. Install the brush bridge on the rotor shaft and replace the brushes.

23. Fit the commutator bearing shield into position and install the retaining screws.
24. Install the adjusting washers and snap a new lockwasher into position on the end of the shaft. Make sure that the rotor axial clearance does not exceed 0.12 in. If necessary, adjust the clearance with washers, maintaining a minimum clearance of 0.002 in.
25. Replace the small cover over the front end of the shaft and install the two retaining screws.
26. Install the starter in the car as outlined in "Starter Removal and Installation."

SOLENOID REPLACEMENT

Before replacing the solenoid when the starter will not crank, see if the battery has sufficient charge. If the no-crank condition persists when the battery is known to be good, connect a jumper wire between the positive terminal of the battery and the contact screw for the solenoid lead. If the solenoid engages the starter pinion, the starter switch or leads are at fault. If the starter still does not crank, replace the solenoid. To remove the solenoid, remove the starter from the car. The solenoid may be removed from the starter while installed in the car, but then aligning the solenoid is as follows.

1. Remove the starter from the car as outlined in "Starter Removal and Installation."
2. Unscrew the two solenoid-to-starter housing retaining screws and remove the solenoid.
3. As a final test, wipe the solenoid clean and press in the armature. Test its operation by connecting it to a battery. If the solenoid still does not function, replace it with a new unit.
4. Position the new solenoid so that the eyelet on the end of the plunger fits into the engaging arm. Tighten the retaining screws.
5. Replace the starter in the car as outlined in "Starter Removal and Installation."

ENGINE MECHANICAL

Four basic engines are covered here—the four basic engines Volvo has used since 1976. They are the B21F (2127cc), which is the basic inline four-cylinder, overhead cam engine; the B27F (2664cc), an alloy overhead cam V6 with iron liners first introduced in 1976 and phased out in 1980; the B28F (2849cc), which is almost identical in design to the B27F, except with a larger bore and slightly shorter stroke (new in 1980); and the D24 Diesel (2383cc), which is a Volkswagen-manufactured inline six first introduced in Volvo cars in 1980. The D24 is also a single overhead cam design.

Engine

REMOVAL AND INSTALLATION

B21F (Includes B21FLH, B21FT, B21A)

1. On cars equipped with manual transmission, remove the four retaining clips and lift up the shifter boot. Then, remove the snap-ring from the shifter.
2. Remove the battery.
3. Disconnect the windshield washer hose, engine compartment light wire and remove the hood.
4. Remove the overflow tank cap. Drain the cooling system by disconnecting the lower radiator hose and opening the engine drain cock (beneath the exhaust manifold).
5. Remove the upper and lower radiator hoses. Disconnect the overflow hoses at the radiator. Disconnect the overflow hoses at the radiator. Disconnect the PCV hose at the cylinder head.
6. On cars equipped with automatic transmission, disconnect the oil cooler lines at the radiator.
7. Remove the radiator and fan shroud.
8. Remove the air cleaner assembly and hoses.

9. Disconnect the hoses at the air pump. Remove the air pump and drive belt, if equipped.
10. Disconnect the vacuum pump hoses and remove the vacuum pump. Disconnect the power brake booster vacuum hose.
11. Remove the power steering pump, drive belt and bracket. Position to one side.
12. On cars equipped with air conditioning, remove the crankshaft pulley (5 mm Allen wrench), and compressor drive belt. Then, install the pulley again for reference. Remove the AC wire connector and the compressor from its bracket and position to one side. Remove the bracket.
13. Disconnect the vacuum hoses from the engine. Disconnect the carbon canister hoses.
14. Disconnect the distributor wire connector, high tension lead, starter cables, and the clutch cable clamp.
15. Disconnect the wiring harness at the voltage regulator. Disconnect the throttle cable at the pulley, and the wire for the AC at the intake manifold solenoid.
16. Remove the gas cap. Disconnect the fuel lines at the filter and return pipe.
17. At the firewall, disconnect the electrical connectors for the ballast resistor, and relays. Disconnect the heater hoses.
18. Disconnect the micro switch connectors at the intake manifold, and all remaining harness connectors to the engine.
19. Drain the crankcase.
20. Remove the exhaust manifold flange retaining nuts. Loosen the exhaust pipe clamp bolts and remove the bracket for the front exhaust pipe mount. On B21FT (Turbo) models, disconnect the turbo from the intake hose, disconnect the other hoses from the turbo unit, and disconnect the turbocharger from the exhaust system.
21. From underneath, remove the front motor mount bolts.
22. On cars equipped with automatic transmission, place the gear selector lever in "Park" and disconnect the gear shift control rod from the transmission.
23. On manual transmission cars, disconnect the clutch cable. Then, loosen the set screw, drive out the pivot pin, and remove the shifter from the control rod.
24. Disconnect the speedometer and the driveshaft from the transmission.

25. On overdrive equipped models, disconnect the control wire from the shifter.
26. Jack up the front of the car and place jack stands beneath the reinforced box member areas to the rear of each front jacking attachment. Then, using a floor jack and a wooden block, support the weight of the engine beneath the transmission.
27. Remove the bolts for the rear transmission mount. Remove the transmission support crossmember.
28. Lift out the engine.
29. Reverse the above procedure to install.

B27F and B28F

1. On cars equipped with manual transmission, remove the shifter assembly. From underneath, loosen the set screw and drive out the pivot pin. Then, pull up the boot, remove the reverse pawl bracket, and snap-ring for the shifter, and lift out the shifter.
2. Remove the battery.
3. Disconnect the windshield washer hose, engine compartment light wire and remove the hood.
4. Remove the air cleaner assembly.
5. Remove the splash guard under the engine.
6. Drain the cooling system by disconnecting the lower radiator hose and open the drain cocks on both sides of the cylinder block.
7. Remove the overflow tank cap. Remove the upper and lower radiator hoses, and disconnect the overflow hoses at the radiator.
8. On cars equipped with automatic transmission, disconnect the transmission cooler lines at the radiator.
9. Remove the radiator and fan shroud.
10. Disconnect the heater hoses, power brake hose at the intake manifold and the vacuum pump hose at the pump. Remove the vacuum pump and O-ring in the valve cover. Remove the gas cap.
11. At the firewall disconnect the fuel lines (**CAUTION: High pressure**) at the filter and return pipe, disconnect the relay connectors and all other wire connectors. Disconnect the distributor wires.
12. Disconnect the evaporative control

Removing the front engine mounts—B21F series

Removing the transmission support member—B21F series (V6 similar)

four bolts M7-30
10-15 Nm

11 mm hex

7-11 lb.ft.

spark plugs
17.5-20 Nm

16 mm hex

13-15 lb.ft.

Molybdenum
disulphide
grease on
threads

AC brackets
M10
15-25

17 mm hex

11-18 lb.ft.

four bolts M8-20
15-25 Nm

13 mm hex

11-14 lb.ft.

ten bolts M7-25
ten bolts M7-50
10-15 Nm

11 mm hex

7-11 lb.ft.

exhaust pipe
nuts
31-51 Nm

15 mm hex

22-37 lb.ft.

6+6 nuts
10-15 Nm

11 mm hex

7-11 lb.ft.

two M10 nuts
15-25 Nm

17 mm hex

11-18 lb.ft.

B27F and B28F series (V6) engines

carbon canister hoses and the vacuum hose at the EGR valve.

13. Disconnect the voltage regulator wire connector.

14. Disconnect the throttle cable (and kickdown cable on automatic transmission cars), the vacuum amplifier hose at the T-pipe, and the hoses at the wax thermostat.

15. Disconnect the air pump hose at the backfire valve, the solenoid valve wire, and the micro switch wire.

16. Remove the exhaust manifold flange retaining nuts (both sides).

17. On cars equipped with air conditioning, remove the compressor and drive belt, and place it to one side. Do not disconnect the refrigerant hoses.

18. Drain the crankcase.

19. Remove the power steering pump, drive belt, and bracket. Position to one side.

20. From underneath, remove the retaining nuts for the front motor mounts.

21. On models equipped with a catalytic converter, remove the front exhaust pipe.

22. On 49 states models, remove the front exhaust pipe hangers and clamps and allow the system to hang.

23. On cars equipped with automatic transmission, place the shift lever in "Park". Disconnect the shift control lever at the transmission.

24. On manual transmission cars, disconnect the clutch cylinder from the bell housing. Leave the cylinder connected (secure it to the car).

25. Disconnect the speedometer cable and driveshaft at the transmission.

26. Jack up the front of the car and place jack stands beneath the reinforced box member area to the rear of each front jacking attachment. Then, using a floor jack and a thick, wide wooden block, support the weight of the engine beneath the oil pan.

27. Remove the bolts for the rear transmission mount. Remove the transmission support crossmember.

28. Lift out the engine.

29. Reverse the above procedure to install.

D-24

1. Remove the hood.
2. Disconnect the negative battery terminal.
3. Drain the radiator coolant.
4. Remove the four clips and pull up the rubber boot on the shift lever.
5. Disconnect the back-up light and overdrive connector if so equipped.
6. Remove the bracket for the reverse inhibitor.
7. Release the lock ring on the shift lever.
8. Move the lock ring, rubber ring, and plastic journal up on the lever.

NOTE: On cars with automatic transmissions place the shift lever in Park before disconnecting.

9. Disconnect the top and bottom radiator hoses.

Sectional view of the D24 Diesel

10. Disconnect the lower hose at the cold start device, and drain the coolant into a suitable container.

11. On vehicles with automatic transmissions remove the cooling lines from the radiator.

12. Disconnect the expansion tank hose.

13. Unbolt and remove the radiator.

14. Disconnect the electrical connection at the firewall.

15. Remove the heater hoses at the control valve.

16. Disconnect the hose from the vacuum pump.

17. Disconnect the accelerator cable from the pulley and bracket.

18. Disconnect the vacuum line to the brake booster.

19. Disconnect the fuel lines.

NOTE: Thoroughly clean all connections prior to disconnecting them.

20. Plug all fuel lines to prevent dirt from entering them.

21. Disconnect the wires at the main terminal.

22. Disconnect the glow plug relay.

23. Remove the relay retaining screws and hang the relay and the wire bundle on the engine.

24. Remove the steering pump and brackets, and tie it out of the way.

25. Remove the starter wires and the battery ground strap.

26. Remove the fan, spacer, pulley and drive belts.

27. Remove the air cleaner and all necessary hoses.

28. Disconnect the alternator wires.

29. Disconnect the exhaust pipe at the front exhaust manifold.

30. Drain the engine oil.

31. Disconnect the exhaust pipe at the rear exhaust manifold.

32. Disconnect the clutch cable, return spring, vibration damper, and rubber buffer.

33. Pull out the clutch cable from the clutch lever and housing.

34. Disconnect the speedometer from the transmission.

NOTE: On cars with automatic transmissions disconnect the shift lever.

35. Disconnect the shift lever and push it up into the car.

36. Remove the driveshaft from the transmission.

37. Support the transmission with a jack and remove the rear crossmember.

38. Remove the engine mounts.
   a. Left side: Remove the nuts from the front axle member.
   b. Right side: Remove the lower nut from the rubber pad.

39. Gently put tension on your engine removal hoist.

40. Remove the left engine mount assembly.

41. Remove the engine.

42. Installation is the reverse of removal.

Cylinder Head

REMOVAL AND INSTALLATION

NOTE: To prevent warpage of the

head, removal should be attempted only on a cold engine.

B21F

1. Disconnect the battery.
2. Remove the overflow tank cap and drain the coolant. Disconnect the upper radiator hose.
3. Remove the distributor cap and wires.
4. Remove the PCV hoses.
5. Remove the EGR valve and vacuum pump.
6. Remove the air pump, if equipped, and air injection manifold. Disconnect and remove all hoses to the turbocharger if equipped.
7. Remove the exhaust manifold and header pipe bracket.
8. Remove the intake manifold. Disconnect the manifold brace and the hose clamp to the bellows for the fuel injection air/flow unit. Disconnect the throttle cable, and all vacuum hoses and electrical connectors to the fuel injection unit.
9. Remove the fuel injectors.
10. Remove the valve cover.
11. Loosen the fan shroud and remove

Oil feed hole in head

Guide stud installation

the fan. Remove the shroud. Remove the upper belts and pulleys.

12. Remove the timing belt cover. Remove the timing belt as described later in this section.
13. Remove the camshaft (if so desired) as outlined later in this section.
14. Remove the cylinder head (10 mm Allen head bolts).
15. To install, reverse the removal procedure. Oil the head bolts. Tighten the head bolts in the prescribed torque sequence first to 44 ft. lbs., then to 81 ft. lbs. After the engine has been run 30 minutes, slacken the bolts to relieve any pretension, and then retorque to 81 ft. lbs. To set the valve timing, follow the steps for timing belt installation later in this section.

B27F and B28F

1. Disconnect the battery. Drain the coolant.
2. Remove the air cleaner assembly and all attaching hoses.
3. Disconnect the throttle cable. On automatic transmission equipped cars, disconnect the kick-down cable.
4. Disconnect the EGR vacuum hose and remove the pipe between the EGR valve and manifold.
5. Remove the oil filler cap, and cover the hole with a rag. Disconnect the PCV pipe(s) from the intake manifold.
6. Remove the front section of the intake manifold.
7. Disconnect the electrical connector and fuel line at the cold start injector. Disconnect the vacuum hose, both fuel lines, and the electrical connector from the control pressure regulator.
8. Disconnect the hose, pipe, and electrical connector from the auxiliary air valve. Remove the auxiliary air valve.
9. Disconnect the electrical connector from the fuel distributor. Remove the wire looms from the intake manifolds. Disconnect the spark plug wires.
10. Disconnect the fuel injectors from their holders.
11. Disconnect the distributor vacuum hose, carbon filter hose, and diverter valve hose from the intake manifold. Also, disconnect the power brake hose and heater hose at the intake manifold.
12. Disconnect the throttle control link from its pulley.
13. On cars equipped with an EGR vacuum amplifier, disconnect the wires from the throttle micro switch and solenoid valve.
14. At the firewall, disconnect the fuel lines from the fuel filter and return line.
15. Remove the two attaching screws and lift out the fuel distributor and throttle housing assembly.
16. On cars not equipped with an EGR vacuum amplifier, disconnect the EGR valve hose from underneath the throttle housing.
17. Remove the cold start injector, rubber ring, and pipe.
18. Remove the four retaining bolts and

B21 cylinder head assembly

one M6 bolt per head
5-7.5 Nm

10 mm hex
3.6-5.4 lb.ft.

eight bolts
M12x1.5 per head
19 mm hex
For torquing
procedure see
Op.F10-F15 in
Group 20.

distributor
retaining
nut M7x1
10-15 Nm

11 mm hex
7-11 lb.ft.

two bolts M7-16
10-15 Nm

11 mm hex
7-11 lb.ft.

2+2 M6-12
5-7.5 Nm

10 mm hex
3.6-5.4 lb.ft.

M7 studs
5-10 Nm
3.5-7 lb.ft.

M7 nuts
10-15 Nm

11 mm hex
7-11 lb.ft.

spark plugs
17.5-20 Nm

16 mm hex
13-15 lb.ft.

Molybdenum
disulphide
grease on
threads

B27, 28 cylinder head assembly

B27, 28 cylinder head removal

lift off the intake manifold. Remove the rubber rings.

19. Remove the splash guard beneath the engine.

20. If removing the left cylinder head, remove the air pump from its bracket.

21. Remove the vacuum pump and O-ring in the valve cover. Remove the vacuum hoses from the wax thermostat.

22. If removing the right cylinder head, disconnect the upper radiator hose.

23. On air conditioned models, remove the AC compressor and secure it to one side. *Do not disconnect the refrigerant lines.*

24. Disconnect the distributor leads and remove the distributor. Remove the EGR valve, bracket and pipe. At the firewall, disconnect the electrical connectors at the relays.

25. On air conditioned models, remove the rear compressor bracket.

26. Disconnect the coolant hose(s) from the water pump to the cylinder head(s). If removing the left cylinder head, disconnect the lower radiator hose at the water pump.

27. Disconnect the air injection system supply hose from the applicable cylinder head. Separate the air manifold at the rear of the engine. If removing the left cylinder head, remove the backfire valve and air hose.

28. Remove the valve cover(s).

29. On the left cylinder head, remove the Allen head screw and four upper bolts to the timing gear cover. On the right cylinder head, remove the four upper bolts to the timing gear cover and the front cover plate.

30. From beneath the car, remove the exhaust pipe clamps for both header pipes.

31. If removing the right cylinder head, remove the retainer bracket bolts and pull the dipstick tube out of the crankcase.

32. Remove the applicable exhaust manifold(s).

33. Remove the cover plate at the rear of the cylinder head.

34. Rotate the camshaft sprocket (for the applicable cylinder head) into position so that the large sprocket hole aligns with the rocker arm shaft. With the camshaft in this position, loosen the cylinder head bolts in sequence (same sequence as tightening), and remove the rocker arm and shaft assembly.

35. Loosen the camshaft retaining fork bolt (directly in back of sprocket) and slide the fork away from the camshaft.

36. Next, it is necessary to hold the cam chain stretched during camshaft removal. Otherwise, the chain tensioner will automatically take up the slack, making it impossible to reinstall the sprocket on the cam without removing the timing chain cover to loosen the tensioner device. To accomplish this, a special sprocket retainer tool (Volve #999 5104) is installed over the sprocket with two bolts in the top of the timing chain cover. A bolt is then screwed into the sprocket to hold it in place.

37. Remove the camshaft sprocket cen-

**Final step of cylinder head tightening sequence
is protractor torquing to 116-120 degrees
(1/3 of a full turn)**

Aligning camshaft for cylinder head removal, B27, 28

ter bolt and push the camshaft to the rear, so it clears the sprocket.

38. Remove the cylinder head.

NOTE: Do not remove the cylinder head by pulling straight up. Instead, lever the head off by inserting two spare head bolts into the front and rear inboard cylinder head bolt holes, and pulling toward the applicable wheel housing. Otherwise, the cylinder liners may be pulled up, breaking the lower liner seal and leaking coolant into the crankcase. If any do pull up, new liner seals must be used, and the crankcase completely drained. If the head(s) seem stuck, gently tap around the edges of the head(s) with a rubber mallet, to break the joint.

39. Remove the head gasket. Clean the contact surfaces with a plastic scraper and lacquer thinner.

40. If the head is going to be off for any length of time, install liner holders (Volvo special tool #999 5093) or two strips of thick stock steel with holes for the head bolts, so that the liners stay pressed down against their seals. Install the holders widthwise between the middle four head bolt holes.

41. Reverse the above procedure to install, using the following installation notes:

a. There are a pair of guide dowels at both outboard corners of the head. If they fell down during removal, pull them back out with a puller hammer. They can be propped up with a ⅛ in. drill shank.

b. Remove the liner holders.

c. The right and left head gaskets are different.

d. Check the timing chain cover gasket. If damaged, replace only the upper section.

e. Oil the head bolt threads. Position the head on the dowels and install (hand tight) one center head bolt. Then, slide the camshaft forward into position against the sprocket and install the sprocket center bolts, and remove the retainer tool.

f. Before installing the head bolts, remove the guide dowel shanks, if used.

g. Using the correct tightening sequence, tighten the head bolts to 7 ft. lbs., then 22 ft. lbs., and then 44 ft. lbs. Next slacken the head bolts (in the tightening sequence) to relieve any pre-tension. Now, tighten the bolts to 11–14 ft. lbs. *Finally, tighten the head bolts exactly one-third of a full 360° turn (116–120°) in the tightening sequence. This is critical for proper piston liner O-ring sealing. If necessary, use a protractor to ensure accuracy.*

h. Adjust the valves after completing assembly.

i. After running the engine to operating temperature, allow to cool for 30 minutes, and retorquing the head bolts. Following the tightening sequence slacken the bolts to relieve any pre-tension, then tighten to 11–14 ft. lbs. *and finally protractor torque them to 113–117° (one-third of a full turn).*

D-24

1. Disconnect the negative battery terminal.

2. Remove the engine splash guard.

3. Disconnect the exhaust pipe from the transmission bracket.

4. Disconnect the exhaust pipe from the rear exhaust manifold.

5. Disconnect the exhaust pipe from the front exhaust manifold.

6. Remove the air cleaner and all necessary hoses.

7. Drain the radiator.

Cylinder liner holders installed

B27, 28 camshaft sprocket retainer tool

Head bolt removal sequence D24 engine start at bolt 14, end at bolt 1

8. Remove the bottom and top radiator hoses.

9. Remove the bottom hose from the cold start device and drain it into a suitable container.

10. Remove the top cold start hose.

11. Remove the vacuum pump and the plunger.

12. Remove all the fuel lines and plug the fuel line connections.

NOTE: Carefully remove all dirt from the fuel line connections to prevent dirt from entering the system.

13. Remove the glow plug wires and temperature sender wire.

14. Remove the rear injector return line hose.

15. Remove the valve cover.

16. Remove the front and rear timing belt covers.

17. Set the engine at top dead center and the fuel pump to the injection position for the Number one cylinder.

18. Remove the timing belt shield from the head.

NOTE: Be careful not to drop the washers or bolts into the lower cover.

19. Loosen the bolts on the water pump and the belt idler pulley.

20. Remove the belt from the camshaft.

21. Use special tool #5199 or a suitable replacement to hold the cam gear steady while removing it. This tool is available from your Volvo dealer.

NOTE: Do not allow the camshaft to turn.

22. Loosen the fuel pump bracket retaining screws to loosen the belt tension.

23. Remove the belt.

24. Remove the rear camshaft gear; see Step #21 for this procedure.

25. Remove the head bolts, and remove the head.

26. Installation is the reverse of removal.

NOTE: From late 1980, new type cylinder head bolts are used on the D24 Diesel. They are longer and 1mm wide. Torquing these bolts is a six-step procedure:

1. Torque to 30 ft. lbs.
2. Torque to 44 ft. lbs.
3. Torque to 55 ft. lbs.
4. Tighten 180°, in one movement, without stopping.
5. Run engine until oil temperature is minimum 120°F.
6. Tighten 90°, in one movement, without stopping.

NOTE: Always use a new gasket when replacing the head.

The following special tools are needed for reinstallation of the head: Belt tension gauge #5197, Camshaft position gauge #5190.

OVERHAUL

Refer to "Cylinder Head Reconditioning" in the "Engine Rebuilding" section.

Rocker Shafts

REMOVAL AND INSTALLATION

B27F and B28F

1. Disconnect the battery.
2. Remove the air cleaner assembly.
3. Disconnect the air pump bracket.
4. Remove the left valve cover (if so desired).
5. Tie the upper radiator hose out of the way and remove the oil filler cap and carbon canister hose.
6. On air conditioned models, remove the AC compressor from its bracket. Do not disconnect the hoses.
7. Remove the EGR valve.
8. Remove the AC compressor rear bracket.
9. Remove the control pressure regulator.
10. Disconnect any hoses or wires in the way. Remove the right valve cover (if so desired).
11. The rocker arm bolts double as cylinder head bolts. When loosening, follow the cylinder head bolt tightening sequence

diagram. If removing both rocker shafts, mark them left and right.

NOTE: Do not jar or strike head while rockers and bolts are out, as cylinder liner O-ring seals may break, necessitating teardown of engine to clean coolant out of crankcase and installation of new seals.

12. To install, reverse removal procedure. Follow cylinder head installation procedure for proper torque sequence.

Intake and Exhaust Manifolds

REMOVAL AND INSTALLATION

Inlet Duct

1. Disconnect the negative battery cable.
2. Disconnect the throttle and downshift linkage. Remove from the inlet duct, the positive crankcase ventilation, distributor advance, pressure sensor (electronic fuel-injection models only) and power brake hoses.
3. On electronic fuel-injected models, disconnect the contact for the throttle valve switch, and remove the ground cable for the inlet duct.
4. Remove the bolts for the inlet duct stay. Remove the inlet duct-to-cylinder head retaining nuts and slide the inlet duct off the studs. Discard the old gasket.
5. To install, reverse the above procedure. Use a new inlet duct gasket. Torque the nuts to 13–16 ft. lbs.

Intake Manifold

B27F and B28F

1. Remove the air cleaner and all necessary hoses.
2. Drain the radiator coolant.
3. Remove the throttle cable from the pulley and bracket.
4. On automatic transmission cars re-

Camshaft position gauge

B27F/B28F intake manifold securing bolts

move the throttle cable that is connected to the transmission.

5. Remove the EGR pipe from the EGR valve to the manifold.

6. Disconnect the EGR vacuum line.

7. Remove the oil filler cap and PCV valve.

NOTE: Cover the oil cap opening with a rag to keep dirt out.

8. Remove the front manifold bolts and remove the front section of the manifold.

9. Disconnect the cold start connector, fuel line, and injector.

10. Disconnect the pressure control regulator vacuum lines, fuel lines, and the connector.

11. Remove the auxiliary valve and its necessary piping.

12. Disconnect the electrical connections at the air-fuel control unit.

13. Remove all six spark plug wires.

14. Remove all six injectors.

15. Move the wiring harness to the outside of the manifold.

16. Disconnect the vacuum hose at the distributor and the intake manifold.

17. Disconnect the heater hose at the intake manifold.

18. Disconnect the hose to the diverter valve.

19. Disconnect the vacuum hose to the power brake booster.

20. Disconnect the throttle cable link.

21. Disconnect the wires to the micro switch.

22. Pull the wires away from the intake manifold.

23. Remove the fuel filter line and the return line.

24. Remove the air control unit.

25. Disconnect the vacuum hose from the throttle valve housing.

26. Remove the pipe and cold start injector assembly.

27. Remove the intake assembly.

28. Installation is the reverse of removal.

NOTE: Always use new gaskets when reinstalling the manifold.

29. Torque the manifold bolts to 7–11 ft. lbs.

B21F

1. Remove the air cleaner and all necessary hoses.

2. Remove the PCV valve.

3. Remove the connector at the cold start injector.

4. Remove the fuel hose from the cold start injector.

5. Remove the cold start injector.

6. Remove the connector on the auxiliary valve.

7. Disconnect the hoses at the auxiliary valve.

8. Remove the auxiliary valve.

9. Remove the intake manifold brace.

10. Disconnect the distributor vacuum hose at the intake manifold.

11. Loosen the clamp for the rubber connecting pipe on the air-fuel control unit.

12. Remove the manifold bolts and remove the manifold.

13. Installation is the reverse of removal.

NOTE: Remember to install new manifold gaskets before replacing the manifold.

14. Torque the manifold bolts to 15 ft. lbs.

D24 DIESEL

1. Disconnect the negative battery terminal.

2. Remove the air cleaner and all necessary hoses.

3. Remove any other necessary vacuum or electrical lines.

4. Remove the intake manifold bolts and remove the manifold.

5. Installation is the reverse of removal.

NOTE: Always use a new gasket when reinstalling the intake manifold.

6. Torque the intake bolts to 18 ft. lbs.

Exhaust Manifold

B27F and B28F

Depending upon the type of optional equipment your particular vehicle has the exhaust manifolds may be removed from underneath the car.

1. Jack up your vehicle and support it with jack stands.

2. Unbolt the crossover pipe from the left and right side of your exhaust manifolds, (if so equipped).

NOTE: If your car has the "Y" type exhaust pipe disconnect this pipe at the left and right manifolds.

3. Remove any other necessary hardware.

4. Remove the left and right side manifolds.

5. Installation is the reverse of removal.

NOTE: Always use new gaskets when reinstalling the manifolds.

6. Torque the manifold bolts to 7–11 ft. lbs.

B21F

1. Remove the air cleaner and all necessary hoses.

2. Remove the EGR valve pipe from the manifold.

3. Remove the exhaust pipe from the exhaust manifold.

4. Remove the manifold bolts and remove the manifold.

NOTE: Remember to install new manifold gaskets before installing the manifold.

5. Installation is the reverse of removal.

6. Torque the manifold bolts to 10–20 ft. lbs.

D24 DIESEL

1. Disconnect the negative battery terminal.

2. Remove the air cleaner and all necessary hoses.

3. Remove the exhaust pipes from the manifolds.

NOTE: The exhaust manifold is made in two separate sections.

4. Remove any other necessary hardware.

5. Remove the intake manifold. See the intake manifold removal section.

6. Remove the exhaust manifold in two sections.

7. Installation is the reverse of removal.

NOTE: Always use new gaskets when reinstalling the exhaust manifold.

8. Torque the bolts to 18 ft. lbs.

Turbocharger

REMOVAL AND INSTALLATION

B21FT

NOTE: Due to the complexity and close tolerances involved with the turbocharger unit, we recommend that any service other than removal and installation be performed by an experienced turbo technician.

1. Disconnect battery ground cable.

2. Disconnect expansion tank from retainer. Remove expansion tank retainer.

3. Remove preheater hose to the air cleaner. Remove the pipe and rubber bellows between the air/fuel control unit and the turbocharger unit. Pull out the crankcase ventilation hose from the pipe.

4. Remove the pipe and pipe connector between the turbocharger unit and the intake manifold.

NOTE: Cover the turbocharger intake and outlet ports to keep dirt out of the system.

5. Disconnect the exhaust pipe and secure it aside.

6. Disconnect the spark plug wires at the plugs.

7. Remove the upper heat shield. Remove the brace between the turbocharger unit and the manifold.

8. Remove the lower heat shield by removing the one retaining screw underneath the manifold.

9. Remove the oil pipe clamp, retaining screws on the turbo unit and the pipe connection screw in the cylinder block under the manifold. DO NOT allow any dirt to enter the oilways.

10. Remove the manifold retaining

Disconnect the turbocharger unit from the exhaust system

screws and washers. Let one nut remain in position to keep the manifold in position.

11. Remove the oil delivery pipe. Cover the opening on the turbo unit.

12. Disconnect the air/fuel contro unit by loosening the clamps. Move the unit with the lower section of the air cleaner up to the right side wheel housing. Place a cover over the wheel housing as protection.

13. Remove the air cleaner filter.

14. Remove the remaining nut and washer on the manifold. Lift the assembly forward and up. Remove the manifold gaskets. Dis-

connect the return oil pipe O-ring from the cylinder block.

15. Disconnect the turbocharger unit from the manifold.

16. Installation is the reverse of removal. Be sure to use a new gasket for the exhaust manifold and a new O-ring to the return oil pipe. Keep everything clean during assembly, and use extreme care in keeping dirt out of the various turbo inlet and outlet pipes and hoses.

Timing Belt Cover

REMOVAL AND INSTALLTION

B21F

1. Loosen the fan shroud and remove the fan. Remove the shroud.

2. Loosen the alternator, air pump, power steering pump (if so equipped), and AC compressor (if so equipped) and remove their drive belts.

3. Remove the water pump pulley.

4. Remove the four retaining bolts and lift off the timing belt cover.

5. Reverse the above procedure to install.

D24

1. Drain the engine coolant.

2. Remove the splash guard under the engine. Disconnect the lower hose at the radiator. Remove the expansion tank cap.

3. Remove the radiator.

4. Remove the cooling fan with spacer and pulley.

5. Remove the fan belt. Remove the drive belt for the power steering pump.

6. Remove the valve cover.

7. Remove the front and rear timing gear covers.

8. Installation is the reverse of removal.

Timing Belt

REMOVAL AND INSTALLATION

B21F

1. Remove the timing belt cover as outlined previously.

2. To remove the tension from the belt, loosen the nut for the tensioner and press the idler roller back. The tension spring can be locked in this position by inserting the

Turbocharger system component location

1. Engine front cover
2. Oil seal (intermediate shaft)
3. Oil seal (crankshaft)
4. Engine cover gasket
5. Timing belt guard
6.–7. Bolt and washer
8. Pivot stud
9–13. Belt tensioner
14. Timing belt
15. Crankshaft timing belt gear
16. Intermediate gear
17. Camshaft gear
18. Timing belt cover
19–23. Timing belt cover attachments

B21F series timing belt assembly

Make sure all marks are lined up including marks on new belt—B21F series

B21F series timing belt tensioner

shank end of a 3 mm drill through the pusher rod.

3. Remove the six retaining bolts and the crankshaft pulley.

4. Remove the belt, taking care not to bend it at any sharp angles. The belt should be replaced at 45,000 mile intervals, if it becomes oil soaked or frayed, or if it is on a car that has been sitting idle for any length of time.

5. If the crankshaft, idler shaft, or camshaft were disturbed while the belt was out, align each shaft with its corresponding index mark to assure proper valve timing and ignition timing, as follows:

    a. Rotate the crankshaft so that the notch in the convex crankshaft gear belt guide aligns with the embossed mark on the front cover (12 o'clock position).

    b. Rotate the idler shaft so that the dot on the idler shaft drive sprocket aligns with the notch on the timing belt rear cover (four o'clock position).

    c. Rotate the camshaft so that the notch in the camshaft sprocket inner belt guide

aligns with the notch in the forward edge of the valve cover (12 o'clock position).

6. Install the timing belt (don't use any sharp tools) over the sprockets, and then over the tensioner roller. New belts have yellow marks. The two lines on the drive belt should fit toward the crankshaft marks. The next mark should then fit toward the intermediate shaft marks, etc. Loosen the tensioner nut and let the spring tension automatically take up the slack. Tighten the tensioner nut to 37 ft. lbs.

7. Rotate the crankshaft one full revolution clockwise, and make sure the timing marks still align.

8. Reverse Steps 1-3 to install.

D24

1. Remove the timing belt cover as previously outlined.

2. Set cylinder No. 1 to Top Dead Center and injection, using a 27 mm (1 1/16 in.) socket on the vibration damper bolt to turn the engine to position for No. 1 cylinder

injection. Both cam lobes should point up at equally large angles. The flywheel timing mark should be set at 0.

3. Remove the vibration damper center bolt. It may be necessary to use Volvo special wrenches 5187 (to hold) and 5188 (to remove). You may have to turn the engine slightly to allow the holding wrench to rest temporarily on the cooling fan.

4. Check to make sure No. 1 cylinder is at TDC. If necessary, adjust the flywheel to the 0 mark.

5. Remove the vibration damper by removing the four 6mm Allen bolts.

NOTE: The vibration damper and the crankshaft gear may be stuck together. You may have to tap them apart.

6. Remove the camshaft gear belt by removing the lower belt shield, and releasing the retaining bolts for coolant pump.

7. Pull the gear belt straight out and off of the gears.

8. Installation is the reverse of removal.

Locking the tensioner spring with drill bit shank

Setting No. 1 cylinder to TDC and injection position—D24. Cam lobes are "up", flywheel on 0

NOTE: The idler pulley MUST be replaced when replacing the timing gear belt. Remove the center bolt using a puller. Tap the new idler pulley into position, and install the center bolt.

Timing Chain Cover

REMOVAL AND INSTALLATION

B27F and B28F

1. Remove the air cleaner and valve covers.
2. Loosen the fan shroud and remove the fan. Remove the shroud.
3. Loosen the alternator, air pump, power steering pump, and AC compressor (if so equipped) and remove their drive belts.
4. Block the flywheel from turning, remove the crankshaft pulley nut (36 mm) and the pulley.

NOTE: Do not drop the pulley key into the crankcase.

5. Remove the power steering pump and place to one side. Remove the pump bracket.

6. Remove the timing chain cover retaining bolts (25 11 mm hex bolts), tap and remove the cover.
7. Clean the gasket contact surfaces. Place the upper gasket on the cover and the lower gasket on the block. Install the cover and tighten to 7–11 ft. lbs. Trim the gaskets flush with the valve cover.
8. Install a new crankshaft seal.
9. Block the flywheel, install the pulley, (and key) and tighten the 36 mm nut to 118–132 ft. lbs.
10. Reverse Steps 1–5 to install.

Relieving chain tension

Timing Chain

REMOVAL AND INSTALLATION

B27F and B28F

1. Remove the timing chain cover and adjacent engine accessories as outlined previously.
2. Remove the oil pump sprocket and drive chain.
3. Slacken the tension in both camshaft timing chains by rotating each tensioner lock ¼ turn counterclockwise and pushing the rubbing block piston.
4. Remove both chain tensioners. Remove the two curved and the two straight chain damper/runners.
5. Remove the camshaft sprocket retaining bolt (10 mm Allen head) and the sprocket and chain assembly. Repeat for other side.
6. Install the chain tensioners and tighten to 5 ft. lbs. Install the curved chain damper/runners and tighten to 7–11 ft. lbs. Install the straight chain damper/runners and torque to 5 ft. lbs.
7. First install the left (driver) side camshaft sprocket and chain. Rotate the crankshaft (use crankshaft nut, if necessary) until No. 1 cylinder is at TDC. At this point, the crankshaft key is pointing directly to the left side camshaft, and the left side camshaft key groove is pointing straight up (12 o'clock). Place the chain on the left side sprocket so that the sprocket notchmark is centered precisely between the two white lines on the chain. Then, position the chain on the crankshaft sprocket (inner), making sure that the other white line on the

Left side camshaft timing chain installation sequence

6 bolts M7-40
18 bolts M7-40
1 bolt M7-55
10-15 Nm

11 mm hex
7-11 lb.ft.

two bolts
M7-16
10-15 Nm

11 mm hex
7-11 lb.ft.

two bolts M6-12
5-7.5 Nm

10 mm hex
3.6-5.4 lb.ft.

four bolts
M6-35
5-7.5 Nm

10 mm hex
3.6-5.4 lb.ft.

four bolts
M6-14
5-7 Nm

10 mm hex
3.6-5.4 lb.ft.

two bolts M7-30
10-15 Nm

11 mm hex
7-11 lb.ft.

B27, 28 timing chain assembly

chain aligns with the crankshaft sprocket notch. While holding the left side chain and sprockets in this position, install the sprocket and chain on the left side camshaft (chain stretched on tension side) so that the sprocket pin fits into the camshaft recess. Tighten

the sprocket center bolt to 51–59 ft. lbs. (use screwdriver to keep cam from turning).

8. To install the right side camshaft sprocket and chain, rotate the crankshaft clockwise until the crankshaft key points straight down (6 o'clock). Align the cam-

shaft key groove so that it is pointing half-way between the 8 and 9 o'clock positions (at this position, the No. 6 cylinder rocker arms will rock). Place the chain on the right side sprocket so that the sprocket notch-mark is centered precisely between the two

Right side camshaft timing chain installation sequence

white lines on the chain. Then, position the chain on the middle crankshaft sprocket, making sure that the other white line aligns with the crankshaft sprocket notch. Then, install the sprocket and chain on the camshaft so that the sprocket notch fits into the camshaft recess. Tighten the sprocket nut to 51–59 ft. lbs.

9. Rotate the chain tensioners ¼ turn clockwise eash. The chains are tensioned by rotating the crankshaft two full turns clockwise. Recheck to make sure the alignment marks coincide.

10. Install the oil pump sprocket and chain.

Aligning (top to bottom) crankshaft sprocket, idler shaft sprocket, and camshaft sprocket with their respective timing index marks prior to installing timing belt

11. Install the timing chain cover and engine accessories as outlined previously.

Camshaft

REMOVAL AND REPLACEMENT

B21F

1. Remove the timing belt cover and timing belt as outlined in their appropriate sections.

2. Remove the valve cover.

3. Remove the camshaft center bearing cup. Install special camshaft press tool (Volvo #5021) over the center bearing journal to hold the camshaft in place while removing the other bearing caps.

4. Remove the four remaining bearing caps.

5. Remove the seal from the forward edge of the camshaft.

6. Release camshaft press tool, and lift out the camshaft.

7. Reverse the above procedure to install. Make sure the camshaft and followers are well oiled before installation.

B21 camshaft press tool installed

B27F and B28F

1. Remove the cylinder head as outlined previously.

2. Remove the camshaft rear cover plate.

3. Remove the camshaft retaining fork at the front of the cylinder head.

4. Pull the camshaft out the rear of the head.

5. Reverse the above to install. Oil the camshaft and followers before installation.

D24 Diesel

1. Disconnect the negative battery terminal.

2. Drain the radiator.

3. Remove the expansion tank hose.

4. Remove the top and bottom radiator hoses.

5. Remove the fan with the spacer and pulley.

6. Remove all the drive belts.

7. Remove the valve cover.

8. Remove the timing gear belt cover.
9. Set the Number 1 cylinder to top dead center.

NOTE: This is accomplished by turning the crankshaft pulley with an 1¹⁄₁₆ socket. The flywheel timing mark should be set at zero.

10. Remove the crankshaft pulley bolt.
11. Remove the four Allen head bolts in the center of the pulley and remove the pulley.

NOTE: The pulley and the crankshaft gear may be stuck together. Gently tap them apart with a rubber hammer.

12. Remove the lower belt shield.
13. Loosen and remove the timing belt.
14. Remove the front camshaft gear.

NOTE: Use tool #5199 available from Volvo or another suitable tool to prevent the camshaft from turning.

15. Remove the rear timing belt cover.
16. Loosen the injection pump bracket to release tension from the injection pump drive belt.
17. Remove the timing belt.
18. Remove the rear camshaft gear.

NOTE: See Step #14 for this procedure.

19. Installation is the reverse of removal.
The following torque specifications are needed: Front camshaft gear 33 ft. lbs., Rear camshaft gear 73 ft. lbs., Crankshaft pulley 330 ft. lbs., Crankshaft pulley Allen bolts 15 ft. lbs.

D24 Diesel

1. Follow the procedure for the camshaft gear removal.
2. Remove the first and fourth bearing caps.
3. Remove the second and third bearing caps.

NOTE: Loosen the bearing cap nuts on an alternating basis to prevent cam distortion.

4. Remove the camshaft and discard the seals.
5. Installation is the reverse of removal, with the following suggestions.
1. When reinstalling the cam you must use special tool #5190 available from your Volvo dealer.
2. Place grease on the oil seal lips before installation. The seals must be driven into place with Volvo tool #5200 or a suitable substitute.
3. Torque the cam bearing caps to 15 ft. lbs.
4. The second and third bearing caps should be installed first.

Pistons and Connecting Rods

PISTON AND CONNECTING ROD POSITIONING

On all engines, the notch or arrow stamped on top of the piston must face the front of the engine. On the B21 the connecting rod marking must face the front of the engine.

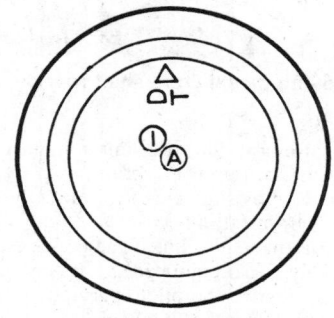

B27, 28 piston positioning. Arrowhead faces forward

B21F series piston positioning. Notch faces forward

Correct B27, 28 piston liner height "A" above block face is 0.0091 in. Shims are available for installation at point "B" and should be uniform for all cylinders

When installing B27 and B28 liner shims, color marking "A" must face up and be positioned where shown. Inside tabs "B" fit into liner groove

ENGINE LUBRICATION

Oil Pan

REMOVAL AND INSTALLATION

B21F

1. Attach a chain/pulley hoist to the lifting eye on the thermostat housing.
2. On air conditioned models, remove the compressor from its bracket to gain access to the motor mount.
3. Remove the retaining bolts for the left (drive side) motor mount at the cylinder block.
4. Drain the crankcase.
5. Remove the splash guard.
6. Raise the engine slightly.
7. Remove the left motor mount from the chassis.
8. Remove the engine-to-clutch housing brace.

Steering yoke removal; arrows indicate retaining nuts

Pan support bracket—B21F series engines (view from under car)

9. Remove the oil pan retaining bolts. Tap the pan loose, swivel and remove.

10. Reverse the removal procedure to install.

B21F Late 79–83

A new oil pan was introduced in May 1979. It is deeper with a lowered oil baffle, and designed to insure oil supply during rapid acceleration and provide less engine noise.

1. Jack up your vehicle and support it with jack stands.

2. Drain the engine oil.

3. Remove the splash guard.

4. Remove the engine mount retaining nuts.

5. Remove the lower bolt and loosen the top bolt on the steering column yoke.

6. Slide the yoke assembly up on the steering shaft.

7. Jack up the front of the engine.

8. Remove the retaining bolts for the front axle crossmember.

9. Remove the crossmember.

10. Remove the left engine mount.

11. Remove the pan support bracket.

12. Remove the pan bolts and remove the pan.

13. Installation is the reverse of removal.

NOTE: Always use a new pan gasket when reinstalling the pan.

The following torque specifications are needed: Pan bolts 8 ft. lbs. Steering yoke lower bolt, 18 ft. lbs.

B27F and B28F

1. Remove the splash guard.

2. Drain the crankcase.

3. Remove the oil pan retaining bolts. Swivel the pan past the stabilizer bar and remove.

4. Reverse the above to install.

REAR MAIN OIL SEAL REPLACEMENT

D24

1. Disconnect the negative battery terminal.

Removing diesel crankshaft rear oil seal

2. Remove the transmission, (see the transmission removal section).

3. Remove all but one starter bolt to keep it from falling out.

4. Remove the clutch and pressure plate assembly (if so equipped).

5. Remove the pilot bearing.

6. Remove the flywheel.

NOTE: Use special tool #5112 or a suitable replacement to keep the flywheel from turning while removing the bolts.

7. Remove the oil seal with a screwdriver.

8. Check the contact surfaces on the seal holder and crankshaft.

9. Installation is the reverse of removal.

When reinstalling a new seal use special tool #5208 available from Volvo or a suitable replacement. Coat the seal with oil before installation. Torque the flywheel bolts to 55 ft. lbs. Use a liquid sealer (Loctite® or similar product) on the bolts prior to installing them.

B27F and B28F

1. Disconnect the negative battery terminal.

2. Remove the transmission (see the transmission removal section).

3. Remove the clutch and pressure plate (if so equipped).

4. Remove the flywheel (drive plate on automatic transmissions).

NOTE: On automatic transmissions remove the crankshaft spacer.

5. Remove the two rear pan bolts.

6. Remove the bolts in the seal housing and then the housing.

NOTE: Gently remove the housing so as not to damage the oil pan gasket.

7. Use special tool #5107 to remove the old seal and install the new one. This tool is available from Volvo or use a suitable replacement.

8. Installation is the reverse of removal.

The following torque specifications are needed; Flywheel 33–37 ft. lbs., Seal housing 7–11 ft. lbs.

B21F

1. Disconnect the negative battery terminal.

2. Remove the transmission (see the transmission removal section).

3. Remove the clutch and pressure plate (if so equipped).

4. Remove the pilot bearing snap-ring and remove the bearing.

5. Remove the flywheel or driveplate which ever is applicable.

NOTE: Be careful not to press in the activator pins for the timing device.

6. Remove the rear oil pan brace.

7. Remove the two center bolts from the pan that bolt into the seal housing.

8. Loosen two bolts on either side of the two in the seal housing.

9. Remove the six seal housing bolts, and remove the seal housing.

NOTE: Be careful not to damage the oil pan gasket when removing the seal housing.

10. Remove the seal using special tool #2817 or a suitable replacement.

Flywheel installation B21 engine

11. Installation is the reverse of removal.

NOTE: Use a new gasket on the seal housing and coat the seal with oil prior to installation.

Torque the flywheel to 47–54 ft. lbs. When installing the flywheel turn the crankshaft to bring the No. 1 piston to top dead center. The lower flywheel pin should be installed approximately 15° from the horizontal and opposite the starter. Install the bolts.

Oil Pump

REPLACEMENT

B21F

1. Remove the oil pan as described previously.
2. Remove the two oil pump retaining bolts, and pull the delivery tube from the block.
3. When installing, use new sealing rings at either end of the delivery tube. Also, make sure you "prime" the pump (remove all air) by filling it with clean engine oil and operating the pump by hand, before installation.

NOTE: On 1980 and later, the oil pump has been redesigned to position the suction pipe and strainer further forward in the oil pan.

B27F and B28F

The oil pump body is cast integrally with the cylinder block. It is chain driven by a separate sprocket on the crankshaft and is

1. Pump body
2. Spring for relief valve
3. Gear
4. Valve ball
5. Hole for oil pipe

Oil pump—B21F (V6 similar)

located behind the timing chain cover. The pick-up screen and tube are serviced by removing the oil pan. To check the pump gears or remove the oil pump cover:

1. Remove the air cleaner and valve covers.
2. Loosen the fan shroud and remove the fan. Remove the shroud.
3. Loosen the alternator, air pump, power steeing pump, and AC compressor (if so equipped) and remove their drive belts.
4. Block the flywhell from turning, and remove the 36 mm bolt and the crankshaft pulley.

NOTE: Do not drop key into crankcase.

5. Remove the timing gear cover (25 bolts).
6. Remove the oil pump drive sprocket and chain.
7. Remove the oil pump cover, and gears.
8. Reverse the removal procedure to install. Prime the pump (remove all air) by filling it with clean engine oil and operating the pump by hands, before installation.

D24

The oil pan can not be removed without removing the engine. Refer to the Engine Removal section. This procedure requires quite a few special tools, and without them this job should be left to your Volvo dealer or a professional mechanic.

1. Remove the engine from the car.
2. Remove the oil pan and the oil suction pipe.
3. Remove the front timing belt cover, timing belt, vibration damper, and lower timing belt cover.

NOTE: Do not allow the crankshaft to turn when disconnected from the camshaft. If this should happen the fuel injection timing must be reset.

4. Remove the crankshaft gear and seal with a puller.
5. Remove the timing belt inner shield.
6. Remove the oil pump bolts and remove the pump.

NOTE: The oil pump can not be repaired. It must be replaced as a unit.

7. When installing the oil pump the triangular mark on the pump outer gear must face the oil pump rear cover.
8. Installation is the reverse of removal. Fill the oil pump with clean engine oil and "prime" the pump by operating it by hand prior to installation.

OIL PUMP CLEARANCE

After removing the oil pump from the engine, place the pump body in a vise. Remove the four bolts which retain the pick-up screen housing to the pump body, exposing the oil pump gears, relief valve, ball and spring. To measure the tooth flank clearance, insert a proper size feeler gauge

between the engaging teeth of the oil pump gears. Proper tooth flank clearance is 0.006–0.014 in. If the clearance is not within specifications the pump must be replaced. To measure the oil pump gear end-float, place a straightedge ruler over top of the two pump gears so that it lies flat on the pump housing at both ends, and insert a proper size feeler gauge between the top of the pump gear and the straightedge. Proper gear end float is 0.0008–0.0040 in. If all clearances are within specifications, reassemble the oil pump taking care to install the relief valve, ball, and spring in their original locations.

ENGINE COOLING

Radiator

REMOVAL AND INSTALLATION

1. Remove the radiator and expansion tank caps, disconnect the lower radiator hose, and drain the cooling system.
2. Remove the expansion tank and hose, and drain the coolant. Remove the upper radiator hose. On cars with automatic transmissions, disconnect and plug the transmission oil cooler lines at the radiator.
3. Remove the retaining bolts for the radiator and fan shroud, if so equipped, and lift out the radiator.
4. To install, place the radiator and fan shroud in position and install the retaining bolts.
5. On automatic transmission cars, connect the oil cooler lines.
6. Install the lower and upper radiator hoses.
7. Install the expansion tank with its hose. Make sure that the overflow hose is clear of the fan and is free of any sharp bends.
8. Fill the cooling system with a 50 percent ethylene glycol, 40 percent water solution. Replace the caps.
9. Start the engine and check for leaks. After the engine has reached operating temperature make sure that the coolant level in the expansion tank is between the maximum and minimum marks.

Water Pump

REMOVAL AND INSTALLATION

B21F

1. Remove the overflow tank cap. Drain the cooling system by opening the cylinder block drain cock (beneath the exhaust

B21F water pump bolts

mainfold) and disconnecting the lower radiator hose.

2. Remove the fan and fan shroud.

3. Remove the alternator and air pump drive belts. Remove the water pump pulley.

4. Remove the timing belt cover.

5. Remove the lower radiator hose.

6. Remove the retaining bolt for the coolant pipe (beneath exhaust manifold) and pull the pipe rearward.

7. Remove the six retaining bolts and lift off the water pump.

8. Clean the gasket contact surfaces thoroughly, and use a new gasket and O-rings (especially between the cylinder head and top of water pump).

9. Reverse Steps 1–7 to install.

B27F and B28F

1. Remove the front and main sections of the intake manifold.

2. Remove the overflow tank cap and drain the cooling system.

3. Disconnect both radiator hoses. On automatic transmission cars, disconnect the transmission cooler lines at the radiator. Disconnect the fan shroud. Remove the radiator and fan shroud.

4. Remove the fan.

5. Remove the hoses from the water pump to each cylinder head.

6. Remove the fan belts. Remove the water pump pulley.

7. Loosen the hose clamps at the rear of the water pump.

8. Transfer the thermal time sender and temperature sensor to the new pump.

9. Remove the water pump from the block (three bolts).

10. Transfer the thermostat cover, thermostat, and rear pump cover to the new pump.

11. Reverse the removal procedure to install.

D24

1. Drain the radiator.

2. Remove the splash gear under the engine.

3. Remove the expansion tank.

4. Remove the top and bottom radiator hoses.

NOTE: On cars with automatic transmissions remove the cooler lines from the radiator.

5. Remove the radiator (and shroud if so equipped).

6. Remove all the drive belts.

7. Remove the fan with the spacer and pulley.

8. Remove the front timing gear cover.

9. Disconnect the cold start device.

10. Loosen screw #1 and push the lever forward, rotate the lever 90° and push it backward against the stop.

NOTE: Do not touch the second screw. If it becomes loosened, the cold start device must be reset on a test bench.

11. Remove the injection pump plug and install a dial indicator gauge with a measuring range of 0–.118 in.

NOTE: This gauge must have adapter #5194, available from Volvo attached to it.

12. Set the gauge to approximately .078 in.

13. Set the Number 1 cylinder to top dead center.

14. The marking on the injection pump gear should coincide with the marking on the injection pump bracket.

15. The flywheel timing mark should be at zero.

Make sure the O-ring around the lower lip of water pump is in good condition. Replace if there is any damage

16. Turn the engine ¼ turn past zero and then back to zero again. This is done in order to place slack in the timing belt on the drive side. Otherwise the engine setting would be incorrect.

NOTE: The gauge must not move during the remainder of the work. If it does the engine must be completely retimed.

17. Loosen the water pump bolts to release the belt tension.

18. Remove the timing bolt from the camshaft gear.

19. Remove the camshaft gear.

20. Remove the vibration damper.

21. Remove the lower belt guard.

22. Loosen the bracket for the fan and alternator.

23. Remove the lower retaining bolt and move the bracket away from the engine.

24. Remove the inner belt shield and water pump.

25. Installation is the reverse of removal.

NOTE: Grease the O-ring before installing it in the water pump.

The following torque specifications are needed. Vibration damper screws 15 ft. lbs., crankshaft center bolt 255 ft. lbs., camshaft gear 33 ft. lbs., pump setting 0.0256–.0287 in.

B27F/B28F water pump mounting bolts

Removing front cover and water pump bolts—Diesel D24

Thermostat

REMOVAL AND INSTALLATION

1. Disconnect the lower radiator hose and drain the cooling system.

2. Remove the two bolts securing the thermostat housing to the cylinder head and carefully lift the housing free.

3. Remove all old gasket material from the mating surfaces and remove the thermostat.

4. Test the operation of the thermostat by immersing it in a container of heated water. Replace any thermostat that does not open at the correct temperature.

5. Place the thermostat, with a new gasket, in the cylinder head. Fit the thermostat housing to the head and hand-tighten the two bolts until snug. Do not tighten the bolts more than ¼ turn past snug.

6. Connect the lower radiator hose and replace the coolant.

Remove the two top water pump bolts for access to the V6 thermostat

EMISSION CONTROLS

PCV System

Volvos have been equipped with positive crankcase ventilation (PCV) systems to control crankcase vapors since the early 1960s. The present system is a closed one; it is sealed to the atmosphere. A metal filter located inline between the fresh air source and the crankcase prevents engine backfire from reaching the crankcase and oil from being drawn into the induction system.

Evaporative Control System

All model Volvos are equipped with an evaporative control system to prevent un-

PCV valves and lines—V6

burnt fuel vapors in the fuel tank from escaping into the atmosphere. An expansion tank above the fuel tank provides for thermal expansion of fuel vapors in warm weather.

NOTE: All models have the expansion tank inside the fuel tank.

Those vapors which do not condense and return to the fuel tank are displaced and drawn into an activated charcoal canister in the engine compartment. The charcoal canister then absorbs and stores these fuel tank vapors when the engine is shut off or is idling. Throttling the engine causes the vapors to be drawn out of the canister into the inlet duct and then into the combustion chambers where they are burned.

NOTE: All 1980 and later B21F and B28F engines are equipped with a rollover valve. It is designed to close at 45° from horizontal. This valve will prevent a fuel spill through the carbon filter, if the car is involved in a rollover.

Exhaust Emission Control

Various measures have been taken to limit exhaust emissions of hydrocarbons, carbon monoxide, and more revently, oxides of nitrogen. Basic modifications include a distributor which retards the timing from its basic setting during idle, and the installation of a "hotter" 190°F thermostat in the cooling system. Fuel injection, which is inherently cleaner due to its precise regulation of the air-fuel mixture under varying rpm, engine load, and ambient temperature conditions, has been available since 1970.

PRE-HEATING AIR INTAKE
B28F

This system is designed to improve cold engine performance. Its advantages are as follows:

1. Improved cold engine performance.
2. Ambient temperatures do not influence engine performance.

3. Icing has been eliminated.

The pre-heating device consists of a heater on the left side of the manifold, a thermostat controlled air mixer, and hoses.

The thermostat senses the intake air temperature and controls the air mixture.

Exhaust Gas Recirculation (EGR) System

In order to control emissions of NO$_x$, 1976–79 models are equipped with an exhaust gas recirculation system.

NOTE: Models equipped with the Lambda Sond oxygen sensor system do not have EGR valves. These include 78–80 California and all 1980 and later vehicles.

The system consists of a metering valve, a tubular pipe running from the exhaust manifold to the valve, another tubular pipe running from the valve to the inlet duct, and a vacuum hose running from the valve's diaphragm to the inlet duct in front of the air regulator shutter. The valve permits a regulated amount of exhaust gases to enter the inlet duct and mix with the incoming intake air when the throttle is partly open. Every 12 months or 15,000 miles (1976), the system must be disassembled and cleaned. Every 30,000 miles (1976), the valve must be replaced with a new one.

On 1976 B21 and B27 models sold in California, and all later models with EGR valves, the EGR system is modified to improve cold start driveability by the addition of a venturi vacuum amplifier system. The EGR system with vacuum amplifier works as follows: Venturi vacuum at the air intake is used to measure the total air flow. This weak vacuum signal controls the vacuum amplifier which regulates the EGR valve via a solenoid valve. The vacuum amplifier receives inputs both from the strong intake manifold source which is used as a power source, and from the weak air intake source which is to be amplified. The intake vacuum is stored in the vacuum reservoir and is controlled by a check valve in the amplifier. This allows a generous amount of vacuum on tap regardless of variations in engine manifold vacuum. The amplifier then continues to supply adequate vacuum at higher speeds and moderate throttle openings, when manifold vacuum normally would drop to an insufficient amount. The EGR system functions as before, except that the exhaust gases are prevented from recirculation at idle and full throttle by a throttle angle sensing microswitch and an electrically operated solenoid valve, rather than simple vacuum. On 1976 models and later, a wax thermostat blocks exhaust gas recirculation until the engine warns to 140°F.

All Volvos are equipped with an EGR service reminder light which is actuated by

Without vacuum amplifier

EXHAUST RETURN PIPE
from EGR valve
to intake manifold

WAX THERMOSTAT

EGR VALVE

EXHAUST RETURN PIPE
from exhaust manifold
to EGR valve

manifold nipple

**With vacuum amplifier
(California)**

MICRO SWITCH

VENTURI TUBE

WAX THERMOSTAT

EXHAUST RETURN PIPE
from EGR valve
to intake manifold

VACUUM AMPLIFIER

SOLENOID VALVE

EGR VALVE

EXHAUST RETURN PIPE
from exhaust manifold
to EGR valve

manifold nipple

B27F/B28F EGR system

Without vacuum amplifier

WAX THERMOSTAT

manifold nipple

EXHAUST RETURN PIPE
from EGR valve
to intake manifold

EXHAUST RETURN PIPE
from exhaust manifold
to EGR valve

EGR VALVE

MICRO SWITCH

WAX THERMOSTAT

**With vacuum amplifier
(California)**

VENTURI TUBE

VACUUM AMPLIFIER

SOLENOID VALVE

manifold nipple

EXHAUST RETURN PIPE
from EGR valve
to intake manifold

EGR VALVE

EXHAUST RETURN PIPE
from exhaust manifold
to EGR valve

B21 EGR system

EGR, catalytic converter service reminder light reset button

the odometer at 15,000 mile intervals. The light may be reset by pressing a white button at the rear of the odometer.

Air Injection Reactor System

All 1976 and later Volvos (except Canadian B21A engines, which are equipped with a Pulsar system) are equipped with an air injection reactor system except the diesel. Basically, the system injects filtered air into the exhaust manifold in order to reduce emissions of carbon monoxide and hydrocarbons. The oxygen in the air reacts with the exhaust gas and promotes further combustion in the exhaust manifold.

The system consists of an air pump (belt-driven), a diverter valve, a backfiring valve, and an air manifold which is attached to the exhaust manifold. Under normal conditions, air is pumped from the air pump via the diverter valve, the backfiring valve and the air manifold into the exhaust manifold ports. The air pump takes in filtered air which is then compressed and discharged to the diverter valve. The diverter valve sends the air through to the backfiring valve, except during deceleration. The diverter valve also releases some of the air into the atmosphere if the pressure is too great. The backfiring valve is a one-way valve which prevents the exhaust gases from flowing back towards the air injection components, but allows the pump air to pass into the air manifold and exhaust manifold.

CHECKING THE AIR SYSTEM

Service the AIR system every 15,000 miles. Make sure the drive belt is in good condition on the air pump. If the belt breaks, the backfire valve must be checked.

Make sure all attaching nuts and bolts for the air pump and bracket are secure.

To check the air pump, use the following procedure.

Start the engine and listen for excessive

B21F AIR system—V6 similar except has an air manifold for each cylinder bank

noise from the pump. Remember, though, that the air pump is not normally completely noiseless, and it can make a bit of a racket when its cold. Under normal circumstances, the noise rises in pitch as engine speed increases. Do not attempt to lubricate or repair the pump: it must be replaced.

To check the backfire valve, use the following procedure.

1. Disconnect the hose from the diverter valve.

2. Apply a vacuum to the hose: no air should come through. If it does, replace the backfire valve.

To check the diverter valve, use the following procedure.

1. Disconnect and plug the hose from the diverter valve.

2. Run the engine at idle. Air should only be coming out of point "A" in the illustration.

3. Increase the engine speed to 3000–3500 rpm, then quickly release the throttle. Air should now flow from points "B" in the illustration. If not, replace the diverter valve.

1976–79 Models Equipped with Vacuum Amplifier

NOTE: Use the illustration to identify the vacuum amplifier. It is located in the engine compartment.

1. With a cold engine (below 130°F coolant temperature), check the operation of the wax thermostat. Disconnect the vacuum hose at the solenoid valve and disconnect the vacuum hose at the vacuum amplifier connection "S". Suck one of the disconnected hoses. If any air passes, one

of the hoses has a vacuum leak or the wax thermostat is faulty. Connect the hoses.

2. Start the engine and warm to operating temperature (176°F). Stop the engine. Disconnect the two hoses again, and apply a vacuum through either of the hoses. This time the thermostat should be open, and air should pass through. If not, replace the wax thermostat.

3. Connect the hoses. Check the throttle position sensing micro-switch next. Connect a 12v test light in series between the upper wire connector and its upper terminal. Switch the ignition to the "on" position. Pull back the throttle lever and insert a 0.006 in. feeler gauge between the screw and the lever stop. When the lever is released and the throttle screw makes contact with the switch plunger, the test light should illuminate. This indicates that current is reaching the solenoid valve, the micro-switch is activating, and the fuse is good. Then, repeat by inserting an 0.008 in. feeler gauge between the screw and lever stop. This time, the test light should not light and the throttle screw should not make contact with the switch plunger. Adjust as necessary by loosening the locknut on the stopscrew and adjusting for 0.006 in. clearance.

4. Check the solenoid valve next. Start the engine and idle. Disconnect the hose from connection "1", and create a vacuum. With the engine idling, the EGR valve should remain closed (no change in rpm). If not, the solenoid valve is defective.

5. With the vacuum pump still connected, and engine idling, check that the vacuum reading does not change for 10 seconds. If the reading changes, this indicates a bad amplifier or leaking hoses.

6. Finally, with the engine idling, increase the rpm while observing the EGR

valve. If the EGR valve rod does not open, check for a clogged venturi or leaking venturi vacuum hose. Then, suddenly release the throttle and check that the EGR valve rod closes. If not, the solenoid valve is faulty.

Pulsair System

SYSTEM CHECK

Canadian 240 Series with B21A and B21F Engines

Beginning in 1979, Canadian B21A and some B21F engines were fitted with the then then-new "Pulsair" air injection system. In the Pulsair, the natural pressure pulses in the engine's exhaust system help to draw air into the exhaust system. The air is then injected into the end of the exhaust port, as in the air pump system, and the oxygen in the injected air aids in the further burning of emissions. The air pump is eliminated in the Pulsair system. Check valves in the system exhaust gases from entering the air cleaner during the pressure pulses.

To check the operation of the system, disconnect the air hose at the air cleaner. With the engine idling, check that air is being drawn in with the palm of your hand and that no back pressure exists.

Pulsair system—Canadian B21A/F models. Box at right is intake

Catalytic Converter System

All 1976–83 Volvos are equipped with a catalytic converter. The converters are installed to further control emissions of carbon monoxide and hydrocarbons which have resisted the treatment of the air injection system.

The converter is installed in the exhaust system ahead of the muffler. The catalytic converter on 1980 and later B28F engines is located closer to the engine compartment. This design allows quicker warm-up and reduced emissions. The converter uses platinum and palladium metals in a substrate or beaded form as the catalyst. The catalyst and the oxygen supplied by the air pump then react with the exhaust gases producing harmless carbon dioxide and water vapor, as well as a minute amount of sulphur dioxide or sulphuric acid.

The 1977 California 240 series, all 1978–80 260 California series, all 1979 49 states 260 series and the 1979 49 states 242 GT are equipped with three way catalytic converters.

NOTE: All 1980 and later models use the three way catalytic converter.

The purpose of the three way catalytic converter is to neutralize carbon monoxide, hydrocarbons and oxides of nitrogen in the exhaust gases. The main difference between this catalytic converter and the oxidation converter is that the three way converter is able to process large amounts of oxides of nitrogen (NO_x), while the oxidation catalyst cannot.

The operating range of the three way catalyst is limited to a narrow band around the ideal air/fuel mixture for the engine. To keep the mixture within this narrow band, an oxygen sensor is used to monitor the amount of oxygen in the exhaust gases and fine tune the air/fuel mixture. See "Oxygen Sensor Feedback System (Lambda Sond)" for more information on the oxygen sensor system.

The converter is designed, if properly maintained, to last 50,000 miles as long as leaded gasoline is not used. The lead in gasoline will coat the catalytic substrate or beads, thereby preventing the reaction process, rendering the converter ineffective.

At 15,000 mile intervals the retaining bolts for the converter must be checked for tightness. A service reminder light on the dashboard lights at 15,000 mile intervals. To extinguish the light, press the white reset buttom at the rear of the odometer.

NOTE: The 1980–83 diesel engine is not equipped with a catalytic converter.

Oxygen Sensor Feedback System (Lambda Sond)

This is a self-tuning engine controlled system, designed to reduce emissions and improve fuel economy. An exhaust gas sensor (oxygen sensor or lambda sensor) located in the exhaust manifold, monitors the composition of the exhaust gases leaving the engine. This analysis is fed into a closed loop feedback system. This continuously adjusts the air-fuel mixture to provide op-

Instrument pick–up

Electronic module

Frequency valve

timum conditions for combustion and efficient breakdown of all three major pollutants by a three-way catalytic converter.

The major components of the system are: the oxygen sensor, the electronic module and the frequency valve. The oxygen sensor is a platinum coated ceramic tube. It is located in the exhaust manifold. The inside is vented to the atmosphere while the outside is connected to the exhaust gas flow. The output from the sensor is fed to the electronic module. This device supplies a control current to the frequency valve. The frequency valve alters the flow of fuel in the CI system by activating a diaphragm in the fuel pressure regulating valve. The frequency valve, so called because it operates on a set frequency, functions during what is called its duty cycle. This duty cycle corresponds to the ratio of closed-to-open circuit impulses from the electronic module. The cycle can be measured in terms of

Checking wax thermostat

Oxygen sensor

oxygen sensor

frequency valve

pump relay

test instrument
pick-up point

electronic module

main relay,
oxygen sensor
feedback system

Typical Lambda-sond system wiring

Replace oxygen sensor (Lambda-sond) every 15,000 miles. Apply an anti-locking compound before installation

degrees by using an ordinary ignition system dwell meter. The dwell meter is connected to an instrument pick-up connector located on a wire coming from the electronic module. The pick-up connector is located on the firewall, in the engine compartment to the left of the master cylinder. The duty cycle of the B21F system is 54° while that of the B27F system is 40–50°. The B28F (1980 and later) cycle is 49–59°.

NOTE: 1980 and later B28F engines have a micro-switch at the throttle cable pulley. It closes a circuit at full throttle and grounds the electronic module of the Lambda Sond allowing a richer mixture at full throttle.

All other tests on the system are made with extremely sophisticated equipment and should be performed by trained service men only.

If the oxygen sensor in the manifold is obviously damaged, it can be replaced by simply disconnecting it and unscrewing it from the manifold. When installing a new sensor, the threads must be coated with anti-seize compound. The unit should be torqued to 40 ft. lbs.

NOTE: The oxygen sensor should be replaced every 30,000 miles.

Component Testing and Adjustment

EGR SYSTEM CHECKING

49 States Models—B21, B27

1. With a cold engine, check the operation of the wax thermostat. Start the engine and idle. Manipulate the throttle by hand and check that the EGR valve rod does not move in and out. If it does, the thermostat is faulty. It should not operate the EGR valve until the the coolant reaches 130–140°F.

2. With the engine warmed up (176°F), check that the EGR valve rod does move

in and out when the throttle is opened and closed. If not, the wax thermostat, hoses or EGR valve may be at fault.

3. Stop the engine. Disconnect the vacuum hose from the EGR valve. Blow through the hose. If no air passes, the wax thermostat is faulty. If air does pass, either the hose is incorrectly installed or the EGR valve is defective.

4. Finally, connect the EGR vacuum hose and start the engine. Open the throttle to 3000–4000rpm and then quickly release. The EGR valve rod should close. If not, replace the EGR valve.

California Models-B21, B27 and B28F

1. With a cold engine (below 130°F coolant temperature), check the operation of the wax thermostat. Disconnect the vacuum hose at the solenoid valve and disconnect the vacuum hose at the vacuum amplifier connection "S". Apply vacuum to one of the disconnected hoses. If any air passes, one of the hoses has a vacuum leak or the wax thermostat is faulty. Connect the hoses.

2. Start the engine and warm to operating temperature (176°F). Stop the engine. Disconnect the two hoses again, and apply vacuum through either of the hoses. This time the thermostat should be open, and air should pass through. If not, replace the wax thermostat.

3. Connect the hoses. Check the throttle position sensing micro-switch next. Connect a 12v test light in series between the upper wire connector and its upper terminal. Switch the ignition to the "on" position. Pull back the throttle lever and insert a 0.006 in. feeler gauge between the screw and the lever stop. When the lever is released and the throttle screw makes contact with the switch plunger, the test light should illuminate. This indicates that current is reaching the solenoid valve, the micro-switch is activating, and the fuse is good. Then, repeat by inserting an 0.008 in. feeler gauge between the screw and lever stop. This time, the test light should not light and the throttle screw should not make contact with the switch plunger. Adjust as necessary by loosening the locknut on the stopscrew and adjusting for 0.006 in. clearance.

4. Check the solenoid valve next. Start the engine and idle. Disconnect the hose from connection "1", and create a vacuum. With the engine idling, the EGR valve should remain closed (no change in rpm). If not, the solenoid valve is defective.

5. With the vacuum pump still connected, and engine idling, check that the vacuum reading does not change for 10 seconds. If the reading changes, this indicates a bad amplifier or leaking hoses.

6. Finally, with the engine idling, increase the rpm while observing the EGR valve. If the EGR valve rod does not open, check for a clogged venturi or leaking venturi vacuum hose. Then, suddenly release

the throttle and check that the EGR valve rod closes. If not, the solenoid valve is faulty.

Component Service

POSITIVE CRANKCASE VENTILATION SYSTEM

The only service required for the PCV system is the cleaning of the hoses, nipples, and metal filter every 15,000 miles (1976–79), 60,000 miles 1980 and later gasoline engines; 15,000 miles 1980 and later diesel engines.

Checking micro-switch—1976

Checking solenoid valve

FUEL EVAPORATIVE CONTROL SYSTEM

The only items requiring service in the evaporative control system are the foam plastic filter in the bottom of the charcoal canister. The canister filter is replaced every 45,000 miles (all models and years).

FUEL SYSTEM

NOTE: All Volvos manufactured for sale in the U.S. are equipped with fuel injection. One Canadian engine, the B21A, is equipped with a one-barrel carburetor.

Fuel Pump

All pumps are electrical.

NOTE: Volvo states that a "no-start" condition may occasionally occur when the car has not been started for an extended period of time. This may be due to the fuel pump sticking in one position because of foreign matter entering the pump, or corrosion forming on the rotor shaft or commutator and brushes. It is, therefore, very important to clean the fuel tank pick-up screen every 12 months or 12,000 miles to prevent corrosion causing water condensation and foreign matter from entering the pump. As an additional corrosion prevention measure, add an alcohol solution or "dry gas" to the fuel, especially in winter months. If, however, the pump does become "stuck" in one position for any of the above reasons, it may be "unstuck" by lightly rapping on the pump casing with a length of hardwood such as a hammer handle, while the ignition is switched on.

NOTE: 1980–and later fuel tank filters require replacement at 60,000 miles.

TESTING AND ADJUSTMENT

No adjustments or repairs may be made to the fuel pump. If the pump is not functioning properly, it must be discarded and replaced. To check the function of the fuel pump, the pump should be connected to a pressure gauge. Be careful not to switch the electrical leads. If the pump fails to pump its normal capacity, or if it cannot pump that capacity at its specified rate of current consumption, it must be replaced.

REPLACEMENT

1. Remove the filler cap. Remove the electrical lead from the pump as well as the template to which the pump is mounted.

2. Clean around the hose connections. Pinch shut the fuel lines, loosen the hose clamps, and disconnect the lines.

3. Loosen the retaining nuts and remove the pump from its rubber mounts.

4. Install the new pump on its rubber mounts and tighten the retaining nuts.

5. Reconnect the fuel lines, tighten the hose clamps, and remove the pinchers.

6. Mount the template beneath the car and connect the electrical lead.

7. Start the engine and check for leaks.

Fuel Filters

REMOVAL AND INSTALLATION

NOTE: The fuel filter should be replaced every 30,000 miles, or less under extremely dusty or smoggy conditions. The entire filter canister is replaced on both systems.

L-Jetronic fuel pump and filter location on bracket under left side of car

controlled by the Electronic Control Unit, and are only spraying when told to do so. The control unit is supplied information from the various sensors, which constantly respond to changes in the engine's operating environment (such as coolant temperature, ambient air temperature, etc.). **For all fuel injection system repair and service procedures not detailed below, please refer to "Fuel Injection" in the Unit Repair section.**

FUEL INJECTION SYSTEM PRECAUTIONS

Due to the highly sensitive nature of the Bosch electronic fuel injection system, the following special precautions must be strictly adhered to in order to avoid damage to the system.

1. Do not operate the engine with the battery disconnected.

2. Do not utilize a high-speed battery charger as a starting aid.

CIS fuel filter located on the firewall

1. Loosen the fuel cap.
2. Clean the filter connections carefully before removing.
3. Disconnect the nipples and remove the seals.
4. Remove the filter and clamp.
5. Transfer the nipples and clamp to the new filter.

NOTE: Fuel flow direction arrow is marked on the new (and old) filter. Arrow follows direction from fuel tank to engine.

Bosch Electronic Fuel Injection

The Bosch L-Jetronic electronic fuel injection system became available on the B21F engine in 1982. The complete system contains the following components: L-Jetronic control unit (brain), airflow sensor, system relay, fuel pump relay, Landa-sond oxygen sensor, vacuum switch, electric fuel pump, coolant temperature sensor fuel injectors, and the electronic control unit terminal for the Constant Idle System (CIS) (if equipped). The L-Jetronic system differs from the CIS system in that the injectors are individually

B21FLH L-Jetronic system—1982 and later

The impulse relay on 1982 and later B21F Turbo is wired in parallel to the thermal time switch, providing enrichment on cold starts

L-Jetronic fuel and electrical flow diagram

welding wire to disconnect the main plug contact. Insert the puller in the rear of the control unit and pull out the plug carefully.

4. Press the plug contact firmly into the new or reconditioned control unit. Fit the plastic cover strip, retaining cap, and screw.

. 5. Fit the control unit into place and install its retaining screws.

Fuel Injectors

1. Remove the air cleaner hoses.

2. Pinch shut the fuel hose to the header pipe.

3. Loosen the hose clamps for the injectors and lift up the heade pipe.

4. Remove the plug contacts from the injectors. Disconnect the cable harness from the distributing pipe.

5. Turn the lock rings on the injectors counterclockwise so that they loosen from their bayonet fittings. Lift out the injectors.

6. Place the new injectors, with *new* washers and rubber sealing rings, in position and secure them by turning the lock-rings clockwise.

7. Connect the cable harness at the distributing pipe. Connect the plug contacts to the injectors.

8. Place the header pipe in position, and tighten the hose clamps. Remove the pinch clamps.

9. Install the air cleaner hoses.

L-Jetronic fuel injector

Cold-Start Valve

1. Remove the air cleaner assembly.

2. Pinch shut the fuel line to the valve.

3. Remove the plug contact and the fuel hose from the valve.

3. When using a high-speed battery charger to charge the battery while it is installed in the vehicle, at least one battery cable must be disconnected.

4. Do not allow the control unit to be subjected to temperatures exceeding 185°F, such as when the vehicle is being banked after painting. If there is a risk of the temperature exceeding 185°F, the control unit must be removed.

5. The engine must not be started when the ambient temperature exceeds 158°F, or damage to the control unit will result.

6. The ignition must be in the off position when disconnecting or connecting the control unit.

7. When working on the fuel system, take care not to allow dirt to enter the system. Small dust particles may jam fuel injectors.

COMPONENT REPLACEMENT

The fuel injection system is repaired simply by replacing the defective component. There are some adjustments that can be made to some components, but these require a high level of experience and special test equipment. To make resistance checks, use an ohmmeter, and for continuity checks, a 12V test light. If the control unit is defective, return it to a qualified repair agency and install a new unit.

Control Unit

1. Disconnect the defroster hose, remove the control unit bracket retaining screws, and lower the unit to the floor, move the passenger's front seat all the way back, unscrew the bolt securing the seat's front, move the seat forward while folding the seat bottom to the rear, remove the control unit retaining screws, and draw out the unit.

2. Remove the screw for the cap holding the cable harness to the unit. Pull out the plastic cover strip.

3. Construct a puller out of 5/64 in.

Connected   Disconnected

Cold start device

Diverter valve check

4. Remove the two retaining screws and the cold-start valve from the inlet duct.

5. Place the new cold-start valve in position with packing and install the retaining screws.

6. Connect the plug contact and fuel hose to the valve. Remove the pinch clamp.

7. Install the air cleaner assembly.

Continuous Fuel Injection

Continuous fuel injection is standard on all 240 and 260 models with both the 4 and V6 engines. It differs from electronic fuel injection in that injection takes place continuously; controlled throgh a variation of the fuel flow rate through the injectors, rather than variation of the fuel injection duration. This system has no electronic computer. It is an electro-mechanical system that will provide suitable air/fuel mixtures to accommodate differing driving conditions.

The complete system consists of the following components: air/fuel control unit (housing both air flow sensor and fuel distributor), electric fuel pump (and fuel pressure accumulator), fuel filter, control pressure regulator, continuous fuel injectors, auxiliary air valve, cold-start injector, thermal time switch, main relay, and a fuel pump relay.

The heart of the system is the air/fuel control Unit. It consists of an air flow sensor and a fuel distributor. Intake air flows past the air cleaner and through the air venturi raising (four cylinder) or lowering (V6) the counterbalanced air flow sensor plate. The plate is connected to a pivoting lever which moves the control plunger in the fuel distributor in direct proportion to the intake air flow.

The fuel distributor, which controls and distributes the amount of fuel to the injectors consists of a line pressure regulator, a control plunger, and (4 or 6) pressure regulator valves (one for each injector).

NOTE: There is no CO adjustment on the 1980 and later fuel distributor.

The line pressure regulator maintains the fuel distributor inlet pressure at about 65 psi., and will recirculate fuel to the tank if pressure exceeds this valve. The control plunger, which is connected to the air flow sensor plate, controls the amount of fuel available to each of the pressure regulator valves. The pressure regulator valves maintain a constant fuel pressure differential (1.4 psi) between the inlet and outlet sides of the control plunger. This is independent of the amount of fuel passing through the valves, which varies according to plunger height.

The injectors themselves are spring loaded and calibrated to open at 47–51 psi. They are not electrically operated as on the electronic fuel injection system.

The control pressure regulator, located on the intake manifold, acts to regulate the fuel/air mixture according to engine temperature. When the engine is cold, the control pressure regulator richens the mixture (4-5 minutes max.). This is accomplished in the following manner; a certain amount of fuel is bled off into a separate control pressure system. The control pressure regulator maintains this fuel at about 52.5 psi. The regulator is connected to the upper side of the fuel distributor control plunger. When the engine temperature is below operating parameters, a bi-metal spring in the regulator senses this and reduces the fuel pressure on top of the plunger. This allows the

plunger to rise further and channel more fuel to the regulator valves and injectors, thereby richeining the mixture. When the engine warms, the bi-metal spring in the regulator increases the pressure back to 52.5 psi, leaning the mixture back to its normal operation ratio. On V6 models, a vacuum feature is added to the regulator, whereby low vacuum situations, such as acceleration, temporarily lowers the control pressure and richens the mixture. At idle, full throttle, and steady state conditions, the vacuum is high and the mixture returns to normal.

The auxiliary air valve provides extra air to mix with the richer mixture during warm-up, thus raising the engine speed and improving cold-start driveability. The auxiliary air valve, which also has a temperature sensitive bi-metal spring, works directly with the control pressure regulator. At cold start-up, the valve is fully open. As the engine warms, an electric coil slowly closes the valve (4–5 minutes max.), blocking off the extra air and fast idle speed.

The cold start injector, located on the inlet duct, sprays extra fuel into the intake air stream during starter motor operation when the engine coolant temperature is below 95°F. It has a maximum spraying duration of about 12 seconds.

The thermal time switch, located on the cylinder head, actuates the cold start injector. It has a bi-metal spring which senses coolant temperature and an electric coil which limits the cold start injector spray to 12 seconds.

The fuel accumulator, located adjacent to the fuel tank mounted electric fuel pump, has a check valve which keeps residual fuel pressure from dropping below 28 psi when the engine or fuel pump are shut off. Therefore, the system is always pressurized, preventing vapor lock in hot start situations.

Continuous injection system electrical schematic

auxiliary
air valve

cold start
injector

fuel filter

injector

charcoal canister
(evaporative
emission
control)

idle adjustment screw

control
pressure
regulator

fuel distributor

air flow sensor

air filter element

Continuous injection system components—B21

CIS components—V6 engines

Diesel Fuel System

The Volvo diesel engine has indirect fuel injection, which means that the fuel is not injected directly into the combustion chamber (as is common diesel practice), but rather is fed into a small pre-combustion chamber in the head. During the compression stroke, air is forced up into the swirl chamber, which is connected to the combustion chamber by a narrow channel in the head. The shape of the swirl chamber causes the air to rotate rapidly. This air speed in the swirl chamber promotes even combustion and is the reason the engine can reach fairly high engine speeds.

Fuel is injected into the swirl chamber just before the piston reaches top dead center and the fuel mixes with the turbulent air. As the piston reaches TDC, it compresses the air/fuel mixture to a ration of 23.0:1. This ratio is over twice that of a gasoline engine. The mere act of compressing air to this level generates tremendous heat (1400°F), and it is this heat which ignites the air/fuel mixture.

FUEL FILTER

The fuel filter must be drained every 7,500 miles. Place a drain pan under the drain screw (#2 in the illustration) to collect the condensate. Loosen the bleeder screw (#1) several turns. Loosen the drain screw and drain until clean fuel flows out. Tighten the drain screw and the bleeder screw.

COMPONENT TESTING AND ADJUSTING

For any fuel injection system repair and service procedures not detailed below, please refer to "Fuel Injection" in the Unit Repair section.

Fuel Injectors

REMOVAL AND INSTALLATION

The fuel injectors on all Volvo CI systems are very close fit in the intake manifold. They are a "plug in" fit—they do not screw into the manifold by threads.

1. Grasp the injector body (see arrow in illustration). DO NOT grasp and pull on the fuel line. Pull injector straight out of manifold.
2. Protect injector tip—it is a precision instrument and is easily damaged. Proceed to next injector and so on.
3. Moisten a new rubber seal with gasoline before reinstalling injectors.
4. Press each injector in fully until seated.

TESTING

1. Remove the injector but leave it connected to the fuel line.
2. Point the injector into a container.
3. Remove the fuel pump relay and

bridge the relay with a fused (8 amp) jumper wire.
4. Remove the air duct from the air flow sensor.
5. Have an assistant turn the ignition switch on.
6. Lift the air flow sensor plate with a magnet and observe the injector nozzle spray pattern. The spray pattern must be cone shaped and even; if it is not, replace the injector.
7. Turn the ignition off and hold the injector horizontally. It should not drip.

NOTE: One or more injectors may be checked at the same time.

8. Moisten the rubber seals with gasoline before installings.
9. Press the injectors firmly into place.

Remove all fuel injectors (CIS Pictured) by pulling on the injector body, not on the fuel line

Diesel fuel filter service location. #1 is bleeder screw, #2 is drain

FUEL PUMP/INJECTION PUMP

The fuel pump is also the injection pump and is located on the left rear side of the engine and is driven by a belt running off the rear of the camshaft. The pump supplies

Return   Injector   Cold start   Gear   Injection
          pipe   device   belt   pump

Supply
line

Injector   Glow plug   Fuel filter

D24 Diesel showing injection system component location

the engine with more fuel than it can use, the excess fuel being returned to the fuel tank through suction-return lines. The system constantly bleeds itself of air. Because the pump constantly moves such large amounts of fuel, it tends to stay cool and this reduces the chances of vapor lock. The pump is lubricated by the fuel passing through it. Do not use fuel additives unless specifically recommended by Volvo for fear of damaging the pump.

The pump contains a single piston which rotates and distributes fuel to each injector in the correct sequence, much in the same way the distributor on a gasoline engine distributes the spark to the spark plugs.

Removal and Installation

NOTE: Several special tools are needed to remove and install the pump and to set its timing. If these tools are not available do not attempt to remove the pump. The tool numbers are given in the procedure.

1. Pinch off and remove the two coolant hoses running to the cold-start device on the fuel pump.
2. Disconnect the accelerator linkage at the pump and disconnect the wire from the stop valve on the top of the pump.
3. Remove the rear timing belt cover and thoroughly clean the fuel lines, and their connections at the injection pump.
4. Disconnect the fuel lines at the pump and plug the open connections to prevent dirt from entering the fuel system.
5. Remove the vacuum pump and its plunger.

6. Clean and remove the delivery lines at the fuel injectors. Plug all connections.
7. Set cylinder No. 1 to TDC injection stroke. At this position, the 0 mark on the flywheel aligns with the pointer and the notch on the injection pump pulley aligns with the notch on the pump housing. Both valves on No. 1 cylinder are closed and their camshaft lobes are pointing up at equally large angles.
8. Loosen the retaining bolts for the injection pump and push the pump up, then remove the pump drive belt. Tighten one bolt to hold the pump in the upper position.
9. Loosen the center bolt in the rear camshaft gear while using wrench 5199 to hold the gear. The bolts will be easily accessible if wrench 5201 is used.

NOTE: The camshaft must not rotate. Loosen the bolt only enough to rotate the gear on the camshaft.

10. Insert pin number 5193 into the injection pump gear to lock it in position and remove the injection pump gear nut.
11. With the pin still in position, use a puller to remove the pump gear.
12. Remove the bolts retaining the front injection pump bracket to the engine, then remove the inhex screws retaining the pump and remove the pump from the engine.
13. Install the pump on the engine and tighten the bolts only fingertight so that pump position can be adjusted.
14. Set the injection pump so that the mark on pump and the pump bracket align, then tighten the retaining bolts.
15. Make sure the shaft key is correctly installed and install the injection pump gear,

washer and nut. Use pin 5193 to hold the gear while tightening the nut.

16. Proceed to "Setting the Injection Pump Timing," below.

17. After the injection pump timing is set, fill the pump with clean diesel fuel through the fuel line connection *only* if a new fuel pump is being installed or if the old pump was drained and rebuilt.

18. Install the rear timing gear cover. Connect the fuel lines and fuel delivery pipes. Tighten the fuel delivery line cap nuts and the fuel line banjo bolts to 18 ft. lbs.

When installing the fuel line on the pump, do not mix the banjo bolts: the bolt for the fuel return line has a small hole in it and is marked OUT.

19. Install the vacuum pump and all remaining components in the reverse order of removal. Adjust the accelerator linkage.

Setting the Injection Pump Timing

This procedure requires many special tools and gauges. We recommend the procedure be handled by a professional fuel injection technician.

FUEL INJECTORS

REMOVAL AND INSTALLATION

1. Thoroughly clean the fuel delivery line connections around each fitting before removing.
2. Unscrew each fitting from its injector. Plug or tape the end of each fitting to prevent any dirt or grit from entering the fuel system.
3. Using a box-end wrench, unscrew the injector from the cylinder head. Remove the small heat shield and discard. Use care not to damage any part of the injector (especially the nozzle tip) while it is out of the engine. Plug each injector hole in the head with a piece of clean rag to prevent dirt from entering.
4. Installation is the reverse of removal. Be sure to use *new* heat shields with each injector. Note the proper way to install the heat shields as in the illustration.

Diesel injector. Make sure you install new heat shields in the manner shown

MANUAL TRANSMISSION

REMOVAL AND INSTALLATION

The transmission or the transmission-overdrive assembly may be removed with the engine installed in the vehicle.

1976 and Later 240 and 260 Series

1. Disconnect the battery. At the firewall, disconnect the back-up light connector.

2. Jack up the front of the car and install jack stands. Loosen the set screw and drive out the pin for the shifter rod. Disconnect the shift lever from the rod.

3. Inside the car, pull up the shift boot. Remove the fork for the reverse gear detent. Remove the snap-ring and lift up the shifter. If overdrive-equipped, disconnect the engaging switch wire.

4. On 240 Series models, disconnect the clutch cable and return spring at the throw-out fork and flywheel housing. On 260 series models, remove the bolts retaining the slave cylinder to the flywheel housing and tie the cylinder back out of the way (do not disconnect).

5. Disconnect the exhaust pipe bracket(s) from the flywheel cover. Remove the oil pan splash guard.

6. Using a floor jack and a block of wood, support the engine beneath the oil pan. Remove the transmission support crossmember.

7. Disconnect the driveshaft. Disconnect the speedometer cable. If so equipped, disconnect the overdrive wire.

8. Remove the starter retaining bolts and pull free of the flywheel housing.

9. Support beneath the transmission using another floor jack. Remove the flywheel (bell) housing-to-engine bolts and remove the transmission.

10. Reverse Steps 1–9 to install. Tighten the flywheel housing-to-engine bolts to 25–35 ft. lbs.

Transmission guide pins installed

M45 manual transmission plugs

LINKAGE ADJUSTMENT

Adjustments are not necessary.

TRANSMISSION LUBRICATION

The M45 transmission uses Automatic Transmission Fluid type F or G. The oil level should be up to the filler plug hole.

OVERDRIVE

The overdrive unit for the M46 transmission is a planetary gear type and is mounted on the rear of the transmission. When the overdrive is in the direct drive position (overdrive switched off) and the car is driven forward, power from the transmission mainshaft is transmitted through the freewheel rollers and uni-directional clutch to the overdrive output shaft. When the car is backing up or during periods of engine braking, torque is transmitted through the clutch sliding member which is held by spring pressure against the tapered portion of the output shaft. When the overdrive is actuated, the clutch sliding member is pressed by hydraulic pressure against the brake disc (ring), which locks the sun wheel. As a result, the output shaft of the overdrive rotates at a higher speed than the mainshaft thereby accomplishing a 20° reduction in engine speed in relation to vehicle speed.

M46 overdrive bottom cover

REMOVAL AND INSTALLATION

To facilitate removal, the vehicle should first be driven in 4th gear with the overdrive engaged, and then coasted for a few seconds with the overdrive disengaged and the clutch pedal depressed.

1. Remove the transmission from the vehicle as outlined in the applicable "Transmission Removal and Installation" section.

2. Disconnect the solenoid cables.

3. If the overdrive unit has not already been drained, remove the six bolts and the overdrive oil pan.

4. Remove the bolts which retain the overdrive unit to the transmission intermediate flange. Pull the unit straight to the rear until it clears the transmission mainshaft.

5. Reverse the above procedure to install. Install the overdrive oil pan with a new gasket. After installation of the transmission (which automatically fills the overdrive) to the proper level with Automatic Transmission Fluid type F or G. Check the lubricant level in the transmission after driving 6–9 miles. The oil level should be up to the filler plug hole.

CLUTCH

All Volvos are equipped with Borg and Beck or Fichtel and Sachs diaphragm spring clutches. The 240, DL, GL and GT Diesel series use an 8½ in. disc. The 260 uses a 9 in. disc. The 260 series, GLE and Coupe use a hydraulically-operated clutch, incorporating a clutch master cylinder and slave cylinder. There is no effective adjustment in this type of system.

CLUTCH ADJUSTMENT

240 Series and DL, GL, GLT

The play in the manually-operated clutches in these four cylinder Volvos can be adjusted. Clutch play is adjusted underneath the car at the clutch fork. Loosen the lock nut on the fork side of the cable bracket, then turn the adjusting nut until the proper play is achieved. Tighten the lock nut. Clutch play for all 4-cylinder engines except Turbo is 3–5mm (⅛ in.–³⁄₁₆ in.). Turbo clutch play (free movement rearward) is 1–3mm (about ⁵⁄₆₄ in.).

Clutch Master Cylinder

REMOVAL AND INSTALLATION

260 Series, GLE and Coupe

1. Drain the clutch reservoir with a bulb

260 series clutch linkage—GLE and Coupe (all V6) similar

Clutch master cylinder and slave cylinder location—V6 models. Clutch travel is about 6.7 in. (170 mm)

syringe. Be careful not to drip brake fluid (used in the clutch cylinders) on any painted surfaces.

2. Remove the fluid pipe from the master cylinder.

3. Remove the two retaining bolts and remove the master cylinder.

4. Install in the reverse order. Fill the reservoir with fluid and bleed the system at the slave cylinder on the flywheel housing.

Clutch Slave Cylinder

REMOVAL AND INSTALLATION

260 Series, GLE and Coupe

The slave cylinder is unbolted from the flywheel housing after its fluid tube is disconnected and plugged. Be sure to bleed the system after installation.

REMOVAL AND INSTALLATION

M45 and M46

1. Remove the transmission as outlined under M45 and M46 Removal and Installation.

2. Scribe alignment marks on the clutch and flywheel. In order to prevent warpage, slowly loosen the bolts which retain the clutch to the flywheel diagonally in rotation. Remove the bolts and lift off the clutch and pressure plate.

3. Inspect the clutch assembly as outlined under "Clutch Inspection."

4. When ready to install, wash the pressure plate and flywheel with solvent to remove any traces of oil, and wipe them clean with a cloth.

5. Position the clutch assembly (the longest side of the hub facing backwards) to the flywheel and align the bolt holes. Insert a pilot shaft (centering mandrel or drift), or an input shaft from an old transmission of the same type, through the clutch

Clutch free-play clearance—B21F Turbo

assembly and flywheel so that the flywheel pilot bearing is centered.

6. Install the six bolts which retain the clutch assembly to the flywheel and tighten them diagonally in rotation, a few turns at a time. After all the bolts are tightened, remove the pilot shaft (centering mandrel).

7. Install the transmission as outlined under M45 and M46 Removal and Installation.

8. On the 260 (GLE, etc.), bleed the clutch hydraulic system, if necessary.

Clutch fork play adjustment—B21F series. Locknut at center, adjusting nut at left

CLUTCH INSPECTION

Check the pressure plate for heat damage, cracks, scoring, or other damage to the friction surface. Check the curvature of the pressure plate with a steel ruler. Place the ruler diagonally over the pressure plate friction surface and measure the distance between the straight edge of the ruler and the inner diameter of the pressure plate. The measurement must not be greater than 0.0012 in. In addition, there must be no clearance between the straight edge of the ruler and the outer diameter of the pressure points. Replace the clutch as a unit if it proves faulty.

Check the throwout bearing by rotating it several times while applying finger pressure, so that the ball bearings roll against the inside of the races. If the bearing does not turn easily or if it binds at any point, replace it as a unit. Also make sure that the bearing slides easily on the guide sleeve from the transmission.

AUTOMATIC TRANSMISSION

Volvos 1976 and later are available with four different automatic transmissions. The Borg-Warner BW55 (and its Japanese made counterpart the Aisin-Warner AW55) have been used since 1976. These transmissions are three-speed dual-range automatics with a three element torque converter. The AW70 and heavy-duty AW71 are 4-speed automatics available since 1982. The AW71 is

240 series—clutch linkage

also used with the higher-torque B21F Turbo engine.

REMOVAL AND INSTALLATION

240 Series

1. Remove the dipstick and filler pipe clamp.
2. Remove the bracket and throttle cable from the dashboard and throttle control, respectively.
3. Disconnect the exhaust pipe at the manifold.
4. Raise the car and support it on jack stands at the front and rear axles.
5. Drain the fluid into a clean container.
6. Disconnect the driveshaft from the transmission flange.
7. Disconnect the selector lever controls and remove the reinforcing bracket from the pan.
8. Remove the torque converter attaching bolts.
9. Support the transmission with a jack equipped with a holding fixture.
10. Remove the car crossmember.
11. Disconnect the exhaust pipe brackets and remove the speedometer cable from the case.
12. Remove the filler pipe.
13. Place a wooden block between the engine and firewall and lower the jack until the engine is against the block.

NOTE: If the battery cable appears to stretch too much, remove it.

14. Disconnect the starter wires, remove the converter housing bolts and pull the transmission backwards to clear the guide pins.
15. Install in the reverse of removal. Torque all 14 mm bolts to 35 ft. lbs.

260 Series

1. Remove air cleaner.
2. Disconnect throttle cable.
3. Remove the two upper converter housing bolts.
4. Remove the filler pipe.
5. Raise the vehicle, support it front and rear with jack stands and drain the transmission into a clean container.
6. Remove the splash shield (8 bolts).
7. Disconnect the front muffler from the rubber suspensor.
8. Disconnect the driveshaft from the transmission flange.
9. Remove the exhaust pipe brackets at the rear of the transmission.
10. Remove the rear crossmember.
11. Remove the rear engine support and exhaust pipe bracket.
12. Remove the speedometer cable.
13. Disconnect the cooler lines at the transmission.
14. Remove the electrical connections from transmission.
15. Remove neutral start switch.

| 6–9 Nm |
| 10 mm hex |
| 4.4–6.6 lb.ft. |

| 41–50 Nm |
| 17 mm hex |
| 30–37 lb.ft. |

| 41–50 Nm |
| 17 mm hex |
| 30–37 lb.ft. |

| 41–50 Nm |
| 14 mm hex |
| 30–37 lb.ft. |

BW55, AW55 mountings and controls—AW70 and AW71 similar

16. Remove shift control rod.
17. Remove the engine-to-transmission cover plate.
18. Remove starter motor and cover.
19. Remove converter-to-drive plate bolts.
20. Position jack, with holding fixture, under transmission.

21. Remove the two lower converter housing bolts.
22. Pull the transmission back and down to clear the guide pins.
23. Installation is the reverse of removal. Torque the converter housing bolts to 35 ft. lbs. Torque filler pipe nut to 70 ft. lbs. Torque converter-to-drive plate bolts to 35 ft. lbs. Adjust control rod so that 1⅛" of thread is visible. Torque crossmember bolts to 35 ft. lbs.

FLuid Pan

REMOVAL AND INSTALLATION

1. Raise the car and place jack stands underneath.

Neutral start switch adjustment—1976-77

2. The dipstick tube doubles as the filler tube, and when removed, the drain plug. Disconnect the tube from the side of the pan, and drain the transmission.

3. Remove the 14 pan bolts, and lower the pan and gasket (some fluid will remain in the pan).

4. Inspect the magnet (located adjacent to the filter screen) for metal particles. Check the filter screen for the pump. Remove any gum or sludge from the bottom of the pan. Clean and dry the pan and install a new gasket.

5. Position the pan and install the bolts fingertight. Then, stop torque, diagonally in rotation, to 4.4–7.4 ft. lbs.

6. Connect the dipstick tube and tighten to 59–74 ft. lbs.

7. Remove the jack stands and lower the car. Refer to the capacities chart and fill the transmission to the proper level with ATF Type F.

PUMP STRAINER SERVICE

1. Remove the pan as outlined in the "Pan Removal and Installation" section.

2. Remove the bolts which retain the front pump wire-mesh strainer to the valve body, and lower the strainer.

3. Clean the strainers in an alcohol based solvent solution.

4. Position the strainers to the valve body and install the retaining screws and bolts. Torque the bolts to 3.7–4.4 ft. lbs.

5. Install the pan with a new gasket as outlined in the "Pan Removal and Installation" section.

BAND ADJUSTMENTS— ALL TRANSMISSIONS

The BW55 and AW55, AW70 and AW71 transmissions are equipped with a multi-disc brake (band) system which does not require any adjustment. No provision is made for band adjustment, even at overhaul.

NEUTRAL START SWITCH ADJUSTMENT

Some early production 1976 models have a nonadjustable neutral start switch located on the side of the case. All subsequent production models have an adjustable switch, located beneath the shifter quadrant on the tunnel. To adjust:

1. Remove the shifter quadrant cover.

2. Place the shifter lever in Park. Check that the round switch contact centers over the indicating line for "P" (park). If not, loosen the two switch mounting screws and align the switch.

3. Place the shifter lever in Neutral. Repeat the check and adjust as necessary.

4. Finally, check that the engine starts only in Park or Neutral, and check that the back-up lights work only in Reverse.

GEAR SELECTOR LINKAGE ADJUSTMENT

240, 260 Series

NOTE: The gear selector shift console has been moved forward on cars equipped with the AW70/AW71 transmissions. The shift linkage is also shortened on these cars.

1. Disconnect the shift rod from the transmission lever. Place both the transmission lever and the gear selector lever in the "2" position.

2. Adjust the length of the shift control rod so that a small clearance of 0.04 in. is obtained between the gear selector lever inhibitor and the inhibitor plate, when the shift control rod is connected to the transmission lever.

3. Position the gear selector lever in Drive and make sure that a similar small clearance of 0.04 in. exists between the lever inhibitor and the inhibitor plate. Disconnect the shift control rod from the transmission lever and adjust, if necessary.

4. Lock the control rod bolt with its safety clasp and tighten the locknut. Make sure that the control rod lug follows with the transmission lever.

Adjusting automatic transmission gear selector. Clearance in position D toward position N is the same as the clearance in position 2 toward position 1. Adjust at the bottom end of the gear selector.

5. After moving the transmission lever to the Park and "1" positions, make sure that the clearances remain the same. In addition, make sure that the output shaft is locked with the selector lever in the Park position.

1976 and Later BW55

1. With the engine off, check that the distance between the "D" position and its forward stop is equal to the distance between the "2" position and its rearward stop, when the gear selector is moved. If you are not sure, remove the gear quadrant cover, and measure.

2. If adjustment is necessary, a rough setting is made by loosening the locknut and rotating the clevis on the control rod to the transmission. A fine adjustment can be made by rotating the knurled sleeve between the control rod locknut and the pivot for the gear selector lever. Increasing the rod length will decrease clearance between the "D" position and its forward stop, and vice versa. Maximum permissable length of exposed thread between the locknut and the control rod is 1.1 in.

THROTTLE AND DOWNSHIFT CABLE ADJUSTMENT

1. First, adjust the throttle plate angle and throttle cable. Disconnect the cable at the control pulley and the linkage rod at the throttle shaft. Set the throttle plate angle by loosening the adjusting screw locknut and backing off the screw. Then, turn in the screw until it just makes contact and then one additional turn. Tighten the locknut. Adjust the linkage rod so that it fits onto the throttle shaft pulley ball without moving the cable pulley. Attach the throttle cable to the pulley and adjust the cable sheath so that the cable is stretched but does not move the cable pulley. Finally, fully depress the gas pedal and check that the pulley contacts the full throttle abutment.

Shortened shaft linkage and closer control console—AW70/AW71 automatics

Throttle and downshaft cable adjustment—1976-77 models

2. With the transmission cable hooked up, check that there is 0.010–0.040 in. clearance between the cable clip and the adjusting sheath. The cable should be stretched at idle. Pull out the cable about ½ in. and release. A distinct click should be heard from the transmission as the throttle can returns to its initial position. Depress the gas pedal again to wide open throttle. Check that the transmission cable moves about 2 in. Adjust as necessary at the adjusting sheath.

DRIVELINE

Driveshaft and U-Joints

The driveshaft is a two-piece, tubular unit, connected by an intermediate universal joint. The rear end of the front section of the driveshaft forms a splined sleeve. A splined shaft forming one of the yokes for the intermediate U-joints fits into this sleeve. The front section is supported by a ball bearing contained in an insulated rubber housing which is attached to the bottom of the drive-shaft tunnel. The front section is connected to the transmission flange, and the rear section is connected to the differential housing flange by universal joints. Each joint consists of a spider with four ground trunnions carried in the flange yokes by needle bearings.

DRIVESHAFT AND UNIVERSAL JOINT REMOVAL AND INSTALLATION

1. Jack up the vehicle and install safety stands.

2. Mark the relative positions of the driveshaft yokes and transmission and differential housing flanges for purposes of assembly. Remove the nuts and bolts which retain the front and rear driveshaft sections to the transmission and differential housing flanges, respectively. Remove the support bearing housing from the driveshaft tunnel, and lower the driveshaft and universal joint assembly as a unit.

3. Pry up the lock washer and remove the support bearing retaining nut. Pull off the rear section of the driveshaft with the intermediate universal joint and splined shaft

of the front section. The support bearing may now be pressed off the driveshaft.

4. Remove the support from its housing.

5. For removal of the universal joints from the driveshaft, consult "Universal Joint Overhaul."

6. Inspect the driveshaft sections for straightness. Using a dial indicator, or rolling the shafts along a flat surface, make sure that the driveshaft out-of-round does not exceed 0.010 in. Do not attempt to straighten a damaged shaft. Any shaft exceeding 0.010 in. out-of-round will cause substantial vibration, and must be replaced. Also, inspect the support bearing by pressing the races against each other by hand, and turning them in opposite directions. If the bearing binds at any point, it must be discarded and replaced.

7. Install the support bearing into its housing.

8. Press the support bearing and housing onto the front driveshaft section. Push the splined shaft of the front section, with the intermediate universal joint and rear driveshaft section, into the splined sleeve of the front section. Install the retaining nut and lock washer for the support bearing.

9. Taking note of the alignment marks made prior to removal, position the driveshaft and universal joint assembly to its flange connections and install but do not tighten its retaining nuts and bolts. Position the support bearing housing to the driveshaft tunnel and install the retaining nut. Tighten the nuts which retain the driveshaft sections to the transmission and differential housing flanges to a torque of 25–30 ft. lbs.

10. Remove the safety stands and lower the vehicle. Road test the car and check for driveline vibrations and noise.

Universal joint disassembled

UNIVERSAL JOINT OVERHAUL

1. Remove the driveshaft and universal joint assembly as outlined in "Driveshaft and Universal Joint Assembly Removal and Installation."

2. Place the driveshaft section in a vise so that the joint being removed comes as close as possible to the vise jaws. Do not tighten the vise any more than is necessary as the driveshaft is of tubular construction, and easily deformed.

3. Remove the snap-rings, which se-

1. Flange on transmission
2. Front universal joint
3. Front section of driveshaft
4. Support bearing

5. Intermediate universal joint
6. Rear section of driveshaft
7. Rear universal joint
8. Flange on rear axle

Driveshaft with support bearing

cure the needle bearings in the yokes, with snap-ring pliers.

4. With a hammer and a metal punch, drive the spider as far as it will go in one direction. The needle bearing should come about half-way out. Then, drive the spider as far as it will go in the other direction.

5. Drive out one of the needle bearings with a thinner punch. Remove the spider, and then drive out the other needle bearing.

6. Clean the spider and needle bearings completely. Check the frictional surfaces for wear. Replace any worn or broken parts. If the old needle bearings and spider are to be reused, fill them with molybdenum disulphide chassis grease, and make sure that the rubber seals are not damaged. If new needle bearings are used, fill them half-way with the grease.

7. To install, position the spider in the yoke and push the spider in one direction as far as it will go, so that the needle bearing can be fitted onto the spider trunnion. Then, using a drift of a slightly smaller diameter than the needle bearing sleeve, press the needle bearing in until the bearing sleeve and snap-ring can be fitted.

8. Install the other needle bearing, bearing sleeve, and snap-ring as outlined in Step 7.

9. Remove the driveshaft section from the vise and repeat Steps 2–8 for the other universal joints.

10. Install the driveshaft and universal joint assembly as outlined under "Driveshaft and Universal Joint Removal and Installation."

REAR AXLE

All Volvos utilize a solid rear axle housing carried in two support arms. Two torque rods, connected between the axle shaft tubes and the body, limit the rear axle wind-up. A track bar controls lateral movement of the axle housing. Final drive is of the hypoid design, with the drive pinion lying below the ring gear. Each axle shaft is indexed into a splined sleeve for the different side gears, and supported at its outer end in a tapered roller bearing. Bearing clearance is not adjustable by use of shims as on earlier model Volvos, but instead is determined by bearing thickness. Both sides of the axles bearings are protected by oil seals.

NOTE: Some Volvos are equipped with a limited slip differential that requires a special type lubricant available from your Volvo dealer.

Limited Slip Differential

Except for the differential assembly the design is the same as the standard differential.

Two shafts make up the spider for the differential pinion gears. On the side where it is against the differential carrier, each shaft has a V-shaped bevel. The differential carrier is similarly designed. When power from the engine starts to drive the vehicle, the shafts (A) glide up the beveled recess in the differential carrier. This compresses the friction plates behind the differential side gears so that the differential assembly brakes. The bevel angle on the differential carrier is designed and chosen in such a way that the differential gears are not entirely locked, but a maximum of 75% of engine torque can be transmitted to a driveshaft.

NOTE: Never attempt to run your vehicle with only one wheel jacked up. Both rear wheels must be off the ground before running your vehicle or serious damage could result.

AXLE SHAFT REMOVAL AND INSTALLATION BEARING AND OIL SEAL REPLACEMENT

1. Raise the vehicle and install safety stands.

2. Remove the applicable wheel and tire assembly.

3. Place a wooden block beneath the brake pedal, plug the master cylinder reservoir vent hole, and remove and plug the brake line from the caliper. *Be careful not to allow any brake fluid to spill onto the disc or pads.* Remove the two bolts which retain brake caliper to the axle housing, and lift off the caliper. Lift off the brake disc.

4. Remove the thrust washer bolts through the holes in the axle shaft flange. Using a slide hammer, remove the axle shaft, bearing and oil seal assembly.

5. Using an arbor press, remove the axle shaft bearing and its locking ring from the axle shaft. Remove and discard the old oil seal.

6. Fill the space between the lips of the new oil seal with wheel bearing grease. Position the new seal on the axle shaft.

Correct tooth contact

Using an arbor press, install the bearing with a new locking ring, onto the axle shaft.

7. Thoroughly pack the bearing with wheel bearing grease. Install the axle shaft into the housing, rotating it so that it indexes with the differential. Install the bolts for the thrust washer and tighten to 36 ft. lbs.

8. Install the brake disc. Position the brake caliper to its retainer on the axle housing and install the two retaining bolts. Torque the caliper retaining bolts to 45–50 ft. lbs.

9. Unplug the brake line and connect it to the caliper. Bleed the caliper of all air trapped in the system.

10. Position the wheel and tire assembly on its lugs and hand-tighten the lug nuts. Remove the jack stands and lower the vehicle. Torque the lug nuts to 70–100 ft. lbs.

Differential

REMOVAL

1. Block the front wheels. Unscrew the rear wheel nuts. Jack up the rear of the vehicle. Place blocks in front of the rear jack attachments and lower the jack slightly. Remove the rear wheels.

2. Unscrew the upper bolts for the shock absorbers. Disconnect the handbrake cables from the lever arms and brackets on the brake backing plates.

3. Disconnect the driveshaft from the flange (yoke) on the pinion. Remove the brake line union from the differential carrier.

4. Loosen the front attaching bolt for the support arms about 1 turn. Remove the rear screws for the torque rods. Disconnect the track rod from the bracket on the differential carrier. Remove the lower attaching bolts for the springs.

5. Lower the jack until the support arms release from the springs. Remove the bolts which secure the differential carrier to the support arms. Lower the jack and pull the rear axle forward.

OVERHAUL

Due to the high degree of experience needed in disassembling a differential (and in the repair of the same), we recommend all rear axle work be handled by a professional. Also, in many cases, it is easier and less costly to replace the entire axle unit with one from a salvage yard. The Volvo owner should examine all options before attempting any internal differential repair.

INSTALLATION

1. Place the rear axle on a garage jack. Move the axle in under the car and install the bolts for the support arms and torque rods.

2. Raise the jack until the track rod

attachment on the shaft is at the level with the attachment on the body. Install the track rod.

3. Install the attaching bolts for the springs. Tighten the nuts for the torque rods and support arms.

4. Install the bracket, union, and brake hoses. Connect the universal joint to the flange.

5. Install the upper bolts for the shock absorbers. Install the handbrake cable in the brackets and at the levers. Adjust the handbrake and bleed the brake system. Fill with oil.

6. Install the wheels and nuts. Lower the car. Tighten the wheel nuts to 70–100 ft. lbs. Fill with oil. Use only hypoid oil, 80w/90.

and axle housing until the spring is fully extended. Remove the spring.

4. To install, position the retaining bolt and inner washer, for the upper attachment, inside the spring and then, while holding the outer washer and rubber spacer to the upper body attachment, install the spring and inner washer to the upper attachment (sandwiching the rubber spacer), and tighten the retaining bolt.

5. Raise the jack and secure the bottom of the spring to its lower attachment with the washer and retaining bolt.

6. Connect the shock absorber to its upper attachment. Install the wheel and tire assembly.

7. Remove the jack stands and lower the car. Tighten the lug nuts to 70–100 ft. lbs. and install the hub cap.

Shock Absorbers

REMOVAL AND INSTALLATION

1. Remove the hub cap and loosen the lug nuts a few turns. Place blocks in front of the front wheels. Jack up the rear of the car and place jack stands in front of the rear jacking points. Remove the wheel and tire assembly.

2. Remove the nuts and bolts which retain the shock absorber to its upper and lower attachments and remove the shock absorber. Make sure that the spacing sleeve, inside the axle support arm for the lower attachment, is not misplaced.

3. The damping effect of the shock ab-

REAR SUSPENSION

All Volvos use a coil spring rear suspension. The solid rear axle is suspended from the rigid frame member by a pair of support arms and damped by a pair of double-acting telescopic shock absorbers. A pair of torque rods control rear axle wind-up and a track rod limits the lateral movement of the rear axle in relation to the car. A rear stabilizer bar, attached to both rear support (trailing) arms, is installed on 240 and 260 models.

Springs

REMOVAL AND INSTALLATION

1. Remove the hub cap and loosen the lug nuts a few turns. Jack up the car and place jack stands in front of the rear jacking points. Remove the wheel and tire assembly.

2. Place a hydraulic jack beneath the rear axle housing and raise the housing sufficiently to compress the spring. Loosen the nuts for the upper and lower spring attachments.

—— CAUTION ——
Due to the fact that the spring is compressed under several hundred pounds of pressure, when it is freed from its lower attachment, it will attempt to suddenly spring back to its extended position. It is therefore imperative that the axle housing be lowered with extreme care until the spring is fully extended. As an added safety measure, a chain may be attached to the lower spring coil and secured to the axle housing.

3. Disconnect the shock absorber at its upper attachment. Carefully lower the jack

Rear suspension—240, 260 series

sorber may be tested by securing the lower attachment in a vise and extending and compressing it. A properly operating shock absorber should offer approximately three times as much resistance to extending the unit as compressing it. Replace the shock absorber if it does not function as above, or if its fixed rubber bushings are damaged. Replace any leaking shock absorber.

4. To install, position the shock absorber to its upper and lower attachments. Make sure that the spacing sleeve is installed inside the axle support (trailing) arm and is aligned with the lower attachment bolt hole. Install the retaining nuts and bolts. On 240 series models, the shock fits *inside* the support arm. On all 164 models, the shock attaches on the *outboard* side of the support arm.

5. Install the wheel and tire assembly. Remove the jack stands and lower the car. Tighten the lug nuts to 70–100 ft. lbs., and install the hub cap.

FRONT SUSPENSION

All Volvos use a coil spring independent front suspension utilizing a pair of Mac-Pherson-type struts located between a sheet metal tower at the top and a lower control arm at the bottom. The MacPherson strut design incorporates the coil spring, shock absorber and wheel spindle into a single assembly, eliminating the need for an upper suspension control arm. The MacPherson strut design provides for generous vertical suspension travel allowing the use of softer springs. The strut design is extremely sensitive to front wheel imbalance; the slightest imbalance often leading to front end wobble. Finally, the caster angle of the front suspension is preset and cannot be adjusted. If the caster angle is not up to specifications, the damaged components must be replaced as a unit.

Strut

REMOVAL AND INSTALLATION

1. Remove the hub cap and loosen the lug nuts a few turns.

2. Firmly apply the parking brake and place blocks in back of the rear wheels.

3. Jack up the front of the car with a hoist or using a floor jack at the center of the front crossmember. When the wheels are 2–3 in. off the ground, the car is high enough. Place jack stands beneath the front jacking points. Then, remove the floor jack from the crossmember (if used), and reposition it beneath the applicable lower

1. Strut assembly
2. Lower spring support
3. Shock absorber
4. Rubber bumper
5. Upper attachment
6. Coil spring
7. Ruber sleeve, protecting the shock absorber
8. Stabilizer bar
9. Stabilizer bar attachment
10. Stabilizer link

Front suspension—240, 260 series

control arm to provide support at the outer end. Remove the wheel and tire assembly.

4. Using a ball joint puller, disconnect the steering rod from the steering arm.

5. Disconnect the stabilizer bar at the link upper attachment.

6. Remove the bolt retaining the brake line bracket to the fender well.

7. Open the hood and remove the cover for the strut assembly upper attachment.

8. While keeping the strut from turning, loosen and remove the nut for the upper attachment.

9. Before lowering the strut assembly, wire or tie the strut to some stationary component, or use a holding fixture such as SVO 5045, to prevent the strut from traveling down too far and damaging the hydraulic brake lines. Then lower the jack supporting the lower arm and allow the strut to tilt out to about a 60 degree angle. At this angle, the top of the strut assembly should just protrude past the wheel well, allowing removal of the strut from the top.

10. Carefully lift and guide the strut assembly into its upper attachment in the spring tower. Connect the stabilizer bar to the stabilizer link. Guide the shock absorber spindle into the upper attachment and raise the

Spring–type lower ball joint maximum allowable length

Non-spring type lower ball joint maximum allowable length

jack beneath the lower control arm. Install the washer and nut on top of the shock absorber spindle. While holding the spindle from turning, tighten the nut to 15–25 ft. lbs. Install the cover.

11. Attach the brake line bracket to its mount. Tighten the nut retaining the stabilizer bar to the link. Connect the steering rod at the steering arm.

12. Install the wheel and tire assembly. Remove the jack stands and lower the car. Jounce the suspension a few times and then road test.

OVERHAUL

For all spring and shoch absorber removal and installation procedures and any other strut overhaul procedures, please refer to "Strut Overhaul" in the Unit Repair section.

Lower Control Arm

REPLACEMENT

1. Jack up car, support on stands and remove wheels.

Suspending the top of the strut from the body with a wire while removing the lower ball joint

Late type lower ball joint-to-strut retaining bolts

2. Remove stabilizer bar.
3. Remove ball joint from control arm.
4. Remove control arm front retaining bolt.
5. Remove control arm rear attachment plate.
6. Remove attachment plate from control arm.
7. Remove stabilizer link from control arm.
8. Install in reverse of removal.

NOTE: Right and left bushings are not interchangeable. The right side bushing should be turned so that the small slots point horizontally when installed. Torque the front retaining bolt to 55 ft. lbs., the rear bushing to 4 ft. lbs. and the rear attachment bolts to 30 ft. lbs.

Lower Ball Joint

REMOVAL AND INSTALLATION

Early Production Models

1. Follow Steps 1–9 under "Strut Removal and Installation" for the 240, 260 series.

2. While grasping the strut outer tube (casing) with a pair of locking pliers, loosen and remove the shock absorber retaining nut.
3. Pull the shock absorber unit out of the outer tube.
4. Loosen the ball joint retaining nut. Grasp the outer tube at the weld with a pair of channel-lock pliers and loosen the nut with a 19 mm socket and a long extension, until the joint bracket comes loose.
5. Using a drift and hammer, loosen the conical part of the ball joint from the strut assembly.
6. Using the 19 mm socket coated on the inside with vaseline or wheel bearing grease, remove the ball joint retaining nut.

The grease should keep the nut from falling down into the strut tube.
7. Wire the top of the strut assembly to the sheet metal tower, and allow the strut to hang vertically. Disconnect the ball joint from the bottom of the strut assembly. Take care not to damage the brake hoses. Then, disconnect the ball joint from the lower control arm.
8. Attach the new ball joint to the lower control arm.

NOTE: Make sure the new ball joint stud is free of grease, or the stud could be tightened too far into the cone making the rubber bellows stick to the strut.

9. Remove the securing wire and lift

Front suspension strut—240, 260 series

the strut assembly into position. Install the ball joint nut, and torque to 30–50 ft. lbs. Stop the outer tube from turning with locking pliers at the weld.

10. Install the shock absorber and retaining nut. Tighten as in Step 8. Pull the shock absorber spindle to its uppermost position.

11. Follow Steps 10–12 under ''Strut Removal and Installation'' for the 240, 260 series.

1979–83 Models

1. Jack up the front of the car and install jack stands beneath the front jacking attachments.

2. Remove the tire and wheel assembly.

3. Reach in between the spring coils and loosen the shock absorber cap nut a few turns.

4. Remove the four bolts (12 mm) retaining the ball joint seat to the bottom of the strut.

5. Remove the three nuts (19 mm) retaining the ball joint to the lower control arm.

6. Place the ball joint and attachment assembly in a vise and remove the 19 mm nut from the ball joint stud. Then, drive out the old ball joint.

7. Install the new ball joint in the attachment and tighten the stud nut to 35–50 ft. lbs.

8. Attach the ball joint assembly to the strut. Tighten to 15–20 ft. lbs.

9. Attach the ball joint assembly to the control arm. Tighten to 70–95 ft. lbs.

10. Tighten the shock absorber cap nut. Install the wheel and tire. Lower the car and road-test.

NOTE: On 1979 and later models with power steering, the ball joints are different for the left and right side.

Compared to previous years, the ball joint is .393 in. forward in control rod attachment. It is therefore most important that these ball joints are installed on the correct side.

Wheel Alignment

CASTER AND CAMBER ADJUSTMENT

Caster angle is fixed by suspension design and cannot be adjusted. If caster is not within specifications, check front end parts for damage and replace as necessary.

Camber angle, however, may be adjusted. At the strut upper attachment to the body, two of the three bolts holes are eccentric, allowing the upper end of the strut to tilt out or in as necessary. A special pivot lever tool SVO #5038, which attaches to the tops of the strut upper attachment retaining bolt threads is recommended for this job. To adjust, loosen the three retaining

nuts, install the pivot lever tool, and adjust to specifications. After adjusting, torque the nuts to 15–25 ft. lbs.

TOE-IN ADJUSTMENT

Toe-in may be adjusted after performing the caster and camber adjustments. With a wheel spreader, measure the distance (X) between the rear of the right and left front tires, at spindle (hub) height, and then measure the distance (Y) between the front of the right and left front tires, also at spindle (hub) height. Subtract the front distance (Y) from the rear distance (X), and compare that to the specifications table. X ∞s Y = toe-in. If the adjustment is not correct, loosen the locknuts on both sides of the tie rod, and rotate the tie rod itself. Toe-in is increased by turning the tie rod in the normal forward rotation of the wheels, and reduced by turning it in the opposite direction. After the final adjustment is made, torque the locknuts to 55–65 ft. lbs., being careful not to disturb the adjustment.

STEERING

All Volvos use divided steering columns that protect the driver during front end collisions. The manual steering gear used on the 240 series is a rack and pinion type of either Cam or ZF manufacture. Both units are fully enclosed, with the steering rods attached directly to the rack piston and protected by rubber bellows. However, the Cam unit is filled with steering gear oil while the ZF unit is grease-filled. Power steering is available on all 240 series models and standard equipment on the 260. Power assist is integral with the steering rear unit, and is supplied by an engine driven pump of ZF or Saginaw manufacture. The Saginaw pump is used in the 260 series, while the ZF pump is used in the 240.

Steering Wheel

REMOVAL AND INSTALLATION

NOTE: The use of a knock-off type steering wheel puller, or the use of a hammer may damage the collapsible column and is not recommended.

240 Series (DL and GL)

1. Disconnect the negative battery cable.

2. Remove the retaining screws for the upper half of the molded turn signal housing and lift off the housing.

3. Pry off the steering wheel impact pad.

Loosen the upper strut nuts to adjust the camber of 240 and 260 series

4. Disconnect the horn plug contact.
5. Remove the steering wheel nut.

NOTE: Due to a change in the cone angle of this steering shaft, a puller is not needed on 1979 and later models.

6. With the front wheels pointing straight ahead, and the steering wheel centered, install a steering wheel puller. On 240 and 260 models, use a universal type puller, such as SVO 2263.

7. To install, make sure that the front wheels are pointing straight ahead, then place the centered steering wheel on the column with the plug contact to the left. Install the nut and tighten to 20–30 ft. lbs.

8. Connect the horn plug contact and install the impact pad.

9. Install the upper turn signal housing half.

10. Connect the negative battery cable and test the operation of the horn.

TURN SIGNAL SWITCH REPLACEMENT

See ''Steering Wheel Removal and Installation.''

Ignition Lock and Switch

REPLACEMENT

1. Remove noise insulation panel and center side panel.
2. Disconnect the wires from the switch.
3. Pry out the switch with a short screwdriver.
4. Install in reverse of removal.

Manual Steering Gear

REMOVAL AND INSTALLATION

240 (DL and GL) Series

1. Remove the lock bolt and nut from

aligned in the plate slots. Install flat washers and nuts.

10. Install the splash guard.

11. Connect the steering rods to the steering arms.

12. Install the front wheels and lower the vehicle.

13. Install the lock bolt for the steering shaft flange.

PITMAN ARM ADJUSTMENT

On a steering gear with a marked pitman arm and pitman arm shaft (on the steering gear), make sure that the marks align.

On a steering gear without the marks, lift up the front of the vehicle so that the front wheels are free. Turn the steering wheel to its center position (count the number of turns). Lower the vehicle. If the vehicle is correctly loaded, the wheels should now point straight forward. If the wheels do not, remove the pitman arm from the shaft with a puller. Then set the left wheel straight ahead should be in its center position. Tighten the pitman arm nut to 100–120 ft. lbs.

Power Steering Gear
REMOVAL AND INSTALLATION

1. Loosen the steering column shaft flange from the pinion shaft. Remove the lock bolt and bend apart the flange slightly.

2. Jack up the front end. Position jack stands at the front jack supports. Remove the front wheels.

3. Disconnect the steering rods from the steering arms, with a ball joint puller.

4. Remove the splash guard.

5. Disconnect the hoses at the settering gear. Install protective plugs in the hose connections.

6. Remove the steering gear from the front axle member.

7. Remove the steering gear by pulling down until it is free from the steering shaft flange. Then remove the unit on the left side of the vehicle.

8. Position the steering gear and attach the pinion shaft to the steering shaft flange. Take care to align the recess for the lock bolt.

9. Install right side U-bolt and bracket, but do *NOT* tighten the nuts.

10. Install left side retaining bolts, and tighten. Tighten the U-bolt nuts.

11. Connect the steering rods to the steering arms.

12. Install the lock bolt on the steering column flange.

13. Connect the return and pressure hoses to the steering gear.

Power Steering Pump
REMOVAL AND INSTALLATION

1. Remove all dirt and grease from

1. Bolt
2. Adjusting screw
3. Locknut
4. Pitman arm shaft bushing
5. Cover
6. Lock ring
7. Tab washer
8. Upper steering cam bearing

9. Oil seal, steering column
10. Steering cam
11. Pitman arm shaft bushing
12. Pitman arm shaft seal
13. Pitman arm
14. Nut

15. Housing
16. Lower bearing cap
17. Steering column cover
18. Lower cam bearing
19. Washer
20. Shims
21. Pitman arm shaft with roller

Manual steering gear—worm and roller

the column flange. Bend apart the flange slightly with a screwdriver.

2. Jack up the front end. The stands should be positioned at the jack supports. Remove the front wheels.

3. Disconnect the steering rods from the steering arms, using a ball joint puller.

4. Remove the splash guard.

5. Disconnect the steering gear from the front axle member.

6. Disconnect the steering gear from

the steering gear flange. Remove steering gear.

7. Install rubber spacers and plates for the steering gear attachment points.

8. Position the steering gear, and guide the pinion shaft into the steering shaft flange. The recess on the pinion shaft should be aligned towards the lock bolt opening in the flange.

9. Attach the steering gear to the front axle member. Check that the U-bolts are

around the suction line connections and from around the delivery line on the pump-housing.

2. Using a container to catch any power steering fluid that might run out, disconnect the lines, and plug them to prevent dirt from entering the system.

3. Remove the tensioning bolt and the attaching bolts.

4. Clear the pump free of the fan belt and lift it out.

5. If a new pump is to be used, the old brackets, fittings, and pulley must be transferred from the old unit. The pulley may be removed with a puller, and pressed on the pump shaft with a press tool. Under no circumstances should the pulley be hammered on, as this will damage the pump bearings.

6. To install, place the pump in position and loosely fit the attaching bolts. Connect the lines to the pump with new seals.

7. Place the fan belt onto the pulley and adjust the fan belt tension as outlined in Chapter one.

8. Tighten the tensioning bolt and the attaching bolts.

9. Fill the reservoir with Type "A" automatic transmission fluid and bleed the system as outlined under "Power Steering System Bleeding."

POWER STEERING SYSTEM BLEEDING

1. Fill the reservoir up to the edge with Automatic Transmission Fluid Type "A". Raise the front wheels off the ground, and install safety stands. Place the transmission in neutral and apply the parking brake.

2. Keeping a can of ATF Type "A" within easy reach, start the engine and fill the reservoir as the level drops.

3. When the reservoir level has stopped dropping, slowly turn the steering wheel from lock to lock several times. Fill the reservoir if necessary.

4. Locate the bleeder screw on the power steering gear. Open the bleeder screw ½–1 turn, and close it when oil starts flowing out.

5. Continue to turn the steering wheel slowly until the fluid in the reservoir is free of air bubbles.

6. Stop the engine and observe the oil level in the reservoir. If the oil level rises more than ¼ in. past the level mark, air still remains in the system. Continue bleeding until the level rise is correct.

7. Remove the safety stands and lower the car.

STEERING AND TIE ROD SERVICE

Bent or otherwise damaged steering rods and tie rods must be replaced, never straightened. All components of the steering linkage, including the pitman arm and idler arm (on worm and roller steering types),

1. Housing
2. Pinion
3. Seal
4. Pinion cover
5. Spacer sleeve
6. Upper Pinion bearing
7. Rack
8. Steering rod
9. Inner ball joint
10. Rubber bellow
11. Pre-tensioning piston
12. O-ring
13. Spring
14. Cover
15. Bushing

Manual steering gear assembly (cam gear)—rack and pinion type

Rack and pinion steering gear disassembled

Adjusting thrust rod

are connected by means of ball joints. Ball joints cannot be disassembled or adjusted, so they must be replaced when damaged. They should also be replaced if the rubber seal is broken and the joint contaminated.

The ball joints of the steering rods are made in unit with the rods, therefore the entire rod assembly must be replaced when their ball joints become unserviceable. Maximum permissible axial (vertical) play is .120 in. After removing the cotter pins and ball stud nuts at the rod's connections, press the ball joint out of its connecting socket.

The ball joints of the tie rod may be replaced individually. After the ball joint is disconnected, the locknut on the tie rod is loosened and the clamp bolt released. The ball joint is then screwed out of the tie rod, taking note of the number of turns. The new ball joint is screwed in the same number of turns, and the clamp bolt and locknut tightened. The ball joint is locked to the rod with 55–65 ft. lbs. of torque. The new ball joint is pressed into its connection and the ball stud not tightened to 23–27 ft. lbs.

After reconditioning of the rods and joints, the wheel alignment must be adjusted.

BRAKE SYSTEM

All Volvos are equipped with a four wheel power-assisted disc brake system. The four wheel disc system utilizes a pair of four-piston, fixed calipers at the rear. The calipers are either Girling or ATE manufacture, so when ordering disc pads or caliper rebuilding kits, you must identify which you have. The discs are one-piece castings.

NOTE: All models except DL2/4 door models have ventilated front brake discs.

Whenever adding to or replacing brake fluid, it is imperative that the fluid be of SAE 70 R3 (SAE J 1703) quality or better. Fluid meeting DOT 3 or DOT 4 specifications is also acceptable. Avoid mixing brake fluids from different manufacturers and never reuse old brake fluid.

For all brake system repair and adjustment procedures not detailed below, please refer to "Brakes" in the Unit Repair section.

Disc Brake Adjustment

Disc brakes require no adjustment. They should, however, be checked frequently for wear. Consult the specifications table for new pad thickness. Pads should never be allowed to wear down to less than 0.125 in., or disc damage may occur.

Master Cylinder

REMOVAL AND INSTALLATION

1. To prevent brake fluid from spilling onto and damaging the paint, place a protective cover over the fender apron, and rags beneath the master cylinder.
2. Disconnect and plug the brake lines from the master cylinder.
3. Remove the nuts which retain the master cylinder and reservoir assembly to the vacuum booster, and lift the assembly forward, being careful not to spill any fluid on the fender. Empty out and discard the brake fluid.

— CAUTION —
Do not depress the brake pedal while the master cylinder is removed.

4. In order for the master cylinder to function properly when installed to the vacuum booster, the adjusting nut for the thrust rod of the booster must not prevent the primary piston of the master cylinder from returning to its resting position. A clearance (C) of 0.004–0.04 in. is required between the thrust rod and primary piston with the master cylinder installed. The clearance may be adjusted by rotating the adjusting nut for the booster thrust rod in the required direction. To determine what the clearance (C) will be when the master cylinder and booster are connected, first measure the distance (A) between the face of the attaching flange and the center of the primary piston on the master cylinder, then measure the distance (B) that the thrust rod protrudes from the fixed surface of the booster (making sure that the thrust rod is depressed fully

with a partial vacuum existing in the booster). When measurement is subtracted from measurement (A), clearance (C) should be obtained. If not, adjust the length of the thrust rod by turning the adjusting screw to suit. After the final adjustment is obtained, apply a few drops of locking compound, such as Loctite®, to the adjusting nut.

5. Position the master cylinder and reservoir assembly onto the studs for the booster, and install the washers and nuts. Tighten the nuts to 17 ft. lbs.
6. Remove the plugs and connect the brake lines.
7. Bleed the entire brake system.

Brake System Warning Valve

The brake system warning valve is located near the master cylinder in the engine compartment. On 1976–77 models. On 1978 and later models it is located under a bolt on the front axle member. The value is centered by hydraulic pressure from the primary circuit on one side and the secondary circuit on the other. When a hydraulic imbalance exists, such as a leak in one of the calipers, the valve will move off-center toward the system with the leak and, therefore, the lowest pressure. When the valve moves off-center, it closes a circuit to a warning light on the dashboard, warning the driver of the imbalance. Sometimes, the valve will actuate the warning light when one of the systems is bled during normal maintenance. When this happens, the valve has to be reset.

VALVE RESETTING

1. Disconnect the plug contact and screw out the warning switch so that the pistons inside the valve may return to their normal position.
2. Repair and bleed the faulty hydraulic circuit.
3. Screw in the warning switch and tighten it to a torque of 10–14 ft. lbs. Connect the plug contact.

REPLACEMENT

1. Placing a rag beneath the valve to catch the brake fluid, loosen the pipe connections, and disconnect the sic brake lines. Disconnect the electrical plug contact, and lift out the valve.
2. Connect the new warning valve in the reverse order of removal, and connect the plug contact.
3. Bleed the entire brake system.

Brake System Proportioning Valves

Each of the brake circuits has a proportioning (relief) valve located inline between the rear wheels. The purpose of these valves is to ensure that brake pressure on all four wheels compensates for the change in weight distribution under varied braking conditions. The harder the brakes are applied, the more weight there is on the front wheels. The valves regulate the hydraulic pressure to the rear wheels so that under hard braking conditions, they receive a smaller percentage of the total braking effort. This prevents premature rear wheel lock-up when the brakes are applied in emergency situations.

REPLACEMENT

Sophisticated pressure testing equipment is required to troubleshoot the dual hydraulic system in order to determine if the proportioning valve(s) are in need of replacement. However, if the car is demonstrating signs of rear wheel lock-up under moderate to heavy braking pressure, and other variables such as tire pressure, tread depth, etc., have been ruled out, the valve(s) may be at fault. The valves are not rebuildable, and must be replaced as a unit.

1. Unscrew, disconnect and plug the brake pipe from the master cylinder, at the valve connection.
2. Slacken the connection for the flexible brake hose to the rear wheel a *maximum* of ¼ turn.
3. Remove the bolt(s) which retain the valve to the underbody, and unscrew the valve from the rear brake hose.
4. To install the valve, place a new seal on it, and screw the valve onto the rear brake hose and hand tighten. Secure the valve to the underbody with the retaining bolt(s).
5. Connect the brake pipe and tighten both connections, making sure that there is no tension on the flexible rear hose.
6. Bleed the brake system.

Front Wheel Bearings

REPLACEMENT AND ADJUSTMENT

1. Remove the hub cap, and loosen the lug nuts a few turns.
2. Firmly apply the parking brake. Jack up the front of the car and place jack stands beneath the lower control arms. Remove the wheel and tire assembly.
3. Remove the front caliper.
4. Pry off the grease cap. Remove the cotter pin and castle nut. Use a hub puller to pull off the hub. If the inner bearing remains lodged on the stub axle, remove it with a puller.
5. Using a drift, remove the inner and outer bearing rings.
6. Thoroughly clean the hub, brake disc, and grease cap.
7. Press in the new inner and outer bearing rings with a drift.

8. Press grease into both bearings with a bearing packer. If one is not available, pack the bearings with as much wheel bearing grease as possible by hand. Also coat the outsides of the bearings and the outer rings pressed into the hub. Fill the recess in the hub with grease up to the smallest diameter on the outer ring for the outer bearing. Place the inner bearing in position in the hub and press its seal in with a drift. The felt ring should be thoroughly coated with light engine oil.
9. Place the hub onto the stub axle. Install the outer bearing washer, and castle nut.
10. Adjust the front wheel bearings by tightening the castle nut to 50 ft. lbs. to seat the bearings. Then, back off the nut ⅓ of a turn counterclockwise. If the nut slot does not align with the hole in the stub axle, loosen the nut until the cotter pin may be installed. Make sure that the wheel spins freely without any side play.
11. Fill the grease cap halfway with wheel bearing grease, and install it on the hub.
12. Install the front caliper.
13. Install the wheel and tire assembly. Remove the jack stand and lower the car. Tighten the lug nuts to 70–100 ft. lbs. and install the hub cap.

Parking Brake

The parking brake is mechanically actuated by a cable which is connected, by means of a pull rod and linkage, to a lever mounted on the floor to the left of the driver's seat. The brake consists of two miniature duo-servo drum brakes, one mounted at each end of the rear axle housing inside the hub of the rear brake discs.

ADJUSTMENT

1. Remove the rear ashtray (between the front seat backs).
2. Tighten the parking brake cable adjusting screw so that the brake is fully applied when pulled up 2–3 notches.
3. If one cable is stretched more than the other, they can be individually adjusted by removing the parking brake cover (2 screws) and turning the individual cable adjusting nut at the front of each yoke pivot.

Adjusting the parking brake through the access hole in the rear hub

4. Install the ashtray, and parking brake cover (if equipped).

CABLE REPLACEMENT

1. Apply the parking brake. Remove the hub caps for the rear wheels and loosen the lug nuts a few turns.
2. Place blocks in front of the front wheels. Jack up the rear end and place jackstands beneath the rear axle. Remove the wheel and tire assembly. Release the parking brake.

Adjust the 1981 and later parking brake if it is not fully applied after pulling the lever 10–11 notches. After adjusting, good braking power should be obtained after pulling the lever 2–3 notches

3. Remove the bolt and the wheel from the pulley.
4. Remove the rubber cover for the front attachment of the cable sleeve and nut, as well as the attachment for the rubber suspension ring on the frame. Remove the cable from the other side of the attachment in the same manner.
5. Hold the return spring in position. Pry up the lock and remove the lock pin so that the cable releases from the lever.
6. Remove the return spring with washers. Loosen the nut for the rear attachment of the cable sleeve. Lift the cable forward, after loosening both sides of the attachments, and remove it.
7. To install, first adjust the rear brake shoes of the parking brake as outlined in Steps 3, 4 and 5 under "Parking Brake Adjustment."
8. Install new rubber cable guides for the cable suspension. Place the cable in position in the rear attachment and tighten the nut. Install the washers and return spring. Oil the lock pin and install it, together with the cable, on the lever. Install the attachment and rubber cable guide on the frame.
9. Install the cable in the same manner on the side of the vehicle.
10. Place the cable sleeve in position in the front attachments and install the rubber covers.
11. Lubricate and install the pulley on the pull rod. Adjust the pulley so that the parking brake is fully engaged with the lever at the third or fourth notch.
12. Install the wheel and tire assemblies. Remove the jack stands and lower the vehicle. Tighten the lug nut to 70–100 ft. lbs. and install the hub caps.

YOKE
should be approx. perpendicular to the lever

MAIN ADJUSTING SCREW

CABLE INDIVIDUAL ADJUSTMENT NUT
adjust yoke to correct position

Parking brake cable adjustment—1976–80

PARKING BRAKE SHOE REPLACEMENT

1. Remove the rear ashtray and back off the adjusting screw so that the cable goes slack.
2. Jack up and support the rear end.
3. Remove the wheels.
4. Remove the brake line-to-axle clamp.
5. Remove the caliper retaining bolts and suspend the caliper out of the way.
6. Unbolt and remove the brake drum.
7. Unhook the return springs and remove the shoes.
8. Install in reverse of the above. Adjust the parking brake.

CHASSIS ELECTRICAL

Heater

REMOVAL AND INSTALLATION

STANDARD HEATING SYSTEM

1. Remove the lower radiator hose, open the engine drain plug, and drain the cooling system. Disconnect the negative battery cable.
2. Remove the center panel and the lefthand defroster hose.
3. Lift up the driveshaft tunnel mat, disconnect the front and rear attaching screws of the rear seat heater ducts, and then remove the ducts from the heater.
4. Disconnect the heater control valve and air-mix cables from their shutters.
5. Disconnect and plug the pressure hose at the heater. Also plug the heater pipes to prevent residual coolant from spilling onto the carpet.
6. Remove the attaching screws which secure the left-hand upper bracket to the dashboard and the left-hand lower bracket to the transmission tunnel.
7. Remove the glovebox by unscrewing the four attaching screws, removing the glovebox door stop, and disconnecting the wires from the glovebox courtesy light.

8. Disconnect the defroster and floor heating cables from their levers.
9. Disconnect the fan motor wires at the switch contact plate.
10. Remove the attaching screws which secure the right-hand upper bracket to the dashboard and the right-hand lower bracket to the transmission tunnel.
11. Remove the right-hand defroster hose. Disconnect the hose between the heater and the dashboard circular vents. Lift the heater unit to the right, and then out of the vehicle.
12. Reverse the above procedure to install, taking care to ensure that the air vent rubber seal is properly located, and that the fan motor ground cable is attached to the upper righthand bracket attaching screw.

COMBINATION HEATER— AIR CONDITIONER SYSTEM

— CAUTION —
When working on this system, DO NOT disconnect any refrigerant lines. The refrigerant, R-12, is dangerous when released and can burn your skin. Leave all air conditioning repairs to an air conditioning specialist.

1. Remove the lower radiator hose, open the engine drain plug, and drain the cooling system. Disconnect the negative battery cable.
2. Remove the heater hoses from the heater pipes at the engine side of the firewall. Plug the heater pipes.
3. Remove the evaporator hose brackets from their body mounts and disconnect the dryer from its bracket. Position the dryer as close to the firewall as the evaporator hose permits.
4. Remove the instrument cluster by removing the steering column molded casings, removing the bracket retaining screw and lowering it toward the steering column, removing the four instruments cluster retaining screws, disconnecting the speedometer cable, tilting the speedometer out of its snap fitting, moving the electrical plug contacts, then lifting the cluster out of the vehicle.
5. Remove the air hose between the central unit and the left inner air vent. Remove the hose from the vacuum motor for the left defroster nozzle.

6. Remove the left-side panel from the central unit.
7. Lift up the driveshaft tunnel mat and disconnect the rear seat heater duct from the central unit.
8. Remove the heater pipes from the passenger side of the firewall.
9. Remove the upper and lower attaching screws for the left support leg. Remove the attaching screws which secure the upper bracket to the dashboard and the lower bracket to the transmission tunnel.

NOTE: If the upper bracket screw holes are slotted, the screws need only be slackened a few turns.

10. Remove the right-side panel from the central unit.
11. Remove the glovebox by unscrewing the four attaching screws, removing the glovebox door stop, and disconnecting the glovebox courtesy light wires.
12. Remove the right defroster nozzle, and also the air hose between the central unit and the right inner air vent.
13. Lift up the driveshaft tunnel mat and disconnect the rear seat heater duct from the central unit.
14. Remove the upper and lower attaching screws for the right support leg. Remove the lower attaching screws for the control panel.
15. Disconnect the fan motor wires and the ground wires from the control panel.
16. Disconnect the yellow lead cable from its plug contact.
17. Separate the havles of the vacuum hose connector and disconnect the vacuum tank hose at the connector.
18. Position the control panel as far back on the transmission tunnel as the cables permit.
19. Remove the screws which attach the upper brackets to the firewall and the lower brackets to the transmission tunnel.
20. Remove the thermostat clamp from the central unit, and the two evaporator cover retaining clamps.
21. Without disconnecting any of the refrigerant lines, remove the evaporator from the central unit, placing it on the right-hand side of the firewall.
22. Remove the molded dashboard padding from beneath the glovebox.
23. Remove the retaining clamps for the right outer vent duct, and remove the duct. Pry off the locking retainer for the blower, and remove the turbine. Remove the clamps which retain the blower housing (inner end) to the central unit and remove the housing.
24. Remove the passenger's front seat cushion and lift the central unit forward and onto the floor of the vehicle. Be careful not to place undue stress on the connected refrigerant lines.
25. Reverse the above procedure to install, taking care to ensure that the evaporator pipes and thermostat capillary are enclosed in sealing compound, that the drainage tubes are inserted in the respective

transmission tunnel holes, and that the ground cables are connected.

Blower

REMOVAL AND INSTALLATION

STANDARD HEATING SYSTEM

1. Remove the heater unit as outlined in "Heater Unit Removal and Installation."
2. Place the unit on its side with the control valve facing upward. Remove the spring clips and separate the housing halves.
3. Lift out the old fan motor and replace it with a new unit, making sure that the support leg without the "foot" points to the output for the defroster channel.
4. Assemble the heater housing halves with new spring clips, and seal the joint without clips with soft sealing compound.
5. Install the heater unit as outlined in "Heater Unit Removal and Installation."

COMBINATION HEATER– AIR CONDITIONER SYSTEM

In order to remove the blower motor, both the right and left blower wheels must first be removed. The heater unit does not have to be removed.

1. Disconnect the negative battery cable.
2. Lift the carpet and remove the central unit side panels.
3. Remove the retaining screws for the control panel and move the panel as far back on the transmission tunnel as the electrical cables will permit.
4. Remove the attaching screws for the rear seat heater ducts and disconnect the ducts from the central unit.
5. Remove the instrument cluster as outlined in "Instrument Cluster Removal and Installation."
6. Remove the glovebox by unscrewing the four attaching screws, removing the glovebox door stop, and disconnecting the wires from the glovebox courtesy light. Remove the molded dashboard padding from beneath the glovebox.
7. Disconnect the vacuum hoses to the left and right defroster nozzle vacuum motors, then remove the nozzles and the left and right air ducts.
8. Remove the air hoses between the left and right inside air vents.
9. Remove the clamps on the central unit outer ends, and remove the ends.
10. Pry off the locking retainer for the turbines (blower wheels), and remove both left and right blower wheels.
11. Position the heater control valve capillary tube to one side.
12. Remove the left inner end (blower housing) from the central unit.
13. Unscrew the three retaining screws and remove the fan motor retainer.

14. Disconnect the plug contact from the fan motor control panel. Release the tabs of electric cables from the plug contact, and, removing the rubber grommet, pull the electrical cables down through the central unit right opening.
15. Remove the fan motor from the left opening.
16. Reverse the above procedure to install.

Heater Core

REMOVAL AND INSTALLATION

STANDARD HEATING SYSTEM

1. Remove the heater unit as outlined in "Heater Unit Removal and Installation."
2. Place the unit on its side with the control valve facing upward. Remove the spring clips and separate the housing halves.
3. Disconnect the capillary tube from the heater core and then lift out the core.
4. Reverse the above procedure to install, being careful to transfer the foam plastic packing to the new heater core, and to install the fragile capillary tube carefully on the core.

COMBINATION HEATER– AIR CONDITIONER SYSTEM

——————— **CAUTION** ———————
Do not disconnect the refrigerant lines from the air conditioning system. These lines carry a dangerous refrigerant, the gas R-12. All air conditioning service should be left to a certified air conditioning specialist.
—————————————————————

1. Remove the combination heater-air conditioner unit as outlined under "Heater Unit Removal and Installation."
2. Remove the left outer end of the central unit. Remove the locking retainer and the turbine (blower wheel).
3. Remove the two retaining screws for the left transmission tunnel bracket.
4. Remove the lockring for the left intake shutter shaft.
5. Remove the three retaining screws and lift off the inner end.
6. Remove the three retaining screws for the fan motor retainer.
7. Disconnect the heater hoses at the heater core.
8. Remove the clamps which retain the central unit halves together, lift off the left half, and remove the heater core.
9. Reverse the above procedure to install, taking care to transfer the foam plastic packing to the new heater core.

Radio

REMOVAL AND INSTALLATION

1. Disconnect the negative battery cable.
2. Remove the radio control knobs by pulling them straight out. Remove the control shaft retaining nuts.
3. Disconnect the speaker wires, the power lead (either at the fuse box or the inline fuse connection), and the antenna cable from its jack on the radio.
4. Remove the hardware which attaches the radio to its mounting (support) bracket(s), and slide it back and down from the dash.
5. Reverse the above procedure to install.

Windshield Wipers

MOTOR REMOVAL AND INSTALLATION

1. Disconnect the negative battery cable.
2. Disconnect the drive link from the wiper motor lever by unsnapping the locking tab underneath the dashboard.
3. Open the hood and disconnect the plug contact from the motor, located on the firewall.
4. Remove the three attaching screws and lift out the motor.
5. Reverse the above procedure to install, taking care to transfer the rubber seal, rubber damper, and spacer sleeves to the new motor.

Installing the cable for the drive link and parallel drive link (left side)—240 series and DL, GL, and GLT

Tailgate Window Wiper

MOTOR REMOVAL AND INSTALLATION

1. Disconnect the negative battery cable.
2. Remove the upholstered finish panel on the inside of the tailgate.
3. Remove the screws which retain the reinforcing bracket beneath the wiper motor.

4. Disconnect the wiper link arm. Bend the reinforcing bracket to one side and lower the wiper motor until it is clear of the bracket.

5. Disconnect the electrical wires from the motor and remove the motor.

6. Reverse the above procedure to install.

Instrument Cluster

REMOVAL AND INSTALLATION

A voltage stabilizer feeds a 10 V current to both the temperature and the fuel gauges. Electrical malfunctions in these gauges must be checked with an ohmmeter, not a 12 V

test light. If malfunctions occur simultaneously in all three of the gauges that are fed by the stabilizer, the stabilizer itself is probably malfunctioning. When replacing the voltage stabilizer, the new unit must fit in the same position as the old one. If the stabilizer is not located correctly in the dash, the voltage output may be altered.

1. Disconnect the negative battery cable.

2. Remove the molded plastic casings from the steering column.

3. Remove the bracket retaining screw and lower the bracket toward the steering column.

4. Remove the cluster attaching screws.

5. Disconnect the speedometer cable.

6. Tilt the cluster out of its snap fitting and disconnect the plug contact. On vehi-

cles equipped with a tachometer, disconnect the tachometer sending wire.

7. Lift the cluster out of the dashboard.

8. Reverse the above procedure to install.

Fuses

On 240, 260 series (all DL, GL, GLE, GLT and Coupe models), the fuse box is located beneath a protective cover, below the dashboard, in front of the driver's door.

On electronic fuel-injected models, an additional fuse box is located in the engine compartment on the left wheel well. It houses a single fuse protecting the electrical fuel pump.

Unit Repair Section

Tools and Equipment

The service procedures in this book presuppose a familiarity with hand tools and their proper use. However, it is possible that you may have a limited amount of experience with the sort of equipment needed to work on an automobile. This section is designed to help you assemble a basic set of tools that will handle the majority of jobs you may undertake.

In addition to the normal assortment of screwdrivers and pliers, automotive service work requires an investment in wrenches, sockets and the handles needed to drive them, and various measuring tools such as torque wrenches and feeler gauges.

The best approach to gathering the required equipment is to proceed slowly, buying high-quality tools as they are needed. An initial investment should be made in a set of quality wrenches, ranging in size from ¼ inch to one inch, if your car has standard bolts, or from 5 mm to 19 mm if your car has metric fasteners. High quality forged wrenches are available in three styles: open end, box end, and combination open/box end. The combination tools are generally the most desirable as a starter set; the wrenches shown in the illustration are of the combination type.

The other set of tools inevitably required is a ratchet handle and socket set. This set should have the same size range as your wrench set. The ratchet, extension, and flex drives for the sockets are available in many sizes; it is advisable to choose a ⅜ inch drive set initially. One break in the inch/metric sizing war is that metric-sized sockets sold in the U.S. have inch-sized drive (¼, ⅜, ½, etc.). Sockets are available in six and twelve point versions; six point types are generally cheaper and are a good choice for a first set. The choice of a drive handle for the sockets should be made with some care. If this is your first set, take the plunge and invest in a flex-head ratchet; it will get into many places otherwise accessible only through a long chain of universal joints,

extensions and adapters. An alternative is a flex handle; such a tool is shown in the illustration, below the ratchet handle. In addition to the range of sockets mentioned, a rubber-lined spark plug socket should be purchased. Spark plugs have either a ¹³⁄₁₆ or a ⅝ inch hex; get the correct socket for the plugs in your car.

The most important thing to consider when purchasing hand tools is quality. Don't be misled by the low cost of ''bargain'' tools. Forged wrenches, tempered screwdriver blades, and fine tooth ratchets are a much better investment than their less expensive counterparts. The skinned knuckles and frustration inflicted by poor quality tools make any job an unhappy chore. Another consideration is that quality tools sold by reputable firms come with an on-the-spot replacement guarantee—if the tool breaks, you get a new one, no questions asked.

The tools needed for basic maintenance jobs, in addition to those just mentioned, include:

1. Jackstands, for support
2. Oil filter wrench
3. Oil filler spout or funnel
4. Grease gun
5. Battery hydrometer
6. Battery post and clamp cleaner
7. Container for draining oil
8. Lots of rags for the inevitable spills

In addition to these items there are several others which are not absolutely necessary, but handy to have around. These include a transmission funnel and filler tube, a drop (trouble) light on a long cord, an adjustable wrench (crescent wrench), and slip joint pliers.

A more extensive list of tools, suitable for tune-up work, can be drawn up easily. While the tools involved are slightly more sophisticated, they need not be outrageously expensive. For example, there are several inexpensive tach/dwell meters on the market that are every bit as good for the average mechanic as a $100.00 profes-

sional model. The key to these purchases is to make them with an eye towards adaptability and wide range. Using the tach/dwell meter example again, if the model you buy runs up to at least 1,500 rpm on the tachometer scale, the dwell meter works on 4, 6, or 8 cylinder engines, and the tachometer unit is adaptable to both conventional and electronic ignitions, it will serve for a long time on a variety of automobiles. A basic list of tune-up tools could include:

1. A tach/dwell meter
2. Spark plug gauge and gapping tool
3. Feeler blades
4. Timing light

In this list, the choice of a timing light should be made carefully. A light which works on the DC current supplied by the car battery is the best choice; it should have a xenon tube for brightness. If your car has electronic ignition, the light should have an inductive pick-up (the timing light illustrated has one of these), and since nearly all cars will have electronic ignition in the future, this feature is a reasonable one to look for.

In addition to these basic tools, there are several other tools and gauges you may find useful. These include:

1. A compression gauge. The screw-in type is slower to use, but eliminates the possibility of a faulty reading due to escaping pressure.
2. A manifold vacuum gauge
3. A test light
4. An induction meter. This is used to determine whether or not there is current flowing in a wire, and thus is extremely helpful in electrical troubleshooting.

Finally, you will probably find a torque wrench necessary for all but the most basic of work. The beam type models are perfectly adequate, although the newer click (breakaway) type are more precise. Whichever type you choose, plan on having it recalibrated every once in a while.

WIRE TYPE FEELER GAUGES

FLAT TYPE FEELER GAUGES

TORQUE WRENCH (BEAM TYPE)

JACKSTAND

TIMING LIGHT (WITH INDUCTIVE PICKUP)

VACUUM GAUGE

COMPRESSION GAUGE

DWELL TACHOMETER

A basic tool collection will handle almost any automotive repair work

SERVICING YOUR CAR SAFELY

It is virtually impossible to anticipate all of the hazards involved with automotive maintenance and service, but care and common sense will prevent most accidents.

The rules of safety for mechanics range from ''don't smoke around gasoline,'' to ''use the proper tool for the job.'' The trick to avoiding injuries is to develop safe work habits and take every possible precaution.

DO'S

●DO keep a fire extinguisher and first aid kit within easy reach.

●DO wear safety glasses or goggles when cutting, drilling, grinding, or prying, even if you have 20-20 vision. If you wear glasses for the sake of vision, they should be made of hardened glass that can serve also as safety glasses, or wear safety goggles over your regular glasses.

●DO shield your eyes whenever you work around the battery. Batteries contain sulphuric acid. In case of contact with the eyes or skin, flush the area with water or a mixture of water and baking soda and get medical attention immediately.

●DO use safety stands for any undercar service. Jacks are for raising vehicles; safety stands are for making sure the vehicle stays raised until you want it to come down. Whenever the car is raised, block the wheels remaining on the ground and set the parking brake.

Always support the car securely with jackstands; never use cinder blocks, tire changing jacks or the like

●DO use adequate ventilation when working with any chemicals or hazardous materials. Follow the manufacturer's directions for usage. Brake fluid, anti-freeze, solvents, paints, etc. are all deadly poisons if taken internally. Seal the containers tightly after use and store them safely, out of the reach of children.

●DO use caution when working on clutches or brakes. The asbestos used in the friction material will cause lung cancer if inhaled. Wipe the component with a damp rag to remove dust, and dispose of the rag after use.

●DO disconnect the negative battery cable when working on the electrical system. The secondary ignition system can contain up to 40,000 volts.

●DO properly maintain your tools. Loose hammerheads, mushroomed punches and chisels, frayed or poorly grounded electrical cords, excessively worn screwdrivers, spread open-end wrenches, cracked sockets, slipping ratchets, or faulty droplight sockets can cause accidents.

●DO use the proper size and type of tool for the job being done.

●DO when possible, pull on a wrench handle rather than push on it, and adjust your stance to prevent a fall.

●DO be sure that adjustable wrenches are tightly closed on the nut or bolt and pulled so that the face is on the side of the fixed jaw.

●DO select a wrench or socket that fits the nut or bolt. The wrench or socket should sit straight, not cocked.

●DO strike squarely with a hammer; avoid glancing blows.

●DO set the parking brake and block the drive wheels if the work requires the engine running.

DONT'S

●DON'T run an engine in a garage or anywhere else without proper ventilation— EVER! Carbon monoxide is poisonous; it takes a long time to leave the human body and you can build up a deadly supply of it in your system by simply breathing in a little every day. You may not realize you are slowly poisoning yourself. Always use power vents, windows, fans or open the garage doors.

●DON'T work around moving parts while wearing a necktie or other loose clothing. Short sleeves are much safer than long, loose sleeves; hard-toed shoes with neoprene soles protect your toes and give a better grip on slippery surfaces. Jewelry such as watches, fancy belt buckles, beads or body adornment of any kind is not safe working around a car. Long hair should be hidden under a hat or cap.

●DON'T use pockets for toolboxes. A fall or bump can drive a screwdriver deep into your body. Even a wiping cloth hanging from the back pocket can wrap around a spinning shaft or fan.

●DON'T smoke when working around gasoline, cleaning solvent or other flammable material.

●DON'T smoke when working around the battery. When the battery is being charged, it gives off explosive hydrogen gas.

●DON'T use gasoline to wash your hands; there are excellent soaps available. Gasoline may contain lead, and lead can enter the body through a cut, accumulating in the body until you are very ill. Gasoline also removes all the natural oils from the skin so that bone dry hands will suck up oil and grease.

●DON'T service the air conditioning system unless you are equipped with the necessary tools and training. The refrigerant, R-12, is extremely cold when compressed, and when released into the air will instantly freeze any surface it contacts, including your eyes. Although the refrigerant is normally non-toxic, R-12 becomes a deadly poisonous gas in the presence of an open flame. One good whiff of the vapors from burning refrigerant can be fatal.

Basic Maintenance

INTRODUCTION

Routine maintenance is probably the most important part of automobile care and the easiest to neglect. A regular program aimed at monitoring essential systems ensures that all components are in good and safe working order, and can prevent small problems from developing into major headaches. Routine maintenance also pays big dividends in keeping major repair costs at a minimum and extending the life of the car.

The owner's manual that came with your car includes a maintenance schedule, indicating service intervals in numbers of months or thousand of miles. This schedule should always be followed. We have provided, in each section, a guide to service intervals based on an averaging of manufacturer's recommendations. In most cases, the suggested interval offered here will be close to that given by the manufacturer of your car, but the manufacturer's schedule should always take precedence.

We have divided the maintenance work to be done into three categories: Under Hood, Under Car, and Exterior. The checks in each section require only a few minutes of attention every few weeks; the services to be performed can be easily accomplished in a morning. The most important part of any maintenance program is regularity. The few minutes or occasional morning spent on these seemingly trivial tasks will forestall or eliminate major problems later.

UNDER HOOD
Automatic Transmission, Automatic Transaxle

The fluid level in the automatic transmission or transaxle should be checked every three months or 6000 miles. All automatic transmissions have a dipstick for fluid level checks.

1. Drive the car until it is at normal operating temperature. The level should not be checked immediately after the car has been driven for a long time at high speed, or in city traffic in hot weather; in those cases, the transmission should be given a half hour to cool down.

2. Stop the car, apply the parking brake, then shift slowly through all gear positions, ending in Park. Leave the engine running.

3. Remove the dipstick, wipe it clean, then reinsert it, pushing it fully home.

4. Pull the dipstick again and, holding it horizontally, read the fluid level.

5. Cautiously feel the end of the dipstick to determine the temperature. Most dipsticks are marked with both cool and hot levels. If the fluid is not up to the correct level, more will have to be added.

6. Fluid is added through the dipstick tube. You will probably need the aid of a spout or a long-necked funnel. Be sure that whatever you pour through is perfectly clean and dry. Fluid recommendations can be found in the owner's manual.

Add fluid slowly, and in small amounts, checking the level frequently between additions. Do not overfill, which will cause foaming, fluid loss, slippage, and possible transmission damage.

Check the automatic transmission fluid level with the dipstick provided

Fill the automatic transmission through the dipstick tube

Battery

FLUID LEVEL (EXCEPT "MAINTENANCE FREE" BATTERIES)

Check the battery electrolyte level at least once a month, or more often in hot weather or during periods of extended car operation. The level can be checked through the case on translucent polypropylene batteries; the cell caps must be removed on other models. The electrolyte level in each cell should be kept filled to the split ring inside, or the line marked on the outside of the case.

If the level is low, add only distilled water, or colorless, odorless drinking water, through

Fill the battery cell to the bottom of the split ring

the opening until the level is correct. Each cell is completely separate from the others, so each must be checked and filled individually.

If water is added in freezing weather, the car should be driven several miles to allow the water to mix with the electrolyte. Otherwise, the battery could freeze.

SPECIFIC GRAVITY (EXCEPT "MAINTENANCE FREE" BATTERIES)

While not technically exact, a practical measurement of the chemical condition of the battery is indicated by measuring the specific gravity of the acid (electrolyte) contained in each cell. The electrolyte in a fully charged battery is usually between 1.260 and 1.280 times as heavy as pure water at the same temperature (80°F). Variations in the specific gravity readings for a fully charged battery may differ. Therefore, it is most important that all battery cells produce an equal reading.

As a battery discharges, a chemical change takes place within each cell. The sulfate factor of the electrolyte combines chemically with the battery plates, reducing the weight of the electrolyte. A reading of the specific gravity of the acid, or electrolyte, of any partially charged battery, will therefore be less than that taken in a fully charged one.

The hydrometer is the instrument used for determining the specific gravity of liquids. The battery hydrometer is readily available from many sources, including local auto replacement parts stores. The following chart gives an indication of specific gravity value, related to battery charge condition. If, after charging, the specific gravity between any two cells varies more than 50 points (.050), the battery is probably bad.

Specific Gravity Reading	Charged Condition
1.260–1.280	Fully charged
1.230–1.250	Three-quarter charged
1.200–1.220	One-half charged
1.170–1.190	One-quarter charged
1.140–1.160	Just about flat
1.110–1.130	All the way down

CABLES AND CLAMPS

Once a year, the battery terminals and the cable clamps should be cleaned. Loosen the clamps and remove the cables, negative cable first. On batteries with posts on top, the use of a puller specially made for the purpose is recommended. These are inexpensive, and available in auto parts stores. Side terminal battery cables are secured with a bolt.

Use a puller to remove the clamp on post-type batteries

Clean the cable clamps and the battery terminal with a wire brush until all corrosion, grease, etc. is removed and the metal is shiny. It is especially important to clean the inside of the clamp thoroughly, since a small deposit of foreign material or oxidation there will prevent a sound electrical connection and inhibit either starting or charging. Special tools are available for cleaning these parts, one type for conventional batteries and another type for side terminal batteries.

Before installing the cables, loosen the battery hold-down clamp or strap, remove the battery and check the battery tray. Clear it of any debris, and check it for soundness. Rust should be wire brushed away, and the metal given a coat of anti-rust paint. Replace the battery and tighten the hold-down clamp or strap securely, but be careful not to overtighten, which will crack the battery case.

Clean the clamp with a wire brush

The posts are easily cleaned with a wire brush, or the battery post tool shown

After the clamps and terminals are clean, reinstall the cables, negative cable last; do not hammer on the clamps to install. Tighten the clamps securely, but do not distort them. Give the clamps and terminals a thin external coat of grease after installation, to retard corrosion.

Check the cables at the same time that the terminals are cleaned. If the cable insulation is cracked or broken, or if the ends are frayed, the cable should be replaced with a new cable of the same length and gauge.

NOTE: Keep flame or sparks away from the battery; it gives off explosive hydrogen gas. Battery electrolyte contains sulphuric acid. If you should splash any on your skin or in your eyes, flush the affected area with plenty of clear water; if it lands in your eyes, get medical help immediately.

Testing battery specific gravity

Check the belts for wear

To either adjust or remove a belt, loosen the driven component's adjusting bolt

A special tool is required to clean the terminals and clamps on side terminal batteries

Brake Fluid

Once a month, the fluid level in the brake master cylinder should be checked.

1. Park the car on a level surface.

2. Clean off the master cylinder cover before removal. Some covers are retained by a bolt. Some of the newer master cylinders with plastic reservoirs have screw caps. Remove the cover, being careful not to drop or tear the rubber diaphragm which will probably be underneath. Be careful also not to drip any brake fluid on painted surfaces, as it eats paint.

NOTE: Brake fluid absorbs moisture from the air, which reduces effectiveness and will corrode brake parts once in the system. Never leave the master cylinder or the brake fluid container uncovered for any longer than necessary.

3. The fluid level should be about ¼ inch below the lip of the master cylinder well.

4. If fluid addition is necessary, use only extra heavy duty disc brake fluid meeting DOT 3 or DOT 4 specifications. The fluid should be reasonably fresh, because brake fluid deteriorates with age.

5. Replace the cover, making sure that the diaphragm is correctly seated.

If the brake fluid is constantly low, the system should be checked for leaks. However, it is normal for the fluid level to fall gradually as the disc brake pads wear; expect the fluid level to drop about ⅛ inch for every 10,000 miles of wear.

Belt Tension

Every six months or 12,000 miles, check

the water pump, alternator, power steering pump, air pump, and air conditioning compressor drive belts for proper tension. Also look for signs of wear, fraying, separation, glazing and so on, and replace the belts as required.

Belt tension should be checked with a gauge made for the purpose. If a gauge is not available, tension can be checked with moderate thumb pressure applied to the belt at its longest span midway between pulleys. If the belt has a free span less than twelve inches, it should deflect approximately ⅛–¼ inch. If the span is longer than twelve inches, deflection can range between ⅛ and ⅜ inches.

Check the belt tension at the middle of the longest span between pulleys

To adjust or replace belts:

1. Loosen the driven accessory's pivot and mounting bolts. Some air conditioning compressor belts are tensioned by an idler pulley; in this case, loosen the idler pulley and use a ½ in. drive ratchet in the square hole provided to lever the idler pulley up or down.

2. Move the accessory toward or away from the engine until the tension is correct. You can use a wooden hammer handle or broomstick as a lever, but do not use anything metallic.

3. Tighten the bolts and recheck the tension. If new bolts have been installed, run the engine for a few minutes, then recheck and readjust as necessary.

Push the component toward the engine to remove the belt

Pull outwards on the component to tension the belt, then tighten the bolts; recheck the belt tension after tightening

Slip the replacement belt over the pulley

NOTE: If the driven component has two drive belts, the belts should be replaced in pairs to maintain proper tension.

It is better to have belts too loose than too tight, because overtight belts will lead to bearing failure, particularly in the water pump and alternator. However, loose belts place an extremely high impact load on the driven components due to the whipping action of the belt.

Carburetor and Choke Linkage

Every 12 months or 6000 miles, examine the carburetor linkage and choke plate for free movement. The choke plate action can generally be freed, if necessary, with the application of a solvent made for the purpose to the ends of the choke shaft. This solvent will also clean grease and dirt from the throttle linkage.

Use a spray solvent on the choke shaft, but do not apply any lubricants

Cooling System

Once a month, the engine coolant level should be checked. On cars without a cool-

ant recovery system, this should only be done when the engine is cold. Remove the radiator cap; the coolant level should be about one inch below the radiator filler neck.

── CAUTION ──

To avoid injury when working with a hot engine, cover the radiator cap with a thick cloth. Wear a heavy glove to protect your hand. Turn the radiator cap slowly to the first stop, and allow all the pressure to vent (indicated when the hissing noise stops). When the pressure has been released, remove the cap the rest of the way.

COLD FILL

HOT LEVEL
COLD LEVEL

Fill level mark on crossflow radiator.

Hot and cold level fill marks, constant-full system.

Proper coolant level is about one inch below the radiator neck, or between the lines on the recovery tank

On cars with a coolant recovery tank, coolant should be visible within the tank; as long as the coolant is between the markings on the tank, the level is correct.

If coolant is needed, a 50/50 mix of ethylene glycol-based antifreeze and water should always be used, both winter and summer. This is imperative on cars with air conditioning; without the antifreeze, the heater core could freeze when the air conditioning is used. Add coolant to the radiator if the car does not have a coolant recovery system. Add coolant to the recovery tank on cars so equipped.

The radiator hoses and clamps and the radiator cap should be checked at the same time as the coolant level. Hoses which are brittle, cracked, or swollen should be replaced. Clamps should be checked for tightness (screwdriver tight only—do not allow the clamp to cut into the hose or crush the fitting). The radiator cap gasket should

GASKET

SEAL

Check the radiator cap gasket and sealing surface

be checked for any obvious tears, cracks or swelling, or any signs of incorrect seating in the radiator neck.

The cooling system should be drained, flushed and refilled after the first 24 months or 24,000 miles, and every year thereafter.

1. Drain the radiator by opening the drain cock at the bottom. Some radiators do not have these; the lower radiator hose must be disconnected at the radiator instead. If the engine block has drain plugs, they should be opened to speed draining.

2. Close the drain cocks and fill the system with clear water. A cooling system flushing additive can be used, if desired.

3. Run the engine until it is hot. The heater should be turned on to its maximum heat position so that the core is flushed out.

4. Drain the system, then flush with water until it runs clear.

5. Clean out the coolant recovery tank, if equipped.

6. Fill the system with a 50/50 mix of ethylene glycol-based antifreeze and water. Fill the coolant recovery tank midway between the marks with this mixture also.

7. Run the engine until it is hot, then let it cool and top up the radiator or coolant recovery tank as necessary with the antifreeze/water mixture.

Heat Riser

The heat riser is a thermostatically or vacuum operated valve in the exhaust manifold (not all cars have one). It closes when the engine is warming up, in order to preheat the incoming fuel/air mixture. If it sticks open, the result will be frequent stalling during warmup, especially in cold and damp weather. If it sticks shut, the result will be a rough idle after the engine is warm.

POWER ACTUATOR

ACTUATOR ROD

BRACKET

EXHAUST HEAT VALVE

EXHAUST PIPE

Exploded view of a vacuum-operated heat riser

The heat riser should move freely. It can be checked easily when the engine is cold by giving the counterweight on the valve shaft a twirl, or pulling the vacuum rod to open and shut the valve. If the valve is sticking or binding, a quick shot of solvent made for the purpose will free it up. This solvent should be applied every six months or 6000 miles to keep the valve free. If the valve is still stuck after application of the solvent, sometimes rapping the end of the

Thermostatically-operated heat control valve

shaft lightly with a hammer will break it loose. Otherwise, the components will have to be removed for further repairs.

Ignition Cables

The ignition system (points, condenser, rotor, spark plugs, etc.) receives regular attention in the form of a tune-up, and thus is not covered here. But one of the most commonly overlooked components is the ignition cable, or spark plug wire.

Inspect the ignition cables for cracks or breaks in the insulation

Although they rarely show any visible signs of deterioration, the ignition cables should be checked at every tune-up, and replaced at least every 50,000 miles. Cracking and embrittlement are of course obvious signs of wear, but most newer ca-

Test the ignition cables with an ohmmeter. Conventional ignition cables should be removed from the distributor cap, but electronic ignition wires should first be tested through the cap

bles have silicone insulation and thus are not prone to display these conditions.

The most reliable way to check the cables is with an ohmmeter. On conventional ignitions, the resistance should be less than 7,000 ohms per foot (wire removed). On cars with electronic ignitions, it is generally recommended to leave the wire attached to the distributor cap; test with one lead from the ohmmeter connected to the corresponding terminal in the distributor cap, the other lead touched to the disconnected end of the cable at the spark plug. Then, if resistance seems close to the limit, remove the wire from the cap and retest. In general, the spark plug wires on electronic ignitions should be replaced if the total resistance is over 36,000 ohms.

Always replace the cables with new ones of the same type. Replace the wires one at a time, working from the longest to the shortest.

Oil Level

The engine oil should be checked on a regular basis, ideally at each fuel stop, or once a week. It is best to check when the engine is at operating temperature, but checking the level immediately after shutting off the engine will give a false reading, because all of the oil will not yet have drained back into the crankcase. The car should be parked on a level surface to obtain an accurate reading.

Check the engine oil level with the dipstick

1. Remove the oil dipstick. Wipe it clean, then replace it, seating it firmly.
2. Remove the dipstick again and hold it horizontally to prevent the oil from running. The level should be between the "Add" and "Full" marks on the dipstick. The dipstick may be marked "Add" and "Full," "Add" and "Safe," or may have lines scribed on it; in any case, the oil level should be above the lower marking.
3. If the oil is below the lower mark, enough oil should be added to the engine to raise the level to the upper mark. The markings are usually spaced so that one quart of oil will raise the level from the "Add" mark to the "Full" mark. Oil is added through the capped opening in the valve cover. Only oils labeled SF (gasoline engines) or CC (diesel engines) should be

Add oil through the valve cover

used; select a viscosity that will be compatible with the temperatures expected until the next drain interval.

4. Replace the dipstick, then check the level again after any additions of oil. Be careful not to overfill, which will lead to leakage and seal damage.

Power Steering

The power steering fluid level is usually checked with a dipstick inserted into the pump reservoir. The dipstick may be attached to the reservoir cap, or inserted into a tube on the pump body. The level should be checked at every oil change. On some models, the power steering reservoir is translucent, allowing the level to be checked through the sides of the container without removing the cap. On others, the reservoir is a metal canister with a wingnut-attached

The power steering fluid level on many models is checked by means of a dipstick installed in the reservoir

cap. After the cap is removed, the level is checked with the scribed lines on the inside of the container.

On most models, the fluid level may be checked with the fluid either warm or cold. If checked with the fluid cold, the level will be slightly lower than with the fluid warm. If doubts arise about the specific procedures

Typical power steering dipstick markings

"HOT" MARK

"COLD" MARK

"ADD"

for the car being checked, consult the owner's manual.

1. On all models, with the engine off, remove the dipstick, remove the cap or check the level through the side of the reservoir. If warm, the level should be between the "Hot" and "Cold" marks or even with the scribed line in the reservoir. If the fluid is cold, the level should be slightly lower.

NOTE: On some Volvos and other makes the level should be checked with the engine running. Consult the owner's manual.

2. If the level is low, add power steering fluid until the correct level is reached. Do not overfill the reservoir.

Windshield Washer Fluid

Check the fluid level in the windshield washer tank at every oil level check. The fluid can be mixed in a 50% solution with water, if desired, as long as temperatures remain above freezing. Below freezing, the fluid should be used full strength. Never add engine coolant antifreeze to the washer fluid, because it will damage the car's paint.

UNDER CAR

Axle

The fluid level in the rear axle should be checked every 12 months or 12,000 miles.

1. With the car parked on a level surface, remove the filler plug. The plug can be found either in the rear cover of the differential, or on the front of the pinion housing.

2. If lubricant trickles out when the plug is removed, the level is correct. If not, stick your finger in the hole (watch out for sharp threads); the fluid level should be even with edge of the filler hole.

3. If lubricant is needed, use SAE 80W-90 GL-5 gear oil (SAE 80W GL-5 in very cold climates) to fill standard axles. Limited

FILLER PLUG

Rear axle filler plug locations

slip axles require a special lubricant, available in auto parts stores.

4. When the level is correct, install the plug and tighten until snug. Do not overtighten.

Standard axles should be drained and refilled with fresh lubricant every 15,000 miles when the car is used to pull a trailer. Limited slip axles should be drained and refilled at the first 7500 miles; the limited slip lubricant should be changed every 7500 miles when the car is used for trailer pulling. The axle may be drained by removing the drain plug at the bottom of the differential housing, if present. Otherwise, the rear cover must be removed, or a suction gun used through the filler hole. When installing a rear cover which does not use a gasket,

SEALANT

Apply a bead of silicone sealer to the rear cover if no gasket is used

apply a thin bead of silicone sealer to the cover, running the bead around the inside of the bolt holes. Install the cover, then tighten the bolts a few turns at a time in a crisscross pattern.

NOTE: On many later models, the rear axle is filled for life and fluid does not have to be replaced.

Exhaust System

The exhaust system should be checked twice a year for general soundness. Inspect the pipes for holes, broken welds, leaking seams, or loose connections. Leaks at connections can sometimes be successfully repaired with the use of a commercial exhaust pipe sealer, but holes or breaks warrant replacement of the part. The exhaust pipe hangers and straps should be examined for any breaks or cracks; replace these as necessary. Some slight cracking of rubber hangers is normal, but deep cracks or cuts are cause for replacement.

CAUTION
Check the exhaust system only when it is cold. The temperature on an exhaust system using a catalytic converter can reach 1000°F after only a short period of engine operation.

Manual Transmission, Manual Transaxle

The fluid level in the manual transmission (or transaxle on front wheel drive cars) should be checked twice a year, or every 6000 miles.

1. Park the car on a level surface. The transmission should be cool to the touch.

2. Remove the filler plug from the side of the transmission or transaxle. If lubricant trickles out as the plug is removed, the fluid level is correct. If not, stick your finger into

FILL PLUG

MANUAL TRANSMISSION
FILL TO BOTTOM OF FILLER HOLE WITH VEHICLE ON LEVEL GROUND.

Typical manual transmission filler plug location

the hole (watch out for sharp threads); the lubricant should be right up to the edge of the filler hole.

3. If lubricant is needed, consult the owner's manual for the correct weight and type of fluid.

Lubricate the parking brake cable with white waterproof grease

NOTE: Some manual transmission/transaxle assemblies are filled with automatic transmission fluid rather than gear oil. Consult the owner's manual for lubricant information.

4. When the level is correct, install the filler plug and tighten until snug.

Parking Brake Linkage

The parking brake cable assembly should be inspected twice a year for fraying, kinks, and binding. A smooth white waterproof lubricant should be applied at the same time to all pivot points and areas in sliding contact.

Suspension Lubrication

Depending on the year of manufacture, there may be as many as twelve grease fittings on the suspension parts, or as few as two. Typical locations for grease nipples are on the ball joints, control arm pivot points, steering linkage, and the tie rod ends.

Lubricate these fittings with a small hand operated grease gun filled with EP chassis lubricant. Pump grease into the fitting slowly, until it begins to ooze out around the joint, or until the grease begins to expand the rubber boot around the fitting. Be extremely careful not to rupture any seals or boots, as this will lead to lubricant loss and contamination of the parts involved.

Occasionally, the grease nipples may become clogged with dirt or hardened grease. If so, unscrew them with a wrench of the proper size and clean them out with solvent. When reinstalled, they may be covered with plastic caps made for the purpose, or a piece of aluminum foil.

The chassis and suspension parts should be lubricated once a year, or every 7500 miles, whichever comes first.

Transfer Case

The transfer case on the four wheel drive Subaru shares a common lubricant supply with the transmission, therefore the transfer case lubricant supply does not have to be checked separately.

EXTERIOR

Drain Holes and Underbody

Most cars have drain holes spaced along the lower edge of the rocker panels and doors. These holes should be cleared of any debris or rust twice a year. A small screwdriver can be used to open plugged drain holes.

Use engine oil to lubricate the door, hood, and trunk hinges

Every spring, the underbody should be flushed with clear water to remove deposits of mud, road salt, and debris. It is advisable to loosen any packed-in sediment before flushing to assure a more thorough cleaning.

Hinges and Locks

Once a year, the door, hood, and trunk hinges, and all locks should be lubricated to ensure smooth operation. The hinge points should be lightly oiled. Lock cylinders may be easily lubricated with a shot of silicone spray directed into the keyhole. Silicone lubricant also works well on the door latch mechanisms, and keeps the door, trunk, and window weatherseals pliable when applied in a light film.

Tires

Tires should be checked weekly for proper air pressure. A chart, located either in the glove compartment or on the driver's or passenger's door, gives the recommended inflation pressures. Maximum fuel economy and tire life will result if the pressure is maintained at the highest figure given on the chart. Pressures should be checked before driving since pressure can increase as

Tire tread depth can be checked with a penny. If the top of Lincoln's head is visible, the tires are due for replacement

much as six pounds per square inch (psi) due to heat buildup. It is a good idea to have your own accurate pressure gauge, because not all gauges on service station air pumps can be trusted. When checking pressures, do not neglect the spare tire. Note that some spare tires require pressures considerably higher than those used in the other tires.

While you are about the task of checking air pressure, inspect the tire treads for cuts, bruises and other damage. Check the air valves to be sure that they are tight. Replace any missing valve caps.

Check the tires for uneven wear that might indicate the need for front end alignment or tire rotation. Tires should be replaced when a tread wear indicator appears as a solid band across the tread.

Tread wear indicators will appear as a band across the tire when the tread has worn out.

When buying new tires, give some thought to the following points, especially if you are considering a switch to larger tires or a different profile series:

1. All four tires must be of the same construction type. This rule cannot be violated. Radial, bias, and bias-belted tires must not be mixed.

2. The wheels should be the correct width for the tire. Tire dealers have charts of tire and rim compatibility. A mismatch will cause sloppy handling and rapid tire wear. The tread width should match the rim width (inside bead to inside bead) within an inch. For radial tires, the rim width should be 80% or less of the tire (not tread) width.

3. The height (mounted diameter) of the new tires can change speedometer accuracy, engine speed at a given road speed, fuel mileage, acceleration, and ground clearance. Tire manufacturers furnish full measurement specifications.

4. The spare tire should be usable, at least for short distance and low speed operation, with the new tires.

5. There shouldn't be any body interference when loaded, on bumps, or in turns.

TIRE ROTATION

Tire rotation is recommended every 6000 miles or so, to obtain maximum tire wear. The pattern you use depends on whether or not your car has a usable spare. Radial tires should not be cross-switched (from one side of the car to the other); they last longer if their direction of rotation is not changed. Snow tires sometimes have directional arrows molded onto the side of their carcass; the arrow shows the direction of rotation. They will wear very rapidly if the rotation is reversed. Studded tires will lose their studs if their rotational direction is reversed.

NOTE: Mark the wheel position or direction of rotation on radial tires or studded snow tires before removing them.

STORAGE

Store the tires at proper inflation pressure if they are mounted on wheels. Keep them in a cool dry place, laid on their sides. If the tires are stored in the garage or basement, do not let them stand on a concrete floor; set them on strips of wood.

Windshield Wipers and Washers

For maximum effectiveness, and longest element life, the windshield and wiper blades should be kept clean. Dirt, tree sap, road tar and so on will cause streaking, smearing and blade deterioration if left on the glass. It is advisable to wash the windshield carefully with a commercial glass cleaner at least once a month. Wipe off the rubber blades with the wet rag afterwards. For access to the blades on wiper systems which park below the hood line, turn the ignition key to "On" and run the wipers to the center of the windshield. Shut the wipers off with the ignition key, not the wiper switch. Do not attempt to move the wipers by hand; damage to the motor and drive mechanism will result.

If the blades are found to be cracked, broken or torn, they should be replaced immediately. Replacement intervals will vary with usage, although ozone deterioration usually limits blade life to about one year. If the wiper pattern is smeared or streaked, or if the blade chatters across the glass, the elements should be replaced. It is easiest and most sensible to replace the elements

| BIAS PLY TIRE 4-WHEEL ROTATION | BIAS PLY TIRE 5-WHEEL ROTATION | RADIAL PLY TIRES 4-WHEEL ROTATION | RADIAL PLY TIRES 5-WHEEL ROTATION |

Tire rotation diagrams; note that radials should not be cross-switched

TRICO

BLADE FRAME LEVER

RUBBER BLADE ELEMENT ASSY.

SQUEEZE SIDES OF RETAINER

LEVER JAWS

LATCH LOCK RELEASE

METAL BACKING IS WIDER

HOLD FRAME FROM TWISTING

METAL BACKING STRIP

RETAINING TABS

METAL BACKING STRIP

FRAME

INSERT SCREWDRIVER BEHIND TAB AND PUSH HANDLE DOWN.

ANCO

LATCH-PIN

YOKE JAWS

RUBBER BLADE ELEMENT ASSY.

YOKE JAWS

POLYCARBONATE

UNLOCKED

LOCKED

TRIDON

PLASTIC BACKING STRIP

NOTCH

FRAME

PULL UP & TWIST

PRESSURE DOWN

RUBBER BLADE

RETAINING TABS

16

16.5

FIRM SURFACE

FRAME

THE LENGTH OF THE 16" AND 16.5" TRIDON BLADES ARE MOLDED IN EACH END. REPLACE ONLY WITH IDENTICAL BLADES OR REFILLS.

Windshield wiper blade replacement methods

in pairs.

There are basically three different types of refills, which differ in their method of replacement. One type has two release buttons, approximately one-third of the way up from the ends of the blade frame. Pushing the buttons down releases a lock and allows the rubber filler to be removed from the frame. The new filler slides back into the frame and locks in place.

The second type of refill has two metal tabs which are unlocked by squeezing them together. The rubber filler can then be withdrawn from the frame jaws. A new refill is installed by inserting the refill into the front frame jaws and sliding it rearward to engage the remaining frame jaws. There are usually four jaws; be certain when installing that the refill is engaged in all of them. At the end of its travel, the tabs will lock into place on the front jaws of the wiper blade frame.

The third type is a refill made from polycarbonate. The refill has a simple locking device at one end which flexes downward out of the groove into which the jaws of the holder fit, allowing easy release. By sliding the new refill through all the jaws and pushing through the slight resistance when it reaches the end of its travel, the refill will lock into position.

Regardless of the type of refill used, make sure that all of the frame jaws are engaged as the refill is pushed into place and locked. The metal blade holder and frame will scratch the glass if allowed to touch it.

WASHER NOZZLE ADJUSTMENT

Centered Single Post–Non-Adjustable Nozzles

This type is usually located on the rear center of the hood panel, directly in front of the windshield. By loosening the body retaining nut from under the hood, the nozzle body can be turned to provide the best spray discharge to cover the windshield. Tighten the retaining nut while holding the nozzle in position.

Centered Single Post–Adjustable Nozzles

This nozzle is adjusted with a wrench, screwdriver, or pliers. If the nozzle has no gripping area, the adjustment is made by inserting a stiff wire into the nozzle opening and moving the nozzle in the direction desired. When using the wire as an adjuster tool, do not force the nozzle; the wire can be broken within the nozzle opening.

Individual Nozzles

A tab is usually fastened to the nozzle stem to assist in turning the nozzle in the desired direction. If a tab is not present, use a pair of pliers to gently move the nozzle.

Wiper Arm Nozzles

No adjustment is necessary on this type of nozzle, because the opening is centered on the wiper arm and moves along with the arm.

Diesel Service

NOTE: Most procedures associated with diesel engined cars are similar to gas engined cars, although many parts of the diesel engine are unique compared to their gas engine counterparts. Standard maintenance and service procedures are given here while component removal, installation and adjustment procedures unique to diesel engines can be found in the appropriate car section.

HOW THE DIESEL ENGINE WORKS

Four-stroke diesels require four piston strokes for the complete cycle of actions, exactly like a gasoline engine. The difference lies in how the fuel mixture is ignited. A diesel engine does not rely on a conventional spark ignition to ignite the fuel mixture for the power stroke. Instead, a diesel relies on the heat produced by compressing air in the combustion chamber to ignite the fuel and produce a power stroke. This is known as a compression-ignition engine. No fuel enters the cylinder on the intake stroke, only air. At the end of the compression stroke, fuel is sprayed into the precombustion chamber (prechamber). The mixture ignites and spreads out into the main combustion chamber, forcing the piston downward (power stroke). The fuel/air mixture ignites because of the very high combustion chamber temperatures generated by the extraordinarily high compression ratios used in diesel engines. Typically, the compression ratios used in automotive diesels run any-where from 16:1 to 23:1. A typical spark-ignition engine has a ratio of about 8:1. This is why a spark-ignition engine which continues to run after you have shut off the engine is said to be "dieseling". It is running on combustion chamber heat alone.

Designing an engine to ignite on its own combustion chamber heat poses certain problems. For instance, although a diesel engine has no need for a coil, spark plugs, or a distributor, it does need what are known as "glow plugs". These superficially resemble spark plugs, but are only used to warm the combustion chambers when the engine is cold. Without these plugs, cold starting would be impossible, due to the enormously high compression ratios and the characteristics of the diesel fuel itself.

All diesel engines use fuel injection, be-

4-stroke diesel engine cycle. At *air intake* (1), rotation of the crankshaft drives a toothed belt that turns the camshaft, opening the intake valve. As the piston moves down, a vacuum is created, sucking fresh air into the cylinder, past the open intake valve. *Air compression* (2): As the piston moves up, both valves are closed, and the air is compressed about 23 times smaller than its original volume. The compressed air reaches a temperature of about 1,650°F., far above the temperature needed to ignite diesel fuel. *Fuel injection and compression* (3): As the piston reaches the top of the stroke, the air temperature is at its maximum. A fine mist of fuel is sprayed into the prechamber, where it ignites, and the flame front spreads rapidly into the combustion chamber. The piston is forced downward by the pressure (about 500 psi) of expanding gases. *Exhaust* (4): As the energy of combustion is spent and the piston begins to move upward again, the exhaust valve opens, and burnt gases are forced out past the open valve. As the piston starts down, the exhaust valve closes, the intake valve opens, and the air intake stroke begins again.

Increasingly, modern diesel engines are being equipped with turbochargers, exhaust gas–driven devices that force more air into the engine to increase power output

Maintenance and Service Procedures

Maintenance procedures for the diesel engine generally fall into three categories:
1. Fuel system
2. Starting system
3. Engine mechanical systems

Of these, the fuel system is usually the most likely source of engine troubles, and should be high on the list for regular maintenance attention.

FUEL SYSTEM

The typical diesel engine fuel system consists of fuel tank, fuel feed and return lines, mechanical fuel injection pump, fuel injectors and lines, and a large capacity fuel filter. On some models, the engine may also be equipped with a small, low pressure fuel pump which feeds the injection pump.

In addition to these, the air intake system (air cleaner, inlet manifold) should be checked over regularly to insure unrestricted air flow into the cylinders.

In operation, fuel is sucked out of the fuel tank by the injection pump (or its feed pump) and fed by the injection pump to the injectors in the cylinder head at a very high pressure. Before the fuel is allowed to enter the main injection pump, it passes through a specially built fuel filter which traps solid particles (and water on some models) in the fuel. Fuel that is not used is pumped back to the fuel tank through the fuel return lines. This recirculated fuel helps cool the injection pump.

Air Cleaner

On a gasoline engine, the volume of air taken in by the engine is controlled by throttle valves. When the throttle valves are closed (engine idling), air intake is restricted. When the throttle valves are wide open (accelerator pedal to the floor), the engine draws

cause unlike spark-ignited engines, the fuel cannot be drawn through the intake tract

Cutaway view of typical 4-cylinder diesel engine.

and into the cylinders. The introduction of fuel into a diesel engine must be precisely timed so that each cylinder "fires" at the proper moment. Also, the fuel injection pressure (at the cylinder) must be great enough to overcome the high compression pressures, and properly atomize the fuel without the aid of a moving air mass (as in a carbureted gas engine). It is not uncommon for diesel engine fuel injection pressures to be set at 1500–1700 psi.

Diesel engines share many of their basic mechanical components with gasoline engines, though the cylinder block, head(s), crankshaft, connecting rods, pistons, etc., are manufactured to be much stronger for use in diesel engines. The additional strength of the components is necessary due to the very high cylinder pressure generated within the diesel engine.

Typical diesel engine fuel system schematic

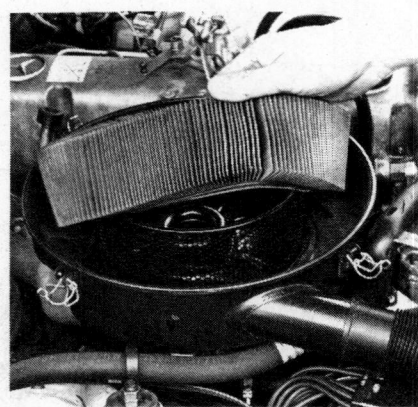

Because a greater quantity of air passes through the diesel engine, air filter maintenance is particularly important. Most diesel air filters on passenger cars are similar to their counterparts on gasoline engines.

in the maximum amount of air it possibly can. This applies to both carbureted and fuel injected gasoline engines.

The speed (rpm) of a diesel engine is controlled by the quantity of fuel which is injected into the engine; no air metering restrictions (throttle valves) are used. Because of this, diesel engines ingest as much air as they possibly can under all conditions. A much greater volume of air passes through the air cleaner of a diesel per mile, therefore, diesel air filters must either be larger or the filter replacement intervals more frequent than those of a similarly sized gasoline engine.

One word of caution: never remove the air cleaner on a diesel with the engine running, and never run the engine with the air cleaner removed. The volume of air drawn through the inlet manifold is very great, and, because the inlet manifold is unobstructed, anything drawn into the inlet manifold (air cleaner wing nut, etc.) goes straight to the combustion chambers, where it can cause major engine damage.

Fuel Filter

The diesel engine fuel filter is usually larger than the filter used on gasoline engines. The extra capacity is needed to trap the suspended particles in diesel fuel, which is generally "dirtier" than gasoline.

Many diesel engines use a spin-on type primary fuel filter.

On some engines, the fuel filter looks like a second engine oil filter, and is removed and installed in the same manner as the canister-type oil filter.

The fuel filter must be changed according to the manufacturer's suggested interval. See the owner's manual for information.

After installing the fuel filter start the engine and check for leaks. Run the engine for about two minutes, then stop the engine for the same amount of time to allow any air trapped in the injection system to bleed off.

Many diesels also have a small, in-tank filter which is usually maintenance-free.

A smaller, in-line secondary filter is used on many engines.

Check the tightness of the clamps securing the injector lines. Note that the injector lines are all the same length.

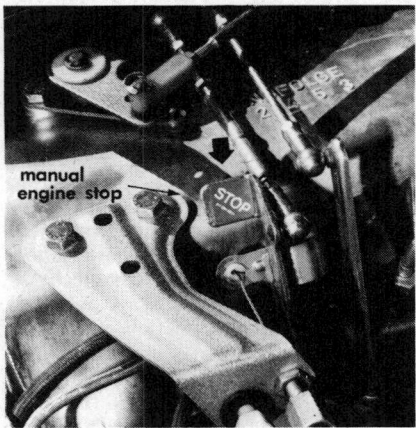

manual engine stop

Mercedes-Benz diesel engines use this stop switch, which shuts off fuel delivery

Water In Fuel

Diesel fuel is a hydrophilic fluid, that is, it naturally attracts water. Since diesel fuel and water do not mix, the water remains floating beneath the fuel at the bottom of the tank. This water must be removed every now and then, or it will be sucked into the fuel circuit and pass through the injection system, causing corrosion and possible component failure (injection pumps can cost up to $1,000). Water in the fuel system will also cause the engine to run poorly, if at all.

Most diesel fuel tanks are equipped with

a separator which can isolate from 1 to 3 gallons of water from the fuel.

Many diesels are also equipped with "Water in Fuel" lights in the dashboard which warn of the presence of water in the fuel tank. These warning systems can be installed on models not so equipped.

On some diesels, there is a water catcher in the bottom of the fuel filter which can easily be bled off. In addition, there are several bolt-on water filters on the market which attach to the fuel line under the hood and separate water from the fuel. Depending on which kind you buy, draining water from the system is simply a matter of opening the petcock at the bottom of the filter and letting the water drain out, or, if money is no object, a separator is available on which water is drained from the filter simply by activating a switch on the dashboard.

REMOVING WATER FROM THE FUEL TANK

Treat diesel fuel with the same respect you would gasoline, and after the procedure, properly dispose of the fuel.

1. Remove the fuel tank cap.
2. Connect a pump or siphon hose to the ¼ in. fuel return hose (smaller of the two fuel hoses) above the rear axle, or under the hood near the fuel pump (on the passenger's side of the engine, near the front).
3. Siphon until all water is removed from the tank. Do not use your mouth to create siphon vacuum, EVER! The best method is to siphon the water into a large capacity see-through container. The water will collect at the bottom of the container.
4. When all water has been removed from the tank, be sure to reinstall the fuel return hose and fuel cap.

NOTE: If the entire fuel system (not just the tank) is contaminated by water, the vehicle must be stopped immediately and the fuel system must be purged. This includes draining and removing the fuel tank, blowing low pressure compressed air backwards through the fuel feed and return lines, and bleeding the water out of all injection components. This job should be referred to a qualified technician.

Cold Weather Fuel System Maintenance

——— CAUTION ———
NEVER use "starting aids" (e.g.—ether) to help start a diesel engine—serious engine damage will result.

As will be explained later under "Fuel Recommendations", diesel fuel tends to become "cloudy", or thicker, as the temperature drops. The thicker the diesel fuel becomes, the slower it flows through the fuel system, until finally it stops flowing altogether somewhere near the bottom of the thermometer.

One way to fight sluggish fuel flow is to use winterized blends of diesel fuel, straight No. 1 diesel fuel or add cold weather additives to the fuel to improve flow in cold weather.

NOTE: Consult your owners manual for recommendations and be sure to use a fuel conditioner compatible with water separators.

Another way is to install an aftermarket fuel system pre-heater. These are generally canisters which connect into the fuel line and use coolant from the engine cooling system to heat the fuel before it reaches the injection pump. The one drawback with this system is the engine must be started before the pre-heater begins to work. Also available are electric fuel warmers. These pre-heat the fuel going into the filter and can be used in conjunction with the coolant-type fuel heater.

Cold weather additives and fuel conditioners can help improve cold weather flow of diesel fuel.

Some manufacturers offer an optional electric diesel fuel heater and engine block heaters. The fuel heater is thermostatically controlled to heat the fuel before it enters the fuel filter when fuel temperature is 20°F or lower. The fuel heater works only when the ignition key is in the RUN position. On these models, the fuel tank filter has a by-pass valve which allows fuel to flow to the heater when the tank filter is covered with fuel wax. The engine block heater is equipped with an electrical cord wrapped up in the engine compartment. The cord

Some diesel engines come equipped with a built-in heating system to keep the engine warm in cold temperatures.
Most OEM heaters work from 110-volt house current.

plugs into regular 110 volt household current. The block heater can be used, according to the type of oil in the crankcase, up to eight hours or overnight to warm up the block.

Some aftermarket diesel fuel warmers are thermostatically controlled heat exchangers that use engine coolant to keep diesel fuel above its "cloud point," the temperature at which it gels and forms wax that can clog a fuel system.

STARTING SYSTEM

The diesel starting system includes one (sometimes two) heavy duty batteries, the starter, and the glow plug circuit. In addition to the heavy duty battery(ies), the majority of diesel engines also have starters and battery cables designed specifically as heavy duty items for diesel usage only. Because of the high compression of any diesel, the torque required to turn the engine is much greater than a gasoline engine. The starter must be powerful enough to handle the increased load; the battery cables must be thick enough to withstand the heat generated by the starter load.

For battery maintenance, see the regular "Maintenance" section. Jump starting procedures for a dual battery car are given below. Starter maintenance is included in the appropriate car section.

The glow plug circuit is used on the diesel to initially start the engine. When the ignition switch is turned to the ON position, a light will come on in the instrument panel signalling that the glow plugs are preheating the combustion chambers. After a certain interval (depending on how cold the engine is), the light will go off. This signals that the starter may be engaged and the engine started. If the glow plug circuit mal-

functions, especially in cold weather, the engine will be almost impossible to start.

— **CAUTION** —
NEVER use "starting aids" (e.g.—ether) to help start a diesel engine—serious engine damage will result.

Glow Plug Testing

To test each individual glow plug, disconnect the busbar and/or wire connector from the glow plug and connect a test light between the glow plug terminal and the positive battery terminal. If the test light lights, the glow plug is working. Replace individual glow plugs which do not work.

NOTE: Some diesel engines are equipped with either "slow glow" or "fast glow" glow plugs. Do not attempt to interchange any parts of these two glow plug systems.

To test the glow plug circuit, connect a test light to the terminal of one of the glow plugs (glow plug wiring still attached) and turn the ignition to the heating position. The test light should light for a short while. If not, the glow plug circuit is malfunctioning and must be diagnosed and repaired.

NOTE: Perform this operation on a cold engine only.

Jump-Starting a Dual Battery Diesel

Some diesels are equipped with two 12 volt batteries. The batteries are connected in parallel circuit (positive terminal to positive terminal, negative terminal to negative terminal). Hooking the batteries up in parallel circuit increases battery cranking power without increasing total battery voltage output (12 volts). On the other hand, hooking two 12 volt batteries up in a series circuit (positive terminal to negative terminal, positive terminal to negative terminal) increases total battery output to 24 volts (12 volts + 12 volts).

— **CAUTION** —
NEVER hook the batteries up in a series circuit; SEVERE electrical system damage will result.

In the event that a dual battery diesel must be jumped started, use the following procedure.
1. Open the hood and locate the batteries.
2. Position the donor car so that the jumper cables will reach from its battery (must be 12 volt, negative ground) to the appropriate battery in the diesel. Do not allow the cars to touch.
3. Shut off all electrical equipment on both vehicles. Turn off the engine of the donor car, set the parking brakes on both vehicles and block the wheels. Also, make sure both vehicles are in Neutral (manual

transmission models) or Park (automatic transmission models).

4. Using the jumper cables, connect the positive (+) terminal of the donor car battery to the positive terminal of one (not both) of the diesel batteries.

5. Using the second jumper cable, connect the negative (−) terminal of the donor battery to a solid, stationary, metallic point on the diesel (alternator bracket, engine block, etc.). Be very careful to keep the jumper cables away from moving parts (cooling fan, alternator belt, etc.) on both vehicles.

6. Start the engine of the donor car and run it at moderate speed.

7. Start the engine of the diesel.

8. When the diesel starts, disconnect the battery cables in the reverse order of attachment.

ENGINE MECHANICAL SYSTEMS

Included are engine lubrication and engine compression.

Although diesel engines are very low in carbon monoxide (CO) and hydrocarbon (HC) emissions, ''particulate'' emission output is very high from diesel engines. This is evident from the black smoke emitted by diesels, which is most noticeable during hard acceleration or high engine loads. The particulates are made up of mostly soot (carbon) and sulpher particles. The majority of these particulates are released into the atmosphere. However, some of the particulate matter, because it is produced within the engines cylinders, is left inside the engine and gradually contaminates the engine oil. This contamination makes the oil corrosive, due to the sulpher, and abrasive, due to the carbon. Serious engine damage will result if these contaminants continue to accumulate in the oil. Engine oil and filters of diesel engines must be changed more frequently than those of gasoline engines, due to the increased rate at which the contaminants form in the diesel. Consult the ''Maintenance'' section for oil and filter change procedures. The manufacturer's recommended oil change interval will be given in the owner's manual. An explanation of diesel engine oils is given at the end of this section.

As explained earlier, very high cylinder compression is the key to the operation of the diesel engine. The normal compression of most gasoline engines will rarely exceed 180 psi; whereas with diesel engines, compression pressures of 350–400 psi are commonplace.

───── CAUTION ─────
DO NOT attempt to check the compression of a diesel engine with a standard compression gauge—personal injury could result. A special, high pressure compression gauge is needed to safely check the compression of any diesel.

A diesel compression tester kit with adaptors for Volvo, Audi and VW cars (upper right) and Mercedes-Benz cars (top center). (Courtesy S & G Tools).

Compression Test

1. Remove the air cleaner.

2. Disconnect the wire from the fuel shutoff solenoid terminal of the injection pump.

3. Disconnect the wires from the glow plugs and remove all glow plugs.

4. Screw compression gauge into the glow plug hole in the cylinder being checked.

5. Crank the engine, allowing six ''puffs'' for each cylinder.

The lowest reading cylinder should not be less than 70% of the highest, and no cylinder should be less than 275 pounds.

Idle Speed Adjustments

Idle speed adjustment procedures for individual diesel engines are given in the car section. Consult the following section for procedures to measure idle speed

Connecting a Tachometer to a Diesel Engine

As mentioned earlier, the diesel engine does not require an electrical ignition system. Because of this, problems arise when attempts are made to connect a tachometer to the engine for the purpose of idle adjustments, etc. The average gasoline engine tachometer senses the ignition spark pulses and converts them into a readable engine rpm signal. This type of tachometer is use-

less on the diesel engine, because of the diesel's compression ignition system.

There are several magnetic and photoelectric tachometers available from various tool manufacturers which were designed specifically for use with the diesel engine. These units can run into a little more money than the average do-it-yourselfer may be willing to spend, in which case any adjustments requiring the monitoring of engine rpm should be performed by a competent service technician.

The newest equipment for measuring idle speed on a diesel engine includes (clockwise from lower left) a digital diesel tach display, photomagnetic pick-up with display input, magnetic swivel base (holder), DC power source for the display unit and a roll of magnetic tape.

The magnetic tape is attached to any moving part (such as the balancer). The pieces of tape must be at least 6 inches apart. Aim the photomagnetic pick-up at the moving object and adjust the position of the pick-up until the "on-target" light is lit. Flip the switch to TACH and read the rpm.

Diesel Engine Precautions

- Never run the engine with the air cleaner removed: if anything is sucked into the inlet manifold it will go straight to the combustion chambers, or jam behind a valve.
- Never wash a diesel engine: the reaction of a warm fuel injection pump to cold (or even warm) water can ruin the pump.
- Never operate a diesel engine with one or more fuel injectors removed unless fully familiar with injector testing procedures: some diesel injection pumps spray fuel at up to 1400 psi—enough pressure to allow the fuel to penetrate your skin.
- Do not skip engine oil and filter changes.
- Strictly follow the manufacturer's oil and fuel recommendations as given in the owner's manual.
- Do not use home heating oil as fuel for your diesel.
- Do not use "starting aids" (e.g.—ether) in the automotive diesel engine, as these "aids" can cause severe internal engine damage.
- Do not run a diesel engine with the "Water in Fuel" warning light on in the dashboard.
- If removing water from the fuel tank yourself, use the same caution you would use when working around gasoline engine fuel components.
- Do not allow diesel fuel to come in contact with rubber hoses or components on the engine, as it can damage them.

Fuel and Oil Recommendations

FUEL

Fuel makers produce two grades of diesel fuel, No. 1 and No. 2, for use in automotive diesel engines. Generally speaking, No. 2 fuel is recommended over No. 1 for driving in temperatures above 20°F. In fact, in many areas, No. 2 diesel is the only fuel available. By comparison, No. 2 diesel fuel is less volatile than No. 1 fuel, and gives better fuel economy. No. 2 fuel is also a better injection pump lubricant.

Two important characteristics of diesel fuel are its cetane number and its viscosity.

The cetane number of a diesel fuel refers to the ease with which a diesel fuel ignites. High cetane numbers mean that the fuel will ignite with relative ease or that it ignites well at low temperatures. Naturally, the lower the cetane number, the higher the temperature must be to ignite the fuel. Most commercial fuels have cetane numbers that range from 35 to 65. No. 1 diesel fuel generally has a higher cetane rating than No. 2 fuel.

Cetane (diesel engine) versus octane (gasoline engine) ratings. The higher the cetane number, the faster the fuel burns

Viscosity is the ability of a liquid, in this case diesel fuel, to flow. Using straight No. 2 diesel fuel below 20°F can cause problems, because this fuel tends to become cloudy, meaning wax crystals begin forming in the fuel. In extreme cold weather, No. 2 fuel can stop flowing altogether. In either case, fuel flow is restricted, which can result in a "no start" condition or poor engine performance. Fuel manufacturers often "winterize" No. 2 diesel fuel by using various fuel additives and blends (No. 1 diesel fuel, kerosene, etc.) to lower its winter-time viscosity. Generally speaking, though, No. 1 diesel fuel is more satisfactory in extremely cold weather.

NOTE: No. 1 and No. 2 diesel fuels will mix and burn with no ill effects, although the engine manufacturer will undoubtedly recommend one or the other. Consult the owner's manual for information.

Depending on local climate, most fuel manufacturers make winterized No. 2 fuel available seasonally.

Many automobile manufacturers publish pamphlets giving the locations of diesel fuel stations nationwide. Contact the local dealer for information.

Do not substitute home heating oil for automotive diesel fuel. While in some cases, home heating oil refinement levels equal those of diesel fuel, many times they are far below diesel engine requirements. The result of using "dirty" home heating oil will be a clogged fuel system, in which case the entire system may have to be dismantled and cleaned.

One more word on diesel fuels. Don't thin diesel fuel with gasoline in cold weather. The lighter gasoline, which is more explosive, will cause rough running at the very least, and may cause extensive engine damage if enough is used.

OIL

Diesel engines require different engine oil from those used in gasoline engines. Besides doing the things gasoline engine oil does, diesel oil must also deal with increased engine heat and the diesel blow-by gases, which create sulphuric acid, a high corrosive.

Under the American Petroleum Institute (API) classifications, gasoline engine oil codes begin with an "S", and diesel engine oil codes begin with a "C". This first letter designation is followed by a second letter code which explains what type of service (heavy, moderate, light) the oil is meant for. For example, the top of a typical oil can will include: "API SERVICES SC, SD, SE, CA, CB, CC". This means the oil in the can is a good, moderate duty engine oil when used in a diesel engine.

It should be noted here that the further

COMPARISON OF #1 AND #2 DIESEL FUEL

Requirement	1-D	2-D
Flash Point, °F minimum	100	125
Cetane Number, minimum	40	40
Viscosity at 100°F, Centistokes		
Minimum	1.4	2.0
Maximum	2.5	4.3
Water and Sediment, % by volume maximum	Trace	0.05
Sulfur, % by weight maximum	0.5	0.5
Ash, % by weight maximum	0.01	0.01

Flash Point: The temperature at which diesel fuel ignites when exposed to a flame *in the open air*.

Cetane Number: See text

down the alphabet the second letter of the API classification is, the greater the oil's protective qualities are (CD is the severest duty diesel engine oil, CA is the lightest duty oil, etc.). The same is true for gasoline engine oil classifications (SF is the severest duty gasoline engine oil, SA is the lightest duty oil, etc.).

Many diesel manufacturers recommend an oil with both gasoline and diesel engine API classifications. Consult the owner's manual for specifications.

The top of the oil can will also contain an SAE (Society of Automotive Engineers) designation, which gives the oil's viscosity. A typical designation will be: SAE 10W-30, which means the oil is a "winter" viscosity oil, meaning it will flow and give protection at low temperatures.

On the diesel engine, oil viscosity is critical, because the diesel is much harder to start (due to its higher compression) than a gasoline engine. Obviously, if you fill the crankcase with a very heavy oil during winter (SAE 20W-50, for example), the starter is going to require a lot of current from the battery to turn the engine. And, since batteries don't function well in cold weather in the first place, you may find yourself stranded some morning. Consult the owner's manual for recommended oil specifications for the climate you live in.

LUBE OIL ANALYSIS

From an oil sample a laboratory can diagnose many potential engine problems—from piston wear to impending bearing failure. What's more, the laboratory can spot them quicker, and with greater accuracy. Just as easily, the lab can give the diesel a clean bill of health, saving the car owner unnecessary servicing and other routine preventive maintenance, costly in time and money.

There's nothing new about engine lube oil analysis. Thousands of the nation's trucks and buses regularly have their engine's lube oil analyzed by laboratories specializing in this type of work. What is new is the availability of lube oil analysis to individual vehicle owners rather than, as before, almost exclusively to companies operating fleets of diesel equipment.

Lube oil analysis can be a valuable indicator of internal engine condition.

Here's how lube oil analysis works. You write one of the several laboratories that offer individual diesel vehicle owners lube analysis service. By return mail you'll receive an oil sampling kit. It will probably contain a two-ounce plastic oil sampling container with a screw-on plastic top. Instructions tell you how to take the sample. Usually, a lab-bound sample of diesel lube oil may be taken in any of three ways, but always right after the engine has been shut off, so that the sampled oil is as close as possible to normal engine operating temperature. That's important to assure that the lab's test will be accurate. Oil samples can be taken during normal oil changes, when lube oil is drained anyway. Between oil changes, a sample can be drawn from the engine through the dipstick tube (where you normally check the oil's level). In drawing an oil sample from the dipstick tube, a small suction bulb fitted with a length of disposable tubing is used. The tubing is merely inserted into the dipstick tube, the suction bulb depressed, and the oil sample drawn. The third method of sampling is by loosening the drain plug on the engine's bypass oil filter (if your diesel has one). A little oil is caught in the lube sampling container. In all cases, extreme cleanliness is a must, so as not to contaminate the sample with dirt, grease, or other substances not actually found inside the engine. For example, using a rag that contains solvents, metal filings, or other impurities can contaminate the oil sample, leading to false and even alarming lab reports. A bit of technique is required: In taking a sample of lube oil during a routine oil drain, about half of the crankcase's lube oil should be allowed to drain out before the sample is taken. The sample taken, the date, make and model of the engine, its mileage, mileage since last oil change, and sometimes oil type are noted on the container's label, and the container is mailed to the laboratory.

Shortly, you'll receive the lab's report, which, based on a number of tests, including spectrochemical analysis (using a spectrometer, which can detect the presence of virtually all basic elements and contaminants), tells what's in the oil in what quantities and analyzes both the probable source of what was found and whether it indicates trouble. For one example, the finding of more than trace amounts of copper in an oil sample may strongly point to excessive bearing wear in a particular diesel whose bearings contain copper. Some analyses report on as many as eighteen basic elements that may be found in a diesel's lube oil sample, and in the report's "recommendation" may pinpoint their probable source—as, "indicates piston ring wear." Also indicated is the presence of such contaminants as water, solids (the products of oxidation and engine blow-by), and fuel dilution. Noted, too, is the lubricity of the sample—whether, or not, in the lab's opinion, it is still doing its internal engine lubricating job.

NOTE: Never use lube analysis and a lab's report of "good oil" to extend, beyond the manufacturer's recommendation, the mileage period between oil changes. Follow the manufacturers recommendations.

The more frequently an engine is lube-sampled, the more accurate and meaningful the lab's reports. Infrequent samplings, although they can spot sudden, unusual changes in internal engine condition, may fail to show the gradual deterioration of engine parts. Ideally, you should have the laboratory analyze a lube sample every other oil change. For most automobile diesels, that's every 6,000 miles. Analysis costs from $7 to $11 per sample. Drive an average 18,000 miles a year and you'd change your diesel's oil three times. In that time, you'd submit three samples to the lab at an annual lube analysis cost of $21 to $33.

Aftermarket Fuel System Accessories

Due to reasons described previously, most diesel engine problems can be attributed to either fuel contamination or cold weather fuel performance characteristics. Diesel-engined vehicle manufacturers have designed and installed various systems to combat these problems, but ultimately, their best efforts are limited by cost.

Inconvenience is a major concern to diesel owners. If water accumulates (in substantial quantities) in the diesel fuel system, the fuel and water must be siphoned from the fuel tank and purged from the remainder of the fuel system. It goes without saying that this operation is a messy, time-consuming process. Even if the vehicle is equipped with a water/fuel separator having a drain valve, the owner must manually open the valve from either under the hood or beneath the vehicle.

Although the fuel filter installed by the manufacturer offers adequate performance when maintained properly, the addition of another, separate diesel fuel filter is a wise improvement.

If you live in an extremely cold climate, you've probably experienced cold starting problems due to fuel "waxing", plugged filters, "gelled" fuel, etc. If your vehicle is not factory-equipped with the optional fuel line or cylinder block heaters, these

Aftermarket fuel filter/water separator and fuel line heater

heaters can be purchased from the aftermarket (retail auto parts manufacturers). The installation of either of these items can improve cold-starting dramatically.

WATER/FUEL SEPARATORS

Centrifugal Action

Sometimes referred to as a "cyclonic" water/fuel separator, this device uses baffles which spin the fuel as it comes through the separator inlet. Since water is heavier than diesel fuel, the water will spin away from the fuel, sink to the bottom of the separator, and collect in the sediment bowl.

This type of separator is most efficient in dealing with large water droplets. If the water is in emulsion with the fuel, that is, if the water is equally dispersed through the fuel in very small droplets, some of the water will remain with the fuel to travel through the fuel system.

Coalescing Action

In this type of separator, the fuel must pass through a coalescent filtering media before proceeding through the fuel system. The idea behind the coalescent media is to trap even the smallest droplets of water on the media. As the small droplets combine into larger, heavier droplets, gravity acts on the droplets to pull them downward, off of the media and into the sediment bowl.

FUEL FILTER/SEPARATOR COMBINATION UNITS

Most separators of either the centrifugal or coalescent types are available with disposeable fuel filtering elements which are built into the separator unit. If your car already has a large, disposeable filter, it would probably be more cost-effective to stay with a separator only, and to change the factory-equipped filter at the recommended intervals. Should your vehicle have a fairly small filter, and/or an inconveniently located water drain (or none at all), choose the filter/separator combination. The filter/separator offers both increased fuel filtering ability and efficient water separation.

Convenience Add-Ons

Available with many separators and filter/separators are items such as dash-mounted water-in-fuel indicator lamps, audible water-in-fuel alarms, and dash-controlled water ejection systems. A properly chosen system would warn you of water in the fuel, and allow you to eject the water by simply "flipping" a dash-mounted switch.

Installing a Separator

Clear installation instructions and the necessary installation parts will be provided with the separator kit. Follow those instructions exactly. A general list of suggestions follows:

1. Fuel additives should not be used unless approved by the separator manufacturer.

2. Do not install a separator within 4″ of any exhaust system component.

3. If plastic fittings are supplied with the kit, do not replace them with metal fittings. Also, use extreme caution when tightening the fittings, especially those made of plastic.

4. Use a fuel-proof sealer on all fitting threads, only if the threads are not factory-coated with sealer.

5. Use only fuel-proof hoses for the installation.

6. Do not eliminate the original equipment fuel filter, even if a filter/separator is installed.

7. For new car warranty purposes, a filter/separator should be located BEFORE the original equipment filter. The fuel must pass through the original filter last, before entering the fuel injection pump.

8. If any type of fuel line heater is installed, it is best to position the heater between the fuel tank and the separator inlet.

9. To ease the job of the separator, the separator should be installed between the fuel transfer pump and the tank (unless the separator manufacturer specifies otherwise). Fuel and water which have been churned through the fuel transfer pump will be more difficult to separate.

10. Be sure that any wiring (for warning lamps, water ejection, etc.) is routed and connected properly. If the wiring must pass through a drilled hole, be sure to use a rubber grommet between the drilled component(s) and the wire to prevent damage to the wire.

FUEL LINE HEATERS

Two popular types of fuel line heaters are available for diesel passenger cars. Both types raise the temperature of the fuel to prevent "waxing" and "gelling" of the fuel in the lines during cold weather operation. One type uses engine coolant as a heating source. In order for this type to heat the fuel, the engine must first be started and allowed to run until the coolant temperature increases. Though this type of heater will usually increase fuel mileage, it offers no aid in starting ability.

The other type of heater uses a 12VDC electric heating element. This type is recommended, due to its ability to warm the fuel BEFORE the engine is started. This type of heater will also usually increase the overall fuel mileage.

Installation

Follow the manufacturer's instructions exactly. Also, see suggestions 5, 8, and 9 under Separator Installation.

CYLINDER BLOCK HEATERS

A cylinder block heater electrically (usually 110V house current) heats the engine coolant, which in turn warms the cylinder block, heads, and engine oil. In this case, the warmth is not used to alter the characteristics of the fuel. Block heaters offer two main advantages when starting a diesel in cold weather:

1. The reduced viscosity (thinning) of the engine oil from the warmth allows the engine to be "turned over" easier (and faster) by the starter. Less strain is imposed on the starting system.

2. Because the diesel relies on the heat of compression to ignite the fuel, the increase in the base combustion chamber temperature results in a higher tempeature during compression. This allows the fuel to ignite easier than if just the glow plugs were used.

Installation

Most cylinder block heaters replace one of the existing freeze (or expansion) plugs of the cylinder block. Follow the manufacturers installation instructions exactly. Also, refer to the manufacturers recommendations for usage.

Carburetor Service

FUNCTIONS

Gasoline is the source of fuel for power in the automobile engine and the carburetor is the mechanism which automatically mixes liquid fuel with air in the correct proportions to provide the desired power output from the engine. The carburetor performs this function by metering, atomizing, and mixing fuel with air flowing through the engine.

A carburetor also regulates the volume of air-to-fuel mixture which enters the engine. It is the carburetor's regulation of the mixture flow which gives the operator control of the engine speed.

Metering

The automotive internal combustion engine operates efficiently within a relatively small range of air-to-fuel ratios. It is the function of the carburetor to meter the fuel in exact proportions to the air flowing into the engine, so that the optimum ratio of air-to-fuel is maintained under all operating conditions. Regulations governing exhaust gas emissions have made the proper metering of fuel by the carburetor an increasingly important factor. Too rich a mixture will result in poor fuel economy and increased emissions, while too lean a mixture will result in loss of power and generally poor performance.

Carburetors are matched to engines so that metering can be accomplished by using carefully calibrated metering jets which allow fuel to enter the engine at a rate proportional to the engine's ability to draw air.

Atomization

The liquid fuel must be broken up into small particles so that it will more readily mix with air and vaporize. The more contact the fuel has with the air, the better the vaporization. Atomization can be accomplished in two ways: air may be drawn into a stream of fuel which will cause a turbulence and break the solid stream of fuel into smaller particles; or a nozzle can be positioned at the point of highest air velocity in the carburetor and the fuel will be torn into a fine spray as it enters the air stream.

Distribution

The carburetor is the primary device involved in the distribution of fuel to the engine. The more efficiently fuel and air are combined in the carburetor, the smoother the flow of vaporized mixture through the intake manifold to each combustion chamber. Hence, the importance of the carburetor in fuel distribution.

PRINCIPLES

Vacuum

All carburetors operate on the basic principle of pressure difference. Any pressure less than atmospheric pressure is considered vacuum or a low pressure area. In the engine, as the piston moves down on the intake stroke with the intake valve open, a partial vacuum is created in the intake manifold. The farther the piston travels downward, the greater the vacuum created in the manifold. As vacuum increases in the manifold, a difference in pressure occurs between the carburetor and cylinder. The carburetor is positioned in such a way that the high pressure above it, and the vacuum or low pressure beneath it, causes air to be drawn through it. Fuel and air always move from high to low pressure areas.

Venturi Principle

To obtain greater pressure drop at the tip of the fuel nozzle so that fuel will flow, the principle of increasing the air velocity to create a low pressure area is used. The device used to increase the velocity of the air flowing through the carburetor is called a venturi. A venturi is a specially designed restriction placed in the air flow. In order for the air to pass through the restriction, it must accelerate, causing a pressure drop or vacuum as it passes.

CIRCUITS

Float Circuit

The float circuit includes the float, float bowl, and a needle valve and seat. This circuit controls the amount of gas allowed to flow into the carburetor.

As the fuel level rises, it causes the float to rise which pushes the needle valve into its seat. As soon as the valve and seat make contact, the flow of gas is cut off from the fuel inlet. When the level of fuel drops, the float sinks and releases the needle valve from its seat which allows the gas to flow

Typical float circuit

in. In actual operation, the fuel is maintained at practically a constant level. The float tends to hold the needle valve partly closed so that the incoming fuel just balances the fuel being withdrawn.

Idle and Low Speed Circuit

When the throttle is closed or only slightly opened, the air speed is low and practically no vacuum develops in the venturi. This means that the fuel nozzle will not feed. Thus, the carburetor must have another circuit to supply fuel during operation with a closed or slightly opened throttle.

This circuit is called the idle and low speed circuit. It consists of passages in which air and gas can flow beneath the throttle plate. With the throttle plate closed, there

Typical idle and low speed circuit

is high vacuum from the intake manifold. Atmospheric pressure pushes the air/fuel mixture through the passages of the idle and low speed circuit and past the tapered point of the idle adjustment screw, which regulates engine idle mixture volume.

High Speed Partial Load Circuit

When the throttle plate is opened sufficiently, there is little difference in vacuum between the upper and lower part of the air horn. Thus, little air/fuel mixture will discharge from the low speed and idle circuit. However, under this condition enough air is moving through the air horn to produce vacuum in the venturi to cause the main nozzle or high speed nozzle to discharge fuel. The circuit from the float bowl to the main nozzle is called the high speed partial load circuit. A nearly constant air/fuel ratio is maintained by this circuit from part to full-throttle.

High Speed Full Power Circuit

For high-speed, full-power, wide open

Typical power circuit

throttle operation, the air/fuel mixture must be enriched; this is done either mechanically or by intake manifold vacuum.

Full Power Circuit (Mechanical)

This circuit includes a metering rod jet and a metering rod. The rod has two steps of different diameters and is attached to the throttle linkage.

When the throttle is wide open, the metering rod is lifted, bringing the smaller diameter of the rod into the jet. When the throttle is partly closed, the larger diameter of the metering rod is in the jet. This restricts fuel flow to the main nozzle but adequate amounts of fuel do flow for part-throttle operation.

Full Power Circuit (Vacuum)

This circuit is operated by intake manifold vacuum. It includes a vacuum diaphragm or piston linked to a valve.

When the throttle is opened so that intake manifold vacuum is reduced, the spring raises the diaphragm or piston. This allows more fuel to flow in, either by lifting a metering rod or by opening a power valve.

Accelerator Pump Circuit

For acceleration, the carburetor must deliver additional fuel. A sudden inrush of air is caused by rapid acceleration or applying full throttle.

Typical accelerator pump circuit

When the throttle is opened, the pump lever pushes the plunger down and this forces fuel to flow through the accelerator pump circuit and out the pump jet. This fuel enters the air passage through the carburetor to supply additional fuel demands.

Choke

When starting an engine, it is necessary to increase the amount of fuel delivered to the intake manifold. This increase is controlled by the choke.

The choke consists of a valve in the top of the air horn controlled mechanically by an automatic device. When the choke valve is closed, only a small amount of air can get past it. When the engine is cranked, a fairly high vacuum develops in the air horn. This vacuum causes the main nozzle to dis-

Typical choke system

charge a heavy stream of fuel. The quantity delivered is sufficient to produce the correct air/fuel mixture needed for starting the engine. The choke is released either manually or by heat from the engine.

OVERHAUL

Generally, when a carburetor requires major service, a rebuilt one is purchased on an exchange basis, or a kit may be bought for overhauling the carburetor.

The kit contains the necessary parts and some form of instructions for carburetor rebuilding. The instructions may vary between a simple exploded view and detailed step-by-step rebuilding instructions. Unless you are familiar with carburetor overhaul, the latter should be used.

There are some general overhaul procedures which should always be observed:

Efficient carburetion depends greatly on careful cleaning and inspection during overhaul since dirt, gum, water, or varnish in or on the carburetor parts are often responsible for poor performance.

Overhaul your carburetor in a clean, dust-free area. Carefully disassemble the carburetor, referring often to the exploded views. Keep all similar and lookalike parts segregated during disassembly and cleaning to avoid accidental interchange during assembly. Make a note of all jet sizes.

When the carburetor is disassembled, wash all parts except diaphragms, electric choke units, pump plunger, and any other plastic, leather, fiber, or rubber parts in clean carburetor solvent. Do not leave parts in the solvent any longer than is necessary to sufficiently loosen the deposits. Excessive cleaning may remove the special finish from the float bowl and choke valve bodies, leaving these parts unfit for service. Rinse all parts in clean solvent and blow them dry with compressed air or allow them to air dry. Wipe clean all cork, plastic, leather, and fiber parts with a clean, lint-free cloth.

Blow out all passages and jets with compressed air and be sure that there are no restrictions or blockages. Never use wire or similar tools to clean jets, fuel passages, or air bleeds. Clean all jets and valves separately to avoid accidental interchange.

Check all parts for wear or damage. If

wear or damage is found, replace the defective parts. Especially check the following:

1. Check the float needle and seat for wear. If wear is found, replace the complete assembly.

2. Check the float hinge pin for wear and the float(s) for dents or distortion. Replace the float if fuel has leaked into it.

3. Check the throttle and choke shaft bores for wear or an out-of-round condition. Damage or wear to the throttle arm, shaft, or shaft bore will often require replacement of the throttle body. These parts require a close tolerance of fit; wear may allow air leakage, which could affect starting and idling.

NOTE: Throttle shafts and bushings are not included in overhaul kits. They can be purchased separately.

4. Inspect the idle mixture adjusting needles for burrs or grooves. Any such condition requires replacement of the needle, since you will not be able to obtain a satisfactory idle.

5. Test the accelerator pump check valves. They should pass air one way but not the other. Test for proper seating by blowing and sucking on the valve. Replace the valve if necessary. If the valve is satisfactory, wash the valve again to remove breath moisture.

6. Check the bowl cover for warped surfaces with a straightedge.

7. Closely inspect the valves and seats for wear and damage, replacing as necessary.

8. After the carburetor is assembled, check the choke valve for freedom of operation.

Carburetor overhaul kits are recommended for each overhaul. These kits contain all gaskets and new parts to replace those that deteriorate most rapidly. Failure to replace all parts supplied with the kit (especially gaskets) can result in poor performance later.

Some carburetor manufacturers supply overhaul kits of three basic types: minor repair; major repair; and gasket kits. Basically, they contain the following:

Minor Repair Kits:
All gaskets
Float needle valve
Volume control screw
All diaphragms
Spring for the pump diaphragm

Major Repair Kits:
All jets and gaskets
All diaphragms
Float needle valve
Volume control screw
Pump ball valve
Main jet carrier
Float
Complete intermediate rod
Intermediate pump lever
Complete injector tube
Some cover hold-down screws and washers

Gasket Kits:
All gaskets

After cleaning and checking all components, reassemble the carburetor, using new parts and referring to the exploded view. When reassembling, make sure that all screws and jets are tight in their seats, but do not overtighten, as the tips will be distorted. Tighten all screws gradually, in rotation. Do not tighten needle valves into their seats; uneven jetting will result. Always use new gaskets. Be sure to adjust the float level when reassembling.

STROMBERG CARBURETORS ONLY

The preceding information applies to Stromberg carburetors also, but the following, additional suggestions should be followed.

1. Soak the small cork gaskets (jet gland washers) in penetrating oil or hot water for at least a half hour prior to assembly, or they will invariably split.

2. When the jet is fully assembled, the jet tube should be a close fit without any lateral play, but it should be free to move smoothly. A few drops of oil, or polishing of the tube may be necessary to achieve this.

3. If the jet sealing ring washer is made of cork, soak it in hot water for a minute or two prior to installation.

4. Adjust the float height.

5. Center the jet so that the piston will fall freely (when raised) and seat with a distinct click. If the jet is not centered properly, it will hang up in the tube.

TROUBLESHOOTING

NOTE: Carburetor problems cannot be isolated effectively unless all other engine systems are functioning correctly and the engine is properly tuned.

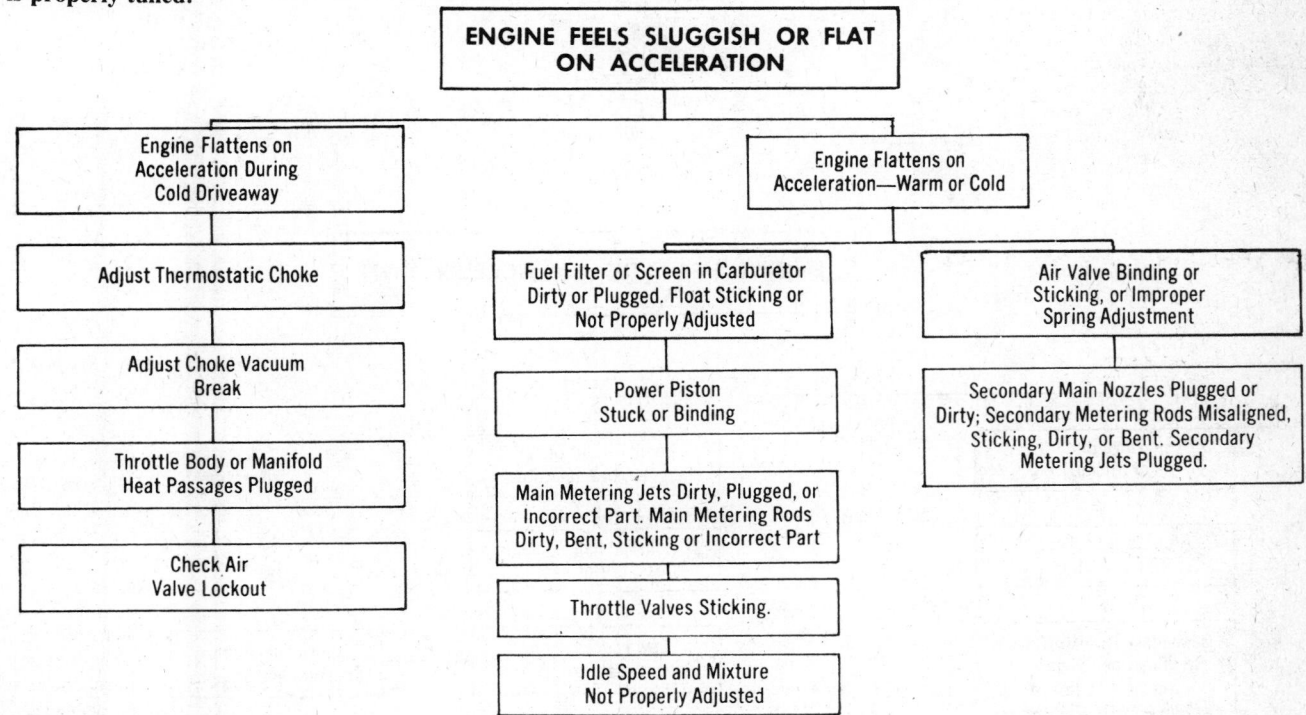

ENGINE CRANKS
NO START

No Start Cold

No Start Hot

Use Proper
Starting
Procedure

Correct Starting
Procedure Used
—Still No Start

Use Proper
Starting
Procedure

Correct Starting
Procedure Used
—Still No Start

Check Under
No Start Cold

Engine
Flooded

Choke Valve
Not Closing

No Fuel
in Carburetor

Choke Valve
Not Unloading

Check Automatic Choke
Coil Adjustment

No Fuel in Tank

Check Throttle Linkage
for Full Travel

Check for Binding
or Stuck Choke
Valve or Linkage

Fuel Lines or Filters
Plugged

Check Float Needle
and Seat for Leakage

Check and Adjust Choke
Rod and Vacuum Break

Defective Fuel Pump.
Run Pressure and
Volume Test

Check Float Adjustment

Check Float Needle
for Sticking in Seat
or Binding Float

ENGINE HESITATES ON ACCELERATION

Air Valve Binding
or Sticking

Pump Circuit Dirty,
Plugged, or Inoperative

Air Valve Lockout
Not Operating

Discharge Ball Sticking,
Dirty, or Not Seating

Secondary Throttle Valves
Sticking Open Slightly—
Check for Damage

Low Fuel Level in
Float Bowl

Check Fuel Pump
Pressure and Volume

CARBURETOR FLOODING

Run Fuel Pump Test—
Check Pressure and
Volume

Check Float Needle and Seat for
Dirt, Wear, Damage, or Loose Part.
Clean All Fuel Screens and Filters

Check and Adjust Float Level.
Check for Distorted Float Arms.

Check for Float Bowl Leaks.
(Fill Bowl with Fuel on Bench
and Observe for Leaks)
Check Seal on All Bowl Gaskets

ENGINE RUNS UNEVENLY OR SURGES

Check Fuel Pump Pressure
and Volume

Fuel Filter or Screen
Plugged or Dirty

Main Metering Jets
Plugged, Loose,
or Wrong Part

Primary Metering Rods
Bent, Altered, or
Incorrect Part

Power Piston Sticking,
Dirty, Spring Missing,
or Incorrect Part

Float Adjustment Incorrect

Adjust Idle Speed
and Mixture

Check Idle System for
Dirty or Plugged Passages.

Gaskets Not Sealing—
May Be Hard or Brittle
Check for Loose Screws

Secondary Throttle Valves
Sticking Open or Misaligned

ROUGH ENGINE IDLE AND STALLING

Adjust Idle Speed

If Rough Idle Continues After
Proper Idle Adjustment, Check
As Follows:

Tighten All Carburetor Screws.
Torque Carburetor to Manifold
and Manifold to Engine Bolts.

Carburetor Idle Passages
Dirty or Plugged

Idle Mixture Adjusting
Needles Dirty,
Bent, or Scored

Throttle Valves
Sticking Open

Clean or Replace Float
Needle and Seat.

Float Needle Seat Leaking
Float Not Properly Adjusted

Check for Binding
or Leaking Float

Check Air Horn to Bowl and
Throttle Body Gaskets for
Air Leaks Between Castings

Check Power Piston
Passages for Air Leaks

POOR ECONOMY

Run Mileage Test
Check Driver Habits

If Mileage Is Poor,
Proceed to Check the
Following:

Check Choke Valve and Linkage
for Binding or Sticking

Check Power Piston
Spring for Distortion

Check Power Piston
for Sticking or Being Bent

Check Power Piston
Vacuum Passages for Leaks
or Being Plugged

Check Metering Rods
for Being
Bent or Wrong Part

Check Main Metering Jets
for Being Plugged, Loose,
or Incorrect Part

Make Sure Gaskets
Seal Properly on
All Vacuum Passages

Carburetor Flooding

Adjust Float

Check Float Needle Seat
for Leakage from Dirt,
Wear, Damage, Looseness.

Check and Adjust Idle
Speed

Float Bent, Loaded,
Sticking, or Misaligned

Pump Discharge Ball Not
Seating—Check for Dirt,
Defective Seat or
Discharge Spring

**LACK OF HIGH SPEED
PERFORMANCE OR POWER**

Check for Full Throttle
Opening at Carburetor.
Adjust Throttle Linkage
As Necessary

Air Valve Binding, Sticking
or Wrong Tension.

Power Piston Stuck or Binding—
Check for Distorted Spring

Air Valve
Not Unlocking.

Float Setting Incorrect

Float Sticking Misaligned
or Leaking

Secondary Metering Rods
Bent or Incorrect Part, or
Not Adjusted Properly

Main Metering Jets Plugged,
Dirty, or Incorrect Part

Metering Rods Altered,
Bent, or Incorrect Part

Gaskets Not Sealing.
May Be Hard or Brittle.
Check for Loose Screws

Fuel Injection

GASOLINE FUEL INJECTION CHART

	D-Jetronic	L-Jetronic	K-Jetronic
Audi			
100			1976–77
Fox			1976–79
4000, Coupe			1980 and later
5000, Turbo, Quattro			1978 and later
BMW			
3.0Si, CSi		1976	
320i			1977 and later
528i		1979–81	
528e		②	
530i		1976–78	
630CSi		1977–78	
633CSi		1978 and later②	
733i		1978 and later②	
Datsun			
200SX		1982 and later	
280Z, ZX		1976 and later	
810		1977 and later	
Fiat			
Spider 2000, Turbo		1980 and later	
Strada		1980 and later	
X1/9		1980 and later	
Brava		1980–81	
Jaguar ③			
XJS, XJ12	1976–79		
Mercedes Benz			
280E, SE, CE			1977–81
450SL, 450SLC			1976–80
450SE, 450SEL			1976–80
6.9			1978–79
380SL, SLC, SEL, SEC			1981 and later
Peugeot			
505			1980 and later

GASOLINE FUEL INJECTION CHART

	D-Jetronic	L-Jetronic	K-Jetronic
Porsche			
911, 911S			1976–77
911SC			1978 and later
Turbo			1976–79
912E		1976	
914 1.8		1976	
914 2.0	1976		
924, 924 Turbo			1976–81
928		1980 and later	1978–79
944		②	
Renault			
18i		1981 and later	
Fuego		1982 and later	
SAAB			
99			1976–78
99 Turbu			1978
900			1979 and later
900 Turbo			1979 and later
Toyota			
Supra		1979 and later	
Cressida		1980 and later	
Triumph			
TR-7, TR-8		1980–81	
Volkswagen			
Beetle (Type 1)		1976–79	
Bus (Type 2), Vanagon		1976 and later	
Dasher			1976–81
Jetta			1980 and later
Rabbit			1977 and later①
Scirocco			1976 and later
Quantum			1982 and later
Volvo			
242, 244, 245			1976–79
262, 264, 265			1976–79
DL, GL, GLE, GT, Coupe			1980 and later

①Except for certain 1980 and later
  engines which were carbureted
②1982 and later: Bosch Motronic
  Injection System—No information
  available at time of publication
③Bosch-Lucas System

NOTE: This section is basically concerned with troubleshooting and problem diagnosis on various fuel injection systems. Location of parts may vary on individual car lines, but the operation of the system is similar and an understanding of its operation is critical to effective problem diagnosis. See the individual manufacturer's car section for schematics and parts replacement.

The use of fuel injection on a large scale in the U.S. more or less began with the Bosch system used by VW on its 1968 Type

3 Squareback and Fastback models. Since then, many different systems have been used, but aside from diesel and mechanical, gasoline fuel injection systems, used primarily on older Mercedes and Porsche models, there are really only 3 basic types in current use. All are manufactured by Bosch or are manufactured under a Bosch licensing agreement and are used on many and varied import car applications. The 3 systems are known as D, L and K-Jetronic. The D and L-Jetronic systems are electronic and are sometimes called, respectively MPC (Manifold Pressure Controlled) and AFC (Air

Flow Controlled). The K-Jetronic system is a continuous injection system sometimes known by the letters CIS.

Comparing Carburetor Circuits to EFI Components

It makes electronic fuel injection a little easier to understand if we compare the functions of major systems in the carburetor to those of an EFI system. It quickly becomes apparent the EFI is basically just a more sophisticated way of doing the same thing.

Carburetor	EFI
Accelerator pump	Throttle switch
Fast idle cam	Thermo-time switch
Float	Fuel pressure regulator
Power valve/ metering rod(s)	Manifold pressure sensor (D-Jetronic) Airflow sensor (L-Jetronic)
Metering jets & idle fuel system	Injector valves/ electronic control unit

Allen wrench with long handle makes mixture adjustment easier

Electronic harness repair kit

Zelenda Machine & Tool Corp.
66-02 Austin St.
Forest Hills, NY 11374

SAFETY PRECAUTIONS— L-JETRONIC

Observe the following precautions to avoid damaging components of the L-Jetronic EFI system.

1. Never start the engine without the battery cables connected.
2. Never jump the battery to start the car.
3. Never remove the cables from the battery with the engine running.
4. Always remove the cables from the battery before charging the battery.
5. Never remove or attach the wiring harness plug to the control unit with the ignition ON.
6. When checking compression, unplug the red cable from the battery to the relays.

TOOLS AND EQUIPMENT

Most of the tools necessary to work on D, L and K-Jetronic fuel injection systems are part of a well-equipped tool box. Box wrenches, screwdrivers, a jumper wire and a volt-ohmmeter are usually in the tool box or available. Specialized equipment includes a pressure tester that reads to at least 100 psi, and includes connecting lines and tees and a 3-way valve to select different pressure tests. The other required tool, especially for K-Jetronic, is a 3 mm Allen wrench for adjusting fuel mixture. A fuel injection harness repair kit is also invaluable

Bosch injection valve tester

able in repairing the electric wiring harness. The kit contains prewired contacts and housings that are replacements for the OEM (original equipment manufacturer) pieces.

Several companies make off-car injector testers, a device for testing individual injectors and observing the spray pattern.

Tool Suppliers

Check with your local jobber or distributor for the testers and tools you need.
Robert Bosch Corp.
2800 S. 25th Ave.
Broadview, IL 60153

RAM Products Inc.
150 Ludlow Ave.
Northvale, NJ 07647

Snap-on Tools Corp.
8036-D 28th Ave.
Kenosha, WI 53140

L (EUROPEAN CARS ONLY) AND D– JETRONIC

Operation

D and L-Jetronic are electronically controlled, intermittent fuel injection systems. Both operate in a similar manner, the basic difference being that D uses intake manifold pressure as the measure of engine load and L uses the flow of air going into the engine. An electronic control unit (ECU) is the "brain" of the system. The ECU processes electric signals from the engine sensors, figures out the fuel requirement, and then tells the injectors when and how much fuel to spray.

D and L fuel supply is handled by an electric pump and a pressure regulator. Both systems use a time and temperature sensor controlled cold start valve for additional fuel and an auxiliary air device to provide an enriched mixture for cold starting and warmup. Fuel injectors are solenoid operated valves for each cylinder. On D-Jetronic, injectors are split into groups of two (2 on 4-cyl., 3 on 6-cyl., and 4 on V8 engines). Each injector group is parallel wired so that injectors in a group open at the same time, L injectors are all grouped

CIS pressure tester for K-Jetronic only

Fuel injection pressure gauge for K-, D- and L-Jetronic systems

1. Electronic control unit
2. Injection valve
3. Pressure sensor
4. Temperature sensor
5. Thermo-switch or thermo-time switch
6. Start valve
7. Electric fuel pump
8. Fuel filter
9. Fuel pressure regulator
10. Auxiliary air device
11. Throttle valve switch
12. Trigger contacts

D-Jetronic injection system schematic

together. Engine speed information for D and L is sent by a special set of contacts in the distributor. Both systems have engine and air temperature sensors. Throttle valve switches supply the D and L ECU with throttle position information.

D-Jetronic works by measuring intake manifold pressure, engine speed, air and engine temperature, and supplying this information to its ECU, which then decides how much fuel is needed. L-Jetronic measures air flow, engine and air temperature, engine speed, and throttle position and passes these inputs to the ECU to be translated into injection signals.

Troubleshooting

WATER IN FUEL

Water is one of the biggest killers of EFI components, regardless of the type of system. The high pressures generated by the fuel pump can and will push water and fuel right through the fuel filter into the rest of the system.

Water problems can be minimized by changing filters regularly, at least every 7500–10,000 miles, using water absorbing fuel additives (especially in colder weather), staying away from cheapo gas stations that

are more susceptible to water in the fuel supply and by installing a water filter.

Several companies manufacture water separation/filtration systems which electronically detect the presence of water in the fuel. They can be used in all environments under the hood, with all fuels, and are packaged with all fittings, brackets and hardware for easy installation.

PRELIMINARY CHECKS

Before assuming that the EFI system is at fault, make the standard preliminary checks of ignition system and engine condition before going any further.

Also, check the electrical connections. EFI electrical systems won't tolerate corrosion or sloppy connections. Clean those connections with one of the electrical cleaners available and be absolutely certain that spaded terminals snap tightly into their plastic connector bodies. Carefully crimp these where necessary with needlenose pliers. Also, check the main harness connector that plugs into the ECU for dirt, corrosion, or bent or spread-out terminals. This check alone has solved many intermittent EFI performance problems.

Is the battery OK?

A bad set of ignition wires will cause just about all the same symptoms as a bad pressure regulator, so check the ignition system first. Steady vacuum that's within specs is a must on these cars. A vacuum leak unbalances the system throughout its entire operating range. A leaky engine will start, idle, and run poorly.

FUEL PUMP

Fuses and Relays

Both the D and L-Jetronic systems are fed by chassis-mounted electric fuel pumps. Usually, these pumps just quit running. Probably the most common symptom of a bad fuel pump is the no-start or dies-out-completely condition. If you don't hear the pump buzz for a second or two when you hit the key, first check the pump fuse. All EFI fuel pumps are fused *somewhere* in the vehicle. On some cars such as Volvos and Saabs, the fuse could be under the hood. Watch for corrosion in the contacts of the fuseholder. Often, an electric fuel pump is so worn that it tries to draw too much current and blows the fuse. You can liken this action to a dragging starter that draws too much cranking amperage. In colder weather, moisture in the gas can cause an electric pump to freeze. The frozen pump will also draw enough current to blow the pump fuse.

If the electric pump on an EFI-equipped car quits on the road, you can sometimes get the car back to the shop simply by rapping on the pump with the wooden handle of your hammer. Sometimes this rap will start the pump again and it'll run long enough to get the car in.

After the fuse, check the pump relay or

1. Electronic control unit
2. Injection valve
3. Air-flow sensor
4. Temperature sensor
5. Thermo-time switch
6. Start valve
7. Electric fuel pump
8. Fuel filter
9. Fuel pressure regulator
10. Auxiliary air device
11. Throttle valve switch
12. Relay set

L-Jetronic injection system schematic

Water separation/filtration systems come in different sizes and applications. See text for more information (Photo Courtesy Ram Products)

dual relay assembly. As is the case with the fuse, these relays could be anywhere. Datsun hides a dual relay inside the kick panel; VW may have it under the dashboard; and others may have their pump relays under the hood. On a D-Jetronic car, the only way you can run the pump without starting the car is to by-pass the relay. Locate the hot wire feeding the relay and connect it directly to the pump wire with a jumper wire. Exercise caution with the dual relays used in L-Jetronic cars. Refer to a wiring diagram because the main-relay side and the pump-relay side of the dual relay are seldom labeled by the manufacturer. Be sure you're connecting that jumper across

On most L-Jetronic systems, you can check fuel pump operation by reaching into the air-flow meter and moving the flap by hand. Relay should click and pump should buzz. That flap has to move freely and smoothly; biggest problem with L system is the fact that these air-flow meter flaps begin to stick—then you have to replace the entire unit. Engine backfiring sometimes dislodges or damages intake air hoses on L system, causing no-start condition.

the *pump-relay* side of the dual relay. Remember, too, that all EFI electric fuel pumps use a separate ground wire. So don't neglect to ground check during your pump troubleshooting.

Volume Test

A pressure test alone won't reveal trouble with an EFI fuel pump. It's imperative that you perform a volume test as well as a pressure test. With 12 volts at the pump and at least half a tank of gas in the car, a typical D or L-Jetronic pump should deliver a quart (almost a liter) of fuel in 30 seconds.

Pressure Test

To test the D and L-Jetronic systems, you must have an extremely accurate pressure gauge that reads 0–50 psi in 0.5-psi increments. Also, remember that high operating pressures mean that connections must be tight. 30–40 psi pressures won't tolerate those haphazard connections. Don't risk a fire—use a reinforced fuel line hose that'll withstand 30–40 psi and use worm-gear type clamps to secure the hose. Keep an eye out for leakage in the fuel plumbing and check even the braided hose used as OEM equipment.

Fuel pressure test—D-Jetronic

When you're taking your fuel pressure reading at idle, normal injector pulsation will cause the gauge to fluctuate. You'll find that this pulsation is most pronounced on 4-cylinder engines. Watch the needle carefully and take the *average* pressure value. At idle, simply take your pressure reading as being the mid-point between the highest and lowest fluctuations of the pressure gauge needle. D and L-Jetronic systems should have 28.5 psi at idle.

If fuel pressure isn't within specs at idle, you could have a clogged fuel filter or either a restricted fuel line or fuel return line. Be sure to change fuel filters at least every 7500–10,000 miles in conjunction with gas additives. The gas additive will minimize water build-up in the fuel system (see the section on water in the fuel).

Provided everything else is right, you can bring the pressure on a D-Jetronic system back into specs by adjusting the pressure regulator. If system pressure doesn't change when you turn the adjustment bolt on the regulator, then the regulator is defective. Under these same circumstances on an L-Jetronic system, you'll have to replace the pressure regulator because L-type regulators aren't adjustable.

After taking the idle pressure reading, shut off the engine and watch the pressure gauge. The system should hold 17–20 psi. If the pressure drops to zero, there's a leak in the system. On a car with a conventional fuel system, such a pressure loss would suggest that either the fuel pump or the carburetor inlet valve were leaking. But assuming that they're not leaking fuel *externally*, there are four places a D or L-Jetronic system can leak *internally*:

1. The check valve in the output side of the electric fuel pump
2. The pressure regulator
3. One or more injectors
4. The cold start injector

To begin isolating a leak, crimp the hose connecting the fuel pressure regulator to the fuel tank. Turn the ignition switch off and on to cycle the fuel pump so you build up pressure in the system again. If the system now holds pressure, then the regulator is leaking. If the pressure still drops, keep your locking pliers on the regulator hose and have someone cycle the fuel pump with the ignition switch. Then quickly crimp the hose connecting the pump to the main fuel rail. If the pressure holds steady, the check valve in the output side of the fuel pump is defective. A bad pump check valve usually causes a hard-start condition on an EFI car when the engine's hot.

LEAKING INJECTORS

If the system doesn't hold pressure after you've crimped both the regulator and pump hoses, then an injector is leaking. You can remove the entire fuel rail from the engine and switch the pump on and off again. Then watch for the injector that's leaking fuel. To give you an idea of how well an injector should hold pressure, Bosch instructions state that "the injector orifice may become wet, but no more than two drops should form on the valve (injector) per minute."

DEAD OR PLUGGED INJECTORS

You can spot a dead or plugged injector several ways. We indicated that you must perform a routine ignition and engine condition test on any EFI-equipped engine before digging into its fuel system. If the ignition's sound and you're getting little or no rpm drop when you short a cylinder, you could have a vacuum leak at the nozzle seal.

Some cars seem to eat up these nozzle seals. Injector O-rings are a potential vacuum leak on any EFI-equipped engine.

To determine if you've got a leaking O-ring, use the same technique you use on standard intake manifold leaks: spritz the O-ring with some carb and choke cleaner and watch for a response on your vacuum gauge. And don't assume that EFI systems are immune from the loose-and-leaking intake syndrome.

If the O-rings are sealing properly, then a bad injector is probably responsible for the weak cylinder. You can place your finger on a good injector and feel it clicking open and closed. If you put a stethoscope on a good injector, you'll hear it opening and closing. If you don't hear an injector clicking, you may have a poor electrical connection at that injector. Try switching injector wires with an adjacent good injector. If swapping wires brings the dead injector to life, look for a corroded or loose connection or a broken injector wire.

Be wary of smelling gasoline first thing in the morning after starting your car. EFI injectors have a bad habit of allowing fuel to gush out from the seam where the black plastic part of the injector mates with the colored plastic part. But as soon as they warm up, the leak stops.

COLD START INJECTORS

Another source of leakage is the cold start injector. On a cold engine, you should get a squirt of fuel from the cold start injector when you crank the engine with the ignition disabled. Of course, the cold start injector must not leak after you've cycled it open and closed. If you suspect that it's opening when the engine's hot, crank the engine when it's at operating temperature and take a pressure reading. If the pressure drops when you crank the engine, you know the thermo-time switch controlling the cold start injector is defective because it's allowing that injector to open when the engine's hot.

Pen points to seam where leaks occur on cold injectors. Watch out for external fuel leakage from those braided hose connections between the fuel rail and the injectors. You can get an aftermarket repair kit that'll enable you to make your own OE-type crimped hose connections on the injectors

SENSORS

In general, you'll find that coolant and cylinder head temperature sensors have a fairly

Because it's under constant use, throttle valve switch is probably the fastest wearing component in D-Jetronic system. Besides bad electrical connections, a worn throttle valve switch often causes intermittent cut-out conditions. Zig-zagging circuit path at lower right on each switch constitutes the D-Jetronic "accelerator pump." the acceleration enrichment circuit. If mixture doesn't change when you turn the CO-adjuster knob on the ECU, then this switch is worn, dirty, or out of adjustment

L-Jetronic throttle switch is much simpler—and therefore more reliable—than D-type switch. Rotating cam there opens and closes those contacts, providing either an idle or an enriched wide-open-throttle signal. The L-Jetronic throttle switch works like a big variable resistor, signaling the ECU as to what the throttle position is at any moment

Some ECUs have provision for CO adjustment, some don't. Whenever an EFI system lacks the CO adjustment, the integrity of the intake system and the precision of your sensor adjustments become more critical than ever. Because they're so well isolated from the harsh underhood environment, ECU failure really isn't that common. Usually, a sensor, switch, or mechanical problem cause EFI breakdowns

high mortality rate on EFI systems. VW's, for example, use up their cylinder head sensors pretty often. On L-Jetronic systems, the intake air temperature sensor is incorporated into the air flow meter. If it dies, you'll have to replace the air flow meter. And you'll soon discover that it's impossible to tune or adjust and EFI-equipped engine if one of its sensors is bad.

On the D-system, the trigger points *inside* the distribution are a high-wear item.

On many EFI cars, you have to readjust the throttle stop screw. Turn the screw in until it just touches the stop, give it another ½–¾ turn, and then tighten the lock-nut. Then readjust the throttle switch. If someone has fooled with that stop screw, you can be sure that both the mixture and the throttle switch will require adjustment.

CHILTON TIP

You can ease throttle switch adjustments on many D-Jetronic systems by arming yourself with a 0.014 in. and an 0.018 feeler gauge. Back the throttle stop all the way out and then thread it in until it just touches the throttle level. Give it another ¼–½ turn and place your 0.014 in. feeler gauge between the screw and the lever. Loosen and rotate the throttle switch until your ohmmeter reads zero. When you put the 0.018 in. gauge between the lever and the screw, your meter should read infinity. It's touchy, so carefully rotate the switch until you get the correct resistance readings with each feeler gauge.

Finally, the L-Jetronic systems tend to be so "mixture sensitive" that crankcase air leaks will upset them. If the sealing ring around the oil filler cap is broken or missing, a VW for instance, with L-Jetronic just won't perform.

L-JETRONIC— JAPANESE CARS

Operation

The fuel injection system used on these cars is an adaption of the Bosch L-Jetronic seen on many European cars. Japanese L-Jet injection works basically the same way, with a few variations.

We can break the L-Jetronic into three basic systems: air intake, fuel supply, and electronic control. Some components like the air flow meter are part of two systems. The air intake system consists of the air cleaner, air flow meter, throttle housing, connecting hoses, air valve (air regulator) and the manifold. The fuel system includes tank, fuel pump, fuel damper, filter, fuel rail, cold start injector, fuel injectors, and connecting lines. European L-Jet systems don't use a fuel damper. Both Datsun and Toyota employ dampers to reduce pulsation from pump output. Dampers have what looks like an adjusting screw, but don't attempt any adjustment. The 200SX injection system doesn't use a cold start injector.

The electronic control system is made up of the electronic control unit (ECU) and several sensors. Each sensor signals mea-

1. Air Flow Meter
2. Fuel Pump Check Connector
3. Oxygen Sensor
4. Computer
5. Throttle Position Sensor
6. Cold Start Injector
7. Service Connector
8. Fuel Pump
9. Circuit Opening Relay
10. HAC Sensor
11. Resistor
12. No. 2 Main Relay
13. Air Valve
14. No. 1 Main Relay
15. Injector
16. Water Thermo Sensor
17. Cold Start Injector Time Switch

Electronic Controls on Toyota Supra

Datsun 200SX EFI component location

ECU is located near kick panel on most cars. These rarely go bad and are expensive. Make sure large ECU connector is snapped on tight

Datsun 200SX air valve or air regulator supplies extra air to throttle housing for higher idle during warm-up. Pinching off air hose should cause an rpm drop when engine's cold

Arrow points to throttle switch on Supra throttle valve housing. These switches are relatively troublefree. Check linkage for smoothness

Toyota Supra No. 1 EFI Relay (1), No. 2 relay (2) and injector solenoid resistor

surements on engine condition to the ECU, which then computes fuel needs. Injectors are then opened and closed by ECU command to feed the needed amount of fuel. Injectors are connected in parallel. All supply fuel at the same time. They open twice for each rotation of the engine camshaft, injecting ½the needed fuel each time.

The big sensor, and the one that gives the system its name, is the air flow sensor. This is located in the large airbox. A flap in the box opens and closes in response to air being drawn into the engine. The ECU is then signalled the amount of air being taken in. An air temperature sensor in the box sends that information to the ECU. Engine rpm is picked up from the negative side of the coil. A throttle valve switch tells the control unit how much the throttle is open. Engine temperature is transmitted from a coolant temperature sensor. Later model Datsuns use a cylinder head temperature sensor instead of coolant temperature sensor. A signal from the ignition switch tells the ECU when the engine is being started. An O2 sensor has been added to Datsuns and Toyotas to feed exhaust gas oxygen content to the ECU.

Troubleshooting

WATER IN FUEL

See the section on ''Water in the Fuel'' under the European L-Jetronic system.

PRELIMINARY CHECKS

In general follow the same checks as you would for the European L-Jetronic systems.

NO-START

If an EFI-equipped Japanese car doesn't start, there's a good chance it might be the fuel pump or its circuit. First, visually check all the pump and relay wiring, it could be nothing more than a bad connection. Be sure that the fuel pump is grounded. All Datsun and Toyota fuel pumps are located back near the tank. Check the EFI fuse and look to see if the fusible link near the battery is burned. Don't forget the battery cables, the pump calls for 12 volts. If the link or fuse is burned, it could be a worn out pump. Or it could be watered gas, which will freeze the pump up in winter. The last item to try is by-passing the relay. If it works, then the relay's bad. Toyotas have a convenient fuel pump check connector under the air box. Pry the cap off and, with a jumper wire, you can run the pump without starting the engine. If you can feel fuel pressure at the cold start injector and hear fuel returning through the regulator, the pump's working.

Trouble-shooting guide for L-Jetronic fuel injection

SYMPTOM →	Engine cranks but does not start	Engine starts but then dies	Rough or unstable idle	Idle speed incorrect	CO value incorrect	Erratic running	Engine misses when driving	Fuel consumption too high	No maximum power	CAUSE	REMEDY
	●	●	●	●		●	●	●	●	Defect in ignition system	Check battery, distributor, plugs, coil and timing
	●	●	●			●	●	●	●	Mechanical defect in engine	Check compression, valve adj. and oil pressure
	●	●	●	●	●	●	●	●		Leaks in air intake system (false air)	Check all hoses and connections; eliminate leaks
	●	●	●						●	Blockage in fuel system	Check fuel tank, filter and lines for free flow
	●	●								Relay defective; wire to injector open	Test relay; check wiring harness
	●									Fuel pump not operating	Check pump fuse, pump relay and pump
			●	●			●	●	●	Fuel system pressure incorrect	Check pressure regulator
	●									Cold start valve not operating	Test for spray, check wiring and thermo-time switch
	●	●	●		●			●		Cold start valve leaking	Check valve for leakage
	●									Thermo-time switch defective	Test for resistance readings vs. temperature
	●									Auxiliary air valve not operating correctly	Must be open with cold engine; closed with warm
	●	●	●				●			Temperature sensor defective	Test for 2-3 kΩ at 68° F.
	●	●				●	●	●	●	Air flow meter defective	Check pump contacts; test flap for free movement
			●	●					●	Throttle butterfly does not completely close or open	Readjust throttle stops
				●					●	Throttle valve switch defective	Check with ohmmeter and adjust
				●						Idle speed incorrectly adjusted	Adjust idle speed with bypass screw
			●		●	●	●		●	Defective injection valve	Check valves individually for spray
					●			●		CO concentration incorrectly set	Readjust CO with screw on air flow meter
	●	●	●	●		●	●			Loose connection in wiring harness or system ground	Check and clean all connections
	●	●	●						●	Control unit defective	Use known good unit to confirm defect

NO-START OR POOR COLD START

No starts or poor cold starting can be caused by a malfunctioning cold start injector. Cranking a cold engine with the coil wire grounded should produce a nice, cone-shaped spray from the cold start injector. Cranking a warm engine should produce no fuel, if the injector dribbles gas, replace it.

PRESSURE TEST

To pressure test Datsun and Toyota L-Jet systems, you'll need an accurate pressure gauge. Since pressures are in the 30–40 psi, the gauge should read to 50 psi. Tee the pressure gauge into the line between the fuel rail and the filter on Datsuns. Use a container to catch fuel when a line is opened. You can hook up the gauge to the cold start injector connection on the Toyota fuel rail.

Banjo fittings are used throughout the Toyota EFI system. An adapter with a banjo fitting at one end will be needed to hook up the gauge. Take a good look at the hoses on these cars. Hoses must be in decent shape and fittings (Toyota) or clamps (Datsun) tight.

Start the engine and, on a Toyota, disconnect and plug the vacuum line to the pressure regulator. Pressure at idle should be 33–38 psi on Toyotas and approximately 30 psi on Datsuns. A bad pressure regulator is indicated by pressure that's too high. Look for kinked fuel lines, restrictive fuel filter, or a faulty pump or pump check valve, if the pressure is too low. If you've got a Toyota, connect the vacuum hose to the pressure regulator. Watch the gauge. Pressure should drop to 28 psi. A reading over 33 psi means the regulator's bad. On a Datsun, check pressure at full throttle. Pressure should climb to 37 psi as soon as the throttle is wide open. On both Datsuns and Toyotas, pressure should hold when the engine is shut off. An immediate pressure drop means an internally leaking injector(s), pressure regulator, or fuel pump.

INJECTOR CHECK

See the section on injectors in the D and L-Jetronic system.

Using a mechanic's stethoscope or a screwdriver, you can listen to each injector. A regular clicking means it's working. The interval between clicks should shorten as engine speed is increased.

Air flow meter is in air box, Datsun shown here. Check air flap movement by operating it by hand. If flap sticks, replace air box

Pressure gauge hooked up to 280ZX. System must hold pressure when engine's shut down. A quick drop is indicative of an external or internal leak

Datsun cylinder head temperature sensor. These connections should be clean and tight. Corroded contacts here can cause an engine miss. Ram Products makes harness repair kits to fix faulty wiring

K-JETRONIC

Operation

K-Jetronic is an independent mechanical system. That is, no pump or other component is driven by the engine. The basic operating principle is to continuously inject fuel into the intake side of the engine by means of an electric pump. The amount of fuel delivered is metered by an air flow measuring device. K is a mechanical system, there is no electronic brain deciding when or how much fuel to inject as is done on the D and L-Jetronic systems.

The primary fuel circuit consists of an electric pump, which pulls fuel from the tank. Fuel then passes through an accumulator. The accumulator is basically a container in the fuel line. It houses a spring-loaded diaphragm that provides fuel damping and delays pressure build-up when the engine is first started. When the engine is shut down, the expanded chamber in the accumulator keeps the system under enough pressure for good hot restarts with no vapor locking. Fuel flows through a large, paper element filter to the mixture control assembly.

The mixture control assembly is the K-Jet heart. It houses the air flow sensor and the fuel distributor. The air sensor is a round plate attached to a counterbalanced lever. The plate and lever are free to move up-and-down on a fulcrum. Accelerator pedal linkage connects to a throttle butterfly, which is upstream (closer to the manifold and intake valves) of the air sensor. If you're following this far, stepping on the gas opens the throttle valve. Increased air, demanded by the engine, is sucked through the air cleaner and around the air sensor plate.

In the air funnel, where the air sensor plate is located, the quantity of intake air lifts the plate until an equlibrium is reached between air flow and hydraulic counter-pressure acting on the lever through a plunger. This is the control plunger. In this balanced position, the plunger stays at a level in the fuel distributor to open small metering slits, one for each cylinder in the engine. Fuel under controlled pressure from the pump goes through the slits to the injectors. The slit determines the right amount of fuel rather than the injectors as on the D and L-Jetronic systems.

In order to maintain a precise fuel pressure, a pressure regulator, or pressure relief valve, is located in the primary fuel circuit of the fuel distributor. Excess fuel is diverted back to the tank through a return line. To make sure the amount of fuel going through the control plunger slits depends only on their area, an exact pressure differential must always be maintained at the openings. This pressure is controlled by a differential-pressure valve. There's one valve for each cylinder. The valve consists of a spring loaded steel diaphragm and an outlet

1. Mixture-control unit
1a. Air-flow sensor
1b. Fuel distributor
1c. Idle-mixture adjusting screw
2. Fuel tank
3. Electric fuel pump
4. Fuel accumulator
5. Fuel filter
6. Primary-pressure regulator
6a. Push-up valve
7. Fuel injection valve
8. Idle speed adjusting screw
9. Battery
10. Ignition and starting switch
11. Control relay
12. Ignition distributor
13. Start valve
14. Thermo-time switch
15. Auxiliary air device
16. Warm-up regulator
16a. Full-load diaphragm

K-Jetronic injection system schematic

to the injectors. The diaphragm separates the upper and lower chambers.

The valve keeps an exact pressure differential of 1.42 psi between upper chamber pressure and lower chamber pressure. Both pressures act on the spring loaded steel diaphragm which opens the outlet to the injectors. The size of the outlet opening is always just enough to maintain that 1.42 psi pressure differential at the metering slit. The diaphragm opens more if a larger amount of fuel flows. If less fuel enters the upper chamber, the diaphragm opens less and less fuel goes to the injectors. An exact pressure differential between upper and lower chamber is kept constant. Diaphragm movement is actually only a few thousandths of an inch.

A warm-up regulator can alter the pressure on the control plunger according to engine and outside air temperature. For warm-up running, it lowers the pressure so that the air sensor plate can go higher for the same air flow. This exposes more metering slit area, and more fuel flows for a richer mixture. An auxiliary-air valve passes extra air to create a richer (than throttle valve position calls for) mixture. For cold starts, a separate injector is used to squirt fuel into the intake manifold. This injector is electronically controlled. A thermo-time switch limits the amount of time the valve is open and at high temperatures, cuts it off. The thermo-time switch screws into the water jacket of a water cooled engine or the cylinder head on the air cooled Porsche 911.

Troubleshooting

WATER IN THE FUEL

Water in the fuel, and the resulting rust, are the number one enemies of any fuel injection system, especially CIS. Rust particles inflict more casualties more often on K-Jetronic than any other Bosch injection system. Because normal operating pressure on K systems ranges from 65–85 psi, the fuel pump usually pushes any water right through the fuel filter. A little plastic filter in the center of the fuel distributor traps the water. The trapped water then rusts out the fuel distributor! Not only will the rust block the tiny metering slits in the fuel distributor, it can also flow into the injectors and warm-up compensator. So if you find rust in one

part, you can bet there's rust in the other. When rust particles block a metering slit, the cylinder fed by that slit will either die completely or else develop an intermittent misfire closely resembling the conditions created by a bad plug. If the plug is known to be good, look for rust or water in the fuel. Disconnect the injector lines and spread some fresh white paper towels on the workbench. Remove the entire fuel distributor and tap it against the bench. Shake it and tap it again. If you're able to shake rust particles out of those injector-line openings, it's time for a new fuel distributor.

Water contamination can be prevented with regular, and the emphasis is on regular, fuel filter changes. Filters for these cars are expensive, but a fresh filter is much cheaper than a set of injectors, warm-up regulator, or worse, a fuel distributor. A rusty fuel distributor can't be fixed, and they're very expensive. Not to mention the headaches you will experience with lousy performance, intermittent cut-out, and other nonsense. Change the filter regularly, add water-chasing fuel additives, and don't frequent cheapo gas stations that sell watered down fuel.

See the discussion of water separators/filtration systems under the D and L-Jetronic section.

PRELIMINARY CHECKS

Always make a complete ignition check first and then perform all the injection pressure tests in sequence. The worst return you could get on the time spent hooking up the gauge would be that you'll find the problem quickly or you'll discover there's nothing wrong with the injection system.

The cause of many CIS complaints is the old fashioned vacuum leak. Vacuum leaks fool the fuel metering system and foul up the mixture. This gives poor gas economy and poor performance. Look for leaks at:
1. EGR valve
2. Intake manifold
3. Cold start injector
4. Air sensor boot
5. Brake booster vacuum lines
6. Air ducts

Rust can ruin an expensive fuel distributor

Here's where a good percentage of K-Jet problems start. Water and dirt in fuel ruin pump, warm-up regulator, fuel distributor, and injectors. Change filters!

Symptoms

Engine does not start or starts poorly when **cold**	Engine does not start or starts poorly when **warm**	Irregular idle (engine shakes) during warm-up	Irregular idle (engine shakes) with engine **warm**	Engine misfires (engine shakes) with engine **warm**	Engine does not draw fuel smoothly (backfires)	Insufficient power under full load	Engine runs on (diesels)	Excessive fuel consumption	Flat spot during acceleration	Idle CO value too **high**	Idle CO value too **low**	Idle speed cannot be adjusted (too high)	Engine stalls immediately after starting	Cause(s)
►	►	►	►		►			►		►				Vacuum system leaking (see *Vacuum Leaks*)
►	►		►			►	►		►	►	►			Air flow sensor plate and/or control plunger not moving smoothly (see *Air Flow Sensor Movement*)
	►					►								Air flow sensor plate stop incorrectly set (see *Air Flow Sensor Position*)
►		►												Auxiliary air valve does not open (see *Auxiliary Air Valve*)
												►		Auxiliary air valve does not close (see *Auxiliary Air Valve*)
►	►			►									►	Electric fuel pump not operating (see *Fuel Pump*)
►														Defective cold start system (see *Cold Start System*)
		►	►			►	►		►					Leaking cold start valve (see *Cold Start System*)
►		►												Incorrect cold control pressure (see *Warm-up Regulator*)
	►		►	►	►	►			►				►	Warm control pressure too high (see *Warm-up Regulator*)
			►	►		►		►	►	►			►	Warm control pressure too low (see *Warm-up Regulator*)
				►	►				►				►	Incorrect system pressure (see *System Pressure*)
	►													Fuel system pressure leakage (see *Fuel Leaks*)
	►	►	►		►		►							Injection valve(s) leaking, opening pressure too low (see *Testing Injectors*)
		►	►		►			►						Unequal fuel delivery between cylinders (see *Comparative Test*)
	►	►	►				►	►	►	►	►			Basic idle and/or CO adjustment incorrect (see *Idle and CO Adjustment*)
					►									Throttle plate does not open completely

Check K-Jetronic systems for vacuum leaks at arrows

This residual pressure is called rest pressure. The valve functions are: *valve open—control pressure; valve closed—primary pressure; valve open and engine off—rest pressure.*

On the D and L-Jetronic systems, you locate internal leakage by pinching a hose shut and noting if the system holds rest pressure after you pinch that hose. On K-Jetronic cars, all you have to do is close that valve on the pressure gauge to isolate a leak inside the *feed* side of the system from a leak inside the *return* side.

Primary Pressure

When you close the 3-way valve with the engine idling and the primary pressure reads low, you could have a fuel pump problem or a primary regulator problem. To isolate one from the other, locate the return line leading from the fuel distributor back to the gas tank. Now plug the return line securely at some convenient point. Have an assistant switch on the pump *just long enough* to get

Rubber boot must be tight. Always give air ducts the once-over for leaks or cracks. Vacuum leaks will upset system and the engine will never run correctly

And, don't forget the less obvious vacuum limiter, evaporative canister, and A/C door actuator.

To quick test the system for leaks, disconnect the auxiliary air valve hose, block open the throttle, and apply shop air pressure to the hose. Use a spray bottle of soapy water to hit all the fittings where leaks could occur.

FUEL PUMP POWER CHECK

Tracing K-Jetronic fuel pump problems is very similar to checking an electric pump on a D or L-Jetronic system. K-type pumps need 12 volts and a good ground. A relay located somewhere in the pump's power wire operates the pumps. And like D and L systems, the relay may be a hide-and-seek item. All K-Jetronic pumps are fused someplace in the car, usually right in the vehicle's fuse panel.

If the pump's dead, check the fuse, the ground, and try bridging the relay with a jumper wire. During winter months, water

CIS electronic fuel pumps are found back near the tank. Filter is on pressure side of pump because it would be ruined if allowed to run "dry", since fuel cools it

in the gas can cause the pump to freeze and then blow a fuse.

PRESSURE TESTS

It's impossible to test any K-Jetronic system without an accurate 100-psi gauge and a 3-way valve such as the one illustrated.

Diagnose a K-Jetronic system in this order: check cold control pressure first, hot control pressure next, then primary pressure, and finally rest pressure. The gauge for testing K-Jetronic always tees into the line running between the fuel distributor and the warm-up compensator. With the 3-way valve open, the gauge remains teed-in and therefore reads control pressure. Remember that control pressure is derived or fed from the primary circuit pressure so a pressure change in one circuit means a change in the other.

Closing the valve shuts off fuel flow to the warm-up compensator and forces the gauge to read only one circuit—the primary circuit.

When you shut the engine off and leave the 3-way valve open, the teed-in gauge should show the system's holding pressure.

Fuel pressure test points with push valve (top) and without push valve (bottom). In general, vehicles since 1978 have push valves, recognizable by 2 fuel lines connecting to the warm-up regulator

a pressure reading. If the pump is good, the pressure will jump almost instantly to 100 psi or higher. Should the primary pressure exceed 116 psi during this momentary test, the check valve in the intake side of the fuel pump will vent the pressure back into the gas tank.

If the fuel pump produces good pressure with the return line plugged, then you know that the primary pressure regulator is causing your low primary pressure reading. If that little O-ring you find around the inboard end of the primary regulator starts leaking or becomes dislodged, it'll lower primary pressure. Install a primary regulator repair kit from your Bosch supplier. If installing this kit doesn't bring primary pressure within specs, you'll have to shim the primary pressure regulator. For every 0.1 mm shim you install, the primary pressure should increase about 2 psi (0.15 bar.). Some Bosch suppliers stock these shims and import car dealers should stock shims for the fuel distributors on any CIS-equipped cars they sell. If you can't get the shims, you'll have to replace the entire fuel distributor.

What if primary pressure is higher than specs? The car probably won't run, but look for a kinked fuel return line under the car.

Rest Pressure

Good rest pressure enables a K-Jetronic engine to start easily when it's hot. If the K system loses rest pressure for any reason, the injector lines will literally vapor lock. Then the driver has to crank the engine until the pump can replenish the lines with liquid fuel.

REST PRESSURE DROPS QUICKLY

Suppose you shut off the engine and the rest pressure drops off too quickly. Start the engine and run it long enough to build the system pressure back up. Then kill the engine, pull the electrical connector off the cold start injector and remove the injector from the intake manifold. If the cold start injector is dripping, replace it and re-check rest pressure.

If the cold-start valve is holding pressure, reinstall it and run the engine again to build up pressure. Kill the engine and close the 3-way valve. If the pressure reading remains steady now, you know the return side of the system—the warm-up compensator—is leaking. Replace the compensator. If the rest pressure still drops rapidly after you've closed the 3-way valve, the leak's in the feed side of the system. This could mean a bad fuel pump, bad accumulator, or a bad primary pressure regulator.

Shoot for the easy stuff first. The fuel pump's intake hose is flexible. Clamp this hose shut and recheck rest pressure. If the system holds pressure, then the check ball in the output side of the pump is leaking.

A sharp eye and a healthy ear will help you isolate a bad accumulator. Watch your

pressure gauge as your helper shuts off the engine. If the accumulator's good, the pressure will drop, stop for a second, and then the gauge needle will actually rise—pressure will increase for a moment—before the pressure stabilizes. If you don't see that slight upward needle movement, the accumulator is leaking rest pressure. Furthermore, a bad accumulator will cause a loud, tell-tale groaning noise at the fuel pump. If you're still in doubt about that accumulator, try blocking off its return line.

The same primary pressure regulator that can cause low primary pressure can also leak *rest* pressure. If you've eliminated the fuel pump and the accumulator, then install a primary regulator repair kit.

AIR FLOW SENSOR PLATE

The air flow sensor plate in the fuel distributor must operate smoothly in order to do a good job of measuring air. Remove the air boot and check the sensor plate movement. When released, the plate should fall freely with one or two bounces. If the plate sticks, loosen the mounting screws and retighten them uniformly. If it feels as if the plunger is sticking, remove it and clean it in solvent. Be very careful not to drop it. Clean the funnel and sensor plate too, as these can get dirty from PCV fumes.

The sensor plate should sit flat and rest even in the narrowest part of the funnel. It shouldn't touch the sides of the funnel. If it's out of position, loosen the center screw and using a Bosch guide plate or 0.10 mm feeler gauge, center the plate.

When the sensor plate moves, fuel is delivered. Check the sensor plate for free movement. You should feel even resistant through it's full travel

FUEL PUMP

Volume Test

The fuel pump is sometimes a source of trouble. Dirt in the fuel can quickly ruin a pump. Check the pump after being sure the fuel filter isn't clogged, the ground connections are good, and at least 11.5 volts are supplied to the pump.

1. Disconnect the return line at the fuel distributor.

2. Run the pump for 30 seconds and

compare fuel quantity against specifications in the car section.

3. Check fuel delivery at the warm-up regulator. Disconnect the regulator and auxiliary air valve, as we don't want them controlling pressure during the test.

4. Jump the safety circuit to run the pump for 30 seconds. Compare the fuel delivered against specifications in the car section. A K-Jetronic system should deliver the quantity of fuel shown in the "Tune-Up Specifications" chart in the manufacturer's car section. If no volume specification is given, a typical K-Jetronic system will deliver approximately 1 quart of gas in about 30 seconds.

If the filter's good, pump's getting close to 12 volts, and the fuel line and tank strainer are OK—replace the pump.

ACCUMULATOR DIAPHRAGM

If the pump flunks a volume test, raise the car and trace the fuel feed line back to the pump. Look for mashed or crimped lines from a carelessly-placed jack. Next, plug the accumulator return hose and repeat the volume test. If this yields good fuel volume, you know the accumulator diaphragm is ruptured. If the accumulator trick does no good, douse a new fuel filter with clean gas and install it. A fresh fuel filter every 10—12,000 miles is cheap protection for any K-Jetronic system. Just remember to wet the filter beforehand. When 80 psi worth of incoming fuel hits a dry filter, it can tear off some of the element and carry the paper debris into the rest of the system. If the pump fails a volume test after you change the fuel filter, replace it.

COLD START INJECTOR

The cold start injector can be checked by removing it. Ground one terminal and connect the second to the positive side of the coil. When you run the pump, 10–30 seconds is plenty, you should get a good, cone-shaped spray. Dry the injector, disconnect your jumpers, and energize the pump again. There shouldn't be any fuel. If it drips, replace it. Check the thermo-time switch when it's below 95°F. Disconnect the cold start injector and hook up a test light across its connector. Ground No. 1 coil terminal and run the starter. The light should glow for several seconds and then go out. If not, replace the thermo-time switch.

INJECTOR SPRAY PATTERN

A bad injection valve can cause a number of problems:

1. Hot restart troubles
2. Rough idle
3. Hesitation
4. Poor power

If the engine ever blows off this rubber boot (arrow) connecting air flow sensor to the manifold, the engine won't start. Cold start valve is nearly identical to D- or L-Jetronic electrical injectors. If you can't find a rest-pressure leak anywhere else, warm up engine, pull wiring connector off cold start valve, and shut engine off. Then pull cold start valve out of manifold and see if it's dribbling fuel

Use your vacuum gauge. O-ring seals on K-Jetronic injectors often dry out and create intake vacuum leaks, rough idling, etc.

Hot starting complaints can come from an injector or injectors that are leaking fuel droplets when they're supposed to be completely shut. The next three problems can be caused by a bad spray pattern from one or more of the injectors. Dribble patterns, fire hose shots, and uneven sprays will produce hesitation, stumbling and general lack of power.

On-Car Testing

With care, you can check injectors without a tester, but if you suspect injector problems, it's worth having them checked on a test stand. To watch spray patterns on the

K-Jet fuel injector pulled from head. You can test these on the car by switching ignition ON and then lifting and releasing sensor plate. Spray should be cone-like

car, switch the ignition on, pull an injector out of the head, and lift the air sensor plate with your fingers (carefully). When you let the plate down quickly, you should get a fine, cone-shaped spray of fuel. If not, the injector should come off and be cleaned or replaced. Repeat the test for each injector. Hot start complaints call for a different procedure. Crank the starter and pull each injector in turn. If an injector drips fuel, it's defective and should be replaced.

Off-Car Testing

Testing injectors out of the car is the most accurate method for determining whether or not they're causing performance problems. Individual injectors are expensive items, and immediately trashing suspect injection valves is not wise. New and old injectors can be mixed in the set for that engine, so only defective units need be replaced.

Bosch manufactures a valve tester KDJE 7452. This tester is only for K-Jet injectors, the tester shown in the photos here is another Bosch unit that also tests mechanical fuel and diesel injection valves. The K-Jet only tester reads to 142.2 psi and comes with a hand pump, pressure gauge, test-fluid bottle, and test line. All you need do is bolt it to a stand.

On the test stand, you can operate the valve as much as you like and watch the pattern. Use kerosene as a test fluid, not gasoline! With the injector filled with fluid and bled, tighten the test line fitting. Slowly

work the handle, without going over 21 psi. Pressure should build up and the injector shouldn't leak. Next, build up pressure with the test valve open until the injector squirts. Opening pressure for all K-Jet cars except Mercedes-Benz is 35–52 psi Mercedes injectors open at 42–58 psi.

IDLE ADJUSTMENTS

The idle speed screw (called a by-pass screw by some manufacturers) on the throttle-body housing of a K system bleeds air into the manifold when you increase idle speed—or cuts it off to slow the engine down. When you change idle speed, the idle mixture always changes to some degree, and vice-versa. Therefore, you'll have to juggle the speed and mixture adjustments back and forth to get the specified idle speed within the right range of CO. Tweak that mixture screw a wee bit at a time. It's so sensitive that you can just *touch* it with the 3mm Allen wrench and the CO changes! And unlike a carburetor, changing the idle CO changes the mixture throughout the entire rpm range. Never rev the engine with the Allen wrench sitting in the mixture screw or you may damage the air sensor plate.

Engine oil temperature is the most critical factor in getting an accurate CO adjustment on any K-Jetronic system. Don't touch the mixture screw until the oil temperature is between 140–176°F (60–80°C). If you try adjusting mixture when the engine oil's hotter than 176°F, you'll end up with a lean-running engine. If the engine's

Mixture adjustment on CIS is especially critical, since it effects the air/fuel ratio throughout the operating range, not just at idle. Adjustment is made with Allen wrench (arrow)

Uneven spray

Fire hose

Off center

Correctly atomized

Fuel injector spray patterns

K-Jetronic in its Lambda guise. Components are like earlier K-Jets, with the addition of an electronic control unit (ECU), oxygen sensor, and frequency valve. This system is used with a 3-way converter. Oxygen sensor signals ECU to have frequency valve enrichen or lean mixture according to exhaust O₂ content

too cold, your mixture setting will give you a rich-running guzzler.

Companies such as Sun Electric and Siemens include oil temperature probes with their equipment. These probes slip into the dipstick tube. Mercedes offers an oil thermometer among their shop tools.

Final advice? Other than servicing the primary pressure regulator, don't fool around with a fuel distributor! Opening a fuel distributor would be like opening Pandora's Box all over again.

LAMBDA (CLOSED LOOP) SYSTEM

With the advent of the 3-way catalytic converter, the K-Jetronic system has undergone modification. Three new components have been integrated with the system, an oxygen sensor, an electronic control unit (ECU), and a frequency valve. These convert K-Jet into a closed loop fuel system. In order for the 3-way converter to work effectively, the air/fuel mixture must be kept within a very precise range. Between 15 and 14 parts of air to one part of fuel, there's an ideal ratio called stoichiometric where

HC, CO, and NO_x emissions are all at a minimum. Bosch calls this ratio, or point, Lambda. Combined with an oxygen, or Lambda, sensor, the air/fuel ratio in a fuel injected system can be controlled within a tolerance of 0.02%

The oxygen sensor in the exhaust system monitors the oxygen content of the exhaust gases. It produces a small amount of voltage that varies depending on the amount of oxygen present in the exhaust. This voltage signal is sent to the ECU. The ECU, in turn, then signals the frequency valve to enrichen or lean the mixture. The voltage signal is approximately one volt. The frequency valve is located between the fuel distributor and the fuel return line. It does not change control pressure in the K-Jet system; it alters system pressure in the lower chamber of the fuel distributor for each cylinder's differential pressure valve.

Duty Cycle

When the oxygen sensor signals a rich mixture to the ECU, it will close the frequency valve. This causes pressure in the lower chamber of the fuel distributor to increase and push the diaphragm up to reduce fuel quantity. If the air/fuel mixture is too lean,

the frequency valve will be open and reduce pressure in the lower chamber. The diaphragm is then pushed down and the amount of fuel is increased. The valve opens and closes many times per second. The average pressure is determined by the ratio of valve openings and closings. A higher open-to-closed ratio would provide a richer mixture, a lower open-to-closed ratio would give a leaner mixture. This is called the duty cycle of the frequency valve.

Bosch makes a tester for the Lambda system that measures the open-to-closed ratio, or duty cycle. The Bosch KDJE 7453 tester reads out the duty cycle on a percentage meter. A reading of 60, for instance, would be a frequency valve pulse rate of 60% You can also use a sensitive dwell meter that reads to at least 70° to measure duty cycle on the 4-cyl. scale. Manufacturers using K-Jet with Lambda provide a test socket, so that a duty cycle tester can easily be hooked up. Audi's test connection, for instance, is located behind the throttle valve housing. Saab and most other makers locate the test socket in the wiring harness right near the underhood relay box.

The following is a general procedure for checking the duty cycle with a dwell meter.

1. Disconnect the thermo switch wiring. Shorting the switch will enrich the mixture to about 60% for a cold engine. The meter needle should stay steady, which indicates an "open loop." This means the system isn't being affected by the oxygen sensor. Reconnect the thermo switch.

2. Disconnect the oxygen sensor with a warm engine. The meter should register a 50% signal.

3. Reconnect the oxygen sensor. You should see a change from open to closed loop. The needle will stay steady in the middle at 50% for about a minute. When the oxygen sensor warms up, it should signal the frequency valve for closed loop operation. That will be shown by a swinging needle on the meter, when the system is working correctly.

Turbocharging

DESCRIPTION

A turbocharger is an exhaust-driven turbine which drives a centrifugal compressor wheel. The compressor is usually located between the air cleaner and the engine's intake manifold, while the turbine is located between the exhaust manifold and the muffler. Primarily, the turbocharger compresses the air entering the engine, forcing more air into the cylinders. This allows the engine to efficiently burn more fuel, thereby producing more horsepower.

All of the exhaust gases pass through the turbine housing. The expansion of these gases, acting on the turbine wheel, causes it to turn. After passing through the turbine the exhaust gases are routed to the atmosphere through the exhaust system. On some non-automotive applications, the turbocharger provides sufficient muffling of the exhaust noises to eliminate the need for a muffler.

1. V-band coupling
2. Compressor housing
3. Bolt, turbine
4. Lockplate, turbine
5. Clamp, turbine
6. Turbine housing
7. Nut, shaft
8. Turbine shaft wheel
9. Compressor wheel
10. Lockplate, backplate
11. Bolt, backplate
12. Backplate (vaneless on some models)
13. O-ring (used on vaned backplate)
14. Seal ring
15. Seal spacer
16. Piston ring
17. Thrust collar
18. Inboard thrust washer
19. Bearing retainer
20. Bearing washer
21. Bearing
22. Center housing
23. Shroud, turbine
24. Drive screw
25. Nameplate
26. Piston ring, turbine
27. Pin

Typical turbocharger exploded view

Typical turbocharger air flow schematic

The turbine also functions as a spark arrester. For example, the US Department of Agriculture recognizes the turbocharger as an adequate spark arrester for forestry operations.

OPERATION

The compressor and turbine are each enclosed in their own housings and are directly connected by a shaft. The housings are constructed of light alloy and are designed for maximum heat dissipation. The only power loss from the turbine to the compressor is the slight friction of the shaft journal bearings. Air is drawn in through the filtered intake system, compressed by the compressor wheel and discharged into the intake manifold. The extra charge of air provided by the turbocharger allows more fuel to be burned, providing more power.

As engine speed increases, the length of time the intake valves are open decreases, giving the air less time to fill the cylinders. On an engine running at 2500 rpm, the intake valves are open less than 0.017 second. The air drawn into a naturally aspirated engine's cylinder is less than atmospheric pressure. Turbochargers pack air into the cylinder at greater than atmospheric pressure at all speeds. The flow of exhaust gas from each cylinder occurs intermittantly as the exhaust valve opens. This results in fluctuating gas pressures, also known as pulse energy, at the turbine inlet. With a conventional turbine housing, only a small amount of pulse energy is used.

To better utilize these impulses, one design has an internal division in the turbine housing and the exhaust manifold which directs these exhaust gases to the turbine wheel. There is a

Altitude compensator

separate passage for each half of the engine cylinder exhaust.

On some four and six cylinder engines built to accommodate turbochargers, there is a separate passage for the front two or three cylinders and another for the rear half.

By using a fully divided exhaust system combined with a dual scroll turbine housing, the result is a highly effective nozzle velocity. This produces higher turbine speeds and manifold pressures than can be obtained with an undivided system.

At high altitudes, a naturally aspirated engine drops 3% in horsepower per 1000 feet elevation due to a 3% decrease in air density per 1000 feet.

With a turbocharged engine, an increase in altitude also increases the pressure drop

1.	Bellows	15.	Drive screw
2.	Capscrew	16.	Adjusting screw
3.	Capscrew, seal type	17.	Lead seal
4.	Side cover	18.	Upper shaft
5.	Bellows cover	19.	Lower shaft
6.	Screw seal	20.	Bellows spring
7.	Air filter	21.	Lever
8.	Housing	22.	O-ring
9.	Lockwasher	23.	Lever, pin
10.	Nut	24.	Shaft valve
11.	Piston	25.	Check valve
12.	Dataplate	26.	Bellows washer
13.	Plug	27.	Washer
14.	Pipe plugs		

Aneroid exploded view

across the turbine. Inlet turbine pressure remains the same, but the outlet pressure decreases as the altitude increases. Turbine speed also increases as the pressure difference increases. The compressor wheel turns faster, providing approximately the same inlet pressure as at sea level, even though the incoming air is less dense.

There are, however, limitations to the actual amount of compensation for altitude provided by the turbocharger. These limitations are primarily a result of varying amounts of boost pressure and turbocharger-to-engine match. To make up for the difference in altitude compensation, an altitude compensator

Basic parts of the turbocharger

is added to the system. During rapid acceleration or rapid engine load changes, the turbocharger speed, reflected in manifold pressure, inherently lags behind the power or fuel demand exercised by the opening of the throttle. This lag does not exist in the fuel system, so an overly rich mixture accompanied by heavy smoke occurs until the turbocharger catches up.

On diesel engines, two types of altitude compensators are used. One is a compressed air type which is very similar in appearance to the turbocharger. This type supplies compressed air to the intake manifold at a pressure about equal to sea level pressure. There is no increase of fuel for combustion and consequently no horsepower increase. However, the extra air provided by the altitude compensator usually increases combustion efficiency, thereby increasing fuel economy and reducing smoke levels.

The second type is the aneroid type unit. The function of the aneroid is to create a lag in the fuel system response equal to that of the turbocharger, thereby control the mixture problem and eliminating the smoke. The aneroid system is widely used on diesel engines and on some gasoline engines.

Fuel from the outlet side of the fuel pump enters the aneroid and goes through the starting check valve area. On others, it must be located in the supply line. The starting check valve prevents the aneroid from bypassing fuel at the engine during cranking. For speeds above cranking, fuel pressure forces the check valve open, allowing fuel to flow to the valve port of the aneroid shaft. The shaft and its bore form the bypass valve. This shaft and bore allow passage or restriction of fuel flow in a manner similar to that of a pressure/time type injection pump.

Fuel allowed to pass through the bypass valve is returned to the suction side of the injection pump. The bypassed fuel manifold pressure in proportion to the bypass rate. The shaft and sleeve are bypassing fuel when the control arm on the aneroid is resting against the adjusting screw. The amount of fuel bypassed is regulated by this screw which is located at the bottom of the aneroid body. The control lever, which is connected to a piston in the aneroid body by an actuating shaft, rotates the shaft closing the valve port. The lever is actuated by manifold pressure against the piston and diaphragm. Anytime the manifold pressure is above a present air actuating pressure, the aneroid is effectively out of the system. When pressure drops below the preset figure, the aneroid comes into the system.

In modern automotive gasoline engine applications with their stricter emission control standards, turbocharger lag is compensated for by means of modified spark control and/or an enrichment vacuum regulator system. The spark control system changes the ignition timing on demand and the vacuum regulator system regulates vacuum flow at the carburetor through a remote power enrichment port.

Some engines, particularly passenger car applications, in which boost pressure must be held at low levels, utilize a wastegate unit. Since turbocharger operation is self-perpetuating, unchecked operation will increase boost pressure beyond the operating capabilities of these engines. Some method of limiting this boost increases must be used. The principle means is by the inclusion of a wastegate in the system. The wastegate, usually located in the outlet elbow assembly, is activated when boost pressure reaches a predetermined level (usually 3-7 psi depending on application). The wastegate opens and bypasses exhaust flow around the turbine.

LUBRICATION

Since turbine speeds routinely reach 140,000 rpm, adequate lubrication is vitally important. Turbochargers are lubricated by engine oil. Depending on the application, the lubrication may be either pressure-fed or gravity-fed. In areas of very heavy load or when shut-down after peak operation is routine, pressure feeding, sometimes with a separate oil pump, is used. In cases where a separate oil pump is used, the pump continues operating during spin-down. Since all parts of the rotating assemblies are protected by a film of oil, no metal-to-metal contact occurs. Consequently, no appreciable wear should occur. If a constant supply of clean engine oil is maintained, bearing life should be indefinite. If the unit has floating sleeve type bearings, they provide oil clearance between the bearing and housing as well as between the bearing and shaft. When the turbocharger is operating, this allows the bearing

Twin passage turbine

to turn as the shaft turns. All clearances in the turbocharger are closely controlled and carefully machined. Any dirt in the oil will adversely affect service life of the working parts. Oil and filter changes should occur regularly. Some manufacturers recommend more frequent oil changes for turbocharged engines. In any case, on turbocharged engines, the oil filter(s) should ALWAYS be changed with the engine oil. ALWAYS use oil of the recommended viscosity for that particular engine application. Check the owner's manual for your engine or vehicle for recommended intervals and proper viscosity.

TWO-CYCLE APPLICATIONS

Turbochargers may be used in addition to the regular scavenging process. In these cases, the air is drawn into the blower or scavenging pump and then transferred to the turbocharger where it is compressed and forced into the engine.

At light loads, there is little energy available to drive the turbocharger. The mechanically driven blower alone supplies scavenging air to cylinders. At increased loads, the turbocharger speeds up and takes in a sufficient amount of additional air to allow the inlet

pressure to drop to atmospheric levels, causing the blower check valve to open. At this engine speed, the blower becomes unloaded, saving engine power, and the turbocharger enters the load range where it alone can provide scavenging and turbocharging. Under ideal conditions, the engine starting air contains enough energy to start the turbocharger and also supply enough air for combustion. In some applications, however, turbochargers can be equipped with additional methods for supplying necessary scavenging air while the engine is being started. This can be accomplished either mechanically by coupling the turbocharger to the crankshaft in such a manner that it is mechanically driven during starting and automatically disconnects when exhaust pressure is high enough or by jet air starting, where air is blown through jets into the turbocharger turbine or compressor. The air passing through the compressor also aids in scavenging during starting.

INTERCOOLERS

When the air passing through the compressor is compressed it becomes heated and expands. Expanding air is less dense, therefore less air is forced into the engine. This helps defeat the turbocharging process. To overcome this condition, some engine applications use a heat exchanger, also known as an inter-

Turbocharger oil flow

ENGINE EXHAUST GAS FLOW
COMPRESSED AIR FLOW

Two cycle air flow

cooler or after cooler. The intercooler reduces intake air temperature by as much as 90° F.

Located between the turbocharger and the intake manifold, the intercooler is a series of connected tubes, finned to provide dissipation, through which engine coolant is circulated. The carrying off of heat from the air makes the air denser, allowing more air to be forced into the engine. This provides more power, greater economy and quieter combustion.

GENERAL OPERATING INSTRUCTIONS FOR TURBOCHARGED ENGINES

1. After starting the engine, make sure there is sufficient oil pressure before accelerating or applying load.

2. When starting in cold weather, allow the engine to run a sufficient length of time (up to five minutes for diesel engines in extreme cold) before applying load or accelerating. This will insure adequate lubrication.

3. Should the engine stall at normal operating temperature, restart it immediately. This will prevent a rapid rise in the turbocharger

known as "temperature soaking". Also, the turbocharger, running hot during operation, may experience coking due to hot oil build-up in the center section. This coking will cause a blockage of the oil passages leading to failure of the unit.

4. Before stopping the engine, allow it to run for a short length of time (up to two or three minutes for some diesels) to allow internal engine temperatures to normalize or equalize. Failure to allow temperature normalization can lead to heat fatigue and/or blockage of oil passages due to coking.

— CAUTION —
When transporting an engine equipped with a turbocharger, always cover the exhaust outlet. This will prevent entrance of foreign material and/or the rotation of the turbine. Turbine rotation on a stopped engine could lead to bearing failure since no lubricating oil will be provided.

PREVENTIVE MAINTENANCE

1. Inspect all mountings and connections regularly to make sure they are secure and no leakage is present.

2. Make certain that there is no restriction in air flow at the crankcase ventilation system.

3. Run the engine at various, normal operating speeds and listen for unusual noises at the turbocharger.

Turbochargers normally emit a shrill whistle or whine. Bearings about to fail also emit a shrill whine, somewhat different from normal turbocharger noise. Try to distinguish between the two.

NOTE: After engine shut-off, the turbocharger will whine during rundown. Don't confuse this with bearing failure noise. Grating or scraping noises could indicate improper turbine or compressor wheel-to-housing clearances. If any such noises are heard, the unit should be removed for inspection.

4. Check the unit for unusual vibrations during operation.

5. Check for unusual smoking under load conditions. Excessive smoke means an incorrect air/fuel ratio.

6. Inspect and replace the air filter according to your owner's manual recommendations.

TROUBLE-SHOOTING

The turbocharger is a relatively simple unit. Most problems occur in other parts of the engine such as the lubrication system or the fuel system. With proper routine maintenance, the unit should give troublefree operation.

TURBOCHARGER TROUBLESHOOTING CHART

Trouble	Possible Cause	Remedy
Noisy operation or vibration.	Bearings not being lubricated.	Supply required oil pressure. Clean or replace oil line. If trouble persists, overhaul the turbocharger.
	Leak in engine intake or exhaust manifold.	Tighten loose connections or replace manifold gaskets.
Engine will not deliver rated power.	Clogged manifold system.	Clear all ducting.
	Foreign matter lodged in compressor, impeller, or turbine.	Disassemble and clean.
	Excessive buildup in compressor.	Thoroughly clean compressor assembly. Clean air cleaner and check for leaks.
	Leak in engine intake or exhaust manifold.	Tighten loose connections or replace manifold gaskets.
	Rotating assembly bearing seizure.	Overhaul turbocharger.
Oil seal leakage.	Failure of seal.	Overhaul turbocharger.
	Restriction in air cleaner or air intake creating suction.	Remove the restriction.

Manual Transmissions

MANUAL TRANSMISSIONS APPLICATION CHART

Make	Year	Vehicle Model	Transmission Model	Speeds	Reference Type No.	Page
BMW	'76	2002	232	4	6	U62
			235/5	5	7	U65
	'76	3.0Si	262/8, 9	4	4	U57
			ZF-S4-18/3	4	8	U67
	'77–'82	320i	242/9, 18, 18.50	4	5	U59
	'77–'83	528i, 530i	262/8, 9, 9.20	4	4	U57
		630CSi, 633CSi	262/8, 9, 9.20, 9.90 ①	4	4	U57
		733i	262/8, 9, 9.10, 9.30, 9.35	4	4	U57
Capri	'76–'77	All	—	4	9	U69
Chrysler Corp./ Mitsubishi	'76–'78	Arrow	KM110	4	1	U51
	'77–'80	Arrow	KM119	5	2	U53
			KM132	5	3	U56
	'76–'78	Colt/Champ	KM110	4	1	U51
	'76–'79	Colt/Champ	KM119	5	2	U53
			KM132	5	3	U56
	'76–'80	Colt/Champ Wagon	KM110	4	1	U51
			KM119	5	2	U53
			KM132	5	3	U56
	'78–'83	Challenger/Sapporo Starion	KM119	5	2	U53
			KM132	5	3	U56
Datsun/Nissan	'76–'78	B210	F4W60L	4	17	U88
	'78–'82	210	F4W60L	4	17	U88
			F4W56A	4	13	U75
			FS5W60A,L	5	16	U84
	'78–'81	510	F4W63L	4	10, 15 ②	U70, U81
			FS5W63A	5	14	U77
	'76–'77	610, 710	F4W63L	4	10, 15 ②	U70, U81
	'77–'83	810, Maxima	F4W71B	4	11	U72
			FS5W71B	5	12	U73
	'77–'79	200SX	FS5W63A	5	14	U77

MANUAL TRANSMISSIONS APPLICATION CHART

Make	Year	Vehicle Model	Transmission Model	Speeds	Reference Type No.	Page
	'80–'83	200SX	FS5W71B	5	12	U73
	'76–'83	280Z, ZX	F4W71B	4	11	U72
			FS5W71B	5	12	U73
Fiat	'76–'83	124, Spider	—	4 & 5	18	U91
	'76–'81	131, Brava	—	5	19	U93
Isuzu	'81–'83	All	—	4	26	U107
			—	5	27	U109
Mazda	'76–'78	Cosmo	—	5	22	U100
	'77–'80	GLC	—	4 & 5	21	U98
	'76–'78	RX-3	—	4	20	U95
	'76–'78	RX-4	—	4	20	U95
			—	5	22	U100
	'79–'83	RX-7	—	5	22	U100
	'79–'82	626	—	4 & 5	21	U98
	'76–'78	808	—	4	20	U95
			—	5	22	U100
Mercedes-Benz	'76–'83	All	—	4	23	U103
MG	'76–'79	Midget	—	4	25	U104
	'76–'80	MGB	—	4	24	U104
Peugeot	'76–'83	504	BA-7, BA-10, BA-10/4	4	28	U111
	'80–'83	505	BA-7, BA-10, BA-10/4	4	28	U111
			BA-10/5	5	37	U137
	'77–'80	604	BA-7, BA-10, BA-10/4	4	28	U111
	'82–'83	604	BA-10/5	5	37	U137
Toyota	'76–'83	Celica, Supra	W40	4	34	U128
			W50, P51, W55, W58③	5	35	U130
	'76–'79	Corolla	K40, K50	4 & 5	32	U123
	'80–'83	Corolla	T40, T41, T50	4 & 5	33	U126
	'76–'82	Corona	W40	4	34	U128
			W50, P51	5	35	U130
	'81–'83	Starlet	K40, K50, K51	4 & 5	32	U123
Triumph	'76–'81	Spitfire	—	4	30	U120
	'76	TR-6	—	4	31	U121
	'76–'81	TR-7, TR-8	—	4	30	U120
			—	5	29	U118
Volvo	'76–'83	All	M45, M46	4	36	U135

NOTE: Although certain late model transmissions may differ slightly from the earlier models; certain basic similarities will usually exist, thus enabling overhaul of the newest models with the guidelines given within the text.

① 262/9.90 is the model designation for 1982–83 Calif. transmissions

② Two different versions of the same model were imported; use the illustrations to identify the transmission being overhauled

③ The W55 and W58 transmissions used in 1981 and later models are similar to the W50 and P51

TYPE 1

4 Speed Transmission–Model KM 110

Chrysler Corp./ Mitsubishi

DISASSEMBLY

1. Using a ³/₁₆ in. punch, drive out the clutch spring pins. Remove the clutch shaft with release fork and springs.

2. Remove the speedometer gear assembly and the lockplate. Remove the clutch and the back-up light switches.

3. The extension housing can be removed by tapping lightly with a hammer.

4. With the transmission inverted remove the bottom cover.

5. Remove the speedometer drive snap-rings, and gear. Remove the main drive gear retainer. Remove the countershaft stopper.

6. Remove the countershaft rearward. Remove the countergear, 40 roller bearings, spacers, and front and rear washers.

7. Lift out the thrust washer, rear idler gear, needle bearings, and spacer located on the reverse idler gear shaft.

8. Withdraw the gear shaft bolt and pull the shaft from the case. Remove the front idler gear.

9. Locate the three plugs on the left case side. Remove them and the poppet springs and balls.

10. Loosen the reverse shift bar and reverse locking bolt. Pull out the reverse shift bar. Remove the reverse shaft fork and spacer.

11. Using a ³/₁₆ in. punch, drive the fork spring pins and shift bar from the mount. Remove the shift bar and the shaft fork. Do not disassemble the shift bar.

12. Remove the reverse gear from the case.

13. Remove the mainshaft and the main drive gear synchronizer ring.

14. Pull the main drive gear assembly from the case front. Remove all snap-rings.

15. Remove the shifter assembly.

TRANSMISSION SPECIFICATIONS:

Helical gear backlash: 0.002-0.006 in.

Shift fork to sleeve clearance: 0.004-0.008 in.

Spur gear backlash: 0.004-0.008 in.

Gear change lever-selector groove clearance: 0.004-0.012 in.

Reverse shift fork-reverse gear groove clearance: 0.004-0.012 in.

ASSEMBLY

1. Press the bearing onto the main drive gear.

2. Secure it with the snap-ring of appropriate thickness to give an end-play of 0.002 in.

Snap-Ring Code (in.):
White 0.091
None 0.093
Red 0.094
Yellow 0.098

3. Assemble the hub and synchronizer ring.

Synchronizer inspection—Dimension A = 0.059 in.

4. Place the front and rear springs on the shaft in opposite directions.

5. Assemble the second gear synchronizer hub with the stepped gear end (narrow toothed side rearward).

6. Install the needle bearings and third gear onto the mainshaft from the front end.

7. Install the snychronizer assembly.

8. Assemble the first-second synchronizer in the same direction it was removed.

9. Fit the snap-rings to give a proper end-play of 0.0012-0.0075 in. Third-fourth gear hub end-play is 0.00-0.0043 in.

Snap-Ring Code (in.):
None 0.085
Yellow 0.087
Green 0.090
Blue 0.093

10. Place the needle bearings and the second gear on the mainshaft from the rear.

11. Install the synchronizer assembly.

1. Flywheel
2. Transmission case
3. Main drive gear
4. Synchronizer sleeve (for third-fourth speed)
5. Third-speed gear
6. Second-speed gear
7. Synchronizer sleeve (for first-second speeds)
8. First-speed gear
9. Rear bearing retainer
10. Reverse gear
11. Control shaft
12. Gearshift lever assembly
13. Pressure plate assembly
14. Counter gear
15. Under cover
16. Mainshaft
17. Reverse idler gear
18. Extension housing
19. Shift fork (reverse)
20. Speedometer drive gear

Cross section of 4-speed transmission model, KM 110

1. Snap-ring
2. Synchronizer ring
3. Synchronizer hub (3rd-4th speeds)
4. Synchronizer spring
5. Synchronizer piece
6. Synchronizer sleeve (3rd-4th speeds)
7. Needle bearing

8. 3rd-speed gear
9. Mainshaft
10. 2nd-speed gear
11. Synchronizer hub (1st-2nd speeds)
12. Synchronizer sleeve (1st-2nd speeds)
13. Low-speed gear
14. Spacer bushing

15. Spacer
16. Snap-ring
17. Ball bearing
18. Locknut
19. Reverse gear
20. Speedometer drive gear

Exploded view of mainshaft components

12. Check and adjust the end-play to 0.0012-0.0075 in.

13. Place the first gear spacer, middle bearings, synchronizer, and first gear on the shaft.

14. Adjust end-play to 0.0012-0.0075 in.

15. Spacer must be installed with the I mark in the direction of the ball bearing.

16. Install the mainshaft bearing with a suitable driver and tighten the locknut.

17. Install the snap-ring and retainer.

18. Adjust to give a mainshaft bearing end-play of 0.00-0.006 in.

Snap-Ring Code (in.):
None 0.057
Red 0.060
White 0.064
Yellow 0.067
Blue 0.071

19. Invert the transmission case.

20. Install the main drive gear assembly into the transmission case.

21. Place the needle bearings on the main drive gear front end.

22. Install the synchronizer ring.

23. Be certain that all synchronizer rings are in proper mesh.

24. Install the rear bearing retainer in the case.

25. Place the reverse gear in position on the mainshaft. Install the shift fork into the shift fork groove in the synchronizer sleeve. While holding the forks, place the third-fourth shift bar assembly into the case through the lower rear hole.

26. Insert the first interlock plunger in the case; drive the plunger into position with the use of an appropriate driver.

27. Place the first-second gear shift bar assembly into the case. Position the shift forks so that the pin holes are aligned with the shift

bar holes. Secure the shift forks to the shift bars with spring pins into position with the slot of the centerline of the shift bar.

28. Insert the second interlock plunger into the case.

29. Place the reverse shift fork ends in the reverse gear groove. Insert the reverse gear bar into the fork. Install the spacer on the shift bar and place the reverse shift bar assembly into the case. Secure the fork to the bar with a locking bolt.

30. Position the poppet balls and springs. Insert the plugs with commercial sealant. Be certain to install the tapered end of the poppet spring toward the poppet balls.

To install the reverse idler gear:
Place the needle bearings and spacers in position on the rear reverse idler gear. Insert the assembly into the rear of the case. Place the front idler gear with the thrust washer onto the rear shaft end. Insert the gear shaft in the case and secure with a bolt.

31. Measure the size from the rear surface of the transmission case to the rear of the reverse idler gear.

32. Measure the depth from the extension housing end to the idler gear shaft end. Add 0.004 in. This figure is the extension housing packing thickness.

33. Subtract NO. 2 from NO. 1. Subtract 0.009-0.012 in. (thrust washer clearance) from the result. (This figure is the thickness of the thrust washer required.)

Thrust Washer Identification (in.):
A-0.078
B-0.085
C-0.093
D-0.100

To install the countergear:

34. Insert the needle roller bearings (20 front, 20 rear) and spacers in the front and rear holes of the countergear.

35. Be sure the spacers are installed on the outside of the roller bearings.

36. Install a 1.378 in. OD thrust washer on the rear end.

37. Install a 1.181 in. ID thrust washer on the rear end.

38. Holding the countergear cluster inside the case, install the countergear shaft from the rear and properly mesh the gears.

39. Select a tear thrust washer to give 0.002-0.007 in. countergear end-play.

40. Secure the rear shaft end with a stopper plate.

41. Place the front bearing retainer in position and install the front bearing.

42. Bearing-to-retainer clearance should be 0.002-0.0012 in.

43. Place the speedometer drive gear on the mainshaft.

44. There should be no clearance between the speedometer gear and the snap-ring.

45. Shim if necessary.

46. Connect the extension housing to the transmission case.

47. When installing the washers, install with the bulged side toward the bolt head.

48. Install the transmission and backup light switch.

49. Next, install the locking plate and the transmission driven gear.

50. Finally, secure the under-cover to the transmission.

51. Place the gear lever in the first gear gate.

52. Be sure the nylon bushing is in the vertical position.

1. Shift rail (3rd-4th speed)
2. Shift rail (1st-2nd speed)
3. Shift fork (3rd-4th speed)
4. Shift fork (1st-2nd speed)
5. Spring pin
6. Selector (3rd-4th speed)

7. Selector (1st-2nd speed)
8. Shift fork (Reverse)
9. Shift rail (Reverse)
10. Distance piece
11. Interlock plunger

Exploded view of shift rail components

53. With the transmission in the car, apply sealant to the packings and grease bushings.

54. Insert the clutch control shaft into the transmission from the left-hand side.

55. Assemble the shift fork and springs onto the shaft.

56. Align the shift fork with the clutch control shaft.

57. Drive the spring pin into the pin hole and set the spring.

58. Be certain that the spring pin has its slot on the centerline of the clutch control shaft.

TYPE 2

5 Speed Transmission—Model KM 119

Chrysler Corp./ Mitsubishi

DISASSEMBLY

1. Remove the clutch assembly.
2. Remove the under cover.
3. Remove the backup lamp switch. Remove the steel ball from the extension housing.
4. Remove the extension housing assem-

---

1. Transmission case
2. Main drive pinion
3. Synchronizer assy (3-4 speed)
4. 3rd speed gear
5. 2nd speed gear
6. Synchronizer assy (1-2 speed)
7. 1st speed gear
8. Rear bearing retainer
9. Synchronizer assy (overdrive)
10. Overdrive gear
11. Control finger
12. Neutral return finger
13. Control shaft
14. Control level cover
15. Control lever assy
16. Stopper plate
17. Control housing
18. Change shifter
19. Mainshaft
20. Speedometer drive gear
21. Extension housing
22. Counter overdrive gear
23. Counter reverse gear
24. Reverse idler gear
25. Reverse idler gear shaft
26. Under cover
27. Counter gear
28. Front bearing retainer
29. Clutch shift arm
30. Release bearing carrier
31. Clutch control shaft
32. Return spring

Cross section of 5-speed transmission, model KM 119

1. 3rd speed gear
2. 2nd speed gear
3. 1st speed gear
4. Mainshaft
5. Snap ring
6. Synchronizer ring (3-4 speed)
7. Synchronizer piece
8. Synchronizer sleeve (3-4 speed)
9. Synchronizer spring (3-4 speed)
10. Synchronizer hub (3-4 speed)
11. Needle bearing (3rd speed gear)
12. Needle bearing (2nd speed gear)
13. Synchronizer ring (1-2 speed)
14. Synchronizer piece
15. Synchronizer sleeve (1-2 speed)
16. Synchronizer spring (1-2 speed)
17. Synchronizer hub (1-2 speed)
18. Needle bearing (1st speed gear)
19. 1st gear bearing sleeve
20. Bearing spacer

Assembled view of mainshaft

bly, with the gearshift lever placed in the reverse and overtop position.

5. Remove the snap-ring. Remove the speedometer drive gear and the steel ball. Also remove the gear front snap-ring.

6. Remove the mainshaft rear bearing. Remove the bearing front snap-ring.

7. Remove the reverse idler gear and related parts.

8. Loosen and remove the mainshaft intermediate locknut and the countershaft gear rear end locknut. The mainshaft intermediate locknut cannot be removed and therefore is to be loosened only.

9. Remove the three poppet springs from the right-hand side of the transmission case, and then remove three poppet springs and three balls.

10. Remove the cotter pin retaining the 1-2 and 3-4 speed shift forks.

11. Pull the 1-2 speed shift rail toward the rear of the case. Remove the counter overdrive gear and the ball bearing simultaneously with the rail.

12. Pull the 3-4 speed shift rail out toward the rear of the case.

13. Remove the mainshaft nut.

14. Remove the overdrive-reverse synchronizer assembly, the overdrive gear, and the overdrive-reverse shift rail and shift fork at the same time. Pull off the spacer also.

15. Remove two interlock plungers.

16. Remove the spacer and the counter reverse gear.

17. Remove the rear retainer.

18. Remove the front bearing retainer and spacer.

19. Insert rear stopper plate special tool between the clutch gear and synchronizer ring of the 3rd speed gear, and the front stopper plate between the clutch gear and the synchronizer ring of the main drive gear.

NOTE: The front and rear stopper plates inserted are special tools used to prevent the 3-4 speed synchronizer from damage by the main drive gear bearing when these bearings are removed or installed.

20. Remove the mainshaft bearing snapring. Remove the ball bearing. After removal of the bearing, slide special tool Mainshaft Support in place of the bearing over the mainshaft to support the mainshaft.

21. Remove the main drive gear bearing snap-rings. Pull off the bearing.

22. Remove special tools.

23. Remove the countershift gear front bearing snap-ring, of the countershaft gear front bearing.

24. Remove the countershaft gear rear bearing snap-ring, and remove the countershaft rear bearing.

25. Remove mainshaft adapter special tool. Lower the mainshaft assembly and at the same time take the 1st speed gear rear bearing spacer out of the case.

Shift the 3-4 speed synchronizer sleeve to the 3rd speed side to permit easy removal of the countershaft gear without interference with the sleeve.

26. Remove the countershaft gear.

27. Remove the 1-2 speed and 3-4 speed shift forks.

28. Remove the main drive gear.

29. Remove the mainshaft. Disassemble the mainshaft related parts. The synchronizer hub, sleeve, piece and spring, and the bearings for the 3-4 speed should be so laid as to prevent confusion with the 1-2 speed parts.

ASSEMBLY

1. Slide the 3rd speed gear and the needle bearing over the mainshaft from the front.

2. Install the synchronizer ring.

3. Assemble the 3-4 speed synchronizer hub and sleeve. Insert the synchronizer pieces, then install the synchronizer springs.

4. Install the assembled 3-4 speed synchronizer assembly on the mainshaft, with the synchronizer piece fitted into the ring groove in the synchronizer. Install a selected snapring so that the synchronizer hub will have end-play of 0-.003 in.

Thickness:	Identification Color:
.085 in.	Blue
.087 in.	None
.090 in.	Brown
.093 in.	White

5. Slide the 2nd speed gear and needle bearing over the mainshaft from the rear end.

6. Install the synchronizer ring.

7. Assemble the 1-2 speed synchronizer hub and sleeve. Insert the synchronizer piece and install the synchronizer spring. The synchronizer spring should be installed in the same manner as the 3-4 speed synchronizer spring.

Spring installation

8. Install the assembled 1-2 speed synchronizer assembly on the mainshaft, fitting the synchronizer piece into the groove in the synchronizer.

9. Install the synchronizer ring. Install the 1st speed gear, needle bearing and sleeve.

10. Install the bearing spacer. Check to see if, when the bearing spacer is pressed firmly forward, the 1st and 2nd speed gears have an end-play in excess of 0.001-0.007 in. Check the gear and hub ends for wear.

11. Install the mainshaft.

12. Install the synchronizer ring and the needle bearing to the main drive gear, and install the main drive gear.

Assembled view of synchronizers

Thickness:	Identification Color:
.033 in.	Black
.037 in.	None
.040 in.	Red
.044 in.	White
.047 in.	Yellow
.051 in.	Blue
.054 in.	Green

24. Install the front bearing retainer in the transmission case.

25. Install the rear retainer.

26. Install the counter reverse gear and the spacer with the relieved side toward the bearing.

27. Install two interlock plungers.

28. Assemble the overdrive-reverse synchronizer.

NOTE: The synchronizer spring should be installed in the same manner as the 3-4 speed synchronizer.

29. Install the spacer on the mainshaft from the rear. Install the synchronizer ring, overdrive gear, needle bearing and sleeve to the synchronizer assembly assembled above.

30. Install the mainshaft locknut.

31. Insert the 3-4 speed shift rail into the case from the rear and further into the 1-2 speed and 3-4 speed shift forks.

32. Insert the 1-2 speed shift rail into the case from the rear and further into the shift forks. At the same time, align the counter-overdrive gear with the relieved portion of the shift rail and install both parts simultaneously since they cannot be installed individually.

33. Install the spring pins into the holes. In this case the pin must not project out of the fork, and the slit of the pin must be in the direction of the axis of the shift rail.

34. Install the poppet balls and springs. Install the plugs until their heads are flush with the case surface and then apply sealant to them. The springs must be installed with their tapered ends directed inside (on the ball side).

35. Tighten the mainshaft and countershaft gear nuts.

36. Insert the reverse idler shaft into the case. Install the spacer bushing, gear, needle bearing and thrust washer. The thrust washer must be installed with the ground side on the gear side.

37. Install the rear ball bearing on the mainshaft. Install the snap-ring. There should be 0-0.007 in. clearance.

Thickness:	Identification Color:
.0591 in.	Red
.0630 in.	White

38. Install the speedometer drive gear and snap-ring.

39. Assemble the extension housing.

40. Install the extension housing assembly in the case.

When installing the extension housing, tilt the change shifter fully down to the left and install the change lever in the groove provided in the selector. Install the back-up light switch.

41. Install neutral return plungers A and B, springs and steel ball, and spring.

42. Install the under cover and gasket.

43. Install the transmission control lever.

---

13. Install the 1-2 speed and 3-4 speed shift forks. Shift the 3-4 speed synchronzier sleeve to 3rd speed side until the 1st speed gear rear bearing spacer is out of the case.

14. Install the countershaft gear.

15. Insert countershaft gear support special tool into the case to support the countergear.

16. After installing the snap-ring, install the countershaft gear bearing.

17. To install the countershaft gear front bearing, first install the outer race only into the transmission case and then install the needle bearing. The outer race and needle bearing, if assembled before installation, will damage the countershaft at the time of installation. To install the countershaft gear bearing, attach the snap-ring to the outer race and, using an aluminum rod, drive the bearing into place while tapping the circumference of the outer race evenly. Do not attempt to force the outer race into position.

18. Support the rear of the mainshaft.

19. Insert front stopper plate tool between the main drive gear and the synchronizer ring and insert the rear stopper plate tool between the 3rd speed gear and the synchronizer ring, with the stamped tool number on the tools directed to the front of the transmission.

20. To install the main drive gear bearing,

3-4-speed synchronizer

first install the snap-ring to the bearing, and then using a bearing installer, drive the bearing into position. Subsequently, install the snap-ring (small) on the main drive gear. This snap-ring must be selected and installed to obtain 0-.002 in. clearance between the bearing inner race and the snap-ring.

Thickness:	Identification Color:
.087 in.	Dark Blue
.089 in.	Brown
.090 in.	Orange
.092 in.	Blue
.093 in.	Green

21. Install the snap-ring to the mainshaft bearing. Drive the bearing into proper position. Remove front and rear stopper plates.

22. Install the oil seal in the front bearing retainer.

23. Before installing the front bearing retainer, check the clearance between front bearing retainer and main drive gear. Select and install a spacer to obtain 0-0.004 in. To measure the clearance, check the amount of bearing projection (A) from the front end of the case and the depth (B) of the retainer. The thickness of the spacer to be installed can be obtained from the formula (B + .3 (thickness of gasket) − A = Clearance). (0-.004 in.)

1-2-speed synchronizer

TYPE 3

5 Speed Transmission—Model KM 132

Chrysler Corp./ Mitsubishi

DISASSEMBLY

1. Remove the clutch release bearing and carrier.
2. Remove the spring pin and the clutch control shaft. Remove the felt, return spring and clutch shift arm.
3. Remove the case cover.
4. Remove the back-up light switch.
5. Remove the extension housing.
6. Remove the speedometer drive gear.
7. Remove the ball bearing from the mainshaft rear end.
8. Loosen three poppet spring plugs, then remove three poppet springs and three balls.

9. Remove the 3-4 and 1-2 speed shift fork spring pins. Pull off each shift rail toward the rear of the transmission case, then remove the shift fork. Remove the interlock plunger.
10. Remove the overdrive and reverse shift forks spring pins, shift rails and forks.
11. Loosen the locknuts (mainshaft and countershaft rear ends).
12. Pull off the counter overdrive gear and the ball bearing at the same time using a puller. Remove the spacer and the counter reverse gear.
13. Remove the overdrive gear and sleeve from the mainshaft. Remove the overtop synchronizer assembly and spacer.
14. Remove the reverse idler gear.
15. Remove the rear bearing retainer.
16. Drive the reverse idler gear shaft from inside the case.
17. Remove the front bearing retainer.
18. With the countergear pressed to the rear, remove the rear bearing snap-ring. Remove the counter rear bearing.
19. Remove the counter front bearing.
20. Remove the countergear from the inside of the case.
21. Remove the main drive pinion from the front of the case. Remove the main drive pinion bearing.
22. Remove the mainshaft bearing snap-ring. Remove the ball bearing.

23. Pull the mainshaft assembly from the case.
24. Disassemble the mainshaft in the following order:
   a. Remove the 1st gear, the 1-2 speed synchronizer and the 2nd speed gear toward the rear of the mainshaft.
   b. Remove the snap-ring from the forward end of the mainshaft. Remove the 3-4 speed synchronizer and the 3rd gear.
25. Disassemble the extension housing.
   a. Remove the lock plate and the speedometer driven gear.
   b. Remove the plug, spring and neutral return plunger.
   c. When removing the control shaft assembly, pull off the lock pin locking the gear shifter. To remove the lock pin, press the gear shifter forward and pull it off.

ASSEMBLY

1. Install the ball bearing on the main drive pinion. Install a selective snap-ring so that there will be 0-0.002 in. clearance between the snap-ring and the bearing.

Thickness of Snap-Ring:	Identification Color:
.0906 in.	White
.0925 in.	None
.0945 in.	Red

1. Transmission case
2. Main drive pinion
3. Synchronizer assy (3-4 speed)
4. 3rd speed gear
5. 2nd speed gear
6. Synchronizer assy (1-2 speed)
7. 1st speed gear
8. Rear bearing retainer
9. Synchronizer assy (overtop)
10. Overtop gear
11. Control finger
12. Neutral return finger
13. Control shaft
14. Control lever cover
15. Control lever assy
16. Stopper plate
17. Control housing
18. Change shifter
19. Mainshaft
20. Speedometer drive gear
21. Extension housing
22. Counter overtop gear
23. Counter reverse gear
24. Reverse idler gear
25. Reverse idler gear shaft
26. Case cover
27. Counter gear
28. Front bearing retainer
29. Clutch shift arm
30. Release bearing carrier
31. Clutch control shaft
32. Return spring

Cross section of 5-speed transmission, model KM 132

.0965 in.	Blue
.0984 in.	Yellow

2. Install the mainshaft in the following order:

a. Assemble the 3-4 speed and 1-2 speed synchronizers. The front and rear ends of the synchronizer sleeve and hub can be identified as shown. The synchronizer spring can be installed as shown.

b. Install the needle bearing, the 3rd speed gear, the synchronizer ring, and the 3-4 speed synchronizer assembly on to the mainshaft from the front end. Select and install a snap-ring of proper size so that the 3-4 speed synchronizer hub end-play will be 0-0.003 in.

Thickness of Snap-Ring:	Identification Color:
.0846 in.	None
.0874 in.	Yellow
.0902 in.	Green
.0929 in.	White

c. Check the 3rd gear end-play (.0016-0079 in.)

d. Install the needle bearing, the 2nd speed gear, the synchronizer assembly, the bearing sleeve, the needle bearing, the 1st speed gear, and the bearing spacer on the mainshaft from the rear. With the bearing spacer pressed forward, check the 2nd and 1st gear end-play (0.0016-0.0079 in.).

3. Install the mainshaft into the transmission case and drive in the mainshaft center bearing.

4. Install the needle bearing and the synchronizer ring. Install the main drive pinion assembly into the case from the front.

5. Install the countershaft gear into the case. Drive the front bearing into the case.

6. Install the snap-ring on the countershaft rear bearing.

7. Install the front bearing retainer. Select and install a spacer of proper size so that the clearance will be 0-0.0039 in.

Thickness of Spacer:	Identification Color:
.0030 in.	Black
.0366 in.	None
.0402 in.	Red
.0437 in.	White
.0472 in.	Yellow
.0508 in.	Blue
.0543 in.	Green

Replace the front bearing retainer oil seal.

8. Install the rear bearing retainer.

9. Install the reverse idler gear shaft.

10. Install the needle bearing, the reverse idler gear and the thrust washer. Check the reverse idler gear end-play (.0047-.0110 in.). Install the thrust washer with the ground side toward the gear side.

11. Assemble the overdrive synchronizer.

12. Install the spacer, the stop plate, the overdrive synchronizer assembly, the overdrive gear bearing sleeve, the needle bearing, the synchronizer ring and the overdrive gear in the written order on to the mainshaft from the rear end. Check the overdrive gear end-play.

13. Install the spacer, the counter reverse gear, the spacer, the counter overdrive gear and the ball bearing on to the countershaft gear from the rear end.

14. Insert the 3-4 and 1-2 speed shift forks into respective synchronizer sleeves. Insert

each shift rail from the rear of the case. Lock the shift forks and rails with spring pins. Install an interlock plunger between shift rails. The pin should be installed with the slit in the axial direction of the shift rail.

15. Insert the ball and poppet spring into each shift rail. Install the poppet spring with the small end on the ball side.

16. Install the ball bearing on to the rear end of the mainshaft.

17. Install the speedometer drive gear.

18. Install the extension housing. Turn the change shifter fully down to the left. Make sure the forward end of the control finger is snugly fitted in the slot of the shift lug.

19. Install the neutral return plungers (A) and (B), the spring, and resistance spring and ball. Tighten each plug till its top is flush with the boss top surface.

20. Install the speedometer driven gear sleeve into the extension housing and into mesh with the drive gear.

21. Install the back-up light switch. Remember the steel ball.

22. Install the under cover.

23. Insert the clutch control shaft. Install the packing (felt), the return spring and the clutch shift arm. The spring pin should be installed in such a manner that the slip will be at right angles with the axis of the control shaft.

24. Install the transmission control level assembly. Fill the gear shifter area with grease.

25. After reassembly, rotate the drive pinion to see if it rotates smoothly.

TYPE 4

4 Speed Transmission— Model 262/8, 9 BMW

DISASSEMBLY

1. Remove the console bracket from the rear of the transmission housing.

2. Remove the rear crossmember and the exhaust system bracket.

3. Slide the spring sleeve cover from the selector rod nonnector and drive the round pin from the coupler. Remove the selector rod connector.

4. Mount the transmission securely and drain the lubricating oil.

5. Remove the front cover retaining bolts and remove the cove with shims.

NOTE: Observe the difference in the length of the bolts and mark them for assembly.

6. Remove the circlip, spacer and support disc from the input shaft.

7. Using a bearing puller tool, remove the front bearing from the input shaft.

8. Using a bearing puller tool, remove the countershaft bearing.

9. Remove the selector lever lockpin cover, the lockpin and spring from the upper front side of the transmission case.

10. Remove the back-up light switch from the left front side of the transmission case.

11. Remove the front transmission case retaining bolts and remove the case from over the gear train.

12. Loosen the reverse gear selector lever holding bolt from outside the rear surface of the case, far enough so that the lever can be removed.

13. Using a pin punch, remove the lockpins from the 3rd-4th and reverse selector rods and forks.

14. Pull the reverse gear selector rod from the rear case. Do not lose the detent balls.

15. Turn the selector shaft so that the 3rd-4th gear selector rod can be pulled from the rear case. Do not lose the detent balls.

16. Install an output flange holding tool or equivalent on the output shaft flange, straight the retaining nut lock-washer and remove the retaining nut from the shaft.

NOTE: Certain transmissions will have a collared nut without a lock washer and will require the use of a thread-lock compound.

17. Remove the rear bearing cover retaining bolts and remove the cover.

NOTE: The speedometer driven gear should have been removed during the transmission R & R procedure. If not, remove it before the rear bearing housing is taken from the case.

18. Heat the rear transmission case to approximately 175° F (80° C). Remove the input shaft, countershaft, reverse gear, 1st-2nd gear selector rod and the selector forks from the case.

NOTE: The use of wet hot towels placed over the case is recommended, rather than the use of open heat. Do not lose the balls and spring from the selector rod detents.

19. Remove the rollers from the selector shaft and remove the shaft from the case.

20. Remove all selector rod sealing covers from the case.

21. Remove the input shaft and its needle bearing cage. Remove the circlip, support disc, synchronizer assembly with the synchronizer (baulk) rings attached, the needle bearing cage and the 3rd gear.

22. Place the output shaft in a press or equivalent tool and remove the 2nd gear, synchronizer assembly with the synchronizer (baulk) rings, 1st gear, support ring, ball bearing, support disc and the speedometer drive gear from the shaft.

CAUTION

Mark the synchronizer assemblies so that they can be reassembled with their respective gears.

---

23. The 4th and 3rd gears can be pressed from the countergear assembly. A circlip must be removed before the 3rd gear can be pressed off.

Cross section of 4-speed transmission, model 262/8, 9 (Getrag)

— **CAUTION** —

Note the direction of the gears during the removal.

24. Remove the sliding sleeve from the synchronizer hub. Do not lose the balls, springs and pressure pads from the hub.

25. The seals, gaskets, necessary replacement parts should be renewed in preparation for assembly.

ASSEMBLY

1. Assemble the synchronizer sliding sleeve to the synchronizer hub, halfway, and install the springs, pressure pads and the balls in their positions on the hub. Press the balls in until the sleeve can be slid over the hub completely.

NOTE: The convex face of the pressure pads must face the sliding sleeve.

1. Input shaft
2. Needle bearing cage
3. Circlip
4. Support disc
5. Synchronizer ring
6. Hub with sliding sleeve
7. Synchronizer ring
8. Needle bearing cage
9. Gear wheel
10. 2nd gear
11. Needle bearing cage
12. Synchronizer ring
13. Hub with sliding sleeve
14. Synchronizer ring
15. 1st gear
16. Needle bearing cage
17. Spacer
18. Reverse gear
19. Support ring
20. Ball bearing
21. Support disc
22. Speedometer drive gear

Input and mainshaft components

2. Install the synchronizer (baulk) rings in place on the synchronizer assembly and measure the distance between the ring and the body, in the area of the ring stops. The clearance should not be less than 0.031 inch (0.8 mm) for used rings, nor less than 0.039 inch (1.0 mm) for new rings.

3. Assemble the countergear assembly by pressing the 3rd gear in place, after heating the gear to approximately 250-300° F (120-150° C). Install the circlip in place on the shaft.

4. Press the 4th gear in place on the shaft after heating the gear to the same temperatures as the 3rd gear.

NOTE: Both the 3rd and 4th gears must be installed with the raised collar on the gear bore, facing the 2nd gear.

5. Install the 2nd speed gear and needle cage on the rear of the output shaft and press into place. Position the 1st/2nd synchronizer assembly in place on the shaft and press into place.

NOTE: Assemble the synchronizer (baulk) rings so that they are reused with the same gears.

6. Install the 1st gear, the needle cage, spacer, reverse gear, support ring, ball bearing, support disc and the speedometer gear in place on the shaft.

7. Install the 3rd gear, needle cage, synchronizer assembly, support disc and circlip in place on the front of the output shaft.

NOTE: Assemble the synchronizer (baulk) rings so that they are reused with the same gears.

8. Install the needle bearing in the bore of the input shaft and install the input shaft onto the front of the output shaft.

The rear bearing shim size must be determined before the transmission is reassembled. The following procedure should be followed:

a. Measure the case depth to the bearing seat with a depth gauge.

b. Measure the bearing seat depth of the bearing bracket with a depth gauge.

c. Measure the bearing outer race thickness in width.

d. Add the results of the case and bracket together and subtract the thickness of the bearing race from the results to obtain the desired thickness of the shim.

9. Install two guide pins into the rear bearing holder and with the use of both hands, install the output shaft, countershaft and reverse gear assemblies into the transmission rear case. Heat the case to 175° F (80° C).

— CAUTION —
Do not drop the gear assemblies during the installation.

10. Install the remaining bolts into the rear bearing holder and tighten securely. Remove the guide pins.

11. Mount the reverse gear selector lever to the selector rod and secure with the rolled pin.

12. Install the selector rod into the transmission case. Install the rollers on the selector shaft.

---

13. Place the selector forks on their respective sliding sleeves.

NOTE: The high selector fork is the 3rd-4th.

14. Install the detent balls as the selector rods are installed.

15. Turn the selector shaft to the reverse position and install the 1st-2nd gear selector shaft.

16. Install the 3rd-4th selector rod. Secure the selector rods to the shifting forks with the rolled pins.

17. Install the shifting rod covers in the case and seal with a sealing compound.

18. Install and secure the selector lever for the reverse gear arm. Install the bolt into the lever and do not cross thread.

19. Install the output shaft flange, the nut and tighten securely. Lock the washer, if so equipped.

20. Install a new gasket and install the transmission front case. Secure the case to the rear case with the retaining bolts and tighten securely.

21. Install the back-up light switch and the lockpin and spring.

22. Heat the grooved inner races of the countershaft and input shaft bearings and install them on their respective shafts with a bearing installing tool.

NOTE: Heat the inner races to approximately 175° F (80° C).

— CAUTION —
Be sure the bearings are seated to the shafts tightly.

---

23. Install the support disc, spacer and circlip on the input shaft. Be sure the circlip is engaged in its groove on the shaft.

24. To find the proper shims to be used on the front bearings, measure as outlined:

a. Measure the distance from the front of the transmission case to the outer surface of the bearing race on the input shaft and record the reading.

b. Measure the distance from the front of the transmission case to the outer surface of the bearing race on the countershaft. Record the reading.

c. Attach the gasket to the front bearing housing and measure with a depth gauge, the distance from the surface of the gasket and the inner surface of the front bearing housing seat, for both the input shaft bearing and the countershaft bearing. Record each measurement.

d. Subtract the measurement reading of the transmission case to bearing results from the results of the depth measurement of the bearing seats in the front bearing housing.

e. The difference is the size of the shims needed to properly control the end-play of the input and countershaft bearings.

25. Install the shims and retain with a coating of grease, in the front bearing cover. Install the cover on the front case and secure with the retaining bolts.

NOTE: Be sure the guide flange is installed with the front cover.

— CAUTION —
Install the bolts in their original positions.

---

26. Install the selector rod connector and install the round pin into the coupler. Slide the spring sleeve cover into its place on the coupler.

27. Install the exhaust system bracket and the rear crossmember to the transmission case.

28. Install the console bracket to the rear of the transmission case.

TYPE 5

4 Speed Transmission—Models 242/9, 18, 18.50

BMW

DISASSEMBLY

1. Remove the crossmember and exhaust system bracket from the rear of the transmission.

2. Mount the transmission securely and drain the lubricating oil from the unit. Remove the console from the transmission.

3. Remove the clutch release bearing assembly and release lever from the front of the transmission.

4. Remove the front guide sleeve and retaining bolts. Do not lose the shims.

5. Remove the circlip and shim from the input shaft.

6. Remove the case cover mounting bolts and drive the two dowel pins from the case cover.

7. Using a special case puller or equivalent, remove the case cover from the transmission case.

NOTE: The input shaft bearing will remain with the case cover as the cover is removed from the transmission case.

8. Remove the front bearing from the case cover by driving it from the rear to the front. Do not lose the accompanying shim.

9. Remove the lockpin and spring from the case.

NOTE: The lockpin maintains the selector shaft positioning.

10. Move the 3rd/4th selector lever and rod to the third speed position. Drive the fork retaining pin downward very carefully until the rod can be pulled out.

— CAUTION —
The fork retaining pin must be driven downward between the teeth of the synchronizer body. The pin should remain in the lower part of the selector fork.

---

11. Slide the locking sleeve away from the pin of the selector shaft coupler and drive the pin from the coupler.

Cross section of 4-speed transmission, model 242/9 (Getrag)

12. Remove the selector rod by pulling it forward and out of the shifting fork.

13. Move the gear sleeve back to the neutral position and remove the selector fork.

14. Remove the bushing and the speedometer driven gear.

15. Straighten the bend in the lockplate on the output flange retaining nut. Install a flange holding tool and remove the locknut. Pull the flange from the output shaft.

16. Remove the rear bearing support ring and shims.

17. Using a special bearing puller or equivalent, remove the rear bearing from the transmission cover.

NOTE: A 0.078 inch (2.0 mm) metal strip must be placed between the 2nd and 3rd gears to prevent the pressing off of the 2nd gear synchronizer body during the removal of the rear bearing from the shaft and cover.

18. Lift the input and output shaft assemblies slightly and remove the countergear assembly from the end bearing and out of the cover.

19. Pull the selector fork, the reverse gear and the selector rod from the transmission cover. Do not lose the detent balls.

20. Remove the input and output shaft as-

semblies, along with the 1st/2nd selector rod and fork, from the transmission cover. Do not lose the detent balls.

21. Remove the back-up lamp switch and the end cap for the 1st/2nd selector shaft.

22. Remove the input shaft from the output shaft and remove the 4th speed synchronizer (baulk) ring.

23. Remove the circlip from the front of the output shaft and remove the support disc, synchronizer body assembly, 3rd gear synchronizer (baulk) ring, needle bearing race and the 3rd gear from the shaft.

24. Place the output shaft into a press or equivalent, and remove the speedometer drive gear, washer, reverse gear, spacer, needle bearing race, 1st gear, synchronizer (baulk) ring, synchronizer body with the sliding sleeve, synchronizer (baulk) ring, needle bearing race and the 2nd speed gear from the shaft.

25. The 3rd and 4th gears can be pressed from the countershaft gear assembly, along with the roller bearing.

26. The pilot bearing can be removed from the bore of the input shaft.

27. The synchronizer unit can be disassembled by sliding the sleeve off the hub. The pressure pads will drop from the unit as the sleeve is removed.

28. Replace all worn, damaged or broken parts, along with new gaskets and seals.

ASSEMBLY

1. Install the synchronizer springs onto the hub with the hooked ends of the springs in different pressure pads.

2. Install the pressure pads in place and slide the sleeve, with the flat teeth locations, over the pressure pads.

3. If the 3rd and 4th gears have been removed from the countershaft, reinstall or replace the gears back on to the shaft. Heat the gears to 250 to 300° F (120 to 150° C) and install. The high collar on the bore of the 3rd and 4th gears should face the 2nd gear. Install the bearing and race onto the shaft.

4. Place the output shaft in an upright position with the rear of the shaft up. Place the 2nd speed gear and needle bearing assembly onto the shaft. Install the 1st/2nd synchronizer assembly with the two synchronizer (baulk) rings onto the shaft, followed by the 1st speed gear, needle bearing, spacer, reverse gear wheel, washer and complete the assembly by pressing the speedometer gear onto the shaft.

NOTE: The end-play of the gear train should be 0.003 inch (0.09 mm). Adjust by changing the selective washer between the speedometer gear and the reverse gear.

5. Invert the output shaft and install the

1. Synchronizer ring
2. Circlip
3. Support disc
4. Hub and sliding sleeve
5. 3rd gear synchronizer ring
6. Needle bearing cage
7. 3rd gear

8. Speedometer drive gear
9. Washer
10. Reverse gear
11. Spacer
12. Needle bearing cage
13. 1st gear

14. Synchronizer ring
15. Hub and sliding sleeve
16. Synchronizer ring
17. Needle bearing cage
18. 2nd gear
19. Output shaft

Output shaft components

3rd gear onto the shaft. Install the synchronizer assembly less the 4th speed synchronizer (baulk) ring onto the shaft and retain with the support disc and circlip.

Measurements Prior to Transmission Assembly

Washer type shims are used to control the end-play of the shafts and gears, while maintaining gear positioning, so that tooth contact is in proper relationship with each other. It is most important to inspect, measure and correct the shim packs to obtain the necessary preloads and clearances.

INPUT SHAFT

1. Install a 0.039 inch (1.0 mm) shim and the ball bearing into the case bore.
2. With a depth gauge, measure the distance, A, from the sealing surface of the case to the surface of the bearing race.
3. A numerical figure is electrically engraved on the input shaft and represents column B in the accompanying chart.
4. The thickness of the shim, X, needed on the input shaft can be determined by corresponding the measurements A and B to the

chart and locating the proper shim from column X.

COUNTERSHAFT ASSEMBLY

1. Measure the distance, A, from the sealing surface of the case housing to the circlip in the bottom of the housing.
2. Install the countershaft into the transmission case bearing and measure the dis-

tance, B, from the top of the large bearing race to the sealing surface of the case, with the gasket installed.
3. Determine the thickness of the shim, C, by subtracting distance B from distance A. The result is shim C.

NOTE: The "C" shims can be used to change tooth engagement.

"A"	"B"	"X"
153.9 mm 6.059"	45 . . . 50 mm 1.772 . . . 1.968"	0.5 mm / 0.020"
	35 . . . 40 mm 1.378 . . . 1.575"	0.6 mm / 0.024"
	25 . . . 30 mm 0.984 . . . 1.181"	0.7 mm / 0.027"
153.8 mm 6.055"	45 . . . 50 mm 1.772 . . . 1.968"	0.4 mm / 0.016"
	35 . . . 40 mm 1.378 . . . 1.575"	0.5 mm / 0.020"
	25 . . . 30 mm 0.984 . . . 1.181"	0.6 mm / 0.024"
153.7 mm 6.051"	45 . . . 50 mm 1.772 . . . 1.968"	0.3 mm / 0.012"
	35 . . . 40 mm 1.378 . . . 1.575"	0.4 mm / 0.016"
	25 . . . 30 mm 0.984 . . . 1.181"	0.5 mm / 0.020"
153.6 mm 6.047"	45 . . . 50 mm 1.722 . . . 1.968"	0.2 mm / 0.008"
	35 . . . 40 mm 1.378 . . . 1.575"	0.3 mm / 0.012"
	25 . . . 30 mm 0.984 . . . 1.181"	0.4 mm / 0.016"

Measurement of extension case and gear assembly to determine shim "X" thickness

Location of shim "X" and engraved measurement "B".

Measurement of distance between extension case edge and ball bearing. "C" equals distance.

Measurement of case edge to ball bearing ... "A" equals distance.

SPEEDOMETER GEAR TO TRANSMISSION CASE

1. Measure the thickness, B, of the speedometer gear.
2. Press the ball bearing into the transmission case and measure the distance, C, from the sealing surface of the case to the race of the bearing, without the gasket installed.
3. The nominal distance, A, is a predetermined distance and is used to arrive at the proper sized shim.
4. Subtract distance B from the nominal distance A. Subtract the result of A minus B

from distance C, which is the proper sized shim, X, to be used between the speedometer gear and the ball bearing of the case.

5. An example is as follows;

$$
\begin{array}{rl}
\text{Example:} & \text{A} \quad 22.0 \text{ mm } (0.866'') \\
& \quad \text{nominal distance} \\
+ & \text{B} \quad 14.8 \text{ mm } (0.582'') \\
\hline
& \quad 36.8 \text{ mm } (1.488'') \\
& \text{C} \quad 37.0 \text{ mm } (1.456'') \\
- & \quad 36.8 \text{ mm } (1.448'') \\
\hline
& \text{X} \quad 0.2 \text{ mm } (0.008'')
\end{array}
$$

Transmission Assembly After Basic Measurements

1. Have the transmission case in a secure support.
2. Insert the selector rod detent balls and springs. Install the reverse gear selector rod with the reverse gear, into the case until the 1st lock is engaged.
3. Install the countershaft into the roller bearing, mounted in the case.
4. Install the input shaft on the output shaft and install the assembly into its position on the transmission case.
5. Install the predetermined shim between the speedometer gear and the ball bearing. Install the bearing into the case, but do not seat completely.
6. Using a special bearing installer tool or equivalent, seat the bearing on the output shaft and into the transmission case.
7. Check the tooth engagement of the input, output and countergear assemblies. Tooth engagement can be changed by movement of shims.
8. Install the speedometer bushing and driven gear.
9. Set the transmission assembly in the upright position with the output shaft pointing upward. Measure the distance A, from the case to the ball bearing race.
10. Measure the distance B, from the shoulder height of the sealing cover, to the surface of the gasket on the cover.
11. Subtract distance B from distance A and the result is the thickness of the needed shim between the ball bearing and the sealing cover.

— CAUTION —
There should be no end-play between the ball bearing race and the sealing

cover. Remeasure and remove play with shims.

12. Secure the sealing cover and install the output flange. Install the locknut and washer. Jam the lockplate washer into the groove of the flange.
13. Install the 1st-2nd gear selector rod and fork into place. Insert the locking detent balls and springs. Secure the fork to the rod with the rolled pin.
14. Install the 3rd-4th selector fork into place on the sliding sleeve. Install the main selector rod. Install the lockpin and spring into the tapered bushing. Install the locking detent balls and springs.
15. Install the 3rd-4th gear selector rod and secure to the fork with the rolled pin. (Remove pin and reinstall from the top of the fork.)
16. Install the back-up lamp switch and the selector rod cap.
17. Install the gasket on the mating surfaces of the transmission case and housing. Install the predetermined shims on their respective locations and install the transmission housing over the gear assembly.
18. Bolt the housing to the case securely.

NOTE: It may be necessary to heat the transmission area of the input shaft to install the front bearing.

19. Install the shim and bearing onto the input shaft and housing. Install washer and circlip.
20. Install the clutch release guide sleeve and install a shim to eliminate any existing play between the guide and the bearing.
21. Measure the distance between the case and the ball bearing. This distance is A. Measure the distance from the top of the shoulder of the guide sleeve to the mating surface, with the gasket installed. This distance is B.
22. Subtract distance B from distance A and the result is the thickness of shim needed to remove the existing play between the guide and the bearing.
23. Install the selector rod coupler and secure with the pin. Slide the sleeve over the pin location.
24. Install the console onto the transmission case.
25. Fill the unit with the proper level of lubricating oil.
26. Install the clutch release bearing assembly and the operating lever.
27. Install the crossmember and the exhaust system bracket.

TYPE 6

4 Speed Transmission– Model 232

BMW

DISASSEMBLY

1. Remove the exhaust system bracket from the rear of the transmission.

2. Mount the transmission securely and drain the lubricating oil.

3. Remove the clutch release bearing guide sleeve, the ball bearing circlip retainer and the shim(s).

4. Using a special puller, remove the front ball bearing from the input shaft and housing.

NOTE: Should a ball bearing with a plastic cage be encountered that would restrict the use of the special bearing puller, it would be necessary to remove the transmission housing with the use of a special housing removal tool or equivalent.

5. Remove the retaining bolts from the transmission housing and drive the dowel pins from the housing.

6. Heat the housing in the area of the countershaft bearing so that when the housing is removed, the countershaft bearing will slide from the housing easily.

───── CAUTION ─────
It is recommended to use hot, wet towels instead of an open flame to heat the transmission housing.

7. Carefully remove the transmission housing from the cover assembly.

8. Remove the locking pin, spring and retaining cap from the cover.

9. Move the 3rd/4th selector rod to the 4th gear position. Rotate the guide sleeve until the rolled pin can be driven from the fork and rod. Pull the selector lever from the cover assembly.

───── CAUTION ─────
Do not drop or lose the detent balls.

10. Turn the main selector rod until the selector bar is up and remove the selector rod from the cover assembly.

───── CAUTION ─────
Do not drop or lose the detent balls and sleeve.

11. Move the 3rd/4th selector fork to the neutral position and remove the fork from the sliding sleeve.

12. Move the 1st/2nd selector fork and rod into the 2nd gear position. Remove the roll pin from the selector fork and slide the rod from the cover assembly. Remove the fork from the sleeve and push the sliding sleeve into the neutral position.

───── CAUTION ─────
Do not drop or lose the detent balls.

13. Remove the speedometer driven gear and bushing.

14. Straighten the output flange locking plate and with the use of special holding tools or equivalent, remove the nut and flange from the output shaft.

15. Remove the rear bearing support ring and the shim(s) from the rear of the cover assembly.

16. Install a metal strip between the 2nd and 3rd gears to prevent the synchronizer assembly from being forced off when the rear ball bearing is removed. The metal strip size should be 0.079 inch (2.0 mm).

17. Using a special bearing remover or equivalent, remove the rear bearing from the cover and output shaft.

18. Remove the input and output shaft assembly by moving the assembly away from the selector rod and pulling the unit from the cover.

19. Relieve the weight of the countergear assembly and drive the unit from the cover with a plastic hammer.

NOTE: Two types of bearings are used in the cover for the countershaft. If the shaft is equipped with a ball bearing, it will come out of the cover with the shaft. If the shaft is equipped with a roller bearing, the roller bearing will remain in the cover and must be removed separately.

20. Pull the selector rod with the lever from the cover, along with the reverse gear pinion.

───── CAUTION ─────
Do not drop or lose the detent balls.

NOTE: Observe the reverse gear and pinion for a groove around the outer face of the gears. If the groove is present, the gears are of a later design with a 15° mesh angle, instead of an earlier mesh angle of 20°. The gears are not to be interchanged. The new designed mesh angle was incorporated when the synchronizer assemblies were changed from the Porsche type to the Borg-Warner type.

21. Separate the input shaft from the output shaft by pulling the two assemblies apart. The needle roller cage will remain on the output shaft.

22. Remove the circlip from the output shaft, along with the support disc, shim, sliding sleeve and the 3rd speed gear with the synchronizer assembly. Remove the needle bearing cage.

23. Place the output shaft into a press or equivalent tool and press the shaft from the gear train.

───── CAUTION ─────
Mark the sequence of gear and bearing removal from the shaft and the type of synchronizer unit used.

24. The 4th and 3rd gears can be pressed from the countershaft. Remove the circlip from the 3rd speed gear location before the 3rd speed gear is pressed off.

25. Replace all necessary gears, bearings, seals and gaskets.

ASSEMBLY

1. If the counter 3rd and 4th gears were removed, heat the replacement gears to 248 to 302° F (120 to 150° C) and press the gears onto the shaft. Install the bearings.

───── CAUTION ─────
After pressing the 3rd speed gear on the countershaft, be sure to install the circlip.

2. Replace the necessary bearings or races on the countershaft assembly.

3. Assemble the output shaft, depending upon the type synchronizer unit used, as follows:

a. Porsche Type—Place the needle cage bearing and the 2nd speed gear onto the rear of the shaft. Install the guide sleeve, the selector sleeve, the distance bushing, the needle cage bearing, 1st speed gear, the reverse gear, thrust washer and the speedometer drive gear.

NOTE: The ground side of the reverse gear must face the 1st gear.

Install the 3rd speed gear with the needle bearing onto the front of the input shaft, followed by the guide sleeve, the thrust washer and the circlip. Determine the gap between the thrust washer and the guide sleeve with a feeler gauge and change the shim until zero clearance is obtained.

b. Borg Warner Type—Install the 3rd speed gear and needle bearing onto the front of the input shaft, followed by the synchronizer assembly with rings, the thrust washer and the circlip. From the rear of the shaft, install the 2nd speed gear and needle bearing, the synchronizer assembly with rings, the 1st speed gear and needle bearing, the reverse gear, washer and speedometer drive gear.

NOTE: When installing the 3rd/4th speed gear sliding sleeve, face the

1. Speedometer drive gear
2. Thrust washer
3. Reverse gear
4. 1st gear
5. Needle bearing cage
6. Spacer
7. Selector sleeve
8. Guide sleeve
9. 2nd Gear
10. Needle bearing cage

Output shaft components—Porsche type synchronizer units

groove in the sleeve towards the 3rd gear.

Measurements Prior to Assembly
OUTPUT SHAFT ASSEMBLY (PORSCHE TYPE SYNCHRONIZERS)

1. After the synchronizer assemblies are installed on the output shaft, determine the actual distance from the machined surface of the guide sleeve on the front of the shaft, to the face of the reverse gear hub on the rear of the shaft.

2. The nominal distance should be 5.433 ± 0.039 inch (138.0 ± 0.1 mm). Subtract the actual measured distance from the nominal distance and install a shim behind the reverse gear to provide the correct clearance.

MAINSHAFT END CLEARANCE IN COVER

1. Measure the thickness of the speedometer drive gear.

2. Install the ball bearing into the transmission cover and measure the distance from the face of the bearing race to the top of the cover's mating surface, with the sealing gasket in place. This distance is known as C.

3. Using the nominal measurement A, representing 5.433 inch (138.0 mm), add the measurement B, representing the thickness of the speedometer gear, to measurement A. Subtract the measurement C from the results of A + B, which represents the actual measurement of the gear train above the mating surface of the cover with the gasket installed. This measurement is considered to be D. The nominal measurement of D is 4.567 inch (116.0 mm). To find the thickness of the shim X, subtract the actual measurement D from the nominal measurement D. Shim X is installed between the speedometer drive gear and the ball bearings in the transmission cover.

4. An example is given to assist the repairman in determining shim X thickness.

Nominal
  Measurement A = 5.433 inch (138.0 mm)
Add
  Measurement B = 0.583 inch (14.8 mm)
Results =   6.016 inch (152.8 mm)
Subtract
  Measurement C = 1.457 inch (37.0 mm)
Results =   4.559 inch (115.8 mm)

Nominal
  Measurement D = 4.567 inch (116.0 mm)
Subtract Actual
  Measurement D = 4.559 inch (115.8 mm)
Results
  (Shim X Thickness)= 0.008 inch (0.2 mm)

NOTE: Nominal measurements represent theoretical measurements, determined by the manufacturer at time of design.

COUNTERSHAFT END-PLAY

1. Measure the distance, A, from the mating surface of the housing to the top of the bearing bore circlip in the base of the housing.

2. Place the assembled countergear assembly into the cover and measure the distance, B, from the mating surface of the cover, with the gasket in place, to the top of the bearing race on the countergear assembly.

3. Subtract distance B, from distance A and the result is the width of the shim, C, needed to control the end-play of the countergear.

NOTE: The tooth engagement of the output shaft and the countershaft gears can be altered by splitting the shim C, between the front and the rear bearing seats.

CAUTION
When rotating the gear train and a noise is heard, check the reverse gear teeth and the support disc on the countershaft for signs of contact. If necessary, the points of contact can be ground down no more than 0.051 inch (1.3 mm) on the support disc and no more than 0.055 inch (1.4 mm) on the reverse gear teeth.

Transmission Assembly After the Basic Measurement

1. Install the detent ball and spring, insert the reverse gear selector rod with the reverse pinion gear into the cover, while holding the detent ball downward and engage the ball to detent groove.

2. Place the predetermined shim C, into the housing and install the countershaft assembly.

3. Assemble the input shaft to the output shaft while engaging the 4th speed synchronizer (baulk) ring grooves to the lugs of

the guide sleeve (Porsche Type), or on the pressure plates (Borg Warner Type).

4. Install the input-output shaft assembly into the cover and install the predetermined shim X on the output shaft and install the rear bearing until it seats.

5. Check the tooth engagement of the output shaft and the countershaft gears.

NOTE: The tooth engagement can be altered with shim C.

6. Measure the distance, A, from the housing cover to the grooved ball bearing race.

7. Measure the flange height, B, of the sealing cover with the gasket in place.

8. Subtract distance B from distance A and the result is the width shim needed to reduce the end-play to zero. Install the shim, the sealing cover and secure the cover with retaining bolts.

9. Install the output flange and secure it to the output shaft.

10. Install the gear selector fork into 1st/2nd sliding sleeve. Install the detent ball and spring. Install the selector rod into the fork and the cover. Push the detent ball downward and engage the ball with the detent groove on the rod. Install the retaining roll pin in the selector fork to rod.

11. Install the 3rd/4th gear selector fork into the sliding sleeve.

12. Install the primary selector shaft into the housing. Note the position of the tapered bushing. Install the locking pin, spring and the threaded retainer.

13. Install the detent ball and spring. Install the 3rd/4th selector rod and secure it to the fork with a rolled pin.

14. Fit the sealing cap into the selector rod hole and install the back-up lamp switch. Install the speedometer driven gear assembly.

15. Install the circlip into the input bearing bore groove of the housing and from the front, seat a 0.039 inch (1.0 mm) shim and ball bearing on the circlip.

16. Invert the housing and measure the distance, A, from the housing mating surface to the inner race of the input shaft bearing.

17. Distance B is electrically engraved on the input shaft. Locate and record.

18. From the following chart, determine the size of the shim needed to control the input-output shaft end-play.

19. Place the required shim, X, on the output shaft and the shim C, on the bearing of the countershaft.

20. Install the gasket on the housing and install the housing over the gear assembly.

21. Use a special pressure tool or equivalent, to force the housing into place on the cover assembly.

22. Secure the housing with the retaining bolts.

23. Measure the thickness of the circlip needed to retain the front bearing on the input shaft. This measurement is considered A. Install the circlip into its groove.

24. Determine the distance, B, from the circlip to the face of the ball bearing. This distance is the size of the shim, C, needed to remove the end-play from between the circlip and the ball bearing.

25. Install the shim and the circlip in their respective places on the input shaft.

Measurement points to determine shim "x"

A	B	ins.	X mm
153.9	45-50	(0.0196)	0.5
(6.059)	35-40	(0.0236)	0.6
	25-30	(0.0276)	0.7
153.8	45-50	(0.0157)	0.4
(6.055)	35-40	(0.0196)	0.5
	25-30	(0.0236)	0.6
153.7	45-50	(0.0118)	0.3
(6.051)	35-40	(0.0157)	0.4
	25-30	(0.0196)	0.5
153.6	45-50	(0.0078)	0.2
(6.047)	35-40	(0.0118)	0.3
	25-30	(0.0157)	0.4

26. Install the guide sleeve for the clutch release bearing.

27. Install the exhaust system bracket to the rear of the transmission assembly.

TYPE 7

5 Speed Transmission–Model 235/5 BMW

DISASSEMBLY

1. Remove the exhaust system support, the gear lever coupler and the bracket from the rear of the transmission.

2. Mount the transmission securely and drain the lubricating oil.

3. Compress the clutch release lever retaining spring and remove the lever assembly from the pivot ball stud.

4. Remove the clutch release bearing guide sleeve from the front of the transmission.

5. Remove the circlip and shim from the input shaft, retaining the front bearing.

6. Remove the retaining bolts from the transmission cover, freeing the intermediate housing and the front housing.

7. Mount a special pressing tool on the front housing, contacting the input shaft, and press the front housing away from the intermediate housing.

NOTE: Do not lose the shims from the input and countershafts.

8. Lift the locking plate from the output shaft flange. Using a special holding tool or equivalent, remove the retaining nut and the output flange.

9. Remove the rear bearing support ring and the retaining bolts.

NOTE: Do not lose the bolts.

10. Hold the cover assembly and the intermediate housing together with two bolts and nuts.

11. With a special bearing remover or equivalent, remove the rear ball bearing and bushing.

12. Place the transmission in the neutral position and remove the locking pin threaded cap, spring and the locking pin.

13. Remove the speedometer driven gear from the cover assembly.

14. Place the transmission in the 5th gear and turn the guide sleeve until the roll pin can be removed.

15. Remove the 4th/5th gear selector rod from the fork and the intermediate housing and cover assembly.

CAUTION

During the removal of the selector rods from the intermediate housing and the cover assembly, do not lose the detent balls and springs.

---

16. Engage the third gear and turn the guide sleeve until the rolled pin can be driven out of the 2nd/3rd fork and rod.

17. Remove the 2nd/3rd selector rod from the intermediate housing and cover assembly.

18. Position the selector sleeve in the neutral position and drive the dowel pins from the intermediate housing. Remove the two retaining bolts and nuts.

19. Pull the gear assembly with the intermediate housing, selector shaft and selector rod of the 1st/reverse gear, from the transmission cover.

CAUTION

Do not lose the ball bearing from the cover.

---

20. Place the intermediate housing in a vise or other holding tool and remove the speedometer drive gear and the reverse gear with the needle bearing cage.

NOTE: Mark the speedometer drive gear before removal.

21. Remove the rolled pins from the fork for the 1st and reverse gears.

22. Pull the 1st/reverse selector rod from the intermediate housing, toward the rear.

23. Remove the selector forks of the 2nd/3rd and 4th/5th gears from the sliding sleeves.

24. Move the output shaft towards the rear until it is to the stop in the housing. Pull the selector hinion of the 1st gear with the guide sleeve and spacer bushing.

NOTE: Use a puller with extra long arms to grip gear.

25. Move the output shaft carefully forward until the synchronizer unit of the 3rd speed contacts the 3rd gear of the countershaft.

26. From the rear of the intermediate housing, remove the Allen headed screws and the retaining keys.

NOTE: Shims are used to obtain a good fit on the keys, as necessary. Do not lose them.

27. Position the gear and housing assembly into a press. Position a long tube on the countershaft so that it is even with the output shaft end. Lay a flat bar, horizontally on the output shaft and the extension for the countershaft, and press the two shafts from the housing with the gear assemblies attached.

28. Separate the input shaft from the output shaft assembly, along with the selector sleeve and the needle bearing.

29. Remove the circlip from the front of the

1. Spacer bushing	6. 2nd Gear
2. Shim	7. Sliding sleeve
3. Roller bearing	8. Hub (Porsche Type)
4. Spacer bushing	9. 3rd gear
5. Needle bearing	10. Needle bearing

Output shaft components from the machined collar to the rear of the shaft

output shaft and remove the support disc, the shim, sliding sleeve and the 4th gear with the needle bearing cage.

30. Invert the output shaft and press the spacer bushing, shim, roller bearing, spacer bushing, needle bearing 2nd gear, selector sleeve, 3rd gear and the needle bearing from the shaft.

─── **CAUTION** ───
Do not drop the gears.

31. The 5th and 4th gears may be pressed from the countershaft, if necessary. If the 1st gear and or bearing must be replaced on the countershaft, the retaining screw, support disc and shim must be removed.

32. Replace any bearings, seals, broken or worn gears, as required.

Synchronizer Assembly Overhaul
PORSCHE TYPE

1. Remove the lock washer, the synchronizer baulk ring, the baulk strap, the block and the stop.

NOTE: The synchronizer ring for the 1st speed is more oval in shape than the rings for the second, third and fourth gears.

Identification marks for these are as follows; 1st gear—white spot of paint, 2nd, 3rd and 4th—blue spot of paint.

2. Examine the synchronizer and replace the defective parts.

3. Install the synchronizer ring into the selector sleeve. Install the stop, the block, the baulk strap and install the lock washer.

4. The synchronizer ring must be able to easily turn.

Borg-Warner Type

1. Press the selector sleeve from the synchronizer hub. Catch the pressure plates as the sleeve is removed.

2. Remove the synchronizer springs from the hub. Note the installed position.

3. Measure the synchronizer rings to the hub.
Service limit—0.032 inch (0.8 mm).
New limit —0.039 inch (1.0 mm)

4. Reassemble the synchronizer springs to the hub in a staggered manner. Attach the pressure plates to the springs.

5. Press the selector sleeve over the hub assembly, with the flat teeth of the selector sleeve in line with the pressure plates.

NOTE: The teeth in the selector sleeves are recessed for 1st, 2nd and 3rd speeds. When assembling, the groove in the selector sleeve for the 3rd speed, must be visible.

ASSEMBLY

1. From the rear of the output shaft, install the needle bearing and 3rd gear, the selector sleeve, 2nd gear pinion and needle bearing, the spacer bushing, roller bearing, shim and spacer bushing.

NOTE: A press will have to be used on certain parts during the installation.

2. From the front of the output shaft, install the 4th gear and needle bearing, the

sliding sleeve, shim and the support disc. Install the circlip.

3. Check output shaft end-play as follows:
a. Front of shaft: Check the clearance between the support disc and the guide sleeve with a feeler gauge. Replace the shim with one of proper thickness to eliminate end-play.
b. Rear of shaft: Install the guide sleeve for the 1st speed and determine the end-play between the spacer bushing and the guide sleeve. Adjust the size of the shim to remove the end-play. Remove shim, spacer bushing and guide sleeve.

4. Assemble the 4th and 5th speed gears on the countershaft, if removed. The 1st speed gear should be removed before the shaft is installed in the housing.

5. Install the roller bearings of the output and countershafts into the intermediate housing. Install the retaining keys and Allen headed screws to retain the output shaft bearing.

NOTE: Do not tilt the retaining keys. Use shims to obtain a parallel fit to the bearing and housing.

6. Install the output and countershaft into the roller bearings. Install the 1st speed gear onto the countershaft and install the support disc and bolt. Measure the distance between the gear and the support disc and install a shim of the proper size between the support disc and the 1st speed gear. Secure the bolt with a locking substance.

7. Install the previously determined shim on the output shaft and press the spacer bushing into place.

8. Install the 1st speed gear and the guide sleeve, with the long bars of the sleeve towards the gear.

9. Install the selector forks on the selector sleeves for the 2nd/3rd and 4th/5th gears.

10. Push the selector rod for the 1st/reverse gear, along with the selector, into the intermediate housing.

11. Install the selector sleeve into the selector fork, install on the selector rod and slide the selector sleeve onto the guide sleeve for the 1st/reverse gear.

12. Install the rolled pins into the selector fork and the selector rod.

13. Install the reverse gear pinion onto the output shaft and adjust the tooth engagement of the output and countershaft with shims between the speedometer drive gear and the ball bearing. To accomplish this measurement, proceed as follows:
a. Place the roller bearing into the transmission cover bore and set the speedometer gear on top of the bearing inner race. Measure the distance, C, from the cover sealing surface to the top of the speedometer drive gear.
b. The tooth engagement is set correctly when the distance C, is 0.866 ± 0.0039 inch (22.0 ± 0.1 mm). Remove the ball bearing from the cover.

14. Remove the back-up lamp switch and the selector sealing cap, if not already done.

15. Install the double pinion gear and the thrust washer onto the shaft in the cover. Place the sealing gasket on the cover.

16. Fit the intermediate housing and gear assemblies to the cover. Loosely secure the housing to the cover with two bolts.

17. Install the detent balls and springs in their respective bores, holding them down while installing the selector rods.

NOTE: The locking balls have to be installed as the selector rods are installed in the housing and cover.

18. Install the 5th gear locking ball and detent ball in the bore, with the 1st/reverse selector rod in the Neutral position.

19. Install the 2nd/3rd selector rod through the fork and into the housing. Install the rolled pin through the fork and rod.

20. Position the selector sleeve of the 4th/5th gear to the neutral position and install the locking and detent balls. Install the selector rod and secure it to the fork with the rolled pin.

21. Install the back-up light switch and the sealing cap into their respective bores.

22. Install the dowel pins into the bores of the intermediate housing.

23. Fit the locking pin and the speedometer driven gear assembly.

24. Install the bushing onto the output shaft and drive the ball bearing on the shaft until it is fully seated.

25. Determine distance A, which is the dis-

1. Correct installation
2. Incorrect installation
3. Shim
Proper use of retaining keys and shims

Measuring from intermediate housing to top of countershaft for dimension "D"

A	B	C
150.6 (5.929)	23.6 (0.9291)	0. (0)
	23.5 (0.9252)	0.1 (0.0039)
	23.4 (0.9212)	0.2 (0.0078)
150.7 (5.933)	23.6 (0.9291)	0.1 (0.0039)
	23.5 (0.9252)	0.2 (0.0078)
	23.4 (0.9212)	0.3 (0.0118)
150.8 (5.937)	23.6 (0.9291)	0.2 (0.0078)
	23.5 (0.9252)	0.3 (0.0118)
	23.4 (0.9212)	0.4 (0.0157)
150.9 (5.941)	23.6 (0.9291)	0.3 (0.0118)
	23.5 (0.9252)	0.4 (0.0157)
	23.4 (0.9212)	0.5 (0.0196)
151.0 (5.945)	23.6 (0.9291)	0.4 (0.0157)
	23.5 (0.9252)	0.5 (0.0196)
	23.4 (0.9212)	0.6 (0.0236)
151.1 (5.949)	23.6 (0.9291)	0.5 (0.0196)
	23.5 (0.9252)	0.6 (0.0236)
	23.4 (0.9212)	0.7 (0.0275)
151.2 (5.953)	23.6 (0.9291)	0.6 (0.0236)
	23.5 (0.9252)	0.7 (0.0275)
	23.4 (0.9212)	0.8 (0.0315)
151.3 (5.957)	23.6 (0.9291)	0.7 (0.0275)
	23.5 (0.9252)	0.8 (0.0315)
	23.4 (0.9212)	0.8 (0.0315)

Example: A = 150.90 mm (5.941 in.)
B =   0.42 mm (0.017 in.)
C =   0.50 mm (0.020 in.)

tance from the outer face of the ball bearing and the face of the transmission cover.

26. Install the gasket on the sealing bearing cover and measure the distance B, from the top of the seal to the bearing contact surface of the cover.

27. Determine the thickness of the shim by subtracting distance B from distance A. The result is the size of the shim needed between the bearing cover and the bearing to obtain zero end-play.

28. Install the shim and the sealing cover. Install the retaining bolts. Install the output shaft flange.

29. Rotate the transmission assembly so that the gears are in an upright position. Remove the retaining bolts from the intermediate housing to the cover. Install the gasket on the intermediate housing mating surface and measure the distance from the gasket area to the top of the countershaft gear. This distance is considered D.

30. Measure the distance, known as E, from the mating surface of the front housing to the surface of the countershaft ball bearing, in its bore of the housing.

31. Determine the thickness of the shim, known as F, that is needed on the end of the countershaft, to allow 0.0079 inch (0.2 mm) end-play between the end of the shaft and the front housing.

32. Determine distance A, from the front housing mating surface to the input ball bearing, seated in its bore.

33. Install the input shaft, needle bearing and selector sleeve onto the output shaft. Locate the electrically engraved number on the machined surface of the input shaft. This number represents distance B. Locate the proper shim from the following chart.

NOTE The engraved number always denotes the digit after 23, as taken from the accompanying chart.

34. Install the proper shim on the input shaft. Carefully install the front housing over the gear assembly. Install a pulling tool or equivalent, and pull the input shaft into the ball bearing and the front housing to the mating surface of the intermediate housing. Secure the housings with the retaining bolts.

35. After the front bearing and housing are

pulled into position, measure the distance, E, from the circlip to the ball bearing.

36. Measure the thickness, D, of the circlip.

37. Select a shim to provide the needed zero clearance between the circlip and the bearing, with the support disc in place.

38. Install the guide sleeve gasket and install the guide to the transmission housing. Retain with the retaining bolts.

39. Install the clutch release lever and bearing, the exhaust support, the gear lever, stay and the bracket assembly.

40. Fill the transmission to the proper level with lubricating oil.

TYPE 8

4 Speed Transmission–Model ZF-S4-18/3

BMW

DISASSEMBLY

1. Mount the transmission securely and drain the lubricating oil.

2. Remove the gearshift upper housing with the torsion spring and centering spring, mounted on the shift plate.

3. Remove the shift control housing from the rear of the transmission.

4. Remove the vibration damper, located between the shift control housing and the transmission case.

5. Slide the shifting bars guide piece from the shifting bars.

6. Remove the front bearing cover from the front of the transmission.

NOTE: Do not lose the shims.

7. Remove the small circlip from the input shaft and remove the shims.

8. With the aid of a bearing puller or equivalent, remove the front bearing from the input shaft.

NOTE: Do not lose the shims between the bearing and the shaft.

9. Remove the bearing pins from the 3rd/4th selector fork. The pins are retained by bolts on the left and right sides of the front housing.

10. Remove the front housing retaining bolts and separate the front housing from the rear housing.

11. Remove the shift rails for the 3rd/4th and 1st/2nd gears towards the front of the transmission.

12. Remove the reverse shift rail from the rear of the transmission.

Removing the reverse gear by pressing the 1st/2nd gear against notch

Removing the 1st/2nd shift forks bearing bolts

NOTE: The deep shift rail cutouts should be towards the shift lever side.

13. Engage the 1st speed gear and remove the 3rd/4th selector fork.

14. Remove the output shaft flange locking plate, the locking nut and remove the flange from the shaft.

15. Remove the rear bearing cover and shims from the rear of the transmission.

16. Remove the speedometer drive gear and washer.

17. Using a special bearing puller or equivalent, remove the countershaft ball bearing.

18. Remove the input shaft and the countershaft gear assemblies from the rear housing.

19. Engage 2nd gear and remove the bearing pins from the 1st/2nd selector fork.

20. Remove the bearing pin for the reverse selector fork and remove the fork from the housing.

21. Press the 1st/2nd selector fork against the notch in housing and pull the reverse gear out.

22. Remove the rear output shaft bearing by either pulling the bearing from the shaft or pressing the shaft from the bearing. Remove the bearing from the housing, if remaining.

Do not lose the shim from under the large circlip.

23. Remove the output shaft gear assembly from the housing and remove the 1st/2nd selector fork from the sliding sleeve.

24. Press the 1st and reverse gears from the output shaft. Remove the needle bearing and remove the snap-ring. Remove the synchronizer ring.

25. Press the synchronizer assembly and the 2nd speed gear from the shaft and remove the needle bearing.

26. Remove the front snap-ring and remove the synchronizer assembly and the 3rd gear from the shaft.

27. If necessary, the 3rd and 4th countershaft gears can be replaced, by removing the circlip and pulling the ball bearing from the shaft to expose the gears. Remove the circlip from between the gears.

28. Replace any worn or defective parts, seals and gaskets, in preparation for the reassembly.

ASSEMBLY

1. Check the synchronizer rings to the clutch body gap and renew the rings if the gap is less than 0.0157 inch (0.4 mm).

Removing or installing input, output and countershaft assemblies from transmission rear housing

2. Assemble the synchronizer assembly with the springs and pressure plates in position. Install the sliding sleeve over the hub assembly.

NOTE: The sliding sleeve for the 1st/2nd gears has equal serrations all around. The sliding sleeve for the 3rd/4th gears has interrupted serrations. The hub for the 1st/2nd gears is equal on both sides while the hub for the 3rd/4th gears is lower on the side facing the 4th gear.

3. Install the needle bearing and the 3rd gear onto the front of the output shaft. Install the 3rd/4th synchronizer assembly on the shaft with the higher side towards the 3rd gear. Install the circlip of a size that no end-play is present.

4. Install the needle bearing and the 2nd gear onto the rear of the output shaft. Assemble the 1st/2nd synchronizer assembly and install on the shaft. Install the retaining snap-ring of a size to prevent end-play.

NOTE: Be sure the synchronizer rings are in place on the synchronizer hub.

5. Install the needle bearing and the 1st gear onto the shaft and press the reverse gear in place with its thicker hub side facing to the outside.

6. Measure the distance, A, from the hub of the front synchronizer, less snap-ring, to the machined surface on the rear of the reverse gear.

7. Install the rear bearing into the rear housing and measure the distance, B, from the housing mating surface, less gasket, to the ball bearing inner race.

8. Add distance A and B together and the result is the actual measurement, C, from the face of the inner race of the ball bearing to the front of the synchronizer hub. A theoretical measurement is given for this distance and is noted as 2.106 inch (53.5 mm).

NOTE: The theoretical measurement is obtained at time of transmission design and the difference is in the machining of the various internal part, which represents the actual measurement.

Measurement locations to determine shim "D"

9. Subtract the theoretical measurement, C, from the actual measurement, C, and the result is the size shim needed, known as D, between the rear bearing and the transmission case for the output shaft. Remove the rear bearing and install the shim D, and reinstall the bearing in its bore.

10. Place the 1st/2nd selector fork into the sliding sleeve of the 1st/2nd synchronizer assembly.

NOTE: Play between the fork follower and the sliding sleeve should be 0.0629 inch (1.6 mm) so as to avoid vibration of the shift lever.

11. Position and press the output shaft into the rear bearing, seated in the rear housing.

12. Engage the 2nd gear and press the selector fork against the stop. Position the reverse gear pinion with the relieved tooth face side towards the housing and install on the shaft.

13. Install the reverse gear selector fork and secure with the bearing pin.

14. Secure the 1st/2nd selector fork with the bearing pins. Place the gear train into the Neutral position.

15. Place the transmission gear train in the upright position and install the 3rd/4th sliding sleeve and synchronizer ring, if not previously done. Position the roller bearing on the front of the output shaft and install the input shaft. Be sure the synchronizer rings fit into their respective notches.

16. Install the countershaft assembly and support the assembly until the rear bearing can be pressed on to the shaft and into the housing. Allow the bearing to project from the face of the housing, 0.196 inch (5.0 mm) and is known as dimension D.

17. Install the gasket on the rear of the housing and measure the distance A, from the face of the gasket to the height of the output shaft bearing.

18. Measure the distance B, from the surface of the bearing cover to the seat of the bearing bore within the cover.

19. Determine the thickness of shim C by subtracting distance A from distance B.

NOTE: The shimming accuracy should be ± 0.002 inch (0.06 mm).

20. Install the washer and the speedometer drive gear onto the output shaft.

21. Hold shim C with grease to the bearing cover and install the cover to the rear of the transmission case. Install the retaining bolts and secure. Install the output shaft flange, the locking nut and the locking plate.

22. Install the selector fork to the 3rd/4th sliding sleeve. Install the shift rails, reverse from the rear of the transmission and the 1st/2nd or 3rd/4th from the front of the transmission.

23. Install the front housing to the rear housing and secure. Install the 3rd/4th bearing pins, vibration damper and shift arm.

24. Measure the distance A, from the front face of the housing to the contact face on the input shaft for the front bearing.

25. Measure the distance from the ball bearing edge (facing inward), to the lock-ring on the ball bearing. This measurement is known as distance B.

26. Subtract distance A from distance B. The result is known as C. Subtract 0.019 inch (0.5 mm) from distance C and the results are the thickness of shim D.

NOTE: A range of 0.019 to 0.031 inch (0.5 to 0.8 mm) is given to subtract from distance C.

27. Install shim D on the input shaft and press the bearing into place on the shaft and into the bore of the housing.

28. Shim the clearance between the ball bearing inner race and the circlip to zero by adding the proper sized shim.

29. Install the gasket on the front of the transmission.

30. Measure the distance between the top of the countershaft bearing and the gasket surface. This distance is known as A.

31. Distance B is the end-play of the countershaft, 0.004 to 0.008 inch (0.1 to 0.2 mm). Subtract distance B from distance A to obtain the thickness of shim C.

32. Measure distance D between the mating face and the machined bore bottom of the guide sleeve. (Input shaft).

33. Measure the distance E from the ball bearing top face to the gasket on the housing. (Input shaft.)

34. Subtract distance E from distance D

and the result is shim size F, ± 0.002 inch (± 0.05 mm).

35. Install the shims on the respective bearings and install the guide sleeve and secure it with the retaining bolts.

36. Fill the transmission with lubricating oil to its proper level.

TYPE 9

4 Speed Transmission Capri

DISASSEMBLY

1. Remove the retaining clips and the flat washers from the shift rods at the shift levers. Remove the rods.

2. Remove the shift linkage cover. Remove the shifter forks from the gear box.

3. Remove the bolts which hold the tailshaft to the gear box and twist the tailshaft until the countershaft becomes fully visible.

4. Remove the countershaft by driving it from the front of the gear box toward the rear using a brass drift. The countershaft should just clear the front of the case. Push the countershaft out the rest of the way with a dummy shaft. Lower the cluster gear to the bottom of the gear box.

5. Remove the snap-ring which secures the input shaft bearing and press off the bearing.

6. Remove the tailshaft and the output shaft assembly from the gear box.

7. Disassemble the cluster gear by allowing the dummy countershaft to fall out. Remove the needle bearings and the spacers from the cluster gear.

Removing third gear snap-ring—2000, 2300, and V6 transmissions

Installing caged roller bearing—2000, 2300, and V6 transmissions

EXTENSION HOUSING AND
OUTPUT SHAFT ASSEMBLY

REVERSE
IDLER
GEAR

Removing tailshaft—2000, 2300, and V6 transmission

8. Drive out the reverse idler gear shaft toward the rear of the gear box.

9. Remove the snap-ring in front of the third and fourth gear synchronizer, from the output shaft assembly. Remove the synchronizer assembly including third gear.

10. Remove the snap-ring and the thrust washer in front of the second gear. Remove second gear and the blocking ring.

11. Remove the first and second gear synchronizer sleeve and remove the synchronizer inserts.

12. Remove the speedometer drive gear.

13. Remove the snap-ring which retains the output bearing in the tailshaft.

14. Remove the output shaft from the tailshaft.

15. Remove the snap-ring from the output shaft and press off the bearing using an arbor press. Remove the spacer and first gear with the blocking ring and insert spring.

ASSEMBLY

1. Slide the insert spring, blocking ring, first gear, and the spacer onto the rear of the output shaft. Make sure that the broad side of the spacer is pointing toward the shaft bearing.

2. Install a new snap-ring on the tailshaft output shaft.

When installing a new bearing on the tailshaft, a new snap-ring should be selected as follows: Place a dummy bearing into the tailshaft and determine the distance between the top face of the bearing and the outer edge of the retaining groove, using a feeler gauge.

The thickness of the dummy bearing (0.688 in.) plus the feeler gauge blades is the total width between the stop for the bearing, and the outer edge of the snap-ring retaining groove. Measure the width of the new bearing and subtract that number from the total width just obtained. This figure is the thickness that the new snap-ring should be.

3. Install the speedometer gear along the output shaft by pressing it into place.

4. Position the first and second gear synchronizer springs in the synchronizer hub by placing one end of each spring into the same groove.

5. Position the inserts in their grooves and then slide the first and second gear synchronizer sleeve onto the synchronizer hub.

6. Slide the blocking ring, second gear and the thrust washer onto the output shaft. Install the snap-ring.

7. Heat the tailshaft. A pan of hot water is recommended. Install the output shaft and bearing into the tailshaft.

8. Install the snap-ring which you had previously measured in the tailshaft.

9. Position the synchronizer springs as described in Step 4. Install the inserts in their groove. Slide the third and fourth gear synchronizer sleeve onto the hub.

10. Install the third and fourth gear synchronizer assembly by sliding it onto the output shaft and install the snap-ring.

11. Press the input shaft bearing onto the input shaft and install a snap-ring that gives the least possible end-play.

12. Install the input shaft and gear to the gear box using a brass drift.

13. Install the front bearing retainer to the gear box with the gasket in place. The oil groove in the retainer should be in line with the oil passage in the gear box.

14. Install the reverse idler gear, with the collar for the selector fork facing rearward, then drive the idler gear shaft into position until it is flush against the case.

15. With a dummy pinion installed in the bottom of the gear box, install the countershaft. Position the thrust washers in the gear box.

16. Install the tailshaft using sealer on both ends. Slide the tailshaft and the output shaft into position.

17. Using cords, raise the cluster gear into mesh with the main gear train and install the countershaft. The offset lug on the rear of the countershaft must be positioned to allow final installation of the tailshaft.

18. Use a sealer and install the tailshaft bolts. Install the speedometer driven gear.

19. Install the shifter forks for first/second and third/fourth gears so that the numbers stamped on the forks face the front of the transmission. Install the reverse fork with the number facing the rear.

20. Install the retaining clips and the flat washers on the shift levers and install the shift rods to the shift levers.

TYPE 10

4 Speed Transmission–Model F4W63L

Datsun

DISASSEMBLY

The reverse and reverse idler drive gears are contained in the extension housing of this transmission. On late units, the cast, ribbed bottom cover is replaced by a stamped steel cover. Virtually all of these transmissions imported to the U.S. have a modified extension housing incorporating a floorshift mechanism.

1. Drain the transmission.

2. Remove the clutch throughout lever and release bearing.

3. Remove the clevis pin which connects the striker rod to the shift lever.

4. Remove the speedometer drive pinion assembly.

5. Unbolt and remove the extension housing, disengaging the striker rod from the shift rod gates.

6. Remove the bottom and front covers.

7. Remove the three detent plugs, springs and balls.

8. Drive out the shift fork retaining pins. Remove the rods and forks.

9. Move the first/second and third/fourth coupling sleeves into gear at the same time to lock the mainshaft.

10. Pull out the countershaft and countergear with the two needle roller bearings and spacers.

11. Remove the snap-ring, reverse idler gears, and shaft.

12. Unbolt the mainshaft rear bearing retainer.

13. Pull out the mainshaft assembly to the rear. Pull out the clutch shaft to the front.

14. To disassemble the mainshaft, remove the snap-ring, third/ fourth synchronizer hub and coupling sleeve. Remove third gear, with the roller bearing. Remove the mainshaft nut, lock-plate, speedometer drive gear, and steel ball. Take off reverse gear, and the hub. Press off the bearing and retainer.

ASSEMBLY

1. Assembly procedures are generally the reverse of disassembly, however the following special instructions are required.

2. On the clutch shaft, there should be no end-play between the bearing and the snap-ring. Snap-rings are available in sizes from 0.0598 in. (1.52 mm) to 0.0697 in. (1.77 mm).

3. Some of these transmissions use a servo type synchronizer which utilizes brake bands. To assemble these synchronizers, place each

Transmission case components, model F4W63L

1. Case	13. Oil seal	25. Lockwasher	37. Pinion sleeve
2. Needle bearing	14. Breather	26. Drain plug	38. Pin
3. Dowel pin	15. Striker bushing	27. Bearing retainer	39. Lockplate
4. Plug assembly	16. Gasket	28. Detent ball	40. Lockwasher
5. Front cover	17. Bolt	29. Detent spring	41. Bolt
6. Oil seal	18. Lockwasher	30. Interlock plunger	42. Bolt
7. Gasket	19. Bearing retainer	31. Interlock pin	43. Lockwasher
8. Bolt	20. Bolt	32. Detent plug	44. Bolt
9. Bolt	21. Lockwasher	33. Detent plug	45. Lockwasher
0. Lockwasher	22. Bottom cover	34. Not used	46. Nut
11. Extension housing	23. Gasket	35. Washer	47. Plug for backup light switch
12. Bushing	24. Bolt	36. Speedometer pinion	

Exploded view of gear train components

1. Reverse idler gear	15. Snap-ring	30. Third gear
2. Reverse idler shaft	16. Mainshaft	31. Baulk ring
3. Main reverse idler gear	17. 5/32″ steel ball	32. Shifting insert
4. Snap-ring	18. Thrust washer	33. Spreader ring
5. Thrust washer	19. Needle bearing	34. Third/fourth synchro hub
6. Countergear	20. First gear bushing	35. Coupling sleeve
7. Countershaft	21. First gear	36. Snap-ring
8. Spacer	22. Baulk ring	37. Pilot bearing
9. Needle bearing	23. Shifting insert	38. Bearing
10. Front countershaft thrust washer	24. Spreader ring	39. Snap-ring
11. Rear countershaft thrust washer	25. First/second synchro hub	40. Reverse gear
12. Main drive gear	26. Coupling sleeve	41. Reverse gear hub
13. Main drive gear bearing	27. Needle bearing	42. Speedometer drive gear
14. Washer	28. Second gear	43. Lockwasher
	29. Needle bearing	44. Nut
		45. Steel ball

Shift rod and fork details, four speed bottom cover transmission

1. First/second shift fork
2. Third/fourth shift fork
3. First/second shift rod
4. Interlock plunger
5. Third/fourth shift rod
6. Interlock plunger
7. Interlock pin
8. Reverse shift fork
9. Reverse shift rod
10. Fork retaining pin

gear on a flat surface. Install the synchronizer ring into the clutch gear. Place the thrust block and anchor block and install the circlip into the groove.

4. Third gear should be adjusted to give an end-play of 0.0020-0.0059 in. Snap-rings for adjustment are available in sizes from 0.0551 in. to 0.0630 in.

5. Install the reverse idler driving gear on the reverse shaft and fasten with a snap-ring. Install the shaft and gear into the case, placing a thrust washer between the gear and case. Place a thrust washer, idler gear, and snap-ring on the inside end of the shaft. Idler gear end-play should be 0.0039-0.0118 in. Snap-rings are available in sizes from 0.0433 in. to 0.0591 in.

6. Countergear end-play should be 0.0020-0.0059 in. Thrust washers for adjustment are available from 0.0945 in. to 0.1024 in.

7. To assemble the shift mechanism, place the first/second and third/fourth forks onto their sleeves. Insert the first/second shift rod. Install an interlock plunger and then the third/forth shift rod with the interlock pin. Install the other interlock plunger and then

Servo type synchronizer assembly details

Shift rod interlock details for four speed bottom cover transmission

the reverse shift fork and rod. Place a detent ball and spring into each detent hole. Use sealant on the plug threads.

8. Install the extension housing, engaging the striker rod with the shift rod.

TYPE 11

4 Speed Transmission—Model F4W71B

Datsun

DISASSEMBLY

This transmission is constructed in three sections: clutch housing, transmission housing and extension housing. There are no case cover plates. There is a cast iron adapter plate between the transmission and extension housings.

1. Remove the clutch housing dust cover. Remove the retaining spring, release bearing sleeve, and throwout lever.

2. Remove the backup light/neutral safety switch.

3. Unbolt and remove the clutch housing, rapping with a soft hammer if necessary. Remove the gasket, mainshaft bearing shim, and countershaft bearing shim.

4. Remove the speedometer pinion sleeve.

5. Remove the striker rod pin from the rod. Separate the striker rod from the shift lever bracket.

6. Unbolt and remove the rear extension. It may be necessary to rap the housing with a soft hammer.

7. Remove the mainshaft bearing snap-ring.

8. Remove the adapter plate and gear assembly from the transmission case.

9. Punch out the shift fork retaining pins. Remove the shift rod snap-rings. Remove the detent plugs, springs and balls from the adapter plate. Remove the shift rods, being careful not to lose the interlock balls.

10. Remove the snap-ring, speedometer drive gear and locating ball.

11. Remove the nut, lockwasher, thrust washer, reverse hub and reverse gear.

12. Remove the snap-ring and countershaft

1. Pilot bearing	8. 2nd gear, mainshaft	15. Needle bearing
2. 3rd & 4th synchromesh assembly	9. 1st & 2nd synchromesh assembly	16. Bushing, 1st gear
3. Baulk ring	10. Coupling sleeve	17. Thrust washer, mainshaft
4. 3rd gear, mainshaft	11. Shifting insert	18. Mainshaft bearing
5. Needle bearing	12. Spread spring	19. Reverse gear, mainshaft
6. Mainshaft	13. Synchronizer hub	10. Thrust washer
7. Needle bearing	14. 1st gear, mainshaft	21. Nut
		22. Steel ball

Mainshaft—280Z

reverse gear. Remove the snap-ring, reverse idler gear, thrust washer and needle bearing.

13. Support the gear assembly while rapping on the rear of the mainshaft wih a soft hammer.

14. Remove the setscrew from the adapter plate. Remove the shaft nut, spring washer, plain washer and reverse idler shaft.

15. Remove the bearing retainer and the mainshaft rear bushing.

16. To disassemble the mainshaft (rear section), remove the front snap-ring, third/fourth synchronizer assembly, third gear and needle bearing. From the rear, remove the thrust washer, locating ball, first gear, needle bearing, first gear bushing, first/second synchronizer assembly, second gear, and needle bearing.

17. To disassemble the clutch shaft, re-

move the snap-ring and bearing spacer and press off the bearing.

18. To disassemble the countershaft, press off the front bearing. Press off the rear bearing, press off the gears and remove the keys.

19. Remove the retaining pin, control arm pin and shift control arm from the rear of the extension housing.

ASSEMBLY

1. Place the O-ring in the front cover. Install the front cover to the clutch housing with a press. Put in the front cover oil seal.

2. Install the rear extension oil seal.

3. Assemble the first/second and third/fourth synchronizer assemblies. Make sure that the ring gaps are not both on the same side of the unit.

1. Countershaft front bearing
2. Counter drive gear
3. Countershaft
4. Countershaft rear bearing
5. Countershaft reverse gear
6. Countershaft front bearing shim
7. Snap ring
8. Woodruff key
9. Snap ring

Countershaft—280Z and 620

FORK ROD (1st & 2nd)

FORK ROD (3rd & 4th)

FORK ROD (REV.)

Interlock and detent plunger—280Z and 620

4. On the rear end of the mainshaft, install the needle bearing, second gear, baulk ring, first/second synchronizer assembly, baulk ring, first gear bushing, needle bearing, first gear, locating ball and thrust washer.

5. Drive or press on the mainshaft rear bearing.

6. Install the countershaft rear bearing to the adapter plate. Drive or press the mainshaft rear bearing into the adapter plate until the bearing snap-ring groove comes through the rear side of the plate. Install the snapring. If it is not tight against the plate, press the bearing back in slightly.

7. Insert the countershaft bearing ring between the countershaft rear bearing and bearing retainer. Install the bearing retainer to the adapter plate. Stake both ends of the screws.

8. Insert the reverse idler shaft from the rear of the adapter plate. Install the spring washer and plain washer to the idler shaft.

9. Place the two keys on the countershaft and oil the shaft lightly. Press on third gear and install a snap-ring.

10. Install the countershaft into its rear bearing.

11. From the front of the mainshaft, install the needle bearing, third gear, baulk ring, third/fourth synchronizer assembly and snap-ring. Snap-rings are available in thicknesses from 0.0561 in. to 0.0640 in. to adjust gear end-play.

12. Press the main drive bearing onto the clutch shaft. Install the main drive gear spacer and a snap-ring. Snap-rings are available in thicknesses from 0.0710 in. to 0.0820 in. to adjust gear end-play.

13. Insert a key into the countershaft drive gear with fourth gear and drive on the countershaft fourth gear with a drift. The rear end of the countershaft should be held steady while driving on the gear, to prevent rear bearing damage.

14. Install the reverse hub, reverse gear, thrust washer, and lock tab on the rear of the mainshaft. Install the shaft nut temporarily.

15. Install the needle bearing, reverse idler gear, thrust washer, and snap-ring.

16. Place the countershaft reverse gear and snap-ring on the rear of the countershaft. Snap-rings are available in thicknesses from 0.0433 in. to 0.0590 in. to adjust gear end-play.

17. Engage both first and second gears to lock the shaft.

18. On the rear of the mainshaft, install the snap-ring, locating ball, speedometer drive gear, and snap-ring. Snap-rings are available in thicknesses from 0.0433 in. to 0.0590 in.

19. Recheck end-play and backlash of all gears.

20. Place the reverse shift fork on the reverse gear and install the reverse shift rod. Install the detent ball, spring and plug. Install the fork retaining pin. Place two interlock balls between the reverse shift rod and the third/fourth shift rod location. Install the third/fourth shift fork and rod. Install the detent ball, spring and plug. This plug is shorter than the other two. Install the fork retaining pin. Place two interlock balls between the first/second shift rod location and the third/fourth shift rod. Install the first/second shift fork and rod. Install the detent ball, spring and plug.

21. Install the shift rod snap-rings.

22. Apply sealant sparingly to the adapter plate and transmission housing. Install the transmission housing to the adapter plate and bolt it down temporarily.

23. Drive in the countershaft front bearing with a drift. Place the snap-ring in the mainshaft front bearing.

24. Apply sealant sparingly to the adapter plate and extension housing. Align the shift rods in the neutral positions. Position the striker rod to the shift rods and bolt down the extension housing.

25. Insert the striker rod pin, connect the rod to the shift lever bracket and install the striker rod pin retaining ring. Replace the shift control arm.

26. To select the proper mainshaft bearing shim, first measure the amount the bearing protrudes from the front of the transmission case. This is measurement (B). Then measure the depth of the bearing recess in the rear of the clutch housing. This is measurement (A). Required shim thickness is found by subtracting (B) from (A). Shims are available in thicknesses of 0.0551 in. and 0.0630 in.

27. To select the proper countershaft front bearing shim, measure the amount that the bearing is recessed into the transmission case. Shim thickness should equal this measurement. Shims are available in thicknesses from 0.0157 in. (.4 mm) to 0.0394 in. (1.0 mm).

28. Apply sealant sparingly to the clutch and transmission housing mating surfaces.

29. Replace the clutch operating mechanism.

30. Install the shift lever temporarily and check shifting action.

TYPE 12

5 Speed Transmission—Model FS5W71B

Datsun

This transmission is similar to the 4 speed transmission, model F4W71B and the overhaul can be accomplished by following the outline for the disassembly and assembly of the model F4W71B transmission.

Servo type synchromesh is used, instead of the Borg-Warner type in the four speed. Shift linkage and interlock arrangements are the same, except the reverse shift rod also operates fifth gear. Most service procedures are identical to those for the four speed unit. Those unique to the five-speed follow.

DISASSEMBLY

To disassemble the synchronizers, remove the circlip, synchronizer ring, thrust block, brake band, and anchor block. Be careful not to mix parts of the different synchronizer assemblies.

ASSEMBLY

1. The synchronizer assemblies for second, third, and fourth are identical. When assembling the first gear synchronizer, be sure to install the 0.0866 in. thick brake band at the bottom.

2. When assembling the mainshaft, select a third gear synchronizer hub snap-ring to minimize hub end-play. Snap-rings are available in thicknesses of 0.061-0.630 in. 0.0591-0.0610 in. and 0.0571-0.0591 in. The synchronizer hub must be installed with the longer boss to the rear.

3. When reassembling the gear train, install the mainshaft, countershaft, and gears to the adapter plate. Hold the rear nut and force the front nut against it to a torque of 217 ft/lbs. Select a snap-ring to minimize end-play of the fifth gear bearing at the rear of the mainshaft. Snap-rings are available in thicknesses from 0.0433 in. to 0.0551 in.

1. Main drive gear
2. Baulk ring
3. Shifting insert
4. Shifting insert spring
5. Synchronizer hub
6. Coupling sleeve
7. 3rd main gear
8. Needle bearing
9. Mainshaft
10. 2nd main gear
11. Bushing
12. 1st main gear
13. OD-reverse synchronizer hub
14. Reverse gear
15. Circlip
16. Thrust block
17. Brake band
18. Synchronizer ring
19. Overdrive main gear
20. Overdrive gear bushing
21. Washer
22. Mainshaft nut
23. Overdrive mainshaft bearing
24. Speedometer drive gear
25. Countershaft front bearing shim
26. Countershaft front bearing
27. Countershaft drive gear
28. Countershaft
29. Countershaft bearing
30. Reverse counter gear spacer
31. Reverse counter gear
32. Overdrive counter gear
33. Countershaft rear bearing
34. Countershaft nut
35. Reverse idler shaft
36. Reverse idler thrust washer
37. Reverse idler gear
38. Reverse idler gear bearing
39. Reverse idler thrust washer

Exploded view of gear train components

1. Front cover
2. Front cover oil seal
3. Front cover gasket
4. Transmission case
5. Adapter plate
6. Mainshaft bearing
7. Bearing retainer
8. Rear extension
9. Breather
10. Rear extension oil seal
11. Sleeve yoke dust cover

Component parts of model FS5C71 transmission case

TYPE 13

4 Speed Transmission–Model F4W56A Datsun

This transmission is constructed in two sections: a combined clutch and transmission housing, and an extension housing. There is a cast iron adapter plate between the housings. There are no case cover plates.

DISASSEMBLY

1. Drain the oil.
2. Remove the dust cover, spring, clutch throwout lever, and release bearing.
3. Remove the front cover from inside the clutch housing.
4. Remove the speedometer drive pinion from the extension housing. Remove the striker rod return spring plug, spring, plunger, and bushing. Remove the striker rod pin and separate the striker rod from the shift lever bracket.
5. Remove the extension housing. Tap it with a soft hammer, if necessary.
6. Separate the adapter plate from the transmission case, being careful not to lose the countershaft bearing washer.
7. Clamp the adapter plate in a vise with the reverse idler gear up.

8. Drive out the retaining pin and remove the reverse shift fork and reverse idler gear.
9. Remove the mainshaft rear snap-ring, washer, and reverse gear.
10. Drive out the remaining shift fork retaining pins. Remove all three detent plugs, springs, and balls. Remove the forks and shift rods. Be careful not to lose the interlock plungers.
11. Tap the rear of the mainshaft with a soft hammer to separate the mainshaft and countershaft from the adapter plate. Be careful not to drop the shafts. Separate the clutch shaft from the mainshaft.
12. From the front of the mainshaft, remove the needle bearing, synchronizer hub thrust washer, steel locating ball, third/fourth synchronizer, baulk ring, third gear, and needle bearing.
13. Press off the mainshaft bearing to the rear. Remove the thrust washer, first gear, needle bearing, baulk ring, first/second synchronizer, snap-ring and bearing.

ASSEMBLY

1. Press on the countershaft bearings. Install the countershaft assembly to the transmission case and replace the adapter plate temporarily. Countershaft end-play should be 0-0.0079 in. Front bearing shims are available for adjustment in thicknesses from 0.0315 in. to 0.0512 in. Remove the countershaft assembly from the case.
2. Install the coupling sleeve, shifting inserts, and spring on the synchronizer hub. Be

careful not to hook the front and rear ends of the spring to the same insert.
3. Install the needle bearing from the rear of the mainshaft. Install second gear, the baulk ring, and synchronizer hub assembly. Align the shifting insert to the baulk ring groove. Install the first gear side needle bearing, baulk ring, and first gear. Install the mainshaft thrust washer and press on the rear bearing.

On the mainshaft front end, replace the needle bearing, third gear, baulk ring, synchronizer hub assembly, steel locating ball, thrust washer, and pilot bearing. Be sure to grease the sliding surface of the steel ball and thrust washer. The dimpled side of the thrust washer must face to the front and the oil grooved side to the rear.
4. Replace the main bearing, washer, and snap-ring onto the clutch shaft. The web side of the washer must face the bearing. Place the baulk ring on the clutch shaft and assemble the clutch shaft to the mainshaft.
5. Align the mainshaft assembly with the countershaft assembly and install them to the adapter plate by lightly tapping on the clutch shaft with a soft hammer.
6. Place the first/second and third/fourth shift forks on the shift rods, being careful that the forks are not reversed. Install all three shift rods and the detent and interlock parts. Apply locking agent to the detent plug threads and screw the plugs in flush. Make sure the shift forks are in their grooves and drive in the retaining pins.
7. Install the mainshaft reverse gear,

1. Front cover
2. Front cover oil seal
3. Front cover O-ring
4. Front cover adjusting shim
5. Welch plug
6. Top detecting switch
7. Reverse lamp switch
8. Transmission case assembly
9. Adapter plate
10. Striking rod bushing
11. Breather
12. Filler plug
13. Rear extension dowel pin
14. Rear extension assembly
15. Drain plug
16. Rear extension dust cover with oil seal
17. Retaining pin
18. Speedometer pinion O-ring
19. Speedometer sleeve
20. Speedometer pinion

Transmission case components—model F4W56A

1. Main drive bearing
2. Main drive gear
3. 3rd & top synchronizer
4. 3rd gear, mainshaft
5. Mainshaft
6. 2nd gear, mainshaft
7. 1st & 2nd synchronizer
8. 1st gear, mainshaft
9. Mainshaft bearing
10. Reverse gear, mainshaft
11. Counter gear assembly
12. Idler gear assembly

Exploded view of the gear train components

thrust washer, and snap-ring. Face the web side of the thrust washer to the gear.

8. Replace the reverse idler gear and pin on the reverse shift fork. Check interlock action by attempting to shift two shift rods at once.

9. Install the adapter plate to the transmission case. Make sure to install the countergear front shim selected in Step 1. Use sealant on the joint and seat the plate by tapping with a soft hammer.

10. Align the striker lever and install the extension housing. Use sealant on the joint. Install the bushing, plunger, return spring, and plug. Use sealant on the plug threads. Install the striker rod pin and the speedometer drive pinion.

11. Select clutch shaft bearing shim(s) by measuring the amount the bearing outer race is recessed below the machined surface for the front cover. The depth should be 0.1969-0.2028 in. Shims are available for adjustment in thicknesses of 0.0039 in., 0.0079 in., and 0.0197 in.

12. Place the oil seal in the front cover, grease the seal lip, and install the cover and O-ring with the shim(s) selected in Step 11.

13. Replace the clutch release bearing, return spring, and withdrawal lever.

14. Check shifting action. Rotate the clutch shaft slowly in neutral. The rear of the mainshaft should not turn.

TYPE 14

5 Speed Transmission–Model FS5W63A, L

Datsun

DISASSEMBLY

1. Secure the transmission and drain the lubricant.

2. Remove the dust cover, the clutch release bearing and the operating lever.

3. Remove the electrical switches from the case.

4. Remove the speedometer driven gear assembly.

5. Remove the front main drive gear bearing cover and detach the countershaft front bearing shim.

6. Remove the main drive gear bearing snap-ring from the outer race.

7. Remove the return spring plug, the return spring and plunger from the rear extension.

8. Remove the rear extension housing retaining bolts and with the use of a puller, remove the housing from the transmission case and adapter plate.

9. Separate the adapter plate from the transmission case by lightly tapping the case from the adapter plate.

10. Mount the adapter plate assembly into a holding fixture, either purchased or fabricated, and mount in a vise or similar tool.

11. Drive the retaining pins from the shifting forks and selector shaft rods with a pin punch.

1. 1st & 2nd fork rod	11. Stopper ring	21. O-ring
2. 3rd & top fork rod	12. Shift rod A bracket	22. Stopper pin bolt
3. Reverse fork rod	13. Reverse shift fork	23. Striking guide assembly
4. Retaining pin	14. Lock pin	24. Striking guide oil seal
5. 1st & 2nd shift fork	15. Striking lever	25. Control lever bushing
6. 3rd & top shift fork	16. Striking rod	26. Expansion plug
7. Checking ball plug	17. Return spring plug	27. Control pin bushing
8. Check ball spring	18. Reverse check spring	28. Control arm pin
9. Check ball	19. Return spring	29. Control lever
10. Interlock plunger	20. Plunger	

Exploded view of shift selector rod and fork components

1. Front cover
2. Front cover oil seal
3. Withdrawal lever ball pin
4. Transmission case
5. Breather
6. Reverse lamp switch
7. Top switch (U.S.A. models)
8. Sleeve yoke dust cover
9. Rear extension oil seal
10. Speedometer pinion
11. Speedometer sleeve
12. Rear extension
13. Adapter plate

Transmission case components, model FS5W63A

12. Remove the three selector rod check ball plugs. Remove the check balls and springs.

13. Remove the selector rods from the front to the rear by lightly tapping on the rods with a soft-faced hammer. Remove the interlock plungers.

14. Remove the mainshaft bearing snap-ring and with the aid of a puller, remove the mainshaft bearing from the shaft. Remove the second snap-ring from the mainshaft.

15. Engage two gears to lock the gear train and remove the mainshaft locking nut, from the rear extension side.

16. After the nut has been removed, remove the speedometer drive gear and steel ball, the synchronizer hub with reverse gear, 1st gear with the needle bearing and the bushing, the idler gear and needle bearing. Remove the thrust washer and the second steel ball.

17. From the rear extension housing end of the adapter plate, remove the snap-ring and thrust washer, 1st gear using a puller tool, from the countershaft.

18. Attaching a special pushing tool or equivalent, to the adapter plate and push the mainshaft approximately 0.39 inch (10 mm) from the adapter plate. Remove the main drive gear and the countergear. Holding the mainshaft gear assembly by hand, remove the mainshaft and mainshaft gears as an assembly.

19. After the mainshaft has been removed, take the thrust washer, the steel ball, 2nd gear and the needle bearing from the mainshaft.

20. Using a press or similar tool, remove the 2nd gear mainshaft bushing, 3rd gear and

the 2nd/3rd synchronizer assembly from the mainshaft.

21. Remove the snap-ring on the front end of the mainshaft and remove the 4th/5th speed synchronizer and the 5th gear.

22. The bearing can be removed from the maindrive gear by the removal of the snap-ring and spacer. The bearing should be pressed from the shaft.

23. Remove the front and rear bearings from the countergear by using a press or similar tool.

24. To disassemble the synchronizers, remove the spread springs and the shift inserts. Separate the coupling sleeve from the hub.

25. With the adapter plate still in the holding fixture, remove the bearing retainer bolts with an appropriate tool. Remove the bearing from the rear extension side of the adapter plate. The outer race of the counter gear rear bearing can be removed from the adapter plate with the aid of a brass punch.

26. The rear extension housing can be disassembled by the removal of the lock pin from the striking lever and the main selector shift rod (striking rod). The rod can then be removed from the housing.

27. Replace all necessary parts, seals and gaskets.

ASSEMBLY

1. With the adapter plate in the holding fixture and locked in a vise or appropriate tool, install the countergear bearing outer race. Install the mainshaft bearing. Install the bearing retainer and screws. Torque the screws to 5.8 to 9.4 ft/lbs (0.8 to 1.3 Kg-m). Stake each screw head to the retainer at two points.

2. Assemble the synchronizers by placing the hubs into the coupling sleeves. Fit the inserts into their respective grooves and install the spread springs so that the ends of the springs are not in the same insert.

3. Install the 5th speed needle bearing, 5th gear, synchronizer (baulk) ring and the 4th/5th speed synchronizer assembly on the front of the mainshaft.

4. Install a selective snap-ring onto the mainshaft so that the minimum clearance exists between the end face of the hub and the snap-ring. The snap-ring can be selected from the following list:

No.	Thickness	
	mm	(in.)
1	1.40 to 1.45	(0.0551 to 0.0571)
2	1.45 to 1.50	(0.0571 to 0.0591)
3	1.50 to 1.55	(0.0591 to 0.0610)
4	1.55 to 1.60	(0.0610 to 0.0630)
5	1.60 to 1.65	(0.0630 to 0.0650)

Exploded view of gear train components

1. Main drive bearing
2. Main drive gear
3. 4th and 5th synchronizer
4. 5th gear, mainshaft
5. Mainshaft
6. 3rd gear, mainshaft
7. 3rd and 2nd synchronizer
8. 2nd gear, mainshaft
9. Mainshaft bearing
10. 1st gear, mainshaft
11. Reverse and 1st synchronizer
12. Reverse gear, mainshaft
13. Mainshaft end bearing
14. Counter gear assembly
15. Idler gear assembly

5. Install the 3rd gear needle bearing, 3rd gear, 3rd gear synchronizer (baulk) ring, 2nd/3rd gear synchronizer, fit the 2nd gear bushing to the mainshaft, along with the mainshaft bearing thrust washer.

6. Install the 2nd speed synchronizer (baulk) ring, needle bearing, 2nd gear, steel ball and the thrust washer.

7. Press the main drive gear bearing on to the main drive gear and install the spacer and secure with a snap-ring that will eliminate end-play between the spacer and the snap-ring. A selective snap-ring can be selected from the following list:

8. Press the front and rear bearings onto the countergear with appropriate tools.

9. Place the mainshaft assembly into the adapter plate and place the mainshaft nut onto the shaft.

10. Using a puller type tool, move the mainshaft into the adapter plate until the thrust washer to bearing clearance is approximately 0.39 inch (10. mm).

11. Install the pilot bearing into the main drive gear bore and install the main drive gear and the synchronizer (baulk) ring onto the mainshaft assembly.

12. Assemble the countergear assembly to the mainshaft gear assembly.

13. Continuing the pulling effort, move the mainshaft and countergear assemblies into the adapter plate.

14. Place the 1st countergear on the countergear assembly and press into position. Install the spacer on the rear of the 1st countergear and secure it with a new snap-ring.

	Thickness	
No.	mm	(in.)
1	1.49 to 1.55	(0.0587 to 0.0610)
2	1.56 to 1.62	(0.0614 to 0.0638)
3	1.62 to 1.68	(0.0638 to 0.0661)
4	1.68 to 1.74	(0.0661 to 0.0685)
5	1.74 to 1.80	(0.0685 to 0.0709)
6	1.80 to 1.86	(0.0709 to 0.0732)
7	1.86 to 1.92	(0.0732 to 0.0756)

15. Install the steel ball and the thick thrust washer on the end of the mainshaft, install the synchronizer with the reverse gear, 1st gear along with the needle bearing and bushing, the idler gear and the needle bearing.

16. Install the mainshaft nut and tighten it snugly. Lock two gears at the same time to lock the gear train, and tighten the locknut to 101 to 123 ft/lbs (14 to 17 Kg-m). Stake the nut to the groove of the mainshaft with a punch.

17. Check the gear end-play, which should conform to the following specifications:

1st gear
  0.27 to 0.37 mm
  (0.0106 to 0.0146 in.)
2nd gear
  0.20 to 0.30 mm
  (0.0079 to 0.0118 in.)
3rd gear
  0.05 to 0.15 mm
  (0.0020 to 0.0059 in.)
5th gear
  0.05 to 0.20 mm
  (0.0020 to 0.0079 in.)
Reverse idler gear
  0.15 to 0.40 mm
  (0.0059 to 0.0157 in.)

18. Fit a 0.043 inch (1.1 mm) thick snapring to the front side of the mainshaft end bearing. Install the mainshaft end bearing and fit another snap-ring to the mainshaft on the rear side of the bearing, to eliminate end-play. A list of selective snap-rings are available as follows:

No.	Thickness	
	mm	(in)
1	1.1	(0.043)
2	1.2	(0.047)
3	1.3	(0.051)
4	1.4	(0.055)

19. Place the 1st/reverse selector rod into the adapter plate, position the 1st/reverse fork into its gear position, and slide the selector rod into the fork.

20. Place the 1st/reverse selector rod in the neutral position and install the interlock plunger into the adapter plate.

21. Insert the 2nd/3rd selector rod into the adapter plate, position the 2nd/3rd and 4th/5th forks in their respective gear grooves and slide the 2nd/3rd selector rod through the 2nd/3rd and 4th/5th forks.

22. Place the 2nd/3rd selector rod in the neutral position and insert the interlock plunger in the adapter plate.

23. Install the 4th/5th selector rod into the adapter plate and through the 4th/5th fork.

24. Secure the forks to the selector rods with the retaining pins.

25. Install the check balls and springs in their respective bores of the adapter plate.

26. Apply sealer to the check ball plugs and install the plugs in the adapter plate.

NOTE: The check ball plug for the 1st/reverse selector rod is longer than the other plugs.

27. To insure that the interlock plungers are operating properly, slide the 2nd/3rd selector rod into gear and attempt to move the other selector rods into gear. The gears should not mesh. Continue to check the remaining selector rods.

28. Remove the adapter plate from the holder tool. Apply sealer to the mating surfaces of the transmission case and the adapter plate.

29. Slide the transmission case onto the adapter plate by lightly tapping on the case with a soft hammer until the case and the adapter plate meet. Be sure the dowel pin is properly aligned.

30. As the case is being installed to the adapter plate, the front drive gear bearing and the countergear front bearing must be aligned to the transmission case.

31. Install the front drive gear bearing snap-ring into the bearing groove.

32. Assemble the main selector rod to the rear extension housing in the reverse of its removal. Apply sealer to the mating surfaces of the extension housing and the transmission case. Place the transmission gear train in the

1. 4th and 5th fork rod	8. Interlock plunger	15. Control lever bushing
2. 2nd and 3rd fork rod	9. Striking rod	16. Expansion plug
3. 1st and reverse fork rod	10. Striking lever	17. Control lever knob
4. Retaining pin	11. Lock pin	18. Control pin bushing
5. Checking ball	12. O-ring	19. Control arm pin
6. Check ball spring	13. Striking guide	20. Control lever
7. Check ball plug	14. Striking guide oil seal	21. Control lever boot

22. Striking pin	
23. Shift arm	
24. Shift arm bracket	
25. Arm bracket O-ring	
26. Arm bracket plain washer	
27. 1st and reverse shift fork	
28. 2nd and 3rd shift fork	
29. 4th and 5th shift fork	

Exploded view of shift selector rod and fork components

No.	"H" mm	(in)	Thickness of countershaft front bearing shim mm	(in)
1	1.200 to 1.225	(0.0472 to 0.0482)	1.350	(0.0531)
2	1.225 to 1.250	(0.0482 to 0.0492)	1.375	(0.0541)
3	1.250 to 1.275	(0.0492 to 0.0502)	1.400	(0.0551)
4	1.275 to 1.300	(0.0502 to 0.0512)	1.425	(0.0561)
5	1.300 to 1.325	(0.0512 to 0.0522)	1.450	(0.0571)
6	1.325 to 1.350	(0.0522 to 0.0531)	1.475	(0.0581)
7	1.350 to 1.375	(0.0531 to 0.0541)	1.500	(0.0591)
8	1.375 to 1.400	(0.0541 to 0.0551)	1.525	(0.0600)
9	1.400 to 1.425	(0.0551 to 0.0561)	1.550	(0.0610)
10	1.425 to 1.450	(0.0561 to 0.0571)	1.575	(0.0620)
11	1.450 to 1.475	(0.0571 to 0.0581)	1.600	(0.0630)
12	1.475 to 1.500	(0.0581 to 0.0591)	1.625	(0.0640)
13	1.500 to 1.525	(0.0591 to 0.0600)	1.650	(0.0650)
14	1.525 to 1.550	(0.0600 to 0.0610)	1.675	(0.0659)
15	1.550 to 1.575	(0.0610 to 0.0620)	1.700	(0.0669)
16	1.575 to 1.600	(0.0620 to 0.0630)	1.725	(0.0679)
17	1.600 to 1.625	(0.0630 to 0.0640)	1.750	(0.0689)
18	1.625 to 1.650	(0.0640 to 0.0650)	1.775	(0.0699)

37. Using a special measuring tool or equivalent, measure the clearance between the measuring tool, mounted on the countergear, and the transmission case, using a thickness gauge.

38. When the correct shim is selected, install the front cover. Apply sealant to the threads of the bolts and torque to 9 to 13 ft/lbs (1.3 to 1.8 Kg-m).

39. Install the speedometer driven gear assembly, install the electrical switches that were removed during the disassembly.

40. Install the operating lever, the clutch release bearing and the return spring.

41. Install the dust cover, fill the transmission to the proper level with lubricant.

TYPE 15

4 Speed Transmission–Model F4W63L

Datsun

DISASSEMBLY

1. Secure the transmission and drain the lubricant.

5th gear and install the rear extension into place.

33. During the installation of the rear extension housing, align the striking lever into the selector rods.

34. Install the rear extension bolts and torque to 9 to 13 ft/lbs. (1.3 to 1.8 Kg-m).

35. Install the plunger into the rear extension. Install the reverse check spring and the return spring. Apply sealer to the return spring plug and install the plug in place.

36. Support the transmission assembly with its front side up. Rotate the main drive gear until the bearings are settled.

1. Front cover
2. Front cover oil seal
3. Front cover gasket
4. Bottom cover
5. Bottom cover gasket
6. Filler plug
7. Transmission case assembly
8. Rear extension gasket
9. Mainshaft bearing retainer
10. Rear extension dowel pin

11. Breather
12. Control arm O-ring
13. Striking rod bushing
14. Control arm
15. Control arm O-ring
16. Oil seal
17. Rear extension assembly
18. Rear extension oil seal
19. Reverse lamp switch
20. Top switch (U.S.A. models)

Transmission case components, model F4W63L

Exploded view of gear train components

1. Main drive bearing
2. Main drive gear
3. 3rd & 4th synchronizer
4. 3rd gear, mainshaft
5. Mainshaft

6. 2nd gear, mainshaft
7. 1st & 2nd synchronizer
8. 1st gear, mainshaft
9. Mainshaft bearing

10. Reverse gear, mainshaft
11. Counter gear assembly
12. Countershaft
13. Idler gear assembly

2. Remove the dust cover from the transmission case.

3. Remove the release bearing and the operating lever. Remove the electrical switches from the case.

4. Remove the speedometer driven gear assembly.

5. Remove the front cover and the bottom cover from the transmission assembly.

6. Position the gearshift into the neutral position and pull out the striking rod (main shift control rod) pin bolt.

7. Remove the rear extension housing retaining bolts and tap the housing with a soft hammer to remove it from the transmission case.

8. Remove the striking rod (main shift control rod).

9. Drive the shifting fork retaining pins from the forks and selector shafts.

10. Remove the three check ball plugs. Do not lose the check balls and springs. Remove the two interlock plungers.

11. Remove the selector rods and shifting forks from the transmission. Keep in their proper order for installation.

12. Lock the gear train by meshing two gears at the same time. Straighten the lock washer and loosen the nut on the mainshaft.

Place the gear train back in the neutral position.

13. Use a dummy countershaft tool or equivalent, and push the countershaft from the transmission case, from the rear to the front. Do not drop the needle bearings or thrust washers into the transmission.

14. Remove the counter gear assembly from the case.

15. Remove the snap-ring retaining the reverse idler counter gear in place and remove the shaft from the rear of the case. Do not remove the needle bearing.

16. Remove the mainshaft bearing retainer and bolts. Remove the mainshaft assembly from the rear of the transmission case. Remove the loose synchronizer (baulk) ring from the front of the mainshaft.

17. Remove the pilot bearing located between the main drive gear and the mainshaft.

18. Using a wooden shaft, drive the main drive gear and bearing from the transmission case. Do not allow the gear to drop.

19. The main drive gear bearing can be removed after the retaining snap-ring is removed. A press or bearing puller should be used.

20. Remove the front retaining snap-ring from the mainshaft and remove the 3rd/4th

synchronizer assembly, the 3rd gear and mainshaft needle bearing from the shaft.

21. Remove the locknut from the mainshaft and remove the reverse gear, reverse gear hub and the speedometer drive gear.

NOTE: Do not lose the steel ball locating the speedometer drive gear to the mainshaft.

22. Install a suitable puller or set in a press and remove the 1st speed gear, along with the bearing and retainer.

— **CAUTION** —
Do not attach pulling or press tool to the 2nd gear as damage to the 1st gear mainshaft bushing can result. Do not remove the needle bearing with the 1st gear bearing as the needle bearing could be damaged by the second steel ball on the mainshaft.

23. Remove the second steel ball on the mainshaft and install a puller or set in a press and remove the 1st gear bushing, along with the 1st/2nd synchronizer assembly and the 2nd gear.

24. To disassemble the synchronizers, remove the spread springs and take out the

shifting inserts. Separate the coupling sleeve from the synchronizer hub.

25. Clean the assemblies, replace the necessary parts and replace the necessary seals and gaskets.

ASSEMBLY

1. Install the synchronizer hub into the coupling sleeve and fit the three shift inserts in their respective grooves.

2. Install the spread springs on each side of the coupling sleeve and hooked into the shift inserts.

NOTE: Do not hook the spread spring ends in the same shift insert.

3. Assemble the 2nd gear needle bearing, 2nd gear, 2nd gear synchronizer (baulk) ring and the 1st/2nd speed synchronizer assembly onto the mainshaft.

4. Install the 1st gear bushing onto the mainshaft by using a brass drift. Install the 1st gear synchronizer (baulk) ring, needle bearing, steel ball and the thrust washer onto the mainshaft.

5. Press the mainshaft bearing and the reverse hub onto the mainshaft.

6. Install the 3rd gear needle roller bearing, 3rd synchronizer (baulk) ring, 3rd/4th speed synchronizer assembly onto the mainshaft.

7. Install a new snap-ring onto the mainshaft so that a minimum of clearance exists between the face of the hub and the snap-ring groove.

8. Install the reverse gear, the steel ball, the speedometer gear, lock plate and the nut onto the mainshaft.

9. Install the mainshaft assembly into the rear of the transmission case and install the mainshaft bearing retainer plate and bolts. Torque to 5.8 to 7.2 ft/lbs (7.8 to 9.8 Nm).

10. Install the main drive gear bearing in place, using a press or bearing installer. Install the spacer and the retaining selector snap-ring, so that a mimimum of clearance exists between the spacer and the snap-ring. Available selections are as follows:

No.	Thickness	
	mm	(in.)
1	1.40 to 1.45	(0.0551 to 0.0571)
2	1.45 to 1.50	(0.0571 to 0.0591)
3	1.50 to 1.55	(0.0591 to 0.0610)
4	1.55 to 1.60	(0.0610 to 0.0630)
5	1.60 to 1.65	(0.0630 to 0.0650)

No.	Thickness	
	mm	(in.)
1	1.49 to 1.55	(0.0587 to 0.0610)
2	1.56 to 1.62	(0.0614 to 0.0638)
3	1.62 to 1.68	(0.0638 to 0.0661)
4	1.68 to 1.74	(0.0661 to 0.0685)
5	1.74 to 1.80	(0.0685 to 0.0709)
6	1.80 to 1.86	(0.0709 to 0.0732)
7	1.86 to 1.92	(0.0732 to 0.0756)

No.	Thickness	
	mm	(in.)
1	1.15 to 1.25	(0.0453 to 0.0492)
2	1.35 to 1.45	(0.0531 to 0.0571)
3	1.25 to 1.35	(0.0492 to 0.0531)
4	1.45 to 1.55	(0.0571 to 0.0610)
5	1.05 to 1.15	(0.0413 to 0.0453)

No.	Thickness	
	mm	(in.)
1	2.35 to 2.40	(0.0925 to 0.0945)
2	2.40 to 2.45	(0.0945 to 0.0965)
3	2.45 to 2.50	(0.0965 to 0.0984)
4	2.50 to 2.55	(0.0984 to 0.1004)
5	2.55 to 2.60	(0.1004 to 0.1024)

11. Install the pilot bearing into the bore of the main drive gear. Install the main drive gear assembly into the transmission case front.

12. Install the reverse idler shaft into the transmission case from the rear, with the identification mark facing towards the rear.

13. Assemble the thrust washer and the reverse idler (helical) gear and seat the snap-ring in its groove in the top of the reverse idler shaft.

14. Insert a 0.004 inch (0.1 mm) feeler gauge blade between the gear and the thrust washer. With the shaft pushed fully to the rear, install the thrust washer and the spur gear and fit the snap-ring, selected to obtain the proper end-play for the reverse idler gear.

15. The reverse idler gear end-play is 0.0039 to 0.0118 inch (0.10 to 0.30 mm).

NOTE: Install the thrust washers so that the grooved sides are facing towards the gears.

16. Install a dummy shaft or equivalent into the countergear and install the inner washers into the gear. Apply grease to the needle bearings and install 21 bearings on each end of the gear. Install the outer washers and the thrust washers in place on the gear assembly. Place the gear assembly into the transmission case.

NOTE: If a dummy countershaft is used, the shaft should only be as long as the gear assembly and the diameter smaller than the original countershaft.

17. Install the retaining pin in the front of the countershaft and push the shaft into the transmission case, from the front to the rear, engaging the thrust washer, the countergear and forcing the dummy shaft (if used) out through the hole in the back of the case.

18. The rear thrust washer is used to determine the countergear end-play. The end-play is 0.0020 to 0.0059 inch (0.05 to 0.15 mm).

19. After the end-play has been determined, locate the countershaft pin in its indent at the front of the transmission case.

20. Mesh two gears so that the transmission gear train is locked. Tighten the mainshaft locknut to 58 to 80 ft/lbs (8.0 to 11.0 Kg-m). Secure the mainshaft locknut washer by bending over the nut.

21. Align the 1st/2nd shift fork and the 3rd/4th shift fork with the grooves of the coupling sleeves.

22. Install the 1st/2nd selector shift rod into the case and through the selector fork. Install the retaining pin through the fork and rod.

23. Place the 1st/2nd shift fork and gear in the Neutral position. Install the interlock plunger and install the 3rd/4th selector shift rod into the case and the 3rd/4th shift fork. Install the retaining pin in the fork and rod.

24. Place the 3rd/4th selector rod in the Neutral position and install the interlock plunger.

25. Install the reverse shift selector rod through the reverse shift fork and install the retaining pin.

26. Install the check balls and the check ball springs. Install sealer on the plugs and install them into their respective bores.

NOTE: The check ball plug for the

1. Check ball plug		23. Control lever rubber
2. Check ball spring		24. 1st and 2nd fork rod
3. Check ball	9. Reverse fork pin	16. Control bushing	25. 3rd and 4th fork rod
4. Interlock plunger	10. Reverse pin return spring	17. Control lever bracket	26. Reverse fork rod
5. Interlock plunger	11. Roller pin	18. Control spring	27. Reverse shift fork
6. Check ball	12. Retaining pin	19. Striking pin C-ring	28. 1st and 2nd shift fork
7. Check ball spring	13. Control arm pin	20. Control lever	29. 3rd and 4th fork rod
8. Check ball plug	14. Striking rod pin	21. Control lever upper washer	30. Control arm
	15. Thrust washer	22. Control lever upper washer	

Exploded view of shift selector rod and fork components

3rd/4th fork and shift rod is shorter than those for the reverse and 1st/2nd fork and shift rods.

— CAUTION —
To insure that the interlock plungers are properly installed, slide the 3rd/ 4th fork selector rod into gear and try to operate the other selector rods. All other gears should not mesh. Operate the other selector rods and check in the same manner.

---

27. Place all gears in the Neutral position and install the rear extension to the transmission case, using sealer on the mating surfaces.

28. As the rear extension housing is being installed, align the striking lever to the shift rod brackets.

29. Install the front main shaft cover. Apply sealer to the threads of the bolts and torque to 5.8 to 7.2 ft/lbs (0.8 to 1.0 Kg-m).

30. Install the clutch release bearing and the operating shaft to the front of the case. Install the dust cover.

31. Install the electrical switches that were removed during the disassembly.

32. Install the speedometer driven gear assembly.

33. Install the bottom cover to the case and fill the unit with the proper level of lubricant.

TYPE 16

5 Speed Transmission–Model FS5W60A, L Datsun

DISASSEMBLY

1. Secure the transmission and drain the lubricating oil.

2. Remove the dust cover from the transmission case.

3. Remove the clutch release bearing and withdraw the pivot lever.

4. Remove the electrical switches from the case.

5. Remove the speedometer driven gear assembly.

6. Remove the shift selector stopper pin bolt and nut from the boss of the rear extension housing.

7. Remove the shift selector return spring plug, return spring and plunger from the rear extension.

8. Remove the reverse check sleeves assembly.

9. Remove the front bearing cover, O-ring and front cover adjusting shim.

10. Remove the main bearing snap-ring from the groove in the bearing outer race.

11. Remove the rear extension retaining bolts and turn the shift selector rod clockwise.

12. Using a special puller, remove the rear extension housing from the output shaft.

13. Separate the transmission case from the adapter plate by tapping evenly around the transmission case.

NOTE: Do not pry the units apart with a prybar. Damage can occur to the mating surfaces.

14. A special type holding tool should be

1. Front cover
2. Front cover oil seal
3. Front cover O-ring
4. Front cover adjusting shim
5. Welch plug
6. Top gear switch
7. O.D. gear switch
8. Reverse lamp switch
9. Neutral switch
10. Transmission case assembly
11. Adapter plate
12. Breather
13. Return spring bushing
14. Filler plug
15. Bearing retainer
16. Rear extension assembly
17. Drain plug
18. Reverse check sleeve
19. Rear extension dust cover
    with oil seal
20. Speedometer pinion
21. Speedometer sleeve
22. Retaining pin

Transmission case components, model FS5W60A

used to hold the adapter plate so that it can be held in a vise or other holding tool. This plate can be purchased or fabricated.

15. Mount the unit in the holding tool and remove the countergear thrust washer.

16. Using a pin punch, remove the retaining pins from the forks and selector rods.

17. Remove the check ball plugs (3).

18. Remove the selector rods from the adapter plate and detach the forks from the rods.

─────── CAUTION ───────

Do not lose the check balls, springs and the two interlock plungers.

NOTE: Each gear and shaft can be removed from the adapter plate independently of the other shaft and without the removal of the selector rods and forks.

19. Remove the outer snap-ring of the mainshaft end bearing with a bearing puller. Remove the second bearing snap-ring from the shaft.

20. Engage the 1st and reverse speeds so that the gear train is locked in two gears at the same time. Remove the countergear nut after releasing the staking.

21. From the rear extension side of the adapter plate, remove the mainshaft holding snap-ring, C-ring holder, C-ring and the thrust washer.

22. Remove the O.D. main gear with the needle bearings and the O.D. countergear together.

23. Remove the synchronizer (baulk) ring, the coupling sleeve, the O.D. and reverse

synchronizer hub snap-ring, the O.D. and reverse synchronizer hub and the reverse gear together with the needle bearing and bushing, and the reverse countergear at one time.

24. Remove the bearing retainer screws from the adapter plate. Remove the bearing retainer.

25. Remove the snap-ring from the mainshaft rear bearing and remove the mainshaft assembly together with the countergear by lightly tapping on the rear shaft while holding the front of the mainshaft and countergear assembly by hand to avoid dropping the assembly.

26. Remove the snap-ring and spacer from the reverse idler shaft and tap the idler shaft outward slightly.

27. Using a pin punch, remove the retaining pin from the reverse idler shaft and remove the shaft. Remove the thrust washers, spacer and reverse idler gear with the needle bearing.

28. Disassemble the mainshaft assembly by removing the snap-ring from the shaft front end. Remove the 3rd/4th synchronizer assembly, synchronizer (baulk) rings, 3rd gear and the mainshaft needle bearing toward the front side.

29. Remove the mainshaft bearing with a puller.

30. Remove the thrust washer and 1st gear, together with the needle bearing and bushing, synchronizer (baulk) rings, coupling sleeve, 1st/2nd synchronizer hub and the 2nd gear with the needle bearing.

31. Remove the snap-ring and spacer from the maindrive gear and remove the bearing with a press or puller.

32. The countershaft rear bearing can be removed with the use of a press.

33. The synchronizers can be disassembled for repairs by removing the spread spring and removing the shifting insert. Separate the coupling sleeve from the synchronizer hub.

ASSEMBLY

1. Replace any bearings, seals or worn parts as required.

2. Install the synchronizer hub into the coupling sleeve and fit the shifting inserts into their respective grooves on the assembly.

3. Install the spread springs to the inserts so that the insert is securely attached to the inner side of the coupling sleeve.

─────── CAUTION ───────

Do not hook the ends of the spread springs to the same insert. The hub and sleeve should operate smoothly when moved by hand.

4. Install the 2nd gear needle bearing, 2nd gear, synchronizer (baulk) ring, 1st/2nd speed synchronizer assembly, 1st gear synchronizer (baulk) ring, 1st gear bushing, needle bearing, 1st gear and thrust washer onto the mainshaft.

5. Press the bearing onto the mainshaft, using a pressor bearing installer.

6. Install the 3rd gear needle bearing, 3rd gear, synchronizer (baulk) ring, 3rd/4th synchronizer assembly on the front side of the mainshaft.

7. Install a selective snap-ring on the mainshaft so that a minimum clearance exists between the face of the hub and the ring.

CAUTION

Be sure the snap-ring is fully seated in its groove.

8. Install the main drive gear bearing onto the shaft. Install the main drive bearing spacer on the main drive bearing and secure the bearing with a proper sized snap-ring that will eliminate any end play.

9. Install the countergear thrust washer and countergear into the transmission case and select the countergear thrust washer of proper thickness, by using a straightedge, from the countergear face to the transmission case, allowing for standard end play of 0.0039 to 0.0079 inch (0.10 mm to 0.20 mm).

10. Remove the countergear from the transmission and keep the thrust washer with the gear.

11. Install the thrust washers, needle bearing, reverse idler gear and inner thrust washer in place on the reverse idler shaft. Install a new retaining pin in the reverse idler shaft.

12. Install the reverse idler shaft into the adapter plate. Position a thrust washer and install a new snap-ring so that the minimum clearance exists between the adapter plate and the thrust washer.

13. Install a synchronizer (baulk) ring on the main drive gear and place with the mainshaft to complete this portion of the assembly.

No.	Thickness	
	mm	(in)
1	1.55-1.60	(0.0610-0.0630)
2	1.60-1.65	(0.0630-0.0650)
3	1.65-1.70	(0.0650-0.0669)

No.	Thickness	
	mm	(in)
1	1.34-1.40	(0.0528-0.0551)
2	1.40-1.46	(0.0551-0.0575)
3	1.46-1.52	(0.0575-0.0598)
4	1.52-1.58	(0.0598-0.0622)
5	1.58-1.64	(0.0622-0.0646)
6	1.64-1.70	(0.0646-0.0669)
7	1.70-1.76	(0.0669-0.0693)

No.	Thickness	
	mm	(in)
1	2.20-2.25	(0.0866-0.0886)
2	2.25-2.30	(0.0886-0.0906)
3	2.30-2.35	(0.0906-0.0925)
4	2.35-2.40	(0.0925-0.0945)
5	2.40-2.45	(0.0945-0.0965)
6	2.45-2.50	(0.0965-0.0984)
7	2.50-2.55	(0.0984-0.1004)
8	2.55-2.60	(0.1004-0.1024)

Exploded view of gear train components

NOTE: Install the pilot bearing in place before coupling the main drive gear to the mainshaft.

14. Combine the mainshaft assembly with the countergear assembly and place them into the adapter plate as a unit.

NOTE: Use a puller tool to move the mainshaft into the adapter plate. Carefully hold the gears to avoid dropping them until in position.

——— CAUTION ———
Be sure the snap-ring groove on the mainshaft rear bearing clears the adapter plate.

15. Install the rear bearing snap-ring into its groove. Install the bearing retainer and install the retaining screws. Torque to 5.1 to 7.2 ft/lbs (6.9 to 9.8 Nm).

IMPORTANT: Stake each screw at two points with a center punch.

The selective snap-rings are as follows:

No.	Thickness	
	mm	(in)
1	1.1	(0.043)
2	1.2	(0.047)

16. Place the thrust washer, reverse gear bushing, needle bearing and the reverse main drive gear on the end of the mainshaft.

17. Install the reverse countergear on the end of the countershaft.

18. Install the O.D. and reverse synchronizer assembly and install a new snap-ring so that the minimum amount of clearance exists between the end face of the hub and the snap-ring.

The selective snap-rings are as follows:

No.	Thickness	
	mm	(in)
1	1.32	(0.0520)
2	1.38	(0.0543)
3	1.46	(0.0575)
4	1.54	(0.0606)
5	1.62	(0.0638)

19. Position the synchronizer (baulk) ring, O.D. gear needle bearing and the O.D. main gear on the end of the mainshaft.

20. Install the O.D. countergear on the end of the mainshaft.

21. Place the thrust washer in place so that a minimum of clearance exists between the C-holder and the ring. Position the C-ring and the C-ring holder and fit a new mainshaft holder snap-ring.

The selective snap-rings are as follows:

No.	Thickness	
	mm	(in.)
1	7.87	(0.3098)
2	7.94	(0.3126)
3	8.01	(0.3154)
4	8.08	(0.3181)
5	8.15	(0.3209)
6	8.22	(0.3236)

22. Engage the 1st and reverse gears and tighten the countershaft nut to 36 to 43 ft/lbs (49 to 59 Nm).

23. Stake the countershaft nut to the groove in the countershaft with a punch.

24. Measure the gear end-play. The measurements are as follows:

1st main gear
0.15-0.25 mm
(0.0059-0.0098 in.)
2nd main gear
0.30-0.40 mm
(0.0118-0.0157 in.)
3rd main gear
0.15-0.35 mm
(0.0059-0.0138 in.)
O.D. (5th) main gear
0.30-0.40 mm
(0.0118-0.0157 in.)

Exploded view of shift selector rod and fork components

Reverse main gear
0.30-0.55 mm
(0.0118-0.0217 in.)
Countergear
0.10-0.20 mm
(0.0039-0.0079 in.)
Reverse idler gear
0-0.20 mm
(0-0.0079 in.)

25. Place a snap-ring to the front of the mainshaft end bearing, measuring 0.0453 inch (1.15 mm).

26. Install the mainshaft end bearing using a bearing installer. Fit a snap-ring to the rear side of the bearing to eliminate any end-play. The available snap-rings are as follows:

No.	Thickness	
	mm	(in.)
1	1.15	(0.0453)
2	1.02	(0.047)

27. Install the O.D. and reverse fork and selector rod into the adapter plate. Place the rod in the neutral position and install the interlock plunger into its bore in the adapter plate.

28. Install the 3rd/4th selector rod into the fork and install a new snap-ring. Install the selector rod and fork into the adapter plate.

29. Insert the interlock plunger into the adapter plate with the selector rods in the neutral position.

30. Install the 1st/2nd selector rod into the fork and install both into the adapter plate.

31. Secure all the selector rods and forks with new retaining pins.

IMPORTANT: Properly align the groove in the assembled selector rod with the interlock plunger, during the assembly. Align the shift forks with their respective coupling sleeves before installing.

32. Install the check balls and springs into the proper bores. Seal and install the check ball plugs.

33. Align the center notch in each fork selector rod with the check balls, as required.

NOTE: The selector rod for the 1st/2nd gear is longer than the 3rd/4th or the O.D./Reverse selector rods.

— CAUTION —
To make sure the interlock plunger is installed properly, slide the 1st/2nd selector rod into gear and operate the other selector rods. All other gears should not mesh. Check all other rods in the same manner.

34. Prepare the adapter plate and transmission case by installing a sealer to the mating surfaces.

35. Apply grease to the sliding surface of the thrust washer for the countergear, that was selected previously. The oil groove should face to the front while the dimpled side should face towards the thrust side.

36. Place the clutch housing end of the transmission case flat on a surface and level the housing. Position the adapter plate assembly into the transmission housing and tap

No.	"A"		Adjusting shim	
	mm	(in.)	mm	(in.)
1	6.05-6.09	(0.2382-0.2398)	0.50	(0.0197)
2	6.10-6.14	(0.2402-0.2417)	0.55	(0.0217)
3	6.15-6.19	(0.2421-0.2437)	0.60	(0.0236)
4	6.20-6.24	(0.2441-0.2457)	0.65	(0.0256)
5	6.25-6.29	(0.2461-0.2476)	0.70	(0.0276)
6	6.30-6.34	(0.2480-0.2496)	0.75	(0.0295)
7	6.35-6.39	(0.2500-0.2516)	0.80	(0.0315)

the plate into the transmission housing. Line the dowel pin to its proper position.

37. Carefully install the main drive bearing and countergear front needle bearing.

NOTE: Be sure the mainshaft rotates freely.

38. Install the main drive bearing snap-ring in its groove in the bearing.

39. Apply sealant to the mating surfaces of the adapter plate and the rear extension housing.

40. Place the selector rods in the O.D. position on the transmission, while placing the main selector rod in the neutral position. Turn the striking guide clockwise and then adjust the main selector rod and the shift arm. Align the shift arm pin with the groove in the selector rods and assemble the rear extension housing to the adapter plate. Install the retaining bolts and torque to 12 to 16 ft/lbs (16 to 22 Nm).

41. Install grease to the plunger and install it into the rear extension. Install the return spring, apply sealer to the return spring plug and install it.

42. Turn the transmission assembly so that the front is up. Measure the distance from the front end of the transmission case to the main drive bearing outer race with a depth gauge. Select a shim to correspond to the dimension or thickness "A". The front cover adjusting shim can be one of seven shims.

43. Install the front cover with the adjusting shim and the O-ring in place.

44. Install the speedometer driven gear and install the securing bolt and nut.

45. Install a new O-ring in the groove of the reverse check sleeve and tighten the bolts.

46. Replace the electrical switches that were removed during the disassembly.

47. Install the pivot lever, the release bearing and sleeve. Connect the holding spring and install the dust cover.

TYPE 17

4 Speed Transmission–Model F4W60L Datsun

DISASSEMBLY

1. Secure the transmission and drain the lubricating oil.

2. Remove the dust cover from the transmission case.

3. Remove the clutch release bearing and the pivot lever.

4. Remove the electrical switches from the transmission case.

5. Remove the speedometer driven gear assembly from the rear extension housing.

6. Remove the stopper pin bolt and nut from the rear extension housing. Remove the return spring plug, the return spring, reverse check spring and the plunger from the rear extension housing.

7. Remove the front cover along with the O-ring and the front cover adjusting shim.

8. Remove the main drive bearing snapring from the bearing groove.

9. Remove the rear extension housing retaining bolts and rotate the striking rod (main shift control shaft) clockwise.

10. Drive the rear extension housing rearward by lightly tapping on the housing to separate the housing from the transmission.

11. Separate the transmission case from the adapter plate by lightly tapping the case from the plate.

— CAUTION —
Do not pry the transmission assembly apart with a pry bar. The mating surfaces can be damaged.

12. A special type holding tool should be used to hold the adapter plate so that it can be held in a vise or other holding tool. The plate can be purchased or fabricated.

13. Remove the countergear thrust washer and drive the shift fork retaining pins from the selector shafts.

14. Remove the reverse gear shift fork and the reverse idler gear.

15. Remove the three check ball plugs. The check balls and the springs will be exposed for removal. Visually check the spring lengths for proper installation and mark accordingly.

16. Drive the selector rods from the adapter plate by tapping on the front end of the rods. Do not lose the interlock plungers from between the selector shift rods. Remove the shifting forks as necessary.

IMPORTANT: Measure the end-play of the mainshaft before disassembly of the shaft. Measure between the end face of the 3rd/4th synchronizer hub and the snap-ring. Record the clearance.

17. Remove the reverse gear snap-ring from the rear of the shaft and remove the thrust washer and mainshaft reverse gear.

18. Remove the four bearing retainer at-

1. Front cover
2. Front cover oil seal
3. Front cover O-ring
4. Front cover adjusting shim
5. Welch plug
6. Transmission case assembly
7. Filler plug
8. Adapter plate
9. Breather
10. Bearing retainer
11. Rear extension dowel pin
12. Reverse lamp switch
13. Rear extension assembly
14. Drain plug
15. Return spring bushing
16. Rear extension dust cover
    with oil seal
17. Top detecting switch

Transmission case components, model F4W60L

taching screws and remove the bearing retainer.

19. Remove the snap-ring from the mainshaft rear bearing.

20. Remove the mainshaft gear assembly along with the countergear assembly by lightly tapping on the rear of the shafts with a soft hammer while holding the gears by hand to avoid their dropping to the floor.

21. Separate the countergear, main drive gear and mainshaft assembly.

22. The mainshaft gear assembly can be disassembled by removal of the retaining snap-ring from the front of the shaft.

23. The mainshaft bearing must be pressed from the shaft and the remaining gears and hubs can be removed.

IMPORTANT: Observe the sequence and direction of the gear and hubs during the disassembly. Mark as required.

24. The main drive gear bearing can be pressed from the shaft after the removal of the retaining snap-ring. The pilot bearing can be removed from the shaft bore.

25. Remove the snap-ring from the rear of the countershaft and press out the counter reverse gear, using a suitable puller.

26. Remove the countergear rear bearing by the use of the bearing puller.

27. The synchronizers can be disassembled by removing the spread springs and removing the shifting inserts. Remove the coupling sleeves from the synchronizer hubs.

IMPORTANT: Note the direction of the coupling sleeves in relation to the hubs.

28. The reverse idler shaft snap-ring is re-

moved and the shaft is removed from the adapter plate by lightly tapping on the shaft with a soft hammer.

29. The rear extension housing can be disassembled by removing the lock pin nut and lock pin from the striking lever (main shift control shaft). Remove the lever and the shaft can be removed from the housing.

30. Replace the necessary parts, clean the assembly, install new seal and prepare to reassemble.

ASSEMBLY

1. Assemble the rear extension housing by installing the striking lever shaft (mainshaft control shaft) into the housing. Fit the striking lever to the shaft and install the retaining pin.

2. Install the reverse idler shaft into the adapter plate and install the retaining snap-ring.

3. Assemble the synchronizers by installing the coupling sleeves over the synchronizer hubs. Install the shifting inserts and the spread springs, being careful not to connect the spread spring ends to the same insert.

4. Assemble the mainshaft by installing the 2nd gear needle bearing, 2nd gear, the

synchronizer (baulk) ring, 1st-2nd speed synchronizer assembly, the 1st gear synchronizer (baulk) ring, 1st gear bushing, needle bearing, 1st gear and the thrust washer.

5. Press the mainshaft bearing in place with a bearing installer.

6. Position the 3rd gear needle bearing, 3rd gear, synchronizer (baulk) ring and the 3rd-4th synchronizer assembly onto the front side of the mainshaft.

7. Fit a new snap-ring in place on the shaft so that a minimum of clearance exists between the end face of the hub and the snap-ring.

8. Install the main drive gear bearing in place on the shaft by the use of a bearing installer tool or press. Install the bearing spacer and a snap-ring to provide a minimum of clearance between the snap-ring and the bearing spacer.

9. Using a bearing press, install the countergear bearing onto the countergear.

10. Install a countergear thrust washer and the countergear with bearing into the transmission case and with a special height gauge or equivalent, select a thrust washer from the accompanying chart to provide a standard end-play of 0.0039 to 0.0079 inch (0.10 to 0.20 mm).

No.	Thickness	
	mm	**(in.)**
1	1.55 to 1.60	(0.0610 to 0.0630)
2	1.60 to 1.65	(0.0630 to 0.0650)
3	1.65 to 1.70	(0.0650 to 0.0669)

Thickness		
No.	mm	(in.)
1	1.34 to 1.40	(0.0528 to 0.0551)
2	1.40 to 1.46	(0.0551 to 0.0575)
3	1.46 to 1.52	(0.0575 to 0.0598)
4	1.52 to 1.58	(0.0598 to 0.0622)
5	1.58 to 1.64	(0.0622 to 0.0646)
6	1.64 to 1.70	(0.0646 to 0.0669)
7	1.70 to 1.76	(0.0669 to 0.0693)

Thickness		
No.	mm	(in.)
1	2.20 to 2.25	(0.0866 to 0.0886)
2	2.25 to 2.30	(0.0886 to 0.0906)
3	2.30 to 2.35	(0.0906 to 0.0925)
4	2.35 to 2.40	(0.0925 to 0.0945)
5	2.40 to 2.45	(0.0945 to 0.0965)
6	2.45 to 2.50	(0.0965 to 0.0984)
7	2.50 to 2.55	(0.0984 to 0.1004)
8	2.55 to 2.60	(0.1004 to 0.1024)

10. Remove the countergear assembly from the transmission and press the counter reverse gear onto the countergear assembly, using a press or equivalent tool.

11. Install a new snap-ring into the groove at the end of the countergear.

12. Install a synchronizer (baulk) ring on the main drive gear and install it onto the mainshaft to complete the mainshaft assembly.

NOTE: Be sure to install the pilot bearing into the main drive gear bore.

13. Place the adapter plate in the holding device and assemble the mainshaft and countershaft and place them into the adapter plate as a unit. Hold the gears by hand so as not to drop them.

14. A puller should be used to pull the mainshaft into the adapter plate. The countershaft can be installed at the same time by tapping lightly with a soft hammer.

IMPORTANT: Make sure the snap-ring groove on the mainshaft clears the adapter plate.

15. Install the snap-ring on to the mainshaft.

16. Install the bearing retainer plate on the adapter plate and install the retaining screws.

1. Main drive bearing
2. Main drive gear
3. 3rd & top synchronizer
4. 3rd gear, mainshaft
5. Mainshaft
6. 2nd gear, mainshaft
7. 1st & 2nd synchronizer
8. 1st gear, mainshaft
9. Mainshaft bearing
10. Reverse gear, mainshaft
11. Counter gear assembly
12. Idler gear assembly

Exploded view of gear train components

Torque the screws to 5.1 to 7.2 ft/lbs (6.9 to 9.8 Nm) and stake each screw in two places with a center punch.

17. Install the mainshaft reverse gear and thrust washer on the rear of the mainshaft and secure with a new snap-ring.

NOTE: Install the thrust washer with its concave side towards the mainshaft reverse gear.

18. Install the 1st/2nd selector rod into the adapter plate and install the shifting fork onto the rod.

19. Place the 1st/2nd selector rod in the neutral position and install the interlock plunger into the adapter plate.

20. Insert the 3rd/4th selector rod into the adapter plate and install the shifting fork.

21. Set the 3rd/4th selector rod in the neutral position and install the interlock plunger into the adapter plate.

22. Install the reverse selector rod into the adapter plate.

NOTE: Be sure to install the interlock plungers into the adapter plate between each adjacent selector rod. Align the shifting forks with the sliding sleeves before installation.

23. Install the check balls and springs in their respective bores in the adapter plate. Install sealer to the check ball plugs and install in place.

NOTE: The check ball plug for 1st/2nd selector rod is longer than the plugs for the 3rd/4th and reverse rods.

24. Install the reverse idler gear together with the reverse shift fork.

25. Install new retaining pins in the shifting forks to the selector rods.

NOTE: To insure the interlock plunger is installed properly, slide the 3rd/4th fork and selector rod into gear and try to operate the other rods. Only the 3rd/4th gears should mesh. Operate the remaining selector rods in the same manner.

26. With all the gears assembled to the adapter plate, remove the assembly from the vise and remove the holder.

27. Clean all the mating surfaces of the transmission assembly. Install sealer to the surfaces of the adapter plate and the transmission surfaces.

28. Install the previously selected countergear thrust washer into the transmission case.

NOTE: The smooth side with the oil groove goes to the front of the transmission case, while the dimpled side goes towards the gear side.

29. Slide the transmission case onto the adapter plate assembly by lightly tapping the adapter plate with a soft hammer. Be sure the dowel pin is properly lined up.

30. Carefully install the main drive bearing and the front countergear needle bearing. Be sure the mainshaft rotates.

31. Install the main drive bearing snap-ring into its groove on the bearing outer race.

32. Apply sealant to the rear extension housing and the adapter plate. Place the selector rods in the neutral position and turn

No.	"A" mm	(in.)	Adjusting shim mm	(in.)
1	6.05 to 6.09	(0.2382 to 0.2398)	0.50	(0.0197)
2	6.10 to 6.14	(0.2402 to 0.2417)	0.55	(0.0271)
3	6.15 to 6.19	(0.2421 to 0.2437)	0.60	(0.0236)
4	6.20 to 6.24	(0.2441 to 0.2457)	0.65	(0.0256)
5	6.25 to 6.29	(0.2461 to 0.2476)	0.70	(0.0276)
6	6.30 to 6.34	(0.2480 to 0.2496)	0.75	(0.0295)
7	6.35 to 6.39	(0.2500 to 0.2516)	0.80	(0.0315)

the striking rod (main shift selector rod) clockwise and gradually slide the rear extension onto the adapter plate, being sure the striking lever engages the fork rod brackets correctly.

33. Install the retaining bolts and tighten to 12 to 16 ft/lbs (16 to 22 Nm).

34. Install the stopper pin bolt into the rear extension and tighten to 3.6 to 5.8 ft/lbs (4.9 to 7.8 Nm).

35. Lubricate the plunger and install it into the rear extension. Install the reverse check spring and return spring. Apply sealer to the return spring plug and install it in place.

36. Turn the transmission assembly so that the front is up. Measure the distance from the front end of the transmission case to the main drive bearing outer race with a depth gauge. Select a shim to correspond to the dimension or thickness "A". The front cover adjusting shim can be one of seven shims.

37. Install the front cover to the transmission case with the O-ring and the shim in place.

38. Install the speedometer driven gear and install the securing bolt.

39. Install the electrical switches onto the case assembly.

40. Install the operating lever, the clutch release bearing and the dust cover. Install the proper level of lubricant to the transmission.

TYPE 18

4 and 5 Speed Transmissions Fiat

DISASSEMBLY

1. Remove the oil filler plug.
2. Place the transmission upside down and remove the lower cover and gasket.
3. Remove the clutch release fork and slide the thrust bearing and control sleeve from the central support.
4. Remove the bellhousing and gasket. At the same time remove the center cover of the direct driveshaft with the oil seal and spring washer.
5. It may be necessary to remove the seal on the bench.
6. Remove the bolts which secure the 3rd and 4th gear selector forks.

NOTE: When the bolts have been

removed the fork can be removed along the bar and the two gears can be engaged simultaneously.

7. Slide the rubber dust cover from the end of the mainshaft.

8. Remove the snap-ring and flexible coupling ring.

9. Lock the mainshaft by proceeding according to the note above, and remove the spider from the mainshaft.

10. Remove the speedometer drive support and gasket from the rear transmission cover.

11. Remove the selector rod detent ball spring cover plate from the main casing.

12. Remove the springs from the recesses, followed by the detent balls.

NOTE: The reverse gear selector rod ball spring is not of the same compression as the other two springs. Keep this one separate from the other two.

13. Remove the rear cover complete with gear lever, by proceeding as follows:

14. Remove the stop screw which limits the side movement of the lever.

15. Remove the nuts which retain the cover to the main body.

16. Move the gear lever to the left to disengage it from the selector rods and remove the rear cover.

17. Remove the gear lever from the rear cover.

18. Slide the rear ball bearing and speedometer drive gear from the mainshaft.

19. Slide the reverse gear selector rod, complete with fork, from its seat in the main case and, at the same time, remove reverse gear from its spindle.

20. Remove the snap-ring which retains the reverse driving gear and remove the gear from the end of the layshaft.

21. Remove the snap-ring which retains the driven gear from the reverse gear train.

22. Remove the spring washers, driven gear of the reverse gear train, and remove the Woodruff key from its seat.

NOTE: Before removing the retaining clip of the reverse gear driven train, the spring washer must be compressed.

23. Engage the two gears to prevent the shafts from turning and remove the retaining bolt and front ball bearing from the layshaft.

24. Tilt the layshaft and remove it from the main case.

25. Remove the 3rd and 4th gear selector rods from the case and remove the bolt and spring washer holding the 1st and 2nd gear selector forks to the rod.

26. Remove the rod, followed by the 1st/

1. Inner cover seal
2. Bearing snap-ring
3. Spring washer
4. Direct drive shaft bearing
5. Needle roller bearing
6. Mainshaft intermediate bearing
7. Bearing retaining plate
8. Retaining screw
9. Retaining screw washer
10. Key
11. Mainshaft rear bearing
12. Rear cover oil seal
13. Flexible coupling
14. Retaining nut
15. Sealing ring
16. Centering ring
17. Snap-ring
18. Lock washer

19. Mainshaft
20. Spring washer
21. Retaining snap-ring
22. Direct drive and 4th gear shaft
23. 3rd/4th gear sliding sleeve hub
24. Sliding sleeve
25. Lock ring
26. Synchronizer ring
27. Synchronizer spring
28. Cup
29. 3rd speed driven gear
30. 2nd speed driven gear
31. Cup
32. Synchronizer spring
33. Synchronizer ring
34. Lock ring
35. 1st/2nd gear sliding sleeve hub
36. Sliding sleeve

37. 1st speed driven gear
38. 1st gear bushing
39. Reverse driven gear
40. Spring washer
41. Retaining snap-ring
42. Snap-ring
43. Reverse driving gear
44. Spring washer
45. Countershaft rear roller bearing
46. Countershaft with 1st, 2nd and 3rd speed gears
47. Countershaft front double row bearing
48. Flat washer
49. Spring washer
50. Countershaft front bearing
51. Reverse idler gear spindle
52. Reverse idler gear bushing
53. Reverse idler gear

Exploded view of gear train components, 4-speed transmission without intermediate housing

2nd and 3rd/4th gear forks. The three safety rollers will be released as the selector rods are removed.

27. Remove the plate which retains the mainshaft intermediate ball bearing.

28. Withdraw the bearing from its housing.

29. Withdraw the reverse gear spindle from the main case.

30. Remove the direct drive and 4th gear shaft from the mainshaft, complete with ball bearing and 4th gear synchronizing ring.

31. Tilt the mainshaft and remove it from the case, complete with gears, hubs, sliding sleeves and synchronizing rings.

32. Remove the following parts from the mainshaft: 1st gear with synchronizer and bushing. 1st and 2nd gear hub and sliding sleeve, 2nd gear and synchronizer assembly.

33. Remove the snap-ring from its seat in the front end of the mainshaft and remove the following parts: spring washer, 3rd/4th gear hub, 3rd gear, and synchronizer assembly.

34. Remove the snap-ring from the direct drive and 4th gear shaft and remove the spring washer and ball bearing.

ASSEMBLY

1. Assemble the following parts on the front of the mainshaft, in the order given: 3rd gear and synchronizing ring, 3rd/4th gears and spring washer.

2. Insert the snap-ring in the groove, securing the parts listed above to the front of the mainshaft.

1. Hub
2. Synchronizing ring
3. Blocker ring
4. 3rd gear pinion
5. Cup ring
6. Spring
7. Circlip
8. Sliding sleeve

Third gear synchronizer—4 and 5-speed

3. Slide the 2nd gear and synchronizing ring, 1st/2nd gear sliding sleeve and hub and 1st speed synchronizing ring and gear with bushing onto the rear end of the shaft.

4. Tilt the mainshaft and insert it into the transmission case.

5. Working from the rear end of the mainshaft, use a driver and insert the intermediate ball bearing.

6. Install the reverse idler gear shaft, then fit the shaft and bearing retaining plate.

7. Secure the plate to the main case and stake the nuts in place.

8. Fit the ball bearing and spring washer to the direct driveshaft and 4th gear shaft, and insert the spring retaining clip of the bearing in the groove.

9. Install the direct drive roller bearing onto the mainshaft.

10. Insert the direct driveshaft in the main case and slide it onto the end of the mainshaft.

11. Install the 1st and 2nd gear selector fork to the sliding sleeve and slide the corresponding selector rod into the fork from outside.

12. Replace the locating roller of this bar to its seat and secure the fork to the rod.

13. Install the 3rd/4th gear selector fork and rod in the same manner.

NOTE: Do not lock the fork to the rod at this point, since it will be necessary to use this fork to lock the transmission at a later time.

14. Insert the layshaft into the main case.

15. Replace the front ball bearing and rear ball bearing of the layshaft.

16. Lock the shafts by engaging two gears at the same time.

17. Use the flat washer, spring washer and bolt to secure the front bearing to the layshaft.

18. Fit the key to the mainshaft and install the reverse driving gear and spring washer.

19. Retain these with a snap-ring.

NOTE: When installing the reverse driven gear snap-ring, center the spring washer so that the snap-ring cannot snap into the groove of the shaft. Fit the spring washer and reverse driving gear to the rear end of the layshaft and secure them with a snap-ring.

20. Insert the reverse selector rod locating roller in its seating, and fit the selector fork to the rod.

21. Retain this with a bolt and spring washer.

22. Install the selector rod in its guide and at the same time, fit the reverse idler gear to its spindle.

23. Install the speedometer drive gear and rear ball bearing on the mainshaft.

24. Fit the gear shifting assembly to the rear transmission cover, as follows.

25. Drive a new oil seal with inner spring into place.

26. Fit the gear shifting lever to the cover.

27. Attach the gear lever return spring to the lever and replace the screw in the cover.

28. Mount the lever assembly on the rear cover and fit the rear cover to the main transmission case. Be sure to fit a gasket between the two cases. Install the back-up light switch.

29. Replace the speedometer drive support

| 1A. 1st gear | 3A. 3rd gear | 5A. 5th gear |
| 2A. 2nd gear | 4A. 4th gear | RM. Reverse gear |

Fifth speed gear train

with a gasket under it. It is held in place by a nut on a stud in the cover.

30. Install the flexible spider and flat washer on the tail of the mainshaft.

31. Lock the gears and tighten the nut, bending up the tab washer.

32. Install the dust cover on the mainshaft and drive the coupling centering ring into place and insert the snap-ring in the groove.

33. Drive an oil seal into the cover of the direct drive and 4th gear shaft and attach this cover to the front of the transmission body (bellhousing).

34. Insert a sealing ring between them.

35. Install the spring washer of the cover and fit the bellhousing to the main case, with a gasket.

36. Fit the 3rd and 4th gear selector fork to the selector rod and secure with a bolt and washer.

37. Replace the three selector rod detent balls and springs in their proper bores. Note that the reverse spring is different from the other two.

38. Fit the lower cover and gasket to the main case.

39. Install the oil drain plug.

40. Fit the clutch release sleeve and thrust bearing to the cover of the direct driveshaft and install the fork lever.

41. Turn the transmission right side up, and fill with 2.75 pints of oil. The oil must come to the brim of the filler hole.

42. Replace the filler plug.

124 (5-Speed)

This transmission is used on 124 Spider and 2000 Spider Coupe models. Basically, it is the same unit as the 4-speed, with the addition of a fifth gear or overdrive. The transmission is in three parts. The front body is bolted to the crankcase and houses the clutch and withdrawal sleeve, with a thrust bearing. The center body is bolted to the front body and contains the 1st, 2nd, 3rd and 4th gears. The rear cover is bolted to the center body and carries 5th and reverse gears, along with the selector bars. It also contains the mainshaft roller bear-

ing and countershaft ball bearing. The upper part of the rear cover holds the gearshift extension mechanism which is slightly different from the 4-speed unit.

Disassembly and assembly are basically the same procedures as those outlined for the 124 (4-speed). Specifications remain identical to those for the 4-speed unit.

When assembling a synchronizer, be sure that the returned ends of the spring are inserted in the slots in the blocker ring, without distorting the normal diameter of the spring. This should be done before the circlip is fitted.

TYPE 19

5 Speed Transmission Fiat

DISASSEMBLY

1. Pull the output yoke off of the output shaft.

2. Remove the speedometer driven gear retainer and gasket.

3. Remove the gearshift support and gasket from the rear housing.

4. Remove the seven bolts and washers retaining the rear housing to the main case. Tap lightly with wooden or plastic hammer and pull off to the rear.

5. Disconnect clutch release lever from ball joint pivot. Remove release bearing support and release lever.

6. Inside bellhousing, remove the seven bolts retaining bellhousing to main case. Tap lightly and remove bellhousing.

7. Remove snap-ring for speedometer drive gear and slide gear off output shaft.

8. Remove snap-ring in front of input shaft bearing.

9. Apply pressure to spring washer behind snap-ring at rear of output shaft and remove snap-ring. Remove spring washer.

10. Remove bolt retaining reverse shifting fork to shifting rod, and remove fork and reverse idler gear. Remove shifting rod spacer. Remove reverse gear from the mainshaft.

11. Remove bolt retaining extension for 3rd and 4th gear shifting rod. Remove extension.

12. Remove snap-ring retaining reverse drive gear onto auxiliary shaft, and remove the gear.

13. Remove two bolts retaining detent ball cover. Remove cover, springs and balls.

14. Remove Woodruff key from output shaft. Slide main case off of shafts. Remove magnet for front housing slot.

15. Remove bolt retaining fork to shifting rod, and remove rod. Assemble fork to rod for reference. Repeat for other shifting rods.

16. Remove mainshaft and auxiliary shaft from housing.

17. Disconnect input shaft from mainshaft. Remove inside input shaft.

18. Position mainshaft in vise with protective jaws. Using two screwdrivers, pry outer bearing race off of shaft. Then, slide 1st gear, outer race for thrust bearing, thrust bearing, inner race, and thrust washer off of mainshaft.

19. Remove roller bearing (122 rollers) and separator for bearings.

20. Remove snap-ring retaining 1st and 2nd gear synchronizer hub. Place mainshaft in press with block beneath 2nd gear. Press off hub, synchronizer ring, gear, and washers. Remove roller bearing (134 rollers) from shaft.

21. Invert mainshaft. Depress spring washer and remove snap-ring and washer from other end. Pull the 3rd and 4th gear

synchronizer hub from shaft. Remove 3rd gear.

22. Remove snap-ring retaining 5th gear synchronizer hub. Pull off hub. Remove 5th gear.

23. Depress spring washer and remove snap-ring. Pull bearing from mainshaft.

ASSEMBLY

1. Press bearing on input shaft. Position spring washer and snap-ring on shaft. Depress spring washer and install snap-ring in groove.

2. Place 5th gear and synchronizer ring on mainshaft. Tap hub for 5th gear synchronizer down with brass drift until ring seats correctly in hub. Secure with snap-ring. Position sliding sleeve on hub with beveled teeth facing 5th gear.

3. Place 3rd gear and synchronizer on mainshaft. Tap hub down with brass drift. Install sliding sleeve on hub with grooved side down. Position spring washer and snap-ring on shaft. Depress spring washer and install snap-ring in groove.

4. Invert mainshaft. Position two rows of 67 roller bearings on shaft and retain with clean wheel bearing grease.

5. Place 2nd gear and synchronizer ring and hub for 1st and 2nd gear on mainshaft.

1. Input shaft
2. Bearing
3. 4th gear
4. 3rd and 4th gear synchronizer
5. 3rd gear
6. 5th gear synchronizer
7. 5th gear
8. 2nd gear
9. 1st and 2nd gear synchronizer
10. 1st gear
11. Bearing outer race
12. Main shaft
13. Auxiliary shaft

Main and auxiliary shafts—131 and Brava 5-speed transmission

1. Hub
2. Sliding sleeve
3. Synchronizer ring
4. 5th gear

Third gear and synchronizer—131 and Brava

1. Snap ring
2. Spring washer
3. Outer race
4. Bearing
5. Outer race
6. Input shaft
7. Synchronizer ring
8. Bearing

Input shaft—131 and Brava

1. 3rd gear
2. Synchronizer ring
3. Sliding sleeve
4. Hub
5. Spring washer
6. Snap ring

Fifth gear synchronizer—131 and Brava

1. Spacer
2. Roller bearings
3. Synchronizer ring
4. 1st gear
5. Flat washer
6. Thrust washer
7. Thrust bearing
8. Outer race

First gear and synchronizer—131 and Brava

Tap hub down with brass drift. Retain with snap-ring.

6. Position flat washer on mainshaft. Place a row of 61 roller bearings on the shaft, install a spacer, and then a second row of 61 bearings, forming a ring. Retain with grease.

7. Position sliding sleeve on hub with grooved side down. Place 1st gear on mainshaft, then install thrust washer, thrust bearing and washer.

8. Press bearing onto input shaft. Position flat washer and outer bearing race on shaft. Tap outer race down with brass drift.

9. Place lockwasher on bearing in front housing for auxiliary shaft. Position magnet in case with magnetic face toward gears.

10. Install input shaft in mainshaft. Mesh together mainshaft and auxiliary shaft gears and install in front housing.

11. Remove Allen bolt from front housing. Position 5th gear shifting fork on rod in case with fork on 5th gear sliding sleeve. Install detent ball in front housing adjacent to 5th gear shifting rod.

12. Position 3rd and 4th gear shifting fork on rod. Install rod in case with fork on 3rd and 4th gear sliding sleeve. Install detent ball in front housing adjacent to 3rd and 4th gear shifting rod.

13. Position 1st and 3rd gear shifting fork on rod. Install rod in case with fork on 1st and 2nd gear sliding sleeve. Install Allen bolt. Tighten shifting fork bolts to 14.5 ft/lbs.

14. Coat auxiliary shaft bearing retainer with grease. Position retainer on bearing in case with grooved surface facing away from bearing.

15. Install main case and gasket over shafts and shifting rods. Position outer race for mainshaft bearing on shaft, and tap down with brass drift. Position washer and retainer plate on shaft.

16. Place reverse gear idle shaft in case. Position retainer plate tab in shaft groove. Secure with 4 bolts.

17. Position detent balls and springs in case, and retain plate with 2 bolts. Tighten to 18 ft/lbs.

18. Install reverse drive gear on auxiliary shaft with washer and secure with snap-ring.

19. Position 3rd and 4th gear shifting rod extension on rod. Install extension retaining bolt and lockwasher and tighten.

20. Install Woodruff key in mainshaft.

21. Install reverse gear on mainshaft. Place spacer on reverse shifting rod. Position shifting fork with reverse idler gear on shifting rod and idler shaft. Secure fork to rod with bolt and lockwasher.

22. Position spring washer and snap-ring on mainshaft. Depress spring washer and install snap-ring in groove.

23. Install speedometer drive gear on mainshaft and secure with snap-ring.

24. Install input shaft outer bearing retaining snap-ring.

25. Position bellhousing with gasket to main case, and secure with seven bolts and washers. Install clutch release lever and release bearing on input shaft and connect lever to ball joint pivot.

26. Position rear housing with gasket to main case and secure with seven bolts and washers.

27. Place both ends of shifter spring in rear housing slotted plate. Then, flip spring over and install over spring support boss.

28. Install gearshift support with gasket on rear housing. Install retaining bolts and check shifting action.

29. Install speedometer driven gear housing and gasket.

30. Slide output shaft yoke onto shaft.

TYPE 20

4 Speed Transmission

Mazda

DISASSEMBLY

1. Install the transmission on a workstand.

2. Drain the oil.

3. Remove the fork and throwout bearing from the housing.

4. Remove the bellhousing.

5. Remove the adjusting shim from the bellhousing bearing bore.

6. Remove the shift lever tower and gasket.

7. Remove the extension housing. Set the control lever end in the neutral position, press the control lever end as far left as possible, and slide the extension housing off the transmission.

8. Remove the neutral switch from the transmission (models with seat belt interlock).

9. Remove the gearshift yoke from the central lever.

10. Remove the speedometer sleeve and driven gear. Remove the back-up light switch.

11. Unfasten the speedometer drive gear snap-ring, slide the drive gear off of the output shaft, and remove the lockball.

12. Remove the bottom cover and gasket.

13. Remove the cap bolts, the detent springs, and detent balls.

14. Remove the blind covers and gaskets from the transmission case.

15. Remove the reverse shift rod and idler gear from the rear of the transmission case. Remove the reverse shift fork.

16. Unfasten third/fourth shift fork securing bolt and remove the third/fourth shift rod from the rear of the case.

17. Repeat Step 16 for the first/second shift rod.

18. Straighten out the output shaft lockwasher. Hold the output shaft to keep it from turning, and loosen the locknut. Slide the reverse gear and key off the end of the output shaft.

19. Remove the countershaft snap-ring (rear) and remove the reverse countergear.

20. Remove the bearing cover.

21. Remove the reverse idler gear.

22. Hold the fourth synchronizer ring and gear on the output shaft.

23. Remove the countershaft front bearing snap-ring. Remove the front bearing. Remove the adjusting shim from the case bearing bore.

24. Remove the countershaft rear bearing.

Installing shifter spring—131 and Brava

Remove the adjusting shim from the case bearing bore.

25. Remove the input shaft bearing snap-ring and remove the bearing with the puller.

26. Lift the countershaft out.

27. Separate the input and output shafts. Remove the input shaft. Remove the fourth synchronizer ring and needle bearing from the input shaft.

28. Remove the output shaft gear assembly.

29. Remove first/second and third/fourth shift forks from the case. Withdraw the shift interlock pins.

30. Remove the third/fourth clutch hub snap-ring, then slide the clutch hub sleeve, third synchronizer ring and third gear off the front of the output shaft. Be careful not to mix up the synchronizer rings.

31. Slide the first gear and synchronizer ring off the rear of the output shaft.

32. Slide the first gear sleeve, second gear, second synchronizer ring and first/second clutch hub/sleeve assembly off the output shaft.

ASSEMBLY

1. Install the first/second clutch hub on its sleeve, place the three shift keys in the clutch hub key slots, and install the key springs. Be sure to keep the open ends of the key springs 120° apart.

2. Repeat Step 1 for the third/fourth synchronizer assembly.

3. Place the synchronizer ring on second gear and then slide second gear on the output shaft, so that the synchronizer ring faces the rear of the shaft.

4. Slide the first/second clutch hub and sleeve on the output shaft so that the clutch oil grooves face forward. Be sure that the three synchronizer keys engage the notches on the second gear synchronizer ring.

5. Install the first gear sleeve in the output shaft.

6. Install the synchronizer ring in the first gear and install the gear on the output shaft so that the ring faces the front of the shaft.

7. Install the same thrust washer on the output shaft that was removed.

8. Repeat Step 6 for third gear.

9. Install the third/fourth clutch hub and sleeve on the output shaft, being sure to engage the three synchronizer keys with the notches in the ring.

NOTE: The larger boss on the third/fourth clutch hub goes toward the front.

10. Install the snap-ring on the front of the output shaft. Install the output shaft/gear set assembly in the case. Fit the needle bearing on the front of the output shaft.

11. Place the synchronizer ring on the input shaft gear (fourth) and install the gear on the front of the output shaft. Be sure that the synchronizer keys engage the notches in the synchronizer ring.

12. Position the first/second and third/fourth shift forks in groove on the clutch hub/sleeve assembly.

13. Install the countergear assembly in the case, being careful to engage each countergear with its respective output shift gear.

14. Check the output shaft bearing end-play as follows:

1. Adjusting shim	17. Thrust washer
2. Main driveshaft bearing	18. Mainshaft bearing
3. Main driveshaft and gear	19. Adjusting shim
4. Needle bearing	20. Bearing cover plate
5. Synchronizer ring	21. Key
6. Third-and-fourth clutch hub	22. Gearshift lever retainer
7. Synchronizer key	23. Cover
8. Clutch sleeve	24. Shim
9. Third gear	25. Boot
10. Second gear	26. Gearshift lever
11. Synchronizer ring	27. Gearshift lever knob
12. Synchronizer key	28. Bush
13. First-and-second clutch hub	29. Control lever end
14. Clutch sleeve	30. Gearshift control lever
15. First gear	31. Adjusting shim
16. First gear sleeve	32. Transmission case

33. Countershaft front bearing
34. Gasket
35. Transmission under cover
36. Countershaft
37. Drain plug
38. Gasket
39. Countershaft rear bearing
40. Counter reverse gear
41. Reverse gear
42. Lock washer
43. Locknut
44. Mainshaft
45. Speedometer drive gear
46. Lock ball
47. Extension housing
48. Mainshaft oil seal

Cross section of Mazda 4-speed transmission without intermediate housing

a. Measure the depth of the transmission case output shaft bearing bore.

b. Measure the height of the bearing.

c. The difference between these two measurements indicates the correct thickness of the adjusting shim to be used. The amount of end-play permitted is 0-0.0039 in.

d. Shims are available in thicknesses of 0.0039 or 0.0118 in.

15. Hold the fourth synchronizer ring off the input shaft synchronizer gear.

16. Install the input and output shaft bearings in their respective bores with a press.

17. Install the input shaft bearing snap-ring.

18. Check the countershaft bearing end-play, as outlined in Step 14 for the input shaft. The amount of end-play allowed and available shim size are the same for both bearings.

19. Repeat Step 15.

20. Press the countershaft front and rear bearings into their respective bores. Install the snap-ring on the front bearing.

21. Install the reverse countergear on the rear of the countershaft.

22. Install the reverse gear idler shaft in the transmission case.

23. Install the bearing cover on the case.

24. Secure the reverse gear on the output shaft with its key.

25. Hold the output shaft to keep it from turning and tighten to 150-180 ft/lbs.

26. Install the first/second shift rod into the case and secure it to the shift fork with the lockbolt. Place the shift rod in Neutral. Drive the interlock pin into its bore.

27. Repeat Step 26 for the third/fourth shift rod.

28. Slide the reverse shift rod, complete with the reverse idler gear, in from the rear of the case. Secure the shift rod to the reverse fork with its lockbolt.

29. Install the detent balls and springs in their bores and secure them with their cap bolts.

30. Check the synchronizer key-to-exposed edge of the synchronizer ring clearance with a feeler gauge; it should be 0.026-0.079 in. If the clearance is greater, the synchronizer key could pop out. If the clearance is greater than specified, replace the selective-fit thrust washer with one of the three available sizes.

31. Install the blind covers over their gaskets.

32. Install the lockball, speedometer drive gear, and snap-ring, in that order, on the rear of the output shaft.

33. Install the gearshift control lever through the holes in the front of the extension housing. Install the Woodruff key on the control lever and install the yoke over it. Secure the yoke with its setbolt.

34. Thread the Neutral switch (for seat belt interlock) into the extension housing.

35. Fit the spring and plunger in the extension housing and secure them with the capbolt.

36. Install the back-up light switch.

37. Secure the speedometer driven gear in its extension housing bore with the lockplate and bolt.

38. Push the gearshift control lever over to the left as far as possible. Place a gasket on the rear of the transmission case and install the extension housing over it.

39. Install the bottom cover.

40. Insert the select lockpin and spring in the shift tower. Align the slot in the pin with the lockball bore. Drop the lockball and spring into the bore; secure with the capbolt.

41. Install the shift tower on the extension housing and secure it with its bolts.

42. Repeat Step 14 for the input shaft bearing and clutch housing bore. The end-play and shim thickness are the same as in Step 14.

43. Lubricate the lip of the bellhousing oil seal.

44. Put a gasket on the front of the transmission case, and install the bell housing.

45. Install the throwout bearing, release fork and boot in the bellhousing.

1. Adjusting shim
2. Snap-ring
3. Input shaft bearing
4. Input shaft
5. Synchronizer ring
6. Needle bearing
7. Synchronizer key spring
8. Third-and-Fourth clutch hub
9. Synchronizer key
10. Clutch hub sleeve
11. Third gear
12. Output shaft
13. Second gear
14. First-and-Second clutch hub
15. Clutch hub sleeve
16. Gear sleeve
17. First gear
18. Thrust washer
19. Adjust shim
20. Ball bearing and clip
21. Bearing stop
22. Bolt
23. Key
24. Reverse gear
25. Lockwasher
26. Locknut
27. Steel ball
28. Speedometer drive gear
29. Snap-ring
30. Ball bearing and clip
31. Adjusting shim
32. Countershaft
33. Needle bearing
34. Reverse countergear
35. Reverse idler gear
36. Reverse idler gear shaft

Exploded view of gear train components—Mazda 4-speed transmission without intermediate housing

TYPE 21

4 and 5 Speed Transmission Mazda

The 4 and 5 speed transmissions are basically the same, with an added housing located between the adapter plate and the rear extension housing, to carry the 5th and reverse gears. Added roller bearings are used in the housing to prevent shaft misalignment.

DISASSEMBLY

1. Remove the throwout bearing return spring, throwout bearing, and the release fork.
2. Remove the bearing housing.
3. Remove the input shaft and countershaft snap-rings.
4. Remove the floorshift lever retainer, complete with gasket.
5. Unfasten the cap bolt and withdraw the spring, steel ball, select lock pin and spring from the retainer.
6. Remove the extension housing. Turn the control lever as far left as it will go and slide the extension housing off the output shaft.
7. Remove the spring seat and spring from the end of the shift control lever.
8. Loosen the spring cap and withdraw the spring and plunger from their bore.

9. Remove the control rod and boss from the extension housing.
10. Remove the speedometer driven gear. Remove the back-up light switch.
11. Remove the speedometer drive gear.
12. Tap the front ends of the input shaft and countershaft with a plastic hammer; then remove the intermediate housing assembly from the transmission case.
13. Remove the three cap bolts; then withdraw the springs and lockballs.
14. Remove the reverse shift rod, reverse idler gear, and shift lever.
15. Remove the setscrews from all the shift forks and push the shift rods rearward to remove them. Remove the shift forks.
16. Withdraw the reverse shift rod lockball, spring, and interlock pins from the intermediate housing.
17. Remove reverse gear and key from the output shaft.
18. Remove the reverse countergear.
19. Remove the countershaft and output shaft from the intermediate housing.
20. Remove the bearings from the intermediate housing and transmission case.
21. Remove the snap-ring from the output shaft.
22. Slide the third/fourth clutch hub, sleeve, synchronizer ring, and third gear off the output shaft.
23. Remove the thrust washer, first gear, sleeve, synchronizer ring, and second gear from the rear of the output shaft.

ASSEMBLY

1. Install the third/fourth synchronizer

clutch hub on the sleeve. Place the three synchronizer keys in the clutch hub key slots. Install the key springs with their open ends 120° apart.
2. Install third gear and the synchronizer ring on the front of the output shaft. Install the third/fourth clutch hub assembly on the output shaft. Be sure that the larger boss faces the front of the shaft.
3. Secure the gear and synchronizer with the snap-ring.
4. Repeat Step 1 for the first/second synchronizer assembly.
5. Position the synchronizer ring on second gear. Slide second gear on the output shaft so that the synchronizer ring faces the rear of the shaft.
6. Install the first/second clutch hub assembly on the output shaft so that its oil grooves face the front of the shaft. Engage the keys in the notches on the second gear synchronizer ring.
7. Slide the first gear sleeve onto the output shaft. Position the synchronizer ring on first gear. Install the first gear on the output shaft so that the synchronizer ring faces frontward. Rotate the first gear as required to engage the notches in the synchronizer ring with the keys in the clutch hub.
8. Slip the thrust washer on the rear of the output shaft. Install the needle bearing on the front of the output shaft.
9. Install the synchronizer ring on fourth gear and install the input shaft on the front of the output shaft.
10. Press the countershaft rear bearing and shim into the intermediate housing, then press the countershaft into the rear bearing.

1. Snap-ring
2. Speedometer drive gear
3. Ball
4. Locknut
5. Lock washer
6. Reverse gear
7. Key
8. Snap-ring
9. Counter reverse gear
10. Bolt/bearing cover
11. Countershaft
12. Countershaft rear bearing
13. Shim

Gear train position in 4-speed transmission with intermediate housing

11. Keep the thrust washer and first gear from falling off the output shaft by supporting the shaft. Install the output shaft on the intermediate housing. Be sure that each output shaft gear engages with its opposite number on the countershaft.

12. Tap the output shaft bearing and shim into the intermediate housing with a plastic hammer. Install the cover.

13. Install reverse gear on the output shaft and secure it with its key.

NOTE: The chamfer on the teeth of both the reverse gear and the reverse countergear should face rearward.

14. Install the reverse countergear.

15. Install the lockball and spring into the bore in the intermediate housing. Depress the ball with a screwdriver.

16. Install the reverse shift rod, lever, and idler gear at the same time. Place the reverse shift rod in the neutral position.

17. Align the bores and insert the shift interlock pin.

18. Install the third/fourth shift rod into the intermediate housing and shift bores. Place the shift rod in Neutral.

19. Install the next interlock pin in the bore.

20. Install the first/second shift rod.

21. Install the lockballs and springs in their bores. Install the cap bolt.

22. Install the speedometer drive gear and lockball on the output shaft, and install its snap-ring.

23. Apply sealer to the mating surfaces of

1. Spring cap bolt/packing/ spring/locking ball
2. Spring cap bolt/packing/ spring/locking ball
3. Spring cap bolt/packing/ spring/locking ball
4. Bolt/washer
5. Shift fork (Reverse)/rod/ reverse idler gear

6. Spring/locking ball
7. Bolt/washer
8. Shift rod (3rd & 4th)
9. Shift rod (1st & 2nd)
10. Interlock pin
11. Shift fork (3rd & 4th)
12. Shift fork (1st & 2nd)

Exploded view of shift selector rods and forks, 4-speed with intermediate housing

MAIN DRIVE SHAFT

CLUTCH HUB ASSEMBLY

MAIN SHAFT

COUNTER SHAFT

CLUTCH RELEASE FORK

Cross section of 5-speed transmission showing added housing

the intermediate housing. Install the intermediate housing in the transmission case.

24. Install the input shaft and countershaft front bearings in the transmission case.

25. Secure the speedometer driven gear.

26. Install the control rod through the holes in the front of the extension housing.

27. Align the key with the keyway and install the yoke on the end of the control rod. Install the yoke lockbolt.

28. Fit the plunger and spring into the extension housing bore and secure with the spring cap.

29. Turn the control rod all the way to the left and install the extension housing on the intermediate housing.

30. Insert the spring and select lockpin inside the gearshift retainer. Align the steel ball and spring with the lockpin slot, and secure it with the spring cap.

31. Install the spring and spring seat in the control rod yoke.

32. Install the gearshift lever retainer over its gasket on the extension housing.

33. Lubricate the lip of the front bearing cover oil seal and secure the cover on the transmission case.

34. Check the clearance between the front bearing cover and bearing. It should be less than 0.006 in. If it is not within specifications insert additional adjusting shims. The shims are available in 0.006 in. or 0.012 in. sizes.

35. Install the throwout bearing, return spring and release fork.

5 Speed

The disassembly and assembly of the rear extension housing, selector levers and forks are completed in the same manner as the 4 speed transmission. After this has been done, the added housing can be removed by taking out the retaining bolts. The housing will have to be lightly tapped with a soft-faced hammer. The removal of the housing exposes the 5th/reverse synchronizer assembly, the reverse countergear, the countershaft and mainshaft bearings. The bearings are pulled from the shafts and then the gears can be removed. The assembly is in the reverse of the removal procedure.

TYPE 22

5 Speed Transmission
Mazda

DISASSEMBLY

1. Pull the release fork outward until the

Cross section of Mazda 5-speed transmission

1. Adjusting shim
2. Main driveshaft bearing
3. Main driveshaft gear
4. Needle bearing
5. Synchronizer ring
6. Synchronizer key
7. 3rd-and-4th clutch hub
8. Clutch sleeve
9. 3rd gear
10. 2nd gear
11. Synchronizer ring
12. Synchronizer key
13. 1st-and-2nd clutch hub
14. Clutch sleeve
15. 1st gear
16. Needle bearing
17. Needle bearing inner race
18. Thrust washer
19. Mainshaft front bearing
20. Adjusting shim
21. Bearing cover plate
22. Spacer

23. Reverse gear and clutch sleeve assembly
24. Synchronizer key
25. Synchronizer ring
26. Lock washer
27. Locknut
28. 5th gear
29. Needle bearing
30. Thrust washer
31. Gearshift lever retainer
32. Cover
33. Gasket
34. Boot
35. Gearshift lever
36. Gearshift lever knob
37. Bush
38. Gearshift control lever end
39. Gearshift control lever

40. Adjusting shim
41. Transmission case
42. Countershaft front bearing
43. Countershaft
44. Transmission under cover
45. Gasket
46. Drain plug
47. Gasket
48. Countershaft center bearing
49. Counter reverse gear
50. Drain plug
51. Spacer
52. Counter 5th gear
53. Countershaft rear bearing
54. Thrust washer
55. Mainshaft rear bearing
56. Thrust washer
57. Speedometer drive gear
58. Lock ball
59. Mainshaft
60. Extension housng
61. Mainshaft oil seal

spring clip of the fork releases from the ball pivot.

2. Remove the fork and release bearing.

3. Remove the clutch housing shim and gasket.

4. Remove the gearshift lever retainer and gasket.

5. Remove the spring and steel ball, select lock spindle and spring from the gearshift lever retainer.

6. Remove the extension housing with the control lever end down to the left as far as it will go.

7. Remove the control lever end, key and control rod.

8. Remove the lock plate and speedometer gear.

9. Remove the back-up light switch.

10. Remove the snap-ring and slide the speedometer drive gear from the mainshaft.

11. Remove the bottom cover and gasket.

12. Remove the shift rod ends.

13. Remove the rear bearing housing.

14. Remove the snap-ring and remove the mainshaft rear bearing, thrust washer and race.

15. Using the puller, remove the washer and countershaft rear bearing.

16. Remove the counter fifth gear.

17. Remove the intermediate housing.

18. Remove the springs and shift locking balls.

19. Remove the two blind covers and gaskets from the case.

20. Remove the reverse/fifth shift rod, fork and interlock pin.

21. Remove the first/second and third/fourth shift forks, rods and interlock pins.

22. Remove the snap-ring and slide the washer, fifth gear and synchronizer ring from the mainshaft. Also, remove the steel ball and needle bearing.

23. Lock the rotation of the mainshaft with second and reverse.

24. Remove the locknut and slide the reverse/fifth clutch hub and sleeve assembly, synchronizer ring, reverse gear and needle bearing from the mainshaft.

25. Remove the spacer and counter reverse gear from the countershaft.

26. Remove the reverse idler gear, thrust washers and shaft from the transmission case.

27. Remove the bearing rear cover plate.

28. Remove the snap-ring from the front end of the countershaft and install Mazda tool number 49 0839 445 synchronizer ring holder or its equivalent between the fourth synchronizer ring and the synchromesh gear on the main driveshaft.

29. Remove the countershaft front bearing.

30. Remove the adjusting shim from the countershaft front bearing bore.

31. Remove the countershaft center bearing outer race.

32. With a special puller and attachment, remove the mainshaft front bearing, thrust washer and inner race along with the adjusting shim from the mainshaft front bearing bore.

33. Remove the snap-ring, and remove the main driveshaft bearing.

34. Remove the countershaft center bearing inner race with the puller.

35. Separate the input shaft from the mainshaft and remove the input shaft.

36. Remove the synchronizer ring and needle bearing from the input shaft.

37. Remove the mainshaft assembly.

38. Remove the first/second and third/fourth shift forks from the case.

39. Remove the snap-ring and slide the third/fourth clutch hub and sleeve assembly, synchronizer ring and third gear from the mainshaft.

40. Remove the thrust washer, first gear and needle bearing from the rear of the mainshaft.

41. Press out the needle bearing inner race, synchronizer ring, first and second clutch hub, sleeve assembly, synchronizer ring and second gear from the mainshaft.

ASSEMBLY

1. Install the third/fourth clutch hub into the sleeve, place the three keys into the clutch hub slots and install the springs onto the hub.

2. Assemble the first/second and reverse/fifth clutch hub and sleeve as described in Step 1.

3. Install the needle bearing, second gear, synchronizer ring, and first/second clutch assembly on the rear section of the mainshaft.

4. Press on the first gear needle bearing inner race.

5. Install the third gear and synchronizer ring onto the front section of the mainshaft.

6. Install the third/fourth clutch assembly onto the mainshaft.

7. Install the snap-ring on the mainshaft.

8. Install the needle bearing, synchronizer ring, first gear and thrust washer on the mainshaft.

9. Install the mainshaft assembly.

10. Install the needle bearing on the front end of the mainshaft.

11. Install the first/second and third/fourth shift forks in their respective clutch sleeves.

12. Check the mainshaft bearing end-play. Check the depth of the mainshaft bearing bore in the case. Measure the mainshaft bearing height. The difference indicates the required adjusting shim to give a total end-play of less than 0.0039 in.

13. Install the synchronizer ring holder tool between the fourth synchronizer ring and the synchromesh gear on the input shaft.

14. Position the shims and mainshaft bearing in the bore and install with a press.

15. Install the input shaft bearing in the same way.

16. Check the countershaft front bearing end-play in the same way as the mainshaft bearing end-play.

17. Install the front bearing snap-ring.

18. Press the countershaft center bearing into position.

19. Install the bearing cover plate.

20. Install the reverse idler gearshaft, thrust washers and reverse idler gear.

21. Install the counter reverse gear and spacer on the rear end on the countershaft.

22. Install the thrust washer and press the needle bearing inner race of the reverse gear on the mainshaft.

23. Install the needle bearing, reverse gear, synchronizer ring, reverse/fifth clutch assembly and new mainshaft locknut on the mainshaft.

24. Lock the mainshaft with the second and reverse gears. Tighten the locknut.

25. Install the needle bearing, synchronizer ring and fifth gear on the mainshaft.

26. Install the thrust washer, steel ball and snap-ring on the mainshaft.

27. Check the thrust washer-to-snap-ring clearance. It should be 0.0039-0.0118 in.

1. Shift fork
2. Shift fork
3. Shift fork
4. 3rd-and-4th shift rod
5. 1st-and-2nd shift rod
6. Rev.-and-5th shift rod
7. Stop ring
8. Shift rod end
9. Shift rod end
10. Shift rod end
11. Detent ball
12. Detent spring
13. Washer
14. Spring cap bolt
15. Interlock pin

Mazda 5-speed shift rod and forks

Mazda 5-speed gear train

1. Shim	15. 2nd gear	29. Stop ring	43. Counter shaft
2. Snap ring	16. 1st-and-2nd clutch hub	30. Rev.-and-5th clutch hub	44. Counter shaft center bearing
3. Main drive shaft bearing	17. Clutch sleeve	31. Clutch sleeve	45. Counter reverse gear
4. Main drive shaft gear	18. Bearing inner race	32. Main shaft lock nut	46. Spacer
5. Synchronizer ring	19. Needle bearing	33. Needle bearing	47. Reverse gear
6. Synchronizer key	20. 1st gear	34. 5th gear	48. Counter shaft rear bearing
7. Synchronizer key spring	21. Thrust washer	35. Thrust washer	49. Thrust washer
8. 3rd-and-4th clutch hub	22. Shim	36. Lock ball	50. Thrust washer
9. Clutch sleeve	23. Main shaft front bearing	37. Main shaft rear bearing	51. Reverse idler gear
10. 3rd gear	24. Bearing cover	38. Thrust washer	52. Idler gear shaft
11. Needle bearing	25. Thrust washer	39. Lock ball	53. Thrust washer
12. Needle bearing	26. Bearing inner race	40. Speedometer drive gear	
13. Main shaft	27. Needle bearing	41. Counter shaft front bearing	
14. Needle bearing	28. Reverse gear	42. Shim	

28. Install the first/second shift rod through the holes in the case and fork.

29. Install the interlock pin with a special installer and guide.

30. Install the third/fourth shift rod through the holes in the case and fork.

31. Align the holes and install the lockbolts of each shift fork and rod.

32. Install the interlock pin as above.

33. Position the reverse/fifth shift fork on the clutch sleeve and install the shift rod.

34. Tighten the lockbolt.

35. Install the three shift locking balls, springs and cap bolts.

36. Place the third/fourth clutch sleeve in third gear.

37. Check the clearance between the synchronizer key and the exposed edge of the synchronizer ring with a feeler gauge. The gap should be 0.026-0.079 in. Adjust by varying thrust washers.

38. Install the two blind covers and gaskets.

39. Install the undercover and gasket.

40. Apply a thin coat of sealer to the mating edges and install the intermediate housing on the transmission case. Align the lockbolt holes of the housing and reverse idler gearshaft, install and tighten the lockbolt.

41. Position the counter fifth gear and bearing to the rear end of the countershaft and install with a press.

42. Install the thrust washer and snap-ring.

43. Check the clearance between the washer and snap-ring. Clearance should be less than 0.0039 in.

44. Install the mainshaft rear bearing.

45. Install the thrust washer and snap-ring.

46. Check the thrust washer-to-snap-ring clearance. Clearance should be less than 0.0059 in.

47. Apply a thin coat of sealing agent to the mating surfaces and install the bearing housing on the intermediate housing.

48. Install the shift rod ends on their respective rods.

49. Install the speedometer drive gear and steel ball on the mainshaft. Secure it with a snap-ring.

50. Install a speedometer driven gear assembly on the extension housing and secure it with the bolt and lock plate.

51. Insert the control rod through the holes from the front side of the extension housing.

52. Align the key and insert the control lever end in the control rod.

53. Install the bolt and tighten it to 20-30 ft/lbs.

54. Install the back-up light switch.

55. Place the gasket on the case and install the extension housing with the control lever end down and as far to the left as it will go.

56. Insert the select lock spindle and spring from the underside of the shift lever retainer.

57. Install the steel ball and spring in alignment with the spindle groove and install the spring cap bolt.

58. Install the gearshift lever retainer and gasket on the extension housing.

59. Check the bearing end-play. Measure the depth of the bearing bore in the housing.

Measure the height of the bearing protrusion. The difference indicates the thickness of the shim needed. The end-play should be less than 0.0039 in.

60. Place the gasket on the front side of the case. Apply lubricant to the lip of the oil seal and install the clutch housing on the case.

61. Install the release bearing and fork on the clutch housing.

TYPE 23

4 Speed Transmission

Mercedes-Benz

DISASSEMBLY AND ASSEMBLY

The G 76/18, G 76/18A, G 76/18B, G 76/27 end G 76/27A 4-speed manual transmissions are all very much alike. Overhaul is predominantly given for the G 76/18C since only minor modifications have been made.

1. Remove the throwout bearing and fork.

2. Remove the clutch housing with the slave cylinder.

3. Remove the reverse shift lever clamp.

4. Remove the reverse shift lever.

5. Remove the side cover.

6. Remove the shift forks.

1. Input shaft bearing
2. Input shaft
3. 3rd gear
4. 3rd gear needle bearing
5. Mainshaft
6. 2nd gear needle bearing
7. 2nd gear
8. 1st gear needle bearing
9. Reverse slide gear
10. 1st gear
11. Rear bearing
12. Rear bearing holder
13. Reverse gear, mainshaft
14. Speedometer drive gear
15. Drive flange
16. Countershaft front bearing
17. Countershaft gear, constant speed
18. Countershaft gear, 3rd speed
19. Countershaft gear, 2nd and 1st speed
20. Countershaft rear bearing
21. Countershaft gear, reverse
22. Transmission case
23. Speedometer driven gear
24. Side cover

Exploded view of typical Mercedes-Benz 4-speed

7. Disassemble the side cover and forks.

8. Unbolt and remove the transmission front cover.

9. Remove the bearing housing.

10. Remove the rear transmission cover.

11. Press out the speedometer drive gear.

12. Remove the tachometer drive seal.

13. Remove the reverse gear from the mainshaft.

14. Remove the reverse sliding gear shaft from the housing while holding the sliding gear.

15. Unlock the nut on the rear of the countershaft.

16. Remove reverse gear from the countershaft.

17. Knock the pin from reverse shifter shaft and move the shaft as far forward as possible.

18. Remove the shift rod from the housing.

19. Unlock the slotted nut.

20. Remove the front countershaft bearing. On G 76/27A transmissions, the bearing is beveled and is removed toward the inside of the case.

21. Remove the rear countershaft bearing.

22. Lift the mainshaft at the rear and pull the input shaft out of the housing.

23. Push the mainshaft completely rearward and remove it at an angle.

24. Remove the countershaft from the housing.

25. Disassemble the mainshaft, if necessary.

26. If necessary, disassemble the countershaft.

27. Assembly is basically the reverse of disassembly. Try to obtain 0 end-play on the main and input shafts.

TYPE 24

4 Speed Transmission–British Leyland Model

MG

DISASSEMBLY

1. Remove the driveshaft flange.

2. Remove the shift linkage housing.

3. Withdraw the selector interlock arm and plate assembly.

4. Remove the extension and mainshaft shims.

At this point, if it is desired to rebuild the shift linkage, the extension components can be disassembled.

5. Remove the snap-ring and oil seal from the rear of the extension and press the bearing out if it is to be replaced.

6. Remove the shift lever locating bolt.

7. Remove the retaining cap, damper and spring at the base of the shift lever.

8. Remove the shift lever.

9. Remove the linkage shaft.

10. Remove the clutch release bearing and release lever.

11. Remove the front cover and bearing shims.

12. Remove the side cover.

13. Remove the selector detent plunger plugs and springs.

14. Remove the selector fork and selector lever retaining bolts.

15. Remove the selector rods and selector forks.

16. Remove the reverse shaft and gear.

17. Carefully drive the countershaft out of the case.

18. Drive the input shaft assembly forward out of the case, making sure it is clear of the clustergear.

19. Remove the spacer and shims from the mainshaft.

20. Remove the rear extension mounting studs from the rear of the transmission case.

21. Check that the mainshaft components are clear of the clustergear teeth, and press the mainshaft assembly out the back of the transmission. Remove the clustergear.

ASSEMBLY

1. Transmission assembly is in reverse order of disassembly. The following points should be noted:

2. When the rear extension housing or any mainshaft components have been replaced, the shim thickness for the rear extension must be checked. Temporarily install the extension with the gasket, to allow the gasket to be compressed. Remove the extension and measure the amount that the bearing is recessed from the transmission case mating surface, and add to this the thickness from the extension bearing surface. Use the number of shims required to make the second distance equal to or 0.001 in. less than the first distance.

3. If the front cover or any of the input shaft components have been replaced, the shim thickness for the front cover must be checked. Temporarily install the cover with the gasket, to allow the gasket to be compressed. Measure the amount that the bearing protrudes from the transmission case. Measure the distance from the cover mating surface to the face of the cover bearing surface and add to this the thickness of the gasket. Use the number of shims required to make the second distance equal to or 0.001 in. less than the first distance.

TYPE 25

4 Speed Transmission–British Leyland Model

MG

DISASSEMBLY

1. Remove the top cover from the transmission.

2. Twist and release the cap at the base of the gearshift lever. Remove the nyloc nut and bolt to release the shaft from the gearshift lever.

3. Lift the gearshift lever assembly from the rear extension and remove the cups along with the outer spring.

4. Remove the snap-ring from the gearshift lever, then remove the inner spring and the nylon ball.

5. Remove the reverse stop plate.

6. Remove the reverse stop bolt from the gearshift lever.

7. Remove the threaded and tapered locking pin and extract the shaft from the extension housing and selector.

8. Remove the rubber O-rings from the bores of the extension housing.

9. Remove the retaining nut and withdraw the pivot bolt from the coupling fork. Extract the shaft and fiber washers from the coupling. Remove the steel pin, releasing the coupling fork from the shaft.

10. Disassemble the selector shaft and fork assemblies.

11. Remove the threaded, tapered locking pins from the selector shafts and forks. Release the 1st/2nd selector fork, spacer washer and sleeve by pushing the 1st/2nd selector shaft out of the cover.

12. Remove the two interlock balls and plunger.

13. Release the 3rd/4th selector fork by pushing the 3rd/4th selector shaft out of the cover.

14. Release the reverse selector by pushing the reverse selector shaft out of the cover. Remove the detent plungers and springs from the cover.

15. Disassemble the clutch housing. Remove the release lever from its pivot pin and remove the lever and bearing. Remove the retaining bolts, releasing the clutch housing, and remove the springs.

16. Disassemble the rear extension. Remove the retaining nut and extract the driving flange from the mainshaft. Remove the retaining bolts and carefully withdraw the extension from the transmission. The operation may be facilitated by lightly tapping the mounting lugs with a soft-headed hammer.

17. Remove the paper washer and spacer washer from the mainshaft.

18. Remove the bolt and extract the reverse spindle and spacer.

19. If necessary, withdraw the ball bearing and oil seal from the extension.

20. Withdraw the countershaft, retaining the needle roller bearing. Using a special tool, withdraw the input shaft assembly from the transmission case. Shake out the roller bearing and remove the baulk ring.

21. Remove the circlip and snap-ring and use the special tool and adaptor to extract the ball race and oil thrower.

22. With an abutment plate installed, remove the snap-ring, circlip, and spacer washer. Withdraw the ball bearing and speedometer gear, using the special tool and adaptors used for the first ball race.

23. Remove the abutment plate, tilt the mainshaft assembly and remove it from the transmission case.

24. Disassemble the mainshaft as follows: Remove the 3rd/4th synchronizer unit, 3rd

1. Side cover
2. Gasket
3. Dust cover
4. Pivot bolt for clutch withdrawal lever
5. Bush for clutch withdrawal lever
6. Clutch withdrawal lever
7. Front cover
8. Gasket
9. Oil seal
10. Gearbox case
11. First motion shaft
12. Spigot bearing
13. Bearing
14. Circlip for bearing
15. Shim
16. Nut and lock washer
17. Locking screw and lock washer
18. Reverse shaft
19. Bush for reverse wheel
20. Reverse wheel
21. Breather
22. Layshaft
23. Laygear
24. Bearing for laygear
25. Distance tube
26. Circlip for laygear
27. Front thrust washer for laygear
28. Rear thrust washer for laygear
29. Third motion shaft front nut and lock washer
30. Baulk ring
31. Third/fourth synchronizer coupling
32. Third/fourth synchronizer hub
33. Synchronizer ball and spring
34. Sleeve for third speed gear

35. Third speed gear
36. Bush for third speed gear
37. Thrust washer for third speed gear
38. Second speed gear
39. Bush for second speed gear
40. Thrust washer for second speed gear
41. First/second speed synchronizer coupling
42. First/second speed synchronizer hub
43. Third motion shaft
44. Reverse light switch
45. First speed gear
46. Bush for first speed gear
47. Reverse gear
48. Bearing housing
49. Roller bearing
50. Circlip for bearing
51. Shim
52. Distance piece
53. Speedometer drive gear
54. Distance tube
55. Shim
56. Bearing
57. Circlip for bearing
58. Oil seal
59. Drive flange
60. Nut and lock washer
61. Selector lever
62. Bush for selector lever
63. Selector lever shaft
64. Locking screw and lock washer
65. Spring for reverse plunger
66. Locating pin
67. Reverse plunger
68. Detent plug and washer

69. Detent spring and plunger
70. Interlock arm
71. First/second speed selector fork
72. First/second speed selector rod
73. First/second speed selector
74. Third/fourth speed selector fork
75. Third/fourth speed selector rod
76. Third/fourth speed selector
77. Reverse selector fork
78. Reverse selector rod
79. Reverse selector
80. Drain plug
81. Detent plug and washer
82. Detent spring and plunger
83. Rear extension
84. Gasket
85. Change speed lever
86. Seating cone
87. Change speed lever knob and retaining nut
88. Change speed lever retainer
89. Retaining cap for plunger
90. Damper plunger and spring for change speed lever
91. Remote control housing
92. Gasket
93. Dowel
94. Locating pin for change speed lever
95. Bush for change speed lever
96. Retaining cap for plunger
97. Damper plunger and spring for remote control shaft
98. Remote control shaft
99. Selector lever
100. Key for selector lever

Exploded view of MGB transmission

gear baulk ring, thrust washer, 1st gear and 1st gear baulk ring. Remove the circlip, washer, 3rd gear, bushing, thrust washer, 2nd gear, bushing, thrust washer, 2nd gear baulk ring, 1st/2nd synchronizer unit, and split collars.

25. Disassemble each synchronizer unit by pressing the hub through the sleeve. During this operation, the synchronizer unit should be placed in a container to prevent the loss of the spring-loaded balls.

26. Withdraw the countershaft assembly from the case and lift out the thrust washers.

The countershaft may be further disassembled by removing the needle rollers and the retaining rings.

27. Disassemble the reverse idler gear and actuator by taking out the idler gear, removing the securing nut, and removing the actuator and pivot pin.

ASSEMBLY

1. Replace the needle rollers, smearing them with grease, and insert the retaining tube.

2. With the steel face of the front thrust washer smeared with grease, locate the washer in the transmission case. The tag should engage the recess provided.

3. Insert the end of the countershaft spindle through the case to centralize the thrust washer.

4. With the countershaft gear cluster assembly lowered into the case, install the rear thrust washer and insert the spindle.

5. Measure the end clearance of the countershaft and adjust if necessary to 0.007-0.013 in. by using thrust washers of selected thick-

1. Gearbox case	27. Speedometer pinion
2. Oil filter level plug	28. Gear lever yoke
3. Spacer	29. Seat
4. Joint gaskets	30. Spring
5. Top cover	31. Anti-rattle plunger
6. Top cover bolt	32. Lower gear-change lever
7. Joint gasket	33. Upper gear-change lever
8. Plug	34. Dust cover washer
9. Detent plunger	35. Dust cover
10. Detent spring	36. Knob
11. Rear extension	37. Drain plug
12. End cover	38. Reverse idler spindle locating screw
13. Reverse light switch	39. Reverse idler spindle
14. Reverse lift plate	40. Reverse idler gear bushing
15. Oil seal	41. Reverse idler gear
16. Interlock spool	42. Reverse idler spacer
17. Selector shaft roll pin	43. 3rd and 4th speed selector forks
18. Reverse operating lever pin	44. 1st and 2nd speed selector forks
19. Reverse operating lever	45. Selector fork shaft
20. Gear selector shaft	46. Circlip
21. Magnet	47. Backing washer
22. Interlock spool plate	48. Snap-ring
23. Retaining clip	49. Ball bearing
24. Seal	50. Synchromesh cup
25. Housing	51. Ball
26. "O"-ring	52. Spring
	53. 3rd and 4th speed synchromesh hub
	54. 3rd and 4th speed operating sleeve
	55. Synchromesh cup
	56. Mainshaft circlip
	57. 3rd speed gear thrust washer
	58. 3rd speed gear
	59. Gear bushing
	60. Selective washer
	61. Gear bushing
	62. 2nd speed gear
	63. Thrust washer
	64. Synchromesh cup
	65. Ball
	66. Spring
	67. 1st and 2nd speed operating sleeve
	68. Mainshaft reverse gear
	69. Synchromesh cup
	70. Split collar
	71. 1st speed gear
	72. Thrust washer
	73. Mainshaft center bearing
	74. Snap-ring
	75. Selective washer
	76. Circlip
	77. Speedometer wheel
	78. Oil flinger
	79. Front thrust washer
	80. Bearing outer retaining ring
	81. 1st motion shaft
	82. Needle-roller bearing
	83. Mainshaft
	84. Washer
	85. Ball bearing
	86. Drive flange
	87. Washer
	88. Self-locking nut
	89. Countershaft gear cluster
	90. Bearing inner retaining ring
	91. Needle rollers
	92. Rear thrust washer
	93. Layshaft
	94. Layshaft dowel
	95. Laygear pre-load springs

MG Midget 4-speed case and gear train

ness. If the thickness of a thrust washer must be reduced, do not remove metal from the bronze face.

6. Insert the needle roller retaining tube and remove the countershaft spindle. Allow the gear cluster assembly to drop to the bottom of the transmission case.

7. Assemble the reverse idle gear mechanism by screwing the pivot pin into the actuator until a thread protrudes through the boss of the lever. Install it into the transmission case and secure it with a nut and washer.

8. Position the reverse idler gear in the case.

9. Install the synchronizer springs and balls to the 3rd/4th synchronizer hub and install the outer sleeve.

10. Repeat the preceding with the 1st/2nd synchronizer unit and test the axial release loads, which should be between 19 and 21 pounds for each unit. The axial release load may be adjusted by the installation of new springs or the addition/subtraction of shims to/from the position beneath each synchronizer spring.

11. Measure the end clearance of each mainshaft gear on its respective bushing. Correct end clearance is 0.002-0.006 in. End clearance may be increased by the installation of a new bushing and decreased by the reduction of the length of the bushing.

NOTE: The reduction of bushing length will increase the end clearance of the bushings on the mainshaft.

12. Install the thrust washer, bushing, thrust washer, bushing and washer to the mainshaft.

13. With the assembly secured with half a circlip, measure the total end clearance of the bushings and thrust washers on the mainshaft. The end clearance may be adjusted to the correct range of 0.004-0.010 in. through the use of thrust washers of various thicknesses.

14. Determine the required thickness of the circlip washer by installing the split collars, 1st gear thrust washer, bearing inner race or spacer tube, spacer washer and half circlip to the mainshaft, then insert a feeler gauge as shown in the illustration. Use washers of proper thicknesses to obtain the correct clearance of 0.000-0.002 in.

15. Install the following components on the mainshaft: 1st/2nd synchronizer unit, and washer. Use a special tool to install the circlip, and install the 3rd/4th synchronizer unit, split collars, 1st gear baulk ring, and 1st gear.

16. Position the mainshaft assembly in the transmission case, install an abutment plate tool or its equivalent, and install the thrust washer.

17. With the transmission positioned vertically, and the abutment plate held in a vise, install the snap-ring to the ball bearing and position the ball bearing over the mainshaft.

18. Being sure that the mainshaft is correctly located in the abutment plate, drive the ball bearing into position, using the special tool and adapter or their equivalents.

19. Install the speedometer drive gear and remove the abutment plate from the transmission.

20. Assemble the input shaft components: Position the 4th gear baulk ring into the 3rd/4th synchronizer unit.

21. Using the special tool and adapter or their equivalents, press the ball bearing and oil thrower onto the input shaft and secure the ball bearing with the circlip.

22. Install the snap-ring onto the ball bearing and place the roller bearing in the bore of the input shaft.

23. Ensuring that the baulk ring is correctly located, drive the input shaft assembly into the transmission case.

24. Assemble the countershaft by inverting the transmission, lining up the countershaft thrust washers and gearcluster, and inserting the spindle from the rear. With the reverse idler gear correctly positioned, insert the spindle and install the spacer.

25. Assemble the rear extension. Replace the ball bearing and seal to the rear extension. Install a new gasket at the rear of the transmission and place the washer over the end of the mainshaft. Install the rear extension assembly and secure it with bolts. Replace and secure the driving flange.

26. Assemble the bearing, oil seal, O-rings and driven gear and install the assembly to the extension housing, securing it with the bolt.

27. Insert the three springs into their holes in the front face of the transmission case.

28. Replace, if necessary, the oil seal in the clutch housing and install a new gasket to the front face of the transmission.

29. Replace the clutch throwout bearing and sleeve and the release lever.

30. Reassemble the top cover as follows: Insert the plungers and springs into the cover and slide the 3rd/4th selector shaft into the front end of the cover. While the shaft is being slid into position, press down on the selector plunger so that the shaft will be able to pass over it and through the selector fork. The shaft should be inserted until its middle indentation engages the plunger, achieving the neutral position. Repeat the above procedure with the reverse shaft and selector.

31. With the interlock plunger inserted into the 1st/2nd selector shaft, install the selector fork, sleeve and washer into the corner in similar fashion, ensuring that the shaft also passes through the 3rd/4th selector fork. Before the 1st/2nd selector shaft is pushed to its neutral position, insert the two interlock balls into the transverse bore which connects the shaft bores at the rear of the casting and then push the shaft further into the cover until the selector plunger engages the middle identation and the balls and plunger are retained by the shafts.

32. Use new tapered locking pins to secure the selector and forks to the shafts.

33. Use sealing compound around the edges of the plugs before driving them into the ends of the selector shaft bores.

34. Use a new pin to secure the fork to the shaft. If necessary, replace the "Metalistik" bushing in the shaft. Using new fiber washers, secure the shaft to the fork with the bolt and nut.

35. Install new O-rings to the case and install the shaft through the bores of the case and through the selector.

36. Use a new tapered locking pin when securing the selector to the shaft.

37. Install the reverse stop bolt, locknut, nylon ball, spring and snap-ring to the gearshift lever.

38. Install the reverse stop plate to the cover and secure with the retaining screws. With the gearshift lever assembly positioned in the cover, install two new bushings to the lever, install the spacer tube, and secure the lever to the shaft with the retaining bolt and nut.

39. Install the spring, cups, and cap over the gearshift lever.

40. Adjust the reverse stop plate and bolt with the gearshift lever in the neutral position of the 1st/2nd gate. The clearance between the reverse stop plate and bolt should be, as shown in the diagram, 0.010-0.050 in. (0.26-1.27 mm).

41. Reinstall the top cover on the transmission.

TYPE 26

4 Speed Transmission

Isuzu

DISASSEMBLY

1. Remove the boot, clutch fork and throwout bearing.

2. Remove bearing retainer, gasket and spring washer.

3. Remove the speedometer gear and bushing.

4. Remove the shifter cover and gasket.

5. Remove the back-up switch on California vehicles and both back-up and CRS switches on all others.

6. Remove the rear extension and gasket.

7. Remove the thrust washers and reverse idler gear.

8. Remove the snap-rings, speedometer drive gear and key from the mainshaft.

9. Remove the spring pin from the reverse shifter fork and reverse gear.

10. Remove the snap-ring from the outer circumference of the clutch gear shaft ball bearing.

11. Remove the center support assembly from the transmission case.

12. Drive out the spring pins from the third and fourth and first and second shift forks.

NOTE: When removing the spring pin, hold a round bar against the end of the shifter rods to prevent damage.

13. Remove the detent spring plate from the center support, then remove the detent springs and balls.

14. Remove the first and second and the third and fourth shifter rods from the center support, then remove the shifter forks.

15. Remove the reverse shifter rod forward as it is fitted with a stopper pin.

NOTE: Be careful not to loose the detent interlock plugs located between the shifter rods in the center support.

1. Case, w/center support
2. Pin, guide
3. Bearing, needle
4. Plug, shift rod
5. Stud.
6. Plug, oil filler
7. O-ring, oil filler
8. Dust cover, shift fork
9. Ring, snap, mainshaft
10. Ring, snap counter gear
11. Gasket, case and rear cover
12. Ball stud
13. Washer, lock
14. Washer, plain
15. Plug, screw
16. Gasket, plug (Calif. spec.)
17. Plug, screw (Calif. spec.)
18. Gasket, plug (Calif. spec.)
19. Shaft, clutch gear
20. Bearing, ball
21. Ring, snap
22. Ring, snap
23. Spring, belleville
24. Bearing, needle
25. Bearing retainer
26. Seal, oil, bearing retainer
27. Gasket, bearing retainer
28. Bolt
29. Extension Assy., rear, w/bushing and seal
30. Bushing
31. Seal, oil, rear extension
32. Breather assy.
33. Plug, oil drain
34. O-ring, oil drain
35. Bolt
37. Shaft main
38. Ring, snap

39. Hub, synchronizer, 3rd-4th
40. Sleeve, synchronizer
41. Key, synchronizer
42. Spring, synchronizer
43. Ring, blocker
44. Gear assy., 3rd
45. Gear assy., 2nd
46. Hub, synchronizer, 1st-2nd
47. Sleeve, synchronizer
48. Key, synchronizer
49. Spring, synchronizer
50. Ring blocker
51. Gear assy., 1st
52. Bearing, needle, 1st
53. Bearing, needle, 2nd
54. Collar, needle bearing
55. Washer, thrust, 1st
56. Bearing, mainshaft
57. Washer, lock, mainshaft
58. Nut, mainshaft
59. Gear, reverse
60. Gear, speed drive
61. Ring, snap, drive gear
62. Key
63. Gear, counter
64. Bearing, angular ball
65. Gear, counter reverse
66. Spacer
67. Washer, plain
68. Nut, self lock
69. Shaft, reverse idle
70. Plate, lock
71. Bolt, lock
72. Washer, spring
73. Gear, reverse idle
74. Washer, thrust
75. Synchronizer assy., 3rd-4th
76. Synchronizer assy., 1st-2nd

Isuzu 4-speed manual transmission

16. Move both synchronizers rearward to prevent turning of the mainshaft.

NOTE: It may be necessary to tap the synchronizers with the hammer handle to get them engaged.

17. Remove the locknut and washer from the mainshaft.

18. Remove the nut, washer, countershaft reverse gear and collar from the rear of the countergear.

19. Remove the center support counter-gear bearing snap-ring.

20. Remove the center support.

21. Separate the clutch gear, needle bearings and blocker ring from the mainshaft assembly.

22. Press the rear bearing from the mainshaft.

23. Remove the thrust washer, 1st speed gear, needle roller bearing, a collar and blocker ring.

24. Remove the 1st and 2nd gear synchronizer assembly.

25. Remove the 2nd gear, blocker ring and needle roller bearing from the mainshaft.

26. Remove the snap-ring, 3rd and 4th synchronizer assembly and blocker ring from the mainshaft.

27. Remove the 3rd gear and needle bearings.

28. Remove the snap-ring and press off the clutch bearing and countergear bearing from the shaft.

ASSEMBLY

1. Stand the front of the mainshaft upward and install the 3rd speed gear and needle roller bearing with the tapered side of the gear facing the front of the mainshaft.

2. Install a blocker ring with the clutching teeth upward over the synchronizing surface of the 3rd speed gear.

3. If it is necessary to reassemble the synchronizer assembly turn the face of the synchronizer hub with the heavy boss to the face of the sleeve with the light chamfering on the outer rim.

4. Fit the keys into the key groove and position the synchronizer springs into the hole in the side face of the hub.

5. Install the 3rd and 4th synchronizer assembly on the mainshaft with the face of the sleeve with the light chamfer rearward.

6. Turn the rear of the mainshaft upward and install the 2nd speed gear and needle roller bearing on the mainshaft with the tapered surface of the gear facing the rear of the mainshaft.

7. Install a blocker ring with the clutching teeth downward over the synchronizing surface of the 2nd speed gear.

8. Install the 1st and 2nd synchronizer assembly with the chamfer on the sleeve facing the front of the mainshaft.

9. Install a blocker ring with the clutching teeth rearward.

10. Install the colllr, needle roller bearing and 1st speed gear on the mainshaft.

NOTE: The tapered side of the gear should be facing the front of the mainshaft.

11. Install the 1st speed gear thrust washer on the mainshaft with the grooved side facing 1st gear.

12. Press the rear bearing on the mainshaft with the snap-ring groove facing the front of the mainshaft.

13. If removed, press the ball bearing on the clutch gearshaft with the snap-ring groove on the bearing facing the front of the transmission. Install the snap-ring on the clutch gear shaft.

14. Assemble the needle roller bearing, blocker ring and clutch gear to the front of the mainshaft.

15. If removed, press on the countergear ball bearing with the snap-ring groove facing the rear of the transmission.

16. If removed, install the snap-rings in the inner circumference of the mainshaft and countergear holes of the center support.

17. If removed, insert the idler gear shaft with the lock plate groove side into the center support from the rear, then install the lock plate.

18. Mesh the countergear with the mainshaft assembly and install a holding tool on the mainshaft and countergear.

19. Install the center support.

20. Press the center support onto the shaft until the countergear bearing is brought into contact with its snap-ring.

21. Expand the countergear bearing snap-ring and press the center support further until the mainshaft and countergear snap-rings are fitted into their grooves.

22. Remove the holding tool from the mainshaft and countergear.

23. Move both synchronizers rearward to prevent turning of the mainshaft.

24. Install the collar, countershaft reverse gear, washer and nut on the rear of the countergear.

NOTE: Install the locknut so that the chamfered side if facing the lockwasher.

25. Install the locknut and lock washer on the mainshaft.

NOTE: Install the locknut so that the chamfered side is facing the lockwasher.

26. Apply grease to the two detent plugs and insert them into their detent holes from the middle hole of the center support.

27. Install the 1st and 2nd shifter forks and the 3rd and 4th into their grooves in the synchronizer assembly.

28. Install 3rd and 4th shifter rod from the rear of the center support through the middle hole and into the 1st and 2nd, 3rd and 4th shifter forks. Align the spring pin hole in the shifter fork with the hole in the shifter rod.

NOTE: Identify the 3rd and 4th shifter rod by the two detent grooves on the side of the rod.

29. Install the 1st and 2nd shifter rod from the rear of the center support through the 1st and 2nd shifter fork and align the hole in the rod to the hole in the shifter fork.

30. If removed, install the stopper pin in the reverse shifter rod and the front of the center support.

31. Install the two spring pins in the 1st/2nd and 3rd/4th shifter forks.

32. Install the detent balls, spring, gasket and retainer on the center support.

33. Install the center support assembly and gasket.

34. Assemble the reverse shifter fork to the reverse reverse gear and install these parts into position from the rear side of the mainshift, then connect them to the reverse shifter rod.

35. Install the spring pin in the reverse shifter fork.

36. Install the thrust washer and reverse idler gear on the idler shaft.

NOTE: The reverse idler gear should be installed with undercut teeth forward.

37. Install the speedometer drive gear snap-ring and key on the mainshaft.

38. Install a new oil seal in the rear extension.

39. Apply grease to the outer thrust washer of the reverse idler shaft and insert it in the rear extensions.

40. Install the rear extension and gasket.

41. Install the back-up lamp switch and CRS switch.

42. Install the shifter cover and gasket.

43. Install the oil O-ring to the speedometer drive gear and install the gear.

44. Install the front bearing retainer seal.

45. Install a snap-ring in the outer circumference of the clutch gear bearing.

46. Apply grease to the bearing retainer spring washer and place it in the bearing retainer with the dished face turned to the bearing outer race.

47. Install the bearing retainer to the front of the transmission case.

NOTE: The shorter bolts are used on countergear front bearing side of the bearing retainer.

48. Install the ball stud to the bearing retainer.

49. Install the boot clutch fork and throw-out bearing, then install the retaining spring.

TYPE 27

5 Speed Transmission Isuzu

DISASSEMBLY

1. Drain the gear box of lubrication.

2. Remove the clutch release bearing and yoke assembly from the bell housing. Remove the clutch fork ball stud, if necessary, for removal clearance of the front bearing retainer.

3. Remove the front bearing retainer and Belleville spring.

4. Remove the speedometer driven gear and shift lever quadrant from the extension housing.

NOTE: Remove the Coasting Richer System switch from the quadrant on California models.

5. Remove the back-up lamp switch and the extension housing from the gear box.

6. Remove the snap-rings, speedometer drive gear, key, spacer and bearing from the mainshaft.

7. Remove the snap-ring, thrust washer and lock ball from the fifth gear on the mainshaft.

8. Remove the large snap-ring from the front bearing.

9. Remove the center support plate from the transmission case, with the mainshaft, countergear and drive gear as an assembly.

10. Support the ends of the 1st and 2nd, 3rd and 4th and 5th and reverse shift forks and drive the retaining pins from the forks.

11. Remove the detent spring plate from the center support plate and remove the three springs and balls.

12. Remove the shifter shafts from the center support plate and remove the shift forks and interlock pins.

13. To prevent the turning of the mainshaft and countergear while removing the locking nuts from the gear assembly, engage the synchronizers in 1st and 3rd gears.

14. Remove the nut and washer retaining the countergear and by using a puller, remove the ball bearing and the fifth gear from the rear of the countershaft.

15. Remove the fifth gear, blocker ring and needle bearing from the mainshaft.

16. Remove the nut from the reverse idler gearshaft and remove the thrust washers and gear from the idler gearshaft.

17. Straighten the mainshaft locking retainer tab and remove the nut and retainer from the mainshaft.

18. Remove the synchronizer assembly, reverse gear, needle bearing, collar and thrust washer.

19. Remove the reverse gear from the countergear and reposition the synchronizers to the neutral position.

20. Expand the countergear bearing snap-ring and move the center support plate by gently tapping on its front.

21. Expand the mainshaft bearing snap-ring and move the mainshaft inward. Remove the mainshaft and countergear.

22. Remove the drive gear, needle bearing and blocker ring from the mainshaft.

23. Remove the rear bearing from the mainshaft with the aid of a puller or press.

24. Remove the thrust washer, 1st speed gear, needle bearings and spacer.

25. Remove the 1st and 2nd synchronizer, 2nd speed gear and needle bearing.

26. Remove the snap-ring from the front of the mainshaft that holds the 3rd and 4th synchronizer. Remove the 3rd speed gear and needle bearing.

27. Remove the snap-ring from the drive gearshaft and with the use of a puller or a press, remove the front bearing.

ASSEMBLY

1. Place the coned side of the 3rd speed gear towards the front of the transmission and install it and the needle bearing on the front of the mainshaft.

2. Install the 3rd and 4th synchronizer on mainshaft with the chamfered end towards the front of the transmission. Retain with a snap-ring.

3. Install the 2nd speed gear and needle bearing on the rear of the mainshaft with the coned end of the gear towards the rear of the transmission.

4. Install the 1st and 2nd synchronizer on the mainshaft with the large chamfered end towards the rear on the transmission.

5. Install the spacer, needle bearings and 1st speed gear on the mainshaft, with the coned end of the gear towards the front of the transmission.

6. Install the first gear thrust washer with the slots towards the gear.

7. Press the rear bearing onto the mainshaft with the snap-ring groove towards the front of the transmission.

8. Install the center support plate snap-rings and reverse idler shaft. Torque bolts to 14 ft-lbs.

9. Install the drive gear on the front of the mainshaft and engage with the countergear to install the center support plate.

10. Install countergear and mainshaft bearings into the center support plate and while expanding the snap-rings, move the bearings into place on the support plate and engage the snap-rings in the bearing grooves.

11. Engage the gears in 1st and 3rd to prevent turning and install the reverse gear on the countergear.

12. Install the thrust washer on the main-

1. Drive gear
2. Release bearing
3. Drive gear bearing retainer
4. Shift fork
5. Drive gear bearing
6. Shifter shaft
7. 3rd & 4th shift fork
8. 1st & 2nd shift fork
9. Mainshaft bearing
10. Center support
11. Shift lever quadrant
12. Shift lever
13. 5th & reverse shift fork
14. Mainshaft rear bearing
15. Extension housing
16. Rear seal
17. Speedometer drive gear
18. 5th gear assy
19. Counter gear rear bearing
20. 5th counter gear
21. Needle bearing
22. Reverse counter gear
23. Reverse idler shaft
24. Reverse idler gear
25. Counter gear bearing
26. Needle bearing
27. Counter gear
28. Mainshaft
29. Counter gear front bearing
30. Needle gearing

Cross section of Opel Isuzu 5-speed transmission

shaft with the oil grooves turned towards the reverse gear. Install the collar, needle bearings and reverse gear on the mainshaft.

13. Install the synchronizer assembly so that the face of the clutch hub boss is turned to the reverse gear side.

14. Install the locking retainer and nut on the front of the mainshaft. Torque the nut to 94 ft/lbs. Bend the retainer tab to lock the nut in place.

15. Install the thrust washers and reverse idler gear on the reverse idler shaft and tighten the nut to 80 ft/lbs.

NOTE: Install new self-locking nut on countergear.

16. Install the blocker ring, needle bearing and 5th gear on the mainshaft.

17. Install the countergear 5th gear, ball bearing, washer and selflocking nut on the rear of the countergear. Torque the nut to 80 ft/lbs.

NOTE: Install new self-locking nut on countergear.

18. Reposition the synchronizers to the neutral position.

19. Lubricate the interlock pins and install in the center support plate.

20. Place the shift forks on the synchronizer sleeves and install the 3rd and 4th shifter

shaft through the center support plate and into the shift fork for 3rd and 4th gear.

21. Install the 1st and 2nd shifter shaft through the center support plate and through the 1st and 2nd shift fork.

22. Install the reverse and 5th shifter shaft through the center support plate and into the reverse and 5th shifter fork.

23. Install the three detent balls and springs in the center support plate and retain with the detent plate and gasket. Torque the bolts to 14 ft/lbs.

24. Install the retaining pins in the shifter forks to the shifter shafts while supporting the ends of the shaft with a bar or block of wood.

25. Install the countergear needle bearing in the front of the transmission case.

26. Install a new gasket on the transmission case and install the center support plate assembly into the transmission case.

27. Install the large snap-ring on the front bearing of the mainshaft.

28. Install the lock ball and thrust washer on the mainshaft and retain with a snap-ring.

29. Measure the clearance between the 5th gear and the thrust washer on the mainshaft. The clearance should be 0.010 to 0.016 in.

30. If the clearance is out of specifications, replace the thrust washer with one of the following:

Part Number	Thickness (inches)	(Millimeters)
94025579	0.3014	7.656
94025580	0.3073	7.805
94025581	0.3132	7.955
94025582	0.3191	8.105

31. Install the speedometer drive gear front snap-ring, ball bearing and key onto the mainshaft.

32. Align the groove in the speedometer drive gear with the key on the mainshaft and install the gear. Retain with a snap-ring.

33. Install the rear extension housing with a new gasket on to the center support plate. Torque the bolts to 27 ft/lbs.

34. Install the shift lever quadrant with gasket on the extension housing. Torque the bolts to 14 ft/lbs.

35. Install the speedometer driven gear and torque the retaining bolt to 14 ft/lbs.

36. California Models only: Install the CRS switch on the extension housing.

37. Install the Belleview washer with the dished side towards the drive gear bearing and install the bearing retainer and gasket. Torque the bolts to 14 ft/lbs.

NOTE: Seal the lower left bolt with a non-hardening sealer or equivalent.

38. Install the clutch release bearing and yoke assembly on the bell housing.

NOTE: The gearshift lever is installed when the transmission is in the vehicle.

TYPE 28

4 Speed Transmission—Models BA-7, BA-10, BA-10/4 Peugeot

DISASSEMBLY

BA-7

1. Drain the lubricating oil from the gear box and mount the assembly upside down in the support tool or its equivalent.
2. Remove the clutch release fork, the clutch housing and the back-up lamp switch.
3. Remove the speedometer drive gear socket bushing and the retaining screw from the rear extension.

NOTE: To pull the socket bushing from the housing, an expanding set of pliers will be needed.

4. Invert the transmission on the support tool or its equivalent and secure.
5. Move the control lever to the neutral

position and pull the selector lever fully to the rear.

6. Remove the rear extension housing retaining bolts and separate the rear housing from the transmission case.

NOTE: A rubber mallet may be needed to loosen the rear extension housing from the transmission case.

7. Remove the four Allen screws from the rear bearing lock plate.
8. Remove the eight half housing retaining bolts and remove the upper half housing from the lower half housing, with the gear train remaining in the lower housing.
9. Lift the gear train assembly from the lower half housing as a unit.

BA-10, BA-10/4

1. Mount the gear box by its left housing in the support tool or its equivalent and drain the lubricating oil, if not previously done.
2. Remove the set screw and the speedometer driven socket bushing from the rear extension housing.

NOTE: An expanding set of pliers will be needed to pull the socket bushing from the housing.

3. Move the selector and control levers into the neutral position.

BA-7

Remove the return spring and its support from the extension housing.

NOTE: The return spring support is mounted on a rear extension housing bolt.

BA-10, BA-10/4

Remove the return spring and the reverse gear plunger from the rear extension housing.

NOTE: The return spring support is bolted to the rear of the extension housing.

4. Remove the retaining bolts and loosen the rear extension housing with a rubber mallet. Remove the housing from the transmission.
5. Engage the 4th gear and place an output shaft holding tool or its equivalent on the output shaft splines.
6. Hold the output shaft securely and remove the nut from the countershaft. Remove the reverse idling pinion gear.
7. Remove the clutch release bearing fork rubber protection cover, the clutch release fork and the clutch release bearing. Remove the retaining bolts from the clutch housing and remove the housing from the transmission case.
8. Engage the reverse gear and remove the rear bearing thrust plate retaining screws.
9. Remove the retaining bolts from the half housings and separate the two halfs by the removal of the right hand housing.
10. Lift the countershaft assembly from the left half housing. Mark the bearing outer races, in case they are to be reused.
11. Remove the input and mainshaft assembly from the half housing as a unit. Do not separate.
12. Set the reverse semi-synchronizer to the neutral position.

Countershaft
BA-7

1. Place the countershaft in a holding tool or vise and remove the snap-ring from the reverse idler gear. Remove the washer and the gear from the countershaft.

Gear train position and shift direction of synchronizers—Model BA-7

Gear train position in half housing and shift direction of synchronizers—Model BA-10

2. Remove the outer race from the bearing and with the use of a press, remove the front and rear bearings.

NOTE: Do not lose the adjusting shim located behind the front bearing.

BA-10, BA-10/4

1. Place the countershaft in a press and remove the front bearing and adjusting shim.

2. Invert the countershaft and press the rear bearing from the shaft.

Separation of Input and Mainshaft—All Models

1. Place the 3rd/4th synchronizer assembly in the 3rd speed position and pull the input

Position of gear train in half housing and the shift direction of the synchronizers—Model BA-10/4

shaft from the mainshaft. Do not lose the needle bearing from the input shaft bore.

Mainshaft
BA-7

1. Remove the grease from the 3rd/4th synchronizer assembly. Place the mainshaft assembly in a holding tool or vise.

2. Mark the position of the 3rd/4th sliding gear on the 3rd/4th hub, using a sharp brass rod or its equivalent. Remove the sliding gear.

3. Remove the snap-ring and spring washer retaining the 3rd/4th speed hub to the mainshaft.

4. While holding the reverse pinion with a holding tool or equivalent, and the mainshaft still in the vise or holding tool, fully unscrew the reverse pinion retaining nut from the mainshaft threads.

NOTE: The nut is retained on the shaft by the speedometer gear.

5. Remove the 3rd/4th synchronizer hub and 3rd speed gear from the mainshaft. A puller or a press may have to be used.

6. Place the mainshaft assembly into a press and press the mainshaft downward to free the rear bearing from its seat on the mainshaft.

CAUTION
Be sure the retaining nut is free of its threads on the mainshaft, before the press pressure is applied.

7. Continue the downward pressure on the mainshaft and remove the speedometer drive gear from the mainshaft.

8. Remove the assembly from the press and remove the parts from the mainshaft in the following order:
    a. Speedometer drive gear
    b. Nut
    c. Reverse pinion gear
    d. Rear bearing and retainer plate
    e. Rear bearing and adjusting shims
    f. 1st speed gear spacer bushing
    g. Needle bearing cage
    h. 1st speed gear
    i. 1st/2nd speed gear synchronizer and hub.
    j. 2nd speed gear.

NOTE: Observe the direction of gear position on the mainshaft.

BA-10, BA-10/4

1. Degrease the 3rd/4th synchronizer assembly and mark the positioning of the sliding gear to the hub assembly with a sharp piece of brass welding rod.

2. Remove the sliding gear from the mainshaft.

3. Remove the circlip and spring washer from the front end of the mainshaft, holding the 3rd/4th synchronizer hub in place.

4. Holding the mainshaft in a vise or other holding fixture, remove the reverse gear nut from its threads on the mainshaft, while holding the reverse gear stationary.

5. Using a press or a puller, remove the 3rd gear synchronizer hub and the 3rd gear from the mainshaft.

6. Place the mainshaft assembly into a press with the rear of the mainshaft pointing

upward. Using press pressure, force the mainshaft downward to unseat the rear bearing from its seat on the mainshaft.

CAUTION
Be sure the nut is free of its threads on the mainshaft, before the press pressure is applied.

7. Continue the downward pressure of the press on the mainshaft and remove the speedometer drive gear from the mainshaft.

8. Remove the assembly from the press and remove the parts from the mainshaft in the following order:
    a. Speedometer drive gear
    b. Retaining nut
    c. Reverse gear driven pinion
    d. Rear bearing thrust plate
    e. Rear bearing and adjusting shims
    f. 1st gear spacer collar
    g. Needle bearing
    h. 1st gear driven pinion
    i. 1st/2nd synchronizer assembly with hub.
    j. 2nd gear driven pinion
    k. Needle bearing

NOTE: Observe the direction of gear position on the mainshaft.

Input Shaft
ALL MODELS

1. Remove the large and small circlips from the bearing and the shaft. Remove the spring washer from under the small circlip.

2. Using a press, force the input shaft from the bearing. Do not lose the oil defector or the adjusting shims.

Shifting Rails and Forks
BA-7

1. Place the 1st/2nd shifting mechanism in the 2nd speed position.

2. Using a drift of proper size, remove the roll pin from the 1st/2nd gear shift fork.

3. Return the 1st/2nd shift mechanism to the neutral position, and position the 3rd/4th shift rail to the 4th speed location. Remove the roll pin from 3rd/4th shifting fork.

4. Return the 3rd/4th shift rail to the neutral position.

5. Remove the detent ball locking plug from the outside of the transmission case. An Allen key type tool is used.

6. Remove the 1st/2nd gear shift rail and the 3rd/4th gear shift rail from the transmission case.

7. Invert the transmission case and remove the reverse shifting detent ball locking plug with the Allen key tool.

8. Remove the shift rail and fork with the countershaft pinion from the transmission case.

9. Locate and remove from the case, the three locking springs, four balls and the one locking finger.

NOTE: If the balls are stuck in the passages, use a long rod to free them.

10. Remove the locking needle from the 3rd/4th speed shifting rail.

11. Using a drift, remove the roll pin from the reverse pinion shaft and move the shaft towards the inside of the case and remove.

BA-10

1. Place the 1st/2nd shift fork in the neutral position and remove the roll pin with a proper sized drift.

2. Move the 3rd/4th shift rail into the 4th speed position and remove the roll pin from the fork.

3. Remove the 1st/2nd locking spring plug and remove the spring and ball from the outside of the transmission case.

4. Remove the shift rail and the shift fork.

5. Remove the reverse detent spring plug, the spring and the ball. If not done previously, remove the back-up light switch.

6. Remove the reverse shift fork and idler gear assembly. Remove the indent and spring (Operating spigot).

7. Remove the 3rd/4th detent plug, spring and ball from the outside of the transmission case.

8. Remove the 3rd/4th shift rail. Remove the fork, the interlock pin, the detent ball and interlock finger from the bearing block.

Diagram of detent and interlock components—Model BA-7

Diagram of detent and interlock components—Model BA-10

9. Using a drift, remove the roll pin from the reverse shaft and push the shaft towards the outside of the housing.

BA-10/4

1. Remove the 3rd/4th detent spring from the hole in the bearing seat at the rear of the transmission half housing.

2. Place the selector rail into 4th gear and remove the roll pins from the 1st/2nd and 3rd/4th rails and forks.

3. If not done previously, remove the back-up light switch from the case.

4. Remove the 1st/2nd detent ball plug and spring from the outside of the case.

5. Remove the 1st/2nd shift rail and the 1st/2nd shift fork.

6. Remove the 3rd/4th shift rail and fork. Remove the detent balls and recover the interlock pins.

7. Remove the roll pin from the reverse gearshaft.

8. Remove the remaining detent plugs and springs from the outside of the case.

9. Remove the reverse gear assembly, consisting of the gear, shaft, fork and shifting rail and the semi-synchronizer bushing.

10. Obtain the detent balls and the interlock pins from the passages in the transmission case.

Neutral Ball Detent—Rear Extension Housing
ALL MODELS

1. Check the operation of the neutral position ball detent by pushing and pulling the selector lever in and out of the housing.

2. If the detent is found to be defective, remove the detent plug and check the condition of the spring and ball. Replace the necessary parts.

ASSEMBLY
General

1. When reassembling the gearboxes, replace the following parts as standard procedure.
   a. Shaft circlips
   b. Spring washers
   c. Roll pins
   d. Mainshaft nut
   e. Output shaft oil seal
   f. Input shaft oil seal
   g. Speedometer driven socket bushing
   h. Thrust washers

2. Oil the various gears, shafts and components before installation.

3. When joining the housings, apply a thin coat of jointing compound to seal the units.

4. Inspect the clutch housing to be sure the front and rear surfaces are parallel to each other. If a difference of more than 0.004 inch (0.10 mm) exists, the housing should be replaced.

5. Replace the thrust guide in the clutch housing by removing the oil seal, the circlip and pressing the guide from the housing.

6. Replace the thrust guide by applying a grease to the tube and pressing it into place in the housing. Install the circlip and the oil seal.

NOTE: To avoid damage to the seal, do not install it into the clutch housing until the adjustment operations are made during the assembly of the unit.

7. Remove the rear oil seal in the extension housing by prying it from the housing bore. Remove the needle bearing with the aid of a press.

8. Install the needle bearing with the aid of a press and install the seal in its bore.

NOTE: The needle bearing assembly and seal should be replaced any time the transmission is disassembled.

When installing the needle bearing, position the bearings wih the markings on it towards the outside.

Installation of Shift Rails, Forks and Detents
BA-7

1. Place the left hand transmission housing in the holding tool or equivalent.

2. Install the reverse pinion shaft and align the roll pin holes. Install the roll pin into the pre-aligned holes.

3. Turn the housing on its side so that the drain plug is upward and install the reverse gear along with the shifting fork.

NOTE: The shift fork collar on the gear should be towards the rear.

4. Install the ball and the spring detent into its passage, from the outside of the case. Install a sealer on the plug threads and install the plug into the case. Torque to 9.4 ft/lb. Locate the reverse shift rail to the neutral position.

5. Rotate the housing to the opposite side to expose the lock ng passage and install the 3rd/4th locking finger (indent) into the passage.

6. Install the locking needle on the 3rd/4th shifting rail and hold with grease. Install the rail into its respective bore.

7. Rotate the housing until it is in its upright position and install the 1st/2nd shift fork into the case and 3rd/4th shift fork onto the shift rail. Push the rail inward until it is flush with the ball lock hole in the front of the case.

NOTE: The 1st/2nd shift fork will be along side the shift rail.

8. Insert a ball and spring into the hole and compress the spring and ball. Push the rail forward and over the ball and spring.

9. Set the shaft into the neutral position and secure the 3rd/4th shifting fork to the shift rail with a new roll pin.

10. Rest the housing on its side and install a locking ball into the passage to rest against the 3rd/4th shift rail.

11. Install the 1st/2nd shift rail into its respective bore until the neutral position is reached, and entering the 1st/2nd shift fork.

12. Install the locking ball and spring into its bore, sealing the plug and installing it into the housing. Torque to 9.4 ft/lb. Secure the 1st/2nd shifting fork with a new roll pin.

BA-10

1. Install the reverse gear shaft and align the pin holes. Install a new roll pin into the pre-aligned holes.

2. Install the reverse gear, the shift fork and the shifting rail into the transmission case.

NOTE: The shifting fork collar of the reverse gear should face to the rear.

3. Install the ball and spring into the reverse lock hole and install the locking plug, after coating it with a sealer, into the transmission case.

4. Position the shifting shaft into the neutral position.

5. Place the 3rd/4th and reverse indent

Diagram of detent and interlock components—Model BA-10/4

pin into the passage to contact the reverse shift rail.

6. Lubricate the interlock pin and place it in its position on the 3rd/4th shift rail.

7. Place the operating indent and spring on the reverse shift fork.

NOTE: The indent is commonly called "spigot".

8. Position the 3rd/4th shift fork rail into the case with the operating clevis horizontal and pointing to the left. Engage the rail by compressing the drive interlock pin (spigot) until the locking flat is opposite the indent.

9. Place the 3rd/4th shift fork in position with its collar towards the rear and engage the rail into the fork. Secure the shifting fork to the rail with a new roll pin.

IMPORTANT: Be assured that the interlock pin is in its proper position in the passage, located in the strut of the case.

10. Rotate the transmission case and install the detent ball in the passage to locate the ball between the 3rd/4th and the 1st/2nd shift rails.

11. Install the 1st/2nd shift rail and the 1st/2nd shift fork into the transmission case, with the shift collar of the gear towards the front. Engage the shift rail into the shift fork and install a new roll pin.

12. Install a ball and spring into the 1st/2nd speed detent passage and after coating the plug with sealer, install the plug into the passageway. Torque to 9.4 ft/lb.

13. Install the ball and spring into the 3rd/4th detent passage.

14. Coat the plug with a sealer and install into the transmission case. Torque to 9.4 ft/lb.

BA-10/4

1. Install the reverse gear assembly consisting of the gear, shaft, fork and rail and the semi-synchronizer ring, into the transmission housing.

2. Align the holes in the reverse gear shaft and the transmission case strut and install a new roll pin.

3. Install the detent balls and springs into the detent passages in the following order.
Rear passage—A detent ball and the 50 mm long spring.
Intermediate passage—A detent ball and a 30 mm long spring.

4. Coat the plugs with a sealer and install in the case. Torque to 9.4 ft/lbs. Set the reverse rail to neutral position.

5. Install the interlock pin into the passage towards the front of the case.

6. Install the interlock pin into the hole in the 3rd/4th shift rail and hold in position with grease.

7. Place the 3rd/4th shifting fork in the case with the boss to the rear. Slide the 3rd/4th shifting rail into position, through the case and into the shifting fork.

8. Install a detent ball into the open passage, towards the front of the case.

9. Install the 1st/2nd shifting fork with the boss towards the front of the case. Install the 1st/2nd shifting rail into the case and the fork.

10. Install a detent ball and a 30 mm long spring into the open detent passage, closest to the front, and coat the plug with sealer and install it into the case. Torque to 9.4 ft/lbs.

1. Position of 4th speed synchronizer cone
2. Position of 2nd speed synchronizer cone
3. Countershaft taper roller bearing preload

Location of adjusting shims needed during the transmission assembly—Models BA-7, BA-10, BA-10/4

11. Align the holes in the 1st/2nd and 3rd/4th shifting forks and rails and install new roll pins to secure them.

Adjustment Prior to Assembly

Three major adjustments should be made prior to the assembly of the gear box components. The adjustments are as follows.

a. Position of the 4th speed synchronizer cone.

b. Position of the 2nd speed synchronizer cone.

c. Countershaft taper roller bearing preload.

Special tools are needed for the adjustments and should be attained prior to transmission repairs.

An explanation of the adjustments are outlined, with the use of the special tools included in the outline.

ADJUSTMENT OF THE 4TH SPEED SYNCHRONIZER CONE

1. Install the input shaft and bearing, less shims and oil deflector, into the clutch housing, inverted on a flat surface.

2. Install the right hand half of the transmission housing to the clutch housing and install two bolts. Torque the bolts to 14.5 ft/lbs.

CAUTION

Be sure the bearing is properly seated in the clutch housing bore and in the right transmission housing bore.

3. Seat the special tool gauge block (8.0314 G or equivalent) countershaft front bearing bore of the right transmission housing and the clutch housing.

4. Install the dial indictor (8.0310 FZ or equivalent), into the hole on its block base. Retain the dial indicator with the thumb screw.

5. Align the dial indicator stem with the edge of the 4th speed synchronizer cone. Rotate the shaft and cone, one turn, and obtain an average reading. Adjust the dial indicator to zero at the average reading height of the cone.

6. Reposition the dial indicator base to the tool gauge block so that the stem is resting on

Position of dial indicator, input shaft and bearing, clutch housing and half housing during 4th speed synchronizer cone measurement

the gauge block surface. Record the measurement.

7. The measurement result represents the thickness of the shim or shims needed to be inserted between the input shaft and the front bearing. The measured value should be rounded off to the nearest 0.05 mm. Shims are available from 0.15 to 0.50 mm, in increments of 0.05 mm.

NOTE: Model BA-7, shims available—0.15 to 0.35 mm.

Prepare the shim stacks as follows;
Model BA-7
Example
Dial indicator reading	0.58 mm
Total shim pack needed (rounded off)	0.60 mm

Use—Oil deflector washer
(constant size)	0.15 mm
Shim	0.20 mm
Shim	0.25 mm
Total	0.60 mm

Model BA-10 (Synchronizer cone diameter—91. mm)
Example
Dial indicator reading	0.43 mm
Total shim thickness needed (rounded off)	0.45 mm

NOTE: Remove the oil deflector washer and discard. Do not include it in the shim pact measurement.

Model BA-10/4 (Synchronizer cone diameter—96. mm)
Example
Dial indicator reading	0.87 mm
Subtract from obtained reading (constant)	0.50 mm
Result	0.37 mm
Shim required (rounded off)	0.35 mm

NOTE: Remove the oil deflector washer and discard. Do not include it in the shim pack measurement.

ADJUSTMENT OF THE 2ND SPEED SYNCHRONIZER CONE

1. With the input shaft and bearing in the same position as in the 1st measurement procedure, install a needle bearing into the bore of the input shaft.
2. Install the mainshaft, with the 2nd speed gear and needle bearing, the 1st/2nd speed synchronizer hub and the spacer. Be sure the 2nd speed gear is seated properly.
3. Install the rear bearing temporarily to steady the mainshaft.
4. Install the tool gauge block, (8.0314 K or equivalent) in the countershaft front bearing bore.
5. Place the dial indicator and block base, on the upper part of the transmission half case housing. Using a long dial indicator stem, place the end on the surface of the tool gauge block and set the dial indicator to zero.
6. Position the long dial indicator stem on the rim of the 2nd speed synchronizer cone and record the measurement.
7. The dial indicator reading represents the thickness of the shim or shims needed between the spacer and the rear bearing. Round the results off to the nearest 0.05 mm. Prepare the shim pack as follows;

Model BA-7
Example
Dial indicator reading	0.47 mm
Shims required (rounded off)	0.45 mm

NOTE: Shim available from 0.15 to 0.50 mm in increments of 0.05 mm.

Model BA-10
Example
Dial indicator reading	2.82 mm
Shim required (rounded off)	2.80 mm

Model BA-10/4
Example
Dial indicator reading	2.91 mm
Add to obtained reading (constant)	0.50 mm
Result	3.41 mm
Shim required (rounded off)	3.40 mm

NOTE: Shims are available for models BA-10 and BA-10/4 in steps of 0.05 mm, from 2.35 to 3.65 mm.

8. Remove the dial indicator unit, the mainshaft, the right hand housing and the input shaft.

ADJUSTMENT OF THE COUNTERSHAFT TAPERED ROLLER BEARING PRELOAD

1. Place the left hand half housing in the holding stand or its equivalent.
2. Install the countershaft with its bearings and the thrust plate into the housing. Engage the reverse position.
3. Place the right hand half housing on the left housing, with the dowel pins in position, and install two bearing center bolts and four thrust plate bolts. Hand-tighten only.
4. Position the gearbox housing in an upright position, with the front pointing up.
5. With tool number 8.0314 or equivalent, apply pressure to the countershaft bearings. Rotate the shaft to seat the bearings properly.
6. Tighten the previously hand-tightened bolts to a torque of 7.2 ft/lb. (Bearing center bolts and the thrust plate bolts.)
7. Place the dial indicator and its base on the countershaft end, with the indicator stem contacting the front bearing outer race. Turn the indicator and base in a complete circle and record the average measurement.
8. Move the dial indicator and base to have the stem contact the face of the half housing and again turn the indicator and base in a complete circle. Record the average measurement.
9. The difference between the two measurements is the run-out between the outer race and the front of the half housings. This measurement should not exceed 0.003 mm.
10. Should the measurement of the run-out exceed specifications, tap gently with a mallet on the outer bearing race, be sure the effort to turn the countershaft has not increased, and recheck the run-out.
11. If necessary, loosen and retighten the front bearing center bolt.
12. Position the dial indicator on the countershaft end with the stem resting on the bearing race. Set the dial indicator hands on 2 and 0.
13. Move the dial indicator so that the stem moves from the race to the front face of the housings. Note and record the dial indicator movement.
14. Add 0.10 mm to this measurement to provide for the bearing preload, and round off to the nearest 0.05 mm.
Example
Measurement to housing	4.27 mm
Preset measurement on race	2.00 mm
Difference	2.27 mm
Add preload	0.10 mm
Necessary shim	2.37 mm
Round off to nearest 0.05 mm	2.35 mm

NOTE: Available shims for the Model BA-7 range from 2.25 to 3.25 mm in increments of 0.05 mm. Available shims for the models BA-10 and BA-10/4 range from 2.15 to 3.30 mm in increments of 0.05 mm.

Position of dial indicator and base for measuring preload of countershaft tapered roller bearing

15. Remove the retaining bolts from the thrust plate and the bearing areas of the half housings and separate the two housings. Remove the countershaft and bearings.
16. Remove the front bearing from the countershaft and install the shim of proper thickness, as determined in the previous adjustment procedure, between the bearing and the gear. The shim chamfer should be facing the gear. Press the bearing in place on the countershaft.

Mainshaft Assembly

BA-7
1. Install the following components in order, aligning the previously marked reference points, made during the disassembly, on the mainshaft, from rear to front.
   a. 2nd gear
   b. Synchronizer hub and sliding sleeve
   c. 1st gear
   d. Needle bearing
   e. Spacer
   f. Adjusting shims
   g. Rear bearing with snap-ring groove towards the rear

NOTE: The bearing should be pressed on the shaft, not to exceed 3 tons with the parts bottomed.

   h. The thrust plate with the machined surface towards bearing

1. Speedometer drive gear
2. Nut
3. Reverse gear
4A. Rear bearing thrust plate
4. Rear bearing
5. Adjusting shim pack
6. 1st speed spacer bushing
7. Needle bearing
8. 1st speed gear
9. Synchronizer cage
10. Synchronizer hub
11. 2nd speed gear

Main shaft components—Model BA-7

1. Speedometer drive gear
2. Nut
3. Reverse gear
4. Rear bearing thrust plate
5. Rear bearing
6. Shim washer
7. 1st gear spacer collar
8. Needle bearing
9. 1st gear
10. Synchronizer cage
11. Synchronizer hub
12. 2nd gear
13. Needle bearing

Mainshaft components—Models BA-10, BA-10/4

i. Reverse gear with chamfered edge of teeth towards the rear

j. A new nut. Tighten to 40 ft-lbs and lock

k. Press speedometer drive gear onto mainshaft

2. Install the following components in order, onto the mainshaft from front to rear, following the reference marks made previously.

a. 3rd gear

b. 3rd/4th gear synchronizer hub (press if necessary)

c. Spring washer

d. Snap-ring

e. 3rd/4th sliding gear and engage 3rd gear

BA-10, BA-10/4

1. Install the following components on the mainshaft from rear to front, following the reference marks made during the disassembly.

a. 2nd speed gear with needle bearing (length—31 mm)

b. 1st/2nd synchronizer hub and cage, with the marking groove towards the 1st gear

c. 1st speed gear

d. Needle bearing (length—29 mm)

e. Spacer ring

f. Adjustment shims

g. Rear bearing. Press the bearing onto the shaft and do not exceed 3 tons of pressure when bearing bottoms.

h. Thrust plate

i. Reverse drive gear with the flat face towards the rear

j. New nut, torque to 39 ft/lbs and lock in place

k. Speedometer drive gear. Press on shaft with the undercut towards the front

2. Install the following components on the front of the mainshaft, following the reference marks made during the disassembly.

a. 3rd speed gear and needle bearing

b. 3rd/4th synchronizer hub. Press on if necessary

c. Spring washer

d. Snap-ring (Install with components under pressure, if necessary)

Input Shaft
ALL MODELS

1. Install the predetermined shims (with oil deflector on model BA-7) on the input shaft.

2. Position the bearing with the outer snap-ring groove facing the front of the shaft, and press the bearing into place on the shaft.

3. Install a new spring washer and snap-ring while the pressure is on the bearing.

4. Install the outer snap-ring in the outer bearing race groove.

5. Install the needle bearing in the bore of the input shaft.

6. Position the 3rd/4th synchronizer cage to the reference marks, made during the disassembly, on the mainshaft.

7. Install the input shaft to the mainshaft, again aligning the reference marks made during the disassembly.

8. Set both synchronizers to the neutral position.

Assembly of Components to the Half Housings
BA-7

1. Secure the half housing with the shifting forks to the support base or equivalent.

2. Install the countershaft assembly to the mainshaft/input shaft assembly by passing the reverse gear on the countershaft through the opening in the thrust plate Mesh the gear teeth together and install the assembly into the left hand housing, aligning the shifting forks to the synchronizer sliding sleeves.

3. Install the countershaft front bearing outer race to the bearing.

4. Apply sealer to the housing mating surfaces and install the right housing to the left housing.

5. Install the four housing retaining bolts and torque to 3.6 ft/lbs. (Two bolts at the rear and two bolts at the front.)

6. Apply sealer to the rear face of the clutch housing and install on the transmission case.

7. Secure the housing with the six bolts and torque to 20 ft/lbs.

8. Install the four Allen screws and secure the rear bearing thrust plate. Torque to 7.2 ft/lbs.

9. Loosen the four housing retaining bolts and strike the housings with a rubber mallet while turning the mainshaft. Retighten and torque the bolts to 11 ft/lbs.

10. Use a dial indicator and base block to check the "out of Flush" of the two half housings at their rear mating surfaces. The housings should not be out of flush more than 0.02 mm.

11. Install the four assembly bolts and nuts to the half housings and torque to 7.2 ft/lbs.

12. Apply sealer to the rear housing mating surface and install the housing to the transmission.

13. Tighten the seven studs and bolts to 11 ft/lbs after pulling the selector lever fully rearward.

14. Install the speedometer drive socket bushing with a lubricated O-ring. Install the stop screw and locknut.

15. Install the clutch release bearing and fork. Install the back-up lamp and fill with lubricant.

BA-10, BA-10/4

1. Place the left hand housing in the support tool or equivalent.

2. BA-10/4—Install a detent ball and a 30 mm long spring in the detent passage of the rear bearing seat.

3. Set the reverse gear semi-synchronizer to the neutral position. Set the assembled input and mainshaft synchronizers to the neutral position.

4. Install the gear trains into the half housing while engaging the shifting forks to their respective synchronizer sleeves.

5. Install the outer races to the countershaft bearings and install the countershaft into the housing. Mate the gears of the countershaft and the mainshaft.

6. Coat the half housing mating surfaces with sealer and install the right housing to the left, being sure the dowel pins are properly located.

7. Install the six end housing retaining bolts and torque to 3.5 ft/lbs.

8. Engage the reverse gear and install the four thrust plate bolts. Torque to 9.4 ft/lbs.

9. Fit the reverse idler gear to the countershaft with the boss of the gear to the front. Install a new nut.

10. Engage 4th gear, hold the mainshaft with a special holding tool or equivalent, and tighten the nut to 18 ft/lbs.

11. Lock the skirt of the nut to the countershaft by crimping the skirt with a pair of lock pliers.

--- CAUTION ---
Never hammer the nut to lock the skirt.

12. Install the oil seal in the clutch housing if not previously done. Coat the clutch housing mating surface with sealer and install on the transmission case. Tighten the seven securing nuts to a torque of 20 ft/lbs.

NOTE: Turn the mainshaft while tightening the clutch housing bolts.

13. Loosen the six bolts at the front and the rear of the transmission case. Tap the housing with a rubber mallet while turning the mainshaft. Retighten the six bearing bolts to a torque of 10 ft/lbs.

14. Install the remaining six bolts in the flanges of the assembled housings. Tighten to a torque of 7 ft/lbs.

15. Reset the reverse gear synchronizer to the neutral position. Apply sealer to the rear extension housing mating surface.

16. Turn the selector lever to the left (counterclockwise) as far as it will go and fit the rear housing to the transmission assembly. Tighten the bolts and nut to 10 ft/lbs.

17. Install the shift control return spring bracket and attach the spring.

18. BA-10/4—Install special tool 8.0310 V or equivalent between the jack lever and the housing. Install the reverse gear plunger until it touches the selector lever. Tighten the two bolts and connect the spring. Remove the gauge tool.

19. Install the speedometer driven gear socket bushing and a lubricated O-ring. Install the set screw and tighten.

20. Install the clutch release fork and bearing assembly, along with the rubber protector.

21. Install the back-up light switch and fill the transmission with lubricant.

DISASSEMBLY

1. Secure the transmission and drain the lubricating oil from the unit.

2. Remove the clutch release lever pivot bolt and remove the clutch release lever complete with the pivot bolt and the bearing slippers.

3. Remove the release bearing and the slippers from the clutch release bearing, as required.

4. Remove the bell housing retaining bolts and carefully remove the bell housing from the transmission case.

5. Remove the nut and connecting pin that connects the selector shaft to the remote control shaft.

6. Remove the remote control housing from the transmission rear extension.

7. Remove the nut and washer securing the drive flange to the output shaft. Remove the flange.

NOTE: It is necessary to hold the input shaft while the transmission gear train is in gear, during the removal of the nut and washer from the output shaft.

8. Remove the speedometer driven gear and housing.

9. Remove the two locating boss bolts for the selector rear spool and remove the selector boss.

10. Remove the retaining bolts and remove the rear extension housing from the transmission case.

11. Remove the oil pump driveshaft from the countergear assembly.

12. Remove the 5th gear selector fork and bracket by the removal of the two retaining bolts.

13. Remove the circlip from the selector shaft and remove the 5th gear selector spool.

NOTE: The longer cam of the selector spool is positioned towards the bottom of the transmission.

14. Remove the circlip retaining the 5th gear synchronizer assembly to the output shaft and remove the assembly, the 5th gear (driven) and the spacer from the shaft.

15. Remove the circlip retaining the 5th gear (drive) from the countershaft. Remove the gear and spacer from the countershaft.

16. Remove the front cover and gasket from the transmission, along with the input shaft selective washer, bearing race, countershaft selector washer and the bearing race.

17. Remove the retaining bolts for the locating boss of the selector shaft front spool and withdraw the locating boss.

18. Remove the selector plug, spring and ball from the center plate.

19. Support the gearbox assembly on the

Cross section of Triumph 5-speed transmission

5th speed synchronizer assembly

center plate and remove the case assembly upward from the center plate and gear assembly.

20. Remove the input shaft and the 1st gear synchronizer cone.

21. Remove the countergear assembly from the center plate.

22. Place the center plate assembly in a vise with protected jaws or in a similar holding tool.

23. Remove the reverse lever pivot pin circlip and the pivot pin.

24. Remove the reverse lever and the slipper pad.

25. Slide the reverse shaft towards the rear and remove the reverse gear spacer, the mainshaft, the selector shaft, selector shaft fork and spool in a forward direction to clear the center plate.

26. Remove the selector shaft fork and spool.

NOTE: The shorter cam of the spool is fitted towards the bottom of the transmission.

27. Remove the retaining nut for the re-

verse gear pivot shaft and remove the pivot shaft, if replacement of the pivot shaft and/or the center plate is necessary.

28. With an appropriate bearing puller, remove the bearings from the input shaft and the race from the front cover assembly. Remove the oil seal from the front cover.

29. Remove the countershaft bearings, using a bearing puller as required.

30. Remove the following from the mainshaft;

   a. Remove the pilot bearing and spacer.

   b. Remove the 3rd/4th speed synchronizer hub and sleeve.

   c. Remove the 3rd speed gear.

   d. Remove the circlip securing the mainshaft bearing and remove the bearing, 1st gear and bushing, 1st and 2nd speed hub, sleeve and synchronizer cones and the 2nd gear.

31. Remove the oil seal, bearing, speedometer drive gear, circlip, sleeve and the oil sleeve from the rear extension housing. Remove the oil pump drive, pump cover and gears.

32. Replace the necessary parts, seals and gaskets as required.

ASSEMBLY

1. Install the bearings on the countershaft with an appropriate bearing installer.

2. Install the 2nd gear, synchronizer (baulk) ring and the 1st/2nd speed synchronizer sleeve and hub on the rear of the mainshaft.

NOTE: Assembly the 1st/2nd speed synchronizer so that the short splines on the inner member are towards the 2nd speed gear and the sleeve fork groove is towards the rear of the transmission.

3. Install the synchronizer (baulk) ring, the 1st speed gear, the selective bushing (collars of different thicknesses), the bearing and a new circlip on the mainshaft.

NOTE: End play of from 0.0002 to 0.002 inch (0.005 to 0.055 mm) should exist between the selective bushing and the assembled gear train.

4. Install the 3rd gear, synchronizer (baulk) ring and the synchronizer hub and sleeve onto the front of the mainshaft.

NOTE: The longer boss of the synchronizer hub should be towards the front of the transmission.

5. Install the spacer and the bearing to the front of the mainshaft.

6. Install the bearing race into the centerplate for the countershaft bearing.

7. Install the countergear assembly into the center plate and install the 5th gear onto the shaft. Install the spacer and a new circlip.

8. Install the mainshaft bearing race into the center plate. Place the center plate into a vise with soft jaws or into a similar holding tool.

9. Assemble the selector shaft with the 1st/2nd and 3rd/4th forks and spool and place the assembly onto the mainshaft in their respective synchronizer sleeves.

10. Install the mainshaft and selector shaft

assembly into the center plate. Install the spacer, the 5th gear, the synchronizer (baulk) ring, the synchronizer hub and sleeve, end plate, the selective spacer and a new circlip.

NOTE: The end play for the 5th gear should be from 0.0002 to 0.002 inch (0.005 to 0.055 mm).

11. Install the reverse gear, with the lip for the slipper pad to the front of the transmission, the front and rear spacers and the reverse shaft.

12. Install the reverse lever, slipper pad, pivot pin and circlip.

13. Remove the center plate assembly from the holding vise or other tool and set the assembly in an upright position with the front of the mainshaft up.

14. Install the centerplate gasket. Install the external bearing and the internal bearing race onto the input shaft.

15. Install the input shaft into the transmission case.

16. Carefully slide the transmission case and input shaft over the gear assembly. Be sure that the center plate dowels and the selector shaft are both engaged in their respective locations.

17. Install the countershaft and input shaft bearing races in place.

18. Evenly draw the transmission case into position with seven bolts and *flat* washers, to avoid damage to the rear face of the center plate.

19. Install a countershaft spacer of a thickness of 0.040 inch (1.02 mm) on the countershaft bearing race and install the front cover and gasket. Secure the cover with bolts.

20. Check the end play of the countershaft with a dial indicator gauge. The required end play is 0.0002 to 0.002 inch (0.005 to 0.050 mm).

21. Remove the front cover and the provisional spacer. The spacer thickness required is the provisional spacer thickness plus the end play obtained, minus 0.002 inch (0.055 mm).

22. Select the correct spacer and reinstall the front cover and retaining bolts. Recheck the countershaft end play to be certain it is correct.

23. Place a ball bearing into the center of the input shaft and mount a dial indicator with the stylus resting on the bearing. Zero the gauge.

24. Check the mainshaft and output shaft end play combined by lifting the rear of the mainshaft until all play is measured. Total should be 0.0002 to 0.002 inch (0.005 to 0.055 mm).

NOTE: Care must be exercised when checking end play that only the end play is measured and not side play.

25. When the end play measurement is taken, the selective washer can be determined as follows; End play measurement minus 0.002 inch (0.055 mm). Remove the front cover and install the spacer, reinstall the cover and recheck the mainshaft and input shaft endplay. Remove the front cover again.

26. Install the front seal in the front cover and lubricate the seal lips. Protect the seal lips from the input shaft splines and reinstall the front cover and bolt into place.

27. Place the gearbox assembly on a flat surface and remove the seven bolts and flat washers from the center plate to the transmission case.

28. Install the 5th gear spool and circlip to the selector shaft.

NOTE: The longer cam of the spool is fitted towards the bottom of the transmission.

29. Install the 5th gear selector fork and bracket. Renew the selector shaft O-ring in the rear cover and install the oil ring bushing.

30. Install the rear center plate gasket in place and install the oil pump driveshaft in place on the countershaft.

31. Install the oil pump gears and the cover in place on the rear extension housing.

32. Install the rear extension housing over the output shaft and make sure the oil pump driveshaft engages the oil pump gears.

33. Install the selector shaft ball, spring and plug to the center plate.

34. Install the spool locating bosses (2) to the 1st/2nd spool and the 5th gear spool. Install the speedometer drive gear to engage the mainshaft flats.

35. Install the bell housing with the clutch release bearing and operating lever, with the pivot bolt in place.

36. Install the shifting mechanism to the transmission.

37. Install the proper lubrication to the level and secure the fill plug.

TYPE 30

4 Speed Transmission Triumph

DISASSEMBLY

1. Remove the transmission.
2. Remove the bellhousing and clutch lever.
3. Take out the top cover retaining bolts.
4. Lift off the top cover and extension and the joint washer.
5. Unscrew the output flange nut and remove the washer.
6. Withdraw the output flange.
7. Unscrew the bolts retaining the rear extension to the case.
8. Remove the rear extension and joint washer.
9. Unscrew the retaining bolt, for the reverse idler spindle.
10. Withdraw the reverse idler spindle and spacer.
11. Insert the needle-roller retaining tube and remove the layshaft spindle to the rear. Allow the layshaft cluster to drop to the bottom of the transmission.
12. Remove the constant pinion assembly.
13. Remove the top gear baulk ring.

14. Remove the circlip retaining the speedometer drive gear.
15. Remove the speedometer drive gear and ball.
16. Remove the snap-ring from the mainshaft ballrace.
17. Remove the circlip from the mainshaft ballrace.
18. Withdraw the ballrace using special tools S4221A and S4221A—19/1.
19. Tilt the mainshaft and remove it from the transmission.
20. Remove the 3rd/top synchro unit.
21. Remove the 3rd gear baulk ring.
22. From the rear of the mainshaft; remove the thrust washer.
23. Remove the 1st speed gear.
24. Remove the 1st gear baulk ring.
25. Remove the circlip.
26. Withdraw the washer.
27. Remove the 3rd speed gear and bushing.
28. Remove the thrust washer.
29. Remove the 2nd speed gear and bushing.
30. Remove the 2nd gear baulk ring.
31. Remove the thrust washer.
32. Remove the 1st/2nd synchro unit.
33. Remove the split collars.
34. Lift out the jackshaft cluster.
35. Take out the jackshaft thrust washer.
36. Remove the reverse idler gear.
37. Unscrew the nut retaining the reverse actuator.
38. Remove the reverse actuator and pivot pin.

ASSEMBLY

1. Screw the pivot pin into the reverse actuator until one full thread protrudes through the lever boss.
2. Install the actuator and pivot pin into the gear casing.
3. Install the plain washer and tighten the nut.
4. Smear the front face of the jackshaft front thrust washer with grease and stick it in position in the gear casing. Insert one end of the jackshaft spindle through the casing to centralize the washer.
5. Lower the jackshaft cluster assembly into the transmission.
6. Install the rear thrust washer in position.
7. Insert the jackshaft spindle and eject the needle-roller retaining tube.
8. Measure the jackshaft cluster end-play. Adjust the layshaft end-float to 0.007 to 0.013 in. (0.18 to 0.33 mm), by selective use of thrust washers.
9. Insert the needle-roller retaining tube, eject the layshaft spindle and allow the cluster to drop to the bottom of the transmission.
10. Install the split collars to the mainshaft.
11. Slide the 1st/2nd synchro unit onto the shaft.
12. Reinstall the thrust washer.
13. Fit the 2nd gear baulk ring.
14. Check the end-play of the second gear on the bushing, which if correct will be 0.002 to 0.006 in. (0.0508 to 0.1524 mm). Reduce the length of the bushing to reduce the end-play.

13. Mainshaft bearing circlip
14. Mainshaft bearing snap-ring
16. Mainshaft bearing

18. Countergear cluster
19. Reverse shift fork

Triumph manual transmission—typical

TYPE 31

4 Speed Transmission Triumph

DISASSEMBLY

1. Disassemble the top cover. Remove the bolts, washers, top cover, and paper gasket. Remove the nut, cross pin, cover, and withdraw the gear shift lever assembly from the top cover. With the cover inverted, remove the plugs, spacer, springs, plunger, and balls. Detach the peg bolts. With the selector shafts in the neutral position, withdraw the 3rd/4th gear selector shaft, being careful to remove the interlock plunger and balls as they are released. Remove the 3rd/4th selector fork and spacer tube from the top cover. Repeat the preceding operation for the 1st/2nd and reverse gear selector shifts. Remove the retaining screws and take out the retaining plate. Remove the sealing rings from their recesses. If necessary, remove the peg bolts and remove the selectors from their shafts.

2. Disassemble the front cover. Remove the tapered bolt, bolt, and spring washer. Withdraw the cross-shaft along with the release spring, release bearing, sleeve and fork. Remove the retaining bolts and remove the front cover, bolts, and plate.

3. Disassemble the rear extension. Remove the peg bolt and withdraw the speedometer drive gear assembly. Remove the cotter pin, slotted nut, and withdraw the flange. Remove the retaining bolts and detach the rear extension, using an extractor.

4. Remove the countershaft and reverse pinion shaft by removing the retaining screw and plate.

5. Withdraw the input shaft assembly from the transmission.

6. Remove the circlips, spacer washer, and withdraw the bearing.

7. Detach the disc and, if necessary, remove the needle roller bearing.

8. Remove the circlip, spacer washer, and circlip, and remove the mainshaft rear bearing.

9. After maneuvering the mainshaft assembly through the transmission top cover opening, lift out the countershaft assembly, thrust washers, and reverse gear.

10. Remove the countershaft gears from the hub and, if necessary, remove the needle roller assemblies from the hub bore.

11. Remove the circlip by driving a special tool beneath the circlip and then levering the 3rd gear forward to remove the circlip from its groove.

12. Remove all mainshaft components and remove the 1st/2nd and 3rd/4th synchronizer inner hubs from the outer sleeves (being careful not to catch the springs and balls).

ASSEMBLY

1. Install the reverse gear in the transmission, with the selector groove to the rear.

---

15. Install the second gear bushing to the shaft.
16. Reinstall the thrust washer.
17. Check the end-play of the 3rd gear on the bushing, which if correct will be 0.002 to 0.006 in.
18. Install the 3rd gear bushing to the shaft.
19. Install the washer.
20. Secure the assembly using a discarded half circlip.
21. Measure the end-play of the bushing on the mainshaft and adjust by selective use of thrust washers until an end-play of 0.000 to 0.006 in. is obtained. Dismantle the mainshaft.
22. Install the split collars to the mainshaft.
23. Install the 1st speed gear.
24. Install the thrust washer.
25. Install a discarded bearing inner race to spacer 0.784 to 0.750 in. long.
26. Measure the thickness of the circlip washer and assemble to the shaft.
27. Install a discarded half circlip.
28. Measure the 1st gear end-play and determine the thickness of the circlip washer required to provide an end-play of 0.000 to 0.002 in.
29. Dismantle the mainshaft. Assemble components to the mainshaft as follows:
First/second synchro unit
Second gear baulk ring
Thrust washer
Second speed gear and bushing
Thrust washer
Third speed gear and bushing
Washer
Circlip, offset outermost
Split collars
First gear baulk ring
First speed gear
Third/top synchro unit
30. Position the reverse idler gear in the casing.

31. Place the mainshaft assembly in the transmission.
32. Install the abutment plate on the case and mount in a vise.
33. Install the thrust washer over the mainshaft.
34. Assemble the snap-ring to the ball race.
35. Place the ball race over the mainshaft and drive into position.
36. Install the circlip washer selected. (See Step 28.)
37. Install a new circlip.
38. Install the speedometer drive gear, ball and circlip.
39. Remove the transmission from the vise and take off the abutment plate.
40. Place the top gear baulk ring in the 3rd/top synchro unit.
41. Install the constant pinion assembly using Tool No. S314/1 and adapter S4221A—19/3.
42. Invert the transmission and align the jackshaft cluster and thrust washer.
43. Insert the jackshaft spindle from the gear and remove the needle-roller retaining tube.
44. Position the reverse idler gear and fit the spindle and spacer. Install the locating bolt.
45. Locate the washer on the end of the mainshaft.
46. Refit the rear extension assembly and a new joint washer.
47. Install the bolts and washers.
48. Replace the drive flange.
49. Install and tighten the nut and washer and secure the cotter pin.
50. Refit the bellhousing assembly and a new joint washer. Install the clutch lever.
51. Install and tighten the bottom bolt and copper washer.
52. Select 1st gear on the top cover and the transmission.
53. Install the top cover and a new washer.

2. Install the reverse gear shaft, securing it with string to prevent it from sliding into the transmission.

3. Use a stepped drift to drive a new needle roller bearing (with lettered face outward) into each end of the countershaft hub.

4. Install the gears, spacer, and gear to the countershaft hub.

5. Using grease to retain the countershaft thrust washers, install the washers into the transmission and lower the gear cluster into position. With the countershaft temporarily installed, measure the cluster gear end-play, which should be 0.007-0.012 in. End clearance may be adjusted to within this range through the use of thrust washers of larger or smaller thickness. Remove the countershaft and drop the gear cluster to the bottom of the transmission case.

6. Assemble the synchronizer springs, balls and shims to the 3rd/4th synchronizer hub. Install the outer sleeve. Repeat the preceding operations with the 1st/2nd synchronizer unit. Check the axial release loads. The points of release should be as follows:

3rd/4th: 19/21 lbs.
1st/2nd: 25/27 lbs.

If the actual release loads observed are greater or less than those specified above, the correct loading may be achieved by adjusting the number of shims beneath each synchronizer spring.

7. Using a straightedge and a feeler gauge, measure the end clearance of each mainshaft gear on its bushing. The end clear-

ance measured should be 0.004-0.006 in., and may be increased by installing a new bushing and decreased by reducing bushing length. In the preceding adjustments, take care, as reduction of bushing length will cause the end clearance of the bushings on the mainshaft to increase.

8. Install the thrust washer, bushings and thrust washer to the mainshaft, secure the assembly and measure the total end clearance of the bushings and thrust washers on the mainshaft. This measurement should be 0.003-0.009 in. (0.08-0.23 mm), and may be adjusted by using thrust washers available.

9. Install the thrust washer, bushing, and thrust washer to the mainshaft.

10. Using a special tool, assemble the race into position and install the washer and circlip. The race should be driven toward the rear to ensure that it is firmly against the circlip.

11. Measure the 1st gear end clearance by gauging the distance between the washer and bushing. The end clearance should be 0.003-0.009 in. and is adjustable by use of the various thrust washers (Step 8).

12. Prior to final assembly, all components should be removed from the mainshaft.

13. Assemble the mainshaft as follows. With the components placed in their proper relative positions, install them in the following order: thrust washer, gear and bushing, gear and bushing, thrust washer, a new circlip, 3rd/4th synchronizer unit with baulk ring at each side. Install a baulk ring to each side of

the 1st/2nd synchronizer unit, slide the unit over the rear of the mainshaft and onto the larger splines. Install the washer, gear and bushing, and washer to the rear of the mainshaft.

14. Pass the rear of the mainshaft through the rear bearing housing and position the shaft.

15. With the mainshaft in position, a special tool is installed in place of the front cover. This tool consists of a plate that holds the front of the mainshaft in position.

16. Install the circlip to the bearing and drive the bearing into position. Install the washer and cirlip.

17. Tap the rear of the mainshaft with a soft-headed mallet to take up the clearance between the circlip, washer, and bearing.

18. Install the disc, bearing (with circlip groove to the front), washer, and circlip to the input shaft. If necessary, a new bearing should be installed to the bore of the input shaft, with the lettered face of the bearing facing outwards.

19. Install the circlip to the bearing and install the assembly.

20. Install the front cover as follows. With the lip of the seal toward the gears, use a special tool to drive a new seal into the front cover.

21. With a seal protector protecting the oil seal, install the gasket and cover and secure with the retaining washers and bolts.

22. With a tapered pilot tool inserted to align the countershaft gears and thrust

1. Thrust washer
2. Bushing—1st speed gear
3. 1st speed gear
4. Thrust washer
5. 1st speed synchro cup
6. 1st/2nd speed synchro hub
7. Synchro ball
8. Spring
9. Reverse mainshaft gear and synchro outer sleeve
10. 2nd speed synchro cup
11. Thrust washer
12. 2nd speed gear
13. Bushing—2nd speed gear
14. Bushing—3rd speed gear
15. 3rd speed gear
16. Thrust washer
17. Circlip
18. 3rd speed synchro cup
19. Synchro ball
20. Spring
21. 3rd/top synchro hub
22. Synchro sleeve
23. Top gear synchro cup
24. Circlip
25. Spacer washer
26. Circlip
27. Ball race
28. Oil deflector plate
29. Input shaft
30. Needle roller bearing
31. Mainshaft

32. Ball race
33. Circlip
34. Spacer washer
36. Spacer washer
37. Rear ball race
38. Flange
39. Plain washer
40. Slotted nut
41. Cotter pin
42. Rear thrust washer

43. Needle roller bearing
44. Countershaft hub
45. 2nd speed countershaft gear
46. 3rd speed countershaft gear
47. Spacer piece
48. Countershaft gear
49. Needle roller bearing
50. Front thrust washer

51. Countershaft
52. Reverse gear shaft
53. Pivot stud
54. Nyloc nut and washer
55. Reverse gear operating lever
56. Reverse gear
57. Reverse gear bushing
58. Locating plate
59. Screw

TR-6 transmission components

washers, insert the countershaft, pushing out the pilot tool.

23. With the ends of the countershaft and reverse gear shafts engaged at the retaining plate, secure with the Phillips head screw.

24. Install and secure the countershaft cover gasket and cover plate.

25. Assemble the rear extension as follows. Install a new gasket and the rear extension to the transmission and secure with the retaining bolts.

26. Install a spacer washer to the mainshaft and drive the extension ball bearing into position. With its sealing face forward, install a new oil seal.

27. With the driving flange positioned on the mainshaft, install the washer and slotted nut.

28. Install the speedometer drive gear assembly, and secure with a retaining bolt.

29. Reassemble the top cover. Install the selectors to their shafts and secure with the retaining bolts.

30. Install the new O-rings to the recesses in the rear of the top cover and install the retaining plate and secure bolts.

31. With the interlock plunger positioned in the 3rd/4th selector shaft, insert the shaft into the top cover.

32. Install the selector fork, spacer tube, and retaining bolt.

33. Install the interlock ball between the bores of the reverse and 3rd/4th selector shafts, using grease to retain the ball. Slide the reverse selector shaft into the top cover and engage it with the reverse selector fork and spacer.

34. Install the retaining bolt to the selector fork.

35. With the reverse and 3rd/4th selector shafts in the neutral position, install the other interlock ball, using grease to retain it.

36. Install the 1st/2nd selector shaft into the top cover, inserting the shaft through the 1st/2nd selector fork and spacer tube.

37. Install the balls and long springs to the 1st/2nd and 3rd/4th selector shaft detents.

38. The springs may be retained by screwing the plugs so that they are flush with the machined lower face of the top cover.

NOTE: From transmission number CT.9899, the 3rd/4th selector shaft ball and long spring have been replaced by a plunger and short spring identical to those of the reverse selector shaft.

39. Install the plunger, short spring, and shim to the reverse selector shaft detent, and use the plug to retain the assembly.

40. Use a spring balance to check the selector shaft release loads. If necessary, the spring loads may be adjusted by grinding the end of the spring (to reduce the release load) or by installing shims between the spring and plunger (to increase the load).

41. Replace the spring and plunger to the gearshift lever.

42. Assemble the gearshift lever, spring and plate to the top cover, pressing the plunger with a screwdriver as the end of the gearshift lever engages the selectors.

43. Retain the gearshift lever with the cap, cross pin, and nut.

44. Install a new gasket and replace the top cover assembly to the transmission. Be sure

that the reverse selector fork engages the actuating lever. Install the strap beneath the head of the rear mounting bolt.

NOTE: With the modified gearshift lever installed in TR-6 models, the position of the gearshift lever is adjusted as follows: With the gearshift lever positioned into the 1st and 2nd gate, screw the locating pin clockwise until it just causes the gearshift lever to move, then turn the locating pin one-half turn in the counterclockwise direction and tighten the locknut. Move the gearshift lever into the reverse gate position and adjust the other locating pin in the same manner.

TYPE 32

4 and 5 Speed Transmissions— Models K40, K50, K51 Toyota

DISASSEMBLY

1. Secure the transmission and drain the lubricant from the unit.

2. Remove the clutch release bearing, fork, boot and spring.

3. Remove the countershaft cover from the front of the transmission. (K40).

4. Remove the front bearing retainer and bolts. (K40).

5. Remove the shifting locking ball and spring retainer on top of the transmission case. (K40).

6. Remove the back-up light switch.

7. Remove the speedometer driven gear assembly.

8. Remove the restricting pins from the shift control opening and the shift lever retainer.

9. Remove the rear extension housing bolts and the extension housing. Disengage the selector shaft from the shift fork shafts by moving the housing towards the bottom of the case.

10. Locate and retain the countergear thrust washer when the extension housing is removed. (K50).

11. Remove the lower pan from the case assembly.

Case Disassembly: K40

1. Remove the lockbolt and remove the reverse idler gear and shaft.

2. Remove the countershaft by driving it from the front to the rear.

3. Remove the countergear, bearings and thrust washers from the case.

4. Shift the number one shift fork shaft to the neutral position and using a pin punch, remove the slotted spring pins from the shift forks and shafts.

5. Set each fork shaft to the neutral position and pull the shaft from the case.

6. Shift the number one clutch hub sleeve into 2nd gear and remove the shift fork from inside the case.

7. Arrange the three interlock pins and slotted spring pins and lay aside for the assembly.

8. Remove the output shaft from the rear of the transmission with the gear intact. Remove the input shaft and bearing.

9. Remove the snap-rings at the speedometer drive gear and remove the gear from the shaft.

10. Release the staked parts of the locknut on the mainshaft and remove the nut from the shaft with a holding tool and special wrench.

11. Remove the rear bearing and housing from the mainshaft.

12. Remove the 1st gear, bushing, needle bearing and locking ball from the shaft.

13. Remove the synchronizer (baulk) ring, 1st/2nd clutch hub and sleeve, synchronizer (baulk) ring and the 2nd speed gear from the shaft.

14. Remove the snap-ring from the front of the shaft and remove the 3rd/4th synchronizer assembly and the 3rd speed gear, with spacer.

Case Disassembly: K50

1. Remove the snap-rings and speedometer drive gear from the output or mainshaft.

2. Remove the 5th gearshift arm bracket, arm and the number 3 shift fork.

3. Remove the snap-ring and the shifting key retainer from the mainshaft.

4. Remove the number three clutch hub and sleeve, the synchronizer (baulk) ring and the 5th gear with its needle roller bearing.

5. Remove the snap-ring from the countergear and remove the counter 5th gear, the countergear rear bearing and sleeve. The sleeve is retained with a snap-ring.

6. Remove the locking bolt and pull the reverse idler shaft from the case. Remove the reverse idler gear.

7. Remove the countergear, thrust washer and the front bearing from the case as a unit.

8. Remove the locking balls and springs cover from the top of the transmission case. Remove the springs and balls.

9. Using a pin punch, drive the slotted spring pins from the forks and shafts.

10. Place each shaft into the neutral position and remove from the case.

11. Arrange the slotted spring pins, the interlock pins, and locking ball for easier assembly.

12. Shift the number one clutch into 2nd gear and remove the shift fork from inside the case.

13. Remove the input shaft and front bearing retainer from the front of the case.

14. Secure the pilot bearing rollers and the 4th speed synchronizer (baulk) ring.

15. Spread the expanding snap-ring on the rear bearing and remove the output shaft assembly from the front of the transmission case.

16. Disassemble the mainshaft by removing the rear snap-ring and removing the rear bearing, bushing, needle roller bearing and locating ball. Continue by removing the 1st gear, synchronizer (baulk) ring, number one

A B C D E F G H I J K E L M N O P Q R S T U V W X Y Z AA AB AC AD AE AF

AG AH AI   AJ AK AL AM   AN AO AG

(a)—Shaft snap-ring
(b)—Bearing (transmission front)
(c)—Input shaft
(d)—Needle roller bearing
(e)—Synchronizer ring No. 3
(f)—Transmission hub sleeve
(g)—Shaft snap-ring
(h)—Transmission clutch hub No. 2
(i)—Clutch hub spacer
(j)—Synchromesh shifting key spring No. 2
(k)—Synchromesh shifting key No. 2
(l)—Side gear
(m)—Second gear
(n)—Synchronizer ring No. 2

(o)—Reverse gear
(p)—Transmission clutch hub No. 1
(q)—Synchromesh shifting key spring No. 1
(r)—Synchromesh shifting key No. 1
(s)—Synchronizer ring No. 1
(t)—First gear
(u)—Ball
(v)—First gear bushing
(w)—Bearing (transmission rear)
(x)—Shaft snap-ring
(y)—Shim
(z)—Nut
(aa)—Woodruff key
(ab)—Speedometer drive gear

(ac)—Shaft snap-ring
(ad)—Slotted split pin
(ae)—Output shaft rear retainer
(af)—Output shaft
(ag)—Countergear thrust washer (case side)
(ah)—Needle roller bearing
(ai)—Countergear
(aj)—Shaft retaining bolt
(ak)—Reverse idler gear shaft
(al)—Reverse idler gear
(am)—Spacer
(an)—Counter shaft
(ao)—Countergear thrust washer (gear side)

Corolla 1200 transmission components

clutch hub, sleeve, synchronizer (baulk) ring and the second gear.

17. Remove the front snap-ring, the number two clutch hub, sleeve, synchronizer (baulk) ring and the second gear.

NOTE: During the disassembly and assembly of the K40 and K50 transmissions, the need to press bearings or gears from and back onto the shafts will exist. Govern the disassembly and assembly procedures accordingly.

INSPECTION

Inspect the gears, shafts, bearings and other internal components and replace or repair the necessary parts. Install new seals and gaskets during the reassembly.

ASSEMBLY

Case Assembly K40

1. Place the mainshaft in an upright position with the rear of the shaft pointing up. Place the 2nd speed gear and the synchronizer (baulk) ring onto the shaft, followed by the number one clutch hub and sleeve. Ring identification: Narrow insert gap for 1st gear and wide insert gap for 2nd gear.

2. Install the second synchronizer (baulk) ring, the 1st gear, the locking ball, the needle roller bearing and the bushing.

3. Install the rear bearing and housing onto the shaft and retain it with a washer and locknut. Tighten the locknut to a torque of 33 to 72 ft/lbs (4.5 to 10.0 Kg-m) with the special wrench and the shaft holding tool. Stake the nut to the shaft.

4. Measure the thrust clearance of the 1st and 2nd speed gears:

1st gear—0.0071 to 0.0110 inch (0.18 to 0.28 mm)

2nd gear—0.0039 to 0.0098 inch (0.10 to 0.25 mm)

5. Install the 3rd gear on the front of the shaft. Line up the shifting key inserts with the insert slots in the synchronizer (baulk) ring and install the number two clutch hub and sleeve.

6. Push the number two clutch hub inward as far as it will go and measure the 3rd gear thrust clearance:

3rd gear—0.0020 to 0.0079 inch (0.05 to 0.20 mm)

Limit—0.0018 inch (0.30 mm)

7. When the 3rd gear thrust clearance is not within specifications, select a spacer from the following list;

Thickness	
mm	(in.)
4.30-4.35	(0.1693-0.1713)
4.35-4.40	(0.1713-0.1732)
4.40-4.45	(0.1732-0.1752)

8. Select a snap-ring that will control the clearance to zero between the snap-ring and the clutch hub, from the following list:

Thickness	
mm	(in.)
2.05-2.10	(0.0807-0.0827)
2.10-2.15	(0.0827-0.0846)
2.15-2.20	(0.0846-0.0866)
2.20-2.25	(0.0866-0.0886)
2.25-2.30	(0.0886-0.0906)
2.30-2.35	(0.0906-0.0925)
2.35-2.40	(0.0925-0.0945)
2.40-2.45	(0.0945-0.0965)

9. Install the snap-ring in place on the mainshaft.

10. If not previously done, install the front

bearing on the input shaft. Install the needle roller bearings into the bore of the mainshaft and hold in place with a grease.

11. Install the input shaft into the transmission case and select a front bearing retainer gasket in the following manner.

    a. If the bearing face extends outside of the case machined surface, use a bearing retainer gasket of 0.020 inch (0.5 mm) in thickness.

    b. If the bearing face is below the case machined surface, use a bearing retainer gasket of 0.012 inch (0.3 mm) in thickness.

12. Lubricate the front bearing retainer oil seal and install the retainer to the case. Torque the bolts 11 to 15 ft/lbs (1.5 to 2.2 Kg-m).

13. Set the transmission case upright with the input shaft on the bottom. Be sure the needle bearings remain in their proper position in the input shaft bore.

14. Carefully insert the mainshaft assembly into the transmission case and align the shifting key inserts with the slots in the synchronizer (baulk) ring.

15. Align the pin on the rear bearing housing with the groove in the transmission case. Be sure the mainshaft and the input shaft rotate freely.

16. Temporarily, install a holding tool over the rear bearing retainer so that the gear train is held securely. Place the transmission with the bottom up.

17. Shift the synchronizer assembly sleeve into the 2nd speed position. Install the reverse shift fork, the 1st/2nd shift fork and the 3rd/4th shift fork in their respective sleeve grooves.

18. Insert the shift shafts into the transmission case and through their respective shifting forks. Place the center shaft in the neutral position, along with the reverse shifting shaft in the neutral position.

19. Install the 1st-2nd shifting shaft to the point where the shaft dummy hole and the case hole line up.

20. Insert a probe into the case hole and be sure the outer two shaft holes line up and the probe touches the inner shaft.

21. Install the interlock pins and push the inner shaft to the neutral position. Move the center shift shaft to the third speed position. The other shafts should not move.

22. Align the forks to the holes in the shafts and install the slotted spring pins.

23. Coat the countergear thrust washers with a grease and place them on the inner walls of the transmission case. Insert the countershaft from the rear of the case until the shaft end is even with the rear thrust washer.

24. Carefully install the countergear and push the countershaft into the transmission case and the countergear bearings. Measure the thrust clearance and correct by selecting a proper sized thrust washer. The thrust clearance should be 0.0020 to 0.0098 inch (0.05 to 0.25 mm).

25. Install the reverse idler gear and shaft. An adjustment can be made to prevent the gear from contacting the case surface. A spacer can be installed between the gear and the case. A clearance of 0.039 to 0.079 inch (1.0 to 2.0 mm) should exist between the teeth of the reverse gear and the teeth of the countergear. A pivot screw and locknut are pro-

Thickness	
mm	(in.)
1.30-1.35	(0.0512-0.0531)
1.40-1.45	(0.0551-0.0571)
1.50-1.55	(0.0591-0.0610)
1.60-1.65	(0.0630-0.0650)

vided on the case to help in the adjustment of the reverse gear clearance.

26. Set the transmission upright with the output shaft horizontal position and the pan opening down.

27. Install the three balls and springs into the holes in the case top and install the locking ball and spring cover.

28. Install the countergear shaft cover on the front of the transmission case.

29. Shift the fork shafts and be sure the shifting of the gear sleeves, forks and linkage is proper.

Case Assembly: K50

1. Position the mainshaft with the rear of the shaft pointing upward. Install the 2nd speed gear and the synchronizer (baulk) ring onto the shaft, followed by the number one clutch hub and sleeve.

Ring identification: Narrow insert gap for 1st gear and the wide insert gap for the 2nd gear.

2. Install the second synchronizer (baulk) ring, the 1st gear, the locking ball, the needle roller bearing and the bushing.

3. Install the rear bearing and select a selective snap-ring that will allow zero thrust clearance. The snap-ring thicknesses are as follows:

Thickness	
mm	(in.)
2.05-2.10	(0.0807-0.0827)
2.10-2.15	(0.0827-0.0846)
2.15-2.20	(0.0846-0.0866)
2.20-2.25	(0.0866-0.0886)
2.25-2.30	(0.0886-0.0906)
2.30-2.35	(0.0906-0.0925)
2.35-2.40	(0.0925-0.0945)
2.40-2.45	(0.0945-0.0965)
2.45-2.50	(0.0965-0.0984)
2.50-2.55	(0.0984-0.1004)

Install the snap-ring on the mainshaft in its groove.

4. Check the thrust clearances of the 1st and 2nd gears. The clearances should be as follows:

    1st gear—0.0071 to 0.0110 inch (0.18 to 0.28 mm)

    2nd gear—0.0039 to 0.0098 inch (0.10 to 0.25 mm)

    Limit—0.0118 inch (0.30 mm)

5. Install the 3rd gear onto the front of the shaft and install the synchronizer hub and sleeve, along with the inner synchronizer (baulk) ring in place on the gear unit.

6. Push inward on the number two clutch hub and measure the 3rd gear thrust clearance. The clearance should be as follows:

    3rd gear—0.0020 to 0.0079 inch (0.05 to 0.20 mm)

    Limit—0.0118 inch (0.30 mm)

Install one of the following spacers as required:

Thickness	
mm	(in.)
4.30-4.35	(0.1693-0.1713)
4.35-4.40	(0.1713-0.1732)
4.40-4.45	(0.1732-0.1752)

7. Select a snap-ring of proper thickness to provide zero clearance between the snap-ring and the clutch hub, and install on the shaft. A list of available snap-rings are as follows:

Thickness	
mm	(in.)
2.05-2.10	(0.0807-0.0827)
2.10-2.15	(0.0827-0.0846)
2.15-2.20	(0.0846-0.0866)
2.20-2.25	(0.0866-0.0886)
2.25-2.30	(0.0886-0.0906)
2.30-2.35	(0.0906-0.0925)
2.35-2.40	(0.0925-0.0945)
2.40-2.45	(0.0945-0.0965)

8. Install the mainshaft assembly into the transmission case from the front. Stand the case assembly upright and pull the mainshaft assembly upward, seating the bearing into the case bore, while having the bearing snap-ring expanded in the case. Secure the bearing in the case with the snap-ring.

9. Install the roller bearing and housing on the input shaft, if not previously done. Install the needle bearings in the bore of the input shaft, holding them in place with grease. Place the synchronizer (baulk) ring on the input shaft and install the shaft assembly into the front of the case. Align the shifting key insert slots properly during the installation.

10. Install the front bearing retainer bolts and torque to 11 to 15 ft/lb.

11. Shift the transmission gear train into the 2nd gear. Install the shift forks in their respective sleeve grooves.

12. Install the reverse shift shaft and fork. Install the interlock ball (coated with grease) into the hole in the reverse shift fork. Push it into position into the shaft groove.

13. Position the three shafts into their respective bores in the transmission case and position in the neutral mode, having entered the bores of the shifting forks. Move the 1st/2nd speed shaft until the dummy hole on the shaft is lined up with the case hole. Insert a probe in the hole to be sure the shafts are aligned.

14. Install the grease coated interlock pins and push them into position with a probe. Move the three fork shafts in the neutral position. Shift the number two or center shaft into the 3rd gear position and check that the remaining shafts do not move.

15. Align the pin holes in the shift forks and shift fork shafts and secure with the slotted spring pins.

16. Assemble the countergear and shaft with the thrust washer oil groove facing the countergear side, and install into the transmission case. Install the rear bearing and outer race into position in the case. The outer snap-ring must be expanded during this operation.

17. Install the reverse idler gear and shaft. Have the shift arm engaged with the hub of the reverse idler gear.

18. Install the 5th gear on the countershaft with the stepped side of the gear hub facing the case. Secure the gear to the shaft with a snap-ring of a selected size to provide zero clearance, as taken from the following list:

Thickness	
mm	(in.)
2.25-2.35	(0.0886-0.0925)
2.35-2.45	(0.0925-0.0965)
2.45-2.55	(0.0965-0.1004)

19. Select a countergear thrust washer by installing a thrust washer in place on the countergear and installing the rear extension housing and torquing the retaining bolts 22 to 32 ft/lbs (3.0 to 4.5 Kg-m) and measuring the thrust clearance of the countergear to case.

NOTE: Position the thrust washer with the oil groove facing the 5th gear.

20. The thrust clearance should be 0.0031 to 0.0157 inch (0.08 to 0.40 mm). Select the proper sized thrust washer from the following list:

Thickness	
mm	(in.)
1.71-1.81	(0.0673-0.0713)
1.83-1.93	(0.0720-0.0760)
1.95-2.05	(0.0768-0.0807)

21. Remove the extension housing and install the proper thrust washer in place on the counter 5th gear.

22. Align the shifting key insert slots and install the 5th gear and the 5th synchronizer assembly onto the output shaft. Tap the output shaft to the front of the transmission and with a snap-ring retainer pressed against the hub, select a snap-ring to provide a thrust clearance of 0.008 to 0.012 inch (0.2 to 0.3 mm) between the 5th gear hub and the rear bearing face.

23. Install the snap-ring and recheck the thrust clearance. Push up on the reverse idler gear until the fork shaft is in a position with the groove above the case.

24. Install the 5th gearshift arm bracket in place on the rear of the case and engage the bracket in the reverse shaft fork. Position the fork claw in the hub sleeve groove and the

Thickness	
mm	(in.)
2.05-2.10	(0.0807-0.0827)
2.10-2.15	(0.0827-0.0846)
2.15-2.20	(0.0846-0.0866)
2.20-2.25	(0.0866-0.0886)
2.25-2.30	(0.0886-0.0906)
2.30-2.35	(0.0906-0.0925)
2.35-2.40	(0.0925-0.0945)
2.40-2.45	(0.0945-0.0965)
2.45-2.50	(0.0965-0.0984)
2.50-2.55	(0.0984-0.1004)
2.55-2.60	(0.1004-0.1024)
2.60-2.65	(0.1024-0.1043)
2.65-2.70	(0.1043-0.1063)
2.70-2.75	(0.1063-0.1083)
2.75-2.80	(0.1083-0.1102)

shift arm shaft in the gearshift head 1st groove.

25. Install the three locking balls and springs in the bores of the case. Install the cover and the retaining bolts.

26. Install the inner snap-ring, the speedometer drive gear and the outer snap-ring on the mainshaft. Be sure the locking ball is placed between the gear and the shaft.

27. Adjust the reverse idler gear position so that a clearance of 0.039 to 0.079 inch (1.0 to 2.0 mm) exists between the gear teeth of the countergear and the reverse idler gear teeth by the adjustment of the pivot bolt and locknut, located on the outside of the case.

28. Adjust the 5th speed synchronizer sleeve position so that the bottom of the sleeve groove is 0.039 to 0.059 inch (1.0 to 1.5 mm) above the rear face of the counter 5th gear.

K40, K50

1. Install the thrust washer on the counter 5th gear with the oil groove towards the gear side. (K50). Install the rear gaskets.

2. Align the shifting fork shafts in the neutral position and install the rear extension housing. Engage the selector shaft to the shift fork shafts. Install the housing retaining bolts and torque to 22-32 ft/lbs.

3. Install the shift control restricting pins and torque to the following values:

K40—Black = 1st and 2nd
　　　White = Reverse
K50—Black = 1st and 2nd
　　　White = 5th and Reverse
All—27 to 31 ft/lbs (3.7 to 4.3 Kg-m)

4. Install the speedometer driven gear assembly.

5. Install the back-up light switch.

6. Install the clutch release bearing, fork, boot and spring.

7. Install the bottom cover and gasket. Fill the transmission with lubricant to its proper level.

8. Attach the shift lever and make sure the shifting of the gear train is proper.

TYPE 33

4 and 5 Speed Transmissions— Models T40, T41, T50 Toyota

DISASSEMBLY

— CAUTION —
The clutch housing, split transmission case, and extension housing are all made of aluminum.

1. Drain the oil.

2. Remove the clutch housing, bearing retainer, release bearing, and release fork.

3. Remove the speedometer shaft sleeve and driven gear.

4. Remove the extension housing.

5. Remove the back-up light switch.

6. Separate the case halves. Do not pry apart.

7. Measure gear backlash. The backlash for all gears should be 0.004-0.008 in.

8. Remove the countergear set from the right-hand half of the case.

9. Use a magnet to remove the ball from the second countergear bearing.

10. Withdraw the input and the output shafts as a unit.

11. Use a punch to drive the three slotted spring pins out of the shift forks and shift fork shafts.

NOTE: The slotted pin cannot always be fully removed from the first/second shift fork; however, the shift fork can still be withdrawn. Do not try to force the pin out, as damage to the transmission case could result.

12. Remove the case cover and the three detent balls and springs.

13. Remove the shift fork shafts in the following order:
　a. First/second shaft
　b. Pin
　c. Reverse shift fork shaft
　d. Third/fourth shaft
　e. Pin

14. Measure the thrust clearance of the reverse idler gear. The specified clearance is 0.002-0.020 in.

15. Remove the idler shaft. Remove the gear and washer.

16. Measure the thrust clearance of the gears on the output shaft.

1st, 2nd, 5th	0.006-0.010 in.
3rd	0.006-0.012 in.
Reverse	0.008-0.012 in.

5th gear is optional

17. Disassemble the components of the output shaft. Five-speed transmissions have an extra gearset and related parts.

Replace the front bearing, if it is rough or noisy. Use a drift and a press. Remove the snap-ring first.

For bearing installation, replacement snap-rings are available in a range of sizes (0.0925-0.1024 in.) to obtain *minimum* axial play between the input shaft and the bearing.

4-Speed (T40) 5-Speed (T50)

Cross section of models T 40 and T 50 transmissions

Five Speed T/M

Five Speed T/M

1. Conical spring	18. Clutch hub
2. Shaft snap-ring	19. Hub sleeve
3. Ball bearing	20. First gear assembly
4. Input shaft	21. Needle roller bearing
5. Roller	22. Ball
6. Snap-ring	23. First gear bushing
7. Shaft snap-ring	24. Ball bearing
8. Synchronizer ring	25. Reverse gear bushing
9. Shift-key spring	26. Shift-key spring*
10. Shift-key	27. Shift-key*
11. Clutch hub	28. Synchronizer ring*
12. Hub sleeve	29. Fifth gear assembly*
13. Third gear assembly	30. Needle roller bearing*
14. Second gear assembly	31. Ball*
15. Synchronizer ring	32. Fifth gear bushing*
16. Shift-key spring	33. Ball bearing*
17. Shift-key	

34. Reverse gear	51. Ball
35. Clutch hub	52. Roller bearing
36. Hub sleeve	53. Reverse countergear
37. Spacer	54. Snap-ring
38. Spacer (long)	55. Thrust washer—reverse idler gear
39. Shim	56. Reverse idler gear
40. Nut	57. Bushing
41. Shaft snap-ring	58. Reverse idler gear shaft
42. Ball	59. Shaft retaining bolt
43. Speedometer drive gear	60. Countergear*
44. Shim	61. Fifth-speed countergear*
45. Conical spring	62. Ball bearing*
46. Output shaft	63. Shim*
47. Bolt and washer	64. Nut*
48. Plate washer	
49. Ball bearing	* Five-speed transmission only
50. Countergear	

Corolla and Carina 4 and 5-speed transmission components

ASSEMBLY

1. Assemble the components of the synchronizer hubs, and the output shaft.

2. Install the rear bushing on the output shaft, being careful to install it in the proper direction.

3. Install the ball into the groove of the bushing and slide the bushing over the shaft.

4. Install the needle roller bearing, reverse gear, the ball and the reverse gear synchronizer hub.

5. Install the following items on the output shaft of the four-speed transmission, in the order indicated:
   a. Large-diameter reverse gear spacer
   b. Long spacer
   c. Shims

6. Install the following items on the output shaft of the five-speed transmission in the order indicated:
   a. Ball
   b. Fifth gear synchronizer ring
   c. Fifth gear
   d. Needle roller bearing
   e. Bushing
   f. Rear support ball bearing.

7. Install the shims and the nut on the end of the output shaft.

NOTE: If the original nut is being used, change the number of shims to alter the locking portion of the nut.

8. Check the thrust clearance of each gear.

9. Working from the rear of the output shaft, install 3rd gear, synchronizer, spacer, and 3rd/4th synchronizer hub (should face forward).

10. Select a snap-ring to obtain a thrust clearance of less than 0.002 in. for the 3rd/4th synchronizer hub.

11. Assemble the following from the rear of the output shaft:
   a. Snap-ring
   b. Key
   c. Speedometer drive gear
   d. Snap-ring

12. Check thrust clearance of gears.

13. Install the fork and shaft assembly in the transmission case.

14. Insert the straight pins in the grooves on either side of the third/fourth shift shaft.

15. Assemble the first/second gear shaft and fork.

16. Perform Step 11 for the reverse shift fork shaft.

17. Insert the three detent balls, followed by their springs.

18. Place the cover gasket on the case and install the cover.

19. Use a punch to drive a slotted spring pin into each shift fork to secure it.

20. Assemble the input and output shafts.

21. Install the shift forks into their respective grooves on the input/output shaft assembly.

22. Install the shaft assembly in the right-hand half of the transmission case, so that the snap-ring is positioned firmly against the front surface of the transmission case.

23. Apply grease to the countergear rear bearing lockball. Insert the ball into the hole in the rear bearing outer race.

24. Place the countergear assembly into the right-hand half of the transmission case. Mate the lockball with the hole in the transmission case. Place the bearing snap-ring firmly against the front surface of the transmission case.

25. Install the reverse idler gear.

26. Install the washers, so that their protrusions align with the grooves in the transmission case.

27. Install the shaft into the case and through the gears and washers.

28. Align the grooves in the idler shaft with the hole in the shaft boss. Install the retaining bolt and washer into the boss.

29. Apply a light coating of liquid sealer over the joint surfaces of the transmission case halves.

CAUTION
Do not apply sealer to the ½ in. hole for the back-up light switch.

30. Align the transmission case locating pins with their holes and assemble the halves of the case.

NOTE: There are four different bolt lengths, do not install the wrong bolt in the wrong hole.

31. Insert the ball, spring, and washer in the back-up light switch hole. Screw in the switch assembly.

32. Install the gasket and bolt the extension housing to the rear of the transmission.

33. Install the speedometer shaft sleeve and drive gear.

34. Apply grease to the conical springs. Install one spring over the input shaft bearing and the other over the countershaft bearing. Install the spacer over the countershaft bearing spring, after coating the spacer with grease.

35. Install the gasket and the clutch housing.

10. Remove the snap-rings from the input and countershaft bearings.

11. Remove the intermediate plate.

12. When removing the intermediate plate, leave all of the gears and other parts attached.

13. Remove the speedometer driven gear.

14. Punch the slotted pin out of the reverse shift arm bracket bolt and remove the bracket, complete with the shift arm.

15. Remove the reverse idler shaft stop and withdraw the idler gear and shaft assembly away from the intermediate plate.

16. Remove the output shaft rear bearing retainer.

17. Remove the screw plug and spring from each shift fork and shaft.

18. Drive the slotted interlock pins out of each shaft.

19. Remove the shift fork shafts in the following order:
   a. Reverse
   b. First/second
   c. Third/fourth

Once the shafts have been removed, slide the shift forks off them.

20. Remove the snap-ring from the output shaft rear bearing. Push the output shaft and countershaft out as an assembly, working from the rear side of the plate.

21. Separate the input shaft and the front synchronizer ring from the output shaft.

22. Remove the hub and synchronizer ring, followed by third gear.

23. Press off the rear bearing.

24. Remove the following items from the output shaft, in the order listed:
   a. First gear
   b. Roller bearing with inner race
   c. Synchronizer ring
   d. Reverse gear
   e. Clutch hub
   f. Second gear
   g. Synchronizer ring

ASSEMBLY

1. Apply a thin coating of gear oil to all rotating or sliding surfaces, prior to assembly.

2. Assemble the 3rd/4th synchronizer hub:
   a. Install key springs in the hub.
   b. Place the 3 keys in the hub slots.
   c. Install the 2nd clutch hub in the sleeve.

To maintain uniform spring pressure, keep the open end of the key springs 120° apart.

3. Assemble the synchronizer ring to third gear, and fit both of them on the output shaft.

4. Insert the third/fourth synchronizer hub on the output shaft, until it contacts the shoulder of the shaft.

5. Select a snap-ring to provide 0.002 in. axial play for the synchronizer hub and fit it onto the shaft. Snap-rings are available in a range of sizes.

6. Measure third gear thrust clearance with a feeler gauge. The clearance should be 0.004-0.010 in. Replace third gear if the clearance exceeds the limit of 0.012 in.

7. Install the synchronizer ring for second gear to the gear and install the assembly on the output shaft.

TYPE 34

4 Speed Transmission– Model W-40 Toyota

DISASSEMBLY

1. Drain the oil.

2. Remove the clutch housing, with the release fork, bearing and hub still attached.

3. Remove the back-up light switch.

4. Remove the gearshift lever retainer.

5. Rotate the shift rod housing counterclockwise (viewed from behind) and then disconnect the rod from the shift fork shafts.

6. Unbolt and remove the extension housing.

7. Drive out the slotted pin and separate the shift rod, housing and spring.

8. Remove the front bearing retainer.

9. Take off both of the front countershaft covers and the spacer.

Cross section of model W 40 transmission

hub and the groove on the inner race aligns with the locking ball.

13. Press the rear bearing onto the output shaft.

14. Measure first gear thrust clearance; it should be 0.004-0.010 in. Replace the gear if the clearance exceeds 0.012 in.

15. Select a snap-ring for the rear output shaft bearing that will provide 0.002 in. axial play for it.

16. Use a press to insert the straight pin into the intermediate plate, until it protrudes ¼-⁵/₁₆ in. from the cover front side.

17. Coat the roller bearing with grease and install it over the input shaft.

18. Apply gear oil to the front synchronizer ring on the output shaft.

19. Assemble the output shaft and the input shaft.

20. Assemble the output shaft and countergear, then fit them through the holes in the intermediate plate. Push them in until the snap-ring sticks out beyond the plate. Install the snap-ring and then push the shafts back until the snap-ring is flush with the intermediate plate.

21. Install the shaft through the reverse idler gear. Insert the end of the shaft into the end of the intermediate plate.

22. Install the spacer on the idler shaft and secure it with a snap-ring.

23. Install the idler shaft stop.

24. Install the first/second and third/fourth shift forks into the grooves on the hub sleeves, so that the longer parts of their bosses face each other.

25. Assemble the ends of the three shift fork shafts and insert them into the intermediate plate. Install the interlock pins, after coating them with grease.

26. Install the shafts through the forks and drive in the slotted spring pins to secure them.

27. Insert the lockballs, followed by their springs.

28. Install the output shaft rear bearing retainer.

NOTE: There should be zero clearance between the rear bearing snap-ring and the surface of the intermediate plate.

29. Assemble the reverse shift arm to its bracket. Install on the intermediate cover.

30. Drive the slotted mounting pin in, so that it protrudes 0.08-0.16 in. beyond the intermediate cover.

31. Shift the gears so that reverse is selected. Check the gear contact. If the gears are meshing properly, the front face of the idler gear will align with the front face of the reverse gear.

32. If necessary, adjust the gear mesh at the pivot.

NOTE: When the gears are meshing properly, the slot in the pivot should be perpendicular to the intermediate plate.

33. Tighten the pivot nut and install the lockpin. Be careful not to change gear contact.

34. Install the shift rod from the front end of the extension housing. Install the spring and housing onto the end of the shift rod.

35. Clean the gasket surfaces of the rear

8. Install the reverse gear over its clutch hub.

9. Install the reverse gear and hub on the output shaft so that they contact the shoulder.

10. Measure second gear thrust clearance; it should be between 0.004-0.010 in. Replace the gear if the clearance is more than 0.012 in.

11. Coat the locking ball with grease. Insert it, and the roller bearing inner race, on the output shaft.

12. Assemble first gear with its synchronizer ring, bearing and bearing inner race. Install them on the output shaft, so that the end of the inner race contacts the clutch

1. Ring, shaft snap
2. Bearing, radial ball
3. Ring, shaft snap
4. Shaft subassy., input
5. Bearing, needle roller
6. Ring, synchronizer, No. 2
7. Spring, synchromesh shifting key
8. Hub, transmission clutch, No. 2
9. Key, synchromesh shifting, No. 2
10. Spring, transmission hub, No. 2
11. Gear subassy., third
12. Gear subassy., second
13. Key, synchromesh shifting, No. 1
14. Hub, transmission clutch, No. 1
15. Gear, reverse
16. Ring, synchronizer, No. 1
17. Gear subassy., first
18. Bearing, needle roller
19. Race, first gear bearing inner
20. Bearing, radial ball
21. Ring, shaft snap

22. Shaft, output
23. Ball, reverse shaft restrict
24. Ring, shaft snap
25. Ring, shaft snap
26. Gear, speedometer drive
27. Cover, counter shaft, No. 1
28. Cover, counter shaft, No. 2
29. Spacer
30. Ring, shaft snap
31. Bearing, radial ball
32. Ring, shaft snap
33. Gear, counter
34. Bearing, radial ball
35. Ring, shaft snap
36. Ring, shaft snap
37. Spacer
38. Bushing, bimetal formed
39. Gear, reverse idler
40. Shaft, reverse idler
41. Stopper, reverse idler gear shaft

Exploded view of model W 40 gear train

cover and transmission case. Install the intermediate plate.

36. Install the input shaft and countergear front bearing snap-rings.

37. Install the extension housing and gasket over the intermediate cover, after cleaning both gasket mounting surfaces.

38. Screw the securing bolts through the extension housing, the intermediate cover and into the transmission case.

39. Install the reverse restrictor pin and gasket.

40. Push the countergear rearward, as far as it will go and measure the distance (E) in the illustration. Select a spacer to yield the *minimum* clearance which is closest to the measurement obtained.

41. Install the spacer and then the countershaft end covers.

42. Align the front bearing retainer gasket with the oil holes. Install the bearing retainer over the gasket.

43. Bolt the clutch housing onto the front of the transmission case.

44. Attach the shift lever retainer to the extension housing.

45. Install the speedometer driven gear.

46. Install the back-up light switch.

TYPE 35

5 Speed Transmissions— Models W50, P51, W55, W58 Toyota

DISASSEMBLY

NOTE: The Model P-51 transmission disassembly and assembly, is basically the same as the W-50 transmission, with only minor variations.

1. Drain the oil.

2. Remove the clutch housing, with the release fork, bearing and hub still attached.

3. Remove the back-up light switch.

4. Remove the gearshift lever retainer.

5. Rotate the shift rod housing counterclockwise (viewed from behind) and then disconnect the rod from the shift fork shafts.

6. Unbolt and remove the extension housing.

7. Drive out the slotted pin and separate the shift rod, housing and spring.

8. Remove the front bearing retainer.

9. Take off both of the front countershaft covers, and the spacer.

10. Remove the snap-rings from the input and countershaft bearings.

11. Remove the intermediate plate.

12. When removing the intermediate plate, leave all the gears and other parts attached.

13. Remove the speedometer driven gear.

NOTE: There are two reverse restrictor pins. The pins are located underneath plugs on the extension housing.

14. Remove the straight screw plugs from the shift forks and withdraw the springs.

15. Drive the slotted spring pins out of each shift fork.

16. Slide the gear shift fork shafts back and remove the forks.

17. Remove the speedometer drive gear snap-ring and remove the drive gear.

18. Remove the output shaft bearing.

19. Remove the countershaft bearing.

20. Remove the fifth and reverse gears from the countershaft.

21. Remove the snap-ring, fifth gear, its synchronizer ring, needle roller bearing, and fifth gear bearing inner race from the output shaft.

22. Remove the reverse gear and clutch hub from the output shaft.

23. Loosen the bolt and remove the reverse idler gear stop from the rear cover. Withdraw the reverse idler shaft from the rear; remove the reverse idler gear and spacer.

24. Remove the output shaft rear bearing retainer. Remove the rear bearing snap-ring.

25. Push the countergear bearing outer race rearward, and remove the bearing. Separate the countergear from the intermediate plate.

26. Separate the input shaft and synchronizer ring from the output shaft.

27. Remove the output shaft from the intermediate plate.

28. Remove the hub and synchronizer ring, followed by third gear.

29. Press off the rear bearing.

30. Remove the following items from the output shaft, in the order listed:
   a. First gear
   b. Roller bearing with inner race
   c. Synchronizer ring
   d. Reverse gear
   e. Clutch hub
   f. Second gear
   g. Synchronizer ring

ASSEMBLY

1. Install the sleeve over the third gear synchronizer hub. Insert the three shift keys into the hub and sleeve keyways install the hub two springs.

2. Assemble the synchronizer ring to third gear, and fit both of them on the output shaft.

3. Insert the third/fourth synchronizer hub on the output shaft, until it contacts the shoulder of the shaft.

4. Select a snap-ring to provide 0.002 in. axial play for the synchronizer hub and fit it onto the shaft. Snap-rings are available in a range of sizes.

5. Measure third gear thrust clearance with a feeler gauge. The clearance should be 0.004-0.010 in. Replace third gear if the clearance exceeds the limit of 0.010 in.

6. Install the synchronizer ring for second gear to the gear and install the assembly on the output shaft.

7. Install the reverse gear over its clutch hub.

8. Install the reverse gear and hub on the output shaft so that they contact the shoulder.

9. Measure second gear thrust clearance; it should be between 0.004-0.010 in. Replace the gear if the clearance is more than 0.010 in.

10. Coat the locking ball with grease. Insert it, and the roller bearing inner race, on the output shaft.

11. Assemble first gear with its synchronizer ring, bearing and bearing inner

Cross section of model W 50 transmission

Cross section of model P-51 transmission

13. Synchromesh shifting key, No. 1
14. Transmission clutch hub, No. 1
15. Reverse gear
16. First gear
17. Bearing
18. First gear bearing inner race
19. Reverse gear
20. Snap-ring
21. Transmission clutch hub, No. 3
22. Synchromesh shifting key spring
23. Synchromesh shifting key, No. 3
24. Fifth gear
25. Bearing
26. Fifth gear bushing
27. Bearing
28. Snap-ring
29. Ball
30. Snap-ring
31. Output shaft
32. Snap-ring
33. Spacer
34. Speedometer drive gear
35. Countershaft cover
36. Spacer
37. Snap-ring
38. Bearing
39. Snap-ring
40. Counter gear
41. Bearing
42. Countershaft reverse gear
43. Countershaft fifth gear
44. Bearing
45. Snap-ring
46. Stopper
47. Bimetal formed bushing
48. Reverse idler gear
49. Reverse idler gear shaft spacer
50. Reverse idler gear shaft

1. Snap-ring
2. Bearing
3. Snap-ring
4. Input shaft
5. Bearing
6. Synchronizer ring, No. 2

7. Synchromesh shifting key spring
8. Transmission clutch hub, No. 2
9. Synchromesh shifting key, No. 2

10. Transmission hub sleeve, No. 2
11. Third gear
12. Second gear sub-assembly

Exploded view of gear train, model W 50 transmission

25. Hub sleeve No. 2
26. Third gear
27. Second gear
28. Synchronizer ring No. 1
29. Thrust block No. 2
30. Anchor block No. 2
31. Brake band No. 1
32. Snap-ring
33. Clutch hub No. 1
34. Hub sleeve No. 1
35. Thrust block No. 1
36. First gear
37. Clutch hub No. 3
38. Reverse gear
39. Fifth gear
40. Countershaft cover
41. Spacer
42. Snap-ring
43. Bearing
44. Snap-ring
45. Counter gear
46. Roller bearing
47. Countershaft reverse gear
48. Spacer
49. Countershaft fifth gear
50. Bearing
51. Spacer
52. Nut
53. Lock washer
54. Bushing
55. Spacer
56. Reverse idler gear
57. Reverse idler gear shaft
58. Anchor block No. 1
59. Bolt
60. Spacer
61. Counter gear plate
62. Pin
63. Spring

1. Snap-ring
2. Snap-ring
3. Bearing
4. Needle roller bearing
5. Snap-ring
6. Needle roller bearing
7. Needle roller bearing
8. Bearing inner race

9. Thrust washer
10. Bearing inner race
11. Snap-ring
12. Snap-ring
13. Bearing
14. Spacer
15. Speedometer drive gear
16. Input shaft

17. Output shaft
18. Ball
19. Synchronizer ring No. 2
20. Thrust block No. 3
21. Anchor block No. 3
22. Brake band No. 2
23. Snap-ring
24. Clutch hub No. 2

Exploded view of gear train, model P-51 transmission

race. Install them on the output shaft, so that the end of the inner race contacts the clutch hub and the groove on the inner race aligns with the locking ball.

12. Press the rear bearing onto the output shaft.

13. Measure first gear thrust clearance.

NOTE: The thrust clearance of all gears in the W-50 5-speed transmission should be between 0.006-0.010 in.; the thrust clearance limit for all gears is 0.012 in.

14. Use a press to insert the straight pin into the intermediate plate, until it protrudes ¼-⁵/₁₆ in. from the cover front side.

15. Install the output shaft on the intermediate plate.

16. Coat the roller bearing with grease and install it over the input shaft.

17. Apply gear oil to the front synchronizer ring on the output shaft.

18. Assemble the output shaft and the input shaft.

19. Install the countergear on the intermediate plate.

20. Install the cylindrical roller bearing into the intermediate plate, and then install the spacer.

21. Assemble the output shaft and countergear, then fit them through the holes in the intermediate plate. Push them in until the snap-ring sticks out beyond the intermediate plate. Install the snap-ring and then push the shafts back until the snap-ring is flush with the intermediate plate surface.

22. Install the shaft through the reverse idler gear. Insert the end of the shaft into the end of the intermediate plate.

23. Install the spacer on the idler shaft and secure it with a snap-ring.

24. Lock the reverse idler shaft on the intermediate plate with its stop. Check the reverse idler gear thrust clearance, it should be 0.006-0.010 in.

25. Install the reverse clutch hub on the reverse gear.

26. Install the three shift keys into the hub keyways and secure them with the two springs and a snap-ring.

27. Slide the reverse gear hub over the output shaft until it registers against the inner race of the intermediate plate bearing.

28. Insert the inner race lockball into the output shaft bore, after greasing it so that it can't fall out.

29. Assemble fifth gear, its synchronizer ring, needle roller bearing, and race. Slide the assembly onto the output shaft until the inner bear face rests against the reverse clutch hub. Be sure that the inner race groove is aligned with the lockball.

30. Secure fifth gear with a snap-ring.

31. Measure fifth gear thrust clearance; it should be 0.004 to 0.010 in. The thrust clearance limit is 0.012 in.

32. Install the countershaft reverse gear so that it just rests against the bearing inner race. Install the countershaft fifth gear and then install the countershaft bearing with a brass drift.

33. Install a snap-ring on the countershaft; select a snap-ring from one of the four available sizes.

34. Install a snap-ring on the output shaft,

and drive its bearing into place with a brass drift. Coat the bearing with grease first.

35. Install the spacer, ball, and speedometer drive gear on the output shaft.

36. Install the three shift forks in their hub sleeve grooves. Install the first and third shift fork shafts and secure them with their interlock pins. Install the second shift fork shaft next.

NOTE: Place each shift fork shaft in Neutral during assembly.

37. Secure the shift fork shafts to the end cover by inserting the lockballs into their bores, followed by the lockball springs.

38. Use a new gasket between the transmission case and the intermediate plate. Slide the case into place.

39. Fit snap-rings on the input shaft and countershaft front bearings.

40. Install the shift lever housing on the end of the shifter shaft. Slide the shifter shaft into the extension housing and secure it with a slotted spring pin.

41. Install a new gasket and slide the extension housing into place, until there is about an inch of clearance between it and the intermediate plate.

42. Rotate the shift lever housing clockwise (as viewed from the rear) to engage the shifter

1. Gear shift fork, No. 2	16. Shift lever knob sub-assembly
2. Gear shift fork, No. 1	17. Shift lever
3. Gear shift fork, No. 3	18. Shift and select lever boot
4. Slotted spring pin	19. Transmission shift lever ball seat
5. Gear shift fork shaft, No. 1	20. Conical spring
6. Gear shift fork shaft, No. 2	21. Control shift lever retainer gasket, No. 2
7. Gear shift fork shaft, No. 3	22. Control shift lever retainer
8. Shift interlock pin	23. Extension housing oil baffle
9. Ball	24. Shift lever housing
10. Compression spring	25. Shift lever shaft, No. 1
11. Plug	26. Plug
12. Plug	27. Gasket
13. Reverse restrict pin	28. Compression spring
14. Compression spring	29. Restrict pin
15. Cotter pin	

Exploded view of model W 50 shift linkage—typical of model P-51

Snap Ring

Center Bearing Retainer

Reverse Gear

Fifth Gear

Snap Ring

Snap Ring

Rear Bearing

Speedometer Drive Gear

Input Shaft

Synchronizer Ring

Output Shaft

Counter Center Bearing Outer Race

Rear Bearing

Counter Gear

Snap Ring

Clutch Hub No.3

Center Bearing

Synchronizer Ring

Counter Fifth Gear Assembly

Clutch Hub No.2

Third Gear and Synchronizer Ring

Output Shaft

Clutch Hub No.1

Center Bearing

Second Gear, Needle Roller Bearing and Synchronizer Ring

First Gear, Inner Race, Needle Roller Bearing and Synchronizer Ring

Steel Ball

Exploded view of the gear train—model W55 transmission

Clutch Housing

Front Bearing Retainer

Speedometer Driven Gear

Restrict Pin

Shift Lever Retainer

Extension Housing

Restrict Pin

Intermediate Plate

Snap Ring

Transmission Case

Back-up Light Switch

Input Shaft

Output Shaft

Straight Screw Plugs, Springs and Balls

Counter Gear

Reverse Idler Gear and Shaft

Shift Fork No.1

Shift Fork Shaft No.1

Interlock Pin No.1

Reverse Shift Arm

Shift Fork Shaft No.2

Slotted Spring Pin

Interlock Pin No.2

Shift Fork No.2

Interlock Pin No.3

Shift Fork No.3

Lock Washers and Bolts

Shift Fork Shaft No.3

Shift Fork Shaft No.4

Reverse Idler Gear Shaft Stopper

Detailed view of the W58 transmission

shaft with the selector lever and the shift fork shaft.

43. Slide the extension housing the rest of the way.

44. Install the spacer and then the countershaft end covers.

45. Align the front bearing retainer gasket with the oil holes. Install the bearing retainer over the gasket.

46. Bolt the clutch housing onto the front of the transmission case.

47. Fit the restrictor pins and springs into their extension housing bores.

48. Install the shift lever retainer over the oil baffle on the extension housing.

49. Install the shift lever conical spring, large side down, and install the ball seat in the shift lever retainer.

50. Attach the shift lever retainer to the extension housing.

51. Install the speedometer driven gear.

52. Install the back-up light switch.

53. Check to see that the input shaft has no more than 0.020 in. end-play. Put the transmission in Neutral and see if the output shaft can be rotated freely by hand.

TYPE 36

4 Speed
Transmission–Models
M-45 (4 spd.)
M-46 (4 spd. w/OD)

Volvo

DISASSEMBLY

1. Remove the transmission.

2. Remove the gearshift bracket extension assembly. Remove the gearshift joint sleeve. Drive out the front pin for the gearshift joint and remove the rear gearshift extension rod.

3. On the M45, block the output shaft flange from turning, and remove the rear flange.

4. On the M46, unbolt the overdrive unit. Attach a slide hammer to the output shaft of the overdrive unit and disconnect and remove the overdrive. Unbolt the intermediate housing.

5. On the M45, remove the speedometer driven gear. Remove the transmission rear cover, noting placement of bearing shims (if so equipped). Remove the speedometer drive gear.

6. Remove the back-up light switch.

7. Remove the top cover and gasket. Use a magnet to remove the spring detent balls.

8. Knock out the lockpins for the shift forks and shift rails.

NOTE: The forward gear shifters should be separated so that the pins do not damage the gears when driven out.

9. Remove the shift rails, shift forks and shifters for all forward speeds.

10. On the M46, remove the snap-ring and oil pump eccentric for the overdrive from the output shaft. Remove the eccentric retaining key.

11. Remove the mainshaft (output shaft) bearing inner and outer snap-rings. Before removing the mainshaft bearing, place a metal spacer (guard plate Volvo # 2985) between the input shaft and the front synchronizer ring to prevent damage to the ring during bearing removal. Remove the mainshaft bearing ring and pull off the bearing. Remove the bearing thrust washer.

12. Remove the flywheel (bell) housing.

13. Remove the snap-ring and spacer rings retaining the input shaft bearing. With the front synchronizer ring protective spacer still in place, pull out the input shaft bearing. Remove the protective plate.

14. Knock the intermediate shaft back and remove the rear outer race for the intermediate shaft. Then, knock the shaft forward and remove the front intermediate shaft outer race.

15. Remove the input shaft.

16. Lift out the 4th gear synchronizer ring.

17. Lift out the mainshaft.

18. Lift out the intermediate shaft.

19. Drive back the reverse gear sliding shaft and remove the gear shift rail, unhook and remove the reverse gear shift fork. Remove the reverse gear shift rail.

20. Pull off the intermediate shaft bearing.

21. Remove 1st gear and its synchronizer ring from the mainshaft. Remove the snap-ring for the 1-2 synchronizer hub. Press off the synchronizer hub and gear. Remove the 3-4 synchronizer hub snap-ring and press off that gear and hub.

22. If the shift mechanism needs repair, unhook the detent plate spring, remove the three retaining bolts, and remove the detent

Volvo M45, M46 gear train

plate. Remove the shifter shaft. If necessary, remove the shaft seal at the rear of the cover.

23. If leaking, remove the bell housing seal and the rear cover seal.

24. Push the two synchronizer hubs out of their sleeves and inspect for wear.

ASSEMBLY

1. Install new seals in the bell housing, shift cover and rear cover as required. Install the shifter assembly in the cover. The detent plate is installed with the flat washers between the plate and C-clips.

2. Connect the 3rd and 4th gear synchronizer hubs. The dogs must be positioned in the grounded slots in the hub. The sleeve end with the turned groove must face in the same direction as the hub flat end.

3. Assemble the mainshaft: install the 3rd gear and synchronizer ring, 3rd/4th synchronizer hubs, and snap-ring; install the 2nd gear and synchronizer ring, 1st/2nd synchronizer hubs, and snap-ring; install the 1st gear and synchronizer ring.

4. Press on the two intermediate shaft bearings.

5. Press on the input shaft bearing, and install its snap-ring.

NOTE: Do not install the spacer ring yet.

6. Install the reverse gear shift rail (without lockpin), shift fork and shifter. Install the reverse gear and shaft. Check that the reverse gear shaft aligns flush with the outside of the case. Also, check that the clearance between the reverse gear and shift fork is 0.004 0.08 in. Adjust as necessary by knocking the shift fork pivot in axially with a punch.

7. Lay the intermediate shaft at the bottom of the case. Slip the thrust washer, ball bearing and positioning ring over the output end of the mainshaft. Press the mainshaft bearing into place, taking care not to damage the reverse gear. When the bearing seats properly, the positioning ring will butt against the case.

8. Grease and install the input shaft inner roller bearing.

9. On the M46, install the snap-ring for the mainshaft bearing. Install the Woodruff key, overdrive oil pump eccentric and snap-ring on the mainshaft extension.

10. Position the 4th gear synchronizer ring in its hub.

11. Push the input shaft into the case all the way, so it makes contact with the mainshaft.

12. Lift up the intermediate shaft so that both bearings locate in the case.

13. Pull out the input shaft slightly to install the spacer ring. Then push the input shaft back in so that the spacer rings contact the case.

14. Install the intermediate shaft outer bearing races.

15. Determine the shim thickness required between the bell housing and the input shaft bearing. Measure how much the input shaft bearing protrudes from the case, and measure the depth of the bearing seat in the bell housing. Subtract bell housing seat depth and bell housing gasket thickness (0.25 mm) from the input shaft bearing protrusion height, and then subtract from this the allowable clearance (0.01-0.15 mm), and you have your required shim clearance. Shims come in 0.10, 0.15 and 0.20 mm sizes.

16. Install the bell housing.

17. Install the shift forks on the synchronizer hubs (the forks are identical). Install the forward shift rails and shifters (not interchangeable) and secure with the lock pins. Drive in the pins until flush.

18. Determine the shim thickness required between the rear cover and the intermediate shaft outer race, and the shim thickness between the rear cover and the mainshaft bearing. Allowable clearance is 1.98 mm for the intermediate shaft outer race, and 0.24 mm for the mainshaft bearing. Gasket thickness is 0.25 mm. When measuring, turn the transmission case vertical with the input shaft facing down, to take any slack out of the intermediate or mainshafts.

19. On the M45, install the speedometer drive gear.

20. Install the rear cover (or intermediate housing on the M46) with shims and a new gasket.

21. On the M45, install the output shaft flange. Install the speedometer driven gear and new O-ring. Install the gear retainer and bolt.

22. Position the top cover gasket with shifter detent balls and springs. Install the cover. Install the back-up light switch. Check gear operation by inserting a punch through the shift rod eye and rotating the mainshaft.

23. On the M46, install the overdrive assembly.

24. Install a new rubber O-ring in the gearshift rod joint. Connect the gearshift rod and drive in the locking pin. Install the cover sleeve.

25. Install the gearshift bracket extension assembly with the spacers, rubber washers, and flat washers as shown to eliminate vibration. First install the two upper bolts flush with the spacer sleeve, and then the two lower bolts. Then, tighten all four bolts to 15-18 lbs.

Volvo M45, M46 case and overdrive

overdrive unit (M46)

26. Fill the transmission with 0.8 qts. (2.4 qts. with overdrive M46) of 80W/90 hypoid gear oil. Install the plug(s).

TYPE 37

5 Speed Transmission– Model BA-10/5

Peugeot

DISASSEMBLY

1. Mount the transmission in a holding fixture or equivalent and drain the lubricant.

2. Remove the speedometer driven gear socket set screw and remove the driven gear socket from the rear extension housing.

3. Position the transmission in the vertical position with the rear upward. Set the gear selectors in the neutral position. Remove the selection lever return spring.

4. Remove the 5th gear cover plate and its gasket. Remove the extension housing bolts.

5. Place an extractor plate tool or equivalent to the rear housing, using the three bolts of the cover plate. Remove the rear housing from the transmission.

6. Remove the 5th speed gear from the mainshaft with an appropriate puller. The rear bearing will be removed as part of the 5th speed gear.

7. Remove the 5th speed drive gear shim washer, the spacer washer, the 5th gear and its needle bearing from the 5th gear stub shaft.

8. Mark the direction of rotation of the 5th/reverse synchronizer and the position of the cage and hub, in relation to each other.

9. Engage the 5th gear and drive the 5th/reverse selector fork roll pin from the fork and rail.

— CAUTION —

Do not damage the mating surface of the housing.

10. Reset the rail to the neutral position and remove the 5th/ reverse synchronizer cage and selector fork assembly, the synchronizer hub and the 5th gear subshaft.

11. Disengage the selection lever finger from the selector forks spindles. Remove the intermediate housing and retaining bolts.

12. Place the transmission in a horizontal position with the right side up. Remove the clutch fork and release bearing assembly from the front of the transmission. Remove the clutch housing and bolts.

13. Remove the six Allen headed screws from the rear bearing thrust plate. Remove the right hand housing retaining bolts and the housing.

14. Remove the countershaft from the exposed left hand housing.

NOTE: Mark and set aside the bearing races, if to be used again.

15. Lift the input and mainshaft assembly from the case as a unit. Do not separate while removing.

16. Separate the input and the mainshaft when the assembly is on a work bench. Remove the needle bearing from the bore of the input shaft. Hold the mainshaft in the 3rd gear position.

17. To disassemble the input shaft, remove the circlips, the spring washer and press the bearing from the shaft. Do not lose the adjusting shims.

18. To disassemble the mainshaft, mark the direction of rotation of the 3rd/4th synchronizer cage in relation to the synchronizer hub.

NOTE: Mark the components with a sharp piece of brass welding rod.

19. Remove the front synchronizer ring, the circlip and the spring washer from the front of the mainshaft.

20. Remove the 3rd/4th gear synchronizer hub and 3rd gear with an appropriate puller.

21. Invert the mainshaft and lock in a holding device such as a vise. Unscrew the reverse driven gear locknut from the mainshaft. Remove the reverse gear from the shaft.

22. Position the mainshaft and the remaining gears on a press bench and press the mainshaft through the rear bearing. Remove the gear components from the mainshaft in the following order;
    a. Rear bearing
    b. Bearing spacer
    c. Adjustment shim washer
    d. 1st speed driven gear
    e. Needle bearing
    f. 1st gear bushing
    g. 1st/2nd gear synchronizer and hub
    h. 2nd speed driven gear
    i. Needle bearing

23. Using a press, remove the front bearing and the shim adjusting washers. Remove the rear bearing.

24. To disassemble the rear housing, the ball bearing, the oil seal and the bearing race is pressed from the housing. Locate the shim washer in the race bore.

— CAUTION —

The press ram should be no bigger than 24 mm in diameter.

Selector Forks and Shift Rail Removal

1. Remove the spring and the 4th speed locking ball from the rear bearing bore of the half case.

2. Move the 4th gearfork and rail to the engaged position and drive the roll pins from the 1st/2nd and 3rd/4th selector forks. Return the 3rd/4th shift rail to the neutral position.

3. Remove the 1st/2nd locking ball plug, spring and ball from the passage on the center of the outer side of the case.

4. Pivot the 3rd/4th selector rail and remove the 1st/2nd rail from the case. Remove the fork.

5. Remove the reverse gear locking ball plug, spring and ball from the opposite side from the 3rd/4th locking ball passage.

6. Disengage the reverse fork and rail assembly and withdraw it from the case.

7. Remove the 3rd/4th shifting rail and remove the fork, interlock pin, the ball and the interlock plunger from the bearing bore.

8. Remove the roll pin from the reverse fork and rail. Push the shifting rail outward. Remove the fork.

Engagement Lever in the Intermediate Cover

Remove the circlip and washer. Remove the engagement lever spindle and recover the washer, spring, thrust plate and the operating fingers from the inside of the housing.

Clutch Housing

The thrust guide sleeve can be pressed from the housing after the oil seal has been removed.

ASSEMBLY
General

Always replace the following components when overhauling the transmission:
    a. Shaft circlips
    b. Spring washers
    c. Roll pins
    d. Mainshaft nut
    e. Output and input seals
    f. O-ring on speedometer driven bushing
    g. Thrust washers
    h. Necessary gaskets
    i. Sealing compound to mating surfaces

Diagram of the detent and interlock components—model BA-10/5

Position of the gear train in the half housing and the shift direction of the synchronizers—Model BA-10/5

Engagement Levers

Install the lever spindle while fitting the operating fingers, the spring thrust plate, the spring and the washer. Install the washer and the circlip on the lever spindle, exposed on the side of the intermediate housing.

Forks, Shift Rails and Interlocks

1. Install the reverse gear sliding shift rail into the case and into the bracket. Align the roll pin holes and install a new roll pin.

2. Install the reverse sliding gear with the 5th/reverse fork and shifting rail into the case.

3. Install in the reverse interlock passage on the outside of the case, a ball and spring. Coat the plug with a sealer and install it into the passage. Torque to 9.5 ft/lbs. Move the shift rail to the neutral position.

4. Install the 3rd/4th and 5th/reverse interlock plunger into its passage in the case.

5. Install an interlock pin in the 3rd/4th shift rail and retain with grease. Install the shifting rail into the case. Align the holes in the fork and the rail. Be sure the interlock pin is in the correct position and install a new roll pin.

6. Install an interlock ball in the passage between the 3rd/4th and the 1st/2nd fork rails. Install the 1st/2nd gear fork in the case with the boss towards the front. Install the shifting rail and engage the shifting fork. Align the holes in the fork and the shifting rail and install a new roll pin.

7. Install an interlock ball and spring in the 3rd/4th/2nd/1st interlock passage. Coat plug with sealer and install it in the passage. Torque to 9.5 ft/lbs.

8. Install the ball and spring in the passage of the rear bearing bore, for the 3rd/4th shifting rail.

Preparing the Input Shaft and Mainshaft for Adjustment

INPUT SHAFT

Press the front bearing on the input shaft with the snap-ring groove to the front. Do not install any shims.

MAINSHAFT

1. Install the 2nd speed gear and its needle bearing, the 1st/2nd synchronizer hub, the 1st speed gear spacer and washer. Install the rear bearing along with a new circlip.

NOTE: The bearing will have to be pressed on the shaft.

Do not exceed 3 metric tons pressure after the bearing is seated.

2. Install the adjustment shim removed during the disassembly, the spacer and a new nut on the shaft following the rear bearing. Tighten the nut to 39 ft/lbs.

COUNTERSHAFT

Press the new bearings onto the countershaft, beginning with the rear bearing and then the front.

CLUTCH HOUSING

1. Install the thrust guide sleeve and new circlip in its groove.

NOTE: Do not install an oil seal in the housing until all adjustments are completed.

2. Verify the front and rear faces of the clutch housing are parallel with the use of a dial indicator. If out of parallel more than 0.10 mm, replace the housing.

Adjustments Prior to Assembly

Five adjustments are necessary, prior to the complete assembly of the transmission. The adjustments are as follows.

1. Position of the 4th gear synchronizer cone (prior to assembly).

2. Position of the 2nd gear synchronizer cone (prior to assembly).

3. Preload of the countershaft tapered roller bearings (prior to assembly).

4. Preload of the mainshaft tapered roller bearings (during assembly).

5. End play of the 5th/reverse sub-shaft (during assembly).

Special tools are available through the manufacturer and other sources for the measurement procedures needed during the adjustment phases. References will be made to the special tools needed.

Position of the 4th Gear Synchronizer Cone

1. Place the clutch housing, front down on a flat surface, and install the input shaft and bearing.

2. Install the right hand housing onto the clutch housing and secure with two bolts. Tighten to 14 ft/lbs.

--- **CAUTION** ---

Be sure the bearing fits into the bore of the clutch housing and the half housing.

---

3. Install the special setting gauge tool, 80314G or equivalent, into the clutch housing, in place of the countershaft front bearing.

4. Place the dial indicator and the special tool base, 80310FZ or equivalent, on the top of the setting tool.

5. Align the dial indicator stem on the edge of the synchronizer cone and rotate the input shaft one complete turn and obtain an average reading. Adjust the indicator to zero at the average reading point on the cone edge.

6. Reposition the dial indicator and base on the setting gauge block and record the measurement.

7. The measurement obtained represents the thickness of shims needed between the input shaft and the front bearing, minus 0.5 mm and rounded off to the nearest 0.05 mm.

Example:

Indicator reading	1.12 mm
Minus	0.50 mm
Result	0.62 mm
Rounded off to nearest 0.05 mm	0.60 mm

Therefore, a shim pack of 0.60 mm is needed between the input shaft and the front bearing to properly position the 4th speed synchronizer cone, in this hypothetical example.

NOTE: Shims are available in steps of 0.05 mm, from 0.15 to 0.50 mm.

Position of dial indicator and special tools for the measurements of the 4th gear synchronizer cone

Position of the 2nd Gear Synchronizer Cone

1. Install the needle bearing into the bore of the input shaft. Install the mainshaft and prepared components into the input shaft, with the rear bearing seated in its bore on the right hand housing.

NOTE: Be sure the bearing circlip is installed in the half housing groove.

2. Install the larger setting tool, 80314K or equivalent, into the countershaft front bearing bore of the clutch housing.

3. Install a longer stem, 80310 J or equivalent, onto the dial indicator. Place the dial indicator and special base on the top of the right hand half housing, in a position to touch both the setting tool and the 2nd synchronizer cone.

4. With the dial indicator set to zero, position the stem on the top of the setting tool.

5. Reposition the indicator stem to the edge of the 2nd synchronizer cone and record the measurement reading. The amount of movement noted, represents the thickness of

shims needed between the 1st gear spacer and the rear bearing, plus 0.50 mm, rounded off to the nearest 0.05 mm.

Example:

Indicator reading	2.51 mm
Plus	0.50 mm
Result	3.01 mm
Rounded off to nearest 0.05 mm	3.00 mm

6. Remove the input and mainshaft assemblies. Separate the clutch housing and the half housing.

Preload of the Countershaft Tapered Roller Bearings

1. Place the left half housing in the support stand or equivalent. Install the countershaft and its bearings into the housing.

2. Place the right housing in place on the left housing, making sure the dowel pins are in position.

3. Install two bearing center bolts into the housings and hand tighten the bolts. Install bolts into the rear bearing thrust plate and hand tighten the bolts.

4. Position the transmission with the front of the housings upward. Apply a downward pressure to the countershaft front bearing while rotating the countershaft, in order to seat the bearings.

5. Tighten the bearing center bolts and the bearing thrust plate bolts to 7 ft/lb.

6. By placing the dial indicator on the end of the countershaft and rotating it one complete turn with the stem contacting the housings, the run-out between the outer race and the face of the half housings must not exceed 0.03 mm.

7. Should the run-out exceed the specifications, the race must be realigned by tapping with a mallet. Should the countershaft be difficult to turn, the bearing center bolts and the bearing thrust plate bolts must be loosened and retightened and the run-out rechecked.

8. If the run-out is within specifications, set the dial indicator with a short stem, to number 2 and zero, with the stem resting on the side of the outer race. Move the indicator until the stem is contacting the face of the housing and record the measurement of the movement. Add 0.10 mm to the results for the preload of the bearings and round the results to the nearest 0.05 mm.

1. Position of 4th gear synchro cone
2. Position of 2nd gear synchro cone
3. Preloading of countershaft taper roller bearings
4. Preloading of mainshaft taper roller bearings
5. End float of 5th/R sub-shaft

Location of the adjustment shims needed during the assembly

Example:

Housing reading	4.27 mm
Bearing reading (preset)	2.00 mm
Result	2.27 mm
Plus preload	0.10 mm
Shim pack needed	2.37 mm
Rounded off to nearest 0.05 mm	2.35 mm

NOTE: Shims are available from 2.15 to 3.30 mm, in increments of 0.05 mm.

9. Remove the countershaft and the front bearing from the countershaft. Install the predetermined shim with the chamfer facing the gear, between the gear and the bearing. Press the bearing in place.

NOTE: The 4th and 5th adjustments are made during the assembly of the transmission as noted in the adjustment list.

Final Assembly
INPUT SHAFT

1. Remove the bearing from the shaft and install the predetermined shim pack between the shaft and the bearing.

2. Reinstall the bearing, with the groove for the large circlip to the front. Press the bearing into position and install the spring washer and circlip on the input shaft. Be sure the circlip engages the groove completely.

MAINSHAFT

1. Remove the rear bearing and shims from the mainshaft, used in the measurement check.

2. Install in the following order, from the rear to the front of the shaft, the components as listed;

   a. The second gear and its needle bearing (31 mm wide).

   b. The synchronizer hub and cage.

   c. The 1st gear and needle bearing (29 mm wide).

   d. The spacer and adjusting shim (from measurement check).

   e. The bearing spacer.

   f. Press the bearing onto the shaft with the circlip to the rear.

   g. Install the reverse driven gear with the plain face to the rear.

h. Install a new nut and tighten to 39 ft/lbs and lock the collar to the shaft.

3. Invert the mainshaft and install the following in order.

    a. 3rd gear along with its needle bearing (31 mm wide).

    b. 3rd-4th synchronizer hub.

4. Install a new spring washer and circlip on the end of the mainshaft. Be sure circlip is in the groove.

5. Insert the needle bearing in the bore of the input shaft, fit the 3rd-4th synchronizer cage and assemble the input and mainshaft together. Set the synchronizers to neutral positions.

INSTALLING GEAR TRAINS INTO TRANSMISSION CASES

1. Be sure the reverse synchronizer is in the neutral position and the 3rd-4th gear locking ball and spring is in position in the bearing bore.

2. Install the input and mainshaft assembly into the left half housing, engaging the selector forks with the synchronizer cages.

3. Install the outer races to the countershaft and install the countershaft into the housing. Be sure the teeth of both gear trains mate properly.

4. Be sure the alignment dowel pins are in place. Coat the mating surfaces of the half housings with sealer and position the right hand housing onto the left. Position the rear bearing thrust plate.

5. Install the six bearing bolts and tighten to 3 ft/lbs. Install the two thrust plate bolts and tighten to 7 ft/lbs.

6. Be sure the oil seal is installed in the clutch cover and install the clutch cover in place on the transmission housing.

7. Tighten the seven securing bolts to 19 ft/lbs. Rotate the input shaft during the clutch cover retaining bolt tightening.

8. Loosen the six bearing bolts in the housings and tap the half housings with a rubber mallet while rotating the input shaft. Retighten the six bearing bolts to 11 ft/lbs.

9. Install the six assembly bolts in the housing and torque to 7 ft/lbs.

10. Invert the transmission with the rear of the mainshaft upward. Be sure the alignment dowels are in place, coat the mating surfaces of the transmission housing and the intermediate housing with sealing compound and install the intermediate housing in place, while engaging the finger in the selector fork detents.

11. Tighten the five nuts and two bolts to 13 ft/lbs. Place the 5th/reverse spindle to the 5th gear position.

12. Install the 5th/reverse stub shaft and the 5th/reverse synchronizer hub.

NOTE: If a new hub is used, the marking groove should be towards the reverse gear.

13. As a unit, install the 5th/reverse synchronizer cage and the selector fork, bringing together the marks on the synchronizer hub and the cage.

14. Align the holes and install a new roll pin. Set the unit to the neutral position.

15. Install the 5th gear and needle bearing, along with the spacer.

5TH GEAR ASSEMBLY AND PREPARATION FOR MEASUREMENTS 4TH AND 5TH

1. Press the bearing on to the gear pinion.

------ **CAUTION** ------
When new parts are used, match the pinion gear to the mainshaft by green or yellow color.

2. Place the 5th gear pinion with the bearing fitted, on a hot plate and place a small piece of solder on the pinion. When the solder melts, place the pinion gear onto the shaft.

NOTE: A drift may have to be used to seat the gear.

3. Remove the alignment dowels from the rear housing and set them aside for later use. Install a shim pack, 4.0 mm thick and the bearing race, into the rear housing.

PRELOAD OF THE MAINSHAFT TAPERED ROLLER BEARING (NUMBER 4 MEASUREMENT)

1. Place the rear housing in position on the transmission case. Fit three bolts to hold housing and hand tighten.

2. Rotate the mainshaft, loosen the three bolts of the rear housing and retighten hand tight only.

3. A gap will exist between the two housings. Measure the gap to check for parallelism and to calculate the shim thickness needed to preload the mainshaft bearing.

Example

Thickness of basic shim	4.00 mm
Measurement of gap	1.85 mm
Difference	2.15 mm
Plus preload	0.10 mm
Shim thickness required	2.25 mm

NOTE: Shims are available in increments of 0.05 mm from 1.5 mm to 2.95 mm.

4. Remove the rear housing and remove the rear bearing outer race and the basic 4.00 mm shim pack.

Manual Transaxles

MANUAL TRANSAXLE APPLICATION CHART

Make	Year	Vehicle Model	Transmission Model	Speeds	Reference Type No.	Page
Audi	'76	100	—	4	1	U142
	'76–'79	Fox	—	4	2	U145
	'80–'83	4000	—	4	2	U145
			—	5	19	U193
	'78–'83	5000	—	4	1	U142
			—	5	19	U193
Chrysler Corp./ Mitsubishi	'80–'83	Colt, Champ, Tredia, Cordia①	KM160	4	3	U149
			KM165	4 (twinstick)	3	U149
Datsun/Nissan	'77–'81	f10, 310	F4WF60A	4	4	U152
			F5WF60A	5	4	U152
Fiat	'76–'83	128, X1/9, Strada	—	4 & 5	5	U155
Fiesta	'78–'80	All	—	4	6	U157
Honda	'76–'83	All	—	4 & 5	7	U161
Mazda	'81–'83	GLC	—	4 & 5	20	U198
Porsche	'76–'83	911, 912, 914, 930	—	4 & 5	8	U162
	'76–'78	924	—	4②	2	U145
	'78–'83	928	G 28.03	5	9	U166
Renault	'76–'83	Le Car	—	4③	10	U168
	'78–'83	18i	—	4③	11	U170
SAAB	'76–'83	All	—	4③	12	U172
Subaru	'76–'83	All ex. 4WD	—	4	13	U174
			—	5	14	U176
	'77–'83	All 4WD	—	4	15	U178
Toyota	'80–'83	Tercel	Z40	4	16	U179
			Z50	5	16	U179

MANUAL TRANSAXLE APPLICATION CHART

Make	Year	Vehicle Model	Transmission Model	Speeds	Reference Type No.	Page
Volkswagen	'76–'83	Types 1 & 2	002, 091	4	18	U188
	'76–'83	Rabbit, Scirocco, Jetta, Quantum	—	4 & 5	17	U184
	'76–'81	Dasher	—	4	2	U145

NOTE: Although certain late model transaxles may differ slightly from their predecessors, certain basic similarities continue to exist; thus enabling overhaul procedures for these newer models to be compatible with those given within the text.
① Cordia: twinstick only
② Information on the 1979 and later 924 and 944 with 5 speed transaxle was not available at the time of publication
③ Information on the new 5 speed models not available at the time of publication

TYPE 1

4 Speed Transaxle
Audi

DISASSEMBLY

1. Mount the transaxle in a holding fixture.
2. Block the drive flange with a drift and remove the center bolt. Remove both drive flanges.
3. Remove the differential cover and O-ring. Remove the differential.

—————— CAUTION ——————
If the tapered roller bearings on the pinion shaft are to be replaced, it is necessary to measure the pinion position before the transaxle is disassembled. Both pinion shaft bearings must be replaced at the same time with bearings of the same make. The pinion must be set to its original position when the transaxle is assembled.

4. Remove the bolts holding the gear carrier to the final drive housing.
5. Remove the dowel pin from the gear carrier.
6. Remove the selector shaft spring and cap. Push the selector shaft into the final drive housing.
7. Separate the gear carrier and the final drive housing.
8. Remove the end cap from the gear carrier. Remove the mainshaft bolt and washer.
9. Remove the shift rod stop-screws, springs, and interlock plungers.
10. Drive the spring pin out of the third/fourth gear shaft fork.
11. Pull the third/fourth gear selector rod out of the gear carrier. The shift fork will stay on the mainshaft.
12. Press the mainshaft out of the bearing. Guide the mainshaft and pinion shaft with the selector rod and fork for first/second gear.

13. Remove the main and pinion shafts together with the selector rod and shift forks. Swing the pinion shaft slightly to clear the reverse sliding gear.
14. Remove the speedometer drive gear.
15. Pry the oil seal from the differential cover.
16. Remove the bearing race from the differential cover. Remove the shim and record the size.
17. Remove the drive flange oil seal.
18. Pull the differential bearing outer race out of the final drive housing. Remove the shim and record the size.
19. Remove the selector shaft and oil seal.
20. Remove the clutch release shaft, bearing springs, and bushings. Remove the clutch bearing guide sleeve.
21. Remove the mainshaft oil seal.
22. Remove the pinion shaft needle bearings from the final drive housing.
23. Remove the mainshaft needle bearings.
24. Remove the reverse gear relay lever and the reverse selector rod.
25. Remove the reverse shaft and gear.
26. Press the synchronizer assembly (with third gear) off the mainshaft. Remove the needle bearings.
27. Remove the pinion shaft bolt.

28. Press the bearing (along with first gear and synchronizer ring) off the pinion shaft. Remove the needle bearings.
29. Remove the circlip from the synchronizer.
30. Press the synchronizer assembly (along with second gear and synchronizer ring) off the pinion shaft. Remove the needle bearings.
31. Remove the third gear circlip and press third gear off the pinion shaft.
32. Remove the circlip from fourth gear and press it off the pinion shaft.
33. Press the large tapered roller bearing off the pinion shaft.
34. Remove the spring pin from the pinion gear shaft in the differential housing and drive the shaft out. Remove the thrust washers and pinion gears.
35. Remove the side gears, threaded washers, and shims. Record the shim size.
36. Remove the differential bearings and speedometer drive gear.
37. Remove the ring gear.

ASSEMBLY

1. Heat the ring gear to 212° F. and install it.
2. Heat the differential housing bearings

Gear carrier with gear train and selector components

to 212° F and press them on. Install the speedometer drive gear.

3. Install the side gears with a 0.5 mm shims. Install the pinion gears and thrust washers.

4. Press the small gears outward and check the side gear play. Insert shims for the side gears until the play does not exceed 0.003 in. Install the threaded washers.

NOTE: The adjustment is correct when no play can be felt and the gears turn easily by hand without jamming.

5. Install the pinion gear shaft.

6. Press the large tapered roller bearing onto the pinion shaft.

7. Heat the fourth gear to 250° F and press it onto the pinion shaft. The shoulder on the gear faces third gear.

CAUTION
The pinion shaft and fourth gear must be absolutely free of oil and grease.

8. Install the circlip on fourth gear and measure the end-play. Play should be 0-0.0007 in. with the lower limit preferred.

9. Install the third gear needle bearings.

10. Heat third gear to 250° F and press onto the pinion shaft.

CAUTION
The pinion shaft and third gear must be absolutely free of grease or oil.

11. Install the third gear circlip. Measure the end-play with a feeler gauge and install a circlip that will give a play between 0-0.001 in. The lower limit is preferred.

12. Press the synchronizer rings on the first and second gears. Check the gap between the gears and synchronizer rings. On new parts the gap should be 0.039-0.066 in. The wear limit is 0.019 in.

13. Install the keys on the synchronizer hub. Install the synchronizer sleeve over the hub aligning the matchmarks. Install the springs on the synchronizer assembly 120° offset from each other. The angled spring end is hooked in the key hollow.

14. Press the synchronizer assembly onto the pinion shaft. Turn the synchronizing ring of the second gear so that the grooves align with the keys in the synchronizer hub. Install the circlip on the synchronizer assembly and measure the end-play with a feeler gauge. Play should be 0-0.0007 in. with the lower limit preferred.

15. Press the small tapered roller bearing onto the pinion shaft. Install the washer and bolt.

16. Install the third gear needle bearings.

17. Install the synchronizer rings on third and fourth gears. The gap between new gears should be 0.039-0.066 in.

18. Assemble the third/fourth synchronizer.

19. Align the grooves in the synchronizer ring for third gear with the keys in the synchronizer hub. Press the synchronizer assembly, synchronizer ring, and third gear onto the mainshaft.

20. Install the synchronizer assembly circlip and measure the end-play. End-play should be 0-0.001 in.

21. Install the fourth gear bearings.

Components of the final drive housing

Shim S₄

Gear carrier

Outer race/pinion bearing

Plug

Bushing

Spring

Gear detent

Interlock plungers

Backup light switch

Reverse selector rod

Reverse gear shaft

Reverse sliding gear

Mainshaft bearing

Circlip

Gear carrier housing

Bolt

Inner race, small bearing

1st gear

1st gear needle bearing

Circlip

1st/2 nd gear synchro ring

2nd gear

Pinion

Sleeve/hub for 1st/2nd gear

2nd gear needle bearing

Circlip

3rd gear

Circlip

4th gear

Inner race, large bearing

Pinion shaft assembly

22. Install fourth gear and thrust washer on the mainshaft. Play should be 0.007-0.013 in.

23. Drive the mainshaft bearing into the gear carrier (closed side out).

24. Install the shim and pinion bearing outer race.

25. Install reverse gear shaft and reverse gear.

26. Install the interlock plungers in the gear carrier. Install the reverse selector shaft. Install the reverse relay lever through the gear carrier and into the threaded portion of the lever. Press the lever toward the center of the carrier and tighten the bolt in until it touches the relay lever. Press the lever against the bolt and turn back until the thread starts to engage.

27. Install the interlock plungers, bushings, springs and plugs.

28. Install the differential bearing shim and outer race.

29. Install the mainshaft needle bearings. The lettering on the bearing should be toward the drift.

30. Heat the final drive housing *completely* to 212° F and press the pinion bearing outer race and shim into the housing. Hold the pressure on the race for 1-2 minutes until heat transfer has taken place.

31. Install the mainshaft bushing. The bushing should be driven in 0.452 in. from the surface of the clutch bearing guide sleeve flange.

32. Install the mainshaft oil seal.

33. Drive the selector shaft oil seal into the final drive housing. Install the selector shaft.

34. Install the clutch bearing guide sleeve, the clutch release shaft bushings, spring, shaft, oil seal, and release bearing.

35. Drive the drive flange oil seals into the differential cover and the final drive housing.

36. Install the main and pinion shafts along with the shift forks and first/second gear selector rod. These components must be installed as an assembly. Hook the hole in web of third/fourth gear fork over the reverse selector rod.

NOTE: Make sure the interlock plungers engage the shift selector rod.

37. Pull the mainshaft into the bearing with an 8 mm bolt. When fully seated install the mainshaft bolt.

38. Move the selector rods for first/second and reverse into neutral.

39. Slide the third/fourth selector rod into the shift fork and gear carrier. Make sure that the interlock plungers engage. Secure the shift fork to the rod with a new spring pin.

40. Install the shift rod stop screws.

41. Press the mainshaft cap and O-ring into the gear carrier. The recess in the cap points toward the oil drilling in gear carrier.

42. Install the gear carrier.

43. Assemble the measuring bar and measure the pinion location.

NOTE: Refer to Differential and Rear Axle section.

If the measurement is not the same as previously recorded, proceed as follows:

a. If the reading is smaller, a thinner shim must be installed between the pinion shaft outer race and final drive housing.

b. If the reading is the same or very close

to the original reading, proceed to the next step.

c. If the reading is larger, a thicker shim must be installed between the final drive housing. Install new shim if necessary.

44. Install the dowel pin between the final drive housing and gear carrier.

45. Install the differential.

46. Install the differential cover.

47. Install the drive flanges.

48. Install the selector shaft spring and cover.

TYPE 2

4 Speed Transaxle

VW, Porsche, Audi

DISASSEMBLY

Certain variations are used in the application of this basic transaxle. The gear arrangement remains the same, the shifting mechanism differs in the shaping of various fingers and forks. The case is modified to adapt to the various vehicles in which it is used. Roller bearings are used in the majority of applications, while tapered bearings are used in the remainder. Needle caged bearings may be found as split, one piece or with a foldable cage. A pinion nut is used on varied models, while a bolt and washer are used on others.

A completely new five speed transaxle assembly is available for the 924 models, beginning with the 1980 model year. No service information is available at time of printing on this transaxle model. A modified version of this transaxle is used on the 1980 924 Turbo models.

1. Mount the transaxle in a holding fixture.

2. Separate the shift housing from the transaxle.

3. Mount a dial gauge and zero the gauge with a 3 mm preload.

CAUTION

The greatest care must be taken when determining the thickness of the gasket and shim used between the shift housing and the gear carrier. The thickness of these two parts influence the position of the drive pinion. If the bearings for the mainshaft, pinion shaft are replaced or if the shift housing or gear carrier housing are replaced, the measurements must be remade and new shim and gasket sizes selected.

Spring loaded inner shift lever

4. Measure the distance between the main shaft bearing and the gear carrier (a). Record this reading. Make sure that the bearing is fully seated.

5. Measure the distance between the pin-

- a — between main shaft bearing and gear carrier
- b — between pinion bearing and gear carrier
- c — between end face of gearshift housing and shim contact in gearshift housing
- d — gasket thickness
- s — shim thickness

End cover gasket and shim dimensions

Gear carrier housing and shift rod interlock components

ion bearing and the gear carrier (b). Record the reading. Make sure that the bearing is fully seated.

6. Measure the distance between the end face and the shim contact surface on the gear carrier (c). Record the reading.

7. Determine the shim thickness as follows; add the measurements from Step 4 (a) and 6 (c), then subtract step 5 (b). This will give the shim thickness required.

8. (Fox only.) The gasket thickness is determined by the mainshaft bearing projection obtained in step 4.

Bearing projection (mm)	Gasket size (mm)
0.20-0.26	0.30
0.27-0.32	0.40

NOTE: When replacing the transmission housing, gear carrier, first gear needle bearing or the pinion bearing the exact location of the pinion must be determined before disassembly. Once the new parts have been installed, it will be necessary to set the pinion to its original position.

9. Block the drive flange and remove the bolt.

Mainshaft assembly

Pinion ball bearing/inner race

Needle bearing when replacing measure position of drive pinion and restore.

Shim S₃ determine new shim if following parts have been replaced: gear carrier, transmission housing, drive pinion ball bearing, 1st gear needle bearing, gear set.

1st gear

Synchronizer ring 1st and 2nd gear

Synchronizer hub 1st/2nd gear (complete)

2nd gear

Circlip

3rd gear

4th gear

Pinion shaft assembly

10. Remove the final drive cover. Remove the differential assembly.

NOTE: To perform the following operation, it is necessary to have special Volkswagen tools or equivalent.

11. Assemble the tool universal bar. Zero the dial indicator with a 2 mm preload.

12. Install the measuring plate tool on the pinion and install the measuring bar in the final drive housing.

13. Install the final drive cover and tighten the retaining nuts to 18 ft/lbs.

14. Move the second centering disc outward with the movable setting ring until the measuring bar can be turned by hand.

15. Turn the measuring bar until the measuring pin extension touches the plate on the pinion. Note the indicator needle at the point of maximum deflection. Record the reading.

NOTE: After parts have been replaced, this setting must be reproduced as closely as possible.

16. Separate the gear carrier from the final drive housing.

17. Drive the spring pin out of the 3rd/4th shift fork in the direction of the pinion.

18. Move the shift fork along the selector shaft and engage 3rd gear. *Do not move the shaft.*

19. Engage reverse gear. Place the gear carrier in the final drive housing. Loosen the pinion nut. Remove the gear carrier from the final drive housing. Remove the 3rd/4th shift fork.

20. Remove the mainshaft bearing using a suitable bearing puller. Remove the mainshaft.

21. Drive the reverse gear shaft out of the gear carrier.

22. Place the remaining gears in neutral and press the pinion shaft out of the gear carrier along with the 1st/2nd selector shaft and shift fork.

23. Remove the inner shift lever spring from the shift housing, remove the shift lever.

24. Press the transmission rear mount off the shift housing.

25. Pry the inner shift lever oil seal out of the shift housing.

26. Drive the inner shift lever rear bushing out of the shift housing.

27. Press the inner shift lever front bushing out of the shift housing.

28. Pry the mainshaft oil seal out of the final drive housing.

29. Drive the mainshaft sleeve out of the final drive housing from the gear carrier end.

30. Drive the mainshaft needle bearings out of the final drive housing from the front (flywheel side).

31. Remove the dowel pin from the pinion bearing and drive out of the final drive housing.

32. Using a slide hammer, pull the clutch release shaft bushing out of the final drive housing.

33. Pull the starter bushing out of the final drive housing.

34. Drive the pinion bearing out of the gear carrier.

35. Remove the pin from the reverse gear selector shaft.

36. Drive the 1st/2nd and 3rd/4th interlock plungers through the gear carrier and remove through the access hole in the rear of the gear carrier.

37. Tap the remaining interlock plunger plug out.

38. Remove the circlip from the mainshaft which holds the 4th gear and the synchronizer ring. Remove the parts from the shaft.

39. Remove the circlip retaining the synchronizer hub, synchronizer ring, and third gear from the main shaft.

40. Press the synchronizer hub and third gear off the mainshaft.

41. Press the pinion bearing inner race along with the first gear off the pinion shaft.

42. Press the synchronizer hub for 1st/2nd gear along with second gear off the pinion shaft.

43. Remove the third gear circlip from the pinion shaft.

44. Press the third gear off the pinion shaft.

45. Press the fourth gear off the pinion shaft.

46. Remove the drive flange oil seal from the final drive housing by prying.

47. Drive the differential outer bearing race and shim out of the final drive cover.

48. Using a suitable puller, remove the differential bearing inner race/cage from the side opposite the ring gear.

49. Pull the bearing from the ring gear side of the differential assembly, along with the speedometer drive gear and bushing.

50. Remove the bolts holding the ring gear to the differential housing and drive the housing and gear apart.

51. Remove the circlip from the pinion gear shaft. Slide the shaft out of the differential housing.

52. Remove the pinion gears, side gears and the drive flange nuts.

ASSEMBLY

1. Insert the side gears and drive flange nuts. Bolt the drive flanges to the side gears.

2. Insert the pinion gears and move the drive flange until the pinion gears are aligned. Install the pinion shaft. Remove the drive flanges.

NOTE: The drive pinion and the ring gears are matched units and can be replaced only as a matched set.

Components of differential housing

Exploded view of 1st/2nd synchronizer

3. Heat the ring gear to approximately 212° F and center on the differential housing with a drift.

4. Install the bearing opposite to the ring gear by heating to 212° F and pressing onto the differential housing.

5. Install the bearing on the ring gear side of the differential housing by heating to 212° F and pressing onto the differential housing.

6. Insert 1.8 mm shim onto differential housing and press drive gear bushing on.

7. Insert the shim into the final drive cover and drive the outer bearing race into place and insert the shim in the final drive housing.

8. Drive the right side drive flange oil seal into place in the final drive housing.

9. Press the 4th gear onto the pinion shaft while holding the bearing with the wide shoulder facing the pinion head.

10. Press the third gear onto the pinion shaft.

11. Measure with a feeler gauge the space between the third gear and the pinion shaft. Install a circlip of the correct size.

12. Position the three keys in the slots in the 1st/2nd gear synchronizer hub.

13. Place the synchronizer sleeve over the synchronizer hub and align marks.

14. Install the springs 120° offset with the angled ends engaged in the hollow of a key.

15. Position the shift fork slot and the groove in the synchronizer hub so that they face the first gear and press the synchronizer assembly onto the pinion shaft.

16. Press the synchronizer ring onto the first gear and measure the gap between the parts with a feeler gauge. New parts should be between 0.042-0.066 in. and a used part should be no more than 0.023 in.

17. Install the first gear on the pinion shaft, slide on bearing and shim.

18. Press the inner race onto the pinion shaft.

19. Assemble the 3rd/4th gear synchronizer in the same way as the 1st/2nd synchronizer.

20. Press the synchronizer rings onto the third and fourth gears. Check the gap between the synchronizer rings and the gears. New parts should measure 0.053-0.075 in. and used parts should be no more than 0.023 in.

21. Install needle bearing on mainshaft.

22. Press the synchronizer hub along with the third gear onto the mainshaft. The chamfer on the synchronizer hub inner splines faces third gear.

23. Install the circlip on the mainshaft for the synchronizer assembly.

24. Install the needle bearing.

25. Install the spring pin in the mainshaft and align the pin with the slot in the 4th gear.

26. Install the fourth gear and shim, secure with the circlip.

CAUTION

Before measuring end-play, press the synchronizer and third gear against the circlip located against the synchronizer hub.

---

27. Measure the end-play between the shim and fourth gear. If the measurement is not between 0.10-0.40 mm remove the circlip and install a shim that will bring the measurement within limits.

28. Install the plunger and spring for the first second shift selector shaft. Install the interlock plunger (between the 1st/2nd and the 3rd/4th shafts) from the top of the case.

29. Install the plunger and spring for the 3rd/4th selector shaft. Hold down the plunger and install the 3rd/4th shift selector shaft.

30. Install the pin for the reverse gear selector shaft.

31. Install the second interlock plunger from the top of the gear carrier.

32. Install the reverse gear selector shaft. Install the remaining spring and plunger. Install the reverse lever pin in selector shaft.

NOTE: The first/second shift selector shaft is not installed until the gear train is in place.

33. Install the plugs in the interlock plunger bores.

34. Install the reverse sliding gear. Insert the reverse lever with the shift segment.

35. Install the bolt and washer and press the reverse lever toward the center of the gear carrier.

36. Turn the bolt in until it touches the reverse lever. Press the lever against the bolt and make certain that the threads engage smoothly. Continue until the bolt is seated in the gear carrier. Tighten the bolt to 25 ft/lbs.

37. Check the operation of the reverse selector several times. Make sure that the lever moves easily in all positions. Remove the reverse sliding gear.

38. Press the pinion bearing into the gear carrier.

39. Drive a new starter bushing into the final drive housing.

40. Drive a new clutch release shaft bushing into the final drive housing.

41. Align the pinion bearing outer race with the hole in the final drive housing drive

into place. The groove on the side must be toward the gear carrier. Install the dowel pin.

42. Drive the mainshaft needle bearings into place in the final drive housing.

43. Drive the mainshaft sleeve into position in the final drive housing.

44. Drive the mainshaft oil seal into position.

45. Install the clutch bearing guide sleeve, the clutch release shaft and spring and the clutch release bearing.

46. Press the inner shift lever rear bushing into the shift lever housing until it is flush with shoulder.

47. Press the shift lever oil seal into the shift lever housing until it is flush with the housing.

48. Press the transmission rear mount onto the shift housing.

49. Press the inner shift lever front bushing into the housing until it is flush.

50. Install the inner shift lever and install the spring.

51. Press the pinion shaft assembly into the ball bearing in the gear carrier.

52. Drive the mainshaft bearing into the gear carrier assembly.

53. Position the 1st/2nd selector shaft and fork on the assembled pinion shaft assembly.

54. Press the pinion shaft assembly into the gear carrier assembly. Guide the shift selector shaft into the operating sleeve. Make sure that the selector shaft does not jam.

55. Place the pinion shaft in a vise and tighten the pinion nut to 14-21 ft/lbs. Install the gear carrier in the final drive housing and secure with four nuts.

56. Repeat the measurements from Steps 11 thru 15 of disassembly. If the measurements are not the same as previously recorded, proceed as follows:

   a. If the second measurement is smaller, a thinner shim must be installed (between the pinion shaft inner bearing race and needle bearing on the pinion shaft).

   b. If the measurement is the same or very close to the original reading proceed to the next step.

   c. If the measurement is larger, a thicker shim must be installed.

57. Remove the gear carrier from the final drive housing, install new shim if needed.

58. Place the mainshaft assembly in the gear carrier. Install the shim and circlip.

59. Install the 3rd/4th shift fork with the wider shoulder facing toward fourth gear. Secure the shift fork with a new spring pin.

60. Block the gear train and tighten the pinion nut to 72 ft/lbs.

61. Install the first/second gear selector dog.

62. Install the gear carrier assembly on the final drive housing. Install the dowel pins before tightening the nuts or bolts.

63. Install the differential assembly into the final drive housing.

64. Install the final drive cover.

65. Install the drive flanges and block with suitable drift.

66. Repeat the measurements from Steps 3 thru 8 of Disassembly. Select the proper shim and gasket to be installed between the gear carrier and shift housing.

67. Install the shift housing on the gear carrier assembly.

TYPE 3
4 Speed Transaxle–Model KM 160
4 Speed Transaxle w/Twin Stick–Model KM 165
Chrysler Corp./Mitsubishi

DISASSEMBLY

1. Mount the transaxle securely and drain the lubricating oil.
2. Remove the clutch operating bracket and the transaxle mounting bracket.
3. Remove the backup lamp switch and the steel ball from inside the transaxle case.
4. Remove the rear cover from the transaxle case. Remove the two spacers from the rear of the tapered roller bearings.
5. Remove the transaxle case, exposing the gear train assembly.

6. Locate all the shift rails in the neutral position.

NOTE: The shift rails would be locked if any one of the shift rails are in a position other than neutral.

7. Remove the three poppet plugs and remove the springs and balls (three each).
8. Remove the reverse idler shaft and the reverse idler gear.

NOTE: The reverse idler shaft sometimes will come off with the removal of the transaxle case.

9. Remove the reverse shift lever assembly.
10. Remove the reverse shift rail and the 3rd/4th speed shift rail spacer collar.
11. Using a pin punch and light hammer, remove the spring pins from the 1st/2nd and 3rd/4th speed shift forks.

--- **CAUTION** ---
Support the shift forks before attempting to remove the spring pins.

12. Pull the 1st/2nd speed shift rail upward from the case, sliding the rail through the fork.

NOTE: The 1st/2nd speed shift rail and fork cannot be removed until after Step 13.

13. Pull the 3rd/4th speed shift rail from the case and remove the 1st/2nd and 3rd/4th speed shift rails and forks together.
14. Move the 3rd/4th speed synchronizer into the 4th speed position and remove the output shaft assembly.
15. Remove the differential assembly from the case.
16. **KM 165 models:** Remove the plug, poppet and spring for the two-speed shift rail and fork.
17. Remove the bolts from the input shaft bearing retainer and remove the input shaft assembly.
18. **KM 165 models:** Remove the shift rail and fork, along with the intermediate shaft assembly, when the input shaft is removed.
19. Remove the shift shaft spring retainer and pull out the spring pin with pliers.
20. Move the shift shaft towards the outside of the case by using a pin punch in the pin

1. Clutch housing
2. Bearing retainer
3. Transaxle
4. Input shaft
5. Intermediate gear
6. Rear cover
7. Clutch release bearing
8. Clutch release fork
9. Output shaft
10. Differential side gear
11. Differential pinion
12. Pinion shaft
13. Differential drive gear
14. Differential case
15. 4th speed gear
16. 3rd and 4th speed synchronizer assembly
17. 3rd speed gear
18. 2nd speed gear
19. 1st and 2nd speed synchronizer assembly
20. 1st speed gear

Cross section of model KM 160 transaxle

1. Clutch housing
2. Input shaft
3. Bearing retainer
4. Input low gear
5. Synchronizer assembly
6. Input high gear
7. Transaxle case
8. Intermediate gear
9. Rear cover
10. Clutch release bearing
11. Clutch release fork
12. Output shaft
13. Differential side gear
14. Differential pinion
15. Pinion shaft
16. Differential drive gear
17. Differential case
18. 4th speed gear
19. 3rd and 4th speed synchronizer assembly
20. 3rd speed gear
21. 2nd speed gear
22. 1st and 2nd speed synchronizer assembly
23. 1st speed gear

Cross section of model KM 165 transaxle (twin-stick)

1. Control shaft
2. Control lug
3. Lock pin
4. Control finger
5. Steel ball
6. Spring
   [Length; 18.9 mm (.74 in.)]
7. Neutral return spring
8. Spacer collar
9. Reverse restrict spring
10. Shift shaft
11. O-ring
12. Spring pin
13. Spring retainer
14. 1st and 2nd speed shift rail

15. Shift lug
16. Shift fork
17. 3rd and 4th speed shift rail
18. Shift lug
19. Shift fork
20. Lock pin
21. Spring pin
22. Spacer collar
23. Reverse shift rail
24. Reverse shift lever
    assembly
25. Steel ball
26. Reverse spring
    [Length; 16.6 mm (.65 in.)]
27. Spring

[Length; 18.9 mm (.74 in.)]
28. Gasket
29. Plug
30. Interlock plunger A
31. Interlock plunger B
*32. Selector shaft
*33. O-ring
*34. Selector finger
*35. Lock pin
*36. Shift rail
*37. Shift fork
*38. Lock pin
*39. Steel ball
*40. Spring
*41. Plug

NOTE: Part marked * is applicable
to KM165.

Exploded view of shift mechanism

hole. Pull the shaft from the case and remove the control finger, two springs, spacer collar, poppet spring and ball.

--------- **CAUTION** ---------
During removal of the shift shaft from the case, the poppet ball will jump out of the control finger hole. Close the hole with an object of finger tip to prevent loss of the ball.

21. Put an identifying mark on the tapered roller bearing outer race and remove it from the case.
22. Remove the lock and the speedometer driven gear assembly.

Input Shaft
KM 160
1. Remove the front bearing snap-ring and using a special puller, remove the front bearing from the input shaft.
2. Straighten the locking washer and remove the locknut at the rear of the input shaft.
3. Using a press or a special puller, remove the rear bearing from the shaft.

KM 165
1. Remove the front bearing snap-ring and emove the front bearing with a special puller.
2. Straighten the locking washer and remove the locknut at the rear of the input shaft.
3. Using a press and supporting the low

gear of the input shaft, press on the rear of the input shaft and remove the input high gear, gear sleeve, synchronizer assembly, input low gear and the rear bearing.

NOTE: To remove the rear bearing only, use a special puller. The input high gear will come off with the rear bearing.

ASSEMBLY
KM 160
1. Install the front bearing on the input shaft, using a bearing installer tool.
2. Install the front bearing selective snap-ring into the snap-ring groove.

3. Install a spacer to the rear of the input shaft with the stepped side towards the rear bearing.

4. Install the rear bearing on the input shaft, using a bearing installer tool.

5. Install the locknut to the end of the input shaft and tighten to 66 to 79 ft/lbs (89 to 107 Nm). Stake the locknut into the notch of the input shaft only. Lock the lock plate, if reused.

CAUTION

The shaft end will interfere with the breather if it is deformed by staking, resulting in breakage.

KM 165

1. Install the front bearing on the input shaft, using a bearing installer.

2. Install the front bearing selective snap-ring into the snap-ring groove.

3. Install the synchronizer hub with the .16 inch (4 mm) diameter slot in the oil groove, facing the clutch or engine side.

4. The synchronizer sleeve must be installed with the 30° chamfer on the clutch or engine side.

NOTE: The opposite side of the synchronizer sleeve is machined at a 45° angle.

5. Install the synchronizer spring with its stepped part positioned on the synchronizer key. Alternate the stepped parts of the front and rear springs to avoid having the stepped parts on the same key.

6. Install the sub-gear to the input high gear and lubricate the entire surface.

7. Install the cone spring and install a new snap-ring, making sure the inner side of the cone spring is not in the snap-ring groove.

8. Install the input low gear and the needle bearing on the input shaft.

9. Install the synchronizer ring.

10. Using a special installer tool, press fit the synchronizer assembly onto the input shaft with the synchronizer key correctly aligned with the synchronizer ring keyway.

11. Install the input high gear sleeve with a special installer tool. The input low gear should rotate smoothly. Install the synchronizer ring, the input high gear and needle bearing.

12. Install the spacer with the stepped side facing the rear bearing side.

13. Install the rear bearing with a special installer tool.

14. Install and tighten the input shaft rear nut to 66 to 79 ft/lbs (89 to 107 Nm.) and stake in place into the notch on the input shaft. Should the lockplate be reused, bend the plate over a shoulder of the locknut.

Output Shaft
DISASSEMBLY

1. Unlock the rear locknut plate and remove the locknut from the shaft.

2. Remove the front and rear tapered bearings from the output shaft, using special bearing puller tools.

3. Using a puller tool, remove the 1st speed gear, gear sleeve, 1st and 2nd speed synchronizer assembly and the 2nd speed gear.

4. Remove the 2nd speed gear sleeve, 3rd speed gear, 3rd speed gear sleeve, 3rd/4th speed synchronizer assembly and the 4th speed gear.

ASSEMBLY

1. Assemble the synchronizers in the following manner;

a. 3rd/4th synchronizer: Position the sleeve over the hub with the fork groove on the same side as the .160 inch (4 mm) oil groove on the hub.

b. 1st/2nd synchronizer: Position the sleeve over the hub with the 30° chamfer on the same side as the .160 inch (4 mm) oil groove on the hub.

c. Install the synchronizer springs into the 3rd/4th and 1st/2nd synchronizer unit with the stepped part of the springs on the synchronizer key.

NOTE: Do not have the stepped part of the front and rear springs on the same key. Alternate between keys.

2. Assemble the 4th speed gear onto the output shaft and install the synchronizer ring.

NOTE: Lubricate the contact surfaces with gear oil.

3. Press fit the 3rd/4th synchronizer unit to the output shaft with the oil grooves on the hub and the fork groove in the sleeve facing towards the clutch (engine) side. Align the synchronizer ring keyway with the synchronizer ring key. After the installation, be sure the 4th speed gear rotates freely.

4. Install the 3rd speed gear sleeve by pressing into place. Install the 3rd speed gear assembly.

5. Install the 2nd speed gear sleeve by pressing into place. Be sure the 3rd speed gear rotates freely.

6. Install the 2nd speed gear and the 1st/2nd synchronizer ring.

7. Install the 1st/2nd speed synchronizer assembly onto the output shaft by pressing with the proper tools. Be sure the 2nd speed gear rotates freely.

8. Install the 1st/2nd synchronizer ring. Press the 1st/2nd speed synchronizer assembly into place on the output shaft. Be sure the 2nd speed gear rotates freely.

9. Install the 1st/2nd speed synchronizer ring with the keyways properly aligned with the keys.

10. Install the 1st gear to the gear sleeve and press the unit onto the output shaft. Be sure the 1st speed gear rotates freely.

11. Install the front and rear tapered bearings on the front and the rear of the shaft.

12. Install the locknut on the rear of the shaft and torque to 66 to 79 ft/lbs. (89 to 107 Nm). Lock the locking plate to the nut, if used. Stake the locknut securely to the output shaft.

Intermediate Shaft
DISASSEMBLY

1. Remove the front tapered bearing with a press unit.

2. Remove the sub-gear and the spring assembly.

3. Remove the rear tapered bearing with the use of a press.

ASSEMBLY

1. Assemble the sub-gear spring assembly to the intermediate shaft gear with the longer end of the spring fitted to the .160 inch (4 mm) diameter hole in the sub-gear.

2. Install the sub-gear and insert the remaining end of the sub-gear spring into the smallest hole in the sub-gear, .160 inch (4 mm).

3. Install the front and rear tapered roller bearings on the shaft with a press tool.

Speedometer Driven Gear
NOTE: The speedometer driven gear assembly cannot be removed without disassembly of the transaxle.

DISASSEMBLY

1. Using a pin punch, remove the spring pin from the sleeve and driven gear shaft.

2. Separate the driven gear from the sleeve and remove the O-rings.

ASSEMBLY

1. Install new O-rings and lubricate the driven gearshaft.

2. Insert the driven gearshaft into the sleeve.

3. Align the sleeve hole with the pin slot in the driven gear.

4. Install the spring pin in such a manner so as not to contact the gearshaft with the slit in the spring pin.

Control Shaft or Control Lug
REMOVAL

1. A centering hole is located on a 16 mm boss, on the engine side of the lower part of the clutch housing.

2. Drill through the centering hole with a drill with a diameter of .470 inch (12 mm).

3. Remove the lock pin from the control shaft and lug. Remove the control shaft and lug.

INSTALLATION

1. Install the control shaft and lug. Install a new lock pin through the control lug and shaft.

2. Install a .470 inch (12 mm) cup plug in the drilled hole and seal the plug with a bonding sealant.

Differential
The overhaul of the differential assembly is confined to the replacement of the side bearings, ring gear and the differential and pinion gears. The replacement is done in the conventional manner. Necessary measurements during the assembly is given in the transaxle assembly procedures.

ASSEMBLY OF TRANSAXLE

NOTE: Lubricate all seals and O-rings during the assembly.

1. Prepare the transaxle case for component assembly by replacing all oil seals and case internal small parts that were removed during the disassembly.

2. Install the speedometer driven gear assembly into the clutch housing. Install the locking plate into the groove cut into the sleeve.

3. **Model KM 165:** Install an O-ring onto the selector shaft and lubricate the ring and the bore in the case. Install the shaft into the case and install the selector finger. Install the

lock pin so that it is flush on the clutch housing side of the selector finger.

4. Install the poppet spring and steel ball into the control finger and with the use of a special tool, force the poppet ball into its bore. Leave the tool in position.

5. Install a new O-ring onto the shift shaft and install the shaft into the clutch housing and engage the reverse restrict spring and the control finger.

6. Press the shift shaft inward until the special tool, used to hold the poppet ball and spring, is forced out. Recover and lay aside. Install the spacer collar and the neutral return spring and force the shift shaft to its bore in the opposite side of the case opening.

7. Align the spring pin holes and install the spring pins.

8. Install the spring retainer in place over the control finger assembly.

9. Install the differential gear assembly into the clutch housing. Adjust the differential case end-play as follows:

a. Place two pieces of plastic type gauge material, approximately ¾ inch in length, on the differential ball bearing outer race, 180° apart.

b. Install the transaxle case and gasket. Tighten the mounting bolts to 26 to 30 ft/lbs. (35 to 41 Nm). Remove the bolts and the transaxle case. Lay the case aside for later installation.

c. Measure the thickness of the plastic type gauge material and select a spacer of the proper thickness to provide the standard end-play. The end-play should range between 0.000 to 0.0059 inch (0.0 to 0.15 mm).

d. Spacer thicknesses are as follows:

Inch	MM	I.D. Mark
0.0516	1.31	E
0.0551	1.40	None
0.0587	1.49	C
0.0622	1.58	B
0.0657	1.67	A
0.0693	1.76	F

10. Turn the sub gear in the direction of the embossed arrow to align the .310 inch (8 mm) hole in the intermediate gear with that in the sub-gear. Insert a bar or bolt in the holes to maintain alignment.

11. Install the input shaft assembly and the intermediate shaft assembly into the clutch housing as a unit.

NOTE: KM 165 models—Install the selector shift rail and fork assembly at the same time.

12. Install the selector shaft poppet ball, poppet spring and plug. Apply a sealer to the plug and seat it flush with the housing surface.

13. Install the input shaft bearing retainer and remove the bar or bolt used to retain the alignment of the sub-gear to the intermediate gear.

14. Install the output shaft assembly.

15. Install the interlock plungers into the housing. Reassemble the 1st/2nd and 3rd/4th speed shift rails and forks in the reverse order of removal, into the housing.

16. Align the holes in the shift rail and the shift fork and install the pin. The pin must have its slit on the shift rail center line. Even the spring pin protrusion on both sides.

17. Install the reverse shift rail and install the three poppet balls, springs and plugs.

NOTE: The poppet spring with the white paint I.D. must be installed in the poppet hole of the reverse shift rail. Install the small diameter ends of the springs towards the steel balls.

18. Install the reverse shift lever assembly, the reverse idler gear and shaft and apply lubricate to the gear and shaft.

19. Measure the height of the reverse idler gear. The height from the face of the case to the upper flat of the gear should be 1.4429 to 1.5374 inch (37.85±1.2 mm). If less than specified, replace the reverse shift lever assembly.

20. Apply a sealer to the gasket and install on to the clutch housing.

21. Install the selected spacer on the differential side bearing and install the transaxle case. Install the bolts and torque to 26 to 30 ft/lbs (35 to 41 Nm).

22. Install the intermediate and output shaft rear tapered bearing outer races and press them in by hand.

23. Install the oil seal into the axle output shaft case hole, if not previously done.

NOTE: The oil seal hole must be chamfered before the seal is installed into the case, to prevent periphery damage to the seal and to cause leakages.

24. To select the outer race end spacer, use the following procedure:

a. Seat the outer races properly and measure the depths of the transaxle case to the races, using a depth micrometer.

b. Select a spacer for each race 0.004 inch (0.4 mm) thicker than the measured value.

c. Install the spacers in their respective bores and install the rear cover. Torque the bolts to 14 to 16 ft/lbs (19 to 22 Nm).

d. Using the special tool seal installer or equivalent, shift the transaxle to any desired gear, while rotating the input shaft.

NOTE: The input shaft may turn hard and the installation of the clutch plate may be necessary to assist in turning the shaft.

e. Remove the rear cover after setting the transaxle in a position with the rear cover up.

f. Remove the spacers and remeasure the depth as was done in Step a.

g. Reselect spacers of proper thickness so that an end-play of 0.000 to 0.0020 inch (0.0 to 0.05 mm) exists at the tapered roller bearing outer races.

h. Spacer thicknesses are as follows:

Inch	MM	I.D. Mark
.0724	1.84	84
.0736	1.87	87
.0748	1.90	90
.0760	1.93	93

Inch	MM	I.D. Mark
.0772	1.96	96
.0783	1.99	99
.0795	2.02	02
.0807	2.05	05
.0819	2.08	08
.0831	2.11	11
.0843	2.14	14
.0854	2.17	17
.0866	2.20	20
.0878	2.23	23
.0890	2.26	26
.0902	2.29	29
.0913	2.32	32
.0925	2.35	35
.0937	2.38	38
.0949	2.41	41
.0961	2.44	44
.0972	2.47	47
.0984	2.50	50
.0996	2.53	53
.1008	2.56	56
.1020	2.59	59
.1031	2.62	62
.1043	2.65	65
.1055	2.68	68

25. Apply sealer to the gasket and reinstall the rear cover. Torque the bolts to 14 to 16 ft/lbs (19 to 22 Nm).

26. Install the back-up lamp switch with washer and steel ball in place.

27. Verify the transaxle shifts and the internal gear rotate smoothly.

TYPE 4

4 and 5 Speed Transaxle–Models F4WF60A, F5WF60A Datsun

DISASSEMBLY

1. Remove the reverse light switch and drain the transmission.

2. Remove the bearing housing and primary gear as a unit.

3. Remove the primary gear cover.

4. Take the bottom cover off the transmission. Put reverse and 1st gears into position (to keep the shaft from turning) and remove the main gear locknut.

5. Remove the primary gear cover.

6. Remove the clutch housing.

7. If necessary, drive out the drive and idler bearing with a puller. Then press the bearing out of the main drive input gear.

8. Remove the differential side flanges.

9. Remove the speedometer pinion gear.

1. Primary drive gear
2. Primary idler gear
3. Sub gear
4. Main drive input gear
5. Main drive gear
6. Baulk ring
7. Spread spring
8. Coupling sleeve
9. Shifting insert
10. Synchronizer hub
11. 3rd main gear
12. Main gear bushing
13. Main gear spacer
14. 2nd main gear
15. 1st main gear
16. Reverse main gear
17. Main shaft
18. Final gear
19. Counter gear
20. Thrust washer
21. Thrust spring
22. Counter shaft
23. Reverse idler gear
24. Reverse idler shaft
25. Bearing retainer

4-speed gear components

1. Bearing housing
2. Primary gear cover
3. Clutch housing
4. Transmission case
5. Transmission case cover
6. Bottom cover

Transaxle case components

10. Remove the differential case as a unit.

11. Pull the differential side bearings and remove the ring gear mounting bolts.

12. Remove the differential case and withdraw the pinion shaft and remove the side gear and pinion mate.

13. Loosen bolts D1 and D2 and remove the reverse fork lever and bracket. Loosen double nuts E1 and bolts D3 and remove the bearing retainer.

NOTE: Double nuts E1 should be loosened before bolts D3.

14. Remove the reverse idler gear and shaft and drive out the countergear and countershaft guide.

NOTE: Needle bearing on countergear is not a retainer type. When removing gear, do not allow the bearing to come off.

15. Remove the transmission case service plug. This will allow access to the roll pin on the 1st/2nd shift fork.

Using a punch drive the roll pins out of the shift forks. Withdraw the fork rods and remove the shift forks.

NOTE: When driving out the roll pin from the 3rd/4th shift fork, shift the rod to 3rd gear before starting. Also be careful of the placement of the interlock plungers.

16. Remove the mainshaft gear assembly and the main drive gear toward the final drive gear side.

1. Primary drive gear
2. Primary idler gear
3. Sub gear
4. Main drive input gear
5. Main drive gear
6. Baulk ring
7. Spread spring
8. Coupling sleeve
9. Shifting insert
10. Synchronizer hub
11. 4th main gear
12. 4th gear bushing

1. Baulk ring
2. Spread spring
3. Coupling sleeve
4. Shifting insert
5. Synchronizer hub

Exploded view of synchronizer unit

NOTE: The locknut is caulked, but you do not have to remove the caulking for loosening.

17. Remove the mainshaft components in this order: 3rd/4th synchronizer, 3rd gear, main gear bushing, main gear spacer, 2nd gear, main gear bushing, 1st/2nd synchronizer, 1st gear, main gear bushing and reverse gear.

NOTE: The 3rd main gear bushing and mainshaft are press-fit. Remove the bushing with the main gear spacer and the 2nd main gear with a puller.

18. Press out the bearing from the mainshaft.

19. To disassemble a synchronizer, remove the spread springs and the shifting inserts, then separate the coupling sleeve from the synchro-hub.

ASSEMBLY

Generally, the procedures for assembly are the reverse of removal. However, there are certain steps you must observe.

1. Slide the synchro-hub into the coupling sleeve and fit the shifting inserts into their grooves.

2. Put one spread spring on the lower side of the shifting inserts to hold them to the inner side of the coupling sleeve. Put the other spread spring on the opposite side of the synchro-hub.

NOTE: Make sure the spread springs are opposite each other.

3. Press ball bearing onto the mainshaft and assemble reverse gear. Assemble the main gear bushing and 1st gear.

NOTE: Be sure to align the oil hole in the bushing with the one on the mainshaft.

4. Assemble baulk ring, synchronizer, main gear bushing, baulk ring, 2nd gear, main gear spacer, main gear bushing, 3rd gear, baulk ring, synchronizer and locknut on the mainshaft.

5. Put the spacers and needles into both sides of the countergear. Be sure to grease the needles before inserting.

13. Main gear spacer
14. 3rd main gear
15. 2nd main gear
16. Reverse main gear
17. Main shaft
18. Final gear
19. 1st main gear
20. Counter gear
21. 1st-reverse counter gear
22. Reverse idler gear
23. Reverse idler input gear

5-speed gear components

6. Insert a countershaft guide into the countergear.

7. Press the differential side bearing into the differential case.

8. Put the pinion mates, side gears, thrust washers and pinion shaft in the case.

9. Select the proper thrust washer to adjust side gear end-play to 0.008 in., then apply oil to gear teeth and thrust surfaces.

10. Put the ring gear onto the differential case.

11. Press in the differential side flange oil seals after lubricating their lips with grease.

12. Assemble the main drive gear and mainshaft in the transmission case.

13. Put in the 1st/2nd shift fork and the 3rd/4th fork. Make sure they are into their grooves in the coupling sleeves.

14. Slide the 3rd/4th fork rod through the transmission case and the 3rd/4th shift fork. Secure it with a new retaining pin.

15. Assemble the check ball, spring and check ball plug. Before tightening, apply sealer to the plug. Be sure to align the notch in the 3rd/4th rod with the check ball. Place the unit in Neutral. Assemble the 1st/2nd and reverse fork rod similarly.

16. With the countershaft guide in place in the countergear, install the countergear, thrust washers and thrust spring on the transmission case. Insert countershaft into countergear and drive out the guide.

NOTE: Pay attention to the direction of thrust washer assembly. Align the cut out portion of the countershaft with the bearing retainer.

17. Assemble the reverse idler shaft, reverse idler gear, bearing retainer, reverse fork and fork bracket with the cutout portion of the reverse idler shaft aligned with the bearing retainer.

18. Before installing the differential case, measure bearing height "H".

If it is 4.720 to 4.730 in., a shim is not needed.

If it is 4.715 to 4.719 in., use a 0.0078 shim.

If it is 4.710 to 4.714 in., use a 0.0118 shim.

19. With the fork rods in Neutral, put the case cover onto the transmission.

NOTE: Make sure the shifter engages with the fork rod brackets correctly. If the resin-coating comes off the bolt threads, the bolt should not be reused.

20. Assemble the differential side flanges.

21. Put the clutch housing on the transmission case and press the bearings onto primary and main drive input gears. Assemble the sub-gear on the idler gear. Insert both ends of the ring spring into 0.197 in. hole on the primary idler gear and sub-gear. Install the spacer and press the bearing onto the idler gear.

NOTE: Select a spacer that will insure the sub-gear end-play is less than 0.004 in.

22. Put the idler gear into the clutch housing and assemble the main drive gear, setting the idler sub-gear by inserting a bar into the hole in the idler gear through the sub-gear.

23. Put the thrust washer, lock washer and drive gear together in that order.

NOTE: As in removal, mesh two gears to keep the mainshaft from turning while tightening.

24. Assemble the primary gear cover and install the bearing housing assembly and drive gear. Rotate the drive gear while assembling.

25. Assemble the bottom cover, speedometer gear, reverse light switch, drain plug and service hole plug.

5-Speed Transmission

Most of the procedures described in the 4-speed section apply to the 5-speed, with the following exceptions:

When removing the mainshaft and drive gear, you may have to tap the end of the mainshaft with a hammer.

When assembling the 3rd main gear bushing, make sure the claw is lined up with the main gear spacer and that the thinner spline tooth side of the 2nd/3rd synchro-hub must point towards 3rd gear.

When installing the main gear spacer, make sure that the uneven side is pointed toward 4th gear. The 4th gear bushing is the same as the 4-speed main gear bushing.

TYPE 5

4 and 5 Speed Transaxle Fiat

DISASSEMBLY

NOTE: The five speed transaxle case and gear arrangement is basically the

same as the four speed transaxle, except the rear extension housing is extended to include the fifth gear on the input and output shafts and shift forks are controlled by the fifth and reverse selector rail.

1. Remove the drain plug and drain the lubricant from the transmission/differential.

2. Remove the screws securing the oil boots and remove the axle shafts together with the oil boots.

3. Remove the nuts retaining the cover and remove the cover and gasket.

4. Remove the snap-ring from the mainshaft bearing.

5. Compress the spring washer in the countershaft and remove the snap-ring from the countershaft.

6. Remove the detent ball spring cover and gasket for the shift control rods. Remove the three ball spring and balls.

7. Remove the two ball bearings from the mainshaft and countershaft.

8. Remove the nuts attaching the transmission housing to the main case and lift the case off of the studs.

9. Remove the screws retaining the gearshift forks and dogs to the rods. Remove the rods, forks, and dogs from their seats in the housing.

10. Remove the gear selector and engagement lever support.

11. Remove the gasket between the maincase and the housing.

12. Remove the nut securing the reverse gearshaft retaining plate and remove the plate and the reverse gearshaft.

13. Remove the mainshaft and countershaft assemblies together with the differential assembly.

14. Remove the screw retaining the shift lever and remove the gear shift control rod.

1. Bushing	11. Spring	21. Spring
2. Driven gear	12. Synchronizer	22. Pad
3. Driven gear	13. Bushing	23. Pad
4. Bushing	14. Driven gear	24. Snap ring
5. Countershaft	15. Gear	25. Hub
6. Bearing	16. Bushing	26. Sleeve
7. Synchronizer	17. Bearing	27. Synchronizer
8. Spring	18. Spring washer	28. Spring
9. Hub	19. Snap ring	29. Snap ring
10. Pad	20. Synchronizer	30. Sleeve

Drive gear assembly on countershaft

ASSEMBLY

1. Clean all of the parts with solvent and check the maincase, housing, and cover for cracks and wear or damage to the bearing seats. Check all of the seals for deterioration or wear. Check all shafts for chipping or excessive wear. Check the splines for wear or damage.

Check and make sure that the sliding sleeve hubs for the engagement of first/second and third/fourth gears are not nicked. Check the sleeve sliding surface.

Check the synchronizer rings for signs of deterioration on the inside surface and on the teeth that mesh with the sliding sleeves. The rings must not be loose in its gear seat.

If splined parts do not slide easily and smoothly, remove the cause with a very fine file or replace the defective parts.

2. Install the bearing for the countershaft into the clutch cover end of the transmission case.

3. Install the outer bearing race for the differential bearing onto the case.

4. Install the gear shift control rod in the housing with the spring, gasket, cover, and boot. Next install the control lever.

5. Install the differential assembly in the housing.

6. Install the countershaft assembly in the housing.

7. Install the mainshaft assembly in the housing.

1. Bushing	4. Bearing	7. Mainshaft	10. Lockwasher
2. Gear	5. Snap ring	8. Shaft	11. Stud
3. Seal	6. Bearing	9. Nut	12. Plate

Mainshaft and reverse and reverse idler gear

8. Install the reverse gearshaft with its gasket in the housing. Secure the reverse gear shaft assembly with the plate and nut.

9. Install the gasket onto the housing mating surface.

10. Make sure that the gear selector and engagement lever is sealed on the control lever attached to the gear control rod. Install the support for the selector and engagement lever on the housing. Secure the support with the nut.

11. Install the rod detent rollers in their seats on the support.

12. Install the gear selector rods, forks, and dogs.

13. Install the transmission case on the housing.

14. Secure the two halves of the transmission case together with the washers and nuts.

1. Cover	11. Dowel	21. Seal	31. Gasket
2. Bolt and washer	12. Stud	22. Stud	32. Magnet
3. Plug	13. Lockwasher	23. Lockwasher	33. Gasket
4. Bolt and washer	14. Nut	24. Nut	34. Cover
5. Gasket	15. Stud	25. Flange	35. Bolt
6. Cover	16. Bolt and washer	26. Plug	36. Plug
7. Seal	17. Lockwasher	27. Nut	37. Case
8. Plug	18. Nut	28. Lockwasher	38. Gasket
9. Cover	19. Vent	29. Stud	39. Plug
10. Plug	20. Gasket	30. Cover	

Transaxle case assembly

15. Install the three detent balls and springs in the transmission case.

16. Install the gasket and spring retainer cover. Secure the cover with the two bolts.

17. Install the bearing on the countershaft. Install the two spring washers and snap-ring on the countershaft. Install the snap-ring on the mainshaft.

18. Install the gasket and cover on the transmission.

19. Set the differential bearing. (See differential overhaul.)

20. Install the clutch release forked lever and sliding sleeve.

TYPE 6

4 Speed Transaxle

Fiesta

Special tools are needed in the overhaul of the transaxle gear box.

It would be most advantageous for the repairman to obtain the special tools or their equivalent before the overhaul work is begun.

A list of special tools needed and their reference numbers are given for the convenience of the repairman.

1.	Differential bearing cone replacer	T77F-4220
2.	Differential bearing cone remover and adapter	T77F-4220B
3.	Differential bearing cup installer	T77F-4222A
4.	Differential bearing cup remover	T77F-4222B
5.	Bearing collet (2.675 OD)	T77F-7025A
6.	Bearing collet (2.440 OD)	T77F-7025B
7.	Bearing collet sleeve	T77F-7025C
8.	Transmission output shaft bearing replacer	T77F-7025E
9.	Output shaft rear and input shaft front bearing replacer	T71P-7025A
10.	Transaxle output shaft bearing replacer	T77F-7025E
11.	Selector shaft seal tool	T77F-7288A
12.	Input shaft seal replacer	T77F-7050A
13.	Input shaft seal remover	T77F-7050B
14.	Forcing screw	T75L-7025J
15.	Stub shaft remover adapter	T77F-3617A
16.	Threaded drawbar assembly	T77F-1176A
17.	Slide hammer assembly	T50T-100A
18.	Driver handle	T73T-815A
19.	Input shaft rear bearing replacer	T62F-4621A
20.	Input shaft front bearing remover	T71P-4621B
21.	Transaxle output shaft seal remover	T73C-6700A

TRANSAXLE

Disassembly

1. Mount the removed transaxle on a work stand and drain all oil from the unit.

2. Remove the clutch release lever, fork and release bearing.

3. Remove the selector shaft locking retainer nut with the locking pin and spring.

A — Output shaft (mainshaft)
B — 4th speed gears
C — Input shaft
D — 3rd speed gears
E — 2nd speed gears
F — Reverse gear
G — Reverse idler gear
H — 1st speed gears
J — 1st/2nd speed synchronizer sleeve (Selector ring)
K — Differential drive pinion
L — U-joint
M — Differential case

N — Oil seal
O — Speedometer drive gear
P — Differential side gear
Q — C.V. joint snap ring
R — Differential drive gear
S — Differential side bearing
T — Diaphragm springs
U — 1st/2nd speed synchronizer assy
V — 3rd/4th speed synchronizer hub
W — 3rd/4th speed synchronizer sleeve (Selector Ring)
X — Bearings
Y — C.V. joint

Cross section of Fiesta transaxle assembly

4. Remove the housing end cover plate.

5. Remove the C-clips from the main and input shaft bearings.

6. Remove the small housing section by carefully tapping the housing with a soft headed hammer and lifting upward.

7. Remove the magnetic disc, located on the differential gear side of the unit.

NOTE: Do not drop the disc, as breakage will occur.

8. Remove the selector fork guide shaft, the fork, shift locking plate and spring.

9. Remove the complete mainshaft assembly from the housing, including input shaft and reverse gear.

10. Lift the differential gear from the housing.

11. Remove the mainshaft bearings and disassemble the plastic bearing cage. Remove the rollers and cage. Remove the oil slinger. With the mainshaft bearing remover and slide hammer special tools or equivalent, remove the bearing race from the housing.

12. Remove the input shaft seal with the special tool or equivalent.

NOTE: During the removal of the seal, do not damage the housing.

13. Remove the stubshaft seal from the large housing with the output shaft seal remover or equivalent.

14. Remove the differential gear bearing race from the large housing.

15. Remove the stubshaft from the small

Removing or installing transaxle gears

housing with the stubshaft remover or equivalent.

16. Remove the differential bearing race and cup springs (large and small) from the small housing, with the use of a suitable driver.

TRANSMISSION MAINSHAFT

Disassembly

1. Remove snap-ring from mainshaft end and reinstall the C-clip into the bearing outer race groove. Use a puller and remove the bearing from the shaft, using the C-clip as a pulling base.

2. Remove the fourth gear from the shaft.

3. Remove the retaining ring and remove the third gear synchronizer unit from the shaft.

4. Remove the second speed gear after removing the support ring and locking plate halves.

5. Remove the retaining ring and remove the first/second synchromesh clutch assembly, complete with the first gear.

6. To disassemble the synchronizer clutches, remove the retaining springs with the blocker bars and withdraw the selector ring from the hub.

Assembly

1. Install the first/second gear clutch assembly, complete with the first gear, onto the shaft and secure with the retaining ring.

   NOTE: The selector groove of the clutch assembly must face towards the first gear.

2. Slide the second gear on to the shaft and fit the locking plate halves and secure with a retaining clip.

3. Install the third/fourth synchronizer clutch assembly, complete with third gear and secure with a retainer.

4. Install the fourth gear and install the mainshaft bearing with the groove facing upward, with a suitable press tool and secure with a retaining clip.

COUNTERSHAFT CLUSTER

Disassembly and Assembly

1. Remove the input shaft bearing retainer and reinstall the C-clip in the bearing outer groove to use as a pulling base and remove the bearing with a suitable puller.

2. Remove the small input shaft bearing from the shaft, using a suitable puller.

3. The assembly of the countershaft is the installation of the bearings. Use a suitable installer to press the bearings in place.

DIFFERENTIAL GEAR

Disassembly

1. Remove both differential side gears from the case by turning the side gears laterally.

2. Remove the retaining clip from the differential pinion shaft and push the shaft from the housing. The differential pinions can then be removed.

3. With the aid of a puller, remove the differential tapered roller bearings from the gear housing. Remove the speedometer drive gear from the housing.

4. Remove the axle drive gear (ring gear) from the differential gear housing. Use a soft faced hammer to tap the gear from the housing, after the bolts are removed.

Assembly

1. Position the axle drive gear with the chamfered edge of the gear ring towards the differential gear location. Align the axle drive gear bolt holes with the threaded bolt holes in the housing and tighten the new bolts securely.

2. Press the speedometer drive gear on the differential housing.

3. Press the differential taper roller bearings on the housing with the special tool or equivalent.

4. Install the differential pinions and insert the pinion shaft through the pinions and the housing. Install the retaining clip on the pinion shaft.

5. Install the differential side gears by fitting the side gears into the teeth of the pinion gears and turning the gears simultaneously to position the side gears at the axle openings of the housing.

Exploded view of synchronizer assembly

A—Synchronizer blocking ring
B—Synchronizer insert retaining springs
C—Synchronizer inserts (3)
D—Synchronizer hub
E—Synchronizer sleeve

A — Output shaft with drive gear
B — 1st speed gear
C — 1st/2nd speed blocking rings
D — 1st/2nd speed synchronizer sleeve with reverse gear

E — Retaining (snap) ring
F — 2nd speed gear
G — Locking plate halves (2)
H — Locking plate support ring
J — 3rd speed gear

K — 3rd/4th speed blocking rings
L — 3rd/4th speed synchronizer sleeve
M — Retaining (snap) ring
N — 4th speed gear
O — Output shaft bearing (ball)
P — Snap ring

Exploded view of mainshaft assembly

A — Outer snap ring
B — Countershaft cluster with driving gears 1 through 4 and reverse gear
C — Small ball bearing
D — Large ball bearing
E — Snap ring

Exploded view of input shaft and cluster gear

TRANSAXLE

Assembly

1. Seat the tapered roller bearing cup into the large housing section with the aid of the cup installer tool or equivalent.

2. Install the bearing cup with the large and small springs into the small housing section.

NOTE: Install the small spring with the outside diameter facing the housing and then insert the large spring.

3. Secure the bearing race with a center punch mark on the housing to avoid having the bearing race drop out during the assembly of the two housings.

4. Install a new input shaft seal with the special seal installer tool or equivalent.

5. Install the mainshaft bearing into the housing and install a new oil slinger.

6. Install the roller bearing with the rear of the cage facing downward with the special installer tool or equivalent.

7. Install the differential assembly with the axle drive gear into the large housing.

8. Slide the reverse idler gear onto the shaft and at the same time, insert the selector lever into the selector groove.

NOTE: Raise the selector lever with the idler gear and support on the selector shaft detent for better installation of the mainshaft and input shaft.

9. Install the mainshaft and input shaft cluster simultaneously and carefully into the housing by pairing up the mainshaft and input shaft gears.

10. Install the selector lever and the reverse idler gear.

—————— CAUTION ——————
During the installation of the input and mainshaft, do not damage seals.

11. Install the selector lock plate and fit the

Shifting locking plate in position

selector forks, (first/ second gear with a short actuating lever, third/fourth gear with a long actuating lever).

12. Install the springs in the housing bore and install the selector fork guide shaft with the long pin pointing downward.

NOTE: Engage fourth gear for later selector lever adjustment.

13. Install the magnetic disc into the housing recess.

14. Install the small housing onto the large housing, using new gasket and install the bolts.

15. Raise the shafts slightly with a screwdriver and install the C-clip in the outer bearing race grooves.

NOTE: The C-clips are available in three different sizes. Select the one that just fits into the groove of the bearing race.

16. Install the cover and new gasket on the housing and install the bolts.

17. Install the detent pin with spring and the retaining nut for the selector shaft detent.

18. Install the stubshaft seals into the large and small housing halves with the seal installer special tool or equivalent.

19. Install the clutch release shaft and link with the release bearing on the housing.

SELECTOR MECHANISM

Removal (Transmission Disassembled)

1. Remove the retainer and remove the reverse gear selector from the shaft.

2. Remove the selector lever retaining plate complete with the lever and remove the guide shaft.

3. Remove the guide lever from the retainer plate by removal of two clips.

4. Remove the rubber collar from the control shaft and unscrew the selector gate from the control shaft and press out the shaft.

5. Remove the shaft seal with the seal remover special tool or equivalent.

Installation

1. Install the seal with the special seal installer or equivalent.

2. Install the control shaft and attach the gearshift gate. Install the rubber boot.

3. Attach the guide lever with clips to the retainer plate.

4. Install the guide shaft and fit retainer plate complete with the guide lever.

5. Install the reverse selector lever on the shaft and install the retainer clip.

A — Reverse gearshift lever
B — Shift lever retainer
C — Guide lever retaining plate
D — Guide levers (2)
E — Control shaft boot
F — Control shaft oil seal
G — Control shaft
H — Selector block
J — Selector block
K — Guide shaft

Exploded view of internal shift linkage

TYPE 7

4 and 5 Speed Transaxle Honda

DISASSEMBLY

1. Remove the transmission end cover. Check the transmission mainshaft and countershaft end-play. End-play should be between 0.002-0.003 in. If the clearance is excessive, inspect the ball bearings after transmission disassembly.

2. Remove the locking tab from the mainshaft locknut. The mainshaft locknut has left hand threads. Place the transmission in gear and place the proper size wrench on countershaft to keep it from moving. Remove the mainshaft locknut.

3. Remove the mainshaft bearing and the large snap-ring.

4. Loosen the three shift detent lock ball screws. Remove the screws, springs and balls.

5. Remove the transmission case bolts. Lightly tap the case with a hammer and drift and separate case. Do not pry case apart with a screwdriver.

6. Remove the reverse idler gear and shaft. Remove the reverse shift fork.

7. Remove the shift selector assembly. If repair to the shift selector is necessary, disassemble as follows:

    a. Remove two screws and retaining plate. Stake screws when reinstalling.

    b. Push the shift arm into the reverse position (towards the large spring). Then release it.

    c. The pivot shaft holds a spring loaded detent. Do not lose the detent ball and spring when removing. Remove the pivot shaft.

    d. Remove the interlock bar and shift arms.

    e. During reassembly, insert a screwdriver into the reverse side (large spring end) of the arm assembly to hold down the detent ball, while inserting the pivot shaft.

8. Remove the shift fork retaining bolts and pull the shift shafts up until they clear the case. Remove the forks and shafts.

NOTE: When reinstalling the fork retaining bolts turn the shaft so the threaded portion of the hole is facing away from the bolt.

9. Remove the mainshaft and countershaft at the same time by holding the two shafts and lightly tapping the flywheel end of the mainshaft.

10. Remove the shift rod boot, shift arm, lock washer and bolt. Remove the shift rod and shift arm.

NOTE: During installation of the shift arm retaining bolt, turn the shaft so that the threaded portion of the hole is facing away from the bolt.

11. Measure the side clearance of the low gear with a feeler gauge, if the clearance is excessive, replace the thrust plate. Perform the same measurement on the remaining gears, if the clearance is beyond the service

1. Blocking ring

Measuring the clearance between the synchronizer ring and gear hub

limit, replace the bearing race (spacer). See chart for specifications.

12. If the countershaft must be disassembled to adjust clearances, or replace gears, remove the locknut by installing the shaft in the case and holding the differential securely.

NOTE: Place the end lugs of the holder in the case and center the lug in the hole of the differential carrier.

13. Remove the two screws and retaining plate which hold the countershaft bearing. Remove the countershaft bearing with a bearing puller.

14. Clean all component parts thoroughly in the proper solvent.

15. Inspect the surfaces of each gear and blocking ring for roughness or damage. Apply a thin coat of oil to the tapered surfaces of each gear and push them together with a rotating motion. Measure the distance between the ring and gear. Replace all necessary parts. Clearance should be between 0.120-0.139 in.

16. Measure the clearance between the

1. Needle roller bearing set plate
2. Needle roller bearing
3. Clutch case
4. Reverse gear shaft
5. Reverse idle gear
6. Reverse shift fork
7. Shift selector assembly
8. Countershaft gear assembly
9. Main shaft
10. First/second fork shaft
11. Reverse fork shaft
12. Third/fourth fork shaft
13. Steel ball
14. Ball set spring
15. Drain plug washer
16. Set ball spring screw
17. Ball bearing
18. Needle roller bearing
19. 48 mm snap ring
20. Ball bearing
21. 62 mm snap ring
22. 23 mm lock nut
23. 20 mm lock nut
24. Transmission rear cover
25. Speedometer gear

Exploded view of typical Honda manual transmission

Exploded view of housing and cover assemblies

1 Housing, transmission
2 Spacer, transmission housing
3 Cover, transmission
4 Cover, right side
5 Plate, oil barrier
6 Tube, breather
7 Gasket, transmission housing
8 Cap, breather
9 Gasket, transmission case

10 Bolt, flanged, 6 x 85 mm
11 Bolt, oil check
12 Bolt, plug 25 mm
13 Washer, sealing, 25 mm
14 Washer, 8 mm
15 Oil seal, 35 x 56 x 9 mm
16 O-ring, 9.4 x 2.4
17 O-ring, 64.5 x 3
18 O-ring, 42 x 2.4

19 Bracket, wire harness
20 Bolt, drain plug, 14 mm
21 Washer, drain plug, 14 mm
22 Pin, dowel, 14 x 20 mm
23 Pin, dowel, 8 x 14 mm
24 Bolt, flanged, 6 x 20 mm
25 Bolt, flanged, 6 x 45 mm
26 Bolt, flanged, 8 x 40 mm
27 Bolt, flanged, 8 x 45 mm

shift forks and synchronizer sleeves. The clearance should be between 0.039-0.018. If clearances are excessive, replace the shift forks, synchronizers or both.

17. Ensure that there are no restrictions in the oil holes on the countershaft. Check the splines for wear.

18. Inspect the condition of the mainshaft and countershaft bearing surfaces. Check run-out, gear tooth and spline condition.

19. Check the condition of all the gears. Check the condition of all bearing surfaces.

20. Inspect the bearing race (spacer) of each gear.

21. Replace all questionable parts.

ASSEMBLY

1. Transmission should be assembled in the reverse order of disassembly. During assembly, note the following points.

2. Check the differential bearing clearance.

3. Apply a thin coat of oil to all parts before they are installed.

4. Be certain that hub and synchronizer teeth match when they are assembled.

5. The mainshaft and countershaft must be installed at the same time. Next, install the third/fourth shift fork and shaft, first/second shift fork and shaft, and then the reverse shaft.

6. When the shift selector assembly is installed, there are two special bolts which must be inserted first. These bolts locate the assembly.

7. Lock the mainshaft and countershaft locknuts with a punch.

8. Make sure that the mainshaft and coun-

tershaft turn smoothly and that all gears engage freely. Check and be certain that all bolts are properly torqued.

TYPE 8

4 and 5 Speed Transaxle

Porsche

NOTE: Turbo (930) transaxle similar.

When disassembling and assembling a four speed transaxle, the procedures described in the five speed overhaul should be followed. The gear arrangement, 1st through 4th, on the pinion shaft in the four speed transaxle, is the same as the gear arrangement, 2nd through 5th, in the five speed unit, with the front cover housing only the reverse gear.

Because of the reverse action of the 1st speed synchronizer in the four speed unit, as compared to the five speed unit, the synchronizer components have to be installed directly opposite each other. When installing the synchronizer components for the 1st speed in the four speed transaxle, it should be remembered to insert only one brake band.

The Sportomatic transaxle unit is not covered in the manual transaxle section.

External shifting controls have been relocated from the front of the transaxle to the side on one model and the case has been

modified from a tunnel type to a removable gear housing type on an other model. The gear trains remain basically the same in all models.

DISASSEMBLY

1. Mount the transaxle securely and drain the lubricating fluid.

2. Remove the starter assembly and the center caps from the drive flanges.

3. Remove the retaining bolts from the drive flanges and remove the flanges from the inner axle stub shafts.

NOTE: Place the transaxle in gear and block the input shaft to prevent turning.

4. Remove the side cover assembly and withdraw the differential assembly.

5. Remove the crossmember from the front cover, if not previously done, and remove the front cover assembly.

— CAUTION —

During the front cover removal, the reverse gear components may drop. Prevent from falling to the floor.

6. Remove the 1st/reverse selector fork retaining screw and remove the gear with the fork.

7. Remove the retaining bolt from the pinion shaft.

8. Remove the roll pin from the castled nut on the input shaft. Remove the castle nut and the 1st speed gear.

9. Place the transaxle gears in the neutral position and remove the retaining nut from the plate of the inner shift rod guide fork and remove the guide fork.

10. Remove the inner shift rod through the rear access hole. Shift the gears into the 5th speed position with a suitable bar and remove the intermediate plate with the gear clusters.

NOTE: A plastic hammer may be needed to lightly tap the plate loose.

— CAUTION —

The gear cluster can be installed or removed from the housing only when the transaxle gears are in the 5th speed gear position.

Intermediate Plate and Gear Cluster
DISASSEMBLY

1. Install the intermediate plate assembly in a vise or similar holder and remove the 1st/reverse hub gear, using two suitable prybars.

2. Remove the gear Number two of the 1st speed, along with the needle bearing cage.

3. Shift the gear assembly into neutral position. Remove the selector shaft detent plug and remove the detent spring.

4. Remove the 1st/reverse selector shaft, along with the detent ball.

NOTE: Mark all selector forks and rails during the disassembly to avoid assembly problems.

5. Remove the 2nd/3rd selector fork retaining screw. Remove the selector shaft, fork and detent.

Tunnel type transaxle

6. Remove the 4th and 5th selector fork retaining screw. Remove the selector shaft, fork and detent ball.

7. Remove the detent ball, spring and detent.

8. The input and pinion shafts must be pressed from the intermediate plate.

NOTE: To allow the intermediate plate to lay flat on the press, drive the aligning dowels into the plate and remove the throttle linkage.

9. Remove the bearing plate assembly. Heat the intermediate plate to 248° F (120° C)

and press the bearings from the plate. Remove the detent bushings as necessary.

ASSEMBLY

1. Install the detent bushings, if removed.

───── **CAUTION** ─────
Do not allow the bushings to protrude into the selector shaft bores.

2. Heat the intermediate plate to 248° F (120° C) and press the two bearings into place.

3. Install the bearing brace plate assembly. Torque the retaining bolts to 18 ft/lbs (2.5 Mkp) and lock the bolt heads in place with the lock plates.

4. Insert the input shaft and pinion shaft assemblies into the intermediate plate assembly.

5. Reposition the aligning dowels and the throttle linkage.

Housing Assembly
DISASSEMBLY AND ASSEMBLY

1. Before any attempt is made to install the bearing races, heat the housing to 248° F (120° C).

2. The bearing races can be installed with installer tools and a hammer. Replace the necessary seal or seals.

3. To prevent damages to the housing, install the bearing races squarely in to the housing.

Pinion Shaft
DISASSEMBLY AND ASSEMBLY

1. Remove the retaining bolt with the

Non-tunnel type transaxle

Side shift type transaxle

L. Four-point ballbearing
1. Gear II for 1st speed (Freewheeling)
2. Spider
3. Brake band
4. Gear II for 2nd speed (Freewheeling)
5. Gear II for 3rd speed (Fixed)
6. Gear II for 4th speed (Fixed)
7. Spacer
8. Roller bearing
9. Pinion shaft

10. Thrust washer (6.6 mm thickness)
11. Needle bearing inner race (gear speeds 1 thru 4)
12. Needle bearing cage (gear speeds 1 thru 4)
13. Sliding sleeve
14. Synchronizing ring
15. Needle bearing inner race
16. Needle bearing cage
17. Spacers
18. Retaining ring

Cross section of 4-speed pinion shaft assembly

Correct assembly of 1st speed synchronizer for the 5-speed gear train

Correct assembly of 1st speed synchronizer for the 4-speed gear train

speedometer gear attached, from the pinion shaft.

2. The gear assemblies are removed by pressing the shaft from the gears.

3. Mark and identify all components so as to maintain proper assembly sequence.

CAUTION

Note the number and thickness of spacers between the roller bearings and thick spacers to avoid recomputing spacer thickness during reassembly.

NOTE: Later transaxles have the thrust washer and spacer replaced with a single, beveled thrust washer.

Input Shaft
DISASSEMBLY AND ASSEMBLY

1. Straighten the locking tabs from the hex nut. Remove the retaining hex nut from the shaft, using the necessary special tools.

2. Press the roller bearing from the shaft, using special tools as necessary.

3. Remove the gears and components from the input shaft.

NOTE: Mark the needle bearing cages to properly install them during the installation procedure.

4. To remove the inner half of the ball bearing race from the stub end of the shaft, drive the race away from its seat with a drift punch or similar tool, and remove with a puller.

5. The reassembly of the shaft and components should be done in the reverse of the removal procedure.

6. The locknut should be torqued to 72 to 86 ft/lbs (10 to 12 Mkp). Be sure to secure the nut with the locking tabs of the lock plate edge.

Differential Assembly

The differential assembly is overhauled in the conventional manner. Special measuring tools are needed to measure the preload, tooth contact and to determine the thickness of necessary shims and spacers.

TRANSAXLE REASSEMBLY

1. Having the transaxle case overhauled as required and the intermediate plate as-

sembled, place the gears in the 5th speed and prepare to install the assembly into the case.

2. Guide the intermediate plate assembly into the case and lightly tighten at four housing studs.

3. Install gear one of 1st speed on the input shaft. Install the spacer and tighten the castellated nut to a torque of 43 to 47 ft/lbs (6.0 to 6.5 Mkp). Secure the nut with a spiral pin.

4. Install the thrust washer on the pinion shaft with the small collar facing the bearing. Guide the needle bearing in place with a suitable tool.

5. Install the needle bearing and gear two of 1st speed. Install the spider wheel of the 1st/reverse gear.

6. Tighten the pinion shaft bolt (with extension for tachometer) to 80 to 86 ft/lbs (11 to 12 Mkp). Block the gear train to prevent turning.

7. Remove the intermediate plate assembly from the case assembly. Place the intermediate plate assembly into a holder so that the selector shafts can be installed.

8. Install the shafts in the following order:

a. Place the selector sleeve of the 4th/5th speed onto its respective slide and position the 4th/5th speed selector shaft through the fork and through the intermediate plate. Tighten the fork retaining screw.

b. Install into the detent bore, one ball, detent pin, one long spring and one more ball.

c. Place the selector fork of 2nd/3rd speeds onto the respective sliding sleeve and push the selector shaft through the fork and into the intermediate plate.

NOTE: The 4th/5th selector shaft must be in the neutral position and the detent ball pressed down.

d. Tighten the fork retaining screw and move the selector lever to the neutral position. Insert the detent.

e. Install the 1st/reverse selector shaft into the intermediate plate and install the detent ball and short spring. Tighten the detent cap screw to 18 ft/lbs (2.5 Mkp).

f. Slide the selector fork and the sliding gear for the 1st/ reverse speed together onto the spider wheel and selector shaft. Install and tighten the fork retaining screw.

NOTE: The sliding sleeves must be adjusted to a position in the exact center in relation to the synchronizer rings when in the neutral position. The forks can be moved by loosening the retaining bolts. A special gauge block is available for this operation, but normally not available to the average repair shop.

g. When the adjustment of the forks are completed, torque the retaining bolts to 18 ft/lbs (2.5 Mkp).

9. Install the inner shift rod into the transaxle housing, after having installed the shift finger onto the shaft and securing it with the retaining pin and cotter pin.

10. Guide the intermediate plate assembly into the transaxle housing with gaskets attached, carefully to avoid damage to the input shaft seal.

NOTE: The gear train assembly must be in the 5th speed position.

11. Shift the gear train into Neutral. Guide the inner shift rod into its proper position at the selector shaft tabs and into the rear rod bore.

12. Install the guide fork of the inner shift rod, using a new gasket and be sure the inner shift rod enters the guide fork.

13. Assemble the front cover and install on the transaxle assembly.

a. Install the bearing cages and the spacer bushings.

b. Install the reverse gear, axial thrust needle bearing and the thrust washer.

c. Install the tachometer elbow unit drive unit into the cover and align the indent for the set screw with the hole in the cover.

d. Install a new gasket and install the front cover. Pull the reverse gear and its axial thrust needle bearing with the thrust washer as far to the end of the shaft as possible to clear the sliding gear of the 1st/reverse speed gear.

NOTE: The machined recess in the thrust washer must align with the outer collar of the pinion shaft bearing.

14. Install the retaining nuts and torque to 15.2 to 16.6 ft/lbs (2.1 to 2.8 Mkp).

15. Install the transaxle support.

Location of 1st/reverse sliding gear with selector fork in place—5-speed

Gear train assembled in the intermediate plate—typical

TYPE 9

5 Speed Transaxle (Model G 28.03) Porsche

DISASSEMBLY

1. Mount transaxle assembly securely and drain the lubricating oil.

2. Remove the rear cover and top cover from the transaxle case.

3. Remove the right and left axle flange retaining bolts and remove the axle flanges.

4. Remove the right and left side cover retaining bolts and carefully separate the side covers, with shims, from the transaxle case. Carefully remove the differential carrier assembly.

5. Drive the main shift rod pin from the shift finger with a pin punch or other suitable tool. Remove the lockout spring and pin from the shaft. Remove the shaft from the transaxle case.

6. Remove the shift shaft interlock mechanism by removing the screw plugs, located on the left and right sides of the case, near the front upper sides.

7. Drive the pins from the shift fingers and shift forks with a pin punch or other suitable tool. Remove the shafts to the rear of the transaxle case, being careful not to exert undue force. Remove the interlock detents and springs as the shafts are removed. Remove the shift fingers and forks from the case.

8. Remove the input shaft oil seal holder by pulling outward while turning.

9. Remove the countershaft retaining circlip from the transaxle case. From the rear of the case, tap the countershaft forward and out of the case.

NOTE: The pinion shaft bearing plate may have to be loosened.

— CAUTION —
To avoid damage to the case or gears, hold the countergears from falling into the case with wire as a support.

10. With the use of a special puller to maintain straightness, remove the input shaft from the case.

11. Remove the pinion shaft bearing retainer plate bolts and remove the pinion shaft assembly by using a puller.

12. Lift the countergear assembly from the case.

13. Using an appropriate driver, remove the reverse idler shaft from the gear and case.

14. Remove shift shaft oil seals from the case.

Input Shaft
DISASSEMBLY

1. Remove the synchronizer ring, shift band, stop and thrust block from the input shaft.

2. Remove the front ball bearing circlip and press the bearing from the input shaft.

3. With an appropriate puller, remove the two needle bearings and spacer from the input shaft.

ASSEMBLY

1. Install one needle bearing into the input shaft, followed by the spacer and the second needle bearing.

2. Heat the ball bearing assembly to 212° F (100° C) and drive it on to the input shaft. Install the retaining circlip.

3. Install the thrust block, stop, shift band

1. Bolt	18. Spring	31. Oil seal
2. Washer	19. Detent plunger	32. Input shaft
3. Upper cover	20. Shift rod with shift fork for 4th and 5th gear	33. O-ring
4. Gasket	21. Detent/interlock plungers	34. Bolt
5. Vent	22. Spring	35. Serrated lock washer
6. Roll pin	23. Shift rod with shift fork for 2nd and 3rd gear	36. Pinion shaft assembly
7. Split pin	24. Shift rod with shift fork for 1st and reverse gear	37. Shim
8. Main shift rod	25. Interlock pin	38. Needle bearing
9. Shift finger	26. Circlip	39. Spacer
10. U-spring	27. Countershaft	40. Countershaft hub/gears
11. Lockout spring	28. O-ring	41. Needle bearing
12. Backup light switch	29. Circlip	42. Thrust washer
13. Plunger	30. Input shaft oil seal holder	43. Reverse idler shaft
14. Plug		44. Reverse idler gear
15. Seal		45. Oil seal
16. Plug		46. Magnetic drain plug
17. Seal		

Exploded view of shifting mechanism and gear train—928

1. Circlip	
2. Shim (distance y)	
3. Shift sleeve	
4. Hub	
5. Needle bearing	
6. Inner race	
7. Gear, 4th speed	
8. Thrust washer	
9. Needle bearing	
10. Inner race	
11. Gear, 3rd speed	

12. Shift sleeve	
13. Hub	
14. Needle bearing	
15. Inner race	
16. Gear, 2nd speed	
17. Thrust washer	
18. Needle bearing	
19. Inner race	
20. Gear, 1st speed	
21. Shift sleeve	
22. Hub	

23. Shim (distance x)	
24. Locknut	
25. Reverse gear	
26. Tapered roller bearing inner race	
27. Shim	
28. Bearing retaining plate	
29. Tapered roller bearing inner race	
30. Pinion shaft	

Exploded view of pinion shaft gear assembly—928

and secure with the synchronizer ring on the input shaft.

Mainshaft
DISASSEMBLY

1. Remove the circlip and shims from the front of the mainshaft. Note the number and thickness of the shims for reassembly.

2. Using a press, remove the gears, bearings and races from the mainshaft, noting the direction of each gear and component for reassembly. Mark the disassembled parts as required. Note the location of all shims for reassembly.

3. Remove the locknut from the mainshaft with appropriate tools and remove the reverse gear. Press the front tapered bearing and bearing retaining plate from the mainshaft. Press the rear tapered bearing from the mainshaft.

ASSEMBLY

1. Heat the rear tapered bearing to 212° F (100° C) and drive on to the mainshaft.

2. Place the bearing retaining plate on the mainshaft and heat the front tapered bearing as was done to the rear bearing, and drive the front bearing on to the mainshaft.

3. Install the reverse gear with the small depression on the hub towards the front of the mainshaft. Install the locknut and torque to 109 to 130 ft/lbs (15 to 18 Mkg). Stake the locknut collar to the small depression in the reverse gear hub.

4. To properly position the gears on the mainshaft, selective shims must be used in conjunction with the locknut. To obtain the proper specification, the following formula must be used.

Measuring Formula

The design specification is 108.80 mm from the rear face of the pinion gear to the front face of the selective shim and should be measured with a sliding caliper or micrometer. To obtain the proper specifications without the needed shim, use the formula by substituting the resulting readings, as illustrated by the example.

108.80 = Design specifications

A = Distance from rear face of pinion to the locknut bearing surface.

B = Distance A + r

X = Shim thickness required

r = Pinion shaft and gear deviation during manufacture

Example

Distance A = 106.90 mm

Distance B = A + r

$$A = 106.90 \text{ mm}$$
$$r = +0.12 \text{ mm}$$
$$B = 107.02 \text{ mm}$$

Distance X = 108.80 mm — B
$$\underline{\begin{array}{l} 108.80 \text{ mm} \\ 107.02 \text{ mm} \end{array}}$$

1.78 mm is the thickness of the selective shim needed (Distance X)

5. Following the disassembly order, replace the gears, spacers, bearings and circlips on the mainshaft.

NOTE: The inner races for the needle bearing have to be heated to 212° F (100° C) before installation on the mainshaft.

Determining Shim Thickness

1. Place the gear train of the mainshaft in a press, under approximately 5 ton, and measure the space between the front circlip and the 4th/5th gear hub.

2. Select a shim with maximum thickness to remove all play between the circlip and the gear hub.

3. Remove the unit from the press, remove the circlip and install the shim. Reinstall the circlip.

Determining Input Shaft Clearance (During Assembly)

1. The clearance between the input shaft and the 4th/5th gear hub can be determined by inserting a feeler gauge between the shaft end and the gear hub. The clearance should be 0.2 to 0.3 mm.

2. Should this clearance not be obtained, the mainshaft will have to be disassembled and the shim thickness at the locknut be rechecked and corrected.

3. Reassemble the mainshaft and recheck the clearance, again under pressure, between

the circlip and the 4th/5th gear hub. Correct as required.

4. Recheck the clearance between the input shaft and the 4th/5th gear hub.

Synchronizer Component Identification

1ST GEAR

Synchronizer ring—One groove on face.
Thrust block—Two beveled sides.
Shift band—Uneven shift bands.
Stop—Two straight sides.
Installation note: Short side of shift band must be to the right of the thrust block.

2ND GEAR

Synchronizer ring—Two grooves on the face or a red dot.
Thrust block—Two beveled sides.
Shift band—Even shift bands.
Stop—One straight and one beveled side.
Installation note: Beveled side of stop must be faced to the right as seen from the top view.

3RD GEAR

Synchronizer ring—Two grooves on the face or a red dot.
Thrust block—Two beveled sides.
Shift band—Two separate shift bands.
Stop—Beveled sides.

4TH GEAR

Synchronizer ring—No grooves.
Thrust block—Two beveled sides.
Shift band—Two separate shift bands.
Stop—Beveled sides.

5TH GEAR

Synchronizer ring—No grooves (0.6 mm wider).
Thrust block—Two beveled sides.
Shift band—Two separate shift bands.
Stop—Beveled sides.

NOTE: All synchronizers should have an installed diameter of 86.0 ±0.24 mm, measured at the highest point of the ring.

Countershaft
DISASSEMBLY

1. Remove the circlip from the countershaft hub.
2. Press the 3rd, 4th and 5th gears from the countershaft hub.

INSTALLATION

1. Heat the gears to approximately 212° F (100° C) and press them into their proper position.
2. Install the circlip on the countershaft hub.

TRANSMISSION ASSEMBLY

1. Place the assembled countershaft assembly into the transmission case with lift wires attached.
2. Install the mainshaft into the case and install the bolts in the bearing retaining plate to case.
3. Install the input shaft assembly in the front of the transmission case.
4. With the lifting wire, raise the countershaft hub assembly in place and insert the countershaft from the front of the transmission case and towards the rear, engaging the notched portion of the shaft into the slot pro-

vided by the installation of the mainshaft bearing retainer plate.

NOTE: The bearing retaining plate may have to be loosened to allow the entry of the countershaft into its position in the rear of the case. Retighten the bearing retaining plate.

5. Check the gear train for freeness of rotation and proper clearances.
6. Install the shift rods, forks and finger in their proper locations and install the retaining pins through the forks and fingers to engage the shift rods. Install the necessary detent plungers and springs during the shift rod installation.
7. Install the detent plugs, necessary circlips and the input shaft oil seal holder.
8. Install the main shift rod and shift finger. Install the retaining pin into the finger and through the shaft.
9. Install the differential carrier assembly and the side covers with the removed shims.

NOTE: Should the differential need to be adjusted, refer to the individual car section.

10. Install the left and right axle flanges and retain with the retaining bolts.
11. Install the top and rear cover, using new gaskets.
12. Fill the transmission and the differential with hypoid type oil, 90 weight. Each must be filled separately.

TYPE 10

4 Speed Transaxle Renault

DISASSEMBLY

1. Mount the transaxle assembly securely and drain the lubricating oil.
2. Remove the clutch housing assembly.
3. Remove the locking washers and bolts from the differential adjusting ring nuts and with the use of a special wrench or equivalent, remove the adjusting ring nuts.
4. Release the clutch shaft roll pin retaining spring and remove the pin. Remove the clutch shaft and the differential assembly.

5. Remove the top cover retaining bolts and the cover.
6. Remove the selector fork shaft springs and the locking balls.
7. Remove the front cover retaining bolts and the top cover.
8. Remove the primary shaft adjusting shims.
9. Remove the primary shaft rear bearing retaining plate and bolts.
10. Using a pin punch, remove the two roll pins holding the reverse gear pinion shaft. Remove the reverse gear selector shaft and the locking disc between the shifting shafts.
11. Engage the gears in one speed, unlock and remove the speedometer end nut from the final drive pinion, along with the rubber washer.
12. Move the gears to the neutral position, move the final drive pinion in towards the differential and remove the tapered bearing. Remove the final drive pinion.
13. Push the primary shaft towards the differential and free the rear bearing cage.
14. Remove the front bearing (freefitting), the primary shaft, the reverse gear shaft and the reverse gear.
15. Remove the 1st/2nd and 3rd/4th gear fork roll pins, using a pin punch. Remove the shafts and selector forks.
16. Remove the lock plate for the secondary bearing adjusting nut and remove the nut.
17. Remove the 4th speed gear thrust washer and push out the primary shaft front bearing assembly.
18. Lift the secondary shaft and the synchronizer assembly from the transaxle.

Differential

The differential assembly is overhauled in the conventional manner. Special tools are needed to measure the bearing preload, tooth contact and to determine the thickness of various shims, when used. To aid the repairman when differential repairs do not need to be done, all necessary measurements should be made of the differential assembly before disassembly and providing no internal parts were installed that would affect the differential measurements, reassemble to the original measurements.

Cross section of Renault 4-speed transaxle

Bearings and Races
REMOVAL AND INSTALLATION

A press and puller is needed to remove and replace the transaxle bearings and races from the case, adjusting ring nuts and the shafts. Caution must be exercised when removing the races because of a lip on varied races. Do not press in the wrong direction. Replace all seals during the overhaul of the transaxle assembly.

Primary Shaft

The disassembly and assembly of the primary shaft is limited to the replacement of the bearings, which should be pressed on and off as necessary.

Secondary Shaft (Pinion)
DISASSEMBLY

1. Mark the position of each sliding gear in relation to its hub, before disassembly.
2. Move each gear, hub and bearing from the shaft, keeping each in its proper order.
3. Remove the pinion gear end bearing by pressing the shaft from the bearing.

ASSEMBLY

1. Install the pinion gear end bearing onto the shaft.
2. Install the gears, hubs and bearings onto the shaft in the order of their removal.

Top Cover
DISASSEMBLY

1. Remove the reverse gear selector and the two roll pins securing the selector finger.
2. Remove the control shaft assembly. Mark the location of the springs, stops and bellows.
3. If necessary, remove the bushing and the seal from the cover.

ASSEMBLY

1. Install the bushing and the seal, if removed.
2. Install the control shaft assembly. Position the spring, spring stops and the bellows.
3. Install the roll pins securing the selector finger.
4. Install the reverse gear selector and retaining bolt.

Synchronizers

When new synchronizers are installed, match the sliding sleeve over the hub assembly until a free fit is felt. Mark the assembly and install on the shaft in its proper turn.

1ST/2ND SYNCHRONIZER

1. Place the springs so that the three slots are covered on the hub assembly.

3RD/4TH SYNCHRONIZER

1. Place the springs into the hub so that the two springs are approximately 180° apart on each side of the hub.
2. Install the three keys and push the sliding sleeve over the hub, with the grooves on the sleeve facing towards the low part of the hub with the biggest offset.
3. Mark the unit for installation.

Reassembly of the Transaxle
SECONDARY (PINION) SHAFT

1. Have the case assembly in a vertical position and place the secondary gear stack, less

the 4th speed driven gear, in the transaxle case.
2. Slide the final drive pinion shaft into the casing, mating the shaft splines to the 1st/2nd and 3rd/4th speed synchronizer hubs.

NOTE: A block can be used to hold the pinion shaft in the upright position while completing the assembly of the gear train.

3. Install the 4th speed gear and gear ring onto the shaft. Install the caged two needle bearing and the 4th gear sleeve.
4. Place the 4th speed thrust washer with the large diameter facing the gear and screw the bearing ring adjusting nut into place until snug.
5. Install the tapered roller bearing on the final drive pinion, hand tight.
6. Hold the sliding gear in place with a special wrench or equivalent tool and tighten the speedometer drive pinion with a properly fitted wrench, so that the tapered roller bearing is drawn into position.
7. Remove the speedometer drive pinion and insert the spring washer. Reinstall the drive pinion and torque to 75 to 90 ft/lbs (10 to 12 Nm). Lock the pinion into position.

PINION SHAFT BEARING ADJUSTMENT

1. Unscrew the adjusting ring nut until the race touches the rollers.
2. When using original bearings, no end-play should exist between the rollers and the race and no preload is required. When adjusted, install the lock plate.
3. When installing new bearings, a preload must be obtained. Perform the following operation.
   a. Unscrew the ring nut while turning the secondary (pinion) shaft by hand.
   b. When the shaft becomes hard to turn, preload has developed. Continue to rotate the shaft several times to seat the bearings.
   c. Tie a piece of string around the 3rd/4th sliding sleeve groove and wrap it several times around the sleeve.
   d. Using a spring scale, pull the string and measure the rotating force. The torque preload should be 1 to 3½ lbs (0.5 to 1.7 N).
   e. Adjust the ring nut as necessary to obtain the proper preload.
   f. When the preload is correct, lock the ring nut with the lock plate.

INSTALLATION OF SELECTOR FORKS

NOTE: During the installation of the retaining roll pins, the slots must face towards the differential.

1. Place the 1st/2nd speed selector fork in the case and slide the selector shaft through the case bracket and into the selector fork.
2. Install the retaining roll pin through the fork and shaft.
3. Install the 3rd/4th selector fork into the case and slide the selector shaft through the case bracket and into the selector fork.
4. Install the retaining roll pin through the fork and shaft.

Primary Shaft
INSTALLATION

1. Position the transaxle case in the upright with the differential housing on top.

2. Place the primary shaft into the case with the 4th speed gear setting on the transaxle case.
3. From the differential side, install the tapered roller bearing, using a length of pipe stock, fitted to the inner race of the bearing.
4. Position the reverse gear in the case, with the groove facing towards the differential housing. Install the reverse shaft and secure with a roll pin.

NOTE: The roll pin should protrude equally from both sides of the shaft.

5. Install the primary shaft bearing race onto the rear of the shaft and install the race retaining plate and lockplate.
6. Tighten the lockplate bolts and bend the lockplate tabs over the bolt heads.
7. Install the primary shaft front bearing. The bearing should slide onto the shaft.
8. Install the outer race onto the shaft until it is flush with the case.

PRIMARY SHAFT BEARING ADJUSTMENT

NOTE: The end-play of the primary shaft should be adjusted to 0.001 to 0.005 inch (0.02 to 0.12 mm). Shims are used to adjust the end-play.

1. Mount a dial indicator gauge on the speedometer drive pinion end of the case. Push the bearing race inward to reduce the end-play of the shaft, measured by the dial indicator on the shaft end.
2. When the proper amount of end-play has been obtained, place the adjusting shims in position on the bearing race, so that the last shim extends beyond the gasket face by 0.012 inch (0.30 mm).

Front Cover
INSTALLATION

1. Install the locking disc between the selector shafts and slide the reverse gear shaft in place.
2. Install the lock balls and springs into the bores in the transaxle case.

NOTE: The longest spring is for the 1st/2nd gear selector shaft.

3. Install the speedometer gear sleeve in position, with its O-ring in place.
4. Install the speedometer driven gear, the primary shaft adjusting shims and the paper gasket.
5. Install the front cover and secure it with the retaining bolts.

Top Cover
INSTALLATION

1. Place the transaxle gear train in the neutral position. Slide the reverse gear on the shaft until it rests on the 4th speed gear of the primary shaft.
2. Invert the top cover and space the long end of the selector lever ⅜ inch (10 mm) from the center line of the stop on the top cover.
3. Again, invert the cover and with its sealing gasket, place it onto the transaxle.
4. Move the cover so that the ends of the gear lever engages in the selector fork notches and the ends of the reverse selector lever engages the notch on the selector shaft and the groove in the gear.

5. Secure the cover with the retaining bolts.

Differential
INSTALLATION

1. Install the differential assembly into the housing. Install the clutch shaft and secure with a roll pin. Install the retaining spring.

2. Seal the threads of the differential adjusting nuts and install into the housing, matching the disassembly marks.

3. The backlash is adjusted by the movement of the adjusting ring nuts and should measure 0.005 to 0.010 inch (0.12 to 0.25 mm).

4. Install the lock plates to lock the adjusting rings.

Clutch Housing
INSTALLATION

1. Install the oil seal in the clutch housing and install the gasket.

2. Install a seal protector tool over the clutch shaft and install the clutch housing.

3. Install the retaining bolts for the clutch housing. Torque to 30 ft/lbs (4 Nm).

4. Remove the seal protector tool from the clutch shaft.

TYPE 11

4 Speed Transaxle
Renault

DISASSEMBLY

NOTE: The shifting control linkage arm can be located at either the top or bottom of the front cover, depending upon the transaxle model.

1. Mount the transaxle securely and drain the lubricating oil.

2. Remove the clutch housing retaining bolts and remove the cover assembly.

3. Remove the back-up light switch and the front cover assembly. Remove the spacer and the primary shaft bearing adjusting shims. Measure the ring and pinion backlash and

mark the differential adjusting locknuts for installation purposes.

4. Remove the right and left differential bearing adjusting locknuts, using the appropriate tools.

5. Remove the half housing assembly retaining bolts and separate the half housings.

6. Lift the pinion shaft assembly from the half housing, along with the stop peg which is used to lock the double tapered roller bearing outer cage.

7. Lift the primary shaft and the differential from the half housing.

8. Using a drift, remove the roll pin from the 3rd/4th speed fork. Remove the fork and shaft, while retaining the locking ball and spring. Remove the locking disc located between the shafts.

9. Move the selector lever into the 1st gear position and slide the reverse gear shaft as far as possible back on the control rod side.

10. Using a drift, remove the roll pin from the 1st/2nd gear fork. Remove the fork and shaft while retaining the locking ball and spring.

11. Unscrew the reverse gear swivel lever bolt and remove the swivel lever.

12. Using a drift, remove the reverse gear positioning shaft roll pin. Remove the shaft and fork.

NOTE: The roll pin will touch the housing and must be turned and the pin removed completely with a pair of pliers.

Remove the circlip from the reverse idler gear and shaft. Remove the shaft, the gear, thrust washer and the guide. Retain the locking ball and spring.

14. Necessary replacement of half housing parts and seals can now be accomplished.

Primary Shaft
DISASSEMBLY

1. Separate the clutch shaft from the primary shaft by removal of the roll pin with a drift.

2. Remove the bearings from the shaft, using appropriate pullers.

ASSEMBLY

1. Using a press or its equivalent, install the tapered bearing onto the primary shaft.

2. Install the clutch shaft onto the primary shaft, using a new roll pin.

Pinion Shaft (Secondary)
DISASSEMBLY

1. Place the pinion shaft assembly in a vise and secure on the 1st speed gear. Place the 1st/2nd synchronizer in the 1st speed position.

2. Release the speedometer drive gear locking tabs and unscrew the gear from the shaft.

3. Remove the double tapered roller bearing, the adjusting washer, the 4th speed gear and ring, along with the 3rd/4th speed synchronizer sliding sleeve and keys.

─── CAUTION ───
Mark the position of the sliding sleeve with reference to its position on the hub.

.4 Using a press and appropriate tools, remove the 3rd/4th speed synchronizer hub from the shaft.

5. Remove the 3rd gear stop washer and retaining key. Remove the 3rd gear and synchronizer ring.

6. Remove the 2nd speed gear stop washer, the 2nd speed gear and synchronizer ring. Remove the 1st/2nd synchronizer sliding gear.

─── CAUTION ───
Mark the position of the sliding sleeve with reference to its position on the hub.

7. Remove the stop washer from the shaft for the 1st/2nd synchronizer hub.

8. Using a press or equivalent tool, remove the 1st/2nd gear synchronizer hub from the shaft.

9. Remove the 1st gear synchronizer ring, the stop washer and the 1st speed gear.

10. Install a retaining clip onto the strengthen crown wheel and pinion assemblies to prevent the tapered roller bearing from falling out. This clip is supplied with new crown wheel and pinion assemblies.

NOTE: The bearing inner track (race) is bonded to the final drive pinion shaft and cannot be replaced.

ASSEMBLY

1. Install a new crown wheel and pinion assembly, if required.

2. Install the 1st speed gear, the stop washer and the 1st speed gear onto the shaft.

3. The 1st/2nd synchronizer hub should be heated to 482° F (250° C) maximum, when installed on the pinion shaft.

4. Install the 1st/2nd gear synchronizer stop washer, the 1st/2nd synchronizer sliding gear to its original position in reference to the hub, the 2nd speed gear and its ring and the 2nd speed gear stop washer.

5. Install the 3rd speed gear and synchronizer ring, the 3rd speed gear stop washer and the stop washer retaining key.

6. Install the 3rd/4th speed synchronizer hub.

NOTE: The hub can be heated or pressed onto the shaft.

7. Install the 3rd/4th speed synchronizer

Cross section of Renault split case transaxle

Positioning of the gears on the primary shaft

Position (A) of the three reversed nuts for clutch control clearance

sliding gear and keys to their original positions as per the previous marks.

8. Install the 4th speed gear and synchronizer ring, the pinion sleeve adjusting washer and the double tapered roller bearing.

9. Install the speedometer drive gear and screw it on to the shaft. Place the pinion shaft in a vise, and secure the 1st speed gear. Place the synchronizer sliding sleeve into the 1st speed position.

10. Tighten the speedometer drive gear to 75 to 85 ft/lbs. Lock the tabs of the locking ring unless the pinion depth adjustment is to be made.

Differential

The differential assembly is overhauled in the conventional manner. Refer to the general instruction in the rear axle repair unit section. Special measuring tools are needed to measure the pinion depth, ring gear backlash adjustment and differential bearing preload adjustment.

Positioning the Primary and Pinion Shaft

1. Place the primary and the pinion (secondary) shafts into the left half housing.

2. The position of the 3rd speed gear on the primary shaft should be offset with reference to the 3rd speed gear of the pinion (secondary) shaft, by the same amount as the 4th speed gear on the primary shaft in reference to the 4th speed gear on the pinion (secondary) shaft.

3. To achieve the proper distance, the positioning is accomplished by using adjusting washers in selective sizes on the primary shaft.

Adjusting Primary Shaft Bearings

1. Place the primary shaft assembly into the left half housing and fit the right half housing in place, but do not secure it.

2. Fit the spacer and shim pack into the 4th gear side bearing bore.

3. The shaft should turn freely, without any end-play and the spacer should project past the housing 0.008 inch (0.2 mm), which represents the thickness of the front housing paper gasket.

4. Should the clearance be wrong, increase or decrease the shim sizes by selecting one of proper size.

5. Upon obtaining the proper clearance, remove the right half housing and the primary shaft.

ASSEMBLY

1. Install the reverse shaft and position the fork on the shaft. Retain the fork to the shaft by the roll pin.

2. Place the reverse shaft swivel lever in position and retain with the bolt. Torque to 20 ft/lbs.

3. Install the 1st/2nd shaft locking ball and spring. Insert the 1st/2nd speed selector

shaft. Fit the reverse end fitting and retain it with a roll pin. Install the 1st/2nd speed gear fork and retain it with a roll pin.

4. Position the locking disc in place between the shafts and install the 3rd/4th selector shaft locking ball and spring.

5. Install the shaft and fit the 3rd/4th gear fork with the hub towards the differential end and retain it with a roll pin.

6. Install the locking ball and spring, the reverse idler shaft and gear, (with the hub towards the differential end) and the thrust washer into the right half housing. The thrust washer bronze face should be against the gear.

7. Install the guide from inside the bore and push the shaft fully into place. Install the gear retaining circlip.

8. Place the differential, the primary shaft with the clutch shaft in place and the secondary shaft assembly into the left half housing.

9. Install a sealing compound on the joint faces of the half housings and fit the right housing to the left housing, being sure the end of the reverse idler lever enters the slot in the reverse gear shaft.

10. Install the retaining bolts and nuts.

--- **CAUTION** ---

The nuts are located on the right half housing, except three under the differential assembly, reversed to allow clearance for the clutch controls.

11. Fit the primary shaft bearing adjusting shims and the spacer.

12. Install the shift fork shaft control lever.

13. Install a new gasket on the front housing and install in place on the transaxle, while engaging the shaft into the control lever.

14. Install the retaining pin with a drift. Install the cover retaining nuts but do not tighten.

15. Tighten the half housing bolts to the following torque;
   0.276 inch (7 mm)—15 ft/lbs
   0.315 inch (8 mm)—20 ft/lbs

16. Tighten the front cover nuts.

17. Install the differential carriers and tighten to the original positions as marked during the disassembly.

18. Install a new gasket on the clutch housing and install the housing. Fill the transaxle with lubricating oil after the unit is installed in the vehicle.

Positioning of gear train in the half case

TYPE 12

4 Speed Transaxle
SAAB

DISASSEMBLY

NOTE: The disassembly and assembly of the transaxle gear train can be accomplished without separating the engine and gearbox. However, the engine flywheel must be removed.

— CAUTION —

Before the transaxle disassembly is begun, measure the backlash of the differential ring and pinion gears, so that the same backlash is obtained during the reassembly, providing no affected components for the differential are replaced. Upon removal of the differential bearing seats, measure and mark the shims for later installation.

1. Secure the transaxle and drain the lubricating oil. Remove the side and end plates from the case.
2. Remove the differential bearing seat retaining bolts and with the aid of a puller type tool, remove the left and right seats. Remove the spring and plunger on each end of the inner driveshaft, along with the adjusting shims.

NOTE: The inner driveshafts will be removed with the seats as an assembly.

3. Remove the differential assembly from the housing.
4. Remove the lock plate that holds the intermediate and reverse gear shafts in place.
5. Using a special pulling tool or equivalent, pull the intermediate gear shaft from the housing and allow the intermediate gear set to drop downward.
6. Remove the primary gear housing retaining bolts and separate the primary gear housing from the transaxle housing.
7. With the primary gear housing separated from the transaxle housing, the intermediate gear set can be removed from the transaxle.
8. Remove the transaxle side cover, if not already removed, and take out the spring and ball catch for the gear selector rod.
9. Remove the reverse gear selector shaft retaining screw, turn the gear selector rod so the driver is detached from the reverse gear shift and pull out the shaft.
10. Remove the shift shaft for the 1st/2nd gear, 3rd top gear and shift forks. Remove the shift fork and the sliding sleeve for the 3rd speed gear.

NOTE: The reverse lever does not need to be removed from the gear shift shaft when the shaft is removed.

11. Remove the reverse gear shaft and lift the reverse idler gear from the housing.
12. Remove the needle bearing from the pinion shaft and install a special holding tool or equivalent, as a lock on the reverse gear of the pinion shaft. Remove the pinion nut from the shaft.
13. Remove the gear holding tool and re-move the 3rd/4th gear synchronizer hub and 3rd gear.
14. Remove the four pinion shaft bearing housing screws. Install a special pushing tool or equivalent, and remove the pinion shaft from the housing. Remove the gears, sleeves, washers and shims from the housing, noting each component's location.

Pinion Shaft and Housing
DISASSEMBLY

1. To remove the pinion shaft from the pinion shaft housing, the pinion bearing nut must be removed. The pinion shaft can then be pressed from the housing and the front bearing removed.
2. Place the pinion shaft and rear bearing in a press and remove the rear bearing from the shaft.
3. Remove the outer races from the pinion shaft housing as required, with a press and the necessary special tools.

ASSEMBLY

1. Install the outer races in the pinion shaft housing and seat firmly.
2. Press the rear bearing onto the pinion shaft. Fit the spacer and bearing housing onto the shaft.

NOTE: The bearings should be lightly oiled before assembly.

3. Place the shaft assembly in a press or equivalent tool, install the front bearing and force into place on the shaft, while turning the housing until a resistance is felt.
4. Install a "locking" substance on the shaft threads and install the locking nut.
5. Wrap a cord around the pinion housing and attach a pull scale to the cord.
6. Tighten the locking nut until a pull torque of 10 to 15 lbs. (47 to 71 N-4.7 to 7.0 kp) is attained for new bearings, or a pull torque of 4.2 to 9.2 lbs. (19 to 43 N-1.9 to 4.3

Exploded view of transaxle, chain driven primary gear train

kp) is reached for bearings having more than 1200 miles (2,000 KM), considered to be used bearings.

7. When the bearing pull torque is correct, lock the pinion nut in place on the shaft with a center punch or drift.

Primary Gear Case (Up to and Including Transaxle Number 817000, Gear Driven)
DISASSEMBLY

1. Remove the retaining bolts for the bearing housing and separate the bearing housing from the primary gear case.

2. Remove the center gear shaft from the bearing housing and remove the center gear nut so that the center gear can be removed.

3. The roller bearings and races can be pressed from the center gear as required.

4. Remove the cap from the bearing housing for the output shaft and press the output shaft from the housing, after removal of the snap-ring from the shaft.

5. Press the input gear assembly from the bearing housing, complete with the bearing.

6. Remove the snap-ring and press the bearing from the input shaft.

7. Remove the bearing support that retains the 4th speed input gear with the bearing.

8. Press the primary gear housing 4th speed input gear out of the housing. Remove the snap-ring and remove the bearing from the shaft.

9. If necessary, remove the oil collector and the needle bearing from the primary gear housing.

NOTE: The needle bearing in the primary gear housing has been discontinued from the 1976 and later models and need not be replaced during the overhaul of early designed gear boxes. When gears in the primary gear assembly of earlier designed transaxles are to be replaced, the needle bearing must be removed and discarded because the replacement shaft has not been machined for it.

ASSEMBLY

1. Position the oil collector into the primary gear housing, if removed.

2. Install the bearing on the primary gear housing 4th speed gear. Install the snap-ring and press the 4th speed gear assembly into the primary gear housing.

3. Mount the support for the bearing of the primary gear housing input shaft to the primary gear housing and secure the bolts with a locking substance.

4. Install the bearing onto the input gear and install the snap-ring.

5. Press the primary input gear and bearing into the bearing housing. The bearing must be flush with the mating surface of the bearing housing.

6. Press the output gear ball bearing into the bearing housing, and then press the output gear into the bearing. Install the washer and spring.

7. Install the roller bearing races, bearings and the shaft into the center gear. Install the locknut and snug.

8. Position the gear in a holding device and wrap a cord around the gear teeth so that the gear can be rotated on the bearings.

9. Pull the cord and cause the gear to rotate with a spring scale attached to the cord. A turning torque reading of 1.3 to 1.8 lbs. (6 to 8 N-0.6 to 0.8 kp). Obtain the correct reading by adjusting the locknut. Secure the locknut to the shaft with center punch of drift.

10. Fit the center gear into the bearing housing and secure with the attaching bolt.

11. Install the primary input gear bearing into the primary housing, if previously removed.

12. Install the bearing housing onto the primary gear housing and secure with the retaining bolts.

Primary Gear Case (Up to and Including Transaxle Number 817000, Gear Driven)
DISASSEMBLY

1. Remove the retaining bolts for the bearing housing and separate the bearing housing from the primary gear case.

2. Remove the center gear shaft from the bearing housing and remove the center gear nut so that the center gear can be removed.

3. The roller bearings and races can be pressed from the center gear as required.

4. Remove the cap from the bearing housing for the output shaft and press the output shaft from the housing, after removal of the snap-ring from the shaft.

5. Press the input gear assembly from the bearing housing, complete with the bearing.

6. Press the primary input gear and bearing into the bearing housing. The bearing must be flush with the mating surface of the bearing housing.

7. Press the output gear ball bearing into the bearing housing, and then press the output gear into the bearing. Install the washer and spring.

8. Install the roller bearing races, bearings and the shaft into the center gear. Install the locknut and snug.

9. Position the gear in a holding device and wrap a cord around the gear teeth so that the gear can be rotated on the bearings.

10. Pull the cord and cause the gear to rotate with a spring scale attached to the cord. A turning torque reading of 1.3 to 1.8 lbs (6 to 8 N-0.6 to 0.8 kp). Obtain the correct reading by adjusting the locknut. Secure the locknut to the shaft with center punch of drift.

11. Fit the center gear into the bearing housing and secure with the attaching bolt.

12. Install the primary input gear bearing into the primary housing, if previously removed.

13. Install the bearing housing onto the primary gear housing and secure with the retaining bolts.

Primary Gear Case (From Transaxle Numbers 900001 and S00001, Chain Driven)
DISASSEMBLY

1. Remove the retaining bolts and separate the cover from the primary gear housing.

2. Remove the chain tensioner assembly.

3. Remove the circlip from the lower gear sprocket and the circlip from the upper gear, through the opening in the gear sprocket.

4. Remove the gear sprockets and the chain at the same time. It may be necessary to apply pressure to the sprockets.

5. Remove the upper gear sprocket circlip and remove the sprocket bearing, if necessary.

6. Remove the four screws and bearing retainer at the input gear to the gearbox.

7. Press the input shaft from the primary gear case.

8. Remove the circlip and press the bearing from the input shaft.

9. Remove the needle bearing circlip and remove the needle bearing from the primary gear case.

10. Remove the clutch shaft seal.

ASSEMBLY

Install a new clutch shaft seal.

2. Install the needle bearing and circlip into the primary gear case.

NOTE: The mark on the needle bearing should be facing out.

3. Install the ball bearing onto the input shaft and fit the circlip on the shaft.

4. Press the input shaft assembly into the primary gear case.

5. Place the bearing retainer onto the primary gear case and apply a sealing compound to the screw threads.

6. Install the bearing, race and circlip into the upper gear sprocket.

1. Input gear
2. Center wheel
3. Output gear

Primary gear train using gears to drive transaxle

NOTE: The chamfer of the circlip must face outward when the gear is installed.

Install the chain on the sprocket gears and install onto the splines and stud in the primary gear case. Install the two circlips.

8. Install the chain tensioner with the oil passage at the top and place the backing plate so that its top edge is in line with the top edge of the chain tensioner housing. Apply thread sealant to the chain tensioner bolts and install.

9. Install the primary gear cover and new gasket.

ASSEMBLY OF TRANSAXLE

1. Install the guide studs into the transaxle housing and install the pinion assembly into the case, with the original shims between the bearing housing and the transaxle housing.

NOTE: Should new components be installed that would change the pinion depth, special tools would have to be used to correct the components to the proper pinion depth setting.

2. Remove the guide studs and install the four retaining bolts into the bearing housing.

NOTE: Any measurement operations and adjustments must be done before the bolts are secured with a "locking" substance.

3. The distance between the connecting surface for the primary gear housing and the pinion shaft nut should be checked before installing the reverse gear on the pinion shaft. The distance should be 7.677 to 7.681 inches (195.0 to 195.1 mm). Adjust a depth gauge to the measurement and measure the clearance with a feeler gauge. Install the necessary shims to close the clearance, between the pinion nut and the reverse gear.

NOTE: If the pinion shaft depth was not changed, the original shims can be reused.

4. After the necessary shims have been selected and installed on the pinion shaft, install the reverse gear on the shaft.

NOTE The gears will have to be driven on the pinion shaft with a sleeve and a plastic tipped hammer.

5. Install the 1st gear on the bearing sleeve of the reverse gear.

6. Install the 1st/2nd synchronizer hub in place on the pinion shaft. Place the 1st/2nd gear shift fork into the sliding sleeve and mount on the synchronizer hub.

7. Install the 2nd gear sleeve and mount the 2nd gear onto the sleeve.

8. Install the spacer and sleeve for the 3rd gear. Install the 3rd gear on the sleeve.

9. Install the 3rd/4th synchronizer hub. Place the 3rd/4th shifting fork into the sliding sleeve of the 3rd/4th gear and install on the synchronizer hub.

10. Lock the reverse gear so that the pinion shaft does not turn. Install and torque the pinion shaft nut to 30 to 45 ft/lbs. (40 to 60 Nm—4 to 6 KPM).

11. Secure the nut to the pinion shaft.

12. Install the pinion shaft needle bearing and its locking ring. Remove the shaft locking tool.

13. Locate the sliding sleeves in the neutral position and install the shift shaft for the 1st, 2nd, 3rd and 4th gear shift forks.

14. Turn the gear selector shaft clockwise to gain clearance to install the reverse gear shift shaft. Install the shaft and lock with the stop screw.

15. Mount the needle bearings into the intermediate gear assembly, using grease to hold them in place. Install the gear set into the bottom of the gear box housing.

16. Have the thrust washer located in the correct position for the intermediate gear assembly, on the primary gear housing. Be sure the connecting tube is fitted to the output shaft of the primary gear.

17. Seal the mating surface of the primary gear housing and mount it to the transaxle case.

NOTE: Do not tighten the primary gear housing screws until the intermediate gear shaft is installed.

18. Insert the intermediate gear shaft into position. Move the intermediate gear assembly in order that the shaft can be installed. Align the thrust washer so the shaft can be installed through it. Tighten the primary gear housing retaining screws.

19. Install the reverse gear and shaft. Be sure the reverse lever is fitted into the groove on the reverse gear. Install the lock plate over the reverse gear and the intermediate gear shaft ends. Secure the screw.

20. Install the spring and lock ball for the gear selector rod and fit the housing cover in place and secure with the retaining bolts.

21. Install the differential assembly into the housing.

22. Using the shims that were removed during the disassembly, install the inner drive shaft assemblies in place on the housing. Measure the differential gear backlash and adjust to the measurements obtained before the disassembly.

23. Complete the assembly by installing the cover onto the housing and filling the unit with lubricating oil to the specified level.

TYPE 13

4 Speed Transaxle

Subaru

DISASSEMBLY

1. Disconnect the return springs from the release bearing holder and remove the clutch fork and release bearing holder.

2. Remove the transmission cover.

3. Wind vinyl tape on the spline of the right and left axle drive shafts to prevent the oil seals from being damaged when separating the case.

4. Separate the transmission case by removing the seventeen bolts.

NOTE: The case will separate easily if the two areas around the knock pins are tapped upward with a plastic hammer.

5. Use a shank of a hammer and remove the drive pinion.

6. Remove the transmission mainshaft.

7. Remove the differential.

8. Remove the three shifter rail spring plugs.

9. Remove the shifter forks and rails.

NOTE: When pulling out a rail, keep the other rails placed in Neutral. Pull the rail for the 4th/3rd by turning 90°.

10. Remove the one screw on the right and left side of the transmission case and remove the oil seal holder lock plate. Using a special oil seal holder wrench remove the oil seal holder and O-rings.

11. Remove the speedometer driven gear. Knock the speedometer shaft outside the case by tapping lightly.

12. Pull the knock pins out and then pull out the reverse idler gear shaft, reverse idler gear and shifter lever.

13. Disassemble the transmission mainshaft.
    a. Remove the snap-ring.
    b. Press off the ball bearing, main shaft collar, 4th drive gear, synchronizer hub, 4th drive gear bushing and the 3rd drive gear.

NOTE: The 3rd drive gear bushing may be left installed but if replacement is necessary, cut a groove with a grinder and drive it off with a chisel. When the bushing moves a little remove it with a press.

14. Disassemble the drive pinion.
    a. Unscrew the drive pinion locknut.
    b. Remove the ball bearing and the 4th/3rd driven gear with a press then remove the 2nd gear and needle bearing by hand.
    c. Remove the 1st driven gear, needle bearing race, synchronizer hub and needle bearing by using a press.
    d. Remove the needle bearing race, drive pinion spacer and roller bearing by using a press.

15. Disassemble the transmission cover.
    a. Remove the back-up light switch and remove the reverse accent spring, ball and straight pin.
    b. Remove the plug in the upper part of the cover and then remove the reverse accent shaft and reverse return spring.

16. Disassemble the differential assembly.
    a. Remove the right and left snap-rings and then remove the two axle driveshafts.
    b. Remove the ring gear.
    c. Drive out the straight pin toward the ring gear.
    d. Pull out the differential pinion shaft, and then remove the differential pinion, side gear and washer.
    e. Remove the roller bearing by using a puller.

ASSEMBLY

1. Reassemble the transmission mainshaft.

1. Reverse idle gear complete
2. Reverse idler gear bushing
3. Reverse idler gear shaft
4. Knock pin
5. Reverse shifter rail
6. Shifter fork rail
7. Shifter fork rail 2
8. Shifter rail plunger 2
9. Shifter rail plunger
10. Shifter fork
11. Shifter fork set screw
12. Reverse shifter rail arm
13. Reverse shifter lever complete
14. Shifter fork 2
15. Transmission main shaft collar 2
16. Snap-ring (outer)
17. Ball bearing
18. Transmission main shaft collar
19. Gear set
20. Synchronizer ring
21. 4th drive gear bushing
22. Synchronizer sleeve
23. Synchronizer hub spring
24. Synchronizer hub
25. Synchronizer hub insert
26. Third drive gear bushing
27. Transmission main shaft
28. Needle bearing
29. Oil seal
30. Drive pinion lock nut
31. Drive pinion lock washer
32. Ball bearing
33. Bolt
34. Spring washer
35. Drive pinion shim
36. Second driven gear
37. Synchronizer ring 2
38. Needle bearing
39. Needle bearing inner race
40. Reverse driven gear
41. Synchronizer hub spring 2
42. Synchronizer hub 2
43. Synchronizer hub insert 2
44. Low (1st) driven gear
45. Drive pinion spacer
46. Roller bearing
47. Key

Exploded view of 4-speed transaxle gear assemblies

NOTE: Install the hub so that the end of the spline having the narrower tooth width is on the 3rd gear side. The shorter insert is for the 4th/3rd synchronizer and the longer insert is for the 1st/2nd synchronizer.

2. Reassemble the drive pinion.
  a. Install the roller bearing in the drive pinion and press on the spacer.
  b. Install the three synchronizer inserts, reverse driven gear and the two springs on the hub.

NOTE: Install the reverse driven gear so that its toothed side and the side of the synchronizer hub has its lower boss face in the same direction.

  c. Install the needle bearing race with a press.
  d. Install the needle bearing. 1st driven gear, synchronizer rings and hub which was sub-assembled in (c).
  e. Install the needle bearing race with a press.
  f. Install the 2nd driven gear and insert a key into the groove on the drive pinion.
  g. Install the 4th/3rd driven gear with a press.
  h. Install the ball bearing with a press.
  i. Install the drive pinion lockwasher.

NOTE: Stake the locknut in two places.

3. Reassemble the differential.
  a. Install the side and pinion gears on the case and then insert the pinion shaft.

  b. Measure the backlash between the gear and pinion and make adjustment using the proper washers.
  c. Align the differential pinion shaft with the holes on the differential case and drive the straight pin in from the ring gear side. Drive it in until it falls in about 0.039 in. then stake the pin.
  d. Press on the roller bearing on the differential case.
  e. Using new lockwashers, clamp the ring gear on the case.
  f. Install the axle driveshafts and lock it with snap-rings.
  g. Measure the clearance between the pinion shaft and the tip of the axle drive shaft. Clearance should be 0-0.0079 in. Make adjustment by selecting the proper snap-ring.

NOTE: The figure of the lower three digits marked on the drive pinion end face is the match number for combining it with the ring gear. The upper figure is for the shim adjustment. The first three digits on the ring gear indicates a number for combination with the drive pinion. The following digits indicates a value of appropriate backlash.

  h. Adjust the drive pinion shim, place the drive pinion on the transmission case without a shim and tighten the pinion.
  i. Press on the oil seal into the axle shaft oil seal holder.
4. Position the transmission case on the stand and screw the axle shaft oil seal holder into the case using the special wrench.

NOTE: Make sure the holder marked "R" is installed on the right side and holder marked "L" is installed on the left side.

5. Install the outer snap-ring and washer on the speedometer shaft, then install them into the transmission case. Install the speedometer driven gear on the shaft. Install oil seal.

NOTE: Install the outer snap-ring on the speedometer driveshaft from the driven gear side.

6. Install the reverse shifter lever into the transmission case. Install the reverse idler gear and shaft.
7. Install the reverse shifter rail arm to the end of the reverse shifter lever. Install the reverse shifter rail.
8. Install the shifter fork rail spring, ball and gasket in the case and tighten the shifter rail spring plug.
9. Shift the reverse shifter rail and select the reverse shifter rail arm so that the clearance between the reverse idler gear and the wall of the case is 0.059-0.079 in.
10. Install the shifter rail plunger into the hold of the case.
11. Wind tape around the splines of the axle driveshafts of the differential assembly to prevent damage to the oil seals.
12. Install the differential on the axle shaft oil seal holder.
13. Install the needle bearing on the transmission mainshaft and install the case.

NOTE: Make sure the knock pin of the case is fitted into the hole in the needle bearing outer race. To prevent damage to the roller bearing place the open end of the roving plunger on the bearing.

14. Install the shifter fork. Install the shifter rail plunger in the shifter fork rail.

15. Install the shims in the drive pinion selected in Step "k" under reassembling the differential assembly, and then install into the transmission case.

16. When installing the roller bearing outer race knock hole to the knock pin of the case, position the knock hole to the edge of the transmission case and put a mark on top of the outer race. Turn the outer race so that the mark comes to the edge of the transmission case while slightly up the drive pinion, then slightly move the outer race right and left and front and rear until the knock pin fits into the knock hole.

17. Install the shifter rail plunger.

18. Install the shifter fork and shifter fork rail.

19. Install the shifter fork rail spring, ball and gasket into the case.

20. Select the shifter forks so that the synchronizer sleeve and reverse driven gear come to the center of the gears when the mainshaft and drive pinion are placed in the normal position (both the shaft and drive pinion are forced against the forward side without any clearance).

21. Check clearance A at the end of each rail. If dimension A is not within the range of 0.012 to 0.063 in., replace the rail, fork and set screw so that the proper dimension is obtained.

22. Install the mainshaft oil seal with its end surface A as shown in the illustration.

NOTE: When joining the cases from above be careful not to let the oil seal tilt. Apply liquid gasket to the case surfaces, remove the outer race of the roller bearings and make sure the speedometer gear tooth is meshed.

23. Clamp the clutch cable bracket, and back-up lamp wire clip together.

24. Install the drive pinion onto the case.

25. Install the outer race of the roller bearing.

26. Check and adjust the backlash of the ring gear and check the adjustment of preload on the roller bearing. Special tools are necessary unless it is done by trial-and-error. Backlash is as specified between 0.0039 to 0.0059 in.

27. Check the tooth contact of the hypoid gear as follows. To reduce backlash, loosen the holder on the upper case side and turn in the holder on the lower case side by the same amount. To increase backlash, loosen the lower and turn in the upper.

The drive pinion shim selected earlier may be too thick or thin. Increase or reduce its thickness.

28. Remove the lock plate (driveshaft holder). Loosen the driveshaft holder until the O-ring groove appears, install the O-ring into the groove and tighten the holder into position where the holder has been tightened in. Do this on both upper and lower heads.

29. Tighten the lock plate. Remove the protective vinyl tape wound on the axle shafts.

30. Reassemble the transmission cover.

31. Install the transmission cover.

a. Adjust the bearing side clearance 0-0.0118 in. using collar (transmission mainshaft). For adjustment, insert collar if required.

b. Install the shifter arm in the cover (and install the cover to the thransmission).

c. Adjust the transmission cover by inserting a bar through the hole of the shifter arm and shift the gear into 4th. Move the shifter arm from 4th position to 2nd and reverse position. The arm will move lightly toward 2nd side but heavy to reverse side because of the function of the return spring, and the arm will come into contact with the stopper at the end. To adjust, remove the plug on the cover and change the thickness of the aluminum gasket, so that the light stroke and heavy stroke become the same.

32. Install the clutch release fork and release bearing holder and secure them with return springs.

NOTE: Fill the internal groove of the holder with grease.

TYPE 14

5 Speed Transaxle
Subaru

DISASSEMBLY

1. Remove the transmission.
2. Remove the clutch release fork and release bearing holder.

1. Roller bearing
2. Bolt
3. Crown gear lock washer
4. Differential pinion shaft
5. Differential case
6. Straight pin
7. Axle drive shaft
8. Axle shaft oil seal holder
9. O-ring
10. Oil seal (RH)
11. Pinion & crown gear set (AT)
12. Pinion & crown gear set (4WD)
13-1. Pinion & crown gear set (4-speed)
13-2. Pinion & crown gear set (5-speed)
14. Washer
15. Differential side gear
16. Differential pinion
17. Snap-ring
18. Oil seal (LH)

Exploded view of differential assembly and the three pinion gear lengths

1. Washer	18. Shifter rail plunger 2	30. Synchronizer hub spring	47. Drive pinion shim
2. Reverse idler gear bushing	19. Reverse shifter rail arm	31. Synchronizer hub	48. Snap ring
3. Reverse idler gear complete	20. Reverse shifter lever complete	32. Synchronizer hub insert	49. Low (1st) driven gear washer
4. Reverse idler gear shaft	21. Shifter fork 2	33. Woodruff key	50. Second driven spring gear
5. Knock pin	22. Transmission main shaft	34. Transmission main shaft	51. Second driven gear
6. Spring pin	collar 2	35. Needle bearing	52. Synchronizer ring 2
7. Shifter fork 3	23. Transmission main shaft lock	36. Oil seal	53. Needle bearing
8. Reverse shifter rail	nut	37. Needle bearing	54. Needle bearing inner race
9. Shifter fork rail	24. Transmission main shaft	38. Drive pinion lock nut	55. Bolt
10. Shifter fork rail 2	lock washer	39. Drive pinion lock washer	56. Spring washer
11. Shifter rail plunger 2	25. Ball bearing	40. Synchronizer stopper 2	57. Reverse driven gear
12. Shifter rail plunger	26. Transmission main shaft	41. Synchronizer stopper	58. Synchronizer hub spring 2
13. Snap ring (outer)	collar	42. Fifth gear set	59. Synchronizer hub 2
14. Shifter fork	27. Synchronizer ring	43. Third and fourth gear set	60. Synchronizer hub insert 2
15. Shifter fork set screw	28. 4th drive gear bushing	44. Needle bearing inner race 5	61. Low (1st) driven gear
16. Ball	28. 3rd drive gear bushing	45. Drive pinion spacer 2	62. Low (1st) driven spring gear
17. Shifter fork rail spring 2	29. Synchronizer sleeve	46. Ball bearing	63. Drive pinion spacer
			64. Roller bearing

Exploded view of 5-speed transaxle gear assemblies

3. Remove the transmission rear cover.

4. Drive out the spring pin on the shifter fork.

5. Shift the gears into first gear, install the mainshaft stopper (special tool), release the staking on the drive pinion locknut and remove the nut.

6. Remove the synchronizer hub and shifter fork together.

7. Remove the 5th driven gear, needle bearing inner race, needle bearing and drive pinion spacer.

8. Remove the three bolts retaining the drive pinion assembly to the case.

9. Separate the left and right sections of the transmission case.

10. Remove the drive pinion assembly mainshaft assembly and differential assembly.

11. Remove the three shifter rail spring plugs.

12. Remove the shifter fork setscrew, shift-er fork and shifter fork rail of 3rd/4th and 1st/2nd.

   a. To remove the shifter fork rail position the rest of the rails in neutral.

   b. To remove the 3rd and 4th rails, turn them 90 degrees and let the shifter rail plunger fall in the groove of the reverse shifter rail.

13. Take out the lock pin and the reverse idler gear shaft then, remove the reverse idler gear and the reverse shifter lever as a unit.

14. Remove the outer snap-ring and take out the reverse shifter rail arm from the rail then remove the ball and spring.

15. Disassemble the mainshaft.

   a. Using the special wrench and holder, remove the locknut and remove the 5th drive gear with a press.

   b. Remove the Woodruff key.

   c. Remove the ball bearing and 4th drive gear using a press.

   d. Disassemble the synchronizer hub, third drive gear and 4th drive gear bushing using a press.

   e. Remove the outer snap-ring, 1st driven gear washer, 1st driven gear spring and 2nd driven gear spring, from the 1st driven gear and 2nd driven gear which were removed from the drive pinion.

16. The procedure for disassembling the main shaft differential gear, shifter fork, etc., is the same as the 4 speed transmission disassembly Steps 14 thru 16.

ASSEMBLY

NOTE: Since some assembly procedures are the same as the 4-speed transmission, refer to that section where noted.

1. Reassemble the drive pinion components parts following the procedure in the four

speed transmission section until the ball bearing, then install the spacer, needle bearing race, needle bearing, fifth driven gear, synchronizer hub, stopper, lockwasher and nut. Tighten the locknut to 60 ft-lbs.

2. Select a drive pinion shim (see Step 3—4 speed assembly procedures).

3. Put the shifter rail spring and ball in the reverse shifter rail arm. Insert the reverse shifter rail.

4. Install the outer snap-ring.

5. Put the shifter fork rail spring, ball and gasket in the case.

6. Select the reverse shifter lever so that the gap between the reverse idler gear and the case wall becomes 0.06 to 0.118 in. by shifting the reverse shifter rail.

7. Shift it to the neutral position, then select the right size washer so that the gap between the case wall becomes 0 to 0.02 in.

8. Put the shifter rail plunger into the grooves of the case and the reverse shifter rail arm.

9. Install the 1st driven gear spring (sub-gear) with the outer snap-ring and 1st driven gear washer to the 2nd driven gear.

NOTE: The clearance between the tooth tops of the gear and spring (sub-gear) is 0.0039-0.0197 in.

10. Reassemble the transmission mainshaft as given in Step 1 under assembly of 4 speed transmission. Then install a key, 5th drive gear, lock washer and locknut to the mainshaft.

11. Fit the differential assembly into the case.

12. Attach the mainshaft assembly.

13. Insert a shifter rail plunger and install a shifter fork and rail.

14. Install the adjustment shim selected before with the drive pinion assembly and then install them to the case.

15. Insert the shifter rail plunger.

16. Install the shifter fork and shifter rail.

17. Install the shifter fork rail spring and ball in the case.

18. Select the shifter fork so that the synchronizer sleeve comes to the center of the 3rd and 4th drive gears.

19. Select the next shifter fork so that the reverse driven gear comes to the center of the 1st and 2nd driven gears.

20. Apply a liquid gasket to the mating surfaces of the case halves and put them together.

21. Tighten the drive pinion on to the transmission case.

22. Inspect the ring gear backlash and the tooth contact as described under 4 speed transmission assembly Steps 26 and 27.

23. Remove the locknut of the drive pinion assembly to remove the lockwasher, stoppers and hub.

24. Install the hub, fork and rail using the spring pin.

25. Install the synchronizer stoppers and drive pinion lockwasher. Using the mainshaft stopper tool tighten the pinion locknut to 58 ft/lbs.

NOTE: Shift the gear to 1st position when tightening the drive pinion locknut.

26. Select the last shifter fork so that the clearance between the sleeve and the 5th driven gear becomes 0.008 to 0.020 when the gear is in the 5th position.

27. Stake the drive pinion locknut.

28. Check the clearance between the edges of each rail. If the clearance is not within 0.012-0.063 in. replace the rail, fork and setscrew as necessary.

29. Select the correct mainshaft collar.

30. Install the rear cover.

TYPE 15

4 Speed Transaxle Subaru
DISASSEMBLY

NOTE: Since some of the overhaul procedures are the same as the 4 speed transmission refer to that section when noted.

1. Remove the transmission.

2. Drive out the straight pin and pull out the shifter fork rail, fork, ball and spring.

3. Remove the case assembly.

4. Shift the gear to the 1st position, release the staked part of the nut, then using a main shaft stopper, remove the locknut and take out the rear shaft drive gear from the drive pinion.

5. Remove the case assembly.

6. Remove the race, needle bearing collar and washer from the drive pinion.

7. Shift the sleeve into the drive position and using a holder, remove the mainshaft locknut.

8. Remove the ball bearing assembly.

9. Remove the mainshaft spacer, rearshaft driven gear, sleeve, synchronizer hub and rear drive spacer from the rear driveshaft.

10. Remove the snap-ring from the case.

11. Punch out the rear driveshaft and using a press, remove the ball bearing.

12. Take out the O-ring from the shifter arm and remove the shifter arm.

13. Remove the back-up lamp switch from the case and the reverse accent spring ball and straight pin.

14. Remove the plug from the case and

1. Shifter fork rail 2
2. Shifter fork rail
3. Reverse shifter rail
4. Transmission main shaft lock nut
5. Transmission main shaft lock washer
6. Ball bearing
7. Transmission main shaft collar
8. Rear shaft driven gear
9. Synchronizer ring
10. Rear shaft driven gear bushing
11. Synchronizer sleeve
12. Synchronizer hub spring
13. Synchronizer hub
14. Synchronizer hub insert
15. Rear drive spacer
16. Snap ring
17. Ball bearing
18. Rear drive shaft
19. Washer
20. Drive pinion collar
21. Needle bearing race 5
22. Rear shaft drive gear

Exploded view of added gears and shafts for the 4 wheel drive unit

take out the reverse accent shaft and turn spring.

15. Remove the needle bearing from the case.

16. Remove the rear extension oil seal.

17. For the remainder of the transmission disassembly procedures refer to the 4 speed transmission section.

ASSEMBLY

1. Assemble the main transmission unit.
   a. The drive pinion assembly is assembled by fitting the ball bearing, washer collar, needle bearing inner race, rear drive shaft gear, lockwasher and locknut. Do not stake the nut at this time.

2. Assemble the transmission case without the transfer system.

NOTE: After assembling, remove the locknut, lockwasher and rear shaft drive gear from the drive pinion.

3. Press fit the needle bearing into the case.

4. Insert the reverse return spring and the reverse accent shaft into the case. Install an adjusting aluminum gasket on the plug.

5. Set the ball reverse accent spring, straight pin and aluminum washer on the back-up lamp switch.

6. Install the shifter arm on the transmission case.

7. Assemble the three synchronizer inserts, sleeve and two springs on the synchronizer hub.

NOTE: Make sure the hub is installed so that the spline with the smaller width is on the rear drive spacer side.

8. Press fit the ball bearing to the rear driveshaft.

9. Hammer the rear driveshaft into the transmission case and install the inner snapring.

10. Install the snap-ring rear drive spacer, synchronizer hub, rear shaft driven gear sleeve, synchronizer ring, rear shaft driven gear and mainshaft spacer to the shaft.

11. Press fit the ball bearing to the rear driveshaft.

12. Shift the sleeve to be fitted with a transmission mainshaft lockwasher to the drive position.

13. Adjust the bearing side clearance to 0-0.012 in. using a mainshaft collar.

14. Mount the case assembly on the main transmission unit.

15. Install the washer, drive pinion collar and needle bearing race to the drive pinion. Shift the gear in 1st then tighten the locknut.

16. Install the O-ring into the groove of the shifter arm.

17. Mount the case assembly and tighten the bolts.

NOTE: When installing, the rear shift drive and 4th drive gears should engage each other. Before tightening each bolt, make sure that the shifter arm shifts smoothly in each direction.

18. Install the 3rd shifter fork, spring, ball and rail into the case.

NOTE: To install the ball, press it down by using the end of the shifter fork rail while forcing the rail into the case with the round side down. Rotate the rail by 180° to its proper position.

19. Drive in the straight pin, then move the shifter fork rail and check the accent.

20. Install the transmission case cover.

21. Adjust the selecting direction and position of the shifter arm shaft.
   a. Install the gear shift system.
   b. Shift the gear into 4th.
   c. Shift the shifter arm from the 4th/3rd position to the 1st and reverse position.
   d. The arm moves lightly to the 1st position while it moves heavily to the reverse position and hits the stopper as the force of the return spring is applied.
   e. Adjust so that the light travel becomes the same as the heavy travel by removing the plug on the top of the transmission case and change the thickness of aluminum gasket.

22. When mounting the transmission on the car body, the gearshift system should be removed first.

23. For reassembly of the remaining transmission parts refer to the 4 speed transmission section.

TYPE 16

4 and 5 Speed Transaxle—Models Z-40 and Z-50

Toyota

DISASSEMBLY

1. Support the transaxle securely and drain the lubricating oil.

2. Remove the reverse shift arm pivot and the backup lamp switch.

3. Remove the mounting brackets from the transaxle extension housing.

4. Remove the speedometer driven gear assembly.

5. Remove the shifting restricting pins, springs and screw caps from the extension housing.

6. Remove the extension housing retaining bolts and carefully remove the housing from the transaxle case.

7. Remove the speedometer drive gear retaining snap-ring and remove the gear and the locating ball.

8. Drive the roll pins from the gear shifting arms with a pin punch.

9. Remove the shifting rod detent balls, springs and threaded caps from the transaxle case.

NOTE: A magnet is used to remove the balls from their bores.

10. Remove the input shaft cover retaining bolts and remove the cover, shaft and bearing assemblies.

11. Remove the snap-ring from the countershaft bearing.

12. Remove the extension housing retaining bolts and carefully tap the housing loose from the intermediate plate.

13. Remove the case from the intermediate plate and remove the reverse shift arm from the pivot shaft.

14. Remove the rolled pins from the gear shift head and the shift forks. Pull the Number three shift rod from the intermediate plate. Remove the Number three shift fork from the coupling sleeve.

15. Remove the interlock pin and pull the Number two shift rod from the intermediate plate. Remove the shift fork from the coupling sleeve.

16. Remove the interlock pin and pull the Number one rod from the intermediate plate. Remove the Number one shift fork from the coupling sleeve. Remove the reverse shift fork.

17. To remove the gear assemblies from the intermediate plate, perform the following procedures as applies to each transaxle.
   a. Z-50—Measure the 5th gear thrust clearance which should be 0.0059 to 0.0128 inch (0.15 to 0.325 mm), and with a service limit of 0.016 inch (0.4 mm). Remove the retaining snap-ring and remove the 5th gear, clutch hub and synchronizer ring with a puller type tool. Remove the roller bearing cage, the spacer and the steel locater ball.
   b. Z-40—Remove the countergear plate, bolt and lock washer.

18. Remove the output shaft bearing retainer and bolts from the intermediate plate. Remove the two ball bearing snap-rings and with a plastic hammer or equivalent, force the output shaft, the reverse gearshaft and idler gear halfway out from the plate.

——— **CAUTION** ———
Support the shafts by hand.

19. Remove the idler gear and the reverse gearshaft as an assembly.

20. Remove the countergear and the output shaft together.

21. Measure the thrust clearances of the 1st, 2nd, 3rd and 4th gears before disassembly of the output shaft. Record the clearances for reference during the assembly.

22. Using a puller type tool, remove the sleeve yoke from the end of the output shaft.

23. Z-50—Remove the snap-ring from the shaft and remove the 5th gear with the puller type tool. Remove the ball bearing snap-ring.

24. Z-40—Remove the snap-ring from the shaft that locates the sleeve yoke and the snap-ring that retains the ball bearing in position on the shaft.

25. Using the puller type tool, remove the ball bearing from the shaft. Remove the spacer from the shaft, along with the thrust bearing.

——— **CAUTION** ———
Do not drop the thrust bearing.

26. Remove the 4th gear and the half needle bearing cages from the shaft.

27. Remove the snap-ring from the shaft and remove the Number two clutch hub, synchronizer ring and the 3rd speed gear from the shaft with the puller type tool.

Z50

Z40

Cross section of models Z50 and Z40 transaxles

Exploded view of transaxle gear housing, cover and intermediate plate

1. Reverse shift arm pivot
2. Back-up light switch
3. Mounting stay
4. Speedometer driven gear
5. Restrict pin
6. Extension housing
7. Speedometer drive gear
8. Gear shift head
9. Locking ball
10. Input shaft
11. Snap-ring
12. Transmission case

28. Remove the snap-ring from the front of the shaft and remove the bushing needle bearing, 1st gear and the synchronizer ring. Using a magnet, remove the locating locking ball from the shaft.

29. Remove the Number one clutch hub, synchronizer ring and the second gear from the shaft.

30. Inspect the gears, bearings, case, housing, plate, synchronizers, shafts and the remaining parts of the transaxle for wear and damage. Replace the necessary parts before the assembly.

ASSEMBLY

1. Begin the assembly by placing the 2nd gear on the output shaft, followed by the synchronizer ring and the Number one clutch hub. Install the locking ball in place on the shaft and install the synchronizer ring, the 1st gear, bearing and the bushing. Install the snap-ring of a thickness to obtain a thrust clearance of zero. The following snap-rings are available.

SNAP-RING SIZES

Mark	Thickness mm	(in.)
1	2.15-2.20	(0.0846-0.0866)
2	2.20-2.25	(0.0866-0.0886)
3	2.25-2.30	(0.0886-0.0906)
4	2.30-2.35	(0.0906-0.0925)
5	2.35-2.40	(0.0925-0.0945)
6	2.40-2.45	(0.0945-0.0965)
7	2.45-2.50	(0.0965-0.0984)
8	2.50-2.55	(0.0984-0.1004)
9	2.55-2.60	(0.1004-0.1024)

2. Check the thrust clearances of the 1st and 2nd gears. The clearances should be as listed.

1st gears—0.0059 to 0.0108 inch (0.15 to 0.275 mm)
   Service limit—0.0118 inch (0.30mm)
2nd gears—0.0059 to 0.0004 inch (0.15 to 0.25 mm)
   Service limit—0.0118 inch (0.30 mm)

3. Install the number two clutch hub on the shaft and align the shifting keys with the key slots in the synchronizer rings.

4. Install the widest thrust bearing against the number two clutch hub. Install the half needle bearing cages, synchronizer ring and the 4th speed gear.

5. Install the spacer and the snap-ring to the front side of the 4th gear.

6. Install the smaller thrust washer into the spacer and install the assembly onto the shaft with the thrust washer facing the 4th speed gear.

NOTE: The spacer will have to be pressed onto the shaft.

7. Press the ball bearing onto the shaft with the groove on the bearing facing towards the front.

8. Select a snap-ring of a thickness to obtain a thrust clearance of zero from the following list of available snap-rings.

SNAP-RING SIZES

Mark	Thickness	
	mm	(in.)
2	2.10-2.15	(0.0827-0.0846)
3	2.15-2.20	(0.0846-0.0866)

SNAP-RING SIZES

Mark	Thickness	
	mm	(in.)
4	2.20-2.25	(0.0866-0.0886)
5	2.25-2.30	(0.0886-0.0906)
6	2.30-2.35	(0.0906-0.0925)
7	2.35-2.40	(0.0925-0.0945)
8	2.40-2.45	(0.0945-0.0965)
9	2.45-2.50	(0.0965-0.0984)
10	2.50-2.55	(0.0984-0.1004)

9. With the selected snap-ring installed, measure the thrust clearance of the 3rd and 4th gears.

The clearance should be as follows.

3rd gear—0.0059 to 0.0098 inch (0.15 to 0.25 mm)

Service limit—0.0118 inch (0.30 mm)

4th gear—0.0008 to 0.0094 inch (0.02 to 0.24 mm)

Service limit—0.0118 inch (0.30 mm)

10. Z-50—Install the 5th gear and select a snap-ring of a thickness to obtain a clearance of zero from the following list of snap-rings.

SNAP-RING SIZES

Mark	Thickness	
	mm	(in.)
2	2.10-2.15	(0.0827-0.0846)
3	2.15-2.20	(0.0846-0.0866)
4	2.20-2.25	(0.0866-0.0886)
5	2.25-2.30	(0.0886-0.0906)
6	2.30-2.35	(0.0906-0.0925)

11. Z-40—Install the snap-ring in the groove on the shaft near the end.

13. Reverse shift arm	17. No. 3 shift fork	21. Interlock pin
14. Slotted spring pin	18. Interlock pin	22. No. 1 shift fork shaft
15. Gear shift head	19. No. 2 shift fork shaft	23. No. 1 shift fork
16. No. 3 shift fork shaft	20. No. 2 shift fork	24. Reverse shift fork

Exploded view of shift mechanism, typical of models Z50 and Z40 transaxles

12. Press the sleeve yoke onto the shaft until the yoke touches the first snap-ring and that zero clearance exists between the snap-ring and the shaft groove.

13. Place the intermediate plate in a holder and place the assembled output shaft and the countershaft gear assembly into the intermediate plate, approximately half-way.

14. Align the idler gear with the notched portion of the reverse idler gearshaft. Tap the idler gearshaft bearing approximately half way into the intermediate plate.

NOTE: Be sure the idler gear and the output shaft spacers are not in contact with each other.

15. Tap each gearshaft until the bearings are seated in the intermediate plate. Install the retaining snap-rings on the bearings.

16. Install the bearing retainer and secure the retaining bolts.

17. a. Z-40—Align the countergear plate with the countershaft protrusion and install the bolt and lockwasher. Torque to 8 to 11 ft-lbs. (1.0 to 1.6 Kg-m).

NOTE: Mesh the gears to lock the shaft.

b. Z-50—Align the synchronizer shifting slots and keys on the synchronizer ring and install the number three clutch hub. Install a selective snap-ring of a thickness that will reduce the thrust clearance to zero, selected from the following chart.

SNAP-RING SIZES

Thickness	
mm	(in.)
1.80-1.85	(0.0709-0.0728)
1.85-1.90	(0.0728-0.0748)
1.90-1.95	(0.0748-0.0768)
1.95-2.00	(0.0768-0.0787)
2.00-2.05	(0.0787-0.0807)
2.05-2.10	(0.0807-0.0827)
2.10-2.15	(0.0827-0.0846)

18. Measure the 5th gear thrust clearance. The clearance should be 0.0059 to 0.0128 inch (0.15 to 0.325 mm), with a service limit of 0.0157 inch (0.40 mm).

19. Fit the shifting forks into their respective coupling sleeves. Insert the number one shift rod into the number one shifting fork, the reverse shift fork and into the intermediate plate bore.

20. Install the number two shift rod into the lower hole of the number one shift fork and through the number two shift fork, and on into the intermediate plate bore.

21. Install the number three shift rod into the number four gear shift head and into the number three shift fork. Continue inward with the shifting rod until the pin hole of the number three shift fork is aligned with the interlock pin hole.

22. Insert a piece of wire into the interlock pin hole to a length of 4.7 inches (120 mm) from the ouside of the intermediate plate.

23. Assemble the interlock pins so that a long pin is inserted first, followed by the small pin and then the same sized pin as the first one, for a total of three. Push the pins inward with a piece of wire and verify the distance is 3.1 inches (80 mm) from the outside of the intermediate plate.

24. In the transaxle of the Z-50, install the number three shaft into the fork controlling the 5th speed synchronizer.

25. Place the shift rods in the neutral position. Move the number two shift rod into the 3rd gear position and the number one and two shafts should not move.

26. Apply a sealer to the plug for the interlocks and tighten into place.

27. Align the pin holes in the shift forks and shift fork shafts. Drive the roll pins into place and secure the forks to the shafts.

28. Install the gasket to the intermediate plate and carefully install the case to the plate.

29. Install the countershaft snap-ring to the ball bearing. Install the detent locking balls and springs. Apply sealer to the detent plugs and install.

30. Install the reverse shift arm pivot bolt through the under side of the reverse shift arm.

1. Snap-ring
2. No. 3 clutch hub, synchronizer ring and 5th gear
3. Bearing
4. Spacer & steel ball
5. Counter gear plate
6. Bearing retainer
7. Snap-ring
8. Snap-ring
9. Idler gear & reverse idler gear
10. Output gear & counter gear

Exploded view of intermediate plate and gears—model Z40 and Z50 parts illustrated

31. Install the gear shift heads to the shift rods and install the roll pins to retain the heads.

32. Install the locating ball, the speedometer drive gear and the snap-ring.

33. Apply the gasket and sealer to the mating surface of the case and engage the end of the shift lever shaft and the number two shift head, on the extension housing. Install the retaining bolts and secure.

34. Install the restricting pins in their proper positions as follows.
Green—1st and 2nd gears
Red—5th and reverse

35. Install the mounting brackets to their marked positions.

36. Fill the transaxle with lubricating oil to its proper level.

37. Be sure the transaxle gear shifts smoothly in all positions.

38. Install the input shaft, gasket and retainer. Secure with the retaining bolts.

39. Install the speedometer driven gear assembly and electrical switch.

TYPE 17

4 and 5 Speed Transaxle Volkswagen

DISASSEMBLY

NOTE: A five speed transaxle is available for use in later vehicles. The disassembly and assembly procedures remain basically the same and the same precautions and care should be exercised during the overhaul procedure as is done in the overhaul of the four speed unit.

1. Mount the transaxle assembly in a holding fixture.

2. Remove the end cover and gasket.

3. Remove the circlips from the clutch release shaft. Slide the shaft out of the gear carrier and remove the clutch lever and return spring.

4. Remove the clutch release bearing and clutch pushrod.

5. Mount a bar with a locknut and spacer across the final drive housing to support the mainshaft.

6. Remove the selector shaft cover. Remove the interlock plunger springs, and the selector shaft.

7. Remove the circlip from the gear carrier side drive flange. Install the special tool with two bolts on the drive flange. Remove the drive flange.

8. Remove the plastic caps covering the clamping screws. Remove the clamping screw nuts.

9. Remove the reverse shaft retaining bolt.

10. Mount the special tool on the gear carrier assembly and lift the gear carrier off the final drive assembly while threading the special tool bolt in.

11. Drive the drive flange oil seal out of the gear carrier housing.

12. Pry the clutch operating shaft oil seal out of the carrier housing.

13. Pull the pinion shaft needle bearing out of the gear carrier.

14. Remove the shift fork assembly and the mainshaft from the final drive housing.

15. Remove the remaining drive flange as outlined in Step 7.

16. Remove the needle bearing stop and the first circlip from the pinion shaft. Lift fourth gear off the shaft.

Stop
for needle bearing

Circlip
always replace

4th gear
replace as matched set only
collar faces up

Circlip
always replace

3rd gear
replace as matched set only

2nd gear

Needle bearing and inner race for 2nd gear

Synchronizer hub for 1st/2nd gear

Synchronizer ring for 1st/2nd gear

Reverse gear
collar faces down

Bushing for reverse gear

1st gear

Shaft for reverse gear

Thrust washer
recess faces tapered
roller bearing

Exploded view of pinion shaft gear assembly

Shim

Circlip
always replace

Bearing

Thrust washer
must fit tightly
when replacing
readjust main shaft

4th gear
replace as matched set only

Synchronizer ring 3rd/4th gear

Circlip
always replace

Synchronizer hub 3rd/4th gear

3rd gear
replace as matched set only

Main shaft
when replacing readjust

Bushing for clutch push rod

Exploded view of mainshaft assembly

17. Remove the second circlip from the pinion shaft. Lift third gear, second gear, second gear inner race and needle bearing off the shaft.

18. Remove the reverse shaft and gear.

19. Using a gear puller, remove the synchronizer hub and first/second gear from the pinion shaft.

20. Remove the pinion bearing cover and outer bearing race. Remove the pinion shaft.

21. Remove the differential assembly.

22. Pry the mainshaft oil seal out of the final drive housing.

23. Drive the drive flange oil seal out of the final drive housing.

24. Pull the starter bushing out of the final drive housing.

25. Pull the pinion outer bearing race out of the final drive housing.

26. Drive the differential outer bearing race out of the final drive housing.

27. Pull the mainshaft needle bearing out of the final drive housing.

28. Remove the two circlips from the shift fork shaft and slide the components off the shaft.

29. Remove the first circlip from the mainshaft and discard. Press the bearing off the shaft.

30. Mount the separator assembly on fourth gear and press the gear off the mainshaft. Remove the needle bearings.

31. Remove the second circlip from the mainshaft and discard. Press third gear and the synchronizer assembly off the shaft. Remove the needle bearings.

32. Slide a ⅜ in. rod in the mainshaft and drive the clutch pushrod out.

33. Press the two tapered roller bearings off the pinion shaft.

34. Remove the circlips from the differential pinion shaft and drive out.

35. Remove the differential pinion gears and thrust washers.

36. Remove the circlips from the drive flange shafts. Remove the side gears and thrust washers.

37. Press the tapered roller bearing off the housing side of the differential.

38. Remove the tapered roller bearing from the ring gear side of the differential.

39. Remove the ring gear. On 1976-77 models, the ring gear is riveted in place. Drill out rivets and replace with special bolts.

ASSEMBLY

NOTE: The ring gear and pinion shaft can be replaced only as a matched set.

1. Heat the pinion shaft small tapered bearing to 212° F and press onto the shaft.

2. Heat the pinion shaft large tapered bearing to 212° F and press onto the shaft.

3. Place a 0.75 mm shim in the pinion bore in the final drive housing and press the small bearing outer position.

4. Install the pinion shaft and cover.

5. Assemble the pinion adjustment fixture tools. Place the end plate on the pinion shaft. Attach the dial indicator and zero with a 1 mm preload.

— **CAUTION** —
Do not turn the pinion shaft while measuring because the bearings will settle and give incorrect reading.

6. Move the pinion shaft up and down and note the reading.

7. Specified bearing preload is obtained by adding the constant figure of 0.20 mm to the measured reading and the shim thickness (0.75 mm).

Example:

Shim installed	0.75 mm
reading	0.30 mm
preload (constant figure)	+0.20 mm
shim size	1.25 mm

8. Remove the pinion shaft cover and the pinion shaft. Pull the pinion shaft small bearing outer race of the final drive housing.

9. Install the correct shim and press the pinion shaft small bearing outer race into the final drive housing.

Pinion shaft gears
must be removed to take out pinion shaft

2.0 mkg (14 ft lb)

Main shaft

Shift fork set
disassemble only to replace individual parts

Ring gear
when removing, pinion shaft must be removed

2 Circlips
removing with screwdriver

Drive flange

Circlip for drive shaft
always replace

Gear train assembly and final drive housing

NOTE: If new bearings have been installed on the pinion shaft, check the pinion shaft turning torque. Reading should be 4.4-13.1 in/lbs.

10. Install the side gears and thrust washers in the differential housing.

11. Install the pinion gears and thrust washers. Drive the pinion shaft into the differential housing.

12. Install centering pins on the differential housing. Heat the ring gear to 212° F and press onto the differential housing.

13. Heat the housing side differential bearing to 212° F and press the bearing into place.

14. Heat the ring gear side bearing to 212° F and press the bearing into place.

NOTE: If new bearings have been installed, the differential must be adjusted.

15. Slide the drive flange shafts into the side gears. Determine the thickness of the circlip by pressing the drive flange shaft against the pinion gearshaft, while pressing the side gears against the housing. Insert the thickest possible circlip. The circlip should not be jammed sideways.

CAUTION

The differential inner and outer bearing races are matched to their bearings and cannot be interchanged.

---

16. If new differential bearings have been installed, proceed as follows:

a. Install the race in the final drive housing with a 1 mm shim.

b. Install the race in the gear carrier without a shim.

c. Place the differential assembly in the final drive housing. Install the gear carrier on the final drive housing, with the gasket.

d. Install the dial indicator fixture on the gear carrier tool and place the end plate on the drive flange. Install the dial indicator with a 1 mm preload.

CAUTION

Do not turn the differential when making the measurements because the bearings will settle and give incorrect readings.

---

e. Move the differential up and down and note the reading.

f. The correct bearing preload is determined by adding a constant figure or .40 mm to the measured reading.

Measuring clearance (A) between pinion shaft third gear and mainshaft third gear

Example:

measured reading	0.90 mm
preload (constant figure)	+0.40 mm
shim (for gear carrier side)	1.30 mm

g. Remove the gear carrier from the final drive housing.

h. Pull the bearing race out of the gear carrier housing with a suitable extractor.

i. Install the shims (determined in Step f) in the gear carrier starting with the thickest. Install the bearing race.

17. With the differential in the final drive housing, install the pinion shaft and tighten the nuts on the cover plate to 14 ft/lbs.

NOTE: Synchronizers can be replaced only as a matched unit.

18. Position the keys in the slots in the synchronizer hub. Place the synchronizer sleeve over the hub and align the marks. Install the springs 120° offset with the angled ends engaged in the hollow of a key.

19. Press the synchronizer rings onto the first and second gears. Check the gap between the ring and gear with a feeler gauge. The gap on new parts should be between 0.042-0.066 in. and no less than 0.019 in. on used parts.

20. Install the thrust washer and needle bearing for first gear on the pinion shaft. The recess in the thrust washer faces the roller bearing.

21. Align the grooves in the first gear synchronizer ring with the synchronizer shift keys. Position the shift fork slot in the operating sleeve toward second gear. The groove on the synchronizer hub should face toward first gear.

22. Heat the first gear and synchronizer as an assembly to 250° F and press onto the pinion shaft.

23. Drive the second gear needle bearing race onto the pinion shaft.

24. Install the second gear needle bearings and second gear.

25. Install third gear on the pinion shaft with the collar facing toward second gear. Secure third gear with the selective circlip which will give an axial play between 0.00-0.20 mm. Measure the play with a feeler gauge between the circlip and third gear.

26. Warm the reverse gear bushing and press it on the reverse shaft until the top of the bushing is 41 mm (1.614 in.) from the bottom of the shaft.

27. Install the reverse gear shaft retaining bolt in the shaft. Center the shaft and drive it in until the collar makes contact with the final drive housing. Remove the retaining bolt.

28. Assemble the third/fourth synchronizer in the same way outlined in Step 57.

29. Press the synchronizer rings onto third and fourth gear. The gap between the gear and synchronizer ring should be as follows:

	New Part in. (mm)	Wear Limit in. (mm)
Third	0.045-0.068	0.019
	(1.15-1.75)	(0.5)
Fourth	0.051-0.074	0.19
	(1.3-1.9)	(0.5)

30. Press the clutch pushrod bushing into the mainshaft until it is flush.

31. Install third gear needle bearings on the mainshaft.

32. Turn the synchronizer ring on third gear until the grooves align with the shift keys

in the synchronizer hub. The chamfer on the synchronizer hub inner splines must face toward third gear.

33. Press the third gear and synchronizer onto the mainshaft as a unit. Install the circlip.

NOTE: If the mainshaft thrust washer is replaced, the mainshaft position must be readjusted.

34. Install the fourth gear needle bearings on the mainshaft. Install fourth gear.

35. Press the mainshaft thrust washer on until it contacts fourth gear.

36. Drive the mainshaft oil seal into the final drive housing. Drive the mainshaft needle bearings into the final drive housing.

37. Make sure that the mainshaft support bar, locknut and spacer are in place. Insert the mainshaft. Install the shift fork assembly and secure with the circlips. Make sure that the gears are in Neutral.

38. Lift the shaft with the spindle until the play between second gear on the pinion shaft and third gear on the mainshaft can be checked. Measure the end-play with a feeler gauge. Measurement should be 0.039 in. (1.0 mm). Lock the spindle at the support bar and check the measurement to make sure it has not changed.

39. Install the measuring sleeve tool on the mainshaft. Place a new gasket on the final drive housing and install the gear carrier. Tighten the bolts to 14 ft/lbs.

40. Mount a dial indicator in a holding assembly and zero the indicator with a 3 mm preload. Move the measuring sleeve up and down, and record the indicator reading.

Mainshaft Play mm	Shim Size mm Used
0.00-0.46	No Shim Used
0.47-0.75	0.30
0.76-1.04	0.60
1.05-1.45	0.90

41. Remove the gear carrier from the final drive housing.

42. Install the shim (determined in Step 40) in the mainshaft bearing bore. Press the mainshaft bearing into the gear carrier, and secure with the clamping screws and nuts. Tighten the nuts to 11 ft/lbs.

43. Drive the drive flange oil seal into the final drive housing until it bottoms against the bearing race.

44. Install the drive flange on the final drive housing side, with the special tool (VW391), secure with a new circlip.

45. Drive the starter bushing into the final drive housing.

46. Drive the selector shaft oil seal into the gear carrier.

47. Drive the clutch operating lever oil seal into the gear carrier.

48. Drive the pinion shaft needle bearings into the gear carrier.

49. Drive the drive flange oil seal into the gear carrier cover until it bottoms on the differential bearing race.

50. Position the gasket on the final drive housing. Install the gear carrier housing on the final drive housing. Make sure that the reverse gear shaft is aligned with the hole in the gear carrier, install the reverse shaft retaining screw.

51. Install the gear carrier to final drive housing bolts and tighten to 14 ft/lbs.

52. Install the mainshaft circlip through the

clutch release bearing opening in the gear carrier.

53. Install the remaining driveshaft flange and circlip using special tools.

54. Remove the mainshaft support bar. Insert the clutch pushrod.

55. Insert the clutch release bearing assembly. Insert the clutch operating lever through the spring and clutch bearing lever. The bent end of the spring must contact the gear carrier. The center part of the spring is hooked over the end of the clutch bearing lever. Install the two circlips. Install the gasket and cover.

56. Insert the selector shaft and springs into the selector opening in the gear carrier assembly. Lubricate the selector with a multi-purpose grease before assembly. Install the selector shaft cover.

57. Install the interlock plunger assembly in the gear carrier assembly. Adjust the interlock plunger as follows:

a. Turn the slotted screw (interlock plunger) in until the nut starts to move out (bottoms).

b. Back the slotted screw out ¼ turn.

c. Install the plastic cap.

58. Install the plastic caps over the bearing clamping screws.

TYPE 18

4 Speed Transaxle— Models 002 and 091

Volkswagen

NOTE: Many special tools are required in the overhaul procedures of these transaxles. Use only recommended or equivalent tools to prevent personal injury or damage to the units.

DISASSEMBLY

MODELS 002 AND 091

1. Mount the transaxle securely and drain the lubricating oil from the unit.

2. Pry the caps from the center of the left and right drive flanges and remove the circlips from the stub axles. Using a puller, remove the drive flanges.

3. Mark the positions of the differential adjusting rings and measure the distance or depth to which the rings are screwed into the transaxle case. Record the readings for the assembly references.

4. Loosen the left differential adjusting ring to relieve the tension within the transaxle housing and remove the clutch housing assembly. Remove the rear driveshaft by unscrewing the shaft from the front drive or mainshaft. Remove the reverse drive gear.

5. Remove the left and right differential adjusting rings and lift the differential assembly from the case.

6. Remove the pinion gear assembly retaining ring from the differential side of the transaxle case.

NOTE: The retaining ring is peened, so that extra effort must be used to remove the ring.

7. Remove the gear shift housing from the gear carrier housing carefully to avoid damaging the housing mating surfaces.

8. Remove the gear carrier housing from the transaxle case and press the gear train from the transaxle case.

NOTE: Locate the shims from between the tapered roller bearing and the transaxle case for reuse during the reassembly.

9. The pinion and mainshaft must be pressed from the gear carrier housing.

——— CAUTION ———
Remove the circlips before attempting press work.

Thrust washer 4th gear

3rd/4th gear synchro ring

4th speed gear

Circlip

Sleeve/synchro hub 3rd/ 4th gears

Needle bearing 3rd/4th gears

3rd speed gear

Drive shaft

Exploded view of driveshaft (mainshaft) assembly—model 002

Ball joint

Intermediate shift lever

Intermediate shift lever

Intermediate shift lever shaft

Spring

Spring

Stop plate

Bracket for intermediate shift lever

Intermediate pin

3rd/4th gear selector shaft

Interlock pin

Reverse gear selector shaft

Detent ball

Spring

1st/2nd gear selector shaft

Sleeve

Drive shaft bearing

Plug

Pinion needle bearing

Lock plate

Gear carrier

Clamp sleeve

Circlip

Union nut

Support, rocker lever

Bracket, relay shaft

Rocker lever

Relay shaft

Exploded view of model 091 gear carrier housing and shift mechanism—typical of model 002

4th speed gear

3rd/4th gear synchro ring

Circlip

Sleeve/synchro hub 3rd/4th gears

Needle bearing 3rd/4th gears

3rd speed gear

Drive shaft

Exploded view of driveshaft (mainshaft) assembly—model 091

Mainshaft (Driveshaft)
DISASSEMBLY
MODEL 002

1. Press the 4th gear and thrust washer from the mainshaft.
2. Remove the caged roller bearing and the circlip.
3. Press the synchronizer hub from the shaft and remove the lower circlip.
4. Remove the 3rd speed gear and the split caged bearing.

MODEL 091

1. Remove the 4th speed gear and roller bearing.

2. Remove the circlip and press the 3rd/4th synchronizer hub from the shaft. Remove the lower circlip.
3. Remove the 3rd speed gear and the caged needle bearing from the shaft.

ASSEMBLY
MODEL 002

1. Install the split caged roller bearing and the 3rd speed gear.

NOTE: Use only the split caged bearings with the needle bearings in pairs.

2. Install the lower circlip in its groove on the shaft.

3. Press the 3rd/4th gear assembly into position on the shaft. Install the upper circlip.
4. Install the roller bearing and the 4th speed gear on the shaft.
5. Heat the thrust washer to 212° F (100° C) and press it on to the shaft with the oil grooves towards the 4th gear.

MODEL 091

1. Install the caged needle bearing on to the shaft and install the 3rd speed gear. Install the circlip.
2. Install the sleeve and hub for the 3rd and 4th gears. Install the second circlip.

NOTE: The identify groove on the synchronizer ring should be towards the 4th speed gear.

3. Install the roller bearing and the 4th speed gear assembly.

Pinion Shaft
DISASSEMBLY
MODEL 002

1. Remove the upper circlip by applying pressure against the 4th speed gear to compress the spacer spring. Remove the gear and the spacer spring.

—————— CAUTION ——————

The pressure tool should be firmly seated on the 4th gear to avoid personal injury due to the spacer spring tension.

2. Remove the circlip holding the 3rd gear in place and remove the 3rd gear, 2nd gear and 1st gear assemblies from the pinion shaft.

—————— CAUTION ——————

Observe the location and direction of the gear train components.

3. Remove the shim from the bearing surface of the round nut. Using a special tool, remove the round nut from the pinion shaft.

4. Using a press, remove the tapered roller bearing assembly from the shaft, along with the inner needle bearing race.

MODEL 091

1. Remove the upper circlip by applying pressure against the 4th speed gear to compress the spacer spring. Remove the pressure cautiously to avoid personal injury.

2. Remove the second circlip, the 3rd speed gear and the 2nd speed gear with needle bearing.

3. Remove the third circlip and remove the 1st/2nd speed gear assembly.

4. Remove the anti-rotation ring from the synchronizer hub with a punch.

5. Unscrew the inner race from the pinion shaft with a special tool. Press the tapered bearing assembly from the pinion shaft.

ASSEMBLY

NOTE: Should the pinion shaft or the tapered bearing be replaced, the pinion depth should be checked before total assembly is completed. Special tools are needed for the measurements.

MODEL 002

1. Heat the tapered bearing assembly to 212° F (100° C) and press into place on the pinion shaft.

2. Oil the bearing with hypoid oil and install the pinion and bearing assembly into the transaxle case. Install the retaining ring and torque to 159 ft/lbs (22 mkg).

3. Install an inch/pound torque wrench or equivalent on to the end of the pinion shaft and turn the shaft in both directions, approximately 15 to 20 turns and read the turning torque. The torque should be between 2.7 to 18.2 in/lbs (3.0 to 21.0 cmkg) for new bearings and 2.7 to 6.1 in/lbs (2.7 to 7.0 cmkg) for used bearings or for bearings that have been run at least 30 miles (50 km).

Circlip

Inner race, needle bearing

4th speed gear

Spacer spring

Cirlip

3rd speed gear

2nd speed gear

2nd gear synchro ring

1st gear synchro ring

Sleeve/hub 1st/2nd gear

1st speed gear

Shim

Round nut

Needle bearing

Inner race, needle bearing

Tapered roller bearing

Pinion

Exploded view of pinion shaft assembly—model 002

4. Remove the tapered bearing assembly and pinion shaft from the case and continue the assembly.

5. Install the needle bearing inner race and the needle bearing assembly. Install the round nut and torque it to 144 ft/lbs (20 mkg). Peen locking shoulder into spline.

6. Install the shim and the 1st gear and preassembled synchronizer as a unit, on the shaft and measure the axial play with a feeler gauge between the tapered bearing and the gear. The play should be 0.004 to 0.010 inch (0.10 to 0.25 mm). Adjust with selective shims.

7. Assemble the 2nd and 3rd speed gears to the shaft and install the circlip. Measure the clearance between the 3rd gear and the circlip. The clearance should be 0.004 to 0.010 inch (0.10 to 0.25 mm). Adjust by installing selective sized circlips.

8. Install the spacer spring, 4th gear and securely press downward with a press.

9. Heat the inner race to 212° F (100° C) and install on the shaft. Install the circlip on the shaft end.

Anti-rotation ring

bearing

Inner race/needle bearing

Tapered roller bearing

Pinion

Circlip

4th speed gear

Spacer spring

Circlip

3rd speed gear

2nd speed gear

Needle bearing

2nd gear synchro ring

Circlip

Sleeve/hub for 1st/2nd gear

1st gear synchro ring

1st speed gear

Exploded view of pinion shaft assembly—model 091

MODEL 091

1. Heat the tapered bearing assembly to 212° F (100° C) and press into position on the pinion shaft.

2. Oil the bearing with hypoid oil and install the pinion and bearing assembly into the transaxle case. Install the retaining ring and torque to 159 ft/lbs (22 mkg).

3. Install an inch/pound torque wrench or equivalent on to the end of the pinion shaft and turn the shaft in both directions, approximately 15 to 20 turns and read the turning torque. The torque should be between 2.7 to 18.2 in/lbs (3.0 to 21.0 cmkg) for new bearings and 2.7 to 6.1 in/lbs (2.7 to 7.0 cmkg) for used bearings or for bearings that have been run at least 30 miles (50 km).

4. Remove the tapered bearing assembly and pinion shaft from the case and continue the assembly.

5. Install the inner race and torque to 144 ft/lbs (20 mkg). Peen locking shoulder into gear spline.

6. Install the inner race of the 1st gear needle bearing and a new anti-rotation ring.

7. Install the 1st speed gear, the sleeve and hub for the 1st/2nd gear. Install the retaining circlip.

8. Install the 2nd speed gear needle bearing, the 2nd speed gear and the 3rd speed gear on the shaft and retain with a circlip. Measure the play between the circlip and the 3rd speed gear. The clearance should be 0.002 to 0.008 inch (0.5 to 0.20 mm).

9. Install the spacer spring and the 4th speed gear on the shaft. Safely depress the gear and spring and install the end circlip.

Gear Carrier Housing
DISASSEMBLY AND ASSEMBLY
MODELS 002 AND 091

1. The mainshaft bearing and pinion shaft bearings are pressed both in and out.

2. The detent springs and interlock pins must be removed before the shift rods can be removed.

3. The bracket for the intermediate shift lever is removable by removing attaching bolts.

4. The relay rod, rocker lever, relay shaft bracket and small components are removable. Note the location and direction of the individual parts for ease of reassembly.

Synchronizer Rings
MARKINGS ON RINGS
MODEL 002

1. 1st gear ring has no notch on the outer surface.

2. 2nd gear ring has three notches on the outer surface.

3. No identification on 3rd/4th gear rings.

4. Clearance between ring and cone of gear under pressure.

1st and 2nd gears—0.042 to 0.070 inch (1.1 to 1.8 mm).

3rd and 4th gears—0.039 to 0.074 inch (1.0 to 1.9 mm).

5. The sleeves and hubs are not matched and may be renewed separately. They should slide smoothly and have minimum backlash. The springs should be fitted with the end offset at 120° with the angled ends fitted over the keys.

MODEL 091

1. 1st gear ring has no notch on the outer surface, is made of brass and the friction surface is treated with molybdenum.

2. The 2nd, 3rd and 4th gear rings have three notches on the outer surface or three depressions on the end face of the rings.

3. The 2nd gear ring is made of brass and has the friction surface coated with molybdenum.

4. The 3rd gear ring is steel and the friction surface is treated with molybdenum.

5. The 4th gear ring is made of brass and has no special coating.

6. The clearance between the ring and gear cone while under pressure is:

1st and 2nd gear—0.040 to 0.064 inch (1.0 to 1.6 mm).

3rd and 4th gear—0.040 to 0.066 inch (1.0 to 1.7 mm).

7. The sleeves and the hubs are not matched and may be replaced separately. They must slide smoothly and have minimum backlash.

Reverse Drive Gear and Shaft
MODELS 002 AND 091

The reverse gear and shaft assemblies are removed and installed as a unit. The disassembly can be accomplished with the gear and shaft assemblies out of the case. Both the 002 and 091 model transaxles use basically the same gear and shaft arrangement with differences in gear teeth and shaft splines.

ASSEMBLY
MODELS 002 AND 091
Before Assembly

1. Should a new tapered roller bearing assembly be installed without a peening notch, one must be made by grinding a notch into the bearing housing.

----- CAUTION -----
Prevent metal particals from entering the bearings by using standard safety precautions.

----

2. Replacement of the transaxle housing, tapered roller bearing, ring and pinion or differential side bearings necessitate the measuring of the pinion depth and carrier adjustment. Special tools must be used for these operations.

ASSEMBLY

1. Press the mainshaft (driveshaft) and pinion shaft into the gear carrier housing bearings and secure as required. Locate the shift forks and shift fingers properly.

2. Place the removed shims into place on the transaxle housing. Using a new gasket, install the gear carrier housing assembly into the transaxle housing. Position the assembly into place by tapping on the pinion shaft with a plastic hammer.

NOTE: A special tool jig is used to adjust the shift forks and fingers before the gear train is installed. Since this type of tool is not always available, caution must be exercised so that the shift forks do not rub or exert pressure, but have clearance on the sides of the grooves in the operating sleeves, when in Neutral or while engaged in gear.

3. Install the tapered bearing retaining ring and torque to 159 ft/lbs (22 mkg), back off and retighten to 159 ft/lbs.

4. Peen the retaining ring into the notch on the tapered bearing housing.

5. Using a new gasket, install the gearshift housing by guiding the inner shift lever into the ball joint on the intermediate lever.

6. Install the differential into the case and install the adjusting rings and necessary spacers with new seals and O-rings.

7. Using the disassembly marks and depth measurements, adjust the left and right adjusting rings and check for proper gear backlash and tooth contact.

8. Install the rear driveshaft and the reverse gear. Tighten the rear driveshaft stud into the forward driveshaft (mainshaft) snugly and back off one spline. Install the reverse drive gear.

NOTE: Lengths of the rear driveshafts differ with certain engine usage.

9. Loosen the left adjusting ring and carefully install the clutch housing assembly into place and install the retaining washers or nuts. Some units will use bolts with washers. Retighten the left adjusting ring to the previously marked position.

10. Install the drive flanges on the axle stubs and install the circlips. Install new center plugs in the drive flange centers.

11. Fill the unit with lubricating oil and rotate by hand to allow oil to cover the internal components.

TYPE 19

5 Speed Transaxle

Audi

DISASSEMBLY

1. Mount the transaxle assembly into a holder securely and drain the lubricating oil.

2. Mark and remove the gear selector lever and the gear selector shaft assembly.

NOTE: If necessary, replace the gear selector shaft assembly rather than repairing it.

3. Remove the gear carrier housing cover/gear carrier housing assembly, the mainshaft and the pinion from the final drive housing.

NOTE: Dowel pins are used to align the gear carrier housing to the final drive housing. If the dowel pins are to be removed, drive them from the gear carrier.

4. Remove the gear carrier housing end plug with a sharp ended tool, by driving the tool into the center of the plug and prying the cover outward.

5. Place the mainshaft into a vise with soft jaw covers and remove the bolt from the mainsahft, in the cover cap opening.

6. Reposition the gear carrier housing so

1. Main shaft	7. 5th gear
2. 4th gear	8. Pinion
3. 3rd gear	9. Final drive housing
4. 2nd gear	10. Gear carrier housing
5. Reverse gear	11. Gear carrier housing cover
6. 1st gear	

Cross section of 5-speed Audi transaxle

that the vise soft jaws are holding the housing instead of the mainshaft.

7. Remove the twelve retaining bolts from the gear carrier housing cover and separate the cover from the gear housing.

8. Remove the mainshaft bearing inner race from gear carrier housing.

9. Remove the 5th gear clutch hub and mainshaft bearing inner race from the cover end of the mainshaft.

10. Remove the 5th gear synchronizer ring.

11. Drive the 5th gear shift fork roll pin from the fork with a pin punch.

--- **CAUTION** ---
Support the selector rod and fork to avoid damage to the gear carrier housing.

12. Remove the circlip, the 5th speed gear with the synchronizer hub, needle bearing and the 5th speed gear shift fork.

NOTE: The 5th/reverse gear selector rod will remain in the gear carrier housing.

13. Remove the selector rod stop screws from the outside of the gear carrier housing.

14. Reposition the gear carrier housing assembly in the jaws of the vise, with the soft jaw covers, and clamp the 4th speed gear in the vise.

15. Remove the bolt from the pinion shaft and remove the 5th gear and the adjustment shim.

16. Reposition the gear carrier housing in the soft jawed vise and drive the 1st/2nd gear selector fork roll pin from the fork.

--- **CAUTION** ---
Support the selector rod and fork to avoid damage to the gear carrier housing.

17. Remove the 3rd/4th gear selector fork roll pin.

--- **CAUTION** ---
Support the selector rod and fork to avoid damage to the gear carrier housing.

18. Remove the 3rd/4th selector rod from the gear carrier housing. The shifting fork should remain in the synchronizer hub.

NOTE: Do not lose the indent or interlock pin.

19. Remove the relay lever bolt from the reverse gear relay lever.

20. Pull the pinion and mainshaft partially from the gear carrier housing and remove the mainshaft with the 3rd/4th gear shift fork on the synchronizer hub.

21. Pull the pinion from the housing, far enough so that the selector rod and shift fork of the 1st/2nd gears can be removed, after the reverse gear spring clip on the pinion side is unhooked and turned.

22. Remove the pinion from the housing.

23. Inspect the transaxle components, replace all seals and gaskets, gears that are damaged or worn, and bearings, both needle and ball.

Mainshaft and Pinion Shaft

The mainshaft and pinion shaft gears can be disassembled by the removal of the end bearings or circlips. Certain gears will have to be removed either with a puller or a press. Mark the gears before the removal to avoid backward installation. The synchronizers are of the Borg Warner type and should be match-marked before disassembly.

During the reassembly of the shafts, the following clearances should be observed.

MAINSHAFT
3rd/4th Synchronizer Rings to Hub Clearance

New rings—0.039 to 0.067 inch (1.0 to 1.7 mm)

Wear limit—0.020 inch (0.5 mm)

5th Gear Synchronizer Ring to Hub Clearance

New ring—0.039 to 0.075 inch (1.0 to 1.9 mm)

Wear limit—0.020 inch (0.5 mm)

1. 5th and reverse gear selector rod	9. Selector shaft
2. Selector shaft assembly	10. Final drive housing
3. Reverse gear shift fork	11. Mounting plate
4. Relay lever	12. Reverse gear synchronizer
5. Reverse gear interlock	13. Reverse gear
6. 5th gear synchronizer ring	14. Gear carrier housing
7. 5th gear clutch sleeve	15. 5th gear
8. Main shaft	16. 5th gear shift fork
	17. 5th gear synchronizer hub

5th and reverse shift linkage viewed from the top

1. Bolt
2. Main shaft bearing outer race
3. Main shaft bearing
4. Circlip
5. Baffle plate
6. Main shaft bearing inner race
7. 5th gear clutch hub
8. 5th gear synchronizer ring
9. Circlip

10. 5th gear with synchronizer hub and sleeve
11. Sleeve
12. Hollow key
13. Spring
14. 5th gear with synchronizer hub
15. 5th gear needle bearing
16. Main shaft bearing
17. Circlip
18. Mainshaft bearing inner race
19. Mainshaft
20. 3rd gear needle bearing
21. 3rd gear

22. 3rd gear synchronizer ring
23. 3rd & 4th gear synchronizer hub
24. Circlip
25. 4th gear synchronizer ring
26. 4th gear needle bearing
27. 4th gear
28. 4th gear thrust washer
29. Circlip
30. Main shaft needle bearing
31. Spring
32. Sleeve
33. Hub
34. Hollow key

Exploded view of mainshaft assembly

3rd/4th Synchronizer Hub End-Play
0.000 to 0.002 inch (0.00 to 0.05 mm)
Correct by selective circlips
4th Gear End-Play
0.008 to 0.013 inch (0.20 to 0.35 mm)
PINION SHAFT
4th Gear End-Play
Limit—0.0008 (0.02 mm)
Correct by selective circlip
3rd Gear End-Play
0.000 to 0.0016 inch (0.00 to 0.04 mm)
1st/2nd Synchronizer Rings to Hub Clearance
New rings—0.039 to 0.067 inch (1.0 to 1.7 mm)
Wear limit—0.020 inch (0.5 mm)
1st/2nd Synchronizer Hub End-Play
0.000 to 0.0016 inch (0.00-0.04 mm)
Correct by selective circlip

Reverse Gear Synchronizer Clearance
New ring—0.029 to 0.090 inch (0.75 to 2.3 mm)
Wear limit—0.007 inch (0.2 mm)

Differential Assembly

The differential assembly is removed from the final drive housing after removal of the drive flange and the final drive cover. Methods of repairs are found in the Unit Overhaul section.

ASSEMBLY

1. Have the reverse gear engaged and the spring clip is unhooked on the one side and turned away from the pinion bore.
2. Install the pinion shaft assembly par-
tially into the carrier housing. Install the 1st/2nd gear shift rod and press the pinion into the housing until it is fully seated.
3. Connect the unhooked spring clip and disengage the reverse gear.
4. Install the 3rd/4th gearshift fork with the slot into the 5th/reverse gearshift rod.
5. If the mainshaft bearing inner race is on the mainshaft, it must be removed before the shaft is installed into the gear carrier.
6. Install the mainshaft partially into the housing and insert the 3rd/4th shift fork into the sliding sleeve and install the mainshaft until fully seated.
7. Move all the shifting rods to the neutral position and check for the correct position of the interlock pins.
8. Install the 3rd/4th gear shift rod into

1. Pinion
2. Shim
3. Pinion bearing outer race
4. Pinion bearing
5. 4th gear
6. Circlip
7. Circlip
8. 3rd gear

9. Circlip
10. 2nd gear needle bearing
11. 2nd gear
12. 2nd gear synchronizer ring
13. Synchronizer sleeve/hub for 1st and 2nd gears
14. Spring
15. Synchronizer sleeve
16. Synchronizer hub
17. Hollow keys
18. Circlip

19. 1st gear synchronizer ring
20. 1st gear needle bearing
21. 1st gear
22. Pinion bearing
23. Pinion bearing outer race
24. Shim
25. Shim for 5th gear
26. 5th gear
27. Bolt

Exploded view of pinion shaft assembly

Exploded view of gear carrier housing and cover components

1. Bolt
2. Sleeve
3. Spring clip
4. Mounting plate
5. Reverse gear shaft
6. Spring
7. Reverse gear synchronizer
8. Reverse gear
9. Reverse gear relay lever
10. Reverse gear interlock plunger
11. 5th/reverse gear selector rod
12. Reverse gear shift fork
13. Plungers
14. Pinion bearing outer race
15. Shim
16. Main shaft bearing
17. Gear carrier housing
18. Relay lever bolt
19. 5th gear interlock mechanism
20. 1st to 4th gear interlock mechanism
21. Spring
22. Plunger
23. Gasket
24. Stop screw
25. Baffle plate
26. Circlip
27. Mainshaft bearing
28. Gear carrier housing cover
29. Magnet

the gear carrier housing and the shift fork. Install the interlock pin and secure the fork to the rod with the roll pin.

——— CAUTION ———
Support the shift rod and fork when installing the roll pin.

9. Install the roll pin into the 1st/2nd gear selector rod and fork.

——— CAUTION ———
Support the shift rod and fork when installing the roll pin.

10. Install the detent balls and springs. Place new gaskets on the stop screws and install them into the housing.

11. Clamp the 4th gear of the pinion shaft into a vise with soft jaw covers.

12. With the gear carrier housing/cover mating surface facing upward, measure the distance from the housing surface to the top of the pinion bearing outer race or to the shim. Selective shims are available as follows.

NOTE: Measurements are in mm. Convert to inches as required.

Depth (mm)	Shim Thickness (mm)
8.35-8.64	1.1
8.65-8.94	1.4
8.95-9.24	1.7
9.25-9.54	2.0
9.55-9.84	2.3

13. Heat the 5th gear to 250° F (120° C) and drive on the pinion shaft until seated on the selected shim.

NOTE: Be sure the collar of the gear faces the pinion head.

14. Install the washer and bolt and torque to 36 ft/lbs (50 Nm).

15. Heat the main bearing inner race to 250° F (120° C) and drive on the mainshaft. Select a circlip of proper thickness to fit tightly in the groove on the mainshaft.

16. Install the 5th gear with the synchronizer hub, needle bearing and shift rod. Support the shift rod and install the roll pin.

17. Install the retaining circlip and install the 5th gear synchronizer ring.

18. Heat the 5th gear clutch hub to 250° F (120° C) and drive on the mainshaft. Drive on the mainshaft inner bearing race with a driving sleeve type tool.

19. Install the dowel pins and a new gasket to the mating surface.

20. Carefully install the gear carrier housing cover, and drive the second mainshaft inner bearing race onto the shaft.

21. Install the washer and bolt onto the mainshaft and tighten to 36 ft/lbs (50 Nm).

22. Install the cover retaining bolts and tighten to 18 ft/lbs (25 Nm).

23. Install a new cover cap into the end of the gear carrier housing cover.

24. Assemble the gear carrier housing/cover assembly to the final drive housing and install the retaining bolts. Tighten to 18 ft/lbs (25 Nm).

25. Install the selector shaft housing into the final drive housing and retain with the retaining bolts. Tighten to 7 ft/lbs (10 Nm).

26. Install the selector shaft lever, flush with the toothed end of the selector shaft. Tighten the clamping bolt.

27. Fill the unit to its proper level with lubricating oil and check for proper shifting of the internal gears.

TYPE 20

4 And 5 Speed Transaxle

Mazda

DISASSEMBLY AND ASSEMBLY

NOTE: The procedures described are for both the four speed and the five speed transaxle. The five speed unit has a rear cover which easily distinguishes it from the other unit.

Disassembly (Fifth Gear)

1. Remove the rear cover. Remove the roll pin that secures the fifth gear shift fork to the selector shaft. Shift the transaxle unit into either first or second gear.

NOTE: Do not shift into fourth gear as, by doing this you may cause damage to the gears.

2. Move the fifth gear clutch sleeve, to engage fifth gear and double lock the transmission.

3. Straighten the tab of the locknut on both the primary and secondary shafts. Remove the locknuts from the shafts.

4. Pull the fifth gear clutch hub assembly out along with the shift fork.

NOTE: Remove the fork to gain access to the primary shaft locknut.

5. Reinstall the fifth gear clutch hub and move the sleeve to the fifth gear position in order to lock the transmission.

Mazda GLC manual transaxle—exploded view

6. Remove the primary shaft locknut and remove the fifth gear from the transmission case.

Assembly (Fifth Gear)

1. Install the fifth gear on the primary shaft. Be sure that the marked boss is facing toward the locknut. Install the bush and the fifth gear on the secondary shaft.

2. Install the synchronizer ring and clutch hub and the selector fork. Do not install the shift fork pin.

NOTE: The stop washer or plate for the clutch hub must be installed between the locknut and clutch hub to prevent overtravel of the clutch when shifting into reverse gear to prevent the synchronizer keys from falling out.

3. Install the locknuts on both shafts and tighten them slightly.

4. Shift into first or second gear only, using the control rod. Shift into fifth gear to double lock the transmission.

5. Tighten the primary shaft locknut and lock the tub.

NOTE: Do not tighten the secondary shaft locknut until the selector fork is installed. Remove the locknut and clutch hub from the secondary gear shaft and reassemble it with the selector fork. Do not insert the drive pin at this time.

6. Move the fifth gear selector clutch to engage the fifth gear in order to lock the transmission.

7. Shift the unit into either first or second gear.

8. Install the roll pin securing the fifth gear shift fork to the selector shaft. Install the cover.

Primary Shaft

The Mazda manual transaxle uses two types of primary shafts, one for the four speed transaxle and one for the five speed transaxle. Both shafts are made as a cluster with reverse, first, second, third and fourth gears integral. The fifth gear (when equipped) is splined into the end of the shaft, thus distinguishing between the four and five speed unit.

Secondary Shaft

The secondary shaft assembly consists of the secondary shaft, gears, clutch hub and

FOUR SPEED

20   19   18

FIVE SPEED

20   19

DIFFERENTIAL RING GEAR

77   78   79

FINAL GEAR RATIO

3.850   4.105   4.388

Secondary shaft identification

sleeve assemblies, synchro rings and bearings. The secondary shaft is manufactured integrally with the final drive gear.

There are three different types of secondary shafts used in the four speed transaxle and two different types used in the five speed transaxle. All of these shafts vary by the number of gear teeth on the final drive gears.

NOTE: The combination of the final drive gear on the secondary shaft and ring gear are identified by the groove provided in the construction of each individual gear.

Disassembly and Assembly (Secondary Gears)

1. Install a suitable bearing puller in the grooves between the gear and the gear spline of fourth gear. Remove the bearing and the fourth gear from the assembly.

2. Remove the snap-ring on the third and fourth clutch hub. Slide out the clutch hub and the sleeve assembly.

3. Remove the third gear, the thrust washer and the second gear.

4. Remove the snap-ring, and slide out the clutch hub and reverse gear assembly and first gear.

5. Install the bearing remover tool under the rollers and press out the shaft.

6. Assembly is the reverse of disassembly.

Synchronizer Rings

Bridge type synchronizer rings are used in the Mazda transaxle. There are three different synchronizer rings; one for second, third and fourth speed, another for first and third speed and one for fifth speed if the vehicle is so equipped. The first speed synchro ring can be identified from the other two because it has less teeth.

Thrust Clearance

The thrust clearance of each gear is checked by using a feeler gauge. The specification for thrust clearance is .5 mm (.020 in.).

Reverse Idler Shaft and Shift Rod

The reverse idler shaft has an integral mounting post which is secured to the case with a bolt. When installing the idler shaft, align the holes of the shaft with the notch in the transaxle case. When installing the reverse shift rod to the shift gate, be sure that the screw holes are aligned and that the hole of the shift rod is not 180 degrees out of phase.

Reverse idler shaft alignment

Checking thrust clearance

Checking thrust clearance—fifth gear

Bearing Preload Adjustment

NOTE: When the clutch housing, transaxle case, primary shaft, secondary shaft, bearings or differential case are replaced the bearing preload should be checked and adjusted.

1. Remove the oil seal and the differential bearing outer race. Adjust the shim from the transaxle case.

2. Remove the bearing outer races from the primary and secondary shafts. Adjust the shims from the transaxle case and the clutch housing.

3. Reinstall the outer races to the transaxle case.

4. Install the outer races (removed in Step 2) to their respective selectors. Install the selectors, primary shaft assembly and the secondary shaft assembly to the clutch housing.

5. Install the transaxle case and place the ten collars between the transaxle case and the clutch housing.

Collar positioning

NOTE: The collars should be positioned as shown in the illustration.

6. To properly settle each bearing, using the tool turn the selector in a direction where the gap is widened until it cannot be turned by hand. Then turn the selector in the opposite direction until the gap is eliminated. Manually turn the selector to a direction where the gap becomes wider until the selector cannot be turned.

NOTE: Make sure that the shaft turns smoothly.

7. Measure the gap of the selector with a feeler gauge.

Checking differential bearing preload

NOTE: This measurement should be taken at several places along the circumference of the selector.

8. Take the maximum reading and determine the shim to be used as follows.

9. For the primary shaft bearing, first subtract 1.00 mm (thickness of the diaphragm spring) from the gap (determined in Step 7).

e.g.: Measurement 1.39 mm minus 1.00 mm equals .39 mm, so you select the next larger and closer shim which would be .40 mm.

NOTE: Do not use more than two shims.

10. For the secondary shaft bearing, select a shim which has a thickness that is larger and closer to the gap (determined in Step 7).

e.g.: Measurement .42 mm, so you select the next larger and closer shim which would be .45 mm.

NOTE: Do not use more than two shims to accomplish this task.

11. For the differential bearing, set the preload adapters (tool # 49-0180-510A and # 49-FT01-515 or equivalent) to the pinion shaft through the hole for the driveshaft of the transaxle case. Hook a spring scale to the adapter and check the bearing preload.

NOTE: While checking the preload, turn the selector until the reading of the spring scale becomes 1.1-1.5 lb.

12. Then measure the gap of the selector on the differential using a feeler gauge.

NOTE: This measurement should be taken in several places along the circumference of the selector.

Selected shim installation

13. Select a shim that has a thickness larger and closer to the maximum reading that was taken in the previous step.

e.g.: Measurement .54 mm, so you select the next larger and closer shim which would be .60 mm.

NOTE: Do not use more than three shims to accomplish this task.

14. Remove the shim selectors and each bearing outer race. Install the shims selected in previous steps between the transaxle case and bearing outer race.

15. A diaphragm spring is used to keep the bearing preload as specified and also to maintain low level gear noise. So when installing the diaphragm spring, be sure it is in the proper direction.

16. When installing the oil funnel on the clutch housing, be sure that it is in the proper position.

17. After assembling the transaxle, recheck the preloads of the differential bearing and the primary shaft bearing.

18. The differential bearing preload should be .3-6.6 in/lbs., and the reading on the spring scale should be .07-1.7 lb.

19. The primary shaft preload should be 1.7-3.5 in/lbs., and the reading on the spring scale should be .4-.9 lb.

Differential

The final gear is helical cut with the same tooth design as that used in the transmission. No adjustments are required.

There are three different ring gears in numbers of gear teeth on the manual transaxle. They are identified by the marks (grooves) provided on the gear outer surface.

The backlash between the differential side gear and pinion gear is adjusted by the thrust washer installed behind the side gear teeth. There are three different thicknesses of thrust washers available.

When checking the backlash, insert both driveshafts into the side gears.

Strut Overhaul

STRUT SERVICE AND REPAIR

MacPherson struts are appearing on the front (and rear) wheels of more and more cars. The strut design takes up less room in the engine compartment, compared to a conventional upper and lower arm with shock absorber arrangement. The trend toward smaller, lighter and more efficient packaging mandates the use of a strut suspension to permit more room for engine accessories and front wheel drive components.

Strut Suspension Design

In a conventional front suspension, the wheel is attached to a spindle, which is in turn, connected to upper and lower control arms through upper and lower ball joints. A coil spring between the control arms (sometimes on top of the upper arm) supports the weight of the vehicle and a shock absorber controls rebound and dampens oscillations.

In a strut type suspension, the strut performs a shock dampening function, like a shock absorber, but unlike a conventional shock absorber, the strut is a structural part of the vehicle's suspension.

The strut assembly usually contains a spring seat to retain the coil spring that supports the vehicle's weight. The shock absorber is built into the body of the strut housing. The strut is normally attached at the bottom to the lower control arm and at the top to the car body. The upper mount usually features a bearing that permits the coil spring to rotate as the wheels turn for

Conventional upper and lower arm suspension

Strut with concentric coil spring (rear wheel drive)

Strut with concentric coil spring (front wheel drive)

smoother steering. The entire design eliminates the need for the upper control arm, upper ball joint and many of the conventional suspension bushings. The lower ball joint is no longer a load carrying unit, because it is isolated from the weight of the vehicle.

Serviceability

Struts fall into 2 broad categories—serviceable and sealed units. A sealed strut is designed so that the top closure of the strut assembly is permanently sealed. There is no access to the shock absorber cartridge inside the strut housing and no means of replacing the cartridge. It is necessary to replace the entire strut unit.

A serviceable strut is designed so that the cartridge inside the housing, that provides the shock absorbing function, can be replaced with a new cartridge. Serviceable struts use a threaded body nut in place of a sealed cap to retain the cartridge.

The shock absorber device inside a serviceable strut is generally "wet". This means that the shock absorber contains oil that contacts and lubricates the inner wall of the

strut body. The oil is sealed inside the strut by the body nut, O-ring and piston rod seal.

Servicing a "wet" strut with the equivalent components involves a thorough cleaning of the inside of the strut body, absolute cleanliness and great care in reassembly.

Cartridge inserts were developed to simplify servicing "wet" struts. The insert is a factory sealed replacement for the strut shock absorber. The replacement cartridge is simply substituted for the original shock absorber cartridge and retained with the body nut, avoiding the near laboratory-like conditions required to service a "wet" strut with "wet" service components.

Import cars use predominantly concentric coil spring units and, for the most part are serviceable, meaning that they can be removed from the vehicle, disassembled and the shock absorber cartridge replaced in the old housing. Both OEM and aftermarket replacement cartridges can be used in these struts if they are serviceable. Exceptions to the serviceable struts include Ford Fiesta and some later Fiats and Hondas, but even on these cars OEM struts can be replaced with aftermarket units, which are serviceable once the aftermarket unit is installed.

A sealed strut has no body nut and is serviceable by replacement

Serviceable struts have a removeable body nut to allow replacement of the strut cartridge

WHEEL ALIGNMENT

It is not always necessary to re-align the wheels after struts are serviced. If care is taken matchmarking affected components and in reassembling, alignment may be unaffected. However, if wheels were not in proper alignment prior to service, or if the entire strut assembly was replaced, a wheel alignment check should be made. Generally, only camber is adjustable, and then only within a narrow range.

NOTE: Do not attempt to bend components to correct wheel alignment.

On most serviceable import struts, the position of the upper bearing plate or lower mount can be matchmarked and wheel alignment will be maintained during reassembly.

Tools

Without the right tools, a strut job will take longer than necessary and can be dangerous.

A normal selection of hand tools such as open end and box wrenches, sockets, pliers, screwdrivers and hammers are necessary to work on struts. Extensions and universal joints will help reach tight spots. Be sure to have both metric and inch-sized wrenches on hand. Two big time-savers are "crows-feet" and ratcheting box wrenches in assorted sizes. Torx fasteners are also showing up more and more in chassis fasteners.

In addition to the normal handtools, some sort of spanner is necessary to remove the body nut on serviceable struts. Sometimes a pipe wrench can be used successfully.

Strut and cartridge replacement requires a spring compressor.

--- CAUTION ---
Makeshift tools for compressing coil springs—threaded rod, chains, wire or other methods—should never be used. The coil spring is under tremendous compression and can fly off causing personal injury and damage to equipment. Use only a good quality spring compressor such as described below.

Economy, or manual, spring compressors are the least expensive but more time consuming to use. Angle hooks grasp the spring coils and must be compressed with a wrench. For those who service struts infrequently, this is probably the wisest investment for purchase.

Other manual spring compressors (jaws type) are faster to operate, have a more positive gripping action and can be used on or off the car. These types are probably not cost effective for the do-it-yourselfer, but can be rented from auto supply stores for single-time use.

For volume work, compressors that are pneumatically or hydraulically operated are best. Air operated compressors are suitable

Exploded view of a typical strut

MAINTAINING WHEEL ALIGNMENT

The location and method of adjusting wheel alignment determines the components that must be match-marked to maintain wheel alignment. There are 4 basic methods of adjusting wheel alignment. Almost all cars use one of these or a slight variation.

Mark the eccentric (camber adjusting bolt) relative to the clevis mounting bracket.

Mark the mounting stud that faces the front of the vehicle. This type of bracket is reversible for varying applications.

Mark the upper support housing relative to the inner fender before removing the strut from the upper mount.

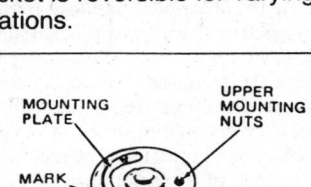

Mark the location of the mounting plate relative to the location on the inner fender.

An economical manual spring compressor

"Jaws" type spring compressor

Lightweight, air operated, portable spring compressor can be used on or off the vehicle. Extra shoes are available to handle all strut applications

A simple spanner wrench designed for use with body nuts equipped with recessed lugs. A pipe wrench is a frequent substitute

Spanner wrench with adaptor inserts for various applications of body nuts. This type of spanner can be used with a torque wrench for retorqueing the body nut

A manual spring compressor with plates or hooks for servicing virtually any strut

STRUT OVERHAUL

Stationary, universal pneumatic spring compressor

for all types of struts (through use of adaptors), are lightweight and can be used on or off the vehicle. Bench mounted hydraulically operated units are probably the safest, but are also the most expensive and require that the strut be removed from the vehicle, which means separating brake lines and other connections which can be time consuming.

There are also universal kits that fit all struts in either the manual or air operated types.

Repair Tips

1. Make sure you have all the tools you'll need. NEVER IMPROVISE A SPRING COMPRESSOR.

2. Normally both front struts should be repaired or replaced at the same time.

3. The easiest way to work on most struts is to remove the entire unit from the vehicle, unless you have access to an air operated spring compressor. Some struts, however, can, and should, be repaired while installed on the vehicle.

4. Always read the instructions packaged with any replacement parts. In particular, note whether the body nut is supplied new or re-used.

5. Mark the position(s) of any bearing plate nuts or cam bolts to assure proper alignment after installation.

6. Be sure to protect the rubber boot on the drive axle of front wheel drive cars.

7. If necessary to remove the brake caliper, do not let the caliper hang by the brake hose. Suspend the caliper from a wire hook or rope.

8. Be careful in clamping a strut in a vise. Special fixtures are available to hold struts in a vise, but are not necessary if care is used to be sure the housing is not crushed or dented. A block of soft wood on either side of the housing will prevent most damage.

9. Use a spring compressor to relieve tension from the spring. Be sure to clean and lubricate the screw threads, particularly on hand operated (manual) spring compressors.

NOTE: Some springs have a special coating that should not be scuffed.

10. If you are replacing the strut cartridge, clean the inside of the strut housing and the body nut threads before replacing the oil and installing a new cartridge.

11. Be sure to use OEM quality fasteners any time a fastener is replaced.

Mark the position of the attachments that control wheel alignment. See Maintaining Wheel Alignment earlier in this section

STRUT OVERHAUL (OFF-CAR)

Following is a typical overhaul procedure of a serviceable MacPherson strut, after having removed the strut from the vehicle. The vehicle should be firmly supported. If it is necessary, to separate the brake line from the strut for strut removal, the brakes will have to be bled after reinstallation. See the manufacturer's car section for specific MacPherson strut removal and installation procedures.

Photos Courtesy Gabriel Div., Maremont Corp.

Examine the strut assembly for damage, dented strut body, spring seat, broken or missing strut mounting parts. Any of these will require replacement of the complete assembly. Also inspect other suspension components for wear or damage

Matchmark the upper end of the coil spring and bearing plate to avoid confusion during reassembly

To make servicing easier, clamp the strut in a strut vise. The strut vise is designed to clamp the strut tight without damage to strut cylinder. It is very handy for strut work and can be used in your shop vise or mounted to any bench

Before using the manual spring compressor, lubricate both sides of the thrust washers and the threads with a light coat of grease

Install the compressor hooks on opposite sides of the coil spring with the hooks attached to the upper-most and lower-most spring coils. To avoid possible slippage, use tape or small hose clamps on either side of the compressor hooks

Alternately tighten the bolts a few turns at a time until all tension is removed from the spring seat

Remove the piston rod nut and disassemble the upper mounting parts, keeping them in order for reassembly. Remove the coil spring. There is no need to remove the compressor from the coil spring

An alternative to the manual compressor is the "jaws" type. Turn the load screw to open or close the compressor until the maximum number of spring coils can be engaged

Tighten the load screw until the coil spring is loose from the spring seats. There is no need to compress the spring any further

Remove the piston rod nut and disassemble the upper mounting parts

Like the manual compressor, there is no need to remove the compressor from the coil spring. Remove the coil spring and compressor.

Keep the upper mounting parts in order of their removal. They'll be re-assembled in reverse order

A spanner wrench is necessary to remove body nuts although a pipe wrench will do the job

Use the spanner wrench or pipe wrench to loosen the body nut

Remove the body nut and discard if a new body nut came with the replacement cartridge. If not, save the body nut

Use a scribe or suitable tool to remove the O-ring from the top of the housing

Grasp the piston rod and pull cartridge out of the housing. Remove it slowly to avoid splashing oil. Be sure all pieces come out of the housing

Pour all of the strut fluid into a suitable container, clean the inside of the strut cylinder, and inspect the cylinder for dents and to insure that all loose parts have been removed from inside of strut body

Refill the cylinder with one ounce (a shot glass) of the original oil or fresh oil. The oil helps dissipate internal cartridge heat during operation and results in a cooler running, longer lasting unit. Do not put too much oil in—otherwise the oil may leak at the body nut after it expands when heated

Insert the new replacement cartridge into the strut body

Push the piston road *all* the way down, to avoid damage to the piston rod if the spanner wrench slips, and start the body nut by hand. Be sure it is not cross-threaded

Tighten the body nut securely

⟍ STRUT OVERHAUL

Inspect the loose parts prior to re-assembly. Note the chalk mark location for proper seating of the upper spring seat

Re-assemble the coil spring and upper mounting parts in re-verse order. Tighten the piston rod nut and remove the spring compressor. Install the dust cap. Install the strut in the vehicle. See the car section for details

STRUT OVERHAUL (ON-CAR)

On some cars, it is best not to completely remove the strut for service. Removal or reassembly of some parts may be difficult without special equipment. Datsun Z-cars are among these. The service methods shown in the following procedure are typical of on-car strut overhaul, although parts or assembly sequences may vary. Refer to the individual manufacturer's car section for details of installations.

Photos Courtesy Gabriel Div., Maremont Corp.

Raise the car to the desired working height and place jack stands under the crossmember, not under the lower control arm. Mark wheel rim and mating lug to assure that wheel balance is not disturbed

Disconnect brake line at frame bracket

Disconnect the emergency brake cable from actuator arm (Datsun uses a cotter key)

Remove emergency brake cable from bracket by removing the spring clip

Remove nut, retainer and bushing securing sway bar to its vertical link

Mark the driveshaft flange and hub to assure proper reassembly. Remove the nuts, bolts, and lock washers securing the driveshaft to the hub

Loosen, but do not remove the nut securing the bottom of the strut to the lower control arm

From inside the vehicle remove the nuts and lockwashers securing the upper support housing to vehicle fender.

Press down on lower control arm with pry bar and swing strut from under fender. (Note: *A slit hose can be used to protect wheel well fender edge.*)

Either a manual or pneumatic spring compressor can be used to compress the spring. A pneumatic compressor is illustrated. Compress the spring and remove upper mounting parts. Remove the spring from the strut.

Remove body nut. For convenience, the strut can be propped up while removing body nut

Remove O-ring using a small pick or an awl and remove the cartridge.

Tilt strut down to allow all the oil to drain into a suitable container. Inspect cylinder for dents and to insure all loose parts have been removed from inside of strut body

Pour about one ounce (a shot glass) of oil back into the strut body for heat transfer. Avoid over-filling or the oil may leak past the body nut

Insert the new replacement cartridge into the strut body

Install the body nut and tighten securely

Re-install compression bumper, coil spring, spring seat and upper support housing. Be sure to position the support housing studs relative to the holes in the vehicle's inner fender. Install the piston rod nut. Tighten securely. Relieve the spring tension

Push the strut back under fender and install the nuts and lockwasher securing the upper support housing to the inner fender

Reconnect the brake line

Re-assemble the emergency brake cable in the bracket

Re-assemble brake cable to actuator arm and install cotter pin

Re-install the bushing retainer and nut on sway bar link

Align marks made earlier, then install and tighten the four nuts and bolts that secure the driveshaft to the hub

Bleed the brakes and install the tire and lower *the car to the ground*. Tighten the two nuts securing the strut to the lower control arm. Note: *Torqueing the nuts while the car is not on the ground can cause a hard, choppy ride due to incorrect bushing preload*

MACPHERSON STRUT PROBLEM DIAGNOSIS

Problems with MacPherson struts generally fall into 3 main categories: suspension, tire wear and steering. In general, the symptoms encountered are not significantly different from those encountered on conventional suspensions.

Suspension

Sag

Vehicle "sag" is a visible tilt of the car from one side to the other or one end to the other while parked on a level surface.

Weak or damaged strut springs could cause this condition and should be repaired immediately.

Sag will also cause steering and tire wear problems to be more pronounced and vehicle instability on rough roads. Front wheel alignment will not solve the problem.

Weak strut springs increase vehicle sag. See "Tire Cupping".

Cartridge Leaks

Strut cartridge leaks (not seepage) indicate the need for cartridge or strut replacement. Be sure the leakage is coming from the strut, and not from elsewhere on the vehicle.

Check For Leaks

Strut

Abnormal Tire Wear

Wear on One Side

One sided tire wear indicates incorrect camber. Check the causes in the accompanying illustration and be sure the wheel alignment is correct.

COIL SPRING WEAK OR BROKEN

STRUT HOUSING BENT

CONTROL ARM BUSHING(S) WORN OR MISSING

BALL JOINTS LOOSE

STRUT ROD BUSHINGS WORN OR MISSING

Tire "Cupping"

Cupped tires indicate any or all of the following problems.

1. A weak strut cartridge can be verified by bouncing each corner of the car vigorously and letting go. The car should not bounce more than once, if the shock absorber cartridges are good.

2. Weak strut springs allow sag to increase with only a slight amount of downward pressure. A visual inspection will reveal any broken springs or shiny spots.

3. Check for loose or worn wheel bearings with the weight of the car off of the wheel.

4. Check the wheel balance.

Tread Edge Wear

Wear along tread edges (feathering) indicates a suspension or steering system problem.

1. Strut rod bushings are worn or missing.

2. Tie rod end wear can be determined by grabbing the tie rod end firmly and forcing it up, down or sideways to check for lost motion.

— MACPHERSON STRUT PROBLEM DIAGNOSIS —

Problems with MacPherson struts generally fall into 3 main categories: suspension, tire wear and steering. In general, the symptoms encountered are not significantly different from those encountered on conventional suspensions.

Steering

Tires

Both front tires should match and both rear tires should match. Be sure air pressure is correct.

Ball Joints

Support the car under the frame or crossmember so that the jack does not interfere with the control arm. Rock the tire in and out and up and down. Excessive movement means that both ball joints should be replaced.

Struts with lower weight-carrying ball joints should be supported at the outer edge of the lower control arm. These vehicles usually have wear indicating ball joints that can be checked visually.

WORN   NORMAL

Stabilizer Bar Bushings

Check for worn bushings or lost motion with the vehicle level and the weight evenly distributed on all wheels.

WEAR POINTS

Strut Rod Bushings

Grasp the strut rod and shake it. Any noticeable play indicates excessive wear and need for parts replacement.

Control Arm Bushings

Support the car under the frame or body and remove the weight from the wheel and control arm. Check for free-play in the bushings at the pivot point, using a pry bar.

NOTE: Some control arm bushings are serviceable only by replacing the entire arm.

Strut Assembly

Check the strut assembly for cracks or dents in the housing. Look for worn, bent or loose piston rods or dents that will inhibit piston rod movement.

Steering Gear

Check for worn steering gear or loose or worn mounting bolts and bushings.

WEAR POINTS

ROAD TEST TROUBLESHOOTING

Following are possible solutions to common potential problems which might be noticed during the road test after strut service is completed. Many are not exclusively strut service related.

Problem	Correction

Brake pedal low or soft	Bleed brakes
	Check for leaks
	  Brake lines
	  Wheel cylinder
	  Caliper piston seal

Erratic steering	Check upper support housing components for proper assembly Check spring assembly right side up Check for spring helix riding correctly on spring seat Check wheel alignment

Noises and rattles	Check torques
	  Piston rod nut
	  Upper support housing nuts & bolts
	  Lower mounting nuts & bolts
	  Body nut
	Check cartridge assembly in the body
	  Spacer used
	  Centering collar used

Brakes

BRAKE SYSTEM

Understanding the Brakes

HYDRAULIC SYSTEM

Basic Operating Principles

Hydraulic systems are used to actuate the brakes of all modern automobiles. The system transports the power required to force the frictional surfaces of the braking system together from the pedal to the individual brake units at each wheel. A hydraulic system is used for two reasons. First, fluid under pressure can be carried to all parts of an automobile by small hoses—some of which are flexible—without taking up a significant amount of room or posing routing problems. Second, a great mechanical advantage can be given to the brake pedal end of the system, and the foot pressure required to actuate the brakes can be reduced by making the surface area of the master cylinder pistons smaller than that of any of the pistons in the wheel cylinders of calipers.

The master cylinder consists of a fluid reservoir and either a single or double cylinder and piston assembly. Double type master cylinders are designed to separate

Dual braking system—front-to-rear split

Dual braking system—diagonally split

two two–wheel braking systems hydraulically in case of a leak. The standard approach has been to utilize two separate two–wheel circuits; one for the front wheels and another for the rear wheels.

Most newer models now use a diagonally split system; i.e. one front wheel and the opposite side rear wheel make up one braking circuit, while the remaining circuit consists of the other front wheel and its opposite side rear wheel.

Steel lines carry the brake fluid to a point on the vehicle's frame near each of the vehicle's wheels. The fluid is then carried to the slave cylinders by flexible tubes in order to allow for suspension and steering movements.

In drum brake systems, the slave cylinders are called wheel cylinders. Each wheel cylinder contains two pistons, one at either end, which push outward in opposite directions. In disc brake systems, the slave cylinders are part of the calipers. One, two or four cylinders are used to force the brake pads against the disc. All slave cylinder pistons employ some type of seal, usually made of rubber, to minimize the leakage of fluid around the piston. A rubber dust boot seals the outer end of the cylinder against dust and dirt. The boot fits around the outer end of the piston on disc brake calipers, and around the brake actuating rod on wheel cylinders.

The hydraulic system operates as follows: When at rest, the entire system, from the piston(s) in the master cylinder to those in the wheel cylinders or calipers, is full of brake fluid. Upon application of the brake pedal, fluid trapped in front of the master cylinder piston(s) is forced through the lines to the slave cylinders (wheel cylinders or calipers). Here, it forces the pistons outward, in the case of drum brakes, and inward toward the disc, in the case of disc brakes. The motion of the pistons is opposed by return springs mounted outside the cylinders in drum brakes, and by internal springs or spring seals, in disc brakes.

Upon release of the brake pedal, a spring located inside the master cylinder immediately returns the master cylinder pistons to the normal position. The pistons contain check valves and the master cylinder has compensating ports drilled in to it. These are uncovered as the pistons reach their normal position. The piston check valves allow fluid to flow toward the wheel cylinders or calipers as the pistons withdraw. Then, as the return springs force the brake pads or shoes into the released position, the excess fluid reservoir through the compensating ports. It is during the time the pedal is in the released position that any fluid that has leaked out of the system will be replaced through the compensating ports.

Dual circuit master cylinders employ two pistons, located one behind the other, in the same cylinder. The primary piston is actuated directly by mechanical linkage from the brake pedal. The secondary piston is actuated by fluid trapped between the two pistons. If a leak develops in front of the secondary piston, it moves forward until it bottoms against the front of the master cylinder, and the fluid trapped between the pistons will operate one side of the split system. If the other side of the system develops a leak, the primary piston will move forward until direct contact with the secondary piston takes place, and it will force the secondary piston to actuate the other side of the split system. In either case, the brake pedal moves farther when the brakes are applied, and less braking power is available.

All dual-circuit systems use a distributor switch to warn the driver when only half of the brake system is operational. This switch is located in a valve body which is mounted on the firewall or the frame below the master cylinder. A hydraulic piston receives pressure from both circuits, each circuit's pressure being applied to one end of the piston. When the pressures are in balance, the piston remains stationary. When one circuit has a leak, however, the greater pressure in that circuit during application of the brakes will push the piston to one side, closing the distributor switch and activating the brake warning light.

In disc brake systems, this valve body also contains a metering valve and, in some cases, a proportioning valve (or valves). The metering valve keeps pressure from traveling to the disc brakes on the front wheels until the brake shoes or pads on the rear wheels have contacted the drums or rotors, ensuring that the front brakes will never be used alone. The proportioning valve throttles the pressure to the rear brakes so as to avoid rear wheel lock-up during very hard braking.

These valves may be tested by removing the lines to the front and rear brake systems and installing special brake pressure testing gauges. Front and rear system pressures are then compared as the pedal is gradually depressed. Specifications vary with the manufacturer and design of the brake system.

Brake system warning lights may be tested by depressing the brake pedal and holding it while opening one of the wheel cylinder bleeder screws. If this does not cause the light to go on, substitute a new lamp, make continuity checks, and, finally, replace the switch as necessary.

The hydraulic system may be checked for leaks by applying pressure to the pedal gradually and steadily. If the pedal sinks very slowly to the floor, the system has a leak. This is not to be confused with a springy or spongy feel due to the compression of air within the lines. If the system leaks, there will be a gradual change in the position of the pedal with a constant pressure.

Check for leaks along all lines and at wheel cylinders. If no external leaks are apparent, the problem is inside the master cylinder.

DISC BRAKES

Basic Operating Principles

Instead of the traditional expanding brakes that press outward against a circular drum, disc brakes systems utilize a cast iron disc with brake pads positioned on either side of it. Braking effect is achieved in a manner similar to the way you would squeeze a

Typical disc brake assembly

spinning phonograph record between your fingers. The disc (rotor) is a one-piece casting which may be equipped with cooling fins between the two braking surfaces. The fins (if equipped) enable air to circulate between the braking surfaces making them less sensitive to heat buildup and more resistant to fade. Dirt and water do not affect braking action since contaminants are thrown off by the centrifugal action of the rotor or scraped off by the pads. Also, the equal clamping action of the two brake pads tends to ensure uniform, straightline stops. All disc brakes are inherently self-adjusting.

There are three general types of disc brake:
1. A fixed caliper, two or four-piston type.
2. A floating caliper, single piston or double piston back–to–back type.
3. A sliding caliper, single piston or double piston back–to–back type.

The fixed caliper design uses one or two pistons mounted on either side of the rotor

Typical fixed caliper disc brake (four piston shown)

Typical floating caliper disc brake (sliding caliper similar)

(in each side of the caliper). The caliper is mounted rigidly and does not move.

The sliding and floating designs are quite similar. In fact, these two types are often lumped together. In both designs, the pad on the inside of the rotor is moved into contact with the rotor by hydraulic force. The caliper, which is not held in a fixed position, moves slightly, bringing the outside pad into contact with the rotor. There are various methods of attaching floating calipers. Some pivot at the bottom or top, and some slide on mounting bolts. In any event, the end result is the same.

DRUM BRAKES

Basic Operating Principles

Drum brakes employ two brake shoes mounted on a stationary backing plate. These shoes are positioned inside a circular cast iron (or aluminum) drum which rotates with the wheel assembly. The shoes are held in place by springs; this allows them to slide toward the drums (when they are applied) while keeping the linings and drums in alignment. The shoes are actuated by a wheel cylinder which is mounted at the top of the backing plate. When the brakes are applied, hydraulic pressure forces the wheel cylinder's two actuating links outward. Since these links bear directly against the top of the brake shoes, the tops of the shoes are then forced outward against the inner side of the drum. This action forces the bottoms of the two shoes to contact the brake drum by rotating the entire assembly slightly (known as servo action). When pressure within the wheel cylinder is relaxed, return springs pull the shoes back away from the drum.

Most modern drum brakes are designed to self-adjust themselves during application when the vehicle is moving in reverse. This motion causes both shoes to rotate very slightly with the drum, rocking an adjusting lever, thereby causing rotation of the adjusting screw by means of a star wheel.

POWER BRAKE BOOSTERS

Power brakes operate just as standard brake systems except in the actuation of the master cylinder pistons. A vacuum diaphragm is located on the front of the master cylinder and assists the driver in applying the brakes, reducing both the effort and travel he must put into moving the brake pedal.

The vacuum diaphragm housing is connected to the intake manifold by a vacuum hose. A check valve is placed at the point where the hose enters the diaphragm housing, so that during periods of low manifold vacuum brake assist vacuum will not be lost.

Depressing the brake pedal closes off the vacuum source and allows atmospheric pressure to enter on one side of the diaphragm. This causes the master cylinder pistons to move and apply the brakes. When the brake pedal is released, vacuum is applied to both sides of the diaphragm, and return springs return the diaphragm and master cylinder pistons to the released position. If the vacuum fails, the brake pedal rod will butt against the end of the master cylinder actuating rod, and direct mechanical application will occur as the pedal is depressed.

HYDRAULIC CYLINDERS AND VALVES

Master Cylinders

The master cylinder is a type of hydraulic pump that is operated by a push rod attached to the brake pedal or by a push rod that is part of the power brake booster. The cylinder provides a means of converting mechanical force into hydraulic pressure. Two general types of master cylinders are in use on passenger cars; single system and dual system master cylinders.

SINGLE SYSTEM MASTER CYLINDER

This type master cylinder was used on many passenger car models. It has one fluid reservoir and one piston connected directly to the push rod. In a full pedal stroke, the single system pedal is stopped by the floorboard or other external stop before the cylinder can bottom-out. Fluid circulates between the single reservoir and the cylinder bore through the vent and replenishing ports. Fluid leakage past the secondary cup may be observed by pulling back the push rod boot or loosening the cylinder on its mount. Some seepage (dampness) is not unusual

1. Reservoir cap
2. Strainer
3. Stopper ring
4. Stopper screw
5. Stopper
6. Primary piston
7. Spring
8. Secondary piston
9. Spring
10. Plug
11. Check valve

Exploded view of a dual system master cylinder

but leaks affecting the fluid level require correction.

Single system master cylinders used on four wheel drum brake equipped cars usually contain a residual pressure check valve in the outlet port. This valve maintains a slight pressure in the line at all times to keep air from entering the system past the lips of the wheel cylinder cups when the pedal is released, and fluid returns from the wheel cylinder to the master cylinder.

Cars with front disc, rear drum brakes and a single system master cylinder may have the residual valve in the line leading to the rear brakes.

Single system master cylinder operation is the same as explained under tandem mas-

ter cylinder operation, except movement of only the primary piston is involved.

DUAL SYSTEM TANDEM MASTER CYLINDER

In this type there are two separate hydraulic pressure systems. One of the hydraulic systems may be connected to the front brakes, and the other to the rear brakes, or the systems may connect diagonal wheels. If one system fails, the other system remains operational, thus providing an additional safety measure. There are two distinct fluid reservoirs and each has a vent and replenishing port that leads into the cylinder bore. These ports have been called compensating and inlet ports or bypass ports, and the terms have been used inconsistently causing confusion. The terms ''vent'' and ''replenishing'' ports are now standardized S.A.E. terms. An airtight seal for the reservoir is provided in the form of a rubber diaphragm, which is held in place by a metal cover. A bail type retainer or a bolt usually holds the cover on the reservoirs. The cover is vented to permit atmospheric pressure to enter above the diaphragm. The diaphragm prevents moisture and debris from contaminating the fluid. The cylinder bore contains the return springs, two pistons, and the seals. The piston stop bolt (if present) may be assembled in a threaded hole in the bottom of the cylinder.

Some master cylinders have the piston stop bolt assembled in a threated hole in the side of the bore or in the bottom of the front reservoir, and others do not have stop

1. Cylinder and supply tank assembly
2. Filler cap
3. Seal
4. Valve assembly
5. Spring
6. Spring retainer
7. Main cup
8. Washer
9. Piston
10. Secondary cup
11. Pushrod
12. Circlip
13. Boot
14. Mounting bolt
15. Mounting bolt
16. Lockwasher
17. Nut
18. Banjo
19. Bolt
20. Gasket
21. Gasket

Exploded view of a single system master cylinder

bolts at all. Do not install a stop bolt in the reservoir of a master cylinder if one was not originally there. Some cylinders have a tapped hole, but no bolt was ever installed in production. *This was done on purpose, and is not an error.*

A retaining ring fits into a groove near the end of the bore and holds the piston assemblies in the cylinder bore.

Dual System—Applied

When the brake pedal is depressed, the push rod moves the primary piston forward in the cylinder bore. The primary vent port is sealed off by the lip of the primary cup. As a result, a solid column of fluid is created between the primary and secondary pistons.

Dual system—applied

With the help of the primary piston return spring, this column moves the secondary piston forward in the cylinder bore. This closes the secondary vent port. When both ports are closed, any further movement of the push rod and pistons serves to increase the hydraulic pressure in the area ahead of each piston. This pressure is then transmitted through the two hydraulic brake systems to the brakes at each wheel.

Dual System—Released

When the brake pedal is released, the piston return springs move both pistons to their normal released position. The piston may move faster than the fluid can return from the wheel cylinders, creating a low pressure ahead of the piston.

To allow rapid pedal return, this low pressure must be relieved. Fluid flows from the reservoir through the replenishing port.

Dual system—released

It then flows around the outside of the piston and cup lips to the area ahead of the piston. Another design has this flow pass through small drilled holes in the piston face, then around the cup lips. This flow relieves the low pressure area ahead of the piston.

Due to this action, the area in the front of the pistons is kept full of brake fluid at all times. Any excess fluid is returned to the master cylinder reservoirs through the vent ports after the pistons reach their fully released positions. Tandem master cylinders on cars equipped with four wheel drum brakes may contain two residual check valves, one in each outlet port. Those on cars with front disc/rear drum brakes may contain one in the rear (drum) brake outlet port.

Partial System Failure

If a failure occurs in the hydraulic system served by the primary piston, this piston will move forward but will not develop pressure. The piston extension contacts the secondary piston and pedal effort is transmitted directly to that piston to build hydraulic pressure to operate the brakes in the secondary system.

Primary system failure

If the secondary system suffers a leak or failure, both pistons move forward until the secondary piston bottoms out at the end of the master cylinder bore. Then the primary piston develops hydraulic pressure to operate the brakes in the primary system.

Secondary system failure

The loss of about half the pedal stroke is usually experienced when a half system failure occurs.

OTHER VARIATIONS

Dual Bore Type Master Cylinder

The housing of this type of master cylinder accomodates two cylinders side by side. Only one cylinder functions in the brake system, the other is used for hydraulic clutch actuation, and a common fluid reservoir with an internal partition is used. The clutch system does not have a residual pressure check valve. Each hydraulic system must be bled separately.

Dual bore type master cylinder

Step Bore Dual System Master Cylinder

This cylinder is the same as other cylinders except that the forward part of the bore is slightly smaller in diameter than the rear part. This difference contributes to correct brake balance.

Step bore type master cylinder

Volvo has incorporated a step bore master cylinder into a sophisticated brake system which provides automatic brake proportioning, no pedal loss on half system failure, and automatically increases pressure on the remaining system during half system failure.

Disc Brake Master Cylinder

These are similar to drum brake master cylinders, the principal difference being the unequal size of the two reservoirs.

Since the disc brakes require greater fluid reserve, a large fluid reservoir is provided.

The outlet connected to the disc brakes does not contain a residual pressure check valve, however the drum brake outlet may have one.

Manual and Power Brake Master Cylinders

Both types are mostly the same except that

DRUM BRAKE RESERVOIR   DISC BRAKE RESERVOIR

Disc brake master cylinder

#6-32 SELF TAPPING SCREW

SCREWDRIVER   SCREWDRIVER

TUBE SEAT INSERT   CHECK VALVE

CHECK VALVE SPRING

Removing the inserts from the master cylinder ports

manual brake cylinders normally include a dust boot, push rod, and push rod retainer. The push rod used with power brake master cylinders is usually a part of the power brake booster.

DUST BOOT

PUSH ROD

OUTLET PORTS

Manual brake master cylinder

Aluminum and Composite Tandem Master Cylinders.

Aluminum body master cylinders have been used on special applications for many years. Today its use is becoming more widespread due to the weight advantage over cast iron. The machined aluminum bore is usually anodized to resist corrosion, prevent galling, and provide better wear resistance. Aluminum master cylinder bores are not serviced if scored or pitted, but must be replaced. A ''composite master cylinder'' is a common phrase used to describe units with a plastic reservoir attached to a metal barrel. Composites offer reduced weight, lower material costs and greater application flexibility.

MASTER CYLINDER SERVICING

Just like any other brake parts, master cylinders require periodic service. The usual reason for a master cylinder failure is that the cups don't seal any more. Fluid leaks past cups internally, and sometimes shows up as an external leak as well. A common symptom is a ''spongy'' brake pedal that goes all the way to the floor when all other brake system components are in good shape. The rubber parts wear with usage or may deteriorate with age or fluid contamination. Corrosion or deposits formed in the bore due to moisture or dirt in the hydraulic system may result in wear of the cylinder bore or the parts therein. Also, the fluid level in the reservoirs should be checked periodically. Whenever needed, clean brake fluid should be added to maintain the fluid level ¼" to ½" (6 to 13 mm) from the top of the reservoir.

Removal and Disassembly

1. Clean the area around the master cylinder to prevent dirt and grease from contaminating the cylinder or the hydraulic lines. Disconnect the tubes, remove nuts or bolts that secure the master cylinder to fire wall or power brake, and remove the master cylinder from the car. (For further details, refer appropriate car section).

On cars with manual brakes, the push rod must be disconnected from the brake pedal before removing the master cylinder from the car.

2. Remove the reservoir cover, and drain the brake fluid from the reservoir. Then remove the piston stop bolt, if present, from the master cylinder. Remove boot and snap ring, then slide the primary piston assembly out of the master cylinder. Next, remove the secondary piston assembly by tapping the master cylinder, or by using needle nose pliers to pull it from its bore, or by carefully using compressed air. Disassemble the secondary piston assembly.

3. Clamp the master cylinder in a vise with the outlet ports facing up. Test for presence of check valve by probing with wire through hole in tube seats. Replace tube seat(s) and check valve(s) only if check valve is present and supplied in rebuild kit. Remove the tube seat inserts, if required, by partially threading a self-tapping screw into each tube seat and using two screwdrivers to pry each seat out of the master cylinder. Remove the residual check valve and the spring from the outlet(s) (if present).

Plastic Reservoir Cleaning and Removal

Plastic reservoirs need to be removed only for the following reasons:

a. Reservoir is damaged or the rubber grommet(s) between the reservoir and bore is leaking.

b. Removal of the stop pin from Chrysler style plastic reservoir master cylinders to allow for the removal of pistons. Pin is located underneath front reservoir nipple.

The reservoir should be removed by first clamping the flange in a vice. Next remove the reservoir for the Chrysler style. Grasp the reservoir base on one end and pull away from the body. Some must be removed by prying between the reservoir and casting with a pry bar. Grommets can be reused if

they are in good condition. Whether or not the reservoir is removed, it and the cover or caps should be thoroughly cleaned.

Cleaning and Inspection

Thoroughly clean the master cylinder and any other parts to be reused in clean alcohol. DO NOT USE PETROLEUM PRODUCTS FOR CLEANING. If the bore is not badly scored, rusted or corroded, it is possible to rebuild the master cylinder in some cases. A slight bit of honing is permissible to clean cups are facing.

——— CAUTION ———
Aluminum cylinder bores cannot be honed. The cylinder MUST be replaced if the bore is scored.

Lubricate all new rubber parts with brake fluid or brake system assembly lubricant.

CAST IRON BORE CLEAN-UP

Crocus cloth or an approved cylinder hone should be used to remove lightly pitted, scored, or corroded areas from the bore.

——— CAUTION ———
If an aluminum master cylinder has pits or scratches in the bore, it must be replaced.

Brake fluid can be used as a lubricant while honing lightly. The master cylinder should be replaced if it cannot be cleaned up readily. After using the crocus cloth or a hone, the master cylinder should be thoroughly washed in clean alcohol or brake fluid to remove all dust and grit. If alcohol is used, dry parts thoroughly before reinstalling.

——— CAUTION ———
Other solvents should not be used.

Then the clearance between the bore wall and the piston (primary piston of a dual system master cylinder) should be checked. If a narrow (⅛" (3.2 mm) to ¼" (6.4 mm) wide) 0.006" (0.15 mm) feeler gauge can be inserted between the wall and a new piston, the clearance is excessive, and the master cylinder should be replaced. The maximum clearance allowed for units containing pistons without replenishing holes is .009" (0.23 mm).

ALUMINUM BORE CLEAN-UP

Inspect the bore for scoring, corrosion and pitting. If the bore is scored or badly pitted and corroded the assembly should be replaced. *Under no conditions should the bore be cleaned with an abrasive material.* This will remove the wear and corrosion resistant anodized surface. Clean the bore with a clean piece of cloth around a wooden dowel and wash thoroughly with alcohol. Do not confuse bore discoloration or staining with corrosion.

Reassembly and Installation

1. Carefully install the new cups or seals in the same positions and in reverse order of removal.

2. Use brake fluid or assembly fluid very generously to keep from damaging the seals.

3. Placing the small end of the pressure spring into the secondary piston retainer, slide the assembly into the cylinder bore, taking care not to nick or gouge any rubber part.

4. Place the spring retainer of the primary piston assembly over the secondary piston shoulder and push both assemblies into the bore.

5. Install and tighten the piston retaining screw and gasket, while holding the pistons in their seated positions. At the same time, reinstall any piston snap rings.

6. Install the residual check valve and spring in the proper master cylinder outlet (or both outlets, if originally present). If the tube seat inserts were removed, install new seats in both fluid outlets making sure that they are securely seated.

Bleeding and Checking

1. Bleed the hydraulic system as described later in this section.

NOTE: Be sure to bench bleed a rebuilt or new master cylinder before installation.

2. Check master cylinder vent port clearance by watching for a spurt of brake fluid in both reservoir vent holes when brake pedal is slightly depressed, indicating proper port clearance.

Master Cylinder Push Rod Adjustment

After assembly of the master cylinder to the power section, the piston cup in the hydraulic cylinder should just clear the compensating port hole when the brake pedal is fully released. If the push rod is too long, it will hold the piston over the port.

A push rod that is too short, will give too much loose travel (excessive pedal play).

Apply the brakes and release the pedal all the way observing the brake fluid flow back into the master cylinder.

A full flow indicates the piston is coming back far enough to release the fluid.

A slow return of the fluid indicates the piston is not coming back far enough to clear the ports. The push rod adjustment is too tight, and should be shortened.

Wheel Cylinders

DRUM BRAKE WHEEL CYLINDER

The wheel cylinder performs in response to the master cylinder. It receives fluid from the hydraulic hose through its inlet port. As the pressure increases the wheel cylinder cups and pistons are forced apart. As a result, the hydraulic pressure is converted into mechanical force acting on the brake shoes. The wheel cylinder size may vary from front to rear. The variation in wheel cylinder size (diameter) is one of the factors controlling the distribution of braking force in a vehicle. Larger diameter wheel cylinders are normally specified for the front brakes of front engine passenger cars equipped with drum brakes. Bleeder screws are provided to remove air or vapor trapped in the system.

Three types of wheel cylinders are normally used with drum brakes.

Single Piston or "Single-end" Type

A single piston wheel cylinder has only one cup, piston, and dust boot and spring. It may also contain a cup filler or cup expander.

Single piston wheel cylinder

Double piston wheel cylinder

Double Piston or "Double-end" Straight Bore Type

This type is most commonly used on modern automobile brakes. It carries two opposed pistons, two cups and two boots.

Double Piston or "Double-end" Step Bore Type

This type is used on some of the non-servo brakes and has the same components as the straight bore type. Two different dust boots, cups, and pistons are used. Opposed pistons of different diameters exert different amounts of force.

Step bore wheel cylinder

WHEEL CYLINDER OPERATION

The space between the cups in the cylinder bore must remain filled with fluid at all times. After depressing the brake pedal, additional brake fluid is forced into the cylinder bore. As a result of this, cups and pistons move outward in the cylinder bore pushing the shoe links and the brake shoes outward to contact the drum and apply the brakes.

On some designs, the end of the shoe web bears directly against the pistons and therefore, shoe links are not used.

Typical wheel cylinder components

SERVICE PROCEDURES

Wheel cylinders may need reconditioning or replacement whenever the brake shoes are replaced or when required to correct a leak condition. On many designs, the wheel cylinders can be disassembled without removing them from the backing plate. On some designs, however, the cylinder is mounted in an indention in the backing plate or a cylinder piston stop is welded to the backing plate. When servicing brakes or this type, the cylinder must be removed from the backing plate before being disassembled.

Diagnostic Inspection and Cleaning

Leaks which coat the boot and the cylinder with fluid, or result in a dropped reservoir fluid level, or dampen and stain the brake linings are dangerous. Such leaks can cause the brakes to ''grab'' or fail and should be immediately corrected. A leakage, not immediately apparent, can be detected by pulling back the cylinder boot. A small amount of fluid seepage dampening the interior of the boot is normal; a dripping boot is not. Unless other conditions causing a brake to pull, grab, or drag becomes obvious, the wheel cylinder is a suspect and should be included in general reconditioning.

Cylinder binding may be caused by rust, deposits, grime, or swollen cups due to fluid contamination, or by a cup wedged into an excessive piston clearance. If the clearance between the pistons and the bore wall exceeds allowable values, a condition called ''heel drag'' may exist. It can result in rapid cup wear and can cause the pistons to retract very slowly when the brakes are released.

A typical example of a scored, pitted or corroded cylinder bore is shown in the accompanying illustration. A ring of a hard, crystal-like substance is sometimes noticed in the cylinder bore where the piston stops after the brakes are released.

Light roughness or deposits can be removed with crocus cloth or an approved cylinder hone. While honing lightly, brake fluid can be used as a lubricant. If the bore cannot be cleaned up readily, the cylinder must be replaced.

NOTE: Aluminum wheel cylinders must not be honed.

Some front wheel cylinders have a baffle located between the opposed pistons. The baffle contains a small hole which causes the cylinder to act as a fluid shock absorber damping servo brake shoes as they become energized. These cylinders cannot be honed and should be replaced if the bore is pitted or corroded.

—————— **CAUTION** ——————
Hydraulic system parts should not be allowed to come in contact with oil or grease, neither should those be handled with greasy hands. Even a trace of any petroleum based

product is sufficient to cause damage to the rubber parts.

Reconditioning Wheel Cylinders

It is a common practice to recondition a wheel cylinder without dismounting it, however some brakes are equipped with external piston stops which prevent disassembly unless the cylinder is removed. In order to dismount, remove the shoe springs and spread the shoes apart, disconnect the brake line, remove the mounting bolts or retaining clips, and pull the cylinder free.

Most wheel cylinders are attached to the backing plate with bolts and are easily removed for service or replacement. In recent years, some cars use a retaining clip for this purpose. To remove this type cylinder, use a special service tool, or this alternate method: Insert ⅛" diameter or less awls or pins into the slots between wheel cylinder pilot and retainer locking tabs. Bend both tabs away at the same time until tabs spring over the shoulder, releasing the cylinder. DISCARD old retainer.

To replace cylinder, use a new retainer and the following procedure:

1. Hold wheel cylinder against the backing plate by inserting a block between the wheel cylinder and axle shaft flange.
2. Position the wheel cylinder retainer clip so the tabs will be away from and in horizontal position with the backing plate when installing.
3. Press the new retaining clip over the wheel cylinder abutment and into position using a 1⅛ inch 12 point socket. Retainer is in place when the tabs are snapped under the retainer abutment. Examine closely to be sure both retainer tabs are properly engaged.

Another variation of retainer clip is used on some vehicles. The retainer usually consists of two or three separate pieces which when slid together will lock themselves and the wheel cylinder in place. The retainers can be carefully removed without incurring damage which allows them to be reused. If they are damaged or corroroded, however, they must be replaced.

Pull the protective dust boots off the cylinder. Internal parts should slide out, or be picked out easily. Parts can be driven out with a wooden dowel, or blown out at low pressure by applying compressed air to the fluid inlet port. Parts which cannot be removed easily indicate they are damaged beyond repair and the cylinder should be replaced.

Clean the cylinder and the parts in alcohol and/or brake fluid. (Do NOT use gasoline or other petroleum based products). Use only lint-free wiping cloths. Crocus cloth can be used to clean minute scratches, signs of rust, corrosion or discoloration from the cylinder bore and pistons. Slide the cloth in a circular rather than a lengthwise motion. A clean-up hone may be used. After a cylinder has been honed, inspect it for excessive piston clearance and remove any

FEELER SHIM

Checking the maximum piston clearance

burrs formed on the edge of fluid intake or bleeder screw ports.

—————— **CAUTION** ——————
Do not rebuild aluminun cylinders.

To check the maximum piston clearance, place a ¼" (6 mm) wide strip of feeler shim lengthwise in the cylinder bore.

If the piston can be inserted with the shim in place, the cylinder is oversize, and should be discarded. Depending upon the cylinder bore diameter, the shim (or the feeler gauge) thickness can vary as follows:

Cyl. Bore	¾"–1³⁄₁₆" (19–30 mm)	1¼"–1⁷⁄₁₆" (32–37 mm)	1½" up (38 mm)
Shim	.006" (.15 mm)	.007" (.18 mm)	.008" (.2 mm)

Assemble the cylinder with the internal parts, making sure that the cylinder wall is wet with brake fluid. Insert the cups and pistons from each end of a double-end cylinder; do not slide them through the cylinder. Cup lips should always face inward.

Hydraulic Control Valves

PRESSURE DIFFERENTIAL VALVE

The pressure differential valve activates a dash panel warning light if pressure loss in the brake system occurs. If pressure loss occurs in one half of the split system, the other system's normal pressure causes the piston in the switch to compress a spring until it touches an electrical contact. This causes the warning lamp on the dash panel to light, thus warning the driver of possible brake failure.

On some cars the spring balance piston automatically recenters as the brake pedal is released, warning the driver only upon brake application. On other cars, the light remains on until manually cancelled.

Valves may be located separately or as part of a combination valve. On certain front wheel drive cars, the valve and switch are usually incorporated into the master cylinder.

Re-setting Valves

On some cars, the valve piston(s) remain off center after failure, until necessary repairs are made. The valve will automatically reset itself (after repairs) when pressure is equal on both sides of the system.

If the light does not go out, bleed the brake system that is opposite the failed system. If front brakes failed, bleed the rear brakes, this should force the light control piston toward center.

If this fails, remove the terminal switch. If brake fluid is present in the electrical area, the seals are gone, replace the complete valve assembly.

METERING VALVE

The metering valve's function is to improve braking balance between the front and rear brakes, especially during light brake application.

The metering valve prevents application of the front disc brakes until the rear brakes overcome the return spring pressure. Thus, when the front disc pads contact the rotor, the rear shoes will contact the brake drum at the same time.

Typical pressure metering valve

Inspect the metering valve each time the brakes are serviced. A slight amount of moisture inside the boot does not indicate a defective valve, however, fluid leakage indicates a damaged or worn valve. If fluid leakage is present, the valve must be replaced.

The metering valve can be checked very simply. With the car stopped, gently apply the brakes. At about an inch of travel a very small change in pedal effort (lke a small bump) will be felt if the valve is operating properly. Metering valves are not serviceable, and must be replaced if defective.

PROPORTIONING VALVE

The proportioning (pressure control) valve is used, on some cars, to reduce the hydraulic pressure to the rear wheels to prevent skid during heavy brake application and to provide better brake balance. It is usually mounted in line to the rear wheels.

Whenever the brakes are serviced, the valve should be inspected for leakage. Pre-

Typical proportioning valve

mature rear brake application during light braking can mean a bad proportioning valve. Repair is by replacement of the valve. Make sure the valve port marked "R" is connected toward the rear wheels.

On some front wheel drive cars, the proportioning valve(s) is (are) screwed into the master cylinder. Since these cars usually have a diagonally split brake system, two valves are required. One rear brake line screws into each valve. The early type valves were steel, an occasional "clunking" noise was encountered on some early models, but does not affect brake efficiency. Replacement valves are now made of aluminum. Never mix an aluminum valve with a steel valve, always use two aluminum valves.

COMBINATION VALVE

The combination valve may perform two or three functions. They are; metering, proportioning and brake failure warning.

Variations of the two-way combination valve are; proportioning and brake failure warning or metering and brake failure warning.

Two—way combination valve (metering and brake warning light switch)

3—way combination valve

A three-way combination valve directs the brake fluid to the appropriate wheel, performs necessary valving and contains a brake failure warning.

The combination valve is usually mounted under the hood close to the master cylinder, where the brake lines can easily be connected and routed to the front or rear wheels.

The combination valve is nonserviceable and must be replaced if malfunctioning.

Brake Bleeding

The hydraulic brake system must be free of air to operate properly. Air can enter the system when hydraulic parts are disconnected for servicing or replacement, or when the fluid level in the master cylinder reservoir(s) is very low. Air in the system will give the brake pedal a spongy feeling upon application.

The quickest and easiest of the two ways for system bleeding is the pressure method, but special equipment is needed to externally pressurize the hydraulic system. The other, more commonly used method of brake bleeding is done manually.

BLEEDING SEQUENCE

Bleeding may be required at only one or two wheels or at the master cylinder, depending upon what point the system was opened to air. If after bleeding the cylinder/caliper that was rebuilt or replaced, the pedal still has a spongy feeling upon application, it will be necessary to bleed the entire system.

Bleed the system in the following order:

1. **Master cylinder:** If the cylinder is not equipped with bleeder screws, open the brake line(s) to the wheels slightly while pressure is applied to the brake pedal. Be sure to tighten the line before the brake pedal is released. The procedure for bench bleeding the master cylinder is in the following section.

2. **Power Brake Booster:** If the unit is equipped with bleeder screws, it should be bled after the master cylinder. The car engine should be off and the brake pedal applied several times to exhaust any vacuum in the booster. If the unit is equipped with two bleeder screws, always bleed the higher one first.

3. **Combination Valve:** If equipped with a bleeder screw.

4. **Front/Back Split Systems:** Start with the wheel farthest away from the master cylinder, usually the right rear wheel. Bleed the other rear wheel, right front and then the left front.

NOTE: If you are unsuccessful in bleeding the front wheels, it may be necessary to deactivate the metering valve. This is accomplished by either pushing in, or pulling out a button or stem on the valve. The valve may be held by hand, with a special tool or taped, it should remain deactivated while the front brakes are bled.

5. **Diagonally Split System:** Start with the right rear then the left front. The left rear than the right front.

6. **Rear Disc Brakes:** If the car is equipped with rear disc brakes and the calipers have two bleeder screws, bleed the inner first and then the outer.

——— **CAUTION** ———

Do not allow brake fluid to spill on the car's finish, it will remove the paint. Flush the area with water.

MANUAL BLEEDING

1. Clean the bleeder screw at each wheel.

2. Start with the wheel farthest from the master cylinder (right rear).

3. Attach a small rubber hose to the bleeder screw and place the end in a clear container of brake fluid.

4. Fill the master cylinder with brake fluid. (Check often during bleeding). Have an assistant slowly pump up the brake pedal and hold pressure.

Manual bleeding drum brakes

5. Open the bleed screw about one-quarter turn, press the brake pedal to the floor, close the bleed screw and slowly release the pedal. Continue until no more air bubbles are foced from the cylinder on application of the brake pedal.

6. Repeat procedure on remaining wheel cylinders and calipers.

Master cylinders equipped with bleed screws may be bled independently. When bleeding the Bendix-type dual master cylinder it is necessary to solidly cap one reservoir section while bleeding the other to prevent pressure loss through the cap vent hole.

NOTE: The disc should be rotated to make sure that the piston has returned to the unapplied position when bleeding is completed and the bleed screw closed.

——— **CAUTION** ———

The bleeder valve at the wheel cylinder must be closed at the end of each stroke, and before the brake pedal is released, to insure that no air can enter the system. It is also important that the brake pedal be returned to the full up position so the piston in the master cylinder moves back enough to clear the bypass outlets.

PRESSURE BLEEDING DISC BRAKES

Pressure bleeding disc brakes will close the metering valve and the front brakes will not bleed. For this reason it is necessary to manually hold the metering valve open during pressure bleeding. Never use a block or clamp to hold the valve open, and never force the valve stem beyond its normal position. Two different types of valves are used. The most common type requires the valve stem to be held in which bleeding the brakes, while the second type requires the valve stem to be held out (.060 in. minimum travel.) Determine the type of visual inspection.

——— **CAUTION** ———

Special adapters are required when pressure bleeding cylinders with plastic reservoirs.

Pressure bleeding equipment should be diaphragm type; placing a diaphragm between the pressurized air supply and the brake fluid. This prevents moisture and other contaminants from entering the hydraulic system.

NOTE: Front disc/rear drum equipped vehicles use a metering valve which closes off pressure to the front brakes under certain conditions. These systems contain manual release actuators which must be engaged to pressure bleed the front brakes.

1. Connect the tank hydraulic hose and adapter to the master cylinder.

2. Close hydraulic valve on the bleeder equipment.

3. Apply air pressure to the bleeder equipment.

——— **CAUTION** ———

Follow equipment manufacturer's recommendations for correct air pressure.

4. Open the valve to bleed air out of the pressure hose to the master cylinder.

NOTE: Never bleed this system using the secondary piston stopscrew on the bottom of many master cylinders.

5. Open the hydraulic valve and bleed each wheel cylinder and caliper. Bleed rear brake system first when bleeding both front and rear systems.

FLUSHING HYDRAULIC BRAKE SYSTEMS

Hydraulic brake systems must be totally flushed if the fluid becomes contaminated with water, dirt or other corrosive chemicals. To flush, simply bleed the entire system until *all* fluid has been replaced with the correct type of new fluid.

BENCH BLEEDING MASTER CYLINDER

Bench bleeding the master cylinder before installing it on the car reduces the possibility of air getting into the lines.

1. Connect two short pieces of brake line to the outlet fittings, bend them until the free end is below the fluid level in the master cylinder reservoir(s).

2. Fill the reservoirs with fresh brake fluid. Pump the piston until no more air bubbles appear in the reservoir(s).

3. Disconnect the two short lines, refill the master cylinder and securely install the cylinder cap(s).

4. Install the master cylinder on the car. Attach the lines but do not completely tighten them. Force any air that might have been trapped in the connection by slowly depressing the brake pedal. Tighten the lines before releasing the brake pedal.

POWER BRAKES

Vacuum Operated Booster

Power brakes operate just as standard brake systems except in the actuation of the master cylinder pistons. A vacuum diaphragm is located on the front of the master cylinder and assists the driver in applying the brakes, reducing both the effort and travel he must put into moving the brake pedal.

The vacuum diaphragm housing is connected to the intake manifold by a vacuum hose. A check valve is placed at the point where the hose enters the diaphragm housing, so that during periods of low manifold vacuum brake assist vacuum will not be lost.

Depressing the brake pedal closes off the vacuum source and allows atmospheric pressure to enter on one side of the diaphragm. This causes the master cylinder pistons to move and apply the brakes. When the brake pedal is released, vacuum is applied to both sides of the diaphragm, and return springs return the diaphragm and master cylinder pistons to the released position. If the vacuum fails, the brake pedal rod will butt against the end of the master cylinder actuating rod, and direct mechanical application will occur as the pedal is depressed.

The hydraulic and mechanical problems that apply to conventional brake systems also apply to power brakes, and should be checked for if the tests and chart below do not reveal the problem.

Tests for a system vacuum leak as described below:

1. Operate the engine at idle with the transmission in Neutral without touching the brake pedal for at least one minute.

2. Turn off the engine, and wait one minute.

3. Test for the presence of assist vacuum by depressing the brake pedal and releasing it several times. Light application will produce less and less pedal travel, if vacuum was present. If there is no vacuum, air is leaking into the system somewhere. Test for system operation as follows:

1. Pump the brake pedal (with engine off) until the supply vacuum is entirely gone.

2. Put a light, steady pressure on the pedal.

3. Start the engine, and operate it at idle with the transmission in Neutral. If the system is operating, the brake pedal should fall toward the floor if constant pressure is maintained on the pedal.

Power brake systems may be tested for hydraulic leaks just as ordinary systems are tested, except that the engine should be idling with the transmission in Neutral throughout the test.

POWER BRAKE BOOSTER TROUBLESHOOTING CHART

The following items are in addition to those listed in the General Troubleshooting Section. Check those items first.

Hard Pedal

1. Faulty vacuum check valve.
2. Vacuum hose kinked, collapsed, plugged, leaky, or improperly connected.
3. Internal leak in unit.
4. Damaged vacuum cylinder.
5. Damaged valve plunger.
6. Broken or faulty springs.
7. Broken plunger stem.

Grabbing Brakes

1. Damaged vacuum cylinder.
2. Faulty vacuum check valve.
3. Vacuum hose leaky or improperly connected.
4. Broken plunger stem.

Pedal Goes to Floor

Generally, when this problem occurs, it is not caused by the power brake booster. In rare cases, a broken plunger stem may be at fault.

Overhaul

Most power brake boosters are services by replacement only. In many cases, repair parts are not available. A good many special tools are required for rebuilding these units. For these reasons, it would be most practical to replace a failed booster with a new or remanufactured unit.

SERVICING DISC BRAKES

Disc Brake Caliper

An integral part of the caliper, the caliper bore(s) contains the piston(s) that direct thrust against the brake pads supported within the caliper. Since all braking forces (pad application force) are applied on each side of the rotor with no self energization, the cylinder and piston are large in comparison to a drum brake wheel cylinder.

Fixed–Type

A fixed type caliper is mounted solidly to the spindle bracket.

Pistons are located on both sides of the rotor, in inboard and outboard caliper halves. Fluid passes between caliper halves through an external crossover tube or through internal passages. A bleeder screw is located in the inboard caliper half. A dust boot protecting each cylinder fits in a circumferential groove on the piston.

Fixed caliper disc brake

Floating–Type

Floating or sliding calipers are free to move in a fixed bracket or support.

The piston(s) is located only on the inboard side of the caliper housing, which straddles the rotor. The cylinder piston(s) applies the inboard brake shoe directly, and simultaneously hydraulic pressure slides the caliper in a clamping action which forces the caliper to apply the outboard brake shoe. The actual applying movement is small.

Floating caliper disc brake (sliding caliper similar)

The unit merely grips during application, relaxes upon release, and the shoes do not retract an appreciable distance from the rotor. The fluid inlet port and the bleeder screw are located on the inboard side of the caliper. A dust boot is fitted into a circumferential groove on the piston and into a recess at or near the outer end of the cylinder bore.

A scratched piston, nicked seal, or a sludge or varnish deposit which limits the sealing edge away from the piston will cause a fluid leak. A serious leak could develop if calipers are not reconditioned when new pads are installed. Then dust and road grime, gradually accumulating behind the dust boot, could be carried into the seal when the piston is shoved inward to accommodate new thick linings. Old seals may have taken a "set," thus preventing proper seating in the retainer groove and on the piston. Therefore, when reconditioning calipers, new seals should be installed.

OVERHAUL PROCEDURES

Before servicing, syphon or syringe about ⅔ of the fluid from the master cylinder reservoir; do not, however, lower the fluid level below the cylinder intake port.

1. To prevent a gravity loss of fluid, plug the brake line after disconnecting from the caliper.

2. To overhaul, remove the caliper from the vehicle, allow the unit to drain, and remove the brake shoes.

Removing the fixed caliper bridge bolts

3. For benchwork, clamp the caliper housing in a soft jawed vice.

4. On fixed-caliper types, remove the bridge bolts and separate the caliper into halves. Remove the sealing O-rings at crossover points, if the unit has internal fluid passages across the halves.

5. Whenever required, use special tools to remove pistons, dust boots, and seals. If compressed air is used, apply it gradually, gently ease the pistons from the cylinders, and trap them in a clean cloth; do not allow them to pop out. *Take care to avoid pinching hands or fingers.*

6. While removing stroking type seals and boots, work the lip of the boot from the groove in the caliper. After the boot is

Removing a hollow-end piston with compressed air (top) or the special tool (bottom)

Removing a fixed position rectangular ring seal

free, pull the piston, and strip the seal and boot from the piston.

7. While removing fixed position (rectangular ring) seals and boots, pull the piston through the boot. *Do not use a metal tool which would scratch the piston.* Use a small pointed wooden or plastic tool to lift the boots and seals from the grooves in the cylinder bore.

Cleaning, Inspection, and Installation

Use only alcohol and/or brake fluid and a lint free wiping cloth to clean the caliper and parts.

Checking maximum piston clearance

──────── **CAUTION** ────────

Other solvents should not be used. Blow out passages with compressed air. Always wear eye protection when using compressed air or cleaning calipers.

1. To correct minor inperfections in the cylinder bore, polish with a fine grade of crocus coth cloth working in a circular rather than a lengthwise motion. Do not use any form of abrasive on a plated piston. Discard a piston which is pitted or has signs of plating wear.

2. Inspect the new seal. It should lie flat and be round. If it has suffered a distorted "set" during its shelf life, do not use it. Lubricate the cylinder wall and parts with brake fluid.

3. While installing stroking type seals and boots, stretch the boot and the seal over the piston and seat them in position.

4. Use special alignment tools for inserting lip culp seals.

5. Install the fixed position (rectangular ring) seals and be sure the ring does not twist or roll in the groove.

6. Where the boot lip is retained inside the cylinder bore, the following method works well:

a. Lubricate the bottom inside edge of the piston and brake seal in caliper with brake fluid.

Typical boot installation

b. Pull the boot over the bottom end of the piston so that boot is positioned on the bottom of the piston with the lip about ¼ inch up from bottom end.

c. Hold piston suspended over bore.

d. Insert the back boot lip into the groove in the caliper.

e. Tuck the sides of the boot into the groove and work forward until only one bulge remains.

f. Tuck the final bulge into the front of the groove.

g. Push the piston carefully through the seal and boot to the bottom of the bore. The inside of the boot should slide on the piston and come to rest in the boot groove.

If the boot lip is retained outside the cylinder bore, first stretch the boot over the piston and seat it in its groove, then press the piston through the seal.

Fully depress the piston. You'll need 50 to 100 of pounds force to fasten the boot lip in place. On some designs, it is necessary to use a wooden drift or a special tool to seat the metal boot in the caliper counterbore below the face of the caliper.

Installing Fixed Caliper Bridge Bolts

If tbe caliper contains internal fluid cross-over passages, be sure to install the new O-ring seals at the joints.

Install high tensile strength bridge bolts on the mated caliper halves.

Never replace the bridge bolts with ordinary standard hardware bolts; order the bolts by part numbers only. Tighten the bridge bolts, using a specified torque wrench as follows specified by the manufacturer.

Replacing the O-rings in the internal cross-over passages

OVERHAUL NOTES

Field reports indicate that two factors determine whether to replace or rebuild calipers:

1. Can the piston or pistons be removed?

2. Will the bleed screw break off when removal is attempted? (Rebuilders will not accept a caliper with a broken bleed screw.) Since there is no way to predict how a bleed screw will react, follow this porcedure to attempt removal.

1. Insert a drill shank into the bleed screw hole (snug fit).

2. Tap the screw on all sides.

3. With a six point wrench apply pressure gently while working the drill up and down slightly.

4. If the drill starts to bind, the screw is beginning to collapse and cannot be removed intact.

Heating the caliper is another successful, but time consuming, bleed screw removal technique.

1. Remove the caliper from the car.

2. Heat the caliper.

3. Shrink the bleed screw by applying dry ice, and attempt removal.

BLEEDER SCREW REPLACEMENT

1. Using the existing hole in the bleeder screw for a pilot, drill ¼ in. hole completely through the existing bleeder.

Replacing a disc brake bleeder screw

2. Increase the hole to 7/16 in.
3. Tap hole using a 1/4 in. (18-national pipe tap) 1/2 in. deep-(full thread.)
4. Install bleeder repair kit.
5. Test for leaks and full brake pedal pressure.

FROZEN PISTONS

Sliding or Floating Caliper

1. **Hydraulic Removal:** remove the caliper assembly from the rotor.
2. Remove the brake pads and dust seal. With flexible brake line connected and the bleed screw closed, apply enough pedal pressure to move the piston most of the way out of the bore. (Brake fluid will begin to ooze past the piston inner seal.)
1. **Pneumatic Removal:** remove the caliper from the car.
2. With the bleed screw closed, apply air pressure to force the piston out.

--- CAUTION ---
Hydraulic and pneumatic methods of piston removal should be done carefully to prevent personal injury or piston damage.

Fixed Caliper

NOTE: The hydraulic or pneumatic methods which apply to the single piston type caliper will not work on the multiple type caliper will not work on the multiple piston type brake caliper.

1. Remove the caliper from the car with the two halves separated.
2. Mount in a vise and use a piston puller (many types available) to remove the pistons.

Brake Disc (Rotor)
ROTOR RUNOUT

Manufacturers differ widely on permissible runout, but too much can sometimes be felt as a pulsation at the brake pedal. A wobble pump effect is created when a rotor is not perfectly smooth and the pad hits the high spots forcing fluid back into the master cylinder. This alternating present causes a pulsating feeling which can be felt at the pedal when the brakes are applied. This excessive runout also causes the brakes to be out of adjustment because disc brakes are self-adjusting; they are designed so that the pads drag on the rotor at all times and therefore automatically compensate for wear.

NOTE: For illustration purposes a dial gauge is shown making rotor measurements. There are several other more convenient types of measurement tools. (Disc illustrations are exaggerated views to more clearly emphasize the conditions.)

Excessive runout

To check the actual runout of the rotor, first tighten the wheel spindle nut to a snug bearing adjustment, end-play removed. Fasten a dial indicator on the suspension at a convenient place so that the indicator stylus contacts the rotor face approximately one inch from its outer edge. Set the dial at zero. Check the total indicator reading while turning the rotor one full revolution. If the rotor is warped beyond the runout specification, it is likely that it can be successfully remachined.

Lateral Runout: A wobbly movement of the rotor from side to side as it rotates. Excessive lateral runout causes the rotor faces to knock back the disc pads and can result in chatter, excessive pedal travel, pumping or fighting pedal and vibration during the breaking action.

Parallelism

Parallelism (lack of): Refers to the amount of variation in the thickness of the rotor. Excessive variation can cause pedal vibration or fight, front end vibrations and possible "grab" during the braking action; a condition comparable to an "out-of-round brake drum." Check parallelism with a micrometer. "mike" the thickness at eight or more equally spaced points, equally distant from the outer edge of the rotor, preferably at mid-points of the braking surface. Parallelism then is the amount of variation between maximum and minimum measurements.

Surface or Micro-inch finish, flatness, smoothness: Different from parallelism, these terms refer to the degree of perfection of the flat surface on each side of the rotor; that is, the minute hills, valleys and swirls inherent in machining the surface. In a visual inspection, the remachined surface should have a fine ground polish with, at most, only a faint trace of nondirectional swirls.

TYPE 1

Kelsey-Hayes Floating Caliper

This unit is a single piston, one-piece caliper which floats on two guide pins screwed into the adapter (anchor plate). The adaptor, in turn, is held to the steering knuckle with two bolts. As the brake pads wear, the caliper floats along the adapter and guide pins during braking.

PAD REPLACEMENT

1. Raise the front of the vehicle and support it with jackstands. Remove the wheel.
2. Siphon some brake fluid from the master cylinder reservoir to prevent its overflowing when the piston is retracted into the cylinder bore.

Kelsey–Hayes floating caliper disc brake assembly

DISC BRAKE APPLICATION CHART

Make	Year/Model	Reference Number	Caliper Design
Audi	'76–'77 100	6	Sliding Yoke
	'76–'77 Fox	6	Sliding Yoke
	'78–'79 Fox	4	Floating
	'80–'83 4000	4	Floating
	'78–'80 5000	6	Sliding Yoke
	'81–'83 5000	4	Floating
	'80–'83 Turbo Front	4	Floating
	Rear	4	Floating
	'82–'83 Quattro Front	4	Floating
	Rear	4	Floating
BMW	'76 2002	2	Fixed
	'76–'83 3.0Si, 528i, 530i, 630CSi, Front 633CSi, 733i Rear	2 2	Fixed Fixed
	'77–'83 320i	2	Fixed
	'82–'83 528e Front	4	Floating
	Rear	4	Floating
Capri	'76–'78 All	2	Fixed
Chrysler/Mitsubishi	'76–'83 Colt/Champ (ex. Sta. Wag.)	3	Floating
	(Sta. Wag.)	5	Sliding
	'76–'80 Arrow (w/Rear Drums)	3	Floating
	(w/Rear Discs)	5②	Sliding
	'76–'83 Challenger/ Sapporo Front	5	Sliding
	Rear	5	Sliding
Datsun/Nissan	'76–'83 B210, 210, 310, 510, 610, 710, f10	7	Sliding Yoke
	'77–'81 200SX Front	7	Sliding Yoke
	Rear	7	Sliding Yoke
	'82–'83 200SX Front	7	Sliding Yoke
	Rear	4	Floating
	'77–'80 810 Front	7	Sliding Yoke
	Rear	7	Sliding Yoke
	'81–'83 810 Front	4	Floating
	Rear	4③	Floating
	'76–'78 280Z	2	Fixed
	'79–'81 280ZX Front	4	Floating
	Rear	7	Sliding Yoke
	'82–'83 280ZX Front	4	Floating
	Rear	4	Floating
	'82–'83 Sentra, Stanza	4	Floating
Fiat	'76–'83 All	5②	Sliding
Fiesta	'78–'80 All	5	Sliding
Honda	'76–'79 Civic (ex. Sta. Wag.)	7	Sliding Yoke
	(Sta. Wag.)	3	Floating
	'80–'83 Civic (ex. Sta. Wag.)	4	Floating
	(Sta. Wag.)	5	Sliding

DISC BRAKE APPLICATION CHART

Make	Year/Model	Reference Number	Caliper Design
Honda	'76–'81 Accord	5	Sliding
	'82–'83 Accord	4	Floating
	'79–'83 Prelude	4	Floating
Isuzu	'80–'83 All	2	Fixed
Mazda	'76–'79 808, RX-3	3	Floating
	'79–'82 626	4	Floating
	'76–'83 RX-4, Cosmo, GLC	5④	Sliding
	'79 RX-7	5	Sliding
	'80–'83 RX-7	4	Floating
Mercedes-Benz	'76–'83 All (ex. 300SEC) Front	2	Fixed
	Rear	2	Fixed
	'82–'83 300SEC Front	5	Sliding
	Rear	5	Sliding
MG	'76–'80 All	2	Fixed
Peugeot	'76–'83 504	7	Floating
	'80–'83 505 Front	6	Sliding Yoke
	Rear	7	Sliding Yoke
	'77–'83 604 Front	7	Sliding Yoke
	Rear	6	Sliding Yoke
Porsche	'76–'83 911, 912, Front	2	Fixed
	914, 930 Rear	2	Fixed
	'77–'82 924	6	Sliding Yoke
	'78–'83 928, 944 Front	6	Sliding Yoke
	Rear	6	Sliding Yoke
Renault	'76–'83 Le Car	5	Sliding
	'81–'83 18i, Fuego	8	Floating
SAAB	'76–'83 All Front	7	Sliding
	Rear	2	Fixed
Subaru	'76–'79 All	5	Sliding
	'80–'83 All	9	Floating
Toyota	'76–'82 Corona, MkII	2	Fixed
	'76–'79 Corolla (ex. 1200)	5	Sliding
	(1200)	3	Floating
	'80–'83 Corolla	3	Floating
	'80–'83 Tercel, Starlet	4	Floating
	'78–'80 Cressida	2	Fixed
	'81–'83 Cressida	5	Sliding
	'76–'81 Celica, Supra	5⑤	Sliding
	'82–'83 Celica, Supra	4⑤	Floating
Triumph	'76–'81 All	2	Fixed
Volkswagen	'76–'83 Types 1 & 2	2	Fixed
	'76–'77 Dasher	6, 7	Sliding, Sliding Yoke
	'78–'81 Dasher	4	Floating
	'76–'83 Rabbit, Scirocco, Jetta, Quantum	1, 6, 7②	Floating, Sliding, Sliding Yoke

DISC BRAKE APPLICATION CHART

Make	Year/Model	Reference Number	Caliper Design
Volvo	'76–'83 All Front	2	Fixed
	Rear	2	Fixed

① All applications are for front discs only unless otherwise noted
② Applies to both front and rear
③ 1981: 7, Sliding Yoke
④ Also applies to Cosmo w/rear discs
⑤ Also applies to Supra w/rear discs

3. Disconnect the brake pad warning indicator if so equipped.

4. Using a pair of needlenose pliers or the like, remove the anti-rattle springs.

5. Using an Allen wrench, back out the two guide pins that attach the caliper to the anchor plate.

NOTE: When replacing pads only, it is not necessary to remove the guide pins completely from the rubber bushings, as they may be difficult to reinstall.

6. Lift off the caliper and position it out of the way with some wire—you need not remove the brake lines.

--- CAUTION ---
Never allow the caliper to hand by its brake lines.

7. Slide the outer pad out of the anchor plate and then remove the inner pad. Check the rotor as detailed in the appropriate section. Check the caliper for fluid leaks or cracked boots. If any damage is found, the caliper will require overhauling or replacement.

8. Carefully clean the anchor plate with a wire brush or some other abrasive material. Install the new brake pads into po-

sition on the anchor plate. The inner pad usually has chamfered edges.

NOTE: When replacing brade pads, always replace both pads on both sides of the vehicle. Mixed pads will cause uneven braking.

9. Slowly and carefully push the piston into its bore until it's bottomed and then position the caliper onto the anchor plate. Install the guide pins and tighten them to 25–30 ft. lbs.

NOTE: The upper guide pin is usually longer than the lower one.

--- CAUTION ---
Use extreme care so as not to cross–thread the guide pins when tightening.

10. Install the anti–rattle springs between the anchor plate and brake pads ears. The loops on the springs should be positioned inboard.

11. Fill the reservoir with brake fluid and pump the brake pedal several times to set the piston. It should not be necessary to bleed the system; however, if a firm pedal cannot be obtained, the system must be bled (see "Bleeding the Brakes" in this section).

12. Install the wheel and lower the vehicle.

TYPE 2

ATE, Girling, Sumitomo Fixed Caliper

These units are either two or four piston, two-piece calipers that are fixed directly to the steering knuckle or spindle.

Brake pads may be changed without removing the caliper on all of these models. There may be some differences in retainers or anti-rattle springs from the illustrations, but all versions are basically the same. Before removing any parts, carefully note the position of any springs, retainers or clips. Change pads on one wheel at a time and use the other as a reference.

Typical fixed caliper disc brake assembly

All pads on all models are held in position by either retaining pins or retainer plates. The retainer plates are bolted to the caliper housing and need only be loosened and rotated out of the way for pad removal.

PAD REPLACEMENT

1. Raise the front (or rear) of the vehicle and support it with jackstands. Remove the wheel.

Exploded view of a Kelsey–Hayes floating caliper

BLEEDER SCREW AND CAP

CALIPER HOUSING BOLTS

CALIPER OUTER HOUSING

HOUSING SEAL

PISTON

DUST BOOT

PISTON SEAL

SPRING RING

SPREADER SPRING

BRAKE PAD

PISTON RETAINING PLATE

BRAKE PAD

RETAINING PIN

HOUSING BOLT NUTS

CALIPER INNER HOUSING

Exploded view of a two–piston fixed caliper

2. Siphon a sufficient quantity of brake fluid from the master cylinder reservoir to prevent the brake fluid from overflowing the master cylinder when removing or installing new pads. This is necessary as the pistons must be forced into the cylinder bore to provide sufficient clearance to remove the pads.

3. Some models may use a cover plate over the access hole for the pads, if so, remove it. Disconnect the brake pad lining wear indicator wire on models so equipped.

4. Carefully clean the exterior of the caliper with a wire brush and note the position of any dampening shims or anti–rattle springs.

5. Remove the pad retaining pins and any retaining clips holding them. Remove the anti–rattle springs if so equipped. Some pads may be held in position by a plate with a retaining bolt. If so, loosen the bolt and swing the plate away. Lift out the spreader spring if so equipped.

NOTE: It is a good idea to remove one retaining spring or plate and then remove the anti–rattle springs or spreader spring. Remove the second retaining pin or plate last.

6. Force the old pads away from the rotor for easy withdrawal and remove the pads from the caliper.

7. If so equipped, remove the lower anti–rattle springs and dampening shims using needlenose pliers.

8. Check the brake disc (rotor) as detailed in the appropriate section.

9. Examine the dust boot for cracks or damage and push the pistons back into the cylinder bores. If the pistons are frozen or if the caliper is leaking hydraulic fluid, it must be overhauled.

10. Install the anti–rattle spring or damping shims and slip the new pads into the caliper. If damping shims are used, be sure that the directional arrow on the hims face the forward rotation of the rotor.

11. Install one pad retaining pin and hairpin clip. Position the anti–rattle springs and/or spreader spring and then install the other pad retaining pin and clip.

12. Refill the master cylinder to the correct level with the proper brake fluid.

13. Replace the wheel and lower the vehicle. Pump the brake pedal several times to bring the pads into correct adjustment. Road test the vehicle.

NOTE: If a firm pedal cannot be obtained, the system will require bleeding (see "Bleeding the Brakes" in this section).

TYPE 3

Sumitomo Torque Plate Floating Caliper

This unit is a single piston, two–piece caliper which floats on torque plate pins. The torque plate itself is bolted to the steering knuckle. The outer caliper half may be sep-

CALIPER HOUSING BOLTS

BLEEDER SCREWS

BRAKE PADS

ANTI-RATTLE SPRINGS

INNER CALIPER HOUSING

PISTON SEAL

PISTON

DUST BOOT

DUST BOOT RETAINER

PAD RETAINING PIN

HAIRPIN TYPE CLIP

DUST BOOT RETAINER

DUST BOOT

PISTON

PISTON SEAL

CALIPER HOUSING SEAL

OUTER CALIPER HOUSING

Exploded view of a four–piston fixed caliper

ROTOR

CALIPER ASSEMBLY

PAD PROTECTOR

BLEEDER SCREW

Typical Sumitomo Torque Plate floating caliper disc brake assembly

arated from the inner half although the caliper need not be separated or removed for pad replacement.

PAD REPLACEMENT

1. Raise the front of the vehicle and support it on jackstands. Remove the wheel.

2. Siphon a sufficient quantity of brake fluid from the master cylinder reservoir to prevent the brake fluid from overflowing the master cylinder when removing or installing new pads. This is necessary as the piston must be forced into the cylinder bore to provide sufficient clearance to remove the pads.

3. Use a small prybar or other suitable tool and pry the pad protector off of the retaining pins.

4. Remove the center of the 'M' clip from the hole in the outboard pad and its ends from the retaining pins.

NOTE: To facilitate the reassembly operation later on, note how the 'M' clip and the 'K' spring are positioned in the caliper.

5. Pull out the retaining pins and remove the 'K' spring from the inboard pad.

6. Remove the inner and outer pads.

7. Check the brake disc (rotor) as detailed in the appropriate section.

8. Examine the dust boot for cracks or damage and then push the piston back into the cylinder bore. Use a C-clamp or other suitable tool to bottom the piston. If the piston is frozen, or if the caliper is leaking hydraulic fluid, the caliper must be overhauled or replaced.

9. Install new pads into the caliper.

10. Install one retaining pin.

Spring and clip installation

11. Install the inboard pad 'K' spring. Hook one end of the 'K' spring under the retaining pin and the center of the 'K' spring over the top of the inboard pad. Insert the other retaining pin through the outboard pad, over the 'K' spring and through the inboard pad.

12. Insert the ends of the 'M' clip into the holes in the retaining pins and press the center of the spring into the hole in the outboard pad.

13. Install the pad protector.

14. Refill the master cylinder with fresh brake fluid.

15. Install the tire and wheel assembly and then pump the brake pedal several times

BRIDGE BOLTS
BLEEDER SCREW
INNER CALIPER
TORQUE PLATE BUSHING
RUBBER SPACER
TORQUE PLATE
INNER PAD
PAD PROTECTOR
OUTER PAD
OUTER CALIPER
WIPER SEAL
SEAL RETAINER
PISTON SEAL
PISTON
DUST BOOT
DUST BOOT RETAINER
M-CLIP
K-SPRING
RETAINING PINS

Exploded view of a Sumitomo Torque Plate floating caliper

to bring the pads into adjustment. Road test the vehicle.

NOTE: If a firm pedal cannot be obtained, bleed the system as detailed in "Bleeding the Brakes".

TYPE 4

ATE, Girling, etc. Floating Caliper

Although similar in many respects to a sliding caliper, this single piston unit floats on guide pins and bushings which are threaded into a mounting bracket. The mounting bracket is bolted to the steering knuckle.

Variations in pad retainers, shims, anti-rattle and retaining springs will be encountered but the service procedures are all basically the same. Note the position of all springs, clips or shims when removing the pads. Work on one side at a time and use the other for reference.

PAD REPLACEMENT

1. Raise and support the front (or rear) of the vehicle on jackstands. Remove the wheel.

BLEEDER DUST CAP
BLEEDER SCREW
BRAKE CALIPER CYLINDER
DUST CAP
DUST BOOT
PISTON SEAL
PISTON
GUIDE PIN
BRAKE PAD CARRIER
BRAKE PADS

Exploded view of a typical Type 4 floating caliper

Exploded view of a Type 4 floating caliper with parking brake (Datsun shown, others similar)

2. Siphon a sufficient quantity of brake fluid from the master cylinder reservoir to prevent the brake fluid from overflowing the master cylinder when removing or installing new pads. This is necessary as the piston must be forced into the cylinder bore to provide sufficient clearance to remove the pads.

3. Grasp the cliper from behind and pull it toward you. This will push the piston back into the cylinder bore.

4. Disconnect the brake pad lining wear indicator if so equipped. Remove any anti-rattle springs or clips if so equipped.

On some models, the caliper cylinder may be pivoted upwards to remove the pads

Using needle-nosed pliers to turn the piston before pushing it into the cylinder bore

NOTE: Depending on the model and year of the particular caliper, you may not have to remove it entirely to get at the brake pads. If the caliper is the "swing" type, remove the lower guide bolt, pivot the caliper on the upper bolt and swing it upward exposing the brake pads. If this method is employed, skip to Step 7.

5. Remove the caliper guide pins.

6. Remove the caliper from the rotor by slowly sliding it out and away from the rotor. Position the caliper out of the way and support it with wire so that it doesn't hang by the brake line.

7. Slide the outboard pad out of the adapter.

8. Remove the inboard pad. Remove any shims or shields behind the pads and note their positions.

9. Install the anti-rattle hardware and then the pads (in their proper positions!).

10. On Audis (or Datsuns) with rear disc brakes, use an Allen wrench (or needle-nosed pliers) to turn the piston to the right and then push it back into the cylinder bore.

11. Install any pad shims or heat shields.

12. Reposition the caliper and install the guide pins.

NOTE: If the caliper is the "swing" type, you need only pivot it back into position and install the lower guide pin.

13. Refill the master cylinder with fresh brake fluid.

14. Install the tire and wheel assembly and then pump the brake pedal several times to bring the pads into adjustment. Road test the vehicle.

NOTE: After installing new pads on Audis with rear disc brakes, depress the brake pedal firmly, approximately 40 times with the engine turned off to permit automatic adjusting. Check the parking brake adjustment.

NOTE: If a firm pedal cannot be obtained, bleed the system as detailed in "Bleeding the Brakes".

TYPE 5

Akebono, Girling, etc. Sliding Caliper

This unit is a single piston, one-piece caliper that slides on a mounting bracket or frame which bolts to the steering knuckle. The caliper is retained in the mounting bracket by caliper guides (retaining keys) and support springs. Narrow support plates under each brake pad are utilized to eliminate rattle. One or two caliper guides may be used—it is imperative that they are replaced as originally found.

PAD REPLACEMENT

1. Raise and support the front (or rear) of the vehicle on jackstands. Remove the front wheel.

2. Siphon a sufficient quantity of brake fluid from the master cylinder reservoir to prevent the brake fluid from overflowing the master cylinder when removing or installing pads. This is necessary as the piston must be forced into the cylinder bore to provide sufficient clearance to remove the pads.

NOTE: On Subarus (and Fiats, Supras and Chryslers with rear disc brakes) only, remove the outer cable clip and then remove the parking brake cable.

3. Remove the clips or pins that hold the caliper guides in position.

4. Lightly tap out the guides—there may only be one, so remember the correct positioning.

5. Lift the caliper off of the mounting bracket.
It may be necessary to rock it back and forth a bit in order to seat the piston so it will clear the brake pads. Position the cal-

Typical sliding caliper disc brake assembly

iper out of the way and support it with wire so it doesn't hang by the brake lines.

6. Remove the brake pads from the mounting bracket. *Do not remove the support springs.*

7. A support plate is under each pad; they are not interchangeable and must be replaced correctly. Remove the support plates.

8. Inspect the brake disc (rotor) as detailed in the appropriate section.

9. Inspect the caliper and piston assembly for breaks, cracks or other damage. Overhaul or replace the caliper as necessary.

10. Replace the support plates in their *original* positions.

11. Place the new pads in the support bracket over the support springs.

12. Push the piston all the way back into its bore (a C–clamp may be necessary for this operation).

13. Position the caliper over the pads and onto the mounting bracket.

14. Install the caliper guides (retaining keys) and then install the guide retaining pins or clips. Install the parking brake cable and its clip on all Subarus (and Fiats, Supras and Chrysler/Mitsubishi cars, with rear disc brakes).

15. Refill the master cylinder with fresh brake fluid.

16. Install the tire and wheel assembly and then pump the brake pedal several times

to bring the pads into adjustment. Road test the vehicle.

NOTE: If a firm pedal cannot be obtained, bleed the system as detailed in ''Bleeding the Brakes''.

TYPE 6

ATE Sliding Yoke Caliper

This unit is a single piston, two–piece caliper. It has a fixed mounting frame which is bolted to the steering knuckle. The pads are retained in the fixed frame. A floating frame, or yoke, slides on the fixed frame. The cylinder attaches to this yoke, creating a caliper. Braking pressure forces tbe piston against the inner pad. The reaction causes

Typical ATE sliding yoke disc brake assembly

1. Bleeder screw cap
2. Bleeder screw
3. Brake pads
4. Spring
5. Caliper fastener spring
6. Caliper support bracket

7. Caliper locking block
8. Cotter pin
9. Piston seal
10. Piston dust boot
11. Assembled caliper

Exploded view of a Type 5 sliding caliper

1. Brake disc
2. Caliper mounting frame
3. Pads
4. Cross spring
5. Retaining pins
6. Clamp ring
7. Boot
8. Piston
9. Seal
10. Cylinder
11. Bleeder nipple
12. Guide spring

Exploded view of an ATE sliding yoke caliper

1. Pad (disc brake F)	9. Lever & spindle ass'y (RH)	14. Bushing (hand brake)
2. Spring (caliper)		15. Retaining spring
3. Bracket (mounting)	10. Bracket (hand brake)	16. Spindle ass'y
4. Pin (caliper)	11. Spring (hand brake lever return LH)	17. Connecting link
5. Stopper (plug)		18. Cap (air bleeder)
6. Spring (pad)	12. Spring (hand brake lever return RH)	19. Cap (lever)
7. Body caliper ass'y		20. Brake disc (F)
8. Lever & spindle ass'y (LH)	13. Bleeder screw (wheel cylinder)	21. Cover (disc)

Exploded view of a Type 5 sliding caliper with parking brake (Subaru shown, others similar)

the yoke to move in the opposite direction, applying pressure to the outer pad.

PAD REPLACEMENT

1. Raise the front (or rear) of the vehicle and support it with jackstands. Remove the wheel.

2. Siphon a sufficient quantity of brake fluid from the master cylinder reservoir to prevent the brake fluid from overflowing the master cylinder when removing or installing new pads. This is necessary as the piston must be forced into the cylinder bore to provide sufficient clearance to remove the pads.

3. Disconnect the wire connector leading to the brake pad wear indicator.

4. Remove the brake pad retaining clips on the inside of the caliper and then drive out the retaining pins. Don't lose the pad positioner (spreader) that is held down by the pins.

5. Pull out the inner brake pad.

6. The outer pads are secured by a notch at the top of the pad. Grasp the caliper assembly from the inside and pull it toward yourself. Remove the pad and detach the wear indicator.

7. Check the brake disc (rotor) as detailed in the appropriate section.

8. Inspect the caliper and piston assem-

bly for breaks, cracks or other damage. Overhaul or replace the caliper as necessary.

9. Use a C–clamp and press the piston back into the cylinder bore.

10. Install the wear indicator on the outer pad and then install both pads.

11. Installation of the remaining components is the reverse order or removal.

12. Top off the master cylinder with fresh brake fluid.

13. Pump the brake pedal several times to bring the pads into adjustment. Road test the vehicle. If a firm pedal cannot be obtained, bleed the brakes as detailed in "Bleeding the Brakes".

TYPE 7

Girling/Annette Sliding Yoke Caliper

This unit is a double piston, one–piece caliper. The cylinder body contains two pistons, back–to–back, in a thru–bore. The cylinder body is bolted to the steering knuckle, with both pistons inboard of the rotor. A yoke, which slides on the cylinder body, is installed over the rotor and the caliper.

When the brakes are applied, hydraulic pressure forces the pistons apart in the double ended bore. The piston closest to the rotor applies force directly to the inboard pad. The other piston applies force to the yoke, which transmitts the force to the outer pad, creating a friction force on each side of the rotor.

One variation has a yoke that floats on guide pins screwed into the cylinder body.

Some designs incorporate parking brake mechanisms which are actuated by a lever and cam working between the piston and the yoke.

The yokes do not have to be removed to replace the brake pads.

Typical Type 7 sliding yoke caliper disc brake assembly

PAD REPLACEMENT

1. Raise and support the front (or rear) of the vehicle on jackstands. Remove the wheel.

2. Siphon a sufficient quantity of brake fluid from the master cylinder reservoir to prevent the brake fluid from overflowing the master cylinder when removing or installing new pads. This is necessary as the piston must be forced into the cylinder bore to provide sufficient clearance to remove the pads.

3. Disconnect the brake pad lining wear indicator if so equipped.

4. Remove the dust cover and/or anti–rattle (damper) clip if so equipped.

5. Lift off the wire clip(s) which hold the guide pins or retaining pin in place.

6. Remove the upper guide pin and the two hanger springs. Carefully tap out the lower guide pin.

7. Slide the yoke outward and remove the outer brake pad and the anti–noise shim (if so equipped).

8. Slide the yoke inward and repeat Step 7.

9. Check the rotor as detailed in the appropriate section.

10. Inspect the caliper and piston assembly for breaks, cracks or other damage. Overhaul or replace the caliper as necessary.

11. Push the piston next to the rotor back into the cylinder bore until the end of the piston is flush with the boot retaining ring.

12. Retract the piston farthest from the rotor by pulling the yoke toward the outside of the vehicle.

13. Install the outboard pad. Anti–noise shims (if so equipped) must be located on the plate side of the pad with the triangular cutout pointing toward the top of the caliper.

14. Install the inboard pad with the shims (if so equipped) in the correct position.

15. Replace the lower guide pin and the anti–rattle coil spring.

16. Hook the hanger springs under the pin and over the brake pads.

17. Install the upper guide pin over the ends of the hanger springs.

NOTE: If a single two–sided retaining pin is used, install the pin and then install the hanger springs as in Steps 16–17.

18. Insert the wire clip locks into the holes in the guide pins or retaining pin.

19. Refill the master cylinder with fresh brake fluid.

20. Install the tire and wheel assembly. Pump the brake pedal several times to bring the pads into adjustment. Road test the vehicle. If a firm pedal cannot be obtained, refer to "Bleeding the Brakes".

Exploded view of a Type 7 sliding yoke caliper

TYPE 8

Bendix Floating Caliper

This is a single piston unit that floats on guide pins and bellows bushings which are threaded into a mounting bracket. The mounting bracket is bolted to the stub axle

1. Yoke
2. Yoke spring
3. Clip
4. Pad pin
5. Anti-squeal spring
6. Pad
7. Retaining ring
8. Dust seal
9. Outer piston
10. Oil seal
11. Adjusting nut
12. Bearing
13. Spacer
14. Wave washer
15. Snap ring B
16. Piston seal
17. Cylinder body
18. Retainer
19. Snap ring A
20. Spring cover
21. Spring
22. Spring seat
23. Snap ring C
24. Key plate
25. Push rod
26. O-ring
27. Strut
28. Inner piston
29. Cam
30. Toggle lever
31. Spring
32. Washer
33. Nut

Exploded view of a Type 7 sliding yoke caliper with parking brake

Typical Bendix floating caliper disc brake assembly

carrier. This caliper is unique in that it is mounted on the leading edge of the brake disc, where most are mounted on the trailing edge.

The caliper does not have to be removed when replacing the brake pads.

PAD REPLACEMENT

1. Raise and support the front of the vehicle on jackstands. Remove the wheel.
2. Siphon a sufficient quantity of brake fluid from the master cylinder reservoir to prevent the brake fluid from overflowing the master cylinder when removing or installing new pads. This is necessary as the piston must be forced into the cylinder bore to provide sufficient clearance to remove the pads.
3. Grasp the cylinder from behind and carefully pull it toward you. This will push the piston back into the cylinder bore.
4. Disconnect the brake pad lining wear indicator wires. Remove the anti-rattle springs.

5. Remove the retaining key clip on the upper side of the caliper. Remove the retaining key.
6. Lift out the brake pads.
7. Inspect the brake disc (rotor) as detailed in the appropriate section.
8. Inspect the caliper and piston assembly for breaks, cracks or other damage. Overhaul or replace the caliper as necessary.
9. Push the piston all the way back into its bore (a C-clamp may be necessary for this operation).

Exploded view of the Bendix floating caliper

10. Slide the new pads into their original positions.
11. Slide the retaining key into position and replace the clip.
12. Reinstall the anti-rattle springs and the wear indicator.
13. Refill the master cylinder with fresh brake fluid.
14. Install the tire and wheel assembly and then pump the brake pedal several times to bring the pads into adjustment. Road test the vehicle.

NOTE: If a firm pedal cannot be obtained, bleed the system as detailed in "Bleeding the Brakes".

TYPE 9

Akebono Floating Caliper W/Parking Brake

This is a single piston unit that floats on guide pins and bushings which are threaded into a mounting bracket. The mounting bracket is bolted to the steering knuckle. This unit also incorporates a parking brake into the caliper.

The caliper does not have to be removed completely in order to remove the brake pads.

PAD REPLACEMENT

1. Raise and support the front of the vehicle on jackstands. Remove the wheel.
2. Siphon a sufficient quantity of brake fluid from the master cylinder reservoir to prevent the brake fluid from overflowing the master cylinder when removing or installing new pads. This is necessary as the piston must be forced into the cylinder bore to provide sufficient clearance to remove the pads.
3. Release the parking brake and disconnect the cable from the caliper lever.
4. Remove the 6 mm lock pin bolt (lower front of the caliper). Loosen and remove the lock pin.

NOTE: Do not pull out the lock pin until it is loosened to the position shown in the illustration.

5. The caliper will now pivot on its upper support, swing it up and out of the way.
6. Remove the pads. Note the positions of the pad shims and the inner and outer pad clips.
7. Inspect the brake disc (rotor) as detailed in the appropriate section.

6 mm bolt
Lock pin

Removing the lock pin

1 Caliper body	13 Gutter spring	25 Outer pad
2 Boot ring	14 Return spring	26 Inner pad
3 Piston boot	15 Connecting link	27 Rubber bushing
4 Piston seal	16 Bolt assembly	28 Retainer
5 Piston	17 Bracket	29 Lock pin boot
6 Guide pin boot	18 Spindle	30 Cone spring
7 Air bleeder screw	19 O-ring	31 Lock pin
8 Air bleeder cap	20 Cone spring	32 Shim
9 Lever & spindle	21 Snap ring	33 Outer pad clip
10 Spring pin	22 Spring washer	34 Inner pad clip
11 Cap ring	23 Bolt	35 Lever cap (upper)
12 Lever cap	24 Support	

Exploded view of the Type 9 floating caliper

8. Inspect the caliper and piston assembly for breaks, cracks or other damage. Overhaul or replace the caliper as necessary.

9. Turn the caliper piston clockwise into the cylinder bore and align the notches.

NOTE: Do not force the piston into the cylinder bore. The piston is mounted on a threaded spindle which will bend under pressure.

10. Insert the new pads making sure that all shims and clips are in their original positions.

11. Swing the caliper down into position and install the lock pin and the 6 mm bolt.

12. Reconnect the parking brake.

13. Refill the master cylinder with fresh brake fluid.

14. Install the tire and wheel assembly and then pump the brake pedal several times to bring the pads into adjustment. Road test the vehicle.

NOTE: If a firm pedal cannot be obtained, bleed the system as detailed in "Bleeding the Brakes".

SERVICING DRUM BRAKES

A typical drum brake assembly includes a backing or support plate, with one or two wheel cylinders attached to it. Mounted on the backing plate are two lined brake shoes with shoe return springs and hold-down parts, and a means of adjusting the shoes to compensate for lining wear. A brake drum encloses these parts. The drum brakes on the rear of most vehicles also normally include the parts required for parking brakes. All of the drum brakes used on modern vehicles have these components but there is a variety of configurations for each.

Drum brakes are designed to be either "servo" or "non-servo" acting.

Servo Type Brakes

In these brakes the shoes are assembled to form a compound, "primary" and "secondary" shoe unit joined at one end by an adjustable floating link. The drag of a normal (forward) drum rotation causes the primary shoe to leave its anchor and holds the secondary shoe anchored.

All of the forces applying and anchoring the primary shoe are transmitted through the shoe link, in a servo action, and also apply the secondary shoe, thus compounding its braking effect. When the drum is rotated backward, this compounding action of the shoes is reversed. When equipped with a double-end wheel cylinder (two opposed pistons), brake effectiveness can be substantially the same with either forward or reverse movement of the vehicle. With a single-end wheel cylinder (one piston), the brake is energized in only one direction. Since the secondary shoe performs more of the work in forward movement, it shows more lining wear. A longer or thicker lining is often used to offset this wear.

Non-Servo Type Brakes

In these brakes each shoe is separately anchored and their action is not compounded. On single cylinder brakes a "forward" or "leading" shoe is self-energized by the usual (forward) drum rotation while a "reverse" or "trailing" shoe is de-energized. When the drum is rotated backward, this action reverses, thus energizing the reverse shoe and de-energizing the forward shoe. The lining wear is unbalanced because the shoes perform different amounts of work; the wear is more rapid on the forward acting shoe during a forward stop.

Large two cylinder non-servo brakes, found on certain models, make use of two double-end wheel cylinders which enable the shoes to be anchored or actuated at either

Servo brakes

Non-servo brakes

end. This arrangement is non-directional in effectiveness. With two-cylinder brakes, lining wear is balanced on both shoes.

MECHANICAL COMPONENTS

To be sure of restoring the brake components correctly after servicing, closely observe the arrangement of shoe hook-up parts as the brake is disassembled. These arrangements may vary on different models. Usually the brake shoes are held in a sliding fit by spring tensions, at rest upon their anchor by the return springs, and against support pads by spring or clip type hold-downs. Opposite the anchor, a star wheel adjuster links the shoe webs and provides a threaded adjustment which permits the shoes to be expanded or contracted. Some rear brakes have adjustable links. The shoes are held against the adjuster by a spring.

Different types of shoe hold-downs

Shoe Hold-Downs

Various shoe hold-downs are shown in the illustration.

To unlock or lock the straight pin hold-downs, depress the locking cup and coil spring, or the spring clip, and rotate the pin or lock 90 degrees. On certain lever type adjusters, the inner (bottom) cup has a sleeve which aligns the adjuster lever.

Shoe Anchors

As shown in the illustration, there are various types of anchors such as the fixed non-adjustable type, or self-centering shoe sliding type, or, on some earlier models, adjustable fixed type providing either an eccentric or a slotted adjustment. On some front brakes, fixed anchors are threaded into or are bolted through the steering knuckle and also support the wheel cylinder.

On adjustable anchors, when necessary to re-center the shoes in the drum or drum gauge, loosen the locknut enough to permit the anchor to slip out not so much that it can tilt.

On the eccentric type anchors, tighten the star wheel to heavy brake drag. Rotate the eccentric anchor in the direction which frees the brake until drag cannot be relieved. Tighten the anchor nut. Back off the star wheel to a normal manual adjustment.

On the slotted type anchor, tighten the star wheel to heavy drag. Tap the support plate until the anchor slips and frees the brake. Repeat this sequence until drag cannot be relieved. Tighten the locknut to the

NON-DIRECTIONAL ACTING

Two cylinder, non-servo brake

Different types of shoe anchors

ADJUSTABLE FIXED ANCHORS
ECCENTRIC

ECCENTRIC TYPE

Anchor adjustment—fixed and eccentric

SLOTTED HOLE

SLOTTED TYPE

PIVOT PIN — SLOTTED HOLE

PIVOTED SLOTTED TYPE

Anchor adjustment—slotted type

proper torque. Back off the star wheel to a normal manual adjustment.

Brake Shoes

In the same brake sizes, there can be differences in web thickness, shape of web cut-outs and positions of any reinforcements. Some vehicles require shoes made of higher tensile strength steels. Higher strength shoes usually are coded with a letter symbol stamped on the shoe web. Shoes with extra web holes or table nibs or tabs which do not cause interference generally are considered interchangeable with other shoes.

Stops

An eccentric stop under the primary or secondary shoe web on tilted front brakes prevents the shoes from bumping against the drum. Before adjusting the star wheel, loosen the lock nut on the support plate and rotate the eccentric in the forward direction until the shoe drags. Back-off until drag is relieved and tighten the lock nut.

PISTON STOPS

If the brake is equipped with piston stops, the wheel cylinder must be dismounted for reconditioning.

BASIC SERVICE

———— CAUTION ————
Do not blow the brake dust out of the drums with compressed air or lung power; always use a damp cloth and wipe it out. Brake linings contain asbestos, a known cancer causing substance. Dispose of the cloth after use.

NOTE: Never work on a car supported only on a jack. Use a hydraulic lift or jack stands to support the vehicle while working.

Raising both front or rear wheels at once and supporting them on jack stands also allows comparison of the brake being serviced to the brake on the opposite side.

Check for Leaks

Press the brake pedal to ensure that there are no leaks in the hydraulic system. If the pedal does not remain hard, and drops to the floor, it is an indication of a leak in the master cylinder, hoses, wheel cylinders, or disc brake calipers. When performing this test, the engine should be running if the car is equipped with power brakes. With power brakes it is normal for the pedal to drop slightly when the engine starts. If it continues to drop, start looking for a leak.

Drum Removal

Safely support the car and release the parking brake if working on the rear axle. Remove the lug nuts, the wheel/tire assembly and then pull off the drums. If the brake shoes have expanded too tightly against the drum, or have cut into the friction surface of the brake drum, the drums may be too tight for removal. In such a case, adjust the shoes inward before the brake drum is removed. On cars with self-adjusting mechanisms, reach through the adjusting slot with a very small prybar (or similar tool) and

ADJUSTER HOLE

ADJUSTER LEVER PUSH BACK 1/16" MAX. (1.5 mm)

MOVE HANDLE UPWARD TO RETRACT BRAKE SHOES DOWNWARD TO EXPAND

Some drums can be removed by backing off the self–adjuster

DRUM

Hard or chill spots

DRUM

Heat checks

Sanding the drum

carefully push the self-adjusting lever away from the star wheel by a maximum of 1/16" (1.5 mm). While holding the lever back, insert a brake adjusting tool into the slot and turn the star wheel in the proper direction until the brake drum can be removed. On cars with manual adjusting mechanisms, try lightly tapping the drum with a rubber mallet. If this does not work, simply reverse the manual adjustment procedures given later in this section until the drum can be removed.

Drum Inspection

Check the drums for any cracks, scores, grooves, or an out-of-round condition. Replace if cracked. Slight scores can be removed with fine emery cloth while extensive scoring requires turning the drum on a lathe.

If the friction surface of the brake drum appears scored or otherwise damaged beyond repair, it will require reconditioning.

Scored drum

Bellmouth drum

Concave drum

After machining, the drum diameter must not exceed the diameter cast on the drum or 0.060″ (1.5 mm) over the original nominal diameter. Carefully look for signs of grease or oil at the center of the assembly. If any leak is noticed, the seal should be replaced.

Rebuild the Cylinders

It is *always* a good idea to rebuild or replace the wheel cylinders when relining the brakes.

Convex drum

This will help assure a properly operating brake system.

Remove Brake Shoes

It is convenient to disassemble one wheel at a time so the opposite side serves as a reference. Carefully note the colors and locations of different springs and parts. This is necessary to distinguish different springs that appear to be the same but have different tensions. If there are extra unused holes close to the ones in which the springs are located, use a dab of paint or other marking on the new shoes to identify the holes to be used. Replace any discolored springs and other parts found corroded or distorted. Use special tools whenever necessary. Examine the springs for signs of stretching or other defects and replace if their condition is at all questionable. Examine the flexible brake hoses and replace any that show signs of cracking or other damage.

Clean and Lubricate Brake Shoes

With all the brake parts off, clean the backing plate with a damp cloth to avoid raising any asbestos dust, and dispose of the rag after use. Clean any rust with wire brush. File smooth any ridges or rough edges on the contact points on the backing plate, and lubricate with approved brake lubricant. Clean and lightly lubricate the adjuster threads, and screw the adjuster all the way together to facilitate reassembly later on. Wash the wheel bearings with solvent and repack them with the proper grease. Check backing plate bolts to make sure they are tight.

Reassemble and Install Brake Shoes

Reassemble the brakes in the reverse order

of disassembly. Make sure all parts are in their proper locations and that both brake shoes are properly positioned in either end of the adjuster. Also, both brake shoes should correctly engage the wheel cylinder push rods and parking brake links, and should be centered on the backing plate. Parking brake links and levers should be in place on the rear brakes. With all the parts in place, try the fit of the brake drum over the new shoes. If not slightly snug, pull it off and turn the star wheel until a slight drag is felt when sliding the drum on. The use of a brake preset gauge will make this job easy. This makes final brake adjustment simpler. Then install the brake drum, wheel bearings, spindle nuts, cotter pins, dust caps, and wheel/tire assemblies, and make final brake adjustments as specified. Torque spindle and lug nuts to specifications.

Bleed and Road-Test

Bleed the brakes to make sure of a high, hard brake pedal, and road-test the car. Most self-adjusting mechanisms are activated only during the rearward motion of a car. So, whenever servicing self-adjusting brakes, make sure that the road test includes enough stops, traveling in reverse, to allow the self-adjusters to perform the proper match-up of all wheels. Or, operate the parking brake several times if that activates the automatic adjuster.

CHILTON TIPS

- The primary brake shoe is the one toward the front of the car, and its lining is usually shorter than that on the secondary (rearward) shoe.
- Self-adjusting mechanisms are usually mounted on the secondary shoe.
- The star wheel part of an adjuster usually (but not always) goes toward the rear of the car.
- Different color springs belong in different locations.
- Self-adjusters and related parts are not interchangeable from one side of a car to the other since the direction of adjuster rotation varies from one side of a car to the other. Most adjusters on one side of a car have right hand threads, and the adjusters on the other side have left hand threads.
- Never press the brake pedal when one or more brake drums are off, or a wheel cylinder will pop apart.

DRUM BRAKE APPLICATION CHART

Make	Year/Model	Reference Number	Adjuster Type
Audi	'76–'77 100	5	Manual (cam type)
	'76–'79 Fox '78 5000	13	Manual (star wheel)
	'80–'83 4000 '79–'83 5000	12	Automatic

DRUM BRAKE APPLICATION CHART

Make	Year/Model	Reference Number	Adjuster Type
BMW	'76–'83 2002, 320i	5	Manual (cam type)
Capri	'76–'78 All	7	Automatic
Chrysler/Mitsubishi	'76–'83 Challenger/Sapporo, Arrow, Colt (rear wheel drive)	9	Automatic
	'79–'83 Colt/Champ (front wheel drive)	14	Automatic
Datsun/Nissan	'76–'77 610, 710	2	Manual (bolt type)
	'76–'78 280Z	7	Automatic
	'82–'83 Sentra	14	Automatic
	'76–'83 All Others	15	Automatic
Fiat	'76–'82 128, 131, Strada	5, 6②	Manual (cam type), Automatic
Fiesta	'78–'80 All	11	Automatic
Honda	'76–'83 All	8	Manual (bolt type)
Isuzu	'80–'83 All	9	Automatic
Mazda	'76–'83 RX-3, RX-4, RX-7 626	13	Automatic
	'76–'80 808, GLC	1	Manual
	'81–'83 GLC	15	Automatic
MG	'76–'80 All	8	Manual (bolt type)
Porsche	'77–'82 924	1	Manual
Renault	'81–'83 18i, Fuego	9	Automatic
	'76–'83 Le Car	5	Manual (cam type)
Subaru	'76–'83 All	8	Manual (bolt type)
Toyota	'76–'83 Celica/Supra	3	Semi-Automatic
	'76–'83 All Others	3, 4, 5, 6, 14②	Semi-Automatic, Manual (star wheel), Manual (bolt type), Automatic, Automatic
Triumph	'76–'81 TR-6, Spitfire	2	Manual (bolt type)
	'76–'81 TR-7, TR-8	11	Automatic
Volkswagen	'76–'83 Types 1 & 2	1	Manual
	'76–'83 Rabbit, Scirocco, Jetta, Dasher, Quantum	10, 12②	Manual (star wheel), Automatic

①Due to the large number of different models covered in each section, slight differences in brake hardware and/or appearance may occur. The basic procedure as given, though, will apply to all models covered.

②When more than one reference number is given, compare the brake being serviced with those illustrated in each section until the correct one is found.

TYPE 1

Lockheed Non–Servo—Manual Adjuster

This brake consists of non-servo forward and reverse shoes with double-end type wheel cylinder. The shoes anchor upon the slotted adjusting screws which permit them a sliding self centering action. Brakes are mounted with cylinder and adjuster horizontally (VW front), or with the cylinder at the top and the adjuster at the bottom.

REMOVAL AND INSTALLATION

1. Raise the front/rear of the vehicle and support it on jackstands. Remove the tire and wheel.

2. Remove the drums (some vehicles may require special pullers).

3. Detach both retracting springs.

4. Remove the hold-down springs and lift the brake shoes from backing plate. On the rear wheels, unhook the parking brake cable from parking brake lever. Before shoe removal.

5. Clean and lubricate the backing plate as detailed earlier.

6. Check the wheel cylinder for frozen pistons or fluid leaks. If any are found, rebuild or replace the cylinder. Disassemble the adjusters and clean and lubricate them.

7. Install the parking brake lever on a new reverse shoe (only on rear wheel brakes).

8. Place new brake shoes on the backing plate and attach the hold-down springs.

1. Cotter pin	8. Clip
2. Castle nut	9. Return spring
3. Brake drum	10. Pressure rod
4. Spring retainer	11. Brake shoe
5. Spring	12. Brake lever
6. Pin	13. Adjusting screw
7. Return spring	14. Adjusting nut

15. Plug	22. Bolt
16. Bolt	23. Washer
17. Lockwasher	24. Plain washer
18. Holder	25. Cover
19. Bolt	26. Spacer
20. Lockwasher	27. Brake carrier
21. Wheel brake cylinder	28. Seal

Exploded view of a Type 1 drum brake

NOTE: Slots in the adjusting screws must be slanted toward the center of the assembly.

The ends of the shoes should engage the wheel cylinder piston slots, and the adjuster slots. If the adjuster screw ends have a slot with a bevel on one side. Make sure the bevel lines up with the bevel on the shoe web.

The end of the shoe with a slot for the parking strut should be installed near the wheel cylinder.

9. For rear wheels, hook the parking brake lever on the parking brake cable and then install the parking brake strut.

10. Install the heavier retracting spring between the toe or cylinder ends of the brake shoes.

Rear drum brake shoe adjusters are found behind the two lower rubber plugs on the backing plate. The two higher plugs (if so equipped) are removed to check brake shoe wear

11. Attach the lighter retracting spring to the heel or anchor ends of the shoes.

12. Replace drums, bleed and adjust the assembly and road test the car.

ADJUSTMENT

Insert an adjusting spoon or a small screwdriver through the adjusting hole in the backing plate and expand the shoe assembly by revolving the notched adjusting wheel in a clockwise direction when facing the end of the wheel cylinder. Adjust the shoe until a heavy drag is felt when turning the wheel and drum; then, back off the adjustment until the wheel spins freely. Adjust one shoe at a time and repeat this procedure at all brake shoes.

Front wheel brake   **Rear wheel brake**

FRONT
1. Adjusting screw
2. Anchor block
3. Front return spring
4. Adjusting nut
5. Guide spring with cup and pin
6. Cylinder
7. Rear return spring

8. Back plate
9. Brake shoe with lining

REAR
1. Cylinder
2. Brake shoe with lining
3. Upper return spring
4. Spring with cup and pin

5. Lower return spring
6. Adjusting screw
7. Back plate
8. Connecting link
9. Lever
10. Brake cable
11. Adjusting nut
12. Anchor block

Typical Lockhead non–servo drum brake assembly (left—front brakes; right—rear brakes)

TYPE 2

Girling Non–Servo Sliding Cylinder— Manual Adjuster

This brake consists of non–servo forward and reverse shoes with a single–end type sliding wheel cylinder. The brakes are mounted with the cylinder at the bottom and the anchor plate/adjuster at the top.

REMOVAL AND INSTALLATION

1. Raise the rear of the vehicle and support it with jackstands. Remove the tire and wheel.
2. Remove the brake drums.
3. Remove the brake shoes by prying one shoe out of the groove in the wheel cylinder (use a small prybar). Both shoes and retracting springs can now be removed from backing plate.
4. Check the wheel cylinder for a frozen piston or leaks. If any are found, rebuild or replace the wheel cylinder.
5. Clean component parts and lubricate backing plate.

Typical Girling sliding cylinder brake assembly

1. Brake disc
2. Return spring adjuster side
3. Brake shoe adjuster
4. Brake shoe assembly-fore
5. Anti-rattler pin
6. Lever
7. Rear wheel cylinder
8. Return spring cylinder side
9. Bleeder
10. Lock plate A
11. Lock plate B
12. Lock plate C and D
13. Dust cover
14. Brake shoe assembly-after

Exploded view of a Type 2 drum brake

6. To replace lined shoes on the backing plate, hook the retracting springs to the shoes and mount in the adjuster and wheel cylinder slots.
7. Back off all adjustment on the adjusting mechanism.
8. Replace the drums. Center the brake shoes in the drum by depressing the brake pedal a few times.
9. Adjust and bleed brakes.
10. Road test the car.

ADJUSTMENT

Jack up the car and release the hand brake. Turn the square-headed adjuster (backing plate side at the top) in a clockwise direction until a heavy drag is felt on the wheel and drum, then back off until wheel spins freely.

Brake adjuster—Type 2

TYPE 3

Non–Servo—Semi– Automatic Adjuster

This brake consists of non–servo forward and reverse shoes with a double–ended type wheel cylinder. The brake shoes are adjusted automatically whenever the parking brake is applied.

REMOVAL AND INSTALLATION

1. Raise the rear of the vehicle and support it with jackstands. Remove the tire and wheel.
2. Remove the brake drum. Tap the drum lightly with a mallet in order to free it. If the drum cannot be removed easily, insert a screwdriver into the hole in the backing plate and hold the automatic adjusting lever away from the adjusting bolt. Using another screwdriver, relieve the brake shoe tension by turning the adjusting bolt clockwise. If the drum still will not come off, use a puller; but first make sure that the parking brake is released.

— **CAUTION** —
Do not depress the brake pedal once the brake drum has been removed.

3. Unhook the shoe tension springs from the shoes with the aid of a brake spring removing tool.
4. Remove the brake shoe securing springs.
5. Disconnect the parking brake cable at the parking brake shoe lever.
6. Withdraw the shoes, complete with the parking brake shoe lever.
7. Unfasten the C-clip and remove the adjuster assembly from the shoes.

Typical Type 3 drum brake assembly

8. Inspect the shoes for wear and scoring.

9. Check the wheel cylinder for frozen pistons or fluid leaks. If any are found, rebuild or replace the wheel cylinder.

10. Clean and inspect all parts. Lubricate the backing plate bosses and anchor plate.

11. Check the tension springs to see if they are weak, distorted or rusted.

12. Inspect the teeth on the automatic adjuster wheel for chipping or other damage.

Installation is performed in the following order:

NOTE: Grease the point of the shoe with slides against the backing plate. Do not get grease on the linings.

1. Attach the parking brake shoe lever and the automatic adjuster lever to the rear side of the shoe.

2. Fasten the parking brake cable to the lever on the brake shoe.

3. Install the automatic adjuster and fit the tension spring on the adjuster lever.

4. Install the securing spring on the *rear* shoe and then install the securing spring on the *front* shoe.

Backing off the brake shoes to remove the brake drum—Type 3

NOTE: The tension spring should be installed on the anchor, before performing Step 4.

5. Hook one end of the tension spring over the rear shoe with the tool used during removal; hook the other end over the front shoe.

—————— CAUTION ——————
Be sure that the wheel cylinder boots are not being pinched in the ends of the shoes.

6. Test the automatic adjuster by operating the parking brake shoe lever.

7. Install the drum and adjust the brakes.

ADJUSTMENT

These brakes are equipped with automatic adjusters actuated by the parking brake mechanism. No periodic adjustment of the drum brakes is necessary if this mechanism is working properly. If the brake shoe to drum clearance is incorrect, and applying and releasing the parking brake a few times does not adjust it properly, the parts will have to be disassembled for repair.

Exploded view of a Type 3 drum brake

TYPE 4

Non–Servo—Manual Adjuster

This brake is a non–servo unit with two single-piston wheel cylinders that act upon an individual shoe.

REMOVAL AND INSTALLATION

1. Raise the rear of the vehicle and support it with jackstands. Remove the tire and wheel.

2. Remove the brake drum as previously detailed.

3. Remove the retracting springs and hold down spring clips.

4. Lift the shoes off of the backing plate.

Typical Type 4 drum brake assembly

5. Check the wheel cylinders for frozen pistons or leaks. If any are found, the wheel cylinder must be rebuilt or replaced.

6. Clean the backing plate and lubricate the bosses and bearing ends of the new shoes.

7. Place the new shoes in the slots of the wheel cylinders and the adjusters. Install the hold down spring clips.

8. Install the retracting springs. The blue, lighter weight spring is installed to the piston side of the shoe; the black, heavier weight spring to the adjuster side of shoe.

9. The shoes must slide freely in the slots.

10. Replace the drum and wheel; bleed and adjust the brake.

11. Road test the car.

ADJUSTMENT

Adjust each shoe individually by rotating the notched adjuster (backing plate side) until a heavy drag is felt when turning the wheel and drum in a forward direction. Back off the adjuster until the wheel spins freely.

TYPE 5

Bendix Non–Servo, Self–Centering— Manual Adjuster

This brake consists of non–servo forward and reverse shoes with a double–ended type wheel cylinder. The brake shoes are self–centering by means of an anchor block and two adjusting cams.

REMOVAL AND INSTALLATION

1. Raise the rear of the vehicle and support it with jackstands. Remove the tire and wheel.

2. Remove the brake drums as previously detailed.

3. Remove the retracting spring (and hold-down springs, if used) and lift the shoe assembly from the backing plate. On the rear wheels, unhook the parking brake cable from the parking brake lever.

4. Separate the shoes by removing the connecting spring.

5. Check the wheel cylinder for frozen pistons or leaks. If any are found, rebuild or replace the cylinder.

6. Clean and lubricate the backing plate bosses and hold down clips.

7. Install the parking brake lever on the new reverse shoe.

8. Attach the connecting spring to the heel ends of the shoes.

9. Mount the shoes on the backing plate.

Typical Bendix drum brake assembly with self–centering shoes

For the rear wheels, hook the parking plate lever on the parking brake cable and install the parking brake strut.

10. Attach the retracting spring to the toe ends of the shoes.

11. Replace the drums. Center the shoes in the drums by depressing the pedal.

12. Bleed and adjust the brakes.

13. Road test the car.

ADJUSTMENT

Because of the self-centering feature of this brake, only minor adjustments to compensate for lining wear are necessary.

1. Jack up the car and support it with jackstands.

2. See that the parking brake lever is in the fully released position. Check the rear brake shoes to make certain they have not been moved away from the adjusting cams (partially applied) by improper adjustment of the cable (or cables) or by a sticking cable. If the shoes are not resting against the adjusting cams, back off or disconnect the parking brake cable.

3. Expand the brake shoes by turning the adjusting cams. If the adjusting cams have lock nuts, loosen the lock nut. Spin the wheel, while turning the adjusting cam in the proper direction, until a heavy drag is reached and then back the cam off gradually in the opposite direction until the wheel spins freely. When adjusting the forward

Adjustment of the Type 5 brake shoes is made by means of adjusting cams found on the backing plate

shoe, spin the wheel in the forward direction. When adjusting the reverse shoe, spin the wheel in the reverse direction.

4. Apply the brake pedal firmly a few times and check all wheels to be sure that they spin freely. If a brake drag is noticed at this point, readjust the brake in accordance with Step 3.

TYPE 6

Bendix Non–Servo— Automatic Adjuster

This brake consists of non–servo forward and reverse shoes with a double–ended type wheel cylinder. The shoes anchor to the slotted anchor plate permitting them a sliding self–centering action.

REMOVAL AND INSTALLATION

1. Raise the rear of the vehicle and support it with jackstands, Remove the tire and wheel.

2. Before removing the brake drum, remove the rubber grommet from the adjustment release hole in the backing plate. Insert a small prybar and push down on the adjustment latch. This will allow the shoes to retract and will eliminate possible interference between the brake shoes and brake drum.

3. Remove the brake drum and disengage the automatic adjuster spring from the strut and the reverse shoe. Remove the anti-noise spring.

4. Remove the upper shoe-to-shoe spring.

5. Remove the strut and disengage the shoes from the hold down springs. Check the springs for cracks or fatigue.

6. Unhook the lower shoe-to-shoe spring. Remove spring and forward shoe assembly.

7. Disconnect the parking brake cable and remove the parking brake lever from the reverse shoe.

8. Remove the adjusting latch and the automatic adjusting lever from the forward shoe. Check for worn or damaged teeth.

To install:

1. Clean and inspect all parts. Replace if necessary.

2. Lubricate the shoe guide pads on the backing plate and the curved edges of anchor plate.

3. Lubricate the latch pin (long pin) and attach the latch to the outer surface of the forward shoe web.

4. Lubricate the adjustment lever pin (short pin) and attach the adjustment lever to the web of the forward shoe.

5. Lubricate the parking brake lever pin and attach the parking brake lever to the web of the reverse shoe. The reverse shoe has a short lining.

6. Attach the parking brake cable.

7. Attach the lower shoe-to-shoe spring to the forward and reverse shoes.

8. Place the forward and reverse shoes in position on the backing plate and install the parking brake strut. Engage the tab on the strut in the slot of the adjustment lever and place the upper ends of the shoe webs against the wheel cylinder pistons.

9. Install the upper shoe-to-shoe spring.

10. Install the automatic adjustment spring. The spring must hold the strut tight against the parking brake lever.

11. Lubricate the inner surfaces of the shoe hold down springs and install the springs over the shoe webs.

12. Install the latch spring over the latch pivot pin. With the adjustment lever against the shoe rim, hook the spring over the latch.

13. Attach the anti-noise spring between the anchor plate and reverse shoe.

14. Install the drum and wheel. Bleed the system if necessary and then road test the vehicle.

ADJUSTMENT

An initial adjustment can be made after the brake drum has been removed and replaced by applying the handbrake several times. Aside from this initial adjustment, the brakes are self–adjusting and no further adjustment should ever be required.

TYPE 7

Non–Servo— Automatic Adjuster

This brake consists of non–servo forward and reverse shoes with a single–end type wheel cylinder. The anchor plate is mounted at the top of the brake plate while the wheel cylinder is at the bottom.

Backing off the adjusting wheel to remove the drum

REMOVAL AND INSTALLATION

1. Raise the rear of the vehicle and support it with jackstands. Remove the tire and wheel assembly.

2. Remove the brake drum. If it is necessary to retract the shoes in order to remove a worn drum: disconnect the parking brake cable; remove the adjusting hole plug located in the drum; insert a small prybar and pry the adjusting lever away from the adjusting wheel. While holding the adjusting lever away from the adjusting wheel, turn the adjusting wheel with the suitable tool to retract the shoes.

3. Remove the upper shoe-to-shoe return spring.

DRUM ROTATION

UPPER SHOE TO SHOE SPRING
WHEEL CYLINDER
AUTOMATIC ADJUSTING LEVER
PARKING BRAKE LEVER
PARKING BRAKE STRUT
AUTOMATIC ADJUSTMENT SPRING
FORWARD SHOE
REVERSE SHOE
HOLD DOWN CLIP
HOLD DOWN CLIP
ANTI-NOISE SPRING
ADJUSTMENT RELEASE HOLE
LATCH PIN
ANCHOR PLATE
AUTOMATIC ADJUSTMENT LATCH
LOWER SHOE TO SHOE SPRING
LATCH SPRING

Typical Type 6 drum brake assembly

4. Remove the brake shoe hold-down springs by compressing and rotating the spring 90° while holding the guide pin.

5. Pivot the shoes out of the slots in the upper anchor plate and remove the shoes along with the lower shoe-to-shoe return spring.

6. Check the wheel cylinder for frozen pistons or fluid leaks. If any are found, rebuild or replace the wheel cylinder.

7. Inspect the old springs. If the old springs are damaged or have been overheated, they should be replaced. Indications of overheated springs are paint discoloration and distortion.

8. Inspect the drum and recondition or replace if necessary.

9. Clean and lubricate the bosses on the backing plate which make contact with the brake shoe. Apply a light coat of lubricant to the upper and lower web of the new shoes.

10. Back off all remaining adjustment on the slotted adjuster screw. Position the adjuster lever under the adjuster wheel, so that it points toward the backing plate.

11. Hook the lower shoe-to-shoe spring into the new shoes.

12. Place the lower end of the shoes in the slots of the wheel cylinder. Be sure that the parking brake lever is properly positioned in the square hole of the forward shoe. Place the upper end of the shoes in the slots of the anchor plate.

13. Install the hold-down springs and upper shoe-to-shoe return spring.

14. Reconnect the parking brake cable.

15. Install the drum and wheel.

Typical Type 7 drum brake assembly

NOTE: The drum may not fit if the adjustment has not been backed off sufficiently or if the shoes are not centered properly on the backing plate.

16. Adjust the brakes by applying the parking brake several times.

17. Bleed the system if necessary and road test the vehicle.

ADJUSTMENT

Other than the initial adjustment with the parking brake described previously, no further adjustments are either necessary or possible.

TYPE 8

Non–Servo–Manual Adjuster

This brake consists of non–servo forward and reverse shoes with a double–ended wheel cylinder. The shoes are held in position by an adjuster/anchor plate and are manually adjusted.

REMOVAL AND INSTALLATION

1. Raise the rear of the vehicle and support it with jackstands. Remove the tire and wheel assembly.

2. Remove the brake drum. If it is necessary to retract the shoes in order to remove a worn drum, remove the dust cover and back off on the adjusting bolt located on the inboard of the backing plate.

3. Remove the upper and lower shoe-to-shoe return springs.

4. Remove the brake shoe hold-down springs and lift the shoes from the backing plate.

5. Check the wheel cylinder for frozen pistons or fluid leaks. If any are found, rebuild or replace the wheel cylinder.

6. Clean and inspect all parts. Lubricate the backing plate bosses and the adjuster assembly.

7. Apply a thin coat of grease to the adjuster.

8. Back off all adjustment on the adjusting bolt located behind the backing plate.

9. Mount the new shoes to the backing plate and install the brake shoe hold-down

1. Anti-rattle pin	7. Return spring
2. Brake backing plate	8. Wheel cylinder
3. Anchor block	9. Fore shoe assembly
4. After shoe assembly	10. Retaining shim
5. Return spring	11. Dust cover
6. Anti-rattle spring	

Exploded view of the Type 7 drum brake

Typical Type 8 drum brake assembly

springs. Be sure that the webs of the shoes are properly engaged in the parking brake mechanism, adjuster assembly and wheel cylinder.

10. Install the upper and lower shoe-to-shoe return springs.

NOTE: The upper and lower shoe-to-shoe return springs are not interchangeable and must be installed in the proper direction. Use the other wheel for reference if necessary when installing these springs.

11. Install the drum and then install the wheel and tire assembly.

NOTE: The drum may not fit if the adjustment bolt has not been backed off sufficiently or if the shoes are not centered properly on the backing plate.

12. Bleed the system if necessary and then road test the vehicle.

ADJUSTMENT

1. Block the front wheels, release the parking brake, raise the rear of the vehicle and support it with jackstands.

2. Depress the brake pedal several times and then release it.

1. Pin
2. Backing plate
3. Return spring
4. Brake shoe
5. Return spring
6. Retainer spring
7. Wheel cylinder
8. Boot
9. Piston
10. Cup
11. Bleeder
12. Cap
13. Adjuster

Exploded view of the Type 8 drum brake

3. Locate the adjuster on the inboard side of the brake backing plate and turn it clockwise until the wheel will no longer spin.

4. Back off the adjuster (counterclockwise) approximately two (2) turns or until the wheel just begins to turn freely.

TYPE 9

Non–Servo— Automatic Adjuster

This brake consists of non–servo forward and reverse shoes with a double–ended wheel cylinder. The shoes are held in position by an anchor plate and are automatically adjusted.

REMOVAL AND INSTALLATION

1. Raise the rear of the vehicle and support it with jackstands. Remove the tire and wheel assembly.

2. Remove the drum. If it is necessary to retract the shoes in order to remove a worn drum, insert a small prybar through the hole in the backing plate and press down on the adjusting latch.

3. Remove the brake shoe hold-down springs.

4. Remove the upper strut-to-shoe spring and the upper shoe-to-shoe return spring.

5. Remove the reverse shoe along with the lower shoe-to-shoe return spring.

6. Holding the adjusting latch on the forward shoe downward, pull the adjusting lever toward the center of the brake and then remove the leading shoe assembly.

7. Check the wheel cylinder for frozen pistons or leaks. If any are found, rebuild or replace the cylinder.

8. Inspect old springs. If old springs are damaged or have been overheated, they should be replaced. Indications of overheated springs are paint discoloration and distortion.

9. Inspect the drum and recondition or replace if necessary.

10. Check the adjusting lever and adjusting latch for wear and damage. Replace damaged parts.

11. Clean and lubricate the backing plate bosses.

12. Remove the adjusting lever and latch from the forward shoe and install them on a new forward shoe.

13. Before mounting the forward shoe, rotate the adjusting lever outward away from the rim of the new shoe. Engage the adjusting lever with the parking brake strut. Rotate the adjusting lever inward until it touches the rim of the shoe and place the shoe against the backing plate.

14. Install the brake shoe hold-down

Typical Type 9 drum brake assembly

WHEEL CYLINDER

UPPER SHOE TO SHOE RETURN SPRING

STRUT TO SHOE RETURN SPRING

HOLD DOWN SPRING

REVERSE SHOE

ANCHOR PLATE

LOWER SHOE TO SHOE RETURN SPRING

PARKING BRAKE STRUT

FORWARD SHOE

HOLD DOWN SPRING

ADJUSTING LEVER

ADJUSTING LATCH

and the upper strut-to-shoe spring. Be sure that the web of the shoes are properly engaged with the slots in the wheel cylinder piston and parking brake lever.

17. Install the drum and wheel.

NOTE: The drum may not fit if the shoes are partially adjusted outward or if they are not centered properly on the backing plate.

18. Apply the brake pedal a few times to bring the brake shoes into adjustment.

19. Bleed the system and road test the vehicle.

ADJUSTMENT

This brake is automatically adjusted; no adjustment is either necessary or possible.

TYPE 10

Non–Servo—Manual Adjuster

This brake consists of non–servo forward and reverse shoes with a double–ended wheel cylinder. The shoes are held in position by an anchor plate and are manually adjusted.

spring to the forward shoe. Be sure that the web of the shoe is engaged with the slot in the wheel cylinder piston.

15. Hook one end of the lower shoe-to-shoe spring to the forward shoe and the other end to a new reverse shoe. Place the

lower part of the reverse shoe on the anchor. Using the lower anchor as a pivot, rotate the reverse shoe upward toward the wheel cylinder and secure it to the backing plate with the hold-down spring.

16. Install the upper shoe-to-shoe spring

Bleeder screw cap

Bleeder screw (right rear wheel cylinder only)
7 to 9 Nm (5 to 7 ft-lbs.)

Rear wheel cylinder boot

Rear wheel cylinder piston

Rear wheel cylinder cup

Rear wheel cylinder body

8 to 12 Nm (6 to 9 ft-lbs.)

Shoe hold-down pin

Strut

Shoe-to-shoe spring

Strut-to-shoe spring

Parking lever

Rear brake shoe and lining

Backing plate assembly

Retainer

Shoe hold-down spring

Shoe-return spring

Adjusting lever

Latch

Stopper

Spring

Pin

Brake drum

Exploded view of a Type 9 drum brake

DRUM ROTATION

SHOE TO BACKING PLATE SPRINGS

FORWARD SHOE

HOLD DOWN CLIPS

ADJUSTER SCREW ASSEMBLY

REVERSE SHOE

PARKING BRAKE LEVER

PARKING BRAKE CABLE

SHOE TO ANCHOR SPRING

SHOE TO ANCHOR SPRING

ANCHOR PLATE

Typical Type 10 drum brake assembly

REMOVAL AND INSTALLATION

1. Raise the rear of the vehicle and support it with jackstands. Remove the tire and wheel assembly.

2. Remove the plug from the brake adjusting hole. Using a small prybar or other suitable tool, release the brake shoes by rotating the shoe adjuster downward on the right side of the vehicle and upward on the left side of the vehicle.

3. Remove the brake drum.

4. Remove the parking brake cable from the parking brake lever by compressing the cable return spring.

5. Remove the shoe-to-anchor springs located at the bottom.

6. Remove the brake shoe hold-down clips and pins.

7. Remove the adjuster screw assembly by spreading the shoes apart making sure that the adjuster screw is fully backed off.

8. Pull the reverse shoe away from the anchor plate to release the tension on the

6. Brake shoe with parking brake lever
7. Return spring
8. Wheel cylinder
9. Hold-down spring
10. Adjuster
11. Brake shoe

Exploded view of a Type 10 drum brake

upper return spring. Disengage the shoe and remove the spring. To facilitate the reassembly operation, note how the upper return spring is positioned on the shoe and how it is connected to the hole in the anchor plate.

9. Remove the forward shoe in the same manner as above.

10. Inspect the wheel cylinder and recondition or replace if necessary.

11. Clean and inspect the adjuster screw assembly. Apply a thin coat of lubricant to the adjuster threads.

12. Inspect the old springs. If old springs are damaged or have been overheated, they should be replaced. Indications of overheated springs are paint discoloration or distortion.

13. Lubricate the bosses on the anchor plate which make contact with the brake shoe tabs.

To install:

1. Remove the parking brake lever and attach the parking brake lever to the web of a new reverse shoe.

2. Position the upper return spring on the forward shoe and hook the other end of the spring into the hole in the backing plate.

3. Rotate the shoe outward with the upper part of the shoe against the wheel cylinder piston and insert the bottom part of the shoe under the anchor plate.

4. Repeat the above procedure for the reverse shoe.

5. With the adjuster screw fully retracted, position the straight forked end of the adjuster screw assembly on the parking brake lever. Make sure that the spring lock on the adjuster screw is on the outside and away from the adjusting hole.

6. Rotate the bottom of the forward shoe off the anchor plate and insert the curved fork end of the adjuster screw assembly into the web of the forward shoe.

NOTE: Make sure that the curved portion of the forked end is facing down-

ward and that the spring lock is on the outside and away from the adjusting hole.

7. Insert the pins for the hold-down clips through the backing plate and web of the shoes. Install the hold-down clips.

8. Install the shoe-to-anchor springs.

9. Compress the brake cable return spring and attach the cable to the bottom of the parking brake lever.

10. Install the brake drum.

11. Install the wheel and tire assembly.

12. Adjust the brakes.

13. Bleed the system and road test the car.

ADJUSTMENT

Adjust the brakes through the adjusting hole located in the backing plate. Adjustment is made manually by spreading the adjuster screw assembly which is located directly under the wheel cylinder. Insert a small prybar or other suitable tool through the hole in the backing plate and rotate the adjuster wheel clockwise until the brakes drag as you turn the wheel in a forward direction. Turn the adjuster in the opposite direction until you just pass the point of drag. Repeat the procedure on the other wheel.

Adjusting the brake shoes—Type 10

TYPE 11

Non–Servo— Automatic Adjuster

These brakes are a leading-trailing shoe design with a ratchet type self-adjusting mechanism. The shoes are held against the anchors at the top by a shoe to shoe spring. At the bottom the shoe webs are held against the wheel cylinder piston ends by a return spring.

The self-adjusting mechanism consists of a spacer strut and a pair of toothed ratchets attached to the primary brake shoe. The parking brake actuating lever is pivoted on the spacer strut.

The self-adjusting mechanism automatically senses the correct lining to drum

A—Secondary shoe | D—Primary shoe
B—Cylinder | E—Pivot position
C—Spring—weaker | F—Spring—stronger

Typical Type 11 drum brake assembly

clearance. As the linings wear, the clearance is adjusted by increasing the effective length of the spacer strut. This strut has projections to engage the inner edge of the secondary shoe via the handbrake lever and the inner edge of the large ratchet on the primary shoe. As wear on the linings increases, the movement of the shoes to bring them in contact with the drums becomes greater than the gap. The spacer strut, bearing on the shoe web, is moved together with the secondary shoe to close the gap. Further movement causes the large ratchet, behind the primary shoe, to rotate inwards against the spring-loaded small ratchet, and the serrations on the mating edges maintain this new setting until further wear on the shoes results in another readjustment. On releasing brake pedal pressure, the return springs cause the shoes to move into contact with the shoulders of the spacer strut/handbrake actuating lever, thus restoring the clearance between the linings and the drum proportionate to the gap shown.

REMOVAL AND INSTALLATION

1. Raise the rear of the vehicle and support it with jackstands. Remove the wheel and tire assembly.
2. Disconnect the brake cable from the operating lever at the back of the backing plate. Remove the dust boot from the operating lever.
3. Remove the brake drum. If it is necessary to retract the shoes in order to remove a worn drum, insert a small prybar through the hole in the backing plate and lift the small ratchet lever on the adjuster assembly.
4. Remove the hold-down spring from the reverse shoe by depressing and rotating the washer. Remove the washer, spring and hold-down pin.
5. Twist the reverse shoe outwards and upwards away from the backing plate, taking care not to damage the wheel cylinder dust boot.
6. Unfasten the upper and lower shoe-to-shoe return springs and remove the shoe and springs.
7. Remove the hold-down spring from the forward shoe.
8. Lift the forward shoe along with the

parking brake lever and spacer strut assembly away from the anchor plate. The operating lever should slide out of the hole in the backing plate.

NOTE: To facilitate the reassembly operation later on, note how the parking brake lever is attached to the forward shoe.

9. Disengage the parking brake lever and spacer strut assembly from the forward shoe by twisting inward to remove the tension on the spring.
10. Disassemble the ratchet assembly from the reverse shoe by first removing the retaining washers. Note how the ratchet levers are assembled so that you can put them back on a new shoe in the same way.

A—Spacer strut
B—Slot

Removing the spacer strut from the carrier plate

11. Rotate the large ratchet lever outward from under the tension spring and remove the ratchet lever from the shoe.
12. Remove the pressure spring and the small ratchet lever.
13. Check the wheel cylinder for frozen pistons or leaks. If any are found, rebuild or replace the wheel cylinder.
14. Inspect the old springs. If the old springs are damaged or have been overheated, they should be replaced. Indications of overheated springs are paint discoloration and distortion.
15. Inspect the drum and recondition or replace if necessary.

A—Secondary shoe
B—Spacer strut
C—Handbrake lever return spring

Assembling the secondary shoe components

16. Check the adjusting lever and adjusting latch for wear and damage. Replace damaged parts.
17. Clean and lubricate backing plate bosses.
18. Install the large ratchet on a new reverse shoe and secure it with a new retaining washer.
19. Install the small ratchet and pressure spring on the pivot of the new reverse shoe and secure with a new retaining washer. Be sure that the ratchet rotates and returns freely with spring pressure.
20. Pull back the small ratchet and rotate the large ratchet inward toward the rim of the shoe. Release the small ratchet and slowly rotate the large ratchet lever outward until the hole in the brake shoe web for the hold-down spring becomes completely exposed.
21. Attach the parking brake lever and spacer strut assembly to a new forward shoe. Hook the short side of the lever and strut tension spring to the slotted hole in the shoe. Hook the long end of the spring to the spacer strut part of the brake lever assembly and rotate the lever assembly until it is attached to the new shoe.
22. Place the forward shoe on the backing plate by inserting the operating lever through the hole in the backing plate. Insert the forked end of the spacer strut into the slotted carrier plate. Rest the upper part of the shoe against the anchor plate and the lower part against the wheel cylinder piston.

Self–adjusting mechanism

23. Insert the hold-down pin through the backing plate and web of the shoe. Install the hold-down spring and washer.

24. Before mounting the reverse shoe, note the slot in the long ratchet lever. The spacer strut must be engaged in the slotted hole in the long ratchet lever when the shoe is mounted to the backing plate.

25. Hook the stronger (thicker) shoe-to-shoe spring through the hole at the top of the already installed forward shoe.

26. Hook the reverse shoe to the other end of the shoe spring. Place the upper part of the shoe against the anchor plate and using the anchor plate as a pivot, rotate the bottom part of the shoe outward. Position the lower part of the shoe against the wheel cylinder piston making sure that the spacer strut is engaged in the hole in the ratchet lever.

27. Insert the hold-down pin through backing plate. Install the hold-down spring and washer.

28. Install the lower shoe-to-shoe spring (the weaker of the two springs) using a pair of pliers or other suitable tool.

29. Before installing the brake drum, lift the small ratchet lever upwards against the spring. This will allow the long ratchet lever to rotate inward toward the rim of the shoe and provide clearance needed to install the drum.

30. Replace the dust boot over the operating lever behind the backing plate.

31. Reconnect the brake cable to the operating lever.

32. Install the brake drum and wheel.

NOTE: The drum may not fit if the shoes are partially adjusted outward or if they are not centered properly on the backing plate.

33. Apply the brake pedal a few times to bring the brake shoe into adjustment.

34. Bleed the system and road test the vehicle.

TYPE 12

Non–Servo– Automatic Adjuster

This brake consists of non–servo forward and reverse shoes with a double–ended wheel cylinder. The shoes are mounted by means of hold-down springs and an anchor plate. Adjustment is performed automatically.

REMOVAL AND INSTALLATION

1. Raise the rear of the vehicle and support it with jackstands. Remove the tire and wheel assembly.

2. Remove the brake drum.

Exploded view of the Type 12 drum brake assembly

NOTE: If it is necessary to retract the shoes in order to remove a worn drum, insert a small prybar through one of the stud holes in the brake drum. Retract the adjuster wedge upward by pressing down on the prybar.

3. Remove the adjusting wedge spring.

4. Remove the upper and lower return springs.

5. Remove the hold-down springs.

6. Lift the shoes from the backing plate and disconnect the parking brake cable from the lever.

7. Disconnect the rear shoe from the push bar.

8. Clamp the push bar in a vise and remove the tensioning spring and adjusting wedge.

9. Check the wheel cylinder for frozen pistons or leaks. If any are found, rebuild or replace the wheel cylinder.

10. Inspect old springs. If old springs are damaged or have been overheated, they should be replaced. Indications of overheated springs are paint discoloration and distortion.

11. Inspect the brake drum and recondition or replace if necessary.

12. Clean and lubricate all contact points on the backing plate.

13. Attach the push bar and tensioning spring to the new front shoe.

14. Insert the adjusting wedge so that its lug is pointing toward the backing plate.

15. Remove the parking brake lever from the old rear shoe and attach it onto the new rear brake shoe.

16. Install the push bar onto the rear brake shoe and parking brake lever assembly.

17. Connect the parking brake cable to the lever and place the whole assembly onto the backing plate.

18. Install the hold-down springs.

19. Install the upper and lower return springs.

20. Install the adjusting wedge spring.

21. Center the brake shoes on the backing plate making sure the adjusting wedge is fully released before installing the drum.

22. Install the drum and wheel assembly and torque the wheel lugs to the manufacturer's specifications.

23. Apply the brake pedal several times to bring the brake shoes into adjustment.

24. Bleed the system and road test the vehicle.

ADJUSTMENT

This brake adjusts itself automatically; aside from the initial adjustments given in the previous section, no adjustments are either necessary or possible.

TYPE 13

Non–Servo—Manual Adjuster

This brake consists of non–servo forward and reverse shoes with a double–ended wheel cylinder. The brake shoes are retained in position by an anchor plate and retaining springs.

REMOVAL AND INSTALLATION

1. Raise the rear of the car and support it with jackstands.

Exploded view of the Type 13 drum brake assembly

Adjusting the brake shoes—Type 13

4. Back off the adjusting wheel 6–8 teeth and replace the rubber plug.

TYPE 14

Non–Servo— Automatic Adjuster

This brake consists of non–servo forward and reverse shoes with a double–ended type wheel cylinder. The brake shoes are held in position by an anchor plate and two hold down springs. The brakes are self–adjusting.

REMOVAL AND INSTALLATION

1. Raise the rear of the vehicle and support it with jackstands. Remove the wheel and tire assembly.

2. Remove the brake drums.

3. Remove the lower pressed metal spring clip, the shoe return spring (the large one piece spring between the two shoes), and the two shoe hold-down springs.

4. Remove the shoes and adjuster as an assembly, Disconnect the parking brake cable from the lever, remove the spring between the shoes and the lever from the rear (trailing) shoe. Disconnect the adjuster retaining spring and remove the adjuster, turn the star wheel in to the adjuster body after cleaning and lubricating the threads.

5. The wheel cylinder may be removed for service or replacement, if necessary.

6. Clean the backing plate with a wire brush. Install the wheel cylinder if it was removed. Lubricate all contact points on the backing plate, anchor plate, wheel cylinder–to-shoe contact and parking brake strut joints and contacts. Installation of the brake shoes, from this point, is the reverse of removal after the lever has been transferred to the new rear (trailing) shoe.

7. Pre-adjustment of the brake shoe can be made by turning the adjuster star wheel out until the drum will just slide on over the brake shoes. Before installing the drum

2. Remove the wheels and then remove the brake drum.

NOTE: If the drum does not come off easily, the brakes will have to be backed off. First, push the lever on the proportioning valve toward the rear axle to relieve the residual brake pressure. Next remove the plug on the backing plate and turn the adjusting wheel to back off the brake shoes.

3. Use brake pliers to remove the upper and lower return springs.

4. Turn and remove the washers to release the brake shoe retaining springs.

5. Disconnect the parking brake cable by pressing the spring toward the front of the car and unhooking the cable from the brake lever.

6. Lift out the brake shoes. Make sure you take note of how the adjuster mechanism fits into the brake shoe web.

Press the proportioning valve lever in the direction of the rear axle (Audi shown)

7. Check the wheel cylinder for frozen pistons or leaks. If any are found, rebuild or replace the wheel cylinder.

8. Inspect old springs. If old springs are damaged or have been overheated, they should be replaced. Indications of overheated springs are paint discoloration and distortion.

9. Inspect the brake drum and recondition or replace if necessary.

10. Clean and lubricate all contact points on the backing plate.

11. Fit the adjuster mechanism into the brake shoe web and then position the shoes onto the brake backing plate.

12. Push the retaining pin springs in and turn the washers onto the retaining pins.

13. Squeeze the spring and hook the parking brake cable to the parking brake lever.

14. Install the upper and lower retaining springs.

15. Install the brake drums and wheels and then lower the vehicle.

16. Bleed (if necessary) and adjust the brakes. Road test the vehicle.

ADJUSTMENT

1. Press the lever of the proportioning valve in the direction of the rear axle to relieve the residual brake pressure.

2. Remove the rubber plug from the brake backing plate.

3. Insert a small prybar into the hole and turn the adjusting wheel until the brake linings are just touching the drum.

make sure the parking brake is not adjusted too tightly, if it is, loosen, or the adjustment of the rear brakes will not be correct.

8. If the wheel cylinders were serviced, bleed the brake system. The brake shoes are then adjusted by pumping the brake pedal and applying and releasing the parking brake. Adjust the parking brake stroke. Road test the car.

ADJUSTMENT

The brakes are self-adjusting. Aside from the initial adjustments given in the "Removal and Installation" section, no adjustments are either necessary or possible.

TYPE 15

Non-Servo—Automatic Adjuster

This brake consists of non-servo forward and reverse shoes with a double-ended type wheel cylinder. The shoes are held in position by an anchor plate and anti-rattle springs. The wheel cylinder is located at the top or bottom of the brake backing plate depending upon the particular application. These brakes are self-adjusting.

REMOVAL AND INSTALLATION

1. Raise the rear of the vehicle and support it with jackstands. Remove the tire and wheel assembly.
2. Engage the parking brake. Pull the pin out and then remove the stopper from the toggle lever. Release the parking brake.
3. Remove the brake drum.

NOTE: If the brake drum cannot be easily removed, install two (2) bolts (8 mm) in the holes and drive it out.

Removing the anti-rattle spring and pin

Tightening torque Nm (ft-lbs.)

1. Backing plate
2. Spring
3. Adjuster
4. Parking lever
5. Shoe and lining assembly
6. Piston
7. Wheel cylinder body
8. Shoe hold spring pin
9. Shoe hold-down spring
10. Shoe to shoe spring
11. Shoe return spring
12. Clip spring

Exploded view of the Type 14 drum brake

4. Remove the return springs.
5. Push the anti-rattle spring retainers in and turn them so they can be removed from the pins.
6. Remove the brake shoes.
7. Clean the brake backing plate and check the wheel cylinder for leaks or other damage; replace as necessary.
8. Hook the return springs into the new shoes. The springs should be between the shoes and the backing plate. The longer return spring must be adjacent to the wheel cylinder. A very thin film of grease may be applied to the pivot points at the ends of the brake shoes. Grease the shoe locating buttons on the backing plate, also. Be careful not to get grease on the linings or drums.
9. Place one shoe in the adjuster and

piston slots, and pry the other shoe into position.
10. Press and turn the anti-rattle spring retainers onto the pins.
11. Replace the drums and wheels. Adjust the brakes. Bleed the hydraulic system of air if the brake lines were disconnected.
12. Reconnect the handbrake, making sure that it does not cause the shoes to drag when it is released.

ADJUSTMENT

These brakes adjust themselves automatically with each application of the brake pedal or the parking brake; other than this, no adjustments are either necessary or possible.

Engine Rebuilding

This section describes, in detail, the procedures involved in rebuilding a typical engine. The procedures are basically identical to those used in rebuilding engines of nearly all design and configurations.

The section is divided into two parts. The first, Cylinder Head Reconditioning, assumes that the cylinder head is removed from the engine, all manifolds are removed, and the cylinder head is on a workbench. The camshaft should be removed from overhead cam cylinder heads. The second section, Cylinder Block Reconditioning, covers the block, pistons, connecting rods and crankshaft. It is assumed that the engine is mounted on a work stand, and the cylinder head and all accessories are removed.

Procedures are identified as follows:

Unmarked—Basic procedures that must be performed in order to successfully complete the rebuilding process.

Starred (*)—Procedures that should be performed to ensure maximum performance and engine life.

Double starred (**)—Procedures that may be performed to increase engine performance and reliability.

In many cases, a choice of methods is also provided. Methods are identified in the same manner as procedures. The choice of method for a procedure is at the discretion of the user.

The tools required for the basic rebuilding procedure should, with minor exceptions, be those included in a mechanic's tool kit. An accurate torque wrench, and a dial indicator (reading in thousandths) mounted on a universal base should be available. Special tools, where required, all are readily available from the major tool suppliers. The services of a competent automotive machine shop must also be readily available.

When assembling the engine, any parts that will be in frictional contact must be pre-lubricated, to provide protection on initial start-up. Any product specifically formulated for this purpose may be used. NOTE: *Do not use engine oil.* Where semi-permanent (locked but removable) installation of bolts or nuts is desired, threads should be cleaned and coated with Loctite® or a similar product (non-hardening).

Aluminum has become increasingly popular for use in engines, due to its low weight and excellent heat transfer characteristics. The following precautions must be observed when handling aluminum engine parts:
—Never hot-tank aluminum parts.
—Remove all aluminum parts (identification tags, etc.) from engine parts before hot-tanking (otherwise they will be removed during the process).
—Always coat threads lightly with engine oil or anti-seize compounds before installation, to prevent seizure.
—Never over-torque bolts or spark plugs in aluminum threads. Should stripping occur, threads can be restored using any of a number of thread repair kits available (see next section).

Magnaflux and Zyglo are inspection techniques used to locate material flaws, such as stress cracks. Magnafluxing coats the part with fine magnetic particles, and subjects the part to a magnetic field. Cracks cause breaks in the magnetic field, which are outlined by the particles. Since Magnaflux is a magnetic process, it is applicable only to ferrous materials. The Zyglo process coats the material with a fluorescent dye penetrant, and then subjects it to blacklight inspection, under which cracks glow brightly. Parts made of any material may be tested using Zyglo. While Magnaflux and Zyglo are excellent for general inspection, and locating hidden defects, specific checks of suspected cracks may be made at lower cost and more readily using spot check dye. The dye is sprayed onto the suspected area, wiped off, and the area is then sprayed with a developer. Cracks then will show up brightly. Spot check dyes will only indicate surface cracks; therefore, structural cracks below the surface may escape detection. When questionable, the part should be tested using Magnaflux or Zyglo.

REPAIRING DAMAGED THREADS

Several methods of repairing damaged threads are available. Heli-Coil® (shown here), Keenserts® and Microdot® are among the most widely used. All involve basically the same principle—drilling out stripped threads, tapping the hole and installing a pre-wound insert— making welding, plugging and oversize fasteners unnecessary.

Two types of thread repair inserts are usually supplied—a standard type for most Inch Coarse, Inch Fine, Metric Coarse and Metric Fine thread sizes and a spark plug type to fit most spark plug port sizes. Consult the individual manufacturer's catalog to determine exact applications. Typical thread repair kits will contain a selection of prewound threaded inserts, a tap (corresponding to the outside diameter threads of the insert) and an installation tool. Most manufacturers also supply blister-packed thread repair inserts separately and a master kit with a variety of taps and inserts plus installation tools.

Before effecting a repair to a threaded hole, remove any snapped, broken or damaged bolts or studs. Penetrating oil can be used to free frozen threads; the offending item can be removed with locking pliers or with a screw or stud extractor. After the hole is clear, the thread can be repaired as follows.

A. Drill out the damaged threads with the specified drill. Drill completely through the hole or to the bottom of a blind hole.

B. With the tap supplied tap the hole to receive the threaded insert. Keep the tap well oiled and back it out frequently to avoid clogging the threads.

C. Screw the threaded insert onto the installation tool until the tang engages the slot. Screw the insert into the tapped hole until it is ¼–½ turn below the top surface. After installation, break the tang off with a hammer and punch.

ENGINE REBUILDING

STANDARD TORQUE SPECIFICATIONS AND CAPSCREW MARKINGS

Newton-Meter has been designated as the world standard for measuring torque and will gradually replace the foot-pound and kilogram-meter torque measuring standard. Torquing tools are still being manufactured with foot-pounds and kilogram-meter scales, along with the new Newton-Meter standard. To assist the repairman, foot-pounds, kilogram-meter and Newton-Meter are listed in the following charts, and should be followed as applicable.

U.S. BOLTS

SAE Grade Number	1 or 2			5			6 or 7			8		
Capscrew Head Markings (Manufacturer's marks may vary. Three-line markings on heads below indicate SAE Grade 5.)												
Usage	Used Frequently			Used Frequently			Used at Times			Used at Times		
Quality of Material	Indeterminate			Minimum Commercial			Medium Commercial			Best Commercial		
Capacity Body Size	Torque			Torque			Torque			Torque		
(inches)−(thread)	Ft-Lb	kgm	Nm	Ft-Lb	kgm	Nm	Ft-Lb	kgm	Nm	Ft-Lb	kgm	Nm
1/4−20	5	0.6915	6.7791	8	1.1064	10.8465	10	1.3630	13.5582	12	1.6596	16.2698
−28	6	0.8298	8.1349	10	1.3830	13.5582				14	1.9362	18.9815
5/16−18	11	1.5213	14.9140	17	2.3511	23.0489	19	2.6277	25.7605	24	3.3192	32.5396
−24	13	1.7979	17.6256	19	2.6277	25.7605				27	3.7341	36.6071
3/8−16	18	2.4894	24.4047	31	4.2873	42.0304	34	4.7022	46.0978	44	6.0852	59.6560
−24	20	2.7660	27.1164	35	4.8405	47.4536				49	6.7767	66.4351
7/16−14	28	3.8132	37.9629	49	6.7767	66.4351	55	7.6065	74.5700	70	9.6810	94.9073
−20	30	4.1490	40.6745	55	7.6065	74.5700				78	10.7874	105.7538
1/2−13	39	5.3937	52.8769	75	10.3725	101.6863	85	11.7555	115.2445	105	14.5215	142.3609
−20	41	5.6703	55.5885	85	11.7555	115.2445				120	16.5860	162.6960
9/16−12	51	7.0533	69.1467	110	15.2130	149.1380	120	16.5960	162.6960	155	21.4365	210.1490
−18	55	7.6065	74.5700	120	16.5960	162.6960				170	23.5110	230.4860
5/8−11	83	11.4789	112.5329	150	20.7450	203.3700	167	23.0961	226.4186	210	29.0430	284.7180
−18	95	13.1385	128.8027	170	23.5110	230.4860				240	33.1920	325.3920
3/4−10	105	14.5215	142.3609	270	37.3410	366.0660	280	38.7240	379.6240	375	51.8625	508.4250
−16	115	15.9045	155.9170	295	40.7985	399.9610				420	58.0860	568.4360
7/8−9	160	22.1280	216.9280	395	54.6285	535.5410	440	60.8520	596.5520	605	83.6715	820.2590
−14	175	24.2025	237.2650	435	60.1605	589.7730				675	93.3525	915.1650
1−8	236	32.5005	318.6130	590	81.5970	799.9220	660	91.2780	894.8280	910	125.8530	1233.7780
−14	250	34.5750	338.9500	660	91.2780	849.8280				990	136.9170	1342.2420

METRIC BOLTS

Description	Torque ft-lbs. (Nm)			
Thread for general purposes (size x pitch (mm))	Head Mark 4		Head Mark 7	
6 x 1.0	2.2 to 2.9	(3.0 to 3.9)	3.6 to 5.8	(4.9 to 7.8)
8 x 1.25	5.8 to 8.7	(7.9 to 12)	9.4 to 14	(13 to 19)
10 x 1.25	12 to 17	(16 to 23)	20 to 29	(27 to 39)
12 x 1.25	21 to 32	(29 to 43)	35 to 53	(47 to 72)
14 x 1.5	35 to 52	(48 to 70)	57 to 85	(77 to 110)
16 x 1.5	51 to 77	(67 to 100)	90 to 120	(130 to 160)
18 x 1.5	74 tc 110	(100 to 150)	130 to 170	(180 to 230)
20 x 1.5	110 to 140	(150 to 190)	190 to 240	(160 to 320)
22 x 1.5	150 to 190	(200 to 260)	250 to 320	(340 to 430)
24 x 1.5	190 to 240	(260 to 320)	310 to 410	(420 to 550)

CAUTION: Bolts threaded into aluminum require much less torque

NOTE: This engine rebuilding section is a guide to accepted rebuilding procedures. Typical examples of standard rebuilding procedures are illustrated.

CYLINDER HEAD RECONDITIONING

Procedure	Method
Identify the valves:	Invert the cylinder head, and number the valve faces front to rear, using a permanent felt-tip marker.
Remove the rocker arms (OHV engines only):	Remove the rocker arms with shaft(s) or balls and nuts. Wire the sets of rockers, balls and nuts together, and identify according to the corresponding valve.
Remove the camshaft (OHC engines only):	See the engine service procedures earlier in this book for details concerning specific engines.
Remove the valves and springs:	Using an appropriate valve spring compressor (depending on the configuration of the cylinder head), compress the valve springs. Lift out the keepers with needlenose pliers, release the compressor, and remove the valve, spring, and spring retainer.
Remove glow plugs and fuel injectors (Diesel engines only):	Label and remove all fuel injectors and glow plugs from the head. Glow plugs unscrew. See the appropriate car section for injector removal. Inspect glow plugs for bulges, cracks or signs of melting. Clean injector tips with a steel brush, then inspect for evidence of melting.
**Remove pre-combustion chamber inserts (Diesel engines only):	**Remove the pre-combustion chambers using a hammer and a thin, blunt brass drift, inserted through the injector hole (or glow plug hole, whichever is more convenient). If chamber is to be reused, carefully remove all carbon from it. NOTE: *Remove chamber only if being replaced, if a glow plug tip has broken off and must be removed, or if chamber is obviously damaged or loose.*

Removing pre-combustion chamber with a drift (© G.M. Corp.)

Check the valve stem-to-guide clearance:	Clean the valve stem with lacquer thinner or a similar solvent to remove all gum and varnish. Clean the valve guides using solvent and an expanding wire-type valve guide cleaner. Mount a dial indicator so that the stem is at 90° to the valve stem, as close to the valve guide as possible. Move the valve off its seat, and measure the valve guide-to-stem clearance by rocking the stem back and forth to actuate the dial indicator. Measure the valve stems using a micrometer, and compare to specifications, to determine whether stem or guide wear is responsible for excessive clearance.

DIAL INDICATOR

VALVE STEM

Checking the valve stem-to-guide clearance

CYLINDER HEAD RECONDITIONING

Procedure	Method

De-carbon the cylinder head and valves:

Chip carbon away from the valve heads, combustion chambers, and ports, using a chisel made of hardwood. Remove the remaining deposits with a stiff wire brush.
NOTE: *Ensure that the deposits are actually removed, rather than burnished.*

Removing carbon from the cylinder head

Hot-tank the cylinder head (cast iron heads only):
CAUTION: *Do not hot-tank aluminum parts.*

Have the cylinder head hot-tanked to remove grease, corrosion, and scale from the water passages.
NOTE: *In the case of overhead cam cylinder heads, consult the operator to determine whether the camshaft bearings will be damaged by the caustic solution.*

Degrease the remaining cylinder head parts:

Using solvent (i.e., Gunk), clean the rockers, rocker shaft(s) (where applicable), rocker balls and nuts, springs, spring retainers, and keepers. Do not remove the protective coating from the springs.

Check the cylinder head for warpage:

Place a straight-edge across the gasket surface of the cylinder head. Using feeler gauges, determine the clearance at the center of the straight-edge. Measure across both diagonals, along the longitudinal centerline, and across the cylinder head at several points. If warpage exceeds .003' in a 6' span, or .006' over the total length, the cylinder head must be resurfaced.
NOTE: *If warpage exceeds the manufacturer's maximum tolerance for material removal, the cylinder head must be replaced.*
When milling the cylinder heads of V-type engines, the intake manifold mounting position is altered, and must be corrected by milling the manifold flange a proportionate amount.

1 & 3 CHECK DIAGONALLY
2 CHECK ACROSS CENTER

Checking cylinder head for warpage

**Porting and gasket matching:

**Coat the manifold flanges of the cylinder head with Prussian blue dye. Glue intake and exhaust gaskets to the cylinder head in their installed position using rubber cement and scribe the outline of the ports on the manifold flanges. Remove the gaskets. Using a small cutter in a hand-held power tool gradually taper the walls of the port out to the scribed outline of the gasket. Further enlargement of the ports should include the removal of sharp edges and radiusing of sharp corners. Do not alter the valve guides.
NOTE: *The most efficient port configuration is determined only by extensive testing. Therefore, it is best to consult someone experienced with the head in question to determine the optimum alterations.*

CYLINDER HEAD RECONDITIONING

Procedure	Method

*Knurling the valve guides:

Cut-away view of a knurled valve guide

*Valve guides which are not excessively worn or distorted may, in some cases, be knurled rather than replaced. Knurling is a process in which metal is displaced and raised, thereby reducing clearance. Knurling also provides excellent oil control. The possibility of knurling rather than replacing valve guides should be discussed with a machinist.

Replacing the valve guides:
NOTE: *Valve guides should only be replaced if damaged or if an oversize valve stem is not available.*

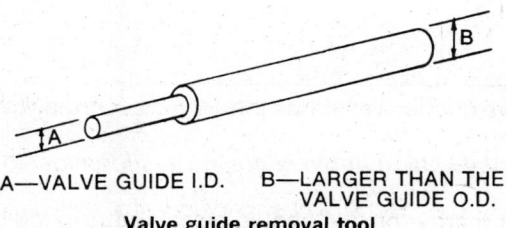

A—VALVE GUIDE I.D. B—LARGER THAN THE VALVE GUIDE O.D.
Valve guide removal tool

WASHERS

A—VALVE GUIDE I.D. B—LARGER THAN THE VALVE GUIDE O.D.
Valve guide installation tool (with washers used for installation)

Depending on the type of cylinder head, valve guides may be pressed, hammered, or shrunk in. In cases where the guides are shrunk into the head, replacement should be left to an equipped machine shop. In other cases, the guides are replaced as follows: Press or tap the valve guides out of the head using a stepped drift (see illustration). Determine the height above the boss that the guide must extend, and obtain a stack of washers, their I.D. similar to the guide's O.D., of that height. Place the stack of washers on the guide, and insert the guide into the boss.
NOTE: *Valve guides are often tapered or beveled for installation.*
Using the stepped installation tool (see illustration), press or tap the guides into position. Ream the guides according to the size of the valve stem.

Replacing valve seat inserts:

Replacement of valve seat inserts which are worn beyond resurfacing or broken, if feasible, must be done by a machine shop.

Resurfacing the valve seats using reamers:

45° VALVE MARGIN

SEAT WIDTH

CORRECT

NO MARGIN

INCORRECT

Valve seat width and centering

Reaming the valve seat

Select a reamer of the correct seat angle, slightly larger than the diameter of the valve seat, and assemble it with a pilot of the correct size. Install the pilot into the valve guide, and using steady pressure, turn the reamer clockwise.
CAUTION: *Do not turn the reamer counterclockwise.*
Remove only as much material as necessary to clean the seat. Check the concentricity of the seat (see below). If the dye method is not used, coat the valve face with Prussian blue dye, install and rotate it on the valve seat. Using the dye marked area as a centering guide, center and narrow the valve seat to specifications with correction cutters.
NOTE: *When no specifications are available, minimum seat width for exhaust valves should be 5/64", intake valves 1/16".*
After making correction cuts, check the position of the valve seat on the valve face using Prussian blue dye.
NOTE: *Do not cut induction hardened seats; they must be ground.*

CYLINDER HEAD RECONDITIONING

Procedure	Method

*Resurfacing the valve seats using a grinder:

Grinding a valve seat

*Select a pilot of the correct size, and a coarse stone of the correct seat angle. Lubricate the pilot if necessary, and install the tool in the valve guide. Move the stone on and off the seat at approximately two cycles per second, until all flaws are removed from the seat. Install a fine stone, and finish the seat. Center and narrow the seat using correction stones, as described above.

Resurfacing (grinding) the valve face:

Using a valve grinder, resurface the valves according to specifications.
CAUTION: *Valve face angle is not always identical to valve seat angle.*
A minimum margin of 1/32″ should remain after grinding the valve. The valve stem top should also be squared and resurfaced, by placing the stem in the V-block of the grinder, and turning it while pressing lightly against the grinding wheel.
NOTE: *Do not grind sodium filled exhaust valves on a machine. These should be hand lapped.*

Critical valve dimensions

Valve grinding by machine

CYLINDER HEAD RECONDITIONING

Procedure	Method

Checking the valve seat concentricity:

Checking valve seat concentricity using a dial gauge

Coat the valve face with Prussian blue dye, install the valve, and rotate it on the valve seat. If the entire seat becomes coated, and the valve is known to be concentric, the seat is concentric.
*Install the dial gauge pilot into the guide, and rest the arm on the valve seat. Zero the gauge, and rotate the arm around the seat. Run-out should not exceed .002″.

---

*Lapping the valves:
NOTE: *Valve lapping is done to ensure efficient sealing of resurfaced valves and seats.*

HAND DRILL

ROD

SUCTION CUP

Hand lapping the valves

Home made mechanical valve lapping tool

*Invert the cylinder head, lightly lubricate the valve stems, and install the valves in the head as numbered. Coat valve seats with fine grinding compound, and attach the lapping tool suction cup to a valve head.
NOTE: *Moisten the suction cup.*
Rotate the tool between the palms, changing position and lifting the tool often to prevent grooving. Lap the valve until a smooth, polished seat is evident. Remove the valve and tool, and rinse away all traces of grinding compound.
**Fasten a suction cup to a piece of drill rod, and mount the rod in a hand drill. Proceed as above, using the hand drill as a lapping tool.
CAUTION: *Due to the higher speeds involved when using the hand drill, care must be exercised to avoid grooving the seat.* Lift the tool and change direction of rotation often.

Check the valve springs:

NOT MORE THAN ⁵⁄₆₄″

CLOSED COIL END DOWNWARD

Checking valve spring free length and squareness

Measuring valve spring test pressure

Place the spring on a flat surface next to a square. Measure the height of the spring, and rotate it against the edge of the square to measure distortion. If spring height varies (by comparison) by more than 1/16″ or if distortion exceeds 1/16″, replace the spring.
**In addition to evaluating the spring as above, test the spring pressure at the installed and compressed (installed height minus valve lift) height using a valve spring tester. Springs used on small displacement engines (up to 3 liters) should be ∓ 1 lb. of all other springs in either position. A tolerance of ∓ 5 lbs. is permissible on larger engines.

CYLINDER HEAD RECONDITIONING

Procedure	Method
Install pre-combustion chambers (Diesel engines only) **Align the notches to install the pre-combustion chamber (© G.M. Corp.)**	Pre-combustion chambers are press-fit into the head. The chambers will fit only one way: on G.M. V8, align the notches in the chamber and head; on 1.8L 4 cyl., install lock ball into groove in chamber, then align lock ball in chamber with groove in cylinder head. Press the chamber into the head. Fit a piece of metal against the chamber face for protection. On 1.8L, after installation, grind the face of the chamber flush with the face of the cylinder head. On G.M. V8, use a 1¼ in. socket to install the chamber (the chamber should be flush ± .003 in. to the face of the head).
Install fuel injectors and glow plugs (Diesel engines)	Before installing glow plugs, check for continuity across plug terminals and body. If no continuity exists, the heater wire is broken and the plug should be replaced.
*Install valve stem seals: **Valve stem seal installation**	*Due to the pressure differential that exists at the ends of the intake valve guides (atmospheric pressure above, manifold vacuum below), oil is drawn through the valve guides into the intake port. This has been alleviated somewhat since the addition of positive crankcase ventilation, which lowers the pressure above the guides. Several types of valve stem seals are available to reduce blow-by. Certain seals simply slip over the stem and guide boss, while others require that the boss be machined. Recently, Teflon guide seals have become popular. Consult a parts supplier or machinist concerning availability and suggested usages. NOTE: *When installing seals, ensure that a small amount of oil is able to pass the seal to lubricate the valve guides; otherwise, excessive wear may result.*
Install the valves:	Lubricate the valve stems, and install the valves in the cylinder head as numbered. Lubricate and position the seals (if used, see above) and the valve springs. Install the spring retainers, compress the springs, and insert the keys using needlenose pliers or a tool designed for this purpose. NOTE: *Retain the keys with wheel bearing grease during installation.*

CYLINDER HEAD RECONDITIONING

Procedure	Method

Check valve spring installed height:

Valve spring installed
height dimension

Measuring valve spring
installed height

Measure the distance between the spring pad and the lower edge of the spring retainer, and compare to specifications. If the installed height is incorrect, add shim washers between the spring pad and the spring.
CAUTION: *Use only washers designed for this purpose.*

Install the camshaft (OHC engines only) and check end play:

See the engine service procedures earlier in this book for details concerning specific engines.

Inspect the rocker arms, balls, studs, and nuts (OHV engines only):

Stress cracks in the rocker nuts

Visually inspect the rocker arms, balls, studs, and nuts for cracks, galling, burning, scoring or wear. If all parts are intact, liberally lubricate the rocker arms and balls, and install them on the cylinder head. If wear is noted on a rocker arm at the point of valve contact, grind it smooth and square, removing as little material as possible. Replace the rocker arm if excessively worn. If a rocker stud shows signs of wear, it must be replaced (see below). If a rocker nut shows stress cracks, replace it. If an exhaust ball is galled or burned, substitute the intake ball from the same cylinder (if it is intact), and install a new intake ball.
NOTE: *Avoid using new rocker balls on exhaust valves.*

Replacing rocker studs (OHV engines only):

AS STUB BEGINS TO PULL UP, IT WILL BE NECESSARY TO REMOVE THE NUT AND ADD MORE WASHERS

⅜″ NUT

FLAT WASHERS

Extracting a pressed-in rocker stud

In order to remove a threaded stud, lock two nuts on the stud, and unscrew the stud using the lower nut. Coat the lower threads of the new stud with Loctite®, and install.
Two alternative methods are available for replacing pressed in studs. Remove the damaged stud using a stack of washers and a nut (see illustration). In the first, the boss is reamed .005–.006″ oversize, and an oversize stud pressed in. Control the stud extension over the boss using washers, in the same manner as valve guides. Before installing the stud, coat it with white lead and grease. To retain the stud more positively drill a hole through the stud and boss, and install a roll pin. In the second method, the boss is tapped, and a threaded stud installed. Retain the stud using Loctite® Stud and Bearing Mount.

Reaming the stud bore for oversize rocker studs

CYLINDER HEAD RECONDITIONING

Procedure	Method

Inspect the rocker shaft(s) and rocker arms (OHV engines only):

Disassemble the rocker shaft for inspection

Remove rocker arms, springs and washers from rocker shaft. NOTE: *Lay out parts in the order as they are removed.* Inspect rocker arms for pitting or wear on the valve contact point, or excessive bushing wear. Bushings need only be replaced if wear is excessive, because the rocker arm normally contacts the shaft at one point only. Grind the valve contact point of rocker arm smooth if necessary, removing as little material as possible. If excessive material must be removed to smooth and square the arm, it should be replaced. Clean out all oil holes and passages in rocker shaft. If shaft is grooved or worn, replace it. Lubricate and assemble the rocker shaft.

Rocker arm-to-rocker shaft contact area

Inspect the camshaft bushings and the camshaft (OHC engines):

See next section.

Inspect the pushrods (OHV engines only):

Remove the pushrods, and, if hollow, clean out the oil passages using fine wire. Roll each pushrod over a piece of clean glass. If a distinct clicking sound is heard as the pushrod rolls, the rod is bent, and must be replaced.

*The length of all pushrods must be equal. Measure the length of the pushrods, compare to specifications, and replace as necessary.

Inspect the valve lifters (OHV engines only):

CHECK FOR CONCAVE WEAR ON FACE OF TAPPET USING TAPPET FOR STRAIGHT EDGE

Checking the lifter face

Remove lifters from their bores, and remove gum and varnish, using solvent. Clean walls of lifter bores. Check lifters for concave wear as illustrated. If face is worn concave, replace lifter, and carefully inspect the camshaft. Lightly lubricate lifter and insert it into its bore. If play is excessive, an oversize lifter must be installed (where possible). Consult a machinist concerning feasibility. If play is satisfactory, remove, lubricate, and reinstall the lifter.
NOTE: *1981 and later G.M. diesel V8 valve lifters have roller cam followers. Check these for smooth operation and wear. The roller should rotate freely, but without excessive play. Check the rollers for missing or broken needle bearings. If the roller is pitted or rough, check the camshaft lobe for wear.*

---

*Testing hydraulic lifter leak down (OHV gasoline engines only):

Typical exploded view of hydraulic valve lifter

Submerge lifter in a container of kerosene. Chuck a used pushrod or its equivalent into a drill press. Position container of kerosene so pushrod acts on the lifter plunger. Pump lifter with the drill press, until resistance increases. Pump several more times to bleed any air out of lifter. Apply very firm, constant pressure to the lifter, and observe rate at which fluid bleeds out of lifter. If the fluid bleeds very quickly (less than 15 seconds), lifter is defective. If the time exceeds 60 seconds, lifter is sticking. In either case, recondition or replace lifter. If lifter is operating properly (leak down time 15–60 seconds), lubricate and install it.

CYLINDER HEAD RECONDITIONING

Procedure	Method
Bleed the hydraulic lifters (diesel engines only):	After the cylinder heads are installed on G.M. V8 diesels, the valve lifters must be bled down before the crankshaft is turned. Failure to bleed down the lifters will cause damage to the valve train. See diesel engine rocker arm replacement procedure in Oldsmobile 88, 98, etc. car section for procedures. NOTE: *When installing new lifters, prime by working the lifter plunger while submerged in clean kerosene or diesel fuel.*

CYLINDER BLOCK RECONDITIONING

Procedure	Method
Checking the main bearing clearance: **Plastigage® installed on the lower bearing shell** **Measuring Plastigage® to determine bearing clearance**	Invert engine, and remove cap from the bearing to be checked. Using a clean, dry rag, thoroughly clean all oil from crankshaft journal and bearing insert. NOTE: *Plastigage is soluble in oil; therefore, oil on the journal or bearing could result in erroneous readings.* Place a piece of Plastigage along the full length of journal, reinstall cap, and torque to specifications. Remove bearing cap, and determine bearing clearance by comparing width of Plastigage to the scale on Plastigage envelope. Journal taper is determined by comparing width of the Plastigage strip near its ends. Rotate crankshaft 90° and retest, to determine journal eccentricity. NOTE: *Do not rotate crankshaft with Plastigage installed.* If bearing insert and journal appear intact, and are within tolerances, no further main bearing service is required. If bearing or journal appear defective, cause of failure should be determined before replacement. *Remove crankshaft from block (see below). Measure the main bearing journals at each end twice (90° apart) using a micrometer, to determine diameter, journal taper and eccentricity. If journals are within tolerances, reinstall bearing caps at their specified torque. Using a telescope gauge and micrometer, measure bearing I.D. parallel to piston axis and at 30° on each side of piston axis. Subtract journal O.D. from bearing I.D. to determine oil clearance. If crankshaft journals appear defective, or do no meet tolerances, there is no need to measure bearings; for the crankshaft will require grinding and/or undersize bearings will be required. If bearing appears defective, cause for failure should be determined prior to replacement.
Checking the connecting rod bearing clearance:	Connecting rod bearing clearance is checked in the same manner as main bearing clearance, using Plastigage. Before removing the crankshaft, connecting rod side clearance also should be measured and recorded. *Checking connecting rod bearing clearance, using a micrometer, is identical to checking main bearing clearance. If no other service is required, the piston and rod assemblies need not be removed.

CYLINDER BLOCK RECONDITIONING

Procedure	Method

Removing the crankshaft:

Using a punch, mark the corresponding main bearing caps and saddles according to position (i.e., one punch on the front main cap and saddle, two on the second, three on the third, etc.). Using number stamps, identify the corresponding connecting rods and caps, according to cylinder (if no numbers are present). Remove the main and connecting rod caps, and place sleeves of plastic tubing over the connecting rod bolts, to protect the journals as the crankshaft is removed. Lift the crankshaft out of the block.

Connecting rod matched to cylinder with a number stamp

Scribe connecting rod matchmarks

Remove the ridge from the top of the cylinder:

In order to facilitate removal of the piston and connecting rod, the ridge at the top of the cylinder (unworn area; see illustration) must be removed. Place the piston at the bottom of the bore, and cover it with a rag. Cut the ridge away using a ridge reamer, exercising extreme care to avoid cutting to deeply. Remove the rag, and remove cuttings that remain on the piston.

CAUTION: *If the ridge is not removed, and new rings are installed, damage to rings will result.*

RIDGE CAUSED BY CYLINDER WEAR

CYLINDER WALL

TOP OF PISTON

Cylinder bore ridge

Removing the piston and connecting rod:

Invert the engine, and push the pistons and connecting rods out of the cylinders. If necessary, tap the connecting rod boss with a wooden hammer handle, to force the piston out.

CAUTION: *Do not attempt to force the piston past the cylinder ridge* (see above).

Removing the piston

CYLINDER BLOCK RECONDITIONING

Procedure	Method
Service the crankshaft:	Ensure that all oil holes and passages in the crankshaft are open and free of sludge. If necessary, have the crankshaft ground to the largest possible undersize. **Have the crankshaft Magnafluxed, to locate stress cracks. Consult a machinist concerning additional service procedures, such as surface hardening (e.g., nitriding, Tuftriding) to improve wear characteristics, cross drilling and chamfering the oil holes to improve lubrication, and balancing.
Removing freeze plugs:	Drill a small hole in the middle of the freeze plugs. Thread a large sheet metal screw into the hole and remove the plug with a slide hammer.
Remove the oil gallery plugs:	Threaded plugs should be removed using an appropriate (usually square) wrench. To remove soft, pressed in plugs, drill a hole in the plug, and thread in a sheet metal screw. Pull the plug out by the screw using pliers.
Hot-tank the block: NOTE: *Do not hot-tank aluminum parts.*	Have the block hot-tanked to remove grease, corrosion, and scale from the water jackets. NOTE: *Consult the operator to determine whether the camshaft bearings will be damaged during the hot-tank process.*

Check the block for cracks:	Visually inspect the block for cracks or chips. The most common locations are as follows:
	    Adjacent to freeze plugs.
	    Between the cylinders and water jackets.
	    Adjacent to the main bearing saddles.
	    At the extreme bottom of the cylinders.
	Check only suspected cracks using spot check dye (see introduction). If a crack is located, consult a machinist concerning possible repairs.
	
	**Magnaflux the block to locate hidden cracks. If cracks are located, consult a machinist about feasibility of repair.

Install the oil gallery plugs and freeze plugs:	Coat freeze plugs with sealer and tap into position using a piece of pipe, slightly smaller than the plug, as a driver. To ensure retention, stake the edges of the plugs. Coat threaded oil gallery plugs with sealer and install. Drive replacement soft plugs into block using a large drift as a driver. *Rather than reinstalling lead plugs, drill and tap the holes, and install threaded plugs.
*Check the deck height:	*The deck height is the distance from the crankshaft centerline to the block deck. To measure, invert the engine, and install the crankshaft, retaining it with the center main cap. Measure the distance from the crankshaft journal to the block deck, parallel to the cylinder centerline. Measure the diameter of the end (front and rear) main journals, parallel to the centerline of the cylinders, divide the diameter in half, and subtract it from the previous measurement. The results of the front and rear measurements should be identical. If the difference exceeds .005″, the deck height should be corrected. NOTE: *Block deck height and warpage should be corrected at the same time.*

CYLINDER BLOCK RECONDITIONING

Procedure	Method

Check the block deck for warpage:

Using a straightedge and feeler gauges, check the block deck for warpage in the same manner that the cylinder head is checked (see Cylinder Head Reconditioning). If warpage exceeds specifications, have the deck resurfaced.

NOTE: *In certain cases a specification for total material removal (Cylinder head and block deck) is provided. This specification must not be exceeded.*

Check the bore diameter and surface:

Measuring the cylinder bore with a dial gauge

Visually inspect the cylinder bores for roughness, scoring, or scuffing. If evident, the cylinder bore must be bored or honed oversize to eliminate imperfections, and the smallest possible oversize piston used. The new pistons should be given to the machinist with the block, so that the cylinders can be bored or honed exactly to the piston size (plus clearance). If no flaws are evident, measure the bore diameter using a telescope gauge and micrometer, or dial guage, parallel and perpendicular to the engine centerline, at the top (below the ridge) and bottom of the bore. Subtract the bottom measurements from the top to determine taper, and the parallel to the centerline measurements from the perpendicular measurements to determine eccentricity. If the measurements are not within specifications, the cylinder must be bored or honed, and an oversize piston installed. If the measurements are within specifications the cylinder may be used as is, with only finish honing (see below).

NOTE: *Prior to boring, check the block deck warpage, height and bearing alignment.*

CAUTION: *The 4 cyl. 140 G.M. engine cylinder walls are impregnated with silicone. Boring or honing can be done only by a shop with the proper equipment.*

TELESCOPE GAUGE 90° FROM PISTON PIN

Measuring cylinder bore with a telescope gauge

← CENTERLINE OF ENGINE →

A—AT RIGHT ANGLE TO CENTERLINE OF ENGINE
B—PARALLEL TO CENTERLINE OF ENGINE
Cylinder bore measuring points

TELESCOPE GAUGE

MICROMETER

Determining cylinder bore by measuring telescope gauge with a micrometer

Check the cylinder block bearing alignment:

Checking main bearing saddle alignment

Remove the upper bearing inserts. Place a straightedge in the bearing saddles along the centerline of the crankshaft. If clearance exists between the straightedge and the center saddle, the block must be alignbored.

CYLINDER BLOCK RECONDITIONING

Procedure

Method

Clean and inspect the pistons and connecting rods:

Using a ring expander, remove the rings from the piston. Remove the retaining rings (if so equipped) and remove piston pin.
NOTE: *If the piston pin must be pressed out, determine the proper method and use the proper tools; otherwise the piston will distort.*
Clean the ring grooves using an appropriate tool, exercising care to avoid cutting too deeply. Thoroughly clean all carbon and varnish from the piston with solvent.
CAUTION: *Do not use a wire brush or caustic solvent on pistons.*
Inspect the pistons for scuffing, scoring, cracks, pitting, or excessive ring groove wear. If wear is evident, the piston must be replaced. Check the connecting rod length by measuring the rod from the inside of the large end to the inside of the small end using calipers (see illustration). All connecting rods should be equal length. Replace any rod that differs from the others in the engine.

*Have the connecting rod alignment checked in an alignment fixture by a machinist. Replace any twisted or bent rods.

*Magnaflux the connecting rods to locate stress cracks. If cracks are found, replace the connecting rod.

RING EXPANDER

Removing the piston rings

RING GROOVE CLEANER

Cleaning the piston ring grooves

Check the connecting rod length (arrow)

Fit the pistons to the cylinders:

Using a telescope gauge and micrometer, or a dial gauge, measure the cylinder bore diameter perpendicular to the piston pin, 2½° below the deck. Measure the piston perpendicular to its pin on the skirt. The difference between the two measurements is the piston clearance. If the clearance is within specifications or slightly below (after boring or honing), finish honing is all that is required. If the clearance is excessive, try to obtain a slightly larger piston to bring clearance within specifications. Where this is not possible, obtain the first oversize piston, and hone (or if necessary, bore) the cylinder to size.

90°

Measuring the piston prior to fitting

Assemble the pistons and connecting rods:

Inspect piston pin, connecting rod small end bushing, and piston bore for galling, scoring, or excessive wear. If evident, replace defective part(s). Measure the I.D. of the piston boss and connecting rod small end, and the O.D. of the piston pin. If within specifications, assemble piston pin and rod.
CAUTION: *If piston pin must be pressed in, determine the proper method and use the proper tools; otherwise the piston will distort.*

CYLINDER BLOCK RECONDITIONING

Procedure	Method

Installing piston pin lock rings

Install the lock rings; ensure that they seat properly. If the parts are not within specifications, determine the service method for the type of engine. In some cases, piston and pin are serviced as an assembly when either is defective. Others specify reaming the piston and connecting rods for an oversize pin. If the connecting rod bushing is worn, it may in many cases be replaced. Reaming the piston and replacing the rod bushing are machine shop operations.

Clean and inspect the camshaft:

Checking the camshaft for straightness

Degrease the camshaft, using solvent, and clean out all oil holes. Visually inspect cam lobes and bearing journals for excessive wear. If a lobe is questionable, check all lobes as indicated below. If a journal or lobe is worn, the camshaft must be reground or replaced.

NOTE: *If a journal is worn, there is a good chance that the bushings are worn.*

If lobes and journals appear intact, place the front and rear journals in V-blocks, and rest a dial indicator on the center journal. Rotate the camshaft to check straightness. If deviation exceeds .001°, replace the camshaft.

*Check the camshaft lobes with a micrometer, by measuring the lobes from the nose to base and again at 90° (see illustration). The lift is determined by subtracting the second measurement from the first. If all exhaust lobes and all intake lobes are not identical, the camshaft must be reground or replaced.

Camshaft lobe measurement

Replace the camshaft bearings (OHV engines only):

Camshaft removal and installation tool (typical)

If excessive wear is indicated, or if the engine is being completely rebuilt, camshaft bearings should be replaced as follows: Drive the camshaft rear plug from the block. Assemble the removal puller with its shoulder on the bearing to be removed. Gradually tighten the puller nut until bearing is removed. Remove remaining bearings, leaving the front and rear for last. To remove front and rear bearings, reverse position of the tool, so as to pull the bearings in toward the center of the block. Leave the tool in this position, pilot the new front and rear bearings on the installer, and pull them into position: Return the tool to its original position and pull remaining bearings into postion.

NOTE: *Ensure that oil holes align when installing bearings.*
Replace camshaft rear plug, and stake it into position to aid retention.

CYLINDER BLOCK RECONDITIONING

Procedure	Method

Finish hone the cylinders:

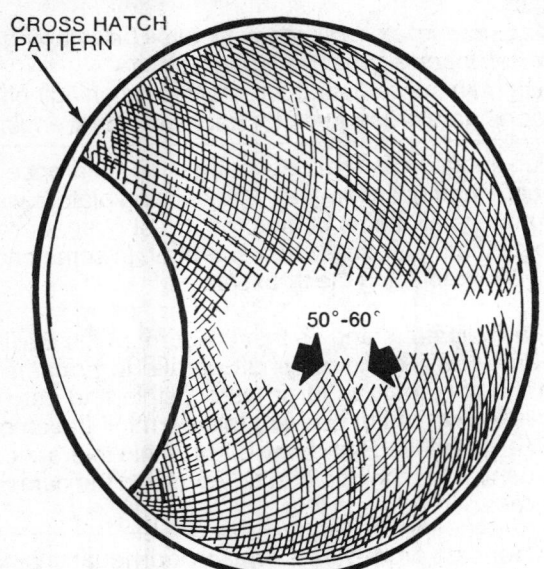

CROSS HATCH PATTERN

50°-60°

Chuck a flexible drive hone into a power drill, and insert it into the cylinder. Start the hone, and move it up and down the cylinder at a rate which will produce approximately a 60° cross-hatch pattern (see illustration).

NOTE: *Do not extend the hone below the cylinder bore.*

After developing the pattern, remove the hone and recheck piston fit. Wash the cylinders with a detergent and water solution to remove abrasive dust, dry, and wipe several times with a rag soaked in engine oil.

Check piston ring end-gap:

Checking ring end-gap

Compress the piston rings to be used in a cylinder, one at a time, into that cylinder, and press them approximately 1″ below the deck with an inverted piston. Using feeler gauges, measure the ring end-gap, and compare to specifications. Pull the ring out of the cylinder and file the ends with a fine file to obtain proper clearance.

CAUTION: *If inadequate ring end-gap is utilized, ring breakage will result.*

Install the piston rings:

PISTON RING

FEELER GAUGE

RING GROOVE

Checking ring side clearance

Inspect the ring grooves in the piston for excessive wear or taper. If necessary, recut the groove(s) for use with an over-width ring or a standard ring and spacer. If the groove is worn uniformly, overwidth rings, or standard rings and spacers may be installed without recutting. Roll the outside of the ring around the groove to check for burrs or deposits. If any are found, remove with a fine file. Hold the ring in the groove, and measure side clearance. If necessary, correct as indicated above.

NOTE: *Always install any additional spacers above the piston ring.*

The ring groove must be deep enough to allow the ring to seat below the lands (see illustration). In many cases, a "go-no-go" depth gauge will be provided with the piston rings. Shallow grooves may be corrected by recutting, while deep grooves require some type of filler or expander behind the piston. Consult the piston ring supplier concerning the suggested method. Install the rings on the piston, lowest ring first, using a ring expander.

NOTE: *Position the ring markings as specified by the manufacturer (see car section).*

CYLINDER BLOCK RECONDITIONING

Procedure	Method

Install the camshaft (OHV engines only):

Liberally lubricate the camshaft lobes and journals, and install the camshaft.

CAUTION: *Exercise extreme care to avoid damaging the bearings when inserting the camshaft.*

Install and tighten the camshaft thrust plate retaining bolts. See the appropriate procedures for each individual engine.

Check camshaft end-play (OHV engines only):

DIAL INDICATOR CAMSHAFT

Checking camshaft end-play with a feeler gauge

Checking camshaft end-play with a dial indicator

Using feeler gauges, determine whether the clearance between the camshaft boss (or gear) and backing plate is within specifications. Install shims behind the thrust plate, or reposition the camshaft gear and retest end-play. In some cases, adjustment is by replacing the thrust plate.

*Mount a dial indicator stand so that the stem of the dial indicator rests on the nose of the camshaft, parallel to the camshaft axis. Push the camshaft as far in as possible and zero the gauge. Move the camshaft outward to determine the amount of camshaft endplay. If the endplay is not within tolerance, install shims behind the thrust plate, or reposition the camshaft gear and retest.

Install the rear main seal (where applicable):

See the appropriate procedures for each individual engine.

Install the crankshaft:

INSTALLING BEARING SHELL

REMOVING BEARING SHELL

Removal and installation of upper bearing insert using a roll-out pin

60°

5"/8

Home-made bearing roll-out pin

Thoroughly clean the main bearing saddles and caps. Place the upper halves of the bearing inserts on the saddles and press into position.

NOTE: *Ensure that the oil holes align.*

Press the corresponding bearing inserts into the main bearing caps. Lubricate the upper main bearings, and lay the crankshaft in position. Place a strip of Plastigage on each of the crankshaft journals, install the main caps, and torque to specifications. Remove the main caps, and compare the Plastigage to the scale on the Plastigage envelope. If clearances are within tolerances, remove the Plastigage, turn the crankshaft 90°, wipe off all oil and retest. If all clearances are correct, remove all Plastigage, thoroughly lubricate the main caps and bearing journals, and install the main caps. If clearances are not within tolerance, the upper bearing inserts may be removed, without removing the crankshaft, using a bearing roll out pin (see illustration). Roll in a bearing that will provide proper clearance, and retest. Torque all main caps, excluding the thrust bearing cap, to specifications. Tighten the thrust bearing cap finger tight. To properly align the thrust bearing, pry the crankshaft the extent of its axial travel several times, the last movement held toward the front of the engine, and torque the thrust bearing cap to specifications. Determine the crankshaft end-play (see below), and bring within tolerance with thrust washers.

PRY CRANKSHAFT FORWARD — THRUST BEARING

PRY CAP BACKWARD — THRUST BEARING

TIGHTEN CAP — THRUST BEARING

Aligning the thrust bearing

CYLINDER BLOCK RECONDITIONING

Procedure	Method

Measure crankshaft end-play:

NO. 3
MAIN BEARING
CAP

DIAL
INDICATOR

Checking crankshaft end-play with a dial indicator

Mount a dial indicator stand on the front of the block, with the dial indicator stem resting on the nose of the crankshaft, parallel to the crankshaft axis. Pry the crankshaft the extent of its travel rearward, and zero the indicator. Pry the crankshaft forward and record crankshaft end-play.

NOTE: *Crankshaft end-play also may be measured at the thrust bearing, using feeler gauges* (see illustration).

Checking crankshaft end-play with a feeler gauge

Install the pistons:

USE A SHORT
PIECE OF 3/8"
HOSE AS A
GUIDE

Tubing used to protect crankshaft journals and cylinder walls during piston installation

Press the upper connecting rod bearing halves into the connecting rods, and the lower halves into the connecting rod caps. Position the piston ring gaps according to specifications (see car section), and lubricate the pistons. Install a ring compressor on a piston, and press two long (8") pieces of plastic tubing over the rod bolts. Using the tubes as a guide, press the pistons into the bores and onto the crankshaft with a wooden hammer handle. After seating the rod on the crankshaft journal, remove the tubes and install the cap finger tight. Install the remaining pistons in the same manner. Invert the engine and check the bearing clearance at two points (90° apart) on each journal with Plastigage.

NOTE: *Do not turn the crankshaft with Plastigage installed.* If clearance is within tolerances, remove *all* Plastigage, thoroughly lubricate the journals, and torque the rod caps to specifications. If clearance is not within specifications, install different thickness bearing inserts and recheck.

CAUTION: *Never shim or file the connecting rods or caps.* Always install plastic tube sleeves over the rod bolts when the caps are not installed, to protect the crankshaft journals.

RING COMPRESSOR

Installing a piston

CYLINDER BLOCK RECONDITIONING

Procedure	Method
Check connecting rod side clearance: Checking connecting rod side clearance	Determine the clearance between the sides of the connecting rods and the crankshaft, using feeler gauges. If clearance is below the minimum tolerance, the rod may be machined to provide adequate clearance. If clearance is excessive, substitute an unworn rod, and recheck. If clearance is still outside specifications, the crankshaft must be welded and reground, or replaced.
Inspect the timing chain (or belt):	Visually inspect the timing chain for broken or loose links, and replace the chain if any are found. If the chain will flex sideways, it must be replaced. Install the timing chain as specified. Be sure the timing belt is not stretched, frayed or broken. NOTE: *If the original timing chain is to be reused, install it in its original position.*
Check timing gear backlash and runout (OHV engines): Checking camshaft gear backlash Checking camshaft gear runout	Mount a dial indicator with its stem resting on a tooth of the camshaft gear (as illustrated). Rotate the gear until all slack is removed, and zero the indicator. Rotate the gear in the opposite direction until slack is removed, and record gear backlash. Mount the indicator with its stem resting on the edge of the camshaft gear, parallel to the axis of the camshaft. Zero the indicator, and turn the camshaft gear one full turn, recording the runout. If either backlash or runout exceed specifications, replace the worn gear(s).

Completing the Rebuilding Process

Following the above procedures, complete the rebuilding process as follows:

Fill the oil pump with oil, to prevent cavitating (sucking air) on initial engine start up. Install the oil pump and the pickup tube on the engine. Coat the oil pan gasket as necessary, and install the gasket and the oil pan. Mount the flywheel and the crankshaft vibration damper or pulley on the crankshaft. NOTE: *Always use new bolts when installing the flywheel.*

Inspect the clutch shaft pilot bushing in the crankshaft. If the bushing is excessively worn, remove it with an expanding puller and a slide hammer, and tap a new bushing into place.

Position the engine, cylinder head side up. Lubricate the lifters, and install them into their bores. Install the cylinder head, and torque it as specified. Insert the pushrods (where applicable), and install the rocker shaft(s) (if so equipped) or position the rocker arms on the pushrods. Adjust the valves.

Install the intake and exhaust manifolds, the carburetor(s), the distributor and spark plugs. Adjust the point gap and the static ignition timing. Mount all accessories and install the engine in the car. Fill the radiator with coolant, and the crankcase with high quality engine oil.

Break-in Procedure

Start the engine, and allow it to run at low speed for a few minutes, while checking for leaks. Stop the engine, check the oil level, and fill as necessary. Restart the engine, and fill the cooling system to capacity. Check the point dwell angle and adjust the ignition timing and the valves. Run the engine at low to medium speed (800–2500 rpm) for approximately ½ hour, and retorque the cylinder head bolts. Road test the car, and check again for leaks.

Follow the manufacturer's recommended engine break-in procedure and maintenance schedule for new engines.

Troubleshooting is an exercise in logic. The experienced troubleshooter realizes an automobile is composed of a series of systems which many times are interrelated. Besides a fundamental understanding of the systems involved, effective trouble-shooting requires an attention to detail (making sure all wires are connected properly, etc.) and an awareness of the interrelated systems of the automobile (rapid front tire wear could indicate steering misalignment, possibly caused by a bent suspension part, etc.).

This section is designed to aid both amateur and experienced mechanics in troubleshooting all major automotive systems.

ENGINE
Gasoline Engine Troubleshooting

See applicable Car or Unit Repair section for specific service procedures

INDEX TO SYSTEMS

System	To Test	Group
Battery	Engine need not be running	1
Starting system	Engine need not be running	2
Primary electrical system	Engine need not be running	3
Secondary electrical system	Engine need not be running	4
Fuel system	Engine need not be running	5
Engine compression	Engine need not be running	6
Engine vacuum	Engine must be running	7
Secondary electrical system	Engine must be running	8
Valve train	Engine must be running	9
Exhaust system	Engine must be running	10
Cooling system	Engine must be running	11
Engine lubrication	Engine must be running	12

INDEX TO PROBLEMS

Problem Symptom	Begin at Specific Diagnosis, Number
Engine Won't Start	
Starter doesn't turn	1.1, 2.1
Starter turns, engine doesn't	2.1
Starter turns engine very slowly	1.1, 2.4
Starter turns engine normally	3.1, 4.1
Starter turns engine very quickly	6.1
Engine fires intermittently	4.1
Engine fires consistently	5.1, 6.1
Engine Runs Poorly	
Hard starting	3.1, 4.1, 5.1, 8.1
Rough idle	4.1, 5.1, 8.1
Stalling	3.1, 4.1, 5.1, 8.1
Engine dies at high speeds	4.1, 5.1
Hesitation (on acceleration from standing stop)	5.1, 8.1
Poor pickup	4.1, 5.1, 8.1
Lack of power	3.1, 4.1, 5.1, 8.1
Backfire through the carburetor	4.1, 8.1, 9.1
Backfire through the exhaust	4.1, 8.1, 9.1
Blue exhaust gases	6.1, 7.1
Black exhaust gases	5.1
Running on (after the ignition is shut off)	3.1, 8.1
Susceptible to moisture	4.1
Engine misfires under load	4.1, 7.1, 8.4, 9.1
Engine misfires at speed	4.1, 8.4
Engine misfires at idle	3.1, 4.1, 5.1, 7.1, 8.4

SAMPLE SECTION

Test and Procedure	Results and Indications	Proceed to
4.1 Check for spark: Hold each spark plug wire approximately ¼″ from ground with gloves or a heavy, dry rag. Crank the engine and observe the spark.	If no spark is evident	**4.2**
	If spark is good in some cases	**4.3**
	If spark is good in all cases	**4.6**

SPECIFIC DIAGNOSIS

This section is arranged so that following each test, instructions are given to proceed to another, until a problem is diagnosed.

SECTION 1—BATTERY

Test and Procedure	Results and Indications	Proceed to
1.1 Inspect the battery visually for case condition (corrosion, cracks) and water level.	If case is cracked, replace battery.	**1.4**
	If the case is intact, remove corrosion with a solution of baking soda and water. **(CAUTION: Do not get the solution into the battery).** Fill with water.	**1.2**

DIRT ON TOP OF BATTERY
CORROSION
PLUGGED VENT
LOOSE CABLE OR POSTS
CRACKS
LOW WATER LEVEL

Inspect the battery case

Test and Procedure	Results and Indications	Proceed to
1.2 Check the battery cable connections: Insert a screwdriver between the battery post and the cable clamp. Turn the headlights on high beam, and observe them as the screwdriver is gently twisted to ensure good metal to metal contact.	If the lights brighten, remove and clean the clamp and post; coat the post with petroleum jelly, install and tighten the clamp.	**1.4**
	If no improvement is noted	**1.3**

TESTING BATTERY CABLE CONNECTIONS USING A SCREWDRIVER

Test and Procedure	Results and Indications	Proceed to
1.3 Test the state of charge of the battery using an individual cell tester or hydrometer.	If indicated, charge the battery. **NOTE: If no obvious reason exists for the low state of charge (i.e., battery age, prolonged storage), proceed to:**	**1.4**

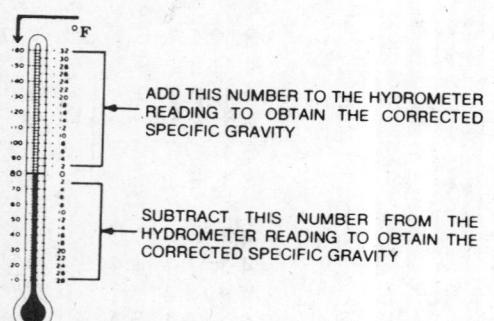

°F

ADD THIS NUMBER TO THE HYDROMETER READING TO OBTAIN THE CORRECTED SPECIFIC GRAVITY

SUBTRACT THIS NUMBER FROM THE HYDROMETER READING TO OBTAIN THE CORRECTED SPECIFIC GRAVITY

Specific Gravity (@ 80° F.)

Minimum	Battery Charge
1.260	100% Charged
1.230	75% Charged
1.200	50% Charged
1.170	25% Charged
1.140	Very Little Power Left
1.110	Completely Discharged

The effects of temperature on battery specific gravity (left) and amount of battery charge in relation to specific gravity (right)

Test and Procedure	Results and Indications	Proceed To
1.4 Visually inspect battery cables for cracking, bad connection to ground, or bad connection to starter.	If necessary, tighten connections or replace the cables.	2.1

SECTION 2—STARTING SYSTEM

Test and Procedure	Results and Indications	Proceed to
Note: Tests in Group 2 are performed with coil high tension lead disconnected to prevent accidental starting.		
2.1 Test the starter motor and solenoid: Connect a jumper from the battery post of the solenoid (or relay) to the starter post of the solenoid (or relay).	If starter turns the engine normally	2.2
	If the starter buzzes, or turns the engine very slowly	2.4
	If no response, replace the solenoid (or relay).	3.1
	If the starter turns, but the engine doesn't, ensure that the flywheel ring gear is intact. If the gear is undamaged, replace the starter drive.	3.1
2.2 Determine whether ignition override switches are functioning properly (clutch start switch, neutral safety switch), by connecting a jumper across the switch(es), and turning the ignition switch to "start".	If starter operates, adjust or replace switch.	3.1
	If the starter doesn't operate	2.3
2.3 Check the ignition switch "start" position: Connect a 12V test lamp or voltmeter between the starter post of the solenoid (or relay) and ground. Turn the ignition switch to the "start" position, and jiggle the key.	If the lamp doesn't light or the meter needle doesn't move when the switch is turned, check the ignition switch for loose connections, cracked insulation, or broken wires. Repair or replace as necessary.	3.1
	If the lamp flickers or needle moves when the key is jiggled, replace the ignition switch.	3.3

Checking the ignition switch "start" position

2.4 Remove and bench test the starter, according to specifications in the car section.	If the starter does not meet specifications, repair or replace as needed	3.1
	If the starter is operating properly	2.5

Test and Procedure	Results and Indications	Proceed To
2.5 Determine whether the engine can turn freely: Remove the spark plugs, and check for water in the cylinders. Check for water on the dipstick, or oil in the radiator. Attempt to turn the engine using an 18″ flex drive and socket on the crankshaft pulley nut or bolt.	If the engine will turn freely only with the spark plugs out, and hydrostatic lock (water in the cylinders) is ruled out, check valve timing.	9.2
	If engine will not turn freely, and it is known that the clutch and transmission are free, the engine must be disassembled for further evaluation.	**See Car Section**

SECTION 3—PRIMARY ELECTRICAL SYSTEM

Test and Procedure	Results and Indications	Proceed to
3.1 Check the ignition switch "on" position: Connect a jumper wire between the distributor side of the coil and ground, and a 12V test lamp between the switch side of the coil and ground. Remove the high tension lead from the coil. Turn the ignition switch on and jiggle the key.	If the lamp lights	3.2
	If the lamp flickers when the key is jiggled, replace the ignition switch.	3.3
	If the lamp doesn't light, check for loose or open connections. If none are found, remove the ignition switch and check for continuity. If the switch is faulty, replace it.	3.3

Checking the ignition switch "on" position

3.2 Check the ballast resistor or resistance wire for an open circuit, using an ohmmeter.	Replace the resistor or resistance wire if the resistance is zero. **NOTE: Some ignition systems have no ballast resistor.**	3.3

RESISTOR BLOCK

CALIBRATED RESISTANCE LEAD

Two types of resistors

3.3 On point-type ignition systems, visually inspect the breaker points for burning, pitting or excessive wear. Gray coloring of the point contact surfaces is normal. Rotate the crankshaft until the contact heel rests on a high point of the distributor cam and adjust the point gap to specifications. On electronic ignition models, remove the distributor cap and visually inspect the armature. Ensure that the armature pin is in place, and that the armature is on tight and rotates when the engine is cranked. Make sure there are no cracks, chips or rounded edges on the armature.	If the breaker points are intact, clean the contact surfaces with fine emery cloth, and adjust the point gap to specifications. If the points are worn, replace them. On electronic systems, replace any parts which appear defective. If condition persists	3.4

Test and Procedure	Results and Indications	Proceed To
3.4 On point-type ignition systems, connect a dwell-meter between the distributor primary lead and ground. Crank the engine and observe the point dwell angle. On electronic ignition systems, conduct a stator (magnetic pickup assembly) test. See Electronic Ignition Unit Repair Section.	On point-type systems, adjust the dwell angle if necessary. **NOTE: Increasing the point gap decreases the dwell angle and vice-versa.**	3.6
	If the dwell meter shows little or no reading	3.5
	On electronic ignition systems, if the stator is bad, replace the stator. If the stator is good, proceed to the other tests in The Electronic Ignition Unit Repair Section.	

Dwell is a function of point gap

Test and Procedure	Results and Indications	Proceed To
3.5 On the point-type ignition systems, check the condenser for short: connect an ohmeter across the condenser body and the pigtail lead.	If any reading other than infinite is noted, replace the condenser	3.6

Checking the condenser for short

Test and Procedure	Results and Indications	Proceed To
3.6 Test the coil primary resistance: On point-type ignition systems, connect an ohmmeter across the coil primary terminals, and read the resistance on the low scale. Note whether an external ballast resistor or resistance wire is used. On electronic ignition systems, test the coil primary resistance.	Point-type ignition coils utilizing ballast resistors or resistance wires should have approximately 1.0 ohms resistance. Coils with internal resistors should have approximately 4.0 ohms resistance. If values far from the above are noted, replace the coil.	4.1

Checking the coil primary resistance

SECTION 4—SECONDARY ELECTRICAL SYSTEM

Test and Procedure	Results and Indications	Proceed to
4.1 Check for spark: Hold each spark plug wire approximately ¼″ from ground with gloves or heavy, dry rag. Crank the engine, and observe the spark.	If no spark is evident	**4.2**
	If spark is good in some cylinders	**4.3**
	If spark is good in all cylinders	**4.6**

Check for spark at the plugs

Test and Procedure	Results and Indications	Proceed to
4.2 Check for spark at the coil high tension lead: Remove the coil high tension lead from the distributor and position it approximately ¼″ from ground. Crank the engine and observe spark. **CAUTION: This test should not be performed on engines equipped with electronic ignition.**	If the spark is good and consistent	**4.3**
	If the spark is good but intermittent, test the primary electrical system starting at 3.3.	**3.3**
	If the spark is weak or non-existent, replace the coil high tension lead, clean and tighten all connections and retest. If no improvement is noted	**4.4**

Test and Procedure	Results and Indications	Proceed to
4.3 Visually inspect the distributor cap and rotor for burned or corroded contacts, cracks, carbon tracks, or moisture. Also check the fit of the rotor on the distributor shaft (where applicable).	If moisture is present, dry thoroughly, and retest per 4.1.	**4.1**
	If burned or excessively corroded contacts, cracks, or carbon tracks are noted, replace the defective part(s) and retest per 4.1.	**4.1**
	If the rotor and cap appear intact, or are only slightly corroded, clean the contacts thoroughly (including the cap towers and spark plug wire ends) and retest per 4.1.	
	If the spark is good in all cases	**4.6**
	If the spark is poor in all cases	**4.5**

CORRODED OR LOOSE WIRE
HIGH RESISTANCE CARBON
EXCESSIVE WEAR OF BUTTON
ROTOR TIP BURNED AWAY

Inspect the distributor cap and rotor

Test and Procedure	Results and Indications
4.4 Check the coil secondary resistance: On point-type systems connect an ohmmeter across the distributor side of the coil and the coil tower. Read the resistance on the high scale of the ohmmeter. On electronic ignition systems, see The Electronic Ignition Unit Repair Section for specific tests.	The resistance of a satisfactory coil should be between 4,000 and 10,000 ohms. If resistance is considerably higher (i.e., 40,000 ohms) replace the coil and retest per 4.1. **NOTE: This does not apply to high performance coils.**

Testing the coil secondary resistance

Spark Plug Analysis

Normal

APPEARANCE

This plug is typical of one operating normally. The insulator nose varies from a light tan to grayish color with slight electrode wear. The presence of slight deposits is normal on used plugs and will have no adverse effect on engine performance. The spark plug heat range is correct for the engine and the engine is running normally.

CAUSE

Properly running engine

RECOMMENDATION

Before reinstalling this plug, the electrodes should be cleaned and filed square. Set the gap to specifications. If the plug has been in service for more than 10–12,000 miles, the entire set should probably be replaced with a fresh set of the same heat range.

Incorrect Heat Range

APPEARANCE

The effects of high temperature on a spark plug are indicated by clean white, often blistered insulator. This can also be accompanied by excessive wear of the electrode, and the absence of deposits.

CAUSE

Check for the correct spark plug heat range. A plug which is too hot for the engine can result in overheating. A car operated mostly at high speeds may require a colder plug. Also check ignition timing, cooling system level, fuel mixture and leaking intake manifold.

RECOMMENDATION

If all ignition and engine adjustments are known to be correct, and no other malfunction exists, install spark plugs one heat range colder.

Oil Deposits

APPEARANCE

The firing end of the plug is covered with a wet, oily coating.

CAUSE

The problem is poor oil control. On high mileage engines, oil is leaking past the rings or valve guides into the combustion chamber. A common cause is also a plugged PCV valve, and a ruptured fuel pump diaphragm can also cause this condition. Oil fouled plugs such as these are often found in new or recently overhauled engines, before normal oil control is achieved, and can be cleaned and reinstalled.

RECOMMENDATION

A hotter spark plug may temporarily relieve the problem, but the engine is probably in need of engine work.

Carbon Deposits

APPEARANCE

Carbon fouling is easily identified by the presence of dry, soft, black, sooty deposits.

CAUSE

Changing the heat range can often lead to carbon fouling, as can prolonged slow, stop-and-start driving. If the heat range is correct, carbon fouling can be attributed to a rich fuel mixture, sticking choke, clogged air cleaner, worn breaker points, retarded timing or low compression. If only one or two plugs are carbon fouled, check for corroded or cracked wires on the affected plugs. Also look for cracks in the distributor cap between the towers of affected cylinders.

RECOMMENDATION

After the problem is corrected, these plugs can be cleaned and reinstalled if not worn severely.

Ash Deposits

APPEARANCE

Ash deposits are characterized by light brown or white colored deposits crusted on the side or center electrodes. In some cases it may give the plug a rusty appearance.

CAUSE

Ash deposits are normally derived from oil or fuel additives burned during normal combustion. Normally they are harmless, though excessive amounts can cause misfiring. If deposits are excessive in short mileage, the valve guides may be worn. Reddish or rusty deposits are caused by manganese, an anti-knock compound replacing lead in unleaded gas. No engine malfunction is indicated.

RECOMMENDATION

Ash-fouled plugs can be cleaned, gapped and reinstalled.

Splash Deposits

APPEARANCE

Splash deposits occur in varying degrees as spotty deposits on the insulator.

CAUSE

These usually occur after a long delayed tune-up. By-products of combustion have accumulated on pistons and valves because of a delayed tune-up. Following tune-up or during hard acceleration, the deposits loosen and are thrown against the hot surface of the plug. If the deposits accumulate sufficiently, misfiring can occur.

RECOMMENDATION

These plugs can be cleaned, gapped and reinstalled.

High Speed Glazing

APPEARANCE

Glazing appears as shiny coating on the plug, either yellow or tan in color.

CAUSE

During hard, fast acceleration, plug temperatures rise suddenly. Deposits from normal combustion have no chance to fluff-off; instead, they melt on the insulator forming an electrically conductive coating which causes misfiring.

RECOMMENDATION

Glazed plugs are not easily cleaned. They should be replaced with a fresh set of plugs of the correct heat range. If the condition recurs, using plugs with a heat range one step colder may cure the problem.

Detonation

APPEARANCE

Detonation is usually characterized by a broken plug insulator.

CAUSE

A portion of the fuel charge will begin to burn spontaneously, from the increased heat following ignition. The explosion that results applies extreme pressure to engine components, frequently damaging spark plugs and pistons.

Detonation can result by over-advanced ignition timing, inferior gasoline (low octane) lean air fuel mixture, poor carburetion, engine lugging or an increase in compression ratio due to combustion chamber deposits or engine modification.

RECOMMENDATION

Replace the plugs after correcting the problem.

Test and Procedure	Results and Indications	Proceed To

4.5 Visually inspect the spark plug wires for cracking or brittleness. Ensure that no two wires are positioned so as to cause induction firing (adjacent and parallel). Remove each wire, one by one, and check resistance with an ohmmeter.

Replace any cracked or brittle wires. If any of the wires are defective, replace the entire set. Replace any wires with excessive resistance (over 8000 Ω per foot for suppression wire), and separate any wires that might cause induction firing.

4.6

Misfiring can be the result of spark plug leads to adjacent, consecutively firing cylinders running parallel and too close together

On point-type ignition systems, check the spark plug wires as shown. On electronic ignitions, do not remove the wire from the distributor cap terminal; instead, test through the cap

Spark plugs wires can be checked visually by bending them in a loop over your finger. This will reveal any cracks, burned or broken insulation. Any wire with cracked insulation should be replaced

4.6 Remove the spark plugs, noting the cylinders from which they were removed, and evaluate according to the chart in this section.

See chart.

See Chart

4.7 Reinstall the spark plugs.
NOTE: Modern electronic ignition systems generate extremely high voltages and high heats. The spark plug boots can soften and actually fuse to the ceramic insulator of the spark plugs after long exposures to high temperature and voltage. If this happens, the boot (and possibly the wire) must be replaced.

To help alleviate this condition, many manufacturers are recommending new silicone compounds to slow the deterioration. The compounds are generally nonconductive, protective lubricants that will not dry out, harden, or melt away. They form a weather-tight seal between rubber or plastic and metal and are found in several typical locations: Inside the insulating boots of spark plug wires, inside primary ignition circuit cable connectors, on distributor and rotor cap electrodes.

4.8

Test and Procedure	Results and Indications	Proceed To
4.8 Examine the location of all the plugs.	The following diagrams illustrate some of the conditions that the location of plugs will reveal.	4.9

Two adjacent plugs are fouled in a 6-cylinder engine, 4-cylinder engine or either bank of a V-8. This is probably due to a blown head gasket between the two cylinders.

An unbalanced carburetor is indicated. Following the fuel flow on this particular design shows that the cylinders fed by the right-hand barrel are fouled from overly rich mixture, while the cylinders fed by the left-hand barrel are normal.

Finding one plug overheated may indicate an intake manifold leak near the affected cylinder. If the overheated plug is the second of two adjacent, consecutively firing plugs, it could be the result of ignition cross-firing. Separating the leads to these two plugs will eliminate cross-fire.

The two center plugs in a 6-cylinder engine are fouled. Raw fuel may be "boiled" out of the carburetor into the intake manifold after the engine is shut-off. Stop-start driving can also foul the center plugs, due to overly rich mixture. Proper float level, a new float needle and seat or use of an insulating spacer may help this problem.

If the four rear plugs are overheated, a cooling system problem is suggested. A thorough cleaning of the cooling system may restore coolant circulation and cure the problem.

Occasionally, the two rear plugs in large, lightly used V-8's will become oil fouled. High oil consumption and smoky exhaust may also be noticed. It is probably due to plugged oil drain holes in the rear of the cylinder head, causing oil to be sucked in around the valve stems. This usually occurs in the rear cylinders first, because the engine slants that way.

Test and Procedure	Results and Indications	Proceed To
4.9 Determine the static ignition timing. Using the crankshaft pulley timing marks as a guide, locate top dead center on the compression stroke of the number one cylinder.	The rotor should be pointing toward the No. 1 tower in the distributor cap, and, on electronic ignitions, the armature spoke for that cylinder should be lined up with the stator.	4.10
4.10 Check coil polarity: Connect a voltmeter negative lead to the coil high tension lead, and the positive lead to ground. **NOTE: Reverse the hook-up for positive ground systems.** Crank the engine momentarily.	If the voltmeter reads up-scale, the polarity is correct.	5.1
	If the voltmeter reads down-scale, reverse the coil polarity (switch the primary leads).	5.1

Checking coil polarity

SECTION 5—FUEL SYSTEM

Test and Procedure	Results and Indications	Proceed to
5.1 Determine that the air filter is functioning efficiently: Hold paper elements up to a strong light, and attempt to see light through the filter.	Clean permanent air filters in solvent (or manufacturer's recommendation), and allow to dry. Replace paper elements through which light cannot be seen.	5.2
5.2 Determine whether a flooding condition exists: Flooding is identified by a strong gasoline odor, and excessive gasoline present in the throttle bore(s) of the carburetor.	If flooding is not evident	5.3
	If flooding is evident, permit the gasoline to dry for a few moments and restart.	
	If flooding doesn't recur	5.7
	If flooding is persistent	5.5

If the engine floods repeatedly, check the choke butterfly flap

5.3 Check that fuel is reaching the carburetor: Detach the fuel line at the carburetor inlet. Hold the end of the line in a cup (not styrofoam), and crank the engine.	If fuel flows smoothly	5.7
	If fuel doesn't flow	5.4
	If fuel flows erratically.	
	NOTE: Make sure that there is fuel in the tank	

Check the fuel pump by disconnecting the output line (fuel pump-to-carburetor) at the carburetor and operating the starter briefly

Test and Procedure	Results and Indications	Proceed To
5.4 Test the fuel pump: Disconnect all fuel lines from the fuel pump. Hold a finger over the input fitting, crank the engine (with electric pump, turn the ignition or pump on); and feel for suction.	If suction is evident, blow out the fuel line to the tank with low pressure compressed air until bubbling is heard from the fuel filler neck. Also blow out the carburetor fuel line (both ends disconnected).	5.7
	If no suction is evident, replace or repair the fuel pump. **NOTE: Repeated oil fouling of the spark plugs, or a no-start condition, could be the result of a ruptured vacuum booster pump diaphragm, through which oil or gasoline is being drawn into the intake manifold (where applicable).**	5.7
5.5 Occasionally, small specks of dirt will clog the small jets and orifices in the carburetor. With the engine cold, hold a flat piece of wood or similar material over the carburetor, where possible, and crank the engine.	If the engine starts, but runs roughly the engine is probably not run enough.	
	If the engine won't start.	5.9
5.6 Check the needle and seat: Tap the carburetor in the area of the needle and seat.	If flooding stops, a gasoline additive (e.g., Gumout) will often cure the problem.	5.7
	If flooding continues, check the fuel pump for excessive pressure at the carburetor (according to specifications). If the pressure is normal, the needle and seat must be removed and checked, and/or the float level adjusted.	5.7
5.7 Test the accelerator pump by looking into the throttle bores while operating the throttle.	If the accelerator pump appears to be operating normally	5.8
	If the accelerator pump is not operating, the pump must be reconditioned. Where possible, service the pump with the carburetor(s) installed on the engine. If necessary, remove the carburetor. Prior to removal	5.8

Check for gas at the carburetor by looking down the carburetor throat while someone moves the accelerator

Test and Procedure	Results and Indications	Proceed To
5.8 Determine whether the carburetor main fuel system is functioning: Spray a commercial starting fluid into the carburetor while attempting to start the engine.	If the engine starts, runs for a few seconds, and dies	5.9
	If the engine doesn't start	6.1
5.9 Uncommon fuel system malfunctions: See below:	If the problem is solved	6.1
	If the problem remains, remove and recondition the carburetor.	

Condition	Indication	Test	Prevailing Weather Conditions	Remedy
Vapor lock	Engine will not re-start shortly after running.	Cool the components of the fuel system until the engine starts. Vapor lock can be cured faster by draping a wet cloth over a mechanical fuel pump.	Hot to very hot	Ensure that the exhaust manifold heat control valve is operating. Check with the vehicle manufacturer for the recommended solution to vapor lock on the model in question.
Carburetor icing	Engine will not idle, stalls at low speeds.	Visually inspect the throttle plate area of the throttle bores for frost.	High humidity, 32–40° F.	Ensure that the exhaust manifold heat control valve is operating, and that the intake manifold heat riser is not blocked.
Water in the fuel	Engine sputters and stalls; may not start.	Pump a small amount of fuel into a glass jar. Allow to stand, and inspect for droplets of a layer of water.	High humidity, extreme temperature changes.	For droplets, use one or two cans of commercial gas line anti-freeze. For a layer of water, the tank must be drained, and the fuel lines blown out with compressed air.

SECTION 6—ENGINE COMPRESSION

Test and Procedure	Results and Indications	Proceed to
6.1 Test engine compression: Remove all spark plugs. Block the throttle wide open. Insert a compression gauge into a spark plug port, crank the engine to obtain the maximum reading, and record.	If compression is within limits on all cylinders	7.1
	If gauge reading is extremely low on all cylinders	6.2
	If gauge reading is low on one or two cylinders: (If gauge readings are identical and low on two or more adjacent cylinders, the head gasket must be replaced.)	6.2

Checking compression

6.2 Test engine compression (wet): Squirt approximately 30 cc. of engine oil into each cylinder, and retest per 6.1.	If the readings improve, worn or cracked rings or broken pistons are indicated:	See Car Section
	If the readings do not improve, burned or excessively carboned valves or a jumped timing chain are indicated.	7.1
	NOTE: A jumped timing chain is often indicated by difficult cranking.	

SECTION 7—ENGINE VACUUM

Test and Procedure	Results and Indications	Proceed to
7.1 Attach a vacuum gauge to the intake manifold beyond the throttle plate. Start the engine, and observe the action of the needle over the range of engine speeds.	See below.	See below

INDICATION: Normal engine in good condition

Proceed to: 8.1

Normal engine

Gauge reading: Steady, from 17–22 in./Hg.

INDICATION: Sticking valves or ignition miss

Proceed to: 9.1, 8.3

Sticking valves

Gauge reading: Intermittent fluctuation at idle

INDICATION: Late ignition or valve timing, low compression, stuck throttle valve, leaking carburetor or manifold gasket

Proceed to: 6.1

Incorrect valve timing

Gauge reading: Low (10–15 in./Hg) but steady

INDICATION: Improper carburetor adjustment or minor intake leak.

Proceed to: 7.2

Carburetor requires adjustment

Gauge reading: Drifting needle

INDICATION: Ignition miss, blown cylinder head gasket, leaking valve or weak valve spring

Proceed to: 8.3, 6.1

Blown head gasket

Gauge reading: Needle fluctuates as engine speed increases

INDICATION: Burnt valve or faulty valve clearance: Needle will fall when defective valve operates

Proceed to: 9.1

Burnt or leaking valves

Gauge reading: Steady needle, but drops regularly

INDICATION: Choked muffler, excessive back pressure in system

Proceed to: 10.1

Clogged exhaust system

Gauge reading: Gradual drop in reading at idle

INDICATION: Worn valve guides

Proceed to: 9.1

Worn valve guides

Gauge reading: Needle vibrates excessively at idle, but steadies as engine speed increases

White pointer = steady gauge hand

Black pointer = fluctuating gauge hand

 U 288

Test and Procedure	Results and Indications	Proceed To
7.2 Attach a vacuum gauge per 7.1, and test for an intake manifold leak. Squirt a small amount of oil around the intake manifold gaskets, carburetor gaskets, plugs and fittings. Observe the action of the vacuum gauge.	If the reading improves, replace the indicated gasket, or seal the indicated fitting or plug:	8.1
	If the reading remains low:	7.3
7.3 Test all vacuum hoses and accessories for leaks as described in 7.2. Also check the carburetor body (dashpots, automatic choke mechanism, throttle shafts) for leaks in the same manner.	If the reading improves, service or replace the offending part(s):	8.1
	If the reading remains low:	6.1

SECTION 8—SECONDARY ELECTRICAL SYSTEM

Test and Procedure	Results and Indications	Proceed to
8.1 Remove the distributor cap and check to make sure that the rotor turns when the engine is cranked. Visually inspect the distributor components.	Clean, tighten or replace any components which appear defective.	8.2
8.2 Connect a timing light (per manufacturer's recommendation) and check the dynamic ignition timing. Disconnect and plug the vacuum hose(s) to the distributor if specified, start the engine, and observe the timing marks at the specified engine speed.	If the timing is not correct, adjust to specifications by rotating the distributor in the engine: (Advance timing by rotating distributor opposite normal direction of rotor rotation, retard timing by rotating distributor in same direction as rotor rotation.)	8.3
8.3 Check the operation of the distributor advance mechanism(s): To test the mechanical advance, disconnect the vacuum lines from the distributor advance unit and observe the timing marks with a timing light as the engine speed is increased from idle. If the mark moves smoothly, without hesitation, it may be assumed that the mechanical advance is functioning properly. To test vacuum advance and/or retard systems, alternately crimp and release the vacuum line, and observe the timing mark for movement. If movement is noted, the system is operating.	If the systems are functioning	8.4
	If the systems are not functioning, remove the distributor, and test on a distributor tester.	8.4
8.4 Locate an ignition miss: With the engine running, remove each spark plug wire, one at a time, until one is found that doesn't cause the engine to roughen and slow down. **CAUTION: Do not pull on the wire to remove the boot from the plug. Be sure your hand is insulated from the wire.**	When the missing cylinder is identified	4.1

SECTION 9—VALVE TRAIN

Test and Procedure	Results and Indications	Proceed to
9.1 Evaluate the valve train: Remove the valve cover, and ensure that the valves are adjusted to specifications. A mechanic's stethoscope may be used to aid in the diagnosis of the valve train. By pushing the probe on or near push rods or rockers, valve noise often can be isolated. A timing light also may be used to diagnose valve problems. Connect the light according to manufacturer's recommendations, and start the engine. Vary the firing moment of the light by increasing the engine speed (and therefore the ignition advance), and moving the trigger from cylinder to cylinder. Observe the movement of each valve.	Sticking valves or erratic valve train motion can be observed with the timing light. The cylinder head must be disassembled for repairs.	**See Car Section**
9.2 Check the valve timing: Locate top dead center of the No. 1 piston, and install a degree wheel or tape on the crankshaft pulley or damper with zero corresponding to an index mark on the engine. Rotate the crankshaft in its direction of rotation, and observe the opening of the No. 1 cylinder intake valve. The opening should correspond with the correct mark on the degree wheel according to specifications.	If the timing is not correct, the timing cover must be removed for further investigation.	**See Car Section**

SECTION 10—EXHAUST SYSTEM

Test and Procedure	Results and Indications	Proceed to
10.1 Determine whether the exhaust manifold heat control valve is operating: Operate the valve by hand to determine whether it is free to move. If the valve is free, run the engine to operating temperature and observe the action of the valve, to ensure that it is opening.	If the valve sticks, spray it with a suitable solvent, open and close the valve to free it, and retest. If the valve functions properly	10.2
	If the valve does not free, or does not operate, replace the valve.	10.2
10.2 Ensure that there are no exhaust restrictions: Visually inspect the exhaust system for kinks, dents, or crushing. Also note that gases are flowing freely from the tailpipe at all engine speeds, indicating no restriction in the muffler or resonator.	Replace any damaged portion of the system.	11.1

SECTION 11—COOLING SYSTEM

Test and Procedure	Results and Indications	Proceed to
11.1 Visually inspect the fan belt for glazing, cracks, and fraying, and replace if necessary. Tighten the belt so that the longest span has approximately ½″ play at its midpoint under thumb pressure (see Maintenance Section).	Replace or tighten the fan belt as necessary.	**11.2**

Checking belt tension

Test and Procedure	Results and Indications	Proceed to
11.2 Check the fluid level of the cooling system.	If full or slightly low, fill as necessary.	**11.5**
	If extremely low	**11.3**
11.3 Visually inspect the external portions of the cooling system (radiator, radiator hoses, thermostat elbow, water pump seals, heater hoses, etc.) for leaks. If none are found, pressurize the cooling system to 14–15 psi.	If cooling system holds the pressure	**11.5**
	If cooling system loses pressure rapidly, reinspect external parts of the system for leaks under pressure. If none are found, check dipstick for coolant in crankcase. If no coolant is present, but pressure loss continues	**11.4**
	If coolant is evident in crankcase, remove cylinder head(s), and check gasket(s). If gaskets are intact, block and cylinder head(s) should be checked for cracks or holes.	
	If the gasket(s) is blown, replace, and purge the crankcase of coolant.	**12.6**
	NOTE: Occasionally, due to atmospheric and driving conditions, condensation of water can occur in the crankcase. This causes the oil to appear milky white. To remedy, run the engine until hot, and change the oil and oil filter.	
11.4 Check for combustion leaks into the cooling system: Pressurize the cooling system as above. Start the engine, and observe the pressure gauge. If the needle fluctuates, remove each spark plug wire, one at a time, noting which cylinder(s) reduce or eliminate the fluctuation.	Cylinders which reduce or eliminate the fluctuation, when the spark plug wire is removed, are leaking into the cooling system. Replace the head gasket on the affected cylinder bank(s).	**See Car Section**

Pressurizing the cooling system

Test and Procedure	Results and Indications	Proceed To
11.5 Check the radiator pressure cap: Attach a radiator pressure tester to the radiator cap (wet the seal prior to installation). Quickly pump up the pressure, noting the point at which the cap releases.	If the cap releases within ±1 psi of the specified rating, it is operating properly.	**11.6**
	If the cap releases at more than ±1 psi of the specified rating, it should be replaced.	**11.6**

Checking radiator pressure cap

Test and Procedure	Results and Indications	Proceed To
11.6 Test the thermostat: Start the engine cold, remove the radiator cap, and insert a thermometer into the radiator. Allow the engine to idle. After a short while, there will be a sudden, rapid increase in coolant temperature. The temperature at which this sharp rise stops is the thermostat opening temperature.	If the thermostat opens at or about the specified temperature	**11.7**
	If the temperature doesn't increase (If the temperature increases slowly and gradually, replace the thermostat.)	**11.7**
11.7 Check the water pump: Remove the thermostat elbow and the thermostat, disconnect the coil high tension lead (to prevent starting), and crank the engine momentarily.	If coolant flows, replace the thermostat and retest per 11.6.	**11.6**
	If coolant doesn't flow, reverse flush the cooling system to alleviate any blockage that might exist. If system is not blocked, and coolant will not flow, replace the water pump.	**See Car Section**

SECTION 12—LUBRICATION

Test and Procedure	Results and Indications	Proceed to
12.1 Check the oil pressure gauge or warning light: If the gauge shows low pressure, or the light is on for no obvious reason, remove the oil pressure sender. Install an accurate oil pressure gauge and run the engine momentarily.	If oil pressure builds normally, run engine for a few moments to determine that it is functioning normally, and replace the sender.	—
	If the pressure remains low	12.2
	If the pressure surges	12.3
	If the oil pressure is zero	12.3
12.2 Visually inspect the oil: If the oil is watery or very thin, milky, or foamy, replace the oil and oil filter.	If the oil is normal	12.3
	If after replacing oil the pressure remains low	12.3
	If after replacing oil the pressure becomes normal	—
12.3 Inspect the oil pressure relief valve and spring, to ensure that it is not sticking or stuck. Remove and thoroughly clean the valve, spring, and the valve body.	If the oil pressure improves	—
	If no improvement is noted	12.4

Test and Procedure	Results and Indications	Proceed To
12.4 Check to ensure that the oil pump is not cavitating (sucking air instead of oil): See that the crankcase is neither over nor underfull, and that the pickup in the sump is in the proper position and free from sludge.	Fill or drain the crankcase to the proper capacity, and clean the pickup screen in solvent if necessary. If no improvement is noted	**12.5**
12.5 Inspect the oil pump drive and the oil pump:	If the pump drive or the oil pump appear to be defective, service as necessary and retest per 12.1. If the pump drive and pump appear to be operating normally, the engine should be disassembled to determine where blockage exists.	**12.1**
12.6 Purge the engine of ethylene glycol coolant: Competely drain the crankcase and the oil filter. Obtain a commercial butyl cellosolve base solvent, designated for this purpose, and follow the instructions precisely. Following this, install a new oil filter and refill the crankcase with the proper weight oil. The next oil and filter change should follow shortly thereafter (1000 miles).		

Diesel Engine Troubleshooting

NOTE: The following troubleshooting procedures cover problems usually associated with diesel engines. Those problems common to both gasoline and diesel engines are covered in the gasoline engine troubleshooting procedures.

INDEX TO PROBLEMS

SECTION 1—Fuel System

Test and Procedure		Results and Indication	Proceed To
1.1a	Check for pressure at the outlet of the feed pump	If pressure exists, there is a clog in the supply line. Clean or replace it. If there is little or no pressure at the outlet, the filter is clogged. Clean or replace the filter. If the filter is clear, the feed pump piston is inoperative. Relace it.	1.1b
1.1b	Check the feed pump valves	If the inlet and outlet valves do not operate, the check valve or spring is broken. Replace it.	1.2a
1.2a	Check for fuel leakage at the overflow or return line	A clogged filter can result in high pressure causing leakage. Replace the filter.	1.2b
1.2b	Check for fuel in the filter leaking at the overflow valve	If leakage is found, the overflow valve is damaged. Replace it.	1.2c
1.2c	Check for leakage at the injection pump overflow valve	If leakage is found, it is caused by: damaged overflow valve, sticking plunger, or sticking delivery valve. Replace the defective part(s).	1.2d
1.2d	Check the injection pump plunger feed pressures.	If pressure at the plungers is low, replace the plunger(s).	1.2e

Test and Procedure		Results and Indication	Proceed To
1.2e	Check to make sure the injection pump is operating	An inoperative pump is caused by: a damaged or missing shaft key, or a damaged drive gear train.	1.3a
1.3a	Check that the pump timing marks are correctly aligned in the gear train	Incorrect timing marks alignment must be corrected.	1.3b
1.3b	Check that the injection pump is properly mounted	Remove and install the pump correctly	1.4a
1.4a	Install an injection nozzle on a tester and make sure that fuel is continuously ejected	A broken or intermittent stream is caused by a damaged spring or a sticking nozzle needle	1.4b
1.4b	With the nozzle on the tester as in 1.4a, check that shutoff is clean with no dribble or afterdrip	Dribble is caused by a defective nozzle valve seat. Replace the nozzle.	1.4c
1.4c	Using a tester, check injection pressure	Low pressure is a result of a weak spring. Replace the spring or adjust the initial injection pressure.	1.5a
1.5a	See 1.2a	Proceed as in 1.2a	1.5b
1.5b	Check for water in the fuel	Drain and clean the tank	1.5c
1.5c	Check for air in the fuel lines	Air can be introduced through a damaged fuel inlet line, a loose inlet line connector or a damaged gasket	1.5d
1.5d	Check for insufficient fuel feed	Insufficient fuel feed is caused by: a damaged feed pump, a clogged tank vent, or a clogged filter. Replace or repair as necessary.	1.6a
1.6a	Check the control rack action for smooth operation	Uneven control rack operation is caused by: a sticking plunger, improper meshing of the rack and pinion, poor seating of the plunger spring, insufficient clearance between the plunger and lower spring seat, or an overly tight delivery valve holder. Replace or adjust as necessary.	1.6b
1.6b	Check that the injection pump discharge is uniform	If the output is uneven, adjust as necessary	1.6c
1.6c	Check that the injection pump discharge volume is adequate	An inadequate discharge volume is caused by a worn plunger or a broken spring	1.6d
1.6d	Check for even low speed engine performance	If the engine performs unevenly or erratically at low speed only, a worn feed pump piston or defective feed pump valve is the cause.	1.6e
1.6e	Check for smooth engine operation throughout the operating range	This problem is usually caused by mechanical governor defects such as: a defective low speed spring, defective damper spring, or excessive friction among moving parts. Replace the defective parts.	1.6f
1.6f	Check the injectors on a tester	Improper nozzle operation should be corrected accordingly	1.7a
1.7a	Check the operating governor	A broken or weak spring in the governor will prevent full speed operation.	1.7b
1.7b	Check the injectors on a tester for a drop in injector output	A drop in output is caused by a sticking needle or a dirty nozzle. Replace or clean as necessary.	1.8a

Test and Procedure		Results and Indications	Proceed To
1.8a	Check the injection pump for proper rack and pinion action	A catching or dirty rack and pinion will cause overspeeding.	1.8b
1.8b	Check the governor adjustment	An improperly adjusted governor will cause overspeeding. Adjust.	1.9a
1.9a	Check the injection pump output	Low output can be caused by: Incorrect adjustment—Adjust Loose delivery valve—Tighten Broken delivery valve seal—Replace Poor valve seat contact—Replace Broken/weak delivery valve spring—Replace	1.9b
1.9b	Check for unusual noise at the injection pump	A noisy pump is an indication of a broken plunger spring	1.9c
1.9c	Check plunger operation	A sticking injection pump plunger will cause power loss. Replace.	1.9d
1.9d	Check the injection timer	A lag in injection timing is caused by large clearances in the timer due to wear. Replace.	1.9e
1.9e	Check for air or water in the fuel	Bleed the air or drain the fuel and clean the tank and lines	1.9f
1.9f	Check the injection timing	Readjust timing if necessary	1.10a
1.10a	Check the initial injection timing	Adjust if necessary	1.10b
1.10b	Check the injection pressure	High pressure will cause knock. Adjust as necessary	1.10c
1.10c	Check the injector nozzle	A clogged nozzle causes knock. Clean or replace the nozzle.	1.11a
1.11a	Check the injection pump output and timing	Excessive output, coupled with incorrect timing causes knock. Adjust as necessary	1.11b
1.11b	Check the delivery valve seat	Replace a defective seat	1.11c
1.11c	Check the pump plungers	Replace badly worn plungers	1.11d
1.11d	Check injector opening pressure on a tester	Adjust as necessary	1.11e
1.11e	Check the injector	Replace a broken nozzle spring or sticking needle.	

SECTION 2—ENGINE MECHANICAL

Test and Procedure		Results and Indications	Proceed To
2.1a	Check for piston seizing	Seized pistons are caused by low oil pressure, oil breakdown, or overheating. Replace the pistons and liners.	2.1b
2.1b	Check for a damaged flywheel ring gear	A damaged ring gear will cause poor meshing with the starter. Replace the ring gear.	2.1c
2.1c	Make a compression check	Low compression can be caused by: sticking rings, worn rings, worn liners. Replace the rings or liners.	2.2a
2.2a	A knocking noise at idle or during acceleration can be caused by a variety of wear problems.	Use a stethoscope or similar listening device to try to pinpoint the source of the noise. Among other reasons for knocking are: piston pins, rod bearings, loose rod caps, crankshaft journals and/or bearings, crankshaft thrust washer. Replace any worn parts.	2.2b
2.2b	An infrequently encountered noise is a continuous growl during acceleration	This problem is usually caused by problems in the engine timing gears. Poor contact, excessive backlash or loose gears are usually at fault.	2.2c
2.2c	Intermittent noises are the hardest to find. They are usually caused by broken moving parts.	Check the gear train for a chipped or cracked gear; the oil pan for broken parts or foreign objects or the cylinder head for a broken valve or valve spring.	2.3
2.3	Check for oil in the combustion chambers	Oil entering the combustion chambers will cause the engine to overspeed if the amount of oil is too great, or run unevenly. Check for broken or sticking rings, bad head gasket(s) or worn valve guides.	2.4
2.4	Check the compression	Low compression is the main cause of power loss. The main causes for low compression are: worn rings or liners, cracked valves, warped head or block, and bad head gasket.	2.5
2.5	A large amount of black exhaust is caused by low compression	See 2.4 above	2.6
2.6	If the engine stops suddenly during operation, the cause is usually sudden damage	Check the pistons, main bearings or rod bearings for lack of lubrication. A seized camshaft is also a result of low or no lubrication. Check the timing gears for damage.	2.7
2.7	Check for excessive clearance between the bearings and journals on both the mains and rod bearings. Check the oil pressure.	Replace as necessary. Replace the pump as necessary.	2.8
2.8	Aside from the usual leaking gasket problems, check the condition of the combustion chamber O-rings.	Replace as necessary	2.9
2.9	Compression leakage is usually caused by a seal defect between the head and the block	Check the head gasket; check for loose head bolts; check for head or block warpage. Replace or repair as necessary.	

Engine Overheating Troubleshooting

NOTE: THIS CHART IS DESIGNED TO AID IN THE DIAGNOSIS AND CORRECTION OF ENGINE OVERHEATING PROBLEMS. THE POSSIBILITY OF MULTIPLE MALFUNCTIONS SHOULD NOT BE OVERLOOKED.

OVERHEAT SHOWN ON GAUGE, WITH BOILING, COOLANT LOSS OR STEAM

CHECK RADIATOR FAN MOTOR, RELAY AND FAN SWITCH

CHECK ALTERNATOR AND WATER PUMP BELT TENSION

ADJUST/REPLACE BELT AS NECESSARY

CHECK FOR RESTRICTED AIR FLOW THROUGH RADIATOR AND/OR AIR CONDITIONING CONDENSER

RESTRICTED AIR FLOW – BUGS, LEAVES, GRASS, BUG SCREEN, NONPRODUCTION BUMPER GUARDS. FOG LIGHTS

NO RESTRICTION

CHECK ENGINE OIL LEVEL – CHANGE OR ADD AS REQUIRED

CLEAN FINS OF RADIATOR AND/OR AIR CONDITIONING CONDENSER, REMOVE OR REPOSITION ACCESSORIES

CHECK LEVEL OF COOLANT IN RESERVE TANK AND RADIATOR TANK

COOLANT LEVEL LOW

CHECK COOLANT FOR EVIDENCE OF FOAMING

IN RADIATOR TOP TANK NOT IN RESERVE TANK

IN COOLANT RESERVE TANK

CHECK RESERVE TANK SYSTEM FOR LEAKS

ADD COOLANT

COOLANT LEVEL NOT LOW

CHECK COOLANT ANTI-FREEZE PROTECTION

PROTECTION O.K. TO AT LEAST −34°F

NO ANTI-FREEZE OR INADEQUATE ANTI-FREEZE PROTECTION

ADD ANTI-FREEZE OR FLUSH SYSTEM AND REFILL WITH 50/50 SOLUTION

CHECK FOR MISSING AND/OR OUT OF PLACE AIR SEALS

ALL AIR SEALS IN PLACE

AIR SEALS MISSING AND/OR OUT OF PLACE

REPLACE MISSING SEALS AND/OR ADJUST MISPLACED SEALS

OVERHEAT SHOWN ON GAUGE ONLY NO COOLANT LOSS

CHECK GAUGE AND SENDING UNIT

REPAIR AS NECESSARY

Engine Overheating Troubleshooting

NO EVIDENCE OF EXCESSIVE FOAMING

CHECK SYSTEM FOR LEAKS, INCLUDING RADIATOR CAP, PRESSURE TEST COOLING SYSTEM

EXCESSIVE FOAMING EVIDENT

DRAIN AND FLUSH COOLING SYSTEM REFILL WITH NEW 50/50 SOLUTION

SYSTEM DOES NOT LEAK

SYSTEM LEAKS

REPAIR LEAKS AS NECESSARY

CIRCULATION POOR

CHECK FOR COLLAPSED LOWER RADIATOR HOSE

CHECK COOLANT CIRCULATION IN RADIATOR OR UPPER RADIATOR HOSE

CIRCULATION GOOD

CORRECT OR REPAIR AS NECESSARY

CHECK IGNITION TIMING

CHECK EXHAUST HEAT VALVE FOR FREE MOVEMENT

HOSE NOT COLLAPSED

VISUALLY CHECK RADIATOR TUBES FOR EVIDENCE OF PLUGGED OR RESTRICTED RADIATOR

HOSE COLLAPSED

REPLACE HOSE

PLUGGED RADIATOR OR RESTRICTED TUBES EVIDENT

REMOVE RADIATOR AND THOROUGHLY CLEAN BY RODDING. DIP IN 30/70 SOLDER

NO EVIDENCE OF PLUGGED RADIATOR

THERMOSTAT FAULTY

TEST THERMOSTAT

REPLACE THERMOSTAT

THERMOSTAT OK

CHECK WATER PUMP IMPELLER FOR LOOSENESS

IMPELLER LOOSE

REPLACE WATER PUMP

IMPELLER NOT LOOSE

REMOVE HEAD AND CLEAN OUT BLOCKED PASSAGES AS REQUIRED

CHECK HEAD AND/OR BLOCK FOR INTERNAL RESTRICTION

Low Engine Temperature Troubleshooting

Metric Tables

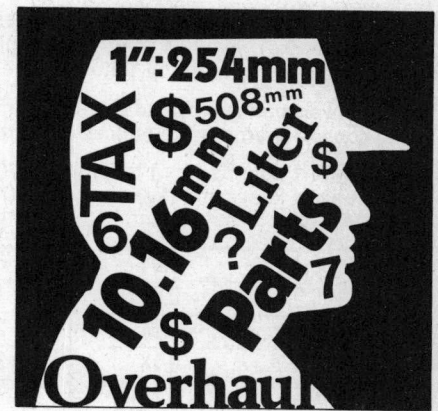

SI METRIC TABLES

The following tables are given in SI (International System) metric units. SI units replace both customary (English) and the older gavimetric units. The use of SI units as a new world-wide standard was set by the International Committee of Weights and Measures in 1960. SI has since been adopted by most countries as their national standard.

These tables are general conversion tables which will allow you to convert customary units, which appear in the text, into SI units.

The following are a list of SI units and the customary units, used in this book, which they replace:

To measure:	Use SI units:	Which replace (customary units):
mass	kilograms (kg)	pounds (lbs)
temperature	Celsius (°C)	Fahrenheit (°F)
length	millimeters (mm)	inches (in.)
force	newtons (N)	pounds force (lbs)
capacities	liters (l)	pints/quarts/gallons (pts/qts/gals)
torque	newton-meters (N·m)	foot pounds (ft lbs)
pressure	kilopascals (kPa)	pounds per square inch (psi)
volume	cubic centimeters (cm³)	cubic inches (cu in.)
power	kilowatts (kW)	horsepower (hp)

If you have had any prior experience with the metric system, you may have noticed units in this chart which are not familiar to you. This is because, in some cases, SI units differ from the older gravimetric units which they replace. For example, newtons (N) replace kilograms (kg) as a force unit, kilopascals (kPa) replace atmospheres or bars as a unit of pressure, and, although the units are the same, the name Celsius replaces centigrade for temperature measurement.

If you are not using the SI tables, have a look at them anyway; you will be seeing a lot more of them in the future.

METRIC TABLES

ENGLISH TO METRIC CONVERSION: MASS (WEIGHT)

Current **mass** measurement is expressed in pounds and ounces (lbs. & ozs.). The metric unit of mass (or weight) is the kilogram (kg). Even although this table does not show conversion of masses (weights) larger than 15 lbs, it is easy to calculate larger units by following the data immediately below.

To convert ounces (oz.) to grams (g): multiply th number of ozs. by 28
To convert grams (g) to ounces (oz.): multiply the number of grams by .035

To convert pounds (lbs.) to kilograms (kg): multiply the number of lbs. by .45
To convert kilograms (kg) to pounds (lbs.): multiply the number of kilograms by 2.2

lbs	kg	lbs	kg	oz	kg	oz	kg
0.1	0.04	0.9	0.41	0.1	0.003	0.9	0.024
0.2	0.09	1	0.4	0.2	0.005	1	0.03
0.3	0.14	2	0.9	0.3	0.008	2	0.06
0.4	0.18	3	1.4	0.4	0.011	3	0.08
0.5	0.23	4	1.8	0.5	0.014	4	0.11
0.6	0.27	5	2.3	0.6	0.017	5	0.14
0.7	0.32	10	4.5	0.7	0.020	10	0.28
0.8	0.36	15	6.8	0.8	0.023	15	0.42

ENGLISH TO METRIC CONVERSION: TEMPERATURE

To convert Fahrenheit (°F) to Celsius (°C): take number of °F and subtract 32; multiply result by 5; divide result by 9

To convert Celsius (°C) to Fahrenheit (°F): take number of °C and multiply by 9; divide result by 5; add 32 to total

Fahrenheit (F)		Celsius (C)		Fahrenheit (F)		Celsius (C)		Fahrenheit (F)		Celsius (C)	
°F	°C	°C	°F	°F	°C	°C	°F	°F	°C	°C	°F
−40	−40	−38	−36.4	80	26.7	18	64.4	215	101.7	80	176
−35	−37.2	−36	−32.8	85	29.4	20	68	220	104.4	85	185
−30	−34.4	−34	−29.2	90	32.2	22	71.6	225	107.2	90	194
−25	−31.7	−32	−25.6	95	35.0	24	75.2	230	110.0	95	202
−20	−28.9	−30	−22	100	37.8	26	78.8	235	112.8	100	212
−15	−26.1	−28	−18.4	105	40.6	28	82.4	240	115.6	105	221
−10	−23.3	−26	−14.8	110	43.3	30	86	245	118.3	110	230
−5	−20.6	−24	−11.2	115	46.1	32	89.6	250	121.1	115	239
0	−17.8	−22	−7.6	120	48.9	34	93.2	255	123.9	120	248
1	−17.2	−20	−4	125	51.7	36	96.8	260	126.6	125	257
2	−16.7	−18	−0.4	130	54.4	38	100.4	265	129.4	130	266
3	−16.1	−16	3.2	135	57.2	40	104	270	132.2	135	275
4	−15.6	−14	6.8	140	60.0	42	107.6	275	135.0	140	284
5	−15.0	−12	10.4	145	62.8	44	112.2	280	137.8	145	293
10	−12.2	−10	14	150	65.6	46	114.8	285	140.6	150	302
15	−9.4	−8	17.6	155	68.3	48	118.4	290	143.3	155	311
20	−6.7	−6	21.2	160	71.1	50	122	295	146.1	160	320
25	−3.9	−4	24.8	165	73.9	52	125.6	300	148.9	165	329
30	−1.1	−2	28.4	170	76.7	54	129.2	305	151.7	170	338
35	1.7	0	32	175	79.4	56	132.8	310	154.4	175	347
40	4.4	2	35.6	180	82.2	58	136.4	315	157.2	180	356
45	7.2	4	39.2	185	85.0	60	140	320	160.0	185	365
50	10.0	6	42.8	190	87.8	62	143.6	325	162.8	190	374
55	12.8	8	46.4	195	90.6	64	147.2	330	165.6	195	383
60	15.6	10	50	200	93.3	66	150.8	335	168.3	200	392
65	18.3	12	53.6	205	96.1	68	154.4	340	171.1	205	401
70	21.1	14	57.2	210	98.9	70	158	345	173.9	210	410
75	23.9	16	60.8	212	100.0	75	167	350	176.7	215	414

ENGLISH TO METRIC CONVERSION: LENGTH

To convert inches (ins.) to millimeters (mm): multiply number of inches by 25.4

To convert millimeters (mm) to inches (ins.): multiply number of millimeters by .04

Inches	Decimals	Milli-meters	Inches to millimeters inches	mm	Inches	Decimals	Milli-meters	Inches to millimeters inches	mm
	1/64 0.051625	0.3969	0.0001	0.00254		33/64 0.515625	13.0969	0.6	15.24
1/32	0.03125	0.7937	0.0002	0.00508	17/32	0.53125	13.4937	0.7	17.78
	3/64 0.046875	1.1906	0.0003	0.00762		35/64 0.546875	13.8906	0.8	20.32
1/16	0.0625	1.5875	0.0004	0.01016	9/16	0.5625	14.2875	0.9	22.86
	5/64 0.078125	1.9844	0.0005	0.01270		37/64 0.578125	14.6844	1	25.4
3/32	0.09375	2.3812	0.0006	0.01524	19/32	0.59375	15.0812	2	50.8
	7/64 0.109375	2.7781	0.0007	0.01778		39/64 0.609375	15.4781	3	76.2
1/8	0.125	3.1750	0.0008	0.02032	5/8	0.625	15.8750	4	101.6
	9/64 0.140625	3.5719	0.0009	0.02286		41/64 0.640625	16.2719	5	127.0
5/32	0.15625	3.9687	0.001	0.0254	21/32	0.65625	16.6687	6	152.4
	11/64 0.171875	4.3656	0.002	0.0508		43/64 0.671875	17.0656	7	177.8
3/16	0.1875	4.7625	0.003	0.0762	11/16	0.6875	17.4625	8	203.2
	13/64 0.203125	5.1594	0.004	0.1016		45/64 0.703125	17.8594	9	228.6
7/32	0.21875	5.5562	0.005	0.1270	23/32	0.71875	18.2562	10	254.0
	15/64 0.234375	5.9531	0.006	0.1524		47/64 0.734375	18.6531	11	279.4
1/4	0.25	6.3500	0.007	0.1778	3/4	0.75	19.0500	12	304.8
	17/64 0.265625	6.7469	0.008	0.2032		49/64 0.765625	19.4469	13	330.2
9/32	0.28125	7.1437	0.009	0.2286	25/32	0.78125	19.8437	14	355.6
	19/64 0.296875	7.5406	0.01	0.254		51/64 0.796875	20.2406	15	381.0
5/16	0.3125	7.9375	0.02	0.508	13/16	0.8125	20.6375	16	406.4
	21/64 0.328125	8.3344	0.03	0.762		53/64 0.828125	21.0344	17	431.8
11/32	0.34375	8.7312	0.04	1.016	27/32	0.84375	21.4312	18	457.2
	23/64 0.359375	9.1281	0.05	1.270		55/64 0.859375	21.8281	19	482.6
3/8	0.375	9.5250	0.06	1.524	7/8	0.875	22.2250	20	508.0
	25/64 0.390625	9.9219	0.07	1.778		57/64 0.890625	22.6219	21	533.4
13/32	0.40625	10.3187	0.08	2.032	29/32	0.90625	23.0187	22	558.8
	27/64 0.421875	10.7156	0.09	2.286		59/64 0.921875	23.4156	23	584.2
7/16	0.4375	11.1125	0.1	2.54	15/16	0.9375	23.8125	24	609.6
	29/64 0.453125	11.5094	0.2	5.08		61/64 0.953125	24.2094	25	635.0
15/32	0.46875	11.9062	0.3	7.62	31/32	0.96875	24.6062	26	660.4
	31/64 0.484375	12.3031	0.4	10.16		63/64 0.984375	25.0031	27	690.6
1/2	0.5	12.7000	0.5	12.70					

ENGLISH TO METRIC CONVERSION: TORQUE

To convert foot-pounds (ft. lbs.) to Newton-meters: multiply the number of ft. lbs. by 1.3

To convert inch-pounds (in. lbs.) to Newton-meters: multiply the number of in. lbs. by .11

in lbs	N·m	in lbs	N·m	in lbs	N·m	in lbs	N·m	in lbs	N·m
0.1	0.01	1	0.11	10	1.13	19	2.15	28	3.16
0.2	0.02	2	0.23	11	1.24	20	2.26	29	3.28
0.3	0.03	3	0.34	12	1.36	21	2.37	30	3.39
0.4	0.04	4	0.45	13	1.47	22	2.49	31	3.50
0.5	0.06	5	0.56	14	1.58	23	2.60	32	3.62
0.6	0.07	6	0.68	15	1.70	24	2.71	33	3.73
0.7	0.08	7	0.78	16	1.81	25	2.82	34	3.84
0.8	0.09	8	0.90	17	1.92	26	2.94	35	3.95
0.9	0.10	9	1.02	18	2.03	27	3.05	36	4.07

ENGLISH TO METRIC CONVERSION: TORQUE

Torque is now expressed as either foot-pounds (ft./lbs.) or inch-pounds (in./lbs.). The metric measurement unit for torque is the Newton-meter (Nm). This unit—the Nm—will be used for all SI metric torque references, both the present ft./lbs. and in./lbs.

ft lbs	N-m	ft lbs	N-m	ft lbs	N-m	ft lbs	N-m
0.1	0.1	33	44.7	74	100.3	115	155.9
0.2	0.3	34	46.1	75	101.7	116	157.3
0.3	0.4	35	47.4	76	103.0	117	158.6
0.4	0.5	36	48.8	77	104.4	118	160.0
0.5	0.7	37	50.7	78	105.8	119	161.3
0.6	0.8	38	51.5	79	107.1	120	162.7
0.7	1.0	39	52.9	80	108.5	121	164.0
0.8	1.1	40	54.2	81	109.8	122	165.4
0.9	1.2	41	55.6	82	111.2	123	166.8
1	1.3	42	56.9	83	112.5	124	168.1
2	2.7	43	58.3	84	113.9	125	169.5
3	4.1	44	59.7	85	115.2	126	170.8
4	5.4	45	61.0	86	116.6	127	172.2
5	6.8	46	62.4	87	118.0	128	173.5
6	8.1	47	63.7	88	119.3	129	174.9
7	9.5	48	65.1	89	120.7	130	176.2
8	10.8	49	66.4	90	122.0	131	177.6
9	12.2	50	67.8	91	123.4	132	179.0
10	13.6	51	69.2	92	124.7	133	180.3
11	14.9	52	70.5	93	126.1	134	181.7
12	16.3	53	71.9	94	127.4	135	183.0
13	17.6	54	73.2	95	128.8	136	184.4
14	18.9	55	74.6	96	130.2	137	185.7
15	20.3	56	75.9	97	131.5	138	187.1
16	21.7	57	77.3	98	132.9	139	188.5
17	23.0	58	78.6	99	134.2	140	189.8
18	24.4	59	80.0	100	135.6	141	191.2
19	25.8	60	81.4	101	136.9	142	192.5
20	27.1	61	82.7	102	138.3	143	193.9
21	28.5	62	84.1	103	139.6	144	195.2
22	29.8	63	85.4	104	141.0	145	196.6
23	31.2	64	86.8	105	142.4	146	198.0
24	32.5	65	88.1	106	143.7	147	199.3
25	33.9	66	89.5	107	145.1	148	200.7
26	35.2	67	90.8	108	146.4	149	202.0
27	36.6	68	92.2	109	147.8	150	203.4
28	38.0	69	93.6	110	149.1	151	204.7
29	39.3	70	94.9	111	150.5	152	206.1
30	40.7	71	96.3	112	151.8	153	207.4
31	42.0	72	97.6	113	153.2	154	208.8
32	43.4	73	99.0	114	154.6	155	210.2

ENGLISH TO METRIC CONVERSION: FORCE

Force is presently measured in pounds (lbs.). This type of measurement is used to measure spring pressure, specifically how many pounds it takes to compress a spring. Our present force unit (the pound) will be replaced in SI metric measurements by the Newton (N). This term will eventually see use in specifications for electric motor brush spring pressures, valve spring pressures, etc.

To convert pounds (lbs.) to Newton (N): multiply the number of lbs. by 4.45

lbs	N	lbs	N	lbs	N	oz	N
0.01	0.04	21	93.4	59	262.4	1	0.3
0.02	0.09	22	97.9	60	266.9	2	0.6
0.03	0.13	23	102.3	61	271.3	3	0.8
0.04	0.18	24	106.8	62	275.8	4	1.1
0.05	0.22	25	111.2	63	280.2	5	1.4
0.06	0.27	26	115.6	64	284.6	6	1.7
0.07	0.31	27	120.1	65	289.1	7	2.0
0.08	0.36	28	124.6	66	293.6	8	2.2
0.09	0.40	29	129.0	67	298.0	9	2.5
0.1	0.4	30	133.4	68	302.5	10	2.8
0.2	0.9	31	137.9	69	306.9	11	3.1
0.3	1.3	32	142.3	70	311.4	12	3.3
0.4	1.8	33	146.8	71	315.8	13	3.6
0.5	2.2	34	151.2	72	320.3	14	3.9
0.6	2.7	35	155.7	73	324.7	15	4.2
0.7	3.1	36	160.1	74	329.2	16	4.4
0.8	3.6	37	164.6	75	333.6	17	4.7
0.9	4.0	38	169.0	76	338.1	18	5.0
1	4.4	39	173.5	77	342.5	19	5.3
2	8.9	40	177.9	78	347.0	20	5.6
3	13.4	41	182.4	79	351.4	21	5.8
4	17.8	42	186.8	80	355.9	22	6.1
5	22.2	43	191.3	81	360.3	23	6.4
6	26.7	44	195.7	82	364.8	24	6.7
7	31.1	45	200.2	83	369.2	25	7.0
8	35.6	46	204.6	84	373.6	26	7.2
9	40.0	47	209.1	85	378.1	27	7.5
10	44.5	48	213.5	86	382.6	28	7.8
11	48.9	49	218.0	87	387.0	29	8.1
12	53.4	50	224.4	88	391.4	30	8.3
13	57.8	51	226.9	89	395.9	31	8.6
14	62.3	52	231.3	90	400.3	32	8.9
15	66.7	53	235.8	91	404.8	33	9.2
16	71.2	54	240.2	92	409.2	34	9.4
17	75.6	55	244.6	93	413.7	35	9.7
18	80.1	56	249.1	94	418.1	36	10.0
19	84.5	57	253.6	95	422.6	37	10.3
20	89.0	58	258.0	96	427.0	38	10.6

ENGLISH TO METRIC CONVERSION: LIQUID CAPACITY

Liquid or fluid capacity is presently expressed as pints, quarts or gallons, or a combination of all of these. In the metric system the liter (l) will become the basic unit. Fractions of a liter would be expressed as deciliters, centiliters, or most frequently (and commonly) as milliliters.

To convert pints (pts.) to liters (l): multiply the number of pints by .47
To convert liters (l) to pints (pts.): multiply the number of liters by 2.1
To convert quarts (qts.) to liters (l): multiply the number of quarts by .95

To convert liters (l) to quarts (qts.): multiply the number of liters by 1.06
To convert gallons (gals.) to liters (l): multiply the number of gallons by 3.8
To convert liters (l) to gallons (gals.): multiply the number of liters by .26

gals	liters	qts	liters	pts	liters
0.1	0.38	0.1	0.10	0.1	0.05
0.2	0.76	0.2	0.19	0.2	0.10
0.3	1.1	0.3	0.28	0.3	0.14
0.4	1.5	0.4	0.38	0.4	0.19
0.5	1.9	0.5	0.47	0.5	0.24
0.6	2.3	0.6	0.57	0.6	0.28
0.7	2.6	0.7	0.66	0.7	0.33
0.8	3.0	0.8	0.76	0.8	0.38
0.9	3.4	0.9	0.85	0.9	0.43
1	3.8	1	1.0	1	0.5
2	7.6	2	1.9	2	1.0
3	11.4	3	2.8	3	1.4
4	15.1	4	3.8	4	1.9
5	18.9	5	4.7	5	2.4
6	22.7	6	5.7	6	2.8
7	26.5	7	6.6	7	3.3
8	30.3	8	7.6	8	3.8
9	34.1	9	8.5	9	4.3
10	37.8	10	9.5	10	4.7
11	41.6	11	10.4	11	5.2
12	45.4	12	11.4	12	5.7
13	49.2	13	12.3	13	6.2
14	53.0	14	13.2	14	6.6
15	56.8	15	14.2	15	7.1
16	60.6	16	15.1	16	7.6
17	64.3	17	16.1	17	8.0
18	68.1	18	17.0	18	8.5
19	71.9	19	18.0	19	9.0
20	75.7	20	18.9	20	9.5
21	79.5	21	19.9	21	9.9
22	83.2	22	20.8	22	10.4
23	87.0	23	21.8	23	10.9
24	90.8	24	22.7	24	11.4
25	94.6	25	23.6	25	11.8
26	98.4	26	24.6	26	12.3
27	102.2	27	25.5	27	12.8
28	106.0	28	26.5	28	13.2
29	110.0	29	27.4	29	13.7
30	113.5	30	28.4	30	14.2

ENGLISH TO METRIC CONVERSION: PRESSURE

The basic unit of pressure measurement used today is expressed as pounds per square inch (psi). The metric unit for psi will be the kilopascal (kPa). This will apply to either fluid pressure or air pressure, and will be frequently seen in tire pressure readings, oil pressure specifications, fuel pump pressure, etc.

To convert pounds per square inch (psi) to kilopascals (kPa): multiply the number of psi by 6.89

Psi	kPa	Psi	kPa	Psi	kPa	Psi	kPa
0.1	0.7	37	255.1	82	565.4	127	875.6
0.2	1.4	38	262.0	83	572.3	128	882.5
0.3	2.1	39	268.9	84	579.2	129	889.4
0.4	2.8	40	275.8	85	586.0	130	896.3
0.5	3.4	41	282.7	86	592.9	131	903.2
0.6	4.1	42	289.6	87	599.8	132	910.1
0.7	4.8	43	296.5	88	606.7	133	917.0
0.8	5.5	44	303.4	89	613.6	134	923.9
0.9	6.2	45	310.3	90	620.5	135	930.8
1	6.9	46	317.2	91	627.4	136	937.7
2	13.8	47	324.0	92	634.3	137	944.6
3	20.7	48	331.0	93	641.2	138	951.5
4	27.6	49	337.8	94	648.1	139	958.4
5	34.5	50	344.7	95	655.0	140	965.2
6	41.4	51	351.6	96	661.9	141	972.2
7	48.3	52	358.5	97	668.8	142	979.0
8	55.2	53	365.4	98	675.7	143	985.9
9	62.1	54	372.3	99	682.6	144	992.8
10	69.0	55	379.2	100	689.5	145	999.7
11	75.8	56	386.1	101	696.4	146	1006.6
12	82.7	57	393.0	102	703.3	147	1013.5
13	89.6	58	399.9	103	710.2	148	1020.4
14	96.5	59	406.8	104	717.0	149	1027.3
15	103.4	60	413.7	105	723.9	150	1034.2
16	110.3	61	420.6	106	730.8	151	1041.1
17	117.2	62	427.5	107	737.7	152	1048.0
18	124.1	63	434.4	108	744.6	153	1054.9
19	131.0	64	441.3	109	751.5	154	1061.8
20	137.9	65	448.2	110	758.4	155	1068.7
21	144.8	66	455.0	111	765.3	156	1075.6
22	151.7	67	461.9	112	772.2	157	1082.5
23	158.6	68	468.8	113	779.1	158	1089.4
24	165.5	69	475.7	114	786.0	159	1096.3
25	172.4	70	482.6	115	792.9	160	1103.2
26	179.3	71	489.5	116	799.8	161	1110.0
27	186.2	72	496.4	117	806.7	162	1116.9
28	193.0	73	503.3	118	813.6	163	1123.8
29	200.0	74	510.2	119	820.5	164	1130.7
30	206.8	75	517.1	120	827.4	165	1137.6
31	213.7	76	524.0	121	834.3	166	1144.5
32	220.6	77	530.9	122	841.2	167	1151.4
33	227.5	78	537.8	123	848.0	168	1158.3
34	234.4	79	544.7	124	854.9	169	1165.2
35	241.3	80	551.6	125	861.8	170	1172.1
36	248.2	81	558.5	126	868.7	171	1179.0

ENGLISH TO METRIC CONVERSION: PRESSURE

The basic unit of pressure measurement used today is expressed as pounds per square inch (psi). The metric unit for psi will be the kilopascal (kPa). This will apply to either fluid pressure or air pressure, and will be frequently seen in tire pressure readings, oil pressure specifications, fuel pump pressure, etc.

To convert pounds per square inch (psi) to kilopascals (kPa): multiply the number of psi by 6.89

Psi	kPa	Psi	kPa	Psi	kPa	Psi	kPa
172	1185.9	216	1489.3	260	1792.6	304	2096.0
173	1192.8	217	1496.2	261	1799.5	305	2102.9
174	1199.7	218	1503.1	262	1806.4	306	2109.8
175	1206.6	219	1510.0	263	1813.3	307	2116.7
176	1213.5	220	1516.8	264	1820.2	308	2123.6
177	1220.4	221	1523.7	265	1827.1	309	2130.5
178	1227.3	222	1530.6	266	1834.0	310	2137.4
179	1234.2	223	1537.5	267	1840.9	311	2144.3
180	1241.0	224	1544.4	268	1847.8	312	2151.2
181	1247.9	225	1551.3	269	1854.7	313	2158.1
182	1254.8	226	1558.2	270	1861.6	314	2164.9
183	1261.7	227	1565.1	271	1868.5	315	2171.8
184	1268.6	228	1572.0	272	1875.4	316	2178.7
185	1275.5	229	1578.9	273	1882.3	317	2185.6
186	1282.4	230	1585.8	274	1889.2	318	2192.5
187	1289.3	231	1592.7	275	1896.1	319	2199.4
188	1296.2	232	1599.6	276	1903.0	320	2206.3
189	1303.1	233	1606.5	277	1909.8	321	2213.2
190	1310.0	234	1613.4	278	1916.7	322	2220.1
191	1316.9	235	1620.3	279	1923.6	323	2227.0
192	1323.8	236	1627.2	280	1930.5	324	2233.9
193	1330.7	237	1634.1	281	1937.4	325	2240.8
194	1337.6	238	1641.0	282	1944.3	326	2247.7
195	1344.5	239	1647.8	283	1951.2	327	2254.6
196	1351.4	240	1654.7	284	1958.1	328	2261.5
197	1358.3	241	1661.6	285	1965.0	329	2268.4
198	1365.2	242	1668.5	286	1971.9	330	2275.3
199	1372.0	243	1675.4	287	1978.8	331	2282.2
200	1378.9	244	1682.3	288	1985.7	332	2289.1
201	1385.8	245	1689.2	289	1992.6	333	2295.9
202	1392.7	246	1696.1	290	1999.5	334	2302.8
203	1399.6	247	1703.0	291	2006.4	335	2309.7
204	1406.5	248	1709.9	292	2013.3	336	2316.6
205	1413.4	249	1716.8	293	2020.2	337	2323.5
206	1420.3	250	1723.7	294	2027.1	338	2330.4
207	1427.2	251	1730.6	295	2034.0	339	2337.3
208	1434.1	252	1737.5	296	2040.8	240	2344.2
209	1441.0	253	1744.4	297	2047.7	341	2351.1
210	1447.9	254	1751.3	298	2054.6	342	2358.0
211	1454.8	255	1758.2	299	2061.5	343	2364.9
212	1461.7	256	1765.1	300	2068.4	344	2371.8
213	1468.7	257	1772.0	301	2075.3	345	2378.7
214	1475.5	258	1778.8	302	2082.2	346	2385.6
215	1482.4	259	1785.7	303	2089.1	347	2392.5